O
1994 NCAA®
BASKETBALL

NATIONAL COLLEGIATE ATHLETIC ASSOCIATION

THE NATIONAL COLLEGIATE ATHLETIC ASSOCIATION
6201 College Boulevard
Overland Park, Kansas 66211-2422
913/339-1906

November 1993

[ISSN 0267-1017]

Compiled By: Gary K. Johnson, *Assistant Statistics Coordinator;* Richard M. Campbell, *Assistant Statistics Coordinator;* John D. Painter, *Assistant Statistics Coordinator;* Sean W. Straziscar, *Assistant Statistics Coordinator;* James F. Wright, *Assistant Director of Communications.*

Edited By: Laura E. Bollig, *Publications Editor.*

Designed By: Victor M. Royal, *Director of Graphics.*

Cover Photography By: Young Company, *Kansas City, Missouri.*

NCAA 9412-11/93

Contents

DIVISION I
MEN'S RECORDS

Tennessee's Allan Houston ended his career with 2,801 points–14th on the NCAA career scoring list. He became the Volunteers' all-time leading scorer and finished second in scoring in the Southeastern Conference.

DIVISION I MEN'S INDIVIDUAL RECORDS

Basketball records are confined to the "modern era," which began with the 1937-38 season, the first without the center jump after each goal scored. Official weekly statistics rankings in scoring and shooting began with the 1947-48 season; individual rebounds were added for the 1950-51 season, although team rebounds were not added until 1954-55. Assists were added in 1983-84, blocked shots and steals were added in 1985-86 and three-point field goals were added in 1986-87. Scoring, rebounding, assists, blocked shots and steals are ranked on total number and on per-game average; shooting, on percentage. In statistical rankings, the rounding of percentages and/or averages may indicate ties where none exist. In these cases, the numerical order of the rankings is accurate. In 1973, freshmen became eligible to compete on the varsity level.

SCORING

Points

Game
100—Frank Selvy, Furman vs. Newberry, Feb. 13, 1954 (41 FGs, 18 FTs)

Season
1,381—Pete Maravich, Louisiana St., 1970 (522 FGs, 337 FTs, 31 games)

Career
3,667—Pete Maravich, Louisiana St., 1968-70 (1,387 FGs, 893 FTs, 83 games)

Points vs. Division I Opponent

Game
72—Kevin Bradshaw, U.S. Int'l vs. Loyola (Cal.), Jan. 5, 1991

Average Per Game

Season
44.5—Pete Maravich, Louisiana St., 1970 (1,381 in 31)

Career
44.2—Pete Maravich, Louisiana St., 1968-70 (3,667 in 83)

Most Combined Points, Two Teammates

Game
125—Frank Selvy (100) and Darrell Floyd (25), Furman vs. Newberry, Feb. 13, 1954

Most Combined Points, Two Teammates vs. Division I Opponent

Game
92—Kevin Bradshaw (72) and Isaac Brown (20), U.S. Int'l vs. Loyola (Cal.), Jan. 5, 1991

Most Combined Points, Two Opposing Players on Division I Teams

Game
115—Pete Maravich (64), Louisiana St. and Dan Issel (51), Kentucky, Feb. 21, 1970

Games Scoring At Least 50 Points

Season
10—Pete Maravich, Louisiana St., 1970

Season—Consecutive Games
3—Pete Maravich, Louisiana St., Feb. 10 to Feb. 15, 1969

Career
28—Pete Maravich, Louisiana St., 1968-70

Most Games Scoring in Double Figures

Career
132—Danny Manning, Kansas, 1985-88

Consecutive Games Scoring in Double Figures

Career
115—Lionel Simmons, La Salle, 1987-90

FIELD GOALS

Field Goals

Game
41—Frank Selvy, Furman vs. Newberry, Feb. 13, 1954 (66 attempts)

Season
522—Pete Maravich, Louisiana St., 1970 (1,168 attempts)

Career
1,387—Pete Maravich, Louisiana St., 1968-70 (3,166 attempts)

Consecutive Field Goals

Game
16—Doug Grayson, Kent vs. North Caro., Dec. 6, 1967 (18 of 19)

Season
25—Ray Voelkel, American, 1978 (during nine games, Nov. 24-Dec. 16)

Field-Goal Attempts

Game
71—Jay Handlan, Wash. & Lee vs. Furman, Feb. 17, 1951 (30 made)

Season
1,168—Pete Maravich, Louisiana St., 1970 (522 made)

Career
3,166—Pete Maravich, Louisiana St., 1968-70 (1,387 made)

Field-Goal Percentage

Game
(Min. 14 made) 100%—Cornelius Holden, Louisville vs. Southern Miss., March 3, 1990 (14 of 14); Dana Jones, Pepperdine vs. Boise St., Nov. 30, 1991 (14 of 14)
(Min. 20 made) 95.5%—Bill Walton, UCLA vs. Memphis St., March 26, 1973 (21 of 22)

***Season**
74.6%—Steve Johnson, Oregon St., 1981 (235 of 315)

Career
(Min. 400 made) 68.5%—Stephen Scheffler, Purdue, 1987-90 (408 of 596)
(Min. 600 made) 67.8%—Steve Johnson, Oregon St., 1976-81 (828 of 1,222)

* *Based on qualifiers for national championship.*

THREE-POINT FIELD GOALS

Three-Point Field Goals

Game

14—Dave Jamerson, Ohio vs. Charleston, Dec. 21, 1989 (17 attempts)

Season

158—Darrin Fitzgerald, Butler, 1987 (362 attempts)

Career

363—Jeff Fryer, Loyola (Cal.), 1987-90 (940 attempts)

Three-Point Field Goals Made Per Game

Season

5.6—Darrin Fitzgerald, Butler, 1987 (158 in 28)

Career

(Min. 200 made) 4.6—Timothy Pollard, Mississippi Val., 1988-89 (256 in 56)

Consecutive Three-Point Field Goals

Game

11—Gary Bossert, Niagara vs. Siena, Jan. 7, 1987

Season

15—Todd Leslie, Northwestern, 1990 (during four games, Dec. 15-28)

Consecutive Games Making a Three-Point Field Goal

Season

38—Steve Kerr, Arizona, Nov. 27, 1987, to April 2, 1988

Career

73—Wally Lancaster, Virginia Tech, Dec. 30, 1986, to March 4, 1989

Three-Point Field-Goal Attempts

Game

26—Lindsey Hunter, Jackson St. vs. Kansas, Dec. 27, 1992 (11 made)

Season

362—Darrin Fitzgerald, Butler, 1987 (158 made)

Career

940—Jeff Fryer, Loyola (Cal.), 1987-90 (363 made)

Three-Point Field-Goal Attempts Per Game

Season

12.9—Darrin Fitzgerald, Butler, 1987 (362 in 28)

Career

7.8—Wally Lancaster, Virginia Tech, 1987-89 (694 in 89)

Three-Point Field-Goal Percentage

Game

(Min. 8 made) 100%—Tomas Thompson, San Francisco vs. Loyola (Cal.), March 7, 1992 (8 of 8)

(Min. 12 made) 85.7%—Gary Bossert, Niagara vs. Siena, Jan. 7, 1987 (12 of 14)

Season

(Min. 50 made) 63.4%—Glenn Tropf, Holy Cross, 1988 (52 of 82)

(Min. 100 made) 57.3%—Steve Kerr, Arizona, 1988 (114 of 199)

Career

(Min. 200 made) 49.7%—Tony Bennett, Wis.-Green Bay, 1989-92 (290 of 584)

(Min. 300 made) 43.9%—Andy Kennedy, North Caro. St. and Ala.-Birmingham, 1987, 1989-91 (330 of 752)

FREE THROWS

Free Throws

Game

30—Pete Maravich, Louisiana St. vs. Oregon St., Dec. 22, 1969 (31 attempts)

Season

355—Frank Selvy, Furman, 1954 (444 attempts)

Career

(3 yrs.) 893—Pete Maravich, Louisiana St., 1968-70 (1,152 attempts)

(4 yrs.) 905—Dickie Hemric, Wake Forest, 1952-55 (1,359 attempts)

Consecutive Free Throws

Game

24—Arlen Clark, Oklahoma St. vs. Colorado, March 7, 1959 (24 of 24)

Season

64—Joe Dykstra, Western Ill., 1981-82 (during eight games, Dec. 1-Jan. 4)

Free-Throw Attempts

Game

36—Ed Tooley, Brown vs. Amherst, Dec. 4, 1954 (23 made)

Season

444—Frank Selvy, Furman, 1954 (355 made)

Career

(3 yrs.) 1,152—Pete Maravich, Louisiana St., 1968-70 (893 made)

(4 yrs.) 1,359—Dickie Hemric, Wake Forest, 1952-55 (905 made)

Free-Throw Percentage

Game

(Min. 24 made) 100% —Arlen Clark, Oklahoma St. vs. Colorado, March 7, 1959 (24 of 24)

***Season**

95.9%—Craig Collins, Penn St., 1985 (94 of 98)

Career

(Min. 300 made) 90.9%—Greg Starrick, Kentucky and Southern Ill., 1969, 1970-72 (341 of 375)

(Min. 600 made) 88.5%—Ron Perry, Holy Cross, 1976-80 (680 of 768)

(Min. 2.5 made per game) 92.3%—Dave Hildahl, Portland St., 1979-81 (131 of 142)

* *Based on qualifiers for national championship.*

REBOUNDS

Rebounds

Game

51—Bill Chambers, William & Mary vs. Virginia, Feb. 14, 1953

Season

734—Walt Dukes, Seton Hall, 1953 (33 games)

Career

(3 yrs.) 1,751—Paul Silas, Creighton, 1962-64 (81 games)

(4 yrs.) 2,201—Tom Gola, La Salle, 1952-55 (118 games)

Average Per Game

Season

25.6—Charlie Slack, Marshall, 1955 (538 in 21)

Career

(Min. 800) 22.7—Artis Gilmore, Jacksonville, 1970-71 (1,224 in 54)

ASSISTS

Assists

Game

22—Tony Fairley, Charleston So. vs. Armstrong St., Feb. 9, 1987; Avery Johnson, Southern-B.R. vs. Texas Southern, Jan. 25, 1988; Sherman Douglas, Syracuse vs. Providence, Jan. 28, 1989

Season

406—Mark Wade, Nevada-Las Vegas, 1987 (38 games)

Career

1,076—Bobby Hurley, Duke, 1990-93 (140 games)

Average Per Game

Season

13.3—Avery Johnson, Southern-B.R., 1988 (399 in 30)

Career

8.9—Avery Johnson, Cameron and Southern-B.R., 1985 and 1987-88 (838 in 94)

BLOCKED SHOTS

Blocked Shots

Game

14—David Robinson, Navy vs. N.C.-Wilmington, Jan. 4, 1986; Shawn Bradley, Brigham Young vs. Eastern Ky., Dec. 7, 1990

Season

207—David Robinson, Navy, 1986 (35 games)

Career

453—Alonzo Mourning, Georgetown, 1989-92 (120 games)

Average Per Game

Season

5.9—David Robinson, Navy, 1986 (207 in 35)

Career

(Min. 200) 5.2—David Robinson, Navy, 1986-87 (351 in 67)

STEALS

Steals

Game

13—Mookie Blaylock, Oklahoma vs. Centenary, Dec. 12, 1987; and vs. Loyola (Cal.), Dec. 17, 1988

Season

150—Mookie Blaylock, Oklahoma, 1988 (39 games)

Career

376—Eric Murdock, Providence, 1988-91 (117 games)

Average Per Game

Season

5.0—Darron Brittman, Chicago St., 1986 (139 in 28)

Career

(Min. 200) 3.8—Mookie Blaylock, Oklahoma, 1988-89 (281 in 74)

(Min. 300) 3.2—Eric Murdock, Providence, 1988-91 (376 in 117)

GAMES

Games Played (Since 1947-48)

Season

40—Mark Alarie, Tommy Amaker, Johnny Dawkins, Danny Ferry and Billy King, Duke, 1986; Larry Johnson, Nevada-Las Vegas, 1990

Career

148—Christian Laettner, Duke, 1989-92

GENERAL

Averaging 20 Points and 20 Rebounds

Career

Walt Dukes, Seton Hall, 1952-53 (23.5 points and 21.1 rebounds)

Bill Russell, San Francisco, 1954-56 (20.7 points and 20.3 rebounds)

Paul Silas, Creighton, 1962-64 (20.5 points and 21.6 rebounds)

Julius Erving, Massachusetts, 1970-71 (26.3 points and 20.2 rebounds)

Artis Gilmore, Jacksonville, 1970-71 (24.3 points and 22.7 rebounds)

Kermit Washington, American, 1971-73 (20.1 points and 20.2 rebounds)

DIVISION I MEN'S TEAM RECORDS

Note: Where records involve both teams, each team must be an NCAA Division I member institution.

SINGLE-GAME SCORING

Most Points

186—Loyola (Cal.) vs. U.S. Int'l (140), Jan. 5, 1991

Most Points by Losing Team

150—U.S. Int'l vs. Loyola (Cal.) (181), Jan. 31, 1989

Most Points, Both Teams

331—Loyola (Cal.) (181) vs. U.S. Int'l (150), Jan. 31, 1989

Most Points in a Half

97—Oklahoma vs. U.S. Int'l, Nov. 29, 1989 (1st)

Most Points in a Half, Both Teams

172—Loyola (Cal.) (86) vs. Gonzaga (86), Feb. 18, 1989 (2nd)

Largest Lead Before the Opponent Scores at the Start of a Game

32-0—Connecticut vs. New Hampshire, Dec. 12, 1990

Largest Deficit Overcome to Win Game
29—Duke (74) vs. Tulane (72), Dec. 30, 1950 (trailed 27-56 at half time)

Largest Deficit Before Scoring Overcome to Win Game
28—New Mexico St. (117) vs. Bradley (109), Jan. 27, 1977 (trailed 0-28 with 13:49 left in first half)

Largest Half-Time Deficit Overcome to Win Game
29—Duke (74) vs. Tulane (72), Dec. 30, 1950 (trailed 27-56 at half time)

Fewest Points Allowed (Since 1938)
6—Tennessee (11) vs. Temple, Dec. 15, 1973; Kentucky (75) vs. Arkansas St., Jan. 8, 1945

Fewest Points, Both Teams (Since 1938)
17—Tennessee (11) vs. Temple (6), Dec. 15, 1973

Widest Margin of Victory
95—Oklahoma (146) vs. Northeastern Ill. (51), Dec. 2, 1989

SINGLE-GAME FIELD GOALS

Most Field Goals
74—Houston vs. Valparaiso, Feb. 24, 1968 (112 attempts)

Most Field Goals, Both Teams
130—Loyola (Cal.) (67) vs. U.S. Int'l (63), Jan. 31, 1989

Most Field Goals in a Half
42—Oklahoma vs. U.S. Int'l, Nov. 29, 1989 (90 attempts) (1st)

Most Field-Goal Attempts
147—Oklahoma vs. U.S. Int'l, Nov. 29, 1989 (70 made)

Most Field-Goal Attempts, Both Teams
245—Loyola (Cal.) (124) vs. U.S. Int'l (121), Jan. 7, 1989

Most Field-Goal Attempts in a Half
90—Oklahoma vs. U.S. Int'l, Nov. 29, 1989 (42 made) (1st)

Fewest Field Goals (Since 1938)
2—Duke vs. North Caro. St., March 8, 1968 (11 attempts); Arkansas St. vs. Kentucky, Jan. 8, 1945

Fewest Field-Goal Attempts (Since 1938)
9—Pittsburgh vs. Penn St., March 1, 1952 (3 made)

Highest Field-Goal Percentage
(Min. 15 made) 83.3%—Maryland vs. South Caro., Jan. 9, 1971 (15 of 18)
(Min. 30 made) 81.4%—New Mexico vs. Oregon St., Nov. 30, 1985 (35 of 43)

Highest Field-Goal Percentage, Half
94.1%—North Caro. vs. Virginia, Jan. 7, 1978 (16 of 17) (2nd)

SINGLE-GAME THREE-POINT FIELD GOALS

Most Three-Point Field Goals
23—Lamar vs. Louisiana Tech, Feb. 28, 1993 (49 attempts)

Most Three-Point Field Goals, Both Teams
33—Temple (19) vs. Geo. Washington (14), March 4, 1992

Consecutive Three-Point Field Goals Made Without a Miss
11—Niagara vs. Siena, Jan. 7, 1987; Eastern Ky. vs. N.C.-Asheville, Jan. 14, 1987

Highest Number of Different Players to Score a Three-Point Field Goal, One Team
8—Kentucky vs. Furman, Dec. 19, 1989

Most Three-Point Field-Goal Attempts
53—Kentucky vs. Southwestern La., Dec. 23, 1989 (15 made)

Most Three-Point Field-Goal Attempts, Both Teams
84—Kentucky (53) vs. Southwestern La. (31), Dec. 23, 1989

Highest Three-Point Field-Goal Percentage
(Min. 10 made) 90.9%—Duke vs. Clemson, Feb. 1, 1988 (10 of 11); Hofstra vs. Rhode Island, Jan. 16, 1993 (10 of 11)
(Min. 15 made) 83.3%—Eastern Ky. vs. N.C.-Asheville, Jan. 14, 1987 (15 of 18)

Highest Three-Point Field-Goal Percentage, Both Teams
(Min. 10 made) 83.3%—Lafayette (7 of 8) vs. Marist (3 of 4), Dec. 6, 1986 (10 of 12)
(Min. 15 made) 76.2%—Florida (10 of 14) vs. California (6 of 7), Dec. 27, 1986 (16 of 21)
(Min. 20 made) 72.4%—Princeton (12 of 15) vs. Brown (9 of 14), Feb. 20, 1988 (21 of 29)

SINGLE-GAME FREE THROWS

Most Free Throws
53—Morehead St. vs. Cincinnati, Feb. 11, 1956 (65 attempts); Miami (Ohio) vs. Central Mich., Jan. 29, 1992 (64 attempts)

Most Free Throws, Both Teams
88—Morehead St. (53) vs. Cincinnati (35), Feb. 11, 1956 (111 attempts)

Most Free-Throw Attempts
79—Northern Ariz. vs. Arizona, Jan. 26, 1953 (46 made)

Most Free-Throw Attempts, Both Teams
130—Northern Ariz. (79) vs. Arizona (51), Jan. 26, 1953 (78 made)

Fewest Free Throws
0—Many teams

Fewest Free-Throw Attempts
0—Many teams

Highest Free-Throw Percentage
(Min. 30 made) 100.0%—UC Irvine vs. Pacific (Cal.), Feb. 21, 1981 (34 of 34); Samford vs. Central Fla., Dec. 20, 1990 (34 of 34)
(Min. 35 made) 97.2%—Vanderbilt vs. Mississippi St., Feb. 26, 1986 (35 of 36); Butler vs. Dayton, Feb. 21, 1991 (35 of 36); Marquette vs. Memphis St., Jan. 23, 1993 (35 of 36)
(Min. 40 made) 95.5%—Nevada-Las Vegas vs. San Diego St., Dec. 11, 1976 (42 of 44)

Highest Free-Throw Percentage, Both Teams
100%—Purdue (25 of 25) vs. Wisconsin (22 of 22), Feb. 7, 1976 (47 of 47)

SINGLE-GAME REBOUNDS

Most Rebounds
108—Kentucky vs. Mississippi, Feb. 8, 1964

Most Rebounds, Both Teams
152—Indiana (95) vs. Michigan (57), March 11, 1961

Highest Rebound Margin
84—Arizona (102) vs. Northern Ariz. (18), Jan. 6, 1951

SINGLE-GAME ASSISTS

Most Assists
41—North Caro. vs. Manhattan, Dec. 27, 1985; Weber St. vs. Northern Ariz., March 2, 1991

Most Assists, Both Teams
65—Dayton (34) vs. Central Fla. (31), Dec. 3, 1988

SINGLE-GAME BLOCKED SHOTS

Most Blocked Shots
20—Iona vs. Northern Ill., Jan. 7, 1989

Most Blocked Shots, Both Teams
29—Rider (17) vs. FDU-Teaneck (12), Jan. 9, 1989

SINGLE-GAME STEALS

Most Steals
34—Oklahoma vs. Centenary, Dec. 12, 1987; Northwestern (La.) vs. LeTourneau, Jan. 20, 1992

Most Steals, Both Teams
44—Oklahoma (34) vs. Centenary (10), Dec. 12, 1987

SINGLE-GAME PERSONAL FOULS

Most Personal Fouls
50—Arizona vs. Northern Ariz., Jan. 26, 1953

Most Personal Fouls, Both Teams
84—Arizona (50) vs. Northern Ariz. (34), Jan. 26, 1953

Most Players Disqualified
8—St. Joseph's (Pa.) vs. Xavier (Ohio), Jan. 10, 1976

Most Players Disqualified, Both Teams
12—Nevada-Las Vegas (6) vs. Hawaii (6), Jan. 19, 1979 (ot); Arizona (7) vs. West Tex. A&M (5), Feb. 14, 1952

SINGLE-GAME OVERTIMES

Most Overtime Periods
7—Cincinnati (75) at Bradley (73), Dec. 21, 1981

Most Points in One Overtime Period
25—Texas A&M vs. North Caro., March 9, 1980; Wis.-Green Bay vs. Cleveland St., Feb. 27, 1988; Old Dominion vs. William & Mary, Feb. 1, 1992

Most Points in One Overtime Period, Both Teams
40—Old Dominion (25) vs. William & Mary (15), Feb. 1, 1992

Most Points in Overtime Periods
37—Iona vs. Fairfield, Feb. 20, 1982 (5 ot)

Most Points in Overtime Periods, Both Teams
72—Iona (37) vs. Fairfield (35), Feb. 20, 1982 (5 ot)

Largest Winning Margin in Overtime Game
18—Nebraska (85) vs. Iowa St. (67), Dec. 30, 1949

SEASON SCORING

Most Points
4,012—Oklahoma, 1988 (39 games)

Highest Average Per Game
122.4—Loyola (Cal.), 1990 (3,918 in 32)

Highest Average Scoring Margin
30.3—UCLA, 1972 (94.6 offense, 64.3 defense)

Most Games at Least 100 Points
28—Loyola (Cal.), 1990

Most Consecutive Games at Least 100 Points
12—Nevada-Las Vegas, 1977; Loyola (Cal.), 1990

SEASON FIELD GOALS

Most Field Goals
1,533—Oklahoma, 1988 (3,094 attempts)

Most Field Goals Per Game
46.3—Nevada-Las Vegas, 1976 (1,436 in 31)

Most Field-Goal Attempts
3,094—Oklahoma, 1988 (1,533 made)

Most Field-Goal Attempts Per Game
98.5—Oral Roberts, 1973 (2,659 in 27)

Highest Field-Goal Percentage
57.2%—Missouri, 1980 (936 of 1,635)

SEASON THREE-POINT FIELD GOALS

Most Three-Point Field Goals
340—Kentucky, 1993 (862 attempts)

Most Three-Point Field Goals Per Game
10.0—Lamar, 1993 (271 in 27)

Most Three-Point Field-Goal Attempts
888—Kentucky, 1992 (317 made)

Most Three-Point Field-Goal Attempts Per Game
28.9—Kentucky, 1990 (810 in 28)

Highest Three-Point Field-Goal Percentage
(Min. 100 made) 50.8%—Indiana, 1987 (130 of 256)
(Min. 150 made) 50.0%—Mississippi Val., 1987 (161 of 322)
(Min. 200 made) 49.2%—Princeton, 1988 (211 of 429)

ALL-TIME THREE-POINT FIELD GOALS

Consecutive Games Scoring a Three-Point Field Goal
242—Nevada-Las Vegas, Nov. 26, 1986 to present

SEASON FREE THROWS

Most Free Throws
865—Bradley, 1954 (1,263 attempts)

Most Free Throws Per Game
28.9—Morehead St., 1956 (838 in 29)

Most Consecutive Free Throws
49—Indiana St., 1991 (during two games, Feb. 13-18)

Most Free-Throw Attempts
1,263—Bradley, 1954 (865 made)

Most Free-Throw Attempts Per Game
41.0—Bradley, 1953 (1,107 in 27)

Highest Free-Throw Percentage
82.2%—Harvard, 1984 (535 of 651)

SEASON REBOUNDS

Most Rebounds
2,074—Houston, 1968 (33 games)

Highest Average Per Game
70.0—Connecticut, 1955 (1,751 in 25)

Highest Average Rebound Margin
25.0—Morehead St., 1957 (64.3 offense, 39.3 defense)

SEASON ASSISTS

Most Assists
926—Nevada-Las Vegas, 1990 (40 games)

Highest Average Per Game
24.7—Nevada-Las Vegas, 1991 (863 in 35)

SEASON BLOCKED SHOTS

Most Blocked Shots
309—Georgetown, 1989 (34 games)

Highest Average Per Game
9.1—Georgetown, 1989 (309 in 34)

SEASON STEALS

Most Steals
486—Oklahoma, 1988 (39 games)

Highest Average Per Game
14.8—Texas-San Antonio, 1991 (430 in 29)

SEASON PERSONAL FOULS

Most Personal Fouls
966—Providence, 1987 (34 games)

Most Personal Fouls Per Game
29.3—Indiana, 1952 (644 in 22)

Fewest Personal Fouls
253—Air Force, 1962 (23 games)

Fewest Personal Fouls Per Game
11.0—Air Force, 1962 (253 in 23)

SEASON DEFENSE

Lowest Scoring Average Per Game Allowed (Since 1938)
25.7—Oklahoma St., 1939 (693 points in 27 games)

Lowest Scoring Average Per Game Allowed (Since 1965)
47.1—Fresno St., 1982 (1,412 points in 30 games)

Lowest Field-Goal Percentage Allowed (Since 1978)
36.4%—Nevada-Las Vegas, 1992 (628 of 1,723)

SEASON OVERTIMES

Most Overtime Games
8—Western Ky., 1978 (won 5, lost 3); Portland, 1984 (won 4, lost 4); Valparaiso, 1993 (won 4, lost 4)

Most Consecutive Overtime Games
4—Jacksonville, 1982 (won 3, lost 1); Illinois St., 1985 (won 3, lost 1); Dayton, 1988 (won 1, lost 3)

GENERAL RECORDS

Most Games in a Season (Since 1947-48)
40—Duke, 1986 (37-3); Nevada-Las Vegas, 1990 (35-5)

Most Victories in a Season
37—Duke, 1986 (37-3); Nevada-Las Vegas, 1987 (37-2)

Most Victories in a Perfect Season
32—North Caro., 1957; Indiana, 1976

Most Consecutive Victories
88—UCLA, from Jan. 30, 1971, through Jan. 17, 1974 (ended Jan. 19, 1974, at Notre Dame, 71-70; last UCLA defeat before streak also came at Notre Dame, 89-82)

Most Consecutive Home-Court Victories
129—Kentucky, from Jan. 4, 1943, to Jan. 8, 1955 (ended by Georgia Tech, 59-58)

Most Consecutive Regular-Season Victories (NCAA, NIT, CCA tourneys not included)
76—UCLA, 1971-74

Most Defeats in a Season
28—Prairie View, 1992 (0-28)

Most Consecutive Defeats in a Season
28—Prairie View, 1992 (0-28)

Most Consecutive Defeats
37—Citadel, from Jan. 16, 1954, to Dec. 12, 1955

Most Consecutive Home-Court Defeats
32—New Hampshire, from Feb. 9, 1988, to Feb. 2, 1991 (ended vs. Holy Cross, 72-56)

Most Consecutive Winning Seasons
46—Louisville, 1945-90

Most Consecutive 20-Win Seasons
23—North Caro., 1971-93

Most Consecutive Non-Losing Seasons
60—Kentucky, 1928-88¢

¢ *Did not play in 1953.*

Unbeaten Teams (Since 1938; number of victories in parentheses)
1939 LIU-Brooklyn (24)†
1940 Seton Hall (19)††
1944 Army (15)††
1954 Kentucky (25)††
1956 San Francisco (29)*
1957 North Caro. (32)*
1964 UCLA (30)*
1967 UCLA (30)*
1972 UCLA (30)*
1973 UCLA (30)*
1973 North Caro. St. (27)††
1976 Indiana (32)*

Unbeaten in Regular Season But Lost in NCAA (*) or NIT (†)
1939 Loyola (Ill.) (20; 21-1)†
1941 Seton Hall (19; 20-2)†
1951 Columbia (21; 21-1)*
1961 Ohio St. (24; 27-1)*
1968 Houston (28; 31-2)*
1968 St. Bonaventure (22; 23-2)*
1971 Marquette (26; 28-1)*
1971 Pennsylvania (26; 28-1)*
1975 Indiana (29; 31-1)*
1976 Rutgers (28; 31-2)*
1979 Indiana St. (27; 33-1)*
1979 Alcorn St. (25; 28-1)†
1991 Nevada-Las Vegas (30; 34-1)*

30-Game Winners (Since 1938)
37—Duke, 1986; Nevada-Las Vegas, 1987.
36—Kentucky, 1948.
35—Arizona, 1988; Georgetown, 1985; Kansas, 1986; Nevada-Las Vegas, 1990; Oklahoma, 1988.
34—Arkansas, 1991; Duke, 1992; Georgetown, 1984; Kentucky, 1947; Nevada-Las Vegas, 1991; North Caro., 1993.
33—Indiana St., 1979; Louisville, 1980; Nevada-Las Vegas, 1986.
32—Arkansas, 1978; Bradley, 1950, 1951 & 1986; Duke, 1991; Houston, 1984; Indiana, 1976; Kentucky, 1949, 1951 & 1986; Louisville, 1983 & 1986; Marshall, 1947; North Caro., 1957, 1982 & 1987; Temple, 1987 & 1988.
31—Connecticut, 1990; Houston, 1968 & 1983; Illinois, 1989; Indiana, 1975 & 1993; Louisiana St., 1981; Memphis St., 1985; Michigan, 1993; Oklahoma, 1985; Oklahoma St., 1946; Rutgers, 1976; St. John's (N.Y.), 1985 & 1986; Seton Hall, 1953 & 1989; Syracuse, 1987; Wyoming, 1943.
30—Arkansas, 1990; Georgetown, 1982; Indiana, 1987; Iowa, 1987; Kansas, 1990; Kentucky, 1978 & 1993; La Salle, 1990; Massachusetts, 1992; Michigan, 1989; Navy, 1986; North Caro., 1946; North Caro. St., 1951 & 1974; Oklahoma, 1989; Oregon, 1946; Syracuse, 1989; UCLA, 1964, 1967, 1972 & 1973; Utah, 1991; Virginia, 1982; Western Ky., 1938.

* *NCAA champion.* † *NIT champion.* †† *Not in either tourney.*

DIVISION I MEN'S ALL-TIME INDIVIDUAL LEADERS

SINGLE-GAME SCORING HIGHS VS. DIVISION I OPPONENT

Pts.	Player, Team vs. Opponent	Date
72	Kevin Bradshaw, U.S. Int'l vs. Loyola (Cal.)	Jan. 5, 1991
69	Pete Maravich, Louisiana St. vs. Alabama	Feb. 7, 1970
68	Calvin Murphy, Niagara vs. Syracuse	Dec. 7, 1968
66	Jay Handlan, Wash. & Lee vs. Furman	Feb. 17, 1951
66	Pete Maravich, Louisiana St. vs. Tulane	Feb. 10, 1969
66	Anthony Roberts, Oral Roberts vs. North Caro. A&T	Feb. 19, 1977
65	Anthony Roberts, Oral Roberts vs. Oregon	Mar. 9, 1977
65	Scott Haffner, Evansville vs. Dayton	Feb. 18, 1989
64	Pete Maravich, Louisiana St. vs. Kentucky	Feb. 21, 1970
63	Johnny Neumann, Mississippi vs. Louisiana St.	Jan. 30, 1971
63	Hersey Hawkins, Bradley vs. Detroit Mercy	Feb. 22, 1988

SINGLE-GAME SCORING HIGHS VS. NON-DIVISION I OPPONENT

Pts.	Player, Team vs. Opponent	Date
100	Frank Selvy, Furman vs. Newberry	Feb. 13, 1954
85	Paul Arizin, Villanova vs. Philadelphia NAMC	Feb. 12, 1949
81	Freeman Williams, Portland St. vs. Rocky Mountain	Feb. 3, 1978
73	Bill Mlkvy, Temple vs. Wilkes	Mar. 3, 1951
71	Freeman Williams, Portland St. vs. Southern Ore.	Feb. 9, 1977
67	Darrell Floyd, Furman vs. Morehead St.	Jan. 22, 1955
66	Freeman Williams, Portland St. vs. George Fox	Jan. 13, 1978
65	Bob Zawoluk, St. John's (N.Y.) vs. St. Peter's	Mar. 30, 1950
63	Sherman White, LIU-Brooklyn vs. John Marshall	Feb. 1950
63	Frank Selvy, Furman vs. Mercer	Feb. 11, 1953

SINGLE-GAME FIELD-GOAL PERCENTAGE

(Minimum 13 field goals made)

Pct.	Player, Team vs. Opponent (FG-FGA)	Date
100	Cornelius Holden, Louisville vs. Southern Miss. (14 of 14)	Mar. 3, 1990
100	Dana Jones, Pepperdine vs. Boise St. (14 of 14)	Nov. 30, 1991
100	Rick Dean, Syracuse vs. Colgate (13 of 13)	Feb. 14, 1966
100	Kevin King, N.C.-Charlotte vs. South Ala. (13 of 13)	Feb. 20, 1978
100	Ted Guzek, Butler vs. Michigan (13 of 13)	Dec. 15, 1978
100	Steve Johnson, Oregon St. vs. Hawaii-Hilo (13 of 13)	Dec. 5, 1979
100	Antoine Carr, Wichita St. vs. Abilene Christian (13 of 13)	Nov. 28, 1980
100	Brad Daugherty, North Caro. vs. UCLA (13 of 13)	Nov. 24, 1985
100	Rafael Solis, Brooklyn vs. Wagner (13 of 13)	Dec. 11, 1991
95.5	Bill Walton, UCLA vs. Memphis St. (21 of 22)	Mar. 26, 1973

SINGLE-GAME THREE-POINT FIELD GOALS MADE

3FG	Player, Team vs. Opponent	Date
14	Dave Jamerson, Ohio vs. Charleston	Dec. 21, 1989
12	Gary Bossert, Niagara vs. Siena	Jan. 7, 1987
12	Darrin Fitzgerald, Butler vs. Detroit Mercy	Feb. 9, 1987
11	Dennis Scott, Georgia Tech vs. Houston	Dec. 28, 1988
11	Scott Haffner, Evansville vs. Dayton	Feb. 18, 1989
11	Bobby Phills, Southern-B.R. vs. Alcorn St.	Feb. 3, 1990
11	Dave Jamerson, Ohio vs. Kent	Feb. 24, 1990
11	Jeff Fryer, Loyola (Cal.) vs. Michigan	Mar. 18, 1990
11	Terry Brown, Kansas vs. North Caro. St.	Jan. 5, 1991
11	Marc Rybczyk, Central Conn. St. vs. LIU-Brooklyn	Nov. 26, 1991
11	Mark Alberts, Akron vs. Wright St.	Feb. 8, 1992
11	Mike Alcorn, Youngstown St. vs. Pitt.-Bradford	Feb. 24, 1992
11	Doug Day, Radford vs. Morgan St.	Dec. 9, 1992
11	Lindsey Hunter, Jackson St. vs. Kansas	Dec. 27, 1992
11	Keith Veney, Lamar vs. Prairie View	Feb. 2, 1993
11	Keith Veney, Lamar vs. Ark.-Lit. Rock	Feb. 11, 1993

SINGLE-GAME REBOUNDING HIGHS

(Before 1973)

Reb.	Player, Team vs. Opponent	Date
51	Bill Chambers, William & Mary vs. Virginia	Feb. 14, 1953
43	Charlie Slack, Marshall vs. Morris Harvey	Jan. 12, 1954
42	Tom Heinsohn, Holy Cross vs. Boston College	Mar. 1, 1955
40	Art Quimby, Connecticut vs. Boston U.	Jan. 11, 1955
39	Maurice Stokes, St. Francis (Pa.) vs. John Carroll	Jan. 28, 1955
39	Dave DeBusschere, Detroit Mercy vs. Central Mich.	Jan. 30, 1960
39	Keith Swagerty, Pacific (Cal.) vs. UC Santa Barb.	Mar. 5, 1965
38	Jerry Koch, St. Louis vs. Bradley	Mar. 5, 1954
38	Charlie Tyra, Louisville vs. Canisius	Dec. 10, 1955
38	Paul Silas, Creighton vs. Centenary	Feb. 19, 1962
38	Tommy Woods, East Tenn. St. vs. Middle Tenn. St.	Mar. 1, 1965

SINGLE-GAME REBOUNDING HIGHS

(Since 1973)

Reb.	Player, Team vs. Opponent	Date
34	David Vaughn, Oral Roberts vs. Brandeis	Jan. 8, 1973
33	Robert Parish, Centenary vs. Southern Miss.	Jan. 22, 1973
32	Durand Macklin, Louisiana St. vs. Tulane	Nov. 26, 1976
31	Jim Bradley, Northern Ill. vs. Wis.-Milwaukee	Feb. 19, 1973
31	Calvin Natt, Northeast La. vs. Ga. Southern	Dec. 29, 1976
30	Marvin Barnes, Providence vs. Assumption	Feb. 3, 1973
30	Brad Robinson, Kent vs. Central Mich.	Feb. 9, 1974
29	Robert Parish, Centenary vs. Texas-Arlington	Feb. 5, 1973
29	Donald Newman, Ark.-Lit. Rock vs. Centenary	Jan. 24, 1984
29	Hank Gathers, Loyola (Cal.) vs. U.S. Int'l	Jan. 31, 1989

SINGLE-GAME ASSISTS

Ast.	Player, Team vs. Opponent	Date
22	Tony Fairley, Charleston So. vs. Armstrong St.	Feb. 9, 1987
22	Avery Johnson, Southern-B.R. vs. Texas Southern	Jan. 25, 1988
22	Sherman Douglas, Syracuse vs. Providence	Jan. 28, 1989
21	Mark Wade, Nevada-Las Vegas vs. Navy	Dec. 29, 1986
21	Kelvin Scarborough, New Mexico vs. Hawaii	Feb. 13, 1987
21	Anthony Manuel, Bradley vs. UC Irvine	Dec. 19, 1987
21	Avery Johnson, Southern-B.R. vs. Alabama St.	Jan. 16, 1988
20	Grayson Marshall, Clemson vs. Md.-East. Shore	Nov. 25, 1985
20	James Johnson, Middle Tenn. St. vs. Freed-Hardeman	Jan. 2, 1986
20	Avery Johnson, Southern-B.R. vs. Texas Southern	Mar. 6, 1987
20	Avery Johnson, Southern-B.R. vs. Mississippi Val.	Feb. 8, 1988
20	Howard Evans, Temple vs. Villanova	Feb. 10, 1988
20	Chris Corchiani, North Caro. St. vs. Maryland	Feb. 27, 1991
20	Dana Harris, Md.-Balt. County vs. St. Mary's (Md.)	Dec. 12, 1992
20	Sam Crawford, New Mexico St. vs. Sam Houston St.	Dec. 21, 1992

SINGLE-GAME BLOCKED SHOTS

Blk.	Player, Team vs. Opponent	Date
14	David Robinson, Navy vs. N.C.-Wilmington	Jan. 4, 1986
14	Shawn Bradley, Brigham Young vs. Eastern Ky.	Dec. 7, 1990
13	Kevin Roberson, Vermont vs. New Hampshire	Jan. 9, 1992
13	Jim McIlvaine, Marquette vs. Northeastern Ill.	Dec. 9, 1992
12	David Robinson, Navy vs. James Madison	Jan. 9, 1986
12	Derrick Lewis, Maryland vs. James Madison	Jan. 28, 1987
12	Rodney Blake, St. Joseph's (Pa.) vs. Cleveland St.	Dec. 2, 1987
12	Walter Palmer, Dartmouth vs. Harvard	Jan. 9, 1988
12	Alan Ogg, Ala.-Birmingham vs. Florida A&M	Dec. 16, 1988
12	Dikembe Mutombo, Georgetown vs. St. John's (N.Y.)	Jan. 23, 1989
12	Shaquille O'Neal, Louisiana St. vs. Loyola (Cal.)	Feb. 3, 1990
12	Cedric Lewis, Maryland vs. South Fla.	Jan. 19, 1991
12	Ervin Johnson, New Orleans vs. Texas A&M	Dec. 29, 1992

SINGLE-GAME STEALS

Stl.	Player, Team vs. Opponent	Date
13	Mookie Blaylock, Oklahoma vs. Centenary	Dec. 12, 1987
13	Mookie Blaylock, Oklahoma vs. Loyola (Cal.)	Dec. 17, 1988
12	Kenny Robertson, Cleveland St. vs. Wagner	Dec. 3, 1988
12	Terry Evans, Oklahoma vs. Florida A&M	Jan. 27, 1993
11	Darron Brittman, Chicago St. vs. McKendree	Jan. 24, 1986
11	Darron Brittman, Chicago St. vs. St. Xavier	Feb. 8, 1986
11	Marty Johnson, Towson St. vs. Bucknell	Feb. 17, 1988
11	Aldwin Ware, Florida A&M vs. Tuskegee	Feb. 24, 1988
11	Mark Macon, Temple vs. Notre Dame	Jan. 29, 1989
11	Carl Thomas, Eastern Mich. vs. Chicago St.	Feb. 20, 1991
11	Ron Arnold, St. Francis (N.Y.) vs. Mt. St. Mary's (Md.)	Feb. 4, 1993

SEASON POINTS

Player, Team	Season	G	FG	3FG	FT	Pts.
Pete Maravich, Louisiana St.	1970	31	522	—	337	1,381
Elvin Hayes, Houston	1968	33	519	—	176	1,214
Frank Selvy, Furman	1954	29	427	—	355	1,209
Pete Maravich, Louisiana St.	1969	26	433	—	282	1,148
Pete Maravich, Louisiana St.	1968	26	432	—	274	1,138

Player, Team	Season	G	FG	3FG	FT	Pts.
Bo Kimble, Loyola (Cal.)	1990	32	404	92	231	1,131
Hersey Hawkins, Bradley	1988	31	377	87	284	1,125
Austin Carr, Notre Dame	1970	29	444	—	218	1,106
Austin Carr, Notre Dame	1971	29	430	—	241	1,101
Otis Birdsong, Houston	1977	36	452	—	186	1,090
Dwight Lamar, Southwestern La.	1972	29	429	—	196	1,054
Kevin Bradshaw, U.S. Int'l	1991	28	358	60	278	1,054
Hank Gathers, Loyola (Cal.)	1989	31	419	0	177	1,015
Oscar Robertson, Cincinnati	1960	30	369	—	273	1,011
Freeman Williams, Portland St.	1977	26	417	—	176	1,010
Billy McGill, Utah	1962	26	394	—	221	1,009
Rich Fuqua, Oral Roberts	1972	28	423	—	160	1,006

SEASON SCORING AVERAGE

Player, Team	Season	G	FG	3FG	FT	Pts.	Avg.
Pete Maravich, Louisiana St.	†1970	31	522	—	337	1,381	44.5
Pete Maravich, Louisiana St.	†1969	26	433	—	282	1,148	44.2
Pete Maravich, Louisiana St.	†1968	26	432	—	274	1,138	43.8
Frank Selvy, Furman	†1954	29	427	—	355	1,209	41.7
Johnny Neumann, Mississippi	†1971	23	366	—	191	923	40.1
Freeman Williams, Portland St.	†1977	26	417	—	176	1,010	38.8
Billy McGill, Utah	†1962	26	394	—	221	1,009	38.8
Calvin Murphy, Niagara	1968	24	337	—	242	916	38.2
Austin Carr, Notre Dame	1970	29	444	—	218	1,106	38.1
Austin Carr, Notre Dame	1971	29	430	—	241	1,101	38.0
Kevin Bradshaw, U.S. Int'l	†1991	28	358	60	278	1,054	37.6
Rick Barry, Miami (Fla.)	†1965	26	340	—	293	973	37.4
Elvin Hayes, Houston	1968	33	519	—	176	1,214	36.8
Marshall Rogers, Tex.-Pan American	†1976	25	361	—	197	919	36.8
Howard Komives, Bowling Green	†1964	23	292	—	260	844	36.7

† *National champion.*

SEASON FIELD-GOAL PERCENTAGE

(Based on qualifiers for annual championship)

Player, Team	Season	G	FG	FGA	Pct.
Steve Johnson, Oregon St.	†1981	28	235	315	74.6
Dwayne Davis, Florida	†1989	33	179	248	72.2
Keith Walker, Utica	†1985	27	154	216	71.3
Steve Johnson, Oregon St.	†1980	30	211	297	71.0
Oliver Miller, Arkansas	†1991	38	254	361	70.4
Alan Williams, Princeton	†1987	25	163	232	70.3
Mark McNamara, California	†1982	27	231	329	70.2
Warren Kidd, Middle Tenn. St.	1991	30	173	247	70.0
Pete Freeman, Akron	1991	28	175	250	70.0
Joe Senser, West Chester	†1977	25	130	186	69.9
Lee Campbell, Southwest Mo. St.	†1990	29	192	275	69.8
Stephen Scheffler, Purdue	1990	30	173	248	69.8
Lester James, St. Francis (N.Y.)	1991	29	149	215	69.3
Murray Brown, Florida St.	†1979	29	237	343	69.1
Joe Senser, West Chester	†1978	25	135	197	68.5

† *National champion.*

SEASON THREE-POINT FIELD GOALS MADE PER GAME

(Based on qualifiers for annual championship)

Player, Team	Season	G	3FG	Avg.
Darrin Fitzgerald, Butler	†1987	28	158	5.64
Timothy Pollard, Mississippi Val.	†1988	28	132	4.71
Dave Jamerson, Ohio	†1990	28	131	4.68
Sydney Grider, Southwestern La.	1990	29	131	4.52
Timothy Pollard, Mississippi Val.	†1989	28	124	4.43
Bobby Phills, Southern-B.R.	†1991	28	123	4.39
Mark Alberts, Akron	1990	28	122	4.36
Jeff Fryer, Loyola (Cal.)	1990	28	121	4.32
Sydney Grider, Southwestern La.	1989	29	122	4.21
Bernard Haslett, Southern Miss.	†1993	26	109	4.19

Player, Team	Season	G	3FG	Avg.
Stevin Smith, Arizona St.	1993	27	113	4.19
Mark Alberts, Akron	1993	26	107	4.12
Jeff Fryer, Loyola (Cal.)	1989	31	126	4.06
Doug Day, Radford	†1992	29	117	4.03
Ronnie Schmitz, Mo.-Kansas City	1991	29	116	4.00

† *National champion.*

SEASON THREE-POINT FIELD-GOAL PERCENTAGE

(Based on qualifiers for annual championship)

Player, Team	Season	G	3FG	3FGA	Pct.
Glenn Tropf, Holy Cross	†1988	29	52	82	63.4
Sean Wightman, Western Mich.	†1992	30	48	76	63.2
Keith Jennings, East Tenn. St.	†1991	33	84	142	59.2
Dave Calloway, Monmouth (N.J.)	†1989	28	48	82	58.5
Steve Kerr, Arizona	1988	38	114	199	57.3
Reginald Jones, Prairie View	†1987	28	64	112	57.1
Joel Tribelhorn, Colorado St.	1989	33	76	135	56.3
Mike Joseph, Bucknell	1988	28	65	116	56.0
Christian Laettner, Duke	1992	35	54	97	55.7
Reginald Jones, Prairie View	1988	27	85	155	54.8
Eric Rhodes, Stephen F. Austin	1987	30	58	106	54.7
Dave Orlandini, Princeton	1988	26	60	110	54.5
Mike Joseph, Bucknell	1989	31	62	115	53.9
John Bays, Towson St.	1989	29	71	132	53.8
Jeff Anderson, Kent	†1993	26	44	82	53.7

† *National champion.*

SEASON FREE-THROW PERCENTAGE

(Based on qualifiers for annual championship)

Player, Team	Season	G	FT	FTA	Pct.
Craig Collins, Penn St.	†1985	27	94	98	95.9
Rod Foster, UCLA	†1982	27	95	100	95.0
Carlos Gibson, Marshall	†1978	28	84	89	94.4
Jim Barton, Dartmouth	†1986	26	65	69	94.2
Jack Moore, Nebraska	1982	27	123	131	93.9
Rob Robbins, New Mexico	†1990	34	101	108	93.5
Tommy Boyer, Arkansas	†1962	23	125	134	93.3
Damon Goodwin, Dayton	1986	30	95	102	93.1
Brian Magid, Geo. Washington	†1980	26	79	85	92.9
Mike Joseph, Bucknell	1990	29	144	155	92.9
Steve Kaplan, Rutgers	†1970	23	102	110	92.7
Dave Hildahl, Portland St.	†1981	21	76	82	92.7
Greg Starrick, Southern Ill.	†1972	26	148	160	92.5
Steve Henson, Kansas St.	†1988	34	111	120	92.5
Randy Nesbit, Citadel	1980	27	74	80	92.5
Michael Smith, Brigham Young	†1989	29	160	173	92.5
Robert Smith, Nevada-Las Vegas	†1977	32	98	106	92.5

† *National champion.*

SEASON REBOUNDS

(Before 1973)

Player, Team	Ht.	Season	G	Reb.
Walt Dukes, Seton Hall	6-10	†1953	33	734
Leroy Wright, Pacific (Cal.)	6-8	†1959	26	652
Tom Gola, La Salle	6-6	†1954	30	652
Charlie Tyra, Louisville	6-8	†1956	29	645
Paul Silas, Creighton	6-7	†1964	29	631
Elvin Hayes, Houston	6-8	†1968	33	624
Artis Gilmore, Jacksonville	7-2	†1970	28	621
Tom Gola, La Salle	6-6	†1955	31	618
Ed Conlin, Fordham	6-5	1953	26	612
Art Quimby, Connecticut	6-5	1955	25	611
Bill Russell, San Francisco	6-9	1956	29	609
Jim Ware, Oklahoma City	6-8	†1966	29	607
Joe Holup, Geo. Washington	6-6	1956	26	604
Artis Gilmore, Jacksonville	7-2	†1971	26	603
Elton Tuttle, Creighton	6-5	1954	30	601

† *National champion.*

SEASON REBOUNDS
(Since 1973)

Player, Team	Ht.	Season	G	Reb.
Marvin Barnes, Providence	6-9	†1974	32	597
Marvin Barnes, Providence	6-9	†1973	30	571
Kermit Washington, American	6-8	1973	25	511
Bill Walton, UCLA	6-11	1973	30	506
Larry Bird, Indiana St.	6-9	†1979	34	505
Larry Kenon, Memphis St.	6-9	†1973	30	501
Akeem Olajuwon, Houston	7-0	†1984	37	500
Glenn Mosley, Seton Hall	6-8	†1977	29	473
Popeye Jones, Murray St.	6-8	†1991	33	469
Pete Padgett, Nevada	6-8	†1973	26	462
Xavier McDaniel, Wichita St.	6-8	†1985	31	460
Larry Johnson, Nevada-Las Vegas	6-7	†1990	40	457
Anthony Bonner, St. Louis	6-8	1990	33	456
Bill Cartwright, San Francisco	7-1	1979	29	455
David Robinson, Navy	6-11	†1986	35	455

† *National champion.*

SEASON REBOUND AVERAGE
(Before 1973)

Player, Team	Ht.	Season	G	Reb.	Avg.
Charlie Slack, Marshall	6-5	†1955	21	538	25.6
Leroy Wright, Pacific (Cal.)	6-8	†1959	26	652	25.1
Art Quimby, Connecticut	6-5	1955	25	611	24.4
Charlie Slack, Marshall	6-5	1956	22	520	23.6
Ed Conlin, Fordham	6-5	†1953	26	612	23.5
Joe Holup, Geo. Washington	6-6	††1956	26	604	23.2
Artis Gilmore, Jacksonville	7-2	†1971	26	603	23.2
Art Quimby, Connecticut	6-5	†1954	26	588	22.6
Paul Silas, Creighton	6-7	1962	25	563	22.5
Leroy Wright, Pacific (Cal.)	6-8	†1960	17	380	22.4
Walt Dukes, Seton Hall	6-10	1953	33	734	22.2
Charlie Tyra, Louisville	6-8	1956	29	645	22.2
Charlie Slack, Marshall	6-5	1954	21	466	22.2
Artis Gilmore, Jacksonville	7-2	†1970	28	621	22.2
Bill Chambers, William & Mary	6-4	1953	22	480	21.8
Bob Pelkinton, Xavier (Ohio)	6-7	†1964	26	567	21.8
Dick Cunningham, Murray St.,	6-10	†1967	22	479	21.8
Paul Silas, Creighton	6-7	1964	29	631	21.8

† *National champion.* †† *From 1956 through 1962, individual champions were determined by percentage of all recoveries; Holup led in percentage of recoveries and Slack led in average in 1956.*

SEASON REBOUND AVERAGE
(Since 1973)

Player, Team	Ht.	Season	G	Reb.	Avg.
Kermit Washington, American	6-8	†1973	25	511	20.4
Marvin Barnes, Providence	6-9	1973	30	571	19.0
Marvin Barnes, Providence	6-9	†1974	32	597	18.7
Pete Padgett, Nevada	6-8	1973	26	462	17.8
Jim Bradley, Northern Ill.	6-10	1973	24	426	17.8
Bill Walton, UCLA	6-11	1973	30	506	16.9
Larry Kenon, Memphis St.	6-9	1973	30	501	16.7
Glenn Mosley, Seton Hall	6-8	†1977	29	473	16.3
John Irving, Hofstra	6-9	1977	27	440	16.3
Carlos McCullough, Tex.-Pan American	6-7	1974	22	358	16.3
Brad Robinson, Kent	6-7	1974	26	423	16.3
Monti Davis, Tennessee St.	6-7	†1979	26	421	16.2
Sam Pellom, Buffalo	6-8	†1976	26	420	16.2
Robert Elmore, Wichita St.	6-10	1977	28	441	15.8
Bill Cartwright, San Francisco	7-1	1979	29	455	15.7

† *National champion.*

SEASON ASSISTS

Player, Team	Season	G	Ast.
Mark Wade, Nevada-Las Vegas	†1987	38	406
Avery Johnson, Southern-B.R.	†1988	30	399
Anthony Manuel, Bradley	1988	31	373
Avery Johnson, Southern-B.R.	1987	31	333
Mark Jackson, St. John's (N.Y.)	†1986	32	328
Sherman Douglas, Syracuse	†1989	38	326
Greg Anthony, Nevada-Las Vegas	†1991	35	310
Sam Crawford, New Mexico St.	†1993	34	310
Reid Gettys, Houston	†1984	37	309
Carl Golston, Loyola (Ill.)	†1985	33	305
Craig Neal, Georgia Tech	1988	32	303
Keith Jennings, East Tenn. St.	1991	33	301
Chris Corchiani, North Caro. St.	1991	31	299
Keith Jennings, East Tenn. St.	†1990	34	297
Howard Evans, Temple	1988	34	294

† *National champion.*

SEASON ASSIST AVERAGE

Player, Team	Season	G	Ast.	Avg.
Avery Johnson, Southern-B.R.	†1988	30	399	13.3
Anthony Manuel, Bradley	1988	31	373	12.0
Avery Johnson, Southern-B.R.	†1987	31	333	10.7
Mark Wade, Nevada-Las Vegas	1987	38	406	10.7
Glenn Williams, Holy Cross	†1989	28	278	9.9
Chris Corchiani, North Caro. St.	†1991	31	299	9.6
Tony Fairley, Charleston So.	1987	28	270	9.6
Tyrone Bogues, Wake Forest	1987	29	276	9.5
Ron Weingard, Hofstra	†1985	24	228	9.5
Craig Neal, Georgia Tech	1988	32	303	9.5
Craig Lathan, Ill.-Chicago	†1984	29	274	9.4
Andre Van Drost, Wagner	1987	28	260	9.3
Todd Lehmann, Drexel	†1990	28	260	9.3
Danny Tirado, Jacksonville	1991	28	259	9.3
Carl Golston, Loyola (Ill.)	1985	33	305	9.2

† *National champion.*

SEASON BLOCKED SHOTS

Player, Team	Season	G	Blk.
David Robinson, Navy	†1986	35	207
Shawn Bradley, Brigham Young	†1991	34	177
Alonzo Mourning, Georgetown	†1989	34	169
Alonzo Mourning, Georgetown	†1992	32	160
Shaquille O'Neal, Louisiana St.	1992	30	157
Dikembe Mutombo, Georgetown	1991	32	151
David Robinson, Navy	†1987	32	144
Cedric Lewis, Maryland	1991	28	143
Shaquille O'Neal, Louisiana St.	1991	28	140
Kevin Roberson, Vermont	1992	28	139
Alan Ogg, Ala.-Birmingham	1989	34	129
Dikembe Mutombo, Georgetown	†1990	31	128
Derrick Coleman, Syracuse	1989	37	127
Duane Causwell, Temple	1989	30	124
Kenny Green, Rhode Island	1990	26	124
Theo Ratliff, Wyoming	†1993	28	124
Sharone Wright, Clemson	†1993	30	124

† *National champion.*

SEASON BLOCKED-SHOT AVERAGE

Player, Team	Season	G	Blk.	Avg.
David Robinson, Navy	†1986	35	207	5.91
Shaquille O'Neal, Louisiana St.	†1992	30	157	5.23
Shawn Bradley, Brigham Young	†1991	34	177	5.21
Cedric Lewis, Maryland	1991	28	143	5.11
Shaquille O'Neal, Louisiana St.	1991	28	140	5.00

Player, Team	Season	G	Blk.	Avg.
Alonzo Mourning, Georgetown	1992	32	160	5.00
Alonzo Mourning, Georgetown	†1989	34	169	4.97
Kevin Roberson, Vermont	1992	28	139	4.96
Kenny Green, Rhode Island	†1990	26	124	4.77
Dikembe Mutombo, Georgetown	1991	32	151	4.72
David Robinson, Navy	†1987	32	144	4.50
Theo Ratliff, Wyoming	†1993	28	124	4.43
Derrick Lewis, Maryland	1987	26	114	4.38
Duane Causwell, Temple	1989	30	124	4.13
Dikembe Mutombo, Georgetown	1990	31	128	4.13
Sharone Wright, Clemson	1993	30	124	4.13

† *National champion.*

SEASON STEALS

Player, Team	Season	G	Stl.
Mookie Blaylock, Oklahoma	†1988	39	150
Aldwin Ware, Florida A&M	1988	29	142
Darron Brittman, Chicago St.	†1986	28	139
Nadav Henefeld, Connecticut	†1990	37	138
Mookie Blaylock, Oklahoma	†1989	35	131
Ronn McMahon, Eastern Wash.	1990	29	130
Marty Johnson, Towson St.	1988	30	124
Jim Paguaga, St. Francis (N.Y.)	1986	28	120
Tony Fairley, Charleston So.	†1987	28	114
Scott Burrell, Connecticut	†1991	31	112
Kenny Robertson, Cleveland St.	1989	28	111
Lance Blanks, Texas	1989	34	111
Eric Murdock, Providence	1991	32	111
Jason Kidd, California	†1993	29	110
Robert Dowdell, Coastal Caro.	1990	29	109
Keith Jennings, East Tenn. St.	1991	33	109
Mark Woods, Wright St.	1993	30	109

† *National champion.*

SEASON STEAL AVERAGE

Player, Team	Season	G	Stl.	Avg.
Darron Brittman, Chicago St.	†1986	28	139	4.96
Aldwin Ware, Florida A&M	†1988	29	142	4.90
Ronn McMahon, Eastern Wash.	†1990	29	130	4.48
Jim Paguaga, St. Francis (N.Y.)	1986	28	120	4.29
Marty Johnson, Towson St.	1988	30	124	4.13
Tony Fairley, Charleston So.	†1987	28	114	4.07
Kenny Robertson, Cleveland St.	†1989	28	111	3.96
Mookie Blaylock, Oklahoma	1988	39	150	3.85
Jason Kidd, California	†1993	29	110	3.79
Jay Goodman, Utah St.	1993	27	102	3.78
Robert Dowdell, Coastal Caro.	1990	29	109	3.76
Mookie Blaylock, Oklahoma	1989	35	131	3.74
Nadav Henefeld, Connecticut	1990	37	138	3.73
Van Usher, Tennessee Tech	†1991	28	104	3.71
Mark Woods, Wright St.	1993	30	109	3.63

† *National champion.*

TOP SEASONAL PERFORMANCES BY CLASS

SCORING AVERAGE

Class	Player, Team	Year	G	FG	3FG	FT	Pts.	Avg.
Senior	Pete Maravich, Louisiana St.	1970	31	522	—	337	1,381	44.5
Junior	Pete Maravich, Louisiana St.	1969	26	433	—	282	1,148	44.2
Sophomore	Pete Maravich, Louisiana St.	1968	26	432	—	274	1,138	43.8
Freshman	Chris Jackson, Louisiana St.	1989	32	359	84	163	965	30.2

FIELD-GOAL PERCENTAGE

Class	Player, Team	Year	G	FG	FGA	Pct.
Senior	Steve Johnson, Oregon St.	1981	28	235	315	74.6
Junior	Steve Johnson, Oregon St.	1980	30	211	297	71.0
Sophomore	Dwayne Davis, Florida	1989	33	179	248	72.2
Freshman	Sidney Moncrief, Arkansas	1976	28	149	224	66.5

THREE-POINT FIELD GOALS MADE PER GAME

Class	Player, Team	Year	G	3FG	Avg.
Senior	Darrin Fitzgerald, Butler	1987	28	158	5.64
Junior	Timothy Pollard, Mississippi Val.	1988	28	132	4.71
Sophomore	Mark Alberts, Akron	1990	28	122	4.36
Freshman	Keith Veney, Lamar	1993	27	106	3.93

THREE-POINT FIELD-GOAL PERCENTAGE

Class	Player, Team	Year	G	3FG	3FGA	Pct.
Senior	Keith Jennings, East Tenn. St.	1991	33	84	142	59.2
Junior	Glenn Tropf, Holy Cross	1988	29	52	82	63.4
Sophomore	Dave Calloway, Monmouth (N.J.)	1989	28	48	82	58.5
Freshman	Jay Edwards, Indiana	1988	23	59	110	53.6

FREE-THROW PERCENTAGE

Class	Player, Team	Year	G	FT	FTA	Pct.
Senior	Craig Collins, Penn St.	1985	27	94	98	95.9
Junior	Rod Foster, UCLA	1982	27	95	100	95.0
Sophomore	Steve Kaplan, Rutgers	1970	23	102	110	92.7
Freshman	Jim Barton, Dartmouth	1986	26	65	69	94.2

REBOUND AVERAGE

Class	Player, Team	Year	G	Reb.	Avg.
Senior	Art Quimby, Connecticut	1955	25	611	24.4
Junior	Charlie Slack, Marshall	1955	21	538	25.6
Sophomore	Ed Conlin, Fordham	1953	26	612	23.5
Freshman	Pete Padgett, Nevada	1973	26	462	17.8

ASSIST AVERAGE

Class	Player, Team	Year	G	Ast.	Avg.
Senior	Avery Johnson, Southern-B.R.	1988	30	399	13.30
Junior	Anthony Manuel, Bradley	1988	31	373	12.03
Sophomore	Anthony Manuel, Bradley	1987	27	237	8.78
Freshman	Orlando Smart, San Francisco	1991	29	237	8.17

BLOCKED-SHOT AVERAGE

Class	Player, Team	Year	G	Blk.	Avg.
Senior	Cedric Lewis, Maryland	1991	28	143	5.11
Junior	David Robinson, Navy	1986	35	207	5.91
Sophomore	Shaquille O'Neal, Louisiana St.	1991	28	140	5.00
Freshman	Shawn Bradley, Brigham Young	1991	34	177	5.21

STEAL AVERAGE

Class	Player, Team	Year	G	Stl.	Avg.
Senior	Darron Brittman, Chicago St.	1986	28	139	4.96
Junior	Kenny Robertson, Cleveland St.	1989	28	111	3.96
Sophomore	Scott Burrell, Connecticut	1991	31	112	3.61
Freshman	Jason Kidd, California	1993	29	110	3.79

SEASON POINTS BY A FRESHMAN

Player, Team	Season	G	FG	3FG	FT	Pts.
Chris Jackson, Louisiana St.	1989	32	359	84	163	965
James Williams, Austin Peay	1973	29	360	—	134	854
Wayman Tisdale, Oklahoma	1983	33	338	—	134	810
Alphonso Ford, Mississippi Val.	1990	27	289	104	126	808
Mark Aguirre, DePaul	1979	32	302	—	163	767

SEASON SCORING AVERAGE BY A FRESHMAN

Player, Team	Season	G	FG	3FG	FT	Pts.	Avg.
Chris Jackson, Louisiana St.	1989	32	359	84	163	965	30.2
Alphonso Ford, Mississippi Val.	1990	27	289	104	126	808	29.9
James Williams, Austin Peay	1973	29	360	—	134	854	29.4
Harry Kelly, Texas Southern	1980	26	313	—	127	753	29.0
Bernard King, Tennessee	1975	25	273	—	115	661	26.4

SEASON FIELD-GOAL PERCENTAGE BY A FRESHMAN

Player, Team	Season	G	FG	FGA	Pct.
Sidney Moncrief, Arkansas	1976	28	149	224	66.5
Gary Trent, Ohio	1993	27	194	298	65.1
Ed Pinckney, Villanova	1982	32	169	264	64.0
Jimmy Lunsford, Alabama St.	1993	22	142	223	63.7
Cedric Robinson, Nicholls St.	1983	24	146	231	63.2

SEASON THREE-POINT FIELD-GOAL PERCENTAGE BY A FRESHMAN

Player, Team	Season	G	3FG	3FGA	Pct.
Jay Edwards, Indiana	1988	23	59	110	53.6
Ross Richardson, Loyola (Cal.)	1991	25	61	116	52.6
Lance Barker, Valparaiso	1992	26	61	117	52.1
Ed Peterson, Yale	1989	28	53	104	51.0
Willie Brand, Texas-Arlington	1988	29	65	128	50.8

SEASON THREE-POINT FIELD GOALS MADE BY A FRESHMAN

Player, Team	Season	G	3FG	Avg.
Keith Veney, Lamar	1993	27	106	3.93
Alphonso Ford, Mississippi Val.	1990	27	104	3.85
Tony Ross, San Diego St.	1987	28	104	3.71
Ronnie Schmitz, Mo.-Kansas City	1990	28	90	3.21
Eddie Benton, Vermont	1993	26	82	3.15

SEASON FREE-THROW PERCENTAGE BY A FRESHMAN

Player, Team	Season	G	FT	FTA	Pct.
Jim Barton, Dartmouth	1986	26	65	69	94.2
Steve Alford, Indiana	1984	31	137	150	91.3
Jay Edwards, Indiana	1988	23	69	76	90.8
LaBradford Smith, Louisville	1988	35	143	158	90.5
Mike Waitkus, Brown	1983	26	97	108	89.8

SEASON REBOUNDS BY A FRESHMAN

Player, Team	Season	G	Reb.
Pete Padgett, Nevada	1973	26	462
Kenny Miller, Loyola (Ill.)	1988	29	395
Shaquille O'Neal, Louisiana St.	1990	32	385
Ralph Sampson, Virginia	1980	34	381
Michael Cage, San Diego St.	1981	27	355

SEASON REBOUND AVERAGE BY A FRESHMAN

Player, Team	Season	G	Reb.	Avg.
Pete Padgett, Nevada	1973	26	462	17.8
Glenn Mosley, Seton Hall	1974	21	299	14.2
Ira Terrell, Southern Methodist	1973	25	352	14.1
Kenny Miller, Loyola (Ill.)	1988	29	395	13.6
Bob Stephens, Drexel	1976	23	307	13.3

SEASON ASSISTS BY A FRESHMAN

Player, Team	Season	G	Ast.
Bobby Hurley, Duke	1990	38	288
Kenny Anderson, Georgia Tech	1990	35	285
Andre LaFleur, Northeastern	1984	32	252
Orlando Smart, San Francisco	1991	29	237
Chris Corchiani, North Caro. St.	1988	32	235

SEASON ASSIST AVERAGE BY A FRESHMAN

Player, Team	Season	G	Ast.	Avg.
Orlando Smart, San Francisco	1991	29	237	8.17
Kenny Anderson, Georgia Tech	1990	35	285	8.14
Taurence Chisholm, Delaware	1985	28	224	8.00
Andre LaFleur, Northeastern	1984	32	252	7.88
Marc Brown, Siena	1988	29	222	7.66
Jason Kidd, California	1993	29	222	7.66

SEASON BLOCKED SHOTS BY A FRESHMAN

Player, Team	Season	G	Blk.
Shawn Bradley, Brigham Young	1991	34	177
Alonzo Mourning, Georgetown	1989	34	169
Shaquille O'Neal, Louisiana St.	1990	32	115
Dwayne Schintzius, Florida	1987	34	96
Pervis Ellison, Louisville	1986	39	92
Jim McIlvaine, Marquette	1991	28	92

SEASON BLOCKED-SHOT AVERAGE BY A FRESHMAN

Player, Team	Season	G	Blk.	Avg.
Shawn Bradley, Brigham Young	1991	34	177	5.21
Alonzo Mourning, Georgetown	1989	34	169	4.97
Shaquille O'Neal, Louisiana St.	1990	32	115	3.59
Jim McIlvaine, Marquette	1991	28	92	3.29
Derek Stewart, Augusta	1990	28	82	2.93

SEASON STEALS BY A FRESHMAN

Player, Team	Season	G	Stl.
Nadav Henefeld, Connecticut	1990	37	138
Jason Kidd, California	1993	29	110
Eric Murdock, Providence	1988	28	90
Pat Baldwin, Northwestern	1991	28	90
Clarence Ceasar, Louisiana St.	1992	31	90

SEASON STEAL AVERAGE BY A FRESHMAN

Player, Team	Season	G	Stl.	Avg.
Jason Kidd, California	1993	29	110	3.79
Nadav Henefeld, Connecticut	1990	37	138	3.73
Eric Murdock, Providence	1988	28	90	3.21
Pat Baldwin, Northwestern	1991	28	90	3.21
Jeff Myers, St. Francis (N.Y.)	1993	26	81	3.12

CAREER POINTS

Player, Team	Ht.	Last Year	Yrs.	G	FG	3FG#	FT	Pts.
Pete Maravich, Louisiana St.	6-5	1970	3	83	1,387	—	893	3,667
Freeman Williams, Portland St.	6-4	1978	4	106	1,369	—	511	3,249
Lionel Simmons, La Salle	6-7	1990	4	131	1,244	56	673	3,217
Alphonso Ford, Mississippi Val.	6-2	1993	4	109	1,121	333	590	3,165
Harry Kelly, Texas Southern	6-7	1983	4	110	1,234	—	598	3,066
Hersey Hawkins, Bradley	6-3	1988	4	125	1,100	118	690	3,008
Oscar Robertson, Cincinnati	6-5	1960	3	88	1,052	—	869	2,973
Danny Manning, Kansas	6-10	1988	4	147	1,216	10	509	2,951
Alfredrick Hughes, Loyola (Ill.)	6-5	1985	4	120	1,226	—	462	2,914
Elvin Hayes, Houston	6-8	1968	3	93	1,215	—	454	2,884
Larry Bird, Indiana St.	6-9	1979	3	94	1,154	—	542	2,850
Otis Birdsong, Houston	6-4	1977	4	116	1,176	—	480	2,832
Kevin Bradshaw, Bethune-Cookman & U.S. Int'l	6-6	1991	4	111	1,027	132	618	2,804
Allan Houston, Tennessee	6-5	1993	4	128	902	346	651	2,801
Hank Gathers, Southern Cal & Loyola (Cal.)	6-7	1990	4	117	1,127	0	469	2,723
Reggie Lewis, Northeastern	6-7	1987	4	122	1,043	30(1)	592	2,708
Daren Queenan, Lehigh	6-5	1988	4	118	1,024	29	626	2,703
Byron Larkin, Xavier (Ohio)	6-3	1988	4	121	1,022	51	601	2,696
David Robinson, Navy	7-1	1987	4	127	1,032	1	604	2,669
Wayman Tisdale, Oklahoma	6-9	1985	3	104	1,077	—	507	2,661
Michael Brooks, La Salle	6-7	1980	4	114	1,064	—	500	2,628
Calbert Cheaney, Indiana	6-6	1993	4	132	1,018	148	429	2,613
Mark Macon, Temple	6-5	1991	4	126	980	246	403	2,609
Don MacLean, UCLA	6-10	1992	4	127	943	11	711	2,608
Joe Dumars, McNeese St.	6-3	1985	4	116	941	(5)	723	2,605
Terrance Bailey, Wagner	6-2	1987	4	110	985	42	579	2,591
Dickie Hemric, Wake Forest	6-6	1955	4	104	841	—	905	2,587
Calvin Natt, Northeast La.	6-5	1979	4	108	1,017	—	547	2,581
Derrick Chievous, Missouri	6-7	1988	4	130	893	30	764	2,580
Skip Henderson, Marshall	6-2	1988	4	125	1,000	133	441	2,574
Austin Carr, Notre Dame	6-3	1971	3	74	1,017	—	526	2,560
Sean Elliott, Arizona	6-8	1989	4	133	896	140	623	2,555
Rodney Monroe, North Caro. St.	6-3	1991	4	124	885	322	459	2,551
Calvin Murphy, Niagara	5-10	1970	3	77	947	—	654	2,548
Frank Selvy, Furman	6-3	1954	3	78	922	—	694	2,538
Johnny Dawkins, Duke	6-2	1986	4	133	1,026	(19)	485	2,537
Willie Jackson, Centenary	6-6	1984	4	114	995	(18)	545	2,535
Steve Rogers, Alabama St.	6-5	1992	4	113	817	187	713	2,534
Steve Burtt, Iona	6-2	1984	4	121	1,003	—	528	2,534
Joe Jakubick, Akron	6-5	1984	4	108	973	(53)	584	2,530

Player, Team	Ht.	Last Year	Yrs.	G	FG	3FG#	FT	Pts.
Andrew Toney, Southwestern La.	6-3	1980	4	107	996	—	534	2,526
Ron Perry, Holy Cross	6-2	1980	4	109	922	—	680	2,524
Mike Olliver, Lamar	6-1	1981	4	122	1,130	—	258	2,518
Bryant Stith, Virginia	6-5	1992	4	131	856	114	690	2,516
Bill Bradley, Princeton	6-5	1965	3	83	856	—	791	2,503
Jeff Grayer, Iowa St.	6-5	1988	4	125	974	27	527	2,502
Elgin Baylor, Col. Idaho & Seattle	6-6	1958	3	80	956	—	588	2,500

 # Listed is the number of three-pointers scored since it became the national rule in 1987; the number in the parenthesis is number scored prior to 1987—these counted as three points in the game but counted as two-pointers in the national rankings. The three-pointers in the parenthesis are not included in total points.

Note: Dwight Lamar of Southwestern Louisiana scored 3,493 points in 112 games (1973), and Rich Fuqua of Oral Roberts scored 3,004 points in 111 games (1973); however, each played only two seasons in Division I. Also, Gerald Glass of Mississippi scored 2,813 points in 124 games (1990); however, he played his first two years at Division II Delta State.

2,000-POINT SCORERS

A total of 310 players in Division I history have scored at least 2,000 points over their careers. The first was Jim Lacy, Loyola (Md.), with 2,154 over four seasons ending with 1949. The first to reach 2,000 in a three-season career was Furman's Frank Selvy, 2,538 through 1954. The 310 come from 178 different colleges. Duke leads with seven 2,000-pointers: Jim Spanarkel (last season was 1979), Mike Gminski (1980), Gene Banks (1981), Mark Alarie (1986), Johnny Dawkins (1986), Danny Ferry (1989) and Christian Laettner (1992). North Carolina and Tennessee are next with five apiece.

CAREER SCORING AVERAGE

Player, Team	Last Year	Yrs.	G	FG	3FG	FT	Pts.	Avg.
Pete Maravich, Louisiana St.	1968	3	83	1,387	—	893	3,667	44.2
Austin Carr, Notre Dame	1971	3	74	1,017	—	526	2,560	34.6
Oscar Robertson, Cincinnati	1960	3	88	1,052	—	869	2,973	33.8
Calvin Murphy, Niagara	1970	3	77	947	—	654	2,548	33.1
Dwight Lamar, Southwestern La.†	1973	2	57	768	—	326	1,862	32.7
Frank Selvy, Furman	1954	3	78	922	—	694	2,538	32.5
Rick Mount, Purdue	1970	3	72	910	—	503	2,323	32.3
Darrell Floyd, Furman	1956	3	71	868	—	545	2,281	32.1
Nick Werkman, Seton Hall	1964	3	71	812	—	649	2,273	32.0
Willie Humes, Idaho St.	1971	2	48	565	—	380	1,510	31.5
William Averitt, Pepperdine	1973	2	49	615	—	311	1,541	31.4
Elgin Baylor, Col. Idaho & Seattle	1958	3	80	956	—	588	2,500	31.3
Elvin Hayes, Houston	1968	3	93	1,215	—	454	2,884	31.0
Freeman Williams, Portland St.	1978	4	106	1,369	—	511	3,249	30.7
Larry Bird, Indiana St.	1979	3	94	1,154	—	542	2,850	30.3
Bill Bradley, Princeton	1965	3	83	856	—	791	2,503	30.2
Rich Fuqua, Oral Roberts†	1973	2	54	692	—	233	1,617	29.9
Wilt Chamberlain, Kansas	1958	2	48	503	—	427	1,433	29.9
Rick Barry, Miami (Fla.)	1965	3	77	816	—	666	2,298	29.8
Doug Collins, Illinois St.	1973	3	77	894	—	452	2,240	29.1
Alphonso Ford, Mississippi Val.	1993	4	109	1,121	333	590	3,165	29.0
Chris Jackson, Louisiana St.	1990	2	64	664	172	354	1,854	29.0
Dave Schellhase, Purdue	1966	3	74	746	—	582	2,074	28.8
Dick Wilkinson, Virginia	1955	3	78	783	—	665	2,233	28.6
James Williams, Austin Peay	1974	2	54	632	—	277	1,541	28.5

† Each played two years of non-Division I (Lamar—four years, 3,493 points and 31.2 average; Fuqua—four years, 3,004 points and 27.1 average).

CAREER FIELD-GOAL PERCENTAGE

(Minimum 400 field goals made)

Player, Team	Ht.	Last Year	Yrs.	G	FG	FGA	Pct.
Stephen Scheffler, Purdue	6-9	1990	4	110	408	596	68.5
Steve Johnson, Oregon St.	6-10	1981	4	116	828	1,222	67.8
Murray Brown, Florida St.	6-8	1980	4	106	566	847	66.8
Lee Campbell, Southwest Mo. St.	6-7	1990	3	88	411	618	66.5
Warren Kidd, Middle Tenn. St.	6-9	1993	3	83	496	747	66.4
Joe Senser, West Chester	6-5	1979	4	96	476	719	66.2
Kevin Magee, UC Irvine	6-8	1982	2	56	552	841	65.6
Orlando Phillips, Pepperdine	6-7	1983	2	58	404	618	65.4
Bill Walton, UCLA	6-11	1974	3	87	747	1,147	65.1
William Herndon, Massachusetts	6-3	1992	4	100	472	728	64.8

Player, Team	Ht.	Last Year	Yrs.	G	FG	FGA	Pct.
Larry Stewart, Coppin St.	6-8	1991	3	91	676	1,046	64.6
Larry Johnson, Nevada-Las Vegas	6-7	1991	2	75	612	952	64.3
Dwayne Davis, Florida	6-7	1991	4	124	572	892	64.1
Lew Alcindor, UCLA	7-2	1969	3	88	943	1,476	63.9
Akeem Olajuwon, Houston	7-0	1984	3	100	532	833	63.9
Oliver Miller, Arkansas	6-9	1992	4	137	680	1,069	63.6
Mike Coleman, Liberty	6-7	1992	4	105	421	663	63.5
Jeff Ruland, Iona	6-10	1980	4	89	717	1,130	63.5
Mark McNamara, California	6-10	1982	4	107	709	1,119	63.4
Marro Hawkins, Centenary	6-7	1990	4	115	459	725	63.3
Cherokee Rhone, Centenary	6-8	1982	3	63	421	667	63.1
Brian Hill, Evansville	6-7	1990	4	120	424	672	63.1
Bobby Lee Hurt, Alabama	6-9	1985	4	126	646	1,024	63.1
Keith Walker, Utica	6-5	1985	4	99	429	681	63.0
Felton Spencer, Louisville	7-0	1990	4	134	409	651	62.8
Riley Smith, Idaho	6-8	1990	2	62	455	725	62.8

CAREER THREE-POINT FIELD GOALS MADE

Player, Team	Ht.	Last Year	Yrs.	G	3FG
Doug Day, Radford	6-1	1993	4	117	401
Ronnie Schmitz, Mo.-Kansas City	6-3	1993	4	112	378
Mark Alberts, Akron	6-1	1993	4	107	375
Jeff Fryer, Loyola (Cal.)	6-2	1990	4	112	363
Dennis Scott, Georgia Tech	6-8	1990	3	99	351
Allan Houston, Tennessee	6-5	1993	4	128	346
Alphonso Ford, Mississippi Val.	6-2	1993	4	109	333
Andy Kennedy, North Caro. St. & Ala.-Birmingham	6-8	1991	4	121	330
Rodney Monroe, North Caro. St.	6-3	1991	4	124	322
Terry Dehere, Seton Hall	6-3	1993	4	128	315
Henry Williams, N.C.-Charlotte	6-2	1992	4	118	308
Lindsey Hunter Jackson St.	6-2	1993	4	120	297
Mark Mocnik, Campbell	6-6	1993	4	116	295
Dana Barros, Boston College	5-11	1989	3	91	291
Jack Hurd, La Salle	6-6	1992	4	124	291
Willie Brand, Texas-Arlington	6-1	1991	4	113	290
Tony Bennett, Wis.-Green Bay	6-0	1992	4	118	290
Scott Draud, Vanderbilt	6-2	1991	4	130	288
Tony Petrarca, Duquesne	6-2	1991	5	120	287
Raymond Dudley, Air Force	6-0	1990	4	109	285
Todd Lehmann, Drexel	5-11	1990	4	112	285
Brent Price, South Caro. & Oklahoma	6-0	1992	4	124	284
Anderson Hunt, Nevada-Las Vegas	6-2	1991	3	109	283
Bobby Phills, Southern-B.R.	6-4	1991	4	113	282
Randy Woods, La Salle	6-0	1992	3	88	278

CAREER THREE-POINT FIELD GOALS MADE PER GAME

(Minimum 200 three-point field goals made)

Player, Team	Ht.	Last Year	Yrs.	G	3FG	Avg.
Timothy Pollard, Mississippi Val.	6-3	1989	2	56	256	4.57
Sydney Grider, Southwestern La.	6-3	1990	2	58	253	4.36
Dave Mooney, Coastal Caro.	6-4	1988	2	56	202	3.61
Dennis Scott, Georgia Tech	6-8	1990	3	99	351	3.55
Mark Alberts, Akron	6-1	1993	4	107	375	3.50
Doug Day, Radford	6-1	1993	4	117	401	3.43
Ronnie Schmitz, Mo.-Kansas City	6-3	1993	4	112	378	3.38
Jeff Fryer, Loyola (Cal.)	6-2	1990	4	112	363	3.24
Dana Barros, Boston College	5-11	1989	3	91	291	3.20
Tony Ross, San Diego St.	6-3	1989	3	85	270	3.18
Randy Woods, La Salle	6-0	1992	3	88	278	3.16
Wally Lancaster, Virginia Tech	6-5	1989	3	82	257	3.13
Jim Barton, Dartmouth	6-4	1989	3	78	242	3.10
Alphonso Ford, Mississippi Val.	6-2	1993	4	109	333	3.06
Terry Brown, Kansas	6-2	1991	2	70	200	2.86
Scott Haffner, Evansville	6-4	1989	3	87	245	2.82
Gerald Paddio, Nevada-Las Vegas	6-7	1988	2	73	205	2.81
Andy Kennedy, North Caro. St. & Ala.-Birmingham	6-8	1991	4	121	330	2.73
Allan Houston, Tennessee	6-5	1993	4	128	346	2.70
Marc Rybczyk, Central Conn. St.	6-1	1993	4	89	235	2.64

Player, Team	Ht.	Last Year	Yrs.	G	3FG	Avg.
Raymond Dudley, Air Force	6-0	1990	4	109	285	2.61
Henry Williams, N.C.-Charlotte	6-2	1992	4	118	308	2.61
Rodney Monroe, North Caro. St.	6-3	1991	4	124	322	2.60
Michael Strickland, Texas Christian	6-5	1992	3	90	231	2.57
Willie Brand, Texas-Arlington	6-1	1991	4	113	290	2.57

CAREER THREE-POINT FIELD-GOAL PERCENTAGE

(Minimum 200 three-point field goals made)

Player, Team	Ht.	Last Year	Yrs.	G	3FG	3FGA	Pct.
Tony Bennett, Wis.-Green Bay	6-0	1992	4	118	290	584	49.7
Keith Jennings, East Tenn. St.	5-7	1991	4	127	223	452	49.3
Kirk Manns, Michigan St.	6-1	1990	4	120	212	446	47.5
Tim Locum, Wisconsin	6-4	1991	4	118	227	446	47.2
David Olson, Eastern Ill.	6-4	1992	4	111	262	562	46.6
Sean Jackson, Ohio & Princeton	5-11	1992	4	104	243	528	46.0
Barry Booker, Vanderbilt	6-3	1989	3	98	246	535	46.0
Kevin Booth, Mt. St. Mary's (Md.)	6-0	1993	5	110	265	577	45.9
Dave Calloway, Monmouth (N.J.)	6-3	1991	4	115	260	567	45.9
Tony Ross, San Diego St.	6-3	1992	3	85	270	589	45.8
Jason Matthews, Pittsburgh	6-3	1991	4	123	259	567	45.7
Jim Barton, Dartmouth	6-4	1989	3	78	242	532	45.5
Carlton Becton, North Caro. A&T	6-6	1989	3	84	209	462	45.2
Steve Henson, Kansas St.	6-1	1990	4	127	240	537	44.7
Jeff McCool, New Mexico St.	6-5	1989	3	92	201	450	44.7
Mark Alberts, Akron	6-1	1993	4	107	375	853	44.0
Andy Kennedy, North Caro. St. & Ala.-Birmingham	6-8	1991	4	121	330	752	43.9
Scott Draud, Vanderbilt	6-2	1991	4	130	288	657	43.8
Willie Brand, Texas-Arlington	6-1	1991	4	113	290	665	43.6
Rodney Monroe, North Caro. St.	6-3	1991	4	124	322	739	43.6
Craig Davis, Pepperdine	6-4	1990	4	121	274	629	43.6
Mark Daly, Boston U.	6-3	1992	4	110	202	465	43.4
Scott Shepherd, Robert Morris	6-3	1991	3	88	207	477	43.4
Davor Marcelic, Southern Utah	6-7	1992	4	112	226	521	43.4
Norm Grevey, Dayton	6-3	1991	4	113	208	481	43.2
Dana Barros, Boston College	5-11	1989	3	91	291	674	43.2

CAREER FREE-THROW PERCENTAGE

(Minimum 300 free throws made)

Player, Team	Last Year	Yrs.	G	FT	FTA	Pct.
Greg Starrick, Kentucky & Southern Ill.	1972	4	72	341	375	90.9
Jack Moore, Nebraska	1982	4	105	446	495	90.1
Steve Henson, Kansas St.	1990	4	127	361	401	90.0
Steve Alford, Indiana	1987	4	125	535	596	89.8
Bob Lloyd, Rutgers	1967	3	77	543	605	89.8
Jim Barton, Dartmouth	1989	4	104	394	440	89.5
Tommy Boyer, Arkansas	1963	3	70	315	353	89.2
Rob Robbins, New Mexico	1991	4	133	309	348	88.8
Sean Miller, Pittsburgh	1992	4	128	317	358	88.5
Ron Perry, Holy Cross	1980	4	109	680	768	88.5
Joe Dykstra, Western Ill.	1983	4	117	587	663	88.5
Mike Joseph, Bucknell	1990	4	115	397	449	88.4
Kyle Macy, Purdue & Kentucky	1980	5	125	416	471	88.3
Jimmy England, Tennessee	1971	3	81	319	362	88.1
Rod Foster, UCLA	1983	4	113	309	351	88.0
Michael Smith, Brigham Young	1989	4	122	431	491	87.8
Jason Matthews, Pittsburgh	1991	4	123	481	548	87.8
Mike Iuzzolino, Penn St. & St. Francis (Pa.)	1991	4	112	402	458	87.8
Rick Suder, Duquesne	1986	4	105	342	390	87.7
Bill Bradley, Princeton	1965	3	83	791	903	87.6
William Lewis, Monmouth (N.J.)	1992	4	112	317	362	87.6

CAREER REBOUNDS

Player, Team	Ht.	Last Year	Yrs.	G	Reb.
Tom Gola, La Salle	6-6	1955	4	118	2,201
Joe Holup, Geo. Washington	6-6	1956	4	104	2,030
Charlie Slack, Marshall	6-5	1956	4	88	1,916
Ed Conlin, Fordham	6-5	1955	4	102	1,884
Dickie Hemric, Wake Forest	6-6	1955	4	104	1,802
Paul Silas, Creighton	6-7	1964	3	81	1,751
Art Quimby, Connecticut	6-5	1955	4	80	1,716
Jerry Harper, Alabama	6-8	1956	4	93	1,688
Jeff Cohen, William & Mary	6-7	1961	4	103	1,679
Steve Hamilton, Morehead St.	6-7	1958	4	102	1,675
Charlie Tyra, Louisville	6-8	1957	4	95	1,617
Bill Russell, San Francisco	6-9	1956	3	79	1,606
Elvin Hayes, Houston	6-8	1968	3	93	1,602
Marvin Barnes, Providence	6-9	1974	3	89	1,592
Elgin Baylor, Col. Idaho & Seattle	6-6	1958	3	80	1,559
Ernie Beck, Pennsylvania	6-4	1953	3	82	1,557
Dave DeBusschere, Detroit Mercy	6-5	1962	3	80	1,552
Wes Unseld, Louisville	6-8	1968	3	82	1,551

CAREER REBOUNDS

(For careers beginning in 1973 or after)

Player, Team	Ht.	Last Year	Yrs.	G	Reb.
Derrick Coleman, Syracuse	6-9	1990	4	143	1,537
Ralph Sampson, Virginia	7-4	1983	4	132	1,511
Pete Padgett, Nevada	6-8	1976	4	104	1,464
Lionel Simmons, La Salle	6-7	1990	4	131	1,429
Anthony Bonner, St. Louis	6-7	1990	4	133	1,424
Tyrone Hill, Xavier (Ohio)	6-9	1990	4	126	1,380
Popeye Jones, Murray St.	6-8	1992	4	123	1,374
Michael Brooks, La Salle	6-7	1980	4	114	1,372
Xavier McDaniel, Wichita St.	6-7	1985	4	117	1,359
John Irving, Arizona & Hofstra	6-9	1977	4	103	1,348
Sam Clancy, Pittsburgh	6-6	1981	4	116	1,342
Keith Lee, Memphis St.	6-10	1985	4	128	1,336
Larry Smith, Alcorn St.	6-8	1980	4	111	1,334
Clarence Weatherspoon, Southern Miss.	6-7	1992	4	117	1,320
Michael Cage, San Diego St.	6-9	1984	4	112	1,317
Bob Stephens, Drexel	6-7	1979	4	99	1,316
Patrick Ewing, Georgetown	7-0	1985	4	143	1,316
David Robinson, Navy	7-1	1987	4	127	1,314

CAREER REBOUND AVERAGE

(Minimum 800 rebounds)

Player, Team	Ht.	Last Year	Yrs.	G	Reb.	Avg.
Artis Gilmore, Jacksonville	7-2	1971	2	54	1,224	22.7
Charlie Slack, Marshall	6-5	1956	4	88	1,916	21.8
Paul Silas, Creighton	6-7	1964	3	81	1,751	21.6
Leroy Wright, Pacific (Cal.)	6-8	1960	3	67	1,442	21.5
Art Quimby, Connecticut	6-5	1955	4	80	1,716	21.5
Walt Dukes, Seton Hall	6-10	1953	2	59	1,247	21.1
Bill Russell, San Francisco	6-9	1956	3	79	1,606	20.3
Kermit Washington, American	6-8	1973	3	73	1,478	20.2
Julius Erving, Massachusetts	6-6	1971	2	52	1,049	20.2
Joe Holup, Geo. Washington	6-6	1956	4	104	2,030	19.5
Elgin Baylor, Col. Idaho & Seattle	6-6	1958	3	80	1,559	19.5
Dave DeBusschere, Detroit Mercy	6-5	1962	3	80	1,552	19.4
Ernie Beck, Pennsylvania	6-4	1953	3	82	1,557	19.0
Wes Unseld, Louisville	6-8	1968	3	82	1,551	18.9
Tom Gola, La Salle	6-6	1955	4	118	2,201	18.7
Ed Conlin, Fordham	6-5	1955	4	102	1,884	18.5
Wilt Chamberlain, Kansas	7-0	1958	2	48	877	18.3
Jerry Harper, Alabama	6-8	1956	4	93	1,688	18.2

CAREER REBOUND AVERAGE

(For careers beginning in 1973 or after)

(Minimum 650 rebounds)

Player, Team	Ht.	Last Year	Yrs.	G	Reb.	Avg.
Glenn Mosley, Seton Hall	6-8	1977	4	83	1,263	15.2
Bill Campion, Manhattan	6-10	1975	3	74	1,070	14.2
Pete Padgett, Nevada	6-8	1976	4	104	1,464	14.1
Bob Warner, Maine	6-6	1976	4	96	1,304	13.6
Shaquille O'Neal, Louisiana St.	7-1	1992	3	90	1,217	13.5
Cornelius Cash, Bowling Green	6-8	1975	3	79	1,068	13.5
Larry Knight, Loyola (Ill.)	6-7	1979	2	54	729	13.5
Ira Terrell, Southern Methodist	6-8	1976	3	80	1,077	13.5
Lionel Garrett, Southern-B.R.	6-9	1979	2	56	748	13.4
Bob Stephens, Drexel	6-7	1979	4	99	1,316	13.3
Larry Bird, Indiana St.	6-9	1979	3	94	1,247	13.3
Bernard King, Tennessee	6-7	1977	3	76	1,004	13.2

CAREER ASSISTS

Player, Team	Ht.	Last Year	Yrs.	G	Ast.
Bobby Hurley, Duke	6-0	1993	4	140	1,076
Chris Corchiani, North Caro. St.	6-1	1991	4	124	1,038
Keith Jennings, East Tenn. St.	5-7	1991	4	127	983
Sherman Douglas, Syracuse	6-0	1989	4	138	960
Greg Anthony, Portland & Nevada-Las Vegas	6-1	1991	4	138	950
Gary Payton, Oregon St.	6-2	1990	4	120	939
Andre LaFleur, Northeastern	6-3	1987	4	128	894
Jim Les, Bradley	5-11	1986	4	118	884
Frank Smith, Old Dominion	6-0	1988	4	120	883
Taurence Chisholm, Delaware	5-7	1988	4	110	877
Grayson Marshall, Clemson	6-2	1988	4	122	857
Anthony Manuel, Bradley	5-11	1989	4	108	855
Avery Johnson, Cameron & Southern-B.R.	5-11	1988	3	94	838
Pooh Richardson, UCLA	6-1	1989	4	122	833
Butch Moore, Southern Methodist	5-10	1986	4	125	828
Mark Woods, Wright St.	6-1	1993	4	113	811
Drafton Davis, Marist	6-0	1988	4	115	804
Marc Brown, Siena	5-11	1991	4	123	796
Tyrone Bogues, Wake Forest	5-3	1987	4	119	781
Jeff Timberlake, Boston U.	6-2	1989	4	121	778
Kenny Smith, North Caro.	6-3	1987	4	127	768
Bruce Douglas, Illinois	6-3	1986	4	130	765
Andre Turner, Memphis St.	5-10	1986	4	132	763
Howard Evans, Temple	6-1	1988	4	132	748
Sean Miller, Pittsburgh	6-1	1992	4	128	744

CAREER ASSIST AVERAGE

(Minimum 550 assists)

Player, Team	Ht.	Last Year	Yrs.	G	Ast.	Avg.
Avery Johnson, Cameron & Southern-B.R.	5-11	1988	3	94	838	8.91
Sam Crawford, New Mexico St.	5-8	1993	2	67	592	8.84
Mark Wade, Oklahoma & Nevada-Las Vegas	6-0	1987	3	79	693	8.77
Chris Corchiani, North Caro. St.	6-1	1991	4	124	1,038	8.37
Taurence Chisholm, Delaware	5-7	1988	4	110	877	7.97
Van Usher, Tennessee Tech	6-0	1992	3	85	676	7.95
Anthony Manuel, Bradley	5-11	1989	4	108	855	7.92
Gary Payton, Oregon St.	6-2	1990	4	120	938	7.82
Keith Jennings, East Tenn. St.	5-7	1991	4	127	983	7.74
Bobby Hurley, Duke	6-0	1993	4	140	1,076	7.69
Chuck Evans, Old Dominion & Mississippi St.	5-11	1993	3	85	648	7.62
Jim Les, Bradley	5-11	1986	4	118	884	7.49
Frank Smith, Old Dominion	6-0	1988	4	120	883	7.36
Doug Wojcik, Navy	6-1	1987	3	99	714	7.21
Mark Woods, Wright St.	6-1	1993	4	113	811	7.18

Player, Team	Ht.	Last Year	Yrs.	G	Ast.	Avg.
Grayson Marshall, Clemson	6-2	1988	4	122	857	7.02
Drafton Davis, Marist	6-0	1988	4	115	804	6.99
Andre LaFleur, Northeastern	6-3	1987	4	128	894	6.98
Sherman Douglas, Syracuse	6-0	1989	4	138	960	6.96
Greg Anthony, Portland & Nevada-Las Vegas	6-1	1991	4	138	950	6.88
Pooh Richardson, UCLA	6-1	1989	4	122	833	6.83
Dwayne Washington, Syracuse	6-2	1986	3	95	637	6.71
Tony Coner, Alabama	6-3	1987	4	100	664	6.64
Butch Moore, Southern Methodist	5-10	1986	4	125	828	6.62
Tyrone Bogues, Wake Forest	5-3	1987	4	119	781	6.56

CAREER BLOCKED SHOTS

Player, Team	Ht.	Last Year	Yrs.	G	Blk.
Alonzo Mourning, Georgetown	6-10	1992	4	120	453
Rodney Blake, St. Joseph's (Pa.)	6-8	1988	4	116	419
Shaquille O'Neal, Louisiana St.	7-1	1992	3	90	412
Kevin Roberson, Vermont	6-7	1992	4	112	409
Tim Perry, Temple	6-9	1988	4	130	392
Pervis Ellison, Louisville	6-9	1989	4	136	374
Acie Earl, Iowa	6-10	1993	4	116	365
Dikembe Mutombo, Georgetown	7-2	1991	3	96	354
David Robinson, Navy	6-11	1987	2	67	351
Charles Smith, Pittsburgh	6-10	1988	4	122	346
Rik Smits, Marist	7-4	1988	4	107	345
Oliver Miller, Arkansas	6-9	1992	4	137	345
Derrick Lewis, Maryland	6-7	1988	4	127	339
Luc Longley, New Mexico	7-2	1991	4	132	336
David Van Dyke, UTEP	6-8	1992	4	127	336
Kenny Green, Rhode Island	6-8	1990	4	122	335
Elden Campbell, Clemson	6-10	1990	4	123	334
Rony Seikaly, Syracuse	6-10	1988	4	136	319
Derrick Coleman, Syracuse	6-9	1990	4	143	318
Ervin Johnson, New Orleans	6-11	1993	4	123	294
Robert Horry, Alabama	6-9	1992	4	133	286
Vin Baker, Hartford	6-11	1993	4	112	279
Anthony Cook, Arizona	6-9	1989	4	133	278
Mike Butts, Bucknell	6-9	1989	4	114	278
Dwayne Schintzius, Florida	7-2	1990	4	110	272

CAREER BLOCKED-SHOT AVERAGE

(Minimum 200 blocked shots)

Player, Team	Ht.	Last Year	Yrs.	G	Blk.	Avg.
David Robinson, Navy	6-11	1987	2	67	351	5.24
Shaquille O'Neal, Louisiana St.	7-1	1992	3	90	412	4.58
Alonzo Mourning, Georgetown	6-10	1992	4	120	453	3.78
Lorenzo Williams, Stetson	6-9	1991	2	63	234	3.71
Dikembe Mutombo, Georgetown	7-2	1991	3	96	354	3.69
Kevin Roberson, Vermont	6-7	1992	4	112	409	3.65
Rodney Blake, St. Joseph's (Pa.)	6-8	1988	4	116	419	3.61
Lester Fonville, Jackson St.	7-2	1987	2	58	205	3.53
Charles Outlaw, Houston	6-9	1993	2	61	211	3.46
Rik Smits, Marist	7-4	1988	4	107	345	3.22
Acie Earl, Iowa	6-10	1993	4	116	365	3.15
Tim Perry, Temple	6-9	1988	4	130	392	3.02
Charles Smith, Pittsburgh	6-10	1988	4	122	346	2.84
Damon Lopez, Fordham	6-9	1991	3	93	258	2.77
Pervis Ellison, Louisville	6-9	1989	4	136	374	2.75
Kenny Green, Rhode Island	6-8	1990	4	122	335	2.75
Elden Campbell, Clemson	6-10	1990	4	123	334	2.72
Derrick Lewis, Maryland	6-7	1988	4	127	339	2.67
David Van Dyke, UTEP	6-8	1992	4	127	336	2.65
Walter Palmer, Dartmouth	7-1	1990	4	87	225	2.59
Luc Longley, New Mexico	7-2	1991	4	132	336	2.55
Cedric Lewis, Maryland	6-9	1991	4	95	239	2.52
Monty Henderson, Siena	6-7	1989	4	94	235	2.50
Vin Baker, Hartford	6-11	1993	4	112	279	2.49
Dwayne Schintzius, Florida	7-2	1990	4	110	272	2.47
Khari Jaxon, New Mexico	6-8	1993	3	89	220	2.47

CAREER STEALS

Player, Team	Ht.	Last Year	Yrs.	G	Stl.
Eric Murdock, Providence	6-2	1991	4	117	376
Michael Anderson, Drexel	5-11	1988	4	115	341
Kenny Robertson, Cleveland St.	6-0	1990	4	119	341
Keith Jennings, East Tenn. St.	5-7	1991	4	127	334
Greg Anthony, Portland & Nevada-Las Vegas	6-1	1991	4	138	329
Chris Corchiani, North Caro. St.	6-1	1991	4	124	328
Gary Payton, Oregon St.	6-2	1990	4	120	321
Mark Woods, Wright St.	6-1	1993	4	113	314
Scott Burrell, Connecticut	6-7	1993	4	119	310
Elliot Perry, Memphis St.	6-0	1991	4	126	304
Aldwin Ware, Florida A&M	6-2	1988	4	110	301
Drafton Davis, Marist	6-0	1988	4	115	301
Gary Grant, Michigan	6-3	1988	4	129	300
Taurence Chisholm, Delaware	5-7	1988	4	110	298
Frank Smith, Old Dominion	6-0	1988	4	120	295
D'Wayne Tanner, Rice	5-9	1990	4	109	291
Lee Mayberry, Arkansas	6-2	1992	4	139	291
Mike Bright, Bucknell	6-6	1993	4	117	286
Michael Williams, Baylor	6-2	1988	4	115	282
Mookie Blaylock, Oklahoma	6-0	1989	2	74	281
Mark Macon, Temple	6-5	1991	4	126	281
Terry Giles, Florida A&M	5-9	1990	4	115	278
Doug Overton, La Salle	6-3	1991	4	123	277
Randy Brown, Houston & New Mexico St.	6-3	1991	4	116	271
Van Usher, Tennessee Tech	6-0	1992	3	85	270
Brent Price, South Caro. & Oklahoma	6-1	1992	4	124	270

CAREER STEAL AVERAGE

(Minimum 200 steals)

Player, Team	Ht.	Last Year	Yrs.	G	Stl.	Avg.
Mookie Blaylock, Oklahoma	6-0	1989	2	74	281	3.80
Ronn McMahon, Eastern Wash.	5-9	1990	3	64	225	3.52
Eric Murdock, Providence	6-2	1991	4	117	376	3.21
Van Usher, Tennessee Tech	6-0	1992	3	85	270	3.18
Michael Anderson, Drexel	5-11	1988	4	115	341	2.97
Haywoode Workman, Oral Roberts	6-3	1989	3	85	250	2.94
Kenny Robertson, Cleveland St.	6-0	1990	4	119	341	2.87
Darnell Mee, Western Ky.	6-3	1993	3	91	259	2.85
Mark Woods, Wright St.	6-1	1993	4	113	314	2.78
Aldwin Ware, Florida A&M	6-2	1988	4	110	301	2.74
Taurence Chisholm, Delaware	5-7	1988	4	110	298	2.71
Chuck Evans, Mississippi St.	5-11	1993	3	85	229	2.69
Gary Payton, Oregon St.	6-2	1990	4	120	321	2.68
D'Wayne Tanner, Rice	5-9	1990	4	109	291	2.67
Chris Corchiani, North Caro. St.	6-1	1991	4	124	328	2.65
Keith Jennings, East Tenn. St.	5-7	1991	4	127	334	2.63
Drafton Davis, Marist	6-0	1988	4	115	301	2.62
Scott Burrell, Connecticut	6-7	1993	4	119	310	2.61
Randy Woods, La Salle	6-0	1992	3	88	220	2.50
Frank Smith, Old Dominion	6-0	1988	4	120	295	2.46
Michael Williams, Baylor	6-2	1988	4	115	282	2.45
Mike Bright, Bucknell	6-6	1993	4	117	286	2.44
Darryl Owens, Nevada	6-0	1989	3	82	200	2.44
Terry Giles, Florida A&M	5-9	1990	4	115	278	2.42
Elliot Perry, Memphis St.	6-0	1991	4	126	304	2.41

CAREER 2,000 POINTS & 1,000 REBOUNDS

Player, Team	Ht.	Last Year	Yrs.	G	Pts.	Reb.
Lionel Simmons, La Salle	6-7	1990	4	131	3,217	1,429
Harry Kelly, Texas Southern	6-7	1983	4	110	3,066	1,085
Oscar Robertson, Cincinnati	6-5	1960	3	88	2,973	1,338
Danny Manning, Kansas	6-10	1988	4	147	2,951	1,187
Elvin Hayes, Houston	6-8	1968	3	93	2,884	1,602

Player, Team	Ht.	Last Year	Yrs.	G	Pts.	Reb.
Larry Bird, Indiana St.	6-9	1979	3	94	2,850	1,247
Hank Gathers, Southern Cal & Loyola (Cal.)	6-7	1990	4	117	2,723	1,128
Daren Queenan, Lehigh	6-5	1988	4	118	2,703	1,013
David Robinson, Navy	7-1	1987	4	127	2,669	1,314
Wayman Tisdale, Oklahoma	6-9	1985	3	104	2,661	1,048
Michael Brooks, La Salle	6-7	1980	4	114	2,628	1,372
Dickie Hemric, Wake Forest	6-6	1955	4	104	2,587	1,802
Calvin Natt, Northeast La.	6-5	1979	4	108	2,581	1,285
Willie Jackson, Centenary	6-6	1984	4	114	2,535	1,013
Bill Bradley, Princeton	6-5	1965	3	83	2,503	1,008
Elgin Baylor, Col. Idaho & Seattle	6-6	1958	3	80	2,500	1,559
Tom Gola, La Salle	6-6	1955	4	118	2,462	2,201
Christian Laettner, Duke	6-11	1992	4	148	2,460	1,149
Keith Lee, Memphis St.	6-11	1985	4	128	2,408	1,336
Phil Sellers, Rutgers	6-5	1976	4	114	2,399	1,115
Byron Houston, Oklahoma St.	6-7	1992	4	127	2,379	1,190
Ron Harper, Miami (Ohio)	6-6	1986	4	120	2,377	1,119
Lew Alcindor, UCLA	7-2	1969	3	88	2,325	1,367
Mike Gminski, Duke	6-11	1980	4	122	2,323	1,242
Billy McGill, Utah	6-9	1962	3	86	2,321	1,106
Adam Keefe, Stanford	6-9	1992	4	125	2,319	1,119
Jerry West, West Va.	6-3	1960	3	93	2,309	1,240
Jonathan Moore, Furman	6-8	1980	4	117	2,299	1,242
Rick Barry, Miami (Fla.)	6-7	1965	3	77	2,298	1,274
Gary Winton, Army	6-5	1978	4	105	2,296	1,168
Kenneth Lyons, North Texas	6-7	1983	4	111	2,291	1,020
Tom Davis, Delaware St.	6-6	1991	4	95	2,274	1,013
Nick Werkman, Seton Hall	6-3	1964	3	71	2,273	1,036
Jim McDaniels, Western Ky.	7-0	1971	3	81	2,238	1,118
Joe Holup, Geo. Washington	6-6	1956	4	104	2,226	2,030
Ralph Sampson, Virginia	7-4	1983	4	132	2,225	1,511
Patrick Ewing, Georgetown	7-0	1985	4	143	2,184	1,316
Doug Smith, Missouri	6-10	1991	4	128	2,184	1,054
Kenny Sanders, George Mason	6-5	1989	4	107	2,177	1,026
Joe Barry Carroll, Purdue	7-1	1980	4	123	2,175	1,148
Reggie King, Alabama	6-6	1979	4	118	2,168	1,279
Len Chappell, Wake Forest	6-8	1962	3	87	2,165	1,213
Danny Ferry, Duke	6-10	1989	4	143	2,155	1,003
Xavier McDaniel, Wichita St.	6-7	1985	4	117	2,152	1,359
Derrick Coleman, Syracuse	6-9	1990	4	143	2,143	1,537
Joe Binion, North Caro. A&T	6-8	1984	4	116	2,143	1,194
Pervis Ellison, Louisville	6-9	1989	4	136	2,143	1,149
Dan Issel, Kentucky	6-9	1970	3	83	2,138	1,078
Jesse Arnelle, Penn St.	6-5	1955	4	102	2,138	1,238
Sam Perkins, North Caro.	6-10	1984	4	135	2,133	1,167
Bob Elliott, Arizona	6-10	1977	4	114	2,131	1,083
Clarence Weatherspoon, Southern Miss.	6-7	1992	4	117	2,130	1,320
Greg Grant, Utah St.	6-7	1986	4	115	2,124	1,003
Bill Cartwright, San Francisco	6-11	1979	4	111	2,116	1,137
Bob Harstad, Creighton	6-6	1991	4	128	2,110	1,126
B. B. Davis, Lamar	6-8	1981	4	119	2,084	1,122
Durand Macklin, Louisiana St.	6-7	1981	5	123	2,080	1,276
Ralph Crosthwaite, Western Ky.	6-9	1959	4	103	2,076	1,309
Sidney Green, Nevada-Las Vegas	6-9	1983	4	119	2,069	1,276
Bob Lanier, St. Bonaventure	6-11	1970	3	75	2,067	1,180
Fred West, Texas Southern	6-9	1990	4	118	2,066	1,136
Sidney Moncrief, Arkansas	6-4	1979	4	122	2,066	1,015
Popeye Jones, Murray St.	6-8	1992	4	123	2,057	1,374
Mark Acres, Oral Roberts	6-11	1985	4	110	2,038	1,051
Fred Hetzel, Davidson	6-8	1965	3	79	2,032	1,094
Bailey Howell, Mississippi St.	6-7	1959	3	75	2,030	1,277
Larry Krystkowiak, Montana	6-9	1986	4	120	2,017	1,105
Greg Kelser, Michigan St.	6-7	1979	4	115	2,014	1,092
Herb Williams, Ohio St.	6-10	1981	4	114	2,011	1,111
Stacey Augmon, Nevada-Las Vegas	6-8	1991	4	145	2,011	1,005
Jeff Cohen, William & Mary	6-7	1961	4	103	2,003	1,679
Tyrone Hill, Xavier (Ohio)	6-9	1990	4	126	2,003	1,380
Alonzo Mourning, Georgetown	6-10	1992	4	120	2,001	1,032
Josh Grant, Utah	6-9	1993	5	131	2,000	1,066

DIVISION I MEN'S ANNUAL INDIVIDUAL CHAMPIONS

SCORING AVERAGE

Year	Player, Team	Ht.	Cl.	G	FG	FT	Pts.	Avg.
1948	Murray Wier, Iowa	5-9	Sr.	19	152	95	399	21.0
1949	Tony Lavelli, Yale	6-3	Sr.	30	228	215	671	22.4
1950	Paul Arizin, Villanova	6-3	Sr.	29	260	215	735	25.3
1951	Bill Mlkvy, Temple	6-4	Sr.	25	303	125	731	29.2
1952	Clyde Lovellette, Kansas	6-9	Sr.	28	315	165	795	28.4
1953	Frank Selvy, Furman	6-3	Jr.	25	272	194	738	29.5
1954	Frank Selvy, Furman	6-3	Sr.	29	427	*355	1,209	41.7
1955	Darrell Floyd, Furman	6-1	Jr.	25	344	209	897	35.9
1956	Darrell Floyd, Furman	6-1	Sr.	28	339	268	946	33.8
1957	Grady Wallace, South Caro.	6-4	Sr.	29	336	234	906	31.2
1958	Oscar Robertson, Cincinnati	6-5	So.	28	352	280	984	35.1
1959	Oscar Robertson, Cincinnati	6-5	Jr.	30	331	316	978	32.6
1960	Oscar Robertson, Cincinnati	6-5	Sr.	30	369	273	1,011	33.7
1961	Frank Burgess, Gonzaga	6-1	Sr.	26	304	234	842	32.4
1962	Billy McGill, Utah	6-9	Sr.	26	394	221	1,009	38.8
1963	Nick Werkman, Seton Hall	6-3	Jr.	22	221	208	650	29.5
1964	Howard Komives, Bowling Green	6-1	Sr.	23	292	260	844	36.7
1965	Rick Barry, Miami (Fla.)	6-7	Sr.	26	340	293	973	37.4
1966	Dave Schellhase, Purdue	6-4	Sr.	24	284	213	781	32.5
1967	Jim Walker, Providence	6-3	Sr.	28	323	205	851	30.4
1968	Pete Maravich, Louisiana St.	6-5	So.	26	432	274	1,138	43.8
1969	Pete Maravich, Louisiana St.	6-5	Jr.	26	433	282	1,148	44.2
1970	Pete Maravich, Louisiana St.	6-5	Sr.	31	*522	337	*1,381	*44.5
1971	Johnny Neumann, Mississippi	6-6	So.	23	366	191	923	40.1
1972	Dwight Lamar, Southwestern La.	6-1	Jr.	29	429	196	1,054	36.3
1973	William Averitt, Pepperdine	6-1	Sr.	25	352	144	848	33.9
1974	Larry Fogle, Canisius	6-5	So.	25	326	183	835	33.4
1975	Bob McCurdy, Richmond	6-7	Sr.	26	321	213	855	32.9
1976	Marshall Rodgers, Tex.-Pan American	6-2	Sr.	25	361	197	919	36.8
1977	Freeman Williams, Portland St.	6-4	Jr.	26	417	176	1,010	38.8
1978	Freeman Williams, Portland St.	6-4	Sr.	27	410	149	969	35.9
1979	Lawrence Butler, Idaho St.	6-3	Sr.	27	310	192	812	30.1
1980	Tony Murphy, Southern-B.R.	6-3	Sr.	29	377	178	932	32.1
1981	Zam Fredrick, South Caro.	6-2	Sr.	27	300	181	781	28.9
1982	Harry Kelly, Texas Southern	6-7	Jr.	29	336	190	862	29.7
1983	Harry Kelly, Texas Southern	6-7	Sr.	29	333	169	835	28.8
1984	Joe Jakubick, Akron	6-5	Sr.	27	304	206	814	30.1
1985	Xavier McDaniel, Wichita St.	6-8	Sr.	31	351	142	844	27.2
1986	Terrance Bailey, Wagner	6-2	Jr.	29	321	212	854	29.4

Year	Player, Team	Ht.	Cl.	G	FG	3FG	FT	Pts.	Avg.
1987	Kevin Houston, Army	5-11	Sr.	29	311	63	268	953	32.9
1988	Hersey Hawkins, Bradley	6-3	Sr.	31	377	87	284	1,125	36.3
1989	Hank Gathers, Loyola (Cal.)	6-7	Jr.	31	419	0	177	1,015	32.7
1990	Bo Kimble, Loyola (Cal.)	6-5	Sr.	32	404	92	231	1,131	35.3
1991	Kevin Bradshaw, U.S. Int'l	6-6	Sr.	28	358	60	278	1,054	37.6
1992	Brett Roberts, Morehead St.	6-8	Sr.	29	278	66	193	815	28.1
1993	Greg Guy, Tex.-Pan American	6-1	Jr.	19	189	67	111	556	29.3

* *Record.*

FIELD-GOAL PERCENTAGE

Year	Player, Team	Cl.	G	FG	FGA	Pct.
1948	Alex Peterson, Oregon St.	Jr.	27	89	187	47.6
1949	Ed Macauley, St. Louis	Sr.	26	144	275	52.4
1950	Jim Moran, Niagara	Jr.	27	98	185	53.0
1951	Don Meineke, Dayton	Jr.	32	240	469	51.2
1952	Art Spoelstra, Western Ky.	So.	31	178	345	51.6
1953	Vernon Stokes, St. Francis (N.Y)	Sr.	24	147	247	59.5
1954	Joe Holup, Geo. Washington	So.	26	179	313	57.2
1955	Ed O'Connor, Manhattan	Sr.	23	147	243	60.5
1956	Joe Holup, Geo. Washington	Sr.	26	200	309	64.7
1957	Bailey Howell, Mississippi St.	So.	25	217	382	56.8
1958	Ralph Crosthwaite, Western Ky.	Jr.	25	202	331	61.0
1959	Ralph Crosthwaite, Western Ky.	Sr.	26	191	296	64.5
1960	Jerry Lucas, Ohio St.	So.	27	283	444	63.7
1961	Jerry Lucas, Ohio St.	Jr.	27	256	411	62.3
1962	Jerry Lucas, Ohio St.	Sr.	28	237	388	61.1

Year	Player, Team	Cl.	G	FG	FGA	Pct.
1963	Lyle Harger, Houston	Sr.	26	193	294	65.6
1964	Terry Holland, Davidson	Sr.	26	135	214	63.1
1965	Tim Kehoe, St. Peter's	Sr.	19	138	209	66.0
1966	Julian Hammond, Tulsa	Sr.	29	172	261	65.9
1967	Lew Alcindor, UCLA	So.	30	346	519	66.7
1968	Joe Allen, Bradley	Sr.	28	258	394	65.5
1969	Lew Alcindor, UCLA	Sr.	30	303	477	63.5
1970	Willie Williams, Florida St.	Sr.	26	185	291	63.6
1971	John Belcher, Arkansas St.	Jr.	24	174	275	63.3
1972	Kent Martens, Abilene Christian	Sr.	21	136	204	66.7
1973	Elton Hayes, Lamar	Sr.	24	146	222	65.8
1974	Al Fleming, Arizona	So.	26	136	204	66.7
1975	Bernard King, Tennessee	Fr.	25	273	439	62.2
1976	Sidney Moncrief, Arkansas	Fr.	28	149	224	66.5
1977	Joe Senser, West Chester	So.	25	130	186	69.9
1978	Joe Senser, West Chester	Jr.	25	135	197	68.5
1979	Murray Brown, Florida St.	Jr.	29	237	343	69.1
1980	Steve Johnson, Oregon St.	Jr.	30	211	297	71.0
1981	Steve Johnson, Oregon St.	Sr.	28	235	315	*74.6
1982	Mark McNamara, California	Sr.	27	231	329	70.2
1983	Troy Lee Mikel, East Tenn. St.	Sr.	29	197	292	67.5
1984	Akeem Olajuwon, Houston	Jr.	37	249	369	67.5
1985	Keith Walker, Utica	Sr.	27	154	216	71.3
1986	Brad Daugherty, North Caro.	Sr.	34	284	438	64.8
1987	Alan Williams, Princeton	Sr.	25	163	232	70.3
1988	Arnell Jones, Boise St.	Sr.	30	187	283	66.1
1989	Dwayne Davis, Florida	So.	33	179	248	72.2
1990	Lee Campbell, Southwest Mo. St.	Sr.	29	192	275	69.8
1991	Oliver Miller, Arkansas	Jr.	38	254	361	70.4
1992	Charles Outlaw, Houston	Jr.	31	156	228	68.4
1993	Charles Outlaw, Houston	Sr.	30	196	298	65.8

* *Record.*

THREE-POINT FIELD GOALS MADE PER GAME

Year	Player, Team	Cl.	G	3FG	Avg.
1987	Darrin Fitzgerald, Butler	Sr.	28	158	*5.64
1988	Timothy Pollard, Mississippi Val.	Jr.	28	132	4.71
1989	Timothy Pollard, Mississippi Val.	Sr.	28	124	4.43
1990	Dave Jamerson, Ohio	Sr.	28	131	4.68
1991	Bobby Phills, Southern-B.R.	Sr.	28	123	4.39
1992	Doug Day, Radford	Jr.	29	117	4.03
1993	Bernard Haslett, Southern Miss.	Jr.	26	109	4.19

* *Record.*

THREE-POINT FIELD-GOAL PERCENTAGE

Year	Player, Team	Cl.	G	3FG	3FGA	Pct.
1987	Reginald Jones, Prairie View	Jr.	28	64	112	57.1
1988	Glenn Tropf, Holy Cross	Jr.	29	52	82	*63.4
1989	Dave Calloway, Monmouth (N.J.)	So.	28	48	82	58.5
1990	Matt Lapin, Princeton	Sr.	27	71	133	53.4
1991	Keith Jennings, East Tenn. St.	Sr.	33	84	142	59.2
1992	Sean Wightman, Western Mich.	Jr.	30	48	76	63.2
1993	Jeff Anderson, Kent	Jr.	26	44	82	53.7

* *Record.*

FREE-THROW PERCENTAGE

Year	Player, Team	Cl.	G	FT	FTA	Pct.
1948	Sam Urzetta, St. Bonaventure	So.	22	59	64	92.2
1949	Bill Schroer, Valparaiso	So.	24	59	68	86.8
1950	Sam Urzetta, St. Bonaventure	Sr.	22	54	61	88.5
1951	Jay Handlan, Wash. & Lee	Jr.	22	148	172	86.0
1952	Sy Chadroff, Miami (Fla.)	Sr.	22	99	123	80.5
1953	John Weber, Yale	Sr.	24	117	141	83.0
1954	Dick Daugherty, Arizona St.	Sr.	23	75	86	87.2
1955	Jim Scott, West Tex. A&M	Sr.	23	153	171	89.5
1956	Bill Von Weyhe, Rhode Island	Jr.	25	180	208	86.5
1957	Ernie Wiggins, Wake Forest	Sr.	28	93	106	87.7

Year	Player, Team	Cl.	G	FT	FTA	Pct.
1958	Semi Mintz, Davidson	Sr.	24	105	119	88.2
1959	Arlen Clark, Oklahoma St.	Sr.	25	201	236	85.2
1960	Jack Waters, Mississippi	Jr.	24	103	118	87.3
1961	Stew Sherard, Army	Jr.	24	135	154	87.7
1962	Tommy Boyer, Arkansas	Jr.	23	125	134	93.3
1963	Tommy Boyer, Arkansas	Sr.	24	147	161	91.3
1964	Rick Park, Tulsa	Jr.	25	121	134	90.3
1965	Bill Bradley, Princeton	Sr.	29	273	308	88.6
1966	Bill Blair, Providence	Sr.	27	101	112	90.2
1967	Bob Lloyd, Rutgers	Sr.	29	255	277	92.1
1968	Joe Heiser, Princeton	Sr.	26	117	130	90.0
1969	Bill Justus, Tennessee	Sr.	28	133	147	90.5
1970	Steve Kaplan, Rutgers	So.	23	102	110	92.7
1971	Greg Starrick, Southern Ill.	Jr.	23	119	132	90.2
1972	Greg Starrick, Southern Ill.	Sr.	26	148	160	92.5
1973	Don Smith, Dayton	Jr.	26	111	122	91.0
1974	Rickey Medlock, Arkansas	Jr.	26	87	95	91.6
1975	Frank Oleynick, Seattle	Sr.	26	135	152	88.8
1976	Tad Dufelmeier, Loyola (Ill.)	Jr.	25	71	80	88.8
1977	Robert Smith, Nevada-Las Vegas	Sr.	32	98	106	92.5
1978	Carlos Gibson, Marshall	Jr.	28	84	89	94.4
1979	Darrell Mauldin, Campbell	Jr.	26	70	76	92.1
1980	Brian Magid, Geo. Washington	Sr.	26	79	85	92.9
1981	Dave Hildahl, Portland St.	Sr.	21	76	82	92.7
1982	Rod Foster, UCLA	Jr.	27	95	100	95.0
1983	Rob Gonzalez, Colorado	Sr.	28	75	82	91.5
1984	Steve Alford, Indiana	Fr.	31	137	150	91.3
1985	Craig Collins, Penn St.	Sr.	27	94	98	*95.9
1986	Jim Barton, Dartmouth	Fr.	26	65	69	94.2
1987	Kevin Houston, Army	Sr.	29	268	294	91.2
1988	Steve Henson, Kansas St.	So.	34	111	120	92.5
1989	Michael Smith, Brigham Young	Sr.	29	160	173	92.5
1990	Rob Robbins, New Mexico	Jr.	34	101	108	93.5
1991	Darin Archbold, Butler	Jr.	29	187	205	91.2
1992	Don MacLean, UCLA	Sr.	32	197	214	92.1
1993	Josh Grant, Utah	Sr.	31	104	113	92.0

* *Record.*

REBOUND AVERAGE

Year	Player, Team	Ht.	Cl.	G	Reb.	Avg.
1951	Ernie Beck, Pennsylvania	6-4	So.	27	556	20.6
1952	Bill Hannon, Army	6-3	So.	17	355	20.9
1953	Ed Conlin, Fordham	6-5	So.	26	612	23.5
1954	Art Quimby, Connecticut	6-5	Jr.	26	588	22.6
1955	Charlie Slack, Marshall	6-5	Jr.	21	538	*25.6
1956	Joe Holup, Geo. Washington	6-6	Sr.	26	604	†.256
1957	Elgin Baylor, Seattle	6-6	Jr.	25	508	†.235
1958	Alex Ellis, Niagara	6-5	Sr.	25	536	†.262
1959	Leroy Wright, Pacific (Cal.)	6-8	Jr.	26	652	†.238
1960	Leroy Wright, Pacific (Cal.)	6-8	Sr.	17	380	†.234
1961	Jerry Lucas, Ohio St.	6-8	Jr.	27	470	†.198
1962	Jerry Lucas, Ohio St.	6-8	Sr.	28	499	†.211
1963	Paul Silas, Creighton	6-7	Sr.	27	557	20.6
1964	Bob Pelkington, Xavier (Ohio)	6-7	Sr.	26	567	21.8
1965	Toby Kimball, Connecticut	6-8	Sr.	23	483	21.0
1966	Jim Ware, Oklahoma City	6-8	Sr.	29	607	20.9
1967	Dick Cunningham, Murray St.	6-10	Jr.	22	479	21.8
1968	Neal Walk, Florida	6-10	Jr.	25	494	19.8
1969	Spencer Haywood, Detroit Mercy	6-8	So.	22	472	21.5
1970	Artis Gilmore, Jacksonville	7-2	Jr.	28	621	22.2
1971	Artis Gilmore, Jacksonville	7-2	Sr.	26	603	23.2
1972	Kermit Washington, American	6-8	Jr.	23	455	19.8
1973	Kermit Washington, American	6-8	Sr.	22	439	20.0
1974	Marvin Barnes, Providence	6-9	Sr.	32	597	18.7
1975	John Irving, Hofstra	6-9	So.	21	323	15.4
1976	Sam Pellom, Buffalo	6-8	So.	26	420	16.2
1977	Glenn Mosley, Seton Hall	6-8	Sr.	29	473	16.3
1978	Ken Williams, North Texas	6-7	Sr.	28	411	14.7
1979	Monti Davis, Tennessee St.	6-7	Jr.	26	421	16.2
1980	Larry Smith, Alcorn St.	6-8	Sr.	26	392	15.1

Year	Player, Team	Ht.	Cl.	G	Reb.	Avg.
1981	Darryl Watson, Mississippi Val.	6-7	Sr.	27	379	14.0
1982	LaSalle Thompson, Texas	6-10	Jr.	27	365	13.5
1983	Xavier McDaniel, Wichita St.	6-7	So.	28	403	14.4
1984	Akeem Olajuwon, Houston	7-0	Jr.	37	500	13.5
1985	Xavier McDaniel, Wichita St.	6-8	Sr.	31	460	14.8
1986	David Robinson, Navy	6-11	Jr.	35	455	13.0
1987	Jerome Lane, Pittsburgh	6-6	So.	33	444	13.5
1988	Kenny Miller, Loyola (Ill.)	6-9	Fr.	29	395	13.6
1989	Hank Gathers, Loyola (Cal.)	6-7	Jr.	31	426	13.7
1990	Anthony Bonner, St. Louis	6-8	Sr.	33	456	13.8
1991	Shaquille O'Neal, Louisiana St.	7-1	So.	28	411	14.7
1992	Popeye Jones, Murray St.	6-8	Sr.	30	431	14.4
1993	Warren Kidd, Middle Tenn. St.	6-9	Sr.	26	386	14.8

** Record. † From 1956 through 1962, championship was determined on highest individual recoveries out of total by both teams in all games.*

ASSIST AVERAGE

Year	Player, Team	Cl.	G	Ast.	Avg.
1984	Craig Lathen, Ill.-Chicago	Jr.	29	274	9.45
1985	Rob Weingard, Hofstra	Sr.	24	228	9.50
1986	Mark Jackson, St. John's (N.Y.)	Jr.	36	328	9.11
1987	Avery Johnson, Southern-B.R.	Jr.	31	333	10.74
1988	Avery Johnson, Southern-B.R.	Sr.	30	399	*13.30
1989	Glenn Williams, Holy Cross	Sr.	28	278	9.93
1990	Todd Lehmann, Drexel	Sr.	28	260	9.29
1991	Chris Corchiani, North Caro. St.	Sr.	31	299	9.65
1992	Van Usher, Tennessee Tech	Sr.	29	254	8.76
1993	Sam Crawford, New Mexico St.	Sr.	34	310	9.12

** Record.*

BLOCKED-SHOT AVERAGE

Year	Player, Team	Cl.	G	Blk.	Avg.
1986	David Robinson, Navy	Jr.	35	207	*5.91
1987	David Robinson, Navy	Sr.	32	144	4.50
1988	Rodney Blake, St. Joseph's (Pa.)	Sr.	29	116	4.00
1989	Alonzo Mourning, Georgetown	Fr.	34	169	4.97
1990	Kenny Green, Rhode Island	Sr.	26	124	4.77
1991	Shawn Bradley, Brigham Young	Fr.	34	177	5.21
1992	Shaquille O'Neal, Louisiana St.	Jr.	30	157	5.23
1993	Theo Ratliff, Wyoming	Jr.	28	124	4.43

** Record.*

STEAL AVERAGE

Year	Player, Team	Cl.	G	Stl.	Avg.
1986	Darron Brittman, Chicago St.	Sr.	28	139	*4.96
1987	Tony Fairley, Charleston So.	Sr.	28	114	4.07
1988	Aldwin Ware, Florida A&M	Sr.	29	142	4.90
1989	Kenny Robertson, Cleveland St.	Jr.	28	111	3.96
1990	Ronn McMahon, Eastern Wash.	Sr.	29	130	4.48
1991	Van Usher, Tennessee Tech	Jr.	28	104	3.71
1992	Victor Snipes, Northeastern Ill.	So.	25	86	3.44
1993	Jason Kidd, California	Fr.	29	110	3.79

** Record.*

DIVISION I MEN'S ALL-TIME TEAM LEADERS

SINGLE-GAME SCORING HIGHS

Pts.	Team vs. Opponent (Opp. Pts.)	Date
186	Loyola (Cal.) vs. U.S. Int'l (140)	Jan. 5, 1991
181	Loyola (Cal.) vs. U.S. Int'l (150)	Jan. 31, 1989
173	Oklahoma vs. U.S. Int'l (101)	Nov. 29, 1989
172	Oklahoma vs. Loyola (Cal.) (112)	Dec. 15, 1990
166	Arkansas vs. U.S. Int'l (101)	Dec. 9, 1989
164	Nevada-Las Vegas vs. Hawaii-Hilo (111)	Feb. 19, 1976
164	Loyola (Cal.) vs. Azusa-Pacific (138)	Nov. 28, 1988
162	Loyola (Cal.) vs. U.S. Int'l (144)	Jan. 7, 1989
162	Loyola (Cal.) vs. Chaminade (129)	Nov. 25, 1990
162	Oklahoma vs. Angelo St. (99)	Dec. 1, 1990

Pts.	Team vs. Opponent (Opp. Pts.)	Date
159	Southern-B.R. vs. Texas College (65)	Dec. 6, 1990
159	Louisiana St. vs. Northern Ariz. (86)	Dec. 28, 1991
157	Loyola (Cal.) vs. San Francisco (115)	Feb. 5, 1990
156	Southern-B.R. vs. Baptist Christian (91)	Dec. 14, 1992
155	Oral Roberts vs. Union (Tenn.) (113)	Feb. 24, 1972
155	Southern-B.R. vs. Prairie View (91)	Feb. 22, 1993
154	Texas-Arlington vs. Huston-Tillotson (85)	Nov. 29, 1990
152	Jacksonville vs. St. Peter's (106)	Dec. 3, 1970
152	Oklahoma vs. Centenary (84)	Dec. 12, 1987
152	Oklahoma vs. Oral Roberts (122)	Dec. 10, 1988
152	Loyola (Cal.) vs. U.S. Int'l (137)	Dec. 7, 1989
152	Northeastern vs. Loyola (Cal.) (123)	Nov. 24, 1990
151	Loyola (Cal.) vs. U.S. Int'l (107)	Jan. 11, 1986
151	Oklahoma vs. Dayton (99)	Dec. 24, 1987
151	Alabama St. vs. Grambling (97)	Jan. 21, 1991

SINGLE-GAME SCORING HIGHS BY LOSING TEAM

Pts.	Team vs. Opponent (Opp. Pts.)	Date
150	U.S. Int'l vs. Loyola (Cal.) (181)	Jan. 31, 1989
144	U.S. Int'l vs. Loyola (Cal.) (162)	Jan. 7, 1989
141	Loyola (Cal.) vs. Oklahoma (136)	Dec. 23, 1989
141	Loyola (Cal.) vs. Louisiana St. (148) (ot)	Feb. 3, 1990
140	Utah St. vs. Nevada-Las Vegas (142) (3 ot)	Jan. 2, 1985
140	U.S. Int'l vs. Loyola (Cal.) (186)	Jan. 5, 1991
137	U.S. Int'l vs. Loyola (Cal.) (152)	Dec. 7, 1989
136	Gonzaga vs. Loyola (Cal.) (147)	Feb. 18, 1989
127	Pepperdine vs. Loyola (Cal.) (142)	Feb. 20, 1988
125	Nevada vs. Loyola (Cal.) (130)	Dec. 30, 1988
123	San Francisco vs. Loyola (Cal.) (137)	Feb. 9, 1990
123	Loyola (Cal.) vs. Pepperdine (148)	Feb. 17, 1990
123	Loyola (Cal.) vs. Northeastern (152)	Nov. 24, 1990
122	Oral Roberts vs. Oklahoma (152)	Dec. 10, 1988

SINGLE-GAME SCORING HIGHS BOTH TEAMS COMBINED

Pts.	Team (Pts.) vs. Team (Pts.)	Date
331	Loyola (Cal.) (181) vs. U.S. Int'l (150)	Jan. 31, 1989
326	Loyola (Cal.) (186) vs. U.S. Int'l (140)	Jan. 5, 1991
306	Loyola (Cal.) (162) vs. U.S. Int'l (144)	Jan. 7, 1989
289	Loyola (Cal.) (152) vs. U.S. Int'l (137)	Dec. 7, 1989
289	Louisiana St. (148) vs. Loyola (Cal.) (141) (ot)	Feb. 3, 1990
284	Oklahoma (172) vs. Loyola (Cal.) (112)	Dec. 15, 1990
283	Loyola (Cal.) (147) vs. Gonzaga (136)	Feb. 18, 1989
282	Nevada-Las Vegas (142) vs. Utah St. (140) (3 ot)	Jan. 2, 1985
275	Northeastern (152) vs. Loyola (Cal.) (123)	Nov. 24, 1990
274	Oklahoma (152) vs. Oral Roberts (122)	Dec. 10, 1988
274	Oklahoma (173) vs. U.S. Int'l (101)	Nov. 29, 1989
272	Loyola (Cal.) (157) vs. San Francisco (115)	Feb. 4, 1990
269	Loyola (Cal.) (142) vs. Pepperdine (127)	Feb. 20, 1988
269	Loyola (Cal.) (150) vs. St. Mary's (Cal.) (119)	Feb. 1, 1990

SINGLE-GAME SCORING HIGHS IN A HALF

Pts.	Team vs. Opponent (Half)	Date
97	Oklahoma vs. U.S. Int'l (1st)	Nov. 29, 1989
96	Southern-B.R. vs. Texas College (2nd)	Dec. 6, 1990
94	Loyola (Cal.) vs. U.S. Int'l (1st)	Jan. 31, 1989
94	Oklahoma vs. Northeastern Ill. (2nd)	Dec. 2, 1989
94	Loyola (Cal.) vs. U.S. Int'l (1st)	Jan. 5, 1991
93	Loyola (Cal.) vs. U.S. Int'l (1st)	Jan. 7, 1989
93	Oklahoma vs. Loyola (Cal.) (2nd)	Dec. 15, 1990
92	Loyola (Cal.) vs. U.S. Int'l (2nd)	Jan. 5, 1991
92	Alabama St. vs. Grambling (2nd)	Jan. 21, 1991
91	Oklahoma vs. Angelo St. (2nd)	Dec. 1, 1990
87	Oklahoma vs. Oral Roberts (2nd)	Dec. 10, 1988
87	Loyola (Cal.) vs. U.S. Int'l (2nd)	Jan. 31, 1989
86	Jacksonville vs. St. Peter's (2nd)	Dec. 3, 1970
86	Lamar vs. Portland St. (2nd)	Jan. 12, 1980
86	Loyola (Cal.) vs. Gonzaga (2nd)	Feb. 18, 1989
86	Gonzaga vs. Loyola (Cal.) (2nd)	Feb. 18, 1989

SINGLE-GAME SCORING HIGHS IN A HALF BOTH TEAMS COMBINED

Pts.	Team (Pts.) vs. Team (Pts.) (Half)	Date
172	Loyola (Cal.) (86) vs. Gonzaga (86) (2nd)	Feb. 18, 1989
170	Loyola (Cal.) (94) vs. U.S. Int'l (76) (1st)	Jan. 31, 1989
164	Loyola (Cal.) (94) vs. U.S. Int'l (70) (1st)	Jan. 5, 1991
162	Loyola (Cal.) (92) vs. U.S. Int'l (70) (2nd)	Jan. 5, 1991
161	Loyola (Cal.) (93) vs. U.S. Int'l (68) (1st)	Jan. 7, 1989
161	Loyola (Cal.) (87) vs. U.S. Int'l (74) (2nd)	Jan. 31, 1989
160	Oklahoma (87) vs. Oral Roberts (73) (2nd)	Dec. 10, 1988

SINGLE-GAME FIELD-GOAL PERCENTAGE

Pct.	Team (FG-FGA) vs. Opponent	Date
83.3	Maryland (15-18) vs. South Caro.	Jan. 9, 1971
81.4	New Mexico (35-43) vs. Oregon St.	Nov. 30, 1985
81.0	Fresno St. (34-42) vs. Portland St.	Dec. 3, 1977
81.0	St. Peter's (34-42) vs. Utica	Dec. 4, 1984
80.5	Fordham (33-41) vs. Fairfield	Feb. 27, 1984
80.0	Holy Cross (32-40) vs. Vermont	Nov. 30, 1981
80.0	Oklahoma St. (28-35) vs. Tulane	Mar. 22, 1992
79.4	Arkansas (27-34) vs. Texas Tech	Feb. 20, 1979
79.4	Columbia (27-34) vs. Dartmouth	Mar. 2, 1984
79.0	North Caro. (49-62) vs. Loyola (Cal.)	Mar. 19, 1988
78.6	Villanova (22-28) vs. Georgetown	Apr. 1, 1985
78.6	St. Peter's (22-28) vs. Army	Jan. 9, 1982
78.4	Western Ky. (29-37) vs. Dayton	Jan. 24, 1979
78.1	Army (25-32) vs. Manhattan	Jan. 20, 1979
77.8	Samford (35-45) vs. Loyola (La.)	Dec. 12, 1992
77.5	Nicholls St. (31-40) vs. Samford	Dec. 30, 1983
77.4	Richmond (24-31) vs. Citadel	Feb. 8, 1976

SINGLE-GAME THREE-POINT FIELD GOALS MADE

3FG	Team vs. Opponent	Date
23	Lamar vs. Louisiana Tech	Feb. 28, 1993
21	Kentucky vs. North Caro.	Dec. 27, 1989
21	Loyola (Cal.) vs. Michigan	Mar. 18, 1990
21	Nevada-Las Vegas vs. Nevada	Dec. 8, 1990
20	Navy vs. Mt. St. Mary's (Md.)	Nov. 26, 1990
20	Lamar vs. Prairie View	Feb. 3, 1993
19	Valparaiso vs. Butler	Feb. 6, 1989
19	St. Francis (Pa.) vs. LIU-Brooklyn	Feb. 25, 1989
19	Kentucky vs. Furman	Dec. 19, 1989
19	Loyola (Cal.) vs. Chaminade	Nov. 25, 1990
19	New Mexico St. vs. Morgan St.	Dec. 29, 1990
19	Southern-B.R. vs. Southeastern La.	Feb. 14, 1991
19	Temple vs. Geo. Washington	Mar. 4, 1992
18	Eight tied	

SINGLE-GAME REBOUNDS

Reb.	Team vs. Opponent	Date
108	Kentucky vs. Mississippi	Feb. 8, 1964
103	Holy Cross vs. Boston College	Mar. 1, 1956
102	Arizona vs. Northern Ariz.	Jan. 6, 1951
101	Weber St. vs. Idaho St.	Jan. 22, 1966
100	William & Mary vs. Virginia	Feb. 14, 1954
95	Indiana vs. Michigan	Mar. 11, 1961
95	Murray St. vs. MacMurray	Jan. 2, 1967
92	Santa Clara vs. St. Mary's (Cal.)	Feb. 15, 1971
92	Oral Roberts vs. Brandeis	Jan. 8, 1973
91	Notre Dame vs. St. Norbert	Dec. 7, 1965
91	Southern Miss. vs. Tex.-Pan American	Feb. 9, 1970
91	Houston vs. Rice	Mar. 7, 1974
90	Vanderbilt vs. Sewanee	Dec. 4, 1954

SINGLE-GAME ASSISTS

Ast.	Team vs. Opponent	Date
41	North Caro. vs. Manhattan	Dec. 27, 1985
41	Weber St. vs. Northern Ariz.	Mar. 2, 1991
40	Loyola (Cal.) vs. U.S. Int'l	Jan. 5, 1991
40	New Mexico vs. Texas-Arlington	Nov. 23, 1990
40	Southern Utah vs. Texas Wesleyan	Jan. 25, 1992
40	Lamar vs. Prairie View	Feb. 2, 1993
39	Southern Miss. vs. Virginia Tech	Jan. 16, 1988
39	Nevada-Las Vegas vs. Pacific (Cal.)	Feb. 8, 1990
39	Nevada-Las Vegas vs. Rutgers	Feb. 3, 1991
39	Davidson vs. Warren Wilson	Dec. 9, 1991
38	New Mexico vs. U.S. Int'l	Dec. 3, 1985
38	Pepperdine vs. U.S. Int'l	Jan. 7, 1986
38	UCLA vs. Loyola (Cal.)	Dec. 2, 1990
38	Arizona vs. Northern Ariz.	Dec. 18, 1991
37	Eight tied (most recent: Tex.-San Antonio vs. Schreiner, Dec. 1, 1992)	

SINGLE-GAME BLOCKED SHOTS

Blk.	Team vs. Opponent	Date
20	Iona vs. Northern Ill.	Jan. 7, 1989
18	North Caro. vs. Stanford	Dec. 20, 1985
17	Maryland vs. Md.-East. Shore	Feb. 27, 1987
17	Rider vs. FDU-Teaneck	Jan. 9, 1989
17	Georgetown vs. Providence	Feb. 22, 1989
17	Georgetown vs. Hawaii-Loa	Nov. 23, 1990
17	Brigham Young vs. Eastern Ky.	Dec. 7, 1990
17	Northwestern (La.) vs. Oauchita Baptist	Nov. 30, 1991
17	New Orleans vs. Texas A&M	Dec. 29, 1992
16	UTEP vs. Fort Lewis	Nov. 26, 1988
16	Maryland vs. Md.-East. Shore	Dec. 1, 1988
16	Oklahoma St. vs. Oklahoma	Feb. 14, 1989
16	Clemson vs. Radford	Dec. 9, 1989
16	Villanova vs. Drexel	Dec. 16, 1989
16	Louisiana St. vs. Texas	Jan. 2, 1990
16	UCLA vs. UC Irvine	Nov. 23, 1990
16	Kentucky vs. Georgia	Feb. 3, 1991
16	Rutgers vs. St. Bonaventure	Jan. 16, 1992

SINGLE-GAME STEALS

Stl.	Team vs. Opponent	Date
34	Oklahoma vs. Centenary	Dec. 12, 1987
34	Northwestern (La.) vs. LeTourneau	Jan. 20, 1992
33	Connecticut vs. Pittsburgh	Jan. 6, 1990
32	Manhattan vs. Lehman	Dec. 14, 1987
32	Oklahoma vs. Angelo St.	Dec. 1, 1990
30	Southern-B.R. vs. Baptist Christian	Dec. 14, 1992
29	Cleveland St. vs. Canisius	Dec. 28, 1986
29	Oklahoma vs. U.S. Int'l	Nov. 19, 1989
29	Centenary vs. East Texas Baptist	Dec. 12, 1992
28	Oklahoma vs. Morgan St.	Dec. 21, 1991
28	Memphis St. vs. Southeastern La.	Jan. 11, 1993
28	Oklahoma vs. Florida A&M	Jan. 27, 1993
27	Oregon St. vs. Hawaii-Loa	Dec. 22, 1985
27	Cal St. Fullerton vs. Lamar	Nov. 24, 1989
27	Texas-San Antonio vs. Samford	Jan. 19, 1991
27	Iowa St. vs. Bethune-Cookman	Dec. 31, 1992

SEASON WON-LOST PERCENTAGE

Team	Season	Won	Lost	Pct.
North Caro.	1957	32	0	1.000
Indiana	1976	32	0	1.000
UCLA	1964	30	0	1.000
UCLA	1967	30	0	1.000
UCLA	1972	30	0	1.000
UCLA	1973	30	0	1.000
San Francisco	1956	29	0	1.000
North Caro. St.	1973	27	0	1.000
Kentucky	1954	25	0	1.000
LIU-Brooklyn	1939	24	0	1.000

Team	Season	Won	Lost	Pct.
Seton Hall	1940	19	0	1.000
Army	1944	15	0	1.000
Nevada-Las Vegas	1991	34	1	.971
Indiana St.	1979	33	1	.971
Indiana	1975	31	1	.969
North Caro. St.	1974	30	1	.968
UCLA	1968	29	1	.967
UCLA	1969	29	1	.967
UCLA	1971	29	1	.967
San Francisco	1955	28	1	.966
UTEP	1966	28	1	.966
Marquette	1971	28	1	.966
Pennsylvania	1971	28	1	.966
Alcorn St.	1979	28	1	.966
Ohio St.	1961	27	1	.964

SEASON MOST-IMPROVED TEAMS

(Since 1974)

Team	Year	W-L Record	Previous Yr. W-L	Games Up
North Caro. A&T	1978	20-8	3-24	16½
Murray St.	1980	23-8	4-22	16½
Liberty	1992	22-7	5-23	16½
North Texas	1976	22-4	6-20	16
Radford	1991	22-7	7-22	15
Tulsa	1981	26-7	8-19	15
Utah St.	1983	20-9	4-23	15
Western Mich.	1992	21-9	5-22	14½
Tennessee St.	1993	19-10	4-24	14½
Fresno St.	1978	21-6	7-20	14
James Madison	1987	20-10	5-23	14
Loyola (Cal.)	1988	28-4	12-16	14
Michigan St.	1978	25-5	10-17	13½
Kansas	1974	23-7	8-18	13
Wagner	1979	21-7	7-19	13
Xavier (Ohio)	1983	22-8	8-20	13
Arizona	1988	35-3	18-12	13
Ball St.	1989	29-3	14-14	13
Nebraska	1991	26-8	10-18	13
Wagner	1992	16-12	4-26	13

SEASON SCORING OFFENSE

Team	Season	G	Pts.	Avg.
Loyola (Cal.)	†1990	32	3,918	122.4
Loyola (Cal.)	†1989	31	3,486	112.5
Nevada-Las Vegas	†1976	31	3,426	110.5
Loyola (Cal.)	†1988	32	3,528	110.3
Nevada-Las Vegas	†1977	32	3,426	107.1
Oral Roberts	†1972	28	2,943	105.1
Southern-B.R.	†1991	28	2,924	104.4
Loyola (Cal.)	1991	31	3,211	103.6
Oklahoma	1988	39	4,012	102.9
Oklahoma	1989	36	3,680	102.2
Oklahoma	1990	32	3,243	101.3
Jacksonville	†1970	28	2,809	100.3
Jacksonville	†1971	26	2,598	99.9
Arkansas	1991	38	3,783	99.6
Southern-B.R.	1990	31	3,078	99.3

† *National leader.*

SEASON SCORING DEFENSE

Team	Season	G	Pts.	Avg.
Oklahoma St.	†1948	31	1,006	32.5
Oklahoma St.	†1949	28	985	35.2
Oklahoma St.	†1950	27	1,059	39.2
Alabama	1948	27	1,070	39.6
Creighton	1948	23	925	40.2

Team	Season	G	Pts.	Avg.
Wyoming	1948	27	1,101	40.8
Wyoming	1950	36	1,491	41.4
Siena	1948	28	1,161	41.5
St. Bonaventure	1948	22	921	41.9
Siena	1949	29	1,215	41.9
Tulane	1948	26	1,102	42.4
Wyoming	1949	35	1,509	43.1
Texas	1948	25	1,079	43.2
Utah	1948	20	868	43.4
Minnesota	1949	21	912	43.4

† *National leader.*

SEASON SCORING DEFENSE

(Since 1965)

Team	Season	G	Pts.	Avg.
Fresno St.	†1982	30	1,412	47.1
Princeton	†1992	28	1,349	48.2
Princeton	†1991	27	1,320	48.9
North Caro. St.	1982	32	1,570	49.1
Princeton	1982	26	1,277	49.1
Princeton	†1984	28	1,403	50.1
St. Peter's	1980	31	1,563	50.4
Fresno St.	1981	29	1,470	50.7
Princeton	†1990	27	1,378	51.0
Princeton	1981	28	1,438	51.4
St. Peter's	1981	26	1,338	51.5
Wyoming	1982	30	1,545	51.5
Princeton	†1977	26	1,343	51.7
Princeton	†1983	29	1,507	52.0
James Madison	1982	30	1,559	52.0

† *National leader.*

SEASON SCORING MARGIN

Team	Season	Off.	Def.	Mar.
UCLA	†1972	94.6	64.3	30.3
North Caro. St.	†1948	75.3	47.2	28.1
Kentucky	†1954	87.5	60.3	27.2
Kentucky	†1952	82.3	55.4	26.9
Nevada-Las Vegas	†1991	97.7	71.0	26.7
UCLA	†1968	93.4	67.2	26.2
UCLA	†1967	89.6	63.7	25.9
Houston	1968	97.8	72.5	25.3
Kentucky	1948	69.0	44.4	24.6
Kentucky	†1949	68.2	43.9	24.3
Bowling Green	1948	70.5	46.7	23.8
Loyola (Ill.)	†1963	91.8	68.1	23.7
N.C.-Charlotte	†1975	88.9	65.2	23.7
Arizona St.	†1962	90.1	67.6	22.5
St. Bonaventure	†1970	88.4	65.9	22.5

† *National leader.*

SEASON FIELD-GOAL PERCENTAGE

Team	Season	FG	FGA	Pct.
Missouri	†1980	936	1,635	57.2
Michigan	†1989	1,325	2,341	56.6
Oregon St.	†1981	862	1,528	56.4
UC Irvine	†1982	920	1,639	56.1
Michigan St.	†1986	1,043	1,860	56.1
North Caro.	1986	1,197	2,140	55.9
Kansas	1986	1,260	2,266	55.6
Kentucky	†1983	869	1,564	55.6
Notre Dame	1981	824	1,492	55.2
Houston Baptist	†1984	797	1,445	55.2
Maryland	1980	985	1,789	55.1
Idaho	1981	816	1,484	55.0
UC Irvine	1981	934	1,703	54.8
Navy	†1985	946	1,726	54.8
Stanford	1983	752	1,373	54.8

† *National leader.*

SEASON FIELD-GOAL PERCENTAGE DEFENSE

(Since 1978)

Team	Season	FG	FGA	Pct.
Nevada-Las Vegas	†1992	628	1,723	36.5
Georgetown	†1991	680	1,847	36.8
Princeton	1992	445	1,169	38.1
Northern Ill.	1991	616	1,587	38.8
Connecticut	1991	682	1,753	38.9
Temple	†1988	777	1,981	39.2
Marquette	†1993	634	1,613	39.3
Georgetown	†1984	799	2,025	39.5
Montana	1992	685	1,736	39.5
Geo. Washington	1993	708	1,794	39.5
New Orleans	1991	725	1,837	39.5
Middle Tenn. St.	1991	793	2,007	39.5
Wyoming	†1982	584	1,470	39.7
Arizona	1991	903	2,272	39.7
Connecticut	1992	734	1,843	39.8
Charleston	1992	592	1,486	39.8

† *National leader.*

SEASON THREE-POINT FIELD GOALS MADE PER GAME

Team	Season	G	3FG	Avg.
Lamar	†1993	27	271	10.037
Kentucky	†1990	28	281	10.036
Kentucky	1993	34	340	10.00
La Salle	†1992	31	294	9.48
Arizona St.	1993	28	263	9.39
Loyola (Cal.)	1990	32	298	9.31
Loyola (Cal.)	†1989	31	287	9.26
Northwestern (La.)	1992	28	259	9.25
Texas-Arlington	†1991	29	265	9.14
East Tenn. St.	1991	33	301	9.12
Valparaiso	1989	29	257	8.86
Dayton	1991	29	256	8.83
North Caro. St.	1992	30	265	8.83
Kentucky	1992	36	317	8.81
Texas-Arlington	1992	29	255	8.79

† *National leader.*

SEASON THREE-POINT FIELD-GOAL PERCENTAGE

Team	Season	G	3FG	3FGA	Pct.
Indiana	†1987	34	130	256	50.8
Mississippi Val.	1987	28	161	322	50.0
Stephen F. Austin	1987	30	120	241	49.8
Princeton	†1988	26	211	429	49.2
Prairie View	1988	27	129	266	48.5
Kansas St.	1988	34	179	370	48.4
Arizona	1988	38	254	526	48.3
Indiana	†1989	35	121	256	47.3
Bucknell	1988	28	154	328	47.0
Holy Cross	1988	29	158	337	46.9
Michigan	1989	37	196	419	46.8
Wis.-Green Bay	†1992	30	204	437	46.7
Citadel	1989	28	153	328	46.6
Niagara	1987	31	128	275	46.5
Eastern Mich.	1987	29	144	310	46.5

† *National leader.*

SEASON FREE-THROW PERCENTAGE

Team	Season	FT	FTA	Pct.
Harvard	†1984	535	651	82.2
Brigham Young	†1989	527	647	81.5
Harvard	†1985	450	555	81.1
Ohio St.	†1970	452	559	80.9
Vanderbilt	†1974	477	595	80.2

Travis Ford and his Kentucky teammates averaged 10.00 three-point field goals per game in 1993. The Wildcats hold three of the top 15 performances in season three-pointers made per game.

Team	Season	FT	FTA	Pct.
Michigan St.	†1986	490	613	79.9
Butler	†1988	413	517	79.9
Miami (Fla.)	†1975	642	807	79.6
Tulane	†1963	390	492	79.3
Tennessee	†1971	538	679	79.2
Auburn	†1966	476	601	79.2
Oklahoma St.	†1958	488	617	79.1
Duke	†1978	665	841	79.1
Utah	†1993	476	602	79.1
Gonzaga	1989	485	614	79.0

† *National leader.*

SEASON REBOUND MARGIN

(Since 1973)

Team	Season	Off.	Def.	Margin
Manhattan	†1973	56.5	38.0	18.5
American	1973	56.7	40.3	16.4
Alcorn St.	†1978	52.3	36.0	16.3
Oral Roberts	1973	66.9	50.3	15.6
Alcorn St.	†1980	49.2	33.8	15.4
UCLA	1973	49.0	33.9	15.1
Houston	1973	54.7	40.8	13.9
Massachusetts	†1974	44.5	30.7	13.8

Team	Season	Off.	Def.	Margin
Alcorn St.	†1979	50.1	36.3	13.8
Minnesota	1973	49.0	36.0	13.0
Va. Commonwealth	1974	55.1	42.1	13.0
Northeastern	†1981	44.9	32.0	12.9
Stetson	†1975	47.1	34.7	12.4
Notre Dame	†1976	46.3	34.1	12.2
Harvard	1973	53.5	41.3	12.2
Tennessee St.	1980	46.5	34.3	12.2

† *National leader.*

SEASON ASSISTS PER GAME

Team	Season	G	Ast.	Avg.
Nevada-Las Vegas	†1991	35	863	24.7
Loyola (Cal.)	†1990	32	762	23.8
North Caro.	†1986	34	800	23.5
Nevada-Las Vegas	1990	40	926	23.2
Southern Methodist	†1987	29	655	22.6
Southern Methodist	†1988	35	786	22.5
Oklahoma	†1985	37	828	22.4
Oklahoma	1988	39	862	22.1
Northwestern (La.)	†1993	26	570	21.9
Nevada-Las Vegas	1987	39	853	21.9
Kansas	1990	35	763	21.8
North Caro.	1987	36	782	21.7
Iowa St.	1988	32	694	21.7
Arkansas	1991	38	819	21.6
North Caro.	†1989	37	788	21.3
Georgia Tech	1988	32	680	21.3

† *National leader.*

SEASON BLOCKED SHOTS PER GAME

Team	Season	G	Blk.	Avg.
Georgetown	†1989	34	309	9.09
Nevada-Las Vegas	†1991	35	266	7.60
Georgetown	†1990	31	233	7.52
Georgetown	1991	32	235	7.34
Brigham Young	1991	34	246	7.24
Louisiana St.	1990	32	225	7.03
Vermont	†1992	29	198	6.83
Clemson	1990	35	235	6.71
Navy	†1986	35	233	6.66
Siena	†1988	29	193	6.66
Louisiana St.	1992	31	206	6.65
Maryland	1991	28	185	6.61
Louisiana St.	1991	30	198	6.60
Wyoming	†1993	28	184	6.57
Siena	†1987	29	188	6.48

† *National leader.*

SEASON STEALS PER GAME

Team	Season	G	Stl.	Avg.
Texas-San Antonio	†1991	29	430	14.8
Cleveland St.	†1987	33	473	14.3
Centenary	†1993	27	380	14.1
Loyola (Cal.)	†1990	32	450	14.1
Cleveland St.	†1986	33	436	13.2
Florida A&M	†1988	30	395	13.2
Connecticut	1990	37	484	13.1
N.C.-Charlotte	1991	28	363	13.0
Northeastern Ill.	†1992	28	358	12.8
Oklahoma	1993	32	405	12.7
Southern-B.R.	1991	28	352	12.6
Cleveland St.	1988	30	376	12.5

Team	Season	G	Stl.	Avg.
Tulane	1992	31	388	12.5
Southern-B.R.	1993	31	387	12.5
Oklahoma	1988	39	486	12.5

† *National leader.*

DIVISION I MEN'S ANNUAL TEAM CHAMPIONS

WON-LOST PERCENTAGE

Year	Team	Won	Lost	Pct.
1948	Western Ky.	28	2	.933
1949	Kentucky	32	2	.941
1950	Holy Cross	27	4	.871
1951	Columbia	21	1	.956
1952	Kansas	26	2	.929
1953	Seton Hall	31	2	.939
1954	Kentucky	25	0	1.000
1955	San Francisco	28	1	.966
1956	San Francisco	29	0	1.000
1957	North Caro.	32	0	1.000
1958	West Va.	26	2	.929
1959	Kansas St.	25	2	.926
1960	California	28	2	.933
	Cincinnati	28	2	.933
1961	Ohio St.	27	1	.964
1962	Cincinnati	29	2	.935
1963	Loyola (Ill.)	29	2	.935
1964	UCLA	30	0	1.000
1965	UCLA	28	2	.933
1966	UTEP	28	1	.966
1967	UCLA	30	0	1.000
1968	UCLA	29	1	.967
1969	UCLA	29	1	.967
1970	UCLA	28	2	.933
1971	UCLA	29	1	.967
1972	UCLA	30	0	1.000
1973	UCLA	30	0	1.000
	North Caro. St.	27	0	1.000
1974	North Caro. St.	30	1	.968
1975	Indiana	31	1	.969
1976	Indiana	32	0	1.000
1977	San Francisco	29	2	.935
1978	Kentucky	30	2	.938
1979	Indiana St.	33	1	.971
1980	Alcorn St.	28	2	.933
1981	DePaul	27	2	.931
1982	North Caro.	32	2	.941
1983	Houston	31	3	.912
1984	Georgetown	34	3	.919
1985	Georgetown	35	3	.921
1986	Duke	37	3	.925
1987	Nevada-Las Vegas	37	2	.949
1988	Temple	32	2	.941
1989	Ball St.	29	3	.906
1990	La Salle	30	2	.938
1991	Nevada-Las Vegas	34	1	.971
1992	Duke	34	2	.944
1993	North Caro.	34	4	.895

MOST-IMPROVED TEAMS

Year	Team	W-L Record	Previous Yr. W-L	Games Up
1974	Kansas	23-7	8-18	13
1975	Holy Cross	20-8	8-18	11
1976	North Texas	22-4	6-20	16
1977	Southwestern La.	21-8	7-19	12½
1978	North Caro. A&T	20-8	3-24	16½

Year	Team	W-L Record	Previous Yr. W-L	Games Up
1979	Wagner	21-7	7-19	13
1980	Murray St.	23-8	4-22	16½
1981	Tulsa	26-7	8-19	15
1982	Cal St. Fullerton	18-14	4-23	11½
1983	Utah St.	20-9	4-23	15
1984	Northeastern	27-5	13-15	12
	Loyola (Md.)	16-12	4-24	12
1985	Cincinnati	17-14	3-25	12½
1986	Bradley	32-3	17-13	12½
1987	James Madison	20-10	5-23	14
1988	Loyola (Cal.)	28-4	12-16	14
1989	Ball St.	29-3	14-14	13
1990	South Fla.	20-11	7-21	11½
	Geo. Washington	14-17	1-27	11½
1991	Radford	22-7	7-22	15
1992	Liberty	22-7	5-23	16½
1993	Tennessee St.	19-10	4-24	14½

SCORING OFFENSE

Year	Team	G	(W-L)	Pts.	Avg.
1948	Rhode Island	23	(17-6)	1,755	76.3
1949	Rhode Island	22	(16-6)	1,575	71.6
1950	Villanova	29	(25-4)	2,111	72.8
1951	Cincinnati	22	(18-4)	1,694	77.0
1952	Kentucky	32	(29-3)	2,635	82.3
1953	Furman	27	(21-6)	2,435	90.2
1954	Furman	29	(20-9)	2,658	91.7
1955	Furman	27	(17-10)	2,572	95.3
1956	Morehead St.	29	(19-10)	2,782	95.9
1957	Connecticut	25	(17-8)	2,183	87.3
1958	Marshall	24	(17-7)	2,113	88.0
1959	Miami (Fla.)	25	(18-7)	2,190	87.6
1960	Ohio St.	28	(25-3)	2,532	90.4
1961	St. Bonaventure	28	(24-4)	2,479	88.5
1962	Loyola (Ill.)	27	(23-4)	2,436	90.2
1963	Loyola (Ill.)	31	(29-2)	2,847	91.8
1964	Detroit Mercy	25	(14-11)	2,402	96.1
1965	Miami (Fla.)	26	(22-4)	2,558	98.4
1966	Syracuse	28	(22-6)	2,773	99.0
1967	Oklahoma City	26	(16-10)	2,496	96.0
1968	Houston	33	(31-2)	3,226	97.8
1969	Purdue	28	(23-5)	2,605	93.0
1970	Jacksonville	28	(26-2)	2,809	100.3
1971	Jacksonville	26	(22-4)	2,598	99.9
1972	Oral Roberts	28	(26-2)	2,943	105.1
1973	Oral Roberts	27	(21-6)	2,626	97.3
1974	Md.-East. Shore	29	(27-2)	2,831	97.6
1975	South Ala.	26	(19-7)	2,412	92.8
1976	Nevada-Las Vegas	31	(29-2)	3,426	110.5
1977	Nevada-Las Vegas	32	(29-3)	3,426	107.1
1978	New Mexico	28	(24-4)	2,731	97.5
1979	Nevada-Las Vegas	29	(21-9)	2,700	93.1
1980	Alcorn St.	30	(28-2)	2,729	92.0
1981	UC Irvine	27	(17-10)	2,332	86.4
1982	LIU-Brooklyn	30	(20-10)	2,605	86.8
1983	Boston College	32	(25-7)	2,697	84.3
1984	Tulsa	31	(27-4)	2,816	90.8
1985	Oklahoma	37	(31-6)	3,328	89.9
1986	U.S. Int'l	28	(8-20)	2,542	90.8
1987	Nevada-Las Vegas	39	(37-2)	3,612	92.6
1988	Loyola (Cal.)	32	(28-4)	3,528	110.3
1989	Loyola (Cal.)	31	(20-11)	3,486	112.5
1990	Loyola (Cal.)	32	(26-6)	3,918	*122.4
1991	Southern-B.R.	28	(19-9)	2,924	104.4
1992	Northwestern (La.)	28	(15-13)	2,660	95.0
1993	Southern-B.R.	31	(21-10)	3,011	97.1

* *Record.*

SCORING DEFENSE

Year	Team	G	(W-L)	Pts.	Avg.
1948	Oklahoma St.	31	(27-4)	1,006	*32.5
1949	Oklahoma St.	28	(23-5)	985	35.2
1950	Oklahoma St.	27	(18-9)	1,059	39.2
1951	Texas A&M	29	(17-12)	1,275	44.0
1952	Oklahoma St.	27	(19-8)	1,228	45.5
1953	Oklahoma St.	30	(23-7)	1,614	53.8
1954	Oklahoma St.	29	(24-5)	1,539	53.1
1955	San Francisco	29	(28-1)	1,511	52.1
1956	San Francisco	29	(29-0)	1,514	52.2
1957	Oklahoma St.	26	(17-9)	1,420	54.6
1958	San Francisco	27	(25-2)	1,363	50.5
1959	California	29	(25-4)	1,480	51.0
1960	California	30	(28-2)	1,486	49.5
1961	Santa Clara	27	(18-9)	1,314	48.7
1962	Santa Clara	25	(19-6)	1,302	52.1
1963	Cincinnati	28	(26-2)	1,480	52.9
1964	San Jose St.	24	(14-10)	1,307	54.5
1965	Tennessee	25	(20-5)	1,391	55.6
1966	Oregon St.	28	(21-7)	1,527	54.5
1967	Tennessee	28	(21-7)	1,511	54.0
1968	Army	25	(20-5)	1,448	57.9
1969	Army	28	(18-10)	1,498	53.5
1970	Army	28	(22-6)	1,515	54.1
1971	FDU-Teaneck	23	(16-7)	1,236	53.7
1972	Minnesota	25	(18-7)	1,451	58.0
1973	UTEP	26	(16-10)	1,460	56.2
1974	UTEP	25	(18-7)	1,413	56.5
1975	UTEP	26	(20-6)	1,491	57.3
1976	Princeton	27	(22-5)	1,427	52.9
1977	Princeton	26	(21-5)	1,343	51.7
1978	Fresno St.	27	(21-6)	1,417	52.5
1979	Princeton	26	(14-12)	1,452	55.8
1980	St. Peter's	31	(22-9)	1,563	50.4
1981	Fresno St.	29	(25-4)	1,470	50.7
1982	Fresno St.	30	(27-3)	1,412	47.1
1983	Princeton	29	(20-9)	1,507	52.0
1984	Princeton	28	(18-10)	1,403	50.1
1985	Fresno St.	32	(23-9)	1,696	53.0
1986	Princeton	26	(13-13)	1,429	55.0
1987	Southwest Mo. St.	34	(28-6)	1,958	57.6
1988	Ga. Southern	31	(24-7)	1,725	55.6
1989	Princeton	27	(19-8)	1,430	53.0
1990	Princeton	27	(20-7)	1,378	51.0
1991	Princeton	27	(24-3)	1,320	48.9
1992	Princeton	28	(22-6)	1,349	48.2
1993	Princeton	26	(15-11)	1,421	54.7

* *Record.*

SCORING MARGIN

Year	Team	Off.	Def.	Margin
1949	Kentucky	68.2	43.9	24.3
1950	Holy Cross	72.6	55.4	17.2
1951	Kentucky	74.7	52.5	22.2
1952	Kentucky	82.3	55.4	26.9
1953	La Salle	80.1	61.8	18.3
1954	Kentucky	87.5	60.3	27.2
1955	Utah	79.0	59.9	19.1
1956	San Francisco	72.2	52.2	20.0
1957	Kentucky	84.2	69.4	14.8
1958	Cincinnati	86.5	65.9	20.6
1959	Idaho St.	74.2	53.7	20.5
1960	Cincinnati	86.7	64.7	22.0
1961	Memphis St.	85.0	64.2	20.8
1962	Arizona St.	90.1	67.6	22.5
1963	Loyola (Ill.)	91.8	68.1	23.7

Year	Team	Off.	Def.	Margin
1964	Davidson	89.3	70.5	18.8
1965	Connecticut	85.1	66.5	18.6
1966	Loyola (Ill.)	97.5	76.6	20.9
1967	UCLA	89.6	63.7	25.9
1968	UCLA	93.4	67.2	26.2
1969	UCLA	84.7	63.8	20.9
1970	St. Bonaventure	88.4	65.9	22.5
1971	Jacksonville	99.9	79.0	20.9
1972	UCLA	94.6	64.3	*30.3
1973	North Caro. St.	92.9	71.1	21.8
1974	N.C.-Charlotte	90.2	69.4	20.8
1975	N.C.-Charlotte	88.9	65.2	23.7
1976	Nevada-Las Vegas	*110.5	89.0	21.5
1977	Nevada-Las Vegas	107.1	87.7	19.4
1978	UCLA	85.3	67.4	17.9
1979	Syracuse	88.7	71.5	17.2
1980	Alcorn St.	91.0	73.6	17.4
1981	Wyoming	73.6	57.5	16.1
1982	Oregon St.	69.6	55.0	14.6
1983	Houston	82.4	64.9	17.4
1984	Georgetown	74.3	57.9	16.4
1985	Georgetown	74.3	57.3	17.1
1986	Cleveland St.	88.9	69.6	19.3
1987	Nevada-Las Vegas	92.6	75.5	17.1
1988	Oklahoma	102.9	81.0	21.9
1989	St. Mary's (Cal.)	76.1	57.6	18.5
1990	Oklahoma	101.3	80.4	21.0
1991	Nevada-Las Vegas	97.7	71.0	26.7
1992	Indiana	83.4	65.8	17.6
1993	North Caro.	86.1	68.3	17.8

* *Record.*

FIELD-GOAL PERCENTAGE

Year	Team	FG	FGA	Pct.
1948	Oregon St.	668	1,818	36.7
1949	Muhlenberg	593	1,512	39.2
1950	Texas Christian	476	1,191	40.0
1951	Maryland	481	1,210	39.8
1952	Boston College	787	1,893	41.6
1953	Furman	936	2,106	44.4
1954	Geo. Washington	744	1,632	45.6
1955	Geo. Washington	867	1,822	47.6
1956	Geo. Washington	725	1,451	50.0
1957	Manhattan	679	1,489	45.6
1958	Fordham	693	1,440	48.1
1959	Auburn	593	1,216	48.8
1960	Auburn	532	1,022	52.1
1961	Ohio St.	939	1,886	49.8
1962	Florida St.	709	1,386	51.2
1963	Duke	984	1,926	51.1
1964	Davidson	894	1,644	54.4
1965	St. Peter's	579	1,089	53.2
1966	North Caro.	838	1,620	51.7
1967	UCLA	1,082	2,081	52.0
1968	Bradley	927	1,768	52.4
1969	UCLA	1,027	1,999	51.4
1970	Ohio St.	831	1,527	54.4
1971	Jacksonville	1,077	2,008	53.6
1972	North Caro.	1,031	1,954	52.8
1973	North Caro.	1,150	2,181	52.7
1974	Notre Dame	1,056	1,992	53.0
1975	Maryland	1,049	1,918	54.7
1976	Maryland	996	1,854	53.7
1977	Arkansas	849	1,558	54.5
1978	Arkansas	1,060	1,943	54.6
1979	UCLA	1,053	1,897	55.5
1980	Missouri	936	1,635	*57.2

Year	Team	FG	FGA	Pct.
1981	Oregon St.	862	1,528	56.4
1982	UC Irvine	920	1,639	56.1
1983	Kentucky	869	1,564	55.6
1984	Houston Baptist	797	1,445	55.2
1985	Navy	946	1,726	54.8
1986	Michigan St.	1,043	1,860	56.1
1987	Princeton	601	1,111	54.1
1988	Michigan	1,198	2,196	54.6
1989	Michigan	1,325	2,341	56.6
1990	Kansas	1,204	2,258	53.3
1991	Nevada-Las Vegas	1,305	2,441	53.5
1992	Duke	1,108	2,069	53.6
1993	Indiana	1,076	2,062	52.2

* *Record.*

FIELD-GOAL PERCENTAGE DEFENSE

Year	Team	FG	FGA	Pct.
1977	Minnesota	766	1,886	40.6
1978	Delaware St.	733	1,802	40.7
1979	Illinois	738	1,828	40.4
1980	Penn St.	543	1,309	41.5
1981	Wyoming	637	1,589	40.1
1982	Wyoming	584	1,470	39.7
1983	Wyoming	599	1,441	41.6
1984	Georgetown	799	2,025	39.5
1985	Georgetown	833	2,064	40.4
1986	St. Peter's	574	1,395	41.1
1987	San Diego	660	1,645	40.1
1988	Temple	777	1,981	39.2
1989	Georgetown	795	1,993	39.9
1990	Georgetown	713	1,929	37.0
1991	Georgetown	680	1,847	36.8
1992	Nevada-Las Vegas	628	1,723	*36.4
1993	Marquette	634	1,613	39.3

* *Record.*

THREE-POINT FIELD GOALS MADE PER GAME

Year	Team	G	3FG	Avg.
1987	Providence	34	280	8.24
1988	Princeton	26	211	8.12
1989	Loyola (Cal.)	31	287	9.26
1990	Kentucky	28	281	10.04
1991	Texas-Arlington	29	265	9.14
1992	La Salle	31	294	9.48
1993	Lamar	27	271	*10.04

* *Record.*

THREE-POINT FIELD-GOAL PERCENTAGE

Year	Team	G	3FG	3FGA	Pct.
1987	Indiana	34	130	256	*50.8
1988	Princeton	26	211	429	49.2
1989	Indiana	35	121	256	47.3
1990	Princeton	27	208	460	45.2
1991	Wis.-Green Bay	31	189	407	46.4
1992	Wis.-Green Bay	30	204	437	46.7
1993	Valparaiso	28	214	500	42.8

* *Record.*

FREE-THROW PERCENTAGE

Year	Team	FT	FTA	Pct.
1948	Texas	351	481	73.0
1949	Davidson	347	489	71.0

Year	Team	FT	FTA	Pct.
1950	Temple	342	483	70.8
1951	Minnesota	287	401	71.6
1952	Kansas	491	707	69.4
1953	Geo. Washington	502	696	72.1
1954	Wake Forest	734	1,010	72.7
1955	Wake Forest	709	938	75.6
1956	Southern Methodist	701	917	76.4
1957	Oklahoma St.	569	752	75.7
1958	Oklahoma St.	488	617	79.1
1959	Tulsa	446	586	76.1
1960	Auburn	424	549	77.2
1961	Tulane	459	604	76.0
1962	Southern Methodist	552	718	76.9
1963	Tulane	390	492	79.3
1964	Miami (Fla.)	593	780	76.0
1965	Miami (Fla.)	642	807	79.6
1966	Auburn	476	601	79.2
1967	West Tex. A&M	400	518	77.2
1968	Vanderbilt	527	684	77.0
1969	Jacksonville	574	733	78.3
1970	Ohio St.	452	559	80.9
1971	Tennessee	538	679	79.2
1972	Lafayette	656	844	77.7
1973	Duke	496	632	78.5
1974	Vanderbilt	477	595	80.2
1975	Vanderbilt	530	692	76.6
1976	Morehead St.	452	577	78.3
1977	Utah	499	638	78.2
1978	Duke	665	841	79.1
1979	St. Francis (Pa.)	350	446	78.5
1980	Oral Roberts	481	610	78.9
1981	Connecticut	487	623	78.2
1982	Western Ill.	447	569	78.6
1983	Western Ill.	526	679	77.5
1984	Harvard	535	651	*82.2
1985	Harvard	450	555	81.1
1986	Michigan St.	490	613	79.9
1987	Alabama	521	662	78.7
1988	Butler	413	517	79.9
1989	Brigham Young	527	647	81.5
1990	Lafayette	461	588	78.4
1991	Butler	725	922	78.6
1992	Northwestern	497	651	76.3
1993	Utah	476	602	79.1

* *Record.*

REBOUNDING

Year	Team	G	Reb.	Pct.
1955	Niagara	26	1,507	.624
1956	Geo. Washington	26	1,451	.616
1957	Morehead St.	27	1,735	.621
1958	Manhattan	26	1,437	.591
1959	Mississippi St.	25	1,012	.589
1960	Iona	18	1,054	.607
1961	Bradley	26	1,330	.592
1962	Cornell	25	1,463	.590
1963	UTEP	26	1,167	.591
1964	Iona	20	1,071	.640
1965	Iona	23	1,191	.628
1966	UTEP	29	1,430	.577
1967	Florida	25	1,275	.600

Year	Team	G	Reb.	Avg.
1968	Houston	33	2,074	62.8
1969	Middle Tenn. St.	26	1,685	64.8
1970	Florida St.	26	1,451	55.8
1971	Pacific (Cal.)	28	1,643	58.7
1972	Oral Roberts	28	1,686	60.2

Year	Team	Off.	Def.	Margin
1973	Manhattan	56.5	38.0	*18.5
1974	Massachusetts	44.5	30.7	13.8
1975	Stetson	47.1	34.7	12.4
1976	Notre Dame	46.3	34.1	12.2
1977	Notre Dame	42.4	31.6	10.8
1978	Alcorn St.	52.3	36.0	16.3
1979	Alcorn St.	50.1	36.3	13.8
1980	Alcorn St.	49.2	33.8	15.4
1981	Northeastern	44.9	32.0	12.9
1982	Northeastern	41.2	30.8	10.4
1983	Wichita St.	42.4	33.6	8.8
1984	Northeastern	40.1	30.3	9.8
1985	Georgetown	39.6	30.5	9.1
1986	Notre Dame	36.4	27.8	8.6
1987	Iowa	43.1	31.5	11.5
1988	Notre Dame	36.0	26.2	9.9
1989	Iowa	41.4	31.8	9.6
1990	Georgetown	44.8	34.0	10.8
1991	New Orleans	41.7	32.4	9.3
1992	Delaware	42.1	33.8	8.3
1993	Massachusetts	43.9	32.8	11.2

Note: From 1955 through 1967, the rebounding champion was determined on the basis of highest team recoveries out of the total by both teams in all games. From 1968 through 1972, the champion was determined on the basis of rebound average per game. Beginning with the 1973 season, the champion has been determined on the basis of rebounding margin.

* *Record.*

ASSISTS

Year	Team	G	Ast.	Avg.
1984	Clemson	28	571	20.4
1985	Oklahoma	37	828	22.4
1986	North Caro.	34	800	23.5
1987	Southern Methodist	29	655	22.6
1988	Southern Methodist	35	786	22.5
1989	North Caro.	37	788	21.3
1990	Loyola (Cal.)	32	762	23.8
1991	Nevada-Las Vegas	35	863	*24.7
1992	Arkansas	34	674	19.8
1993	Northwestern (La.)	26	570	21.9

* *Record.*

BLOCKED SHOTS

Year	Team	G	Blk.	Avg.
1986	Navy	35	233	6.66
1987	Siena	29	188	6.48
1988	Siena	29	193	6.66
1989	Georgetown	34	309	*9.09
1990	Georgetown	31	233	7.52
1991	Nevada-Las Vegas	35	266	7.60
1992	Vermont	29	198	6.83
1993	Wyoming	28	184	6.57

* *Record.*

STEALS

Year	Team	G	Stl.	Avg.
1986	Cleveland St.	33	436	13.2
1987	Cleveland St.	33	473	14.3
1988	Florida A&M	30	395	13.2
1989	Arkansas	32	372	11.6
1990	Loyola (Cal.)	32	450	14.1
1991	Texas-San Antonio	29	430	*14.8
1992	Northeastern Ill.	28	358	12.8
1993	Centenary	27	380	14.1

* *Record.*

DIVISION I MEN'S STATISTICAL TRENDS

Year	Games	FG Made	FG Att.	Pct.	FT Made	FT Att.	Pct.	PF	Pts.
1948	3,945	40.6	138.7	29.3	25.3	42.2	59.8	36.9	106.5
1949	3,737	41.4	134.7	30.8	26.7	43.3	61.6	38.7	109.5
1950	3,659	43.2	136.8	31.6	28.7	46.5	61.8	39.0	115.1
1951	3,974	45.6	137.8	33.1	30.2	48.1	62.8	42.7	121.4
1952	4,009	47.5	*140.6	33.7	31.6	50.5	62.6	*44.9	126.6
1953	3,754	48.0	138.1	34.7	42.1	*65.8	64.0	42.5	138.1
1954	3,933	48.8	135.5	35.4	41.9	64.3	65.2	42.0	137.9
1955	3,829	51.1	138.6	36.9	*43.1	64.7	66.5	37.9	145.3
1956	4,098	52.1	139.0	37.5	42.3	63.3	66.8	37.7	146.5
1957	4,113	51.6	135.1	38.2	40.8	60.6	67.3	36.5	144.0
1958	4,153	51.6	134.2	38.4	33.6	50.5	66.4	36.4	136.8
1959	4,234	51.7	132.3	39.1	34.0	50.7	67.1	36.3	137.4
1960	4,295	52.6	132.3	39.8	34.7	51.5	67.4	36.7	139.9
1961	4,238	53.3	131.1	40.7	34.7	50.9	68.2	36.4	141.3
1962	4,341	54.0	134.5	40.2	33.0	48.6	67.9	36.1	141.0
1963	4,180	53.2	127.6	41.7	32.6	47.8	68.2	36.4	139.0
1964	4,347	57.3	134.7	42.5	34.2	50.1	68.3	38.1	148.8
1965	4,520	58.3	135.4	43.1	34.7	50.3	69.0	38.5	151.4
1966	3,986	60.0	137.6	43.6	35.0	50.5	69.2	38.4	154.9
1967	4,602	57.7	131.9	43.8	34.4	49.8	69.0	38.3	149.8
1968	4,739	58.1	133.1	43.7	34.7	50.2	69.1	38.0	150.9
1969	4,883	58.2	132.8	43.8	34.8	50.8	68.4	37.9	151.2
1970	4,979	59.9	135.5	44.2	35.3	51.4	68.7	38.6	155.1
1971	5,232	60.2	135.6	44.4	35.0	51.3	68.1	38.5	*155.4
1972	5,404	60.2	134.3	44.8	35.0	51.1	68.6	38.4	155.3
1973	5,582	62.3	139.2	44.8	26.2	38.3	68.4	38.4	150.9
1974	6,060	62.0	136.5	45.4	25.6	37.4	68.4	38.4	149.5
1975	6,147	*62.9	136.7	46.0	27.4	39.7	69.0	40.3	153.1
1976	6,240	61.9	132.5	46.7	27.6	39.8	69.2	40.4	151.3
1977	6,676	60.7	129.8	46.7	28.4	41.0	69.4	40.2	149.7
1978	6,901	60.2	127.2	47.3	28.6	41.4	69.2	40.4	148.9
1979	7,131	59.2	124.1	47.7	29.5	42.2	*69.7	41.1	147.9
1980	7,304	57.2	119.3	47.9	29.7	42.6	69.6	40.3	144.0
1981	7,407	55.6	115.9	48.0	29.0	42.0	68.9	40.2	140.1
1982	7,646	53.3	111.2	47.9	28.5	41.6	68.6	38.7	135.1
1983	7,957	54.3	114.0	47.7	29.0	42.3	68.5	39.7	138.6
1984	8,029	53.4	111.1	*48.1	29.5	42.8	68.9	39.9	136.3
1985	8,269	54.5	113.9	47.9	29.3	42.5	68.9	39.3	138.3
1986	8,360	54.7	114.6	47.7	29.4	42.5	69.1	39.1	138.7

Year	Games	FG Made	FG Att.	Pct.	3FG Made	3FG Att.	Pct.	FT Made	FT Att.	Pct.	PF	Pts.
1987	8,580	54.4	117.3	46.4	7.0	18.3	*38.4	29.7	43.0	69.1	39.3	145.5
1988	8,587	54.8	116.6	47.0	8.0	20.8	38.2	30.2	43.8	68.9	39.4	147.8
1989	8,677	55.7	118.5	47.0	8.9	23.6	37.6	31.1	45.0	69.1	40.2	151.4
1990	8,646	54.7	118.9	46.0	9.4	25.7	36.7	31.1	45.1	68.9	39.6	149.8
1991	8,720	55.6	121.3	45.8	10.0	27.6	36.1	31.7	46.3	68.5	39.2	152.9
1992	*8,803	53.0	116.6	45.5	9.9	28.0	35.5	31.6	46.4	68.1	40.0	147.6
1993	8,528	52.9	117.2	45.2	*10.5	*29.8	35.4	30.8	45.5	67.7	39.1	147.2

** All-time high.*

Note: Averages and percentages are for both teams, per game.

DIVISION I MEN'S WINNING STREAKS

LONGEST—FULL SEASON

Team	No. of Games	Seasons	Ended By
UCLA	88	1971-74	Notre Dame (71-70)
San Francisco	60	1955-57	Illinois (62-33)
UCLA	47	1966-68	Houston (71-69)
Nevada-Las Vegas	45	1990-91	Duke (79-77)

Team	No. of Games	Seasons	Ended By
Texas	44	1913-17	Rice (24-18)
Seton Hall	43	1939-41	LIU-Brooklyn (49-26)
LIU-Brooklyn	43	1935-37	Stanford (45-31)
UCLA	41	1968-69	Southern Cal (46-44)
Marquette	39	1970-71	Ohio St. (60-59)
Cincinnati	37	1962-63	Wichita St. (65-64)
North Caro.	37	1957-58	West Va. (75-64)
North Caro. St.	36	1974-75	Wake Forest (83-78)
Arkansas	35	1927-29	Texas (26-25)

LONGEST—REGULAR SEASON

Team	No. of Games	Seasons	Ended By
UCLA	76	1971-74	Notre Dame (71-70)
Indiana	57	1975-77	Toledo (59-57)
Marquette	56	1970-72	Detroit Mercy (70-49)
Kentucky	54	1952-55	Georgia Tech (59-58)
San Francisco	51	1955-57	Illinois (62-33)
Pennsylvania	48	1970-72	Temple (57-52)
Ohio St.	47	1960-62	Wisconsin (86-67)
Texas	44	1913-17	Rice (24-18)
UCLA	43	1966-68	Houston (71-69)
LIU-Brooklyn	43	1935-37	Stanford (45-31)
Seton Hall	42	1939-41	LIU-Brooklyn (49-26)

LONGEST—HOME COURT

Team	Games	Start	End
Kentucky	129	1943	1955
St. Bonaventure	99	1948	1961
UCLA	98	1970	1976
Cincinnati	86	1957	1964
Arizona	81	1945	1951
Marquette	81	1967	1973
Lamar	80	1978	1984
Long Beach St.	75	1968	1974
Nevada-Las Vegas	72	1974	1978
Arizona	71	1987	1992

DIVISION I MEN'S ALL-TIME WINNINGEST TEAMS

VICTORIES

(Minimum 20 years in Division I)

No.	School	First Year	Yrs.	Won	Lost	Tied	Pct.
1.	North Caro.	1911	83	1,570	564	0	.736
2.	Kentucky	1903	90	1,561	506	1	.755
3.	Kansas	1899	95	1,515	689	0	.687
4.	St. John's (N.Y.)	1908	86	1,482	635	0	.700
5.	Duke	1906	88	1,435	703	0	.671
6.	Oregon St.	1902	92	1,415	888	0	.614
7.	Temple	1895	97	1,393	761	0	.647
8.	Notre Dame	1898	88	1,362	701	1	.660
8.	Pennsylvania	1902	92	1,362	785	0	.634
10.	Syracuse	1901	92	1,360	644	0	.679
11.	Indiana	1901	93	1,329	711	0	.651
12.	Washington	1896	91	1,318	821	0	.616
13.	UCLA	1920	74	1,294	577	0	.692
14.	Western Ky.	1915	74	1,284	605	0	.680
15.	Princeton	1901	93	1,279	810	0	.612
16.	Fordham	1903	90	1,275	906	0	.585
17.	West Va.	1904	84	1,262	762	0	.624
18.	Purdue	1897	95	1,275	720	0	.636

No.	School	First Year	Yrs.	Won	Lost	Tied	Pct.
19.	North Caro. St.	1913	81	1,254	698	0	.642
20.	Utah	1909	85	1,248	697	0	.642
21.	Illinois	1906	88	1,245	690	0	.643
22.	Bradley	1903	89	1,236	778	0	.614
23.	Washington St.	1902	92	1,232	1,091	0	.530
24.	Louisville	1912	79	1,230	655	0	.653
25.	Ohio St.	1899	94	1,217	808	0	.601

PERCENTAGE

(Minimum 20 years in Division I)

No.	School	First Year	Yrs.	Won	Lost	Tied	Pct.
1.	Nevada-Las Vegas	1961	33	747	227	0	.767
2.	Kentucky	1903	90	1,561	506	1	.755
3.	North Caro.	1911	83	1,570	564	0	.736
4.	St. John's (N.Y.)	1908	86	1,482	635	0	.700
5.	UCLA	1920	74	1,294	577	0	.692
6.	Kansas	1899	95	1,515	689	0	.687
7.	Western Ky.	1915	74	1,284	605	0	.680
8.	Syracuse	1901	92	1,360	644	0	.679
9.	Duke	1906	88	1,435	703	0	.671
10.	DePaul	1924	70	1,134	557	0	.671
11.	Notre Dame	1898	88	1,362	701	1	.660
12.	Louisville	1912	79	1,230	655	0	.653
13.	La Salle	1931	63	1,045	559	0	.651
14.	Indiana	1901	93	1,329	711	0	.651
15.	Houston	1946	48	867	467	0	.650
16.	Arkansas	1924	70	1,141	623	0	.647
17.	Temple	1895	97	1,393	761	0	.647
18.	Weber St.	1963	31	564	309	0	.646
19.	Illinois	1906	88	1,245	690	0	.643
20.	North Caro. St.	1913	81	1,254	698	0	.642
21.	Utah	1909	85	1,248	697	0	.642
22.	Purdue	1897	95	1,257	720	0	.636
23.	Villanova	1921	73	1,161	668	0	.635
24.	Pennsylvania	1902	92	1,362	785	0	.634
25.	Northeastern	1973	21	374	218	0	.632

FINAL NATIONAL POLLS

(Polls are final regular-season rankings; AP is the writers' poll; UPI and USA TODAY/CNN are the coaches' polls.)

1949

AP

1. Kentucky
2. Oklahoma St.
3. St. Louis
4. Illinois
5. Western Ky.
6. Minnesota
7. Bradley
8. San Francisco
9. Tulane
10. Bowling Green

1950

AP

1. Bradley
2. Ohio St.
3. Kentucky
4. Holy Cross
5. North Caro. St.
6. Duquesne
7. UCLA
8. Western Ky.
9. St. John's (N.Y.)
10. La Salle
11. Villanova
12. San Francisco
13. LIU-Brooklyn
14. Kansas St.
15. Arizona
16. Wisconsin
17. San Jose St.
18. Washington St.
19. Kansas
20. Indiana

1951

AP

1. Kentucky
2. Oklahoma St.
3. Columbia
4. Kansas St.
5. Illinois
6. Bradley
7. Indiana
8. North Caro. St.
9. St. John's (N.Y.)
10. St. Louis
11. Brigham Young
12. Arizona
13. Dayton
14. Toledo
15. Washington
16. Murray St.
17. Cincinnati
18. Siena
19. Southern Cal
20. Villanova

UPI

1. Kentucky
2. Oklahoma St.
3. Kansas St.
4. Illinois
5. Columbia
6. Bradley
7. North Caro. St.
8. Indiana
9. St. John's (N.Y.)
10. Brigham Young
11. St. Louis
12. Arizona
13. Washington
14. Beloit
    Villanova
16. UCLA
17. Cincinnati
18. Dayton
    St. Bonaventure
    Seton Hall
    Texas A&M

1952

AP
1. Kentucky
2. Illinois
3. Kansas St.
4. Duquesne
5. St. Louis
6. Washington
7. Iowa
8. Kansas
9. West Va.
10. St. John's (N.Y.)
11. Dayton
12. Duke
13. Holy Cross
14. Seton Hall
15. St. Bonaventure
16. Wyoming
17. Louisville
18. Seattle
19. UCLA
20. Southwest Tex. St.

UPI
1. Kentucky
2. Illinois
3. Kansas
4. Duquesne
5. Washington
6. Kansas St.
7. St. Louis
8. Iowa
9. St. John's (N.Y.)
10. Wyoming
11. St. Bonaventure
12. Seton Hall
13. Texas Christian
14. West Va.
15. Holy Cross
16. Western Ky.
17. La Salle
18. Dayton
19. Louisville
20. UCLA
    Indiana

1953

AP
1. Indiana
2. Seton Hall
3. Kansas
4. Washington
5. Louisiana St.
6. La Salle
7. St. John's (N.Y.)
8. Oklahoma St.
9. Duquesne
10. Notre Dame
11. Illinois
12. Kansas St.
13. Holy Cross
14. Seattle
15. Wake Forest
16. Santa Clara
17. Western Ky.
18. North Caro. St.
19. DePaul
20. Southwest Mo. St.

UPI
1. Indiana
2. Seton Hall
3. Washington
4. La Salle
5. Kansas
6. Louisiana St.
7. Oklahoma St.
8. North Caro. St.
9. Kansas St.
10. Illinois
11. Western Ky.
12. California
13. Notre Dame
14. DePaul
    Wyoming
16. St. Louis
17. Holy Cross
18. Oklahoma City
19. Brigham Young
20. Duquesne

1954

AP
1. Kentucky
2. La Salle
3. Holy Cross
4. Indiana
5. Duquesne
6. Notre Dame
7. Bradley
8. Western Ky.
9. Penn St.
10. Oklahoma St.
11. Southern Cal
12. Geo. Washington
13. Iowa
14. Louisiana St.
15. Duke
16. Niagara
17. Seattle
18. Kansas
19. Illinois
20. Maryland

UPI
1. Indiana
2. Kentucky
3. Duquesne
4. Oklahoma St.
5. Notre Dame
6. Western Ky.
7. Kansas
8. Louisiana St.
9. Holy Cross
10. Iowa
11. La Salle
12. Illinois
13. Colorado St.
14. North Caro. St.
    Southern Cal
16. Oregon St.
17. Seattle
    Dayton
19. Rice
20. Duke

1955

AP
1. San Francisco
2. Kentucky
3. La Salle
4. North Caro. St.
5. Iowa
6. Duquesne
7. Utah
8. Marquette
9. Dayton
10. Oregon St.
11. Minnesota
12. Alabama
13. UCLA
14. Geo. Washington
15. Colorado
16. Tulsa
17. Vanderbilt
18. Illinois
19. West Va.
20. St. Louis

UPI
1. San Francisco
2. Kentucky
3. La Salle
4. Utah
5. Iowa
6. North Caro. St.
7. Duquesne
8. Oregon St.
9. Marquette
10. Dayton
11. Colorado
12. UCLA
13. Minnesota
14. Tulsa
15. Geo. Washington
16. Illinois
17. Niagara
18. St. Louis
19. Holy Cross
20. Cincinnati

1956

AP
1. San Francisco
2. North Caro. St.
3. Dayton
4. Iowa
5. Alabama
6. Louisville
7. Southern Methodist
8. UCLA
9. Kentucky
10. Illinois
11. Oklahoma City
12. Vanderbilt
13. North Caro.
14. Holy Cross
15. Temple
16. Wake Forest
17. Duke
18. Utah
19. Oklahoma St.
20. West Va.

UPI
1. San Francisco
2. North Caro. St.
3. Dayton
4. Iowa
5. Alabama
6. Southern Methodist
7. Louisville
8. Illinois
9. UCLA
10. Vanderbilt
11. North Caro.
12. Kentucky
13. Utah
14. Temple
15. Holy Cross
16. Oklahoma St.
    St. Louis
18. Seattle
    Duke
    Canisius

1957

AP
1. North Caro.
2. Kansas
3. Kentucky
4. Southern Methodist
5. Seattle
6. Louisville
7. West Va.
8. Vanderbilt
9. Oklahoma City
10. St. Louis
11. Michigan St.
12. Memphis St.
13. California
14. UCLA
15. Mississippi St.
16. Idaho St.
17. Notre Dame
18. Wake Forest
19. Canisius
    Oklahoma St.

UPI
1. North Caro.
2. Kansas
3. Kentucky
4. Southern Methodist
5. Seattle
6. California
7. Michigan St.
8. Louisville
9. UCLA
   St. Louis
11. West Va.
12. Dayton
13. Bradley
14. Brigham Young
15. Indiana
16. Vanderbilt
    Xavier (Ohio)
    Oklahoma City
19. Notre Dame
20. Kansas St.

1958

AP
1. West Va.
2. Cincinnati
3. Kansas St.
4. San Francisco
5. Temple
6. Maryland
7. Kansas
8. Notre Dame
9. Kentucky
10. Duke
11. Dayton
12. Indiana
13. North Caro.
14. Bradley
15. Mississippi St.
16. Auburn
17. Michigan St.
18. Seattle
19. Oklahoma St.
20. North Caro. St.

UPI
1. West Va.
2. Cincinnati
3. San Francisco
4. Kansas St.
5. Temple
6. Maryland
7. Notre Dame
8. Kansas
9. Dayton
10. Indiana
11. Bradley
12. North Caro.
13. Duke
14. Kentucky
15. Oklahoma St.
16. Oregon St.
    North Caro. St.
18. St. Bonaventure
19. Michigan St.
    Wyoming
    Seattle

1959

AP
1. Kansas St.
2. Kentucky
3. Mississippi St.
4. Bradley
5. Cincinnati
6. North Caro. St.
7. Michigan St.
8. Auburn
9. North Caro.
10. West Va.
11. California
12. St. Louis
13. Seattle
14. St. Joseph's (Pa.)
15. St. Mary's (Cal.)
16. Texas Christian
17. Oklahoma City
18. Utah
19. St. Bonaventure
20. Marquette

UPI
1. Kansas St.
2. Kentucky
3. Michigan St.
4. Cincinnati
5. North Caro. St.
6. North Caro.
    Mississippi St.
8. Bradley
9. California
10. Auburn
11. West Va.
12. Texas Christian
13. St. Louis
14. Utah
15. Marquette
16. Tennessee Tech
17. St. John's (N.Y.)
18. Navy
    St. Mary's (Cal.)
20. St. Joseph's (Pa.)

1960

AP
1. Cincinnati
2. California
3. Ohio St.
4. Bradley
5. West Va.
6. Utah
7. Indiana
8. Utah St.
9. St. Bonaventure
10. Miami (Fla.)
11. Auburn
12. New York U.
13. Georgia Tech
14. Providence
15. St. Louis
16. Holy Cross
17. Villanova
18. Duke
19. Wake Forest
20. St. John's (N.Y.)

UPI
1. California
2. Cincinnati
3. Ohio St.
4. Bradley
5. Utah
6. West Va.
7. Utah St.
8. Georgia Tech
9. Villanova
10. Indiana
11. St. Bonaventure
12. New York U.
13. Texas
14. North Caro.
15. Duke
16. Kansas St.
17. Auburn
18. Providence
19. St. Louis
20. Dayton

1961

AP
1. Ohio St.
2. Cincinnati
3. St. Bonaventure
4. Kansas St.
5. North Caro.
6. Bradley
7. Southern Cal
8. Iowa
9. West Va.
10. Duke
11. Utah
12. Texas Tech
13. Niagara
14. Memphis St.
15. Wake Forest
16. St. John's (N.Y.)
17. St. Joseph's (Pa.)
18. Drake
19. Holy Cross
20. Kentucky

UPI
1. Ohio St.
2. Cincinnati
3. St. Bonaventure
4. Kansas St.
5. Southern Cal
6. North Caro.
7. Bradley
8. St. John's (N.Y.)
9. Duke
10. Wake Forest
    Iowa
12. West Va.
13. Utah
14. St. Louis
15. Louisville
16. St. Joseph's (Pa.)
17. Dayton
18. Kentucky
    Texas Tech
20. Memphis St.

1962

AP
1. Ohio St.
2. Cincinnati
3. Kentucky
4. Mississippi St.
5. Bradley
6. Kansas St.
7. Utah
8. Bowling Green
9. Colorado
10. Duke
11. Loyola (Ill.)
12. St. John's (N.Y.)
13. Wake Forest
14. Oregon St.
15. West Va.
16. Arizona St.
17. Duquesne
18. Utah St.
19. UCLA
20. Villanova

UPI
1. Ohio St.
2. Cincinnati
3. Kentucky
4. Mississippi St.
5. Kansas St.
6. Bradley
7. Wake Forest
8. Colorado
9. Bowling Green
10. Utah
11. Oregon St.
12. St. John's (N.Y.)
13. Duke
    Loyola (Ill.)
15. Arizona St.
16. West Va.
17. UCLA
18. Duquesne
19. Utah St.
20. Villanova

1963

AP
1. Cincinnati
2. Duke
3. Loyola (Ill.)
4. Arizona St.
5. Wichita St.
6. Mississippi St.
7. Ohio St.
8. Illinois
9. New York U.
10. Colorado

UPI
1. Cincinnati
2. Duke
3. Arizona St.
4. Loyola (Ill.)
5. Illinois
6. Wichita St.
7. Mississippi St.
8. Ohio St.
9. Colorado
10. Stanford
11. New York U.
12. Texas
13. Providence
14. Oregon St.
15. UCLA
16. St. Joseph's (Pa.)
    West Va.
18. Bowling Green
19. Kansas St.
    Seattle

1964

AP
1. UCLA
2. Michigan
3. Duke
4. Kentucky
5. Wichita St.
6. Oregon St.
7. Villanova
8. Loyola (Ill.)
9. DePaul
10. Davidson

UPI
1. UCLA
2. Michigan
3. Kentucky
4. Duke
5. Oregon St.
6. Wichita St.
7. Villanova
8. Loyola (Ill.)
9. UTEP
10. Davidson
11. DePaul
12. Kansas St.
13. Drake
    San Francisco
15. Utah St.
16. Ohio St.
    New Mexico
18. Texas A&M
19. Arizona St.
    Providence

1965

AP
1. Michigan
2. UCLA
3. St. Joseph's (Pa.)
4. Providence
5. Vanderbilt
6. Davidson
7. Minnesota
8. Villanova
9. Brigham Young
10. Duke

UPI
1. Michigan
2. UCLA
3. St. Joseph's (Pa.)
4. Providence
5. Vanderbilt
6. Brigham Young
7. Davidson
8. Minnesota
9. Duke
10. San Francisco
11. Villanova
12. North Caro. St.
13. Oklahoma St.
14. Wichita St.
15. Connecticut
16. Illinois
17. Tennessee
18. Indiana
19. Miami (Fla.)
20. Dayton

1966

AP
1. Kentucky
2. Duke
3. UTEP
4. Kansas
5. St. Joseph's (Pa.)
6. Loyola (Ill.)
7. Cincinnati
8. Vanderbilt
9. Michigan
10. Western Ky.

UPI
1. Kentucky
2. Duke
3. UTEP
4. Kansas
5. Loyola (Ill.)
6. St. Joseph's (Pa.)
7. Michigan
8. Vanderbilt
9. Cincinnati
10. Providence
11. Nebraska
12. Utah
13. Oklahoma City
14. Houston
15. Oregon St.
16. Syracuse
17. Pacific (Cal.)
18. Davidson
19. Brigham Young
    Dayton

1967

AP
1. UCLA
2. Louisville
3. Kansas
4. North Caro.
5. Princeton
6. Western Ky.
7. Houston
8. Tennessee
9. Boston College
10. UTEP

UPI
1. UCLA
2. Louisville
3. North Caro.
4. Kansas
5. Princeton
6. Houston
7. Western Ky.
8. UTEP
9. Tennessee
10. Boston College
11. Toledo
12. St. John's (N.Y.)
13. Tulsa
14. Vanderbilt
    Utah St.
16. Pacific (Cal.)
17. Providence
18. New Mexico
19. Duke
20. Florida

1968

AP
1. Houston
2. UCLA
3. St. Bonaventure
4. North Caro.
5. Kentucky
6. New Mexico
7. Columbia
8. Davidson
9. Louisville
10. Duke

UPI
1. Houston
2. UCLA
3. St. Bonaventure
4. North Caro.
5. Kentucky
6. Columbia
7. New Mexico
8. Louisville
9. Davidson
10. Marquette
11. Duke
12. New Mexico St.
13. Vanderbilt
14. Kansas St.
15. Princeton
16. Army
17. Santa Clara
18. Utah
19. Bradley
20. Iowa

1969

AP
1. UCLA
2. La Salle
3. Santa Clara
4. North Caro.
5. Davidson
6. Purdue
7. Kentucky
8. St. John's (N.Y.)
9. Duquesne
10. Villanova
11. Drake
12. New Mexico St.
13. South Caro.
14. Marquette
15. Louisville
16. Boston College
17. Notre Dame
18. Colorado
19. Kansas
20. Illinois

UPI
1. UCLA
2. North Caro.
3. Davidson
4. Santa Clara
5. Kentucky
6. La Salle
7. Purdue
8. St. John's (N.Y.)
9. New Mexico St.
10. Duquesne
11. Drake
12. Colorado
13. Louisville
14. Marquette
15. Villanova
    Boston College
17. Weber St.
    Wyoming
19. Colorado St.
20. South Caro.
    Kansas

1970

AP

1. Kentucky
2. UCLA
3. St. Bonaventure
4. Jacksonville
5. New Mexico St.
6. South Caro.
7. Iowa
8. Marquette
9. Notre Dame
10. North Caro. St.
11. Florida St.
12. Houston
13. Pennsylvania
14. Drake
15. Davidson
16. Utah St.
17. Niagara
18. Western Ky.
19. Long Beach St.
20. Southern Cal

UPI

1. Kentucky
2. UCLA
3. St. Bonaventure
4. New Mexico St.
5. Jacksonville
6. South Caro.
7. Iowa
8. Notre Dame
9. Drake
10. Marquette
11. Houston
12. North Caro. St.
13. Pennsylvania
14. Florida St.
15. Villanova
    Long Beach St.
17. Western Ky.
    Utah St.
    Niagara
20. Cincinnati
    UTEP

1971

AP

1. UCLA
2. Marquette
3. Pennsylvania
4. Kansas
5. Southern Cal
6. South Caro.
7. Western Ky.
8. Kentucky
9. Fordham
10. Ohio St.
11. Jacksonville
12. Notre Dame
13. North Caro.
14. Houston
15. Duquesne
16. Long Beach St.
17. Tennessee
18. Villanova
19. Drake
20. Brigham Young

UPI

1. UCLA
2. Marquette
3. Pennsylvania
4. Kansas
5. Southern Cal
6. South Caro.
7. Western Ky.
8. Kentucky
9. Fordham
10. Ohio St.
11. Jacksonville
    Brigham Young
13. North Caro.
14. Notre Dame
    Long Beach St.
16. Drake
17. Villanova
18. Duquesne
    Houston
20. Weber St.

1972

AP

1. UCLA
2. North Caro.
3. Pennsylvania
4. Louisville
5. Long Beach St.
6. South Caro.
7. Marquette
8. Southwestern La.
9. Brigham Young
10. Florida St.
11. Minnesota
12. Marshall
13. Memphis St.
14. Maryland
15. Villanova
16. Oral Roberts
17. Indiana
18. Kentucky
19. Ohio St.
20. Virginia

UPI

1. UCLA
2. North Caro.
3. Pennsylvania
4. Louisville
5. South Caro.
6. Long Beach St.
7. Marquette
8. Southwestern La.
9. Brigham Young
10. Florida St.
11. Maryland
12. Minnesota
13. Memphis St.
14. Kentucky
15. Villanova
16. Kansas St.
17. UTEP
18. Marshall
19. Missouri
    Weber St.

1973

AP

1. UCLA
2. North Caro. St.
3. Long Beach St.
4. Providence
5. Marquette
6. Indiana
7. Southwestern La.
8. Maryland
9. Kansas St.
10. Minnesota
11. North Caro.
12. Memphis St.
13. Houston
14. Syracuse
15. Missouri
16. Arizona St.
17. Kentucky
18. Pennsylvania
19. Austin Peay
20. San Francisco

UPI

1. UCLA
2. North Caro. St.
3. Long Beach St.
4. Marquette
5. Providence
6. Indiana
7. Southwestern La.
   Kansas St.
9. Minnesota
10. Maryland
11. Memphis St.
12. North Caro.
13. Arizona St.
14. Syracuse
15. Kentucky
16. South Caro.
17. Missouri
18. Weber St.
    Houston
20. Pennsylvania

1974

AP

1. North Caro. St.
2. UCLA
3. Marquette
4. Maryland
5. Notre Dame
6. Michigan
7. Kansas
8. Providence
9. Indiana
10. Long Beach St.
11. Purdue
12. North Caro.
13. Vanderbilt
14. Alabama
15. Utah
16. Pittsburgh
17. Southern Cal
18. Oral Roberts
19. South Caro.
20. Dayton

UPI

1. North Caro. St.
2. UCLA
3. Notre Dame
4. Maryland
5. Marquette
6. Providence
7. Vanderbilt
8. North Caro.
9. Indiana
10. Kansas
11. Long Beach St.
12. Michigan
13. Southern Cal
14. Pittsburgh
15. Louisville
16. South Caro.
17. Creighton
18. New Mexico
19. Alabama
    Dayton

1975

AP

1. UCLA
2. Kentucky
3. Indiana
4. Louisville
5. Maryland
6. Syracuse
7. North Caro. St.
8. Arizona St.
9. North Caro.
10. Alabama
11. Marquette
12. Princeton
13. Cincinnati
14. Notre Dame
15. Kansas St.
16. Drake
17. Nevada-Las Vegas
18. Oregon St.
19. Michigan
20. Pennsylvania

UPI

1. Indiana
2. UCLA
3. Louisville
4. Kentucky
5. Maryland
6. Marquette
7. Arizona St.
8. Alabama
9. North Caro. St.
10. North Caro.
11. Pennsylvania
12. Southern Cal
13. Utah St.
14. Nevada-Las Vegas
    Notre Dame
16. Creighton
17. Arizona
18. New Mexico St.
19. Clemson
20. UTEP

1976

AP
1. Indiana
2. Marquette
3. Nevada-Las Vegas
4. Rutgers
5. UCLA
6. Alabama
7. Notre Dame
8. North Caro.
9. Michigan
10. Western Mich.
11. Maryland
12. Cincinnati
13. Tennessee
14. Missouri
15. Arizona
16. Texas Tech
17. DePaul
18. Virginia
19. Centenary
20. Pepperdine

UPI
1. Indiana
2. Marquette
3. Rutgers
4. Nevada-Las Vegas
5. UCLA
6. North Caro.
7. Alabama
8. Notre Dame
9. Michigan
10. Washington
11. Missouri
12. Arizona
13. Maryland
14. Tennessee
15. Virginia
16. Cincinnati
    Florida St.
18. St. John's (N.Y.)
19. Western Mich.
    Princeton

1977

AP
1. Michigan
2. UCLA
3. Kentucky
4. Nevada-Las Vegas
5. North Caro.
6. Syracuse
7. Marquette
8. San Francisco
9. Wake Forest
10. Notre Dame
11. Alabama
12. Detroit Mercy
13. Minnesota
14. Utah
15. Tennessee
16. Kansas St.
17. N.C.-Charlotte
18. Arkansas
19. Louisville
20. Va. Military

UPI
1. Michigan
2. San Francisco
3. North Caro.
4. UCLA
5. Kentucky
6. Nevada-Las Vegas
7. Arkansas
8. Tennessee
9. Syracuse
10. Utah
11. Kansas St.
12. Cincinnati
13. Louisville
14. Marquette
15. Providence
16. Indiana St.
17. Minnesota
18. Alabama
19. Detroit Mercy
20. Purdue

1978

AP
1. Kentucky
2. UCLA
3. DePaul
4. Michigan St.
5. Arkansas
6. Notre Dame
7. Duke
8. Marquette
9. Louisville
10. Kansas
11. San Francisco
12. New Mexico
13. Indiana
14. Utah
15. Florida St.
16. North Caro.
17. Texas
18. Detroit Mercy
19. Miami (Ohio)
20. Pennsylvania

UPI
1. Kentucky
2. UCLA
3. Marquette
4. New Mexico
5. Michigan St.
6. Arkansas
7. DePaul
8. Kansas
9. Duke
10. North Caro.
11. Notre Dame
12. Florida St.
13. San Francisco
14. Louisville
15. Indiana
16. Houston
17. Utah St.
18. Utah
19. Texas
20. Georgetown

1979

AP
1. Indiana St.
2. UCLA
3. Michigan St.
4. Notre Dame
5. Arkansas
6. DePaul
7. Louisiana St.
8. Syracuse
9. North Caro.
10. Marquette
11. Duke
12. San Francisco
13. Louisville
14. Pennsylvania
15. Purdue
16. Oklahoma
17. St. John's (N.Y.)
18. Rutgers
19. Toledo
20. Iowa

UPI
1. Indiana St.
2. UCLA
3. North Caro.
4. Michigan St.
5. Notre Dame
6. Arkansas
7. Duke
8. DePaul
9. Louisiana St.
10. Syracuse
11. Iowa
12. Georgetown
13. Marquette
14. Purdue
15. Texas
16. Temple
17. San Francisco
18. Tennessee
19. Louisville
20. Detroit Mercy

1980

AP
1. DePaul
2. Louisville
3. Louisiana St.
4. Kentucky
5. Oregon St.
6. Syracuse
7. Indiana
8. Maryland
9. Notre Dame
10. Ohio St.
11. Georgetown
12. Brigham Young
13. St. John's (N.Y.)
14. Duke
15. North Caro.
16. Missouri
17. Weber St.
18. Arizona St.
19. Iona
20. Purdue

UPI
1. DePaul
2. Louisiana St.
3. Kentucky
4. Louisville
5. Oregon St.
6. Syracuse
7. Indiana
8. Maryland
9. Ohio St.
10. Georgetown
11. Notre Dame
12. Brigham Young
13. St. John's (N.Y.)
14. Missouri
15. North Caro.
16. Duke
17. Weber St.
18. Texas A&M
19. Arizona St.
20. Kansas St.

1981

AP
1. DePaul
2. Oregon St.
3. Arizona St.
4. Louisiana St.
5. Virginia
6. North Caro.
7. Notre Dame
8. Kentucky
9. Indiana
10. UCLA
11. Wake Forest
12. Louisville
13. Iowa
14. Utah
15. Tennessee
16. Brigham Young
17. Wyoming
18. Maryland
19. Illinois
20. Arkansas

UPI
1. DePaul
2. Oregon St.
3. Virginia
4. Louisiana St.
5. Arizona St.
6. North Caro.
7. Indiana
8. Kentucky
9. Notre Dame
10. Utah
11. UCLA
12. Iowa
13. Louisville
14. Wake Forest
15. Tennessee
16. Wyoming
17. Brigham Young
18. Illinois
19. Kansas
20. Maryland

1982

AP	UPI
1. North Caro.	1. North Caro.
2. DePaul	2. DePaul
3. Virginia	3. Virginia
4. Oregon St.	4. Oregon St.
5. Missouri	5. Missouri
6. Georgetown	6. Minnesota
7. Minnesota	7. Georgetown
8. Idaho	8. Idaho
9. Memphis St.	9. Memphis St.
10. Tulsa	10. Fresno St.
11. Fresno St.	11. Tulsa
12. Arkansas	12. Alabama
13. Alabama	13. Arkansas
14. West Va.	14. Kentucky
15. Kentucky	15. Wyoming
16. Iowa	16. Iowa
17. Ala.-Birmingham	17. West Va.
18. Wake Forest	18. Kansas St.
19. UCLA	19. Wake Forest
20. Louisville	20. Louisville

1983

AP	UPI
1. Houston	1. Houston
2. Louisville	2. Louisville
3. St. John's (N.Y.)	3. St. John's (N.Y.)
4. Virginia	4. Virginia
5. Indiana	5. Indiana
6. Nevada-Las Vegas	6. Nevada-Las Vegas
7. UCLA	7. UCLA
8. North Caro.	8. North Caro.
9. Arkansas	9. Arkansas
10. Missouri	10. Kentucky
11. Boston College	11. Villanova
12. Kentucky	12. Missouri
13. Villanova	13. Boston College
14. Wichita St.	14. North Caro. St.
15. Tenn.-Chatt.	15. Georgia
16. North Caro. St.	16. Tenn.-Chatt.
17. Memphis St.	17. Memphis St.
18. Georgia	18. Illinois St.
19. Oklahoma St.	19. Oklahoma St.
20. Georgetown	20. Georgetown

1984

AP	UPI
1. North Caro.	1. North Caro.
2. Georgetown	2. Georgetown
3. Kentucky	3. Kentucky
4. DePaul	4. DePaul
5. Houston	5. Houston
6. Illinois	6. Illinois
7. Oklahoma	7. Arkansas
8. Arkansas	8. Oklahoma
9. UTEP	9. UTEP
10. Purdue	10. Maryland
11. Maryland	11. Purdue
12. Tulsa	12. Tulsa
13. Nevada-Las Vegas	13. Nevada-Las Vegas
14. Duke	14. Duke
15. Washington	15. Washington
16. Memphis St.	16. Memphis St.
17. Oregon St.	Syracuse
18. Syracuse	18. Indiana
19. Wake Forest	19. Auburn
20. Temple	20. Oregon St.

1985

AP	UPI
1. Georgetown	1. Georgetown
2. Michigan	2. Michigan
3. St. John's (N.Y.)	3. St. John's (N.Y.)
4. Oklahoma	4. Memphis St.
5. Memphis St.	5. Oklahoma
6. Georgia Tech	6. Georgia Tech
7. North Caro.	7. North Caro.
8. Louisiana Tech	8. Louisiana Tech
9. Nevada-Las Vegas	9. Nevada-Las Vegas
10. Duke	10. Illinois
11. Va. Commonwealth	11. Va. Commonwealth
12. Illinois	12. Duke
13. Kansas	13. Kansas
14. Loyola (Ill.)	14. Tulsa
15. Syracuse	15. Syracuse
16. North Caro. St.	16. Texas Tech
17. Texas Tech	17. Loyola (Ill.)
18. Tulsa	18. North Caro. St.
19. Georgia	19. Louisiana St.
20. Louisiana St.	20. Michigan St.

1986

AP	UPI
1. Duke	1. Duke
2. Kansas	2. Kansas
3. Kentucky	3. St. John's (N.Y.)
4. St. John's (N.Y.)	4. Kentucky
5. Michigan	5. Michigan
6. Georgia Tech	6. Georgia Tech
7. Louisville	7. Louisville
8. North Caro.	8. North Caro.
9. Syracuse	9. Syracuse
10. Notre Dame	10. Nevada-Las Vegas
11. Nevada-Las Vegas	11. Notre Dame
12. Memphis St.	12. Memphis St.
13. Georgetown	13. Bradley
14. Bradley	14. Indiana
15. Oklahoma	15. Georgetown
16. Indiana	16. UTEP
17. Navy	17. Oklahoma
18. Michigan St.	18. Michigan St.
19. Illinois	19. Alabama
20. UTEP	20. Illinois

1987

AP	UPI
1. Nevada-Las Vegas	1. Nevada-Las Vegas
2. North Caro.	2. Indiana
3. Indiana	3. North Caro.
4. Georgetown	4. Georgetown
5. DePaul	5. DePaul
6. Iowa	6. Purdue
7. Purdue	7. Iowa
8. Temple	8. Temple
9. Alabama	9. Alabama
10. Syracuse	10. Syracuse
11. Illinois	11. Illinois
12. Pittsburgh	12. Pittsburgh
13. Clemson	13. UCLA
14. Missouri	14. Missouri
15. UCLA	15. Clemson
16. New Orleans	16. Texas Christian
17. Duke	17. Wyoming
18. Notre Dame	18. Notre Dame
19. Texas Christian	19. New Orleans
20. Kansas	Oklahoma
	UTEP

1988

AP	UPI
1. Temple	1. Temple
2. Arizona	2. Arizona
3. Purdue	3. Purdue
4. Oklahoma	4. Oklahoma
5. Duke	5. Duke
6. Kentucky	6. Kentucky
7. North Caro.	7. Pittsburgh
8. Pittsburgh	8. North Caro.
9. Syracuse	9. Syracuse
10. Michigan	10. Michigan
11. Bradley	11. Nevada-Las Vegas
12. Nevada-Las Vegas	12. Bradley
13. Wyoming	13. North Caro. St.
14. North Caro. St.	14. Wyoming
15. Loyola (Cal.)	15. Illinois
16. Illinois	16. Loyola (Cal.)
17. Iowa	17. Brigham Young
18. Xavier (Ohio)	18. Iowa
19. Brigham Young	19. Indiana
20. Kansas St.	20. Kansas St.

1989

AP	UPI
1. Arizona	1. Arizona
2. Georgetown	2. Georgetown
3. Illinois	3. Illinois
4. Oklahoma	4. North Caro.
5. North Caro.	5. Oklahoma
6. Missouri	6. Indiana
7. Syracuse	7. Duke
8. Indiana	8. Missouri
9. Duke	9. Syracuse
10. Michigan	10. Michigan
11. Seton Hall	11. Seton Hall
12. Louisville	12. Stanford
13. Stanford	13. Louisville
14. Iowa	14. Nevada-Las Vegas
15. Nevada-Las Vegas	15. Iowa
16. Florida St.	16. Florida St.
17. West Va.	17. Arkansas
18. Ball St.	18. North Caro. St.
19. North Caro. St.	19. West Va.
20. Alabama	20. Alabama

1990

AP	UPI
1. Oklahoma	1. Oklahoma
2. Kansas	2. Kansas
3. Nevada-Las Vegas	3. Nevada-Las Vegas
4. Syracuse	4. Syracuse
5. Georgetown	5. Missouri
6. Missouri	6. Georgetown
7. Michigan St.	7. Connecticut
8. Connecticut	8. Michigan St.
9. Arkansas	9. Purdue
10. Purdue	10. Arkansas
11. La Salle	11. Duke
12. Duke	12. La Salle
13. Michigan	13. Georgia Tech
14. Georgia Tech	14. Michigan
15. Arizona	15. Clemson
16. Louisiana St.	16. Arizona
17. Clemson	17. New Mexico
18. Louisville	18. Louisville
19. Minnesota	19. Minnesota
20. Illinois	Illinois
21. Loyola (Cal.)	
22. Oregon St.	
23. New Mexico	
24. Xavier (Ohio)	
25. Georgia	

1991

AP	UPI
1. Nevada-Las Vegas	1. Nevada-Las Vegas
2. Arkansas	2. Arkansas
3. Indiana	3. Indiana
4. North Caro.	4. North Caro.
5. Ohio St.	5. Ohio St.
6. Duke	6. Duke
7. Syracuse	7. Arizona
8. Arizona	8. Syracuse
9. Kentucky	9. Nebraska
10. Utah	10. Utah
11. Nebraska	11. Seton Hall
12. Kansas	12. Kansas
13. Seton Hall	13. Oklahoma St.
14. Oklahoma St.	14. UCLA
15. New Mexico St.	15. East Tenn. St.
16. UCLA	16. Alabama
17. East Tenn. St.	17. New Mexico St.
18. Princeton	18. Mississippi St.
19. Alabama	19. St. John's (N.Y.)
20. St. John's (N.Y.)	20. Princeton
21. Mississippi St.	21. Louisiana St.
22. Louisiana St.	22. Michigan St.
23. Texas	23. Georgetown
24. DePaul	24. North Caro. St.
25. Southern Miss.	25. Texas

1992

AP	UPI
1. Duke	1. Duke
2. Kansas	2. Kansas
3. Ohio St.	3. UCLA
4. UCLA	4. Ohio St.
5. Indiana	5. Arizona
6. Kentucky	6. Indiana
7. Nevada-Las Vegas	7. Southern Cal
8. Southern Cal	8. Arkansas
9. Arkansas	9. Kentucky
10. Arizona	10. Oklahoma St.
11. Oklahoma St.	11. Michigan St.
12. Cincinnati	12. Missouri
13. Alabama	13. Alabama
14. Michigan St.	14. Cincinnati
15. Michigan	15. North Caro.
16. Missouri	16. Florida St.
17. Massachusetts	17. Michigan
18. North Caro.	18. Seton Hall
19. Seton Hall	19. Georgetown
20. Florida St.	20. Syracuse
21. Syracuse	21. Massachusetts
22. Georgetown	22. Oklahoma
23. Oklahoma	23. DePaul
24. DePaul	24. St. John's (N.Y.)
25. Louisiana St.	25. Tulane

1993

AP	USA TODAY/CNN
1. Indiana	1. Indiana
2. Kentucky	2. North Caro.
3. Michigan	3. Kentucky
4. North Caro.	4. Michigan
5. Arizona	5. Arizona
6. Seton Hall	6. Seton Hall
7. Cincinnati	7. Cincinnati
8. Vanderbilt	8. Kansas
9. Kansas	9. Vanderbilt
10. Duke	10. Duke
11. Florida St.	11. Florida St.
12. Arkansas	12. Arkansas
13. Iowa	13. Iowa
14. Massachusetts	14. Louisville
15. Louisville	15. Wake Forest
16. Wake Forest	16. Utah
17. New Orleans	17. Massachusetts
18. Georgia Tech	18. New Orleans
19. Utah	19. Nevada-Las Vegas
20. Western Ky.	20. Georgia Tech
21. New Mexico	21. Purdue
22. Purdue	Virginia
23. Oklahoma St.	23. Oklahoma St.
24. New Mexico St.	24. New Mexico St.
25. Nevada-Las Vegas	25. Western Ky.

NUMBER 1 vs. NUMBER 2

(Since 1980)

Date	No. 1, Score	W-L	No. 2, Score	Site
Dec. 26, 1981	North Caro. 82	W	Kentucky 69	East Rutherford, N.J.
Jan. 9, 1982	North Caro. 65	W	Virginia 60	Chapel Hill, N.C.
April 2, 1983	Houston 94	W	Louisville 81	Albuquerque, N.M.
Dec. 15, 1984	Georgetown 77	W	DePaul 57	Landover, Md.
Feb. 27, 1985	St. John's (N.Y.) 69	L	Georgetown 85	New York, N.Y.
Mar. 9, 1985	Georgetown 92	W	St. John's (N.Y.) 80	New York, N.Y.
Feb. 4, 1986	North Caro. 78	W (ot)	Georgia Tech 77	Atlanta, Ga.
Feb. 13, 1990	Kansas 71	L	Missouri 77	Lawrence, Kan.
Mar. 10, 1990	Oklahoma 95	W	Kansas 77	Kansas City, Mo.
Feb. 10, 1991	Nevada-Las Vegas 112	W	Arkansas 105	Fayetteville, Ark.

DIVISION II
MEN'S RECORDS

California (Pennsylvania) guard Ray Gutierrez led the nation in three-point field goals made per game in 1992-93. Gutierrez made 142 three-pointers in 29 games for an average of 4.9 per contest.

DIVISION II MEN'S INDIVIDUAL RECORDS

Basketball records are confined to the "modern era," which began with the 1937-38 season, the first without the center jump after each goal scored. Official weekly statistics rankings in scoring and shooting began with the 1947-48 season. Individual rebounds were added for the 1950-51 season, while team rebounds were added for the 1959-60 season. Assists were added for the 1988-89 season. Scoring and rebounding are ranked on per-game average; shooting, on percentage. Beginning with the 1967-68 season, Division II rankings were limited only to NCAA members. The 1973-74 season was the first under a three-division reorganization plan adopted by the special NCAA Convention of August 1973. In statistical rankings, the rounding of percentages and/or averages may indicate ties where none exist. In these cases, the numerical order of the rankings is accurate.

SCORING

Points

Game
113—Clarence "Bevo" Francis, Rio Grande vs. Hillsdale, Feb. 2, 1954

Season
1,329—Earl Monroe, Winston-Salem, 1967 (31 games)

Career
4,045—Travis Grant, Kentucky St., 1969-72 (121 games)

Average Per Game

Season
†46.5—Clarence "Bevo" Francis, Rio Grande, 1954 (1,255 in 27)

Career
(Min. 1,400) 33.4—Travis Grant, Kentucky St., 1969-72 (4,045 in 121)

Games Scoring at Least 50 Points

Season
†8—Clarence "Bevo" Francis, Rio Grande, 1954

Career
†14—Clarence "Bevo" Francis, Rio Grande, 1953-54

Most Games Scoring in Double Figures

Career
130—Lambert Shell, Bridgeport, 1989-92

† *Season and career figures for Francis limited only to his 39 games (27 in 1954) against four-year colleges.*

FIELD GOALS

Field Goals

Game
38—Clarence "Bevo" Francis, Rio Grande vs. Alliance, Jan. 16, 1954 (71 attempts) and vs. Hillsdale, Feb. 2, 1954 (70 attempts)

Season
539—Travis Grant, Kentucky St., 1972 (869 attempts)

Career
1,760—Travis Grant, Kentucky St., 1969-72 (2,759 attempts)

Consecutive Field Goals

Game
20—Lance Berwald, North Dak. St. vs. Augustana (S.D.), Feb. 17, 1984

Season
28—Don McAllister, Hartwick, 1980 (during six games, Jan. 26-Feb. 9); Lance Berwald, North Dak. St., 1984 (during three games, Feb. 13-18)

Field-Goal Attempts

Game
71—Clarence "Bevo" Francis, Rio Grande vs. Alliance, Jan. 16, 1954 (38 made)

Season
925—Jim Toombs, Stillman, 1965 (388 made)

Career
3,309—Bob Hopkins, Grambling, 1953-56 (1,403 made)

Field-Goal Percentage

Game
(Min. 20 made) 100%—Lance Berwald, North Dak. St. vs. Augustana (S.D.), Feb. 17, 1984 (20 of 20)

***Season**
75.2%—Todd Linder, Tampa, 1987 (282 of 375)

* *Based on qualifiers for annual championship.*

Career
(Min. 400 made) 70.8%—Todd Linder, Tampa, 1984-87 (909 of 1,284)

THREE-POINT FIELD GOALS

Three-Point Field Goals

Game
14—Andy Schmidtmann, Wis.-Parkside vs. Lakeland, Feb. 14, 1989 (32 attempts)

Season
167—Alex Williams, Cal St. Sacramento, 1988 (369 attempts)

Career
431—Tony Smith, Pfeiffer, 1989-92 (1,047 attempts)

Three-Point Field Goals Made Per Game

Season
5.6—Alex Williams, Cal St. Sacramento, 1988 (167 in 30)

Career

4.3—Alex Williams, Cal St. Sacramento, 1987-88 (247 in 58)

Consecutive Three-Point Field Goals

Game

10—Duane Huddleston, Missouri-Rolla vs. Northeast Mo. St., Jan. 23, 1988

Season

13—Barry Randles, Livingston (during three games, Nov. 28 to Dec. 11, 1987)

Consecutive Games Making a Three-Point Field Goal

Season

32—Reggie Evans, Central Okla., Nov. 23, 1991, to March 26, 1992

Career

79—Bryan Williams, Tampa, Jan. 11, 1989, to March 9, 1991

Three-Point Field-Goal Attempts

Game

32—Andy Schmidtmann, Wis.-Parkside vs. Lakeland, Feb. 14, 1989 (14 made)

Season

369—Alex Williams, Cal St. Sacramento, 1988 (167 made)

Career

1,047—Tony Smith, Pfeiffer, 1989-92 (431 made)

Three-Point Field-Goal Attempts Per Game

Season

12.3—Alex Williams, Cal St. Sacramento, 1988 (369 in 30)

Career

9.3—Alex Williams, Cal St. Sacramento, 1987-88 (541 in 58)

Three-Point Field-Goal Percentage

Game

(Min. 9 made) 100%—Steve Divine, Ky. Wesleyan vs. Wayne St. (Mich.), March 14, 1992 (9 of 9)

***Season**

(Min. 35 made) 65.0%—Ray Lee, Hampton, 1988 (39 of 60)

(Min. 50 made) 59.0%—Aaron Baker, Mississippi Col., 1989 (69 of 117)

(Min. 100 made) 56.7%—Scott Martin, Rollins, 1991 (114 of 201)

(Min. 150 made) 45.3%—Alex Williams, Cal St. Sacramento, 1988 (167 of 369)

* *Based on qualifiers for annual championship.*

Career

(Min. 200 made) 51.3%—Scott Martin, Rollins, 1988-91 (236 of 460)

FREE THROWS

Free Throws

Game

37—Clarence "Bevo" Francis, Rio Grande vs. Hillsdale, Feb. 2, 1954 (45 attempts)

Season

401—Joe Miller, Alderson-Broaddus, 1957 (496 attempts)

Career

1,130—Joe Miller, Alderson-Broaddus, 1954-57 (1,460 attempts)

Consecutive Free Throws

Game

23—Carl Hartman, Alderson-Broaddus vs. Salem, Dec. 6, 1954

Season

74—Mike Hall, Adams St., 1992 (during 13 games, Jan. 11-Feb. 15)

Free-Throw Attempts

Game

45—Clarence "Bevo" Francis, Rio Grande vs. Hillsdale, Feb. 2, 1954 (37 made)

Season

†510—Clarence "Bevo" Francis, Rio Grande, 1954 (367 made)

Career

1,460—Joe Miller, Alderson-Broaddus, 1954-57 (1,130 made)

† *Season figure for Francis limited to 27 games against four-year colleges.*

Free-Throw Percentage

Game

(Min. 20 made) 100%—Forrest "Butch" Meyeraan, Mankato St. vs. Wis.-River Falls, Feb. 21, 1961 (20 of 20)

***Season**

94.4%—Kent Andrews, McNeese St., 1968 (85 of 90); Billy Newton, Morgan St., 1976 (85 of 90)

* *Based on qualifiers for annual championship.*

Career

(Min. 250 made) 91.6%—Kent Andrews, McNeese St., 1967-69 (252 of 275)

(Min. 500 made) 87.9%—Steve Nisenson, Hofstra, 1963-65 (602 of 685)

REBOUNDS

Rebounds

Game

46—Tom Hart, Middlebury vs. Trinity (Conn.), Feb. 5, 1955, and vs. Clarkson, Feb. 12, 1955

Season

799—Elmore Smith, Kentucky St., 1971 (33 games)

Career

(4 yrs.) 2,334—Jim Smith, Steubenville, 1955-58 (112 games)

(3 yrs.) 1,917—Elmore Smith, Kentucky St., 1969-71 (85 games)

Average Per Game

Season

29.5—Tom Hart, Middlebury, 1956 (620 in 21)

Career

(Min. 900) 27.6—Tom Hart, Middlebury, 1953, 55-56 (1,738 in 63)

ASSISTS

Assists

Game

25—Ali Baaqar, Morris Brown vs. Albany St. (Ga.), Jan. 26, 1991; Adrian Hutt, Metropolitan St. vs. Cal St. Sacramento, Feb. 9, 1991

Season

400—Steve Ray, Bridgeport, 1989 (32 games)

Career

1,044—Demetri Beekman, Assumption, 1990-93 (119 games)

Average Per Game

Season
12.5—Steve Ray, Bridgeport, 1989 (400 in 32)

Career
(Min. 550) 12.1—Steve Ray, Bridgeport, 1989-90 (785 in 65)

GAMES

Games Played

Season
36—Bill Reigel, Frank Glenn, Jesse Perry and Ruble Scarborough, McNeese St., 1956

Career
133—Pat Morris, Bridgeport, 1989-92

DIVISION II MEN'S TEAM RECORDS

Note: Where records involve both teams, each team must be an NCAA Division II member institution.

SINGLE-GAME SCORING

Most Points
258—Troy St. vs. DeVry (Ga.) (141), Jan. 12, 1992

Most Points vs. Division II Team
169—Stillman vs. Miles (123), Feb. 17, 1966

Most Points by Losing Team
146—Mississippi Col. vs. Livingston (160), Dec. 2, 1969

Most Points, Both Teams
306—Livingston (160) and Mississippi Col. (146), Dec. 2, 1969

Most Points in a Half
135—Troy St. vs. DeVry (Ga.), Jan. 12, 1992

Fewest Points Allowed (Since 1938)
4—Albion (76) vs. Adrian, Dec. 12, 1938; Tennessee St. (7) vs. Oglethorpe, Feb. 16, 1971

Fewest Points, Both Teams (Since 1938)
11—Tennessee St. (7) and Oglethorpe (4), Feb. 16, 1971

Widest Margin of Victory
118—Mississippi Col. (168) vs. Dallas Bible (50), Dec. 9, 1971

SINGLE-GAME FIELD GOALS

Most Field Goals
102—Troy St. vs. DeVry (Ga.), Jan. 12, 1992 (190 attempts)

Most Field-Goal Attempts
190—Troy St. vs. DeVry (Ga.), Jan. 12, 1992 (102 made)

Fewest Field Goals (Since 1938)
0—Adrian vs. Albion, Dec. 12, 1938 (28 attempts)

Fewest Field-Goal Attempts
7—Mansfield vs. West Chester, Dec. 8, 1984 (4 made)

Highest Field-Goal Percentage
81.6%—Youngstown St. vs. Northern Iowa, Jan. 26, 1980 (31 of 38)

Highest Field-Goal Percentage, Half
95.0%—Abilene Christian vs. Cameron, Jan. 21, 1989 (19 of 20)

SINGLE-GAME THREE-POINT FIELD GOALS

Most Three-Point Field Goals
51—Troy St. vs. DeVry (Ga.), Jan. 12, 1992 (109 attempts)

Most Three-Point Field Goals, Both Teams
39—Columbus (22) vs. Troy St. (17), Feb. 14, 1991

Consecutive Three-Point Field Goals Made Without a Miss
12—Pace vs. Medgar Evers, Nov. 27, 1991

Highest Number of Different Players to Score a Three-Point Field Goal, One Team
10—Troy St. vs. DeVry (Ga.), Jan. 12, 1992

Most Three-Point Field-Goal Attempts
109—Troy St. vs. DeVry (Ga.), Jan. 12, 1992 (51 made)

Most Three-Point Field-Goal Attempts, Both Teams
95—Columbus (52) vs. Troy St. (43), Feb. 14, 1991

Highest Three-Point Field-Goal Percentage
(Min. 10 made) 90.9%—Phila. Textile vs. Spring Garden, Nov. 24, 1987 (10 of 11); Armstrong St. vs. Columbus, Feb. 24, 1990 (10 of 11)

Highest Three-Point Field-Goal Percentage, Both Teams
(Min. 10 made) 83.3%—Tampa (9 of 10) vs. St. Leo (1 of 2), Jan. 21, 1987 (10 of 12)
(Min. 20 made) 75.9%—Indiana (Pa.) (11 of 15) vs. Cheyney (11 of 14), Jan. 26, 1987 (22 of 29)

SINGLE-GAME FREE THROWS

Most Free Throws
64—Wayne St. (Mich.) vs. Grand Valley St., Feb. 13, 1993 (79 attempts); Baltimore vs. Washington (Md.), Feb. 9, 1955 (84 attempts)

Most Free Throws, Both Teams
89—Baltimore (64) and Washington (Md.) (25), Feb. 9,1955

Most Free-Throw Attempts
84—Baltimore vs. Washington (Md.), Feb. 9, 1955 (64 made)

Most Free-Throw Attempts, Both Teams
121—Illinois Tech (70) and Illinois Col. (51), Dec. 13, 1952 (66 made)

Fewest Free Throws
0—Many teams

Fewest Free-Throw Attempts
0—Many teams

Highest Free-Throw Percentage
(Min. 31 made) 100%—Dowling vs. LIU-Southampton, Feb. 6, 1985 (31 of 31)

Highest Free-Throw Percentage, Both Teams
(Min. 30 made) 97.0%—Hartford (17 of 17) vs. Bentley (15 of 16), Feb. 22, 1983 (32 of 33)

SINGLE-GAME REBOUNDS

Most Rebounds
111—Central Mich. vs. Alma, Dec. 7, 1963

Most Rebounds, Both Teams
141—Loyola (Md.) (75) vs. Western Md. (66), Dec. 6, 1961; Concordia (Ill.) (72) vs. Concordia (Neb.) (69), Feb. 26, 1965

Highest Rebound Margin
65—Moravian (100) vs. Drew (35), Feb. 18, 1969

SINGLE-GAME ASSISTS

Most Assists
65—Troy St. vs. DeVry (Ga.), Jan. 12, 1992

Most Assists, Both Teams
65—Central Okla. (34) vs. Stonehill (31), Dec. 29, 1990

SINGLE-GAME PERSONAL FOULS

Most Personal Fouls
50—Steubenville vs. West Liberty, 1952

Most Personal Fouls, Both Teams (Including Overtimes)
75—Edinboro (47) vs. Calif. (Pa.) (28) (5 ot), Feb. 4, 1989

Most Personal Fouls, Both Teams (Regulation Time)
74—Bentley (36) vs. Mass.-Boston (38), Jan. 23, 1971

Most Players Disqualified
7—Illinois Col. vs. Illinois Tech, Dec. 13, 1952; Steubenville vs. West Liberty, 1952; Washington (Md.) vs. Baltimore, Feb. 9, 1955; Southern Colo. vs. Air Force, Jan. 12, 1972; Edinboro vs. Calif. (Pa.) (5 ot), Feb. 4, 1989

Most Players Disqualified, Both Teams
12—Alfred (6) and Rensselaer (6), Jan. 9, 1971

SINGLE-GAME OVERTIMES

Most Overtime Periods
7—Yankton (79) at Black Hills (80), Feb. 18, 1956

Most Points in One Overtime Period
27—Southern Ind. vs. Central Mo. St., Jan. 5, 1985

Most Points in One Overtime Period, Both Teams
42—Southern Ind. (27) vs. Central Mo. St. (15), Jan. 5, 1985

Most Points in Overtime Periods
60—Calif. (Pa.) vs. Edinboro (5 ot), Feb. 4, 1989

Most Points in Overtime Periods, Both Teams
114—Calif. (Pa.) (60) vs. Edinboro (54) (5 ot), Feb. 4, 1989

Largest Winning Margin in Overtime Game
22—Pfeiffer (72) vs. Belmont Abbey (50), Dec. 8, 1960

SEASON SCORING

Most Points
3,566—Troy St., 1993 (32 games); Central Okla., 1992 (32 games)

Highest Average Per Game
121.1—Troy St., 1992 (3,513 in 29)

Highest Average Scoring Margin
31.4—Bryan, 1961 (93.8 offense, 62.4 defense)

Most Games at Least 100 Points
25—Troy St., 1993 (32-game season)

Most Consecutive Games at Least 100 Points
17—Norfolk St., 1970

SEASON FIELD GOALS

Most Field Goals
1,455—Kentucky St., 1971 (2,605 attempts)

Most Field Goals Per Game
46.9—Lincoln (Mo.), 1967 (1,267 in 27)

Most Field-Goal Attempts
2,853—Ark.-Pine Bluff, 1967 (1,306 made)

Most Field-Goal Attempts Per Game
108.2—Stillman, 1968 (2,814 in 26)

Highest Field-Goal Percentage
62.4%—Kentucky St., 1976 (1,093 of 1,753)

SEASON THREE-POINT FIELD GOALS

Most Three-Point Field Goals
444—Troy St., 1992 (1,303 attempts)

Most Three-Point Field Goals Made Per Game
15.3—Troy St., 1992 (444 in 29)

Most Three-Point Field-Goal Attempts
1,303—Troy St., 1992 (444 made)

Most Three-Point Field-Goal Attempts Per Game
44.9—Troy St., 1992 (1,303 in 29)

Highest Three-Point Field-Goal Percentage
(Min. 90 made) 53.8%—Winston-Salem, 1988 (98 of 182)
(Min. 200 made) 50.2%—Oakland City, 1992 (244 of 486)

SEASON FREE THROWS

Most Free Throws
896—Ouachita, 1965 (1,226 attempts)

Most Free Throws Per Game
36.1—Baltimore, 1955 (686 in 19)

Most Free-Throw Attempts
1,226—Ouachita, 1965 (896 made)

Most Free-Throw Attempts Per Game
49.6—Baltimore, 1955 (943 in 19)

Highest Free-Throw Percentage
81.5%—South Ala., 1971 (422 of 518)

SEASON REBOUNDS

Most Rebounds
1,570—Alabama A&M, 1985 (31 games)

Highest Average Per Game
65.8—Bentley, 1964 (1,513 in 23)

Highest Average Rebound Margin
24.4—Mississippi Val., 1976 (63.9 offense, 39.5 defense)

SEASON ASSISTS

Most Assists
736—New Hamp. Col., 1993 (33 games)

Highest Average Per Game
25.5—Morris Brown, 1989 (663 in 26)

SEASON PERSONAL FOULS

Most Personal Fouls
947—Seattle, 1952 (37 games)

Most Personal Fouls Per Game
29.9—Shaw, 1987 (748 in 25)

Fewest Personal Fouls
184—Sewanee, 1962 (17 games)

Fewest Personal Fouls Per Game
10.0—Ashland, 1969 (301 in 30)

SEASON DEFENSE

Lowest Points Per Game Allowed
20.2—Alcorn St., 1941 (323 in 16)

Lowest Points Per Game Allowed (Since 1948)
29.1—Miss. Industrial, 1948 (436 in 15)

Lowest Field-Goal Percentage Allowed (Since 1978)
37.0—Virginia Union, 1992 (766 of 2,069)

SEASON OVERTIMES

Most Overtime Games
8—Belmont Abbey, 1983 (won 4, lost 4)

Most Consecutive Overtime Games
3—eight times

Most Multiple-Overtime Games
5—Cal St. Dom. Hills, 1987 (four 2 ot, one 3 ot; won 2, lost 3)

GENERAL RECORDS

Most Games in a Season
39—Regis (Colo.), 1949 (36-3)

Most Victories in a Season
36—Regis (Colo.), 1949 (36-3)

Most Victories in a Perfect Season
33—Cal St. Bakersfield, 1993

Most Consecutive Victories
52—Langston (from 1943-44 opener through fifth game of 1945-46 season)

Most Consecutive Home-Court Victories
79—Denver (from Feb. 12, 1980, to Jan. 8, 1985)

Most Consecutive Regular-Season Victories (postseason tournaments not included)
52—Langston (from 1943-44 opener through fifth game of 1945-46 season)

Most Defeats in a Season
27—Colorado Mines, 1992 (0-27); Bowie St., 1985 (1-27)

Most Consecutive Defeats in a Season
27—Colorado Mines, 1992 (0-27)

Most Consecutive Defeats
46—Olivet, Feb. 21, 1959, to Dec. 4, 1961; Southwest St. (Minn.), Dec. 11, 1971, to Dec. 1, 1973

Most Consecutive Winning Seasons
31—Norfolk St., 1963-93

Most Consecutive Non-Losing Seasons
31—Norfolk St., 1963-93

††Unbeaten teams
(Since 1938; number of victories in parentheses)
1938 Glenville St. (28)
1941 Milwaukee St. (16)
1942 Indianapolis (16)
1942 Rochester (16)
1944 Langston (23)
1945 Langston (24)
1948 West Va. St. (23)
1949 Tennessee St. (24)
1956 Rochester Inst. (17)
1959 Grand Canyon (20)
1961 Calvin (20)
1964 Bethany (W. Va.) (18)
1965 Central St. (Ohio) (30)
1965 Evansville (29)#
1993 Cal St. Bakersfield (33)#

†† *At least 15 victories.*

Division II NCAA champion.

DIVISION II MEN'S ALL-TIME INDIVIDUAL LEADERS

SINGLE-GAME SCORING HIGHS

Pts.	Player, Team vs. Opponent	Season
113	Clarence "Bevo" Francis, Rio Grande vs. Hillsdale	1954
84	Clarence "Bevo" Francis, Rio Grande vs. Alliance	1954
82	Clarence "Bevo" Francis, Rio Grande vs. Bluffton	1954
80	Paul Crissman, Southern Cal. Col. vs. Pacific Christian	1966
77	William English, Winston-Salem vs. Fayetteville St.	1968
75	Travis Grant, Kentucky St. vs. Northwood	1970
72	Nate DeLong, Wis.-River Falls vs. Winona St.	1948
72	Lloyd Brown, Aquinas vs. Cleary	1953
72	Clarence "Bevo" Francis, Rio Grande vs. Calif. (Pa.)	1953
72	John McElroy, Youngstown St. vs. Wayne St. (Mich.)	1969
71	Clayborn Jones, L. A. Pacific vs. L. A. Baptist	1965
70	Paul Wilcox, Davis & Elkins vs. Glenville	1959
70	Bo Clark, Central Fla. vs. Fla. Memorial	1977

SEASON SCORING AVERAGE

Player, Team	Season	G	FG	FT	Pts.	Avg.
Clarence "Bevo" Francis, Rio Grande	†1954	27	444	367	1,255	*46.5
Earl Glass, Miss. Industrial	†1963	19	322	171	815	42.9
Earl Monroe, Winston-Salem	†1967	32	509	311	*1,329	41.5
John Rinka, Kenyon	†1970	23	354	234	942	41.0
Willie Shaw, Lane	†1964	18	303	121	727	40.4
Travis Grant, Kentucky St.	†1972	33	*539	226	1,304	39.5
Thales McReynolds, Miles	†1965	18	294	118	706	39.2
Bob Johnson, Fitchburg St.	1963	18	213	277	703	39.1
Roger Kuss, Wis.-River Falls	†1953	21	291	235	817	38.9
Florindo Vieira, Quinnipiac	1954	14	191	138	520	37.1

† *National champion.* * *Record.*

SEASON FIELD-GOAL PERCENTAGE

(Based on qualifiers for annual championship)

Player, Team	Season	G	FG	FGA	Pct.
Todd Linder, Tampa	†1987	32	282	375	*75.2
Maurice Stafford, North Ala.	†1984	34	198	264	75.0
Matthew Cornegay, Tuskegee	†1982	29	208	278	74.8
Brian Moten, West Ga.	†1992	26	141	192	73.4
Ed Phillips, Alabama A&M	†1968	22	154	210	73.3
Ray Strozier, Central Mo. St.	†1980	28	142	195	72.8
Harold Booker, Cheyney	†1965	24	144	198	72.7
Tom Schurfranz, Bellarmine	†1991	30	245	339	72.3
Marv Lewis, LIU-Southampton	†1969	24	271	375	72.3
Louis Newsome, North Ala.	†1988	29	192	266	72.2
Ed Phillips, Alabama A&M	†1971	24	159	221	71.9
Gregg Northington, Alabama St.	1971	26	324	451	71.8

† *National champion.* * *Record.*

SEASON THREE-POINT FIELD GOALS MADE PER GAME

Player, Team	Season	G	3FG	Avg.
Alex Williams, Cal St. Sacramento	†1988	30	*167	*5.6
Jason Garrow, Augustana (S.D.)	†1992	27	135	5.0
Ray Gutierrez, Calif. (Pa.)	†1993	29	142	4.9
John Boyd, LeMoyne-Owen	1992	26	123	4.7
Duane Huddleston, Missouri-Rolla	1988	25	118	4.7
Shawn Williams, Central Okla.	†1991	29	129	4.4
Robert Martin, Cal St. Sacramento	1988	30	128	4.3
Bill Harris, Northern Mich.	†1987	27	117	4.3
Robert Martin, Cal St. Sacramento	†1989	28	118	4.2
Louis Smart, Tuskegee	1989	25	103	4.1
Kwame Morton, Clarion	1993	26	107	4.1
Mike Sinclair, Bowie St.	1988	28	115	4.1
Andy Schmidtmann, Wis.-Parkside	1989	28	114	4.1
Scott Martin, Rollins	1991	28	114	4.1

† *National champion.* * *Record.*

SEASON THREE-POINT FIELD-GOAL PERCENTAGE

(Based on qualifiers for annual championship)

Player, Team	Season	G	3FG	3FGA	Pct.
Ray Lee, Hampton	†1988	24	39	60	*65.0
Steve Hood, Winston-Salem	1988	28	42	67	62.7
Mark Willey, Fort Hays St.	†1990	29	49	81	60.5
Aaron Baker, Mississippi Col.	†1989	27	69	117	59.0
Walter Hurd, Johnson Smith	1989	27	49	84	58.3
Scott Martin, Rollins	†1991	28	114	201	56.7
Charles Byrd, West Tex. A&M	†1987	31	95	168	56.5
Jay Nolan, Bowie St.	1987	27	70	124	56.5
Tony Harris, Dist. Columbia	1987	30	79	141	56.0
Rickey Barrett, Ala.-Huntsville	1987	26	63	113	55.8
Erik Fisher, San Fran. St.	1991	28	80	144	55.6
Mike Doyle, Phila. Textile	1988	30	82	149	55.0

† *National champion.* * *Record.*

SEASON FREE-THROW PERCENTAGE

(Based on qualifiers for annual championship)

Player, Team	Season	G	FT	FTA	Pct.
Billy Newton, Morgan St.	†1976	28	85	90	*94.4
Kent Andrews, McNeese St.	†1968	24	85	90	*94.4
Mike Sanders, Northern Colo.	†1987	28	82	87	94.3
Joe Cullen, Hartwick	†1969	18	96	103	93.2
Charles Byrd, West Tex. A&M	†1988	29	92	99	92.9
Brian Koephick, Mankato St.	1988	28	104	112	92.9
Jon Hagen, Mankato St.	†1963	25	76	82	92.7
Carl Gonder, Augustana (S.D.)	†1982	27	86	93	92.5
Hal McManus, Lander	†1992	28	110	119	92.4
Terry Gill, New Orleans	†1974	30	97	105	92.4
Emery Sammons, Phila. Textile	†1977	28	145	157	92.4

† *National champion.* * *Record.*

SEASON REBOUND AVERAGE

Player, Team	Season	G	Reb.	Avg.
Tom Hart, Middlebury	†1956	21	620	*29.5
Tom Hart, Middlebury	†1955	22	649	29.5
Frank Stronczek, American Int'l	†1966	26	717	27.6
R. C. Owens, College of Idaho	†1954	25	677	27.1
Maurice Stokes, St. Francis (Pa.)	1954	26	689	26.5
Roman Turmon, Clark Atlanta	1954	23	602	26.2
Pat Callahan, Lewis	1955	20	523	26.2
Hank Brown, Lowell Tech	1966	19	496	26.1
Maurice Stokes, St. Francis (Pa.)	1955	28	726	25.9

† *National champion.* * *Record.*

SEASON ASSISTS

Player, Team	Season	G	Ast.
Steve Ray, Bridgeport	†1989	32	*400
Steve Ray, Bridgeport	†1990	33	385
Tony Smith, Pfeiffer	†1992	35	349
Jim Ferrer, Bentley	1989	31	309
Brian Gregory, Oakland	1989	28	300
Charles Jordan, Erskine	1992	34	298
Adrian Hutt, Metropolitan St.	†1991	28	285
Patrick Boen, Stonehill	1989	32	278
Demetri Beekman, Assumption	1992	32	271
Gallagher Driscoll, St. Rose	1991	29	267

† *National champion.* * *Record.*

SEASON ASSIST AVERAGE

Player, Team	Season	G	Ast.	Avg.
Steve Ray, Bridgeport	†1989	32	*400	*12.5
Steve Ray, Bridgeport	†1990	33	385	11.7
Demetri Beekman, Assumption	†1993	23	264	11.5
Brian Gregory, Oakland	1989	28	300	10.7
Adrian Hutt, Metropolitan St.	†1991	28	285	10.2

Player, Team	Season	G	Ast.	Avg.
Tony Smith, Pfeiffer	†1992	35	349	10.0
Jim Ferrer, Bentley	1989	31	309	10.0
Paul Beaty, Miles	1992	26	248	9.5
Lawrence Jordan, IU/PU-Ft. Wayne	1990	28	266	9.5
Hal Chambers, Columbus	1993	24	227	9.5
Gallagher Driscoll, St. Rose	1991	29	267	9.2
David Daniels, Colo. Christian	1993	29	264	9.1

*† National champion. * Record.*

CAREER POINTS

Player, Team	Seasons	Pts.
Travis Grant, Kentucky St.	1969-72	*4,045
Bob Hopkins, Grambling	1953-56	3,759
Tony Smith, Pfeiffer	1989-92	3,350
Earnest Lee, Clark Atlanta	1984-87	3,298
Joe Miller, Alderson-Broaddus	1954-57	3,294
Henry Logan, Western Caro.	1965-68	3,290
John Rinka, Kenyon	1967-70	3,251
Dick Barnett, Tennessee St.	1956-59	3,209
Willie Scott, Alabama St.	1966-69	3,155
Johnnie Allen, Bethune-Cookman	1966-69	3,058
Bennie Swain, Texas Southern	1955-58	3,008
Lambert Shell, Bridgeport	1989-92	3,001
Carl Hartman, Alderson-Broaddus	1952-55	2,959
Earl Monroe, Winston-Salem	1964-67	2,935
Bo Clark, Central Fla.	1975-77, 78-80	2,886

** Record.*

CAREER SCORING AVERAGE

(Minimum 1,400 points)

Player, Team	Seasons	G	FG	3FG	FT	Pts.	Avg.
Travis Grant, Kentucky St.	1969-72	121	*1,760	—	525	*4,045	*33.4
John Rinka, Kenyon	1967-70	99	1,261	—	729	3,251	32.8
Florindo Vieira, Quinnipiac	1954-57	69	761	—	741	2,263	32.8
Willie Shaw, Lane	1961-64	76	960	—	459	2,379	31.3
Mike Davis, Virginia Union	1966-69	89	1,014	—	730	2,758	31.0
Henry Logan, Western Caro.	1965-68	107	1,263	—	764	3,290	30.7
Willie Scott, Alabama St.	1966-69	103	1,277	—	601	3,155	30.6
George Gilmore, Chaminade	1991-92	51	485	174	387	1,531	30.0
Bob Hopkins, Grambling	1953-56	126	1,403	—	953	3,759	29.8
Rod Butler, Western New Eng.	1968-70	59	697	—	331	1,725	29.2
Gregg Northington, Alabama St.	1970-72	75	894	—	403	2,191	29.2
Isaiah Wilson, Baltimore	1969-71	67	731	—	471	1,933	28.9

** Record.*

CAREER FIELD-GOAL PERCENTAGE

(Minimum 400 field goals made)

Player, Team	Seasons	G	FG	FGA	Pct.
Todd Linder, Tampa	1984-87	122	909	1,284	*70.8
Tom Schurfranz, Bellarmine	1987-88, 91-92	112	742	1,057	70.2
Ed Phillips, Alabama A&M	1968-71	95	610	885	68.9
Otis Evans, Wayne St. (Mich.)	1989-92	106	472	697	67.7
Ulysses Hackett, S.C.-Spartanburg	1989-92	119	1,026	1,529	67.1
Matthew Cornegay, Tuskegee	1979-82	105	524	783	66.9
Ray Strozier, Central Mo. St.	1978-81	110	563	843	66.8
James Morris, Central Okla.	1990-93	76	532	798	66.7
Lance Berwald, North Dak. St.	1983-84	58	475	717	66.2
Harold Booker, Cheyney	1965-67, 69	108	662	1,002	66.1
Larry Tucker, Lewis	1980-83	112	841	1,277	65.9

** Record.*

CAREER THREE-POINT FIELD GOALS MADE

Player, Team	Seasons	G	3FG
Tony Smith, Pfeiffer	1989-92	126	*431
Gary Duda, Merrimack	1989-92	122	389
Columbus Parker, Johnson Smith	1990-93	115	354
Gary Paul, Indianapolis	1987-90	111	354
Mike Ziegler, Colorado Mines	1987-90	118	344

Player, Team	Seasons	G	3FG
Jon Cronin, Stonehill	1989-92	117	308
Bryan Williams, Tampa	1988-91	123	303
Steve Schieppe, Northeast Mo. St.	1988-91	105	300
Mike Sinclair, Bowie St.	1987-89	82	299
Kevin McCarthy, New Hamp. Col.	1989-92	117	297
Robert Martin, Cal St. Sacramento	1987-89	85	294

** Record.*

CAREER THREE-POINT FIELD GOALS MADE PER GAME

(Minimum 200 three-point field goals made)

Player, Team	Seasons	G	3FG	Avg.
Alex Williams, Cal St. Sacramento	1987-88	58	247	*4.26
Shawn Williams, Central Okla.	1990-91	57	212	3.72
Mike Sinclair, Bowie St.	1987-89	82	299	3.65
Robert Martin, Cal St. Sacramento	1987-89	85	294	3.46
Tony Smith, Pfeiffer	1989-92	126	*431	3.42
@Jeff deLaveaga, Cal Lutheran	1989-92	80	272	3.40
Gary Paul, Indianapolis	1987-90	111	354	3.19
Gary Duda, Merrimack	1989-92	122	389	3.19
Rod Harris, LIU-Southampton	1987-89	78	241	3.09
Columbus Parker, Johnson Smith	1990-93	115	354	3.08

** Record. @ Played in Division III in 1992 season.*

CAREER THREE-POINT FIELD-GOAL PERCENTAGE

(Minimum 200 three-point field goals made)

Player, Team	Seasons	G	3FG	3FGA	Pct.
Scott Martin, Rollins	1988-91	104	236	460	*51.3
Matt Markle, Shippensburg	1989-92	101	202	408	49.5
Lance Gelnett, Millersville	1989-92	109	266	547	48.6
Keith Abeyta, Southern Colo.	1990-92	88	234	489	47.9
Mark Willey, Fort Hays St.	1989-92	117	224	478	46.9
Todd Bowden, Randolph-Macon	1987-89	84	229	491	46.6
Gary Paul, Indianapolis	1987-90	111	*354	768	46.1
Alex Williams, Cal St. Sacramento	1987-88	58	247	541	45.7
Boyd Printy, Northeast Mo. St.	1990-92	77	201	447	45.0
Buck Williams, North Ala.	1987-89	84	238	535	44.5

** Record.*

CAREER FREE-THROW PERCENTAGE

(Minimum 250 free throws made)

Player, Team	Seasons	G	FT	FTA	Pct.
Kent Andrews, McNeese St.	1967-69	67	252	275	*91.6
Jon Hagen, Mankato St.	1963-65	73	252	280	90.0
Dave Reynolds, Davis & Elkins	1986-89	107	383	429	89.3
Tony Budzik, Mansfield	1989-92	107	367	416	88.2
Terry Gill, New Orleans	1972-74	79	261	296	88.2
Bryan Vacca, Randolph-Macon	1980-83	94	262	298	87.9
Steve Nisenson, Hofstra	1963-65	83	602	685	87.9
Jack Sparks, Bentley	1976-80	99	253	288	87.8
Jeff Gore, St. Rose	1990-93	120	349	398	87.7
Wayne Profitt, Lynchburg	1965-67	57	482	551	87.5
Clyde Briley, McNeese St.	1962-65	101	561	642	87.4
Foy Ballance, Armstrong St.	1978-81	108	351	402	87.3
Jehu Brabham, Mississippi Col.	1969-71	72	452	518	87.3
Pete Chambers, West Chester	1966-68	67	267	306	87.3

** Record.*

CAREER REBOUND AVERAGE

(Minimum 900 rebounds)

Player, Team	Seasons	G	Reb.	Avg.
Tom Hart, Middlebury	1953, 55-56	63	1,738	*27.6
Maurice Stokes, St. Francis (Pa.)	1953-55	72	1,812	25.2
Frank Stronczek, American Int'l	1965-67	62	1,549	25.0
Bill Thieben, Hofstra	1954-56	76	1,837	24.2
Hank Brown, Lowell Tech	1965-67	49	1,129	23.0

Player, Team	Seasons	G	Reb.	Avg.
Elmore Smith, Kentucky St.	1969-71	85	1,917	22.6
Charles Wrinn, Trinity (Conn.)	1951-53	53	1,176	22.2
Roman Turmon, Clark Atlanta	1952-54	60	1,312	21.9
Tony Missere, Pratt	1966-68	62	1,348	21.7
Ron Horton, Delaware St.	1966-68	64	1,384	21.6

** Record.*

CAREER ASSISTS

Player, Team	Seasons	G	Ast.
Demetri Beekman, Assumption	1990-93	119	*1,044
Gallagher Driscoll, St. Rose	1989-92	121	878
Tony Smith, Pfeiffer	1989-92	126	828
Steve Ray, Bridgeport	1989-90	65	785
Charles Jordan, Erskine	1989-92	119	727
Pat Madden, Jacksonville St.	1989-91	88	688
Mark Benson, Texas A&I	1989-91	86	674
Mike Buscetto, Quinnipiac	1990-93	99	624
Orlando Vandross, American Int'l	1989-92	111	597
John Haas, Le Moyne	1990-93	112	561
C. Russell, Slippery Rock	1989-91	89	543
Brian Gregory, Oakland	1989-90	56	531
Brandy Monks, Bellarmine	1989-91	87	521
Lawrence Jordan, IU/PU-Ft. Wayne	1989-90	56	515
Adrian Hutt, Metropolitan St.	1990-91	60	512

** Record.*

CAREER ASSIST AVERAGE

(Minimum 550 assists)

Player, Team	Seasons	G	Ast.	Avg.
Steve Ray, Bridgeport	1989-90	65	785	*12.1
Demetri Beekman, Assumption	1990-93	119	1,044	8.8
Mark Benson, Texas A&I	1989-91	86	674	7.8
Pat Madden, Jacksonville St.	1989-91	88	688	7.8
Gallagher Driscoll, St. Rose	1989-92	121	*878	7.3
Tony Smith, Pfeiffer	1989-92	126	828	6.6
Mike Buscetto, Quinnipiac	1990-93	99	624	6.3
Charles Jordan, Erskine	1989-92	119	727	6.1

** Record.*

DIVISION II MEN'S ANNUAL INDIVIDUAL CHAMPIONS

SCORING AVERAGE

Year	Player, Team	G	FG	FT	Pts.	Avg.
1948	Nate DeLong, Wis.-River Falls	22	206	206	618	28.1
1949	George King, Charleston (W. Va.)	26	289	179	757	29.1
1950	George King, Charleston (W. Va.)	31	354	259	967	31.2
1951	Scott Seagall, Millikin	31	314	260	888	28.6
1952	Harold Wolfe, Findlay	22	285	101	671	30.5
1953	Roger Kuss, Wis.-River Falls	21	291	235	817	38.9
1954	Clarence "Bevo" Francis, Rio Grande	27	444	367	1,255	*46.5
1955	Bill Warden, North Central	13	162	127	451	34.7
1956	Bill Reigel, McNeese St.	36	425	370	1,220	33.9
1957	Ken Hammond, West Va. Tech	27	334	274	942	34.9
1958	John Lee Butcher, Pikeville	27	330	210	870	32.2
1959	Paul Wilcox, Davis & Elkins	23	289	195	773	33.6
1960	Don Perrelli, Southern Conn. St.	22	263	168	694	31.5
1961	Lebron Bell, Bryan	14	174	114	462	33.0
1962	Willie Shaw, Lane	18	239	115	593	32.9
1963	Earl Glass, Miss. Industrial	19	322	171	815	42.9
1964	Willie Shaw, Lane	18	303	121	727	40.4
1965	Thales McReynolds, Miles	18	294	118	706	39.2
1966	Paul Crissman, Southern Cal College	23	373	90	836	36.3
1967	Earl Monroe, Winston-Salem	32	509	311	*1,329	41.5

Year	Player, Team	G	FG	FT	Pts.	Avg.
1968	Mike Davis, Virginia Union	25	351	206	908	36.3
1969	John Rinka, Kenyon	26	340	202	882	33.9
1970	John Rinka, Kenyon	23	354	234	942	41.0
1971	Bo Lamar, Southwestern La.	29	424	196	1,044	36.0
1972	Travis Grant, Kentucky St.	33	*539	226	1,304	39.5
1973	Claude White, Elmhurst	18	248	101	597	33.2
1974	Aaron James, Grambling	27	366	137	869	32.2
1975	Ron Barrow, Southern-B.R.	23	296	115	707	30.7
1976	Ron Barrow, Southern-B.R.	27	318	136	772	28.6
1977	Ed Murphy, Merrimack	28	369	158	896	32.0
1978	Harold Robertson, Lincoln (Mo.)	28	408	149	965	34.5
1979	Bo Clark, Central Fla.	23	315	97	727	31.6
1980	Bill Fennelly, Central Mo. St.	28	337	189	863	30.8
1981	Gregory Jackson, St. Paul's	26	267	183	717	27.6
1982	John Ebeling, Fla. Southern	32	286	284	856	26.8
1983	Danny Dixon, Alabama A&M	27	379	152	910	33.7
1984	Earl Jones, Dist. Columbia	22	215	200	630	28.6
1985	Earnest Lee, Clark Atlanta	29	380	230	990	34.1
1986	Earnest Lee, Clark Atlanta	28	314	191	819	29.3

Year	Player, Team	G	FG	3FG	FT	Pts.	Avg.
1987	Earnest Lee, Clark Atlanta	29	326	35	174	861	29.7
1988	Daryl Cambrelen, LIU-Southampton	25	242	32	170	686	27.4
1989	Steve deLaveaga, Cal Lutheran	28	278	79	151	786	28.1
1990	A. J. English, Virginia Union	30	333	65	270	1,001	33.4
1991	Gary Mattison, St. Augustine's	26	277	53	159	766	29.5
1992	George Gilmore, Chaminade	28	280	82	238	880	31.4
1993	Darrin Robinson, Sacred Heart	26	313	75	130	831	32.0

* *Record.*

FIELD-GOAL PERCENTAGE

Year	Player, Team	G	FG	FGA	Pct.
1949	Vern Mikkelson, Hamline	30	203	377	53.8
1950	Nate DeLong, Wis.-River Falls	29	287	492	58.3
1951	Johnny O'Brien, Seattle	33	248	434	57.1
1952	Forrest Hamilton, Southwest Mo. St.	30	147	246	59.8
1953	Bob Buis, Carleton	21	149	246	60.6
1954	Paul Lauritzen, Augustana (Ill.)	19	158	251	62.9
1955	Jim O'Hara, UC Santa Barb.	24	140	214	65.4
1956	Logan Gipe, Ky. Wesleyan	22	134	224	59.8
1957	John Wilfred, Winston-Salem	30	229	381	60.1
1958	Bennie Swain, Texas Southern	35	363	587	61.8
1959	Dick O'Meara, Babson	18	144	225	64.0
1960	Edwin Cox, Howard Payne	26	126	194	64.9
1961	Tony Solomon, St. Paul's	20	94	149	63.1
1962	Tom Morris, St. Paul's	17	108	168	64.3
1963	Howard Trice, Howard Payne	26	168	237	70.9
1964	Robert Springer, Howard Payne	24	119	174	68.4
1965	Harold Booker, Cheyney	24	144	198	72.7
1966	Harold Booker, Cheyney	27	170	240	70.8
1967	John Dickson, Arkansas St.	24	214	308	69.5
1968	Edward Phillips, Alabama A&M	22	154	210	73.3
1969	Marvin Lewis, LIU-Southampton	24	271	375	72.3
1970	Travis Grant, Kentucky St.	31	482	688	70.1
1971	Edward Phillips, Alabama A&M	24	159	221	71.9
1972	Don Manley, Otterbein	23	146	207	70.5
1973	Glynn Berry, LIU-Southampton	26	191	302	63.2
1974	Kirby Thurston, Western Caro.	25	242	367	65.9
1975	Gerald Cunningham, Kentucky St.	29	280	411	68.1
1976	Thomas Blue, Elizabeth City St.	24	270	388	69.6
1977	Kelvin Hicks, New York Tech	24	161	232	69.4
1978	Ron Ripley, Wis.-Green Bay	32	162	239	67.8
1979	Carl Bailey, Tuskegee	27	210	307	68.4
1980	Ray Strozier, Central Mo. St.	28	142	195	72.8
1981	Matthew Cornegay, Tuskegee	26	177	247	71.7
1982	Matthew Cornegay, Tuskegee	29	208	278	74.8
1983	Rudy Burton, Elizabeth City St.	24	142	201	70.6
1984	Maurice Stafford, North Ala.	34	198	264	75.0
1985	Todd Linder, Tampa	31	219	306	71.6
1986	Todd Linder, Tampa	28	204	291	70.1
1987	Todd Linder, Tampa	32	282	375	*75.2
1988	Louis Newsome, North Ala.	29	192	266	72.2

Year	Player, Team	G	FG	FGA	Pct.
1989	Tom Schurfranz, Bellarmine	28	164	240	68.2
1990	Ulysses Hackett, S.C.-Spartanburg	32	301	426	70.7
1991	Tom Schurfranz, Bellarmine	30	245	339	72.3
1992	Brian Moten, West Ga.	26	141	192	73.4
1993	Chad Scott, Calif. (Pa.)	28	173	245	70.6

* *Record.*

THREE-POINT FIELD GOALS MADE PER GAME

Year	Player, Team	G	3FG	Avg.
1987	Bill Harris, Northern Mich.	27	117	4.3
1988	Alex Williams, Cal St. Sacramento	30	*167	*5.6
1989	Robert Martin, Cal St. Sacramento	28	118	4.2
1990	Gary Paul, Indianapolis	28	110	3.9
1991	Shawn Williams, Central Okla.	29	129	4.4
1992	Jason Garrow, Augustana (S.D.)	27	135	5.0
1993	Ray Gutierrez, Calif. (Pa.)	29	142	4.9

* *Record.*

THREE-POINT FIELD-GOAL PERCENTAGE

Year	Player, Team	G	3FG	3FGA	Pct.
1987	Charles Byrd, West Tex. A&M	31	95	168	56.5
1988	Ray Lee, Hampton	24	39	60	*65.0
1989	Aaron Baker, Mississippi Col.	27	69	117	59.0
1990	Mark Willey, Fort Hays St.	29	49	81	60.5
1991	Scott Martin, Rollins	28	114	201	56.7
1992	Jeff Duvall, Oakland City	30	49	91	53.8
1993	Greg Wilkinson, Oakland City	32	82	152	53.9

* *Record.*

FREE-THROW PERCENTAGE

Year	Player, Team	G	FT	FTA	Pct.
1948	Frank Cochran, Delta St.	22	36	43	83.7
1949	Jim Walsh, Spring Hill	25	62	75	82.7
1950	Dean Ehlers, Central Methodist	33	186	213	87.3
1951	Jim Hoverder, Central Mo. St.	23	75	85	88.2
1952	Jim Fenton, Akron	24	104	121	86.0
1953	Dick Parfitt, Central Mich.	22	93	105	88.6
1954	Bill Parrott, David Lipscomb	24	174	198	87.9
1955	Pete Kovacs, Monmouth (Ill.)	20	175	199	87.9
1956	Fred May, Loras	22	127	146	87.0
1957	Jim Sutton, South Dak. St.	22	127	138	92.0
1958	Arnold Smith, Allen	22	103	113	91.2
1959	Bill Reece, Lenoir-Rhyne	27	84	92	91.3
1960	Ron Slaymaker, Emporia St.	20	80	88	90.9
1961	Harvey Rosen, Wilkes	22	105	115	91.3
1962	Wayne Mahone, Stephen F. Austin	26	76	84	90.5
1963	Jon Hagen, Mankato St.	25	76	82	92.7
1964	Steve Nisenson, Hofstra	28	230	252	91.3
1965	Jon Hagen, Mankato St.	23	103	112	92.0
1966	Jack Cryan, Rider	25	182	198	91.9
1967	Kent Andrews, McNeese St.	22	101	110	91.8
1968	Kent Andrews, McNeese St.	24	85	90	*94.4
1969	Joe Cullen, Hartwick	18	96	103	93.2
1970	John Rinka, Kenyon	23	234	263	89.0
1971	Ed Roeth, Defiance	26	138	152	90.8
1972	Jeff Kuntz, St. Norbert	25	142	155	91.6
1973	Bob Kronisch, Brooklyn	30	93	105	88.6
1974	Terry Gill, New Orleans	30	97	105	92.4
1975	Clarence Rand, Alabama St.	29	91	101	90.1
1976	Billy Newton, Morgan St.	28	85	90	*94.4
1977	Emery Sammons, Phila. Textile	28	145	157	92.4
1978	Dana Skinner, Merrimack	28	142	154	92.2
1979	Jack Sparks, Bentley	28	76	84	90.5
1980	Grey Giovanine, Central Mo. St.	28	75	83	90.4
1981	Ted Smith, SIU-Edwardsville	26	67	73	91.8
1982	Carl Gonder, Augustana (S.D.)	27	86	93	92.5

Year	Player, Team	G	FT	FTA	Pct.
1983	Joe Sclafani, New Haven	28	86	98	87.8
1984	Darrell Johnston, New Hamp. Col.	29	74	81	91.4
1985	Tom McDonald, South Dak. St.	33	88	97	90.7
1986	Todd Mezzulo, Alas. Fairbanks	27	114	125	91.2
1987	Mike Sanders, Northern Colo.	28	82	87	94.3
1988	Charles Byrd, West Tex. A&M	29	92	99	92.8
1989	Mike Boschee, North Dak.	28	71	77	92.2
1990	Mike Morris, Ala.-Huntsville	28	114	125	91.2
1991	Ryun Williams, South Dak.	30	114	125	91.2
1992	Hal McManus, Lander	28	110	119	92.4
1993	Jason Williams, New Haven	27	115	125	92.0

** Record.*

REBOUND AVERAGE

Year	Player, Team	G	Reb.	Avg.
1951	Walter Lenz, Frank. & Marsh.	17	338	19.9
1952	Charley Wrinn, Trinity (Conn.)	19	486	25.6
1953	Ellerbe Neal, Wofford	23	609	26.5
1954	R. C. Owens, College of Idaho	25	677	27.1
1955	Tom Hart, Middlebury	22	649	29.5
1956	Tom Hart, Middlebury	21	620	*29.5
1957	Jim Smith, Steubenville	26	651	25.0
1958	Marv Becker, Widener	18	450	25.0
1959	Jim Davis, King's (Pa.)	17	384	22.6
1960	Jackie Jackson, Virginia Union	19	424	†.241
1961	Jackie Jackson, Virginia Union	26	641	24.7
1962	Jim Ahrens, Buena Vista	28	682	24.4
1963	Gerry Govan, St. Mary's (Kan.)	18	445	24.7
1964	Ernie Brock, Virginia St.	24	597	24.9
1965	Dean Sandifer, Lakeland	23	592	25.7
1966	Frank Stronczek, American Int'l	26	717	27.6
1967	Frank Stronczek, American Int'l	25	602	24.1
1968	Ron Horton, Delaware St.	23	543	23.6
1969	Wilbert Jones, Albany St. (Ga.)	28	670	23.9
1970	Russell Jackson, Southern-B.R.	22	544	24.7
1971	Tony Williams, St. Francis (Me.)	24	599	25.0
1972	No rankings			
1973	No rankings			
1974	Larry Johnson, Prairie View	23	519	22.6
1975	Major Jones, Albany St. (Ga.)	27	608	22.5
1976	Major Jones, Albany St. (Ga.)	24	475	19.8
1977	Andre Means, Sacred Heart	32	516	16.1
1978	Scott Mountz, Calif. (Pa.)	24	431	18.0
1979	Keith Smith, Shaw	20	329	16.5
1980	Ricky Mahorn, Hampton	31	490	15.8
1981	Earl Jones, Dist. Columbia	25	333	13.3
1982	Donnie Carter, Tuskegee	29	372	12.8
1983	David Binion, N.C. Central	25	400	16.0
1984	Jerome Kersey, Longwood	27	383	14.2
1985	Charles Oakley, Virginia Union	31	535	17.3
1986	Raheem Muhammad, Wayne St. (Mich.)	31	428	13.8
1987	Andre Porter, LIU-Southampton	23	309	13.4
1988	Anthony Ikeobi, Clark Atlanta	27	380	14.1
1989	Toby Barber, Winston-Salem	24	327	13.6
1990	Leroy Gasque, Morris Brown	24	375	15.6
1991	Sheldon Owens, Shaw	27	325	12.0
1992	David Allen, Wayne St. (Neb.)	28	362	12.9
1993	James Hector, American Int'l	28	389	13.9

** Record. † Championship determined by highest individual recoveries out of total by both teams in all games.*

ASSIST AVERAGE

Year	Player, Team	G	Ast.	Avg.
1989	Steve Ray, Bridgeport	32	*400	*12.5
1990	Steve Ray, Bridgeport	33	385	11.7
1991	Adrian Hutt, Metropolitan St.	28	285	10.2
1992	Tony Smith, Pfeiffer	35	349	10.0
1993	Demetri Beekman, Assumption	23	264	11.5

** Record.*

BLOCKED-SHOT AVERAGE

Year	Player, Team	G	Blk.	Avg.
1993	Antonio Harvey, Pfeiffer	29	155	5.3

STEAL AVERAGE

Year	Player, Team	G	Stl.	Avg.
1993	Marcus Stubblefield, Queens (N.C.)	28	110	3.9

DIVISION II MEN'S ANNUAL TEAM CHAMPIONS

WON-LOST PERCENTAGE

Year	Team	Won	Lost	Pct.
1968	Monmouth (N.J.)	27	2	.931
1969	Alcorn St.	26	1	.963
1970	Central Wash.	31	2	.939
1971	Kentucky St.	31	2	.939
1972	Olivet	22	1	.957
1973	Coe	24	1	.960
1974	West Ga.	29	4	.879
1975	Bentley	23	2	.920
1976	Phila. Textile	25	3	.893
1977	Clarion	27	3	.900
	Kentucky St.	27	3	.900
	Towson St.	27	3	.900
1978	Wis.-Green Bay	30	2	.938
1979	Roanoke	25	3	.893
1980	Alabama St.	32	2	.941
1981	Mt. St. Mary's (Md.)	28	3	.903
1982	Cheyney	28	3	.903
1983	Dist. Columbia	29	3	.906
1984	Norfolk St.	29	2	.935
1985	Jacksonville St.	31	1	.969
	Virginia Union	31	1	.969
1986	Wright St.	28	3	.903
1987	Norfolk St.	28	3	.903
1988	Fla. Southern	31	3	.912
1989	UC Riverside	30	4	.882
1990	Ky. Wesleyan	31	2	.939
1991	Southwest Baptist	29	3	.906
1992	Calif. (Pa.)	31	2	.939
1993	Cal St. Bakersfield	33	0	1.000

SCORING OFFENSE

Year	Team	G	(W-L)	Pts.	Avg.
1948	St. Anselm	19	(12-7)	1,329	69.9
1949	Charleston (W. Va.)	26	(18-8)	2,023	77.8
1950	Charleston (W. Va.)	31	(22-9)	2,477	79.9
1951	Beloit	23	(18-5)	1,961	85.3
1952	Lambuth	22	(17-5)	1,985	90.2
1953	Arkansas Tech	21	(20-1)	1,976	94.1
1954	Montclair St.	22	(18-4)	2,128	96.7
1955	West Va. Tech	20	(15-5)	2,150	107.5
1956	West Va. Tech	22	(16-6)	2,210	100.5
1957	West Va. Tech	29	(26-3)	2,976	102.6
1958	West Va. Tech	29	(24-5)	2,941	101.4
1959	Grambling	29	(28-1)	2,764	95.3
1960	Mississippi Col.	19	(15-4)	2,169	114.2
1961	Lawrence Tech	25	(19-6)	2,409	96.4
1962	Troy St.	25	(20-5)	2,402	96.1
1963	Miles	21	(17-4)	2,011	95.8
1964	Benedict	27	(19-8)	2,730	101.1
1965	Ark.-Pine Bluff	26	(22-4)	2,655	102.1
1966	Southern Cal College	23	(15-8)	2,480	107.8
1967	Lincoln (Mo.)	27	(24-3)	2,925	108.3

Year	Team	G	(W-L)	Pts.	Avg.
1968	Stillman	26	(17-9)	2,898	111.5
1969	Norfolk St.	25	(21-4)	2,653	106.1
1970	Norfolk St.	26	(19-7)	2,796	107.5
1971	Savannah St.	29	(18-11)	3,051	105.2
1972	Florida A&M	28	(18-10)	2,869	102.5
1973	Md.-East. Shore	31	(26-5)	2,974	95.9
1974	Texas Southern	28	(15-13)	2,884	103.0
1975	Prairie View	26	(16-10)	2,774	106.7
1976	Southern-B.R.	27	(13-14)	2,637	97.7
1977	Virginia Union	30	(25-5)	2,966	98.9
1978	Merrimack	28	(22-6)	2,606	93.1
1979	Armstrong St.	27	(21-6)	2,626	97.3
1980	Ashland	27	(11-16)	2,514	93.1
1981	Virginia St.	31	(20-11)	2,761	89.1
1982	Alabama St.	28	(22-6)	2,429	86.8
1983	Virginia St.	29	(19-10)	2,802	96.6
1984	New Hamp. Col.	29	(18-11)	2,564	88.4
1985	Alabama A&M	31	(21-10)	2,881	92.9
1986	Alabama A&M	32	(23-9)	2,897	90.5
1987	Alabama A&M	30	(23-7)	2,826	94.2
1988	Oakland	28	(19-9)	2,685	95.9
1989	Stonehill	32	(23-9)	3,244	101.4
1990	Jacksonville St.	29	(24-5)	2,872	99.0
1991	Troy St.	30	(22-8)	3,259	108.6
1992	Troy St.	29	(23-6)	3,513	*121.1
1993	Central Okla.	29	(23-6)	3,293	113.6

* *Record.*

SCORING DEFENSE

Year	Team	G	(W-L)	Pts.	Avg.
1948	Miss. Industrial	15	(13-2)	436	‡29.1
1949	Gordon	20	(16-4)	655	32.8
1950	Corpus Christi	26	(25-1)	1,030	39.6
1951	St. Martin's	24	(11-13)	1,137	47.4
1952	Northeast Mo. St.	19	(12-7)	876	46.1
1953	Cal St. Sacramento	26	(18-8)	1,381	53.1
1954	Cal St. Sacramento	18	(9-9)	883	49.1
1955	Amherst	22	(16-6)	1,233	56.0
1956	Amherst	22	(16-6)	1,277	58.0
1957	Stephen F. Austin	26	(23-3)	1,337	51.4
1958	McNeese St.	23	(19-4)	1,068	46.4
1959	Humboldt St.	23	(14-9)	1,166	50.7
1960	Wittenberg	24	(22-2)	1,122	46.8
1961	Wittenberg	29	(25-4)	1,270	43.8
1962	Wittenberg	26	(21-5)	1,089	41.9
1963	Wittenberg	28	(26-2)	1,285	45.9
1964	Wittenberg	23	(18-5)	1,186	51.6
1965	Cheyney	25	(24-1)	1,393	55.7
1966	Chicago	16	(12-4)	894	55.9
1967	Ashland	24	(21-3)	1,025	42.7
1968	Ashland	30	(23-7)	1,164	38.8
1969	Ashland	30	(26-4)	1,017	33.9
1970	Ashland	27	(23-4)	1,118	41.4
1971	Ashland	28	(25-3)	1,523	54.4
1972	Chicago	20	(16-4)	1,132	56.6
1973	Steubenville	29	(22-7)	1,271	43.8
1974	Steubenville	26	(14-12)	1,336	51.4
1975	Cal Poly SLO	26	(15-11)	1,590	61.2
1976	Wis.-Green Bay	29	(21-8)	1,768	61.0
1977	Wis.-Green Bay	29	(26-3)	1,682	58.0
1978	Wis.-Green Bay	32	(30-2)	1,682	52.6
1979	Wis.-Green Bay	32	(24-8)	1,612	50.4
1980	Wis.-Green Bay	27	(15-12)	1,577	58.4
1981	San Fran. St.	26	(17-9)	1,463	56.3
1982	Cal Poly SLO	29	(23-6)	1,537	53.0
1983	Cal Poly SLO	28	(18-10)	1,553	55.5
1984	Cal Poly SLO	28	(20-8)	1,458	52.1
1985	Cal Poly SLO	27	(16-11)	1,430	53.0
1986	Lewis	30	(24-6)	1,702	56.7
1987	Denver	29	(20-9)	1,844	63.6

Year	Team	G	(W-L)	Pts.	Avg.
1988	N.C. Central	29	(26-3)	1,683	58.0
1989	N.C. Central	32	(28-4)	1,791	56.0
1990	Humboldt St.	31	(20-11)	1,831	59.1
1991	Minn.-Duluth	32	(27-5)	1,899	59.3
1992	Pace	30	(23-7)	1,517	50.6
1993	Phila. Textile	32	(30-2)	1,898	59.3

‡ *Record since 1948.*

SCORING MARGIN

Year	Team	Off.	Def.	Margin
1950	Montana	77.4	57.7	19.7
1951	Eastern Ill.	84.7	57.9	26.8
1952	Southwest Tex. St.	77.4	48.9	28.5
1953	Arkansas Tech	94.7	74.3	20.4
1954	Texas Southern	89.2	63.3	25.9
1955	Mt. St. Mary's (Md.)	95.2	73.3	21.9
1956	Western Ill.	92.5	72.1	20.4
1957	West Va. Tech	102.6	77.2	25.4
1958	Tennessee St.	88.7	64.1	24.6
1959	Grambling	95.3	73.3	22.0
1960	Mississippi Col.	*114.2	92.9	21.3
1961	Bryan	93.8	62.4	*31.4
1962	Mansfield	87.6	64.7	22.9
1963	Gorham St.	94.7	69.7	25.0
1964	Central Conn. St.	94.5	67.7	26.8
1965	Cheyney	80.7	55.7	25.0
1966	Cheyney	90.0	64.4	25.6
1967	Lincoln (Mo.)	108.3	82.2	26.1
1968	Western New Eng.	104.7	76.8	27.9
1969	Indiana (Pa.)	88.6	64.5	24.1
1970	Husson	106.1	79.0	27.1
1971	Kentucky St.	103.5	78.2	25.3
1972	Brockport St.	93.8	70.3	23.5
1973	Wis.-Green Bay	71.2	52.1	19.1
1974	Alcorn St.	96.9	79.8	17.1
1975	Bentley	95.2	78.7	16.5
1976	Central Fla.	94.8	78.4	16.4
1977	Texas Southern	88.4	71.9	16.5
1978	Wis.-Green Bay	68.8	52.6	16.2
1979	Roanoke	77.8	60.8	17.0
1980	Central Fla.	91.7	72.1	19.6
1981	West Ga.	88.5	70.2	18.3
1982	Minn.-Duluth	81.7	64.8	16.9
1983	Minn.-Duluth	84.8	69.8	15.0
1984	Chicago St.	85.9	70.2	15.7
1985	Virginia Union	87.6	67.8	19.8
1986	Mt. St. Mary's (Md.)	80.0	65.7	14.3
1987	Ky. Wesleyan	92.4	72.9	19.8
1988	Fla. Southern	89.6	70.5	19.1
1989	Virginia Union	88.2	69.6	18.6
1990	Ky. Wesleyan	97.3	76.8	20.5
1991	Ashland	99.8	78.2	21.6
1992	Oakland City	99.5	77.1	22.4
1993	Phila. Textile	78.8	59.3	19.4

* *Record.*

FIELD-GOAL PERCENTAGE

Year	Team	FG	FGA	Pct.
1948	East Tex. St.	445	1,119	39.8
1949	Southwest Mo. St.	482	1,106	43.6
1950	Corpus Christi	555	1,290	43.0
1951	Beloit	773	1,734	44.6
1952	Southwest Mo. St.	890	1,903	46.8
1953	Lebanon Valley	637	1,349	47.2
1954	San Diego St.	675	1,502	44.9
1955	UC Santa Barb.	672	1,383	48.6
1956	UC Santa Barb.	552	1,142	48.3
1957	Alderson-Broaddus	1,006	2,094	48.0

Year	Team	FG	FGA	Pct.
1958	North Caro. A&T	552	1,072	51.5
1959	Grambling	1,048	2,048	51.2
1960	William Carey	708	1,372	51.6
1961	Virginia Union	908	1,735	52.3
1962	West Va. Tech	871	1,575	55.3
1963	Lenoir-Rhyne	869	1,647	52.8
1964	LeMoyne-Owen	844	1,520	55.5
1965	Southern-B.R.	1,036	1,915	54.1
1966	Howard Payne	932	1,710	54.5
1967	Alabama St.	874	1,555	56.2
1968	South Caro. St.	588	1,010	58.2
1969	LIU-Southampton	846	1,588	53.3
1970	Savannah St.	1,145	1,969	58.2
1971	Alabama St.	1,196	2,100	57.0
1972	Florida A&M	1,194	2,143	55.7
1973	Wis.-Green Bay	929	1,700	54.6
1974	Kentucky St.	1,252	2,266	55.3
1975	Kentucky St.	1,121	1,979	56.6
1976	Kentucky St.	1,093	1,753	*62.4
1977	Merrimack	1,120	2,008	55.8
1978	Wis.-Green Bay	840	1,509	55.7
1979	Morris Brown	980	1,763	55.6
1980	Pembroke St.	849	1,544	55.0
1981	Bellarmine	851	1,561	54.5
1982	Fla. Southern	943	1,644	57.4
1983	Lewis	807	1,448	55.7
1984	Lewis	851	1,494	57.0
1985	Virginia Union	1,132	1,967	57.5
1986	Tampa	856	1,546	55.4
1987	Johnson Smith	995	1,817	54.8
1988	Fla. Southern	1,118	2,026	55.2
1989	Millersville	1,119	2,079	53.8
1990	S.C.-Spartanburg	954	1,745	54.7
1991	S.C.-Spartanburg	923	1,631	56.6
1992	S.C.-Spartanburg	898	1,664	54.0
1993	Cal St. Bakersfield	1,002	1,849	54.2

* *Record.*

FIELD-GOAL PERCENTAGE DEFENSE

Year	Team	FG	FGA	Pct.
1978	Wis.-Green Bay	681	1,830	37.2
1979	Wis.-Green Bay	639	1,709	37.4
1980	Wis.-Parkside	688	1,666	41.3
1981	Central St. (Ohio)	675	1,724	39.2
1982	Mankato St.	699	1,735	40.3
1983	Central Mo. St.	746	1,838	40.6
1984	Norfolk St.	812	1,910	42.5
1985	Central Mo. St.	683	1,660	41.1
1986	Norfolk St.	782	1,925	40.6
1987	Denver	691	1,709	40.4
1988	Minn.-Duluth	702	1,691	41.5
1989	N.C. Central	633	1,642	38.6
1990	Central Mo. St.	696	1,757	39.6
1991	Southwest Baptist	758	1,942	39.0
1992	Virginia Union	766	2,069	*37.0
1993	Pfeiffer	767	2,028	37.8

* *Record.*

THREE-POINT FIELD GOALS MADE PER GAME

Year	Team	G	3FG	Avg.
1987	Northern Mich.	27	187	6.9
1988	Cal St. Sacramento	30	303	10.1
1989	Central Okla.	27	280	10.4
1990	Stonehill	27	259	9.6
1991	Hillsdale	27	318	11.8
1992	Troy St.	29	*444	*15.3
1993	Hillsdale	28	366	13.1

* *Record.*

THREE-POINT FIELD-GOAL PERCENTAGE

Year	Team	G	3FG	3FGA	Pct.
1987	St. Anselm	30	97	189	51.3
1988	Winston-Salem	28	98	182	*53.8
1989	Mississippi Col.	27	144	276	52.2
1990	Shaw	27	74	143	51.7
1991	Rollins	28	278	585	47.5
1992	Oakland City	30	244	486	50.2
1993	Oakland City	32	215	465	46.2

* *Record.*

FREE-THROW PERCENTAGE

Year	Team	FT	FTA	Pct.
1948	Charleston (W. Va.)	446	659	67.7
1949	Linfield	276	402	68.7
1950	Jacksonville St.	452	613	73.7
1951	Millikin	603	846	71.3
1952	Eastern Ill.	521	688	75.7
1953	Upsala	513	69	74.0
1954	Central Mich.	376	509	73.9
1955	Mississippi Col.	559	733	76.3
1956	Wheaton (Ill.)	625	842	74.2
1957	Wheaton (Ill.)	689	936	73.6
1958	Wheaton (Ill.)	517	689	75.0
1959	Wabash	418	545	76.7
1960	Allen	225	297	75.8
1961	Southwest Mo. St.	453	605	74.9
1962	Lenoir-Rhyne	477	599	79.6
1963	Hampden-Sydney	442	559	79.1
1964	Western Caro.	492	621	79.2
1965	Mississippi Col.	529	663	79.8
1966	Athens St.	631	802	78.7
1967	Northwestern (La.)	528	678	77.9
1968	Kenyon	684	858	79.7
1969	Kenyon	583	727	80.2
1970	Wooster	571	714	80.0
1971	South Ala.	422	518	*81.5
1972	Clark Atlanta	409	520	78.7
1973	Rockford (Ill.)	367	481	76.3
1974	New Orleans	537	701	76.6
1975	Alabama St.	456	565	80.7
1976	Alabama St.	451	576	78.3
1977	Puget Sound	495	637	77.7
1978	Merrimack	508	636	79.9
1979	Bentley	506	652	77.6
1980	Phila. Textile	436	549	79.4
1981	Coppin St.	401	514	78.0
1982	Fla. Southern	726	936	77.6
1983	Transylvania	463	606	76.4
1984	Transylvania	491	639	76.8
1985	Mankato St.	349	445	78.4
1986	New Hamp. Col.	507	672	75.4
1987	Columbus	339	433	78.3
1988	Rollins	631	795	79.4
1989	Rollins	477	607	78.6
1990	Rollins	449	582	77.1
1991	Lenoir-Rhyne	441	564	78.2
1992	Adams St.	397	512	77.5
1993	Phila. Textile	491	630	77.9

* *Record.*

REBOUND MARGIN

Year	Team	Off.	Def.	Margin
1976	Mississippi Val.	63.9	39.5	*24.4
1977	Phila. Textile	38.7	24.1	14.6
1978	Mass.-Lowell	49.0	37.5	11.5
1979	Dowling	48.2	32.6	15.6
1980	Ark.-Pine Bluff	40.3	25.9	14.4

Year	Team	Off.	Def.	Margin
1981	Wis.-Green Bay	40.6	26.5	14.1
1982	Central St. (Ohio)	48.0	37.2	10.8
1983	Hampton	50.2	38.5	11.8
1984	Calif. (Pa.)	46.4	33.1	13.3
1985	Virginia Union	44.1	32.0	12.1
1986	Tampa	39.9	28.0	11.8
1987	Millersville	44.7	33.8	10.9
1988	Clark Atlanta	44.7	32.5	12.1
1989	Hampton	46.7	36.3	10.3
1990	Fla. Atlantic	41.0	29.4	11.6
1991	Calif. (Pa.)	44.6	32.0	12.6
1992	Oakland City	43.4	31.8	11.6
1993	Metropolitan St.	45.5	32.0	13.5

* *Record.*

DIVISION II MEN'S ALL-TIME WINNINGEST TEAMS

Includes records as a senior college only; minimum 10 seasons of competition.
Postseason games are included.

PERCENTAGE

Team	1st Year	Yrs.	Won	Lost	Pct.
Norfolk St.	1954	40	807	293	.734
Phila. Textile	1920	69	907	391	.699
Jacksonville St.	1919	84	944	423	.691
LeMoyne-Owen	1960	34	647	294	.688
Cal St. Bakersfield	1972	22	426	205	.675
Sacred Heart	1966	28	536	269	.666
New Hamp. Col.	1964	30	555	280	.665
Ky. Wesleyan	1908	83	1,094	569	.658
Carson-Newman	1959	35	705	374	.653
Grand Canyon	1949	45	754	414	.646
Bentley	1964	30	504	279	.644
LIU-C. W. Post	1956	37	589	328	.642
Fla. Southern	1957	37	651	373	.636
Gannon	1945	49	791	454	.635
Fort Hays St.	1917	75	996	575	.634
North Dak.	1905	88	1,171	710	.623
New Haven	1962	30	494	303	.620
Central Mo. St.	1906	88	1,178	731	.617
Millersville	1929	63	846	527	.616
Drury	1909	84	1,102	705	.610
Minn.-Duluth	1930	62	869	559	.609
Southern Colo.	1964	30	500	323	.608
West Tex. A&M	1921	72	1,056	683	.607
Grand Valley St.	1967	27	454	295	.606
S.C.-Spartanburg	1975	19	332	218	.604
St. Cloud St.	1923	69	875	589	.598
Springfield	1906	83	1,064	717	.597
Northern Mich.	1906	87	918	629	.593
Indiana (Pa.)	1928	54	781	539	.592
Troy St.	1950	33	678	473	.589
Assumption	1924	64	831	584	.587
Indianapolis	1923	68	938	660	.587
Lewis	1949	43	667	473	.585
Valdosta St.	1955	43	538	382	.585
Delta St.	1928	63	829	595	.582
Johnson Smith	1929	53	733	543	.574
Stonehill	1949	44	630	467	.574
South Dak. St.	1906	85	996	740	.574
Lenoir-Rhyne	1920	72	986	748	.569
Longwood	1977	17	254	194	.567

VICTORIES

Team	Wins
Central Mo. St.	1,178
North Dak.	1,171
Drury	1,102
Ky. Wesleyan	1,094
Elon	1,093
Springfield	1,064
West Tex. A&M	1,056
Fort Hays St.	996
South Dak. St.	996
Lenoir-Rhyne	986
Pittsburg St.	958
Jacksonville St.	944
Denver	938
Indianapolis	938
East Tex. St.	924
Neb.-Kearney	919
Northern Mich.	918
Phila. Textile	907
Northwest Mo. St.	906
Wayne St. (Neb.)	890
St. Cloud St.	875
Wofford	872
Minn.-Duluth	869
Chapman	868
Erskine	854
Abilene Christian	853
Northeast Mo. St.	847
Millersville	846
Central Okla.	845
Northern Colo.	838
Assumption	831
Delta St.	829
Ashland	824
Mankato St.	809
Norfolk St.	807
Gannon	791
Indiana (Pa.)	781
St. Michael's	776
Ferris St.	757
Grand Canyon	754

PERCENTAGE

Team	1st Year	Yrs.	Won	Lost	Pct.
Cal St. Dom. Hills	1978	16	244	187	.566
Alas. Anchorage	1972	22	337	259	.565
Mankato St.	1921	68	809	622	.565
Erskine	1914	68	854	662	.563
Neb.-Kearney	1906	85	919	722	.560
Pembroke St.	1940	54	719	582	.553
Southern Ind.	1970	24	352	286	.552
Northwest Mo. St.	1917	77	906	737	.551
East Tex. St.	1916	78	924	775	.544
Pittsburg St.	1917	76	958	805	.543
North Ala.	1932	60	692	582	.543
Northeast Mo. St.	1920	74	847	713	.543
Chapman	1922	68	868	732	.543
Ferris St.	1926	64	757	644	.540
Wayne St. (Neb.)	1912	78	890	762	.539

VICTORIES

Team	Wins
Johnson Smith	733
Slippery Rock	722
Pembroke St.	719
Eastern Mont.	717
Carson-Newman	705
North Ala.	692
Troy St.	678
Seattle Pacific	675
St. Anselm	668
Lewis	667
Fla. Southern	651
Morningside	648
LeMoyne-Owen	647
Stonehill	630
Regis (Colo.)	627

DIVISION III
MEN'S RECORDS

Drew's Dave Shaw led the nation in 1993 with 663 points in 23 games – an average of 28.8 points per game.

DIVISION III MEN'S INDIVIDUAL RECORDS

Division III men's basketball records are based on the performances of Division III teams since the three-division reorganization plan was adopted by the special NCAA Convention in August 1973. Assists were added for the 1988-89 season. In statistical rankings, the rounding of percentages and/or averages may indicate ties where none exist. In these cases, the numerical order of the rankings is accurate.

SCORING

Points

Game
63—Joe DeRoche, Thomas vs. St. Joseph's (Me.), Feb. 1, 1988

Season
1,044—Greg Grant, Trenton St., 1989 (32 games)

Career
2,940—Andre Foreman, Salisbury St., 1988-89, 91-92 (109 games)

Average Per Game

Season
36.2—Rickey Sutton, Lyndon St., 1976 (507 in 14)

Career
(Min. 1,400) 29.7—Rickey Sutton, Lyndon St., 1976-79 (2,379 in 80)

Most Points Scored With No Time Elapsing Off of the Clock

Game
24—Rob Rittgers, UC San Diego vs. Menlo, Jan. 16, 1988 (made 24 consecutive free throws due to 12 bench technical fouls)

Games Scoring at Least 50 Points

Season
2—Dana Wilson, Husson, 1974

Career
2—Dana Wilson, Husson, 1974; Mark Veenstra, Calvin, 1974-77; Dwain Govan, Bishop, 1974-75; Greg Grant, Trenton St., 1987-89

Most Games Scoring in Double Figures

Career
116—Lamont Strothers, Chris. Newport, 1988-91

Consecutive Games Scoring in Double Figures

Career
116—Lamont Strothers, Chris. Newport, from Nov. 20, 1987, to March 8, 1991

FIELD GOALS

Field Goals

Game
29—Shannon Lilly, Bishop vs. Southwest Assembly of God, Jan. 31, 1983 (36 attempts)

Season
394—Dave Russell, Shepherd, 1975 (687 attempts)

Career
1,140—Andre Foreman, Salisbury St., 1988-89, 91-92 (2,125 attempts)

Consecutive Field Goals

Game
17—Fennell Fowlkes, Ramapo vs. FDU-Madison, Jan. 23, 1980

Season
21—Tod Hart, Ithaca, 1982 (during three games, Feb. 20-24); Mark Jones, Binghamton, 1986 (during three games, Jan. 29-Feb. 4)

Field-Goal Attempts

Game
38—Brett Wyatt, Jersey City St. vs. Mercy, Feb. 11, 1979 (24 made)

Season
742—Greg Grant, Trenton St., 1989 (387 made)

Career
2,149—Lamont Strothers, Chris. Newport, 1988-91 (1,016 made)

Field-Goal Percentage

Game
(Min. 13 made) 100%—Bruce Merklinger, Susquehanna vs. Drew, Jan. 22, 1986 (13 of 13); Antonio Randolph, Averett vs. Methodist, Jan. 26, 1991 (13 of 13); Pat Holland, Randolph-Macon vs. East. Mennonite, Feb. 9, 1991 (13 of 13); Todd Seifferlein, DePauw vs. Franklin, Jan. 18, 1992 (13 of 13)

***Season**
75.3—Pete Metzelaars, Wabash, 1982 (271 of 360)

* *Based on qualifiers for annual championship.*

Career
(Min. 400 made) 72.4—Pete Metzelaars, Wabash, 1979-82 (784 of 1,083)

THREE-POINT FIELD GOALS

Three-Point Field Goals

Game
12—Kirk Anderson, Augustana (Ill.) vs. Wis.-Platteville, March 13, 1993 (19 attempts); Mike Webster, Rose-Hulman vs. Eureka, Dec. 13, 1986 (20 attempts); Todd Hennink, Calvin vs. Malone, Nov. 24, 1990 (14 attempts); Craig Studer, Grinnell vs. Knox, Dec. 7, 1990 (17 attempts)

Season
133—Chris Jans, Loras, 1991 (340 attempts)

Career
354—Ray Wilson, UC Santa Cruz, 1989-92 (960 attempts)

Three-Point Field Goals Made Per Game

Season
5.3—Chris Jans, Loras, 1991 (133 in 25)

Career
3.5—Ray Wilson, UC Santa Cruz, 1989-92 (354 in 100)

Consecutive Three-Point Field Goals

Game
10—Brad Block, Aurora vs. Rockford, Feb. 20, 1988; Jim Berrigan, Framingham St. vs. Western New Eng., Feb. 27, 1988

Season
16—John Richards, Sewanee (during five games, Feb. 10 to Feb. 25, 1990)

Consecutive Games Making a Three-Point Field Goal

Season
31—Troy Greenlee, DePauw, Nov. 17, 1989, to March 17, 1990

Career
65—Rob Hayward, Gordon, Nov. 16, 1990, to Jan. 19, 1993

Three-Point Field-Goal Attempts

Game
28—Lamont Strothers, Chris. Newport vs. Ferrum, Feb. 11, 1989 (9 made)

Season
340—Chris Jans, Loras, 1991 (133 made)

Career
960—Ray Wilson, UC Santa Cruz, 1989-92 (354 made)

Three-Point Field-Goal Attempts Per Game

Season
13.6—Chris Jans, Loras, 1991 (340 in 25)

Career
9.6—Ray Wilson, UC Santa Cruz, 1989-92 (960 in 100)

Three-Point Field-Goal Percentage

Game
(Min. 9 made) 100%—Jim Durrell, Colby-Sawyer vs. Southern Vt., Jan. 15, 1991 (9 of 9)

Season
(Min. 40 made) 67.0%—Reggie James, New Jersey Tech, 1989 (59 of 88)
(Min. 90 made) 56.9%—Eric Harris, Bishop, 1987 (91 of 160)

Career
(Min. 200 made) 51.3%—Jeff Seifriz, Wis.-Whitewater, 1987-89 (217 of 432)

FREE THROWS

Free Throws

Game
30—Rob Rittgers, UC San Diego vs. Menlo, Jan. 16, 1988 (30 attempts)

Season
249—Dave Russell, Shepherd, 1975 (293 attempts)

Career
792—Matt Hancock, Colby, 1987-90 (928 attempts)

Consecutive Free Throws

Game
30—Rob Rittgers, UC San Diego vs. Menlo, Jan. 16, 1988

Season
59—Mike Michelson, Coast Guard (during 13 games, Jan. 16 to Feb. 27, 1990)

Free-Throw Attempts

Game
30—Rob Rittgers, UC San Diego vs. Menlo, Jan. 16, 1988 (30 made)

Season
293—Dave Russell, Shepherd, 1975 (249 made)

Career
928—Matt Hancock, Colby, 1987-90 (792 made)

Free-Throw Percentage

Game
(Min. 30 made) 100%—Rob Rittgers, UC San Diego vs. Menlo, Jan. 16, 1988 (30 of 30)

***Season**
95.3%—Andy Enfield, Johns Hopkins, 1991 (123 of 129)

* *Based on qualifiers for annual championship.*

Career
(Min. 250 made) 92.5%—Andy Enfield, Johns Hopkins, 1988-91 (431 of 466)
(Min. 500 made) 85.9%—Kevin Brown, Emory & Henry, 1984-87 (507 of 590)

REBOUNDS

Rebounds

Game
36—Mark Veenstra, Calvin vs. Southern Colo., Feb. 3, 1976; Clinton Montford, Methodist vs. Warren Wilson, Jan. 21, 1989

Season
579—Joe Manley, Bowie St., 1976 (29 games)

Career
1,628—Michael Smith, Hamilton, 1989-92 (107 games)

Average Per Game

Season
20.0—Joe Manley, Bowie St., 1976 (579 in 29)

Career
(Min. 900) 17.4—Larry Parker, Plattsburgh St., 1975-78 (1,482 in 85)

ASSISTS

Assists

Game
26—Robert James, Kean vs. New Jersey Tech, March 11, 1989

Season
391—Robert James, Kean, 1989 (29 games)

Career
909—Steve Artis, Chris. Newport, 1990-93 (112 games)

Average Per Game

Season
13.5—Robert James, Kean, 1989 (391 in 29)

Career
(Min. 550) 8.1—Steve Artis, Chris. Newport, 1990-93 (909 in 112)

GAMES

Games Played

Season
34—Thane Anderson, Matt Benedict, Tim Blair, Lanse Carter, Mike Johnson, Todd Oehrlein, Mike Prasher and Derrick Shelton, Wis.-Eau Claire, 1990

Career
119—Steve Honderd, Calvin, 1990-93; Chris Finch, Frank. & Marsh., 1989-92; Chris Fite, Rochester, 1989-92; Jim Clausen, North Park, 1978-81

DIVISION III MEN'S TEAM RECORDS

Note: Where records involve both teams, each team must be an NCAA Division III member institution.

SINGLE-GAME SCORING

Most Points
168—Bishop vs. Southwest Assembly of God (76), Jan. 31, 1983

Most Points by Losing Team
132—Stillman vs. Philander Smith (134), Dec. 12, 1977

Most Points, Both Teams
277—Methodist (150) vs. Salisbury St. (127), Nov. 18, 1989

Most Points in a Half
92—Wis.-Platteville vs. Mt. St. Clare, Dec. 14, 1989 (first)

Most Points Scored With No Time Elapsing Off of the Clock
24—UC San Diego vs. Menlo, Jan. 16, 1988 (made 24 consecutive free throws due to 12 bench technical fouls)

Fewest Points Allowed
6—Dickinson (15) vs. Muhlenberg, Feb. 3, 1982

Fewest Points Allowed in a Half
0—Dickinson (2) vs. Muhlenberg (first), Feb. 3, 1982

Fewest Points, Both Teams
21—Dickinson (15) vs. Muhlenberg (6), Feb. 3, 1982

Fewest Points, Half, Both Teams
2—Dickinson (2) vs. Muhlenberg (0) (first), Feb. 3, 1982

Widest Margin of Victory
112—Eureka (149) vs. Barat (37), Nov. 29, 1989

SINGLE-GAME FIELD GOALS

Most Field Goals
78—Bishop vs. Southwest Assembly of God, Jan. 31, 1983 (103 attempts)

Most Field-Goal Attempts
132—Mercy vs. Cathedral, Dec. 9, 1978 (69 made)

Fewest Field Goals
3—Muhlenberg vs. Dickinson, Feb. 3, 1982 (11 attempts)

Fewest Field-Goal Attempts
11—Muhlenberg vs. Dickinson, Feb. 3, 1982 (3 made)

Highest Field-Goal Percentage
83.8%—Wabash vs. Anderson, Feb. 10, 1990 (31 of 37)

Highest Field-Goal Percentage, Half
91.3%—Wis.-Stevens Point vs. Wis.-La Crosse, Feb. 12, 1980 (21 of 23)

SINGLE-GAME THREE-POINT FIELD GOALS

Most Three-Point Field Goals
27—Catholic vs. St. Joseph's (N.Y.), Nov. 25, 1991 (62 attempts)

Most Three-Point Field Goals, Both Teams
28—Carleton (18) vs. Macalester (10), Jan. 6, 1993; Wilkes (15) vs. Lycoming (13), Feb. 4, 1989

Consecutive Three-Point Field Goals Made Without a Miss
11—Willamette vs. Western Baptist, Jan. 8, 1987

Highest Number of Different Players to Score a Three-Point Field Goal, One Team
8—Bates vs. Brandeis, Feb. 10, 1988; Central (Iowa) vs. Iowa Wesleyan, Jan. 8, 1991

Most Three-Point Field-Goal Attempts
62—Catholic vs. St. Joseph's (N.Y.), Nov. 25, 1991 (27 made)

Most Three-Point Field-Goal Attempts, Both Teams
87—Knox (47) vs. Grinnell (40), Feb. 15, 1991

Highest Three-Point Field-Goal Percentage
(Min. 10 made) 100%—Willamette vs. Western Baptist, Jan. 8, 1987 (11 of 11); Kean vs. Ramapo, Feb. 11, 1987 (10 of 10)
(Min. 15 made) 83.3%—Rockford vs. Trinity (Ill.), Jan. 21, 1989 (15 of 18)

Highest Three-Point Field-Goal Percentage, Both Teams
(Min. 10 made) 92.9%—Luther (8 of 8) vs. Wartburg (5 of 6), Feb. 14, 1987 (13 of 14)
(Min. 15 made) 75.0%—Anna Maria (4 of 6) vs. Nichols (11 of 14), Feb. 10, 1987 (15 of 20)
(Min. 20 made) 62.2%—Beloit (13 of 23) vs. Rockford (10 of 14), Jan. 18, 1988 (23 of 37)

SINGLE-GAME FREE THROWS

Most Free Throws
53—UC San Diego vs. Menlo, Jan. 16, 1988 (59 attempts)

Most Free Throws, Both Teams
77—Waynesburg (41) vs. Thiel (36), Feb. 3, 1993

Most Free-Throw Attempts
71—Earlham vs. Oberlin, Dec. 5, 1992 (46 made)

Most Free-Throw Attempts, Both Teams
105—Earlham (71) vs. Oberlin (34), Dec. 5, 1992

Fewest Free Throws
0—Many teams

Fewest Free-Throw Attempts
0—Many teams

Highest Free-Throw Percentage
(Min. 24 made) 100.0%—Guilford vs. Wash. & Lee, Feb. 14, 1991 (24 of 24)
(Min. 30 made) 97.1%—Rochester Inst. vs. Rensselaer, Feb. 16, 1980 (34 of 35)
(Min. 45 made) 89.8%—UC San Diego vs. Menlo, Jan. 16, 1988 (53 of 59)

Highest Free-Throw Percentage, Both Teams
(Min. 20 made) 95.5%—Baldwin-Wallace (13 of 13) vs. Muskingum (8 of 9), Dec. 29, 1977 (21 of 22)
(Min. 30 made) 94.9%—Muskingum (30 of 31) vs. Ohio Wesleyan (7 of 8), Jan. 10, 1981 (37 of 39)

SINGLE-GAME REBOUNDS

Most Rebounds
98—Alma vs. Marion, Dec. 28, 1973

Most Rebounds, Both Teams
124—Ill. Wesleyan (62) vs. North Central (62), Feb. 8, 1977; Rochester Inst. (72) vs. Thiel (52), Nov. 18, 1988

Highest Rebound Margin
56—MIT vs. Emerson-MCA (18), Feb. 21, 1990 (74)

SINGLE-GAME ASSISTS

Most Assists
48—Me.-Farmington vs. Lyndon St., Feb. 11, 1991

Most Assists, Both Teams
60—Staten Island (43) vs. CCNY (17), Jan. 14, 1989

SINGLE-GAME PERSONAL FOULS

Most Personal Fouls
47—Concordia (Ill.) vs. Trinity Christian, Feb. 26, 1988

Most Personal Fouls, Both Teams
76—Bates (42) vs. Norwich (34), Feb. 14, 1988

Most Players Disqualified
6—Union (N.Y.) vs. Rochester, Feb. 15, 1985; Haverford vs. Drew, Jan. 10, 1990; Manhattanville vs. Drew, Jan. 11, 1992

Most Players Disqualified, Both Teams
11—Union (N.Y.) (6) vs. Rochester (5), Feb. 15, 1985

SINGLE-GAME OVERTIMES

Most Overtime Periods
5—Capital (86) vs. Muskingum (89), Jan. 5, 1980; Carnegie Mellon (81) vs. Allegheny (76), Feb. 12, 1983; Rochester (99) vs. Union (N.Y.) (98), Feb. 15, 1985

Most Points in One Overtime Period
25—Williams vs. Bates, Jan. 25, 1991

Most Points in One Overtime Period, Both Teams
39—Williams (25) vs. Bates (14), Jan. 25, 1991

Most Points in Overtime Periods
39—Rochester vs. Union (N.Y.) (5 ot), Feb. 15, 1985

Most Points in Overtime Periods, Both Teams
77—Rochester (39) vs. Union (N.Y.) (38) (5 ot), Feb. 15, 1985

SEASON SCORING

Most Points
3,073—Franklin Pierce, 1980 (31 games)

Highest Average Per Game
112.5—Me.-Farmington, 1991 (2,701 in 24)

Highest Average Scoring Margin
31.1—Husson, 1976 (98.7 offense, 67.6 defense)

Most Games at Least 100 Points
17—Me.-Farmington, 1991 (in 24-game season)

Most Consecutive Games at Least 100 Points
8—Bishop, 1975 (dates not available); St. Joseph's (Me.), from Jan. 24, 1991, to Feb. 10, 1991

SEASON FIELD GOALS

Most Field Goals
1,323—Shepherd, 1975 (2,644 attempts)

Most Field Goals Per Game
42.5—Mercy, 1977 (1,062 in 25)

Most Field-Goal Attempts
2,644—Shepherd, 1975 (1,323 made)

Most Field-Goal Attempts Per Game
90.1—Stillman, 1975 (2,342 in 26)

Highest Field-Goal Percentage
60.0—Stony Brook, 1978 (1,033 of 1,721)

SEASON THREE-POINT FIELD GOALS

Most Three-Point Field Goals
335—Catholic, 1992 (877 attempts)

Most Three-Point Field Goals Made Per Game
12.9—Catholic, 1992 (335 in 26)

Most Three-Point Field-Goal Attempts
877—Catholic, 1992 (335 made)

Most Three-Point Field-Goal Attempts Per Game
33.7—Catholic, 1992 (877 in 26)

Highest Three-Point Field-Goal Percentage
(Min. 100 made) 62.0%—New Jersey Tech, 1989 (124 of 200)
(Min. 150 made) 49.0%—Kenyon, 1988 (175 of 357)

SEASON FREE THROWS

Most Free Throws
698—Ohio Wesleyan, 1988 (888 attempts)

Most Free Throws Per Game
21.9—Queens (N.Y.), 1981 (636 in 29)

Most Free-Throw Attempts
930—Queens (N.Y.), 1981 (636 made)

Most Free-Throw Attempts Per Game
32.1—Queens (N.Y.), 1981 (930 in 29)

Highest Free-Throw Percentage
80.2%—Colby, 1990 (485 of 605)

SEASON REBOUNDS

Most Rebounds
1,616—Keene St., 1976 (29 games)

Highest Average Per Game
56.3—Mercy, 1977 (1,408 in 25)

Highest Average Rebound Margin
17.0—Hamilton, 1991 (49.6 offense, 32.5 defense)

SEASON ASSISTS

Most Assists
861—Salisbury St., 1991 (29 games)

Highest Average Per Game
31.2—Me.-Farmington, 1991 (748 in 24)

SEASON PERSONAL FOULS

Most Personal Fouls
737—Jersey City St., 1986 (32 games)

Most Personal Fouls Per Game
26.8—Alfred, 1988 (696 in 26)

Fewest Personal Fouls
239—Yeshiva, 1990 (22 games)

Fewest Personal Fouls Per Game
10.9—Yeshiva, 1990 (239 in 22)

SEASON DEFENSE

Fewest Points Per Game Allowed
47.7—Fredonia St., 1974 (1,049 in 22)

Lowest Field-Goal Percentage Allowed (Since 1978)
36.5—Scranton, 1993 (659 of 1,806)

SEASON OVERTIMES

Most Overtime Games
7—Albany (N.Y.), 1981 (won 5, lost 2); Trenton St., 1982 (won 6, lost 1); St. John's (Minn.), 1983 (won 4, lost 3)

Most Consecutive Overtime Games
3—Ithaca, 1987 (won 3, lost 0); Cortland St., 1989 (won 1, lost 2); Oberlin, 1989 (won 1, lost 2); Susquehanna, 1989 (won 3, lost 0)

GENERAL RECORDS

Most Games in a Season
34—LeMoyne-Owen, 1980 (26-8); Wis.-Eau Claire, 1990 (30-4)

Most Victories in a Season
32—Potsdam St., 1986 (32-0)

Most Consecutive Victories
60—Potsdam St. (from first game of 1985-86 season to March 14, 1987)

Most Consecutive Home-Court Victories
62—North Park (from Feb. 8, 1984, to Feb. 3, 1988)

Most Consecutive Regular Season Victories
59—Potsdam St. (from Nov. 22, 1985, to Dec. 12, 1987)

Most Defeats in a Season
26—Otterbein, 1988 (1-26); Maryville (Mo.), 1991 (0-26)

Most Consecutive Defeats in a Season
26—Maryville (Mo.), 1991 (0-26)

Most Consecutive Defeats
47—Rutgers-Newark (from November 1983 to December 1985)

Most Consecutive Winning Seasons
25—Wis.-Eau Claire, 1969-93

Most Consecutive Non-Losing Seasons
25—Wis.-Eau Claire, 1969-93

Unbeaten Teams (Number of victories in parentheses)
1986 Potsdam St. (32)

DIVISION III MEN'S ALL-TIME INDIVIDUAL LEADERS

SINGLE-GAME SCORING HIGHS

Pts.	Player, Team vs. Opponent	Season
63	Joe DeRoche, Thomas vs. St. Joseph's (Me.)	1988
62	Shannon Lilly, Bishop vs. Southwest Assembly of God	1983
61	Steve Honderd, Calvin vs. Kalamazoo	1993
61	Dana Wilson, Husson vs. Ricker	1974
56	Mark Veenstra, Calvin vs. Adrian	1976
55	Dwain Govan, Bishop vs. Texas Southern	1975
54	Bill Simpson, Elmhurst vs. Wheaton (Ill.)	1975
54	Victor Harp, Thiel vs. Penn St.-Behrend	1985
54	David Peach, Framingham St. vs. Westfield St.	1986
53	Moses Jean-Pierre, Plymouth St. vs. Southern Me.	1993
53	Eric Harris, Bishop vs. Dallas	1986
52	Dwain Govan, Bishop vs. Texas Lutheran	1974
52	Dana Wilson, Husson vs. Me.-Presque Isle	1974
52	Mark Veenstra, Calvin vs. Biola	1977
52	Cedric Oliver, Hamilton vs. Cortland St.	1979
52	Brett Wyatt, Jersey City St. vs. Mercy	1979
52	Dick Hempy, Otterbein vs. Baldwin-Wallace	1987
52	Tony Tucker, Shenandoah vs. Frostburg St.	1987
52	Greg Grant, Trenton St. vs. Wilmington (Ohio)	1988
52	Andre Foreman, Salisbury St. vs. Wesley	1992

SEASON SCORING AVERAGE

Player, Team	Season	G	FG	3FG	FT	Pts.	Avg.
Rickey Sutton, Lyndon St.	†1976	14	207	—	93	507	*36.2
Shannon Lilly, Bishop	†1983	26	345	—	218	908	34.9
Dana Wilson, Husson	†1974	20	288	—	122	698	34.9
Rickey Sutton, Lyndon St.	†1977	16	223	—	112	558	34.9
Dwain Govan, Bishop	†1975	29	392	—	179	963	33.2
Clarence Caldwell, Greensboro	1976	22	306	—	111	723	32.8
Greg Grant, Trenton St.	†1989	32	387	76	194	*1,044	32.6
Dave Russell, Shepherd	1975	32	*394	—	*249	1,037	32.4
Dwain Govan, Bishop	1974	26	358	—	126	842	32.4
Ron Stewart, Otterbein	1983	24	297	—	166	760	31.7

† *National champion.* * *Record.*

SEASON FIELD-GOAL PERCENTAGE

(Based on qualifiers for annual championship)

Player, Team	Season	G	FG	FGA	Pct.
Pete Metzelaars, Wabash	†1982	28	271	360	*75.3
Tony Rychlec, Mass. Maritime	†1981	25	233	311	74.9
Tony Rychlec, Mass. Maritime	1982	20	193	264	73.1
Russ Newnan, Menlo	1991	26	130	178	73.0
Ed Owens, Hampden-Sydney	†1979	24	140	192	72.9
Scott Baxter, Capital	†1991	26	164	226	72.6
Maurice Woods, Potsdam St.	1982	30	203	280	72.5
Earl Keith, Stony Brook	1979	24	164	227	72.2
Pete Metzelaars, Wabash	1981	25	204	283	72.1
Jon Rosner, Yeshiva	1991	22	141	196	71.9
Pete Metzelaars, Wabash	1979	24	122	170	71.8
Anthony Farley, Miles	1982	26	168	235	71.5

† *National champion.* * *Record.*

SEASON THREE-POINT FIELD GOALS MADE PER GAME

Player, Team	Season	G	3FG	Avg.
Chris Jans, Loras	†1991	25	*133	*5.3
Chris Geruschat, Bethany (W. Va.)	1991	24	111	4.6
Jeff deLaveaga, Cal Lutheran	†1992	28	122	4.4
Brad Block, Aurora	†1989	26	112	4.3
Mike Miller, Beloit	1989	24	103	4.3

Player, Team	Season	G	3FG	Avg.
Everett Foxx, Ferrum	1992	29	124	4.3
Jeff Jones, Lycoming	†1988	23	97	4.2
Joe Trent, Stevens Tech	1991	23	96	4.2
Mike Connelly, Catholic	†1993	27	111	4.1
Kirk Anderson, Augustana (Ill.)	1993	30	123	4.1
Chris Hamilton, Blackburn	†1990	24	98	4.1

† *National champion.* * *Record.*

SEASON THREE-POINT FIELD-GOAL PERCENTAGE

(Based on qualifiers for annual championship)

Player, Team	Season	G	3FG	3FGA	Pct.
Reggie James, New Jersey Tech	†1989	29	59	88	*67.0
Chris Miles, New Jersey Tech	†1987	26	41	65	63.1
Chris Miles, New Jersey Tech	1989	29	46	75	61.3
Matt Miota, Lawrence	†1990	22	33	54	61.1
Mike Bachman, Alma	†1991	26	46	76	60.5
Ray Magee, Stockton St.	†1988	26	41	71	57.7
Keith Orchard, Whitman	1988	26	42	73	57.5
Brian O'Donnell, Rutgers-Camden	1988	24	65	114	57.0
Eric Harris, Bishop	1987	26	91	160	56.9
Rick Brown, Muskingum	1988	30	71	125	56.8
Jamie Eichel, Fredonia St.	1989	24	51	90	56.7
Todd Bartlett, Monmouth (Ill.)	1987	20	42	75	56.0

† *National champion.* * *Record.*

SEASON FREE-THROW PERCENTAGE

(Based on qualifiers for annual championship)

Player, Team	Season	G	FT	FTA	Pct.
Andy Enfield, Johns Hopkins	†1991	29	123	129	*95.3
Chris Carideo, Widener	†1992	26	80	84	95.2
Yudi Teichman, Yeshiva	†1989	21	119	125	95.2
Mike Scheib, Susquehanna	†1977	22	80	85	94.1
Jerry Prestier, Baldwin-Wallace	†1978	25	125	134	93.3
Jeff Bowers, Southern Me.	†1988	29	95	102	93.1
Eric Jacobs, Scranton	1986	29	81	87	93.1
Jim Durrell, Colby-Sawyer	†1993	25	67	72	93.1
Joe Purcell, King's (Pa.)	†1979	26	66	71	93.0
Todd Reinhardt, Wartburg	†1990	26	91	98	92.9
Reiner Kolodinski, Occidental	1979	24	65	70	92.9
Shannon Lilly, Bishop	†1982	22	142	153	92.8
Andy Enfield, Johns Hopkins	1990	28	137	148	92.6
Tim Mieure, Hamline	†1976	25	88	95	92.6
Scott Anderson, Wis.-Stevens Point	1990	28	86	93	92.5

† *National champion.* * *Record.*

SEASON REBOUND AVERAGE

Player, Team	Season	G	Reb.	Avg.
Joe Manley, Bowie St.	†1976	29	*579	*20.0
Fred Petty, New Hamp. Col.	†1974	22	436	19.8
Larry Williams, Pratt	†1977	24	457	19.0
Charles Greer, Thomas	1977	17	318	18.7
Larry Parker, Plattsburgh St.	†1975	23	430	18.7
John Jordan, Southern Me.	†1978	29	536	18.5
Keith Woolfolk, Upper Iowa	1978	26	479	18.4
Michael Smith, Trinity (Conn.)	†1990	22	398	18.1
Mike Taylor, Pratt	1978	23	414	18.0
Walt Edwards, Husson	1976	26	467	18.0
Dave Kufeld, Yeshiva	†1979	20	355	17.8

† *National champion.* * *Record.*

SEASON ASSISTS

Player, Team	Season	G	Ast.
Robert James Kean	†1989	29	*391
Ricky Spicer, Wis.-Whitewater	1989	31	295
Ron Torgalski, Hamilton	1989	26	275
Albert Kirchner, Mt. St. Vincent	†1990	24	267
Steve Artis, Chris. Newport	1991	29	262

Player, Team	Season	G	Ast.
Steve Artis, Chris. Newport	1990	28	251
Russell Springman, Salisbury St.	1990	27	246
Tom Genco, Manhattanville	1990	26	244
Mark Cottom, Ferrum	1991	25	242
Tim Lawrence, Maryville (Tenn.)	1992	29	241

† *National champion.* * *Record.*

SEASON ASSIST AVERAGE

Player, Team	Season	G	Ast.	Avg.
Robert James, Kean	†1989	29	*391	*13.5
Albert Kirchner, Mt. St. Vincent	†1990	24	267	11.1
Ron Torgalski, Hamilton	1989	26	275	10.6
Louis Adams, Rust	1989	22	227	10.3
Eric Johnson, Coe	†1991	24	238	9.9
Mark Cottom, Ferrum	1991	25	242	9.7
Ricky Spicer, Wis.-Whitewater	1989	31	295	9.5
Pat Heldman, Maryville (Tenn.)	1989	25	236	9.4
Tom Genco, Manhattanville	1990	26	244	9.4
Justin Culhane, Suffolk	1992	24	225	9.4

† *National champion.* * *Record.*

CAREER POINTS

Player, Team	Seasons	Pts.
Andre Foreman, Salisbury St.	1988-89, 91-92	*2,940
Dwain Govan, Bishop	1972-75	2,796
Dave Russell, Shepherd	1972-75	2,761
Lamont Strothers, Chris. Newport	1988-91	2,709
Matt Hancock, Colby	1987-90	2,678
Greg Grant, Trenton St.	1987-89	2,611
Wil Peterson, St. Andrews	1980-83	2,553
Ron Stewart, Otterbein	1980-83	2,549
Scott Tedder, Ohio Wesleyan	1985-88	2,501
Steve Honderd, Calvin	1990-93	2,469
Herman Alston, Kean	1988-91	2,457
Dick Hempy, Otterbein	1984-87	2,439
Kevin Moran, Curry	1983-86	2,415
Ray Buckland, Mass.-Boston	1978-81	2,413
Keith Moran, Curry	1983-86	2,406
Rickey Sutton, Lyndon St.	1976-79	2,379
Frank Wachlarowicz, St. John's (Minn.)	1975-79	2,357
Cedric Oliver, Hamilton	1976-79	2,349
Dana Janssen, Neb. Wesleyan	1983-86	2,333
Kevin Brown, Emory & Henry	1984-87	2,322

* *Record.*

CAREER SCORING AVERAGE

(Minimum 1,400 points)

Player, Team	Seasons	G	FG	3FG	FT	Pts.	Avg.
Rickey Sutton, Lyndon St.	1976-79	80	960	—	459	2,379	*29.7
John Atkins, Knoxville	1976-78	70	845	—	322	2,012	28.7
Steve Peknik, Windham	1974-77	76	816	—	467	2,099	27.6
Andre Foreman, Salisbury St.	1988-89, 91-92	109	1,140	68	592	*2,940	27.0
Luis Frias, Anna Maria	1980-83	60	676	—	265	1,617	27.0
Matt Hancock, Colby	1987-90	102	844	198	*792	2,678	26.3
Terrence Dupree, Polytechnic (N.Y.)	1990-92	70	700	22	407	1,829	26.1
Dave Russell, Shepherd	1972-75	108	1,072	—	617	2,761	25.6
Mark Veenstra, Calvin	1974-77	89	960	—	341	2,261	25.4
Ron Swartz, Hiram	1984-87	90	883	78	408	2,252	25.0
Dwain Govan, Bishop	1972-75	112	1,137	—	522	2,796	25.0
Clarence Caldwell, Greensboro	1974-77	93	971	—	363	2,309	24.8
James Rehnquist, Amherst	1975-77	61	614	—	284	1,512	24.8

* *Record.*

CAREER FIELD-GOAL PERCENTAGE

(Minimum 400 field goals made)

Player, Team	Seasons	G	FG	FGA	Pct.
Pete Metzelaars, Wabash	1979-82	103	784	1,083	*72.4
Maurice Woods, Potsdam St.	1980-82	93	559	829	67.4
Earl Keith, Stony Brook	75-76, 78-79	94	777	1,161	66.9
Wade Gugino, Hope	1989-92	97	664	1,010	65.7
Rick Batt, UC San Diego	1989-92	106	558	855	65.2
Kevin Ryan, Trenton St.	1987-90	102	619	955	64.8
Scott Baxter, Capital	1988-91	104	505	782	64.6
Tod Hart, Ithaca	1980-83	97	726	1,133	64.1
Tony Seay, Averett	1989-90	55	465	726	64.0
Dick Hempy, Otterbein	1984-87	112	923	1,447	63.8
Mike Johnson, Wis.-Eau Claire	1989-91	89	402	636	63.2
Damon Forney, Greensboro	1978-81	92	586	928	63.1
Bob Richardson, Hamline	1975-77	83	560	887	63.1
Jeff Hrubes, Coe	1986-88	62	459	728	63.0
Doug Blessing, Allentown	1979-82	96	458	728	62.9

* *Record.*

CAREER THREE-POINT FIELD GOALS MADE

Player, Team	Seasons	G	3FG
Ray Wilson, UC Santa Cruz	1989-92	100	*354
Chris Hamilton, Blackburn	1988-91	101	334
Jason Valant, Colorado Col.	1990-93	103	315
Everett Foxx, Ferrum	1989-92	104	315
Chris Geruschat, Bethany (W. Va.)	1989-92	89	307
Mike Connelly, Catholic	1990-93	103	292
Scott Lamond, Gettysburg	1988-91	98	284
Brad Alberts, Ripon	1989-92	95	277
Dan Lenert, Ill. Benedictine	1990-93	104	276
Chris Sullivan, Wheaton (Mass.)	1990-93	100	275
Perry Junius, Allegheny	1988-91	93	275
Dave Levesque, Plymouth St.	1989-92	102	272
Eli Haskell, Colorado Col.	1990-93	99	263
Rick Brown, Muskingum	1987-90	112	263
Travis Aronson, New England Col.	1990-93	100	256

* *Record.*

CAREER THREE-POINT FIELD GOALS MADE PER GAME

(Minimum 200 three-point field goals made)

Player, Team	Seasons	G	3FG	Avg.
Ray Wilson, UC Santa Cruz	1989-92	100	*354	*3.54
Chris Geruschat, Bethany (W. Va.)	1989-92	89	307	3.45
Chris Hamilton, Blackburn	1988-91	101	334	3.31
Jeff Jones, Lycoming	1987-89	71	232	3.27
Jason Valant, Colorado Col.	1990-93	103	315	3.06
Everett Foxx, Ferrum	1989-92	104	315	3.03
Perry Junius, Allegheny	1988-91	93	275	2.96
Brad Alberts, Ripon	1989-92	95	277	2.92
Scott Lamond, Gettysburg	1988-91	98	284	2.90
Kelvin Richardson, Maryville (Tenn.)	1990-93	82	236	2.88
Mike Connelly, Catholic	1990-93	103	292	2.83
Mike Miller, Beloit	1988-91	78	220	2.82
Kirk Anderson, Augustana (Ill.)	1990-93	85	237	2.79
Mario Pritchett, Shenandoah	1989-91	84	232	2.76

* *Record.*

CAREER THREE-POINT FIELD-GOAL PERCENTAGE

(Minimum 200 three-point field goals made)

Player, Team	Seasons	G	3FG	3FGA	Pct.
Jeff Seifriz, Wis.-Whitewater	1987-89	85	217	423	*51.3
Everett Foxx, Ferrum	1989-92	104	315	630	50.0
Brad Alberts, Ripon	1989-92	95	277	563	49.2
Jeff Jones, Lycoming	1987-89	71	232	472	49.2
Troy Greenlee, DePauw	1988-91	106	232	473	49.0
David Todd, Pomona-Pitzer	1987-90	84	212	439	48.3

* *Record.*

CAREER FREE-THROW PERCENTAGE

(Minimum 250 free throws made)

Player, Team	Seasons	G	FT	FTA	Pct.
Andy Enfield, Johns Hopkins	1988-91	108	431	466	*92.5
Doug Brown, Elizabethtown	1976-80	96	252	279	90.3
Tim McGraw, Hartwick	1985-88	107	330	371	88.9
Eric Jacobs, Wilkes & Scranton	1984-87	106	303	343	88.3
Todd Reinhardt, Wartburg	1988-91	105	283	322	87.9
Jeff Thomas, King's (Pa.)	1989-92	110	466	532	87.6
Brian Andrews, Alfred	1984-87	101	306	350	87.4
Eric Elliott, Hope	1988-91	103	350	403	86.8
Pat Pruitt, Albright	1989-92	87	261	301	86.7
Mike Johnson, Wis.-Eau Claire	1989-91	89	421	486	86.6
Ron Barczak, Kalamazoo	1988-91	98	360	416	86.5
Scott Smith, Salisbury St.	1981-85	106	290	336	86.3
Roy Mosser, Millikin	1973-77	105	274	318	86.2

* *Record.*

CAREER REBOUND AVERAGE

(Minimum 900 rebounds)

Player, Team	Seasons	G	Reb.	Avg.
Larry Parker, Plattsburgh St.	1975-78	85	1,482	*17.4
Charles Greer, Thomas	1975-77	58	926	16.0
Willie Parr, LeMoyne-Owen	1974-76	76	1,182	15.6
Michael Smith, Hamilton	1989-92	107	*1,628	15.2
Dave Kufeld, Yeshiva	1977-80	81	1,222	15.1
Ed Owens, Hampden-Sydney	1977-80	77	1,160	15.1
John Jordan, Southern Me.	1978-81	105	1,504	14.4
Kevin Clark, Clark (Mass.)	1978-81	101	1,450	14.4
Mark Veenstra, Calvin	1974-77	89	1,260	14.2

* *Record.*

CAREER ASSISTS

Player, Team	Seasons	G	Ast.
Steve Artis, Chris. Newport	1990-93	112	*909
Lance Andrews, New Jersey Tech	1990-93	113	664
Dennis Jacobi, Bowdoin	1989-92	93	662
Tim Lawrence, Maryville (Tenn.)	1989-92	106	660
Pat Skerry, Tufts	1989-92	95	650
Eric Johnson, Coe	1989-92	90	637
John Snyder, King's (Pa.)	1989-92	107	631
Jerry Dennis, Otterbein	1989-92	118	613
James Braxton, Averett	1989-92	106	583
Kevin Root, Eureka	1989-91	81	579
Keith Newman, Bethel (Minn.)	1989-92	96	560

* *Record.*

CAREER ASSIST AVERAGE

(Minimum 550 assists)

Player, Team	Seasons	G	Ast.	Avg.
Steve Artis, Chris, Newport	1990-93	112	909	*8.1
Kevin Root, Eureka	1989-91	81	579	7.1
Dennis Jacobi, Bowdoin	1989-92	93	662	7.1
Eric Johnson, Coe	1989-92	90	637	7.1
Pat Skerry, Tufts	1989-92	95	650	6.8
Tim Lawrence, Maryville (Tenn.)	1989-92	106	660	6.2
John Snyder, King's (Pa.)	1989-92	107	631	5.9
Lance Andrews, New Jersey Tech	1990-93	113	664	5.9
Keith Newman, Bethel (Minn.)	1989-92	96	560	5.8
James Braxton, Averett	1989-92	106	583	5.5
Jerry Dennis, Otterbein	1989-92	118	613	5.2

* *Record.*

DIVISION III MEN'S ANNUAL INDIVIDUAL CHAMPIONS

SCORING AVERAGE

Year	Player, Team	G	FG	3FG	FT	Pts.	Avg.
1974	Dana Wilson, Husson	20	288		122	698	34.9
1975	Dwain Govan, Bishop	29	392		179	963	33.2
1976	Rickey Sutton, Lyndon St.	14	207		93	507	*36.2
1977	Rickey Sutton, Lyndon St.	16	223		112	558	34.9
1978	John Atkins, Knoxville	25	340		103	783	31.3
1979	Scott Rogers, Kenyon	24	289		109	687	28.6
1980	Ray Buckland, Mass.-Boston	25	271		153	695	27.8
1981	Gerald Reece, William Penn	27	306		145	757	28.0
1982	Ashley Cooper, Ripon	22	256		89	601	27.3
1983	Shannon Lilly, Bishop	26	345		218	908	34.9
1984	Mark Van Valkenburg, Framingham St.	25	312		133	757	30.3
1985	Adam St. John, Maine Maritime	18	193		135	521	28.9
1986	John Saintignon, UC Santa Cruz	22	291		104	686	31.2
1987	Rod Swartz, Hiram	23	232	78	133	675	29.3
1988	Matt Hancock, Colby	27	275	56	247	853	31.6
1989	Greg Grant, Trenton St.	32	387	76	194	*1,044	32.6
1990	Grant Glover, Rust	23	235	1	164	635	27.6
1991	Andre Foreman, Salisbury St.	29	350	39	175	914	31.5
1992	Jeff deLaveaga, Cal Lutheran	28	258	122	187	825	29.5
1993	Dave Shaw, Drew	23	210	74	169	663	28.8

* *Record.*

FIELD-GOAL PERCENTAGE

Year	Player, Team	G	FG	FGA	Pct.
1974	Fred Waldstein, Wartburg	28	163	248	65.7
1975	Dan Woodard, Elizabethtown	23	190	299	63.5
1976	Paul Merlis, Yeshiva	21	145	217	66.8
1977	Brent Cawelti, Trinity (Conn.)	20	107	164	65.2
1978	Earl Keith, Stony Brook	29	228	322	70.8
1979	Ed Owens, Hampden-Sydney	24	140	192	72.9
1980	E. D. Schechterley, Lynchburg	25	184	259	71.0
1981	Tony Rychlec, Mass. Maritime	25	233	311	74.9
1982	Pete Metzelaars, Wabash	28	271	360	*75.3
1983	Mike Johnson, Drew	23	138	205	67.3
1984	Mark Van Valkenburg, Framingham St.	25	312	467	66.8
1985	Reinout Brugman, Muhlenberg	26	176	266	66.2
1986	Oliver Kyler, Frostburg St.	28	183	266	68.8
1987	Tim Ervin, Albion	21	127	194	65.5
1988	Matt Strong, Hope	27	163	232	70.3
1989	Kevin Ryan, Trenton St.	32	246	345	71.3
1990	Bill Triplett, New Jersey Tech	28	169	237	71.3
1991	Scott Baxter, Capital	26	164	226	72.6
1992	Brett Grebing, Redlands	23	125	176	71.0
1993	Jim Leibel, St. Thomas (Minn.)	28	141	202	69.8

* *Record.*

THREE-POINT FIELD GOALS MADE PER GAME

Year	Player, Team	G	3FG	Avg.
1987	Scott Fearrin, MacMurray	25	96	3.8
1988	Jeff Jones, Lycoming	23	97	4.2
1989	Brad Block, Aurora	26	112	4.3
1990	Chris Hamilton, Blackburn	24	109	4.5
1991	Chris Jans, Loras	25	*133	*5.3
1992	Jeff deLaveaga, Cal Lutheran	28	122	4.4
1993	Mike Connelly, Catholic	27	111	4.1

* *Record.*

THREE-POINT FIELD-GOAL PERCENTAGE

Year	Player, Team	G	3FG	3FGA	Pct.
1987	Chris Miles, New Jersey Tech	26	41	65	63.1
1988	Ray Magee, Stockton St.	26	41	71	57.7
1989	Reggie James, New Jersey Tech	29	59	88	*67.0
1990	Matt Miota, Lawrence	22	33	54	61.1
1991	Mike Bachman, Alma	26	46	76	60.5
1992	John Kmack, Plattsburgh St.	26	44	84	52.4
1993	Brad Apple, Greensboro	26	49	91	53.8

* *Record.*

FREE-THROW PERCENTAGE

Year	Player, Team	G	FT	FTA	Pct.
1974	Bruce Johnson, Plymouth St.	17	73	81	90.1
1975	Harold Howard, Austin	24	83	92	90.2
1976	Tim Mieure, Hamline	25	88	95	92.6
1977	Mike Scheib, Susquehanna	22	80	85	94.1
1978	Jerry Prestier, Baldwin-Wallace	25	125	134	93.3
1979	Joe Purcell, King's (Pa.)	26	66	71	93.0
1980	David Whiteside, N.C.-Greensboro	28	120	132	90.9
1981	Jim Cooney, Elmhurst	26	65	72	90.3
1982	Shannon Lilly, Bishop	22	142	153	92.8
1983	Mike Sain, Eureka	26	66	72	91.7
1984	Chris Genian, Redlands	24	71	78	91.0
1985	Bob Possehl, Coe	22	59	65	90.8
1986	Eric Jacobs, Scranton	29	81	87	93.1
1987	Chris Miles, New Jersey Tech	26	70	76	92.1
1988	Jeff Bowers, Southern Me.	29	95	102	93.1
1989	Yudi Teichman, Yeshiva	21	119	125	95.2
1990	Todd Reinhardt, Wartburg	26	91	98	92.9
1991	Andy Enfield, Johns Hopkins	29	123	129	*95.3
1992	Chris Carideo, Widener	26	80	84	95.2
1993	Jim Durrell, Colby-Sawyer	25	67	72	93.1

* *Record.*

REBOUND AVERAGE

Year	Player, Team	G	Reb.	Avg.
1974	Fred Petty, New Hamp. Col.	22	436	19.8
1975	Larry Parker, Plattsburgh St.	23	430	18.7
1976	Joe Manley, Bowie St.	29	*579	*20.0
1977	Larry Williams, Pratt	24	457	19.0
1978	John Jordan, Southern Me.	29	536	18.5
1979	Dave Kufeld, Yeshiva	20	355	17.8
1980	Dave Kufeld, Yeshiva	20	353	17.7
1981	Kevin Clark, Clark (Mass.)	27	465	17.2
1982	Len Washington, Mass.-Boston	23	361	15.7
1983	Luis Frias, Anna Maria	23	320	13.9
1984	Joe Weber, Aurora	27	370	13.7
1985	Albert Wells, Rust	22	326	14.8
1986	Russell Thompson, Westfield St.	22	338	15.4
1987	Randy Gorniak, Penn St.-Behrend	25	410	16.4
1988	Mike Nelson, Hamilton	26	349	13.4
1989	Clinton Montford, Methodist	27	459	17.0
1990	Michael Stubbs, Trinity (Conn.)	22	398	18.1
1991	Mike Smith, Hamilton	27	435	16.1
1992	Jeff Black, Fitchburg St.	22	363	16.5
1993	Steve Lemmer, Hamilton	27	404	15.0

* *Record.*

ASSIST AVERAGE

Year	Player, Team	G	Ast.	Avg.
1989	Robert James, Kean	27	*391	*13.5
1990	Albert Kirchner, Mt. St. Vincent	24	267	11.1
1991	Eric Johnson, Coe	24	238	9.9
1992	Edgar Loera, La Verne	23	202	8.8
1993	David Genovese, Mt. St. Vincent	27	237	8.8

* *Record.*

BLOCKED-SHOT AVERAGE

Year	Player, Team	G	Blk.	Avg.
1993	Matt Cusano, Scranton	29	145	5.0

STEAL AVERAGE

Year	Player, Team	G	Stl.	Avg.
1993	Moses Jean-Pierre, Plymouth St.	25	114	4.6

DIVISION III MEN'S ANNUAL TEAM CHAMPIONS

WON-LOST PERCENTAGE

Year	Team	Won	Lost	Pct.
1974	Calvin	21	2	.913
1975	Calvin	22	1	.957
1976	Husson	25	1	.961
1977	Mass.-Boston	25	3	.893
1978	North Park	29	2	.935
1979	Stony Brook	24	3	.889
1980	Franklin Pierce	29	2	.935
1981	Potsdam St.	30	2	.938
1982	St. Andrews	27	3	.900
1983	Roanoke	31	2	.939
1984	Roanoke	27	2	.931
1985	Colby	22	3	.880
1986	Potsdam St.	32	0	1.000
1987	Potsdam St.	28	1	.966
1988	Scranton	29	3	.906
1989	Trenton St.	30	2	.938
1990	Colby	26	1	.963
1991	Hamilton	26	1	.963
1992	Calvin	31	1	.969
1993	Rowan	29	2	.935

SCORING OFFENSE

Year	Team	G	(W-L)	Pts.	Avg.
1974	Bishop	26	(14-12)	2,527	97.2
1975	Bishop	29	(25-4)	2,932	101.1
1976	Husson	26	(25-1)	2,567	98.7
1977	Mercy	25	(16-9)	2,587	103.5
1978	Mercy	26	(16-10)	2,602	100.1
1979	Ashland	25	(14-11)	2,375	95.0
1980	Franklin Pierce	31	(29-2)	*3,073	99.1
1981	Husson	23	(20-3)	2,173	94.5
1982	Husson	26	(19-7)	2,279	87.7
1983	Bishop	26	(18-8)	2,529	97.3
1984	St. Joseph's (Me.)	29	(24-5)	2,666	91.9
1985	St. Joseph's (Me.)	30	(22-8)	2,752	91.7
1986	St. Joseph's (Me.)	30	(26-4)	2,837	94.6
1987	Bishop	26	(13-13)	2,534	97.5
1988	St. Joseph's (Me.)	29	(20-9)	2,785	96.0
1989	Redlands	25	(15-10)	2,507	100.3
1990	Salisbury St.	27	(14-13)	2,822	104.5
1991	Redlands	26	(15-11)	2,726	104.8
1992	Redlands	25	(18-7)	2,510	100.4
1993	Salisbury St.	26	(18-8)	2,551	98.1

SCORING DEFENSE

Year	Team	G	(W-L)	Pts.	Avg.
1974	Fredonia St.	22	(13-9)	1,049	*47.7
1975	Chicago	15	(9-6)	790	52.7
1976	Fredonia St.	23	(10-13)	1,223	53.2
1977	Hamline	30	(22-8)	1,560	52.0
1978	Widener	31	(26-5)	1,693	54.6

Year	Team	G	(W-L)	Pts.	Avg.
1979	Coast Guard	24	(21-3)	1,160	48.3
1980	John Jay	27	(10-17)	1,411	52.3
1981	Wis.-Stevens Point	26	(19-7)	1,394	53.6
1982	Wis.-Stevens Point	28	(22-6)	1,491	53.3
1983	Ohio Northern	26	(18-8)	1,379	53.0
1984	Wis.-Stevens Point	32	(28-4)	1,559	48.7
1985	Wis.-Stevens Point	30	(25-3)	1,438	47.9
1986	Widener	27	(15-12)	1,356	50.2
1987	Muskingum	27	(16-11)	1,454	53.9
1988	Ohio Northern	30	(21-9)	1,734	57.8
1989	Wooster	28	(21-7)	1,600	57.1
1990	Randolph-Macon	29	(24-5)	1,646	56.8
1991	Ohio Northern	27	(14-13)	1,508	55.9
1992	Wittenberg	29	(23-6)	1,651	56.9
1993	St. Thomas (Minn.)	28	(19-9)	1,599	57.1

* *Record.*

SCORING MARGIN

Year	Team	Off.	Def.	Margin
1974	Fisk	83.3	65.7	17.6
1975	Monmouth (Ill.)	83.9	66.0	17.9
1976	Husson	98.7	67.6	*31.1
1977	Husson	101.2	78.6	22.6
1978	Stony Brook	86.6	68.7	17.9
1979	North Park	84.4	67.3	17.1
1980	Franklin Pierce	99.1	76.5	22.6
1981	Husson	94.5	70.1	24.4
1982	Hope	83.9	70.0	13.8
1983	Trinity (Conn.)	79.8	61.4	18.4
1984	Wis.-Stevens Point	68.4	48.7	19.7
1985	Hope	85.4	66.0	19.4
1986	Potsdam St.	81.5	57.3	24.2
1987	New Jersey Tech	90.8	63.9	26.9
1988	Cal St. San B'dino	89.4	69.4	20.0
1989	Trenton St.	92.3	68.5	23.8
1990	Colby	94.7	71.9	22.8
1991	Hamilton	89.8	66.2	23.6
1992	New Jersey Tech	95.0	73.4	21.6
1993	New Jersey Tech	90.4	65.7	24.7

* *Record.*

FIELD-GOAL PERCENTAGE

Year	Team	FG	FGA	Pct.
1974	Muskingum	560	1,056	53.0
1975	Savannah St.	1,072	1,978	54.2
1976	Stony Brook	778	1,401	55.5
1977	Stony Brook	842	1,455	57.9
1978	Stony Brook	1,033	1,721	*60.0
1979	Stony Brook	980	1,651	59.4
1980	Framingham St.	924	1,613	57.3
1981	Averett	845	1,447	58.4
1982	Lebanon Valley	608	1,098	55.4
1983	Bishop	1,037	1,775	58.4
1984	Framingham St.	849	1,446	58.7
1985	Me.-Farmington	751	1,347	55.8
1986	Frostburg St.	971	1,747	55.6
1987	New Jersey Tech	969	1,799	53.9
1988	Rust	878	1,493	58.8
1989	Bridgewater (Va.)	650	1,181	55.0
1990	Wartburg	792	1,474	53.7
1991	Otterbein	1,104	2,050	53.9
1992	Bridgewater (Va.)	706	1,315	53.7
1993	St. John's (Minn.)	744	1,415	52.6

* *Record.*

FIELD-GOAL PERCENTAGE DEFENSE

Year	Team	FG	FGA	Pct.
1978	Grove City	589	1,477	39.9
1979	Coast Guard	464	1,172	39.6
1980	Calvin	552	1,364	40.5
1981	Wittenberg	670	1,651	40.6
1982	Tufts	622	1,505	41.3
1983	Trinity (Conn.)	580	1,408	41.2
1984	Widener	617	1,557	39.6
1985	Colby	679	1,712	39.7
1986	Widener	531	1,344	39.5
1987	Widener	608	1,636	37.2
1988	Rust	603	1,499	40.2
1989	Wooster	595	1,563	38.1
1990	Rochester	760	1,990	38.2
1991	Hamilton	679	1,771	38.3
1992	Scranton	589	1,547	38.1
1993	Scranton	659	1,806	*36.5

* *Record.*

THREE-POINT FIELD GOALS MADE PER GAME

Year	Team	G	3FG	Avg.
1987	Grinnell	22	166	7.5
1988	Southern Me.	29	233	8.0
1989	Redlands	25	261	10.4
1990	Augsburg	25	266	10.6
1991	Redlands	26	307	11.8
1992	Catholic	26	*335	*12.9
1993	Anna Maria	27	302	11.2

* *Record.*

THREE-POINT FIELD-GOAL PERCENTAGE

Year	Team	G	3FG	3FGA	Pct.
1987	Mass.-Dartmouth	28	102	198	51.5
1988	Stockton St.	26	122	211	57.8
1989	New Jersey Tech	29	124	200	*62.0
1990	Western New Eng.	26	85	167	50.9
1991	Ripon	26	154	331	46.5
1992	Dickinson	27	126	267	47.2
1993	DePauw	26	191	419	45.6

* *Record.*

FREE-THROW PERCENTAGE

Year	Team	FT	FTA	Pct.
1974	Lake Superior St.	369	461	80.0
1975	Muskingum	298	379	78.6
1976	Case Reserve	266	343	77.6
1977	Hamilton	491	640	76.7
1978	Case Reserve	278	351	79.2
1979	Marietta	364	460	79.1
1980	Denison	377	478	78.9
1981	Ripon	378	494	76.5
1982	Otterbein	458	589	77.8
1983	DePauw	368	475	77.5
1984	Redlands	426	534	79.8
1985	Wis.-Stevens Point	363	455	79.8
1986	Heidelberg	375	489	76.7
1987	Denison	442	560	78.9
1988	Capital	377	473	79.7
1989	Colby	464	585	79.3
1990	Colby	485	605	*80.2
1991	Wartburg	565	711	79.5
1992	Thiel	393	491	80.0
1993	Colby	391	506	77.3

* *Record.*

REBOUND MARGIN

Year	Team	Off.	Def.	Margin
1976	Bowie St.	54.0	37.5	16.5
1977	Husson	51.6	35.0	16.7
1978	Gallaudet	46.3	33.0	13.3
1979	St. Lawrence	43.2	28.7	14.5
1980	Elmira	41.4	28.7	12.7
1981	Clark (Mass.)	40.0	25.0	15.0
1982	Maryville (Mo.)	41.0	26.7	14.4
1983	Framingham St.	38.0	22.2	15.8
1984	New England Col.	43.3	29.3	14.0
1985	Bethel (Minn.)	45.0	32.2	12.8
1986	St. Joseph's (Me.)	43.7	29.5	14.2
1987	Elmira	40.6	29.3	11.3
1988	Cal St. San B'dino	46.6	29.7	16.9
1989	Yeshiva	49.8	34.6	15.2
1990	Bethel (Minn.)	42.2	30.3	12.0
1991	Hamilton	49.6	32.5	*17.0
1992	Bethel (Minn.)	42.3	31.0	11.3
1993	Eureka	33.9	22.2	11.7

* *Record.*

DIVISION III MEN'S ALL-TIME WINNINGEST TEAMS

Includes records as a senior college only; minimum 10 seasons of competition. Postseason games are included.

PERCENTAGE

Team	1st Year	Yrs.	Won	Lost	Pct.
Wittenberg	1912	82	1,232	543	.694
Jersey City St.	1935	58	571	271	.678
Calvin	1920	73	928	475	.661
Wis.-Eau Claire	1917	77	1,050	*554	.655
Hope	1901	87	1,069	578	.649
North Park	1959	35	573	315	.645
Nazareth (N.Y.)	1978	16	263	146	.643
St. Joseph's (Me.)	1972	22	368	206	.641
Beloit	1906	86	1,003	582	.633
Stockton St.	1973	21	344	201	.631
Roanoke	1911	80	999	597	.626
Wooster	1901	93	1,106	675	.621
St. Thomas (Minn.)	1917	76	1,081	663	.620
Wartburg	1936	57	833	511	.620
Ill. Wesleyan	1910	83	1,139	706	.617
New York U.	1906	75	893	555	.617
Hamline	1910	83	1,064	683	.609
Williams	1901	92	958	616	.609
Capital	1907	87	963	638	.601
Augustana (Ill.)	1901	88	1,047	695	.601
Albany (N.Y.)	1910	80	860	571	.601
Colby	1938	54	737	496	.598
Scranton	1917	76	1,048	711	.596
Chris. Newport	1968	26	396	270	.595
Wis.-Stevens Point	1897	94	983	672	.594
Randolph-Macon	1910	80	1,031	721	.588
Muskingum	1903	89	1,006	711	.586
Neb. Wesleyan	1906	88	1,081	769	.584
Ithaca	1930	62	737	533	.580
St. John Fisher	1964	30	413	300	.579
Stony Brook	1960	33	439	331	.570
Widener	1906	86	876	666	.568
Rochester	1902	92	945	723	.567
Loras	1909	85	1,001	769	.566
Redlands	1917	76	828	651	.560

VICTORIES

Team	Wins
Wittenberg	1,232
Ill. Wesleyan	1,139
Wooster	1,106
St. Thomas (Minn.)	1,081
Neb. Wesleyan	1,081
Hope	1,069
Hamline	1,064
Wis.-Eau Claire	1,050
Scranton	1,048
Augustana (Ill.)	1,047
Randolph-Macon	1,031
Muskingum	1,006
Beloit	1,003
Wheaton (Ill.)	1,002
Loras	1,001
Roanoke	999
Gust. Adolphus	997
Ohio Wesleyan	987
Wis.-Stevens Point	983
Millikin	974
Mount Union	968
Capital	963
Williams	958
Rochester	945
Wash. & Lee	942
DePauw	940
Calvin	928
Muhlenberg	922
Wabash	912
Chicago	911
Frank. & Marsh.	903
Kalamazoo	894
New York U.	893
Allegheny	882
Ohio Northern	882

PERCENTAGE

Team	1st Year	Yrs.	Won	Lost	Pct.
Gust. Adolphus	1904	82	997	786	.559
Montclair St.	1931	64	790	625	.558
Wis.-Platteville	1905	82	852	677	.557
King's (Pa.)	1947	47	622	496	.556
Eureka	1920	72	821	661	.554
Millikin	1904	86	974	787	.553
Frank. & Marsh.	1900	89	903	739	.550
DePauw	1904	87	940	**771	.549
Allegheny	1896	98	882	726	.549
Kalamazoo	1907	86	894	748	.544
Ohio Northern	1911	81	882	745	.542
Wash. & Lee	1907	75	942	*797	.542
Ill. Benedictine	1966	27	371	315	.541
Mount Union	1896	96	968	822	.541
Ohio Wesleyan	1906	88	987	841	.540
Ripon	1898	95	849	726	.539

* *Includes one tie.* ** *Includes two ties.*

VICTORIES

Team	Wins
Widener	876
CCNY	868
Hampden-Sydney	861
Albany (N.Y.)	860
Wis.-Platteville	852
Ripon	849
Wartburg	833
Redlands	828
Wesleyan	826
Eureka	821
Wis.-Whitewater	796
Montclair St.	790
Wash. & Jeff.	759
Knox	752
Colby	737
Ithaca	737

AWARD WINNERS

Calbert Cheaney of Indiana was selected as the 1993 Division I player of the year by The Associated Press, United Press International and the U.S. Basketball Writers Association. Cheaney [illegible]

DIVISION I MEN'S CONSENSUS ALL-AMERICAN SELECTIONS

(1929-1993)

1929

Charley Hyatt, Pittsburgh; Joe Schaaf, Pennsylvania; Charles Murphy, Purdue; Vern Corbin, California; Thomas Churchill, Oklahoma; John Thompson, Montana St.

1930

Charley Hyatt, Pittsburgh; Charles Murphy, Purdue; Branch McCracken, Indiana; John Thompson, Montana St.; Frank Ward, Montana St.; John Wooden, Purdue.

1931

John Wooden, Purdue; Joe Reiff, Northwestern; George Gregory, Columbia; Wes Fesler, Ohio St.; Elwood Romney, Brigham Young.

1932

Forest Sale, Kentucky; Ed Krause, Notre Dame; John Wooden, Purdue; Louis Berger, Maryland; Les Witte, Wyoming.

1933

Forest Sale, Kentucky; Don Smith, Pittsburgh; Elliott Loughlin, Navy; Joe Reiff, Northwestern; Ed Krause, Notre Dame; Jerry Nemer, Southern Cal.

1934

Claire Cribbs, Pittsburgh; Ed Krause, Notre Dame; Les Witte, Wyoming; Hal Lee, Washington; Norman Cottom, Purdue.

1935

Jack Gray, Texas; Lee Guttero, Southern Cal; Claire Cribbs, Pittsburgh; Bud Browning, Oklahoma; Leroy Edwards, Kentucky.

1936

Bob Kessler, Purdue; Paul Nowak, Notre Dame; Hank Luisetti, Stanford; Vern Huffman, Indiana; John Moir, Notre Dame; Ike Poole, Arkansas; Bill Kinner, Utah.

1937

Hank Luisetti, Stanford; Paul Nowak, Notre Dame; Jules Bender, LIU-Brooklyn; John Moir, Notre Dame; Jewell Young, Purdue.

1938

Hank Luisetti, Stanford; John Moir, Notre Dame; Fred Pralle, Kansas; Jewell Young, Purdue; Paul Nowak, Notre Dame; Meyer Bloom, Temple.

1939

FIRST TEAM—Irving Torgoff, LIU-Brooklyn; Urgel Wintermute, Oregon; Chet Jaworski, Rhode Island; Ernie Andres, Indiana; Jimmy Hull, Ohio St.
SECOND TEAM—Bob Calihan, Detroit Mercy; Michael Novak, Loyola (Ill.); Bernard Opper, Kentucky; Robert Anet, Oregon; Bob Hassmiller, Fordham.

1940

FIRST TEAM—Ralph Vaughn, Southern Cal; John Dick, Oregon; Bill Hapac, Illinois; George Glamack, North Caro.; Gus Broberg, Dartmouth.
SECOND TEAM—Jack Harvey, Colorado; Marvin Huffman, Indiana; James McNatt, Oklahoma; Jesse Renick, Oklahoma St.

1941

FIRST TEAM—Gus Broberg, Dartmouth; John Adams, Arkansas; Howard Engleman, Kansas; George Glamack, North Caro.; Gene Englund, Wisconsin.
SECOND TEAM—Frank Baumholtz, Ohio; Paul Lindeman, Washington St.; Oscar Schechtman, LIU-Brooklyn; Robert Kinney, Rice; Stan Modzelewski, Rhode Island.

1942

FIRST TEAM—John Kotz, Wisconsin; Price Brookfield, West Tex. A&M; Bob Kinney, Rice; Andrew Phillip, Illinois; Robert Davies, Seton Hall.
SECOND TEAM—Robert Doll, Colorado; Wilfred Doerner, Evansville; Donald Burness, Stanford; George Munroe, Dartmouth; Stan Modzelewski, Rhode Island; John Mandic, Oregon St.

1943

FIRST TEAM—Andrew Phillip, Illinois; George Senesky, St. Joseph's (Pa.); Ken Sailors, Wyoming; Harry Boykoff, St. John's (N.Y.); Charles Black, Kansas; Ed Beisser, Creighton; William Closs, Rice.
SECOND TEAM—Gerald Tucker, Oklahoma; Bob Rensberger, Notre Dame; Gene Rock, Southern Cal; John Kotz, Wisconsin; Otto Graham, Northwestern; Gale Bishop, Washington St.

1944

FIRST TEAM—George Mikan, DePaul; Audley Brindley, Dartmouth; Otto Graham, Northwestern; Robert Brannum, Kentucky; Alva Paine, Oklahoma; Robert Kurland, Oklahoma St.; Leo Klier, Notre Dame.
SECOND TEAM—Arnold Ferrin, Utah; Dale Hall, Army; Don Grate, Ohio St.; Bob Dille, Valparaiso; William Henry, Rice; Dick Triptow, DePaul.

1945

FIRST TEAM—George Mikan, DePaul; Robert Kurland, Oklahoma St.; Arnold Ferrin, Utah; Walton Kirk, Illinois; William Hassett, Notre Dame; William Henry, Rice; Howard Dallmar, Pennsylvania; Wyndol Gray, Bowling Green.
SECOND TEAM—Richard Ives, Iowa; Vince Hanson, Washington St.; Dale Hall, Army; Max Morris, Northwestern; Don Grate, Ohio St.; Herb Wilkinson, Iowa.

1946

FIRST TEAM—George Mikan, DePaul; Robert Kurland, Oklahoma St.; Leo Klier, Notre Dame; Max Norris, Northwestern; Sid Tanenbaum, New York U.
SECOND TEAM—Jack Parkinson, Kentucky; John Dillon, North Caro.; Ken Sailors, Wyoming; Charles Black, Kansas; Tony Lavelli, Yale; William Hassett, Notre Dame.

1947

FIRST TEAM—Ralph Beard, Kentucky; Gerald Tucker, Oklahoma; Alex Groza, Kentucky; Sid

Tanenbaum, New York U.; Ralph Hamilton, Indiana.
SECOND TEAM—George Kaftan, Holy Cross; John Hargis, Texas; Don Barksdale, UCLA; Arnold Ferrin, Utah; Andrew Phillip, Illinois; Ed Koffenberger, Duke; Vern Gardner, Utah.

1948

FIRST TEAM—Murray Wier, Iowa, 5-9, Muscatine, Iowa; Ed Macauley, St. Louis, 6-8, St. Louis, Mo.; Jim McIntyre, Minnesota, 6-10, Minneapolis, Minn.; Kevin O'Shea, Notre Dame, 6-1, San Francisco, Calif.; Ralph Beard, Kentucky, 5-10, Louisville, Ky.
SECOND TEAM—Dick Dickey, North Caro. St.; Arnold Ferrin, Utah; Alex Groza, Kentucky; Harold Haskins, Hamline; George Kaftan, Holy Cross; Duane Klueh, Indiana St.; Tony Lavelli, Yale; Jack Nichols, Washington; Andy Wolfe, California.

1949

FIRST TEAM—Tony Lavelli, Yale, 6-3, Somerville, Mass.; Vince Boryla, Denver, 6-5, East Chicago, Ind.; Ed Macauley, St. Louis, 6-8, St. Louis, Mo.; Alex Groza, Kentucky, 6-7, Martin's Ferry, Ohio; Ralph Beard, Kentucky, 5-10, Louisville, Ky.
SECOND TEAM—Bill Erickson, Illinois; Vern Gardner, Utah; Wallace Jones, Kentucky; Jim McIntyre, Minnesota; Ernie Vandeweghe, Colgate.

1950

FIRST TEAM—Dick Schnittker, Ohio St., 6-5, Sandusky, Ohio; Bob Cousy, Holy Cross, 6-1, St. Albans, N.Y.; Paul Arizin, Villanova, 6-3, Philadelphia, Pa.; Paul Unruh, Bradley, 6-4, Toulon, Ill.; Bill Sharman, Southern Cal, 6-2, Porterville, Calif.
SECOND TEAM—Charles Cooper, Duquesne; Don Lofgran, San Francisco; Kevin O'Shea, Notre Dame; Don Rehfeldt, Wisconsin; Sherman White, LIU-Brooklyn.

1951

FIRST TEAM—Bill Mlkvy, Temple, 6-4, Palmerton, Pa.; Sam Ranzino, North Caro. St., 6-1, Gary, Ind.; Bill Spivey, Kentucky, 7-0, Macon, Ga.; Clyde Lovellette, Kansas, 6-9, Terre Haute, Ind.; Gene Melchiorre, Bradley, 5-8, Highland Park, Ill.
SECOND TEAM—Ernie Barrett, Kansas St.; Bill Garrett, Indiana; Dick Groat, Duke; Mel Hutchins, Brigham Young; Gale McArthur, Oklahoma St.

1952

FIRST TEAM—Cliff Hagan, Kentucky, 6-4, Owensboro, Ky.; Rod Fletcher, Illinois, 6-4, Champaign, Ill.; Chuck Darling, Iowa, 6-8, Denver, Colo.; Clyde Lovellette, Kansas, 6-9, Terre Haute, Ind.; Dick Groat, Duke, 6-0, Swissvale, Pa.
SECOND TEAM—Bob Houbregs, Washington; Don Meineke, Dayton; Johnny O'Brien, Seattle; Mark Workman, West Va.; Bob Zawoluk, St. John's (N.Y.).

1953

FIRST TEAM—Ernie Beck, Pennsylvania, 6-4, Philadelphia, Pa.; Bob Houbregs, Washington, 6-7, Seattle, Wash.; Walt Dukes, Seton Hall, 6-11, Rochester, N.Y.; Tom Gola, La Salle, 6-6, Philadelphia, Pa.; Johnny O'Brien, Seattle, 5-8, South Amboy, N.J.
SECOND TEAM—Dick Knostman, Kansas St.; Bob Pettit, Louisiana St.; Joe Richey, Brigham Young; Don Schlundt, Indiana; Frank Selvy, Furman.

1954

FIRST TEAM—Frank Selvy, Furman, 6-3, Corbin, Ky.; Tom Gola, La Salle, 6-6, Philadelphia, Pa.; Don Schlundt, Indiana, 6-10, South Bend, Ind.; Bob Pettit, Louisiana St., 6-9, Baton Rouge, La.; Cliff Hagan, Kentucky, 6-4, Owensboro, Ky.
SECOND TEAM—Bob Leonard, Indiana; Tom Marshall, Western Ky.; Bob Mattick, Oklahoma St.; Frank Ramsey, Kentucky; Dick Ricketts, Duquesne.

1955

FIRST TEAM—Tom Gola, La Salle, 6-6, Philadelphia, Pa.; Dick Ricketts, Duquesne, 6-8, Pottstown, Pa.; Bill Russell, San Francisco, 6-9, Oakland, Calif.; Si Green, Duquesne, 6-3, Brooklyn, N.Y.; Dick Garmaker, Minnesota, 6-3, Hibbing, Minn.
SECOND TEAM—Darrell Floyd, Furman; Robin Freeman, Ohio St.; Dickie Hemric, Wake Forest; Don Schlundt, Indiana; Ron Shavlik, North Caro. St.

1956

FIRST TEAM—Tom Heinsohn, Holy Cross, 6-7, Union City, N.J.; Ron Shavlik, North Caro. St., 6-9, Denver, Colo.; Bill Russell, San Francisco, 6-9, Oakland, Calif.; Si Green, Duquesne, 6-3, Brooklyn, N.Y.; Robin Freeman, Ohio St., 5-11, Cincinnati, Ohio.
SECOND TEAM—Bob Burrow, Kentucky; Darrell Floyd, Furman; Rod Hundley, West Va.; K. C. Jones, San Francisco; Willie Naulls, UCLA; Bill Uhl, Dayton.

1957

FIRST TEAM—Rod Hundley, West Va., 6-4, Charleston, W. Va.; Lenny Rosenbluth, North Caro., 6-5, New York, N.Y.; Jim Krebs, Southern Methodist, 6-8, Webster Groves, Mo.; Wilt Chamberlain, Kansas, 7-0, Philadelphia, Pa.; Charlie Tyra, Louisville, 6-8, Louisville, Ky.; Chet Forte, Columbia, 5-9, Hackensack, N.J.
SECOND TEAM—Elgin Baylor, Seattle; Frank Howard, Ohio St.; Guy Rodgers, Temple; Gary Thompson, Iowa St.; Grady Wallace, South Caro.

1958

FIRST TEAM—Bob Boozer, Kansas St., 6-8, Omaha, Neb.; Elgin Baylor, Seattle, 6-6, Washington, D.C.; Wilt Chamberlain, Kansas, 7-0, Philadelphia, Pa.; Oscar Robertson, Cincinnati, 6-5, Indianapolis, Ind.; Guy Rodgers, Temple, 6-0, Philadelphia, Pa.; Don Hennon, Pittsburgh, 5-9, Wampum, Pa.
SECOND TEAM—Pete Brennan, North Caro.; Archie Dees, Indiana; Dave Gambee, Oregon St.; Mike Farmer, San Francisco; Bailey Howell, Mississippi St.

1959

FIRST TEAM—Bailey Howell, Mississippi St., 6-7, Middleton, Tenn.; Bob Boozer, Kansas St., 6-8, Omaha, Neb.; Oscar Robertson, Cincinnati, 6-5, Indianapolis, Ind.; Jerry West, West Va., 6-3, Cabin Creek, W. Va.; Johnny Cox, Kentucky, 6-4, Hazard, Ky.
SECOND TEAM—Leo Byrd, Marshall; Johnny Green, Michigan St.; Tom Hawkins, Notre Dame; Don Hennon, Pittsburgh; Alan Seiden, St. John's (N.Y.).

1960

FIRST TEAM—Oscar Robertson, Cincinnati, 6-5, Indianapolis, Ind.; Jerry West, West Va., 6-3, Cabin Creek, W. Va.; Jerry Lucas, Ohio St., 6-8, Middletown, Ohio; Darrall Imhoff, California, 6-10; Alhambra, Calif.; Tom Stith, St. Bonaventure, 6-5, Brooklyn, N.Y.

SECOND TEAM—Terry Dischinger, Purdue; Tony Jackson, St. John's (N.Y.); Roger Kaiser, Georgia Tech; Lee Shaffer, North Caro.; Len Wilkens, Providence.

1961

FIRST TEAM—Jerry Lucas, Ohio St., 6-8, Middletown, Ohio; Tom Stith, St. Bonaventure, 6-5, Brooklyn, N.Y.; Terry Dischinger, Purdue, 6-7, Terre Haute, Ind.; Roger Kaiser, Georgia Tech, 6-1, Dale, Ind.; Chet Walker, Bradley, 6-6, Benton Harbor, Mich.
SECOND TEAM—Walt Bellamy, Indiana; Frank Burgess, Gonzaga; Tony Jackson, St. John's (N.Y.); Billy McGill, Utah; Larry Siegfried, Ohio St.

1962

FIRST TEAM—Jerry Lucas, Ohio St., 6-8, Middletown, Ohio; Len Chappell, Wake Forest, 6-8, Portage Area, Pa.; Billy McGill, Utah, 6-9, Los Angeles, Calif.; Terry Dischinger, Purdue, 6-7, Terre Haute, Ind.; Chet Walker, Bradley, 6-6, Benton Harbor, Mich.
SECOND TEAM—Jack Foley, Holy Cross; John Havlicek, Ohio St.; Art Heyman, Duke; Cotton Nash, Kentucky; John Rudometkin, Southern Cal; Rod Thorn, West Va.

1963

FIRST TEAM—Art Heyman, Duke, 6-5, Rockville Center, N.Y.; Ron Bonham, Cincinnati, 6-5, Muncie, Ind.; Barry Kramer, New York U., 6-4, Schenectady, N.Y.; Jerry Harkness, Loyola (Ill.), 6-3, New York, N.Y.; Tom Thacker, Cincinnati, 6-2, Covington, Ky.
SECOND TEAM—Gary Bradds, Ohio St.; Bill Green, Colorado St.; Cotton Nash, Kentucky; Rod Thorn, West Va.; Nate Thurmond, Bowling Green.

1964

FIRST TEAM—Bill Bradley, Princeton, 6-5, Crystal City, Mo.; Dave Stallworth, Wichita St., 6-7, Dallas, Tex.; Gary Bradds, Ohio St., 6-8, Jamestown, Ohio; Walt Hazzard, UCLA, 6-2, Philadelphia, Pa.; Cotton Nash, Kentucky, 6-5, Leominster, Mass.
SECOND TEAM—Ron Bonham, Cincinnati; Mel Counts, Oregon St.; Fred Hetzel, Davidson; Jeff Mullins, Duke; Cazzie Russell, Michigan.

1965

FIRST TEAM—Bill Bradley, Princeton, 6-5, Crystal City, Mo.; Rick Barry, Miami (Fla.), 6-7, Roselle Park, N.J.; Fred Hetzel, Davidson, 6-8, Washington, D.C.; Cazzie Russell, Michigan, 6-5, Chicago, Ill.; Gail Goodrich, UCLA, 6-1, North Hollywood, Calif.
SECOND TEAM—Bill Buntin, Michigan; Wayne Estes, Utah St.; Clyde Lee, Vanderbilt; Dave Schellhase, Purdue; Dave Stallworth, Wichita St.

1966

FIRST TEAM—Dave Bing, Syracuse, 6-3, Washington, D.C.; Dave Schellhase, Purdue, 6-4, Evansville, Ind.; Clyde Lee, Vanderbilt, 6-9, Nashville, Tenn.; Cazzie Russell, Michigan, 6-5, Chicago, Ill.; Jim Walker, Providence, 6-3, Boston, Mass.
SECOND TEAM—Lou Dampier, Kentucky; Matt Guokas, St. Joseph's (Pa.); Jack Marin, Duke; Dick Snyder, Davidson; Bob Verga, Duke; Walt Wesley, Kansas.

1967

FIRST TEAM—Lew Alcindor, UCLA, 7-2, New York, N.Y.; Elvin Hayes, Houston, 6-8, Rayville, La.; Wes Unseld, Louisville, 6-8, Louisville, Ky.; Jim Walker, Providence, 6-3, Boston, Mass.; Clem Haskins, Western Ky., 6-3, Campbellsville, Ky.; Bob Lloyd, Rutgers, 6-1, Upper Darby, Pa.; Bob Verga, Duke, 6-0, Sea Girt, N.J.
SECOND TEAM—Mel Daniels, New Mexico; Sonny Dove, St. John's (N.Y.); Larry Miller, North Caro.; Don May, Dayton; Lou Dampier, Kentucky.

1968

FIRST TEAM—Wes Unseld, Louisville, 6-8, Louisville, Ky.; Elvin Hayes, Houston, 6-8, Rayville, La.; Lew Alcindor, UCLA, 7-2, New York, N.Y.; Pete Maravich, Louisiana St., 6-5, Raleigh, N.C.; Larry Miller, North Caro., 6-4, Catasauga, Pa.
SECOND TEAM—Lucius Allen, UCLA; Bob Lanier, St. Bonaventure; Don May, Dayton; Calvin Murphy, Niagara; Jo Jo White, Kansas.

1969

FIRST TEAM—Lew Alcindor, UCLA, 7-2, New York, N.Y.; Spencer Haywood, Detroit Mercy, 6-8, Detroit, Mich.; Pete Maravich, Louisiana St., 6-5, Raleigh, N.C.; Rick Mount, Purdue, 6-4, Lebanon, Ind.; Calvin Murphy, Niagara, 5-10, Norwalk, Conn.
SECOND TEAM—Dan Issel, Kentucky; Mike Maloy, Davidson; Bud Ogden, Santa Clara; Charlie Scott, North Caro.; Jo Jo White, Kansas.

1970

FIRST TEAM—Pete Maravich, Louisiana St., 6-5, Raleigh, N.C.; Rick Mount, Purdue, 6-4, Lebanon, Ind.; Bob Lanier, St. Bonaventure, 6-11, Buffalo, N.Y.; Dan Issel, Kentucky, 6-9, Batavia, Ill.; Calvin Murphy, Niagara, 5-10, Norwalk, Conn.
SECOND TEAM—Austin Carr, Notre Dame; Jim Collins, New Mexico St.; John Roche, South Caro.; Charlie Scott, North Caro.; Sidney Wicks, UCLA.

1971

FIRST TEAM—Austin Carr, Notre Dame, 6-3, Washington, D.C.; Sidney Wicks, UCLA, 6-8, Los Angeles, Calif.; Artis Gilmore, Jacksonville, 7-2, Dothan, Ala.; Dean Meminger, Marquette, 6-1, New York, N.Y.; Jim McDaniels, Western Ky., 7-0, Scottsdale, Ky.
SECOND TEAM—John Roche, South Caro.; Johnny Neumann, Mississippi; Ken Durrett, La Salle; Howard Porter, Villanova; Curtis Rowe, UCLA.

1972

FIRST TEAM—Bill Walton, UCLA, 6-11, La Mesa, Calif.; Dwight Lamar, Southwestern La., 6-1, Columbus, Ohio; Ed Ratleff, Long Beach St., 6-6, Columbus, Ohio; Bob McAdoo, North Caro., 6-8, Greensboro, N.C.; Tom Riker, South Caro., 6-10, Oyster Bay, N.Y.; Jim Chones, Marquette, 6-11, Racine, Wis.; Henry Bibby, UCLA, 6-1, Franklinton, N.C.
SECOND TEAM—Barry Parkhill, Virginia; Jim Price, Louisville; Bud Stallworth, Kansas; Henry Willmore, Michigan; Rich Fuqua, Oral Roberts.

1973

FIRST TEAM—Doug Collins, Illinois St., 6-6, Benton, Ill.; Ed Ratleff, Long Beach St., 6-6, Columbus, Ohio; Dwight Lamar, Southwestern La., 6-1, Columbus, Ohio; Bill Walton, UCLA, 6-11, La Mesa, Calif.; Ernie DiGregorio, Providence, 6-0, North Providence, R.I.; David Thompson, North Caro. St., 6-4, Shelby, N.C.; Keith Wilkes, UCLA, 6-6, Santa Barbara, Calif.
SECOND TEAM—Jim Brewer, Minnesota; Kevin

Joyce, South Caro.; Kermit Washington, American; Tom Burleson, North Caro. St.; Larry Finch, Memphis St.; Tom McMillen, Maryland.

1974

FIRST TEAM—Keith Wilkes, UCLA, 6-6, Santa Barbara, Calif.; John Shumate, Notre Dame, 6-9, Elizabeth, N.J.; Bill Walton, UCLA, 6-11, La Mesa, Calif.; David Thompson, North Caro. St., 6-4, Shelby, N.C.; Marvin Barnes, Providence, 6-9, Providence, R.I.
SECOND TEAM—Len Elmore, Maryland; Bobby Jones, North Caro.; Bill Knight, Pittsburgh; Larry Fogle, Canisius; Campy Russell, Michigan.

1975

FIRST TEAM—David Thompson, North Caro. St., 6-4, Shelby, N.C.; Adrian Dantley, Notre Dame, 6-5, Washington, D.C.; Scott May, Indiana, 6-7, Sandusky, Ohio; John Lucas, Maryland, 6-4, Durham, N.C.; Dave Meyers, UCLA, 6-8, La Habra, Calif.
SECOND TEAM—Luther Burden, Utah; Kevin Grevey, Kentucky; Leon Douglas, Alabama; Gus Williams, Southern Cal; Ron Lee, Oregon.

1976

FIRST TEAM—Scott May, Indiana, 6-7, Sandusky, Ohio; Richard Washington, UCLA, 6-10, Portland, Ore.; John Lucas, Maryland, 6-4, Durham, N.C.; Kent Benson, Indiana, 6-11, New Castle, Ind.; Adrian Dantley, Notre Dame, 6-5, Washington, D.C.
SECOND TEAM—Mitch Kupchak, North Caro.; Phil Sellers, Rutgers; Phil Ford, North Caro.; Earl Tatum, Marquette; Bernard King, Tennessee.

1977

FIRST TEAM—Otis Birdsong, Houston, 6-4, Winter Haven, Fla.; Marques Johnson, UCLA, 6-7, Los Angeles, Calif.; Kent Benson, Indiana, 6-11, New Castle, Ind.; Rickey Green, Michigan, 6-2, Chicago, Ill.; Phil Ford, North Caro., 6-2, Rocky Mount, N.C.; Bernard King, Tennessee, 6-7, Brooklyn, N.Y.
SECOND TEAM—Phil Hubbard, Michigan; Mychal Thompson, Minnesota; Ernie Grunfield, Tennessee; Greg Ballard, Oregon; Rod Griffin, Wake Forest; Butch Lee, Marquette; Bill Cartwright, San Francisco.

1978

FIRST TEAM—Phil Ford, North Caro., 6-2, Rocky Mount, N.C.; Butch Lee, Marquette, 6-2, Bronx, N.Y.; David Greenwood, UCLA, 6-9, Los Angeles, Calif.; Mychal Thompson, Minnesota, 6-10, Nassau, Bahamas; Larry Bird, Indiana St., 6-9, French Lick, Ind.
SECOND TEAM—Jack Givens, Kentucky; Freeman Williams, Portland St.; Rick Robey, Kentucky; Ron Brewer, Arkansas; Rod Griffin, Wake Forest.

1979

FIRST TEAM—Larry Bird, Indiana St., 6-9, French Lick, Ind.; David Greenwood, UCLA, 6-9, Los Angeles, Calif.; Earvin Johnson, Michigan St., 6-8, Lansing, Mich.; Sidney Moncrief, Arkansas, 6-4, Little Rock, Ark.; Mike Gminski, Duke, 6-11, Monroe, Conn.
SECOND TEAM—Bill Cartwright, San Francisco; Calvin Natt, Northeast La.; Kelly Tripucka, Notre Dame; Mike O'Koren, North Caro.; Jim Spanarkel, Duke; Jim Paxson, Dayton; Sly Williams, Rhode Island.

1980

FIRST TEAM—Mark Aguirre, DePaul, 6-7, Chicago, Ill.; Michael Brooks, La Salle, 6-7, Philadelphia, Pa.; Joe Barry Carroll, Purdue, 7-1, Denver, Colo.; Kyle Macy, Kentucky, 6-3, Peru, Ind.; Darrell Griffith, Louisville, 6-4, Louisville, Ky.
SECOND TEAM—Albert King, Maryland; Mike Gminski, Duke; Mike O'Koren, North Caro.; Sam Worthen, Marquette; Kelvin Ransey, Ohio St.

1981

FIRST TEAM—Mark Aguirre, DePaul, 6-7, Chicago, Ill.; Danny Ainge, Brigham Young, 6-5, Eugene, Ore.; Steve Johnson, Oregon St., 6-11, San Bernardino, Calif.; Ralph Sampson, Virginia, 7-4, Harrisonburg, Va.; Isiah Thomas, Indiana, 6-1, Chicago, Ill.
SECOND TEAM—Sam Bowie, Kentucky; Jeff Lamp, Virginia; Durand Macklin, Louisiana St.; Kelly Tripucka, Notre Dame; Danny Vranes, Utah; Al Wood, North Caro.

1982

FIRST TEAM—Terry Cummings, DePaul, 6-9, Chicago, Ill.; Quintin Dailey, San Francisco, 6-4, Baltimore, Md.; Eric Floyd, Georgetown, 6-3, Gastonia, N.C.; Ralph Sampson, Virginia, 7-4, Harrisonburg, Va.; James Worthy, North Caro., 6-9, Gastonia, N.C.
SECOND TEAM—Dale Ellis, Tennessee; Kevin Magee, UC Irvine; John Paxson, Notre Dame; Sam Perkins, North Caro.; Paul Pressey, Tulsa.

1983

FIRST TEAM—Dale Ellis, Tennessee, 6-7, Marietta, Ga.; Patrick Ewing, Georgetown, 7-0, Cambridge, Mass.; Michael Jordan, North Caro., 6-6, Wilmington, N.C.; Sam Perkins, North Caro., 6-9, Latham, N.Y.; Ralph Sampson, Virginia, 7-4, Harrisonburg, Va.; Wayman Tisdale, Oklahoma, 6-9, Tulsa, Okla.; Keith Lee, Memphis St., 6-9, West Memphis, Ark.
SECOND TEAM—Clyde Drexler, Houston; John Paxson, Notre Dame; Steve Stipanovich, Missouri; Jon Sundvold, Missouri; Darrell Walker, Arkansas; Sidney Green, Nevada-Las Vegas; Randy Wittman, Indiana.

1984

FIRST TEAM—Wayman Tisdale, Oklahoma, 6-9, Tulsa, Okla.; Sam Perkins, North Caro., 6-10, Latham, N.Y.; Patrick Ewing, Georgetown, 7-0, Cambridge, Mass.; Akeem Olajuwon, Houston, 7-0, Lagos, Nigeria; Michael Jordan, North Caro., 6-5, Wilmington, N.C.
SECOND TEAM—Chris Mullin, St. John's (N.Y.); Devin Durrant, Brigham Young; Leon Wood, Cal St. Fullerton; Keith Lee, Memphis St.; Melvin Turpin, Kentucky; Michael Cage, San Diego St.

1985

FIRST TEAM—Wayman Tisdale, Oklahoma, 6-9, Tulsa, Okla.; Patrick Ewing, Georgetown, 7-0, Cambridge, Mass.; Keith Lee, Memphis St., 6-10, West Memphis, Ark.; Chris Mullin, St. John's (N.Y.), 6-6, Brooklyn, N.Y.; Xavier McDaniel, Wichita St., 6-7, Columbia, S.C.; Johnny Dawkins, Duke, 6-2, Washington, D.C.
SECOND TEAM—Kenny Walker, Kentucky; Jon Koncak, Southern Methodist; Len Bias, Maryland; Mark Price, Georgia Tech; Dwayne Washington, Syracuse.

1986

FIRST TEAM—Len Bias, Maryland, 6-8, Landover, Md.; Kenny Walker, Kentucky, 6-8, Roberta, Ga.;

Walter Berry, St. John's (N.Y.), 6-8, Bronx, N.Y.; Johnny Dawkins, Duke, 6-2, Washington, D.C.; Steve Alford, Indiana, 6-2, New Castle, Ind.
SECOND TEAM—Dell Curry, Virginia Tech; Brad Daugherty, North Caro.; Danny Manning, Kansas; Ron Harper, Miami (Ohio); Scott Skiles, Michigan St.; David Robinson, Navy.

1987

FIRST TEAM—David Robinson, Navy, 7-1, Woodbridge, Va.; Danny Manning, Kansas, 6-11, Lawrence, Kan.; Reggie Williams, Georgetown, 6-7, Baltimore, Md.; Steve Alford, Indiana, 6-2, New Castle, Ind.; Kenny Smith, North Caro., 6-3, Queens, N.Y.
SECOND TEAM—Armon Gilliam, Nevada-Las Vegas; Dennis Hopson, Ohio St.; Mark Jackson, St. John's (N.Y.); Ken Norman, Illinois; Horace Grant, Clemson.

1988

FIRST TEAM—Gary Grant, Michigan, 6-3, Canton, Ohio; Hersey Hawkins, Bradley, 6-3, Chicago, Ill.; J. R. Reid, North Caro., 6-9, Virginia Beach, Va.; Sean Elliott, Arizona, 6-8, Tucson, Ariz.; Danny Manning, Kansas, 6-11, Lawrence, Kan.
SECOND TEAM—Mark Macon, Temple; Rony Seikaly, Syracuse; Danny Ferry, Duke; Jerome Lane, Pittsburgh; Mitch Richmond, Kansas St.; Michael Smith, Brigham Young.

1989

FIRST TEAM—Sean Elliott, Arizona, 6-8, Sr., Tucson, Ariz.; Pervis Ellison, Louisville, 6-9, Sr., Savannah, Ga.; Danny Ferry, Duke, 6-10, Sr., Bowie, Md.; Chris Jackson, Louisiana St., 6-1, Fr., Gulfport, Miss.; Stacey King, Oklahoma, 6-11, Sr., Lawton, Okla.
SECOND TEAM—Mookie Blaylock, Oklahoma, 6-1, Sr.; Sherman Douglas, Syracuse, 6-0, Sr.; Jay Edwards, Indiana, 6-4, So.; Todd Lichti, Stanford, 6-4, Sr.; Glen Rice, Michigan, 6-7, Sr.; Lionel Simmons, La Salle, 6-6, Jr.

1990

FIRST TEAM—Derrick Coleman, Syracuse, 6-10, Sr., Detroit, Mich.; Chris Jackson, Louisiana St., 6-1, So., Gulfport, Miss.; Larry Johnson, Nevada-Las Vegas, 6-7, Jr., Dallas, Tex.; Gary Payton, Oregon St., 6-3, Sr., Oakland, Calif.; Lionel Simmons, La Salle, 6-6, Sr., Philadelphia, Pa.
SECOND TEAM—Hank Gathers, Loyola (Cal.), 6-7, Sr.; Kendall Gill, Illinois, 6-5, Sr.; Bo Kimble, Loyola (Cal.), 6-5, Sr.; Alonzo Mourning, Georgetown, 6-10, So.; Rumeal Robinson, Michigan, 6-2, Sr.; Dennis Scott, Georgia Tech, 6-8, Jr.; Doug Smith, Missouri, 6-10, Jr.

1991

FIRST TEAM—Kenny Anderson, Georgia Tech, 6-2, So., Rego Park, N.Y.; Jim Jackson, Ohio St., 6-6, So., Toledo, Ohio; Larry Johnson, Nevada-Las Vegas, 6-7, Sr., Dallas, Tex.; Shaquille O'Neal, Louisiana St., 7-1, So., San Antonio, Tex.; Billy Owens, Syracuse, 6-9, Jr., Carlisle, Pa.
SECOND TEAM—Stacey Augmon, Nevada-Las Vegas, 6-8, Sr.; Keith Jennings, East Tenn. St., 5-7, Sr.; Christian Laettner, Duke, 6-11, Jr.; Eric Murdock, Providence, 6-2, Sr.; Steve Smith, Michigan St., 6-6, Sr.

1992

FIRST TEAM—Jim Jackson, Ohio St., 6-6, Jr., Toledo, Ohio; Christian Laettner, Duke, 6-11, Sr., Angola, N.Y.; Harold Miner, Southern Cal, 6-5, Jr., Inglewood, Calif.; Alonzo Mourning, Georgetown, 6-10, Sr., Chesapeake, Va.; Shaquille O'Neal, Louisiana St., 7-1, Jr., San Antonio, Tex.
SECOND TEAM—Byron Houston, Oklahoma St., 6-7, Sr.; Don MacLean, UCLA, 6-10, Sr.; Anthony Peeler, Missouri, 6-4, Sr.; Malik Sealy, St. John's (N.Y.), 6-7, Sr.; Walt Williams, Maryland, 6-8, Sr.

1993

FIRST TEAM—Calbert Cheaney, Indiana, 6-7, Sr., Evansville, Ind.; Anfernee Hardaway, Memphis St., 6-7, Jr., Memphis, Tenn.; Bobby Hurley, Duke, 6-0, Sr., Jersey City, N.J.; Jamal Mashburn, Kentucky, 6-8, Jr., New York, N.Y.; Chris Webber, Michigan, 6-9, So., Detroit, Mich.
SECOND TEAM—Terry Dehere, Seton Hall, 6-3, Sr.; Grant Hill, Duke, 6-7, Jr.; Billy McCaffrey, Vanderbilt, 6-3, Jr.; Eric Montross, North Caro., 7-0, Jr.; J. R. Rider, Nevada-Las Vegas , 6-7, Sr.; Glenn Robinson, Purdue, 6-9, So.; Rodney Rogers, Wake Forest, 6-8, Jr.

Teams used for consensus selections:
Helms Foundation—1929-48
Converse Yearbook—1932-48
College Humor Magazine—1929-33, 1936
Christy Walsh Syndicate—1929-30
Literary Digest Magazine—1934
Madison Square Garden—1937-42
Omaha World Newspaper—1937
Newspaper Enterprises Assn.—1938, 1953-63
Colliers (Basketball Coaches)—1939, 1949-56
Pic Magazine—1942-44
Sporting News—1943-46
Argosy Magazine—1945
True Magazine—1946-47
International News Service—1950-58
Look Magazine—1949-63
Associated Press—1948-93
United Press International—1949-93
National Assn. of Basketball Coaches—1957-93
U.S. Basketball Writers Assn.—1960-93

DIVISION I MEN'S CONSENSUS ALL-AMERICANS BY COLLEGE

ARIZONA
88—Sean Elliott
89—Sean Elliott

ARKANSAS
36—Ike Poole
41—John Adams
79—Sidney Moncrief

BOWLING GREEN
45—Wyndol Gray

BRADLEY
50—Paul Unruh
51—Gene Melchiorre
61—Chet Walker
62—Chet Walker
88—Hersey Hawkins

BRIGHAM YOUNG
31—Elwood Romney
81—Danny Ainge

CALIFORNIA
29—Vern Corbin
60—Darrall Imhoff

CINCINNATI
58—Oscar Robertson
59—Oscar Robertson
60—Oscar Robertson
63—Ron Bonham
Tom Thacker

COLUMBIA
31—George Gregory
57—Chet Forte

CREIGHTON
43—Ed Beisser

DARTMOUTH
40—Gus Broberg
41—Gus Broberg
44—Audley Brindley

DAVIDSON
65—Fred Hetzel

DENVER
49—Vince Boryla

DEPAUL
44—George Mikan
45—George Mikan
46—George Mikan
80—Mark Aguirre
81—Mark Aguirre
82—Terry Cummings

DETROIT MERCY
69—Spencer Haywood

DUKE
52—Dick Groat
63—Art Heyman
67—Bob Verga
79—Mike Gminski
85—Johnny Dawkins
86—Johnny Dawkins
89—Danny Ferry
92—Christian Laettner
93—Bobby Hurley

DUQUESNE
55—Dick Ricketts
Si Green
56—Si Green

FURMAN
54—Frank Selvy

GEORGETOWN
82—Eric Floyd
83—Patrick Ewing
84—Patrick Ewing
85—Patrick Ewing
87—Reggie Williams
92—Alonzo Mourning

GEORGIA TECH
61—Roger Kaiser
91—Kenny Anderson

HOLY CROSS
50—Bob Cousy
56—Tom Heinsohn

HOUSTON
67—Elvin Hayes
68—Elvin Hayes
77—Otis Birdsong
84—Akeem Olajuwon

ILLINOIS
40—Bill Hapac
42—Andrew Phillip
43—Andrew Phillip
45—Walton Kirk
52—Rod Fletcher

ILLINOIS ST.
73—Doug Collins

INDIANA
30—Branch McCracken
36—Vern Huffman
39—Ernie Andres
47—Ralph Hamilton
54—Don Schlundt
75—Scott May
76—Scott May
Kent Benson
77—Kent Benson
81—Isiah Thomas
86—Steve Alford
87—Steve Alford
93—Calbert Cheaney

INDIANA ST.
78—Larry Bird
79—Larry Bird

IOWA
48—Murray Wier
52—Chuck Darling

JACKSONVILLE
71—Artis Gilmore

KANSAS
38—Fred Pralle
41—Howard Engleman
43—Charles Black
51—Clyde Lovellette
52—Clyde Lovellette
57—Wilt Chamberlain
58—Wilt Chamberlain
87—Danny Manning
88—Danny Manning

KANSAS ST.
58—Bob Boozer
59—Bob Boozer

KENTUCKY
32—Forest Sale
33—Forest Sale
35—Leroy Edwards
44—Robert Brannum
47—Ralph Beard
Alex Groza
48—Ralph Beard
49—Ralph Beard
Alex Groza
51—Bill Spivey
52—Cliff Hagan
54—Cliff Hagan
59—Johnny Cox
64—Cotton Nash
70—Dan Issel
80—Kyle Macy
86—Kenny Walker
93—Jamal Mashburn

LA SALLE
53—Tom Gola
54—Tom Gola
55—Tom Gola
80—Michael Brooks
90—Lionel Simmons

LONG BEACH ST.
72—Ed Ratleff
73—Ed Ratleff

LIU-BROOKLYN
37—Jules Bender
39—Irving Torgoff

LOUISIANA ST.
54—Bob Pettit
68—Pete Maravich
69—Pete Maravich
70—Pete Maravich
89—Chris Jackson
90—Chris Jackson
91—Shaquille O'Neal
92—Shaquille O'Neal

LOUISVILLE
57—Charlie Tyra
67—Wes Unseld
68—Wes Unseld
80—Darrell Griffith
89—Pervis Ellison

LOYOLA (ILL.)
63—Jerry Harkness

MARQUETTE
71—Dean Meminger
72—Jim Chones
78—Butch Lee

MARYLAND
32—Louis Berger
75—John Lucas
76—John Lucas
86—Len Bias

MEMPHIS ST.
83—Keith Lee
85—Keith Lee
93—Anfernee Hardaway

MIAMI (FLA.)
65— Rick Barry

MICHIGAN
65—Cazzie Russell
66—Cazzie Russell
77—Rickey Green
88—Gary Grant
93—Chris Webber

MICHIGAN ST.
79—Earvin Johnson

MINNESOTA
48—Jim McIntyre
55—Dick Garmaker
78—Mychal Thompson

MISSISSIPPI ST.
59—Bailey Howell

MONTANA ST.
29—John Thompson
30—John Thompson
Frank Ward

NAVY
33—Elliott Loughlin
87—David Robinson

NEVADA-LAS VEGAS
90—Larry Johnson
91—Larry Johnson

NEW YORK U.
46—Sid Tanenbaum
47—Sid Tanenbaum
63—Barry Kramer

NIAGARA
69—Calvin Murphy
70—Calvin Murphy

NORTH CARO.
40—George Glamack
41—George Glamack
57—Lenny Rosenbluth
68—Larry Miller
72—Bob McAdoo
77—Phil Ford
78—Phil Ford
82—James Worthy
83—Michael Jordan
Sam Perkins
84—Michael Jordan
Sam Perkins
87—Kenny Smith
88—J. R. Reid

NORTH CARO. ST.
51—Sam Ranzino
56—Ron Shavlik
73—David Thompson

74—David Thompson
75—David Thompson

NORTHWESTERN
31—Joe Reiff
33—Joe Reiff
44—Otto Graham
46—Max Norris

NOTRE DAME
32—Ed Krause
33—Ed Krause
34—Ed Krause
36—Paul Nowak
John Moir
37—Paul Nowak
John Moir
38—Paul Nowak
John Moir
44—Leo Klier
45—William Hassett
46—Leo Klier
48—Kevin O'Shea
71—Austin Carr
74—John Shumate
75—Adrian Dantley
76—Adrian Dantley

OHIO ST.
31—Wes Fesler
39—Jimmy Hull
50—Dick Schnittker
56—Robin Freeman
60—Jerry Lucas
61—Jerry Lucas
62—Jerry Lucas
64—Gary Bradds
91—Jim Jackson
92—Jim Jackson

OKLAHOMA
29—Thomas Churchill
35—Bud Browning
44—Alva Paine
47—Gerald Tucker
83—Wayman Tisdale
84—Wayman Tisdale
85—Wayman Tisdale
89—Stacey King

OKLAHOMA ST.
44—Robert Kurland
45—Robert Kurland
46—Robert Kurland

OREGON
39—Urgel Wintermute
40—John Dick

OREGON ST.
81—Steve Johnson
90—Gary Payton

PENNSYLVANIA
29—Joe Schaaf
45—Howard Dallmar
53—Ernie Beck

PITTSBURGH
29—Charley Hyatt
30—Charley Hyatt
33—Don Smith
34—Claire Cribbs
35—Claire Cribbs
58—Don Hennon

PRINCETON
64—Bill Bradley
65—Bill Bradley

PROVIDENCE
66—Jim Walker
67—Jim Walker
73—Ernie DiGregorio
74—Marvin Barnes

PURDUE
29—Charles Murphy
30—Charles Murphy
John Wooden
31—John Wooden
32—John Wooden
34—Norman Cottom
36—Bob Kessler
37—Jewell Young
38—Jewell Young
61—Terry Dischinger
62—Terry Dischinger
66—Dave Schellhase
69—Rick Mount
70—Rick Mount
80—Joe Barry Carroll

RHODE ISLAND
39—Chet Jaworski

RICE
42—Bob Kinney
43—William Closs
45—William Henry

RUTGERS
67—Bob Lloyd

ST. BONAVENTURE
60—Tom Stith
61—Tom Stith
70—Bob Lanier

ST. JOHN'S (N.Y.)
43—Harry Boykoff
85—Chris Mullin
86—Walter Berry

ST. JOSEPH'S (PA.)
43—George Senesky

ST. LOUIS
48—Ed Macauley
49—Ed Macauley

SAN FRANCISCO
55—Bill Russell
56—Bill Russell
82—Quintin Dailey

SEATTLE
53—Johnny O'Brien
58—Elgin Baylor

SETON HALL
42—Robert Davies
53—Walt Dukes

SOUTH CARO.
72—Tom Riker

SOUTHERN CAL
33—Jerry Nemer
35—Lee Guttero
40—Ralph Vaughn
50—Bill Sharman
92—Harold Miner

SOUTHERN METHODIST
57—Jim Krebs

SOUTHWESTERN LA.
72—Dwight Lamar
73—Dwight Lamar

STANFORD
36—Hank Luisetti
37—Hank Luisetti
38—Hank Luisetti

SYRACUSE
66—Dave Bing
90—Derrick Coleman
91—Billy Owens

TEMPLE
38—Meyer Bloom
51—Bill Mlkvy
58—Guy Rodgers

TENNESSEE
77—Bernard King
83—Dale Ellis

TEXAS
35—Jack Gray

UCLA
64—Walt Hazzard
65—Gail Goodrich
67—Lew Alcindor
68—Lew Alcindor
69—Lew Alcindor
71—Sidney Wicks
72—Bill Walton
Henry Bibby
73—Bill Walton
Keith Wilkes
74—Bill Walton
Keith Wilkes
75—Dave Meyers
76—Richard Washington
77—Marques Johnson
78—David Greenwood
79—David Greenwood

UTAH
36—Bill Kinner
45—Arnold Ferrin
62—Billy McGill

VANDERBILT
66—Clyde Lee

VILLANOVA
50—Paul Arizin

VIRGINIA
81—Ralph Sampson
82—Ralph Sampson
83—Ralph Sampson

WAKE FOREST
62—Len Chappell

WASHINGTON
34—Hal Lee
53—Bob Houbregs

WEST TEX. A&M
42—Price Brookfield

WEST VA.
57—Rod Hundley
59—Jerry West
60—Jerry West

WESTERN KY.
67—Clem Haskins
71—Jim McDaniels

WICHITA ST.
64—Dave Stallworth
85—Xavier McDaniel

WISCONSIN
41—Gene Englund
42—John Kotz

WYOMING
32—Les Witte
34—Les Witte
43—Ken Sailors

YALE
49—Tony Lavelli

TEAM LEADERS IN CONSENSUS ALL-AMERICANS

(Ranked on total number of selections)

Team	No.	Players	Team	No.	Players
Kentucky	18	13	Georgetown	6	4
UCLA	17	11	Pittsburgh	6	4
Notre Dame	17	9	DePaul	6	3
Purdue	15	9	Southern Cal	5	5
North Caro.	14	10	Bradley	5	4
Indiana	13	10	Illinois	5	4
Ohio St.	10	7	Louisville	5	4
Duke	9	8	Cincinnati	5	3
Kansas	9	6	La Salle	5	3
Oklahoma	8	6	Michigan	5	3
Louisiana St.	8	4	North Caro. St.	5	3

DIVISION I ACADEMIC ALL-AMERICANS BY COLLEGE

AIR FORCE
68—Cliff Parsons
70—Jim Cooper
78—Tom Schneeberger

AMERICAN
72—Kermit Washington
73—Kermit Washington
87—Patrick Witting

ARIZONA
76—Bob Elliott
77—Bob Elliott

ARIZONA ST.
64—Art Becker

ARKANSAS
78—Jim Counce

ARMY
64—Mike Silliman

BOSTON COLLEGE
68—Terry Driscoll

BRIGHAM YOUNG
80—Danny Ainge
81—Danny Ainge
83—Devin Durrant
84—Devin Durrant
87—Michael Smith
88—Michael Smith
89—Michael Smith
90—Andy Toolson

BROWN
86—Jim Turner

CALIFORNIA
87—David Butler

CENTRAL MICH.
93—Sander Scott

CINCINNATI
67—Mike Rolf

CLEVELAND ST.
73—Pat Lyons

CONNECTICUT
67—Wes Bialosuknia

CREIGHTON
64—Paul Silas
78—Rick Apke

DARTMOUTH
84—Paul Anderson

DAVIDSON
88—Derek Rucker

DAYTON
79—Jim Paxson
81—Mike Kanieski
82—Mike Kanieski

DEPAUL
91—Stephen Howard
92—Stephen Howard

DUKE
63—Jay Buckley
64—Jay Buckley
71—Dick DeVenzio
72—Gary Melchionni
75—Bob Fleischer
78—Mike Gminski
Jim Spanarkel
79—Mike Gminski
Jim Spanarkel
80—Mike Gminski

DUQUESNE
69—Bill Zopf
70—Bill Zopf

EVANSVILLE
89—Scott Haffner

FDU-TEANECK
78—John Jorgensen

FORDHAM
75—Darryl Brown

GEO. WASHINGTON
76—Pat Tallent
86—Steve Frick

GEORGIA
88—Alec Kessler
89—Alec Kessler
90—Alec Kessler

GEORGIA TECH
64—Jim Caldwell
69—Rich Yunkus
70—Rich Yunkus
71—Rich Yunkus

GONZAGA
84—Bryce McPhee
John Stockton
85—Bryce McPhee
92—Jarrod Davis
93—Jeff Brown

HARVARD
85—Joe Carrabino
87—Arne Duncan

HOLY CROSS
69—Ed Siudut
78—Ronnie Perry
79—Ronnie Perry
80—Ronnie Perry
91—Jim Nairus

ILLINOIS
68—Dave Scholz
69—Dave Scholz
71—Rich Howatt
74—Rick Schmidt
75—Rick Schmidt

ILLINOIS ST.
73—Doug Collins

INDIANA
64—Dick Van Arsdale
65—Dick Van Arsdale
65—Tom Van Arsdale
73—John Ritter
74—Steve Green
75—Steve Green
76—Kent Benson
77—Kent Benson
78—Wayne Radford
82—Randy Wittman
83—Randy Wittman
85—Uwe Blab
89—Joe Hillman

JACKSONVILLE
71—Vaughan Wedeking
83—Maurice Roulhac

KANSAS
71—Bud Stallworth
74—Tom Kivisto
77—Ken Koenigs
Chris Barnthouse
78—Ken Koenigs
79—Darnell Valentine
80—Darnell Valentine
81—Darnell Valentine
82—David Magley

KANSAS ST.
68—Earl Seyfert
82—Tim Jankovich
Ed Nealy

KENTUCKY
66—Lou Dampier
67—Lou Dampier
69—Larry Conley
70—Dan Issel
Mike Pratt

71—Mike Casey
75—Bob Guyette
Jimmy Dan Conner
79—Kyle Macy

LA SALLE
77—Tony DiLeo
88—Tim Legler
92—Jack Hurd

LEWIS
89—Jamie Martin

LOUISVILLE
76—Phil Bond

LOYOLA (CAL.)
73—Steve Smith

MARQUETTE
82—Marc Marotta
83—Marc Marotta
84—Marc Marotta

MARSHALL
72—Mike D'Antoni
73—Mike D'Antoni

MARYLAND
72—Tom McMillen
73—Tom McMillen
74—Tom McMillen
91—Matt Roe

MIAMI (OHIO)
93—Craig Michaelis

MICHIGAN
76—Steve Grote
81—Marty Bodnar

MICHIGAN ST.
70—Ralph Simpson
79—Greg Kelser

MISSISSIPPI
75—Dave Shepherd

MISSOURI
83—Steve Stipanovich

MONTANA
81—Craig Zanon
85—Larry Krystkowiak
86—Larry Krystkowiak

MURRAY ST.
85—Mike Lahm

NEBRASKA
84—John Matzke

NEVADA-LAS VEGAS
83—Danny Tarkanian
84—Danny Tarkanian

NEW MEXICO
69—Ron Becker
70—Ron Becker

NORTH CARO.
65—Billy Cunningham
70—Charlie Scott
72—Dennis Wuycik
Steve Previs
76—Tommy LaGarde
86—Steve Hale

NORTH CARO. ST.
84—Terry Gannon
85—Terry Gannon

NORTHEASTERN
77—David Caligaris
78—David Caligaris

NORTHERN ILL.
84—Tim Dillion

NORTHERN IOWA
84—Randy Kraayenbrink

NORTHWESTERN
67—Jim Burns
80—Mike Campbell
87—Shon Morris
88—Shon Morris

NOTRE DAME
67—Bob Arnzen
68—Bob Arnzen
69—Bob Arnzen
74—Gary Novak
79—Kelly Tripucka
80—Rich Branning
82—John Paxson
83—John Paxson

OHIO
71—Craig Love
77—Steve Skaggs
90—Dave Jamerson

OHIO ST.
68—Bill Hosket

OKLAHOMA
74—Alvin Adams
75—Alvin Adams
80—Terry Stotts

OKLAHOMA ST.
64—Gary Hassmann
69—Joe Smith

PACIFIC (CAL.)
67—Keith Swagerty

PENNSYLVANIA
72—Robert Morse

PRINCETON
65—Bill Bradley
91—Kit Mueller

PURDUE
65—Dave Schellhase
66—Dave Schellhase
72—Robert Ford
81—Brian Walker
82—Keith Edmonson
83—Steve Reid
85—Steve Reid

ST. FRANCIS (PA.)
90—Michael Iuzzolino
91—Michael Iuzzolino

ST. LOUIS
68—Rich Niemann

SAN DIEGO ST.
76—Steve Copp

SANTA CLARA
68—Dennis Awtrey
69—Dennis Awtrey
70—Dennis Awtrey

SIENA
85—Doug Peotzch
92—Bruce Schroeder

SOUTH CARO.
70—John Roche
71—John Roche

SOUTHERN ILL.
76—Mike Glenn
77—Mike Glenn

SOUTHERN METHODIST
77—Pete Lodwick

SYRACUSE
81—Dan Schayes

TENNESSEE
68—Bill Justus
93—Lang Wiseman

TEXAS
79—Jim Krivacs

TEXAS A&M
64—Bill Robinette

UCLA
67—Mike Warren
69—Kenny Heitz
71—Sidney Wicks
72—Bill Walton
Keith Wilkes
Greg Lee
73—Bill Walton
Keith Wilkes
Greg Lee
74—Bill Walton
Keith Wilkes
Greg Lee
75—Ralph Drollinger
77—Marques Johnson
79—Kiki Vandeweghe
80—Kiki Vandeweghe

UTAH
70—Mike Newlin
71—Mike Newlin
77—Jeff Jonas

UTAH ST.
64—Gary Watts
80—Dean Hunger
82—Larry Bergeson

VANDERBILT
75—Jeff Fosnes
76—Jeff Fosnes
93—Bruce Elder

VILLANOVA
73—Tom Inglesby
82—John Pinone
83—John Pinone
86—Harold Jensen
87—Harold Jensen

VIRGINIA
76—Wally Walker
81—Jeff Lamp
Lee Raker

VA. MILITARY
80—Andy Kolesar
81—Andy Kolesar

WASHINGTON
82—Dave Henley

WASHINGTON ST.
89—Brian Quinnett

WEBER ST.
85—Randy Worster

WICHITA ST.
67—Jamie Thompson
69—Ron Mendell

WILLIAM & MARY
85—Keith Cieplicki

WISCONSIN
74—Dan Anderson

WIS.-GREEN BAY
92—Tony Bennett

NCAA POSTGRADUATE SCHOLARSHIP WINNERS BY COLLEGE

AIR FORCE
70—James Cooper
73—Thomas Blase
74—Richard Nickelson
78—Thomas Schneeberger
92—Brent Roberts
93—Brad Boyer

ALBANY (N.Y.)
88—John Carmello

ALLEGHENY
76—Robert Del Greco

ALLENTOWN
85—George Bilicic Jr.

ALMA
76—Stuart TenHoor

AMERICAN
73—Kermit Washington

ARIZONA
88—Steve Kerr
91—Matt Muehlebach

ARIZONA ST.
65—Dennis Dairman

ARKANSAS ST.
75—J. H. Williams

ARMY
65—John Ritch III
72—Edward Mueller
73—Robert Sherwin Jr.
85—Randall Cozzens

ASSUMPTION
75—Paul Brennan
77—William Wurm

AUBURN
76—Gary Redding

AUGUSTANA (ILL.)
75—Bruce Hamming

AUGUSTANA (S.D.)
75—Neil Klutman
92—Jason Garrow

BALL ST.
89—Richard Hall

BATES
84—Herbert Taylor

BELLARMINE
92—Tom Schurfranz

BENTLEY
80—Joseph Betley

BOSTON COLLEGE
67—William Wolters
70—Thomas Veronneau
72—James Phelan
80—James Sweeney

BOWDOIN
66—Howard Pease

BOWLING GREEN
65—Robert Dwors

BRANDEIS
72—Donald Fishman
78—John Martin

BRIDGEWATER (VA.)
70—Frederick Wampler

BRIGHAM YOUNG
66—Richard Nemelka
83—Gregory Kite
84—Devin Durrant
87—Brent Stephenson
89—Michael Smith
90—Andy Toolson
91—Steve Schreiner

BROWN
72—Arnold Berman

BUTLER
77—Wayne Burris
91—John Karaffa

CALIFORNIA
87—David Butler

UC DAVIS
70—Thomas Cupps
77—Mark Ford
83—Preston Neumayr
91—Matt Cordova

UC IRVINE
75—Carl Baker

UC RIVERSIDE
75—Randy Burnett

UC SANTA BARB.
73—Robert Schachter
93—Michael Meyer

CAL POLY POMONA
78—Thomas Ispas

CAL ST. DOM. HILLS
87—John Nojima

CAL ST. STANISLAUS
83—Richard Thompson

CAL TECH
66—Alden Holford
67—James Pearson
68—James Stanley
71—Thomas Heinz

CALIF. (PA.)
84—William Belko

CALVIN
77—Mark Veenstra
93—Steve Honderd

CARLETON
69—Thomas Weaver
82—James Tolf

CARNEGIE MELLON
80—Lawrence Hufnagel

CASE RESERVE
71—Mark Estes

CATHOLIC
72—Joseph Good

CENTRAL (IOWA)
73—Dana Snoap
80—Jeffrey Verhoef

CENTRAL MICH.
93—Sander Scott

CENTRE
85—Thomas Cowens

CHAPMAN
70—Anthony Mason

CHICAGO
69—Dennis Waldon
74—Gerald Clark
85—Keith Libert

CINCINNATI
77—Gary Yoder

CLAREMONT-M-S
72—Jeffrey Naslund

CLARION
73—Joseph Sebestyen

CLEMSON
67—James Sutherland
80—Robert Conrad Jr.

COE
65—Gary Schlarbaum

COLBY
72—Matthew Zweig

COLORADO
66—Charles Gardner
85—Alex Stivrins

COLORADO MINES
91—Hank Prey

COLORADO ST.
86—Richard Strong Jr.

COLUMBIA
68—William Ames

CORNELL COLLEGE
67—David Crow
79—Robert Wisco
81—Eric Reitan
87—Jefferson Fleming

CREIGHTON
71—Dennis Bresnahan Jr.
78—Richard Apke

DARTMOUTH
68—Joseph Colgan
76—William Healey
84—Paul Anderson

DAVIDSON
69—Wayne Huckel
83—Clifford Tribus

DAYTON
79—Jim Paxson
85—Larry Schellenberg

DELAWARE
78—Brian Downie

DENISON
68—William Druckemiller Jr.
88—Kevin Locke
93—Kevin Frye

DENVER
68—Richard Callahan

DEPAUL
92—Stephen Howard

DEPAUW
69—Thomas McCormick
70—Richard Tharp
73—Gordon Pittenger
86—Phillip Wendel

DICKINSON
82—David Freysinger
87—Michael Erdos

DREW
89—Joe Novak

DUKE
75—Robert Fleischer

EMORY
93—Kevin Felner

EVANSVILLE
89—Scott Haffner

FDU-TEANECK
78—John Jorgensen
93—Kevin Conway

FLORIDA
70—Andrew Owens Jr.
73—Anthony Miller

FLA. SOUTHERN
69—Richard Lewis
79—Larry Tucker
89—Kris Kearney

GEO. WASHINGTON
76—Pat Tallent
87—Steve Frick

GEORGETOWN
68—Bruce Stinebrickner

GEORGIA
65—McCarthy Crenshaw Jr.
87—Chad Kessler
90—Alec Kessler

GONZAGA
92—Jarrod Davis

GRAMBLING
83—William Hobdy

GRINNELL
68—James Schwartz
76—John Haigh

HAMILTON
69—Brooks McCuen
78—John Klauberg

HAMLINE
89—John Banovetz

HAMPDEN-SYDNEY
83—Christopher Kelly

HARVARD
79—Glenn Fine

HAVERFORD
66—Hunter Rawlings III
67—Michael Bratman
77—Richard Voith

HIRAM
77—Edwin Niehaus

HOLY CROSS
69—Edward Siudut
77—William Doran Jr.
79—John O'Connor
80—Ronnie Perry

HOUSTON BAPTIST
85—Albert Almanza

IDAHO
67—Michael Wicks

IDAHO ST.
93—Corey Bruce

ILLINOIS
71—Rich Howat

ILLINOIS ST.
88—Jeffrey Harris

ILLINOIS TECH
69—Eric Wilson

ILL. WESLEYAN
88—Brian Coderre

INDIANA
75—Steven Green
82—Randy Wittman
85—Uwe Blab

INDIANA ST.
72—Danny Bush
81—Steven Reed

IOWA
66—Dennis Pauling
76—G. Scott Thompson
81—Steven Waite

IOWA ST.
89—Marc Urquhart

ITHACA
73—David Hollowell

JACKSONVILLE
71—Vaughn Wedeking
83—Maurice Roulhac
86—Thomas Terrell

JAMES MADISON
78—Sherman Dillard

JAMESTOWN
81—Peter Anderson

JOHNS HOPKINS
65—Robert Smith
75—Andrew Schreiber
91—Andy Enfield
92—Jay Gangemi

KALAMAZOO
65—Thomas Nicolai
73—James Van Sweden
79—David Dame
82—John Schelske

KANSAS
74—Thomas Kivisto
78—Kenneth Koenigs

KANSAS ST.
68—Earl Seyfert

KENTUCKY
75—Robert Guyette

KING'S (PA.)
81—James Shea

KNOX
65—James Jepson

LA SALLE
92—John Hurd

LAFAYETTE
72—Joseph Mottola
80—Robert Falconiero
91—Bruce Stankavage

LAKE FOREST
68—Frederick Broda

LAMAR
70—James Nicholson

LEWIS
89—James Martin

LONG BEACH ST.
90—Tyrone Mitchell

LORAS
71—Patrick Lillis
72—John Buri

LOUISVILLE
77—Phillip Bond

LOYOLA (CAL.)
73—Stephen Smith

LOYOLA (MD.)
79—John Vogt

LUTHER
68—David Mueller
74—Timothy O'Neill
82—Douglas Kintzinger
86—Scott Sawyer

MAINE
90—Dean Smith

MARQUETTE
84—Marc Marotta

MARSHALL
73—Michael D'Antoni

MARYLAND
74—Tom McMillen
81—Gregory Manning
91—Matt Roe

MASS.-LOWELL
70—Alfred Spinell Jr.

MIT
66—John Mazola
67—Robert Hardt
68—David Jansson
71—Bruce Wheeler
91—David Tomlinson

MCNEESE ST.
78—John Rudd

MIAMI (OHIO)
82—George Sweigert

MICHIGAN
81—Martin Bodnar
93—Rob Pelinka

MICHIGAN TECH
78—Michael Trewhella
81—Russell Van Duine

MIDDLEBURY
75—David Pentkowski
82—Paul Righi

MINNESOTA
70—Michael Regenfuss

MISSISSIPPI ST.
76—Richard Knarr

MISSOURI
72—Gregory Flaker

MISSOURI-ROLLA
77—Ross Klie

MO.-ST. LOUIS
77—Robert Bone

MONMOUTH (ILL.)
92—Steve Swanson

MONTANA
68—Gregory Hanson
81—Craig Zanon
86—Larry Krystkowiak
92—Daren Engellant

MONTANA ST.
88—Ray Willis Jr.

MOORHEAD ST.
80—Kevin Mulder

MORNINGSIDE
86—John Kelzenberg

MT. ST. MARY'S (MD.)
76—Richard Kidwell

MUHLENBERG
76—Glenn Salo

MUSKINGUM
74—Gary Ferber
83—Myron Dulkoski Jr.

NAVY
79—Kevin Sinnett
84—Clifford Maurer

NEBRASKA
72—Alan Nissen
86—John Matzke
87—William Jackman
91—Beau Reid

NEBRASKA-OMAHA
81—James Gregory

NEVADA-LAS VEGAS
84—Danny Tarkanian

NEW MEXICO
73—Breck Roberts

NEW YORK POLY
68—Charles Privalsky

NORTH CARO.
66—Robert Bennett Jr.
74—John O'Donnell
77—Bruce Buckley
86—Steve Hale

NORTH CARO. ST.
66—Peter Coker
85—Terrence Gannon

NORTH DAK. ST.
89—Joe Regnier

NORTHEASTERN
78—David Caligaris

NORTHERN ARIZ.
79—Troy Hudson

NORTHERN COLO.
68—Dennis Colson
90—Toby Moser

NORTHERN ILL.
84—Timothy Dillion

NORTHERN IOWA
79—Michael Kemp

NORTHWEST MO. ST.
89—Robert Sundell

NORTHWESTERN
73—Richard Sund
80—Michael Campbell
90—Walker Lambiotte

NOTRE DAME
69—Robert Arnzen
74—Gary Novak
83—John Paxson

OAKLAND
90—Brian Gregory

OBERLIN
72—Victor Guerrieri

OCCIDENTAL
73—Douglas McAdam
81—Miles Glidden

OGLETHORPE
92—David Fischer

OHIO
67—John Hamilton
68—Wayne Young
79—Steven Skaggs

OHIO ST.
68—Wilmer Hosket

OKLAHOMA
72—Scott Martin
75—Robert Pritchard
80—Terry Stotts
88—Dave Sieger

OKLAHOMA CITY
67—Gary Gray

OKLAHOMA ST.
65—Gary Hassmann
69—Joseph Smith

OLD DOMINION
75—Gray Eubank

OREGON
71—William Drozdiak
88—Keith Balderston

OREGON ST.
67—Edward Fredenburg

PACIFIC (CAL.)
67—Bruce Parsons Jr.
79—Terence Carney
86—Richard Anema
92—Delano Demps

PENNSYLVANIA
72—Robert Morse

PENN ST.
82—Michael Edelman

PITTSBURGH
76—Thomas Richards
86—Joseph David
92—Darren Morningstar

POMONA-PITZER
66—Gordon Schloming
70—Douglas Covey
86—David Di Cesaris

PORTLAND ST.
66—John Nelson

PRINCETON
69—Christopher Thomforde

PRINCIPIA
79—William Kelsey

PUGET SOUND
74—Richard Brown

PURDUE
71—George Faerber
81—Brian Walker

REDLANDS
90—Robert Stone

REGIS (COLO.)
88—John Nilles

RENSSELAER
67—Kurt Hollasch

RICHMOND
86—John Davis Jr.

RIPON
78—Ludwig Wurtz

ROLLINS
93—David Wolf

RUTGERS
85—Stephen Perry

ST. ANSELM
80—Sean Canning

ST. JOHN'S (N.Y.)
81—Frank Gilroy

ST. JOSEPH'S (IND.)
75—James Thordsen

ST. JOSEPH'S (PA.)
66—Charles McKenna

ST. LAWRENCE
69—Philip McWhorter

ST. LEO
81—Kevin McDonald

ST. LOUIS
67—John Kilo

ST. MARY'S (CAL.)
80—Calvin Wood

ST. NORBERT
87—Andris Arians

ST. OLAF
66—Eric Grimsrud
71—David Finholt

ST. THOMAS (MINN.)
67—Daniel Hansard

SAN DIEGO
78—Michael Strode

SAN DIEGO ST.
76—Steven Copp

SAN FRANCISCO
90—Joel DeBortoli

SCRANTON
74—Joseph Cantafio
84—Michael Banas
85—Daniel Polacheck
88—John Andrejko
93—Matt Cusano

SETON HALL
69—John Suminski

SEWANEE
67—Thomas Ward Jr.
76—Henry Hoffman Jr.
82—James Sherman

SIENA
92—Bruce Schroeder

SIMPSON
80—John Hines

SLIPPERY ROCK
75—Clyde Long

SOUTH DAK.
76—Rick Nissen

SOUTH DAK. ST.
73—David Thomas

SOUTH FLA.
92—Radenko Dobras

SOUTHERN CAL
74—Daniel Anderson
75—John Lambert

SOUTHERN ILL.
77—Michael Glenn

SOUTHERN METHODIST
77—Peter Lodwick

SOUTHERN UTAH
91—Peter Johnson
93—Richard Barton

SOUTHWEST MO. ST.
71—Tillman Williams

STANFORD
76—Edward Schweitzer
80—Kimberly Belton

SUSQUEHANNA
86—Donald Harnum

SWARTHMORE
65—Cavin Wright
87—Michael Dell

SYRACUSE
81—Dan Schayes

TENNESSEE
93—Lang Wiseman

TENN.-MARTIN
76—Michael Baker

TEXAS
74—Harry Larrabee
79—Jim Krivacs

TEXAS A&M
70—James Heitmann

TEXAS-ARLINGTON
80—Paul Renfor

TEXAS CHRISTIAN
70—Jeffrey Harp
81—Larry Frevert

TEX.-PAN AMERICAN
76—Jesus Guerra Jr.

TEXAS TECH
85—Brooks Jennings Jr.
86—Tobin Doda

TOLEDO
67—William Backensto
80—Timothy Selgo

TRANSYLVANIA
72—Robert Jobe Jr.
80—Lawrence Kopczyk

TRINITY (CONN.)
71—Howard Greenblatt

TRINITY (TEX.)
75—Phillip Miller

TUFTS
81—Scott Brown

UCLA
69—Kenneth Heitz
71—George Schofield
80—Kiki Vandeweghe

UTAH
68—Lyndon MacKay
71—Michael Newlin
77—Jeffrey Jonas

VANDERBILT
76—Jeffrey Fosnes

VILLANOVA
83—John Pinone

VIRGINIA
73—James Hobgood

VA. MILITARY
69—John Mitchell
71—Jan Essenburg
77—William Bynum III
81—Andrew Kolesar
87—Gay Elmore Jr.

VIRGINIA TECH
72—Robert McNeer

WABASH
76—Len Fulkerson

WAKE FOREST
69—Jerry Montgomery

WARTBURG
72—David Platte
74—Fred Waldstein
91—Dan Nettleton

WASHINGTON
70—Vincent Stone
74—Raymond Price
87—Rodney Ripley

WASHINGTON (MD.)
79—Joseph Wilson
90—Mike Keehan

WASHINGTON (MO.)
91—Jed Bargen

WASH. & JEFF.
70—Terry Evans
81—David Damico

WASH. & LEE
83—Brian Hanson
84—John Graves

WEBER ST.
80—Mark Mattos
85—Kent Hagan

WESLEYAN
73—Brad Rogers
74—Richard Fairbrother
77—Steve Malinowski
82—Steven Maizes
85—Gregory Porydzy

WESTERN CARO.
82—Gregory Dennis
87—Richard Rogers

WESTERN ILL.
84—Todd Hutcheson

WESTERN MD.
83—Douglas Pinto

WESTMINSTER (PA.)
67—John Fontanella

WHITTIER
77—Rodney Snook

WICHITA ST.
69—Ronald Mendell
91—Paul Guffrovich

WIDENER
83—Louis DeRogatis

WILLIAM & MARY
85—Keith Cieplicki

WILLIAMS
65—Edgar Coolidge III
86—Timothy Walsh

WISCONSIN
87—Rodney Ripley

WIS.-PLATTEVILLE
93—T. J. Van Wie

WIS.-STEVENS POINT
83—John Mack

WITTENBERG
84—Jay Ferguson

WRIGHT ST.
78—Alan McGee

XAVIER (OHIO)
75—Peter Accetta
81—Gary Massa

YALE
67—Richard Johnson
68—Robert McCallum Jr.

DIVISION I MEN'S PLAYER OF THE YEAR

Year	United Press International	Associated Press	U.S. Basketball Writers Assn.	Wooden Award
1955	Tom Gola La Salle			
1956	Bill Russell San Francisco			
1957	Chet Forte Columbia			
1958	Oscar Robertson Cincinnati			
1959	Oscar Robertson Cincinnati		Oscar Robertson Cincinnati	
1960	Oscar Robertson Cincinnati		Oscar Robertson Cincinnati	
1961	Jerry Lucas Ohio St.	Jerry Lucas Ohio St.	Jerry Lucas Ohio St.	
1962	Jerry Lucas Ohio St.	Jerry Lucas Ohio St.	Jerry Lucas Ohio St.	
1963	Art Heyman Duke	Art Heyman Duke	Art Heyman Duke	
1964	Gary Bradds Ohio St.	Gary Bradds Ohio St.	Walt Hazzard UCLA	
1965	Bill Bradley Princeton	Bill Bradley Princeton	Bill Bradley Princeton	
1966	Cazzie Russell Michigan	Cazzie Russell Michigan	Cazzie Russell Michigan	
1967	Lew Alcindor UCLA	Lew Alcindor UCLA	Lew Alcindor UCLA	

Year	United Press International	Associated Press	U.S. Basketball Writers Assn.	Wooden Award
1968	Elvin Hayes Houston	Elvin Hayes Houston	Elvin Hayes Houston	
1969	Lew Alcindor UCLA	Lew Alcindor UCLA	Lew Alcindor UCLA	
1970	Pete Maravich Louisiana St.	Pete Maravich Louisiana St.	Pete Maravich Louisiana St.	
1971	Austin Carr Notre Dame	Austin Carr Notre Dame	Sidney Wicks UCLA	
1972	Bill Walton UCLA	Bill Walton UCLA	Bill Walton UCLA	
1973	Bill Walton UCLA	Bill Walton UCLA	Bill Walton UCLA	
1974	Bill Walton UCLA	David Thompson North Caro. St.	Bill Walton UCLA	
1975	David Thompson North Caro. St.	David Thompson North Caro. St.	David Thompson North Caro. St.	
1976	Scott May Indiana	Scott May Indiana	Adrian Dantley Notre Dame	
1977	Marques Johnson UCLA	Marques Johnson UCLA	Marques Johnson UCLA	M. Johnson UCLA
1978	Butch Lee Marquette	Butch Lee Marquette	Phil Ford North Caro.	Phil Ford North Caro.
1979	Larry Bird Indiana St.	Larry Bird Indiana St.	Larry Bird Indiana St.	Larry Bird Indiana St.
1980	Mark Aguirre DePaul	Mark Aguirre DePaul	Mark Aguirre DePaul	Darrell Griffith Louisville
1981	Ralph Sampson Virginia	Ralph Sampson Virginia	Ralph Sampson Virginia	Danny Ainge Brigham Young
1982	Ralph Sampson Virginia	Ralph Sampson Virginia	Ralph Sampson Virginia	Ralph Sampson Virginia
1983	Ralph Sampson Virginia	Ralph Sampson Virginia	Ralph Sampson Virginia	Ralph Sampson Virginia
1984	Michael Jordan North Caro.	Michael Jordan North Caro.	Michael Jordan North Caro.	Michael Jordan North Caro.
1985	Chris Mullin St. John's (N.Y.)	Patrick Ewing Georgetown	Chris Mullin St. John's (N.Y.)	Chris Mullin St. John's (N.Y.)
1986	Walter Berry St. John's (N.Y.)	Walter Berry St. John's (N.Y.)	Walter Berry St. John's (N.Y.)	Walter Berry St. John's (N.Y.)
1987	David Robinson Navy	David Robinson Navy	David Robinson Navy	David Robinson Navy
1988	Hersey Hawkins Bradley	Hersey Hawkins Bradley	Hersey Hawkins Bradley	Danny Manning Kansas
1989	Danny Ferry Duke	Sean Elliott Arizona	Danny Ferry Duke	Sean Elliott Arizona
1990	Lionel Simmons La Salle	Lionel Simmons La Salle	Lionel Simmons La Salle	Lionel Simmons La Salle
1991	Shaquille O'Neal Louisiana St.	Shaquille O'Neal Louisiana St.	Larry Johnson Nevada-Las Vegas	Larry Johnson Nevada-Las Vegas
1992	Jim Jackson Ohio St.	Christian Laettner Duke	Christian Laettner Duke	Christian Laettner Duke
1993	Calbert Cheaney Indiana	Calbert Cheaney Indiana	Calbert Cheaney Indiana	Calbert Cheaney Indiana

Year	Nat'l Assn. of Basketball Coaches	Naismith Award	Frances Pomeroy Naismith Award
1969		Lew Alcindor UCLA	Billy Keller Purdue
1970		Pete Maravich Louisiana St.	John Rinka Kenyon
1971		Austin Carr Notre Dame	Charlie Johnson California
1972		Bill Walton UCLA	Scott Martin Oklahoma
1973		Bill Walton UCLA	Bobby Sherwin Army
1974		Bill Walton UCLA	Mike Robinson Michigan St.
1975	David Thompson North Caro. St.	David Thompson North Caro. St.	Monty Towe North Caro. St.
1976	Scott May Indiana	Scott May Indiana	Frank Alagia St. John's (N.Y.)

Year	Nat'l Assn. of Basketball Coaches	Naismith Award	Frances Pomeroy Naismith Award
1977	Marques Johnson UCLA	Marques Johnson UCLA	Jeff Jonas Utah
1978	Phil Ford North Caro.	Butch Lee Marquette	Mike Schib Susquehanna
1979	Larry Bird Indiana St.	Larry Bird Indiana St.	Alton Byrd Columbia
1980	Michael Brooks La Salle	Mark Aguirre DePaul	Jim Sweeney Boston College
1981	Danny Ainge Brigham Young	Ralph Sampson Virginia	Terry Adolph West Tex. A&M
1982	Ralph Sampson Virginia	Ralph Sampson Virginia	Jack Moore Nebraska
1983	Ralph Sampson Virginia	Ralph Sampson Virginia	Ray McCallum Ball St.
1984	Michael Jordan North Caro.	Michael Jordan North Caro.	Ricky Stokes Virginia
1985	Patrick Ewing Georgetown	Patrick Ewing Georgetown	Bubba Jennings Texas Tech
1986	Walter Berry St. John's (N.Y.)	Johnny Dawkins Duke	Jim Les Bradley
1987	David Robinson Navy	David Robinson Navy	Tyrone Bogues Wake Forest
1988	Danny Manning Kansas	Danny Manning Kansas	Jerry Johnson Fla. Southern
1989	Sean Elliott Arizona	Danny Ferry Duke	Tim Hardaway UTEP
1990	Lionel Simmons La Salle	Lionel Simmons La Salle	Boo Harvey St. John's (N.Y.)
1991	Larry Johnson Nevada-Las Vegas	Larry Johnson Nevada-Las Vegas	Keith Jennings East Tenn. St.
1992	Christian Laettner Duke	Christian Laettner Duke	Tony Bennett Wis.-Green Bay
1993	Calbert Cheaney Indiana	Calbert Cheaney Indiana	Sam Crawford New Mexico St.

DIVISIONS II AND III MEN'S FIRST-TEAM ALL-AMERICANS BY COLLEGE

Current Division I member denoted by (*). Non-NCAA member denoted by (†).

ABILENE CHRISTIAN
68—John Godfrey

AKRON*
67—Bill Turner
72—Len Paul

ALA.-HUNTSVILLE
78—Tony Vann

ALAS. ANCHORAGE
87—Jesse Jackson
87—Hansi Gnad
89—Michael Johnson
90—Todd Fisher

ALBANY ST. (GA.)
75—Major Jones

ALCORN ST.*
76—John McGill

AMERICAN*
60—Willie Jones

AMERICAN INT'L
69—Greg Hill
70—Greg Hill

AMHERST
70—Dave Auten
71—James Rehnquist

ARKANSAS ST.*
65—Jerry Rook

ARMSTRONG ST.
75—Ike Williams

ASSUMPTION
70—Jake Jones
71—Jake Jones
73—Mike Boylan
74—John Grochowalski
75—John Grochowalski
76—Bill Wurm

AUGUSTANA (ILL.)
73—John Laing

BABSON
92—Jim Pierrakos

BENTLEY
74—Brian Hammel
75—Brian Hammel

BISHOP
83—Shannon Lilly

BRIDGEPORT
69—Gary Baum
76—Lee Hollerbach
85—Manute Bol
91—Lambert Shell
92—Lambert Shell

BRYANT
81—Ernie DeWitt

CALIF. (PA.)
93—Ray Gutierrez

UC RIVERSIDE
89—Maurice Pullum

CALVIN
93—Steve Honderd

CAMERON
74—Jerry Davenport

CARLETON
93—Gerrick Monroe

CENTENARY*
57—Milt Williams

CENTRAL CONN. ST.*
69—Howie Dickenman

CENTRAL FLA.*
79—Bo Clark
80—Bo Clark

CENTRAL MO. ST.
81—Bill Fennelly
85—Ron Nunnelly
91—Armando Becker

CENTRAL OKLA.
93—Alex Wright

CENTRAL WASHINGTON
67—Mel Cox

CHEYNEY
79—Andrew Fields
81—George Melton
82—George Melton

CHRIS. NEWPORT
91—Lamont Strothers

CLAREMONT-M-S
92—Chris Greene

CLARK (MASS.)
80—Kevin Clark
81—Kevin Clark
88—Kermit Sharp

COLBY
77—Paul Harvey
78—Paul Harvey
89—Matt Hancock
90—Matt Hancock

DAVID LIPSCOMB†
88—Phillip Hutcheson
89—Phillip Hutcheson
90—Phillip Hutcheson
92—John Pierce

DAVIS & ELKINS
59—Paul Wilcox

DELTA ST.
69—Sammy Little

DEPAUW
87—David Galle

DIST. COLUMBIA
82—Earl Jones
83—Earl Jones
Michael Britt
84—Earl Jones

EASTERN MICH.*
71—Ken McIntosh
72—George Gervin

EMORY
90—Tim Garrett

EVANSVILLE*
59—Hugh Ahlering
60—Ed Smallwood
65—Jerry Sloan
Larry Humes
66—Larry Humes

FLA. SOUTHERN
81—John Ebeling
82—John Ebeling
88—Jerry Johnson
Kris Kearney
89—Kris Kearney
90—Donolly Tyrell

FRAMINGHAM ST.
84—Mark Van Valkenburg

FRANK. & MARSH.
92—Will Lasky

GANNON
85—Butch Warner

GEORGETOWN (KY.)†
64—Cecil Tuttle

GRAMBLING*
61—Charles Hardnett
62—Charles Hardnett
64—Willis Reed
66—Johnny Comeaux
76—Larry Wright

GRAND CANYON
76—Bayard Forest

GUILFORD
68—Bob Kauffman
75—Lloyd Free

HAMILTON
77—Cedric Oliver
78—Cedric Oliver
79—Cedric Oliver
87—John Cavanaugh

HAMPDEN-SYDNEY
92—Russell Turner

HARTFORD*
79—Mark Noon

HARTWICK
77—Dana Gahres
83—Tim O'Brien

HAVERFORD
77—Dick Vioth

HOPE
84—Chip Henry

ILLINOIS ST.*
68—Jerry McGreal

ILL. WESLEYAN
77—Jack Sikma
89—Jeff Kuehl

INDIANA ST.*
68—Jerry Newsome

JACKSON ST.*
74—Eugene Short
75—Eugene Short
77—Purvis Short

JACKSONVILLE*
62—Roger Strickland
63—Roger Strickland

JERSEY CITY ST.
79—Brett Wyatt

KEAN
93—Fred Drains

KENTUCKY ST.
71—Travis Grant
Elmore Smith
72—Travis Grant
75—Gerald Cunningham
77—Gerald Cunningham

KY. WESLEYAN
57—Mason Cope
67—Sam Smith
68—Dallas Thornton
69—George Tinsley
84—Rod Drake
Dwight Higgs
88—J. B. Brown
90—Corey Crowder
91—Corey Crowder

KENYON
69—John Rinka
70—John Rinka
79—Scott Rogers
80—Scott Rogers

LEWIS & CLARK†
63—Jim Boutin
64—Jim Boutin

LINCOLN (MO.)
78—Harold Robertson

LIU-BROOKLYN*
68—Luther Green
Larry Newbold

LONGWOOD
84—Jerome Kersey

LOUISIANA COLLEGE†
79—Paul Poe

LOUISIANA TECH*
73—Mike Green

MAINE*
61—Tom Chappelle

MASS.-DARTMOUTH
93—Steve Haynes

MASS.-LOWELL
89—Leo Parent

MERCHANT MARINE
90—Kevin D'Arcy

MERRIMACK
77—Ed Murphy
78—Ed Murphy
Dana Skinner
83—Joe Dickson

MO.-ST. LOUIS
77—Bob Bone

MORGAN ST.
74—Marvin Webster
75—Marvin Webster

MT. ST. MARY'S (MD.)*
57—Jack Sullivan

MUSKINGUM
92—Andy Moore

NEB. WESLEYAN
86—Dana Janssen

NEBRASKA-OMAHA
92—Phil Cartwright

NEW HAVEN
88—Herb Watkins

NEW ORLEANS*
71—Xavier Webster

NEW YORK TECH
80—Kelvin Hicks

NICHOLLS ST.*
78—Larry Wilson

NORFOLK ST.
79—Ken Evans
84—David Pope
87—Ralph Talley

NORTH ALA.
80—Otis Boddie

NORTH DAK.
66—Phil Jackson
67—Phil Jackson
91—Dave Vonesh
93—Scott Guldseth

NORTH DAK. ST.
60—Marvin Bachmeier

NORTH PARK
79—Mike Harper
80—Mike Harper
81—Mike Thomas

NORTHERN MICH.
87—Bill Harris

NORTHWOOD
73—Fred Smile

OHIO NORTHERN
82—Stan Mories

OHIO WESLEYAN
87—Scott Tedder
88—Scott Tedder

OKLAHOMA CITY†
92—Eric Manuel

OLD DOMINION*
72—Dave Twardzik
74—Joel Copeland
76—Wilson Washington

OTTERBEIN
66—Don Carlos
82—Ron Stewart
83—Ron Stewart
85—Dick Hempy
86—Dick Hempy

87—Dick Hempy
91—James Bradley

PACIFIC LUTHERAN†
59—Chuck Curtis

PFEIFFER
92—Tony Smith

PHILA. TEXTILE
76—Emory Sammons
77—Emory Sammons

POTSDAM ST.
80—Derrick Rowland
81—Derrick Rowland
82—Maurice Woods
83—Leroy Witherspoon
84—Leroy Witherspoon
86—Roosevelt Bullock
86—Brendan Mitchell
87—Brendan Mitchell
88—Steve Babiarz
89—Steve Babiarz

PRAIRIE VIEW*
62—Zelmo Beaty

PUGET SOUND
79—Joe Leonard

RANDOLPH-MACON
83—Bryan Vacca

ROANOKE
72—Hal Johnston
73—Jay Piccola
74—Jay Piccola
83—Gerald Holmes
84—Reggie Thomas
85—Reggie Thomas

ROCHESTER
91—Chris Fite
92—Chris Fite

SACRED HEART
72—Ed Czernota
78—Hector Olivencia
Andre Means
82—Keith Bennett
83—Keith Bennett
86—Roger Younger
93—Darrin Robinson

ST. CLOUD ST.
57—Vern Baggenstoss
86—Kevin Catron

ST. JOSEPH'S (IND.)
60—Bobby Williams

ST. MICHAEL'S
65—Richie Tarrant

ST. NORBERT
63—Mike Wisneski

SALEM (W. VA.)†
76—Archie Talley

SALISBURY ST.
91—Andre Foreman
92—Andre Foreman

SAM HOUSTON ST.
73—James Lister

SCRANTON
63—Bill Witaconis
77—Irvin Johnson
78—Irvin Johnson
84—Bill Bessoir
85—Bill Bessoir
93—Matt Cusano

SLIPPERY ROCK
91—Myron Brown

SOUTH DAK.
58—Jim Daniels

SOUTH DAK. ST.
61—Don Jacobsen
64—Tom Black

SE OKLAHOMA†
57—Jim Spivey

SOUTHERN ILL.*
66—George McNeil
67—Walt Frazier

SOUTHWEST TEX. ST.*
59—Charles Sharp
60—Charles Sharp

SOUTHWESTERN LA.*
65—Dean Church
70—Marvin Winkler
71—Dwight Lamar

SPRINGFIELD
70—Dennis Clark
86—Ivan Olivares

STEPHEN F. AUSTIN*
70—Surry Oliver

STETSON*
70—Ernie Killum

STEUBENVILLE†
58—Jim Smith

STONEHILL
79—Bill Zolga
80—Bill Zolga
82—Bob Reitz

STONY BROOK
79—Earl Keith

SUSQUEHANNA
86—Dan Harnum

TAMPA
85—Todd Linder
86—Todd Linder
87—Todd Linder

TENN.-CHATT.*
77—Wayne Golden

TENNESSEE ST.*
58—Dick Barnett
59—Dick Barnett
71—Ted McClain
72—Lloyd Neal
74—Leonard Robinson

TEX.-PAN AMERICAN*
64—Lucious Jackson
68—Otto Moore

TEXAS SOUTHERN*
58—Bennie Swain
77—Alonzo Bradley

TRENTON ST.
88—Greg Grant
89—Greg Grant

TRINITY (TEX.)
68—Larry Jeffries
69—Larry Jeffries

TROY ST.*
93—Terry McCord

UPSALA
81—Steve Keenan
82—Steve Keenan

VIRGINIA UNION
85—Charles Oakley
90—A. J. English

WABASH
82—Pete Metzelaars

WASH. & LEE
78—Pat Dennis

WEST GA.
74—Clarence Walker

WESTERN CARO.*
68—Henry Logan

WESTMINSTER (PA.)†
62—Ron Galbreath

WESTMINSTER (UTAH)†
69—Ken Hall

WHEATON (ILL.)
58—Mel Peterson

WIDENER
78—Dennis James
88—Lou Stevens

WILLIAMS
61—Bob Mahland
62—Bob Mahland

WINSTON-SALEM
67—Earl Monroe
80—Reginald Gaines

WIS.-EAU CLAIRE
72—Mike Ratliff

WIS.-GREEN BAY*
78—Tom Anderson
79—Ron Ripley

WIS.-PARKSIDE
76—Gary Cole

WIS.-PLATTEVILLE
92—T. J. Van Wie

WIS.-STEVENS POINT
85—Terry Porter

WIS.-WHITEWATER
90—Ricky Spicer

WITTENBERG
61—George Fisher
63—Al Thrasher
80—Brian Agler
81—Tyrone Curtis
85—Tim Casey
89—Steve Allison
90—Brad Baldridge
91—Brad Baldridge

WRIGHT ST.
81—Rodney Benson
86—Mark Vest

XAVIER (LA.)†
73—Bruce Seals

YOUNGSTOWN ST.*
77—Jeff Covington
78—Jeff Covington

Teams used for selections:
AP Little All-America—1957-79
NABC College Division—1967-76
NABC Division II, III—1977-93

DIVISIONS II AND III ACADEMIC ALL-AMERICANS BY COLLEGE

AKRON
72—Wil Schwarzinger

ALBION
79—John Nibert

ALBANY (N.Y.)
88—John Carmello

ARKANSAS TECH
90—Gray Townsend

ASHLAND
67—Jim Basista
70—Jay Franson

ASSUMPTION
67—George Ridick

AUGUSTANA (ILL.)
73—Bruce Hamming
74—Bruce Hamming
75—Bruce Hamming
79—Glen Heiden

AUGUSTANA (S.D.)
74—John Ritterbusch
75—John Ritterbusch

BALDWIN-WALLACE
85—Bob Scelza

BARRINGTON
82—Shawn Smith

BATES
83—Herb Taylor
84—Herb Taylor

BEMIDJI ST.
76—Steve Vogel
77—Steve Vogel
78—Steve Vogel

BENTLEY
80—Joe Betley

BLOOMSBURG
78—Steve Bright

BRANDEIS
78—John Martin

BRIAR CLIFF
89—Chad Neubrand

BRIDGEWATER (VA.)
85—Sean O'Connell

BRYAN
81—Dean Ropp

CAL LUTHERAN
83—Bill Burgess

CALIF. (PA.)
93—Raymond Guttierez

UC DAVIS
70—Tom Cupps
83—Preston Neumayr

UC RIVERSIDE
71—Kirby Gordon

CALVIN
92—Steve Honderd
93—Steve Honderd

CAPITAL
73—Charles Gashill

CARNEGIE MELLON
73—Mike Wegener
79—Larry Hufnagel
80—Larry Hufnagel

CASTLETON ST.
85—Bryan DeLoatch

CENTRAL FLA.
82—Jimmie Farrell

CENTRAL MICH.
67—John Berends
71—Mike Hackett

CENTRAL ST. (OHIO)
71—Sterling Quant

CHADRON ST.
92—Josh Robinson

COAST GUARD
71—Ken Bicknell

COLORADO MINES
91—Daniel McKeon
Hank Prey

CORNELL COLLEGE
74—Randy Kuhlman
77—Dick Grant
78—Robert Wisco
79—Robert Wisco
87—Jeff Fleming

DAVID LIPSCOMB
89—Phil Hutcheson
90—Phil Hutcheson
92—Jerry Meyer

DELTA ST.
72—Larry MaGee

DENISON
67—Bill Druckemiller
70—Charles Claggett
87—Kevin Locke
88—Kevin Locke

DENVER
87—Joe Fisher

DEPAUW
70—Richard Tharp
73—Gordon Pittenger
87—David Galle

DICKINSON
71—Lloyd Bonner
81—David Freysinger
82—David Freysinger

DREXEL
67—Joe Hertrich

ELON
88—Brian Branson
88—Steve Page

FORT HAYS ST.
78—Mike Pauls

GETTYSBURG
75—Jeffrey Clark

GRINNELL
76—John Haigh

GROVE CITY
79—Mike Donahoe
84—Curt Silverling
85—Curt Silverling

GUST. ADOLPHUS
83—Mark Hanson

HAMILTON
78—John Klauberg

HAMLINE
86—Paul Westling
89—John Banovetz

HAMPDEN-SYDNEY
92—Russell Turner

HARDING
85—Kenneth Collins
86—Kenneth Collins

HOWARD PAYNE
73—Garland Bullock
74—Garland Bullock

ILL. WESLEYAN
72—Dean Gravlin
73—Dean Gravlin
75—Jack Sikma
Bob Spear
76—Jack Sikma
Bob Spear
77—Jack Sikma
Bob Spear
79—Al Black
81—Greg Yess
82—Greg Yess
87—Brian Coderre

INCARNATE WORD
93—Randy Henderson

JAMES MADISON
76—Sherman Dillard

JAMESTOWN
80—Pete Anderson
81—Pete Anderson

JOHNS HOPKINS
91—Andy Enfield

KENYON
70—John Rinka
77—Tim Appleton
85—Chris Coe Russell

LAGRANGE
80—Todd Whitsitt

LIBERTY
80—Karl Hess

LIU-C. W. POST
73—Ed Fields

LUTHER
81—Doug Kintzinger
82—Doug Kintzinger

MACMURRAY
70—Tom Peters

MANHATTAN
90—Peter Runge

MARIETTA
82—Rick Clark
83—Rick Clark

MASS.-LOWELL
70—Alfred Spinell
84—John Paganetti

MCGILL
83—Willie Hinz

MCNEESE ST.
72—David Wallace

MERRIMACK
83—Joseph Dickson
84—Joseph Dickson

MICHIGAN TECH
81—Russ VanDuine
85—Wayne Helmila

MILLIKIN
77—Roy Mosser
Dale Wills
78—Gregg Finigan
79—Rich Rames

Gary Jackson
80—Gary Jackson
81—Gary Jackson
89—Brian Horst

MILWAUKEE SCHOOL OF ENGINEERING
83—Jeffrey Brezovar

MISSOURI-ROLLA
84—Todd Wentz

MO.-ST. LOUIS
75—Bobby Bone
76—Bobby Bone
77—Bobby Bone

MIT
80—Ray Nagem
91—David Tomlinson

MONMOUTH (ILL.)
90—S. Juan Mitchell

MOUNT UNION
71—Jim Howell

MUHLENBERG
79—Greg Campisi
81—Dan Barletta

NEB.-KEARNEY
74—Tom Kropp
75—Tom Kropp

NEBRASKA-OMAHA
81—Jim Gregory

NEB. WESLEYAN
84—Kevin Cook
86—Kevin Cook

N.C.-ASHEVILLE
74—Randy Pallas

NORTHEAST MO. ST.
84—Mark Campbell

NORTHERN COLO.
67—Dennis Colson

OBERLIN
71—Vic Guerrieri
72—Vic Guerrieri

OHIO WESLEYAN
90—Mark Slayman

OLD DOMINION
74—Gray Eubank
75—Gray Eubank

OTTERBEIN
80—Mike Cochran

PACIFIC LUTHERAN
67—Doug Leeland

POINT PARK
86—Richard Condo

ROCHESTER
84—Joe Augustine

ROCKFORD
76—John Morrissey
77—John Morrissey

ST. JOSEPH'S (IND.)
75—James Thordsen

ST. LEO
77—Ralph Nelson

ST. THOMAS (FLA.)
76—Arthur Collins
77—Mike LaPrete

ST. THOMAS (MINN.)
67—Dan Hansard
78—Terry Fleming

SCRANTON
83—Michael Banas
84—Michael Banas
85—Dan Polacheck
93—Matt Cusano

SHIPPENSBURG
79—John Whitmer
81—Brian Cozzens
82—Brian Cozzens

SLIPPERY ROCK
71—Robert Wiegand
79—Mike Hardy
83—John Samsa

SOUTH DAK.
70—Bill Hamer
75—Rick Nissen
76—Rick Nissen
78—Jeff Nannen
80—Jeff Nannen
85—Rob Swanhorst

SOUTH DAK. ST.
71—Jim Higgins
72—Jim Higgins

SOUTHERN COLO.
72—Jim Von Loh

SUSQUEHANNA
86—Donald Harnum

TENNESSEE TEMPLE
77—Dan Smith
78—Dan Smith

UNION (N.Y.)
70—Jim Tedisco

VIRGINIA TECH
68—Ted Ware

WABASH
73—Joe Haklin

WARTBURG
71—Dave Platte
72—Dave Platte
74—Fred Waldstein
90—Dan Nettleton
91—Dan Nettleton

WASHINGTON (MO.)
88—Paul Jackson

WASH. & JEFF.
80—David Damico

WESLEYAN
72—James Akin
74—Rich Fairbrother
82—Steven Maizes

WESTERN MD.
83—Douglas Pinto
85—David Malin

WESTERN ST. (COLO.)
70—Michael Adams
73—Rod Smith

WESTMINSTER (PA.)
67—John Fontanella

WIS.-EAU CLAIRE
72—Steven Johnson
75—Ken Kaiser
76—Ken Kaiser

WIS.-GREEN BAY
74—Tom Jones

WIS.-PLATTEVILLE
92—T. J. Van Wie
93—T. J. Van Wie

WITTENBERG
67—Jim Appleby

COACHES' RECORDS

Roy Williams (left) and Dean Smith rank first and second, respectively, in winning percentage among active Division I coaches. In five seasons at Kansas, Williams has won 78.1 percent of his games. Smith has amassed 774 wins in 32 years at North Carolina for a winning percentage of .776. Williams was Smith's assistant for 10 years before taking over at Kansas.

WINNINGEST ACTIVE 1993-94 DIVISION I MEN'S COACHES

BY PERCENTAGE

(Minimum five years as a Division I head coach; includes record at four-year colleges only.)

	Coach, College	Yrs.	Won	Lost	Pct.
1.	Roy Williams, Kansas	5	132	37	.781
2.	Dean Smith, North Caro.	32	774	223	.776
3.	Jim Boeheim, Syracuse	17	411	133	.756
4.	John Chaney, Temple	21	478	156	.754
5.	Bob Knight, Indiana	28	619	214	.743
6.	Nolan Richardson, Arkansas	13	308	109	.739
7.	Ralph Underhill, Wright St.	15	317	114	.735
8.	John Thompson, Georgetown	21	484	178	.731
9.	Denny Crum, Louisville	22	518	192	.730
10.	Pete Gillen, Xavier (Ohio)	8	180	67	.729
11.	Steve Fisher, Michigan	5	99	37	.728
12.	Eddie Sutton, Oklahoma St.	23	502	189	.726
13.	Lute Olson, Arizona	20	429	173	.713
14.	Bob Huggins, Cincinnati	12	262	108	.708
15.	Rick Majerus, Utah	9	181	76	.704
16.	Speedy Morris, La Salle	7	153	65	.702
17.	Don Haskins, UTEP	32	627	276	.694
18.	Pat Foster, Nevada	13	276	122	.693
19.	Billy Tubbs, Oklahoma	19	424	189	.692
20.	Mike Krzyzewski, Duke	18	394	177	.690
21.	Lefty Driesell, James Madison	31	621	279	.690
22.	Tom Asbury, Pepperdine	5	106	48	.688
23.	Ben Jobe, Southern-B.R.	22	422	193	.686
24.	Rick Pitino, Kentucky	11	228	105	.685
25.	Gale Catlett, West Va.	21	429	201	.681
26.	Charlie Spoonhour, St. Louis	10	209	98	.681
27.	Neil McCarthy, New Mexico St.	18	370	179	.674
28.	Lou Henson, Illinois	31	609	295	.674
29.	Gene Keady, Purdue	15	306	149	.673
30.	Norm Stewart, Missouri	32	612	306	.667
31.	Mack McCarthy, Tenn.-Chatt.	8	162	81	.667
32.	Jim Harrick, UCLA	14	283	143	.664
33.	Pat Kennedy, Florida St.	13	268	136	.663
34.	Joey Meyer, DePaul	9	184	94	.662
35.	Paul Evans, Pittsburgh	20	379	194	.661
36.	Tim Floyd, New Orleans	7	142	73	.660
37.	James Phelan, Mt. St. Mary's (Md.)	39	706	365	.659
38.	Tom Davis, Iowa	22	426	222	.657
39.	Pete Carril, Princeton	27	469	248	.654
40.	Gene Bartow, Ala.-Birmingham	31	595	315	.654
41.	Butch van Breda Kolff, Hofstra	27	473	252	.652
42.	Mike Jarvis, Geo. Washington	8	157	84	.651
43.	Frank Kerns, Ga. Southern	20	366	196	.651
44.	Bill Frieder, Arizona St.	13	260	140	.650
45.	Bob Hallberg, Ill.-Chicago	22	436	.237	.648
46.	Mike Vining, Northeast La.	12	230	126	.646
47.	Dick Bennett, Wis.-Green Bay	17	312	173	.643
48.	Larry Finch, Memphis St.	7	145	81	.642
49.	James Oliver, Alabama St.	18	330	185	.641
50.	Eddie Fogler, South Caro.	7	142	80	.640
51.	John Calipari, Massachusetts	5	101	57	.639
52.	Hugh Durham, Georgia	27	495	284	.635
53.	Mike Deane, Siena	9	165	95	.635
54.	Dale Brown, Louisiana St.	21	403	233	.634
55.	Bobby Dye, Boise St.	19	339	198	.631
56.	Jim Calhoun, Connecticut	21	381	223	.631
57.	Jim Crews, Evansville	8	148	87	.630
58.	Cliff Ellis, Clemson	18	332	197	.628
59.	Mike Montgomery, Stanford	15	279	168	.624
60.	Bobby Cremins, Georgia Tech	18	340	205	.624
61.	Jerry Pimm, UC Santa Barb.	19	339	208	.620
62.	Tom Green, FDU-Teaneck	10	182	112	.619
63.	Paul Westhead, George Mason	14	247	153	.618
64.	Bill Foster, Virginia Tech	26	451	283	.614
65.	Stew Morrill, Colorado St.	7	128	81	.612

	Coach, College	Yrs.	Won	Lost	Pct.
66.	Rollie Massimino, Nevada-Las Vegas	22	410	265	.607
67.	Nelson Catalina, Arkansas St.	9	165	107	.607
68.	Bill Hodges, Mercer	11	201	133	.602
69.	Charles Woollum, Bucknell	18	308	204	.602
70.	Benny Dees, Western Caro.	10	171	114	.600

(Coaches with less than five years as a Division I head coach; includes record at four-year colleges only.)

	Coach, College	Yrs.	Won	Lost	Pct.
1.	John Kresse, Charleston	14	340	95	.782
2.	Dan Peters, Youngstown St.	7	160	53	.751
3.	Jerry Welsh, Iona	24	485	168	.743
4.	Larry Hunter, Ohio	17	365	127	.742
5.	Ron Shumate, Southeast Mo. St.	19	402	164	.710
6.	Ron Abegglen, Weber St.	7	145	66	.687
7.	Mark Adams, Tex.-Pan American	10	210	99	.680
8.	Don Maestri, Troy St.	11	210	107	.662
9.	Kevin Bannon, Rider	11	204	106	.658
10.	Darrel Johnson, Baylor	8	167	90	.650
11.	Jim Wooldridge, Southwest Tex. St.	8	151	82	.648
12.	Alan LeForce, East Tenn. St.	12	201	112	.642
13.	Ron Bradley, Radford	7	131	76	.633
14.	John Beilein, Canisius	11	193	118	.621
15.	Kevin Eastman, N.C.-Wilmington	6	106	65	.620

BY VICTORIES

(Minimum five years as a Division I head coach; includes record at four-year colleges only.)

	Coach, College	Wins
1.	Dean Smith, North Caro.	774
2.	James Phelan, Mt. St. Mary's (Md.)	706
3.	Don Haskins, UTEP	627
4.	Lefty Driesell, James Madison	621
5.	Bob Knight, Indiana	619
6.	Norm Stewart, Missouri	612
7.	Lou Henson, Illinois	609
8.	Gene Bartow, Ala.-Birmingham	595
9.	Gary Colson, Fresno St.	529
10.	Denny Crum, Louisville	518
11.	Eldon Miller, Northern Iowa	504
12.	Eddie Sutton, Oklahoma St.	502
13.	Hugh Durham, Georgia	495
14.	John Thompson, Georgetown	484
15.	John Chaney, Temple	478
16.	Butch van Breda Kolff, Hofstra	473
17.	Pete Carril, Princeton	469
18.	Johnny Orr, Iowa St.	452
19.	Bill Foster, Virginia Tech	451
20.	Calvin C. Luther, Tenn.-Martin	443
21.	Bob Hallberg, Ill.-Chicago	436
22.	Lute Olson, Arizona	429
23.	Gale Catlett, West Va.	429
24.	Tom Davis, Iowa	426
25.	Billy Tubbs, Oklahoma	424
26.	Ben Jobe, Southern-B.R.	422
27.	Jim Boeheim, Syracuse	411
28.	Rollie Massimino, Nevada-Las Vegas	410
29.	George Blaney, Holy Cross	407
30.	Dale Brown, Louisiana St.	403
31.	Mike Krzyzewski, Duke	394
32.	Jim Calhoun, Connecticut	381
33.	Paul Evans, Pittsburgh	379
34.	Tom Penders, Texas	376
35.	Jud Heathcote, Michigan St.	375
36.	Neil McCarthy, New Mexico St.	370
37.	Frank Kerns, Ga. Southern	366
38.	Bobby Cremins, Georgia Tech	340
39.	Bobby Dye, Boise St.	339
40.	Jerry Pimm, UC Santa Barb.	339
41.	Don DeVoe, Navy	336
42.	Cliff Ellis, Clemson	332
43.	James Oliver, Alabama St.	330
44.	Dave Bliss, New Mexico	325
45.	George Raveling, Southern Cal	320
46.	Ralph Underhill, Wright St.	317
47.	Dick Bennett, Wis.-Green Bay	312
48.	Nolan Richardson, Arkansas	308
49.	Charles Woollum, Bucknell	308
50.	Gene Keady, Purdue	306
51.	Homer Drew, Valparaiso	305
52.	Tom Apke, Appalachian St.	295
53.	Russ Bergman, Coastal Caro.	291
54.	Robert Moreland, Texas Southern	288
55.	Hank Egan, San Diego	285
56.	Jim Harrick, UCLA	283
57.	Paul Lizzo, LIU-Brooklyn	282
58.	Mike Montgomery, Stanford	279
59.	Pat Foster, Nevada	276
60.	P. J. Carlesimo, Seton Hall	274
61.	Ben Braun, Eastern Mich.	273
62.	Pat Kennedy, Florida St.	268
62.	Gary Williams, Maryland	268
64.	Bob Huggins, Cincinnati	262
64.	Sonny Smith, Va. Commonwealth	262
66.	Jim Brovelli, San Francisco	261
67.	Bill Frieder, Arizona St.	260
68.	Bob Donewald, Western Mich.	259
69.	Nick Macarchuk, Fordham	259
70.	M. K. Turk, Southern Miss.	256
71.	Les Robinson, North Caro. St.	253
72.	Tates Locke, Indiana St.	251

	Coach, College	Wins
73.	Paul Westhead, George Mason	247
74.	Bobby Paschal, South Fla.	240
75.	Bruce Parkhill, Penn St.	236
76.	Danny Nee, Nebraska	233
77.	Moe Iba, Texas Christian	232
78.	Mike Vining, Northeast La.	230
79.	Billy Lee, Campbell	230
80.	Rick Pitino, Kentucky	228
81.	Stan Morrison, San Jose St.	227
82.	Joe Harrington, Colorado	221
83.	Butch Estes, Furman	217
84.	Clem Haskins, Minnesota	212
85.	Charlie Spoonhour, St. Louis	209
86.	Bill Hodges, Mercer	201

(Coaches with less than five years as a Division I head coach; includes record at four-year colleges only.)

	Coach, College	Wins
1.	Jerry Welsh, Iona	485
2.	Ron Shumate, Southeast Mo. St.	402
3.	Larry Hunter, Ohio	365
4.	John Kresse, Charleston (S.C.)	340
5.	Pete Cassidy, Cal St. Northridge	311
6.	Rees Johnson, Northeastern Ill.	263
7.	Mark Adams, Tex.-Pan American	210
7.	Don Maestri, Troy St.	210
9.	Kevin Bannon, Rider	204
10.	Steve Antrim, Wis.-Milwaukee	202
11.	Alan LeForce, East Tenn. St.	201

WINNINGEST DIVISION I MEN'S COACHES ALL-TIME

BY PERCENTAGE

(Minimum 10 head coaching seasons in Division I)

	Coach (College coached, tenure)	Yrs.	Won	Lost	Pct.
1.	Jerry Tarkanian (Long Beach St. 69-73, Nevada-Las Vegas 74-92)	24	+625	122	.837
2.	Clair Bee (Rider 29-31, LIU-Brooklyn 32-45, and 46-51)	21	412	87	.826
3.	Adolph Rupp (Kentucky 31-72)	41	$875	190	.822
4.	John Wooden (Indiana St. 47-48, UCLA 49-75)	29	664	162	.804
5.	Dean Smith (North Caro. 62-93)*	32	774	223	.776
6.	Harry Fisher (Columbia 07-16, Army 22-23, 25)	13	147	44	.770
7.	Frank Keaney (Rhode Island 21-48)	27	387	117	.768
8.	George Keogan (St. Louis 16, Allegheny 19, Valparaiso 20-21, Notre Dame 24-43)	24	385	117	.767
9.	Jack Ramsay [St. Joseph's (Pa.) 56-66]	11	+231	71	.765
10.	Vic Bubas (Duke 60-69)	10	213	67	.761
11.	Jim Boeheim (Syracuse 77-93)*	17	411	133	.756
12.	John Chaney (Cheyney 73-82, Temple 83-93)*	21	478	156	.754
13.	Charles "Chick" Davies (Duquesne 25-43 and 47-48)	21	314	106	.748
14.	Ray Mears (Wittenberg 57-62, Tennessee 63-77)	21	399	135	.747
15.	Bob Knight (Army 66-71, Indiana 72-93)*	28	##619	214	.743
16.	Al McGuire (Belmont Abbey 58-64, Marquette 65-77)	20	#405	143	.739
17.	Everett Case (North Caro. St. 47-64)	18	376	133	.739
18.	F. C. "Phog" Allen (Baker 06-08, Kansas 08-09, Haskell 09, Central Mo. St. 13-19, Kansas 20-56)	48	746	264	.739
19.	Nolan Richardson (Tulsa 81-85, Arkansas 86-93)*	13	308	109	.739
20.	John Thompson (Georgetown 73-93)*	21	484	178	.738
21.	Walter Meanwell (Wisconsin 12-17 and 21-34, Missouri 18, 20)	22	280	101	.735
22.	Cam Henderson (Muskingum 21-23, Davis & Elkins 24-35, Marshall 36-55)	35	583	216	.730
23.	Denny Crum (Louisville 72-93)*	22	518	192	.730
24.	Eddie Sutton (Creighton 70-74, Arkansas 75-85, Kentucky 86-89, Oklahoma St. 91-93)*	23	502	189	.726
25.	Lew Andreas (Syracuse 25-43 and 45-50)	25	355	134	.726
26.	Lou Carnesecca [St. John's (N.Y.) 66-70 and 74-92]	24	526	200	.725
27.	Fred Schaus (West Va. 55-60, Purdue 73-78)	12	#251	96	.723
28.	Hugh Greer (Connecticut 47-63)	17	290	112	.721
29.	Joe Lapchick [St. John's (N.Y.) 37-47 and 57-65]	20	335	130	.720
30.	Donald "Dudey" Moore (Duquesne 49-58, La Salle 59-63)	15	270	107	.716
31.	Ed Diddle (Western Ky. 23-64)	42	759	302	.715
32.	Tom Blackburn (Dayton 48-64)	17	352	141	.714
33.	John Lawther (Westminster 27-36, Penn St. 37-49)	23	317	127	.714
34.	Clarence "Hec" Edmundson (Idaho 17-18, Washington 21-47)	29	508	204	.713
35.	Lute Olson (Long Beach St. 74, Iowa 75-83, Arizona 84-93)*	20	##429	173	.713
36.	Harlan "Pat" Page (Chicago 13-20, Butler 21-26)	14	242	99	.710
37.	Ward "Piggy" Lambert (Purdue 17 and 19-45)	29	371	152	.709
38.	Peck Hickman (Louisville 45-67)	23	443	183	.708
39.	Lee Rose (Transylvania 65-75, N.C.-Charlotte 76-78, Purdue 79-80, South Fla. 81-86)	19	388	162	.705

Coach (College coached, tenure)	Yrs.	Won	Lost	Pct.
40. Joe Hall (Regis 60-64, Central Mo. St. 65, Kentucky 73-85)	19	373	156	.705
41. Frank McGuire [St. John's (N.Y.) 48-52, North Caro. 53-61, South Caro. 65-80]	30	549	236	.699
42. Boyd Grant (Fresno St. 78-86, Colorado St. 88-91)	13	275	120	.696
43. Doug Mills (Illinois 37-47)	11	151	66	.696
44. Don Haskins (UTEP 62-93)*	32	627	276	.694
45. Henry Iba (Northwest Mo. St. 30-33, Colorado 34, Oklahoma St. 35-70)	41	767	338	.694
46. Pat Foster (Lamar 81-86, Houston 87-93)*	13	276	122	.693
47. John "Honey" Russell (Seton Hall 37-43, Manhattan 46, Seton Hall 50-60)	19	308	137	.692
48. Wimp Sanderson (Alabama 81-92)	12	265	118	.692
49. Larry Weise (St. Bonaventure 62-73)	12	202	90	.692
50. Billy Tubbs [Southwestern (Tex.) 72-73, Lamar 77-80, Oklahoma 81-93]*	19	424	189	.692
51. Gene Smithson (Illinios St. 76-78, Wichita St. 79-86)	11	221	99	.691
52. Harold Anderson (Toledo 35-42, Bowling Green 42-63)	29	504	226	.690
53. Nat Holman (CCNY 20-52 and 55-56 and 59-60)	37	423	190	.690
54. Mike Krzyzewski (Army 76-80, Duke 81-93)*	18	394	177	.690
55. Charles "Lefty" Driesell (Davidson 61-69, Maryland 70-86, James Madison 89-93)*	31	621	279	.690
56. Rick Pitino (Boston U. 79-83, Providence 86-87, Kentucky 90-93)*	11	228	105	.685
57. Dana Kirk (Tampa 67-71, Va. Commonwealth 77-79, Memphis St. 80-86)	15	+281	131	.682
58. Gale Catlett (Cincinnati 73-78, West Va. 79-93)*	21	429	201	.681
59. Charlie Spoonhour (Southwest Mo. St. 84-92, St. Louis 93)*	10	209	98	.681
60. Ozzie Cowles (Carleton 25-30, Wis.-River Falls 34-36, Dartmouth 37-43 and 45-46, Michigan 47-48, Minnesota 49-59)	31	421	198	.680
61. Guy Lewis (Houston 57-86)	30	592	279	.680
62. Johnny Oldham (Tennessee Tech 56-64, Western Ky. 65-71)	16	+260	123	.679
63. Harry Combes (Illinois 48-67)	20	316	150	.678
64. Richard "Digger" Phelps (Fordham 71, Notre Dame 72-91)	21	419	200	.677
65. Bob King (New Mexico 63-72, Indiana St. 76-78)	13	236	113	.676
66. Jack Gardner (Kansas St. 40-42 and 47-53, Utah 54-71)	28	486	235	.674
67. Neil McCarthy (Weber St. 76-85, New Mexico St. 86-93)*	18	370	179	.674
68. Lou Henson (Hardin-Simmons 63-66, New Mexico St. 67-75, Illinois 76-93)*	31	##609	295	.674
69. Roy Skinner (Vanderbilt 59 and 62-76)	16	278	135	.673
70. Alex Severance (Villanova 37-61)	25	413	201	.673
71. Gene Keady (Western Ky. 79-80, Purdue 81-93)*	15	306	149	.673
72. Ray Meyer (DePaul 43-84)	42	724	354	.672
73. Herbert Read (Western Mich. 23-49)	27	351	172	.671
74. Don Corbett [Lincoln (Mo.) 72-79, North Caro. A&T 80-93]*	22	413	204	.669
75. Norm Stewart (Northern Iowa 62-67, Missouri 68-93)*	32	612	306	.667
75. Charles Moir (Roanoke 68-73, Tulane 74-76, Virginia Tech 77-87)	20	392	196	.667
75. Joel Eaves (Auburn 50-64)	15	224	112	.667
75. Jack Gray (Texas 37-42 and 46-51)	12	194	97	.667
79. Harold Bradley (Hartwick 48-50, Duke 51-59, Texas 60-67)	20	337	169	.666
80. Jim Harrick (Pepperdine 80-88, UCLA 89-93)*	14	283	143	.664
81. Pat Kennedy (Iona 81-86, Florida St. 87-93)*	13	268	136	.663
82. Paul Evans (St. Lawrence 74-80, Navy 81-86, Pittsburgh 87-93)*	20	379	194	.661
83. Branch McCracken (Ball St. 30-37, Indiana 39-43 and 47-65)	32	450	231	.661
84. Dave Gavitt (Dartmouth 68-69, Providence 70-79)	12	227	117	.660
85. Terry Holland (Davidson 70-74, Virginia 75-90)	21	418	216	.659
86. Harry Litwack (Temple 53-73)	21	373	193	.659
87. Tom Davis (Lafayette 72-77, Boston College 78-82, Stanford 83-86, Iowa 87-93)*	22	426	222	.657
88. Pete Newell (San Francisco 47-50, Michigan St. 51-54, California 55-60)	14	234	123	.655
89. Dick Tarrant (Richmond 82-93)	12	239	126	.655
90. Pete Carril (Lehigh 67, Princeton 68-93)*	27	469	248	.654
91. Jack Kraft (Villanova 62-73, Rhode Island 74-81)	20	+361	191	.654
92. Gene Bartow (Central Mo. St. 62-64, Valparaiso 65-70, Memphis St. 71-74, Illinois 75, UCLA 76-77, Ala.-Birmingham 79-93)*	31	%595	315	.654
93. Jack Hartman (Southern Ill. 63-70, Kansas St. 71-86)	24	#439	233	.653

	Coach (College coached, tenure)	Yrs.	Won	Lost	Pct.
94.	Eddie Hickey (Creighton 36-43 and 47, St. Louis 48-58, Marquette 59-64)	26	435	231	.653
95.	Fred Taylor (Ohio St. 59-76)	18	297	158	.653
96.	Butch van Breda Kolff (Lafayette 52-55, Hofstra 56-62, Princeton 63-67, New Orleans 78-79, Lafayette 85-88, Hofstra 89-93)*	27	473	252	.652
97.	George King (Charleston 57, West Va. 61-65, Purdue 66-72)	13	223	119	.652
98.	Frank Kerns (Spring Hill 72-79, Ga. Southern 1982-93)*	20	366	196	.651
99.	Bill Frieder (Michigan 81-89, Arizona St. 90-93)*	13	260	140	.650

BY VICTORIES

(Minimum 10 head coaching seasons in Division I)

	Coach	Wins
1.	Adolph Rupp	876
2.	Dean Smith*	774
3.	Henry Iba	767
4.	Ed Diddle	759
5.	F. C. "Phog" Allen	746
6.	Ray Meyer	724
7.	John Wooden	664
8.	Ralph Miller (Wichita St., Iowa, Oregon St.)	+**657
9.	Marv Harshman (Pacific Lutheran, Washington St., Washington)	%642
10.	Don Haskins*	627
10.	Norm Sloan (Presbyterian, Citadel, North Caro. St., Florida)	627
12.	Jerry Tarkanian	+625
13.	Charles "Lefty" Driesell*	621
14.	Bob Knight*	##619
15.	Norm Stewart*	612
16.	Lou Henson*	##609
17.	Amory "Slats" Gill (Oregon St.)	599
15.	Abe Lemons (Oklahoma City, Tex.-Pan American, Oklahoma City)	597
19.	Gene Bartow*	%595
20.	Guy Lewis	592
21.	Cam Henderson	583
22.	Paul "Tony" Hinkle (Butler)	557
23.	Glenn Wilkes (Stetson)	551
24.	Frank McGuire	549
25.	Harry Miller [Western St. (Colo.), Fresno St., Eastern N. Mex., North Texas, Wichita St., Stephen F. Austin]	534
26.	Gary Colson (Valdosta St., Pepperdine, New Mexico, Fresno St.)*	529
27.	Lou Carnesecca	526
28.	Fred Enke (Louisville, Arizona)	525
29.	Tom Young (Catholic, American, Rutgers, Old Dominion)	524
30.	Denny Crum*	518
31.	C. M. Newton (Transylvania, Alabama, Vanderbilt)	509
32.	Clarence "Hec" Edmundson	508
33.	Eldon Miller (Wittenberg, Western Mich., Ohio St., Northern Iowa)*	##504
33.	Harold Anderson	504
35.	Eddie Sutton*	502
36.	Hugh Durham (Florida St., Georgia)*	495
36.	Ned Wulk [Xavier (Ohio), Arizona St.]	495
38.	Jack Friel (Washington St.)	494
38.	Everett Shelton (Phillips, Wyoming, Cal St. Sacramento)	494
40.	Jack Gardner	486
41.	John Thompson*	484
42.	John Chaney*	478
43.	Butch van Breda Kolff*	473
44.	Pete Carril*	469
45.	Bill E. Foster (Bloomsburg, Rutgers, Utah, Duke, South Caro., Northwestern)*	467
46.	John "Taps" Gallagher (Niagara)	465
47.	Bill Reinhart (Oregon, Geo. Washington)	464
48.	Clarence "Nibs" Price (California)	463
49.	Tex Winter (Marquette, Kansas St., Washington, Northwestern, Long Beach St.)	##454
50.	Johnny Orr (Massachusetts, Michigan, Iowa St.)*	452
51.	Bill Foster [Shorter, N.C.-Charlotte, Clemson, Miami (Fla.), Virginia Tech]*	451
52.	Branch McCracken	450
52.	Davey Whitney (Texas Southern, Alcorn St.)	450
54.	Peck Hickman	443
54.	Shelby Metcalf (Texas A&M)	443
54.	Calvin Luther (DePauw, Murray St., Longwood, Tenn.-Martin)*	443
57.	Jack Hartman	#439
58.	Don Donoher (Dayton)	437
59.	Eddie Hickey	435
60.	Gale Catlett*	429
60.	Lute Olson*	429
62.	Tom Davis*	426
63.	Billy Tubbs*	424
64.	Nat Holman	423
65.	Ozzie Cowles	421
66.	Richard "Digger" Phelps	419
67.	Terry Holland	418
68.	Alex Severance	413
68.	Don Corbett	413
70.	Clair Bee	412
71.	Jim Boeheim*	411
72.	Rollie Massimino (Stony Brook, Villanova, Nevada-Las Vegas)*	410
73.	Howard Cann (New York U.)	409
74.	George Blaney (Stonehill, Dartmouth, Holy Cross)*	407
75.	Al McGuire	405
76.	Dale Brown (Louisiana St.)*	403
77.	Howard Hobson (Southern Ore., Oregon, Yale)	400

** Active coaches. % Includes one forfeit over Oregon State. # One, ## two forfeits over Minnesota, both by action of NCAA Council under restitution provisions of Section 10, Official Procedure Governing NCAA Enforcement Program (adopted by NCAA membership at 69th annual Convention, January 1975).*

*Restitution may be applied when a student-athlete has been permitted to participate while ineligible due to a court order against his institution or the NCAA, if the court order subsequently is overturned. ** Miller lost 15 victories and Dutcher 24 in those cases; Miller 674-370, .646, and Dutcher 314-172, .646, without voids and forfeits. $ Kentucky played no varsity schedule in 1953—under NCAA suspension. + NCAA tournament record voided: Alabama 2-1 from 1987, Memphis State 9-5 from 1982-86, Florida 3-2 from 1987-88, Georgia 1-1 in 1985, Long Beach State 6-3 from 1971-73, Western Kentucky 4-1 in 1971, Villanova 4-1 in 1971, St. Joseph's (Pa.) 3-1 in 1961, Austin Peay 1-2 in 1973, and Oregon State 2-3 from 1980-82. (Tarkanian was head coach at Long Beach State in 1971-73.)*

DIVISION I MEN'S COACHES—TOP 10 BEST CAREER STARTS—BY PERCENTAGE

(Head Coaches With At Least Half Their Seasons at Division I)

1 Season	Season	W	L	Pct.
Norman Shepard, North Caro.	1924	23	0	1.000
Bill Hodges, Indiana St.	1979	33	1	.970
Tom Gola, La Salle	1969	23	1	.958
Lou Rossini, Columbia	1951	21	1	.955
Earl Brown, Dartmouth	1944	19	2	.905
Phil Johnson, Weber St.	1969	27	3	.900
Gary Cunningham, UCLA	1978	25	3	.893
Bob Davies, Seton Hall	1947	24	3	.889
Jerry Tarkanian, Long Beach St.	1969	23	3	.885
John Castellani, Seattle	1957	22	3	.880

2 Seasons	Seasons	W	L	Pct.
Lew Andreas, Syracuse	1925-26	33	3	.917
Everett Case, North Caro. St.	1947-48	55	8	.873
Buck Freeman, St. John's (N.Y.)	1928-29	41	6	.872
Gary Cunningham, UCLA	1978-79	50	8	.862
Nibs Price, California	1925-26	25	4	.862
Denny Crum, Louisville	1972-73	49	8	.860
Adolph Rupp, Kentucky	1931-32	30	5	.857
Jerry Tarkanian, Long Beach St.	1969-70	47	8	.855
John Castellani, Seattle	1957-58	45	9	.833
Hugh Greer, Connecticut	1947-48	29	6	.829

3 Seasons	Seasons	W	L	Pct.
Nibs Price, California	1925-27	38	4	.905
Buck Freeman, St. John's (N.Y.)	1928-30	64	7	.901
Lew Andreas, Syracuse	1925-27	48	7	.873
Adolph Rupp, Kentucky	1931-33	51	8	.864
Jerry Tarkanian, Long Beach St.	1969-71	71	13	.845
Jim Boeheim, Syracuse	1977-79	74	14	.841
Everett Case, North Caro. St.	1947-49	80	16	.833
Ben Carnevale, North Caro. & Navy	1945-47	68	14	.829
Phil Johnson, Weber St.	1969-71	68	16	.810
Fred Taylor, Ohio St.	1959-61	63	15	.808

4 Seasons	Seasons	W	L	Pct.
Buck Freeman, St. John's (N.Y.)	1928-31	85	8	.914
Adolph Rupp, Kentucky	1931-34	67	9	.882
Jerry Tarkanian, Long Beach St.	1969-72	96	17	.850
Jim Boeheim, Syracuse	1977-80	100	18	.847
Fred Taylor, Ohio St.	1959-62	89	17	.840
Everett Case, North Caro. St.	1947-50	107	22	.829
Nibs Price, California	1925-28	47	10	.825
Nat Holman, CCNY	1920-23	46	10	.821
Denny Crum, Louisville	1972-75	98	22	.817
Lew Andreas, Syracuse	1925-28	58	13	.817

5 Seasons	Seasons	W	L	Pct.
Buck Freeman, St. John's (N.Y.)	1928-32	107	12	.899
Adolph Rupp, Kentucky	1931-35	86	11	.887
Jerry Tarkanian, Long Beach St. & Nevada-Las Vegas	1969-73	122	20	.859
Nat Holman, CCNY	1920-24	58	11	.841
Fred Taylor, Ohio St.	1959-63	109	21	.838
Nibs Price, California	1925-29	64	13	.831
Everett Case, North Caro. St.	1947-51	137	29	.825
Buster Sheary, Holy Cross	1949-53	110	27	.803
Jim Boeheim, Syracuse	1977-81	122	30	.803
Lew Andreas, Syracuse	1925-29	69	17	.802

6 Seasons	Seasons	W	L	Pct.
Buck Freeman, St. John's (N.Y.)	1928-33	130	16	.890
Adolph Rupp, Kentucky	1931-36	101	17	.856
Jerry Tarkanian, Long Beach St. & Nevada-Las Vegas	1969-74	142	26	.845
Nat Holman, CCNY	1920-25	70	13	.843
Buster Sheary, Holy Cross	1949-54	136	29	.824
Lew Andreas, Syracuse	1925-30	87	19	.821
Everett Dean, Carleton & Indiana	1922-27	82	18	.820
Clair Bee, Rider & LIU-Brooklyn	1929-34	101	23	.815
Fred Taylor, Ohio St.	1959-64	125	29	.812
Everett Case, North Caro. St.	1947-52	161	39	.805

7 Seasons	Seasons	W	L	Pct.
Buck Freeman, St. John's (N.Y.)	1928-34	146	19	.885
Jerry Tarkanian, Long Beach St. & Nevada-Las Vegas	1969-75	166	31	.843
Adolph Rupp, Kentucky	1931-37	118	22	.843
Clair Bee, Rider & LIU-Brooklyn	1929-35	125	25	.833
Everett Dean, Carleton & Indiana	1922-28	97	20	.829
Lew Andreas, Syracuse	1925-31	103	23	.817
Nat Holman, CCNY	1920-26	79	18	.814
Buster Sheary, Holy Cross	1949-55	155	36	.812
Everett Case, North Caro. St.	1947-53	187	45	.806
Vic Bubas, Duke	1960-66	158	39	.802

8 Seasons	Seasons	W	L	Pct.
Clair Bee, Rider & LIU-Brooklyn	1929-36	150	25	.857
Buck Freeman, St. John's (N.Y.)	1928-35	159	27	.855
Jerry Tarkanian, Long Beach St. & Nevada-Las Vegas	1969-76	195	33	.855
Adolph Rupp, Kentucky	1931-38	131	27	.829
Nat Holman, CCNY	1920-27	88	21	.807
Everett Case, North Caro. St.	1947-54	213	52	.804
Hugh Greer, Connecticut	1947-54	151	38	.799
Lew Andreas, Syracuse	1925-32	116	30	.795
Henry Iba, Northwest Mo. St., Colorado & Oklahoma St.	1930-37	157	42	.789
Vic Bubas, Duke	1960-67	176	48	.786
Denny Crum, Louisville	1972-79	186	52	.782

9 Seasons	Seasons	W	L	Pct.
Clair Bee, Rider & LIU-Brooklyn	1929-37	177	28	.863
Jerry Tarkanian, Long Beach St. & Nevada-Las Vegas	1969-77	224	36	.862
Buck Freeman, St. John's (N.Y.)	1928-36	177	31	.851
Adolph Rupp, Kentucky	1931-39	147	31	.826
Everett Case, North Caro. St.	1947-55	241	56	.811
Lew Andreas, Syracuse	1925-33	130	32	.802
Henry Iba, Northwest Mo. St., Colorado & Oklahoma St.	1930-38	182	45	.802
Denny Crum, Louisville	1972-80	219	55	.799
Hugh Greer, Connecticut	1947-55	171	43	.799
Nat Holman, CCNY	1920-28	99	25	.798

10 Seasons	Seasons	W	L	Pct.
Clair Bee, Rider & LIU-Brooklyn	1929-38	200	32	.862
Jerry Tarkanian, Long Beach St. & Nevada-Las Vegas	1969-78	244	44	.847
Everett Case, North Caro. St.	1947-56	265	60	.815
Adolph Rupp, Kentucky	1931-40	162	37	.814
Lew Andreas, Syracuse	1925-34	145	34	.810
Henry Iba, Northwest Mo. St., Colorado & Oklahoma St.	1930-39	201	53	.791
Denny Crum, Louisville	1972-81	240	64	.789
Harold Anderson, Toledo & Bowling Green	1935-44	182	50	.784
Nat Holman, CCNY	1920-29	108	30	.783
Joseph Lapchick, St. John's (N.Y.)	1937-46	165	47	.778

11 Seasons	Seasons	W	L	Pct.
Clair Bee, Rider & LIU-Brooklyn	1929-39	223	32	.875
Jerry Tarkanian, Long Beach St. & Nevada-Las Vegas	1969-79	259	49	.841
Lew Andreas, Syracuse	1925-35	160	36	.816
Henry Iba, Northwest Mo. St., Colorado & Oklahoma St.	1930-40	227	56	.802
Adolph Rupp, Kentucky	1931-41	179	45	.799
Everett Case, North Caro. St.	1947-57	280	71	.798
Harold Anderson, Toledo & Bowling Green	1935-45	206	54	.792
Nat Holman, CCNY	1920-30	119	33	.783
Denny Crum, Louisville	1972-82	263	74	.780
Joe Mullaney, Norwich & Providence	1955-65	221	63	.778

12 Seasons	Seasons	W	L	Pct.
Clair Bee, Rider & LIU-Brooklyn	1929-40	242	36	.871
Jerry Tarkanian, Long Beach St. & Nevada-Las Vegas	1969-80	282	58	.829
Lew Andreas, Syracuse	1925-36	172	41	.806
Harold Anderson, Toledo & Bowling Green	1935-46	233	59	.798
Henry Iba, Northwest Mo. St., Colorado & Oklahoma St.	1930-41	245	63	.795
Adolph Rupp, Kentucky	1931-42	198	51	.795
Everett Case, North Caro. St.	1947-58	298	77	.795
Denny Crum, Louisville	1972-83	295	78	.791
Joe Mullaney, Norwich & Providence	1955-66	243	68	.781
Nat Holman, CCNY	1920-31	131	37	.780

13 Seasons	Seasons	W	L	Pct.
Clair Bee, Rider & LIU-Brooklyn	1929-41	267	38	.875
Jerry Tarkanian, Long Beach St. & Nevada-Las Vegas	1969-81	298	70	.810
Lew Andreas, Syracuse	1925-37	185	45	.804
Harold Anderson, Toledo & Bowling Green	1935-47	261	66	.798
Everett Case, North Caro. St.	1947-59	320	81	.798
Nat Holman, CCNY	1920-32	147	38	.795
Henry Iba, Northwest Mo. St., Colorado & Oklahoma St.	1930-42	265	69	.793
Adolph Rupp, Kentucky	1931-43	215	57	.790
Denny Crum, Louisville	1972-84	319	89	.782
Joe Mullaney, Norwich & Providence	1955-67	264	75	.779

14 Seasons	Seasons	W	L	Pct.
Clair Bee, Rider & LIU-Brooklyn	1929-42	291	41	.877
Nat Holman, CCNY	1920-33	160	39	.804
Harold Anderson, Toledo & Bowling Green	1935-48	288	72	.800
Jerry Tarkanian, Long Beach St. & Nevada-Las Vegas	1969-82	318	80	.799
Adolph Rupp, Kentucky	1931-44	234	59	.799
Lew Andreas, Syracuse	1925-38	198	50	.798
Henry Iba, Northwest Mo. St., Colorado & Oklahoma St.	1930-43	279	79	.779
Everett Case, North Caro. St.	1947-60	331	96	.775
Jim Boeheim, Syracuse	1977-90	343	108	.761
Denny Crum, Louisville	1972-85	338	107	.760
Ray Mears, Wittenberg & Tennessee	1957-70	266	84	.760

15 Seasons	Seasons	W	L	Pct.
Clair Bee, Rider & LIU-Brooklyn	1929-43	304	47	.866
Nat Holman, CCNY	1920-34	174	40	.813
Jerry Tarkanian, Long Beach St. & Nevada-Las Vegas	1969-83	346	83	.807
Adolph Rupp, Kentucky	1931-45	256	63	.803
Harold Anderson, Toledo & Bowling Green	1935-49	312	79	.798
Lew Andreas, Syracuse	1925-39	212	54	.797
Henry Iba, Northwest Mo. St., Colorado & Oklahoma St.	1930-44	306	85	.783
Everett Case, North Caro. St.	1947-61	347	105	.768
Denny Crum, Louisville	1972-86	370	114	.764
Jim Boeheim, Syracuse	1977-91	369	114	.764

16 Seasons	Seasons	W	L	Pct.
Clair Bee, Rider & LIU-Brooklyn	1929-43, 46	318	56	.850
Adolph Rupp, Kentucky	1931-46	284	65	.814
Jerry Tarkanian, Long Beach St. & Nevada-Las Vegas	1969-84	375	89	.808
Nat Holman, CCNY	1920-35	184	46	.800
Henry Iba, Northwest Mo. St., Colorado & Oklahoma St.	1930-45	333	89	.789
Harold Anderson, Toledo & Bowling Green	1935-50	331	90	.786
Lew Andreas, Syracuse	1925-40	222	62	.782
Everett Case, North Caro. St.	1947-62	358	111	.763
Ray Mears, Wittenberg & Tennessee	1957-72	306	97	.759
Jim Boeheim, Syracuse	1977-92	391	124	.759

17 Seasons	Seasons	W	L	Pct.
Clair Bee, Rider & LIU-Brooklyn	1929-43, 46-47	335	61	.850
Adolph Rupp, Kentucky	1931-47	318	68	.824
Jerry Tarkanian, Long Beach St. & Nevada-Las Vegas	1969-85	403	93	.813
Henry Iba, Northwest Mo. St., Colorado & Oklahoma St.	1930-46	364	91	.800
Nat Holman, CCNY	1920-36	194	50	.795
Harold Anderson, Toledo & Bowling Green	1935-51	341	94	.784
Lew Andreas, Syracuse	1925-41	236	67	.779
Jim Boeheim, Syracuse	1977-93	411	133	.756
Joseph Lapchick, St. John's (N.Y.)	1937-47, 57-62	291	95	.754
Ray Mears, Wittenberg & Tennessee	1957-73	321	106	.752

18 Seasons	Seasons	W	L	Pct.
Clair Bee, Rider & LIU-Brooklyn	1929-43, 46-48	352	65	.844
Adolph Rupp, Kentucky	1931-48	354	71	.833
Jerry Tarkanian, Long Beach St. & Nevada-Las Vegas	1969-86	436	98	.816
Henry Iba, Northwest Mo. St., Colorado & Oklahoma St.	1930-47	388	99	.797
Nat Holman, CCNY	1920-37	204	56	.785
Harold Anderson, Toledo & Bowling Green	1935-52	358	104	.775
Lew Andreas, Syracuse	1925-42	251	73	.775
Dean Smith, North Caro.	1962-79	386	127	.752
John Thompson, Georgetown	1973-90	423	142	.749
Lou Carnesecca, St. John's (N.Y.)	1966-70, 74-86	402	136	.747
Denny Crum, Louisville	1972-89	436	148	.747

19 Seasons	Seasons	W	L	Pct.
Adolph Rupp, Kentucky	1931-49	386	73	.841
Clair Bee, Rider & LIU-Brooklyn	1929-43, 46-49	370	77	.828
Jerry Tarkanian, Long Beach St. & Nevada-Las Vegas	1969-87	473	100	.825
Henry Iba, Northwest Mo. St., Colorado & Oklahoma St.	1930-48	415	103	.801
Nat Holman, CCNY	1920-38	217	59	.786
Lew Andreas, Syracuse	1925-43	259	83	.757
Harold Anderson, Toledo & Bowling Green	1935-53	370	119	.757
Dean Smith, North Caro.	1962-80	407	135	.751
Frank Keaney, Rhode Island	1922-40	244	82	.748
Denny Crum, Louisville	1972-90	463	156	.748

20 Seasons	Seasons	W	L	Pct.
Adolph Rupp, Kentucky	1931-50	411	78	.840
Clair Bee, Rider & LIU-Brooklyn	1929-43, 46-50	390	82	.826
Jerry Tarkanian, Long Beach St. & Nevada-Las Vegas	1969-88	501	106	.825
Henry Iba, Northwest Mo. St., Colorado & Oklahoma St.	1930-49	438	108	.802
Phog Allen, Baker, Kansas, Haskell, Central Mo. St. & Kansas	1906-09, 13-28	325	89	.785
Nat Holman, CCNY	1920-39	228	65	.778
John Chaney, Cheyney & Temple	1973-92	458	143	.762
Frank Keaney, Rhode Island	1922-41	265	86	.755
Harold Anderson, Toledo & Bowling Green	1935-54	387	126	.754
Dean Smith, North Caro.	1962-81	436	143	.753

21 Seasons	Seasons	W	L	Pct.
Adolph Rupp, Kentucky	1931-51	443	80	.847
Clair Bee, Rider & LIU-Brooklyn	1929-43, 46-51	410	86	.827
Jerry Tarkanian, Long Beach St. & Nevada-Las Vegas	1969-89	530	114	.823
Henry Iba, Northwest Mo. St., Colorado & Oklahoma St.	1930-50	456	117	.796

	Seasons	W	L	Pct.
Nat Holman, CCNY	1920-40	236	73	.764
Dean Smith, North Caro.	1962-82	468	145	.763
Phog Allen, Baker, Kansas, Haskell, Central Mo. St. & Kansas	1906-09, 13-29	328	104	.759
Frank Keaney, Rhode Island	1922-42	283	90	.759
John Chaney, Cheyney & Temple	1973-93	478	156	.754
Chick Davies, Duquesne	1925-40, 47-48	314	106	.748

22 Seasons	Seasons	W	L	Pct.
Adolph Rupp, Kentucky	1931-52	472	83	.850
Jerry Tarkanian, Long Beach St. & Nevada-Las Vegas	1969-90	565	119	.826
Henry Iba, Northwest Mo. St., Colorado & Oklahoma St.	1930-51	485	123	.798
Nat Holman, CCNY	1920-41	253	78	.764
Dean Smith, North Caro.	1962-83	496	153	.764
Frank Keaney, Rhode Island	1922-43	299	93	.763
Phog Allen, Baker, Kansas, Haskell, Central Mo. St. & Kansas	1906-09, 13-30	342	108	.760
John Wooden, Indiana St. & UCLA	1947-68	464	151	.754
Lew Andreas, Syracuse	1925-47	308	105	.746
Bob Knight, Army & Indiana	1966-87	468	169	.735

23 Seasons	Seasons	W	L	Pct.
Adolph Rupp, Kentucky	1931-52, 54	497	83	.857
Jerry Tarkanian, Long Beach St. & Nevada-Las Vegas	1969-91	599	120	.833
Henry Iba, Northwest Mo. St., Colorado & Oklahoma St.	1930-52	504	131	.794
Dean Smith, North Caro.	1962-84	524	156	.771
Nat Holman, CCNY	1920-42	269	81	.769
John Wooden, Indiana St. & UCLA	1947-69	493	152	.764
Phog Allen, Baker, Kansas, Haskell, Central Mo. St. & Kansas	1906-09, 13-31	357	111	.763
Frank Keaney, Rhode Island	1922-44	313	99	.760
Ed Diddle, Western Ky.	1923-45	395	134	.747
Bob Knight, Army & Indiana	1966-88	487	179	.731

24 Seasons	Seasons	W	L	Pct.
Adolph Rupp, Kentucky	1931-52, 54-55	520	86	.858
Jerry Tarkanian, Long Beach St. & Nevada-Las Vegas	1969-92	625	122	.837
Henry Iba, Northwest Mo. St., Colorado & Oklahoma St.	1930-53	527	138	.792
John Wooden, Indiana St. & UCLA	1947-70	521	154	.772
Dean Smith, North Caro.	1962-85	551	165	.770
Frank Keaney, Rhode Island	1922-45	333	104	.762
Phog Allen, Baker, Kansas, Haskell, Central Mo. St. & Kansas	1906-09, 13-32	370	116	.761
Nat Holman, CCNY	1920-43	277	91	.753
Bob Knight, Army & Indiana	1966-89	514	187	.733
Lew Andreas, Syracuse	1925-49	337	125	.729

25 Seasons	Seasons	W	L	Pct.
Adolph Rupp, Kentucky	1931-52, 54-56	540	92	.854
Henry Iba, Northwest Mo. St., Colorado & Oklahoma St.	1930-54	551	143	.794
John Wooden, Indiana St. & UCLA	1947-71	550	155	.780
Dean Smith, North Caro.	1962-86	579	171	.772
Frank Keaney, Rhode Island	1922-46	354	107	.768
Phog Allen, Baker, Kansas, Haskell, Central Mo. St. & Kansas	1906-09, 13-33	383	120	.761
Nat Holman, CCNY	1920-44	283	102	.735
Ed Diddle, Western Ky.	1923-47	435	157	.735
Bob Knight, Army & Indiana	1966-90	532	198	.729
Lew Andreas, Syracuse	1925-50	355	134	.726

26 Seasons	Seasons	W	L	Pct.
Adolph Rupp, Kentucky	1931-52, 54-57	563	97	.853
John Wooden, Indiana St. & UCLA	1947-72	580	155	.789
Henry Iba, Northwest Mo. St., Colorado & Oklahoma St.	1930-55	563	156	.783
Dean Smith, North Caro.	1962-87	611	175	.777
Frank Keaney, Rhode Island	1922-47	371	110	.771
Phog Allen, Baker, Kansas, Haskell, Central Mo. St. & Kansas	1906-09, 13-34	399	121	.767
Ed Diddle, Western Ky.	1923-48	463	159	.744
Nat Holman, CCNY	1920-45	295	106	.736
Bob Knight, Army & Indiana	1966-91	561	203	.734
Frank McGuire, St. John's (N.Y.), North Caro. & South Caro.	1948-76	489	188	.722

27 Seasons	Seasons	W	L	Pct.
Adolph Rupp, Kentucky	1931-52, 54-58	586	103	.851
John Wooden, Indiana St. & UCLA	1947-73	610	155	.797
Henry Iba, Northwest Mo. St., Colorado & Oklahoma St.	1930-56	581	165	.779
Dean Smith, North Caro.	1962-88	638	182	.778
Frank Keaney, Rhode Island	1922-48	387	117	.768
Phog Allen, Baker, Kansas, Haskell, Central Mo. St. & Kansas	1906-09, 13-35	414	126	.767

	Seasons	W	L	Pct.
Ed Diddle, Western Ky.	1923-49	488	163	.750
Nat Holman, CCNY	1920-46	309	110	.737
Bob Knight, Army & Indiana	1966-92	588	210	.737
Frank McGuire, St. John's (N.Y.), North Caro. & South Caro.	1948-77	503	200	.716

28 Seasons	Seasons	W	L	Pct.
Adolph Rupp, Kentucky	1931-52, 54-59	610	106	.852
John Wooden, Indiana St. & UCLA	1947-74	636	159	.800
Dean Smith, North Caro.	1962-89	667	190	.778
Henry Iba, Northwest Mo. St., Colorado & Oklahoma St.	1930-57	598	174	.775
Phog Allen, Baker, Kansas, Haskell, Central Mo. St. & Kansas	1906-09, 13-36	435	128	.773
Ed Diddle, Western Ky.	1923-50	513	169	.752
Bob Knight, Army & Indiana	1966-93	619	214	.743
Nat Holman, CCNY	1920-47	326	116	.738
Frank McGuire, St. John's (N.Y.), North Caro. & South Caro.	1948-78	519	212	.710
Don Haskins, UTEP	1962-89	542	232	.700

29 Seasons	Seasons	W	L	Pct.
Adolph Rupp, Kentucky	1931-52, 54-60	628	113	.848
John Wooden, Indiana St. & UCLA	1947-75	664	162	.804
Phog Allen, Baker, Kansas, Haskell, Central Mo. St. & Kansas	1906-09, 13-37	450	132	.773
Henry Iba, Northwest Mo. St., Colorado & Oklahoma St.	1930-58	619	182	.773
Dean Smith, North Caro.	1962-90	688	203	.772
Ed Diddle, Western Ky.	1923-51	532	179	.748
Nat Holman, CCNY	1920-48	344	119	.743
Frank McGuire, St. John's (N.Y.), North Caro. & South Caro.	1948-79	534	224	.704
Don Haskins, UTEP	1962-90	563	243	.699
Lefty Driesell, Davidson, Maryland & James Madison	1961-86, 89-91	579	259	.691

30 Seasons	Seasons	W	L	Pct.
Adolph Rupp, Kentucky	1931-52, 54-61	647	122	.841
Phog Allen, Baker, Kansas, Haskell, Central Mo. St. & Kansas	1906-09, 13-38	468	134	.777
Dean Smith, North Caro.	1962-91	717	209	.774
Henry Iba, Northwest Mo. St., Colorado & Oklahoma St.	1930-59	630	196	.763
Ed Diddle, Western Ky.	1923-52	558	184	.752
Nat Holman, CCNY	1920-49	361	127	.740
Frank McGuire, St. John's (N.Y.), North Caro. & South Caro.	1948-80	550	235	.701

	Seasons	W	L	Pct.
Don Haskins, UTEP	1962-91	579	256	.693
Lefty Driesell, Davidson, Maryland & James Madison	1961-86, 89-92	600	270	.690
Guy Lewis, Houston	1957-86	592	279	.680

31 Seasons	Seasons	W	L	Pct.
Adolph Rupp, Kentucky	1931-52, 54-62	670	125	.843
Phog Allen, Baker, Kansas, Haskell, Central Mo. St. & Kansas	1906-09, 13-39	481	141	.773
Dean Smith, North Caro.	1962-92	740	219	.772
Ed Diddle, Western Ky.	1923-53	583	190	.754
Henry Iba, Northwest Mo. St., Colorado & Oklahoma St.	1930-60	640	211	.752
Nat Holman, CCNY	1920-50	385	132	.745
Don Haskins, UTEP	1962-92	606	263	.697
Lefty Driesell, Davidson, Maryland & James Madison	1961-86, 89-93	621	279	.690
Lou Henson, Hardin-Simmons & Illinois	1963-93	609	295	.674
Norm Stewart, Northern Iowa & Missouri	1962-92	593	292	.670

32 Seasons	Seasons	W	L	Pct.
Adolph Rupp, Kentucky	1931-52, 54-63	686	134	.837
Dean Smith, North Caro.	1962-93	774	223	.776
Phog Allen, Baker, Kansas, Haskell, Central Mo. St. & Kansas	1906-09, 13-40	500	147	.773
Ed Diddle, Western Ky.	1923-54	612	193	.760
Henry Iba, Northwest Mo. St., Colorado & Oklahoma St.	1930-61	655	221	.748
Nat Holman, CCNY	1920-51	397	139	.741
Don Haskins, UTEP	1962-93	627	276	.694
Norm Stewart, Northern Iowa & Missouri	1962-93	612	306	.667
Fred Enke, Louisville & Arizona	1926-55	463	250	.649
Abe Lemons, Oklahoma City, Tex.-Pan American, Texas, & Oklahoma City	1956-82, 84-88	567	317	.641

33 Seasons	Seasons	W	L	Pct.
Adolph Rupp, Kentucky	1931-52, 54-64	707	140	.835
Phog Allen, Baker, Kansas, Haskell, Central Mo. St. & Kansas	1906-09, 13-41	512	153	.770
Ed Diddle, Western Ky.	1923-55	630	203	.756
Henry Iba, Northwest Mo. St., Colorado & Oklahoma St.	1930-62	669	232	.743
Nat Holman, CCNY	1920-52	405	150	.730
Fred Enke, Louisville & Arizona	1926-56	474	265	.641

	Seasons	W	L	Pct.
Abe Lemons, Oklahoma City, Tex.-Pan American, Texas, & Oklahoma City	1956-82, 84-89	579	331	.636
Ralph Miller, Wichita St., Iowa & Oregon St.	1952-84	562	328	.631
Ray Meyer, DePaul	1943-75	509	303	.627
Tony Hinkle, Butler	1927-42, 46-62	455	288	.612

34 Seasons	Seasons	W	L	Pct.
Adolph Rupp, Kentucky	1931-52, 54-65	722	150	.828
Phog Allen, Baker, Kansas, Haskell, Central Mo. St. & Kansas	1906-09, 13-42	529	158	.770
Ed Diddle, Western Ky.	1923-56	646	215	.750
Henry Iba, Northwest Mo. St., Colorado & Oklahoma St.	1930-63	685	241	.740
Nat Holman, CCNY	1920-52, 55	413	160	.721
Fred Enke, Louisville & Arizona	1926-57	487	278	.637
Abe Lemons, Oklahoma City, Tex.-Pan American, Texas, & Oklahoma City	1956-82, 84-90	597	344	.634
Ralph Miller, Wichita St., Iowa & Oregon St.	1952-85	584	337	.634
Ray Meyer, DePaul	1943-76	529	312	.629
Tony Hinkle, Butler	1927-42, 46-63	471	298	.612

35 Seasons	Seasons	W	L	Pct.
Adolph Rupp, Kentucky	1931-52, 54-66	749	152	.831
Phog Allen, Baker, Kansas, Haskell, Central Mo. St. & Kansas	1906-09, 13-43	551	164	.771
Ed Diddle, Western Ky.	1923-57	663	224	.747
Henry Iba, Northwest Mo. St., Colorado & Oklahoma St.	1930-64	700	251	.736
Nat Holman, CCNY	1920-52, 55-56	417	174	.706
Fred Enke, Louisville & Arizona	1926-58	497	293	.629
Ralph Miller, Wichita St., Iowa & Oregon St.	1952-86	596	352	.629
Ray Meyer, DePaul	1943-77	544	324	.627
Norm Sloan, Presbyterian, Citadel, Florida, North Caro. St. & Florida	1952-55, 57-87	583	370	.612
Tony Hinkle, Butler	1927-42, 46-64	484	311	.609

36 Seasons	Seasons	W	L	Pct.
Adolph Rupp, Kentucky	1931-52, 54-67	762	165	.822
Phog Allen, Baker, Kansas, Haskell, Central Mo. St. & Kansas	1906-09, 13-44	568	173	.767
Ed Diddle, Western Ky.	1923-58	677	235	.742
Henry Iba, Northwest Mo. St., Colorado & Oklahoma St.	1930-65	720	258	.736
Nat Holman, CCNY	1920-52, 55-56, 59	423	186	.695
Ray Meyer, DePaul	1943-78	571	327	.636
Ralph Miller, Wichita St., Iowa & Oregon St.	1952-87	615	363	.629
Fred Enke, Louisville & Arizona	1926-59	501	315	.614
Norm Sloan, Presbyterian, Citadel, Florida, North Caro. St. & Florida	1952-55, 57-88	606	382	.613
Slats Gill, Oregon St.	1929-64	599	393	.604

37 Seasons	Seasons	W	L	Pct.
Adolph Rupp, Kentucky	1931-52, 54-68	784	170	.822
Phog Allen, Baker, Kansas, Haskell, Central Mo. St. & Kansas	1906-09, 13-45	580	178	.765
Ed Diddle, Western Ky.	1923-59	693	245	.739
Henry Iba, Northwest Mo. St., Colorado & Oklahoma St.	1930-66	724	279	.722
Nat Holman, CCNY	1920-52, 55-56, 59-60	423	190	.690
Ray Meyer, DePaul	1943-79	597	333	.642
Ralph Miller, Wichita St., Iowa & Oregon St.	1952-88	635	374	.629
Norm Sloan, Presbyterian, Citadel, Florida, North Caro. St. & Florida	1952-55, 57-89	627	395	.614
Fred Enke, Louisville & Arizona	1926-60	511	329	.608
Tony Hinkle, Butler	1927-42, 46-66	511	336	.603

38 Seasons	Seasons	W	L	Pct.
Adolph Rupp, Kentucky	1931-52, 54-69	807	175	.822
Phog Allen, Baker, Kansas, Haskell, Central Mo. St. & Kansas	1906-09, 13-46	599	180	.769
Ed Diddle, Western Ky.	1923-60	714	252	.739
Henry Iba, Northwest Mo. St., Colorado & Oklahoma St.	1930-67	731	297	.711
Ray Meyer, DePaul	1943-80	623	335	.650
Ralph Miller, Wichita St., Iowa & Oregon St.	1952-89	657	382	.632
Fred Enke, Louisville & Arizona	1926-61	522	344	.603
Tony Hinkle, Butler	1927-42, 46-67	520	353	.596
Marv Harshman, Pacific Lutheran, Washington St. & Washington	1946-83	596	431	.580

39 Seasons	Seasons	W	L	Pct.
Adolph Rupp, Kentucky	1931-52, 54-70	833	177	.825

	Seasons	W	L	Pct.
Phog Allen, Baker, Kansas, Haskell, Central Mo. St. & Kansas	1906-09, 13-47	607	185	.766
Ed Diddle, Western Ky.	1923-61	732	260	.740
Henry Iba, Northwest Mo. St., Colorado & Oklahoma St.	1930-68	741	313	.703
Ray Meyer, DePaul	1943-81	650	337	.659
Tony Hinkle, Butler	1927-42, 46-68	531	367	.591
Marv Harshman, Pacific Lutheran, Washington St. & Washington	1946-84	620	438	.586

40 Seasons	Seasons	W	L	Pct.
Adolph Rupp, Kentucky	1931-52, 54-71	855	183	.824
Phog Allen, Baker, Kansas, Haskell, Central Mo. St. & Kansas	1906-09, 13-48	616	200	.755
Ed Diddle, Western Ky.	1923-62	749	270	.735
Henry Iba, Northwest Mo. St., Colorado & Oklahoma St.	1930-69	753	326	.698
Ray Meyer, DePaul	1943-82	676	339	.666
Marv Harshman, Pacific Lutheran, Washington St. & Washington	1946-85	642	448	.589
Tony Hinkle, Butler	1927-42, 46-69	542	382	.587

41 Seasons	Seasons	W	L	Pct.
Adolph Rupp, Kentucky	1931-52, 54-72	876	190	.822
Phog Allen, Baker, Kansas, Haskell, Central Mo. St. & Kansas	1906-09, 13-49	628	212	.748
Ed Diddle, Western Ky.	1923-63	754	286	.725
Henry Iba, Northwest Mo. St., Colorado & Oklahoma St.	1930-70	767	338	.694
Ray Meyer, DePaul	1943-83	697	351	.665
Tony Hinkle, Butler	1927-42, 46-70	557	393	.586

42 Seasons	Seasons	W	L	Pct.
Phog Allen, Baker, Kansas, Haskell, Central Mo. St. & Kansas	1906-09, 13-50	642	223	.742
Ed Diddle, Western Ky.	1923-64	759	302	.715
Ray Meyer, DePaul	1943-84	724	354	.672

DIVISION I MEN'S COACHES—TOP 10 BEST CAREER STARTS—BY WINS

(Head Coaches With At Least Half Their Seasons at Division I)

1 Season	Season	W	L	Pct.
Bill Hodges, Indiana St.	1979	33	1	.970
John Warren, Oregon	1945	30	13	.698
Phil Johnson, Weber St.	1969	27	3	.900
Blaine Taylor, Montana	1992	27	4	.871
Jim Boeheim, Syracuse	1977	26	4	.867
Everett Case, North Caro. St.	1947	26	5	.839
Denny Crum, Louisville	1972	26	5	.839
Pete Herrmann, Navy	1987	26	6	.813
Nolan Richardson, Tulsa	1981	26	7	.788
Dick Hunsaker, Ball St.	1990	26	7	.788
Larry Finch, Memphis St.	1987	26	8	.765
Everett Case, North Caro. St.	1947	26	5	.839
Denny Crum, Louisville	1972	26	5	.839
Pete Herrmann, Navy	1987	26	6	.813

2 Seasons	Seasons	W	L	Pct.
Everett Case, North Caro. St.	1947-48	55	8	.873
Ben Carnevale, North Caro.	1945-46	52	11	.825
Gary Cunningham, UCLA	1978-79	50	8	.862
Kermit Davis Jr., Idaho	1989-90	50	12	.806
Nolan Richardson, Tulsa	1981-82	50	13	.794
Stan Watts, Brigham Young	1950-51	50	21	.704
Denny Crum, Louisville	1972-73	49	8	.860
Bill Hodges, Indiana St.	1979-80	49	12	.803
Peter Barry, San Francisco	1981-82	49	13	.790
Roy Williams, Kansas	1989-90	49	17	.742

3 Seasons	Seasons	W	L	Pct.
Everett Case, North Caro. St.	1947-49	80	16	.833
Roy Williams, Kansas	1989-91	76	25	.752
Jim Boeheim, Syracuse	1977-79	74	14	.841
Jerry Tarkanian, Long Beach St.	1969-71	71	13	.845
Dick Hunsaker, Ball St.	1990-92	71	26	.732
Denny Crum, Louisville	1972-74	70	19	.787
Don Donoher, Dayton	1965-67	70	19	.787
Pat Foster, Lamar	1981-83	70	20	.777
Pete Gillen, Xavier (Ohio)	1986-88	70	22	.761
Randy Ayers, Ohio St.	1990-92	70	23	.753
Speedy Morris, La Salle	1987-89	70	29	.707

4 Seasons	Seasons	W	L	Pct.
Everett Case, North Caro. St.	1947-50	107	22	.829
Bruce Stewart, West Va. Wesleyan & Middle Tenn. St.	1983-86	104	34	.754
Roy Williams, Kansas	1989-92	103	30	.774
Jim Boeheim, Syracuse	1977-80	100	18	.847
Speedy Morris, La Salle	1987-90	100	31	.763
Denny Crum, Louisville	1972-75	98	22	.817
Dick Hunsaker, Ball St.	1990-93	97	34	.740
Jerry Tarkanian, Long Beach St.	1969-72	96	17	.850
Pat Foster, Lamar	1981-84	96	25	.793
Nolan Richardson, Tulsa	1981-84	96	29	.768

5 Seasons	Seasons	W	L	Pct.
Everett Case, North Caro. St.	1947-51	137	29	.825

	Season	W	L	Pct.
Roy Williams, Kansas	1989-93	132	37	.781
Bruce Stewart, West Va. Wesleyan & Middle Tenn. St.	1983-87	126	41	.754
Forddy Anderson, Drake & Bradley	1947-51	123	42	.745
Jerry Tarkanian, Long Beach St. & Nevada-Las Vegas	1969-73	122	20	.859
Jim Boeheim, Syracuse	1977-81	122	30	.803
Fred Schaus, West Va.	1955-59	120	32	.789
Larry Brown, UCLA & Kansas	1980-81, 84-86	120	38	.759
Nolan Richardson, Tulsa	1981-85	119	37	.763
Speedy Morris, La Salle	1987-91	119	41	.744
Pete Gillen, Xavier (Ohio)	1986-90	119	39	.753

6 Seasons	Seasons	W	L	Pct.
Everett Case, North Caro. St.	1947-52	161	39	.805
Bruce Stewart, West Va. Wesleyan & Middle Tenn. St.	1983-88	149	52	.741
Fred Schaus, West Va.	1955-60	146	37	.798
Larry Brown, UCLA & Kansas	1980-81, 84-87	145	49	.747
Jerry Tarkanian, Long Beach St. & Nevada-Las Vegas	1969-74	142	26	.845
Pete Gillen, Xavier (Ohio)	1986-91	141	49	.742
Forddy Anderson, Drake & Bradley	1947-52	140	54	.722
Denny Crum, Louisville	1972-77	139	37	.790
Speedy Morris, La Salle	1987-92	139	52	.728
Jim Boeheim, Syracuse	1977-82	138	43	.762

7 Seasons	Seasons	W	L	Pct.
Everett Case, North Caro. St.	1947-53	187	45	.806
Larry Brown, UCLA & Kansas	1980-81, 84-88	172	60	.741
Bruce Stewart, West Va. Wesleyan & Middle Tenn. St.	1983-89	172	60	.741
Jerry Tarkanian, Long Beach St. & Nevada-Las Vegas	1969-75	166	31	.843
Denny Crum, Louisville	1972-78	162	44	.786
Fred Schaus, West Va. & Purdue	1955-60, 73	161	46	.778
Howard Hobson, Southern Ore. & Oregon	1933-39	161	48	.770
Jim Boeheim, Syracuse	1977-83	159	53	.750
Vic Bubas, Duke	1960-66	158	39	.802
Boyd Grant, Fresno St.	1978-84	156	50	.757
Pete Gillen, Xavier (Ohio)	1986-92	156	61	.719

8 Seasons	Seasons	W	L	Pct.
Everett Case, North Caro. St.	1947-54	213	52	.804
Jerry Tarkanian, Long Beach St. & Nevada-Las Vegas	1969-76	195	33	.855
Denny Crum, Louisville	1972-79	186	52	.782
Bruce Stewart, West Va. Wesleyan & Middle Tenn. St.	1983-90	184	75	.710
Fred Schaus, West Va. & Purdue	1955-60, 73-74	182	55	.768
Jim Boeheim, Syracuse	1977-84	182	62	.745
Howard Hobson, Southern Ore. & Oregon	1933-40	180	60	.750
Pete Gillen, Xavier (Ohio)	1986-93	180	67	.729
Boyd Grant, Fresno St.	1978-85	179	59	.752
Charlie Spoonhour, Southwest Mo. St.	1984-91	174	73	.704
Forddy Anderson, Drake & Bradley	1947-54	174	79	.688

9 Seasons	Seasons	W	L	Pct.
Everett Case, North Caro. St.	1947-55	241	56	.811
Jerry Tarkanian, Long Beach St. & Nevada-Las Vegas	1969-77	224	36	.862
Denny Crum, Louisville	1972-80	219	55	.799
Jim Boeheim, Syracuse	1977-85	204	71	.742
Fred Schaus, West Va. & Purdue	1955-60, 73-75	199	66	.751
Vic Bubas, Duke	1960-68	198	54	.786
Howard Hobson, Southern Ore. & Oregon	1933-41	198	78	.717
Tom Blackburn, Dayton	1948-56	198	74	.728
Charlie Spoonhour, Southwest Mo. St.	1984-92	197	81	.709
Nolan Richardson, Tulsa & Arkansas	1981-89	196	83	.703

10 Seasons	Seasons	W	L	Pct.
Everett Case, North Caro. St.	1947-56	265	60	.815
Jerry Tarkanian, Long Beach St. & Nevada-Las Vegas	1969-78	244	44	.847
Denny Crum, Louisville	1972-81	240	64	.789
Jim Boeheim, Syracuse	1977-86	230	77	.749
Nolan Richardson, Tulsa & Arkansas	1981-90	226	88	.720
Tom Blackburn, Dayton	1948-57	217	83	.723
Boyd Grant, Fresno St. & Colorado St.	1978-86, 88	216	87	.713
Gene Keady, Western Ky. & Purdue	1979-88	216	88	.711
Wimp Sanderson, Alabama	1981-90	216	99	.686
Fred Schaus, West Va. & Purdue	1955-60, 73-76	215	77	.736

11 Seasons	Seasons	W	L	Pct.
Everett Case, North Caro. St.	1947-57	280	71	.798
Denny Crum, Louisville	1972-82	263	74	.780
Jim Boeheim, Syracuse	1977-87	261	84	.757
Nolan Richardson, Tulsa & Arkansas	1981-91	260	92	.739
Jerry Tarkanian, Long Beach St. & Nevada-Las Vegas	1969-79	259	49	.841
Tom Blackburn, Dayton	1948-58	242	87	.736

	Seasons	W	L	Pct.
Boyd Grant, Fresno St. & Colorado St.	1978-86, 88-89	239	97	.711
Wimp Sanderson, Alabama	1981-91	239	109	.687
Fred Schaus, West Va. & Purdue	1955-60, 73-77	235	85	.734
Bob Huggins, Walsh, Akron & Cincinnati	1981-92	235	103	.695

12 Seasons	Seasons	W	L	Pct.
Everett Case, North Caro. St.	1947-58	298	77	.795
Denny Crum, Louisville	1972-83	295	78	.791
Jim Boeheim, Syracuse	1977-88	287	93	.755
Nolan Richardson, Tulsa & Arkansas	1981-92	286	100	.741
Jerry Tarkanian, Long Beach St. & Nevada-Las Vegas	1969-80	282	58	.829
Wimp Sanderson, Alabama	1981-92	265	118	.692
John Thompson, Georgetown	1973-84	262	104	.716
Bob Huggins, Walsh, Akron & Cincinnati	1981-93	262	108	.708
Boyd Grant, Fresno St. & Colorado St.	1978-86, 88-90	260	106	.710
Peck Hickman, Louisville	1945-56	256	79	.764
Lou Carnesecca, St. John's (N.Y.)	1966-70, 74-80	256	90	.740
Tom Blackburn, Dayton	1948-59	256	99	.721

13 Seasons	Seasons	W	L	Pct.
Everett Case, North Caro. St.	1947-59	320	81	.798
Denny Crum, Louisville	1972-84	319	89	.782
Jim Boeheim, Syracuse	1977-89	317	101	.758
Nolan Richardson, Tulsa & Arkansas	1981-93	308	109	.739
Jerry Tarkanian, Long Beach St. & Nevada-Las Vegas	1969-81	298	70	.810
John Thompson, Georgetown	1973-85	297	107	.735
Peck Hickman, Louisville	1945-57	277	84	.767
Tom Blackburn, Dayton	1948-60	277	106	.723
Pat Foster, Lamar & Houston	1981-93	276	122	.693
Lou Carnesecca, St. John's (N.Y.)	1966-70, 74-81	273	101	.730

14 Seasons	Seasons	W	L	Pct.
Jim Boeheim, Syracuse	1977-90	343	108	.761
Denny Crum, Louisville	1972-85	338	107	.760
Everett Case, North Caro. St.	1947-60	331	96	.775
John Thompson, Georgetown	1973-86	321	115	.736
Jerry Tarkanian, Long Beach St. & Nevada-Las Vegas	1969-82	318	80	.799
Billy Tubbs, Southwest Tex. St., Lamar & Oklahoma	1972-73, 77-88	306	142	.683
Tom Blackburn, Dayton	1948-61	297	115	.721
Eddie Sutton, Creighton, Arkansas & Kentucky	1970-83	295	105	.738

	Seasons	W	L	Pct.
Lou Carnesecca, St. John's (N.Y.)	1966-70, 74-82	294	110	.728
Gale Catlett, Cincinnati & West Va.	1973-86	292	124	.702

15 Seasons	Seasons	W	L	Pct.
Denny Crum, Louisville	1972-86	370	114	.764
Jim Boeheim, Syracuse	1977-91	369	114	.764
John Thompson, Georgetown	1973-87	350	120	.745
Everett Case, North Caro. St.	1947-61	347	105	.768
Jerry Tarkanian, Long Beach St. & Nevada-Las Vegas	1969-83	346	83	.807
Billy Tubbs, Southwest Tex. St., Lamar & Oklahoma	1972-73, 77-89	336	148	.694
Lou Carnesecca, St. John's (N.Y.)	1966-70, 74-83	322	115	.737
Tom Blackburn, Dayton	1948-62	321	121	.726
Eddie Sutton, Creighton, Arkansas & Kentucky	1970-84	320	112	.741
Gale Catlett, Cincinnati & West Va.	1973-87	315	132	.705

16 Seasons	Seasons	W	L	Pct.
Jim Boeheim, Syracuse	1977-92	391	124	.759
Denny Crum, Louisville	1972-87	388	128	.752
Jerry Tarkanian, Long Beach St. & Nevada-Las Vegas	1969-84	375	89	.808
John Thompson, Georgetown	1973-88	370	130	.740
Billy Tubbs, Southwest Tex. St., Lamar & Oklahoma	1972-73, 77-90	363	153	.703
Everett Case, North Caro. St.	1947-62	358	111	.763
Eddie Sutton, Creighton, Arkansas & Kentucky	1970-85	342	125	.732
Dean Smith, North Caro.	1962-77	340	113	.751
Lou Carnesecca, St. John's (N.Y.)	1966-70, 74-84	340	127	.728
Murray Arnold, Birmingham Southern, Tenn.-Chatt. & Western Ky.	1971-78, 80-88	338	142	.704

17 Seasons	Seasons	W	L	Pct.
Denny Crum, Louisville	1972-88	412	139	.748
Jim Boeheim, Syracuse	1977-93	411	133	.756
Jerry Tarkanian, Long Beach St. & Nevada-Las Vegas	1969-85	403	93	.813
John Thompson, Georgetown	1973-89	399	135	.747
Billy Tubbs, Southwest Tex. St., Lamar & Oklahoma	1972-73, 77-91	383	168	.695
Eddie Sutton, Creighton, Arkansas & Kentucky	1970-86	374	129	.744
Lou Carnesecca, St. John's (N.Y.)	1966-70, 74-85	371	131	.739
Mike Krzyzewski, Army & Duke	1976-92	370	169	.686

	Seasons	W	L	Pct.
Everett Case, North Caro. St.	1947-63	368	122	.751
Henry Iba, Northwest Mo. St., Colorado & Oklahoma St.	1930-46	364	91	.800

18 Seasons	Seasons	W	L	Pct.
Jerry Tarkanian, Long Beach St. & Nevada-Las Vegas	1969-86	436	98	.816
Denny Crum, Louisville	1972-89	436	148	.747
John Thompson, Georgetown	1973-90	423	142	.749
Billy Tubbs, Southwest Tex. St., Lamar & Oklahoma	1972-73, 77-92	404	177	.695
Lou Carnesecca, St. John's (N.Y.)	1966-70, 74-86	402	136	.747
Mike Krzyzewski, Army & Duke	1976-93	394	177	.690
Eddie Sutton, Creighton, Arkansas & Kentucky	1970-87	392	140	.740
Henry Iba, Northwest Mo. St., Colorado & Oklahoma St.	1930-47	388	99	.797
Dean Smith, North Caro.	1962-79	386	127	.752
Lute Olson, Long Beach St., Iowa & Arizona	1974-91	381	162	.702

19 Seasons	Seasons	W	L	Pct.
Jerry Tarkanian, Long Beach St. & Nevada-Las Vegas	1969-87	473	100	.825
Denny Crum, Louisville	1972-90	463	156	.748
John Thompson, Georgetown	1973-91	442	155	.740
Billy Tubbs, Southwest Tex. St., Lamar & Oklahoma	1972-73, 77-93	424	189	.692
Lou Carnesecca, St. John's (N.Y.)	1966-70, 74-87	423	145	.745
Eddie Sutton, Creighton, Arkansas & Kentucky	1970-88	417	145	.742
Henry Iba, Northwest Mo. St., Colorado & Oklahoma St.	1930-48	415	103	.801
Dean Smith, North Caro.	1962-80	407	135	.751
Lute Olson, Long Beach St., Iowa & Arizona	1974-92	405	169	.706
Bob Knight, Army & Indiana	1966-84	398	143	.736

20 Seasons	Seasons	W	L	Pct.
Jerry Tarkanian, Long Beach St. & Nevada-Las Vegas	1969-88	501	106	.825
Denny Crum, Louisville	1972-91	477	172	.735
John Thompson, Georgetown	1973-92	464	165	.738
John Chaney, Cheyney & Temple	1973-92	458	143	.762
Lou Carnesecca, St. John's (N.Y.)	1966-70, 74-88	440	157	.737
Henry Iba, Northwest Mo. St., Colorado & Oklahoma St.	1930-49	438	108	.802
Dean Smith, North Caro.	1962-81	436	143	.753
Eddie Sutton, Creighton, Arkansas & Kentucky	1970-89	430	164	.724
Lute Olson, Long Beach St., Iowa & Arizona	1974-93	429	173	.713
Bob Knight, Army & Indiana	1966-85	417	157	.726

21 Seasons	Seasons	W	L	Pct.
Jerry Tarkanian, Long Beach St. & Nevada-Las Vegas	1969-89	530	114	.823
Denny Crum, Louisville	1972-92	496	183	.730
John Thompson, Georgetown	1973-93	484	178	.731
John Chaney, Cheyney & Temple	1973-93	478	156	.754
Dean Smith, North Caro.	1962-82	468	145	.763
Lou Carnesecca, St. John's (N.Y.)	1966-70, 74-89	460	170	.730
Henry Iba, Northwest Mo. St., Colorado & Oklahoma St.	1930-50	456	117	.796
Eddie Sutton, Creighton, Arkansas, Kentucky & Oklahoma St.	1970-89, 91	454	172	.725
Adolph Rupp, Kentucky	1931-51	443	80	.847
Bob Knight, Army & Indiana	1966-86	438	165	.726

22 Seasons	Seasons	W	L	Pct.
Jerry Tarkanian, Long Beach St. & Nevada-Las Vegas	1969-90	565	119	.826
Denny Crum, Louisville	1972-93	518	192	.730
Dean Smith, North Caro.	1962-83	496	153	.764
Henry Iba, Northwest Mo. St., Colorado & Oklahoma St.	1930-51	485	123	.798
Lou Carnesecca, St. John's (N.Y.)	1966-70, 74-90	484	180	.729
Eddie Sutton, Creighton, Arkansas, Kentucky & Oklahoma St.	1970-89, 91-92	482	180	.728
Adolph Rupp, Kentucky	1931-52	472	83	.850
Bob Knight, Army & Indiana	1966-87	468	169	.735
John Wooden, Indiana St. & UCLA	1947-68	464	151	.754
Lefty Driesell, Davidson & Maryland	1961-82	436	180	.708

23 Seasons	Seasons	W	L	Pct.
Jerry Tarkanian, Long Beach St. & Nevada-Las Vegas	1969-91	599	120	.833
Dean Smith, North Caro.	1962-84	524	156	.771
Lou Carnesecca, St. John's (N.Y.)	1966-70, 74-91	507	189	.728
Henry Iba, Northwest Mo. St., Colorado & Oklahoma St.	1930-52	504	131	.794
Eddie Sutton, Creighton, Arkansas, Kentucky & Oklahoma St.	1970-89, 91-93	502	189	.726
Adolph Rupp, Kentucky	1931-52, 54	497	83	.857

	Seasons	W	L	Pct.
John Wooden, Indiana St. & UCLA	1947-69	493	152	.764
Bob Knight, Army & Indiana	1966-88	487	179	.731
Lefty Driesell, Davidson & Maryland	1961-83	456	190	.706
Peck Hickman, Louisville	1945-67	443	183	.708

24 Seasons	Seasons	W	L	Pct.
Jerry Tarkanian, Long Beach St. & Nevada-Las Vegas	1969-92	625	122	.837
Dean Smith, North Caro.	1962-85	551	165	.770
Henry Iba, Northwest Mo. St., Colorado & Oklahoma St.	1930-53	527	138	.792
Lou Carnesecca, St. John's (N.Y.)	1966-70, 74-92	526	200	.725
John Wooden, Indiana St. & UCLA	1947-70	521	154	.772
Adolph Rupp, Kentucky	1931-52, 54-55	520	86	.858
Bob Knight, Army & Indiana	1966-89	514	187	.733
Lefty Driesell, Davidson & Maryland	1961-84	480	198	.708
Lou Henson, Hardin-Simmons & Illinois	1963-86	458	226	.670
Gene Bartow, Central Mo. St., Valparaiso, Memphis St., Illinois, UCLA, & Ala.-Birmingham	1962-77, 78-86	455	232	.662

25 Seasons	Seasons	W	L	Pct.
Dean Smith, North Caro.	1962-86	579	171	.772
Henry Iba, Northwest Mo. St., Colorado & Oklahoma St.	1930-54	551	143	.794
John Wooden, Indiana St. & UCLA	1947-71	550	155	.780
Adolph Rupp, Kentucky	1931-52, 54-56	540	92	.854
Bob Knight, Army & Indiana	1966-90	532	198	.729
Lefty Driesell, Davidson & Maryland	1961-85	505	220	.706
Lou Henson, Hardin-Simmons & Illinois	1963-87	481	234	.673
Gene Bartow, Central Mo. St., Valparaiso, Memphis St., Illinois, UCLA, & Ala.-Birmingham	1962-77, 78-87	476	243	.662
Guy Lewis, Houston	1957-81	474	235	.669
Frank McGuire, St. John's (N.Y.), North Caro. & South Caro.	1948-61, 65-75	471	179	.725

26 Seasons	Seasons	W	L	Pct.
Dean Smith, North Caro.	1962-87	611	175	.777
John Wooden, Indiana St. & UCLA	1947-72	580	155	.789
Henry Iba, Northwest Mo. St., Colorado & Oklahoma St.	1930-55	563	156	.783
Adolph Rupp, Kentucky	1931-52, 54-57	563	97	.853
Bob Knight, Army & Indiana	1966-91	561	203	.734
Lefty Driesell, Davidson & Maryland	1961-86	524	224	.701
Lou Henson, Hardin-Simmons & Illinois	1963-88	504	244	.674
Guy Lewis, Houston	1957-82	499	243	.673
Don Haskins, UTEP	1962-87	493	215	.696
Gene Bartow, Central Mo. St., Valparaiso, Memphis St., Illinois, UCLA, & Ala.-Birmingham	1962-77, 78-88	492	258	.656

27 Seasons	Seasons	W	L	Pct.
Dean Smith, North Caro.	1962-88	638	182	.778
John Wooden, Indiana St. & UCLA	1947-73	610	155	.797
Bob Knight, Army & Indiana	1966-92	588	210	.737
Adolph Rupp, Kentucky	1931-52 54-58	586	103	.851
Henry Iba, Northwest Mo. St., Colorado & Oklahoma St.	1930-56	581	165	.779
Lefty Driesell, Davidson, Maryland & James Madison	1961-86, 89	540	238	.694
Lou Henson, Hardin-Simmons & Illinois	1963-89	535	249	.682
Guy Lewis, Houston	1957-83	530	246	.683
Don Haskins, UTEP	1962-88	516	225	.696
Gene Bartow, Central Mo. St., Valparaiso, Memphis St., Illinois, UCLA, & Ala.-Birmingham	1962-77, 78-89	514	270	.656

28 Seasons	Seasons	W	L	Pct.
Dean Smith, North Caro.	1962-89	667	190	.778
John Wooden, Indiana St. & UCLA	1947-74	636	159	.800
Bob Knight, Army & Indiana	1966-93	619	214	.743
Adolph Rupp, Kentucky	1931-52, 54-59	610	106	.852
Henry Iba, Northwest Mo. St., Colorado & Oklahoma St.	1930-57	598	174	.775
Guy Lewis, Houston	1957-84	562	251	.691
Lefty Driesell, Davidson, Maryland & James Madison	1961-86, 89-90	560	249	.692
Lou Henson, Hardin-Simmons & Illinois	1963-90	556	257	.684
Don Haskins, UTEP	1962-89	542	232	.700
Gene Bartow, Central Mo. St., Valparaiso, Memphis St., Illinois, UCLA, & Ala.-Birmingham	1962-77, 78-90	536	279	.658

29 Seasons	Seasons	W	L	Pct.
Dean Smith, North Caro.	1962-90	688	203	.772
John Wooden, Indiana St. & UCLA	1947-75	664	162	.804
Adolph Rupp, Kentucky	1931-52, 54-60	628	113	.848
Henry Iba, Northwest Mo. St., Colorado & Oklahoma St.	1930-58	619	182	.773

	Seasons	W	L	Pct.
Lefty Driesell, Davidson, Maryland & James Madison	1961-86, 89-91	579	259	.691
Guy Lewis, Houston	1957-85	578	265	.686
Lou Henson, Hardin-Simmons & Illinois	1963-91	577	267	.684
Don Haskins, UTEP	1962-90	563	243	.699
Gene Bartow, Central Mo. St., Valparaiso, Memphis St., Illinois, UCLA, & Ala.-Birmingham	1962-77, 78-91	554	292	.655
Norm Stewart, Northern Iowa & Missouri	1962-90	552	273	.669

30 Seasons	**Seasons**	**W**	**L**	**Pct.**
Dean Smith, North Caro.	1962-91	717	209	.774
Adolph Rupp, Kentucky	1931-52, 54-61	647	122	.841
Henry Iba, Northwest Mo. St., Colorado & Oklahoma St.	1930-59	630	196	.763
Lefty Driesell, Davidson, Maryland & James Madison	1961-86, 89-92	600	270	.690
Guy Lewis, Houston	1957-86	592	279	.680
Lou Henson, Hardin-Simmons & Illinois	1963-92	590	282	.677
Don Haskins, UTEP	1962-91	579	256	.693
Gene Bartow, Central Mo. St., Valparaiso, Memphis St., Illinois, UCLA, & Ala.-Birmingham	1962-77, 78-92	574	301	.656
Norm Stewart, Northern Iowa & Missouri	1962-91	572	283	.669
Ed Diddle, Western Ky.	1923-52	558	184	.752

31 Seasons	**Seasons**	**W**	**L**	**Pct.**
Dean Smith, North Caro.	1962-92	740	219	.772
Adolph Rupp, Kentucky	1931-52, 54-62	670	125	.843
Henry Iba, Northwest Mo. St., Colorado & Oklahoma St.	1930-60	640	211	.752
Lefty Driesell, Davidson, Maryland & James Madison	1961-86, 89-93	621	279	.690
Lou Henson, Hardin-Simmons & Illinois	1963-93	609	295	.674
Don Haskins, UTEP	1962-92	606	263	.697
Gene Bartow, Central Mo. St., Valparaiso, Memphis St., Illinois, UCLA, & Ala.-Birmingham	1962-77, 78-93	595	315	.654
Norm Stewart, Northern Iowa & Missouri	1962-92	593	292	.670
Ed Diddle, Western Ky.	1923-53	583	190	.754
Abe Lemons, Oklahoma City, Tex.-Pan American, Texas, & Oklahoma City	1956-87	548	305	.642

32 Seasons	**Seasons**	**W**	**L**	**Pct.**
Dean Smith, North Caro.	1962-93	774	223	.776
Adolph Rupp, Kentucky	1931-52, 54-63	686	134	.837
Henry Iba, Northwest Mo. St., Colorado & Oklahoma St.	1930-61	655	221	.748
Don Haskins, UTEP	1962-93	627	276	.694
Ed Diddle, Western Ky.	1923-54	612	193	.760
Norm Stewart, Northern Iowa & Missouri	1962-93	612	306	.667
Abe Lemons, Oklahoma City, Tex.-Pan American, Texas & Oklahoma City	1956-82, 84-88	567	317	.641
Ralph Miller, Wichita St., Iowa & Oregon St.	1952-83	540	321	.627
Gary Colson, Valdosta St., Pepperdine, New Mexico & Fresno St.	1959-79, 81-88, 91-93	529	359	.596
Norm Sloan, Presbyterian, Citadel, Florida, North Caro. St. & Florida	1952-55, 57-84	523	333	.611

33 Seasons	**Seasons**	**W**	**L**	**Pct.**
Adolph Rupp, Kentucky	1931-52, 54-64	707	140	.835
Henry Iba, Northwest Mo. St., Colorado & Oklahoma St.	1930-62	669	232	.743
Ed Diddle, Western Ky.	1923-55	630	203	.756
Abe Lemons, Oklahoma City, Tex.-Pan American, Texas & Oklahoma City	1956-82, 84-89	579	331	.636
Ralph Miller, Wichita St., Iowa & Oregon St.	1952-84	562	328	.631
Norm Sloan, Presbyterian, Citadel, Florida, North Caro. St. & Florida	1952-55, 57-85	541	345	.611
Marv Harshman, Pacific Lutheran, Washington St. & Washington	1946-78	518	367	.585
Phog Allen, Baker, Kansas, Haskell, Central Mo. St. & Kansas	1906-09, 13-41	512	153	.770
Glenn Wilkes, Stetson	1958-90	512	389	.568
Ray Meyer, DePaul	1943-75	509	303	.627

34 Seasons	**Seasons**	**W**	**L**	**Pct.**
Adolph Rupp, Kentucky	1931-52, 54-65	722	150	.828
Henry Iba, Northwest Mo. St., Colorado & Oklahoma St.	1930-63	685	241	.740
Ed Diddle, Western Ky.	1923-56	646	215	.750
Abe Lemons, Oklahoma City, Tex.-Pan American, Texas & Oklahoma City	1956-82, 84-90	597	344	.634
Ralph Miller, Wichita St., Iowa & Oregon St.	1952-85	584	337	.634
Norm Sloan, Presbyterian, Citadel, Florida, North Caro. St. & Florida	1952-55, 57-86	560	359	.609

	Seasons	W	L	Pct.
Phog Allen, Baker, Kansas, Haskell, Central Mo. St. & Kansas	1906-09, 13-42	529	158	.770
Ray Meyer, DePaul	1943-76	529	312	.629
Marv Harshman, Pacific Lutheran, Washington St. & Washington	1946-79	529	383	.580
Glenn Wilkes, Stetson	1958-91	527	405	.565

35 Seasons	Seasons	W	L	Pct.
Adolph Rupp, Kentucky	1931-52, 54-66	749	152	.831
Henry Iba, Northwest Mo. St., Colorado & Oklahoma St.	1930-64	700	251	.736
Ed Diddle, Western Ky.	1923-57	663	224	.747
Ralph Miller, Wichita St., Iowa & Oregon St.	1952-86	596	352	.629
Norm Sloan, Presbyterian, Citadel, Florida, North Caro. St. & Florida	1952-55, 57-87	583	370	.612
Phog Allen, Baker, Kansas, Haskell, Central Mo. St. & Kansas	1906-09, 13-43	551	164	.771
Marv Harshman, Pacific Lutheran, Washington St. & Washington	1946-80	547	393	.582
Ray Meyer, DePaul	1943-77	544	324	.627
Glenn Wilkes, Stetson	1958-92	538	422	.560
Fred Enke, Louisville & Arizona	1926-58	497	293	.629

36 Seasons	Seasons	W	L	Pct.
Adolph Rupp, Kentucky	1931-52, 54-67	762	165	.822
Henry Iba, Northwest Mo. St., Colorado & Oklahoma St.	1930-65	720	258	.736
Ed Diddle, Western Ky.	1923-58	677	235	.742
Ralph Miller, Wichita St., Iowa & Oregon St.	1952-87	615	363	.629
Norm Sloan, Presbyterian, Citadel, Florida, North Caro. St. & Florida	1952-55, 57-88	606	382	.613
Slats Gill, Oregon St.	1929-64	599	393	.604
Ray Meyer, DePaul	1943-78	571	327	.636
Phog Allen, Baker, Kansas, Haskell, Central Mo. St. & Kansas	1906-09, 13-44	568	173	.767
Marv Harshman, Pacific Lutheran, Washington St. & Washington	1946-81	561	406	.580
Glenn Wilkes, Stetson	1958-93	551	436	.558

37 Seasons	Seasons	W	L	Pct.
Adolph Rupp, Kentucky	1931-52, 54-68	784	170	.822
Henry Iba, Northwest Mo. St., Colorado & Oklahoma St.	1930-66	724	279	.722
Ed Diddle, Western Ky.	1923-59	693	245	.739
Ralph Miller, Wichita St., Iowa & Oregon St.	1952-88	635	374	.629
Norm Sloan, Presbyterian, Citadel, Florida, North Caro. St. & Florida	1952-55, 57-89	627	395	.614
Ray Meyer, DePaul	1943-79	597	333	.642
Phog Allen, Baker, Kansas, Haskell, Central Mo. St. & Kansas	1906-09, 13-45	580	178	.765
Marv Harshman, Pacific Lutheran, Washington St. & Washington	1946-82	580	416	.582
Fred Enke, Louisville & Arizona	1926-60	511	329	.608
Tony Hinkle, Butler	1927-42, 46-66	511	336	.603

38 Seasons	Seasons	W	L	Pct.
Adolph Rupp, Kentucky	1931-52, 54-69	807	175	.822
Henry Iba, Northwest Mo. St., Colorado & Oklahoma St.	1930-67	731	297	.711
Ed Diddle, Western Ky.	1923-60	714	252	.739
Ralph Miller, Wichita St., Iowa & Oregon St.	1952-89	657	382	.632
Ray Meyer, DePaul	1943-80	623	335	.650
Phog Allen, Baker, Kansas, Haskell, Central Mo. St. & Kansas	1906-09, 13-46	599	180	.769
Marv Harshman, Pacific Lutheran, Washington St. & Washington	1946-83	596	431	.580
Fred Enke, Louisville & Arizona	1926-61	522	344	.603
Tony Hinkle, Butler	1927-42, 46-67	520	353	.596

39 Seasons	Seasons	W	L	Pct.
Adolph Rupp, Kentucky	1931-52, 54-70	833	177	.825
Henry Iba, Northwest Mo. St., Colorado & Oklahoma St.	1930-68	741	313	.703
Ed Diddle, Western Ky.	1923-61	732	260	.740
Ray Meyer, DePaul	1943-81	650	337	.659
Marv Harshman, Pacific Lutheran, Washington St. & Washington	1946-84	620	438	.586
Phog Allen, Baker, Kansas, Haskell, Central Mo. St. & Kansas	1906-09, 13-47	607	185	.766
Tony Hinkle, Butler	1927-42, 46-68	531	367	.591

40 Seasons	Seasons	W	L	Pct.
Adolph Rupp, Kentucky	1931-52, 54-71	855	183	.824
Henry Iba, Northwest Mo. St., Colorado & Oklahoma St.	1930-69	753	326	.698
Ed Diddle, Western Ky.	1923-62	749	270	.735
Ray Meyer, DePaul	1943-82	676	339	.666
Marv Harshman, Pacific Lutheran, Washington St. & Washington	1946-85	642	448	.589

	Seasons	W	L	Pct.
Phog Allen, Baker, Kansas, Haskell, Central Mo. St. & Kansas	1906-09, 13-40	616	200	.755
Tony Hinkle, Butler	1927-42, 46-69	542	382	.587

41 Seasons	Seasons	W	L	Pct.
Adolph Rupp, Kentucky	1931-52, 54-72	876	190	.822
Henry Iba, Northwest Mo. St., Colorado & Oklahoma St.	1930-70	767	338	.694
Ed Diddle, Western Ky.	1923-63	754	286	.725
Ray Meyer, DePaul	1943-83	697	351	.665

	Seasons	W	L	Pct.
Phog Allen, Baker, Kansas, Haskell, Central Mo. St. & Kansas	1906-09, 13-49	628	212	.748
Tony Hinkle, Butler	1927-42, 46-70	557	393	.586

42 Seasons	Seasons	W	L	Pct.
Ed Diddle, Western Ky.	1923-64	759	302	.715
Ray Meyer, DePaul	1943-84	724	354	.672
Phog Allen, Baker, Kansas, Haskell, Central Mo. St. & Kansas	1906-09, 13-50	642	223	.742

ACTIVE DIVISION I MEN'S COACHING RECORDS FOR LONGEVITY

(Minimum five years as a Division I head coach)

MOST GAMES

No.	Coach, School and Years
1,071	James Phelan, Mt. St. Mary's (Md.) 1955-93
997	Dean Smith, North Caro. 1962-93
918	Norm Stewart, Northern Iowa 1962-67, Missouri 68-93
910	Gene Bartow, Central Mo. St. 1962-64, Valparaiso 65-70, Memphis St. 71-74, Illinois 75, UCLA 76-77, Ala.-Birmingham 79-93
904	Lou Henson, Hardin-Simmons 1963-66, New Mexico St. 67-75, Illinois 76-93
903	Don Haskins, UTEP 1962-93
900	Lefty Driesell, Davidson 1961-69, Maryland 70-86, James Madison 89-93
888	Gary Colson, Valdosta St. 1959-68, Pepperdine 69-79, New Mexico 81-88, Fresno St. 91-93
848	Eldon Miller, Wittenberg 1963-70, Western Mich. 71-76, Ohio St. 77-86, Northern Iowa 87-93
833	Bob Knight, Army 1966-71, Indiana 72-93
795	Calvin Luther, DePauw 1955-58, Murray St. 59-73, Longwood 82-90, Tenn. Martin 91-93
785	Johnny Orr, Massachusetts 1964-66, Michigan 69-80, Iowa St. 81-93
779	Hugh Durham, Florida St. 1967-78, Georgia 79-93
734	Bill C. Foster, Shorter 1963-67, N.C.-Charlotte 71-75, Clemson 76-84, Miami (Fla.) 86-90, Virginia Tech 93
727	George Blaney, Stonehill 1968-69, Dartmouth 70-72, Holy Cross 73-93
725	Butch van Breda Kolff, Lafayette 1952-55, Hofstra 56-62, Princeton 63-67, New Orleans 78-79, Lafayette 85-88, Hofstra 89-93
717	Pete Carril, Lehigh 1967, Princeton 68-93
710	Denny Crum, Louisville 1972-93
691	Eddie Sutton, Creighton 1970-74, Arkansas 75-85, Kentucky 86-89, Oklahoma St. 91-93
675	Rollie Massimino, Stonybrook 1970-71, Villanova 74-92, Nevada-Las Vegas 93
673	Bob Hallberg, St. Xavier (Ill.) 1972-77, Chicago St. 78-87, Ill.-Chicago 88-93
662	John Thompson, Georgetown, 1973-93
648	Tom Davis, Lafayette 1972-77, Boston College 78-82, Stanford 83-86, Iowa 87-93
641	Tom Penders, Tufts, 1972-74, Columbia 75-78, Fordham 79-86, Rhode Island 87-88, Texas 89-93
636	Dale Brown, Louisiana St. 1973-93
634	John Chaney, Cheyney 1973-82, Temple 83-93
632	Jud Heathcote, Montana 1972-76, Michigan St. 77-93
630	Gale Catlett, Cincinnati 1973-78, West Va. 79-93
615	Ben Jobe, Talladega 1965-67, Alabama St. 68, South Caro. St. 69-73, Denver 79-80, Alabama A&M 83-86, Southern-B.R. 87-93
613	Billy Tubbs, Southwestern Tex. St. 1972-73, Lamar 77-80, Oklahoma 81-93
604	Jim Calhoun, Northeastern 1973-86, Connecticut 87-93
602	Lute Olson, Long Beach St. 1974, Iowa 75-83, Arizona 84-93
600	George Raveling, Washington St. 1973-83, Iowa 84-86, Southern Cal 87-93

MOST YEARS

No.	Coach, School and Years
39	James Phelan, Mt. S. Mary's (Md.) 1955-93
32	Gary Colson, Valdosta St. 1959-68, Pepperdine 69-79, New Mexico 81-88, Fresno St. 91-93
32	Don Haskins, UTEP 1962-93
32	Dean Smith, North Caro. 1962-93
32	Norm Stewart, Northern Iowa 1962-67, Missouri 68-93

No.	Coach, School and Years
31	Gene Bartow, Central Mo. St. 1962-64, Valparaiso 65-70, Memphis St. 71-74, Illinois 75, UCLA 76-77, Ala.-Birmingham 79-93
31	Lefty Driesell, Davidson 1961-69, Maryland 70-86, James Madison 89-93
31	Lou Henson, Hardin-Simmons 1963-66, New Mexico St. 67-75, Illinois 76-93
31	Eldon Miller, Wittenberg 1963-70, Western Mich. 71-76, Ohio St. 77-86, Northern Iowa 87-93
28	Bob Knight, Army 1966-71, Indiana 72-93
28	Johnny Orr, Massachusetts 1964-66, Michigan 69-80, Iowa St. 81-93
27	Pete Carril, Lehigh 1967, Princeton 68-93
27	Hugh Durham, Florida St. 1967-78, Georgia 79-93
27	Butch van Breda Kolff, Lafayette 1952-55, Hofstra 56-62, Princeton 63-67, New Orleans 78-79, Lafayette 85-88, Hofstra 89-93
26	George Blaney, Stonehill 1968-69, Dartmouth 70-72, Holy Cross 73-93
26	Bill C. Foster, Shorter 1963-67, N.C.-Charlotte 71-75, Clemson 76-84, Miami (Fla.) 86-90, Virginia Tech 93
23	Eddie Sutton, Creighton 1970-74, Arkansas 75-85, Kentucky 86-89, Oklahoma St. 91-93
22	Denny Crum, Louisville 1972-93
22	Tom Davis, Lafayette 1972-77, Boston College 78-82, Stanford 83-86, Iowa 87-93
22	Hank Egan, Air Force 1972-84, San Diego 85-93
22	Bob Hallberg, St. Xavier (Ill.) 1972-77, Chicago St. 78-87, Ill.-Chicago 88-93
22	Jud Heathcote, Montana 1972-76, Michigan St. 77-93
22	Ben Jobe, Talladega 1965-67, Alabama St. 68, South Caro. St. 69-73, Denver 79-80, Alabama A&M 83-86, Southern-B.R. 87-93
22	Paul Lizzo, FDU-Madison 1972-75, LIU-Brooklyn 76-93
22	Rollie Massimino, Stonybrook 1970-71, Villanova 74-92, Nevada-Las Vegas 93
22	Tom Penders, Tufts, 1972-74, Columbia 75-78, Fordham 79-86, Rhode Island 87-88, Texas 89-93

MOST YEARS AT CURRENT SCHOOL

No.	Coach, School and Years
39	James Phelan, #Mt. St. Mary's (Md.) 1955-93
32	Don Haskins, #UTEP 1962-93
32	Dean Smith, #North Caro. 1962-93
26	Pete Carril, Princeton 1968-93
26	Norm Stewart, Missouri 1968-93
22	Denny Crum, #Louisville 1972-93
22	Bob Knight, Indiana 1972-93
21	George Blaney, Holy Cross 1973-93
21	Dale Brown, Louisiana St. 1973-93
21	John Thompson, Georgetown 1973-93

 # Has coached only at this school.

MOST 20-WIN SEASONS

No.	Coach, School and Years
26	Dean Smith, North Caro. 1962-93
19	Lefty Driesell, Davidson 1961-69, Maryland 70-86, James Madison 89-93
18	Denny Crum, Louisville 1972-93
18	Bob Knight, Army 1966-71, Indiana 72-93
17	Lou Henson, Hardin-Simmons 1963-66, New Mexico St. 67-75, Illinois 76-93
16	Jim Boeheim, Syracuse 1977-93
16	John Chaney, Cheyney 1973-82, Temple 83-93
16	Don Haskins, UTEP 1962-93
16	John Thompson, Georgetown, 1973-93
15	Norm Stewart, Northern Iowa 1962-67, Missouri 68-93
15	Gene Bartow, Central Mo. St. 1962-64, Valparaiso 65-70, Memphis St. 71-74, Illinois 75, UCLA 76-77, Ala.-Birmingham 79-93
15	Lute Olson, Long Beach St. 1974, Iowa 75-83, Arizona 84-93
15	Eddie Sutton, Creighton 1970-74, Arkansas 75-85, Kentucky 86-89, Oklahoma St. 91-93
14	Billy Tubbs, Southwestern (Tex.) 1972-73, Lamar 77-80, Oklahoma 81-93
12	Gale Catlett, Cincinnati 1973-78, West Va. 79-93
12	Bob Hallberg, St. Xavier (Ill.) 1972-77, Chicago St. 78-87, Ill.-Chicago 88-93
12	Neil McCarthy, Weber St. 1976-85, New Mexico St. 86-93
11	Tom Davis, Lafayette 1972-77, Boston College 78-82, Stanford 83-86, Iowa 87-93
11	Mike Krzyzewski, Army 1976-80, Duke 81-93
11	Butch van Breda Kolff, Lafayette 1952-55, Hofstra 56-62, Princeton 63-67, New Orleans 78-79, Lafayette 85-88, Hofstra 89-93

MOST SCHOOLS

No.	Coach, School and Years
6	Gene Bartow, Central Mo. St. 1962-64, Valparaiso 65-70, Memphis St. 71-74, Illinois 75, UCLA 76-77, Ala.-Birmingham 79-93

No.	Coach, School and Years
6	Ben Jobe, Talladega 1965-67, Alabama St. 68, South Caro. St. 69-73, Denver 79-80, Alabama A&M 83-86, Southern-B.R. 87-93
5	Don DeVoe, Virginia Tech 1972-76, Wyoming 77-78, Tennessee 79-89, Florida 90, Navy 93
5	Bill C. Foster, Shorter 1963-67, N.C.-Charlotte 71-75, Clemson 76-84, Miami (Fla.) 86-90, Virginia Tech 93
5	Tates Locke, Army 1964-65, Miami (Ohio) 67-70, Clemson 71-75, Jacksonville 79-81, Indiana St. 91-93
5	Tom Penders, Tufts 1972-74, Columbia 75-78, Fordham 79-86, Rhode Island 87-88, Texas 89-93
4	Gary Colson, Valdosta St. 1959-68, Pepperdine 69-79, New Mexico 81-88, Fresno St. 91-93
4	Tom Davis, Lafayette 1972-77, Boston College 78-82, Stanford 83-86, Iowa 87-93
4	Joe Harrington, Hofstra 1980, George Mason 81-87, Long Beach St. 88-90, Colorado 91-93
4	Eldon Miller, Wittenberg 1963-70, Western Mich. 71-76, Ohio St. 77-86, Northern Iowa 87-93
4	Lynn Nance, Iowa St. 1977-80, Central Mo. St. 81-85, St. Mary's (Cal.) 87-89, Washington 91-93
4	Eddie Sutton, Creighton 1970-74, Arkansas 75-85, Kentucky 86-89, Oklahoma St. 91-93
4	Butch van Breda Kolff, Lafayette 1952-55, Hofstra 56-62, Princeton 63-67, New Orleans 78-79, Lafayette 85-88, Hofstra 89-93
4	Gary Williams, American 1979-82, Boston College 83-86, Ohio State 87-89, Maryland 91-93

ALL-TIME DIVISION I MEN'S COACHING RECORDS FOR LONGEVITY

(Minimum 10 head coaching seasons in Division I)

MOST GAMES

No.	Coach, School and Years
1,105	Henry Iba, Northwest Mo. St. 1930-33, Colorado 34, Oklahoma St. 35-70
1,090	Marv Harshman, Pacific Lutheran 1946-58, Washington St. 59-71, Washington 72-85
1,078	Ray Meyer, DePaul 1943-84
1,066	Adolph Rupp, Kentucky 1931-72
1,061	Ed Diddle, Western Ky. 1923-64
1,039	Ralph Miller, Wichita St. 1952-64, Iowa 65-70, Oregon St. 71-89
1,017	Norm Sloan, Presbyterian 1952-55, Citadel 57-60, Florida 61-66, North Caro. St. 67-80, Florida 81-89
1,010	Phog Allen, Baker 1906-08, Kansas 08-09, Haskell 09, Central Mo. St. 13-19, Kansas 20-56
997	Dean Smith, North Caro. 1962-93*
991	Slats Gill, Oregon St. 1929-64
987	Glenn Wilkes, Stetson 1958-93*
950	Tony Hinkle, Butler 1927-42, 46-70
941	Abe Lemons, Oklahoma City 1956-73, Tex.-Pan American 74-76, Texas 77-82, Oklahoma City 84-90
918	Norm Stewart, Northern Iowa 1962-67, Missouri 68-93*
910	Gene Bartow, Central Mo. St. 1962-64, Valparaiso 65-70, Memphis St. 71-74, Illinois 75, UCLA 76-77, Ala.-Birmingham 79-93*
908	Harry Miller, Western St. 1953-58, Fresno St. 61-65, Eastern N. Mex. 66-70, North Texas 71, Wichita St. 72-78, Stephen F. Austin 79-88
904	Lou Henson, Hardin-Simmons 1963-66, New Mexico St. 67-75, Illinois 76-93*
903	Don Haskins, UTEP 1962-93*
900	Lefty Driesell, Davidson 1961-69, Maryland 70-86, James Madison 89-93*
888	Gary Colson, Valdosta St. 1959-68, Pepperdine 69-79, New Mexico 81-88, Fresno St. 91-93*
884	C. M. Newton, Transylvania 1956-64 and 66-68, Alabama 69-80, Vanderbilt 82-89
876	Bill E. Foster, Bloomsburg 1961-63, Rutgers 64-71, Utah 72-74, Duke 75-80, South Caro. 81-86, Northwestern 87-93
872	Jack Friel, Washington St. 1929-58
871	Guy Lewis, Houston 1957-86
866	Fred Enke, Louisville 1924-25, Arizona 26-61
852	Tom Young, Catholic 1959-67, American 70-73, Rutgers 74-85, Old Dominion 86-91
848	Eldon Miller, Wittenberg 1963-70, Western Mich. 71-76, Ohio St. 77-86, Northern Iowa 87-93*
837	Ned Wulk, Xavier (Ohio) 1952-57, Arizona St. 58-82
833	Bob Knight, Army 1966-71, Indiana 72-93*
826	John Wooden, Indiana St. 1947-48, UCLA 49-75

* *Active.*

MOST YEARS

No.	Coach, School and Years
48	Phog Allen, Baker 1906-08, Kansas 08-09, Haskell 09, Central Mo. St. 13-19, Kansas 20-56
42	Ed Diddle, Western Ky. 1923-64
42	Ray Meyer, DePaul 1943-84
41	Tony Hinkle, Butler 1927-42, 46-70
41	Henry Iba, Northwest Mo. St. 1930-33, Colorado 34, Oklahoma St. 35-70

No.	Coach, School and Years
41	Adolph Rupp, Kentucky 1931-72
40	Marv Harshman, Pacific Lutheran 1946-58, Washington St. 59-71, Washington 72-85
38	Fred Enke, Louisville 1924-25, Arizona 26-61
38	Ralph Miller, Wichita St. 1952-64, Iowa 65-70, Oregon St. 71-89
37	Nat Holman, CCNY 1920-52 and 55-56 and 59-60
37	Norm Sloan, Presbyterian 1952-55, Citadel 57-60, Florida 61-66, North Caro. St. 67-80, Florida 81-89
36	Slats Gill, Oregon St. 1929-64
36	William Reinhart, Oregon 1924-35, Geo. Washington 36-42 and 50-66
36	Glenn Wilkes, Stetson 1958-93
35	Cam Henderson, Muskingum 1921-23, Davis & Elkins 24-35, Marshall 36-55
35	Abe Lemons, Oklahoma City 1956-73, Tex.-Pan American 74-76, Texas 77-82, Oklahoma City 84-90
34	Harry Miller, Western St. 1953-58, Fresno St. 61-65, Eastern N. Mex. 66-70, North Texas 71, Wichita St. 72-78, Stephen F. Austin 79-88
33	Donald White, Washington (Mo.) 1924-35, Connecticut 37-45, Rutgers 46-56 and 63
33	Bill E. Foster, Bloomsburg 1961-63, Rutgers 64-71, Utah 72-74, Duke 75-80, South Caro. 81-86, Northwestern 87-93
32	Gary Colson, Valdosta St. 1959-68, Pepperdine 69-79, New Mexico 81-88, Fresno St. 91-93*
32	Don Haskins, UTEP 1962-93*
32	John Mauer, Kentucky 1928-30, Miami (Ohio) 31-38, Tennessee 39-47, Army 48-51, Florida 52-60
32	Branch McCracken, Ball St. 1930-37, Indiana 39-43 and 47-65
32	C. M. Newton, Transylvania 1956-64 and 66-68, Alabama 69-80, Vanderbilt 82-89
32	Dean Smith, North Caro. 1962-93*
31	Norm Stewart, Northern Iowa 1962-67, Missouri 68-93*
31	Gene Bartow, Central Mo. St. 1962-64, Valparaiso 65-70, Memphis St. 71-74, Illinois 75, UCLA 76-77, Ala.-Birmingham 79-93*
31	Ozzie Cowles, Carleton 1925-30, Wis.-River Falls 34-36, Dartmouth 37-43 and 45-46, Michigan 47-48, Minnesota 49-59
31	Lefty Driesell, Davidson 1961-69, Maryland 70-86, James Madison 89-93*
31	Taps Gallagher, Niagara 1932-43 and 47-65
31	Lou Henson, Hardin-Simmons 1963-66, New Mexico St. 67-75, Illinois 76-93*
31	Doggie Julian, Albright 1928-29, Muhlenberg 37-45, Holy Cross 46-48, Dartmouth 51-67
31	Cy McClairen, Bethune-Cookman 1962-66 and 68-93
31	Eldon Miller, Wittenberg 1963-70, Western Mich. 71-76, Ohio St. 77-86, Northern Iowa 87-93*
31	Ned Wulk, Xavier (Ohio) 1952-57, Arizona St. 58-82
31	Tom Young, Catholic 1959-67, American 70-73, Rutgers 74-85, Old Dominion 86-91
30	Jack Friel, Washington St. 1929-58
30	Guy Lewis, Houston 1957-86
30	Ed Martin, South Caro. St. 1956-68, Tennessee St. 69-85
30	Frank McGuire, St. John's (N.Y.) 1948-52, North Caro. 53-61, South Caro. 65-80
30	Nibs Price, California 1925-54

* *Active.*

MOST YEARS AT ONE SCHOOL

No.	Coach, School and Years
42	Ed Diddle, #Western Ky. 1923-64
42	Ray Meyer, #DePaul 1943-84
41	Tony Hinkle, #Butler 1927-42, 46-70
41	Adolph Rupp, #Kentucky 1931-72
39	Phog Allen, Kansas 1908-09 and 20-56
37	Nat Holman, #CCNY 1920-52 and 55-56 and 59-60
36	Fred Enke, Arizona 1926-61
36	Slats Gill, #Oregon St. 1929-64
36	Henry Iba, Oklahoma St. 1935-70
36	Glenn Wilkes, #Stetson 1958-93
32	Don Haskins, #UTEP 1962-93*
32	Dean Smith, #North Caro. 1962-93*
31	Taps Gallagher, #Niagara 1932-43 and 47-65
31	Cy McClairen, #Bethune-Cookman 1962-66 and 68-93
30	Jack Friel, #Washington St. 1929-58
30	Guy Lewis, #Houston 1957-86
30	Nibs Price, #California 1925-54
29	Piggy Lambert, #Purdue 1917 and 19-46
29	Harry Rabenhorst, #Louisiana St. 1926-42 and 46-57
28	Frank Keaney, #Rhode Island 1921-48
27	Hec Edmundson, Washington 1921-47
27	Shelby Metcalf, #Texas A&M 1964-90
27	Herbert Read, #Western Mich. 1923-49

No.	Coach, School and Years
27	John Wooden, UCLA 1949-75
26	Pete Carril, Princeton 1968-93*
26	Jim McDermott, #Iona 1948-73
26	Norm Stewart, Missouri 1968-93*
26	Jim Williams, #Colorado St. 1955-80
25	Lew Andreas, #Syracuse 1925-43 and 45-50
25	John Brooks, #East Tenn. St. 1949-73
25	Don Donoher, #Dayton 1965-89
25	Bud Foster, #Wisconsin 1935-59
25	Alex Severance, #Villanova 1937-61
25	Jim Snyder, #Ohio 1950-74
25	Ned Wulk, Arizona St. 1958-82

* *Active.* # *Has coached only at this school.*

MOST 20-WIN SEASONS

No.	Coach, School and Years
26	Dean Smith, North Caro. 1962-93*
23	Adolph Rupp, Kentucky 1931-72
23	Jerry Tarkanian, Long Beach St. 1969-73, Nevada-Las Vegas 74-92
19	Lefty Driesell, Davidson 1961-69, Maryland 70-86, James Madison 89-93*
18	Lou Carnesecca, St. John's (N.Y.) 1966-70, 74-92
18	Denny Crum, Louisville 1972-93*
18	Ed Diddle, Western Ky. 1923-64
18	Henry Iba, Northwest Mo. St. 1930-33, Colorado 34, Oklahoma St. 35-70
18	Bob Knight, Army 1966-71, Indiana 72-93*
18	John Wooden, Indiana St. 1947-48, UCLA 49-75
17	Lou Henson, Hardin-Simmons 1963-66, New Mexico St. 67-75, Illinois 76-93*
16	Jim Boeheim, Syracuse 1977-93*
16	John Chaney, Cheyney 1973-82, Temple 83-93*
16	Don Haskins, UTEP 1962-93*
16	John Thompson, Georgetown, 1973-93*
15	Gene Bartow, Central Mo. St. 1962-64, Valparaiso 65-70, Memphis St. 71-74, Illinois 75, UCLA 76-77, Ala.-Birmingham 79-93*
15	Cam Henderson, Muskingum 1921-23, Davis & Elkins 24-35, Marshall 36-55
15	Lute Olson, Long Beach St. 1974, Iowa 75-83, Arizona 84-93*
15	Norm Stewart, Northern Iowa 1962-67, Missouri 68-93*
15	Eddie Sutton, Creighton 1970-74, Arkansas 75-85, Kentucky 86-89, Oklahoma St. 91-93*
14	Guy Lewis, Houston 1957-86
14	Digger Phelps, Fordham 1971, Notre Dame 72-91
14	Billy Tubbs, Southwestern (Tex.) 1972-73, Lamar 77-80, Oklahoma 81-93*

* *Active.*

MOST SCHOOLS

No.	Coach, School and Years
7	Elmer Ripley, Wagner 1923-25, Georgetown 28-29, 39-43 and 47-49, Yale 30-35, Columbia 44-45, Notre Dame 46, John Carroll 50-51, Army 52-53
7	Bob Vanatta, Central Mo. St. 1943 and 48-50, Southwest Mo. St. 51-53, Army 54, Bradley 55-56, Memphis St. 57-62, Missouri 63-67, Delta St. 73
6	Gene Bartow, Central Mo. St. 1962-64, Valparaiso 65-70, Memphis St. 71-74, Illinois 75, UCLA 76-77, Ala.-Birmingham 79-93*
6	Bill E. Foster, Bloomsburg 1961-63, Rutgers 64-71, Utah 72-74, Duke 75-80, South Caro. 81-86, Northwestern 87-93
6	Robert Hopkins, Prairie View 1965, Alcorn St. 67-69, Xavier (La.) 70-74, Southern-B.R. 85-86, Grambling 87-89, Md.-East. Shore 91-92
6	Ben Jobe, Talladega 1965-67, Alabama St. 68, South Caro. St. 69-73, Denver 79-80, Alabama A&M 83-86, Southern-B.R. 87-93*
6	Press Maravich, West Va. Wesleyan 1950, Davis & Elkins 51-52; Clemson 57-62, North Caro. St. 65-66, Louisiana St. 67-72, Appalachian St. 73-75
6	Harry Miller, Western St. 1953-58, Fresno St. 61-65, Eastern N. Mex. 66-70, North Texas 71, Wichita St. 72-78, Stephen F. Austin 79-88
6	Hal Wissel, Trenton St. 1965-67, Lafayette 68-71, Fordham 72-76, Fla. Southern 78-82, N.C.-Charlotte 83-85, Springfield 87-90
5	J. D. Barnett, Lenoir-Rhyne 1970, High Point 71, Louisiana Tech 78-79, Va. Commonwealth 80-85, Tulsa 86-91
5	Ozzie Cowles, Carleton 1925-30, Wis.-River Falls 34-36, Dartmouth 37-43 and 45-46, Michigan 47-48, Minnesota 49-59
5	Don DeVoe, Virginia Tech 1972-76, Wyoming 77-78, Tennessee 79-89, Florida 90, Navy 93*
5	Bill C. Foster, Shorter 1963-67, N.C.-Charlotte 71-75, Clemson 76-84, Miami (Fla.) 86-90, Virginia Tech 93*

No.	Coach, School and Years
5	Blair Gullion, Earlham 1928-35, Tennessee 36-38, Cornell 39-42, Connecticut 46-47, Washington (Mo.) 48-59
5	Tates Locke, Army 1964-65, Miami (Ohio) 67-70, Clemson 71-75, Jacksonville 79-81, Indiana St. 91-93*
5	John Mauer, Kentucky 1928-30, Miami (Ohio) 31-38, Tennessee 39-47, Army 48-51, Florida 52-60
5	Tom Penders, Tufts 1972-74, Columbia 75-78, Fordham 79-86, Rhode Island 87-88, Texas 89-93*
5	Gordon Stauffer, Washburn 1967, Indiana St. 68-75, IU/PU-Ft. Wayne 76-79, Geneva 80-81, Nicholls 82-90
5	Tex Winter, Marquette 1952-53, Kansas St. 54-68, Washington 69-71, Northwestern 74-78, Long Beach St. 79-83

* *Active.*

ALL COACHES WHO HAVE WON AT LEAST 500 GAMES AT FOUR-YEAR COLLEGES, REGARDLESS OF CLASSIFICATION OR ASSOCIATION

	Coach (Alma Mater) Colleges Coached, Tenure	Yrs.	Won	Lost	Pct.
$1.	Adolph Rupp (Kansas '23) Kentucky 31-72	41	876	190	.822
2.	Clarence "Big House" Gaines (Morgan St. '45) Winston-Salem 47-93	47	828	447	.649
*3.	Dean Smith (Kansas '53) North Caro. 62-93	32	774	223	.776
4.	Henry Iba (Northwest Mo. St. '28) Northwest Mo. St. 30-33, Colorado 34, Oklahoma St. 35-70	41	767	338	.694
5.	Ed Diddle (Centre '21) Western Ky. 23-64	42	759	302	.715
6.	F. C. "Phog" Allen (Kansas '06) Baker 06-08, Kansas 08-09, Haskell 09, Central Mo. St. 13-19, Kansas 20-56	48	746	264	.739
7.	Ray Meyer (Notre Dame '38) DePaul 43-84	42	724	354	.672
*8.	Jim Phelan (La Salle '51) Mt. St. Mary's (Md.) 55-93	39	706	365	.659
9.	John Wooden (Purdue '32) Indiana St. 47-48, UCLA 49-75	29	664	162	.804
10.	Bloomer Sullivan (Southeastern Okla. '33) Southeastern Okla. 37-67	31	662	235	.738
@+11.	Ralph Miller (Kansas '42) Wichita St. 52-64, Iowa 65-70, Oregon St. 71-89	38	657	382	.632
12.	Ed Adams (Tuskegee '33) N.C. Central 35-36, Tuskegee 37-49, Texas Southern 50-58	24	645	153	.808
*12.	Jerry Johnson (Fayetteville St. '51) LeMoyne-Owen 59-93	35	645	296	.685
14.	John Lance (Pittsburg St. '18) Southwestern Okla. 19-22, Pittsburg St. 23-63	45	643	345	.651
%15.	Marv Harshman (Pacific Lutheran '42) Pacific Lutheran 46-58, Washington St. 59-71, Washington 72-85	40	642	448	.589
*16.	Dick Sauers (Slippery Rock '51) Albany St. (N.Y.) 56-87, 89-93	37	630	294	.682
*17.	Don Haskins (Oklahoma St. '53) UTEP 62-93	32	627	276	.694
18.	Jerry Tarkanian (Fresno St. '56) Long Beach St. 69-73, Nevada-Las Vegas 74-92	24	625	122	.837
+19.	Norm Sloan (North Caro. St. '51) Presbyterian 52-55, Citadel 57-60, Florida 61-66, North Caro. St. 67-80, Florida 81-89	37	624	393	.614
*20.	Charles "Lefty" Driesell (Duke '54) Davidson 61-69, Maryland 70-86, James Madison 89-93	31	621	279	.690
*21.	Bob Knight (Ohio St. '62) Army 66-71, Indiana 72-93	28	619	214	.743
*22.	Norm Stewart (Missouri '56) Northern Iowa 62-67, Missouri 68-93	32	612	306	.667
*23.	Ed Messbarger (Northwest Mo. St. '56) Benedictine Heights 57-60, Dallas 61-63, St. Mary's (Tex.) 63-78, Angelo St. 79-93	36	610	439	.582
24.	Dean Nicholson (Central Wash. '50) Central Wash. 65-90	26	609	219	.736
*24.	Lou Henson (New Mexico St. '56) Hardin-Simmons 63-66, New Mexico St. 67-75, Illinois 76-93	31	609	295	.674
26.	Don Dyer (Henderson St. '55) Henderson St. 63-78, Central Ark. 79-93	29	606	278	.686
27.	Amory "Slats" Gill (Oregon St. '25) Oregon St. 29-64	36	599	392	.604
28.	Ken Anderson (Wis.-Eau Claire '55) Wis.-Eau Claire 69-93	25	597	136	.814
28.	Abe Lemons (Oklahoma City '49) Oklahoma City 56-73, Tex.-Pan American 74-76, Texas 77-82, Oklahoma City 84-90	34	597	344	.634

	Coach (Alma Mater) Colleges Coached, Tenure	Yrs.	Won	Lost	Pct.
*30.	Gene Bartow (Northeast Mo. St. '53) Central Mo. St. 62-64, Valparaiso 65-70, Memphis St. 71-74, Illinois 75, UCLA 76-77, Ala.-Birmingham 79-93	31	595	315	.654
31.	Guy Lewis (Houston '47) Houston 57-86	30	592	279	.680
32.	Dom Rosselli (Geneva '59) Youngstown St. 41-42, 47-82	38	591	384	.606
33.	Joe Hutton (Carleton '24) Hamline 31-65	35	590	208	.739
34.	Cam Henderson [Salem (W. Va.) '17] Muskingum 21-23, Davis & Elkins 24-35, Marshall 36-55	35	583	216	.730
35.	Floyd McBride (Oklahoma '26) East Central Okla. 28-41, 45-67	37	577	312	.649
*36.	Harry Statham (McKendree '60) McKendree 67-93	27	575	245	.701
37.	Fred Hobdy (Grambling '49) Grambling 57-86	30	571	287	.666
38.	Cliff Hamlow (Azusa Pacific '56) Azusa Pacific 55-82, 85-88	32	570	414	.579
39.	Paul "Tony" Hinkle (Chicago '21) Butler 27-42, 46-70	41	557	393	.586
40.	Bill Vining (Ouachita Baptist '51) Ouachita Baptist 55-89	34	554	391	.586
41.	Glenn Wilkes (Mercer '50) Stetson 58-93	36	551	436	.558
42.	Frank McGuire [St. John's (N.Y.) '36] St. John's (N.Y.) 48-52, North Caro. 53-61, South Caro. 65-80	30	550	235	.701
43.	Jim Gudger (Western Caro. '42) Western Caro. 51-69, East Tex. St. 70-83	33	547	365	.600
*44.	Herb Magee (Phila. Textile '63) Phila. Textile 68-93	26	544	205	.72
45.	Chet Kammerer (Grace '64) Grace 66-75, Westmont (Cal.) 76-92	27	542	256	.679
*46.	Don Callan (Taylor '55) Cedarville 61-93	33	537	397	.575
47.	Duane Woltzen (Illinois St. '57) Lakeland (Wis.) 65-87	23	535	229	.700
48.	Harry Miller (Eastern N. Mex. '51) Western St. (Colo.) 53-58, Fresno St. 61-65, Eastern N. Mex. 66-70, North Tex. St. 71, Wichita St. 72-78, Stephen F. Austin 79-88	34	534	374	.588
49.	Rankin Williams (Southwestern Okla. '22) Southwestern Okla. 28-64	37	533	325	.621
50.	Bob Wachs (Northern Colo. '47) Northern St. (S.D.) 56-85	30	532	286	.650
*51.	Marvin Hohenberger (MacMurray '62) Defiance 66-93	28	530	247	.682
*52.	Don Myer, David Lipscomb 73-93	21	529	178	.748
*52.	Gary Colson (David Lipscomb '56) Valdosta St. 59-68, Pepperdine 69-79, New Mexico 81-88, Fresno St. 91-93	32	529	359	.596
*52.	Sam Moir (Appalachian St. '50) Catawba 61-93	33	529	389	.576
55.	Lou Carnesecca [St. John's (N.Y.) '46] St. John's (N.Y.) 66-70, 74-92	24	526	200	.725
56.	Tom Young (Maryland '58) Catholic 59-67, American 70-73, Rutgers 74-85, Old Dominion 86-91	31	524	328	.615
57.	John McClendon Jr. (Kansas '36) N.C. Central 41-52, Hampton 53-54, Tennessee St. 55-59, Kentucky St. 64-66, Cleveland St. 67-69	25	523	165	.760
58.	Bob Davis [Georgetown (Ky.) '50] High Point 52-53, Georgetown (Ky.) 54-73, Auburn 74-78	27	522	266	.662
58.	Fred Enke (Minnesota '21) Louisville 24-25, Arizona 26-61	38	522	344	.603
*60.	Bruce MacGregor, Husson 68-93	26	520	176	.747
*61.	Denny Crum (UCLA '58) Louisville 1972-93	22	518	192	.730
62.	Paul Webb (William & Mary '51) Randolph-Macon 57-75, Old Dominion 76-85	29	511	257	.665
*63.	Lewis Levick (Drake '58) Wartburg 1966-93	28	510	225	.694
63.	Aubrey Bonham (Northern Iowa '27) Whittier 38-43, 46-68	29	510	285	.642
*63.	Bill Knapton (Wis.-La Crosse '52) Beloit 1958-93	36	510	298	.631
66.	Clarence "Hec" Edmundson (Idaho '09) Idaho 17-18, Washington 21-47	29	508	204	.711
*66.	Bob Erickson, Doane 63-93	31	508	402	.558
68.	Leo Nicholson (Washington '25) Central Wash. 30-43, 46-64	33	505	281	.642
69.	Harold Anderson (Otterbein '24) Toledo 35-42, Bowling Green 43-63	29	504	226	.690
*69.	Eldon Miller (Wittenberg '61) Wittenberg 1963-70, Western Mich. 71-76, Ohio St. 77-86, Northern Iowa 87-93	31	504	344	.594
*71.	Eddie Sutton (Oklahoma St. '58) Creighton 1970-74, Arkansas 75-85, Kentucky 86-89, Oklahoma St. 91-93	23	502	189	.726
72.	Ed Martin (North Caro. A&T '51) South Caro. 56-68, Tennessee St. 69-85	30	501	253	.664
72.	Robert Vaughan (Virginia St. '48) Elizabeth City St. 52-86	34	501	363	.580

** Active. $ Kentucky played no varsity schedule 1953—under NCAA suspension. % Includes one forfeit over Oregon State. @ Miller lost 15 wins by action of NCAA Council (see note under all-time coaches victories). + Tournament participation voided by NCAA Executive Committee (see note under all-time coaches victories).*

DIVISION I MEN'S COACH OF THE YEAR

Year	United Press International	Associated Press	U.S. Basketball Writers Assn.	National Assn. of Basketball Coaches
1955	Phil Woolpert San Francisco			
1956	Phil Woolpert San Francisco			
1957	Frank McGuire North Caro.			
1958	Tex Winter Kansas St.			
1959	Adolph Rupp Kentucky		Eddie Hickey Marquette	
1960	Pete Newell California		Pete Newell California	
1961	Fred Taylor Ohio St.		Fred Taylor Ohio St.	
1962	Fred Taylor Ohio St.		Fred Taylor Ohio St.	
1963	Ed Jucker Cincinnati		Ed Jucker Cincinnati	
1964	John Wooden UCLA		John Wooden UCLA	
1965	Dave Strack Michigan		Bill van Breda Kolff Princeton	
1966	Adolph Rupp Kentucky		Adolph Rupp Kentucky	
1967	John Wooden UCLA	John Wooden UCLA	John Wooden UCLA	
1968	Guy Lewis Houston	Guy Lewis Houston	Guy Lewis Houston	
1969	John Wooden UCLA	John Wooden UCLA	Maury John Drake	John Wooden UCLA
1970	John Wooden UCLA	John Wooden UCLA	John Wooden UCLA	John Wooden UCLA
1971	Al McGuire Marquette	Al McGuire Marquette	Al McGuire Marquette	Jack Kraft Villanova
1972	John Wooden UCLA	John Wooden UCLA	John Wooden UCLA	John Wooden UCLA
1973	John Wooden UCLA	John Wooden UCLA	John Wooden UCLA	Gene Bartow Memphis St.
1974	Digger Phelps Notre Dame	Norm Sloan North Caro. St.	Norm Sloan North Caro. St.	Al McGuire Marquette
1975	Bob Knight Indiana	Bob Knight Indiana	Bob Knight Indiana	Bob Knight Indiana
1976	Tom Young Rutgers	Bob Knight Indiana	Bob Knight Indiana	Johnny Orr Michigan
1977	Bob Gaillard San Francisco	Bob Gaillard San Francisco	Eddie Sutton Arkansas	Dean Smith North Caro.
1978	Eddie Sutton Arkansas	Eddie Sutton Arkansas	Ray Meyer DePaul	Bill Foster Duke; Abe Lemons Texas
1979	Bill Hodges Indiana St.	Bill Hodges Indiana St.	Dean Smith North Caro.	Ray Meyer DePaul
1980	Ray Meyer DePaul	Ray Meyer DePaul	Ray Meyer DePaul	Lute Olson Iowa
1981	Ralph Miller Oregon St.	Ralph Miller Oregon St.	Ralph Miller Oregon St.	Ralph Miller Oregon St.; Jack Hartman Kansas St.
1982	Norm Stewart Missouri	Ralph Miller Oregon St.	John Thompson Georgetown	Don Monson Idaho
1983	Jerry Tarkanian Nevada-Las Vegas	Guy Lewis Houston	Lou Carnesecca St. John's (N.Y.)	Lou Carnesecca St. John's (N.Y.)
1984	Ray Meyer DePaul	Ray Meyer DePaul	Gene Keady Purdue	Marv Harshman Washington

Year	United Press International	Associated Press	U.S. Basketball Writers Assn.	National Assn. of Basketball Coaches
1985	Lou Carnesecca St. John's (N.Y.)	Bill Frieder Michigan	Lou Carnesecca St. John's (N.Y.)	John Thompson Georgetown
1986	Mike Krzyzewski Duke	Eddie Sutton Kentucky	Dick Versace Bradley	Eddie Sutton Kentucky
1987	John Thompson Georgetown	Tom Davis Iowa	John Chaney Temple	Rick Pitino Providence
1988	John Chaney Temple	John Chaney Temple	John Chaney Temple	John Chaney Temple
1989	Bob Knight Indiana	Bob Knight Indiana	Bob Knight Indiana	P. J. Carlesimo Seton Hall
1990	Jim Calhoun Connecticut	Jim Calhoun Connecticut	Roy Williams Kansas	Jud Heathcote Michigan St.
1991	Rick Majerus Utah	Randy Ayers Ohio St.	Randy Ayers Ohio St.	Mike Krzyzewski Duke
1992	Perry Clark Tulane	Roy Williams Kansas	Perry Clark Tulane	George Raveling Southern Cal
1993	Eddie Fogler Vanderbilt	Eddie Fogler Vanderbilt	Eddie Fogler Vanderbilt	Eddie Fogler Vanderbilt

Note: The Naismith Coach of the Year: 1987—Bob Knight, Indiana; 1988—Larry Brown, Kansas; 1989—Mike Krzyzewski, Duke; 1990—Bobby Cremins, Georgia Tech; 1991—Randy Ayers, Ohio St; 1992—Mike Krzyzewski, Duke; 1993—Dean Smith, North Caro.

DIVISION I HEAD COACHING CHANGES

Year	Teams	Changes	Pct.	1st Yr.	Year	Teams	Changes	Pct.	1st Yr.
1950	154	22	14.3	11	1972	210	37	17.6	21
1951	156	28	17.9	15	1973	217	38	17.5	24
1952	159	23	14.5	18	1974	234	41	17.5	23
1953	165	20	12.1	13	1975	235	44	18.7	30
1954	165	12	7.3	7	1976	235	34	14.5	20
1955	165	21	12.7	9	1977	245	39	15.9	21
1956	169	18	10.7	12	1978	254	39	15.4	24
1957	170	18	10.6	9	1979	257	53	20.6	28
1958	174	14	8.0	8	1980	261	43	16.5	23
1959	177	20	11.3	10	1981	264	42	15.9	21
1960	177	23	13.0	15	1982	272	37	13.6	20
1961	176	15	8.5	11	1983	274	37	13.5	18
1962	179	15	8.4	14	1984	276	38	13.8	21
1963	180	24	13.3	15	1985	282	26	9.2	15
1964	180	23	12.8	17	1986	283	56	19.8	21
1965	185	15	8.1	8	1987	290	66	22.8	35
1966	185	24	13.0	20	1988	290	39	13.4	16
1967	186	33	17.7	18	1989	293	42	14.3	24
1968	192	26	13.5	16	1990	292	54	18.5	29
1969	196	29	14.8	19	1991	295	41	13.9	16
1970	197	29	14.7	17	1992	298	39	13.1	15
1971	203	30	14.8	17	1993	298	34	11.4	15

WINNINGEST ACTIVE 1993-94 DIVISION II MEN'S COACHES

BY PERCENTAGE

(Minimum five years as a head coach; includes record at four-year colleges only.)

	Coach, College	Yrs.	Won	Lost	Pct.
1.	Dave Robbins, Virginia Union	15	371	90	.805
2.	Rick Cooper, West Tex. A&M	6	152	48	.760
3.	John Kochan, Millersville	10	224	72	.757
4.	Bill Morse, Mercyhurst	16	381	130	.746
5.	Bob Chipman, Washburn	14	331	115	.742
6.	Jim Boone, Calif. (Pa.)	7	152	53	.741
7.	Pat Douglass, Cal St. Bakersfield	12	274	97	.739
8.	Tom Galeazzi, LIU-C.W. Post	12	261	92	.739
9.	L. Vann Pettaway, Alabama A&M	7	155	57	.731
10.	Herb Magee, Phila. Textile	26	544	205	.726
11.	Richard Schmidt, Tampa	12	260	101	.720
12.	William S. Jones, Dist. Columbia	9	179	71	.716
13.	Jerry Kirksey, Southwest Baptist	10	206	82	.715
14.	Brian Beaury, St. Rose	7	155	62	.714

	Coach, College	Yrs.	Won	Lost	Pct.
15.	Jerry Waters, S.C.-Spartanburg	15	308	124	.713
16.	John Masi, UC Riverside	14	288	116	.713
17.	Stanley Spirou, New Hamp. Col.	8	174	72	.707
18.	Bill Jones, Jacksonville St.	21	404	169	.705
19.	Mike Jones, Mississippi Col.	5	96	41	.701
20.	Dale Race, Minn.-Duluth	13	282	124	.695
21.	Andy Piazza, IU/PU-Ft. Wayne	6	116	53	.686
22.	Jerry Johnson, LeMoyne-Owen	35	645	296	.685
23.	Royce Waltman, Indianapolis	6	112	52	.683
24.	Michael Bernard, Norfolk St.	8	156	76	.672
25.	Jerry Hueser, Neb.-Kearney	23	458	230	.666
26.	Jerry Schmutte, Morningside	12	222	113	.663
27.	Ron Spry, Paine	13	285	146	.661
28.	Dave Boots, South Dak.	11	203	105	.659
29.	Charles Chronister, Bloomsburg	22	393	205	.657
30.	Dave Bike, Sacred Heart	15	296	158	.652
31.	Tom Villemure, Grand Valley St.	22	407	220	.649
32.	Tom Ludwig, Ferris St.	16	272	147	.649
33.	Dick Peth, Denver	8	150	81	.649
34.	Bob Hull, Metropolitan St.	8	147	81	.645
35.	Bob Dukiet, Gannon	14	257	144	.641
36.	Wayne Boultinghouse, Ky. Wesleyan	10	177	101	.637
37.	Brad Soderberg, South Dak. St.	5	79	45	.637
38.	Bob Lutz, Pfeiffer	7	131	75	.636
39.	Rich Glas, North Dak.	15	266	153	.635
40.	Bob Olson, Northern St.	8	158	91	.635
41.	Dan McCarrell, Mankato St.	26	447	262	.630
42.	Denny Alexander, Shepherd	12	221	130	.630
43.	Tom Klusman, Rollins	13	227	134	.629
44.	Bruce Webster, Bridgeport	28	498	295	.628
45.	John Jones, Cal St. Stanislaus	5	88	54	.620
46.	Earl Diddle, Eastern N. Mex.	9	164	101	.619
47.	Steve Dodd, Alderson-Broaddus	9	155	96	.618
48.	Doug Schakel, Mesa St.	14	254	165	.606
49.	Steve Rives, Delta St.	8	137	89	.606
50.	Lewis Hill, Francis Marion	23	396	259	.605
51.	Zeke Avery, Hampton	6	98	64	.605
52.	Dave Blank, Lock Haven	5	84	55	.604
53.	Bill Carter, Texas A&M-Kingsville	8	135	89	.603
54.	Stu Grove, New Haven	18	300	198	.602
55.	Steve Joyner, Johnson Smith	6	104	69	.601

BY VICTORIES

(Minimum five years as a head coach; includes record at four-year colleges only.)

	Coach, College	Wins
1.	Jerry Johnson, LeMoyne-Owen	645
2.	Ed Messbarger, Angelo St.	610
3.	Herb Magee, Phila. Textile	544
4.	Sam Moir, Catawba	529
5.	Bruce Webster, Bridgeport	498
6.	Jerry Steele, High Point	467
7.	Jerry Hueser, Neb.-Kearney	458
8.	Dan McCarrell, Mankato St.	447
9.	Finis Horne, Lander	415
10.	Arthur McAfee, Morehouse	408
11.	Tom Villemure, Grand Valley St.	407
12.	Ron Slaymaker, Emporia St.	407
13.	Bill Jones, Jacksonville St.	404
14.	Richard Meckfessel, Mo.-St. Louis	403
15.	Lewis Hill, Francis Marion	396
16.	Paul Peak, East Tex. St.	396
17.	Charles Chronister, Bloomsburg	393
18.	Butch Raymond, St. Cloud St.	383
19.	Bill Morse, Mercyhurst	381
20.	Bob Hanson, Nebraska-Omaha	378
21.	Dave Robbins, Virginia Union	371
22.	Jim Harley, Eckerd	364
23.	James Dominey, Valdosta St.	348

	Coach, College	Wins
24.	Joe Reibel, Bellarmine	335
25.	Bob Chipman, Washburn	331
26.	A. Craig Drennon, Limestone	328
27.	Robert Pratt, Saginaw Valley	327
28.	Oliver Jones, Albany St. (Ga.)	322
29.	Robert Wilson, Hawaii-Hilo	311
30.	Jerry Waters, S.C.-Spartanburg	308
31.	Harvey Heartley, St. Augustine's	304
32.	Stu Grove, New Haven	300
33.	Jim Seward, Central Okla	297
34.	Dave Bike, Sacred Heart	296
35.	John Masi, UC Riverside	288
36.	Ron Spry, Paine	285
37.	Dale Race, Minn.-Duluth	282
38.	Pat Sullivan, St. Francis (Ill.)	280
39.	Tom Smith, Mo. Western St.	278
40.	Rodger Goodling, Shippensburg	276
41.	Pat Douglass, Cal St. Bakersfield	274
41.	Willard Sims, Northeast Mo. St.	274
43.	Tom Ludwig, Ferris St.	272
44.	Rich Glas, North Dak.	266
45.	Tom Galeazzi, LIU-C.W. Post	261

	Coach, College	Wins
45.	Lonnie Porter, Regis (Colo.)	261
45.	Robert Lovell, IU/PU-Indianapolis	261
48.	Richard Schmidt, Tampa	260
49.	Bob Dukiet, Gannon	257
49.	Dave Schellhase, Moorhead St.	257
51.	Frank Evans, Colo. Christian	256
52.	Doug Schakel, Mesa St.	254
53.	Les Wothke, Winona St.	254
54.	Gary Bays, Eastern Mont.	249
55.	Harold Deane, Virginia St.	245
56.	Dave Yanai, Cal St. Dom. Hills	244
57.	Mike Sandifar, Oakland City	242
58.	Terry Brown, Bluefield St.	241
59.	Jim Powell, American Int'l	236
60.	Jack Margenthaler, SIU-Edwardsville	235
61.	Herbert Greene, Columbus	231
62.	Tom Klusman, Rollins	227
63.	John Kochan, Millersville	224
64.	Jerry Schmutte, Morningside	222
65.	Denny Alexander, Shepherd	221
66.	Ed Murphy, West Ga.	220
67.	Terry Layton, Adams St.	215
68.	Tom Sutherland, West Va. Tech	209
69.	Jerry Kirksey, Southwest Baptist	206
70.	Dave Boots, South Dak.	203
71.	Ajac Triplett, Morris Brown	203
72.	Dick Walker, Sonoma St.	203

WINNINGEST ACTIVE 1993-94 DIVISION III MEN'S COACHES

BY PERCENTAGE

(Minimum five years as a head coach; includes record at four-year colleges only.)

	Coach, College	Yrs.	Won	Lost	Pct.
1.	Ken Anderson, Wis.-Eau Claire	25	597	136	.814
2.	Bob Campbell, Western Conn. St.	9	189	54	.778
3.	Bo Ryan, Wis.-Platteville	9	192	63	.753
4.	James Catalano, New Jersey Tech	14	286	99	.743
5.	Glenn Van Wieren, Hope	16	299	104	.742
6.	Richard Bihr, Buffalo St.	14	272	100	.731
7.	Brian Baptiste, Mass.-Dartmouth	10	201	75	.728
8.	Gerald Matthews, Stockton St.	8	161	61	.725
9.	Charles Brown, Jersey City St.	11	226	86	.724
10.	Bosko Djurickovic, North Park	9	180	70	720
11.	Dave Vander Meulen, Wis.-Whitewater	15	298	118	.716
12.	Glenn Robinson, Frank. & Marsh.	22	427	171	.714
13.	Rick Simonds, St. Joseph's (Me.)	13	265	108	.710
14.	Dave Darnall, Eureka	19	356	146	.709
15.	Bob Bessoir, Scranton	21	430	177	.708
16.	Tom Murphy, Hamilton	23	405	168	.707
17.	Joe Nesci, New York U.	5	83	35	.703
18.	Nick Lambros, Hartwick	16	291	125	.700
19.	Al Sokaitis, Southern Me.	6	111	48	.698
20.	Lewis Levick, Wartburg	28	510	225	.694
21.	Ed Douma, Calvin	20	366	162	.693
22.	Terry Glasgow, Monmouth (Ill.)	21	328	145	.693
23.	Dick Whitmore, Colby	23	382	175	.686
24.	Richard Sauers, Albany (N.Y.)	37	630	294	.682
25.	Marvin Hohenberger, Defiance	28	530	247	.682
26.	John Dzik, Cabrini	13	256	120	.681
27.	Stan Ogrodnik, Trinity (Conn.)	12	192	90	.681
28.	Harry Sheehy, Williams	10	162	76	.681
29.	Dave Gunther, Buena Vista	21	402	190	.679
30.	Bob Gillespie, Ripon	13	205	98	.677
31.	Ray Amalbert, Hunter	5	95	46	.674
32.	Bob Parker, Wis.-Stevens Point	9	166	81	.672
33.	David Buss, St. Olaf	20	368	184	.667
34.	Steve Moore, Wooster	12	212	106	.667
35.	Dick Reynolds, Otterbein	21	381	193	.664
36.	Rudy Marisa, Waynesburg	24	407	207	.663
37.	Hal Nunnally, Randolph-Macon	18	331	173	.657
38.	Jim Todd, Salem St.	8	141	75	.653
39.	Joe Haklin, Kalamazoo	6	99	53	.651
40.	Bob Ward, St. John Fisher	6	102	55	.650
41.	Dennis Bridges, Ill. Wesleyan	28	486	274	.639
42.	C. J. Woollum, Chris. Newport	9	163	92	.639
43.	Bill Nelson, Johns Hopkins	13	217	123	.638
44.	C. Alan Rowe, Widener	28	465	268	.634
45.	Bill Knapton, Beloit	36	510	298	.631
46.	Bill Harris, Wheaton (Ill.)	8	150	89	.628
47.	Tony Shaver, Hampden-Sydney	7	117	70	.626
48.	Bill Fenlon, DePauw	8	126	76	.624

	Coach, College	Yrs.	Won	Lost	Pct.
49.	Herb Hilgeman, Rhodes	17	255	158	.617
50.	David Hixon, Amherst	16	234	146	.616
51.	Peter Barry, Coast Guard	11	198	124	.615
52.	Tom Marshall, UC San Diego	10	161	101	.615
53.	Steve Fritz, St. Thomas (Minn.)	13	212	133	.614
54.	Ken Atkins, King's (Pa.)	10	160	101	.613
55.	Tom Baker, Ithaca	15	255	162	.612
56.	Gene Mehaffey, Ohio Wesleyan	25	460	297	.608
57.	Bill Chambers, N.C. Wesleyan	7	115	74	.608
58.	Paul Phillips, Anna Maria	7	110	71	.608
59.	Chuck Mancuso, Mt. St. Vincent	12	179	118	.603
60.	Randy Lambert, Maryville (Tenn.)	13	203	134	.602
61.	Jim Burson, Muskingum	26	391	261	.600
62.	Mike Neer, Rochester	17	266	177	.600

BY VICTORIES

(Minimum five years as a head coach; includes record at four-year colleges only.)

	Coach, College	Wins
1.	Richard Sauers, Albany (N.Y.)	630
2.	Ken Anderson, Wis.-Eau Claire	597
3.	Marvin Hohenberger, Defiance	530
4.	Lewis Levick, Wartburg	510
5.	Bill Knapton, Beloit	510
6.	Dennis Bridges, Ill. Wesleyan	486
7.	C. Alan Rowe, Widener	465
8.	Jim Smith, St. John's (Minn.)	465
9.	Gene Mehaffey, Ohio Wesleyan	460
10.	Verne Canfield, Wash. & Lee	441
11.	Bob Bessoir, Scranton	430
11.	Glenn Robinson, Frank. & Marsh.	427
13.	Rudy Marisa, Waynesburg	407
14.	Tom Murphy, Hamilton	405
15.	Dave Gunther, Buena Vista	402
16.	Jim Burson, Muskingum	391
17.	Leon Richardson, William Penn	390
18.	Dick Whitmore, Colby	382
19.	Dick Reynolds, Otterbein	381
20.	Jon Davison, Dubuque	370
21.	David Buss, St. Olaf	368
22.	Tony LaScala, Ill. Benedictine	368
23.	Ed Douma, Calvin	366
24.	Dave Darnall, Eureka	356
25.	Tom Bryant, Centre	355
26.	Cliff Garrison, Hendrix	353
27.	Jack Walvoord, Central (Iowa)	342
28.	Jack Jensen, Guilford	340
29.	Hal Nunnally, Randolph-Macon	331
30.	Terry Glasgow, Monmouth (Ill.)	328
31.	Roland Wierwille, Berea	323
32.	Ward Lambert, Salisbury St.	322
33.	Clarence Burch, Lycoming	314
34.	Bill Merris, Illinois Col.	313
35.	Tom Pope, Geneseo St.	306
36.	Dave Jacobs, Whittier	306
37.	Glenn Van Wieren, Hope	299
38.	Dave Vander Meulen, Wis.-Whitewater	298
39.	Gary Smith, Redlands	297
40.	Tom Finnegan, Washington (Md.)	296
41.	Nick Lambros, Hartwick	291
42.	Herb Kenny, Wesleyan	290
43.	James Catalano, New Jersey Tech	286
44.	Joe Ramsey, Millikin	283
45.	Bill Scanlon, Union (N.Y.)	278
46.	Richard Bihr, Buffalo St.	272
47.	Mac Petty, Wabash	271
48.	Doug Bolstorff, Macalester	270
49.	Mike Turner, Albion	269
50.	Mike Neer, Rochester	266
51.	Rick Simonds, St. Joseph's (Me.)	265
52.	John Dzik, Cabrini	256
53.	Gary Morrison, Olivet	256
54.	Herb Hilgeman, Rhodes	255
55.	Tom Baker, Ithaca	255
56.	John Hill, Heidelberg	255
57.	Lee McKinney, Fontbonne	254
58.	John Barr, Grove City	253
59.	David Wells, Claremont-M-S	249
60.	William C. Sudeck, Case Reserve	245
61.	Jack Berkshire, Oglethorpe	242
62.	David Hixon, Amherst	234
63.	Charles Brown, Jersey City St.	226
64.	Ken Kaufman, Worcester Tech	222
65.	Bill Nelson, Johns Hopkins	217
66.	James Walker, Moravian	216
67.	Steve Moore, Wooster	212
68.	Steve Fritz, St. Thomas (Minn.)	212
69.	Bob Gillespie, Ripon	205
70.	Mike Beitzel, Hanover	204
71.	Bob Gay, MacMurray	204
72.	Randy Lambert, Maryville (Tenn.)	203
73.	Charlie Titus, Mass.-Boston	202
74.	Brian Baptiste, Mass.-Dartmouth	201
74.	Jeff Gamber, York (Pa.)	201
76.	Dan Switchenko, Eastern Conn. St.	200

MEN'S CHAMPIONSHIPS

D'Artis Jones scored 21 points in the title game to lead Ohio Northern past Augustana (Illinois) in the 1993 Division III Men's Basketball Championship. It was the Polar Bears' first NCAA team championship.

DIVISION I MEN'S CHAMPIONSHIP

1993 DIVISION I MEN'S CHAMPIONSHIP RESULTS

FIRST ROUND
Kentucky 96, Rider 52
Utah 86, Pittsburgh 65
Wake Forest 81, Tenn.-Chatt. 58
Iowa 82, Northeast La. 69
Tulane 55, Kansas St. 53
Florida St. 82, Evansville 70
Western Ky. 55, Memphis St. 52
Seton Hall 81, Tennessee St. 59
Michigan 84, Coastal Caro. 53
UCLA 81, Iowa St. 70
Geo. Washington 82, New Mexico 68
Southern-B.R. 93, Georgia Tech 78
Illinois 75, Long Beach St. 72
Vanderbilt 92, Boise St. 72
Temple 75, Missouri 61
Santa Clara 64, Arizona 61
North Caro. 85, East Caro. 65
Rhode Island 74, Purdue 68
St. John's (N.Y.) 85, Texas Tech 67
Arkansas 94, Holy Cross 64
Virginia 78, Manhattan 66
Massachusetts 54, Pennsylvania 50
New Mexico St. 93, Nebraska 79
Cincinnati 93, Coppin St. 66
Indiana 97, Wright St. 54
Xavier (Ohio) 73, New Orleans 55
Oklahoma St. 74, Marquette 62
Louisville 76, Delaware 70
California 66, Louisiana St. 64
Duke 105, Southern Ill. 70
Brigham Young 80, Southern Methodist 71
Kansas 94, Ball St. 72

SECOND ROUND
Kentucky 83, Utah 62
Wake Forest 84, Iowa 78
Florida St. 94, Tulane 63
Western Ky. 72, Seton Hall 68
Michigan 86, UCLA 84 (ot)
Geo. Washington 90, Southern-B.R. 80
Vanderbilt 85, Illinois 68
Temple 68, Santa Clara 57
North Caro. 112, Rhode Island 67
Arkansas 80, St. John's (N.Y.) 74
Virginia 71, Massachusetts 56
Cincinnati 92, New Mexico St. 55
Indiana 73, Xavier (Ohio) 70
Louisville 78, Oklahoma St. 63
California 82, Duke 77
Kansas 90, Brigham Young 76

REGIONAL SEMIFINALS
Kentucky 103, Wake Forest 69
Florida St. 81, Western Ky. 78 (ot)
Michigan 72, Geo Washington 64
Temple 67, Vanderbilt 59
North Caro. 80, Arkansas 74
Cincinnati 71, Virginia 54
Indiana 82, Louisville 69
Kansas 93, California 76

REGIONAL CHAMPIONSHIPS
Kentucky 106, Florida St. 81
Michigan 77, Temple 72
North Caro. 75, Cincinnati 68 (ot)
Kansas 83, Indiana 77

SEMIFINALS
North Caro. 78, Kansas 68
Michigan 81, Kentucky 78 (ot)

CHAMPIONSHIP
North Caro. 77, Michigan 71

FINAL FOUR BOX SCORES

SEMIFINALS

North Caro. 78, Kansas 68

Kansas	FG-FGA	FT-FTA	RB	PF	TP
Darrin Hancock	2- 5	2- 2	5	1	6
Richard Scott	3- 5	2- 2	1	5	8
Eric Pauley	2- 5	1- 1	9	3	5
Rex Walters	7-15	0- 0	0	2	19
Adonis Jordan	7-13	0- 0	1	1	19
Calvin Rayford	0- 0	0- 0	0	0	0
Steve Woodberry	2- 5	0- 0	2	4	4
Patrick Richey	1- 4	0- 0	2	1	2
Greg Ostertag	0- 2	2- 2	2	3	2
Greg Gurley	1- 2	0- 0	0	0	3
Sean Pearson	0- 1	0- 0	0	0	0
Team			2		
TOTALS	25-57	7- 7	24	20	68

North Caro.	FG-FGA	FT-FTA	RB	PF	TP
Brian Reese	3- 5	1- 2	4	0	7
George Lynch	5-12	4- 6	10	3	14
Eric Montross	9-14	5- 8	4	4	23
Derrick Phelps	1- 3	1- 2	5	2	3
Donald Williams	7-11	6- 6	3	1	25
Pat Sullivan	0- 2	0- 0	1	1	0
Henrik Rodl	0- 0	0- 0	0	2	0
Kevin Salvadori	3- 5	0- 0	3	0	6
Dante Calabria	0- 0	0- 0	0	0	0
Scott Cherry	0- 0	0- 0	2	0	0
Larry Davis	0- 0	0- 0	0	0	0
Travis Stephenson	0- 0	0- 0	0	0	0
Ed Geth	0- 0	0- 0	0	0	0
Matt Wenstrom	0- 0	0- 0	0	0	0
Team			3		
TOTALS	28-52	17-24	35	13	78

Half time: North Caro. 40, Kansas 36. Three-point field goals: Kansas 11-20 (Jordan 5-7, Walters 5-9, Gurley 1-1, Pearson 0-1, Woodberry 0-2); North Caro. 5-7 (Williams 5-7). Officials: John Clougherty, Jim Burr, Ted Valentine. Attendance: 64,151.

Michigan 81, Kentucky 78 (ot)

Michigan	FG-FGA	FT-FTA	RB	PF	TP
Chris Webber	10-17	7- 9	13	3	27
Ray Jackson	4- 7	3- 5	8	4	11
Juwan Howard	6-12	5- 7	3	4	17
Jalen Rose	6-16	6- 7	6	3	18
Jimmy King	1- 3	0- 0	3	5	2
Eric Riley	2- 4	0- 0	4	2	4
Rob Pelinka	0- 1	2- 2	1	3	2
James Voskuil	0- 0	0- 0	0	0	0
Team			2		
TOTALS	29-60	23-30	40	24	81

Kentucky	FG-FGA	FT-FTA	RB	PF	TP
Jamal Mashburn	10-18	5- 9	6	5	26
Jared Prickett	1- 6	7- 7	7	5	9
Rodney Dent	2- 6	2- 2	3	4	6
Travis Ford	3-10	4- 4	5	2	12
Dale Brown	6-10	0- 0	1	2	16
Rodrick Rhodes	0- 1	1- 2	1	4	1

	FG-FGA	FT-FTA	RB	PF	TP
Andre Riddick	2- 4	0- 0	2	2	4
Gimel Martinez ...	0- 3	0- 0	1	3	0
Jeff Brassow	0- 0	0- 0	0	0	0
Tony Delk	1- 3	2- 2	3	0	4
Junior Braddy	0- 0	0- 0	0	0	0
Team			5		
TOTALS	25-61	21-26	34	27	78

Half time: Michigan 40, Kentucky 35. End of regulation: Tied at 71. Three-point field goals: Michigan 0-4 (Webber 0-1, Pelinka 0-1, Rose 0-2); Kentucky 7-21 (Brown 4-6, Ford 2-6, Mashburn 1-3, Prickett 0-1, Rhodes 0-1, Martinez 0-2, Delk 0-2). Officials: Gerry Donaghy, Dick Paparo, Larry Rose. Attendance: 64,151.

CHAMPIONSHIP

North Caro. 77, Michigan 71

North Caro.	FG-FGA	FT-FTA	RB	PF	TP
Brian Reese	2- 7	4- 4	5	1	8
George Lynch ...	6-12	0- 0	10	3	12
Eric Montross	5-11	6- 9	5	2	16
Derrick Phelps ...	4- 6	1- 2	3	0	9
Donald Williams ..	8-12	4- 4	1	1	25
Pat Sullivan	1- 2	1- 2	1	2	3
Kevin Salvadori ..	0- 0	2- 2	4	1	2
Henrik Rodl	1- 4	0- 0	0	0	2
Dante Calabria ...	0- 0	0- 0	0	0	0
Matt Wenstrom ...	0- 1	0- 0	0	0	0
Scott Cherry	0- 0	0- 0	0	0	0
Team			0		
TOTALS	27-55	18-23	29	10	77

Michigan	FG-FGA	FT-FTA	RB	PF	TP
Chris Webber	11-18	1- 2	11	2	23
Ray Jackson	2- 3	2- 2	1	5	6
Juwan Howard ...	3- 8	1- 1	7	3	7
Jalen Rose	5-12	0- 0	1	3	12
Jimmy King	6-13	2- 2	6	2	15
Eric Riley	1- 3	0- 0	3	1	2
Rob Pelinka	2- 4	0- 0	2	1	6
Michael Talley	0- 0	0- 0	0	1	0
James Voskuil	0- 1	0- 0	0	0	0
Team			2		
TOTALS	30-62	6- 7	33	18	71

Half time: North Caro. 42, Michigan 36. Three-point field goals: North Caro. 5-11 (Williams 5-7, Reese 0-1, Phelps 0-1, Rodl 0-2); Michigan 5-15 (Pelinka 2-3, Rose 2-6, King 1-5, Webber 0-1). Officials: Ed Hightower, Tom Harrington, Jim Stupin. Attendance: 64,151.

DIVISION I MEN'S CHAMPIONSHIP RECORDS

ALL-TIME RESULTS

Year	Champion	Score	Runner-Up	Third Place	Fourth Place
1939	Oregon	46-33	Ohio St.	+Oklahoma	+Villanova
1940	Indiana	60-42	Kansas	+Duquesne	+Southern Cal
1941	Wisconsin	39-34	Washington St.	+Pittsburgh	+Arkansas
1942	Stanford	53-38	Dartmouth	+Colorado	+Kentucky
1943	Wyoming	46-34	Georgetown	+Texas	+DePaul
1944	Utah	42-40†	Dartmouth	+Iowa St.	+Ohio St.
1945	Oklahoma St.	49-45	New York U.	+Arkansas	+Ohio St.
1946	Oklahoma St.	43-40	North Caro.	Ohio St.	California
1947	Holy Cross	58-47	Oklahoma	Texas	CCNY
1948	Kentucky	58-42	Baylor	Holy Cross	Kansas St.
1949	Kentucky	46-36	Oklahoma St.	Illinois	Oregon St.
1950	CCNY	71-68	Bradley	North Caro. St.	Baylor
1951	Kentucky	68-58	Kansas St.	Illinois	Oklahoma St.
1952	Kansas	80-63	St. John's (N.Y.)	Illinois	Santa Clara
1953	Indiana	69-68	Kansas	Washington	Louisiana St.
1954	La Salle	92-76	Bradley	Penn St.	Southern Cal
1955	San Francisco	77-63	La Salle	Colorado	Iowa
1956	San Francisco	83-71	Iowa	Temple	Southern Meth.
1957	North Caro.	54-53‡	Kansas	San Francisco	Michigan St.
1958	Kentucky	84-72	Seattle	Temple	Kansas St.
1959	California	71-70	West Va.	Cincinnati	Louisville
1960	Ohio St.	75-55	California	Cincinnati	New York U.
1961	Cincinnati	70-65†	Ohio St.	*St. Joseph's (Pa.)	Utah
1962	Cincinnati	71-59	Ohio St.	Wake Forest	UCLA
1963	Loyola (Ill.)	60-58†	Cincinnati	Duke	Oregon St.
1964	UCLA	98-83	Duke	Michigan	Kansas St.
1965	UCLA	91-80	Michigan	Princeton	Wichita St.
1966	UTEP	72-65	Kentucky	Duke	Utah
1967	UCLA	79-64	Dayton	Houston	North Caro.
1968	UCLA	78-55	North Caro.	Ohio St.	Houston
1969	UCLA	92-72	Purdue	Drake	North Caro.
1970	UCLA	80-69	Jacksonville	New Mexico St.	St. Bonaventure
1971	UCLA	68-62	*Villanova	*Western Ky.	Kansas
1972	UCLA	81-76	Florida St.	North Caro.	Louisville
1973	UCLA	87-66	Memphis St.	Indiana	Providence
1974	North Caro. St.	76-64	Marquette	UCLA	Kansas
1975	UCLA	92-85	Kentucky	Louisville	Syracuse
1976	Indiana	86-68	Michigan	UCLA	Rutgers
1977	Marquette	67-59	North Caro.	Nevada-Las Vegas	N.C.-Charlotte
1978	Kentucky	94-88	Duke	Arkansas	Notre Dame

Year	Champion	Score	Runner-Up	Third Place	Fourth Place
1979	Michigan St.	75-64	Indiana St.	DePaul	Penn
1980	Louisville	59-54	*UCLA	Purdue	Iowa
1981	Indiana	63-50	North Caro.	Virginia	Louisiana St.
1982	North Caro.	63-62	Georgetown	+Houston	+Louisville
1983	North Caro. St.	54-52	Houston	+Georgia	+Louisville
1984	Georgetown	84-75	Houston	+Kentucky	+Virginia
1985	Villanova	66-64	Georgetown	+St. John's (N.Y.)	+*Memphis St.
1986	Louisville	72-69	Duke	+Kansas	+Louisiana St.
1987	Indiana	74-73	Syracuse	+Nevada-Las Vegas	+Providence
1988	Kansas	83-79	Oklahoma	+Arizona	+Duke
1989	Michigan	80-79†	Seton Hall	+Duke	+Illinois
1990	Nevada-Las Vegas	103-73	Duke	+Arkansas	+Georgia Tech
1991	Duke	72-65	Kansas	+Nevada-Las Vegas	+North Caro.
1992	Duke	71-51	Michigan	+Cincinnati	+Indiana
1993	North Caro.	77-71	Michigan	+Kansas	+Kentucky

*† Overtime. + Tied for third place. ‡ Three overtimes. * Record later vacated.*

Year	Site of Finals	Coaches of Team Champions	Outstanding Player Award
1939	Evanston, Ill.	Howard Hobson, Oregon	None Selected
1940	Kansas City, Mo.	Branch McCracken, Indiana	Marvin Huffman, Indiana
1941	Kansas City, Mo.	Harold Foster, Wisconsin	John Kotz, Wisconsin
1942	Kansas City, Mo.	Everett Dean, Stanford	Howard Dallmar, Stanford
1943	New York City	Everett Shelton, Wyoming	Ken Sailors, Wyoming
1944	New York City	Vadal Peterson, Utah	Arnold Ferrin, Utah
1945	New York City	Henry Iba, Oklahoma St.	Bob Kurland, Oklahoma St.
1946	New York City	Henry Iba, Oklahoma St.	Bob Kurland, Oklahoma St.
1947	New York City	Alvin Julian, Holy Cross	George Kaftan, Holy Cross
1948	New York City	Adolph Rupp, Kentucky	Alex Groza, Kentucky
1949	Seattle, Wash.	Adolph Rupp, Kentucky	Alex Groza, Kentucky
1950	New York City	Nat Holman, CCNY	Irwin Dambrot, CCNY
1951	Minneapolis, Minn.	Adolph Rupp, Kentucky	None Selected
1952	Seattle, Wash.	Forrest Allen, Kansas	Clyde Lovellette, Kansas
1953	Kansas City, Mo.	Branch McCracken, Indiana	B. H. Born, Kansas
1954	Kansas City, Mo.	Kenneth Loeffler, La Salle	Tom Gola, La Salle
1955	Kansas City, Mo.	Phil Woolpert, San Francisco	Bill Russell, San Francisco
1956	Evanston, Ill.	Phil Woolpert, San Francisco	Hal Lear, Temple
1957	Kansas City, Mo.	Frank McGuire, North Caro.	Wilt Chamberlain, Kansas
1958	Louisville, Ky.	Adolph Rupp, Kentucky	Elgin Baylor, Seattle
1959	Louisville, Ky.	Pete Newell, California	Jerry West, West Va.
1960	San Francisco, Calif.	Fred Taylor, Ohio St.	Jerry Lucas, Ohio St.
1961	Kansas City, Mo.	Edwin Jucker, Cincinnati	Jerry Lucas, Ohio St.
1962	Louisville, Ky.	Edwin Jucker, Cincinnati	Paul Hogue, Cincinnati
1963	Louisville, Ky.	George Ireland, Loyola (Ill.)	Art Heyman, Duke
1964	Kansas City, Mo.	John Wooden, UCLA	Walt Hazzard, UCLA
1965	Portland, Ore.	John Wooden, UCLA	Bill Bradley, Princeton
1966	College Park, Md.	Don Haskins, UTEP	Jerry Chambers, Utah
1967	Louisville, Ky.	John Wooden, UCLA	Lew Alcindor, UCLA
1968	Los Angeles, Calif.	John Wooden, UCLA	Lew Alcindor, UCLA
1969	Louisville, Ky.	John Wooden, UCLA	Lew Alcindor, UCLA
1970	College Park, Md.	John Wooden, UCLA	Sidney Wicks, UCLA
1971	Houston, Texas	John Wooden, UCLA	*Howard Porter, Villanova
1972	Los Angeles, Calif.	John Wooden, UCLA	Bill Walton, UCLA
1973	St. Louis, Mo.	John Wooden, UCLA	Bill Walton, UCLA
1974	Greensboro, N.C.	Norm Sloan, North Caro. St.	David Thompson, North Caro. St.
1975	San Diego, Calif.	John Wooden, UCLA	Richard Washington, UCLA
1976	Philadelphia, Pa.	Bob Knight, Indiana	Kent Benson, Indiana
1977	Atlanta, Ga.	Al McGuire, Marquette	Butch Lee, Marquette
1978	St. Louis, Mo.	Joe Hall, Kentucky	Jack Givens, Kentucky
1979	Salt Lake City, Utah	Jud Heathcote, Michigan St.	Earvin Johnson, Michigan St.
1980	Indianapolis, Ind.	Denny Crum, Louisville	Darrell Griffith, Louisville
1981	Philadelphia, Pa.	Bob Knight, Indiana	Isiah Thomas, Indiana
1982	New Orleans, La.	Dean Smith, North Caro.	James Worthy, North Caro.
1983	Albuquerque, N.M.	Jim Valvano, North Caro. St.	Akeem Olajuwon, Houston
1984	Seattle, Wash.	John Thompson, Georgetown	Patrick Ewing, Georgetown
1985	Lexington, Ky.	Rollie Massimino, Villanova	Ed Pinckney, Villanova
1986	Dallas, Texas	Denny Crum, Louisville	Pervis Ellison, Louisville
1987	New Orleans, La.	Bob Knight, Indiana	Keith Smart, Indiana
1988	Kansas City, Mo.	Larry Brown, Kansas	Danny Manning, Kansas
1989	Seattle, Wash.	Steve Fisher, Michigan	Glen Rice, Michigan
1990	Denver, Colo.	Jerry Tarkanian, Nevada-Las Vegas	Anderson Hunt, Nevada-Las Vegas

Year	Site of Finals	Coaches of Team Champions	Outstanding Player Award
1991	Indianapolis, Ind.	Mike Krzyzewski, Duke	Christian Laettner, Duke
1992	Minneapolis, Minn.	Mike Krzyzewski, Duke	Bobby Hurley, Duke
1993	New Orleans, La.	Dean Smith, North Caro.	Donald Williams, North Caro.

** Record later vacated.*

LEADING SCORER

Year	Player, School	G	FG	FT	Pts.	Avg.
1939	Jim Hull, Ohio St.	3	22	14	58	19.3
1940	Howard Engleman, Kansas	3	18	3	39	13.0
1941	John Adams, Arkansas	2	21	6	48	24.0
1942	Jim Pollard, Stanford	2	19	5	43	21.5
	Chet Palmer, Rice	2	20	3	43	21.5
1943	John Hargis, Texas	2	21	17	59	29.5
1944	Aud Brindley, Dartmouth	3	24	4	52	17.3
1945	Bob Kurland, Oklahoma St.	3	30	5	65	21.7
1946	Bob Kurland, Oklahoma St.	3	28	16	72	24.0
1947	George Kaftan, Holy Cross	3	25	13	63	21.0
1948	Alex Groza, Kentucky	3	23	8	54	18.0
1949	Alex Groza, Kentucky	3	31	20	82	27.3
1950	Sam Ranzino, North Caro. St.	3	25	25	75	25.0
1951	Don Sunderlage, Illinois	4	28	27	83	20.8
1952	Clyde Lovellette, Kansas	4	53	35	141	35.3
1953	Bob Houbregs, Washington	4	57	25	139	34.8
1954	Tom Gola, La Salle	5	38	38	114	22.8
1955	Bill Russell, San Francisco	5	49	20	118	23.6
1956	Hal Lear, Temple	5	63	34	160	32.0
1957	Len Rosenbluth, North Caro.	5	53	34	140	28.0
1958	Elgin Baylor, Seattle	5	48	39	135	27.0
1959	Jerry West, West Va.	5	57	46	160	32.0
1960	Oscar Robertson, Cincinnati	4	47	28	122	30.5
1961	Billy McGill, Utah	4	49	21	119	29.8
1962	Len Chappell, Wake Forest	5	45	44	134	26.8
1963	Mel Counts, Oregon St.	5	50	23	123	24.6
1964	Jeff Mullins, Duke	4	50	16	116	29.0
1965	Bill Bradley, Princeton	5	65	47	177	35.4
1966	Jerry Chambers, Utah	4	55	33	143	35.8
1967	Elvin Hayes, Houston	5	57	14	128	25.6
1968	Elvin Hayes, Houston	5	70	27	167	33.4
1969	Rick Mount, Purdue	4	49	24	122	30.5
1970	Austin Carr, Notre Dame	3	68	22	158	52.7
1971	*Jim McDaniels, Western Ky.	5	61	25	147	29.4
	Austin Carr, Notre Dame	3	48	29	125	41.7
1972	Jim Price, Louisville	4	41	21	103	25.8
1973	Ernie DiGregorio, Providence	5	59	10	128	25.6
1974	David Thompson, North Caro. St.	4	38	21	97	24.3
1975	Jim Lee, Syracuse	5	51	17	119	23.8
1976	Scott May, Indiana	5	45	23	113	22.6
1977	Cedric Maxwell, N.C.-Charlotte	5	39	45	123	24.6
1978	Mike Gminski, Duke	5	45	19	109	21.8
1979	Tony Price, Pennsylvania	6	58	26	142	23.7
1980	Joe Barry Carroll, Purdue	6	63	32	158	26.3
1981	Al Wood, North Caro.	5	44	21	109	21.8
1982	Rob Williams, Houston	5	30	28	88	17.6
1983	Dereck Whittenburg, North Caro. St.	6	47	26	120	20.0
1984	Roosevelt Chapman, Dayton	4	35	35	105	26.3
1985	Chris Mullin, St. John's (N.Y.)	5	39	32	110	22.0
1986	Johnny Dawkins, Duke	6	66	21	153	25.5

Year	Player, School	G	FG	3FG	FT	Pts.	Avg.
1987	Steve Alford, Indiana	6	42	21	33	138	23.0
	Rony Seikaly, Syracuse	6	87	0	32	138	23.0
1988	Danny Manning, Kansas	6	69	2	23	163	27.2
1989	Glen Rice, Michigan	6	75	27	7	184	30.7
1990	Dennis Scott, Georgia Tech	5	51	24	27	153	30.6
1991	Christian Laettner, Duke	6	37	2	49	125	20.8
1992	Christian Laettner, Duke	6	39	7	30	115	19.2
1993	Donald Williams, North Caro.	6	40	22	16	118	19.7

** Record later vacated.*

HIGHEST SCORING AVERAGE

(Minimum: 50% of maximum tournament games)

Year	Player, School	G	FG	FT	Pts.	Avg.
1939	Jim Hull, Ohio St.	3	22	14	58	19.3
1940	Howard Engleman, Kansas	3	18	3	39	13.0
	Bob Kinney, Rice	2	12	2	26	13.0
1941	John Adams, Arkansas	2	21	6	48	24.0
1942	Chet Palmer, Rice	2	19	5	43	21.5
	Jim Pollard, Stanford	2	20	3	43	21.5
1943	John Hargis, Texas	2	21	17	59	29.5
1944	Nick Bozolich, Pepperdine	2	17	11	45	22.5
1945	Dick Wilkins, Oregon	2	19	6	44	22.0
1946	Bob Kurland, Oklahoma St.	3	28	16	72	24.0
1947	George Kaftan, Holy Cross	3	25	13	63	21.0
1948	Jack Nichols, Washington	2	13	13	39	19.5
1949	Alex Groza, Kentucky	3	31	20	82	27.3
1950	Sam Ranzino, North Caro. St.	3	25	25	75	25.0
1951	William Kukoy, North Caro. St.	3	25	19	69	23.0
1952	Clyde Lovellette, Kansas	4	53	35	141	35.3
1953	Bob Houbregs, Washington	4	57	25	139	34.8
1954	John Clune, Navy	3	30	19	79	26.3
1955	Terry Rand, Marquette	3	31	11	73	24.3
1956	Hal Lear, Temple	5	63	34	160	32.0
1957	Wilt Chamberlain, Kansas	4	40	41	121	30.3
1958	Wayne Embry, Miami (Ohio)	3	32	19	83	27.7
1959	Jerry West, West Va.	5	57	46	160	32.0
1960	Jerry West, West Va.	3	35	35	105	35.0
1961	Billy McGill, Utah	4	49	21	119	29.8
1962	Len Chappell, Wake Forest	5	45	44	134	26.8
1963	Barry Kramer, New York U.	3	31	28	100	33.3
1964	Jeff Mullins, Duke	4	50	16	116	29.0
1965	Bill Bradley, Princeton	5	65	47	147	35.4
1966	Jerry Chambers, Utah	4	55	33	143	35.8
1967	Lew Alcindor, UCLA	4	39	28	106	26.5
1968	Elvin Hayes, Houston	5	70	27	167	33.4
1969	Rick Mount, Purdue	4	49	24	122	30.5
1970	Austin Carr, Notre Dame	3	68	22	158	52.7
1971	Austin Carr, Notre Dame	3	48	29	125	41.7
1972	*Dwight Lamar, Southwestern La.	4	41	18	100	33.3
	Jim Price, Louisville	4	41	21	103	25.8
1973	Larry Finch, Memphis St.	4	34	39	107	26.8
1974	John Shumate, Notre Dame	3	35	16	86	28.7
1975	Adrian Dantley, Notre Dame	3	29	34	92	30.7
1976	Willie Smith, Missouri	3	38	18	94	31.3
1977	Cedric Maxwell, N.C.-Charlotte	5	39	45	123	24.6
1978	Dave Corzine, DePaul	3	33	16	82	27.3
1979	Larry Bird, Indiana St.	5	52	32	136	27.2
1980	Joe Barry Carroll, Purdue	6	63	32	158	26.3
1981	Al Wood, North Caro.	5	44	21	109	21.8
1982	Oliver Robinson, Ala.-Birmingham	3	27	12	66	22.0
1983	Greg Stokes, Iowa	3	24	13	61	20.3
1984	Roosevelt Chapman, Dayton	4	35	35	105	26.3
1985	Kenny Walker, Kentucky	3	28	19	75	25.0
1986	David Robinson, Navy	4	35	40	110	27.5

Year	Player, School	G	FG	3FG	FT	Pts.	Avg.
1987	Fennis Dembo, Wyoming	3	25	11	23	84	28.0
1988	Danny Manning, Kansas	6	69	2	23	163	27.2
1989	Glen Rice, Michigan	6	75	27	7	184	30.7
1990	Bo Kimble, Loyola (Cal.)	4	51	15	26	143	35.8
1991	Terry Dehere, Seton Hall	4	34	12	17	97	24.3
1992	Jamal Mashburn, Kentucky	4	34	6	22	96	24.0
1993	Calbert Cheaney, Indiana	4	40	3	23	106	26.5

CAREER SCORING

Player, School (Years Competed)	G	FG	3FG	FT	Pts.	Avg.
Christian Laettner, Duke (1989-90-91-92)	23	128	9	142	407	17.7
Elvin Hayes, Houston (1966-67-68)	13	152	—	54	358	27.5
Danny Manning, Kansas (1985-86-87-88)	16	140	2	46	328	20.5
Oscar Robertson, Cincinnati (1958-59-60)	10	117	—	90	324	32.4
Glen Rice, Michigan (1986-87-88-89)	13	128	35	17	308	23.7

Player, School (Years Competed)	G	FG	3FG	FT	Pts.	Avg.
Lew Alcindor, UCLA (1967-68-69)	12	115	—	74	304	25.3
Bill Bradley, Princeton (1963-64-65)	9	108	—	87	303	33.7
Austin Carr, Notre Dame (1969-70-71)	7	117	—	55	289	41.3
Calbert Cheaney, Indiana (1990-91-92-93)	13	108	13	50	279	21.5
Jerry West, West Va. (1958-59-60)	9	97	—	81	275	30.6
Danny Ferry, Duke (1986-87-88-89)	19	101	10	57	269	14.2
Jerry Lucas, Ohio St. (1960-61-62)	12	104	—	58	266	22.2
Reggie Williams, Georgetown (1984-85-86-87)	17	96	11	57	260	15.3
Patrick Ewing, Georgetown (1982-83-84-85)	18	104	—	48	256	14.2
Bill Walton, UCLA (1972-73-74)	12	109	—	36	254	21.2
Stacey King, Oklahoma (1987-88-89)	12	102	0	42	246	20.5
Stacey Augmon, Nevada-Las Vegas (1988-89-90-91)	17	98	12	34	242	14.2
Todd Day, Arkansas (1989-90-91-92)	13	86	25	43	240	18.5
Bobby Hurley, Duke (1990-91-92-93)	20	69	42	59	239	12.0
Sam Perkins, North Caro. (1981-82-83-84)	15	86	—	65	237	15.8
Sean Elliott, Arizona (1986-87-88-89)	10	88	18	42	236	23.6
Gail Goodrich, UCLA (1963-64-65)	10	84	—	67	235	23.5
Marques Johnson, UCLA (1974-75-76-77)	16	96	—	42	234	14.6

BEST SINGLE-GAME SCORING PERFORMANCES

Player, School vs. Opponent, Year	Round	FG	3FG	FT	Pts.
Austin Carr, Notre Dame vs. Ohio, 1970	1st	25	—	11	61
Bill Bradley, Princeton vs. Wichita St., 1965	N3d	22	—	14	58
Oscar Robertson, Cincinnati vs. Arkansas, 1958	R3d	21	—	14	56
Austin Carr, Notre Dame vs. Kentucky, 1970	RSF	22	—	8	52
Austin Carr, Notre Dame vs. Texas Christian, 1971	1st	20	—	12	52
David Robinson, Navy vs. Michigan, 1987	1st	22	0	6	50
Elvin Hayes, Houston vs. Loyola (Ill.), 1968	1st	20	—	9	49
Hal Lear, Temple vs. Southern Methodist, 1956	N3d	17	—	14	48
Austin Carr, Notre Dame vs. Houston, 1971	R3d	17	—	13	47
Dave Corzine, DePaul vs. Louisville, 1978	RSF	18	—	10	46
Bob Houbregs, Washington vs. Seattle, 1953	RSF	20	—	5	45
Austin Carr, Notre Dame vs. Iowa, 1970	R3d	21	—	3	45
Bo Kimble, Loyola (Cal.) vs. New Mexico St., 1990	1st	17	5	6	45
Clyde Lovellette, Kansas vs. St. Louis, 1952	RF	16	—	12	44
Bill Walton, UCLA vs. Memphis St., 1973	CH	21	—	2	44
Rod Thorn, West Va. vs. St. Joseph's (Pa.), 1963	RSF	16	—	12	44
Dan Issel, Kentucky vs. Notre Dame, 1970	RSF	17	—	10	44
Hersey Hawkins, Bradley vs. Auburn, 1988	1st	15	6	8	44
Travis Mays, Texas vs. Georgia, 1990	1st	10	1	23	44
Oscar Robertson, Cincinnati vs. Kansas, 1960	RF	19	—	5	43
Jeff Mullins, Duke vs. Villanova, 1964	RSF	19	—	5	43
Willie Smith, Missouri vs. Michigan, 1976	RF	18	—	7	43

[Key: 1st—first round; 2nd—second round; RSF—regional semifinal; RF—regional final; R3d—regional third place; N3d—national third place; CH—national championship.]

LEADING REBOUNDER

Year	Player, School	G	Reb.	Avg.
1951	Bill Spivey, Kentucky	4	65	16.3
1957	John Green, Michigan St.	4	77	19.3
1958	Elgin Baylor, Seattle	5	91	18.2
1959	Jerry West, West Va.	5	73	14.6
1960	Tom Sanders, New York U.	5	83	16.6
1961	Jerry Lucas, Ohio St.	4	73	18.3
1962	Len Chappell, Wake Forest	5	86	17.2
1963	Nate Thurmond, Bowling Green	3	70	23.3
	Vic Rouse, Loyola (Ill.)	5	70	14.0
1964	Paul Silas, Creighton	3	57	19.0
1965	Bill Bradley, Princeton	5	57	11.4
1966	Jerry Chambers, Utah	4	56	14.0
1967	Don May, Dayton	5	82	16.4
1968	Elvin Hayes, Houston	5	97	19.4
1969	Lew Alcindor, UCLA	4	64	16.0
1970	Artis Gilmore, Jacksonville	5	93	18.6
1971	*Clarence Glover, Western Ky.	5	89	17.8
	Sidney Wicks, UCLA	4	52	13.0
1972	Bill Walton, UCLA	4	64	16.0
1973	Bill Walton, UCLA	4	58	14.5

Year	Player, School	G	Reb.	Avg.
1974	Tom Burleson, North Caro. St.	4	61	15.3
1975	Richard Washington, UCLA	5	60	12.0
1976	Phil Hubbard, Michigan	5	61	12.2
1977	Cedric Maxwell, N.C.-Charlotte	5	64	12.8
1978	Eugene Banks, Duke	5	50	10.0
1979	Larry Bird, Indiana St.	5	67	13.4
1980	Mike Sanders, UCLA	6	60	10.0
1981	Cliff Levingston, Wichita St.	4	53	13.3
1982	Clyde Drexler, Houston	5	42	8.4
1983	Akeem Olajuwon, Houston	5	65	13.0
1984	Akeem Olajuwon, Houston	5	57	11.4
1985	Ed Pinckney, Villanova	6	48	8.0
1986	Pervis Ellison, Louisville	6	57	9.5
1987	Derrick Coleman, Syracuse	6	73	12.2
1988	Danny Manning, Kansas	6	56	9.3
1989	Daryll Walker, Seton Hall	6	58	9.7
1990	Larry Johnson, Nevada-Las Vegas	6	75	12.5
1991	Larry Johnson, Nevada-Las Vegas	5	51	10.2
1992	Chris Webber, Michigan	6	58	9.7
1993	Chris Webber, Michigan	6	68	11.3

* *Record later vacated.*

HIGHEST REBOUNDING AVERAGE

Year	Player, School	G	Reb.	Avg.
1951	Bill Spivey, Kentucky	4	65	16.3
1957	John Green, Michigan St.	4	77	19.3
1958	Elgin Baylor, Seattle	5	91	18.2
1959	Oscar Robertson, Cincinnati	4	63	15.8
1960	Howard Jolliff, Ohio	3	64	21.3
1961	Jerry Lucas, Ohio St.	4	73	18.3
1962	Mel Counts, Oregon St.	3	53	17.7
1963	Nate Thurmond, Bowling Green	3	70	23.3
1964	Paul Silas, Creighton	3	57	19.0
1965	James Ware, Oklahoma City	3	55	18.3
1966	Elvin Hayes, Houston	3	50	16.7
1967	Don May, Dayton	5	82	16.4
1968	Elvin Hayes, Houston	5	97	19.4
1969	Lew Alcindor, UCLA	4	64	16.0
1970	Artis Gilmore, Jacksonville	5	93	18.6
1971	*Clarence Glover, Western Ky.	5	89	17.8
	Collis Jones, Notre Dame	3	49	16.3
1972	Bill Walton, UCLA	4	64	16.0
1973	Bill Walton, UCLA	4	58	14.5
1974	Marvin Barnes, Providence	3	51	17.0
1975	Mike Franklin, Cincinnati	3	49	16.3
1976	Al Fleming, Arizona	3	39	13.0
1977	Phil Hubbard, Michigan	3	45	15.0
1978	Greg Kelser, Michigan St.	3	37	12.3
1979	Larry Bird, Indiana St.	5	67	13.4
1980	Durand Macklin, Louisiana St.	3	31	10.3
1981	Cliff Levingston, Wichita St.	4	53	13.3
1982	Ed Pinckney, Villanova	3	30	10.0
1983	Akeem Olajuwon, Houston	5	65	13.0
1984	*Keith Lee, Memphis St.	3	37	12.3
	Akeem Olajuwon, Houston	5	57	11.4
1985	Karl Malone, Louisiana Tech	3	40	13.3
1986	David Robinson, Navy	4	47	11.8
1987	Derrick Coleman, Syracuse	6	73	12.2
1988	Pervis Ellison, Louisville	3	33	11.0
1989	Pervis Ellison, Louisville	3	31	10.3
	Stacey King, Oklahoma	3	31	10.3
1990	Dale Davis, Clemson	3	44	14.7
1991	Byron Houston, Oklahoma St.	3	36	12.0
	Perry Clark, Ohio St.	3	36	12.0
1992	Doug Edwards, Florida St.	3	32	10.7
1993	Chris Webber, Michigan	6	68	11.3

* *Record later vacated.*

CAREER REBOUNDING

Player, School (Years Competed)	G	Reb.	Avg.
Elvin Hayes, Houston (1966-67-68)	13	222	17.1
Lew Alcindor, UCLA (1967-68-69)	12	201	16.8
Jerry Lucas, Ohio St. (1960-61-62)	12	197	16.4
Bill Walton, UCLA (1972-73-74)	12	176	14.7
Christian Laettner, Duke (1989-90-91-92)	23	169	7.3
Paul Hogue, Cincinnati (1960-61-62)	12	160	13.3
Sam Lacey, New Mexico St. (1968-69-70)	11	157	14.3
Derrick Coleman, Syracuse (1987-88-89-90)	14	155	11.1
Akeem Olajuwon, Houston (1982-83-84)	15	153	10.2
Patrick Ewing, Georgetown (1982-83-84-85)	18	144	8.0
Marques Johnson, UCLA (1974-75-76-77)	16	138	8.6
George Lynch, North Caro. (1990-91-92-93)	17	138	8.1
Len Chappell, Wake Forest (1961-62)	8	137	17.1
Ed Pinckney, Villanova (1982-83-84-85)	14	135	9.6
Oscar Robertson, Cincinnati (1958-59-60)	10	131	13.1
Curtis Rowe, UCLA (1969-70-71)	12	131	10.9
Danny Ferry, Duke (1986-87-88-89)	19	131	6.9
Sam Perkins, North Caro. (1981-82-83-84)	15	129	8.6
Mel Counts, Oregon St. (1962-63-64)	9	127	14.1
Larry Johnson, Nevada-Las Vegas (1990-91)	11	126	11.5
Chris Webber, Michigan (1992-93)	12	126	10.5
Jerry West, West Va. (1958-59-60)	9	124	13.8
Pervis Ellison, Louisville (1986-88-89)	12	121	10.1
John Green, Michigan St. (1957, 1959)	6	118	19.7
Danny Manning, Kansas (1985-86-87-88)	16	117	7.3

BEST SINGLE-GAME REBOUNDING PERFORMANCES

Player, School vs. Opponent, Year	Round	Reb.
Fred Cohen, Temple vs. Connecticut, 1956	RSF	34
Nate Thurmond, Bowling Green vs. Mississippi St., 1963	R3d	31
Jerry Lucas, Ohio St. vs. Kentucky, 1961	RF	30
Toby Kimball, Connecticut vs. St. Joseph's (Pa.), 1965	1st	29
Elvin Hayes, Houston vs. Pacific (Cal.), 1966	R3d	28
Bill Russell, San Francisco vs. Iowa, 1956	CH	27
John Green, Michigan St. vs. Notre Dame, 1957	2nd	27
Paul Silas, Creighton vs. Oklahoma City, 1964	1st	27
Elvin Hayes, Houston vs. Loyola (Ill.), 1968	1st	27
Howard Jolliff, Ohio vs. Georgia Tech, 1960	RSF	26
Phil Hubbard, Michigan vs. Detroit Mercy, 1977	RSF	26
Jerry Lucas, Ohio St. vs. Western Ky., 1960	RSF	25
Elvin Hayes, Houston vs. Texas Christian, 1968	RF	25
K. E. Kirchner, Texas Christian vs. DePaul, 1959	R3d	24
Paul Silas, Creighton vs. Memphis St., 1962	1st	24
Eddie Jackson, Oklahoma City vs. Creighton, 1964	1st	24
Elvin Hayes, Houston vs. UCLA, 1967	NSF	24
Elvin Hayes, Houston vs. Louisville, 1968	RSF	24
Sam Lacey, New Mexico St. vs. Drake, 1970	RF	24
Tom Burleson, North Caro. St. vs. Providence, 1974	RSF	24

[Key: 1st—first round; 2nd—second round; RSF—regional semifinal; RF—regional final; R3d—regional third place; NSF—national semifinal; CH—national championship.]

INDIVIDUAL RECORDS—SINGLE GAME

Most Points
61, Austin Carr, Notre Dame vs. Ohio, SE 1st, 1970

Most Points by Two Teammates
85, Austin Carr (61) and Collis Jones (24), Notre Dame vs. Ohio, SE 1st, 1970

Most Points by Two Opposing Players
96, Austin Carr (52), Notre Dame, and Dan Issel (44), Kentucky, SE RSF, 1970

Most Field Goals
25, Austin Carr, Notre Dame vs. Ohio, SE 1st, 1970

Most Field Goals Attempted
44, Austin Carr, Notre Dame vs. Ohio, SE 1st, 1970

Highest Field-Goal Percentage (minimum 11 made)
100% (11-11), Kenny Walker, Kentucky vs. Western Ky., SE 2nd, 1986

Most Three-Point Field Goals
11, Jeff Fryer, Loyola (Cal.) vs. Michigan, West 2nd, 1990

Most Three-Point Field Goals Attempted
22, Jeff Fryer, Loyola (Cal.) vs. Arkansas, MW 1st, 1989

Highest Three-Point Field-Goal Percentage (minimum 7 made)
100% (7-7) Sam Cassell, Florida St. vs. Tulane, SE 2nd, 1993

Most Free Throws
23, Bob Carney, Bradley vs. Colorado, MW RSF, 1954; Travis Mays, Texas vs. Georgia, MW 1st, 1990

Most Free Throws Attempted
27, David Robinson, Navy vs. Syracuse, East 2nd, 1986; Travis Mays, Texas vs. Georgia, MW 1st, 1990

Highest Free-Throw Percentage (minimum 16 made)
100% (16-16), Bill Bradley, Princeton vs. St. Joseph's (Pa.), East 1st, 1963; Fennis Dembo, Wyoming vs. UCLA, West 2nd, 1987

Most Rebounds
34, Fred Cohen, Temple vs. Connecticut, East RSF, 1956

Most Assists
18, Mark Wade, Nevada-Las Vegas vs. Indiana, NSF, 1987

Most Blocked Shots
11, Shaquille O'Neal, Louisiana St. vs. Brigham Young, West 1st, 1992

Most Steals
8, Darrell Hawkins, Arkansas vs. Holy Cross, East 1st, 1993; Grant Hill, Duke vs. California, MW 2nd, 1993

INDIVIDUAL RECORDS—SERIES

(Three-game minimum for averages and percentages)

Most Points
184, Glen Rice, Michigan, 1989 (6 games)

Highest Scoring Average
52.7, Austin Carr, Notre Dame, 1970 (158 points in 3 games)

Most Field Goals
75, Glen Rice, Michigan, 1989 (6 games)

Most Field Goals Attempted
138, *Jim McDaniels, Western Ky., 1971 (5 games)
137, Elvin Hayes, Houston, 1968 (5 games)

Highest Field-Goal Percentage (minimum 5 made per game)
78.8% (26-33), Christian Laettner, Duke, 1989 (5 games)

Most Three-Point Field Goals
27, Glen Rice, Michigan, 1989 (6 games)

Most Three-Point Field Goals Attempted
65, Freddie Banks, Nevada-Las Vegas, 1987 (5 games)

Highest Three-Point Field-Goal Percentage (minimum 1.5 made per game)
100% (6-6), Ranzino Smith, North Caro., 1987 (4 games)

Most Free Throws
55, Bob Carney, Bradley, 1954 (5 games)

Most Free Throws Attempted
71, Jerry West, West Va., 1959 (5 games)

Highest Perfect Free-Throw Percentage (minimum 2.5 made per game)
100% (23-23), Richard Morgan, Virginia, 1989 (4 games)

Most Rebounds
97, Elvin Hayes, Houston, 1968 (5 games)

Highest Rebound Average
23.3, Nate Thurmond, Bowling Green, 1963 (70 rebounds in 3 games)

Most Assists
61, Mark Wade, Nevada-Las Vegas, 1987 (5 games)

Most Blocked Shots
23, David Robinson, Navy, 1986 (4 games)

Most Steals
23, Mookie Blaylock, Oklahoma, 1988 (6 games)

INDIVIDUAL RECORDS—CAREER

Most Points
407, Christian Laettner, Duke, 1989-90-91-92 (23 games)

Highest Scoring Average
41.3, Austin Carr, Notre Dame, 1969-70-71 (289 points in 7 games)

Most Field Goals
152, Elvin Hayes, Houston, 1966-67-68

Most Field Goals Attempted
310, Elvin Hayes, Houston, 1966-67-68

Highest Field-Goal Percentage (minimum 60 made)
68.6% (109-159), Bill Walton, UCLA, 1972-74

Most Three-Point Field Goals
42, Bobby Hurley, Duke, 1990-91-92-93 (20 games)

Most Three-Point Field Goals Attempted
103, Anderson Hunt, Nevada-Las Vegas, 1989-90-91 (15 games)

Highest Three-Point Field-Goal Percentage
(Minimum 30 made)
56.5% (35-62), Glen Rice, Michigan, 1986-87-88-89 (13 games)
(Minimum 20 made)
65.0% (26-40), William Scott, Kansas St., 1987-88 (5 games)

Most Free Throws
142, Christian Laettner, Duke, 1989-90-91-92 (23 games)

Most Free Throws Attempted
167, Christian Laettner, Duke, 1989-90-91-92 (23 games)

Highest Free-Throw Percentage
(Minimum 50 made)
90.6% (87-96), Bill Bradley, Princeton, 1963-64-65 (9 games)
(Minimum 30 made)
95.7% (45-47), LaBradford Smith, Louisville, 1988-89-90 (8 games)

Most Rebounds
222, Elvin Hayes, Houston, 1966-67-68 (13 games)

Highest Rebounding Average
19.7, John Green, Michigan St., 1957-59 (118 rebounds in 6 games)

Most Assists
145, Bobby Hurley, Duke, 1990-91-92-93 (20 games)

Most Blocked Shots
37, Alonzo Mourning, Georgetown, 1989-90-91-92 (10 games)

Most Steals
32, Mookie Blaylock, Oklahoma, 1988-89 (9 games); Christian Laettner, Duke, 1989-90-91-92 (23 games)

Most Games Played
23, Christian Laettner, Duke, 1989-90-91-92

TEAM RECORDS—SINGLE GAME

Most Points
149, Loyola (Cal.) vs. Michigan, West 2nd, 1990

Fewest Points
20, North Caro. vs. Pittsburgh (26), East RF, 1941

Largest Winning Margin
69, Loyola (Ill.) (111) vs. Tennessee Tech (42), SE 1st, 1963

Smallest Winning Margin
1, 115 tied (most recent: two in 1992)

Most Points Scoring by Losing Team
120, Utah vs. *St. Joseph's (Pa.) (127), N3d, 1961 (4 ot)

Most Field Goals
52, Iowa vs. Notre Dame, SE R3d, 1970

Fewest Field Goals
8, Springfield vs. Indiana, East 1st, 1940

Most Field Goals Attempted
112, Marshall vs. Southwestern La., MW 1st, 1972

Highest Field-Goal Percentage
80.0% (28-35), Oklahoma St. vs. Tulane, SE 2nd, 1992

Lowest Field-Goal Percentage
12.7% (8-63), Springfield vs. Indiana, East RSF, 1940

Most Three-Point Field Goals
21, Loyola (Cal.) vs. Michigan, West 2nd, 1990

Most Three-Point Field Goals Attempted
41, Loyola (Cal.) vs. Nevada-Las Vegas, West RF, 1990

Highest Three-Point Field-Goal Percentage (minimum 7 made)
88.9% (8-9), Kansas St. vs. Georgia, West 1st, 1987

Most Free Throws
41, Utah vs. Santa Clara, West R3d, 1960; Navy vs. Syracuse, East 2nd, 1986

Most Free Throws Attempted
55, UTEP vs. Tulsa, West 1st, 1985

Highest Free-Throw Percentage (minimum 22 made)
100% (22-22), Fordham vs. South Caro., East R3d, 1971

Most Rebounds
86, Notre Dame vs. Tennessee Tech, SE 1st, 1958

Largest Rebound Margin
42, Notre Dame (86) vs. Tennessee Tech (44), SE 1st, 1958

Most Assists
36, North Caro. vs. Loyola (Cal.), West 2nd, 1988

Most Blocked Shots
13, Louisville vs. Illinois, MW RSF, 1989; Brigham Young vs. Virginia, West 1st, 1991

Most Steals
19, Providence vs. Austin Peay, SE 2nd, 1987; Connecticut vs. Boston U., East 1st, 1990

Most Personal Fouls
41, Dayton vs. Illinois, East RSF, 1952

Most Players Disqualified
6, Kansas vs. Notre Dame, MW 1st, 1975

TEAM RECORDS—SINGLE GAME, BOTH TEAMS

Most Points
264, Loyola (Cal.) (149) vs. Michigan (115), West 2nd, 1990

Most Field Goals
97, Iowa (52) vs. Notre Dame (45), SE R3d, 1970

Most Field Goals Attempted
204, Utah (103) vs. *St. Joseph's (Pa.) (101), N3d, 1961 (4 ot)

Most Three-Point Field Goals
25, Loyola (Cal.) (21) vs. Michigan (4), West 2nd, 1990

Most Three-Point Field Goals Attempted
59, Loyola (Cal.) (41) vs. Nevada-Las Vegas (18), West RF, 1990

Most Free Throws
69, Morehead St. (37) vs. Pittsburgh (32), SE 1st, 1957

Most Free Throws Attempted
105, Iowa (52) vs. Morehead St. (53), MW RSF, 1956

Most Rebounds
134, Marshall (68) vs. *Southwestern La. (66), MW 1st, 1972

Most Assists
58, Nevada-Las Vegas (35) vs. Loyola (Cal.) (23), West RF, 1990

Most Blocked Shots
18, Iowa (10) vs. Duke (8), East 2nd, 1992

Most Steals
27, Loyola (Cal.) (14) vs. Nevada-Las Vegas (13), West 2nd, 1990

Most Personal Fouls
65, Seattle (36) vs. UCLA (29), West RSF, 1964

TEAM RECORDS—SERIES

(Three-game minimum for averages and percentages)

Most Points
571, Nevada-Las Vegas, 1990 (6 games)

Highest Scoring Average
105.8, Loyola (Cal.), 1990 (423 points in 4 games)

Most Field Goals
218, Nevada-Las Vegas, 1977 (5 games)

Most Field Goals Attempted
442, *Western Ky., 1971 (5 games)
441, Nevada-Las Vegas, 1977 (6 games)

Highest Field-Goal Percentage
60.4% (113-187), North Caro., 1975 (3 games)

Most Three-Point Field Goals
56, Loyola (Cal.), 1990 (4 games)

Most Three-Point Field Goals Attempted
137, Loyola (Cal.), 1990 (4 games)

Highest Three-Point Field-Goal Percentage (minimum 3 made per game)
60.9% (14-23), Indiana, 1989 (3 games)

Highest Three-Point Field-Goal Percentage (minimum 30 made)
51.9% (40-77), Kansas, 1993 (5 games)

Most Free Throws
146, Bradley, 1954 (5 games)

Most Free Throws Attempted
194, Bradley, 1954 (5 games)

Highest Free-Throw Percentage
87.0% (47-54), St. John's (N.Y.), 1969 (3 games)

Most Rebounds
306, Houston, 1968 (5 games)

Most Assists
140, Nevada-Las Vegas, 1990 (6 games)

Most Blocked Shots
33, Nevada-Las Vegas, 1990 (6 games)

Most Steals
72, Oklahoma, 1988 (6 games)

Most Personal Fouls
150, Pennsylvania, 1979 (6 games)

CH-National championship game
NSF-National semifinal game
N3d-National third-place game
RF-Regional final game
RSF-Regional semifinal game
R3d-Regional third-place game
2nd-Second-round game
1st-First-round game
Op-Opening-round game
East-East region
SE-Southeast/Mideast region
MW-Midwest region
West-West/Far West region
*Record later vacated

NCAA DIVISION I MEN'S TOURNAMENT

ALL-TIME RECORD OF EACH COLLEGE COACH-BY-COACH, 1939-1993

(242 COLLEGES)

	Yrs	Won	Lost	CH	2d	3d%	4th	RR
AIR FORCE								
Bob Spear (DePauw '41) 60, 62	2	0	2	0	0	0	0	0
TOTAL	2	0	2	0	0	0	0	0
AKRON								
Bob Huggins (West Va. '77) 86	1	0	1	0	0	0	0	0
TOTAL	1	0	1	0	0	0	0	0
ALABAMA*								
C. M. Newton (Kentucky '52) 75, 76	2	1	2	0	0	0	0	0
Wimp Sanderson (North Ala. '59) 82, 83, 84, 85, 86, 87, 89, 90, 91, 92	10	12	10	0	0	0	0	0
TOTAL	12	13	12	0	0	0	0	0
ALA.-BIRMINGHAM								
Gene Bartow (Northeast Mo. St. '53) 81, 82RR, 83, 84, 85, 86, 87, 90	8	6	8	0	0	0	0	1
TOTAL	8	6	8	0	0	0	0	1
ALCORN ST.								
Davey Whitney (Kentucky St. '53) 80, 82, 83, 84	4	3	4	0	0	0	0	0
TOTAL	4	3	4	0	0	0	0	0
APPALACHIAN ST.								
Bobby Cremins (South Caro. '70) 79	1	0	1	0	0	0	0	0
TOTAL	1	0	1	0	0	0	0	0
ARIZONA								
Fred Enke (Minnesota '21) 51	1	0	1	0	0	0	0	0
Fred Snowden [Wayne St. (Mich.) '58] 76RR, 77	2	2	2	0	0	0	0	1
Luther "Lute" Olson (Augsburg '57) 85, 86, 87, 88-tie 3d, 89, 90, 91, 92, 93	9	9	9	0	0	1	0	0
TOTAL	12	11	12	0	0	1	0	1
ARIZONA ST.								
Ned Wulk (Wis.-La Crosse '42) 58, 61RR, 62, 63RR, 64, 73, 75RR, 80, 81	9	8	10	0	0	0	0	3
Bill Frieder (Michigan '64) 91	1	1	1	0	0	0	0	0
TOTAL	10	9	11	0	0	0	0	3
ARKANSAS								
Eugene Lambert (Arkansas '29) 45-tie 3d, 49RR	2	2	2	0	0	1	0	1
Glen Rose (Arkansas '28) 41-tie 3d, 58	2	1	3	0	0	1	0	0
Eddie Sutton (Oklahoma St. '59) 77, 78-3d, 79RR, 80, 81, 82, 83, 84, 85	9	10	9	0	0	1	0	1
Nolan Richardson (UTEP '65) 88, 89, 90-tie 3d, 91RR, 92, 93	6	11	6	0	0	1	0	1
TOTAL	19	24	20	0	0	4	0	3

	Yrs	Won	Lost	CH	2d	3d%	4th	RR
ARK.-LIT. ROCK								
Mike Newell (Sam Houston St. '73) 86, 89, 90	3	1	3	0	0	0	0	0
TOTAL	3	1	3	0	0	0	0	0
AUBURN								
Sonny Smith (Milligan '58) 84, 85, 86RR, 87, 88	5	7	5	0	0	0	0	1
TOTAL	5	7	5	0	0	0	0	1
AUSTIN PEAY*								
Lake Kelly (Georgia Tech '56) 73, 74, 87	3	2	4	0	0	0	0	0
TOTAL	3	2	4	0	0	0	0	0
BALL ST.								
Steve Yoder (Ill. Wesleyan '62) 81	1	0	1	0	0	0	0	0
Al Brown (Purdue '64) 86	1	0	1	0	0	0	0	0
Rick Majerus (Marquette '70) 89	1	1	1	0	0	0	0	0
Dick Hunsaker (Weber St. '77) 90, 93	2	2	2	0	0	0	0	0
TOTAL	5	3	5	0	0	0	0	0
BAYLOR								
R. E. "Bill" Henderson (Howard Payne '25) 46RR, 48-2d, 50-4th..	3	3	5	0	1	0	1	1
Gene Iba (Tulsa '63) 88.................................	1	0	1	0	0	0	0	0
TOTAL	4	3	6	0	1	0	1	1
BOISE ST.								
Doran "Bus" Connor (Idaho St. '55) 76.................	1	0	1	0	0	0	0	0
Bob Dye (Idaho St. '62) 88, 93	2	0	2	0	0	0	0	0
TOTAL	3	0	3	0	0	0	0	0
BOSTON COLLEGE								
Donald Martin (Georgetown '41) 58....................	1	0	1	0	0	0	0	0
Bob Cousy (Holy Cross '48) 67RR, 68	2	2	2	0	0	0	0	1
Bob Zuffelato (Central Conn. St. '59) 75	1	1	2	0	0	0	0	0
Tom Davis (Wis.-Platteville '60) 81, 82RR...............	2	5	2	0	0	0	0	1
Gary Williams (Maryland '67) 83, 85....................	2	3	2	0	0	0	0	0
TOTAL	8	11	9	0	0	0	0	2
BOSTON U.								
Matt Zunic (Geo. Washington '42) 59RR	1	2	1	0	0	0	0	1
Rick Pitino (Massachusetts '74) 83	1	0	1	0	0	0	0	0
Mike Jarvis (Northeastern '68) 88, 90..................	2	0	2	0	0	0	0	0
TOTAL	4	2	4	0	0	0	0	1
BOWLING GREEN								
Harold Anderson (Otterbein '24) 59, 62, 63.............	3	1	4	0	0	0	0	0
Bill Fitch (Coe '54) 68	1	0	1	0	0	0	0	0
TOTAL	4	1	5	0	0	0	0	0
BRADLEY								
Forrest "Forddy" Anderson (Stanford '42) 50-2d, 54-2d	2	6	2	0	2	0	0	0
Bob Vanatta (Central Methodist '45) 55RR	1	2	1	0	0	0	0	1
Dick Versace (Wisconsin '64) 80, 86....................	2	1	2	0	0	0	0	0
Stan Albeck (Bradley '55) 88	1	0	1	0	0	0	0	0
TOTAL	6	9	6	0	2	0	0	1
BRIGHAM YOUNG								
Stan Watts (Brigham Young '38) 50RR, 51RR, 57, 65, 69, 71, 72	7	4	10	0	0	0	0	2
Frank Arnold (Idaho St. '56) 79, 80, 81RR	3	3	3	0	0	0	0	1
Ladell Anderson (Utah St. '51) 84, 87, 88..............	3	2	3	0	0	0	0	0
Roger Reid (Weber St. '67) 90, 91, 92, 93..............	4	2	4	0	0	0	0	0
TOTAL	17	11	20	0	0	0	0	3
BROWN								
George Allen (West Va. '35) 39RR.....................	1	0	1	0	0	0	0	1
Mike Cingiser (Brown '62) 86	1	0	1	0	0	0	0	0
TOTAL	2	0	2	0	0	0	0	1
BUCKNELL								
Charles Woollum (William & Mary '62) 87, 89	2	0	2	0	0	0	0	0
TOTAL	2	0	2	0	0	0	0	0
BUTLER								
Paul "Tony" Hinkle (Chicago '21) 62	1	2	1	0	0	0	0	0
TOTAL	1	2	1	0	0	0	0	0
CALIFORNIA								
Clarence "Nibs" Price (California '14) 46-4th	1	1	2	0	0	0	1	0
Pete Newell [Loyola (Cal.) '40] 57RR, 58RR, 59-CH, 60-2d	4	10	3	1	1	0	0	2
Lou Campanelli (Montclair St. '60) 90	1	1	1	0	0	0	0	0
Todd Bozeman (Rhode Island '86) 93	1	2	1	0	0	0	0	0
TOTAL	7	14	7	1	1	0	1	2

	Yrs	Won	Lost	CH	2d	3d%	4th	RR
UC SANTA BARB.								
Jerry Pimm (Southern Cal '61) 88, 90	2	1	2	0	0	0	0	0
TOTAL	2	1	2	0	0	0	0	0
CAL ST. FULLERTON								
Bob Dye (Idaho St. '62) 78RR	1	2	1	0	0	0	0	1
TOTAL	1	2	1	0	0	0	0	1
CAL ST. LOS ANGELES								
Bob Miller (Occidental '53) 74	1	0	1	0	0	0	0	0
TOTAL	1	0	1	0	0	0	0	0
CAMPBELL								
Billy Lee (Barton '71) 92	1	0	1	0	0	0	0	0
TOTAL	1	0	1	0	0	0	0	0
CANISIUS								
Joseph Curran (Canisius '43) 55RR, 56RR, 57	3	6	3	0	0	0	0	2
TOTAL	3	6	3	0	0	0	0	2
CATHOLIC								
John Long (Catholic '28) 44RR	1	0	2	0	0	0	0	1
TOTAL	1	0	2	0	0	0	0	1
CENTRAL MICH.								
Dick Parfitt (Central Mich. '53) 75, 77	2	2	2	0	0	0	0	0
Charlie Coles [Miami (Ohio) '65] 87	1	0	1	0	0	0	0	0
TOTAL	3	2	3	0	0	0	0	0
CINCINNATI								
George Smith (Cincinnati '35) 58, 59-3d, 60-3d	3	7	3	0	0	2	0	0
Ed Jucker (Cincinnati '40) 61-CH, 62-CH, 63-2d	3	11	1	2	1	0	0	0
Tay Baker (Cincinnati '50) 66	1	0	2	0	0	0	0	0
Gale Catlett (West Va. '63) 75, 76, 77	3	2	3	0	0	0	0	0
Bob Huggins (West Va. '77) 92-tie 3d, 93 RR	2	7	2	0	0	1	0	1
TOTAL	12	27	11	2	1	3	0	1
CCNY								
Nat Holman (Savage School of Phys. Ed. '17) 47-4th, 50-CH	2	4	2	1	0	0	1	0
TOTAL	2	4	2	1	0	0	1	0
CLEMSON								
William C. "Bill" Foster (Carson-Newman '58) 80RR	1	3	1	0	0	0	0	1
Cliff Ellis (Florida St. '68) 87, 89, 90	3	3	3	0	0	0	0	0
TOTAL	4	6	4	0	0	0	0	1
CLEVELAND ST.								
Kevin Mackey (St. Anselm '67) 86	1	2	1	0	0	0	0	0
TOTAL	1	2	1	0	0	0	0	0
COASTAL CARO.								
Russ Bergman (Louisiana St. '70) 91, 93	2	0	2	0	0	0	0	0
TOTAL	2	0	2	0	0	0	0	0
COLORADO								
Forrest "Frosty" Cox (Kansas '30) 40RR, 42-tie 3d, 46RR	3	2	4	0	0	1	0	2
Horace "Bebe" Lee (Stanford '38) 54, 55-3d	2	3	3	0	0	1	0	0
Russell "Sox" Walseth (Colorado '48) 62RR, 63RR, 69	3	3	3	0	0	0	0	2
TOTAL	8	8	10	0	0	2	0	4
COLORADO ST.								
Bill Strannigan (Wyoming '41) 54	1	0	2	0	0	0	0	0
Jim Williams (Utah St. '47) 63, 65, 66, 69RR	4	2	4	0	0	0	0	1
Boyd Grant (Colorado St. '57) 89, 90	2	1	2	0	0	0	0	0
TOTAL	7	3	8	0	0	0	0	1
COLUMBIA								
Gordon Ridings (Oregon '29) 48RR	1	0	2	0	0	0	0	1
Lou Rossini (Columbia '48) 51	1	0	1	0	0	0	0	0
John "Jack" Rohan (Columbia '53) 68	1	2	1	0	0	0	0	0
TOTAL	3	2	4	0	0	0	0	1
CONNECTICUT								
Hugh Greer (Connecticut '26) 51, 54, 56, 57, 58, 59, 60	7	1	8	0	0	0	0	0
George Wigton (Ohio St. '56) 63	1	0	1	0	0	0	0	0
Fred Shabel (Duke '54) 64RR, 65, 67	3	2	3	0	0	0	0	1
Donald "Dee" Rowe (Middlebury '52) 76	1	1	1	0	0	0	0	0
Dom Perno (Connecticut '64) 79	1	0	1	0	0	0	0	0
Jim Calhoun (American Int'l '68) 90RR, 91, 92	3	6	3	0	0	0	0	1
TOTAL	16	10	17	0	0	0	0	2

	Yrs	Won	Lost	CH	2d	3d%	4th	RR
COPPIN ST.								
Ron Mitchell (Edison '84) 90, 93	2	0	2	0	0	0	0	0
TOTAL	2	0	2	0	0	0	0	0
CORNELL								
Royner Greene (Illinois '29) 54	1	0	2	0	0	0	0	0
Mike Dement (East Caro. '76) 88	1	0	1	0	0	0	0	0
TOTAL	2	0	3	0	0	0	0	0
CREIGHTON								
Eddie Hickey (Creighton '27) 41RR	1	1	1	0	0	0	0	1
John "Red" McManus (St. Ambrose '49) 62, 64	2	3	3	0	0	0	0	0
Eddie Sutton (Oklahoma St. '59) 74	1	2	1	0	0	0	0	0
Tom Apke (Creighton '65) 75, 78, 81	3	0	3	0	0	0	0	0
Tony Barone (Duke '68) 89, 91	2	1	2	0	0	0	0	0
TOTAL	9	7	10	0	0	0	0	1
DARTMOUTH								
Osborne "Ozzie" Cowles (Carleton '22) 41RR, 42-2d, 43RR	3	4	3	0	1	0	0	2
Earl Brown (Notre Dame '39) 44-2d	1	2	1	0	1	0	0	0
Alvin "Doggie" Julian (Bucknell '23) 56, 58RR, 59	3	4	3	0	0	0	0	1
TOTAL	7	10	7	0	2	0	0	3
DAVIDSON								
Charles "Lefty" Driesell (Duke '54) 66, 68RR, 69RR	3	5	4	0	0	0	0	2
Terry Holland (Davidson '64) 70	1	0	1	0	0	0	0	0
Bobby Hussey (Appalachian St. '62) 86	1	0	1	0	0	0	0	0
TOTAL	5	5	6	0	0	0	0	2
DAYTON								
Tom Blackburn [Wilmington (Ohio) '31] 52	1	1	1	0	0	0	0	0
Don Donoher (Dayton '54) 65, 66, 67-2d, 69, 70, 74, 84RR, 85	8	11	10	0	1	0	0	1
Jim O'Brien [St. Joseph's (Pa.)] 90	1	1	1	0	0	0	0	0
TOTAL	10	13	12	0	1	0	0	1
DELAWARE								
Steve Steinwedel (Mississippi St. '75) 92, 93	2	0	2	0	0	0	0	0
TOTAL	2	0	2	0	0	0	0	0
DEPAUL								
Ray Meyer (Notre Dame '38) 43-tie 3d, 53, 56, 59, 60, 65, 76, 78RR, 79-3d, 80, 81, 82, 84	13	14	16	0	0	2	0	1
Joey Meyer (DePaul '71) 85, 86, 87, 88, 89, 91, 92	7	6	7	0	0	0	0	0
TOTAL	20	20	23	0	0	2	0	1
DETROIT MERCY								
Robert Calihan (Detroit Mercy '40) 62	1	0	1	0	0	0	0	0
Dick Vitale (Seton Hall '62) 77	1	1	1	0	0	0	0	0
Dave "Smokey" Gaines (LeMoyne-Owen '63) 79	1	0	1	0	0	0	0	0
TOTAL	3	1	3	0	0	0	0	0
DRAKE								
Maurice John (Central Mo. St. '41) 69-3d, 70RR, 71RR	3	5	3	0	0	1	0	2
TOTAL	3	5	3	0	0	1	0	2
DREXEL								
Eddie Burke (La Salle '67) 86	1	0	1	0	0	0	0	0
TOTAL	1	0	1	0	0	0	0	0
DUKE								
Harold Bradley (Hartwick '34) 55	1	0	1	0	0	0	0	0
Vic Bubas (North Caro. St. '51) 60RR, 63-3d, 64-2d, 66-3d	4	11	4	0	1	2	0	1
William E. "Bill" Foster (Elizabethtown '54) 78-2d, 79, 80RR	3	6	3	0	1	0	0	1
Mike Krzyzewski (Army '69) 84, 85, 86-2d, 87, 88-tie 3d, 89-tie 3d, 90-2nd, 91-CH, 92-CH, 93	10	34	8	2	2	2	0	0
TOTAL	18	51	16	2	4	4	0	2
DUQUESNE								
Charles "Chick" Davies (Duquesne '34) 40-tie 3d	1	1	1	0	0	1	0	0
Donald "Dudey" Moore (Duquesne '34) 52RR	1	1	1	0	0	0	0	1
John "Red" Manning (Duquesne '51) 69, 71	2	2	2	0	0	0	0	0
John Cinicola (Duquesne '55) 77	1	0	1	0	0	0	0	0
TOTAL	5	4	5	0	0	1	0	1
EAST CARO.								
Tom Quinn (Marshall '54) 72	1	0	1	0	0	0	0	0
Eddie Payne (Wake Forest '73) 93	1	0	1	0	0	0	0	0
TOTAL	2	0	2	0	0	0	0	0

	Yrs	Won	Lost	CH	2d	3d%	4th	RR
EAST TENN. ST.								
J. Madison Brooks (Louisiana Tech '37) 68	1	1	2	0	0	0	0	0
Les Robinson (North Caro. St. '64) 89, 90	2	0	2	0	0	0	0	0
Alan LeForce (Cumberland '57) 91, 92	2	1	2	0	0	0	0	0
TOTAL	5	2	6	0	0	0	0	0
EASTERN ILL.								
Rick Samuels (Chadron St. '71) 92	1	0	1	0	0	0	0	0
TOTAL	1	0	1	0	0	0	0	0
EASTERN KY.								
Paul McBrayer (Kentucky '30) 53, 59	2	0	2	0	0	0	0	0
Jim Baechtold (Eastern Ky. '52) 65	1	0	1	0	0	0	0	0
Guy Strong (Eastern Ky. '55) 72	1	0	1	0	0	0	0	0
Ed Byhre [Augustana (S.D.) '66] 79	1	0	1	0	0	0	0	0
TOTAL	5	0	5	0	0	0	0	0
EASTERN MICH.								
Ben Braun (Wisconsin '75) 88, 91	2	2	2	0	0	0	0	0
TOTAL	2	2	2	0	0	0	0	0
EVANSVILLE								
Dick Walters (Illinois St. '69) 82	1	0	1	0	0	0	0	0
Jim Crews (Indiana '76) 89, 92, 93	3	1	3	0	0	0	0	0
TOTAL	4	1	4	0	0	0	0	0
FAIRFIELD								
Mitch Buonaguro (Boston College '75) 86, 87	2	0	2	0	0	0	0	0
TOTAL	2	0	2	0	0	0	0	0
FDU-TEANECK								
Tom Green (Syracuse '71) 85, 88	2	0	2	0	0	0	0	0
TOTAL	2	0	2	0	0	0	0	0
FLORIDA*								
Norm Sloan (North Caro. St. '51) 87, 88, 89	3	3	3	0	0	0	0	0
TOTAL	3	3	3	0	0	0	0	0
FLORIDA ST.								
Hugh Durham (Florida St. '59) 68, 72-2d, 78	3	4	3	0	1	0	0	0
Joe Williams (Southern Methodist '56) 80	1	1	1	0	0	0	0	0
Pat Kennedy [King's (Pa.) '76] 88, 89, 91, 92, 93RR	5	6	5	0	0	0	0	1
TOTAL	9	11	9	0	1	0	0	1
FORDHAM								
John Bach (Fordham '48) 53, 54	2	0	2	0	0	0	0	0
Richard "Digger" Phelps (Rider '63) 71	1	2	1	0	0	0	0	0
Nick Macarchuk (Fairfield '63) 92	1	0	1	0	0	0	0	0
TOTAL	4	2	4	0	0	0	0	0
FRESNO ST.								
Boyd Grant (Colorado St. '61) 81, 82, 84	3	1	3	0	0	0	0	0
TOTAL	3	1	3	0	0	0	0	0
FURMAN								
Joe Williams (Southern Methodist '56) 71, 73, 74, 75, 78	5	1	6	0	0	0	0	0
Eddie Holbrook (Lenoir-Rhyne '62) 80	1	0	1	0	0	0	0	0
TOTAL	6	1	7	0	0	0	0	0
GEORGE MASON								
Ernie Nestor (Alderson-Broaddus '68) 89	1	0	1	0	0	0	0	0
TOTAL	1	0	1	0	0	0	0	0
GEO. WASHINGTON								
Bill Reinhart (Oregon '23) 54, 61	2	0	2	0	0	0	0	0
Mike Jarvis (Northeastern '68) 93	1	2	1	0	0	0	0	0
TOTAL	3	2	3	0	0	0	0	0
GEORGETOWN								
Elmer Ripley (No college) 43-2d	1	2	1	0	1	0	0	0
John Thompson (Providence '64) 75, 76, 79, 80RR, 81, 82-2d, 83, 84-CH, 85-2d, 86, 87RR, 88, 89RR, 90, 91, 92	16	28	15	1	2	0	0	3
TOTAL	17	30	16	1	3	0	0	3
GEORGIA*								
Hugh Durham (Florida St. '59) 83-tie 3d, 85, 87, 90, 91	5	4	5	0	0	1	0	0
TOTAL	5	4	5	0	0	1	0	0
GA. SOUTHERN								
Frank Kerns (Alabama '57) 83, 87, 92	3	0	3	0	0	0	0	0
TOTAL	3	0	3	0	0	0	0	0
GEORGIA ST.								
Bob Reinhart (Indiana '61) 91	1	0	1	0	0	0	0	0
TOTAL	1	0	1	0	0	0	0	0

	Yrs	Won	Lost	CH	2d	3d%	4th	RR
GEORGIA TECH								
John "Whack" Hyder (Georgia Tech) 60RR	1	1	1	0	0	0	0	1
Bobby Cremins (South Caro. '70) 85RR, 86, 87, 88, 89, 90-tie 3d, 91, 92, 93	9	13	9	0	0	1	0	1
TOTAL	10	14	10	0	0	1	0	2
HARDIN-SIMMONS								
Bill Scott (Hardin-Simmons '47) 53, 57	2	0	2	0	0	0	0	0
TOTAL	2	0	2	0	0	0	0	0
HARVARD								
Floyd Stahl (Illinois '26) 46RR	1	0	2	0	0	0	0	1
TOTAL	1	0	2	0	0	0	0	1
HAWAII								
Ephraim "Red" Rocha (Oregon St. '50) 72	1	0	1	0	0	0	0	0
TOTAL	1	0	1	0	0	0	0	0
HOFSTRA								
Roger Gaeckler (Gettysburg '65) 76, 77	2	0	2	0	0	0	0	0
TOTAL	2	0	2	0	0	0	0	0
HOLY CROSS								
Alvin "Doggie" Julian (Bucknell '23) 47-CH, 48-3d	2	5	1	1	0	1	0	0
Lester "Buster" Sheary (Catholic '33) 50RR, 53RR	2	2	3	0	0	0	0	2
Roy Leenig [Trinity (Conn.) '42] 56	1	0	1	0	0	0	0	0
George Blaney (Holy Cross '61) 77, 80, 93	3	0	3	0	0	0	0	0
TOTAL	8	7	8	1	0	1	0	2
HOUSTON								
Alden Pasche (Rice '32) 56	1	0	2	0	0	0	0	0
Guy Lewis (Houston '47) 61, 65, 66, 67-3d, 68-4th, 70, 71, 72, 73, 78, 81, 82-tie 3d, 83-2d, 84-2d	14	26	18	0	2	2	1	0
Pat Foster (Arkansas '61) 87, 90, 92	3	0	3	0	0	0	0	0
TOTAL	18	26	23	0	2	2	1	0
HOUSTON BAPTIST								
Gene Iba (Tulsa '63) 84	1	0	1	0	0	0	0	0
TOTAL	1	0	1	0	0	0	0	0
HOWARD								
A. B. Williamson (North Caro. A&T '68) 81	1	0	1	0	0	0	0	0
Alfred "Butch" Beard (Louisville '72) 92	1	0	1	0	0	0	0	0
TOTAL	2	0	2	0	0	0	0	0
IDAHO								
Don Monson (Idaho '55) 81, 82	2	1	2	0	0	0	0	0
Kermit Davis Jr. (Mississippi St. '82) 89, 90	2	0	2	0	0	0	0	0
TOTAL	4	1	4	0	0	0	0	0
IDAHO ST.								
Steve Belko (Idaho '39) 53, 54, 55, 56	4	2	4	0	0	0	0	0
John Grayson (Oklahoma '38) 57, 58, 59	3	4	5	0	0	0	0	0
John Evans (Idaho '48) 60	1	0	1	0	0	0	0	0
Jim Killingsworth (Northeastern Okla. '48) 74, 77RR	2	2	2	0	0	0	0	1
Jim Boutin (Lewis & Clark '64) 87	1	0	1	0	0	0	0	0
TOTAL	11	8	13	0	0	0	0	1
ILLINOIS								
Doug Mills (Illinois '30) 42RR	1	0	2	0	0	0	0	1
Harry Combes (Illinois '37) 49-3d, 51-3d, 52-3d, 63RR	4	9	4	0	0	3	0	1
Lou Henson (New Mexico St. '55) 81, 83, 84RR, 85, 86, 87, 88, 89-tie 3d, 90, 93	10	12	10	0	0	1	0	1
TOTAL	15	21	16	0	0	4	0	3
ILLINOIS ST.								
Bob Donewald (Hanover '64) 83, 84, 85	3	2	3	0	0	0	0	0
Bob Bender (Duke '80) 90	1	0	1	0	0	0	0	0
TOTAL	4	2	4	0	0	0	0	0
INDIANA								
Branch McCracken (Indiana '30) 40-CH, 53-CH, 54, 58	4	9	2	2	0	0	0	0
Lou Watson (Indiana '50) 67	1	1	1	0	0	0	0	0
Bob Knight (Ohio St. '62) 73-3d, 75RR, 76-CH, 78, 80, 81-CH, 82, 83, 84RR, 86, 87-CH, 88, 89, 90, 91, 92-tie 3d, 93RR	17	38	14	3	0	2	0	3
TOTAL	22	48	17	5	0	2	0	3
INDIANA ST.								
Bill Hodges (Marian '70) 79-2d	1	4	1	0	1	0	0	0
TOTAL	1	4	1	0	1	0	0	0

	Yrs	Won	Lost	CH	2d	3d%	4th	RR
IONA*								
Jim Valvano (Rutgers '67) 79, 80	2	1	2	0	0	0	0	0
Pat Kennedy [King's (Pa.) '76] 84, 85	2	0	2	0	0	0	0	0
TOTAL	4	1	4	0	0	0	0	0
IOWA								
Frank "Bucky" O'Connor (Drake '38) 55-4th, 56-2d	2	5	3	0	1	0	1	0
Ralph Miller (Kansas '42) 70	1	1	1	0	0	0	0	0
Luther "Lute" Olson (Augsburg '57) 79, 80-4th, 81, 82, 83	5	7	6	0	0	0	1	0
George Raveling (Villanova '60) 85, 86	2	0	2	0	0	0	0	0
Tom Davis (Wis.-Platteville '60) 87RR, 88, 89, 91, 92, 93	6	9	6	0	0	0	0	1
TOTAL	16	22	18	0	1	0	2	1
IOWA ST.								
Louis Menze (Central Mo. St. '28) 44-tie 3d	1	1	1	0	0	1	0	0
Johnny Orr (Beloit '49) 85, 86, 88, 89, 92, 93	6	3	6	0	0	0	0	0
TOTAL	7	4	7	0	0	1	0	0
JACKSONVILLE								
Joe Williams (Southern Methodist '56) 70-2d	1	4	1	0	1	0	0	0
Tom Wasdin (Florida '57) 71, 73	2	0	2	0	0	0	0	0
Tates Locke (Ohio Wesleyan '59) 79	1	0	1	0	0	0	0	0
Bob Wenzel (Rutgers '71) 86	1	0	1	0	0	0	0	0
TOTAL	5	4	5	0	1	0	0	0
JAMES MADISON								
Lou Campanelli (Montclair St. '60) 81, 82, 83	3	3	3	0	0	0	0	0
TOTAL	3	3	3	0	0	0	0	0
KANSAS								
Forrest C. "Phog" Allen (Kansas '06) 40-2d, 42RR, 52-CH, 53-2d	4	10	3	1	2	0	0	1
Dick Harp (Kansas '40) 57-2d, 60RR	2	4	2	0	1	0	0	1
Ted Owens (Oklahoma '51) 66RR, 67, 71-4th, 74-4th, 75, 78, 81	7	8	9	0	0	0	2	1
Larry Brown (North Caro. '63) 84, 85, 86-tie 3d, 87, 88-CH	5	14	4	1	0	1	0	0
Roy Williams (North Caro. '72) 90, 91-2d, 92, 93-tie 3d	4	11	4	0	1	1	0	0
TOTAL	22	47	22	2	4	2	2	3
KANSAS ST.								
Jack Gardner (Southern Cal '32) 48-4th, 51-2d	2	4	3	0	1	0	1	0
Fred "Tex" Winter (Southern Cal '47) 56, 58-4th, 59RR, 61RR, 64-4th, 68	6	7	9	0	0	0	2	2
Lowell "Cotton" Fitzsimmons (Midwestern St. '55) 70	1	1	1	0	0	0	0	0
Jack Hartman (Oklahoma St. '49) 72RR, 73RR, 75RR, 77, 80, 81RR, 82	7	11	7	0	0	0	0	4
Lon Kruger (Kansas St. '74) 87, 88, 89, 90	4	4	4	0	0	0	0	1
Dana Altman (Eastern N. Mex. '80) 93	1	0	1	0	0	0	0	0
TOTAL	21	27	25	0	1	0	3	7
KENTUCKY*								
Adolph Rupp (Kansas '23) 42-tie 3d, 45RR, 48-CH, 49-CH, 51-CH, 52RR, 55, 56RR, 57RR, 58-CH, 59, 61RR, 62RR, 64, 66-2d, 68RR, 69, 70RR, 71, 72RR	20	30	18	4	1	1	0	9
Joe Hall (Sewanee '51) 73RR, 75-2d, 77RR, 78-CH, 80, 81, 82, 83RR, 84-tie 3d, 85	10	20	9	1	1	1	0	3
Eddie Sutton (Oklahoma St. '59) 86RR, 87, 88	3	5	3	0	0	0	0	1
Rick Pitino (Massachusetts '74) 92RR, 93-tie 3d	2	7	2	0	0	1	0	1
TOTAL	35	62	32	5	2	3	0	14
LA SALLE								
Ken Loeffler (Penn St. '24) 54-CH, 55-2d	2	9	1	1	1	0	0	0
Jim Harding (Iowa '49) 68	1	0	1	0	0	0	0	0
Paul Westhead [St. Joseph's (Pa.) '61] 75, 78	2	0	2	0	0	0	0	0
Dave "Lefty" Ervin (La Salle '68) 80, 83	2	1	2	0	0	0	0	0
Bill "Speedy" Morris [St. Joseph's (Pa.) '73] 88, 89, 90, 92	4	1	4	0	0	0	0	0
TOTAL	11	11	10	1	1	0	0	0
LAFAYETTE								
George Davidson (Lafayette '51) 57	1	0	2	0	0	0	0	0
TOTAL	1	0	2	0	0	0	0	0
LAMAR								
Billy Tubbs (Lamar '58) 79, 80	2	3	2	0	0	0	0	0
Pat Foster (Arkansas '61) 81, 83	2	2	2	0	0	0	0	0
TOTAL	4	5	4	0	0	0	0	0

	Yrs	Won	Lost	CH	2d	3d%	4th	RR
LEBANON VALLEY								
George "Rinso" Marquette (Lebanon Valley '48) 53	1	1	2	0	0	0	0	0
TOTAL	1	1	2	0	0	0	0	0
LEHIGH								
Tom Schneider (Bucknell '69) 85	1	0	1	0	0	0	0	0
Fran McCaffery (Pennsylvania '82) 88	1	0	1	0	0	0	0	0
TOTAL	2	0	2	0	0	0	0	0
LONG BEACH ST.*								
Jerry Tarkanian (Fresno St. '56) 70, 71RR, 72RR, 73 ...	4	7	5	0	0	0	0	2
Dwight Jones (Pepperdine '65) 77	1	0	1	0	0	0	0	0
Seth Greenberg (FDU-Teaneck '78) 93	1	0	1	0	0	0	0	0
TOTAL	6	7	7	0	0	0	0	2
LIU-BROOKLYN								
Paul Lizzo (Northwest Mo. St. '63) 81, 84	2	0	2	0	0	0	0	0
TOTAL	2	0	2	0	0	0	0	0
LOUISIANA ST.								
Harry Rabenhorst (Wake Forest '21) 53-4th, 54	2	2	4	0	0	0	1	0
Dale Brown (Minot St. '57) 79, 80RR, 81-4th, 84, 85, 86-tie 3d, 87RR, 88, 89, 90, 91, 92, 93	13	15	14	0	0	1	1	2
TOTAL	15	17	18	0	0	1	2	2
LOUISIANA TECH								
Andy Russo (Lake Forest '70) 84, 85	2	3	2	0	0	0	0	0
Tommy Eagles (Louisiana Tech '71) 87, 89	2	1	2	0	0	0	0	0
Jerry Lloyd (LeTourneau '76) 91	1	0	1	0	0	0	0	0
TOTAL	5	4	5	0	0	0	0	0
LOUISVILLE								
Bernard "Peck" Hickman (Western Ky. '35) 51, 59-4th, 61, 64, 67	5	5	7	0	0	0	1	0
John Dromo (John Carroll '39) 68	1	1	1	0	0	0	0	0
Denny Crum (UCLA '59) 72-4th, 74, 75-3d, 77, 78, 79, 80-CH, 81, 82-tie 3d, 83-tie 3d, 84, 86-CH, 88, 89, 90, 92, 93	17	35	17	2	0	3	1	0
TOTAL	23	41	25	2	0	3	2	0
LOYOLA (CAL.)*								
John Arndt [Loyola (Cal.) '50] 61	1	1	1	0	0	0	0	0
Ron Jacobs (Southern Cal '64) 80	1	0	1	0	0	0	0	0
Paul Westhead [St. Joseph's (Pa.) '61] 88, 89, 90RR	3	4	3	0	0	0	0	1
TOTAL	5	5	5	0	0	0	0	1
LOYOLA (ILL.)								
George Ireland (Notre Dame '36) 63-CH, 64, 66, 68	4	7	3	1	0	0	0	0
Gene Sullivan (Notre Dame '53) 85	1	2	1	0	0	0	0	0
TOTAL	5	9	4	1	0	0	0	0
LOYOLA (LA.)								
Jim McCafferty [Loyola (La.) '42] 54, 57	2	0	2	0	0	0	0	0
Jim Harding (Iowa '49) 58	1	0	1	0	0	0	0	0
TOTAL	3	0	3	0	0	0	0	0
MANHATTAN								
Ken Norton (LIU-Brooklyn '39) 56, 58	2	1	3	0	0	0	0	0
Fran Fraschilla (Brooklyn Col. '80) 93	1	0	1	0	0	0	0	0
TOTAL	3	1	4	0	0	0	0	0
MARIST								
Matt Furjanic (Point Park '73) 86	1	0	1	0	0	0	0	0
Dave Magarity [St. Francis (Pa.) '74] 87	1	0	1	0	0	0	0	0
TOTAL	2	0	2	0	0	0	0	0
MARQUETTE								
Jack Nagle (Marquette '40) 55RR	1	2	1	0	0	0	0	1
Eddie Hickey (Creighton '27) 59, 61	2	1	3	0	0	0	0	0
Al McGuire [St. John's (N.Y.) '51] 68, 69RR, 71, 72, 73, 74-2d, 75, 76RR, 77-CH	9	20	9	1	1	0	0	2
Hank Raymonds (St. Louis '48) 78, 79, 80, 82, 83	5	2	5	0	0	0	0	0
Kevin O'Neill (McGill '79) 93	1	0	1	0	0	0	0	0
TOTAL	18	25	19	1	1	0	0	3
MARSHALL*								
Jule Rivlin (Marshall '40) 56	1	0	1	0	0	0	0	0
Carl Tacy (Davis & Elkins '56) 72	1	0	1	0	0	0	0	0
Rick Huckabay (Louisiana Tech '67) 84, 85, 87	3	0	3	0	0	0	0	0
TOTAL	5	0	5	0	0	0	0	0

	Yrs	Won	Lost	CH	2d	3d%	4th	RR
MARYLAND*								
H. A. "Bud" Millikan (Oklahoma St. '42) 58	1	2	1	0	0	0	0	0
Charles "Lefty" Driesell (Duke '54) 73RR, 75RR, 80, 81, 83, 84, 85, 86	8	10	8	0	0	0	0	2
Bob Wade (Morgan St. '67) 88	1	1	1	0	0	0	0	0
TOTAL	10	13	10	0	0	0	0	2
MASSACHUSETTS								
Matt Zunic (Geo. Washington '42) 62	1	0	1	0	0	0	0	0
John Calipari (Clarion St. '82) 92, 93	2	3	2	0	0	0	0	0
TOTAL	3	3	3	0	0	0	0	0
McNEESE ST.								
Steve Welch (Southeastern La. '71) 89	1	0	1	0	0	0	0	0
TOTAL	1	0	1	0	0	0	0	0
MEMPHIS ST.*								
Eugene Lambert (Arkansas '29) 55, 56	2	0	2	0	0	0	0	0
Bob Vanatta (Central Methodist '45) 62	1	0	1	0	0	0	0	0
Gene Bartow (Northeast Mo. St. '53) 73-2d	1	3	1	0	1	0	0	0
Wayne Yates (Memphis St. '61) 76	1	0	1	0	0	0	0	0
Dana Kirk (Marshall '60) 82, 83, 84, 85-tie 3d, 86	5	9	5	0	0	1	0	0
Larry Finch (Memphis St. '73) 88, 89, 92RR, 93	4	4	4	0	0	0	0	1
TOTAL	14	16	14	0	1	1	0	1
MERCER								
Bill Bibb (Ky. Wesleyan '57) 81, 85	2	0	2	0	0	0	0	0
TOTAL	2	0	2	0	0	0	0	0
MIAMI (FLA.)								
Bruce Hale (Santa Clara '41) 60	1	0	1	0	0	0	0	0
TOTAL	1	0	1	0	0	0	0	0
MIAMI (OHIO)								
Bill Rohr (Ohio Wesleyan '40) 53, 55, 57	3	0	3	0	0	0	0	0
Dick Shrider (Ohio '48) 58, 66	2	1	3	0	0	0	0	0
Tates Locke (Ohio Wesleyan '59) 69	1	1	2	0	0	0	0	0
Darrell Hedric [Miami (Ohio) '55] 71, 73, 78, 84	4	1	4	0	0	0	0	0
Jerry Peirson [Miami (Ohio) '66] 85, 86	2	0	2	0	0	0	0	0
Joby Wright (Indiana '72) 92	1	0	1	0	0	0	0	0
TOTAL	13	3	15	0	0	0	0	0
MICHIGAN#								
Osborne "Ozzie" Cowles (Carleton '22) 48RR	1	1	1	0	0	0	0	1
Dave Strack (Michigan '46) 64-3d, 65-2d, 66RR	3	7	3	0	1	1	0	1
Johnny Orr (Beloit '49) 74RR, 75, 76-2d, 77RR	4	7	4	0	1	0	0	2
Bill Frieder (Michigan '64) 85, 86, 87, 88	4	5	4	0	0	0	0	0
Steve Fisher (Illinois St. '67) 89-CH, 90, 92-2d, 93-2d	4	17	3	1	2	0	0	0
TOTAL	16	37	15	1	4	1	0	4
MICHIGAN ST.								
Forrest "Forddy" Anderson (Stanford '42) 57-4th, 59RR	2	3	3	0	0	0	1	1
George "Jud" Heathcote (Washington St. '50) 78RR, 79-CH, 85, 86, 90, 91, 92	7	13	6	1	0	0	0	1
TOTAL	9	16	9	1	0	0	1	2
MIDDLE TENN. ST.								
Jimmy Earle (Middle Tenn. St. '59) 75, 77	2	0	2	0	0	0	0	0
Stan Simpson (Ga. Southern '61) 82	1	1	1	0	0	0	0	0
Bruce Stewart (Jacksonville St. '75) 85, 87, 89	3	1	3	0	0	0	0	0
TOTAL	6	2	6	0	0	0	0	0
MINNESOTA*								
Bill Musselman (Wittenberg '61) 72	1	1	1	0	0	0	0	0
Jim Dutcher (Michigan '55) 82	1	1	1	0	0	0	0	0
Clem Haskins (Western Ky. '67) 89, 90RR	2	5	2	0	0	0	0	1
TOTAL	4	7	4	0	0	0	0	1
MISSISSIPPI								
Bob Weltlich (Ohio St. '67) 81	1	0	1	0	0	0	0	0
TOTAL	1	0	1	0	0	0	0	0
MISSISSIPPI ST.								
James "Babe" McCarthy (Mississippi St. '49) 63	1	1	1	0	0	0	0	0
Richard Williams (Mississippi St. '67) 91	1	0	1	0	0	0	0	0
TOTAL	2	1	2	0	0	0	0	0
MISSISSIPPI VAL.								
Lafayette Stribling (Mississippi Industrial '57) 86, 92	2	0	2	0	0	0	0	0
TOTAL	2	0	2	0	0	0	0	0

	Yrs	Won	Lost	CH	2d	3d%	4th	RR
MISSOURI#								
George Edwards (Missouri '13) 44RR	1	1	1	0	0	0	0	1
Norm Stewart (Missouri '56) 76RR, 78, 80, 81, 82, 83, 86, 87, 88, 89, 90, 92, 93	13	8	13	0	0	0	0	1
TOTAL	14	9	14	0	0	0	0	2
MONTANA								
George "Jud" Heathcote (Washington St. '50) 75	1	1	2	0	0	0	0	0
Stew Morrill (Gonzaga '74) 91	1	0	1	0	0	0	0	0
Blaine Taylor (Montana '82) 92	1	0	1	0	0	0	0	0
TOTAL	3	1	4	0	0	0	0	0
MONTANA ST.								
John Breeden (Montana St. '29) 51	1	0	1	0	0	0	0	0
Stu Starner (Minn.-Morris '65) 86	1	0	1	0	0	0	0	0
TOTAL	2	0	2	0	0	0	0	0
MOREHEAD ST.								
Robert Laughlin (Morehead St. '37) 56, 57, 61	3	3	4	0	0	0	0	0
Wayne Martin (Morehead St. '68) 83, 84	2	1	2	0	0	0	0	0
TOTAL	5	4	6	0	0	0	0	0
MURRAY ST.								
Cal Luther (Valparaiso '51) 64, 69	2	0	2	0	0	0	0	0
Steve Newton (Indiana St. '63) 88, 90, 91	3	1	3	0	0	0	0	0
Edgar Scott (Pitt.-Johnstown '78) 92	1	0	1	0	0	0	0	0
TOTAL	6	1	6	0	0	0	0	0
NAVY								
Ben Carnevale (New York U. '38) 47RR, 53, 54RR, 59, 60	5	4	6	0	0	0	0	2
Paul Evans (Ithaca '67) 85, 86RR	2	4	2	0	0	0	0	1
Pete Herrmann (Geneseo St. '70) 87	1	0	1	0	0	0	0	0
TOTAL	8	8	9	0	0	0	0	3
NEBRASKA								
Moe Iba (Oklahoma St. '62) 86	1	0	1	0	0	0	0	0
Danny Nee (St. Mary of the Plains '71) 91, 92, 93	3	0	3	0	0	0	0	0
TOTAL	4	0	4	0	0	0	0	0
NEVADA								
Sonny Allen (Marshall '59) 84, 85	2	0	2	0	0	0	0	0
TOTAL	2	0	2	0	0	0	0	0
NEVADA-LAS VEGAS								
Jerry Tarkanian (Fresno St. '56) 75, 76, 77-3d, 83, 84, 85, 86, 87-tie 3d, 88, 89RR, 90-CH, 91-tie 3d	12	30	11	1	0	3	0	1
TOTAL	12	30	11	1	0	3	0	1
NEW MEXICO								
Bob King (Iowa '47) 68	1	0	2	0	0	0	0	0
Norm Ellenberger (Butler '55) 74, 78	2	2	2	0	0	0	0	0
Dave Bliss (Cornell '65) 91, 93	2	0	2	0	0	0	0	0
TOTAL	5	2	6	0	0	0	0	0
NEW MEXICO ST.								
George McCarty (New Mexico St. '50) 52	1	0	2	0	0	0	0	0
Presley Askew (Southeastern Okla. St. '30) 59, 60	2	0	2	0	0	0	0	0
Lou Henson (New Mexico St. '55) 67, 68, 69, 70-3d, 71, 75	6	7	7	0	0	1	0	0
Ken Hayes (Northeastern Okla. St. '56) 79	1	0	1	0	0	0	0	0
Neil McCarthy (Sacramento St. '65) 90, 91, 92, 93	4	3	4	0	0	0	0	0
TOTAL	14	10	16	0	0	1	0	0
NEW ORLEANS								
Benny Dees (Wyoming '58) 87	1	1	1	0	0	0	0	0
Tim Floyd (Louisiana Tech '77) 91, 93	2	0	2	0	0	0	0	0
TOTAL	3	1	3	0	0	0	0	0
NEW YORK U.								
Howard Cann (New York U. '20) 43RR, 45-2d, 46RR	3	3	4	0	1	0	0	2
Lou Rossini (Columbia '48) 60-4th, 62, 63	3	6	5	0	0	0	1	0
TOTAL	6	9	9	0	1	0	1	2
NIAGARA								
Frank Layden (Niagara '55) 70	1	1	2	0	0	0	0	0
TOTAL	1	1	2	0	0	0	0	0

	Yrs	Won	Lost	CH	2d	3d%	4th	RR
NORTH CARO.								
Bill Lange (Wittenberg '21) 41RR	1	0	2	0	0	0	0	1
Ben Carnevale (New York U. '38) 46-2d	1	2	1	0	1	0	0	0
Frank McGuire [St. John's (N.Y.) '36] 57-CH, 59	2	5	1	1	0	0	0	0
Dean Smith (Kansas '53) 67-4th, 68-2d, 69-4th, 72-3d, 75, 76, 77-2d, 78, 79, 80, 81-2d, 82-CH, 83RR, 84, 85RR, 86, 87RR, 88RR, 89, 90, 91-tie 3d, 92, 93-CH	23	55	23	2	3	2	2	4
TOTAL	27	62	27	3	4	2	2	5
NORTH CARO. A&T								
Don Corbett [Lincoln (Mo.) '65] 82, 83, 84, 85, 86, 87, 88	7	0	7	0	0	0	0	0
TOTAL	7	0	7	0	0	0	0	0
N.C.-CHARLOTTE								
Lee Rose (Transylvania '58) 77-4th	1	3	2	0	0	0	1	0
Jeff Mullins (Duke '64) 88, 92	2	0	2	0	0	0	0	0
TOTAL	3	3	4	0	0	0	1	0
NORTH CARO. ST.*								
Everett Case (Canterbury 16-18, Wisconsin '23) 50-3d, 51RR, 52, 54, 56	5	6	6	0	0	1	0	1
Press Maravich (Davis & Elkins '41) 65	1	1	1	0	0	0	0	0
Norm Sloan (North Caro. St. '51) 70, 74-CH, 80	3	5	2	1	0	0	0	0
Jim Valvano (Rutgers '67) 82, 83-CH, 85RR, 86RR, 87, 88, 89	7	14	6	1	0	0	0	2
Les Robinson (North Caro. St. '64) 91	1	1	1	0	0	0	0	0
TOTAL	17	27	16	2	0	1	0	3
NORTH TEXAS								
Jimmy Gales (Alcorn St. '63) 88	1	0	1	0	0	0	0	0
TOTAL	1	0	1	0	0	0	0	0
NORTHEAST LA.								
Mike Vining (Northeast La. '67) 82, 86, 90, 91, 92, 93	6	0	6	0	0	0	0	0
TOTAL	6	0	6	0	0	0	0	0
NORTHEASTERN								
Jim Calhoun (American Int'l '66) 81, 82, 84, 85, 86	5	3	5	0	0	0	0	0
Karl Fogel (Colby '68) 87, 91	2	0	2	0	0	0	0	0
TOTAL	7	3	7	0	0	0	0	0
NORTHERN ILL.								
John McDougal (Evansville '50) 82	1	0	1	0	0	0	0	0
Jim Molinari (Ill. Wesleyan '77) 91	1	0	1	0	0	0	0	0
TOTAL	2	0	2	0	0	0	0	0
NORTHERN IOWA								
Eldon Miller (Wittenberg '61) 90	1	1	1	0	0	0	0	0
TOTAL	1	1	1	0	0	0	0	0
NOTRE DAME								
John Jordan (Notre Dame '35) 53RR, 54RR, 57, 58RR, 60, 63	6	8	6	0	0	0	0	3
Johnny Dee (Notre Dame '46) 65, 69, 70, 71	4	2	6	0	0	0	0	0
Richard "Digger" Phelps (Rider '63) 74, 75, 76, 77, 78-4th, 79RR, 80, 81, 85, 86, 87, 88, 89, 90	14	15	16	0	0	0	1	1
TOTAL	24	25	28	0	0	0	1	4
OHIO								
James Snyder (Ohio '41) 60, 61, 64RR, 65, 70, 72, 74	7	3	8	0	0	0	0	1
Danny Nee (St. Mary of the Plains '71) 83, 85	2	1	2	0	0	0	0	0
TOTAL	9	4	10	0	0	0	0	1
OHIO ST.								
Harold Olsen (Wisconsin '17) 39-2d, 44-tie 3d, 45-tie 3d, 46-3d	4	6	4	0	1	3	0	0
William H. H. "Tippy" Dye (Ohio St. '37) 50RR	1	1	1	0	0	0	0	1
Fred Taylor (Ohio St. '50) 60-CH, 61-2d, 62-2d, 68-3d, 71RR	5	14	4	1	2	1	0	1
Eldon Miller (Wittenberg '61) 80, 82, 83, 85	4	3	4	0	0	0	0	0
Gary Williams (Maryland '67) 87	1	1	1	0	0	0	0	0
Randy Ayers [Miami (Ohio) '78] 90, 91, 92RR	3	6	3	0	0	0	0	1
TOTAL	18	31	17	1	3	4	0	3
OKLAHOMA								
Bruce Drake (Oklahoma '29) 39-tie 3d, 43RR, 47-2d	3	4	3	0	1	1	0	1
Dave Bliss (Cornell '65) 79	1	1	1	0	0	0	0	0
Billy Tubbs (Lamar '58) 83, 84, 85RR, 86, 87, 88-2d, 89, 90, 92	9	15	9	0	1	0	0	1
TOTAL	13	20	13	0	2	1	0	2

	Yrs	Won	Lost	CH	2d	3d%	4th	RR
OKLAHOMA CITY								
Doyle Parrack (Oklahoma St. '45) 52, 53, 54, 55	4	1	5	0	0	0	0	0
A. E. "Abe" Lemons (Oklahoma City '49) 56RR, 57RR 63, 64, 65, 66, 73	7	7	8	0	0	0	0	2
TOTAL	11	8	13	0	0	0	0	2
OKLAHOMA ST.								
Henry Iba [Westminster (Mo.) '28] 45-CH, 46-CH, 49-2d, 51-4th, 53RR, 54RR, 58RR, 65RR	8	15	7	2	1	0	1	4
Paul Hansen (Oklahoma City '50) 83	1	0	1	0	0	0	0	0
Eddie Sutton (Oklahoma St. '59) 91, 92, 93	3	5	3	0	0	0	0	0
TOTAL	12	20	11	2	1	0	1	4
OLD DOMINION								
Paul Webb (William & Mary '51) 80, 82, 85	3	0	3	0	0	0	0	0
Tom Young (Maryland '58) 86	1	1	1	0	0	0	0	0
Oliver Purnell (Old Dominion '75) 92	1	0	1	0	0	0	0	0
TOTAL	5	1	5	0	0	0	0	0
ORAL ROBERTS								
Ken Trickey (Middle Tenn. St. '54) 74RR	1	2	1	0	0	0	0	1
Dick Acres (UC Santa Barb.) 84	1	0	1	0	0	0	0	0
TOTAL	2	2	2	0	0	0	0	1
OREGON								
Howard Hobson (Oregon '26) 39-CH	1	3	0	1	0	0	0	0
John Warren (Oregon '28) 45RR	1	1	1	0	0	0	0	1
Steve Belko (Idaho '39) 60RR, 61	2	2	2	0	0	0	0	1
TOTAL	4	6	3	1	0	0	0	2
OREGON ST.*								
Amory "Slats" Gill (Oregon St. '25) 47RR, 49-4th, 55RR, 62RR, 63-4th, 64	6	8	8	0	0	0	2	3
Paul Valenti (Oregon St. '42) 66RR	1	1	1	0	0	0	0	1
Ralph Miller (Kansas '42) 75, 80, 81, 82RR, 84, 85, 88, 89	8	3	9	0	0	0	0	1
Jim Anderson (Oregon St. '59) 90	1	0	1	0	0	0	0	0
TOTAL	16	12	19	0	0	0	2	5
PACIFIC (CAL.)								
Dick Edwards (Culver-Stockton '52) 66, 67RR, 71	3	2	4	0	0	0	0	1
Stan Morrison (California '62) 79	1	0	1	0	0	0	0	0
TOTAL	4	2	5	0	0	0	0	1
PENN ST.								
John Lawther [Westminster (Pa.) '19] 42RR	1	1	1	0	0	0	0	1
Elmer Gross (Penn St. '42) 52, 54-3d	2	4	3	0	0	1	0	0
John Egli (Penn St. '47) 55, 65	2	1	3	0	0	0	0	0
Bruce Parkhill (Lock Haven '71) 91	1	1	1	0	0	0	0	0
TOTAL	6	7	8	0	0	1	0	1
PENNSYLVANIA								
Howie Dallmar (Stanford '48) 53	1	1	1	0	0	0	0	0
Dick Harter (Pennsylvania '53) 70, 71RR	2	2	2	0	0	0	0	1
Chuck Daly (Bloomsburg '53) 72RR, 73, 74, 75	4	3	5	0	0	0	0	1
Bob Weinhauer (Cortland St. '61) 78, 79-4th, 80, 82	4	6	5	0	0	0	1	0
Craig Littlepage (Pennsylvania '73) 85	1	0	1	0	0	0	0	0
Tom Schneider (Bucknell '69) 87	1	0	1	0	0	0	0	0
Fran Dunphy (La Salle '70) 93	1	0	1	0	0	0	0	0
TOTAL	14	12	16	0	0	0	1	2
PEPPERDINE								
Al Duer (Emporia St. '29) 44RR	1	0	2	0	0	0	0	1
R. L. "Duck" Dowell (Northwest Mo. St. '33) 62	1	1	1	0	0	0	0	0
Gary Colson (David Lipscomb '56) 76, 79	2	2	2	0	0	0	0	0
Jim Harrick [Charleston (W. Va.) '60] 82, 83, 85, 86	4	1	4	0	0	0	0	0
Tom Asbury (Wyoming '67) 91, 92	2	0	2	0	0	0	0	0
TOTAL	10	4	11	0	0	0	0	1
PITTSBURGH								
Henry Carlson (Pittsburgh '17) 41-tie 3d	1	1	1	0	0	1	0	0
Bob Timmons (Pittsburgh '33) 57, 58, 63	3	1	4	0	0	0	0	0
Charles "Buzz" Ridl [Westminster (Pa.) '42] 74RR	1	2	1	0	0	0	0	1
Roy Chipman (Maine '61) 81, 82, 85	3	1	3	0	0	0	0	0
Paul Evans (Ithaca '67) 87, 88, 89, 91, 93	5	3	5	0	0	0	0	0
TOTAL	13	8	14	0	0	1	0	1
PORTLAND								
Al Negratti (Seton Hall '43) 59	1	0	1	0	0	0	0	0
TOTAL	1	0	1	0	0	0	0	0

	Yrs	Won	Lost	CH	2d	3d%	4th	RR
PRINCETON#								
Franklin Cappon (Michigan '24) 52, 55, 60	3	0	5	0	0	0	0	0
J. L. "Jake" McCandless (Princeton '51) 61	1	1	2	0	0	0	0	0
Bill van Breda Kolff (Princeton '47) 63, 64, 65-3d, 67	4	7	5	0	0	1	0	0
Pete Carril (Lafayette '52) 69, 76, 77, 81, 83, 84, 89, 90, 91, 92	10	3	10	0	0	0	0	0
TOTAL	18	11	22	0	0	1	0	0
PROVIDENCE								
Joe Mullaney (Holy Cross '49) 64, 65RR, 66	3	2	3	0	0	0	0	1
Dave Gavitt (Dartmouth '59) 72, 73-4th, 74, 77, 78	5	5	6	0	0	0	1	0
Rick Pitino (Massachusetts '74) 87 tie-3d	1	4	1	0	0	1	0	0
Rick Barnes (Lenoir-Rhyne '77) 89, 90	2	0	2	0	0	0	0	0
TOTAL	11	11	12	0	0	1	1	1
PURDUE								
George King [Charleston (W. Va.) '50] 69-2d	1	3	1	0	1	0	0	0
Fred Schaus (West Va. '49) 77	1	0	1	0	0	0	0	0
Lee Rose (Transylvania '58) 80-3d	1	5	1	0	0	1	0	0
Gene Keady (Kansas St. '58) 83, 84, 85, 86, 87, 88, 90, 91, 93	9	5	9	0	0	0	0	0
TOTAL	12	13	12	0	1	1	0	0
RHODE ISLAND								
Ernie Calverley (Rhode Island '46) 61, 66	2	0	2	0	0	0	0	0
Jack Kraft [St. Joseph's (Pa.) '42] 78	1	0	1	0	0	0	0	0
Tom Penders (Connecticut '67) 88	1	2	1	0	0	0	0	0
Al Skinner (Massachusetts '74) 93	1	1	1	0	0	0	0	0
TOTAL	5	3	5	0	0	0	0	0
RICE								
Byron "Buster" Brannon (Texas Christian '33) 40RR, 42RR	2	1	3	0	0	0	0	2
Don Suman (Rice '44) 54	1	1	1	0	0	0	0	0
Don Knodel [Miami (Ohio) '53] 70	1	0	1	0	0	0	0	0
TOTAL	4	2	5	0	0	0	0	2
RICHMOND								
Dick Tarrant (Fordham '51) 84, 86, 88, 90, 91	5	5	5	0	0	0	0	0
TOTAL	5	5	5	0	0	0	0	0
RIDER								
John Carpenter (Penn St. '58) 84	1	0	1	0	0	0	0	0
Kevin Bannon (St. Peter's '79) 93	1	0	1	0	0	0	0	0
TOTAL	2	0	2	0	0	0	0	0
ROBERT MORRIS								
Matt Furjanic (Point Park '73) 82, 83	2	1	2	0	0	0	0	0
Jarrett Durham (Duquesne '71) 89, 90, 92	3	0	3	0	0	0	0	0
TOTAL	5	1	5	0	0	0	0	0
RUTGERS								
Tom Young (Maryland '58) 75, 76-4th, 79, 83	4	5	5	0	0	0	1	0
Bob Wenzel (Rutgers '71) 89, 91	2	0	2	0	0	0	0	0
TOTAL	6	5	7	0	0	0	1	0
ST. BONAVENTURE								
Eddie Donovan (St. Bonaventure '50) 61	1	2	1	0	0	0	0	0
Larry Weise (St. Bonaventure '58) 68, 70-4th	2	4	4	0	0	0	1	0
Jim Satalin (St. Bonaventure '69) 78	1	0	1	0	0	0	0	0
TOTAL	4	6	6	0	0	0	1	0
ST. FRANCIS (PA.)								
Jim Baron (St. Bonaventure '77) 91	1	0	1	0	0	0	0	0
TOTAL	1	0	1	0	0	0	0	0
ST. JOHN'S (N.Y.)								
Frank McGuire [St. John's (N.Y.) '36] 51RR, 52-2d	2	5	2	0	1	0	0	1
Joe Lapchick (No college) 61	1	0	1	0	0	0	0	0
Frank Mulzoff [St. John's (N.Y.) '51] 73	1	0	1	0	0	0	0	0
Lou Carnesecca [St. John's (N.Y.) '46] 67, 68, 69, 76, 77, 78, 79RR, 80, 82, 83, 84, 85-tie 3rd, 86, 87, 88, 90, 91RR, 92	18	17	20	0	0	1	0	2
Brian Mahoney (Manhattan '71) 93	1	1	1	0	0	0	0	0
TOTAL	23	23	25	0	1	1	0	3

	Yrs	Won	Lost	CH	2d	3d%	4th	RR
ST. JOSEPH'S (PA.)*								
John "Jack" Ramsay [St. Joseph's (Pa.) '49] 59, 60, 61-3d, 62, 63RR, 65, 66	7	8	11	0	0	1	0	1
John "Jack" McKinney [St. Joseph's (Pa.) '57] 69, 71, 73, 74	4	0	4	0	0	0	0	0
Jim Lynam [St. Joseph's (Pa.) '64] 81RR	1	3	1	0	0	0	0	1
Jim Boyle [St. Joseph's (Pa.) '64] 82, 86	2	1	2	0	0	0	0	0
TOTAL	14	12	18	0	0	1	0	2
ST. LOUIS								
Eddie Hickey (Creighton '27) 52RR, 57	2	1	3	0	0	0	0	1
TOTAL	2	1	3	0	0	0	0	1
ST. MARY'S (CAL.)								
James Weaver (DePaul '47) 59RR	1	1	1	0	0	0	0	1
Lynn Nance (Washington '65) 89	1	0	1	0	0	0	0	0
TOTAL	2	1	2	0	0	0	0	1
ST. PETER'S								
Ted Fiore (Seton Hall '62) 91	1	0	1	0	0	0	0	0
TOTAL	1	0	1	0	0	0	0	0
SAN DIEGO								
Jim Brovelli (San Francisco '64) 84	1	0	1	0	0	0	0	0
Hank Egan (Navy '60) 87	1	0	1	0	0	0	0	0
TOTAL	2	0	2	0	0	0	0	0
SAN DIEGO ST.								
Tim Vezie (Denver '67) 75, 76	2	0	2	0	0	0	0	0
Dave "Smokey" Gaines (LeMoyne-Owen '63) 85	1	0	1	0	0	0	0	0
TOTAL	3	0	3	0	0	0	0	0
SAN FRANCISCO								
Phil Woolpert [Loyola (Cal.) '40] 55-CH, 56-CH, 57-3d, 58	4	13	2	2	0	1	0	0
Peter Peletta (Cal St. Sacramento '50) 63, 64RR, 65RR	3	3	3	0	0	0	0	2
Bob Gaillard (San Francisco '62) 72, 73RR, 74RR, 77, 78	5	4	5	0	0	0	0	2
Dan Belluomini (San Francisco '64) 79	1	1	1	0	0	0	0	0
Peter Barry (San Francisco '70) 81, 82	2	0	2	0	0	0	0	0
TOTAL	15	21	13	2	0	1	0	4
SAN JOSE ST.								
Walter McPherson (San Jose St. '40) 51	1	0	1	0	0	0	0	0
Bill Berry (Michigan St. '65) 80	1	0	1	0	0	0	0	0
TOTAL	2	0	2	0	0	0	0	0
SANTA CLARA								
Bob Feerick (Santa Clara '41) 52-4th, 53RR, 54RR, 60	4	6	6	0	0	0	1	2
Dick Garibaldi (Santa Clara '57) 68RR, 69RR, 70	3	3	3	0	0	0	0	2
Carroll Williams (San Jose St. '55) 87, 93	2	1	2	0	0	0	0	0
TOTAL	9	10	11	0	0	0	1	4
SEATTLE#								
Al Brightman [Charleston (W. Va.)] 53, 54, 55, 56	4	4	6	0	0	0	0	0
John Castellani (Notre Dame '52) 58-2d	1	4	1	0	1	0	0	0
Vince Cazzetta (Arnold '50) 61, 62	2	0	2	0	0	0	0	0
Clair Markey (Seattle '63) 63	1	0	1	0	0	0	0	0
Bob Boyd (Southern Cal '53) 64	1	2	1	0	0	0	0	0
Lionel Purcell (UC Santa Barb. '52) 67	1	0	1	0	0	0	0	0
Morris Buckwalter (Utah '56) 69	1	0	1	0	0	0	0	0
TOTAL	11	10	13	0	1	0	0	0
SETON HALL								
P. J. Carlesimo (Fordham '71) 88, 89-2d, 91RR, 92, 93	5	12	5	0	1	0	0	1
TOTAL	5	12	5	0	1	0	0	1
SIENA								
Mike Deane (Potsdam St. '74) 89	1	1	1	0	0	0	0	0
TOTAL	1	1	1	0	0	0	0	0
SOUTH ALA.								
Cliff Ellis (Florida St. '68) 79, 80	2	0	2	0	0	0	0	0
Ronnie Arrow (Southwest Tex. St. '69) 89, 91	2	1	2	0	0	0	0	0
TOTAL	4	1	4	0	0	0	0	0
SOUTH CARO.								
Frank McGuire [St. John's (N.Y.) '36] 71, 72, 73, 74	4	4	5	0	0	0	0	0
George Felton (South Caro. '75) 89	1	0	1	0	0	0	0	0
TOTAL	5	4	6	0	0	0	0	0
SOUTH CARO. ST.								
Cy Alexander (Catawba '75) 89	1	0	1	0	0	0	0	0
TOTAL	1	0	1	0	0	0	0	0

	Yrs	Won	Lost	CH	2d	3d%	4th	RR
SOUTH FLA.								
Bobby Paschal (Stetson '64) 90, 92	2	0	2	0	0	0	0	0
TOTAL	2	0	2	0	0	0	0	0
SOUTHERN-B.R.								
Carl Stewart (Grambling '54) 81	1	0	1	0	0	0	0	0
Robert Hopkins (Grambling '56) 85	1	0	1	0	0	0	0	0
Ben Jobe (Fisk '56) 87, 88, 89, 93	4	1	4	0	0	0	0	0
TOTAL	6	1	6	0	0	0	0	0
SOUTHERN CAL								
Justin "Sam" Barry (Lawrence '12-13, Wisconsin '16) 40-tie 3d	1	1	1	0	0	1	0	0
Forrest Twogood (Iowa '29) 54-4th, 60, 61	3	3	5	0	0	0	1	0
Bob Boyd (Southern Cal '53) 79	1	1	1	0	0	0	0	0
Stan Morrison (California '62) 82, 85	2	0	2	0	0	0	0	0
George Raveling (Villanova '60) 91, 92	2	1	2	0	0	0	0	0
TOTAL	9	6	11	0	0	1	1	0
SOUTHERN ILL.								
Paul Lambert (William Jewell '56) 77	1	1	1	0	0	0	0	0
Rich Herrin (McKendree '56) 93	1	0	1	0	0	0	0	0
TOTAL	2	1	2	0	0	0	0	0
SOUTHERN METHODIST								
E. O. "Doc" Hayes (North Texas '27) 55, 56-4th, 57, 65, 66, 67RR	6	7	8	0	0	0	1	1
Dave Bliss (Cornell '65) 84, 85, 88	3	3	3	0	0	0	0	0
John Shumate (Notre Dame '74) 93	1	0	1	0	0	0	0	0
TOTAL	10	10	12	0	0	0	1	1
SOUTHERN MISS.								
M. K. Turk (Livingston '64) 90, 91	2	0	2	0	0	0	0	0
TOTAL	2	0	2	0	0	0	0	0
SOUTHWEST MO. ST.								
Charlie Spoonhour (School of Ozarks '61) 87, 88, 89, 90, 92	5	1	5	0	0	0	0	0
TOTAL	5	1	5	0	0	0	0	0
SOUTHWESTERN LA.*								
Beryl Shipley (Delta St. '51) 72, 73	2	3	3	0	0	0	0	0
Bobby Paschal (Stetson '64) 82, 83	2	0	2	0	0	0	0	0
Marty Fletcher (Maryland '73) 92	1	1	1	0	0	0	0	0
TOTAL	5	4	6	0	0	0	0	0
SPRINGFIELD								
Ed Hickox (Ohio Wesleyan '05) 40RR	1	0	1	0	0	0	0	1
TOTAL	1	0	1	0	0	0	0	1
STANFORD								
Everett Dean (Indiana '21) 42-CH	1	3	0	1	0	0	0	0
Mike Montgomery (Long Beach St. '68) 89, 92	2	0	2	0	0	0	0	0
TOTAL	3	3	2	1	0	0	0	0
SYRACUSE								
Marc Guley (Syracuse '36) 57RR	1	2	1	0	0	0	0	1
Fred Lewis (Eastern Ky. '46) 66RR	1	1	1	0	0	0	0	1
Roy Danforth (Southern Miss. '62) 73, 74, 75-4th, 76	4	5	5	0	0	0	1	0
Jim Boeheim (Syracuse '66) 77, 78, 79, 80, 83, 84, 85, 86, 87-2d, 88, 89RR, 90, 91, 92	14	19	14	0	1	0	0	1
TOTAL	20	27	21	0	1	0	1	3
TEMPLE								
Josh Cody (Vanderbilt '20) 44RR	1	1	1	0	0	0	0	1
Harry Litwack (Temple '30) 56-3d, 58-3d, 64, 67, 70, 72	6	7	6	0	0	2	0	0
Don Casey (Temple '70) 79	1	0	1	0	0	0	0	0
John Chaney (Bethune-Cookman '55) 84, 85, 86, 87, 88RR, 90, 91RR, 92, 93 RR	9	13	9	0	0	0	0	3
TOTAL	17	21	17	0	0	2	0	4
TENNESSEE								
Ramon "Ray" Mears [Miami (Ohio) '49] 67, 76, 77	3	0	4	0	0	0	0	0
Don DeVoe (Ohio St. '64) 79, 80, 81, 82, 83, 89	6	5	6	0	0	0	0	0
TOTAL	9	5	10	0	0	0	0	0
TENN.-CHATT.								
Murray Arnold (American '60) 81, 82, 83	3	1	3	0	0	0	0	0
Mack McCarthy (Virginia Tech '74) 88, 93	2	0	2	0	0	0	0	0
TOTAL	5	1	5	0	0	0	0	0
TENNESSEE ST.								
Frankie Allen (Roanoke '71) 93	1	0	1	0	0	0	0	0
TOTAL	1	0	1	0	0	0	0	0

	Yrs	Won	Lost	CH	2d	3d%	4th	RR
TENNESSEE TECH								
Johnny Oldham (Western Ky. '48) 58, 63	2	0	2	0	0	0	0	0
TOTAL	2	0	2	0	0	0	0	0
TEXAS								
H. C. "Bully" Gilstrap (Texas '22) 43-tie 3d	1	1	1	0	0	1	0	0
Jack Gray (Texas '35) 39RR, 47-3d	2	2	3	0	0	1	0	1
Harold Bradley (Hartwick '34) 60, 63	2	2	3	0	0	0	0	0
Leon Black (Texas '53) 72, 74	2	1	3	0	0	0	0	0
A. E. "Abe" Lemons (Oklahoma City '49) 79	1	0	1	0	0	0	0	0
Tom Penders (Connecticut '67) 89, 90RR, 91, 92	4	5	4	0	0	0	0	1
TOTAL	12	11	15	0	0	2	0	2
TEXAS A&M								
John Floyd (Oklahoma St. '41) 51	1	0	1	0	0	0	0	0
Shelby Metcalf (East Tex. St. '53) 64, 69, 75, 80, 87	5	3	6	0	0	0	0	0
TOTAL	6	3	7	0	0	0	0	0
TEXAS CHRISTIAN								
Byron "Buster" Brannon (Texas Christian '33) 52, 53, 59	3	3	3	0	0	0	0	0
Johnny Swaim (Texas Christian '53) 68RR, 71	2	1	2	0	0	0	0	1
Jim Killingsworth (Northeastern Okla. '48) 87	1	1	1	0	0	0	0	0
TOTAL	6	5	6	0	0	0	0	1
TEXAS-SAN ANTONIO								
Ken Burmeister [St. Mary's (Tex.) '71] 88	1	0	1	0	0	0	0	0
TOTAL	1	0	1	0	0	0	0	0
TEXAS SOUTHERN								
Robert Moreland (Tougaloo '62) 90	1	0	1	0	0	0	0	0
TOTAL	1	0	1	0	0	0	0	0
TEXAS TECH								
Polk Robison (Texas Tech '35) 54, 56, 61	3	1	3	0	0	0	0	0
Gene Gibson (Texas Tech '50) 62	1	1	2	0	0	0	0	0
Gerald Myers (Texas Tech '59) 73, 76, 85, 86	4	1	4	0	0	0	0	0
James Dickey (Central Ark. '76) 93	1	0	1	0	0	0	0	0
TOTAL	9	3	10	0	0	0	0	0
TOLEDO								
Jerry Bush [St. John's (N.Y.) '38] 54	1	0	1	0	0	0	0	0
Bob Nichols (Toledo '53) 67, 79, 80	3	1	3	0	0	0	0	0
TOTAL	4	1	4	0	0	0	0	0
TOWSON ST.								
Terry Truax (Maryland '68) 90, 91	2	0	2	0	0	0	0	0
TOTAL	2	0	2	0	0	0	0	0
TRINITY (TEX.)								
Bob Polk (Evansville '39) 69	1	0	1	0	0	0	0	0
TOTAL	1	0	1	0	0	0	0	0
TUFTS								
Richard Cochran (Tufts '34) 45RR	1	0	2	0	0	0	0	1
TOTAL	1	0	2	0	0	0	0	1
TULANE								
Perry Clark (Gettysburg '74) 92, 93	2	2	2	0	0	0	0	0
TOTAL	2	2	2	0	0	0	0	0
TULSA								
Clarence Iba (Panhandle St. '36) 55	1	1	1	0	0	0	0	0
Nolan Richardson (UTEP '65) 82, 84, 85	3	0	3	0	0	0	0	0
J. D. Barnett (Winona St. '66) 86, 87	2	0	2	0	0	0	0	0
TOTAL	6	1	6	0	0	0	0	0
UCLA*								
John Wooden (Purdue '32) 50RR, 52, 56, 62-4th, 63, 64-CH, 65-CH, 67-CH, 68-CH, 69-CH, 70-CH, 71-CH, 72-CH, 73-CH, 74-3d, 75-CH	16	47	10	10	0	1	1	1
Gene Bartow (Northeast Mo. St. '53) 76-3d, 77	2	5	2	0	0	1	0	0
Gary Cunningham (UCLA '62) 78, 79RR	2	3	2	0	0	0	0	1
Larry Brown (North Caro. '63) 80-2d, 81	2	5	2	0	1	0	0	0
Larry Farmer (UCLA '73) 83	1	0	1	0	0	0	0	0
Walt Hazzard (UCLA '64) 87	1	1	1	0	0	0	0	0
Jim Harrick [Charleston (W. Va.) '60] 89, 90, 91, 92RR, 93	5	7	5	0	0	0	0	1
TOTAL	29	68	23	10	1	2	1	3

	Yrs	Won	Lost	CH	2d	3d%	4th	RR
UTAH								
Vadal Peterson (Utah '20) 44-CH, 45RR	2	3	2	1	0	0	0	1
Jack Gardner (Southern Cal '32) 55, 56RR, 59, 60, 61-4th, 66-4th	6	8	9	0	0	0	2	1
Jerry Pimm (Southern Cal '61) 77, 78, 79, 81, 83	5	5	5	0	0	0	0	0
Lynn Archibald (Fresno St. '68) 86	1	0	1	0	0	0	0	0
Rick Majerus (Marquette '70) 91, 93	2	3	2	0	0	0	0	0
TOTAL	16	19	19	1	0	0	2	2
UTAH ST.								
E. L. "Dick" Romney (Utah '17) 39RR	1	1	1	0	0	0	0	1
Ladell Anderson (Utah St. '51) 62, 63, 64, 70RR, 71	5	4	7	0	0	0	0	1
Gordon "Dutch" Belnap (Utah St. '58) 75, 79	2	0	2	0	0	0	0	0
Rod Tueller (Utah St. '59) 80, 83, 88	3	0	3	0	0	0	0	0
TOTAL	11	5	13	0	0	0	0	2
UTEP								
Don Haskins (Oklahoma St. '53) 63, 64, 66-CH, 67, 70, 75, 84, 85, 86, 87, 88, 89, 90, 92	14	14	13	1	0	0	0	0
TOTAL	14	14	13	1	0	0	0	0
VANDERBILT								
Roy Skinner (Presbyterian '52) 65RR, 74	2	1	3	0	0	0	0	1
C. M. Newton (Kentucky '52) 88, 89	2	2	2	0	0	0	0	0
Eddie Fogler (North Caro. '70) 91, 93	2	2	2	0	0	0	0	0
TOTAL	6	5	7	0	0	0	0	1
VILLANOVA*								
Alex Severance (Villanova '29) 39-tie 3d, 49RR, 51, 55	4	4	4	0	0	1	0	1
Jack Kraft [St. Joseph's (Pa.) '42] 62RR, 64, 69, 70RR, 71-2d, 72	6	11	7	0	1	0	0	2
Rollie Massimino (Vermont '56) 78RR, 80, 81, 82RR, 83RR, 84, 85-CH, 86, 88, 90, 91	11	20	10	1	0	0	0	4
TOTAL	21	35	21	1	1	1	0	7
VIRGINIA								
Terry Holland (Davidson '64) 76, 81-3d, 82, 83RR, 84-tie 3d, 86, 87, 89RR, 90	9	15	9	0	0	2	0	2
Jeff Jones, (Virginia '82) 91, 93	2	2	2	0	0	0	0	0
TOTAL	11	17	11	0	0	2	0	2
VA. COMMONWEALTH								
J. D. Barnett (Winona St. '66) 80, 81, 83, 84, 85	5	4	5	0	0	0	0	0
TOTAL	5	4	5	0	0	0	0	0
VA. MILITARY								
Louis "Weenie" Miller (Richmond '47) 64	1	0	1	0	0	0	0	0
Bill Blair (Va. Military '64) 76RR	1	2	1	0	0	0	0	1
Charlie Schmaus (Va. Military '66) 77	1	1	1	0	0	0	0	0
TOTAL	3	3	3	0	0	0	0	1
VIRGINIA TECH								
Howard Shannon (Kansas St. '48) 67RR	1	2	1	0	0	0	0	1
Don DeVoe (Ohio St. '64) 76	1	0	1	0	0	0	0	0
Charles Moir (Appalachian St. '52) 79, 80, 85, 86	4	2	4	0	0	0	0	0
TOTAL	6	4	6	0	0	0	0	1
WAKE FOREST								
Murray Greason (Wake Forest '26) 39RR, 53	2	1	2	0	0	0	0	1
Horace "Bones" McKinney (North Caro. '46) 61RR, 62-3d	2	6	2	0	0	1	0	1
Carl Tacy (Davis & Elkins '56) 77RR, 81, 82, 84RR	4	5	4	0	0	0	0	2
Dave Odom (Guilford '65) 91, 92, 93	3	3	3	0	0	0	0	0
TOTAL	11	15	11	0	0	1	0	4
WASHINGTON								
Clarence "Hec" Edmundson (Idaho '09) 43RR	1	0	2	0	0	0	0	1
Art McLarney (Washington St. '32) 48RR	1	1	1	0	0	0	0	1
William H. H. "Tippy" Dye (Ohio St. '37) 51RR, 53-3d	2	5	2	0	0	1	0	1
Marv Harshman (Pacific Lutheran '42) 76, 84, 85	3	2	3	0	0	0	0	0
Andy Russo (Lake Forest '70) 86	1	0	1	0	0	0	0	0
TOTAL	8	8	9	0	0	1	0	3
WASHINGTON ST.								
Jack Friel (Washington St. '23) 41-2d	1	2	1	0	1	0	0	0
George Raveling (Villanova '60) 80, 83	2	1	2	0	0	0	0	0
TOTAL	3	3	3	0	1	0	0	0
WAYNE ST. (MICH.)								
Joel Mason (Western Mich. '36) 56	1	1	2	0	0	0	0	0
TOTAL	1	1	2	0	0	0	0	0

	Yrs	Won	Lost	CH	2d	3d%	4th	RR
WEBER ST.								
Dick Motta (Utah St. '53) 68	1	0	1	0	0	0	0	0
Phil Johnson (Utah St. '53) 69, 70, 71	3	2	3	0	0	0	0	0
Gene Visscher (Weber St. '66) 72, 73	2	1	3	0	0	0	0	0
Neil McCarthy (Cal St. Sacramento '65) 78, 79, 80, 83	4	1	4	0	0	0	0	0
TOTAL	10	4	11	0	0	0	0	0
WEST TEX. A&M								
W. A. "Gus" Miller (West Tex. A&M '27) 55	1	0	1	0	0	0	0	0
TOTAL	1	0	1	0	0	0	0	0
WEST VA.								
Fred Schaus (West Va. '49) 55, 56, 57, 58, 59-2d, 60	6	6	6	0	1	0	0	0
George King [Charleston (W. Va.) '50] 62, 63, 65	3	2	3	0	0	0	0	0
Raymond "Bucky" Waters (North Caro. St. '57) 67	1	0	1	0	0	0	0	0
Gale Catlett (West Va. '63) 82, 83, 84, 86, 87, 89, 92	7	3	7	0	0	0	0	0
TOTAL	17	11	17	0	1	0	0	0
WESTERN KY.*								
Ed Diddle (Centre '21) 40RR, 60, 62	3	3	4	0	0	0	0	1
Johnny Oldham (Western Ky. '48) 66, 67, 70, 71-3d	4	6	4	0	0	1	0	0
Jim Richards (Western Ky. '59) 76, 78	2	1	2	0	0	0	0	0
Gene Keady (Kansas St. '58) 80	1	0	1	0	0	0	0	0
Clem Haskins (Western Ky. '67) 81, 86	2	1	2	0	0	0	0	0
Murray Arnold (American '60) 87	1	1	1	0	0	0	0	0
Ralph Willard (Holy Cross '67) 93	1	2	1	0	0	0	0	0
TOTAL	14	14	15	0	0	1	0	1
WESTERN MICH.								
Eldon Miller (Wittenberg '61) 76	1	1	1	0	0	0	0	0
TOTAL	1	1	1	0	0	0	0	0
WICHITA ST.								
Ralph Miller (Kansas '42) 64RR	1	1	1	0	0	0	0	1
Gary Thompson (Wichita St. '54) 65-4th	1	2	2	0	0	0	1	0
Harry Miller (Eastern N. Mex. '51) 76	1	0	1	0	0	0	0	0
Gene Smithson (North Central '61) 81RR, 85	2	3	2	0	0	0	0	1
Eddie Fogler (North Caro. '70) 87, 88	2	0	2	0	0	0	0	0
TOTAL	7	6	8	0	0	0	1	2
WILLIAMS								
Alex Shaw (Michigan '32) 55	1	0	1	0	0	0	0	0
TOTAL	1	0	1	0	0	0	0	0
WISCONSIN								
Harold "Bud" Foster (Wisconsin '30) 41-CH, 47RR	2	4	1	1	0	0	0	1
TOTAL	2	4	1	1	0	0	0	1
WIS.-GREEN BAY								
Dick Bennett (Ripon '65) 91	1	0	1	0	0	0	0	0
TOTAL	1	0	1	0	0	0	0	0
WRIGHT ST.								
Ralph Underhill (Tennessee Tech '64) 93	1	0	1	0	0	0	0	0
TOTAL	1	0	1	0	0	0	0	0
WYOMING								
Everett Shelton (Phillips '23) 41RR, 43-CH, 47RR, 48RR, 49RR, 52RR, 53, 58	8	4	12	1	0	0	0	5
Bill Strannigan (Wyoming '41) 67	1	0	2	0	0	0	0	0
Jim Brandenburg (Colorado St. '58) 81, 82, 87	3	4	3	0	0	0	0	0
Benny Dees (Wyoming '58) 88	1	0	1	0	0	0	0	0
TOTAL	13	8	18	1	0	0	0	5
XAVIER (OHIO)								
Jim McCafferty [Loyola (La.) '42] 61	1	0	1	0	0	0	0	0
Bob Staak (Connecticut '71) 83	1	0	1	0	0	0	0	0
Pete Gillen (Fairfield '68) 86, 87, 88, 89, 90, 91, 93	7	5	7	0	0	0	0	0
TOTAL	9	5	9	0	0	0	0	0
YALE								
Howard Hobson (Oregon '26) 49RR	1	0	2	0	0	0	0	1
Joe Vancisin (Dartmouth '44) 57, 62	2	0	2	0	0	0	0	0
TOTAL	3	0	4	0	0	0	0	1

% *National third-place games did not start until 1946 and ended in 1981; in other years, two teams tied for third and both listed this column.* RR *Regional runner-up, or one victory from Final Four, thus in top eight.*

NOTES ON TEAMS AND COACHES:

MICHIGAN: Steve Fisher coached Michigan in the 1989 tournament; Bill Frieder was the coach during the regular season.

MISSOURI: Rich Daly coached Missouri in the 1989 tournament due to Norm Stewart's illness; Missouri credits the entire 1989 season and tournament to Stewart.

PRINCETON: J. L. McCandless coached Princeton in 1961 NCAA; Franklin Cappon suffered a heart attack after 11 games; Princeton credits entire 1961 season to Cappon.

SEATTLE: Clair Markey coached Seattle in 1963 NCAA due to Vince Cazetta's resignation.

***TEAMS WITH VACATED NCAA TOURNAMENT ACTION, YEARS & RECORDS:**

Teams	Years	Rec.	Place	Conference
Alabama	1987	2-1		Southeastern
Austin Peay	1973	1-2		Ohio Valley
Florida	1987-88	3-2		Southeastern
Georgia	1985	1-1		Southeastern
Iona	1980	1-1		Metro Atlantic
Kentucky	1988	2-1		Southeastern
Long Beach St.	1971-72-73	6-3	2RR	Big West
Loyola (Cal.)	1980	0-1		West Coast
Marshall	1987	0-1		Southern
Maryland	1988	1-1		Atlantic Coast
Memphis St.	1982-83-84-85-86	9-5	3rd	Metro
Minnesota	1972	1-1		Big Ten
North Caro. St.	1987-88	0-2		Atlantic Coast
Oregon St.	1980-81-82	2-3		Pacific-10
St. Joseph's (Pa.)	1961	3-1	3rd	Atlantic 10
Southwestern La.	1972-73	3-3		Independent
UCLA	1980	5-1	2nd	Pacific-10
Villanova	1971	4-1	2nd	Big East
Western Ky.	1971	4-1	3rd	Ohio Valley
19 teams	30 years	48-32	2 2nd, 3 3rd, 2RR	

Official NCAA Records:	Yrs	Won	Lost	CH	2d	3d	4th	RR
Alabama	11	11	11	0	0	0	0	0
Austin Peay	2	1	2	0	0	0	0	0
Florida	1	0	1	0	0	0	0	0
Georgia	4	3	4	0	0	1	0	0
Iona	3	0	3	0	0	0	0	0
Kentucky	33	56	30	5	2	2	0	13
Long Beach St.	2	1	3	0	0	0	0	0
Loyola (Cal.)	4	5	4	0	0	0	0	0
Marshall	4	0	4	0	0	0	0	0
Maryland	9	12	9	0	0	0	0	2
Memphis St.	8	7	8	0	1	0	0	1
Minnesota	3	6	3	0	0	0	0	1
North Caro. St.	15	27	14	2	0	1	0	2
Oregon St.	13	10	16	0	0	0	2	3
St. Joseph's (Pa.)	13	9	17	0	0	0	0	2
Southwestern La.	3	1	3	0	0	0	0	0
UCLA	27	62	21	10	0	2	1	2
Villanova	20	31	20	1	0	1	0	6
Western Ky.	12	8	13	0	0	0	0	0

FINAL FOUR ALL-TOURNAMENT TEAMS

(First player listed on each team was the outstanding player in the Final Four)

1939—Not chosen.

1940—Marvin Huffman, Indiana
Howard Engleman, Kansas
Bob Allen, Kansas
Jay McCreary, Indiana
William Menke, Indiana

1941-51—Not chosen.

1952—Clyde Lovellette, Kansas
Bob Zawoluk, St. John's (N.Y.)
John Kerr, Illinois
Ron MacGilvray, St. John's (N.Y.)
Dean Kelley, Kansas

1953—B. H. Born, Kansas
Bob Houbregs, Washington
Bob Leonard, Indiana
Dean Kelley, Kansas
Don Schlundt, Indiana

1954—Tom Gola, La Salle
Chuck Singley, La Salle
Jesse Arnelle, Penn St.
Roy Irvin, Southern Cal
Bob Carney, Bradley

1955—Bill Russell, San Francisco
Tom Gola, La Salle

K. C. Jones, San Francisco
Jim Ranglos, Colorado
Carl Cain, Iowa

1956—Hal Lear, Temple
Bill Russell, San Francisco
Carl Cain, Iowa
Hal Perry, San Francisco
Bill Logan, Iowa

1957—Wilt Chamberlain, Kansas
Len Rosenbluth, North Caro.
John Green, Michigan St.
Gene Brown, San Francisco
Pete Brennan, North Caro.

1958—Elgin Baylor, Seattle
John Cox, Kentucky
Guy Rodgers, Temple
Charley Brown, Seattle
Vern Hatton, Kentucky

1959—Jerry West, West Va.
Oscar Robertson, Cincinnati
Darrall Imhoff, California
Don Goldstein, Louisville
Denny Fitzpatrick, California

1960—Jerry Lucas, Ohio St.
Oscar Robertson, Cincinnati
Mel Nowell, Ohio St.
Darrall Imhoff, California
Tom Sanders, New York U.

1961—Jerry Lucas, Ohio St.
Bob Wiesenhahn, Cincinnati
Larry Siegfried, Ohio St.
Carl Bouldin, Cincinnati
Vacated†

1962—Paul Hogue, Cincinnati
Jerry Lucas, Ohio St.
Tom Thacker, Cincinnati
John Havlicek, Ohio St.
Len Chappell, Wake Forest

1963—Art Heyman, Duke
Tom Thacker, Cincinnati
Les Hunter, Loyola (Ill.)
George Wilson, Cincinnati
Ron Bonham, Cincinnati

1964—Walt Hazzard, UCLA
Jeff Mullins, Duke
Bill Buntin, Michigan
Willie Murrell, Kansas St.
Gail Goodrich, UCLA

1965—Bill Bradley, Princeton
Gail Goodrich, UCLA
Cazzie Russell, Michigan
Edgar Lacey, UCLA
Kenny Washington, UCLA

1966—Jerry Chambers, Utah
Pat Riley, Kentucky
Jack Marin, Duke
Louie Dampier, Kentucky
Bobby Joe Hill, UTEP

1967—Lew Alcindor, UCLA
Don May, Dayton
Mike Warren, UCLA
Elvin Hayes, Houston
Lucius Allen, UCLA

1968—Lew Alcindor, UCLA
Lynn Shackleford, UCLA
Mike Warren, UCLA
Lucius Allen, UCLA
Larry Miller, North Caro.

1969—Lew Alcindor, UCLA
Rick Mount, Purdue
Charlie Scott, North Caro.
Willie McCarter, Drake
John Vallely, UCLA

1970—Sidney Wicks, UCLA
Jimmy Collins, New Mexico St.
John Vallely, UCLA
Artis Gilmore, Jacksonville
Curtis Rowe, UCLA

1971—Vacated†
Vacated†
Vacated†
Steve Patterson, UCLA
Sidney Wicks, UCLA

1972—Bill Walton, UCLA
Keith Wilkes, UCLA
Robert McAdoo, North Caro.
Jim Price, Louisville
Ron King, Florida St.

1973—Bill Walton, UCLA
Steve Downing, Indiana
Ernie DiGregorio, Providence
Larry Finch, Memphis St.
Larry Kenon, Memphis St.

1974—David Thompson, North Caro. St.
Bill Walton, UCLA
Tom Burleson, North Caro. St.
Monte Towe, North Caro. St.
Maurice Lucas, Marquette

1975—Richard Washington, UCLA
Kevin Grevey, Kentucky
Dave Myers, UCLA
Allen Murphy, Louisville
Jim Lee, Syracuse

1976—Kent Benson, Indiana
Scott May, Indiana
Rickey Green, Michigan
Marques Johnson, UCLA
Tom Abernethy, Indiana

1977—Butch Lee, Marquette
Mike O'Koren, North Caro.
Cedric Maxwell, N.C.-Charlotte
Bo Ellis, Marquette
Walter Davis, North Caro.
Jerome Whitehead, Marquette

1978—Jack Givens, Kentucky
Ron Brewer, Arkansas
Mike Gminski, Duke
Rick Robey, Kentucky
Jim Spanarkel, Duke

1979—Earvin Johnson, Michigan St.
Greg Kelser, Michigan St.
Larry Bird, Indiana St.
Mark Aguirre, DePaul
Gary Garland, DePaul

1980—Darrell Griffith, Louisville
Vacated†
Joe Barry Carroll, Purdue
Vacated†
Rodney McCray, Louisville

1981—Isiah Thomas, Indiana
Jeff Lamp, Virginia
Jim Thomas, Indiana
Landon Turner, Indiana
Al Wood, North Caro.

1982—James Worthy, North Caro.
Patrick Ewing, Georgetown
Eric Floyd, Georgetown
Michael Jordan, North Caro.
Sam Perkins, North Caro.

1983—Akeem Olajuwon, Houston
Thurl Bailey, North Caro. St.
Sidney Lowe, North Caro. St.

Milt Wagner, Louisville
Dereck Whittenburg, North Caro. St.

1984—Patrick Ewing, Georgetown
Michael Graham, Georgetown
Akeem Olajuwon, Houston
Michael Young, Houston
Alvin Franklin, Houston

1985—Patrick Ewing, Georgetown
Ed Pinckney, Villanova
Dwayne McClain, Villanova
Harold Jensen, Villanova
Gary McLain, Villanova

1986—Pervis Ellison, Louisville
Billy Thompson, Louisville
Johnny Dawkins, Duke
Mark Alarie, Duke
Tommy Amaker, Duke

1987—Keith Smart, Indiana
Sherman Douglas, Syracuse
Derrick Coleman, Syracuse
Armon Gilliam, Nevada-Las Vegas
Steve Alford, Indiana

1988—Danny Manning, Kansas
Milt Newton, Kansas
Stacey King, Oklahoma
Dave Sieger, Oklahoma
Sean Elliott, Arizona

1989—Glen Rice, Michigan
Rumeal Robinson, Michigan
Danny Ferry, Duke
Gerald Greene, Seton Hall
John Morton, Seton Hall

1990—Anderson Hunt, Nevada-Las Vegas
Stacey Augmon, Nevada-Las Vegas
Larry Johnson, Nevada-Las Vegas
Phil Henderson, Duke
Dennis Scott, Georgia Tech

1991—Christian Laettner, Duke
Bobby Hurley, Duke
Bill McCaffrey, Duke
Mark Randall, Kansas
Anderson Hunt, Nevada-Las Vegas

1992—Bobby Hurley, Duke
Grant Hill, Duke
Christian Laettner, Duke
Jalen Rose, Michigan
Chris Webber, Michigan

1993—Donald Williams, North Caro.
Eric Montross, North Caro.
George Lynch, North Caro.
Chris Webber, Michigan
Jamal Mashburn, Kentucky

† The following student-athletes and the institutions they represented were declared ineligible subsequent to the tournament. Under NCAA rules, the teams' and student-athletes' records were deleted and the teams' places in the final standings were vacated: 1961—John Egan, St. Joseph's (Pa.); 1971—Howard Porter, Villanova; Hank Siemiontkowski, Villanova; Jim McDaniels, Western Kentucky; 1980—Kiki Vandeweghe, UCLA; Rod Foster, UCLA.

DIVISION II MEN'S CHAMPIONSHIP

1993 DIVISION II MEN'S CHAMPIONSHIP RESULTS

REGIONALS
N.C. Central 93, Alabama A&M 84
Virginia Union 67, Fayetteville St. 38
Alas. Anchorage 72, Cal St. Chico 70
Cal St. Bakersfield 98, Grand Canyon 68
Northern Mich. 86, Southern Ind. 85
Wayne St. (Mich.) 78, IU/PU-Ft. Wayne 72
Millersville 86, Calif. (Pa.) 77
Phila. Textile 70, Gannon 56
Delta St. 73, Tampa 61
Troy St. 75, Fla. Southern 72
Washburn 92, Central Okla. 88
Eastern N. Mex. 76, Mo. Southern St. 73
Franklin Pierce 95, Bentley 74
New Hamp. Col. 67, St. Anselm 63
North Dak. 80, Western St. 61
South Dak. 78, Colo. Christian 60

REGIONAL THIRD PLACE
Alabama A&M 79, Fayetteville St. 62
Grand Canyon 103, Cal St. Chico 98
Southern Ind. 95, IU/PU-Ft. Wayne 93
Tampa 79, Fla. Southern 73
Central Okla. 116, Mo. Southern St. 109
Bentley 109, St. Anselm 90
Western St. 81, Colo. Christian 71

REGIONAL CHAMPIONSHIPS
N.C. Central 93, Virginia Union 81
Cal St. Bakersfield 78, Alas. Anchorage 59
Wayne St. (Mich.) 90, Northern Mich. 58
Phila. Textile 70, Millersville 62
Troy St. 110, Delta St. 93
Washburn 79, Eastern N. Mex. 78
New Hamp. Col. 83, Franklin Pierce 73
South Dak. 66, North Dak. 64 (ot)

QUARTERFINALS
Cal St. Bakersfield 86, N.C. Central 80
Wayne St. (Mich.) 78, Phila. Textile 76
Troy St. 94, Washburn 82
New Hamp. Col. 100, South Dak. 96 (3 ot)

SEMIFINALS
Cal St. Bakersfield 61, Wayne St. (Mich.) 57
Troy St. 126, New Hamp. Col. 123

CHAMPIONSHIP
Cal St. Bakersfield 85, Troy St. 72

DIVISION II MEN'S CHAMPIONSHIP BOX SCORES

SEMIFINALS

Cal St. Bakersfield 61, Wayne St. (Mich.) 57

Wayne St. (Mich.)	FG-FGA	FT-FTA	RB	PF	TP
Mike Moscato	0- 1	0- 0	0	0	0
Mark Herron	0- 1	0- 0	1	3	0
Derek Hardy	7-18	2- 5	2	1	17
Scott Armstrong	3- 8	0- 0	2	1	6
Danny Lewis	7-20	6- 8	13	2	24
Andy Ayrault	0- 2	3- 4	3	4	3
Will Paige	2- 5	0- 1	5	3	4

	FG-FGA	FT-FTA	RB	PF	TP
Randy Calcaterra	0- 0	0- 0	0	0	0
Brian Koscielski..	1- 1	1- 3	8	1	3
Team.............			7		
TOTALS..........	20-56	12-21	41	15	57

Cal St. Bakersfield	FG-FGA	FT-FTA	RB	PF	TP
Kenny Warren....	1- 9	0- 0	4	2	3
Erin Vines........	1-11	0- 0	5	4	2
Tyrone Pollard ...	2- 2	0- 0	0	1	4
Reggie Phillips ...	4-15	3- 4	3	5	11
Tyrone Davis.....	6-10	3- 5	4	4	15
Roheen Oats.....	7-16	5- 6	19	1	19
Eric Williams.....	0- 1	0- 0	2	0	0
Jeff Kuehl........	3- 4	1- 1	7	1	7
Team.............			3		
TOTALS..........	24-68	12-16	47	18	61

Half time: Wayne St. (Mich.) 32, Cal St. Bakersfield 31. Three-point field goals: Wayne St. (Mich.) 5-23 (Lewis 4-12, Hardy 1-6, Moscato 0-1, Herron 0-1, Armstrong 0-3); Cal St. Bakersfield 1-7 (Warren 1-6, Vines 0-1). Officials: John Jaworski, Don Winterton, Barry Spears. Attendance: 2,699.

Troy St. 126, New Hamp. Col. 123

Troy St.	FG-FGA	FT-FTA	RB	PF	TP
Dandrea Evans...	7-12	1- 2	4	2	19
Chris Williams....	9-13	1- 2	8	3	19
Steve Hunt.......	2- 6	0- 1	1	1	5
Tommy Davis	7-15	5- 5	3	5	24
Bryant Johnson..	3- 4	0- 0	0	2	6
Fred Bryant......	1- 4	0- 0	3	2	2
Terry McCord	7-11	1- 2	8	4	20
Chris Greasham .	7-11	2- 2	5	3	21
Brian Simpson ...	3- 5	1- 4	1	0	10
Team.............			2		
TOTALS..........	46-81	11-18	35	22	126

New Hamp. Col.	FG-FGA	FT-FTA	RB	PF	TP
Wayne Robertson	14-17	3- 6	15	4	31
Matt Ripaldi......	1- 3	0- 0	0	0	2
Baris Kacar......	8-10	1- 3	9	2	18
Waymon Boone..	2- 7	2- 3	3	0	6
Rob Paternostro .	9-21	4- 4	1	3	25
Will Flowers......	8- 9	5- 6	9	4	21
Joey Castronovo.	5-12	1- 2	3	4	12
Artay Drinks	3- 8	2- 2	4	2	8
Team.............			3		
TOTALS..........	50-87	18-26	47	19	123

Half time: Troy St. 67, New Hamp. Col. 65. Three-point field goals: Troy St. 23-44 (McCord 5-6, Greasham 5-8, Davis 5-12, Evans 4-8, Simpson 3-5, Hunt 1-3, Williams 0-1, Johnson 0-1); New Hamp. Col. 5-16 (Paternostro 3-8, Kacar 1-2, Castronovo 1-4, Ripaldi 0-2). Officials: John Hannon, James Green, Robert Pugh. Attendance: 2,699.

CHAMPIONSHIP

Cal St. Bakersfield 85, Troy St. 72

Troy St.	FG-FGA	FT-FTA	RB	PF	TP
Dandrea Evans...	3-10	0- 0	3	5	7
Chris Williams....	3-10	7-10	13	2	13
Steve Hunt.......	1- 4	0- 0	0	4	2
Tommy Davis	2-12	3- 4	6	3	8
Bryant Johnson..	2- 2	4- 4	2	5	8
Fred Bryant......	0- 0	0- 0	1	1	0
Terry McCord	8-17	4- 5	6	5	23
Chris Greasham .	2- 9	0- 2	4	2	4
Brian Simpson ...	1- 2	5- 5	2	2	7
Team.............			6		
TOTALS..........	22-66	23-30	43	29	72

Cal St. Bakersfield	FG-FGA	FT-FTA	RB	PF	TP
Kenny Warren....	2- 6	5- 6	5	2	11
Justin Hutson	1- 1	0- 0	0	0	2
Erin Vines........	3- 5	2- 3	1	4	8
Tyrone Pollard ...	0- 5	0- 0	1	1	0
Reggie Phillips ...	8-12	7- 8	2	4	23
Tyrone Davis.....	9-16	9-15	6	3	27
Roheen Oats.....	4- 7	2- 2	8	3	10
Eric Williams.....	0- 0	0- 0	0	1	0
Jeff Kuehl........	1- 3	2- 5	11	3	4
Team.............			5		
TOTALS..........	28-55	27-39	39	21	85

Half time: Cal St. Bakersfield 34, Troy St. 30. Three-point field goals: Troy St. 5-23 (McCord 3-8, Evans 1-4, Davis 1-5, Hunt 0-1, Simpson 0-1, Greasham 0-4); Cal St. Bakersfield 2-6 (Warren 2-5, Oats 0-1). Officials: Leroy Hendricks, Jeffrey Plunkett, Michael Cabral. Attendance: 5,653.

DIVISION II MEN'S CHAMPIONSHIP RECORDS

ALL-TIME RESULTS

Year	Champion	Score	Runner-Up	Third Place	Fourth Place
1957	Wheaton (Ill.)	89-65	Ky. Wesleyan	Mt. St. Mary's (Md.)	Cal St. Los Angeles
1958	South Dak.	75-53	St. Michael's	Evansville	Wheaton (Ill.)
1959	Evansville	83-67	Southwest Mo. St.	North Caro. A&T	Cal St. Los Angeles
1960	Evansville	90-69	Chapman	Ky. Wesleyan	Cornell College
1961	Wittenberg	42-38	Southeast Mo. St.	South Dak. St.	Mt. St. Mary's (Md.)
1962	Mt. St. Mary's (Md.)	58-57†	Cal St. Sacramento	Southern Ill.	Neb. Wesleyan
1963	South Dak. St.	44-42	Wittenberg	Oglethorpe	Southern Ill.
1964	Evansville	72-59	Akron	North Caro. A&T	Northern Iowa
1965	Evansville	85-82†	Southern Ill.	North Dak.	St. Michael's
1966	Ky. Wesleyan	54-51	Southern Ill.	Akron	North Dak.
1967	Winston-Salem	77-74	Southwest Mo. St.	Ky. Wesleyan	Illinois St.
1968	Ky. Wesleyan	63-52	Indiana St.	Trinity (Tex.)	Ashland
1969	Ky. Wesleyan	75-71	Southwest Mo. St.	**Vacated	Ashland
1970	Phila. Textile	76-65	Tennessee St.	UC Riverside	Buffalo St.
1971	Evansville	97-82	Old Dominion	**Vacated	Ky. Wesleyan
1972	Roanoke	84-72	Akron	Tennessee St.	Eastern Mich.
1973	Ky. Wesleyan	78-76†	Tennessee St.	Assumption	Brockport St.
1974	Morgan St.	67-52	Southwest Mo. St.	Assumption	New Orleans
1975	Old Dominion	76-74	New Orleans	Assumption	Tenn.-Chatt.
1976	Puget Sound	83-74	Tenn.-Chatt.	Eastern Ill.	Old Dominion
1977	Tenn.-Chatt.	71-62	Randolph-Macon	North Ala.	Sacred Heart
1978	Cheyney	47-40	Wis.-Green Bay	Eastern Ill.	Central Fla.
1979	North Ala.	64-50	Wis.-Green Bay	Cheyney	Bridgeport

Year	Champion	Score	Runner-Up	Third Place	Fourth Place
1980	Virginia Union	80-74	New York Tech	Fla. Southern	North Ala.
1981	Fla. Southern	73-68	Mt. St. Mary's (Md.)	Cal Poly SLO	Wis.-Green Bay
1982	Dist. Columbia	73-63	Fla. Southern	Ky. Wesleyan	Cal St. Bakersfield
1983	Wright St.	92-73	Dist. Columbia	*Cal St. Bakersfield	*Morningside
1984	Central Mo. St.	81-77	St. Augustine's	*Ky. Wesleyan	*North Ala.
1985	Jacksonville St.	74-73	South Dak. St.	*Ky. Wesleyan	*Mt. St. Mary's (Md.)
1986	Sacred Heart	93-87	Southeast Mo. St.	*Cheyney	*Fla. Southern
1987	Ky. Wesleyan	92-74	Gannon	*Delta St.	*Eastern Mont.
1988	Mass.-Lowell	75-72	Alas. Anchorage	Fla. Southern	Troy St.
1989	N.C. Central	73-46	Southeast Mo. St.	UC Riverside	Jacksonville St.
1990	Ky. Wesleyan	93-79	Cal St. Bakersfield	North Dak.	Morehouse
1991	North Ala.	79-72	Bridgeport	*Cal St. Bakersfield	*Virginia Union
1992	Virginia Union	100-75	Bridgeport	*Cal St. Bakersfield	*Calif. (Pa.)
1993	Cal St. Bakersfield	85-72	Troy St.	*Wayne St. (Mich.)	*New Hamp. Col.

*† Overtime. * Indicates tied for third. ** Student-athletes representing American International in 1969 and Southwestern Louisiana in 1971 were declared ineligible subsequent to the tournament. Under NCAA rules, the teams' and ineligible student-athletes' records were deleted, and the teams' places in the final standings were vacated.*

Year	Site of Finals	Coaches of Team Champions	Outstanding Player Award
1957	Evansville, Ind.	Lee Pfund, Wheaton (Ill.)	Mel Peterson, Wheaton (Ill.)
1958	Evansville, Ind.	Duane Clodfelter, South Dak.	Ed Smallwood, Evansville
1959	Evansville, Ind.	Arad McCutchan, Evansville	Hugh Ahlering, Evansville
1960	Evansville, Ind.	Arad McCutchan, Evansville	Ed Smallwood, Evansville
1961	Evansville, Ind.	Ray Mears, Wittenberg	Don Jacobsen, South Dak. St.
1962	Evansville, Ind.	Jim Phelan, Mt. St. Mary's (Md.)	Ron Rohrer, Cal. St. Sacramento
1963	Evansville, Ind.	Jim Iverson, South Dak. St.	Wayne Rasmussen, South Dak. St.
1964	Evansville, Ind.	Arad McCutchan, Evansville	Jerry Sloan, Evansville
1965	Evansville, Ind.	Arad McCutchan, Evansville	Jerry Sloan, Evansville
1966	Evansville, Ind.	Guy Strong, Ky. Wesleyan	Sam Smith, Ky. Wesleyan
1967	Evansville, Ind.	C. E. Gaines, Winston-Salem	Earl Monroe, Winston-Salem
1968	Evansville, Ind.	Bob Daniels, Ky. Wesleyan	Jerry Newsom, Indiana St.
1969	Evansville, Ind.	Bob Daniels, Ky. Wesleyan	George Tinsley, Ky. Wesleyan
1970	Evansville, Ind.	Herb Magee, Phila. Textile	Ted McClain, Tennessee St.
1971	Evansville, Ind.	Arad McCutchan, Evansville	Don Buse, Evansville
1972	Evansville, Ind.	Charles Moir, Roanoke	Hal Johnston, Roanoke
1973	Evansville, Ind.	Bob Jones, Ky. Wesleyan	Mike Williams, Ky. Wesleyan
1974	Evansville, Ind.	Nathaniel Frazier, Morgan St.	Marvin Webster, Morgan St.
1975	Evansville, Ind.	Sonny Allen, Old Dominion	Wilson Washington, Old Dominion
1976	Evansville, Ind.	Don Zech, Puget Sound	Curt Peterson, Puget Sound
1977	Springfield, Mass.	Ron Shumate, Tenn.-Chatt.	Wayne Golden, Tenn.-Chatt.
1978	Springfield, Mo.	John Chaney, Cheyney	Andrew Fields, Cheyney
1979	Springfield, Mo.	Bill Jones, North Ala.	Perry Oden, North Ala.
1980	Springfield, Mass.	Dave Robbins, Virginia Union	Keith Valentine, Virginia Union
1981	Springfield, Mass.	Hal Wissel, Fla. Southern	John Ebeling, Fla. Southern
1982	Springfield, Mass.	Wil Jones, Dist. Columbia	Michael Britt, Dist. Columbia
1983	Springfield, Mass.	Ralph Underhill, Wright St.	Gary Monroe, Wright St.
1984	Springfield, Mass.	Lynn Nance, Central Mo. St.	Ron Nunnelly, Central Mo. St.
1985	Springfield, Mass.	Bill Jones, Jacksonville St.	Mark Tetzlaff, South Dak. St.
1986	Springfield, Mass.	Dave Bike, Sacred Heart	Roger Younger, Sacred Heart
1987	Springfield, Mass.	Wayne Chapman, Ky. Wesleyan	Sam Smith, Ky. Wesleyan
1988	Springfield, Mass.	Don Doucette, Mass.-Lowell	Leo Parent, Mass.-Lowell
1989	Springfield, Mass.	Michael Bernard, N.C. Central	Miles Clarke, N.C. Central
1990	Springfield, Mass.	Wayne Chapman, Ky. Wesleyan	Wade Green, Cal St. Bakersfield
1991	Springfield, Mass.	Gary Elliott, North Ala.	Lambert Shell, Bridgeport
1992	Springfield, Mass.	Dave Robbins, Virginia Union	Derrick Johnson, Virginia Union
1993	Springfield, Mass.	Pat Douglass, Cal St. Bakersfield	Tyrone Davis, Cal St. Bakersfield

INDIVIDUAL RECORDS

Most Points, One Game

54—Willie Jones, American (91) vs. Evansville (101), 1960; Bill Fennelly, Central Mo. St. (112) vs. Jacksonville St. (91), 1980.

Most Points, Series

185—Jack Sullivan, Mt. St. Mary's (Md.), 1957 (36 vs. CCNY, 48 vs. N.C. Central, 39 vs. Rider, 19 vs. Ky. Wesleyan, 43 vs. Cal St. Los Angeles).

Most Field Goals, One Game

22—Phil Jackson, North Dak. (107) vs. Parsons (56), 1967.

Most Field Goals, Series

71—Jack Sullivan, Mt. St. Mary's (Md.), 1957 (14 vs. CCNY, 19 vs. N.C. Central, 16 vs. Rider, 8 vs. Ky. Wesleyan, 14 vs. Cal St. Los Angeles).

Most Three-Point Field Goals, One Game
11—Kenny Warren, Cal St. Bakersfield (98) vs. Grand Canyon (68), 1993.
Most Three-Point Field Goals, Series
22—Kenny Warren, Cal St. Bakersfield, 1993 [11 vs. Grand Canyon, 3 vs. Alas. Anchorage, 5 vs. N.C. Central, 1 vs. Wayne St. (Mich.), 2 vs. Troy St.].
Most Free Throws, One Game
24—Dave Twardzik, Old Dominion (102) vs. Norfolk St. (97), 1971.
Most Free Throws, Series
55—Don Jacobsen, South Dak. St., 1961 [9 vs. Cornell College, 22 vs. Prairie View, 9 vs. UC Santa Barb., 11 vs. Southeast Mo. St., 4 vs. Mt. St. Mary's (Md.)].
Highest Free-Throw Percentage, One Game (minimum 18 made)
100%—Ralph Talley, Norfolk St. (70) vs. Virginia Union (60), 1986 (18-18).
Most Assists, One Game
20—Steve Ray, Bridgeport (132) vs. Stonehill (127) (ot), 1989.
Most Assists, Series
41—Derrick Russell, Bridgeport, 1992 [5 vs. Merrimack, 9 vs. New Hamp. Col., 16 vs. Central Okla., 6 vs. Calif. (Pa.), 5 vs. Virginia Union].

TEAM RECORDS

Most Points, One Game
132—Bridgeport vs. Stonehill (127) (ot), 1989; Central Okla. vs. Washburn (114), 1992.
Most Points, Series
500—Brockport St., 1973 (78 vs. Jersey City St., 93 vs. LIU-C.W. Post, 70 vs. Hartwick, 79 vs. UC Riverside, 90 vs. Ky. Wesleyan, 90 vs. Assumption).
Most Field Goals, One Game
54—Bentley (129) vs. Stonehill (118), 1989.
Most Field Goals, Series
188—Assumption, 1973; Assumption, 1974 (38 vs. St. Michael's, 36 vs. Bentley, 43 vs. Coe, 29 vs. Tennessee St., 42 vs. Brockport St.); Tenn.-Chatt., 1976 (41 vs. Rollins, 37 vs. Valdosta St., 42 vs. Nicholls St., 35 vs. Eastern Ill., 33 vs. Puget Sound).
Most Three-Point Field Goals, One Game
23—Troy St. (126) vs. New Hamp. Col. (123), 1993.
Most Three-Point Field Goals, Series
57—Troy St., 1993 (9 vs. Fla. Southern, 14 vs. Delta St., 6 vs. Washburn, 23 vs. New Hamp. Col., 5 vs. Cal St. Bakersfield).
Most Free Throws, One Game
46—Evansville (110) vs. North Caro. A&T (92), 1959.
Most Free Throws, Series
142—Mt. St. Mary's (Md.), 1957.
Most Assists, One Game
36—Troy St. (126) vs. New Hamp. Col. (123), 1993.
Most Assists, Series
120—North Dak., 1990.

DIVISION II MEN'S ALL-TOURNAMENT TEAMS

(First player listed on each team was the outstanding player of the championship.)

1957—Mel Peterson, Wheaton (Ill.)
Jack Sullivan, Mt. St. Mary's (Md.)
Mason Cope, Ky. Wesleyan
Bob Whitehead, Wheaton (Ill.)
Jim Daniels, South Dak.

1958—Ed Smallwood, Evansville
Jim Browne, St. Michael's
Jim Daniels, South Dak.
Mel Peterson, Wheaton (Ill.)
Dick Zeitler, St. Michael's

1959—Hugh Ahlering, Evansville
Joe Cotton, North Caro. A&T
Jack Israel, Southwest Mo. St.
Paul Benes, Hope
Leo Hill, Cal St. Los Angeles

1960—Ed Smallwood, Evansville
Dale Wise, Evansville
Tom Cooke, Chapman
Gary Auten, Ky. Wesleyan
William Jones, American

1961—Don Jacobsen, South Dak. St.
John O'Reilly, Mt. St. Mary's (Md.)
George Fisher, Wittenberg
Vivan Reed, Southeast Mo. St.
Carl Ritter, Southeast Mo. St.

1962—Ron Rohrer, Cal St. Sacramento
Jim Mumford, Neb. Wesleyan
Ed Spila, Southern Ill.
John O'Reilly, Mt. St. Mary's (Md.)
Ed Pfeiffer, Mt. St. Mary's (Md.)

1963—Wayne Rasmussen, South Dak. St.
Tom Black, South Dak. St.
Bob Cherry, Wittenberg
Bill Fisher, Wittenberg
Al Thrasher, Wittenberg

1964—Jerry Sloan, Evansville
Maurice McHartley, North Caro. A&T
Larry Humes, Evansville
Bill Stevens, Akron
Buster Briley, Evansville

1965—Jerry Sloan, Evansville
Richard Tarrant, St. Michael's
Walt Frazier, Southern Ill.
George McNeil, Southern Ill.
Larry Humes, Evansville

1966—Sam Smith, Ky. Wesleyan
Clarence Smith, Southern Ill.
George McNeil, Southern Ill.
David Lee, Southern Ill.
Phil Jackson, North Dak.

1967—Earl Monroe, Winston-Salem
Lou Shepherd, Southwest Mo. St.
Sam Smith, Ky. Wesleyan
Danny Bolden, Southwest Mo. St.
Dallas Thornton, Ky. Wesleyan

1968—Jerry Newsom, Indiana St.
Larry Jeffries, Trinity (Tex.)
George Tinsley, Ky. Wesleyan
Fred Hardman, Indiana St.
Dallas Thornton, Ky. Wesleyan

1969—George Tinsley, Ky. Wesleyan
Curtis Perry, Southwest Mo. St.
Tommy Hobgood, Ky. Wesleyan
Mert Bancroft, Southwest Mo. St.
Bob Rutherford, American Int'l

1970—Ted McClain, Tennessee St.
Randy Smith, Buffalo St.
Carl Poole, Phila. Textile
Howard Lee, UC Riverside
John Pierantozzi, Phila. Textile

1971—Don Buse, Evansville
Vacated*
Rick Coffey, Evansville
John Duncan, Ky. Wesleyan
Skip Noble, Old Dominion

1972—Hal Johnston, Roanoke
Leonard Robinson, Tennessee St.
Lloyd Neal, Tennessee St.
Jay Piccola, Roanoke
Len Paul, Akron

1973—Mike Williams, Ky. Wesleyan
Ron Gilliam, Brockport St.
Mike Boylan, Assumption
Leonard Robinson, Tennessee St.
Roger Zornes, Ky. Wesleyan

1974—Marvin Webster, Morgan St.
John Grochowalski, Assumption
Randy Magers, Southwest Mo. St.
William Doolittle, Southwest Mo. St.
Alvin O'Neal, Morgan St.

1975—Wilson Washington, Old Dominion
Wilbur Holland, New Orleans
John Grochowalski, Assumption
Joey Caruthers, Old Dominion
Paul Brennan, Assumption

1976—Curt Peterson, Puget Sound
Wayne Golden, Tenn.-Chatt.
Jeff Fuhrmann, Old Dominion
Jeff Furry, Eastern Ill.
Brant Gibler, Puget Sound

1977—Wayne Golden, Tenn.-Chatt.
Joe Allen, Randolph-Macon
Otis Boddie, North Ala.
William Gordon, Tenn.-Chatt.
Hector Olivencia, Sacred Heart

1978—Andrew Fields, Cheyney
Kenneth Hynson, Cheyney
Tom Anderson, Wis.-Green Bay
Charlie Thomas, Eastern Ill.
Jerry Prather, Central Fla.

1979—Perry Oden, North Ala.
Carlton Hurdle, Bridgeport
Ron Ripley, Wis.-Green Bay
Ron Darby, North Ala.
Rory Lindgren, Wis.-Green Bay

1980—Keith Valentine, Virginia Union
Larry Holmes, Virginia Union
Bobby Jones, New York Tech
John Ebeling, Fla. Southern
Johnny Buckmon, North Ala.

1981—John Ebeling, Fla. Southern
Mike Hayes, Fla. Southern
Durelle Lewis, Mt. St. Mary's (Md.)
Jim Rowe, Mt. St. Mary's (Md.)
Jay Bruchak, Mt. St. Mary's (Md.)

1982—Michael Britt, Dist. Columbia
John Ebeling, Fla. Southern
Dwight Higgs, Ky. Wesleyan
Earl Jones, Dist. Columbia
Wayne McDaniel, Cal St. Bakersfield

1983—Gary Monroe, Wright St.
Anthony Bias, Wright St.
Fred Moore, Wright St.
Earl Jones, Dist. Columbia
Michael Britt, Dist. Columbia

1984—Ron Nunnelly, Central Mo. St.
Brian Pesko, Central Mo. St.
Kenneth Bannister, St. Augustine's
Rod Drake, Ky. Wesleyan
Robert Harris, North Ala.

1985—Mark Tetzlaff, South Dak. St.
Dave Bennett, Ky. Wesleyan
Melvin Allen, Jacksonville St.
Robert Spurgeon, Jacksonville St.
Darryle Edwards, Mt. St. Mary's (Md.)

1986—Roger Younger, Sacred Heart
Kevin Stevens, Sacred Heart
Keith Johnson, Sacred Heart
Riley Ellis, Southeast Mo. St.
Ronny Rankin, Southeast Mo. St.

1987—Sam Smith, Ky. Wesleyan
Andra Whitlow, Ky. Wesleyan
John Worth, Ky. Wesleyan
Mike Runski, Gannon
Jerome Johnson, Eastern Mont.

1988—Leo Parent, Mass.-Lowell
Bobby Licare, Mass.-Lowell
Averian Parrish, Alas. Anchorage
Jerry Johnson, Fla. Southern
Darryl Thomas, Troy St.

1989—Miles Clarke, N.C. Central
Dominique Stephens, N.C. Central
Antoine Sifford, N.C. Central
Earnest Taylor, Southeast Mo. St.
Maurice Pullum, UC Riverside

1990—Wade Green, Cal St. Bakersfield
LeRoy Ellis, Ky. Wesleyan
Corey Crowder, Ky. Wesleyan
Dave Vonesh, North Dak.
Vincent Mitchell, Ky. Wesleyan

1991—Lambert Shell, Bridgeport
Pat Morris, Bridgeport
Fred Stafford, North Ala.
Allen Williams, North Ala.
Carl Wilmer, North Ala.

1992—Derrick Johnson, Virginia Union
Reggie Jones, Virginia Union
Winston Jones, Bridgeport
Steve Wills, Bridgeport
Kenney Toomer, Calif. (Pa.)

1993—Tyrone Davis, Cal St. Bakersfield
Roheen Oats, Cal St. Bakersfield
Terry McCord, Troy St.
Wayne Robertson, New Hamp. Col.
Danny Lewis, Wayne St. (Mich.)

** The participation of Dwight Lamar (Southwestern Louisiana) in the 1971 tournament was voided by action of the NCAA Council.*

DIVISION III MEN'S CHAMPIONSHIP

1993 DIVISION III MEN'S CHAMPIONSHIP RESULTS

FIRST ROUND
Ithaca 71, Fredonia St. 56
Otterbein 80, Defiance 66
Rhodes 71, Va. Wesleyan 62
Lebanon Valley 53, Johns Hopkins 49
Stockton St. 106, Catholic 91
Augustana (Ill.) 79, DePauw 66
St. John's (Minn.) 80, Wartburg 75 (ot)
Wis.-Whitewater 84, Manchester 68

SECOND ROUND
New York U. 75, Ithaca 61
Eastern Conn. St. 81, Salem St. 71
Geneseo St. 80, Buffalo St. 69
Mass.-Dartmouth 90, Westfield St. 81
Calvin 90, Otterbein 68
Emory & Henry 85, Maryville (Tenn.) 61
Ohio Northern 88, Wooster 62
Chris. Newport 84, Rhodes 74
Scranton 58, Lebanon Valley 56
Hunter 83, New Jersey Tech 70
Frank. & Marsh. 78, Elizabethtown 64
Rowan 84, Stockton St. 61
La Verne 67, Cal Lutheran 56
Augustana (Ill.) 92, Beloit 66
St. Thomas (Minn.) 75, St. John's (Minn.) 61
Wis.-Platteville 88, Wis.-Whitewater 72

SECTIONAL SEMIFINALS
Eastern Conn. St. 78, New York U. 73 (2 ot)
Mass.-Dartmouth 68, Geneseo St. 66
Calvin 101, Emory & Henry 67
Ohio Northern 83, Chris. Newport 67
Scranton 78, Hunter 62
Rowan 69, Frank. & Marsh. 68
Augustana (Ill.) 87, La Verne 84
Wis.-Platteville 70, St. Thomas (Minn.) 60

SECTIONAL CHAMPIONSHIPS
Mass.-Dartmouth 75, Eastern Conn. St. 64
Ohio Northern 67, Calvin 56
Rowan 80, Scranton 73
Augustana (Ill.) 100, Wis.-Platteville 86

SEMIFINALS
Ohio Northern 74, Mass.-Dartmouth 73
Augustana (Ill.) 83, Rowan 81

THIRD PLACE
Rowan 95, Mass.-Dartmouth 74

CHAMPIONSHIP
Ohio Northern 71, Augustana (Ill.) 68

DIVISION III MEN'S CHAMPIONSHIP BOX SCORES

SEMIFINALS

Ohio Northern 74, Mass.-Dartmouth 73

Ohio Northern	FG-FGA	FT-FTA	RB	PF	TP
Mark Gooden	6-14	4-6	5	0	16
Jon Lepinski	2-6	0-0	5	2	5
Tom Nation	0-1	0-0	0	3	0
Aaron Madry	10-19	5-6	9	2	29
D'Artis Jones	5-14	5-6	5	2	15
Kevin Wysocki	1-1	0-0	1	1	3
Jody May	0-0	0-0	0	0	0
Tony Vogel	1-1	0-0	3	5	2
Nick Bertke	2-7	0-2	5	2	4
Team			6		
TOTALS	27-63	14-20	39	17	74

Mass.-Dartmouth	FG-FGA	FT-FTA	RB	PF	TP
Stefan Pagios	4-9	2-3	3	4	10
Jason Correiro	5-10	0-0	1	2	15
Aaron Lee	2-8	0-0	3	1	5
Jon Dunlap	2-2	0-0	3	2	4
Steven Haynes	13-21	6-9	13	5	32
Eric Eaton	0-1	0-0	1	0	0
Paul Brewer	0-1	0-0	0	0	0
Ted Sisson	3-3	1-2	3	3	7
Team			2		
TOTALS	29-55	9-14	29	17	73

Half time: Ohio Northern 39, Mass.-Dartmouth 35. Three-point field goals: Ohio Northern 6-16 (Madry 4-7, Wysocki 1-1, Lepinski 1-3, Gooden 0-5); Mass.-Dartmouth 6-15 (Correiro 5-8, Lee 1-4, Eaton 0-1, Haynes 0-2). Officials: Pete Hansen, Randy Bruns. Attendance: 1,800.

Augustana (Ill.) 83, Rowan 81

Augustana (Ill.)	FG-FGA	FT-FTA	RB	PF	TP
Tom Wise	3-4	0-0	3	1	6
Aben Cooper	4-9	4-4	11	4	12
Josh Thompson	4-11	1-2	4	2	10
Rick Kelley	2-3	4-4	1	4	9
Kirk Anderson	10-20	3-5	4	3	29
Layne Pitzer	1-3	2-2	3	0	4
Cardenal Collins	0-2	0-0	0	2	0
Mike Radue	0-0	0-0	1	0	0
Brent Shreeves	1-1	0-0	0	1	3
Brian Moe	5-7	0-1	5	2	10
Team			4		
TOTALS	30-60	14-18	36	19	83

Rowan	FG-FGA	FT-FTA	RB	PF	TP
Omar Foote	5-9	4-6	7	3	15
Lonnie McCoy	2-7	0-0	2	2	4
Michael Burden	5-8	3-8	12	1	13
Paul Wiedeman	2-4	0-0	5	2	6
Keith Wood	10-20	3-4	5	3	27
Shea Harvey	0-0	1-2	0	0	1
Terrence Stewart	1-4	0-0	0	1	2
Tyrone McCloud	0-1	0-0	0	0	0
Adrian Matthew	5-18	2-2	5	1	13
James Battersby	0-0	0-0	1	1	0
Team			5		
TOTALS	30-71	13-22	42	14	81

Half time: Rowan 46, Augustana (Ill.) 43. Three-point field goals: Augustana (Ill.) 9-15 (Anderson 6-7, Kelley 1-1, Shreeves 1-1, Thompson 1-5, Wise 0-1); Rowan 8-18 (Wood 4-8, Wiedeman 2-2, Foote 1-1, Matthew 1-6, Stewart 0-1). Officials: David Chambers, Mike Alvaro. Attendance: 1,800.

THIRD PLACE

Rowan 95, Mass.-Dartmouth 74

Rowan	FG-FGA	FT-FTA	RB	PF	TP
Greg Harris	2-3	0-0	1	1	4
Lonnie McCoy	6-12	6-6	2	2	18
Omar Foote	3-5	1-1	10	2	7
Paul Wiedeman	1-5	2-2	9	1	5
Keith Wood	7-14	2-2	4	0	19
Shea Harvey	1-1	0-0	0	1	3
Bill Lange	0-0	1-2	0	0	1
Terrence Stewart	3-6	1-4	6	1	7
Adrian Matthew	6-10	0-0	4	2	15
Michael Burden	4-5	0-0	4	1	8
James Battersby	1-3	0-0	2	3	2

	FG-FGA	FT-FTA	RB	PF	TP
Tyrone McCloud	3- 4	0- 0	2	0	6
Team			3		
TOTALS	37-68	13-17	47	14	95

Mass.-Dartmouth	FG-FGA	FT-FTA	RB	PF	TP
Stefan Pagios	3-14	2- 2	2	1	9
Jason Correiro	5-13	0- 0	0	1	14
Aaron Lee	3-12	0- 0	0	3	7
Jon Dunlap	2- 6	1- 2	7	3	5
Steven Haynes	13-18	2- 4	17	1	30
Paul Brewer	1- 2	0- 0	0	1	2
Byron Andrews	0- 1	0- 0	1	0	0
Matt McConnell	1- 3	1- 2	0	2	3
Aaron Berger	0- 2	0- 0	0	0	0
Ted Sisson	0- 3	0- 0	3	1	0
Mark Holmes	0- 0	0- 0	0	0	0
Jason Youngquist	1- 2	0- 0	0	0	2
Darius Modestow	0- 0	2- 2	1	2	2
Team			3		
TOTALS	29-76	8-12	34	15	74

Half time: Rowan 43, Mass.-Dartmouth 36. Three-point field goals: Rowan 8-17 (Matthew 3-5, Wood 3-6, Harvey 1-1, Wiedeman 1-3, Stewart 0-1, Foote 0-1); Mass.-Dartmouth 8-34 (Correiro 4-11, Haynes 2-4, Pagios 1-6, Lee 1-9, Andrews 0-1, McConnell 0-1, Berger 0-1, Dunlap 0-1). Officials: Roger MacTavish, Pat Cannon. Attendance: 2,120.

CHAMPIONSHIP

Ohio Northern 71, Augustana (Ill.) 68

Augustana (Ill.)	FG-FGA	FT-FTA	RB	PF	TP
Tom Wise	2- 4	0- 0	3	2	5
Aben Cooper	8-16	1- 2	11	5	17
Josh Thompson	2-10	3- 4	4	5	8
Kirk Anderson	8-25	0- 0	7	2	20
Rick Kelley	1- 4	0- 0	7	3	3
Layne Pitzer	1- 2	0- 0	1	0	2
Cardenal Collins	1- 1	0- 0	0	1	2
Mike Radue	2- 3	0- 0	1	1	5
Eric Rowell	0- 0	0- 0	0	0	0
Brent Shreeves	0- 1	0- 0	1	0	0
Brian Moe	3- 5	0- 2	5	2	6
Team			5		
TOTALS	28-71	4- 8	45	21	68

Ohio Northern	FG-FGA	FT-FTA	RB	PF	TP
Aaron Madry	6-13	0- 2	4	1	14
D'Artis Jones	9-17	3- 4	6	4	21
Tom Nation	2- 4	0- 0	6	3	4
Mark Gooden	3-11	15-17	5	0	21
Jon Lepinski	1- 3	0- 0	3	0	2
Kevin Wysocki	0- 0	0- 0	0	1	0
Jody May	0- 0	0- 0	0	0	0
Tony Vogel	2- 3	0- 0	4	1	4
Nick Bertke	2- 6	1- 2	7	2	5
Team			2		
TOTALS	25-57	19-25	37	12	71

Half time: Ohio Northern 41, Augustana (Ill.) 31. Three-point field goals: Augustana (Ill.) 8-27 (Anderson 4-16, Wise 1-1, Radue 1-2, Thompson 1-4, Kelley 1-4); Ohio Northern 2-8 (Madry 2-4, Gooden 0-4). Officials: Mike Lonski, Carmen Urzetta. Attendance: 2,120.

DIVISION III MEN'S CHAMPIONSHIP RECORDS

ALL-TIME RESULTS

Year	Champion	Score	Runner-Up	Third Place	Fourth Place
1975	LeMoyne-Owen	57-54	Rowan	Augustana (Ill.)	Brockport St.
1976	Scranton	60-57	Wittenberg	Augustana (Ill.)	Plattsburgh St.
1977	Wittenberg	79-66	Oneonta St.	Scranton	Hamline
1978	North Park	69-57	Widener	Albion	Stony Brook
1979	North Park	66-62	Potsdam St.	Frank. & Marsh.	Centre
1980	North Park	83-76	Upsala	Wittenberg	Longwood
1981	Potsdam St.	67-65†	Augustana (Ill.)	Ursinus	Otterbein
1982	Wabash	83-62	Potsdam St.	Brooklyn	Cal St. Stanislaus
1983	Scranton	64-63	Wittenberg	Roanoke	Wis.-Whitewater
1984	Wis.-Whitewater	103-86	Clark (Mass.)	DePauw	Upsala
1985	North Park	72-71	Potsdam St.	Neb. Wesleyan	Widener
1986	Potsdam St.	76-73	LeMoyne-Owen	Neb. Wesleyan	Jersey City St.
1987	North Park	106-100	Clark (Mass.)	Wittenberg	Stockton St.
1988	Ohio Wesleyan	92-70	Scranton	Neb. Wesleyan	Hartwick
1989	Wis.-Whitewater	94-86	Trenton St.	Southern Me.	Centre
1990	Rochester	43-42	DePauw	Washington (Md.)	Calvin
1991	Wis.-Platteville	81-74	Frank. & Marsh.	Otterbein	Ramapo
1992	Calvin	62-49	Rochester	Wis.-Platteville	Jersey City St.
1993	Ohio Northern	71-68	Augustana (Ill.)	Rowan	Mass.-Dartmouth

† *Overtime.*

Year	Site of Finals	Coaches of Team Champions	Outstanding Player Award
1975	Reading, Pa.	Jerry Johnson, LeMoyne-Owen	Bob Newman, LeMoyne-Owen
1976	Reading, Pa.	Bob Bessoir, Scranton	Jack Maher, Scranton
1977	Rock Island, Ill.	Larry Hunter, Wittenberg	Rick White, Wittenberg
1978	Rock Island, Ill.	Dan McCarrell, North Park	Michael Harper, North Park
1979	Rock Island, Ill.	Dan McCarrell, North Park	Michael Harper, North Park
1980	Rock Island, Ill.	Dan McCarrell, North Park	Michael Thomas, North Park
1981	Rock Island, Ill.	Jerry Welsh, Potsdam St.	Maxwell Artis, Augustana (Ill.)
1982	Grand Rapids, Mich.	Mac Petty, Wabash	Pete Metzelaars, Wabash
1983	Grand Rapids, Mich.	Bob Bessoir, Scranton	Bill Bessoir, Scranton
1984	Grand Rapids, Mich.	Dave Vander Meulen, Wis.-Whitewater	Andre McKoy, Wis.-Whitewater
1985	Grand Rapids, Mich.	Bosko Djurickovic, North Park	Earnest Hubbard, North Park
1986	Grand Rapids, Mich.	Jerry Welsh, Potsdam St.	Roosevelt Bullock, Potsdam St.

Year	Site of Finals	Coaches of Team Champions	Outstanding Player Award
1987	Grand Rapids, Mich.	Bosco Djurickovic, North Park	Michael Starks, North Park
1988	Grand Rapids, Mich.	Gene Mehaffey, Ohio Wesleyan	Scott Tedder, Ohio Wesleyan
1989	Springfield, Ohio	Dave Vander Meulen, Wis.-Whitewater	Greg Grant, Trenton St.
1990	Springfield, Ohio	Mike Neer, Rochester	Chris Fite, Rochester
1991	Springfield, Ohio	Bo Ryan, Wis.-Platteville	Shawn Frison, Wis.-Platteville
1992	Springfield, Ohio	Ed Douma, Calvin	Steve Honderd, Calvin
1993	Buffalo, New York	Joe Campoli, Ohio Northern	Kirk Anderson, Augustana (Ill.)

INDIVIDUAL RECORDS

Most Points, One Game
49—Gerald Reece, William Penn (85) vs. North Park (81), 1981.

Most Points, Series
167—Greg Grant, Trenton St., 1989 (30 vs. Shenandoah, 28 vs. Jersey City St., 38 vs. Potsdam St., 36 vs. Southern Me., 35 vs. Wis.-Whitewater).

Most Field Goals, One Game
21—Gerald Reece, William Penn (85) vs. North Park (81), 1981.

Most Field Goals, Series
68—Greg Grant, Trenton St., 1989 (11 vs. Shenandoah, 11 vs. Jersey City St., 16 vs. Potsdam St., 16 vs. Southern Me., 14 vs. Wis.-Whitewater).

Most Three-Point Field Goals, One Game
12—Kirk Anderson, Augustana (Ill.) (100) vs. Wis.-Platteville (86), 1993.

Most Three-Point Field Goals, Series
35—Kirk Anderson, Augustana (Ill.), 1993 (4 vs. DePauw, 5 vs. Beloit, 4 vs. La Verne, 12 vs. Wis.-Platteville, 6 vs. Rowan, 4 vs. Ohio Northern).

Most Free Throws, One Game
21—Tom Montsma, Calvin (88) vs. Wabash (76), 1980.

Most Free Throws, Series
45—Andre McKoy, Wis.-Whitewater, 1984 [11 vs. Ill. Wesleyan, 8 vs. St. Norbert, 4 vs. Neb. Wesleyan, 9 vs. DePauw, 13 vs. Clark (Mass.)].

Most Assists, One Game
16—Tim Brack, Centre (124) vs. Cal St. Stanislaus (123) (2 ot), 1989; James Bradley, Otterbein (113) vs. Ramapo (84), 1991.

Most Assists, Series
62—Ricky Spicer, Wis.-Whitewater, 1989.

TEAM RECORDS

Most Points, One Game
124—Centre vs. Cal St. Stanislaus (123) (2 ot), 1989.

Most Points, Series
509—Augustana (Ill.), 1993 (79 vs. DePauw, 92 vs. Beloit, 87 vs. La Verne, 100 vs. Wis.-Platteville, 83 vs. Rowan, 68 vs. Ohio Northern).

Most Field Goals, One Game
50 vs. Cal St. Stanislaus (123) vs. Centre (124) (2 ot), 1989.

Most Field Goals, Series
190—Wis.-Platteville, 1991 (39 vs. Ripon, 44 vs. Chris. Newport, 43 vs. Ill. Benedictine, 36 vs. Otterbein, 28 vs. Frank. & Marsh.).

Most Three-Point Field Goals, One Game
15—Hope (107) vs. Ohio Wesleyan (110) (2 ot), 1988.

Most Three-Point Field Goals, Series
59—Augustana (Ill.), 1993 (6 vs. DePauw, 11 vs. Beloit, 11 vs. LaVerne, 14 vs. Wis.-Platteville, 9 vs. Rowan, 8 vs. Ohio Northern).

Most Free Throws, One Game
43—Capital (103) vs. Va. Wesleyan (93), 1982; Potsdam St. (91) vs. Jersey City St. (89), 1986.

Most Free Throws, Series
130—North Park, 1987 [28 vs. Ripon, 26 vs. Ill. Wesleyan, 28 vs. Wartburg, 17 vs. Wittenberg, 31 vs. Clark (Mass.)].

Most Assists, One Game
33—Centre (124) vs. Cal St. Stanislaus (123) (2 ot), 1989

Most Assists, Series
108—Augustana (Ill.), 1993 (12 vs. DePauw, 21 vs. Beloit, 18 vs. La Verne, 13 vs. Wis.-Platteville, 26 vs. Rowan, 18 vs. Ohio Northern).

DIVISION III MEN'S ALL-TOURNAMENT TEAMS

(First player listed on each team was the outstanding player of the championship.)

1975—Robert Newman, LeMoyne-Owen
Clint Jackson, LeMoyne-Owen
Dan Panaggio, Brockport St.
Bruce Hamming, Augustana (Ill.)
Greg Ackles, Rowan

1976—Jack Maher, Scranton
Tom Dunn, Wittenberg
Bob Heubner, Wittenberg
Ronnie Wright, Plattsburgh St.
Terry Lawrence, Augustana (Ill.)

1977—Rick White, Wittenberg
Phil Smyczek, Hamline
Paul Miernicki, Scranton
Clyde Eberhardt, Wittenberg
Ralph Christian, Oneonta St.

1978—Michael Harper, North Park
Dennis James, Widener
John Nibert, Albion
Earl Keith, Stony Brook
Tom Florentine, North Park

1979—Michael Harper, North Park
Don Marsh, Frank. & Marsh.
Derrick Rowland, Potsdam St.
Michael Thomas, North Park
Modzel Greer, North Park

1980—Michael Thomas, North Park
Ellonya Green, Upsala
Steve Keenan, Upsala
Tyronne Curtis, Wittenberg
Keith French, North Park

1981—Max Artis, Augustana (Ill.)
Bill Rapier, Augustana (Ill.)
Ed Jachim, Potsdam St.
Derrick Rowland, Potsdam St.
Ron Stewart, Otterbein

1982—Pete Metzelaars, Wabash
Doug Cornfoot, Cal St. Stanislaus
Rick Davis, Brooklyn
Merlin Nice, Wabash
Leroy Witherspoon, Potsdam St.
Maurice Woods, Potsdam St.

1983—Bill Bessoir, Scranton
Mickey Banas, Scranton
Jay Ferguson, Wittenberg
Mark Linde, Wis.-Whitewater
Gerald Holmes, Roanoke

1984—Andre McKoy, Wis.-Whitewater
Mark Linde, Wis.-Whitewater
James Gist, Upsala
Dan Trant, Clark (Mass.)
David Hathaway, DePauw

1985—Earnest Hubbard, North Park
Justyne Monegain, North Park
Dana Janssen, Neb. Wesleyan
Brendan Mitchell, Potsdam St.
Lou Stevens, Widener

1986—Roosevelt Bullock, Potsdam St.
Barry Stanton, Potsdam St.
Johnny Mayers, Jersey City St.
Michael Neal, LeMoyne-Owen
Dana Janssen, Neb. Wesleyan

1987—Michael Starks, North Park
Mike Barach, North Park
Steve Iannarino, Wittenberg
Kermit Sharp, Clark (Mass.)
Donald Ellison, Stockton St.

1988—Scott Tedder, Ohio Wesleyan
Lee Rowlinson, Ohio Wesleyan
J. P. Andrejko, Scranton
Charlie Burt, Neb. Wesleyan
Tim McGraw, Hartwick

1989—Greg Grant, Trenton St.
Danny Johnson, Centre
Jeff Bowers, Southern Me.
Ricky Spicer, Wis.-Whitewater
Elbert Gordon, Wis.-Whitewater
Jeff Seifriz, Wis.-Whitewater

1990—Chris Fite, Rochester
Brett Crist, DePauw
Chris Brandt, Washington (Md.)
Brett Hecko, DePauw
Steve Honderd, Calvin

1991—Shawn Frison, Wis.-Platteville
James Bradley, Otterbein
Robby Jeter, Wis.-Platteville
Will Lasky, Frank. & Marsh.
David Wilding, Frank. & Marsh.

1992—Steve Honderd, Calvin
Matt Harrison, Calvin
Mike LeFebre, Calvin
Chris Fite, Rochester
Kyle Meeker, Rochester

1993—Kirk Anderson, Augustana (Ill.)
Mark Gooden, Ohio Northern
Aaron Madry, Ohio Northern
Steven Haynes, Mass.-Dartmouth
Keith Wood, Rowan

STATISTICAL LEADERS

Augustana (Illinois) senior Kirk Anderson was the nation's ninth-leading scorer in 1992-93, averaging 24.5 points a game. Anderson averaged 4.1 three-point shots a contest last year, second in the country. Anderson led Augustana (Illinois) to a second-place finish in the Division III Men's Basketball Championship. He was named the tournament's most outstanding player.

1993 DIVISION I MEN'S INDIVIDUAL LEADERS

SCORING

	CL	HT	G	TFG	FGA	PCT.	3FG	FGA	PCT.	FT	FTA	PCT.	REB	AVG.	PTS.	AVG.
1. Greg Guy, Tex.-Pan American ..	Jr	6-1	19	189	459	41.2	67	184	36.4	111	127	87.4	88	4.6	556	29.3
2. J. R. Rider, Nevada-Las Vegas .	Sr	6-5	28	282	548	51.5	55	137	40.1	195	236	82.6	250	8.9	814	29.1
3. John Best, Tennessee Tech	Sr	6-8	28	296	535	55.3	4	18	22.2	203	271	74.9	235	8.4	799	28.5
4. Vin Baker, Hartford	Sr	6-11	28	305	639	47.7	32	119	26.9	150	240	62.5	300	10.7	792	28.3
5. Lindsey Hunter, Jackson St. ...	Sr	6-2	34	320	777	41.2	112	328	34.1	155	201	77.1	115	3.4	907	26.7
6. Alphonso Ford, Mississippi Val.	Sr	6-2	28	252	578	43.6	76	216	35.2	148	187	79.1	147	5.3	728	26.0
7. Bill Edwards, Wright St.	Sr	6-8	30	288	556	51.8	43	114	37.7	138	176	78.4	289	9.6	757	25.2
8. Billy Ross, Appalachian St.	Sr	6-6	28	232	536	43.3	93	230	40.4	126	170	74.1	162	5.8	683	24.4
9. Glenn Robinson, Purdue	So	6-8	28	246	519	47.4	32	80	40.0	152	205	74.1	258	9.2	676	24.1
10. Kenneth Sykes, Grambling	So	6-4	27	242	482	50.2	37	86	43.0	123	165	74.5	136	5.0	644	23.9
11. Tony Dumas, Mo.-Kansas City .	Jr	6-5	27	238	487	48.9	45	127	35.4	122	170	71.8	148	5.5	643	23.8
12. Eddie Benton, Vermont	Fr	6-0	26	176	425	41.4	82	196	41.8	185	221	83.7	79	3.0	619	23.8
13. Tony Dunkin, Coastal Caro.	Sr	6-7	32	263	506	52.0	64	136	47.1	169	216	78.2	203	6.3	759	23.7
14. D. Johnson, Central Conn. St. ..	Sr	6-3	26	236	497	47.5	0	5	0.0	133	185	71.9	101	3.9	605	23.3
15. Stan Rose, Weber St.	Sr	6-7	28	240	390	61.5	0	0	0.0	170	275	61.8	232	8.3	650	23.2
16. Jesse Ratliff, North Texas	Jr	6-6	26	207	493	42.0	60	178	33.7	127	171	74.3	269	10.3	601	23.1
17. Lucious Harris, Long Beach St..	Sr	6-5	32	251	478	52.5	73	177	41.2	164	212	77.4	169	5.3	739	23.1
18. Darnell Sneed, Charleston So...	Sr	6-4	27	218	494	44.1	25	85	29.4	161	186	86.6	177	6.6	622	23.0
18. Devin Boyd, Towson St.	Sr	6-1	27	177	441	40.1	54	171	31.6	214	272	78.7	105	3.9	622	23.0
#20. A. Hardaway, Memphis St.	Jr	6-7	32	249	522	47.7	73	220	33.2	158	206	76.7	273	8.5	729	22.8
21. Brian Gilgeous, American	Sr	6-6	28	205	419	48.9	49	111	44.1	177	211	83.9	201	7.2	636	22.7
22. Demetrius Dudley, Hofstra	Sr	6-4	26	184	417	44.1	81	171	47.4	141	178	79.2	137	5.3	590	22.7
23. Kareem Townes, La Salle	So	6-3	27	203	550	36.9	97	301	32.2	104	149	69.8	95	3.5	607	22.5
24. Calbert Cheaney, Indiana	Sr	6-7	35	303	552	54.9	47	110	42.7	132	166	79.5	223	6.4	785	22.4
25. Tyrone Phillips, Marshall	Sr	6-6	26	228	419	54.4	0	4	0.0	125	180	69.4	153	5.9	581	22.3
26. Orlando Lightfoot, Idaho	Jr	6-7	32	288	582	49.5	37	114	32.5	102	143	71.3	276	8.6	715	22.3
27. Devon Lake, Southeast Mo. St. .	Sr	6-3	27	198	429	46.2	45	126	35.7	162	205	79.0	99	3.7	603	22.3
28. Allan Houston, Tennessee	Sr	6-6	30	211	454	46.5	82	198	41.4	165	188	87.8	145	4.8	669	22.3
29. Buck Jenkins, Columbia	Sr	6-6	26	188	433	43.4	56	146	38.4	146	193	75.6	84	3.2	578	22.2
30. Darrick Suber, Rider	Sr	6-4	30	246	520	47.3	63	161	39.1	110	157	70.1	120	4.0	665	22.2
31. Michael Finley, Wisconsin	So	6-7	28	223	478	46.7	63	173	36.4	111	144	77.1	161	5.8	620	22.1
32. Kenny Brown, Mercer	Sr	6-3	26	192	428	44.9	67	153	43.8	124	161	77.0	150	5.8	575	22.1
33. Terry Dehere, Seton Hall	Sr	6-4	35	242	525	46.1	84	212	39.6	202	247	81.8	105	3.0	770	22.0
34. Tucker Neale, Colgate	So	6-3	28	201	429	46.9	69	162	42.6	141	173	81.5	124	4.4	612	21.9
35. Kenny Williams, Ill.-Chicago ...	Jr	5-10	32	254	523	48.6	88	209	42.1	99	130	76.2	104	3.3	695	21.7
36. Chuck Penn, Lehigh	Sr	6-4	27	208	462	45.0	28	78	35.9	138	189	73.0	118	4.4	582	21.6
37. DeLon Turner, Florida A&M	Sr	6-5	26	220	408	53.9	8	29	27.6	112	162	69.1	287	11.0	560	21.5
38. Hank Washington, S'eastrn La..	Sr	6-4	27	203	389	52.2	48	115	41.7	126	154	81.8	85	3.1	580	21.5
39. Jamaine Williams, N.C. A&T ...	Jr	6-8	26	214	439	48.7	37	94	39.4	92	126	73.0	232	8.9	557	21.4
40. Tyler Rullman, Harvard	Sr	6-7	26	206	456	45.2	39	118	33.1	105	132	79.5	151	5.8	556	21.4
41. Tracy Gipson, Valparaiso	Sr	5-10	28	217	467	46.5	28	61	45.9	133	159	83.6	100	3.6	595	21.3
#42. Rodney Rogers, Wake Forest ..	Jr	6-7	30	239	431	55.5	24	67	35.8	134	187	71.7	221	7.4	636	21.2
43. Ryan Stuart, Northeast La.	Sr	6-4	29	254	430	59.1	2	12	16.7	103	175	58.9	274	9.4	613	21.1
44. Curt Smith, Drake	Jr	5-10	28	219	517	42.4	46	146	31.5	107	137	78.1	87	3.1	591	21.1
#45. Jamal Mashburn, Kentucky	Jr	6-8	34	259	526	49.2	66	180	36.7	130	194	67.0	284	8.4	714	21.0
46. Tanoka Beard, Boise St.	Sr	6-9	27	199	339	58.7	0	0	0.0	168	209	80.4	208	7.7	566	21.0
47. Michael Allen, S'western La. ...	Jr	6-0	30	212	492	43.1	67	190	35.3	135	165	81.8	70	2.3	626	20.9
48. Eric Kubel, Northwestern (La.) .	Jr	6-8	26	195	356	54.8	5	18	27.8	144	193	74.6	252	9.7	539	20.7
49. Doug Bentz, Morehead St.	Sr	6-9	26	171	351	48.7	5	23	21.7	191	259	73.7	256	9.8	538	20.7
50. Leonard White, Southern-B.R. ..	Sr	6-7	30	218	484	45.0	59	129	45.7	124	178	69.7	302	10.1	619	20.6
#51. James Robinson, Alabama	Jr	6-1	29	202	481	42.0	78	222	35.1	116	170	68.2	130	4.5	598	20.6
52. Aaron McKie, Temple	Jr	6-5	33	240	555	43.2	77	196	39.3	123	156	78.8	195	5.9	680	20.6
53. Billy McCaffrey, Vanderbilt	Jr	6-4	34	241	436	55.3	83	162	51.2	134	154	87.0	90	2.6	699	20.6
54. Reggie Jackson, Nicholls St. ...	So	6-6	26	199	336	59.2	0	1	0.0	134	202	66.3	325	12.5	532	20.5
55. Tony Tolbert, Detroit Mercy	Sr	6-4	27	198	447	44.3	52	127	40.9	104	152	68.4	107	4.0	552	20.4
56. Chris Mills, Arizona	Sr	6-6	28	211	406	52.0	56	116	48.3	92	110	83.6	222	7.9	570	20.4
57. Robert Gaines, Western Caro. ..	Sr	6-5	26	199	419	47.5	62	178	34.8	69	96	71.9	153	5.9	529	20.3
58. Richard Barton, Southern Utah .	Sr	6-9	27	188	322	58.4	15	32	46.9	158	206	76.7	180	6.7	549	20.3
59. Carlos Rogers, Tennessee St. ..	Jr	6-11	29	239	385	62.1	0	3	0.0	111	178	62.4	339	11.7	589	20.3
60. Will Flemons, Texas Tech	Sr	6-7	30	214	344	62.2	14	28	50.0	165	224	73.7	324	10.8	607	20.2
61. Michael Richardson, Texas	Sr	6-3	27	195	489	39.9	33	99	33.3	122	174	70.1	168	6.2	545	20.2
62. Jackie Robinson, South Caro. St.	Sr	6-8	29	193	369	52.3	10	27	37.0	189	272	69.5	217	7.5	585	20.2
63. Shawn Respert, Michigan St. ..	So	6-3	28	192	399	48.1	60	140	42.9	119	139	85.6	111	4.0	563	20.1
#64. Parrish Casebier, Evansville ...	Jr	6-3	27	170	371	45.8	16	49	32.7	186	239	77.8	178	6.6	542	20.1
65. Al Hamilton, Weber St.	Sr	6-7	27	213	454	46.9	11	38	28.9	104	140	74.3	174	6.4	541	20.0
66. Joe Griffin, LIU-Brooklyn	Jr	6-5	28	217	362	59.9	1	4	25.0	126	184	68.5	200	7.1	561	20.0
67. Stevin Smith, Arizona St.	Jr	6-2	27	171	405	42.2	113	300	37.7	85	109	78.0	75	2.8	540	20.0
68. Derrick Alston, Duquesne	Jr	6-11	28	214	380	56.3	1	1	100.0	128	223	57.4	261	9.3	557	19.9
69. Bob Sura, Florida St.	So	6-5	34	241	533	45.2	73	220	33.2	120	188	63.8	209	6.1	675	29.9
70. Randolph Childress, Wake Forest	So	6-2	30	184	380	48.4	96	217	44.2	128	158	81.0	84	2.8	592	19.7

Entered NBA draft.

FIELD-GOAL PERCENTAGE

(Min. 5 FG Made Per Game)	CL	HT	G	FG	FGA	PCT.
1. Charles Outlaw, Houston	Sr	6-8	30	196	298	65.8
2. Brian Grant, Xavier (Ohio)	Jr	6-8	30	223	341	65.4
3. Harry Hart, Iona	Sr	6-9	26	151	231	65.4

(Min. 5 FG Made Per Game)	CL	HT	G	FG	FGA	PCT.
4. Cherokee Parks, Duke	So	6-11	32	161	247	65.2
5. Gary Trent, Ohio	Fr	6-8	27	194	298	65.1
6. Mike Nahar, Wright St.	Jr	7-0	30	190	296	64.2
7. Mike Peplowski, Michigan St.	Sr	6-11	28	161	252	63.9
8. Jimmy Lunsford, Alabama St.	Fr	6-8	22	142	223	63.7
9. Warren Kidd, Middle Tenn. St.	Sr	6-9	26	167	265	63.0
10. Eddie Gay, Winthrop	Sr	6-9	30	194	309	62.8
11. Fred Shepherd, Arkansas St.	Sr	6-6	26	145	232	62.5
12. Alex Holcombe, Baylor	Sr	6-9	27	191	306	62.4
13. Mike Lovelace, Detroit Mercy	Sr	6-6	27	136	218	62.4
14. Will Flemons, Texas Tech	Sr	6-7	30	214	344	62.2
15. Bryant Reeves, Oklahoma St.	So	7-0	29	210	338	62.1
16. Carlos Rogers, Tennessee St.	Jr	6-11	29	239	385	62.1
17. Dana Jones, Pepperdine	Jr	6-6	31	207	334	62.0
18. Ervin Johnson, New Orleans	Sr	6-11	29	208	336	61.9
#19. Chris Webber, Michigan	So	6-9	36	281	454	61.9
20. Stan Rose, Weber St.	Sr	6-7	28	240	390	61.5
21. Julius Nwosu, Liberty	Sr	6-10	30	203	330	61.5
22. Eric Montross, North Caro.	Jr	7-0	38	222	361	61.5
23. Lee Matthews, Siena	Sr	6-7	29	193	317	60.9
24. Deon Thomas, Illinois	Jr	6-9	32	225	371	60.6
25. Johnny McDowell, Texas-Arlington	Sr	6-5	28	190	315	60.3
26. Erik Martin, Cincinnati	Sr	6-6	31	164	272	60.3
27. Aaron Swinson, Auburn	Jr	6-5	27	183	305	60.0
27. David Ardayfio, Army	Jr	6-4	26	147	245	60.0
29. Joe Griffin, LIU-Brooklyn	Jr	6-5	28	217	362	59.9
30. Mike VandeGarde, Illinois St.	Jr	6-8	29	171	288	59.4
31. Brent Scott, Rice	Sr	6-10	28	184	310	59.4

Entered NBA draft.

THREE-POINT FIELD GOALS MADE PER GAME

	CL	HT	G	NO.	AVG.
1. Bernard Haslett, Southern Miss.	Jr	6-3	26	109	4.2
2. Stevin Smith, Arizona St.	Jr	6-2	27	113	4.2
3. Mark Alberts, Akron	Sr	6-0	26	107	4.1
4. Keith Veney, Lamar	Fr	6-3	27	106	3.9
5. Doug Day, Radford	Sr	6-1	31	116	3.7
6. Ronnie Schmitz, Mo.-Kansas City	Sr	6-4	27	98	3.6
7. Kareem Townes, La Salle	So	6-3	27	97	3.6
8. Greg Guy, Tex.-Pan American	Jr	6-1	19	67	3.5
9. Matt Maloney, Pennsylvania	So	6-3	27	91	3.4
10. Billy Ross, Appalachian St.	Sr	6-6	28	93	3.3
10. Charlton Young, Ga. Southern	Sr	6-1	28	93	3.3
12. Don Leary, Cal St. Fullerton	Jr	6-2	27	89	3.3
13. Lindsey Hunter, Jackson St.	Sr	6-2	34	112	3.3
14. Pat Easterlin, Wis.-Milwaukee	Jr	6-3	27	87	3.2
14. Jay Goodman, Utah St.	Sr	6-0	27	87	3.2
16. Rob West, Tennessee Tech	Jr	6-3	28	90	3.2
17. Phil Glenn, Southern Cal	Sr	6-1	29	93	3.2
18. Randolph Childress, Wake Forest	So	6-2	30	96	3.2
19. Eddie Benton, Vermont	Fr	6-0	26	82	3.2
20. Demetrius Dudley, Hofstra	Sr	6-4	26	81	3.1
21. Dwayne Hackett, Southern Cal	Sr	6-1	30	91	3.0
22. Johnny Murdock, Southwest Mo. St.	So	6-1	31	94	3.0
23. Aundre Branch, Baylor	So	6-3	27	81	3.0
23. Shannon Washington, Centenary	Sr	5-10	24	72	3.0
25. Travis Ford, Kentucky	Jr	5-9	34	101	3.0
26. LaShawn Coulter, Winthrop	So	6-2	30	89	3.0
27. Marquis Hicks, Coastal Caro.	So	6-1	28	83	3.0
28. Steve Edwards, Miami (Fla.)	Fr	6-5	27	79	2.9
29. Roosevelt Moore, Sam Houston St.	Jr	5-10	25	73	2.9
30. Chris Whitney, Clemson	Sr	6-0	30	87	2.9

THREE-POINT FIELD-GOAL PERCENTAGE

(Min. 1.5 3FG Made Per Game and 40%)	CL	HT	G	FG	FGA	PCT.
1. Jeff Anderson, Kent	Jr	6-4	26	44	82	53.7
2. Roosevelt Moore, Sam Houston St.	Jr	5-10	25	73	137	53.3
3. Dwayne Morton, Louisville	Jr	6-6	31	51	96	53.1
4. Travis Ford, Kentucky	Jr	5-9	34	101	191	52.9
5. Greg Graham, Indiana	Sr	6-4	35	57	111	51.4
6. Billy McCaffrey, Vanderbilt	Jr	6-4	34	83	162	51.2
7. Brad Divine, Eastern Ky.	Fr	6-0	27	43	85	50.6
8. Sean Wightman, Western Mich.	Sr	6-5	29	63	129	48.8
9. Chris Mills, Arizona	Sr	6-6	28	56	116	48.3
10. Sam Brown, Toledo	Jr	5-10	28	68	141	48.2
11. Darryl Cheeley, North Caro. A&T	Sr	6-0	24	44	92	47.8
12. LaSalle Thompson, Indiana St.	So	5-10	27	43	90	47.8
13. Casey Schmidt, Valparaiso	Jr	6-5	27	71	149	47.7
14. Brian Holden, Drexel	So	6-4	29	58	122	47.5
15. Kevin Booth, Mt. St. Mary's (Md.)	Sr	6-1	28	67	141	47.5

(Min. 1.5 3FG Made Per Game and 40%)	CL	HT	G	FG	FGA	PCT.
16. Doug Harris, San Diego	So	6-0	27	54	114	47.4
16. Demetrius Dudley, Hofstra	Sr	6-4	26	81	171	47.4
18. Jonathan Pixley, Samford	Fr	6-4	26	42	89	47.2
19. Tony Dunkin, Coastal Caro.	Sr	6-7	32	64	136	47.1
20. Tony Miller, Marquette	So	5-11	28	46	98	46.9
20. Chris Mooney, Princeton	Jr	6-6	26	46	98	46.9
22. Darryl Davis, Central Fla.	So	6-5	27	45	96	46.9
23. Jeremy Lake, Montana	So	6-3	28	49	105	46.7
23. Keith Adkins, N.C.-Wilmington	Sr	6-0	28	70	150	46.7
25. Wesley Person, Auburn	Jr	6-6	27	58	125	46.4
26. Phil Dixon, Utah	Jr	6-5	31	56	122	45.9
27. Ken Gibson, Nevada-Las Vegas	Jr	6-2	29	55	120	45.8
28. Ike Williams, New Mexico	Sr	6-4	31	71	155	45.8
29. Andy Kilbride, Wisconsin	So	6-3	27	49	107	45.8
30. Andy Holderman, Wright St.	Jr	6-1	30	81	177	45.8

FREE-THROW PERCENTAGE

(Min. 2.5 FT Made Per Game)	CL	HT	G	FT	FTA	PCT.
1. Josh Grant, Utah	Sr	6-9	31	104	113	92.0
2. Roger Breslin, Holy Cross	Sr	6-2	30	100	111	90.1
3. Jeremy Lake, Montana	So	6-3	28	71	79	89.9
4. Casey Schmidt, Valparaiso	Jr	6-5	27	70	78	89.7
5. Scott Hartzell, N.C.-Greensboro	Fr	6-0	27	72	81	88.9
6. Greg Holman, Kent	Sr	6-4	27	69	78	88.5
7. Travis Ford, Kentucky	Jr	5-9	34	104	118	88.1
8. Pat Baldwin, Northwestern	Jr	6-1	25	66	75	88.0
9. Don Burgess, Radford	Jr	6-6	31	109	124	87.9
10. Allan Houston, Tennessee	Sr	6-6	30	165	188	87.8
11. Jeff Gaca, Cornell	Sr	6-3	26	91	104	87.5
12. Greg Guy, Tex.-Pan American	Jr	6-1	19	111	127	87.4
13. Sander Scott, Central Mich.	Sr	6-0	25	104	119	87.4
14. Rex Walters, Kansas	Sr	6-4	36	110	126	87.3
15. Russell Ponds, Southwest Tex. St.	Jr	6-0	27	109	125	87.2
16. Billy McCaffrey, Vanderbilt	Jr	6-4	34	134	154	87.0
17. Damon Key, Marquette	Jr	6-8	27	93	107	86.9
18. Mark Bass, St. Joseph's (Pa.)	Fr	5-9	29	73	84	86.9
19. Janko Narat, Davidson	Jr	6-6	28	85	98	86.7
20. Greg Thomas, Indiana St.	Sr	6-0	28	111	128	86.7
21. Ryan Yoder, Colorado St.	Jr	5-10	29	78	90	86.7
22. Darnell Sneed, Charleston So.	Sr	6-4	27	161	186	86.6
23. Ron Bayless, Iowa St.	Sr	6-1	31	81	94	86.2
24. Mark Pope, Washington	So	6-9	27	112	130	86.2
25. Deonte Hursey, Maine	Jr	5-11	27	87	101	86.1
26. Matthew Hildebrand, Liberty	Jr	6-3	30	86	100	86.0
27. Shawn Respert, Michigan St.	So	6-3	28	119	139	85.6
28. Jonathan Pixley, Samford	Fr	6-4	26	71	83	85.5
29. Jay Goodman, Utah St.	Sr	6-0	27	117	137	85.4
30. Geoff Goss, Gonzaga	Jr	6-0	28	122	143	85.3
31. Jamie Matthews, Ball St.	Sr	5-10	34	132	155	85.2

REBOUNDING

	CL	HT	G	NO.	AVG.
1. Warren Kidd, Middle Tenn. St.	Sr	6-9	26	386	14.8
2. Jervaughn Scales, Southern-B.R.	Jr	6-6	31	393	12.7
3. Reggie Jackson, Nicholls St.	So	6-6	26	325	12.5
4. Spencer Dunkley, Delaware	Sr	6-11	30	367	12.2
5. Dan Callahan, Northeastern	Jr	6-8	28	340	12.1
6. Ervin Johnson, New Orleans	Sr	6-11	29	346	11.9
7. Carlos Rogers, Tennessee St.	Jr	6-11	29	339	11.7
8. Malik Rose, Drexel	Fr	6-7	29	330	11.4
9. Michael Smith, Providence	Jr	6-8	33	375	11.4
10. Darren Brown, Colgate	Sr	6-7	28	317	11.3
11. Keith Bullock, Manhattan	Sr	6-7	30	332	11.1
12. DeLon Turner, Florida A&M	Sr	6-5	26	287	11.0
13. Clifford Rozier, Louisville	So	6-9	31	338	10.9
14. Will Flemons, Texas Tech	Sr	6-7	30	324	10.8
15. Lee Matthews, Siena	Sr	6-7	29	313	10.8
16. Ashraf Amaya, Southern Ill.	Sr	6-8	33	354	10.7
17. Vin Baker, Hartford	Sr	6-11	28	300	10.7
18. Josh Grant, Utah	Sr	6-9	31	331	10.7
19. Sascha Hupmann, Evansville	Sr	7-1	23	244	10.6
20. Sharone Wright, Clemson	So	6-10	30	314	10.5
21. Jesse Ratliff, North Texas	Jr	6-6	26	269	10.3
22. Glen Whisby, Southern Miss.	So	6-9	27	279	10.3
23. Yinka Dare, Geo. Washington	Fr	7-1	30	308	10.3
24. Malcolm Mackey, Georgia Tech	Sr	6-11	30	306	10.2
25. Geert Hammink, Louisiana St.	Sr	7-0	32	325	10.2
26. Leonard White, Southern-B.R.	Sr	6-7	30	302	10.1
#27. Chris Webber, Michigan	So	6-9	36	362	10.1
28. Bryant Reeves, Oklahoma St.	So	7-0	29	291	10.0

	CL	HT	G	NO.	AVG.
29. Charles Outlaw, Houston	Sr	6-8	30	301	10.0
30. Johnny McDowell, Texas-Arlington	Sr	6-5	28	280	10.0
31. Mike Peplowski, Michigan St.	Sr	6-11	28	279	10.0

Entered NBA draft.

ASSISTS

	CL	HT	G	NO.	AVG.
1. Sam Crawford, New Mexico St.	Sr	5-8	34	310	9.1
2. Dedan Thomas, Nevada-Las Vegas	Jr	6-0	29	248	8.6
3. Mark Woods, Wright St.	Sr	6-1	30	253	8.4
4. Bobby Hurley, Duke	Sr	6-0	32	262	8.2
5. Chuck Evans, Mississippi St.	Sr	5-11	29	235	8.1
6. Jason Kidd, California	Fr	6-4	29	222	7.7
7. Tony Miller, Marquette	So	5-11	28	213	7.6
8. Nelson Haggerty, Baylor	So	6-0	26	189	7.3
9. Atiim Browne, Lamar	Jr	6-1	27	195	7.2
10. Marcell Capers, Arizona St.	Jr	6-2	28	200	7.1
11. Roger Breslin, Holy Cross	Sr	6-2	30	214	7.1
12. David Cain, St. John's (N.Y.)	Sr	5-11	30	213	7.1
13. Orlando Smart, San Francisco	Jr	6-0	31	220	7.1
14. Ray Kelly, UC Santa Barb.	Sr	5-11	29	205	7.1
15. Ryan Yoder, Colorado St.	Jr	5-10	29	204	7.0
16. Marc Mitchell, Wis.-Milwaukee	Sr	6-0	27	189	7.0
17. Brian Schmall, Radford	Sr	6-2	31	216	7.0
18. Jay Goodman, Utah St.	Sr	6-0	27	185	6.9
19. Maurice Houston, Tennessee Tech	Jr	5-10	26	178	6.8
20. Quincy Lewis, Wagner	Sr	6-0	30	204	6.8
21. Gerald Lewis, Southern Methodist	Sr	6-3	27	180	6.7
22. David Edwards, Texas A&M	Jr	5-9	27	177	6.6
23. Bryan Parker, Pepperdine	Jr	6-2	31	203	6.5
24. Dana Harris, Md.-Balt. County	Sr	6-0	26	168	6.5
25. Chris Whitney, Clemson	Sr	6-0	30	193	6.4
26. Tracy Webster, Wisconsin	Jr	5-11	28	179	6.4
#27. Anfernee Hardaway, Memphis St.	Jr	6-7	32	204	6.4
28. Tim Brooks, Tenn.-Chatt.	Sr	6-0	33	209	6.3
29. Kenny Harris, Va. Commonwealth	Jr	6-3	30	188	6.3
29. Jay Fazande, Fordham	Sr	6-0	30	188	6.3
31. Kevin McLinton, Maryland	Sr	6-3	28	175	6.3

Entered NBA draft.

BLOCKED SHOTS

	CL	HT	G	NO.	AVG.
1. Theo Ratliff, Wyoming	So	6-10	28	124	4.4
2. Sharone Wright, Clemson	So	6-10	30	124	4.1
3. Charles Outlaw, Houston	Sr	6-8	30	114	3.8
4. Carlos Rogers, Tennessee St.	Jr	6-11	29	93	3.2
5. Theron Wilson, Eastern Mich.	So	6-9	30	96	3.2
5. Spencer Dunkley, Delaware	Sr	6-11	30	96	3.2
7. Rodney Dobard, Florida St.	Sr	6-9	35	111	3.2
8. Constantin Popa, Miami (Fla.)	So	7-3	27	85	3.1
9. Harry Hart, Iona	Sr	6-9	26	80	3.1
10. Shelby Thurman, Western Ill.	Jr	6-9	27	83	3.1
11. Khari Jaxon, New Mexico	Sr	6-8	31	88	2.8
12. Godfrey Thompson, Jackson St.	Jr	6-7	34	96	2.8
13. Jim McIlvaine, Marquette	Jr	7-1	28	79	2.8
14. Yinka Dare, Geo. Washington	Fr	7-1	30	84	2.8
15. Acie Earl, Iowa	Sr	6-10	32	88	2.8
15. Jason Whatley, Colgate	Jr	6-10	28	77	2.8
17. Conrad McRae, Syracuse	Sr	6-10	28	76	2.7
18. Crawford Palmer, Dartmouth	Sr	6-10	26	70	2.7
19. Ervin Johnson, New Orleans	Sr	6-11	29	77	2.7
20. Vin Baker, Hartford	Sr	6-11	28	74	2.6
21. Sean Williams, Cal St. Fullerton	Sr	6-10	26	66	2.5
#22. Chris Webber, Michigan	So	6-9	36	91	2.5
23. Odell Hodge, Old Dominion	Fr	6-9	29	73	2.5
24. John James, Towson St.	Jr	6-8	26	63	2.4
25. Martin Yokum, McNeese St.	Jr	6-10	27	65	2.4
25. John Amaechi, Penn St.	So	6-10	27	65	2.4
27. Ricky Nedd, Appalachian St.	Jr	6-7	28	67	2.4
28. Chuck Weiler, Rutgers	Sr	6-9	28	65	2.3
29. Glen Whisby, Southern Miss.	So	6-9	27	61	2.3
30. Luther Wright, Seton Hall	Jr	7-2	34	76	2.2

Entered NBA draft.

STEALS

	CL	HT	G	NO.	AVG.
1. Jason Kidd, California	Fr	6-4	29	110	3.8
2. Jay Goodman, Utah St.	Sr	6-0	27	102	3.8
3. Mark Woods, Wright St.	Sr	6-1	30	109	3.6
4. Mike Bright, Bucknell	Sr	6-7	29	94	3.2

	CL	HT	G	NO.	AVG.
5. Darnell Mee, Western Ky.	Sr	6-5	32	100	3.1
6. Jeff Myers, St. Francis (N.Y.)	Fr	6-1	26	81	3.1
7. Marcus Woods, Charleston	So	6-2	27	84	3.1
8. Dana Johnson, Canisius	Jr	6-1	26	79	3.0
9. Russell Peyton, Bucknell	Sr	6-1	29	88	3.0
10. Terry Evans, Oklahoma	Sr	6-0	32	97	3.0
11. Gerald Walker, San Francisco	Fr	6-1	29	87	3.0
11. Cedric Yelding, South Ala.	Sr	6-1	28	84	3.0
11. Marcus Walton, Alcorn St.	So	6-2	26	78	3.0
11. Vince Langston, Morgan St.	Jr	5-10	24	72	3.0
15. Pat Baldwin, Northwestern	Jr	6-1	25	74	3.0
16. Hank Washington, Southeastern La.	Sr	6-4	27	79	2.9
16. Gerald Lewis, Southern Methodist	Sr	6-3	27	79	2.9
18. Pointer Williams, Tulane	So	6-0	31	90	2.9
19. Marc Mitchell, Wis.-Milwaukee	Sr	6-0	27	78	2.9
20. John Giraldo, Monmouth (N.J.)	Fr	6-0	27	77	2.9
21. Vernell Brent, Loyola (Ill.)	Jr	5-9	26	74	2.8
22. Chuck Evans, Mississippi St.	Sr	5-11	29	82	2.8
23. Robert Shepherd, Arkansas	Sr	6-1	31	87	2.8
24. Devon Chambers, Buffalo	Jr	6-3	27	75	2.8
25. Keith Johnson, Northeast La.	Sr	6-1	31	86	2.8
26. Sam Cassell, Florida St.	Sr	6-4	35	97	2.8
27. Dana Harris, Md.-Balt. County	Sr	6-0	26	72	2.8
28. Damian Johnson, Central Conn. St.	Sr	6-3	26	71	2.7
29. Angelo Hamilton, Oklahoma	Sr	6-5	30	81	2.7
30. Curt Smith, Drake	Jr	5-10	28	75	2.7

1993 DIVISION I MEN'S BASKETBALL GAME HIGHS

INDIVIDUAL HIGHS

SCORING

Pts.	Player, Team vs. Opponent	Date
49	Alphonso Ford, Mississippi Val. vs. Alabama St.	Jan. 23
49	Alphonso Ford, Mississippi Val. vs. Southern-B.R.	Feb. 8
48	Lindsey Hunter, Jackson St. vs. Kansas	Dec. 27
47	Will Flemons, Texas Tech vs. Oral Roberts	Feb. 15
46	Reggie Kemp, Youngstown St. vs. Wright St.	Feb. 6
46	Devin Boyd, Towson St. vs. Md.-Balt. County	Feb. 27
45	Bill Edwards, Wright St. vs. Morehead St.	Dec. 8
44	Parrish Casebier, Evansville vs. Illinois St.	Dec. 12
44	Orlando Lightfoot, Idaho vs. Boise St.	Feb. 6
44	Demetrius Dudley, Hofstra vs. Central Conn. St.	Feb. 9
44	J. R. Rider, Nevada-Las Vegas vs. Nevada	Feb. 25

THREE-POINT FIELD GOALS

3FG	Player, Team vs. Opponent	Date
11	Doug Day, Radford vs. Morgan St.	Dec. 9
11	Lindsey Hunter, Jackson St. vs. Kansas	Dec. 27
11	Keith Veney, Lamar vs. Prairie View	Feb. 3
11	Keith Veney, Lamar vs. Ark.-Little Rock	Feb. 11
10	Theon Dotson, Texas Southern vs. Tex.-San Antonio	Dec. 5
10	Stevin Smith, Arizona St. vs. Oregon	Jan. 30
10	Bernard Haslett, Southern Miss. vs. Memphis St.	Feb. 10
9	Kenny McMillan, Northwestern (La.) vs. Tex.-San Antonio	Feb. 20
9	Mike Bright, Bucknell vs. Loyola (Md.)	Feb. 24
9	Bennie Seltzer, Washington St. vs. Stanford	Feb. 27
9	Quincy Dockins, Lamar vs. Louisiana Tech	Feb. 28

FREE THROWS

FT	Player, Team vs. Opponent	Date
26	Greg Graham, Indiana vs. Purdue	Feb. 21
22	Devin Boyd, Towson St. vs. Md.-Balt. County	Feb. 27
20	Tanoka Beard, Boise St. vs. George Mason	Dec. 29
19	Demetrius Dudley, Hofstra vs. Central Conn. St.	Feb. 9
19	Eddie Benton, Vermont vs. New Hampshire	Feb. 18
18	Darnell Sneed, Charleston So. vs. Md.-Balt. County	Jan. 23
17	10 tied.	

REBOUNDS

Reb.	Player, Team vs. Opponent	Date
27	Ervin Johnson, New Orleans vs. Lamar	Feb. 18
26	Malik Rose, Drexel vs. Vermont	Jan. 29
25	Malik Rose, Drexel vs. Vermont	Feb. 11
25	Spencer Dunkley, Delaware vs. Md.-Balt. County	Jan. 6
24	Todd Cauthorn, William & Mary vs. Citadel	Dec. 5
24	Ervin Johnson, New Orleans vs. Jacksonville	Jan. 2
24	Yinka Dare, Geo. Washington vs. St. Bonaventure	Feb. 6
23	Malik Rose, Drexel vs. St. Francis (Pa.)	Dec. 12
23	James White, Morgan St. vs. Bethune-Cookman	Jan. 23
23	Ervin Johnson, New Orleans vs. Tex.-Pan American	Feb. 11

ASSISTS

Ast.	Player, Team vs. Opponent	Date
20	Dana Harris, Md.-Balt. County vs. St. Mary's (Md.)	Dec. 12
20	Sam Crawford, New Mexico St. vs. Sam Houston St.	Dec. 21
19	Nelson Haggerty, Baylor vs. Oral Roberts	Feb. 27
18	B. J. Tyler, Texas vs. Oral Roberts	Dec. 1
17	Gary Robb, Tenn.-Chatt. vs. Southern-B.R.	Dec. 29
17	Bryan Parker, Pepperdine vs. Oral Roberts	Jan. 9
17	Sam Crawford, New Mexico St. vs. San Jose St.	Jan. 14
17	Gerald Lewis, Southern Methodist vs. Texas	Mar. 6
16	10 tied.	

BLOCKED SHOTS

Blk.	Player, Team vs. Opponent	Date
13	Jim McIlvaine, Marquette vs. Northeastern Ill.	Dec. 9
12	Ervin Johnson, New Orleans vs. Texas A&M	Dec. 29
10	Sharone Wright, Clemson vs. N.C.-Greensboro	Dec. 12
10	Sharone Wright, Clemson vs. Maryland	Jan. 27
10	Charles Outlaw, Hosuton vs. Texas A&M	Feb. 17
10	Theo Ratliff, Wyoming vs. San Diego St.	Feb. 25
9	Shelby Thurmond, Western Ill. vs. Chicago St.	Dec. 9
9	Theo Ratliff, Wyoming vs. Marshall	Dec. 21
9	Antoine Teague, Murray St. vs. Pikeville	Jan. 2
9	Theo Ratliff, Wyoming vs. UTEP	Feb. 11
9	Andre Riddick, Kentucky vs. Louisiana St.	Mar. 14

STEALS

St.	Player, Team vs. Opponent	Date
12	Terry Evans, Oklahoma vs. Florida A&M	Jan. 27
11	Ron Arnold, St. Francis (N.Y.) vs. Mt. St. Mary's (Md.)	Feb. 4
10	Michael Finley, Wisconsin vs. Purdue	Feb. 13
9	Robert Shepherd, Arkansas vs. Arizona	Dec. 6
9	Darius Minns, Southern-B.R. vs. Baptist Christian	Dec. 14
9	Cam Johnson, Northern Iowa vs. St. Bonaventure	Dec. 19
9	Hank Washington, Southeastern La. vs. Tex.-Pan American	Dec. 19
9	Angelo Hamilton, Oklahoma vs. Brigham Young	Dec. 21
9	Acie Earl, Iowa vs. Texas Southern	Dec. 28
9	Darnell Mee, Western Ky. vs. Jacksonville	Feb. 11
9	Jay Goodman, Utah St. vs. San Jose St.	Feb. 20
9	Darnell Mee, Western Ky. vs. Louisiana Tech	Feb. 25
9	Corey Taylor, Iona vs. Loyola (Md.)	Feb. 27

TEAM HIGHS

SCORING

Pts.	Team vs. Opponent	Date
156	Southern-B.R. vs. Baptist Christian	Dec. 14
146	Oklahoma vs. Florida A&M	Jan. 27
143	Lamar vs. Prairie View	Feb. 3
140	Kansas vs. Oral Roberts	Jan. 14
138	Lamar vs. Prairie View	Dec. 28
136	Texas vs. Oral Roberts	Dec. 1
136	Charleston So. vs. Allen	Dec. 11
136	Wright St. vs. Chicago St.	Jan. 6
132	Rutgers vs. Keene St.	Dec. 7
130	Washington vs. Cal St. Chico	Dec. 1

FIELD-GOAL PERCENTAGE

Pct.		Team vs. Opponent	Date
77.8	(34-45)	Samford vs. Loyola (La.)	Dec. 12
75.4	(43-57)	North Caro. vs. Old Dominion	Dec. 1
73.7	(28-38)	Oklahoma St. vs. Tulsa	Dec. 12
71.4	(40-56)	Rider vs. St. Francis (N.Y.)	Jan. 5
70.0	(35-50)	Louisville vs. Tulane	Feb. 27
69.6	(32-46)	Southern Utah vs. Cal St. Northridge	Jan. 30
69.5	(41-59)	Duke vs. Canisius	Dec. 1
69.1	(38-55)	Brigham Young vs. Arizona St.	Dec. 1
68.6	(24-35)	Charleston vs. Charleston So.	Jan. 14
68.2	(30-44)	Texas Tech vs. Texas Christian	Feb. 27

THREE-POINT FIELD GOALS

3FG	Team vs. Opponent	Date
*23	Lamar vs. Louisiana Tech	Feb. 28
20	Lamar vs. Prairie View	Feb. 3
17	Northwestern (La.) vs. Tex.-San Antonio	Jan. 21
17	Old Dominion vs. James Madison	Feb. 17
17	Morehead St. vs. Tennessee Tech	Feb. 22
16	Eight tied.	

*Record.

1993 DIVISION I MEN'S TEAM LEADERS

SCORING OFFENSE

	G	W-L	PTS.	AVG.
1. Southern-B.R.	31	21-10	3011	97.1
2. Northwestern (La.)	26	13-13	2357	90.7
3. Nevada-Las Vegas	29	21-8	2592	89.4
4. Wright St.	30	20-10	2674	89.1
5. Oklahoma	32	20-12	2850	89.1
6. Lamar	27	15-12	2384	88.3
7. Alabama St.	27	14-13	2378	88.1
8. Kentucky	34	30-4	2975	87.5
9. Northeast La.	31	26-5	2702	87.2
10. Tennessee Tech	28	15-13	2440	87.1
11. Baylor	27	16-11	2352	87.1
12. Arkansas	31	22-9	2695	86.9
13. Indiana	35	31-4	3028	86.5
14. Duke	32	24-8	2766	86.4
15. Florida St.	35	25-10	3020	86.3
16. North Caro.	38	34-4	3272	86.1
17. Tenn.-Chatt.	33	26-7	2820	85.5
18. Holy Cross	30	23-7	2563	85.4
19. Western Ky.	32	26-6	2723	85.1
20. Jackson St.	34	25-9	2884	84.8
21. Murray St.	30	18-12	2536	84.5
22. Arizona St.	28	18-10	2366	84.5
23. Kansas	36	29-7	3037	84.4
24. Old Dominion	29	21-8	2445	84.3
25. Centenary	27	9-18	2272	84.1
26. Texas-Arlington	28	16-12	2354	84.1
27. Winthrop	30	14-16	2508	83.6
28. Arizona	28	24-4	2340	83.6
29. Grambling	27	13-14	2254	83.5
30. East Tenn. St.	29	19-10	2413	83.2

SCORING DEFENSE

	G	W-L	PTS.	AVG.
1. Princeton	26	15-11	1421	54.7
2. Yale	26	10-16	1444	55.5
3. Miami (Ohio)	31	22-9	1775	57.3
4. Cincinnati	32	27-5	1871	58.5
5. Southwest Mo. St.	31	20-11	1813	58.5
6. Charleston	27	19-8	1631	60.4
7. Marquette	28	20-8	1692	60.4
8. New Orleans	30	26-4	1835	61.2
9. Bradley	27	11-16	1656	61.3
10. Montana	28	17-11	1723	61.5
11. Pennsylvania	27	22-5	1686	62.4
12. Georgetown	33	20-13	2062	62.5
13. UC Santa Barb.	29	18-11	1830	63.1
14. Wis.-Green Bay	27	13-14	1705	63.1
15. New Mexico	31	24-7	1960	63.2
16. Illinois St.	29	19-10	1839	63.4
17. Pacific (Cal.)	27	16-11	1719	63.7
18. Massachusetts	31	24-7	1986	64.1
19. Ball St.	34	26-8	2185	64.3
20. Ala.-Birmingham	35	21-14	2254	64.4
21. Pepperdine	31	23-8	1998	64.5
22. Providence	33	20-13	2137	64.8
23. Xavier (Ohio)	30	24-6	1954	65.1
24. Washington St.	27	15-12	1762	65.3
25. Florida Int'l	30	20-10	1959	65.3
26. Evansville	30	23-7	1960	65.3
27. Iowa	32	23-9	2093	65.4
28. Gonzaga	28	19-9	1833	65.5
29. Arkansas St.	28	16-12	1834	65.5
30. Akron	26	8-18	1709	65.7

SCORING MARGIN

	OFF.	DEF.	MAR.
1. North Caro.	86.1	68.3	17.8
2. Kentucky	87.5	69.8	17.7
3. Cincinnati	74.5	58.5	16.0
4. Duke	86.4	71.2	15.2
5. Indiana	86.5	71.6	14.9
6. Kansas	84.4	69.7	14.6
7. Western Ky.	85.1	71.7	13.4
8. Marquette	73.8	60.4	13.4
9. Tenn.-Chatt.	85.5	72.3	13.2
10. Vanderbilt	83.0	69.9	13.1
11. Northeast La.	87.2	74.2	13.0
12. Iowa	78.3	65.4	12.9
13. Arizona	83.6	71.4	12.2
14. Southern-B.R.	97.1	85.5	11.6
15. Iowa St.	81.3	69.6	11.6
16. Utah	77.1	65.8	11.4
17. New Orleans	72.5	61.2	11.3

	OFF.	DEF.	MAR.
18. Seton Hall	77.9	66.9	10.9
19. Wright St.	89.1	78.4	10.7
20. Michigan	81.9	71.8	10.1
21. Oklahoma	89.1	79.0	10.1
22. Pennsylvania	72.2	62.4	9.8
23. Wis.-Milwaukee	79.7	70.0	9.7
24. Evansville	75.0	65.3	9.7
25. Arkansas	86.9	77.5	9.4
26. Bucknell	81.0	71.8	9.3
27. Gonzaga	74.7	65.5	9.3
28. Xavier (Ohio)	74.3	65.1	9.2
29. James Madison	80.4	71.3	9.1
30. Brigham Young	81.0	71.9	9.1
31. Massachusetts	73.0	64.1	8.9

WON-LOST PERCENTAGE

	W-L	PCT.
1. North Caro.	34-4	.895
2. Indiana	31-4	.886
3. Kentucky	30-4	.882
4. New Orleans	26-4	.867
5. Michigan	31-5	.861
6. Arizona	24-4	.857
7. Wis.-Milwaukee	23-4	.852
8. Cincinnati	27-5	.844
9. Northeast La.	26-5	.839
10. Vanderbilt	28-6	.824
11. Pennsylvania	22-5	.815
12. Western Ky.	26-6	.813
13. Kansas	29-7	.806
14. Seton Hall	28-7	.800
14. Xavier (Ohio)	24-6	.800
16. Bucknell	23-6	.793
17. Tenn.-Chatt.	26-7	.788
18. Cleveland St.	22-6	.786
19. Massachusetts	24-7	.774
19. New Mexico	24-7	.774
19. Utah	24-7	.774
22. Evansville	23-7	.767
22. Holy Cross	23-7	.767
22. Manhattan	23-7	.767
22. Niagara	23-7	.767
26. Ball St.	26-8	.765
26. New Mexico St.	26-8	.765
28. Drexel	22-7	.759
29. Duke	24-8	.750
29. Idaho	24-8	.750
31. Pepperdine	23-8	.742

FIELD-GOAL PERCENTAGE

	FG	FGA	PCT.
1. Indiana	1076	2062	52.2
2. Northeast La.	1015	1946	52.2
3. James Madison	848	1634	51.9
4. Wright St.	987	1912	51.6
5. Kansas	1109	2154	51.5
6. Oklahoma St.	807	1571	51.4
7. Duke	989	1950	50.7
8. Michigan St.	806	1591	50.7
9. North Caro.	1219	2407	50.6
10. Gonzaga	724	1435	50.5
11. UCLA	985	1960	50.3
12. Auburn	815	1627	50.1
13. Xavier (Ohio)	841	1679	50.1
14. Vanderbilt	986	1971	50.0
15. Michigan	1131	2269	49.8
16. Louisville	917	1841	49.8
17. Brigham Young	948	1905	49.8
18. Southern Utah	726	1459	49.8
19. Nevada-Las Vegas	909	1833	49.6
20. Florida St.	1145	2315	49.5
21. Georgia Tech	905	1833	49.4
22. Pepperdine	820	1661	49.4
23. Utah	863	1752	49.3
24. Niagara	854	1736	49.2
25. Texas-Arlington	867	1765	49.1
26. Wake Forest	834	1699	49.1
27. Columbia	647	1320	49.0
28. N.C.-Wilmington	814	1663	48.9
29. Weber St.	799	1634	48.9
30. Iowa St.	946	1935	48.9

FIELD-GOAL PERCENTAGE DEFENSE

	FG	FGA	PCT.
1. Marquette	634	1613	39.3
2. Geo. Washington	708	1794	39.5
3. Arizona	710	1776	40.0
4. Utah	737	1831	40.3
5. New Orleans	680	1689	40.3
6. Michigan St.	705	1748	40.3
7. Montana	595	1472	40.4
8. Missouri	759	1877	40.4
9. Seton Hall	853	2107	40.5
10. Virginia	789	1947	40.5
11. Wyoming	727	1794	40.5
12. Pennsylvania	608	1493	40.7
13. Georgetown	729	1790	40.7
14. Cincinnati	655	1604	40.8
15. Evansville	701	1708	41.0
16. Temple	785	1911	41.1
17. Brigham Young	827	2013	41.1
18. Iowa	795	1930	41.2
19. Jackson St.	948	2298	41.3
20. North Caro.	978	2370	41.3
21. Manhattan	700	1693	41.3
22. Michigan	943	2275	41.5
23. Oklahoma St.	741	1783	41.6
24. Tennessee St.	762	1833	41.6
25. Dartmouth	633	1522	41.6
26. New Mexico	755	1812	41.7
27. Delaware	786	1882	41.8
28. Massachusetts	731	1747	41.8
29. West Va.	693	1656	41.8
30. Montana St.	664	1585	41.9

THREE-POINT FIELD GOALS MADE PER GAME

	G	NO.	AVG.
1. Lamar	27	271	10.0
2. Kentucky	34	340	10.0
3. Arizona St.	28	263	9.4
4. N.C.-Asheville	27	235	8.7
5. Southern Cal	30	259	8.6
6. Campbell	27	228	8.4
7. Southern-B.R.	31	258	8.3
8. Vermont	27	222	8.2
9. Tennessee Tech	28	226	8.1
10. Dayton	30	240	8.0
10. Nevada-Las Vegas	29	232	8.0
12. Baylor	27	215	8.0
13. Samford	27	214	7.9
14. Centenary	27	213	7.9
14. Morehead St.	27	213	7.9
16. La Salle	27	212	7.9
17. Princeton	26	204	7.8
18. Wisconsin	28	219	7.8
19. Northwestern (La.)	26	203	7.8
20. Southern Miss.	27	209	7.7
21. Vanderbilt	34	262	7.7
22. New Mexico	31	238	7.7
23. Valparaiso	28	214	7.6
24. Wis.-Milwaukee	27	206	7.6
25. North Texas	26	192	7.4
26. Tulsa	29	213	7.3
27. Sam Houston St.	25	183	7.3
28. East Tenn. St.	29	212	7.3
29. Va. Commonwealth	30	219	7.3
30. Pennsylvania	27	197	7.3

THREE-POINT FIELD-GOAL PERCENTAGE

(Min. 3.0 3FG Made Per Game)	G	FG	FGA	PCT.
1. Valparaiso	28	214	500	42.8
2. Princeton	26	204	479	42.6
3. Indiana	35	197	464	42.5
4. Kent	27	162	384	42.2
5. Miami (Ohio)	31	218	522	41.8
6. Louisville	31	188	452	41.6
7. Vanderbilt	34	262	636	41.2
8. Old Dominion	29	184	447	41.2
9. Wis.-Green Bay	27	151	367	41.1
10. Utah	31	189	461	41.0

(Min. 3.0 3FG Made Per Game)	G	FG	FGA	PCT.
11. Wagner	30	179	438	40.9
12. Kansas	36	215	527	40.8
13. Indiana St.	28	155	380	40.8
14. N.C.-Wilmington	28	166	409	40.6
15. Drexel	29	142	350	40.6
16. Md.-Balt. County	28	161	397	40.6
17. Samford	27	214	528	40.5
18. Hofstra	27	134	331	40.5
19. Coastal Caro.	32	195	482	40.5
20. Gonzaga	28	127	314	40.4
21. Washington St.	27	195	483	40.4
22. Wake Forest	30	181	450	40.2
23. Pennsylvania	27	197	491	40.1
24. Xavier (Ohio)	30	138	345	40.0
25. Marquette	28	131	328	39.9
26. Toledo	28	165	415	39.8
27. Duke	32	184	463	39.7
28. James Madison	30	162	408	39.7
29. Richmond	27	148	373	39.7
30. Boston College	31	180	454	39.6

FREE-THROW PERCENTAGE

	FT	FTA	PCT.
1. Utah	476	602	79.1
2. Charleston So.	408	526	77.6
3. Valparaiso	412	532	77.4
4. Indiana St.	445	580	76.7
5. Brigham Young	697	909	76.7
6. Iowa St.	465	613	75.9
7. Seton Hall	683	905	75.5
8. Tex.-Pan American	284	377	75.3
9. Creighton	409	543	75.3
10. Cornell	416	553	75.2
11. Old Dominion	565	752	75.1
12. Tenn.-Chatt.	595	792	75.1
13. Evansville	549	735	74.7
14. Boston College	443	594	74.6
15. Marquette	476	641	74.3
16. Samford	473	638	74.1
17. Niagara	526	712	73.9
18. Idaho St.	457	620	73.7
19. Furman	451	612	73.7
20. Tennessee	467	634	73.7
21. Holy Cross	629	854	73.7
22. Tenn.-Martin	431	586	73.5
23. Tennessee Tech	514	699	73.5
24. Monmouth (N.J.)	364	496	73.4
25. Vermont	439	600	73.2
26. Drake	421	576	73.1
27. Vanderbilt	588	807	72.9
28. Washington	386	530	72.8
29. St. Louis	419	576	72.7
30. James Madison	555	763	72.7

REBOUND MARGIN

	OFF.	DEF.	MAR.
1. Iowa	42.8	31.7	11.1
2. Idaho	39.6	29.3	10.3
3. Arizona	43.1	34.2	9.0
4. North Caro.	41.1	32.2	8.9
5. Oklahoma St.	38.8	30.8	8.0
6. Michigan	41.5	33.6	7.8
7. Providence	39.9	32.6	7.3
8. Southwest Tex. St.	39.9	32.7	7.2
9. Massachusetts	39.7	32.8	7.0
10. Southern Ill.	39.7	32.8	6.8
11. Brigham Young	38.9	32.3	6.6
12. Michigan St.	39.1	32.6	6.5
13. Marquette	36.9	30.5	6.4
14. Wright St.	37.9	31.6	6.3
15. Delaware	42.0	35.7	6.3
16. Northeastern	41.3	35.1	6.2
17. Pepperdine	36.6	30.5	6.1
18. N.C.-Charlotte	41.9	35.8	6.1
19. Kentucky	40.1	34.1	6.0
20. Georgetown	38.8	33.1	5.8
21. New Orleans	37.9	32.1	5.7
22. Rice	38.9	33.3	5.6
23. Kansas St.	37.2	32.1	5.2
24. UC Irvine	38.2	33.0	5.1
25. Southeastern La.	42.0	36.9	5.1
26. South Ala.	40.8	35.8	5.0
27. Navy	36.3	31.4	4.9
28. Manhattan	37.9	33.0	4.8
29. Wake Forest	36.8	32.0	4.8
30. Old Dominion	38.9	34.1	4.8

1993 TOP RETURNEES—CAREER TOTALS

DIVISION I

MOST POINTS

Seniors	Ht.	Yrs.	G	FG	3FG	FT	Pts.	Avg.
1. Tony Dumas, Mo.-Kansas City	6-5	3	83	615	103	373	1706	20.6
2. Bernard Blunt, St. Joseph's (Pa.)	6-3	3	87	567	127	375	1636	18.8
3. Jeff Webster, Oklahoma	6-8	3	97	645	3	308	1601	16.5
4. Deon Thomas, Illinois	6-9	3	90	959	0	389	1581	17.6
5. Jesse Ratliff, North Texas	6-6	3	85	561	83	355	1560	18.4
6. Wesley Person, Auburn	6-6	3	80	555	169	166	1445	18.1
7. Bill Curley, Boston College	6-9	3	92	509	0	403	1421	15.4
8. Myron Walker, Robert Morris	6-4	3	77	52	278	416	1402	18.2
9. Kenny Williams, Ill.-Chicago	5-10	3	92	516	148	221	1401	15.2
10. Jamaine Williams, North Caro. A&T	6-8	3	81	556	63	224	1399	17.3
Juniors								
1. Jalen Rose, Michigan	6-8	2	70	409	69	265	1152	16.5
2. Terrence Rencher, Texas	6-3	2	60	408	74	254	1144	19.1
3. Lawrence Moten, Syracuse	6-5	2	61	384	89	244	1101	18.0
4. Bob Sura, Florida St.	6-5	2	65	365	112	214	1056	16.2
5. Shawn Respert, Michigan St.	6-3	2	58	365	120	187	1037	17.9
6. Michael Finley, Wisconsin	6-7	2	59	353	89	206	1001	17.0

HIGHEST FIELD-GOAL PERCENTAGE

Seniors (Min. 300 Made)	Ht.	Yrs.	G	FG	FGA	FG%
1. Ricky Nedd, Appalachian St.	6-7	3	86	313	450	69.6
2. Brian Grant, Xavier (Ohio)	6-8	3	88	475	780	60.9
3. Richard Scott, Kansas	6-7	3	103	378	622	60.8
4. Eric Montross, North Caro.	7-0	3	104	443	743	59.6
5. Aaron Swinson, Auburn	6-5	2	54	340	572	59.4
6. Dana Jones, Pepperdine	6-6	3	91	483	813	59.4
7. Carlos Rogers, Tennessee St.	6-11	2	48	303	511	59.3
8. Deon Thomas, Illinois	6-9	3	90	596	1009	59.1
9. Joe Griffin, LIU-Brooklyn	6-5	3	81	428	748	57.2
10. Jeff Brown, Gonzaga	6-9	3	65	386	675	57.2

Juniors (Min. 250 Made)

	Ht.	Yrs.	G	FG	FGA	FG%
1. Bryant Reeves, Oklahoma St.	7-0	2	65	321	551	58.3
2. Reggie Jackson, Nicholls St.	6-6	2	54	368	636	57.9
3. Clifford Rozier, Louisville	6-9	2	65	256	478	53.6
4. Sharone Wright, Clemson	6-10	2	58	315	589	53.5
5. Miladin Mutavdzic, Wagner	6-10	2	58	359	705	50.9

MOST THREE-POINT FIELD GOALS MADE

Seniors

	Ht.	Yrs.	G	3FG	Avg.
1. Stevin Smith, Arizona St.	6-2	3	87	227	2.61
2. Bernard Haslett, Southern Miss.	6-3	3	83	204	2.46
3. Phil Dixon, Utah	6-5	4	106	182	1.72
4. Skip Saunders, Md.-Balt. County	6-0	3	86	178	2.07
5. Wesley Person, Auburn	6-6	3	80	169	2.11
5. Robb Logterman, Marquette	6-3	3	86	169	1.97

Juniors

	Ht.	Yrs.	G	3FG	Avg.
1. Randolph Childress, Wake Forest	6-2	2	59	160	2.71
2. Tim Roberts, Southern-B.R.	6-5	2	59	128	2.17
3. Matt Maloney, Pennsylvania	6-3	2	57	120	2.11
4. Shawn Respert, Michigan St.	6-3	2	58	120	2.07
5. Johnny Murdock, Southwest Mo. St.	6-1	2	62	120	1.94

HIGHEST THREE-POINT FIELD-GOAL PERCENTAGE

Seniors (Min. 120 Made)

	Ht.	Yrs.	G	3FG	3FGA	3FG%
1. Roosevelt Moore, Sam Houston St.	5-10	3	53	139	294	47.3
2. Curtis Shelton, Southeast Mo. St.	5-9	3	80	129	290	44.5
3. Travis Ford, Kentucky	5-9	3	97	151	341	44.3
4. Wesley Person, Auburn	6-6	3	80	169	384	44.0
5. Bobby Hopson, Wagner	5-10	3	69	129	298	43.3

Juniors (Min. 90 Made)

	Ht.	Yrs.	G	3FG	3FGA	3FG%
1. Lance Barker, Valparaiso	6-1	2	53	91	186	48.9
2. Shawn Respert, Michigan St.	6-3	2	58	120	272	44.1
3. Matt Maloney, Pennsylvania	6-3	2	57	120	274	43.8
4. Randolph Childress, Wake Forest	6-2	2	59	160	383	41.8
5. Johnny Murdock, Southwest Mo. St.	6-1	2	62	120	299	40.1

HIGHEST FREE-THROW PERCENTAGE

Seniors (Min. 180 Made)

	Ht.	Yrs.	G	FT	FTA	3FT%
1. Travis Ford, Kentucky	5-9	3	97	196	225	87.1
2. Matt Hildebrand, Liberty	6-2	3	87	249	290	85.9
3. Don Burgess, Radford	6-6	3	89	226	265	85.3
4. Doremus Bennerman, Siena	5-11	3	92	331	388	85.3
5. Billy McCaffrey, Vanderbilt	6-4	3	110	287	342	83.9
6. Deonte Hursey, Maine	5-11	3	88	216	265	81.5
7. Andre Chevalier, Cal St. Northridge	5-11	3	83	259	318	81.4
8. Damon Key, Marquette	6-8	3	84	263	324	81.2
9. Michael Allen, Southwestern La.	6-0	2	61	195	244	79.9
10. Jason Zimmerman, Davidson	6-2	3	85	198	248	79.8

Juniors (Min. 120 Made)

	Ht.	Yrs.	G	FT	FTA	3FT%
1. Shawn Respert, Michigan St.	6-3	2	58	187	217	86.2
2. Mark Pope, Washington	6-9	2	56	186	222	83.8
3. Randolph Childress, Wake Forest	6-2	2	59	223	281	79.4

MOST REBOUNDS

Seniors

	Ht.	Yrs.	G	Reb.	Avg.
1. Brian Grant, Xavier (Ohio)	6-8	3	88	793	9.0
2. Dana Jones, Pepperdine	6-6	3	91	740	8.1
3. Jervaughn Scales, Southern-B.R.	6-6	2	61	715	11.7
4. Kendrick Warren, Va. Commonwealth	6-8	3	79	713	9.0
5. Joe Spinks, Campbell	6-7	3	83	709	8.5
6. Michael Smith, Providence	6-8	2	64	694	10.8
7. Bill Curley, Boston College	6-9	3	92	691	7.5
8. Jesse Ratliff, North Texas	6-6	3	85	678	8.0
9. Derrick Alston, Duquesne	6-11	3	84	661	7.9
10. Eric Montross, North Caro.	7-0	3	104	656	6.3

Juniors

	Ht.	Yrs.	G	Reb.	Avg.
1. Reggie Jackson, Nicholls St.	6-6	2	54	635	11.8
2. Miladin Mutavdzic, Wagner	6-10	2	58	556	9.6
3. Sharone Wright, Clemson	6-10	2	58	541	9.3
4. Juwan Howard, Michigan	6-9	2	70	479	6.8
5. Bryant Reeves, Oklahoma St.	7-0	2	65	473	7.3

MOST ASSISTS

Seniors

	Ht.	Yrs.	G	Ast.	Avg.
1. Orlando Smart, San Francisco	6-0	3	89	698	7.8
2. Atiim Brown, Lamar	6-1	3	86	530	6.2
3. David Edwards, Texas A&M	5-9	3	86	487	5.7
4. Derrick Phelps, North Caro.	6-4	3	99	461	4.7
5. Sinua Phillips, Central Fla.	6-1	3	81	439	5.4

Juniors

	Ht.	Yrs.	G	Ast.	Avg.
1. Tony Miller, Marquette	6-0	2	57	434	7.6
2. Marcus Walton, Alcorn St.	6-2	2	55	305	5.5
3. Jeremy Livingston, Jacksonville	6-0	2	53	281	5.3

MOST BLOCKED SHOTS

Seniors	Ht.	Yrs.	G	Blk.	Avg.
1. Jim McIlvaine, Marquette	7-1	3	85	257	3.0
2. Godfrey Thompson, Jackson St.	6-7	3	91	203	2.2
3. Chuck Weiler, Rutgers	6-9	3	81	175	2.2
4. John James, Towson St.	6-8	3	85	162	1.9
5. Jason Whatley, Colgate	6-10	3	77	143	1.9
Juniors					
1. Sharone Wright, Clemson	6-10	2	58	187	3.2
2. Theo Ratliff, Wyoming	6-10	2	55	165	3.0
3. Constantin Popa, Miami (Fla.)	7-3	2	59	149	2.5

MOST STEALS

Seniors	Ht.	Yrs.	G	St.	Avg.
1. Pat Baldwin, Northwestern	6-1	3	67	213	3.2
2. Orlando Smart, San Francisco	6-0	3	89	213	2.4
3. Rap Curry, St. Joseph's (Pa.)	6-3	3	79	203	2.6
4. Charlie Ward, Florida St.	6-1	3	75	194	2.6
5. David Edwards, Texas A&M	5-9	3	86	190	2.2
Juniors					
1. Clarence Ceasar, Louisiana St.	6-7	2	63	164	2.6
2. Pointer Williams, Tulane	6-0	2	60	146	2.4
3. Marcus Walton, Alcorn St.	6-2	2	55	138	2.5

1993 DIVISION II MEN'S INDIVIDUAL LEADERS

SCORING

	CL	G	TFG	3FG	FT	PTS.	AVG.
1. Darrin Robinson, Sacred Heart	Sr	26	313	75	130	831	32.0
2. Alex Wright, Central Okla.	Sr	28	293	97	165	848	30.3
3. Ray Gutierrez, Calif. (Pa.)	Sr	29	235	142	165	777	26.8
4. David Eaker, Fort Valley St.	Jr	27	257	23	176	713	26.4
5. Kwame Morton, Clarion	Jr	26	220	107	108	655	25.2
6. Terrance Jordan, Livingstone	Sr	24	214	0	166	594	24.8
7. Ed Wheeler, Angelo St.	Jr	26	263	1	111	638	24.5
8. Jason Williams, New Haven	Sr	27	237	66	115	655	24.3
9. Terry McCord, Troy St.	Sr	32	274	71	156	775	24.2
10. Chad Briscoe, Grand Canyon	Sr	31	278	96	95	747	24.1
11. Derrick Myers, Pitt.-Johnstown	Sr	20	183	32	83	481	24.0
12. DeCarlo Deveaux, Tampa	Jr	30	243	63	166	715	23.8
13. Michael Williams, Saginaw Valley	Jr	25	215	24	135	589	23.6
14. Corey Ward, Lake Superior St.	Jr	22	169	69	102	509	23.1
15. Raul Varela, Colorado Mines	Fr	27	213	32	166	624	23.1
16. Columbus Parker, Johnson Smith	Sr	26	173	84	169	599	23.0
17. Nate Higgs, Elizabeth City St.	Jr	28	224	19	167	634	22.6
18. Bill Jolly, Missouri-Rolla	Sr	27	162	88	193	605	22.4
19. Jeff Campbell, Shaw	Jr	27	195	77	136	603	22.3
20. Shon Crosby, Lock Haven	Jr	26	194	21	164	573	22.0
21. Rashe Reviere, Mercyhurst	Jr	27	228	38	100	594	22.0
22. Tim Fitzpatrick, Fort Lewis	Sr	27	185	66	153	589	21.8
23. Bill Hanford, Lander	Jr	24	224	0	75	523	21.8
24. Jamie Anderson, Keene St.	So	25	188	70	94	540	21.6
24. Mike Grove, New Haven	Sr	25	195	86	64	540	21.6
26. Ken Francis, Molloy	Jr	27	208	57	106	579	21.4
27. Corey Warner, Lincoln (Mo.)	Jr	26	208	16	124	556	21.4
28. Ali Travis, Catawba	Sr	25	178	52	125	533	21.3
29. David Norwood, Morehouse	Sr	26	215	17	98	545	21.0
30. John Adams, Lewis	Sr	26	210	0	124	544	20.9
31. Winston Jones, Bridgeport	Jr	25	206	13	98	523	20.9
32. Sean Gibson, IU/PU-Ft. Wayne	Sr	29	194	10	208	606	20.9
33. Derek Stewart, Augusta	Sr	28	215	15	140	585	20.9
34. Paul Beaty, Miles	Sr	22	163	60	73	459	20.9
35. Chuck Gholston, Bowie St.	Sr	27	185	62	131	563	20.9
36. Lawrence Williams, San Fran St.	So	26	219	0	104	542	20.8
37. Joey Haythorn, Southern Colo.	Sr	28	209	89	76	583	20.8
38. Lamont Jones, Bridgeport	So	29	216	77	94	603	20.8
39. Frank MacIntosh, Wis.-Parkside	Fr	26	183	89	85	540	20.8
40. Samuel Fatoki, Dist. Columbia	Sr	24	180	55	82	497	20.7
41. Chris Bowles, Southern Ind.	Sr	29	242	7	106	597	20.6
42. Teaser Sweeney, Bemidji St.	Sr	26	192	12	137	533	20.5
43. Brent Wichlacz, Grand Valley St.	Sr	26	191	52	97	531	20.4
43. Pete Hoffman, Michigan Tech	Sr	26	176	69	110	531	20.4
45. Todd Kenyon, Colorado Mines	So	26	183	2	161	529	20.3
46. Tim Kissman, Hillsdale	Jr	28	224	37	84	569	20.3
47. DeVelle Walker, Cal St. San B'dino	Sr	25	181	53	93	508	20.3
48. Darian Farmer, Dowling	Jr	28	234	0	100	568	20.3
49. Cederic Fuller, Kentucky St.	Sr	27	183	0	180	546	20.2
50. Chris Williams, Troy St.	Jr	32	268	2	109	647	20.2
51. Earl Elliotte, Springfield	Sr	26	195	18	117	525	20.2
52. James Hector, American Int'l	Jr	28	227	0	109	563	20.1

	CL	G	TFG	3FG	FT	PTS.	AVG.
53. Albert Gates, Henderson St.	Jr	29	243	0	96	582	20.1
54. Shawn Walker, Elizabeth City St.	Jr	28	175	105	106	561	20.0
55. Lance Reinhard, West Ga.	Sr	26	152	100	115	519	20.0
56. Cornelius Muller, Elon	Sr	26	201	29	87	518	19.9
57. Scott Guldseth, North Dak.	Sr	31	213	37	153	616	19.9
58. Antwan Stallworth, SIU-Edwardsville	Sr	25	209	0	78	496	19.8
59. Jeff Gore, St. Rose	Sr	31	198	54	165	615	19.8
60. Rich Aigner, Lewis	Jr	27	184	55	111	534	19.8
61. Tom Eller, Oakland	Jr	26	183	35	113	514	19.8
62. Kenny Brown, Millersville	Sr	30	200	98	95	593	19.8
62. Jon Dunmeyer, Millersville	Sr	30	213	0	167	593	19.8
64. Michael Nowell, Clark Atlanta	Sr	25	192	1	109	494	19.8
65. Leon Morgan, Pembroke St.	Sr	25	162	65	104	493	19.7
66. Trevor Crowe, Southwest Baptist	Sr	28	204	50	91	549	19.6
67. Shonteau Joshua, Eastern N. Mex.	Sr	30	211	41	121	584	19.5
68. Russ Crafton, Chadron St.	Jr	28	181	85	98	545	19.5
69. Trasel Rone, Mo. Western St.	Sr	27	189	44	103	525	19.4
70. Adam Cheek, Edinboro	Sr	29	206	54	96	562	19.4

FIELD-GOAL PERCENTAGE

(Min. 5 FG Made Per Game)	CL	G	FG	FGA	PCT.
1. Chad Scott, Calif. (Pa.)	So	28	173	245	70.6
2. Charles McLemore, Chaminade	Jr	28	148	214	69.2
3. Marcel Boggs, Francis Marion	Sr	28	186	278	66.9
4. James Morris, Central Okla.	Jr	27	176	269	65.4
5. Chris Jones, South Dak.	Jr	30	169	259	65.3
6. Wayne Robertson, New Hamp. Col.	Jr	33	268	411	65.2
7. Antwan Stallworth, SIU-Edwardsville	Sr	25	209	322	64.9
8. Roheen Oats, Cal St. Bakersfield	Jr	33	199	308	64.6
9. Sarran Marshall, Morehouse	So	25	142	222	64.0
10. Tyrone Davis, Cal St. Bakersfield	Jr	33	183	288	63.5
11. Lonnie White, East Stroudsburg	Sr	26	162	255	63.5
12. Reggie Bell, Quincy	Jr	27	195	307	63.5
13. Joachim Jerichow, Chaminade	So	28	153	241	63.5
14. Bill Hanford, Lander	Jr	24	224	354	63.3
15. Tihomir Juric, Wis.-Parkside	Jr	27	175	280	62.5
16. Albert Gates, Henderson St.	Jr	29	243	389	62.5
17. Darian Farmer, Dowling	Jr	28	234	375	62.4
18. Mark Baugh, Eastern N. Mex.	Jr	24	129	207	62.3
19. Andy Uphoff, Emporia St.	Sr	27	143	231	61.9
20. Darrel Davis, Eastern Mont.	Jr	28	143	232	61.6
21. Russell Adams, West Tex. A&M	Sr	27	144	234	61.5
22. Larry Lentz, Lenoir-Rhyne	Sr	32	215	350	61.4
23. Tim Wallen, Elon	Jr	26	135	220	61.4
24. Theodore Gadsden, Sacred Heart	Jr	25	170	278	61.2
25. James Shelton, St. Augustine's	Sr	23	140	229	61.1
26. Terrance Jordan, Livingstone	Sr	24	214	351	61.0
27. Darrell Colbert, Pittsburg St.	Sr	23	175	289	60.6
28. Alex Perine, Southern Colo.	Jr	27	174	288	60.4
29. James Hector, American Int'l	Jr	28	227	377	60.2
30. Sean Gibson, IU/PU-Ft. Wayne	Sr	29	194	323	60.1
31. Nathan Hilt, Notre Dame (Cal.)	Sr	25	178	299	59.5
32. Lawrence Williams, San Fran. St.	So	26	219	368	59.5
33. Todd Holthaus, Grand Canyon	Sr	28	155	261	59.4
34. Robert Edwards, Oakland City	Sr	32	217	366	59.3
35. Robert Torrence, Cameron	Sr	27	189	319	59.2

THREE-POINT FIELD GOALS MADE PER GAME

	CL	G	NO.	AVG.
1. Ray Gutierrez, Calif. (Pa.)	Sr	29	142	4.9
2. Kwame Morton, Clarion	Jr	26	107	4.1
3. Lance Reinhard, West Ga.	Sr	26	100	3.8
4. Shawn Walker, Elizabeth City St.	Jr	28	105	3.8
5. Floyd Patterson, Livingston	Sr	26	96	3.7
6. Alex Wright, Central Okla.	Sr	28	97	3.5
7. Arnold Smith, Columbus	Sr	26	90	3.5
8. Mike Grove, New Haven	Sr	25	86	3.4
9. Frank MacIntosh, Wis.-Parkside	Fr	26	89	3.4
10. Leon Perdue, Pfeiffer	Jr	29	97	3.3
11. Mark Johnson, Pittsburg St.	Sr	25	82	3.3
12. Jason Gay, Eastern N. Mex.	Sr	30	98	3.3
12. Kenny Brown, Millersville	Sr	30	98	3.3
14. Bill Jolly, Missouri-Rolla	Sr	27	88	3.3
15. Columbus Parker, Johnson Smith	Sr	26	84	3.2
16. Joey Haythorn, Southern Colo.	Sr	28	89	3.2
17. Corey Ward, Lake Superior St.	Jr	22	69	3.1
18. Mike Peck, Northwood	Sr	23	72	3.1
19. Ron Gulley, Davis & Elkins	Sr	27	84	3.1
20. Brian Gunnels, Henderson St.	Jr	29	90	3.1
21. Chad Briscoe, Grand Canyon	Sr	31	96	3.1
22. Russ Crafton, Chadron St.	Jr	28	85	3.0

	CL	G	NO.	AVG.
22. Chris Berger, Queens (N.C.)	Sr	28	85	3.0
24. Joe Blankenship, Ferris St.	Sr	24	72	3.0
25. Tommy Davis, Troy St.	Sr	32	95	3.0
26. Ricky Spencer, Mass.-Lowell	Fr	28	83	3.0
27. Hal McManus, Lander	Jr	26	76	2.9
28. Scott Spaanstra, Northern Mich.	Sr	30	87	2.9
28. Anthony Hammond, Miles	Sr	20	58	2.9
30. Darrin Robinson, Sacred Heart	Sr	26	75	2.9
31. Bob Timinski, St. Anselm	Jr	31	89	2.9
32. Mike Hajdukovich, Alas. Fairbanks	Jr	28	80	2.9
33. Kerry Baker, Mercyhurst	Sr	27	77	2.9
33. Jeff Campbell, Shaw	Jr	27	77	2.9
35. Shaw Blackmon, S.C.-Aiken	Sr	29	82	2.8

THREE-POINT FIELD-GOAL PERCENTAGE

(Min. 1.5 3FG Made Per Game)	CL	G	FG	FGA	PCT.
1. Greg Wilkinson, Oakland City	Jr	32	82	152	53.9
2. Ryan Wells, Chaminade	Jr	28	77	143	53.8
3. Trevor Crowe, Southwest Baptist	Sr	28	50	95	52.6
4. Scott Kissell, Colo. Christian	Sr	29	45	87	51.7
5. Joey Haythorn, Southern Colo.	Sr	28	89	173	51.4
6. Paul Turino, Michigan Tech	Sr	26	57	112	50.9
7. Frank MacIntosh, Wis.-Parkside	Fr	26	89	175	50.9
8. Vonzell McGrew, Mo. Western St.	Jr	26	42	83	50.6
9. Kenny Warren, Cal St. Bakersfield	Jr	33	90	180	50.0
9. John Brenegan, South Dak.	Sr	30	52	104	50.0
11. Scott Parker, LIU-C. W. Post	Sr	27	61	124	49.2
12. Brian Gunnels, Henderson St.	Jr	29	90	184	48.9
13. Kyle David, Northern Mich.	Jr	27	57	117	48.7
14. Bob Timinski, St. Anselm	Jr	31	89	183	48.6
15. Travis Tuttle, North Dak.	Fr	31	71	146	48.6
16. Shawn Walker, Elizabeth City St.	Jr	28	105	216	48.6
17. Scott Wadsworth, Western St.	Sr	30	66	136	48.5
18. Jeremy Sampson, Pembroke St.	Sr	26	63	130	48.5
19. Marty Bertolette, Eastern Mont.	Jr	27	47	97	48.5
20. Lance Reinhard, West Ga.	Sr	26	100	207	48.3
21. Andrew Wellman, Presbyterian	Jr	32	81	170	47.6
22. Marcus Stubblefield, Queens (N.C.)	Sr	28	49	104	47.1
23. Jim McClintock, Millersville	Jr	29	65	138	47.1
24. Joe Schuitema, Grand Valley St.	Sr	24	63	135	46.7
25. Matt Forness, Wofford	Jr	26	69	148	46.6
26. Shaw Blackmon, S.C.-Aiken	Sr	29	82	176	46.6
27. Scott Spaanstra, Northern Mich.	Sr	30	87	188	46.3
28. Nai-Te Watson, Phila. Textile	Sr	32	60	130	46.2
28. Eric Plitzweit, Winona St.	So	27	66	143	46.2
30. Byron Roberson, Southern Colo.	So	28	63	137	46.0
31. Jason Bullock, Indiana (Pa.)	Fr	27	70	153	45.8
32. George Yarberry, Hillsdale	So	28	68	149	45.6
33. Wayne Boyette, Franklin Pierce	Jr	30	71	156	45.5
34. Jeff Gore, St. Rose	Sr	31	54	119	45.4
35. Chester Hayes, Grand Canyon	Jr	31	77	170	45.3

FREE-THROW PERCENTAGE

(Min. 2.5 FT Made Per Game)	CL	G	FT	FTA	PCT.
1. Jason Williams, New Haven	Sr	27	115	125	92.0
2. Chad Briscoe, Grand Canyon	Sr	31	95	106	89.6
3. Guy Miller, Mesa St.	Sr	29	115	129	89.1
4. Joey Haythorn, Southern Colo.	Sr	28	76	86	88.4
5. John Brenegan, South Dak.	Sr	30	90	103	87.4
6. Ray Gutierrez, Calif. (Pa.)	Sr	29	165	189	87.3
7. Kenny Warren, Cal St. Bakersfield	Jr	33	96	110	87.3
8. Kenneth Brookins, LeMoyne-Owen	Jr	26	75	86	87.2
9. Scott Guldseth, North Dak.	Sr	31	153	176	86.9
10. Adam Cheek, Edinboro	Sr	29	96	111	86.5
11. Kyle David, Northern Mich.	Jr	27	88	102	86.3
12. Michael Druitt, Longwood	Jr	27	69	80	86.3
13. Derick Brewer, S.C.-Aiken	Jr	29	100	116	86.2
14. David Daniels, Colo. Christian	Sr	29	123	143	86.0
15. Lance Reinhard, West Ga.	Sr	26	115	134	85.8
16. Columbus Parker, Johnson Smith	Sr	26	169	197	85.8
17. Derek Chaney, Northern Colo.	Jr	27	84	98	85.7
18. Tim King, St. Paul's	Jr	27	70	82	85.4
19. Jeff McCaw, Mo. Western St.	Sr	28	87	102	85.3
20. Cameron Rice, St. Rose	Fr	31	81	95	85.3
21. David Fields, Phila. Textile	So	31	121	142	85.2
22. Reggie Paul, Seattle Pacific	Jr	30	103	121	85.1
23. Mike McDowell, Eastern Mont.	Sr	28	97	114	85.1
24. Jeff Gore, St. Rose	Sr	31	165	194	85.1
25. Scott Springer, St. Cloud St.	Sr	27	68	80	85.0

(Min. 2.5 FT Made Per Game)	CL	G	FT	FTA	PCT.
26. Mike Buscetto, Quinnipiac	Sr	28	152	179	84.9
27. Lock Jennings, Kutztown	Sr	25	90	106	84.9
28. Todd Kenyon, Colorado Mines	So	26	161	191	84.3
29. Shawn Walker, Elizabeth City St.	Jr	28	106	126	84.1
30. Ed Malloy, Phila. Textile	Sr	32	110	131	84.0
31. Steve Divine, Ky. Wesleyan	Sr	27	68	81	84.0
31. Ryan Schrand, Northern Ky.	So	27	68	81	84.0
33. Darrin Robinson, Sacred Heart	Sr	26	130	155	83.9
34. Scott Spaanstra, Northern Mich.	Sr	30	93	111	83.8
35. Nai-Te Watson, Phila. Textile	Sr	32	82	98	83.7
35. Samuel Fatoki, Dist. Columbia	Sr	24	82	98	83.7

REBOUNDING

	CL	G	NO.	AVG.
1. James Hector, American Int'l	Jr	28	389	13.9
2. Wayne Robertson, New Hamp. Col.	Jr	33	442	13.4
3. Marcus Allen, Paine	Jr	26	334	12.8
4. Cedric Roach, LeMoyne-Owen	Jr	28	340	12.1
5. Fred Tyler, Central Okla.	Sr	29	337	11.6
6. Andy Uphoff, Emporia St.	Sr	27	302	11.2
7. Ed Malloy, Phila. Textile	Sr	32	351	11.0
8. David Allen, Wayne St. (Neb.)	Sr	26	283	10.9
9. Eric White, East Stroudsburg	Jr	23	250	10.9
10. Lorenzo Poole, Albany St. (Ga.)	Jr	19	205	10.8
11. Nate Higgs, Elizabeth City St.	Jr	28	300	10.7
12. Dan Sandel, Le Moyne	Jr	24	250	10.4
13. Jason Miglionico, Franklin Pierce	Sr	30	311	10.4
14. Steve Ryan, Northwood	So	23	234	10.2
15. Antonio Harvey, Pfeiffer	Sr	29	294	10.1
16. Kevin Wells, Drury	Jr	31	314	10.1
17. Kevin Holleman, Virginia St.	Jr	27	272	10.1
18. Corey Warner, Lincoln (Mo.)	Jr	26	261	10.0
19. Chris Bowles, Southern Ind.	Sr	29	289	10.0
20. Cederic Fuller, Kentucky St.	Sr	27	266	9.9
20. Keelon Lawson, LeMoyne-Owen	Sr	27	266	9.9
22. Ed Wheeler, Angelo St.	Jr	26	256	9.8
23. Kevin Oldenberg, Ferris St.	Sr	27	265	9.8
24. John Adams, Lewis	Sr	26	255	9.8
25. Mauricio Almeida, St. Rose	Sr	31	302	9.7
26. Dennis Kann, Oakland	Sr	26	251	9.7
27. Doug Stahly, Indianapolis	Jr	27	260	9.6
28. Sean Gibson, IU/PU-Ft. Wayne	Sr	29	279	9.6
29. Reggie Bell, Quincy	Jr	27	259	9.6
30. Ty Satterfield, Johnson Smith	Fr	28	266	9.5
31. Chris Tucker, Mo. Southern St.	Jr	31	294	9.5
32. Anthony Sullen, Eastern N. Mex.	Sr	30	284	9.5
33. Aaron Martella, Cal St. Chico	Jr	30	283	9.4
34. James Morris, Central Okla.	Jr	27	248	9.2
35. Jo-ve' Ford, Elizabeth City St.	So	28	256	9.1

ASSISTS

	CL	G	NO.	AVG.
1. Demetri Beekman, Assumption	Sr	23	264	11.5
2. Hal Chambers, Columbus	Jr	24	227	9.5
3. David Daniels, Colo. Christian	Sr	29	264	9.1
4. Darnell White, Calif (Pa.)	Jr	29	249	8.6
5. Greg Fox, Edinboro	Sr	27	222	8.2
6. Chris Franklin, Lock Haven	So	26	205	7.9
6. Aaron Johnson, LIU-C. W. Post	Jr	26	205	7.9
8. Lamont Jones, Bridgeport	So	29	222	7.7
9. Warren Burgess, St. Anselm	Jr	31	234	7.5
10. Mike Buscetto, Quinnipiac	Sr	28	211	7.5
11. Rob Paternostro, New Hamp. Col.	So	32	236	7.4
12. Dan Ward, St. Cloud St.	So	27	199	7.4
13. Joey Brauer, St. Leo	Jr	25	184	7.4
14. Ric Van Scoyoc, Chaminade	Sr	28	195	7.0
15. Derrik Jerman, Stonehill	Sr	27	187	6.9
16. Mike Mitchell, Notre Dame (Cal.)	Jr	25	170	6.8
17. John Haas, Le Moyne	Sr	28	190	6.8
17. Will Brown, Dowling	So	28	190	6.8
19. Paul Beaty, Miles	Sr	22	146	6.6
20. Dave Wojciechowski, Clarion	Jr	26	171	6.6
20. Derrick Powell, Livingston	Sr	26	171	6.6
22. Ben Jacobson, North Dak.	Sr	31	203	6.5
23. Kennedy Stephenson, Alas. Fairbanks	Jr	25	160	6.4
24. Gabriel Moss, Albany St. (Ga.)	Sr	22	139	6.3
25. Greg Pounds, S.C.-Spartanburg	Sr	27	168	6.2
26. Patrick Herron, Winston-Salem	So	23	142	6.2
27. Nelson Fonseca, Barry	So	22	135	6.1
28. Damon Scott, Winona St.	So	29	177	6.1
29. Patrick Chambers, Phila. Textile	Jr	31	189	6.1

	CL	G	NO.	AVG.
30. Spencer Wright, Central Okla.	Jr	28	170	6.1
31. Andre Walton, IU/PU-Ft. Wayne	Sr	29	176	6.1
32. William Johnson, Morris Brown	Sr	26	155	6.0
33. Tom Quinlan, Bentley	Jr	30	177	5.9
33. Steve Fendry, Western St.	Sr	30	177	5.9
35. Gregg Williams, Augusta	Jr	29	168	5.8

BLOCKED SHOTS

	CL	G	NO.	AVG.
1. Antonio Harvey, Pfeiffer	Sr	29	155	5.3
2. Elwood Vines, Bloomsburg	Jr	27	107	4.0
3. Marcellus Stiede, Emporia St.	Sr	27	97	3.6
4. Marcus Allen, Paine	Jr	26	93	3.6
5. Tihomir Juric, Wis.-Parkside	Jr	27	92	3.4
6. Eugene Haith, Phila. Textile	So	31	105	3.4
7. Marvin Childs, Hampton	Jr	26	82	3.2
8. Derek Stewart, Augusta	Sr	28	88	3.1
9. Vonzell McGrew, Mo. Western St.	Jr	26	79	3.0
10. Joachim Jerichow, Chaminade	So	28	72	2.6
11. Chris Gardner, North Dak.	Jr	31	77	2.5
12. Julian Rodriguez, Barry	Jr	24	58	2.4
13. Cedric Roach, LeMoyne-Owen	Jr	28	67	2.4
14. Tony Mallard, Lenoir-Rhyne	Sr	32	76	2.4
15. Victor Pettis, Cheyney	Jr	24	54	2.3
16. LeRon Gittens, Quinnipiac	Jr	29	65	2.2
17. Fred Tyler, Central Okla.	Sr	29	64	2.2
18. Steve Gilbert, Norfolk St.	Sr	29	63	2.2
19. Manuel Ruiz, N. M. Highlands	Sr	30	65	2.2
20. Sam Rowe, Adelphi	Sr	28	58	2.1
21. Jo-ve' Ford, Elizabeth City St.	So	28	57	2.0
22. Chris Waters, Fayetteville St.	Sr	29	58	2.0
22. Jason Wenschlag, North Dak. St.	Sr	29	58	2.0
22. Donald Dillon, Molloy	So	27	54	2.0
22. James McClendon, Livingston	Jr	26	52	2.0
26. Alexander Hall, Bentley	Sr	31	61	2.0
27. Rick Sabec, Mansfield	Sr	21	41	2.0
28. Antwine Moore, Millersville	So	24	46	1.9
29. Chris Herriford, Eastern Mont.	Jr	29	55	1.9
30. Chris Middleton, Mercy	So	26	49	1.9
30. Cedric Mansell, Mars Hill	Jr	26	49	1.9
32. Sarran Marshall, Morehouse	So	25	47	1.9
33. Wayne Robertson, New Hamp. Col.	Jr	33	62	1.9
34. Eric Little, Kentucky St.	Sr	26	48	1.8
34. John Adams, Lewis	Sr	26	48	1.8

STEALS

	CL	G	NO.	AVG.
1. Marcus Stubblefield, Queens (N.C.)	Sr	28	110	3.9
2. Demetri Beekman, Assumption	Sr	23	89	3.9
3. Tyrone McDaniel, Lenoir-Rhyne	Sr	32	116	3.6
4. Rudy Berry, Cal St. Stanislaus	Jr	28	100	3.6
4. Alex Wright, Central Okla.	Sr	28	100	3.6
6. Lamont Jones, Bridgeport	So	29	96	3.3
7. Patrick Herron, Winston-Salem	So	23	74	3.2
8. Gary Walker, Regis (Colo.)	Sr	27	85	3.1
9. Bryan Heaps, Abilene Christian	Jr	27	84	3.1
10. Jesse White, Fla. Southern	Sr	32	99	3.1
11. Ron Williams, Merrimack	Jr	26	79	3.0
11. Darrin Robinson, Sacred Heart	Sr	26	79	3.0
13. Sherman Hamilton, Florida Tech	Fr	26	78	3.0
14. Chad Briscoe, Grand Canyon	Sr	31	90	2.9
15. Kenneth Brookins, LeMoyne-Owen	Jr	26	75	2.9
16. Rashe Reviere, Mercyhurst	Jr	27	77	2.9
17. Danny Lewis, Wayne St. (Mich.)	Sr	24	66	2.8
18. Ken Francis, Molloy	Jr	27	74	2.7
19. Pat Watson, Cal St. Hayward	Jr	25	68	2.7
20. Jimmie Walker, N.C. Central	Jr	30	81	2.7
21. Darnell White, Calif (Pa.)	Jr	29	77	2.7
22. Aaron Johnson, LIU-C. W. Post	Jr	26	69	2.7
22. Earl Elliotte, Springfield	Sr	26	69	2.7
24. Chris Franklin, Lock Haven	So	26	68	2.6
25. Alvin Jones, Assumption	Sr	26	67	2.6
25. Peter Walcott, Florida Tech	So	26	67	2.6
27. Kevin Koch, Western St.	Sr	30	77	2.6
28. Virgil Smith, Mercy	Sr	27	68	2.5
29. Orlando Johnson, Northwest Mo. St.	Sr	27	66	2.4
30. Joey Brauer, St. Leo	Jr	25	61	2.4
31. Bryant Johnson, Troy St.	Jr	32	78	2.4
32. Ty Miller, Ferris St.	Jr	27	65	2.4
32. Paul Brown, Northwest Mo. St.	Jr	27	65	2.4
32. Ben Stephens, Shepherd	Sr	27	65	2.4
35. Gregg Williams, Augusta	Jr	29	69	2.4

1993 DIVISION II MEN'S BASKETBALL GAME HIGHS

INDIVIDUAL HIGHS

SCORING

Pts.	Player, Team vs. Opponent	Date
49	Ali Travis, Catawba vs. Wingate	Feb. 17
48	Russ Crafton, Chadron St. vs. Adams St.	Feb. 5
47	Darrin Robinson, Sacred Heart vs. New Haven	Feb. 17
47	Brent Wichlacz, Grand Valley St. vs. Hillsdale	Jan. 23
45	Michael Willams, Saginaw Valley vs. Ferris St.	Feb. 25
45	Danny Lewis, Wayne St. (Mich.) vs. Michigan Tech	Feb. 20
45	Alex Wright, Central Okla. vs. Eastern N. Mex.	Feb. 15
45	Jeff Gore, St. Rose vs. LIU-C. W. Post	Feb. 13
45	David Fields, Phila. Textile vs. St. Rose	Jan. 3
45	Terry McCord, Troy St. vs. Alabama St.	Dec. 12

THREE-POINT FIELD GOALS

3FG	Player, Team vs. Opponent	Date
13	Danny Lewis, Wayne St. (Mich.) vs. Michigan Tech	Feb. 20
12	Eric Carpenter, Cal St. San B'dino vs. Metropolitan St.	Feb. 19
12	Russ Crafton, Chadron St. vs. Adams St.	Feb. 5
12	Mike Morrison, Keene St. vs. New Hamp. Col.	Nov. 21
11	Kenny Warren, Cal St. Bakersfield vs. Grand Canyon	Mar. 12
10	Hal McManus, Lander vs. Newberry	Feb. 18
10	Ron Gulley, Davis & Elkins vs. Waynesburg	Dec. 12

FREE THROWS

FT	Player, Team vs. Opponent	Date
21	Rudy Berry, Cal St. Stanislaus vs. UC Davis	Mar. 2
21	Jeff Gore, St. Rose vs. Concordia (N.Y.)	Feb. 10
20	Duron Hebron, Southern Ind. vs. Kentucky St.	Feb. 13
20	Yancey Taylor, Indiana (Pa.) vs. Kutztown	Dec. 7
19	Michael Williams, Saginaw Valley vs. Ferris St.	Feb. 25
18	Will Paige, Wayne St. (Mich.) vs. Grand Valley St.	Feb. 13
18	Todd Kenyon, Colorado Mines vs. Denver	Feb. 8
18	Peter Walcott, Florida Tech vs. Fla. Southern	Jan. 27
17	Aaron Martella, Cal St. Chico vs. Grand Canyon	Mar. 13
17	Tim Fitzpatrick, Fort Lewis vs. Adams St.	Feb. 2
17	Nate Higgs, Elizabeth City St. vs. Virginia St.	Jan. 16

REBOUNDS

Reb.	Player, Team vs. Opponent	Date
26	James Hector, American Int'l vs. New Haven	Dec. 10
23	Marcus Allen, Paine vs. Morris Brown	Feb. 13
23	Kris Steele, Bridgeport vs. Teikyo Post	Dec. 3
21	Corey Warner, Lincoln (Mo.) vs. Emporia St.	Feb. 20
21	David Allen, Wayne St. (Neb.) vs. Northwest Mo. St.	Feb. 15
21	Duron Hebron, Southern Ind. vs. Kentucky St.	Feb. 13
21	Aaron Martella, Cal St. Chico vs. Humboldt St.	Jan. 30
21	Marus Allen, Paine vs. Albany St. (Ga.)	Jan. 20
21	Jerry Patterson, Northwood vs. Concordia (Mich.)	Dec. 5
21	Bobby Latham, Barry vs. Nova	Nov. 27
20	Several times	

ASSISTS

Ast.	Player, Team vs. Opponent	Date
20	Demetri Beekman, Assumption vs. Bryant	Feb. 13
18	Will Paige, Wayne St. (Mich.) vs. Grand Valley St.	Feb. 13
17	David Daniels, Colo. Christian vs. Fort Lewis	Feb. 18
16	Cameron Rice, St. Rose vs. Southern Conn. St.	Mar. 12
16	Joey Brauer, St. Leo vs. North Fla.	Feb. 24
16	Adrian Hill, Virginia Union vs. Dist. Columbia	Feb. 20
16	Hal Chambers, Columbus vs. Georgia Col.	Jan. 18
16	Paul Beaty, Miles vs. Fisk	Feb. 13
16	Greg Fox, Edinboro vs. Columbia Union	Jan. 16
16	David Daniels, Colo. Christian vs. Mt. Senario	Jan. 5
16	Nelson Fonscca, Barry vs. Graceland	Dec. 30

BLOCKED SHOTS

Blk.	Player, Team vs. Opponent	Date
12	Antonio Harvey, Pfeiffer vs. Mt. Olive	Feb. 20
11	Antonio Harvey, Pfeiffer vs. Ferrum	Jan. 7
10	Marcus Allen, Paine vs. Morris Brown	Feb. 13
10	Joe Jarldane, Dowling vs. Concordia (N.Y.)	Feb. 3
10	Corey Johnson, Pace vs. LIU-C. W. Post	Dec. 20
10	Antonio Harvey, Pfeiffer vs. LIFE (Ga.)	Dec. 5
9	Several times	

STEALS

St.	Player, Team vs. Opponent	Date
10	Marcus Stubblefield, Queens (N.C.) vs. N'west (Wash.)	Feb. 8
9	Jesse White, Fla. Southern vs. North Central	Dec. 7
8	Several times	

TEAM HIGHS

SCORING

Pts.	Team vs. Opponent	Date
167	Central Okla. vs. Bapt. Christian	Jan. 18
151	Adams St. vs. Fort Lewis	Dec. 8
145	Troy St. vs. Faulkner	Feb. 23
145	Troy St. vs. Talledega	Dec. 14
140	Troy St. vs. Central Wesleyan	Dec. 4
137	Central Okla. vs. Paul Quinn	Dec. 8
136	Oakland City vs. Ind.-Northwest	Feb. 6
133	Cal St. San B'dino vs. Pacific Christian	Dec. 11
133	Missouri-Rolla vs. Ark. Baptist	Nov. 22
132	Grand Canyon vs. Pacific Christian	Jan. 28
132	Troy St. vs. Central Methodist	Dec. 31
132	Central Okla. vs. Tabor	Dec. 18
132	Oakland City vs. Ind. East	Dec. 5
132	Chapman vs. Pacific Christian	Nov. 21

FIELD-GOAL PERCENTAGE

Pct.	Team vs. Opponent	Date
75.0	(36 of 48) Colo. Christian vs. Mt. Senario	Jan. 5
73.0	(53 of 74) Oakland City vs. Ind.-Northwest	Mar. 6
72.6	(45 of 62) Ferris St. vs. Urbana	Dec. 4
72.5	(29 of 40) Francis Marion vs. Newberry	Feb. 22
72.3	(34 of 47) Dist. Columbia vs. Lincoln (Pa.)	Dec. 2
72.3	(34 of 47) S.C.-Spartanburg vs. Elon	Nov. 24
71.7	(38 of 53) Chaminade vs. Hawaii Pacific	Jan. 12
70.8	(34 of 48) Lewis vs. Northern Ky.	Feb. 11
70.2	(33 of 47) Western St. vs. Neb.-Kearney	Nov. 27
69.4	(34 of 49) South Dak. vs. Nebraska-Omaha	Feb. 19

THREE-POINT FIELD-GOALS

3FG	Team vs. Opponent	Date
23	Troy St. vs. New Hamp. Col.	Mar. 26
23	Hillsdale vs. Spring Arbor	Dec. 22
19	Bentley vs. Southern Conn. St.	Dec. 8
19	Missouri-Rolla vs. Ark. Baptist	Nov. 22
19	Hillsdale vs. Grand Valley St.	Jan. 7
18	Troy St. vs. Ala.-Huntsville	Feb. 20
18	Central Okla. vs. Bapt. Christian	Jan. 18
18	Columbus vs. Georgia Col.	Jan. 18
18	Cal St. Stanislaus vs. Notre Dame (Cal.)	Jan. 9
18	Keene St. vs. New Hamp. Col.	Nov. 21

1993 DIVISION II MEN'S TEAM LEADERS

SCORING OFFENSE

	G	W-L	PTS.	AVG.
1. Central Okla.	29	23-6	3,293	113.6
2. Troy St.	32	27-5	3,566	111.4
3. Bridgeport	29	20-9	2,800	96.6
4. Alabama A&M	31	28-3	2,990	96.5
5. New Hamp. Col.	33	29-4	3,119	94.5
6. Oakland City	32	22-10	2,987	93.3
7. New Haven	27	13-14	2,489	92.2
8. Fort Lewis	27	11-16	2,440	90.4
9. Millersville	30	24-6	2,709	90.3
10. Grand Canyon	31	20-11	2,792	90.1
11. Neb.-Kearney	26	20-6	2,340	90.0
12. LeMoyne-Owen	28	19-9	2,519	90.0
13. Southern Ind.	29	22-7	2,603	89.8
14. Johnson Smith	28	20-8	2,497	89.2
15. Elizabeth City St.	28	18-10	2,476	88.4
16. Alas. Fairbanks	28	12-16	2,466	88.1
17. Jacksonville St.	26	16-10	2,279	87.7
18. Kentucky St.	27	16-11	2,353	87.1
19. Franklin Pierce	30	22-8	2,610	87.0
20. IU/PU-Ft. Wayne	29	23-6	2,515	86.7
21. Adams St.	27	11-16	2,340	86.7
22. Missouri-Rolla	27	16-11	2,337	86.6
23. Morehouse	26	15-11	2,248	86.5
24. Tampa	30	25-5	2,593	86.4
25. Calif. (Pa.)	29	23-6	2,505	86.4
26. Pfeiffer	29	23-6	2,495	86.0
27. Clarion	26	17-9	2,226	85.6
28. N.C. Central	30	26-4	2,568	85.6
29. Keene St.	25	2-23	2,138	85.5
30. St. Rose	31	23-8	2,627	84.7

SCORING DEFENSE

	G	W-L	PTS.	AVG.
1. Phila. Textile	32	30-2	1,898	59.3
2. Minn.-Duluth	28	16-12	1,690	60.4
3. Pace	29	17-12	1,816	62.6
4. Gannon	27	20-7	1,703	63.1
5. Cal St. Dom. Hills	26	16-10	1,665	64.0
6. South Dak.	30	25-5	1,954	65.1
7. West Chester	26	18-8	1,702	65.5
8. UC Davis	27	13-14	1,787	66.2
9. Fla. Southern	32	24-8	2,120	66.3
10. Cal St. Bakersfield	33	33-0	2,187	66.3
11. Humboldt St.	26	12-14	1,729	66.5
11. Lincoln Memorial	26	17-9	1,729	66.5
13. Francis Marion	28	19-9	1,866	66.6
14. St. Joseph's (Ind.)	27	21-6	1,804	66.8
15. Mankato St.	27	19-8	1,805	66.9
16. Rollins	27	19-8	1,822	67.5
17. Presbyterian	32	27-5	2,162	67.6
18. Delta St.	30	22-8	2,030	67.7
19. Washburn	32	27-5	2,187	68.3
20. UC Riverside	28	20-8	1,915	68.4
21. Fayetteville St.	29	20-9	1,987	68.5
22. West Tex. A&M	27	17-10	1,871	69.3
23. Mansfield	25	11-14	1,743	69.7
24. Pfeiffer	29	23-6	2,030	70.0
25. Longwood	27	17-10	1,892	70.1
26. Queens (N.Y.)	27	8-19	1,894	70.1
27. Southwest Baptist	28	21-7	1,971	70.4
28. Virginia Union	30	27-3	2,113	70.4
29. Pittsburg St.	26	13-13	1,837	70.7
30. Mars Hill	26	16-10	1,838	70.7

SCORING MARGIN

	OFF.	DEF.	MAR.
1. Phila. Textile	78.8	59.3	19.4
2. Oakland City	93.3	76.4	16.9
3. Central Okla.	113.6	96.8	16.8
4. Pfeiffer	86.0	70.0	16.0
5. Alabama A&M	96.5	81.4	15.0
6. Washburn	82.8	68.3	14.5
7. Cal St. Bakersfield	80.6	66.3	14.4
8. New Hamp. Col.	94.5	80.7	13.8
9. Millersville	90.3	76.6	13.7
10. Troy St.	111.4	98.0	13.4
11. Virginia Union	83.6	70.4	13.1
12. Fla. Southern	79.3	66.3	13.1
13. South Dak.	77.9	65.1	12.8
14. Delta St.	79.8	67.7	12.1
15. Southern Ind.	89.8	77.8	11.9
16. West Tex. A&M	80.9	69.3	11.6
17. Eastern N. Mex.	84.3	72.8	11.4
18. N.C. Central	85.6	74.4	11.2
19. IU/PU-Ft. Wayne	86.7	75.6	11.2
20. St. Rose	84.7	73.9	10.9
21. Presbyterian	77.7	67.6	10.1
22. Calif. (Pa.)	86.4	76.4	10.0
23. Franklin Pierce	87.0	77.1	9.9
24. Bridgeport	96.6	86.8	9.7
25. Ky. Wesleyan	81.4	71.9	9.6
26. Mesa St.	82.2	72.7	9.6
27. Seattle Pacific	83.9	74.5	9.3
28. UC Riverside	77.6	68.4	9.2
29. Tampa	86.4	77.4	9.0
30. St. Joseph's (Ind.)	75.7	66.8	8.9

WON-LOST PERCENTAGE

	W-L	PCT.
1. Cal St. Bakersfield	33-0	1.000
2. Phila. Textile	30-2	.938
3. Alabama A&M	28-3	.903
4. Virginia Union	27-3	.900
5. New Hamp. Col.	29-4	.879
6. N.C. Central	26-4	.867
7. Troy St.	27-5	.844
7. Presbyterian	27-5	.844
7. Washburn	27-5	.844
10. South Dak.	25-5	.833
10. Tampa	25-5	.833
10. Western St.	25-5	.833
13. Millersville	24-6	.800
14. Calif. (Pa.)	23-6	.793
14. IU/PU-Ft. Wayne	23-6	.793
14. Pfeiffer	23-6	.793
14. Central Okla.	23-6	.793
18. Lenoir-Rhyne	25-7	.781
19. Ky. Wesleyan	21-6	.778
19. St. Joseph's (Ind.)	21-6	.778
21. Bentley	24-7	.774
22. Neb.-Kearney	20-6	.769
23. Cal St. Chico	23-7	.767
23. Eastern N. Mex.	23-7	.767
25. Southern Ind.	22-7	.759
25. S.C.-Aiken	22-7	.759
27. Fla. Southern	24-8	.750
27. Southwest Baptist	21-7	.750
27. Mo. Western St.	21-7	.750
30. North Dak.	23-8	.742
30. St. Rose	23-8	.742

FIELD-GOAL PERCENTAGE

	FG	FGA	PCT.
1. Cal St. Bakersfield	1,002	1,849	54.2
2. Francis Marion	722	1,337	54.0
3. Oakland City	1,129	2,100	53.8
4. Chaminade	847	1,580	53.6
5. Colo. Christian	859	1,616	53.2
6. Presbyterian	904	1,716	52.7
7. IU/PU-Ft. Wayne	906	1,723	52.6
8. Fla. Southern	942	1,794	52.5
9. New Hamp. Col.	1,158	2,206	52.5
10. Bridgeport	1,062	2,042	52.0
11. Delta St.	890	1,722	51.7
12. Lenoir-Rhyne	966	1,874	51.5
13. Calif. (Pa.)	855	1,666	51.3
14. Rollins	719	1,401	51.3
15. West Tex. A&M	789	1,542	51.2
16. Seattle Pacific	940	1,844	51.0
17. S.C.-Aiken	844	1,657	50.9
18. Michigan Tech	764	1,500	50.9
19. Regis (Colo.)	803	1,581	50.8
20. North Dak.	883	1,742	50.7
21. Millersville	969	1,918	50.5
22. Dowling	819	1,635	50.1
23. Washburn	1,006	2,016	49.9
24. Queens (N.C.)	828	1,660	49.9

	FG	FGA	PCT.
25. Winona St.	794	1,594	49.8
26. LeMoyne-Owen	913	1,833	49.8
27. Northern Mich.	895	1,800	49.7
28. Lincoln Memorial	686	1,384	49.6
29. Johnson Smith	848	1,713	49.5
30. Notre Dame (Cal.)	715	1,445	49.5

FIELD-GOAL PERCENTAGE DEFENSE

	FG	FGA	PCT.
1. Pfeiffer	767	2,028	37.8
2. Delta St.	699	1,741	40.1
3. St. Joseph's (Ind.)	632	1,554	40.7
4. Livingston	659	1,620	40.7
5. Paine	661	1,617	40.9
6. Assumption	713	1,742	40.9
7. Phila. Textile	742	1,805	41.1
8. Virginia Union	787	1,910	41.2
9. Southwest Baptist	710	1,717	41.4
10. Millersville	838	2,017	41.5
11. Bentley	858	2,062	41.6
12. South Dak.	727	1,744	41.7
13. Quinnipiac	836	2,004	41.7
14. Cal St. Bakersfield	788	1,888	41.7
15. Denver	648	1,549	41.8
16. Emporia St.	701	1,675	41.9
17. Oakland City	879	2,094	42.0
18. Cal St. Dom. Hills	583	1,388	42.0
19. North Dak.	778	1,852	42.0
20. Presbyterian	792	1,881	42.1
21. Quincy	797	1,888	42.2
22. Hampton	681	1,611	42.3
23. St. Rose	842	1,991	42.3
24. Gannon	620	1,466	42.3
25. West Chester	629	1,485	42.4
26. Texas A&I	678	1,599	42.4
27. Springfield	653	1,540	42.4
28. Washburn	759	1,789	42.4
29. Kentucky St.	804	1,891	42.5
30. Mankato St.	666	1,565	42.6

THREE-POINT FIELD GOALS MADE PER GAME

	G	NO.	AVG.
1. Hillsdale	28	366	13.1
2. Troy St.	32	394	12.3
3. Central Okla.	29	321	11.1
4. Keene St.	25	241	9.6
5. Livingston	26	241	9.3
6. Cal Poly SLO	26	232	8.9
7. Clarion	26	225	8.7
8. Northern Mich.	30	258	8.6
9. West Ga.	26	216	8.3
10. Pfeiffer	29	237	8.2
11. Cal St. San B'dino	25	202	8.1
12. Grand Valley St.	26	210	8.1
13. Bentley	31	249	8.0
14. Elizabeth City St.	28	224	8.0
15. Columbus	26	207	8.0
16. Denver	26	206	7.9
17. Eastern Mont.	29	229	7.9
18. Michigan Tech	26	204	7.8
19. Grand Canyon	31	243	7.8
20. Henderson St.	29	226	7.8
21. Missouri-Rolla	27	210	7.8
22. West Liberty St.	27	208	7.7
23. Mo. Western St.	28	212	7.6
24. Mo. Southern St.	31	232	7.5
25. Calif. (Pa.)	29	216	7.4
26. Davis & Elkins	27	201	7.4
27. Lake Superior St.	25	186	7.4
28. Wayne St. (Mich.)	32	238	7.4
29. Chadron St.	28	208	7.4
30. Cal St. Stanislaus	28	203	7.3

THREE-POINT FIELD-GOAL PERCENTAGE

(Min. 3.0 3FG Made Per Game)	G	FG	FGA	PCT.
1. Oakland City	32	215	465	46.2
2. Michigan Tech	26	204	445	45.8
3. Calif. (Pa.)	29	216	474	45.6
4. Presbyterian	32	141	311	45.3
5. Chaminade	28	154	340	45.3
6. Southern Colo.	28	173	392	44.1
7. Cal St. Bakersfield	33	139	315	44.1
8. Henderson St.	29	226	514	44.0
9. Northern Mich.	30	258	597	43.2
10. S.C.-Aiken	29	108	250	43.2
11. Pembroke St.	26	177	415	42.7
12. Elizabeth City St.	28	224	526	42.6
13. Johnson Smith	28	145	343	42.3
14. Colo. Christian	29	180	428	42.1
15. Queens (N.C.)	28	181	431	42.0
16. Southwest Baptist	28	180	431	41.8
17. Millersville	30	198	478	41.4
18. St. Rose	31	179	435	41.1
19. North Dak.	31	192	467	41.1
20. Lenoir-Rhyne	32	171	416	41.1
21. LIU-C. W. Post	27	101	247	40.9
22. Bridgeport	29	161	394	40.9
23. Livingston	26	241	590	40.8
24. Denver	26	206	505	40.8
25. St. Cloud St.	27	141	346	40.8
26. Wis.-Parkside	27	188	464	40.5
27. Norfolk St.	29	128	317	40.4
28. St. Michael's	27	187	464	40.3
29. New Hamp. Col.	33	189	469	40.3
30. Phila. Textile	32	181	452	40.0

FREE-THROW PERCENTAGE

	FT	FTA	PCT.
1. Phila. Textile	491	630	77.9
2. Le Moyne	413	546	75.6
3. Wayne St. (Mich.)	565	752	75.1
4. West Liberty St.	452	605	74.7
5. Shepherd	474	639	74.2
6. Catawba	422	573	73.6
7. Northern Ky.	500	680	73.5
8. Western St.	603	822	73.4
9. Mankato St.	401	549	73.0
10. St. Rose	598	819	73.0
11. Missouri-Rolla	565	774	73.0
12. Bentley	479	657	72.9
13. Troy St.	652	896	72.8
14. South Dak.	573	788	72.7
15. Mesa St.	680	937	72.6
16. Mo. Southern St.	531	732	72.5
17. Armstrong St.	462	637	72.5
18. Michigan Tech	388	535	72.5
19. Central Okla.	534	737	72.5
20. Oakland	462	638	72.4
21. Southern Ind.	614	848	72.4
22. Keene St.	367	507	72.4
23. Presbyterian	537	743	72.3
24. Mo. Western St.	404	559	72.3
25. Gannon	375	519	72.3
26. Ky. Wesleyan	462	640	72.2
27. St. Anselm	556	771	72.1
28. Cameron	401	557	72.0
29. New Haven	464	645	71.9
30. Franklin Pierce	491	683	71.9

REBOUND MARGIN

	OFF.	DEF.	MAR.
1. Metropolitan St.	45.5	32.0	13.5
2. LeMoyne-Owen	48.0	36.6	11.4
3. Central Okla.	52.1	40.8	11.4
4. Washburn	43.2	32.3	10.9
5. New Hamp. Col.	45.1	35.5	9.6
6. Southern Ind.	41.7	32.7	9.0
7. Oakland City	42.0	33.5	8.5
8. Ferris St.	39.5	31.2	8.3
9. Virginia Union	42.9	34.8	8.0
10. Oakland	39.0	31.1	7.8
11. UC Davis	37.0	29.2	7.8
12. Delta St.	39.4	31.6	7.7
13. American Int'l	42.6	35.0	7.6
14. Longwood	39.5	32.0	7.5
15. Texas A&I	42.4	35.2	7.3
16. Pfeiffer	47.1	40.0	7.1
17. Columbus	46.7	39.9	6.8
18. Franklin Pierce	41.9	35.2	6.7

	OFF.	DEF.	MAR.
19. Alabama A&M	48.7	42.1	6.6
20. Neb.-Kearney	42.6	36.2	6.4
21. Albany St. (Ga.)	45.9	39.6	6.3
22. Lincoln Memorial	37.0	30.8	6.2
23. Tampa	41.6	35.5	6.1
24. Phila. Textile	37.0	30.9	6.1
25. UC Riverside	37.5	31.5	6.0
26. Millersville	42.1	36.2	5.9
27. Fayetteville St.	38.9	33.0	5.9
28. Cal St. Bakersfield	36.4	30.5	5.8
29. Central Ark.	38.1	32.5	5.6
30. Morningside	38.1	32.9	5.2

1993 DIVISION III MEN'S INDIVIDUAL LEADERS

SCORING

	CL	G	TFG	3FG	FT	PTS.	AVG.
1. Dave Shaw, Drew	Sr	23	210	74	169	663	28.8
2. Dameon Ross, Salisbury St.	Jr	26	268	84	112	732	28.2
3. Alberto Montanez, Rochester Inst.	Sr	28	275	57	137	744	26.6
4. Larry Norman, Clark (Mass.)	Sr	24	222	10	172	626	26.1
5. Vaughn Troyer, East. Mennonite	Sr	25	229	36	157	651	26.0
6. Mike Crnkovich, Wabash	Sr	26	272	4	111	659	25.3
7. Moses Jean-Pierre, Plymouth St.	Jr	25	190	65	169	614	24.6
8. Scott Fitch, Geneseo St.	Jr	27	208	87	160	663	24.6
9. Kirk Anderson, Augustana (Ill.)	Sr	30	237	123	137	734	24.5
10. Al Pettway, Worcester St.	Jr	27	239	71	93	642	23.8
11. Jason Hoppy, Scranton	Sr	29	259	32	138	688	23.7
12. Joe O'Connor, Bri'water (Mass.)	Sr	25	183	81	144	591	23.6
13. Kyle Price, Illinois Col.	Jr	20	172	2	125	471	23.5
14. Gerrick Monroe, Carleton	Sr	24	216	2	124	558	23.3
15. Chris Moore, UC San Diego	Sr	25	206	52	113	577	23.1
16. Rick Hughes, Thomas More	Fr	26	243	0	114	600	23.1
17. Victor Koytikh, Framingham St.	So	25	203	60	108	574	23.0
18. Steve Honderd, Calvin	Sr	28	226	32	157	641	22.9
19. Anthony Cummings, Lynchburg	Jr	20	183	9	77	452	22.6
20. Bill Conlee, Wm. Paterson	Sr	24	194	58	96	542	22.6
21. Steve Haynes, Mass.-Dartmouth	Sr	30	237	44	158	676	22.5
22. Nick Gutman, Otterbein	Jr	29	244	48	106	642	22.1
23. John Bufford, John Carroll	Jr	26	218	20	110	566	21.8
24. Tyler Brown, Upsala	Sr	24	175	58	114	522	21.8
25. Mike Connelly, Catholic	Sr	27	175	111	121	582	21.6
26. Shannon Cloyd, Millikin	So	25	177	16	167	537	21.5
26. Jason Graber, Albany (N.Y.)	Jr	25	196	20	125	537	21.5
28. Billy Collins, Nichols	So	23	176	89	53	494	21.5
29. Sherwin Telford, Binghamton	Jr	27	210	26	133	579	21.4
30. Steve Lemmer, Hamilton	Sr	27	227	0	123	577	21.4
31. Charlie Borsheim, Washington (Mo.)	Sr	25	201	2	129	533	21.3
32. Chris Sullivan, Wheaton (Mass.)	Sr	23	163	79	84	489	21.3
33. Mike Nicholson, York (N.Y.)	So	21	180	2	84	446	21.2
34. John Cooksey, Webster	Jr	24	183	17	126	509	21.2
35. Pat Good, Albertus Magnus	Sr	25	214	46	51	525	21.0
36. Mike Comerford, Rensselaer	Sr	24	176	72	79	503	21.0
37. Kevin Feighery, Merchant Marine	So	18	143	5	83	374	20.8
38. Kelvin Richardson, Maryville (Tenn.)	Sr	26	180	80	98	538	20.7
39. Donny Woodard, Frostburg St.	Jr	26	198	70	71	537	20.7
40. Blair Slattery, Occidental	Jr	19	147	29	69	392	20.6
41. Scott Pritzl, Wis.-Oshkosh	Sr	25	167	85	96	515	20.6
41. Corey Blackwell, Averett	Sr	20	154	11	93	412	20.6
43. Darron Lowe, Concordia (Ill.)	Sr	25	176	43	117	512	20.5
44. Hilliary Scott, Roanoke	Jr	26	187	25	133	532	20.5
45. Jim Petty, Gordon	So	24	171	33	114	489	20.4
46. Joel Dillingham, Lawrence	Sr	22	139	60	110	448	20.4
47. Will Hawkins, Wheaton (Mass.)	Sr	25	196	23	94	509	20.4
48. Troy Tyler, Eureka	Jr	28	212	51	94	569	20.3
49. James President, Framingham St.	Sr	25	190	43	84	507	20.3
50. Rossie Covington, East Conn. St.	Jr	28	233	2	97	565	20.2
51. Derrick Watkins, Fisk	Sr	25	194	42	74	504	20.2
52. Matt Cusano, Scranton	Sr	29	228	0	125	581	20.0
53. Shawn McCartney, Hunter	So	24	173	26	106	478	19.9
54. Josh Hammermesh, Amherst	Jr	23	189	7	72	457	19.9
55. Matt Leary, Wartburg	Sr	26	194	0	126	514	19.8
56. Ryan Buckley, Delaware Valley	Jr	24	166	50	89	471	19.6
56. Richard Hill, Ramapo	So	24	162	21	126	471	19.6
58. David Delnero, Southwestern (Tex.)	Sr	27	200	36	93	529	19.6
59. Daniel Aaron, Yeshiva	Jr	24	201	0	68	470	19.6
60. Bob Croft, Ohio Wesleyan	Jr	25	184	8	113	489	19.6
60. Chris McMahon, Tufts	So	25	196	0	97	489	19.6
62. Demetrius Horne, John Jay	Jr	25	170	33	115	488	19.5
63. Aaron Lee, Mass.-Dartmouth	So	29	192	96	85	565	19.5
64. Rolando Welch, Western Md.	Jr	24	194	5	73	466	19.4
65. Abe Tubbs, Cornell College	Jr	22	183	5	56	427	19.4
66. T. J. Gondek, Colby-Sawyer	So	25	167	71	78	483	19.3
66. Pete Binelas, Wis.-Stout	Jr	25	179	51	74	483	19.3
68. Brian McDonagh, Manhattanville	Jr	24	156	17	134	463	19.3
69. Rick Chalk, Va. Wesleyan	Jr	28	188	7	157	540	19.3
70. Matt Miller, Babson	Sr	21	137	7	123	404	19.2

FIELD-GOAL PERCENTAGE

(Min. 5 FG Made Per Game)	CL	G	FG	FGA	PCT.
1. Jim Leibel, St. Thomas (Minn.)	Jr	28	141	202	69.8
2. Gary Francisco, Utica	Sr	23	115	166	69.3
3. Mike Burden, Rowan	Jr	31	182	268	67.9
4. Marcellus Smith, Marymount (Va.)	Jr	23	145	219	66.2
5. David Otte, Simpson	So	25	139	212	65.6
6. Greg Kemp, Aurora	Jr	25	173	264	65.5
7. Brian Davis, Oglethorpe	Jr	24	163	249	65.5
8. Brett Grebing, Redlands	Sr	24	130	200	65.0
9. Josh Hammermesh, Amherst	Jr	23	189	293	64.5
10. Dan Rush, Bridgewater (Va.)	So	24	160	249	64.3
11. James Boykins, Chris. Newport	Sr	28	212	330	64.2
12. Matt Leary, Wartburg	Sr	26	194	302	64.2
13. Sean Campbell, Mt. St. Vincent	So	26	172	269	63.9
14. Mike McGwin, Nazareth (N.Y.)	Sr	24	179	285	62.8
15. Chris Clark, Maryville (Tenn.)	Jr	26	182	293	62.1
16. Mahlon Williams, Wheaton (Mass.)	So	20	102	165	61.8
17. Doug Cline, Wooster	So	28	150	244	61.5
18. Bill Trump, Lycoming	Jr	23	157	256	61.3
19. Ashley Watson, Bridgewater (Va.)	Sr	23	130	212	61.3
20. Jeff Molisani, Rochester Inst.	Sr	28	168	274	61.3
21. Ed Easley, Neb. Wesleyan	Sr	25	130	214	60.7
22. Justin Wilkins, Neb. Wesleyan	So	25	133	219	60.7
23. John Lampe, Hiram	Sr	25	193	318	60.7
24. Chris Eaton, Eureka	Jr	29	206	340	60.6
25. Anthony Cummings, Lynchburg	Jr	20	183	303	60.4
26. Chris Ratliff, York (N.Y.)	Jr	23	168	279	60.2
27. Bert Gardner, Millsaps	Jr	19	101	168	60.1
28. Jeff Merrill, Binghamton	Jr	28	201	335	60.0
28. Paul Butler, Colby	Sr	25	198	330	60.0
28. William Berry, Carthage	Sr	24	171	285	60.0
31. Steve Honderd, Calvin	Sr	28	226	377	59.9
32. Chris Nicholson, North Park	Sr	25	153	259	59.1
33. Fred Drains, Kean	Sr	26	191	324	59.0
34. Erik Whalen, Rensselaer	Sr	24	142	241	58.9
35. Andrew Daniels, Wm. Paterson	Sr	22	174	296	58.8

THREE-POINT FIELD GOALS MADE PER GAME

	CL	G	NO.	AVG.
1. Mike Connelly, Catholic	Sr	27	111	4.1
2. Kirk Anderson, Augustana (Ill.)	Sr	30	123	4.1
3. Billy Collins, Nichols	So	23	89	3.9
4. David Demarcus, Centre	Jr	24	89	3.7
5. Rodney Lane, Maryville (Tenn.)	Sr	26	92	3.5
6. Chris Sullivan, Wheaton (Mass.)	Sr	23	79	3.4
7. Scott Pritzl, Wis.-Oshkosh	Sr	25	85	3.4
8. Kenny McClain, Oneonta St.	Jr	24	81	3.4
9. Steve Chase, St. Joseph's (Me.)	Sr	29	97	3.3
10. Aaron Lee, Mass.-Dartmouth	So	29	96	3.3
11. Troy Ambers, Rockford	Jr	24	79	3.3
12. Ernie Bray, UC Santa Cruz	Jr	22	72	3.3
13. Doug Dickerson, Baldwin-Wallace	So	26	85	3.3
13. Chris Carideo, Widener	So	26	85	3.3
15. Chad Ford, Averett	Sr	25	81	3.2
15. Joe O'Connor, Bri'water (Mass.)	Sr	25	81	3.2
15. Eli Haskell, Colorado Col.	Sr	25	81	3.2
18. Dameon Ross, Salisbury St.	Jr	26	84	3.2
19. Scott Fitch, Geneseo St.	Jr	27	87	3.2
20. Dave Shaw, Drew	Sr	23	74	3.2
21. Lonnie Brooks, Western Conn. St.	Jr	26	82	3.2
22. Brad Eshoo, Knox	So	22	69	3.1
23. Ryan McKee, Claremont-M-S	Sr	24	75	3.1
24. Rob Hayward, Gordon	Sr	22	68	3.1
25. Kevin Murphy, Frostburg St.	Sr	24	74	3.1
26. Kelvin Richardson, Maryville (Tenn.)	Sr	26	80	3.1
27. Todd Martin, East. Mennonite	Sr	25	75	3.0
28. Tony Balistrere, Susquehanna	Sr	25	75	3.0
28. Mike Comerford, Rensselaer	Sr	24	72	3.0
30. Steve Diekmann, Grinnell	So	22	65	3.0
31. Eddie Peskie, Mt. St. Vincent	So	26	76	2.9
32. Jason Valant, Colorado Col.	Sr	25	73	2.9
33. Seth Heaton, Middlebury	Sr	23	67	2.9
34. Chris Payne, Lomas	Fr	22	64	2.9
35. Jim Durrell, Colby-Sawyer	Jr	25	71	2.8
35. T. J. Gondek, Colby-Sawyer	So	25	71	2.8

THREE-POINT FIELD-GOAL PERCENTAGE

(Min. 1.5 3FG Made Per Game)	CL	G	FG	FGA	PCT.
1. Brad Apple, Greensboro	Jr	26	49	91	53.8
2. Rodney Lane, Maryville (Tenn.)	Sr	26	92	171	53.8
3. Craig Bradley, Wooster	So	27	44	82	53.7

(Min. 1.5 3FG Made Per Game)	CL	G	FG	FGA	PCT.
4. Eddie Peskie, Mt. St. Vincent	So	26	76	144	52.8
5. Joe Kutcka, Gallaudet	Fr	24	41	78	52.6
6. Doug Dickerson, Baldwin-Wallace	So	26	85	162	52.5
7. Jesse Raddabaugh, St. Thomas (Minn.)	Jr	24	46	88	52.3
8. Rob Bice, Williams	Jr	27	69	133	51.9
9. Brian Martin, Ill. Wesleyan	Sr	25	48	93	51.6
10. Justun Lott, Ohio Wesleyan	So	25	40	78	51.3
11. Mark Burgher, DePauw	Sr	26	55	108	50.9
12. Mike Guth, Franklin	So	25	42	83	50.6
13. Felix Rogers, Wis.-Whitewater	Jr	27	45	89	50.6
14. Elgin Holston, Mary Washington	Jr	26	53	105	50.5
15. David Demarcus, Centre	Jr	24	89	177	50.3
16. Chris Peterson, Eureka	Jr	29	67	135	49.6
17. Steve Kuehl, Ill. Wesleyan	Sr	25	57	115	49.6
18. Vince Perrine, Ithaca	Fr	24	50	101	49.5
19. Chris Moore, UC San Diego	Sr	25	52	107	48.6
20. Troy Tyler, Eureka	Jr	28	51	105	48.6
21. John McGovern, Misericordia	Fr	25	40	83	48.2
22. Ryan Vickers, Oglethorpe	Fr	24	50	104	48.1
23. Ken Buskey, Alfred	Jr	24	37	77	48.1
24. Todd Seifferlein, DePauw	Sr	26	71	148	48.0
25. Rob Weedn, Amherst	So	23	56	117	47.9
26. Jay Spearman, Neb. Wesleyan	So	25	43	90	47.8
27. John Francis, Maine Maritime	Fr	19	31	65	47.7
28. Pete Binelas, Wis.-Stout	Jr	25	51	107	47.7
29. Clarence Pierce, New Jersey Tech	So	25	58	122	47.5
30. Brian Carlonas, King's (Pa.)	Jr	22	44	93	47.3
31. Aaron Lee, Mass.-Dartmouth	So	29	96	204	47.1
32. Craig Studer, Grinnell	Jr	22	47	100	47.0
33. John Brownfield, St. Olaf	Jr	25	60	128	46.9
34. Mike Connelly, Catholic	Sr	27	111	237	46.8
35. Willie Green, Wis.-Eau Claire	Jr	26	57	122	46.7

FREE-THROW PERCENTAGE

(Min. 2.5 FT Made Per Game)	CL	G	FT	FTA	PCT.
1. Jim Durrell, Colby-Sawyer	Jr	25	67	72	93.1
2. Bobby Bonjean, Illinois Col.	Jr	21	67	74	90.5
3. Pat Murphy, Wis.-Platteville	Sr	28	134	149	89.9
4. Steve Fleming, Hiram	Jr	25	130	146	89.0
5. Chad Onofrio, Tufts	Fr	25	79	89	88.8
6. Luke Busby, Johns Hopkins	Jr	26	85	96	88.5
6. Dennis Ruedinger, Wis.-Oshkosh	Fr	25	85	96	88.5
8. Noah Clarke, Williams	So	27	68	77	88.3
9. Joe Levesque, MIT	So	24	75	85	88.2
10. Ray Cullinan, Potsdam St.	Fr	23	89	101	88.1
11. Mike Comerford, Rensselaer	Sr	24	79	90	87.8
12. Pat Duquette, Williams	Sr	27	68	78	87.2
13. Steve Dunham, Ithaca	Jr	24	101	116	87.1
14. Jay Moore, Amherst	Jr	18	45	52	86.5
15. Victor Koytikh, Framingham St.	So	25	108	125	86.4
16. Scott Leip, Babson	Sr	24	68	79	86.1
17. John Richards, Sewanee	Sr	25	86	100	86.0
18. Kevin Felner, Emory	Sr	25	98	114	86.0
19. Andy Cook, Centre	So	25	67	78	85.9
20. Tobin Anderson, Wesleyan	So	20	71	83	85.5
21. Derek Elmore, Emory & Henry	Sr	28	97	114	85.1
22. Bob Croft, Ohio Wesleyan	Jr	25	113	133	85.0
23. Vaughn Clark, Colby	Jr	25	79	93	84.9
24. Jason Carpenter, Framingham St.	Sr	25	67	79	84.8
25. Mike Guth, Franklin	So	25	89	105	84.8
26. Jeremy Cole, Kalamazoo	Fr	26	83	98	84.7
27. Adrian Scott, Fisk	Fr	25	121	143	84.6
27. John Spence, UC San Diego	Sr	23	66	78	84.6
29. Mike Rhoades, Lebanon Valley	So	29	145	172	84.3
30. Kevin Ralph, Drew	Jr	23	69	82	84.1
31. Matt Leary, Wartburg	Sr	26	126	150	84.0
32. T.J. Van Wie, Wis.-Platteville	Sr	28	110	131	84.0
33. Bob Brugger, Adrian	Jr	25	67	80	83.8
34. Paul Ferrell, Guilford	Jr	24	103	123	83.7
35. Ben Drake, Brockport St.	Jr	25	82	98	83.7

REBOUNDING

	CL	G	NO.	AVG.
1. Steve Lemmer, Hamilton	Sr	27	404	15.0
2. Rolando Welch, Western Md.	Jr	24	320	13.3
3. Jim Hoopes, Albright	Jr	22	278	12.6
4. Matt Cusano, Scranton	Sr	29	362	12.5
5. William Berry, Carthage	Sr	24	299	12.5
6. Jose Rodriguez, Hunter	Sr	29	357	12.3
7. Andrew South, New Jersey Tech	So	26	319	12.3
8. Shannon Cloyd, Millikin	So	25	301	12.0

	CL	G	NO.	AVG.
9. Mahlon Williams, Wheaton (Mass.)	So	20	236	11.8
10. James Boykins, Chris. Newport	Sr	28	327	11.7
11. Fritz Mardy, Polytechnic (N.Y.)	Sr	17	196	11.5
12. Terry Wilkins, Wash. & Jeff.	Jr	21	242	11.5
13. Tom Dickinson, Wesley	Jr	23	265	11.5
14. Greg Peterson, Bethel (Minn.)	Sr	24	269	11.2
15. Keith Hines, Montclair St.	Jr	24	263	11.0
16. Darryl Taylor, Oneonta St.	Fr	24	261	10.9
17. Paul Butler, Colby	Sr	25	270	10.8
18. Blair Slattery, Occidental	Jr	19	201	10.6
19. Michael Tucker, Old Westbury	Sr	23	237	10.3
20. Jon Selander, Stevens Tech	Jr	23	235	10.2
21. Masio Kinard, Staten Island	Jr	24	244	10.2
22. Steve Haynes, Mass.-Dartmouth	Sr	30	301	10.0
23. Erik Lidecis, Maritime (N.Y.)	Jr	20	200	10.0
24. Peter Deppisch, Salem St.	Sr	26	259	10.0
25. Mike Nicholson, York (N.Y.)	So	21	207	9.9
26. Mark Harris, Coast Guard	Fr	24	235	9.8
26. John Cooksey, Webster	Jr	24	235	9.8
28. Jim Vlogianitis, Brockport St.	Jr	25	244	9.8
29. Chris Sullivan, St. John Fisher	Jr	23	224	9.7
30. Mark Kronk, Fontbonne	So	24	233	9.7
31. Pat Williams, Fitchburg St.	Sr	23	223	9.7
32. John Lampe, Hiram	Sr	25	241	9.6
33. Chris McMahon, Tufts	So	25	238	9.5
33. Khari Brown, Tufts	Jr	25	238	9.5
35. Chris Eaton, Eureka	Jr	29	275	9.5

ASSISTS

	CL	G	NO.	AVG.
1. David Genovese, Mt. St. Vincent	So	27	237	8.8
2. Jeff Molisani, Rochester Inst.	Sr	28	237	8.5
3. Lance Andrews, New Jersey Tech	Sr	26	217	8.3
4. Greg Martin, Westminster (Mo.)	Sr	26	211	8.1
5. Steve Artis, Chris. Newport	Sr	28	220	7.9
6. Jimmy Resvanis, Baruch	Jr	24	186	7.8
7. Jason Franklin, Westfield St.	Sr	27	203	7.5
8. Tres Wolf, Susquehanna	Jr	25	179	7.2
9. Paul Ferrell, Guilford	Jr	24	170	7.1
10. Steve Fleming, Hiram	Jr	25	177	7.1
11. Rodney Lusain, UC San Diego	Jr	24	163	6.8
12. Danny McClain, Rutgers-Camden	Sr	24	153	6.4
13. Fran D'Agata, Hamilton	So	27	169	6.3
14. Jason Simms, Frostburg St.	Jr	26	161	6.2
15. Scott Fitch, Geneseo St.	Jr	27	161	6.0
16. Kevin Shumway, Clarkson	So	23	136	5.9
17. Jeremy Greenberg, Binghamton	Jr	28	164	5.9
18. Moses Jean-Pierre, Plymouth St.	Jr	25	146	5.8
19. Anthony Landry, York (N.Y.)	Jr	22	128	5.8
20. Mike Carlson, Nichols	So	24	136	5.7
21. David Brown, Westfield St.	Jr	28	158	5.6
22. Bobby Bonjean, Illinois Col.	Jr	21	116	5.5
23. Jerry Mackey, Hartwick	Sr	23	126	5.5
23. Jason Bragg, Redlands	Jr	23	126	5.5
25. Scott Leip, Babson	Sr	24	131	5.5
25. Marc Fry, Messiah	Sr	24	131	5.5
27. Derrick Watkins, Fisk	Sr	25	136	5.4
28. Matt Gaudet, Colby	So	25	135	5.4
28. Tom Bowman, New York U.	Jr	25	135	5.4
28. Rowdy Williams, Franklin	Sr	25	135	5.4
31. Kevin Beard, Greensboro	So	26	140	5.4
32. Mike Lauterhahn, Wm. Paterson	Jr	24	129	5.4
33. Derrick Lawson, Hunter	Fr	28	149	5.3
34. Mike Rhoades, Lebanon Valley	So	29	154	5.3
35. Vin Squeglia, Albertus Magnus	Jr	23	122	5.3

BLOCKED SHOTS

	CL	G	NO.	AVG.
1. Matt Cusano, Scranton	Sr	29	145	5.0
2. Andrew South, New Jersey Tech	So	26	111	4.3
3. Khari Brown, Tufts	Jr	25	88	3.5
4. Jason Mekelburg, Bethel (Minn.)	Jr	24	76	3.2
5. John Lampe, Hiram	Sr	25	77	3.1
6. Jack Lothian, Wis.-Stevens Point	Sr	28	83	3.0
7. Ken Beeman, Principia	Sr	24	70	2.9
8. Carlo Williams, La Verne	Sr	21	61	2.9
9. Fred Drains, Kean	Sr	26	75	2.9
10. Doug Wilson, Millsaps	Sr	25	72	2.9
11. Charlie Bartlett, Rochester Inst.	Jr	28	80	2.9
12. Jose Rodriguez, Hunter	Sr	29	80	2.8
13. Jeff Manning, Curry	So	25	66	2.6

	CL	G	NO.	AVG.
14. Eric Hatcher, Framingham St.	Sr	24	59	2.5
15. Mike McGwin, Nazareth (N.Y.)	Sr	24	58	2.4
16. Keith Hines, Montclair St.	Jr	24	57	2.4
17. Pat Quinlan, Monmouth (Ill.)	Sr	23	52	2.3
18. Emmett Highbaugh, FDU-Madison	So	24	54	2.3
19. Adam Fitzgerald, CCNY	Fr	18	40	2.2
20. Wellington Hughes, Widener	Fr	26	56	2.2
21. James Boykins, Chris. Newport	Sr	28	60	2.1
22. Matt Johnson, Wash. & Jeff.	Jr	21	44	2.1
23. Erik Lidecis, Maritime (N.Y.)	Jr	20	41	2.0
24. David Ellison, East. Mennonite	Fr	24	49	2.0
25. Steve Honderd, Calvin	Sr	28	57	2.0
26. Steve Lemmer, Hamilton	Sr	27	53	2.0
27. Blair Slattery, Occidental	Jr	19	37	1.9
28. Dennis McGoldrick, Binghamton	Jr	28	54	1.9
29. Mark Heffernan, MIT	Fr	23	44	1.9
30. David Genovese, Mt. St. Vincent	So	27	51	1.9
31. Pat Smalley, Rhode Island Col.	So	21	38	1.8
32. Robert Clyburn, Kean	So	25	45	1.8
33. Rolando Welch, Western Md.	Jr	24	43	1.8
34. Chris Joyce, Hartwick	Sr	26	46	1.8
35. Mike Kies, Elmhurst	Sr	25	44	1.8

STEALS

	CL	G	NO.	AVG.
1. Moses Jean-Pierre, Plymouth St.	Jr	25	114	4.6
2. Ruben Reyes, Salve Regina	So	25	104	4.2
3. Rodney Lusain, UC San Diego	Jr	24	97	4.0
4. Andre Self, Trenton St.	So	27	107	4.0
5. Eric Bell, New Paltz St.	Fr	24	89	3.7
5. Tom Seeger, Upsala	Sr	24	89	3.7
7. Damon Ridley, Cal Lutheran	Jr	27	96	3.6
8. Garvin Atwell, Utica Tech	Sr	23	77	3.3
9. Tony Abbiati, Bowdoin	Sr	24	78	3.3
10. Rodger Smitherman, Fisk	Sr	24	75	3.1
11. Jeff Molisani, Rochester Inst.	Sr	28	87	3.1
12. Aaron Robinson, N'western Col. (Wis.)	Fr	21	65	3.1
13. Dave Ulloa, Cal Lutheran	Fr	24	73	3.0
14. Jason Franklin, Westfield St.	Sr	27	81	3.0
14. Jeff Landis, York (Pa.)	So	27	81	3.0
14. Jimmy Resvanis, Baruch	Jr	24	72	3.0
14. Ronald Reece, Bard	Fr	24	72	3.0
14. Matt Johnson, Wash. & Jeff.	Jr	21	63	3.0
14. Blair Slattery, Occidental	Jr	19	57	3.0
20. Mark Garnett, Marymount (Va.)	Sr	25	73	2.9
21. Albert Johnson, Rhodes	Fr	27	78	2.9
22. Jeff Jackson, Mass.-Boston	Sr	25	72	2.9
23. Wayne McDowell, York (N.Y.)	Fr	23	66	2.9
24. Adam Machala, Brandeis	Sr	22	63	2.9
25. Victor Koytikh, Framingham St.	So	25	71	2.8
26. Steve Artis, Chris. Newport	Sr	28	79	2.8
27. Scott Rose, Mass.-Boston	Fr	25	70	2.8
28. Rob Carter, Hunter	Jr	29	81	2.8
28. Jamie Header, St. Joseph's (Me.)	Sr	29	81	2.8
30. Paul Wiedeman, Rowan	Sr	31	86	2.8
31. Scott Leip, Babson	Sr	24	66	2.8
32. Brian Scott, Wesley	Fr	23	63	2.7
33. Ernie Peavy, Wis.-Platteville	So	28	76	2.7
34. Garry Murray, Albany (N.Y.)	Jr	24	65	2.7
35. Lance Andrews, New Jersey Tech	Sr	26	70	2.7
35. Dameon Ross, Salisbury St.	Jr	26	70	2.7

1993 DIVISION III MEN'S BASKETBALL GAME HIGHS

INDIVIDUAL HIGHS

SCORING

Pts.	Player, Team vs. Opponent	Date
61	Steve Honderd, Calvin vs. Kalamazoo	Feb. 20
53	Moses Jean-Pierre, Plymouth St. vs. Southern Me.	Jan. 28
48	Alberto Montanez, Rochester Inst. vs. Rensselaer	Jan. 8
48	Larry Norman, Clark (Mass.) vs. Anna Maria	Dec. 2
47	Charlie Borsheim, Washington (Mo.) vs. Emory	Feb. 14
46	Alberto Montanez, Rochester Inst. vs. Hamilton	Mar. 7
46	John Spence, UC San Diego vs. Redlands	Jan. 6
45	Darron Lowe, Concordia (Ill.) vs. Aurora	Feb. 20
45	Moses Jean-Pierre, Plymouth St. vs. Mass.-Boston	Feb. 6
44	Bill Conlee, Wm. Paterson vs. Drew	Feb. 15
44	Al Pettway, Worcester St. vs. Framingham St.	Feb. 11
44	Mike Crnkovich, Wabash vs. Franklin	Feb. 10
44	Craig Instone, Juniata vs. Wash. & Jeff.	Dec. 6

THREE-POINT FIELD GOALS

3FG	Player, Team vs. Opponent	Date
12	Kirk Anderson, Augustana (Ill.) vs. Wis.-Platteville	Mar. 13
10	Scott Krohn, Carleton vs. Macalester	Jan. 6
9	Eli Haskell, Colorado Col. vs. Western St.	Feb. 23
9	Ken McClain, Oneonta St. vs. Cortland St.	Feb. 18
9	Greg Bonczkowski, Hartwick vs. Rochester Inst.	Dec. 8
9	Craig Instone, Juniata vs. Wash. & Jeff.	Dec. 6
9	Mike Connelly, Catholic vs. York (N.Y.)	Dec. 5
9	Troy Ambers, Rockford vs. Marion	Nov. 20
8	Several times	

FREE THROWS

FT	Player, Team vs. Opponent	Date
20	Larry Norman, Clark (Mass.) vs. Anna Maria	Dec. 2
19	Andy Gray, Waynesburg vs. Thiel	Feb. 20
19	Charlie Borsheim, Washington (Mo.) vs. Emory	Feb. 14
17	Steve Honderd, Calvin vs. Kalamazoo	Feb. 20
17	Kevin Frye, Denison vs. Case Reserve	Feb. 6
17	Joe Herman, Defiance vs. Bluffton	Jan. 30
17	Scott Krohn, Carleton vs. Bethel (Minn.)	Jan. 16
17	Rob Novosel, Case Reserve vs. Brandeis	Nov. 28
16	Several times	

REBOUNDS

Reb.	Player, Team vs. Opponent	Date
27	Masio Kinard, Staten Island vs. Mt. St. Vincent	Mar. 6
25	Jose Rodriguez, Hunter vs. York (N.Y.)	Dec. 2
24	Jim Vlogianitis, Brockport St. vs. Catholic	Nov. 21
24	William Berry, Carthage vs. Wis.-Parkside	Nov. 21
23	James Boykins, Chris. Newport vs. York (Pa.)	Jan. 8
23	Yusuf Screen, Skidmore vs. Central Conn. St.	Jan. 6
23	Terry Wilkins, Wash. & Jeff. vs. Juniata	Dec. 5
22	Matt Cusano, Scranton vs. Elizabethtown	Feb. 24
22	Isaiah Johnson, Dubuque vs. Buena Vista	Jan. 30
22	Greg Peterson, Bethel (Minn.) vs. St. Thomas (Minn.)	Jan. 27
22	Chris Weinwurm, Worcester Tech vs. Salve Regina	Jan. 12
22	Matt Cusano, Scranton vs. Catholic	Jan. 6
22	Kirk Daley, Alfred vs. Hobart	Jan. 22
22	William Berry, Carthage vs. Marian	Dec. 30

ASSISTS

Ast.	Player, Team vs. Opponent	Date
16	Steve Evans, Union (N.Y.) vs. St. Lawrence	Feb. 26
16	David Genovese, Mt. St. Vincent vs. Polytechnic (N.Y.)	Feb. 18
15	Jeff Molisani, Rochester Inst. vs. Hamilton	Mar. 7
15	Mike Lautherhahn, Wm. Paterson vs. Stockton St.	Feb. 20
15	Jason Franklin, Westfield St. vs. Framingham St.	Jan. 30

BLOCKED SHOTS

Blk.	Player, Team vs. Opponent	Date
11	Matt Cusano, Scranton vs. Gettysburg	Dec. 28
10	John Lampe, Hiram vs. Thiel	Jan. 25
10	Andrew South, New Jersey Tech vs. Polytechnic (N.Y.)	Jan. 23
10	Jeff Manning, Curry vs. Emerson	Dec. 14
9	Khari Brown, Tufts vs. Anna Maria	Nov. 24
8	Several times	

STEALS

St.	Player, Team vs. Opponent	Date
12	Moses Jean-Pierre, Plymouth St. vs. Rhode Island Col.	Jan. 23
11	Anthony Toner, Gettysburg vs. Messiah	Dec. 12
11	Rich Harding, Fitchburg St. vs. Wentworth Inst.	Nov. 30
10	Jeff Molisani, Rochester Inst. vs. Clarkson	Jan. 30
10	Derek Hamilton, Wis.-Oshkosh vs. Lakeland	Jan. 9
10	Matt Johnson, Wash. & Jeff. vs. Marietta	Dec. 2
10	Justin Brown, Aurora vs. Principia	Nov. 27
9	Several times	

TEAM HIGHS

SCORING

Pts.	Team vs. Opponent	Date
144	Manchester vs. Ind.-Northwest	Dec. 29
141	Mass.-Dartmouth vs. Framingham St.	Dec. 5
137	UC Santa Cruz vs. Simpson (Cal.)	Jan. 9
135	Maryville (Tenn.) vs. Savannah A&D	Nov. 20
133	Cal Lutheran vs. Pacific Union	Nov. 23
132	Washington (Mo.) vs. Emory	Feb. 14
132	Redlands vs. La Sierra	Nov. 23
127	UC San Diego vs. Redlands	Jan. 6
125	Anna Maria vs. Curry	Feb. 2
125	Mt. St. Vincent vs. Bard	Dec. 8

FIELD-GOAL PERCENTAGE

Pct.		Team vs. Opponent	Date
75.5	(37 of 49)	Wheaton (Mass.) vs. Nichols	Jan. 23
73.9	(34 of 46)	St. John's (Minn.) vs. Gust. Adolphus	Jan. 16
73.9	(34 of 46)	Wooster vs. Allegheny	Jan. 13
72.5	(29 of 40)	Ogelthorpe vs. Trinity (Tex.)	Feb. 19
72.0	(36 of 50)	Wis.-Whitewater vs. Wis.-Oshkosh	Jan. 6
71.9	(23 of 32)	Lebanon Valley vs. Frank. & Marsh.	Jan. 23
71.2	(37 of 52)	Kalamazoo vs. Goshen	Dec. 1
70.8	(34 of 48)	Hanover vs. Franklin	Feb. 20
70.5	(31 of 44)	Lebanon Valley vs. Moravian	Jan. 30
69.6	(32 of 46)	Bridgewater (Va.) vs. Guilford	Jan. 16

THREE-POINT FIELD GOALS

3FG	Team vs. Opponent	Date
20	Anna Maria vs. Roger Williams	Feb. 20
20	Colorado Col. vs. Me.-Augusta	Jan. 11
19	Redlands vs. Pomona-Pitzer	Jan. 13
18	Grinnell vs. Vennard	Jan. 11
18	Carleton vs. Macalester	Jan. 6
18	Illinois Col. vs. Maryville (Mo.)	Nov. 25
17	Carroll (Wis.) vs. St. Norbert	Jan. 26
16	Several times	

1993 DIVISION III MEN'S TEAM LEADERS

SCORING OFFENSE

	G	W-L	PTS.	AVG.
1. Salisbury St.	26	18-8	2,551	98.1
2. Worcester St.	27	19-8	2,618	97.0
3. Anna Maria	27	21-6	2,605	96.5
4. Redlands	24	10-14	2,278	94.9
5. St. Joseph's (Me.)	29	22-7	2,637	90.9
6. Hamilton	27	22-5	2,450	90.7
7. New Jersey Tech	26	22-4	2,350	90.4
8. Mass.-Dartmouth	31	25-6	2,773	89.5
9. Maryville (Tenn.)	26	20-6	2,304	88.6
10. Salem St.	26	18-8	2,290	88.1
11. Babson	25	20-5	2,194	87.8
12. Ill. Wesleyan	25	16-9	2,186	87.4
13. Ferrum	25	18-7	2,169	86.8
14. Manchester	28	20-8	2,424	86.6
15. Plymouth St.	25	12-13	2,157	86.3
16. Catholic	27	21-6	2,326	86.1
17. Mt. St. Vincent	27	18-9	2,309	85.5
18. Cal Lutheran	27	20-7	2,305	85.4
19. Westfield St.	28	22-6	2,390	85.4
20. Neb. Wesleyan	25	17-8	2,126	85.0
21. Brandeis	25	8-17	2,125	85.0
22. Wis.-Platteville	28	24-4	2,379	85.0
23. Calvin	28	25-3	2,377	84.9
24. Defiance	27	21-6	2,292	84.9
25. Cabrini	26	20-6	2,201	84.7

	G	W-L	PTS.	AVG.
26. Hunter	29	25-4	2,433	83.9
27. Emory & Henry	28	23-5	2,346	83.8
28. Augustana (Ill.)	31	24-7	2,591	83.6
29. Illinois Col.	21	10-11	1,754	83.5
30. UC San Diego	25	17-8	2,082	83.3

SCORING DEFENSE

	G	W-L	PTS.	AVG.
1. St. Thomas (Minn.)	28	19-9	1,599	57.1
2. Wooster	28	21-7	1,643	58.7
3. Johns Hopkins	26	19-7	1,535	59.0
4. Southwestern (Tex.)	27	18-9	1,600	59.3
5. Randolph-Macon	27	18-9	1,606	59.5
6. Frank. & Marsh.	28	24-4	1,678	59.9
7. St. Olaf	25	17-8	1,499	60.0
8. Ohio Northern	30	28-2	1,821	60.7
9. Eastern Nazarene	26	19-7	1,585	61.0
10. Stony Brook	27	15-12	1,652	61.2
11. DePauw	26	19-7	1,594	61.3
11. Widener	26	14-12	1,594	61.3
13. Buffalo St.	27	21-6	1,660	61.5
14. Scranton	29	27-2	1,784	61.5
15. Wittenberg	26	19-7	1,602	61.6
16. Ithaca	27	20-7	1,664	61.6
17. Rochester	25	11-14	1,541	61.6
18. Rowan	31	29-2	1,919	61.9
19. Kenyon	27	16-11	1,673	62.0
20. Denison	25	11-14	1,565	62.6
21. Eureka	29	24-5	1,821	62.8
22. Kean	26	18-8	1,640	63.1
23. Carleton	24	17-7	1,514	63.1
24. Moravian	24	15-9	1,515	63.1
25. Loras	24	15-9	1,517	63.2
26. Maritime (N.Y.)	24	11-13	1,518	63.3
27. Carnegie Mellon	24	16-8	1,530	63.8
28. Albany (N.Y.)	25	15-10	1,604	64.2
29. Wis.-Eau Claire	26	19-7	1,671	64.3
30. FDU-Madison	24	11-13	1,544	64.3

SCORING MARGIN

	OFF.	DEF.	MAR.
1. New Jersey Tech	90.4	65.7	24.7
2. Rowan	81.7	61.9	19.8
3. Wis.-Platteville	85.0	66.2	18.8
4. Scranton	79.8	61.5	18.3
5. Williams	81.5	64.4	17.1
6. Eureka	79.1	62.8	16.3
7. Anna Maria	96.5	80.4	16.0
8. Cal Lutheran	85.4	69.7	15.7
9. Calvin	84.9	69.3	15.6
10. Manchester	86.6	71.5	15.1
11. Hunter	83.9	69.0	14.9
12. Maryville (Tenn.)	88.6	74.1	14.5
13. New York U.	82.0	68.0	14.0
14. Babson	87.8	74.1	13.7
15. Chris. Newport	83.3	69.7	13.6
16. Geneseo St.	79.1	65.7	13.4
17. St. Joseph's (Me.)	90.9	77.6	13.3
18. Wooster	71.4	58.7	12.7
19. Westfield St.	85.4	73.0	12.4
20. Wittenberg	73.8	61.6	12.2
21. Wis.-Stevens Point	76.5	64.9	11.6
22. Rhodes	80.2	68.6	11.6
23. Ohio Northern	72.3	60.7	11.6
24. Rochester Inst.	83.2	71.8	11.4
25. Emory & Henry	83.8	72.4	11.4
26. Hamilton	90.7	79.5	11.3
27. Frank. & Marsh.	71.1	59.9	11.1
28. Lebanon Valley	75.5	64.4	11.1
29. Mass.-Dartmouth	89.5	78.5	11.0
29. DePauw	72.3	61.3	11.0

WON-LOST PERCENTAGE

	W-L	PCT.
1. Rowan	29-2	.935
2. Ohio Northern	28-2	.933
3. Scranton	27-2	.931
4. Calvin	25-3	.893
5. New York U.	23-3	.885
6. Colby	22-3	.880
7. Hunter	25-4	.862
8. Frank. & Marsh.	24-4	.857
8. Wis.-Platteville	24-4	.857
10. Geneseo St.	23-4	.852
10. Williams	23-4	.852
12. New Jersey Tech	22-4	.846
13. Eureka	24-5	.828
14. Chris. Newport	23-5	.821
14. Emory & Henry	23-5	.821
14. Wis.-Stevens Point	23-5	.821
17. Hamilton	22-5	.815
18. Beloit	21-5	.808
19. Mass.-Dartmouth	25-6	.806
20. Babson	20-5	.800
20. Wheaton (Mass.)	20-5	.800
22. Rochester Inst.	22-6	.786
22. Westfield St.	22-6	.786
24. Anna Maria	21-6	.778
24. Buffalo St.	21-6	.778
24. Catholic	21-6	.778
24. Rhodes	21-6	.778
24. Stockton St.	21-6	.778
24. Defiance	21-6	.778
30. Knox	17-5	.773

FIELD-GOAL PERCENTAGE

	FG	FGA	PCT.
1. St. John's (Minn.)	744	1,415	52.6
2. Bridgewater (Va.)	610	1,170	52.1
3. Scranton	871	1,676	52.0
4. Otterbein	851	1,651	51.5
5. Wartburg	754	1,463	51.5
6. Lebanon Valley	756	1,467	51.5
7. Chris. Newport	909	1,774	51.2
8. Maryville (Tenn.)	805	1,575	51.1
9. Hiram	759	1,491	50.9
10. Eureka	833	1,637	50.9
11. Wooster	735	1,450	50.7
12. Westfield St.	926	1,835	50.5
13. Rochester Inst.	894	1,772	50.5
14. Franklin	717	1,423	50.4
15. Calvin	868	1,723	50.4
16. Kalamazoo	668	1,330	50.2
17. Wis.-Whitewater	792	1,578	50.2
18. Rowan	973	1,942	50.1
19. Amherst	666	1,331	50.0
20. Salem St.	885	1,773	49.9
21. Ill. Wesleyan	755	1,513	49.9
22. Mass.-Dartmouth	959	1,924	49.8
23. Wabash	789	1,584	49.8
24. Guilford	645	1,296	49.8
25. Oglethorpe	692	1,393	49.7
26. Baldwin-Wallace	689	1,389	49.6
27. St. Thomas (Minn.)	651	1,313	49.6
28. Ithaca	699	1,413	49.5
29. Neb. Wesleyan	777	1,571	49.5
30. St. Joseph's (Me.)	989	2,003	49.4

FIELD-GOAL PERCENTAGE DEFENSE

	FG	FGA	PCT.
1. Scranton	659	1,806	36.5
2. Widener	559	1,446	38.7
3. Southwestern (Tex.)	552	1,426	38.7
4. Maine Maritime	499	1,277	39.1
5. New Jersey Tech	668	1,702	39.2
6. Lebanon Valley	660	1,667	39.6
7. Wittenberg	561	1,401	40.0
8. Montclair St.	585	1,460	40.1
9. Binghamton	644	1,604	40.1
10. Wis.-Stevens Point	630	1,567	40.2
11. Old Westbury	669	1,664	40.2
12. FDU-Madison	580	1,438	40.3
13. Kean	622	1,540	40.4
14. Buffalo St.	613	1,517	40.4
15. Monmouth (Ill.)	603	1,492	40.4
16. Hunter	759	1,876	40.5
17. Westminster (Mo.)	641	1,582	40.5
18. Kalamazoo	554	1,364	40.6
19. Dubuque	661	1,625	40.7
20. Ithaca	580	1,423	40.8
21. Bowdoin	589	1,442	40.8

	FG	FGA	PCT.
22. Westfield St.	748	1,831	40.9
23. Neb. Wesleyan	680	1,663	40.9
24. Williams	646	1,575	41.0
25. Maritime (N.Y.)	563	1,371	41.1
26. St. John Fisher	650	1,577	41.2
27. Fredonia St.	672	1,627	41.3
28. Eastern Conn. St.	665	1,604	41.5
29. Millsaps	641	1,543	41.5
30. Beloit	612	1,473	41.5

THREE-POINT FIELD GOALS MADE PER GAME

	G	NO.	AVG.
1. Anna Maria	27	302	11.2
2. Maryville (Tenn.)	26	258	9.9
3. Redlands	24	234	9.8
4. Colby-Sawyer	25	239	9.6
5. Mass.-Dartmouth	31	291	9.4
6. Mary Washington	26	243	9.3
7. Centre	25	221	8.8
7. Colorado Col.	25	221	8.8
7. Sewanee	25	221	8.8
10. Grinnell	22	188	8.5
11. Catholic	27	228	8.4
12. Emory & Henry	28	236	8.4
13. Salisbury St.	26	218	8.4
14. Ill. Wesleyan	25	208	8.3
15. Knox	22	183	8.3
16. Augustana (Ill.)	31	256	8.3
17. Marietta	25	206	8.2
18. New Jersey Tech	26	211	8.1
19. Hamilton	27	214	7.9
20. St. Lawrence	25	197	7.9
21. MacMurray	27	207	7.7
22. Drew	23	176	7.7
23. Eureka	29	217	7.5
24. Plymouth St.	25	187	7.5
25. St. Thomas (Minn.)	28	209	7.5
26. Middlebury	23	169	7.3
27. DePauw	26	191	7.3
28. Colby	25	182	7.3
29. Beloit	26	188	7.2
30. Rensselaer	24	173	7.2

THREE-POINT FIELD-GOAL PERCENTAGE

(Min. 3.0 3FG Made Per Game)	G	FG	FGA	PCT.
1. DePauw	26	191	419	45.6
2. Baldwin-Wallace	26	183	404	45.3
3. Scranton	29	113	253	44.7
4. Eureka	29	217	494	43.9
5. Ill. Wesleyan	25	208	474	43.9
6. Mass.-Dartmouth	31	291	667	43.6
7. Maryville (Tenn.)	26	258	592	43.6
8. Guilford	24	108	249	43.4
9. Ohio Wesleyan	25	111	256	43.4
10. Elizabethtown	26	150	350	42.9
11. Wis.-Whitewater	27	147	344	42.7
12. Greensboro	26	155	366	42.3
13. Ohio Northern	30	157	371	42.3
14. MacMurray	27	207	492	42.1
15. Grinnell	22	188	447	42.1
16. Catholic	27	228	543	42.0
17. Mt. St. Vincent	27	178	424	42.0
18. Gallaudet	24	123	293	42.0
19. Franklin	25	164	392	41.8
20. William Penn	25	96	230	41.7
21. Rensselaer	24	173	415	41.7
22. Cornell College	22	98	237	41.4
23. Colorado Col.	25	221	536	41.2
24. Western New Eng.	21	82	199	41.2
25. Williams	27	154	374	41.2
26. Centre	25	221	539	41.0
27. Middlebury	23	169	415	40.7
28. Ithaca	27	138	339	40.7
29. Kalamazoo	26	107	264	40.5
30. Wis.-Eau Claire	26	157	388	40.5

FREE-THROW PERCENTAGE

	FT	FTA	PCT.
1. Colby	391	506	77.3
2. Wabash	412	534	77.2
3. Franklin	477	624	76.4
4. Dickinson	290	380	76.3
5. Hanover	472	623	75.8
6. Ill. Wesleyan	468	619	75.6
7. Denison	326	433	75.3
8. Moravian	290	387	74.9
9. Rochester	309	413	74.8
10. Carleton	397	531	74.8
11. Manchester	537	720	74.6
12. King's (Pa.)	261	350	74.6
13. Defiance	548	735	74.6
14. Heidelberg	463	621	74.6
15. Illinois Col.	383	515	74.4
16. Ithaca	357	481	74.2
17. DePauw	431	581	74.2
18. Monmouth (Ill.)	352	475	74.1
19. Wartburg	471	636	74.1
20. Johns Hopkins	348	470	74.0
21. Southern Me.	441	596	74.0
22. Oglethorpe	438	592	74.0
23. Williams	440	595	73.9
24. St. Olaf	359	487	73.7
25. Ohio Wesleyan	403	547	73.7
26. Wis.-Platteville	606	825	73.5
27. Framingham St.	364	496	73.4
28. Mass.-Dartmouth	564	772	73.1
29. Rensselaer	365	500	73.0
30. Grinnell	334	459	72.8

REBOUND MARGIN

	OFF.	DEF.	MAR.
1. Eureka	33.9	22.2	11.7
2. Bethel (Minn.)	40.5	28.9	11.6
3. Wis.-Whitewater	42.3	30.9	11.4
4. Wilkes	41.8	31.7	10.1
5. Johns Hopkins	36.6	26.8	9.8
6. Carthage	40.8	31.0	9.8
7. Scranton	41.9	32.6	9.3
8. Williams	40.0	31.3	8.7
9. Wooster	35.0	26.5	8.5
10. Roger Williams	47.3	38.9	8.4
11. Albright	38.1	29.8	8.4
12. Rowan	39.8	31.5	8.2
13. Maritime (N.Y.)	40.0	31.8	8.2
14. Oglethorpe	38.9	30.9	8.0
15. Lebanon Valley	38.2	30.3	7.9
16. Wartburg	37.0	29.2	7.9
17. Trinity (Conn.)	39.3	31.5	7.9
18. Eastern Nazarene	37.4	29.7	7.7
19. Castleton St.	42.6	34.9	7.7
20. Neb. Wesleyan	43.5	36.2	7.3
21. Brockport St.	42.9	35.7	7.2
22. Westfield St.	42.6	35.5	7.1
23. Southwestern (Tex.)	38.5	31.4	7.1
24. Hamilton	46.0	39.1	7.0
25. New Jersey Tech	46.5	39.5	7.0
26. Ithaca	35.1	28.2	6.9
27. Denison	33.1	26.2	6.9
28. St. John's (Minn.)	33.6	26.8	6.8
29. Ferrum	46.5	39.8	6.8
30. New York U.	42.2	35.8	6.3

Reggie Phillips and his Cal State Bakersfield teammates compiled a 14-0 record in the California Collegiate Athletic Association en route to a 33-0 season. The Roadrunners defeated Troy State to claim the Division II Men's Basketball Championship.

1993 MEN'S CONFERENCE STANDINGS

DIVISION I

ATLANTIC COAST CONFERENCE

	CONFERENCE			FULL SEASON		
	W	L	Pct.	W	L	Pct.
North Caro.	14	2	.875	34	4	.895
Florida St.	12	4	.750	25	10	.714
Duke	10	6	.625	24	8	.750
Wake Forest	10	6	.625	21	9	.700
Virginia	9	7	.563	21	10	.677
Georgia Tech #	8	8	.500	19	11	.633
Clemson	5	11	.313	17	13	.567
Maryland	2	14	.125	12	16	.429
North Caro. St.	2	14	.125	8	19	.296

ATLANTIC 10 CONFERENCE

	CONFERENCE			FULL SEASON		
	W	L	Pct.	W	L	Pct.
Massachusetts #	11	3	.786	24	7	.774
Geo. Washington	8	6	.571	21	9	.700
Rhode Island	8	6	.571	19	11	.633
St. Joseph's (Pa.)	8	6	.571	18	11	.621
Temple	8	6	.571	20	13	.606
West Va.	7	7	.500	17	12	.586
Rutgers	6	8	.429	13	15	.464
St. Bonaventure	0	14	.000	10	17	.370

BIG EAST CONFERENCE

	CONFERENCE			FULL SEASON		
	W	L	Pct.	W	L	Pct.
Seton Hall #	14	4	.778	28	7	.800
St. John's (N.Y.)	12	6	.667	19	11	.633
Syracuse	10	8	.556	20	9	.690
Pittsburgh	9	9	.500	17	11	.607
Providence	9	9	.500	20	13	.606
Boston College	9	9	.500	18	13	.581
Connecticut	9	9	.500	15	13	.536
Georgetown	8	10	.444	20	13	.606
Miami (Fla.)	7	11	.389	10	17	.370
Villanova	3	15	.167	8	19	.296

BIG EIGHT CONFERENCE

	CONFERENCE			FULL SEASON		
	W	L	Pct.	W	L	Pct.
Kansas	11	3	.786	29	7	.806
Oklahoma St.	8	6	.571	20	9	.690
Iowa St.	8	6	.571	20	11	.645
Nebraska	8	6	.571	20	11	.645
Kansas St.	7	7	.500	19	11	.633
Oklahoma	7	7	.500	20	12	.625
Missouri #	5	9	.357	19	14	.576
Colorado	2	12	.143	10	17	.370

BIG SKY CONFERENCE

	CONFERENCE			FULL SEASON		
	W	L	Pct.	W	L	Pct.
Idaho	11	3	.786	24	8	.750
Boise St. #	10	4	.714	21	8	.724
Weber St.	10	4	.714	20	8	.714
Montana	8	6	.571	17	11	.607
Idaho St.	5	9	.357	10	18	.357
Montana St.	5	9	.357	9	18	.333
Northern Ariz.	4	10	.286	10	16	.385
Eastern Wash.	3	11	.214	6	20	.231

BIG SOUTH CONFERENCE

	CONFERENCE			FULL SEASON		
	W	L	Pct.	W	L	Pct.
Towson St.	14	2	.875	18	9	.667
Coastal Caro. #	12	4	.750	22	10	.688
Campbell	10	6	.625	12	15	.444
Liberty	9	7	.563	16	14	.533
Radford	8	8	.500	15	16	.484
Md.-Balt. County	7	9	.438	12	16	.429
Winthrop	5	11	.313	14	16	.467
Charleston So.	5	11	.313	9	18	.333
N.C.-Asheville	2	14	.125	4	23	.148

Won conference tournament.

BIG TEN CONFERENCE

	CONFERENCE			FULL SEASON		
	W	L	Pct.	W	L	Pct.
Indiana	17	1	.944	31	4	.886
Michigan	15	3	.833	31	5	.861
Iowa	11	7	.611	23	9	.719
Illinois	11	7	.611	19	13	.594
Minnesota	9	9	.500	22	10	.688
Purdue	9	9	.500	18	10	.643
Ohio St.	8	10	.444	15	13	.536
Michigan St.	7	11	.389	15	13	.536
Wisconsin	7	11	.389	14	14	.500
Northwestern	3	15	.167	8	19	.296
Penn St.	2	16	.111	7	20	.259

BIG WEST CONFERENCE

	CONFERENCE			FULL SEASON		
	W	L	Pct.	W	L	Pct.
New Mexico St.	15	3	.833	26	8	.765
Nevada-Las Vegas	13	5	.722	21	8	.724
Pacific (Cal.)	12	6	.667	16	11	.593
Long Beach St. #	11	7	.611	22	10	.688
UC Santa Barb.	10	8	.556	18	11	.621
Cal St. Fullerton	10	8	.556	15	12	.556
Utah St.	7	11	.389	10	17	.370
Nevada	4	14	.222	9	17	.346
San Jose St.	4	14	.222	7	19	.269
UC Irvine	4	14	.222	6	21	.222

COLONIAL ATHLETIC ASSOCIATION

	CONFERENCE			FULL SEASON		
	W	L	Pct.	W	L	Pct.
Old Dominion	11	3	.786	21	8	.724
James Madison	11	3	.786	21	9	.700
Richmond	10	4	.714	15	12	.556
N.C.-Wilmington	6	8	.429	17	11	.607
William & Mary	6	8	.429	14	13	.519
American	6	8	.429	11	17	.393
East Caro. #	4	10	.286	13	17	.433
George Mason	2	12	.143	7	21	.250

GREAT MIDWEST CONFERENCE

	CONFERENCE			FULL SEASON		
	W	L	Pct.	W	L	Pct.
Cincinnati #	8	2	.800	27	5	.844
Memphis St.	7	3	.700	20	12	.625
Marquette	6	4	.600	20	8	.714
Ala.-Birmingham	5	5	.500	21	14	.600
DePaul	3	7	.300	16	15	.516
St. Louis	1	9	.100	12	17	.414

IVY GROUP

	CONFERENCE			FULL SEASON		
	W	L	Pct.	W	L	Pct.
Pennsylvania	14	0	1.000	22	5	.815
Cornell	10	4	.714	16	10	.615
Columbia	9	5	.643	16	10	.615
Princeton	7	7	.500	15	11	.577
Yale	6	8	.429	10	16	.385
Dartmouth	5	9	.357	11	15	.423
Harvard	3	11	.214	6	20	.231
Brown	2	12	.143	7	19	.269

METRO ATLANTIC ATHLETIC CONFERENCE

	CONFERENCE			FULL SEASON		
	W	L	Pct.	W	L	Pct.
Manhattan #	12	2	.857	23	7	.767
Niagara	11	3	.786	23	7	.767
Iona	9	5	.643	16	11	.593
Siena	8	6	.571	16	13	.552
Fairfield	7	7	.500	14	13	.519
Canisius	5	9	.357	10	18	.357
St. Peter's	3	11	.214	9	18	.333
Loyola (Md.)	1	13	.071	2	25	.074

METROPOLITAN COLLEGIATE ATHLETIC CONFERENCE

	CONFERENCE W	L	Pct.	FULL SEASON W	L	Pct.
Louisville #	11	1	.917	22	9	.710
Tulane	9	3	.750	22	9	.710
Va. Commonwealth	7	5	.583	20	10	.667
N.C.-Charlotte	6	6	.500	15	13	.536
Southern Miss.	6	6	.500	10	17	.370
South Fla.	2	10	.167	8	19	.296
Virginia Tech	1	11	.083	10	18	.357

MID-AMERICAN ATHLETIC CONFERENCE

	CONFERENCE W	L	Pct.	FULL SEASON W	L	Pct.
Ball St. #	14	4	.778	26	8	.765
Miami (Ohio)	14	4	.778	22	9	.710
Western Mich.	12	6	.667	17	12	.586
Ohio	11	7	.611	14	13	.519
Toledo	9	9	.500	12	16	.429
Eastern Mich.	8	10	.444	13	17	.433
Bowling Green	8	10	.444	11	16	.407
Kent	7	11	.389	10	17	.370
Central Mich.	4	14	.222	8	18	.308
Akron	3	15	.167	8	18	.308

MID-CONTINENT CONFERENCE

	CONFERENCE W	L	Pct.	FULL SEASON W	L	Pct.
Cleveland St.	15	1	.938	22	6	.786
Wright St. #	10	6	.625	20	10	.667
Northern Ill.	10	6	.625	15	12	.556
Ill.-Chicago	9	7	.563	17	15	.531
Wis.-Green Bay	9	7	.563	13	14	.481
Valparaiso	7	9	.438	12	16	.429
Eastern Ill.	7	9	.438	10	17	.370
Western Ill.	4	12	.250	7	20	.259
Youngstown St.	1	15	.063	3	23	.115

MID-EASTERN ATHLETIC CONFERENCE

	CONFERENCE W	L	Pct.	FULL SEASON W	L	Pct.
Coppin St. #	16	0	1.000	22	8	.733
South Caro. St.	9	7	.563	16	13	.552
North Caro. A&T	9	7	.563	14	13	.519
Morgan St.	9	7	.563	9	17	.346
Florida A&M	8	8	.500	10	18	.357
Md.-East. Shore	7	9	.438	12	15	.444
Delaware St.	6	10	.375	13	16	.448
Howard	6	10	.375	10	18	.357
Bethune-Cookman	2	14	.125	3	24	.111

MIDWESTERN COLLEGIATE CONFERENCE

	CONFERENCE W	L	Pct.	FULL SEASON W	L	Pct.
Xavier (Ohio)	12	2	.857	24	6	.800
Evansville #	12	2	.857	23	7	.767
La Salle	9	5	.643	14	13	.519
Detroit Mercy	7	7	.500	15	12	.556
Duquesne	5	9	.357	13	15	.464
Butler	5	9	.357	11	17	.393
Loyola (Ill.)	3	11	.214	7	20	.259
Dayton	3	11	.214	4	26	.133

MISSOURI VALLEY CONFERENCE

	CONFERENCE W	L	Pct.	FULL SEASON W	L	Pct.
Illinois St.	13	5	.722	19	10	.655
Southern Ill. #	12	6	.667	23	10	.697
Southwest Mo. St.	11	7	.611	20	11	.645
Tulsa	10	8	.556	15	14	.517
Drake	9	9	.500	14	14	.500
Northern Iowa	8	10	.444	12	15	.444
Bradley	7	11	.389	11	16	.407
Indiana St.	7	11	.389	11	17	.393
Wichita St.	7	11	.389	10	17	.370
Creighton	6	12	.333	8	18	.308

Won conference tournament.

NORTH ATLANTIC CONFERENCE

	CONFERENCE W	L	Pct.	FULL SEASON W	L	Pct.
Drexel #	12	2	.857	22	7	.759
Northeastern	12	2	.857	20	8	.714
Delaware	10	4	.714	22	8	.733
Hartford	7	7	.500	14	14	.500
Maine	4	10	.286	10	17	.370
Vermont	4	10	.286	10	17	.370
New Hampshire	4	10	.286	6	21	.222
Boston U.	3	11	.214	6	21	.222

NORTHEAST CONFERENCE

	CONFERENCE W	L	Pct.	FULL SEASON W	L	Pct.
Rider #	14	4	.778	19	11	.633
Wagner	12	6	.667	18	12	.600
Marist	10	8	.556	14	16	.467
Mt. St. Mary's (Md.)	10	8	.556	13	15	.464
FDU-Teaneck	8	10	.444	11	17	.393
St. Francis (N.Y.)	8	10	.444	9	18	.333
LIU-Brooklyn	7	11	.389	11	17	.393
Monmouth (N.J.)	7	11	.389	11	17	.393
Robert Morris	7	11	.389	9	18	.333
St. Francis (Pa.)	7	11	.389	9	18	.333

OHIO VALLEY CONFERENCE

	CONFERENCE W	L	Pct.	FULL SEASON W	L	Pct.
Tennessee St. #	13	3	.813	19	10	.655
Murray St.	11	5	.688	18	12	.600
Eastern Ky.	11	5	.688	15	12	.556
Southeast Mo. St.	9	7	.563	16	11	.593
Tennessee Tech	9	7	.563	15	13	.536
Morehead St.	6	10	.375	6	21	.222
Middle Tenn. St.	5	11	.313	10	16	.385
Tenn.-Martin	4	12	.250	7	19	.269
Austin Peay	4	12	.250	7	20	.259

PACIFIC-10 CONFERENCE

	CONFERENCE W	L	Pct.	FULL SEASON W	L	Pct.
Arizona	17	1	.944	24	4	.857
California	12	6	.667	21	9	.700
UCLA	11	7	.611	22	11	.667
Arizona St.	11	7	.611	18	10	.643
Southern Cal	9	9	.500	18	12	.600
Washington St.	9	9	.500	15	12	.556
Oregon St.	9	9	.500	13	14	.481
Washington	7	11	.389	13	14	.481
Oregon	3	15	.167	10	20	.333
Stanford	2	16	.111	7	23	.233

PATRIOT LEAGUE

	CONFERENCE W	L	Pct.	FULL SEASON W	L	Pct.
Bucknell	13	1	.929	23	6	.793
Holy Cross #	12	2	.857	23	7	.767
Colgate	9	5	.643	18	10	.643
Fordham	9	5	.643	15	16	.484
Navy	5	9	.357	8	19	.296
Lafayette	4	10	.286	7	20	.259
Army	2	12	.143	4	22	.154
Lehigh	2	12	.143	4	23	.148

SOUTHEASTERN CONFERENCE

Eastern Division	CONFERENCE W	L	Pct.	FULL SEASON W	L	Pct.
Vanderbilt	14	2	.875	28	6	.824
Kentucky #	13	3	.813	30	4	.882
Florida	9	7	.563	16	12	.571
Georgia	8	8	.500	15	14	.517
South Caro.	5	11	.313	9	18	.333
Tennessee	4	12	.250	13	17	.357
Western Division	W	L	Pct.	W	L	Pct.
Arkansas	10	6	.625	22	9	.710
Louisiana St.	9	7	.563	22	11	.667
Auburn	8	8	.500	15	12	.556
Alabama	7	9	.438	16	13	.552
Mississippi St.	5	11	.313	13	16	.448
Mississippi	4	12	.250	10	18	.357

SOUTHERN CONFERENCE

	CONFERENCE			FULL SEASON		
	W	L	Pct.	W	L	Pct.
Tenn.-Chatt. #	16	2	.889	26	7	.788
Ga. Southern	12	6	.667	19	9	.679
East Tenn. St.	12	6	.667	19	10	.655
Marshall	11	7	.611	16	11	.593
Davidson	10	8	.556	14	14	.500
Appalachian St.	8	10	.444	13	15	.464
Furman	8	10	.444	11	17	.393
Citadel	8	10	.444	10	17	.370
Va. Military	3	15	.167	5	22	.185
Western Caro.	2	16	.111	6	21	.222

SOUTHLAND CONFERENCE

	CONFERENCE			FULL SEASON		
	W	L	Pct.	W	L	Pct.
Northeast La. #	17	1	.944	26	5	.839
Nicholls St.	11	7	.611	14	12	.538
Texas-Arlington	10	8	.556	16	12	.571
Texas-San Antonio	10	8	.556	15	14	.517
Southwest Tex. St.	9	9	.500	14	13	.519
McNeese St.	9	9	.500	12	16	.429
Stephen F. Austin	8	10	.444	12	14	.462
Northwestern (La.)	7	11	.389	13	13	.500
North Texas	5	13	.278	5	21	.192
Sam Houston St.	4	14	.222	6	19	.240

SOUTHWEST CONFERENCE

	CONFERENCE			FULL SEASON		
	W	L	Pct.	W	L	Pct.
Southern Methodist	12	2	.857	20	8	.714
Rice	11	3	.786	18	10	.643
Houston	9	5	.643	21	9	.700
Baylor	7	7	.500	16	11	.593
Texas Tech #	6	8	.429	18	12	.600
Texas A&M	5	9	.357	10	17	.370
Texas	4	10	.286	11	17	.393
Texas Christian	2	12	.143	6	22	.214

SOUTHWESTERN ATHLETIC CONFERENCE

	CONFERENCE			FULL SEASON		
	W	L	Pct.	W	L	Pct.
Jackson St.	13	1	.929	25	9	.735
Southern-B.R. #	9	5	.643	21	10	.677
Alabama St.	9	5	.643	14	13	.519
Texas Southern	8	6	.571	12	15	.444
Mississippi Val.	7	7	.500	13	15	.464
Grambling	5	9	.357	13	14	.481
Alcorn St.	5	9	.357	7	20	.259
Prairie View	0	14	.000	1	26	.037

SUN BELT CONFERENCE

	CONFERENCE			FULL SEASON		
	W	L	Pct.	W	L	Pct.
New Orleans	18	0	1.000	26	4	.867
Western Ky. #	14	4	.778	26	6	.813
Arkansas St.	11	7	.611	16	12	.571
Southwestern La.	11	7	.611	17	13	.567
Ark.-Lit. Rock	10	8	.556	15	12	.556
Lamar	9	9	.500	15	12	.556
South Ala.	9	9	.500	15	13	.536
Louisiana Tech	3	15	.167	7	21	.250
Jacksonville	3	15	.167	5	22	.185
Tex.-Pan American	2	16	.111	2	20	.091

Won conference tournament.

TRANS AMERICA ATHLETIC CONFERENCE

	CONFERENCE			FULL SEASON		
	W	L	Pct.	W	L	Pct.
Florida Int'l.	9	3	.750	20	10	.667
Samford	7	5	.583	17	10	.630
Mercer	7	5	.583	13	14	.481
Stetson	6	6	.500	13	14	.481
Georgia St.	5	7	.417	13	14	.481
Southeastern La.	4	8	.333	12	15	.444
Centenary	4	8	.333	9	18	.333

WEST COAST CONFERENCE

	CONFERENCE			FULL SEASON		
	W	L	Pct.	W	L	Pct.
Pepperdine	11	3	.786	23	8	.742
Gonzaga	10	4	.714	19	9	.679
Santa Clara #	9	5	.643	19	12	.613
San Francisco	8	6	.571	19	12	.613
San Diego	7	7	.500	13	14	.481
St. Mary's (Cal.)	6	8	.429	11	16	.407
Portland	3	11	.214	9	18	.333
Loyola (Cal.)	2	12	.143	7	20	.259

WESTERN ATHLETIC CONFERENCE

	CONFERENCE			FULL SEASON		
	W	L	Pct.	W	L	Pct.
Utah	15	3	.833	24	7	.774
Brigham Young	15	3	.833	25	9	.735
New Mexico #	13	5	.722	24	7	.774
UTEP	10	8	.556	21	13	.618
Colorado St.	9	9	.500	17	12	.586
Fresno St.	8	10	.444	13	15	.464
Wyoming	7	11	.389	13	15	.464
Hawaii	7	11	.389	12	16	.429
Air Force	3	15	.167	9	19	.321
San Diego St.	3	15	.167	8	21	.276

DIVISION I INDEPENDENTS

	FULL SEASON		
	W	L	Pct.
Wis.-Milwaukee	23	4	.852
Charleston	19	8	.704
Mo.-Kansas City	15	12	.556
Southern Utah	14	13	.519
Northeastern Ill.	11	16	.407
Cal St. Northridge	10	17	.370
Central Fla.	10	17	.370
N.C.-Greensboro	10	17	.370
Hofstra	9	18	.333
Notre Dame	9	18	.333
Central Conn. St.	8	19	.296
Buffalo	5	22	.185
Chicago St.	4	23	.148
Cal St. Sacramento	3	24	.111

MEN'S CONFERENCE CHAMPIONS YEAR BY YEAR

(Regular-season and conference tournament champions)

DIVISION I

AMERICAN SOUTH

Regular Season

Year	#	School
1988	6	Louisiana Tech
		New Orleans
1989	6	New Orleans
1990	6	Louisiana Tech
		New Orleans
1991	7	New Orleans
		Arkansas St.

Conference Tournament

Year	#	School
1988	6	Louisiana Tech
1989	6	Louisiana Tech
1990	6	New Orleans
1991	7	Louisiana Tech

ATLANTIC COAST

Regular Season

Year	#	School
1954	8	Duke
1955	8	North Caro. St.
1956	8	North Caro. St.
		North Caro.
1957	8	North Caro.
1958	8	Duke
1959	8	North Caro. St.
		North Caro.
1960	8	North Caro.
1961	8	North Caro.
1962	8	Wake Forest
1963	8	Duke

Year	#	Regular Season School
1964	8	Duke
1965	8	Duke
1966	8	Duke
1967	8	North Caro.
1968	8	North Caro.
1969	8	North Caro.
1970	8	South Caro.
1971	8	North Caro.
1972	7	North Caro.
1973	7	North Caro. St.
1974	7	North Caro. St.
1975	7	Maryland
1976	7	North Caro.
1977	7	North Caro.
1978	7	North Caro.
1979	7	Duke
		North Caro.
1980	8	Maryland
1981	8	Virginia
1982	8	North Caro.
		Virginia
1983	8	North Caro.
		Virginia
1984	8	North Caro.
1985	8	Georgia Tech
		North Caro.
		North Caro. St.
1986	8	Duke
1987	8	North Caro.
1988	8	North Caro.
1989	8	North Caro. St.
1990	8	Clemson
1991	8	Duke
1992	9	Duke
1993	9	North Caro.

Year	#	Conference Tournament School
1954	8	North Caro. St.
1955	8	North Caro. St.
1956	8	North Caro. St.
1957	8	North Caro.
1958	8	Maryland
1959	8	North Caro. St.
1960	8	Duke
1961	7	Wake Forest
1962	8	Wake Forest
1963	8	Duke
1964	8	Duke
1965	8	North Caro. St.
1966	8	Duke
1967	8	North Caro.
1968	8	North Caro.
1969	8	North Caro.
1970	8	North Caro. St.
1971	8	South Caro.
1972	7	North Caro.
1973	7	North Caro. St.
1974	7	North Caro. St.
1975	7	North Caro.
1976	7	Virginia
1977	7	North Caro.
1978	7	Duke
1979	7	North Caro.
1980	8	Duke
1981	8	North Caro.
1982	8	North Caro.
1983	8	North Caro. St.
1984	8	Maryland
1985	8	Georgia Tech
1986	8	Duke
1987	8	North Caro. St.
1988	8	Duke
1989	8	North Caro.
1990	8	Georgia Tech
1991	7	North Caro.
1992	9	Duke
1993	9	Georgia Tech

ATLANTIC 10 (Eastern Eight)

Year	#	Regular Season School
1977	8	Rutgers (Eastern)
		West Va. (Western)
		Penn St. (Western)
1978	8	Rutgers
		Villanova
1979	8	Villanova
1980	8	Villanova
		Duquesne
		Rutgers
1981	8	Rhode Island
		Duquesne
1982	8	West Va.
1983	10	Rutgers (Eastern)
		St. Bonaventure (Western)
		West Va. (Western)
1984	10	Temple
1985	10	West Va.
1986	10	St. Joseph's (Pa.)
1987	10	Temple
1988	10	Temple
1989	10	West Va.
1990	10	Temple
1991	10	Rutgers
1992	9	Massachusetts
1993	8	Massachusetts

Year	#	Conference Tournament School
1977	8	Duquesne
1978	8	Villanova
1979	8	Rutgers
1980	8	Villanova
1981	8	Pittsburgh
1982	8	Pittsburgh
1983	10	West Va.
1984	10	West Va.
1985	10	Temple
1986	10	St. Joseph's (Pa.)
1987	10	Temple
1988	10	Temple
1989	10	Rutgers
1990	10	Temple
1991	10	Penn St.
1992	9	Massachusetts
1993	8	Massachusetts

BIG EAST

Year	#	Regular Season School
1980	7	Syracuse
		Georgetown
		St. John's (N.Y.)
1981	8	Boston College
1982	8	Villanova
1983	9	Boston College
		Villanova
		St. John's (N.Y.)
1984	9	Georgetown
1985	9	St. John's (N.Y.)
1986	9	St. John's (N.Y.)
		Syracuse
1987	9	Syracuse
		Georgetown
		Pittsburgh
1988	9	Pittsburgh
1989	9	Georgetown
1990	9	Connecticut
		Syracuse
1991	9	Syracuse
1992	10	Seton Hall
		Georgetown
		St. John's (N.Y.)
1993	10	Seton Hall

Year	#	Conference Tournament School
1980	7	Georgetown
1981	8	Syracuse
1982	8	Georgetown
1983	9	St. John's (N.Y.)
1984	9	Georgetown
1985	9	Georgetown
1986	9	St. John's (N.Y.)
1987	9	Georgetown
1988	9	Syracuse
1989	9	Georgetown
1990	9	Connecticut
1991	9	Seton Hall
1992	10	Syracuse
1993	10	Seton Hall

BIG EIGHT (Big Seven, Big Six, Missouri Valley)

Year	#	Regular Season School
1908	6	Kansas
1909	6	Kansas
1910	6	Kansas
1911	5	Kansas
1912	6	Nebraska
		Kansas
1913	6	Nebraska
1914	7	Kansas
		Nebraska
1915	7	Kansas
1916	7	Nebraska
1917	7	Kansas St.
1918	7	Missouri
1919	8	Kansas St.
1920	8	Missouri
1921	9	Missouri
1922	9	Missouri
		Kansas
1923	9	Kansas
1924	9	Kansas
1925	9	Kansas
1926	10	Kansas
1927	10	Kansas
1928	10	Oklahoma
1929	6	Oklahoma
1930	6	Missouri
1931	6	Kansas
1932	6	Kansas
1933	6	Kansas
1934	6	Kansas
1935	6	Iowa St.
1936	6	Kansas
1937	6	Kansas
		Nebraska
1938	6	Kansas
1939	6	Missouri
		Oklahoma
1940	6	Kansas
		Missouri
		Oklahoma
1941	6	Iowa St.
		Kansas
1942	6	Kansas
		Oklahoma
1943	6	Kansas
1944	6	Iowa St.
		Oklahoma
1945	6	Iowa St.
1946	6	Kansas
1947	6	Oklahoma
1948	7	Kansas St.
1949	7	Nebraska
		Oklahoma
1950	7	Kansas
		Kansas St.
		Nebraska
1951	7	Kansas St.
1952	7	Kansas
1953	7	Kansas
1954	7	Kansas
		Colorado
1955	7	Colorado
1956	7	Kansas St.
1957	7	Kansas
1958	7	Kansas St.
1959	8	Kansas St.
1960	8	Kansas
		Kansas St.
1961	8	Kansas St.
1962	8	Colorado
1963	8	Colorado
		Kansas St.
1964	8	Kansas St.
1965	8	Oklahoma St.
1966	8	Kansas
1967	8	Kansas
1968	8	Kansas St.
1969	8	Colorado
1970	8	Kansas St.
1971	8	Kansas
1972	8	Kansas St.

Regular Season

Year	#	School
1973	8	Kansas St.
1974	8	Kansas
1975	8	Kansas
1976	8	Missouri
1977	8	Kansas St.
1978	8	Kansas
1979	8	Oklahoma
1980	8	Missouri
1981	8	Missouri
1982	8	Missouri
1983	8	Missouri
1984	8	Oklahoma
1985	8	Oklahoma
1986	8	Kansas
1987	8	Missouri
1988	8	Oklahoma
1989	8	Oklahoma
1990	8	Missouri
1991	8	Oklahoma St.
		Kansas
1992	8	Kansas
1993	8	Kansas

Conference Tournament

Year	#	School
1977	8	Kansas St.
1978	8	Missouri
1979	8	Oklahoma
1980	8	Kansas St.
1981	8	Kansas
1982	8	Missouri
1983	8	Oklahoma St.
1984	8	Kansas
1985	8	Oklahoma
1986	8	Kansas
1987	8	Missouri
1988	8	Oklahoma
1989	8	Missouri
1990	8	Oklahoma
1991	8	Missouri
1992	8	Kansas
1993	8	Missouri

BIG SKY

Regular Season

Year	#	School
1964	6	Montana St.
1965	6	Weber St.
1966	6	Weber St.
		Gonzaga
1967	6	Gonzaga
		Montana St.
1968	6	Weber St.
1969	6	Weber St.
1970	6	Weber St.
1971	6	Weber St.
1972	8	Weber St.
1973	8	Weber St.
1974	8	Idaho St.
		Montana
1975	8	Montana
1976	8	Boise St.
		Weber St.
		Idaho St.
1977	8	Idaho St.
1978	8	Montana
1979	8	Weber St.
1980	8	Weber St.
1981	8	Idaho
1982	8	Idaho
1983	8	Weber St.
		Nevada
1984	8	Weber St.
1985	8	Nevada
1986	8	Northern Ariz.
		Montana
1987	8	Montana St.
1988	9	Boise St.
1989	9	Boise St.
		Idaho
1990	9	Idaho
1991	9	Montana
1992	9	Montana
1993	8	Idaho

Conference Tournament

Year	#	School
1976	8	Boise St.
1977	8	Idaho St.
1978	8	Weber St.
1979	8	Weber St.
1980	8	Weber St.
1981	8	Idaho
1982	8	Idaho
1983	8	Weber St.
1984	8	Nevada
1985	8	Nevada
1986	7	Montana St.
1987	8	Idaho St.
1988	9	Boise St.
1989	9	Idaho
1990	9	Idaho
1991	9	Montana
1992	6	Montana
1993	6	Boise St.

BIG SOUTH

Regular Season

Year	#	School
1986	8	Charleston So.
1987	8	Charleston So.
1988	7	Coastal Caro.
1989	7	Coastal Caro.
1990	7	Coastal Caro.
1991	8	Coastal Caro.
1992	8	Radford
1993	9	Towson St.

Conference Tournament

Year	#	School
1986	8	Charleston So.
1987	8	Charleston So.
1988	7	Winthrop
1989	7	N.C.-Asheville
1990	7	Coastal Caro.
1991	8	Coastal Caro.
1992	8	Campbell
1993	9	Coastal Caro.

BIG TEN (Big Nine, Western)

Regular Season

Year	#	School
1906	6	Minnesota
1907	5	Chicago
		Minnesota
		Wisconsin
1908	5	Chicago
		Wisconsin
1909	8	Chicago
1910	8	Chicago
1911	8	Purdue
		Minnesota
1912	8	Wisconsin
1913	9	Wisconsin
1914	9	Wisconsin
1915	9	Illinois
1916	9	Wisconsin
1917	9	Minnesota
		Illinois
1918	10	Wisconsin
1919	10	Minnesota
1920	10	Chicago
1921	10	Michigan
		Wisconsin
		Purdue
1922	10	Purdue
1923	10	Iowa
		Wisconsin
1924	10	Wisconsin
		Illinois
		Chicago
1925	10	Ohio St.
1926	10	Purdue
		Indiana
		Michigan
		Iowa
1927	10	Michigan
1928	10	Indiana
		Purdue
1929	10	Wisconsin
		Michigan
1930	10	Purdue
1931	10	Northwestern
1932	10	Purdue
1933	10	Northwestern
		Ohio St.
1934	10	Purdue
1935	10	Purdue
		Illinois
		Wisconsin
1936	10	Indiana
		Purdue
1937	10	Minnesota
		Illinois
1938	10	Purdue
1939	10	Ohio St.
1940	10	Purdue
1941	10	Wisconsin
1942	10	Illinois
1943	10	Illinois
1944	10	Ohio St.
1945	10	Iowa
1946	10	Ohio St.
1947	9	Wisconsin
1948	9	Michigan
1949	9	Illinois
1950	9	Ohio St.
1951	10	Illinois
1952	10	Illinois
1953	10	Indiana
1954	10	Indiana
1955	10	Iowa
1956	10	Iowa
1957	10	Indiana
		Michigan St.
1958	10	Indiana
1959	10	Michigan St.
1960	10	Ohio St.
1961	10	Ohio St.
1962	10	Ohio St.
1963	10	Ohio St.
		Illinois
1964	10	Michigan
		Ohio St.
1965	10	Michigan
1966	10	Michigan
1967	10	Indiana
		Michigan St.
1968	10	Ohio St.
		Iowa
1969	10	Purdue
1970	10	Iowa
1971	10	Ohio St.
1972	10	Minnesota
1973	10	Indiana
1974	10	Indiana
		Michigan
1975	10	Indiana
1976	10	Indiana
1977	10	Michigan
1978	10	Michigan St.
1979	10	Michigan St.
		Purdue
		Iowa
1980	10	Indiana
1981	10	Indiana
1982	10	Minnesota
1983	10	Indiana
1984	10	Illinois
		Purdue
1985	10	Michigan
1986	10	Michigan
1987	10	Indiana
		Purdue
1988	10	Purdue
1989	10	Indiana
1990	10	Michigan St.
1991	10	Ohio St.
		Indiana
1992	10	Ohio St.
1993	11	Indiana

BIG WEST (Pacific Coast)

Regular Season

Year	#	School
1970	6	Long Beach St.
1971	6	Long Beach St.

Year	#	Regular Season School
1972	7	Long Beach St.
1973	7	Long Beach St.
1974	7	Long Beach St.
1975	6	Long Beach St.
1976	6	Long Beach St.
		Cal St. Fullerton
1977	7	Long Beach St.
		San Diego St.
1978	8	Fresno St.
		San Diego St.
1979	8	Pacific (Cal.)
1980	8	Utah St.
1981	8	Fresno St.
1982	8	Fresno St.
1983	9	Nevada-Las Vegas
1984	10	Nevada-Las Vegas
1985	10	Nevada-Las Vegas
1986	10	Nevada-Las Vegas
1987	10	Nevada-Las Vegas
1988	10	Nevada-Las Vegas
1989	10	Nevada-Las Vegas
1990	10	Nevada-Las Vegas
1991	10	Nevada-Las Vegas
1992	10	Nevada-Las Vegas
1993	10	New Mexico St.

Year	#	Conference Tournament School
1976	4	San Diego St.
1977	7	Long Beach St.
1978	7	Cal St. Fullerton
1979	8	Pacific (Cal.)
1980	7	San Jose St.
1981	7	Fresno St.
1982	7	Fresno St.
1983	8	Nevada-Las Vegas
1984	8	Fresno St.
1985	8	Nevada-Las Vegas
1986	8	Nevada-Las Vegas
1987	8	Nevada-Las Vegas
1988	10	Utah St.
1989	10	Nevada-Las Vegas
1990	10	Nevada-Las Vegas
1991	8	Nevada-Las Vegas
1992	8	New Mexico St.
1993	8	Long Beach St.

BORDER

Year	#	Regular Season School
1932	5	Arizona
1933	6	Texas Tech
1934	6	Texas Tech
1935	6	Texas Tech
1936	7	Arizona
1937	7	New Mexico St.
1938	7	New Mexico St.
1939	7	New Mexico St.
1940	7	New Mexico St.
1941		DNP
1942	9	West Tex. A&M
1943	8	West Tex. A&M
1944	4	Northern Ariz.
1945	9	New Mexico
1946	9	Arizona
1947	9	Arizona
1948	9	Arizona
1949	9	Arizona
1950	9	Arizona
1951	9	Arizona
1952	8	New Mexico St.
		West Tex. A&M
1953	8	Arizona
		Hardin-Simmons
1954	7	Texas Tech
1955	7	Texas Tech
		West Tex. A&M
1956	7	Texas Tech
1957	6	UTEP
1958	6	Arizona St.
1959	6	Arizona St.
		New Mexico St.
		UTEP
1960	6	New Mexico St.
1961	6	Arizona St.
		New Mexico St.
1962	5	Arizona St.

COLONIAL (ECAC South)

Year	#	Regular Season School
1983	6	William & Mary
1984	6	Richmond
1985	8	Navy
		Richmond
1986	8	Navy
1987	8	Navy
1988	8	Richmond
1989	8	Richmond
1990	8	James Madison
1991	8	James Madison
1992	8	Richmond
		James Madison
1993	8	James Madison
		Old Dominion

Year	#	Conference Tournament School
1983	6	James Madison
1984	6	Richmond
1985	8	Navy
1986	8	George Mason
1987	8	Navy
1988	8	Richmond
1989	8	George Mason
1990	8	Richmond
1991	8	Richmond
1992	8	Old Dominion
1993	8	East Caro.

EAST COAST (Middle Atlantic)

Year	#	Regular Season School
1975	12	American (East)
		La Salle (East)
		Lafayette (West)
1976	12	St. Joseph's (Pa.) (East)
		Lafayette (West)
1977	12	Temple (East)
		Hofstra (East)
		Lafayette (West)
1978	12	La Salle (East)
		Lafayette (West)
1979	12	Temple (East)
		Bucknell (West)
1980	12	St. Joseph's (Pa.) (East)
		Lafayette (West)
1981	12	American (East)
		Lafayette (West)
		Rider (West)
1982	12	Temple (East)
		West Chester (West)
1983	10	American (East)
		La Salle (East)
		Hofstra (East)
		Rider (West)
1984	9	Bucknell
1985	8	Bucknell
1986	8	Drexel
1987	8	Bucknell
1988	8	Lafayette
1989	8	Bucknell
1990	8	Towson St.
		Hofstra
		Lehigh
1991	7	Towson St.
1992	7	Hofstra
1993		DNP

Year	#	Conference Tournament School
1975	12	La Salle
1976	12	Hofstra
1977	12	Hofstra
1978	12	La Salle
1979	12	Temple
1980	12	La Salle
1981	12	St. Joseph's (Pa.)
1982	12	St. Joseph's (Pa.)
1983	10	La Salle
1984	9	Rider
1985	8	Lehigh
1986	8	Drexel
1987	8	Bucknell
1988	8	Lehigh
1989	8	Bucknell
1990	8	Towson St.
1991	7	Towson St.
1992	7	Towson St.
1993		DNP

GREAT MIDWEST

Year	#	Regular Season School
1992	6	DePaul
		Cincinnati
1993	6	Cincinnati

Year	#	Conference Tournament School
1992	6	Cincinnati
1993	6	Cincinnati

GULF STAR

Year	#	Regular Season School
1985	6	Southeast La.
1986	6	Sam Houston St.
1987	6	Stephen F. Austin

IVY (Eastern Intercollegiate)

Year	#	Regular Season School
1902	5	Yale
1903	5	Yale
1904	6	Columbia
1905	5	Columbia
1906	6	Pennsylvania
1907	6	Yale
1908	5	Pennsylvania
1909-10		DNP
1911	5	Columbia
1912	6	Columbia
1913	5	Cornell
1914	6	Cornell
		Columbia
1915	6	Yale
1916	6	Pennsylvania
1917	6	Yale
1918	6	Pennsylvania
1919	5	Pennsylvania
1920	6	Pennsylvania
1921	6	Pennsylvania
1922	6	Princeton
1923	6	Yale
1924	6	Cornell
1925	6	Princeton
1926	6	Columbia
1927	6	Dartmouth
1928	6	Pennsylvania
1929	6	Pennsylvania
1930	6	Columbia
1931	6	Columbia
1932	6	Princeton
1933	6	Yale
1934	7	Pennsylvania
1935	7	Pennsylvania
1936	7	Columbia
1937	7	Pennsylvania
1938	7	Dartmouth
1939	7	Dartmouth
1940	7	Dartmouth
1941	7	Dartmouth
1942	7	Dartmouth
1943	7	Dartmouth
1944	5	Dartmouth
1945	4	Pennsylvania
1946	5	Dartmouth
1947	7	Columbia
1948	7	Columbia
1949	7	Yale
1950	7	Princeton
1951	7	Columbia
1952	7	Princeton
1953	7	Pennsylvania
1954	8	Cornell
1955	8	Princeton

Regular Season

Year	#	School
1956	8	Dartmouth
1957	8	Yale
1958	8	Dartmouth
1959	8	Dartmouth
1960	8	Princeton
1961	8	Princeton
1962	8	Yale
1963	8	Princeton
1964	8	Princeton
1965	8	Princeton
1966	8	Pennsylvania
1967	8	Princeton
1968	8	Columbia
1969	8	Princeton
1970	8	Pennsylvania
1971	8	Pennsylvania
1972	8	Pennsylvania
1973	8	Pennsylvania
1974	8	Pennsylvania
1975	8	Pennsylvania
1976	8	Princeton
1977	8	Princeton
1978	8	Pennsylvania
1979	8	Pennsylvania
1980	8	Pennsylvania
1981	8	Princeton
1982	8	Pennsylvania
1983	8	Princeton
1984	8	Princeton
1985	8	Pennsylvania
1986	8	Brown
1987	8	Pennsylvania
1988	8	Cornell
1989	8	Princeton
1990	8	Princeton
1991	8	Princeton
1992	8	Princeton
1993	8	Pennsylvania

METRO

Regular Season

Year	#	School
1976	6	Tulane
1977	7	Louisville
1978	7	Florida St.
1979	7	Louisville
1980	7	Louisville
1981	7	Louisville
1982	7	Memphis St.
1983	7	Louisville
1984	8	Memphis St.
		Louisville
1985	8	Memphis St.
1986	7	Louisville
1987	7	Louisville
1988	7	Louisville
1989	7	Florida St.
1990	8	Louisville
1991	8	Southern Miss.
1992	7	Tulane
1993	7	Louisville

Conference Tournament

Year	#	School
1976	6	Cincinnati
1977	7	Cincinnati
1978	7	Louisville
1979	7	Virginia Tech
1980	7	Louisville
1981	7	Louisville
1982	7	Memphis St.
1983	7	Louisville
1984	8	Memphis St.
1985	8	Memphis St.
1986	7	Louisville
1987	7	Memphis St.
1988	7	Louisville
1989	5	Louisville
1990	8	Louisville
1991	8	Florida St.
1992	7	N.C.-Charlotte
1993	7	Louisville

METRO ATLANTIC

Regular Season

Year	#	School
1982	6	St. Peter's
1983	6	Iona
1984	8	La Salle
		St. Peter's
		Iona
1985	8	Iona
1986	8	Fairfield
1987	8	St. Peter's
1988	8	La Salle
1989	8	La Salle
1990	12	Holy Cross (North)
		La Salle (South)
1991	9	Siena
1992	9	Manhattan
1993	8	Manhattan

Conference Tournament

Year	#	School
1982	6	Fordham
1983	6	Fordham
1984	8	Iona
1985	8	Iona
1986	8	Fairfield
1987	8	Fairfield
1988	8	La Salle
1989	8	La Salle
1990	12	La Salle
1991	9	St. Peter's
1992	9	La Salle
1993	8	Manhattan

METROPOLITAN NEW YORK

Regular Season

Year	#	School
1943	8	St. John's (N.Y.)
1944-45		DNP
1946	7	New York U.
		St. John's (N.Y.)
1947	7	St. John's (N.Y.)
1948	7	New York U.
1949	7	Manhattan
		St. John's (N.Y.)
1950	7	CCNY
1951	7	St. John's (N.Y.)
1952	7	St. John's (N.Y.)
1953	7	Manhattan
1954	7	St. Francis (N.Y.)
1955	7	Manhattan
1956	7	St. Francis (N.Y.)
1957	7	New York U.
1958	7	St. John's (N.Y.)
1959	7	Manhattan
1960	7	New York U.
1961	7	St. John's (N.Y.)
1962	7	St. John's (N.Y.)
1963	7	Fordham

MID-AMERICAN

Regular Season

Year	#	School
1947	5	Butler
		Cincinnati
1948	6	Cincinnati
1949	6	Cincinnati
1950	6	Cincinnati
1951	5	Cincinnati
1952	7	Miami (Ohio)
		Western Mich.
1953	7	Miami (Ohio)
1954	8	Toledo
1955	8	Miami (Ohio)
1956	7	Marshall
1957	7	Miami (Ohio)
1958	7	Miami (Ohio)
1959	7	Bowling Green
1960	7	Ohio
1961	7	Ohio
1962	7	Bowling Green
1963	7	Bowling Green
1964	7	Ohio
1965	7	Ohio
1966	7	Miami (Ohio)
1967	7	Toledo
1968	7	Bowling Green
1969	7	Miami (Ohio)
1970	6	Ohio
1971	6	Miami (Ohio)
1972	6	Ohio
1973	7	Miami (Ohio)
1974	7	Ohio
1975	8	Central Mich.
1976	10	Western Mich.
1977	10	Central Mich.
1978	10	Miami (Ohio)
1979	10	Toledo
1980	10	Toledo
1981	10	Ball St.
		Northern Ill.
		Toledo
		Western Mich.
		Bowling Green
1982	10	Ball St.
1983	10	Bowling Green
1984	10	Miami (Ohio)
1985	10	Ohio
1986	10	Miami (Ohio)
1987	9	Central Mich.
1988	9	Eastern Mich.
1989	9	Ball St.
1990	9	Ball St.
1991	9	Eastern Mich.
1992	8	Miami (Ohio)
1993	10	Ball St.
		Miami (Ohio)

Conference Tournament

Year	#	School
1980	7	Toledo
1981	7	Ball St.
1982	7	Northern Ill.
1983	7	Ohio
1984	7	Miami (Ohio)
1985	7	Ohio
1986	7	Ball St.
1987	7	Central Mich.
1988	7	Eastern Mich.
1989	8	Ball St.
1990	8	Ball St.
1991	8	Eastern Mich.
1992	8	Miami (Ohio)
1993	10	Ball St.

MID-CONTINENT

Regular Season

Year	#	School
1983	8	Western Ill.
1984	8	Ill.-Chicago
1985	8	Cleveland St.
1986	8	Cleveland St.
1987	8	Southwest Mo. St.
1988	8	Southwest Mo. St.
1989	8	Southwest Mo. St.
1990	7	Southwest Mo. St.
1991	9	Northern Ill.
1992	9	Wis.-Green Bay
1993	9	Cleveland St.

Conference Tournament

Year	#	School
1984	8	Western Ill.
1985	8	Eastern Ill.
1986	8	Cleveland St.
1987	8	Southwest Mo. St.
1988		DNP
1989	7	Southwest Mo. St.
1990	7	Northern Iowa
1991	8	Wis.-Green Bay
1992	8	Eastern Ill.
1993	8	Wright St.

MID-EASTERN

Regular Season

Year	#	School
1972	7	North Caro. A&T
1973	7	Md.-East. Shore
1974	7	Md.-East. Shore
		Morgan St.
1975	7	North Caro. A&T
1976	7	North Caro. A&T
		Morgan St.
1977	7	South Caro. St.
1978	7	North Caro. A&T
1979	7	North Caro. A&T

Year	#	Regular Season School
1980	7	Howard
1981	6	North Caro. A&T
1982	7	North Caro. A&T
1983	7	Howard
1984	6	North Caro. A&T
1985	7	North Caro. A&T
1986	8	North Caro. A&T
1987	8	Howard
1988	9	North Caro. A&T
1989	9	South Caro. St.
1990	9	Coppin St.
1991	9	Coppin St.
1992	9	North Caro. A&T
		Howard
1993	9	Coppin St.

Year	#	Conference Tournament School
1972	7	North Caro. A&T
1973	7	North Caro. A&T
1974	7	Md.-East. Shore
1975	7	North Caro. A&T
1976	7	North Caro. A&T
1977	7	Morgan St.
1978	7	North Caro. A&T
1979	7	North Caro. A&T
1980	7	Howard
1981	6	Howard
1982	7	North Caro. A&T
1983	7	North Caro. A&T
1984	6	North Caro. A&T
1985	6	North Caro. A&T
1986	6	North Caro. A&T
1987	7	North Caro. A&T
1988	7	North Caro. A&T
1989	8	South Caro. St.
1990	8	Coppin St.
1991	9	Florida A&M
1992	9	Howard
1993	9	Coppin St.

MIDWESTERN

Year	#	Regular Season School
1980	6	Loyola (Ill.)
1981	7	Xavier (Ohio)
1982	7	Evansville
1983	8	Loyola (Ill.)
1984	8	Oral Roberts
1985	8	Loyola (Ill.)
1986	7	Xavier (Ohio)
1987	7	Evansville
		Loyola (Ill.)
1988	6	Xavier (Ohio)
1989	7	Evansville
1990	8	Xavier (Ohio)
1991	8	Xavier (Ohio)
1992	6	Evansville
1993	8	Evansville
	8	Xavier (Ohio)

Year	#	Conference Tournament School
1980	6	Oral Roberts
1981	7	Oklahoma City
1982	7	Evansville
1983	8	Xavier (Ohio)
1984	8	Oral Roberts
1985	8	Loyola (Ill.)
1986	7	Xavier (Ohio)
1987	7	Xavier (Ohio)
1988	6	Xavier (Ohio)
1989	7	Evansville
1990	8	Dayton
1991	8	Xavier (Ohio)
1992	6	Evansville
1993	8	Evansville

MISSOURI VALLEY

Year	#	Regular Season School
1908	6	Kansas
1909	6	Kansas
1910	6	Kansas
1911	5	Kansas
1912	6	Nebraska
		Kansas
1913	6	Nebraska
1914	7	Kansas
		Nebraska
1915	7	Kansas
1916	7	Nebraska
1917	7	Kansas St.
1918	7	Missouri
1919	8	Kansas St.
1920	8	Missouri
1921	9	Missouri
1922	9	Missouri
		Kansas
1923	9	Kansas
1924	9	Kansas
1925	9	Kansas
1926	10	Kansas
1927	10	Kansas
1928	10	Oklahoma
1929	5	Washington (Mo.)
1930	5	Creighton
		Washington (Mo.)
1931	5	Creighton
		Oklahoma St.
1932	5	Creighton
1933	6	Butler
1934	6	Butler
1935	7	Creighton
		Drake
1936	7	Creighton
		Oklahoma St.
		Drake
1937	7	Oklahoma St.
1938	7	Oklahoma St.
1939	8	Oklahoma St.
		Drake
1940	7	Oklahoma St.
1941	7	Creighton
1942	6	Oklahoma St.
		Creighton
1943	6	Creighton
1944	4	Oklahoma St.
1945	5	Oklahoma St.
1946	7	Oklahoma St.
1947	7	St. Louis
1948	6	Oklahoma St.
1949	6	Oklahoma St.
1950	7	Bradley
1951	8	Oklahoma St.
1952	6	St. Louis
1953	6	Oklahoma St.
1954	6	Oklahoma St.
1955	6	Tulsa
		St. Louis
1956	7	Houston
1957	8	St. Louis
1958	8	Cincinnati
1959	8	Cincinnati
1960	8	Cincinnati
1961	7	Cincinnati
1962	7	Cincinnati
1963	7	Cincinnati
1964	7	Wichita St.
1965	8	Wichita St.
1966	8	Cincinnati
1967	8	Louisville
1968	9	Louisville
1969	9	Louisville
1970	9	Drake
1971	8	Drake
1972	8	Louisville
1973	10	Memphis St.
1974	9	Louisville
1975	8	Louisville
1976	7	Wichita St.
1977	7	Southern Ill.
		New Mexico St.
1978	9	Creighton
1979	9	Indiana St.
1980	9	Bradley
1981	9	Wichita St.
1982	10	Bradley
1983	10	Wichita St.
1984	9	Tulsa
		Illinois St.
1985	9	Tulsa
1986	9	Bradley
1987	8	Tulsa
1988	8	Bradley
1989	8	Creighton
1990	8	Southern Ill.
1991	9	Creighton
1992	10	Southern Ill.
		Illinois St.
1993	10	Illinois St.

Year	#	Conference Tournament School
1977	8	Southern Ill.
1978	9	Creighton
1979	8	Indiana St.
1980	8	Bradley
1981	8	Creighton
1982	8	Tulsa
1983	8	Illinois St.
1984	8	Tulsa
1985	8	Wichita St.
1986	8	Tulsa
1987	7	Wichita St.
1988	8	Bradley
1989	8	Creighton
1990	8	Illinois St.
1991	9	Creighton
1992	8	Southwest Mo. St.
1993	8	Southern Ill.

MOUNTAIN STATES (Skyline Eight, Big Seven)

Year	#	Regular Season School
1938	7	Colorado
		Utah
1939	7	Colorado
1940	7	Colorado
1941	7	Wyoming
1942	7	Colorado
1943	5	Wyoming
1944	7	Utah
1945	7	Utah
1946	7	Wyoming
1947	7	Wyoming
1948	6	Brigham Young
1949	6	Wyoming
1950	6	Brigham Young
1951	6	Brigham Young
1952	8	Wyoming
1953	8	Wyoming
1954	8	Colorado
1955	8	Utah
1956	8	Utah
1957	8	Brigham Young
1958	8	Wyoming
1959	8	Utah
1960	8	Utah
1961	8	Colorado St.
		Utah
1962	8	Utah

NEW ENGLAND

Year	#	Regular Season School
1938	5	Rhode Island
1939	5	Rhode Island
1940	5	Rhode Island
1941	5	Rhode Island
1942	5	Rhode Island
1943	5	Rhode Island
1944	4	Rhode Island
1945		DNP
1946	5	Rhode Island

NEW JERSEY-NEW YORK 7

Year	#	Regular Season School
1977	7	Columbia
		Seton Hall
1978	7	Rutgers
		St. John's (N.Y.)
1979	7	Rutgers

NORTH ATLANTIC (ECAC North Atlantic)

Regular Season

Year	#	School
1980	10	Boston U.
		Northeastern
1981	9	Northeastern
1982	9	Northeastern
1983	9	Boston U.
		New Hampshire
1984	8	Northeastern
1985	9	Northeastern
		Canisius
1986	10	Northeastern
1987	10	Northeastern
1988	10	Siena
1989	10	Siena
1990	7	Northeastern
1991	6	Northeastern
1992	8	Delaware
1993	8	Drexel
		Northeastern

Conference Tournament

Year	#	School
1980	8	Holy Cross
1981	6	Northeastern
1982	6	Northeastern
1983	9	Boston U.
1984	8	Northeastern
1985	9	Northeastern
1986	10	Northeastern
1987	10	Northeastern
1988	10	Boston U.
1989	10	Siena
1990	7	Boston U.
1991	6	Northeastern
1992	8	Delaware
1993	8	Delaware

NORTHEAST (ECAC Northeast, ECAC Metro)

Regular Season

Year	#	School
1982	11	FDU-Teaneck (North)
		Robert Morris (South)
1983	10	LIU-Brooklyn (North)
		Robert Morris (South)
1984	9	LIU-Brooklyn
		Robert Morris
1985	8	Marist
1986	9	FDU-Teaneck
1987	9	Marist
1988	9	FDU-Teaneck
		Marist
1989	9	Robert Morris
1990	9	Robert Morris
1991	9	St. Francis (Pa.)
		FDU-Teaneck
1992	9	Robert Morris
1993	10	Rider

Conference Tournament

Year	#	School
1982	8	Robert Morris
1983	8	Robert Morris
1984	8	LIU-Brooklyn
1985	8	FDU-Teaneck
1986	8	Marist
1987	6	Marist
1988	6	FDU-Teaneck
1989	6	Robert Morris
1990	6	Robert Morris
1991	7	St. Francis (Pa.)
1992	9	Robert Morris
1993	10	Rider

OHIO VALLEY

Regular Season

Year	#	School
1949	8	Western Ky.
1950	7	Western Ky.
1951	7	Murray St.
1952	7	Morehead St.
1953	6	Eastern Ky.
1954	6	Western Ky.
1955	6	Western Ky.
1956	6	Morehead St.
		Tennessee Tech
		Western Ky.
1957	6	Morehead St.
		Western Ky.
1958	7	Tennessee Tech
1959	7	Eastern Ky.
1960	7	Western Ky.
1961	7	Morehead St.
		Western Ky.
		Eastern Ky.
1962	6	Western Ky.
1963	7	Tennessee Tech
		Morehead St.
1964	8	Murray St.
1965	8	Eastern Ky.
1966	8	Western Ky.
1967	8	Western Ky.
1968	8	East Tenn. St.
		Murray St.
1969	8	Murray St.
		Morehead St.
1970	8	Western Ky.
1971	8	Western Ky.
1972	8	Eastern Ky.
		Morehead St.
		Western Ky.
1973	8	Austin Peay
1974	8	Austin Peay
		Morehead St.
1975	8	Middle Tenn. St.
1976	8	Western Ky.
1977	8	Austin Peay
1978	8	Middle Tenn. St.
		Eastern Ky.
1979	7	Eastern Ky.
1980	7	Western Ky.
		Murray St.
1981	8	Western Ky.
1982	8	Murray St.
		Western Ky.
1983	8	Murray St.
1984	8	Morehead St.
1985	8	Tennessee Tech
1986	8	Akron
		Middle Tenn. St.
1987	8	Middle Tenn. St.
1988	8	Murray St.
1989	7	Middle Tenn. St.
		Murray St.
1990	7	Murray St.
1991	7	Murray St.
1992	8	Murray St.
1993	9	Tennessee St.

Conference Tournament

Year	#	School
1949	8	Western Ky.
1950	7	Eastern Ky.
1951	7	Murray St.
1952	7	Western Ky.
1953	6	Western Ky.
1954	6	Western Ky.
1955	6	Eastern Ky.
1956-63		DNP
1964	8	Murray St.
1965	8	Western Ky.
1966	8	Western Ky.
1967	8	Tennessee Tech
1968-74		DNP
1975	4	Middle Tenn. St.
1976	8	Western Ky.
1977	4	Middle Tenn. St.
1978	4	Western Ky.
1979	4	Eastern Ky.
1980	4	Western Ky.
1981	4	Western Ky.
1982	4	Middle Tenn. St.
1983	4	Morehead St.
1984	4	Morehead St.
1985	7	Middle Tenn. St.
1986	7	Akron
1987	7	Austin Peay
1988	7	Murray St.
1989	7	Middle Tenn. St.
1990	7	Murray St.
1991	7	Murray St.
1992	7	Murray St.
1993	6	Tennessee St.

PACIFIC-10 (Pacific 8, Pacific Coast, AAWU)

Regular Season

Year	#	School
1916	3	California
		Oregon St.
1917	6	Washington St.
1918		DNP
1919	6	Oregon
1920	6	Stanford
1921	6	Stanford
1922	8	Idaho
1923	8	Idaho
1924	9	California
1925	8	California
1926	9	California
1927	9	California
1928	10	Southern Cal
1929	10	California
1930	9	Southern Cal
1931	9	Washington
1932	9	California
1933	9	Oregon St.
1934	9	Washington
1935	9	Southern Cal
1936	9	Stanford
1937	9	Stanford
1938	10	Stanford
1939	9	Oregon
1940	9	Southern Cal
1941	9	Washington St.
1942	9	Stanford
1943	9	Washington
1944	8	Washington (North)
		California (South)
1945	8	Oregon (North)
		UCLA (South)
1946	9	California
1947	9	Oregon St.
1948	9	Washington
1949	9	Oregon St.
1950	9	UCLA
1951	9	Washington
1952	9	UCLA
1953	9	Washington
1954	9	Southern Cal
1955	9	Oregon St.
1956	9	UCLA
1957	9	California
1958	9	Oregon St.
		California
1959	9	California
1960	5	California
1961	5	Southern Cal
1962	5	UCLA
1963	5	UCLA
		Stanford
1964	6	UCLA
1965	8	UCLA
1966	8	Oregon St.
1967	8	UCLA
1968	8	UCLA
1969	8	UCLA
1970	8	UCLA
1971	8	UCLA
1972	8	UCLA
1973	8	UCLA
1974	8	UCLA
1975	8	UCLA
1976	8	UCLA
1977	8	UCLA
1978	8	UCLA
1979	10	UCLA
1980	10	Oregon St.
1981	10	Oregon St.
1982	10	Oregon St.
1983	10	UCLA
1984	10	Washington
		Oregon St.

Year	#	Regular Season School
1985	10	Washington
		Southern Cal
1986	10	Arizona
1987	10	UCLA
1988	10	Arizona
1989	10	Arizona
1990	10	Oregon St.
		Arizona
1991	10	Arizona
1992	10	UCLA
1993	10	Arizona

Year	#	Conference Tournament School
1987	10	UCLA
1988	10	Arizona
1989	10	Arizona
1990	10	Arizona

PATRIOT

Year	#	Regular Season School
1990	7	Fordham
1991	7	Fordham
1992	8	Bucknell
		Fordham
1993	8	Bucknell

Year	#	Conference Tournament School
1990	7	Fordham
1991	7	Fordham
1992	8	Fordham
1993	8	Holy Cross

ROCKY MOUNTAIN

Year	#	Regular Season School
1922	6	Colorado Col.
1923	5	Colorado Col.
1924	6	Colorado Col.
1925	12	Colorado Col. (East)
		Brigham Young (West)
1926	12	Colorado St. (East)
		Utah (West)
1927	12	Colorado Col. (East)
		Montana St. (West)
1928	12	Wyoming (East)
		Montana St. (West)
1929	12	Colorado (East)
		Montana St. (West)
1930	12	Colorado (East)
		Montana St. (West)
		Utah St. (West)
1931	12	Wyoming (East)
		Utah (West)
1932	12	Wyoming (East)
		Brigham Young (West)
		Utah (West)
1933	12	Wyoming (East)
		Colorado St. (East)
		Brigham Young (West)
		Utah (West)
1934	12	Wyoming (East)
		Brigham Young (West)
1935	12	Northern Colo. (East)
		Utah St. (West)
1936	12	Wyoming (East)
		Utah (West)
1937	12	Denver (East)
		Colorado (East)
		Montana St. (West)
		Utah (West)
1938	5	Montana St.
1939	5	Northern Colo.
1940	5	Northern Colo.
1941	5	Northern Colo.
1942	5	Northern Colo.
1943	3	Northern Colo.
1944	3	Colorado Col.
1945	3	Colorado Col.
1946	5	Colorado St.
1947	5	Montana St.
1948	4	Colorado St.
1949	5	Colorado St.
1950	6	Montana St.
1951	6	Montana St.

Year	#	Regular Season School
1952	6	Colorado St.
		Montana St.
1953	6	Idaho St.
1954	6	Idaho St.
1955	6	Idaho St.
1956	6	Idaho St.
1957	6	Idaho St.
1958	6	Idaho St.
1959	6	Idaho St.
1960	6	Idaho St.

SOUTHEASTERN

Year	#	Regular Season School
1933	13	Kentucky
1934	13	Alabama
1935	13	Louisiana St.
		Kentucky
1936	13	Tennessee
1937	13	Kentucky
1938	13	Georgia Tech
1939	13	Kentucky
1940	13	Kentucky
1941	12	Tennessee
1942	12	Kentucky
1943	12	Tennessee
1944	6	Kentucky
1945	12	Kentucky
1946	12	Kentucky
1947	12	Kentucky
1948	12	Kentucky
1949	12	Kentucky
1950	12	Kentucky
1951	12	Kentucky
1952	12	Kentucky
1953	11	Louisiana St.
1954	12	Kentucky
		Louisiana St.
1955	12	Kentucky
1956	12	Alabama
1957	12	Kentucky
1958	12	Kentucky
1959	12	Mississippi St.
1960	12	Auburn
1961	12	Mississippi St.
1962	12	Mississippi St.
		Kentucky
1963	12	Mississippi St.
1964	12	Kentucky
1965	11	Vanderbilt
1966	11	Kentucky
1967	10	Tennessee
1968	10	Kentucky
1969	10	Kentucky
1970	10	Kentucky
1971	10	Kentucky
1972	10	Tennessee
		Kentucky
1973	10	Kentucky
1974	10	Vanderbilt
		Alabama
1975	10	Kentucky
		Alabama
1976	10	Alabama
1977	10	Kentucky
		Tennessee
1978	10	Kentucky
1979	10	Louisiana St.
1980	10	Kentucky
1981	10	Louisiana St.
1982	10	Kentucky
		Tennessee
1983	10	Kentucky
1984	10	Kentucky
1985	10	Louisiana St.
1986	10	Kentucky
1987	10	Alabama
1988	10	vacated
1989	10	Florida
1990	10	Georgia
1991	10	Mississippi St.
		Louisiana St.
1992	12	Kentucky (Eastern)
		Arkansas (Western)
1993	12	Vanderbilt (Eastern)
		Arkansas (Western)

Year	#	Conference Tournament School
1933	13	Kentucky
1934	10	Alabama
1935		DNP
1936	9	Tennessee
1937	8	Kentucky
1938	11	Georgia Tech
1939	12	Kentucky
1940	12	Kentucky
1941	12	Tennessee
1942	12	Kentucky
1943	11	Tennessee
1944	6	Kentucky
1945	11	Kentucky
1946	12	Kentucky
1947	12	Kentucky
1948	12	Kentucky
1949	12	Kentucky
1950	12	Kentucky
1951	12	Vanderbilt
1952	12	Kentucky
1953-78		DNP
1979	10	Tennessee
1980	10	Louisiana St.
1981	10	Mississippi
1982	10	Alabama
1983	10	Georgia
1984	10	Kentucky
1985	10	Auburn
1986	10	Kentucky
1987	10	Alabama
1988	10	vacated
1989	10	Alabama
1990	9	Alabama
1991	9	Alabama
1992	11	Kentucky
1993	12	Kentucky

SOUTHERN

Year	#	Regular Season School
1922	13	Virginia
1923	19	North Caro.
1924	21	Tulane
1925	21	North Caro.
1926	22	Kentucky
1927	22	South Caro.
1928	22	Auburn
1929	23	Wash. & Lee
1930	23	Alabama
1931	22	Georgia
1932	23	Kentucky
		Maryland
1933	10	South Caro.
1934	10	South Caro.
1935	10	North Caro.
1936	10	Wash. & Lee
1937	16	Wash. & Lee
1938	15	North Caro.
1939	15	Wake Forest
1940	15	Duke
1941	15	North Caro.
1942	16	Duke
1943	15	Duke
1944	12	North Caro.
1945	14	South Caro.
1946	16	North Caro.
1947	16	North Caro. St.
1948	16	North Caro. St.
1949	16	North Caro. St.
1950	16	North Caro. St.
1951	17	North Caro. St.
1952	17	West Va.
1953	17	North Caro. St.
1954	10	Geo. Washington
1955	10	West Va.
1956	10	Geo. Washington
		West Va.
1957	10	West Va.
1958	10	West Va.
1959	9	West Va.
1960	9	Virginia Tech
1961	9	West Va.
1962	9	West Va.
1963	9	West Va.
1964	9	Davidson

Year	#	Regular Season School
1965	10	Davidson
1966	9	Davidson
1967	9	West Va.
1968	9	Davidson
1969	8	Davidson
1970	8	Davidson
1971	7	Davidson
1972	8	Davidson
1973	8	Davidson
1974	8	Furman
1975	8	Furman
1976	8	Va. Military
1977	10	Furman
		Va. Military
1978	8	Appalachian St.
1979	9	Appalachian St.
1980	9	Furman
1981	9	Appalachian St.
		Davidson
		Tenn.-Chatt.
1982	9	Tenn.-Chatt.
1983	9	Tenn.-Chatt.
1984	9	Marshall
1985	9	Tenn.-Chatt.
1986	9	Tenn.-Chatt.
1987	9	Marshall
1988	9	Marshall
1989	8	Tenn.-Chatt.
1990	8	East Tenn. St.
1991	8	East Tenn. St.
		Furman
		Tenn.-Chatt.
1992	8	East Tenn. St.
		Tenn.-Chatt.
1993	10	Tenn.-Chatt.

Year	#	Conference Tournament School
1921		Kentucky
1922	23	North Caro.
1923	22	Mississippi St.
1924	16	North Caro.
1925	17	North Caro.
1926	16	North Caro.
1927	14	Vanderbilt
1928	16	Mississippi
1929	16	North Caro. St.
1930	16	Alabama
1931	16	Maryland
1932	16	Georgia
1933	8	South Caro.
1934	8	Wash.& Lee
1935	8	North Caro.
1936	8	North Caro.
1937	8	Wash.& Lee
1938	8	Duke
1939	11	Clemson
1940	8	North Caro.
1941	8	Duke
1942	8	Duke
1943	8	Geo. Washington
1944	8	Duke
1945	8	North Caro.
1946	8	Duke
1947	8	North Caro. St.
1948	10	North Caro. St.
1949	8	North Caro. St.
1950	8	North Caro. St.
1951	8	North Caro. St.
1952	8	North Caro. St.
1953	8	Wake Forest
1954	8	Geo. Washington
1955	8	West Va.
1956	8	West Va.
1957	8	West Va.
1958	8	West Va.
1959	8	West Va.
1960	8	West Va.
1961	8	Geo. Washington
1962	8	West Va.
1963	8	West Va.
1964	8	Va. Military
1965	8	West Va.
1966	8	Davidson
1967	8	West Va.
1968	8	Davidson
1969	8	Davidson
1970	8	Davidson
1971	7	Furman
1972	8	East Caro.
1973	8	Furman
1974	8	Furman
1975	8	Furman
1976	8	Va. Military
1977	7	Va. Military
1978	8	Furman
1979	8	Appalachian St.
1980	8	Furman
1981	8	Tenn.-Chatt.
1982	8	Tenn.-Chatt.
1983	8	Tenn.-Chatt.
1984	8	Marshall
1985	8	Marshall
1986	8	Davidson
1987	8	Marshall
1988	8	Tenn.-Chatt.
1989	8	East Tenn. St.
1990	8	East Tenn. St.
1991	8	East Tenn. St.
1992	8	East Tenn. St.
1993	10	Tenn.-Chatt.

SOUTHLAND

Year	#	Regular Season School
1964	5	Lamar
1965	5	Abilene Christian
		Arkansas St.
1966	5	Abilene Christian
1967	5	Arkansas St.
1968	5	Abilene Christian
1969	5	Trinity (Tex.)
1970	5	Lamar
1971	5	Arkansas St.
1972	7	Louisiana Tech
1973	7	Louisiana Tech
1974	3	Arkansas St.
1975	5	McNeese St.
1976	6	Louisiana Tech
1977	6	Southwestern La.
1978	6	McNeese St.
		Lamar
1979	6	Lamar
1980	6	Lamar
1981	6	Lamar
1982	6	Southwestern La.
1983	7	Lamar
1984	7	Lamar
1985	7	Louisiana Tech
1986	7	Northeast La.
1987	6	Louisiana Tech
1988	8	North Texas
1989	8	North Texas
1990	8	Northeast La.
1991	8	Northeast La.
1992	10	Texas-San Antonio
1993	10	Northeast La.

Year	#	Conference Tournament School
1981	6	Lamar
1982	5	Southwestern La.
1983	7	Lamar
1984	7	Louisiana Tech
1985	7	Louisiana Tech
1986	7	Northeast La.
1987	6	Louisiana Tech
1988	6	North Texas
1989	6	McNeese St.
1990	7	Northeast La.
1991	4	Northeast La.
1992	6	Northeast La.
1993	6	Northeast La.

SOUTHWEST

Year	#	Regular Season School
1915	5	Texas
1916	5	Texas
1917	3	Texas
1918	5	Rice
1919	5	Texas
1920	6	Texas A&M
1921	5	Texas A&M
1922	6	Texas A&M
1923	6	Texas A&M
1924	8	Texas
1925	8	Oklahoma St.
1926	7	Arkansas
1927	7	Arkansas
1928	7	Arkansas
1929	7	Arkansas
1930	7	Arkansas
1931	7	Texas Christian
1932	7	Baylor
1933	7	Texas
1934	7	Texas Christian
1935	7	Arkansas
		Rice
		Southern Methodist
1936	7	Arkansas
1937	7	Southern Methodist
1938	7	Arkansas
1939	7	Texas
1940	7	Rice
1941	7	Arkansas
1942	7	Rice
		Arkansas
1943	7	Texas
		Rice
1944	7	Arkansas
		Rice
1945	7	Rice
1946	7	Baylor
1947	7	Texas
1948	7	Baylor
1949	7	Arkansas
		Baylor
		Rice
1950	7	Baylor
		Arkansas
1951	7	Texas A&M
		Texas Christian
		Texas
1952	7	Texas Christian
1953	7	Texas Christian
1954	7	Rice
		Texas
1955	7	Southern Methodist
1956	7	Southern Methodist
1957	7	Southern Methodist
1958	8	Arkansas
		Southern Methodist
1959	8	Texas Christian
1960	8	Texas
1961	8	Texas Tech
1962	8	Southern Methodist
		Texas Tech
1963	8	Texas
1964	8	Texas A&M
1965	8	Southern Methodist
		Texas
1966	8	Southern Methodist
1967	8	Southern Methodist
1968	8	Texas Christian
1969	8	Texas A&M
1970	8	Rice
1971	8	Texas Christian
1972	8	Texas
		Southern Methodist
1973	8	Texas Tech
1974	8	Texas
1975	8	Texas A&M
1976	9	Texas A&M
1977	9	Arkansas
1978	9	Texas
		Arkansas
1979	9	Texas
		Arkansas
1980	9	Texas A&M
1981	9	Arkansas
1982	9	Arkansas
1983	9	Houston
1984	9	Houston
1985	9	Texas Tech
1986	9	Texas Christian
		Texas
		Texas A&M
1987	9	Texas Christian

Regular Season

Year	#	School
1988	9	Southern Methodist
1989	9	Arkansas
1990	9	Arkansas
1991	9	Arkansas
1992	8	Houston
		Texas
1993	8	Southern Methodist

Conference Tournament

Year	#	School
1976	9	Texas Tech
1977	9	Arkansas
1978	9	Houston
1979	9	Arkansas
1980	9	Texas A&M
1981	9	Houston
1982	9	Arkansas
1983	9	Houston
1984	9	Houston
1985	8	Texas Tech
1986	8	Texas Tech
1987	8	Texas A&M
1988	8	Southern Methodist
1989	8	Arkansas
1990	8	Arkansas
1991	9	Arkansas
1992	8	Houston
1993	8	Texas Tech

SOUTHWESTERN

Regular Season

Year	#	School
1957	6	Texas Southern
1958	6	Texas Southern
1959	8	Grambling
1960	8	Grambling
1961	8	Prairie View
1962	7	Prairie View
1963	8	Grambling
1964	8	Grambling
		Jackson St.
1965	8	Southern-B.R.
1966	8	Alcorn St.
		Grambling
1967	8	Alcorn St.
		Arkansas AM&N
		Grambling
1968	8	Alcorn St.
		Jackson St.
1969	8	Alcorn St.
1970	8	Jackson St.
1971	7	Grambling
1972	7	Grambling
1973	7	Alcorn St.
1974	7	Jackson St.
1975	7	Jackson St.
1976	7	Alcorn St.
1977	7	Texas Southern
1978	7	Jackson St.
		Southern-B.R.
1979	7	Alcorn St.
1980	7	Alcorn St.
1981	7	Alcorn St.
		Southern-B.R.
1982	7	Alcorn St.
		Jackson St.
1983	8	Texas Southern
1984	8	Alcorn St.
1985	8	Alcorn St.
1986	8	Alcorn St.
		Southern-B.R.
1987	8	Grambling
1988	8	Southern-B.R.
1989	8	Grambling
		Southern-B.R.
		Texas Southern
1990	8	Southern-B.R.
1991	8	Jackson St.
1992	8	Mississippi Val.
		Texas Southern
1993	8	Jackson St.

Conference Tournament

Year	#	School
1980	7	Alcorn St.
1981	7	Southern-B.R.
1982	7	Alcorn St.
1983	7	Alcorn St.
1984	8	Alcorn St.
1985	4	Southern-B.R.
1986	8	Mississippi Val.
1987	8	Southern-B.R.
1988	8	Southern-B.R.
1989	8	Southern-B.R.
1990	8	Texas Southern
1991	8	Jackson St.
1992	8	Mississippi Val.
1993	8	Southern-B.R.

SUN BELT

Regular Season

Year	#	School
1977	6	N.C.-Charlotte
1978	6	N.C.-Charlotte
1979	6	South Ala.
1980	8	South Ala.
1981	7	Va. Commonwealth
		South Ala.
		Ala.-Birmingham
1982	6	Ala.-Birmingham
1983	8	Va. Commonwealth
		Old Dominion
1984	8	Va. Commonwealth
1985	8	Va. Commonwealth
1986	8	Old Dominion
1987	8	Western Ky.
1988	8	N.C.-Charlotte
1989	8	South Ala.
1990	8	Ala.-Birmingham
1991	8	South Ala.
1992	11	Louisiana Tech
		Southwestern La.
1993	10	New Orleans

Conference Tournament

Year	#	School
1977	6	N.C.-Charlotte
1978	6	New Orleans
1979	6	Jacksonville
1980	8	Va. Commonwealth
1981	7	Va. Commonwealth
1982	6	Ala.-Birmingham
1983	8	Ala.-Birmingham
1984	8	Ala.-Birmingham
1985	8	Va. Commonwealth
1986	8	Jacksonville
1987	8	Ala.-Birmingham
1988	8	N.C.-Charlotte
1989	8	South Ala.
1990	8	South Fla.
1991	8	South Ala.
1992	11	Southwestern La.
1993	9	Western Ky.

TRANS AMERICA

Regular Season

Year	#	School
1979	8	Northeast La.
1980	7	Northeast La.
1981	9	Houston Baptist
1982	9	Ark.-Lit. Rock
1983	8	Ark.-Lit. Rock
1984	8	Houston Baptist
1985	8	Ga. Southern
1986	8	Ark.-Lit. Rock
1987	10	Ark.-Lit. Rock
1988	10	Ark.-Lit. Rock
		Ga. Southern
1989	10	Ga. Southern
1990	9	Centenary
1991	8	Texas-San Antonio
1992	8	Ga. Southern
1993	7	Florida Int'l

Conference Tournament

Year	#	School
1979	6	Northeast La.
1980	7	Centenary
1981	9	Mercer
1982	7	Northeast La.
1983	8	Ga. Southern
1984	8	Houston Baptist
1985	8	Mercer
1986	8	Ark.-Lit. Rock
1987	8	Ga. Southern
1988	8	Texas-San Antonio
1989	8	Ark.-Lit. Rock
1990	8	Ark.-Lit. Rock
1991	8	Georgia St.
1992	8	Ga. Southern
1993		DNP

WEST COAST (California Basketball Association)

Regular Season

Year	#	School
1953	5	Santa Clara
1954	5	Santa Clara
1955	5	San Francisco
1956	8	San Francisco
1957	8	San Francisco
1958	7	San Francisco
1959	7	St. Marys (Cal.)
1960	7	Santa Clara
1961	7	Loyola (Cal.)
1962	7	Pepperdine
1963	7	San Francisco
1964	7	San Francisco
1965	8	San Francisco
1966	8	Pacific (Cal.)
1967	8	Pacific (Cal.)
1968	8	Santa Clara
1969	8	Santa Clara
1970	8	Santa Clara
1971	8	Pacific (Cal.)
1972	8	San Francisco
1973	8	San Francisco
1974	8	San Francisco
1975	8	Nevada-Las Vegas
1976	7	Pepperdine
1977	8	San Francisco
1978	8	San Francisco
1979	8	San Francisco
1980	9	San Francisco
		St. Mary's (Cal.)
1981	8	San Francisco
		Pepperdine
1982	8	Pepperdine
1983	7	Pepperdine
1984	7	San Diego
1985	7	Pepperdine
1986	8	Pepperdine
1987	8	San Diego
1988	8	Loyola (Cal.)
1989	8	St. Mary's (Cal.)
1990	8	Loyola (Cal.)
1991	8	Pepperdine
1992	8	Pepperdine
1993	8	Pepperdine

Conference Tournament

Year	#	School
1987	8	Santa Clara
1988	8	Loyola (Cal.)
1989	8	Loyola (Cal.)
1990		DNP
1991	8	Pepperdine
1992	8	Pepperdine
1993	8	Santa Clara

WESTERN ATHLETIC

Regular Season

Year	#	School
1963	6	Arizona St.
1964	6	New Mexico
		Arizona St.
1965	6	Brigham Young
1966	6	Utah
1967	6	Wyoming
		Brigham Young
1968	6	New Mexico
1969	6	Brigham Young
		Wyoming
1970	8	UTEP
1971	8	Brigham Young
1972	8	Brigham Young
1973	8	Arizona St.
1974	8	New Mexico

Year	#	Regular Season School
1975	8	Arizona St.
1976	8	Arizona
1977	8	Utah
1978	8	New Mexico
1979	7	Brigham Young
1980	8	Brigham Young
1981	9	Utah
		Wyoming
1982	9	Wyoming
1983	9	UTEP
		Utah
1984	9	UTEP
1985	9	UTEP
1986	9	Wyoming
		UTEP
		Utah
1987	9	UTEP
1988	9	Brigham Young
1989	9	Colorado St.
1990	9	Colorado St.
		Brigham Young
1991	9	Utah
1992	9	UTEP
		Brigham Young
1993	10	Brigham Young
		Utah

Year	#	Conference Tournament School
1984	9	UTEP
1985	9	San Diego St.
1986	9	UTEP
1987	9	Wyoming
1988	9	Wyoming
1989	9	UTEP
1990	9	UTEP
1991	9	Brigham Young
1992	8	Brigham Young
1993	10	New Mexico

WESTERN NEW YORK LITTLE THREE

Year	#	Regular Season School
1947	3	Canisius
1948	3	Niagara
1949	3	Niagara
1950	3	Canisius
		Niagara
		St. Bonaventure
1951	3	St. Bonaventure
1952		DNP
1953	3	Niagara
1954	3	Niagara
1955	3	Niagara
1956	3	Canisius
1957	3	Canisius
		St. Bonaventure
1958	3	St. Bonaventure

YANKEE

Year	#	Regular Season School
1947	6	Vermont
1948	6	Connecticut
1949	6	Connecticut
1950	6	Rhode Island
1951	6	Connecticut
1952	6	Connecticut
1953	6	Connecticut
1954	6	Connecticut
1955	6	Connecticut
1956	6	Connecticut
1957	6	Connecticut
1958	6	Connecticut
1959	6	Connecticut
1960	6	Connecticut
1961	6	Rhode Island
1962	6	Massachusetts
1963	6	Connecticut
1964	6	Connecticut
		Rhode Island
1965	6	Connecticut
1966	6	Connecticut
		Rhode Island
1967	6	Connecticut
1968	6	Massachusetts
		Rhode Island
1969	6	Massachusetts
1970	6	Connecticut
		Massachusetts
1971	6	Massachusetts
1972	6	Rhode Island
1973	7	Massachusetts
1974	7	Massachusetts
1975	7	Massachusetts

INDEPENDENTS (Best Record)

Year	#	Regular Season School
1946	30	Yale
1947	32	Duquesne
1948	40	Bradley
1949	34	Villanova
1950	36	Toledo
1951	37	Dayton
1952	42	Seton Hall
1953	42	Seattle
1954	39	Holy Cross
		Seattle
1955	41	Marquette
1956	35	Temple
1957	32	Seattle
1958	29	Temple
1959	32	St. Bonaventure
1960	34	Providence
1961	35	Memphis St.
1962	34	Loyola (Ill.)
1963	47	Loyola (Ill.)
1964	51	UTEP
1965	45	Providence
1966	44	UTEP
1967	47	Boston College
1968	47	Houston
1969	47	Boston College
1970	52	Jacksonville
1971	55	Marquette
1972	59	Oral Roberts
1973	68	Providence
1974	73	Notre Dame
1975	79	Tex.-Pan American
1976	79	Rutgers
1977	73	Nevada-Las Vegas
1978	70	DePaul
1979	68	Syracuse
1980	55	DePaul
1981	54	DePaul
1982	52	DePaul
1983	19	New Orleans
1984	19	DePaul
1985	22	Notre Dame
1986	17	Notre Dame
1987	18	DePaul
1988	18	Akron
1989	22	Akron
1990	19	Wright St.
1991	17	DePaul
1992	12	Penn St.
1993	14	Wis.-Milwaukee

 # Number of schools in the conference or the tournament.

** Note—The Big Eight and Missouri Valley conferences share the same history from 1908 to 1928.*

Consecutive Regular-Season Winner

No.	School	Conference	Years
13	UCLA	Pacific-10	1967-79
10	Connecticut	Yankee	1951-60
10	Nevada-Las Vegas	Big West	1983-92
9	Kentucky	Southeastern	1944-52
8	Idaho St.	Rocky Mountain	1953-60
8	Long Beach St.	Big West	1970-77
7	Dartmouth	Ivy	1938-44
7	Rhode Island	New England	1938-44
6	Arizona	Border	1946-51
6	Cincinnati	Missouri Valley	1958-63
6	Davidson	Southern	1968-73
6	Kansas	Missouri Valley	1922-27
6	Kentucky	Southeastern	1968-73
6	Pennsylvania	Ivy	1970-75
6	Weber St.	Big Sky	1968-73

Consecutive Conference-Tournament Winner

No.	School	Conference	Years
7	Kentucky	Southeastern	1944-50
7	North Caro. A&T	Mid-Eastern	1982-88
6	North Caro. St.	Southern	1947-52
6	West Va.	Southern	1955-60
4	East Tenn. St.	Southern	1989-92
4	Northeast La.	Southland	1990-93
4	Northeastern	North Atlantic	1984-87
3	22 tied		

DIVISION II CONFERENCE STANDINGS

ARKANSAS INTERCOLLEGIATE CONFERENCE

	CONFERENCE W	L	Pct.	FULL SEASON W	L	Pct.
Central Ark.	12	4	.750	20	8	.714
Ozarks (Ark.)	12	4	.750	23	9	.719
Arkansas Tech	12	4	.750	23	10	.697
Henderson St.	9	7	.563	15	14	.517
Ark.-Monticello	7	9	.438	16	15	.516
Ouachita Baptist	7	9	.438	13	14	.481
Arkansas Col.	6	10	.375	11	20	.355
Southern Ark.	4	12	.250	11	15	.423
Harding	3	13	.188	4	23	.148
*John Brown	—	—	—	17	14	.548

* Not eligible for conference title.

CALIFORNIA COLLEGIATE ATHLETIC ASSOCIATION

	CONFERENCE W	L	Pct.	FULL SEASON W	L	Pct.
Cal St. Bakersfield #	14	0	1.000	33	0	1.000
UC Riverside	10	4	.714	20	8	.714
Cal St. Dom. Hills	7	7	.500	16	10	.615
Cal Poly Pomona	7	7	.500	14	13	.519
Cal St. San B'dino	6	8	.429	13	12	.520
Cal St. Los Angeles	5	9	.357	14	11	.560
Chapman	4	10	.286	7	19	.269
Cal Poly SLO	3	11	.214	9	17	.346

CAROLINAS INTERCOLLEGIATE ATHLETIC CONFERENCE

	CONFERENCE W	L	Pct.	FULL SEASON W	L	Pct.
Pfeiffer #	11	1	.917	23	6	.793
Coker	7	5	.583	14	14	.500
High Point	7	5	.583	12	15	.444
Belmont Abbey	6	6	.500	12	16	.429
Barton	4	8	.333	13	15	.464
St. Andrews	4	8	.333	11	16	.407
Mount Olive	3	9	.250	15	14	.517
*Lees-McRae	—	—	—	5	27	.156

* Not eligible for conference title.

CENTRAL INTERCOLLEGIATE ATHLETIC ASSOCIATION

Northern Division	CONFERENCE W	L	Pct.	FULL SEASON W	L	Pct.
Virginia Union #	12	0	1.000	27	3	.900
Elizabeth City St.	8	4	.667	18	10	.643
Norfolk St.	7	5	.583	19	10	.655
Hampton	7	5	.583	15	12	.556
Virginia St.	4	8	.333	12	15	.444
Bowie St.	3	9	.250	9	18	.333
St. Paul's	1	11	.083	6	22	.214
Southern Division						
N.C. Central	11	1	.916	26	4	.867
Fayetteville St.	9	3	.750	20	9	.690
Johnson Smith	8	4	.667	20	8	.714
Shaw	4	8	.333	10	17	.370
St. Augustine's	4	8	.333	9	16	.360
Livingstone	3	9	.250	7	17	.292
Winston-Salem	3	9	.250	6	17	.261

COLORADO ATHLETIC CONFERENCE

	CONFERENCE W	L	Pct.	FULL SEASON W	L	Pct.
Colo. Christian	10	2	.833	20	9	.690
Metropolitan St.	8	4	.667	16	12	.571
Regis (Colo.)	7	5	.583	18	9	.667
Denver	6	6	.500	15	11	.577
Southern Colo.	6	6	.500	14	14	.500
Fort Lewis	4	8	.333	11	16	.407
Colorado-CS	1	11	.083	3	25	.107

\# Won conference tournament.

GREAT LAKES INTERCOLLEGIATE ATHLETIC CONFERENCE

	CONFERENCE W	L	Pct.	FULL SEASON W	L	Pct.
Northern Mich.	12	4	.750	22	8	.733
Ferris St.	10	6	.625	16	11	.593
Wayne St. (Mich.) #	9	7	.563	22	10	.688
Hillsdale	9	7	.563	17	11	.607
Oakland	9	7	.563	15	11	.577
Saginaw Valley	7	9	.438	14	11	.560
Grand Valley St.	7	9	.438	14	12	.538
Michigan Tech	5	11	.313	13	13	.500
Lake Superior St.	4	12	.250	8	17	.320

GREAT LAKES VALLEY CONFERENCE

	CONFERENCE W	L	Pct.	FULL SEASON W	L	Pct.
IU/PU-Ft. Wayne	15	3	.833	23	6	.793
Southern Ind.	14	4	.778	22	7	.759
Ky. Wesleyan	13	5	.722	21	6	.778
St. Joseph's (Ind.)	13	5	.722	21	6	.788
Kentucky St.	10	8	.556	16	11	.593
Indianapolis	8	10	.444	13	14	.481
Lewis	5	13	.278	6	21	.222
Northern Ky.	4	14	.222	11	16	.407
Bellarmine	4	14	.222	7	20	.259
Ashland	4	14	.222	6	21	.222

GULF SOUTH CONFERENCE

	CONFERENCE W	L	Pct.	FULL SEASON W	L	Pct.
Delta St.	9	3	.750	22	8	.733
Livingston	8	4	.667	17	9	.654
Jacksonville St.	6	6	.500	16	10	.615
North Ala.	6	6	.500	16	10	.615
Mississippi Col.	6	6	.500	15	10	.600
Valdosta St.	5	7	.417	12	13	.480
West Ga.	2	10	.167	5	21	.192
*Lincoln Memorial	—	—	—	17	9	.654

* Not eligible for conference title.

LONE STAR CONFERENCE

	CONFERENCE W	L	Pct.	FULL SEASON W	L	Pct.
Central Okla.	10	2	.833	23	6	.793
Eastern N. Mex. #	9	3	.750	23	7	.767
Texas A&M-Kingsville	9	3	.750	17	10	.630
Cameron	4	8	.333	11	17	.393
Abilene Christian	4	8	.333	10	18	.357
Angelo St.	4	8	.333	9	17	.346
East Tex. St.	2	10	.167	3	26	.103

MID-AMERICA INTERCOLLEGIATE ATHLETICS ASSOCIATION

	CONFERENCE W	L	Pct.	FULL SEASON W	L	Pct.
Washburn	13	3	.813	27	5	.844
Mo. Western St.	11	5	.688	21	7	.750
Mo. Southern St. #	11	5	.688	21	10	.677
Southwest Baptist	10	6	.625	21	7	.750
Missouri-Rolla	10	6	.625	16	11	.593
Emporia St.	9	7	.563	18	9	.667
Northwest Mo. St.	6	10	.375	14	13	.519
Pittsburg St.	6	10	.375	13	13	.500
Central Mo. St.	6	10	.375	13	14	.481
Mo.-St. Louis	6	10	.375	11	15	.423
Lincoln (Mo.)	5	11	.313	14	12	.538
Northeast Mo. St.	3	13	.188	6	20	.231

NEW ENGLAND COLLEGIATE CONFERENCE

	CONFERENCE W	L	Pct.	FULL SEASON W	L	Pct.
New Hamp. Col. #	13	1	.929	29	4	.879
Franklin Pierce	10	4	.714	22	8	.733
Le Moyne	7	7	.500	18	10	.643
Mass.-Lowell	7	7	.500	13	15	.464
Sacred Heart	6	8	.429	14	13	.519

	CONFERENCE W	L	Pct.	FULL SEASON W	L	Pct.
Southern Conn. St.	6	8	.429	14	14	.500
New Haven	6	8	.429	13	14	.481
Keene St.	1	13	.071	2	23	.080
*Bridgeport	—	—	—	20	9	.690

* Not eligible for conference title.

NEW YORK COLLEGIATE ATHLETIC CONFERENCE

	CONFERENCE W	L	Pct.	FULL SEASON W	L	Pct.
Phila. Textile #	18	0	1.000	30	2	.938
St. Rose	13	5	.722	23	8	.742
Pace	13	5	.722	17	12	.586
LIU-C. W. Post	11	7	.611	19	8	.704
Adelphi	10	8	.556	14	14	.500
Mercy	7	11	.389	13	14	.482
Queens (N.Y.)	7	11	.389	8	19	.296
Dowling	6	12	.333	8	20	.286
LIU-Southampton	4	14	.222	5	21	.192
Concordia (N.Y.)	1	17	.056	4	23	.148
*Molloy	—	—	—	8	19	.296
*New York Tech	—	—	—	8	19	.296

* Not eligible for conference title.

NORTH CENTRAL INTERCOLLEGIATE ATHLETIC CONFERENCE

	CONFERENCE W	L	Pct.	FULL SEASON W	L	Pct.
South Dak.	16	2	.889	25	5	.833
North Dak. #	13	5	.722	23	8	.742
Mankato St.	11	7	.611	18	9	.667
Morningside	11	7	.611	19	10	.656
South Dak. St.	10	8	.556	19	12	.613
Northern Colo.	9	9	.500	12	15	.444
St. Cloud St.	8	10	.375	15	12	.556
North Dak. St.	7	11	.389	12	17	.414
Augustana (S.D.)	3	15	.167	7	19	.269
Nebraska-Omaha	2	16	.111	5	21	.192

NORTHEAST-10 CONFERENCE

	CONFERENCE W	L	Pct.	FULL SEASON W	L	Pct.
Bentley	15	3	.833	24	7	.774
American Int'l	13	5	.722	19	9	.679
St. Anselm #	13	5	.722	20	11	.645
Quinnipiac	10	8	.556	16	13	.552
Stonehill	9	9	.500	10	17	.370
St. Michael's	8	10	.444	14	13	.519
Springfield	8	10	.444	12	14	.462
Merrimack	7	11	.389	11	16	.407
Bryant	4	14	.222	7	18	.280
Assumption	3	15	.167	7	19	.269

NORTHERN CALIFORNIA ATHLETIC CONFERENCE

	CONFERENCE W	L	Pct.	FULL SEASON W	L	Pct.
Cal St. Chico #	12	2	.857	23	7	.767
Cal St. Stanislaus	11	3	.786	20	8	.714
UC Davis	9	5	.643	13	14	.481
San Fran. St.	7	7	.500	11	15	.423
Humboldt St.	5	9	.357	12	14	.462
Notre Dame (Cal.)	5	9	.357	10	15	.400
Cal St. Hayward	4	10	.286	5	20	.200
Sonoma St.	3	11	.214	6	20	.231

NORTHERN SUN INTERCOLLEGIATE CONFERENCE

	CONFERENCE W	L	Pct.	FULL SEASON W	L	Pct.
Northern St.	11	1	.917	34	2	.944
Winona St.	9	3	.750	19	10	.655
Minn.-Morris	6	6	.500	22	10	.688
Minn.-Duluth	6	6	.500	16	12	.571
Moorhead St.	4	8	.333	14	14	.500
Bemidji St.	4	8	.333	10	17	.370
Southwest St.	2	10	.167	6	21	.222

Won conference tournament.

PACIFIC WEST CONFERENCE

	CONFERENCE W	L	Pct.	FULL SEASON W	L	Pct.
Alas. Anchorage #	7	3	.700	21	10	.677
Seattle Pacific	7	3	.700	20	10	.667
Grand Canyon	7	3	.700	20	11	.645
Eastern Mont.	4	6	.400	10	19	.345
*Chaminade	3	7	.300	16	12	.571
Alas. Fairbanks	2	8	.222	12	16	.429

* Forefeited four conference games (does not affect full-season records).

PEACH BELT ATHLETIC CONFERENCE

	CONFERENCE W	L	Pct.	FULL SEASON W	L	Pct.
S.C.-Aiken #	12	4	.750	22	7	.759
Francis Marion	10	6	.625	19	9	.679
S.C.-Spartanburg	10	6	.625	18	9	.667
Augusta	10	6	.625	17	12	.586
Armstrong St.	8	8	.500	15	12	.517
Columbus	8	8	.500	13	13	.500
Pembroke St.	7	9	.438	10	16	.385
Georgia Col.	6	10	.375	15	13	.536
Lander	1	15	.063	5	24	.172
*Kennesaw St.	—	—	—	19	12	.613

* Did not compete for conference title.

PENNSYLVANIA STATE ATHLETIC CONFERENCE

	CONFERENCE W	L	Pct.	FULL SEASON W	L	Pct.
Eastern Division						
Millersville #	11	1	.917	24	6	.800
Bloomsburg	8	4	.667	17	10	.630
West Chester	7	5	.583	18	8	.692
East Stroudsburg	6	6	.500	13	13	.500
Mansfield	4	8	.333	11	14	.440
Kutztown	3	9	.250	8	17	.320
Cheyney	3	9	.250	8	18	.308
Western Division						
Calif. (Pa.)	11	1	.917	23	6	.793
Indiana (Pa.)	8	4	.667	18	9	.667
Lock Haven	6	6	.500	14	12	.538
Clarion	5	7	.417	17	9	.654
Shippensburg	5	7	.417	13	12	.520
Edinboro	4	8	.333	12	17	.414
Slippery Rock	3	9	.250	10	16	.385

ROCKY MOUNTAIN ATHLETIC CONFERENCE

	CONFERENCE W	L	Pct.	FULL SEASON W	L	Pct.
Western St. #	11	1	.917	25	5	.833
Mesa St.	9	3	.750	21	8	.724
Chadron St.	7	5	.583	12	16	.429
Fort Hays St.	7	5	.583	12	16	.429
Adams St.	3	9	.250	11	16	.407
Colorado Mines	3	9	.250	4	23	.148
N.M. Highlands	2	10	.167	6	24	.200

SOUTH ATLANTIC CONFERENCE

	CONFERENCE W	L	Pct.	FULL SEASON W	L	Pct.
Presbyterian	13	1	.929	27	5	.844
Lenoir-Rhyne #	12	2	.857	25	7	.781
Mars Hill	8	6	.571	16	10	.615
Elon	7	7	.500	13	13	.500
Gardner-Webb	6	8	.429	13	14	.481
Wingate	4	10	.286	11	15	.423
Carson-Newman	3	11	.214	8	18	.308
Catawba	3	11	.214	7	18	.280

SOUTHERN INTERCOLLEGIATE ATHLETIC CONFERENCE

	CONFERENCE W	L	Pct.	FULL SEASON W	L	Pct.
Eastern Region						
Paine	11	4	.733	16	10	.615
Fort Valley St.	10	5	.667	14	14	.500
Savannah St.	7	8	.467	12	15	.444
Albany St. (Ga.)	6	9	.400	10	15	.400
Morris Brown	3	12	.200	3	23	.115
Clark Atlanta	1	14	.067	2	24	.077

Western Region	Conf. W	Conf. L	Conf. Pct.	Full W	Full L	Full Pct.
Alabama A&M #	13	1	.929	28	3	.903
LeMoyne-Owen	10	4	.714	19	9	.679
Tuskegee	8	6	.571	13	14	.481
Morehouse	7	7	.500	15	11	.577
Miles	4	10	.286	7	17	.292

SUNSHINE STATE CONFERENCE

	Conf. W	Conf. L	Conf. Pct.	Full W	Full L	Full Pct.
Tampa	11	1	.917	25	5	.833
Fla. Southern #	9	3	.750	24	8	.750
Rollins	8	4	.667	19	8	.704
Barry	6	6	.500	17	9	.654
Eckerd	4	8	.333	12	14	.462
Florida Tech	3	9	.250	10	16	.385
St. Leo	1	11	.083	4	21	.160
*North Fla.	—	—	—	7	20	.259

* Not eligible for conference title.

WEST VIRGINIA INTERCOLLEGIATE ATHLETIC CONFERENCE

	Conf. W	Conf. L	Conf. Pct.	Full W	Full L	Full Pct.
Salem-Teikyo	18	3	.857	24	6	.800
Glenville St.	17	3	.850	22	5	.815
Bluefield St.	13	6	.684	20	8	.714
Shepherd	15	4	.789	19	8	.704
Alderson-Broaddus	13	8	.619	18	12	.600
Wheeling Jesuit	10	9	.526	16	13	.552
Charleston (W.Va.) #	9	10	.474	14	14	.500
Concord	9	10	.474	13	14	.481
West Va. Wesleyan	9	12	.429	9	17	.346
West Liberty St.	8	11	.421	12	15	.444
Davis & Elkins	5	15	.250	6	21	.222
Fairmont St.	5	16	.238	5	21	.192
West Va. St.	4	15	.211	5	22	.185
West Va. Tech	3	16	.158	5	22	.185

DIVISION II INDEPENDENTS

	Full W	Full L	Full Pct.
Troy St.	27	5	.844
Hardin-Simmons	23	6	.793
Neb.-Kearney	20	6	.769
Gannon	20	7	.741
Queens (N.C.)	20	8	.714
Mercyhurst	19	8	.704
Oakland City	22	10	.688
Wofford	17	9	.654
Longwood	17	10	.630
West Tex. A&M	17	10	.630
Drury	19	12	.613
Quincy	16	11	.593
SIU-Edwardsville	14	12	.538
Limestone	10	17	.370
Pitt.-Johnstown	8	18	.308
Ala.-Huntsville	8	19	.296
Wis.-Parkside	8	19	.296
Erskine	7	20	.259
Wayne St. (Neb.)	7	20	.259
Northwood	5	22	.185
Dist. Columbia	3	22	.120
Newberry	3	23	.115
Fla. Atlantic	3	25	.107

DIVISION III CONFERENCE STANDINGS

ASSOCIATION OF MIDEAST COLLEGES

	Conf. W	Conf. L	Conf. Pct.	Full W	Full L	Full Pct.
Defiance	6	0	1.000	21	6	.778
Thomas More #	3	3	.500	15	11	.577
Wilmington (Ohio)	3	3	.500	6	19	.240
Bluffton	0	6	.000	6	20	.231

CAPITAL ATHLETIC CONFERENCE

	Conf. W	Conf. L	Conf. Pct.	Full W	Full L	Full Pct.
Catholic #	10	2	.833	21	6	.778
York (Pa.)	8	4	.667	19	8	.704
*Marymount (Va.)	8	4	.667	15	10	.600
St. Mary's (Md.)	5	7	.417	10	15	.400
Goucher	4	8	.333	8	16	.333
Mary Washington	4	8	.333	8	18	.308
Gallaudet	3	9	.250	5	19	.208

* Forfeited one conference game (does not affect full-season record).

CITY UNIVERSITY OF NEW YORK ATHLETIC CONFERENCE

North Division	Conf. W	Conf. L	Conf. Pct.	Full W	Full L	Full Pct.
Baruch	4	6	.400	13	13	.500
John Jay	4	6	.400	9	16	.360
CCNY	4	6	.400	7	16	.304
Lehman	0	10	.000	0	25	.000
South Division						
Hunter #	10	0	1.000	25	4	.862
Medgar Evers	7	3	.700	15	13	.536
Staten Island	6	4	.600	14	12	.538
York (N.Y.)	5	5	.500	9	14	.391

\# Won conference tournament.

COLLEGE CONFERENCE OF ILLINOIS AND WISCONSIN

	Conf. W	Conf. L	Conf. Pct.	Full W	Full L	Full Pct.
Augustana (Ill.)	12	2	.857	24	7	.774
Ill. Wesleyan	9	5	.643	16	9	.640
Wheaton (Ill.)	8	6	.571	14	11	.560
North Park	7	7	.500	15	10	.600
Millikin	7	7	.500	13	12	.520
North Central	6	8	.429	8	17	.320
Carthage	4	10	.286	11	13	.458
Elmhurst	3	11	.214	10	15	.400

COMMONWEALTH COAST CONFERENCE

	Conf. W	Conf. L	Conf. Pct.	Full W	Full L	Full Pct.
Anna Maria	13	1	.929	21	6	.778
Eastern Nazarene #	10	4	.714	19	7	.731
Curry	8	6	.571	14	11	.560
Salve Regina	8	6	.571	13	13	.500
Roger Williams	6	8	.429	10	14	.417
Gordon	6	8	.429	8	16	.333
New England Col.	3	11	.214	9	16	.360
Wentworth Inst.	2	12	.143	5	20	.200

CONSTITUTION ATHLETIC CONFERENCE

	Conf. W	Conf. L	Conf. Pct.	Full W	Full L	Full Pct.
Babson #	10	0	1.000	20	5	.800
Worcester Tech	7	3	.700	15	12	.556
Coast Guard	6	4	.600	18	6	.750
Western New Eng.	5	5	.500	8	13	.381
MIT	1	9	.100	5	19	.208
Norwich	1	9	.100	1	23	.042

DIXIE INTERCOLLEGIATE ATHLETIC CONFERENCE

	CONFERENCE W	L	Pct.	FULL SEASON W	L	Pct.
Ferrum	9	1	.900	18	7	.720
Chris. Newport #	8	2	.800	23	5	.821
Greensboro	7	3	.700	17	9	.654
N.C. Wesleyan	3	7	.300	12	14	.462
Methodist	3	7	.300	6	19	.240
Averett	0	10	.000	3	22	.120

EASTERN STATES ATHLETIC CONFERENCE

	CONFERENCE W	L	Pct.	FULL SEASON W	L	Pct.
Lincoln (Pa.)	7	1	.875	16	8	.667
Salisbury St. #	6	2	.750	18	8	.692
Frostburg St.	4	4	.500	14	12	.538
Allentown	2	6	.250	12	15	.444
Shenandoah	1	7	.125	9	16	.360

EMPIRE ATHLETIC ASSOCIATION

	CONFERENCE W	L	Pct.	FULL SEASON W	L	Pct.
Ithaca	12	2	.857	20	7	.741
Rochester Inst.	10	4	.714	22	6	.786
Hartwick	9	5	.643	14	12	.538
Rensselaer	8	6	.571	14	10	.583
Alfred	7	7	.500	9	15	.375
Hobart	6	8	.429	12	13	.480
St. Lawrence	3	11	.214	3	22	.120
Clarkson	1	13	.071	3	22	.120

INDEPENDENT ATHLETIC CONFERENCE

	CONFERENCE W	L	Pct.	FULL SEASON W	L	Pct.
North Division						
Mt. St. Vincent	6	2	.750	18	9	.667
Maritime (N.Y.)	3	5	.375	11	13	.458
Bard	0	8	.000	0	25	.000
South Division						
New Jersey Tech #	9	0	1.000	22	4	.846
Yeshiva	6	3	.667	12	12	.500
Stevens Tech	5	4	.556	8	17	.320
Polytechnic (N.Y.)	1	8	.111	2	20	.091

INDIANA COLLEGIATE ATHLETIC CONFERENCE

	CONFERENCE W	L	Pct.	FULL SEASON W	L	Pct.
DePauw	9	3	.750	19	7	.731
Manchester #	7	5	.583	20	8	.714
Hanover	7	5	.583	16	9	.640
Wabash	6	6	.500	16	10	.615
Franklin	6	6	.500	12	13	.480
Rose-Hulman	5	7	.417	15	10	.600
Anderson	2	10	.167	8	18	.308

IOWA INTERCOLLEGIATE ATHLETIC CONFERENCE

	CONFERENCE W	L	Pct.	FULL SEASON W	L	Pct.
Wartburg	13	3	.813	18	8	.692
Loras	10	6	.625	15	9	.625
Dubuque	10	6	.625	15	10	.600
Simpson	8	8	.500	11	14	.440
Central (Iowa)	7	9	.438	10	15	.400
Luther	6	10	.375	13	12	.520
Upper Iowa	6	10	.375	11	14	.440
Buena Vista	6	10	.375	8	17	.320
William Penn	6	10	.375	8	17	.320

LAKE MICHIGAN CONFERENCE

	CONFERENCE W	L	Pct.	FULL SEASON W	L	Pct.
Edgewood	12	4	.750	21	11	.656
Cardinal Stritch	11	5	.688	21	12	.636
Concordia (Wis.)	11	5	.688	18	8	.692
Marian (Wis.)	11	5	.688	17	17	.500
Lakeland	10	6	.625	17	13	.567
Maranatha	9	7	.563	16	12	.571
Wis. Lutheran	5	11	.313	8	17	.320
Milwaukee Engr.	2	14	.125	3	22	.120
N'western (Wis.)	1	15	.063	2	19	.095

Won conference tournament.

LITTLE EAST CONFERENCE

	CONFERENCE W	L	Pct.	FULL SEASON W	L	Pct.
Mass.-Dartmouth #	10	0	1.000	25	6	.806
Eastern Conn. St.	7	3	.700	21	7	.750
Southern Me.	6	4	.600	13	12	.520
Mass.-Boston	4	6	.400	12	13	.480
Plymouth St.	3	7	.300	12	13	.480
Rhode Island Col.	0	10	.000	4	20	.167

MASSACHUSETTS STATE COLLEGE ATHLETIC CONFERENCE

	CONFERENCE W	L	Pct.	FULL SEASON W	L	Pct.
Salem St. #	11	1	.917	18	8	.692
Westfield St.	9	3	.750	22	6	.786
Worcester St.	8	4	.667	19	8	.704
Framingham St.	6	6	.500	14	11	.560
Bri'water (Mass.)	4	8	.333	7	18	.280
North Adams St.	2	10	.167	4	21	.160
Fitchburg St.	2	10	.167	4	19	.174

MICHIGAN INTERCOLLEGIATE ATHLETIC ASSOCIATION

	CONFERENCE W	L	Pct.	FULL SEASON W	L	Pct.
Calvin #	11	1	.917	25	3	.893
Kalamazoo	9	3	.750	19	7	.731
Albion	7	5	.583	18	8	.692
Hope	7	5	.583	18	8	.692
Alma	4	8	.333	9	16	.360
Olivet	3	9	.250	7	18	.280
Adrian	1	11	.083	7	18	.280

MIDDLE ATLANTIC STATES COLLEGIATE ATHLETIC CONFERENCE

NORTHERN DIVISION	CONFERENCE W	L	Pct.	FULL SEASON W	L	Pct.
Northeast Section						
Scranton *	10	0	1.000	27	2	.931
Wilkes	7	3	.700	16	9	.640
King's (Pa.)	4	6	.400	11	12	.478
FDU-Madison	4	6	.400	11	13	.458
Drew	4	6	.400	7	16	.304
Delaware Valley	1	9	.100	4	20	.167
Northwest Section						
Elizabethtown	8	2	.800	19	7	.731
Susquehanna	8	2	.800	16	9	.640
Albright	6	4	.600	14	10	.583
Juniata	4	6	.400	10	14	.417
Messiah	4	6	.400	7	17	.292
Lycoming	0	10	.000	4	19	.174
SOUTHERN DIVISION						
Southeast Section						
Johns Hopkins	10	0	1.000	19	7	.731
Widener	7	3	.700	14	12	.538
Washington (Md.)	7	3	.700	13	12	.520
Swarthmore	4	6	.400	7	17	.292
Ursinus	2	8	.200	7	17	.292
Haverford	0	10	.000	5	19	.208
Southwest Section						
Frank. & Marsh. *	11	1	.917	24	4	.857
Muhlenberg	8	4	.667	17	8	.680
Lebanon Valley	8	4	.667	18	11	.621
Moravian	6	6	.500	15	9	.625
Dickinson	4	8	.333	11	13	.458
Gettysburg	3	9	.250	9	15	.375
Western Md.	2	10	.167	5	19	.208

* Won divisional tournaments.

MIDWEST COLLEGIATE ATHLETIC CONFERENCE

	CONFERENCE			FULL SEASON		
North Division	W	L	Pct.	W	L	Pct.
Beloit #	13	1	.929	21	5	.808
Ripon	10	4	.714	18	6	.750
Lawrence	7	7	.500	13	9	.591
St. Norbert	5	9	.357	9	13	.409
Carroll (Wis.)	3	11	.214	4	17	.190
Lake Forest	2	12	.143	3	19	.136
South Division						
Knox	13	1	.929	17	5	.773
Monmouth (Ill.)	10	4	.714	13	10	.565
Cornell College	9	5	.643	15	7	.682
Illinois Col.	5	9	.357	10	11	.476
Grinnell	5	9	.357	10	12	.455
Coe	2	12	.143	3	19	.136

MINNESOTA INTERCOLLEGIATE ATHLETIC CONFERENCE

	CONFERENCE			FULL SEASON		
	W	L	Pct.	W	L	Pct.
St. John's (Minn.)	17	3	.850	20	8	.714
Carleton	16	4	.800	17	7	.708
St. Thomas (Minn.) #	15	5	.750	19	9	.679
St. Olaf	14	6	.700	17	8	.680
Augsburg	10	10	.500	12	12	.500
Bethel (Minn.)	10	10	.500	12	12	.500
Gust. Adolphus	10	10	.500	12	12	.500
Hamline	7	13	.350	8	16	.333
St. Mary's (Minn.)	5	15	.250	7	17	.292
Concordia-M'head	4	16	.200	5	19	.208
Macalester	2	18	.100	3	21	.125

NEBRASKA-IOWA ATHLETIC CONFERENCE

	CONFERENCE			FULL SEASON		
	W	L	Pct.	W	L	Pct.
Doane	9	3	.750	18	14	.563
Neb. Wesleyan	8	4	.667	17	8	.680
N'western (Iowa)	7	5	.583	17	10	.630
Concordia (Neb.)	6	6	.500	16	11	.593
Hastings	6	6	.500	12	16	.429
Midland Lutheran	6	6	.500	12	16	.429
Dana	0	12	.000	6	25	.194

NEW ENGLAND SMALL COLLEGE ATHLETIC CONFERENCE

(Did not compete for a regular-season conference title.)

	FULL SEASON		
	W	L	Pct.
Colby	22	3	.880
Williams	23	4	.852
Hamilton	22	5	.815
Amherst	15	8	.652
Tufts	16	9	.640
Bowdoin	14	10	.583
Middlebury	12	11	.522
Trinity (Conn.)	9	12	.429
Bates	10	14	.417
Wesleyan (Conn.)	7	14	.333
Connecticut Col.	6	16	.273

NEW JERSEY ATHLETIC CONFERENCE

	CONFERENCE			FULL SEASON		
	W	L	Pct.	W	L	Pct.
Rowan #	17	1	.944	29	2	.935
Stockton St.	14	4	.778	21	6	.778
Kean	13	5	.722	18	8	.692
Trenton St.	11	7	.611	14	13	.519
Jersey City St.	10	8	.556	15	12	.556
Montclair St.	8	10	.444	11	13	.458
Wm. Paterson	8	10	.444	11	13	.458
Ramapo	6	12	.333	8	16	.333

Won conference tournament.

	CONFERENCE			FULL SEASON		
	W	L	Pct.	W	L	Pct.
Rutgers-Newark	3	15	.167	7	16	.304
Rutgers-Camden	0	18	.000	0	24	.000

NORTH COAST ATHLETIC CONFERENCE

	CONFERENCE			FULL SEASON		
	W	L	Pct.	W	L	Pct.
Allegheny	13	3	.813	19	7	.731
Wittenberg	13	3	.813	19	7	.731
Wooster #	12	4	.750	21	7	.750
Ohio Wesleyan	10	6	.625	12	13	.480
Kenyon	9	7	.563	16	11	.593
Denison	6	10	.375	11	14	.440
Case Reserve	6	10	.375	10	15	.400
Earlham	2	14	.125	4	21	.160
Oberlin	1	15	.063	1	21	.045

NORTHERN ILLINOIS INTERCOLLEGIATE CONFERENCE

	CONFERENCE			FULL SEASON		
	W	L	Pct.	W	L	Pct.
Ill. Benedictine	7	3	.700	15	9	.625
Concordia (Ill.)	7	3	.700	14	11	.560
Aurora	6	4	.600	11	14	.440
Judson	4	6	.400	9	17	.346
Rockford	4	6	.400	8	17	.320
Trinity (Ill.)	2	8	.200	10	16	.385

OHIO ATHLETIC CONFERENCE

	CONFERENCE			FULL SEASON		
	W	L	Pct.	W	L	Pct.
Ohio Northern	17	1	.944	28	2	.933
Hiram	13	5	.722	17	8	.680
Capital	11	7	.611	15	10	.600
Otterbein #	10	8	.556	19	10	.655
John Carroll	8	10	.444	12	14	.462
Muskingum	8	10	.444	11	13	.458
Baldwin-Wallace	7	11	.389	13	13	.500
Heidelberg	7	11	.389	12	16	.429
Mount Union	5	13	.278	9	16	.360
Marietta	4	14	.222	5	20	.200

OLD DOMINION ATHLETIC CONFERENCE

	CONFERENCE			FULL SEASON		
	W	L	Pct.	W	L	Pct.
Emory & Henry	16	2	.889	23	5	.821
Roanoke	14	4	.778	20	6	.769
Va. Wesleyan #	12	6	.667	19	9	.679
Randolph-Macon	12	6	.667	18	9	.667
Bridgewater (Va.)	10	8	.556	12	12	.500
Hampden-Sydney	8	10	.444	12	13	.480
Guilford	7	11	.389	10	14	.417
East. Mennonite	5	13	.278	7	18	.280
Lynchburg	3	15	.167	5	19	.208
Wash. & Lee	3	15	.167	5	19	.208

PENNSYLVANIA ATHLETIC CONFERENCE

	CONFERENCE			FULL SEASON		
	W	L	Pct.	W	L	Pct.
Cabrini #	10	0	1.000	20	6	.769
Alvernia	6	4	.600	13	13	.500
Beaver	5	5	.500	13	13	.500
Eastern	5	5	.500	12	12	.500
Misericordia	3	7	.300	10	15	.400
Gwynedd Mercy	1	9	.100	3	21	.25

PRESIDENTS' ATHLETIC CONFERENCE

	CONFERENCE			FULL SEASON		
	W	L	Pct.	W	L	Pct.
Wash. & Jeff.	6	2	.750	11	10	.524
Bethany (W. Va.)	5	3	.625	10	14	.417
Grove City	5	3	.625	8	14	.364
Waynesburg	2	6	.250	8	16	.333
Thiel	2	6	.250	7	16	.304

ST. LOUIS INTERCOLLEGIATE ATHLETIC CONFERENCE

	CONFERENCE			FULL SEASON		
	W	L	Pct.	W	L	Pct.
MacMurray #	14	0	1.000	20	7	.741
Westminster (Mo.)	10	4	.714	15	11	.400
Fontbonne	8	6	.571	10	15	.400
Maryville (Mo.)	8	6	.571	9	17	.346
Blackburn	6	8	.429	8	17	.320
Parks	4	10	.286	5	18	.217
Principia	3	11	.214	3	21	.125
Webster	3	11	.214	3	22	.120

SKYLINE CONFERENCE

	CONFERENCE			FULL SEASON		
	W	L	Pct.	W	L	Pct.
Hunter	8	2	.800	25	4	.862
New Jersey Tech	8	2	.800	22	4	.846
Stony Brook	6	4	.600	15	12	.556
Manhattanville	4	6	.400	8	17	.320
Staten Island	3	7	.300	14	12	.538
Merchant Marine	1	9	.100	6	18	.250

SOUTHERN CALIFORNIA INTERCOLLEGIATE ATHLETIC CONFERENCE

	CONFERENCE			FULL SEASON		
	W	L	Pct.	W	L	Pct.
Cal Lutheran	12	2	.857	20	7	.741
La Verne	12	2	.857	20	8	.714
Pomona-Pitzer	9	5	.643	16	9	.640
Occidental	9	5	.643	15	9	.640
Claremont-M-S	6	8	.429	10	14	.417
Redlands	6	8	.429	10	14	.417
Whittier	2	12	.143	6	18	.250
Cal Tech	0	14	.000	8	15	.348

SOUTHERN COLLEGIATE ATHLETIC CONFERENCE

	CONFERENCE			FULL SEASON		
	W	L	Pct.	W	L	Pct.
Rhodes	11	3	.786	21	6	.778
Centre	11	3	.786	16	9	.640
Oglethorpe	10	4	.714	15	9	.625
Sewanee	7	7	.500	13	12	.520
Millsaps	6	8	.429	13	12	.520
Hendrix	6	8	.429	9	15	.375
Trinity (Tex.)	5	9	.357	9	16	.360
Fisk	0	14	.000	1	24	.040

STATE UNIVERSITY OF NEW YORK ATHLETIC CONFERENCE

	CONFERENCE			FULL SEASON		
East Division	W	L	Pct.	W	L	Pct.
Binghamton	11	5	.688	19	9	.679
Plattsburgh St.	9	7	.563	15	11	.577
Cortland St.	7	9	.438	10	15	.400
Potsdam St.	6	10	.375	10	15	.400
New Paltz St.	6	10	.375	12	12	.500
Oneonta St.	4	12	.250	6	18	.250
West Division						
Geneseo St.	15	1	.938	23	4	.852
Buffalo St.	14	2	.875	21	6	.778
Fredonia St. #	9	7	.563	18	10	.643
Brockport St.	8	8	.500	12	13	.480
Utica Tech	4	12	.250	7	16	.304
Oswego St.	3	13	.188	5	19	.208

UNIVERSITY ATHLETIC ASSOCIATION

	CONFERENCE			FULL SEASON		
	W	L	Pct.	W	L	Pct.
New York U.	12	2	.857	23	3	.885
Washington (Mo.)	10	4	.714	15	10	.600
Carnegie Mellon	7	7	.500	16	8	.667
Rochester	7	7	.500	11	14	.440
Chicago	5	9	.357	11	14	.440
Emory	4	10	.286	12	13	.480
Brandeis	4	10	.286	8	17	.420
*Johns Hopkins	4	4	.500	19	7	.731
*Case Reserve	4	4	.500	10	15	.400

* Not eligible for conference title.

WESTERN MAINE ATHLETIC CONFERENCE

	CONFERENCE			FULL SEASON		
	W	L	Pct.	W	L	Pct.
St. Joseph's (Me.)	7	1	.875	22	7	.759
Husson	5	3	.625	26	8	.765
New England	5	3	.625	9	16	.360
Thomas	2	6	.250	10	14	.417
Me.-Farmington	1	7	.125	10	13	.435

WISCONSIN STATE UNIVERSITY CONFERENCE

	CONFERENCE			FULL SEASON		
	W	L	Pct.	W	L	Pct.
Wis.-Platteville	13	3	.813	24	4	.857
Wis.-Stevens Point	13	3	.813	23	5	.821
Wis.-Eau Claire	12	4	.750	19	7	.731
Wis.-Whitewater	10	6	.625	18	9	.667
Wis.-Oshkosh	10	6	.625	14	11	.560
Wis.-River Falls	6	10	.375	12	12	.500
Wis.-Stout	5	11	.313	11	14	.440
Wis.-La Crosse	2	14	.125	5	20	.200
Wis.-Superior	1	15	.067	2	22	.083

DIVISION III INDEPENDENTS

	FULL SEASON		
	W	L	Pct.
Eureka	24	5	.828
Wheaton (Mass.)	20	5	.800
Maryville (Tenn.)	20	6	.769
St. John Fisher	20	6	.769
Western Conn. St.	20	6	.769
Colorado Col.	17	8	.680
UC San Diego	17	8	.680
Elmira	18	9	.667
Southwestern (Tex.)	18	9	.667
Utica	17	9	.654
Colby-Sawyer	16	9	.640
Upsala	15	9	.625
Albany (N.Y.)	15	10	.600
UC Santa Cruz	13	12	.528
Rust	12	13	.480
Castleton St.	11	12	.478
Nazareth (N.Y.)	11	13	.458
Old Westbury	11	13	.458
Albertus Magnus	11	14	.440
Maine Maritime	8	11	.421
Menlo	10	14	.417
Skidmore	10	14	.417
Clark (Mass.)	10	15	.400
Penn St.-Behrend	10	15	.400
Union (N.Y.)	10	15	.400
Nichols	9	15	.375
Keuka	8	17	.320
Wiley	8	18	.308
Vassar	6	16	.273
Daniel Webster	4	19	.174
Wesley	4	19	.174

Won conference tournament.

1993 MEN'S ATTENDANCE RECORDS

North Carolina's 78-68 victory over Kansas in the 1993 NCAA Division I semifinals set an attendance record for single-game turnstile count. Both the North Carolina game and Michigan's overtime win over Kentucky were witnessed by 58,903 fans at the Louisiana Superdome.

NATIONAL MEN'S COLLEGE BASKETBALL ATTENDANCE

(For All U.S. Senior-College Men's Varsity Teams)

	Total Teams	Games or Sessions	1993 Attendance	Avg. Per Game or Session	Change@ In Total		Change@ In Avg.	
Home Attendance, NCAA Division I	*298	3,954	21,281,917	5,382	Down	689,829	Down	58
NCAA Championship Tournament		34	*715,246	*21,037	Up	142,071	Up	4,179
Other Division I Neutral-Site Attendance		151	1,324,492	8,771	Down	24,580	Up	392
NCAA DIVISION I TOTAL	*298	4,139	23,321,655	5,635	Down	572,338	Down	8
Home Attendance, NCAA Division II	*220	2,796	3,201,765	1,145	Down	193,919	Down	43
Home Attendance, NCAA Division III	*313	3,544	1,883,283	531	Down	84,920	Down	21
Neutral-Site Attendance for Divisions II & III		20	14,845	742		—		—
NCAA Division II Tournament		20	56,125	2,806	Down	4,504	Down	225
NCAA Division III Tournament		34	49,675	1,461	Down	15,582	Down	458
1993 NATIONAL TOTALS	*831	10,553	28,527,348	2,703	Down	850,813	Down	44

* Record high. @ The 1992 figures used for comparison reflect 1993 changes in association and division lineups to provide parallel comparisons (i.e., 1993 lineups vs. same teams in 1992, whether members or not). Note that the neutral-site attendance for Divisions II and III does not include any tournaments.

ALL DIVISION I CONFERENCES

	Total Teams	Games or Sessions	1993 Attendance	Avg. Per Game or Session	Change@ In Total		Change@ In Avg.	
1. Big Ten #	11	170	+2,163,693	12,728	Up	102,664	Up	460
2. Big East	10	160	1,746,313	10,914	Up	85,262	Down	386
3. Big Eight	8	126	1,345,278	10,677	Up	65,408	Up	272
4. Great Midwest	6	95	1,012,036	*10,653	Up	1,093	Up	337
5. Southeastern	12	173	1,838,259	10,626	Down	114,084	Down	530
6. Atlantic Coast	9	137	1,445,095	10,548	Up	101,910	Up	295
7. Western Athletic #	10	160	1,425,091	8,907	Down	73,928	Down	346
8. Metropolitan Collegiate	7	99	692,068	6,991	Down	81,545	Down	984
9. Pacific-10	10	146	986,982	6,760	Down	144,601	Down	541
10. Midwestern Collegiate #	8	107	687,886	6,429	Down	7,630	Up	219
11. Missouri Valley	10	139	868,286	6,247	Down	5,800	Down	180
12. Big West #	10	139	760,206	5,469	Up	2,453	Up	18
13. Southwest	8	102	535,168	5,247	Down	2,395	Up	270
14. Atlantic 10 #	8	103	520,568	*5,054	Up	46,275	Up	449
15. Big Sky #	8	113	566,737	5,015	Up	22,584	Up	242
16. Colonial Athletic	8	105	*459,174	*4,373	Up	41,921	Up	399
17. Sun Belt #	10	137	560,192	4,089	Down	10,274	Up	43
18. Mid-American #	10	132	525,512	3,981	Down	34,697	Down	169
19. Ohio Valley #	9	110	401,741	3,652	Down	11,707	Down	212
20. Mid-Continent #	9	119	414,880	3,486	Up	3,834	Up	171
21. Southwestern Athletic	8	96	295,333	3,076	Up	45,875	Up	241
22. Southern #	10	131	395,286	3,017	Down	31,061	Down	72
23. Mid-Eastern Athletic	9	99	250,312	2,528	Up	21,851	Up	148
24. Metro Atlantic Athletic #	8	97	241,549	2,490	Up	8,628	Up	64
25. West Coast	8	111	270,547	2,437	Up	1,877	Up	38
26. Ivy	8	159	*356,252	2,241	Up	170,653	Up	224
27. Southland	10	125	236,677	1,893	Up	2,141	Up	2
28. Patriot	8	108	185,573	1,718	Up	14,118	Down	166
29. North Atlantic	8	102	173,258	1,699	Up	11,325	Up	186
30. Big South #	9	117	178,508	1,526	Up	1,772	Up	2
31. Northeast #	10	121	163,742	1,353	Down	17,387	Down	73
32. Trans America #	7	91	113,900	1,252	Down	20,456	Down	193
Division I Independents #	14	174	366,716	2,108	Down	44,256	Down	477

+ National record. * Record high for that conference. @ 1992 figures used in this compilation reflect 1993 changes in conference lineups, to provide parallel comparisons (i.e., 1993 lineups vs. same teams in 1992, whether members or not in 1992); (#) had different lineups in 1992. Note that the conference attendance includes conference tournaments.

LEADING CONFERENCES BELOW DIVISION I

Division II	Total Teams	Games or Sessions	1993 Attendance	Avg. Per Game or Session	Change@ In Total		Change@ In Avg.	
1. North Central Intercollegiate	10	140	408,624	2,919	Down	34,487	Up	42
2. Central Intercollegiate	14	159	356,252	2,241	Up	25,761	Up	226
3. Southern Intercollegiate	11	124	236,175	1,905	Up	7,709	Up	17
4. Mid-America Intercollegiate	12	160	233,206	1,458	Down	38,001	Down	137
5. Great Lakes Valley	10	136	192,293	1,414	Down	39,337	Down	241
6. Gulf South	7	91	128,443	1,411	Down	15,240	Down	12
7. Rocky Mountain	7	86	100,406	1,168	Down	13,173	Down	184
8. South Atlantic	8	91	101,045	1,110	Down	16,619	Down	129
9. Lone Star	7	78	83,131	1,066	Down	8,574	Down	39
10. Pennsylvania	14	176	178,822	1,016	Down	33,673	Down	97

Division III	Total Teams	Games or Sessions	1993 Attendance	Avg. Per Game or Session	Change@ In Total		Change@ In Avg.	
1. Michigan Intercollegiate	7	79	97,624	1,236	Up	8,075	Up	73
2. Wisconsin State University	9	120	130,870	1,091	Down	4,865	Down	31
3. Illinois and Wisconsin	8	89	93,305	1,048	Up	3,669	Up	161
4. Indiana	7	81	76,037	939	Up	1,507	Up	7
5. Ohio Athletic	10	122	99,186	813	Down	1,383	Up	8
6. Minnesota Intercollegiate	11	131	97,823	747	Down	20,681	Down	151
7. Iowa	9	108	75,705	701	Up	7,824	Up	95
8. Southern California	8	92	61,508	669	Up	15,099	Up	227
9. SUNY	12	143	92,623	648	Down	6,233	Down	39
10. Old Dominion	10	115	72,238	628	Down	3,861	Up	24

LEADING TEAMS

NCAA Division I	G/S	1993 Attend.	Avg.	Change in Avg.	
1. Syracuse	16	405,620	25,351	Down	1,752
2. Kentucky	16	382,869	23,929	Up	594
3. Brigham Young	14	296,596	21,185	Up	3,527
4. North Caro.	12	251,428	20,952	Up	1,148
5. Louisville	16	293,043	18,315	Down	806
6. Indiana	15	245,814	16,388	Down	148
7. New Mexico	16	258,308	16,144	Up	539
8. Kansas	15	235,000	15,667	Down	65
9. Tennessee	15	230,498	15,367	Down	806
10. Iowa	16	234,446	15,215	Down	128
11. Vanderbilt	14	212,156	15,154	Up	2,767
12. Memphis St.	17	256,822	15,107	Down	1,035
13. Minnesota	19	282,644	14,876	Up	304
14. Michigan St.	14	207,423	14,816	Up	286
15. Purdue	14	197,722	14,123	Up	658
16. Arizona	15	208,185	13,879	Down	18
17. Seton Hall	18	247,924	13,774	Up	879
18. Michigan	16	219,745	13,734	Up	748
19. Iowa St.	16	217,549	13,597	Up	1,190
20. Marquette	16	215,089	13,443	Up	830
21. Nevada-Las Vegas	16	214,165	13,385	Down	2,210
22. Illinois	16	213,949	13,372	Up	372
23. Nebraska	16	213,715	13,357	Up	360
24. Missouri	16	213,584	13,349	Up	49
25. Utah	15	198,444	13,230	Down	808
26. Ohio St.	16	211,245	13,203	Down	73
27. Connecticut	16	199,969	12,498	Down	65
28. Cincinnati	14	171,337	12,238	Up	2,127
29. Boise St.	15	181,694	12,113	Up	4,577
30. Evansville	13	152,616	11,740	Up	1,542
31. Maryland	15	175,217	11,681	Up	2,118
32. Dayton	15	172,057	11,470	Down	789
33. Texas	10	114,277	11,428	Down	1,639
34. Louisiana St.	18	193,632	10,757	Down	5,164
35. Providence	19	203,484	10,710	Down	70
36. Notre Dame	12	124,658	10,388	Up	1,603
37. Wisconsin	17	176,578	10,387	Up	941
38. St. John's (N.Y.)	12	113,365	9,447	Down	763
39. California	14	130,819	9,344	Up	1,774
40. Duke	16	149,024	9,314		0
41. Florida	11	102,231	9,294	Up	1,985
42. New Mexico St.	15	138,460	9,231	Down	74
43. Florida St.	15	137,863	9,191	Up	729
44. Alabama	14	128,258	9,161	Down	1,477
45. Fresno St.	15	134,894	8,993	Down	777
46. Arkansas	15	134,623	8,975	Up	74
47. Wake Forest	14	125,139	8,939	Down	1,496
48. North Caro. St.	15	130,948	8,730	Down	920
49. Georgia Tech	14	122,154	8,725	Down	101
50. Virginia	15	130,216	8,681	Down	151
51. St. Louis	15	128,864	8,591	Up	894
52. Georgetown	16	135,861	8,491	Down	1,685
53. UTEP	18	151,486	8,416	Up	204
54. Auburn	12	100,291	8,358	Up	841
55. Illinois St.	14	116,232	8,302	Down	393
56. West Va.	15	124,240	8,283	Down	1,488
57. Kansas St.	15	123,943	8,263	Down	153
58. Pittsburgh	15	120,980	8,065	Up	656
59. Oregon St.	12	94,280	7,857	Down	258
60. UCLA	17	132,771	7,810	Down	3,253
61. Southwest Mo. St.	16	124,769	7,798	Down	255
62. Wichita St.	13	101,128	7,779	Up	1,024
63. DePaul	15	116,675	7,778	Down	1,279
64. Oklahoma	16	123,661	7,729	Down	843
65. South Caro.	13	99,107	7,624	Down	2,289
66. Utah St.	13	95,286	7,330	Down	116
67. Bradley	13	94,523	7,271	Up	278
68. Xavier (Ohio)	13	94,073	7,236	Down	1,060
69. Richmond	12	86,571	7,214	Up	210
70. Wright St.	17	121,557	7,150	Down	22
71. Massachusetts	13	92,021	7,079	Up	3,045
72. Clemson	16	111,000	6,938	Down	156
73. Villanova	13	89,368	6,874	Down	755
74. Arizona St.	16	108,092	6,756	Down	838
75. Ball St.	16	106,296	6,644	Down	1,090
76. Southern Ill.	12	78,903	6,575	Up	515
77. Wyoming	15	97,304	6,487	Down	1,350
78. Ala.-Birmingham	17	109,913	6,465	Up	440
79. Arkansas St.	13	82,991	6,384	Up	407
80. Drake	14	88,032	6,288	Up	1,215
81. Oregon	14	87,398	6,243	Up	424
82. Montana	17	105,964	6,233	Down	801
83. Va. Commonwealth	12	74,095	6,175	Down	265

NCAA Division II	G/S	Attend.	Avg.	Change in Avg.	
1. Alabama A&M	15	71,215	4,748	Down	161
2. Norfolk St.	13	58,847	4,527	Down	15
3. South Dak.	14	60,490	4,321	Up	936
4. North Dak.	16	67,345	4,209	Up	734
5. South Dak. St.	15	58,362	3,891	Down	141
6. Ky. Wesleyan	16	55,750	3,484	Up	252
7. North Dak. St.	14	48,514	3,465	Down	305
8. Johnson Smith	10	34,279	3,428	Down	115
9. N.C. Central	12	39,109	3,259	Up	1,150
10. Augustana (S.D.)	14	43,101	3,079	Up	66
11. Virginia Union	12	34,743	2,895	Up	675
12. Morris Brown	11	30,950	2,814	Up	339
13. Jacksonville St.	13	35,272	2,713	Down	475
14. Cal St. Bakersfield	20	52,959	2,648	Up	442
15. St. Cloud St.	14	36,556	2,611	Up	388

NCAA Division III	G/S	Attend.	Avg.	Change in Avg.	
1. Calvin	12	48,215	4,018	Up	1,261
2. Hope	13	27,250	2,096	Up	78
3. Scranton	15	30,300	2,020	Up	20
4. Otterbein	13	24,932	1,918	Down	60
5. Ill. Wesleyan	12	22,850	1,904	Up	31
6. Wis.-Eau Claire	15	28,400	1,893	Down	4
7. Wis.-Stevens Point	15	26,485	1,766	Down	79
8. Wis.-Platteville	16	28,180	1,761	Down	191
9. Binghamton	17	29,650	1,744	Up	721
10. St. John's (Minn.)	16	25,730	1,608	Up	333
11. Messiah	10	14,600	1,460	Up	560
12. Manchester	15	21,223	1,415	Down	385
13. Gust. Adolphus	11	15,075	1,370	Down	403
14. Pomona-Pitzer	11	14,500	1,318	Up	337
15. William Penn	12	14,950	1,246	Up	846

Division I All Games Attendance (Home, Road, Neutral)

1. North Caro. 721,760
2. Kentucky 703,037
3. Syracuse 593,700
4. Michigan 591,704
5. Kansas 586,408
6. Indiana 585,965
7. Louisville 509,522
8. Seton Hall 476,815
9. Brigham Young 474,041
10. Vanderbilt 454,381
11. Minnesota 429,452
12. Cincinnati 416,615
13. Tennessee 412,950
14. Iowa 412,067
15. New Mexico 407,679
16. Illinois 404,007
17. Memphis St. 401,042

ALL-TIME NCAA ATTENDANCE

	Division I		Per Game	Change		All Divisions		Per Game	Change	
Year	Teams	Attendance	Average	In Avg.		Teams	Attendance	Average	In Avg.	
1976	238	15,059,892	4,759	—		—	—	—	—	—
1977	245	16,469,250	5,021	Up	262	717	23,324,040	2,710	—	—
1978	254	17,669,080	5,124	Up	103	726	23,590,952	2,678	Down	32
1979	257	18,649,383	5,271	Up	147	718	24,482,516	2,757	Up	79
1980	261	19,052,743	5,217	Down	54	715	24,861,722	2,765	Up	8
1981	264	19,355,690	5,131	Down	86	730	25,159,358	2,737	Down	28
1982	273	19,789,706	5,191	Up	60	741	25,416,017	2,727	Down	10
1983	274	20,488,437	5,212	Up	21	755	26,122,785	2,706	Down	21
1984	275	20,715,426	5,243	Up	31	750	26,271,613	2,728	Up	22
1985	282	21,394,261	5,258	Up	15	753	26,584,426	2,712	Down	16
1986	283	21,244,519	5,175	Down	83	760	26,368,815	2,654	Down	58
1987	290	21,756,709	5,205	Up	30	760	26,797,644	2,698	Up	44
1988	290	22,463,476	5,443	Up	238	761	27,452,948	2,777	Up	79
1989	293	23,059,429	5,565	Up	122	772	28,270,260	2,814	Up	37
1990	292	23,581,823	5,721	Up	156	767	28,740,819	2,860*	Up	46
1991	295	23,777,437	5,735*	Up	14	796	29,249,583	2,796	Down	64
1992	298*	23,893,993*	5,643	Down	92	813	29,378,161*	2,747	Down	49
1993	298*	23,321,655	5,635	Down	8	831*	28,527,348	2,703	Down	44

* *Record.*

ANNUAL CONFERENCE ATTENDANCE CHAMPIONS

Division I

Year	Conference	Teams	Attendance	P/G Avg.
1976	Atlantic Coast	7	863,082	9,590
1977	Big Ten	10	1,346,889	9,977
1978	Big Ten	10	1,539,589	11,238
1979	Big Ten	10	1,713,380	12,238
1980	Big Ten	10	1,877,048	12,189
1981	Big Ten	10	1,779,892	12,026
1982	Big Ten	10	1,688,834	11,810
1983	Big Ten	10	1,747,910	11,499
1984	Big Ten	10	1,774,140	12,069
1985	Big Ten	10	1,911,325	12,097
1986	Big Ten	10	1,908,629	11,929
1987	Big Ten	10	1,805,263	11,877
1988	Big Ten	10	1,925,617	12,423
1989	Big Ten	10	1,971,110	12,635
1990	Big Ten	10	2,017,407	*13,449
1991	Big Ten	10	2,042,836	13,095
1992	Big Ten	10	1,994,144	12,865
1993	Big Ten	10	*2,163,693	12,728

Division II

Year	Conference	Teams	Attendance	P/G Avg.
1979	Central Intercollegiate	12	375,370	2,760
1980	Mid-Continent	5	189,193	2,782
1981	North Central	8	312,410	2,840
1982	North Central	8	290,995	2,622
1983	North Central	8	356,777	2,567
1984	North Central	10	392,154	2,801
1985	North Central	10	380,087	2,639
1986	North Central	10	379,701	2,601
1987	North Central	10	393,940	2,626
1988	North Central	10	413,956	2,797
1989	North Central	10	438,403	2,923
1990	North Central	10	436,292	2,889
1991	North Central	10	438,746	2,868
1992	North Central	10	*482,213	*3,014
1993	North Central	10	408,624	2,919

Division III

Year	Conference	Teams	Attendance	P/G Avg.
1990	Wisconsin State University	9	*170,276	*1,362
1991	Wisconsin State University	7	84,615	1,128
1992	Michigan Intercollegiate	7	89,549	1,163
1993	Michigan Intercollegiate	7	97,624	1,236

* Record.

ANNUAL TEAM HOME ATTENDANCE CHAMPIONS

Division I

Year	Champion	Games	Attendance	Avg.
1970	Illinois	11	157,206	14,291
1971	Illinois	11	177,408	16,128
1972	Brigham Young	12	261,815	21,818
1973	Brigham Young	14	260,102	18,579
1974	Brigham Young	10	162,510	16,251
1975	Minnesota	13	219,047	16,850
1976	Indiana	12	202,700	16,892
1977	Kentucky	14	312,527	22,323
1978	Kentucky	16	373,367	23,335
1979	Kentucky	15	351,042	23,403
1980	Kentucky	15	352,511	23,501
1981	Kentucky	15	354,996	23,666
1982	Kentucky	16	371,093	23,193
1983	Kentucky	15	356,776	23,785
1984	Kentucky	16	380,453	23,778
1985	Syracuse	15	388,049	25,870
1986	Syracuse	19	498,850	26,255
1987	Syracuse	19	474,214	24,959
1988	Syracuse	16	461,223	28,826
1989	Syracuse	19	*537,949	28,313
1990	Syracuse	16	478,686	*29,918
1991	Syracuse	17	497,179	29,246
1992	Syracuse	17	460,752	27,103
1993	Syracuse	16	405,620	25,351

Division II

Year	Champion	Avg.
1977	Evansville	4,576
1978	Norfolk St.	4,226
1979	Norfolk St.	4,984
1980	Norfolk St.	4,917
1981	North Dak. St.	5,300
1982	North Dak. St.	4,385
1983	North Dak. St.	6,057
1984	Norfolk St.	*6,663
1985	Norfolk St.	6,116
1986	St. Cloud St.	4,539
1987	North Dak. St.	4,820
1988	Southeast Mo. St.	5,227
1989	Southeast Mo. St.	5,052
1990	Southeast Mo. St.	5,287
1991	Southeast Mo. St.	5,370
1992	North Dak.	4,943
1993	Alabama A&M	4,748

Division III

Year	Champion	Avg.
1977	Scranton	2,707
1978	Calvin	*3,630
1979	Savannah St.	2,870
1980	Savannah St.	2,917
1981	Potsdam St.	2,873
1982	Wis.-Stevens Point	2,929
1983	Augustana (Ill.)	3,033
1984	Hope	2,144
1985	Wis.-Stevens Point	2,313
1986	Calvin	2,570
1987	Concordia-M'head	2,869
1988	Calvin	2,627
1989	Calvin	2,544
1990	Calvin	2,622
1991	Hope	2,480
1992	Calvin	2,757
1993	Calvin	4,018

** Record.*

ATTENDANCE RECORDS

Single Game (Paid)

68,112—Louisiana St. (87) vs. Notre Dame (64), January 20, 1990, at Louisiana Superdome, New Orleans, La. (regular-season game)

Single Game (Turnstile)

58,903—North Caro. (78) vs. Kansas (68) and Michigan (81) vs. Kentucky (78), April 3, 1993, at Louisiana Superdome, New Orleans, La. (NCAA semifinals)

Home Court, Single Game

33,048—Syracuse (62) vs. Georgetown (58), March 3, 1991, at Carrier Dome, Syracuse, N.Y.

Home-Court Average, Season
29,918—Syracuse, 1990 (478,686 in 16 games at Carrier Dome)

Home-Court Total, Season
537,949—Syracuse, 1989 (19 games)

Full-Season Average, All Games (home, road, neutral, tournaments)
22,501—Syracuse, 1989 (855,053 in 38 games)

Full-Season Total, All Games (home, road, neutral, tournaments)
855,053—Syracuse, 1989 (38 games)

Top 10 Attendance Games (Paid)*
68,112—Louisiana St. (87) vs. Notre Dame (64), January 20, 1990, at Louisiana Superdome, New Orleans, La.
66,144—Louisiana St. (82) vs. Georgetown (80), January 28, 1989, at Louisiana Superdome, New Orleans, La.
64,959—Indiana (74) vs. Syracuse (73), March 30, 1987, at Louisiana Superdome, New Orleans, La. (NCAA final); Indiana (97) vs. Nevada-Las Vegas (93) and Syracuse (77) vs. Providence (63), March 28, 1987, at Louisiana Superdome, New Orleans, La. (NCAA semifinals)
64,151—North Caro. (77) vs. Michigan (71), April 5, 1993, at Louisiana Superdome, New Orleans, La. (NCAA final); North Caro. (78) vs. Kansas (68) and Michigan (81) vs. Kentucky (78), April 3, 1993, at Louisiana Superdome, New Orleans, La. (NCAA semifinals)
61,612—North Caro. (63) vs. Georgetown (62), March 29, 1982, at Louisiana Superdome, New Orleans, La. (NCAA final); North Caro. (68) vs. Houston (63) and Georgetown (50) vs. Louisville (46), March 27, 1982, at Louisiana Superdome, New Orleans, La. (NCAA semifinals)
61,304—Louisiana St. (84) vs. Texas (83), January 3, 1992, at Louisiana Superdome, New Orleans, La.
52,693—Houston (71) vs. UCLA (69), January 20, 1968, at The Astrodome, Houston, Texas.
50,379—Duke (71) vs. Michigan (51), April 6, 1992, at Hubert H. Humphrey Metrodome, Minneapolis, Minn. (NCAA final); Duke (81) vs. Indiana (78) and Michigan (76) vs. Cincinnati (72), April 4, 1992, at Hubert H. Humphrey Metrodome, Minneapolis, Minn. (NCAA semifinals)
47,100—Duke (72) vs. Kansas (65), April 1, 1991, at Hoosier Dome, Indianapolis, Ind. (NCAA final); Kansas (79) vs. North Caro. (73) and Duke (79) vs. Nevada-Las Vegas (77), March 30, 1991, at Hoosier Dome, Indianapolis, Ind. (NCAA semifinals)
45,214—Louisville (101) vs. Indiana (79) and Notre Dame (81) vs. Kentucky (65), December 3, 1988, at Hoosier Dome, Indianapolis, Ind.

* Note: Figures for games at the Final Four also include the media.

Top Five Attendance Games (Turnstile)
58,903—North Caro. (78) vs. Kansas (68) and Michigan (81) vs. Kentucky (78), April 3, 1993, at Louisiana Superdome, New Orleans, La. (NCAA semifinals)
56,707—Indiana (74) vs. Syracuse (73), March 30, 1987, at Louisiana Superdome, New Orleans, La. (NCAA final)
56,264—North Caro. (77) vs. Michigan (71), April 5, 1993, at Louisiana Superdome, New Orleans, La. (NCAA final)
55,841—Indiana (97) vs. Nevada-Las Vegas (93) and Syracuse (77) vs. Providence (63), March 28, 1987, at Louisiana Superdome, New Orleans, La. (NCAA semifinals)
54,321—Louisiana St. (82) vs. Georgetown (80), January 28, 1989, at Louisiana Superdome, New Orleans, La. (regular-season game)

Top 10 Regular-Season Games (Paid)
68,112—Louisiana St. (87) vs. Notre Dame (64), January 20, 1990, at Louisiana Superdome, New Orleans, La.
66,144—Louisiana St. (82) vs. Georgetown (80), January 28, 1989, at Louisiana Superdome, New Orleans, La.
61,304—Louisiana St. (84) vs. Texas (83), January 3, 1992, at Louisiana Superdome, New Orleans, La.
52,693—Houston (71) vs. UCLA (69), January 20, 1968, at The Astrodome, Houston, Texas.
45,214—Louisville (101) vs. Indiana (79) and Notre Dame (81) vs. Kentucky (65), December 3, 1988, at Hoosier Dome, Indianapolis, Ind.
43,601—Notre Dame (69) vs. Louisville (54) and Kentucky (82) vs. Indiana (76), December 5, 1987, at Hoosier Dome, Indianapolis, Ind.
40,128—Louisville (84) vs. Notre Dame (73) and Indiana (71) vs. Kentucky (69), December 2, 1989, at Hoosier Dome, Indianapolis, Ind.
38,043—Kentucky (98) vs. Notre Dame (90) and Indiana (72) vs. Louisville (52), December 1, 1990, at Hoosier Dome, Indianapolis, Ind.
37,283—Michigan (62) vs. Notre Dame (59), March 4, 1979, at The Silverdome, Pontiac, Mich.
34,704—Kentucky (76) vs. Indiana (74), December 7, 1992, at Hoosier Dome, Indianapolis, Ind.

PLAYING-RULES HISTORY

California freshman Jason Kidd drives to the basket. Beginning in 1993-94, men will have 35 seconds in which to attempt a shot. The 45-second shot clock was introduced in 1985-86 before being reduced to 35 seconds this year by the NCAA Men's Basketball

DR. JAMES NAISMITH'S 13 ORIGINAL RULES OF BASKETBALL

1. The ball may be thrown in any direction with one or both hands.

2. The ball may be batted in any direction with one or both hands (never with the fist).

3. A player cannot run with the ball. The player must throw it from the spot on which he catches it, allowance to be made for a man who catches the ball when running at a good speed if he tries to stop.

4. The ball must be held in or between the hands; the arms or body must not be used for holding it.

5. No shouldering, holding, pushing, tripping, or striking in any way the person of an opponent shall be allowed; the first infringement of this rule by any player shall count as a foul, the second shall disqualify him until the next goal is made, or, if there was evident intent to injure the person, for the whole of the game, no substitute allowed.

6. A foul is striking at the ball with the fist, violation of rules 3, 4, and such as described in rule 5.

7. If either side makes three consecutive fouls, it shall count a goal for the opponents (consecutive means without the opponents in the mean time making a foul).

8. A goal shall be made when the ball is thrown or batted from the grounds into the basket and stays there, providing those defending the goal do not touch or disturb the goal. If the ball rests on the edges, and the opponent moves the basket, it shall count as a goal.

9. When the ball goes out of bounds, it shall be thrown into the field of play by the person first touching it. In case of a dispute, the umpire shall throw it straight into the field. The thrower-in is allowed five seconds; if he holds it longer, it shall go to the opponent. If any side persists in delaying the game, the umpire shall call a foul on that side.

10. The umpire shall be judge of the men and shall note the fouls and notify the refree when three consecutive fouls have been made. He shall have power to disqualify men according to Rule 5.

11. The referee shall be judge of the ball and shall decide when the ball is in play, in bounds, to which side it belongs, and shall keep the time. He shall decide when a goal has been made, and keep account of the goals with any other duties that are usually performed by a referee.

12. The time shall be two 15 minute halves, with five minutes' rest between.

13. The side making the most goals in that time shall be declared the winner. In case of a draw, the game may, by agreement of the captains, be continued until another goal is made.

IMPORTANT RULES CHANGES

1891 - The 13 original rules of basketball are written by Dr. James Naismith in December 1891 in Springfield, Massachusetts.

1894-95 - The free-throw line is moved from 20 to 15 feet.

1895-96 - A field goal changes from three to two points, and free throws from three points to one point.

1896-97 - Backboards first are installed.

1900-01 - A dribbler may not shoot for a field goal and may dribble only once, and then with two hands.

1908-09 - A dribbler is permitted to shoot. The dribble is defined as the "continuous passage of the ball," making the double dribble illegal.
- A second referee is added for games in an effort to curb the rough play.

1910-11 - Players are disqualified upon committing their fourth personal foul.
- No coaching is allowed during the progress of the game by anybody connected with either team. A warning is given for the first violation and a free throw is awarded after that.

1913-14 - The bottom of the net is left open.

1914-15 - College, YMCA and AAU rules are made the same for the first time.

1920-21 - A player can reenter the game once. Before this rule, if a player left the game, he could not reenter for the rest of the game.
- The backboards are moved two feet from the wall of the court. Before this rule, players would "climb" up the padded wall to sink baskets.

1921-22 - Running with the ball changes from a foul to a violation.

1923-24 - The player fouled must shoot his own free throws. Before this rule, one person usually shot all his team's free throws.

1928-29 - The charging foul by the dribbler is introduced.

1930-31 - A "held ball" may be called when a closely guarded player is withholding the ball from play for five seconds. The result will be a jump ball.
- The maximum circumference of the ball is reduced from 32 to 31 inches, and the maximum weight from 23 to 22 ounces.

1932-33 - The 10-second center line is introduced to cut down on stalling.
- No player can stand in the free-throw lane with the ball more than three seconds.

1933-34 - A player may reenter the game twice.

1934-35 - The circumference of the ball again is reduced to between 29½ and 30¼ inches.

1935-36 - No offensive player can remain in the free-throw lane, with or without the ball, for more than three seconds.
- After a made free throw, the team scored upon shall put the ball in play at the end of the court where the goal had been scored.

1937-38 - The center jump after every goal scored is eliminated.

1938-39 - The ball will be thrown in from out of bounds at midcourt by the team shooting a free throw after a technical foul. Before, the ball was put into play with a center jump after a technical foul free throw.
- The circumference of the ball is established as 30 inches.

1939-40 - Teams have the choice of whether to take a free throw or take the ball out of bounds at midcourt. If two or more free throws are awarded, this option applies to the last throw.
- The backboards are moved from two to four feet from the end line to permit freer movement under the basket.

1940-41 - Fan-shaped backboards are made legal.

1942-43 - Any player who is eligible to start an overtime period will be allowed an extra personal foul, upping the total so disqualification is on the fifth foul.

1944-45 - Defensive goaltending is banned.

- Five personal fouls now disqualify a player. An extra foul is not permitted in overtime games.
- Unlimited substitution is introduced.

1946-47 - Transparent backboards are authorized.

1947-48 - The clock is stopped on every dead ball the last three minutes of the second half and of every overtime period. This includes every time a goal is scored because the ball is considered dead until put into play again. (This rule was abolished in 1951.)

1948-49 - Coaches are allowed to speak to players during a timeout.

1951-52 - Games are to be played in four 10-minute quarters. Before this, games were played in two 20-minute halves.

1952-53 - Teams can no longer waive free throws in favor of taking the ball out of bounds.
- The one-and-one free-throw rule is introduced, although the bonus is used only if the first shot is missed. The rule will be in effect the entire game except the last three minutes, when every foul is two shots.

1954-55 - The one-and-one free throw is changed so that the bonus shot is given only if the first shot is made.
- Games are changed back to being played in two 20-minute halves.

1955-56 - The two-shot penalty in the last three minutes of the game is eliminated. The one-and-one is now in effect the entire game.

1956-57 - The free-throw lane is increased from six feet to 12 feet. On the lineup for a free throw, the two spaces adjacent to the end line must be occupied by opponents of the free thrower. In the past, one space was marked "H" for a home team player to occupy, and across the lane the first space was marked "V" for a visiting team player to stand in.
- Grasping the basket is now classified as a technical foul under unsportsmanlike tactics.

1957-58 - Offensive goaltending is now banned, as an addition to the original 1945 rule.
- One free throw for each common foul is taken for the first six personal fouls by one team in each half, and the one-and-one is used thereafter.
- On uniforms, the use of the single digit numbers one and two and any digit greater than five is prohibited.

1964-65 - Coaches must remain seated on the bench except while the clock is stopped or to direct or encourage players on the court. This rule is to help keep coaches from inciting undesirable crowd reactions toward the officials.

1967-68 - The dunk is made illegal during the game and pregame warm-up.

1970-71 - During a jump ball, a nonjumper may not change his position from the time the official is ready to make the toss until after the ball has been tapped.

1972-73 - The free throw on the first six common fouls each half by a team is eliminated.
- Players cannot attempt to create the false impression that they have been fouled in charging-guarding situations or while screening when the contact was only incidental. An official can charge the "actor" with a technical foul for unsportsmanlike conduct if, in the official's opinion, the actor is making a travesty of the game.
- Freshmen are eligible to play varsity basketball. This was the result of a change in the NCAA bylaws, not the basketball playing rules.

1973-74 - Officials may now penalize players for fouls occurring away from the ball, such as grabbing, holding and setting illegal screens.

1974-75 - During a jump ball, a nonjumper on the restraining circle may move around it after the ball has left the official's hands.
- A player charged with a foul is no longer required to raise his hand. (In 1978, however, it was strongly recommended that a player start raising his hand again.)

1976-77 - The dunk is made legal again.

1981-82 - The jump ball is used only at the beginning of the game and the start of each overtime. An alternating arrow will indicate possession in jump-ball situations during the game.

- All fouls charged to bench personnel shall be assessed to the head coach.

1982-83 - When the closely guarded five-second count is reached, it is no longer a jump-ball situation. It is a violation, and the ball is awarded to the defensive team out of bounds.

1983-84 - Two free throws are taken for each common foul committed within the last two minutes of the second half and the entire overtime period, if the bonus rule is in effect. (This rule was rescinded one month into the season.)

1984-85 - The coaching box is introduced, whereby a coach and all bench personnel must remain in the 28-foot-long coaching box unless seeking information from the scorer's table.

1985-86 - The 45-second clock is introduced. The team in control of the ball must now shoot for a goal within 45 seconds after it attains team control.

- If a shooter is fouled intentionally and the shot is missed, the penalty will be two shots and possession of the ball out of bounds to the team that was fouled.

- The head coach may stand throughout the game, while all other bench personnel must remain seated.

1986-87 - The three-point field goal is introduced and set at 19 feet 9 inches from the center of the basket.

- A coach may leave the confines of the bench at any time without penalty to correct a scorer's or timer's mistake. A technical foul is assessed if there is no mistake. (This was changed the next year to a timeout.) Also, a television replay may be used to prevent or rectify a scorer's or timer's mistake or a malfunction of the clock.

1987-88 - Each intentional personal foul carries a two-shot penalty plus possession of the ball.

1988-89 - Any squad member who participates in a fight will be ejected from the game and will be placed on probation. If that player participates in a second fight during the season, he will be suspended for one game. A third fight involving the same person results in suspension for the rest of the season including championship competition.

1990-91 - Beginning with the team's 10th personal foul in a half, two free throws are awarded for each common foul, except player-control fouls.

- Three free throws are awarded when a shooter is fouled during an unsuccessful three-point try.

- The fighting rule is amended. The first time any squad member or bench personnel participates in a fight he will be suspended for the team's next game. If that same person participates in a second fight, he will be suspended for the rest of the season including championship competition.

1991-92 - Contact technical fouls count toward the five fouls for player disqualification and toward the team fouls in reaching bonus free-throw situations.

- The shot clock is reset when the ball strikes the basket ring, not when a shot leaves the shooter's hands as it had been ever since the rule was introduced in 1986.

1992-93 - Unsporting technical fouls, in addition to contact technical fouls, count toward the five fouls for player disqualification and toward the team fouls in reaching bonus free-throw situations.

1993-94 - The shot clock is reduced to 35 seconds from 45. The team in control of the ball must now shoot for a goal within 35 seconds after it gains team control.

- A foul shall be ruled intentional if, while playing the ball, a player causes excessive contact (hard foul) with an opponent.
- The game clock will be stopped after successful field goals in the last minute of the game and the last minute of any overtime period with no substitution allowed.
- The five-second dribbling violation when closely guarded is eliminated.
- The rule concerning the use of profanity is expanded to include abusive and obscene language in an effort to curtail verbal misconduct by players and coaches.

RESULTS/SCHEDULES

Ervin Johnson led New Orleans to a 26-4 record. The Privateers were 18-0 in Sun Belt Conference play and were selected to the Division I Men's Basketball Championship field of 64. New Orleans lost to Xavier (Ohio) in the first round of the tournament.

1993 Men's Basketball Scores

Following is an alphabetical listing of the 1992-93 season's game-by-game scores for the men's teams of the member colleges and universities of the National Collegiate Athletic Association whose records were available at press time.

Squares (■) indicate home games, daggers (†) indicate neutral-site games and section symbols (§) indicate forfeits. Games played and subsequently forfeited do not alter records.

All records are restricted to varsity games between four-year college institutions.

ABILENE CHRISTIAN			**10-18**
76	†	Western N. Mex.	86
98	†	Colorado Mines	80
97		Adams St.	109
90	■	Adams St.	84
69	■	Mississippi Col.	81
76	■	Mary Hardin-Baylor	78
74	†	West Tex. A&M	79
95	†	Neb.-Kearney	99
96	■	Schreiner	85
78	■	Dallas	72
64		UTEP	96
56	†	Livingston	66
64		Mississippi Col.	86
114	■	Concordia (Tex.)	109
59	■	Tex. A&M-Kingsville	91
84	■	East Tex. St.	69
90		Cameron	99
117		Central Okla.	119
71		Angelo St.	83
77		Eastern N. Mex.	87
91	■	Eastern N. Mex.	101
57		East Tex. St.	68
94		Tex. A&M-Kingsville	77
118	■	Central Okla.	128
108	■	Cameron	80
81	■	Angelo St.	80
82	■	Angelo St.	72
81	■	Tex. A&M-Kingsville	91

ADAMS ST.			**11-16**
109	■	Abilene Christian	97
84		Abilene Christian	90
81	†	Angelo St.	71
151	■	Fort Lewis	110
73	■	Southern Colo.	72
86		Metropolitan St.	82
95	†	Central Mo. St.	97
68		Air Force	87
91		Colorado-CS	52
106	■	Colorado-CS	62
64		Westmont	67
100	†	William Jewell	78
85		Mesa St.	96
70		Western St.	81
89	■	N.M. Highlands	83
80		Southern Colo.	108
101	■	Colorado Mines	78
107		Fort Lewis	119
106	■	Chadron St.	116
68	■	Fort Hays St.	72
64		Colorado Mines	67
69		N.M. Highlands	86
82		Chadron St.	83
72		Fort Hays St.	64
89	■	Western St.	98
77	■	Mesa St.	100
73		Fort Hays St.	74

ADELPHI			**14-14**
67		West Chester	73
69		Fordham	85
64	■	New York Tech	49
97	■	Mt. St. Mary (N.Y.)	76
71	■	Southern Conn. St.	78
98		Concordia (N.Y.)	71
96		Central Conn. St.	103
74		St. Rose	93
56		Seton Hall	85
47		Queens (N.Y.)	57
93		Dowling	72
85	■	Mercy	79
80	■	LIU-Southampton	67
96	■	Concordia (N.Y.)	66
78	■	New Jersey Tech	73
58	■	Phila. Textile	65
85	■	St. Rose	90
90		LIU-C.W. Post	82
80	■	Queens (N.Y.)	70
48		Phila. Textile	68
68		LIU-Southampton	51
61	■	Pace	76
59	†	Pace	48
76		Mercy	78
98	■	LIU-C.W. Post	94
81	■	Dowling	86
81		LIU-C.W. Post	74
69		Phila. Textile	101

ADRIAN			**7-18**
67	†	Kenyon	55
71	†	Defiance	85
94	■	Concordia (Mich.)	64
104	■	Wilberforce	82
77	■	Ferris St.	93
67	■	Bluffton	51
63		Franklin	92
74		Western Conn. St.	93
71	†	Jersey City St.	67
57		Bluffton	64
80		Alma	89
58	■	Calvin	97
59	■	Albion	69
64		Hope	80
66		Olivet	77
50	■	Kalamazoo	62
77		Concordia (Mich.)	68
55		Kalamazoo	61
75	■	Olivet	85
73		Siena Heights	82
73	■	Hope	96
52		Calvin	91
53		Albion	73
76	■	Alma	75
46		Kalamazoo	71

AIR FORCE			**9-19**
58		Valparaiso	66
78		Youngstown St.	82
75	■	Regis (Colo.)	64
90	■	Doane	53
88	■	Mesa St.	76
96	■	Portland	65
87	■	Adams St.	68
50		Vanderbilt	95
75	†	Rider	66
69	■	Colorado St.	58
53	■	Wyoming	59
69		UTEP	82
43		New Mexico	63
47	■	Utah	61
68	■	Brigham Young	103
71		Fresno St.	51
51		San Diego St.	59
59		Hawaii	74
62	■	San Diego St.	72
69	■	Hawaii	78
61	■	Fresno St.	58
61		Utah	87
80		Brigham Young	96
46	■	UTEP	68
60	■	New Mexico	80
55		Colorado St.	72
58		Wyoming	64
54	†	Hawaii	62

AKRON			**8-18**
75	■	Mansfield	55
81		Mississippi Val.	93
50		Penn St.	56
82	■	Youngstown St.	66
62	■	Northern Ill.	57
65		Youngstown St.	59
60	†	Wagner	76
60	†	Fla. Atlantic	40
53	■	Bowling Green	51
46	■	Miami (Ohio)	51
62		Eastern Mich.	57
64	■	Western Mich.	67
71		Toledo	87
58	■	Ohio	65
45		Kent	61
62	■	Central Mich.	64
50		Ball St.	60
46		Miami (Ohio)	58
69	■	Eastern Mich.	79
44		Western Mich.	60
67	■	Toledo	75
67		Ohio	75
75	■	Kent	76
59		Central Mich.	75
83	■	Ball St.	70
58		Bowling Green	76

ALABAMA			**16-13**
93	■	Wichita St.	71
70	†	Washington St.	68
86	■	Southern Miss.	76
91		Old Dominion	93
83		Virginia	86
79	†	Rhode Island	78
65		Santa Clara	58
73		Vanderbilt	76
95	■	Tennessee St.	80
77	■	Louisiana St.	67
64	■	Texas A&M	58
66		Arkansas	74
80	■	Mississippi	67
59	■	Kentucky	73
53		Mississippi St.	66
81	■	Auburn	78
59	■	East Caro.	54
59		Florida	69
85		Tennessee	81
93	■	Arkansas	82
70	■	Georgia	73
82		Mississippi	83
68		Louisiana St.	76
97	■	South Caro.	80
70		Auburn	78
92	■	Mississippi St.	80
86	†	South Caro.	79
59	†	Vanderbilt	76
56	■	Ala.-Birmingham	58

ALA.-BIRMINGHAM			**21-14**
63	†	Vanderbilt	81
80	†	Dayton	67
67	†	Tenn.-Chatt.	52
100	■	Southern-B.R.	88
73	■	Mississippi St.	68
100	■	Alcorn St.	70
87	■	Texas-Arlington	68
75	■	Tulane	69
111	■	Prairie View	61
97	■	Nicholls St.	67
103	■	Mississippi Val.	81
68	†	South Caro.	75
83	†	Holy Cross	90
59		Minnesota	74
57		UC Santa Barb.	77
66	■	Marquette	80
50		Memphis St.	47
62	■	DePaul	73
38		Cincinnati	40
75	■	Cal St. Northridge	63
53	■	Memphis St.	69
68	■	Temple	55
74	■	Auburn	86
44		Marquette	38
48		DePaul	55
84	■	St. Louis	45
59		South Fla.	61
67	■	Cincinnati	60
77		St. Louis	57
64	†	DePaul	66
58		Alabama	56
65	■	Clemson	64
61	■	Southwest Mo. St.	52
41	†	Georgetown	45
55	†	Providence	52

ALA.-HUNTSVILLE			**8-19**
97	■	North Ala.	85
72	†	Belhaven	75
84	†	Athens St.	96
75	■	Athens St.	78
81	■	Livingston	72
68		Montevallo	66
82	■	Wofford	77
106	†	Talladega	112
97		Aub.-Montgomery	103
48	■	Montevallo	47
76	†	North Ala.	88
57		Delta St.	78
76		Wofford	78
101		Newberry	102
74		Livingston	66
70		Lincoln Memorial	71
62		Athens St.	67
83	■	West Ga.	82
69		Jacksonville St.	100
86	■	Faulkner	102
93	■	Troy St.	120
72		Alabama A&M	102
70	■	Lincoln Memorial	72
94		West Ga.	103
89		Troy St.	114

83		Birm. Southern	128
103	■	Newberry	82

ALABAMA A&M 28-3

106		Miles	69
123		Alabama St.	120
124	■	Selma	99
83	■	Albany St. (Ga.)	61
84		LeMoyne-Owen	89
61		Paine	59
96		Albany St. (Ga.)	92
104		Jacksonville St.	109
93	■	Savannah St.	86
94	■	Fort Valley St.	88
88	■	Tuskegee	71
100		Clark Atlanta	66
87	■	Morris Brown	65
94		Tuskegee	63
101	■	Miles	70
94	■	Alabama St.	83
92	†	Morehouse	84
95		Morris Brown	81
102	■	Ala.-Huntsville	72
115	■	Talladega	93
103		Morehouse	86
97	■	Clark Atlanta	81
108	■	Paine	93
113	■	Lane	71
100	■	Knoxville	80
109	■	LeMoyne-Owen	96
89	†	Albany St. (Ga.)	76
80	†	Fort Valley St.	78
92	†	LeMoyne-Owen	88
84	†	N.C. Central	93
79	†	Fayetteville St.	62

ALABAMA ST. 14-13

120	■	Alabama A&M	123
83	■	Florida A&M	65
76		Samford	86
121	■	Troy St.	116
93		N.C.-Wilmington	102
73	†	Louisiana Tech	88
107	■	Clark Atlanta	68
75	†	Drexel	83
82	†	Sam Houston St.	75
74		Georgia St.	91
70		Florida A&M	57
89		Texas Southern	91
96		Prairie View	92
92	■	Southern-B.R.	80
97	■	Alcorn St.	87
84		Mississippi Val.	108
90	■	Grambling	74
85	■	Jackson St.	91
83		Alabama A&M	94
83	■	Texas Southern	69
95	■	Prairie View	74
86		Southern-B.R.	82
85		Alcorn St.	81
93	■	Mississippi Val.	87
85		Grambling	91
75		Jackson St.	86
80	†	Alcorn St.	83

ALAS. ANCHORAGE 21-10

89	■	Edinboro	83
116	■	Edinboro	92
73	■	Oregon	96
56	■	Tenn.-Chatt.	110
84	■	Dayton	70
115	■	Colorado-CS	52
95	■	Colorado-CS	62
73	†	Bridgewater (Va.)	60
73	†	Lander	70
64	†	Calvin	69
70	†	Oklahoma	102
80	†	Weber St.	71
79		Arizona St.	80
84	■	East Tex. St.	75
86	■	N.M. Highlands	82
90	■	Southern Colo.	75
82	■	Alas. Fairbanks	68
88		Grand Canyon	92
82		Eastern Mont.	62
71	■	Chaminade	76
91	■	Hawaii-Hilo	83
90	■	Seattle Pacific	79
81		Chaminade	85
83		Alas. Fairbanks	78
79	■	Eastern Mont.	74
76	■	Grand Canyon	74
49		Seattle Pacific	86
65	■	Eastern Mont.	64
86	■	Grand Canyon	78
72	†	Cal St. Chico	70
59		Cal St. Bakersfield	78

ALAS. FAIRBANKS 12-16

71	■	Calvin	81
94	■	Virginia Union	97
99	■	Edinboro	84
85	■	Edinboro	84
89	■	Colorado-CS	67
105	■	Colorado-CS	77
77		Oregon	97
66		Toledo	55
108	†	Bethany (Kan.)	98
92		Cal St. Chico	83
90	†	Emporia St.	102
78	†	Hawaii Pacific	110
95	†	Sheldon Jackson	81
72	†	BYU-Hawaii	82
68		Alas. Anchorage	82
78		Eastern Mont.	82
73		Grand Canyon	110
113	■	Hawaii-Hilo	82
107	■	Chaminade	88
76	■	Seattle Pacific	94
114	■	Queens (N.C.)	108
85	■	Queens (N.C.)	92
78	■	Alas. Anchorage	83
97	■	Grand Canyon	101
111	■	Eastern Mont.	92
68		Seattle Pacific	94
89		Chaminade	101
88		Hawaii-Hilo	90

ALBANY (N.Y.) 15-10

68		Skidmore	52
84	†	Rensselaer	70
55		Binghamton	61
76	■	Castleton St.	55
59	■	Green Mountain	57
54	■	Western Conn. St.	53
54	■	Ithaca	62
84		Hamilton	85
92	■	Upsala	66
77		Plattsburgh St.	90
44		Buffalo St.	69
95		Old Westbury	77
68	■	Oneonta St.	53
61		Union (N.Y.)	69
72	■	Cortland St.	79
78	■	Mt. St. Mary (N.Y.)	70
72	■	Utica Tech	50
56		North Adams St.	51
61	■	Stony Brook	48
60		Skidmore	62
68		Elmira	87
56		Hartwick	65
48	■	Potsdam St.	44
77	■	Elmira	69
65		Rensselaer	60

ALBANY ST. (GA.) 10-15

57	■	Ga. Southwestern	73
88		LeMoyne-Owen	105
61		Alabama A&M	83
71	†	Columbus	88
90	†	Southern Tech	70
84		Clark Atlanta	83
84		Morris Brown	62
92	■	Alabama A&M	96
85	■	LeMoyne-Owen	67
76		Fort Valley St.	80
69		Paine	82
65	■	Morris Brown	63
76		Morehouse	82
73	■	Valdosta St.	66
77	■	Clark Atlanta	66
65	■	Paine	67
77	■	Fort Valley St.	89
86		Valdosta St.	95
81		Miles	84
78		Savannah St.	70
63		Tuskegee	74
91	■	Savannah St.	63
86		Fla. Memorial	75
85		Ga. Southwestern	96
76	†	Alabama A&M	89

ALBERTUS MAGNUS 11-14

79		Wheaton (Mass.)	89
78	†	Elmira	75
65	■	St. Joseph's (N.Y.)	64
54	■	Trinity (Conn.)	68
73		John Jay	72
74	†	Fitchburg St.	63
75		Anna Maria	83
67		Coast Guard	68
54		Eastern Conn. St.	65
67	■	Ramapo	69
60		Colby	85
78	†	Hamilton	108
83	■	Connecticut Col.	78
81	■	Bard	54
87	■	Rivier	61
64		Westfield St.	103
80	■	Mt. St. Vincent	97
77	■	Colby-Sawyer	87
57	■	Western New Eng.	54
64		Wesleyan	66
75		Western Conn. St.	86
79	■	Rivier	81
75	■	Maritime (N.Y.)	52
97		Vassar	70
111		Daniel Webster	79

ALBION 18-8

59	■	Rose-Hulman	73
64		Bluffton	58
81	†	Mich.-Dearborn	68
80	†	Ind.-South Bend	64
87	■	Grand Rapids Bapt.	61
76		Tri-State	89
92	■	Goshen	63
81	†	Bluffton	52
112	†	Olivet	80
68		Calvin	65
81		Olivet	63
69	■	Hope	67
69		Adrian	59
75	■	Kalamazoo	84
79	■	Alma	66
78		Grand Rapids Bapt.	65
67	■	Calvin	70
85	■	Spring Arbor	79
71		Alma	72
64		Kalamazoo	79
55		Hope	76
73	■	Adrian	53
82	■	Olivet	78
79	■	Olivet	71
56	†	Kalamazoo	53
72		Calvin	74

ALBRIGHT 14-10

69	†	Washington (Md.)	60
61		Muhlenberg	59
45	■	Ursinus	58
67		Wilkes	55
55		Lebanon Valley	81
66	■	FDU-Madison	59
64	■	Dickinson	71
77	†	Drew	60
65	†	Scranton	81
80	■	Swarthmore	64
69		King's (Pa.)	59
47	■	Scranton	61
72	■	Allentown	77
57		Juniata	64
81	■	Elizabethtown	85
89		Lycoming	70
78		Messiah	74
77	■	Susquehanna	65
78	■	Juniata	65
62		Moravian	57
74		Elizabethtown	85
89	■	Lycoming	62
60	■	Messiah	44
58		Susquehanna	73

ALCORN ST. 7-20

81		Southeast Mo. St.	86
90	†	Northeast La.	105
76	■	Wis.-Milwaukee	91
70		Ala.-Birmingham	100
67	†	Gonzaga	77
59		Southern Miss.	86
59	†	Ga. Southern	69
85	†	Campbell	61
81		Wisconsin	110
80		Wis.-Milwaukee	94
55	■	Mississippi Val.	56
86	■	Grambling	83
86		Jackson St.	103
87		Alabama St.	97
107		Prairie View	89
85		Texas Southern	72
83		Southern-B.R.	94
79		Mississippi Val.	87
74		Grambling	87
69	■	Jackson St.	83
81	■	Alabama St.	85
63		Mississippi Col.	76
100	■	Prairie View	69
93	■	Texas Southern	91
78	■	Southern-B.R.	89
83	†	Alabama St.	80
75		Southern-B.R.	93

ALFRED 9-15

61		Rochester	79
84		Nazareth (N.Y.)	90
57		Fredonia St.	76
52	†	Penn St.-Behrend	57
64	■	Union (N.Y.)	55
78	■	Houghton	56
87		Elmira	91
76	■	Clarkson	64
100	■	St. Lawrence	108
59		Ithaca	73
46		Penn St.-Behrend	48
86		Hobart	84
70		Rochester Inst.	80
82	■	Rensselaer	79
77	■	Hartwick	61
85		St. Lawrence	70
66		Clarkson	63
59		Hartwick	54
74		Rensselaer	81
83	■	Elmira	94
64	■	Rochester Inst.	81
64	■	Hobart	65
66	■	St. John Fisher	69
62	■	Ithaca	70

ALLEGHENY 19-7

91	†	Wash. & Jeff.	95
60		Grove City	63
70	■	Heidelberg	66
64	■	Buffalo St.	60
83	■	Case Reserve	69
71	■	Ohio Wesleyan	69
77		Oberlin	55
95		Bethany (W.Va.)	74
88		Penn St.-Behrend	62
93		Earlham	59
66	■	Kenyon	51
66		Wittenberg	57
58	■	Wooster	80
70		Denison	63
60		Westminster (Pa.)	65
72		Ohio Wesleyan	71
87	■	Oberlin	77
90	■	Earlham	77

69 Wooster 78
72 ■ Wittenberg 77
76 Case Reserve 73
67 ■ Denison 56
88 ■ St. John Fisher 61
59 Kenyon 52
76 ■ Case Reserve 72
57 † Wooster 67

ALLENTOWN 12-15
65 Moravian 74
81 ■ Centenary (N.J.) 64
65 ■ Muhlenberg 79
75 Widener 72
49 ■ Wilkes 74
83 ■ Lycoming 72
67 Holy Family 53
81 † Millsaps 89
75 † Rensselaer 87
63 Radford 79
80 ■ Drew 81
77 Albright 72
77 Penn St.-Harrisburg 50
87 ■ Wesley 64
86 ■ Salisbury St. 104
62 ■ Lincoln (Pa.) 75
63 Frostburg St. 76
78 Shenandoah 75
58 ■ Cabrini 57
82 Salisbury St. 85
74 Lincoln (Pa.) 83
71 Delaware Valley 74
56 ■ Frostburg St. 62
92 ■ Shenandoah 78
81 † Shenandoah 71
74 † Lincoln (Pa.) 61
93 † Salisbury St. 123

AMERICAN 11-17
87 ■ Mt. St. Mary's (Md.) 71
74 ■ Villanova 86
100 ■ St. Joseph's (Pa.) 81
67 Maryland 98
74 Marquette 90
56 Stanford 57
52 † St. Mary's (Cal.) 61
71 Geo. Washington 82
76 ■ William & Mary 71
88 ■ Old Dominion 95
84 Pennsylvania 89
89 East Caro. 64
75 N.C.-Wilmington 93
71 ■ Coppin St. 56
81 George Mason 67
79 ■ James Madison 83
73 Richmond 74
82 William & Mary 77
85 Old Dominion 86
106 ■ N.C.-Wilmington 99
67 ■ East Caro. 57
82 Mt. St. Mary's (Md.) 89
66 ■ George Mason 73
67 James Madison 90
63 ■ Richmond 69
77 Charleston (S.C.) 68
78 † William & Mary 72
61 † James Madison 70

AMERICAN INT'L 19-9
107 Southern Conn. St. 95
74 Franklin Pierce 99
78 Stonehill 69
79 Mass.-Lowell 73
93 ■ Quinnipiac 77
102 New Haven 96
81 ■ New Hamp. Col. 88
90 † Cal St. Los Angeles 85
73 Cal St. Stanislaus 77
67 St. Michael's 66
93 ■ Merrimack 64
85 ■ Springfield 79
70 St. Anselm 79
82 Assumption 72
89 ■ Bryant 72
81 Quinnipiac 97
72 ■ Bentley 77
97 ■ Stonehill 80
64 Merrimack 62
78 Springfield 67
84 ■ St. Anselm 72
74 ■ Assumption 62
75 Bryant 69
64 Bentley 77
74 ■ St. Michael's 76
79 ■ Springfield 73
78 † St. Anselm 94
73 † Quinnipiac 71

AMHERST 15-8
104 St. Lawrence 95
85 Clarkson 72
62 ■ Williams 74
110 ■ Curry 58
65 ■ Western New Eng. 42
75 ■ Skidmore 77
71 Middlebury 76
79 Babson 74
57 Williams 72
72 Connecticut Col. 69
79 ■ Bowdoin 72
55 ■ Colby 68
77 ■ Clark (Mass.) 63
96 ■ Hamilton 98
83 Framingham St. 71
56 ■ Tufts 71
87 Nichols 79
104 ■ Brandeis 93
70 Wesleyan 58
78 ■ Westfield St. 89
84 Trinity (Conn.) 77
88 ■ Wesleyan 64
74 Worcester Tech 69

ANDERSON 8-18
68 Capital 75
83 † Bethany (W.Va.) 65
113 † Southeastern (Fla.) 49
88 † Central Wesleyan 79
50 Butler 90
74 ■ Cincinnati Bible 53
69 ■ St. Joseph's (Ind.) 74
70 † Marian (Ind.) 88
86 † Huntington 94
84 ■ Ind. Wesleyan 70
63 Manchester 67
98 ■ Franklin 105
74 Hanover 94
79 ■ Rose-Hulman 62
65 ■ DePauw 77
78 Wabash 80
76 ■ Defiance 92
68 Franklin 76
70 ■ Manchester 83
52 Rose-Hulman 71
70 ■ Hanover 62
76 ■ Wabash 85
72 DePauw 103
79 Thomas More 80
75 Hanover 58
55 † Manchester 75

ANGELO ST. 9-17
65 † Mississippi Col. 63
71 † Adams St. 81
79 ■ Neb.-Kearney 75
83 ■ West Tex. A&M 79
75 ■ Incarnate Word 88
91 ■ Sul Ross 66
74 Eastern Mont. 80
63 Western Mont. 75
87 Texas-San Antonio 92
65 † Wayland Baptist 71
72 † Avila 62
55 West Tex. A&M 94
66 Neb.-Kearney 72
74 ■ East Tex. St. 72
69 ■ Tex. A&M-Kingsville 76
84 Central Okla. 104
72 Cameron 96
83 ■ Abilene Christian 71
57 Eastern N. Mex. 93
69 ■ Eastern N. Mex. 78
65 Tex. A&M-Kingsville 71
72 East Tex. St. 69
75 ■ Cameron 57
89 ■ Central Okla. 93
80 Abilene Christian 81
72 Abilene Christian 82

ANNA MARIA 21-6
89 ■ Tufts 93
100 Mass.-Boston 84
114 † Worcester St. 101
108 ■ Worcester St. 118
89 Clark (Mass.) 93
87 ■ Nichols 78
83 ■ Albertus Magnus 75
103 ■ Worcester Tech 90
97 ■ Bates 84
76 Fitchburg St. 67
99 Roger Williams 66
99 Wentworth Inst. 84
73 Gordon 48
90 ■ Salve Regina 66
81 ■ Eastern Nazarene 73
95 New England Col. 75
110 ■ Curry 57
125 ■ Wentworth Inst. 75
108 ■ New England Col. 77
61 Eastern Nazarene 68
95 ■ Gordon 64
101 Salve Regina 74
108 Curry 88
124 ■ Roger Williams 95
125 ■ Wentworth Inst. 88
80 ■ Salve Regina 94
85 Williams 97

APPALACHIAN ST. 13-15
95 ■ Lander 65
90 ■ Montana St. 75
83 Nebraska 93
73 † Clemson 91
80 N.C.-Charlotte 88
76 ■ East Caro. 74
111 ■ Marshall 92
76 Ga. Southern 103
69 Citadel 53
86 ■ Va. Military 93
81 ■ Furman 77
78 ■ Davidson 69
69 Tenn.-Chatt. 89
79 ■ East Tenn. St. 98
89 Western Caro. 80
64 Va. Military 55
79 Marshall 82
80 ■ N.C.-Wilmington 72
84 ■ Western Caro. 71
85 ■ Tenn.-Chatt. 87
88 Tennessee Tech 96
71 ■ Citadel 75
84 ■ Ga. Southern 92
81 Furman 98
79 Davidson 76
78 East Tenn. St. 81
84 † Western Caro. 73
84 † East Tenn. St. 97

ARIZONA 24-4
80 ■ Arkansas 86
89 ■ New Mexico 70
78 ■ Utah 64
66 Providence 81
92 ■ Delaware St. 52
75 ■ West Va. 74
87 ■ Rhode Island 79
82 UCLA 80
81 Southern Cal 73
93 ■ Washington 76
87 ■ Washington St. 63
91 Arizona St. 87
72 New Orleans 69
92 Oregon 60
57 Oregon St. 54
96 ■ Stanford 61
93 ■ California 81
70 Washington St. 64
81 Washington 72
116 ■ Arizona St. 80
70 † Cincinnati 60
81 ■ Oregon St. 70
99 ■ Oregon 68
71 † California 74
94 Stanford 80
87 ■ Southern Cal 76
99 ■ UCLA 80
61 † Santa Clara 64

ARIZONA ST. 18-10
98 Brigham Young 108
67 ■ San Diego St. 64
81 ■ Northern Ariz. 67
93 ■ Northeastern Ill. 84
103 ■ Duquesne 81
100 ■ Detroit Mercy 84
80 ■ Alas. Anchorage 79
79 Southern Cal 87
85 UCLA 89
81 ■ Washington St. 77
94 ■ Washington 85
87 ■ Arizona 91
59 Louisville 85
82 Oregon St. 73
99 Oregon 84
90 ■ California 83
109 ■ Stanford 87
79 Washington 74
67 Washington St. 97
80 Arizona 116
89 † Memphis St. 76
103 ■ Oregon 88
76 ■ Oregon St. 61
75 Stanford 71
67 † California 91
74 ■ UCLA 77
101 ■ Southern Cal 67
68 ■ Georgetown 78

ARKANSAS 22-9
81 ■ Memphis St. 76
90 ■ Tenn.-Martin 69
86 Arizona 80
96 † Southeast Mo. St. 72
73 Missouri 68
123 † Jackson St. 76
101 ■ Tulsa 87
93 † Coastal Caro. 74
78 † Northeast La. 87
72 Southern Methodist 53
90 ■ Mississippi 78
86 South Caro. 76
74 ■ Alabama 66
89 Vanderbilt 102
89 ■ Auburn 100
76 Mississippi St. 80
97 ■ Georgia 79
91 Louisiana St. 79
74 Florida 66
101 ■ Kentucky 94
82 Alabama 93
91 ■ Tennessee 101
115 ■ Mississippi St. 58
85 Mississippi 63
88 ■ Louisiana St. 75
80 Auburn 81
65 † Georgia 60
81 Kentucky 92
94 † Holy Cross 64
80 † St. John's (N.Y.) 74
74 † North Caro. 80

ARK.-LIT. ROCK 15-12
63 ■ Delta St. 59
54 † Idaho 64
60 † Tennessee St. 62
70 ■ Grambling 59
88 ■ Tenn.-Martin 58
62 South Ala. 86

64 Florida St. 95
75 Grambling 63
76 ■ Arkansas St. 64
62 ■ New Orleans 78
60 Lamar 80
56 Western Ky. 92
73 ■ Southwestern La. 71
66 ■ Jacksonville 59
77 Tex.-Pan American 70
74 Southwestern La. 88
77 Jacksonville 61
63 ■ Louisiana Tech 58
53 Arkansas St. 82
84 ■ Lamar 76
85 ■ South Ala. 79
67 Louisiana Tech 60
81 Tenn.-Martin 67
60 New Orleans 86
78 ■ Tex.-Pan American 66
71 ■ Western Ky. 78
60 † Arkansas St. 74

ARKANSAS ST. 16-12

79 † Northeast La. 72
69 Southeast Mo. St. 71
80 ■ Houston Baptist 54
76 † Texas Christian 55
58 Austin Peay 64
100 † North Caro. A&T 102
82 ■ Houston 84
64 Ark.-Lit. Rock 76
64 Louisiana Tech 51
76 ■ South Ala. 61
60 ■ Jacksonville 55
58 New Orleans 60
75 ■ Western Ky. 86
79 Lamar 74
58 ■ St. Louis 45
93 ■ Louisiana Tech 65
59 South Ala. 78
74 Tex.-Pan American 61
82 ■ Ark.-Lit. Rock 53
69 ■ Southwestern La. 71
86 Jacksonville 73
57 ■ Lamar 55
61 Western Ky. 67
66 ■ Tex.-Pan American 57
60 Southwestern La. 59
51 ■ New Orleans 52
74 † Ark.-Lit. Rock 60
59 † New Orleans 73

ARMSTRONG ST. 15-12

58 † Mo. Southern St. 73
85 † Wingate 89
67 † Savannah St. 61
95 ■ Newberry 61
117 ■ Troy St. 106
79 ■ Coker 70
54 Valdosta St. 74
86 † Kennesaw 70
79 † East Stroudsburg 72
70 ■ Georgia Col. 59
45 S.C.-Spartanburg 71
71 Lander 56
68 Columbus 65
86 ■ Augusta 75
67 ■ Pembroke St. 63
60 Francis Marion 63
92 ■ Valdosta St. 73
57 S.C.-Aiken 56
65 Augusta 71
89 ■ S.C.-Spartanburg 76
82 ■ Columbus 86
59 ■ Francis Marion 70
87 ■ Lander 66
87 Pembroke St. 94
60 ■ S.C.-Aiken 77
68 Georgia Col. 74
58 † S.C.-Spartanburg 65

ARMY 4-22

57 Northeastern 90
50 Drexel 64
48 ■ Monmouth (N.J.) 60
51 Manhattan 83
69 ■ Rider 64
66 Mt. St. Mary's (Md.) 70
47 † N.C.-Greensboro 67
58 Brown 70
71 ■ Richmond 89
66 Navy 73
63 ■ Holy Cross 64
52 ■ Hofstra 64
56 Fordham 75
57 Bucknell 83
74 ■ Lehigh 72
58 Colgate 73
60 ■ Lafayette 57
39 ■ Navy 56
73 Holy Cross 110
40 ■ Fordham 42
63 ■ Bucknell 82
61 Lehigh 72
68 ■ Colgate 79
73 ■ Marist 67
67 Lafayette 77
68 Holy Cross 85

ASHLAND 6-21

82 ■ Wayne St. (Mich.) 87
70 † Bloomsburg 99
66 † St. Thomas Aquinas 69
89 ■ Lake Erie 78
63 ■ Hillsdale 60
60 Eastern Mich. 85
52 Gannon 74
81 ■ Northern Ky. 90
72 ■ Indianapolis 77
74 Southern Ind. 121
66 Ky. Wesleyan 121
79 Findlay 91
53 ■ IU/PU-Ft. Wayne 73
72 ■ Kentucky St. 88
68 ■ Bellarmine 64
43 St. Joseph's (Ind.) 66
74 Lewis 88
73 ■ Ky. Wesleyan 85
60 ■ Southern Ind. 91
55 ■ Wooster 75
60 IU/PU-Ft. Wayne 89
74 Bellarmine 70
80 Kentucky St. 93
70 ■ Lewis 92
90 ■ St. Joseph's (Ind.) 92
79 Indianapolis 71
99 Northern Ky. 89

ASSUMPTION 7-19

101 † New York Tech 83
70 St. Rose 65
74 Quinnipiac 76
64 ■ Mass.-Boston 62
63 ■ Springfield 65
64 Franklin Pierce 94
90 ■ Sacred Heart 81
68 ■ New Hamp. Col. 70
73 Merrimack 78
60 Mass.-Lowell 85
82 St. Michael's 64
70 ■ Bentley 79
71 Bryant 79
72 ■ American Int'l 82
76 ■ St. Anselm 83
65 Springfield 84
92 Stonehill 104
84 ■ Bridgeport 89
53 ■ Quinnipiac 65
65 ■ St. Michael's 62
81 Bentley 88
110 ■ Bryant 119
62 American Int'l 74
86 St. Anselm 96
77 ■ Stonehill 79
73 ■ Merrimack 71

AUBURN 15-12

98 ■ Louisiana Col. 60
80 James Madison 89
77 ■ Lincoln Memorial 51
65 † Louisiana Tech 45
80 N.C.-Wilmington 91
86 ■ Centenary 61
96 ■ Old Dominion 85
71 Mississippi St. 77
73 ■ Florida 76
81 Louisiana St. 87
83 South Caro. 81
88 ■ Tennessee 75
100 Arkansas 89
78 Alabama 81
70 ■ Vanderbilt 73
85 Mississippi 74
69 Georgia 96
86 Ala.-Birmingham 74
73 ■ Louisiana St. 75
83 ■ Mississippi St. 77
81 Southern Miss. 75
83 ■ Mississippi 73
78 Kentucky 80
78 ■ Alabama 70
81 ■ Arkansas 80
76 † Tennessee 78
72 Clemson 84

AUGSBURG 12-12

65 North Dak. St. 95
82 ■ Concordia (St. Paul) 58
81 St. Scholastica 63
71 St. John's (Minn.) 95
65 ■ Macalester 63
85 ■ Hamline 71
69 N'western (Minn.) 77
97 ■ St. Mary's (Minn.) 70
58 Concordia-M'head 65
74 ■ Gust. Adolphus 78
73 Bethel (Minn.) 71
92 St. Olaf 75
54 ■ Carleton 52
64 St. Thomas (Minn.) 58
74 ■ St. John's (Minn.) 76
96 Macalester 73
86 Hamline 77
61 St. Mary's (Minn.) 54
82 ■ Concordia-M'head 85
56 Gust. Adolphus 71
60 ■ Bethel (Minn.) 68
44 ■ St. Olaf 75
73 Carleton 89
58 ■ St. Thomas (Minn.) 67

AUGUSTA 17-12

109 † Kennesaw 102
96 † Erskine 80
84 ■ Catawba 85
78 ■ Fla. Memorial 60
87 Tenn.-Chatt. 109
71 Pembroke St. 64
102 ■ Morehouse 100
90 ■ Fla. Southern 81
80 Ga. Southern 85
86 ■ Barry 88
77 Lander 65
80 Francis Marion 75
75 Armstrong St. 86
70 Georgia Col. 74
71 ■ S.C.-Aiken 59
86 ■ Pembroke St. 83
71 ■ Armstrong St. 65
86 S.C.-Spartanburg 93
93 Columbus 87
107 ■ Georgia Col. 85
76 ■ Lander 77
84 S.C.-Aiken 95
76 ■ Francis Marion 73
82 † Paine 86
75 ■ S.C.-Spartanburg 69
84 ■ Columbus 85
70 ■ Pembroke St. 66
69 ■ Francis Marion 68
60 ■ S.C.-Aiken 64

AUGUSTANA (ILL.) 24-7

68 ■ Beloit 71
77 ■ Dubuque 51
84 St. Ambrose 82
88 ■ Aurora 78
86 ■ Teikyo Marycrest 58
74 Rockford 66
98 ■ Central (Iowa) 70
83 Cal Poly SLO 94
70 Cal St. Bakersfield 82
63 ■ Teikyo Marycrest 59
94 ■ Ill. Wesleyan 80
85 ■ North Park 73
100 ■ Wheaton (Ill.) 71
87 Millikin 89
73 St. Louis 86
71 North Central 69
95 Wheaton (Ill.) 76
87 ■ Carthage 70
93 ■ Millikin 67
73 ■ North Central 56
113 Elmhurst 69
82 Carthage 65
79 Ill. Wesleyan 78
64 North Park 65
95 ■ Elmhurst 78
79 ■ DePauw 66
92 Beloit 66
87 † La Verne 84
100 Wis.-Platteville 86
83 † Rowan 81
68 † Ohio Northern 71

AUGUSTANA (S.D.) 7-19

82 ■ Sioux Falls 80
71 ■ Briar Cliff 69
62 ■ Northern St. 81
70 Fla. Southern 90
86 Tampa 95
95 ■ Huron 67
52 Minn.-Duluth 64
69 ■ Dak. Wesleyan 66
65 ■ Nebraska-Omaha 64
64 ■ Northern Colo. 73
76 North Dak. St. 88
63 North Dak. 72
49 ■ South Dak. 65
73 ■ Morningside 61
49 Mankato St. 59
63 St. Cloud St. 73
66 South Dak. St. 71
79 Northern Colo. 84
87 ■ North Dak. 91
53 ■ North Dak. St. 54
49 Morningside 81
65 South Dak. 68
80 ■ St. Cloud St. 60
79 ■ Mankato St. 85
57 Nebraska-Omaha 62
74 ■ South Dak. St. 77

AURORA 11-14

78 † Olivet (Ill.) 103
73 † North Central 86
118 ■ Principia 57
75 ■ Blackburn 55
77 ■ Carthage 97
78 Augustana (Ill.) 88
64 † Ill. Benedictine 76
80 ■ Millikin 79
84 Monmouth (Ill.) 90
70 Wheaton (Ill.) 75
97 † Rust 88
61 Elmhurst 63
53 † Teikyo Marycrest 77
86 † Marian (Wis.) 80
60 ■ Eureka 76
90 ■ Rockford 72
73 Trinity (Ill.) 74
83 ■ Ill. Benedictine 75
66 ■ Concordia (Ill.) 89
83 Judson 82
60 Rockford 64
96 ■ Trinity (Ill.) 80
75 Ill. Benedictine 67

77 Concordia (Ill.) 106
90 ■ Judson 82

AUSTIN PEAY 7-20
73 Mississippi St. 80
96 ■ Christian Bros. 82
61 Indiana 107
72 † Pacific (Cal.) 69
64 ■ Arkansas St. 58
71 ■ Vanderbilt 116
56 UTEP 77
62 † Florida 86
73 ■ Evansville 75
76 ■ Murray St. 82
68 ■ Southeast Mo. St. 90
72 ■ Tennessee Tech 90
73 Eastern Ky. 78
58 Morehead St. 79
71 ■ Tenn.-Martin 74
55 Middle Tenn. St. 73
68 Tennessee St. 93
61 Cincinnati 98
64 ■ Eastern Ky. 65
90 ■ Morehead St. 75
83 Tennessee Tech 92
61 Tenn.-Martin 59
69 Murray St. 88
64 Southeast Mo. St. 77
57 ■ Middle Tenn. St. 51
80 ■ Tennessee St. 77
66 † Murray St. 82

AVERETT 3-22
58 Belmont Abbey 88
46 † Va. Wesleyan 101
59 Randolph-Macon 65
44 Longwood 78
53 Liberty 111
87 ■ Shenandoah 105
89 ■ Clinch Valley 69
70 Maryville (Tenn.) 93
73 Shenandoah 84
81 ■ Clinch Valley 69
78 ■ Ferrum 89
55 ■ N.C. Wesleyan 83
50 ■ Queens (N.C.) 89
65 Newport News App. 61
64 Chris. Newport 88
61 ■ Greensboro 84
58 ■ Methodist 77
47 Queens (N.C.) 85
82 Ferrum 115
71 ■ Maryville (Tenn.) 77
63 N.C. Wesleyan 90
53 ■ Chris. Newport 89
66 Methodist 69
79 Greensboro 105
69 Greensboro 79

BABSON 20-5
85 ■ Wentworth Inst. 56
76 ■ Wesleyan 60
72 MIT 55
87 ■ Worcester Tech 74
75 Western New Eng. 62
64 Harvard 80
72 ■ St. Anselm 99
98 ■ Middlebury 80
105 Brandeis 94
74 ■ Amherst 79
77 Bowdoin 78
79 Coast Guard 70
76 ■ Norwich 59
89 Suffolk 78
102 ■ Bates 78
97 Clark (Mass.) 72
97 Norwich 72
106 Tufts 103
94 ■ Western New Eng. 51
99 Worcester Tech 82
106 ■ Coast Guard 79
94 ■ MIT 49
95 ■ MIT 68
94 ■ Worcester Tech 77

81 Wheaton (Mass.) 97

BALDWIN-WALLACE 13-13
103 ■ Oberlin 80
70 ■ Ohio Dominican 86
91 Grove City 75
59 Ohio Northern 71
75 ■ John Carroll 67
64 Muskingum 69
81 ■ Frostburg St. 62
102 ■ Marietta 63
76 † Randolph-Macon 47
93 Oglethorpe 83
76 Hiram 82
73 ■ Capital 72
62 Mount Union 66
73 ■ Otterbein 65
68 Heidelberg 87
81 ■ Hiram 84
61 John Carroll 75
52 ■ Ohio Northern 60
79 ■ Muskingum 81
77 Marietta 72
78 ■ Heidelberg 54
41 Capital 65
62 ■ Mount Union 45
70 Otterbein 75
61 ■ Mount Union 50
54 Ohio Northern 57

BALL ST. 26-8
72 ■ Simon Fraser 57
81 ■ Lindenwood 57
67 ■ Md.-East. Shore 47
63 ■ St. Peter's 50
78 ■ Xavier (Ohio) 81
66 ■ Indiana St. 64
75 Valparaiso 78
75 ■ Chicago St. 69
49 Butler 63
78 † Marist 64
90 † Liberty 80
81 † San Francisco 72
50 Miami (Ohio) 65
70 ■ Western Mich. 65
78 Ohio 64
73 ■ Central Mich. 48
61 Bowling Green 59
66 ■ Eastern Mich. 62
78 Toledo 81
59 ■ Kent 51
60 ■ Akron 50
55 Western Mich. 66
72 ■ Ohio 52
84 Central Mich. 81
66 ■ Bowling Green 50
77 Eastern Mich. 57
78 ■ Toledo 64
77 Kent 63
70 Akron 83
72 ■ Miami (Ohio) 63
77 † Kent 57
72 † Toledo 64
79 † Western Mich. 64
72 † Kansas 94

BARD 0-25
67 Albany Pharmacy 95
55 ■ Vassar 69
33 ■ Yeshiva 65
51 † Polytechnic (N.Y.) 55
55 ■ Rivier 83
66 ■ Mt. St. Vincent 125
44 Maritime (N.Y.) 74
56 ■ Vassar 70
47 Mt. St. Mary (N.Y.) 84
54 Albertus Magnus 81
75 Molloy 113
59 St. Joseph's (N.Y.) 71
53 ■ St. Mary's (Md.) 81
61 ■ Albany Pharmacy 74
65 ■ Polytechnic (N.Y.) 66
47 Nyack 83
75 Southern Vt. 102
65 Mt. St. Vincent 90

61 Stevens Tech 83
53 ■ St. Joseph's-Suffolk 71
50 ■ Maritime (N.Y.) 81
50 ■ New Jersey Tech 106
71 Mt. St. Vincent 104
68 New Paltz St. 98
53 Vassar 66

BARRY 17-9
128 ■ Nova 122
75 ■ Presbyterian 85
82 Fla. Atlantic 80
75 ■ St. Thomas (Fla.) 70
64 Miami (Fla.) 81
87 ■ Palm Beach Atl. 56
86 ■ Lynchburg 47
106 ■ Graceland (Ind.) 65
88 Augusta 86
83 Fla. Southern 92
65 North Fla. 64
90 ■ Rollins 98
91 Florida Tech 80
83 ■ Yeshiva 58
80 ■ St. Leo 72
63 Eckerd 66
73 ■ Tampa 75
117 ■ North Fla. 96
89 ■ Fla. Atlantic 54
64 Rollins 81
90 ■ Florida Tech 75
83 St. Leo 78
76 ■ Eckerd 63
67 Tampa 89
71 ■ Fla. Southern 69
81 Tampa 98

BATES 10-14
72 New York U. 85
80 † Tufts 81
62 Bowdoin 104
80 New England 75
65 Westbrook 90
64 Merrimack 102
58 † Pace 90
83 ■ Gordon 62
84 Anna Maria 97
73 Colby-Sawyer 85
81 Plymouth St. 74
90 ■ Suffolk 54
70 ■ Colby 78
75 St. Joseph's (Me.) 83
78 Babson 102
100 ■ Me.-Farmington 95
92 ■ Wesleyan 81
80 ■ Trinity (Conn.) 75
79 ■ Bowdoin 60
78 ■ Norwich 68
68 ■ Middlebury 102
73 ■ Tufts 76
90 Connecticut Col. 73
67 Colby 79

BAYLOR 16-11
97 ■ Hardin-Simmons 64
104 ■ Valparaiso 87
94 ■ N.C.-Charlotte 93
88 North Texas 86
75 Oklahoma St. 93
89 Texas-San Antonio 72
100 South Ala. 105
98 ■ Mo.-Kansas City 87
94 ■ Tulsa 85
89 ■ Southwest Tex. St. 81
79 ■ Texas Christian 57
87 Texas 86
77 Houston 83
96 ■ Rice 87
70 DePaul 72
71 Texas A&M 80
92 ■ Southern Meth. 105
105 Texas Tech 102
67 Texas Christian 55
90 ■ Texas A&M 82

77 Rice 84
73 ■ Texas 88
75 ■ Houston 76
124 ■ Oral Roberts 102
74 Southern Methodist 81
91 ■ Texas Tech 90
74 † Texas Tech 83

BELLARMINE 7-20
82 ■ Ind.-Southeast 63
69 † Bethel (Tenn.) 86
67 ■ Union (Ky.) 46
62 ■ Central Mo. St. 59
84 ■ IU/PU-Indianapolis 88
90 Georgetown (Ky.) 93
53 ■ John Carroll 54
64 ■ St. Joseph's (Ind.) 75
79 ■ Lewis 76
70 Indianapolis 73
82 Northern Ky. 87
72 ■ Ky. Wesleyan 86
82 ■ Southern Ind. 93
75 IU/PU-Ft. Wayne 102
64 Ashland 68
68 ■ SIU-Edwardsville 78
63 Kentucky St. 92
72 ■ Northern Ky. 76
61 ■ Indianapolis 55
76 Southern Ind. 105
54 Ky. Wesleyan 77
70 ■ Ashland 74
71 ■ IU/PU-Ft. Wayne 83
75 IU/PU-Indianapolis 76
69 ■ Kentucky St. 65
59 St. Joseph's (Ind.) 81
66 Lewis 54

BELOIT 21-5
73 ■ N'western (Wis.) 56
71 Augustana (Ill.) 68
66 Carthage 82
71 ■ Rockford 66
77 † Trinity (Tex.) 62
76 Washington (Mo.) 73
82 Lake Forest 66
72 ■ Carroll (Wis.) 60
73 BYU-Hawaii 79
58 Hawaii-Hilo 81
66 Marian (Wis.) 61
79 ■ Lawrence 66
80 St. Norbert 67
84 ■ Illinois Col. 61
64 ■ Knox 72
73 Coe 72
79 Grinnell 77
66 ■ Ripon 58
77 Carroll (Wis.) 48
62 Lawrence 58
72 Ripon 50
70 ■ St. Norbert 61
78 ■ Lake Forest 57
79 ■ Monmouth (Ill.) 71
86 ■ Ripon 83
66 ■ Augustana (Ill.) 92

BEMIDJI ST. 10-17
86 Northern Mich. 100
98 Wis.-Parkside 97
86 Lewis 75
68 ■ North Dak. 87
80 ■ Northern Mich. 87
88 ■ Wayne St. (Neb.) 81
97 Mayville St. 108
67 ■ St. Scholastica 61
64 St. Cloud St. 89
64 Mankato St. 81
90 Neb.-Kearney 97
71 † Wayne St. (Neb.) 76
103 ■ Mayville St. 85
65 ■ Wis.-Parkside 64
64 Winona St. 86
76 Southwest St. 82
66 Wayne St. (Neb.) 83
105 ■ Moorhead St. 94

Score	Opponent	Opp.
76	Minn.-Duluth	66
87	■ Northern St.	108
71	■ Minn.-Morris	70
81	Moorhead St.	83
71	Northern St.	103
84	■ Southwest St.	82
76	■ Winona St.	79
71	■ Minn.-Duluth	77
80	Minn.-Morris	91

BENTLEY 24-7

Score	Opponent	Opp.
94	■ Brandeis	75
90	■ Bryant	68
68	Mass.-Lowell	65
78	Merrimack	63
93	Southern Conn. St.	97
118	■ Keene St.	83
81	■ Dowling	58
80	■ Mercy	77
85	St. Leo	89
72	Rollins	69
81	■ Quinnipiac	76
87	St. Anselm	85
79	Assumption	70
65	Springfield	69
59	■ Stonehill	80
89	■ St. Michael's	57
71	■ Merrimack	60
77	American Int'l	72
65	Bryant	56
92	■ St. Anselm	68
88	■ Assumption	81
85	■ Springfield	73
97	Stonehill	87
65	St. Michael's	57
77	■ American Int'l	64
63	Quinnipiac	76
87	■ Merrimack	67
93	■ Quinnipiac	69
74	■ St. Anselm	79
74	† Franklin Pierce	95
109	† St. Anselm	90

BETHANY (W.VA.) 10-14

Score	Opponent	Opp.
72	† Thomas More	83
65	† Anderson	83
54	Mount Union	71
71	Denison	79
51	Radford	79
70	■ Penn St.-Behrend	68
74	■ Allegheny	95
91	■ Frostburg St.	70
92	Marietta	91
78	† Emory & Henry	104
77	Gettysburg	93
97	■ Ohio Belmont	72
51	Penn St.-Behrend	68
66	Frostburg St.	84
61	Grove City	83
74	Thiel	47
85	■ Waynesburg	66
73	■ Oberlin	51
76	■ Wash. & Jeff.	93
84	■ Grove City	65
91	■ Thiel	79
89	Waynesburg	73
89	Wash. & Jeff.	93
79	■ Ohio Valley College	80

BETHEL (MINN.) 12-12

Score	Opponent	Opp.
93	■ N'western (Minn.)	69
66	■ Wis.-River Falls	78
82	■ Macalester	67
107	Concordia (Ore.)	100
64	Pacific Union	85
60	St. Thomas (Minn.)	70
57	Concordia-M'head	56
46	■ St. Olaf	68
70	Gust. Adolphus	74
62	■ St. Mary's (Minn.)	51
71	■ Augsburg	73
76	Carleton	86
61	Hamline	63
67	■ St. John's (Minn.)	83
73	Macalester	66
62	■ St. Thomas (Minn.)	88
79	■ Concordia-M'head	61
59	St. Olaf	74
81	■ Gust. Adolphus	73
82	St. Mary's (Minn.)	78
68	Augsburg	60
69	■ Carleton	64
67	■ Hamline	60
58	St. John's (Minn.)	71

BETHUNE-COOKMAN 3-24

Score	Opponent	Opp.
55	South Fla.	82
81	Stetson	74
45	† Geo. Washington	65
50	Wisconsin	75
55	Wis.-Green Bay	89
63	Jacksonville	84
50	Minnesota	92
57	Iowa St.	115
79	■ Stetson	82
71	■ Delaware St.	74
68	■ Md.-East. Shore	71
68	■ South Caro. St.	83
52	■ North Caro. A&T	68
60	Howard	75
70	Morgan St.	80
61	Coppin St.	73
64	South Caro. St.	66
56	North Caro. A&T	66
54	Miami (Fla.)	78
56	Florida A&M	69
64	■ Howard	66
103	■ Morgan St.	93
65	■ Coppin St.	89
81	Delaware St.	86
58	Md.-East. Shore	74
70	■ Florida A&M	66
72	† Howard	86

BINGHAMTON 19-9

Score	Opponent	Opp.
81	■ Misericordia	68
82	■ Manhattanville	62
61	■ Albany (N.Y.)	55
107	■ Hamilton	95
73	Brockport St.	58
56	Fredonia St.	61
71	■ New Paltz St.	67
83	■ Plattsburgh St.	69
67	† Widener	65
50	Stony Brook	49
77	■ Utica Tech	62
85	Oswego St.	60
79	Cortland St.	70
78	■ Elmira	87
71	■ Oneonta St.	78
79	■ Buffalo St.	85
74	■ Potsdam St.	57
63	Potsdam St.	62
80	Plattsburgh St.	77
64	■ Cortland St.	60
64	St. John Fisher	75
77	■ Geneseo St.	88
67	Oneonta St.	63
65	New Paltz St.	67
70	■ Brockport St.	48
56	■ Buffalo St.	55
54	■ Fredonia St.	57
89	■ Elmira	92

BLACKBURN 8-17

Score	Opponent	Opp.
73	■ Illinois Col.	86
55	Aurora	75
55	Millikin	71
67	■ Greenville	84
75	† Tenn. Wesleyan	72
42	† Berea	98
60	Eureka	103
53	Rose-Hulman	67
38	Northern Ill.	86
91	■ Maryville (Mo.)	65
62	Westminster (Mo.)	67
73	■ Webster	71
94	■ Harris-Stowe	78
74	■ Parks	49
56	MacMurray	75
67	■ Principia	55
70	Fontbonne	74
77	Maryville (Mo.)	88
52	Principia	56
72	■ Westminster (Mo.)	70
82	Webster	79
52	Parks	73
64	■ MacMurray	79
68	■ Fontbonne	87
61	Maryville (Mo.)	84

BLOOMSBURG 17-10

Score	Opponent	Opp.
99	† Ashland	70
90	Clarion	106
96	■ Shippensburg	86
60	■ Phila. Textile	81
104	Dist. Columbia	92
89	Caldwell	84
62	■ Alvernia	60
99	■ Phila. Bible	63
68	■ Edinboro	63
79	■ Lock Haven	64
88	Susquehanna	96
90	■ Millersville	83
76	West Chester	77
78	Cheyney	74
90	■ Kutztown	69
69	■ Indiana (Pa.)	66
72	Mansfield	74
58	■ East Stroudsburg	63
69	Millersville	103
82	■ West Chester	60
93	■ Cheyney	72
97	Kutztown	83
84	Pitt.-Johnstown	85
75	Mercyhurst	76
104	■ Mansfield	84
80	East Stroudsburg	70
79	† Calif. (Pa.)	82

BLUFFTON 6-20

Score	Opponent	Opp.
58	■ Albion	64
48	■ Hanover	66
50	■ Manchester	79
58	Goshen	73
51	Adrian	67
75	■ Olivet	71
72	Concordia (Mich.)	67
52	† Albion	81
55	† Aquinas	93
45	Ohio Northern	68
64	■ Adrian	57
79	■ Goshen	70
53	Defiance	81
52	■ Wilmington (Ohio)	62
61	Alma	64
60	Thomas More	70
50	■ Denison	53
66	■ Defiance	80
69	Bethel (Ind.)	97
74	■ Thomas More	77
58	Manchester	85
63	Wilmington (Ohio)	71
73	■ Findlay	97
78	■ Lake Erie	69
77	† Defiance	95
75	† Wilmington (Ohio)	70

BOISE ST. 21-8

Score	Opponent	Opp.
79	■ Seattle Pacific	63
63	Washington	73
94	† Murray St.	82
70	■ Wyoming	50
99	■ Elizabeth City St.	70
75	■ Georgia St.	64
88	■ Pepperdine	92
83	■ George Mason	76
75	■ Southern Utah	69
61	St. Mary's (Cal.)	68
83	Cal St. Sacramento	69
72	Northern Ariz.	78
68	Weber St.	67
79	■ Cal St. Northridge	64
62	Idaho St.	66
72	■ Montana St.	52
75	■ Montana	66
76	Eastern Wash.	66
99	Idaho	107
92	■ Weber St.	75
58	■ Northern Ariz.	45
82	■ Idaho St.	71
59	Montana	56
68	Montana St.	60
52	■ Idaho	67
85	■ Eastern Wash.	81
69	† Weber St.	63
80	Idaho	68
72	† Vanderbilt	92

BOSTON COLLEGE 18-13

Score	Opponent	Opp.
96	■ Harvard	57
72	■ Temple	79
72	■ FDU-Teaneck	54
69	■ Coastal Caro.	65
70	Notre Dame	73
65	■ Coppin St.	51
97	■ LIU-Brooklyn	62
94	Syracuse	93
84	Holy Cross	63
67	■ Villanova	64
57	Georgetown	56
65	Providence	73
64	■ Connecticut	66
70	■ Pittsburgh	81
65	Villanova	58
71	■ St. John's (N.Y.)	61
71	■ Georgetown	61
63	■ Seton Hall	62
71	Miami (Fla.)	75
61	St. John's (N.Y.)	65
79	Pittsburgh	56
64	■ Syracuse	67
64	Connecticut	69
70	■ Miami (Fla.)	58
61	Seton Hall	79
57	■ Providence	58
74	† Villanova	70
56	† St. John's (N.Y.)	76
87	Niagara	83
101	■ Rice	68
58	■ Providence	75

BOSTON U. 6-21

Score	Opponent	Opp.
79	■ UC Irvine	76
80	† Columbia	83
64	■ Brown	74
78	■ Coastal Caro.	85
77	■ LIU-Brooklyn	80
61	Providence	92
62	Duke	106
59	Harvard	79
42	Massachusetts	90
76	■ Central Conn. St.	72
67	Hartford	70
94	Vermont	97
66	Dartmouth	85
69	■ Delaware	70
63	■ Drexel	75
73	Maine	78
76	■ New Hampshire	66
71	■ Hofstra	69
81	■ Northeastern	88
76	New Hampshire	69
82	■ Maine	73
57	Drexel	71
65	Delaware	83
58	■ Hartford	72
88	■ Vermont	98
58	Northeastern	96
58	Drexel	75

BOWDOIN 14-10

Score	Opponent	Opp.
82	Me.-Farmington	97
104	■ Bates	62
64	Tufts	73
72	■ Thomas	57
99	■ Notre Dame (N.H.)	78
99	Palm Beach Atl.	72

105 Embry-Riddle 111
85 ■ Maine Maritime 51
78 ■ Babson 77
68 Colby 73
72 Amherst 79
66 Williams 94
83 ■ MIT 79
82 Norwich 68
72 Middlebury 56
66 Southern Me. 51
87 Colby-Sawyer 70
60 Bates 79
73 ■ Wheaton (Mass.) 77
83 ■ Connecticut Col. 60
106 ■ Me.-Augusta 56
71 ■ New England 76
91 ■ Emerson-MCA 68
51 ■ Colby 52

BOWIE ST. 9-18
61 † Alvernia 62
72 West Chester 82
70 Winston-Salem 74
99 Shaw 96
85 Livingstone 83
56 ■ Hampton 67
99 ■ St. Augustine's 92
130 ■ Capitol 82
66 ■ Fayetteville St. 77
80 Delaware St. 96
97 † Johnson Smith 91
58 † Hampton 71
97 Virginia St. 79
67 ■ N.C. Central 79
86 ■ Johnson Smith 105
68 ■ St. Paul's 72
81 Virginia St. 86
71 ■ Norfolk St. 78
100 ■ Elizabeth City St. 105
67 ■ Virginia Union 92
90 Elizabeth City St. 102
95 St. Paul's 78
74 Norfolk St. 89
70 Virginia Union 88
92 ■ Virginia St. 84
80 Hampton 79
85 † Johnson Smith 89

BOWLING GREEN 11-16
81 ■ Heidelberg 50
68 Michigan 79
54 Ohio St. 80
59 Cleveland St. 61
79 ■ Detroit Mercy 88
73 ■ Penn St. 65
68 † Rider 62
69 Vanderbilt 96
51 Akron 53
74 Eastern Mich. 73
69 ■ Toledo 61
74 Kent 68
59 ■ Ball St. 61
57 Miami (Ohio) 82
68 ■ Western Mich. 45
67 Ohio 73
105 ■ Central Mich. 99
54 ■ Eastern Mich. 65
49 Toledo 50
49 ■ Kent 48
50 Ball St. 66
44 ■ Miami (Ohio) 50
65 Western Mich. 69
64 ■ Ohio 71
73 Central Mich. 64
76 ■ Akron 58
50 † Miami (Ohio) 63

BRADLEY 11-16
49 ■ Utah 83
69 Loyola (Ill.) 64
54 ■ Manhattan 61
85 ■ Chicago St. 61
54 Maine 56
65 ■ Creighton 42
55 Tenn.-Chatt. 75

74 Fla. Atlantic 54
50 Wichita St. 58
43 Tulsa 66
51 ■ Southwest Mo. St. 46
65 ■ Drake 73
64 ■ Southern Ill. 77
68 Illinois St. 70
70 ■ Indiana St. 74
48 Creighton 59
42 Southern Ill. 77
73 ■ Wichita St. 64
49 Southwest Mo. St. 63
76 Northern Iowa 81
53 Indiana St. 36
72 ■ Tulsa 57
55 ■ Illinois St. 41
47 Drake 56
72 ■ Northern Iowa 46
59 ■ DePaul 53
61 † Southern Ill. 63

BRANDEIS 8-17
75 Bentley 94
91 ■ Case Reserve 99
85 ■ MIT 67
73 Johns Hopkins 83
76 Rochester 90
106 ■ Mass.-Dartmouth 91
66 Chicago 63
66 Washington (Mo.) 97
94 ■ Babson 105
85 Eastern Nazarene 86
114 ■ Suffolk 84
110 ■ Worcester Tech 91
110 ■ New York U. 11
100 ■ Emory 73
76 ■ Carnegie Mellon 86
100 Emory 91
82 New York U. 97
81 Wheaton (Mass.) 85
93 Amherst 104
72 Carnegie Mellon 78
89 Clark (Mass.) 92
71 ■ Washington (Mo.) 81
74 ■ Chicago 69
77 ■ Tufts 86
61 ■ Rochester 63

BRIDGEPORT 20-9
112 Concordia (N.Y.) 98
98 Grand Canyon 110
66 † Cal St. Dom. Hills 85
124 Amer. Indian Bib. 57
108 Teikyo-Post 95
102 † New Haven 105
69 † Eckerd 57
97 ■ Millersville 90
109 Dowling 87
70 † Towson St. 85
78 Hartford 87
115 ■ Virginia Union 109
115 ■ Molloy 73
89 ■ Franklin Pierce 87
104 ■ Teikyo-Post 98
100 ■ Dominican (N.Y.) 74
91 New Hamp. Col. 87
96 New Haven 106
98 ■ Mt. St. Vincent 78
98 Franklin Pierce 100
96 † Western Conn. St. 69
100 † St. Joseph's (Me.) 88
89 Assumption 84
109 Keene St. 102
79 Virginia Union 82
110 ■ Molloy 76
119 Mt. St. Mary (N.Y.) 96
76 ■ Pace 68
83 ■ St. Rose 84

BRI'WATER (MASS.) 7-18
55 † Rowan 98
55 Stockton St. 68
74 ■ Suffolk 63
71 Mass.-Boston 91
60 ■ Mass.-Dartmouth 90

61 Eastern Conn. St. 84
70 Curry 74
78 † St. Joseph (Vt.) 76
70 Plattsburgh St. 85
87 ■ Westfield St. 91
66 Framingham St. 97
74 ■ North Adams St. 70
81 Rhode Island Col. 78
59 Western Conn. St. 91
88 ■ Worcester St. 100
93 Salem St. 98
62 ■ Fitchburg St. 43
84 Westfield St. 103
73 ■ Framingham St. 66
74 North Adams St. 63
58 ■ Eastern Nazarene 75
104 Worcester St. 109
71 ■ Salem St. 91
71 Fitchburg St. 79
82 † Framingham St. 91

BRIDGEWATER (VA.) 12-12
63 Marymount (Va.) 65
54 ■ Wash. & Lee 67
80 ■ Newport News App. 64
66 ■ East. Mennonite 58
61 Hampden-Sydney 56
71 East. Mennonite 75
66 ■ Randolph-Macon 57
71 † Lander 79
60 † Alas. Anchorage 73
55 ■ Emory & Henry 61
87 ■ East. Mennonite 76
65 ■ Hampden-Sydney 64
55 Roanoke 60
84 Guilford 65
56 ■ Va. Wesleyan 57
62 Wash. & Lee 60
71 ■ Lynchburg 58
84 ■ Roanoke 72
58 Emory & Henry 78
53 Randolph-Macon 59
67 Lynchburg 61
66 Va. Wesleyan 74
55 ■ Guilford 51
65 Va. Wesleyan 76

BRIGHAM YOUNG 25-9
108 ■ Arizona St. 98
93 Utah St. 83
77 Weber St. 83
108 ■ Southern Utah 62
74 ■ Georgia 64
89 ■ Utah St. 65
76 † Oklahoma 75
73 † Memphis St. 67
66 † Duke 89
70 † Oregon 76
79 † Oregon St. 93
79 ■ UTEP 73
70 ■ New Mexico 56
53 ■ Utah 54
72 Fresno St. 57
103 Air Force 68
76 ■ San Diego St. 64
84 ■ Hawaii 80
70 Colorado St. 63
77 Wyoming 64
81 ■ Colorado St. 57
75 ■ Wyoming 62
62 Hawaii 56
80 San Diego St. 73
90 ■ Fresno St. 74
96 ■ Air Force 80
128 ■ Cal St. Sacramento 78
83 Utah 89
84 UTEP 63
76 New Mexico 79
85 † Hawaii 71
59 † New Mexico 68
80 † Southern Methodist 71
76 † Kansas 90

BROCKPORT ST. 12-13
89 † Catholic 92
90 † Medgar Evers 85
58 ■ Binghamton 73
65 Geneseo St. 77
54 ■ Buffalo St. 66
77 Oneonta St. 65
94 New Paltz St. 93
86 Nazareth (N.Y.) 78
82 † Rochester Inst. 75
77 † Geneseo St. 82
86 † Nazareth (N.Y.) 78
80 Oswego St. 62
84 ■ Utica Tech 70
100 Fredonia St. 86
68 ■ Plattsburgh St. 71
78 ■ Potsdam St. 69
70 ■ Roberts Wesleyan 76
42 Buffalo St. 48
92 ■ Fredonia St. 82
65 St. John Fisher 78
64 Cortland St. 67
64 ■ Oswego St. 66
68 Utica Tech 67
58 ■ Geneseo St. 68
48 Binghamton 70

BROWN 7-19
57 Providence 87
58 Fairfield 68
59 † Florida Int'l 67
74 Boston U. 64
80 ■ Valparaiso 79
78 ■ Colgate 75
70 ■ Army 58
52 Texas A&M 92
73 Prairie View 70
53 New Hampshire 71
43 Yale 58
70 Rider 82
52 ■ Yale 60
50 Rhode Island 90
63 Cornell 74
53 Columbia 86
54 ■ Pennsylvania 89
48 ■ Princeton 41
60 Dartmouth 70
72 Harvard 71
69 ■ Columbia 72
72 ■ Cornell 79
74 ■ Harvard 77
64 ■ Dartmouth 65
56 Princeton 60
60 Pennsylvania 70

BRYANT 7-18
73 ■ Rhode Island Col. 66
53 ■ Stonehill 61
68 Bentley 90
66 New Hamp. Col. 79
68 Sacred Heart 96
57 ■ Mercy 64
88 ■ Southern Conn. St. 87
73 ■ Mass.-Lowell 71
54 Springfield 67
89 ■ Quinnipiac 85
63 ■ St. Michael's 85
79 ■ Assumption 71
71 St. Anselm 88
72 American Int'l 89
66 Stonehill 88
72 ■ Merrimack 70
84 Teikyo-Post 96
56 ■ Bentley 65
62 Quinnipiac 65
69 St. Michael's 78
119 Assumption 110
62 ■ St. Anselm 69
69 ■ American Int'l 75
78 Merrimack 79
73 ■ Springfield 77

BUCKNELL 23-6
97 ■ Mt. St. Mary's (Md.) 73
60 Montana 63

88 † North Texas 64
83 ■ Delaware 71
73 George Mason 60
57 New Orleans 90
65 Cornell 73
75 Loyola (Md.) 59
68 Canisius 69
92 ■ Colgate 83
69 Fordham 65
87 ■ Lafayette 74
83 ■ Army 57
68 Navy 61
94 ■ Lycoming 62
91 ■ Lehigh 75
86 Holy Cross 88
78 ■ Rider 76
65 Colgate 63
77 ■ Fordham 63
84 Lafayette 65
82 Army 63
93 ■ Navy 64
90 Lehigh 80
116 ■ Loyola (Md.) 85
112 ■ Holy Cross 99
69 ■ Lehigh 65
75 ■ Colgate 73
73 ■ Holy Cross 98

BUFFALO 5-22

36 Iowa St. 106
66 Northern Iowa 96
51 ■ St. Francis (Pa.) 56
60 ■ Jacksonville 75
76 Niagara 92
70 ■ Maine 83
70 Colgate 77
72 ■ Loyola (Cal.) 76
72 Central Fla. 68
82 Stetson 89
70 Jacksonville 63
52 Coppin St. 69
64 ■ N.C.-Greensboro ... 62
50 Colorado 93
89 Youngstown St. ... 104
68 Duquesne 81
64 ■ Wagner 69
74 ■ Niagara 89
54 ■ Colgate 55
76 ■ Youngstown St. 64
74 ■ Central Conn. St. ... 57
52 Maine 81
67 ■ Massachusetts 96
64 Wagner 90
69 ■ Cleveland St. 76
61 ■ Va. Commonwealth 90
78 Central Conn. St. ... 83

BUFFALO ST. 21-6

55 ■ St. Norbert 60
80 ■ Daemen 63
57 † Westminster (Pa.) .. 56
60 Allegheny 64
83 ■ Fredonia St. 78
90 ■ Cortland St. 74
66 Brockport St. 54
84 ■ Utica Tech 76
69 ■ Albany (N.Y.) 44
94 ■ King's (N.Y.) 67
66 ■ Ripon 48
73 Plattsburgh St. 65
86 Potsdam St. 66
40 Geneseo St. 65
71 ■ Oswego St. 55
48 ■ Penn St.-Behrend .. 45
85 Binghamton 79
48 ■ Brockport St. 42
88 Utica Tech 61
101 ■ Oneonta St. 70
76 ■ New Paltz St. 62
61 Fredonia St. 75
68 ■ Geneseo St. 56
67 Oswego St. 47
72 † Cortland St. 52
55 Binghamton 56

69 Geneseo St. 80

BUTLER 11-17

56 Indiana St. 70
90 ■ Anderson 50
53 Illinois St. 69
64 Wis.-Green Bay 76
56 ■ North Caro. 103
63 ■ Ball St. 49
48 † Indiana 90
91 † St. Francis (N.Y.) ... 60
54 Purdue 80
81 ■ Valparaiso 62
64 ■ La Salle 59
62 ■ Evansville 77
70 ■ Notre Dame 56
59 Xavier (Ohio) 63
70 Dayton 66
62 N.C.-Charlotte 70
86 ■ Duquesne 80
82 ■ Detroit Mercy 85
68 ■ Loyola (Ill.) 51
64 Duquesne 78
66 La Salle 88
74 ■ Dayton 59
66 ■ Xavier (Ohio) 80
72 Evansville 84
65 Loyola (Ill.) 66
65 Detroit Mercy 71
77 † La Salle 70
71 † Evansville 74

CABRINI 20-6

91 † Hampden-Sydney .. 78
94 Dickinson 90
77 Lebanon Valley ... 102
75 Elizabethtown 80
88 † Penn St.-Harrisburg 75
78 ■ Rowan 85
103 ■ Gwynedd Mercy 64
106 ■ Wilmington (Del.) ... 91
101 † Rosary 95
86 † Siena Heights 85
89 † St. Rose 76
49 † Xavier (La.) 57
101 Beaver 88
91 ■ Clarion 101
76 ■ Misericordia 59
91 Alvernia 83
105 ■ Eastern (Pa.) 85
64 Gwynedd Mercy 63
104 Wilmington (Del.) ... 95
85 Eastern (Pa.) 70
57 Allentown 58
73 Misericordia 70
87 ■ Beaver 64
75 ■ Alvernia 71
82 ■ Misericordia 73
73 ■ Alvernia 53

CALIFORNIA 21-9

89 ■ Cal St. Sacramento . 65
80 ■ Oklahoma St. 65
89 San Francisco 79
80 Santa Clara 73
81 ■ Wake Forest 65
75 † James Madison 90
54 † Cornell 74
84 ■ Texas Southern 69
82 ■ Oregon 65
63 ■ Oregon St. 64
83 ■ Stanford 66
65 Southern Cal 67
104 UCLA 82
79 ■ Washington 65
75 ■ Washington St. 83
83 Arizona St. 90
81 Arizona 93
92 ■ Cal St. Northridge .. 68
86 Stanford 61
86 ■ Southern Cal 83
71 ■ UCLA 85
76 Washington St. 67
76 Washington 75

74 † Arizona 71
91 † Arizona St. 67
78 Oregon St. 72
79 Oregon 76
66 † Louisiana St. 64
82 † Duke 77
76 † Kansas 93

CALIF. (PA.) 23-6

77 † Wheeling Jesuit 91
85 † Pitt.-Johnstown 77
97 ■ West Liberty St. 69
86 Mercyhurst 89
82 ■ Mansfield 75
96 ■ Southern Conn. St. . 71
87 ■ Davis & Elkins 59
74 † Seattle 65
68 Seattle Pacific 63
76 ■ Geneva 77
97 ■ Columbia Union 56
104 ■ Juniata 48
87 Norfolk St. 80
92 Pitt.-Johnstown 78
91 ■ Clarion 88
79 ■ Indiana (Pa.) 83
82 Slippery Rock 67
84 Shippensburg 74
91 Edinboro 89
76 ■ Lock Haven 63
108 Clarion 91
90 Indiana (Pa.) 89
87 ■ Slippery Rock 85
83 ■ Shippensburg 74
101 ■ Edinboro 83
82 Lock Haven 70
82 † Bloomsburg 79
84 Millersville 97
77 Millersville 86

CAL LUTHERAN 20-7

60 † UC Santa Cruz 61
76 Menlo 62
133 Pacific Union 43
88 ■ UC Santa Cruz 64
116 ■ La Sierra 50
108 ■ Dominican (Cal.) ... 73
92 ■ Westmont 74
82 UC San Diego 97
70 ■ Capital 65
67 Biola 80
120 ■ Pacific Christian 85
78 La Verne 74
91 ■ Claremont-M-S 84
79 ■ Whittier 69
57 Pomona-Pitzer 54
99 ■ Redlands 86
92 Cal Tech 53
89 Occidental 80
75 ■ La Verne 83
78 Claremont-M-S 72
61 Whittier 57
92 ■ Pomona-Pitzer 61
102 Redlands 103
99 ■ Cal Tech 46
66 ■ Occidental 55
79 † La Verne 83
56 La Verne 67

CAL POLY POMONA 14-13

103 ■ Dominican (Cal.) ... 55
78 ■ Biola 69
68 San Diego St. 72
94 ■ Cal St. Hayward 83
80 ■ Sonoma St. 68
80 ■ Notre Dame (Cal.) .. 74
78 San Fran. St. 81
61 UC Davis 72
64 † Humboldt St. 63
91 † Emporia St. 100
81 Cal St. Chico 92
101 ■ Pacific Christian 55
56 Cal St. Dom. Hills .. 74
88 Chapman 107
65 ■ Cal St. San B'dino .. 63

65 UC Riverside 75
77 ■ Cal Poly SLO 59
62 ■ Cal St. Bakersfield . 76
68 Cal St. Los Angeles 61
59 Cal St. Bakersfield . 71
69 Cal Poly SLO 65
76 ■ UC Riverside 80
66 Cal St. San B'dino .. 83
76 ■ Chapman 70
60 ■ Cal St. Dom. Hills .. 56
89 ■ Cal St. Los Angeles 76
48 † UC Riverside 70

CAL POLY SLO 9-17

87 ■ Azusa-Pacific 98
76 Westmont 82
90 UC Davis 83
81 Cal St. Hayward 75
86 ■ La Verne 82
98 ■ Morningside 103
57 ■ Fresno Pacific 74
89 ■ Notre Dame (Cal.) . 100
94 ■ Augustana (Ill.) 83
84 ■ St. Ambrose 62
56 Cal St. Bakersfield . 90
62 UC Riverside 100
74 Cal St. San B'dino .. 87
87 ■ UC Santa Cruz 67
89 ■ Chapman 83
65 ■ Cal St. Dom. Hills .. 68
59 Cal Poly Pomona ... 77
78 Cal St. Los Ang. .. 101
53 ■ Cal St. Bakersfield . 69
69 ■ Cal St. Los Angeles 64
65 ■ Cal Poly Pomona ... 69
63 Cal St. Dom. Hills .. 85
81 Chapman 91
85 ■ Cal St. San B'dino .. 97
80 ■ UC Riverside 79
56 Cal St. Bakersfield . 87

CAL ST. BAKERSFIELD 33-0

100 Cal St. Stanislaus .. 80
92 San Fran. St. 86
71 ■ UC Davis 62
66 ■ Master's 65
73 Fresno Pacific 56
88 ■ Grand Canyon 81
85 ■ Southern Colo. 65
84 ■ Mo. Western St. 63
84 ■ Azusa-Pacific 65
90 ■ St. Ambrose 62
82 ■ Augustana (Ill.) 70
90 ■ Cal Poly SLO 56
81 Cal St. San B'dino .. 62
80 UC Riverside 75
73 ■ Cal St. Dom. Hills .. 69
102 ■ Chapman 81
93 Cal St. Los Angeles 80
76 Cal Poly Pomona ... 62
69 Cal Poly SLO 53
71 ■ Cal Poly Pomona ... 59
75 ■ Cal St. Los Angeles 61
74 Chapman 56
62 Cal St. Dom. Hills .. 60
92 ■ UC Riverside 74
85 ■ Cal St. San B'dino .. 72
87 ■ Cal Poly SLO 56
65 ■ Cal St. Dom. Hills .. 59
64 ■ UC Riverside 61
98 ■ Grand Canyon 68
78 ■ Alas. Anchorage ... 59
86 † N.C. Central 80
61 † Wayne St. (Mich.) .. 57
85 † Troy St. 72

CAL ST. CHICO 23-7

81 Puget Sound 74
99 Southern Ore. St. .. 77
75 UC Santa Cruz 79
67 Washington 130
82 Oregon Tech 80
78 Western Mont. 69

78 Eastern Mont. 75
105 ■ Dominican (Cal.) 74
93 ■ Chapman 92
83 ■ Alas. Fairbanks 92
92 ■ Cal Poly Pomona 81
81 ■ Quincy 77
55 UC Davis 52
92 Sonoma St. 77
90 ■ Notre Dame (Cal.) 81
76 ■ San Fran. St. 73
96 Cal St. Stanislaus 101
84 Cal St. Hayward 83
64 Humboldt St. 59
101 ■ Cal St. Hayward 97
82 ■ Cal St. Stanislaus 66
78 San Fran. St. 73
72 Notre Dame (Cal.) 65
88 ■ Sonoma St. 73
70 ■ UC Davis 75
89 ■ Humboldt St. 83
80 ■ San Fran. St. 77
86 ■ Cal St. Stanislaus 80
70 † Alas. Anchorage 72
98 † Grand Canyon 103

CAL ST. DOM. HILLS 16-10
100 † Central Okla. 123
85 † Bridgeport 66
81 Biola 70
60 ■ Pt. Loma Nazarene 58
84 ■ La Verne 46
68 † Mo. Western St. 71
54 † Southern Colo. 51
56 ■ Cal St. Hayward 40
57 ■ Capital 54
65 ■ Christian Heritage 54
74 ■ Cal Poly Pomona 56
62 ■ Cal St. Los Angeles 65
69 Cal St. Bakersfield 73
68 Cal Poly SLO 65
64 ■ Cal St. San B'dino 53
73 ■ UC Riverside 82
66 Master's 60
92 Chapman 79
51 UC Riverside 64
69 Cal St. San B'dino 66
85 ■ Cal Poly SLO 63
60 ■ Cal St. Bakersfield 62
51 Cal St. Los Angeles 57
56 Cal Poly Pomona 60
70 ■ Chapman 62
59 Cal St. Bakersfield 65

CAL ST. FULLERTON 15-12
82 ■ St. Mary's (Cal.) 62
66 Northern Iowa 55
73 Drake 86
75 Cal St. Northridge 68
86 ■ Eastern Ill. 60
92 ■ Chapman 71
82 UCLA 90
65 Nevada-Las Vegas 78
67 New Mexico St. 78
81 ■ Nevada 62
91 ■ Utah St. 71
61 UC Irvine 59
58 Long Beach St. 72
72 UC Santa Barb. 68
66 ■ San Jose St. 61
71 ■ Pacific (Cal.) 58
61 Utah St. 86
72 Nevada 60
63 ■ Houston 77
86 ■ UC Irvine 88
68 ■ Long Beach St. 61
66 ■ UC Santa Barb. 64
53 Pacific (Cal.) 56
58 San Jose St. 60
70 ■ New Mexico St. 78
84 ■ Nevada-Las Vegas 83
68 Long Beach St. 80

CAL ST. HAYWARD 5-20
83 ■ Fresno Pacific 78
74 Menlo 85

76 Cal St. Los Ang. 104
83 Cal Poly Pomona 94
82 ■ Lewis-Clark St. 97
66 ■ Bethany (Cal.) 79
75 ■ Cal Poly SLO 81
57 ■ Westmont 80
55 ■ UC Riverside 65
40 Cal St. Dom. Hills 56
54 San Diego 78
63 Notre Dame (Cal.) 60
59 ■ San Fran. St. 63
62 ■ UC Davis 56
71 Sonoma St. 76
49 ■ Humboldt St. 52
83 ■ Cal St. Chico 84
79 Cal St. Stanislaus 98
97 Cal St. Chico 101
48 Humboldt St. 64
82 ■ Sonoma St. 66
51 UC Davis 68
72 ■ Notre Dame (Cal.) 65
61 San Fran. St. 82
81 ■ Cal St. Stanislaus 91

CAL ST. NORTHRIDGE 10-17
67 Fresno St. 77
60 UC Santa Barb. 67
60 † Eastern Wash. 61
76 Northern Ariz. 67
66 † Loyola (Cal.) 71
65 † Stetson 61
68 ■ Cal St. Fullerton 75
73 UCLA 80
55 Montana 63
65 Montana St. 64
62 ■ Loyola (Cal.) 53
90 ■ Quincy 79
87 ■ Northern Ariz. 86
92 ■ Tex. Wesleyan 62
65 Wis.-Milwaukee 78
64 Boise St. 79
63 Ala.-Birmingham 75
65 Southern Utah 90
54 Missouri 65
80 ■ Cal St. Sacramento 73
68 California 92
65 ■ Southern Utah 63
74 ■ Wis.-Milwaukee 75
60 Cal St. Sacramento 63
61 ■ St. Mary's (Cal.) 69
81 ■ Long Beach St. 78
51 San Diego 82

CAL ST. SACRAMENTO 3-24
65 California 89
45 Utah 74
65 Drake 86
55 Portland 83
33 Stanford 68
38 ■ Montana 53
61 ■ Loyola (Cal.) 66
57 ■ UC Santa Barb. 64
53 ■ Montana St. 72
61 Idaho 81
56 Washington St. 87
69 ■ Boise St. 83
71 ■ Northern Ariz. 78
63 ■ St. Mary's (Cal.) 62
59 ■ Portland 63
61 N.C.-Greensboro 62
60 N.C.-Wilmington 73
70 Nebraska 86
44 Wis.-Milwaukee 96
68 Southern Utah 87
64 Northern Ariz. 68
73 Cal St. Northridge 80
71 ■ Idaho 76
63 ■ Cal St. Northridge 60
82 ■ UC Davis 76
78 Brigham Young 128
76 ■ Wis.-Milwaukee 78

CAL ST. SAN B'DINO 13-12
100 ■ East Tex. St. 79

75 ■ Humboldt St. 72
106 ■ Master's 90
133 † Pacific Christian 71
75 Notre Dame (Cal.) 69
79 San Fran. St. 84
78 † Central Mo. St. 84
76 Metropolitan St. 79
105 ■ Christian Heritage 80
81 ■ Azusa-Pacific 93
78 ■ Sonoma St. 77
62 ■ Cal St. Bakersfield 81
87 ■ Cal Poly SLO 74
63 Cal Poly Pomona 65
69 ■ Cal St. Los Angeles 72
53 Cal St. Dom. Hills 64
76 Chapman 92
65 ■ UC Riverside 64
90 ■ Chapman 66
66 ■ Cal St. Dom. Hills 69
87 Cal St. Los Angeles 73
83 ■ Cal Poly Pomona 66
97 Cal Poly SLO 85
72 Cal St. Bakersfield 85
75 UC Riverside 100

CAL ST. STANISLAUS 20-8
80 ■ Cal St. Bakersfield 100
98 ■ Azusa-Pacific 105
71 ■ Christ-Irvine 70
87 ■ Christian Heritage 61
73 Sheldon Jackson 51
93 Sheldon Jackson 84
65 Seattle Pacific 85
85 ■ San Jose Christian 59
96 Fresno Pacific 86
84 ■ Dordt 68
77 ■ American Int'l 73
80 Santa Clara 93
105 San Fran. St. 90
102 ■ Notre Dame (Cal.) 107
95 ■ Sonoma St. 78
79 UC Davis 73
101 ■ Cal St. Chico 96
60 ■ Humboldt St. 57
98 ■ Cal St. Hayward 79
80 Humboldt St. 59
66 Cal St. Chico 82
63 ■ UC Davis 66
89 Sonoma St. 79
92 ■ San Fran. St. 63
82 Notre Dame (Cal.) 80
91 Cal St. Hayward 81
85 ■ UC Davis 71
80 Cal St. Chico 86

CAL TECH 7-15
64 ■ LIFE Bible 41
59 ■ Holy Names 45
53 ■ Amer. Indian Bib. 60
77 ■ Southern Ariz. Bible 29
61 ■ La Sierra 55
54 ■ Fontbonne 52
66 Cal Maritime 42
78 Pacific Union 61
49 Whittier 81
30 Pomona-Pitzer 65
33 ■ La Verne 81
41 Claremont-M-S 64
39 ■ Occidental 82
53 ■ Cal Lutheran 92
76 Redlands 94
45 ■ Whittier 65
52 ■ Pomona-Pitzer 65
28 La Verne 76
46 ■ Claremont-M-S 72
46 Cal Lutheran 99
55 Occidental 84
59 ■ Redlands 75

UC DAVIS 13-14
74 ■ Bethany (Cal.) 60
62 Cal St. Bakersfield 71
73 ■ Lewis & Clark 83
83 ■ Cal Poly SLO 90
74 ■ Chapman 69

72 Cal St. Los Angeles 75
60 Fresno Pacific 63
72 ■ Cal Poly Pomona 61
65 Pacific (Cal.) 77
71 ■ Menlo 59
59 ■ UC Santa Cruz 61
52 ■ Cal St. Chico 55
66 ■ Humboldt St. 74
56 Cal St. Hayward 62
73 ■ Cal St. Stanislaus 79
55 Notre Dame (Cal.) 47
76 ■ San Fran. St. 57
87 ■ Sonoma St. 48
62 ■ Notre Dame (Cal.) 64
87 San Fran. St. 75
66 Cal St. Stanislaus 63
68 ■ Cal St. Hayward 51
62 Humboldt St. 50
75 Cal St. Chico 70
76 Cal St. Sacramento 82
71 Sonoma St. 56
71 Cal St. Stanislaus 85

UC IRVINE 6-21
76 Boston U. 79
85 Mo.-Kansas City 86
90 † Mississippi Val. 83
97 Nevada-Las Vegas 115
111 ■ Southern Cal Col. 77
60 ■ Georgetown 64
65 Tulane 86
78 Houston 86
65 ■ Utah St. 70
67 ■ Nevada 71
59 ■ Cal St. Fullerton 61
67 New Mexico St. 72
62 ■ Pacific (Cal.) 68
73 ■ San Jose St. 64
58 ■ UC Santa Barb. 67
82 Nevada 79
70 Utah St. 81
88 Cal St. Fullerton 86
67 UC Santa Barb. 85
74 ■ Long Beach St. 88
67 Hofstra 77
67 San Jose St. 62
56 Pacific (Cal.) 65
67 Long Beach St. 84
74 ■ Nevada-Las Vegas 96
74 ■ New Mexico St. 76
76 † New Mexico St. 87

UC RIVERSIDE 20-8
79 ■ Cal Baptist 65
81 ■ East Tex. St. 64
86 † Fresno Pacific 64
77 † Azusa-Pacific 91
93 ■ UC Santa Cruz 59
86 ■ Christian Heritage 58
65 Cal St. Hayward 55
68 Sonoma St. 58
52 San Diego St. 63
74 ■ Taylor 55
62 † Biola 51
65 Grand Canyon 105
100 ■ Cal Poly SLO 62
75 ■ Cal St. Bakersfield 80
82 Cal St. Los Angeles 79
75 ■ Cal Poly Pomona 65
116 ■ Chapman 77
82 Cal St. Dom. Hills 73
64 Cal St. San B'dino 65
64 ■ Cal St. Dom. Hills 51
77 Chapman 56
80 Cal Poly Pomona 76
87 ■ Cal St. Los Angeles 84
74 Cal St. Bakersfield 92
79 Cal Poly SLO 80
100 ■ Cal St. San B'dino 75
70 † Cal Poly Pomona 48
61 Cal St. Bakersfield 64

UC SAN DIEGO 17-8
88 ■ Occidental 74

65	Pomona-Pitzer	69
74	■ Pt. Loma Nazarene	90
73	■ Christian Heritage	63
66	† Cal Baptist	62
71	† Lewis & Clark	73
71	† Menlo	77
101	Whittier	89
97	■ Cal Lutheran	82
75	■ La Verne	77
39	Oregon St.	97
127	Redlands	112
105	■ Haverford	65
73	■ Rowan	75
73	UC Santa Cruz	62
99	Bethany (Cal.)	96
76	Pt. Loma Nazarene	70
107	■ Dominican (Cal.)	73
91	■ Christian Heritage	85
91	■ UC Santa Cruz	38
79	Menlo	75
102	Dominican (Cal.)	94
75	Christ-Irvine	80
83	■ Bethany (Cal.)	74
81	■ Menlo	66

UC SANTA BARB. 18-11

67	■ Cal St. Northridge	60
70	■ Stephen F. Austin	39
60	Pepperdine	55
79	St. Mary's (Cal.)	37
64	Cal St. Sacramento	57
65	■ Coppin St.	55
59	■ Kansas St.	60
67	Pacific (Cal.)	66
77	■ Ala.-Birmingham	57
69	■ New Mexico St.	71
65	Utah St.	75
58	Nevada	64
61	■ Long Beach St.	60
68	■ Cal St. Fullerton	72
64	New Mexico St.	75
68	Long Beach St.	59
67	UC Irvine	58
69	Nevada-Las Vegas	82
93	■ Nevada	60
75	■ Utah St.	77
85	■ UC Irvine	67
64	Cal St. Fullerton	66
86	■ Nevada-Las Vegas	83
67	San Jose St.	62
73	■ Pacific (Cal.)	65
72	■ San Jose St.	59
57	† Pacific (Cal.)	54
77	† New Mexico St.	82
50	■ Pepperdine	53

CALVIN 25-3

81	Alas. Fairbanks	71
103	† Oklahoma City	107
61	■ North Park	54
80	■ Oakland	71
84	■ Grand Valley St.	70
70	Ferris St.	66
107	† West Va. St.	65
77	Malone	66
91	Aquinas	67
98	† Embry-Riddle	78
69	† Alas. Anchorage	64
65	■ Albion	68
76	Kalamazoo	62
97	Adrian	58
108	■ Alma	55
94	Olivet	71
89	■ Hope	72
70	Albion	67
81	Hope	75
105	■ Olivet	80
91	■ Adrian	52
86	Alma	68
96	■ Kalamazoo	90
77	■ Hope	69
74	■ Albion	72
90	■ Otterbein	68
101	Emory & Henry	67

56	† Ohio Northern	67

CAMERON 11-17

78	† Pittsburg St.	66
96	Fort Hays St.	77
87	■ Oklahoma S&A	88
82	Phillips (Okla.)	88
83	† Mesa St.	94
76	Southern Colo.	89
67	Midwestern St.	90
75	† Okla. Baptist	91
58	Pittsburg St.	78
84	Oklahoma S&A	83
99	■ Central Okla.	121
91	■ Lubbock Chrst.	82
85	Eastern N. Mex.	110
83	Lubbock Chrst.	82
99	■ Abilene Christian	90
96	■ Angelo St.	72
81	■ East Tex. St.	64
85	■ Tex. A&M-Kingsville	75
78	Tex. A&M-Kingsville	96
64	East Tex. St.	67
84	■ Eastern N. Mex.	110
85	■ Midwestern St.	79
57	Angelo St.	75
80	Abilene Christian	108
68	Hardin-Simmons	69
88	Central Okla.	129
76	† East Tex. St.	72
69	† Eastern N. Mex.	75

CAMPBELL 12-15

72	■ N.C.-Greensboro	54
79	■ Methodist	50
48	■ Coker	54
71	Louisiana St.	93
59	Southwestern La.	74
61	† Alcorn St.	85
59	William & Mary	75
70	■ N.C.-Wilmington	87
56	Towson St.	61
87	■ Radford	84
50	■ Liberty	70
75	Md.-Balt. County	70
75	N.C.-Greensboro	77
79	■ Barton	82
75	N.C.-Asheville	62
70	■ Md.-Balt. County	65
63	■ Towson St.	61
89	Radford	84
63	Liberty	73
90	■ N.C.-Asheville	65
81	Charleston So.	64
92	■ Winthrop	84
66	■ Coastal Caro.	71
80	■ Charleston So.	83
96	Winthrop	95
50	Coastal Caro.	80
67	† Md.-Balt. County	85

CANISIUS 10-18

62	Duke	110
67	■ St. Bonaventure	85
61	† Robert Morris	63
74	■ St. Francis (Pa.)	52
77	Colgate	89
66	Northeastern	76
84	■ Loyola (Ill.)	66
69	■ Bucknell	68
53	Loyola (Md.)	48
85	George Mason	67
60	■ Manhattan	64
56	Cornell	63
68	■ Iona	49
62	St. Bonaventure	67
64	Iona	77
59	■ Niagara	70
42	Siena	70
64	■ Loyola (Md.)	53
50	■ Fairfield	51
72	St. Peter's	66
55	Manhattan	75
41	Tulane	63
66	Fairfield	81
62	Niagara	72
67	■ Siena	74
67	■ St. Peter's	55
64	† Iona	62
59	† Niagara	64

CAPITAL 15-10

75	■ Anderson	68
63	■ Thomas More	60
65	Ohio Wesleyan	62
57	■ Mount Union	50
75	Heidelberg	76
65	Otterbein	68
80	■ Muskingum	69
71	■ Wittenberg	69
54	Cal St. Dom. Hills	57
65	Cal Lutheran	70
84	■ John Carroll	66
72	Baldwin-Wallace	73
60	■ Ohio Northern	66
86	■ Hiram	77
65	Marietta	48
79	Mount Union	72
65	■ Heidelberg	78
87	Muskingum	74
61	Hiram	70
74	■ Otterbein	73
63	Ohio Northern	65
65	■ Baldwin-Wallace	41
89	■ Marietta	58
65	John Carroll	61
71	■ John Carroll	75

CARLETON 17-7

78	■ Wis.-Superior	74
86	† Southern Cal Col.	90
64	Pomona-Pitzer	66
49	Gust. Adolphus	46
71	■ St. Mary's (Minn.)	63
75	Concordia-M'head	64
45	St. Olaf	39
95	■ Macalester	68
65	■ St. John's (Minn.)	66
56	St. Thomas (Minn.)	54
86	■ Bethel (Minn.)	76
52	Augsburg	54
75	■ Hamline	62
78	■ Concordia-M'head	61
67	St. Mary's (Minn.)	65
65	■ Gust. Adolphus	50
62	■ St. Olaf	54
69	Macalester	62
49	St. John's (Minn.)	68
56	■ St. Thomas (Minn.)	55
64	Bethel (Minn.)	69
89	■ Augsburg	73
63	Hamline	55
72	■ St. Thomas (Minn.)	80

CARNEGIE MELLON 16-8

60	■ Grove City	49
66	† Wash. & Jeff.	64
67	Case Reserve	76
82	■ Thiel	56
75	■ Clark (Mass.)	73
76	■ John Carroll	65
53	■ Chicago	49
57	■ Johns Hopkins	56
75	Gettysburg	73
68	Thiel	53
70	■ New York U.	80
74	■ Emory	78
62	Washington (Mo.)	76
53	Chicago	59
60	■ Wash. & Jeff.	47
64	Rochester	52
86	Brandeis	76
78	■ Washington (Mo.)	67
59	Haverford	66
47	■ Rochester	54
78	■ Brandeis	72
61	■ Denison	43
65	New York U.	83
81	Emory	63

CARROLL (WIS.) 4-17

68	Wis.-Stevens Point	102
84	† Quincy	95
70	■ Marian (Wis.)	72
72	■ Lake Forest	69
72	Cardinal Stritch	88
60	Beloit	72
88	Webster	75
71	Lawrence	74
62	Ripon	84
73	■ Wheaton (Ill.)	95
82	■ Knox	87
92	■ Illinois Col.	87
99	■ St. Norbert	89
65	Grinnell	90
82	Coe	89
74	Lakeland	85
83	■ Lawrence	84
48	■ Beloit	77
57	St. Norbert	72
50	Lake Forest	64
50	■ Ripon	71

CARSON-NEWMAN 8-18

91	■ Lee	106
77	■ Tusculum	86
98	King (Tenn.)	97
66	Belmont	99
77	■ Lincoln Memorial	56
91	Catawba	83
66	East Tenn. St.	112
81	Tusculum	90
73	■ Gardner-Webb	70
67	■ Wingate	82
55	Mars Hill	68
57	■ Presbyterian	72
48	Lincoln Memorial	68
67	■ Lenoir-Rhyne	69
61	Elon	64
78	Lees-McRae	70
109	■ Catawba	82
66	Gardner-Webb	76
83	Wingate	91
76	■ King (Tenn.)	74
58	■ Mars Hill	68
61	Presbyterian	87
68	Lenoir-Rhyne	92
86	■ Elon	89
101	■ Lees-McRae	84
69	† Lenoir-Rhyne	87

CARTHAGE 11-13

64	■ Wis.-Parkside	59
82	■ Beloit	66
97	Aurora	77
59	Teikyo Marycrest	67
71	North Park	76
61	Loyola (Ill.)	85
82	Wis.-Whitewater	79
80	† Marian (Wis.)	65
74	■ Trinity (Tex.)	51
88	■ Concordia (Ill.)	71
69	■ Millikin	77
55	■ Wheaton (Ill.)	58
76	Ill. Wesleyan	93
77	■ North Central	67
87	Millikin	72
53	■ North Park	45
70	Augustana (Ill.)	87
82	■ Elmhurst	61
71	■ Ill. Wesleyan	79
65	■ Augustana (Ill.)	82
57	North Central	58
61	Elmhurst	66
68	Valparaiso	84
64	Wheaton (Ill.)	74

CASE RESERVE 10-15

76	■ Carnegie Mellon	67
99	Brandeis	91
69	Allegheny	83
53	Rochester	66
77	■ Emory	75
47	■ Wooster	61

57 ■ Wittenberg 65
72 ■ Johns Hopkins 82
74 Ohio Wesleyan 81
72 ■ Denison 63
81 ■ New York U. 78
41 Kenyon 57
80 ■ Earlham 74
74 ■ Oberlin 63
60 Chicago 65
79 Washington (Mo.) 108
43 Wooster 73
65 Wittenberg 82
87 ■ Kenyon 83
65 Denison 67
73 ■ Allegheny 76
75 Earlham 59
80 Oberlin 71
54 ■ Ohio Wesleyan 68
72 Allegheny 76

CASTLETON ST. 11-12
48 Utica 68
62 † Utica Tech 66
85 ■ Norwich 55
55 Albany (N.Y.) 76
75 ■ Westbrook 71
96 ■ North Adams St. 73
100 † Johnson St. 86
73 ■ Plymouth St. 61
63 Me.-Presque Isle 82
91 Me.-Fort Kent 54
74 Westbrook 103
86 Lyndon St. 58
83 Johnson St. 92
55 ■ Green Mountain 56
81 ■ St. Joseph (Vt.) 78
100 ■ Lyndon St. 62
73 St. Joseph (Vt.) 75
45 Green Mountain 55
63 ■ Johnson St. 53
83 Husson 91
73 Colby-Sawyer 70
76 ■ Plattsburgh St. 90
72 St. Joseph's (Me.) 103

CATAWBA 7-18
87 Concord 100
93 † Davis & Elkins 87
75 Wofford 88
85 Augusta 84
79 † Paine 73
96 ■ Concord 100
78 ■ High Point 96
83 ■ Carson-Newman 91
70 ■ Presbyterian 73
74 Lenoir-Rhyne 76
71 ■ Elon 72
74 Mars Hill 92
81 Wingate 77
112 ■ Lees-McRae 89
74 ■ Gardner-Webb 86
77 ■ Wofford 83
82 Carson-Newman 109
61 Presbyterian 72
74 ■ Lenoir-Rhyne 92
62 Lees-McRae 94
77 Elon 91
81 ■ Mars Hill 86
102 ■ Wingate 99
97 Gardner-Webb 80
78 ■ Presbyterian 79

CATHOLIC 21-6
92 † Brockport St. 89
85 Susquehanna 82
115 ■ Capitol 59
101 Wesley 73
81 † York (N.Y.) 71
82 Mt. St. Vincent 67
75 ■ Wittenberg 77
83 Lebanon Valley 82
80 Scranton 94
106 ■ Wheaton (Mass.) 104
91 ■ Elmira 81
107 ■ Marymount (Va.) 106

68 York (Pa.) 80
87 Salisbury St. 105
65 St. Mary's (Md.) 54
86 Gallaudet 71
67 Goucher 58
93 ■ Mary Washington 87
77 ■ Goucher 57
88 Marymount (Va.) 90
93 ■ Gallaudet 73
87 ■ York (Pa.) 66
89 Mary Washington 63
85 ■ St. Mary's (Md.) 71
76 ■ Mary Washington 74
76 ■ York (Pa.) 70
91 ■ Stockton St. 106

CENTENARY 9-18
115 ■ Wiley 79
62 † N.C.-Charlotte 81
92 † Valparaiso 89
100 Texas Christian 85
69 ■ Louisiana Tech 82
90 ■ East Tex. Bapt. 64
102 Northwestern (La.) 113
61 Auburn 86
96 Colorado 117
87 ■ Southeastern La. 84
73 ■ Central Fla. 86
86 Grambling 89
89 ■ Mercer 82
111 ■ Dallas 79
77 Stetson 81
59 Florida Int'l 62
57 ■ Samford 60
111 ■ Georgia St. 107
85 ■ Grambling 106
71 Southeastern La. 76
85 Central Fla. 94
82 Mercer 93
82 ■ Ouachita Bapt. 97
82 ■ Stetson 95
84 ■ Florida Int'l 81
84 Samford 96
80 Georgia St. 97

CENTRAL (IOWA) 10-15
73 BYU-Hawaii 85
73 † Hawaii Pacific 110
86 † Westmont 94
70 ■ Neb. Wesleyan 83
71 ■ Teikyo Marycrest 51
65 N'western (Iowa) 83
75 Dordt 72
70 Augustana (Ill.) 98
80 Coe 66
61 ■ Wartburg 79
73 ■ Buena Vista 75
73 Upper Iowa 69
57 Loras 62
73 Dubuque 82
57 Luther 69
67 ■ William Penn 53
73 ■ Simpson 63
74 Buena Vista 80
71 ■ Luther 61
76 ■ Dubuque 82
66 Wartburg 65
88 Simpson 96
71 ■ Upper Iowa 67
78 William Penn 54
58 ■ Loras 77

CENTRAL ARK. 20-8
65 † Tex. A&M-Kingsville 64
75 Central Mo. St. 86
91 ■ Ark.-Pine Bluff 82
53 † Eastern N. Mex. 71
64 West Tex. A&M 62
88 ■ Ark. Baptist 72
80 East Tex. St. 74
84 ■ Oklahoma City 75
84 ■ East Tex. St. 61
71 Arkansas Tech 86
73 ■ Ouachita Bapt. 68
86 ■ Arkansas Col. 89
90 Ark.-Monticello 92
88 ■ Harding 72
87 Henderson St. 74
81 ■ Ozarks (Ark.) 78
82 Southern Ark. 74
77 ■ Arkansas Tech 63
100 Ouachita Bapt. 88
88 ■ Ark.-Monticello 78
80 Harding 72
83 ■ Henderson St. 70
81 Ark.-Pine Bluff 56
79 Ozarks (Ark.) 96
72 ■ Southern Ark. 68
74 Arkansas Col. 61
57 ■ Arkansas Col. 67
66 † Central Wash. 78

CENTRAL CONN. ST. 8-19
82 ■ Queens (N.Y.) 74
52 Massachusetts 78
93 ■ Liberty 79
62 ■ Maine 83
84 † Va. Military 77
81 Marist 101
103 ■ Adelphi 96
67 ■ Md.-East. Shore 68
58 Iowa 104
93 ■ Winthrop 101
81 ■ Skidmore 66
72 Boston U. 76
53 Hartford 83
92 ■ North Adams St. 44
90 Winthrop 106
53 Louisiana St. 86
56 Kansas St. 81
89 Delaware St. 90
86 ■ Vermont 94
72 ■ Hofstra 80
57 Buffalo 74
87 New Hampshire 77
61 Hofstra 86
88 ■ Colgate 103
81 ■ Delaware St. 82
82 Vermont 95
83 ■ Buffalo 78

CENTRAL FLA. 10-17
99 ■ Winthrop 91
79 ■ Fla. Atlantic 62
81 South Fla. 92
78 ■ Mercer 81
68 Florida A&M 66
66 N.C.-Greensboro 78
81 ■ Grambling 85
73 ■ McNeese St. 77
78 ■ Maine 67
68 ■ Buffalo 72
72 ■ N.C.-Greensboro 66
52 Samford 65
86 Centenary 73
62 ■ Florida A&M 52
81 Stetson 98
63 ■ Samford 69
72 ■ South Fla. 77
91 Southern-B.R. 127
65 Charleston (S.C.) 74
72 ■ Florida Int'l 77
91 Fla. Atlantic 80
94 ■ Centenary 85
84 Mercer 93
59 ■ Charleston (S.C.) 62
100 ■ Southern-B.R. 127
74 Florida Int'l 60
82 ■ Stetson 95

CENTRAL MICH. 8-18
91 ■ Lake Superior St. 62
66 † Geo. Washington 87
84 Stetson 83
74 † Ga. Southern 89
61 † Southeast Mo. St. 74
69 Michigan 94
99 Northeastern Ill. 92
71 ■ Eastern Mich. 64
67 Toledo 81
74 ■ Kent 75
48 Ball St. 73
43 ■ Miami (Ohio) 59
53 Western Mich. 69
86 ■ Siena Heights 84
91 ■ Ohio 81
64 Akron 62
99 Bowling Green 105
109 ■ Toledo 115
71 Kent 105
81 ■ Ball St. 84
68 Miami (Ohio) 87
79 ■ Western Mich. 99
51 Ohio 66
75 ■ Akron 59
64 ■ Bowling Green 73
80 Eastern Mich. 92

CENTRAL MO. ST. 13-14
79 ■ Indianapolis 76
86 ■ Central Ark. 75
65 ■ Rockhurst 69
59 Bellarmine 62
76 ■ Drury 66
88 ■ Monmouth (Ill.) 57
84 † Cal St. San B'dino 78
97 † Adams St. 95
53 Fla. Southern 75
84 Tampa 81
69 Emporia St. 67
82 Lincoln (Mo.) 90
69 ■ Washburn 73
93 ■ Missouri-Rolla 96
81 ■ Northeast Mo. St. 66
81 Northwest Mo. St. 64
75 ■ Emporia St. 83
67 ■ Mo. Western St. 66
60 Washburn 80
90 Mo.-St. Louis 74
60 Northeast Mo. St. 74
67 ■ Northwest Mo. St. 73
53 Mo. Western St. 74
76 ■ Pittsburg St. 58
68 Mo. Southern St. 82
71 ■ Southwest Baptist 88
71 Mo. Western St. 95

CENTRAL OKLA. 23-6
90 ■ Southwestern Okla. 71
123 † Cal St. Dom. Hills 100
108 Grand Canyon 110
104 ■ Midwestern St. 103
137 ■ Paul Quinn 80
92 † Mo. Western St. 100
131 Northwest Mo. St. 88
132 Tabor 113
114 † Millersville 101
123 † Slippery Rock 84
125 ■ Benedictine 116
123 † Troy St. 114
86 † Fla. Atlantic 79
121 Cameron 99
119 Eastern N. Mex. 108
167 ■ Bapt. Christian 77
104 ■ Angelo St. 84
119 ■ Abilene Christian 117
100 Midwestern St. 108
90 ■ Tex. A&M-Kingsville 95
122 ■ East Tex. St. 85
113 East Tex. St. 82
85 Tex. A&M-Kingsville 88
111 ■ Eastern N. Mex. 109
128 Abilene Christian 118
93 Angelo St. 89
129 ■ Cameron 88
88 ■ Washburn 92
116 ■ Mo. Southern St. 109

CENTRE 16-9
81 ■ Rose-Hulman 63
96 ■ Fisk 86
81 ■ DePauw 69
78 Maryville (Tenn.) 79

63 Rose-Hulman 78
72 † Roanoke 98
79 † Hanover 78
79 ■ Maryville (Tenn.) 82
64 † Hanover 80
81 ■ Transylvania 72
72 Trinity (Tex.) 60
96 Hendrix 82
72 Oglethorpe 69
94 Sewanee 75
75 ■ Millsaps 81
72 ■ Rhodes 74
63 Wilmington (Ohio) 74
75 ■ Oglethorpe 70
75 ■ Sewanee 64
81 Transylvania 69
92 Fisk 81
76 Millsaps 69
69 Rhodes 71
107 ■ Trinity (Tex.) 58
85 ■ Hendrix 82

CHADRON ST. 12-16
108 ■ Minot St. 71
95 Minot St. 100
88 † Dickinson St. 84
75 ■ South Dak. Tech 70
80 South Dak. Tech 84
75 ■ Black Hills St. 87
92 Regis (Colo.) 106
73 ■ Denver 69
74 ■ Regis (Colo.) 77
62 Montana St. 106
81 Neb.-Kearney 86
88 Fort Hays St. 91
82 Colorado Mines 62
74 Denver 89
79 ■ Mesa St. 83
75 ■ Western St. 83
56 Black Hills St. 66
116 Adams St. 106
97 N.M. Highlands 71
79 ■ Neb.-Kearney 113
68 Mesa St. 75
72 Western St. 102
83 ■ Adams St. 82
94 ■ N.M. Highlands 91
97 ■ Fort Hays St. 77
83 ■ Colorado Mines 75
95 ■ Colorado Mines 83
62 † Mesa St. 78

CHAMINADE 16-12
84 ■ Oakland City 72
90 ■ South Dak. St. 99
56 † Memphis St. 64
88 † Oklahoma 105
71 † Stanford 63
80 † Idaho 84
55 † Missouri 80
93 Hawaii-Hilo 82
92 ■ Pac. Lutheran 88
93 ■ Neb. Wesleyan 76
88 ■ Simon Fraser 83
86 ■ Metropolitan St. 77
79 Hawaii-Hilo 77
100 Hawaii Pacific 104
78 ■ Eastern Mont. 74
102 ■ Grand Canyon 94
84 ■ Seattle Pacific 77
76 Alas. Anchorage 71
88 Alas. Fairbanks 107
71 ■ Hawaii-Hilo 67
60 BYU-Hawaii 63
85 ■ Alas. Anchorage 81
75 Eastern Mont. 88
80 Grand Canyon 79
75 Seattle Pacific 112
76 ■ Hawaii Pacific 92
80 ■ BYU-Hawaii 100
101 ■ Alas. Fairbanks 89

CHAPMAN 7-19
132 ■ Pacific Christian 79
60 ■ Occidental 63
62 ■ Biola 70
71 Sonoma St. 74
69 UC Davis 74
57 Christ-Irvine 62
106 ■ Southern Cal Col. 105
71 Cal St. Fullerton 92
92 Cal St. Chico 93
99 † Bethany (Cal.) 81
83 † Grand Canyon 106
81 ■ Fresno Pacific 89
83 ■ Cal St. Los Angeles 84
107 ■ Cal Poly Pomona 88
83 Cal Poly SLO 89
81 Cal St. Bakersfield 102
77 UC Riverside 116
92 ■ Cal St. San B'dino 76
79 ■ Cal St. Dom. Hills 92
66 Cal St. San B'dino 90
56 ■ UC Riverside 77
56 ■ Cal St. Bakersfield 74
91 ■ Cal Poly SLO 81
70 Cal Poly Pomona 76
83 Cal St. Los Angeles 77
62 Cal St. Dom. Hills 70

CHARLESTON (S.C.) 19-8
75 ■ Voorhees 50
64 ■ N.C. Wesleyan 42
58 Coppin St. 60
70 ■ Western Caro. 49
68 ■ North Caro. A&T 54
65 ■ Coastal Caro. 60
50 Georgia St. 60
56 Mercer 55
86 ■ Charleston So. 62
84 Georgia Tech 67
97 ■ Md.-Balt. County 61
67 ■ South Caro. St. 62
87 ■ Fla. Atlantic 46
60 ■ N.C.-Greensboro 43
57 Coastal Caro. 58
74 ■ Central Fla. 65
88 ■ Georgia St. 63
76 Charleston So. 73
56 South Caro. St. 77
57 N.C.-Greensboro 70
85 ■ Elon 53
63 N.C.-Wilmington 79
62 ■ Mercer 61
62 Central Fla. 59
55 ■ Citadel 53
68 ■ American 77
58 Virginia 72

CHARLESTON SO. 9-18
54 Citadel 59
35 Marquette 73
136 ■ Allen 52
72 Wisconsin 101
81 ■ Lees-McRae 77
73 ■ Montreat-Anderson 72
70 Radford 95
49 Liberty 60
62 Charleston (S.C.) 86
75 ■ Md.-Balt. County 64
76 ■ Towson St. 87
76 Winthrop 65
67 Md.-Balt. County 82
58 Towson St. 75
74 ■ South Caro. St. 80
58 ■ Liberty 72
60 ■ Radford 71
68 Coastal Caro. 84
92 N.C.-Asheville 99
73 ■ Charleston (S.C.) 76
64 ■ Campbell 81
91 ■ N.C.-Asheville 72
107 ■ Piedmont 71
83 Campbell 80
37 ■ Coastal Caro. 45
94 ■ Winthrop 87
66 ■ Coastal Caro. 79

CHEYNEY 8-18
63 † Lincoln (Pa.) 67
72 ■ LIU-C.W. Post 79
54 † St. Cloud St. 82
82 † Morehouse 83
81 ■ Medgar Evers 66
81 ■ CCNY 52
47 Widener 50
67 Edinboro 86
57 Gannon 66
70 Morehouse 83
88 Morris Brown 63
74 Kutztown 65
74 ■ Bloomsburg 78
83 ■ West Chester 68
68 East Stroudsburg 58
82 ■ New York Tech 83
55 ■ Millersville 66
51 Mansfield 53
91 ■ Columbia Union 81
81 Dist. Columbia 76
60 ■ Kutztown 62
72 Bloomsburg 93
56 West Chester 66
64 ■ East Stroudsburg 72
81 Millersville 101
68 ■ Mansfield 70

CHICAGO 11-14
60 ■ Elmhurst 72
83 Trinity (Ill.) 71
63 Lake Forest 61
50 Northwestern 101
49 Carnegie Mellon 53
75 ■ Illinois Tech 53
72 ■ Concordia (Ill.) 60
72 † Wabash 61
52 Kalamazoo 67
63 Ill. Wesleyan 91
63 ■ Brandeis 66
37 ■ Rochester 53
41 Johns Hopkins 54
54 ■ North Park 56
65 ■ Case Reserve 60
59 ■ Carnegie Mellon 53
49 New York U. 58
62 Emory 32
54 ■ Washington (Mo.) 61
90 ■ Emory 78
63 ■ New York U. 64
60 Rochester 56
69 Brandeis 74
75 ■ Mt. Senario 74
60 Washington (Mo.) 96

CHICAGO ST. 4-23
68 DePaul 103
61 Eastern Mich. 86
61 Illinois 88
91 Western Ill. 106
69 Ball St. 75
76 ■ Western Ill. 74
91 ■ Southeast Mo. St. 71
61 Bradley 85
75 Toledo 82
59 Wis.-Green Bay 81
78 ■ Detroit Mercy 96
70 ■ Northern Ill. 76
91 Wright St. 136
47 Marquette 96
76 Mo.-Kansas City 106
43 Cincinnati 103
84 ■ Central St. (Ohio) 78
54 Evansville 116
60 ■ Wis.-Milwaukee 78
89 ■ N.C.-Greensboro 95
74 ■ Northeastern Ill. 77
64 Wis.-Milwaukee 65
69 ■ Mo.-Kansas City 83
66 St. Louis 116
91 N.C.-Greensboro 88
73 Northeastern Ill. 90
67 ■ Ill.-Chicago 92

CHRIS. NEWPORT 23-5
85 Mary Washington 59
71 ■ Va. Wesleyan 62
92 ■ Piedmont 69
73 ■ Mount Olive 72
85 † King's (Pa.) 49
72 York (Pa.) 75
116 ■ Salisbury St. 91
80 Newport News App. 51
102 Marymount (Va.) 87
95 ■ Shenandoah 92
51 ■ Hampton 53
81 † York (Pa.) 62
66 Frostburg St. 64
103 Greensboro 98
91 Methodist 77
66 ■ Ferrum 67
88 ■ Averett 64
91 ■ Newport News App. 73
90 N.C. Wesleyan 75
101 ■ Methodist 50
87 ■ Greensboro 77
89 Averett 53
68 Ferrum 80
83 ■ N.C. Wesleyan 63
80 ■ Greensboro 62
74 ■ N.C. Wesleyan 69
84 ■ Rhodes 74
67 † Ohio Northern 83

CINCINNATI 27-5
87 ■ Texas Southern 44
83 ■ Southeast Mo. St. 58
91 ■ Ga. Southern 57
64 Indiana 79
68 ■ Temple 45
65 Dayton 55
87 ■ South Ala. 49
79 ■ Tennessee 58
64 † Massachusetts 53
80 St. Louis 65
72 Cleveland St. 63
70 DePaul 64
103 ■ Chicago St. 43
40 ■ Ala.-Birmingham 38
78 ■ Xavier (Ohio) 67
80 ■ DePaul 54
74 Miami (Ohio) 68
98 ■ Austin Peay 61
66 Memphis St. 68
55 ■ Marquette 53
64 ■ St. Louis 39
72 South Fla. 50
60 † Arizona 70
66 Marquette 57
60 Ala.-Birmingham 67
78 ■ Memphis St. 55
78 † DePaul 69
77 Memphis St. 72
93 † Coppin St. 66
92 † New Mexico St. 55
71 † Virginia 54
68 † North Caro. 75

CITADEL 10-17
59 ■ Charleston So. 54
68 William & Mary 72
46 Nebraska 86
70 Winthrop 91
54 Clemson 76
67 Samford 73
58 ■ Ga. Southern 66
69 ■ East Tenn. St. 85
53 ■ Appalachian St. 69
74 Va. Military 76
50 Marshall 62
70 Davidson 80
83 ■ Western Caro. 73
62 ■ Tenn.-Chatt. 95
63 Furman 62
73 Ga. Southern 81
86 ■ Furman 78
68 ■ Davidson 58
53 ■ N.C.-Greensboro 47
75 Appalachian St. 71

54 East Tenn. St. 76
68 ■ Marshall 52
69 ■ Va. Military 53
53 Charleston (S.C.) 55
72 Tenn.-Chatt. 95
79 Western Caro. 70
41 † Ga. Southern 72

CCNY 7-16
90 ■ Pratt 76
72 Old Westbury 97
72 Yeshiva 91
70 John Jay 72
52 Cheyney 81
71 † Susquehanna 86
74 † Stevens Tech 69
80 ■ Baruch 69
84 Lehman 73
77 ■ Medgar Evers 86
69 Mt. St. Vincent 75
72 York (N.Y.) 89
88 St. Joseph's (N.Y.) 52
68 Hunter 105
66 Baruch 91
70 St. Joseph's (N.Y.) 73
80 ■ John Jay 75
58 ■ Lehman 49
62 Dominican (N.Y.) 81
50 ■ Staten Island 71
79 ■ Mt. St. Mary (N.Y.) 98
79 ■ Molloy 80
57 ■ York (N.Y.) 74

CLAREMONT-M-S 10-14
70 † Swarthmore 65
44 † Williams 63
81 ■ Macalester 54
59 ■ North Park 64
69 † Menlo 73
65 † Cal Baptist 73
55 ■ Christ-Irvine 73
71 ■ Wooster 57
68 Azusa-Pacific 91
65 ■ Cal Baptist 54
69 Occidental 75
84 Cal Lutheran 91
81 ■ Redlands 78
64 ■ Cal Tech 41
76 Whittier 65
71 ■ Pomona-Pitzer 77
68 La Verne 83
69 ■ Occidental 96
72 ■ Cal Lutheran 78
105 Redlands 99
72 Cal Tech 46
95 ■ Whittier 86
62 Pomona-Pitzer 69
76 ■ La Verne 86

CLARION 17-9
63 Gannon 79
92 ■ St. Thomas Aquinas 59
106 ■ Bloomsburg 90
89 Millersville 111
85 ■ Pitt.-Johnstown 78
90 ■ Hilbert 55
64 ■ Gannon 59
95 ■ Lake Erie 80
80 ■ Mansfield 74
71 Hilbert 61
92 Messiah 61
95 Phila. Bible 53
101 Cabrini 91
88 Calif. (Pa.) 91
84 ■ Edinboro 72
74 Lock Haven 66
70 Shippensburg 73
90 ■ Slippery Rock 66
95 ■ Indiana (Pa.) 86
91 ■ Calif. (Pa.) 108
96 Lake Erie 72
93 Edinboro 100
78 ■ Lock Haven 57
85 ■ Shippensburg 88
80 Slippery Rock 87

79 Indiana (Pa.) 93

CLARK (MASS.) 10-15
82 † Worcester Tech 81
77 Worcester St. 83
86 ■ North Adams St. 74
86 † Thomas 79
73 Carnegie Mellon 75
93 ■ Anna Maria 89
50 † Worcester Tech 57
91 Framingham St. 83
78 ■ Salem St. 76
74 Mass.-Boston 82
65 ■ Eastern Conn. St. 102
66 ■ Western Conn. St. 69
54 Colby 68
56 Wesleyan 69
66 ■ Mass.-Dartmouth 95
63 Amherst 77
83 Salem St. 103
80 ■ Trinity (Conn.) 68
72 ■ Babson 97
91 ■ Middlebury 79
85 Suffolk 80
75 Colby-Sawyer 90
92 ■ Brandeis 89
65 Tufts 77
75 ■ Wheaton (Mass.) 79

CLARK ATLANTA 2-24
74 ■ Ga. Southwestern 83
60 ■ Fayetteville St. 70
99 ■ Stillman 94
68 Alabama St. 107
62 Norfolk St. 96
73 † Fayetteville St. 82
65 † Wingate 79
83 ■ Albany St. (Ga.) 84
78 ■ LeMoyne-Owen 88
72 Morris Brown 81
79 Georgia St. 94
68 Tuskegee 78
77 Savannah St. 97
66 ■ Alabama A&M 100
62 Paine 74
68 † Morehouse 89
66 Albany St. (Ga.) 77
70 † Morris Brown 61
91 ■ Miles 97
53 ■ Savannah St. 61
48 ■ Paine 66
69 Fort Valley St. 89
71 ■ N.C. Central 88
81 Alabama A&M 97
77 ■ Fort Valley St. 80
82 LeMoyne-Owen 104

CLARKSON 3-22
90 ■ Middlebury 78
72 ■ Amherst 85
74 St. John Fisher 85
57 Utica 67
51 Cornell 96
85 St. Lawrence 89
64 Alfred 76
66 Ithaca 69
75 ■ Elmira 92
75 ■ Keuka 70
42 Hartwick 71
78 Rensselaer 92
73 Potsdam St. 77
61 ■ Hobart 76
73 ■ Rochester Inst. 100
55 ■ Ithaca 90
63 ■ Alfred 66
59 Plattsburgh St. 70
65 Rochester Inst. 86
70 Hobart 92
83 ■ St. Lawrence 62
71 ■ Rensselaer 84
53 ■ Hartwick 67
72 Hamilton 89
64 Union (N.Y.) 80

CLEMSON 17-13
93 ■ Liberty 68
89 ■ Howard 70
88 ■ N.C.-Greensboro 62
82 Furman 59
76 ■ Citadel 54
93 ■ Davidson 77
91 † Appalachian St. 73
87 ■ Mercer 69
80 ■ Furman 72
67 Duke 110
82 Virginia 100
72 ■ North Caro. 82
71 ■ Florida St. 89
56 Wake Forest 74
82 ■ Maryland 72
70 North Caro. St. 72
83 Georgia Tech 80
89 South Caro. 84
84 ■ Duke 93
78 ■ Virginia 83
67 North Caro. 80
92 Florida St. 102
76 ■ Wake Forest 74
81 Maryland 73
92 ■ North Caro. St. 82
59 ■ Georgia Tech 66
87 † Florida St. 75
61 † Georgia Tech 69
84 ■ Auburn 72
64 Ala.-Birmingham 65

CLEVELAND ST. 22-6
75 ■ Eastern Mich. 61
56 Michigan 88
61 ■ Bowling Green 59
69 Middle Tenn. St. 77
77 ■ St. Francis (Pa.) 62
81 Kent 64
73 Florida Int'l 74
74 ■ Eastern Ill. 66
94 ■ Western Ill. 75
63 ■ Cincinnati 72
73 ■ Northern Ill. 66
81 ■ Wis.-Green Bay 66
88 ■ Youngstown St. 48
99 Wright St. 91
86 Ill.-Chicago 73
75 Valparaiso 73
69 Creighton 60
91 ■ Wright St. 85
76 Eastern Ill. 75
96 Western Ill. 82
67 ■ Ill.-Chicago 64
85 ■ Valparaiso 81
96 Youngstown St. 78
76 Buffalo 69
62 Northern Ill. 67
63 Wis.-Green Bay 61
64 † Western Ill. 53
68 † Ill.-Chicago 96

COAST GUARD 18-6
66 Roger Williams 46
73 Wentworth Inst. 68
83 Trinity (Conn.) 80
69 † Colby-Sawyer 67
68 Connecticut Col. 74
68 ■ Albertus Magnus 67
82 MIT 57
77 Norwich 55
71 Norwich 50
70 ■ Babson 79
76 ■ MIT 67
69 Connecticut Col. 68
70 ■ Western New Eng. 74
81 ■ Worcester Tech 66
68 Western New Eng. 67
68 ■ Wesleyan 54
68 ■ Nichols 58
75 Maritime (N.Y.) 61
79 Babson 106
76 Worcester Tech 79
74 ■ Connecticut Col. 66
74 † Norwich 61

81 Worcester Tech 83
85 † Merchant Marine 68

COASTAL CARO. 22-10
101 ■ Methodist 51
112 ■ Bryan 88
85 Boston U. 78
65 Boston College 69
77 † Northeast La. 68
62 Hawaii 66
74 † Arkansas 93
90 ■ South Caro. St. 75
60 Charleston (S.C.) 65
66 Liberty 65
83 Radford 84
115 ■ Md.-Balt. County 98
74 ■ Towson St. 77
69 Missouri 94
74 ■ Liberty 81
65 N.C.-Asheville 59
58 ■ Charleston (S.C.) 57
96 ■ Radford 94
84 ■ Charleston So. 68
69 Towson St. 74
91 Md.-Balt. County 73
93 ■ Belmont Abbey 62
74 Winthrop 70
100 ■ N.C.-Asheville 68
71 Campbell 66
45 Charleston So. 37
79 ■ Winthrop 64
80 ■ Campbell 50
79 Charleston So. 66
66 † Md.-Balt. County 59
78 † Winthrop 65
53 † Michigan 84

COE 3-19
69 Ripon 94
89 † Rockford 92
82 ■ Upper Iowa 86
88 ■ Illinois Col. 102
86 ■ Knox 97
90 ■ Mt. Mercy 84
61 ■ Teikyo Marycrest 62
66 ■ Central (Iowa) 80
75 ■ Monmouth (Ill.) 53
62 Simpson 88
71 ■ Grinnell 74
85 Lawrence 87
80 St. Norbert 92
72 ■ Beloit 73
89 ■ Carroll (Wis.) 82
59 Monmouth (Ill.) 64
56 ■ Cornell College 79
75 Mt. Mercy 81
83 Grinnell 85
68 Illinois Col. 92
69 Knox 82
54 Cornell College 73

COLBY 22-3
81 † Hamline 76
88 Trinity (Tex.) 65
75 Suffolk 58
77 ■ Husson 65
86 Tufts 73
71 ■ Gordon 87
77 ■ Southern Me. 69
85 ■ Albertus Magnus 60
79 ■ Colorado Col. 66
68 ■ Clark (Mass.) 54
73 ■ Bowdoin 68
77 Williams 70
68 Amherst 55
78 Bates 70
72 Middlebury 76
76 Norwich 60
58 ■ Trinity (Conn.) 56
88 ■ Wesleyan 55
60 ■ Wheaton (Mass.) 61
87 ■ Mass.-Boston 73
79 ■ Bates 67
52 Bowdoin 51

121 ■ Worcester St. 105
91 ■ Western Conn. St. 77
80 Williams 75

COLBY-SAWYER 16-9
83 ■ Rivier 61
86 Rhode Island Col. 80
67 ■ New England Col. 71
67 † Coast Guard 69
80 † Swarthmore 73
65 Gordon 67
80 Daniel Webster 78
91 Norwich 68
85 ■ Bates 73
68 Green Mountain 61
89 ■ Notre Dame (N.H.) 34
72 New Hamp. Col. 101
69 Middlebury 96
96 ■ Johnson St. 87
87 Albertus Magnus 77
94 ■ Notre Dame (N.H.) 44
70 ■ Bowdoin 87
80 Rivier 61
70 Western Conn. St. 89
90 ■ Clark (Mass.) 75
70 ■ Castleton St. 73
84 ■ Southern Me. 64
115 ■ Lyndon St. 49
70 Wheaton (Mass.) 85
103 ■ Daniel Webster 73

COLGATE 18-10
76 Nebraska 108
76 † Idaho St. 68
85 ■ Harvard 75
89 ■ Canisius 77
77 ■ Buffalo 70
75 Brown 78
94 ■ Vermont 80
65 ■ Yale 61
83 Bucknell 92
78 ■ Manhattan 85
76 Lafayette 73
74 ■ Navy 65
68 Holy Cross 78
54 Fordham 55
73 ■ Army 58
84 Lehigh 73
73 ■ Cornell 79
63 ■ Bucknell 65
68 ■ Lafayette 55
55 Buffalo 54
67 Navy 57
95 ■ Holy Cross 97
73 ■ Fordham 54
79 Army 68
103 Central Conn. St. 88
90 ■ Lehigh 80
84 ■ Navy 80
73 Bucknell 75

COLORADO 10-17
72 ■ Colorado St. 63
74 ■ Wagner 66
97 ■ Middle Tenn. St. 57
86 ■ Wis.-Green Bay 61
72 Wyoming 79
79 † St. Francis (N.Y.) 61
65 † Indiana 85
63 Georgia 75
59 Mo.-Kansas City 63
117 ■ Centenary 96
87 ■ Missouri 91
93 ■ Buffalo 50
78 Kansas St. 83
88 ■ Mo.-Kansas City 66
51 ■ Kansas 82
67 ■ Nebraska 82
70 Oklahoma 94
61 ■ Oklahoma St. 85
74 Iowa St. 94
59 Oklahoma St. 77
88 ■ Kansas St. 77
84 ■ Oklahoma 80
67 Nebraska 76
68 Kansas 72
66 ■ Iowa St. 67
53 Missouri 70
65 † Kansas 82

COLORADO-CS 3-25
48 Fort Hays St. 102
40 † Pittsburg St. 76
52 West Tex. A&M 86
67 Alas. Fairbanks 89
77 Alas. Fairbanks 105
52 Alas. Anchorage 115
62 Alas. Anchorage 95
49 Colorado Col. 80
57 ■ Mesa St. 71
64 † Hastings 78
58 † Bellevue 49
52 ■ Adams St. 91
62 Adams St. 106
62 Mesa St. 96
51 Southern Colo. 84
91 ■ Fort Lewis 100
48 ■ Denver 69
52 ■ Metropolitan St. 72
70 Colo. Christian 88
57 ■ West Tex. A&M 56
64 Regis (Colo.) 85
75 ■ Southern Colo. 78
80 Fort Lewis 89
56 ■ Colorado Col. 66
72 Denver 82
55 Metropolitan St. 78
64 ■ Colo. Christian 61
58 ■ Regis (Colo.) 75

COLO. CHRISTIAN 20-9
99 ■ Kan. Wesleyan 80
100 ■ Sioux Falls 108
88 ■ Avila 67
77 Montana Tech 100
68 Western St. 91
98 ■ N.M. Highlands 82
74 ■ Western St. 61
79 † Florida Tech 59
60 Washburn 94
72 ■ Tarleton St. 70
101 ■ Mt. Senario 96
91 ■ Phillips (Okla.) 82
69 N.M. Highlands 67
71 Denver 57
87 Southern Colo. 70
66 Regis (Colo.) 74
88 ■ Colorado-CS 70
99 ■ Neb.-Kearney 111
88 ■ Metropolitan St. 70
110 † Fort Lewis 93
90 ■ Denver 85
74 ■ BYU-Hawaii 73
114 ■ Fort Lewis 95
90 ■ Southern Colo. 78
73 ■ Regis (Colo.) 71
61 Colorado-CS 64
70 Metropolitan St. 67
60 † South Dak. 78
71 † Western St. 81

COLORADO COL. 17-8
71 † Tufts 52
64 New York U. 88
94 ■ Hobart 83
81 ■ Washington (Mo.) 68
80 ■ Bethany (Kan.) 54
59 Black Hills St. 78
80 ■ Colorado-CS 49
86 † Wartburg 85
47 † Cornell College 53
101 ■ Maryville (Mo.) 63
68 ■ Gust. Adolphus 81
88 † Hamilton 70
66 Colby 79
120 Me.-Augusta 62
111 Daniel Webster 68
102 Rivier 61
96 Bethany (Kan.) 76
62 ■ Regis (Colo.) 61
98 ■ Fort Lewis 75
65 Western St. 97
64 N.M. Highlands 69
89 ■ N.M. Highlands 73
66 Colorado-CS 56
84 Bellevue 73
80 ■ Western St. 81

COLORADO MINES 4-23
64 Southern Colo. 87
80 † Abilene Christian 98
49 Carroll (Mont.) 59
74 † Rocky Mountain 108
51 Montana Tech 66
75 N.M. Highlands 88
83 Western N. Mex. 91
60 ■ Denver 91
77 ■ Regis (Colo.) 94
83 Regis (Colo.) 98
74 St. Francis (Ill.) 72
65 Mesa St. 89
100 † Fort Lewis 104
62 ■ Chadron St. 82
78 Adams St. 101
81 N.M. Highlands 92
61 Fort Hays St. 69
60 Western St. 100
71 Mesa St. 88
75 Denver 95
67 ■ Adams St. 64
85 ■ N.M. Highlands 84
59 ■ Western St. 68
59 ■ Mesa St. 58
58 ■ Fort Hays St. 77
75 Chadron St. 83
83 Chadron St. 95

COLORADO ST. 17-12
96 ■ Simon Fraser 79
63 Colorado 72
87 ■ Eastern Mont. 75
77 ■ Creighton 59
96 ■ Drake 86
62 Texas Tech 72
68 Idaho St. 62
78 ■ East Caro. 66
119 ■ Fort Lewis 79
79 ■ Rice 75
58 Air Force 69
55 Fresno St. 62
82 ■ Hawaii 66
82 ■ San Diego St. 67
92 ■ Wyoming 77
67 New Mexico 65
61 UTEP 63
63 ■ Brigham Young 70
78 ■ Utah 69
57 Brigham Young 81
71 Utah 84
67 ■ New Mexico 50
82 ■ UTEP 77
66 Wyoming 77
72 Hawaii 86
79 San Diego St. 78
72 ■ Air Force 55
78 ■ Fresno St. 83
65 † UTEP 70

COLUMBIA 16-10
68 † Iona 80
104 † St. Francis (N.Y.) 67
83 † Boston U. 80
98 ■ Pratt 37
70 Geo. Washington 80
58 † St. Francis (N.Y.) 50
72 ■ Lafayette 77
63 Villanova 75
84 ■ Manhattan 80
60 Hofstra 68
79 Lehigh 80
74 Cornell 64
75 ■ Cornell 61
65 ■ Fordham 51
58 ■ Yale 45
86 ■ Brown 53
63 ■ Dartmouth 72
101 ■ Harvard 70
63 Pennsylvania 84
71 Princeton 69
72 Brown 69
47 Yale 46
65 ■ Princeton 57
67 ■ Pennsylvania 74
75 Harvard 82
68 Dartmouth 66

COLUMBUS 13-13
108 ■ Piedmont 66
69 Tuskegee 88
87 Kennesaw 97
88 † Albany St. (Ga.) 71
81 Valdosta St. 84
98 ■ LeMoyne-Owen 97
106 ■ Tuskegee 88
78 ■ S.C.-Aiken 79
72 ■ Francis Marion 73
76 ■ Pembroke St. 67
65 ■ Armstrong St. 68
105 Georgia Col. 91
98 ■ Savannah St. 73
87 S.C.-Spartanburg 89
73 Lander 68
76 Savannah St. 77
95 ■ Georgia Col. 86
87 ■ Augusta 93
86 Armstrong St. 82
60 Francis Marion 73
68 Pembroke St. 82
82 ■ S.C.-Spartanburg 69
96 ■ Lander 86
68 S.C.-Aiken 70
85 Augusta 84
69 † Francis Marion 79

CONCORDIA (ILL.) 14-11
73 ■ Eureka 64
90 ■ Elmhurst 86
78 Wheaton (Ill.) 77
85 ■ Hope 91
70 ■ Ripon 81
103 Concordia (Mich.) 75
60 Chicago 72
63 Mesa St. 89
92 † Western St. 97
80 Regis (Colo.) 93
71 Carthage 88
54 Loyola (Ill.) 83
100 Lake Forest 64
71 ■ Trinity (Ill.) 66
81 ■ Judson 78
71 Rockford 65
89 Aurora 66
77 ■ Concordia (St. Paul) 63
75 ■ Concordia (Neb.) 74
77 ■ Ill. Benedictine 66
79 Trinity (Ill.) 100
79 Judson 82
79 ■ Rockford 73
65 Ill. Benedictine 77
106 ■ Aurora 77

CONCORDIA-M'HEAD 5-19
67 ■ Mt. Senario 80
82 Valley City St. 76
74 Moorhead St. 79
52 ■ Gust. Adolphus 87
85 St. John's (Minn.) 100
64 ■ Carleton 75
56 ■ Bethel (Minn.) 57
43 St. Thomas (Minn.) 69
65 ■ Augsburg 58
55 St. Olaf 63
77 ■ Macalester 53
61 ■ Hamline 72
69 ■ St. Mary's (Minn.) 52
61 Carleton 78
62 Gust. Adolphus 65
64 ■ St. John's (Minn.) 68

61 Bethel (Minn.) 79
45 ■ St. Thomas (Minn.) 50
85 Augsburg 82
77 ■ St. Olaf 88
72 Macalester 87
68 Hamline 73
80 ■ Moorhead St. 88
76 St. Mary's (Minn.) 85

CONNECTICUT 15-13
69 † Purdue 73
81 North Caro. St. 74
74 ■ St. John's (N.Y.) 72
65 ■ Yale 38
90 ■ Fairfield 66
91 ■ Hartford 66
99 ■ Towson St. 66
69 Seton Hall 72
87 Villanova 80
78 ■ Pittsburgh 80
66 Boston College 64
69 ■ Georgetown 86
68 ■ Providence 61
65 Miami (Fla.) 80
59 St. John's (N.Y.) 72
57 ■ Syracuse 60
74 ■ Florida St. 86
82 ■ Villanova 62
88 ■ Miami (Fla.) 72
80 Syracuse 76
81 Pittsburgh 80
108 ■ Maine 72
69 ■ Boston College 64
74 ■ Seton Hall 82
71 Providence 74
56 Georgetown 70
55 † Providence 73
88 ■ Jackson St. 90

CONNECTICUT COL. 6-16
76 ■ Roger Williams 47
105 ■ Swarthmore 75
74 ■ Coast Guard 68
64 Manhattanville 67
80 ■ Wesleyan 66
88 Hamilton 110
65 St. Joseph's (N.Y.) 82
78 Albertus Magnus 83
68 † Eastern Conn. St. 84
56 † Trinity (Conn.) 74
69 ■ Amherst 72
79 ■ Middlebury 84
68 ■ Coast Guard 69
88 Trinity (Conn.) 73
101 MIT 71
54 Williams 107
66 ■ Western New Eng. 85
60 Bowdoin 83
68 ■ Wheaton (Mass.) 80
73 ■ Bates 90
66 Coast Guard 74
86 ■ Tufts 102

COPPIN ST. 22-8
61 Kansas St. 85
76 James Madison 95
68 ■ Md.-Balt. County 76
79 Towson St. 74
60 ■ Charleston (S.C.) 58
51 Boston College 65
55 UC Santa Barb. 65
70 Loyola (Ill.) 80
86 South Caro. St. 58
69 ■ Buffalo 52
85 ■ North Caro. A&T 51
79 Md.-East. Shore 69
56 American 71
69 ■ Florida A&M 63
73 ■ Bethune-Cookman 61
87 ■ Morgan St. 61
76 Howard 60
73 Delaware St. 64
71 ■ Howard 57
88 Morgan St. 74
75 ■ Delaware St. 57

93 Florida A&M 70
89 Bethune-Cookman 65
75 ■ South Caro. St. 69
83 North Caro. A&T 71
75 ■ Md.-East. Shore 51
65 † Howard 57
81 † Florida A&M 69
80 † Delaware St. 53
66 † Cincinnati 93

CORNELL 16-10
65 Syracuse 97
70 ■ St. Francis (Pa.) 61
96 ■ Clarkson 51
72 Pittsburgh 80
59 Seton Hall 75
74 † California 54
73 ■ Bucknell 65
60 North Caro. 98
66 Niagara 80
70 ■ Hofstra 56
64 ■ Columbia 74
63 ■ Canisius 56
61 Columbia 75
74 ■ Brown 63
47 ■ Yale 37
79 Colgate 73
71 ■ Harvard 58
79 ■ Dartmouth 58
50 Princeton 62
62 Pennsylvania 66
81 Yale 72
79 Brown 72
69 ■ Pennsylvania 75
54 ■ Princeton 49
91 Dartmouth 86
108 Harvard 87

CORNELL COLLEGE 15-7
68 ■ Dubuque 62
86 Mt. Mercy 70
73 ■ Monmouth (Ill.) 76
66 Luther 77
67 ■ Grinnell 72
64 ■ Simpson 57
78 Buena Vista 64
53 † Colorado Col. 47
59 † Gust. Adolphus 60
104 † Maryville (Mo.) 80
86 ■ Knox 73
77 ■ Illinois Col. 73
79 Lake Forest 69
50 Ripon 71
75 ■ Lawrence 59
56 ■ St. Norbert 47
62 Grinnell 43
79 Coe 56
65 Knox 70
76 Illinois Col. 71
61 Monmouth (Ill.) 72
73 ■ Coe 54

CORTLAND ST. 10-15
84 ■ Lehman 44
83 Roberts Wesleyan 81
37 Ithaca 63
67 Geneseo St. 77
74 Buffalo St. 90
87 ■ Oneonta St. 78
83 ■ Plattsburgh St. 75
88 ■ Potsdam St. 96
74 † Westfield St. 81
62 † Framingham St. 77
78 ■ Oswego St. 66
85 Utica Tech 92
70 ■ Binghamton 79
61 ■ Utica 72
79 Albany (N.Y.) 72
60 New Paltz St. 85
93 ■ Fredonia St. 82
65 ■ Ithaca 76
76 Plattsburgh St. 89
83 Potsdam St. 87
60 Binghamton 64

67 ■ Brockport St. 64
84 ■ New Paltz St. 71
72 Oneonta St. 69
52 † Buffalo St. 72

CREIGHTON 8-18
58 ■ Iowa St. 69
59 Colorado St. 77
83 Nebraska 100
70 ■ Illinois St. 63
56 Siena 69
42 Bradley 65
64 Southern Ill. 85
84 ■ Montana 78
45 Eastern Ill. 49
73 ■ Drake 78
66 ■ Indiana St. 80
79 ■ Southern Ill. 71
72 ■ Southwest Mo. St. 58
47 Wichita St. 68
85 Drake 90
58 Northern Iowa 60
59 ■ Bradley 48
60 ■ Cleveland St. 69
63 ■ Tulsa 70
88 ■ Mo.-Kansas City 79
62 Southwest Mo. St. 65
59 ■ Northern Iowa 54
53 Illinois St. 59
66 Tulsa 69
58 Indiana St. 71
58 ■ Wichita St. 54

CURRY 14-11
64 Rivier 66
56 Suffolk 74
58 Amherst 110
74 ■ Bri'water (Mass.) 70
81 ■ Nichols 65
83 ■ Emerson-MCA 69
80 MIT 83
82 Roger Williams 69
64 Salve Regina 63
72 ■ Wentworth Inst. 82
54 Eastern Nazarene 53
77 ■ New England Col. 66
61 ■ Eastern Nazarene 75
57 Anna Maria 110
60 ■ Roger Williams 51
72 ■ Rivier 59
79 Emerson-MCA 69
58 ■ Salve Regina 54
63 Wentworth Inst. 68
50 Gordon 78
88 ■ Anna Maria 108
84 New England Col. 75
73 ■ Gordon 63
73 ■ Gordon 70
61 † Eastern Nazarene 69

DARTMOUTH 11-15
61 Hartford 64
90 ■ Middlebury 73
90 ■ Harvard 64
60 † Samford 58
49 New Orleans 73
64 Washington 72
57 Portland 61
77 ■ New Hampshire 67
63 Pennsylvania 88
57 Princeton 76
66 ■ Vermont 60
86 Harvard 70
85 ■ Boston U. 66
62 Holy Cross 83
58 Providence 78
105 Vermont 73
72 Columbia 63
58 Cornell 79
70 ■ Brown 60
42 ■ Yale 51
60 ■ Princeton 63
63 ■ Pennsylvania 82
56 Yale 61

65 Brown 64
86 ■ Cornell 91
66 ■ Columbia 68

DAVIDSON 14-14
98 ■ St. Joseph's (Me.) 78
82 ■ Tenn. Temple 56
82 ■ Lynchburg 47
77 Clemson 93
52 † Wake Forest 71
57 N.C.-Charlotte 95
81 Western Caro. 69
73 Furman 80
58 ■ North Caro. St. 63
67 East Tenn. St. 75
69 Appalachian St. 78
80 ■ Citadel 70
75 ■ Va. Military 64
82 ■ Marshall 69
88 ■ Ga. Southern 81
73 ■ Tenn.-Chatt. 80
82 ■ Western Caro. 63
71 Ga. Southern 83
58 Citadel 68
69 ■ N.C.-Charlotte 80
76 ■ Furman 64
80 Tenn.-Chatt. 95
76 ■ Appalachian St. 79
90 ■ East Tenn. St. 75
63 Marshall 57
84 Va. Military 70
67 † Marshall 65
68 † Tenn.-Chatt. 72

DAVIS & ELKINS 6-21
61 † Lincoln Memorial 79
87 † Catawba 93
87 West Va. St. 77
72 Alderson-Broaddus 84
74 Longwood 97
82 † Dist. Columbia 92
59 Calif. (Pa.) 87
108 ■ Waynesburg 91
87 ■ Concord 83
85 West Va. Tech 84
82 ■ Charleston (W.Va.) 76
61 ■ Glenville St. 90
71 ■ Salem Teikyo 75
61 Wheeling Jesuit 91
93 ■ West Liberty St. 102
75 Shepherd 82
77 ■ West Va. Wesleyan 80
54 Charleston (W.Va.) 87
99 ■ Fairmont St. 88
85 Bluefield St. 104
81 Salem Teikyo 91
71 ■ Alderson-Broaddus 74
95 ■ Wheeling Jesuit 99
87 West Liberty St. 108
82 ■ Shepherd 98
74 West Va. Wesleyan 83
77 † Alderson-Broaddus 87

DAYTON 4-26
78 † Illinois 86
67 † Ala.-Birmingham 80
70 Alas. Anchorage 84
53 ■ Vanderbilt 75
50 Miami (Ohio) 57
70 ■ Louisiana Tech 60
60 Michigan St. 65
61 ■ Tennessee 77
55 ■ Cincinnati 65
63 ■ Mo.-St. Louis 66
44 Marquette 82
66 Notre Dame 71
63 ■ Niagara 66
58 ■ Xavier (Ohio) 85
65 ■ Evansville 73
66 ■ Butler 70
70 Loyola (Ill.) 69
70 Detroit Mercy 88
78 ■ Duquesne 77
64 ■ La Salle 72
69 ■ Notre Dame 79

46 Xavier (Ohio) 53
52 ■ St. Louis 73
59 Butler 74
36 Evansville 71
81 ■ Detroit Mercy 70
56 ■ Loyola (Ill.) 59
51 Duquesne 67
57 La Salle 67
66 † Evansville 69

DEPAUL 16-15
103 ■ Chicago St. 68
65 ■ Houston 82
67 Illinois St. 66
91 ■ San Francisco 61
88 Louisville 93
90 ■ Northeastern Ill. 83
73 † Duke 89
76 † Stanford 67
94 † Oklahoma 108
80 ■ Jacksonville 71
71 Loyola (Cal.) 70
88 Loyola (Ill.) 73
93 ■ Memphis St. 95
45 Georgetown 74
64 ■ Cincinnati 70
73 Ala.-Birmingham ... 62
69 † Massachusetts 79
72 ■ Baylor 70
54 Cincinnati 80
65 ■ St. Louis 63
76 ■ Marquette 87
90 ■ Detroit Mercy 79
57 Memphis St. 79
55 ■ Ala.-Birmingham ... 48
70 ■ Notre Dame 62
79 ■ Texas Christian 68
76 St. Louis 92
53 Bradley 59
75 Marquette 86
66 † Ala.-Birmingham ... 64
69 † Cincinnati 78

DEPAUW 19-7
69 † Washington (Mo.) .. 68
81 Ill. Wesleyan 86
75 Purdue-Calumet ... 62
79 ■ Webster 50
69 Centre 81
89 ■ Earlham 50
75 Millikin 58
71 ■ Principia 36
70 ■ Marian (Ind.) 54
56 ■ Hanover 51
61 ■ Taylor 51
83 Rockford 63
47 Rose-Hulman 70
84 ■ Franklin 62
77 Anderson 65
70 ■ Manchester 64
70 ■ Wabash 57
67 Hanover 76
93 ■ Fontbonne 37
63 Franklin 61
70 ■ Rose-Hulman 67
49 Manchester 51
103 ■ Anderson 72
81 Wabash 57
62 ■ Wabash 66
66 Augustana (Ill.) 79

DEFIANCE 21-6
100 ■ Heidelberg 87
85 † Mt. Vernon Naz. 80
85 † Adrian 71
59 ■ Ohio Northern 74
102 † Methodist 63
63 Penn St.-Behrend .. 81
69 † Eureka 68
90 Franklin 93
105 ■ Grove City 91
82 ■ Ohio Dominican 70
104 Huntington 93
82 Ohio Wesleyan 71
81 ■ Bluffton 53
86 ■ Thomas More 77
74 ■ Findlay 77
69 Wilmington (Ohio) .. 65
92 Anderson 76
80 Bluffton 66
74 ■ Wittenberg 72
104 Malone 78
83 ■ Mt. Vernon Naz. 75
83 Thomas More 73
95 ■ Wilmington (Ohio) .. 52
103 ■ Concordia (Ind.) 65
95 † Bluffton 77
81 Thomas More 82
66 ■ Otterbein 80

DELAWARE 22-8
54 † Seton Hall 75
77 ■ Rutgers 69
84 ■ Widener 55
71 Bucknell 83
81 Delaware St. 64
66 † Xavier (Ohio) 74
71 † Rice 65
67 † N.C.-Greensboro ... 60
73 Mt. St. Mary's (Md.) 55
79 ■ Navy 58
106 ■ Md.-Balt. County ... 98
76 Towson St. 69
65 ■ New Hampshire 54
93 ■ Maine 71
70 Boston U. 69
73 Northeastern 76
73 ■ Vermont 69
71 ■ Hartford 67
63 Drexel 79
69 Hartford 65
88 Vermont 73
68 ■ Northeastern 82
83 ■ Boston U. 65
78 Maine 72
62 New Hampshire 64
92 ■ Drexel 73
70 ■ New Hampshire 65
84 Northeastern 61
67 Drexel 64
70 † Louisville 76

DELAWARE ST. 13-16
80 † Hartford 81
102 † Morgan St. 85
80 ■ St. Francis (N.Y.) ... 71
64 ■ Delaware 81
96 ■ Bowie St. 80
52 Arizona 92
74 † La Salle 83
55 ■ Md.-East. Shore ... 67
74 Bethune-Cookman . 71
74 Florida A&M 71
66 Howard 69
65 Morgan St. 82
65 Marquette 105
64 ■ North Caro. A&T ... 66
73 ■ South Caro. St. 71
90 ■ Central Conn. St. ... 89
64 ■ Coppin St. 73
81 North Caro. A&T ... 80
59 South Caro. St. 87
57 Coppin St. 75
65 † Md.-East. Shore ... 69
90 ■ Morgan St. 93
76 ■ Howard 56
86 ■ Bethune-Cookman . 81
88 ■ Florida A&M 91
82 Central Conn. St. ... 81
88 † North Caro. A&T ... 79
75 † South Caro. St. 64
53 † Coppin St. 80

DELAWARE VALLEY 4-20
64 † Rutgers-Camden ... 62
51 Widener 67
74 ■ Elizabethtown 97
50 FDU-Madison 72
66 ■ Upsala 97
74 ■ Beaver 66
65 Ursinus 73
69 Drew 82
69 ■ Wilkes 87
70 ■ Muhlenberg 83
65 ■ Scranton 102
76 Juniata 107
65 ■ Moravian 78
71 ■ King's (Pa.) 93
71 ■ FDU-Madison 74
77 ■ Lycoming 78
72 Upsala 93
52 Holy Family 95
82 Wilkes 84
81 ■ Drew 76
56 Scranton 104
77 Misericordia 90
74 ■ Allentown 71
73 King's (Pa.) 92

DELTA ST. 22-8
53 Ky. Wesleyan 76
59 Ark.-Lit. Rock 63
103 Pensacola Christian 72
82 ■ Ark.-Monticello 84
79 Henderson St. 77
90 ■ North Ala. 73
111 ■ Bapt. Christian 72
78 ■ Ala.-Huntsville 57
74 Valdosta St. 77
94 West Ga. 68
70 Mississippi Val. 69
56 ■ Henderson St. 58
89 ■ Jacksonville St. 69
80 Ark.-Pine Bluff 66
67 ■ Mississippi Col. 66
57 ■ Livingston 58
80 ■ Ark.-Pine Bluff 56
90 North Ala. 69
118 ■ Ark. Baptist 61
91 Livingston 71
80 Mississippi Col. 83
73 ■ Mississippi Val. 63
81 Jacksonville St. 63
90 Ark.-Monticello 78
89 ■ Valdosta St. 62
65 ■ West Ga. 39
70 ■ Mississippi Col. 43
72 ■ Jacksonville St. 66
74 † Tampa 61
93 Troy St. 110

DENISON 11-14
79 ■ Bethany (W.Va.) 71
81 ■ Oberlin 66
59 Kenyon 44
60 Ohio Dominican 66
59 ■ Wooster 49
72 ■ Wilmington (Ohio) .. 54
74 ■ Marietta 57
51 † Frank. & Marsh. 56
50 † Ursinus 48
56 ■ Ohio Wesleyan 57
57 Wittenberg 72
63 Case Reserve 72
84 Earlham 45
63 ■ Allegheny 70
32 Wooster 67
57 ■ Kenyon 66
53 Bluffton 50
48 Ohio Wesleyan 74
69 ■ Earlham 57
67 ■ Case Reserve 65
85 Oberlin 88
56 Allegheny 67
43 Carnegie Mellon ... 61
54 ■ Wittenberg 64
68 Wooster 79

DENVER 15-11
82 ■ Western St. 71
81 Northern Colo. 66
86 ■ Michigan Tech 73
79 Wyoming 82
91 Colorado Mines 60
79 Western St. 85
69 Chadron St. 73
75 Weber St. 90
69 Northern Ariz. 76
61 ■ Northern Colo. 51
94 ■ Mt. Senario 78
57 ■ Colo. Christian 71
64 Metropolitan St. 68
84 ■ Regis (Colo.) 78
69 Colorado-CS 48
89 ■ Chadron St. 74
105 ■ Fort Lewis 101
104 Southern Colo. 97
100 Neb.-Kearney 88
95 ■ Colorado Mines 75
85 Colo. Christian 90
90 ■ Metropolitan St. 70
89 Regis (Colo.) 93
82 ■ Colorado-CS 72
79 Fort Lewis 86
80 ■ Southern Colo. 97

DETROIT MERCY 15-12
95 ■ Wayne St. (Mich.) .. 85
73 ■ Toledo 52
77 Michigan 92
77 ■ Oakland 50
79 ■ Western Ill. 76
88 Bowling Green 79
86 Wisconsin 108
82 † Richmond 70
84 Arizona St. 100
96 Chicago St. 78
83 ■ Notre Dame 59
97 ■ Xavier (Ohio) 90
73 La Salle 80
73 Duquesne 75
96 Loyola (Ill.) 75
88 ■ Dayton 70
85 Butler 82
58 Evansville 82
79 DePaul 90
65 ■ Loyola (Ill.) 56
72 ■ La Salle 73
73 ■ Duquesne 70
70 Dayton 81
74 Xavier (Ohio) 93
65 ■ Evansville 66
71 ■ Butler 65
57 † Duquesne 59

DICKINSON 11-13
75 ■ Ursinus 48
90 ■ Cabrini 94
76 Gettysburg 70
71 ■ Western Md. 58
78 Swarthmore 54
69 ■ Messiah 53
71 Albright 64
59 ■ Shippensburg 84
70 ■ Messiah 51
31 Frank. & Marsh. 57
68 ■ Muhlenberg 73
68 ■ Elizabethtown 70
58 ■ Moravian 62
61 Frostburg St. 70
70 Juniata 60
58 Lebanon Valley 78
58 ■ Gettysburg 56
62 ■ Susquehanna 74
73 Western Md. 68
56 ■ Frank. & Marsh. 60
60 Muhlenberg 72
54 Moravian 66
79 ■ York (Pa.) 67
48 ■ Lebanon Valley 67

DIST. COLUMBIA 3-22
65 † Queens (N.Y.) 63
79 Mansfield 86
64 ■ Virginia Union 71
81 † Kentucky St. 112
60 Norfolk St. 91
96 ■ Lincoln (Pa.) 97

77 Wingate 81
92 † Davis & Elkins 82
92 ■ Bloomsburg 104
90 ■ Columbia Union 81
55 Lincoln Memorial .. 72
59 † Longwood 79
46 † Mansfield 78
67 † Lake Erie 99
54 Kutztown 97
78 Columbia Union 82
61 N.C. Central 87
72 Virginia St. 92
66 Hampton 86
63 Millersville 115
76 ■ Cheyney 81
83 ■ Central St. (Ohio) . 117
76 ■ Hampton 94
61 Virginia Union 108
69 ■ Longwood 84

DOWLING 8-20
105 ■ Molloy 61
92 ■ New York Tech 98
87 ■ Bridgeport 109
55 ■ Mercy 77
58 Bentley 81
56 † Sacred Heart 74
51 Springfield 76
48 † Pace 58
74 ■ LIU-C.W. Post 77
56 Queens (N.Y.) 70
72 ■ Adelphi 93
53 ■ Pace 66
54 Phila. Textile 80
66 ■ St. Rose 80
88 LIU-Southampton .. 83
68 Mercy 81
108 ■ Concordia (N.Y.) 80
67 LIU-C.W. Post 77
65 ■ Phila. Textile 72
89 ■ Queens (N.Y.) 77
94 ■ LIU-Southampton .. 89
79 St. Rose 112
70 Pace 73
76 New Haven 101
108 Concordia (N.Y.) 88
86 Adelphi 81
78 ■ LIU-Southampton .. 69
61 Phila. Textile 86

DRAKE 14-14
86 ■ Cal St. Sacramento . 65
86 Colorado St. 96
86 ■ Cal St. Fullerton 73
95 ■ Lewis 77
66 ■ San Jose St. 43
86 Louisiana St. 94
65 ■ Iowa 80
78 Creighton 73
66 ■ Wichita St. 62
73 Indiana St. 96
73 Bradley 65
74 Southern Ill. 92
90 ■ Creighton 85
81 Iowa St. 119
57 Illinois St. 60
96 ■ Tulsa 88
69 Northern Iowa 59
87 ■ Southern Ill. 79
76 ■ Indiana St. 74
82 Tulsa 95
67 ■ Southwest Mo. St. . 71
62 ■ Northern Iowa 64
65 Wichita St. 73
56 ■ Bradley 47
54 ■ Illinois St. 55
67 Southwest Mo. St. . 82
63 † Northern Iowa 59
59 † Illinois St. 60

DREW 7-16
87 Muhlenberg 103
81 † Washington (Md.) . 102
88 Upsala 92
56 Wilkes 80
90 ■ Stevens Tech 76
69 ■ Moravian 73
60 † Albright 77
63 † Gettysburg 67
77 Swarthmore 83
60 New York U. 69
81 Allentown 80
82 ■ Delaware Valley 69
47 Scranton 73
71 Skidmore 84
64 ■ King's (Pa.) 59
65 FDU-Madison 62
74 ■ Upsala 88
61 ■ Wilkes 70
51 ■ Scranton 74
76 Delaware Valley 81
101 ■ Wm. Paterson 91
106 King's (Pa.) 103
62 ■ FDU-Madison 71

DREXEL 22-7
86 ■ Lehigh 77
64 ■ Army 50
77 St. Francis (Pa.) 66
47 ■ St. Joseph's (Pa.) .. 52
75 Youngstown St. 62
64 Penn St. 73
83 † Alabama St. 75
78 Gonzaga 91
56 Pepperdine 69
72 Lafayette 58
70 ■ Fordham 65
59 ■ Maine 64
73 ■ New Hampshire 52
79 Northeastern 68
75 Boston U. 63
80 ■ Hartford 68
85 ■ Vermont 82
79 ■ Delaware 63
73 Navy 57
85 Vermont 71
76 Hartford 71
71 ■ Boston U. 57
79 ■ Northeastern 73
65 New Hampshire 63
67 Maine 57
73 Delaware 92
75 ■ Boston U. 58
91 ■ Hartford 80
64 ■ Delaware 67

DRURY 19-12
84 ■ Grace 86
77 ■ Northeast Mo. St. .. 68
71 Evangel 54
67 Pittsburg St. 85
88 ■ Mo. Southern St. 71
66 Central Mo. St. 76
82 Missouri-Rolla 94
78 ■ Southwest Baptist .. 92
77 Mo.-St. Louis 75
64 ■ Northeastern Okla. . 53
70 ■ Midwestern St. 69
67 Lincoln (Mo.) 93
67 Rockhurst 59
82 SIU-Edwardsville ... 61
97 ■ Ozarks (Mo.) 63
60 Wayne St. (Neb.) ... 61
91 ■ McKendree 76
88 ■ Quincy 92
80 Southern Nazarene . 83
87 ■ Evangel 54
77 ■ Rockhurst 60
81 ■ Wayne St. (Neb.) ... 78
84 McKendree 79
95 Ozarks (Mo.) 75
89 ■ SIU-Edwardsville ... 94
83 Tarleton St. 75
76 Quincy 91
97 ■ Park 50
73 ■ John Brown 70
102 ■ Columbia (Mo.) 72
70 † Birm. Southern 76

DUBUQUE 15-10
62 Cornell College 68
82 ■ Mt. Mercy 73
57 ■ Teikyo Marycrest ... 81
90 ■ Clarke 88
51 Augustana (Ill.) 77
67 ■ Rockford 57
57 Wis.-Platteville ... 103
95 ■ Mt. St. Clare 85
72 ■ Clarke 65
72 ■ Upper Iowa 57
68 ■ Simpson 52
71 Wartburg 72
91 Buena Vista 80
82 ■ Central (Iowa) 73
75 ■ Loras 64
69 Luther 71
69 ■ Buena Vista 56
79 ■ Wartburg 69
62 William Penn 69
82 Central (Iowa) 76
73 Upper Iowa 48
79 ■ William Penn 73
66 ■ Luther 70
74 Simpson 93
51 Loras 79

DUKE 24-8
110 ■ Canisius 62
79 ■ Michigan 68
103 ■ Northeastern 72
88 † Rutgers 79
89 † DePaul 73
96 † Louisiana St. 67
89 † Brigham Young 66
106 ■ Boston U. 62
88 ■ Oklahoma 84
110 ■ Clemson 67
79 Georgia Tech 80
86 Wake Forest 59
65 ■ Iowa 56
69 ■ Virginia 77
92 ■ North Caro. St. 56
88 Florida St. 89
117 ■ San Francisco 73
78 Maryland 62
81 ■ North Caro. 67
67 Notre Dame 50
93 Clemson 84
73 ■ Georgia Tech 63
86 ■ Wake Forest 98
55 Virginia 58
91 North Caro. St. 82
98 ■ Florida St. 75
78 ■ UCLA 67
95 ■ Maryland 79
69 North Caro. 83
66 † Georgia Tech 69
105 † Southern Ill. 70
77 † California 82

DUQUESNE 13-15
76 ■ Penn St. 65
97 ■ Robert Morris 79
82 St. Francis (Pa.) 72
71 Kent 73
91 ■ Florida St. 84
91 † Pittsburgh 102
81 Arizona St. 103
70 † Richmond 65
67 West Va. 84
73 ■ St. Bonaventure 78
65 ■ Loyola (Ill.) 67
75 ■ Detroit Mercy 73
78 La Salle 81
81 ■ Buffalo 68
64 Evansville 69
80 Butler 86
77 Dayton 78
79 Xavier (Ohio) 85
78 ■ Butler 64
71 ■ Evansville 74
79 Loyola (Ill.) 71
70 Detroit Mercy 73
80 Notre Dame 76
65 ■ La Salle 68
67 ■ Dayton 51
88 ■ Xavier (Ohio) 72
59 † Detroit Mercy 57
41 † Xavier (Ohio) 67

EARLHAM 4-21
80 ■ Graceland (Ind.) 87
106 ■ Lindenwood 99
112 Dyke 100
78 Manchester 108
66 Wittenberg 113
106 Oberlin 87
50 DePauw 89
65 ■ Kenyon 68
81 Heidelberg 88
80 † Siena Heights 107
59 ■ Allegheny 93
78 Marian (Ind.) 93
52 ■ Wooster 83
45 ■ Denison 84
74 Case Reserve 80
61 ■ Ohio Wesleyan 110
89 ■ Oberlin 73
69 Kenyon 94
77 Allegheny 90
57 Denison 69
56 Wooster 82
51 ■ Wittenberg 80
59 ■ Case Reserve 75
75 Ohio Wesleyan 112
66 Wittenberg 96

EAST CARO. 13-17
65 ■ St. Andrews 48
59 ■ N.C.-Charlotte 62
109 ■ Tennessee Tech ... 94
72 † Southeastern La. ... 65
72 Toledo 61
66 Colorado St. 78
77 Tennessee Tech ... 95
67 Virginia Tech 76
74 Appalachian St. 76
82 James Madison 98
65 Richmond 74
64 ■ American 89
68 ■ George Mason 64
74 ■ Fla. Atlantic 60
60 Old Dominion 80
65 ■ William & Mary 81
72 N.C.-Wilmington ... 77
54 Alabama 59
58 ■ James Madison 57
63 ■ Richmond 72
81 George Mason 51
57 American 67
66 ■ Virginia Tech 49
60 ■ Old Dominion 73
74 William & Mary 53
66 ■ N.C.-Wilmington ... 79
73 † Old Dominion 67
55 † N.C.-Wilmington ... 50
54 † James Madison 49
65 † North Caro. 85

EAST STROUDSBURG 13-13
95 † Gwynedd Mercy 61
62 Phila. Textile 74
64 ■ Pace 59
71 ■ Eckerd 67
64 ■ New Haven 82
85 ■ LIU-Southampton .. 60
77 Alvernia 79
93 † Gardner-Webb 83
72 † Armstrong St. 79
65 Gannon 88
103 † Pracitical Bible 42
90 Mercyhurst 100
83 Le Moyne 98
94 ■ Centenary (N.J.) 70
52 West Chester 67
67 ■ Mansfield 54
77 Millersville 95

58 ■ Cheyney 68
89 ■ Kutztown 75
63 Bloomsburg 58
77 ■ West Chester 67
69 Mansfield 51
66 ■ Millersville 70
72 Cheyney 64
60 Kutztown 69
70 ■ Bloomsburg 80

EAST TENN. ST. 19-10
87 ■ Wofford 76
72 † Eastern Ill. 49
74 Purdue 88
83 Kansas 86
112 ■ Carson-Newman ... 66
69 ■ Michigan St. 80
71 Eastern Ky. 66
71 ■ Va. Military 54
85 Citadel 69
75 Ga. Southern 96
83 ■ Marshall 74
75 ■ Davidson 67
98 ■ Furman 82
98 Appalachian St. 79
77 Tenn.-Chatt. 87
73 Marshall 75
96 Va. Military 70
89 ■ Tenn.-Chatt. 87
79 ■ Western Caro. 76
71 Furman 95
93 ■ Ga. Southern 88
76 ■ Citadel 54
77 Western Caro. 85
75 Davidson 90
117 ■ Oral Roberts 91
81 ■ Appalachian St. 78
97 † Appalachian St. 84
84 † Ga. Southern 76
75 † Tenn.-Chatt. 86

EAST TEX. ST. 3-26
60 ■ Southwest Baptist .. 75
79 Cal St. Los Angeles 98
64 UC Riverside 81
79 Cal St. San B'dino 100
70 Midwestern St. 87
74 ■ Central Ark. 80
70 ■ Henderson St. 77
91 Northwest Mo. St. .. 94
60 † Mo. Western St. 10
69 New Mexico St. 83
59 Henderson St. 78
61 Central Ark. 84
75 Alas. Anchorage ... 84
74 † Southern Colo. 80
76 † N.M. Highlands 54
72 Angelo St. 74
69 Abilene Christian ... 84
72 Tex. A&M-Kingsville 76
71 ■ Eastern N. Mex. 78
64 Cameron 81
85 Central Okla. 122
82 ■ Central Okla. 113
67 ■ Cameron 64
68 ■ Abilene Christian ... 57
69 ■ Angelo St. 72
79 Eastern N. Mex. 85
71 ■ Midwestern St. 82
54 ■ Tex. A&M-Kingsville 84
72 † Cameron 76

EASTERN CONN. ST. 21-7
65 ■ Plattsburgh St. 60
77 ■ Teikyo-Post 62
79 ■ North Adams St. ... 60
84 ■ Bri'water (Mass.) ... 61
69 Worcester St. 63
62 † Stockton St. 72
78 † Rivier 56
65 ■ Albertus Magnus ... 54
102 Clark (Mass.) 65
84 † Connecticut Col. ... 68
74 Wesleyan 55
57 ■ Wheaton (Mass.) ... 60
73 ■ Mass.-Dartmouth .. 75
57 ■ Southern Me. 62
61 ■ Western Conn. St. .. 59
76 ■ Rhode Island Col. .. 70
91 Plymouth St. 85
75 Mass.-Dartmouth .. 96
68 Mass.-Boston 60
75 Rhode Island Col. .. 66
98 ■ Plymouth St. 76
78 ■ Mass.-Boston 60
60 Southern Me. 59
75 Southern Me. 57
73 † Mass.-Dartmouth .. 87
81 Salem St. 71
78 † New York U. 73
64 Mass.-Dartmouth .. 75

EASTERN ILL. 10-17
71 ■ Maine 63
49 † East Tenn. St. 72
51 † Weber St. 61
54 Indiana St. 74
72 ■ Southern Ill. 85
60 Cal St. Fullerton 86
54 Nebraska 70
49 ■ Creighton 45
66 Cleveland St. 74
76 Youngstown St. 75
79 ■ Ill. Benedictine 55
76 Valparaiso 94
71 ■ Ill.-Chicago 57
80 Wright St. 104
65 ■ Northern Ill. 63
70 Western Ill. 76
67 ■ Northeastern Ill. 70
47 Wis.-Green Bay 68
56 Northern Ill. 65
73 ■ Western Ill. 75
75 ■ Cleveland St. 76
82 ■ Youngstown St. 76
87 ■ Wright St. 80
60 ■ Wis.-Green Bay 52
77 ■ Valparaiso 76
77 Ill.-Chicago 87
58 Wright St. 94

EASTERN KY. 15-12
81 ■ Northern Ky. 71
79 ■ Thomas More 51
73 Kentucky 82
75 † Eastern Mich. 61
78 Wright St. 88
90 Howard 87
68 Western Ky. 77
73 Northern Iowa 76
66 ■ East Tenn. St. 71
87 Tennessee Tech ... 95
80 Middle Tenn. St. ... 65
59 ■ Northern Iowa 61
78 ■ Austin Peay 73
75 ■ Tennessee St. 73
92 Murray St. 93
63 Southeast Mo. St. .. 79
79 Morehead St. 87
64 ■ Tenn.-Martin 58
65 Austin Peay 64
84 Tennessee St. 93
76 ■ Morehead St. 66
98 ■ Murray St. 82
86 ■ Southeast Mo. St. .. 65
80 ■ Tennessee Tech ... 66
66 ■ Middle Tenn. St. ... 46
66 Tenn.-Martin 56
73 † Murray St. 74

EAST. MENNONITE 7-18
72 Barton 105
79 † Mount Olive 106
67 Guilford 81
85 † Wesley 62
58 Bridgewater (Va.) .. 66
83 ■ Va. Wesleyan 89
87 ■ Roanoke 102
75 ■ Bridgewater (Va.) .. 71
61 Va. Wesleyan 104
76 ■ Emory & Henry ... 102
76 Bridgewater (Va.) .. 87
70 Newport News App. 64
69 Messiah 79
76 ■ Lynchburg 71
85 ■ Guilford 79
56 Randolph-Macon ... 72
64 Lynchburg 68
69 Hampden-Sydney .. 94
56 ■ Randolph-Macon ... 66
76 Wash. & Lee 69
69 Roanoke 75
74 ■ Hampden-Sydney .. 79
71 ■ Wash. & Lee 68
57 Emory & Henry 89
49 Emory & Henry 62

EASTERN MICH. 13-17
86 ■ Chicago St. 61
60 ■ Rhode Island 68
61 Cleveland St. 75
61 † Eastern Ky. 75
87 † Prairie View 62
85 ■ Ashland 60
89 † Ill.-Chicago 81
66 † Iowa 103
58 † Mississippi St. 74
77 ■ Lake Superior St. .. 68
58 Michigan 88
64 Central Mich. 71
73 ■ Bowling Green 74
57 ■ Akron 62
65 Toledo 62
75 ■ Kent 71
62 Ball St. 66
62 ■ Miami (Ohio) 69
74 Western Mich. 75
74 ■ Ohio 81
65 Bowling Green 54
79 Akron 69
65 ■ Toledo 50
55 Kent 61
57 ■ Ball St. 77
59 Miami (Ohio) 55
89 ■ Western Mich. 71
62 Ohio 71
92 ■ Central Mich. 80
57 † Western Mich. 65

EASTERN MONT. 10-19
90 ■ Northern Mont. 93
96 ■ Western Mont. 83
75 Colorado St. 87
74 ■ Metropolitan St. 68
77 Rocky Mountain 63
80 ■ Angelo St. 74
75 ■ Cal St. Chico 78
93 Montana Tech 60
88 Northern Mont. 92
62 North Dak. 97
77 † North Dak. St. 80
47 Montana 95
63 Hawaii-Hilo 86
74 Chaminade 78
82 Seattle Pacific 87
82 ■ Alas. Fairbanks 78
62 ■ Alas. Anchorage ... 82
77 ■ Rocky Mountain 73
77 ■ Grand Canyon 83
77 Western Mont. 86
76 ■ Carroll (Mont.) 75
75 ■ Hawaii-Hilo 79
88 ■ Chaminade 75
81 ■ Seattle Pacific 74
74 Alas. Anchorage ... 79
92 Alas. Fairbanks ... 111
61 Grand Canyon 94
52 Southern Utah 95
64 Alas. Anchorage ... 65

EASTERN NAZARENE 19-7
67 ■ MIT 56
60 King's (N.Y.) 65
95 ■ Wentworth Inst. 43
73 Suffolk 47
69 Trinity (Conn.) 86
86 ■ Brandeis 85
72 Wentworth Inst. 53
65 New England Col. .. 59
74 ■ Roger Williams 48
73 ■ Gordon 50
53 ■ Curry 54
73 Anna Maria 81
75 Curry 61
76 ■ Salve Regina 74
77 ■ New England Col. .. 52
66 Gordon 60
68 ■ Anna Maria 61
58 Roger Williams 60
75 Bri'water (Mass.) ... 58
57 Salve Regina 61
74 † Bryan 92
77 † Valley Forge Chrst. . 53
60 † Nyack 48
69 ■ New England Col. .. 46
69 † Curry 61
82 † Salve Regina 61

EASTERN N. MEX. 23-7
71 † Central Ark. 53
89 † Henderson St. 77
77 Fort Lewis 79
64 New Mexico St. 73
96 ■ Hardin-Simmons ... 59
56 West Tex. A&M 69
86 ■ Panhandle St. 48
66 ■ Western N. Mex. 55
57 † Wayne St. (Neb.) ... 56
92 Neb.-Kearney 77
110 Panhandle St. 71
115 N.M. Highlands 69
108 ■ Central Okla. 119
110 ■ Cameron 85
71 Tex. A&M-Kingsville 60
78 East Tex. St. 71
77 ■ N.M. Highlands 72
93 ■ Angelo St. 57
87 ■ Abilene Christian ... 77
101 Abilene Christian ... 91
78 Angelo St. 69
82 ■ West Tex. A&M 71
110 Cameron 84
109 Central Okla. 111
85 ■ East Tex. St. 79
55 ■ Tex. A&M-Kingsville 64
75 † Cameron 69
76 † Tex. A&M-Kingsville 68
76 † Mo. Southern St. ... 73
78 † Washburn 79

EASTERN WASH. 6-20
89 ■ Portland 80
60 † Stephen F. Austin .. 72
61 † Cal St. Northridge .. 60
66 Washington St. 83
49 ■ Pacific (Ore.) 40
68 ■ Southern Utah 70
50 Gonzaga 71
58 Northeast La. 84
59 † Long Beach St. 76
56 † Navy 57
68 ■ Gonzaga 73
64 ■ Montana St. 54
75 ■ Montana 68
63 Idaho 87
69 Northern Ariz. 89
57 Weber St. 64
66 ■ Boise St. 76
69 ■ Idaho St. 56
65 Montana 85
58 Montana St. 73
67 Southern Utah 87
80 ■ Idaho 82
52 ■ Northern Ariz. 64
73 ■ Weber St. 83
72 Idaho St. 92
81 Boise St. 85

ECKERD 12-14

89 ■ Franklin 81
77 Nova 73
67 East Stroudsburg 71
57 † Bridgeport 69
74 ■ Webber 73
76 ■ Regis (Colo.) 66
59 † Ga. Southern 70
72 ■ Rose-Hulman 78
92 ■ Quinnipiac 90
76 † St. Andrews 64
61 † Lincoln Memorial 71
72 † St. Leo 67
66 ■ North Fla. 64
94 ■ Florida Tech 88
80 ■ St. Leo 74
63 Rollins 78
86 ■ Tampa 97
66 ■ Barry 63
61 Fla. Southern 80
55 Florida Tech 60
77 St. Leo 64
67 ■ Rollins 79
73 Tampa 81
63 Barry 76
61 ■ Fla. Southern 78
100 North Fla. 101

EDINBORO 12-17

83 Alas. Anchorage 89
92 Alas. Anchorage 116
84 Alas. Fairbanks 99
84 Alas. Fairbanks 85
72 ■ Point Park 80
69 Gannon 65
65 ■ Mercyhurst 79
79 ■ West Va. Wesleyan 53
86 ■ Cheyney 67
91 Fairmont St. 74
114 † Teikyo-Post 83
63 Bloomsburg 68
81 ■ Gannon 82
122 ■ Columbia Union 69
63 ■ Slippery Rock 82
88 ■ Lock Haven 73
72 Clarion 84
110 ■ Pitt.-Johnstown 74
89 ■ Calif. (Pa.) 91
79 Indiana (Pa.) 84
82 ■ Shippensburg 75
77 Slippery Rock 78
75 Lock Haven 79
100 ■ Clarion 93
84 Mercyhurst 75
83 Calif. (Pa.) 101
74 ■ Indiana (Pa.) 75
101 Shippensburg 81
85 Millersville 96

ELIZABETH CITY ST. 18-10

80 † Paine 75
95 North Ala. 90
109 Jacksonville St. 108
83 Fayetteville St. 87
66 ■ Livingstone 63
76 ■ St. Paul's 73
89 Johnson Smith 98
70 Boise St. 99
79 † Idaho 72
90 † Winston-Salem 69
77 † Johnson Smith 79
77 ■ Virginia Union 80
107 ■ Hampton 105
115 ■ Virginia St. 112
71 ■ St. Augustine's 70
80 Norfolk St. 76
105 Bowie St. 100
80 Hampton 86
96 ■ St. Paul's 88
101 St. Paul's 90
102 ■ Bowie St. 90
98 Virginia St. 92
76 Shaw 70
75 N.C. Central 92
85 Virginia Union 95
105 ■ Norfolk St. 110
105 † Winston-Salem 64
84 † Johnson Smith 100

ELIZABETHTOWN 19-7

75 Frank. & Marsh. 78
82 † Lebanon Valley 81
97 Delaware Valley 74
77 King's (Pa.) 68
70 ■ York (Pa.) 77
80 ■ Cabrini 75
76 ■ Alvernia 75
89 Scranton 96
87 ■ Frostburg St. 72
73 ■ Frank. & Marsh. 70
101 ■ Western Md. 85
87 Washington (Md.) 78
70 Dickinson 68
88 ■ Lycoming 81
85 Albright 81
69 Susquehanna 86
99 ■ Juniata 86
89 ■ Lebanon Valley 81
77 ■ Messiah 71
79 Lycoming 70
85 ■ Albright 74
76 ■ Susquehanna 85
89 Juniata 71
82 Messiah 71
61 Scranton 84
64 Frank. & Marsh. 78

ELMHURST 10-15

72 Chicago 60
86 Concordia (Ill.) 90
60 Ill. Benedictine 80
79 Northeastern Ill. 91
81 ■ Judson 76
79 ■ Barat 66
69 Menlo 75
75 ■ Kenyon 69
63 ■ Aurora 61
84 Western Ill. 83
80 ■ Millikin 81
57 ■ North Park 59
67 North Central 78
74 Ill. Wesleyan 85
57 Wheaton (Ill.) 61
57 North Park 58
61 Carthage 82
75 Moody Bible 49
69 ■ Augustana (Ill.) 113
104 ■ Ill. Wesleyan 96
81 Millikin 83
66 ■ Carthage 61
66 ■ Wheaton (Ill.) 68
95 ■ North Central 85
78 Augustana (Ill.) 95

ELMIRA 18-9

68 † Western Conn. St. 71
75 † Albertus Magnus 78
59 Houghton 68
68 ■ Dominican (N.Y.) 49
65 ■ Westfield St. 80
88 Misericordia 73
91 ■ Alfred 87
102 Ferrum 107
78 † Wash. & Jeff. 76
81 Catholic 91
92 Clarkson 75
84 Hartwick 63
87 Binghamton 78
83 ■ Utica 62
101 Nazareth (N.Y.) 88
97 Union (N.Y.) 81
79 ■ St. John Fisher 63
85 Roberts Wesleyan 79
85 ■ Keuka 60
75 ■ Geneseo St. 79
87 ■ Albany (N.Y.) 68
94 Alfred 83
85 Lehman 77
69 Albany (N.Y.) 77
75 Utica 71
92 Binghamton 89
94 Hamilton 108

ELON 13-13

81 ■ Lees-McRae 56
95 ■ Barton 75
72 S.C.-Spartanburg 83
65 Francis Marion 72
80 † High Point 76
79 Wingate 80
70 High Point 79
70 ■ Longwood 66
72 ■ Mars Hill 65
52 ■ Presbyterian 68
72 Catawba 71
57 Lenoir-Rhyne 85
70 ■ Erskine 53
53 ■ Gardner-Webb 73
64 ■ Carson-Newman 61
59 Longwood 62
65 ■ Wingate 60
60 Mars Hill 82
61 Presbyterian 73
91 ■ Catawba 77
66 ■ Lenoir-Rhyne 74
53 Charleston (S.C.) 85
85 Gardner-Webb 76
81 Lees-McRae 67
89 Carson-Newman 86
64 † Gardner-Webb 111

EMORY 12-13

83 ■ Loyola (La.) 63
74 ■ Morehouse 76
79 † Rust 82
92 † Lane 82
71 Oglethorpe 56
73 New York U. 81
75 Case Reserve 77
79 ■ Sewanee 73
78 ■ Johns Hopkins 77
87 Savannah A&D 63
78 Carnegie Mellon 74
106 Atlanta Christian 91
74 Rochester 76
73 Brandeis 100
83 ■ Oglethorpe 64
78 ■ Washington (Mo.) 71
32 ■ Chicago 62
91 ■ Brandeis 100
60 ■ Rochester 58
67 Sewanee 82
78 Chicago 90
111 Washington (Mo.) 132
76 ■ Southwestern (Tex.) 69
63 ■ Carnegie Mellon 81
65 ■ New York U. 75

EMORY & HENRY 23-5

91 ■ Ferrum 77
90 Roanoke 83
76 ■ Otterbein 58
113 ■ Savannah A&D 41
96 Wash. & Lee 80
83 ■ Guilford 81
94 † Frostburg St. 78
104 † Bethany (W.Va.) 78
61 Bridgewater (Va.) 55
102 East. Mennonite 76
59 Ferrum 74
92 Hampden-Sydney 75
92 Lynchburg 67
79 ■ Wash. & Lee 68
95 ■ Hampden-Sydney 73
105 ■ Roanoke 84
78 Va. Wesleyan 99
67 Randolph-Macon 62
82 ■ Lynchburg 77
78 ■ Bridgewater (Va.) 58
99 Guilford 84
70 ■ Va. Wesleyan 64
63 ■ Randolph-Macon 78
89 ■ East. Mennonite 57
62 ■ East. Mennonite 49
76 † Va. Wesleyan 90
83 Maryville (Tenn.) 61
67 ■ Calvin 101

EMPORIA ST. 18-9

65 ■ Friends 62
99 ■ Ottawa 62
116 ■ Baker 60
67 ■ Northwestern Okla. 53
56 Kansas 91
85 Fort Hays St. 79
85 ■ Fort Hays St. 68
81 † Grand Canyon 77
100 † Cal Poly Pomona 91
102 † Alas. Fairbanks 90
67 ■ Central Mo. St. 69
83 Mo. Western St. 92
78 ■ Mo.-St. Louis 74
58 Washburn 66
73 Northeast Mo. St. 74
83 Central Mo. St. 75
84 Northwest Mo. St. 55
68 ■ Mo. Western St. 65
51 Southwest Baptist 65
62 ■ Washburn 69
76 ■ Northeast Mo. St. 53
81 ■ Northwest Mo. St. 76
74 ■ Lincoln (Mo.) 63
73 ■ Mo. Southern St. 52
84 Missouri-Rolla 102
78 Pittsburg St. 72
75 Mo. Southern St. 100

ERSKINE 7-20

79 S.C.-Aiken 96
80 † Augusta 96
74 ■ Lander 68
93 ■ S.C.-Aiken 87
67 Francis Marion 83
66 Presbyterian 85
80 ■ Berry 94
66 † Lincoln Memorial 87
69 † St. Andrews 72
77 † Lees-McRae 87
79 ■ Lincoln Memorial 61
56 ■ Wofford 65
53 Elon 70
72 Lander 67
67 Queens (N.C.) 80
68 Berry 83
54 Limestone 70
81 ■ Newberry 68
60 Wofford 80
77 ■ Kennesaw 91
50 Lincoln Memorial 76
65 Central Wesleyan 86
74 ■ Queens (N.C.) 91
70 Kennesaw 83
74 Newberry 61
84 ■ Limestone 75
73 ■ Central Wesleyan 76

EUREKA 24-5

64 Concordia (Ill.) 73
87 Rockford 86
74 ■ Clarke 66
79 Judson 70
103 ■ Blackburn 60
68 † Defiance 69
82 † Greenville 49
83 Sanford Brown 49
97 ■ Lindenwood 71
76 Aurora 60
106 Harris-Stowe 71
82 ■ Wabash 71
67 ■ McKendree 60
65 Greenville 80
85 ■ Brescia 72
83 Moody Bible 37
46 SIU-Edwardsville 56
85 ■ Trinity (Ill.) 56
77 Barat 69
71 N'western (Wis.) 42

66 St. Norbert 44
104 ■ Iowa Wesleyan 62
90 ■ Mt. St. Clare 73
75 ■ Judson 68
86 ■ Greenville 64
80 ■ Trinity (Ill.) 57
76 ■ Judson 73
63 † Tarleton St. 54
60 † N'west Nazarene 69

EVANSVILLE 23-7
82 ■ Missouri-Rolla 73
70 Notre Dame 76
84 Valparaiso 77
86 ■ Illinois St. 67
55 Indiana St. 58
78 ■ Murray St. 87
92 ■ Southeast Mo. St. 68
64 ■ Indiana St. 46
75 Austin Peay 73
42 Southern Ill. 65
82 ■ La Salle 70
77 Butler 62
73 Dayton 65
68 ■ Xavier (Ohio) 74
116 ■ Chicago St. 54
69 ■ Duquesne 64
72 Northeastern Ill. 62
108 Loyola (Ill.) 70
82 ■ Detroit Mercy 58
63 La Salle 41
74 Duquesne 71
63 Xavier (Ohio) 74
71 ■ Dayton 36
84 ■ Butler 72
66 Detroit Mercy 65
62 ■ Loyola (Ill.) 44
69 † Dayton 66
74 † Butler 71
80 † Xavier (Ohio) 69
70 † Florida St. 82

FAIRFIELD 14-13
77 FDU-Teaneck 60
68 ■ Brown 58
89 ■ N.C.-Wilmington 76
84 Harvard 77
58 † Maine 63
66 Connecticut 90
82 ■ Loyola (Cal.) 75
55 Wisconsin 76
59 Wis.-Milwaukee 75
78 ■ Niagara 85
72 Rice 83
57 ■ Yale 48
79 Iona 80
59 ■ Siena 56
60 Loyola (Md.) 48
61 † Marist 56
59 ■ St. Peter's 57
54 Niagara 72
51 Canisius 50
71 Manhattan 82
61 ■ Loyola (Md.) 57
56 St. Peter's 63
81 ■ Canisius 66
64 Siena 59
71 ■ Manhattan 82
57 ■ Iona 63
61 † Siena 70

FDU-MADISON 11-13
59 † Caldwell 73
72 ■ Delaware Valley 50
52 ■ Scranton 61
68 Beaver 63
59 Albright 66
61 ■ Trenton St. 67
49 Misericordia 50
73 ■ Ursinus 60
53 Moravian 55
46 Stony Brook 64
69 ■ King's (Pa.) 70
66 ■ John Jay 60
50 Wilkes 77
64 Upsala 82
71 ■ Centenary (N.J.) 56
62 ■ Drew 65
74 Delaware Valley 71
62 Scranton 83
91 ■ Stevens Tech 56
68 ■ Wesley 66
74 King's (Pa.) 84
54 ■ Wilkes 53
51 ■ Upsala 50
71 Drew 62

FDU-TEANECK 11-17
60 ■ Fairfield 77
79 ■ Montclair St. 38
54 Boston College 72
60 Florida Int'l 72
61 Seton Hall 81
61 ■ St. Peter's 67
67 Marist 68
60 Mt. St. Mary's (Md.) 57
73 ■ Rider 63
65 ■ St. Francis (N.Y.) 62
73 ■ LIU-Brooklyn 74
72 Wagner 79
69 Monmouth (N.J.) 54
54 ■ Robert Morris 53
67 ■ St. Francis (Pa.) 54
80 N.C.-Greensboro 94
76 ■ Marist 84
58 Rider 68
73 ■ Mt. St. Mary's (Md.) 61
73 LIU-Brooklyn 76
83 St. Francis (N.Y.) 84
52 ■ Monmouth (N.J.) 83
75 ■ Wagner 72
76 ■ Florida Int'l 66
76 St. Francis (Pa.) 84
55 Robert Morris 65
81 Marist 62
63 Rider 93

FAYETTEVILLE ST. 20-9
69 ■ Virginia St. 66
76 ■ Hampton 65
70 ■ Claflin 59
80 St. Augustine's 74
87 ■ Elizabeth City St. 83
106 † Morris Brown 67
70 Clark Atlanta 60
60 Pembroke St. 68
77 Bowie St. 66
82 † Clark Atlanta 73
84 West Ga. 72
65 Norfolk St. 81
47 Virginia Union 94
82 St. Paul's 61
73 Livingstone 51
61 ■ St. Augustine's 62
88 ■ Shaw 69
80 Winston-Salem 60
62 Johnson Smith 55
62 N.C. Central 70
82 ■ Livingstone 62
69 Shaw 62
59 Claflin 55
86 ■ N.C. Central 91
83 ■ Johnson Smith 82
82 ■ Winston-Salem 60
62 † St. Paul's 73
38 † Virginia Union 67
62 † Alabama A&M 79

FERRIS ST. 16-11
89 † Winona St. 74
73 Mankato St. 74
91 Wis.-Parkside 73
66 ■ Calvin 70
105 † Urbana 89
93 Adrian 77
92 Northern Mich. 100
87 Michigan Tech 83
87 Wayne St. (Mich.) 73
98 ■ Wis.-Parkside 73
66 ■ Hillsdale 65
90 Grand Valley St. 83
61 ■ Lake Superior St. 66
68 Saginaw Valley 63
109 ■ Northwood 93
83 ■ Northern Mich. 85
104 ■ Michigan Tech 66
85 Oakland 80
73 ■ Wayne St. (Mich.) 74
85 Northwood 86
72 Hillsdale 87
77 ■ Oakland 73
97 ■ Grand Valley St. 80
77 Lake Superior St. 62
94 ■ Saginaw Valley 98
67 † Wayne St. (Mich.) 72
73 † Hillsdale 78

FERRUM 18-7
83 † Marymount (Va.) 76
83 Roanoke 108
84 ■ Maryville (Tenn.) 82
77 Emory & Henry 91
90 † Lincoln (Pa.) 83
87 N.C. Wesleyan 84
92 ■ Newport News App. 54
115 ■ Shenandoah 73
107 ■ Elmira 102
81 Pfeiffer 92
106 Shenandoah 96
74 ■ Emory & Henry 59
89 Averett 78
92 Maryville (Tenn.) 105
67 Chris. Newport 66
81 N.C. Wesleyan 77
85 ■ Methodist 76
82 Greensboro 83
115 ■ Averett 82
93 ■ N.C. Wesleyan 82
94 Methodist 77
80 ■ Chris. Newport 68
94 ■ Greensboro 83
66 Longwood 100
52 † N.C. Wesleyan 56

FISK 1-24
79 ■ Lane 92
82 ■ Morehouse 98
85 Cumberland (Tenn.) 92
86 Centre 96
76 Rust 102
83 ■ Cumberland (Tenn.) 76
86 ■ Miles 87
59 Lane 115
80 Hendrix 88
44 Trinity (Tex.) 81
70 Sewanee 90
69 Oglethorpe 105
57 Morehouse 73
66 ■ Rhodes 89
61 ■ Millsaps 76
89 ■ Stillman 101
72 ■ Sewanee 88
79 ■ Oglethorpe 92
81 ■ Centre 92
79 Miles 110
56 Rhodes 92
70 Millsaps 100
75 Stillman 113
72 ■ Trinity (Tex.) 75
64 ■ Hendrix 81

FITCHBURG ST. 4-19
58 ■ Western New Eng. 65
74 ■ Wentworth Inst. 65
66 ■ Rhode Island Col. 81
63 † Albertus Magnus 74
86 † Nichols 73
79 Worcester St. 98
67 ■ Anna Maria 76
73 ■ Salem St. 94
78 ■ Mass.-Dartmouth 104
66 Suffolk 69
61 Westfield St. 77
68 ■ Framingham St. 81
58 ■ North Adams St. 57
43 Bri'water (Mass.) 62
82 Nichols 85
92 ■ Worcester St. 119
65 Salem St. 101
69 ■ Rivier 81
58 ■ Westfield St. 79
75 Framingham St. 89
55 North Adams St. 71
79 ■ Bri'water (Mass.) 71
56 Westfield St. 96

FLORIDA 16-12
70 ■ Stetson 52
80 South Fla. 78
82 ■ Jacksonville 75
62 † Temple 67
70 † N.C.-Charlotte 69
54 Texas A&M 57
63 † Purdue 67
86 † Austin Peay 62
89 Florida St. 86
76 Auburn 73
62 ■ Vanderbilt 61
81 Georgia 77
81 Louisiana St. 85
76 ■ South Caro. 81
80 Tennessee 68
83 ■ Wichita St. 58
48 Kentucky 71
69 ■ Alabama 59
66 ■ Arkansas 74
82 ■ Georgia 79
94 ■ Mississippi 47
64 Vanderbilt 82
80 South Caro. 73
84 ■ Tennessee 70
71 Mississippi St. 78
77 ■ Kentucky 85
62 † Mississippi 67
66 Minnesota 74

FLORIDA A&M 10-18
83 Georgia Tech 112
65 Alabama St. 83
43 † Princeton 51
70 † Jackson St. 107
66 ■ Central Fla. 68
83 ■ Old Dominion 104
57 ■ Alabama St. 70
69 ■ Md.-East. Shore 50
71 ■ Delaware St. 74
52 Central Fla. 62
76 ■ North Caro. A&T 73
74 ■ South Caro. St. 84
72 Morgan St. 86
63 Coppin St. 69
85 Howard 84
65 Oklahoma 146
68 North Caro. A&T 84
74 South Caro. St. 86
69 ■ Bethune-Cookman 56
83 ■ Morgan St. 82
70 ■ Coppin St. 93
94 ■ Howard 89
83 Md.-East. Shore 63
91 Delaware St. 88
111 ■ Edward Waters 107
66 Bethune-Cookman 70
90 † Morgan St. 87
69 † Coppin St. 81

FLA. ATLANTIC 3-25
60 ■ St. Thomas (Fla.) 64
80 ■ Barry 82
62 Central Fla. 79
74 ■ Florida Tech 85
87 ■ Nova 74
59 ■ Mankato St. 76
61 Miami (Fla.) 84
56 † Southern Cal 82
72 Iona 88

40	† Akron	60
54	■ Bradley	74
93	■ Troy St.	121
64	Florida Tech	53
79	† Central Okla.	86
60	Stetson	63
55	Virginia Tech	80
60	East Caro.	74
46	Charleston (S.C.)	87
73	■ Webber	75
51	Florida Int'l	67
46	Memphis St.	96
80	■ Central Fla.	91
54	Barry	89
97	Troy St.	122
73	■ Central St. (Ohio)	66
70	Georgia St.	89
62	Tulane	87
46	Iowa St.	89

FLORIDA INT'L		20-10
72	Miami (Fla.)	64
60	† N.C.-Wilmington	61
67	† Brown	59
85	■ North Fla.	63
72	■ FDU-Teaneck	60
79	■ Nova	69
51	† Mississippi St.	58
69	† Radford	65
85	† Ill.-Chicago	87
64	■ Murray St.	68
66	South Fla.	72
74	■ Cleveland St.	73
66	Stetson	63
69	Georgia St.	68
67	Samford	65
68	■ Southeastern La.	61
62	■ Centenary	59
61	Mercer	64
67	■ Fla. Atlantic	51
77	Central Fla.	72
82	■ Stetson	75
57	Virginia Tech	44
60	■ Georgia St.	61
58	■ Samford	47
72	Southeastern La.	67
81	Centenary	84
66	FDU-Teaneck	76
67	■ Mercer	65
60	■ Central Fla.	74
66	Lamar	64

FLA. SOUTHERN		24-8
78	† South Dak. St.	91
83	† Oakland City	72
90	■ Augustana (S.D.)	70
100	■ North Central	62
82	■ Webber	65
81	Augusta	90
65	■ Lewis	59
72	■ Quinnipiac	74
75	■ Central Mo. St.	53
89	■ Merrimack	74
71	■ Houghton	45
78	■ Mass.-Dartmouth	55
86	■ Methodist	56
107	■ Rhode Island Col.	32
92	■ Barry	83
44	Rollins	38
99	■ North Fla.	72
106	St. Leo	70
67	■ Florida Tech	78
70	Tampa	76
80	■ Eckerd	61
84	■ Rollins	66
102	North Fla.	88
66	■ St. Leo	47
71	Florida Tech	62
72	■ Tampa	68
78	Eckerd	61
69	Barry	71
66	† Rollins	60
71	Tampa	67
72	Troy St.	75
73	† Tampa	79

FLORIDA ST.		25-10
89	■ Siena	80
109	■ Iowa St.	86
78	† Indiana	81
83	† UCLA	86
67	■ Massachusetts	64
84	Duquesne	91
63	† N.C.-Charlotte	59
91	† Temple	80
95	■ Ark.-Lit. Rock	64
109	■ Md.-Balt. County	80
94	■ South Fla.	73
86	■ Florida	89
76	Virginia	80
74	Wake Forest	72
105	■ Maryland	85
70	■ North Caro. St.	54
89	Clemson	71
89	■ Duke	88
77	North Caro.	82
96	■ Georgia Tech	77
92	Jacksonville	77
86	Connecticut	74
99	■ Virginia	84
111	■ Wake Forest	94
87	Maryland	84
72	North Caro. St.	71
102	■ Clemson	92
75	Duke	98
76	■ North Caro.	86
83	Georgia Tech	82
75	† Clemson	87
82	† Evansville	70
94	† Tulane	63
81	† Western Ky.	78
81	† Kentucky	106

FLORIDA TECH		10-16
85	■ Missouri-Rolla	103
63	■ Washburn	70
68	South Caro.	91
85	Fla. Atlantic	74
59	† Colo. Christian	79
82	† West Va. Tech	58
55	Mo.-Kansas City	68
79	■ Westbrook	58
85	■ New Haven	81
100	■ St. Joseph's (Me.)	85
53	■ Fla. Atlantic	64
86	■ Troy St.	94
85	■ St. Leo	65
88	Eckerd	94
60	Tampa	61
80	■ Barry	91
78	Fla. Southern	67
105	■ North Fla.	92
50	Rollins	70
60	■ Eckerd	55
76	■ Tampa	79
75	Barry	90
62	■ Fla. Southern	71
86	North Fla.	78
51	■ Rollins	56
86	St. Leo	95

FONTBONNE		10-15
73	■ Hannibal-La Grange	85
76	■ Concordia (Mo.)	67
80	■ Rhodes	90
63	Concordia (Mo.)	69
58	Occidental	91
52	Cal Tech	54
84	La Sierra	89
57	Principia	61
72	Maryville (Mo.)	76
66	■ MacMurray	80
61	Westminster (Mo.)	74
62	Parks	37
67	Rhodes	82
74	■ Blackburn	70
67	■ Principia	51
37	DePauw	93
74	Webster	59
71	MacMurray	76
110	■ Maryville (Mo.)	91
70	■ Westminster (Mo.)	80
69	■ Parks	64
74	■ Webster	63
87	Blackburn	68
72	† Parks	59
86	† Westminster (Mo.)	88

FORDHAM		15-16
59	■ Rhode Island	85
85	■ Adelphi	69
60	■ St. John's (N.Y.)	55
58	Iona	77
67	Manhattan	92
64	Hawaii	83
43	† Jackson St.	67
55	† Nebraska	79
60	■ Hofstra	56
68	■ Siena	70
61	Holy Cross	71
65	Drexel	70
65	■ Bucknell	69
75	■ Army	56
40	■ Marquette	66
87	Lehigh	65
55	■ Colgate	54
51	Columbia	65
83	■ Lafayette	71
59	Navy	52
81	■ Holy Cross	73
63	Bucknell	77
42	Army	40
93	■ Lehigh	74
54	Colgate	73
74	Lafayette	78
73	Loyola (Md.)	70
69	■ Rice	67
57	■ Navy	48
84	■ Lafayette	73
78	Holy Cross	86

FORT HAYS ST.		12-16
102	■ Colorado-CS	48
77	■ Cameron	96
69	■ Tabor	66
90	† Baker	96
71	† Christ-Irvine	83
58	■ Washburn	73
58	Pittsburg St.	64
71	Rockhurst	67
79	■ Emporia St.	85
68	Emporia St.	85
87	■ Baker	69
76	■ Neb.-Kearney	88
79	Neb.-Kearney	98
91	■ Chadron St.	88
69	■ Colorado Mines	61
69	■ Western St.	71
57	■ Mesa St.	48
59	■ Rockhurst	77
73	N.M. Highlands	63
72	Adams St.	68
70	Western St.	74
69	Mesa St.	81
85	■ N.M. Highlands	54
64	■ Adams St.	72
77	Colorado Mines	58
77	Chadron St.	97
74	■ Adams St.	73
78	Western St.	83

FORT LEWIS		11-16
71	■ Western St.	77
76	■ Mesa St.	83
97	■ N.M. Highlands	92
79	■ Eastern N. Mex.	77
89	† Western N. Mex.	79
95	N.M. Highlands	87
110	Adams St.	151
104	Mesa St.	100
79	Colorado St.	119
80	Mesa St.	104
79	† St. Francis (Ill.)	84
104	† Colorado Mines	100
82	Western St.	95
86	Regis (Colo.)	94
100	Colorado-CS	91
91	■ Metropolitan St.	92
101	Denver	105
75	Colorado Col.	98
119	■ Adams St.	107
102	Southern Colo.	101
93	† Colo. Christian	110
67	■ Regis (Colo.)	81
89	■ Colorado-CS	80
95	Colo. Christian	114
103	Metropolitan St.	111
86	■ Denver	79
88	■ Southern Colo.	89

FORT VALLEY ST.		14-14
70	■ Livingston	93
82	■ Georgia Col.	85
85	■ Tuskegee	78
86	Valdosta St.	108
66	Mercer	98
75	South Caro. St.	87
77	■ LeMoyne-Owen	95
79	■ Valdosta St.	76
92	■ Miles	66
79	Savannah St.	70
80	■ Albany St. (Ga.)	76
102	Morris Brown	73
88	Alabama A&M	94
82	Miles	59
84	Georgia Col.	97
92	■ Savannah St.	77
93	Paine	91
47	Livingston	69
89	Albany St. (Ga.)	77
73	LeMoyne-Owen	100
62	Tuskegee	63
89	■ Clark Atlanta	69
77	■ Paine	74
88	■ Morris Brown	89
80	Clark Atlanta	77
87	■ Morehouse	99
88	† Tuskegee	80
78	† Alabama A&M	80

FRAMINGHAM ST.		14-11
101	■ Rhode Island Col.	67
82	Suffolk	71
99	■ Mass.-Dartmouth	141
83	■ Clark (Mass.)	91
77	Tufts	71
69	Western New Eng.	49
54	Williams	80
77	† Cortland St.	62
78	North Adams St.	58
93	Nichols	76
97	■ Bri'water (Mass.)	66
81	Worcester St.	83
85	Plymouth St.	83
83	■ Salem St.	75
81	Fitchburg St.	68
60	Westfield St.	87
71	■ Amherst	83
73	■ North Adams St.	67
66	Bri'water (Mass.)	73
101	■ Worcester St.	112
68	Salem St.	81
89	■ Fitchburg St.	75
92	■ Westfield St.	99
91	† Bri'water (Mass.)	82
73	† Salem St.	80

FRANCIS MARION		19-9
107	† Salisbury St.	83
57	† Guilford	50
72	■ Elon	65
78	■ Limestone	59
83	■ Erskine	67
69	Ga. Southern	76
93	■ Coker	63
76	Pembroke St.	80
73	Columbus	72
75	■ Augusta	80
60	■ Lander	57

54 Coker 62
78 ■ S.C.-Spartanburg 71
63 ■ Armstrong St. 60
64 Newberry 57
73 ■ Georgia Col. 74
49 S.C.-Aiken 62
80 ■ Pembroke St. 83
71 Georgia Col. 53
70 Armstrong St. 59
73 ■ Columbus 60
52 S.C.-Spartanburg 50
73 Augusta 76
85 ■ Newberry 67
93 ■ S.C.-Aiken 83
72 Lander 59
79 † Columbus 69
68 Augusta 69

FRANK. & MARSH. 24-4
78 ■ Elizabethtown 75
79 ■ York (Pa.) 76
64 Western Md. 51
75 ■ Muhlenberg 56
51 Johns Hopkins 50
68 York (Pa.) 71
56 † Denison 51
78 Mount Union 64
104 ■ Old Westbury 72
81 ■ Jersey City St. 56
70 Elizabethtown 73
60 Lincoln (Pa.) 59
57 ■ Dickinson 31
72 Moravian 67
82 Penn St.-Harrisburg 62
50 ■ Lebanon Valley 78
72 Gettysburg 60
79 ■ Western Md. 53
74 Muhlenberg 71
60 Dickinson 56
84 ■ Widener 46
68 ■ Moravian 53
64 Lebanon Valley 61
87 ■ Gettysburg 53
67 ■ Widener 52
68 ■ Lebanon Valley 48
78 ■ Elizabethtown 64
68 Rowan 69

FRANKLIN 12-13
81 Eckerd 89
69 Webber 89
109 † IU/PU-Indianapolis 102
72 † Indianapolis 94
78 Kalamazoo 81
96 ■ Knox 95
77 ■ Greenville 65
93 ■ Defiance 90
71 Millikin 78
92 ■ Adrian 63
92 ■ Rose-Hulman 76
105 Anderson 98
114 ■ Wabash 97
62 DePauw 84
98 ■ Manchester 95
85 Hanover 88
77 Thomas More 85
76 ■ Anderson 68
59 Rose-Hulman 102
61 ■ DePauw 63
78 Wabash 90
103 ■ St. Francis (Ind.) 96
70 Manchester 93
84 ■ Hanover 79
73 Wabash 84

FRANKLIN PIERCE 22-8
107 New Hamp. Col. 95
77 † St. Anselm 76
99 ■ American Int'l 74
102 ■ LIU-Southampton 68
94 ■ Assumption 64
104 New York Tech 83
76 ■ Springfield 62
80 † Mercyhurst 90
78 † New York Tech 68
76 ■ Le Moyne 69
87 Bridgeport 89
98 Sacred Heart 86
82 Southern Conn. St. 57
80 ■ Mass.-Lowell 70
100 ■ Bridgeport 98
87 Keene St. 68
79 Le Moyne 66
106 ■ New Haven 76
83 New Hamp. Col. 99
81 ■ Southern Conn. St. 75
71 Mass.-Lowell 62
74 ■ Sacred Heart 79
86 ■ New Hamp. Col. 94
70 New Haven 76
131 ■ Keene St. 86
88 ■ New Haven 78
75 † Le Moyne 73
71 New Hamp. Col. 76
95 † Bentley 74
73 New Hamp. Col. 83

FREDONIA ST. 18-10
76 ■ Alfred 57
73 ■ Hiram 63
61 ■ Binghamton 56
78 Buffalo St. 83
72 Geneseo St. 77
62 ■ Penn St.-Behrend 58
76 ■ Thiel 47
57 Penn St.-Behrend 60
65 Potsdam St. 63
51 Plattsburgh St. 77
58 ■ St. John Fisher 60
71 ■ Oswego St. 70
83 ■ Utica Tech 74
86 ■ Brockport St. 100
80 Roberts Wesleyan 71
82 Cortland St. 93
84 ■ Nazareth (N.Y.) 53
59 ■ Geneseo St. 60
82 Brockport St. 92
76 ■ New Paltz St. 57
74 ■ Oneonta St. 56
75 ■ Buffalo St. 61
91 Oswego St. 62
75 Utica Tech 70
79 † Plattsburgh St. 70
56 † Geneseo St. 51
57 Binghamton 54
56 Ithaca 71

FRESNO ST. 13-15
77 ■ Cal St. Northridge 67
80 ■ Oregon 78
77 Washington 75
64 Nevada 74
49 ■ Pacific (Cal.) 70
73 ■ San Francisco 67
62 San Jose St. 74
66 ■ Navy 53
61 ■ Long Beach St. 82
68 ■ Wyoming 66
62 ■ Colorado St. 55
64 New Mexico 85
67 UTEP 73
57 ■ Brigham Young 72
83 ■ Utah 103
51 ■ Air Force 71
74 Hawaii 78
72 San Diego St. 67
69 ■ Hawaii 64
78 ■ San Diego St. 70
58 Air Force 61
74 Brigham Young 90
65 Utah 75
71 ■ New Mexico 57
60 ■ UTEP 57
55 Wyoming 77
83 Colorado St. 78
48 † New Mexico 72

FROSTBURG ST. 14-12
100 ■ Valley Forge Chrst. 54
70 ■ Stony Brook 48
76 ■ Washington (Md.) 67
79 Goucher 67
74 Waynesburg 62
70 Bethany (W.Va.) 91
62 Baldwin-Wallace 81
78 † Emory & Henry 94
74 Marietta 84
72 Elizabethtown 87
81 ■ Grove City 68
64 ■ Chris. Newport 66
93 Shenandoah 89
75 Salisbury St. 96
73 Lincoln (Pa.) 77
84 ■ Bethany (W.Va.) 66
70 ■ Dickinson 61
93 Mary Washington 91
76 ■ Allentown 63
82 ■ Shenandoah 84
85 ■ Salisbury St. 82
67 ■ Lincoln (Pa.) 73
86 ■ Waynesburg 61
62 Allentown 56
97 ■ Salisbury St. 106
92 ■ Lincoln (Pa.) 94

FURMAN 11-17
75 James Madison 101
81 ■ South Caro. St. 85
84 ■ Lander 62
59 ■ Clemson 82
77 Tennessee 90
72 Clemson 80
61 Tenn.-Chatt. 71
80 ■ Davidson 73
67 Western Caro. 66
77 Appalachian St. 81
82 East Tenn. St. 98
73 ■ Ga. Southern 75
83 ■ Marshall 92
73 ■ Va. Military 61
62 ■ Citadel 63
74 ■ Western Caro. 65
62 ■ Tenn.-Chatt. 82
65 Samford 55
78 Citadel 86
79 Ga. Southern 72
95 ■ East Tenn. St. 71
64 Davidson 76
58 N.C.-Charlotte 81
98 ■ Appalachian St. 81
85 Va. Military 69
84 Marshall 88
76 † Va. Military 51
69 † Tenn.-Chatt. 85

GALLAUDET 5-19
48 Lincoln (Pa.) 79
59 Wesley 78
71 ■ Haverford 77
97 ■ Neumann 111
50 Rochester Inst. 95
66 † York (N.Y.) 71
50 Gettysburg 79
54 St. Mary's (Md.) 64
69 ■ Marymount (Va.) 79
71 Washington (Md.) 78
56 Mary Washington 74
70 ■ Phila. Pharmacy 77
71 ■ Catholic 86
61 York (Pa.) 83
63 Goucher 77
74 ■ Western Md. 64
64 ■ St. Mary's (Md.) 70
81 ■ Mary Washington 70
63 ■ York (Pa.) 62
73 Catholic 93
109 Capitol 105
63 Marymount (Va.) 88
65 ■ Goucher 53
64 Marymount (Va.) 79

GANNON 20-7
79 ■ Clarion 63
72 ■ Mansfield 61
76 ■ New York Tech 57
81 ■ Mercyhurst 55
65 ■ Edinboro 69
74 ■ Pitt.-Bradford 65
62 ■ Walsh 51
59 Clarion 64
74 ■ Ashland 52
66 ■ Cheyney 57
58 ■ Slippery Rock 61
97 ■ Millersville 83
88 ■ East Stroudsburg 65
66 Indiana (Pa.) 64
93 † Millersville 78
82 Edinboro 81
55 Slippery Rock 56
87 ■ Lake Erie 44
65 Pitt.-Johnstown 58
74 ■ Mercyhurst 72
57 ■ Kutztown 56
70 Mercyhurst 71
78 ■ Pitt.-Johnstown 62
63 Le Moyne 68
69 ■ Wis.-Parkside 67
72 ■ St. Vincent 53
56 † Phila. Textile 70

GARDNER-WEBB 13-14
86 ■ Queens (N.C.) 94
57 ■ Longwood 56
97 † Barton 104
104 † Savannah A&D 47
75 Presbyterian 87
81 ■ Limestone 62
83 † East Stroudsburg 93
85 † Kennesaw 73
70 Carson-Newman 73
71 ■ Mars Hill 73
77 ■ Lenoir-Rhyne 58
59 ■ Wingate 56
69 Longwood 67
73 Elon 53
86 Catawba 74
66 ■ S.C.-Spartanburg 76
58 ■ Presbyterian 68
84 Lees-McRae 77
76 ■ Carson-Newman 66
83 Mars Hill 88
60 Lenoir-Rhyne 82
78 Wingate 68
73 Wofford 101
76 ■ Elon 85
80 ■ Catawba 97
111 † Elon 64
77 † Presbyterian 86

GENESEO ST. 23-4
69 † John Carroll 80
78 † Hilbert 59
77 ■ Cortland St. 67
77 ■ Brockport St. 65
77 ■ Fredonia St. 72
86 New Paltz St. 74
103 Oneonta St. 66
115 ■ Roberts Wesleyan 68
89 ■ Roberts Wesleyan 62
82 † Brockport St. 77
79 † St. John Fisher 75
75 Utica Tech 71
65 ■ Buffalo St. 40
78 Oswego St. 54
80 ■ Potsdam St. 60
110 ■ Plattsburgh St. 84
60 Fredonia St. 59
85 ■ Oswego St. 41
79 Elmira 75
88 Binghamton 77
85 ■ Utica Tech 72
56 Buffalo St. 68
68 Brockport St. 58
78 † Potsdam St. 56
51 † Fredonia St. 56
80 ■ Buffalo St. 69

66 Mass.-Dartmouth 68

GEORGE MASON 7-21
71 UTEP 90
76 ■ Morgan St. 63
92 ■ Washington (Md.) 52
38 Monmouth (N.J.) 65
95 ■ Radford 75
70 St. Peter's 61
60 ■ Bucknell 73
76 Boise St. 83
63 † Loyola (Md.) 55
75 Va. Com'wealth 103
71 Towson St. 78
74 ■ Old Dominion 76
89 William & Mary 92
67 ■ Canisius 85
78 N.C.-Wilmington 98
64 East Caro. 68
67 ■ American 81
71 ■ Northeastern 82
50 ■ James Madison 56
62 ■ Richmond 81
62 Old Dominion 91
78 ■ William & Mary 82
51 ■ East Caro. 81
72 ■ N.C.-Wilmington 69
73 American 66
58 Richmond 61
59 James Madison 75
49 † James Madison 60

GEO. WASHINGTON 21-9
76 Monmouth (N.J.) 54
87 † Central Mich. 66
65 † Bethune-Cookman 45
75 ■ Hartford 55
80 ■ Columbia 70
83 ■ Tennessee St. 63
74 San Diego 60
79 Pepperdine 81
90 N.C.-Charlotte 63
82 ■ American 71
71 James Madison 56
56 West Va. 72
62 ■ Temple 64
68 Massachusetts 76
88 ■ Rhode Island 75
78 ■ St. Joseph's (Pa.) 59
105 Rutgers 100
64 ■ St. Bonaventure 59
75 Temple 72
65 ■ Massachusetts 68
79 ■ Richmond 77
89 St. Bonaventure 72
71 ■ West Va. 68
73 St. Joseph's (Pa.) 74
74 ■ Rutgers 72
72 Rhode Island 75
75 † Rhode Island 86
82 † New Mexico 68
90 † Southern-B.R. 80
64 † Michigan 72

GEORGETOWN 20-13
88 ■ St. Leo 49
96 ■ Southern-N.O. 57
80 ■ Pittsburgh 66
87 ■ Md.-East. Shore 54
103 ■ Morgan St. 85
78 † Hawaii Pacific 65
64 UC Irvine 60
69 Miami (Fla.) 80
64 ■ Syracuse 60
56 ■ Boston College 57
74 ■ DePaul 45
66 Villanova 56
86 Connecticut 69
80 Nevada-Las Vegas 96
73 ■ Seton Hall 62
61 Boston College 71
61 St. John's (N.Y.) 79
58 ■ Providence 66
61 Syracuse 76
50 Providence 68
61 ■ Villanova 52
56 Seton Hall 66
56 ■ St. John's (N.Y.) 61
48 Pittsburgh 51
82 ■ Miami (Fla.) 64
70 ■ Connecticut 56
67 † Miami (Fla.) 40
69 † Seton Hall 83
78 Arizona St. 68
71 ■ UTEP 44
66 † Miami (Ohio) 53
45 † Ala.-Birmingham 41
61 † Minnesota 62

GEORGIA 15-14
65 Kansas 76
104 ■ Georgia Col. 66
80 † Santa Clara 68
64 Brigham Young 74
67 † Georgia Tech 75
63 † UCLA 68
69 ■ Miami (Fla.) 67
75 ■ Colorado 63
75 Mississippi 61
59 ■ Kentucky 74
86 ■ Mississippi St. 73
77 ■ Florida 81
66 Vanderbilt 78
88 ■ Mercer 79
85 South Caro. 86
79 Arkansas 97
77 ■ Tennessee 60
96 ■ Auburn 69
79 Florida 82
78 ■ Texas 70
73 Alabama 70
70 Kentucky 86
83 ■ Vanderbilt 87
81 ■ Louisiana St. 78
88 ■ South Caro. 87
96 Tennessee 83
87 † Mississippi St. 56
60 † Arkansas 65
84 West Va. 95

GEORGIA COL. 15-13
89 ■ Wingate 85
94 ■ Queens (N.C.) 89
85 Fort Valley St. 82
66 Georgia 104
98 St. Leo 92
85 ■ Clayton St. 73
99 Lees-McRae 81
59 Armstrong St. 70
82 ■ Pembroke St. 79
64 ■ Voorhees 69
56 S.C.-Spartanburg 85
76 S.C.-Aiken 97
91 ■ Columbus 105
74 ■ Augusta 70
81 Lander 73
97 ■ Fort Valley St. 84
74 Francis Marion 73
79 ■ S.C.-Spartanburg 90
86 Columbus 95
53 ■ Francis Marion 71
85 Augusta 107
90 Pembroke St. 93
62 ■ S.C.-Aiken 72
85 ■ Lander 70
77 Clayton St. 59
74 ■ Armstrong St. 68
78 † Lander 77
69 † S.C.-Aiken 73

GA. SOUTHERN 19-9
76 ■ Francis Marion 69
82 South Caro. 69
89 † Central Mich. 74
57 Cincinnati 91
70 † Eckerd 59
69 † Alcorn St. 59
82 Southwestern La. 107
85 ■ Augusta 80
66 Citadel 58
103 ■ Appalachian St. 76
96 ■ East Tenn. St. 75
74 Marshall 75
73 Va. Military 70
75 Furman 73
92 ■ Tenn.-Chatt. 103
80 ■ Western Caro. 52
81 Davidson 88
81 ■ Citadel 73
83 ■ Davidson 71
72 ■ Furman 79
88 East Tenn. St. 93
92 Appalachian St. 84
69 ■ Va. Military 63
75 ■ Marshall 72
90 Western Caro. 81
68 Tenn.-Chatt. 91
72 † Citadel 41
76 † East Tenn. St. 84

GEORGIA ST. 13-14
84 ■ Shorter 62
84 ■ North Ga. 69
79 Georgia Tech 102
58 ■ Tenn.-Martin 54
62 Southwest Tex. St. 73
64 † Idaho 70
64 Boise St. 75
60 † Pepperdine 79
83 † Southern-B.R. 79
91 ■ Alabama St. 74
76 Memphis St. 97
69 Mercer 77
60 ■ Charleston (S.C.) 50
68 ■ Florida Int'l 69
93 ■ Stetson 81
94 ■ Clark Atlanta 79
78 Samford 92
82 Southeastern La. 90
107 Centenary 111
58 ■ Mercer 57
63 Charleston (S.C.) 88
61 Florida Int'l 60
100 Stetson 89
89 ■ Fla. Atlantic 70
61 ■ Samford 71
75 ■ Southeastern La. 82
97 ■ Centenary 80

GEORGIA TECH 19-11
112 ■ Florida A&M 83
87 Kentucky 96
102 ■ Georgia St. 79
75 † Georgia 67
87 † Louisville 85
81 Tenn.-Chatt. 74
105 ■ Youngstown St. 85
78 ■ Va. Military 52
85 Maryland 75
80 ■ Duke 79
67 North Caro. 80
67 ■ Charleston (S.C.) 84
58 ■ Wake Forest 81
75 Virginia 71
85 ■ North Caro. St. 74
77 Florida St. 96
80 ■ Clemson 83
93 ■ Maryland 79
63 Duke 73
66 ■ North Caro. 77
65 Richmond 60
69 Wake Forest 58
73 ■ Virginia 61
60 North Caro. St. 68
82 ■ Florida St. 83
66 Clemson 59
69 † Duke 66
69 † Clemson 61
77 † North Caro. 75
78 † Southern-B.R. 93

GETTYSBURG 9-15
66 ■ Wilkes 69
62 ■ Phila. Pharmacy 68
70 ■ Dickinson 76
73 ■ Moravian 59
78 Navy 76
69 Messiah 65
89 Lehigh 83
61 † Scranton 81
67 † Drew 63
73 ■ Carnegie Mellon 75
79 ■ Gallaudet 50
93 ■ Bethany (W.Va.) 77
62 Swarthmore 70
73 ■ Lebanon Valley 77
57 Muhlenberg 75
79 Western Md. 86
60 ■ Frank. & Marsh. 72
56 Dickinson 58
51 Moravian 60
54 ■ York (Pa.) 69
66 Lebanon Valley 60
80 ■ Muhlenberg 94
60 ■ Western Md. 59
53 Frank. & Marsh. 87

GONZAGA 19-9
93 ■ Whitman 57
73 San Jose St. 76
59 Southern Cal 77
87 † Texas-Arlington 95
77 † Alcorn St. 67
106 ■ Carroll (Mont.) 56
64 Idaho 82
71 ■ Eastern Wash. 50
84 ■ Sam Houston St. 66
91 ■ Drexel 78
83 ■ Idaho St. 71
73 Eastern Wash. 68
66 Pepperdine 67
65 Loyola (Cal.) 64
64 ■ Santa Clara 61
79 ■ San Diego 64
71 ■ Portland 53
63 Portland 65
82 St. Mary's (Cal.) 64
74 San Francisco 77
85 ■ San Francisco 64
79 ■ St. Mary's (Cal.) 55
69 San Diego 66
56 Santa Clara 58
87 ■ Loyola (Cal.) 73
63 ■ Pepperdine 52
77 † Portland 57
51 † Santa Clara 53

GORDON 8-16
67 ■ St. Joseph's (Me.) 80
69 MIT 77
87 Colby 71
67 ■ Colby-Sawyer 65
65 Oglethorpe 86
40 † Randolph-Macon 58
44 North Ga. 71
62 Bates 83
61 ■ Salem St. 71
74 ■ Salve Regina 81
48 ■ Anna Maria 73
50 Eastern Nazarene 73
69 ■ Roger Williams 56
83 Wentworth Inst. 71
47 New England Col. 46
31 Salve Regina 54
60 ■ Eastern Nazarene 66
82 ■ Wentworth Inst. 65
64 Anna Maria 95
78 ■ Curry 50
72 ■ New England Col. 65
53 Roger Williams 64
63 Curry 73
70 Curry 73

GOUCHER 8-16
73 Roanoke 88
72 † Marymount (Va.) 54
52 Johns Hopkins 66

67 ■ Frostburg St. 79
92 ■ Lancaster Bible 48
93 ■ Neumann 75
85 Washington (Md.) 88
56 † Dominican (N.Y.) 50
52 Slippery Rock 74
68 St. John Fisher 98
62 † Keuka 69
82 ■ York (Pa.) 73
58 ■ St. Mary's (Md.) 69
62 Mary Washington 79
58 ■ Catholic 67
77 ■ Gallaudet 63
60 York (Pa.) 74
57 Catholic 77
47 ■ Phila. Pharmacy 42
70 ■ Mary Washington 49
61 St. Mary's (Md.) 68
64 ■ Marymount (Va.) 74
53 Gallaudet 65
45 York (Pa.) 67

GRAMBLING 13-14

82 ■ Texas Col. 79
106 ■ Bapt. Christian 94
66 ■ Southeastern La. 72
59 Ark.-Lit. Rock 70
104 ■ Jarvis Christian 63
69 Southeastern La. 72
85 Central Fla. 81
94 † Northeastern 83
63 ■ Ark.-Lit. Rock 75
73 Southern-B.R. 107
83 Alcorn St. 86
89 ■ Centenary 86
103 ■ Prairie View 83
69 ■ Texas Southern 71
75 Jackson St. 91
74 Alabama St. 90
86 ■ Mississippi Val. 69
106 Centenary 85
84 ■ Southern-B.R. 91
87 ■ Alcorn St. 74
89 Prairie View 87
82 Texas Southern 98
76 ■ Jackson St. 89
91 ■ Alabama St. 85
82 ■ Tougaloo 79
82 Mississippi Val. 97
91 Southern-B.R. 105

GRAND CANYON 20-11

110 ■ Bridgeport 98
110 ■ Central Okla. 108
73 ■ St. Thomas (Minn.) 71
76 † Mo.-St. Louis 58
74 Southern Ind. 90
76 Southern Utah 74
81 Cal St. Bakersfield 88
77 † Emporia St. 81
90 † Humboldt St. 71
106 † Chapman 83
124 ■ Winona St. 98
105 ■ UC Riverside 65
75 Seattle Pacific 77
74 Hawaii-Hilo 73
94 Chaminade 102
92 ■ Alas. Anchorage 88
110 ■ Alas. Fairbanks 73
132 ■ Pacific Christian 89
83 Eastern Mont. 77
70 West Tex. A&M 79
107 ■ Seattle Pacific 102
82 ■ Hawaii-Hilo 84
79 ■ Chaminade 80
101 Alas. Fairbanks 97
74 Alas. Anchorage 76
94 ■ West Tex. A&M 84
94 ■ Eastern Mont. 61
80 † Seattle Pacific 73
78 Alas. Anchorage 86
68 Cal St. Bakersfield 98
103 † Cal St. Chico 98

GRAND VALLEY ST. 14-12

70 Lewis 80
86 ■ Olivet (Ill.) 80
93 † Wabash 84
70 Calvin 84
100 ■ Aquinas 79
87 ■ Grand Rapids Bapt. 78
67 Michigan Tech 74
88 Northern Mich. 109
82 ■ Saginaw Valley 76
57 St. Joseph's (Ind.) 68
79 Olivet (Ill.) 75
85 Wayne St. (Mich.) 82
91 ■ Lake Superior St. 67
83 ■ Ferris St. 90
80 Northwood 75
71 ■ Oakland 73
103 Hillsdale 104
61 ■ Michigan Tech 79
81 ■ Northern Mich. 79
64 Saginaw Valley 63
77 Lake Superior St. 76
82 ■ Wayne St. (Mich.) 105
80 Ferris St. 97
81 ■ Northwood 79
61 Oakland 68
105 ■ Hillsdale 101

GREENSBORO 17-9

79 † Hanover 82
82 † Penn St.-Behrend 64
80 ■ Maryville (Tenn.) 93
80 High Point 73
97 ■ Savannah A&D 47
75 Salisbury St. 77
53 † Manhattanville 51
71 Guilford 73
87 ■ Newport News App. 56
66 † Western Conn. St. 67
105 † Lehman 44
71 N.C. Wesleyan 62
98 ■ Chris. Newport 103
91 Methodist 68
98 St. Andrews 76
84 Averett 61
83 ■ Ferrum 82
80 ■ Methodist 62
81 Newport News App. 74
77 Chris. Newport 87
86 ■ Guilford 78
100 ■ N.C. Wesleyan 78
83 Ferrum 94
105 ■ Averett 79
79 ■ Averett 69
62 Chris. Newport 80

GRINNELL 10-12

96 ■ Maryville (Mo.) 83
75 ■ Mt. St. Clare 71
82 ■ Principia 48
55 ■ Luther 57
68 ■ Knox 83
78 ■ Illinois Col. 66
62 Monmouth (Ill.) 70
72 Cornell College 67
121 ■ Vennard 41
69 Barat 70
74 Coe 71
48 St. Norbert 61
67 Lawrence 81
90 ■ Carroll (Wis.) 65
77 ■ Beloit 79
83 ■ Grand View 92
43 ■ Cornell College 62
65 ■ Monmouth (Ill.) 74
85 ■ Coe 83
55 Knox 79
68 Illinois Col. 83
77 Mt. St. Clare 68

GROVE CITY 8-14

49 Carnegie Mellon 60
63 ■ Allegheny 60
59 Mount Union 62
75 ■ Baldwin-Wallace 91
86 ■ Tiffin 93
65 ■ Geneva 79
63 ■ Westminster (Pa.) 70
91 Defiance 105
89 † Hiram 93
65 Penn St.-Behrend 62
68 Frostburg St. 81
63 † York (Pa.) 77
67 Geneva 72
56 Thiel 59
83 ■ Bethany (W.Va.) 61
79 ■ Waynesburg 70
79 Wash. & Jeff. 67
69 ■ Penn St.-Behrend 58
60 ■ Thiel 49
65 Bethany (W.Va.) 84
78 Waynesburg 73
73 ■ Wash. & Jeff. 82

GUILFORD 10-14

75 Methodist 59
50 † Francis Marion 57
78 N.C. Wesleyan 71
81 ■ East. Mennonite 67
67 ■ Lynchburg 53
73 Wash. & Lee 67
73 ■ Greensboro 71
81 Emory & Henry 83
69 Hampden-Sydney 64
69 ■ Va. Wesleyan 81
63 ■ Randolph-Macon 59
65 ■ Bridgewater (Va.) 84
77 ■ Roanoke 80
79 East. Mennonite 85
67 Lynchburg 73
56 Randolph-Macon 71
81 ■ Wash. & Lee 60
82 ■ Hampden-Sydney 76
76 Va. Wesleyan 78
84 ■ Emory & Henry 99
78 Greensboro 86
71 Roanoke 90
51 Bridgewater (Va.) 55
58 Roanoke 71

GUST. ADOLPHUS 12-12

74 Luther 79
53 ■ St. Cloud St. 61
46 ■ Carleton 49
87 Concordia-M'head 52
60 † Cornell College 59
81 Colorado Col. 68
63 ■ Hamline 46
74 ■ Bethel (Minn.) 70
78 Augsburg 74
66 ■ St. Mary's (Minn.) 63
60 St. John's (Minn.) 93
59 ■ St. Thomas (Minn.) 61
64 St. Olaf 67
77 Macalester 65
65 ■ Concordia-M'head 62
50 Carleton 65
92 ■ Macalester 65
69 Hamline 79
73 Bethel (Minn.) 81
71 ■ Augsburg 56
70 St. Mary's (Minn.) 72
62 ■ St. John's (Minn.) 67
76 St. Thomas (Minn.) 67
65 ■ St. Olaf 66

HAMILTON 22-5

92 † Utica Tech 76
72 Utica 75
95 Binghamton 107
89 ■ Hobart 67
74 Hartwick 62
85 ■ Albany (N.Y.) 84
110 ■ Connecticut Col. 88
98 ■ Muhlenberg 76
70 † Colorado Col. 88
108 † Albertus Magnus 78
74 Oswego St. 55
63 ■ Ithaca 55
91 ■ Hilbert 81
74 ■ Nazareth (N.Y.) 86
87 ■ Williams 82
98 Amherst 96
65 ■ Utica 48
99 Oneonta St. 74
78 ■ Rochester 67
92 ■ Union (N.Y.) 71
108 Skidmore 83
91 ■ Utica Tech 81
89 ■ Clarkson 72
134 ■ St. Lawrence 98
105 ■ Plattsburgh St. 98
108 ■ Elmira 94
95 ■ Rochester Inst. 105

HAMLINE 8-16

76 † Colby 81
53 † Wash. & Lee 56
76 ■ Luther 62
81 ■ N'western (Minn.) 82
71 ■ St. Mary's (Minn.) 75
64 ■ St. John's (Minn.) 65
71 Augsburg 85
49 ■ St. Thomas (Minn.) 66
46 Gust. Adolphus 63
63 Macalester 56
58 ■ St. Olaf 63
72 Concordia-M'head 61
63 ■ Bethel (Minn.) 61
62 Carleton 75
74 St. Mary's (Minn.) 64
64 St. John's (Minn.) 78
77 ■ Augsburg 86
49 St. Thomas (Minn.) 61
79 ■ Gust. Adolphus 69
85 ■ Macalester 71
63 St. Olaf 70
73 ■ Concordia-M'head 68
60 Bethel (Minn.) 67
55 ■ Carleton 63

HAMPDEN-SYDNEY 12-13

78 † Cabrini 91
82 † Ursinus 57
90 ■ Marymount (Va.) 77
75 Wash. & Lee 73
56 ■ Bridgewater (Va.) 61
91 ■ Newport News App. 48
66 ■ Berea 68
64 ■ Guilford 69
87 ■ Mary Washington 51
64 Bridgewater (Va.) 65
62 Va. Wesleyan 64
75 ■ Emory & Henry 92
56 Randolph-Macon 63
73 Emory & Henry 95
89 ■ Wash. & Lee 67
94 ■ East. Mennonite 69
90 ■ Lynchburg 61
76 Guilford 82
76 Roanoke 85
76 ■ Va. Wesleyan 75
79 East. Mennonite 74
86 Lynchburg 75
75 ■ Randolph-Macon 49
79 ■ Roanoke 85
58 Randolph-Macon 61

HAMPTON 15-12

65 Fayetteville St. 76
79 Johnson Smith 90
65 ■ St. Augustine's 68
81 ■ Shaw 87
67 Bowie St. 56
76 ■ Winston-Salem 64
65 ■ N.C. Central 70
53 Chris. Newport 51
79 St. Paul's 70
82 † Paul Quinn 49
71 † Bowie St. 58
65 † Norfolk St. 75
105 Elizabeth City St. 107
54 Virginia Union 63

103 ■ Virginia St. 96
76 ■ Virginia Union 85
97 ■ Livingstone 78
86 ■ Elizabeth City St. 80
86 ■ Dist. Columbia 66
62 ■ Norfolk St. 53
86 ■ St. Paul's 77
88 Virginia St. 83
71 Norfolk St. 93
94 Dist. Columbia 76
79 ■ Bowie St. 80
100 † Shaw 87
68 † N.C. Central 72

HANOVER 16-9
82 † Greensboro 79
71 Ohio Wesleyan 63
81 Wilmington (Ohio) 73
66 Bluffton 48
100 ■ Ind.-Southeast 65
81 Webster 59
98 Maryville (Mo.) 81
60 Wittenberg 61
78 † Centre 79
51 DePauw 56
102 ■ Wabash 68
101 ■ Wilmington (Ohio) 50
80 † Centre 64
94 ■ Anderson 74
72 Manchester 68
77 ■ Rose-Hulman 57
88 ■ Franklin 85
76 ■ DePauw 67
88 Wabash 91
85 ■ Manchester 76
62 Anderson 70
51 Rose-Hulman 59
84 Thomas More 91
79 Franklin 84
58 ■ Anderson 75

HARTFORD 14-14
64 ■ Dartmouth 61
81 † Delaware St. 80
69 St. Joseph's (Pa.) 93
55 Geo. Washington 75
70 ■ Siena 74
67 Rhode Island 98
66 Connecticut 91
87 ■ Bridgeport 78
97 Portland 84
69 Oregon 71
83 ■ Central Conn. St. 53
70 ■ Boston U. 67
58 Northeastern 68
65 New Hampshire 77
75 Maine 66
68 Drexel 80
67 Delaware 71
93 ■ Vermont 68
65 ■ Delaware 69
71 ■ Drexel 76
97 ■ Harvard 72
88 ■ Maine 76
69 ■ New Hampshire 56
72 Boston U. 58
62 ■ Northeastern 64
76 Vermont 58
59 ■ Maine 49
80 Drexel 91

HARTWICK 14-12
84 ■ Mass.-Dartmouth 86
70 ■ Oneonta St. 64
56 Skidmore 57
62 ■ Hamilton 74
77 Rochester Inst. 71
44 † Menlo 65
74 † Worcester Tech 54
51 Rensselaer 69
63 ■ Elmira 84
71 ■ Clarkson 42
78 ■ St. Lawrence 74
74 ■ Union (N.Y.) 56
48 Ithaca 42

61 Alfred 77
57 ■ Rochester Inst. 54
69 ■ Hobart 55
60 ■ Utica 58
54 ■ Alfred 59
72 ■ Ithaca 80
65 ■ Albany (N.Y.) 56
65 St. Lawrence 67
67 Clarkson 53
63 Oneonta St. 67
72 ■ Rensselaer 65
75 Hobart 72
71 St. John Fisher 88

HARVARD 6-20
72 ■ Holy Cross 92
57 Boston College 96
80 ■ Babson 64
77 ■ Fairfield 84
94 ■ Lehigh 90
64 Dartmouth 90
75 Colgate 85
65 Vermont 73
69 Santa Clara 80
67 † Rhode Island 80
79 ■ Boston U. 59
39 Princeton 63
74 Pennsylvania 86
70 ■ Dartmouth 86
76 ■ New Hampshire 87
58 Cornell 71
70 Columbia 101
54 ■ Yale 51
71 ■ Brown 72
72 Hartford 97
62 ■ Pennsylvania 81
57 ■ Princeton 63
77 Brown 74
58 Yale 68
82 ■ Columbia 75
87 ■ Cornell 108

HAVERFORD 5-19
66 ■ Williams 74
67 Swarthmore 70
96 Neumann 95
75 Phila. Pharmacy 79
77 Gallaudet 71
77 ■ Gwynedd Mercy 76
97 ■ Phila. Bible 79
80 Penn St.-Harrisburg 89
65 UC San Diego 105
65 † Pomona-Pitzer 95
72 Occidental 115
74 Whittier 93
71 ■ New York U. 99
59 Widener 68
64 ■ Washington (Md.) 82
75 ■ Ursinus 82
57 Swarthmore 58
52 Johns Hopkins 78
54 ■ Widener 70
66 ■ Carnegie Mellon 59
66 Washington (Md.) 77
65 Ursinus 72
65 ■ Swarthmore 82
72 ■ Johns Hopkins 89

HAWAII 12-16
63 ■ Tulsa 68
64 ■ San Diego 65
87 ■ Tulsa 69
79 ■ South Caro. St. 64
66 ■ Coastal Caro. 62
83 ■ Fordham 64
66 ■ Kansas 94
84 ■ North Caro. 101
81 ■ San Diego St. 67
66 Colorado St. 82
62 Wyoming 70
68 ■ UTEP 69
58 ■ New Mexico 61
67 Utah 82
80 Brigham Young 84

78 ■ Fresno St. 74
74 ■ Air Force 59
64 Fresno St. 69
78 Air Force 69
56 ■ Brigham Young 62
60 ■ Utah 62
58 New Mexico 82
67 UTEP 68
86 ■ Colorado St. 72
61 ■ Wyoming 59
72 San Diego St. 58
62 † Air Force 54
71 † Brigham Young 85

HEIDELBERG 12-16
87 Defiance 100
66 Allegheny 70
76 † Westminster (Pa.) 74
50 Bowling Green 81
78 ■ Hiram 82
76 ■ Capital 75
91 ■ Marietta 70
71 Mount Union 76
88 ■ Earlham 81
75 ■ Walsh 101
70 ■ Ohio Northern 75
73 Otterbein 77
60 ■ John Carroll 72
60 Muskingum 79
87 ■ Baldwin-Wallace 68
76 Marietta 77
78 Capital 65
99 ■ Otterbein 100
70 Ohio Northern 71
86 ■ Mount Union 67
54 Baldwin-Wallace 78
88 ■ Muskingum 77
70 John Carroll 82
77 Hiram 76
109 ■ Marietta 69
72 Hiram 68
71 † John Carroll 56
82 † Otterbein 101

HENDERSON ST. 15-14
79 ■ Southwest Baptist 87
47 West Tex. A&M 89
77 † Eastern N. Mex. 89
76 ■ Ark. Baptist 73
58 † Evangel 77
48 Southwest Baptist 57
77 East Tex. St. 70
77 ■ Delta St. 79
78 ■ East Tex. St. 59
78 ■ Ark.-Pine Bluff 60
85 ■ Ozarks (Ark.) 91
100 Southern Ark. 89
86 ■ Arkansas Tech 75
58 Delta St. 56
77 Ouachita Bapt. 80
74 ■ Central Ark. 87
92 Ark.-Monticello 101
71 Harding 89
62 ■ Arkansas Col. 57
71 Ozarks (Ark.) 74
80 Arkansas Tech 79
71 ■ Ouachita Bapt. 68
70 Central Ark. 83
101 ■ Ark.-Monticello 77
82 ■ Harding 81
71 Arkansas Col. 48
71 Southern Ark. 61
95 ■ Ouachita Bapt. 79
63 Arkansas Tech 79

HILLSDALE 17-11
98 ■ Tiffin 68
85 ■ Siena Heights 77
72 IU/PU-Ft. Wayne 89
98 ■ Olivet 61
78 ■ Indianapolis 59
60 Ashland 63
68 ■ Lake Superior St. 63
83 ■ Saginaw Valley 62
95 Oakland 83

108 Spring Arbor 70
65 ■ Wayne St. (Mich.) 85
65 Ferris St. 66
82 ■ Michigan Tech 72
67 ■ Northern Mich. 66
112 Northwood 87
104 ■ Grand Valley St. 103
69 Lake Superior St. 57
64 Saginaw Valley 69
81 ■ Findlay 84
92 ■ Oakland 75
75 Wayne St. (Mich.) 81
87 ■ Ferris St. 72
73 Michigan Tech 89
82 Northern Mich. 103
112 ■ Northwood 92
101 Grand Valley St. 105
93 Northern Mich. 94
78 † Ferris St. 73

HIRAM 17-8
85 † Penn St.-Behrend 64
63 Fredonia St. 73
80 ■ Wooster 70
82 Heidelberg 78
69 Otterbein 75
77 ■ Mount Union 66
68 Ohio Northern 75
70 † Ohio Dominican 82
93 † Grove City 89
82 ■ Baldwin-Wallace 76
77 Marietta 70
75 ■ Muskingum 66
77 Capital 86
87 ■ John Carroll 67
84 Baldwin-Wallace 81
86 Thiel 56
80 ■ Otterbein 77
70 Mount Union 56
70 ■ Capital 61
77 ■ Ohio Northern 61
78 John Carroll 68
84 ■ Marietta 70
88 Muskingum 91
76 ■ Heidelberg 77
68 ■ Heidelberg 72

HOBART 12-13
83 Colorado Col. 94
70 † Trenton St. 67
67 Hamilton 89
105 Union (N.Y.) 106
83 ■ Skidmore 74
77 ■ Rensselaer 84
81 St. John Fisher 100
73 † Rochester 67
86 Rochester Inst. 90
72 Rochester Inst. 82
84 ■ Alfred 86
70 ■ Ithaca 78
93 ■ Roberts Wesleyan 74
76 Clarkson 61
92 St. Lawrence 73
73 Rensselaer 85
55 Hartwick 69
66 ■ Rochester Inst. 63
92 ■ Clarkson 70
83 ■ St. Lawrence 69
61 ■ Rochester 57
87 Ithaca 95
65 Alfred 64
81 ■ St. John Fisher 73
72 ■ Hartwick 75

HOFSTRA 9-18
56 Manhattan 80
61 San Francisco 92
63 † Western Ill. 64
48 ■ Yale 46
78 Lehigh 71
50 † St. Bonaventure 66
56 St. John's (N.Y.) 58
64 Rutgers 91
55 Tulane 64
41 Nevada-Las Vegas 79

56 Fordham 60
68 ■ Columbia 60
54 ■ Iona 67
56 Cornell 70
64 Army 52
68 Rhode Island 80
63 Texas Christian 66
69 South Ala. 83
83 ■ Maine 77
55 St. Joseph's (Pa.) 76
78 ■ Stony Brook 57
69 Boston U. 71
80 Central Conn. St. 72
54 Villanova 92
86 ■ Central Conn. St. 61
77 ■ UC Irvine 67
48 Richmond 79

HOLY CROSS 23-7
92 Harvard 72
96 ■ Siena 95
76 New Hampshire 63
76 Pennsylvania 78
83 ■ Northwestern 73
66 † Massachusetts 81
90 † Ala.-Birmingham 83
63 ■ Boston College 84
83 William & Mary 78
70 Manhattan 74
71 ■ Fordham 61
64 Army 63
94 ■ Lehigh 75
78 ■ Colgate 68
95 Lafayette 79
83 ■ Dartmouth 62
95 ■ Navy 69
88 ■ Bucknell 86
73 Fordham 81
110 ■ Army 73
99 ■ Rutgers 89
104 Lehigh 87
97 Colgate 95
95 ■ Lafayette 68
90 Navy 72
99 Bucknell 112
85 ■ Army 68
86 ■ Fordham 78
98 Bucknell 73
64 † Arkansas 94

HOPE 18-8
84 † Bethel (Ind.) 88
84 † Ind.-South Bend 76
92 ■ Concordia (Mich.) 55
59 North Park 64
91 Concordia (Ill.) 85
78 ■ Wheaton (Ill.) 71
87 † Spring Arbor 77
77 † Aquinas 67
106 ■ Trinity Chrst. (Il.) 80
96 ■ Grand Rapids Bapt. 81
76 ■ Alma 63
97 ■ Aquinas 70
67 Albion 69
101 ■ Olivet 96
80 ■ Adrian 64
68 Kalamazoo 79
72 Calvin 89
87 Alma 90
75 ■ Calvin 81
75 ■ Kalamazoo 72
96 Adrian 73
76 ■ Albion 55
64 Olivet 62
80 ■ Siena Heights 70
72 ■ Alma 71
69 Calvin 77

HOUSTON 21-9
82 DePaul 65
92 ■ Ill.-Chicago 66
76 North Caro. 84
94 ■ Texas-San Antonio 67
84 Arkansas St. 82
76 ■ Stephen F. Austin 75
78 UCLA 87
86 ■ UC Irvine 78
83 ■ Wyoming 56
81 ■ Texas 67
81 Texas A&M 69
83 ■ Baylor 77
85 ■ Southern Methodist 75
74 Texas Tech 78
60 Southern Methodist 70
61 ■ Rice 65
66 Texas Christian 68
92 Nevada 80
77 Cal St. Fullerton 63
93 ■ Texas Tech 76
78 ■ Texas A&M 51
89 ■ Louisville 81
76 Baylor 75
86 Texas 79
78 Rice 89
86 ■ Texas Christian 66
84 † Texas A&M 68
58 † Texas 50
76 † Texas Tech 88
61 UTEP 67

HOWARD 10-18
83 ■ Paine 68
70 Clemson 89
51 Northeastern 73
64 Virginia 100
87 ■ Eastern Ky. 90
46 Stanford 71
62 San Fran. St. 59
62 Long Beach St. 95
69 Maryland 109
83 North Caro. A&T 77
56 South Caro. St. 61
79 Md.-East. Shore 91
69 ■ Delaware St. 66
67 ■ St. Peter's 62
75 ■ Bethune-Cookman 60
84 ■ Florida A&M 85
80 ■ Md.-East. Shore 55
60 ■ Coppin St. 76
58 ■ Morgan St. 67
57 Coppin St. 71
66 Bethune-Cookman 64
89 Florida A&M 94
56 Delaware St. 76
81 ■ North Caro. A&T 90
65 ■ South Caro. St. 62
69 Morgan St. 77
86 † Bethune-Cookman 72
57 † Coppin St. 65

HUMBOLDT ST. 12-14
57 ■ Notre Dame (Cal.) 60
63 ■ Carroll (Mont.) 48
72 Cal St. San B'dino 75
53 San Francisco 80
76 ■ Oregon Tech 57
69 ■ Southern Ore. St. 66
54 ■ UC Santa Cruz 52
64 ■ Minn.-Morris 58
63 † Cal Poly Pomona 64
71 † Grand Canyon 90
80 † Bethany (Cal.) 68
65 ■ Bethany (Cal.) 64
79 Sonoma St. 76
74 UC Davis 66
62 ■ San Fran. St. 63
60 ■ Notre Dame (Cal.) 67
52 Cal St. Hayward 49
57 Cal St. Stanislaus 60
59 ■ Cal St. Chico 64
59 ■ Cal St. Stanislaus 80
64 ■ Cal St. Hayward 48
57 Notre Dame (Cal.) 72
76 San Fran. St. 90
50 ■ UC Davis 62
64 ■ Sonoma St. 61
83 Cal St. Chico 89

HUNTER 25-4
83 ■ York (N.Y.) 70
94 ■ Merchant Marine 78
62 Trenton St. 73
89 † Widener 68
76 King's (Pa.) 67
88 Medgar Evers 63
100 Merchant Marine 77
80 New Jersey Tech 85
95 York (N.Y.) 85
92 ■ Mt. St. Mary (N.Y.) 84
82 Mt. St. Vincent 75
94 ■ Staten Island 79
66 Manhattanville 69
67 ■ Stony Brook 60
105 ■ CCNY 68
74 Lehman 43
75 ■ New Jersey Tech 67
92 Staten Island 69
97 ■ Medgar Evers 86
69 ■ Baruch 49
88 Stony Brook 60
94 ■ Manhattanville 70
86 ■ Bloomfield 64
82 John Jay 76
71 ■ Lehman 45
83 ■ Staten Island 50
104 ■ Medgar Evers 73
83 ■ New Jersey Tech 70
62 † Scranton 78

IDAHO 24-8
93 ■ Simon Fraser 68
64 † Ark.-Lit. Rock 54
52 Southwest Mo. St. 57
65 ■ Washington St. 63
61 Oregon 80
70 † Georgia St. 64
72 † Elizabeth City St. 79
82 ■ Gonzaga 64
84 ■ Seattle 41
84 † Chaminade 80
85 † San Francisco 86
76 † Liberty 74
81 ■ Cal St. Sacramento 61
89 ■ Central Wash. 75
80 ■ Whitman 53
60 ■ Montana 50
63 ■ Montana St. 47
87 ■ Eastern Wash. 63
66 Weber St. 67
59 Northern Ariz. 53
97 ■ Idaho St. 76
107 ■ Boise St. 99
65 Montana St. 63
65 Montana 68
76 Cal St. Sacramento 71
82 Eastern Wash. 80
78 ■ Northern Ariz. 51
63 ■ Weber St. 75
67 Boise St. 52
52 Idaho St. 43
91 ■ Idaho St. 87
68 ■ Boise St. 80

IDAHO ST. 10-18
71 † Kent 83
68 † Colgate 76
59 Oklahoma 112
89 ■ Western Mont. 56
62 ■ Colorado St. 68
88 ■ Portland 64
64 Northern Ill. 73
66 ■ Illinois St. 56
97 ■ Tennessee Tech 77
69 Washington 81
71 Gonzaga 83
63 ■ Southern Utah 79
80 Weber St. 91
68 Northern Ariz. 76
66 ■ Boise St. 62
53 ■ Montana 54
62 ■ Montana St. 64
76 Idaho 97
56 Eastern Wash. 69
88 ■ Northern Ariz. 69
94 ■ Weber St. 89
71 Boise St. 82
68 Montana St. 66
62 Montana 68
92 ■ Eastern Wash. 72
43 ■ Idaho 52
61 † Montana 50
87 Idaho 91

ILLINOIS 19-13
86 † Dayton 78
93 † Vanderbilt 77
94 † New Mexico St. 95
70 ■ Ill.-Chicago 68
88 ■ Chicago St. 61
85 ■ Jackson St. 81
58 ■ Princeton 50
77 ■ Mercer 58
65 † Missouri 66
72 Texas 89
58 ■ Marquette 61
81 Northwestern 71
52 Michigan St. 39
79 ■ Indiana 83
82 ■ Penn St. 66
68 Michigan 76
80 ■ Wisconsin 72
86 Ohio St. 76
78 ■ Iowa 77
82 ■ Northwestern 67
83 ■ Michigan St. 80
79 ■ Pittsburgh 95
72 Indiana 93
74 Penn St. 66
78 ■ Purdue 70
66 Wisconsin 74
65 Minnesota 67
85 ■ Ohio St. 73
97 ■ Michigan 98
53 Iowa 63
75 † Long Beach St. 72
68 † Vanderbilt 85

ILL.-CHICAGO 17-15
92 ■ North Park 62
68 Illinois 70
90 ■ Western Mich. 89
66 Houston 92
75 Michigan St. 79
81 † Eastern Mich. 89
87 † Florida Int'l 85
87 † American (P.R.) 73
71 ■ Western Ky. 82
55 Ohio St. 79
75 Wis.-Green Bay 71
85 ■ Wright St. 82
79 ■ Northeastern Ill. 70
57 Eastern Ill. 71
86 Western Ill. 73
88 Valparaiso 86
64 ■ Northern Ill. 66
73 ■ Cleveland St. 86
89 ■ Youngstown St. 71
94 ■ Valparaiso 101
61 Northern Ill. 63
88 Wright St. 96
72 ■ Wis.-Green Bay 65
64 Cleveland St. 67
88 Youngstown St. 74
92 ■ Western Ill. 77
92 Chicago St. 67
92 Northeastern Ill. 97
87 ■ Eastern Ill. 77
46 † Wis.-Green Bay 43
96 † Cleveland St. 68
88 Wright St. 94

ILL. BENEDICTINE 15-9
93 † Trinity Chrst. (Il.) 73
80 Wheaton (Ill.) 73
70 Ripon 83
77 ■ North Central 59
80 ■ Elmhurst 60

66 † Teikyo Marycrest 70
76 † Aurora 64
64 ■ North Park 65
74 † Grand Rapids Bapt. 82
79 † Trinity Chrst. (Il.) 66
79 † Carroll (Mont.) 75
64 Loras 49
61 † Xavier (La.) 64
55 Eastern Ill. 79
83 Judson 69
71 ■ Rockford 42
75 Aurora 83
84 ■ Trinity (Ill.) 53
66 Concordia (Ill.) 77
85 ■ Judson 66
63 Rockford 58
67 ■ Aurora 75
77 ■ Concordia (Ill.) 65
66 Trinity (Ill.) 64

ILLINOIS COL. 10-11
86 Blackburn 73
85 † Westminster (Mo.) 74
103 Maryville (Mo.) 88
96 ■ Principia 40
102 Coe 88
66 Grinnell 78
82 ■ Millikin 99
78 Knox 96
84 Monmouth (Ill.) 87
73 Cornell College 77
61 Beloit 84
87 Carroll (Wis.) 92
86 ■ Lake Forest 77
96 ■ Ripon 93
82 ■ Greenville 79
79 ■ Knox 80
84 ■ Monmouth (Ill.) 97
71 ■ Cornell College 76
78 MacMurray 100
92 ■ Coe 68
83 ■ Grinnell 68

ILLINOIS ST. 19-10
82 ■ Lewis 69
69 ■ Butler 53
66 ■ DePaul 67
67 Evansville 86
61 Tulsa 74
63 Creighton 70
56 Idaho St. 66
64 St. Mary's (Cal.) 44
65 ■ Southwest Mo. St. 57
60 Indiana St. 63
88 ■ Southern Ill. 74
68 Wichita St. 66
82 Southwest Mo. St. 73
88 ■ Loyola (Ill.) 64
70 ■ Bradley 68
68 Southern Ill. 83
60 ■ Drake 57
64 ■ Indiana St. 48
69 Northern Iowa 49
75 ■ Wichita St. 62
55 ■ Miami (Ohio) 65
72 ■ Tulsa 63
59 ■ Creighton 53
41 Bradley 55
55 Drake 54
71 ■ Northern Iowa 59
73 † Indiana St. 68
60 † Drake 59
59 † Southern Ill. 70

ILL. WESLEYAN 16-9
93 ■ Neb. Wesleyan 81
86 ■ DePauw 81
66 Northern Ill. 86
71 ■ Loras 59
96 † St. Joseph's (Ind.) 72
83 Olivet (Ill.) 93
90 Hawaii Pacific 101
76 BYU-Hawaii 80
91 † Sheldon Jackson 75
91 ■ Chicago 63
80 Augustana (Ill.) 94
90 ■ North Central 54
99 ■ Wheaton (Ill.) 84
93 ■ Carthage 76
85 ■ Elmhurst 74
66 North Park 67
99 North Central 63
89 Millikin 92
83 Wheaton (Ill.) 78
79 Carthage 71
85 ■ North Park 69
96 Elmhurst 104
78 ■ Augustana (Ill.) 79
118 ■ Millikin 94
103 ■ Olivet (Ill.) 98

INDIANA 31-4
103 ■ Murray St. 80
102 ■ Tulane 92
81 † Florida St. 78
78 † Seton Hall 74
69 † Kansas 74
75 Notre Dame 70
107 ■ Austin Peay 61
97 ■ Western Mich. 58
79 ■ Cincinnati 64
105 ■ St. John's (N.Y.) 80
90 † Butler 48
85 † Colorado 65
78 † Kentucky 81
75 ■ Iowa 67
105 ■ Penn St. 57
76 Michigan 75
83 Illinois 79
74 Purdue 65
96 ■ Ohio St. 69
61 ■ Minnesota 57
93 Northwestern 71
73 Iowa 66
88 Penn St. 84
93 ■ Michigan 92
93 ■ Illinois 72
93 ■ Purdue 78
77 Ohio St. 81
86 Minnesota 75
98 ■ Northwestern 69
99 ■ Michigan St. 68
87 Wisconsin 80
97 † Wright St. 54
73 † Xavier (Ohio) 70
82 † Louisville 69
77 † Kansas 83

INDIANA (PA.) 18-9
87 Penn St.-Harrisburg 50
95 Fairmont St. 81
98 ■ Juniata 72
81 ■ Glenville St. 91
91 Kutztown 82
83 ■ Point Park 66
77 † Pace 58
74 Springfield 79
64 ■ Gannon 66
77 ■ High Point 51
109 ■ Wilberforce 83
101 ■ Pitt.-Johnstown 71
83 ■ Mercyhurst 63
71 Lock Haven 72
83 Calif. (Pa.) 79
79 ■ Shippensburg 58
79 ■ Slippery Rock 62
66 Bloomsburg 69
84 ■ Edinboro 79
86 Clarion 95
75 ■ Lock Haven 81
89 ■ Calif. (Pa.) 90
69 Shippensburg 66
72 Slippery Rock 71
75 Edinboro 74
93 ■ Clarion 79
75 Millersville 92

INDIANA ST. 11-17
69 Iowa St. 84
70 ■ Butler 56
71 ■ Oral Roberts 67
74 ■ Eastern Ill. 54
64 Ball St. 66
58 ■ Evansville 55
63 Purdue 92
46 Evansville 64
69 ■ Wichita St. 73
73 Northeastern Ill. 76
63 ■ Illinois St. 60
80 Creighton 66
96 ■ Drake 73
68 Wichita St. 84
84 Tulsa 89
69 ■ Northern Iowa 59
74 Bradley 70
52 Northern Iowa 59
48 Illinois St. 64
60 ■ Southern Ill. 75
73 ■ Southwest Mo. St. 76
74 Drake 76
66 Southern Ill. 78
36 ■ Bradley 53
57 Southwest Mo. St. 72
86 ■ Tulsa 74
71 ■ Creighton 58
68 † Illinois St. 73

IU/PU-FT. WAYNE 23-6
77 St. Francis (Ind.) 68
89 ■ Hillsdale 72
82 Purdue-Calumet 75
82 Tri-State 72
115 ■ Huntington 84
96 ■ North Central 62
116 ■ Quincy 106
90 ■ Indianapolis 71
105 ■ Northern Ky. 88
66 Ky. Wesleyan 69
96 Southern Ind. 107
73 Ashland 53
102 ■ Bellarmine 75
83 ■ Kentucky St. 78
79 Lewis 82
66 St. Joseph's (Ind.) 63
118 ■ Goshen 74
99 ■ Southern Ind. 87
81 ■ Ky. Wesleyan 67
71 Findlay 84
89 ■ Ashland 60
80 Kentucky St. 78
83 Bellarmine 71
74 ■ St. Joseph's (Ind.) 66
89 ■ Lewis 76
87 Northern Ky. 70
62 Indianapolis 60
72 † Wayne St. (Mich.) 78
93 Southern Ind. 95

INDIANAPOLIS 13-14
76 Central Mo. St. 79
48 † Tex. A&M-Kingsville 59
80 Wis.-Parkside 85
61 Marian (Ind.) 55
94 † Franklin 72
69 † St. Francis (Ill.) 55
59 Hillsdale 78
71 IU/PU-Ft. Wayne 90
77 Ashland 72
73 ■ Bellarmine 70
80 ■ Kentucky St. 72
74 Lewis 70
58 St. Joseph's (Ind.) 81
99 Northern Ky. 95
79 ■ Oakland City 73
61 ■ Ky. Wesleyan 78
70 ■ Southern Ind. 81
77 Ind. Wesleyan 70
81 Kentucky St. 89
55 Bellarmine 61
57 ■ St. Joseph's (Ind.) 83
76 ■ Lewis 58
82 ■ Northern Ky. 81
83 Southern Ind. 95
80 Ky. Wesleyan 73
71 ■ Ashland 79
60 ■ IU/PU-Ft. Wayne 62

IONA 16-11
80 † Columbia 68
74 St. John's (N.Y.) 90
65 Old Dominion 78
61 ■ Seton Hall 75
77 ■ Fordham 58
74 † Wagner 67
88 ■ Fla. Atlantic 72
98 ■ Wagner 82
66 North Caro. St. 88
80 Rhode Island 87
67 Hofstra 54
63 Loyola (Md.) 47
80 ■ Fairfield 79
49 Canisius 68
93 Niagara 99
77 ■ Canisius 64
74 Manhattan 83
82 ■ Northeastern 78
91 ■ St. Peter's 73
77 ■ Niagara 75
88 Siena 83
76 ■ Manhattan 89
66 St. Peter's 76
96 ■ Siena 90
79 ■ Loyola (Md.) 61
63 Fairfield 57
62 † Canisius 64

IOWA 23-9
100 ■ Mississippi Val. 69
85 ■ Tex.-Pan American 29
69 ■ Mississippi St. 54
64 ■ Northern Iowa 44
78 ■ Iowa St. 51
101 American (P.R.) 47
103 † Eastern Mich. 66
90 † Southern Ill. 70
91 ■ Texas Southern 70
104 ■ Central Conn. St. 58
80 Drake 65
67 Indiana 75
81 Ohio St. 92
84 ■ Minnesota 77
56 Duke 65
96 Michigan St. 90
88 ■ Michigan 80
77 Illinois 78
66 ■ Indiana 73
85 Minnesota 91
68 ■ Ohio St. 54
75 Northwestern 63
74 Penn St. 58
58 ■ Penn St. 38
66 ■ Michigan St. 64
73 Michigan 82
58 Purdue 69
56 ■ Northwestern 50
91 ■ Wisconsin 65
63 ■ Illinois 53
82 † Northeast La. 69
78 † Wake Forest 84

IOWA ST. 20-11
84 ■ Indiana St. 69
86 Florida St. 109
106 ■ Buffalo 36
69 Creighton 58
74 Northern Iowa 67
51 Iowa 78
87 ■ Mercer 46
72 † Michigan 94
111 ■ Texas Southern 74
99 ■ Minnesota 65
115 ■ Bethune-Cookman 57
71 Kansas 78
81 ■ Oklahoma St. 72
49 Missouri 64
91 ■ Southern Utah 63
81 ■ Oklahoma 74
119 ■ Drake 81

77	Oklahoma St.	94
96	■ Nebraska	69
94	■ Colorado	74
66	Kansas St.	68
77	Oklahoma	81
65	■ Missouri	50
75	■ Kansas	71
89	■ Fla. Atlantic	46
87	Nebraska	91
67	Colorado	66
79	■ Kansas St.	61
69	† Oklahoma	55
63	† Missouri	67
70	† UCLA	81

ITHACA 20-7

65	† Teikyo-Post	71
71	† Plattsburgh St.	63
63	■ Cortland St.	37
68	Keuka	50
62	Albany (N.Y.)	54
78	■ St. Lawrence	64
69	■ Clarkson	66
66	■ Skidmore	52
73	■ Alfred	59
55	Hamilton	63
62	Rochester Inst.	66
78	Hobart	70
76	■ Hilbert	79
42	■ Hartwick	48
67	■ Rensselaer	64
76	Cortland St.	65
90	Clarkson	55
94	St. Lawrence	50
50	■ Union (N.Y.)	53
87	Rensselaer	65
80	Hartwick	72
66	Utica	62
95	■ Hobart	87
58	■ Rochester Inst.	56
70	Alfred	62
71	■ Fredonia St.	56
61	New York U.	75

JACKSON ST. 25-9

63	Tennessee St.	70
69	Western Ky.	87
113	■ Ark. Baptist	54
81	Illinois	85
107	† Florida A&M	70
78	Memphis St.	81
76	† Arkansas	123
92	Tulane	84
85	† Kansas	93
67	† Fordham	43
87	† Southwestern La.	85
88	■ Belhaven	64
97	Prairie View	57
84	Texas Southern	83
103	■ Alcorn St.	86
91	■ Southern-B.R.	86
88	■ Northeastern Ill.	80
91	■ Grambling	75
91	Mississippi Val.	89
91	Alabama St.	85
73	■ Montevallo	71
66	■ Tougaloo	50
93	■ Prairie View	76
74	■ Texas Southern	71
83	Alcorn St.	69
74	Southern-B.R.	87
89	Grambling	76
94	■ Mississippi Val.	92
86	■ Alabama St.	75
103	† Prairie View	70
85	† Mississippi Val.	75
80	Southern-B.R.	101
90	Connecticut	88
52	■ Southwest Mo. St.	70

JACKSONVILLE 5-22

75	Florida	82
75	Buffalo	60
84	■ Bethune-Cookman	63
65	■ Washington	78
71	DePaul	80
69	New Orleans	79
59	■ Oklahoma St.	60
63	■ Buffalo	70
55	Arkansas St.	60
84	■ Southwestern La.	90
86	■ Lamar	80
59	Ark.-Lit. Rock	66
79	Tex.-Pan American	80
88	Lamar	97
50	■ New Orleans	66
61	■ Ark.-Lit. Rock	77
77	■ Florida St.	92
75	Louisiana Tech	78
58	South Ala.	73
58	Western Ky.	66
73	■ Arkansas St.	86
90	■ Tex.-Pan American	85
86	■ South Ala.	109
84	■ Louisiana Tech	71
63	Southwestern La.	87
66	■ Western Ky.	101
62	† Louisiana Tech	63

JACKSONVILLE ST. 16-10

108	■ Elizabeth City St.	109
87	† Athens St.	74
81	† Belhaven	70
106	■ Knoxville	78
93	■ Tampa	80
97	■ Athens St.	76
80	■ Pfeiffer	97
75	Seattle Pacific	82
78	† Seattle	76
97	Athens St.	91
95	■ Livingston	78
76	■ Mississippi Col.	65
109	■ Alabama A&M	104
74	North Ala.	90
69	Delta St.	89
86	■ Valdosta St.	77
109	■ West Ga.	87
100	■ Ala.-Huntsville	69
80	Valdosta St.	89
95	West Ga.	97
63	■ Delta St.	81
109	■ North Ala.	95
73	Mississippi Col.	72
86	Livingston	101
86	† Livingston	76
66	Delta St.	72

JAMES MADISON 21-9

101	■ Furman	75
89	■ Auburn	80
95	■ Coppin St.	76
70	La Salle	83
74	Penn St.	75
89	■ Md.-East. Shore	62
70	■ Oregon St.	56
90	† California	75
66	Seton Hall	87
73	Rutgers	61
56	■ Geo. Washington	71
98	■ East Caro.	82
99	■ N.C.-Wilmington	83
90	William & Mary	72
102	■ Old Dominion	89
90	■ Richmond	70
83	American	79
56	George Mason	50
110	■ Morgan St.	73
57	East Caro.	58
85	N.C.-Wilmington	89
99	■ William & Mary	66
88	Old Dominion	92
78	Richmond	73
90	■ American	67
75	■ George Mason	59
60	† George Mason	49
70	† American	61
49	† East Caro.	54
61	Providence	73

JERSEY CITY ST. 15-12

59	■ Bloomfield	72
66	Rowan	79
52	■ Stockton St.	77
63	Trenton St.	61
93	Rutgers-Camden	75
76	■ Ramapo	68
75	■ Upsala	68
69	† Potsdam St.	72
67	† Adrian	71
65	† Southern Me.	58
56	Frank. & Marsh.	81
69	Rutgers-Newark	54
60	■ Kean	66
78	Wm. Paterson	80
64	■ Trenton St.	71
65	Montclair St.	67
59	■ Rowan	76
64	Stockton St.	68
86	■ Rutgers-Newark	60
72	■ Rutgers-Camden	65
72	Ramapo	65
83	■ Montclair St.	70
92	■ Wm. Paterson	78
72	Kean	70
76	■ Yeshiva	62
88	■ Staten Island	81
66	■ Stony Brook	56

JOHN CARROLL 12-14

80	■ Wash. & Jeff.	89
80	† Geneseo St.	69
67	Nazareth (N.Y.)	56
65	Carnegie Mellon	76
92	Marietta	80
67	Baldwin-Wallace	75
57	■ Ohio Northern	67
90	■ Otterbein	87
109	Spalding	112
54	Bellarmine	53
66	Capital	84
73	■ Muskingum	64
72	Heidelberg	60
66	■ Mount Union	82
67	Hiram	87
67	Ohio Northern	95
75	■ Baldwin-Wallace	61
61	■ Marietta	57
66	Mount Union	49
71	Muskingum	90
68	■ Hiram	78
96	Otterbein	100
82	■ Heidelberg	70
61	■ Capital	65
75	Capital	71
56	† Heidelberg	71

JOHN JAY 9-16

72	■ Montclair St.	75
78	■ Old Westbury	72
57	Mt. St. Mary (N.Y.)	99
72	■ Albertus Magnus	73
88	Baruch	98
72	■ CCNY	70
64	■ Centenary (N.J.)	67
73	New York U.	97
79	Medgar Evers	84
74	■ Staten Island	77
85	■ American (P.R.)	93
79	Centenary (N.J.)	77
78	Molloy	84
60	FDU-Madison	66
71	York (N.Y.)	74
84	Lehman	52
63	Yeshiva	64
75	CCNY	80
72	Old Westbury	71
85	■ Lehman	72
111	■ Pratt	93
79	Baruch	70
80	Vassar	59
76	■ Hunter	82
71	Medgar Evers	78

JOHNS HOPKINS 19-7

105	■ St. Mary's (Md.)	62
76	■ Moravian	65
66	■ Goucher	52
73	■ Western Md.	65
83	■ Brandeis	73
56	Carnegie Mellon	57
50	■ Frank. & Marsh.	51
47	■ Rochester	49
82	Case Reserve	72
74	New York U.	80
77	Emory	78
62	■ Messiah	47
54	■ Chicago	41
68	■ Washington (Mo.)	58
64	Ursinus	57
78	■ Swarthmore	53
68	Washington (Md.)	61
69	Widener	57
78	■ Haverford	52
94	■ Ursinus	59
62	Swarthmore	48
72	■ Washington (Md.)	63
57	■ Widener	52
89	Haverford	72
54	■ Lebanon Valley	58
49	■ Lebanon Valley	53

JOHNSON SMITH 20-8

94	Virginia St.	99
83	St. Augustine's	80
90	■ Hampton	79
80	Virginia Union	85
59	■ Queens (N.C.)	57
98	■ Elizabeth City St.	89
82	■ Norfolk St.	71
90	† St. Paul's	76
79	† Elizabeth City St.	77
76	N.C. Central	90
91	† Bowie St.	97
106	† Paul Quinn	65
84	† St. Augustine's	66
78	■ Livingstone	70
105	Bowie St.	86
100	Winston-Salem	74
94	■ Shaw	85
55	■ Fayetteville St.	62
94	St. Paul's	69
106	■ N.C. Central	81
107	■ Winston-Salem	88
113	■ St. Augustine's	101
82	Fayetteville St.	83
93	Shaw	99
94	Livingstone	90
89	† Bowie St.	85
100	† Elizabeth City St.	84
75	† N.C. Central	82

JUNIATA 10-14

73	† Merchant Marine	81
86	† Green Mountain	70
69	■ King's (Pa.)	80
79	York (Pa.)	80
72	Indiana (Pa.)	98
78	■ Misericordia	72
116	■ Wash. & Jeff.	111
57	■ Lebanon Valley	87
48	Calif. (Pa.)	104
58	■ Wilkes	57
58	Waynesburg	61
64	■ Albright	57
107	■ Delaware Valley	76
71	■ Susquehanna	81
60	■ Dickinson	70
58	Messiah	83
86	Elizabethtown	99
88	■ Lycoming	77
65	Albright	78
84	Susquehanna	77
61	■ Messiah	71
89	Western Md.	76
71	■ Elizabethtown	89
90	Lycoming	84

KALAMAZOO 19-7

80 Concordia (Mich.) 48
73 Grand Rapids Bapt. 62
74 Manchester 85
90 ■ Goshen 69
81 ■ Franklin 78
61 † Ind. Wesleyan 59
74 Wabash 83
64 ■ Spring Arbor 74
74 ■ Ind. Wesleyan 56
67 ■ Chicago 52
64 ■ Purdue-Calumet 47
70 ■ Olivet 55
62 ■ Calvin 76
76 Alma 71
55 ■ Aquinas 54
84 Albion 75
79 ■ Hope 68
62 Adrian 50
88 Olivet 70
61 ■ Adrian 55
72 Hope 75
79 ■ Albion 64
72 ■ Alma 57
90 Calvin 96
71 ■ Adrian 46
53 † Albion 56

KANSAS 29-7

76 ■ Georgia 65
74 † Indiana 69
91 ■ Emporia St. 56
94 † Mississippi Val. 46
108 † Mo.-Kansas City 62
86 ■ East Tenn. St. 83
84 ■ North Caro. St. 64
93 † Jackson St. 85
94 Hawaii 66
74 † Michigan 86
103 ■ Wichita St. 54
78 ■ Iowa St. 71
96 Oklahoma 85
140 ■ Oral Roberts 72
98 Louisville 77
71 Kansas St. 65
82 Colorado 51
49 ■ Long Beach St. 64
103 ■ Rollins 56
86 ■ Missouri 69
64 Nebraska 68
84 ■ Oklahoma St. 72
67 Missouri 63
77 ■ Oklahoma 80
77 ■ Kansas St. 64
71 Iowa St. 75
72 ■ Colorado 68
94 ■ Nebraska 83
74 Oklahoma St. 73
82 † Colorado 65
67 † Kansas St. 74
94 † Ball St. 72
90 † Brigham Young 76
93 † California 76
83 † Indiana 77
68 † North Caro. 78

KANSAS ST. 19-11

85 ■ Coppin St. 61
86 ■ Lafayette 63
73 ■ Ohio 72
86 ■ Sam Houston St. 53
66 Mo.-Kansas City 64
61 Wichita St. 74
82 Nevada 83
60 UC Santa Barb. 59
79 ■ La Salle 59
75 Oklahoma St. 62
97 ■ Northeastern Ill. 68
83 ■ Colorado 78
65 ■ Kansas 71
66 Nebraska 64
81 ■ Central Conn. St. 56
86 ■ Temple 63
62 ■ Oklahoma 61
51 Missouri 67

68 ■ Iowa St. 66
59 ■ Nebraska 80
77 Colorado 88
64 Kansas 77
67 Oklahoma 63
61 ■ Oklahoma St. 78
78 ■ Missouri 67
61 Iowa St. 79
47 † Nebraska 45
74 † Kansas 67
56 † Missouri 68
53 † Tulane 55

KEAN 18-8

78 ■ Wm. Paterson 62
64 Rutgers-Newark 59
54 ■ Rowan 70
74 ■ Trenton St. 55
69 Rutgers-Camden 64
73 † Dominican (N.Y.) 60
58 Washington (Md.) 59
90 Molloy 77
102 ■ Lehman 45
50 ■ Western Conn. St. 64
63 ■ Stockton St. 71
69 Montclair St. 66
66 Jersey City St. 60
70 ■ Ramapo 66
49 Rowan 69
83 ■ Columbia Union 77
75 Wm. Paterson 69
79 ■ Rutgers-Newark 50
76 ■ Montclair St. 71
54 Trenton St. 60
74 ■ Rutgers-Camden 48
65 Stockton St. 63
74 Ramapo 57
70 ■ Jersey City St. 72
70 ■ Stockton St. 63
54 Rowan 63

KEENE ST. 2-23

89 † St. Anselm 111
108 New Hamp. Col. 138
71 Springfield 96
113 ■ LIU-Southampton 111
83 Rutgers 132
101 Quinnipiac 110
97 Stonehill 121
83 Bentley 118
65 Merrimack 81
71 ■ Le Moyne 84
92 Sacred Heart 105
98 Southern Conn. St. 90
85 New Haven 108
63 Le Moyne 85
89 New Hamp. Col. 117
68 ■ Franklin Pierce 87
78 Mass.-Lowell 80
90 ■ Southern Conn. St. 96
92 ■ New Hamp. Col. 122
102 ■ Bridgeport 109
80 ■ Mass.-Lowell 87
84 ■ Sacred Heart 101
86 Franklin Pierce 131
93 ■ New Haven 109
56 New Hamp. Col. 76

KENT 10-17

83 † Idaho St. 71
61 Nebraska 85
56 Xavier (Ohio) 72
73 ■ Duquesne 71
70 Niagara 71
67 ■ Yale 59
68 ■ Siena 72
64 ■ Cleveland St. 81
50 Western Mich. 60
64 ■ Ohio 65
75 Central Mich. 74
68 ■ Bowling Green 74
71 Eastern Mich. 75
65 ■ Toledo 57
61 ■ Akron 45

51 Ball St. 59
55 ■ Miami (Ohio) 69
53 Ohio 58
105 ■ Central Mich. 71
48 Bowling Green 49
61 ■ Eastern Mich. 55
58 Toledo 66
76 Akron 75
63 ■ Ball St. 77
38 Miami (Ohio) 71
81 ■ Western Mich. 64
57 † Ball St. 77

KENTUCKY 30-4

81 ■ Wright St. 65
96 ■ Georgia Tech 87
82 ■ Eastern Ky. 73
88 Louisville 68
108 ■ Morehead St. 65
65 ■ Miami (Ohio) 49
89 † Rutgers 67
86 † St. John's (N.Y.) 77
81 † Indiana 78
74 Georgia 59
84 ■ Tennessee 70
86 Vanderbilt 101
73 Alabama 59
108 South Caro. 82
105 ■ Louisiana St. 67
71 ■ Florida 48
87 ■ Mississippi St. 63
82 ■ Vanderbilt 67
94 Arkansas 101
81 Notre Dame 62
87 ■ South Caro. 66
86 ■ Georgia 70
77 Tennessee 78
80 ■ Auburn 78
98 Mississippi 66
85 Florida 77
101 ■ Tennessee 40
92 ■ Arkansas 81
82 ■ Louisiana St. 65
96 † Rider 52
83 † Utah 62
103 † Wake Forest 69
106 † Florida St. 81
78 † Michigan 81

KENTUCKY ST. 16-11

98 ■ Wilberforce 87
112 † Dist. Columbia 81
87 † Livingstone 71
89 ■ Wis.-Parkside 77
108 ■ Central St. (Ohio) 84
100 Wilberforce 103
68 Wis.-Parkside 80
101 ■ Lewis 87
66 ■ St. Joseph's (Ind.) 78
107 Northern Ky. 95
72 Indianapolis 80
95 ■ Southern Ind. 82
84 ■ Ky. Wesleyan 78
88 Ashland 72
78 IU/PU-Ft. Wayne 83
85 Central St. (Ohio) 81
92 ■ Bellarmine 63
89 ■ Indianapolis 81
99 ■ Northern Ky. 93
93 Transylvania 110
79 Ky. Wesleyan 90
78 Southern Ind. 95
78 ■ IU/PU-Ft. Wayne 80
93 ■ Ashland 80
65 Bellarmine 69
75 Lewis 74
74 St. Joseph's (Ind.) 99

KY. WESLEYAN 21-6

103 ■ Wingate 75
66 ■ Mo. Southern St. 63
76 ■ Delta St. 53
77 ■ Olivet (Ill.) 75
103 ■ Quincy 85

99 ■ SIU-Edwardsville 69
97 ■ Oakland City 78
72 SIU-Edwardsville 69
75 Southern Ind. 84
69 ■ IU/PU-Ft. Wayne 66
121 ■ Ashland 66
86 Bellarmine 72
78 Kentucky St. 84
94 ■ Lewis 68
79 ■ St. Joseph's (Ind.) 72
78 Indianapolis 61
91 Northern Ky. 81
85 Ashland 73
67 IU/PU-Ft. Wayne 81
90 ■ Kentucky St. 79
77 ■ Bellarmine 54
54 St. Joseph's (Ind.) 79
76 Lewis 71
65 ■ Northern Ky. 62
73 ■ Indianapolis 80
65 Oakland City 74
83 ■ Southern Ind. 66

KENYON 16-11

63 Waynesburg 58
82 ■ Marietta 64
55 † Adrian 67
62 † Mt. Vernon Naz. 76
54 Ohio Wesleyan 76
44 ■ Denison 59
62 ■ Thiel 44
57 Thiel 41
68 Earlham 65
69 Elmhurst 75
78 † Rust 71
59 Wooster 54
51 Allegheny 66
64 Oberlin 44
57 ■ Case Reserve 41
59 ■ Wittenberg 56
66 Denison 57
94 ■ Earlham 69
65 ■ Wooster 72
83 Case Reserve 87
85 ■ Oberlin 55
75 ■ Ohio Wesleyan 68
56 Wittenberg 60
52 ■ Allegheny 59
81 Ohio Wesleyan 77
54 † Wittenberg 49
48 † Wooster 64

KEUKA 8-17

44 Rochester 76
78 † Skidmore 86
72 ■ Bapt. Bible (Pa.) 59
50 ■ Ithaca 68
71 ■ Rochester Inst. 78
84 ■ Roberts Wesleyan 91
67 Utica 60
89 Bapt. Bible (Pa.) 108
61 † Hilbert 62
69 † Goucher 62
78 ■ Potsdam St. 89
70 Clarkson 75
58 Roberts Wesleyan 85
57 † Nazareth (N.Y.) 77
59 † Hilbert 63
103 ■ Misericordia 89
62 † Taylor 60
61 Houghton 82
69 Houghton 65
66 ■ St. John Fisher 79
60 Elmira 85
68 Penn St.-Behrend 75
64 ■ Houghton 62
63 ■ Utica 66
75 ■ Penn St.-Behrend 66

KING'S (PA.) 11-12

68 † Moravian 86
57 † St. Mary's (Md.) 53
80 Juniata 69
68 ■ Elizabethtown 77

49 Scranton 77
49 † Chris. Newport 85
86 † Wilmington (Del.) 84
64 ■ Susquehanna 57
88 ■ Beaver 72
67 ■ Hunter 76
73 ■ Ursinus 54
59 ■ Albright 69
59 Wilkes 77
70 FDU-Madison 69
71 ■ Upsala 76
59 Drew 64
93 Delaware Valley 71
60 ■ Scranton 76
59 ■ Wilkes 63
82 Lycoming 72
84 ■ FDU-Madison 74
103 ■ Drew 106
92 ■ Delaware Valley 73

KNOX 17-5
84 ■ Lindenwood 74
103 ■ Alma 78
81 ■ Principia 48
83 Grinnell 68
97 Coe 86
95 Franklin 96
93 Palm Beach Atl. 98
74 ■ Judson 78
96 ■ Illinois Col. 78
73 Cornell College 86
67 Monmouth (Ill.) 65
87 Carroll (Wis.) 82
72 Beloit 64
83 ■ Ripon 80
91 ■ Lake Forest 70
70 MacMurray 58
80 Illinois Col. 79
70 ■ Cornell College 65
69 ■ Monmouth (Ill.) 64
79 ■ Grinnell 55
82 ■ Coe 69
76 † Ripon 91

KUTZTOWN 8-17
56 ■ Phila. Textile 67
54 Pace 60
75 Shippensburg 70
82 ■ Indiana (Pa.) 91
97 Alvernia 96
83 † Pitt.-Johnstown 84
67 † Hilbert 76
95 ■ Messiah 80
55 ■ Shippensburg 61
97 ■ Dist. Columbia 54
71 Lock Haven 72
56 Mansfield 61
65 ■ Cheyney 74
61 ■ West Chester 73
69 Bloomsburg 90
58 Millersville 93
71 Queens (N.Y.) 68
75 East Stroudsburg 89
56 Gannon 57
65 ■ Mansfield 58
62 Cheyney 60
52 West Chester 70
83 ■ Bloomsburg 97
52 ■ Millersville 85
69 ■ East Stroudsburg 60

LA SALLE 14-13
59 ■ Phila. Textile 53
44 ■ Pennsylvania 71
83 ■ James Madison 70
76 ■ Maryland 93
60 † Temple 87
67 † West Va. 80
83 † Delaware St. 74
71 ■ Richmond 61
59 Kansas St. 79
70 Evansville 82
59 Butler 64
80 ■ Detroit Mercy 73
70 ■ Loyola (Ill.) 56
66 † St. Joseph's (Pa.) 53
81 ■ Duquesne 78
63 Notre Dame 72
60 Princeton 65
49 Xavier (Ohio) 56
72 Dayton 64
41 ■ Evansville 63
88 ■ Butler 66
73 Detroit Mercy 72
96 Loyola (Ill.) 90
68 Duquesne 65
58 ■ Xavier (Ohio) 73
67 ■ Dayton 57
70 † Butler 77

LA VERNE 20-8
63 † North Park 67
91 † Macalester 55
103 La Sierra 55
93 ■ Dominican (Cal.) 90
46 Cal St. Dom. Hills 84
71 Pt. Loma Nazarene 65
82 Cal Poly SLO 86
65 ■ Master's 58
77 UC San Diego 75
68 ■ Quincy 72
65 Cal Baptist 67
74 ■ Cal Lutheran 78
104 Redlands 101
81 Cal Tech 33
78 ■ Occidental 76
60 Pomona-Pitzer 70
71 ■ Whittier 62
83 ■ Claremont-M-S 68
83 Cal Lutheran 75
83 ■ Redlands 72
76 ■ Cal Tech 28
60 Occidental 58
101 ■ Pomona-Pitzer 68
74 Whittier 69
86 Claremont-M-S 76
83 † Cal Lutheran 79
67 ■ Cal Lutheran 56
84 † Augustana (Ill.) 87

LAFAYETTE 7-20
48 ■ Princeton 65
42 Yale 53
63 Kansas St. 86
56 ■ Rider 72
60 Marist 62
56 † Va. Military 62
77 Columbia 72
47 Wake Forest 74
89 Vermont 79
58 ■ Drexel 72
89 ■ Swarthmore 75
73 ■ Colgate 76
74 Bucknell 87
50 Navy 53
79 ■ Holy Cross 95
71 Fordham 83
57 Army 60
65 ■ Pennsylvania 89
99 ■ Lehigh 82
55 Colgate 68
65 ■ Bucknell 84
65 ■ Navy 60
68 Holy Cross 95
78 ■ Fordham 74
70 Lehigh 83
77 ■ Army 67
73 Fordham 84

LAKE FOREST 3-19
72 Wheaton (Ill.) 78
62 † Trinity Chrst. (Il.) 69
61 ■ Chicago 63
78 ■ Barat 68
69 Carroll (Wis.) 72
66 ■ Beloit 82
73 Otterbein 90
65 † North Park 84
64 ■ Concordia (Ill.) 100
70 St. Norbert 88
69 ■ Cornell College 79
53 ■ Monmouth (Ill.) 61
57 Wis.-Parkside 80
77 Illinois Col. 86
70 Knox 91
73 ■ Ripon 81
62 ■ St. Norbert 63
98 ■ Lawrence 84
62 Ripon 88
64 ■ Carroll (Wis.) 50
79 Lawrence 93
57 Beloit 78

LAMAR 15-12
94 ■ Union (Tenn.) 75
100 ■ McNeese St. 76
90 ■ San Diego St. 65
138 ■ Prairie View 77
89 McNeese St. 83
92 Oklahoma 109
103 ■ Tex.-Pan American 64
76 Southwestern La. 73
80 ■ Ark.-Lit. Rock 60
89 Western Ky. 114
86 ■ South Ala. 77
80 Jacksonville 86
77 New Orleans 96
74 ■ Arkansas St. 79
97 ■ Jacksonville 88
82 Louisiana Tech 66
88 Tex.-Pan American 52
143 Prairie View 88
88 ■ Western Ky. 95
76 Ark.-Lit. Rock 84
55 Arkansas St. 57
73 ■ New Orleans 84
89 ■ Southwestern La. 78
80 South Ala. 101
113 ■ Louisiana Tech 76
64 ■ Florida Int'l 66
68 † Western Ky. 78

LANDER 5-24
96 Newberry 92
68 Erskine 74
65 Appalachian St. 95
62 Furman 84
54 ■ Presbyterian 63
79 † Bridgewater (Va.) 71
70 † Alas. Anchorage 73
74 † Embry-Riddle 71
65 ■ Augusta 77
56 ■ Armstrong St. 71
75 ■ S.C.-Aiken 106
57 Francis Marion 60
48 Pembroke St. 58
67 ■ Erskine 72
73 ■ Georgia Col. 81
68 ■ Columbus 73
77 S.C.-Spartanburg 89
61 Presbyterian 81
53 Western Caro. 73
78 S.C.-Aiken 80
61 ■ S.C.-Spartanburg 63
77 Augusta 76
66 Armstrong St. 87
110 ■ Newberry 84
70 Georgia Col. 85
86 Columbus 96
59 ■ Francis Marion 72
67 ■ Pembroke St. 70
77 † Georgia Col. 78

LAWRENCE 13-9
71 Wis. Lutheran 73
80 ■ N'western (Wis.) 78
61 ■ Milwaukee Engr. 56
55 Ripon 93
75 Palm Beach Atl. 81
83 † Miami Christian 77
75 Lakeland 59
74 ■ Carroll (Wis.) 71
61 ■ Ripon 74
66 Beloit 79
89 Northland Bapt. 77
87 ■ Coe 85
81 ■ Grinnell 67
83 ■ Barat 79
59 Cornell College 75
52 Monmouth (Ill.) 75
70 ■ St. Norbert 55
84 Carroll (Wis.) 83
84 Lake Forest 98
58 ■ Beloit 62
76 St. Norbert 59
93 ■ Lake Forest 79

LE MOYNE 18-10
92 ■ St. Michael's 76
82 Queens (N.Y.) 69
65 Pace 63
84 ■ Hilbert 51
90 ■ Pitt.-Johnstown 75
71 Syracuse 102
56 Siena 83
84 Keene St. 71
69 Franklin Pierce 76
68 ■ Mass.-Lowell 71
98 ■ East Stroudsburg 83
85 ■ Keene St. 63
94 ■ Sacred Heart 73
106 New Haven 109
75 Southern Conn. St. 78
66 ■ Franklin Pierce 79
67 ■ New Hamp. Col. 68
82 Union (N.Y.) 72
69 Sacred Heart 80
100 Mt. St. Mary (N.Y.) 75
109 ■ New Haven 93
91 Lock Haven 72
68 ■ Gannon 63
78 New Hamp. Col. 75
75 † Mass.-Lowell 74
80 ■ Southern Conn. St. 70
101 ■ Sacred Heart 83
73 † Franklin Pierce 75

LEMOYNE-OWEN 19-9
96 Lane 76
98 ■ Miles 100
105 ■ Albany St. (Ga.) 88
89 ■ Alabama A&M 84
97 Columbus 98
103 ■ Morris Brown 83
91 Savannah St. 96
95 Fort Valley St. 77
86 ■ Morehouse 78
88 Clark Atlanta 78
67 Albany St. (Ga.) 85
86 ■ Tuskegee 83
86 ■ Rust 87
83 Tuskegee 64
101 Miles 76
77 Paine 87
94 ■ Lane 81
71 Ark.-Pine Bluff 77
100 ■ Fort Valley St. 73
80 Rust 63
87 ■ Ark.-Pine Bluff 67
94 Morehouse 88
73 Morris Brown 67
104 ■ Clark Atlanta 82
96 Alabama A&M 109
102 † Savannah St. 70
86 † Paine 75
88 † Alabama A&M 92

LEBANON VALLEY 18-11
70 † York (Pa.) 71
81 † Elizabethtown 82
102 ■ Cabrini 77
67 Moravian 69
81 ■ Albright 55
87 Juniata 57
96 † Redlands 71
55 Wooster 66
82 ■ Catholic 83
80 ■ St. Joseph's (N.Y.) 53
93 ■ Washington (Md.) 69

77 Muhlenberg 69
77 Gettysburg 73
94 ■ Western Md. 57
78 Frank. & Marsh. 50
78 ■ Dickinson 58
82 ■ Moravian 52
81 Elizabethtown 89
69 ■ Muhlenberg 72
60 ■ Gettysburg 66
83 Western Md. 55
72 ■ Susquehanna 62
61 ■ Frank. & Marsh. 64
67 Dickinson 48
102 ■ Muhlenberg 71
58 Johns Hopkins 54
48 Frank. & Marsh. 68
53 Johns Hopkins 49
56 Scranton 58

LEHIGH 4-23
77 Drexel 86
73 † Middle Tenn. St. 89
82 † Wagner 87
71 ■ Hofstra 78
90 Harvard 94
83 ■ Gettysburg 89
66 Villanova 90
68 ■ Pennsylvania 78
66 Northwestern 81
54 Yale 53
80 ■ Columbia 79
57 Navy 81
75 Holy Cross 94
65 ■ Fordham 87
72 Army 74
75 Bucknell 91
73 ■ Colgate 84
82 Lafayette 99
74 ■ Navy 83
70 ■ Towson St. 79
87 ■ Holy Cross 104
74 Fordham 93
72 ■ Army 61
80 ■ Bucknell 90
83 ■ Lafayette 70
80 Colgate 90
65 Bucknell 69

LEHMAN 0-25
44 Cortland St. 84
32 Stony Brook 102
58 ■ Pratt 59
50 ■ Utica Tech 59
84 Mt. St. Vincent 104
67 ■ Yeshiva 91
59 ■ American (P.R.) 89
45 Kean 102
44 † Greensboro 105
60 ■ Montclair St. 84
58 Old Westbury 62
73 ■ CCNY 84
58 ■ Baruch 82
37 Maritime (N.Y.) 49
52 ■ John Jay 84
43 ■ Hunter 74
56 ■ York (N.Y.) 64
60 Baruch 74
49 CCNY 58
72 John Jay 85
50 Medgar Evers 64
56 Staten Island 91
66 ■ Rutgers-Newark 78
77 ■ Elmira 85
45 Hunter 71

LENOIR-RHYNE 25-7
94 ■ High Point 100
86 ■ S.C.-Spartanburg 65
84 Belmont Abbey 47
82 High Point 61
103 † Alderson-Broaddus 92
85 † Bluefield St. 95
72 Shepherd 81
76 ■ Catawba 74
75 Wofford 85
58 Gardner-Webb 77
85 ■ Elon 57
69 Carson-Newman 67
86 Presbyterian 80
81 ■ Wingate 64
83 ■ Mars Hill 73
80 ■ Wofford 77
75 Wingate 66
92 Catawba 74
77 Mars Hill 63
82 ■ Gardner-Webb 60
74 Elon 66
92 ■ Carson-Newman 68
67 ■ Presbyterian 72
87 † Carson-Newman 69
81 † Wingate 72
79 † Presbyterian 70
91 ■ High Point 74
83 Pfeiffer 74
74 Presbyterian 66
77 † Wis.-Stevens Point 74
85 † Oklahoma City 67
76 † Hawaii Pacific 79

LEWIS 6-21
80 ■ Grand Valley St. 70
75 ■ Bemidji St. 86
64 ■ Oakland 68
69 Illinois St. 82
54 St. Francis (Ill.) 75
91 Quincy 93
77 Drake 95
59 Fla. Southern 65
87 Kentucky St. 101
76 Bellarmine 79
71 St. Joseph's (Ind.) 86
70 ■ Indianapolis 74
93 ■ Northern Ky. 81
68 Ky. Wesleyan 94
69 Southern Ind. 81
82 ■ IU/PU-Ft. Wayne 79
88 ■ Ashland 74
63 SIU-Edwardsville 88
63 ■ St. Joseph's (Ind.) 77
97 Northern Ky. 88
58 Indianapolis 76
68 ■ Southern Ind. 78
71 ■ Ky. Wesleyan 76
92 Ashland 70
76 IU/PU-Ft. Wayne 89
74 ■ Kentucky St. 75
54 ■ Bellarmine 66

LIBERTY 16-14
68 Clemson 93
93 ■ Marymount (Va.) 73
79 Central Conn. St. 93
111 ■ Averett 53
96 ■ Covenant 59
75 Hawaii-Hilo 66
80 † Ball St. 90
74 † Idaho 76
75 Va. Commonwealth 88
65 ■ Coastal Caro. 66
60 ■ Charleston So. 49
90 Winthrop 93
72 ■ N.C.-Greensboro 62
70 Campbell 50
73 ■ N.C.-Asheville 50
81 Coastal Caro. 74
71 Virginia Tech 65
94 ■ Radford 74
72 Charleston So. 58
80 N.C.-Asheville 73
73 ■ Campbell 63
58 ■ Winthrop 61
81 ■ Towson St. 86
85 Md.-Balt. County 90
69 Towson St. 75
83 ■ Md.-Balt. County 81
55 N.C.-Greensboro 58
89 ■ Tenn. Temple 56
74 Radford 79
69 † Radford 73

LIMESTONE 10-17
67 St. Andrews 64
80 † High Point 78
59 Francis Marion 78
90 ■ St. Andrews 84
89 ■ Allen 67
62 Gardner-Webb 81
74 Pfeiffer 115
75 Voorhees 95
80 Central Wesleyan 101
79 ■ Claflin 94
70 ■ Voorhees 72
74 Newberry 83
61 Lincoln Memorial 64
81 ■ Barber-Scotia 85
70 ■ Erskine 54
92 Morris 75
60 Benedict 71
87 ■ Morris 71
69 ■ Benedict 71
80 ■ Newberry 65
78 Lees-McRae 89
75 ■ Lincoln Memorial 65
73 ■ Central Wesleyan 83
101 Barber-Scotia 103
75 Erskine 84
71 Claflin 89
93 ■ Lees-McRae 85

LINCOLN (MO.) 14-12
68 North Ala. 76
66 † Paine 61
79 Northeast Mo. St. 78
100 ■ SIU-Edwardsville 89
86 ■ Mo. Baptist 84
99 Columbia (Mo.) 95
78 ■ Missouri Valley 65
88 Mo. Baptist 73
82 Mo.-St. Louis 87
90 ■ Central Mo. St. 82
93 ■ Drury 67
88 Mo. Southern St. 101
75 ■ Mo. Western St. 79
77 Pittsburg St. 87
97 Southwest Baptist 81
84 SIU-Edwardsville 80
71 ■ Mo.-St. Louis 73
92 Missouri-Rolla 97
72 ■ Mo. Southern St. 78
82 ■ Northeast Mo. St. 75
61 ■ Pittsburg St. 63
72 ■ Southwest Baptist 84
86 ■ Missouri-Rolla 84
63 Emporia St. 74
62 Washburn 99
84 Northwest Mo. St. 79

LINCOLN MEMORIAL 17-9
79 † Davis & Elkins 61
80 Concord 83
77 Kennesaw 75
75 ■ Bluefield St. 77
71 ■ Spalding 69
77 ■ Kennesaw 70
78 ■ Concord 44
79 ■ Tusculum 71
56 Carson-Newman 77
51 Auburn 77
72 ■ Dist. Columbia 55
61 ■ Lock Haven 40
87 † Erskine 66
71 † Eckerd 61
54 Queens (N.C.) 66
61 Erskine 79
68 ■ Carson-Newman 48
71 ■ Ala.-Huntsville 70
64 ■ Limestone 61
79 ■ Central St. (Ohio) 64
66 Bluefield St. 77
57 Central St. (Ohio) 78
76 ■ Erskine 50
72 Ala.-Huntsville 70
65 Limestone 75
72 ■ Milligan 65

LIVINGSTON 17-9
93 Fort Valley St. 70
115 Southern Ark. 111
96 Ark.-Monticello 89
74 Middle Tenn. St. 88
74 N.C. Wesleyan 85
93 † Lincoln (Pa.) 68
74 ■ Southern-N.O. 58
72 Ala.-Huntsville 81
66 † Abilene Christian 56
77 † Miles 70
76 Mississippi Col. 70
78 Jacksonville St. 95
85 ■ Miles 50
66 ■ Ala.-Huntsville 74
75 ■ Valdosta St. 62
81 ■ West Ga. 62
71 North Ala. 64
58 Delta St. 57
74 ■ Mississippi Col. 87
69 ■ Fort Valley St. 47
71 ■ Delta St. 91
73 ■ North Ala. 70
113 West Ga. 58
75 Valdosta St. 87
101 ■ Jacksonville St. 86
76 † Jacksonville St. 86

LIVINGSTONE 7-17
75 Norfolk St. 67
71 † Kentucky St. 87
83 ■ Bowie St. 85
63 Elizabeth City St. 66
86 † Allen 67
54 ■ Virginia Union 95
75 St. Augustine's 72
73 Shaw 90
70 Johnson Smith 78
51 ■ Fayetteville St. 73
59 Barber-Scotia 71
85 ■ Shaw 81
78 Hampton 97
76 ■ N.C. Central 109
70 Winston-Salem 73
62 Fayetteville St. 82
68 N.C. Central 91
92 ■ St. Paul's 84
107 ■ Morris 78
57 Virginia St. 75
92 ■ Winston-Salem 90
90 ■ Johnson Smith 94
68 ■ St. Augustine's 83
66 † Norfolk St. 85

LOCK HAVEN 14-12
82 ■ Bapt. Bible (Pa.) 75
62 † Mercyhurst 66
82 † New York Tech 42
84 Millersville 92
105 ■ Phila. Bible 59
84 ■ Cedarville 86
72 † Longwood 69
40 Lincoln Memorial 61
78 Alvernia 65
64 Bloomsburg 79
79 ■ Mansfield 66
72 ■ Kutztown 71
72 ■ Indiana (Pa.) 71
73 Edinboro 88
66 ■ Clarion 74
74 ■ Slippery Rock 63
71 ■ Columbia Union 69
60 Shippensburg 63
63 Calif. (Pa.) 76
81 Indiana (Pa.) 75
79 ■ Edinboro 75
72 ■ Le Moyne 91
57 Clarion 78
69 Slippery Rock 67
72 ■ Shippensburg 46
70 ■ Calif. (Pa.) 82

LONG BEACH ST. 22-10
72 † Tulsa 69

80 † San Diego 74
92 ■ Southern Cal Col. 62
112 ■ Pt. Loma Nazarene 71
95 ■ Howard 62
76 † Eastern Wash. 59
82 Fresno St. 61
88 San Jose St. 73
56 Pacific (Cal.) 68
101 ■ Nevada-Las Vegas 94
97 ■ New Mexico St. 71
84 Nevada 75
75 Utah St. 69
60 UC Santa Barb. 61
72 ■ Cal St. Fullerton 58
61 Va. Commonwealth 95
64 Kansas 49
59 ■ UC Santa Barb. 68
65 New Mexico St. 77
83 Nevada-Las Vegas 95
76 ■ Utah St. 64
91 ■ Nevada 82
61 Cal St. Fullerton 68
88 UC Irvine 74
78 Cal St. Northridge 81
84 ■ UC Irvine 67
103 ■ San Jose St. 87
66 ■ Pacific (Cal.) 69
80 ■ Cal St. Fullerton 68
79 ■ Nevada-Las Vegas 77
70 ■ New Mexico St. 62
72 † Illinois 75

LIU-BROOKLYN 11-17
52 † Mississippi St. 61
60 † Tex.-Pan American 54
69 ■ St. Peter's 71
74 Md.-East. Shore 79
80 Boston U. 77
87 Rutgers 99
62 Boston College 97
86 ■ Mt. St. Mary's (Md.) 95
59 ■ Rider 62
70 Wagner 85
77 ■ Monmouth (N.J.) 62
72 Marist 71
74 FDU-Teaneck 73
76 ■ Robert Morris 77
86 ■ St. Francis (Pa.) 67
120 ■ Molloy 69
98 St. Francis (N.Y.) 107
76 Rider 84
78 Mt. St. Mary's (Md.) 76
64 Monmouth (N.J.) 61
67 ■ Wagner 70
76 ■ FDU-Teaneck 73
97 ■ Marist 105
74 St. Francis (Pa.) 80
66 Robert Morris 84
96 ■ St. Francis (N.Y.) 99
80 Robert Morris 77
85 Rider 92

LIU-C.W. POST 19-8
78 ■ Ramapo 57
79 Cheyney 72
79 ■ Molloy 61
109 ■ New York Tech 81
94 ■ LIU-Southampton 69
85 Pace 93
104 Molloy 40
74 ■ Mass.-Lowell 67
81 ■ York (N.Y.) 66
77 Dowling 74
90 Mercy 76
64 Phila. Textile 78
89 ■ St. Rose 104
70 ■ Queens (N.Y.) 67
81 LIU-Southampton 72
102 Concordia (N.Y.) 86
62 ■ Pace 46
65 Stony Brook 60
82 ■ Adelphi 90
77 ■ Dowling 67
77 Queens (N.Y.) 69
74 St. Rose 111
87 ■ Concordia (N.Y.) 71
55 ■ Phila. Textile 72
94 Adelphi 98
88 ■ Mercy 78
74 ■ Adelphi 81

LIU-SOUTHAMPTON 5-21
60 Shippensburg 90
64 † West Va. Tech 85
95 ■ New York Tech 92
72 ■ Molloy 62
111 Keene St. 113
68 Franklin Pierce 102
60 East Stroudsburg 85
69 LIU-C.W. Post 94
68 ■ Queens (N.Y.) 80
52 ■ Pace 58
70 Concordia (N.Y.) 67
52 ■ Phila. Textile 92
93 ■ St. Rose 88
67 Adelphi 80
72 ■ LIU-C.W. Post 81
83 ■ Dowling 88
62 Queens (N.Y.) 75
63 Mercy 67
46 Pace 68
51 ■ Adelphi 68
88 ■ Concordia (N.Y.) 75
89 Dowling 94
45 St. Rose 73
65 ■ Old Westbury 67
48 Phila. Textile 74
69 Dowling 78

LONGWOOD 17-10
56 Gardner-Webb 57
65 † Pfeiffer 73
91 Barton 82
97 ■ Davis & Elkins 74
71 ■ Wingate 79
86 Marshall 101
78 ■ Averett 44
69 † Lock Haven 72
79 † Dist. Columbia 59
66 Elon 70
94 ■ Queens (N.C.) 71
58 High Point 57
102 ■ Newport News App. 57
72 ■ Newberry 70
67 ■ Gardner-Webb 69
61 Pembroke St. 59
66 Pitt.-Johnstown 61
72 Pfeiffer 68
62 ■ Elon 59
75 ■ Mount Olive 60
80 Wofford 90
72 ■ West Va. Wesleyan 63
76 Queens (N.C.) 69
70 Mount Olive 88
100 ■ Ferrum 66
84 Dist. Columbia 69
79 IU/PU-Indianapolis 105

LORAS 15-9
68 St. John's (Minn.) 80
79 ■ Rockford 69
59 Ill. Wesleyan 71
70 ■ Wis.-La Crosse 60
79 Mt. St. Clare 54
74 ■ St. Scholastica 58
49 ■ Ill. Benedictine 64
67 ■ Rockhurst 66
80 ■ William Penn 55
62 ■ Central (Iowa) 57
68 ■ Luther 63
64 Dubuque 75
61 Simpson 63
66 ■ Wartburg 73
63 Upper Iowa 56
82 ■ Buena Vista 62
75 William Penn 64
57 ■ Simpson 58
85 Buena Vista 96
71 Luther 64
50 Wartburg 51
79 ■ Dubuque 51
52 ■ Upper Iowa 49
77 Central (Iowa) 58

LOUISIANA ST. 22-11
83 ■ McNeese St. 72
92 ■ Southeastern La. 65
82 ■ Mercer 48
75 ■ Nicholls St. 64
93 ■ Campbell 71
72 † Stanford 63
67 † Duke 96
66 † Memphis St. 70
93 ■ Northwestern (La.) 79
90 ■ Tennessee St. 68
94 ■ Drake 86
67 Alabama 77
87 ■ Auburn 81
84 Mississippi St. 76
85 ■ Florida 81
86 ■ Central Conn. St. 53
62 Mississippi 71
67 Kentucky 105
85 ■ South Caro. 62
79 ■ Arkansas 91
84 † Texas 81
92 ■ Mississippi St. 66
75 Auburn 73
66 ■ Vanderbilt 87
81 Tennessee 74
76 ■ Alabama 68
78 Georgia 81
75 Arkansas 88
71 ■ Mississippi 56
89 † Mississippi 70
72 † Vanderbilt 62
65 Kentucky 82
64 † California 66

LOUISIANA TECH 7-21
50 Texas Christian 64
57 ■ Wyoming 75
82 Centenary 69
60 Dayton 70
45 † Auburn 65
88 † Alabama St. 73
66 ■ Texas Christian 49
59 Tex.-Pan American 62
51 ■ Arkansas St. 64
40 Western Ky. 86
48 ■ New Orleans 71
68 ■ South Ala. 85
59 ■ Southwestern La. 65
66 ■ Lamar 82
65 Arkansas St. 93
58 Ark.-Lit. Rock 63
78 ■ Jacksonville 75
74 ■ Tex.-Pan American 59
67 South Ala. 64
59 Southwestern La. 81
41 New Orleans 69
60 ■ Ark.-Lit. Rock 67
53 Oklahoma St. 80
71 Jacksonville 84
54 ■ Western Ky. 76
76 Lamar 113
63 † Jacksonville 62
52 † New Orleans 63

LOUISVILLE 22-9
73 † Michigan St. 69
88 Vanderbilt 90
68 ■ Kentucky 88
93 ■ DePaul 88
85 † Georgia Tech 87
67 Maryland 72
122 ■ Oral Roberts 76
98 South Fla. 75
69 N.C.-Charlotte 57
76 ■ Xavier (Ohio) 73
77 ■ Va. Commonwealth 68
77 ■ Kansas 98
85 Southern Miss. 81
85 ■ Arizona St. 59
76 Virginia Tech 65
90 Va. Commonwealth 88
78 ■ South Fla. 61
86 ■ Southern Miss. 71
60 Tulane 62
90 Nevada-Las Vegas 86
77 ■ Western Ky. 78
81 Houston 89
69 ■ N.C.-Charlotte 64
94 ■ Tulane 67
82 ■ Virginia Tech 61
83 ■ Notre Dame 68
71 ■ N.C.-Charlotte 59
90 ■ Va. Commonwealth 78
76 † Delaware 70
78 † Oklahoma St. 63
69 † Indiana 82

LOYOLA (CAL.) 7-20
80 ■ Notre Dame (Cal.) 77
80 ■ Nevada-Las Vegas 84
71 † Cal St. Northridge 66
70 † Michigan St. 73
73 Southwestern La. 87
66 Cal St. Sacramento 61
65 ■ Nevada 70
75 Fairfield 82
76 Buffalo 72
70 ■ DePaul 71
53 Cal St. Northridge 62
88 ■ Oral Roberts 76
80 ■ Portland 65
64 ■ Gonzaga 65
74 St. Mary's (Cal.) 93
72 San Francisco 94
59 ■ St. Mary's (Cal.) 55
60 ■ San Francisco 64
77 San Diego 87
57 Santa Clara 80
62 ■ Santa Clara 71
58 ■ San Diego 59
66 ■ Pepperdine 78
54 Pepperdine 80
73 Gonzaga 87
66 Portland 69
66 † Pepperdine 80

LOYOLA (ILL.) 7-20
68 ■ Wisconsin 66
50 ■ Notre Dame 52
64 ■ Bradley 69
70 Purdue 84
73 Northwestern 79
85 ■ Carthage 61
80 ■ Coppin St. 70
66 Canisius 84
73 ■ DePaul 88
83 ■ Concordia (Ill.) 54
67 Duquesne 65
56 La Salle 70
64 Illinois St. 88
75 ■ Detroit Mercy 96
69 ■ Dayton 70
64 ■ Xavier (Ohio) 81
70 ■ Evansville 108
51 Butler 68
79 Northern Ill. 89
56 Detroit Mercy 65
71 ■ Duquesne 79
90 ■ La Salle 96
65 Xavier (Ohio) 68
59 Dayton 56
66 ■ Butler 65
44 Evansville 62
50 † Xavier (Ohio) 60

LOYOLA (MD.) 2-25
61 Towson St. 71
50 Rutgers 82
37 Princeton 61
56 ■ Mt. St. Mary's (Md.) 52
71 † Southern Utah 81
55 † George Mason 63
59 ■ Bucknell 75

61 St. Joseph's (Pa.) .. 73
48 ■ Canisius 53
62 Navy 65
47 ■ Iona 63
68 ■ St. Peter's 79
57 Siena 74
72 St. Peter's 58
48 ■ Fairfield 60
62 ■ Manhattan 77
53 Canisius 64
47 Niagara 65
57 ■ Siena 71
57 Fairfield 61
62 Md.-Balt. County ... 77
66 ■ Niagara 72
70 ■ Fordham 73
85 Bucknell 116
61 Iona 79
62 Manhattan 79
37 † Manhattan 57

LUTHER 13-12
79 ■ Gust. Adolphus 74
86 Clarke 71
84 Concordia (St. Paul) 77
62 Hamline 76
57 Grinnell 55
68 Mt. Mercy 74
77 ■ Cornell College 66
84 ■ Iowa Wesleyan 66
91 ■ Wis.-La Crosse 84
78 ■ Simpson 60
62 ■ Upper Iowa 57
92 Buena Vista 82
69 Wartburg 73
63 Loras 68
69 ■ Central (Iowa) 57
71 ■ Dubuque 69
70 ■ William Penn 73
61 Central (Iowa) 71
73 Simpson 74
79 Upper Iowa 80
61 ■ Wartburg 79
64 ■ Loras 71
68 ■ Buena Vista 70
70 Dubuque 66
72 William Penn 79

LYCOMING 4-19
74 Wilkes 89
100 ■ Bapt. Bible (Pa.) 97
72 Allentown 83
55 † New Jersey Tech .. 94
75 † Wesley 76
60 † Washington (Md.) .. 76
72 † St. Joseph's (N.Y.) . 59
64 Misericordia 67
81 ■ Wesley 70
68 Scranton 100
81 Elizabethtown 88
55 ■ Messiah 71
62 Bucknell 94
70 ■ Albright 89
66 Susquehanna 88
78 Delaware Valley 77
77 Juniata 88
70 ■ Elizabethtown 79
72 ■ King's (Pa.) 82
55 Messiah 56
62 Albright 89
58 ■ Susquehanna 83
84 ■ Juniata 90

LYNCHBURG 5-19
86 ■ Mary Washington .. 55
53 Guilford 67
74 ■ Newport News App. 63
63 Winthrop 92
47 Davidson 82
47 Barry 86
54 † St. Thomas (Fla.) ... 66
49 ■ Randolph-Macon ... 70
70 ■ Roanoke 81
77 Wash. & Lee 87
67 ■ Emory & Henry 92

71 East. Mennonite 76
64 ■ Va. Wesleyan 59
73 ■ Guilford 67
68 ■ East. Mennonite 64
58 Bridgewater (Va.) .. 71
61 Hampden-Sydney .. 90
77 Emory & Henry 82
59 Randolph-Macon ... 63
69 Roanoke 73
57 ■ Wash. & Lee 58
61 ■ Bridgewater (Va.) .. 67
75 ■ Hampden-Sydney .. 86
67 Va. Wesleyan 79

MACMURRAY 20-7
72 Millikin 83
63 ■ Monmouth (Ill.) 62
55 Marian (Ind.) 79
51 † Upper Iowa 76
90 ■ Westminster (Mo.) . 70
65 ■ Rhodes 84
67 Parks 49
63 Washington (Mo.) .. 83
81 Principia 41
80 Fontbonne 66
84 ■ Webster 68
75 ■ Blackburn 56
86 Greenville 100
76 Maryville (Mo.) 72
72 Westminster (Mo.) . 71
58 ■ Knox 70
75 ■ Parks 48
76 ■ Fontbonne 71
71 Monmouth (Ill.) 65
82 ■ Principia 61
72 Webster 70
100 ■ Illinois Col. 78
79 Blackburn 64
87 ■ Maryville (Mo.) 61
68 † Principia 62
94 Maryville (Mo.) 64
81 † Westminster (Mo.) . 76

MACALESTER 3-21
75 ■ St. Scholastica 62
54 Claremont-M-S 81
55 † La Verne 91
67 Bethel (Minn.) 82
56 Concordia (St. Paul) 70
63 Augsburg 65
71 ■ St. Olaf 74
68 Carleton 95
56 ■ Hamline 63
77 St. John's (Minn.) .. 90
53 Concordia-M'head . 77
59 ■ St. Thomas (Minn.) . 76
80 St. Mary's (Minn.) .. 67
66 ■ Bethel (Minn.) 73
65 ■ Gust. Adolphus 77
73 ■ Augsburg 96
50 St. Olaf 73
65 Gust. Adolphus 92
62 ■ Carleton 69
71 Hamline 85
68 ■ St. John's (Minn.) .. 72
87 ■ Concordia-M'head . 72
46 St. Thomas (Minn.) . 82
71 ■ St. Mary's (Minn.) .. 74

MAINE 10-17
63 Eastern Ill. 71
59 ■ Northern Ariz. 56
83 Central Conn. St. ... 62
63 † Fairfield 58
83 Buffalo 70
56 ■ Bradley 54
67 Central Fla. 78
72 ■ St. Bonaventure 73
68 San Francisco 70
64 Drexel 59
71 Delaware 93
67 ■ Vermont 63
66 ■ Hartford 75
77 Hofstra 83

78 ■ Boston U. 73
70 ■ Northeastern 72
71 New Hampshire 65
60 Northeastern 77
73 Boston U. 82
81 ■ Buffalo 52
76 Hartford 88
74 Vermont 82
72 Connecticut 108
72 ■ Delaware 78
57 ■ Drexel 67
49 ■ New Hampshire 55
49 Hartford 59

MAINE MARITIME 8-11
33 Emerson-MCA 56
63 † Daniel Webster 54
77 Me.-Augusta 81
88 ■ Me.-Fort Kent 61
84 ■ Unity 76
88 ■ Westbrook 110
51 Bowdoin 85
67 Daniel Webster 72
59 ■ Atlantic Union 96
59 Westbrook 86
75 Me.-Augusta 77
72 ■ Thomas 74
87 Me.-Fort Kent 83
82 Unity 77
57 ■ New England 70
82 ■ Daniel Webster 68
95 ■ Me.-Augusta 72
79 New England 93
88 ■ Emerson-MCA 78

MANCHESTER 20-8
91 ■ Huntington 76
85 ■ Kalamazoo 74
101 ■ Olivet 74
108 ■ Earlham 78
69 Goshen 87
79 Bluffton 50
75 Indiana Tech 84
119 † Graceland (Ind.) ... 100
144 ■ Ind.-Northwest 46
90 ■ Purdue-Calumet ... 62
67 ■ Anderson 63
80 Wabash 94
85 ■ St. Francis (Ind.) ... 66
68 ■ Hanover 72
95 Franklin 98
64 DePauw 70
75 Rose-Hulman 63
91 ■ Wabash 65
83 Anderson 70
76 Hanover 85
85 ■ Bluffton 58
51 ■ DePauw 49
93 ■ Franklin 70
98 ■ Rose-Hulman 72
76 ■ Rose-Hulman 68
75 † Anderson 55
83 † Wabash 75
66 Wis.-Whitewater ... 84

MANHATTAN 23-7
80 ■ Hofstra 56
62 Marquette 85
67 † Texas Christian 42
62 Marist 59
61 Bradley 54
83 ■ Army 51
92 ■ Fordham 67
59 † St. John's (N.Y.) 74
76 † Rutgers 80
80 Columbia 84
74 ■ Holy Cross 70
85 Colgate 78
64 Niagara 83
64 Canisius 60
70 ■ Niagara 69
57 St. Peter's 48
64 ■ Siena 62
83 ■ Iona 74

77 Loyola (Md.) 62
82 ■ Fairfield 71
75 ■ Canisius 55
89 Iona 76
76 Siena 84
89 ■ St. Peter's 77
82 Fairfield 71
79 ■ Loyola (Md.) 62
57 † Loyola (Md.) 37
71 † Siena 70
68 † Niagara 67
66 † Virginia 78

MANHATTANVILLE 8-17
92 † Pracitical Bible 54
62 Binghamton 82
87 Staten Island 81
66 New York U. 84
74 ■ New Jersey Tech .. 91
66 † Walsh 104
51 † Greensboro 53
67 ■ Connecticut Col. ... 64
69 ■ Hunter 66
65 Skidmore 75
84 ■ Wm. Paterson 90
63 ■ Staten Island 66
78 ■ St. Joseph's (Me.) .. 92
55 ■ Western Conn. St. .. 69
60 New Jersey Tech .. 67
41 Stony Brook 39
65 Merchant Marine ... 60
70 Hunter 94
70 ■ Trinity (Conn.) 86
86 Mt. St. Vincent 64
69 ■ Merchant Marine ... 80
56 ■ Stony Brook 81
71 Western Conn. St. .. 94
87 Mt. St. Mary (N.Y.) 100
78 Vassar 63

MANKATO ST. 18-9
79 ■ Black Hills St. 57
74 ■ Ferris St. 73
67 ■ Wis.-River Falls 51
63 Minn.-Duluth 67
73 Wayne St. (Neb.) ... 48
76 Fla. Atlantic 59
81 ■ Bemidji St. 64
80 ■ Dak. Wesleyan 69
65 ■ North Dak. 76
73 ■ North Dak. St. 71
63 Morningside 67
63 South Dak. 86
80 ■ St. Cloud St. 68
74 North Dak. 80
59 ■ Augustana (S.D.) ... 49
94 ■ South Dak. St. 76
72 Nebraska-Omaha .. 63
60 Northern Colo. 69
68 ■ South Dak. 77
76 ■ Morningside 54
62 North Dak. St. 51
86 St. Cloud St. 83
66 South Dak. St. 70
85 Augustana (S.D.) ... 79
82 ■ Northern Colo. 62
85 ■ Nebraska-Omaha .. 69
60 † South Dak. St. 69

MANSFIELD 11-14
81 ■ Concordia (N.Y.) 64
86 ■ Dist. Columbia 79
61 Gannon 72
79 ■ Pitt.-Johnstown 77
55 Akron 75
75 Calif. (Pa.) 82
89 † Charleston (W.Va.) . 81
76 Mercyhurst 81
67 ■ Shippensburg 65
78 † Dist. Columbia 46
74 Clarion 80
61 Pitt.-Bradford 48
66 Lock Haven 79
61 ■ Kutztown 56
48 ■ Millersville 55

54 East Stroudsburg .. 67
45 West Chester 60
74 ■ Bloomsburg 72
53 ■ Cheyney 51
58 Kutztown 65
51 Millersville 75
51 ■ East Stroudsburg .. 69
67 ■ West Chester 72
84 Bloomsburg 104
70 Cheyney 68

MARIETTA 5-20

64 Kenyon 82
62 Wooster 87
68 Wash. & Jeff. 87
80 ■ John Carroll 92
50 Mount Union 81
70 Heidelberg 91
63 Baldwin-Wallace .. 102
57 Denison 74
91 ■ Bethany (W.Va.) 92
84 ■ Frostburg St. 74
55 Muskingum 60
70 ■ Hiram 77
79 ■ Otterbein 72
48 Ohio Northern 84
48 ■ Capital 65
77 ■ Heidelberg 76
64 ■ Mount Union 63
57 John Carroll 61
67 Otterbein 114
72 ■ Baldwin-Wallace ... 77
68 ■ Muskingum 67
70 Hiram 84
58 Capital 89
59 ■ Ohio Northern 78
69 Heidelberg 109

MARIST 14-16

60 ■ Siena 62
61 † Va. Commonwealth 86
78 † Southern Miss. 69
59 ■ Manhattan 62
62 ■ Lafayette 60
101 ■ Central Conn. St. ... 81
64 † Ball St. 78
85 Hawaii-Hilo 78
56 † Missouri 69
68 ■ FDU-Teaneck 67
73 Rider 83
74 Mt. St. Mary's (Md.) 90
71 ■ LIU-Brooklyn 72
77 ■ St. Francis (N.Y.) ... 72
59 Monmouth (N.J.) ... 83
72 ■ Robert Morris 60
51 ■ St. Francis (Pa.) 64
56 † Fairfield 61
57 ■ Wagner 52
84 FDU-Teaneck 76
67 ■ Mt. St. Mary's (Md.) 72
69 ■ Rider 65
89 St. Francis (N.Y.) ... 77
105 LIU-Brooklyn 97
64 Wagner 81
71 ■ Monmouth (N.J.) ... 68
67 Army 73
82 Robert Morris 84
85 St. Francis (Pa.) 66
62 ■ FDU-Teaneck 81

MARITIME (N.Y.) 11-13

71 Vassar 57
101 Baruch 96
64 Stevens Tech 70
51 ■ Mt. St. Vincent 72
58 ■ Molloy 64
59 ■ Yeshiva 66
60 ■ Puerto Rico (R.P.) .. 69
74 ■ Merchant Marine ... 81
55 ■ New Jersey Tech .. 96
64 Mt. St. Vincent 79
48 ■ Polytechnic (N.Y.) .. 39
49 ■ Lehman 37
74 ■ Bard 44
57 ■ Stevens Tech 49
65 ■ Medgar Evers 71
58 Utica 69
49 Yeshiva 48
72 ■ Vassar 41
58 Polytechnic (N.Y.) .. 52
68 ■ St. Joseph's (N.Y.) . 44
61 ■ Coast Guard 75
52 Albertus Magnus ... 75
81 Bard 50
57 Stevens Tech 63

MARQUETTE 20-8

84 ■ North Caro. A&T ... 43
85 ■ Manhattan 62
73 ■ Charleston So. 35
95 ■ Northeastern Ill. 65
90 ■ American 74
83 ■ Western Ill. 59
88 Nevada-Las Vegas . 94
61 Illinois 58
67 ■ Wisconsin 77
82 ■ Dayton 44
80 Ala.-Birmingham ... 66
96 ■ Chicago St. 47
65 ■ St. Louis 53
66 Fordham 40
105 ■ Delaware St. 65
78 ■ Memphis St. 66
65 St. Louis 62
69 South Fla. 54
87 DePaul 76
53 Cincinnati 55
38 ■ Ala.-Birmingham ... 44
69 Notre Dame 61
63 ■ Wis.-Green Bay 46
57 ■ Cincinnati 66
63 Memphis St. 68
86 ■ DePaul 75
57 † St. Louis 63
62 † Oklahoma St. 74

MARS HILL 16-10

86 Western Caro. 74
69 ■ Lees-McRae 62
74 Kennesaw 86
81 ■ Kennesaw 73
83 Hawaii Pacific 111
97 † Bluefield Col. 56
65 Elon 72
73 Gardner-Webb 71
68 ■ Carson-Newman ... 55
92 ■ Catawba 74
71 Presbyterian 76
62 Wingate 78
64 Lees-McRae 45
65 ■ Central Wesleyan .. 51
73 Lenoir-Rhyne 83
93 ■ Clinch Valley 69
82 ■ Elon 60
88 ■ Gardner-Webb 83
63 ■ Lenoir-Rhyne 77
68 Carson-Newman ... 58
86 Catawba 81
69 ■ Presbyterian 74
80 ■ Wingate 71
69 † Wingate 73
66 Coker 54
56 Presbyterian 71

MARSHALL 16-11

80 ■ Pitt.-Johnstown 54
81 Pittsburgh 95
101 ■ Longwood 86
89 ■ Ohio 79
85 Montana St. 77
89 Wyoming 101
91 ■ Robert Morris 65
92 Appalachian St. ... 111
78 ■ Tenn.-Chatt. 77
86 ■ Western Caro. 65
74 East Tenn. St. 83
75 ■ Ga. Southern 74
62 ■ Citadel 50
92 Furman 83
69 Davidson 82
80 ■ Va. Military 66
75 ■ East Tenn. St. 73
82 ■ Appalachian St. 79
78 Va. Military 69
85 Western Caro. 81
69 Tenn.-Chatt. 83
65 † West Va. 72
52 Citadel 68
72 Ga. Southern 75
57 ■ Davidson 63
88 ■ Furman 84
65 † Davidson 67

MARY WASHINGTON 8-18

59 ■ Chris. Newport 85
55 Va. Wesleyan 88
107 ■ Shenandoah 98
55 Lynchburg 86
77 † St. Mary's (Md.) 68
51 Hampden-Sydney .. 87
85 Wash. & Lee 83
76 ■ Western Md. 83
78 ■ Newport News App. 67
88 ■ Marymount (Va.) ... 89
74 ■ Gallaudet 56
79 ■ Goucher 62
71 ■ N.C. Wesleyan 74
91 ■ Frostburg St. 93
77 York (Pa.) 90
87 Catholic 93
66 ■ St. Mary's (Md.) 62
77 Marymount (Va.) ... 93
70 Gallaudet 81
94 Shenandoah 106
49 Goucher 70
63 Newport News App. 65
63 ■ Catholic 89
78 ■ York (Pa.) 81
56 St. Mary's (Md.) 55
74 Catholic 76

MARYLAND 12-16

103 ■ Md.-Balt. County ... 80
72 West Va. 86
94 ■ Md.-East. Shore ... 63
98 ■ American 67
93 La Salle 76
78 ■ Towson St. 68
103 ■ Morgan St. 63
72 ■ Louisville 67
109 ■ Howard 69
75 ■ Georgia Tech 85
73 North Caro. 101
85 Florida St. 105
73 ■ Wake Forest 86
89 † Oklahoma 78
70 North Caro. St. 65
72 Clemson 82
62 ■ Duke 78
68 ■ Virginia 70
79 Georgia Tech 93
63 ■ North Caro. 77
84 ■ Florida St. 87
64 Wake Forest 88
88 ■ North Caro. St. 71
73 ■ Clemson 81
79 Duke 95
74 Virginia 88
76 † North Caro. St. 55
66 † North Caro. 102

MD.-BALT. COUNTY 12-16

80 Maryland 103
88 ■ Washington (Md.) .. 76
76 Coppin St. 68
96 ■ St. Mary's (Md.) 68
86 Syracuse 93
80 Florida St. 109
59 St. Francis (Pa.) 67
98 Delaware 106
91 ■ N.C.-Asheville 82
98 Coastal Caro. 115
64 Charleston So. 75
61 Charleston (S.C.) ... 97
70 ■ Campbell 75
82 ■ Charleston So. 67
99 ■ Winthrop 93
65 Campbell 70
85 Winthrop 79
76 Towson St. 82
73 ■ Coastal Caro. 91
86 Radford 88
90 ■ Liberty 85
102 ■ Radford 98
77 ■ Loyola (Md.) 62
81 Liberty 83
91 N.C.-Asheville 75
92 ■ Towson St. 97
85 † Campbell 67
59 † Coastal Caro. 66

MD.-EAST. SHORE 12-15

61 St. Peter's 73
47 Ball St. 67
75 † Morehead St. 72
63 Maryland 94
86 Salisbury St. 80
54 Georgetown 87
79 ■ LIU-Brooklyn 74
62 James Madison 89
68 Central Conn. St. ... 67
67 Delaware St. 55
50 Florida A&M 69
71 Bethune-Cookman . 68
91 ■ Howard 79
69 Morgan St. 88
69 ■ Coppin St. 79
69 ■ South Caro. St. 66
44 ■ North Caro. A&T ... 52
55 Howard 80
64 ■ Morgan St. 69
72 South Caro. St. 70
65 North Caro. A&T ... 88
69 † Delaware St. 65
99 ■ Bryan 89
63 ■ Florida A&M 83
74 ■ Bethune-Cookman . 58
51 Coppin St. 75
57 † South Caro. St. 59

MARYMOUNT (VA.) 15-10

76 † Ferrum 83
54 † Goucher 72
65 ■ Bridgewater (Va.) .. 63
77 Hampden-Sydney .. 90
73 Liberty 93
86 Western Md. 75
94 Wesley 72
87 ■ Chris. Newport ... 102
82 Newport News App. 67
85 ■ N.C. Wesleyan 88
102 ■ Maryville (Tenn.) .. 101
106 Catholic 107
79 Gallaudet 69
89 Mary Washington .. 88
71 ■ York (Pa.) 79
72 York (Pa.) 66
93 ■ Mary Washington .. 77
90 ■ Catholic 88
75 St. Mary's (Md.) 76
78 ■ Newport News App. 68
64 ■ St. Mary's (Md.) 62
74 Goucher 64
88 ■ Gallaudet 63
79 ■ Gallaudet 64
62 ■ York (Pa.) 71

MARYVILLE (MO.) 9-17

83 Grinnell 96
77 † Buena Vista 121
78 ■ Rhodes 91
88 ■ Illinois Col. 103
70 Rhodes 114
76 † Millsaps 89
77 ■ Washington (Mo.) . 108
76 ■ Westminster (Mo.) . 79
81 ■ Hanover 98

63 Colorado Col. 101
80 † Cornell College 104
65 Blackburn 91
61 Parks 54
76 ■ Fontbonne 72
79 ■ Principia 65
75 ■ Webster 72
72 ■ MacMurray 76
88 ■ Blackburn 77
80 Westminster (Mo.) 93
65 ■ Parks 53
91 Fontbonne 110
84 Principia 75
80 Webster 73
61 MacMurray 87
84 ■ Blackburn 61
64 ■ MacMurray 94

MARYVILLE (TENN.) 20-6
135 ■ Savannah A&D 51
100 ■ Rhodes 92
84 ■ Oglethorpe 67
82 Ferrum 84
93 Greensboro 80
82 ■ Otterbein 84
79 ■ Centre 78
84 † North Park 74
75 Otterbein 81
93 ■ Averett 70
82 Centre 79
95 † Salisbury St. 106
101 Marymount (Va.) 102
85 Knoxville 78
105 ■ Ferrum 92
96 Warren Wilson 46
87 ■ Rust 66
53 Lane 52
84 Rust 71
90 ■ Sewanee 70
77 Averett 71
86 Tenn. Wesleyan 56
117 ■ Warren Wilson 38
76 ■ Knoxville 66
102 ■ Lane 89
61 ■ Emory & Henry 83

MASSACHUSETTS 24-7
64 Florida St. 67
78 ■ Central Conn. St. 52
70 Siena 58
83 Oklahoma 93
81 † Holy Cross 66
84 † South Caro. 66
75 New Hampshire 61
90 ■ Boston U. 42
53 † Cincinnati 64
44 Temple 52
82 Rutgers 78
76 ■ Geo. Washington 68
84 ■ Rhode Island 72
52 ■ Temple 50
79 † DePaul 69
84 ■ Southwestern La. 74
93 St. Bonaventure 78
64 ■ West Va. 59
82 ■ Rutgers 67
81 St. Joseph's (Pa.) 69
68 Geo. Washington 65
96 Buffalo 67
68 † Rhode Island 71
54 West Va. 79
86 St. Bonaventure 62
61 ■ St. Joseph's (Pa.) 43
75 † St. Bonaventure 62
76 † Rhode Island 50
69 ■ Temple 61
54 † Pennsylvania 50
56 † Virginia 71

MASS.-BOSTON 12-13
84 ■ Anna Maria 100
105 ■ Savannah A&D 63
91 ■ Bri'water (Mass.) 71
62 Assumption 64
80 Salem St. 99
62 Westfield St. 73
87 North Adams St. 60
82 ■ Clark (Mass.) 74
70 Tufts 58
56 ■ Southern Me. 64
99 † Emerson-MCA 43
88 † Mt. St. Mary (N.Y.) 68
88 Rhode Island Col. 66
67 Mass.-Dartmouth 103
57 Southern Me. 60
67 Suffolk 71
95 ■ Plymouth St. 89
60 ■ Eastern Conn. St. 68
89 MIT 58
72 ■ Mass.-Dartmouth 114
67 ■ Rhode Island Col. 64
60 Eastern Conn. St. 78
73 Colby 87
77 Plymouth St. 69
74 ■ Plymouth St. 78

MASS.-DARTMOUTH 25-6
86 Hartwick 84
103 † Mt. St. Mary (N.Y.) 83
97 ■ Salve Regina 71
90 Bri'water (Mass.) 60
141 Framingham St. 99
107 ■ Worcester St. 109
91 Brandeis 106
72 Webber 63
82 Tampa 93
55 Fla. Southern 78
113 ■ Salem St. 107
75 ■ Rhode Island Col. 59
72 ■ Southern Me. 60
104 Fitchburg St. 78
75 Eastern Conn. St. 73
95 Clark (Mass.) 66
103 ■ Mass.-Boston 67
89 Rhode Island Col. 77
96 ■ Eastern Conn. St. 75
99 ■ Plymouth St. 79
114 Mass.-Boston 72
77 Southern Me. 63
90 ■ Suffolk 70
103 Plymouth St. 101
74 † Plymouth St. 72
87 † Eastern Conn. St. 73
90 ■ Westfield St. 81
68 ■ Geneseo St. 66
75 ■ Eastern Conn. St. 64
73 † Ohio Northern 74
74 † Rowan 95

MASS.-LOWELL 13-15
76 ■ Stonehill 65
82 ■ Merrimack 76
83 ■ Tufts 66
73 ■ American Int'l 79
65 ■ Bentley 68
69 St. Michael's 72
85 ■ St. Anselm 87
74 New York Tech 63
67 LIU-C.W. Post 74
71 Bryant 73
71 Le Moyne 68
85 ■ Assumption 60
94 ■ New Haven 74
80 ■ Southern Conn. St. 72
70 Franklin Pierce 80
75 Sacred Heart 74
78 ■ New Hamp. Col. 87
74 Southern Conn. St. 84
80 ■ Keene St. 78
78 New Haven 97
62 ■ Franklin Pierce 71
86 † Sacred Heart 75
87 Keene St. 80
76 Quinnipiac 82
74 † Le Moyne 75
84 New Hamp. Col. 95
77 ■ Southern Conn. St. 61
70 New Hamp. Col. 120

MIT 5-19
76 Norwich 77
55 ■ Babson 72
66 Worcester Tech 94
67 Brandeis 85
77 ■ Gordon 69
72 ■ Norwich 62
56 Eastern Nazarene 67
57 ■ Coast Guard 82
76 ■ New England Col. 80
83 ■ Curry 80
61 Nichols 74
57 Western New Eng. 63
67 Coast Guard 76
79 Bowdoin 83
92 Suffolk 79
71 ■ Connecticut Col. 101
69 ■ Wentworth Inst. 74
58 ■ Mass.-Boston 89
71 Tufts 80
46 ■ Western New Eng. 52
73 ■ Worcester Tech 89
49 Babson 94
51 Western New Eng. 49
68 Babson 95

MCNEESE ST. 12-15
72 Louisiana St. 83
103 ■ Ark.-Monticello 77
76 ■ Mississippi 80
76 Lamar 100
80 Stetson 74
72 † Northeastern 78
77 Central Fla. 73
83 ■ Lamar 89
70 ■ Texas-San Antonio 71
64 ■ Southwest Tex. St. 71
64 Northeast La. 94
96 Northwestern (La.) 94
70 ■ Texas-Arlington 72
70 ■ North Texas 67
72 Nicholls St. 76
61 Sam Houston St. 62
68 Stephen F. Austin 62
100 ■ Northwestern (La.) 81
79 Texas-San Antonio 68
77 North Texas 68
75 Texas-Arlington 77
67 ■ Nicholls St. 70
68 ■ Northeast La. 72
74 ■ Stephen F. Austin 70
87 ■ Sam Houston St. 65
65 Southwest Tex. St. 64
68 † Texas-San Antonio 77

MEMPHIS ST. 20-12
76 Arkansas 81
59 Tennessee 70
85 ■ Tulane 86
91 ■ Southwestern La. 85
81 ■ Jackson St. 78
64 † Chaminade 56
67 † Brigham Young 73
70 † Louisiana St. 66
78 ■ Robert Morris 63
55 Minnesota 70
97 ■ Georgia St. 76
84 ■ Vanderbilt 78
95 DePaul 93
109 ■ Southeastern La. 58
47 ■ Ala.-Birmingham 50
101 ■ Tennessee Tech 71
64 Missouri 56
66 Marquette 78
69 Ala.-Birmingham 53
96 ■ Fla. Atlantic 46
68 ■ Cincinnati 66
95 ■ Southern Miss. 82
79 ■ DePaul 57
77 St. Louis 69
76 † Arizona St. 89
58 Temple 65
68 ■ Marquette 63
75 ■ St. Louis 72
55 Cincinnati 78
73 ■ St. Louis 65
72 ■ Cincinnati 77
52 † Western Ky. 55

MENLO 10-14
79 ■ Pomona-Pitzer 83
62 ■ Cal Lutheran 76
85 ■ Cal St. Hayward 74
73 † Claremont-M-S 69
86 Redlands 96
77 † UC San Diego 71
104 ■ Holy Names 49
72 Sonoma St. 57
75 ■ Elmhurst 69
59 UC Davis 71
55 ■ Southwestern (Tex.) 58
65 † Hartwick 44
55 Whittier 54
80 ■ Dominican (Cal.) 91
86 ■ Bethany (Cal.) 89
62 UC Santa Cruz 68
73 Notre Dame (Cal.) 78
85 ■ San Fran. St. 94
69 † Dominican (Cal.) 78
90 ■ San Jose Christian 73
75 ■ UC San Diego 79
80 Bethany (Cal.) 89
76 ■ UC Santa Cruz 56
66 UC San Diego 81

MERCER 13-14
82 ■ Brewton Parker 60
48 Louisiana St. 82
88 ■ Valdosta St. 80
98 ■ Fort Valley St. 66
81 Central Fla. 78
46 Iowa St. 87
58 Illinois 77
69 Clemson 87
66 South Caro. 68
52 ■ Tulane 70
77 ■ Georgia St. 69
81 ■ Samford 68
55 ■ Charleston (S.C.) 56
73 Southeastern La. 58
82 Centenary 89
79 Georgia 88
64 ■ Florida Int'l 61
75 ■ Stetson 70
57 Georgia St. 58
71 Samford 89
98 ■ Southeastern La. 77
93 ■ Centenary 82
93 ■ Central Fla. 84
74 N.C.-Asheville 69
61 Charleston (S.C.) 62
65 Florida Int'l 67
87 Stetson 94

MERCHANT MARINE 6-18
81 † Juniata 73
65 St. John Fisher 97
79 ■ Staten Island 82
78 Hunter 94
73 St. Joseph's (N.Y.) 86
77 ■ Hunter 100
81 Maritime (N.Y.) 74
57 ■ Wheaton (Mass.) 78
68 Staten Island 76
78 ■ New Jersey Tech 94
63 ■ Stony Brook 64
65 ■ Union (N.Y.) 85
43 New Jersey Tech 84
63 ■ Stevens Tech 56
83 Nazareth (N.Y.) 90
65 ■ Williams 90
60 ■ Manhattanville 65
48 Rutgers-Newark 71
105 Molloy 102
86 ■ Yeshiva 65
56 Stony Brook 61
80 Manhattanville 69
68 Bloomfield 79
68 † Coast Guard 85

MERCY		**13-14**
89	† West Va. Tech	66
91	Shippensburg	101
79	New Haven	95
98	■ Molloy	64
101	■ New York Tech	100
64	Bryant	57
76	St. Rose	91
58	Queens (N.Y.)	62
77	Dowling	55
57	† Sacred Heart	55
77	Bentley	80
86	■ Concordia (N.Y.)	81
76	■ LIU-C.W. Post	90
59	■ Phila. Textile	93
79	Adelphi	85
75	Pace	69
63	■ Queens (N.Y.)	60
85	New York Tech	79
81	■ Dowling	68
67	■ LIU-Southampton	63
73	Concordia (N.Y.)	74
57	■ Pace	62
84	Phila. Textile	111
81	■ St. Rose	93
78	■ Adelphi	76
78	LIU-C.W. Post	88
52	St. Rose	69

MERCYHURST		**19-8**
93	■ Glenville St.	72
66	† Lock Haven	62
55	Gannon	81
89	■ Calif. (Pa.)	86
108	■ St. Vincent	97
91	■ Central St. (Ohio)	94
79	Edinboro	65
81	■ Mansfield	76
90	† Franklin Pierce	80
73	St. Michael's	78
93	■ Rio Grande	79
84	■ Holy Family	57
100	■ East Stroudsburg	90
87	Slippery Rock	76
63	Indiana (Pa.)	83
77	Glenville St.	86
74	Oakland	84
93	■ Pitt.-Johnstown	66
72	Gannon	74
90	Central St. (Ohio)	71
71	■ Gannon	70
75	■ Edinboro	84
95	■ Wis.-Parkside	79
76	■ Bloomsburg	75
99	■ Malone	91
109	■ Cedarville	72
93	Pitt.-Johnstown	90

MERRIMACK		**11-16**
69	† Sacred Heart	78
76	Mass.-Lowell	82
75	St. Anselm	78
63	■ Bentley	78
73	■ New Hamp. Col.	77
81	■ Keene St.	65
102	■ Bates	64
94	■ Plymouth St.	91
74	Fla. Southern	89
70	St. Leo	66
78	■ Assumption	73
64	American Int'l	93
76	Stonehill	80
73	■ Quinnipiac	77
58	■ St. Michael's	54
73	■ Springfield	62
60	Bentley	71
70	Bryant	72
71	■ St. Anselm	70
62	■ American Int'l	64
73	■ Stonehill	66
73	Quinnipiac	76
50	St. Michael's	74
84	Springfield	79
79	■ Bryant	78
71	Assumption	73
67	Bentley	87

MESA ST.		**21-8**
83	Fort Lewis	76
89	■ Southern Colo.	84
100	■ Tex. Wesleyan	65
94	† Cameron	83
75	† Notre Dame (Cal.)	81
76	Air Force	88
100	■ Fort Lewis	104
71	Colorado-CS	57
89	■ Concordia (Ill.)	63
68	■ Western St.	79
104	■ Fort Lewis	80
89	■ Colorado Mines	65
93	■ St. Francis (Ill.)	66
96	■ Colorado-CS	62
69	Western St.	81
96	■ Adams St.	85
88	■ N.M. Highlands	77
83	Chadron St.	79
48	Fort Hays St.	57
88	■ Colorado Mines	71
75	■ Chadron St.	68
81	■ Fort Hays St.	69
92	■ Western St.	70
58	Colorado Mines	59
71	N.M. Highlands	59
100	Adams St.	77
68	■ N.M. Highlands	62
78	† Chadron St.	62
64	Western St.	78

MESSIAH		**7-17**
72	† N.C. Wesleyan	84
99	Shenandoah	103
73	■ Western Md.	64
63	■ Wilkes	68
78	■ Eastern (Pa.)	85
53	Dickinson	69
65	■ Gettysburg	69
80	Kutztown	95
59	† Penn St.-Harrisburg	63
51	Dickinson	70
47	Johns Hopkins	62
61	■ Clarion	92
79	■ East. Mennonite	69
46	Susquehanna	60
71	Lycoming	55
72	■ Wesley	71
83	■ Juniata	58
74	■ Albright	78
71	Elizabethtown	77
52	■ Susquehanna	88
56	■ Lycoming	55
71	Juniata	61
44	Albright	60
71	■ Elizabethtown	82

METHODIST		**6-19**
59	■ Guilford	75
81	■ Salisbury St.	120
52	Pembroke St.	80
51	Coastal Caro.	101
63	† Defiance	102
66	† Hilbert	80
50	Campbell	79
56	Fla. Southern	86
74	Flagler	90
77	■ Chris. Newport	91
68	■ N.C. Wesleyan	87
80	■ Shenandoah	82
68	■ Greensboro	91
95	■ Piedmont Bible	62
76	Ferrum	85
77	Averett	58
62	Greensboro	80
50	Chris. Newport	101
63	Newport News App.	47
77	■ Ferrum	94
79	Shenandoah	83
65	N.C. Wesleyan	58
88	■ Newport News App.	66
69	■ Averett	66
54	■ N.C. Wesleyan	71

METROPOLITAN ST.		**16-12**
104	■ Langston	70
92	■ Concordia (Neb.)	73
108	■ Bellevue	67
66	■ Christ-Irvine	62
116	■ Baker	78
68	Eastern Mont.	74
90	■ Northern Colo.	80
93	■ Western St.	84
82	■ Adams St.	86
79	■ Cal St. San B'dino	76
71	Northern Colo.	96
57	Hawaii-Hilo	69
77	Chaminade	86
69	Western St.	75
68	■ Denver	64
75	■ Southern Colo.	76
92	Fort Lewis	91
72	Colorado-CS	52
80	■ Regis (Colo.)	79
93	■ Neb.-Kearney	95
70	Colo. Christian	88
72	■ BYU-Hawaii	76
70	Denver	90
76	Southern Colo.	67
111	■ Fort Lewis	103
78	■ Colorado-CS	55
92	Regis (Colo.)	83
67	■ Colo. Christian	70

MIAMI (FLA.)		**10-17**
64	■ Florida Int'l	72
57	■ Southwest Tex. St.	60
56	Seton Hall	65
81	■ Barry	64
84	■ Fla. Atlantic	61
67	Georgia	69
66	† Southern Cal	86
73	■ N.C.-Wilmington	88
80	■ Georgetown	69
78	Pittsburgh	85
81	Syracuse	89
74	St. John's (N.Y.)	78
75	■ Providence	66
84	■ Pittsburgh	86
80	■ Connecticut	65
69	Villanova	82
78	■ Bethune-Cookman	54
81	■ Syracuse	74
75	■ Boston College	71
72	Connecticut	88
60	Providence	75
82	■ St. John's (N.Y.)	77
73	■ Seton Hall	85
58	Boston College	70
64	Georgetown	82
77	■ Villanova	76
40	† Georgetown	67

MIAMI (OHIO)		**22-9**
88	■ Thomas More	44
81	■ Penn St.	68
57	■ Dayton	50
67	Xavier (Ohio)	70
49	Kentucky	65
75	Wright St.	68
65	■ Ball St.	50
51	Akron	46
52	Western Mich.	69
59	■ Ohio	72
59	Central Mich.	43
82	■ Bowling Green	57
69	Eastern Mich.	62
64	■ Toledo	62
68	■ Cincinnati	74
69	Kent	55
58	■ Akron	46
65	■ Western Mich.	39
65	Illinois St.	55
59	Ohio	54
87	■ Central Mich.	68
50	Bowling Green	44
55	■ Eastern Mich.	59
63	Toledo	57
71	■ Kent	38
63	Ball St.	72
63	† Bowling Green	50
48	† Western Mich.	61
56	Ohio St.	53
60	■ Old Dominion	58
53	† Georgetown	66

MICHIGAN		**31-5**
75	Rice	71
68	Duke	79
92	■ Detroit Mercy	77
79	■ Bowling Green	68
88	■ Cleveland St.	56
94	† Iowa St.	72
94	■ Central Mich.	69
88	† Nebraska	73
79	† North Caro.	78
86	† Kansas	74
88	■ Eastern Mich.	58
80	Purdue	70
98	Wisconsin	73
75	■ Indiana	76
70	■ Notre Dame	55
80	Minnesota	73
76	■ Illinois	68
72	■ Ohio St.	62
80	Iowa	88
73	Michigan St.	69
84	■ Purdue	76
85	■ Wisconsin	66
92	Indiana	93
80	Penn St.	70
84	■ Minnesota	69
66	Ohio St.	64
82	■ Iowa	73
87	■ Michigan St.	81
98	Illinois	97
86	■ Northwestern	60
84	† Coastal Caro.	53
86	† UCLA	84
72	† Geo. Washington	64
77	† Temple	72
81	† Kentucky	78
71	† North Caro.	77

MICHIGAN ST.		**15-13**
121	■ Morehead St.	53
69	† Louisville	73
78	† Stetson	59
73	† Loyola (Cal.)	70
79	■ Ill.-Chicago	75
65	■ Dayton	60
81	■ New Hampshire	51
77	■ Washington St.	61
80	East Tenn. St.	69
57	Minnesota	64
39	■ Illinois	52
77	Ohio St.	60
80	Northwestern	75
66	■ Wisconsin	67
90	■ Iowa	96
72	Purdue	64
69	■ Michigan	73
75	■ Minnesota	63
80	Illinois	83
81	■ Ohio St.	66
81	■ Northwestern	55
62	Wisconsin	65
64	Iowa	66
58	■ Purdue	61
81	Michigan	87
68	Indiana	99
70	■ Penn St.	53
86	Oklahoma	88

MICHIGAN TECH		**13-13**
91	North Dak. St.	57
59	■ Minn.-Duluth	48
73	Denver	86
74	■ Grand Valley St.	67
83	■ Ferris St.	87
123	Northwood	76
73	Lake Superior St.	82

79 Missouri-Rolla 67
81 † SIU-Edwardsville 75
84 ■ Saginaw Valley 78
72 ■ Oakland 75
72 Hillsdale 82
80 Wayne St. (Mich.) 101
94 Northern Mich. 110
79 Grand Valley St. 61
66 Ferris St. 104
127 ■ Northwood 86
82 ■ Lake Superior St. 87
73 ■ Northern Mich. 69
78 Saginaw Valley 81
71 Oakland 84
89 ■ Hillsdale 73
97 ■ Wayne St. (Mich.) 103
73 Minn.-Duluth 75
73 Wis.-Stevens Point 55
74 Wis.-Parkside 65

MIDDLE TENN. ST. 10-16
88 ■ Livingston 74
89 † Lehigh 73
57 Colorado 97
65 Minnesota 88
75 Oral Roberts 78
77 ■ Cleveland St. 69
70 ■ Southern-B.R. 69
65 Mo.-Kansas City 73
76 ■ Morehead St. 65
65 ■ Eastern Ky. 80
70 ■ Tennessee St. 78
67 Tenn.-Martin 71
86 Tennessee Tech 73
73 ■ Austin Peay 55
69 Southeast Mo. St. 80
73 Murray St. 76
93 ■ Oral Roberts 76
70 ■ Tenn.-Martin 60
67 Tennessee St. 84
51 Vanderbilt 81
63 ■ Tennessee Tech 65
59 Morehead St. 81
46 Eastern Ky. 66
51 Austin Peay 57
63 ■ Southeast Mo. St. 67
79 ■ Murray St. 74

MIDDLEBURY 12-11
78 Clarkson 90
81 St. Lawrence 66
93 ■ Wesleyan 66
62 ■ St. Michael's 82
73 Dartmouth 90
87 ■ Rensselaer 85
80 Babson 98
76 ■ Amherst 71
62 Union (N.Y.) 72
89 Tufts 99
66 ■ Williams 82
84 Connecticut Col. 79
96 ■ Colby-Sawyer 69
76 ■ Colby 72
56 ■ Bowdoin 72
83 ■ Skidmore 63
79 Clark (Mass.) 91
69 Norwich 56
89 Thomas 66
102 Bates 68
60 Williams 88
68 ■ Tufts 78
81 ■ Union (N.Y.) 62

MILES 7-17
69 ■ Alabama A&M 106
74 Talladega 88
100 LeMoyne-Owen 98
83 Morris Brown 97
87 Fisk 86
91 ■ Troy St. 124
52 Mississippi Col. 76
70 † Livingston 77
66 Fort Valley St. 92
50 Livingston 85
59 ■ Fort Valley St. 82
76 ■ LeMoyne-Owen 101
97 ■ Talladega 83
79 ■ Tuskegee 90
70 Alabama A&M 101
91 ■ Morehouse 109
97 Clark Atlanta 91
84 ■ Albany St. (Ga.) 81
110 ■ Fisk 79
80 Savannah St. 81
68 ■ Paine 79
55 Tuskegee 95
104 Troy St. 130
87 Morehouse 81

MILLERSVILLE 24-6
110 ■ Trenton St. 72
105 ■ Wheeling Jesuit 88
111 ■ Clarion 89
92 ■ Lock Haven 84
90 Bridgeport 97
101 † Central Okla. 114
83 Gannon 97
78 † High Point 74
78 † Gannon 93
113 ■ Columbia Union 85
95 ■ Holy Family 64
83 Bloomsburg 90
55 Mansfield 48
95 ■ East Stroudsburg 77
93 ■ Kutztown 58
113 ■ Shepherd 96
66 Cheyney 55
92 ■ West Chester 74
115 ■ Dist. Columbia 63
103 ■ Bloomsburg 69
75 ■ Mansfield 51
70 East Stroudsburg 66
85 Kutztown 52
101 ■ Cheyney 81
74 West Chester 71
96 ■ Edinboro 85
92 ■ Indiana (Pa.) 75
97 ■ Calif. (Pa.) 84
86 ■ Calif. (Pa.) 77
62 ■ Phila. Textile 70

MILLIKIN 13-12
83 ■ MacMurray 72
98 † Washington (Mo.) 93
86 Webster 66
71 ■ Blackburn 55
78 Wabash 80
73 ■ Olivet (Ill.) 88
79 Aurora 80
99 Illinois Col. 82
58 ■ DePauw 75
78 ■ Franklin 71
81 Elmhurst 80
77 Carthage 69
51 North Park 71
89 ■ Augustana (Ill.) 87
72 ■ Carthage 87
81 Olivet (Ill.) 92
92 ■ Ill. Wesleyan 89
67 Augustana (Ill.) 93
88 ■ North Park 77
70 Wheaton (Ill.) 69
80 North Central 89
83 ■ Elmhurst 81
94 Ill. Wesleyan 118
61 ■ North Central 64
58 ■ Wheaton (Ill.) 60

MILLSAPS 13-12
68 Southwestern (Tex.) 81
85 ■ LSU-Shreveport 78
122 ■ Savannah A&D 64
63 Loyola (La.) 75
89 † Maryville (Mo.) 76
79 LeTourneau 80
89 † Allentown 81
71 Roanoke 108
72 Wash. & Lee 71
77 Savannah A&D 61
62 ■ Oglethorpe 66
80 ■ Sewanee 59
75 ■ Trinity (Tex.) 65
72 ■ Hendrix 71
81 Centre 75
76 Fisk 61
49 Trinity (Tex.) 61
80 Hendrix 87
71 Rhodes 77
84 ■ Loyola (La.) 80
50 ■ Rhodes 60
69 ■ Centre 76
100 ■ Fisk 70
92 Oglethorpe 103
72 Sewanee 83

MINNESOTA 22-10
108 ■ SIU-Edwardsville 64
88 ■ Middle Tenn. St. 65
93 ■ Texas-San Antonio 75
92 ■ Bethune-Cookman 50
92 ■ Tenn.-Martin 63
87 Santa Clara 63
65 Iowa St. 99
70 ■ Memphis St. 55
74 ■ Ala.-Birmingham 59
64 ■ Michigan St. 57
81 ■ Purdue 60
77 Iowa 84
70 Wisconsin 79
73 ■ Michigan 80
70 ■ Northwestern 55
57 Indiana 61
95 ■ Penn St. 67
63 Michigan St. 75
69 Purdue 75
91 ■ Iowa 85
85 ■ Wisconsin 71
69 Michigan 84
79 Northwestern 60
75 ■ Indiana 86
67 ■ Illinois 65
67 Penn St. 41
58 Ohio St. 69
74 ■ Florida 66
86 ■ Oklahoma 72
76 ■ Southern Cal 58
76 † Providence 70
62 † Georgetown 61

MINN.-DULUTH 16-12
60 Wis.-Superior 48
61 ■ Northern Mich. 64
91 ■ Cincinnati Metro 35
59 ■ St. Scholastica 50
48 Michigan Tech 59
46 † Northwestern Okla. 48
57 † Baker 46
67 ■ Mankato St. 63
51 St. Cloud St. 61
64 ■ Augustana (S.D.) 52
61 ■ Mt. Senario 47
64 Wis.-Parkside 60
39 Northern Mich. 67
48 Southwest St. 45
60 Winona St. 64
65 ■ Wis.-Superior 63
66 ■ Bemidji St. 76
56 ■ Minn.-Morris 53
47 ■ Northern St. 57
62 Northern St. 86
72 Moorhead St. 80
59 ■ Southwest St. 53
50 Minn.-Morris 65
77 Bemidji St. 71
72 Moorhead St. 70
75 ■ Michigan Tech 73
73 ■ Winona St. 68
61 Minn.-Morris 66

MISERICORDIA 10-15
68 Binghamton 81
100 † Pracitical Bible 63
87 Eastern (Pa.) 82
63 Scranton 91
90 † Bapt. Bible (Pa.) 88
67 ■ Susquehanna 92
72 Juniata 78
76 † Ursinus 66
73 ■ Elmira 88
50 ■ FDU-Madison 49
71 ■ Beaver 80
67 ■ Lycoming 64
53 ■ Alvernia 74
59 Cabrini 76
93 ■ Lancaster Bible 43
77 Gwynedd Mercy 83
93 ■ Eastern (Pa.) 80
89 Keuka 103
66 Beaver 75
69 Alvernia 71
70 ■ Cabrini 73
93 Penn St.-Harris. 110
77 ■ Gwynedd Mercy 62
90 ■ Delaware Valley 77
73 Cabrini 82

MISSISSIPPI 10-18
103 ■ Houston Baptist 61
71 ■ Oakland 46
80 McNeese St. 76
87 ■ Southwestern La. 103
78 ■ Southern Ill. 85
61 ■ Georgia 75
65 ■ Murray St. 75
78 Arkansas 90
79 ■ Rice 89
73 South Caro. 88
67 Alabama 80
69 ■ Mississippi St. 53
71 ■ Louisiana St. 62
67 Rice 72
62 ■ Tennessee 75
74 ■ Auburn 85
56 Mississippi St. 53
71 ■ Southeastern La. 61
59 Vanderbilt 89
95 ■ Oral Roberts 79
47 Florida 94
83 ■ Alabama 82
73 Auburn 83
63 ■ Arkansas 85
66 ■ Kentucky 98
56 Louisiana St. 71
67 † Florida 62
70 † Louisiana St. 89

MISSISSIPPI COL. 15-10
73 Arkansas Tech 89
63 † Angelo St. 65
81 Abilene Christian 69
87 ■ Paul Quinn 67
97 ■ Tougaloo 61
73 ■ Arkansas Tech 66
76 ■ Miles 52
86 ■ Abilene Christian 64
70 ■ Livingston 76
65 Jacksonville St. 76
80 ■ West Ga. 76
78 ■ Valdosta St. 76
80 Paul Quinn 60
66 Delta St. 67
56 North Ala. 70
87 Livingston 74
68 UTEP 72
113 ■ North Ala. 86
83 ■ Delta St. 80
99 ■ Texas Col. 63
84 Valdosta St. 90
120 West Ga. 83
76 ■ Alcorn St. 63
72 ■ Jacksonville St. 73
43 Delta St. 70

MISSISSIPPI ST. 13-16
80 ■ Austin Peay 73
61 † LIU-Brooklyn 52
54 Iowa 69

68 Ala.-Birmingham ... 73
75 ■ Northeast Mo. St. .. 48
58 † Florida Int'l 51
64 † Southern Ill. 76
74 † Eastern Mich. 58
75 ■ Birm. Southern 71
77 ■ Auburn 71
110 ■ Tennessee Tech ... 65
73 Georgia 86
76 ■ Louisiana St. 84
75 Tennessee 92
53 Mississippi 69
66 ■ Alabama 53
75 ■ Northeast La. 67
80 ■ Arkansas 76
63 Kentucky 87
53 ■ Mississippi 56
66 Louisiana St. 92
83 ■ South Caro. 63
77 Auburn 83
58 Arkansas 115
87 Mo.-Kansas City ... 89
39 ■ Vanderbilt 80
78 ■ Florida 71
80 Alabama 92
56 † Georgia 87

MISSISSIPPI VAL. 13-15
69 Iowa 100
93 ■ Akron 81
46 † Kansas 94
83 † UC Irvine 90
85 † South Fla. 81
81 Ala.-Birmingham . 103
71 West Va. 88
85 ■ Mo.-Kansas City ... 69
56 Alcorn St. 55
71 Southern-B.R. 77
69 ■ Delta St. 70
70 ■ Texas Southern 72
107 ■ Prairie View 80
108 ■ Alabama St. 84
89 ■ Jackson St. 91
69 Grambling 86
90 ■ Oral Roberts 86
87 ■ Alcorn St. 79
95 ■ Southern-B.R. 94
63 Delta St. 73
64 Texas Southern 69
100 Prairie View 92
87 Alabama St. 93
92 Jackson St. 94
97 ■ Grambling 82
97 Oral Roberts 86
92 † Texas Southern 74
75 † Jackson St. 85

MISSOURI 19-14
103 ■ Slippery Rock 53
81 Texas A&M 55
77 ■ Southern Ind. 62
68 ■ Arkansas 73
66 † Illinois 65
71 † San Francisco 78
80 † Chaminade 55
69 † Marist 56
99 ■ N.C.-Asheville 56
82 ■ Southern Ill. 76
91 Colorado 87
84 Nevada-Las Vegas 101
64 ■ Iowa St. 49
94 ■ Coastal Caro. 69
56 ■ Memphis St. 64
79 ■ Oklahoma St. 63
73 ■ Notre Dame 57
87 Nebraska 88
69 Kansas 86
65 ■ Cal St. Northridge .. 54
67 ■ Kansas St. 51
84 Oklahoma 95
63 ■ Kansas 67
50 Iowa St. 65
75 ■ Nebraska 76
73 Oklahoma St. 77
68 ■ Oklahoma 69

67 Kansas St. 78
70 ■ Colorado 53
81 † Oklahoma St. 62
67 † Iowa St. 63
68 † Kansas St. 56
61 † Temple 75

MO.-KANSAS CITY 15-12
44 ■ Southwest Mo. St. . 47
56 Wichita St. 63
97 ■ Tex. Wesleyan 61
86 ■ UC Irvine 85
62 † Kansas 108
64 ■ Kansas St. 66
68 ■ Florida Tech 55
115 ■ Morehead St. 79
87 Baylor 98
63 ■ Colorado 59
73 ■ Middle Tenn. St. ... 65
69 Mississippi Val. 85
65 ■ Nebraska 66
101 ■ Washington (Mo.) .. 62
106 ■ Chicago St. 76
66 Colorado 88
71 Tennessee St. 84
57 Wis.-Milwaukee 73
83 Morehead St. 75
99 ■ Wis.-Milwaukee 77
70 St. Louis 78
79 Creighton 88
83 Chicago St. 69
99 ■ Grand View 78
94 Northeastern Ill. 64
89 ■ Mississippi St. 87
96 ■ Northeastern Ill. 80

MISSOURI-ROLLA 16-11
133 ■ Ark. Baptist 85
103 Florida Tech 85
74 † S.C.-Spartanburg .. 82
73 Evansville 82
97 Arkansas Col. 85
119 Webster 47
94 ■ Drury 82
95 Northern Ariz. 85
67 ■ Michigan Tech 79
67 ■ West Tex. A&M 84
80 ■ Southwest Baptist .. 68
90 ■ Mo. Western St. 76
86 ■ Mo.-St. Louis 65
96 Central Mo. St. 93
63 Mo. Southern St. ... 90
83 ■ Pittsburg St. 79
63 Southwest Baptist .. 79
97 ■ Lincoln (Mo.) 92
89 Mo.-St. Louis 81
77 ■ Washburn 74
80 ■ Mo. Southern St. ... 85
71 Pittsburg St. 80
84 Lincoln (Mo.) 86
100 Northwest Mo. St. 103
102 ■ Emporia St. 84
80 Northeast Mo. St. .. 66
74 Southwest Baptist .. 91

MO.-ST. LOUIS 11-15
116 Webster 54
71 ■ SIU-Edwardsville ... 78
58 † Grand Canyon 76
79 † Stonehill 75
102 ■ Lindenwood 54
68 ■ Washington (Mo.) .. 58
68 Oregon 101
66 Dayton 63
75 ■ Drury 77
87 ■ Lincoln (Mo.) 82
81 Northeast Mo. St. .. 67
65 Missouri-Rolla 86
74 Emporia St. 78
89 ■ Southwest Baptist .. 83
94 ■ Mo. Southern St. ... 89
73 Lincoln (Mo.) 71
87 ■ Pittsburg St. 72
97 Quincy 102

81 ■ Missouri-Rolla 89
74 ■ Central Mo. St. 90
53 Southwest Baptist .. 54
63 Mo. Southern St. ... 71
68 Pittsburg St. 69
66 ■ Washburn 82
65 ■ Northwest Mo. St. .. 69
83 Mo. Western St. 91

MO. SOUTHERN ST. 21-10
73 † Armstrong St. 58
63 Ky. Wesleyan 66
87 ■ Arkansas Tech 67
94 ■ North Ala. 65
91 ■ Graceland (Iowa) ... 51
71 Drury 88
65 ■ Rockhurst 75
74 ■ Pittsburg St. 58
88 † Concordia (Mich.) .. 41
81 † Thomas More 60
97 † Bethel (Ind.) 87
101 ■ Lincoln (Mo.) 88
74 Northeast Mo. St. .. 85
90 ■ Missouri-Rolla 63
89 Mo.-St. Louis 94
69 Pittsburg St. 58
68 ■ Southwest Baptist .. 66
78 Lincoln (Mo.) 72
73 ■ Northwest Mo. St. .. 69
85 Missouri-Rolla 80
71 ■ Mo.-St. Louis 63
54 Southwest Baptist .. 72
69 Mo. Western St. 75
52 Emporia St. 73
82 ■ Central Mo. St. 68
82 ■ Washburn 80
100 ■ Emporia St. 75
78 Mo. Western St. 73
80 Washburn 77
73 † Eastern N. Mex. 76
109 Central Okla. 116

MO. WESTERN ST. 21-7
74 ■ Avila 56
88 ■ William Penn 61
73 ■ Ark.-Pine Bluff 62
77 ■ William Jewell 63
75 William Jewell 66
100 † Central Okla. 92
107 † East Tex. St. 60
71 † Cal St. Dom. Hills .. 68
63 Cal St. Bakersfield . 84
65 ■ Northeast Mo. St. .. 61
76 Missouri-Rolla 90
92 ■ Emporia St. 83
79 Lincoln (Mo.) 75
66 ■ Northwest Mo. St. .. 60
76 ■ Washburn 95
68 Northeast Mo. St. .. 67
66 Central Mo. St. 67
65 Emporia St. 68
86 ■ Pittsburg St. 66
76 Northwest Mo. St. .. 83
76 Washburn 67
74 ■ Central Mo. St. 53
75 ■ Mo. Southern St. ... 69
88 Southwest Baptist .. 66
79 Rockhurst 66
91 ■ Mo.-St. Louis 83
95 ■ Central Mo. St. 71
73 ■ Mo. Southern St. ... 78

MOLLOY 8-19
65 St. Rose 88
77 † New York Tech 88
71 Baruch 88
61 Dowling 105
64 Mercy 98
62 LIU-Southampton .. 72
71 St. Joseph's-Suffolk 55
61 LIU-C.W. Post 79
64 Maritime (N.Y.) 58
84 † New York Tech ... 105
77 ■ Kean 90
40 ■ LIU-C.W. Post 104

55 West Chester 97
73 Bridgeport 115
76 Mt. St. Vincent 79
83 † Pratt 74
84 ■ John Jay 78
68 ■ Mt. St. Mary (N.Y.) . 73
113 ■ Bard 75
69 LIU-Brooklyn 120
84 St. Joseph's (N.Y.) . 71
88 New York Tech ... 115
102 ■ Merchant Marine . 105
80 CCNY 79
94 ■ Old Westbury 87
76 Bridgeport 110
91 ■ St. Joseph's (N.Y.) 101

MONMOUTH (ILL.) 13-10
70 ■ Alma 63
78 ■ Lindenwood 74
62 MacMurray 63
76 Cornell College 73
70 ■ Grinnell 62
90 ■ Aurora 84
57 Central Mo. St. 88
69 Teikyo Marycrest ... 71
53 Coe 75
87 ■ Illinois Col. 84
65 ■ Knox 67
56 Ripon 70
61 Lake Forest 53
71 Northeastern Ill. 94
88 ■ St. Norbert 67
75 ■ Lawrence 52
64 ■ Coe 59
74 Grinnell 65
65 ■ MacMurray 71
97 Illinois Col. 84
64 Knox 69
72 ■ Cornell College 61
71 Beloit 79

MONMOUTH (N.J.) 11-17
54 ■ Geo. Washington ... 76
73 † Western Ill. 60
66 San Francisco 98
60 Army 48
65 ■ George Mason 38
46 Northeastern 47
47 New Orleans 60
57 Rice 78
58 ■ Robert Morris 66
60 ■ St. Francis (Pa.) 52
67 St. Francis (N.Y.) ... 61
62 LIU-Brooklyn 77
61 ■ Wagner 57
83 ■ Marist 59
54 ■ FDU-Teaneck 69
64 Rider 85
71 ■ Mt. St. Mary's (Md.) 89
54 Robert Morris 46
51 St. Francis (Pa.) 59
61 ■ LIU-Brooklyn 64
85 ■ St. Francis (N.Y.) ... 70
59 Wagner 69
83 FDU-Teaneck 52
68 Marist 71
66 Mt. St. Mary's (Md.) 71
73 ■ Rider 79
91 St. Francis (Pa.) 80
66 Wagner 75

MONTANA 17-11
76 ■ Simon Fraser 63
55 ■ Southern Utah 60
63 ■ Bucknell 60
82 ■ Texas Tech 86
55 ■ San Jose St. 51
74 Portland 66
53 Cal St. Sacramento . 38
58 ■ Pepperdine 68
72 ■ Rocky Mountain 56
63 ■ Cal St. Northridge .. 55
65 Northeastern Ill. 59
78 Creighton 84
95 ■ Eastern Mont. 47

50 Idaho 60
68 Eastern Wash. 75
68 ■ Weber St. 61
74 ■ Northern Ariz. 55
54 Idaho St. 53
66 Boise St. 75
62 ■ Montana St. 65
85 ■ Eastern Wash. 65
68 ■ Idaho 65
54 Northern Ariz. 46
66 Weber St. 74
56 ■ Boise St. 59
68 ■ Idaho St. 62
56 Montana St. 54
50 † Idaho St. 61

MONTANA ST. 9-18
87 ■ Carroll (Mont.) 39
75 Appalachian St. 90
56 Southeast Mo. St. 72
60 ■ San Jose St. 57
77 ■ Marshall 85
72 Cal St. Sacramento 53
70 † Texas Tech 79
64 Wyoming 74
64 ■ Cal St. Northridge 65
70 Southern Utah 79
67 Portland 78
106 ■ Chadron St. 62
54 Eastern Wash. 64
47 Idaho 63
66 ■ Northern Ariz. 60
65 ■ Weber St. 71
52 Boise St. 72
64 Idaho St. 62
65 Montana 62
63 ■ Idaho 65
73 ■ Eastern Wash. 58
79 Weber St. 84
73 Northern Ariz. 64
66 ■ Idaho St. 68
60 ■ Boise St. 68
54 ■ Montana 56
72 † Weber St. 91

MONTCLAIR ST. 11-13
75 John Jay 72
59 † St. Joseph's (Me.) 68
79 Ramapo 51
52 ■ Rowan 64
72 ■ Upsala 75
60 Wm. Paterson 68
53 ■ Stockton St. 48
38 FDU-Teaneck 79
61 Trenton St. 62
84 Lehman 60
66 ■ Kean 69
60 Rutgers-Camden 45
71 Rutgers-Newark 65
72 ■ Wm. Paterson 75
67 ■ Jersey City St. 65
54 ■ Ramapo 58
53 Rowan 79
71 Kean 76
79 ■ Centenary (N.J.) 57
82 ■ Trenton St. 79
70 Jersey City St. 83
60 Stockton St. 79
85 ■ Rutgers-Newark 56
76 ■ Rutgers-Camden 59

MORAVIAN 15-9
86 † King's (Pa.) 68
65 Johns Hopkins 76
74 ■ Allentown 65
69 ■ Lebanon Valley 67
59 Gettysburg 73
73 Drew 69
55 ■ Wilkes 38
48 ■ Swarthmore 39
53 ■ Muhlenberg 48
55 ■ FDU-Madison 53
74 Western Md. 71
67 ■ Frank. & Marsh. 72
62 Dickinson 58
63 ■ Muhlenberg 64
78 Delaware Valley 65
52 Lebanon Valley 82
66 Ursinus 60
60 ■ Gettysburg 51
87 ■ Western Md. 61
57 ■ Albright 62
53 Frank. & Marsh. 68
66 ■ Dickinson 54
59 Muhlenberg 75
60 Scranton 76

MOREHEAD ST. 6-21
53 Michigan St. 121
60 † St. Peter's 81
72 † Md.-East. Shore 75
74 Wright St. 102
64 ■ Union (Ky.) 72
65 Kentucky 108
79 Mo.-Kansas City 115
47 ■ Western Mich. 77
63 ■ Wright St. 129
65 Middle Tenn. St. 76
79 Tennessee Tech 97
75 ■ Tennessee St. 86
79 ■ Austin Peay 58
96 Southeast Mo. St. 107
76 Murray St. 89
87 ■ Eastern Ky. 79
75 ■ Mo.-Kansas City 83
77 ■ Tenn.-Martin 74
72 Tennessee St. 96
75 Austin Peay 90
66 Eastern Ky. 76
92 ■ Southeast Mo. St. 85
80 ■ Murray St. 78
81 ■ Middle Tenn. St. 59
96 ■ Tennessee Tech 101
86 Tenn.-Martin 89
89 † Tennessee Tech 97

MOREHOUSE 15-11
98 Fisk 82
76 Emory 74
105 ■ Savannah St. 91
81 ■ Winston-Salem 70
67 Rollins 79
83 † Cheyney 82
103 † Central St. (Ohio) 118
100 Augusta 102
78 LeMoyne-Owen 86
95 Lane 93
92 Morris Brown 82
80 Tuskegee 83
83 ■ Cheyney 70
63 Paine 80
73 ■ Fisk 57
82 ■ Albany St. (Ga.) 76
89 † Clark Atlanta 68
109 Miles 91
84 † Alabama A&M 92
95 ■ Lane 90
90 ■ Tuskegee 89
86 ■ Alabama A&M 103
88 ■ LeMoyne-Owen 94
99 Fort Valley St. 87
81 ■ Miles 87
68 † Paine 71

MORGAN ST. 9-17
63 George Mason 76
80 St. Joseph's (Pa.) 103
85 † Delaware St. 102
97 Radford 104
76 St. Louis 101
85 Georgetown 103
63 Maryland 103
76 Virginia Tech 87
65 South Caro. St. 91
2 § North Caro. A&T 0
88 ■ Md.-East. Shore 69
82 ■ Delaware St. 65
86 ■ Florida A&M 72
80 ■ Bethune-Cookman 70
61 Coppin St. 87
69 Md.-East. Shore 64
67 Howard 58
73 James Madison 110
74 ■ Coppin St. 88
82 Florida A&M 83
93 Bethune-Cookman 103
93 Delaware St. 90
67 ■ South Caro. St. 82
70 ■ North Caro. A&T 71
77 ■ Howard 69
87 † Florida A&M 90

MORNINGSIDE 19-10
87 † Wayne St. (Neb.) 68
55 † Briar Cliff 56
70 N'western (Iowa) 64
68 ■ Southwest St. 60
96 ■ Grand View 79
81 ■ Dana 55
103 Cal Poly SLO 98
74 † Briar Cliff 78
59 South Dak. 68
67 ■ Mankato St. 63
76 ■ St. Cloud St. 65
72 South Dak. St. 74
61 Augustana (S.D.) 73
80 ■ Nebraska-Omaha 73
87 ■ Northern Colo. 56
81 North Dak. St. 69
87 North Dak. 80
82 St. Cloud St. 87
54 Mankato St. 76
81 ■ Augustana (S.D.) 49
55 ■ South Dak. St. 52
91 ■ South Dak. 77
78 Northern Colo. 94
80 Nebraska-Omaha 84
93 ■ North Dak. 72
100 ■ North Dak. St. 63
74 † Northern Colo. 64
77 † North Dak. 78
92 † South Dak. St. 85

MORRIS BROWN 3-23
70 † St. Paul's 92
59 N.C. Central 97
74 ■ Valdosta St. 75
97 ■ Miles 83
66 † Ga. Southwestern 80
67 † Fayetteville St. 106
97 Troy St. 109
68 ■ Paine 83
83 LeMoyne-Owen 103
62 ■ Albany St. (Ga.) 84
82 ■ Morehouse 92
81 ■ Clark Atlanta 72
73 ■ Fort Valley St. 102
63 ■ Cheyney 88
63 Albany St. (Ga.) 65
54 Valdosta St. 85
65 Alabama A&M 87
80 ■ Troy St. 92
61 † Clark Atlanta 70
81 ■ Alabama A&M 95
70 Savannah St. 96
53 Paine 66
89 Fort Valley St. 88
67 ■ LeMoyne-Owen 73
60 Tuskegee 85
60 ■ Savannah St. 63

MT. ST. MARY'S (MD.) 13-15
73 Bucknell 97
71 American 87
55 Penn St. 60
52 Loyola (Md.) 56
70 ■ Army 66
55 ■ Delaware 73
65 Wake Forest 76
95 LIU-Brooklyn 86
83 St. Francis (N.Y.) 71
57 ■ FDU-Teaneck 60
90 ■ Marist 74
74 St. Francis (Pa.) 70
76 Robert Morris 90
62 ■ Rider 55
69 Wagner 64
89 Monmouth (N.J.) 71
72 ■ St. Francis (N.Y.) 76
76 ■ LIU-Brooklyn 78
72 Marist 67
61 FDU-Teaneck 73
96 ■ Robert Morris 75
69 ■ St. Francis (Pa.) 89
89 ■ American 82
71 Rider 88
71 ■ Monmouth (N.J.) 66
70 ■ Wagner 77
81 ■ St. Francis (N.Y.) 78
48 Wagner 65

MT. ST. VINCENT 18-9
80 Stevens Tech 75
72 Maritime (N.Y.) 51
101 ■ Daniel Webster 82
67 ■ Catholic 82
125 Bard 66
104 ■ Lehman 84
75 Yeshiva 74
93 St. Joseph's (N.Y.) 80
79 ■ Molloy 76
74 ■ Baruch 86
75 ■ Hunter 82
79 ■ Maritime (N.Y.) 64
75 ■ CCNY 69
78 Bridgeport 98
84 ■ Stony Brook 81
97 Albertus Magnus 80
53 ■ Yeshiva 74
101 Pratt 93
95 New Jersey Tech 123
90 ■ Bard 65
98 Vassar 67
83 ■ Stevens Tech 67
64 ■ Manhattanville 86
109 ■ Polytechnic (N.Y.) 83
104 ■ Bard 71
63 Yeshiva 81
91 ■ Staten Island 96

MOUNT UNION 9-16
58 † Phila. Pharmacy 57
57 † Wilkes 58
71 ■ Bethany (W.Va.) 54
62 ■ Grove City 59
50 Capital 57
81 ■ Marietta 50
66 Hiram 77
76 ■ Heidelberg 71
70 ■ Ursinus 61
64 ■ Frank. & Marsh. 78
51 Otterbein 74
59 Ohio Northern 72
66 ■ Baldwin-Wallace 62
82 John Carroll 66
59 ■ Muskingum 56
72 ■ Capital 79
63 Marietta 64
56 ■ Hiram 70
49 ■ John Carroll 66
67 Heidelberg 86
66 ■ Otterbein 85
46 ■ Ohio Northern 68
45 Baldwin-Wallace 62
66 Muskingum 79
50 Baldwin-Wallace 61

MUHLENBERG 17-8
103 ■ Drew 87
59 ■ Albright 61
73 ■ Susquehanna 72
79 Allentown 65
56 Frank. & Marsh. 75
82 ■ Swarthmore 77
79 ■ Widener 47
93 † St. Joseph's (N.Y.) 58
76 Hamilton 98
86 † Centenary (N.J.) 55

48	Moravian	53
69	■ Lebanon Valley	77
73	Dickinson	68
83	Delaware Valley	70
75	■ Gettysburg	57
64	Moravian	63
73	■ Western Md.	55
71	■ Wilkes	53
71	■ Frank. & Marsh.	74
72	Lebanon Valley	69
72	■ Dickinson	60
94	Gettysburg	80
75	■ Moravian	59
66	Western Md.	68
71	Lebanon Valley	102

MURRAY ST.		**18-12**
80	Indiana	103
93	■ Campbellsville	80
78	† Rice	89
82	† Boise St.	94
87	Evansville	78
77	Va. Commonwealth	83
58	St. Louis	94
68	Florida Int'l	64
124	■ Pikeville	71
75	Mississippi	65
82	Austin Peay	76
76	Tennessee St.	80
92	■ Tenn.-Martin	66
111	Southeast Mo. St.	95
74	■ Texas	79
93	■ Eastern Ky.	92
89	■ Morehead St.	76
117	■ Tennessee Tech	112
76	■ Middle Tenn. St.	73
100	■ Southeast Mo. St.	96
100	Tenn.-Martin	74
82	Eastern Ky.	98
78	Morehead St.	80
88	■ Austin Peay	69
75	■ Tennessee St.	82
83	Tennessee Tech	81
74	Middle Tenn. St.	79
82	† Austin Peay	66
74	† Eastern Ky.	73
68	† Tennessee St.	82

MUSKINGUM		**11-13**
71	■ Otterbein	67
71	† Nazareth (N.Y.)	64
50	Ohio Northern	69
69	■ Baldwin-Wallace	64
69	Capital	80
61	■ Urbana	90
62	■ Olivet	70
81	■ Malone	68
80	■ West Liberty St.	75
60	■ Marietta	55
66	Hiram	75
79	■ Heidelberg	60
64	John Carroll	73
56	Mount Union	59
63	Otterbein	84
57	■ Ohio Northern	60
74	■ Capital	87
81	Baldwin-Wallace	79
90	■ John Carroll	71
67	Marietta	68
77	Heidelberg	88
91	■ Hiram	88
79	■ Mount Union	66
71	Otterbein	83

NAVY		**8-19**
74	St. Bonaventure	83
58	■ Pennsylvania	78
54	■ Richmond	73
76	■ Gettysburg	78
53	Fresno St.	66
57	† Eastern Wash.	56
58	Delaware	79
53	■ William & Mary	58
73	■ Army	66
65	■ Loyola (Md.)	62
81	■ Lehigh	57
65	Colgate	74
53	■ Lafayette	50
61	■ Bucknell	68
69	Holy Cross	95
52	■ Fordham	59
56	Army	39
83	Lehigh	74
57	■ Drexel	73
57	■ Colgate	67
60	Lafayette	65
78	■ Wash. & Jeff.	63
64	Bucknell	93
72	■ Holy Cross	90
48	Fordham	57
60	N.C.-Greensboro	72
80	Colgate	84

NAZARETH (N.Y.)		**11-13**
72	Rochester	71
90	■ Alfred	84
105	■ Hilbert	68
56	■ John Carroll	67
87	Hilbert	103
64	† Muskingum	71
68	† St. John Fisher	86
98	■ St. Lawrence	82
95	Roberts Wesleyan	92
78	■ Brockport St.	86
66	† Rochester	65
69	† St. John Fisher	79
78	† Brockport St.	86
77	† Keuka	57
86	Hamilton	74
88	■ Elmira	101
90	■ Merchant Marine	83
53	Fredonia St.	84
82	■ Union (N.Y.)	73
98	Oswego St.	85
79	■ Hilbert	82
73	■ Rochester Inst.	94
63	St. John Fisher	72
63	Utica	81

NEBRASKA		**20-11**
108	■ Colgate	76
85	■ Kent	61
86	■ Citadel	46
100	■ Creighton	83
71	Wichita St.	64
93	■ Appalachian St.	83
116	■ Texas-Arlington	95
64	Southern Cal	74
73	† Michigan	88
80	† Southwestern La.	109
79	† Fordham	55
70	■ Eastern Ill.	54
100	■ Southern Utah	85
66	Mo.-Kansas City	65
89	Oklahoma	102
73	Oklahoma St.	78
86	■ Cal St. Sacramento	70
64	■ Kansas St.	66
82	Colorado	67
88	■ Missouri	87
69	Iowa St.	96
68	■ Kansas	64
80	Kansas St.	59
63	■ Oklahoma St.	73
76	Missouri	75
76	■ Colorado	67
91	■ Iowa St.	87
83	Kansas	94
94	■ Oklahoma	83
45	† Kansas St.	47
79	† New Mexico St.	93

NEB.-KEARNEY		**20-6**
82	■ Nebraska-Omaha	63
83	† Western St.	96
103	■ North Dak. St.	82
75	Angelo St.	79
99	† Abilene Christian	95
71	■ North Dak.	85
83	Hastings	76
65	Nebraska-Omaha	63
93	■ Doane	62
97	■ Bemidji St.	90
77	■ Eastern N. Mex.	92
72	■ Angelo St.	66
88	Fort Hays St.	76
86	■ Chadron St.	81
98	■ Fort Hays St.	79
81	■ West Tex. A&M	73
111	Colo. Christian	99
95	Metropolitan St.	93
106	■ Hastings	88
88	■ Denver	100
113	Chadron St.	79
84	■ Briar Cliff	77
95	Wayne St. (Neb.)	72
113	Midland Lutheran	87
74	West Tex. A&M	98
108	■ Wayne St. (Neb.)	80

NEBRASKA-OMAHA		**5-21**
63	Neb.-Kearney	82
99	■ Doane	76
88	Northeast Mo. St.	93
63	■ Neb.-Kearney	65
51	Northern Iowa	61
96	■ Grand View	79
47	■ Briar Cliff	59
77	■ Wayne St. (Neb.)	37
64	Augustana (S.D.)	65
72	South Dak. St.	82
52	■ Northern Colo.	83
58	■ North Dak. St.	61
65	■ North Dak.	81
73	Morningside	80
57	South Dak.	66
63	■ Mankato St.	72
68	■ St. Cloud St.	84
67	■ South Dak. St.	69
73	Northern Colo.	78
66	North Dak.	90
72	North Dak. St.	80
63	■ South Dak.	95
84	■ Morningside	80
62	■ Augustana (S.D.)	57
68	St. Cloud St.	79
69	Mankato St.	85

NEB. WESLEYAN		**17-8**
81	Ill. Wesleyan	93
64	† Washington (Mo.)	82
96	■ N'western (Minn.)	59
92	■ William Penn	72
87	Concordia (Neb.)	74
83	Central (Iowa)	70
106	■ Bellevue	59
108	■ Simpson	69
69	† Pacific (Ore.)	62
76	Chaminade	93
89	■ Concordia (Neb.)	86
77	Dana	64
58	Doane	59
111	■ Bethany (Kan.)	62
95	■ N'western (Iowa)	78
72	■ Hastings	77
95	Midland Lutheran	72
88	■ Dana	80
86	■ Doane	68
81	Bellevue	73
81	N'western (Iowa)	101
89	■ Dordt	76
65	Peru St.	79
90	■ Midland Lutheran	92
86	Hastings	71

NEVADA		**9-17**
81	■ Col. of Idaho	68
74	■ Fresno St.	64
68	Santa Clara	81
76	San Francisco	78
102	■ North Texas	94
70	Loyola (Cal.)	65
83	■ Kansas St.	82
61	■ Utah St.	84
62	Cal St. Fullerton	81
71	UC Irvine	67
75	■ Long Beach St.	84
64	■ UC Santa Barb.	58
49	Pacific (Cal.)	71
70	San Jose St.	73
95	■ Nevada-Las Vegas	110
89	■ New Mexico St.	96
79	■ UC Irvine	82
60	■ Cal St. Fullerton	72
80	■ Houston	92
60	UC Santa Barb.	93
82	Long Beach St.	91
69	■ Pacific (Cal.)	81
68	■ San Jose St.	64
93	Nevada-Las Vegas	100
66	New Mexico St.	87
97	Utah St.	87

NEVADA-LAS VEGAS		**21-8**
84	Loyola (Cal.)	80
89	San Diego St.	77
115	■ UC Irvine	97
94	■ Marquette	88
79	■ Hofstra	41
78	■ Cal St. Fullerton	65
94	Long Beach St.	101
101	■ Missouri	84
88	■ Pacific (Cal.)	71
84	■ San Jose St.	77
98	■ Texas A&M	96
96	■ Georgetown	80
110	Nevada	95
87	Utah St.	78
56	Pacific (Cal.)	62
82	■ UC Santa Barb.	69
95	■ Long Beach St.	83
80	San Jose St.	74
86	■ Louisville	90
97	■ New Mexico St.	81
83	UC Santa Barb.	86
100	■ Nevada	93
94	■ Utah St.	86
88	New Mexico St.	90
96	UC Irvine	74
83	Cal St. Fullerton	84
104	† Utah St.	86
77	Long Beach St.	79
74	■ Southern Cal	90

NEW ENGLAND COL.		**9-16**
69	New Paltz St.	96
78	† Polytechnic (N.Y.)	39
86	Daniel Webster	75
71	Colby-Sawyer	67
54	Wheaton (Mass.)	80
80	■ Rivier	76
80	MIT	76
89	■ Norwich	74
78	Salve Regina	74
59	■ Eastern Nazarene	65
90	Wentworth Inst.	87
81	■ Roger Williams	84
66	■ Plymouth St.	102
66	Curry	77
75	■ Anna Maria	95
46	■ Gordon	47
52	Eastern Nazarene	77
77	Anna Maria	108
73	Johnson St.	82
95	■ Wentworth Inst.	91
72	Roger Williams	84
65	Gordon	72
75	■ Curry	84
54	■ Salve Regina	70
46	Eastern Nazarene	69

NEW HAMPSHIRE		**6-21**
68	Va. Com'wealth	103
27	Providence	56
63	■ Holy Cross	76
51	Michigan St.	81
60	† Princeton	75
61	■ Massachusetts	75

67 Dartmouth 77
70 ■ Wis.-Milwaukee 86
71 ■ Brown 53
54 Delaware 65
52 Drexel 73
77 ■ Hartford 65
69 Vermont 76
62 ■ Northeastern 75
66 Boston U. 76
87 Harvard 76
65 ■ Maine 71
69 ■ Boston U. 76
45 Northeastern 73
77 ■ Central Conn. St. 87
66 ■ Vermont 65
56 Hartford 69
49 Yale 63
63 ■ Drexel 65
64 ■ Delaware 62
55 Maine 49
65 Delaware 70

NEW HAMP. COL. 29-4
95 ■ Franklin Pierce 107
138 ■ Keene St. 108
117 Husson 76
79 ■ Bryant 66
126 Plymouth St. 82
77 Merrimack 73
88 American Int'l 81
102 ■ Stonehill 84
70 Assumption 68
103 New Haven 102
100 ■ St. Anselm 75
95 ■ Southern Conn. St. 68
87 ■ Bridgeport 91
117 ■ Keene St. 89
101 ■ Colby-Sawyer 72
87 Mass.-Lowell 78
95 ■ Sacred Heart 90
68 Le Moyne 67
99 ■ Franklin Pierce 83
100 ■ New Haven 91
122 Keene St. 92
72 Southern Conn. St. 56
94 Franklin Pierce 86
75 ■ Le Moyne 78
95 ■ Mass.-Lowell 84
72 Sacred Heart 60
76 ■ Keene St. 56
120 ■ Mass.-Lowell 70
76 ■ Franklin Pierce 71
67 ■ St. Anselm 63
83 ■ Franklin Pierce 73
100 † South Dak. 96
123 † Troy St. 126

NEW HAVEN 13-14
95 ■ Mercy 79
73 ■ Quinnipiac 74
105 † Bridgeport 102
82 East Stroudsburg 64
66 Springfield 70
96 ■ American Int'l 102
85 Rollins 92
81 Florida Tech 85
114 ■ New York Tech 82
102 ■ New Hamp. Col. 103
110 Concordia (N.Y.) 66
108 ■ Keene St. 85
74 Mass.-Lowell 94
106 ■ Bridgeport 96
109 ■ Le Moyne 106
82 Southern Conn. St. 91
76 Franklin Pierce 106
88 ■ Sacred Heart 99
91 New Hamp. Col. 100
97 ■ Mass.-Lowell 78
93 Le Moyne 109
96 Sacred Heart 102
76 ■ Franklin Pierce 70
101 ■ Dowling 76
96 ■ Southern Conn. St. 83
109 Keene St. 93

78 Franklin Pierce 88

NEW JERSEY TECH 22-4
83 ■ Yeshiva 52
91 Manhattanville 74
104 ■ Stevens Tech 56
104 ■ Staten Island 72
69 Stony Brook 80
94 † Lycoming 55
78 Western Md. 73
81 ■ American (P.R.) 67
85 ■ Hunter 80
96 Maritime (N.Y.) 55
94 Merchant Marine 78
109 Staten Island 85
115 ■ Polytechnic (N.Y.) 43
84 ■ Merchant Marine 43
73 Adelphi 78
67 Hunter 75
67 ■ Manhattanville 60
123 ■ Mt. St. Vincent 95
123 Polytechnic (N.Y.) 67
82 ■ Stony Brook 62
99 Stevens Tech 54
92 Yeshiva 59
106 Bard 50
90 † Stevens Tech 63
71 Yeshiva 50
70 Hunter 83

NEW MEXICO 24-7
89 ■ N.M. Highlands 54
71 ■ Texas A&M 69
70 Arizona 89
69 New Mexico St. 62
96 ■ Texas Tech 75
71 ■ New Mexico St. 66
64 ■ William & Mary 59
54 ■ Pennsylvania 51
45 Utah 78
56 Brigham Young 70
85 ■ Fresno St. 64
63 ■ Air Force 43
77 San Diego St. 52
61 Hawaii 58
65 ■ Colorado St. 67
77 ■ Wyoming 67
65 UTEP 62
78 ■ Texas Southern 61
60 ■ UTEP 53
50 Colorado St. 67
76 Wyoming 60
82 ■ Hawaii 58
71 ■ San Diego St. 55
57 Fresno St. 71
80 Air Force 60
69 ■ Utah 59
79 ■ Brigham Young 76
72 † Fresno St. 48
68 † Brigham Young 59
76 † UTEP 65
68 † Geo. Washington 82

N.M. HIGHLANDS 6-24
70 ■ Western N. Mex. 72
82 Colo. Christian 98
92 Fort Lewis 97
54 New Mexico 89
88 ■ Colorado Mines 75
87 ■ Fort Lewis 95
67 Western N. Mex. 88
96 † Southern Colo. 97
82 Alas. Anchorage 86
54 † East Tex. St. 76
67 ■ Colo. Christian 69
69 ■ Eastern N. Mex. 115
99 Panhandle St. 69
86 ■ Panhandle St. 63
64 Western St. 73
77 Mesa St. 88
83 Adams St. 89
72 Eastern N. Mex. 77
92 ■ Colorado Mines 81
63 ■ Fort Hays St. 73

71 ■ Chadron St. 97
69 ■ Colorado Col. 64
73 Colorado Col. 89
84 Colorado Mines 85
86 ■ Adams St. 69
54 Fort Hays St. 85
91 Chadron St. 94
59 ■ Mesa St. 71
63 ■ Western St. 64
62 Mesa St. 68

NEW MEXICO ST. 26-8
75 † Tenn.-Chatt. 65
86 † Oregon 75
95 † Illinois 94
73 ■ Eastern N. Mex. 64
63 ■ UTEP 64
75 UTEP 69
62 ■ New Mexico 69
104 ■ Sam Houston St. 76
66 New Mexico 71
83 ■ East Tex. St. 69
78 ■ Cal St. Fullerton 67
71 UC Santa Barb. 69
71 Long Beach St. 97
87 ■ San Jose St. 72
53 ■ Pacific (Cal.) 48
76 ■ Midwestern St. 67
72 ■ UC Irvine 67
75 ■ UC Santa Barb. 64
96 Nevada 89
76 Utah St. 64
77 ■ Long Beach St. 65
68 Pacific (Cal.) 71
60 San Jose St. 55
81 Nevada-Las Vegas 97
82 ■ Utah St. 60
87 ■ Nevada 66
90 ■ Nevada-Las Vegas 88
78 Cal St. Fullerton 70
76 UC Irvine 74
87 † UC Irvine 76
82 † UC Santa Barb. 77
62 Long Beach St. 70
93 † Nebraska 79
55 † Cincinnati 92

NEW ORLEANS 26-4
68 ■ Spring Hill 61
76 ■ Southwest Tex. St. 67
73 ■ Dartmouth 49
43 ■ Notre Dame 45
72 ■ Texas A&M 55
90 ■ Bucknell 57
60 ■ Monmouth (N.J.) 47
79 ■ Jacksonville 69
78 Ark.-Lit. Rock 62
82 Southwestern La. 62
83 ■ Tex.-Pan American 62
60 ■ Arkansas St. 58
71 Louisiana Tech 48
96 ■ Lamar 77
69 ■ Arizona 72
66 Jacksonville 50
79 ■ South Ala. 70
89 ■ Western Ky. 80
73 ■ Southwestern La. 71
81 Tex.-Pan American 63
69 ■ Louisiana Tech 41
84 Lamar 73
71 Western Ky. 67
86 ■ Ark.-Lit. Rock 60
71 South Ala. 62
52 Arkansas St. 51
63 † Louisiana Tech 52
73 † Arkansas St. 59
63 † Western Ky. 72
55 † Xavier (Ohio) 73

NEW PALTZ ST. 12-12
96 ■ New England Col. 69
91 ■ Southern Vt. 70
83 Mt. St. Mary (N.Y.) 75
80 Plattsburgh St. 88
66 Potsdam St. 69

67 Binghamton 71
74 ■ Geneseo St. 86
93 ■ Brockport St. 94
80 ■ American (P.R.) 90
77 Rutgers-Newark 78
96 † Mt. St. Mary (N.Y.) 89
91 † Vassar 51
61 Oneonta St. 73
98 ■ Plattsburgh St. 90
55 ■ Potsdam St. 54
85 ■ Cortland St. 60
62 Utica Tech 78
76 ■ Oswego St. 55
80 ■ Oneonta St. 77
57 Fredonia St. 76
62 Buffalo St. 76
71 Cortland St. 84
67 ■ Binghamton 65
98 ■ Bard 68

NEW YORK TECH 8-19
83 † Assumption 101
88 † Molloy 77
92 LIU-Southampton 95
57 Gannon 76
42 † Lock Haven 82
98 Dowling 92
100 Mercy 101
49 Adelphi 64
81 LIU-C.W. Post 109
83 ■ Franklin Pierce 104
82 St. Michael's 102
68 † Franklin Pierce 78
63 ■ Mass.-Lowell 74
85 Queens (N.Y.) 61
82 New Haven 114
60 Phila. Textile 84
60 West Chester 71
105 † Molloy 84
90 Baruch 101
72 ■ St. Rose 75
79 ■ Mercy 85
83 Cheyney 82
115 ■ Molloy 88
92 ■ Concordia (N.Y.) 68
84 ■ Old Westbury 97
82 Southern Conn. St. 107
110 ■ York (N.Y.) 73

NEW YORK U. 23-3
85 ■ Bates 72
88 ■ Colorado Col. 64
94 Staten Island 79
84 ■ Manhattanville 66
81 ■ Emory 73
90 ■ York (N.Y.) 58
97 ■ John Jay 73
80 ■ Johns Hopkins 74
69 ■ Drew 60
78 Case Reserve 81
80 Carnegie Mellon 70
99 Haverford 71
112 Brandeis 110
50 Rochester 48
58 ■ Chicago 49
83 ■ Washington (Mo.) 78
86 ■ Yeshiva 44
72 ■ Rochester 54
97 ■ Brandeis 82
71 Washington (Mo.) 84
64 Chicago 63
83 ■ Carnegie Mellon 65
109 ■ Vassar 47
75 Emory 65
75 ■ Ithaca 61
73 † Eastern Conn. St. 78

NEWBERRY 3-23
92 ■ Lander 96
72 S.C.-Aiken 95
90 Presbyterian 118
61 Armstrong St. 95
67 † Central Wesleyan 64
58 S.C.-Spartanburg 69

102 ■ Ala.-Huntsville 101
74 ■ Queens (N.C.) 79
70 Longwood 72
81 Queens (N.C.) 113
83 ■ Limestone 74
63 ■ Belmont Abbey 75
57 ■ Francis Marion 64
66 ■ S.C.-Spartanburg 94
68 Erskine 81
70 ■ Central Wesleyan 74
69 ■ Wofford 91
65 Limestone 80
77 Wofford 93
68 ■ Presbyterian 73
84 Lander 110
67 Francis Marion 85
61 ■ Erskine 74
82 Ala.-Huntsville 103
65 ■ S.C.-Aiken 79
83 Central Wesleyan 89

NIAGARA 23-7
71 ■ St. John's (N.Y.) 75
92 ■ Buffalo 76
86 ■ Western Mich. 68
71 ■ Kent 70
102 ■ Valparaiso 68
94 Rider 82
85 Fairfield 78
83 Northeastern 71
80 ■ Cornell 66
66 Dayton 63
83 ■ Manhattan 64
106 ■ St. Bonaventure 96
69 Manhattan 70
99 ■ Iona 93
54 St. Bonaventure 69
70 Canisius 59
89 Buffalo 74
72 ■ Fairfield 54
65 ■ Loyola (Md.) 47
75 Iona 77
93 St. Peter's 81
85 Siena 77
72 Loyola (Md.) 66
72 ■ Canisius 62
77 ■ St. Peter's 63
78 ■ Siena 83
84 † St. Peter's 60
64 † Canisius 59
67 † Manhattan 68
83 ■ Boston College 87

NICHOLLS ST. 14-12
85 ■ Spring Hill 68
54 Tulane 96
64 Louisiana St. 75
67 Ala.-Birmingham 97
94 † South Fla. 84
81 ■ Southwest Tex. St. 75
80 ■ Texas-San Antonio 61
72 Northwestern (La.) 79
64 Northeast La. 105
79 ■ North Texas 76
91 ■ Texas-Arlington 74
99 ■ Loyola (La.) 70
76 ■ McNeese St. 72
64 Stephen F. Austin 75
80 Sam Houston St. 74
77 ■ Northeast La. 86
74 ■ Northwestern (La.) 79
62 Southwest Tex. St. 63
88 Texas-Arlington 99
79 North Texas 77
75 ■ Southeastern La. 76
70 McNeese St. 67
91 ■ Sam Houston St. 72
91 ■ Stephen F. Austin 74
93 Texas-San Antonio 80
67 † Texas-San Antonio 86

NICHOLS 9-15
71 Worcester St. 94
72 † Worcester Tech 82
95 Wentworth Inst. 98
78 Anna Maria 87
73 † Fitchburg St. 86
60 Salve Regina 78
65 Curry 81
76 ■ Framingham St. 93
74 ■ MIT 61
85 ■ Emerson-MCA 70
87 Worcester St. 108
53 Wheaton (Mass.) 94
94 ■ Roger Williams 81
78 ■ Rivier 57
88 Westbrook 107
88 Emerson-MCA 66
85 ■ Fitchburg St. 82
79 ■ Amherst 87
75 ■ Worcester Tech 80
58 Coast Guard 68
101 Mass. Pharmacy 51
72 Rhode Island Col. 76
82 ■ Suffolk 61
80 Western New Eng. 76

NORFOLK ST. 19-10
67 ■ Livingstone 75
91 ■ Dist. Columbia 60
67 N.C. Central 75
67 Virginia St. 65
69 ■ Barber-Scotia 57
71 Johnson Smith 82
96 ■ Clark Atlanta 62
81 ■ Fayetteville St. 65
90 Winston-Salem 73
95 † St. Augustine's 75
93 Virginia St. 76
75 † Hampton 65
80 ■ Calif. (Pa.) 87
88 St. Paul's 76
62 ■ Virginia Union 64
76 ■ Elizabeth City St. 80
78 Bowie St. 71
94 ■ Shaw 64
85 ■ Virginia St. 87
53 Hampton 62
72 Virginia Union 78
89 ■ Bowie St. 74
97 ■ St. Paul's 78
93 ■ Hampton 71
80 St. Augustine's 63
110 Elizabeth City St. 105
85 † Livingstone 66
79 † St. Paul's 63
63 † Virginia Union 71

NORTH ADAMS ST. 4-21
75 Wm. Paterson 80
67 Upsala 84
74 Clark (Mass.) 86
60 Eastern Conn. St. 79
83 ■ Southern Vt. 60
73 Castleton St. 96
63 Williams 94
60 ■ Mass.-Boston 87
58 ■ Framingham St. 78
44 Central Conn. St. 92
70 Bri'water (Mass.) 74
76 Worcester St. 100
62 ■ Salem St. 80
52 ■ Skidmore 50
57 Fitchburg St. 58
69 ■ Westfield St. 74
51 ■ Albany (N.Y.) 56
67 Framingham St. 73
63 ■ Bri'water (Mass.) 74
90 ■ Worcester St. 73
61 Salem St. 75
71 ■ Fitchburg St. 55
82 Westfield St. 97
78 Worcester St. 98
58 ■ Western Conn. St. 83

NORTH ALA. 16-10
76 ■ Lincoln (Mo.) 68
90 ■ Elizabeth City St. 95
85 Ala.-Huntsville 97
64 † Pittsburg St. 77
65 Mo. Southern St. 94
96 Arkansas Col. 91
82 ■ Athens St. 70
97 ■ Knoxville 82
73 Delta St. 90
81 ■ Arkansas Col. 67
88 † Ala.-Huntsville 76
103 † Bapt. Christian 84
91 ■ Tusculum 62
80 West Ga. 76
87 Valdosta St. 80
87 Athens St. 86
90 ■ Jacksonville St. 74
122 ■ Bapt. Christian 92
64 ■ Livingston 71
70 ■ Mississippi Col. 56
69 ■ Delta St. 90
86 Mississippi Col. 113
70 Livingston 73
95 Jacksonville St. 109
78 ■ West Ga. 61
76 ■ Valdosta St. 74

NORTH CARO. 34-4
119 ■ Old Dominion 82
108 † South Caro. 67
104 † Texas 68
78 † Virginia Tech 62
84 ■ Houston 76
103 Butler 56
84 Ohio St. 64
80 † Southwestern La. 59
78 † Michigan 79
101 Hawaii 84
98 ■ Cornell 60
100 North Caro. St. 67
101 ■ Maryland 73
80 ■ Georgia Tech 67
82 Clemson 72
80 ■ Virginia 58
70 Seton Hall 66
82 ■ Florida St. 77
62 Wake Forest 88
67 Duke 81
104 ■ North Caro. St. 58
77 Maryland 63
77 Georgia Tech 66
80 ■ Clemson 67
78 Virginia 58
85 ■ Notre Dame 56
86 Florida St. 76
83 ■ Wake Forest 65
83 ■ Duke 69
102 † Maryland 66
74 † Virginia 56
75 † Georgia Tech 77
85 † East Caro. 65
112 † Rhode Island 67
80 † Arkansas 74
75 † Cincinnati 68
78 † Kansas 68
77 † Michigan 71

N.C.-ASHEVILLE 4-23
69 North Caro. St. 72
67 ■ Milligan 57
46 ■ Western Caro. 73
87 ■ Montreat-Anderson 72
71 Virginia Tech 91
52 South Caro. 89
56 Missouri 99
82 Md.-Balt. County 91
64 Towson St. 85
75 ■ Winthrop 79
72 ■ Radford 69
50 Liberty 73
62 Radford 81
59 ■ Coastal Caro. 65
62 ■ Campbell 75
73 ■ Liberty 80
66 Winthrop 79
99 ■ Charleston So. 92
65 Campbell 90
72 Charleston So. 91
68 Coastal Caro. 100
69 ■ Mercer 74
60 ■ Towson St. 75
75 ■ Md.-Balt. County 91
69 Western Caro. 82
81 N.C.-Greensboro 96
87 † Winthrop 101

N.C.-CHARLOTTE 15-13
85 North Caro. A&T 73
81 † Centenary 62
93 Baylor 94
62 East Caro. 59
56 ■ Pepperdine 65
59 † Florida St. 63
69 † Florida 70
63 ■ Geo. Washington 90
88 ■ Appalachian St. 80
95 ■ Davidson 57
57 ■ Louisville 69
65 Virginia Tech 56
70 Tennessee 80
79 Southern Miss. 77
70 ■ Butler 62
83 ■ South Fla. 65
61 Va. Commonwealth 63
68 ■ Tulane 64
80 Davidson 69
84 ■ Va. Commonwealth 70
81 ■ Furman 58
70 Tulane 75
69 ■ Southern Miss. 76
64 Louisville 69
69 South Fla. 89
89 † Virginia Tech 80
68 † Southern Miss. 60
59 Louisville 71

N.C.-GREENSBORO 10-17
76 ■ William & Mary 81
54 Campbell 72
71 ■ Vermont 86
62 Clemson 88
78 ■ Central Fla. 66
70 ■ Winthrop 84
60 † Delaware 67
67 † Army 47
66 Central Fla. 72
70 Siena 102
62 Buffalo 64
62 ■ Cal St. Sacramento 61
62 Liberty 72
66 ■ Samford 81
56 West Va. 77
77 ■ Campbell 75
43 Charleston (S.C.) 60
72 ■ North Caro. A&T 88
95 Chicago St. 89
94 ■ FDU-Teaneck 80
47 Citadel 53
70 ■ Charleston (S.C.) 57
65 North Caro. St. 87
88 ■ Chicago St. 91
58 ■ Liberty 55
96 ■ N.C.-Asheville 81
72 ■ Navy 60

N.C.-WILMINGTON 17-11
96 North Caro. St. 84
61 † Florida Int'l 60
76 Fairfield 89
107 ■ Barton 86
102 ■ Alabama St. 93
91 ■ Auburn 80
88 Miami (Fla.) 73
87 Campbell 70
83 Richmond 80
83 James Madison 99
73 ■ Cal St. Sacramento 60
98 ■ George Mason 78
93 ■ American 75
63 William & Mary 67
92 Old Dominion 94
77 ■ East Caro. 72

72 Appalachian St. 80
69 ■ Richmond 91
89 ■ James Madison 85
90 ■ Mount Olive 63
99 American 106
69 George Mason 72
79 ■ Charleston (S.C.) 63
85 ■ William & Mary 103
79 ■ Old Dominion 90
79 East Caro. 66
71 Richmond 58
50 † East Caro. 55

NORTH CARO. A&T 14-13
73 ■ N.C.-Charlotte 85
43 Marquette 84
87 † Texas Christian 85
97 ■ Virginia St. 87
51 † Vanderbilt 87
102 † Arkansas St. 100
54 Charleston (S.C.) 68
77 ■ Howard 83
0 § ■ Morgan St. 2
51 Coppin St. 85
73 Florida A&M 76
68 Bethune-Cookman 52
71 ■ N.C. Central 80
66 Delaware St. 64
52 Md.-East. Shore 44
88 N.C.-Greensboro 72
84 ■ Florida A&M 68
66 ■ Bethune-Cookman 56
65 Winston-Salem 62
80 ■ Delaware St. 81
88 ■ Md.-East. Shore 65
68 ■ South Caro. St. 72
90 Howard 81
71 Morgan St. 70
71 ■ Coppin St. 83
76 South Caro. St. 70
79 † Delaware St. 88

N.C. CENTRAL 26-4
103 ■ Barber-Scotia 72
97 ■ Morris Brown 59
75 ■ Norfolk St. 67
80 St. Augustine's 72
84 Virginia St. 78
70 Hampton 65
90 ■ Johnson Smith 76
91 Fayetteville St. 86
76 Shaw 71
79 Bowie St. 67
99 ■ Winston-Salem 76
109 St. Paul's 99
80 North Caro. A&T 71
96 ■ St. Augustine's 72
87 ■ Dist. Columbia 61
109 Livingstone 76
70 ■ Fayetteville St. 62
81 Johnson Smith 106
91 ■ Livingstone 68
83 ■ Shaw 66
67 ■ Virginia Union 73
92 ■ Elizabeth City St. 75
88 Clark Atlanta 71
90 Winston-Salem 82
72 † Hampton 68
82 † Johnson Smith 75
61 † Virginia Union 67
93 † Alabama A&M 84
93 † Virginia Union 81
80 † Cal St. Bakersfield 86

NORTH CARO. ST. 8-19
84 ■ N.C.-Wilmington 96
72 ■ N.C.-Asheville 69
74 ■ Connecticut 81
41 † Princeton 50
69 ■ Oregon St. 68
64 Kansas 84
88 ■ Iona 66
67 ■ North Caro. 100
56 ■ Virginia 73
63 Davidson 58
54 Florida St. 70
56 Duke 92
65 ■ Maryland 70
74 Georgia Tech 85
72 ■ Clemson 70
54 ■ Wake Forest 65
58 North Caro. 104
66 Virginia 75
74 ■ Tennessee 72
87 ■ N.C.-Greensboro 65
71 ■ Florida St. 72
82 ■ Duke 91
71 Maryland 88
68 ■ Georgia Tech 60
82 Clemson 92
68 Wake Forest 80
55 † Maryland 76

NORTH CENTRAL 8-17
65 † Malone 68
86 † Aurora 73
59 Ill. Benedictine 77
62 Fla. Southern 100
58 Rollins 91
85 Tampa 105
62 IU/PU-Ft. Wayne 96
63 ■ Olivet (Ill.) 77
76 ■ Rockford 59
68 † Marian (Wis.) 70
70 Wis.-Whitewater 87
54 Ill. Wesleyan 90
78 ■ Elmhurst 67
67 Carthage 77
69 ■ Augustana (Ill.) 71
63 ■ Ill. Wesleyan 99
51 ■ Wheaton (Ill.) 53
67 North Park 57
56 Augustana (Ill.) 73
89 ■ Millikin 80
58 ■ Carthage 57
87 Wheaton (Ill.) 77
64 Millikin 61
85 Elmhurst 95
66 ■ North Park 77

NORTH DAK. 23-8
83 ■ Grand View 74
87 Bemidji St. 68
90 ■ Mt. Senario 60
85 Neb.-Kearney 71
99 ■ Jamestown 48
83 Hawaii Pacific 84
97 ■ Eastern Mont. 62
86 ■ Troy St. 112
76 Mankato St. 65
70 St. Cloud St. 60
79 ■ South Dak. St. 69
72 ■ Augustana (S.D.) 63
60 Northern Colo. 71
81 Nebraska-Omaha 65
80 ■ Mankato St. 74
55 North Dak. St. 68
59 ■ South Dak. 61
80 ■ Morningside 87
91 Augustana (S.D.) 87
96 South Dak. St. 80
90 ■ St. Cloud St. 88
90 ■ Nebraska-Omaha 66
65 ■ Northern Colo. 46
89 ■ North Dak. St. 76
72 Morningside 93
76 South Dak. 67
68 † St. Cloud St. 64
78 † Morningside 77
72 † North Dak. St. 59
80 ■ Western St. 61
64 ■ South Dak. 66

NORTH DAK. ST. 12-17
95 ■ Augsburg 65
57 ■ Michigan Tech 91
82 Neb.-Kearney 103
81 ■ Northern Mich. 83
73 ■ Mary 68
72 ■ Moorhead St. 74
94 † Troy St. 100
80 † Eastern Mont. 77
61 St. Cloud St. 60
71 Mankato St. 73
88 ■ Augustana (S.D.) 76
69 ■ South Dak. St. 95
61 Nebraska-Omaha 58
64 Northern Colo. 67
65 ■ St. Cloud St. 80
68 ■ North Dak. 55
69 ■ Morningside 81
65 ■ South Dak. 82
60 South Dak. St. 77
54 Augustana (S.D.) 53
51 ■ Mankato St. 62
71 ■ Northern Colo. 61
80 ■ Nebraska-Omaha 72
76 North Dak. 89
57 South Dak. 75
63 Morningside 100
82 † South Dak. 74
68 † South Dak. St. 64
59 † North Dak. 72

NORTH FLA. 7-20
87 Embry-Riddle 93
90 Webber 98
73 ■ Brewton Parker 70
63 Florida Int'l 85
76 Brewton Parker 63
79 San Diego St. 90
72 Azusa-Pacific 87
73 ■ Tri-State 78
75 Savannah St. 79
64 Eckerd 66
64 ■ St. Thomas Aquinas 59
64 ■ Barry 65
84 ■ Edward Waters 87
72 Fla. Southern 99
68 ■ Tampa 86
72 ■ Rollins 86
92 Florida Tech 105
75 Stetson 95
115 ■ St. Leo 81
96 Barry 117
98 ■ Savannah St. 85
88 ■ Fla. Southern 102
93 Tampa 122
72 Rollins 81
78 ■ Florida Tech 86
108 St. Leo 107
101 ■ Eckerd 100

NORTH TEXAS 5-21
70 Tulsa 101
68 † Texas Tech 88
64 † Bucknell 88
86 ■ Baylor 88
79 ■ South Ala. 84
94 Nevada 102
94 Southern Meth. 110
89 ■ Northwestern (La.) 78
79 ■ Northeast La. 77
70 ■ Texas Tech 78
76 Texas-Arlington 81
76 Nicholls St. 79
67 McNeese St. 70
95 ■ Stephen F. Austin 97
76 ■ Sam Houston St. 63
73 Southwest Tex. St. 83
74 Texas-San Antonio 100
87 ■ Texas-Arlington 74
97 Northwestern (La.) 121
68 ■ McNeese St. 77
77 ■ Nicholls St. 79
89 Sam Houston St. 97
70 Stephen F. Austin 84
94 ■ Texas-San Antonio 89
60 ■ Southwest Tex. St. 74
77 Northeast La. 99

NORTHEAST LA. 26-5
89 ■ Ark.-Monticello 75
72 † Arkansas St. 79
105 † Alcorn St. 90
79 Southern Miss. 67
68 † Coastal Caro. 77
97 † South Caro. St. 68
84 ■ Eastern Wash. 58
87 † Arkansas 78
87 Texas-Arlington 71
77 North Texas 79
94 ■ McNeese St. 64
105 ■ Nicholls St. 64
113 ■ Southern Miss. 106
80 Stephen F. Austin 62
102 Sam Houston St. 92
77 ■ Southwest Tex. St. 66
86 ■ Texas-San Antonio 66
67 Mississippi St. 75
89 Northwestern (La.) 79
86 Nicholls St. 77
110 ■ Texas-Arlington 83
85 ■ Sam Houston St. 58
94 ■ Stephen F. Austin 74
85 Texas-San Antonio 80
64 Southwest Tex. St. 63
72 McNeese St. 68
94 ■ Northwestern (La.) 73
99 ■ North Texas 77
106 ■ Texas-Arlington 82
80 ■ Texas-San Antonio 66
69 † Iowa 82

NORTHEAST MO. ST. 6-20
78 ■ Lincoln (Mo.) 79
82 † Tabor 71
68 Drury 77
74 Quincy 80
37 Southern Ill. 76
93 ■ Nebraska-Omaha 88
73 ■ Westminster (Mo.) 57
64 ■ SIU-Edwardsville 66
48 Mississippi St. 75
61 Mo. Western St. 65
67 ■ Mo.-St. Louis 81
75 Northwest Mo. St. 80
85 ■ Mo. Southern St. 74
66 Central Mo. St. 81
74 ■ Emporia St. 73
66 ■ Quincy 89
67 ■ Mo. Western St. 68
65 Washburn 83
53 ■ Northwest Mo. St. 73
75 Lincoln (Mo.) 82
74 ■ Central Mo. St. 60
53 Emporia St. 76
63 ■ Washburn 73
53 Southwest Baptist 73
68 Pittsburg St. 72
66 ■ Missouri-Rolla 80

NORTHEASTERN 20-8
90 ■ Army 57
72 Duke 103
73 ■ Howard 51
47 ■ Monmouth (N.J.) 46
78 † McNeese St. 72
83 † Grambling 94
76 ■ Canisius 66
69 Siena 60
71 ■ Niagara 83
72 ■ Rhode Island 80
82 Vermont 74
68 ■ Hartford 58
68 ■ Drexel 79
76 ■ Delaware 73
82 George Mason 71
75 New Hampshire 62
72 Maine 70
78 Iona 82
88 Boston U. 81
77 ■ Maine 60
73 ■ New Hampshire 45
82 Delaware 68
73 Drexel 79
87 ■ Vermont 67

64 Hartford 62
96 ■ Boston U. 58
91 ■ Vermont 68
61 ■ Delaware 84

NORTHEASTERN ILL. 11-16
71 Western Ill. 73
78 Wis.-Milwaukee 94
91 ■ Elmhurst 79
65 Marquette 95
83 DePaul 90
85 ■ Aquinas 66
84 Arizona St. 93
92 ■ Central Mich. 99
59 ■ Montana 65
72 ■ Samford 73
76 ■ Indiana St. 73
68 Kansas St. 97
70 Ill.-Chicago 79
80 Jackson St. 88
94 ■ Monmouth (Ill.) 71
106 ■ Lakeland 64
70 Eastern Ill. 67
62 ■ Evansville 72
77 Chicago St. 74
57 Southern Utah 80
91 ■ Wis.-Milwaukee 86
75 Samford 79
64 ■ Mo.-Kansas City 94
72 ■ Southern Utah 66
90 ■ Chicago St. 73
80 Mo.-Kansas City 96
97 ■ Ill.-Chicago 92

NORTHERN ARIZ. 10-16
89 ■ St. Mary's (Cal.) 79
56 Maine 59
67 ■ Cal St. Northridge 76
74 Southern Utah 100
67 Arizona St. 81
85 ■ Missouri-Rolla 95
78 ■ Winona St. 71
76 ■ Denver 69
78 Cal St. Sacramento 71
86 Cal St. Northridge 87
78 ■ Boise St. 72
76 ■ Idaho St. 68
60 Montana St. 66
55 Montana 74
89 ■ Eastern Wash. 69
53 ■ Idaho 59
68 ■ Cal St. Sacramento 64
70 ■ Weber St. 74
69 Idaho St. 88
45 Boise St. 58
46 ■ Montana 54
64 ■ Montana St. 73
64 Eastern Wash. 52
51 Idaho 78
84 ■ Southern Utah 75
79 Weber St. 100

NORTHERN COLO. 12-15
81 ■ Regis (Colo.) 86
66 ■ Denver 81
56 Southern Colo. 60
93 ■ Doane 77
80 Metropolitan St. 90
96 ■ Metropolitan St. 71
79 South Dak. St. 64
73 Augustana (S.D.) 64
51 Denver 61
83 Nebraska-Omaha 52
71 ■ North Dak. 60
67 ■ North Dak. St. 64
69 South Dak. 79
56 Morningside 87
77 ■ St. Cloud St. 84
69 ■ Mankato St. 60
84 ■ Augustana (S.D.) 79
95 Regis (Colo.) 85
78 ■ Nebraska-Omaha 73
61 North Dak. St. 71
46 North Dak. 65

94 ■ Morningside 78
45 ■ South Dak. 65
62 ■ South Dak. St. 72
62 Mankato St. 82
63 St. Cloud St. 79
64 † Morningside 74

NORTHERN ILL. 15-12
86 ■ Ill. Wesleyan 66
62 ■ Southern Ill. 91
71 Wis.-Milwaukee 79
86 ■ Blackburn 38
57 Akron 62
73 ■ Idaho St. 64
57 ■ Wis.-Milwaukee 82
73 Texas A&M 85
76 Chicago St. 70
73 ■ Valparaiso 65
66 Cleveland St. 73
88 Youngstown St. 82
53 ■ Wis.-Green Bay 50
63 Eastern Ill. 65
66 Ill.-Chicago 64
75 Western Ill. 84
82 ■ Wright St. 77
65 ■ Eastern Ill. 56
63 ■ Ill.-Chicago 61
89 ■ Loyola (Ill.) 79
61 Valparaiso 72
74 ■ Western Ill. 66
56 Wright St. 98
42 Wis.-Green Bay 57
67 ■ Cleveland St. 62
84 ■ Youngstown St. 80
75 † Valparaiso 83

NORTHERN IOWA 12-15
96 ■ Buffalo 66
67 ■ Iowa St. 74
44 Iowa 64
55 ■ Cal St. Fullerton 66
61 ■ Nebraska-Omaha 51
63 St. Bonaventure 74
76 ■ Eastern Ky. 73
75 Tulsa 66
69 Southern Ill. 88
61 Eastern Ky. 59
61 ■ Tulsa 66
74 ■ Wichita St. 72
59 Indiana St. 69
49 Southwest Mo. St. 72
60 ■ Creighton 58
59 ■ Indiana St. 52
59 ■ Drake 69
49 ■ Illinois St. 69
47 Wichita St. 63
81 ■ Bradley 76
54 ■ Southern Ill. 51
54 Creighton 59
64 Drake 62
54 ■ Southwest Mo. St. 53
46 Bradley 72
59 Illinois St. 71
59 † Drake 63

NORTHERN KY. 11-16
79 ■ Wilmington (Ohio) 65
104 ■ Campbellsville 97
82 ■ Spalding 65
71 Eastern Ky. 81
91 ■ SIU-Edwardsville 78
74 Georgetown (Ky.) 87
88 ■ Bethel (Tenn.) 82
90 Ashland 81
88 IU/PU-Ft. Wayne 105
95 ■ Kentucky St. 107
87 ■ Bellarmine 82
64 St. Joseph's (Ind.) 68
81 Lewis 93
98 Oakland City 94
95 ■ Indianapolis 99
79 ■ Southern Ind. 107
81 ■ Ky. Wesleyan 91
76 Bellarmine 72

93 Kentucky St. 99
88 ■ Lewis 97
75 ■ St. Joseph's (Ind.) 71
67 ■ Oakland City 64
81 Indianapolis 82
62 Ky. Wesleyan 65
59 Southern Ind. 60
70 ■ IU/PU-Ft. Wayne 87
89 ■ Ashland 99

NORTHERN MICH. 22-8
100 ■ Bemidji St. 86
64 Minn.-Duluth 61
94 † Quincy 92
91 Wis.-Stevens Point 96
87 Bemidji St. 80
83 North Dak. St. 81
100 ■ Ferris St. 92
109 ■ Grand Valley St. 88
93 Northwood 91
93 ■ Oakland 66
83 ■ Saginaw Valley 80
67 ■ Minn.-Duluth 39
78 Wayne St. (Mich.) 94
66 Hillsdale 67
110 ■ Michigan Tech 94
85 Ferris St. 83
79 Grand Valley St. 81
68 ■ Wis.-Parkside 72
67 ■ Lake Superior St. 52
88 ■ Northwood 71
69 Michigan Tech 73
72 Oakland 62
66 Saginaw Valley 60
78 Lake Superior St. 73
81 ■ Wayne St. (Mich.) 69
103 ■ Hillsdale 82
94 ■ Hillsdale 93
86 ■ Wayne St. (Mich.) 93
86 Southern Ind. 85
58 † Wayne St. (Mich.) 90

NORTHWEST MO. ST. 14-13
76 ■ Mid-America Naz. 72
99 ■ Dana 68
78 Rockhurst 64
80 Wayne St. (Neb.) 71
78 † William Jewell 87
81 † Ark.-Pine Bluff 70
90 ■ Midland Lutheran 77
94 ■ East Tex. St. 91
88 ■ Central Okla. 131
61 ■ Washburn 85
82 Pittsburg St. 92
80 ■ Northeast Mo. St. 75
79 ■ Southwest Baptist 84
60 Mo. Western St. 66
64 ■ Central Mo. St. 81
71 Washburn 111
55 ■ Emporia St. 84
73 Northeast Mo. St. 53
69 Mo. Southern St. 73
83 ■ Mo. Western St. 76
73 Central Mo. St. 67
83 ■ Wayne St. (Neb.) 60
76 Emporia St. 81
103 ■ Missouri-Rolla 100
69 Mo.-St. Louis 65
79 ■ Lincoln (Mo.) 84
62 Washburn 93

NORTHWESTERN 8-19
101 ■ Chicago 50
66 Vanderbilt 86
87 ■ Youngstown St. 57
71 ■ Texas A&M 60
79 ■ Loyola (Ill.) 73
73 Holy Cross 83
61 † Pennsylvania 64
69 † William & Mary 77
81 ■ Lehigh 66
71 ■ Illinois 81
68 Penn St. 70
75 ■ Michigan St. 80

55 Minnesota 70
73 ■ Purdue 83
71 ■ Indiana 93
87 Wisconsin 101
67 Illinois 82
70 ■ Ohio St. 81
67 ■ Penn St. 58
55 Michigan St. 81
63 ■ Iowa 75
60 ■ Minnesota 79
62 Purdue 59
69 Indiana 98
100 ■ Wisconsin 89
50 Iowa 56
60 Michigan 86

N'WESTERN (WIS.) 2-19
56 Beloit 73
78 Lawrence 80
62 Ripon 75
60 Concordia (Wis.) 91
78 ■ Lakeland 97
76 ■ Wis. Lutheran 93
73 ■ Dr. Martin Luther 63
73 Cardinal Stritch 89
64 Milwaukee Engr. 78
46 ■ Edgewood 69
65 Maranatha 87
70 Marian (Wis.) 85
68 ■ Marian (Wis.) 76
60 ■ Concordia (Wis.) 66
68 Lakeland 81
42 ■ Eureka 71
61 Wis. Lutheran 71
67 ■ Cardinal Stritch 91
67 ■ Maranatha 75
75 ■ Milwaukee Engr. 61
53 Edgewood 71

NORTHWESTERN (LA.) 13-13
93 ■ Dallas 70
118 ■ Tex. Lutheran 68
81 Tulane 91
127 ■ Ark. Baptist 92
113 ■ Centenary 102
91 ■ Tex. A&M-Kingsville 80
79 Louisiana St. 93
78 North Texas 89
75 Texas-Arlington 89
79 ■ Nicholls St. 72
94 ■ McNeese St. 96
68 Stephen F. Austin 65
82 Sam Houston St. 84
99 ■ Texas-San Antonio 105
65 ■ Southwest Tex. St. 67
94 Southeastern La. 71
79 ■ Northeast La. 89
81 McNeese St. 100
79 Nicholls St. 74
121 ■ North Texas 97
79 ■ Stephen F. Austin 73
114 ■ Sam Houston St. 89
87 Southwest Tex. St. 99
117 Texas-San Antonio 108
73 Northeast La. 94
90 ■ Texas-Arlington 93

NORTHWOOD 5-22
75 Tri-State 85
71 Siena Heights 80
83 ■ Concordia (Mich.) 69
89 Spring Arbor 91
60 Saginaw Valley 77
62 Wayne St. (Mich.) 84
76 ■ Michigan Tech 123
91 ■ Northern Mich. 93
65 Alma 85
82 Mich.-Dearborn 88
73 ■ Lake Superior St. 66
65 Oakland 96
75 ■ Grand Valley St. 80
93 Grand Rapids Bapt. 78
87 ■ Hillsdale 112
93 Ferris St. 109

85 ■ Aquinas 76
63 ■ Saginaw Valley 81
68 ■ Wayne St. (Mich.) 93
63 ■ Grand Rapids Bapt. 68
86 Michigan Tech 127
71 Northern Mich. 88
86 ■ Ferris St. 85
59 Lake Superior St. 100
51 ■ Oakland 85
79 Grand Valley St. 81
92 Hillsdale 112

NORWICH 1-23
77 ■ MIT 76
55 Castleton St. 85
62 MIT 72
55 St. Michael's 75
68 ■ Colby-Sawyer 91
57 Plymouth St. 89
74 New England Col. 89
55 ■ Coast Guard 77
50 ■ Coast Guard 71
68 ■ Johnson St. 69
42 Western New Eng. 59
59 Babson 76
67 ■ Lyndon St. 78
68 ■ Bowdoin 82
60 ■ Colby 76
72 ■ Babson 97
51 Worcester Tech 83
56 ■ Middlebury 69
68 Bates 78
66 Thomas 81
46 ■ Western New Eng. 57
61 ■ Worcester Tech 81
69 ■ Skidmore 87
61 † Coast Guard 74

NOTRE DAME 9-18
52 Loyola (Ill.) 50
76 ■ Evansville 70
70 ■ Indiana 75
52 Providence 71
73 ■ Boston College 70
45 New Orleans 43
68 † St. Joseph's (Pa.) 65
74 ■ Southern Cal 77
60 Xavier (Ohio) 75
59 Detroit Mercy 83
71 ■ Dayton 66
67 Stanford 61
55 Michigan 70
56 Butler 70
72 ■ La Salle 63
57 Missouri 73
65 UCLA 68
61 ■ St. Bonaventure 64
50 ■ Duke 67
79 Dayton 69
62 ■ Kentucky 81
61 ■ Marquette 69
62 DePaul 70
56 North Caro. 85
76 ■ Duquesne 80
66 ■ Valparaiso 80
68 Louisville 83

NOTRE DAME (CAL.) 10-15
60 Humboldt St. 57
76 † Western Wash. 82
77 Loyola (Cal.) 80
89 Southern Colo. 84
81 † Mesa St. 75
74 Cal Poly Pomona 80
69 ■ Cal St. San B'dino 75
99 Cal St. Los Ang. 107
100 Cal Poly SLO 89
60 ■ Seattle Pacific 67
60 ■ Cal St. Hayward 63
107 Cal St. Stanislaus 102
81 Cal St. Chico 90
67 Humboldt St. 60
47 ■ UC Davis 55

57 Sonoma St. 62
78 ■ Menlo 73
59 San Fran. St. 64
64 UC Davis 62
68 ■ Sonoma St. 51
72 ■ Humboldt St. 57
65 ■ Cal St. Chico 72
65 Cal St. Hayward 72
80 ■ Cal St. Stanislaus 82
62 ■ San Fran. St. 65

OAKLAND 15-11
71 Calvin 80
97 † Wabash 99
68 Lewis 64
46 Mississippi 71
50 Detroit Mercy 77
83 ■ Lake Superior St. 66
83 ■ Hillsdale 95
89 ■ Spring Arbor 70
106 ■ Mich.-Dearborn 67
66 Northern Mich. 93
75 Michigan Tech 72
96 ■ Northwood 65
62 Saginaw Valley 64
73 Grand Valley St. 71
78 ■ Wayne St. (Mich.) 76
84 ■ Mercyhurst 74
91 Lake Superior St. 82
80 ■ Ferris St. 85
75 Hillsdale 92
62 ■ Northern Mich. 72
84 ■ Michigan Tech 71
73 Ferris St. 77
85 Northwood 51
78 ■ Saginaw Valley 60
68 ■ Grand Valley St. 61
66 Wayne St. (Mich.) 60

OAKLAND CITY 22-10
106 ■ Parks 47
79 ■ Sanford Brown 60
72 Chaminade 84
72 † Fla. Southern 83
71 Tenn.-Martin 82
132 ■ Ind.-East 86
116 ■ St. Louis Christian 57
113 ■ Spalding 103
78 Ky. Wesleyan 97
88 ■ Sanford Brown 55
69 Southeast Mo. St. 108
89 Wilberforce 87
107 ■ Great Lakes Bible 54
90 ■ Ind.-Southeast 86
116 ■ Purdue-North Cent. 71
96 Brescia 74
94 ■ Northern Ky. 98
73 Indianapolis 79
102 St. Louis Christian 82
70 Ind.-Southeast 73
136 ■ Ind.-Northwest 71
77 ■ SIU-Edwardsville 74
90 ■ Wilberforce 77
64 Northern Ky. 67
104 ■ Brescia 100
137 ■ Ind.-East 57
74 ■ Ky. Wesleyan 65
141 ■ Ind.-Northwest 51
89 ■ Sue Bennett 80
93 † Bartlesville Wesl. 90
68 † Bethel (Ind.) 69
81 † Master's 77

OBERLIN 1-21
80 Baldwin-Wallace 103
80 ■ Dyke 82
66 Denison 81
87 ■ Earlham 106
55 ■ Allegheny 77
44 Thiel 71
71 Wash. & Jeff. 83
42 ■ Wooster 90
44 ■ Kenyon 64
68 Ohio Wesleyan 82
58 ■ Wittenberg 86

63 Case Reserve 74
73 Earlham 89
77 Allegheny 87
59 ■ Penn St.-Behrend 70
51 Bethany (W.Va.) 73
70 ■ Ohio Wesleyan 97
55 Kenyon 85
88 ■ Denison 85
41 Wittenberg 113
71 ■ Case Reserve 80
56 Wooster 90

OCCIDENTAL 15-9
74 UC San Diego 88
63 Chapman 60
129 ■ LIFE Bible 65
102 Multnomah Bible 85
64 George Fox 90
69 Concordia (Ore.) 77
73 † Wis.-Platteville 75
91 ■ Fontbonne 58
59 ■ Christ-Irvine 48
115 ■ Haverford 72
75 ■ Claremont-M-S 69
82 Whittier 78
67 ■ Pomona-Pitzer 57
76 La Verne 78
82 Cal Tech 39
111 ■ Redlands 95
80 ■ Cal Lutheran 89
96 Claremont-M-S 69
79 ■ Whittier 71
62 Pomona-Pitzer 60
58 ■ La Verne 60
95 Redlands 97
84 ■ Cal Tech 55
55 Cal Lutheran 66

OGLETHORPE 15-9
110 ■ Atlanta Christian 73
96 ■ Palm Beach Atl. 80
67 Maryville (Tenn.) 84
56 ■ Emory 71
71 Sewanee 70
51 † Marian (Ind.) 64
110 † Principia 58
86 ■ Gordon 65
83 ■ Baldwin-Wallace 93
66 Millsaps 62
59 Rhodes 81
69 ■ Centre 72
105 ■ Fisk 69
64 Emory 83
93 ■ Hendrix 71
78 ■ Trinity (Tex.) 55
70 Centre 75
92 Fisk 79
87 ■ Sewanee 57
93 ■ Savannah A&D 63
75 Trinity (Tex.) 59
65 Hendrix 67
103 ■ Millsaps 92
68 ■ Rhodes 60

OHIO 14-13
61 Ohio St. 77
70 Robert Morris 72
72 Kansas St. 73
79 Marshall 89
98 ■ Charleston (W.Va.) 77
77 ■ Wright St. 80
73 † St. Mary's (Cal.) 61
81 Stanford 76
67 ■ Toledo 61
65 Kent 64
64 ■ Ball St. 78
72 Miami (Ohio) 59
71 ■ Western Mich. 86
65 Akron 58
81 Central Mich. 91
73 ■ Bowling Green 67
81 Eastern Mich. 74
58 ■ Kent 53
52 Ball St. 72
54 ■ Miami (Ohio) 59

51 Western Mich. 66
75 ■ Akron 67
66 ■ Central Mich. 51
71 Bowling Green 64
71 ■ Eastern Mich. 62
73 Toledo 85
84 † Toledo 85

OHIO NORTHERN 28-2
62 † Austin 47
54 † Howard Payne 30
77 Dallas 56
74 Defiance 59
71 ■ Baldwin-Wallace 59
69 ■ Muskingum 50
67 John Carroll 57
75 ■ Hiram 68
68 ■ Bluffton 45
75 Heidelberg 70
72 ■ Mount Union 59
66 Capital 60
84 ■ Marietta 48
89 Otterbein 88
95 ■ John Carroll 67
60 Muskingum 57
60 Baldwin-Wallace 52
71 ■ Heidelberg 70
61 Hiram 77
65 ■ Capital 63
68 Mount Union 46
88 ■ Otterbein 73
78 Marietta 59
57 ■ Baldwin-Wallace 54
79 † Otterbein 81
88 ■ Wooster 62
83 † Chris. Newport 67
67 † Calvin 56
74 † Mass.-Dartmouth 73
71 † Augustana (Ill.) 68

OHIO ST. 15-13
77 ■ Ohio 61
73 ■ Southern Cal 56
80 ■ Bowling Green 54
76 ■ Wright St. 55
69 West Va. 78
64 ■ North Caro. 84
85 † Oregon St. 77
79 † Oregon 75
79 ■ Ill.-Chicago 55
71 Penn St. 68
92 ■ Iowa 81
60 ■ Michigan St. 77
67 Wisconsin 76
69 Indiana 96
62 Michigan 72
76 ■ Illinois 86
57 ■ Purdue 62
62 ■ Penn St. 59
81 Northwestern 70
66 Michigan St. 81
54 Iowa 68
80 ■ Wisconsin 70
81 ■ Indiana 77
64 ■ Michigan 66
73 Illinois 85
69 ■ Minnesota 58
72 Purdue 62
53 ■ Miami (Ohio) 56

OHIO WESLEYAN 12-13
61 ■ Penn St.-Behrend 60
63 ■ Hanover 71
84 Ohio Dominican 94
62 ■ Capital 65
76 ■ Kenyon 54
69 Allegheny 71
65 Wittenberg 79
80 ■ Findlay 83
85 Thomas More 78
57 Denison 56
81 ■ Case Reserve 74
71 ■ Defiance 82
82 ■ Oberlin 68
62 Wooster 60

110 Earlham 61
71 ■ Allegheny 72
62 ■ Wittenberg 76
74 ■ Denison 48
97 Oberlin 70
78 Wilmington (Ohio) 83
68 Kenyon 75
75 ■ Wooster 83
112 ■ Earlham 75
68 Case Reserve 54
77 ■ Kenyon 81

OKLAHOMA 20-12
78 ■ Oregon St. 75
115 ■ Towson St. 73
112 ■ Idaho St. 59
92 ■ South Caro. 76
93 ■ Massachusetts 83
75 † Brigham Young 76
105 † Chaminade 88
108 † DePaul 94
102 † Alas. Anchorage 70
85 † Texas 76
109 ■ Lamar 92
84 Duke 88
121 ■ West Tex. A&M 71
85 ■ Kansas 96
102 ■ Nebraska 89
78 † Maryland 89
74 Iowa St. 81
146 ■ Florida A&M 65
94 ■ Colorado 70
61 Kansas St. 62
76 Oklahoma St. 83
95 ■ Missouri 84
81 ■ Iowa St. 77
80 Kansas 77
80 Colorado 84
63 ■ Kansas St. 67
69 Missouri 68
89 ■ Oklahoma St. 80
83 Nebraska 94
55 † Iowa St. 69
88 ■ Michigan St. 86
72 Minnesota 86

OKLAHOMA ST. 20-9
86 ■ Midwestern St. 74
65 California 80
85 ■ Tulsa 67
93 ■ Baylor 75
93 ■ Houston Baptist 54
65 Texas Christian 47
74 ■ Southwest Mo. St. 59
75 † Southern Methodist 59
60 Jacksonville 59
62 ■ Kansas St. 75
72 Iowa St. 81
78 ■ Nebraska 73
90 Oral Roberts 45
63 Missouri 79
94 ■ Iowa St. 77
85 Colorado 61
83 ■ Oklahoma 76
72 Kansas 84
77 ■ Colorado 59
73 Nebraska 63
80 ■ Louisiana Tech 53
77 ■ Missouri 73
78 Kansas St. 61
80 Oklahoma 89
114 ■ Oral Roberts 85
73 ■ Kansas 74
62 † Missouri 81
74 † Marquette 62
63 † Louisville 78

OLD DOMINION 21-8
82 North Caro. 119
118 ■ Shenandoah 71
78 ■ Iona 65
68 Virginia 90
81 † Va. Commonwealth 65
93 ■ Alabama 91
85 Auburn 96
104 Florida A&M 83
78 South Fla. 76
76 George Mason 74
95 American 88
59 ■ Richmond 75
89 James Madison 102
71 ■ Virginia Tech 61
80 ■ East Caro. 60
94 ■ N.C.-Wilmington 92
81 William & Mary 80
99 ■ Southern Miss. 84
91 ■ George Mason 62
86 ■ American 85
80 Richmond 84
92 ■ James Madison 88
73 East Caro. 60
90 N.C.-Wilmington 79
90 ■ William & Mary 80
113 Southern Miss. 105
67 † East Caro. 73
74 ■ Va. Commonwealth 68
58 Miami (Ohio) 60

OLD WESTBURY 11-13
72 † St. Joseph's (Me.) 95
72 John Jay 78
92 Centenary (N.J.) 78
67 ■ Queens (N.Y.) 73
97 ■ CCNY 72
66 Upsala 85
75 York (N.Y.) 70
90 Medgar Evers 93
72 Frank. & Marsh. 104
50 † Southern Me. 57
77 ■ Albany (N.Y.) 95
96 Pratt 89
62 ■ Lehman 58
81 Polytechnic (N.Y.) 55
92 King's (N.Y.) 98
77 ■ Baruch 65
71 ■ John Jay 72
66 Staten Island 89
97 New York Tech 84
87 Molloy 94
77 ■ Bloomfield 80
78 Mt. St. Mary (N.Y.) 74
67 LIU-Southampton 65
57 † Stony Brook 53

OLIVET 7-18
74 Manchester 101
73 ■ Aquinas 77
61 Hillsdale 98
70 † St. Francis (Ind.) 77
85 Wabash 88
82 † Ind. Wesleyan 79
71 Bluffton 75
88 ■ Goshen 53
70 Muskingum 62
84 † Rio Grande 121
90 † Aquinas 68
80 † Albion 112
55 Kalamazoo 70
63 ■ Albion 81
96 Hope 101
71 ■ Calvin 94
77 ■ Adrian 66
87 Alma 99
70 ■ Kalamazoo 88
99 ■ Alma 87
85 Adrian 75
80 Calvin 105
62 ■ Hope 64
78 Albion 82
71 Albion 79

ONEONTA ST. 6-18
91 † Mt. St. Mary (N.Y.) 93
64 Hartwick 70
64 Potsdam St. 67
81 Plattsburgh St. 94
78 Cortland St. 87
65 ■ Brockport St. 77
66 ■ Geneseo St. 103
57 Stony Brook 69
55 † Widener 54
81 ■ Utica 83
53 Albany (N.Y.) 68
73 ■ New Paltz St. 61
72 ■ Potsdam St. 70
49 ■ Plattsburgh St. 63
78 Binghamton 71
56 Oswego St. 64
91 ■ Utica Tech 78
77 New Paltz St. 80
74 ■ Hamilton 99
70 Buffalo St. 101
56 Fredonia St. 74
63 ■ Binghamton 67
69 ■ Cortland St. 72
67 ■ Hartwick 63

OREGON 10-20
96 Alas. Anchorage 73
75 † New Mexico St. 86
81 † Vanderbilt 83
78 Fresno St. 80
68 Pacific (Cal.) 80
97 ■ Alas. Fairbanks 77
80 ■ Idaho 61
101 ■ Mo.-St. Louis 68
83 ■ Pac. Lutheran 72
76 † Brigham Young 70
75 † Ohio St. 79
71 ■ Hartford 69
65 California 82
66 Stanford 71
87 ■ UCLA 99
58 ■ Southern Cal 69
79 Washington St. 95
53 Washington 70
60 ■ Arizona 92
84 ■ Arizona St. 99
75 Oregon St. 83
67 Southern Cal 73
90 UCLA 97
85 ■ Washington 70
62 ■ Washington St. 60
88 Arizona St. 103
68 Arizona 99
48 ■ Oregon St. 54
84 ■ Stanford 73
76 ■ California 79

OREGON ST. 13-14
79 ■ Pacific (Cal.) 62
75 Oklahoma 78
69 ■ Seattle Pacific 62
48 Southwest Mo. St. 63
68 North Caro. St. 69
56 James Madison 70
77 † Ohio St. 85
93 † Brigham Young 79
97 ■ UC San Diego 39
77 Stanford 66
64 California 63
68 ■ Southern Cal 57
79 ■ UCLA 73
73 Washington 70
51 Washington St. 56
73 ■ Arizona St. 82
54 ■ Arizona 57
83 ■ Oregon 75
75 UCLA 76
60 Southern Cal 69
59 ■ Washington St. 58
51 ■ Washington 61
70 Arizona 81
61 Arizona St. 76
54 Oregon 48
72 ■ California 78
82 ■ Stanford 65

OSWEGO ST. 5-19
88 ■ St. Lawrence 81
58 Centenary (N.J.) 53
64 Mt. St. Mary (N.Y.) 68
50 Utica Tech 76
50 ■ Mt. St. Mary (N.Y.) 75
60 ■ Trinity (Conn.) 91
55 ■ Hamilton 74
66 Cortland St. 78
60 ■ Binghamton 85
62 ■ Brockport St. 80
70 Fredonia St. 71
55 Buffalo St. 71
54 ■ Geneseo St. 78
64 ■ Oneonta St. 56
55 New Paltz St. 76
46 Utica 79
69 ■ Utica Tech 67
41 Geneseo St. 85
85 ■ Nazareth (N.Y.) 98
79 Potsdam St. 85
61 ■ Plattsburgh St. 78
66 Brockport St. 64
62 ■ Fredonia St. 91
47 ■ Buffalo St. 67

OTTERBEIN 19-10
67 Muskingum 71
58 Emory & Henry 76
84 Maryville (Tenn.) 82
67 Transylvania 65
75 ■ Hiram 69
68 ■ Capital 65
70 ■ Wittenberg 54
87 John Carroll 90
90 ■ Lake Forest 73
81 ■ Maryville (Tenn.) 75
74 ■ Mount Union 51
77 ■ Heidelberg 73
72 Marietta 79
65 Baldwin-Wallace 73
88 ■ Ohio Northern 89
84 ■ Muskingum 63
77 Hiram 80
100 Heidelberg 99
114 ■ Marietta 67
73 Capital 74
85 Mount Union 66
100 ■ John Carroll 96
73 Ohio Northern 88
75 ■ Baldwin-Wallace 70
83 ■ Muskingum 71
81 † Ohio Northern 79
101 † Heidelberg 82
80 Defiance 66
68 Calvin 90

PACE 17-12
68 Sacred Heart 77
59 East Stroudsburg 64
60 ■ Kutztown 54
63 ■ Le Moyne 65
93 ■ LIU-C.W. Post 85
75 † Plymouth St. 82
90 † Bates 58
58 † Indiana (Pa.) 77
58 † Dowling 48
58 LIU-Southampton 52
79 ■ Concordia (N.Y.) 68
66 Dowling 53
69 ■ Mercy 75
45 ■ Phila. Textile 64
61 Queens (N.Y.) 50
46 LIU-C.W. Post 62
65 ■ St. Rose 44
68 ■ LIU-Southampton 46
55 ■ Queens (N.Y.) 53
62 Mercy 57
76 Adelphi 61
47 Phila. Textile 62
48 † Adelphi 59
73 ■ Dowling 70
66 St. Rose 65
93 Concordia (N.Y.) 58
71 ■ Concordia (N.Y.) 56
64 † St. Rose 75
68 Bridgeport 76

PACIFIC (CAL.) 16-11

62 Oregon St. 79
80 ■ Oregon 68
65 ■ San Francisco 66
56 † Western Mich. 63
69 † Austin Peay 72
70 Fresno St. 49
77 ■ St. Mary's (Cal.) 57
77 ■ UC Davis 65
66 ■ UC Santa Barb. 67
68 ■ Long Beach St. 56
74 San Jose St. 61
71 Nevada-Las Vegas 88
48 New Mexico St. 53
71 ■ Nevada 49
86 ■ Utah St. 79
68 UC Irvine 62
58 Cal St. Fullerton 71
62 ■ Nevada-Las Vegas 56
50 ■ San Jose St. 54
71 ■ New Mexico St. 68
81 Nevada 69
72 Utah St. 62
56 ■ Cal St. Fullerton 53
65 ■ UC Irvine 56
65 UC Santa Barb. 73
69 Long Beach St. 66
54 † UC Santa Barb. 57

PAINE 16-10
75 † Elizabeth City St. 80
61 † Lincoln (Mo.) 66
85 ■ Morris 72
69 † Fla. Memorial 63
73 † Catawba 79
68 Howard 83
87 Morris 70
83 Morris Brown 68
59 ■ Alabama A&M 61
76 ■ Savannah St. 60
82 ■ Albany St. (Ga.) 69
80 ■ Morehouse 63
86 Savannah St. 82
74 ■ Clark Atlanta 62
87 ■ LeMoyne-Owen 77
91 ■ Fort Valley St. 93
67 Albany St. (Ga.) 65
66 Clark Atlanta 48
60 Tuskegee 62
66 ■ Morris Brown 53
74 Fort Valley St. 77
79 Miles 68
93 Alabama A&M 108
86 † Augusta 82
71 † Morehouse 68
75 † LeMoyne-Owen 86

PARKS 5-18
47 Oakland City 106
74 † St. Louis Christian 95
39 ■ Southwestern (Tex.) 75
63 Lincoln Chrst. 78
53 Lindenwood 81
29 Union (Tenn.) 82
65 Bethel (Tenn.) 103
49 ■ MacMurray 67
54 ■ Maryville (Mo.) 61
49 ■ Westminster (Mo.) 62
64 ■ Lincoln Chrst. 57
49 Blackburn 74
37 ■ Fontbonne 62
53 Principia 60
65 ■ Webster 63
48 MacMurray 75
53 Maryville (Mo.) 65
60 Webster 55
59 Westminster (Mo.) 61
73 ■ Blackburn 52
64 Fontbonne 69
77 ■ Principia 67
59 † Fontbonne 72

PEMBROKE ST. 10-16
80 ■ Methodist 52
74 Coker 77
65 Queens (N.C.) 84
84 Mount Olive 85
64 ■ Augusta 71
68 ■ Fayetteville St. 60
64 ■ St. Andrews 66
80 ■ Francis Marion 76
79 Georgia Col. 82
67 Columbus 76
76 ■ S.C.-Spartanburg 83
58 ■ Lander 48
59 ■ Longwood 61
63 Armstrong St. 67
58 S.C.-Aiken 80
83 Augusta 86
83 Francis Marion 80
62 ■ S.C.-Aiken 82
71 ■ Wofford 73
93 ■ Georgia Col. 90
82 ■ Columbus 68
94 ■ Armstrong St. 87
99 Barton 72
71 S.C.-Spartanburg 84
70 Lander 67
66 Augusta 70

PENNSYLVANIA 22-5
68 ■ Virginia 74
78 Navy 58
71 La Salle 44
78 ■ Holy Cross 76
71 † Villanova 59
64 † Northwestern 61
51 New Mexico 54
78 Lehigh 68
88 ■ Dartmouth 63
86 ■ Harvard 74
89 ■ American 84
58 † Temple 72
72 ■ St. Joseph's (Pa.) 94
64 ■ Princeton 46
89 Lafayette 65
89 Brown 54
51 Yale 50
84 ■ Columbia 63
66 ■ Cornell 62
81 Harvard 62
82 Dartmouth 63
75 Cornell 69
74 Columbia 67
71 ■ Yale 49
70 ■ Brown 60
52 Princeton 51
50 † Massachusetts 54

PENN ST. 7-20
65 Duquesne 76
60 ■ Mt. St. Mary's (Md.) 55
68 Miami (Ohio) 81
56 ■ Akron 50
75 ■ James Madison 74
73 ■ Drexel 64
61 † Temple 70
69 Toledo 60
65 Bowling Green 73
68 ■ Ohio St. 71
57 Indiana 105
70 ■ Northwestern 68
54 ■ Purdue 61
66 Illinois 82
68 ■ Wisconsin 75
67 Minnesota 95
59 Ohio St. 62
84 ■ Indiana 88
58 Northwestern 67
70 ■ Michigan 80
66 ■ Illinois 74
58 ■ Iowa 74
38 Iowa 58
62 Wisconsin 58
41 ■ Minnesota 67
49 Purdue 57
53 Michigan St. 70

PENN ST.-BEHREND 10-15
60 Ohio Wesleyan 61
64 † Greensboro 82
64 † Hiram 85
57 † Alfred 52
78 ■ Hilbert 59
81 ■ Defiance 63
68 Bethany (W.Va.) 70
58 Fredonia St. 62
62 ■ Cedarville 67
71 ■ Houghton 69
62 ■ Allegheny 88
62 ■ Grove City 65
71 Waynesburg 59
56 ■ Daemen 62
60 ■ Fredonia St. 57
68 ■ Bethany (W.Va.) 51
48 ■ Alfred 46
45 Buffalo St. 48
70 Oberlin 59
54 ■ Thiel 55
58 Grove City 69
75 ■ Keuka 68
62 Thiel 64
72 Houghton 82
66 Keuka 75

PEPPERDINE 23-8
69 Texas Tech 72
89 ■ Sonoma St. 64
65 N.C.-Charlotte 56
55 ■ UC Santa Barb. 60
68 Montana 58
92 Boise St. 88
81 ■ Geo. Washington 79
79 † Georgia St. 60
67 Tenn.-Chatt. 80
69 ■ Drexel 56
90 ■ Quincy 60
116 ■ Oral Roberts 76
67 ■ Gonzaga 66
80 ■ Portland 69
71 San Francisco 66
54 St. Mary's (Cal.) 46
65 ■ St. Mary's (Cal.) 53
72 ■ San Francisco 75
73 Santa Clara 71
76 San Diego 64
61 ■ San Diego 57
58 ■ Santa Clara 63
78 Loyola (Cal.) 66
80 ■ Loyola (Cal.) 54
67 Portland 49
52 Gonzaga 63
80 † Loyola (Cal.) 66
88 San Francisco 67
63 ■ Santa Clara 73
53 UC Santa Barb. 50
59 Southern Cal 71

PFEIFFER 23-6
101 ■ West Va. Wesleyan 64
73 † Longwood 65
117 ■ Warren Wilson 30
105 † Trevecca Nazarene 78
57 † LIFE (Ga.) 63
115 ■ Limestone 74
97 Jacksonville St. 80
93 Ga. Southwestern 89
76 Tampa 87
92 ■ Ferrum 81
92 ■ Belmont Abbey 55
93 Coker 61
105 ■ Lees-McRae 82
83 St. Andrews 64
115 ■ Barton 108
68 ■ Longwood 72
87 ■ High Point 62
83 Mount Olive 62
40 ■ Coker 44
79 Belmont Abbey 49
81 Lees-McRae 72
84 ■ St. Andrews 63
86 High Point 82
76 Barton 65
89 ■ Mount Olive 66
84 ■ Belmont Abbey 80
69 ■ Mount Olive 62
74 ■ Lenoir-Rhyne 83
81 † Ozarks (Ark.) 87

PHILA. TEXTILE 30-2
74 ■ East Stroudsburg 62
67 Kutztown 56
53 La Salle 59
81 Bloomsburg 60
103 ■ Eastern (Pa.) 55
72 Holy Family 53
76 ■ West Chester 55
99 ■ Concordia (N.Y.) 63
84 ■ St. Rose 68
84 ■ New York Tech 60
92 LIU-Southampton 52
93 Mercy 59
78 ■ LIU-C.W. Post 64
80 ■ Dowling 54
64 Pace 45
65 Adelphi 58
96 Concordia (N.Y.) 64
94 ■ Queens (N.Y.) 62
72 St. Rose 59
68 ■ Adelphi 48
72 Dowling 65
111 ■ Mercy 84
62 ■ Pace 47
72 LIU-C.W. Post 55
67 Queens (N.Y.) 42
74 ■ LIU-Southampton 48
86 ■ Dowling 61
101 ■ Adelphi 69
85 ■ St. Rose 75
70 † Gannon 56
70 Millersville 62
76 † Wayne St. (Mich.) 78

PITTSBURG ST. 13-13
66 † Cameron 78
76 † Colorado-CS 40
60 Friends 63
77 † North Ala. 64
82 † Arkansas Tech 86
85 ■ William Jewell 65
85 ■ Drury 67
64 ■ Fort Hays St. 58
58 Mo. Southern St. 74
66 ■ Rockhurst 63
78 ■ Cameron 58
92 ■ Northwest Mo. St. 82
54 Southwest Baptist 66
69 Washburn 70
87 ■ Lincoln (Mo.) 77
79 Missouri-Rolla 83
58 ■ Mo. Southern St. 69
72 Mo.-St. Louis 87
68 ■ Southwest Baptist 79
66 Mo. Western St. 86
63 Lincoln (Mo.) 61
80 ■ Missouri-Rolla 71
69 ■ Mo.-St. Louis 68
58 Central Mo. St. 76
72 ■ Northeast Mo. St. 68
72 ■ Emporia St. 78

PITTSBURGH 17-11
89 ■ St. Francis (Pa.) 75
95 ■ Marshall 81
66 Georgetown 80
82 ■ West Va. 78
102 † Duquesne 91
80 ■ Cornell 72
87 ■ Robert Morris 63
91 ■ UCLA 79
91 ■ Providence 85
85 ■ Miami (Fla.) 78
77 St. John's (N.Y.) 85
80 Connecticut 78
76 ■ Seton Hall 73
81 Boston College 70
86 Miami (Fla.) 84
79 ■ Syracuse 95

76 ■ Villanova 82
71 ■ St. John's (N.Y.) 69
73 Seton Hall 91
95 Illinois 79
56 ■ Boston College 79
80 ■ Connecticut 81
48 Providence 53
51 ■ Georgetown 48
77 Villanova 76
74 Syracuse 78
50 † Syracuse 55
65 † Utah 86

PITT.-JOHNSTOWN 8-18
84 † West Liberty St. 86
77 † Calif. (Pa.) 85
77 Mansfield 79
54 Marshall 80
90 ■ Wheeling Jesuit 73
78 Clarion 85
82 West Liberty St. 79
75 Le Moyne 90
84 † Kutztown 83
82 St. Vincent 71
79 ■ Lincoln (Pa.) 76
71 Indiana (Pa.) 101
78 ■ Calif. (Pa.) 92
79 Shippensburg 66
61 ■ Longwood 66
83 Point Park 86
74 Edinboro 110
58 ■ Gannon 65
66 Mercyhurst 93
79 ■ Pitt.-Bradford 80
63 Slippery Rock 75
62 ■ Shippensburg 70
62 Gannon 78
85 ■ Bloomsburg 84
97 ■ Slippery Rock 87
90 ■ Mercyhurst 93

PLATTSBURGH ST. 15-11
60 Eastern Conn. St. 65
63 † Ithaca 71
88 ■ New Paltz St. 80
94 ■ Oneonta St. 81
75 ■ Potsdam St. 66
75 Cortland St. 83
69 Binghamton 83
90 ■ Albany (N.Y.) 77
99 ■ Johnson St. 72
85 ■ Bri'water (Mass.) 70
65 ■ Buffalo St. 73
77 ■ Fredonia St. 51
102 St. Lawrence 78
90 New Paltz St. 98
63 Oneonta St. 49
71 Brockport St. 68
84 Geneseo St. 110
89 ■ Cortland St. 76
77 ■ Binghamton 80
70 ■ Clarkson 59
93 ■ Utica Tech 82
78 Oswego St. 61
79 Potsdam St. 93
90 Castleton St. 76
70 † Fredonia St. 79
98 Hamilton 105

PLYMOUTH ST. 12-13
110 ■ Johnson St. 73
115 Salem St. 111
82 ■ New Hamp. Col. 126
111 ■ Rivier 82
89 ■ Thomas 68
61 Castleton St. 73
82 † Pace 75
91 Merrimack 94
89 ■ Norwich 57
53 Southern Me. 80
71 Rhode Island Col. 70
74 ■ Bates 81
83 ■ Framingham St. 85
90 ■ Rhode Island Col. 74

102 New England Col. 66
104 ■ Southern Me. 102
85 ■ Eastern Conn. St. 91
89 Mass.-Boston 95
79 Mass.-Dartmouth 99
101 New England 91
76 Eastern Conn. St. 98
101 ■ Mass.-Dartmouth 103
69 ■ Mass.-Boston 77
78 Mass.-Boston 74
72 † Mass.-Dartmouth 74

POLYTECHNIC (N.Y.) 2-20
54 † Southern Vt. 62
39 † New England Col. 78
71 St. Joseph's (N.Y.) 88
55 † Bard 51
73 Medgar Evers 113
47 ■ Yeshiva 85
56 ■ St. Joseph's (N.Y.) 82
50 ■ Stevens Tech 61
55 ■ Old Westbury 81
39 Maritime (N.Y.) 48
43 New Jersey Tech 115
62 ■ Vassar 63
75 † Southern Vt. 93
66 Bard 65
70 Stevens Tech 88
67 ■ New Jersey Tech 123
52 ■ Maritime (N.Y.) 58
49 Yeshiva 89
53 Vassar 63
72 ■ Pratt 91
83 Mt. St. Vincent 109
50 Yeshiva 90

POMONA-PITZER 16-9
83 Menlo 79
75 † UC Santa Cruz 37
69 ■ UC San Diego 65
66 ■ Carleton 64
75 Southern Cal Col. 101
70 ■ Christ-Irvine 67
73 Cal Baptist 62
45 ■ Wooster 62
84 Azusa-Pacific 94
62 † Rowan 83
95 † Haverford 65
106 Redlands 105
65 ■ Cal Tech 30
57 Occidental 67
54 ■ Cal Lutheran 57
70 ■ La Verne 60
77 Claremont-M-S 71
78 Whittier 66
74 ■ Redlands 72
65 Cal Tech 52
60 ■ Occidental 62
61 Cal Lutheran 92
68 La Verne 101
69 ■ Claremont-M-S 62
93 ■ Whittier 80

PORTLAND 9-18
80 Eastern Wash. 89
89 ■ Seattle 87
83 ■ Cal St. Sacramento 55
96 ■ Pac. Lutheran 71
66 ■ Montana 74
65 Air Force 96
64 Idaho St. 88
61 ■ Dartmouth 57
84 ■ Hartford 97
78 ■ Montana St. 67
69 Weber St. 86
63 Cal St. Sacramento 59
65 Loyola (Cal.) 80
69 Pepperdine 80
64 ■ San Diego 63
74 ■ Santa Clara 77
53 Gonzaga 71
65 ■ Gonzaga 63
69 San Francisco 94
49 St. Mary's (Cal.) 60

68 ■ St. Mary's (Cal.) 74
88 ■ San Francisco 94
60 Santa Clara 66
71 San Diego 82
49 ■ Pepperdine 67
69 ■ Loyola (Cal.) 66
57 † Gonzaga 77

POTSDAM ST. 10-15
78 ■ Staten Island 82
67 ■ Oneonta St. 64
69 ■ New Paltz St. 66
66 Plattsburgh St. 75
96 Cortland St. 88
72 † Jersey City St. 69
70 Western Conn. St. 82
70 ■ Scranton 79
89 Keuka 78
63 ■ Fredonia St. 65
66 ■ Buffalo St. 86
70 Oneonta St. 72
54 New Paltz St. 55
77 ■ Clarkson 73
60 Geneseo St. 80
69 Brockport St. 78
57 Binghamton 74
62 ■ Binghamton 63
87 ■ Cortland St. 83
90 St. Lawrence 70
85 ■ Oswego St. 79
75 Utica Tech 84
93 ■ Plattsburgh St. 79
44 Albany (N.Y.) 48
56 † Geneseo St. 78

PRAIRIE VIEW 1-26
96 ■ La. Christian 108
90 ■ Ark. Baptist 76
48 St. Bonaventure 92
87 Wright St. 112
62 † Eastern Mich. 87
61 Ala.-Birmingham 111
77 Lamar 138
74 Tulane 107
70 ■ Brown 73
57 ■ Jackson St. 97
92 ■ Alabama St. 96
87 ■ Texas Col. 103
83 Grambling 103
80 Mississippi Val. 107
89 ■ Alcorn St. 107
75 ■ Southern-B.R. 99
77 ■ Texas Southern 104
88 ■ Lamar 143
76 Jackson St. 93
74 Alabama St. 95
82 Oral Roberts 84
87 ■ Grambling 89
92 ■ Mississippi Val. 100
69 Alcorn St. 100
91 Southern-B.R. 155
72 Texas Southern 79
70 † Jackson St. 103

PRESBYTERIAN 27-5
83 ■ Lees-McRae 50
84 † St. Thomas (Fla.) 47
85 Barry 75
118 ■ Newberry 90
62 Belmont Abbey 81
71 ■ Wofford 66
87 ■ Gardner-Webb 75
85 ■ Erskine 66
63 Lander 54
67 S.C.-Aiken 61
73 Catawba 70
68 Elon 52
99 ■ Wingate 56
72 Carson-Newman 57
76 ■ Mars Hill 71
80 ■ Lenoir-Rhyne 86
82 Wofford 70
68 Gardner-Webb 58
81 ■ Lander 61

72 ■ Catawba 61
73 ■ Elon 61
80 Wingate 73
87 ■ Carson-Newman 61
73 Newberry 68
74 Mars Hill 69
72 Lenoir-Rhyne 67
79 Catawba 78
86 † Gardner-Webb 77
70 † Lenoir-Rhyne 79
71 ■ Mars Hill 56
66 ■ Lenoir-Rhyne 74
79 † Georgetown (Ky.) 92

PRINCETON 15-11
65 Lafayette 48
53 † Texas 63
51 † South Caro. 40
61 ■ Loyola (Md.) 37
51 † Florida A&M 43
50 Illinois 58
50 † North Caro. St. 41
49 † Washington St. 72
75 † New Hampshire 60
47 Rutgers 64
63 ■ Harvard 39
76 ■ Dartmouth 57
82 ■ Wash. & Jeff. 60
65 ■ La Salle 60
46 Pennsylvania 64
46 Yale 40
41 Brown 48
62 ■ Cornell 50
69 ■ Columbia 71
63 Dartmouth 60
63 Harvard 57
57 Columbia 65
49 Cornell 54
60 ■ Brown 56
53 ■ Yale 62
51 ■ Pennsylvania 52

PRINCIPIA 3-21
50 ■ Greenville 85
57 Aurora 118
48 Grinnell 82
40 Illinois Col. 96
48 Knox 81
49 ■ Rose-Hulman 84
36 DePauw 71
58 † Oglethorpe 110
55 ■ Rhodes 75
61 ■ Fontbonne 57
73 Webster 75
41 ■ MacMurray 81
65 Maryville (Mo.) 79
61 ■ Westminster (Mo.) 77
55 Blackburn 67
60 ■ Parks 53
51 Fontbonne 67
56 ■ Blackburn 52
53 ■ Webster 64
61 MacMurray 82
75 ■ Maryville (Mo.) 84
67 Westminster (Mo.) 76
67 Parks 77
62 † MacMurray 68

PROVIDENCE 20-13
87 ■ Brown 57
78 ■ Robert Morris 49
56 ■ New Hampshire 27
79 ■ Rhode Island 81
71 ■ Notre Dame 52
81 ■ Arizona 66
92 ■ Boston U. 61
85 Pittsburgh 91
76 St. John's (N.Y.) 86
79 ■ Seton Hall 91
73 ■ Boston College 65
57 ■ Syracuse 69
66 Miami (Fla.) 75
61 Connecticut 68
77 ■ Villanova 66
78 ■ Dartmouth 58

71 Seton Hall 90
66 Georgetown 58
64 ■ St. John's (N.Y.) 73
68 ■ Georgetown 50
75 ■ Miami (Fla.) 60
74 Villanova 59
53 ■ Pittsburgh 48
67 Syracuse 68
74 ■ Connecticut 71
58 Boston College 57
73 † Connecticut 55
60 † Seton Hall 69
73 ■ James Madison 61
68 ■ West Va. 67
75 Boston College 58
70 † Minnesota 76
52 † Ala.-Birmingham 55

PURDUE 18-10

73 † Connecticut 69
85 ■ Weber St. 64
88 ■ East Tenn. St. 74
84 ■ Loyola (Ill.) 70
92 ■ Indiana St. 63
48 Southwest Mo. St. 45
67 † Florida 63
63 UTEP 61
80 ■ Butler 54
70 ■ Michigan 80
60 Minnesota 81
76 ■ Wisconsin 60
61 Penn St. 54
65 ■ Indiana 74
83 Northwestern 73
64 ■ Michigan St. 72
62 Ohio St. 57
76 Michigan 84
75 ■ Minnesota 69
90 Wisconsin 87
78 Indiana 93
70 Illinois 78
59 ■ Northwestern 62
61 Michigan St. 58
69 ■ Iowa 58
57 ■ Penn St. 49
62 ■ Ohio St. 72
68 † Rhode Island 74

QUEENS (N.Y.) 8-19

63 † Dist. Columbia 65
82 † Concordia (N.Y.) 89
69 ■ Medgar Evers 78
73 Old Westbury 67
74 Central Conn. St. 82
69 ■ Le Moyne 82
62 ■ Mercy 58
80 LIU-Southampton 68
61 ■ New York Tech 85
57 ■ Adelphi 47
70 ■ Dowling 56
65 St. Rose 74
72 ■ Concordia (N.Y.) 70
67 LIU-C.W. Post 70
60 Mercy 63
50 ■ Pace 61
75 ■ LIU-Southampton 62
68 ■ Kutztown 71
62 Phila. Textile 94
70 Adelphi 80
53 Pace 55
69 ■ LIU-C.W. Post 77
77 Dowling 89
86 Concordia (N.Y.) 75
42 ■ Phila. Textile 67
53 ■ St. Rose 64
43 ■ Concordia (N.Y.) 45

QUEENS (N.C.) 20-8

94 Gardner-Webb 86
83 ■ Savannah St. 58
84 † Coker 70
89 Georgia Col. 94
84 Winthrop 92
84 ■ Pembroke St. 65
71 ■ Wingate 70

57 Johnson Smith 59
71 Longwood 94
87 ■ Lees-McRae 72
78 ■ St. Leo 74
66 ■ Lincoln Memorial 54
79 Newberry 74
86 ■ Belmont Abbey 61
89 Averett 50
113 ■ Newberry 81
80 ■ Erskine 67
96 Wingate 94
72 ■ Wofford 62
85 ■ Averett 47
108 Alas. Fairbanks 114
92 Alas. Fairbanks 85
67 Northwest Col. 58
69 ■ Longwood 76
79 ■ Wash. & Lee 74
91 Erskine 74
93 Savannah St. 102
81 Wofford 83

QUINCY 16-11

72 ■ St. Francis (Ill.) 74
92 † Northern Mich. 94
95 † Carroll (Wis.) 84
80 ■ Northeast Mo. St. 74
85 Ky. Wesleyan 103
88 ■ Culver-Stockton 59
93 ■ Lewis 91
106 IU/PU-Ft. Wayne 116
67 St. Francis (Ill.) 99
83 ■ Southern Ind. 81
77 Cal St. Chico 81
60 Pepperdine 90
72 La Verne 68
79 Cal St. Northridge 90
62 ■ SIU-Edwardsville 63
81 ■ Wayne St. (Neb.) 69
100 ■ Mo. Baptist 87
78 ■ Wis.-Parkside 68
89 Northeast Mo. St. 66
92 Drury 88
102 ■ Mo.-St. Louis 97
63 Wayne St. (Neb.) 56
76 SIU-Edwardsville 80
92 Wis.-Parkside 87
70 Rockhurst 71
91 ■ Drury 76
96 ■ Saginaw Valley 78

QUINNIPIAC 16-13

76 ■ Assumption 74
74 New Haven 73
78 Sacred Heart 72
77 American Int'l 93
110 ■ Keene St. 101
74 Fla. Southern 72
77 Tampa 91
90 Eckerd 92
67 ■ St. Michael's 65
76 Bentley 81
85 Bryant 89
75 ■ St. Anselm 94
77 Merrimack 73
87 Springfield 79
84 ■ Stonehill 81
97 ■ American Int'l 81
76 St. Michael's 84
65 Assumption 53
65 ■ Bryant 62
74 St. Anselm 87
76 ■ Merrimack 73
82 ■ Mass.-Lowell 76
68 ■ Springfield 87
96 Stonehill 102
73 Southern Conn. St. 74
76 ■ Bentley 63
86 ■ Stonehill 75
69 Bentley 93
71 † American Int'l 73

RADFORD 15-16

62 Wake Forest 81

79 ■ Bethany (W.Va.) 51
91 ■ Va. Military 88
104 ■ Morgan St. 97
75 George Mason 95
82 † Southern Ill. 108
65 † Florida Int'l 69
92 American (P.R.) 85
63 Virginia 82
58 Western Ky. 88
99 ■ Western Md. 74
79 ■ Allentown 63
95 ■ Charleston So. 70
84 ■ Coastal Caro. 83
63 Tennessee 105
84 Campbell 87
69 N.C.-Asheville 72
81 ■ N.C.-Asheville 62
74 Liberty 94
94 Coastal Caro. 96
71 Charleston So. 60
84 ■ Campbell 89
107 ■ Winthrop 88
88 ■ Md.-Balt. County 86
90 Towson St. 98
98 Md.-Balt. County 102
98 Winthrop 87
70 ■ Towson St. 81
79 ■ Liberty 74
73 † Liberty 69
69 † Winthrop 87

RAMAPO 8-16

75 † Staten Island 80
89 Ottawa 87
51 ■ Montclair St. 79
61 ■ Stockton St. 77
57 LIU-C.W. Post 78
73 ■ Rutgers-Newark 70
68 Jersey City St. 76
71 ■ Rutgers-Camden 55
69 Albertus Magnus 67
60 Trenton St. 67
53 Wm. Paterson 62
44 ■ Rowan 62
66 Kean 70
53 Stockton St. 74
58 Montclair St. 54
79 ■ Trenton St. 65
66 Bloomfield 74
62 ■ Wm. Paterson 64
65 ■ Jersey City St. 72
64 Rutgers-Camden 58
57 ■ Kean 74
59 Western Conn. St. 70
61 Rowan 87
65 Rutgers-Newark 56

RANDOLPH-MACON 18-9

71 ■ Shenandoah 81
65 ■ Averett 59
57 Bridgewater (Va.) 66
82 † Berea 80
49 † Newport News App. 37
47 † Baldwin-Wallace 76
58 † Gordon 40
62 ■ Roanoke 64
70 Lynchburg 49
59 Guilford 63
78 Wash. & Lee 61
54 ■ Va. Wesleyan 49
63 ■ Hampden-Sydney 56
44 Roanoke 52
72 ■ East. Mennonite 56
71 ■ Guilford 56
62 ■ Emory & Henry 67
66 East. Mennonite 56
63 ■ Lynchburg 59
60 Va. Wesleyan 53
59 ■ Bridgewater (Va.) 53
78 Emory & Henry 63
49 Hampden-Sydney 75
79 ■ Wash. & Lee 48
61 ■ Hampden-Sydney 58
60 † Roanoke 59

61 † Va. Wesleyan 70

REDLANDS 10-14

132 La Sierra 71
89 † Christian Heritage 79
116 † Pt. Loma Nazarene 133
96 ■ Menlo 86
102 ■ Lewis & Clark 134
118 ■ LIFE Bible 65
104 ■ Azusa-Pacific 122
71 † Lebanon Valley 96
102 † Wilmington (Ohio) 111
112 ■ UC San Diego 127
105 ■ Pomona-Pitzer 106
101 ■ La Verne 104
78 Claremont-M-S 81
88 ■ Whittier 82
86 Cal Lutheran 99
95 Occidental 111
94 ■ Cal Tech 76
72 Pomona-Pitzer 74
72 La Verne 83
99 ■ Claremont-M-S 105
71 Whittier 67
103 ■ Cal Lutheran 102
97 ■ Occidental 95
75 Cal Tech 59

REGIS (COLO.) 18-9

82 ■ Northwestern Okla. 74
120 ■ Langston 84
92 ■ Concordia (Neb.) 81
88 ■ Tex. Wesleyan 52
86 Northern Colo. 81
64 Air Force 75
94 Colorado Mines 77
106 ■ Chadron St. 92
66 Eckerd 76
71 St. Leo 56
98 ■ Colorado Mines 83
93 ■ Concordia (Ill.) 80
77 Chadron St. 74
94 ■ Fort Lewis 86
69 Southern Colo. 79
78 Denver 84
61 Colorado Col. 62
74 ■ Colo. Christian 66
79 Metropolitan St. 80
85 ■ Northern Colo. 95
85 ■ Colorado-CS 64
81 Fort Lewis 67
87 ■ Southern Colo. 81
93 ■ Denver 89
71 Colo. Christian 73
83 ■ Metropolitan St. 92
75 Colorado-CS 58

RENSSELAER 14-10

78 † Union (N.Y.) 76
70 † Albany (N.Y.) 84
71 ■ Williams 63
85 Middlebury 87
85 Skidmore 72
77 Roanoke 79
87 † Allentown 75
71 Rochester Inst. 81
84 Hobart 77
69 ■ Hartwick 51
80 ■ St. Lawrence 79
92 ■ Clarkson 78
79 Alfred 82
64 Ithaca 67
85 ■ Hobart 73
83 ■ Rochester Inst. 86
65 ■ Ithaca 87
81 ■ Alfred 74
99 Union (N.Y.) 97
84 Clarkson 71
104 St. Lawrence 84
96 ■ Utica 83
65 Hartwick 72
60 ■ Albany (N.Y.) 65

RHODE ISLAND 19-11

85 Fordham 59

68 Eastern Mich. 60
81 Providence 79
65 Wake Forest 69
98 ■ Hartford 67
78 † Alabama 79
80 † Harvard 67
79 Arizona 87
87 ■ Iona 80
80 Northeastern 72
86 West Va. 82
96 ■ St. Bonaventure 82
80 ■ Hofstra 68
72 Massachusetts 84
75 Geo. Washington 88
90 ■ Brown 50
67 Temple 69
100 ■ Rutgers 81
65 ■ St. Joseph's (Pa.) 74
69 ■ West Va. 59
83 St. Bonaventure 81
67 ■ Temple 65
71 † Massachusetts 68
63 Rutgers 67
80 St. Joseph's (Pa.) 84
75 ■ Geo. Washington 72
86 † Geo. Washington 75
50 † Massachusetts 76
74 † Purdue 68
67 † North Caro. 112

RHODE ISLAND COL. 4-20
66 Bryant 73
80 ■ Colby-Sawyer 86
67 Framingham St. 101
81 Fitchburg St. 66
78 ■ Roger Williams 63
63 Salve Regina 52
80 ■ Southern Me. 97
79 Embry-Riddle 98
78 Flagler 96
32 Fla. Southern 107
59 Mass.-Dartmouth 75
70 ■ Plymouth St. 71
78 ■ Bri'water (Mass.) 81
79 ■ Westfield St. 89
74 Plymouth St. 90
66 ■ Mass.-Boston 88
70 Eastern Conn. St. 76
77 ■ Mass.-Dartmouth 89
69 Wheaton (Mass.) 78
64 Southern Me. 79
66 ■ Eastern Conn. St. 75
64 Mass.-Boston 67
76 ■ Nichols 72
48 Southern Me. 69

RHODES 21-6
96 † Asbury 74
92 Maryville (Tenn.) 100
104 ■ Savannah A&D 36
91 Maryville (Mo.) 78
89 † Westminster (Mo.) 88
72 ■ Rose-Hulman 93
114 ■ Maryville (Mo.) 70
90 Fontbonne 80
75 Principia 55
84 MacMurray 65
85 ■ Sewanee 72
81 ■ Oglethorpe 59
77 ■ Hendrix 62
66 ■ Trinity (Tex.) 52
82 ■ Fontbonne 67
89 Fisk 66
74 Centre 72
64 Hendrix 61
56 Trinity (Tex.) 58
77 ■ Millsaps 71
60 Millsaps 50
92 ■ Fisk 56
71 ■ Centre 69
76 Sewanee 84
60 Oglethorpe 68
71 ■ Va. Wesleyan 62
74 Chris. Newport 84

RICE 18-10
71 ■ Michigan 75
89 † Murray St. 78
68 Washington 60
65 † Delaware 71
60 † Xavier (Ohio) 75
75 Colorado St. 79
78 ■ Monmouth (N.J.) 57
92 Texas 87
83 ■ Fairfield 72
89 Mississippi 79
66 Texas A&M 65
84 ■ Texas Christian 65
67 ■ Texas Tech 59
87 Baylor 96
72 ■ Mississippi 67
101 ■ Texas 83
65 Houston 61
77 Southern Methodist 78
68 Texas Christian 50
84 ■ Baylor 77
86 Texas Tech 79
67 Fordham 69
90 ■ Southern Methodist 67
89 ■ Houston 78
76 ■ Texas A&M 82
76 † Texas 81
77 Wisconsin 73
68 Boston College 101

RICHMOND 15-12
77 ■ Va. Military 65
73 Navy 54
63 ■ Va. Commonwealth 82
74 Wake Forest 88
70 † Detroit Mercy 82
65 † Duquesne 70
61 La Salle 71
89 Army 71
80 ■ N.C.-Wilmington 83
74 ■ East Caro. 65
69 ■ Siena 67
75 Old Dominion 59
54 ■ William & Mary 53
70 James Madison 90
74 ■ American 73
81 George Mason 62
91 N.C.-Wilmington 69
72 East Caro. 63
84 ■ Old Dominion 80
77 Geo. Washington 79
60 ■ Georgia Tech 65
73 ■ James Madison 78
63 William & Mary 66
61 ■ George Mason 58
69 American 63
79 ■ Hofstra 48
58 ■ N.C.-Wilmington 71

RIDER 19-11
74 Seton Hall 87
72 Lafayette 56
64 Army 69
62 † Bowling Green 68
66 † Air Force 75
82 ■ Niagara 94
99 ■ St. Francis (N.Y.) 61
62 LIU-Brooklyn 59
83 ■ Marist 73
63 FDU-Teaneck 73
68 Robert Morris 59
73 St. Francis (Pa.) 68
82 ■ Brown 70
55 Mt. St. Mary's (Md.) 62
85 ■ Monmouth (N.J.) 64
71 Wagner 67
76 Bucknell 78
84 ■ LIU-Brooklyn 76
78 St. Francis (N.Y.) 102
68 ■ FDU-Teaneck 58
65 Marist 69
67 ■ St. Francis (Pa.) 63
76 ■ Robert Morris 65
88 ■ Mt. St. Mary's (Md.) 71
58 ■ Wagner 54
79 Monmouth (N.J.) 73
92 ■ LIU-Brooklyn 85
93 ■ FDU-Teaneck 63
65 ■ Wagner 64
52 † Kentucky 96

RIPON 18-6
94 ■ Coe 69
92 ■ Marian (Wis.) 64
83 ■ Ill. Benedictine 70
75 ■ N'western (Wis.) 62
93 ■ Lawrence 55
81 Concordia (Ill.) 70
81 ■ Trinity (Tex.) 66
59 † Westminster (Pa.) 56
48 Buffalo St. 66
74 Lawrence 61
84 ■ Carroll (Wis.) 62
70 ■ Monmouth (Ill.) 56
71 ■ Cornell College 50
80 Knox 83
93 Illinois Col. 96
81 Lake Forest 73
58 Beloit 66
68 St. Norbert 53
88 ■ Lake Forest 62
50 ■ Beloit 72
71 Carroll (Wis.) 50
62 ■ St. Norbert 54
91 † Knox 76
83 Beloit 86

ROANOKE 20-6
88 ■ Goucher 73
108 ■ Ferrum 83
83 ■ Emory & Henry 90
102 East. Mennonite 87
98 † Centre 72
73 Wittenberg 90
79 ■ Rensselaer 77
108 ■ Millsaps 71
64 Randolph-Macon 62
90 Wash. & Lee 73
81 Lynchburg 70
60 ■ Bridgewater (Va.) 55
87 Va. Wesleyan 91
80 Guilford 77
52 ■ Randolph-Macon 44
65 ■ Va. Wesleyan 50
84 Emory & Henry 105
72 Bridgewater (Va.) 84
85 ■ Hampden-Sydney 76
73 ■ Lynchburg 69
75 ■ East. Mennonite 69
82 ■ Wash. & Lee 64
90 ■ Guilford 71
85 Hampden-Sydney 79
71 ■ Guilford 58
59 † Randolph-Macon 60

ROBERT MORRIS 9-18
56 West Va. 76
49 Providence 78
72 ■ Ohio 70
79 Duquesne 97
63 † Canisius 61
63 Pittsburgh 87
63 Memphis St. 78
65 Marshall 91
59 Wagner 68
66 Monmouth (N.J.) 58
50 ■ St. Francis (Pa.) 53
59 ■ Rider 68
90 ■ Mt. St. Mary's (Md.) 76
77 LIU-Brooklyn 76
60 Marist 72
53 FDU-Teaneck 54
77 St. Francis (N.Y.) 78
46 ■ Monmouth (N.J.) 54
48 ■ Wagner 51
74 St. Francis (Pa.) 76
75 Mt. St. Mary's (Md.) 96
65 Rider 76
81 ■ St. Francis (N.Y.) 73
84 ■ LIU-Brooklyn 66
84 ■ Marist 82
65 ■ FDU-Teaneck 55
77 ■ LIU-Brooklyn 80

ROCHESTER 11-14
79 ■ Alfred 61
71 ■ Nazareth (N.Y.) 72
76 ■ Keuka 44
78 ■ Skidmore 54
66 ■ Case Reserve 53
90 ■ Brandeis 76
49 Johns Hopkins 47
67 Washington (Mo.) 77
53 Chicago 37
65 † Nazareth (N.Y.) 66
67 † Hobart 73
70 † Roberts Wesleyan 57
76 ■ Emory 74
48 ■ New York U. 50
50 St. John Fisher 51
52 ■ Carnegie Mellon 64
63 ■ Rochester Inst. 66
54 New York U. 72
58 Emory 60
67 Hamilton 78
54 Carnegie Mellon 47
57 Hobart 61
56 ■ Chicago 60
79 ■ Washington (Mo.) 80
63 Brandeis 61

ROCHESTER INST. 22-6
77 Baruch 78
78 Keuka 71
71 ■ Hartwick 77
95 ■ Gallaudet 50
76 ■ Roberts Wesleyan 69
81 ■ Rensselaer 71
75 † Brockport St. 82
92 ■ Roberts Wesleyan 69
90 ■ Hobart 86
82 ■ Hobart 72
66 ■ Ithaca 62
80 ■ Alfred 70
73 St. John Fisher 63
83 ■ Houghton 82
103 St. Lawrence 81
100 Clarkson 73
66 Rochester 63
54 Hartwick 57
86 Rensselaer 83
63 Hobart 66
86 ■ Clarkson 65
123 ■ St. Lawrence 82
94 Nazareth (N.Y.) 73
81 Alfred 64
56 Ithaca 58
97 ■ Utica 74
97 † St. John Fisher 74
105 Hamilton 95

ROCKFORD 8-17
66 † Marian (Wis.) 70
92 † Coe 89
86 ■ Eureka 87
72 ■ Rosary 70
66 Beloit 71
69 Loras 79
57 Dubuque 67
67 Barat 50
66 ■ Augustana (Ill.) 74
59 North Central 76
97 Mt. St. Clare 91
69 ■ Concordia (Wis.) 94
72 Aurora 90
63 ■ DePauw 83
42 Ill. Benedictine 71
65 ■ Concordia (Ill.) 71
65 ■ Judson 61
67 Trinity (Ill.) 55
64 St. Ambrose 78
64 ■ Aurora 60
58 ■ Ill. Benedictine 63

73 Concordia (Ill.) 79
68 ■ Wheaton (Ill.) 71
67 Judson 73
50 ■ Trinity (Ill.) 47

ROGER WILLIAMS 10-14
46 ■ Coast Guard 66
72 Emerson-MCA 58
47 Connecticut Col. 76
86 ■ Mass. Pharmacy 57
78 ■ Wentworth Inst. 70
63 Rhode Island Col. 78
66 ■ Anna Maria 99
69 ■ Curry 82
48 Eastern Nazarene 74
84 New England Col. 81
81 Nichols 94
56 Gordon 69
65 Salve Regina 68
65 ■ Wentworth Inst. 59
51 Curry 60
63 ■ Salve Regina 66
48 ■ Suffolk 89
60 ■ Eastern Nazarene 58
84 ■ New England Col. 72
85 Wentworth Inst. 74
64 ■ Gordon 53
83 ■ Johnson & Wales 79
95 Anna Maria 124
73 Salve Regina 77

ROLLINS 19-8
90 ■ Flagler 68
74 Embry-Riddle 78
79 ■ Morehouse 67
72 ■ St. Cloud St. 65
91 ■ North Central 58
98 ■ Milwaukee Engr. 42
92 ■ New Haven 85
75 ■ Tri-State 61
69 ■ Bentley 72
81 ■ Wesley 48
87 ■ Caldwell 68
76 Tampa 79
38 ■ Fla. Southern 44
98 Barry 90
78 ■ Eckerd 63
86 North Fla. 72
56 Kansas 103
70 ■ Florida Tech 50
66 Fla. Southern 84
81 ■ Barry 64
79 Eckerd 67
71 ■ St. Leo 62
81 ■ North Fla. 72
81 St. Leo 78
56 Florida Tech 51
62 ■ Tampa 65
60 † Fla. Southern 66

ROSE-HULMAN 15-10
73 Albion 59
71 ■ Warner Southern 50
63 Centre 81
93 Rhodes 72
54 ■ Upper Iowa 50
71 ■ Marian (Ind.) 63
84 Principia 49
67 ■ Blackburn 53
78 ■ Centre 63
75 Tampa 78
78 Eckerd 72
76 Franklin 92
70 ■ DePauw 47
62 Anderson 79
88 ■ Concordia (Wis.) 70
72 ■ Wabash 70
57 Hanover 77
63 ■ Manchester 75
102 ■ Franklin 59
71 ■ Anderson 52
67 DePauw 70
59 ■ Hanover 51
64 Wabash 72
72 Manchester 98
68 Manchester 76

ROWAN 29-2
98 † Bri'water (Mass.) 55
111 † Bapt. Bible (Pa.) 89
79 ■ Jersey City St. 66
64 Montclair St. 52
70 Kean 54
112 ■ Wm. Paterson 55
63 Stockton St. 55
96 Rutgers-Newark 55
85 Cabrini 78
83 † Pomona-Pitzer 62
75 UC San Diego 73
85 ■ Trenton St. 58
62 Ramapo 44
89 ■ Rutgers-Camden 48
69 ■ Kean 49
76 Jersey City St. 59
79 ■ Montclair St. 53
57 Trenton St. 75
90 Wm. Paterson 67
79 ■ Stockton St. 76
103 ■ Wesley 64
89 Rutgers-Camden 65
87 ■ Ramapo 61
86 ■ Rutgers-Newark 39
73 ■ Trenton St. 54
63 ■ Kean 54
84 ■ Stockton St. 61
69 ■ Frank. & Marsh. 68
80 ■ Scranton 73
81 † Augustana (Ill.) 83
95 † Mass.-Dartmouth 74

RUST 12-13
96 ■ Ark. Baptist 88
77 David Lipscomb 124
82 † Emory 79
84 Stillman 79
73 ■ Philander Smith 69
102 ■ Fisk 76
74 Ark. Baptist 76
74 Wiley 69
75 Philander Smith 73
80 ■ Southern-N.O. 78
68 ■ Wiley 62
65 ■ Xavier (La.) 69
71 † Kenyon 78
88 † Aurora 97
74 ■ Knoxville 80
87 Lane 94
60 Xavier (La.) 63
87 LeMoyne-Owen 86
96 Knoxville 104
66 Maryville (Tenn.) 87
71 ■ Maryville (Tenn.) 84
106 ■ Stillman 101
63 ■ LeMoyne-Owen 80
75 ■ Lane 69
76 Stillman 92

RUTGERS 13-15
79 ■ Tennessee 87
69 Delaware 77
82 ■ Loyola (Md.) 50
132 ■ Keene St. 83
79 † Duke 88
99 ■ LIU-Brooklyn 87
91 ■ Hofstra 64
67 † Kentucky 89
80 † Manhattan 76
61 ■ James Madison 73
64 ■ Princeton 47
90 St. Bonaventure 87
86 St. Joseph's (Pa.) 93
78 ■ Massachusetts 82
113 ■ Utah St. 93
80 ■ Temple 72
71 ■ West Va. 67
81 Rhode Island 100
100 ■ Geo. Washington 105
67 Massachusetts 82
89 Holy Cross 99
66 West Va. 77
90 ■ St. Joseph's (Pa.) 81
82 ■ St. Bonaventure 61
67 ■ Rhode Island 63
72 Geo. Washington 74
75 Temple 89
70 † St. Joseph's (Pa.) 71

RUTGERS-CAMDEN 0-24
59 † York (N.Y.) 60
62 † Delaware Valley 64
53 ■ Trenton St. 76
75 Wm. Paterson 89
78 Rutgers-Newark 83
75 ■ Jersey City St. 93
64 ■ Kean 69
55 Ramapo 71
46 Lincoln (Pa.) 75
62 Stockton St. 86
52 Virginia St. 80
45 ■ Montclair St. 60
48 Rowan 89
67 Wilmington (Del.) 91
64 ■ Rutgers-Newark 79
40 Trenton St. 61
66 ■ Wm. Paterson 83
53 ■ Phila. Pharmacy 67
69 ■ Stockton St. 91
65 Jersey City St. 72
48 Kean 74
58 ■ Ramapo 64
65 ■ Rowan 89
59 Montclair St. 76

RUTGERS-NEWARK 7-16
59 Stockton St. 86
59 ■ Kean 64
82 ■ Baruch 79
83 ■ Rutgers-Camden 78
70 Ramapo 73
68 Wm. Paterson 78
55 ■ Rowan 96
78 ■ New Paltz St. 77
54 ■ Jersey City St. 69
63 Trenton St. 98
65 ■ Montclair St. 71
79 Rutgers-Camden 64
73 Bloomfield 82
66 ■ Stockton St. 93
50 Kean 79
60 Jersey City St. 86
71 ■ Merchant Marine 48
81 ■ Wm. Paterson 68
78 Lehman 66
56 Montclair St. 85
59 ■ Trenton St. 66
39 Rowan 86
56 ■ Ramapo 65

SACRED HEART 14-13
78 † Merrimack 69
83 † Stonehill 66
70 St. Michael's 73
77 ■ Pace 68
72 ■ Quinnipiac 78
96 ■ Bryant 68
99 St. Anselm 97
93 ■ Stonehill 77
55 † Mercy 57
74 † Dowling 56
81 Assumption 90
83 ■ Springfield 75
105 ■ Keene St. 92
86 ■ Franklin Pierce 98
73 Le Moyne 94
80 Southern Conn. St. 83
74 ■ Mass.-Lowell 75
90 New Hamp. Col. 95
99 New Haven 88
80 ■ Le Moyne 69
74 ■ Southern Conn. St. 78
75 † Mass.-Lowell 86
79 Franklin Pierce 74
102 ■ New Haven 96
101 Keene St. 84
60 ■ New Hamp. Col. 72
83 Le Moyne 101

SAGINAW VALLEY 14-11
82 ■ Spring Arbor 70
75 ■ Findlay 67
70 ■ St. Francis (Ill.) 69
82 Siena Heights 78
86 ■ Wayne St. (Mich.) 71
77 ■ Northwood 60
62 Hillsdale 83
76 Grand Valley St. 82
50 Western Mich. 65
76 ■ Aquinas 73
78 Michigan Tech 84
80 Northern Mich. 83
64 ■ Oakland 62
63 ■ Ferris St. 68
77 Lake Superior St. 58
81 Northwood 63
69 ■ Hillsdale 64
66 Wayne St. (Mich.) 92
63 ■ Grand Valley St. 64
81 ■ Michigan Tech 78
60 ■ Northern Mich. 66
60 Oakland 78
98 Ferris St. 94
64 ■ Lake Superior St. 54
78 Quincy 96

ST. ANSELM 20-11
111 † Keene St. 89
76 † Franklin Pierce 77
78 ■ Merrimack 75
79 ■ St. Rose 88
81 St. Michael's 84
87 Mass.-Lowell 85
97 ■ Sacred Heart 99
93 ■ Southern Conn. St. 76
99 Babson 72
79 ■ Stonehill 76
75 New Hamp. Col. 100
85 ■ Bentley 87
94 Quinnipiac 75
79 ■ American Int'l 70
88 ■ Bryant 71
83 Assumption 76
74 ■ St. Michael's 56
95 ■ Springfield 77
70 Merrimack 71
68 Bentley 92
87 ■ Quinnipiac 74
72 American Int'l 84
69 Bryant 62
96 ■ Assumption 86
82 Springfield 72
95 Stonehill 74
91 ■ St. Michael's 73
94 † American Int'l 78
79 Bentley 74
63 New Hamp. Col. 67
90 † Bentley 109

ST. AUGUSTINE'S 9-16
80 ■ Johnson Smith 83
81 ■ Virginia St. 76
103 ■ Morris 68
74 ■ Fayetteville St. 80
68 Hampton 65
72 ■ N.C. Central 80
92 Bowie St. 99
72 ■ Livingstone 75
75 † Norfolk St. 95
70 † West Va. St. 59
66 † Johnson Smith 84
78 ■ Winston-Salem 80
80 Shaw 81
70 Elizabeth City St. 71
62 Fayetteville St. 61
72 N.C. Central 96
80 Voorhees 78
71 ■ Virginia Union 82
92 Winston-Salem 90

101 Johnson Smith ... 113
102 ■ Shaw ... 93
63 ■ Norfolk St. ... 80
72 St. Paul's ... 104
83 Livingstone ... 68
95 † Virginia St. ... 97

ST. BONAVENTURE 10-17

83 ■ Navy ... 74
85 Canisius ... 67
92 ■ Prairie View ... 48
66 † Hofstra ... 50
74 ■ Northern Iowa ... 63
68 ■ Walsh ... 75
73 Maine ... 72
87 ■ Rutgers ... 90
78 Duquesne ... 73
82 Rhode Island ... 96
58 ■ Temple ... 74
96 Niagara ... 106
67 ■ Canisius ... 62
69 ■ Niagara ... 54
56 West Va. ... 92
78 ■ Massachusetts ... 93
64 Notre Dame ... 61
59 Geo. Washington ... 64
60 St. Joseph's (Pa.) ... 73
81 ■ Rhode Island ... 83
72 ■ Geo. Washington ... 89
61 Rutgers ... 82
69 ■ St. Joseph's (Pa.) ... 70
49 Temple ... 68
62 ■ Massachusetts ... 86
67 ■ West Va. ... 82
62 † Massachusetts ... 75

ST. CLOUD ST. 15-12

61 Gust. Adolphus ... 53
82 † Cheyney ... 54
65 Rollins ... 72
85 ■ Mt. Senario ... 68
61 ■ Minn.-Duluth ... 51
78 ■ Winona St. ... 69
89 ■ Bemidji St. ... 64
88 ■ Moorhead St. ... 68
60 ■ North Dak. St. ... 61
60 ■ North Dak. ... 70
68 South Dak. ... 83
65 Morningside ... 76
68 Mankato St. ... 80
80 North Dak. St. ... 65
90 ■ South Dak. St. ... 83
73 ■ Augustana (S.D.) ... 63
84 Northern Colo. ... 77
84 Nebraska-Omaha ... 68
87 ■ Morningside ... 82
72 ■ South Dak. ... 80
88 North Dak. ... 90
83 ■ Mankato St. ... 86
60 Augustana (S.D.) ... 80
50 South Dak. St. ... 68
79 ■ Nebraska-Omaha ... 68
79 ■ Northern Colo. ... 63
64 † North Dak. ... 68

ST. FRANCIS (N.Y.) 9-18

68 St. John's (N.Y.) ... 101
67 † Columbia ... 104
62 Yale ... 61
71 Delaware St. ... 80
73 † Tennessee St. ... 79
50 † Columbia ... 58
61 † Colorado ... 79
60 † Butler ... 91
61 Rider ... 99
71 ■ Mt. St. Mary's (Md.) ... 83
61 ■ Monmouth (N.J.) ... 67
73 ■ Wagner ... 78
62 FDU-Teaneck ... 65
72 Marist ... 77
81 ■ St. Francis (Pa.) ... 77
107 ■ LIU-Brooklyn ... 98
78 ■ Robert Morris ... 77
76 Mt. St. Mary's (Md.) ... 72
102 ■ Rider ... 78

78 Wagner ... 81
70 Monmouth (N.J.) ... 85
77 ■ Marist ... 89
84 ■ FDU-Teaneck ... 83
73 Robert Morris ... 81
71 St. Francis (Pa.) ... 66
99 LIU-Brooklyn ... 96
78 Mt. St. Mary's (Md.) ... 81

ST. FRANCIS (PA.) 9-18

75 Pittsburgh ... 89
61 Cornell ... 70
56 Buffalo ... 51
72 ■ Duquesne ... 82
66 ■ Drexel ... 77
52 Canisius ... 74
62 Cleveland St. ... 77
67 ■ Md.-Balt. County ... 59
52 Monmouth (N.J.) ... 60
60 Wagner ... 76
53 Robert Morris ... 50
70 ■ Mt. St. Mary's (Md.) ... 74
68 ■ Rider ... 73
77 St. Francis (N.Y.) ... 81
67 LIU-Brooklyn ... 86
64 Marist ... 51
54 FDU-Teaneck ... 67
68 ■ Wagner ... 69
59 ■ Monmouth (N.J.) ... 51
76 ■ Robert Morris ... 74
63 Rider ... 67
89 Mt. St. Mary's (Md.) ... 69
80 ■ LIU-Brooklyn ... 74
66 ■ St. Francis (N.Y.) ... 71
84 ■ FDU-Teaneck ... 76
66 ■ Marist ... 85
80 ■ Monmouth (N.J.) ... 91

ST. JOHN FISHER 20-6

89 ■ Green Mountain ... 55
97 ■ Merchant Marine ... 65
90 Houghton ... 70
85 ■ Clarkson ... 74
111 ■ Roberts Wesleyan ... 73
86 † Nazareth (N.Y.) ... 68
98 ■ Goucher ... 68
75 ■ Hilbert ... 61
100 ■ Hobart ... 81
79 † Nazareth (N.Y.) ... 69
75 † Geneseo St. ... 79
60 Fredonia St. ... 58
82 Waynesburg ... 70
63 ■ Rochester Inst. ... 73
51 ■ Rochester ... 50
63 Elmira ... 79
79 Keuka ... 66
78 ■ Brockport St. ... 65
75 ■ Binghamton ... 64
61 Allegheny ... 88
72 ■ Nazareth (N.Y.) ... 63
69 Alfred ... 66
73 Hobart ... 81
88 Utica ... 71
88 ■ Hartwick ... 71
74 † Rochester Inst. ... 97

ST. JOHN'S (MINN.) 20-8

65 Wis.-River Falls ... 67
80 ■ Loras ... 68
95 ■ Augsburg ... 71
61 ■ Minn.-Morris ... 77
65 Hamline ... 64
100 ■ Concordia-M'head ... 85
78 ■ Wis.-La Crosse ... 89
70 St. Mary's (Minn.) ... 76
66 Carleton ... 65
90 ■ Macalester ... 77
54 St. Thomas (Minn.) ... 57
93 ■ Gust. Adolphus ... 60
63 ■ St. Olaf ... 54
83 Bethel (Minn.) ... 67
76 Augsburg ... 74
78 ■ Hamline ... 64
68 Concordia-M'head ... 64

74 ■ St. Mary's (Minn.) ... 71
68 ■ Carleton ... 49
72 Macalester ... 68
63 ■ St. Thomas (Minn.) ... 66
67 Gust. Adolphus ... 62
57 St. Olaf ... 49
71 ■ Bethel (Minn.) ... 58
65 ■ St. Olaf ... 53
56 ■ St. Thomas (Minn.) ... 57
80 ■ Wartburg ... 75
61 St. Thomas (Minn.) ... 75

ST. JOHN'S (N.Y.) 19-11

101 ■ St. Francis (N.Y.) ... 68
90 ■ Iona ... 74
75 Niagara ... 71
72 Connecticut ... 74
55 Fordham ... 60
58 ■ Hofstra ... 56
80 Indiana ... 105
74 † Manhattan ... 59
77 † Kentucky ... 86
86 ■ Providence ... 76
85 ■ Pittsburgh ... 77
76 Villanova ... 70
78 ■ Miami (Fla.) ... 74
78 Syracuse ... 71
61 Boston College ... 71
72 ■ Connecticut ... 59
79 ■ Georgetown ... 61
69 Pittsburgh ... 71
73 Providence ... 64
65 ■ Boston College ... 61
85 ■ Seton Hall ... 95
77 Miami (Fla.) ... 82
61 Georgetown ... 56
65 ■ Villanova ... 62
90 † Syracuse ... 70
73 Seton Hall ... 92
76 † Boston College ... 56
72 † Syracuse ... 84
85 † Texas Tech ... 67
74 † Arkansas ... 80

ST. JOSEPH'S (IND.) 21-6

81 Trinity (Ill.) ... 61
64 ■ St. Francis (Ill.) ... 58
80 † Brescia ... 54
74 Anderson ... 69
74 ■ Purdue-Calumet ... 54
72 † Ill. Wesleyan ... 96
80 Olivet (Ill.) ... 75
74 ■ IU/PU-Indianapolis ... 66
68 ■ Grand Valley St. ... 57
75 Bellarmine ... 64
78 Kentucky St. ... 66
86 ■ Lewis ... 71
68 ■ Northern Ky. ... 64
81 ■ Indianapolis ... 58
69 Southern Ind. ... 85
72 Ky. Wesleyan ... 79
66 ■ Ashland ... 43
63 ■ IU/PU-Ft. Wayne ... 66
77 Lewis ... 63
83 Indianapolis ... 57
71 Northern Ky. ... 75
79 ■ Ky. Wesleyan ... 54
77 ■ Southern Ind. ... 73
66 IU/PU-Ft. Wayne ... 74
92 Ashland ... 90
81 ■ Bellarmine ... 59
99 ■ Kentucky St. ... 74

ST. JOSEPH'S (ME.) 22-7

95 † Old Westbury ... 72
68 † Montclair St. ... 59
80 Gordon ... 67
104 ■ Me.-Farmington ... 82
78 Davidson ... 98
91 New England ... 77
91 ■ Thomas ... 74
75 Stetson ... 82
85 Florida Tech ... 100
87 ■ Husson ... 74

107 ■ Johnson St. ... 65
118 ■ Lyndon St. ... 81
119 ■ New England ... 84
94 Me.-Farmington ... 105
83 ■ Bates ... 75
92 Manhattanville ... 78
88 † Bridgeport ... 100
103 ■ Atlantic Union ... 73
60 Green Mountain ... 67
114 St. Joseph (Vt.) ... 71
92 Southern Me. ... 75
104 ■ Me.-Presque Isle ... 79
92 Thomas ... 57
87 Husson ... 74
81 Me.-Machias ... 65
103 ■ Castleton St. ... 72
90 † Husson ... 86
79 † Green Mountain ... 68
74 † N'west Nazarene ... 80

ST. JOSEPH'S (PA.) 18-11

103 ■ Morgan St. ... 80
93 ■ Hartford ... 69
81 American ... 100
52 Drexel ... 47
64 † Texas A&M ... 50
65 † Notre Dame ... 68
71 Temple ... 66
73 ■ Loyola (Md.) ... 61
93 ■ Rutgers ... 86
80 St. Peter's ... 63
70 ■ West Va. ... 67
53 † La Salle ... 66
81 West Va. ... 82
94 Pennsylvania ... 72
76 ■ Hofstra ... 55
59 Geo. Washington ... 78
74 Rhode Island ... 65
77 † Villanova ... 66
73 ■ St. Bonaventure ... 60
69 ■ Massachusetts ... 81
81 Rutgers ... 90
65 ■ Temple ... 66
70 St. Bonaventure ... 69
74 ■ Geo. Washington ... 73
84 ■ Rhode Island ... 80
43 Massachusetts ... 61
71 † Rutgers ... 70
60 † Temple ... 71
34 Southwest Mo. St. ... 56

ST. LAWRENCE 3-22

95 ■ Amherst ... 104
66 ■ Middlebury ... 81
81 Oswego St. ... 88
64 † Western Conn. St. ... 82
82 † Green Mountain ... 99
82 Nazareth (N.Y.) ... 98
89 ■ Clarkson ... 85
64 Ithaca ... 78
108 Alfred ... 100
78 ■ Plattsburgh St. ... 102
79 Rensselaer ... 80
74 Hartwick ... 78
67 Utica ... 89
81 ■ Rochester Inst. ... 103
73 ■ Hobart ... 92
70 ■ Alfred ... 85
50 ■ Ithaca ... 94
70 ■ Potsdam St. ... 90
82 Rochester Inst. ... 123
69 Hobart ... 83
62 Clarkson ... 83
67 ■ Hartwick ... 65
84 ■ Rensselaer ... 104
63 Union (N.Y.) ... 112
98 Hamilton ... 134

ST. LEO 4-21

89 ■ Webber ... 94
49 Georgetown ... 88
69 ■ St. Thomas (Fla.) ... 75
92 ■ Georgia Col. ... 98

92 Flagler 90
56 ■ Regis (Colo.) 71
89 ■ Bentley 85
66 ■ Merrimack 70
93 † Barton 84
74 Queens (N.C.) 78
67 † Eckerd 72
65 Florida Tech 85
74 ■ Tampa 76
74 Eckerd 80
70 ■ Fla. Southern 106
72 Barry 80
81 North Fla. 115
81 Tampa 108
64 ■ Eckerd 77
47 Fla. Southern 66
62 Rollins 71
78 ■ Barry 83
78 ■ Rollins 81
107 ■ North Fla. 108
95 ■ Florida Tech 86

ST. LOUIS 12-17
54 UCLA 68
86 ■ Slippery Rock 42
66 South Ala. 68
101 ■ Morgan St. 76
44 Southern Ill. 57
94 ■ Southern Cal 79
83 ■ Tennessee St. 61
94 ■ Murray St. 58
52 Southwest Mo. St. 63
56 ■ Southern Methodist 63
65 ■ Cincinnati 80
59 Southern Methodist 66
53 Marquette 65
86 ■ Augustana (Ill.) 73
45 Arkansas St. 58
62 ■ Marquette 65
63 DePaul 65
78 ■ Mo.-Kansas City 70
116 ■ Chicago St. 66
39 Cincinnati 64
73 Dayton 52
69 ■ Memphis St. 77
45 Ala.-Birmingham 84
87 ■ Southern Ill. 78
92 ■ DePaul 76
72 Memphis St. 75
57 ■ Ala.-Birmingham 77
63 † Marquette 57
65 Memphis St. 73

ST. MARY'S (CAL.) 11-16
79 Northern Ariz. 89
62 Cal St. Fullerton 82
65 ■ Villanova 64
43 ■ San Fran. St. 39
37 ■ UC Santa Barb. 79
57 Pacific (Cal.) 77
61 † Ohio 73
61 † American 52
44 ■ Illinois St. 64
68 ■ Boise St. 61
62 Cal St. Sacramento 63
51 San Diego 70
53 Santa Clara 63
93 ■ Loyola (Cal.) 74
46 ■ Pepperdine 54
53 Pepperdine 65
55 Loyola (Cal.) 59
64 ■ Gonzaga 82
60 ■ Portland 49
74 Portland 68
55 Gonzaga 79
82 San Francisco 78
76 ■ San Francisco 74
69 Cal St. Northridge 61
77 ■ Santa Clara 76
65 ■ San Diego 72
68 † Santa Clara 79

ST. MARY'S (MD.) 10-15
62 Johns Hopkins 105
53 † King's (Pa.) 57
72 ■ Salisbury St. 89
59 Washington (Md.) 82
75 † Caldwell 82
104 † Capitol 65
69 ■ Wesley 64
68 Md.-Balt. County 96
68 † Mary Washington 77
64 ■ Gallaudet 54
98 Capitol 71
65 Centenary (N.J.) 69
69 Goucher 58
54 ■ Catholic 65
60 ■ York (Pa.) 73
81 Bard 53
62 Mary Washington 66
70 Gallaudet 64
70 ■ Western Md. 58
76 ■ Marymount (Va.) 75
45 York (Pa.) 86
68 ■ Goucher 61
62 Marymount (Va.) 64
71 Catholic 85
55 ■ Mary Washington 56

ST. MICHAEL'S 14-13
73 ■ Sacred Heart 70
76 Le Moyne 92
82 Middlebury 62
84 ■ St. Anselm 81
72 ■ Mass.-Lowell 69
75 ■ Norwich 55
52 Springfield 64
102 ■ New York Tech 82
78 ■ Mercyhurst 73
65 Quinnipiac 67
66 ■ American Int'l 67
64 ■ Assumption 82
85 Bryant 63
74 ■ Stonehill 59
54 Merrimack 58
57 Bentley 89
56 St. Anselm 74
84 ■ Quinnipiac 76
71 ■ Springfield 66
62 Assumption 65
78 ■ Bryant 69
79 Stonehill 85
74 ■ Merrimack 50
57 ■ Bentley 65
74 Vermont 76
76 American Int'l 74
73 St. Anselm 91

ST. NORBERT 9-13
60 Buffalo St. 55
74 † Mich.-Dearborn 66
40 ■ Wis.-Stevens Point 76
71 Wis.-Oshkosh 99
76 ■ Wheaton (Ill.) 73
67 Edgewood 57
50 Marian (Wis.) 67
89 Carroll (Wis.) 99
88 ■ Lake Forest 70
67 ■ Beloit 80
61 ■ Grinnell 48
92 ■ Coe 80
67 Monmouth (Ill.) 88
47 Cornell College 56
55 Lawrence 70
63 Lake Forest 62
44 ■ Eureka 66
53 ■ Ripon 68
72 ■ Carroll (Wis.) 57
59 ■ Lawrence 76
61 Beloit 70
54 Ripon 62

ST. OLAF 17-8
98 ■ Pillsbury 57
82 † Wis.-Superior 63
56 † Viterbo 74
82 N'western (Minn.) 66
45 St. Thomas (Minn.) 52
74 Macalester 71
39 ■ Carleton 45
68 Bethel (Minn.) 46
69 St. Mary's (Minn.) 54
63 ■ Concordia-M'head 55
63 Hamline 58
75 ■ Augsburg 92
54 St. John's (Minn.) 63
67 ■ Gust. Adolphus 64
65 ■ St. Thomas (Minn.) 29
73 ■ Macalester 50
54 Carleton 62
74 ■ Bethel (Minn.) 59
78 ■ St. Mary's (Minn.) 68
88 Concordia-M'head 77
70 ■ Hamline 63
75 Augsburg 44
49 ■ St. John's (Minn.) 57
66 Gust. Adolphus 65
53 St. John's (Minn.) 65

ST. PAUL'S 6-22
79 ■ Benedict 94
92 † Morris Brown 70
79 † Barber-Scotia 76
117 † Allen 66
73 Elizabeth City St. 76
63 ■ Winston-Salem 75
76 † Johnson Smith 90
64 † Winston-Salem 67
70 ■ Hampton 79
88 Shaw 97
55 Virginia Union 68
61 ■ Fayetteville St. 82
76 ■ Norfolk St. 88
99 ■ N.C. Central 109
72 Bowie St. 68
75 ■ Virginia St. 91
73 ■ Virginia Union 88
88 Elizabeth City St. 96
69 ■ Johnson Smith 94
90 ■ Elizabeth City St. 101
78 ■ Bowie St. 95
77 Hampton 86
84 Livingstone 92
78 Norfolk St. 97
66 Virginia St. 82
104 ■ St. Augustine's 72
73 † Fayetteville St. 62
63 † Norfolk St. 79

ST. PETER'S 9-18
73 ■ Md.-East. Shore 61
81 † Morehead St. 60
50 Ball St. 63
71 LIU-Brooklyn 69
54 Seton Hall 88
61 ■ George Mason 70
81 ■ Youngstown St. 68
67 FDU-Teaneck 61
57 San Diego 67
79 Youngstown St. 67
63 ■ St. Joseph's (Pa.) 80
79 Loyola (Md.) 68
62 Howard 67
48 ■ Manhattan 57
58 ■ Loyola (Md.) 72
52 Siena 57
57 Fairfield 59
51 ■ Siena 64
73 Iona 91
66 ■ Canisius 72
81 ■ Niagara 93
63 ■ Fairfield 56
76 ■ Iona 66
77 Manhattan 89
63 Niagara 77
55 Canisius 67
60 † Niagara 84

ST. ROSE 23-8
88 ■ Molloy 65
65 ■ Assumption 70
88 St. Anselm 79
91 ■ Mercy 76
93 ■ Adelphi 74
68 Phila. Textile 84
121 † Mt. Mercy 73
93 † Cardinal Stritch 78
76 † Cabrini 89
74 ■ Queens (N.Y.) 65
88 LIU-Southampton 93
104 LIU-C.W. Post 89
123 ■ Concordia (N.Y.) 69
80 Dowling 66
75 New York Tech 72
86 Nyack 77
90 Adelphi 85
44 Pace 65
59 ■ Phila. Textile 72
99 Concordia (N.Y.) 85
111 ■ LIU-C.W. Post 74
93 Mercy 81
112 ■ Dowling 79
73 ■ LIU-Southampton 45
65 ■ Pace 66
64 Queens (N.Y.) 53
69 ■ Mercy 52
75 † Pace 64
75 Phila. Textile 85
101 † Southern Conn. St. 82
84 Bridgeport 83

ST. THOMAS (MINN.) 19-9
80 ■ Concordia (St. Paul) 56
42 Viterbo 43
54 Biola 70
71 Grand Canyon 73
52 ■ St. Olaf 45
70 ■ Bethel (Minn.) 60
67 St. Mary's (Minn.) 54
66 Hamline 49
69 ■ Concordia-M'head 43
54 ■ Carleton 56
57 ■ St. John's (Minn.) 54
76 Macalester 59
61 Gust. Adolphus 59
58 ■ Augsburg 64
29 St. Olaf 65
88 Bethel (Minn.) 62
67 ■ St. Mary's (Minn.) 35
61 ■ Hamline 49
50 Concordia-M'head 45
55 Carleton 56
66 St. John's (Minn.) 63
82 ■ Macalester 46
67 ■ Gust. Adolphus 76
67 Augsburg 58
80 Carleton 72
57 St. John's (Minn.) 56
75 ■ St. John's (Minn.) 61
60 Wis.-Platteville 70

SALEM ST. 18-8
101 ■ Southern Me. 95
111 ■ Plymouth St. 115
99 ■ Mass.-Boston 80
88 Wheaton (Mass.) 94
76 Clark (Mass.) 78
89 ■ Rivier 61
83 ■ Stockton St. 93
107 Mass.-Dartmouth 113
71 Gordon 61
94 Fitchburg St. 73
85 ■ Westfield St. 84
68 Tufts 72
75 Framingham St. 83
80 North Adams St. 62
103 ■ Clark (Mass.) 83
98 ■ Bri'water (Mass.) 93
108 Worcester St. 91
101 ■ Fitchburg St. 65
82 Westfield St. 77
81 ■ Framingham St. 68
75 ■ North Adams St. 61
91 Bri'water (Mass.) 71
108 ■ Worcester St. 82
80 † Framingham St. 73

67 † Westfield St. 63
71 ■ Eastern Conn. St. 81

SALISBURY ST. 18-8
83 † Francis Marion 107
120 Methodist 81
89 St. Mary's (Md.) 72
88 ■ Va. Wesleyan 104
77 ■ Greensboro 75
69 ■ Walsh 80
80 ■ Md.-East. Shore 86
91 Chris. Newport 116
102 ■ N.C. Wesleyan 109
106 † Maryville (Tenn.) 95
104 † N.C. Wesleyan 95
91 ■ Washington (Md.) 69
96 ■ Frostburg St. 75
111 ■ Shenandoah 99
105 ■ Catholic 87
104 Allentown 86
123 ■ Wesley 76
101 ■ Lincoln (Pa.) 79
82 Frostburg St. 85
121 Shenandoah 116
85 ■ Allentown 82
96 Trenton St. 69
111 Wesley 76
87 Lincoln (Pa.) 99
106 Frostburg St. 97
123 † Allentown 93

SALVE REGINA 13-13
67 † Daniel Webster 53
83 Emerson-MCA 68
71 Mass.-Dartmouth 97
77 ■ Worcester St. 97
59 Suffolk 64
78 ■ Nichols 60
52 ■ Rhode Island Col. 63
62 Worcester Tech 75
74 ■ New England Col. 78
81 Gordon 74
63 ■ Curry 64
66 Anna Maria 90
81 Wentworth Inst. 75
68 ■ Roger Williams 65
74 Eastern Nazarene 76
54 ■ Gordon 31
66 Roger Williams 63
86 ■ Westbrook 89
54 Curry 58
74 ■ Anna Maria 101
61 ■ Eastern Nazarene 57
90 ■ Wentworth Inst. 72
70 New England Col. 54
77 ■ Roger Williams 73
94 Anna Maria 80
61 † Eastern Nazarene 82

SAM HOUSTON ST. 6-19
100 ■ St. Edward's 71
105 ■ Tex. Wesleyan 75
53 Kansas St. 86
77 UTEP 89
76 New Mexico St. 104
66 Gonzaga 84
75 † Alabama St. 82
68 Stephen F. Austin 79
79 Southwest Tex. St. 92
78 Texas-San Antonio 80
92 ■ Northeast La. 102
84 ■ Northwestern (La.) 82
67 Texas-Arlington 76
63 North Texas 76
62 ■ McNeese St. 61
74 ■ Nicholls St. 80
65 ■ Texas-San Antonio 71
86 ■ Southwest Tex. St. 74
84 ■ Stephen F. Austin 87
58 Northeast La. 85
89 Northwestern (La.) 114
97 ■ North Texas 89
78 ■ Texas-Arlington 100
72 Nicholls St. 91

65 McNeese St. 87

SAMFORD 17-10
73 ■ Belhaven 59
59 Tenn.-Martin 75
86 ■ Alabama St. 76
101 ■ Loyola (La.) 47
58 † Dartmouth 60
71 † Southwest Tex. St. 75
62 Southwestern La. 71
73 ■ Citadel 67
73 Northeastern Ill. 72
65 ■ Central Fla. 52
68 Mercer 81
88 ■ Stetson 71
65 ■ Florida Int'l 67
81 N.C.-Greensboro 66
69 Central Fla. 63
92 ■ Georgia St. 78
60 Centenary 57
64 Southeastern La. 56
55 ■ Furman 65
89 ■ Mercer 71
57 Stetson 76
47 Florida Int'l 58
79 ■ Northeastern Ill. 75
85 ■ Tenn.-Martin 63
71 Georgia St. 61
96 ■ Centenary 84
58 ■ Southeastern La. 66

SAN DIEGO 13-14
85 San Diego St. 60
65 Hawaii 64
74 † Long Beach St. 80
63 UCLA 90
73 ■ Weber St. 87
60 ■ Geo. Washington 74
78 ■ Cal St. Hayward 54
71 Southern Meth. 106
88 Oral Roberts 92
67 ■ St. Peter's 57
112 ■ Oral Roberts 78
59 Santa Clara 57
70 ■ St. Mary's (Cal.) 51
60 ■ San Francisco 68
63 Portland 64
64 Gonzaga 79
63 ■ Santa Clara 62
87 ■ Loyola (Cal.) 77
64 ■ Pepperdine 76
57 Pepperdine 61
59 Loyola (Cal.) 58
66 ■ Gonzaga 69
82 ■ Portland 71
81 San Francisco 85
72 St. Mary's (Cal.) 65
82 ■ Cal St. Northridge 51
93 San Francisco 96

SAN DIEGO ST. 8-21
60 ■ San Diego 85
72 ■ Cal Poly Pomona 68
64 Arizona St. 67
106 ■ Westmont 91
77 ■ Nevada-Las Vegas 89
90 ■ North Fla. 79
51 ■ Washington St. 73
65 Lamar 90
63 ■ UC Riverside 52
67 Hawaii 81
54 Wyoming 77
67 Colorado St. 82
54 ■ UTEP 76
52 ■ New Mexico 77
64 Brigham Young 76
53 Utah 78
59 ■ Air Force 51
67 ■ Fresno St. 72
72 Air Force 62
70 Fresno St. 78
77 ■ Utah 88
73 ■ Brigham Young 80
60 UTEP 77

55 New Mexico 71
64 ■ Wyoming 62
78 ■ Colorado St. 79
58 ■ Hawaii 72
59 † Wyoming 57
64 Utah 85

SAN FRANCISCO 19-12
80 ■ Humboldt St. 53
92 ■ Hofstra 61
98 ■ Monmouth (N.J.) 66
79 ■ California 89
66 Pacific (Cal.) 65
61 DePaul 91
78 ■ Nevada 76
67 Fresno St. 73
78 † Missouri 71
86 † Idaho 85
72 † Ball St. 81
70 ■ Texas Christian 62
97 ■ Sonoma St. 67
70 ■ Maine 68
80 Santa Clara 91
68 San Diego 60
66 ■ Pepperdine 71
94 ■ Loyola (Cal.) 72
73 Duke 117
75 Pepperdine 72
64 Loyola (Cal.) 60
94 ■ Portland 69
77 ■ Gonzaga 74
64 Gonzaga 85
94 Portland 88
78 ■ St. Mary's (Cal.) 82
74 St. Mary's (Cal.) 76
85 ■ San Diego 81
76 ■ Santa Clara 77
96 ■ San Diego 93
67 ■ Pepperdine 88

SAN FRAN. ST. 11-15
86 ■ Cal St. Bakersfield 92
48 Southern Cal 69
78 ■ Lewis & Clark 91
39 St. Mary's (Cal.) 43
84 ■ Cal St. San B'dino 79
57 Santa Clara 89
81 ■ Cal Poly Pomona 78
59 ■ Howard 62
69 ■ Southwestern (Tex.) 80
90 ■ Cal St. Stanislaus 105
63 Cal St. Hayward 59
84 Dominican (Cal.) 78
63 Humboldt St. 62
73 Cal St. Chico 76
69 ■ Sonoma St. 79
57 UC Davis 76
94 Menlo 85
64 ■ Notre Dame (Cal.) 59
63 Sonoma St. 58
75 ■ UC Davis 87
73 ■ Cal St. Chico 78
90 ■ Humboldt St. 76
63 Cal St. Stanislaus 92
82 ■ Cal St. Hayward 61
65 Notre Dame (Cal.) 62
77 Cal St. Chico 80

SAN JOSE ST. 7-19
56 ■ Santa Clara 71
56 ■ Stanford 52
76 ■ Gonzaga 73
51 Montana 55
57 Montana St. 60
43 Drake 66
74 ■ Fresno St. 62
47 Utah 60
73 ■ Long Beach St. 88
61 ■ Pacific (Cal.) 74
72 New Mexico St. 87
77 Nevada-Las Vegas 84
73 ■ Nevada 70
80 ■ Utah St. 79
61 Cal St. Fullerton 66
64 UC Irvine 73

54 Pacific (Cal.) 50
74 ■ Nevada-Las Vegas 80
55 ■ New Mexico St. 60
64 Nevada 68
79 Utah St. 92
62 ■ UC Irvine 67
60 ■ Cal St. Fullerton 58
62 ■ UC Santa Barb. 67
87 Long Beach St. 103
59 UC Santa Barb. 72

SANTA CLARA 19-12
71 San Jose St. 56
60 UCLA 69
68 † Georgia 80
85 † Southern Utah 76
81 ■ Nevada 68
89 ■ San Fran. St. 57
73 ■ California 80
63 ■ Minnesota 87
80 ■ Harvard 69
58 ■ Alabama 65
35 Stanford 66
93 ■ Cal St. Stanislaus 80
57 ■ San Diego 59
91 ■ San Francisco 80
63 ■ St. Mary's (Cal.) 53
61 Gonzaga 64
77 Portland 74
62 San Diego 63
71 ■ Pepperdine 73
80 ■ Loyola (Cal.) 57
71 Loyola (Cal.) 62
63 Pepperdine 58
66 ■ Portland 60
58 ■ Gonzaga 56
76 St. Mary's (Cal.) 77
77 San Francisco 76
79 † St. Mary's (Cal.) 68
53 † Gonzaga 51
73 Pepperdine 63
64 † Arizona 61
57 † Temple 68

SAVANNAH ST. 12-15
59 ■ Fla. Memorial 55
58 Queens (N.C.) 83
91 Morehouse 105
61 † Armstrong St. 67
64 Fla. Memorial 66
96 ■ LeMoyne-Owen 91
79 ■ North Fla. 75
72 ■ Wofford 61
60 Paine 76
70 ■ Fort Valley St. 79
86 Alabama A&M 93
73 Columbus 98
97 ■ Clark Atlanta 77
82 ■ Paine 86
77 ■ Columbus 76
77 Fort Valley St. 92
66 Tuskegee 64
61 Clark Atlanta 53
85 North Fla. 98
96 ■ Morris Brown 70
70 ■ Albany St. (Ga.) 78
81 ■ Miles 80
63 Albany St. (Ga.) 91
73 Wofford 84
102 ■ Queens (N.C.) 93
63 Morris Brown 60
70 † LeMoyne-Owen 102

SCRANTON 27-2
91 ■ Misericordia 63
66 ■ Wilkes 71
77 ■ King's (Pa.) 49
61 FDU-Madison 52
96 ■ Elizabethtown 89
77 ■ Susquehanna 60
81 † Gettysburg 61
81 † Albright 65
94 ■ Catholic 80
79 Potsdam St. 70
61 Albright 47

91 Upsala 66
73 ■ Drew 47
100 ■ Lycoming 68
102 Delaware Valley 65
81 ■ Wilkes 59
76 King's (Pa.) 60
83 ■ FDU-Madison 62
91 ■ Upsala 58
73 Susquehanna 64
74 Drew 51
104 ■ Delaware Valley 56
64 Wilkes 58
76 ■ Moravian 60
84 ■ Elizabethtown 61
69 Susquehanna 44
58 ■ Lebanon Valley 56
78 † Hunter 62
73 Rowan 80

SEATTLE PACIFIC 20-10
101 ■ Cal Baptist 56
88 ■ Sonoma St. 71
63 Boise St. 79
71 ■ Whitworth (Wash.) 69
62 Oregon St. 69
81 Seattle 82
85 ■ Cal St. Stanislaus 65
82 ■ Jacksonville St. 75
63 ■ Calif. (Pa.) 68
76 Utah St. 88
67 Notre Dame (Cal.) 60
83 Puget Sound 63
73 ■ Central Wash. 62
92 ■ Grace 84
97 ■ Northwest Col. 67
77 ■ Grand Canyon 75
87 ■ Eastern Mont. 82
80 Western Wash. 73
77 Chaminade 84
101 ■ Western Wash. 95
91 ■ Seattle 63
79 Alas. Anchorage 90
94 Alas. Fairbanks 76
105 ■ Lewis & Clark 80
102 Grand Canyon 107
74 Eastern Mont. 81
112 ■ Chaminade 75
94 ■ Alas. Fairbanks 68
86 ■ Alas. Anchorage 49
73 † Grand Canyon 80

SETON HALL 28-7
75 † Delaware 54
72 † Tennessee 64
73 † UCLA 64
74 † Indiana 78
87 ■ Rider 74
65 ■ Miami (Fla.) 56
75 Iona 61
88 ■ St. Peter's 54
81 ■ FDU-Teaneck 61
85 ■ Adelphi 56
75 ■ Cornell 59
87 ■ James Madison 66
72 ■ Connecticut 69
91 Providence 79
80 ■ Syracuse 73
73 Pittsburgh 76
66 ■ Villanova 61
66 ■ North Caro. 70
62 Georgetown 73
67 Syracuse 76
90 ■ Providence 71
62 Boston College 63
91 ■ Pittsburgh 73
65 Villanova 59
95 St. John's (N.Y.) 85
66 ■ Georgetown 56
85 Miami (Fla.) 73
82 Connecticut 74
79 ■ Boston College 61
92 ■ St. John's (N.Y.) 73
83 † Georgetown 69
69 † Providence 60
103 † Syracuse 70
81 † Tennessee St. 59
68 † Western Ky. 72

SEWANEE 13-12
84 ■ Loyola (La.) 58
75 ■ Wash. & Lee 85
60 Loyola (La.) 75
70 ■ Oglethorpe 71
91 ■ Free Will Baptist 53
43 Tenn.-Chatt. 98
73 Emory 79
83 Cumberland (Tenn.) 78
108 Savannah A&D 74
72 Rhodes 85
59 Millsaps 80
90 ■ Fisk 70
75 ■ Centre 94
109 ■ Cumberland (Tenn.) 87
87 ■ Hendrix 62
85 ■ Trinity (Tex.) 70
70 Maryville (Tenn.) 90
88 Fisk 72
64 Centre 75
82 ■ Emory 67
57 Oglethorpe 87
80 Hendrix 91
87 Trinity (Tex.) 80
84 ■ Rhodes 76
83 ■ Millsaps 72

SHAW 10-17
93 ■ Morris 80
122 Allen 46
96 ■ Bowie St. 99
79 ■ Claflin 91
87 Hampton 81
93 ■ Winston-Salem 98
97 ■ St. Paul's 88
90 ■ Livingstone 73
71 ■ N.C. Central 76
72 Voorhees 80
81 ■ St. Augustine's 80
70 Virginia Union 79
81 Livingstone 85
69 Fayetteville St. 88
85 Johnson Smith 94
64 Norfolk St. 94
84 Winston-Salem 80
75 ■ Benedict 65
76 ■ Allen 59
62 ■ Fayetteville St. 69
66 N.C. Central 83
70 ■ Elizabeth City St. 76
93 St. Augustine's 102
99 ■ Johnson Smith 93
83 Claflin 87
79 ■ Virginia St. 90
87 † Hampton 100

SHENANDOAH 9-16
76 ■ Belmont Abbey 85
103 ■ Messiah 99
98 Mary Washington 107
71 Old Dominion 118
81 Randolph-Macon 71
70 † Va. Wesleyan 91
73 Ferrum 115
105 Averett 87
92 Chris. Newport 95
74 William & Mary 102
84 ■ Averett 73
96 ■ Ferrum 106
89 ■ Frostburg St. 93
84 Lincoln (Pa.) 104
99 Salisbury St. 111
82 Methodist 80
101 N.C. Wesleyan 89
75 ■ Allentown 78
84 Frostburg St. 82
87 ■ Lincoln (Pa.) 98
116 ■ Salisbury St. 121
106 ■ Mary Washington 94
83 ■ Methodist 79
78 Allentown 92
71 † Allentown 81

SHEPHERD 19-8
72 ■ Shippensburg 75
66 West Liberty St. 65
82 Wheeling Jesuit 72
91 ■ West Va. St. 71
93 Columbia Union 82
81 ■ Lenoir-Rhyne 72
83 Charleston (W.Va.) 65
91 Glenville St. 78
100 ■ Columbia Union 71
100 ■ West Va. Tech 79
75 West Va. Wesleyan 61
56 Shippensburg 65
91 ■ Alderson-Broaddus 55
91 Fairmont St. 80
82 ■ Davis & Elkins 75
80 Salem Teikyo 93
92 ■ Bluefield St. 94
96 Millersville 113
80 ■ Wheeling Jesuit 62
90 Concord 75
81 ■ West Liberty St. 78
71 Alderson-Broad. 110
71 ■ Fairmont St. 62
98 Davis & Elkins 82
76 ■ Salem Teikyo 87
88 † West Va. Tech 50
80 † Wheeling Jesuit 81

SHIPPENSBURG 13-12
90 ■ LIU-Southampton 60
101 ■ Mercy 91
75 Shepherd 72
86 Bloomsburg 96
70 ■ Kutztown 75
59 ■ West Chester 61
65 Mansfield 67
84 Dickinson 59
90 † Penn St.-Harrisburg 48
61 Kutztown 55
65 ■ Shepherd 56
66 ■ Pitt.-Johnstown 79
67 Slippery Rock 63
58 Indiana (Pa.) 79
74 ■ Calif. (Pa.) 84
73 ■ Clarion 70
63 ■ Lock Haven 60
75 Edinboro 82
70 Pitt.-Johnstown 62
74 ■ Slippery Rock 67
66 ■ Indiana (Pa.) 69
74 Calif. (Pa.) 83
88 Clarion 85
46 Lock Haven 72
81 ■ Edinboro 101

SIENA 16-13
80 Florida St. 89
62 Marist 60
95 Holy Cross 96
58 ■ Massachusetts 70
74 Hartford 70
69 ■ Creighton 56
83 ■ Le Moyne 56
72 Kent 68
60 ■ Northeastern 69
70 Fordham 68
102 ■ N.C.-Greensboro 70
67 Richmond 69
42 Va. Commonwealth 57
56 Fairfield 59
74 ■ Loyola (Md.) 57
62 Manhattan 64
57 ■ St. Peter's 52
70 ■ Canisius 42
64 St. Peter's 51
71 Loyola (Md.) 57
83 ■ Iona 88
77 ■ Niagara 85
84 ■ Manhattan 76
59 ■ Fairfield 64
90 Iona 96
74 Canisius 67
83 Niagara 78
70 † Fairfield 61
70 † Manhattan 71

SIMPSON 11-14
69 ■ St. Ambrose 80
72 Teikyo-Westmar 96
66 † Park 57
66 ■ Grand View 69
91 ■ Iowa Wesleyan 84
66 Midland Lutheran 82
69 Neb. Wesleyan 108
57 Cornell College 64
60 Luther 78
52 Dubuque 68
88 ■ Coe 62
69 ■ Buena Vista 66
67 ■ Wartburg 79
63 ■ Loras 61
63 Central (Iowa) 73
71 William Penn 79
60 ■ Upper Iowa 74
74 ■ Luther 73
58 Loras 57
96 ■ Central (Iowa) 88
86 Buena Vista 76
71 Upper Iowa 82
116 ■ William Penn 67
59 Wartburg 64
93 ■ Dubuque 74

SKIDMORE 10-14
52 ■ Albany (N.Y.) 68
81 ■ Union (N.Y.) 75
86 † Keuka 78
54 Rochester 78
57 ■ Hartwick 56
76 ■ St. Joseph's (N.Y.) 57
56 ■ Stony Brook 72
72 ■ Rensselaer 85
74 Hobart 83
77 Amherst 75
66 Central Conn. St. 81
52 Ithaca 66
71 Williams 79
66 ■ Utica 69
84 ■ Drew 71
75 ■ Manhattanville 65
50 North Adams St. 52
76 Wheaton (Mass.) 88
63 Middlebury 83
103 ■ Vassar 53
62 ■ Albany (N.Y.) 60
92 Union (N.Y.) 106
83 ■ Hamilton 108
87 Norwich 69

SLIPPERY ROCK 10-16
74 † Point Park 83
96 † Ohio Valley College 63
53 Missouri 103
42 St. Louis 86
89 ■ Lake Erie 51
74 ■ Goucher 52
61 Gannon 58
84 † Central Okla. 123
78 ■ Point Park 62
76 ■ Mercyhurst 87
56 ■ Gannon 55
54 St. Vincent 56
82 Edinboro 63
63 ■ Shippensburg 67
67 ■ Calif. (Pa.) 82
62 Indiana (Pa.) 79
63 Lock Haven 74
66 Clarion 90
75 ■ Pitt.-Johnstown 63
78 ■ Edinboro 77
67 Shippensburg 74
85 Calif. (Pa.) 87
71 ■ Indiana (Pa.) 72
67 ■ Lock Haven 69

87 Pitt.-Johnstown 97
87 ■ Clarion 80

SONOMA ST. 6-20
70 † Central Wash. 104
71 Seattle Pacific 88
64 Pepperdine 89
68 Cal Poly Pomona ... 80
74 ■ Chapman 71
72 ■ UC Santa Cruz 74
57 ■ Menlo 72
64 ■ Minn.-Morris 61
58 ■ UC Riverside 68
77 Cal St. San B'dino .. 78
67 San Francisco 97
116 ■ San Jose Christian . 91
76 ■ Humboldt St. 79
77 ■ Cal St. Chico 92
78 Cal St. Stanislaus .. 95
76 ■ Cal St. Hayward 71
79 San Fran. St. 69
62 ■ Notre Dame (Cal.) .. 57
48 UC Davis 87
58 ■ San Fran. St. 63
51 Notre Dame (Cal.) .. 68
66 Cal St. Hayward 82
79 ■ Cal St. Stanislaus .. 89
73 Cal St. Chico 88
61 Humboldt St. 64
56 ■ UC Davis 71

SOUTH ALA. 15-13
68 ■ St. Louis 66
107 ■ West Va. 100
77 Texas A&M 85
84 North Texas 79
86 ■ Ark.-Lit. Rock 62
105 ■ Baylor 100
49 Cincinnati 87
83 ■ Western Ky. 88
61 Arkansas St. 76
76 ■ Southwestern La. .. 81
77 Lamar 86
94 ■ Tex.-Pan American . 73
85 Louisiana Tech 68
83 ■ Hofstra 69
101 Western Ky. 98
67 Southern Miss. 68
70 New Orleans 79
78 ■ Arkansas St. 59
81 Southwestern La. .. 90
73 ■ Jacksonville 58
64 ■ Louisiana Tech 67
79 Ark.-Lit. Rock 85
109 Jacksonville 86
101 ■ Lamar 80
62 ■ New Orleans 71
101 Tex.-Pan American . 77
87 † Southwestern La. .. 78
73 † Western Ky. 83

SOUTH CARO. 9-18
91 ■ Florida Tech 68
67 † North Caro. 108
40 † Princeton 51
69 ■ Ga. Southern 82
76 Oklahoma 92
89 ■ N.C.-Asheville 52
75 † Ala.-Birmingham ... 68
66 † Massachusetts 84
68 ■ Mercer 66
95 Tennessee 85
76 ■ Arkansas 86
88 ■ Mississippi 73
81 ■ Auburn 83
81 Florida 76
82 ■ Kentucky 108
86 ■ Georgia 85
62 Louisiana St. 85
72 Vanderbilt 76
84 ■ Clemson 89
111 ■ Tennessee 107
63 Mississippi St. 83
66 Kentucky 87
73 ■ Florida 80

80 Alabama 97
87 Georgia 88
73 ■ Vanderbilt 77
79 † Alabama 86

S.C.-AIKEN 22-7
96 ■ Erskine 79
80 ■ Kennesaw 72
95 ■ Newberry 72
87 Erskine 93
77 ■ S.C.-Spartanburg .. 73
72 Tenn.-Chatt. 95
61 ■ Presbyterian 67
84 Kennesaw 74
79 Columbus 78
106 Lander 75
97 ■ Georgia Col. 76
66 Wofford 64
59 Augusta 71
80 ■ Pembroke St. 58
56 ■ Armstrong St. 57
62 ■ Francis Marion 49
82 Pembroke St. 62
80 ■ Lander 78
65 S.C.-Spartanburg .. 69
95 ■ Augusta 84
72 Georgia Col. 62
96 ■ Wofford 94
77 Armstrong St. 60
83 Francis Marion 93
70 ■ Columbus 68
79 Newberry 65
73 † Georgia Col. 69
77 † S.C.-Spartanburg .. 75
64 Augusta 60

S.C.-SPARTANBURG 18-9
83 ■ Elon 72
69 † Washburn 87
82 † Missouri-Rolla 74
65 Lenoir-Rhyne 86
73 S.C.-Aiken 77
69 ■ Newberry 58
60 ■ Kennesaw 59
71 ■ Armstrong St. 45
85 ■ Georgia Col. 56
83 Pembroke St. 76
71 Francis Marion 78
89 ■ Columbus 87
76 Gardner-Webb 66
89 ■ Lander 77
94 Newberry 66
90 Georgia Col. 79
93 ■ Augusta 86
76 Armstrong St. 89
63 Lander 61
69 ■ S.C.-Aiken 65
50 ■ Francis Marion 52
69 Columbus 82
69 Augusta 75
84 ■ Pembroke St. 71
95 ■ Lees-McRae 64
65 † Armstrong St. 58
75 † S.C.-Aiken 77

SOUTH CARO. ST. 16-13
85 Furman 81
90 ■ Claflin 72
87 ■ Fort Valley St. 75
64 Hawaii 79
68 † Northeast La. 97
58 Southern Cal 98
85 ■ Winthrop 83
75 Coastal Caro. 90
58 ■ Coppin St. 86
91 ■ Morgan St. 65
61 ■ Howard 56
83 Bethune-Cookman . 68
84 Florida A&M 74
62 Charleston (S.C.) ... 67
66 Md.-East. Shore 69
71 Delaware St. 73
80 Charleston So. 74
66 ■ Bethune-Cookman . 64

86 ■ Florida A&M 74
70 ■ Md.-East. Shore ... 72
87 ■ Delaware St. 59
77 ■ Charleston (S.C.) ... 56
72 North Caro. A&T ... 68
69 Coppin St. 75
82 Morgan St. 67
62 Howard 65
70 ■ North Caro. A&T ... 76
59 † Md.-East. Shore ... 57
64 † Delaware St. 75

SOUTH DAK. 25-5
76 † Briar Cliff 84
84 † Wayne St. (Neb.) ... 58
93 ■ Bellevue 57
91 Huron 44
90 ■ Teikyo-Westmar ... 76
84 ■ Midland Lutheran .. 48
87 ■ Doane 69
73 ■ Grand View 42
68 ■ Morningside 59
83 ■ St. Cloud St. 68
86 ■ Mankato St. 63
65 Augustana (S.D.) ... 49
82 South Dak. St. 78
79 ■ Northern Colo. 69
66 ■ Nebraska-Omaha .. 57
61 North Dak. 59
82 North Dak. St. 65
77 Mankato St. 68
80 St. Cloud St. 72
70 ■ South Dak. St. 66
68 ■ Augustana (S.D.) ... 65
77 Morningside 91
95 Nebraska-Omaha .. 63
65 Northern Colo. 45
75 ■ North Dak. St. 57
67 ■ North Dak. 76
74 † North Dak. St. 82
78 † Colo. Christian 60
66 North Dak. 64
96 † New Hamp. Col. .. 100

SOUTH DAK. ST. 19-12
64 ■ Mary 77
65 Hawaii-Hilo 67
91 † Fla. Southern 78
99 Chaminade 90
75 ■ Winona St. 74
106 ■ Wayne St. (Neb.) ... 72
69 Black Hills St. 60
93 ■ Teikyo-Westmar ... 66
73 ■ Dak. Wesleyan 69
94 ■ Doane 81
64 ■ Northern Colo. 79
82 ■ Nebraska-Omaha .. 72
69 North Dak. 79
95 North Dak. St. 69
74 ■ Morningside 72
78 ■ South Dak. 82
83 St. Cloud St. 90
76 Mankato St. 94
71 ■ Augustana (S.D.) ... 66
69 Nebraska-Omaha .. 67
77 ■ North Dak. St. 60
80 ■ North Dak. 96
66 South Dak. 70
52 Morningside 55
70 ■ Mankato St. 66
68 ■ St. Cloud St. 50
72 Northern Colo. 62
77 Augustana (S.D.) ... 74
69 † Mankato St. 60
64 † North Dak. St. 68
85 † Morningside 92

SOUTH FLA. 8-19
82 ■ Bethune-Cookman . 55
78 ■ Florida 80
92 ■ Central Fla. 81
81 † Mississippi Val. 85
84 † Nicholls St. 94
73 Florida St. 94

72 ■ Florida Int'l 66
76 ■ Old Dominion 78
75 ■ Louisville 98
81 ■ Southern Miss. 95
62 Virginia Tech 74
53 Xavier (Ohio) 56
53 ■ Tulane 71
77 Central Fla. 72
65 N.C.-Charlotte 83
54 ■ Marquette 69
61 Louisville 78
59 Va. Commonwealth 79
77 ■ Virginia Tech 50
89 Stetson 73
50 ■ Cincinnati 72
91 ■ Va. Commonwealth 95
61 ■ Ala.-Birmingham ... 59
89 ■ N.C.-Charlotte 69
60 Southern Miss. 90
75 Tulane 91
72 † Va. Commonwealth 79

SOUTHEAST MO. ST. 16-11
67 ■ Wis.-Green Bay 65
86 ■ Alcorn St. 81
71 ■ Arkansas St. 69
72 ■ Montana St. 56
58 Cincinnati 83
74 † Central Mich. 61
72 † Arkansas 96
68 Evansville 92
71 Chicago St. 91
108 ■ Oakland City 69
70 Tennessee St. 95
90 Austin Peay 68
95 ■ Murray St. 111
91 ■ Southern Utah 74
107 ■ Morehead St. 96
79 ■ Eastern Ky. 63
89 Tenn.-Martin 90
80 ■ Middle Tenn. St. ... 69
79 ■ Tennessee Tech ... 74
96 Murray St. 100
85 Morehead St. 92
65 Eastern Ky. 86
94 ■ Tennessee St. 77
77 ■ Austin Peay 64
69 ■ Tenn.-Martin 68
67 Middle Tenn. St. ... 63
99 Tennessee Tech .. 113

SOUTHEASTERN LA. 12-15
99 ■ Bapt. Christian 63
65 Louisiana St. 92
72 Grambling 66
72 ■ Grambling 69
65 † East Caro. 72
87 † Tex.-Pan American . 69
98 ■ La. Christian 95
88 Southern-B.R. 97
108 ■ Texas Col. 94
84 Centenary 87
58 Memphis St. 109
58 ■ Mercer 73
98 ■ Loyola (La.) 82
61 Florida Int'l 68
77 Stetson 83
71 ■ Northwestern (La.) . 94
90 ■ Georgia St. 82
56 ■ Samford 64
85 ■ Southern-B.R. 91
76 ■ Centenary 71
61 Mississippi 71
77 Mercer 98
76 Nicholls St. 75
67 ■ Florida Int'l 72
74 ■ Stetson 79
82 Georgia St. 75
66 Samford 58

SOUTHERN-B.R. 21-10
100 ■ Paul Quinn 83
88 Ala.-Birmingham . 100
102 ■ Xavier (La.) 85
156 ■ Bapt. Christian 91

82 Xavier (La.) 78
102 Tenn.-Chatt. 114
79 † Georgia St. 83
69 Middle Tenn. St. 70
97 ■ Southeastern La. 88
107 ■ Grambling 73
77 ■ Mississippi Val. 71
80 Alabama St. 92
86 Jackson St. 91
90 Texas Southern 88
99 Prairie View 75
127 ■ Central Fla. 91
94 ■ Alcorn St. 83
91 Southeastern La. 85
91 Grambling 84
94 Mississippi Val. 95
82 ■ Alabama St. 86
87 ■ Jackson St. 74
86 ■ Texas Southern 87
155 ■ Prairie View 91
127 Central Fla. 100
89 Alcorn St. 78
105 ■ Grambling 91
93 ■ Alcorn St. 75
101 ■ Jackson St. 80
93 † Georgia Tech 78
80 † Geo. Washington 90

SOUTHERN CAL 18-12
69 ■ San Fran. St. 48
56 Ohio St. 73
77 ■ Gonzaga 59
79 St. Louis 94
98 ■ South Caro. St. 58
74 ■ Nebraska 64
82 † Fla. Atlantic 56
86 † Miami (Fla.) 66
77 Notre Dame 74
87 ■ Arizona St. 79
73 ■ Arizona 81
57 Oregon St. 68
69 Oregon 58
67 ■ California 65
63 ■ Stanford 55
80 ■ UCLA 90
51 Washington St. 73
41 Washington 46
73 ■ Oregon 67
69 ■ Oregon St. 60
83 California 86
62 Stanford 78
72 UCLA 62
56 ■ Washington 55
81 ■ Washington St. 65
76 Arizona 87
67 Arizona St. 101
90 Nevada-Las Vegas 74
71 ■ Pepperdine 59
58 Minnesota 76

SOUTHERN COLO. 14-14
87 ■ Colorado Mines 64
62 ■ Western N. Mex. 48
84 Mesa St. 89
91 † Tex. Wesleyan 77
60 ■ Northern Colo. 56
84 ■ Notre Dame (Cal.) 89
89 ■ Cameron 76
54 Wyoming 79
72 Adams St. 73
65 Cal St. Bakersfield 85
51 † Cal St. Dom. Hills 54
97 † N.M. Highlands 96
80 † East Tex. St. 74
75 Alas. Anchorage 90
84 ■ Colorado-CS 51
79 ■ Regis (Colo.) 69
81 Western St. 86
76 Metropolitan St. 75
70 ■ Colo. Christian 87
108 ■ Adams St. 80
97 ■ Denver 104
101 ■ Fort Lewis 102
78 Colorado-CS 75

81 Regis (Colo.) 87
67 ■ Metropolitan St. 76
78 Colo. Christian 90
97 Denver 80
89 Fort Lewis 88

SOUTHERN CONN. ST. 14-14
95 ■ American Int'l 107
78 ■ Springfield 66
92 Stonehill 90
71 † Charleston (W.Va.) 70
71 Calif. (Pa.) 96
97 ■ Bentley 93
78 Adelphi 71
87 Bryant 88
76 St. Anselm 93
90 ■ Keene St. 98
68 New Hamp. Col. 95
57 ■ Franklin Pierce 82
72 Mass.-Lowell 80
83 ■ Sacred Heart 80
78 ■ Le Moyne 75
91 ■ New Haven 82
84 ■ Mass.-Lowell 74
75 Franklin Pierce 81
96 Keene St. 90
78 Sacred Heart 74
107 ■ New York Tech 82
56 ■ New Hamp. Col. 72
103 ■ Teikyo-Post 96
74 ■ Quinnipiac 73
83 New Haven 96
70 Le Moyne 80
61 Mass.-Lowell 77
82 † St. Rose 101

SOUTHERN ILL. 23-10
76 ■ Northeast Mo. St. 37
85 Eastern Ill. 72
91 Northern Ill. 62
57 ■ St. Louis 44
108 † Radford 82
76 † Mississippi St. 64
70 † Iowa 90
85 Mississippi 78
85 ■ Creighton 64
65 ■ Evansville 42
76 Missouri 82
88 ■ Northern Iowa 69
74 Illinois St. 88
71 Creighton 79
77 Bradley 64
92 ■ Drake 74
85 ■ Wichita St. 67
83 ■ Illinois St. 68
55 Southwest Mo. St. 68
77 ■ Bradley 42
75 Indiana St. 60
79 Drake 87
70 Tulsa 77
78 ■ Indiana St. 66
51 Northern Iowa 54
85 Wichita St. 76
78 St. Louis 87
68 ■ Southwest Mo. St. 60
106 ■ Tulsa 80
63 † Bradley 61
76 † Southwest Mo. St. 68
70 † Illinois St. 59
70 † Duke 105

SIU-EDWARDSVILLE 14-12
78 Mo.-St. Louis 71
89 Lincoln (Mo.) 100
64 Minnesota 108
78 Northern Ky. 91
69 Ky. Wesleyan 99
66 Northeast Mo. St. 64
67 ■ Southern Ind. 77
80 ■ Greenville 61
69 ■ Ky. Wesleyan 72
58 † West Tex. A&M 57
75 † Michigan Tech 81
63 Quincy 62

82 ■ Mo. Baptist 78
61 ■ Drury 82
79 ■ Wis.-Parkside 64
80 ■ Lincoln (Mo.) 84
78 Bellarmine 68
56 ■ Eureka 46
88 ■ Lewis 63
80 ■ Quincy 76
115 ■ IU/PU-Indianapolis 87
74 Oakland City 77
82 ■ Park 61
94 Drury 89
77 Southern Ind. 86
73 Wis.-Parkside 88

SOUTHERN IND. 22-7
116 ■ Indiana Tech 79
104 ■ Union (Ky.) 81
93 ■ Stonehill 72
90 ■ Grand Canyon 74
123 ■ Graceland (Ind.) 76
62 Missouri 77
77 SIU-Edwardsville 67
81 Quincy 83
84 ■ Ky. Wesleyan 75
121 ■ Ashland 74
107 ■ IU/PU-Ft. Wayne 96
82 Kentucky St. 95
93 Bellarmine 82
85 ■ St. Joseph's (Ind.) 69
81 ■ Lewis 69
107 Northern Ky. 79
81 Indianapolis 70
87 IU/PU-Ft. Wayne 99
91 Ashland 60
105 ■ Bellarmine 76
95 ■ Kentucky St. 78
78 Lewis 68
73 St. Joseph's (Ind.) 77
95 ■ Indianapolis 83
60 ■ Northern Ky. 59
86 ■ SIU-Edwardsville 77
66 Ky. Wesleyan 83
85 ■ Northern Mich. 86
95 ■ IU/PU-Ft. Wayne 93

SOUTHERN ME. 13-12
76 ■ Me.-Presque Isle 72
96 ■ Notre Dame (N.H.) 64
78 Thomas 69
95 Salem St. 101
79 ■ New England 68
84 St. Thomas Aquinas 83
68 Husson 76
69 Colby 77
97 Rhode Island Col. 80
58 † Jersey City St. 65
57 † Old Westbury 50
80 ■ Plymouth St. 53
60 Mass.-Dartmouth 72
64 Mass.-Boston 56
62 Eastern Conn. St. 57
102 Plymouth St. 104
60 ■ Mass.-Boston 57
51 ■ Bowdoin 66
79 ■ Rhode Island Col. 64
75 ■ St. Joseph's (Me.) 92
63 ■ Mass.-Dartmouth 77
64 Colby-Sawyer 84
59 ■ Eastern Conn. St. 60
69 ■ Rhode Island Col. 48
57 ■ Eastern Conn. St. 75

SOUTHERN METHODIST 20-8
90 ■ Southwest Tex. St. 69
92 Tulane 103
112 ■ Oral Roberts 73
86 Vanderbilt 95
110 ■ North Texas 94
106 ■ San Diego 71
87 ■ Stetson 77
59 † Oklahoma St. 75
53 ■ Arkansas 72
63 St. Louis 56

102 Texas 92
66 ■ St. Louis 59
61 Texas Tech 59
79 Texas Christian 65
75 Houston 85
68 ■ Texas A&M 65
70 ■ Houston 60
105 Baylor 92
78 ■ Rice 77
78 ■ Texas Tech 75
60 ■ Texas Christian 53
102 Oral Roberts 95
84 Texas A&M 73
67 Rice 90
81 ■ Baylor 74
96 ■ Texas 80
71 ■ Texas Christian 72
71 † Brigham Young 80

SOUTHERN MISS. 10-17
75 Syracuse 103
69 † Marist 78
67 ■ Northeast La. 79
76 Alabama 86
86 ■ Alcorn St. 59
86 ■ Tenn.-Chatt. 83
98 Tennessee Tech 102
74 Va. Commonwealth 85
78 Southwestern La. 69
84 ■ Virginia Tech 82
95 South Fla. 81
106 Northeast La. 113
71 ■ Tulane 84
81 ■ Louisville 85
77 ■ N.C.-Charlotte 79
68 ■ South Ala. 67
52 Tulane 65
84 Old Dominion 99
71 Louisville 86
82 Memphis St. 95
76 N.C.-Charlotte 69
75 ■ Auburn 81
83 Virginia Tech 79
105 ■ Old Dominion 113
90 ■ South Fla. 60
71 ■ Va. Commonwealth 65
60 † N.C.-Charlotte 68

SOUTHERN UTAH 14-13
60 Montana 55
74 ■ Grand Canyon 76
62 Brigham Young 108
76 † Santa Clara 85
62 Weber St. 73
100 ■ Northern Ariz. 74
70 Eastern Wash. 68
81 † Loyola (Md.) 71
69 Boise St. 75
79 ■ Montana St. 70
85 Nebraska 100
79 Idaho St. 63
87 ■ Tex. Wesleyan 63
74 Southeast Mo. St. 91
63 Iowa St. 91
87 ■ Cal St. Sacramento 68
90 ■ Cal St. Northridge 65
80 ■ Northeastern Ill. 57
73 Western Ky. 96
63 Cal St. Northridge 65
87 ■ Eastern Wash. 67
81 ■ Wis.-Milwaukee 80
66 Northeastern Ill. 72
56 Wis.-Milwaukee 66
81 ■ Western N. Mex. 64
95 ■ Eastern Mont. 52
75 Northern Ariz. 84

SOUTHWEST BAPTIST 21-7
75 East Tex. St. 60
87 Henderson St. 79
92 Ozarks (Ark.) 80
80 ■ John Brown 68
57 ■ Henderson St. 48
95 ■ Ark. Baptist 68

107	■ Park	76
91	■ Ozarks (Ark.)	82
104	■ Williams Bapt.	72
92	Drury	78
68	Missouri-Rolla	80
66	■ Pittsburg St.	54
84	Northwest Mo. St.	79
83	Mo.-St. Louis	89
81	■ Lincoln (Mo.)	97
79	■ Missouri-Rolla	63
66	Mo. Southern St.	68
68	Washburn	73
79	Pittsburg St.	68
65	■ Emporia St.	51
54	■ Mo.-St. Louis	53
84	Lincoln (Mo.)	72
72	■ Mo. Southern St.	54
73	■ Northeast Mo. St.	53
66	■ Mo. Western St.	88
88	Central Mo. St.	71
91	■ Missouri-Rolla	74
54	Washburn	73

SOUTHWEST MO. ST.		**20-11**
47	Mo.-Kansas City	44
79	■ Tennessee St.	66
57	■ Idaho	52
71	■ Towson St.	56
63	■ Oregon St.	48
45	■ Purdue	48
59	Oklahoma St.	74
63	■ St. Louis	52
57	Illinois St.	65
62	■ Tulsa	54
46	Bradley	51
73	■ Illinois St.	82
58	Creighton	72
74	Tulsa	77
72	■ Northern Iowa	49
68	■ Southern Ill.	55
54	■ Wichita St.	51
76	Indiana St.	73
63	■ Bradley	49
65	■ Creighton	62
49	Wichita St.	40
71	Drake	67
72	■ Indiana St.	57
53	Northern Iowa	54
60	Southern Ill.	68
82	■ Drake	67
72	† Wichita St.	57
68	† Southern Ill.	76
56	■ St. Joseph's (Pa.)	34
70	Jackson St.	52
52	Ala.-Birmingham	61

SOUTHWEST TEX. ST.		**14-13**
69	Southern Methodist	90
60	Miami (Fla.)	57
65	■ East Central (Okla.)	53
87	■ Tex. Wesleyan	60
73	■ Georgia St.	62
67	New Orleans	76
75	† Samford	71
75	Nicholls St.	81
71	McNeese St.	64
92	■ Sam Houston St.	79
72	■ Stephen F. Austin	63
81	Baylor	89
74	Texas-San Antonio	83
66	Northeast La.	77
67	Northwestern (La.)	65
83	■ North Texas	73
66	■ Texas-Arlington	67
62	Stephen F. Austin	63
74	Sam Houston St.	86
63	■ Nicholls St.	62
65	■ Texas-San Antonio	67
99	■ Northwestern (La.)	87
63	■ Northeast La.	64
78	Texas-Arlington	70
74	North Texas	60
64	■ McNeese St.	65
79	† Texas-Arlington	83

SOUTHWESTERN LA.		**17-13**
85	Memphis St.	91
87	■ Loyola (Cal.)	73
74	■ Campbell	59
107	■ Ga. Southern	82
103	Mississippi	87
71	■ Samford	62
59	† North Caro.	80
109	† Nebraska	80
85	† Jackson St.	87
69	■ Southern Miss.	78
73	■ Lamar	76
62	■ New Orleans	82
81	South Ala.	76
90	Jacksonville	84
71	Ark.-Lit. Rock	73
84	■ Western Ky.	83
65	Louisiana Tech	59
88	■ Ark.-Lit. Rock	74
74	Massachusetts	84
92	Western Ky.	121
90	■ South Ala.	81
71	New Orleans	73
77	■ Tex.-Pan American	63
71	Arkansas St.	69
81	■ Louisiana Tech	59
70	Tex.-Pan American	69
78	Lamar	89
87	■ Jacksonville	63
59	■ Arkansas St.	60
78	† South Ala.	87

SOUTHWESTERN (TEX.)		**18-9**
81	■ Millsaps	68
92	Dallas	90
67	† Howard Payne	62
75	■ Trinity (Tex.)	67
89	Webster	52
75	Parks	39
60	Ambassador	69
80	San Fran. St.	69
58	Menlo	55
67	■ Loyola (La.)	71
72	Hendrix	67
68	■ Dallas	52
50	Austin	53
68	■ Mary Hardin-Baylor	72
62	■ Ambassador	50
55	■ Austin	50
77	■ Concordia (Tex.)	68
85	■ Huston-Tillotson	81
52	Trinity (Tex.)	50
61	Loyola (La.)	70
61	Howard Payne	64
80	■ Hendrix	68
51	■ Howard Payne	48
69	Emory	76
68	Huston-Tillotson	70
77	■ LSU-Shreveport	64
51	Tarleton St.	64

SPRINGFIELD		**12-14**
66	Southern Conn. St.	78
96	■ Keene St.	71
65	Assumption	63
70	■ New Haven	66
64	■ St. Michael's	52
62	Franklin Pierce	76
76	■ Dowling	51
79	■ Indiana (Pa.)	74
75	Sacred Heart	83
67	■ Bryant	54
57	Stonehill	60
79	American Int'l	85
69	■ Bentley	65
79	■ Quinnipiac	87
62	Merrimack	73
84	■ Assumption	65
77	St. Anselm	95
66	St. Michael's	71
87	■ Stonehill	74
67	■ American Int'l	78
73	Bentley	85
87	Quinnipiac	68
79	■ Merrimack	84
72	■ St. Anselm	82
77	Bryant	73
73	American Int'l	79

STANFORD		**7-23**
92	■ Puget Sound	42
52	San Jose St.	56
48	Virginia	72
68	■ Cal St. Sacramento	33
71	■ Howard	46
63	† Louisiana St.	72
67	† DePaul	76
63	† Chaminade	71
57	■ American	56
76	■ Ohio	81
66	■ Santa Clara	35
66	■ Oregon St.	77
71	■ Oregon	66
61	■ Notre Dame	67
66	California	83
76	UCLA	84
55	Southern Cal	63
59	■ Washington St.	64
67	■ Washington	68
61	Arizona	96
87	Arizona St.	109
61	■ California	86
64	■ UCLA	72
78	■ Southern Cal	62
51	Washington	56
54	Washington St.	87
71	■ Arizona St.	75
80	■ Arizona	94
73	Oregon	84
65	Oregon St.	82

STATEN ISLAND		**14-12**
80	† Ramapo	75
82	Potsdam St.	78
81	■ Manhattanville	87
79	■ New York U.	94
76	York (N.Y.)	70
82	Merchant Marine	79
72	New Jersey Tech	104
88	Medgar Evers	90
71	■ Stony Brook	79
76	■ York (N.Y.)	66
77	John Jay	74
76	■ Merchant Marine	68
79	Hunter	94
85	■ New Jersey Tech	109
100	■ Baruch	88
66	Manhattanville	63
82	■ Medgar Evers	96
69	■ Hunter	92
89	■ Old Westbury	66
71	CCNY	50
91	■ Lehman	56
45	Stony Brook	63
67	Baruch	64
50	Hunter	83
96	Mt. St. Vincent	91
81	Jersey City St.	88

STEPHEN F. AUSTIN		**12-14**
92	■ Tex. Wesleyan	72
72	† Eastern Wash.	60
39	UC Santa Barb.	70
75	■ Texas Southern	68
78	■ Oral Roberts	75
70	Texas	83
75	Houston	76
57	Texas Southern	58
79	■ Sam Houston St.	68
64	Texas-San Antonio	77
63	Southwest Tex. St.	72
62	■ Northeast La.	80
65	■ Northwestern (La.)	68
97	North Texas	95
77	Texas-Arlington	78
75	■ Nicholls St.	64
62	■ McNeese St.	68
63	■ Southwest Tex. St.	62
80	■ Texas-San Antonio	71
87	Sam Houston St.	84
73	Northwestern (La.)	79
74	Northeast La.	94
86	■ Texas-Arlington	83
84	■ North Texas	70
70	McNeese St.	74
74	Nicholls St.	91

STETSON		**13-14**
52	Florida	70
74	■ Bethune-Cookman	81
83	■ Central Mich.	84
59	† Michigan St.	78
61	† Cal St. Northridge	65
74	■ McNeese St.	80
77	Southern Methodist	87
82	■ St. Joseph's (Me.)	75
89	■ Buffalo	82
82	Bethune-Cookman	79
63	■ Florida Int'l	66
63	■ Fla. Atlantic	60
71	Samford	88
81	Georgia St.	93
98	■ Central Fla.	81
81	■ Centenary	77
83	■ Southeastern La.	77
70	Mercer	75
95	■ North Fla.	75
75	Florida Int'l	82
76	■ Samford	57
89	■ Georgia St.	100
73	■ South Fla.	89
95	Centenary	82
79	Southeastern La.	74
94	■ Mercer	87
95	Central Fla.	82

STEVENS TECH		**8-17**
40	† Bloomfield	63
75	■ Mt. St. Vincent	80
70	■ Maritime (N.Y.)	64
56	New Jersey Tech	104
76	Drew	90
75	Baruch	101
54	Yeshiva	91
57	Union (N.Y.)	96
69	† CCNY	74
61	Polytechnic (N.Y.)	50
67	■ Pratt	71
76	■ Vassar	56
58	St. Joseph's (N.Y.)	75
48	Centenary (N.J.)	83
49	Maritime (N.Y.)	57
56	Merchant Marine	63
80	■ St. Joseph's-Suffolk	48
88	■ Polytechnic (N.Y.)	70
56	FDU-Madison	91
61	■ Yeshiva	60
83	■ Bard	61
67	Mt. St. Vincent	83
54	■ New Jersey Tech	99
63	■ Maritime (N.Y.)	57
63	† New Jersey Tech	90

STOCKTON ST.		**21-6**
96	■ Bapt. Bible (Pa.)	65
68	■ Bri'water (Mass.)	55
86	■ Rutgers-Newark	59
77	Jersey City St.	52
77	Ramapo	61
48	Montclair St.	53
55	■ Rowan	63
72	† Eastern Conn. St.	62
93	Salem St.	83
86	■ Rutgers-Camden	62
71	Kean	63
85	Lincoln (Pa.)	80
93	■ Wm. Paterson	83
86	■ Trenton St.	71
74	■ Ramapo	53
91	Rutgers-Camden	69
68	■ Jersey City St.	64
92	■ Wesley	64
93	Rutgers-Newark	66

76		Rowan	79
63	■	Kean	65
79	■	Montclair St.	60
84		Trenton St.	83
99		Wm. Paterson	82
63		Kean	70
106		Catholic	91
61		Rowan	84

STONEHILL			**10-17**
65		Mass.-Lowell	76
66	†	Sacred Heart	83
61		Bryant	53
69	■	American Int'l	78
90	■	Southern Conn. St.	92
72		Southern Ind.	93
75	†	Mo.-St. Louis	79
121	■	Keene St.	97
77		Sacred Heart	93
84		New Hamp. Col.	102
76		St. Anselm	79
60	■	Springfield	57
80	■	Merrimack	76
59		St. Michael's	74
80		Bentley	59
81		Quinnipiac	84
88	■	Bryant	66
104	■	Assumption	92
80		American Int'l	97
74		Springfield	87
66		Merrimack	73
85	■	St. Michael's	79
87	■	Bentley	97
102	■	Quinnipiac	96
79		Assumption	77
74	■	St. Anselm	95
75		Quinnipiac	86

STONY BROOK			**15-12**
91	†	Wesley	61
48		Frostburg St.	70
102	■	Lehman	32
72		Skidmore	56
80	■	New Jersey Tech	69
79		Staten Island	71
69	■	Oneonta St.	57
49	■	Binghamton	50
64	■	FDU-Madison	46
64		Merchant Marine	63
60		Hunter	67
81		Mt. St. Vincent	84
73	■	York (N.Y.)	63
57		Hofstra	78
60	■	LIU-C.W. Post	65
39	■	Manhattanville	41
48		Albany (N.Y.)	61
60	■	Hunter	88
62		New Jersey Tech	82
63	■	Staten Island	45
61	■	Merchant Marine	56
81		Manhattanville	56
64	■	Western Conn. St.	58
53	†	Old Westbury	57
66	■	Medgar Evers	59
55		Trenton St.	51
56		Jersey City St.	66

SUSQUEHANNA			**16-9**
87	■	Medgar Evers	58
82	■	Catholic	85
72		Muhlenberg	73
92		Misericordia	67
57		King's (Pa.)	64
60		Scranton	77
86	†	CCNY	71
77		Union (N.Y.)	71
96	■	Bloomsburg	88
60	■	Messiah	46
81		Juniata	71
77		Wilkes	71
86	■	Elizabethtown	69
88	■	Lycoming	66
74		Dickinson	62
65		Albright	77
88		Messiah	52
64	■	Scranton	73
77	■	Juniata	84
85		Elizabethtown	76
62		Lebanon Valley	72
83		Lycoming	58
73	■	Albright	58
70	■	Wilkes	66
44	■	Scranton	69

SWARTHMORE			**7-17**
65	†	Claremont-M-S	70
70	■	Haverford	67
55		Phila. Pharmacy	71
75		Connecticut Col.	105
73	†	Colby-Sawyer	80
54	■	Dickinson	78
77		Muhlenberg	82
64		Albright	80
83	■	Drew	77
39		Moravian	48
56	†	Centenary (N.J.)	78
75		Lafayette	89
70	■	Gettysburg	62
44		Yale	57
64	■	Washington (Md.)	72
53		Johns Hopkins	78
52	■	Widener	65
58	■	Haverford	57
72		Ursinus	60
74		Washington (Md.)	78
48	■	Johns Hopkins	62
42		Widener	53
82		Haverford	65
79	■	Ursinus	65

SYRACUSE			**20-9**
97	■	Cornell	65
103	■	Southern Miss.	75
94	■	Va. Commonwealth	81
87		Tennessee	81
104	■	Texas-San Antonio	78
93	■	Md.-Balt. County	86
85	■	Wagner	52
102	■	Le Moyne	71
93	■	Boston College	94
61	■	Villanova	79
60		Georgetown	64
89	■	Miami (Fla.)	81
73		Seton Hall	80
69		Providence	57
71	■	St. John's (N.Y.)	78
95		Pittsburgh	79
76	■	Seton Hall	67
60		Connecticut	57
74		Miami (Fla.)	81
76	■	Georgetown	61
76	■	Connecticut	80
67		Boston College	64
73		Villanova	72
68	■	Providence	67
70	†	St. John's (N.Y.)	90
78	■	Pittsburgh	74
55	†	Pittsburgh	50
84	†	St. John's (N.Y.)	72
70	†	Seton Hall	103

TAMPA			**25-5**
94	■	Webber	85
86	■	Fla. Memorial	62
108	†	Bapt. Christian	93
80		Jacksonville St.	93
95	■	Augustana (S.D.)	86
105	■	North Central	85
128	■	Edward Waters	94
78	■	Rose-Hulman	75
91	■	Quinnipiac	77
81	■	Central Mo. St.	84
87	■	Pfeiffer	76
93	■	Mass.-Dartmouth	82
79	■	Rollins	76
76		St. Leo	74
61	■	Florida Tech	60
86		North Fla.	68
97		Eckerd	86
76	■	Fla. Southern	70
75		Barry	73
108	■	St. Leo	81
79		Florida Tech	76
122	■	North Fla.	93
81	■	Eckerd	73
68		Fla. Southern	72
89	■	Barry	67
65		Rollins	62
98	■	Barry	81
67	■	Fla. Southern	71
61	†	Delta St.	74
79	†	Fla. Southern	73

TEMPLE			**20-13**
79		Boston College	72
87	†	La Salle	60
67	†	Florida	62
80	†	Florida St.	91
70	†	Penn St.	61
45		Cincinnati	68
66	■	St. Joseph's (Pa.)	71
52	■	Massachusetts	44
64		Geo. Washington	62
74		St. Bonaventure	58
72	†	Pennsylvania	58
50		Massachusetts	52
72		Rutgers	80
69	■	Rhode Island	67
63		Kansas St.	86
55		Ala.-Birmingham	68
69	■	Wake Forest	106
72	■	Geo. Washington	75
79	■	West Va.	62
66		St. Joseph's (Pa.)	65
79	■	Tulane	57
65	■	Memphis St.	58
68	■	St. Bonaventure	49
65		Rhode Island	67
74		West Va.	86
89	■	Rutgers	75
80	†	West Va.	53
71	†	St. Joseph's (Pa.)	60
61		Massachusetts	69
75	†	Missouri	61
68	†	Santa Clara	57
67	†	Vanderbilt	59
72	†	Michigan	77

TENNESSEE			**13-17**
87		Rutgers	79
64	†	Seton Hall	72
96	■	Tennessee Tech	78
70	■	Memphis St.	59
81	■	Syracuse	87
97	■	Western Caro.	55
77		Dayton	61
90	■	Furman	77
58		Cincinnati	79
85	■	South Caro.	95
70		Kentucky	84
105	■	Radford	63
92	■	Mississippi St.	75
80	■	N.C.-Charlotte	70
75		Auburn	88
68	■	Florida	80
65	■	Vanderbilt	82
75		Mississippi	62
60		Georgia	77
81	■	Alabama	85
107		South Caro.	111
72		North Caro. St.	74
101		Arkansas	91
74	■	Louisiana St.	81
78	■	Kentucky	77
70		Florida	84
82		Vanderbilt	90
83	■	Georgia	96
78	†	Auburn	76
40		Kentucky	101

TENN.-CHATT.			**26-7**
65	†	New Mexico St.	75
110		Alas. Anchorage	56
52	†	Ala.-Birmingham	67
109	■	Augusta	87
95	■	S.C.-Aiken	72
98	■	Sewanee	43
83		Southern Miss.	86
74	■	Georgia Tech	81
114	■	Southern-B.R.	102
80	■	Pepperdine	67
75	■	Bradley	55
71	■	Furman	61
77		Marshall	78
71		Va. Military	62
93		Western Caro.	66
89	■	Appalachian St.	69
103		Ga. Southern	92
95		Citadel	62
87	■	East Tenn. St.	77
80		Davidson	73
82		Furman	62
87		East Tenn. St.	89
87		Appalachian St.	85
93	■	Va. Military	70
83	■	Marshall	69
95	■	Davidson	80
85	■	Western Caro.	66
95	■	Citadel	72
91	■	Ga. Southern	68
85	†	Furman	69
72	†	Davidson	68
86	†	East Tenn. St.	75
58	†	Wake Forest	81

TENN.-MARTIN			**7-19**
82	■	Oakland City	71
69		Arkansas	90
75	■	Samford	59
67	†	Texas Christian	75
82	†	Houston Baptist	74
54		Georgia St.	58
58		Ark.-Lit. Rock	88
63		Minnesota	92
66		Murray St.	92
76	■	Tennessee Tech	81
71	■	Middle Tenn. St.	67
74		Austin Peay	71
67		Tennessee St.	85
90	■	Southeast Mo. St.	89
58		Eastern Ky.	64
74		Morehead St.	77
70		Tennessee Tech	87
60		Middle Tenn. St.	70
74	■	Murray St.	100
59	■	Austin Peay	61
70	■	Tennessee St.	79
63		Samford	85
67	■	Ark.-Lit. Rock	81
68		Southeast Mo. St.	69
56	■	Eastern Ky.	66
89	■	Morehead St.	86

TENNESSEE ST.			**19-10**
70	■	Jackson St.	63
62	†	Ark.-Lit. Rock	60
66		Southwest Mo. St.	79
69		David Lipscomb	87
79	†	St. Francis (N.Y.)	73
63		Geo. Washington	83
61		St. Louis	83
68		Louisiana St.	90
80		Alabama	95
95	■	Southeast Mo. St.	70
80	■	Murray St.	76
78		Middle Tenn. St.	70
86		Morehead St.	75
73		Eastern Ky.	75
84	■	Mo.-Kansas City	71
85	■	Tenn.-Martin	67
102		Tennessee Tech	79
93	■	Austin Peay	68
96	■	Morehead St.	72
93	■	Eastern Ky.	84
84	■	Middle Tenn. St.	67
79		Tenn.-Martin	70
77		Southeast Mo. St.	94

82 Murray St. 75
82 ■ Tennessee Tech 78
77 Austin Peay 80
77 † Tennessee Tech 71
82 † Murray St. 68
59 † Seton Hall 81

TENNESSEE TECH 15-13
111 ■ Clinch Valley 60
78 Tennessee 96
99 ■ Western Ky. 92
94 East Caro. 109
102 ■ Southern Miss. 98
95 ■ East Caro. 77
77 Idaho St. 97
65 Mississippi St. 110
95 ■ Eastern Ky. 87
97 ■ Morehead St. 79
90 Austin Peay 72
81 Tenn.-Martin 76
71 Memphis St. 101
73 ■ Middle Tenn. St. 86
79 ■ Tennessee St. 102
112 Murray St. 117
74 Southeast Mo. St. 79
87 ■ Tenn.-Martin 70
96 ■ Appalachian St. 88
92 ■ Austin Peay 83
65 Middle Tenn. St. 63
66 Eastern Ky. 80
101 Morehead St. 96
78 Tennessee St. 82
81 ■ Murray St. 83
113 ■ Southeast Mo. St. 99
97 † Morehead St. 89
71 † Tennessee St. 77

TEXAS 11-17
136 Oral Roberts 97
63 † Princeton 53
68 † North Caro. 104
76 Utah 87
83 ■ Stephen F. Austin 70
89 ■ Illinois 72
104 † Weber St. 96
76 † Oklahoma 85
87 ■ Rice 92
92 ■ Southern Meth. 102
67 Houston 81
86 ■ Baylor 87
79 Murray St. 74
92 ■ Texas Tech 74
83 Rice 101
77 Texas Christian 83
81 † Louisiana St. 84
82 ■ Texas A&M 78
70 Georgia 78
60 ■ Va. Commonwealth 66
88 Baylor 73
57 Texas A&M 77
103 Texas Tech 105
79 ■ Houston 86
102 ■ Texas Christian 84
80 Southern Methodist 96
81 † Rice 76
50 † Houston 58

TEXAS-ARLINGTON 16-12
91 ■ Concordia (Tex.) 86
121 ■ Schreiner 61
105 ■ Sul Ross 91
95 † Gonzaga 87
68 Ala.-Birmingham 87
95 Nebraska 116
79 Wyoming 70
86 † Texas Tech 98
71 ■ Northeast La. 87
89 ■ Northwestern (La.) 75
81 ■ North Texas 76
72 McNeese St. 70
74 Nicholls St. 91
76 ■ Sam Houston St. 67
78 ■ Stephen F. Austin 77
66 Texas-San Antonio 84
67 Southwest Tex. St. 66
74 North Texas 87
83 Northeast La. 110
99 ■ Nicholls St. 88
77 ■ McNeese St. 75
83 Stephen F. Austin 86
100 Sam Houston St. 78
70 ■ Southwest Tex. St. 78
96 ■ Texas-San Antonio 98
93 Northwestern (La.) 90
83 † Southwest Tex. St. 79
82 Northeast La. 106

TEX.-PAN AMERICAN 2-20
29 Iowa 85
54 † LIU-Brooklyn 60
61 Toledo 77
69 † Southeastern La. 87
62 ■ Louisiana Tech 59
64 Lamar 103
62 New Orleans 83
73 South Ala. 94
70 ■ Ark.-Lit. Rock 77
80 ■ Jacksonville 79
49 Western Ky. 105
52 ■ Lamar 88
61 ■ Arkansas St. 74
59 Louisiana Tech 74
63 Southwestern La. 77
63 ■ New Orleans 81
68 ■ Western Ky. 98
85 Jacksonville 90
69 ■ Southwestern La. 70
57 Arkansas St. 66
66 Ark.-Lit. Rock 78
77 ■ South Ala. 101

TEXAS-SAN ANTONIO 15-14
101 ■ Schreiner 82
85 Texas Southern 104
78 Syracuse 104
75 Minnesota 93
67 Houston 94
72 ■ Baylor 89
92 ■ Angelo St. 87
81 ■ Western N. Mex. 64
71 McNeese St. 70
61 Nicholls St. 80
77 ■ Stephen F. Austin 64
80 ■ Sam Houston St. 78
83 ■ Southwest Tex. St. 74
105 Northwestern (La.) 99
66 Northeast La. 86
84 ■ Texas-Arlington 66
100 ■ North Texas 74
71 Sam Houston St. 65
71 Stephen F. Austin 80
68 ■ McNeese St. 79
67 Southwest Tex. St. 65
80 ■ Northeast La. 85
108 ■ Northwestern (La.) 117
89 North Texas 94
98 Texas-Arlington 96
80 ■ Nicholls St. 93
77 † McNeese St. 68
86 † Nicholls St. 67
66 Northeast La. 80

TEXAS A&M 10-17
69 New Mexico 71
55 ■ Missouri 81
85 ■ South Ala. 77
60 Northwestern 71
68 ■ Texas Southern 63
57 ■ Florida 54
50 † St. Joseph's (Pa.) 64
55 New Orleans 72
85 ■ Northern Ill. 73
92 ■ Brown 52
58 Alabama 64
65 ■ Rice 66
69 ■ Houston 81
96 Nevada-Las Vegas 98
60 Texas Christian 58
65 Southern Methodist 68
80 ■ Baylor 71
54 ■ Texas Tech 69
78 Texas 82
82 Baylor 90
51 Houston 78
69 ■ Texas Christian 56
77 ■ Texas 57
73 ■ Southern Methodist 84
53 Texas Tech 72
82 Rice 76
68 † Houston 84

TEX. A&M-KINGSVILLE 17-10
64 † Central Ark. 65
59 † Indianapolis 48
102 ■ Tex. Lutheran 81
71 ■ St. Edward's 64
81 Tex. Lutheran 70
77 St. Mary's (Tex.) 62
62 ■ West Tex. A&M 71
64 Wichita St. 75
80 Northwestern (La.) 91
80 ■ Wayland Baptist 83
90 ■ Concordia (Tex.) 73
68 Oklahoma City 91
67 West Tex. A&M 64
91 Abilene Christian 59
76 Angelo St. 69
76 ■ East Tex. St. 72
60 ■ Eastern N. Mex. 71
95 Central Okla. 90
75 Cameron 85
96 ■ Cameron 78
88 ■ Central Okla. 85
71 ■ Angelo St. 65
77 ■ Abilene Christian 94
64 Eastern N. Mex. 55
84 East Tex. St. 54
91 Abilene Christian 81
68 † Eastern N. Mex. 76

TEXAS CHRISTIAN 6-22
64 ■ Louisiana Tech 50
42 † Manhattan 67
85 † North Caro. A&T 87
85 ■ Centenary 100
75 † Tenn.-Martin 67
55 † Arkansas St. 76
47 ■ Oklahoma St. 65
49 Louisiana Tech 66
62 San Francisco 70
57 Baylor 79
65 Rice 84
66 ■ Hofstra 63
65 ■ Southern Methodist 79
58 ■ Texas A&M 60
66 Tulsa 88
83 Texas Tech 89
83 ■ Texas 77
68 ■ Houston 66
55 ■ Baylor 67
50 ■ Rice 68
53 Southern Methodist 60
56 Texas A&M 69
68 DePaul 79
77 ■ Texas Tech 87
84 Texas 102
66 Houston 86
72 Southern Methodist 71
59 † Texas Tech 76

TEXAS SOUTHERN 12-15
44 Cincinnati 87
104 ■ Texas-San Antonio 85
76 Oral Roberts 82
68 Stephen F. Austin 75
63 Texas A&M 68
74 Iowa St. 111
70 Iowa 91
58 ■ Stephen F. Austin 57
69 California 84
85 ■ Houston Baptist 56
91 ■ Alabama St. 89
83 ■ Jackson St. 84
72 Mississippi Val. 70
71 Grambling 69
88 ■ Southern-B.R. 90
72 ■ Alcorn St. 85
104 Prairie View 77
61 New Mexico 78
69 Alabama St. 83
71 Jackson St. 74
69 ■ Mississippi Val. 64
98 ■ Grambling 82
103 ■ Oral Roberts 80
87 Southern-B.R. 86
91 Alcorn St. 93
79 ■ Prairie View 72
74 † Mississippi Val. 92

TEXAS TECH 18-12
72 ■ Pepperdine 69
88 † North Texas 68
86 Montana 82
65 ■ UTEP 73
72 ■ Colorado St. 62
93 ■ Midwestern St. 69
75 New Mexico 96
79 † Montana St. 70
98 † Texas-Arlington 86
78 North Texas 70
54 Tulane 70
59 ■ Southern Methodist 61
59 Rice 67
74 Texas 92
78 ■ Houston 74
89 ■ Texas Christian 83
69 Texas A&M 54
102 ■ Baylor 105
75 Southern Methodist 78
76 Houston 93
117 ■ Oral Roberts 99
79 ■ Rice 86
105 ■ Texas 103
87 Texas Christian 77
72 ■ Texas A&M 53
90 Baylor 91
83 † Baylor 74
76 † Texas Christian 59
88 † Houston 76
67 † St. John's (N.Y.) 85

THIEL 7-16
63 Roberts Wesleyan 67
92 ■ Ohio Valley College 88
56 Carnegie Mellon 82
59 Thomas 51
44 Kenyon 62
41 ■ Kenyon 57
71 ■ Oberlin 44
47 Fredonia St. 76
53 ■ Carnegie Mellon 68
62 Ohio Valley College 80
83 Bapt. Bible (Pa.) 104
59 ■ Grove City 56
58 Wash. & Jeff. 84
56 ■ Hiram 86
47 ■ Bethany (W.Va.) 74
55 Penn St.-Behrend 54
67 Waynesburg 88
49 Grove City 60
77 Hilbert 89
63 ■ Wash. & Jeff. 67
79 Bethany (W.Va.) 91
64 ■ Penn St.-Behrend 62
96 ■ Waynesburg 86

THOMAS MORE 15-11
83 † Bethany (W.Va.) 72
60 Capital 63
61 ■ Warner Southern 60
44 Miami (Ohio) 88
51 Eastern Ky. 79
80 ■ Ind.-Kokomo 62
78 ■ Ohio Wesleyan 85
84 † Concordia (Mich.) 79
60 † Mo. Southern St. 81
82 † Lake Superior St. 85
56 Wittenberg 68

77 Defiance 86
85 ■ Wilmington (Ohio) 75
70 ■ Bluffton 60
85 ■ Franklin 77
76 Wilmington (Ohio) 82
105 ■ Ky. Christian 95
77 Bluffton 74
107 ■ Berea 88
73 ■ Defiance 83
104 ■ Asbury 106
91 ■ Hanover 84
80 ■ Anderson 79
97 Berea 91
81 ■ Wilmington (Ohio) 64
82 ■ Defiance 81

TOLEDO 12-16
52 Detroit Mercy 73
55 ■ Alas. Fairbanks 66
50 Wis.-Green Bay 62
77 ■ Tex.-Pan American 61
61 ■ East Caro. 72
82 ■ Chicago St. 75
60 ■ Penn St. 69
50 ■ Yale 54
61 Ohio 67
81 ■ Central Mich. 67
61 Bowling Green 69
62 ■ Eastern Mich. 65
87 ■ Akron 71
57 Kent 65
81 ■ Ball St. 78
62 Miami (Ohio) 64
64 ■ Western Mich. 62
115 Central Mich. 109
50 ■ Bowling Green 49
50 Eastern Mich. 65
75 Akron 67
66 ■ Kent 58
64 Ball St. 78
57 ■ Miami (Ohio) 63
57 Western Mich. 75
85 ■ Ohio 73
85 † Ohio 84
64 † Ball St. 72

TOWSON ST. 18-9
71 ■ Loyola (Md.) 61
73 Oklahoma 115
56 Southwest Mo. St. 71
74 ■ Coppin St. 79
68 Maryland 78
85 † Bridgeport 70
66 Connecticut 99
78 ■ George Mason 71
69 ■ Delaware 76
85 ■ N.C.-Asheville 64
61 ■ Campbell 56
77 Coastal Caro. 74
87 Charleston So. 76
93 ■ Winthrop 85
75 ■ Charleston So. 58
78 Winthrop 90
61 Campbell 63
82 ■ Md.-Balt. County 76
74 ■ Coastal Caro. 69
79 Lehigh 70
86 Liberty 81
98 ■ Radford 90
75 ■ Liberty 69
75 N.C.-Asheville 60
81 Radford 70
97 Md.-Balt. County 92
79 † Winthrop 83

TRENTON ST. 14-13
72 Millersville 110
76 Rutgers-Camden 53
93 † Washington (Mo.) 98
67 † Hobart 70
61 ■ Jersey City St. 63
55 Kean 74
73 ■ Hunter 62
62 ■ Montclair St. 61
78 ■ Wm. Paterson 51
67 FDU-Madison 61
67 ■ Ramapo 60
58 Rowan 85
98 ■ Rutgers-Newark 63
71 Stockton St. 86
71 Jersey City St. 64
61 ■ Rutgers-Camden 40
65 Ramapo 79
75 ■ Rowan 57
60 ■ Kean 54
79 Montclair St. 82
68 Wm. Paterson 62
69 ■ Salisbury St. 96
83 ■ Stockton St. 84
66 Rutgers-Newark 59
54 Rowan 73
53 ■ Baruch 47
51 ■ Stony Brook 55

TRINITY (CONN.) 9-12
68 Albertus Magnus 54
80 ■ Coast Guard 83
60 ■ Westfield St. 61
51 † Utica 59
91 Oswego St. 60
86 ■ Eastern Nazarene 69
67 Wesleyan 82
74 † Connecticut Col. 56
76 ■ Wesleyan 58
69 ■ Tufts 71
68 Worcester Tech 59
73 ■ Connecticut Col. 88
96 Vassar 54
68 Clark (Mass.) 80
56 Colby 58
75 Bates 80
58 ■ Williams 80
86 Manhattanville 70
77 ■ Amherst 84
69 ■ Wheaton (Mass.) 84
84 Wesleyan 64

TRINITY (TEX.) 9-16
71 ■ Wash. & Lee 63
65 ■ Colby 88
109 ■ Dallas 70
67 Southwestern (Tex.) 75
62 † Beloit 77
78 † Whittier 81
51 Carthage 74
66 Ripon 81
74 ■ Loyola (La.) 68
78 Hendrix 61
75 Dallas 46
60 ■ Centre 72
81 ■ Fisk 44
65 Millsaps 75
52 Rhodes 66
55 Oglethorpe 78
70 Sewanee 85
50 ■ Southwestern (Tex.) 52
61 ■ Millsaps 49
58 ■ Rhodes 56
52 ■ Hendrix 58
59 ■ Oglethorpe 75
80 ■ Sewanee 87
58 Centre 107
75 Fisk 72

TROY ST. 27-5
104 Faulkner 98
105 ■ Birm. Southern 96
140 Central Wesleyan 100
106 Armstrong St. 117
124 Miles 91
109 ■ Morris Brown 97
116 Alabama St. 121
112 Aub.-Montgomery 107
145 Talladega 115
100 † North Dak. St. 94
112 North Dak. 86
132 ■ Central Meth. 121
113 Valdosta St. 109
121 Fla. Atlantic 93
114 † Central Okla. 123
94 Florida Tech 86
115 ■ Tuskegee 76
85 ■ Aub.-Montgomery 80
125 ■ Kennesaw 109
92 Morris Brown 80
120 Ala.-Huntsville 93
110 ■ Valdosta St. 95
122 ■ Fla. Atlantic 97
84 Tuskegee 87
114 ■ Ala.-Huntsville 89
145 ■ Faulkner 117
130 ■ Miles 104
75 ■ Fla. Southern 72
110 ■ Delta St. 93
94 † Washburn 82
126 † New Hamp. Col. 123
72 † Cal St. Bakersfield 85

TUFTS 16-9
52 † Colorado Col. 71
81 † Bates 80
93 Anna Maria 89
66 Mass.-Lowell 83
73 ■ Colby 86
73 ■ Bowdoin 64
71 ■ Framingham St. 77
99 ■ Middlebury 89
58 ■ Mass.-Boston 70
72 ■ Salem St. 68
71 Trinity (Conn.) 69
61 Wheaton (Mass.) 59
71 Wesleyan 57
99 ■ Suffolk 72
71 Amherst 56
71 Worcester Tech 82
103 ■ Babson 106
80 ■ MIT 71
67 ■ Williams 77
76 Bates 73
78 Middlebury 68
77 ■ Clark (Mass.) 65
86 Brandeis 77
102 Connecticut Col. 86
86 Western Conn. St. 87

TULANE 22-9
70 ■ Wagner 54
92 Indiana 102
96 ■ Nicholls St. 54
103 ■ Southern Methodist 92
86 Memphis St. 85
91 ■ Northwestern (La.) 81
69 Ala.-Birmingham 75
84 ■ Jackson St. 92
64 ■ Hofstra 55
107 ■ Prairie View 74
86 ■ UC Irvine 65
70 Mercer 52
84 ■ Virginia Tech 72
70 ■ Texas Tech 54
84 Southern Miss. 71
84 Va. Commonwealth 76
71 South Fla. 53
65 ■ Southern Miss. 52
72 Virginia Tech 59
64 N.C.-Charlotte 68
62 ■ Louisville 60
63 ■ Canisius 41
75 ■ N.C.-Charlotte 70
87 ■ Fla. Atlantic 62
57 Temple 79
67 Louisville 94
65 ■ Va. Commonwealth 77
91 ■ South Fla. 75
55 † Virginia Tech 64
55 † Kansas St. 53
63 † Florida St. 94

TULSA 15-14
101 ■ North Texas 70
68 Hawaii 63
69 † Long Beach St. 72
69 Hawaii 87
67 Oklahoma St. 85
104 ■ Oral Roberts 81
66 ■ Va. Commonwealth 67
74 ■ Illinois St. 61
87 Arkansas 101
66 ■ Northern Iowa 75
85 Baylor 94
54 Southwest Mo. St. 62
66 ■ Bradley 43
66 Northern Iowa 61
89 ■ Indiana St. 84
77 ■ Southwest Mo. St. 74
103 Oral Roberts 69
88 ■ Texas Christian 66
76 Wichita St. 77
88 Drake 96
70 Creighton 63
77 ■ Southern Ill. 70
95 ■ Drake 82
63 Illinois St. 72
57 Bradley 72
69 ■ Creighton 66
74 Indiana St. 86
80 ■ Wichita St. 63
80 Southern Ill. 106

TUSKEGEE 13-14
61 † Talladega 65
71 Ga. Southwestern 80
71 † Talladega 81
88 ■ Columbus 69
78 Fort Valley St. 85
78 ■ Selma 65
88 Columbus 106
76 Troy St. 115
83 ■ Morehouse 80
83 LeMoyne-Owen 86
78 ■ Clark Atlanta 68
71 Alabama A&M 88
64 ■ LeMoyne-Owen 83
90 Miles 79
63 ■ Alabama A&M 94
72 ■ Talladega 69
64 ■ Savannah St. 66
62 ■ Paine 60
63 ■ Fort Valley St. 62
89 Morehouse 90
87 ■ Troy St. 84
74 ■ Albany St. (Ga.) 63
95 ■ Miles 55
85 ■ Morris Brown 60
79 ■ Ga. Southwestern 69
99 Selma 101
80 † Fort Valley St. 88

UCLA 22-11
68 ■ St. Louis 54
73 ■ UTEP 72
64 † Seton Hall 73
86 † Florida St. 83
69 ■ Santa Clara 60
90 ■ San Diego 63
68 † Georgia 63
80 ■ Cal St. Northridge 73
79 Pittsburgh 91
90 ■ Cal St. Fullerton 82
87 ■ Houston 78
80 ■ Arizona 82
89 ■ Arizona St. 85
99 Oregon 87
73 Oregon St. 79
84 ■ Stanford 76
82 ■ California 104
90 Southern Cal 80
68 ■ Notre Dame 65
67 Washington 81
56 Washington St. 67
76 ■ Oregon St. 75
97 ■ Oregon 90
72 Stanford 64
85 California 71
62 ■ Southern Cal 72
67 Duke 78
71 ■ Washington St. 70
93 ■ Washington 64
77 Arizona St. 74

- 80 Arizona 99
- 81 † Iowa St. 70
- 84 † Michigan 86

UTEP 21-13

- 90 ■ George Mason 71
- 72 UCLA 73
- 64 New Mexico St. 63
- 69 ■ New Mexico St. 75
- 73 Texas Tech 65
- 96 ■ Abilene Christian 64
- 89 ■ Sam Houston St. 77
- 73 ■ Washington 68
- 77 ■ Austin Peay 56
- 61 ■ Purdue 63
- 73 Brigham Young 79
- 54 Utah 75
- 82 ■ Air Force 69
- 73 ■ Fresno St. 67
- 76 San Diego St. 54
- 69 Hawaii 68
- 70 ■ Wyoming 74
- 63 ■ Colorado St. 61
- 62 ■ New Mexico 65
- 72 ■ Mississippi Col. 68
- 53 New Mexico 60
- 81 Wyoming 78
- 77 Colorado St. 82
- 77 ■ San Diego St. 60
- 68 ■ Hawaii 67
- 68 Air Force 46
- 57 Fresno St. 60
- 63 ■ Brigham Young 84
- 79 ■ Utah 70
- 70 † Colorado St. 65
- 90 Utah 85
- 65 † New Mexico 76
- 67 ■ Houston 61
- 44 Georgetown 71

UNION (N.Y.) 10-15

- 76 † Rensselaer 78
- 75 Skidmore 81
- 96 Vassar 52
- 55 Alfred 64
- 62 Wesleyan 70
- 106 ■ Hobart 105
- 58 Williams 80
- 96 ■ Stevens Tech 57
- 71 ■ Susquehanna 77
- 72 ■ Middlebury 62
- 78 Utica 79
- 69 ■ Albany (N.Y.) 61
- 85 Merchant Marine 65
- 56 Hartwick 74
- 81 ■ Elmira 97
- 72 ■ Le Moyne 82
- 73 Nazareth (N.Y.) 82
- 53 Ithaca 50
- 71 Hamilton 92
- 97 ■ Rensselaer 99
- 106 ■ Skidmore 92
- 72 ■ Williams 84
- 62 Middlebury 81
- 112 ■ St. Lawrence 63
- 80 ■ Clarkson 64

UPPER IOWA 11-14

- 73 Iowa Wesleyan 81
- 86 Coe 82
- 50 Rose-Hulman 54
- 76 † MacMurray 51
- 73 Winona St. 92
- 57 ■ Teikyo Marycrest 76
- 89 ■ N'western (Iowa) 57
- 57 Dubuque 72
- 57 Luther 62
- 69 ■ Central (Iowa) 73
- 66 ■ William Penn 61
- 88 ■ Wartburg 80
- 74 Buena Vista 75
- 90 ■ Mt. St. Clare 56
- 87 Mt. Mercy 83
- 56 ■ Loras 63
- 74 Simpson 60
- 80 ■ Buena Vista 58
- 80 ■ Luther 79
- 72 William Penn 76
- 67 Central (Iowa) 71
- 48 ■ Dubuque 73
- 82 ■ Simpson 71
- 49 Loras 52
- 57 Wartburg 87

UPSALA 15-9

- 84 ■ North Adams St. 67
- 101 ■ Centenary (N.J.) 73
- 75 Montclair St. 72
- 92 ■ Drew 88
- 97 Delaware Valley 66
- 85 ■ Old Westbury 66
- 66 Albany (N.Y.) 92
- 68 Jersey City St. 75
- 65 ■ Bloomfield 78
- 66 ■ Scranton 91
- 105 Medgar Evers 89
- 76 King's (Pa.) 71
- 82 ■ FDU-Madison 64
- 108 Pratt 106
- 75 Wilkes 81
- 88 Drew 74
- 93 ■ Delaware Valley 72
- 54 Western Conn. St. 73
- 58 Scranton 91
- 88 Centenary (N.J.) 75
- 83 ■ Caldwell 79
- 50 FDU-Madison 51
- 90 ■ Wilmington (Del.) 75
- 75 ■ Wilkes 77

URSINUS 7-17

- 48 Dickinson 75
- 57 † Hampden-Sydney 82
- 58 Albright 45
- 84 Gwynedd Mercy 66
- 69 † St. Joseph's (N.Y.) 59
- 56 † Phila. Pharmacy 55
- 76 † Wash. & Jeff. 80
- 66 † Misericordia 76
- 61 Mount Union 70
- 48 † Denison 50
- 54 King's (Pa.) 73
- 60 FDU-Madison 73
- 73 ■ Delaware Valley 65
- 57 ■ Johns Hopkins 64
- 48 ■ Widener 65
- 82 Haverford 75
- 51 ■ Washington (Md.) 68
- 60 ■ Moravian 66
- 60 ■ Swarthmore 72
- 59 Johns Hopkins 94
- 39 Widener 70
- 72 ■ Haverford 65
- 41 Washington (Md.) 83
- 65 Swarthmore 79

UTAH 24-7

- 82 ■ Montana Tech 62
- 74 ■ Cal St. Sacramento 45
- 83 Bradley 49
- 86 ■ Utah St. 79
- 64 Arizona 78
- 87 ■ Texas 76
- 75 Utah St. 85
- 96 ■ Wis.-Milwaukee 62
- 60 ■ San Jose St. 47
- 78 ■ New Mexico 45
- 75 ■ UTEP 54
- 54 Brigham Young 53
- 61 Air Force 47
- 103 Fresno St. 83
- 82 ■ Hawaii 67
- 78 ■ San Diego St. 53
- 64 Wyoming 45
- 69 Colorado St. 78
- 88 ■ Wyoming 64
- 84 ■ Colorado St. 71
- 88 San Diego St. 77
- 62 Hawaii 60
- 87 ■ Air Force 61
- 75 ■ Fresno St. 65
- 89 ■ Brigham Young 83
- 59 New Mexico 69
- 70 UTEP 79
- 85 ■ San Diego St. 64
- 85 ■ UTEP 90
- 86 † Pittsburgh 65
- 62 † Kentucky 83

UTAH ST. 10-17

- 80 ■ Montana Tech 49
- 83 ■ Brigham Young 93
- 79 Utah 86
- 80 Weber St. 85
- 65 Brigham Young 89
- 85 ■ Utah 75
- 88 ■ Seattle Pacific 76
- 84 Nevada 61
- 70 UC Irvine 65
- 71 Cal St. Fullerton 91
- 75 ■ UC Santa Barb. 65
- 69 ■ Long Beach St. 75
- 93 Rutgers 113
- 79 Pacific (Cal.) 86
- 79 San Jose St. 80
- 78 ■ Nevada-Las Vegas 87
- 64 ■ New Mexico St. 76
- 86 ■ Cal St. Fullerton 61
- 81 ■ UC Irvine 70
- 64 Long Beach St. 76
- 77 UC Santa Barb. 75
- 62 ■ Pacific (Cal.) 72
- 92 ■ San Jose St. 79
- 60 New Mexico St. 82
- 86 Nevada-Las Vegas 94
- 87 ■ Nevada 97
- 86 † Nevada-Las Vegas 104

UTICA 17-9

- 68 ■ Castleton St. 48
- 75 ■ Hamilton 72
- 66 ■ Utica Tech 55
- 67 ■ Clarkson 57
- 60 ■ Keuka 67
- 59 † Trinity (Conn.) 51
- 66 † Mt. St. Mary (N.Y.) 64
- 83 Oneonta St. 81
- 69 Skidmore 66
- 79 ■ Union (N.Y.) 78
- 72 Cortland St. 61
- 62 Elmira 83
- 104 Pracitical Bible 64
- 89 ■ St. Lawrence 67
- 69 ■ Maritime (N.Y.) 58
- 79 ■ Oswego St. 46
- 48 Hamilton 65
- 58 Hartwick 60
- 71 ■ St. John Fisher 88
- 62 ■ Ithaca 66
- 76 Mt. St. Mary (N.Y.) 74
- 66 Keuka 63
- 83 Rensselaer 96
- 81 ■ Nazareth (N.Y.) 63
- 71 ■ Elmira 75
- 74 Rochester Inst. 97

UTICA TECH 7-16

- 76 † Hamilton 92
- 66 † Castleton St. 62
- 55 Utica 66
- 59 Lehman 50
- 76 ■ Oswego St. 50
- 76 Buffalo St. 84
- 62 Binghamton 77
- 92 ■ Cortland St. 85
- 71 ■ Geneseo St. 75
- 70 Brockport St. 84
- 74 Fredonia St. 83
- 81 ■ Mt. St. Mary (N.Y.) 73
- 78 ■ New Paltz St. 62
- 78 Oneonta St. 91
- 50 Albany (N.Y.) 72
- 67 Oswego St. 69
- 61 ■ Buffalo St. 88
- 82 Plattsburgh St. 93
- 84 ■ Potsdam St. 75
- 72 Geneseo St. 85
- 67 ■ Brockport St. 68
- 70 ■ Fredonia St. 75
- 81 Hamilton 91

VALDOSTA ST. 12-13

- 75 Morris Brown 74
- 80 Mercer 88
- 108 ■ Fort Valley St. 86
- 63 ■ Southern Tech 56
- 84 ■ Columbus 81
- 74 ■ Armstrong St. 54
- 109 ■ Troy St. 113
- 61 West Ga. 69
- 76 Fort Valley St. 79
- 77 ■ Delta St. 74
- 80 ■ North Ala. 87
- 62 Livingston 75
- 76 Mississippi Col. 78
- 77 Jacksonville St. 86
- 85 ■ Morris Brown 54
- 73 Armstrong St. 92
- 66 Albany St. (Ga.) 73
- 91 ■ West Ga. 77
- 89 ■ Jacksonville St. 80
- 95 ■ Albany St. (Ga.) 86
- 95 Troy St. 110
- 90 ■ Mississippi Col. 84
- 87 ■ Livingston 75
- 62 Delta St. 89
- 74 North Ala. 76

VALPARAISO 12-16

- 66 ■ Air Force 58
- 87 Baylor 104
- 89 † Centenary 92
- 77 ■ Evansville 84
- 78 ■ Ball St. 75
- 79 Brown 80
- 68 Niagara 102
- 62 Butler 81
- 78 ■ Wright St. 92
- 65 Northern Ill. 73
- 94 ■ Eastern Ill. 76
- 82 ■ Western Ill. 65
- 86 ■ Ill.-Chicago 88
- 65 Wis.-Green Bay 76
- 85 ■ Youngstown St. 76
- 73 ■ Cleveland St. 75
- 101 Ill.-Chicago 94
- 71 ■ Wis.-Green Bay 78
- 72 ■ Northern Ill. 61
- 67 Wright St. 79
- 93 Youngstown St. 72
- 81 Cleveland St. 85
- 84 ■ Carthage 68
- 76 Eastern Ill. 77
- 104 Western Ill. 100
- 80 Notre Dame 66
- 83 † Northern Ill. 75
- 72 Wright St. 82

VANDERBILT 28-6

- 81 † Ala.-Birmingham 63
- 77 † Illinois 93
- 83 † Oregon 81
- 86 ■ Northwestern 66
- 75 Dayton 53
- 90 ■ Louisville 88
- 95 ■ Southern Methodist 86
- 87 † North Caro. A&T 51
- 116 Austin Peay 71
- 95 ■ Air Force 50
- 96 ■ Bowling Green 69
- 76 ■ Alabama 73
- 78 Memphis St. 84
- 61 Florida 62
- 101 ■ Kentucky 86
- 78 ■ Georgia 66
- 102 ■ Arkansas 89
- 82 Tennessee 65

73 Auburn 70
76 ■ South Caro. 72
67 Kentucky 82
89 ■ Mississippi 59
81 ■ Middle Tenn. St. 51
87 Louisiana St. 66
82 ■ Florida 64
87 Georgia 83
80 Mississippi St. 39
90 ■ Tennessee 82
77 South Caro. 73
76 † Alabama 59
62 † Louisiana St. 72
92 † Boise St. 72
85 † Illinois 68
59 † Temple 67

VASSAR 6-16
57 ■ Maritime (N.Y.) 71
65 ■ Rivier 89
69 Bard 55
52 ■ Union (N.Y.) 96
37 Williams 104
55 † Baruch 80
70 Webb Inst. 14
70 Bard 56
51 † New Paltz St. 91
56 Stevens Tech 76
46 ■ Wesleyan 90
63 Polytechnic (N.Y.) 62
54 ■ Trinity (Conn.) 96
41 Maritime (N.Y.) 72
53 Skidmore 103
67 ■ Mt. St. Vincent 98
59 ■ John Jay 80
63 ■ Polytechnic (N.Y.) 53
70 ■ Albertus Magnus 97
47 New York U. 109
63 ■ Manhattanville 78
66 ■ Bard 53

VERMONT 10-17
82 Yale 70
76 Wake Forest 95
86 N.C.-Greensboro 71
73 ■ Harvard 65
44 Villanova 89
80 Colgate 94
79 ■ Lafayette 89
60 Dartmouth 66
74 ■ Northeastern 82
97 ■ Boston U. 94
63 Maine 67
76 ■ New Hampshire 69
69 Delaware 73
82 Drexel 85
73 ■ Dartmouth 105
94 Central Conn. St. 86
68 Hartford 93
71 ■ Drexel 85
73 ■ Delaware 88
65 New Hampshire 66
82 ■ Maine 74
76 ■ St. Michael's 74
67 Northeastern 87
98 Boston U. 88
95 ■ Central Conn. St. 82
58 ■ Hartford 76
68 Northeastern 91

VILLANOVA 8-19
86 American 74
64 St. Mary's (Cal.) 65
59 † Pennsylvania 71
89 ■ Vermont 44
90 ■ Lehigh 66
75 ■ Columbia 63
79 Syracuse 61
64 Boston College 67
80 ■ Connecticut 87
70 ■ St. John's (N.Y.) 76
56 ■ Georgetown 66
61 Seton Hall 66
58 ■ Boston College 65

66 Providence 77
82 ■ Miami (Fla.) 69
82 Pittsburgh 76
66 † St. Joseph's (Pa.) 77
62 Connecticut 82
92 ■ Hofstra 54
59 ■ Seton Hall 65
52 Georgetown 61
59 ■ Providence 74
72 ■ Syracuse 73
62 St. John's (N.Y.) 65
76 ■ Pittsburgh 77
76 Miami (Fla.) 77
70 † Boston College 74

VIRGINIA 21-10
74 Pennsylvania 68
72 ■ Stanford 48
90 ■ Old Dominion 68
100 ■ Howard 64
86 ■ Alabama 83
82 ■ Radford 63
92 ■ Winthrop 68
80 ■ Florida St. 76
73 North Caro. St. 56
100 ■ Clemson 82
77 Duke 69
58 North Caro. 80
71 ■ Georgia Tech 75
93 William & Mary 84
73 ■ Wake Forest 75
53 † Virginia Tech 59
70 Maryland 68
84 Florida St. 99
75 ■ North Caro. St. 66
83 Clemson 78
58 ■ Duke 55
58 ■ North Caro. 78
61 Georgia Tech 73
56 Wake Forest 58
72 ■ Charleston (S.C.) 58
88 ■ Maryland 74
61 † Wake Forest 57
56 † North Caro. 74
78 † Manhattan 66
71 † Massachusetts 56
54 † Cincinnati 71

VA. COMMONWEALTH 20-10
103 ■ New Hampshire 68
86 † Marist 61
81 Syracuse 94
82 Richmond 63
65 † Old Dominion 81
67 Tulsa 66
78 Western Ky. 84
83 ■ Murray St. 77
85 ■ Southern Miss. 74
103 ■ George Mason 75
88 ■ Liberty 75
68 Louisville 77
57 ■ Siena 42
76 ■ Tulane 84
95 ■ Long Beach St. 61
88 ■ Louisville 90
63 ■ N.C.-Charlotte 61
73 Virginia Tech 54
79 ■ South Fla. 59
70 N.C.-Charlotte 84
66 Texas 60
95 South Fla. 91
86 ■ Virginia Tech 69
90 Buffalo 61
77 Tulane 65
65 Southern Miss. 71
79 † South Fla. 72
85 † Virginia Tech 71
78 Louisville 90
68 Old Dominion 74

VA. MILITARY 5-22
91 ■ Bluefield Col. 63
65 Richmond 77
88 Radford 91

77 † Central Conn. St. 84
62 † Lafayette 56
52 Georgia Tech 78
54 East Tenn. St. 71
67 ■ Western Caro. 56
62 ■ Tenn.-Chatt. 71
93 Appalachian St. 86
76 ■ Citadel 74
70 ■ Ga. Southern 73
64 Davidson 75
61 Furman 73
66 Marshall 80
55 ■ Appalachian St. 64
70 ■ East Tenn. St. 96
67 ■ William & Mary 77
69 ■ Marshall 78
44 Virginia Tech 75
70 Tenn.-Chatt. 93
51 Western Caro. 84
63 Ga. Southern 69
53 Citadel 69
69 ■ Furman 85
70 ■ Davidson 84
51 † Furman 76

VIRGINIA ST. 12-15
66 Fayetteville St. 69
99 ■ Johnson Smith 94
76 St. Augustine's 81
63 ■ Virginia Union 78
65 ■ Norfolk St. 67
78 ■ N.C. Central 84
74 Winston-Salem 50
87 North Caro. A&T 97
84 ■ West Va. St. 55
76 ■ Norfolk St. 93
79 ■ Bowie St. 97
80 ■ Rutgers-Camden 52
112 Elizabeth City St. 115
96 Hampton 103
86 ■ Bowie St. 81
91 St. Paul's 75
92 ■ Dist. Columbia 72
87 Norfolk St. 85
70 Virginia Union 95
92 ■ Elizabeth City St. 98
83 ■ Hampton 88
75 ■ Livingstone 57
84 Bowie St. 92
82 ■ St. Paul's 66
90 Shaw 79
97 † St. Augustine's 95
73 † Virginia Union 90

VIRGINIA TECH 10-18
55 ■ Western Caro. 47
62 † North Caro. 78
91 ■ N.C.-Asheville 71
87 ■ Morgan St. 76
76 ■ East Caro. 67
82 Southern Miss. 84
72 Tulane 84
56 ■ N.C.-Charlotte 65
74 ■ South Fla. 62
80 ■ Fla. Atlantic 55
61 Old Dominion 71
65 ■ Liberty 71
65 ■ Louisville 76
59 † Virginia 53
70 ■ William & Mary 66
59 ■ Tulane 72
54 ■ Va. Commonwealth 73
44 ■ Florida Int'l 57
75 ■ Va. Military 44
50 South Fla. 77
49 East Caro. 66
69 Va. Commonwealth 86
70 West Va. 74
79 ■ Southern Miss. 83
61 Louisville 82
80 † N.C.-Charlotte 89
64 † Tulane 55
71 † Va. Commonwealth 85

VIRGINIA UNION 27-3
86 † Oklahoma City 88
97 Alas. Fairbanks 94
71 Dist. Columbia 64
78 Virginia St. 63
85 ■ Johnson Smith 80
95 Livingstone 54
109 Bridgeport 115
94 ■ Fayetteville St. 47
80 Elizabeth City St. 77
68 ■ St. Paul's 55
63 ■ Hampton 54
79 ■ Shaw 70
64 Norfolk St. 62
85 Hampton 76
88 St. Paul's 73
96 Winston-Salem 72
92 Bowie St. 67
95 ■ Virginia St. 70
82 St. Augustine's 71
78 ■ Norfolk St. 72
73 N.C. Central 67
88 ■ Bowie St. 70
82 ■ Bridgeport 79
95 ■ Elizabeth City St. 85
108 ■ Dist. Columbia 61
90 † Virginia St. 73
71 † Norfolk St. 63
67 † N.C. Central 61
67 † Fayetteville St. 38
81 † N.C. Central 93

VA. WESLEYAN 19-9
88 ■ Mary Washington 55
62 Chris. Newport 71
84 ■ Wash. & Lee 68
104 Salisbury St. 88
91 † Shenandoah 70
101 † Averett 46
89 East. Mennonite 83
63 William & Mary 81
104 ■ East. Mennonite 61
81 Guilford 69
64 ■ Hampden-Sydney 62
91 ■ Roanoke 87
49 Randolph-Macon 54
57 Bridgewater (Va.) 56
59 Lynchburg 64
50 Roanoke 65
99 ■ Emory & Henry 78
77 Wash. & Lee 59
78 ■ Guilford 76
53 ■ Randolph-Macon 60
75 Hampden-Sydney 76
64 Emory & Henry 70
74 ■ Bridgewater (Va.) 66
79 ■ Lynchburg 67
76 ■ Bridgewater (Va.) 65
90 † Emory & Henry 76
70 † Randolph-Macon 61
62 Rhodes 71

WABASH 16-10
121 Ind.-Kokomo 77
84 † Grand Valley St. 93
99 † Oakland 97
80 ■ Millikin 78
107 Webster 66
88 ■ Olivet 85
83 ■ Kalamazoo 74
61 † Chicago 72
87 † Ind. Wesleyan 86
68 Hanover 102
94 ■ Manchester 80
97 Franklin 114
71 Eureka 82
70 Rose-Hulman 72
80 ■ Anderson 78
57 DePauw 70
65 Manchester 91
91 ■ Hanover 88
111 ■ Ind.-Kokomo 36
90 ■ Franklin 78
85 Anderson 76

72 ■ Rose-Hulman 64
57 ■ DePauw 81
84 ■ Franklin 73
66 DePauw 62
75 † Manchester 83

WAGNER 18-12
54 Tulane 70
66 Colorado 74
87 † Lehigh 82
67 † Iona 74
52 Syracuse 85
76 † Akron 60
82 Iona 98
68 ■ Robert Morris 59
76 ■ St. Francis (Pa.) 60
85 ■ LIU-Brooklyn 70
78 St. Francis (N.Y.) 73
57 Monmouth (N.J.) 61
79 ■ FDU-Teaneck 72
69 Buffalo 64
64 ■ Mt. St. Mary's (Md.) 69
67 ■ Rider 71
52 Marist 57
69 St. Francis (Pa.) 68
51 Robert Morris 48
81 ■ St. Francis (N.Y.) 78
70 LIU-Brooklyn 67
69 ■ Monmouth (N.J.) 59
81 ■ Marist 64
72 FDU-Teaneck 75
90 ■ Buffalo 64
54 Rider 58
77 Mt. St. Mary's (Md.) 70
75 ■ Monmouth (N.J.) 66
65 ■ Mt. St. Mary's (Md.) 48
64 Rider 65

WAKE FOREST 21-9
81 ■ Radford 62
95 ■ Vermont 76
69 ■ Rhode Island 65
88 ■ Richmond 74
65 California 81
71 † Davidson 52
74 ■ Lafayette 47
76 ■ Mt. St. Mary's (Md.) 65
99 ■ Winthrop 65
72 ■ Florida St. 74
59 ■ Duke 86
86 Maryland 73
81 Georgia Tech 58
74 ■ Clemson 56
75 Virginia 73
88 ■ North Caro. 62
65 North Caro. St. 54
106 Temple 69
94 Florida St. 111
98 Duke 86
88 ■ Maryland 64
58 ■ Georgia Tech 69
74 Clemson 76
58 ■ Virginia 56
65 North Caro. 83
80 ■ North Caro. St. 68
57 † Virginia 61
81 † Tenn.-Chatt. 58
84 † Iowa 78
69 † Kentucky 103

WARTBURG 18-8
107 ■ North Cent. Bible 53
71 ■ Grand View 82
78 ■ Teikyo-Westmar 86
72 Dordt 70
66 Iowa Wesleyan 64
102 ■ Clarke 80
78 ■ N'western (Minn.) 68
85 † Colorado Col. 86
76 Buena Vista 81
79 Central (Iowa) 61
73 William Penn 61
72 ■ Dubuque 71
73 ■ Luther 69
80 Upper Iowa 88
79 Simpson 67
93 ■ Buena Vista 61
73 Loras 66
69 Dubuque 79
65 ■ Central (Iowa) 66
79 Luther 61
83 ■ William Penn 68
51 ■ Loras 50
113 Buena Vista 87
64 ■ Simpson 59
87 ■ Upper Iowa 57
75 St. John's (Minn.) 80

WASHBURN 27-5
78 ■ Friends 60
87 † S.C.-Spartanburg 69
70 Florida Tech 63
73 Fort Hays St. 58
91 ■ Baker 61
93 Mid-America Naz. 79
103 ■ West Va. Tech 61
94 ■ Colo. Christian 60
108 McPherson 73
85 Northwest Mo. St. 61
73 Central Mo. St. 69
70 ■ Pittsburg St. 69
78 ■ Rockhurst 62
66 ■ Emporia St. 58
95 Mo. Western St. 76
111 ■ Northwest Mo. St. 71
83 ■ Northeast Mo. St. 65
73 ■ Southwest Baptist 68
80 ■ Central Mo. St. 60
74 Missouri-Rolla 77
69 Emporia St. 62
67 ■ Mo. Western St. 76
73 Northeast Mo. St. 63
82 Mo.-St. Louis 66
99 ■ Lincoln (Mo.) 62
80 Mo. Southern St. 82
93 ■ Northwest Mo. St. 62
73 ■ Southwest Baptist 54
77 ■ Mo. Southern St. 80
92 Central Okla. 88
79 † Eastern N. Mex. 78
82 † Troy St. 94

WASHINGTON 13-14
130 ■ Cal St. Chico 67
73 ■ Boise St. 63
60 ■ Rice 68
75 ■ Fresno St. 77
78 Jacksonville 65
68 UTEP 73
76 ■ BYU-Hawaii 48
72 ■ Dartmouth 64
81 ■ Idaho St. 69
59 Washington St. 56
76 Arizona 93
85 Arizona St. 94
70 ■ Oregon St. 73
70 ■ Oregon 53
65 California 79
68 Stanford 67
81 ■ UCLA 67
46 ■ Southern Cal 41
74 ■ Arizona St. 79
72 ■ Arizona 81
70 Oregon 85
61 Oregon St. 51
56 ■ Stanford 51
75 ■ California 76
55 Southern Cal 56
64 UCLA 93
59 ■ Washington St. 72

WASHINGTON (MD.) 13-12
60 † Albright 69
102 † Drew 81
67 Frostburg St. 76
82 ■ St. Mary's (Md.) 59
76 Md.-Balt. County 88
52 George Mason 92
88 ■ Goucher 85
59 ■ Kean 58
76 † Lycoming 60
69 Lebanon Valley 93
78 ■ Elizabethtown 87
69 Salisbury St. 91
73 Western Md. 88
78 ■ Gallaudet 71
72 Swarthmore 64
82 Haverford 64
61 ■ Johns Hopkins 68
68 Ursinus 51
61 Widener 65
78 ■ Swarthmore 74
77 ■ Haverford 66
63 Johns Hopkins 72
83 ■ Ursinus 41
89 ■ Widener 87
51 Widener 68

WASHINGTON (MO.) 15-10
68 † DePauw 69
82 † Neb. Wesleyan 64
93 † Millikin 98
98 † Trenton St. 93
68 Colorado Col. 81
66 ■ Whittier 53
73 ■ Beloit 76
108 Maryville (Mo.) 77
58 Mo.-St. Louis 68
77 ■ Rochester 67
97 ■ Brandeis 66
62 Mo.-Kansas City 101
83 ■ MacMurray 63
58 Johns Hopkins 68
76 ■ Carnegie Mellon 62
108 ■ Case Reserve 79
71 Emory 78
78 New York U. 83
67 Carnegie Mellon 78
61 Chicago 54
84 ■ New York U. 71
132 ■ Emory 111
81 Brandeis 71
80 Rochester 79
96 ■ Chicago 60

WASHINGTON ST. 15-12
87 ■ BYU-Hawaii 60
68 † Alabama 70
63 Idaho 65
83 ■ Eastern Wash. 66
94 † Azusa-Pacific 71
73 San Diego St. 51
72 † Princeton 49
61 Michigan St. 77
87 ■ Cal St. Sacramento 56
56 ■ Washington 59
77 Arizona St. 81
63 Arizona 87
95 ■ Oregon 79
56 ■ Oregon St. 51
64 Stanford 59
83 California 75
73 ■ Southern Cal 51
67 ■ UCLA 56
64 ■ Arizona 70
97 ■ Arizona St. 67
58 Oregon St. 59
60 Oregon 62
67 ■ California 76
87 ■ Stanford 54
70 UCLA 71
65 Southern Cal 81
72 Washington 59

WASH. & JEFF. 11-10
95 † Allegheny 91
64 † Carnegie Mellon 66
89 John Carroll 80
71 St. Vincent 94
87 ■ Marietta 68
80 † Ursinus 76
111 Juniata 116
83 ■ Oberlin 71
76 † Elmira 78
84 † Wheaton (Mass.) 93
67 Waynesburg 69
84 ■ Thiel 58
60 Princeton 82
47 Carnegie Mellon 60
67 ■ Grove City 79
93 Bethany (W.Va.) 76
70 ■ Waynesburg 61
67 Thiel 63
63 Navy 78
82 Grove City 73
93 ■ Bethany (W.Va.) 89

WASH. & LEE 5-19
63 Trinity (Tex.) 71
56 † Hamline 53
85 Sewanee 75
67 Bridgewater (Va.) 54
68 Va. Wesleyan 84
73 ■ Hampden-Sydney 75
67 ■ Guilford 73
80 ■ Emory & Henry 96
71 ■ Millsaps 72
73 ■ Roanoke 90
83 ■ Mary Washington 85
87 ■ Lynchburg 77
61 ■ Randolph-Macon 78
68 Emory & Henry 79
60 ■ Bridgewater (Va.) 62
67 Hampden-Sydney 89
60 Guilford 81
59 ■ Va. Wesleyan 77
69 ■ East. Mennonite 76
58 Lynchburg 57
64 Roanoke 82
74 Queens (N.C.) 79
68 East. Mennonite 71
48 Randolph-Macon 79

WAYNE ST. (MICH.) 22-10
87 Ashland 82
109 ■ Grand Rapids Bapt. 75
85 Detroit Mercy 95
85 ■ Concordia (Mich.) 58
71 Saginaw Valley 86
108 Mich.-Dearborn 86
84 ■ Northwood 62
73 ■ Ferris St. 87
85 Hillsdale 65
82 ■ Grand Valley St. 85
77 ■ Siena Heights 63
94 ■ Northern Mich. 78
101 ■ Michigan Tech 80
64 Lake Superior St. 72
76 Oakland 78
82 Findlay 85
93 Northwood 68
92 ■ Saginaw Valley 66
74 Ferris St. 73
95 ■ Mich.-Dearborn 71
81 ■ Hillsdale 75
105 Grand Valley St. 82
69 Northern Mich. 81
103 Michigan Tech 97
76 ■ Lake Superior St. 63
60 ■ Oakland 66
72 † Ferris St. 67
93 Northern Mich. 86
78 † IU/PU-Ft. Wayne 72
90 † Northern Mich. 58
78 † Phila. Textile 76
57 † Cal St. Bakersfield 61

WAYNE ST. (NEB.) 7-20
70 ■ St. Francis (Ill.) 68
68 † Morningside 87
58 † South Dak. 84
71 ■ Northwest Mo. St. 80
81 Bemidji St. 88
72 South Dak. St. 106
76 ■ Southwest St. 74
48 ■ Mankato St. 73
56 Winona St. 81
42 Viterbo 54

37	Nebraska-Omaha	77
56	† Eastern N. Mex.	57
76	† Bemidji St.	71
59	Southwest St.	53
73	■ Dana	71
69	Quincy	81
83	■ Bemidji St.	66
61	■ Drury	60
73	Briar Cliff	79
55	■ West Tex. A&M	71
56	■ Quincy	63
54	Wis.-Parkside	83
75	■ Briar Cliff	82
78	Drury	81
60	Northwest Mo. St.	83
72	■ Neb.-Kearney	95
80	Neb.-Kearney	108

WAYNESBURG 8-16

58	■ Kenyon	63
62	■ Frostburg St.	74
91	Davis & Elkins	108
82	■ Lake Erie	80
116	Ohio Belmont	98
70	† North Cent. Bible	79
78	Valley Forge Chrst.	70
78	Penn St.-Harrisburg	64
59	■ Penn St.-Behrend	71
66	Dyke	64
61	■ Juniata	58
64	■ Point Park	77
69	■ Wash. & Jeff.	67
70	■ St. John Fisher	82
77	Ohio Valley College	94
70	Grove City	79
66	Bethany (W.Va.)	85
88	■ Thiel	67
61	Wash. & Jeff.	70
69	Lake Erie	71
61	Frostburg St.	86
73	■ Grove City	78
73	■ Bethany (W.Va.)	89
86	Thiel	96

WEBER ST. 20-8

98	■ BYU-Hawaii	80
64	Purdue	85
61	† Eastern Ill.	51
83	■ Brigham Young	77
85	■ Utah St.	80
73	■ Southern Utah	62
87	San Diego	73
90	■ Denver	75
96	† Texas	104
71	† Alas. Anchorage	80
67	■ Lewis-Clark St.	54
86	■ Portland	69
91	■ Idaho St.	80
67	■ Boise St.	68
61	Montana	68
71	Montana St.	65
67	■ Idaho	66
64	■ Eastern Wash.	57
74	Northern Ariz.	70
75	Boise St.	92
89	Idaho St.	94
84	■ Montana St.	79
74	■ Montana	66
83	Eastern Wash.	73
75	Idaho	63
100	■ Northern Ariz.	79
91	† Montana St.	72
63	† Boise St.	69

WEBSTER 3-22

54	■ Mo.-St. Louis	116
66	■ Millikin	86
50	DePauw	79
52	■ Southwestern (Tex.)	89
66	■ Wabash	107
47	■ Missouri-Rolla	119
59	■ Hanover	81
75	■ Carroll (Wis.)	88
63	Bethel (Tenn.)	106

44	Union (Tenn.)	88
75	■ Principia	73
71	Blackburn	73
68	MacMurray	84
72	Maryville (Mo.)	75
72	Westminster (Mo.)	82
63	Parks	65
59	■ Fontbonne	74
64	Principia	53
55	■ Parks	60
79	■ Blackburn	82
70	■ MacMurray	72
73	■ Maryville (Mo.)	80
89	■ Westminster (Mo.)	72
63	Fontbonne	74
64	† Westminster (Mo.)	77

WENTWORTH INST. 5-20

56	Babson	85
82	† Suffolk	83
68	■ Coast Guard	73
65	Fitchburg St.	74
98	■ Nichols	95
78	† Emerson-MCA	75
70	Roger Williams	78
69	■ Worcester Tech	94
43	Eastern Nazarene	95
91	Suffolk	101
53	■ Eastern Nazarene	72
84	■ Anna Maria	99
87	■ New England Col.	90
82	Curry	72
75	■ Salve Regina	81
71	■ Gordon	83
59	Roger Williams	65
75	Anna Maria	125
74	MIT	69
65	Gordon	82
91	New England Col.	95
68	■ Curry	63
74	■ Roger Williams	85
72	Salve Regina	90
88	Anna Maria	125

WESLEY 4-19

61	† Stony Brook	91
86	† Valley Forge Chrst.	60
78	■ Gallaudet	59
73	■ Catholic	101
62	† East. Mennonite	85
73	† Newport News App.	64
64	St. Mary's (Md.)	69
72	■ Marymount (Va.)	94
59	Western Md.	72
76	† Lycoming	75
57	■ York (Pa.)	74
48	Rollins	81
77	Palm Beach Atl.	96
70	Lycoming	81
64	Allentown	87
71	Messiah	72
76	Salisbury St.	123
66	■ Lincoln (Pa.)	90
64	Stockton St.	92
55	■ Holy Family	59
66	FDU-Madison	68
64	Rowan	103
76	■ Salisbury St.	111

WESLEYAN 7-14

73	† Suffolk	62
60	Babson	76
66	Middlebury	93
70	■ Union (N.Y.)	62
66	Connecticut Col.	80
82	■ Trinity (Conn.)	67
55	■ Eastern Conn. St.	74
58	Trinity (Conn.)	76
69	■ Clark (Mass.)	56
90	Vassar	46
57	■ Tufts	71
56	Williams	72
66	■ Albertus Magnus	64
81	Bates	92
55	Colby	88

54	Coast Guard	68
58	■ Amherst	70
80	■ Western New Eng.	69
64	Amherst	88
64	■ Trinity (Conn.)	84
71	■ Williams	77

WEST CHESTER 18-8

54	■ Lincoln (Pa.)	55
82	■ Bowie St.	72
85	■ Gwynedd Mercy	58
73	■ Adelphi	67
61	† Cedarville	84
87	† Phila. Bible	52
61	Shippensburg	59
55	Phila. Textile	76
97	■ Molloy	55
71	■ New York Tech	60
60	Alvernia	46
74	Holy Family	58
90	† Eastern (Pa.)	82
71	Widener	61
67	■ East Stroudsburg	52
77	■ Bloomsburg	76
73	Kutztown	61
68	Cheyney	83
60	■ Mansfield	45
74	Millersville	92
67	East Stroudsburg	77
60	Bloomsburg	82
70	■ Kutztown	52
66	■ Cheyney	56
72	Mansfield	67
71	■ Millersville	74

WEST GA. 5-21

73	■ Brewton Parker	85
92	La Grange	99
53	■ North Ga.	55
79	Talladega	63
77	North Ga.	88
74	Brewton Parker	80
94	■ Wingate	86
72	■ Fayetteville St.	84
75	■ La Grange	77
69	■ Valdosta St.	61
76	■ North Ala.	80
68	■ Delta St.	94
67	■ Wofford	78
76	Mississippi Col.	80
62	Livingston	81
92	Wofford	105
87	Jacksonville St.	109
82	Ala.-Huntsville	83
77	Valdosta St.	91
97	■ Jacksonville St.	95
86	■ Talladega	87
58	■ Livingston	113
83	■ Mississippi Col.	120
103	■ Ala.-Huntsville	94
61	North Ala.	78
39	Delta St.	65

WEST LIBERTY ST. 12-15

86	† Pitt.-Johnstown	84
85	† Wheeling Jesuit	81
69	Calif. (Pa.)	97
65	■ Shepherd	66
79	■ Pitt.-Johnstown	82
73	Wheeling Jesuit	75
75	Muskingum	80
71	■ West Va. Tech	77
97	Charleston (W.Va.)	71
86	■ Glenville St.	90
98	Concord	104
74	Bluefield St.	85
81	■ Fairmont St.	67
102	Davis & Elkins	93
62	■ Salem Teikyo	85
96	Alderson-Broaddus	84
87	■ West Va. Wesleyan	78
104	■ Point Park	97
58	West Va. St.	72
78	Shepherd	81
68	■ Wheeling Jesuit	66

78	Fairmont St.	76
108	■ Davis & Elkins	87
44	Salem Teikyo	79
71	■ Alderson-Broaddus	72
92	† Concord	90
71	† Salem Teikyo	80

WEST TEX. A&M 17-10

111	■ Dallas	61
86	■ Colorado-CS	52
89	■ Henderson St.	47
62	■ Central Ark.	64
79	† Abilene Christian	74
79	Angelo St.	83
69	■ Eastern N. Mex.	56
64	† Western N. Mex.	57
109	† Panhandle St.	84
71	Tex. A&M-Kingsville	62
57	† SIU-Edwardsville	58
84	Missouri-Rolla	67
71	Oklahoma	121
94	■ Angelo St.	55
64	■ Tex. A&M-Kingsville	67
95	■ Huston-Tillotson	62
74	■ Western N. Mex.	75
91	■ Panhandle St.	67
73	Neb.-Kearney	81
71	Wayne St. (Neb.)	55
56	Colorado-CS	57
79	■ Grand Canyon	70
71	Eastern N. Mex.	82
91	■ Lubbock Chrst.	74
84	Grand Canyon	94
98	■ Neb.-Kearney	74
111	Lubbock Chrst.	72

WEST VA. 17-12

76	■ Robert Morris	56
86	■ Maryland	72
100	South Ala.	107
78	Pittsburgh	82
78	■ Ohio St.	69
80	† La Salle	67
74	Arizona	75
88	■ Mississippi Val.	71
84	■ Duquesne	67
72	■ Geo. Washington	56
82	■ Rhode Island	86
67	St. Joseph's (Pa.)	70
77	■ N.C.-Greensboro	56
82	■ St. Joseph's (Pa.)	81
67	Rutgers	71
92	■ St. Bonaventure	56
59	Massachusetts	64
59	Rhode Island	69
77	■ Rutgers	66
62	Temple	79
72	† Marshall	65
68	Geo. Washington	71
74	■ Virginia Tech	70
79	■ Massachusetts	54
86	■ Temple	74
82	St. Bonaventure	67
53	† Temple	80
95	■ Georgia	84
67	Providence	68

WESTERN CARO. 6-21

74	■ Mars Hill	86
47	Virginia Tech	55
73	N.C.-Asheville	46
55	Tennessee	97
73	■ St. Andrews	42
49	Charleston (S.C.)	70
69	■ Davidson	81
56	Va. Military	67
65	Marshall	86
66	■ Furman	67
66	■ Tenn.-Chatt.	93
73	Citadel	83
52	Ga. Southern	80
80	■ Appalachian St.	89
65	Furman	74
63	Davidson	82
73	■ Lander	53

71 Appalachian St. 84
76 East Tenn. St. 79
81 ■ Marshall 85
84 ■ Va. Military 51
85 ■ East Tenn. St. 77
66 Tenn.-Chatt. 85
82 ■ N.C.-Asheville 69
81 ■ Ga. Southern 90
70 ■ Citadel 79
73 † Appalachian St. 84

WESTERN CONN. ST. 20-6
71 † Elmira 68
74 Wheaton (Mass.) 69
72 Westfield St. 89
82 † St. Lawrence 64
53 Albany (N.Y.) 54
76 ■ Wm. Paterson 60
93 ■ Adrian 74
82 ■ Potsdam St. 70
67 † Greensboro 66
64 Kean 50
69 Clark (Mass.) 66
83 North Adams St. 58
91 ■ Bri'water (Mass.) 59
59 Eastern Conn. St. 61
69 † Bridgeport 96
69 Manhattanville 55
90 Mt. St. Mary (N.Y.) 69
73 ■ Upsala 54
86 ■ Albertus Magnus 75
89 ■ Colby-Sawyer 70
70 ■ Ramapo 59
94 ■ Manhattanville 71
106 Teikyo-Post 86
58 Stony Brook 64
87 ■ Tufts 86
77 Colby 91

WESTERN ILL. 7-20
73 ■ Northeastern Ill. 71
60 † Monmouth (N.J.) 73
64 † Hofstra 63
106 ■ Chicago St. 91
76 Detroit Mercy 79
71 Wis.-Milwaukee 92
59 Marquette 83
74 Chicago St. 76
83 ■ Elmhurst 84
67 ■ Wis.-Milwaukee 76
63 Youngstown St. 79
75 Cleveland St. 94
73 Wright St. 87
65 Valparaiso 82
73 ■ Ill.-Chicago 86
64 ■ Wis.-Green Bay 65
76 ■ Eastern Ill. 70
84 ■ Northern Ill. 75
45 Wis.-Green Bay 60
75 Eastern Ill. 73
92 ■ Youngstown St. 78
82 ■ Cleveland St. 96
66 Northern Ill. 74
77 Ill.-Chicago 92
80 ■ Wright St. 81
100 ■ Valparaiso 104
53 † Cleveland St. 64

WESTERN KY. 26-6
87 ■ Jackson St. 69
92 Tennessee Tech 99
84 ■ Va. Commonwealth 78
77 ■ Eastern Ky. 68
82 Ill.-Chicago 71
88 ■ Radford 58
88 South Ala. 83
86 ■ Louisiana Tech 40
114 ■ Lamar 89
92 ■ Ark.-Lit. Rock 56
86 Arkansas St. 75
83 Southwestern La. 84
98 ■ South Ala. 101
105 ■ Tex.-Pan American 49
121 ■ Southwestern La. 92
80 New Orleans 89
95 Lamar 88
96 ■ Southern Utah 73
66 ■ Jacksonville 58
98 Tex.-Pan American 68
78 Louisville 77
67 ■ Arkansas St. 61
67 ■ New Orleans 71
76 Louisiana Tech 54
101 Jacksonville 66
78 Ark.-Lit. Rock 71
78 † Lamar 68
83 † South Ala. 73
72 † New Orleans 63
55 † Memphis St. 52
72 † Seton Hall 68
78 † Florida St. 81

WESTERN MD. 5-19
64 Messiah 73
65 Johns Hopkins 73
51 ■ Frank. & Marsh. 64
58 Dickinson 71
75 ■ Marymount (Va.) 86
72 ■ Wesley 59
73 ■ New Jersey Tech 78
74 Radford 99
85 Elizabethtown 101
83 Mary Washington 76
71 ■ Moravian 74
88 ■ Washington (Md.) 73
57 Lebanon Valley 94
86 ■ Gettysburg 79
55 Muhlenberg 73
53 Frank. & Marsh. 79
64 Gallaudet 74
68 ■ Dickinson 73
61 Moravian 87
58 St. Mary's (Md.) 70
55 ■ Lebanon Valley 83
76 ■ Juniata 89
59 Gettysburg 60
68 ■ Muhlenberg 66

WESTERN MICH. 17-12
75 Wis.-Milwaukee 84
89 Ill.-Chicago 90
63 † Pacific (Cal.) 56
58 Indiana 97
68 Niagara 86
63 ■ Wis.-Milwaukee 74
77 Morehead St. 47
65 ■ Saginaw Valley 50
60 ■ Kent 50
65 Ball St. 70
69 ■ Miami (Ohio) 52
67 Akron 64
86 Ohio 71
69 ■ Central Mich. 53
45 Bowling Green 68
75 ■ Eastern Mich. 74
62 Toledo 64
66 ■ Ball St. 55
39 Miami (Ohio) 65
60 ■ Akron 44
66 ■ Ohio 51
99 Central Mich. 79
69 ■ Bowling Green 65
71 Eastern Mich. 89
75 ■ Toledo 57
64 Kent 81
65 † Eastern Mich. 57
61 † Miami (Ohio) 48
64 † Ball St. 79

WESTERN NEW ENG. 8-13
65 Fitchburg St. 58
79 Daniel Webster 65
64 ■ Westfield St. 78
62 ■ Babson 75
42 Amherst 65
49 ■ Framingham St. 69
52 Worcester Tech 81
63 ■ MIT 57
59 ■ Norwich 42
74 Coast Guard 70
75 ■ Worcester St. 93
54 Albertus Magnus 57
67 ■ Coast Guard 68
85 Connecticut Col. 66
51 Babson 94
52 MIT 46
70 ■ Worcester Tech 83
69 Wesleyan 80
57 Norwich 46
76 ■ Nichols 80
49 ■ MIT 51

WESTERN ST. 25-5
77 Fort Lewis 71
96 † Neb.-Kearney 83
71 Denver 82
91 ■ Colo. Christian 68
85 ■ Denver 79
84 Metropolitan St. 93
61 Colo. Christian 74
97 † Concordia (Ill.) 92
79 Mesa St. 68
95 ■ Fort Lewis 82
75 ■ Metropolitan St. 69
81 ■ Mesa St. 69
86 ■ Southern Colo. 81
73 ■ N.M. Highlands 64
81 ■ Adams St. 70
71 Fort Hays St. 69
83 Chadron St. 75
97 ■ Colorado Col. 65
100 ■ Colorado Mines 60
74 ■ Fort Hays St. 70
102 ■ Chadron St. 72
70 Mesa St. 92
68 Colorado Mines 59
81 Colorado Col. 80
98 Adams St. 89
64 N.M. Highlands 63
83 ■ Fort Hays St. 78
78 ■ Mesa St. 64
61 North Dak. 80
81 † Colo. Christian 71

WESTFIELD ST. 22-6
96 ■ Southern Vt. 49
89 ■ Western Conn. St. 72
78 Western New Eng. 64
97 † Daemen 63
80 Elmira 65
61 Trinity (Conn.) 60
73 ■ Mass.-Boston 62
81 † Cortland St. 74
53 Williams 74
91 Bri'water (Mass.) 87
83 ■ Worcester St. 91
84 Salem St. 85
89 Rhode Island Col. 79
77 ■ Fitchburg St. 61
103 ■ Albertus Magnus 64
87 ■ Framingham St. 60
74 North Adams St. 69
103 ■ Bri'water (Mass.) 84
100 Worcester St. 91
77 ■ Salem St. 82
79 Fitchburg St. 58
89 Amherst 78
99 Framingham St. 92
97 ■ North Adams St. 82
96 ■ Fitchburg St. 56
99 † Worcester St. 87
63 † Salem St. 67
81 Mass.-Dartmouth 90

WESTMINSTER (MO.) 15-11
59 † Cardinal Stritch 67
72 † Moody Bible 46
74 † Illinois Col. 85
88 † Rhodes 89
85 ■ Hannibal-La Grange 74
48 ■ Central Bible (Mo.) 56
57 Northeast Mo. St. 73
70 MacMurray 90
79 Maryville (Mo.) 76
67 ■ Blackburn 62
62 Parks 49
71 Hannibal-La Grange 64
74 ■ Fontbonne 61
77 Principia 61
82 ■ Webster 72
71 ■ MacMurray 72
93 ■ Maryville (Mo.) 80
70 Blackburn 72
65 Central Bible (Mo.) 84
61 ■ Parks 59
80 Fontbonne 70
76 ■ Principia 67
72 Webster 89
77 † Webster 64
88 † Fontbonne 86
76 † MacMurray 81

WHEATON (ILL.) 14-11
78 ■ Lake Forest 72
73 ■ Ill. Benedictine 80
77 ■ Concordia (Ill.) 78
73 St. Norbert 76
71 Hope 78
75 ■ Aurora 70
69 Nova 79
104 Palm Beach Atl. 84
85 Warner Southern 74
84 Ill. Wesleyan 99
58 Carthage 55
71 Augustana (Ill.) 100
95 Carroll (Wis.) 73
61 ■ Elmhurst 57
76 ■ Augustana (Ill.) 95
56 North Park 52
53 North Central 51
78 ■ Ill. Wesleyan 83
69 ■ Millikin 70
49 ■ North Park 47
71 Rockford 68
77 ■ North Central 87
68 Elmhurst 66
60 Millikin 58
74 ■ Carthage 64

WHEATON (MASS.) 20-5
89 ■ Albertus Magnus 79
69 ■ Western Conn. St. 74
101 ■ Emerson-MCA 58
82 † Baruch 67
70 Williams 87
80 ■ New England Col. 54
94 ■ Salem St. 88
104 Catholic 106
93 † Wash. & Jeff. 84
78 Merchant Marine 57
60 Eastern Conn. St. 57
94 ■ Nichols 53
59 ■ Tufts 61
88 ■ Skidmore 76
78 ■ Rhode Island Col. 69
85 ■ Brandeis 81
61 Colby 60
77 Bowdoin 73
80 Connecticut Col. 68
84 Trinity (Conn.) 69
88 ■ Suffolk 61
85 ■ Colby-Sawyer 70
79 Clark (Mass.) 75
97 ■ Babson 81
69 Williams 83

WHEELING JESUIT 16-13
91 † Calif. (Pa.) 77
81 † West Liberty St. 85
88 Millersville 105
73 Pitt.-Johnstown 90
72 ■ Shepherd 82
75 ■ West Liberty St. 73
85 ■ Geneva 78
114 ■ Ohio Belmont 73
104 West Va. Tech 83
86 ■ West Va. Wesleyan 60
74 ■ Ohio Valley College 61

97		Bluefield St.	90
100		Concord	102
91	■	Davis & Elkins	61
70		Salem Teikyo	75
85	■	Alderson-Broaddus	92
97		Fairmont St.	79
64	■	Glenville St.	75
62		Shepherd	80
69	■	Charleston (W.Va.)	65
97	■	West Va. St.	71
66		West Liberty St.	68
99		Davis & Elkins	95
68	■	Salem Teikyo	89
90		Alderson-Broad.	102
90	■	Fairmont St.	75
92	†	Fairmont St.	76
81	†	Shepherd	80
83	†	Charleston (W.Va.)	84

WHITTIER **6-18**

94	■	Pt. Loma Nazarene	78
53		Washington (Mo.)	66
81	†	Trinity (Tex.)	78
71		Azusa-Pacific	108
48		Westmont	79
89	■	UC San Diego	101
59		Christ-Irvine	86
92	■	Worcester Tech	77
54	■	Menlo	55
93	■	Haverford	74
81	■	Cal Tech	49
78	■	Occidental	82
69		Cal Lutheran	79
82		Redlands	88
65	■	Claremont-M-S	76
62		La Verne	71
66	■	Pomona-Pitzer	78
65		Cal Tech	45
71		Occidental	79
57	■	Cal Lutheran	61
67	■	Redlands	71
86		Claremont-M-S	95
69	■	La Verne	74
80		Pomona-Pitzer	93

WICHITA ST. **10-17**

71		Alabama	93
63	■	Mo.-Kansas City	56
64	■	Nebraska	71
75	■	Tex. A&M-Kingsville	64
74	■	Kansas St.	61
54		Xavier (Ohio)	88
73		Indiana St.	69
54		Kansas	103
58	■	Bradley	50
62		Drake	66
66	■	Illinois St.	68
84	■	Indiana St.	68
72		Northern Iowa	74
68	■	Creighton	47
67		Southern Ill.	85
58		Florida	83
77	■	Tulsa	76
51		Southwest Mo. St.	54
64		Bradley	73
62		Illinois St.	75
63	■	Northern Iowa	47
40	■	Southwest Mo. St.	49
76	■	Southern Ill.	85
73	■	Drake	65
63		Tulsa	80
54		Creighton	58
57	†	Southwest Mo. St.	72

WIDENER **14-12**

66	■	York (N.Y.)	40
67	■	Delaware Valley	51
55		Delaware	84
72	■	Allentown	75
68		Phila. Pharmacy	55
47		Muhlenberg	79
50	■	Cheyney	47
68	†	Hunter	89

62	†	Beaver	56
65	†	Binghamton	67
54	†	Oneonta St.	55
92	■	Gwynedd Mercy	53
61	■	West Chester	71
68	■	Haverford	59
65		Ursinus	48
65		Swarthmore	52
57	■	Johns Hopkins	69
65	■	Washington (Md.)	61
70		Haverford	54
46		Frank. & Marsh.	84
70	■	Ursinus	39
53	■	Swarthmore	42
52		Johns Hopkins	57
87		Washington (Md.)	89
68	■	Washington (Md.)	51
52		Frank. & Marsh.	67

WILEY **8-18**

85		S'west Adventist	78
70		Ambassador	96
68	†	LSU-Shreveport	72
93	†	Ark. Baptist	94
79		Centenary	115
64		LSU-Shreveport	73
69	■	Rust	74
62		Rust	68
64	■	Paul Quinn	67
72	■	Ambassador	91
78	■	Ark. Baptist	79
72		Jarvis Christian	64
77		Paul Quinn	87
93	■	East Tex. Bapt.	72
82	■	Texas Col.	98
80		Philander Smith	98
60		Ark. Baptist	62
88	■	S'west Adventist	64
85	■	Philander Smith	77
65		Texas Col.	88
105		La. Christian	96
77	■	Texas Col.	91
78	■	La. Christian	80
77	■	LSU-Shreveport	74
79	†	Ark. Baptist	67
66		Paul Quinn	73

WILKES **16-9**

69		Gettysburg	66
58	†	Mount Union	57
89	■	Lycoming	74
87	†	Bapt. Bible (Pa.)	71
71		Scranton	66
68		Messiah	63
55	■	Albright	67
80	■	Drew	56
74		Allentown	49
38		Moravian	55
57		Juniata	58
77	■	King's (Pa.)	59
87		Delaware Valley	69
77	■	FDU-Madison	50
59		Scranton	81
71	■	Susquehanna	77
81	■	Upsala	75
53		Muhlenberg	71
70		Drew	61
63		King's (Pa.)	59
84	■	Delaware Valley	82
53		FDU-Madison	54
58	■	Scranton	64
77		Upsala	75
66		Susquehanna	70

WILLIAM & MARY **14-13**

81		N.C.-Greensboro	76
72	■	Citadel	68
81	■	Va. Wesleyan	63
102	■	Shenandoah	74
59		New Mexico	64
77	†	Northwestern	69
75	■	Campbell	59
78	■	Holy Cross	83

58		Navy	53
71		American	76
92	■	George Mason	89
72	■	James Madison	90
53		Richmond	54
67	■	N.C.-Wilmington	63
84	■	Virginia	93
81		East Caro.	65
80	■	Old Dominion	81
66		Virginia Tech	70
77		Va. Military	67
77	■	American	82
82		George Mason	78
66		James Madison	99
103		N.C.-Wilmington	85
66	■	Richmond	63
53	■	East Caro.	74
80		Old Dominion	90
72	†	American	78

WM. PATERSON **11-13**

80	■	North Adams St.	75
62		Kean	78
89	■	Rutgers-Camden	75
68	■	Montclair St.	60
55		Rowan	112
78	■	Rutgers-Newark	68
51		Trenton St.	78
60		Western Conn. St.	76
81		Bloomfield	91
102		Medgar Evers	84
62	■	Ramapo	53
83		Stockton St.	93
80	■	Jersey City St.	78
75		Montclair St.	72
90		Manhattanville	84
69	■	Kean	75
83		Rutgers-Camden	66
64		Ramapo	62
67	■	Rowan	90
68		Rutgers-Newark	81
62	■	Trenton St.	68
91		Drew	101
78		Jersey City St.	92
82	■	Stockton St.	99

WILLIAM PENN **8-17**

65	■	Teikyo Marycrest	85
70	†	Hastings	98
72		Neb. Wesleyan	92
61		Mo. Western St.	88
61		Grand View	71
65		Graceland (Iowa)	80
91	■	Iowa Wesleyan	67
86	■	St. Ambrose	79
107	■	Buena Vista	96
61	■	Wartburg	73
55		Loras	80
61		Upper Iowa	66
71	■	Peru St.	88
53		Central (Iowa)	67
73		Luther	70
79	■	Simpson	71
69	■	Dubuque	62
64	■	Loras	75
55		Buena Vista	58
76	■	Upper Iowa	72
68		Wartburg	83
73		Dubuque	79
67		Simpson	116
54	■	Central (Iowa)	78
79	■	Luther	72

WILLIAMS **23-4**

74		Haverford	66
63	†	Claremont-M-S	44
63		Rensselaer	71
74		Amherst	62
104	■	Vassar	37
87	■	Wheaton (Mass.)	70
94	■	North Adams St.	63
80	■	Union (N.Y.)	58
80	■	Framingham St.	54
74	■	Westfield St.	53

79	■	Skidmore	71
72	■	Amherst	57
82		Middlebury	66
70	■	Colby	77
94	■	Bowdoin	66
82		Hamilton	87
72	■	Wesleyan	56
90		Merchant Marine	65
107	■	Connecticut Col.	54
80		Trinity (Conn.)	58
77		Tufts	67
88	■	Middlebury	60
84		Union (N.Y.)	72
77		Wesleyan	71
97	■	Anna Maria	85
83	■	Wheaton (Mass.)	69
75	■	Colby	80

WILMINGTON (OHIO) **6-19**

65		Northern Ky.	79
76	†	Central St. (Ohio)	101
73	■	Hanover	81
62		Wittenberg	95
70		Ohio Dominican	95
53		Wright St.	112
68		Rio Grande	95
86	■	Cedarville	91
54		Denison	72
64		Wooster	93
111	†	Redlands	102
50		Hanover	101
62		Bluffton	52
75		Thomas More	85
65	■	Defiance	69
78	■	Wilberforce	98
82	■	Thomas More	76
74	■	Centre	63
83	■	Ohio Wesleyan	78
93	■	Shawnee St.	94
71	■	Bluffton	63
68		Wooster	83
52		Defiance	95
64		Thomas More	81
70	†	Bluffton	75

WINONA ST. **19-10**

74	†	Ferris St.	89
67	†	Black Hills St.	53
72		Wis.-Stout	69
82	■	St. Mary's (Minn.)	52
74		South Dak. St.	75
92	■	Upper Iowa	73
78		Wis.-Parkside	66
69		St. Cloud St.	78
81	■	Wayne St. (Neb.)	56
71		Northern Ariz.	78
98		Grand Canyon	124
91	†	Biola	84
71	■	Concordia (St. Paul)	48
69	■	Mt. Senario	70
86	■	Bemidji St.	64
64	■	Minn.-Duluth	60
61		Minn.-Morris	55
91		Northern St.	83
72	■	Southwest St.	61
67	■	Moorhead St.	81
83	■	Minn.-Morris	71
87		Southwest St.	84
76	■	Northern St.	87
79		Bemidji St.	76
102		Moorhead St.	91
103	■	St. Scholastica	74
68		Minn.-Duluth	73
72	■	Moorhead St.	61
56	■	Minn.-Morris	58

WINSTON-SALEM **6-17**

74	■	Bowie St.	70
70		Morehouse	81
75		St. Paul's	63
50	■	Virginia St.	74
98		Shaw	93
64		Hampton	76
69	†	Elizabeth City St.	90

67 † St. Paul's 64
73 ■ Norfolk St. 90
80 St. Augustine's 78
76 N.C. Central 99
74 ■ Johnson Smith 100
60 ■ Fayetteville St. 80
72 ■ Virginia Union 96
73 ■ Livingstone 70
80 ■ Shaw 84
62 ■ North Caro. A&T 65
88 Johnson Smith 107
90 ■ St. Augustine's 92
90 Livingstone 92
60 Fayetteville St. 82
82 ■ N.C. Central 90
64 † Elizabeth City St. 105

WINTHROP 14-16
92 ■ Queens (N.C.) 84
91 Central Fla. 99
91 ■ Citadel 70
92 ■ Lynchburg 63
84 N.C.-Greensboro 70
83 South Caro. St. 85
68 Virginia 92
101 Central Conn. St. 93
65 Wake Forest 99
93 ■ Liberty 90
79 N.C.-Asheville 75
106 ■ Central Conn. St. 90
65 ■ Charleston So. 76
85 Towson St. 93
93 Md.-Balt. County 99
90 ■ Towson St. 78
79 ■ Md.-Balt. County 85
79 ■ N.C.-Asheville 66
88 Radford 107
61 Liberty 58
70 ■ Coastal Caro. 74
84 Campbell 92
87 ■ Radford 98
95 ■ Campbell 96
64 Coastal Caro. 79
87 Charleston So. 94
101 † N.C.-Asheville 87
83 † Towson St. 79
87 † Radford 69
65 † Coastal Caro. 78

WISCONSIN 14-14
66 Loyola (Ill.) 68
70 ■ Wis.-Green Bay 65
75 ■ Bethune-Cookman 50
72 ■ Wis.-Milwaukee 77
101 ■ Charleston So. 72
108 ■ Detroit Mercy 86
110 ■ Alcorn St. 81
76 ■ Fairfield 55
77 Marquette 67
73 ■ Michigan 98
60 Purdue 76
79 ■ Minnesota 70
76 ■ Ohio St. 67
67 Michigan St. 66
72 Illinois 80
75 Penn St. 68
101 ■ Northwestern 87
66 Michigan 85
87 ■ Purdue 90
71 Minnesota 85
70 Ohio St. 80
65 ■ Michigan St. 62
74 ■ Illinois 66
58 ■ Penn St. 62
89 Northwestern 100
65 Iowa 91
80 ■ Indiana 87
73 ■ Rice 77

WIS.-EAU CLAIRE 19-7
65 ■ Edgewood 52
66 ■ Briar Cliff 61
67 † Huston-Tillotson 49
78 St. Mary's (Tex.) 68
61 ■ Wis.-Stout 58
83 ■ Wis.-Oshkosh 62
60 ■ Wis.-Whitewater 62
70 Wis.-La Crosse 67
61 ■ Mt. Senario 54
75 ■ Aub.-Montgomery 83
64 ■ St. Mary's (Tex.) 61
68 Wis.-Superior 53
72 ■ Wis.-River Falls 59
55 Wis.-Platteville 78
65 Wis.-Stevens Point 66
73 Briar Cliff 83
113 Wis.-Stout 63
64 ■ Wis.-Superior 39
78 Wis.-Oshkosh 68
88 Wis.-Whitewater 79
73 ■ Wis.-La Crosse 54
85 ■ Wis.-Platteville 73
75 ■ Wis.-Stevens Point 59
63 Wis.-River Falls 65
88 ■ Wis.-Parkside 69
81 ■ Viterbo 86

WIS.-GREEN BAY 13-14
65 Southeast Mo. St. 67
65 Wisconsin 70
61 Colorado 86
89 ■ Bethune-Cookman 55
76 ■ Butler 64
62 ■ Toledo 50
81 ■ Chicago St. 59
71 ■ Ill.-Chicago 75
68 Wis.-Milwaukee 75
81 Youngstown St. 62
66 Cleveland St. 81
50 Northern Ill. 53
65 Western Ill. 64
76 ■ Valparaiso 65
88 ■ Wright St. 90
68 ■ Eastern Ill. 47
60 ■ Western Ill. 45
78 Valparaiso 71
65 Ill.-Chicago 72
76 Wright St. 66
46 Marquette 63
57 ■ Northern Ill. 42
52 Eastern Ill. 60
67 ■ Youngstown St. 47
61 ■ Cleveland St. 63
48 ■ Wis.-Milwaukee 61
43 † Ill.-Chicago 46

WIS.-LA CROSSE 5-20
73 ■ Edgewood 67
56 Minn.-Morris 77
70 ■ Wis.-Superior 67
60 Loras 70
76 Wis.-Stout 86
63 Wis.-River Falls 65
67 ■ Wis.-Eau Claire 70
89 St. John's (Minn.) 78
69 † Iowa Wesleyan 74
63 † St. Scholastica 57
84 Luther 91
68 ■ Wis.-Platteville 85
60 Wis.-Oshkosh 84
59 St. Scholastica 63
63 ■ Wis.-Stevens Point 88
68 Wis.-Superior 70
75 ■ Viterbo 89
55 Wis.-Whitewater 87
66 ■ Wis.-River Falls 51
67 ■ Wis.-Stout 76
54 Wis.-Eau Claire 73
66 ■ Wis.-Whitewater 74
85 ■ Wis.-Oshkosh 102
67 Wis.-Platteville 79
49 Wis.-Stevens Point 101

WIS.-MILWAUKEE 23-4
84 ■ Western Mich. 75
94 ■ Northeastern Ill. 78
91 Alcorn St. 76
98 ■ Wis.-Parkside 71
77 Wisconsin 72
79 ■ Northern Ill. 71
92 ■ Western Ill. 71
74 Western Mich. 63
62 Utah 96
82 Northern Ill. 57
94 ■ Alcorn St. 80
75 ■ Fairfield 59
76 Western Ill. 67
86 New Hampshire 70
75 ■ Wis.-Green Bay 68
78 ■ Cal St. Northridge 65
96 ■ Cal St. Sacramento 44
73 ■ Mo.-Kansas City 57
78 Chicago St. 60
77 Mo.-Kansas City 99
65 ■ Chicago St. 64
86 Northeastern Ill. 91
75 Cal St. Northridge 74
80 Southern Utah 81
66 ■ Southern Utah 56
78 Cal St. Sacramento 76
61 Wis.-Green Bay 48

WIS.-OSHKOSH 14-11
88 Marian (Wis.) 73
111 ■ Wis. Lutheran 85
63 ■ St. Xavier 68
99 ■ St. Norbert 71
79 Wis.-Stevens Point 86
62 Wis.-Eau Claire 83
78 Wis.-Superior 67
68 Viterbo 80
65 ■ Edgewood 77
81 ■ Wis.-Whitewater 91
76 † Lakeland 68
67 Edgewood 81
84 ■ Wis.-La Crosse 60
64 ■ Wis.-River Falls 55
94 ■ Wis.-Stout 77
72 Wis.-Parkside 79
66 Wis.-Platteville 84
70 ■ Wis.-Stevens Point 67
93 Wis.-Whitewater 87
94 Wis.-Stout 90
68 ■ Wis.-Eau Claire 78
90 ■ Wis.-Superior 72
77 Wis.-River Falls 74
102 Wis.-La Crosse 85
75 ■ Wis.-Platteville 85

WIS.-PARKSIDE 8-19
59 Carthage 64
97 ■ Bemidji St. 98
85 ■ Indianapolis 80
65 Wis.-Whitewater 93
73 ■ Ferris St. 91
77 Kentucky St. 89
71 Wis.-Milwaukee 98
50 ■ Wis.-Platteville 94
66 ■ Winona St. 78
80 ■ Kentucky St. 68
62 Wis.-Stevens Point 76
60 ■ Minn.-Duluth 64
73 Ferris St. 98
64 Bemidji St. 65
79 ■ Wis.-Oshkosh 72
68 Quincy 78
64 SIU-Edwardsville 79
80 ■ Lake Forest 57
72 Northern Mich. 68
83 ■ Wayne St. (Neb.) 54
87 ■ Quincy 92
79 Mercyhurst 95
67 Gannon 69
69 Wis.-Eau Claire 88
79 St. Ambrose 71
65 ■ Michigan Tech 74
88 ■ SIU-Edwardsville 73

WIS.-PLATTEVILLE 24-4
100 ■ Concordia (Wis.) 82
82 ■ Teikyo Marycrest 51
88 Judson 47
106 ■ St. Mary's (Minn.) 51
93 Wis.-Whitewater 91
103 ■ Dubuque 57
94 Wis.-Parkside 50
65 Wis.-River Falls 72
75 † Occidental 73
83 † Master's 64
74 ■ Wis.-Stevens Point 56
85 Wis.-La Crosse 68
78 ■ Wis.-Eau Claire 55
76 ■ Wis.-Superior 61
84 ■ Wis.-Oshkosh 66
86 ■ Wis.-Whitewater 67
70 Wis.-Stevens Point 73
74 ■ Marian (Wis.) 50
100 ■ Wis.-Stout 63
90 ■ Wis.-River Falls 59
73 Wis.-Eau Claire 85
89 Wis.-Superior 64
79 ■ Wis.-La Crosse 67
85 Wis.-Oshkosh 75
103 Wis.-Stout 74
88 ■ Wis.-Whitewater 72
70 ■ St. Thomas (Minn.) 60
86 ■ Augustana (Ill.) 100

WIS.-RIVER FALLS 12-12
98 † Jamestown 76
78 Bethel (Minn.) 66
67 ■ St. John's (Minn.) 65
82 ■ Edgewood 96
76 ■ Southwest St. 65
51 Mankato St. 67
47 ■ Wis.-Stevens Point 66
65 ■ Wis.-La Crosse 63
72 ■ Wis.-Platteville 65
87 Wis.-Stout 86
59 Wis.-Eau Claire 72
55 Wis.-Oshkosh 64
57 Wis.-Whitewater 67
109 ■ Wis.-Superior 98
74 ■ Northland 68
62 Mt. Senario 57
59 ■ Wis.-Stout 68
58 Wis.-Stevens Point 65
51 Wis.-La Crosse 66
59 Wis.-Platteville 90
74 ■ Wis.-Oshkosh 77
59 ■ Wis.-Whitewater 77
65 ■ Wis.-Eau Claire 63
69 Wis.-Superior 64

WIS.-STEVENS POINT 23-5
76 St. Norbert 40
102 ■ Carroll (Wis.) 68
96 ■ Northern Mich. 91
72 Viterbo 60
86 ■ Wis.-Oshkosh 79
66 Wis.-River Falls 47
80 Wis.-Stout 68
76 ■ Wis.-Parkside 62
56 Wis.-Platteville 74
83 ■ Wis.-Whitewater 73
75 ■ Wis.-Superior 47
66 ■ Wis.-Eau Claire 65
88 ■ Mt. Senario 69
88 Wis.-La Crosse 63
67 Wis.-Oshkosh 70
73 ■ Wis.-Platteville 70
65 ■ Wis.-River Falls 58
54 ■ Edgewood 52
73 ■ Wis.-Stout 51
98 Wis.-Superior 68
59 Wis.-Eau Claire 75
83 Wis.-Whitewater 79
101 ■ Wis.-La Crosse 49
77 Marian (Wis.) 57
55 ■ Michigan Tech 73
69 ■ Viterbo 63
84 Viterbo 69
74 † Lenoir-Rhyne 77

WIS.-STOUT 11-14
70 † Purdue-Calumet 73
95 † Maranatha 76

73	North Cent. Bible	52
76	■ Mt. Senario	82
69	■ Winona St.	72
58	Wis.-Eau Claire	61
86	■ Wis.-La Crosse	76
68	■ Wis.-Stevens Point	80
60	■ Pillsbury	47
86	■ Wis.-River Falls	87
85	Wis.-Superior	67
57	■ Viterbo	51
71	Wis.-Whitewater	100
77	Wis.-Oshkosh	94
82	St. Scholastica	64
63	■ Wis.-Eau Claire	113
68	Wis.-River Falls	59
90	■ Wis.-Oshkosh	94
63	Wis.-Platteville	100
76	Wis.-La Crosse	67
51	Wis.-Stevens Point	73
75	■ Marian (Wis.)	69
80	■ Wis.-Superior	65
81	■ Wis.-Whitewater	94
74	■ Wis.-Platteville	103

WIS.-SUPERIOR		2-22
48	■ Minn.-Duluth	60
74	Carleton	78
63	† St. Olaf	82
77	† Lakeland	102
67	Wis.-La Crosse	70
86	■ North Cent. Bible	58
51	■ Wis.-Whitewater	80
67	■ Wis.-Oshkosh	78
69	St. Scholastica	94
53	■ Wis.-Eau Claire	68
67	■ Wis.-Stout	85
47	Wis.-Stevens Point	75
61	Wis.-Platteville	76
63	Minn.-Duluth	65
98	Wis.-River Falls	109
70	■ Wis.-La Crosse	68
39	Wis.-Eau Claire	64
65	Wis.-Whitewater	91
72	Wis.-Oshkosh	90
59	■ Northland	72
68	■ Wis.-Stevens Point	98
64	■ Wis.-Platteville	89
65	Wis.-Stout	80
64	■ Wis.-River Falls	69

WIS.-WHITEWATER		18-9
80	■ Maranatha	54
90	■ Purdue-Calumet	78
97	St. Ambrose	77
93	■ Wis.-Parkside	65
87	■ Mt. Senario	86
91	■ Wis.-Platteville	93
80	Wis.-Superior	51
62	Wis.-Eau Claire	60
65	■ Viterbo	53
79	■ Carthage	82
87	■ North Central	70
70	Teikyo Marycrest	71
91	Wis.-Oshkosh	81
73	Wis.-Stevens Point	83
100	■ Wis.-Stout	71
67	■ Wis.-River Falls	57
67	Wis.-Platteville	86
87	■ Wis.-Oshkosh	93
87	■ Wis.-La Crosse	55
91	■ Wis.-Superior	65
79	■ Wis.-Eau Claire	88
74	Wis.-La Crosse	66
77	Wis.-River Falls	59
79	■ Wis.-Stevens Point	83
94	Wis.-Stout	81
84	■ Manchester	66
72	Wis.-Platteville	88

WITTENBERG		19-7
95	■ Wilmington (Ohio)	62
113	■ Earlham	66
62	Wooster	58
79	■ Ohio Wesleyan	65
77	Catholic	75
54	Otterbein	70
69	Capital	71
61	■ Hanover	60
90	■ Roanoke	73
65	Case Reserve	57
72	■ Denison	57
57	■ Allegheny	66
68	■ Thomas More	56
86	Oberlin	58
56	Kenyon	59
45	■ Wooster	54
76	Ohio Wesleyan	62
82	■ Case Reserve	65
72	Defiance	74
77	Allegheny	72
80	Earlham	51
113	■ Oberlin	41
60	■ Kenyon	56
64	Denison	54
96	■ Earlham	66
49	† Kenyon	54

WOFFORD		17-9
88	■ Catawba	75
76	East Tenn. St.	87
66	Presbyterian	71
77	Ala.-Huntsville	82
61	Savannah St.	72
78	■ Ala.-Huntsville	76
85	■ Lenoir-Rhyne	75
78	West Ga.	67
65	Erskine	56
68	■ Belmont Abbey	56
64	■ S.C.-Aiken	66
105	■ West Ga.	92
70	■ Presbyterian	82
83	Catawba	77
62	Queens (N.C.)	72
77	Lenoir-Rhyne	80
80	■ Erskine	60
90	■ Longwood	80
91	Newberry	69
73	Pembroke St.	71
93	■ Newberry	77
101	■ Gardner-Webb	73
94	S.C.-Aiken	96
77	Belmont Abbey	72
84	■ Savannah St.	73
83	■ Queens (N.C.)	81

WOOSTER		21-7
87	■ Marietta	62
70	Hiram	80
58	■ Wittenberg	62
61	Case Reserve	47
49	Denison	59
62	Pomona-Pitzer	45
57	Claremont-M-S	71
93	■ Wilmington (Ohio)	64
66	■ Lebanon Valley	55
54	■ Kenyon	59
90	Oberlin	42
83	Earlham	52
80	Allegheny	58
60	■ Ohio Wesleyan	62
67	■ Denison	32
54	Wittenberg	45
73	■ Case Reserve	43
72	Kenyon	65
78	■ Allegheny	69
82	■ Earlham	56
75	Ashland	55
83	Ohio Wesleyan	75
83	■ Wilmington (Ohio)	68
90	■ Oberlin	56
79	■ Denison	68
67	† Allegheny	57
64	† Kenyon	48
62	Ohio Northern	88

WORCESTER TECH		15-12
81	† Clark (Mass.)	82
82	† Nichols	72
94	■ MIT	66
74	Babson	87
57	† Clark (Mass.)	50
90	Anna Maria	103
94	Wentworth Inst.	69
77	Whittier	92
54	† Hartwick	74
75	■ Salve Regina	62
87	■ Worcester St.	100
81	■ Western New Eng.	52
91	Brandeis	110
59	■ Trinity (Conn.)	68
66	Coast Guard	81
83	■ Norwich	51
93	■ Suffolk	74
82	■ Tufts	71
82	■ Babson	99
83	Western New Eng.	70
89	MIT	73
79	■ Coast Guard	76
81	Norwich	61
69	■ Amherst	74
83	■ Coast Guard	81
77	Babson	94
80	Nichols	75

WORCESTER ST.		19-8
94	■ Nichols	71
83	■ Clark (Mass.)	77
111	† Savannah A&D	72
101	† Anna Maria	114
118	Anna Maria	108
97	Salve Regina	77
63	■ Eastern Conn. St.	69
109	Mass.-Dartmouth	107
102	Emerson-MCA	79
98	■ Fitchburg St.	79
100	Worcester Tech	87
91	Westfield St.	83
83	■ Framingham St.	81
108	■ Nichols	87
100	■ North Adams St.	76
100	Bri'water (Mass.)	88
93	Western New Eng.	75
91	■ Salem St.	108
119	Fitchburg St.	92
91	■ Westfield St.	100
112	Framingham St.	101
73	North Adams St.	90
109	■ Bri'water (Mass.)	104
82	Salem St.	108
98	■ North Adams St.	78
87	† Westfield St.	99
105	Colby	121

WRIGHT ST.		20-10
65	Kentucky	81
112	■ Wilmington (Ohio)	53
102	■ Morehead St.	74
112	■ Prairie View	87
88	■ Eastern Ky.	78
55	Ohio St.	76
80	Ohio	77
68	■ Miami (Ohio)	75
129	Morehead St.	63
136	■ Chicago St.	91
92	Valparaiso	78
82	Ill.-Chicago	85
87	■ Western Ill.	73
104	■ Eastern Ill.	80
100	■ Youngstown St.	65
91	■ Cleveland St.	99
90	Wis.-Green Bay	88
77	Northern Ill.	82
95	Youngstown St.	87
85	Cleveland St.	91
96	■ Ill.-Chicago	88
79	■ Valparaiso	67
66	■ Wis.-Green Bay	76
98	■ Northern Ill.	56
80	Eastern Ill.	87
81	Western Ill.	80
94	■ Eastern Ill.	58
82	■ Valparaiso	72
94	■ Ill.-Chicago	88
54	† Indiana	97

WYOMING		13-15
82	■ Denver	79
75	Louisiana Tech	57
79	■ Southern Colo.	54
50	Boise St.	70
79	■ Colorado	72
101	■ Marshall	89
70	■ Texas-Arlington	79
74	■ Montana St.	64
66	Fresno St.	68
59	Air Force	53
77	■ San Diego St.	54
70	■ Hawaii	62
56	Houston	83
77	Colorado St.	92
74	UTEP	70
67	New Mexico	77
45	■ Utah	64
64	■ Brigham Young	77
64	Utah	88
62	Brigham Young	75
78	■ UTEP	81
60	■ New Mexico	76
77	■ Colorado St.	66
62	San Diego St.	64
59	Hawaii	61
77	■ Fresno St.	55
64	■ Air Force	58
57	† San Diego St.	59

XAVIER (OHIO)		24-6
113	■ Huntington	73
81	Ball St.	78
72	■ Kent	56
70	■ Miami (Ohio)	67
74	† Delaware	66
75	† Rice	60
88	■ Wichita St.	54
75	■ Notre Dame	60
90	Detroit Mercy	97
73	Louisville	76
85	Dayton	58
56	■ South Fla.	53
63	■ Butler	59
74	Evansville	68
67	Cincinnati	78
81	Loyola (Ill.)	64
56	■ La Salle	49
85	■ Duquesne	79
53	■ Dayton	46
74	■ Evansville	63
80	Butler	66
68	■ Loyola (Ill.)	65
93	■ Detroit Mercy	74
73	La Salle	58
72	Duquesne	88
60	† Loyola (Ill.)	50
67	† Duquesne	41
69	† Evansville	80
73	† New Orleans	55
70	† Indiana	73

YALE		10-16
70	■ Vermont	82
53	■ Lafayette	42
61	■ St. Francis (N.Y.)	62
46	Hofstra	48
38	Connecticut	65
59	Kent	67
54	Toledo	50
61	Colgate	65
53	■ Lehigh	54
48	Fairfield	57
58	■ Brown	43
57	■ Swarthmore	44
60	Brown	52
45	Columbia	58
37	Cornell	47
40	■ Princeton	46
50	■ Pennsylvania	51
51	Harvard	54
51	Dartmouth	42

72	■	Cornell	81
46	■	Columbia	47
63	■	New Hampshire	49
61	■	Dartmouth	56
68	■	Harvard	58
49		Pennsylvania	71
62		Princeton	53

YESHIVA 12-12

52		New Jersey Tech	83
65		Bard	33
91	■	CCNY	72
66		Maritime (N.Y.)	59
91	■	Stevens Tech	54
77		Baruch	89
74	■	Mt. St. Vincent	75
85		Polytechnic (N.Y.)	47
58	■	St. Joseph's (N.Y.)	54
91		Lehman	67
58		Barry	83
64	■	John Jay	63
74		Mt. St. Vincent	53
48	■	Maritime (N.Y.)	49
44		New York U.	86
60		Stevens Tech	61
89	■	Polytechnic (N.Y.)	49
65		Merchant Marine	86
71		St. Joseph's (N.Y.)	76
59	■	New Jersey Tech	92
90	■	Polytechnic (N.Y.)	50
81	■	Mt. St. Vincent	63
50	■	New Jersey Tech	71
62		Jersey City St.	76

YORK (PA.) 19-8

71	†	Lebanon Valley	70
76		Frank. & Marsh.	79
80	■	Juniata	79
77		Elizabethtown	70
89	■	Wilmington (Del.)	77
75	■	Chris. Newport	72
71	■	Frank. & Marsh.	68
74		Wesley	57
62	†	Chris. Newport	81
77	†	Grove City	63
73		Goucher	82
80	■	Catholic	68
79		Marymount (Va.)	71
73		St. Mary's (Md.)	60
83	■	Gallaudet	61
90	■	Mary Washington	77
74	■	Goucher	60
66	■	Marymount (Va.)	72
69		Gettysburg	54
62		Gallaudet	63
66		Catholic	87
86	■	St. Mary's (Md.)	45
67		Dickinson	79
81		Mary Washington	78
67	■	Goucher	45
71		Marymount (Va.)	62
70		Catholic	76

YORK (N.Y.) 9-14

40		Widener	66
60	†	Rutgers-Camden	59
70	■	Staten Island	76
70		Hunter	83
71	†	Catholic	81
77	†	Daniel Webster	50
58		New York U.	90
65	†	Roberts Wesleyan	89
71	†	Gallaudet	66
70	■	Old Westbury	75
66		LIU-C.W. Post	81
66		Staten Island	76
85	■	Hunter	95
74	■	John Jay	71
89	■	CCNY	72
93	■	Medgar Evers	85
63		Stony Brook	73
64		Lehman	56
91		Baruch	74
76		Medgar Evers	80
73		New York Tech	110
74		CCNY	57
83		Medgar Evers	84

YOUNGSTOWN ST. 3-23

82	■	Air Force	78
57		Northwestern	87
66		Akron	82
62	■	Drexel	75
68		St. Peter's	81
85		Georgia Tech	105
59	■	Akron	65
79	■	Western Ill.	63
75	■	Eastern Ill.	76
62	■	Wis.-Green Bay	81
82	■	Northern Ill.	88
104	■	Buffalo	89
48		Cleveland St.	88
67	■	St. Peter's	79
65		Wright St.	100
76		Valparaiso	85
71		Ill.-Chicago	89
87	■	Wright St.	95
64		Buffalo	76
78		Western Ill.	92
76		Eastern Ill.	82
72	■	Valparaiso	93
74	■	Ill.-Chicago	88
78	■	Cleveland St.	96
47		Wis.-Green Bay	67
80		Northern Ill.	84

1993-94 MEN'S SCHEDULES

Listed alphabetically in this section are the 1993-94 schedules for men's teams that were available from NCAA member institutions at press time.

Below each institution's name and location appear the name of its head coach and his complete won-lost record as a college head coach.

Divisional designation for each institution is indicated in the lower right-hand corner of each schedule.

Schedules are subject to change.

ABILENE CHRISTIAN .... Abilene, TX 79699

Tony Mauldin (2 YRS. W-27, L-30)

Concordia (Tex.)■	N23
Abilene Christ. Cl.	N26-27
Mississippi	N29
Angelo St. Cl.	D3-4
Texas-Arlington	D 7
UTEP	D18
Tarleton St. Tr.	J3-4
Drury Tr.	J7-8
Angelo St.■	J11
Texas A&M-Kingsville	J15
East Tex. St.	J17
Central Okla.■	J24
West Tex. A&M■	J29
Eastern N. Mex.■	J31
West Tex. A&M	F 5
Eastern N. Mex.	F 7
East Tex. St.■	F12
Texas A&M-Kingsville■	F14
Central Okla.	F19
Cameron	F21
Angelo St.	F26

Colors: Purple & White. Nickname: Wildcats.
AD: Cecil Eager. SID: Garner Roberts. II

ADAMS ST. .... Alamosa, CO 81102

Terry Layton (12 YRS. W-215, L-163)

Adams St. Tr.	N19-20
Denver Cl.	N26-27
Fort Lewis	N30
Alas. Fairbanks	D 3
Alas. Fairbanks	D 4
Alas. Anchorage	D 6
Alas. Anchorage	D 7
Air Force	D11
Boise St.	D22
Colo. Christian Cl.	J5-7
Western St.	J14
Mesa St.	J15
Chadron St.■	J20
Colorado Mines■	J21
Southern Colo.	J26
Colorado Col.	J27
Fort Hays St.■	J29
Colorado Mines	F 3
Chadron St.	F 5
Western St.■	F11
Mesa St.■	F12
N.M. Highlands	F15
Fort Hays St.	F19
Fort Lewis■	F22
N.M. Highlands■	F26

Colors: Green & White. Nickname: Indians.
AD: Vivian Frausto. SID: Lloyd Engen. II

ADELPHI .... Garden City, NY 11530

Jim O'Connor (5 YRS. W-74, L-67)

Fordham	N29
Molloy	D 1
St. Rose■	D 4
Queens (N.Y.)■	D11
Stony Brook☒	D18
Concordia (N.Y.)	J 5
Dowling	J 8
Phila. Textile	J10
Molloy■	J12
LIU-C.W. Post	J15
Mercy■	J19
LIU-Southampton	J22
Phila. Textile■	J24
New York Tech■	J26
St. Rose	J29
Mercy	F 2
New York Tech	F 5
LIU-C.W. Post■	F 7
LIU-Southampton■	F 9
Dowling■	F12
Queens (N.Y.)	F16
Pace ◆	F19
Mt. St. Mary (N.Y.)	F21
Pace	F23
Concordia (N.Y.)■	F26

☒ Uniondale, NY
◆ New York, NY

Colors: Brown & Gold. Nickname: Panthers.
AD: Robert Hartwell. SID: Andrew Baumbach. II

ADRIAN .... Adrian, MI 49221

Buck Riley (11 YRS. W-104, L-161)

Mount Union Cl.	N19-20
Franklin■	N23
Kenyon■	N27
Adrian Cl.	D3-4
Concordia (Mich.)	D 8
Bluffton■	D11
Thomas More■	D18
Ogelthorpe Cl.	D29-30
Calvin	J 5
Albion■	J 8
Olivet■	J12
Alma	J15
Bluffton	J19
Kalamazoo■	J22
Hope	J26
Calvin■	J29
Albion	F 2
Olivet	F 5
Alma■	F 9
Siena Heights■	F14
Kalamazoo	F16
Hope■	F19

Colors: Gold & Black. Nickname: Bulldogs.
AD: Henry Mensing. SID: Darcy Gifford. III

AIR FORCE .... USAF Academy, CO 80840

Reggie Minton (10 YRS. W-105, L-179)

Navy	N27
Mesa St.■	D 1
Doane■	D 4
Navy■	D 6
Adams St.■	D11
Regis (Colo.)■	D13
Valparaiso■	D30
Wyoming	J 3
Colorado St.	J 5
New Mexico■	J 8
UTEP■	J10
Utah	J13
Brigham Young	J15
Cal St. Northridge■	J19
Fresno St.■	J22
Hawaii■	J27
San Diego St.■	J29
Hawaii	F 3
San Diego St.	F 5
Fresno St.	F12
Brigham Young■	F17
Utah■	F19
New Mexico	F24
UTEP	F26
Wyoming■	M 3
Colorado St.■	M 5
Western Ath. Conf.	M9-12

Colors: Blue & Silver. Nickname: Falcons.
AD: Col. Ken Schweitzer. SID: Dave Kellogg. I

AKRON .... Akron, OH 44325

Coleman Crawford (4 YRS. W-55, L-55)

Houston	N27
Carnegie Mellon■	D 1
Iona■	D 4
Penn St.■	D 8
Youngstown St.■	D11
Northern Ill.	D18
Prairie View■	D21
St. Francis (Pa.)■	D30
Eastern Mich.	J 5
Western Mich.	J 8
Toledo■	J12
Ohio	J15
Kent■	J19
Central Mich.	J22
Ball St.■	J26
Bowling Green	J29
Miami (Ohio)■	F 2
Western Mich.■	F 5
Toledo	F 9
Ohio■	F12
Kent	F16
Central Mich.■	F19
Ball St.	F23
Bowling Green■	F26
Miami (Ohio)	M 2
Eastern Mich.■	M 5
Mid-American Conf.	M8-12

Colors: Blue & Gold. Nickname: Zips.
AD: Richard Aynes. SID: Mac Yates. I

ALABAMA .... Tuscaloosa, AL 34587

David Hobbs (1 YR. W-16, L-13)

Tenn.-Chatt.■	D 1
Washington St.☒	D 4
Northwestern (La.)■	D 9
Florida A&M■	D18
Southern Miss.	D21
Charleston (S.C.) Cl	D28-29
South Caro.	J 5
Arkansas■	J 8
Vanderbilt■	J12
Mississippi	J15
Tenn.-Martin■	J17
Louisiana St.	J19
Florida■	J22
Auburn	J25
Mississippi St.■	J29
Kentucky	F 2
Georgia	F 5
Louisiana St.■	F 8
Mercer■	F14
Arkansas	F16
Tennessee■	F19
Tennessee St.■	F23
Mississippi■	F26
Mississippi St.	M 2
Auburn■	M 5
Southeastern Conf.	M10-13

☒ Spokane, WA

Colors: Crimson & White. Nickname: Crimson Tide.
AD: Cecil Ingram. SID: Larry White. I

ALABAMA A&M .... Normal, AL 35762

L. Vann Pettaway (7 YRS. W-155, L-57)

Miles☒	N28
Fla. Memorial■	N30
Lane■	D 2
Albany St. (Ga.)■	D 4
LeMoyne-Owen	D 6
Morris Brown	D11
Savannah St.	J 7
Paine	J 8
Albany St. (Ga.)	J10
Savannah St.■	J14
LeMoyne-Owen■	J19
Tuskegee	J22
Clark Atlanta	J24
Tuskegee■	J29
Fort Valley St.	J31
Miles■	F 2
Morehouse ◆	F 5
Fort Valley St.■	F 7
Clark Atlanta■	F 9
Morris Brown■	F11
Morehouse■	F13
Ala.-Huntsville	F16
Paine■	F19
Knoxville■	F21
Talladega■	F23
Jacksonville St.■	F26

☒ Birmingham, AL
◆ Detroit, MI

Colors: Maroon & White. Nickname: Bulldogs.
AD: Gene Bright. SID: Antoine M. Bell. II

■ Home games on each schedule.

See pages 405–407 for Division I tournament details

ALABAMA ST. .... Montgomery, AL 36101

James Oliver (18 YRS. W-330, L-185)

Pre-Season NIT	N17-26	Mississippi Val.■	J24
Faulkner■	N27	Jackson St.	J29
Ala.-Birmingham	N30	Troy St.■	F 2
Southeast Mo. St. Cl	D3-4	Prairie View	F 5
Georgia St.■	D 8	Texas Southern	F 7
Tuskegee■	D11	Tuskegee	F10
Tenn.-Chatt. Tr.	D29-30	Alcorn St.■	F12
Troy St.	J 6	Southern-B.R.■	F14
Prairie View■	J 8	Grambling■	F19
Texas Southern■	J10	Mississippi Val.	F21
Alcorn St.	J15	Jackson St.■	F26
Southern-B.R.	J17	Southwestern Conf.	M9-13
Grambling	J22		

Colors: Black & Gold. Nickname: Hornets.
AD: Arthur D. Barnett. SID: Peter Forest. I

ALA.-BIRMINGHAM .... Birmingham, AL 35294

Gene Bartow (31 YRS. W-595, L-315)

Texas-Arlington■	N27	Rhode Island■	J22
Alabama St.■	N30	DePaul■	J26
Temple	D 4	Dayton	J30
Mississippi St.	D 7	Marquette	F 2
Hawaii Tip-Off Tr.	D10-11	Cincinnati■	F 5
Auburn	D16	DePaul	F 9
Mississippi Val.■	D18	Memphis St.	F12
South Ala.■	D21	Tulane	F16
South Fla.■	D31	St. Louis	F19
Western Ky.■	J 3	Southern-B.R.■	F24
Cincinnati	J 9	Cal St. Northridge	F26
Cal St. Sacramento■	J12	Dayton■	M 3
Memphis St.■	J16	St. Louis■	M 5
Marquette■	J19	Great Midwest Conf.	M10-12

Colors: Green & Gold. Nickname: Blazers.
AD: Gene Bartow. SID: Grant Shingleton. I

ALA.-HUNTSVILLE .... Huntsville, AL 35899

Joe Baker (7 YRS. W-49, L-144)

Livingston■	N20	Henderson St.	J17
Ala.-Huntsville Tr.	N26-27	Livingston	J22
Valdosta St.	N30	Lincoln Memorial■	J24
Montevallo	D 8	Montevallo■	J26
Middle Tenn. St.	D11	Athens St.■	J31
Athens St.	D15	Central Ark.■	F 5
Faulkner	D18	Henderson St.■	F 7
Birmingham So. Tr.	D30-31	North Ala.■	F12
Tenn.-Martin■	J 5	Alabama A&M■	F16
West Ga.■	J 8	West Ga.	F19
Valdosta St.■	J10	North Ala.	F23
Central Ark.	J15	Lincoln Memorial	F26

Colors: Blue & White. Nickname: Chargers.
AD: Paul Brand. SID: Julie Woltjen. II

ALAS. ANCHORAGE .... Anchorage, AK 99508

Harry Larrabee (12 YRS. W-188, L-163)

Alas. Anchorage Tr.	N12-14	Grand Canyon■	J14
Northern Mich.■	N19	Eastern Mont.■	J15
Northern Mich.■	N20	Hawaii-Hilo	J22
Great Alas. Shootout	N24-27	Chaminade	J24
Adams St.■	D 6	Alas. Fairbanks■	J29
Adams St.■	D 7	Seattle Pacific■	F 4
Western N. Mex.■	D10	Eastern Mont.	F10
Western N. Mex.■	D11	Grand Canyon	F12
Ind.-Southeast	D20	Chaminade■	F17
Ball St.	D29	Hawaii-Hilo■	F19
Washington St.	J 3	Alas. Fairbanks	F26
Seattle Pacific	J 7		

Colors: Green & Gold. Nickname: Seawolves.
AD: Timothy J. Dillon. SID: Dave Mateer. II

ALAS. FAIRBANKS .... Fairbanks, AK 99775

George T. Roderick (8 YRS. W-88, L-134)

Alas. Fairbanks Tr.	N19-20	Eastern Mont.■	J14
Northern Mich.■	N22	Grand Canyon■	J15
Northern Mich.■	N23	Chaminade	J22
Adams St.■	D 3	Hawaii-Hilo	J24
Adams St.■	D 4	Alas. Anchorage	J29
Seattle■	D10	Seattle Pacific■	F 5
Seattle■	D11	Grand Canyon	F10
LSU-Shreveport■	D17	Eastern Mont.	F12
LSU-Shreveport■	D18	Chaminade■	F19
Cal St. Chico Tr.	D28-30	Hawaii-Hilo■	F21
Oregon	J 3	Alas. Anchorage■	F26
Seattle Pacific	J 8		

Colors: Blue & Gold. Nickname: Nanooks.
AD: Tom Wells. SID: Jodi L. Hoatson. II

ALBANY (N.Y.) .... Albany, NY 12222

Richard Sauers (37 YRS. W-630, L-294)

Union (N.Y.) Tr.	N19-20	Plattsburgh St.■	J25
Binghamton■	N23	Mt. St. Mary (N.Y.)	J29
Castleton St.	N30	North Adams St.■	F 3
Union (N.Y.)⊠	D 4	Old Westbury■	F 5
Ithaca	D 7	Oneonta St.	F 8
Buffalo St.■	D12	Elmira■	F12
Staten Island Cl.	D29-30	Hartwick■	F15
Upsala	J 8	Potsdam St.	F19
Cortland St.	J10	St. John Fisher■	F23
Stony Brook	J14	Skidmore■	F26
Rensselaer■	J18	⊠ Albany, NY	
Hamilton■	J20		

Colors: Purple & Gold. Nickname: Great Danes.
AD: Milt Richards. SID: Kyle Serba. III

ALBERTUS MAGNUS .... New Haven, CT 06511

Tom Blake (2 YRS. W-17, L-33)

Norwich	N21	Rivier■	J22
St. Joseph's (N.Y.)	N23	Western Conn. St.■	J27
John Jay■	N29	Western New Eng.	J31
Elmira Tr.	D4-5	Wesleyan■	F 2
Coast Guard■	D 8	Colby-Sawyer	F 5
Salve Regina	D12	Maritime (N.Y.)	F 7
Mass. Pharmacy	D13	Eastern Conn. St.■	F10
Ramapo	J 5	Nichols■	F12
Westfield St.■	J 8	Bard	F16
Tufts■	J11	Daniel Webster■	F19
Trinity (Conn.) Cl.	J14-15	Connecticut Col.	F23
Mt. St. Vincent	J19		

Colors: Royal Blue & White. Nickname: Falcons.
AD: Thomas W. Blake. SID: Joseph Tonelli. III

ALBION .... Albion, MI 49224

Mike Turner (19 YRS. W-269, L-183)

Albion Cl.	N19-20	Kalamazoo■	J12
Concordia (Mich.)	N23	Hope■	J15
Grand Rapids Bapt.■	N30	Calvin	J19
Rose-Hulman Inv.	D3-4	Olivet	J26
Spring Arbor	D 7	Alma	J29
Goshen	D16	Adrian■	F 2
Grand Rapids Bapt.	D20	Kalamazoo	F 5
Albion Tr.	D28-29	Hope	F 9
Alma■	J 5	Calvin■	F12
Adrian	J 8	Olivet■	F19

Colors: Purple & Gold. Nickname: Britons.
AD: Pete Schmidt. SID: Robin Hartman. III

ALBRIGHT .... Reading, PA 19604

Ray Ricketts (5 YRS. W-52, L-74)

Gettysburg Tr.	N19-20	Elizabethtown	J15
Muhlenberg■	N23	Messiah	J18
Widener	N30	Juniata■	J22
Frank. & Marsh.	D 2	Susquehanna■	J26
Lebanon Valley■	D 4	Widener■	J29
FDU-Madison	D 8	Moravian	F 2
King's (Pa.)■	D11	Lebanon Valley	F 5
Drew■	J 5	Messiah■	F 9
Wash. & Jeff. Tr.	J7-8	Elizabethtown■	F12
Moravian■	J11	Susquehanna	F15
Dickinson	J13	Juniata	F19

Colors: Cardinal & White. Nickname: Lions.
AD: William Helm Jr. SID: Elliot Tannenbaum. III

ALCORN ST. .... Lorman, MS 39096

Sam Weaver (1ST YR. AS HEAD COACH)

Memphis St.	N26	Prairie View■	J24
Southern Miss.	D 6	Southern-B.R.■	J29
Mississippi Col.■	D10	Troy St.	J31
Ark.-Lit. Rock	D18	Grambling■	F 5
Toledo	D20	Mississippi Val.■	F 7
Boise St. Tr.	D29-30	Alabama St.	F12
Ark.-Lit. Rock■	J 3	Jackson St.	F14
Grambling	J 8	Texas Southern	F19
Mississippi Val.	J10	Prairie View	F21
Alabama St.■	J15	Troy St.■	F23
Jackson St.■	J17	Southern-B.R.	F26
Texas Southern■	J22	Southwestern Conf.	M9-13

Colors: Purple & Gold. Nickname: Scalping Braves.
AD: Cardell Jones. SID: Gus Howard. I

■ Home games on each schedule.

See pages 405–407 for Division I tournament details

ALDERSON-BROADDUS .... Philippi, WV 26416

Steve Dodd (9 YRS. W-155 , L-96)

Mercyhurst	N20	Glenville St.	J22
David Lipscomb	N27	Wheeling Jesuit■	J24
Davis & Elkins	N30	West Liberty St.	J26
Ohio Valley College■	D 2	West Va. St.■	J29
Fairmont St.	D 4	Fairmont St.■	J31
Coastal Caro.	D 8	Salem Teikyo	F 2
Bluefield St.	J 5	West Va. Tech	F 5
West Va. Wesleyan■	J 8	Ohio Valley College	F 7
Concord	J10	Davis & Elkins■	F 9
West Va. St.	J12	Shepherd	F12
Charleston (W.Va.)■	J15	Glenville St.■	F14
Mercyhurst■	J17	Wheeling Jesuit	F16
Shepherd■	J19	West Liberty St.■	F19

Colors: Blue, Gray & Gold. Nickname: Battlers.
AD: Allen Cassell. SID: Carolyn Mair. II

AMERICAN .... Washington, DC 20016

Chris Knoche (3 YRS. W-37, L-49)

Geo. Washington■	N29	William & Mary■	J24
Villanova	D 1	Old Dominion	J26
Robert Morris■	D 6	George Mason■	J29
Loyola (Md.)■	D 8	Vermont	F 1
Illinios Cl.	D10-11	N.C.-Wilmington■	F 5
St. Peter's	D18	East Caro.■	F 7
Tenn.-Chatt. Tr.	D29-30	Richmond	F12
Towson St.	J 4	James Madison■	F16
East Caro.	J 8	William & Mary	F19
N.C.-Wilmington	J10	Old Dominion■	F23
Niagara■	J13	George Mason	F26
Richmond■	J15	Colonial Conf.	M5-7
James Madison	J19		

Colors: Red, White & Blue. Nickname: Eagles.
AD: Joseph O'Donnell. SID: Joan von Thron. I

ALFRED .... Alfred, NY 14802

Kevin Jones (3 YRS. W-20, L-56)

New York U. Tr.	N20-21	Nazareth (N.Y.)■	J31
Elmira■	N29	St. Lawrence■	F 4
Houghton	D 8	Clarkson■	F 5
Union (N.Y.) Inv.	J7-8	Ithaca	F 8
Clarkson	J14	Hartwick■	F11
St. Lawrence	J15	Rensselaer■	F12
Penn St.-Behrend■	J18	Elmira	F15
Hobart■	J21	Rochester Inst.	F18
Rochester Inst.■	J22	Hobart	F19
Ithaca■	J25	Roberts Wesleyan	F23
Rensselaer	J28	St. John Fisher	F25
Hartwick	J29		

Colors: Purple & Gold. Nickname: Saxons.
AD: Hank Ford. SID: Paul Vecchio. III

AMERICAN (P.R.) .... Bayamon, PR 00621

Osvaldo Santos (1 YR. W-7, L-1)

San Juan Shootout	N26-28	Inter American (PR)■	M 1
Chicharron (P.R.) Tr	D19-21	Turabo (P.R.)■	M 3
Bayamon Central (PR)■	F 8	Halcon (P.R.) Tr.	M3-4
Bayamon Tech (P.R.)	F10	Humacao (P.R.)■	M 7
Puerto Rico (R.P.)	F15	Bayamon Central (PR)	M 9
P.R.-Arecibo■	F17	Bayamon Tech (P.R.)■	M10
Sacred Heart (P.R.)■	F21	Puerto Rico (R.P.)■	M15
Catholic (P.R.)■	F22	P.R.-Arecibo	M17
P.R.-Mayaguez	F24	Sacred Heart (P.R.)	M21
Cayey (P.R.)	F28		

Colors: Royal & Gold. Nickname: Eagles.
AD: Edwin Morales. SID: Osvaldo Santos. III

ALLEGHENY .... Meadville, PA 16335

Phil Ness (4 YRS. W-66, L-40)

Wash. & Jeff.■	N19	Wooster	J12
Grove City■	N20	Denison■	J15
Penn St.-Behrend■	N23	Westminster (Pa.)	J19
Allegheny Cl.	N26-27	Ohio Wesleyan■	J22
Case Reserve	D 1	Oberlin	J26
Ohio Wesleyan	D 4	Earlham	J29
Oberlin■	D 8	Wooster■	F 2
Earlham■	D11	Wittenberg■	F 5
Bethany (W.Va.)■	D15	Case Reserve■	F 9
Ryerson Tr.	D28-30	Denison	F12
Kenyon	J 5	St. John Fisher	F16
Wittenberg	J 8	Kenyon■	F19

Colors: Blue & Gold. Nickname: Gators.
AD: Rick Creehan. SID: To be named. III

AMERICAN INT'L .... Springfield, MA 01109

Jim Powell (14 YRS. W-236, L-169)

Franklin Pierce■	N23	Bentley	J22
Stonehill■	N28	Bryant■	J25
Southern Conn. St.■	N30	Assumption	J27
Springfield	D 4	Stonehill	J29
New Haven■	D 9	Springfield■	F 2
New Hamp. Col.	D11	St. Michael's	F 5
Mass.-Lowell■	D14	Assumption■	F 7
Eckerd	D31	St. Anselm■	F 9
Tampa	J 5	Quinnipiac■	F12
St. Michael's■	J 8	Merrimack	F16
St. Anselm	J12	Bentley■	F19
Quinnipiac	J15	Bryant	F22
Merrimack■	J19		

Colors: Gold & White. Nickname: Yellow Jackets.
AD: Bob Burke. SID: Frank Polera. II

ALLENTOWN .... Center Valley, PA 18034

Scott Coval (1ST YR. AS HEAD COACH)

Stockton St.	N20	Salisbury St.	J15
Moravian■	N23	Rutgers■	J17
Lebanon Valley	N27	Marywood■	J19
Lycoming	N29	Ursinus■	J24
York (Pa.)	D 1	Wesley	J27
Cabrini	D 4	Caldwell	J29
Wilkes	D 6	Drew	J31
Delaware Valley■	D11	Lock Haven■	F 7
Wooster■	D20	Catholic■	F10
Frank. & Marsh. Tr.	J4-5	Holy Family	F16
Marymount Tr.	J8-9	Alvernia■	F19
Muhlenberg	J12		

Colors: Red & Blue. Nickname: Centaurs.
AD: Joy Richman. SID: John Gump. III

AMHERST .... Amherst, MA 01002

David Hixon (16 YRS. W-234, L-146)

Clarkson■	N19	Colby	J21
St. Lawrence■	N20	Bates	J22
Nichols■	N23	Clark (Mass.)	J26
Middlebury■	D 4	Hamilton	J29
Western New Eng.	D 7	Framingham St.■	F 1
Westfield St.	D11	Tufts	F 3
Skidmore	D14	Williams■	F 5
Wash. & Lee	J 2	Wesleyan■	F12
Curry■	J11	Trinity (Conn.)■	F16
Babson■	J13	Wesleyan	F19
Williams	J15	Worcester Tech■	F22
Connecticut Col.■	J18	Brandeis	F26

Colors: Purple & White. Nickname: Lord Jeffs.
AD: Peter Gooding. SID: Kirstin Thorne. III

ALMA .... Alma, MI 48801

Bob Eldridge (11 YRS. W-119, L-165)

North Central Cl.	N19-20	Kalamazoo	J19
Aquinas■	N23	Hope	J22
Oakland■	N27	Calvin■	J26
Concordia (Mich.)■	N30	Albion■	J29
Alma Tr.	D3-4	Olivet	F 2
Bluffton	D 7	Northwood	F 7
Mich.-Dearborn	D11	Adrian	F 9
Palm Beach Atl.	D18	Kalamazoo■	F12
St. Thomas (Fla.)⊠	D20	Hope■	F16
Albion	J 5	Calvin	F19
Olivet■	J 8	⊠ West Palm Beach, FL	
Adrian■	J15		

Colors: Maroon & Cream. Nickname: Scots.
AD: Bob Eldridge. SID: Greg Baadte. III

ANGELO ST. .... San Angelo, TX 76909

Ed Messbarger (36 YRS. W-610, L-439)

Howard Payne■	N20	Central Okla.■	J22
Dallas Christian■	N23	Eastern N. Mex.■	J29
Abilene Christ. Cl.	N26-27	West Tex. A&M■	J31
Angelo St. Cl.■	D 3	Eastern N. Mex.	F 5
McMurry■	D 6	West Tex. A&M	F 7
Texas-Arlington	D 9	Texas A&M-Kingsville■	F12
Texas-San Antonio	D11	East Tex. St.■	F14
Neb.-Kearney Cl.	J6-8	Cameron	F19
Abilene Christian	J11	Central Okla.	F21
East Tex. St.	J15	Abilene Christian■	F26
Texas A&M-Kingsville	J17		

Colors: Blue & Gold. Nickname: Rams.
AD: Jerry Vandergriff. SID: Sean M. Johnson. II

■ Home games on each schedule.

See pages 405–407 for Division I tournament details

ANNA MARIA .... Paxton, MA 01612
Paul Phillips (7 YRS. W-110, L-71)

Tufts N23
Mass.-Boston Inv. N27-28
Worcester St. N29
Clark (Mass.)■ .... D 1
Anna Maria Inv. D4-5
Worcester Tech .... D 7
Bates .... J 8
Fitchburg St.■ J13
Salve Regina■ J15
Gordon■ J18
Roger Williams J20
Eastern Nazarene J22
New England Col.■ J26
Wentworth Inst.■ J29
Curry .... F 1
Salve Regina .... F 3
Gordon .... F 5
Roger Williams■ .... F 9
Wentworth Inst. F12
New England Col. F15
Curry■ F17
Eastern Nazarene■ F19

Colors: Royal Blue & White. Nickname: AMCATS.
AD: Stephen Washkevich. SID: To be named. III

APPALACHIAN ST. .... Boone, NC 28608
Tom Apke (19 YRS. W-295, L-241)

N.C.-Wilmington N26
Nebraska■ .... D 1
N.C.-Charlotte■ .... D 4
Tennessee Tech■ .... D 6
Wingate■ D11
Wake Forest D19
East Caro. D22
Marshall .... J 4
Ga. Southern■ .... J 8
Citadel■ J10
Va. Military J12
Furman J15
Davidson J17
Tenn.-Chatt.■ J20
East Tenn. St.■ J22
Clemson J24
Western Caro.■ J26
Va. Military■ J29
Marshall■ J31
Western Caro. .... F 5
Tenn.-Chatt. .... F 7
Citadel F12
Ga. Southern F14
Furman■ F17
Davidson■ F19
East Tenn. St. F26
Southern Conf. M3-6

Colors: Black & Gold. Nickname: Mountaineers.
AD: Roachel Laney. SID: Rick Covington. I

ARIZONA .... Tucson, AZ 85721
Lute Olson (20 YRS. W-429, L-173)

Baylor■ N29
St. Joseph's (Pa.)■ .... D 1
Oklahoma St.☒ .... D 5
Utah .... D 9
New Orleans■ D14
Santa Clara D18
Maui Inv. D21-23
Arizona Tr. D28-30
Arizona St.■ .... J 5
Marquette■ .... J 8
California■ J13
Stanford■ J15
UCLA J20
Southern Cal J22
Oregon■ J27
Oregon St.■ J29
Washington St. .... F 3
Washington .... F 5
Stanford F10
California F13
Southern Cal■ F17
UCLA■ F19
Oregon St. F24
Oregon F26
Washington■ .... M 3
Washington St.■ .... M 5
Arizona St. M12
☒ Phoenix, AZ

Colors: Cardinal & Navy. Nickname: Wildcats.
AD: Cedric Dempsey. SID: Butch Henry. I

ARIZONA ST. .... Tempe, AZ 85287
Bill Frieder (13 YRS. W-260, L-140)

Brigham Young■ N27
Oklahoma St.☒ .... D 2
Boston College☒ .... D 5
Cal St. Northridge■ D17
Northeastern Ill.■ D18
Southern Methodist■ D22
Arizona St. Cl. D28-29
Arizona .... J 5
St. Louis♦ .... J 8
Stanford■ J13
California■ J15
Southern Cal J20
UCLA J22
Oregon St.■ J27
Oregon■ J29
Washington .... F 3
Washington St. .... F 5
California F10
Stanford F12
UCLA■ F17
Southern Cal■ F19
Oregon F24
Oregon St. F26
Washington St.■ .... M 3
Washington■ .... M 5
Arizona■ M12
☒ Phoenix, AZ
♦ Tucson, AZ

Colors: Maroon & Gold. Nickname: Sun Devils.
AD: Charles Harris. SID: Mark Brand. I

ARKANSAS .... Fayetteville, AR 72701
Nolan Richardson (13 YRS. W-308, L-109)

Murray St.■ N29
Missouri■ .... D 2
Northwestern (La.)■ .... D 4
Memphis St. .... D 8
Delaware St.■ D11
Jackson St.■ D18
Tulsa D23
Texas Southern■ D28
Southern Methodist■ .... J 2
Mississippi■ .... J 5
Alabama .... J 8
Louisiana St.■ J11
Auburn J15
Mississippi St. J19
South Caro.■ J22
Tennessee J29
Vanderbilt■ .... F 1
Montevallo■ .... F 5
Kentucky .... F 9
Florida■ F12
Alabama■ F16
Mississippi F19
Georgia F22
Auburn■ F26
Louisiana St. .... M 2
Mississippi St.■ .... M 5
Southeastern Conf. M10-13

Colors: Cardinal & White. Nickname: Razorbacks.
AD: Frank Broyles. SID: Rick Schaeffer. I

ARKANSAS ST. .... State University, AR 72467
Nelson Catalina (9 YRS. W-165, L-107)

Texas Tech N29
Missouri .... D 6
Arkansas St. Cl. D10-11
Austin Peay■ D18
James Madison D20
Wichita St. Tr. D29-30
New Orleans■ .... J 6
Western Ky. .... J 8
Jacksonville J12
South Ala.■ J15
Louisiana Tech J17
Southwestern La.■ J20
South Ala. J23
Southwestern La. J27
Ark.-Lit. Rock■ J29
Tex.-Pan American■ .... F 3
Lamar■ .... F 5
Louisiana Tech■ .... F 7
New Orleans F10
Ark.-Lit. Rock F12
Lamar F17
Western Ky.■ F19
Tex.-Pan American F23
Jacksonville■ F28
Sun Belt Conf. M4-8

Colors: Scarlet & Black. Nickname: Indians.
AD: Brad Hovious. SID: Jerry Schaeffer. I

ARK.-LIT. ROCK .... Little Rock, AR 72204
Jim Platt (3 YRS. W-42, L-45)

Livingston■ N30
South Ala.■ .... D 4
Tennessee .... D 8
Kansas D11
Alcorn St.■ D18
Grambling D21
Alcorn St. .... J 3
New Orleans■ .... J 8
Western Ky. J10
Southwestern La.■ J13
Louisiana Tech■ J15
Tex.-Pan American J20
Lamar J22
Jacksonville■ J26
Arkansas St. J29
New Orleans J31
Southwestern La. .... F 2
Jacksonville .... F 5
Tex.-Pan American■ F10
Arkansas St.■ F12
Louisiana Tech F14
Western Ky.■ F17
Lamar■ F19
South Ala. F21
Memphis St. F24
Grambling■ F28
Sun Belt Conf. M4-8

Colors: Maroon, White & Gold. Nickname: Trojans.
AD: Mike Hamrick. SID: Will Hancock. I

ARMSTRONG ST. .... Savannah, GA 31419
Griff Mills (2 YRS. W-25, L-23)

Savannah St.☒ N22
Edward Waters■ N24
North Fla. Cl. N26-27
Rollins Inv. D3-4
Coker .... D 8
Kennesaw■ D10
Edward Waters D15
Kennesaw .... J 3
Georgia Col. .... J 6
S.C.-Spartanburg■ .... J 8
Lander■ J10
Columbus■ J15
Augusta■ J17
Pembroke St. J22
Francis Marion J24
S.C.-Aiken■ J29
Augusta J31
S.C.-Spartanburg .... F 5
Columbus .... F 7
Francis Marion■ .... F 9
Lander F14
Pembroke St.■ F19
S.C.-Aiken F21
Georgia Col.■ F26
☒ Savannah, Ga

Colors: Maroon & Gold. Nickname: Pirates.
AD: Roger Counsil. SID: Darrell Stephens. II

ARMY .... West Point, NY 10996
Dino Gaudio (1ST YR. AS HEAD COACH)

Boston U.■ N26
Monmouth (N.J.) N30
Rider .... D 3
Hobart■ .... D 8
Marist D19
Hawaii Rainbow Cl. D27-30
Brown■ .... J 3
Navy■ .... J 8
Drexel■ J10
Holy Cross J12
Fordham■ J15
Bucknell■ J18
Lehigh J22
Colgate■ J25
Lafayette J29
Navy .... F 2
Holy Cross■ .... F 5
Richmond .... F 7
Fordham .... F 9
Bucknell F12
Lehigh■ F15
Colgate F19
Hofstra F22
Lafayette■ F26
Patriot Conf. M4-11

Colors: Black, Gold, Gray. Nickname: Cadets/Black Knights.
AD: Al Vanderbush. SID: Robert Kinney. I

ASBURY .... Wilmore, KY 40390
Winston Smith (1 YR. W-5 , L-21)

Berea N20
Lindsay Wilson N23
Roanoke Tr. N26-27
Alice Lloyd N30
Union (Ky.)■ .... D 2
Shawnee St. .... D 6
Cedarville■ D11
Ind. Wesleyan■ .... J 4
Trevecca Nazarene .... J 8
Alice Lloyd■ J11
Berea■ J13
Pikeville■ J15
Ky. Christian J18
Lindsay Wilson■ J22
Graceland (Ind.) J29
Spalding .... F 3
Maryville (Tenn.)■ .... F 5
Ky. Christian■ .... F 8
Graceland (Ind.)■ F12
Pikeville F15
Thomas More F17
Union (Ky.) F19
Maryville (Tenn.) F23
Spalding■ F26

Colors: Purple & White. Nickname: Eagles.
AD: Rita J. Pritchett. SID: Ken Pickerill. III

■ Home games on each schedule.

See pages 405–407 for Division I tournament details

ASHLAND .... Ashland, OH 44805

Terry Weigand (2 YRS. W-27, L-28)

Opponent	Date	Opponent	Date
Grand Valley St.■	N19	Kentucky St.	J22
Walsh■	N23	Indianapolis■	J27
Taylor■	N27	Northern Ky.■	J29
Wooster	D 1	Lake Erie	F 2
Dyke■	D 4	IU/PU-Ft. Wayne	F 5
Findlay■	D11	Ky. Wesleyan	F10
Walsh	D22	Southern Ind.	F12
St. Joseph's (Ind.)	D28	Kentucky St.■	F17
Lewis	D30	Bellarmine■	F19
IU/PU-Ft. Wayne■	J 8	Northern Ky.	F24
Southern Ind.■	J13	Indianapolis	F26
Ky. Wesleyan■	J15	St. Joseph's (Ind.)■	M 3
Bellarmine	J20	Lewis■	M 5

Colors: Purple & Gold. Nickname: Eagles.
AD: Alan Platt. SID: Al King. II

ASSUMPTION .... Worcester, MA 01615

Jack Renkens (8 YRS. W-130, L-108)

Opponent	Date	Opponent	Date
Springfield■	N19	Bentley	J19
St. Rose	N21	Bryant■	J22
New Hamp. Col.	N23	Stonehill	J25
Wheaton (Mass.)■	N30	American Int'l■	J27
St. Michael's	D 4	Springfield	J29
Franklin Pierce■	D 7	St. Michael's■	F 2
Mass.-Lowell■	D11	St. Anselm	F 5
Bridgeport	J 3	American Int'l	F 7
Quincy■	J 6	Quinnipiac	F 9
St. Anselm■	J 8	Merrimack■	F12
Sacred Heart	J10	Bentley■	F16
Quinnipiac■	J12	Bryant	F19
Merrimack	J15	Stonehill■	F22

Colors: Royal Blue & White. Nickname: Greyhounds.
AD: Rita Castagna. SID: Steve Morris. II

AUBURN .... Auburn University, AL 36831

Tommy Joe Eagles (8 YRS. W-140, L-101)

Opponent	Date	Opponent	Date
N.C.-Wilmington■	N28	Alabama■	J25
Nicholls St.■	N30	Kentucky■	J30
Ball St.■	D 7	Florida	F 2
Troy St.■	D 9	Fla. Atlantic■	F 5
Ala.-Birmingham■	D16	Vanderbilt	F 9
Old Dominion	D18	Louisiana St.■	F12
Arizona Tr.	D28-30	South Caro.■	F16
Georgia■	J 5	Mississippi St.	F19
Louisiana St.	J 8	Southern Miss.■	F22
Mississippi St.■	J12	Arkansas	F26
Arkansas■	J15	Mississippi■	M 2
Mississippi	J19	Alabama	M 5
Tennessee	J22	Southeastern Conf.	M10-13

Colors: Orange & Blue. Nickname: Tigers.
AD: Mike Lude. SID: David Housel. I

AUGSBURG .... Minneapolis, MN 55454

Brian Ammann (5 YRS. W-50, L-74)

Opponent	Date	Opponent	Date
Minn.-Morris	N20	Carleton	J17
St. Scholastica■	N23	St. Thomas (Minn.)■	J19
Concordia (St. Paul)	N30	St. John's (Minn.)	J22
St. John's (Minn.)■	D 4	Macalester■	J26
Macalester	D 8	Hamline■	J29
Hamline	D11	St. Mary's (Minn.)■	J31
N'western (Minn.)■	D16	Concordia-M'head	F 5
St. Mary's (Minn.)	J 3	Gust. Adolphus■	F 9
Concordia-M'head■	J 8	Bethel (Minn.)	F12
Gust. Adolphus	J10	St. Olaf	F14
Bethel (Minn.)■	J12	Carleton■	F16
St. Olaf■	J15	St. Thomas (Minn.)	F19

Colors: Maroon & Gray. Nickname: Auggies.
AD: Paul Grauer. SID: Gene McGivern. III

AUGUSTA .... Augusta, GA 30904

Clint Bryant (5 YRS. W-61, L-82)

Opponent	Date	Opponent	Date
Florida Tech Cl.	N26-27	Pembroke St.■	J29
Savannah St.■	D 5	Armstrong St.■	J31
Francis Marion	D 7	S.C.-Spartanburg■	F 2
Pembroke St.	D 9	Columbus■	F 5
Norfolk St.	D11	Georgia Col.	F 7
Jacksonville St.	D13	Lander■	F12
Augusta Cl.	D29-30	S.C.-Aiken■	F14
Lander	J 4	Francis Marion■	F19
Jacksonville St.■	J15	S.C.-Spartanburg	F23
Armstrong St.	J17	Paine☒	F25
S.C.-Aiken	J22	Columbus	F27
Georgia Col.■	J26	☒ Augusta, GA	

Colors: Blue & White. Nickname: Jaguars.
AD: Clint Bryant. SID: Nicky Zuber. II

AUGUSTANA (ILL.) .... Rock Island, IL 61201

Steve Yount (3 YRS. W-61, L-22)

Opponent	Date	Opponent	Date
Mt. Mercy	N23	North Central■	J15
St. Ambrose■	N30	Millikin	J19
Augustana Inv.	D3-4	Wheaton (Ill.)■	J22
Western Ill.	D 7	North Park■	J25
Loras■	D 9	Carthage	J29
Carthage■	D11	Elmhurst■	F 2
Beloit	D13	Ill. Wesleyan■	F 5
St. Louis	D15	North Central	F 8
Central (Iowa)	D16	Millikin■	F12
Rockford■	D18	Wheaton (Ill.)	F15
Teikyo Marycrest	J 3	North Park	F19
Ill. Wesleyan	J11	Elmhurst	F26

Colors: Gold & Blue. Nickname: Vikings.
AD: John Farwell. SID: Dave Wrath. III

AUGUSTANA (S.D.) .... Sioux Falls, SD 57102

Gary Thomas (1 YR. W-7, L-19)

Opponent	Date	Opponent	Date
Sioux Falls■	N23	Morningside	J15
Wilmington (Ohio)■	N29	Mankato St.■	J21
Bellevue■	D 2	St. Cloud St.■	J22
Northern St.	D 4	South Dak. St.	J29
Dak. Wesleyan	D 9	North Dak.	F 4
Huron■	D11	North Dak. St.	F 5
Teikyo-Westmar■	D13	Northern Colo.■	F 8
Briar Cliff	D30	Morningside■	F11
Northern Colo.	J 2	South Dak.■	F12
Nebraska-Omaha	J 3	St. Cloud St.	F18
North Dak. St.■	J 7	Mankato St.	F19
North Dak.■	J 8	Nebraska-Omaha■	F22
South Dak.	J14	South Dak. St.■	F26

Colors: Reflex Blue & Chrome Yellow. Nickname: Vikings.
AD: Bill Gross. SID: Andy Ludwig. II

AURORA .... Aurora, IL 60506

Don Holler (13 YRS. W-187, L-148)

Opponent	Date	Opponent	Date
Dubuque■	N23	North Central	J 8
Loras■	N24	Eureka	J12
Northern Ill.	N27	Judson■	J15
MacMurray■	D 3	Rockford	J19
Millikin	D 4	Trinity (Ill.)■	J22
Carthage	D 7	Ill. Benedictine	J26
Blackburn	D11	Concordia (Ill.)	F 2
Monmouth (Ill.)■	D14	Judson	F 5
Beloit■	D16	Rockford■	F 9
Ill. Wesleyan■	D18	Trinity (Ill.)	F12
Elmhurst Cl.	D29-30	Concordia (Ill.)■	F16
Washington (Mo.)■	J 6	Ill. Benedictine■	F19

Colors: Royal & White. Nickname: Spartans.
AD: Sam Bedrosian. SID: Dave Beyer. III

AUSTIN PEAY .... Clarksville, TN 37044

Dave Loos (7 YRS. W-115, L-104)

Opponent	Date	Opponent	Date
N.C.-Greensboro■	N29	Eastern Ill.	J19
Evansville	D 1	Murray St.■	J29
Eastern Ill.■	D 4	Southeast Mo. St.■	J31
N.C.-Greensboro	D 6	Tenn.-Martin	F 5
Southern Ill.	D11	Tennessee St.	F 7
Arkansas St.	D18	Eastern Ky.	F12
Vanderbilt	D21	Morehead St.	F14
Bryan■	D29	Tenn.-Martin■	F16
Cincinnati■	D31	Tennessee Tech■	F19
Tennessee St.■	J 4	Middle Tenn. St.■	F22
Tennessee Tech	J 8	Murray St.	F26
Middle Tenn. St.	J12	Southeast Mo. St.	F28
Morehead St.■	J15	Ohio Valley Conf.	M3-5
Eastern Ky.■	J17		

Colors: Red & White. Nickname: Governors.
AD: To be named. SID: Brad Kirtley. I

AVERETT .... Danville, VA 24541

Kirk Chandler (1 YR. W-3, L-22)

Opponent	Date	Opponent	Date
Warren Wilson	N20	Chris. Newport■	J22
Belmont Abbey■	N29	N.C. Wesleyan	J26
Warren Wilson■	D 4	Shenandoah■	J30
Longwood■	D 8	Ferrum■	F 2
Newport News App.■	D10	Greensboro	F 5
Queens (N.C.)	D11	Methodist■	F 9
Liberty	D18	Newport News App.	F11
Queens (N.C.) Cl.	J6-8	Chris. Newport	F12
Ferrum	J12	N.C. Wesleyan■	F16
Greensboro■	J15	Shenandoah	F19
Queens (N.C.)☒	J17	☒ Danville, VA	
Methodist	J19		

Colors: Navy & Gold. Nickname: Cougars.
AD: Vesa Hiltunen. SID: Steve Ballard. III

■ Home games on each schedule.

See pages 405–407 for Division I tournament details

BABSON .... Babson Park, MA 02157
Serge DeBari (13 YRS. W-191, L-131)

Babson Inv. N19-20
MIT■ N23
Harvard N27
Worcester Tech .... D 1
Washington (Mo.) Cl. D3-4
Western New Eng.■ D10
Williams Tr. J7-8
Brandeis■ J11
Amherst J13
Coast Guard■ J19
Norwich J22
Suffolk■ J25
Salem St. J27
Clark (Mass.)■ J29
Tufts■ .... F 1
Norwich■ .... F 5
Western New Eng. F10
Worcester Tech■ F12
Coast Guard F16
MIT F19

Colors: Green & White. Nickname: Beavers.
AD: Steve Stirling. SID: Christine Merlo. III

BALDWIN-WALLACE .... Berea, OH 44017
Steve Bankson (13 YRS. W-179, L-166)

Gettysburg Tr. N19-20
Bethany (W.Va.) N30
Ohio Northern■ .... D 4
John Carroll .... D 8
Muskingum■ D11
Frostburg St. D15
Marietta■ D18
Wittenberg Tr. D29-30
Hiram■ .... J 5
Capital .... J 8
Mount Union■ J12
Otterbein J15
Heidelberg■ J19
Hiram J22
John Carroll■ J26
Ohio Northern J29
Muskingum .... F 2
Marietta .... F 5
Heidelberg .... F 9
Capital■ F12
Mount Union F16
Otterbein■ F19

Colors: Brown & Gold. Nickname: Yellow Jackets.
AD: Steve Bankson. SID: Kevin Ruple. III

BALL ST. .... Muncie, IN 47306
Dick Hunsaker (4 YRS. W-97 , L-34)

Manchester■ N27
Butler■ N30
Ball St. Cardinal Cl D3-4
Auburn .... D 7
Western Ky. D11
Indiana St. D22
Alas. Anchorage■ D29
Ohio■ .... J 5
Central Mich. .... J 8
Bowling Green■ J12
Eastern Mich. J15
Toledo■ J19
Kent J22
Akron J26
Miami (Ohio)■ J29
Western Mich. .... F 2
Central Mich.■ .... F 5
Bowling Green .... F 9
Eastern Mich.■ F12
Toledo F16
Kent■ F19
Akron■ F23
Miami (Ohio) F26
Western Mich.■ .... M 2
Ohio .... M 5
Mid-American Conf. M8-12

Colors: Cardinal & White. Nickname: Cardinals.
AD: Don Purvis. SID: Joe Hernandez. I

BARD .... Annadale-on-Hudson, NY 12504
Kurt James (1 YR. W-0, L-25)

Rivier Tr. N20-21
Vassar■ N23
Merchant Marine■ N29
Yeshiva .... D 2
Lehman■ .... D 5
Mt. St. Vincent .... D 8
Maritime (N.Y.)■ D11
New Paltz St. Tr. J15-16
St. Mary's (Md.) J21
Gallaudet J23
Mt. St. Vincent■ J26
Southern Vt.■ J28
Pratt .... F 3
Bard Tr. F5-6
Stevens Tech■ .... F 9
St. Joseph's-Suffolk F12
Maritime (N.Y.) F14
Albertus Magnus■ F16
New Jersey Tech F19
Vassar F27

Colors: Red, White & Black. Nickname: Blazers.
AD: Joel Tomson. SID: Kristen Hall. III

BARRY .... Miami Shores, FL 33161
Billy Mims (5 YRS. W-62, L-76)

Barry Cl. N26-27
St. Thomas (Fla.)■ N30
California (Pa.) Inv D3-4
Lynn■ .... D 8
Fla. Memorial■ D10
Fla. Memorial D18
Nova■ D30
Lynn .... J 4
North Park■ .... J 8
Eckerd■ J12
Tampa■ J15
Fla. Southern J19
North Fla. J22
Rollins■ J26
Florida Tech J29
St. Leo■ .... F 2
Tampa .... F 5
Fla. Southern■ .... F 9
North Fla.■ F12
Rollins F16
Florida Tech■ F19
St. Leo F23
Eckerd F26

Colors: Red, Black & Silver. Nickname: Buccaneers.
AD: G. Jean Cerra. SID: Robert McKinney. II

BARUCH .... New York, NY 10010
Ray Rankis (10 YRS. W-99, L-159)

Molloy N19
Maritime (N.Y.) N23
New Paltz St.■ N30
John Jay .... D 2
St. Joseph's (N.Y.) .... D 7
Stevens Tech .... D 9
Yeshiva D13
Concordia (Minn.) Tr D29-30
St. Joseph's (N.Y.) .... J 7
CCNY J13
Mt. St. Vincent■ J15
Lehman■ J18
John Jay■ J20
CCNY■ J26
Old Westbury■ J28
Lehman J31
York (N.Y.) .... F 2
Hunter■ .... F 4
Savannah A&D■ .... F 7
Pratt■ F11
Medgar Evers F14
Staten Island■ F16
Centenary (N.J.) F18

Colors: Azure Blue & White. Nickname: Statesmen.
AD: William Eng. SID: Burt Beagle. III

BATES .... Lewiston, ME 04240
Steven Johnson (1 YR. W-10, L-14)

Haverford☒ N19
Swarthmore ◆ N20
Bowdoin■ N30
New England■ .... D 6
Suffolk D11
Southern Cal Col. D29
Cal Baptist D31
Pomona-Pitzer .... J 3
Anna Maria■ .... J 8
Colby-Sawyer■ J12
Hamilton J15
Skidmore J16
Plymouth St.■ J20
Williams■ J21
Amherst■ J22
Colby J25
Me.-Farmington .... F 1
Trinity (Conn.) .... F 4
Wesleyan .... F 5
Bowdoin .... F 8
Norwich F11
Middlebury F12
Tufts F16
Connecticut Col.■ F19
Colby■ F23

☒ Swarthmore, PA
◆ Haverford, PA

Colors: Garnet. Nickname: Bobcats.
AD: Suzanne Coffey. SID: Anne Whittemore. III

BAYLOR .... Waco, TX 76706
Darrel Johnson (8 YRS. W-167, L-90)

North Texas■ N27
Arizona N29
Prairie View■ .... D 1
Nevada .... D 4
Baylor Inv. D10-11
Southwestern La.■ D20
Texas Southern■ D22
Mo.-Kansas City D28
Mississippi Val.■ D30
Oklahoma .... J 5
Texas Tech■ J12
Texas Christian J15
Texas■ J19
Houston■ J22
Rice J26
Oral Roberts J29
Texas A&M■ .... F 2
Southern Methodist .... F 6
Texas Tech .... F 9
Texas Christian■ F12
Texas F15
Houston F19
Rice■ F23
Texas A&M .... M 2
Southern Methodist■ .... M 5
Southwest Conf. M10-12

Colors: Green & Gold. Nickname: Bears.
AD: Richard Ellis. SID: Tommy Newsom. I

BEAVER .... Glenside, PA 19038
Michael G. Holland (4 YRS. W-28, L-78)

Lancaster Bible■ N30
Holy Family .... D 7
FDU-Madison D13
Frank. & Marsh. Tr. J4-5
Salisbury St.■ .... J 8
Alvernia J10
Misericordia■ J12
Cabrini■ J15
Phila. Pharmacy J17
Eastern (Pa.)■ J19
Neumann J22
Marywood J24
Eastern (Pa.) J29
Misericordia .... F 1
Holy Family■ .... F 3
Gwynedd Mercy■ .... F 5
Phila. Pharmacy■ .... F 7
Cabrini F10
Neumann■ F12
Alvernia■ F14
Marywood■ F17
Gwynedd Mercy F21

Colors: Scarlet & Gray. Nickname: Knights.
AD: Shirley M. Liddle. SID: Eric Reynolds. III

BELLARMINE .... Louisville, KY 40205
Joe Reibel (22 YRS. W-335, L-261)

Bellarmine Cl. N26-27
Oakland City■ .... D 1
IU/PU-Indianapolis■ .... D 4
Ind.-Southeast D15
Georgetown (Ky.)■ D18
Kentucky St.■ D22
IU/PU-Indianapolis .... J 3
Indianapolis■ .... J 6
Northern Ky.■ .... J 8
Lewis J13
St. Joseph's (Ind.) J15
Ashland■ J20
IU/PU-Ft. Wayne■ J22
Southern Ind. J27
Ky. Wesleyan J29
Northern Ky. .... F 3
Indianapolis .... F 5
St. Joseph's (Ind.)■ F10
Lewis■ F12
IU/PU-Ft. Wayne F17
Ashland F19
Ky. Wesleyan■ F24
Southern Ind.■ F26
SIU-Edwardsville .... M 2
Kentucky St. .... M 5

Colors: Scarlet & Silver. Nickname: Knights.
AD: James Spalding. SID: Mark Mulloy. II

■ Home games on each schedule.

See pages 405–407 for Division I tournament details

BELMONT ABBEY .... Belmont, NC 28012

Tim Jaeger (1 YR. W-12, L-16)

Catawba Cl.	N19-20	St. Andrews■	J26
Newberry■	N22	Barton	J29
Averett	N29	Pfeiffer	F 2
Queens (N.C.)	D 4	Mount Olive■	F 5
Lees-McRae	D 6	Erskine	F 7
Queens (N.C.)■	J10	Coker■	F 9
Lees-McRae■	J12	St. Andrews	F12
Mount Olive	J15	Newberry	F14
Wofford■	J17	High Point■	F16
Coker	J19	Barton	F19
High Point	J22	Wofford	F21
Erskine■	J24	Pfeiffer■	F26

Colors: Red & White. Nickname: Crusaders.
AD: Mike Reider. SID: Frank Mercogliano. II

BELOIT .... Beloit, WI 53511

Bill Knapton (36 YRS. W-510, L-298)

N'western (Wis.)	N20	Monmouth (Ill.)	J23
Carthage■	N23	Coe■	J29
Rockford	N30	Grinnell■	J30
St. Norbert	D 5	Ill. Benedictine■	F 1
Carroll (Wis.)	D 8	Ripon	F 5
Augustana (Ill.)■	D13	Carroll (Wis.)■	F 9
Aurora	D16	Lawrence	F12
Edgewood Tr.	J7-8	Ripon■	F16
Lake Forest■	J11	St. Norbert■	F19
Lawrence■	J15	Lake Forest	F21
Cornell College	J22		

Colors: Navy Blue & Gold. Nickname: Buccaneers.
AD: Ed DeGeorge. SID: Paul Erickson. III

BEMIDJI ST. .... Bemidji, MN 56601

Karl Salscheider (11 YRS. W-125, L-179)

Mayville St.	N20	Southwest St.	J12
North Dak. St.	N30	Minn.-Morris■	J15
St. Cloud St.■	D 2	Minn.-Duluth	J19
Northern Mich.	D 4	Winona St.■	J22
Mankato St.■	D 8	Moorhead St.	J29
Mayville St.■	D13	Northern St.	F 2
Wis.-Parkside■	D14	Wayne St. (Neb.)■	F 5
St. Scholastica	D16	Southwest St.■	F 9
St. Cloud St.	D18	Minn.-Morris	F12
Wis.-Stevens Point	D20	Minn.-Duluth■	F16
Northern Mich.■	J 3	Winona St.	F19
Northern St.■	J 5	Wis.-Parkside	F21
Wayne St. (Neb.)	J 8	Moorhead St.■	F26

Colors: Green & White. Nickname: Beavers.
AD: Bob Peters. SID: Jeff Swanson. II

BENTLEY .... Waltham, MA 02154

Jay Lawson (2 YRS. W-41, L-17)

Brandeis	N22	Assumption■	J19
St. Anselm■	N28	American Int'l■	J22
Mass.-Lowell■	D 1	Springfield	J25
Quinnipiac	D 4	St. Michael's■	J27
Southern Conn. St.■	D 7	St. Anselm	J29
St. Michael's	D11	Quinnipiac■	F 2
St. Rose	D18	Merrimack	F 5
Bentley Tr.	D28-29	Stonehill■	F 9
Florida Tech	J 2	Bryant■	F12
Rollins	J 5	Assumption	F16
Merrimack■	J 9	American Int'l	F19
Stonehill	J12	Springfield■	F22
Bryant	J15		

Colors: Royal Blue & Gold. Nickname: Falcons.
AD: Bob DeFelice. SID: Dick Lipe. II

BEREA .... Berea, KY 40404

Roland Wierwille (21 YRS. W-323, L-244)

Asbury■	N20	Georgetown (Ky.)	J25
Anderson Inv.	N26-27	Brescia	J29
Brescia■	N30	Lindsay Wilson	F 3
Berea Inv.	D3-4	Cumberland (Ky.)■	F 5
Union (Ky.)	D 7	Pikeville	F 8
Sue Bennett■	D11	Spalding	F10
Cumberland (Ky.)	J 4	Union (Ky.)■	F12
Georgetown (Ky.)■	J 8	Campbellsville	F19
Asbury	J13	Sue Bennett	F21
Lindsay Wilson■	J15	Transylvania	F24
Campbellsville■	J18	Pikeville■	F26
Transylvania■	J22		

Colors: Blue & White. Nickname: Mountaineers.
AD: Roland Wierwille. SID: Roland Wierwille. III

BETHEL (MINN.) .... St. Paul, MN 55112

George Palke (14 YRS. W-194, L-169)

Bethel (Minn.) Cl.	N19-20	St. John's (Minn.)	J19
Wis.-River Falls Cl.	N26-27	Macalester■	J22
Macalester	D 4	St. Thomas (Minn.)	J26
St. Thomas (Minn.)■	D 8	Concordia-M'head	J31
Concordia-M'head■	J 3	St. Olaf■	F 2
St. Olaf	J 5	Gust. Adolphus	F 5
Gust. Adolphus■	J 8	St. Mary's (Minn.)■	F 9
St. Mary's (Minn.)	J10	Augsburg■	F12
Augsburg	J12	Carleton	F14
Carleton■	J15	Hamline	F16
Hamline■	J17	St. John's (Minn.)■	F19

Colors: Royal Blue & Gold. Nickname: Royals.
AD: Dave Klostreich. SID: Leland Christenson. III

BETHUNE-COOKMAN ...... Daytona Beach, FL 32015

Tony Sheals (1ST YR. AS HEAD COACH)

Florida A&M☒	N26	Morgan St.■	J22
Jacksonville	D 1	Coppin St.■	J24
Florida St.	D 5	South Caro. St.■	J29
Georgia	D 7	North Caro. A&T■	J31
Miami (Fla.)	D10	Florida A&M■	F 5
Central Fla.	D13	Howard	F10
Loyola (Ill.)	D20	Morgan St.	F12
Penn St.	D22	Coppin St.	F14
Butler	J 6	Delaware St.■	F19
Delaware St.	J 8	Md.-East. Shore■	F21
Md.-East. Shore	J10	Central Fla.■	F23
North Caro. A&T	J15	Florida A&M	F26
South Caro. St.	J17	Mid-Eastern Conf.	M9-13
Howard■	J20	☒ Tampa, FL	

Colors: Maroon & Gold. Nickname: Wildcats.
AD: Lynn W. Thompson. SID: W. Earl Kitchings. I

BINGHAMTON .... Binghamton, NY 13902

Dick Baldwin (2 YRS. W-38, L-16)

Plattsburgh St. Cl.	N19-20	Cortland St.■	J18
Albany (N.Y.)	N23	Elmira	J20
Hamilton	N29	St. John Fisher■	J22
Brockport St.■	D 3	Oneonta St.	J25
Fredonia St.■	D 4	Buffalo St.	J29
New Paltz St.	D 7	Potsdam St.■	F 4
Potsdam St.	D10	Plattsburgh St.■	F 5
Plattsburgh St.	D11	Cortland St.	F 8
Ithaca	J 8	Geneseo St.	F12
Hartwick■	J11	Oneonta St.■	F15
Utica Tech	J14	New Paltz St.■	F19
Oswego St.■	J15		

Colors: Green & White. Nickname: Colonials.
AD: Joel Thirer. SID: John Hartrick. III

BLACKBURN .... Carlinville, IL 62626

Ira Zeff (3 YRS. W-52, L-32)

Illinois Col.	N20	MacMurray■	J20
St. Louis Pharmacy	N23	Fontbonne■	J22
Sanford Brown■	N27	Westminster (Mo.)■	J25
Millsaps■	N28	Maryville (Mo.)	J27
Rose-Hulman■	N30	Principia■	J29
Hanover Tr.	D4-5	Westminster (Mo.)	F 3
Millikin■	D 8	Webster■	F 5
Aurora■	D11	Parks■	F10
Greenville	D14	MacMurray	F12
Principia	J 6	Fontbonne	F17
Webster	J13	Maryville (Mo.)■	F19
Parks	J15		

Colors: Scarlet & Black. Nickname: Beavers.
AD: Ira Zeff. SID: Tom Emery. III

BLOOMSBURG .... Bloomsburg, PA 17815

Charles Chronister (22 YRS. W-393, L-205)

New York Tech■	N23	Mansfield■	J26
Shippensburg	D 1	West Chester■	J29
Goucher■	D 4	Millersville	F 2
Lock Haven	D 7	Indiana (Pa.)	F 5
Caldwell■	D 9	Pitt.-Johnstown■	F 7
Alvernia	J 5	Cheyney	F 9
Bloomsburg Inv.	J7-8	Kutztown■	F12
Shippensburg■	J10	Mansfield	F16
Cheyney■	J12	East Stroudsburg■	F19
Mercyhurst■	J15	Millersville■	F23
Dist. Columbia■	J17	West Chester	F26
Kutztown	J19	Dist. Columbia	F28
East Stroudsburg	J22		

Colors: Maroon & Gold. Nickname: Huskies.
AD: Mary Gardner. SID: Jim Hollister. II

■ Home games on each schedule.

See pages 405–407 for Division I tournament details

BLUEFIELD ST. .... Bluefield, WV 24701

Terry Brown (14 YRS. W-241, L-179)

Opponent	Date	Opponent	Date
Richlands Tr.	N19-20	West Va. St.	J22
Concord■	N29	Glenville St.■	J24
Rollins Inv.	D3-4	Charleston (W.Va.)	J26
West Va. Tech	D11	Shepherd■	J29
Bluefield St. Cl.	D30-31	Davis & Elkins	F 5
Alderson-Broaddus■	J 5	West Va. Tech■	F 7
Salem Teikyo	J 8	Concord	F 9
Fairmont St.■	J10	West Va. Wesleyan	F12
Wheeling Jesuit	J12	West Va. St.■	F14
West Liberty St.	J15	Glenville St.	F16
West Va. Wesleyan■	J19	Charleston (W.Va.)■	F19

Colors: Blue & Gold. Nickname: Big Blues.
AD: Terry Brown. SID: Terry Brown. II

BLUFFTON .... Bluffton, OH 45817

Guy Neal (4 YRS. W-31, L-73)

Opponent	Date	Opponent	Date
Albion Cl.	N19-20	Wilmington (Ohio)	J15
Bethel (Kan.) Cl.	N26-27	Adrian■	J19
Ohio Northern■	D 1	Thomas More■	J22
Concordia (Mich.)■	D 4	Denison	J26
Alma■	D 7	Defiance	J29
Adrian	D11	Goshen■	F 2
Olivet	D15	Thomas More	F 5
Hanover	D18	Findlay	F 9
Concordia (Mich.)	D30	Wilmington (Ohio)■	F12
Goshen	J 8	Manchester	F16
Defiance■	J12	Lake Erie■	F19

Colors: Northwestern Purple & White. Nickname: Beavers.
AD: Carlin Carpenter. SID: Ron Geiser. III

BOISE ST. .... Boise, ID 83725

Bobby Dye (19 YRS. W-339, L-198)

Opponent	Date	Opponent	Date
Boise St. Cl.	N26-27	Montana St.	J28
Southwestern La.	D 4	Montana	J29
Humboldt St.■	D 7	Eastern Wash.■	F 4
Cincinnati Cl.	D10-11	Idaho■	F 5
Adams St.■	D22	Weber St.	F10
Boise St. Tr.	D29-30	Northern Ariz.	F12
Rice	J 3	Idaho St.■	F18
St. Mary's (Cal.)■	J 8	Montana■	F25
Northern Ariz.■	J13	Montana St.■	F26
Weber St.■	J15	Idaho	M 4
Idaho St.	J21	Eastern Wash.	M 6
Cal St. Sacramento■	J24	Big Sky Conf.	M10-12

Colors: Orange & Blue. Nickname: Broncos.
AD: Gene Bleymaier. SID: Max Corbet. I

BOSTON COLLEGE .... Chestnut Hill, MA 02167

Jim O'Brien (11 YRS. W-162, L-167)

Opponent	Date	Opponent	Date
Hartford■	N27	Providence■	J22
Dartmouth■	N30	St. John's (N.Y.)	J26
Notre Dame■	D 2	Seton Hall■	J29
Arizona St.☒	D 5	Georgetown■	J31
Syracuse	D 9	Villanova	F 5
Buffalo	D11	Connecticut■	F 9
Maui Inv.	D21-23	Miami (Fla.)	F16
LIU-Brooklyn■	D30	Syracuse■	F19
Coppin St.■	J 2	Pittsburgh	F22
Villanova■	J 4	Georgetown	F26
Connecticut	J 8	St. John's (N.Y.)■	M 1
Seton Hall	J12	Providence	M 5
Miami (Fla.)■	J15	Big East Conf.	M10-13
Pittsburgh■	J18	☒ Phoenix, AZ	
Holy Cross■	J20		

Colors: Maroon & Gold. Nickname: Eagles.
AD: Chet S. Gladchuk, Jr. SID: Reid Oslin. I

BOSTON U. .... Boston, MA 02215

Bob Brown (9 YRS. W-129, L-128)

Opponent	Date	Opponent	Date
Army	N26	Drexel	J23
St. Francis (N.Y.)■	N29	Maine■	J27
Syracuse Carrier Cl.	D3-4	New Hampshire	J29
Fordham■	D 8	Hofstra	F 1
Harvard■	D22	Northeastern	F 5
Niagara■	D28	New Hampshire■	F10
Brown	D30	Maine	F12
Michigan	J 3	Drexel■	F18
Central Conn. St.	J 8	Delaware■	F20
Hartford■	J13	Hartford	F24
Vermont■	J15	Vermont	F26
Dartmouth■	J18	Northeastern■	M 1
Delaware	J21	North Atlantic Conf.	M5-9

Colors: Scarlet & White. Nickname: Terriers.
AD: Gary Strickler. SID: Edward Carpenter. I

BOWDOIN .... Brunswick, ME 04011

Timothy Gilbride (8 YRS. W-89, L-100)

Opponent	Date	Opponent	Date
Me.-Augusta■	N23	Rivier■	F 1
Southern Me.■	N27	Clark (Mass.)	F 4
Bates	N30	Trinity (Conn.)	F 5
Tufts■	D 4	Bates■	F 8
Thomas	D 7	Connecticut Col.	F11
Maine Maritime	D11	Wheaton (Mass.)	F12
Skidmore	J15	Me.-Farmington■	F15
Union (N.Y.)	J16	Colby■	F16
Western New Eng.■	J21	New England	F18
Williams■	J22	Colby-Sawyer■	F20
Norwich■	J28	Colby	F26
Middlebury■	J29		

Colors: White. Nickname: Polar Bears.
AD: Sidney Watson. SID: Craig C. Cheslog. III

BOWIE ST. .... Bowie, MD 20715

Tyrone Hart (3 YRS. W-23, L-57)

Opponent	Date	Opponent	Date
Lincoln (Pa.)	N23	Cheyney	J17
Winston-Salem■	N27	Virginia St.■	J20
Shaw■	N29	Norfolk St.	J24
Lincoln (Pa.)	N30	Elizabeth City St.	J25
Morgan St.	D 1	Virginia Union	J29
Livingstone■	D 4	St. Paul's	J31
Hampton	D 7	Elizabeth City St.■	F 3
Delaware St.	D 9	Norfolk St.■	F 7
St. Augustine's	D11	St. Paul's■	F10
Fayetteville St.	D13	Virginia Union■	F12
Virginia St. Cl.	J6-8	Virginia St.	F14
N.C. Central	J13	Hampton■	F18
Johnson Smith	J15		

Colors: Black & Gold. Nickname: Bulldogs.
AD: Charles A. Guilford. SID: Troy Macon. II

BOWLING GREEN .... Bowling Green, OH 43403

Jim Larranaga (9 YRS. W-127, L-126)

Opponent	Date	Opponent	Date
Defiance■	N29	Central Mich.	J26
Findlay■	D 1	Akron■	J29
Loyola (Ill.)	D 4	Eastern Mich.■	F 2
Detroit Mercy	D 8	Kent	F 5
Wis.-Green Bay■	D11	Ball St.■	F 9
Tiffin■	D21	Miami (Ohio)	F12
Michigan St. Cl.	D29-30	Western Mich.■	F16
Toledo	J 5	Ohio	F19
Kent■	J 8	Central Mich.■	F23
Ball St.	J12	Akron	F26
Miami (Ohio)■	J15	Eastern Mich.	M 2
Western Mich.	J19	Toledo■	M 5
Ohio■	J22	Mid-American Conf.	M8-12

Colors: Orange & Brown. Nickname: Falcons.
AD: Jack Gregory. SID: Steve Barr. I

BRADLEY .... Peoria, IL 61625

Jim Molinari (4 YRS. W-60, L-56)

Opponent	Date	Opponent	Date
Maine■	N27	Drake■	J24
Ill. Wesleyan■	D 1	Southern Ill.■	J29
Chicago St.	D 4	Illinois St.	F 2
DePaul	D 7	Tulsa■	F 5
Oregon St.	D16	Northern Iowa	F 7
Fla. Atlantic■	D18	Indiana St.	F12
Drake	D23	Creighton■	F15
Mississippi■	D29	Wichita St.■	F19
Tulsa	J 6	Southwest Mo. St.	F21
Wichita St.	J 8	Loyola (Ill.)■	F23
Indiana St.■	J12	Northern Iowa■	F26
Southern Ill.	J15	Creighton	F28
Illinois St.■	J19	Missouri Valley Conf	M5-7
Southwest Mo. St.■	J22		

Colors: Red & White. Nickname: Braves.
AD: Ron Ferguson. SID: Joseph S. Dalfonso. I

BRANDEIS .... Waltham, MA 02254

Ken Still (2 YRS. W-26, L-27)

Opponent	Date	Opponent	Date
Bentley■	N22	Emory	J23
Case Reserve	N28	Rochester■	J28
MIT	N30	New York U.■	F 1
Johns Hopkins■	D 3	Emory■	F 4
Rochester	D 5	Carnegie Mellon■	F 6
Mass.-Dartmouth	D 7	Wheaton (Mass.)■	F 8
Suffolk	D 9	New York U.	F12
Babson	J11	Clark (Mass.)■	F16
Chicago■	J14	Washington (Mo.)	F18
Washington (Mo.)■	J16	Chicago	F20
Worcester Tech	J19	Tufts	F23
Carnegie Mellon	J21	Amherst■	F26

Colors: Blue & White. Nickname: Judges.
AD: Jeff Cohen. SID: Jack Molloy. III

■ Home games on each schedule.

See pages 405–407 for Division I tournament details

BRIDGEPORT .... Bridgeport, CT 06601

Bruce Webster (28 YRS. W-498, L-295)

Opponent	Date	Opponent	Date
Bridgeport Cl.	N19-20	Sacred Heart	J26
Pace	N23	Keene St.	J29
Husson Tr.	D4-5	Southern Conn. St.■	F 2
New York Tech	D27	Le Moyne■	F 5
Quinnipiac	D30	New Hamp. Col.■	F 7
Assumption■	J 3	New Haven	F 9
Bryant	J 5	Franklin Pierce■	F12
Le Moyne	J10	Mass.-Lowell	F14
Mass.-Lowell■	J12	Southern Conn. St.	F16
New Hamp. Col.	J17	Keene St.■	F19
New Haven■	J19	Sacred Heart■	F23
Franklin Pierce	J22		

Colors: Purple & White. Nickname: Purple Knights.
AD: Ann Fariss. SID: Bob Baird. II

BRI'WATER (MASS.) .... Bridgewater, MA 02324

Joe Farroba (1ST YR. AS HEAD COACH)

Opponent	Date	Opponent	Date
Babson Inv.	N19-20	Rhode Island Col.■	J22
Suffolk	N23	Worcester St.	J25
Eastern Conn. St.■	D 4	Salem St.■	J29
Curry■	D 7	Fitchburg St.■	F 1
Wentworth Inst.	D11	Plymouth St.	F 3
Mass.-Dartmouth	D13	Westfield St.■	F 5
Trenton St. Cl.	J7-8	Framingham St.	F 8
Westfield St.	J11	North Adams St.■	F10
Framingham St.■	J15	Worcester St.■	F15
North Adams St.	J17	Salem St.	F17
Mass.-Boston■	J20	Fitchburg St.	F19

Colors: Crimson & White. Nickname: Bears.
AD: John C. Harper. SID: Mike Storey. III

BRIDGEWATER (VA.) .... Bridgewater, VA 22812

Bill Leatherman (8 YRS. W-115, L-92)

Opponent	Date	Opponent	Date
Marymount (Va.)■	N22	Wash. & Lee	J21
Wash. & Lee■	N27	Va. Wesleyan■	J24
Bridgewater (Va.) Tr	D3-4	Lynchburg	J29
Hampden-Sydney■	D 8	East. Mennonite■	F 1
East. Mennonite	D11	Roanoke	F 3
Randolph-Macon■	D15	Emory & Henry	F 5
Emory & Henry■	J 6	Randolph-Macon	F 9
Marymount Tr.	J8-9	Lynchburg■	F12
Roanoke■	J13	Va. Wesleyan	F16
Guilford■	J15	Guilford	F19
Hampden-Sydney	J17		

Colors: Crimson & Gold. Nickname: Eagles.
AD: Tom Kinder. SID: Rob Marchiony. III

BRIGHAM YOUNG .... Provo, UT 84602

Roger Reid (4 YRS. W-92, L-38)

Opponent	Date	Opponent	Date
Arizona St.	N27	Hawaii	J22
Charlotte Tr.	D3-4	Wyoming■	J27
Brigham Young Cl.	D10-11	Colorado St.■	J29
Utah St.■	D14	Wyoming	F 3
Texas Tech■	D17	Colorado St.	F 5
Weber St.■	D21	San Diego St.■	F10
Western Wash.■	D28	Hawaii■	F12
New Mexico	J 3	Air Force	F17
UTEP	J 5	Fresno St.	F19
Utah	J 8	Utah■	F26
Fresno St.■	J13	New Mexico■	M 3
Air Force■	J15	UTEP■	M 5
San Diego St.	J20	Western Ath. Conf.	M9-12

Colors: Royal Blue & White. Nickname: Cougars.
AD: Clayne Jensen. SID: Ralph Zobell. I

BROCKPORT ST. .... Brockport, NY 14420

Bill Bowe (1 YR. W-12, L-13)

Opponent	Date	Opponent	Date
Susquehanna Tr.	N19-20	Plattsburgh St.	J28
Binghamton	D 3	Potsdam St.	J29
Geneseo St.■	D 4	Buffalo St.■	F 4
Buffalo St.	D 7	Fredonia St.	F 5
Oneonta St.■	D10	St. John Fisher■	F 8
New Paltz St.■	D11	Roberts Wesleyan	F10
Nazareth (N.Y.)■	J 8	Cortland St.■	F12
Rochester Tr.	J12-15	Oswego St.	F15
Oswego St.■	J18	Utica Tech■	F18
Utica Tech	J21	Geneseo St.	F19
Fredonia St.■	J25		

Colors: Green & Gold. Nickname: Golden Eagles.
AD: Edward Matejkovic. SID: Mike Andriatch. III

BROWN .... Providence, RI 02912

Frank Dobbs (2 YRS. W-18, L-34)

Opponent	Date	Opponent	Date
Providence	N27	Yale	J22
Rhode Island■	D 1	Columbia	J28
Lafayette■	D 4	Cornell	J29
Colgate	D 7	Dartmouth	F 4
Holy Cross	D 9	Harvard	F 5
New Hampshire■	D22	Pennsylvania■	F11
Boston U.■	D30	Princeton■	F12
Army	J 3	Cornell■	F18
Valparaiso	J 6	Columbia■	F19
Xavier (Ohio)	J 8	Princeton	F25
Duke	J10	Pennsylvania	F26
Yale■	J15	Harvard■	M 4
Navy	J17	Dartmouth■	M 5

Colors: Seal Brown, Cardinal & White. Nickname: Bears.
AD: David Roach. SID: Chris Humm. I

BRYANT .... Smithfield, RI 02917

Edward Reilly (4 YRS. W-21, L-84)

Opponent	Date	Opponent	Date
Teikyo-Post■	N23	Stonehill■	J19
Mass.-Lowell	N27	Assumption	J22
New Hamp. Col.■	D 2	American Int'l	J25
St. Anselm	D 4	Springfield■	J27
Keene St.	D 6	St. Michael's	J29
Southern Conn. St.	D11	St. Anselm■	F 2
Fla. Southern	D28	Quinnipiac	F 5
Tampa	D30	Springfield	F 7
St. Michael's■	J 3	Merrimack■	F 9
Bridgeport■	J 5	Bentley	F12
Merrimack	J12	Stonehill	F16
Bentley■	J15	Assumption■	F19
Quinnipiac■	J17	American Int'l■	F22

Colors: Black & Gold. Nickname: Indians.
AD: Leon Drury. SID: John Gillooly. II

BUCKNELL .... Lewisburg, PA 17837

Charles Woollum (18 YRS. W-308, L-204)

Opponent	Date	Opponent	Date
Rider	N26	Army	J18
Texas A&M	N28	Navy■	J22
George Mason■	D 1	Lehigh	J26
Marymount (Va.)■	D 4	Holy Cross■	J29
Canisius■	D 7	Colgate■	F 2
Mt. St. Mary's (Md.)	D18	Fordham	F 5
Cornell■	D20	Lafayette■	F 9
Vanderbilt Inv.	D28-29	Army■	F12
Iona■	J 3	Navy	F16
Hartford	J 5	Lehigh■	F19
Colgate	J 8	St. Francis (Pa.)	F21
Fordham■	J12	Holy Cross	F26
Lafayette	J15	Patriot Conf.	M4-11

Colors: Orange & Blue. Nickname: Bison.
AD: Rick Hartzell. SID: Bo Smolka. I

BUENA VISTA .... Storm Lake, IA 50588

Dave Gunther (21 YRS. W-402, L-190)

Opponent	Date	Opponent	Date
Grinnell Tr.	N19-20	Upper Iowa	J22
Teikyo Westmar Tr.	N26-27	Wartburg■	J28
Mt. Marty■	D 4	Dubuque■	J29
Sioux Falls	D11	Central (Iowa)	F 1
Grand View	D18	Loras■	F 4
Buena Vista Tr.	D29-30	Upper Iowa■	F 5
William Penn■	J 7	William Penn	F11
Central (Iowa)■	J 8	Loras	F12
Luther	J14	Simpson	F18
Dubuque	J15	Luther■	F19
Simpson■	J21	Wartburg	F22

Colors: Blue & Gold. Nickname: Beavers.
AD: Jim Hershberger. SID: Jay Miller. III

BUFFALO .... Buffalo, NY 14260

Tim Cohane (11 YRS. W-144, L-145)

Opponent	Date	Opponent	Date
Daemen■	N26	Niagara	J19
Marist■	N27	Northeastern Ill.	J22
Detroit Mercy	N30	Pittsburgh■	J26
Canisius College Cl.	D3-4	Troy St.	J30
Va. Commonwealth	D 7	Jacksonville	F 1
Boston College■	D11	Youngstown St.■	F10
Miami (Fla.)■	D19	Central Conn. St.■	F12
Duquesne■	D22	Massachusetts	F16
Marist Cl.	D29-30	Chicago St.■	F21
Cal St. Northridge	J 4	Daemen■	F23
Loyola (Cal.)	J 7	Central Conn. St.	F28
Youngstown St.	J12	Cleveland St.	M 2
Hofstra	J15	East Coast Conf.	M4-6

Colors: Royal Blue, Red & White. Nickname: Bulls.
AD: Nelson Townsend. SID: Mike Rowland. I

■ Home games on each schedule.

See pages 405–407 for Division I tournament details

BUFFALO ST. .... Buffalo, NY 14222

Richard Bihr (14 YRS. W-272, L-100)

Buffalo St. Cl.	N19-20	Oswego St.	J22
Fredonia St.	D 3	Penn St.-Behrend	J24
Cortland St.	D 4	Binghamton■	J29
Brockport St.■	D 7	Brockport St.	F 4
Utica Tech	D11	Utica Tech■	F 5
Albany (N.Y.)	D12	Oneonta St.	F11
Wittenberg Tr.	D29-30	New Paltz St.	F12
Buffalo St. Tr.	J7-8	Fredonia St.■	F15
Plattsburgh St.■	J14	Geneseo St.	F18
Potsdam St.■	J15	Oswego St.■	F19
Geneseo St.■	J21		

Colors: Orange & Black. Nickname: Bengals.
AD: Fred Hartrick. SID: Keith Bullion. III

BUTLER .... Indianapolis, IN 46208

Barry Collier (4 YRS. W-56, L-60)

Pre-Season NIT	N17-26	Detroit Mercy	J22
Indiana■	N27	North Caro.	J24
Ball St.	N30	Evansville	J29
Valparaiso	D 4	Southern Utah■	F 1
DePauw■	D 6	Detroit Mercy■	F 4
Illinois St.■	D 9	Loyola (Ill.)	F 6
Indiana St.■	D11	Notre Dame	F 8
Jacksonville■	D21	La Salle■	F12
Cal St. Sacramento	D27	Xavier (Ohio)	F16
Santa Clara Cl.	D29-30	Evansville■	F19
Southern Utah	J 3	Mercer	F21
Bethune-Cookman■	J 6	La Salle	F26
Xavier (Ohio)■	J15	Midwestern Conf.	M6-9
Loyola (Ill.)■	J19		

Colors: Blue & White. Nickname: Bulldogs.
AD: John Parry. SID: Jim McGrath. I

CABRINI .... Radnor, PA 19087

John Dzik (13 YRS. W-256, L-120)

Cabrini Tr.	N19-20	Eastern (Pa.)	J22
Radford	N27	Gwynedd Mercy■	J25
Md.-East. Shore	D 1	Marywood■	J27
Allentown■	D 4	Neumann■	F 1
Washington (Md.) Tr.	D10-11	Eastern (Pa.)■	F 4
Nat'l Catholic Tr.	J5-9	Alvernia	F 7
Neumann	J13	Beaver■	F10
Beaver	J15	Marywood	F12
Misericordia■	J18	Gwynedd Mercy	F17
Alvernia■	J20	Misericordia	F19

Colors: Royal Blue & White. Nickname: Cavaliers.
AD: John Dzik. SID: Dennis Wise. III

CALIFORNIA .... Berkeley, CA 94720

Todd Bozeman (1 YR. W-11, L-2)

Pre-Season NIT	N17-26	UCLA■	J30
Texas Southern	D 1	Oregon St.	F 3
Santa Clara■	D 4	Oregon	F 5
California Cl.	D10-12	Arizona St.■	F10
Richmond■	D23	Arizona■	F13
Wake Forest	D30	Stanford■	F17
St. Mary's (Cal.)■	J 2	Cincinnati⊠	F20
Washington St.■	J 6	UCLA	F24
Washington■	J 8	Southern Cal	F26
Arizona	J13	Oregon■	M 3
Arizona St.	J15	Oregon St.■	M 5
Stanford	J20	Washington	M10
Cal St. Northridge■	J22	Washington St.	M12
Southern Cal■	J27	⊠ Orlando, FL	

Colors: Blue & Gold. Nickname: Golden Bears.
AD: To be named. SID: Kevin Reneau. I

CALIF. (PA.) .... California, PA 15419

Jim Boone (7 YRS. W-152, L-53)

Charleston (W.Va.)■	N23	Shippensburg■	J19
Alvernia	N27	Lock Haven	J22
California (Pa.) Inv	D3-4	Pitt.-Johnstown■	J26
Fairmont St.■	D 8	Indiana (Pa.)■	J29
Davis & Elkins	D11	Clarion	F 2
Lake Erie■	D15	Edinboro■	F 5
Detroit Mercy	D18	Slippery Rock	F 9
Gannon Tr.	D29-30	Shippensburg	F12
Mercyhurst■	J 4	Lock Haven■	F19
California (Pa.) Tr.	J8-9	Clarion■	F23
Slippery Rock■	J12	Indiana (Pa.)	F26
Edinboro	J15		

Colors: Red & Black. Nickname: Vulcans.
AD: Tom Pucci. SID: Bruce Wald. II

CAL LUTHERAN .... Thousand Oaks, CA 91360

Mike Dunlop (4 YRS. W-55, L-52)

Menlo Cl.	N19-20	Pomona-Pitzer■	J22
Concordia-M'head■	N26	Claremont-M-S	J26
Pt. Loma Nazarene■	D 4	Cal Tech■	J29
Westmont■	D 8	La Verne	F 2
Christian Heritage■	D21	Occidental	F 5
UC San Diego■	D23	Redlands■	F 9
Cal Lutheran Tr.	D29-30	Whittier	F12
Cal Christian	J 4	Pomona-Pitzer	F16
UC Santa Cruz	J 7	Claremont-M-S■	F19
Occidental■	J12	Cal Tech	F21
Redlands	J15	La Verne■	F24
Whittier■	J19		

Colors: Purple & Gold. Nickname: Kingsmen.
AD: Bob Doering. SID: John Czimbal. III

CAL POLY POMONA .... Pomona, CA 91768

Kevin Patterson (1 YR. W-14, L-13)

Cal Poly Pomona Cl.	N19-20	Cal St. Los Angeles■	J 6
Pt. Loma Nazarene	N23	Cal St. Dom. Hills	J 8
Seattle Pacific Cl.	N26-27	UC Riverside	J13
Master's■	D 2	Cal Poly SLO■	J15
Long Beach St.	D 8	Cal St. Bakersfield■	J22
Sonoma St.	D11	Cal St. San B'dino	J29
Cal St. Hayward	D13	Cal St. Dom. Hills■	F 3
Pacific Christian■	D16	Cal St. Los Angeles	F 5
San Fran. St.■	D18	Cal Poly SLO	F10
Menlo■	D20	UC Riverside■	F12
UC Davis■	D28	Cal St. San B'dino■	F17
San Diego St.	D30	Cal St. Bakersfield	F19

Colors: Green & Gold. Nickname: Broncos.
AD: Karen Miller. SID: Ron Fremont. II

CAL POLY SLO .... San Luis Obispo, CA 93407

Steve Beason (7 YRS. W-111, L-80)

Long Beach St.	N26	Cal St. San B'dino■	J 8
Fresno St.	N28	Cal St. Dom. Hills■	J13
San Francisco	N30	Cal Poly Pomona	J15
Cal St. Hayward■	D 4	Cal St. Bakersfield■	J20
Fresno Pacific	D11	Cal St. Los Angeles	J22
Montana■	D13	UC Riverside■	J29
Master's■	D16	Cal St. San B'dino	F 3
Cal St. Hayward	D18	Cal Poly Pomona■	F10
UC Santa Cruz■	D20	Cal St. Dom. Hills	F12
Keene St.■	D23	UC Riverside	F17
Pt. Loma Nazarene■	D28	Cal St. Los Angeles■	F19
UC Davis■	D30	Cal St. Bakersfield	F26
Northern Ariz.	J 3		

Colors: Green & Gold. Nickname: Mustangs.
AD: John McCutcheon. SID: Eric McDowell. II

CAL ST. BAKERSFIELD .... Bakersfield, CA 93311

Pat Douglass (12 YRS. W-274, L-97)

Cal St. Stanislaus■	N19	Cal St. San B'dino	J13
San Fran. St.■	N20	Cal St. Dom. Hills■	J15
Fresno Pacific■	N26	Cal Poly SLO	J20
Azusa-Pacific	N27	Cal Poly Pomona	J22
UC Davis	D 4	Cal St. Los Angeles■	J29
Southern Colo.	D 9	UC Riverside	F 5
Metropolitan St.	D11	Cal St. Dom. Hills	F10
CS Bakersfield Cl.	D17-18	Cal St. San B'dino■	F12
Keene St.■	D21	Cal St. Los Angeles	F17
Lewis■	D22	Cal Poly Pomona■	F19
Cal St. Chico Tr.	D28-30	Cal Poly SLO■	F26
UC Riverside■	J 6		

Colors: Blue & Gold. Nickname: Roadrunners.
AD: Rudy Carvajal. SID: Joni Jones. II

CAL ST. DOM. HILLS .... Carson, CA 90747

Dave Yanai (12 YRS. W-244, L-187)

Grand Canyon Inv.	N26-27	Cal Poly SLO	J13
Cal St. Hayward	D 3	Cal St. Bakersfield	J15
Notre Dame (Cal.)	D 4	Cal St. Los Angeles■	J20
Pt. Loma Nazarene	D10	UC Riverside	J22
San Diego	D11	Master's■	J28
La Verne	D17	Cal Poly Pomona	F 3
Biola■	D18	Cal St. San B'dino	F 5
Grand Canyon■	D21	Cal St. Bakersfield■	F10
Sonoma St.■	D23	Cal Poly SLO■	F12
Keene St.■	D28	Christian Heritage	F15
St. Anselm■	D30	UC Riverside■	F19
Cal St. San B'dino■	J 6	Cal St. Los Angeles	F26
Cal Poly Pomona■	J 8		

Colors: Cardinal & Gold. Nickname: Toros.
AD: Kay Don. SID: Kevin Gilmore. II

■ Home games on each schedule.

See pages 405–407 for Division I tournament details

CAL ST. FULLERTON .... Fullerton, CA 92634

Brad Holland (1 YR. W-15, L-12)

Wyoming	D 4
St. Mary's (Cal.)	D10
Utah■	D18
Colorado	D21
Colorado St.	D23
Northern Iowa■	D28
Okla. Baptist■	D30
UC Irvine■	J 3
Nevada-Las Vegas■	J 5
New Mexico St.■	J 8
Utah St.	J15
Nevada	J17
San Jose St.■	J20
Pacific (Cal.)■	J22
UC Santa Barb.	J27
Long Beach St.	J29
Pacific (Cal.)	F 3
San Jose St.	F 5
Nevada■	F10
Utah St.■	F12
Nevada-Las Vegas	F17
New Mexico St.	F19
UC Irvine	F24
Long Beach St.■	M 3
UC Santa Barb.■	M 5
Big West Conf.	M10-13

Colors: Blue, Orange & White. Nickname: Titans.
AD: Bill Shumard. SID: Mel Franks. I

CAL ST. HAYWARD .... Hayward, CA 94542

Gary Hulst (13 YRS. W-153, L-206)

Westmont	N19
Fresno Pacific	N20
Menlo■	N27
Cal St. Dom. Hills■	D 3
Cal Poly SLO	D 4
Cal St. San B'dino■	D10
Bethany (Cal.)	D11
Cal Poly Pomona■	D13
Seattle Pacific■	D16
Cal Poly SLO■	D18
Cal St. Los Angeles■	D22
Santa Clara	J 4
Cal St. Chico■	J 7
Humboldt St.■	J 8
UC Davis	J14
Notre Dame (Cal.)■	J15
Sonoma St.	J21
San Fran. St.■	J22
Cal St. Stanislaus	J29
San Fran. St.	F 4
Sonoma St.■	F 5
Notre Dame (Cal.)	F11
UC Davis■	F12
Humboldt St.	F18
Cal St. Chico	F19
Cal St. Stanislaus■	F24

Colors: Red & White. Nickname: Pioneers.
AD: Doug Weiss. SID: Marty Valdez. II

CAL ST. LOS ANGELES .... Los Angeles, CA 90032

Henry Dyer (6 YRS. W-55, L-104)

Master's College Tr.	N19-20
Biola■	N26
Master's■	D10
Seattle Pacific■	D13
UC Davis	D15
CS Bakersfield Cl.	D17-18
Cal St. Hayward	D22
Notre Dame (Cal.)	D23
Keene St.■	D27
CSU Stanislaus Tr.	D28-29
St. Anselm■	J 3
Cal Poly Pomona	J 6
UC Riverside■	J 8
Cal St. San B'dino■	J15
Cal St. Dom. Hills	J20
Cal Poly SLO■	J22
Cal St. Bakersfield	J29
UC Riverside	F 3
Cal Poly Pomona■	F 5
Cal St. San B'dino	F10
Cal St. Bakersfield■	F17
Cal Poly SLO	F19
Cal St. Dom. Hills■	F26

Colors: Black & Gold. Nickname: Golden Eagles.
AD: Carol Dunn. SID: To be named. II

CAL ST. NORTHRIDGE .... Northridge, CA 91330

Pete Cassidy (22 YRS. W-311 , L-279)

Stanford Inv.	N26-27
Long Beach St.	N30
Southwest Mo. St. Cl	D3-4
San Diego■	D 8
UC Irvine■	D11
Arizona St.	D17
San Diego St.■	D21
Fresno St. Cl.	D27-28
Buffalo■	J 4
UC Irvine	J 8
St. Mary's (Cal.)	J11
Colorado	J17
Air Force	J19
California	J22
Northeastern Ill.	J29
Notre Dame	J31
Cal St. Sacramento■	F 5
Northeastern Ill.■	F10
Southern Utah	F12
Grand Canyon■	F15
Cal St. Sacramento	F19
Southern Utah■	F24
Ala.-Birmingham■	F26
San Diego St.	M 3

Colors: Red, White & Black. Nickname: Matadors.
AD: Robert J. Hiegert. SID: Barry Smith. I

CAL ST. SACRAMENTO .... Sacramento, CA 95819

Don Newman (1 YR. W-3, L-24)

Montana	N26
Montana St.	N28
Pacific (Cal.)	D 1
Northern Ariz.■	D 4
Northeastern Ill.	D 6
San Francisco■	D11
Southern Cal	D18
Santa Clara■	D20
Toledo■	D23
Butler■	D27
Idaho■	J 3
Northern Ariz.	J 5
San Francisco	J 8
Ala.-Birmingham	J12
Tulane	J15
St. Mary's (Cal.)	J18
Idaho St.■	J23
Boise St.	J24
Colorado	J26
Southern Utah	J29
Cal St. Northridge	F 5
Eastern Wash.	F14
Idaho	F16
Cal St. Northridge■	F19
Loyola (Cal.)	F22
Southern Utah■	F26
San Diego	M 1

Colors: Green & Gold. Nickname: Hornets.
AD: Lee McElroy. SID: Jeff Minahan. I

CAL ST. SAN B'DINO ..... San Bernardino, CA 92407

Reggie Morris (2 YRS. W-27, L-25)

Christian Heritage	N20
Grand Canyon Inv.	N26-27
Occidental■	D 1
BYU-Hawaii■	D 3
Cal St. Hayward	D10
Cal St. Stanislaus	D12
Pepperdine	D14
San Fran. St.■	D17
Grand Canyon■	D22
Notre Dame (Cal.)■	D30
CS San B'dino Tr.	J2-3
Cal St. Dom. Hills	J 6
Cal Poly SLO	J 8
Cal St. Bakersfield■	J13
Cal St. Los Angeles	J15
UC Riverside	J20
Master's	J25
Cal Poly Pomona■	J29
Cal Poly SLO■	F 3
Cal St. Dom. Hills■	F 5
Cal St. Los Angeles■	F10
Cal St. Bakersfield	F12
Cal Poly Pomona	F17
UC Riverside■	F26

Colors: Light Blue & Brown. Nickname: Coyotes.
AD: David Suenram. SID: Bill Gray. II

CAL ST. STANISLAUS .... Turlock, CA 95380

John Jones (5 YRS. W-88, L-54)

Cal St. Bakersfield	N19
Hawaii-Hilo Cl.	N26-27
San Jose Christian■	D 3
San Francisco	D 8
Fresno Pacific■	D 9
Cal St. San B'dino■	D12
CS Bakersfield Cl.	D17-18
CSU Stanislaus Tr.	D28-29
Nevada	D30
Humboldt St.■	J 7
Cal St. Chico■	J 8
Notre Dame (Cal.)	J14
UC Davis■	J15
San Fran. St.	J21
Sonoma St.■	J22
Cal St. Hayward■	J29
Sonoma St.	F 4
San Fran. St.■	F 5
UC Davis	F11
Notre Dame (Cal.)■	F12
Cal St. Chico	F18
Humboldt St.	F19
Cal St. Hayward	F24

Colors: Red & Gold. Nickname: Warriors.
AD: Joe Donahue. SID: Will Keener. II

CAL TECH .... Pasadena, CA 91125

Gene Victor (6 YRS. W-29, L-111)

Eagle Inv.	N19
Cal Tech Tr.	N26-27
Arizona Bible■	D 4
LIFE Bible■	D10
La Sierra	J 4
Cal Maritime Tr.	J7-8
Pomona-Pitzer■	J12
La Verne	J15
Occidental	J19
Redlands■	J22
Whittier	J26
Cal Lutheran	J29
Claremont-M-S■	F 2
Pomona-Pitzer	F 5
La Verne■	F 9
Occidental■	F12
Redlands	F16
Whittier■	F19
Cal Lutheran■	F21
Claremont-M-S	F24

Colors: Orange & White. Nickname: Beavers.
AD: Dan Bridges. SID: Karen Nelson. III

UC DAVIS .... Davis, CA 95616

Bob Williams (5 YRS. W-79, L-58)

Seattle Pacific Cl.	N26-27
Menlo■	N30
Cal St. Bakersfield■	D 4
Lewis & Clark■	D11
Cal St. Los Angeles■	D15
Oklahoma St.	D18
Pacific (Cal.)	D21
Cal Poly Pomona	D28
Cal Poly SLO	D30
Bethany (Cal.)■	J 3
San Fran. St.■	J 7
Sonoma St.	J 8
Cal St. Hayward■	J14
Cal St. Stanislaus	J15
Humboldt St.■	J21
Cal St. Chico■	J22
Notre Dame (Cal.)■	J29
Cal St. Chico	F 4
Humboldt St.	F 5
Cal St. Stanislaus■	F11
Cal St. Hayward	F12
San Fran. St.	F18
Sonoma St.■	F19
Notre Dame (Cal.)	F24

Colors: Blue & Gold. Nickname: Aggies.
AD: Keith Williams. SID: Doug Dull. II

UC IRVINE .... Irvine, CA 92717

Rod Baker (7 YRS. W-85, L-95)

Salem St.■	N26
Utah	N30
San Diego■	D 2
Cal St. Northridge	D11
Georgetown	D18
St. Mary's (Cal.)	D21
Iowa■	D29
Cal St. Fullerton	J 3
Cal St. Northridge■	J 8
Nevada-Las Vegas■	J11
Nevada	J15
Utah St.	J17
Pacific (Cal.)■	J20
San Jose St.■	J22
Long Beach St.	J27
UC Santa Barb.	J29
San Jose St.	F 3
Pacific (Cal.)	F 5
Utah St.■	F10
Nevada■	F12
New Mexico St.	F17
Nevada-Las Vegas	F19
Cal St. Fullerton■	F24
New Mexico St.■	F26
UC Santa Barb.■	M 3
Long Beach St.■	M 5
Big West Conf.	M10-13

Colors: Blue & Gold. Nickname: Anteaters.
AD: Dan Guerrero. SID: Bob Olson. I

■ Home games on each schedule.

See pages 405–407 for Division I tournament details

UC SAN DIEGO .... La Jolla, CA 92093

Tom Marshall (10 YRS. W-161, L-101)

Pomona-Pitzer■ N19
UC San Diego Tr. N26-27
Redlands Tr. D2-4
Northern Ariz. D18
Redlands■ D20
Cal Lutheran D23
Occidental Tr. D30-31
Whittier■ .... J 4
La Jolla Cl. J7-8
Chapman J11
UC Santa Cruz■ J15
Menlo J21
Dominican (Cal.) J22
Christian Heritage J25
Bethany (Cal.)■ J29
Chapman■ .... F 4
Menlo■ F11
UC Santa Cruz F18
Bethany (Cal.) F19
Dominican (Cal.)■ F25

Colors: Blue & Gold. Nickname: Tritons.
AD: Judith Sweet. SID: Bill Gannon. III

UC SANTA BARB. .... Santa Barbara, CA 93106

Jerry Pimm (19 YRS. W-339, L-208)

Westmont■ N27
St. Mary's (Cal.)■ N30
U.C.-Santa Barb. Tr. D2-4
Ohio St. D14
Loyola (Cal.) D20
Pepperdine■ D22
Hawaii Rainbow Cl. D27-30
New Mexico St. .... J 3
Nevada■ .... J 8
Utah St.■ J10
Pacific (Cal.) J15
San Jose St. J17
Long Beach St. J22
Nevada-Las Vegas J24
Cal St. Fullerton■ J27
UC Irvine■ J29
St. Joseph's (Pa.)■ J31
Long Beach St.■ .... F 5
San Jose St.■ F10
Pacific (Cal.)■ F12
Nevada F17
Utah St. F19
Nevada-Las Vegas■ F24
New Mexico St.■ F28
UC Irvine .... M 3
Cal St. Fullerton .... M 5
Big West Conf. M10-13

Colors: Blue & Gold. Nickname: Gauchos.
AD: John Kasser. SID: Bill Mahoney. I

UC SANTA CRUZ .... Santa Cruz, CA 95064

Duane Garner (2 YRS. W-25, L-24)

Menlo Cl. N19-20
Claremont Tr. N26-27
Pomona-Pitzer .... D 4
La Verne D10
Whittier D11
Cal St. Chico D18
Cal Poly SLO D20
Coast Guard☒ D22
San Jose Christian■ .... J 5
Cal Lutheran■ .... J 7
Chapman J14
UC San Diego J15
Bethany (Cal.)■ J21
Dominican (Cal.)■ J28
Menlo J29
Bethany (Cal.) .... F 4
Dominican (Cal.) F11
San Jose Christian F12
UC San Diego■ F18
Chapman■ F19
Menlo■ F26
☒ Palo Alto, CA

Colors: Blue & Gold. Nickname: Banana Slugs.
AD: Cori Houston. SID: To be named. III

CALVIN .... Grand Rapids, MI 49546

Ed Douma (20 YRS. W-366, L-162)

Grace Tr. N19-20
Wheaton (Ill.)■ N23
Calvin Cl. N26-27
Spring Arbor .... D 4
Siena Heights .... D 8
Trinity Chrst. (Il.)■ D18
Occidental Tr. D30-31
Adrian■ .... J 5
Kalamazoo .... J 8
Hope J12
Albion■ J19
Olivet■ J22
Alma J26
Adrian J29
Kalamazoo■ .... F 2
Hope■ .... F 5
Wayne St. (Mich.)■ .... F 9
Albion F12
Olivet F16
Alma■ F19

Colors: Maroon & Gold. Nickname: Knights.
AD: Ralph Honderd. SID: Phil De Haan. III

CAMERON .... Lawton, OK 73501

Jerry Stone (8 YRS. W-73 , L-136)

Ark. Baptist■ N19
Pittsburg St.■ N23
Abilene Christ. Cl. N26-27
Jarvis Christian■ N30
Angelo St. Cl. D3-4
Phillips (Okla.)■ .... D 8
Lubbock Chrst.■ D11
Stephen F. Austin D31
Oklahoma S&A■ .... J 4
Drury Tr. J7-8
Central Okla. J12
West Tex. A&M■ J15
Eastern N. Mex.■ J17
Lubbock Chrst. J20
Oklahoma S&A J24
East Tex. St. J29
Tarleton St. .... F 3
East Tex. St.■ .... F 7
West Tex. A&M F12
Eastern N. Mex. F14
Tarleton St.■ F17
Angelo St.■ F19
Abilene Christian■ F21
Central Okla.■ F26

Colors: Gold & Black. Nickname: Aggies.
AD: Jerry Hrnciar. SID: David Siegel. II

CAMPBELL .... Buies Creek, NC 27506

Billy Lee (15 YRS. W-230, L-207)

Methodist■ N29
North Caro. St. .... D 4
East Caro. .... D 6
East Caro.■ D18
N.C.-Wilmington D21
Ferrum■ .... J 3
Charleston So.■ .... J 6
N.C.-Greensboro■ .... J 8
William & Mary■ J10
South Caro. J12
Winthrop J15
N.C.-Asheville■ J17
Radford J20
Towson St.■ J22
Md.-Balt. County■ J24
Liberty■ J27
Coastal Caro. J29
Liberty .... F 3
Charleston So. F10
Winthrop■ F12
N.C.-Asheville F14
Radford■ F17
Towson St. F19
Md.-Balt. County F21
N.C.-Greensboro F24
Coastal Caro.■ F26
Big South Conf. M4-7

Colors: Orange & Black. Nickname: Fighting Camels.
AD: Tom Collins. SID: Stan Cole. I

CANISIUS .... Buffalo, NY 14208

John Beilein (11 YRS. W-193, L-118)

St. Bonaventure N29
Canisius College Cl. D3-4
Bucknell .... D 7
St. Francis (Pa.) D19
Colgate■ D22
Wake Forest .... J 3
Siena .... J 5
Northeastern■ .... J 8
Manhattan■ J10
St. Peter's J12
Niagara J15
Cornell■ J18
Loyola (Md.)■ J22
St. Bonaventure■ J25
Tulane■ J29
George Mason■ .... F 1
Manhattan .... F 5
Loyola (Md.) .... F 7
Fairfield■ F10
Iona■ F12
Niagara■ F16
St. Peter's■ F19
Siena☒ F21
Fairfield F25
Iona F27
Metro Atlantic Conf. M5-7
☒ Niagara Falls, NY

Colors: Blue & Gold. Nickname: Golden Griffins.
AD: Daniel P. Starr. SID: John Maddock. I

CAPITAL .... Columbus, OH 43209

Scott Weakley (6 YRS. W-62, L-43)

Capital Cl. N19-20
Ohio Wesleyan■ N27
Tiffin .... D 1
Mount Union■ .... D 4
Heidelberg■ .... D 8
Otterbein■ D11
Muskingum D18
Defiance Tr. D28-29
John Carroll .... J 5
Baldwin-Wallace■ .... J 8
Ohio Northern J12
Hiram J15
Marietta■ J19
Mount Union J22
Heidelberg J26
Muskingum■ J29
Hiram■ .... F 2
Otterbein .... F 5
Ohio Northern■ .... F 9
Baldwin-Wallace F12
Marietta F16
John Carroll■ F19

Colors: Purple & White. Nickname: Crusaders.
AD: Roger Welsh. SID: Dave Graham. III

CARLETON .... Northfield, MN 55057

Guy Kalland (9 YRS. W-111, L-117)

Concordia (St. Paul) N26
Washington (Mo.) Cl. D3-4
Concordia-M'head■ .... D 6
St. Mary's (Minn.) .... D 8
Gust. Adolphus■ D11
St. Cloud St. D29
St. Olaf■ .... J 3
Macalester .... J 5
St. John's (Minn.) .... J 8
St. Thomas (Minn.)■ J10
Bethel (Minn.) J15
Augsburg■ J17
Hamline J19
Concordia-M'head J22
St. Mary's (Minn.)■ J26
Gust. Adolphus J29
St. Olaf J31
Macalester■ .... F 2
St. John's (Minn.)■ .... F 5
St. Thomas (Minn.) .... F 9
Bethel (Minn.)■ F14
Augsburg F16
Hamline■ F19

Colors: Maize & Blue. Nickname: Knights.
AD: Leon Lunder. SID: Joe Hargis. III

CARNEGIE MELLON .... Pittsburgh, PA 15213

Tony Wingen (5 YRS. W-53, L-65)

Grove City☒ N19
Wash. & Jeff.◆ N20
Case Reserve■ N23
Carnegie Mellon Inv. N26-27
Akron .... D 1
Emory .... D 3
Sewanee .... D 4
Denison D18
Rochester■ .... J 7
Stony Brook .... J 9
Johns Hopkins J16
Brandeis■ J21
New York U.■ J23
Wash. & Jeff. J26
Chicago J28
Washington (Mo.) J30
New York U. .... F 4
Brandeis .... F 6
Washington (Mo.)■ F11
Chicago■ F13
Thiel■ F16
Emory■ F20
Rochester F26
☒ Washington, PA
◆ Meadville, PA

Colors: Cardinal, White & Grey. Nickname: Tartans.
AD: John Harvey. SID: Bruce Gerson. III

■ Home games on each schedule.

See pages 405–407 for Division I tournament details

CARROLL (WIS.) .... Waukesha, WI 53186

Jeff Kunz (1 YR. W-4, L-17)

Cardinal Stritch■	N20
Wis.-Whitewater	D 1
Lawrence■	D 4
Beloit■	D 8
St. Norbert	D11
Wooster Cl.	D29-30
Webster■	J 3
Milwaukee Engr.■	J 8
Rockford	J12
Ripon■	J15
Lake Forest■	J19
Monmouth (Ill.)	J22
Cornell College	J23
Lawrence	J26
Grinnell■	J29
Coe■	J30
St. Norbert■	F 5
Beloit	F 9
N'western (Wis.)	F14
Lake Forest	F16
Ripon	F19

Colors: Orange & White. Nickname: Pioneers.
AD: Merle Masonholder. SID: Shawn Ama. III

CARSON-NEWMAN .... Jefferson City, TN 37760

Dale Clayton (5 YRS. W-63, L-79)

Lees-McRae■	N20
Ky. Wesleyan Cl.	N26-27
East Tenn. St.	D 1
Catawba■	D 4
Lincoln Memorial	D 7
Erskine■	D11
Newberry	D14
Augusta Cl.	D29-30
King (Tenn.)■	J 4
Gardner-Webb	J12
Wingate■	J15
Erskine	J17
Mars Hill■	J19
Presbyterian	J22
Lenoir-Rhyne	J26
Elon■	J29
Lincoln Memorial■	F 2
Catawba	F 5
Gardner-Webb■	F 9
Wingate	F12
Mars Hill	F16
Presbyterian■	F19
Lenoir-Rhyne■	F23
Elon	F26

Colors: Orange & Blue. Nickname: Eagles.
AD: David Barger. SID: Eric Trainer. II

CARTHAGE .... Kenosha, WI 53140

Tim Miller (1 YR. W-11, L-13)

St. John's (Minn.)■	N19
Beloit	N23
Wis.-Stevens Pt. Cl.	N26-27
Wis.-Parkside	N29
Aurora■	D 7
Augustana (Ill.)	D11
Marian (Wis.)■	D18
Ill. Wesleyan	J 8
North Park■	J11
Millikin■	J15
Elmhurst	J19
North Central	J22
Augustana (Ill.)■	J29
Wheaton (Ill.)■	F 1
North Park	F 5
Millikin	F 9
Elmhurst■	F12
North Central■	F16
Ill. Wesleyan■	F19
Marycrest■	F24
Wheaton (Ill.)	F26

Colors: Red & White. Nickname: Redmen.
AD: Robert Bonn. SID: Greg Sorenson. III

CASE RESERVE .... Cleveland, OH 44106

William C. Sudeck (30 YRS. W-245, L-390)

Carnegie Mellon	N23
New York U.	N26
Brandeis■	N28
Allegheny■	D 1
Rochester■	D 3
Emory	D 5
Wooster	D 7
Wittenberg	D16
Johns Hopkins	J 3
Ohio Wesleyan■	J 5
Denison	J 8
Kenyon■	J12
Earlham■	J15
Oberlin	J19
Chicago■	J21
Washington (Mo.)■	J23
Wooster■	J26
Wittenberg■	J29
Kenyon	F 2
Denison■	F 5
Allegheny	F 9
Earlham	F12
Oberlin■	F16
Ohio Wesleyan	F19

Colors: Blue, Gray & White. Nickname: Spartans.
AD: Dave Hutter. SID: Sue Herdle Penicka. III

CASTLETON ST. .... Castleton, VT 05735

To be named

Buffalo St. Cl.	N19-20
Norwich	N23
Albany (N.Y.)■	N30
Penn St.-Behrend Tr.	D3-4
North Adams St.	D 7
Atlantic Union	D 9
Westbrook■	D11
Lyndon St.■	D14
Me.-Presque Isle■	J10
Atlantic Union■	J12
Lyndon St.	J15
Westbrook	J16
Johnson St.■	J20
Notre Dame (N.H.)	J22
Plymouth St.	J25
Green Mountain■	J27
St. Joseph (Vt.)	J29
Notre Dame (N.H.)■	F 5
Green Mountain	F 8
Johnson St.	F10
Colby-Sawyer■	F14
Plattsburgh St.■	F19
Husson■	F20

Colors: Green & White. Nickname: Spartans.
AD: To be named. SID: Carrie Zahm. III

CATAWBA .... Salisbury, NC 28144

Sam Moir (33 YRS. W-529, L-389)

Catawba Cl.	N19-20
Lenoir-Rhyne Tr.	N26-27
Lees-McRae■	D 1
Carson-Newman	D 4
Pfeiffer■	D 8
Queens (N.C.) Cl.	J6-8
Presbyterian	J12
Lenoir-Rhyne■	J15
Elon	J19
Mars Hill■	J22
Wingate■	J26
Gardner-Webb	J29
Livingstone■	J31
Barber-Scotia■	F 2
Carson-Newman■	F 5
Presbyterian■	F 9
Lenoir-Rhyne	F12
Lees-McRae	F14
Elon■	F16
Mars Hill	F19
Wingate	F23
Gardner-Webb■	F26

Colors: Blue & White. Nickname: Indians.
AD: Tom Childress. SID: Dennis Davidson. II

CATHOLIC .... Washington, DC 20064

Mike Lonergan (1 YR. W-21, L-6)

Gettysburg Tr.	N19-20
Wesley■	N23
Scranton■	N27
Salisbury St.■	D 6
York (Pa.)	D11
Lebanon Valley■	J 4
Catholic Tr.	J8-9
Marymount (Va.)	J12
York (Pa.)■	J15
Dickinson■	J17
St. Mary's (Md.)■	J19
Wash. & Lee	J23
Gallaudet■	J25
Goucher	J27
Western Md.	J29
Mary Washington■	F 1
Goucher■	F 3
Marymount (Va.)■	F 7
Allentown	F10
Gallaudet	F15
Mary Washington	F17
St. Mary's (Md.)	F19

Colors: Cardinal Red & Black. Nickname: Cardinals.
AD: Bob Talbot. SID: Gabe Romano. III

CENTENARY .... Shreveport, LA 71104

Tommy Vardeman (4 YRS. W-58, L-56)

Tulane	N27
New Mexico Lobo Cl.	D3-4
Wiley■	D 9
LSU-Shreveport■	D11
Louisiana Tech■	D18
Southeastern La.■	J 3
Florida Int'l	J 6
Fla. Atlantic	J 8
Georgia St.■	J13
Samford■	J15
Charleston (S.C.)	J20
Mercer	J22
Central Fla.■	J27
Stetson■	J29
Louisiana Tech	J31
Fla. Atlantic■	F 3
Florida Int'l■	F 5
Rice■	F 8
Samford	F10
Georgia St.	F12
Mercer■	F17
Charleston (S.C.)■	F19
Southeastern La.	F21
Stetson	F26
Central Fla.	F28
Trans America Conf.	M3-5

Colors: Maroon & White. Nickname: Gentlemen.
AD: Tommy Vardeman. SID: Cory Rogers. I

CENTRAL (IOWA) .... Pella, IA 50219

Jack Walvoord (27 YRS. W-342, L-294)

Northeast Mo. St.	N20
Central Inv.	N26-27
N'western (Iowa)■	D 4
Teikyo Marycrest	D 7
Neb. Wesleyan	D11
Augustana (Ill.)■	D16
Wartburg	J 7
Buena Vista	J 8
Upper Iowa■	J14
Loras■	J15
Dubuque■	J21
Luther■	J22
William Penn	J28
Simpson	J29
Buena Vista■	F 1
Luther	F 4
Dubuque	F 5
Wartburg■	F11
Simpson■	F12
Upper Iowa	F15
William Penn■	F25
Loras	F26

Colors: Red & White. Nickname: Flying Dutchmen.
AD: Ron Schipper. SID: Larry Happel. III

CENTRAL ARK. .... Conway, AR 72032

To be named

Tampa	N24
Florida Tech Cl.	N26-27
Southern Ark.■	D 1
Mo. Western Cl.	D3-4
Ark. Baptist	D 6
Harding■	D10
Oklahoma City■	D11
Arkansas Tech Tr.	J4-5
Mississippi Col.	J 8
Livingston	J10
Ala.-Huntsville■	J15
North Ala.■	J17
Ark.-Pine Bluff■	J22
Harding	J24
Henderson St.	J27
Livingston■	J29
Delta St.■	J31
Ala.-Huntsville	F 5
North Ala.	F 7
Ark.-Pine Bluff	F10
Mississippi Col.■	F14
Henderson St.■	F19
Oklahoma City	F22
Delta St.	F26

Colors: Purple & Gray. Nickname: Bears.
AD: Bill Stephens. SID: Darrell Walsh. II

■ Home games on each schedule.

See pages 405–407 for Division I tournament details

CENTRAL CONN. ST. .... New Britain, CT 06050
Mark Adams (9 YRS. W-133, L-128)

Concordia (N.Y.)■ N30
Mt. St. Mary's Tr. D3-4
Liberty .... D 6
Massachusetts .... D 9
Connecticut D11
Maine D13
Dayton D27
Youngstown St. D29
Boston U.■ .... J 8
New Hampshire■ J11
Troy St.■ J15
Northeastern Ill.■ J17
North Adams St.■ J20
CCNY■ J22
Hartford■ J25
Mt. St. Mary's (Md.)■ .... F 1
Hofstra .... F 5
Buffalo F12
Md.-East. Shore F15
Chicago St. F17
Northeastern Ill. F19
Colgate F23
Delaware St.■ F26
Buffalo■ F28
East Coast Conf. M4-6

Colors: Blue & White. Nickname: Blue Devils.
AD: Judith Davidson. SID: Brent Rutkowski. I

CENTRAL FLA. .... Orlando, FL 32816
Kirk Speraw (1ST YR. AS HEAD COACH)

Rollins■ N30
Winthrop .... D 4
Bethune-Cookman■ D13
Fla. Atlantic■ D15
West Fla.■ D17
Florida D20
Maine☒ D30
Florida Int'l■ .... J 3
Samford .... J 6
Georgia St. .... J 8
Charleston (S.C.)■ J13
Mercer■ J15
Fla. Atlantic J19
Stetson J22
Centenary J27
Southeastern La. J29
Georgia St.■ .... F 3
Samford■ .... F 5
South Fla.■ .... F 7
Mercer F10
Charleston (S.C.) F12
Stetson■ F19
Florida Int'l F21
Bethune-Cookman F23
Southeastern La.■ F26
Centenary■ F28
Trans America Conf. M3-5
☒ Augusta, ME

Colors: Black & Gold. Nickname: Golden Knights.
AD: Steve Sloan. SID: Bob Cefalo. I

CENTRAL MICH. .... Mt. Pleasant, MI 48859
Leonard Drake (1ST YR. AS HEAD COACH)

Iona■ N27
Lake Superior St.■ N30
Southwest Mo. St. Cl D3-4
Wis.-Milwaukee■ .... D 8
Northeastern D11
Michigan D20
Northeastern Ill.■ D28
Kent .... J 5
Ball St.■ .... J 8
Miami (Ohio) J12
Western Mich.■ J15
Ohio J19
Akron■ J22
Bowling Green■ J26
Eastern Mich. J29
Toledo■ .... F 2
Ball St. .... F 5
Miami (Ohio)■ .... F 9
Western Mich. F12
Ohio■ F16
Akron F19
Bowling Green F23
Eastern Mich.■ F26
Toledo .... M 2
Kent■ .... M 5
Mid-American Conf. M8-12

Colors: Maroon & Gold. Nickname: Chippewas.
AD: Dave Keilitz. SID: Fred Stabley Jr. I

CENTRAL MO. ST. .... Warrensburg, MO 64093
Bob Sundvold (1 YR. W-13, L-14)

Baker■ N23
Missouri N27
Drury N29
Graceland (Iowa)■ .... D 1
Rockhurst .... D 4
Doane■ .... D 8
Ozarks (Ark.)■ D12
Las Vegas Tr. D27-28
Monmouth (Ill.)■ .... J 2
Pittsburg St.■ .... J 5
Mo. Western St.■ .... J 8
Emporia St. J12
Lincoln (Mo.)■ J15
Mo. Southern St.■ J19
Northeast Mo. St. J22
Missouri-Rolla J26
Southwest Baptist■ J29
Northwest Mo. St.■ .... F 2
Washburn .... F 5
Mo.-St. Louis .... F 9
Mo. Western St. F12
Emporia St.■ F16
Lincoln (Mo.) F19
Mo. Southern St. F23
Northeast Mo. St.■ F26

Colors: Cardinal & Black. Nickname: Mules.
AD: Jerry Hughes. SID: Bill Turnage. II

CENTRAL OKLA. .... Edmond, OK 73034
Jim Seward (19 YRS. W-297, L-231)

Ark. Baptist■ N20
Southwest Baptist■ N23
Barry Cl. N26-27
Emporia St. Cl. D3-4
Paul Quinn■ D10
Gannon Tr. D29-30
Midwestern St.■ .... J 6
Mid-America Naz.■ .... J 8
Cameron■ J12
Eastern N. Mex.■ J15
West Tex. A&M■ J17
Angelo St. J22
Abilene Christian J24
Texas A&M-Kingsville J29
East Tex. St. J31
East Tex. St.■ .... F 5
Texas A&M-Kingsville■ .... F 7
Eastern N. Mex. F12
West Tex. A&M F14
Midwestern St. F17
Abilene Christian■ F19
Angelo St.■ F21
Cameron F26

Colors: Bronze & Blue. Nickname: Bronchos.
AD: John Wagnon SID: Mike Kirk. II

CENTRE .... Danville, KY 40422
Tom Bryant (25 YRS. W-355, L-287)

Rose-Hulman■ N22
DePauw N27
Hanover☒ D11
Rose-Hulman D13
Otterbein Cl. D28-30
Wilmington (Ohio)■ .... J 5
Fisk .... J 9
Transylvania J12
Sewanee■ J14
Oglethorpe■ J16
Maryville (Tenn.) J19
Hendrix■ J21
Trinity (Tex.)■ J23
Rhodes J28
Millsaps J30
Maryville (Tenn.)■ .... F 2
Sewanee .... F 4
Oglethorpe .... F 6
Transylvania■ .... F 9
Rhodes■ F11
Millsaps■ F13
Hendrix F18
Trinity (Tex.) F20
Fisk■ F26
☒ Westerville, OH

Colors: Gold & White. Nickname: Colonels.
AD: To be named. SID: To be named. III

CHADRON ST. .... Chadron, NE 69337
Bob Wood (6 YRS. W-69, L-105)

Regis (Colo.) N20
Minot St. Tr. N26-27
South Dak. Tech .... D 1
Minot St.■ .... D 3
Denver■ .... D 7
Utah St. D11
Denver D20
South Dak. Tech■ .... J 3
Colorado Mines■ .... J 8
Black Hills St.■ J11
Fort Hays St.■ J13
Adams St. J20
N.M. Highlands J21
Mesa St.■ J27
Western St.■ J29
Regis (Colo.)■ J31
N.M. Highlands■ .... F 3
Adams St.■ .... F 5
Black Hills St. .... F 7
Fort Hays St. F11
Neb.-Kearney F12
Mesa St. F18
Western St. F19
Neb.-Kearney■ F22
Colorado Mines F26

Colors: Cardinal & White. Nickname: Eagles.
AD: Brad Smith. SID: Con Marshall. II

CHAMINADE .... Honolulu, HI 96816
Don Doucette (16 YRS. W-161, L-157)

St. Mary's (Tex.)■ N24
BYU-Hawaii Tr. D10-11
Maui Inv. D21-23
Hawaii-Hilo Inv. D28-30
Grand Canyon .... J 6
Eastern Mont. .... J 8
Hawaii-Hilo J15
Seattle Pacific■ J20
Alas. Fairbanks■ J22
Alas. Anchorage■ J24
Hawaii Pacific■ J27
BYU-Hawaii■ .... F 1
Grand Canyon■ .... F 4
Eastern Mont.■ .... F 5
Hawaii Pacific .... F 8
Hawaii-Hilo■ F12
Alas. Anchorage F17
Alas. Fairbanks F19
Seattle Pacific F21
BYU-Hawaii F25

Colors: Royal Blue & White. Nickname: Silverswords.
AD: Chuck English. SID: To be named. II

CHAPMAN .... Orange, CA 92666
Mike Bokosky (1 YR. W-7, L-19)

Claremont Tr. N26-27
Redlands Tr. D2-4
Whittier■ .... D 7
Redlands■ D10
Pomona-Pitzer■ D18
Occidental Tr. D30-31
Claremont-M-S■ .... J 4
Redlands .... J 6
La Verne■ .... J 8
UC San Diego■ J11
UC Santa Cruz■ J14
Fresno Pacific J19
Dominican (Cal.) J21
Menlo J22
Bethany (Cal.)■ J28
UC San Diego .... F 4
Menlo■ F12
Christ-Irvine■ F15
Bethany (Cal.) F18
UC Santa Cruz F19
Dominican (Cal.)■ F26

Colors: Cardinal & Gray. Nickname: Runnin' Panthers.
AD: Dave Currey. SID: Derek Anderson. II

CHARLESTON (S.C.) .... Charleston, SC 29424
John Kresse (14 YRS. W-340, L-95)

Webber■ N27
South Caro. St.■ N29
Charleston So.■ .... D 4
Mount Olive■ D18
South Caro. D22
Charleston (S.C.) Cl D28-29
Samford■ .... J 3
N.C.-Wilmington■ .... J 5
Mercer .... J 8
Central Fla. J13
Stetson J15
Centenary■ J20
Southeastern La.■ J22
Florida Int'l J27
Georgia St. J31
Charleston So. .... F 2
Mercer■ .... F 5
N.C.-Charlotte■ .... F 7
Citadel F10
Central Fla.■ F12
Stetson■ F14
Southeastern La. F17
Centenary F19
Florida Int'l■ F24
Georgia St.■ F26
Samford F28
Trans America Conf. M3-5

Colors: Maroon & White. Nickname: Cougars.
AD: Jerry Baker. SID: Tony Ciuffo. I

■ Home games on each schedule.

See pages 405–407 for Division I tournament details

CHARLESTON SO. .... Charleston, SC 29411
Gary Edwards (9 YRS. W-134, L-133)

Clemson■ ... D 1
Charleston (S.C.) ... D 4
Citadel■ ... D 9
Furman■ ... D18
Iowa St. ... D21
South Caro. St. ... J 3
Campbell ... J 6
N.C.-Asheville■ ... J 8
Winthrop■ ... J10
Md.-Balt. County ... J15
Towson St. ... J17
Liberty■ ... J22
Radford■ ... J24
N.C.-Greensboro ... J29
Coastal Caro.■ ... J31
Charleston (S.C.)■ ... F 2
N.C.-Asheville ... F 5
Winthrop ... F 7
Campbell■ ... F10
Md.-Balt. County■ ... F12
Towson St.■ ... F14
Liberty ... F19
Radford ... F21
Coastal Caro. ... F24
N.C.-Greensboro■ ... F26
Big South Conf. ... M4-7

Colors: Blue & Gold. Nickname: Buccaneers.
AD: Howard Bagwell. SID: Michael Meyer. I

CHEYNEY .... Cheyney, PA 19319
Keith Johnson (4 YRS. W-54, L-54)

Lincoln (Pa.)■ ... N27
Widener Tr. ... D3-4
West Va. St.■ ... D 8
CCNY ... D10
Medgar Evers ... D11
Atlantic City Cl. ... D17-19
Virginia St. Cl. ... J6-8
Bloomsburg ... J12
East Stroudsburg■ ... J15
Bowie St.■ ... J17
West Chester■ ... J19
Mansfield■ ... J22
Dist. Columbia■ ... J24
Millersville ... J26
Kutztown■ ... J29
Columbia Union■ ... J31
East Stroudsburg ... F 5
Bloomsburg■ ... F 9
West Chester ... F12
Millersville■ ... F16
Mansfield ... F19
Dist. Columbia ... F24
Kutztown ... F26

Colors: Blue & White. Nickname: Wolves.
AD: Andy Hinson. SID: To be named. II

CHICAGO .... Chicago, IL 60637
Pat Cunningham (6 YRS. W-56, L-104)

Mount Union Cl. ... N19-20
DePauw■ ... N23
Northwestern ... N27
Ill. Wesleyan■ ... D 4
Illinois Col. ... D 7
Kalamazoo■ ... D10
Concordia (Ill.) ... D18
Washington (Mo.)■ ... J 4
Johns Hopkins■ ... J 7
Brandeis ... J14
New York U. ... J16
Case Reserve ... J21
Rochester ... J23
Carnegie Mellon■ ... J28
Emory■ ... J30
Rochester■ ... F 4
Lake Forest■ ... F 8
Emory ... F11
Carnegie Mellon ... F13
New York U.■ ... F18
Brandeis■ ... F20
Wis.-Parkside ... F23
Washington (Mo.) ... F26

Colors: White & Maroon. Nickname: Maroons.
AD: Tom Weingartner. SID: Dave Hilbert. III

CHICAGO ST. .... Chicago, IL 60628
Rick Pryor (3 YRS. W-15, L-68)

DePaul ... N27
Eastern Ky.■ ... D 1
Bradley■ ... D 4
Southeast Mo. St. ... D 6
St. Louis ... D 8
Utah■ ... D11
Illinois ... D18
Western Ill. ... D20
Eastern Mich.■ ... D22
Wis.-Green Bay ... D27
Northern Ill.■ ... D30
Western Mich. ... J 2
Cincinnati ... J 5
Northeastern Ill.■ ... J13
Northern Iowa ... J18
Mo.-Kansas City■ ... J22
Evansville■ ... J31
N.C.-Wilmington ... F 2
Mo.-Kansas City ... F 7
Troy St. ... F12
Central Conn. St.■ ... F17
Central St. (Ohio)■ ... F19
Buffalo ... F21
Northeastern Ill. ... F24
Hofstra■ ... F26
Wis.-Milwaukee ... M 2
East Coast Conf. ... M4-6

Colors: Green & White. Nickname: Cougars.
AD: Al Avant. SID: Lisette Allison-Moore. I

CHRIS. NEWPORT .... Newport News, VA 23606
C.J. Woollum (9 YRS. W-163, L-92)

Mary Washington■ ... N19
Va. Wesleyan ... N23
Christ. Newport Inv. ... N26-27
Salisbury St. ... D 1
Chowan ... D 6
Washington (Md.) Tr. ... D10-11
Marymount (Va.)■ ... D18
Newport News App. ... D20
Hampton ... D30
N.C. Wesleyan■ ... J12
Shenandoah■ ... J16
Ferrum ... J21
Averett ... J22
Chowan■ ... J25
Methodist■ ... J29
Greensboro■ ... J30
N.C. Wesleyan ... F 2
Shenandoah ... F 6
Ferrum■ ... F 9
Averett■ ... F12
Greensboro ... F18
Methodist ... F19

Colors: Blue & Silver. Nickname: Captains.
AD: C.J. Woollum. SID: Wayne Block. III

CINCINNATI .... Cincinnati, OH 45221
Bob Huggins (12 YRS. W-262, L-108)

Pre-Season NIT ... N17-26
Wyoming■ ... N29
Tennessee St.■ ... D 1
Washington■ ... D 3
Cincinnati Cl. ... D10-11
Temple ... D16
Youngstown St.■ ... D18
Miami (Ohio)■ ... D22
Robert Morris■ ... D29
Austin Peay ... D31
Chicago St.■ ... J 5
Ala.-Birmingham■ ... J 9
Dayton ... J15
Xavier (Ohio) ... J19
Memphis St. ... J23
Massachusetts■ ... J27
DePaul■ ... J29
Memphis St.■ ... F 3
Ala.-Birmingham ... F 5
Marquette■ ... F10
Marquette ... F13
St. Louis■ ... F16
California☒ ... F20
St. Louis ... F23
Dayton■ ... F26
DePaul ... M 2
Great Midwest Conf. ... M10-12
☒ Orlando, FL

Colors: Red & Black. Nickname: Bearcats.
AD: Rick Taylor. SID: Tom Hathaway. I

CITADEL .... Charleston, SC 29409
Pat Dennis (1 YR. W-10, L-17)

Emory■ ... N29
Duke ... D 1
William & Mary■ ... D 4
Charleston So. ... D 9
Clemson ... D18
N.C.-Greensboro■ ... D29
Ga. Southern ... J 5
East Tenn. St. ... J 8
Appalachian St. ... J10
Va. Military■ ... J15
Marshall■ ... J17
Davidson■ ... J19
Western Caro. ... J22
Tenn.-Chatt. ... J24
Furman■ ... J26
Ga. Southern■ ... J29
Erskine■ ... F 1
Furman ... F 5
Davidson ... F 7
Charleston (S.C.)■ ... F10
Appalachian St.■ ... F12
East Tenn. St.■ ... F15
Marshall ... F19
Va. Military ... F21
Tenn.-Chatt.■ ... F26
Western Caro.■ ... F28
Southern Conf. ... M3-6

Colors: Blue & White. Nickname: Bulldogs.
AD: Walt Nadzak. SID: Josh Baker. I

CCNY .... New York, NY 10031
Gary Smith (5 YRS. W-41, L-86)

Pratt ... D 1
Yeshiva■ ... D 6
John Jay ... D 8
Cheyney■ ... D10
Lincoln (Pa.)☒ ... D11
St. Joseph's-Suffolk■ ... J 5
Moravian Tr. ... J7-8
Mt. St. Vincent■ ... J11
Baruch■ ... J13
Lehman■ ... J15
Mt. St. Mary (N.Y.) ... J18
Dominican (N.Y.)■ ... J19
York (N.Y.)■ ... J21
Central Conn. St. ... J22
Hunter■ ... J24
Baruch ... J26
John Jay■ ... J29
Old Westbury■ ... F 1
St. Joseph's (N.Y.)■ ... F 3
Medgar Evers ... F 5
Staten Island ... F 7
York (N.Y.) ... F11
Lehman ... F15
☒ Brooklyn, NY

Colors: Lavender & Black. Nickname: Beavers.
AD: Paul Bobb. SID: Carlos Alejandro. III

CLAREMONT-M-S .... Claremont, CA 91711
David Wells (19 YRS. W-249, L-235)

Christ-Irvine ... N23
Claremont Tr. ... N26-27
Washington (Mo.) Cl. ... D3-4
Cal Baptist ... D 7
Azusa-Pacific■ ... D11
Chapman ... J 4
La Jolla Cl. ... J7-8
La Verne ... J12
Occidental ... J15
Redlands■ ... J19
Whittier■ ... J22
Cal Lutheran■ ... J26
Pomona-Pitzer ... J29
Cal Tech ... F 2
La Verne■ ... F 5
Occidental■ ... F 9
Redlands ... F12
Whittier ... F16
Cal Lutheran ... F19
Pomona-Pitzer■ ... F21
Cal Tech■ ... F24

Colors: Maroon, Gold, White. Nickname: Stags.
AD: John Zinda. SID: Grayle Howlett. III

CLARION .... Clarion, PA 16214
Ron Righter (7 YRS. W-101, L-78)

St. Vincent Tr. ... N19-20
Clarion Cl. ... N26-27
Gannon ... D 1
Pitt.-Johnstown ... D 7
Wheeling Jesuit■ ... D11
Cedarville■ ... D17
Geneva■ ... D31
Clarion Tr. ... J7-8
Edinboro ... J12
Shippensburg■ ... J15
Lock Haven■ ... J19
Indiana (Pa.) ... J22
Slippery Rock ... J26
Phila. Bible■ ... J31
Calif. (Pa.)■ ... F 2
Shippensburg ... F 5
Columbia Union■ ... F 7
Edinboro■ ... F 9
Lock Haven ... F12
Slippery Rock■ ... F16
Indiana (Pa.)■ ... F19
Calif. (Pa.) ... F23

Colors: Blue & Gold. Nickname: Golden Eagles.
AD: Bob Carlson. SID: Rich Herman. II

■ Home games on each schedule.

See pages 405–407 for Division I tournament details

CLARK (MASS.) .... **Worcester, MA 01610**

Larry Mangino (2 YRS. W-23, L-28)

Clark Tr.	N19-20	Worcester Tech■	J22
Anna Maria	D 1	Western New Eng.	J25
North Adams St.	D 4	Amherst■	J26
Framingham St.■	D 7	Babson	J29
Tufts■	D11	Trinity (Conn.)	F 1
New York U.	J 3	Bowdoin■	F 4
John Jay	J 4	Colby■	F 5
Eastern Conn. St.	J 6	Suffolk■	F 9
Southern Me.■	J 8	Colby-Sawyer■	F12
Western Conn. St.	J11	Brandeis	F16
Mass.-Dartmouth	J15	Mass.-Boston■	F22
Wesleyan■	J20	Wheaton (Mass.)	F26

Colors: Scarlet & White. Nickname: Cougars.
AD: Linda Moulton. SID: Kathryn Smith. III

CLARKSON .... **Potsdam, NY 13699**

Jay Murphy (10 YRS. W-64, L-182)

Amherst	N19	Hobart	J28
Middlebury	N20	Rochester Inst.	J29
Utica■	N23	Ithaca	F 4
St. John Fisher■	N30	Alfred	F 5
Cornell	D 7	Plattsburgh St.■	F 8
St. Lawrence■	D 9	Rochester Inst.■	F11
Wilkes Cl.	J7-8	Hobart■	F12
Alfred■	J14	St. Lawrence	F15
Ithaca■	J15	Rensselaer	F18
Hartwick■	J21	Hartwick	F19
Rensselaer■	J22	Hamilton■	F25
Potsdam St.■	J25	Union (N.Y.)■	F26

Colors: Green & Gold. Nickname: Golden Knights.
AD: Bill O'Flaherty. SID: Gary Mikel. III

CLEMSON .... **Clemson, SC 29631**

Cliff Ellis (18 YRS. W-332, L-197)

Texas-Arlington■	N29	Appalachian St.■	J24
Charleston So.	D 1	Maryland	J26
Furman■	D 4	North Caro. St.■	J29
Minnesota	D15	Georgia Tech■	F 2
Citadel■	D18	Duke	F 5
Davidson	D19	South Caro.■	F 9
Hawaii Rainbow Cl.	D27-30	Virginia	F12
Duke■	J 5	North Caro.■	F17
N.C.-Charlotte■	J 8	Florida St.■	F19
Mercer	J10	Wake Forest	F22
Virginia■	J12	Maryland■	F26
North Caro.	J15	North Caro. St.	M 2
Florida St.	J19	Georgia Tech	M 5
Wake Forest■	J22	Atlantic Coast Conf.	M10-13

Colors: Purple & Orange. Nickname: Tigers.
AD: Bobby Robinson. SID: Tim Bourret. I

CLEVELAND ST. .... **Cleveland, OH 44115**

Mike Boyd (3 YRS. W-55, L-46)

Pre-Season NIT	N17-26	Western Ill.■	J29
Michigan	N29	Northern Ill.■	J31
Saginaw Valley■	D 4	Wis.-Milwaukee	F 5
Michigan St.■	D 7	Wis.-Green Bay	F 7
Cincinnati Cl.	D10-11	Wright St.■	F12
Middle Tenn. St.■	D21	Eastern Ill.■	F14
Kent■	D23	Western Ill.	F19
Wright St.	J 5	Northern Ill.	F21
Eastern Ill.	J10	Youngstown St.■	F24
Wis.-Milwaukee■	J15	Valparaiso■	F26
Wis.-Green Bay■	J17	Ill.-Chicago■	F28
Valparaiso	J22	Buffalo■	M 2
Ill.-Chicago	J24	Mid-Continent Conf.	M6-8
Youngstown St.	J27		

Colors: Green & White. Nickname: Vikings.
AD: John Konstantinos. SID: Rick Love. I

COAST GUARD .... **New London, CT 06320**

Peter Barry (11 YRS. W-198, L-124)

Roger Williams■	N19	MIT■	J22
Wentworth Inst.■	N23	Connecticut Col.	J25
Trinity (Conn.)■	N30	Western New Eng.	J27
Coast Guard Cl.	D3-4	Worcester Tech	J29
Albertus Magnus	D 8	Merchant Marine■	F 2
Weber St.	D20	Western New Eng.■	F 5
Notre Dame (Cal.)	D21	Wesleyan	F 8
UC Santa Cruz☒	D22	Nichols	F10
MIT	J 8	Babson■	F16
Norwich■	J14	Worcester Tech■	F19
Norwich■	J15	☒ Palo Alto, CA	
Babson	J19		

Colors: Blue, White & Orange. Nickname: Cadets, Bears.
AD: Chuck Mills. SID: Shaun May. III

COASTAL CARO. .... **Conway, SC 29526**

Russ Bergman (18 YRS. W-291, L-235)

Francis Marion	N30	Liberty■	J24
Virginia Tech	D 4	Campbell■	J29
Alderson-Broaddus■	D 8	Charleston So.	J31
South Caro.	D11	Winthrop■	F 5
South Caro. St.	D18	N.C.-Asheville	F 7
Sugar Bowl Tr.	D27-28	N.C.-Greensboro	F 9
Evansville	J 3	Towson St.■	F12
Winthrop	J 8	Md.-Balt. County■	F14
N.C.-Asheville■	J10	Radford	F19
N.C.-Greensboro■	J12	Liberty	F21
Towson St.	J15	Charleston So.■	F24
Md.-Balt. County	J17	Campbell	F26
Radford■	J22	Big South Conf.	M4-7

Colors: Scarlett & Black. Nickname: Chanticleers.
AD: Andy Hendrick. SID: Davis Fisher. I

COE .... **Cedar Rapids, IA 52402**

Robert Landis (2 YRS. W-15, L-29)

Central Inv.	N26-27	Lake Forest■	J22
Upper Iowa	N30	Ripon■	J23
Knox	D 3	Beloit	J29
Illinois Col.	D 4	Carroll (Wis.)	J30
Mt. Mercy	D 7	Cornell College■	F 5
Mt. St. Clare■	D11	Monmouth (Ill.)	F 8
Luther	D18	Grinnell	F11
Cornell College	J 8	Mt. Mercy■	F14
Simpson■	J11	Knox■	F18
Grinnell■	J14	Illinois Col.■	F19
Monmouth (Ill.)■	J19		

Colors: Crimson & Gold. Nickname: Kohawks.
AD: Barron Bremner. SID: Alice Davidson. III

COKER .... **Hartsville, SC 29550**

Dan Schmotzer (6 YRS. W-90, L-68)

Erskine	N20	Central Wesleyan	J24
Morris■	N23	High Point■	J29
Walsh Tr.	N26-27	Pfeiffer■	J31
Pembroke St.	D 1	Mount Olive	F 2
Franic Marion Cl.	D3-4	Barton	F 5
Western Caro.	D 6	Belmont Abbey	F 9
Armstrong St.■	D 8	Lees-McRae	F12
Erskine■	J10	Morris	F14
Barton■	J15	St. Andrews■	F16
Mount Olive■	J17	High Point	F19
Belmont Abbey■	J19	Pfeiffer	F23
St. Andrews	J22	Lees-McRae■	F26

Colors: Navy Blue & Gold. Nickname: Cobras.
AD: Ed Clark. SID: Greg Grissom. II

COLBY .... **Waterville, ME 04901**

Dick Whitmore (23 YRS. W-382, L-175)

Colby Tr.	N19-20	Bates■	J25
Suffolk■	N27	Middlebury■	J28
Husson	D 1	Norwich■	J29
Tufts■	D 3	Wesleyan	F 4
Southern Me.	D 8	Clark (Mass.)	F 5
Salem St.■	D11	Wheaton (Mass.)	F11
Gordon	J 8	Connecticut Col.	F12
Colby-Sawyer■	J11	Bowdoin	F16
Union (N.Y.)	J15	Mass.-Boston	F19
Hamilton	J16	Bates	F23
Amherst■	J21	Bowdoin■	F26
Western New Eng.■	J22		

Colors: Blue & Gray. Nickname: White Mules.
AD: Dick Whitmore. SID: Jac Coyne. III

COLBY-SAWYER .... **New London, NH 03257**

Bill Foti (1 YR. W-16, L-9)

Norwich■	N20	Southern Me.	J19
Rhode Island Col.■	N23	Suffolk■	J22
Rivier	N30	Middlebury■	J25
New England Col.	D 2	Daniel Webster■	F 2
St. Joseph's (Me.)	D 4	Albertus Magnus■	F 5
Gordon■	D 7	Rivier■	F 7
Lyndon St.	D10	Notre Dame (N.H.)■	F 9
Mt. St. Vincent Cl.	J7-8	Clark (Mass.)	F12
Colby	J11	Castleton St.	F14
Bates	J12	Connecticut Col.■	F18
Suffolk	J15	Bowdoin	F20
Green Mountain■	J17	Wheaton (Mass.)■	F23

Colors: Blue & White. Nickname: Chargers.
AD: Debi McGrath. SID: Bill Warnken. III

■ Home games on each schedule.

See pages 405–407 for Division I tournament details

COLGATE .... Hamilton, NY 13346
Jack Bruen (11 YRS. W-155, L-140)

Yale N27
Harvard N29
San Francisco Cl. D3-4
Brown■ .... D 7
St. John's (N.Y.) Tr D11-12
Canisius D22
Syracuse D29
Vermont .... J 5
Bucknell■ .... J 8
Cornell J10
Lafayette■ J12
Navy J15
Holy Cross■ J18
Fordham■ J22
Army J25
Lehigh■ J29
Bucknell .... F 2
Lafayette .... F 5
Navy■ .... F 9
Holy Cross F12
Fordham F16
Army■ F19
Central Conn. St.■ F23
Lehigh F26
Patriot Conf. M4-11

Colors: Maroon, Gray & White. Nickname: Red Raiders.
AD: Mark Murphy. SID: Bob Cornell. I

COLORADO .... Boulder, CO 80309
Joe Harrington (14 YRS. W-221, L-181)

North Texas■ N29
Colorado Cl. D3-4
Colorado St. .... D 6
Wyoming■ .... D 9
Cal St. Fullerton■ D21
Nevada D28
Md.-East. Shore■ D30
Illinois St. .... J 3
Nebraska .... J 8
Mo.-Kansas City■ J12
Missouri■ J15
Cal St. Northridge■ J17
Nebraska■ J19
Kansas St. J22
Cal St. Sacramento■ J26
Kansas■ J29
Iowa St. .... F 1
Kansas St.■ .... F 5
Missouri .... F 9
Oklahoma F12
Iowa St.■ F19
Oklahoma St.■ F21
Kansas F26
Oklahoma■ .... M 2
Oklahoma St. .... M 5
Big Eight Conf. M11-13

Colors: Silver, Gold & Black. Nickname: Golden Buffaloes.
AD: Bill Marolt. SID: David Plati. I

COLO. CHRISTIAN .... Lakewood, CO 80226
Frank Evans (14 YRS. W-256, L-203)

Colo. Christian Tr. N19-20
Neb.-Kearney N26
Northern Colo.■ N29
N.M. Highlands Tr. D3-4
North Central■ .... D 6
N.M. Highlands■ D11
Northern Colo. D15
Stonehill■ D30
Colo. Christian Cl. J5-7
Metropolitan St. J11
Fort Lewis J14
Colorado-CS■ J20
Southern Colo.■ J22
Denver■ J27
Regis (Colo.) J29
Neb.-Kearney■ .... F 2
Metropolitan St.■ .... F 8
Fort Lewis■ F10
Colorado-CS F17
Southern Colo. F19
Denver F24
Regis (Colo.)■ F26

Colors: Blue & White. Nickname: Cougars.
AD: Frank Evans. SID: Judy M. Vaughn. II

COLORADO COL. .... Colorado Springs, CO 80903
Steve Proefrock (1ST YR. AS HEAD COACH)

Grinnell Tr. N19-20
Colorado College Tr. N26-27
Rose-Hulman Inv. D3-4
Fort Lewis D11
Minn.-Morris■ D13
Hastings Cl. D29-30
Colorado College Inv J2-4
Concordia (Wis.)■ .... J 5
Buffalo St. Tr. J7-8
Bethany (Kan.) J17
Kan. Wesleyan J18
Panhandle St.■ J22
Adams St.■ J27
Colorado-CS .... F 1
Bellevue■ .... F 4
Colorado Mines .... F 8
Kan. Wesleyan■ F12
Panhandle St. F18
Bethany (Kan.)■ F21

Colors: Black & Gold. Nickname: Tigers.
AD: Max Taylor. SID: Dave Moross. III

COLORADO MINES .... Golden, CO 80401
Keith Brown (4 YRS. W-4, L-23)

Colorado-CS■ N20
Jacksonville St.■ N23
Denver Cl. N26-27
Regis (Colo.) N30
Colorado Mines Tr. D3-4
Metropolitan St.■ .... D 8
Minn.-Morris■ D11
Montana St. D17
Idaho St. D18
Colorado-CS D21
Mo.-Rolla Tr. J1-2
Chadron St. .... J 8
Fort Hays St.■ J15
Adams St. J21
N.M. Highlands J22
Western St.■ J27
Mesa St.■ J29
Adams St.■ .... F 3
N.M. Highlands■ .... F 5
Colorado Col.■ .... F 8
Fort Hays St. F12
Western St. F18
Mesa St. F19
Chadron St.■ F26

Colors: Silver & Blue. Nickname: Orediggers.
AD: R. Bruce Allison. SID: Steve Smith. II

COLORADO ST. .... Fort Collins, CO 80523
Stew Morrill (7 YRS. W-128, L-81)

West Tex. A&M■ N27
Utah St.■ .... D 3
Colorado■ .... D 6
North Caro. .... D 9
Toledo D11
Rice D18
Southeast Mo. St.■ D21
Cal St. Fullerton■ D23
Fort Lewis■ D30
Fresno St.■ .... J 3
Air Force■ .... J 5
San Diego St. .... J 8
Hawaii J10
Wyoming J15
New Mexico■ J20
UTEP■ J22
Utah J27
Brigham Young J29
Utah■ .... F 3
Brigham Young■ .... F 5
UTEP F10
New Mexico F12
Wyoming■ F19
San Diego St.■ F24
Hawaii■ F26
Fresno St. .... M 3
Air Force .... M 5
Western Ath. Conf. M9-12

Colors: Green & Gold. Nickname: Rams.
AD: David Ames. SID: Gary Ozzello. I

COLORADO-CS .... Colorado Springs, CO 80933
Mark Felix (2 YRS. W-9, L-47)

Colorado Mines N20
Northern Colo. N23
Eastern Mont. Inv. N26-27
Mesa St.■ N30
Northern Colo.■ .... D 3
Panhandle St. D10
Colorado Mines■ D21
Cal St. Chico Tr. D28-30
Mesa St. .... J 2
Southern Colo. .... J 8
Denver J13
Regis (Colo.)■ J15
Colo. Christian J20
Metropolitan St. J22
Panhandle St.■ J24
Fort Lewis■ J28
Colorado Col.■ .... F 1
Southern Colo.■ .... F 5
Denver■ F10
Regis (Colo.) F12
Colo. Christian■ F17
Metropolitan St.■ F19
Fort Lewis F24

Colors: Gold & Colorado Blue. Nickname: Gold.
AD: Theophilus Gregory. SID: Nanette Anderson. II

COLUMBIA .... New York, NY 10027
Jack Rohan (16 YRS. W-187, L-206)

Haverford■ N27
St. John's (N.Y.) N30
Mt. St. Mary's Tr. D3-4
Lafayette .... D 7
Penn St. D11
Toledo Cl. D29-30
Manhattan .... J 5
Lehigh■ J10
Cornell■ J15
Fordham J17
Cornell J22
Hofstra J25
Brown■ J28
Yale■ J29
Pennsylvania .... F 4
Princeton .... F 5
Dartmouth■ F11
Harvard■ F12
Yale F18
Brown F19
Harvard F25
Dartmouth F26
Princeton■ .... M 4
Pennsylvania■ .... M 5

Colors: Columbia Blue & White. Nickname: Lions.
AD: John Reeves. SID: Bill Steinman. I

COLUMBUS .... Columbus, GA 31907
Herbert Greene (14 YRS. W-231, L-156)

Webber■ N24
Talladega■ N27
Tuskegee .... D 6
Kennesaw■ .... D 8
Tenn.-Chatt. D11
Covenant■ .... J 3
Francis Marion .... J 8
Pembroke St. .... J 9
Armstrong St. J15
Georgia Col.■ J19
S.C.-Spartanburg■ J22
Lander■ J23
West Ga.■ J29
S.C.-Aiken J31
Georgia Col. .... F 3
Augusta .... F 5
Armstrong St.■ .... F 7
West Ga. .... F 9
Francis Marion■ F12
Pembroke St.■ F13
S.C.-Spartanburg F19
Lander F20
S.C.-Aiken■ F26
Augusta■ F27

Colors: Red, White & Blue. Nickname: Cougars.
AD: Herbert Greene. SID: Judy Favor. II

CONCORD .... Athens, WV 24712
Steve Cox (4 YRS. W-84, L-38)

Catawba Cl. N19-20
Bluefield St. N29
West Va. Tech■ .... D 1
Clinch Valley Tr. D3-4
Ohio Valley College .... D 7
Concord Inv. J3-4
Fairmont St. .... J 8
Alderson-Broaddus■ J10
West Liberty St. J14
Wheeling Jesuit J15
Charleston (W.Va.)■ J19
West Va. Wesleyan J22
West Va. St.■ J24
Glenville St. J26
Salem Teikyo■ J29
Davis & Elkins■ J31
West Va. Tech .... F 2
Shepherd .... F 5
Bluefield St.■ .... F 9
Charleston (W.Va.) F12
West Va. Wesleyan■ F14
West Va. St. F16
Glenville St.■ F19

Colors: Maroon & Gray. Nickname: Mountain Lions.
AD: Don Christie. SID: Tom Bone. II

■ Home games on each schedule.

See pages 405–407 for Division I tournament details

CONCORDIA (ILL.) .... River Forest, IL 60305
Keith Peterson (5 YRS. W-49, L-80)

Albion Cl.	N19-20
Elmhurst	N23
Eureka	D 2
Hope	D 4
Loyola (Ill.)	D 8
Concordia (Mich.)■	D11
Chicago■	D18
Concordia (N.Y.)	D27
Western Conn. St. Tr	D29-30
Lake Forest■	J 6
Ill. Benedictine■	J15
Trinity (Ill.)	J19
Judson	J22
Rockford■	J25
Concordia (Minn.) Tr	J28-29
Aurora■	F 2
Ill. Benedictine	F 5
Trinity (Ill.)■	F 9
Judson■	F12
Aurora	F16
Rockford	F19

Colors: Maroon & Gold. Nickname: Cougars.
AD: Conrad Aumann. SID: Jim Egan. III

CONCORDIA-M'HEAD .... Moorhead, MN 56560
Duane Siverson (2 YRS. W-18, L-31)

Pomona-Pitzer	N23
Cal Lutheran	N26
Moorhead St.	D 2
Gust. Adolphus	D 4
Carleton	D 6
St. John's (Minn.)■	D11
Bethel (Minn.)	J 3
St. Thomas (Minn.)■	J 5
Augsburg	J 8
St. Olaf■	J10
Macalester■	J12
Hamline■	J15
St. Mary's (Minn.)	J19
Carleton■	J22
Gust. Adolphus■	J26
St. John's (Minn.)	J29
Bethel (Minn.)■	J31
St. Thomas (Minn.)	F 2
Augsburg■	F 5
Moorhead St.■	F 7
St. Olaf	F 9
Macalester	F12
Hamline	F14
St. Mary's (Minn.)■	F19

Colors: Maroon & Gold. Nickname: Cobbers.
AD: Armin Pipho. SID: Jerry Pyle. III

CONNECTICUT .... Storrs, CT 06269
Jim Calhoun (21 YRS. W-381, L-223)

Towson St.⊠	N27
Virginia	N29
Yale■	D 1
Seton Hall	D 8
Central Conn. St.■	D11
Texas■	D15
Fairfield■	D23
Hawaii-Hilo Inv.	D28-30
Winthrop■	J 2
Georgetown■	J 4
Boston College■	J 8
Syracuse■	J10
St. John's (N.Y.)	J15
Hartford■	J17
Providence	J19
Villanova■	J25
Pittsburgh	J29
Syracuse	F 1
Miami (Fla.)■	F 5
Boston College	F 9
Seton Hall■	F12
Villanova	F15
Providence■	F19
Miami (Fla.)	F22
Pittsburgh■	F26
Georgetown	F28
St. John's (N.Y.)■	M 5
Big East Conf.	M10-13

⊠ Hershey, PA

Colors: Blue & White. Nickname: Huskies.
AD: Lew Perkins. SID: Tim Tolokan. I

CONNECTICUT COL. .... New London, CT 06320
Glen Miller (1ST YR. AS HEAD COACH)

Babson Inv.	N19-20
Roger Williams	N30
Connecticut Col. Cl.	D3-4
Salve Regina■	D 7
Williams	D11
Trinity (Conn.) Cl.	J14-15
Amherst	J18
Middlebury	J22
Coast Guard■	J25
Trinity (Conn.)■	J29
Wheaton (Mass.)	F 1
MIT■	F 3
Manhattanville■	F 5
Western New Eng.	F 8
Bowdoin■	F11
Colby■	F12
Wesleyan	F15
Colby-Sawyer	F18
Bates	F19
Albertus Magnus■	F23
Tufts	F26

Colors: Royal Blue & White. Nickname: Camels.
AD: Robert Malekoff. SID: Martin Schoepfer. III

COPPIN ST. .... Baltimore, MD 21216
Ron Mitchell (7 YRS. W-121, L-83)

San Juan Shootout	N26-28
West Va. St.■	D 1
Kansas St.	D 4
Wichita St.	D 6
Virginia	D 9
Towson St.■	D13
Missouri	D19
Oklahoma	D22
Pittsburgh	D27
Loyola (Ill.)■	D30
Boston College	J 2
South Caro. St.■	J 6
Lincoln (Pa.)■	J 8
North Caro. A&T	J13
Md.-East. Shore■	J17
Florida A&M	J22
Bethune-Cookman	J24
Morgan St.	J27
Howard■	J29
Delaware St.■	F 2
Howard	F 5
Morgan St.■	F 7
Florida A&M■	F12
Bethune-Cookman■	F14
South Caro. St.	F17
North Caro. A&T■	F23
Md.-East. Shore⊠	F26
Delaware St.	M 5
Mid-Eastern Conf.	M9-13

⊠ Salisbury, MD

Colors: Royal Blue & Gold. Nickname: Eagles.
AD: Clayton McNeill. SID: Jesse Batten. I

CORNELL .... Ithaca, NY 14853
Al Walker (5 YRS. W-69, L-60)

Maryland	N27
Syracuse	D 1
St. Louis	D 4
Clarkson■	D 7
Cortland St.■	D19
Bucknell	D20
Michigan St. Cl.	D29-30
Lehigh■	J 5
Hofstra	J 8
Colgate■	J10
Columbia	J15
Canisius	J18
Columbia■	J22
Yale■	J28
Brown■	J29
Princeton	F 4
Pennsylvania	F 5
Harvard■	F11
Dartmouth■	F12
Brown	F18
Yale	F19
Dartmouth	F25
Harvard	F26
Pennsylvania■	M 6
Princeton■	M 7

Colors: Carnelian & White. Nickname: Big Red.
AD: Laing Kennedy. SID: Dave Wohlhueter. I

CORNELL COLLEGE .... Mt. Vernon, IA 52314
Gary Grace (5 YRS. W-60, L-52)

North Central Cl.	N19-20
Mt. Mercy■	N27
Northeastern Ill.	N29
Monmouth (Ill.)	D 3
Grinnell	D10
Luther■	D11
Lakeland■	D18
Clarke■	J 3
Coe■	J 8
Knox■	J14
Illinois Col.■	J15
Grinnell■	J18
Beloit■	J22
Carroll (Wis.)■	J23
Lawrence	J29
St. Norbert	J30
Coe	F 5
Knox	F11
Illinois Col.	F12
Dubuque	F14
Monmouth (Ill.)■	F18

Colors: Purple & White. Nickname: Rams.
AD: Ellen Whale. SID: Mick Kulikowski. III

CORTLAND ST. .... Cortland, NY 13045
John Konowitz (8 YRS. W-104, L-104)

Hartwick Cl.	N19-20
Ithaca■	N30
Geneseo St.■	D 3
Buffalo St.■	D 4
Oneonta St.	D 7
Plattsburgh St.	D10
Potsdam St.	D11
Cornell	D19
Albany (N.Y.)■	J10
Oswego St.	J14
Utica Tech■	J15
Binghamton	J18
Hamilton Inv.	J22-23
New Paltz St.■	J25
Fredonia St.	J29
Ithaca	F 1
Plattsburgh St.■	F 4
Potsdam St.■	F 5
Binghamton■	F 8
Brockport St.	F12
New Paltz St.	F15
Oneonta St.■	F19

Colors: Red & White. Nickname: Red Dragons.
AD: Lee Roberts. SID: Fran Elia. III

CREIGHTON .... Omaha, NE 68178
Rick Johnson (2 YRS. W-17, L-37)

Mo.-Kansas City	N29
Iowa St.	D 1
Nebraska-Omaha■	D 4
St. Louis■	D 6
Nebraska■	D 9
Montana	D19
Florida A&M■	D22
Hawaii-Hilo Inv.	D28-30
Northern Iowa■	J 4
Indiana St.	J 8
Oral Roberts■	J13
Tulsa■	J15
Southern Ill.■	J17
Drake	J20
Northern Iowa	J22
Wichita St.	J24
Southwest Mo. St.■	J29
Southern Ill.	J31
Indiana St.■	F 3
Wichita St.■	F 5
Drake■	F 9
Illinois St.■	F12
Bradley	F15
Illinois St.	F19
Southwest Mo. St.	F24
Tulsa	F26
Bradley■	F28
Missouri Valley Conf	M5-7

Colors: Blue & White. Nickname: Bluejays.
AD: Thomas N. Moore. SID: Kevin Sarver. I

CURRY .... Milton, MA 02186
Gerald Morelli (4 YRS. W-27, L-75)

Babson Inv.	N19-20
Rivier■	N23
Suffolk■	D 4
Bri'water (Mass.)	D 7
Nichols	D 9
Emerson-MCA	D11
Amherst	J11
MIT■	J13
Wentworth Inst.	J15
New England Col.■	J18
Eastern Nazarene	J20
Roger Williams	J22
Emerson-MCA■	J24
Gordon■	J26
Salve Regina	J29
Anna Maria■	F 1
Wentworth Inst.■	F 3
New England Col.	F 5
Eastern Nazarene■	F 9
Salve Regina■	F12
Gordon	F15
Anna Maria	F17
Roger Williams■	F19

Colors: Purple & White. Nickname: Colonels.
AD: Tom Stephens. SID: Joe Hunter. III

■ Home games on each schedule.

See pages 405–407 for Division I tournament details

DANIEL WEBSTER .... **Nashua, NH 03063**

Richard Whitmore (1ST YR. AS HEAD COACH)

Rivier Tr. N20-21
New England Col. N23
Johnson St.■ N28
Thomas N29
Mt. St. Vincent Tr. D4-5
Green Mountain■ .... D 7
Southern Vt. .... D 9
Rivier■ D12
Emerson-MCA D13
Me.-Farmington■ J10
Unity■ J14
Mt. St. Mary Cl. J22-23
Mass. Pharmacy J25
Emerson-MCA■ J26
Atlantic Union■ J29
Southern Vt.■ J30
Colby-Sawyer .... F 2
Maine Maritime■ .... F 5
Unity .... F 6
Johnson St. F13
Mass. Pharmacy■ F15
Rivier F16
Albertus Magnus F19
Maine Maritime■ F20

Colors: Blue, White & Gold. Nickname: Eagles.
AD: Phil Rowe. SID: To be named. III

DARTMOUTH .... **Hanover, NH 03755**

Dave Faucher (2 YRS. W-21, L-31)

New Hampshire N27
Boston College N30
Middlebury■ .... D 1
FDU-Teaneck■ D11
Harvard D14
Valparaiso D18
Iowa D20
Vermont D28
Maine☒ .... J 2
Princeton .... J 7
Pennsylvania .... J 8
Vermont■ J11
Harvard■ J15
Boston U. J18
Hofstra■ J22
Holy Cross■ J31
Brown■ .... F 4
Yale■ .... F 5
Columbia F11
Cornell F12
Pennsylvania■ F18
Princeton■ F19
Cornell■ F25
Columbia■ F26
Yale .... M 4
Brown .... M 5
☒ Portland, ME

Colors: Green & White. Nickname: Big Green.
AD: Dick Jaeger. SID: Kathy Slattery. I

DAVIDSON .... **Davidson, NC 28036**

Bob McKillop (4 YRS. W-39, L-74)

Sewanee■ N27
Samford■ .... D 4
Wake Forest .... D 6
N.C.-Charlotte■ D11
Oglethorpe■ D13
Clemson■ D19
Marshall D30
North Caro. St. .... J 2
Western Caro.■ .... J 5
Furman■ .... J 8
Tenn.-Chatt. J13
East Tenn. St. J15
Appalachian St.■ J17
Citadel J19
Va. Military J22
Ga. Southern J26
Tenn.-Chatt.■ J29
Western Caro. J31
Ga. Southern■ .... F 5
Citadel■ .... F 7
Furman F12
N.C.-Charlotte F15
Appalachian St. F19
East Tenn. St.■ F21
Marshall■ F26
Va. Military■ F28
Southern Conf. M3-6

Colors: Red & Black. Nickname: Wildcats.
AD: Terry Holland. SID: Emil Parker. I

DAVIS & ELKINS .... **Elkins, WV 26241**

Tom Wilson (6 YRS. W-31, L-134)

Edinboro Tr. N19-20
Pitt.-Johnstown N22
Alderson-Broaddus■ N30
Eastern Ky. .... D 4
Salem Teikyo■ .... D 8
Calif. (Pa.)■ D11
Clarion Tr. J7-8
West Va. Tech■ J10
Charleston (W.Va.) J12
Glenville St. J15
Wheeling Jesuit■ J19
West Liberty St. J22
Shepherd■ J24
West Va. Wesleyan J26
Charleston (W.Va.)■ J29
Concord J31
Fairmont St. .... F 2
Bluefield St.■ .... F 5
West Va. St.■ .... F 7
Alderson-Broaddus .... F 9
Wheeling Jesuit F12
West Liberty St.■ F14
Shepherd F16
West Va. Wesleyan■ F19

Colors: Scarlet & White. Nickname: Senators.
AD: Will Shaw. SID: To be named. II

DAYTON .... **Dayton, OH 45469**

Jim O'Brien (9 YRS. W-129, L-135)

Towson St.■ .... D 4
Illinois St. .... D 6
Wright St.■ D11
Western Ill.■ D18
Va. Military■ D22
Central Conn. St.■ D27
Miami (Ohio)■ D30
Murray St.■ .... J 2
Rice■ .... J 5
Wright St. .... J 8
Xavier (Ohio) J12
Cincinnati■ J15
Xavier (Ohio)■ J24
Ala.-Birmingham■ J30
St. Louis .... F 2
Memphis St.■ .... F 5
Memphis St. .... F 9
St. Louis■ F13
DePaul■ F15
DePaul F17
Marquette F20
Marquette■ F23
Cincinnati F26
Detroit Mercy■ .... M 1
Ala.-Birmingham .... M 3
Notre Dame .... M 5
Great Midwest Conf. M10-12

Colors: Red & Blue. Nickname: Flyers.
AD: Ted Kissell. SID: Doug Hauschild. I

DEPAUL .... **Chicago, IL 60614**

Joey Meyer (9 YRS. W-184, L-94)

Chicago St.■ N27
Kansas■ .... D 4
Bradley■ .... D 7
Illinois St.■ D11
Northeastern Ill.■ D14
Jacksonville D18
Texas Christian D21
Houston D30
Maine■ .... J 5
Memphis St. .... J 8
Marquette■ J12
St. Louis■ J15
Massachusetts■ J18
Georgetown■ J22
Ala.-Birmingham J26
Cincinnati J29
Loyola (Ill.)■ .... F 2
St. Louis .... F 6
Ala.-Birmingham■ .... F 9
Detroit Mercy F12
Dayton F15
Dayton■ F17
Notre Dame F20
Marquette F27
Cincinnati■ .... M 2
Memphis St.■ .... M 5
Great Midwest Conf. M10-12

Colors: Scarlet & Blue. Nickname: Blue Demons.
AD: Bill Bradshaw. SID: John Lanctot. I

DEPAUW .... **Greencastle, IN 46135**

Bill Fenlon (8 YRS. W-126, L-76)

Washington (Mo.) Tr. N19-20
Chicago N23
Centre■ N27
Millikin■ N30
Purdue-Calumet■ .... D 2
Webster .... D 4
Butler .... D 6
Elmhurst■ .... D 8
DePauw Inv. D17-18
Earlham D30
Anderson■ .... J 5
Manchester .... J 8
Rockford■ J10
Hanover J15
Rose-Hulman■ J18
Franklin■ J22
Wabash J26
Manchester■ J29
Anderson .... F 1
Hanover■ .... F 5
Franklin F12
Rose-Hulman F16
Wabash■ F19

Colors: Old Gold & Black. Nickname: Tigers.
AD: Ted Katula. SID: Bill Wagner. III

DEFIANCE .... **Defiance, OH 43512**

Marvin Hohenberger (28 YRS. W-530, L-247)

Ohio Wesleyan Tr. N19-20
Heidelberg N23
Ohio Northern N27
Bowling Green N29
Huntington■ .... D 4
Franklin■ .... D 7
Olivet■ D18
Defiance Tr. D28-29
Bahamas Shootout J2-9
Bluffton J12
Thomas More J15
Findlay J19
Wilmington (Ohio)■ J22
Anderson■ J25
Bluffton■ J29
Wittenberg .... F 2
Findlay .... F 7
Thomas More■ F12
Tri-State F14
Wilmington (Ohio) F19

Colors: Purple & Gold. Nickname: Yellow Jackets.
AD: Marvin Hohenberger. SID: Cindy Elliott. III

DELAWARE .... **Newark, DE 19716**

Steve Steinwedel (8 YRS. W-137 , L-93)

Monmouth (N.J.) N27
Washington (Md.)■ N29
Delaware St.■ .... D 4
Widener■ .... D 8
Towson St.■ D11
New Orleans Cl. D20-21
Toledo Cl. D29-30
Loyola (Md.)■ .... J 3
Richmond■ .... J 5
Rutgers .... J 8
New Hampshire J14
Maine J16
Boston U.■ J21
Northeastern■ J23
Vermont J27
Hartford J29
Drexel■ .... F 5
Hartford■ F11
Vermont■ F13
Northeastern F18
Boston U. F20
Maine■ F25
New Hampshire■ F27
Drexel .... M 2
North Atlantic Conf. M5-9

Colors: Blue & Gold. Nickname: Fightin' Blue Hens.
AD: Edgar Johnson. SID: Scott Selheimer. I

DELAWARE ST. .... **Dover, DE 19901**

Jeff Jones (7 YRS. W-83, L-110)

St. Joseph's(Pa.) Tr N26-27
Elizabeth City St.■ .... D 1
Delaware .... D 4
St. Francis (N.Y.) .... D 7
Bowie St.■ .... D 9
Arkansas D11
Charleston (S.C.) Cl D28-29
Bethune-Cookman■ .... J 8
Florida A&M■ J10
Howard■ J15
Morgan St.■ J17
North Caro. A&T J22
South Caro. St. J24
Coppin St. .... F 2
North Caro. A&T■ .... F 5
South Caro. St.■ .... F 7
Md.-East. Shore■ F12
Morgan St. F14
Bethune-Cookman F19
Florida A&M F21
Howard F24
Central Conn. St. F26
Md.-East. Shore .... M 3
Coppin St.■ .... M 5
Mid-Eastern Conf. M9-13

Colors: Red & Coumbia Blue. Nickname: Hornets.
AD: John Martin. SID: Craig Cotton. I

■ Home games on each schedule.

See pages 405–407 for Division I tournament details

DELAWARE VALLEY .... Doylestown, PA 18901

Bill Werkiser (8 YRS. W-59, L-138)

Cabrini Tr.	N19-20	Moravian	J24
Elizabethtown	N23	Upsala	J26
FDU-Madison■	D 1	FDU-Madison	J29
Scranton■	D 4	Alvernia■	J31
Misericordia■	D 9	King's (Pa.)■	F 2
Allentown	D11	Scranton	F 5
Lebanon Valley Tr.	J7-8	Drew	F 9
King's (Pa.)	J12	Juniata■	F11
Wilkes■	J15	Wilkes	F12
Drew■	J18	Holy Family■	F14
Phila. Bible	J20	Upsala■	F16
Lycoming	J22	Lycoming■	F19

Colors: Green & Gold. Nickname: Aggies.
AD: Frank Wolfgang. SID: Matthew Levy. III

DELTA ST. .... Cleveland, MS 38733

Steve Rives (8 YRS. W-137, L-89)

Lane■	D 1	Henderson St.	J29
Lincoln Memorial	D 4	Central Ark.	J31
Ouachita Bapt.■	D 6	Ark.-Pine Bluff	F 2
Ark.-Monticello	D11	Livingston■	F 5
North Ala.■	D17	Mississippi Col.	F 7
Ark.-Pine Bluff■	J 6	Mississippi Val.	F 9
Lincoln Memorial■	J 8	West Ga.■	F12
Ouachita Bapt.	J10	Selma■	F15
Mississippi Val.■	J12	Livingston	F19
West Ga.	J15	North Ala.	F21
Mississippi Col.■	J19	Lane	F23
Ark.-Monticello■	J21	Central Ark.■	F26
Henderson St.■	J22		

Colors: Green & White. Nickname: Statesmen.
AD: Jim Jordan. SID: Jody Correro. II

DENISON .... Granville, OH 43023

Michael Sheridan (2 YRS. W-21, L-30)

Bethany (W.Va.)	N27	Wooster■	J19
Oberlin	D 1	Kenyon	J22
Kenyon■	D 4	Wilmington (Ohio)	J24
Ohio Dominican■	D 8	Bluffton■	J26
Carnegie Mellon■	D18	Ohio Wesleyan■	J29
Hiram	D21	Earlham	F 2
Rollins	D28	Case Reserve	F 5
Ill. Wesleyan☒	D29	Oberlin■	F 9
Ohio Wesleyan	J 2	Allegheny■	F12
Wittenberg■	J 5	Wooster	F16
Case Reserve■	J 8	Wittenberg	F19
Earlham■	J12	☒ Winter Park, FL	
Allegheny	J15		

Colors: Red & White. Nickname: Big Red.
AD: Larry Scheiderer. SID: Jack Hire. III

DENVER .... Denver, CO 80208

Dick Peth (8 YRS. W-150, L-81)

Denver Cl.	N26-27	Fort Lewis■	J22
Wyoming	D 1	Colo. Christian	J27
Colorado Mines Tr.	D3-4	Metropolitan St.■	J29
Chadron St.	D 7	Neb.-Kearney■	F 1
Lincoln (Mo.)■	D10	Regis (Colo.)	F 5
Northern Colo.	D11	Colorado-CS	F10
Chadron St.■	D20	Southern Colo.■	F12
Stonehill■	J 3	Regis (Colo.)■	F15
Valley City St.■	J 4	Fort Lewis	F19
Neb.-Kearney Cl.	J6-8	Colo. Christian■	F24
Colorado-CS■	J13	Metropolitan St.	F26
Southern Colo.	J15		

Colors: Crimson & Gold. Nickname: Pioneers.
AD: Jack McDonald. SID: Amy Turner. II

DETROIT MERCY .... Detroit, MI 48221

Perry Watson (1ST YR. AS HEAD COACH)

Wayne St. (Mich.)■	N27	Butler■	J22
Buffalo■	N30	Xavier (Ohio)	J26
Marquette Tr.	D3-4	La Salle■	J29
Michigan	D 6	Butler	F 4
Bowling Green■	D 8	Evansville	F 6
Michigan St.	D12	Western Ill.	F 9
Calif. (Pa.)■	D18	DePaul■	F12
Fla. Atlantic■	D20	La Salle	F16
Florida A&M Tr.	D28-29	Xavier (Ohio)■	F19
St. Louis	J 2	Loyola (Ill.)	F26
Ferris St.■	J10	Dayton	M 1
Loyola (Ill.)■	J15	Midwestern Conf.	M6-9
Evansville■	J19		

Colors: Red, White & Blue. Nickname: Titans.
AD: Brad Kinsman. SID: Mark Engel. I

DICKINSON .... Carlisle, PA 17013

David Frohman (4 YRS. W-63, L-44)

Dickinson Cl.	N19-20	Ursinus	J22
Swarthmore	D 1	York (Pa.)	J24
Elmira Tr.	D4-5	Frank. & Marsh.■	J29
Western Md.	D 7	Frostburg St.■	J31
Messiah	D 9	Johns Hopkins■	F 2
Haverford	D11	Western Md.■	F 5
Dickinson Tr.	J7-8	Gettysburg	F 9
Albright■	J13	Muhlenberg■	F12
Washington (Md.)■	J15	Frank. & Marsh.	F15
Catholic	J17	Johns Hopkins	F19
Gettysburg■	J19		

Colors: Red & White. Nickname: Red Devils.
AD: Les J. Poolman. SID: Matt Howell. III

DIST. COLUMBIA .... Washington, DC 20005

William S. Jones (9 YRS. W-179, L-71)

Shepherd	N30	Virginia St.■	J26
Shippensburg Tr.	D3-4	Hampton	J29
East Stroudsburg■	D 7	Millersville	J31
Lincoln Memorial Cl.	D18-19	Columbia Union■	F 2
Mansfield■	D21	Longwood■	F 7
Bloomsburg Inv.	J7-8	Millersville■	F 9
East Stroudsburg	J10	Gannon	F12
Longwood	J15	Hampton■	F15
Bloomsburg	J17	Kutztown■	F19
Columbia Union	J19	Cheyney■	F24
Kutztown	J22	Gannon■	F25
Cheyney	J24	Bloomsburg■	F28

Colors: Red & Yellow. Nickname: Firebirds.
AD: Dwight Datcher. SID: Donald Huff. II

DRAKE .... Des Moines, IA 50311

Rudy Washington (3 YRS. W-28, L-56)

Simpson■	N27	Illinois St.	J22
Iowa	N30	Bradley	J24
Toledo■	D 4	Tulsa■	J29
Iowa St.■	D 7	Wichita St.	F 2
Northern Iowa	D12	Indiana St.■	F 5
Bradley■	D23	Creighton	F 9
Florida A&M Tr.	D28-29	Northern Iowa■	F12
Houston	J 3	Indiana St.	F17
San Diego	J 7	Southern Ill.	F19
Southern Ill.■	J10	Illinois St.■	F24
Tulsa	J13	Southwest Mo. St.	F26
Southwest Mo. St.■	J15	Wichita St.■	F28
Creighton■	J20	Missouri Valley Conf	M5-7

Colors: Blue & White. Nickname: Bulldogs.
AD: Lynn King. SID: Mike Mahon. I

DREW .... Madison, NJ 07940

Vincent Masco (7 YRS. W-63, L-113)

Dickinson Cl.	N19-20	Swarthmore■	J20
Gettysburg	N23	FDU-Madison	J22
Caldwell	N28	Scranton■	J26
Lycoming■	D 1	Lycoming	J29
Wilkes	D 4	Allentown■	J31
Stevens Tech	D 6	Upsala■	F 2
Moravian■	D 8	Wilkes■	F 5
Albright	J 5	Delaware Valley■	F 9
Upsala	J10	King's (Pa.)	F12
Haverford	J13	Scranton	F16
King's (Pa.)■	J15	FDU-Madison■	F19
Delaware Valley	J18		

Colors: Lincoln Green & Oxford Blue. Nickname: Rangers.
AD: Vernon Mummert. SID: Ernie Larossa. III

DREXEL .... Philadelphia, PA 19104

Bill Herrion (2 YRS. W-38, L-21)

Widener■	N27	Boston U.■	J23
Lehigh	D 1	Hartford	J27
Fairfield Tr.	D3-4	Vermont	J29
Rider■	D 8	Delaware	F 5
St. Joseph's (Pa.)	D20	Vermont■	F11
Monmouth (N.J.)■	D22	Hartford■	F13
Marist Cl.	D29-30	Boston U.	F18
Md.-Balt. County	J 4	Northeastern	F20
Army	J10	New Hampshire■	F25
Rutgers	J11	Maine■	F27
Maine	J14	Delaware■	M 2
New Hampshire	J16	North Atlantic Conf.	M5-9
Northeastern■	J21		

Colors: Navy Blue & Gold. Nickname: Dragons.
AD: Johnson Bowie. SID: Jan Giel. I

■ Home games on each schedule.

See pages 405–407 for Division I tournament details

DUBUQUE .... **Dubuque, IA 52001**

Jon Davison (27 YRS. W-370, L-321)

Mt. Mercy N20
Aurora N23
Dubuque Cl. N26-27
Rockford .... D 6
Clarke■ D11
Wis.-Whitewater Tr. D29-30
Upper Iowa .... J 7
Simpson .... J 8
Wartburg■ J14
Buena Vista■ J15
Central (Iowa) J21
Loras J22
Luther■ J28
Buena Vista J29
Wartburg .... F 1
William Penn■ .... F 4
Central (Iowa)■ .... F 5
Cornell College■ F14
Upper Iowa■ F18
William Penn F19
Loras■ F22
Luther F25
Simpson■ F26

Colors: Blue and White. Nickname: Spartans.
AD: Jon Davison. SID: Rick Hecker. III

DUKE .... **Durham, NC 27708**

Mike Krzyzewski (18 YRS. W-394, L-177)

Northeastern■ N27
Citadel■ .... D 1
Xavier (Ohio)■ .... D 4
South Caro. St.■ .... D 6
Michigan D11
Iowa D22
Western Caro.■ D30
Clemson .... J 5
Georgia Tech■ .... J 8
Brown■ J10
Wake Forest■ J13
Virginia J15
North Caro. St. J20
Florida St.■ J22
Notre Dame■ J26
Maryland■ J29
North Caro. .... F 3
Clemson■ .... F 5
Georgia Tech .... F 8
Wake Forest F13
Virginia■ F16
North Caro. St.■ F20
Florida St. F23
Temple■ F27
Maryland .... M 2
North Caro.■ .... M 5
Atlantic Coast Conf. M10-13

Colors: Royal Blue & White. Nickname: Blue Devils.
AD: Tom Butters. SID: Mike Cragg. I

DUQUESNE .... **Pittsburgh, PA 15282**

John Carroll (7 YRS. W-88, L-105)

Robert Morris■ N27
N.C.-Charlotte .... D 1
Penn St. .... D 4
St. Francis (Pa.)■ .... D 8
Ohio■ D14
Pittsburgh☒ D18
Buffalo D22
St. Joseph's (Pa.)■ D28
Richmond D30
Rhode Island■ .... J 5
Massachusetts■ .... J 8
Geo. Washington J12
Notre Dame■ J15
Rhode Island J19
West Va. J26
Rutgers J29
Geo. Washington■ .... F 3
Rutgers■ .... F 6
Temple F10
St. Bonaventure F12
Fla. Atlantic■ F15
Fla. Atlantic■ F15
West Va.■ F18
Temple■ F22
St. Bonaventure■ F24
St. Joseph's (Pa.) F26
Massachusetts .... M 2
Atlantic 10 Conf. M5-10
☒ Pittsburgh, PA

Colors: Red & Blue. Nickname: Dukes.
AD: Brian Colleary. SID: Nellie King. I

EARLHAM .... **Richmond, IN 47374**

Tony Gary (1 YR. W-4, L-21)

St. Francis (Ind.)■ N20
Thomas More N23
Wabash N27
Wittenberg■ .... D 1
Oberlin .... D 4
Kenyon .... D 8
Allegheny D11
Rose-Hulman■ D15
Anderson D18
DePauw■ D30
Wooster■ .... J 8
Denison J12
Case Reserve J15
Manchester■ J17
Ohio Wesleyan J19
Oberlin■ J22
Kenyon■ J26
Allegheny■ J29
Denison■ .... F 2
Wooster .... F 5
Wittenberg .... F 9
Case Reserve■ F12
St. Francis (Ind.) F14
Ohio Wesleyan■ F16

Colors: Maroon & White. Nickname: Hustlin' Quakers.
AD: Porter Miller. SID: Pat Thomas. III

EAST CARO. .... **Greenville, NC 27858**

Eddie Payne (7 YRS. W-126, L-86)

N.C.-Charlotte N29
Mt. St. Mary's Tr. D3-4
Campbell■ .... D 6
Furman■ D16
Campbell D18
Appalachian St.■ D22
Wis.-Green Bay Tr. D30-31
Western Caro.■ .... J 3
American■ .... J 8
George Mason■ J10
Old Dominion J15
Fairfield■ J17
William & Mary J19
Richmond J22
James Madison■ J26
N.C.-Wilmington■ J29
Furman .... F 2
George Mason .... F 5
American .... F 7
Old Dominion■ F12
William & Mary■ F14
James Madison F19
Richmond■ F23
N.C.-Wilmington F26
Colonial Conf. M5-7

Colors: Purple & Gold. Nickname: Pirates.
AD: Dave Hart Jr. SID: Charles Bloom. I

EAST STROUDSBURG ..... **E. Stroudsburg, PA 18301**

Sal Mentesana (6 YRS. W-94, L-78)

Le Moyne■ N23
Phila. Textile■ N29
East Stroudsburg Cl. D3-4
Dist. Columbia .... D 7
Pracitical Bible■ .... D 9
LIU-Southampton D14
Holy Family D22
Columbia Union D30
Springfield Cl. J3-4
Lock Haven .... J 7
Dist. Columbia■ J10
Mansfield J12
Cheyney J15
Millersville■ J19
Bloomsburg■ J22
Kutztown J26
Centenary (N.J.)■ J28
West Chester .... F 2
Cheyney■ .... F 5
Mansfield■ .... F 9
Millersville F12
Kutztown■ F16
Bloomsburg F19
West Chester■ F23

Colors: Red & Black. Nickname: Warriors.
AD: Earl W. Edwards. SID: Peter Nevins. II

EAST TENN. ST. .... **Johnson City, TN 37614**

Alan LeForce (12 YRS. W-201, L-112)

Carson-Newman■ .... D 1
Wofford■ .... D 4
Michigan St. .... D 9
Virginia Tech■ D20
Ga. Southern■ D22
Kansas City Cl. D29-30
Xavier (Ohio)■ .... J 3
Citadel■ .... J 8
New Mexico St. J10
Marshall J13
Davidson■ J15
Furman J17
Va. Military J20
Appalachian St. J22
Tenn.-Chatt.■ J26
Marshall■ J29
Va. Military■ .... F 3
Tenn.-Chatt. .... F 5
Western Caro. .... F 7
Furman■ F10
Ga. Southern F12
Citadel F15
Davidson F21
Western Caro.■ F23
Appalachian St.■ F26
Southern Conf. M3-6
San Juan Shootout N26-28

Colors: Blue & Gold. Nickname: Buccaneers.
AD: Janice Shelton. SID: John Cathey. I

EAST TEX. ST. .... **Commerce, TX 75428**

Paul Peak (24 YRS. W-396, L-299)

Henderson St. N19
Southwest Baptist N20
Drury N22
LeTourneau■ .... D 3
Texas-Arlington D11
Tarleton St. J10
Jarvis Christian J13
Angelo St.■ J15
Abilene Christian■ J17
Texas A&M-Kingsville■ J20
West Tex. A&M J22
Eastern N. Mex. J24
Tarleton St.■ J27
Cameron■ J29
Central Okla.■ J31
Drury■ .... F 3
Central Okla. .... F 5
Cameron .... F 7
Jarvis Christian■ F10
Abilene Christian F12
Angelo St. F14
Eastern N. Mex.■ F19
West Tex. A&M■ F21
Texas A&M-Kingsville F24
Henderson St.■ F26

Colors: Blue & Gold. Nickname: Lions.
AD: Margo Harbison. SID: Bill Powers. II

EASTERN CONN. ST. .... **Willimantic, CT 06226**

Dan Switchenko (14 YRS. W-200, L-158)

Eastern Conn. Tr. N19-20
Mass.-Boston Inv. N27-28
North Adams St. .... D 2
Bri'water (Mass.) .... D 4
Worcester St.■ .... D 7
Southern Me. D11
Salem St. Tr. D29-30
Clark (Mass.)■ .... J 6
Rhode Island Col. J11
Plymouth St.■ J15
Western Conn. St. J18
Wheaton (Mass.) J20
Mass.-Boston■ J22
Mass.-Dartmouth J25
Rhode Island Col.■ .... F 1
Southern Me.■ .... F 5
Western Conn. St.■ .... F 8
Albertus Magnus F10
Plymouth St. F12
Mass.-Dartmouth■ F15
Mass.-Boston F17

Colors: Blue & White. Nickname: Warriors.
AD: Sharlene Peter. SID: Bob Molta. III

EASTERN ILL. .... **Charleston, IL 61920**

Rick Samuels (13 YRS. W-193, L-185)

Indiana St.■ .... D 1
Austin Peay .... D 4
Elmhurst■ .... D 9
Northeastern Ill. D11
Maine D19
Western Mich.■ D30
Iowa .... J 2
Youngstown St.■ .... J 8
Cleveland St.■ J10
Ill.-Chicago J15
Northern Ill. J17
Austin Peay■ J19
Western Ill. J22
Wis.-Green Bay■ J24
Wright St. J27
Wis.-Milwaukee■ J29
Valparaiso■ J31
Ill.-Chicago■ .... F 5
Northern Ill.■ .... F 7
Youngstown St. F12
Cleveland St. F14
Wis.-Milwaukee F19
Valparaiso F21
Wright St.■ F24
Western Ill.■ F26
Wis.-Green Bay F28
Mid-Continent Conf. M6-8

Colors: Blue & Gray. Nickname: Panthers.
AD: Mike Ryan. SID: Dave Kidwell. I

■ Home games on each schedule.

See pages 405–407 for Division I tournament details

EASTERN KY. .... Richmond, KY 40475

Mike Calhoun (1 YR. W-15, L-12)

Clinch Valley■	N27	Tenn.-Martin	J15
Chicago St.	D 1	Austin Peay	J17
Davis & Elkins■	D 4	Middle Tenn. St.■	J22
Kentucky	D 8	Tennessee Tech■	J24
Louisville	D11	Morehead St.■	J29
Wright St.■	D14	Murray St.	F 5
Indiana	D18	Southeast Mo. St.	F 7
IU/PU-Indianapolis■	D21	Austin Peay■	F12
Oklahoma Tr.	D29-30	Tennessee St.■	F14
Morehead St.	J 3	Tenn.-Martin■	F21
Southeast Mo. St.■	J 8	Tennessee Tech	F26
Murray St.■	J10	Middle Tenn. St.	F28
Tennessee St.	J13	Ohio Valley Conf.	M3-5

Colors: Maroon & White. Nickname: Colonels.
AD: Roy Kidd. SID: Karl Park. I

EAST. MENNONITE .... Harrisonburg, VA 22801

Tom Baker (1 YR. W-7, L-18)

Muhlenberg Tr.	N19-20	Guilford	J22
Messiah■	N23	Randolph-Macon■	J24
Guilford■	N30	Lynchburg■	J27
Bridgewater (Va.) Tr	D3-4	Hampden-Sydney■	J29
Va. Wesleyan	D 7	Bridgewater (Va.)	F 1
Roanoke	D 9	Randolph-Macon	F 3
Bridgewater (Va.)■	D11	Wash. & Lee	F 5
Emory & Henry■	J 8	Roanoke■	F 9
Shenandoah	J12	Hampden-Sydney	F12
Va. Wesleyan■	J17	Wash. & Lee■	F16
Lynchburg	J20	Emory & Henry	F19

Colors: Royal Blue & White. Nickname: Royals.
AD: R. Mast & Ted Kinder. SID: Larry Guengerich. III

EASTERN MICH. .... Ypsilanti, MI 48197

Ben Braun (16 YRS. W-273, L-207)

Hillsdale■	N29	Ohio	J26
Indianapolis■	D 2	Central Mich.■	J29
Wis.-Milwaukee	D 6	Bowling Green	F 2
Wisconsin	D13	Toledo	F 5
Washington St.	D19	Kent■	F 9
Chicago St.	D22	Ball St.	F12
Wis.-Green Bay Tr.	D30-31	Miami (Ohio)■	F16
Akron■	J 5	Western Mich.	F19
Toledo■	J 8	Ohio■	F23
Kent	J12	Central Mich.	F26
Ball St.■	J15	Bowling Green■	M 2
Miami (Ohio)	J19	Akron	M 5
Western Mich.■	J22	Mid-American Conf.	M8-12

Colors: Green & White. Nickname: Eagles.
AD: Tim Weiser. SID: Jim Streeter. I

EASTERN MONT. .... Billings, MT 59101

Gary Bays (17 YRS. W-249, L-248)

Montana Tech■	N23	Northern Mont.	J19
Eastern Mont. Inv.	N26-27	Grand Canyon■	J22
Rocky Mountain■	D 6	Rocky Mountain	J24
Montana St.	D11	Seattle Pacific	J27
Western Mont.■	D14	Hawaii-Hilo	F 4
Col. of Idaho■	D18	Chaminade	F 5
Cal St. Chico Tr.	D28-30	Alas. Anchorage■	F10
Hawaii-Hilo■	J 6	Alas. Fairbanks■	F12
Chaminade■	J 8	Carroll (Mont.)	F14
Carroll (Mont.)■	J10	Grand Canyon	F19
Alas. Fairbanks	J14	Seattle Pacific■	F24
Alas. Anchorage	J15		

Colors: Black & Gold. Nickname: Yellowjackets.
AD: Gary Nelson. SID: Farrell Stewart. II

EASTERN NAZARENE .... Quincy, MA 02170

Mark E. Fleming (1ST YR. AS HEAD COACH)

Plymouth St. Tr.	N19-20	Anna Maria■	J22
Wentworth Inst.■	D 3	Salve Regina	J26
MIT	D 7	Gordon■	J29
Trinity (Conn.)■	D 9	Roger Williams	F 1
King's (N.Y.)■	D11	New England Col.	F 3
Rhode Island Col.■	J 6	Curry	F 9
Suffolk■	J 8	Gordon	F12
Nyack■	J11	Salve Regina■	F15
New England Col.■	J15	Roger Williams■	F17
Wentworth Inst.	J18	Anna Maria	F19
Curry■	J20		

Colors: Red & White. Nickname: Crusaders.
AD: Carroll Bradley. SID: To be named. III

EASTERN N. MEX. .... Portales, NM 88130

Earl Diddle (9 YRS. W-164, L-101)

Adams St. Tr.	N19-20	Texas A&M-Kingsville■	J22
Fort Lewis■	N23	East Tex. St.■	J24
Tarleton St.	N29	Angelo St.	J29
Tarleton St.■	D 4	Abilene Christian	J31
N.M. Highlands	D10	Angelo St.■	F 5
Western St.	J 3	Abilene Christian■	F 7
Colo. Christian Cl.	J5-7	Central Okla.■	F12
N.M. Highlands■	J11	Cameron■	F14
Central Okla.	J15	East Tex. St.	F19
Cameron	J17	Texas A&M-Kingsville	F21
West Tex. A&M	J20	West Tex. A&M■	F26

Colors: Green & Silver. Nickname: Greyhounds.
AD: Chris Gage. SID: Wendel Sloan. II

EASTERN WASH. .... Cheney, WA 99004

John Wade (3 YRS. W-23, L-57)

Northwest Col.■	N27	Weber St.■	J29
New Mexico Lobo Cl.	D3-4	Boise St.	F 4
Gonzaga	D11	Idaho St.	F 5
Whitworth (Wash.)■	D17	Montana■	F11
Pac. Lutheran■	D20	Montana St.■	F12
Southern Utah	D28	Cal St. Sacramento■	F14
Wis.-Green Bay Tr.	D30-31	Idaho■	F19
Southern Utah■	J10	Weber St.	F24
Montana St.	J14	Northern Ariz.	F26
Montana	J15	Idaho St.■	M 3
Idaho	J21	Boise St.■	M 6
Northern Ariz.■	J27	Big Sky Conf.	M10-12

Colors: Red & White. Nickname: Eagles.
AD: John Johnson. SID: Dave Cook. I

ECKERD .... St. Petersburg, FL 33733

Jim Harley (29 YRS. W-364, L-315)

Palm Beach Atl.■	N23	North Fla.■	J19
Otterbein■	N27	Florida Tech	J22
Flagler■	D 1	St. Leo■	J26
Lewis	D 4	Rollins	J29
Morehouse■	D10	Tampa■	F 2
Nova■	D11	Fla. Southern■	F 5
American Int'l■	D31	North Fla.	F 9
Merrimack■	J 3	Florida Tech■	F12
Monmouth (Ill.)■	J 5	St. Leo	F16
Webber	J 8	Rollins■	F19
Barry	J12	Tampa	F23
Fla. Southern	J15	Barry■	F26

Colors: Red, White & Black. Nickname: Tritons.
AD: James R. Harley. SID: Bill Thornton. II

EDINBORO .... Edinboro, PA 16444

To be named

Edinboro Tr.	N19-20	Gannon■	J19
Fairmont St.■	N23	Shippensburg	J22
Mercyhurst■	D 1	Indiana (Pa.)	J26
Gannon	D 4	Lock Haven	J29
Le Moyne■	D 6	Slippery Rock■	F 2
Point Park■	D 8	Calif. (Pa.)	F 5
Columbia Union■	D18	Clarion	F 9
Lake Erie■	J 5	Mercyhurst	F12
Pitt.-Johnstown	J 8	Indiana (Pa.)■	F16
Clarion■	J12	Shippensburg■	F19
Calif. (Pa.)■	J15	Slippery Rock	F23
Dyke■	J17	Lock Haven■	F26

Colors: Red & White. Nickname: Fighting Scots.
AD: Jim McDonald. SID: Todd Jay. II

ELIZABETH CITY ST. .... Elizabeth City, NC 27909

Claudie Mackey (7 YRS. W-79, L-110)

Delaware St.	D 1	Hampton■	J27
Elizabeth City Inv.	D3-4	St. Paul's	J29
Atlantic City Cl.	D17-19	St. Paul's■	F 1
Smoke on the River	D31-J1	Bowie St.	F 3
Virginia Union	J 8	Virginia St.■	F 5
Hampton	J11	Johnson Smith■	F 7
Virginia St.	J15	Shaw■	F 9
Livingstone	J17	N.C. Central■	F12
St. Augustine's	J18	Fayetteville St.■	F14
Norfolk St.■	J22	Virginia Union■	F16
Bowie St.■	J25	Norfolk St.	F19

Colors: Royal Blue & White. Nickname: Vikings.
AD: Willie Shaw. SID: Glen Mason Jr. II

■ Home games on each schedule.

See pages 405–407 for Division I tournament details

ELIZABETHTOWN .... Elizabethtown, PA 17022

Robert Schlosser (3 YRS. W-43, L-34)

Frank. & Marsh. Cl.	N19-20	Lebanon Valley	J22
Delaware Valley■	N23	Muhlenberg	J25
King's (Pa.)■	N30	Juniata■	J27
Susquehanna■	D 2	Susquehanna	J29
Messiah	D 4	Widener■	F 2
Scranton■	D 7	Messiah■	F 5
Elizabethtown Cl.	D10-11	Moravian■	F 8
LaVerne Tr.	J7-8	Albright	F12
Widener	J12	Juniata	F17
Albright■	J15	Lebanon Valley■	F19
Moravian	J19		

Colors: Blue & Grey. Nickname: Blue Jays.
AD: D. Kenneth Ober. SID: Matt Mackowski. III

ELMHURST .... Elmhurst, IL 60126

Scott Trost (1 YR. W-10, L-15)

Lake Forest	N20	Carthage■	J19
Concordia (Ill.)■	N23	Ill. Wesleyan	J22
Concordia (Wis.)■	N30	North Central	J26
Barat	D 4	Millikin	J29
DePauw	D 8	Augustana (Ill.)	F 2
Eastern Ill.	D 9	Wheaton (Ill.)■	F 4
Regis (Colo.)	D18	North Park	F 9
Metropolitan St.	D20	Carthage	F12
Elmhurst Cl.	D29-30	Ill. Wesleyan■	F15
Judson	J 5	North Central■	F19
Wheaton (Ill.)	J11	Millikin■	F23
North Park■	J15	Augustana (Ill.)■	F26

Colors: Blue & White. Nickname: Bluejays.
AD: Chris Ragdale. SID: John Quigley. III

ELMIRA .... Elmira, NY 14901

Kevin Moore (6 YRS. W-84 , L-77)

Williams Cl.	N19-20	Nazareth (N.Y.)■	J26
Alfred	N29	Union (N.Y.)■	J29
Houghton■	D 1	St. John Fisher	F 1
Elmira Tr.	D4-5	Roberts Wesleyan■	F 3
Misericordia■	D 7	Keuka	F 5
Roanoke Tr.	J3-4	Geneseo St.	F 9
Elmira Inv.	J7-8	Albany (N.Y.)	F12
Keuka■	J12	Alfred■	F15
Hartwick■	J17	Marywood■	F22
Binghamton■	J20	Utica	F26
Utica■	J22		

Colors: Purple & Gold. Nickname: Soaring Eagles.
AD: Patricia Thompson. SID: Jim Scheible. III

ELON .... Elon College, NC 27244

Mark Simons (7 YRS. W-95, L-102)

Wofford	N30	Queens (N.C.)■	J24
Shippensburg Tr.	D3-4	Gardner-Webb	J26
S.C.-Spartanburg■	D 6	Carson-Newman	J29
Lees-McRae■	D 8	Longwood■	F 2
High Point■	D11	Wingate	F 5
Longwood	J 4	Queens (N.C.)	F 7
Barton	J 6	Mars Hill■	F 9
Wingate■	J 8	Presbyterian■	F12
Wofford■	J10	Catawba	F16
Mars Hill	J12	Lenoir-Rhyne	F19
Presbyterian	J15	Gardner-Webb■	F23
Catawba■	J19	Carson-Newman■	F26
Lenoir-Rhyne■	J22		

Colors: Maroon & Gold. Nickname: Fightin' Christians.
AD: Alan J. White. SID: David Hibbard. II

EMERSON-MCA .... Boston, MA 02116

Paul J. Cellucci (1ST YR. AS HEAD COACH)

St. John Fisher Tr.	N20-21	Rivier	J20
Notre Dame (N.H.)■	N30	Curry	J24
Elmira Tr.	D4-5	Daniel Webster	J26
Atlantic Union	D 7	Unity	J30
Lehman■	D10	Atlantic Union■	F 1
Curry■	D11	Notre Dame (N.H.)	F 3
Daniel Webster■	D13	Westbrook	F 5
Mass. Pharmacy■	D15	Nichols	F 8
St. Mary's (Md.)■	J12	Mass. Pharmacy	F10
Unity■	J15	Emerson Inv.	F12-13
Nichols■	J18		

Colors: Purple & Gold. Nickname: Lions.
AD: James Peckham. SID: To be named. III

EMORY .... Atlanta, GA 30322

Pete Manuel (1 YR. W-12, L-13)

Loyola (La.)	N19	Sewanee	J18
West Fla.	N21	New York U.■	J21
Wash. & Lee■	N23	Brandeis■	J23
Oglethorpe■	N27	Oglethorpe	J26
Citadel	N29	Washington (Mo.)	J28
Carnegie Mellon■	D 3	Chicago	J30
Case Reserve■	D 5	Brandeis	F 4
Atlanta Christian■	D 7	New York U.	F 6
Parks■	J 6	Chicago■	F11
Rochester■	J 9	Washington (Mo.)■	F13
Oglethorpe	J11	Rochester	F18
Johns Hopkins	J14	Carnegie Mellon	F20
Swarthmore	J15	Sewanee■	F23

Colors: Blue & Gold. Nickname: Eagles.
AD: Chuck Gordon. SID: John Arenberg. III

EMORY & HENRY .... Emory, VA 24327

Bob Johnson (13 YRS. W-198, L-146)

Va. Intermont■	N22	Roanoke	J26
Allegheny Cl.	N26-27	Va. Wesleyan■	J29
Roanoke■	D 1	Randolph-Macon■	J30
Maryville (Tenn.)■	D 4	Lynchburg■	F 2
Wash. & Lee	D 8	Bridgewater (Va.)■	F 5
Guilford	D11	Maryville (Tenn.)	F 6
Bridgewater (Va.)	J 6	Guilford■	F 8
East. Mennonite	J 8	Va. Wesleyan	F12
Hampden-Sydney	J15	Randolph-Macon	F13
Lynchburg	J16	King (Tenn.)	F16
Wash. & Lee■	J19	East. Mennonite■	F19
Hampden-Sydney■	J22		

Colors: Blue & Gold. Nickname: Wasps.
AD: Lou Wacker. SID: Nathan Graybeal. III

EMPORIA ST. .... Emporia, KS 66801

Ron Slaymaker (23 YRS. W-407, L-288)

Friends■	N20	Mo. Southern St.	J22
Ottawa■	N22	Washburn	J26
Minn.-Duluth Cl.	N26-27	Northwest Mo. St.■	J29
Fort Hays St.■	N29	Missouri-Rolla	F 3
Emporia St. Cl.	D3-4	Mo.-St. Louis	F 5
Fort Hays St.	D11	Pittsburg St.■	F 9
Washburn Tr.	D29-30	Northeast Mo. St.■	F12
Southwest Baptist■	J 5	Central Mo. St.	F16
Northeast Mo. St.	J 8	Mo. Western St.	F19
Central Mo. St.■	J12	Lincoln (Mo.)■	F23
Mo. Western St.■	J15	Mo. Southern St.■	F26
Lincoln (Mo.)	J19		

Colors: Black & Gold. Nickname: Hornets.
AD: Bill Quayle. SID: Dan Ballou. II

ERSKINE .... Due West, SC 29639

Ralph Patterson (1 YR. W-7 , L-20)

Coker■	N20	Belmont Abbey	J24
Western Caro.	N29	Montreat-Anderson■	J27
S.C.-Aiken■	D 4	Citadel	F 1
Carson-Newman	D11	Newberry	F 3
N.C.-Asheville	D18	Belmont Abbey■	F 7
Francis Marion■	J 4	S.C.-Aiken	F 9
Presbyterian■	J 6	Wofford■	F14
Lander	J 8	Central Wesleyan■	F16
Coker	J10	Queens (N.C.)■	F19
Kennesaw	J12	Newberry■	F23
Central Wesleyan	J15	Morris■	F26
Carson-Newman■	J17	Kennesaw■	F28
Lander■	J19	Queens (N.C.)	M 2
Wofford	J22		

Colors: Maroon & Gold. Nickname: The Flying Fleet.
AD: Bill Lesesne. SID: Dick Haldeman. II

EUREKA .... Eureka, IL 61530

Dave Darnall (19 YRS. W-356, L-146)

Capital Cl.	N19-20	McKendree	J18
Rockford■	N23	Barat■	J20
Clarke	N30	Wabash	J22
Concordia (Ill.)■	D 2	Moody Bible■	J25
Judson	D 4	Greenville	J27
Trinity Chrst. (Il.)■	D 7	Judson■	F 3
Wabash Inv.	D10-11	Barat	F 5
Trinity (Ill.)	D17	Westminster (Mo.)■	F 8
Brescia	J 8	SIU-Edwardsville	F12
Harris-Stowe■	J10	Mt. St. Clare	F16
Aurora■	J12	Greenville■	F19
Lindenwood	J15		

Colors: Maroon & Gold. Nickname: Red Devils.
AD: Warner McCollum. SID: Becky Duffield. III

■ Home games on each schedule.

See pages 405–407 for Division I tournament details

EVANSVILLE .... Evansville, IN 47722

Jim Crews (8 YRS. W-148, L-87)

Southeast Mo. St.	N27
Austin Peay■	D 1
Southern Ill.■	D 4
Western Mich.■	D 8
Valparaiso■	D11
Indiana St.■	D14
Kent■	D18
Illinois St.	D21
Hawaii Rainbow Cl.	D27-30
Coastal Caro.■	J 3
Indiana St.	J 5
Walsh■	J 9
La Salle	J15
Detroit Mercy	J19
Xavier (Ohio)■	J22
Tenn.-Martin	J26
Butler■	J29
Chicago St.	J31
Va. Commonwealth■	F 2
Detroit Mercy■	F 6
La Salle■	F10
Loyola (Ill.)■	F12
Loyola (Ill.)	F16
Butler	F19
Mo.-St. Louis■	F21
Xavier (Ohio)	F26
Tenn.-Martin■	M 2
Midwestern Conf.	M6-9

Colors: Purple & White. Nickname: Aces.
AD: Jim Byers. SID: Bob Boxell. I

FAIRFIELD .... Fairfield, CT 06430

Paul Cormier (9 YRS. W-109, L-128)

Toledo	N27
Fairfield Tr.	D3-4
Kent■	D11
Connecticut	D23
Wis.-Milwaukee■	D31
Loyola (Cal.)	J 3
Northern Ariz.	J 7
St. Peter's■	J10
Harvard■	J12
Marist■	J15
East Caro.	J17
St. Peter's	J20
Iona■	J22
Siena	J24
Loyola (Md.)■	J27
Niagara■	J29
Maine■	J31
Manhattan■	F 3
Siena■	F 5
Canisius	F10
Niagara	F12
Manhattan	F16
Iona	F19
Canisius■	F25
Loyola (Md.)	F27
Metro Atlantic Conf.	M5-7

Colors: Cardinal Red. Nickname: Stags.
AD: Harold Menninger. SID: Victor D'Ascenzo. I

FDU-MADISON .... Madison, NJ 07940

Roger Kindel (16 YRS. W-184, L-201)

FDU-Teaneck	N29
Delaware Valley	D 1
King's (Pa.)	D 4
John Jay	D 6
Albright■	D 8
Staten Island■	D11
Beaver■	D13
Trenton St. Cl.	J7-8
Scranton■	J13
Lycoming	J15
Stony Brook■	J17
Upsala■	J19
Drew■	J22
Wilkes	J26
Delaware Valley■	J29
Stevens Tech	J31
Scranton	F 2
King's (Pa.)■	F 5
Upsala	F 9
Lycoming■	F12
Centenary (N.J.)	F14
Wilkes■	F16
Drew	F19

Colors: Columbia, Navy & White. Nickname: Jersey Devils.
AD: Bill Klika. SID: Tom Bonerbo. III

FDU-TEANECK .... Teaneck, NJ 07666

Tom Green (10 YRS. W-182, L-112)

FDU-Madison■	N29
Rutgers	D 1
Pennsylvania■	D 4
Dartmouth	D11
St. Peter's	D14
Long Beach St.■	D22
ECAC Holiday Tr.	D27-29
Rider■	J 4
Mt. St. Mary's (Md.)■	J 6
Marist■	J 8
St. Francis (Pa.)	J13
Robert Morris	J15
St. Francis (N.Y.)■	J18
LIU-Brooklyn■	J20
Monmouth (N.J.)	J22
Wagner	J24
Marist	J29
Robert Morris■	F 3
St. Francis (Pa.)■	F 5
LIU-Brooklyn	F10
St. Francis (N.Y.)	F12
Wagner■	F16
Monmouth (N.J.)■	F18
Rider	F22
Mt. St. Mary's (Md.)	F26
Northeast Conf.	F28-M6

Colors: Maroon, White, Blue. Nickname: Knights.
AD: Roy Danforth. SID: Carmine Faccenda. I

FAIRMONT ST. .... Fairmont, WV 26554

Butch Haswell (1ST YR. AS HEAD COACH)

Edinboro	N23
Pitt.-Johnstown■	N27
Salem Teikyo	N29
Indiana (Pa.)	D 1
Alderson-Broaddus■	D 4
West Va. Wesleyan■	D 6
Calif. (Pa.)	D 8
Westminster (Pa.)■	J 5
Concord■	J 8
Bluefield St.	J10
Glenville St.■	J12
West Va. St.■	J15
West Va. Wesleyan	J17
West Liberty St.■	J19
Shepherd	J22
Charleston (W.Va.)■	J24
Wheeling Jesuit	J26
West Va. Tech■	J29
Alderson-Broaddus	J31
Davis & Elkins■	F 2
Glenville St.	F 5
Salem Teikyo■	F 9
West Liberty St.	F12
Shepherd■	F14
Charleston (W.Va.)	F16
Wheeling Jesuit■	F19

Colors: Maroon & White. Nickname: Falcons.
AD: Colin Cameron. SID: Jim Brinkman. II

FAYETTEVILLE ST. .... Fayetteville, NC 28301

Ricky Dickett (1ST YR. AS HEAD COACH)

Virginia St.	N20
Hampton	N23
N.C. Central Tr.	N26-27
Claflin	N29
Jacksonville St. Cl.	D3-4
Pembroke St.	D11
Bowie St.■	D13
Virginia Union■	J 5
N.C. Central	J 8
St. Paul's■	J13
Livingstone	J15
Norfolk St.■	J17
St. Augustine's	J20
Shaw■	J22
Winston-Salem	J24
Johnson Smith■	J27
N.C. Central■	J29
Livingstone■	F 2
Shaw	F 5
Claflin■	F 7
Johnson Smith	F12
Elizabeth City St.	F14
Winston-Salem■	F17
St. Augustine's■	F19

Colors: White & Blue. Nickname: Broncos.
AD: Ralph Burns. SID: John Hinton. II

FERRIS ST. .... Big Rapids, MI 49307

Tom Ludwig (16 YRS. W-272, L-147)

Indianapolis Tr.	N19-20
Calvin Cl.	N26-27
Mo. Western Cl.	D3-4
Saginaw Valley■	D 9
Northwood	D11
Lake Superior St.	D18
Wis.-Parkside	D30
Northern Mich.■	J 6
Michigan Tech■	J 8
Detroit Mercy	J10
Oakland	J13
Wayne St. (Mich.)■	J15
Wis.-Parkside■	J17
Hillsdale	J22
Grand Valley St.	J27
Lake Superior St.■	J29
Saginaw Valley	F 3
Northwood■	F 5
Northern Mich.	F10
Michigan Tech	F12
Oakland■	F17
Wayne St. (Mich.)	F19
Grand Valley St.■	F21
Hillsdale■	F26

Colors: Crimson & Gold. Nickname: Bulldogs.
AD: Tom Kirinovic. SID: Becky Olsen. II

FERRUM .... Ferrum, VA 24085

Bill Pullen (8 YRS. W-109, L-98)

Roanoke Cl.	N20-21
Chowan	N29
Gallaudet Tr.	D3-4
Newport News App.	D 7
Campbell	J 3
Wheaton (Mass.)☒	J 5
Maryville (Tenn.)	J 8
Averett■	J12
Methodist	J15
N.C. Wesleyan	J18
Chris. Newport■	J21
Greensboro	J25
Chowan■	J27
Shenandoah■	J29
Newport News App.■	J31
Averett	F 2
Methodist■	F 5
Chris. Newport	F 9
N.C. Wesleyan■	F12
Greensboro■	F14
Shenandoah	F16
Maryville (Tenn.)■	F19

☒ Rocky Mount, VA

Colors: Black & Gold. Nickname: Panthers.
AD: Hank Norton. SID: Gary Holden. III

FISK .... Nashville, TN 37203

McKinley Young (13 YRS. W-102, L-237)

Lane■	N20
Knoxville	D 1
Savannah A&D■	D 3
Stillman■	D 4
Tennessee St.	D 6
Centre■	J 9
Lane	J13
Oglethorpe■	J14
Sewanee■	J16
Rust■	J18
Knoxville■	J19
Trinity (Tex.)■	J21
Hendrix■	J23
Savannah A&D	J25
Millsaps	J28
Rhodes	J30
Oglethorpe	F 4
Sewanee	F 6
Stillman	F 8
Millsaps■	F11
Rhodes■	F13
Trinity (Tex.)	F18
Hendrix	F20
Miles	F23
Centre	F26

Colors: Blue & Gold. Nickname: Bulldogs.
AD: McKinley Young. SID: To be named. III

FITCHBURG ST. .... Fitchburg, MA 01420

Robert Bonci (4 YRS. W-26, L-69)

Plymouth St. Tr.	N19-20
Mass.-Boston Inv.	N27-28
Wentworth Inst.	N29
Western New Eng.	D 2
Anna Maria Inv.	D4-5
Worcester St.■	J11
Anna Maria	J13
Salem St.	J15
Suffolk■	J20
Westfield St.■	J22
Framingham St.	J25
North Adams St.	J29
Bri'water (Mass.)	F 1
Nichols■	F 3
Worcester St.	F 5
Salem St.■	F 8
Rivier	F10
Westfield St.	F12
Framingham St.■	F15
North Adams St.■	F17
Bri'water (Mass.)■	F19

Colors: Green, Gold & White. Nickname: Falcons.
AD: Elizabeth Kruczek. SID: Dave Marsh. III

■ Home games on each schedule.

See pages 405–407 for Division I tournament details

FLORIDA .... Gainesville, FL 32604
Lon Kruger (11 YRS. W-179, L-148)

- Florida Int'l■ ... N26
- Texas ... D 4
- South Fla.■ ... D 6
- Jacksonville ... D 8
- Stetson■ ... D11
- Florida St.☒ ... D18
- Central Fla.■ ... D20
- Villanova ... D22
- Hawaii Rainbow Cl. ... D27-30
- Louisiana St.■ ... J 5
- Tennessee ... J 8
- South Fla.◆ ... J11
- South Caro. ... J15
- Kentucky■ ... J18
- Alabama ... J22
- Georgia ... J26
- Vanderbilt■ ... J29
- Auburn■ ... F 2
- Mississippi St.■ ... F 5
- Mississippi ... F 9
- Arkansas ... F12
- Georgia■ ... F16
- South Caro.■ ... F19
- Florida St.■ ... F21
- Vanderbilt ... F26
- Kentucky ... M 2
- Tennessee■ ... M 5
- Southeastern Conf. ... M10-13

☒ Orlando, FL
◆ St. Petersburg, FL

Colors: Orange & Blue. Nickname: Gators.
AD: Jeremy Foley. SID: Joel Glass. I

FLORIDA A&M .... Tallahassee, FL 32307
Ron Brown (1ST YR. AS HEAD COACH)

- Bethune-Cookman☒ ... N26
- Old Dominion ... N29
- Miami (Fla.) ... D 4
- New Orleans ... D 6
- Alabama ... D18
- Nebraska ... D20
- Creighton ... D22
- Florida A&M Tr. ... D28-29
- Tennessee St.■ ... D29
- Md.-East. Shore ... J 8
- Delaware St. ... J10
- South Caro. St. ... J15
- North Caro. A&T ... J17
- Morgan St.■ ... J20
- Coppin St.■ ... J22
- North Caro. A&T■ ... J29
- South Caro. St.■ ... J31
- Bethune-Cookman ... F 5
- Jacksonville ... F 7
- Morgan St. ... F10
- Coppin St. ... F12
- Md.-East. Shore■ ... F19
- Delaware St.■ ... F21
- Bethune-Cookman■ ... F26
- Mid-Eastern Conf. ... M9-13

☒ Tampa, FL

Colors: Orange & Green. Nickname: Rattlers.
AD: Walter Reed. SID: Alvin Hollins. I

FLA. ATLANTIC .... Boca Raton, FL 33431
Tim Loomis (10 YRS. W-132, L-149)

- Miami (Fla.) ... N26
- Nova■ ... N29
- Florida St. ... D 1
- South Fla. ... D 3
- Jacksonville ... D11
- Stetson ... D13
- Central Fla. ... D15
- Bradley ... D18
- Detroit Mercy ... D20
- Virginia Tech■ ... D28
- Navy■ ... D30
- Miami (Fla.)■ ... J 4
- Centenary■ ... J 8
- Florida Int'l■ ... J11
- Florida Int'l ... J14
- Central Fla.■ ... J19
- Georgia St. ... J22
- Iowa St. ... J24
- Tulane■ ... J27
- Centenary ... F 3
- Auburn ... F 5
- Stetson■ ... F 7
- West Va. ... F14
- Duquesne ... F15
- Georgia St.■ ... F20
- North Caro. St. ... F28
- N.C.-Wilmington ... M 1
- Trans America Conf. ... M3-5

Colors: Blue & Gray. Nickname: Owls.
AD: Tom Scott. SID: Katrina McCormick. I

FLORIDA INT'L .... Miami, FL 33199
Bob Weltlich (15 YRS. W-197, L-235)

- Florida ... N26
- Fla. Int'l Inv. ... D3-4
- Murray St. ... D11
- Memphis St. ... D18
- Manhattan ... D21
- Navy■ ... D28
- Virginia Tech■ ... D30
- Central Fla. ... J 3
- Centenary■ ... J 6
- Southeastern La.■ ... J 8
- Fla. Atlantic ... J11
- Fla. Atlantic■ ... J14
- Stetson■ ... J17
- Georgia St. ... J20
- Samford ... J22
- Charleston (S.C.)■ ... J27
- Mercer■ ... J29
- Southeastern La. ... F 3
- Centenary ... F 5
- Stetson ... F10
- Samford■ ... F14
- Georgia St.■ ... F19
- Central Fla.■ ... F21
- Charleston (S.C.) ... F24
- Mercer ... F26
- Trans America Conf. ... M3-5

Colors: Blue & Yellow. Nickname: Golden Panthers.
AD: Ted Aceto. SID: Stuart Davisdon. I

FLA. SOUTHERN .... Lakeland, FL 33802
Gordon Gibbons (3 YRS. W-71, L-23)

- Warner Southern■ ... N22
- Nova■ ... N26
- Franklin Pierce■ ... D 4
- Webber■ ... D 9
- Rollins☒ ... D18
- Neb. Wesleyan■ ... D27
- Bryant■ ... D28
- Shippensburg■ ... D30
- Simpson■ ... J 2
- Merrimack■ ... J 5
- Gardner-Webb■ ... J 7
- Tampa ... J12
- Eckerd■ ... J15
- Barry■ ... J19
- North Fla.■ ... J26
- St. Leo ... J29
- Florida Tech■ ... F 2
- Eckerd ... F 5
- Barry ... F 9
- Rollins■ ... F12
- North Fla. ... F16
- St. Leo■ ... F19
- Florida Tech ... F23
- Tampa■ ... F26

☒ Orlando, FL

Colors: Scarlet & White. Nickname: Moccasins.
AD: Hal Smeltzly. SID: Wayne Koehler. II

FLORIDA ST. .... Tallahassee, FL 32316
Pat Kennedy (13 YRS. W-268 , L-136)

- Fla. Atlantic■ ... D 1
- Bethune-Cookman■ ... D 5
- South Fla. ... D11
- Florida☒ ... D18
- Morgan St.■ ... D20
- Mt. St. Mary's (Md.)■ ... D22
- N.C.-Greensboro■ ... D30
- Lafayette■ ... J 2
- Virginia ... J 6
- Wake Forest■ ... J 8
- Maryland ... J11
- North Caro. St. ... J16
- Clemson■ ... J19
- Duke ... J22
- North Caro.■ ... J26
- Georgia Tech ... J29
- Massachusetts ... F 3
- Virginia■ ... F 6
- Wake Forest ... F10
- Maryland■ ... F12
- North Caro. St.■ ... F16
- Clemson ... F19
- Florida ... F21
- Duke■ ... F23
- North Caro. ... F26
- Georgia Tech■ ... M 2
- Atlantic Coast Conf. ... M10-13

☒ Orlando, FL

Colors: Garnet & Gold. Nickname: Seminoles.
AD: Bob Goin. SID: Rob Wilson. I

FLORIDA TECH .... Melbourne, FL 32901
Andy Russo (11 YRS. W-193, L-133)

- Florida Tech Cl. ... N26-27
- Nova■ ... D 1
- Webber■ ... D 7
- Lynn■ ... D11
- St. Francis (Ill.)■ ... D30
- Bentley■ ... J 2
- Hannibal-La Grange■ ... J 4
- Florida Tech Tr. ... J7-8
- North Fla. ... J12
- Rollins ... J15
- St. Leo■ ... J19
- Eckerd■ ... J22
- Tampa ... J26
- Barry■ ... J29
- Fla. Southern ... F 2
- Rollins■ ... F 5
- Mississippi St. ... F 8
- St. Leo ... F 9
- Eckerd ... F12
- Tampa■ ... F16
- Barry ... F19
- Fla. Southern■ ... F23
- North Fla.■ ... F26

Colors: Crimson & Gray. Nickname: Panthers.
AD: Bill Jurgens. SID: Mike Stern. II

FONTBONNE .... St. Louis, MO 63105
Lee McKinney (15 YRS. W-254, L-200)

- Concordia (Mo.)■ ... N19
- Sanford Brown■ ... N22
- St. Louis Christian■ ... N30
- Southern Cal Col.■ ... D 3
- Wabash■ ... D 4
- Westminster (Mo.)■ ... D 7
- Mo.-St. Louis ... D11
- Concordia (Mo.) ... D14
- Occidental■ ... D15
- Puerto Rico Tr. ... D29-J5
- Maryville (Mo.) ... J11
- Webster■ ... J17
- Parks ... J20
- Blackburn ... J22
- MacMurray ... J25
- Principia■ ... J27
- Webster ... J29
- MacMurray■ ... F 3
- Maryville (Mo.)■ ... F 5
- Greenville■ ... F 7
- Westminster (Mo.) ... F10
- Parks■ ... F12
- Blackburn■ ... F17
- Principia ... F19

Colors: Purple & Gold. Nickname: Griffins.
AD: Lee McKinney. SID: To be named. III

FORDHAM .... Bronx, NY 10458
Nick Macarchuk (16 YRS. W-259, L-208)

- Adelphi■ ... N29
- Manhattan■ ... D 4
- Boston U. ... D 8
- Iona ... D11
- St. John's (N.Y.)☒ ... D18
- Southwest Mo. St.■ ... D21
- Arizona Tr. ... D28-30
- Notre Dame ... J 2
- Holy Cross■ ... J 8
- Bucknell ... J12
- Army ... J15
- Columbia■ ... J17
- Lehigh■ ... J19
- Colgate ... J22
- Lafayette ... J26
- Navy■ ... J29
- Holy Cross ... F 2
- Bucknell■ ... F 5
- Army■ ... F 9
- Lehigh ... F12
- Hofstra ... F14
- Colgate■ ... F16
- Lafayette■ ... F19
- Loyola (Md.)■ ... F21
- Navy ... F26
- Patriot Conf. ... M4-11

☒ Uniondale, NY

Colors: Maroon & White. Nickname: Rams.
AD: Frank McLaughlin. SID: Bill Holtz. I

FORT HAYS ST. .... Hays, KS 67601
Gary Garner (10 YRS. W-139, L-146)

- Fort Hays St. Cl. ... N19-20
- Sterling■ ... N23
- Emporia St. ... N29
- Rockhurst■ ... D 1
- Washburn ... D 4
- Friends■ ... D 7
- Pittsburg St.■ ... D 8
- Emporia St.■ ... D11
- Northeast Mo. St.■ ... D18
- Ottawa■ ... J 6
- Neb.-Kearney■ ... J10
- Chadron St. ... J13
- Colorado Mines ... J15
- Mesa St.■ ... J21
- Western St.■ ... J22
- N.M. Highlands ... J27
- Adams St. ... J29
- Mesa St. ... F 4
- Western St. ... F 5
- Chadron St.■ ... F11
- Colorado Mines■ ... F12
- Neb.-Kearney ... F14
- N.M. Highlands■ ... F18
- Adams St.■ ... F19
- Rockhurst ... F23

Colors: Black & Gold. Nickname: Tigers.
AD: Tom Spicer. SID: Jack Kuestermeyer. II

■ Home games on each schedule.

See pages 405–407 for Division I tournament details

FORT LEWIS .... Durango, CO 81301

Jim Cross (10 YRS. W-116, L-149)

Adams St. Tr. N19-20
N.M. Highlands N22
Eastern N. Mex. N23
Western St.■ N29
Adams St.■ N30
Mesa St.■ .... D 4
Colorado Col.■ D11
N.M. Highlands■ D13
Colorado St. D30
Amer. Indian Bib.■ .... J 4
Western St. .... J 8
Colo. Christian■ J14
Metropolitan St.■ J15
Regis (Colo.) J20
Denver J22
Colorado-CS J28
Southern Colo. J29
Mesa St. .... F 1
Colo. Christian F10
Metropolitan St. F12
Regis (Colo.)■ F18
Denver■ F19
Adams St. F22
Colorado-CS■ F24
Southern Colo.■ F26

Colors: Blue & Gold. Nickname: Raiders.
AD: Bruce Grimes. SID: Chris Aaland. II

FORT VALLEY ST. .... Ft. Valley, GA 31030

To be named

Fla. Memorial■ N20
LeMoyne-Owen N27
Georgia Col.■ N29
Tuskegee .... D 4
Nova D10
Fla. Memorial D11
Georgia Col. D13
Morehouse .... J 5
Savannah St.■ .... J 8
Morris Brown J12
Albany St. (Ga.)■ J15
Paine J17
Miles J19
Savannah St. J22
Morris Brown■ J26
LeMoyne-Owen■ J29
Alabama A&M■ J31
Tuskegee■ .... F 3
Albany St. (Ga.) .... F 4
Alabama A&M .... F 7
Clark Atlanta F12
Paine■ F15
Clark Atlanta■ F19
Morehouse■ F23
Miles■ F26

Colors: Old Gold & Blue. Nickname: Wildcats.
AD: Douglas Porter. SID: Russell Boone, Jr. II

FRAMINGHAM ST. .... Framingham, MA 01701

Togo Palazzi (2 YRS. W-29 , L-22)

Rhode Island Col. N30
Clark (Mass.) .... D 7
Tufts■ .... D 9
Wheaton (Mass.)■ D11
Western New Eng.■ D13
North Adams St.■ J11
Nichols■ J13
Bri'water (Mass.) J15
Worcester St.■ J18
Salem St. J22
Fitchburg St.■ J25
Mass.-Dartmouth J27
Westfield St.■ J29
Amherst .... F 1
North Adams St. .... F 5
Bri'water (Mass.)■ .... F 8
Worcester St. F10
Salem St.■ F12
Fitchburg St. F15
Westfield St. F17

Colors: Black & Gold. Nickname: Rams.
AD: Lawrence Boyd. SID: Kenneth George. III

FRANCIS MARION .... Florence, SC 29501

Lewis Hill (23 YRS. W-396, L-259)

Barton Cl. N19-20
Francis Marion Tr. N26-27
Coastal Caro.■ N30
Franic Marion Cl. D3-4
Augusta■ .... D 7
Erskine .... J 4
Columbus■ .... J 8
S.C.-Aiken■ J10
Pembroke St.■ J12
Lander J15
S.C.-Spartanburg J19
Armstrong St.■ J24
Newberry■ J26
Georgia Col.■ J29
Pembroke St. .... F 2
Georgia Col. .... F 5
Newberry .... F 7
Armstrong St. .... F 9
Columbus F12
S.C.-Spartanburg■ F16
Augusta F19
S.C.-Aiken F23
Lander■ F26

Colors: Red, White & Blue. Nickname: Patriots.
AD: Gerald Griffin. SID: Michael G. Hawkins. II

FRANK. & MARSH. .... Lancaster, PA 17604

Glenn Robinson (22 YRS. W-427, L-171)

Frank. & Marsh. Cl. N19-20
Haverford N23
Albright■ .... D 2
Muhlenberg .... D 4
Johns Hopkins■ .... D 7
York (Pa.)■ .... D 9
Frank. & Marsh. Tr. J4-5
Juniata Tr. J8-9
Lincoln (Pa.)■ J12
Ursinus■ J15
Western Md. J18
Swarthmore■ J22
Princeton J24
Gettysburg J26
Dickinson J29
Lebanon Valley J31
Johns Hopkins .... F 5
Western Md.■ .... F 8
Gettysburg■ F12
Dickinson■ F15
Washington (Md.)■ F19

Colors: Blue & White. Nickname: Diplomats.
AD: William A. Marshall. SID: Tom Byrnes. III

FRANKLIN .... Franklin, IN 46131

Kerry Prather (10 YRS. W-161, L-114)

North Central Cl. N19-20
Adrian N23
IUPU-Indy Tr. N27-29
Kalamazoo■ .... D 4
Defiance .... D 7
Franklin Cl. D10-11
Millikin■ D18
Manchester■ .... J 5
Thomas More .... J 8
Rose-Hulman J12
Anderson■ J15
Knox J17
Wabash■ J19
DePauw J22
Hanover J26
Manchester .... F 2
Anderson .... F 5
Rose-Hulman■ .... F 9
DePauw■ F12
Wabash F16
Hanover■ F19

Colors: Blue & Gold. Nickname: Grizzlies.
AD: Kerry Prather. SID: Kevin Elixman. III

FRANKLIN PIERCE .... Rindge, NH 03461

Arthur Luptowski (4 YRS. W-80, L-39)

Keene St. Cl. N19-20
American Int'l N23
St. Rose■ N29
Tampa .... D 2
Fla. Southern .... D 4
Assumption .... D 7
Springfield D14
New York Tech■ D29
Quincy■ D30
Le Moyne■ .... J 5
Sacred Heart J12
Southern Conn. St. J15
Mass.-Lowell■ J19
Bridgeport■ J22
Keene St. J26
Le Moyne J29
New Haven■ J31
New Hamp. Col. .... F 2
Southern Conn. St.■ .... F 5
Mass.-Lowell .... F 9
Bridgeport F12
Sacred Heart■ F14
New Hamp. Col.■ F16
New Haven F19
Keene St.■ F23

Colors: Crimson & Gray. Nickname: Ravens.
AD: Bruce Kirsh. SID: Jon Tirone. II

FREDONIA ST. .... Fredonia, NY 14063

Gregory Prechtl (16 YRS. W-184, L-214)

Rochester Tip-Off N19-20
Buffalo St.■ .... D 3
Binghamton .... D 4
Geneseo St.■ .... D 7
Penn St.-Behrend D10
Thiel D11
Penn St.-Behrend■ J12
Potsdam St.■ J14
Plattsburgh St.■ J15
St. John Fisher J18
Oswego St. J21
Utica Tech J22
Brockport St. J25
Roberts Wesleyan■ J27
Cortland St.■ J29
Nazareth (N.Y.) .... F 1
Geneseo St. .... F 4
Brockport St.■ .... F 5
New Paltz St. F11
Oneonta St. F12
Buffalo St. F15
Oswego St.■ F18
Utica Tech■ F19

Colors: Blue & White. Nickname: Blue Devils.
AD: Tom Prevet. SID: Donna Hart. III

FRESNO ST. .... Fresno, CA 93740

Gary Colson (32 YRS. W-529, L-359)

Cal Poly SLO■ N28
Pepperdine .... D 1
San Jose St.■ .... D 4
Washington■ .... D 7
Pacific (Cal.) D11
Oregon St.■ D18
Nevada D20
Fresno St. Cl. D27-28
Colorado St. .... J 3
Wyoming .... J 5
UTEP■ .... J 8
New Mexico■ J10
Brigham Young J13
Utah J15
Air Force J22
San Diego St.■ J27
Hawaii■ J29
San Diego St. .... F 3
Hawaii .... F 5
Air Force■ F12
Utah■ F17
Brigham Young■ F19
UTEP F24
New Mexico F26
Colorado St.■ .... M 3
Wyoming■ .... M 5
Western Ath. Conf. M9-12

Colors: Cardinal & Blue. Nickname: Bulldogs.
AD: Gary Cunningham. SID: Scott Johnson. I

FROSTBURG ST. .... Frostburg, MD 21532

Oscar Lewis (8 YRS. W-96, L-96)

Frostburg St. Inv. N19-20
Washington (Md.) N23
Wesley N29
Shenandoah■ .... D 4
Bethany (W.Va.) D13
Baldwin-Wallace■ D15
Shenandoah D18
Wash. & Jeff. .... J 5
Frostburg St. Tr. J7-8
Grove City J12
Lincoln (Pa.) J15
Juniata■ J17
Bethany (W.Va.)■ J20
Goucher■ J24
Salisbury St.■ J29
Dickinson J31
Chowan■ .... F 5
Waynesburg .... F 9
Mary Washington■ F12
Wesley■ F14
Lincoln (Pa.)■ F19
Salisbury St. F24
Chowan F26

Colors: Red, White & Black. Nickname: Bobcats.
AD: Loyal Park. SID: Jeff Krone. III

■ Home games on each schedule.

See pages 405–407 for Division I tournament details

FURMAN .... Greenville, SC 29613

Butch Estes (13 YRS. W-217, L-167)

Wofford■	N29	Va. Military■	J24
Clemson	D 4	Citadel	J26
South Caro. St.■	D 8	Western Caro.	J29
East Caro.	D16	East Caro.■	F 2
Charleston So.	D18	Citadel■	F 5
Kansas	D20	Ga. Southern■	F 7
James Madison■	D28	East Tenn. St.	F10
Tenn.-Chatt.■	J 5	Davidson■	F12
Davidson	J 8	Appalachian St.	F17
Western Caro.■	J13	Tenn.-Chatt.	F23
Appalachian St.■	J15	Va. Military	F26
East Tenn. St.■	J17	Marshall■	F28
Ga. Southern	J19	Southern Conf.	M3-6
Marshall	J22		

Colors: Purple & White. Nickname: Paladins.
AD: Ray Parlier. SID: Hunter Reid. I

GANNON .... Erie, PA 16541

Bob Dukiet (14 YRS. W-257, L-144)

Edinboro Tr.	N19-20	Indiana (Pa.)	J15
Pitt.-Bradford■	N23	Edinboro	J19
Gannon Cl.	N26-27	Lock Haven	J24
Clarion■	D 1	Pitt.-Johnstown	J29
Edinboro■	D 4	Mercyhurst	F 2
St. Vincent■	D 6	Pitt.-Johnstown■	F 5
Lake Erie■	D11	Dist. Columbia■	F12
Kentucky St.■	D17	Le Moyne■	F16
Columbia Union■	D19	Slippery Rock■	F21
Gannon Tr.	D29-30	Dist. Columbia	F25
Springfield Cl.	J3-4	St. Vincent	F28
Mansfield	J 8	Mercyhurst■	M 4

Colors: Maroon & Gold. Nickname: Golden Knights.
AD: Howard Elwell. SID: Bob Shreve. II

GARDNER-WEBB .... Boiling Springs, NC 28017

Jim Johnson (3 YRS. W-47 , L-39)

Gardner-Webb Tr.	N19-20	Wingate	J22
Limestone	N23	Elon■	J26
Pfeiffer Inv.	N26-27	Catawba■	J29
Queens (N.C.)	D 1	Presbyterian	F 5
Longwood Tr.	D3-4	Lees-McRae■	F 7
Presbyterian■	D11	Carson-Newman	F 9
Fla. Southern	J 7	Mars Hill■	F12
Rollins	J 8	Lenoir-Rhyne■	F16
Carson-Newman■	J12	Wingate■	F19
Mars Hill	J15	Elon	F23
Lenoir-Rhyne	J19	Catawba	F26

Colors: Scarlet, White & Black. Nickname: Bulldogs.
AD: Woody Fish. SID: Mark Wilson. II

GENESEO ST. .... Geneseo, NY 14454

Tom Pope (24 YRS. W-306 , L-280)

Ohio Wesleyan Tr.	N19-20	Potsdam St.	J28
Cortland St.	D 3	Plattsburgh St.	J29
Brockport St.	D 4	Fredonia St.■	F 4
Fredonia St.	D 7	Oswego St.	F 5
New Paltz St.■	D10	Elmira■	F 9
Oneonta St.■	D11	St. John Fisher■	F11
Roberts Wesleyan	J 8	Binghamton■	F12
Rochester Tr.	J12-15	Utica Tech	F15
Utica Tech■	J18	Buffalo St.■	F18
Buffalo St.	J21	Brockport St.■	F19
Oswego St.■	J25		

Colors: Blue & White. Nickname: Blue Knights.
AD: John Spring. SID: Fred Bright. III

GEORGE MASON .... Fairfax, VA 22030

Paul Westhead (14 YRS. W-247, L-153)

Troy St.■	N27	Richmond■	J19
Bucknell	D 1	Old Dominion■	J22
Northeastern	D 4	William & Mary	J26
Radford	D 6	American	J29
Niagara■	D 9	Canisius	F 1
St. Peter's■	D11	East Caro.■	F 5
Va. Commonwealth■	D22	N.C.-Wilmington■	F 7
Iona College Tr.	D28-29	James Madison	F12
Morgan St.■	J 2	Richmond	F16
Louisville	J 4	Old Dominion	F19
N.C.-Wilmington	J 8	William & Mary■	F23
East Caro.	J10	American■	F26
James Madison■	J15	Colonial Conf.	M5-7

Colors: Green & Gold. Nickname: Patriots.
AD: Jack Kvancz. SID: Carl Sell. I

GEO. WASHINGTON .... Washington, DC 20052

Mike Jarvis (8 YRS. W-157, L-84)

American	N29	Temple■	J29
Charlotte Tr.	D3-4	West Va.■	F 1
Geo. Washington Tr.	D10-11	Duquesne	F 3
Pepperdine■	D18	St. Joseph's (Pa.)■	F 5
Sugar Bowl Tr.	D27-28	Xavier (Ohio)	F12
St. Bonaventure	J 3	Rutgers	F15
Rutgers■	J 6	St. Bonaventure■	F18
Temple	J 8	Rhode Island■	F21
Duquesne■	J12	N.C.-Charlotte■	F24
West Va.	J16	Massachusetts■	F27
St. Joseph's (Pa.)	J19	Rhode Island	M 2
Massachusetts	J22	Atlantic 10 Conf.	M5-10

Colors: Buff & Blue. Nickname: Colonials.
AD: Steve Bilsky. SID: Betsy Barrett. I

GEORGETOWN .... Washington, DC 20057

John Thompson (21 YRS. W-484, L-178)

Maryland	N26	Miami (Fla.)■	J29
Villanova■	D 4	Boston College	J31
Miami (Fla.)	D 7	Seton Hall■	F 5
Morgan St.■	D10	Syracuse■	F 7
UC Irvine■	D18	Providence	F12
Memphis St.	D30	Pittsburgh■	F16
Connecticut	J 4	St. John's (N.Y.)	F19
Nevada-Las Vegas■	J 8	Villanova	F22
St. John's (N.Y.)■	J12	Boston College■	F26
Providence■	J15	Connecticut■	F28
Seton Hall	J17	Syracuse	M 6
DePaul	J22	Big East Conf.	M10-13
Pittsburgh	J24		

Colors: Blue & Gray. Nickname: Hoyas.
AD: Francis X. Rienzo. SID: Bill Shapland. I

GEORGIA .... Athens, GA 30613

Hugh Durham (27 YRS. W-495, L-284)

Pre-Season NIT	N17-26	Florida■	J26
Western Caro.■	D 4	South Caro.	J29
Bethune-Cookman■	D 7	Stetson■	J31
Georgia Tech⊠	D15	Alabama■	F 5
Kansas⊠	D18	Notre Dame⊠	F 6
Winthrop■	D21	Tennessee■	F12
Washington Tr.	D28-29	Florida	F16
Auburn	J 5	Louisiana St.	F19
Kentucky■	J 8	Arkansas■	F22
Tennessee	J12	Kentucky	F27
Mississippi St.	J15	South Caro.■	M 2
Vanderbilt■	J19	Vanderbilt	M 5
Mississippi■	J22	Southeastern Conf.	M10-13
Texas	J23	⊠ Atlanta, GA	

Colors: Red & Black. Nickname: Bulldogs.
AD: Vince Dooley. SID: Norm Reilly. I

GEORGIA COL. .... Milledgeville, GA 31061

To be named

North Ga.■	N22	Valdosta St.	J24
Kennesaw	N24	Augusta	J26
Ga. Southern	N26	Francis Marion	J29
Fort Valley St.	N29	S.C.-Spartanburg	J31
Voorhees	D10	Columbus■	F 3
Fort Valley St.■	D13	Francis Marion■	F 5
Kennesaw■	D15	Augusta■	F 7
Armstrong St.■	J 6	Pembroke St.■	F12
Pembroke St.	J 8	S.C.-Aiken■	F17
S.C.-Spartanburg■	J13	Lander	F19
S.C.-Aiken	J15	Valdosta St.■	F21
Columbus	J19	North Ga.	F23
Lander■	J22	Armstrong St.	F26

Colors: Brown & Gold. Nickname: Colonials.
AD: Stan Aldridge. SID: Don Carswell. II

GA. SOUTHERN .... Statesboro, GA 30460

Frank Kerns (20 YRS. W-366, L-196)

Georgia Col.■	N26	Tenn.-Chatt.	J22
Presbyterian■	D 3	Western Caro.	J24
South Caro.	D 7	Davidson■	J26
Brewton Parker■	D10	Citadel	J29
Valdosta St.■	D14	Davidson	F 5
Purdue	D18	Furman	F 7
East Tenn. St.	D22	East Tenn. St.■	F12
Michigan St. Cl.	D29-30	Appalachian St.■	F14
Citadel■	J 5	Va. Military	F19
Appalachian St.	J 8	Marshall	F21
Marshall■	J15	Western Caro.■	F26
Va. Military■	J17	Tenn.-Chatt.■	F28
Furman■	J19	Southern Conf.	M3-6

Colors: Blue & White. Nickname: Eagles.
AD: David Wagner. SID: Jim Stephan. I

■ Home games on each schedule.

See pages 405–407 for Division I tournament details

GEORGIA ST. .... Atlanta, GA 30303

Bob Reinhart (8 YRS. W-94, L-134)

Morris Brown■	N27	Fla. Atlantic■	J22
Georgia Tech	D 4	Samford■	J29
Alabama St.	D 8	Charleston (S.C.)■	J31
Memphis St.	D11	Central Fla.	F 3
Tenn.-Martin■	D13	Stetson	F 5
Southwest Tex. St.■	D15	Southeastern La.■	F10
N.C.-Wilmington Cl.	D17-18	Centenary■	F12
Mercer	J 3	Samford	F17
Stetson■	J 6	Florida Int'l	F19
Central Fla.■	J 8	Fla. Atlantic	F20
Centenary	J13	Charleston (S.C.)	F26
Southeastern La.	J15	Mercer■	F28
Florida Int'l■	J20	Trans America Conf.	M3-5

Colors: Royal & Crimson. Nickname: Panthers.
AD: Orby Moss, Jr. SID: Martin Harmon. I

GEORGIA TECH .... Atlanta, GA 30332

Bobby Cremins (18 YRS. W-340, L-205)

Michigan⊠	N26	North Caro. St.	J26
North Caro. A&T■	N30	Florida St.■	J29
Western Caro.■	D 2	Clemson	F 2
Georgia St.■	D 4	Maryland	F 5
Mercer■	D11	Duke■	F 8
Georgia ◆	D15	North Caro.	F12
Vanderbilt ◆	D18	Wake Forest■	F19
Mt. St. Mary's (Md.)■	D20	Virginia	F22
ECAC Holiday Tr.	D27-29	North Caro. St.■	F26
Maryland■	J 4	Florida St.	M 2
Duke	J 8	Clemson■	M 5
North Caro.■	J12	Atlantic Coast Conf.	M10-13
Louisville	J15	⊠ Springfield, MA	
Wake Forest	J19	◆ Atlanta, GA	
Virginia■	J23		

Colors: Old Gold & White. Nickname: Yellow Jackets.
AD: Homer Rice. SID: Mike Finn. I

GETTYSBURG .... Gettysburg, PA 17325

George Petrie (4 YRS. W-37, L-60)

Gettysburg Tr.	N19-20	Swarthmore	J17
Drew■	N23	Dickinson	J19
Ursinus	D 1	Washington (Md.)■	J22
Haverford■	D 4	Frank. & Marsh.■	J26
Goucher	D 8	Johns Hopkins■	J29
Messiah■	D11	Western Md.	F 2
Navy	D22	York (Pa.)	F 5
Bethany (W.Va.)	J 5	Dickinson■	F 9
Moravian Tr.	J7-8	Frank. & Marsh.	F12
Alvernia■	J12	Johns Hopkins	F16
Muhlenberg	J15	Western Md.■	F19

Colors: Orange & Blue. Nickname: Bullets.
AD: Charles Winters. SID: Robert Kenworthy. III

GLENVILLE ST. .... Glenville, WV 26351

Gary Nottingham (11 YRS. W-152, L-138)

Pitt.-Johnstown Tr.	N19-20	Alderson-Broaddus■	J22
St. Vincent■	D 1	Bluefield St.	J24
Indiana (Pa.)■	D 4	Concord■	J26
Salem Teikyo	D 6	Wheeling Jesuit■	J29
Charleston (W.Va.)	D11	West Va. St.	F 2
West Va. Wesleyan■	D13	Fairmont St.■	F 5
Salem Teikyo■	J 5	West Va. Wesleyan	F 9
Shepherd	J 8	West Va. Tech■	F12
West Liberty St.■	J10	Alderson-Broaddus	F14
Fairmont St.	J12	Bluefield St.■	F16
Davis & Elkins■	J15	Concord	F19
West Va. Tech	J19		

Colors: Royal Blue & White. Nickname: Pioneers.
AD: Russell Shepherd. SID: Mark Loudin. II

GONZAGA .... Spokane, WA 99258

Dan Fitzgerald (11 YRS. W-172, L-133)

Stanford Inv.	N26-27	St. Mary's (Cal.)	J22
Canisius College Cl.	D3-4	St. Mary's (Cal.)■	J27
Whitman■	D 7	Santa Clara■	J29
Eastern Wash.■	D11	Loyola (Cal.)	F 4
Western Mont.■	D18	Pepperdine	F 5
Idaho■	D21	Pepperdine■	F10
Shootout Spokane	D27-28	Loyola (Cal.)■	F12
Weber St.■	J 6	Portland■	F16
Idaho St.	J 8	Portland	F19
San Diego■	J13	San Francisco	F24
San Francisco■	J15	San Diego	F26
Santa Clara	J21	West Coast Conf.	M5-7

Colors: Blue, White & Red. Nickname: Bulldogs, Zags.
AD: Dan Fitzgerald. SID: Oliver Pierce. I

GORDON .... Wenham, MA 01984

Steve Heintz (2 YRS. W-25, L-26)

Eastern (Pa.) Tr.	N19-20	Wentworth Inst.■	J22
St. Joseph's (Me.)	N23	Curry	J26
Western New Eng.■	N30	Eastern Nazarene	J29
MIT■	D 2	New England Col.■	F 1
Plymouth St.■	D 4	Roger Williams■	F 3
Colby-Sawyer	D 7	Anna Maria■	F 5
Lehman■	D11	Salve Regina	F 9
Colby■	J 8	Eastern Nazarene■	F12
Salem St.	J12	Curry■	F15
Roger Williams	J15	New England Col.	F17
Anna Maria	J18	Wentworth Inst.	F19
Salve Regina■	J20		

Colors: Blue & White. Nickname: The Fighting Scots.
AD: Walter Bowman. SID: Marc Whitehouse. III

GOUCHER .... Baltimore, MD 21204

Leonard Trevino (3 YRS. W-19 , L-52)

Hampden-Sydney Cl.	N19-20	Mary Washington■	J22
Valley Forge Chrst.	N23	Frostburg St.	J24
Johns Hopkins■	N30	Catholic■	J27
Wesley■	D 2	Marymount (Va.)	J29
Bloomsburg	D 4	York (Pa.)■	J31
Gettysburg■	D 8	Catholic	F 3
Slippery Rock	D11	St. Mary's (Md.)■	F 5
Frank. & Marsh. Tr.	J4-5	Mary Washington	F10
New Paltz St.■	J 9	Gallaudet■	F12
York (Pa.)	J13	Haverford■	F15
St. Mary's (Md.)	J15	Marymount (Va.)■	F17
Gallaudet	J18		

Colors: Blue & Gold. Nickname: Gophers.
AD: William J. Kaiser. SID: Kevin Fillman. III

GRAMBLING .... Grambling, LA 71245

Aaron James (6 YRS. W-57, L-112)

Ark.-Pine Bluff■	N29	Jackson St.■	J24
Texas-San Antonio	D 1	Mississippi Val.	J29
Bapt. Christian■	D 4	Alcorn St.	F 5
Texas-San Antonio■	D 7	Southern-B.R.	F 7
Texas Col.■	D11	Texas Southern■	F12
N.C.-Wilmington Cl.	D17-18	Prairie View■	F14
Ark.-Lit. Rock■	D21	Alabama St.	F19
Wisconsin	D29	Jackson St.	F21
Alcorn St.■	J 8	Southeastern La.■	F23
Southern-B.R.■	J10	Mississippi Val.■	F26
Texas Southern	J15	Ark.-Lit. Rock	F28
Prairie View	J17	Southwestern Conf.	M9-13
Alabama St.■	J22		

Colors: Black & Gold. Nickname: Tigers.
AD: Fred Hobdy. SID: Stanley Lewis. I

GRAND CANYON .... Phoenix, AZ 85017

Leighton McCrary (3 YRS. W-60, L-29)

Grand Canyon Cl.	N26-27	Eastern Mont.	J22
BYU-Hawaii■	N30	Western N. Mex.■	J25
Southern Colo. Tr.	D3-4	Seattle Pacific	J29
Minn.-Duluth■	D16	Chaminade	F 4
Cal St. Dom. Hills	D21	Hawaii-Hilo	F 5
Cal St. San B'dino	D22	Alas. Fairbanks■	F10
South Dak.■	D27	Alas. Anchorage■	F12
Grand Canyon Cl.	D30-31	Cal St. Northridge	F15
Chaminade■	J 6	Eastern Mont.■	F19
Hawaii-Hilo■	J 8	Western N. Mex.	F22
Alas. Anchorage	J14	Seattle Pacific■	F26
Alas. Fairbanks	J15		

Colors: Purple & White. Nickname: Antelopes.
AD: Gil Stafford. SID: ElizaBeth Warner. II

GRAND VALLEY ST. .... Allendale, MI 49401

Tom Villemure (22 YRS. W-407, L-220)

Ashland	N19	Lake Superior St.	J20
St. Joseph's (Ind.)■	N22	Wayne St. (Mich.)■	J22
Lewis■	N23	Ferris St.■	J27
Northwood■	D 4	Northwood	J29
Oakland	D 9	Oakland■	F 3
Hillsdale	D11	Hillsdale■	F 5
Southern Ind. Tr.	D18-19	Michigan Tech	F10
Aquinas	D29	Northern Mich.	F12
Mo.-Rolla Tr.	J1-2	Saginaw Valley■	F19
Michigan Tech■	J 6	Ferris St.	F21
Northern Mich.■	J 8	Lake Superior St.■	F24
Saginaw Valley	J15	Wayne St. (Mich.)	F26

Colors: Blue, Black & White. Nickname: Lakers.
AD: Michael Kovalchik. SID: Don Thomas. II

■ Home games on each schedule.

See pages 405–407 for Division I tournament details

GREENSBORO .... Greensboro, NC 27420

Samuel Hanger (3 YRS. W-36, L-42)

Dickinson Cl. N19-20
Guilford N23
Maryville (Tenn.) N28
Bridgewater (Va.) Tr D3-4
Guilford■ .... D 7
Newport News App.■ D11
Marymount Tr. J8-9
Methodist■ J12
Averett J15
Shenandoah J19
Savannah A&D■ J21
Newport News App. J22
Ferrum■ J25
N.C. Wesleyan J29
Chris. Newport J30
Methodist .... F 2
Averett■ .... F 5
N.C. Wesleyan■ .... F 9
Shenandoah■ F12
Ferrum F14
Chris. Newport■ F18

Colors: Green & White. Nickname: The Pride.
AD: Kim Strable. SID: Samuel Hanger. III

GRINNELL .... Grinnell, IA 50112

David Arseneault (4 YRS. W-31, L-57)

Grinnell Tr. N19-20
Principia N27
Maryville (Mo.) N28
Illinois Col. .... D 3
Knox .... D 4
Cornell College■ D10
William Penn .... J 5
Northeastern Ill. .... J 8
Barat■ J11
Coe J14
Cornell College J18
Ripon■ J22
Lake Forest■ J23
Carroll (Wis.) J29
Beloit J30
Monmouth (Ill.) .... F 4
Grand View .... F 7
Coe■ F11
Monmouth (Ill.)■ F15
Illinois Col.■ F18
Knox■ F19

Colors: Scarlet & Black. Nickname: Pioneers.
AD: Dee Fairchild. SID: Andy Hamilton. III

GROVE CITY .... Grove City, PA 16127

John Barr (21 YRS. W-253, L-239)

Carnegie Mellon☒ N19
Allegheny N20
La Roche N23
Mount Union■ .... D 1
Hilbert .... D 4
Geneva■ .... D 8
Westminster (Pa.) D11
Muskingum Cl. D22-23
Wooster Cl. D29-30
Penn St.-Behrend■ .... J 5
Geneva .... J 8
Frostburg St.■ J12
Malone■ J15
Thiel■ J19
Bethany (W.Va.) J22
Waynesburg J26
Wash. & Jeff.■ J29
Penn St.-Behrend .... F 2
Thiel .... F 5
Bethany (W.Va.)■ .... F 9
Waynesburg■ F12
Wash. & Jeff. F16
☒ Washington, PA

Colors: Crimson & White. Nickname: Wolverines.
AD: R. Jack Behringer. SID: Joe Klimchak. III

GUILFORD .... Greensboro, NC 27410

Jack Jensen (23 YRS. W-340, L-291)

Greensboro■ N23
Christ. Newport Inv. N26-27
East. Mennonite N30
Lynchburg .... D 1
Wash. & Lee■ .... D 4
Greensboro .... D 7
Emory & Henry■ D11
Hampden-Sydney■ .... J 6
Va. Wesleyan .... J 8
Randolph-Macon■ J12
Bridgewater (Va.) J15
Roanoke■ J19
East. Mennonite■ J22
Lynchburg■ J25
Randolph-Macon J28
Wash. & Lee J29
Hampden-Sydney .... F 2
Va. Wesleyan■ .... F 5
Emory & Henry .... F 8
Methodist■ F11
Roanoke F16
Bridgewater (Va.)■ F19

Colors: Crimson & Gray. Nickname: Quakers.
AD: Gayle Currie. SID: Brett Ayers. III

GUST. ADOLPHUS .... St. Peter, MN 56082

Mark Hanson (3 YRS. W-53, L-27)

Luther■ N20
Minn.-Morris .... D 1
Concordia-M'head■ .... D 4
Carleton D11
Cal Lutheran Tr. D29-30
Macalester■ .... J 3
Hamline .... J 5
Bethel (Minn.) .... J 8
Augsburg■ J10
St. Mary's (Minn.) J12
St. John's (Minn.)■ J15
St. Thomas (Minn.) J17
St. Olaf■ J19
Concordia-M'head J26
Carleton■ J29
Macalester J31
Hamline■ .... F 2
Bethel (Minn.)■ .... F 5
Augsburg .... F 9
St. Mary's (Minn.)■ F12
St. John's (Minn.) F14
St. Thomas (Minn.)■ F16
St. Olaf F19

Colors: Black & Gold. Nickname: Golden Gusties.
AD: James Malmquist. SID: Tim Kennedy. III

HAMILTON .... Clinton, NY 13323

Tom Murphy (23 YRS. W-405, L-168)

Hamilton Tr. N20-21
Binghamton■ N29
Hobart .... D 1
Connecticut Col. Cl. D3-4
Hartwick■ D10
Oswego St.■ J11
Bates■ J15
Colby■ J16
Ithaca J18
Albany (N.Y.) J20
Hamilton Inv. J22-23
Williams J25
Amherst■ J29
Utica .... F 2
Oneonta St.■ .... F 5
Rochester .... F 9
Union (N.Y.) F12
Skidmore F19
Utica Tech F23
Clarkson F25
St. Lawrence F26

Colors: Buff & Blue. Nickname: Continentals.
AD: Thomas Murphy. SID: To be named. III

HAMLINE .... St. Paul, MN 55104

Dennis Krishka (1ST YR. AS HEAD COACH)

Luther N23
Minn.-Duluth Cl. N26-27
N'western (Minn.) N30
St. Mary's (Minn.)■ .... D 4
St. John's (Minn.) .... D 8
Augsburg■ D11
St. Thomas (Minn.) .... J 3
Gust. Adolphus■ .... J 5
Macalester■ .... J 8
St. Olaf J12
Concordia-M'head J15
Bethel (Minn.) J17
Carleton■ J19
St. Mary's (Minn.) J22
St. John's (Minn.)■ J26
Augsburg J29
St. Thomas (Minn.)■ J31
Gust. Adolphus .... F 2
Macalester .... F 5
St. Olaf■ F12
Concordia-M'head■ F14
Bethel (Minn.)■ F16
Carleton F19

Colors: Red & Grey. Nickname: Pipers.
AD: Dick Tressel. SID: Tim Cronwell. III

HAMPDEN-SYDNEY .... Hampden-Sydney, VA 23943

Tony Shaver (7 YRS. W-117, L-70)

Hampden-Sydney Cl. N19-20
Mary Washington N23
Marymount (Va.) N29
Wash. & Lee■ .... D 1
Randolph-Macon Tr. D3-4
Bridgewater (Va.) .... D 8
Guilford .... J 6
Lynchburg J10
Va. Wesleyan■ J12
Emory & Henry■ J15
Bridgewater (Va.)■ J17
Randolph-Macon■ J19
Emory & Henry J22
Wash. & Lee J26
East. Mennonite J29
Guilford■ .... F 2
Roanoke■ .... F 5
Va. Wesleyan .... F 9
East. Mennonite■ F12
Lynchburg■ F14
Randolph-Macon F16
Roanoke F19

Colors: Garnet & Grey. Nickname: Tigers.
AD: Joe Bush. SID: Dean Hybl. III

HANOVER .... Hanover, IN 47243

Mike Beitzel (13 YRS. W-204, L-167)

Hanover Cl. N19-20
Wilmington (Ohio) N23
Thomas More■ N27
Ind.-Southeast N30
Hanover Tr. D4-5
Centre☒ D11
Bluffton■ D18
Ill. Wesleyan ◆ D28
Rollins D29
Webster■ .... J 5
Rose-Hulman■ .... J 8
Wabash J12
DePauw■ J15
Anderson J18
Manchester J22
Franklin■ J26
Rose-Hulman J29
DePauw .... F 5
Wabash■ .... F 9
Manchester■ F12
Anderson■ F16
Franklin F19
☒ Westerville, OH
◆ Winter Park, FL

Colors: Red & Blue. Nickname: Panthers.
AD: Dick Naylor. SID: Carter Cloyd. III

HARTFORD .... Hartford, CT 06117

Paul Brazeau (1 YR. W-14, L-14)

Boston College N27
Kent .... D 4
Xavier (Ohio) .... D 6
Siena■ D13
St. Francis (N.Y.) D22
Massachusetts Tr. D28-29
Harvard .... J 3
Bucknell■ .... J 5
Iona .... J 8
Boston U. J13
Northeastern■ J15
Connecticut J17
New Hampshire■ J20
Maine J22
Central Conn. St. J25
Drexel■ J27
Delaware■ J29
Vermont .... F 5
Delaware F11
Drexel F13
Maine■ F17
New Hampshire F19
Boston U.■ F24
Northeastern F26
Vermont■ .... M 2
North Atlantic Conf. M5-9

Colors: Scarlet & White. Nickname: Hawks.
AD: Pat Meiser-McKnett. SID: James R. Keener, Jr. I

■ Home games on each schedule.

See pages 405–407 for Division I tournament details

HARTWICK .... **Oneonta, NY 13820**

Nick Lambros (16 YRS. W-291, L-125)

Hartwick Cl. N19-20
Hilbert■ N23
Skidmore■ .... D 1
Hamilton D10
Hobart■ .... J 7
Rochester Inst.■ .... J 8
Binghamton J11
Rensselaer■ J13
Elmira J17
Clarkson J21
St. Lawrence J22
Union (N.Y.) J25
Ithaca■ J28
Alfred■ J29
Rochester Inst. .... F 4
Hobart .... F 5
Utica .... F 8
Alfred F11
Ithaca F12
Albany (N.Y.) F15
St. Lawrence■ F18
Clarkson■ F19
Oneonta St.■ F21
Rensselaer F24

Colors: Royal Blue & White. Nickname: Warriors.
AD: Ken Kutler. SID: Tim Markey. III

HARVARD .... **Cambridge, MA 02138**

Frank Sullivan (9 YRS. W-126, L-126)

Babson■ N27
Colgate■ N29
St. Francis (N.Y.)■ .... D 4
Holy Cross .... D 7
Lehigh D11
Dartmouth■ D14
Vermont■ D19
Boston U. D22
Vanderbilt Inv. D28-29
Hartford■ .... J 3
Pennsylvania .... J 7
Princeton .... J 8
Fairfield J12
Dartmouth J15
New Hampshire .... F 1
Yale■ .... F 4
Brown■ .... F 5
Cornell F11
Columbia F12
Princeton■ F18
Pennsylvania■ F19
Columbia■ F25
Cornell■ F26
Brown .... M 4
Yale .... M 5

Colors: Crimson, Black & White. Nickname: Crimson.
AD: William Cleary. SID: John Veneziano. I

HAVERFORD .... **Haverford, PA 19041**

David Hooks (5 YRS. W-16, L-105)

Bates☒ N19
Frank. & Marsh.■ N23
Columbia N27
Gettysburg .... D 4
Swarthmore■ .... D 8
Dickinson■ D11
Pennsylvania D18
Johns Hopkins J11
Drew■ J13
Muhlenberg■ J19
Western Md. J22
Washington (Md.) J26
Ursinus■ .... F 2
Swarthmore .... F 5
Muhlenberg .... F 9
Washington (Md.)■ F12
Goucher F15
Ursinus F19
☒ Swarthmore, PA

Colors: Scarlet & Black. Nickname: Fords.
AD: Greg Kannerstein. SID: Jeremy Edwards. III

HAWAII .... **Honolulu, HI 96822**

Riley Wallace (8 YRS. W-105, L-116)

Great Alas. Shootout N24-27
North Caro. .... D 1
Hawaii Tip-Off Tr. D10-11
Hawaii Inv. D17-18
Hawaii Rainbow Cl. D27-30
San Diego St. .... J 3
Wyoming■ .... J 8
Colorado St.■ J10
UTEP J13
New Mexico J15
Utah■ J20
Brigham Young■ J22
Air Force J27
Fresno St. J29
Air Force■ .... F 3
Fresno St.■ .... F 5
Utah F10
Brigham Young F12
UTEP■ F17
New Mexico■ F19
Wyoming F24
Colorado St. F26
San Diego St.■ .... M 5
Western Ath. Conf. M9-12

Colors: Green & White. Nickname: Rainbows.
AD: Hugh Yoshida. SID: Eddie Inouye. I

HAWAII-HILO .... **Hilo, HI 96720**

Robert Wilson (19 YRS. W-311, L-262)

Hawaii-Hilo Cl. N26-27
BYU-Hawaii Tr. D10-11
Azusa-Pacific■ D18
Hawaii-Hilo Inv. D28-30
CS San B'dino Tr. J2-3
Eastern Mont. .... J 6
Grand Canyon .... J 8
Chaminade■ J15
BYU-Hawaii J17
Seattle Pacific■ J21
Alas. Anchorage■ J22
Alas. Fairbanks■ J24
Hawaii Pacific J30
Eastern Mont.■ .... F 4
Grand Canyon■ .... F 5
BYU-Hawaii■ .... F 9
Chaminade F12
Seattle Pacific F17
Alas. Anchorage F19
Alas. Fairbanks F21
Hawaii Pacific■ F27

Colors: Red, White & Blue. Nickname: Vulcans.
AD: William Trumbo. SID: Kelly Leong. II

HEIDELBERG .... **Tiffin, OH 44883**

John Hill (17 YRS. W-255, L-204)

Defiance■ N23
Anderson Inv. N26-27
Wilmington (Ohio)■ N30
Hiram .... D 4
Capital .... D 8
Marietta■ D11
Mount Union D18
Albion Tr. D28-29
Ohio Northern .... J 5
Otterbein■ .... J 8
John Carroll J12
Muskingum■ J15
Baldwin-Wallace J19
Marietta J22
Capital■ J26
Otterbein J29
Ohio Northern■ .... F 2
Mount Union■ .... F 5
Baldwin-Wallace■ .... F 9
Muskingum F12
John Carroll■ F16
Hiram■ F19

Colors: Red, Orange, Black. Nickname: Student Princes.
AD: John Hill. SID: Dick Edmond. III

HENDERSON ST. .... **Arkadelphia, AR 71923**

Eric Bozeman (1ST YR. AS HEAD COACH)

East Tex. St.■ N19
Arkansas Col.■ N22
Arkansas Tech■ N23
Ky. Wesleyan Cl. N26-27
Southern Ark. N29
Southwest Baptist .... D 4
Arkansas Tech .... D 7
Oklahoma City☒ D10
Harding☒ D11
Northwestern (La.) D20
Arkansas Col. .... J 5
Livingston .... J 8
Mississippi Col. J11
North Ala.■ J15
Ala.-Huntsville■ J17
Delta St. J22
Central Ark.■ J27
Delta St.■ J29
Livingston■ J31
North Ala. .... F 5
Ala.-Huntsville .... F 7
Mississippi Col.■ F12
Ark.-Pine Bluff■ F14
Central Ark. F19
Ark.-Pine Bluff F21
East Tex. St. F26
☒ Conway, AR

Colors: Red & Gray. Nickname: Reddies.
AD: Ken Turner. SID: Steve Eddington. II

HENDRIX .... **Conway, AR 72032**

Cliff Garrison (21 YRS. W-353, L-238)

Rhodes Tr. N19-20
LSU-Shreveport■ N22
John Brown N29
John Brown■ .... D 3
Westminster Cl. D10-12
LSU-Shreveport .... J 5
Southwestern (Tex.) .... J 7
Trinity (Tex.) .... J 9
Millsaps■ J14
Rhodes■ J16
Centre J21
Fisk J23
Oglethorpe■ J28
Sewanee■ J30
Millsaps .... F 4
Rhodes .... F 6
Oglethorpe F11
Sewanee F13
Centre■ F18
Fisk■ F20
Trinity (Tex.)■ F26
Southwestern (Tex.)■ F27

Colors: Orange & Black. Nickname: Warriors.
AD: Cliff Garrison. SID: James Eaton. III

HIGH POINT .... **High Point, NC 27262**

Jerry Steele (29 YRS. W-467, L-345)

Gardner-Webb Tr. N19-20
Francis Marion Tr. N26-27
Limestone■ .... D 1
Limestone .... D 8
Elon D11
Indiana (Pa.) Tr. J5-6
California (Pa.) Tr. J8-9
Barton J12
St. Andrews J15
Mount Olive J19
Belmont Abbey■ J22
Pfeiffer■ J26
Coker J29
Lees-McRae .... F 2
St. Andrews■ .... F 5
Mount Olive■ .... F 8
Pfeiffer F12
Belmont Abbey F16
Coker■ F19
Lees-McRae■ F23
Barton■ F26

Colors: Purple & White. Nickname: Panthers.
AD: Jerry Steele. SID: Woody Gibson. II

HILBERT .... **Hamburg, NY 14075**

Mike Cordovano (1ST YR. AS HEAD COACH)

Hamilton Tr. N20-21
Hartwick N23
Nazareth Tr. N27-28
Thiel■ N30
Grove City■ .... D 4
Pitt.-Bradford■ .... D 6
RIT Tr. D10-11
St. John Fisher Inv. J7-8
Houghton■ J20
D'youville■ J24
Pitt.-Bradford J26
Thiel J28
Daemen■ .... F 1
St. John Fisher■ .... F 5
D'youville .... F 9
Le Moyne F10
Nazareth (N.Y.)■ F12
Houghton F15
Penn St.-Behrend F19
Daemen F22
Nazareth (N.Y.) F26

Colors: Blue & White. Nickname: Hawks.
AD: Luke Ruppel. SID: Brian Ackley. III

■ Home games on each schedule.

See pages 405–407 for Division I tournament details

HILLSDALE .... Hillsdale, MI 49242
Bernie Balikian (8 YRS. W-119, L-122)

Hillsdale Cl.	D3-4	Oakland■	J15
St. Francis (Ill.)	N20	Wayne St. (Mich.)	J20
Siena Heights	N22	Ferris St.■	J22
Calvin Cl.	N26-27	Michigan Tech■	J27
Eastern Mich.	N29	Northern Mich.■	J29
IU/PU-Ft. Wayne■	D 1	Northwood	F 3
Northwood■	D 9	Grand Valley St.	F 5
Grand Valley St.■	D11	Lake Superior St.■	F10
Michigan Tech	D18	Saginaw Valley■	F12
Northern Mich.	D20	Oakland	F19
Lake Superior St.	J 6	Wayne St. (Mich.)■	F24
Saginaw Valley	J 8	Ferris St.	F26

Colors: Royal Blue & White. Nickname: Chargers.
AD: Jack McAvoy. SID: Brian Boyse. II

HIRAM .... Hiram, OH 44234
Michael Marcinko (2 YRS. W-31, L-21)

Slippery Rock	N27	Capital■	J15
Thiel■	D 1	John Carroll	J19
Heidelberg■	D 4	Baldwin-Wallace■	J22
Otterbein■	D 8	Otterbein	J26
Mount Union	D11	Mount Union■	J29
Ohio Northern■	D18	Capital	F 2
Denison■	D21	Ohio Northern	F 5
Defiance Tr.	D28-29	John Carroll■	F 9
Baldwin-Wallace	J 5	Marietta	F12
Marietta■	J 8	Muskingum■	F16
Muskingum	J12	Heidelberg	F19

Colors: Red & Blue. Nickname: Terriers.
AD: Cindy McKnight. SID: Renee Mills Arnold. III

HOBART .... Geneva, NY 14456
Brian Streeter (10 YRS. W-100, L-145)

Hamilton■	D 1	Clarkson■	J28
Wheaton (Mass.) Tr.	D4-5	St. Lawrence■	J29
Army	D 8	Union (N.Y.)■	F 1
Skidmore	D11	Rensselaer■	F 4
Hartwick	J 7	Hartwick■	F 5
Rensselaer	J 8	Rochester Inst.	F 8
Rochester Tr.	J12-15	St. Lawrence	F11
Rochester Inst.■	J18	Clarkson	F12
Alfred	J21	Rochester	F15
Ithaca	J22	Ithaca■	F18
Roberts Wesleyan	J25	Alfred■	F19

Colors: Orange & Purple. Nickname: Statesmen.
AD: Michael Hanna. SID: Eric Reuscher. III

HOFSTRA .... Hempstead, NY 11550
Butch van Breda Kolff (27 YRS. W-473, L-252)

Lehigh■	N27	St. Joseph's (Pa.)■	J27
Iona	N30	Boston U.■	F 1
U.C.-Santa Barb. Tr.	D2-4	Central Conn. St.■	F 5
St. John's (N.Y.) Tr	D11-12	St. Francis (N.Y.)■	F 8
Manhattan☒	D18	Notre Dame	F11
Massachusetts Tr.	D28-29	Fordham■	F14
New Hampshire	J 5	Rhode Island■	F17
Cornell■	J 8	Army■	F22
Maine	J11	Chicago St.	F26
Buffalo■	J15	Northeastern Ill.	F28
Troy St.■	J17	East Coast Conf.	M4-6
Dartmouth	J22	☒ Uniondale, NY	
Columbia■	J25		

Colors: Blue, White & Gold. Nickname: Flying Dutchmen.
AD: James Garvey. SID: Jim Sheehan. I

HOLY CROSS .... Worcester, MA 01610
George Blaney (26 YRS. W-407, L-320)

Siena	D 4	Bucknell	J29
Harvard■	D 7	Dartmouth	J31
Brown■	D 9	Fordham■	F 2
Massachusetts☒	D11	Army	F 5
Northwestern	D20	Lehigh	F 9
Santa Clara Cl.	D29-30	Colgate■	F12
William & Mary■	J 5	Lafayette	F16
Fordham	J 8	Navy■	F19
Army■	J12	New Hampshire■	F22
Lehigh■	J15	Rutgers	F24
Colgate	J18	Bucknell■	F26
Boston College	J20	Patriot Conf.	M4-11
Lafayette■	J22	☒ Worcester, MA	
Navy	J26		

Colors: Royal Purple. Nickname: Crusaders.
AD: Ron Perry. SID: Jeff Nelson. I

HOPE .... Holland, MI 49423
Glenn Van Wieren (16 YRS. W-299, L-104)

Grand Rapid Bapt. Tr	N19-20	Albion	J15
Central Inv.	N26-27	Olivet	J19
North Park■	D 1	Alma■	J22
Concordia (Ill.)■	D 4	Adrian■	J26
Wheaton (Ill.)	D 7	Kalamazoo■	J29
Hope Cl.	D10-11	Calvin	F 5
Aquinas	D18	Albion■	F 9
Hope Tr.	D28-29	Olivet■	F12
Kalamazoo	J 5	Alma	F16
Calvin■	J12	Adrian	F19

Colors: Blue & Orange. Nickname: Flying Dutchmen.
AD: Ray Smith. SID: Tom Renner. III

HOUSTON .... Houston, TX 77204
Alvin Brooks (1ST YR. AS HEAD COACH)

Akron■	N27	Texas■	J29
Southwest Mo. St.■	N30	Texas-San Antonio	F 2
Iowa Hawkeye Cl.	D3-4	Rice	F 5
Stephen F. Austin	D 7	Texas Christian	F 8
Purdue☒	D10	Texas Tech■	F12
UCLA■	D20	Texas A&M	F16
Wyoming	D23	Baylor■	F19
DePaul■	D30	Southern Methodist■	F24
Drake■	J 3	Texas	F26
Texas Christian■	J12	Lamar■	M 1
Texas Tech	J15	Rice■	M 5
Texas A&M■	J19	Southwest Conf.	M10-12
Baylor	J22	☒ Indianapolis, IN	
Southern Methodist	J26		

Colors: Scarlet & White. Nickname: Cougars.
AD: Bill Carr. SID: Ted Nance. I

HOWARD .... Washington, DC 20059
Butch Beard (3 YRS. W-35, L-52)

Kentucky St.☒	N27	Md.-East. Shore	J27
James Madison	N30	Coppin St.	J29
St. Peter's	D 7	Morgan St.	J31
Geo. Washington Tr.	D10-11	Coppin St.■	F 5
Northeastern■	D18	Bethune-Cookman■	F10
Southern Cal	D21	North Caro. A&T	F19
Old Dominion	J 5	South Caro. St.	F21
North Caro. A&T■	J 8	Delaware St.■	F24
South Caro. St.■	J10	Louisville■	F28
Md.-East. Shore■	J13	Morgan St.■	M 5
Delaware St.	J15	Mid-Eastern Conf.	M9-13
Bethune-Cookman	J20	☒ Indianapolis, IN	

Colors: Blue, White and Red. Nickname: Bison.
AD: David C. Simmons. SID: Edward Hill, Jr. I

HUNTER .... New York, NY 10021
Ray Amalbert (5 YRS. W-95, L-46)

York (N.Y.)	D 1	CCNY	J24
Old Westbury■	D 3	Merchant Marine■	J26
Trenton St.■	D 6	New Jersey Tech	J29
Merchant Marine	D 8	Staten Island■	J31
Upsala■	D11	Medgar Evers	F 2
Medgar Evers■	J 4	Baruch	F 4
Buffalo St. Tr.	J7-8	Stony Brook	F 7
New Jersey Tech■	J13	Manhattanville	F10
York (N.Y.)■	J15	Lehman■	F12
Staten Island	J18	Mt. St. Mary (N.Y.)	F14
Manhattanville■	J20	John Jay■	F16
Stony Brook■	J22		

Colors: Purple, White & Gold. Nickname: Hawks.
AD: Terry Wansart. SID: Ron Ratner. III

IDAHO .... Moscow, ID 83843
Joe Cravens (1ST YR. AS HEAD COACH)

Seattle■	N26	Weber St.■	J27
Montana Tech■	N29	Northern Ariz.■	J29
San Francisco Cl.	D3-4	Idaho St.	F 4
Washington St.	D 7	Boise St.	F 5
Oregon■	D12	Montana St.■	F11
Washington	D18	Montana■	F12
Gonzaga	D21	Cal St. Sacramento■	F16
Southern Utah	D30	Eastern Wash.	F19
Cal St. Sacramento	J 3	Northern Ariz.	F24
Eastern Ore.■	J 7	Weber St.	F26
Montana	J14	Boise St.■	M 4
Montana St.	J15	Idaho St.■	M 5
Eastern Wash.■	J21	Big Sky Conf.	M10-12

Colors: Silver & Gold. Nickname: Vandals.
AD: Pete Liske. SID: Rance Pugmire. I

■ Home games on each schedule.

See pages 405–407 for Division I tournament details

IDAHO ST. .... Pocatello, ID 83209
Herb Williams (3 YRS. W-30, L-57)

Western Mont.■	N30	Montana	J28
Portland	D 7	Montana St.	J29
Colorado Mines■	D18	Idaho■	F 4
Pacific (Ore.)■	D20	Eastern Wash.■	F 5
Washington■	D23	Northern Ariz.	F10
Wyoming Cowboy Tr.	D28-29	Weber St.	F12
Tennessee Tech	J 3	Boise St.	F18
Gonzaga■	J 8	Montana St.■	F25
Weber St.■	J13	Montana■	F26
Northern Ariz.■	J15	Eastern Wash.	M 3
Southern Utah	J18	Idaho	M 5
Boise St.■	J21	Big Sky Conf.	M10-12
Cal St. Sacramento	J23		

Colors: Orange & Black. Nickname: Bengals.
AD: Randy Hoffman. SID: Glenn Alford. I

ILLINOIS .... Champaign, IL 61820
Lou Henson (31 YRS. W-609, L-295)

La Salle■	D 1	Indiana■	J30
Ill.-Chicago■	D 4	Penn St.	F 2
Marquette	D 7	Michigan St.■	F 9
Illinois Cl.	D10-11	Northwestern	F12
Chicago St.■	D18	Ohio St.■	F15
Jackson St.■	D20	Iowa	F19
Missouri⊠	D22	Michigan	F22
Texas■	J 2	Wisconsin■	F26
Michigan St.	J 8	Indiana	M 1
Northwestern■	J12	Penn St.■	M 5
Ohio St.	J15	Minnesota■	M 9
Iowa■	J19	Purdue	M12
Michigan■	J23	⊠ St. Louis, MO	
Wisconsin	J25		

Colors: Orange & Blue. Nickname: Fighting Illini.
AD: Ron Guenther. SID: Mike Pearson. I

ILL. BENEDICTINE .... Lisle, IL 60532
Tony LaScala (27 YRS. W-368, L-316)

Rosary	N23	Judson■	J19
Lewis	D 1	Rockford	J22
North Park	D 4	Aurora■	J26
Lake Forest	D 7	Trinity (Ill.)	J29
Ill. Wesleyan■	D 9	Beloit	F 1
Anderson■	D10	Concordia (Ill.)■	F 5
North Central	D18	Judson	F 9
Elmhurst Cl.	D29-30	Rockford■	F12
Nat'l Catholic Tr.	J5-9	Aurora	F19
Concordia (Ill.)	J15	Trinity (Ill.)■	F23
Ripon■	J17		

Colors: Cardinal & White. Nickname: Eagles.
AD: Tony Lascala. SID: Keith Bunkenburg. III

ILLINOIS COL. .... Jacksonville, IL 62650
Bill Merris (35 YRS. W-313, L-483)

Blackburn■	N20	Lawrence■	J22
Principia	N30	St. Norbert■	J23
Grinnell■	D 3	Lake Forest	J29
Coe■	D 4	Ripon	J30
Chicago■	D 7	Knox■	F 5
Missouri-Rolla	D11	Millikin	F 7
Webster■	D18	Monmouth (Ill.)■	F11
Knox	J 8	Cornell College■	F12
Monmouth (Ill.)	J14	MacMurray■	F15
Cornell College	J15	Grinnell	F18
Greenville	J18	Coe	F19

Colors: Blue & White. Nickname: Blueboys.
AD: William Anderson. SID: James Murphy. III

ILLINOIS ST. .... Normal, IL 61761
Kevin Stallings (1ST YR. AS HEAD COACH)

Northwestern	D 4	Tulsa	J27
Dayton■	D 6	Wichita St.	J29
Butler	D 9	Bradley■	F 2
DePaul	D11	Northern Iowa	F 5
Northern Iowa■	D19	Tulsa■	F 7
Evansville■	D21	Southwest Mo. St.■	F 9
Vanderbilt Inv.	D28-29	Creighton	F12
Colorado■	J 3	Wichita St.■	F17
Southern Ill.	J 8	Creighton■	F19
Southwest Mo. St.	J12	Indiana St.	F21
Indiana St.■	J15	Drake	F24
Bradley	J19	Southern Ill.■	F27
Drake■	J22	Missouri Valley Conf	M5-7

Colors: Red & White. Nickname: Redbirds.
AD: Rick Greenspan. SID: Kenny Mossman. I

ILL. WESLEYAN .... Bloomington, IL 61701
Dennis Bridges (28 YRS. W-486, L-274)

Washington (Mo.) Tr.	N19-20	North Central	J18
Bradley	D 1	Elmhurst■	J22
Chicago	D 4	North Park	J29
Olivet (Ill.)■	D 7	Millikin■	F 1
Ill. Benedictine	D 9	Augustana (Ill.)	F 5
Rose-Hulman■	D11	Wheaton (Ill.)■	F 8
Aurora	D18	North Central■	F12
Hanover⊠	D28	Elmhurst	F15
Denison⊠	D29	Carthage	F19
Anderson■	J 3	North Park■	F22
Carthage■	J 8	Millikin	F26
Augustana (Ill.)■	J11	⊠ Winter Park, FL	
Wheaton (Ill.)	J15		

Colors: Green & White. Nickname: Titans.
AD: Dennis Bridges. SID: Stew Salowitz. III

ILL.-CHICAGO .... Chicago, IL 60680
Bob Hallberg (22 YRS. W-436, L-237)

Boise St. Cl.	N26-27	Valparaiso	J27
Illinois	D 4	Wright St.■	J29
Northeastern Ill.■	D 9	Wis.-Green Bay	J31
Western Mich.	D11	Eastern Ill.	F 5
Michigan St.	D14	Western Ill.	F 7
North Park■	D29	Wis.-Milwaukee■	F14
Loyola (Ill.)■	J 4	Northern Ill.■	F17
Northern Ill.	J 8	Wright St.	F19
Wis.-Milwaukee	J10	Wis.-Green Bay■	F21
Eastern Ill.■	J15	Valparaiso■	F24
Western Ill.■	J17	Youngstown St.	F26
Youngstown St.■	J22	Cleveland St.	F28
Cleveland St.■	J24	Mid-Continent Conf.	M6-8

Colors: Indigo & Flame. Nickname: Flames.
AD: Tom Russo. SID: Anne Schoenherr. I

INDIANA .... Bloomington, IN 47405
Bob Knight (28 YRS. W-619, L-214)

Butler	N27	Illinois	J30
Kentucky⊠	D 4	Ohio St.■	F 2
Notre Dame■	D 7	Penn St.	F 5
Indiana Cl.	D10-11	Michigan	F 8
Eastern Ky.■	D18	Iowa■	F12
Kansas	D22	Purdue■	F19
Indiana Hoosier Cl.	D27-28	Northwestern	F24
Penn St.■	J 8	Minnesota	F27
Iowa	J11	Illinois■	M 1
Michigan■	J16	Ohio St.	M 6
Purdue	J18	Michigan St.	M 9
Northwestern■	J22	Wisconsin■	M12
Minnesota■	J26	⊠ Indianapolis, IN	

Colors: Cream & Crimson. Nickname: Hoosiers.
AD: Clarence Doninger. SID: Kit Klingelhoffer. I

INDIANA (PA) .... Indiana, PA 15705
Kurt Kanaskie (8 YRS. W-127, L-95)

Point Park■	N23	Slippery Rock	J19
Gannon Cl.	N26-27	Clarion■	J22
Fairmont St.■	D 1	Edinboro■	J26
Glenville St.	D 4	Calif. (Pa.)	J29
Kutztown■	D 6	Lock Haven■	F 2
Columbia Union■	D 8	Bloomsburg■	F 5
Shepherd	D11	Shippensburg■	F 9
Shepherd■	J 3	Slippery Rock■	F12
Indiana (Pa.) Tr.	J5-6	Edinboro	F16
Pitt.-Johnstown	J10	Clarion	F19
Shippensburg	J12	Lock Haven	F23
Gannon■	J15	Calif. (Pa.)■	F26

Colors: Crimson & Gray. Nickname: Indians.
AD: Frank Cignetti. SID: Larry Judge. II

INDIANA ST. .... Terre Haute, IN 47809
Tates Locke (18 YRS. W-251, L-232)

Eastern Ill.	D 1	Southern Ill.■	J25
Purdue Inv.	D3-4	Northern Iowa	J29
Butler	D11	Southwest Mo. St.■	F 1
Evansville	D14	Creighton	F 3
Oral Roberts	D18	Drake	F 5
Ball St.■	D22	Southern Ill.	F 9
Southwest Mo. St.	J 2	Bradley■	F12
Evansville■	J 5	Drake■	F17
Creighton■	J 8	Northern Iowa■	F19
Bradley	J12	Illinois St.■	F21
Illinois St.	J15	Wichita St.	F26
Wichita St.■	J20	Tulsa	F28
Tulsa■	J22	Missouri Valley Conf	M5-7

Colors: Blue & White. Nickname: Sycamores.
AD: Brian Faison. SID: Eric Ruden. I

■ Home games on each schedule.

See pages 405–407 for Division I tournament details

IU/PU-INDIANAPOLIS .... Indianapolis, IN 46260

Robert Lovell (15 YRS. W-261, L-202)

Cumberland (Ky.)	N20	Quincy	J15
IUPU-Indy Tr.	N27-29	Indiana Tech	J18
St. Xavier	D 2	Drury■	J22
Bellarmine	D 4	Taylor	J25
Wis.-Parkside■	D 7	Wis.-Parkside	J29
Ky. Wesleyan	D 9	Tri-State	J31
St. Joseph's (Ind.)■	D18	St. Francis (Ind.)■	F 3
IU/PU-Ft. Wayne	D20	SIU-Edwardsville	F 5
Eastern Ky.	D21	Ind.-Southeast■	F 9
IUPU-Indy Cl.	D28-29	Quincy■	F12
Bellarmine■	J 3	Taylor■	F15
St. Francis (Ill.)■	J 6	Longwood	F19
SIU-Edwardsville■	J 8	Oakland City	F22
Ind.-Southeast	J12	Drury	F26

Colors: Red & Gold. Nickname: Metros.
AD: Hugh Wolf. SID: To be named. II

IU/PU-FT. WAYNE .... Ft. Wayne, IN 46805

Andy Piazza (6 YRS. W-116, L-53)

Wayne St. (Mich.)	N23	Bellarmine	J22
Hillsdale	D 1	Northern Ky.■	J27
Voorhees■	D 4	Indianapolis■	J29
Purdue-Calumet■	D 8	Findlay■	F 2
Quincy	D11	Ashland■	F 5
Madonna■	D18	Southern Ind.	F10
IU/PU-Indianapolis■	D20	Ky. Wesleyan	F12
St. Joseph's (Ind.)	D30	Bellarmine■	F17
Lewis	J 2	Kentucky St.■	F19
Huntington	J 5	Indianapolis	F24
Ashland	J 8	Northern Ky.	F26
Ky. Wesleyan■	J13	Lewis■	M 3
Southern Ind.■	J15	St. Joseph's (Ind.)■	M 5
Kentucky St.	J20		

Colors: Blue & White. Nickname: Mastodons.
AD: Arnie Ball. SID: Matt Delong. II

INDIANAPOLIS .... Indianapolis, IN 46227

Royce Waltman (6 YRS. W-112 , L-52)

Indianapolis Tr.	N19-20	St. Joseph's (Ind.)■	J22
IUPU-Indy Tr.	N27-29	Ashland	J27
Eastern Mich.	D 2	IU/PU-Ft. Wayne	J29
Wis.-Parkside■	D 6	Kentucky St.■	F 3
St. Francis (Ill.)■	D11	Bellarmine■	F 5
Ind. Wesleyan■	D18	Northern Ky.	F12
Southern Ind.■	D30	St. Joseph's (Ind.)	F17
Ky. Wesleyan■	J 1	Lewis	F19
Bellarmine	J 6	IU/PU-Ft. Wayne■	F24
Kentucky St.	J 8	Ashland■	F26
Northern Ky.■	J15	Ky. Wesleyan	M 3
Oakland City■	J17	Southern Ind.	M 5
Lewis■	J20		

Colors: Crimson & Grey. Nickname: Greyhounds.
AD: Bill Bright. SID: Joe Gentry. II

IONA .... New Rochelle, NY 10801

Jerry Welsh (24 YRS. W-485, L-168)

Central Mich.	N27	Manhattan■	J18
Hofstra■	N30	Fairfield	J22
Akron	D 4	Manhattan	J25
Rhode Island■	D 8	Siena■	J31
Fordham■	D11	St. Peter's	F 5
Seton Hall	D14	Niagara	F10
Wagner	D18	Canisius	F12
Iona College Tr.	D28-29	Loyola (Md.)■	F14
Bucknell	J 3	Siena	F17
Loyola (Md.)	J 5	Fairfield■	F19
Hartford■	J 8	Niagara■	F25
Northeastern■	J11	Canisius■	F27
St. Peter's■	J15	Metro Atlantic Conf.	M5-7

Colors: Maroon & Gold. Nickname: Gaels.
AD: Rich Petriccione. SID: David Torromeo. I

IOWA .... Iowa City, IA 52242

Tom Davis (22 YRS. W-426, L-222)

Drake■	N30	Northwestern	J26
Iowa Hawkeye Cl.	D3-4	Michigan St.	J29
Northern Iowa	D 7	Minnesota■	F 2
Iowa St.	D11	Purdue■	F 6
Dartmouth■	D20	Indiana	F12
Duke■	D22	Michigan	F16
UC Irvine	D29	Illinois■	F19
Eastern Ill.■	J 2	Penn St.	F23
Ohio St.	J 4	Northwestern■	F26
Michigan■	J 8	Michigan St.■	M 2
Indiana■	J11	Minnesota	M 5
Illinois	J19	Wisconsin	M 9
Penn St.■	J22	Ohio St.■	M12

Colors: Old Gold & Black. Nickname: Hawkeyes.
AD: Bob Bowlsby. SID: Phil Haddy. I

IOWA ST. .... Ames, IA 50011

Johnny Orr (28 YRS. W-452, L-333)

Creighton■	D 1	Fla. Atlantic■	J24
Northern Iowa■	D 4	Kansas St.	J29
Drake	D 7	Colorado■	F 1
Iowa■	D11	Oklahoma St.	F 5
Texas-Arlington■	D18	St. Louis	F 9
Charleston So.■	D21	Nebraska	F12
UTEP Cl.	D29-30	Missouri■	F16
Nebraska■	J 3	Colorado	F19
Western Ill.■	J 5	Oklahoma	F23
Morningside■	J12	Oklahoma St.■	F26
Oklahoma■	J15	Kansas	M 3
Missouri	J19	Kansas St.■	M 6
Kansas■	J22	Big Eight Conf.	M11-13

Colors: Cardinal & Gold. Nickname: Cyclones.
AD: Gene Smith. SID: Tom Kroeschell. I

ITHACA .... Ithaca, NY 14850

Tom Baker (15 YRS. W-255, L-162)

Johns Hopkins Cl.	N19-20	Hartwick	J28
Cortland St.	N30	Rensselaer	J29
Albany (N.Y.)■	D 7	Cortland St.■	F 1
Union (N.Y.)	D10	Clarkson■	F 4
Binghamton■	J 8	St. Lawrence■	F 5
Skidmore	J11	Alfred■	F 8
St. Lawrence	J14	Rensselaer■	F11
Clarkson	J15	Hartwick■	F12
Hamilton■	J18	Utica■	F15
Rochester Inst.■	J21	Hobart	F18
Hobart■	J22	Rochester Inst.	F19
Alfred	J25	Roberts Wesleyan	F22

Colors: Blue & Gold. Nickname: Bombers.
AD: Robert Deming. SID: Pete Moore. III

JACKSON ST. .... Jackson, MS 39217

Andy Stoglin (6 YRS. W-95, L-83)

Ark. Baptist■	N27	Alcorn St.	J17
Tennessee St.■	N29	Mississippi Val.■	J22
Missouri	D 4	Grambling	J24
Louisiana Tech■	D 7	Alabama St.■	J29
Geo. Washington Tr.	D10-11	Texas Southern	F 5
Arkansas	D18	Prairie View	F 7
Illinois	D20	Southern-B.R.■	F12
Northeastern Ill.	D23	Alcorn St.■	F14
Memphis St.	D27	Mississippi Val.	F19
Wichita St. Tr.	D29-30	Grambling■	F21
Texas Southern■	J 8	Alabama St.	F26
Prairie View■	J10	Southwestern Conf.	M9-13
Southern-B.R.	J15		

Colors: Blue & White. Nickname: Tigers.
AD: W.C. Gorden. SID: Sam Jefferson. I

JACKSONVILLE .... Jacksonville, FL 32211

Matt Kilcullen (5 YRS. W-45, L-86)

Stetson■	N27	Ark.-Lit. Rock	J26
Bethune-Cookman■	D 1	Tex.-Pan American■	J29
Louisiana Tech■	D 4	Buffalo■	F 1
Florida■	D 8	Ark.-Lit. Rock■	F 5
Fla. Atlantic■	D11	Florida A&M■	F 7
DePaul■	D18	Lamar■	F10
Butler	D21	Western Ky.	F12
Southwestern La.■	J 3	New Orleans■	F14
Lamar	J 6	Southwestern La.	F19
Tex.-Pan American	J 8	Louisiana Tech	F21
Arkansas St.■	J12	South Ala.■	F26
Western Ky.■	J15	Arkansas St.	F28
South Ala.	J20	Sun Belt Conf.	M4-8
New Orleans	J22		

Colors: Green & Gold. Nickname: Dolphins.
AD: Tom Seitz. SID: Scott Clark. I

JACKSONVILLE ST. .... Jacksonville, AL 36265

Bill Jones (21 YRS. W-404, L-169)

Southern Colo. Cl.	N19-20	Jacksonville St. Tr.	J7-8
Regis (Colo.)	N22	Paine	J14
Colorado Mines	N23	Augusta	J15
Fla. Memorial■	N27	Miles■	J22
Union (Tenn.)	N30	Shaw■	J24
Jacksonville St. Cl.	D3-4	Oakland City■	F 6
Union (Tenn.)■	D 9	Lee■	F 7
Berry■	D11	Lane■	F14
Augusta■	D13	Clark Atlanta■	F21
CS Bakersfield Cl.	D17-18	Alabama A&M	F26
Paine■	J 3		

Colors: Red & White. Nickname: Gamecocks.
AD: Jerry Cole. SID: Mike Galloway. II

■ Home games on each schedule.

See pages 405–407 for Division I tournament details

JAMES MADISON .... Harrisonburg, VA 22807
Lefty Driesell (31 YRS. W-621, L-279)

Va. Commonwealth	N27	N.C.-Wilmington■	J22
Howard■	N30	East Caro.	J26
Purdue Inv.	D3-4	Richmond	J29
La Salle■	D10	Morgan St.■	F 2
Arkansas St.■	D20	Old Dominion	F 5
Rutgers■	D22	William & Mary	F 7
Furman	D28	George Mason■	F12
Minnesota	D31	American	F16
Liberty■	J 4	East Caro.■	F19
Old Dominion■	J 8	N.C.-Wilmington	F23
William & Mary■	J12	Richmond■	F26
George Mason	J15	N.C.-Charlotte	F28
American■	J19	Colonial Conf.	M5-7

Colors: Purple & Gold. Nickname: Dukes.
AD: Dean Ehlers. SID: Gary Michael. I

JERSEY CITY ST. .... Jersey City, NJ 07305
Charles Brown (11 YRS. W-226, L-86)

Susquehanna Tr.	N19-20	Kean	J14
Rowan■	N23	Wm. Paterson■	J19
Stockton St.	N29	Trenton St.	J22
Trenton St.■	D 1	Rowan	J25
Rutgers-Camden■	D 4	Stockton St.■	J29
Ramapo	D 8	Rutgers-Newark	F 2
Montclair St.■	D11	Rutgers-Camden	F 5
Upsala	D15	Ramapo■	F 9
Salem St. Tr.	D29-30	Montclair St.	F12
Bloomfield	J 8	Wm. Paterson	F16
Rutgers-Newark■	J12	Kean■	F19

Colors: Green & Gold. Nickname: Gothic Knights.
AD: Larry Schiner. SID: John Stallings. III

JOHN CARROLL .... Cleveland, OH 44118
Mike Moran (1 YR. W-12, L-14)

Johns Hopkins	N19-20	Hiram■	J19
Wheeling Jesuit Tr.	N26-27	Ohio Northern■	J22
Wright St.	D 4	Baldwin-Wallace	J26
Baldwin-Wallace■	D 8	Marietta	J29
Ohio Northern	D11	Mount Union■	F 2
Otterbein	D18	Muskingum■	F 5
Marietta⊠	D21	Hiram	F 9
Ky. Wesleyan	D30	Otterbein■	F12
Capital■	J 5	Heidelberg	F16
Muskingum	J 8	Capital	F19
Heidelberg■	J12	⊠ Cleveland, OH	
Mount Union	J15		

Colors: Blue & Gold. Nickname: Blue Streaks.
AD: Tony DeCarlo. SID: Chris Wenzler. III

JOHN JAY .... New York, NY 10019
Jeff Risener (9 YRS. W-99, L-133)

John Jay Tr.	N20-21	York (N.Y.)■	J10
Mt. St. Mary (N.Y.)■	N23	Centenary (N.J.)	J13
Molloy Tr.	N26-28	Baruch	J20
Albertus Magnus	N29	Lehman	J24
Baruch■	D 2	CCNY	J29
FDU-Madison■	D 6	Pratt	J31
CCNY■	D 8	Lehman■	F 4
Centenary (N.J.)■	D10	Yeshiva■	F 6
Clark (Mass.)■	J 4	Old Westbury■	F 9
Medgar Evers■	J 6	Vassar■	F11
Staten Island	J 8	Hunter	F16

Colors: Blue & Gold. Nickname: Bloodhounds.
AD: Susan Larkin. SID: Debra Eckstein. III

JOHNS HOPKINS .... Baltimore, MD 21218
Bill Nelson (13 YRS. W-217, L-123)

Johns Hopkins Cl.	N19-20	Carnegie Mellon■	J16
Ursinus■	N23	Washington (Md.)	J20
Goucher	N30	Muhlenberg	J22
Brandeis	D 3	Western Md.■	J26
New York U.■	D 5	Gettysburg	J29
Frank. & Marsh.	D 7	Dickinson	F 2
Rochester	D10	Frank. & Marsh.■	F 5
Case Reserve■	J 3	Swarthmore■	F 9
Chicago	J 7	Western Md.	F12
Washington (Mo.)	J 9	Gettysburg■	F16
Haverford■	J11	Dickinson■	F19
Emory■	J14		

Colors: Blue & Black. Nickname: Blue Jays.
AD: Robert Scott. SID: Andy Bilello. III

JOHNSON SMITH .... Charlotte, NC 28216
Steve Joyner (6 YRS. W-104, L-69)

Johnson C. Smith Tr.	N19-20	Queens (N.C.)■	J19
St. Paul's■	N23	Winston-Salem■	J22
Virginia St.■	N27	Fayetteville St.	J27
Hampton	N29	Shaw	J29
Jacksonville St. Cl.	D3-4	N.C. Central	F 3
Virginia Union■	D14	Winston-Salem	F 5
N.C. Central■	J 4	Elizabeth City St.	F 7
Norfolk St.	J 8	St. Augustine's■	F 9
Livingstone■	J11	Fayetteville St.■	F12
St. Augustine's	J13	Shaw■	F15
Bowie St.■	J15	Livingstone	F19

Colors: Blue & Gold. Nickname: Golden Bulls.
AD: Horace Small. SID: James Cuthbertson. II

JOHNSON ST. .... Johnson, VT 05656
Buddy Mahar (6 YRS. W-64, L-92)

Plattsburgh St. Cl.	N19-20	Castleton St.	J20
Plymouth St.■	N23	Bishop■	J24
Daniel Webster	N28	Lyndon St.■	J26
St. Joseph (Vt.)	N29	Green Mountain■	J29
Bishop	D 4	St. Joseph (Vt.)■	F 2
New England Col.	D 7	Lyndon St.	F 5
Atlantic Union■	D11	Me.-Farmington	F 7
Me.-Presque Isle■	D12	Castleton St.■	F10
Westbrook	J12	Green Mountain	F12
Notre Dame (N.H.)	J13	Daniel Webster■	F13
St. Joseph's (Me.)■	J15	Notre Dame (N.H.)■	F15
Atlantic Union	J16	Westbrook■	F19
Norwich■	J18		

Colors: Green, Blue & White. Nickname: Badgers.
AD: Peter Albright. SID: To Be Named. III

JUNIATA .... Huntingdon, PA 16652
Jim Zauzig (3 YRS. W-28, L-46)

Johns Hopkins Cl.	N19-20	Albright	J22
King's (Pa.)	N23	Elizabethtown	J27
Allegheny Cl.	N26-27	Messiah	J29
Messiah■	D 1	Lebanon Valley■	F 2
Moravian	D 4	Moravian■	F 5
Lycoming■	D 7	Susquehanna	F 9
Juniata Tr.	J8-9	Delaware Valley	F11
Lebanon Valley	J11	Widener	F12
Widener■	J15	York (Pa.)■	F15
Frostburg St.	J17	Elizabethtown■	F17
Susquehanna■	J19	Albright■	F19

Colors: Yale Blue & Old Gold. Nickname: Indians.
AD: William F. Berrier. SID: Joseph Scialabba. III

KALAMAZOO .... Kalamazoo, MI 49006
Joe Haklin (6 YRS. W-99, L-53)

Concordia (Mich.)■	N20	Olivet	J15
Grand Rapids Bapt.■	N23	Alma■	J19
Franklin	D 4	Adrian	J22
Chicago	D10	Goshen	J26
DePauw Inv.	D17-18	Hope	J29
Spring Arbor	D21	Calvin	F 2
Aquinas	D23	Albion■	F 5
Kalamazoo Tr.	D29-30	Olivet■	F 9
Hope■	J 5	Alma	F12
Calvin■	J 8	Adrian■	F16
Albion	J12		

Colors: Orange & Black. Nickname: Hornets.
AD: Bob Kent. SID: John Greenhoe. III

KANSAS .... Lawrence, KS 66045
Roy Williams (5 YRS. W-132, L-37)

Pre-Season NIT	N17-26	Iowa St.	J22
Temple■	D 1	Oklahoma St.■	J26
DePaul	D 4	Colorado	J29
Washburn■	D 6	Missouri	J31
North Caro. St.	D 8	Nebraska■	F 6
Ark.-Lit. Rock■	D11	Kansas St.	F12
Georgia⊠	D18	Oklahoma St.	F16
Furman■	D20	Missouri■	F20
Indiana■	D22	Nebraska	F23
Kansas City Cl.	D29-30	Colorado■	F26
N.C.-Asheville■	J 5	Iowa St.■	M 3
Southern Methodist■	J 8	Oklahoma	M 6
Oklahoma■	J10	Big Eight Conf.	M11-13
Kansas St.■	J17	⊠ Atlanta, GA	

Colors: Crimson & Blue. Nickname: Jayhawks.
AD: Bob Frederick. SID: Doug Vance. I

■ Home games on each schedule.

See pages 405–407 for Division I tournament details

KANSAS ST. .... Manhattan, KS 66506

Dana Altman (4 YRS. W-63, L-53)

Southern Miss.■	N27	Colorado■	J22
Texas A&M■	D 1	Oklahoma	J26
Coppin St.■	D 4	Iowa St.■	J29
LIU-Brooklyn■	D 7	Oklahoma St.	F 2
Marshall■	D 9	Colorado	F 5
Nevada■	D11	Nebraska■	F 9
Hawaii Inv.	D17-18	Kansas■	F12
Mo.-Kansas City	D22	Western Ky.	F15
Southern Miss.	D30	Oklahoma■	F19
La Salle	J 5	Mo.-Kansas City■	F22
Missouri	J 8	Nebraska	F26
Wichita St.■	J12	Missouri■	M 2
Oklahoma St.■	J15	Iowa St.	M 6
Kansas	J17	Big Eight Conf.	M11-13

Colors: Purple & White. Nickname: Wildcats.
AD: Max Urick. SID: Ben Boyle. I

KEAN .... Union, NJ 07083

Mike Gatley (1 YR. W-18, L-8)

Frostburg St. Inv.	N19-20	Ramapo	J19
Wm. Paterson	N23	Rowan■	J22
Rutgers-Newark■	N27	Wm. Paterson■	J26
Rowan	N30	Rutgers-Newark	J29
Trenton St.	D 4	Montclair St.	F 2
Old Westbury	D 6	Trenton St.■	F 5
Rutgers-Camden■	D 8	Millersville	F 7
Stockton St.	D11	Rutgers-Camden	F 9
Kean Cl.	J8-9	Stockton St.■	F11
Montclair St.■	J12	Ramapo■	F15
Jersey City St.■	J14	Jersey City St.	F19

Colors: Royal Blue & Silver. Nickname: Cougars.
AD: Glenn Hedden. SID: Adam Fenton. III

KEENE ST. .... Keene, NH 03431

Don Kelbick (9 YRS. W-63, L-181)

Keene St. Cl.	N19-20	New Hamp. Col.	J19
Springfield■	D 2	Southern Conn. St.	J23
Bryant■	D 6	Franklin Pierce■	J26
Stonehill■	D11	Bridgeport■	J29
Cal St. Bakersfield	D21	Mass.-Lowell	F 2
Cal Poly SLO	D23	Southern Conn. St.■	F 6
Cal St. Los Angeles	D27	New Hamp. Col.■	F 9
Cal St. Dom. Hills	D28	Mass.-Lowell■	F16
Le Moyne■	J 4	Bridgeport	F19
Sacred Heart	J 8	Sacred Heart■	F21
New Haven	J12	Franklin Pierce	F23
Le Moyne	J15	New Haven■	F26

Colors: Red & White. Nickname: Owls.
AD: Joanne Fortunato. SID: Stuart Kaufman. II

KENNESAW .... Marietta, GA 30061

Phil Zenoni (8 YRS. W-126, L-113)

Lander	N20	Clayton St.	J24
S.C.-Spartanburg■	N22	Valdosta St.■	J26
Georgia Col.■	N24	Southern Tech■	J29
Lander■	D 4	Berry	J31
Columbus	D 8	LIFE (Ga.)	F 5
Armstrong St.	D10	La Grange■	F 7
Georgia Col.	D15	Clayton St.■	F 9
Armstrong St.■	J 3	Newberry■	F12
Valdosta St.	J 5	North Ga.	F16
LIFE (Ga.)■	J 8	Brewton Parker	F19
Erskine■	J12	Southern Tech	F23
Brewton Parker■	J17	Berry■	F26
North Ga.■	J19	Erskine	F28
Newberry	J22		

Colors: Black & Gold. Nickname: Fighting Owls.
AD: Dave Waples. SID: Scott Whitlock. II

KENT .... Kent, OH 44242

Dave Grube (13 YRS. W-181, L-147)

Northern Ill.■	D 1	Miami (Ohio)	J26
Hartford■	D 4	Western Mich.■	J29
Niagara■	D 7	Ohio	F 2
Fairfield	D11	Bowling Green■	F 5
Evansville	D18	Eastern Mich.	F 9
Cleveland St.	D23	Toledo■	F12
Siena	D28	Akron■	F16
Yale	D30	Ball St.	F19
Central Mich.■	J 5	Miami (Ohio)■	F23
Bowling Green	J 8	Western Mich.	F26
Eastern Mich.■	J12	Ohio■	M 2
Toledo	J15	Central Mich.	M 5
Akron	J19	Mid-American Conf.	M8-12
Ball St.■	J22		

Colors: Navy Blue & Gold. Nickname: Golden Flashes.
AD: Paul Amodio. SID: Dale Gallagher. I

KENTUCKY .... Lexington, KY 40506

Rick Pitino (11 YRS. W-228, L-105)

Louisville■	N27	Auburn	J30
Tennessee Tech■	D 1	Alabama■	F 2
Indiana⊠	D 4	Massachusetts@P099	F 6
Eastern Ky.■	D 8	Arkansas■	F 9
Morehead St.■	D17	Syracuse	F12
Maui Inv.	D21-23	Louisiana St.	F15
San Francisco■	D28	Vanderbilt	F19
Robert Morris■	D31	Tennessee	F23
Vanderbilt■	J 4	Georgia■	F27
Notre Dame■	J 6	Florida■	M 2
Georgia	J 8	South Caro.	M 5
Mississippi ◆	J12	Southeastern Conf.	M10-13
Tennessee■	J15	⊠ Indianapolis, IN	
Florida	J18	◆ Louisville, KY	
Mississippi St.	J22	@P099 East Rutherford, NJ	
South Caro.■	J26		

Colors: Blue & White. Nickname: Wildcats.
AD: C.M. Newton. SID: Julie Watson. I

KENTUCKY ST. .... Frankfort, KY 40601

William Graham (4 YRS. W-52, L-59)

Central St. (Ohio)■	N23	Southern Ind.	J29
Howard⊠	N27	Indianapolis	F 3
Clark Atlanta	N29	Northern Ky.	F 5
Rollins Inv.	D3-4	Lewis■	F10
Clark Atlanta■	D 7	St. Joseph's (Ind.)■	F12
Gannon	D17	Ashland	F17
Bellarmine	D22	IU/PU-Ft. Wayne	F19
Northern Ky.■	J 6	Central St. (Ohio)	F22
Indianapolis■	J 8	Southern Ind.■	F24
St. Joseph's (Ind.)	J13	Ky. Wesleyan■	F26
Lewis	J15	Knoxville■	M 2
IU/PU-Ft. Wayne■	J20	Bellarmine■	M 5
Ashland■	J22	⊠ Indianapolis, IN	
Ky. Wesleyan	J27		

Colors: Green & Gold. Nickname: Thorobreds.
AD: Don Lyons. SID: Ron Braden. II

KY. WESLEYAN .... Owensboro, KY 42301

Wayne Boultinghouse (10 YRS. W-177, L-101)

Ky. Wesleyan Cl.	N26-27	Kentucky St.■	J27
IU/PU-Indianapolis■	D 9	Bellarmine■	J29
SIU-Edwardsville	D11	Lewis	F 3
Northern Ky.	D20	St. Joseph's (Ind.)	F 5
John Carroll■	D30	Ashland■	F10
Indianapolis	J 1	IU/PU-Ft. Wayne■	F12
St. Joseph's (Ind.)■	J 6	Quincy	F16
Lewis■	J 8	Southern Ind.■	F19
IU/PU-Ft. Wayne	J13	Bellarmine	F24
Ashland	J15	Kentucky St.	F26
Spalding■	J17	Indianapolis■	M 3
SIU-Edwardsville■	J20	Northern Ky.■	M 5
Southern Ind.	J22		

Colors: Purple & White. Nickname: Panthers.
AD: Wayne Boultinghouse. SID: Roy Pickerill. II

KENYON .... Gambier, OH 43022

Bill Brown (7 YRS. W-71, L-99)

Rochester Tip-Off	N19-20	Waynesburg■	J15
Adrian	N27	Mt. Vernon Naz.■	J17
Ohio Wesleyan■	D 1	Wittenberg	J19
Denison	D 4	Denison■	J22
Thiel	D 6	Earlham	J26
Earlham■	D 8	Wooster	J29
Wooster■	D11	Case Reserve■	F 2
Oberlin■	J 3	Oberlin	F 5
Allegheny■	J 5	Ohio Wesleyan	F 9
Juniata Tr.	J8-9	Wittenberg■	F16
Case Reserve	J12	Allegheny	F19

Colors: Purple & White. Nickname: Lords.
AD: Robert Bunnell. SID: Joe Wasiluk. III

KEUKA .... Keuka Park, NY 14478

David Sweet (8 YRS. W-106, L-96)

Penn St.-Behrend■	N20	Roberts Wesleyan	J18
Mansfield	N23	Hamilton Inv.	J22-23
Pracitical Bible■	N30	Pracitical Bible	J25
Rochester Inst.	D 4	Manhattanville Cl.	J29-30
Utica■	D 8	St. John Fisher	F 3
Nazareth (N.Y.)	D11	Elmira■	F 5
Misericordia	D13	Roberts Wesleyan■	F 7
Bapt. Bible (Pa.)■	J 4	Houghton	F12
Frostburg St. Tr.	J7-8	Penn St.-Behrend	F13
Elmira	J12	Utica	F19
North Adams St.	J15	Houghton■	F24

Colors: Green & Gold. Nickname: Warriors.
AD: David Sweet. SID: Alan Loucks. III

■ Home games on each schedule.

See pages 405–407 for Division I tournament details

KNOX .... Galesburg, IL 61401

Tim Heimann (9 YRS. W-101, L-87)

Rosary■	N27	Franklin■	J17
Rose-Hulman■	N28	St. Norbert■	J22
Coe■	D 3	Lawrence■	J23
Grinnell■	D 4	Ripon	J29
Principia	D 7	Lake Forest	J30
Franklin Cl.	D10-11	Illinois Col.	F 5
MacMurray■	J 5	Cornell College■	F11
Illinois Col.■	J 8	Monmouth (Ill.)■	F12
Mt. St. Clare	J10	Coe	F18
Cornell College	J14	Grinnell	F19
Monmouth (Ill.)	J15		

Colors: Purple & Gold. Nickname: Prairie Fire.
AD: Harlan Knosher. SID: Jay Redfern. III

KUTZTOWN .... Kutztown, PA 19530

Bill Whitney (3 YRS. W-16, L-63)

Pitt.-Johnstown Tr.	N19-20	East Stroudsburg■	J26
Shippensburg	N23	Cheyney	J29
Queens (N.Y.)■	N29	Shippensburg■	J31
Indiana (Pa.)	D 6	Mansfield	F 2
Alvernia■	D11	Millersville■	F 5
Messiah	J 5	New York Tech■	F 7
Clarion Tr.	J7-8	West Chester■	F 9
West Chester	J12	Bloomsburg	F12
Millersville	J15	East Stroudsburg	F16
Lock Haven■	J17	Dist. Columbia	F19
Bloomsburg■	J19	Mansfield■	F23
Dist. Columbia■	J22	Cheyney■	F26

Colors: Maroon & Gold. Nickname: Golden Bears.
AD: Clark Yeager. SID: Matt Santos. II

LA SALLE .... Philadelphia, PA 19141

Speedy Morris (7 YRS. W-153, L-65)

Princeton■	N27	Pennsylvania⊠	J25
Illinois	D 1	Detroit Mercy	J29
Colorado Cl.	D3-4	Xavier (Ohio)■	F 5
Phila. Textile■	D 8	Evansville	F10
James Madison	D10	Butler	F12
Hawaii-Hilo Inv.	D28-30	Detroit Mercy■	F16
Richmond	J 3	Loyola (Ill.)■	F19
Kansas St.■	J 5	Butler■	F26
Notre Dame■	J 8	Villanova⊠	F28
St. Joseph's (Pa.)■	J12	Xavier (Ohio)	M 3
Evansville■	J15	Midwestern Conf.	M6-9
Temple■	J20	⊠ Philadelphia, PA	
Loyola (Ill.)	J22		

Colors: Blue & Gold. Nickname: Explorers.
AD: Bob Mullen. SID: Bob Vetrone. I

LA VERNE .... La Verne, CA 91750

Gary Stewart (6 YRS. W-86, L-71)

Washington (Mo.) Tr.	N19-20	Redlands	J26
UC San Diego Tr.	N26-27	Whittier	J29
La Sierra■	N30	Cal Lutheran■	F 2
UC Santa Cruz■	D10	Claremont-M-S	F 5
Cal St. Dom. Hills■	D17	Cal Tech	F 9
Occidental Tr.	D30-31	Pomona-Pitzer■	F12
Chapman	J 8	Occidental	F16
Claremont-M-S■	J12	Redlands■	F19
Cal Tech■	J15	Whittier■	F21
Pomona-Pitzer	J19	Cal Lutheran	F24
Occidental■	J22		

Colors: Orange & Green. Nickname: Leopards, Leos.
AD: Jim Paschal. SID: Pam Maunakea. III

LAFAYETTE .... Easton, PA 18042

John Leone (5 YRS. W-57, L-84)

Vermont■	N27	Navy■	J19
Princeton	D 1	Holy Cross	J22
Brown	D 4	Fordham■	J26
Columbia■	D 7	Army■	J29
Rider	D11	Lehigh	F 2
Syracuse	D13	Colgate■	F 5
Iona College Tr.	D28-29	Bucknell	F 9
Florida St.	J 2	Navy	F12
Yale■	J 6	Holy Cross■	F16
Swarthmore■	J10	Fordham	F19
Colgate	J12	Lehigh■	F23
Bucknell■	J15	Army	F26
Pennsylvania	J17	Patriot Conf.	M4-11

Colors: Maroon & White. Nickname: Leopards.
AD: Eve Atkinson. SID: Steve Pulver. I

LAKE FOREST .... Lake Forest, IL 60045

Ed Timm (1ST YR. AS HEAD COACH)

Elmhurst■	N20	Grinnell	J23
Barat	N23	Illinois Col.■	J29
Wheaton (Ill.)■	D 1	Knox■	J30
Ripon	D 4	St. Norbert	F 2
Ill. Benedictine■	D 7	Lawrence	F 5
Kalamazoo Tr.	D29-30	Chicago	F 8
Concordia (Ill.)	J 6	Ripon■	F12
Beloit	J11	Carroll (Wis.)■	F16
St. Norbert■	J15	Lawrence■	F19
Carroll (Wis.)	J19	Beloit■	F21
Coe	J22		

Colors: Red & Black. Nickname: Foresters.
AD: Jackie Slaats. SID: To be named. III

LAKE SUPERIOR ST. ...... Sault Ste. Marie, MI 49783

Terry Smith (2 YRS. W-22, L-29)

Tiffin Cl.	N20-21	Grand Valley St.■	J20
Central Mich.	N30	Northwood■	J22
Alma Tr.	D3-4	Ferris St.	J29
Wayne St. (Mich.)	D 9	Wayne St. (Mich.)■	F 3
Saginaw Valley	D11	Saginaw Valley■	F 5
Ferris St.■	D18	Hillsdale	F10
Tiffin Tr.	D29-30	Oakland	F12
Lakeland⊠	J 3	Northern Mich.■	F17
Hillsdale■	J 6	Michigan Tech■	F19
Oakland■	J 8	Grand Valley St.	F24
Northern Mich.	J13	Northwood	F26
Michigan Tech	J15	⊠ Kingsford, MI	

Colors: Royal Blue & Gold. Nickname: Lakers.
AD: Jeff Jackson. SID: Scott Monaghan. II

LAMAR .... Beaumont, TX 77710

Grey Giovanine (1ST YR. AS HEAD COACH)

Concordia (Tex.)■	N27	Western Ky.	J29
Mississippi	D 4	Tex.-Pan American	J31
Houston Baptist■	D 7	South Ala.■	F 3
McNeese St.■	D14	Arkansas St.	F 5
Oklahoma	D18	Jacksonville	F10
McNeese St.	D30	Southwestern La.■	F12
New Orleans	J 3	Arkansas St.■	F17
Jacksonville■	J 6	Ark.-Lit. Rock	F19
Louisiana Tech	J 7	Texas	F21
Southwestern La.	J10	Western Ky.■	F24
New Orleans■	J15	Tex.-Pan American■	F26
South Ala.	J17	Houston	M 1
Ark.-Lit. Rock■	J22	Sun Belt Conf.	M4-8
Louisiana Tech■	J25		

Colors: Red & White. Nickname: Cardinals.
AD: To be named. SID: Joe Lee Smith. I

LANE .... Jackson, TN 38301

J.L. Perry (1ST YR. AS HEAD COACH)

LeMoyne-Owen	N18	Bethel (Tenn.)■	D11
Fisk	N20	Virginia St. Cl.	J6-8
Bethel (Tenn.)	N22	Fisk■	J13
Lambuth■	N23	Oakland City	J22
Norfolk St.	N26-27	Stillman	J25
Freed-Hardeman	N29	Rust■	F 1
Delta St.	D 1	LeMoyne-Owen■	F 8
Alabama A&M	D 2	Oakland City■	F12
Stillman■	D 3	Jacksonville St.	F14
Freed-Hardeman■	D 4	Rust	F19
Lane Tr.	D6-7	Delta St.■	F23
Tuskegee	D 9		

Colors: Blue & Red. Nickname: Dragons.
AD: J.L. Perry. SID: Sherrill Scott. II

LAWRENCE .... Appleton, WI 54911

Mike Gallus (14 YRS. W-137, L-165)

N'western (Wis.)	N23	Knox	J23
Wis. Lutheran■	N29	Carroll (Wis.)■	J26
St. Norbert■	D 1	Cornell College■	J29
Carroll (Wis.)	D 4	Monmouth (Ill.)■	J30
Webster	D11	Ripon	F 2
Parks	D12	Lake Forest■	F 5
Milwaukee Engr.	J 5	Wis. Lutheran	F 8
Lakeland■	J10	Beloit■	F12
Beloit	J15	St. Norbert	F15
Northland Bapt.■	J18	Lake Forest	F19
Illinois Col.	J22	Ripon■	F21

Colors: Navy & White. Nickname: Vikings.
AD: Amy Proctor. SID: Jeff School. III

■ Home games on each schedule.

See pages 405–407 for Division I tournament details

LE MOYNE .... Syracuse, NY 13214

Scott Hicks (1 YR. W-18, L-10)

St. Rose	N19
East Stroudsburg	N23
St. Michael's	N27
Roberts Wesleyan■	N29
Edinboro	D 6
LeMoyne Tr.	D10-11
Keene St.	J 4
Franklin Pierce	J 5
Mass.-Lowell■	J 8
Bridgeport■	J10
New Hamp. Col.■	J12
Keene St.■	J15
Sacred Heart■	J17
Southern Conn. St.	J22
New Haven	J23
Franklin Pierce■	J29
St. Lawrence■	F 2
Bridgeport	F 5
Sacred Heart	F 6
Hilbert■	F10
New Haven■	F12
Gannon	F16
New Hamp. Col.	F19
Mass.-Lowell	F20
Southern Conn. St.■	F26

Colors: Green & Gold. Nickname: Dolphins.
AD: Richard Rockwell. SID: Kim B. McAuliff. II

LEMOYNE-OWEN .... Memphis, TN 38126

Jerry Johnson (35 YRS. W-645, L-296)

Lane■	N18
Miles■	N20
Fort Valley St.■	N27
Savannah St.	N30
Morehouse	D 2
Alabama A&M■	D 6
Albany St. (Ga.)■	D11
Paine■	D13
Atlantic City Cl.	D17-19
Rust■	J12
Savannah St.■	J15
Tuskegee	J17
Alabama A&M	J19
Morris Brown	J21
Tuskegee■	J24
Miles	J27
Fort Valley St.	J29
Morris Brown■	F 5
Lane	F 8
Clark Atlanta	F11
Albany St. (Ga.)	F12
Paine	F14
Rust	F16
Morehouse■	F19
Clark Atlanta■	F23

Colors: Purple & Old Gold. Nickname: Magicians.
AD: E.D. Wilkens. SID: Eddie Cook. II

LEBANON VALLEY .... Annville, PA 17003

Pat Flannery (4 YRS. W-66, L-39)

Frank. & Marsh. Cl.	N19-20
Allentown■	N27
Moravian■	D 1
Albright	D 4
Millersville■	D 8
RIT Tr.	D10-11
Catholic	J 4
Lebanon Valley Tr.	J7-8
Juniata■	J11
Susquehanna	J15
Widener■	J18
Elizabethtown■	J22
Messiah	J26
Moravian	J29
Frank. & Marsh.■	J31
Juniata	F 2
Albright■	F 5
Widener	F 9
Susquehanna■	F12
Messiah■	F16
Elizabethtown	F19

Colors: Royal Blue & White. Nickname: Flying Dutchmen.
AD: Louis Sorrentino. SID: John Deamer. III

LEHIGH .... Bethlehem, PA 18015

Dave Duke (5 YRS. W-65 , L-78)

Hofstra	N27
Drexel■	D 1
Iowa Hawkeye Cl.	D3-4
Towson St.	D 7
Harvard■	D11
Muhlenberg■	D22
Tulane	D29
Pennsylvania	J 3
Cornell	J 5
Yale■	J 8
Columbia	J10
Navy	J12
Holy Cross	J15
Fordham	J19
Army■	J22
Bucknell■	J26
Colgate	J29
Lafayette■	F 2
Navy■	F 5
Holy Cross■	F 9
Fordham■	F12
Army	F15
Bucknell	F19
Lafayette	F23
Colgate■	F26
Patriot Conf.	M4-11

Colors: Brown & White. Nickname: Engineers.
AD: Joe Sterrett. SID: Glenn Hofmann. I

LEHMAN .... Bronx, NY 10468

Kevin McGinniss (1 YR. W-0, L-25)

New Paltz St. Cl.	N19-20
Stevens Tech■	N23
Pac. Lutheran	N29
Webb Inst.■	D 1
Cooper Union■	D 3
Bard	D 5
Mt. St. Mary (N.Y.)■	D 7
Emerson-MCA	D10
Gordon	D11
St. Joseph's-Suffolk	D14
Western Conn. St.■	J 8
St. Joseph's (N.Y.)■	J11
Old Westbury■	J13
CCNY	J15
Baruch	J18
John Jay■	J24
York (N.Y.)	J28
Baruch■	J31
Purchase St.	F 2
John Jay	F 4
Medgar Evers■	F 7
Staten Island■	F 9
Hunter	F12
CCNY■	F15

Colors: Blue, Green & White. Nickname: Lightning.
AD: Kevin McGinniss. SID: Taft Gardner. III

LENOIR-RHYNE .... Hickory, NC 28603

John Lentz (10 YRS. W-172, L-115)

Catawba Cl.	N19-20
Lenoir-Rhyne Tr.	N26-27
S.C.-Spartanburg	D 1
Lincoln Memorial Cl.	D18-19
Wofford	J 3
Wingate	J12
Catawba	J15
Mars Hill■	J17
Gardner-Webb■	J19
Elon	J22
Wofford■	J24
Carson-Newman■	J26
Presbyterian■	J29
Mars Hill	F 5
Wingate■	F 9
Catawba■	F12
Gardner-Webb	F16
Elon■	F19
Carson-Newman	F23
Presbyterian	F26

Colors: Red & Black. Nickname: Bears.
AD: Keith Ochs. SID: Thomas Neff. II

LEWIS .... Romeoville, IL 60441

Jim Whitesell (6 YRS. W-70, L-89)

Parks■	N20
Grand Valley St.	N23
Oakland	N29
Ill. Benedictine■	D 1
Eckerd■	D 4
St. Francis (Ill.)■	D 7
Rosary■	D11
Mt. St. Clare■	D18
Cal St. Bakersfield	D22
Ashland■	D30
IU/PU-Ft. Wayne■	J 2
Southern Ind.	J 6
Ky. Wesleyan	J 8
Bellarmine■	J13
Kentucky St.■	J15
Indianapolis	J20
Northern Ky.	J22
St. Joseph's (Ind.)■	J29
Ky. Wesleyan■	F 3
Southern Ind.■	F 5
Kentucky St.	F10
Bellarmine	F12
Northern Ky.■	F17
Indianapolis■	F19
St. Joseph's (Ind.)	F26
IU/PU-Ft. Wayne	M 3
Ashland	M 5

Colors: Red & White. Nickname: Flyers.
AD: Paul Ruddy. SID: Mark Buerger. II

LIBERTY .... Lynchburg, VA 24506

Jeff Meyer (12 YRS. W-189, L-157)

Va. Commonwealth■	D 3
Central Conn. St.■	D 6
Montreat-Anderson■	D10
Averett■	D18
Western Mich.	D21
Virginia	D30
James Madison	J 4
Md.-Balt. County■	J 8
Towson St.■	J10
N.C.-Asheville	J13
Radford	J15
Virginia Tech	J18
Winthrop■	J20
Charleston So.	J22
Coastal Caro.	J24
Campbell	J27
N.C.-Greensboro■	J31
Campbell■	F 3
Md.-Balt. County	F 5
Towson St.	F 7
N.C.-Asheville■	F10
N.C.-Greensboro	F12
Winthrop	F16
Charleston So.■	F19
Coastal Caro.■	F21
Radford■	F26
Big South Conf.	M4-7

Colors: Red, White & Blue. Nickname: Flames.
AD: Chuck Burch. SID: Mitch Goodman. I

LINCOLN (PA) .... Lincoln University, PA 19352

Robert Byars (7 YRS. W-69, L-108)

Frank. & Marsh. Cl.	N19-20
Bowie St.■	N23
Cheyney	N27
Bowie St.■	N30
Randolph-Macon Tr.	D3-4
Gallaudet	D 7
Medgar Evers ◆	D10
CCNY@	D11
Neumann Cl.	D28-29
Rutgers-Camden	J 5
Coppin St.	J 8
Frank. & Marsh.	J12
Frostburg St.■	J15
Salisbury St.■	J22
Stockton St.	J24
Wesley■	F 1
Salisbury St.	F 5
Frostburg St.	F19

☒

◆ New York, NY

@Brooklyn, NY

Colors: Orange & Blue. Nickname: Lions.
AD: Cyrus Jones. SID: To be named. III

LINCOLN MEMORIAL .... Harrogate, TN 37752

Marc Comstock (4 YRS. W-61, L-52)

Indianapolis Tr.	N19-20
Lincoln Memorial Tr.	N26-27
Milligan■	N30
Delta St.■	D 4
Carson-Newman■	D 7
Knoxville	D10
King (Tenn.)■	D15
Lincoln Memorial Cl.	D18-19
Mississippi Col.	J 6
Delta St.	J 8
Mississippi Col.■	J15
North Ala.	J22
Ala.-Huntsville	J24
Limestone■	J29
Carson-Newman	F 2
West Ga.■	F 5
Limestone	F 7
Valdosta St.■	F12
North Ala.■	F14
Valdosta St.	F19
West Ga.	F21
Knoxville■	F23
Ala.-Huntsville■	F26

Colors: Blue & Gray. Nickname: Railsplitters.
AD: Dave Hyatt. SID: Tom Amis. II

■ Home games on each schedule.

See pages 405–407 for Division I tournament details

LIVINGSTON .... Livingston, AL 35470

Rick Reedy (9 YRS. W-113, L-129)

Opponent	Date	Opponent	Date
Ala.-Huntsville	N20	West Ga.	J17
Winona St.■	N22	Ala.-Huntsville■	J22
Ark.-Monticello■	N27	Mississippi Col.■	J24
Ark.-Lit. Rock	N30	Selma	J27
Faulkner Inv.	D3-4	Central Ark.	J29
Shaw	D 7	Henderson St.	J31
Bapt. Christian■	D11	Delta St.	F 5
Southern-N.O.■	J 4	Valdosta St.■	F 7
Henderson St.■	J 8	Bapt. Christian	F12
Central Ark.■	J10	West Ga.■	F14
Selma■	J11	Delta St.■	F19
Shaw■	J13	Mississippi Col.	F22
Valdosta St.	J15		

Colors: Red & White. Nickname: Tigers.
AD: Billy Slay. SID: Dee Outlaw. II

LOCK HAVEN .... Lock Haven, PA 17745

Dave Blank (5 YRS. W-84, L-55)

Opponent	Date	Opponent	Date
Phila. Bible	N19	Gannon■	J24
Bapt. Bible (Pa.)	N23	Shippensburg■	J26
Mansfield	N29	Edinboro■	J29
Millersville■	D 1	Indiana (Pa.)	F 2
Va. Union Inv.	D3-4	Slippery Rock■	F 5
Bloomsburg■	D 7	Allentown	F 7
East Stroudsburg■	J 7	Mercyhurst	F 9
Mercyhurst■	J12	Clarion■	F12
Mt. St. Mary (N.Y.)■	J13	Shippensburg	F16
Slippery Rock	J15	Calif. (Pa.)	F19
Kutztown	J17	Indiana (Pa.)■	F23
Clarion	J19	Edinboro	F26
Calif. (Pa.)■	J22		

Colors: Crimson & White. Nickname: Bald Eagles.
AD: Sharon Taylor. SID: Pat Donghia. II

LONG BEACH ST. .... Long Beach, CA 90840

Seth Greenberg (3 YRS. W-51, L-39)

Opponent	Date	Opponent	Date
Cal Poly SLO■	N26	Cal St. Fullerton■	J29
Cal St. Northridge■	N30	UC Santa Barb.	F 5
Iowa Hawkeye Cl.	D3-4	Nevada-Las Vegas	F 7
Cal Poly Pomona■	D 8	Pacific (Cal.)■	F10
UCLA	D11	San Jose St.■	F12
FDU-Teaneck	D22	Utah St.	F17
New Mexico St.	J 5	Nevada	F19
Utah St.■	J 8	Memphis St.■	F21
Nevada■	J10	New Mexico St.■	F24
San Jose St.	J15	Nevada-Las Vegas■	F26
Pacific (Cal.)	J17	Cal St. Fullerton	M 3
UC Santa Barb.■	J22	UC Irvine	M 5
UC Irvine■	J27	Big West Conf.	M10-13

Colors: Black & Gold. Nickname: Forty Niners.
AD: Dave O'Brien. SID: Scott Cathcart. I

LIU-BROOKLYN .... Brooklyn, NY 11201

Paul Lizzo (22 YRS. W-282, L-312)

Opponent	Date	Opponent	Date
Md.-East. Shore■	D 4	FDU-Teaneck	J20
Kansas St.	D 7	Robert Morris■	J22
Geo. Washington Tr.	D10-11	St. Francis (Pa.)■	J24
Morgan St.■	D18	Wagner■	J27
Northern Iowa■	D21	Monmouth (N.J.)■	J29
St. Peter's	D23	Mt. St. Mary's (Md.)	F 3
Boston College	D30	Rider	F 5
St. Francis (N.Y.)■	J 4	FDU-Teaneck■	F10
Monmouth (N.J.)	J 8	Marist■	F12
Wagner	J10	St. Francis (Pa.)	F17
Rider■	J13	Robert Morris	F19
Mt. St. Mary's (Md.)■	J15	St. Francis (N.Y.)	F26
Marist	J18	Northeast Conf.	F28-M6

Colors: Blue & White. Nickname: Blackbirds.
AD: Paul Lizzo. SID: Bob Gesslein. I

LIU-C.W. POST .... Greenvale, NY 11548

Tom Galeazzi (12 YRS. W-261, L-92)

Opponent	Date	Opponent	Date
Ramapo■	N29	Pace■	J24
Queens (N.Y.)	D 1	LIU-Southampton	J26
Dowling■	D 4	Dowling◆	J29
St. Rose	D 8	Phila. Textile■	F 2
New York Tech■	D11	LIU-Southampton■	F 5
St. Thomas Aquinas■	D22	Adelphi	F 7
Mercy■	J 5	Concordia (N.Y.)	F 9
Molloy	J 8	Molloy■	F12
Pace	J10	New York Tech	F16
Queens (N.Y.)■	J12	St. Rose■	F23
Adelphi■	J15	Mercy	F26
Phila. Textile	J19	⊠	
Concordia (N.Y.)■	J22	◆ Long Island, NY	

Colors: Green & Gold. Nickname: Pioneers.
AD: Vin Salamone. SID: To be named. II

LIU-SOUTHAMPTON .... Southampton, NY 11968

Mark Dellacave (2 YRS. W-10, L-43)

Opponent	Date	Opponent	Date
Dominican (N.Y.)■	N19	Mercy	J24
Concordia (N.Y.)	D 1	LIU-C.W. Post■	J26
Phila. Textile■	D 4	Phila. Textile	J29
Dowling	D 8	Molloy■	F 2
Pace	D11	LIU-C.W. Post	F 5
East Stroudsburg■	D14	Adelphi	F 9
Queens (N.Y.)	J 5	New York Tech	F12
New York Tech■	J 8	Pace■	F16
Mercy■	J10	St. Rose	F19
Concordia (N.Y.)■	J12	Old Westbury	F21
St. Rose■	J15	Dowling■	F23
Molloy	J19	Queens (N.Y.)■	F26
Adelphi■	J22		

Colors: Blue & Gold. Nickname: Colonials.
AD: Mary Topping. SID: Cindy Corwith. II

LONGWOOD .... Farmville, VA 23901

Ron Carr (3 YRS. W-42, L-41)

Opponent	Date	Opponent	Date
Barton	N22	Limestone	J22
Francis Marion Tr.	N26-27	West Va. Wesleyan	J31
Longwood Tr.	D3-4	Elon	F 2
Marshall	D 6	Queens (N.C.)■	F 5
Averett	D 8	Dist. Columbia	F 7
Lynchburg■	D16	Pitt.-Johnstown■	F12
Pfeiffer■	D19	Mount Olive■	F15
Elon■	J 4	IU/PU-Indianapolis■	F19
Clarion Tr.	J7-8	Queens (N.C.)	F23
Virginia St.	J12	Newberry	F26
Dist. Columbia■	J15	Limestone■	M 2
Barton■	J17		

Colors: Blue & White. Nickname: Lancers.
AD: Emily Harsh. SID: Hoke Currie. II

LORAS .... Dubuque, IA 52001

John Lembezeder (1ST YR. AS HEAD COACH)

Opponent	Date	Opponent	Date
Aurora	N24	Wartburg	J29
Rockford	D 2	Upper Iowa■	F 1
Wis.-La Crosse	D 7	Buena Vista	F 4
Augustana (Ill.)	D 9	William Penn■	F 5
St. John's (Minn.)■	D30	Simpson	F11
Nat'l Catholic Tr.	J5-9	Buena Vista■	F12
William Penn	J14	Luther■	F18
Central (Iowa)	J15	Wartburg■	F19
Luther	J21	Dubuque	F22
Dubuque■	J22	Upper Iowa	F25
Simpson■	J28	Central (Iowa)■	F26

Colors: Purple & Gold. Nickname: Duhawks.
AD: Bob Bierie. SID: Howard Thomas. III

LOUISIANA ST. .... Baton Rouge, LA 70894

Dale Brown (21 YRS. W-403, L-233)

Opponent	Date	Opponent	Date
Texas■	N26	Mississippi St.■	J26
Nicholls St.■	D 4	Mississippi■	J29
Oklahoma St.⊠	D11	South Caro.	F 2
McNeese St.■	D16	Tennessee■	F 5
UCLA	D18	Alabama	F 8
Southeastern La.■	D21	Auburn	F12
Winthrop■	D28	Kentucky■	F15
Radford■	D30	Georgia■	F19
Florida	J 5	Louisville	F23
Auburn■	J 8	Mississippi St.	F26
Arkansas	J11	Arkansas■	M 2
Vanderbilt	J15	Mississippi■	M 5
Alabama■	J19	Southeastern Conf.	M10-13
North Caro.⊠	J22	⊠ New Orleans, LA	

Colors: Purple & Gold. Nickname: Fighting Tigers.
AD: Joe Dean. SID: Herb Vincent. I

LOUISIANA TECH .... Ruston, LA 71272

Jerry Loyd (4 YRS. W-70, L-48)

Opponent	Date	Opponent	Date
Wiley■	D 1	Lamar	J25
Jacksonville	D 4	South Ala.■	J29
Jackson St.	D 7	Centenary■	J31
Centenary	D18	New Orleans■	F 3
Marquette	D21	Arkansas St.	F 7
Texas Christian	D23	Western Ky.■	F10
Nicholls St.■	D30	Tex.-Pan American	F12
Texas Christian⊠	J 3	Ark.-Lit. Rock■	F14
Lamar■	J 7	New Orleans	F17
Tex.-Pan American■	J13	South Ala.	F19
Ark.-Lit. Rock	J15	Jacksonville■	F21
Arkansas St.■	J17	Southwestern La.■	F26
Western Ky.	J20	Sun Belt Conf.	M4-8
Southwestern La.	J22	⊠ Shreveport, LA	

Colors: Red & Blue. Nickname: Bulldogs.
AD: Jerry Stovall. SID: Keith Prince. I

■ Home games on each schedule.

See pages 405–407 for Division I tournament details

LOUISVILLE .... Louisville, KY 40292

Denny Crum (22 YRS. W-518, L-192)

Kentucky	N27
Michigan St.■	D 4
Morehead St.■	D 8
Eastern Ky.■	D11
Wyoming	D18
Western Ky.■	D22
Hawaii Rainbow Cl.	D27-30
George Mason■	J 4
South Fla.■	J 6
Va. Commonwealth■	J 8
Virginia Tech■	J13
Georgia Tech■	J15
Tulane	J20
Southern Miss.■	J22
Virginia Tech	J27
Va. Commonwealth	J29
N.C.-Charlotte■	F 3
Vanderbilt■	F 6
South Fla.	F10
Tulane■	F12
N.C.-Charlotte	F17
Temple⊠	F20
Louisiana St.■	F23
Notre Dame	F26
Howard	F28
Southern Miss.	M 2
UCLA	M 6
Metro Conf.	M11-13

⊠ Orlando, FL

Colors: Red, Black, White. Nickname: Cardinals.
AD: William Olsen. SID: Kenny Klein. I

LOYOLA (CAL.) .... Los Angeles, CA 90045

John Olive (1 YR. W-7, L-20)

UCLA	N27
Southern Cal	N30
Wisconsin■	D 4
San Jose St.	D11
Nevada-Las Vegas	D18
UC Santa Barb.■	D20
San Diego St.■	D23
Texas A&M■	D30
Fairfield■	J 3
Buffalo■	J 7
Oral Roberts	J10
St. Mary's (Cal.)■	J14
Santa Clara■	J15
San Francisco	J20
San Diego	J22
Pepperdine	J26
Pepperdine■	J29
Gonzaga■	F 4
Portland■	F 5
Portland	F10
Gonzaga	F12
San Diego■	F18
San Francisco■	F19
Cal St. Sacramento■	F22
Santa Clara	F25
St. Mary's (Cal.)	F26
West Coast Conf.	M5-7

Colors: Crimson & Blue. Nickname: Lions.
AD: Brian Quinn. SID: Bruce Meyers. I

LOYOLA (ILL.) .... Chicago, IL 60626

Will Rey (4 YRS. W-37, L-77)

Morgan St.■	N27
Morehead St.	D 1
Bowling Green■	D 4
Concordia (Ill.)■	D 8
Northwestern■	D11
Bethune-Cookman■	D20
Morehead St.■	D23
Morgan St.	D28
Coppin St.	D30
Ill.-Chicago	J 4
Miami (Ohio)	J10
Detroit Mercy	J15
Butler	J19
La Salle■	J22
Notre Dame	J24
Xavier (Ohio)	J29
DePaul	F 2
Butler■	F 6
Northern Ill.■	F10
Evansville	F12
Evansville■	F16
La Salle	F19
Bradley	F23
Detroit Mercy■	F26
Xavier (Ohio)■	M 1
Notre Dame■	M 3
Midwestern Conf.	M6-9

Colors: Maroon & Gold. Nickname: Ramblers.
AD: Chuck Schwarz. SID: Traci McCurdy. I

LOYOLA (MD.) .... Baltimore, MD 21210

Skip Prosser (1ST YR. AS HEAD COACH)

William & Mary	N29
Towson St.■	D 1
St. Joseph's (Pa.)■	D 4
American	D 8
Mt. St. Mary's (Md.)	D11
Delaware	J 3
Iona■	J 5
Maine■	J 8
Navy■	J10
Md.-Balt. County■	J12
Siena■	J15
St. Peter's	J17
Canisius	J22
Niagara	J24
Fairfield	J27
William & Mary■	J30
St. Peter's■	F 2
Niagara■	F 5
Canisius■	F 7
Siena	F 9
Manhattan	F12
Iona	F14
Maryland	F19
Fordham	F21
Manhattan■	F23
Fairfield■	F27
Metro Atlantic Conf.	M5-7

Colors: Green & Grey. Nickname: Greyhounds.
AD: Joseph Boylan. SID: Steve Jones. I

LUTHER .... Decorah, IA 52101

Jeff Olinger (2 YRS. W-25, L-26)

Gust. Adolphus	N20
Hamline■	N23
Mt. Mercy■	N30
Iowa Wesleyan	D 4
Clarke■	D 8
Cornell College	D11
Coe■	D18
Elmhurst Cl.	D29-30
Simpson	J 7
Upper Iowa	J 8
Buena Vista■	J14
Wartburg■	J15
Loras■	J21
Central (Iowa)	J22
Dubuque	J28
William Penn	J29
Central (Iowa)■	F 4
Simpson■	F 5
Upper Iowa■	F11
Wartburg	F12
Loras	F18
Buena Vista	F19
Dubuque■	F25
William Penn■	F26

Colors: Blue & White. Nickname: Norse.
AD: Andrea Wickerham. SID: Dave Blanchard. III

LYCOMING .... Williamsport, PA 17701

Clarence Burch (31 YRS. W-314, L-385)

Misericordia■	N23
Allentown■	N29
Drew	D 1
Upsala■	D 4
Juniata	D 7
Elizabethtown Cl.	D10-11
Moravian Tr.	J7-8
Wilkes■	J12
FDU-Madison■	J15
Bapt. Bible (Pa.)	J17
Scranton	J19
Delaware Valley■	J22
King's (Pa.)	J26
Drew■	J29
Susquehanna■	J31
Wilkes	F 2
Upsala	F 5
Scranton■	F 9
FDU-Madison	F12
King's (Pa.)■	F16
Delaware Valley	F19

Colors: Blue & Gold. Nickname: Warriors.
AD: Frank Girardi. SID: Ken Weingartner. III

LYNCHBURG .... Lynchburg, VA 24501

Joe Davis (12 YRS. W-176, L-151)

Mary Washington	N29
Guilford■	D 1
Salisbury St. Cl.	D3-4
Roanoke	D 6
Longwood	D16
Pitt.-Johnstown	J 6
Randolph-Macon	J 8
Hampden-Sydney■	J10
Wash. & Lee■	J12
Pitt.-Johnstown■	J14
Emory & Henry■	J16
East. Mennonite■	J20
Va. Wesleyan	J22
Guilford	J25
East. Mennonite	J27
Bridgewater (Va.)■	J29
Emory & Henry	F 2
Randolph-Macon■	F 5
Roanoke■	F 7
Wash. & Lee	F 9
Bridgewater (Va.)	F12
Hampden-Sydney	F14
Va. Wesleyan■	F19

Colors: Grey & Crimson. Nickname: Hornets.
AD: Jack Toms. SID: Lee Ashby. III

MACALESTER .... St. Paul, MN 55105

Doug Bolstorff (30 YRS. W-270, L-486)

St. Scholastica	N20
Concordia (St. Paul)■	N23
Colorado College Tr.	N26-27
Bethel (Minn.)■	D 4
Augsburg■	D 8
St. Olaf	D11
Gust. Adolphus	J 3
Carleton■	J 5
Hamline	J 8
St. John's (Minn.)■	J10
Concordia-M'head	J12
St. Thomas (Minn.)	J15
St. Mary's (Minn.)■	J17
Bethel (Minn.)	J22
Augsburg	J26
St. Olaf■	J29
Gust. Adolphus■	J31
Carleton	F 2
Hamline■	F 5
St. John's (Minn.)	F 9
Concordia-M'head■	F12
St. Thomas (Minn.)■	F14
St. Mary's (Minn.)	F16

Colors: Orange & Blue. Nickname: Scots.
AD: Ken Andrews. SID: Andy Johnson. III

MACMURRAY .... Jacksonville, IL 62650

Bob Gay (18 YRS. W-204, L-254)

Ripon Tr.	N19-20
Parks■	N30
Aurora	D 3
Monmouth (Ill.)	D 8
Millikin■	D11
Knox	J 5
Rhodes	J 8
Principia■	J13
Webster	J15
Blackburn	J20
Maryville (Mo.)■	J22
Fontbonne■	J25
Westminster (Mo.)	J27
Parks	J29
Washington (Mo.)■	F 1
Fontbonne	F 3
Principia	F 5
Greenville■	F 8
Webster■	F10
Blackburn■	F12
Illinois Col.	F15
Maryville (Mo.)	F17
Westminster (Mo.)■	F19

Colors: Scarlet & Navy. Nickname: Highlanders.
AD: Bob Gay. SID: Tom Lenz. III

MAINE .... Orono, ME 04469

Rudy Keeling (5 YRS. W-60, L-84)

Bradley	N27
Ball St. Cardinal Cl	D3-4
Rhode Island■	D11
Central Conn. St.■	D13
Eastern Ill.■	D19
Central Fla.⊠	D30
Dartmouth ◆	J 2
DePaul	J 5
Loyola (Md.)	J 8
Hofstra■	J11
Drexel■	J14
Delaware■	J16
Vermont	J20
Hartford■	J22
Boston U.	J27
Northeastern	J29
Fairfield	J31
New Hampshire■	F 5
Northeastern■	F10
Boston U.■	F12
Hartford	F17
Vermont■	F19
Delaware	F25
Drexel	F27
New Hampshire	M 2
North Atlantic Conf.	M5-9

⊠ Augusta, ME
◆ Portland, ME

Colors: Blue & White. Nickname: Black Bears.
AD: Michael Ploszek. SID: Matt Bourque. I

■ Home games on each schedule.

See pages 405–407 for Division I tournament details

MAINE MARITIME .... Castine, ME 04420

Chris Murphy (1 YR. W-8, L-11)

Colby Tr. N20-21
Unity .... D 1
Mt. St. Vincent Tr. D4-5
Bowdoin■ D11
Me.-Augusta D13
Thomas D15
Maine Fort Kent Cl. J15-16
Me.-Farmington J20
Thomas J24
Westbrook J26
Me.-Fort Kent J30
Unity .... F 3
Daniel Webster .... F 5
New England .... F 7
Emerson Inv. F12-13
Me.-Augusta F16
Daniel Webster F20

Colors: Royal Blue & Gold. Nickname: Mariners.
AD: Bill Mottola. SID: Holly Daste. III

MANCHESTER .... North Manchester, IN 46962

Steve Alford (2 YRS. W-24, L-24)

Purdue-Calumet■ N20
Huntington N23
Ball St. N27
Olivet N29
Rockford■ .... D 4
Grace■ .... D 7
Thomas More D11
Goshen■ D17
Manchester Cl. D29-30
Franklin .... J 5
DePauw■ .... J 8
Anderson■ J12
Wabash J15
Earlham J17
Hanover■ J22
Rose-Hulman J26
DePauw J29
Franklin■ .... F 2
Wabash■ .... F 5
Anderson .... F 8
Hanover F12
Bluffton■ F16
Rose-Hulman■ F19

Colors: Black & Gold. Nickname: Spartans.
AD: Tom Jarman. SID: Rob Nichols. III

MANHATTAN .... Riverdale, NY 10471

Fran Fraschilla (1 YR. W-23, L-7)

Wagner .... D 1
Fordham .... D 4
Rider■ .... D 6
Monmouth (N.J.)■ D11
Hofstra⊠ D18
Florida Int'l■ D21
Meadowlands Tr. D29-30
Columbia■ .... J 5
Niagara .... J 8
Canisius J10
Siena■ J13
Iona J18
Notre Dame J22
Iona■ J25
Siena J28
St. Peter's■ J30
Fairfield .... F 3
Canisius■ .... F 5
St. Peter's .... F 8
Loyola (Md.)■ F12
Fairfield■ F16
Massachusetts F18
Loyola (Md.) F23
Niagara■ F27
Metro Atlantic Conf. M5-7
⊠ Uniondale, NY

Colors: Kelly Green & White. Nickname: Jaspers.
AD: Robert Byrnes. SID: Jeff Bernstein. I

MANHATTANVILLE .... Purchase, NY 10577

Ralph Tedesco (14 YRS. W-187, L-174)

Rochester Tip-Off N19-20
Staten Island■ N23
New York U.■ N29
St. Thomas Aquin. Tr D3-4
Western Conn. St.■ .... D 8
Maritime (N.Y.) J16
Merchant Marine■ J18
Hunter J20
Skidmore■ J22
Merchant Marine J24
Staten Island J26
Manhattanville Cl. J29-30
New Jersey Tech .... F 1
Stony Brook■ .... F 3
Connecticut Col. .... F 5
Mt. St. Mary (N.Y.)■ .... F 7
Hunter■ F10
Trinity (Conn.) F12
Mt. St. Vincent F14
New Jersey Tech■ F18
Stony Brook F22
Vassar■ F25

Colors: Red & White. Nickname: Valiants.
AD: Ted Kolva. SID: Susan Eichner. III

MANKATO ST. .... Mankato, MN 56001

Dan McCarrell (26 YRS. W-447, L-262)

Mankato St. Cl. N26-27
Wayne St. (Neb.)■ .... D 4
Bemidji St. .... D 8
Minn.-Duluth■ D11
Metro St. Tr. D17-18
Winona St.■ D29
North Dak. St. .... J 2
North Dak. .... J 3
Morningside■ .... J 7
South Dak.■ .... J 8
St. Cloud St. J15
North Dak. St.■ J18
Augustana (S.D.) J21
South Dak. St. J22
Nebraska-Omaha■ J28
Northern Colo.■ J29
South Dak. .... F 4
Morningside .... F 5
St. Cloud St.■ F12
South Dak. St.■ F18
Augustana (S.D.)■ F19
North Dak.■ F22
Northern Colo. F25
Nebraska-Omaha F26

Colors: Purple & Gold. Nickname: Mavericks.
AD: Don Amiot. SID: Paul Allan. II

MANSFIELD .... Mansfield, PA 16933

Tom Ackerman (8 YRS. W-83, L-135)

Mansfield Tr. N19-20
Keuka■ N23
Gannon Cl. N26-27
Lock Haven■ N29
Pitt.-Johnstown .... D 4
Pitt.-Bradford■ .... D 8
Shippensburg D11
Mercyhurst■ D18
Dist. Columbia D21
Indiana (Pa.) Tr. J5-6
Gannon■ .... J 8
East Stroudsburg■ J12
West Chester J15
Cheyney J22
Bloomsburg J26
Millersville J29
Kutztown■ .... F 2
West Chester■ .... F 5
East Stroudsburg .... F 9
Bloomsburg■ F16
Cheyney■ F19
Kutztown F23
Millersville■ F26

Colors: Red & Black. Nickname: Mountaineers.
AD: Roger Maisner. SID: Steve McCloskey. II

MARIETTA .... Marietta, OH 45750

Doug Foote (1 YR. W-5, L-20)

Roanoke Cl. N20-21
Wilmington (Ohio) N27
Xavier (Ohio) N29
Wash. & Jeff.■ .... D 1
Mount Union■ .... D 8
Heidelberg D11
Baldwin-Wallace D18
John Carroll⊠ D21
Marietta Tr. D29
Muskingum■ .... J 5
Hiram .... J 8
Otterbein J12
Ohio Northern■ J15
Capital J19
Heidelberg■ J22
Mount Union J26
John Carroll■ J29
Otterbein■ .... F 2
Baldwin-Wallace■ .... F 5
Muskingum .... F 9
Hiram■ F12
Capital■ F16
Ohio Northern F19
⊠ Cleveland, OH

Colors: Navy Blue & White. Nickname: Pioneers.
AD: Debro Lazorik. SID: Mike McNamara. III

MARIST .... Poughkeepsie, NY 12601

Dave Magarity (12 YRS. W-158, L-179)

Buffalo N27
Siena■ .... D 1
Vermont⊠ .... D 4
Siena .... D 6
St. Francis (Pa.) D11
Army■ D19
Marist Cl. D29-30
Mt. St. Mary's (Md.)■ .... J 4
Rider■ .... J 6
FDU-Teaneck .... J 8
Robert Morris J13
Fairfield J15
LIU-Brooklyn■ J18
St. Francis (N.Y.)■ J20
Wagner J22
Monmouth (N.J.) J24
FDU-Teaneck■ J29
St. Francis (Pa.)■ .... F 3
Robert Morris■ .... F 5
St. Francis (N.Y.) F10
LIU-Brooklyn F12
Monmouth (N.J.)■ F16
Wagner■ F19
Mt. St. Mary's (Md.) F24
Rider F26
Northeast Conf. F28-M6
⊠ Albany, NY

Colors: Red & White. Nickname: Red Foxes.
AD: Gene Doris. SID: Dan Sullivan. I

MARITIME (N.Y.) .... New York, NY 10465

John Dwinell (5 YRS. W-50, L-76)

Vassar N19
Baruch■ N23
Stevens Tech■ N30
Mt. St. Vincent .... D 2
Utica .... D 5
Yeshiva .... D 9
Bard D11
Mt. St. Vincent■ J13
Manhattanville■ J16
St. Joseph's (N.Y.)■ J18
Polytechnic (N.Y.) J20
Stevens Tech J25
Medgar Evers■ J27
Manhattanville Cl. J29-30
Vassar■ .... F 2
St. Joseph's-Suffolk .... F 5
Albertus Magnus■ .... F 7
Merchant Marine .... F 9
Yeshiva■ F12
Bard■ F14
New Jersey Tech F16
Polytechnic (N.Y.)■ F19

Colors: Cardinal Red, Blue & White. Nickname: Privateers.
AD: James Migli. SID: Kathleen Hewitt. III

MARQUETTE .... Milwaukee, WI 53233

Kevin O'Neill (5 YRS. W-79, L-67)

San Juan Shootout N26-28
Marquette Tr. D3-4
Illinois■ .... D 7
Ohio St.■ D12
Wis.-Milwaukee■ D18
Louisiana Tech■ D21
Northern Ill. D28
Wisconsin .... J 2
Memphis St.■ .... J 5
Arizona .... J 8
DePaul J12
Ala.-Birmingham J19
St. Louis■ J22
St. Louis J26
Memphis St. J29
South Fla.■ J31
Ala.-Birmingham■ .... F 2
West Va.■ .... F 5
Cincinnati F10
Cincinnati■ F13
Virginia Tech F15
Notre Dame■ F17
Dayton■ F20
Dayton F23
DePaul■ F27
San Francisco■ F28
Great Midwest Conf. M10-12

Colors: Blue & Gold. Nickname: Warriors.
AD: Bill Cords. SID: Kathleen Hohl. I

■ Home games on each schedule.

See pages 405–407 for Division I tournament details

MARS HILL .... Mars Hill, NC 28754

David Riggins (7 YRS. W-90, L-107)

Lees-McRae■ N29
Berea Inv. D3-4
N.C.-Asheville .... D 8
Clinch Valley D11
Montreat-Anderson■ D18
Queens (N.C.) Cl. J6-8
Elon■ J12
Gardner-Webb■ J15
Lenoir-Rhyne J17
Carson-Newman J19
Catawba J22
Presbyterian■ J26
Wingate■ J29
Lees-McRae J31
Lenoir-Rhyne■ .... F 5
Elon .... F 9
Gardner-Webb F12
Carson-Newman■ F16
Catawba■ F19
Presbyterian F23
Wingate F26

Colors: Blue & Gold. Nickname: Lions.
AD: Ed Hoffmeyer. SID: To be named. II

MARSHALL .... Huntington, WV 25701

Dwight Freeman (3 YRS. W-37, L-47)

Pitt.-Johnstown■ N30
Montana St.■ .... D 4
Longwood■ .... D 6
Kansas St. .... D 9
Oral Roberts D20
Wake Forest D22
Davidson■ D30
North Caro. .... J 2
Appalachian St.■ .... J 4
Tenn.-Chatt. .... J 8
Western Caro. J10
East Tenn. St.■ J13
Ga. Southern J15
Citadel J17
West Va.⊠ J19
Furman■ J22
Va. Military J27
East Tenn. St. J29
Appalachian St. J31
Va. Military■ .... F 5
Western Caro.■ F12
Tenn.-Chatt.■ F14
Citadel■ F19
Ga. Southern■ F21
Davidson F26
Furman F28
Southern Conf. M3-6
⊠ Charleston, WV

Colors: Green & White. Nickname: Thundering Herd.
AD: Lee Moon. SID: Clark Haptonstall. I

MARY WASHINGTON ..... Fredericksburg, VA 22401

Tom Davies (15 YRS. W-154, L-242)

Chris. Newport N19
Va. Wesleyan■ N20
Hampden-Sydney■ N23
Lynchburg■ N29
Shenandoah .... D 2
St. Mary's (Md.) .... J 8
Wash. & Lee■ J10
Western Md. J11
St. Mary's (Md.)■ J13
Newport News App.■ J15
Marymount (Va.)■ J18
Gallaudet J20
Goucher J22
Salisbury St.■ J25
Shenandoah■ J27
York (Pa.)■ J29
Catholic .... F 1
St. Mary's (Md.) .... F 3
Marymount (Va.) .... F 5
Gallaudet■ .... F 8
Goucher■ F10
Frostburg St. F12
Newport News App. F15
Catholic■ F17
York (Pa.) F19

Colors: Navy, Gray & White. Nickname: Eagles.
AD: Ed Hegmann. SID: Vince Benigni. III

MARYLAND .... College Park, MD 20740

Gary Williams (15 YRS. W-268, L-185)

Georgetown■ N26
Cornell■ N27
Rider■ N30
Md.-Balt. County■ .... D 2
Morgan St.■ .... D 4
Oklahoma⊠ .... D 7
Towson St.■ D23
Massachusetts Tr. D28-29
Georgia Tech .... J 4
North Caro.■ .... J 8
Florida St.■ J11
Wake Forest J15
North Caro. St.■ J22
Clemson■ J26
Duke J29
Virginia .... F 2
Georgia Tech■ .... F 5
North Caro. F10
Florida St. F12
Wake Forest■ F16
Loyola (Md.)■ F19
North Caro. St. F23
Clemson F26
Duke■ .... M 2
Virginia■ .... M 5
Atlantic Coast Conf. M10-13
⊠ Oklahoma City, OK

Colors: Red, White, Black & Gold. Nickname: Terps.
AD: Andy Geiger. SID: Herb Hartnett. I

MD.-BALT. COUNTY .... Baltimore, MD 21228

Earl Hawkins (5 YRS. W-58, L-84)

Washington (Md.)■ N27
Maryland .... D 2
Robert Morris■ .... D 4
California Cl. D10-12
Xavier (Ohio)■ D30
Drexel■ .... J 4
Liberty .... J 8
Radford J10
Loyola (Md.) J12
Charleston So.■ J15
Coastal Caro.■ J17
Towson St. J19
N.C.-Greensboro J22
Campbell J24
N.C.-Asheville■ J27
Winthrop■ J29
Liberty■ .... F 5
Radford■ .... F 7
Charleston So. F12
Coastal Caro. F14
Towson St.■ F17
N.C.-Greensboro■ F19
Campbell■ F21
N.C.-Asheville F24
Winthrop F26
Big South Conf. M4-7

Colors: Black & Old Gold. Nickname: Retrievers.
AD: Charles Brown. SID: Steve Levy. I

MD.-EAST. SHORE .... Princess Anne, MD 21853

Rob Chavez (1 YR. W-12, L-15)

Wilmington (Del.)■ N29
Cabrini■ .... D 1
LIU-Brooklyn .... D 4
St. Peter's■ .... D 9
Navy D11
Syracuse D18
Penn St. D20
Colorado D30
North Adams St.■ .... J 6
Florida A&M■ .... J 8
Bethune-Cookman■ J10
Howard J13
Morgan St.■ J15
Coppin St. J17
South Caro. St. J22
North Caro. A&T J24
Howard■ J27
Morgan St. J29
South Caro. St.■ .... F 5
North Caro. A&T■ .... F 7
Delaware St. F12
Central Conn. St.■ F15
Florida A&M F19
Bethune-Cookman F21
Coppin St.⊠ F26
Delaware St.■ .... M 3
Mid-Eastern Conf. M9-13
⊠ Salisbury, MD

Colors: Maroon & Gray. Nickname: Hawks.
AD: Hallie Gregory. SID: Sheila Benton. I

MARYMOUNT (VA.) .... Arlington, VA 22207

Webb Hatch (6 YRS. W-76, L-78)

Bridgewater (Va.) N22
Hampden-Sydney■ N29
Bucknell .... D 4
Western Md.■ .... D 9
Shenandoah D11
Chris. Newport D18
Newport News App. .... J 5
Marymount Tr. J8-9
Catholic■ J12
Gallaudet■ J15
Mary Washington J18
York (Pa.) J20
Wesley■ J22
Shenandoah■ J24
St. Mary's (Md.) J26
Goucher■ J29
York (Pa.)■ .... F 3
Mary Washington■ .... F 5
Catholic .... F 7
St. Mary's (Md.)■ F10
Newport News App.■ F12
Goucher F17
Gallaudet F19

Colors: Royal Blue, White & Green. Nickname: Saints.
AD: Bill Finney. SID: Webb Hatch. III

MARYVILLE (MO.) .... Creve Coeur, MO 63141

Steve Jarvis (2 YRS. W-15, L-43)

Hanover Cl. N19-20
Rhodes■ N23
Grinnell■ N28
Rhodes Cl. D3-4
Mo.-St. Louis .... D 7
Washington (Mo.) D11
BYU-Hawaii D21
Hawaii Pacific D22
Fontbonne■ J11
Principia J15
Webster J20
MacMurray J22
Blackburn■ J27
Westminster (Mo.)■ J29
Parks .... F 3
Fontbonne .... F 5
Parks■ .... F 8
Principia■ F10
Webster■ F12
Westminster (Mo.) F15
MacMurray■ F17
Blackburn F19

Colors: Red & White. Nickname: Saints.
AD: Dave Pierce. SID: Lonnie Folks. III

MARYVILLE (TENN.) .... Maryville, TN 37801

Randy Lambert (13 YRS. W-203, L-134)

Rhodes Tr. N19-20
Covenant N23
Greensboro■ N28
Emory & Henry .... D 4
Tenn. Wesleyan .... D 8
Oglethorpe D11
Tenn. Wesleyan■ D18
Maryville (Tenn.) Tr J3-4
Ferrum■ .... J 8
King (Tenn.)■ J11
Rust J15
Centre■ J19
Knoxville J22
Sewanee J26
Centre .... F 2
Asbury .... F 5
Emory & Henry■ .... F 6
Martin Methodist F10
Rust■ F12
Knoxville■ F16
Ferrum F19
Asbury■ F23
Martin Methodist■ F26

Colors: Orange & Garnet. Nickname: Scots.
AD: Randy Lambert. SID: To be named. III

MASSACHUSETTS .... Amherst, MA 01003

John Calipari (5 YRS. W-101, L-57)

Pre-Season NIT N17-26
Oklahoma N28
St. Bonaventure .... D 4
Central Conn. St.■ .... D 9
Holy Cross⊠ D11
Massachusetts Tr. D28-29
Rutgers .... J 4
Duquesne .... J 8
West Va. J13
St. Bonaventure■ J15
DePaul J18
Rutgers■ J20
Geo. Washington■ J22
Cincinnati J27
Rhode Island■ J30
Florida St.■ .... F 3
Kentucky♦ .... F 6
Rhode Island@ F10
Temple■ F13
St. Joseph's (Pa.) F15
Buffalo■ F16
Manhattan■ F18
West Va.■ F20
St. Joseph's (Pa.)■ F22
Temple F24
Geo. Washington F27
Duquesne■ .... M 2
Atlantic 10 Conf. M5-10
⊠ Worcester, MA
♦ East Rutherford, NJ
@ Providence, RI

Colors: Maroon & White. Nickname: Minutemen.
AD: Frank McInerney. SID: Howard Davis. I

■ Home games on each schedule.

See pages 405–407 for Division I tournament details

MIT .... Cambridge, MA 02139

Leo Osgood (7 YRS. W-64, L-104)

Opponent	Date	Opponent	Date
Trinity (Tex.) Tr.	N19-20	Coast Guard	J22
Babson	N23	Norwich	J25
Worcester Tech■	N27	Suffolk■	J27
Brandeis■	N30	Connecticut Col.	F 3
Gordon	D 2	Wentworth Inst.	F 5
New England Col.	D 4	Tufts■	F 8
Eastern Nazarene■	D 7	Western New Eng.	F12
Coast Guard■	J 8	Norwich■	F15
Curry	J13	Worcester Tech	F17
Nichols■	J15	Babson■	F19
Western New Eng.■	J19		

Colors: Cardinal & Gray. Nickname: Engineers.
AD: Richard Hill. SID: Roger Crosley. III

MASS.-BOSTON .... Boston, MA 02125

Charlie Titus (17 YRS. W-202, L-215)

Opponent	Date	Opponent	Date
Mass.-Boston Inv.	N27-28	Southern Me.	J25
Northeastern	N30	Western Conn. St.	J29
Western Conn. St.■	D 4	Mass.-Dartmouth	F 1
Salem St.■	D 7	Suffolk■	F 5
Westfield St.■	D 9	Plymouth St.■	F 8
North Adams St.■	D11	Tufts■	F10
Mass.-Dartmouth■	J11	Rhode Island Col.	F12
Rhode Island Col.■	J15	Southern Me.■	F15
Plymouth St.	J18	Eastern Conn. St.■	F17
Bri'water (Mass.)	J20	Colby■	F19
Eastern Conn. St.	J22	Clark (Mass.)	F22

Colors: Blue & White. Nickname: Beacons.
AD: Charlie Titus. SID: Kevin Dolan. III

MASS.-LOWELL .... Lowell, MA 01854

Gary Manchel (1 YR. W-13, L-15)

Opponent	Date	Opponent	Date
Merrimack Tr.	N20-21	Franklin Pierce	J19
Bryant■	N27	Sacred Heart	J22
Bentley	D 1	New Hamp. Col.■	J26
St. Michael's■	D 6	Southern Conn. St.	J29
St. Anselm	D 8	Keene St.■	F 2
Assumption	D11	New Haven	F 7
American Int'l	D14	Franklin Pierce■	F 9
New York Tech■	D30	Sacred Heart■	F12
Quinnipiac■	J 3	Bridgeport■	F14
Le Moyne	J 8	Keene St.	F16
Bridgeport	J12	Le Moyne■	F20
New Haven■	J15	New Hamp. Col.	F23
Southern Conn. St.■	J17		

Colors: Red, White & Blue. Nickname: Chiefs.
AD: Wayne Edwards. SID: B.L. Elfring. II

MCNEESE ST. .... Lake Charles, LA 70601

Steve Welch (6 YRS. W-64, L-105)

Opponent	Date	Opponent	Date
Louisiana Col.■	N27	Southwest Tex. St.■	J22
Belhaven■	D 2	Stephen F. Austin	J27
Mississippi	D11	Sam Houston St.	J29
Lamar	D14	Texas-Arlington	F 3
Louisiana St.	D16	North Texas	F 5
Stanford	D20	Northwestern (La.)■	F10
San Francisco	D22	Northeast La.■	F12
Lamar■	D30	Southwest Tex. St.	F17
Nicholls St.■	J 3	Texas-San Antonio	F19
North Texas■	J 6	Sam Houston St.■	F24
Texas-Arlington■	J 8	Stephen F. Austin■	F26
Northeast La.	J13	Nicholls St.	F28
Northwestern (La.)	J15	Southland Conf.	M4-6
Texas-San Antonio■	J20		

Colors: Blue & Gold. Nickname: Cowboys.
AD: Robert Hayes. SID: Louis Bonnette. I

MEDGAR EVERS .... Brooklyn, NY 11225

Bryan Mariner (2 YRS. W-24, L-29)

Opponent	Date	Opponent	Date
New Paltz St. Cl.	N19-20	York (N.Y.)	J24
Queens (N.Y.)	N24	Maritime (N.Y.)	J27
Mt. St. Mary Tr.	D4-5	Staten Island■	J29
Lincoln (Pa.)☒	D10	Hunter■	F 2
Cheyney■	D11	York (N.Y.)■	F 4
Staten Island	D15	CCNY■	F 5
Old Westbury	D17	Lehman	F 7
Hunter	J 4	Pratt	F 8
John Jay	J 6	Baruch■	F14
Mt. St. Vincent Cl.	J7-8	☒ New York, NY	
Ramapo■	J10		

Colors: Brown & Gold. Nickname: Cougars.
AD: Roy Anderson. SID: To be named. III

MEMPHIS ST. .... Memphis, TN 38152

Larry Finch (7 YRS. W-145, L-81)

Opponent	Date	Opponent	Date
Alcorn St.■	N26	Cincinnati■	J23
Tennessee■	D 2	Marquette■	J29
Arkansas■	D 8	Cincinnati	F 3
Georgia St.■	D11	Dayton	F 5
Florida Int'l■	D18	Dayton■	F 9
Texas-San Antonio■	D20	Ala.-Birmingham■	F12
Southwestern La.	D23	Southern Miss.	F16
Jackson St.■	D27	Long Beach St.	F21
Georgetown■	D30	Ark.-Lit. Rock■	F24
Marquette	J 5	St. Louis■	F26
DePaul■	J 8	Southeast Mo. St.■	M 2
St. Louis	J11	DePaul	M 5
Ala.-Birmingham	J16	Great Midwest Conf.	M10-12
Murray St.	J19		

Colors: Blue & Gray. Nickname: Tigers.
AD: Charles Cavagnaro. SID: Mark Owens. I

MENLO .... Menlo Park, CA 94025

Al Klein (1ST YR. AS HEAD COACH)

Opponent	Date	Opponent	Date
Menlo Cl.	N19-20	UC San Diego■	J21
Cal St. Hayward	N27	Chapman■	J22
UC Davis	N30	Notre Dame (Cal.)■	J26
Redlands Tr.	D2-4	UC Santa Cruz■	J29
San Fran. St.	D 8	Dominican (Cal.)■	F 4
Notre Dame (Cal.)	D11	UC San Diego	F11
Christian Heritage	D18	Chapman	F12
Cal Poly Pomona	D20	Dominican (Cal.)	F18
Whittier Cl.	J7-8	Bethany (Cal.)■	F25
San Jose Christian■	J14	UC Santa Cruz	F26
Bethany (Cal.)	J15		

Colors: Blue & White. Nickname: Oaks.
AD: Don Baikie. SID: Mark Majeski. III

MERCER .... Macon, GA 31207

Bill Hodges (11 YRS. W-201, L-133)

Opponent	Date	Opponent	Date
St. Louis	N27	Centenary■	J22
North Ga.■	N30	Samford	J27
Shorter■	D 4	Florida Int'l	J29
Tulane	D 6	Charleston (S.C.)	F 5
Georgia Tech	D11	Central Fla.■	F10
Hawaii Inv.	D17-18	Stetson■	F12
Tennessee	D28	Alabama	F14
Missouri	D30	Centenary	F17
Georgia St.■	J 3	Southeastern La.	F19
Charleston (S.C.)■	J 8	Butler■	F21
Clemson■	J10	Samford■	F24
Stetson	J13	Florida Int'l■	F26
Central Fla.	J15	Georgia St.	F28
Southeastern La.■	J20	Trans America Conf.	M3-5

Colors: Orange & Black. Nickname: Bears.
AD: Bobby Pope. SID: Bobby Pope. I

MERCHANT MARINE .... Kings Point, NY 11024

Andrew Greer (1ST YR. AS HEAD COACH)

Opponent	Date	Opponent	Date
Bard	N29	Manhattanville■	J24
Staten Island	D 1	Hunter	J26
Williams Inv.	D3-4	Nazareth (N.Y.)■	J29
Hunter■	D 8	Williams■	J31
New Jersey Tech■	D10	Coast Guard	F 2
New Jersey Tech	J 5	Montclair St.■	F 7
Trinity (Conn.)■	J11	Maritime (N.Y.)■	F 9
St. Joseph's (N.Y.)■	J13	Skidmore	F12
Staten Island■	J15	Stony Brook■	F14
Manhattanville	J18	Vassar■	F16
Stony Brook	J20	Stevens Tech	F19
Union (N.Y.)	J22	Old Westbury■	F23

Colors: Blue & Gray. Nickname: Mariners.
AD: Susan Petersen Lubow. SID: Chris Brown. III

MERCYHURST .... Erie, PA 16546

Bill Morse (16 YRS. W-381, L-130)

Opponent	Date	Opponent	Date
Alderson-Broaddus■	N20	Bloomsburg	J15
St. Vincent	N23	Alderson-Broaddus	J17
Slippery Rock■	N29	Pitt.-Johnstown■	J19
Edinboro	D 1	Malone■	J22
Mercyhurst Cl.	D3-4	St. Vincent■	J24
Rio Grande	D 7	Gannon■	F 2
LeMoyne Tr.	D10-11	Oakland■	F 7
Salem Teikyo	D14	Lock Haven■	F 9
Mansfield	D18	Edinboro■	F12
Merrimack Inv.	D28-29	Cedarville	F26
Calif. (Pa.)	J 4	Pitt.-Johnstown	M 1
Mercyhurst Tr.	J7-8	Gannon	M 4
Lock Haven	J12		

Colors: Blue & Green. Nickname: Lakers.
AD: Pete Russo. SID: Joe Jordano. II

■ Home games on each schedule.

See pages 405–407 for Division I tournament details

MERRIMACK .... N. Andover, MA 01845

Bert Hammel (13 YRS. W-195, L-176)

Merrimack Tr.	N20-21
Quinnipiac■	N28
Westbrook■	D 1
Stonehill	D 4
New Hamp. Col.	D 8
Quinnipiac■	D11
Merrimack Inv.	D28-29
Eckerd	J 3
Fla. Southern	J 5
Bentley	J 9
Bryant■	J12
Assumption■	J15
American Int'l	J19
Springfield	J22
St. Michael's■	J25
St. Anselm■	J27
Quinnipiac	J29
Stonehill■	F 2
Bentley■	F 5
Bryant	F 9
Assumption	F12
American Int'l■	F16
Springfield■	F19
St. Michael's	F22
St. Anselm	F24

Colors: Navy Blue & Gold. Nickname: Warriors.
AD: Robert DeGregorio, Jr. SID: Jim Seavey. II

MESA ST. .... Grand Junction, CO 81501

Doug Schakel (14 YRS. W-254, L-165)

Adams St. Tr.	N19-20
Mesa St. Cl.	N26-27
Colorado-CS	N30
Air Force	D 1
Fort Lewis	D 4
Western Ore. Tr.	D10-11
Mesa St. Tr.	D29-30
Colorado-CS■	J 2
Western St.	J 7
N.M. Highlands■	J14
Adams St.■	J15
Fort Hays St.	J21
Chadron St.	J27
Colorado Mines	J29
Fort Lewis■	F 1
Fort Hays St.■	F 4
N.M. Highlands	F11
Adams St.	F12
Chadron St.■	F18
Colorado Mines■	F19
Western St.■	F26

Colors: Maroon, White & Gold. Nickname: Mavericks.
AD: Jay Jefferson. SID: Steve Kirkham. II

MESSIAH .... Grantham, PA 17027

Jack Cole (1ST YR. AS HEAD COACH)

Eastern (Pa.) Tr.	N19-20
East. Mennonite	N23
Wilkes	N29
Juniata	D 1
Elizabethtown■	D 4
Dickinson■	D 9
Gettysburg	D11
Kutztown■	J 5
Dickinson Tr.	J7-8
Susquehanna■	J13
Moravian	J15
Albright■	J18
Widener■	J22
Lebanon Valley■	J26
Juniata■	J29
Susquehanna	F 2
Elizabethtown	F 5
Albright	F 9
Moravian■	F12
Lebanon Valley	F16
Widener	F19
Wesley	F22

Colors: Blue & White. Nickname: Falcons.
AD: Layton Shoemaker. SID: Mike D'Virgilio. III

METHODIST .... Fayetteville, NC 28301

Bob McEvoy (8 YRS. W-98, L-115)

Chowan	N22
Campbell	N29
Methodist Inv.	D3-4
Savannah A&D■	D 7
Savannah A&D	J 4
Frostburg St. Tr.	J7-8
Greensboro	J12
Ferrum■	J15
Newport News App.	J17
Averett■	J19
Shenandoah	J22
N.C. Wesleyan■	J24
Chris. Newport	J29
Piedmont Bible	J31
Greensboro■	F 2
Ferrum	F 5
Averett	F 9
Guilford	F11
Shenandoah■	F13
N.C. Wesleyan	F14
Newport News App.■	F18
Chris. Newport■	F19

Colors: Green & Gold. Nickname: Monarchs.
AD: Rita Wiggs. SID: Michael Hogan. III

METROPOLITAN ST. .... Denver, CO 80204

Bob Hull (8 YRS. W-147, L-81)

Bellevue■	N20
Metro St. Cl.	N26-27
North Central■	D 4
Colorado Mines	D 8
Cal St. Bakersfield■	D11
Northern Colo.	D13
Metro St. Tr.	D17-18
Elmhurst■	D20
CS San B'dino Tr.	J2-3
Concordia (Wis.)■	J 8
Colo. Christian■	J11
Fort Lewis	J15
Southern Colo.	J20
Colorado-CS■	J22
Regis (Colo.)■	J27
Denver	J29
Neb.-Kearney	F 5
Colo. Christian	F 8
Fort Lewis■	F12
Southern Colo.■	F17
Colorado-CS	F19
Regis (Colo.)	F24
Denver■	F26

Colors: Navy Blue & Columbia Blue. Nickname: Roadrunners.
AD: William Helman. SID: Gregory Smith. II

MIAMI (FLA.) .... Coral Gables, FL 33124

Leonard Hamilton (6 YRS. W-73, L-106)

Fla. Atlantic■	N26
N.C.-Asheville■	D 1
Florida A&M■	D 4
Georgetown■	D 7
Bethune-Cookman■	D10
Sam Houston St.■	D17
Buffalo	D19
Syracuse	D22
Wagner■	D29
Fla. Atlantic	J 4
Providence	J 8
Pittsburgh	J12
Boston College	J15
St. John's (N.Y.)■	J22
Seton Hall■	J26
Georgetown	J29
Pittsburgh■	F 1
Connecticut	F 5
St. John's (N.Y.)	F 8
Villanova■	F12
Boston College■	F16
Seton Hall	F19
Connecticut■	F22
Providence■	F26
Syracuse■	M 1
Villanova	M 5
Big East Conf.	M10-13

Colors: Orange, Green & White. Nickname: Hurricanes.
AD: Dave Maggard. SID: Linda Venzon. I

MIAMI (OHIO) .... Oxford, OH 45056

Herb Sendek (1ST YR. AS HEAD COACH)

Mt. Vernon Naz.■	N27
San Francisco Cl.	D3-4
Wright St.■	D 8
Xavier (Ohio)■	D11
Cincinnati	D22
Dayton	D30
Western Mich.■	J 5
Ohio	J 8
Loyola (Ill.)■	J10
Central Mich.■	J12
Bowling Green	J15
Eastern Mich.■	J19
Toledo	J22
Kent■	J26
Ball St.	J29
Akron	F 2
Ohio■	F 5
Central Mich.	F 9
Bowling Green■	F12
Eastern Mich.	F16
Toledo■	F19
Kent	F23
Ball St.■	F26
Akron■	M 2
Western Mich.	M 5
Mid-American Conf.	M8-12

Colors: Red & White. Nickname: Redskins.
AD: R.C. Johnson. SID: Brian Teter. I

MICHIGAN .... Ann Arbor, MI 48109

Steve Fisher (5 YRS. W-99, L-37)

Georgia Tech⊠	N26
Cleveland St.■	N29
Tulane■	D 2
Tenn.-Chatt.■	D 4
Detroit Mercy■	D 6
Duke■	D11
Central Mich.■	D20
Arizona Tr.	D28-30
Boston U.■	J 3
Michigan St.■	J 5
Iowa	J 8
Ohio St.■	J13
Indiana	J16
Minnesota	J20
Illinois	J23
Wisconsin■	J29
Purdue	F 1
Michigan St.	F 5
Indiana■	F 8
Ohio St.	F13
Iowa■	F16
Minnesota■	F19
Illinois■	F22
Wisconsin	M 2
Purdue■	M 6
Penn St.■	M 9
Northwestern	M12

⊠ Springfield, MA

Colors: Maize & Blue. Nickname: Wolverines.
AD: Jack Weidenbach. SID: Bruce Madej. I

MICHIGAN ST. .... East Lansing, MI 48824

Jud Heathcote (22 YRS. W-375, L-257)

San Juan Shootout	N26-28
Louisville	D 4
Cleveland St.	D 7
East Tenn. St.■	D 9
Detroit Mercy■	D12
Ill.-Chicago■	D14
Nebraska■	D18
Tennessee	D21
Michigan St. Cl.	D29-30
Michigan	J 5
Illinois■	J 8
Purdue	J12
Northwestern■	J15
Wisconsin■	J19
Minnesota	J22
Ohio St.	J26
Iowa■	J29
Wisconsin	F 2
Michigan■	F 5
Illinois	F 9
Purdue■	F12
Northwestern	F17
Minnesota■	F23
Ohio St.■	F26
Iowa	M 2
Indiana■	M 9
Penn St.	M12

Colors: Green & White. Nickname: Spartans.
AD: Merrily Dean Baker. SID: Ken Hoffman. I

MICHIGAN TECH .... Houghton, MI 49931

Geof Kotila (7 YRS. W-71, L-105)

Minn.-Duluth■	N20
North Dak. St.■	N22
Wis.-Oshkosh Cl.	N26-27
Minn.-Duluth	D 1
Wayne St. (Mich.)■	D 4
Northern Mich.■	D11
Hillsdale■	D18
Southern Cal Col.	D27
Biola	D29
Wis.-Stevens Point■	J 4
Grand Valley St.	J 6
Ferris St.	J 8
Northwood■	J13
Lake Superior St.■	J15
Saginaw Valley	J20
Oakland	J22
Hillsdale	J27
Wayne St. (Mich.)	J29
Northern Mich.	F 5
Grand Valley St.■	F10
Ferris St.■	F12
Northwood	F17
Lake Superior St.	F19
Saginaw Valley■	F24
Oakland■	F26

Colors: Silver & Gold. Nickname: Huskies.
AD: Rick Yeo. SID: Dave Fischer. II

■ Home games on each schedule.

See pages 405–407 for Division I tournament details

MIDDLE TENN. ST. .... Murfreesboro, TN 37132
David Farrar (2 YRS. W-26, L-27)

N.C.-Greensboro■ N27
Oral Roberts■ .... D 1
Minnesota■ .... D 3
Texas Christian .... D 7
Ala.-Huntsville■ D11
Mo.-Kansas City■ D18
Cleveland St. D21
New Mexico Lobo Inv. D29-30
Tenn.-Martin .... J 3
Southern-B.R. .... J 6
Austin Peay■ J12
Murray St. J15
Southeast Mo. St. J17
Tennessee St.■ J19
Eastern Ky. J22
Morehead St. J24
Tennessee Tech■ J29
Tenn.-Martin■ J31
Tennessee St. .... F 5
Murray St.■ F12
Southeast Mo. St.■ F14
Tennessee Tech F17
Austin Peay F22
Morehead St.■ F26
Eastern Ky.■ F28
Ohio Valley Conf. M3-5

Colors: Blue & White. Nickname: Blue Raiders.
AD: John Stanford. SID: Ed Given. I

MIDDLEBURY .... Middlebury, VT 05753
Russell Reilly (16 YRS. W-144, L-197)

St. Lawrence■ N19
Clarkson■ N20
St. Michael's N23
Wesleyan N27
Dartmouth .... D 1
Amherst .... D 4
Vermont .... D 8
Trinity (Conn.)■ D11
Williams Tr. J7-8
Union (N.Y.)■ J13
Tufts■ J15
Williams J18
Connecticut Col.■ J22
Colby-Sawyer J25
Colby J28
Bowdoin J29
Skidmore .... F 2
Norwich■ .... F 8
Bates■ F12
Williams■ F16
Tufts F19
Union (N.Y.) F22

Colors: Blue & White. Nickname: Panthers.
AD: G. Thomas Lawson. SID: Peter Lardner. III

MILLERSVILLE .... Millersville, PA 17551
John Kochan (10 YRS. W-224, L-72)

Edinboro Tr. N19-20
Columbia Union■ N22
Lock Haven .... D 1
Va. Union Inv. D3-4
Lebanon Valley .... D 8
Columbia Union D11
Jacksonville St. Tr. J7-8
Holy Family J12
Kutztown■ J15
East Stroudsburg J19
West Chester J22
Cheyney■ J26
Mansfield■ J29
Dist. Columbia■ J31
Bloomsburg■ .... F 2
Kutztown .... F 5
Kean■ .... F 7
Dist. Columbia .... F 9
East Stroudsburg■ F12
Cheyney F16
West Chester■ F19
Bloomsburg F23
Mansfield F26

Colors: Black & Gold. Nickname: Marauders.
AD: Gene Carpenter. SID: Greg Wright. II

MILLIKIN .... Decatur, IL 62522
Joe Ramsey (20 YRS. W-283, L-234)

Webster■ N20
Washington (Mo.)⊠ N23
DePauw N30
Wabash■ .... D 2
Aurora■ .... D 4
Blackburn .... D 8
MacMurray D11
Franklin D18
La Jolla Cl. J7-8
North Central J12
Carthage J15
Augustana (Ill.)■ J19
North Park J22
Wheaton (Ill.)■ J26
Elmhurst■ J29
Ill. Wesleyan .... F 1
North Central■ .... F 5
Illinois Col.■ .... F 7
Carthage■ .... F 9
Augustana (Ill.) F12
North Park■ F15
Wheaton (Ill.) F19
Elmhurst F23
Ill. Wesleyan■ F26
⊠ Centralia, IL

Colors: Royal & White. Nickname: Big Blue.
AD: Merle Chapman. SID: Mickey Smith. III

MILLSAPS .... Jackson, MS 39210
John Stroud (3 YRS. W-43, L-34)

LeTourneau■ N19
Southwestern (Tex.)■ N20
Welsey (Miss.)■ N22
Webster N27
Blackburn N28
Stillman■ .... D 1
Rhodes Cl. D3-4
Stillman .... D 7
LSU-Shreveport .... J 6
Welsey (Miss.) J11
Hendrix J14
Trinity (Tex.) J16
Sewanee J21
Oglethorpe J23
Fisk■ J28
Centre■ J30
Rhodes■ .... F 1
Hendrix■ .... F 4
Trinity (Tex.)■ .... F 6
Fisk F11
Centre F13
Sewanee■ F18
Oglethorpe■ F20
Rhodes F25

Colors: Purple & White. Nickname: Majors.
AD: Ron Jurney. SID: Trey Porter. III

MINNESOTA .... Minneapolis, MN 55455
Clem Haskins (13 YRS. W-212, L-173)

Pre-Season NIT N17-26
Mississippi Val.■ N29
Middle Tenn. St. .... D 3
Clemson■ D15
Western Caro. D19
San Jose St. D23
Virginia D28
James Madison■ D31
Northeastern Ill.■ .... J 3
Northwestern .... J 8
Wisconsin■ J12
Penn St. J15
Michigan■ J20
Michigan St.■ J22
Indiana J26
Purdue■ J29
St. John's (N.Y.) J30
Iowa .... F 2
Northwestern■ .... F 5
Ohio St.■ .... F 9
Wisconsin F12
Penn St.■ F16
Michigan F19
Michigan St. F23
Indiana■ F27
Purdue .... M 3
Iowa■ .... M 5
Illinois .... M 9

Colors: Maroon & Gold. Nickname: Golden Gophers.
AD: McKinley Boston. SID: Marc Ryan. I

MINN.-DULUTH .... Duluth, MN 55812
Dale Race (13 YRS. W-282, L-124)

Michigan Tech N20
Minn.-Duluth Cl. N26-27
Michigan Tech■ .... D 1
Wis.-Superior■ .... D 4
Northern Mich. .... D 6
Mankato St. D11
Wis.-Parkside■ D13
Amer. Indian Bib. D15
Grand Canyon D16
St. Cloud St.■ D21
Northern Mich.■ .... J 2
Winona St. .... J 8
Moorhead St.■ J12
Northern St. J15
Bemidji St.■ J19
Southwest St. J22
Mt. Senario■ J26
Minn.-Morris J29
Wis.-Superior .... F 1
Winona St.■ .... F 5
Moorhead St. .... F 9
Northern St.■ F12
Bemidji St. F16
Southwest St.■ F19
Minn.-Morris■ F26

Colors: Maroon & Gold. Nickname: Bulldogs.
AD: Bruce McLeod. SID: Bob Nygaard. II

MISERICORDIA .... Dallas, PA 18612
David Martin (3 YRS. W-20, L-55)

King's (Pa.) Tr. N19-20
Lycoming N23
Holy Family■ .... D 1
Elmira .... D 7
Delaware Valley .... D 9
Keuka■ D13
Juniata Tr. J8-9
Beaver J12
Alvernia■ J15
Cabrini J18
Gwynedd Mercy J22
Eastern (Pa.)■ J25
Neumann J27
Marywood■ J29
Beaver■ .... F 1
Alvernia .... F 5
Eastern (Pa.) .... F 8
Neumann■ F10
Gwynedd Mercy■ F12
Marywood F14
Lancaster Bible F17
Cabrini■ F19

Colors: Royal Blue & Gold. Nickname: Cougars.
AD: Michael Mould. SID: Scott Crispell. III

MISSISSIPPI .... University, MS 38677
Rob Evans (1 YR. W-10, L-18)

Abilene Christian■ N29
Loyola (La.)■ .... D 1
Lamar■ .... D 4
Southern Ill. .... D 8
McNeese St.■ D11
Southern Miss.⊠ D18
Murray St. D22
Bradley D29
Arkansas .... J 5
Mississippi St.■ .... J 9
Kentucky◆ J12
Alabama■ J15
Oral Roberts J17
Auburn■ J19
Georgia J22
Rollins■ J24
Louisiana St. J29
South Caro.■ .... F 5
Florida■ .... F 9
Mississippi St. F12
Tennessee F16
Arkansas■ F19
Vanderbilt■ F23
Alabama F26
Auburn .... M 2
Louisiana St. .... M 5
Southeastern Conf. M10-13
⊠ Biloxi, MS
◆ Louisville, KY

Colors: Red & Blue. Nickname: Rebels.
AD: Warner Alford. SID: Jeff Romero. I

MISSISSIPPI COL. .... Clinton, MS 39058
Mike Jones (5 YRS. W-96, L-41)

North Ala. Tr. N19-20
Southern Ark. N23
Miss. College Cl. N26-27
Miss. College Tr. D6-7
Southern Ark.■ .... D 9
Alcorn St. D10
Ark.-Monticello Tr. D17-18
Miss. College Inv. J3-4
Lincoln Memorial■ .... J 6
Central Ark.■ .... J 8
Henderson St.■ J11
Lincoln Memorial J15
Delta St. J19
Livingston J24
Valdosta St.■ .... F 5
Delta St.■ .... F 7
Henderson St. F12
Central Ark. F14
Livingston■ F22
Valdosta St. F26

Colors: Blue & Gold. Nickname: Choctaws.
AD: Terry McMillan. SID: Norman Gough. II

■ Home games on each schedule.

See pages 405–407 for Division I tournament details

MISSISSIPPI ST. .... Mississippi State, MS 39762

Richard Williams (7 YRS. W-98, L-103)

Troy St.■	N30	Alabama	J29
Southern Miss.■	D 4	Mo.-Kansas City■	F 2
Ala.-Birmingham■	D 7	Florida	F 5
Southeastern La.■	D11	Florida Tech■	F 8
Tulane☒	D18	Mississippi■	F12
Northeast La.	D21	Vanderbilt	F16
Arizona St. Cl.	D28-29	Auburn■	F19
Tennessee■	J 5	South Caro.	F23
Mississippi	J 9	Louisiana St.■	F26
Auburn	J12	Alabama■	M 2
Georgia■	J15	Arkansas	M 5
Arkansas■	J19	Southeastern Conf.	M10-13
Kentucky■	J22	☒ Biloxi, MS	
Louisiana St.	J26		

Colors: Maroon & White. Nickname: Bulldogs.
AD: Larry Templeton. SID: David Rosinski. I

MISSISSIPPI VAL. .... Itta Bena, MS 38941

Lafayette Stribling (10 YRS. W-131, L-156)

Oral Roberts	N27	Jackson St.	J22
Minnesota	N29	Alabama St.	J24
Troy St.■	D 6	Grambling■	J29
Talladega■	D 8	Southern Miss.	F 1
Ala.-Birmingham	D18	Southern-B.R.	F 5
Wisconsin	D23	Alcorn St.	F 7
Baylor	D30	Delta St.■	F 9
Troy St.	J 4	Prairie View■	F12
Southern-B.R.■	J 8	Texas Southern■	F14
Alcorn St.■	J10	Jackson St.■	F19
Delta St.	J12	Alabama St.■	F21
Prairie View	J15	Grambling	F26
Texas Southern	J17	Southwestern Conf.	M9-13
Oral Roberts■	J19		

Colors: Green & White. Nickname: Delta Devils.
AD: Charles Prophet. SID: Charles Prophet. I

MISSOURI .... Columbia, MO 65211

Norm Stewart (32 YRS. W-612, L-306)

Central Mo. St.■	N27	Oklahoma St.	J22
Arkansas	D 2	Nebraska	J24
Jackson St.■	D 4	Kansas■	J31
Arkansas St.■	D 6	Oklahoma	F 5
Southern Methodist■	D11	Colorado■	F 9
Coppin St.■	D19	Oklahoma St.■	F12
Illinois☒	D22	Iowa St.	F16
Mercer■	D30	Kansas	F20
Washington■	J 2	Southeast Mo. St.■	F23
Southern Ill.	J 5	Oklahoma■	F26
Kansas St.■	J 8	Kansas St.	M 2
Notre Dame	J12	Nebraska■	M 5
Colorado	J15	Big Eight Conf.	M11-13
Iowa St.■	J19	☒ St. Louis, MO	

Colors: Old Gold & Black. Nickname: Tigers.
AD: Dan Devine. SID: Bob Brendel. I

MO. SOUTHERN ST. .... Joplin, MO 64801

Robert Corn (4 YRS. W-65, L-50)

Pittsburg St.■	N20	Emporia St.■	J22
Mo. Southern Cl.	N26-27	Northwest Mo. St.	J26
Drury■	D 2	Missouri-Rolla■	J29
Rockhurst	D 8	Mo.-St. Louis■	F 2
Christian Bros.	D11	Pittsburg St.	F 5
Southern Ind. Tr.	D18-19	Southwest Baptist	F 8
Grand Canyon Cl.	D30-31	Lincoln (Mo.)	F12
Washburn■	J 5	Mo. Western St.■	F16
Lincoln (Mo.)■	J 8	Northeast Mo. St.	F19
Mo. Western St.	J12	Central Mo. St.■	F23
Northeast Mo. St.■	J15	Emporia St.	F26
Central Mo. St.	J19		

Colors: Green & Gold. Nickname: Lions.
AD: Jim Frazier. SID: Dennis Slusher. II

MO. WESTERN ST. .... St. Joseph, MO 64507

Tom Smith (18 YRS. W-278, L-231)

Fort Hays St. Cl.	N19-20	Lincoln (Mo.)■	J22
Rockhurst■	N27	Pittsburg St.	J26
Mo. Western Cl.	D3-4	Mo.-St. Louis■	J29
Doane■	D 7	Southwest Baptist	F 1
Northwest Mo. St. Cl	D10-11	Missouri-Rolla■	F 5
Las Vegas Tr.	D27-28	Washburn■	F 9
Northwest Mo. St.	J 5	Central Mo. St.■	F12
Central Mo. St.	J 8	Mo. Southern St.	F16
Mo. Southern St.■	J12	Emporia St.■	F19
Emporia St.	J15	Northeast Mo. St.■	F23
Northeast Mo. St.	J19	Lincoln (Mo.)	F26

Colors: Black & Gold. Nickname: Griffons.
AD: Ed Harris. SID: Paul Sweetgall. II

MO.-KANSAS CITY .... Kansas City, MO 64110

Lee Hunt (10 YRS. W-131, L-151)

Southwest Mo. St.	N27	Chicago St.	J22
Creighton■	N29	Texas Tech	J25
Montana Cl.	D3-4	St. Louis■	J29
Southwest Tex. St.■	D 6	Mississippi St.	F 2
Hawaii Tip-Off Tr.	D10-11	Northeastern Ill.	F 5
Middle Tenn. St.	D18	Chicago St.■	F 7
Kansas St.■	D22	Washington (Mo.)■	F 9
Baylor■	D28	Oral Roberts■	F12
Southern Cal■	D31	Southwest Tex. St.	F14
Wichita St.■	J 4	Northeastern Ill.■	F16
Montana■	J 6	Southern Utah■	F19
Texas Tech■	J 8	Kansas St.	F22
Colorado	J12	Southern Utah	M 5
Nebraska	J15		

Colors: Blue & Gold. Nickname: Kangaroos.
AD: Lee Hunt. SID: Jeff Rogers. I

MISSOURI-ROLLA .... Rolla, MO 65401

Dale Martin (6 YRS. W-77, L-79)

Lindenwood■	N22	Southwest Baptist	J22
Quincy■	N29	Central Mo. St.■	J26
Colorado Mines Tr.	D3-4	Mo. Southern St.	J29
Westminster (Mo.)■	D 8	Emporia St.■	F 3
Illinois Col.■	D11	Mo. Western St.	F 5
Drury	D18	Northeast Mo. St.	F 9
Mo.-Rolla Tr.	J1-2	Northwest Mo. St.■	F12
Lincoln (Mo.)■	J 5	Washburn	F16
Northwest Mo. St.	J 8	Mo.-St. Louis	F19
Washburn■	J12	Pittsburg St.■	F23
Mo.-St. Louis■	J15	Southwest Baptist■	F26
Pittsburg St.	J19		

Colors: Silver & Gold. Nickname: Miners.
AD: Mark Mullin. SID: John Kean. II

MOLLOY .... Rockville Centre, NY 11570

Howard Haag (1 YR. W-8, L-19)

Baruch■	N19	New York Tech	J21
Molloy Tr.■	N26	Dowling■	J24
Adelphi■	D 1	Pace■	J26
Concordia (N.Y.)	D 4	Concordia (N.Y.)■	J29
Queens (N.Y.)■	D 8	LIU-Southampton	F 2
St. Rose■	D11	Pace	F 5
Mt. St. Mary (N.Y.)	D13	New York Tech■	F 9
Phila. Textile	J 5	LIU-C.W. Post	F12
LIU-C.W. Post■	J 8	St. Rose	F16
Dowling	J10	Mercy	F19
Adelphi	J12	Queens (N.Y.)	F23
Mercy■	J15	Phila. Textile■	F26
LIU-Southampton■	J19		

Colors: Maroon & White. Nickname: Lions.
AD: Bob Houlihan. SID: Robert Houlihan. II

MONMOUTH (ILL.) .... Monmouth, IL 61462

Terry Glasgow (21 YRS. W-328, L-145)

Rosary■	N27	Beloit■	J23
Cornell College■	D 3	St. Norbert	J29
MacMurray■	D 8	Lawrence	J30
Aurora	D14	Grinnell■	F 4
Teikyo Marycrest■	D19	Coe■	F 8
Central Mo. St.	J 2	Illinois Col.	F11
Eckerd	J 5	Knox	F12
Illinois Col.■	J14	Grinnell	F15
Knox■	J15	Cornell College	F18
Coe	J19	Teikyo Marycrest	F22
Carroll (Wis.)■	J22		

Colors: Crimson & White. Nickname: Fighting Scots.
AD: Terry Glasgow. SID: Chris Pio. III

MONMOUTH (N.J.) .... W. Long Branch, NJ 07764

Wayne Szoke (9 YRS. W-135, L-115)

Delaware■	N27	FDU-Teaneck■	J22
Army■	N30	Marist■	J24
U.C.-Santa Barb. Tr.	D2-4	St. Francis (N.Y.)	J27
Manhattan	D11	LIU-Brooklyn	J29
Drexel	D22	Wagner	F 5
Wichita St. Tr.	D29-30	Rider■	F10
St. Francis (Pa.)	J 4	Mt. St. Mary's (Md.)■	F12
Robert Morris	J 6	Marist	F16
LIU-Brooklyn■	J 8	FDU-Teaneck	F18
St. Francis (N.Y.)■	J10	Robert Morris■	F24
Wagner■	J15	St. Francis (Pa.)■	F26
Rider	J18	Northeast Conf.	F28-M6
Mt. St. Mary's (Md.)	J20		

Colors: Royal Blue & White. Nickname: Hawks.
AD: Wayne Szoke. SID: John Paradise. I

■ Home games on each schedule.

See pages 405–407 for Division I tournament details

MONTANA .... Missoula, MT 59812
Blaine Taylor (2 YRS. W-44, L-15)

Cal St. Sacramento■	N26	Weber St.	J20
Simon Fraser■	N27	Northern Ariz.	J22
Washington	N29	Idaho St.■	J28
Montana Cl.	D3-4	Boise St.■	J29
Western Mont.■	D 9	Montana St.	F 5
Cal Poly SLO	D13	Eastern Wash.	F11
Creighton■	D19	Idaho	F12
Northeastern Ill.■	D21	Northern Ariz.■	F17
Western Ore.■	D28	Weber St.■	F19
Portland■	J 3	Boise St.	F25
Mo.-Kansas City	J 6	Idaho St.	F26
Rice	J 8	Montana St.■	M 5
Idaho■	J14	Big Sky Conf.	M10-12
Eastern Wash.■	J15		

Colors: Copper, Silver, Gold. Nickname: Grizzlies.
AD: William Moos. SID: Dave Guffey. I

MONTANA ST. .... Bozeman, MT 59717
Mick Durham (3 YRS. W-35, L-48)

Cal St. Sacramento■	N28	Weber St.	J22
Rocky Mountain■	D 1	Boise St.■	J28
Marshall	D 4	Idaho St.■	J29
Texas A&M	D 6	Montana■	F 5
Eastern Mont.■	D11	Idaho	F11
Colorado Mines■	D17	Eastern Wash.	F12
Wyoming⊠	D21	Weber St.■	F17
Fresno St. Cl.	D27-28	Northern Ariz.■	F19
San Jose St.	D30	Idaho St.	F25
Portland■	J 5	Boise St.	F26
Southern Utah■	J 8	Montana	M 5
Eastern Wash.■	J14	Big Sky Conf.	M10-12
Idaho■	J15	⊠ Billings, MT	
Northern Ariz.	J20		

Colors: Blue & Gold. Nickname: Bobcats.
AD: Doug Fullerton. SID: Bill Lamberty. I

MONTCLAIR ST. .... Upper Montclair, NJ 07043
Nick DelTufo (2 YRS. W-17, L-31)

Ramapo■	N23	Wm. Paterson	J22
Rowan	N27	Ramapo	J26
Wm. Paterson■	N30	Rowan■	J29
Stockton St.	D 4	Kean■	F 2
Trenton St.■	D 8	Stockton St.■	F 5
Jersey City St.	D11	Merchant Marine	F 7
Upsala	D13	Trenton St.	F 9
Kean	J12	Jersey City St.■	F12
Rutgers-Camden■	J15	Old Westbury	F14
Centenary (N.J.)	J17	Rutgers-Newark■	F16
Rutgers-Newark	J19	Rutgers-Camden	F19

Colors: Scarlet & White. Nickname: Red Hawks.
AD: Gregory Lockard. SID: Al Langer. III

MOORHEAD ST. .... Moorhead, MN 56560
Dave Schellhase (15 YRS. W-257, L-199)

Dakota St.	N22	Winona St.■	J15
Wis.-Stevens Pt. Cl.	N26-27	Wayne St. (Neb.)■	J19
Valley City St.■	N30	Northern St.	J22
Concordia-M'head■	D 2	Bemidji St.■	J29
St. Scholastica	D 4	Mary	J31
North Dak. St.■	D 7	Southwest St.■	F 2
Mayville St.■	D 9	Minn.-Morris	F 5
Minot St.	D13	Concordia-M'head	F 7
St. Cloud St.	D16	Minn.-Duluth■	F 9
Northern St. Inv.	J1-2	Winona St.	F12
Southwest St.	J 5	Northern St.■	F19
Minn.-Morris■	J 8	Bemidji St.	F26
Minn.-Duluth	J12		

Colors: Scarlet & White. Nickname: Dragons.
AD: Katy Wilson. SID: Larry Scott. II

MOREHEAD ST. .... Morehead, KY 40351
Dick Fick (2 YRS. W-20, L-36)

Northern Ky.■	N29	Austin Peay	J15
Loyola (Ill.)■	D 1	Tennessee St.	J17
Thomas More■	D 4	Tennessee Tech■	J22
Louisville	D 8	Middle Tenn. St.■	J24
Illinois Cl.	D10-11	Eastern Ky.	J29
Kentucky	D17	Southeast Mo. St.	F 5
Northern Ill.■	D21	Murray St.	F 7
Loyola (Ill.)	D23	Tennessee St.■	F12
Western Mich.	D27	Austin Peay■	F14
Eastern Ky.■	J 3	Tenn.-Martin■	F19
Murray St.■	J 8	Middle Tenn. St.	F26
Southeast Mo. St.■	J10	Tennessee Tech	F28
Tenn.-Martin	J13	Ohio Valley Conf.	M3-5

Colors: Blue & Gold. Nickname: Eagles.
AD: Steve Hamilton. SID: Randy Stacy. I

MOREHOUSE .... Atlanta, GA 30314
Arthur McAfee (33 YRS. W-408, L-429)

North Ala. Tr.	N19-20	Paine■	J22
New Orleans Tr.	N25-26	Albany St. (Ga.)	J26
LeMoyne-Owen■	D 2	Savannah St.	J28
Albany St. (Ga.)■	D 7	Tuskegee	F 1
Eckerd	D10	Alabama A&M⊠	F 5
Dillard■	D18	Morris Brown■	F 8
Norfolk St.■	D20	Miles■	F11
Augusta Cl.	D29-30	Alabama A&M	F13
Fort Valley St.■	J 5	LeMoyne-Owen	F19
Miles	J12	Talladega■	F21
Tuskegee■	J15	Fort Valley St.	F23
Clark Atlanta■	J19	⊠ Detroit, MI	

Colors: Maroon & White. Nickname: Tigers.
AD: Arthur McAfee. SID: James Nix. II

MORGAN ST. .... Baltimore, MD 21239
Michael Holmes (11 YRS. W-115, L-181)

Loyola (Ill.)	N27	Bethune-Cookman	J22
Bowie St.■	D 1	Coppin St.■	J27
Maryland	D 4	Md.-East. Shore■	J29
Georgetown	D10	Howard■	J31
LIU-Brooklyn	D18	James Madison	F 2
Florida St.	D20	Coppin St.	F 7
Loyola (Ill.)■	D28	Florida A&M■	F10
George Mason	J 2	Bethune-Cookman■	F12
South Caro. St.■	J 8	Delaware St.■	F14
North Caro. A&T■	J10	South Caro. St.	F26
Md.-East. Shore	J15	North Caro. A&T	F28
Delaware St.	J17	Howard	M 5
Florida A&M	J20	Mid-Eastern Conf.	M9-13

Colors: Blue & Orange. Nickname: Bears.
AD: Kenneth McBryde. SID: Joseph McIver. I

MORNINGSIDE .... Sioux City, IA 51106
Jerry Schmutte (12 YRS. W-222, L-113)

Doane■	N22	Nebraska-Omaha	J21
Northern Iowa	N29	Northern Colo.	J22
Briar Cliff	D 4	North Dak. St.■	J28
Wayne St. (Neb.)	D 8	North Dak.■	J29
Midland Lutheran■	D11	St. Cloud St.■	F 4
Dana■	D18	Mankato St.■	F 5
Briar Cliff	D28	Augustana (S.D.)	F11
South Dak.■	J 2	South Dak. St.	F12
Mankato St.	J 7	Northern Colo.■	F18
St. Cloud St.	J 8	Nebraska-Omaha■	F19
Iowa St.	J12	South Dak.	F22
South Dak. St.■	J14	North Dak.	F25
Augustana (S.D.)■	J15	North Dak. St.	F26

Colors: Maroon & White. Nickname: Chiefs.
AD: To be named. SID: Rob Shaw. II

MORRIS BROWN .... Atlanta, GA 30314
Ajac Triplett (15 YRS. W-203, L-202)

Johnson C. Smith Tr.	N19-20	Albany St. (Ga.)■	J22
Georgia St.	N27	Savannah St.	J24
Paine	N30	Fort Valley St.	J26
Clark Atlanta Cl.	D3-4	Paine■	J29
Miles■	D 6	Clark Atlanta	F 2
Albany St. (Ga.)	D 8	LeMoyne-Owen	F 5
Alabama A&M■	D11	Morehouse	F 8
Smoke on the River	D31-J1	Alabama A&M	F11
Fort Valley St.■	J12	Tuskegee■	F14
Clark Atlanta■	J15	Savannah St.	F18
Miles	J17	Tuskegee	F22
LeMoyne-Owen■	J21		

Colors: Purple & Black. Nickname: Wolverines.
AD: Gregory Thompson. SID: Cecil McKay. II

MOUNT OLIVE .... Mount Olive, NC 28365
Bill Clingan (3 YRS. W-48, L-41)

Barton Cl.	N19-20	High Point■	J19
Lenoir-Rhyne Tr.	N26-27	Lees-McRae■	J22
Newport News App.	D 3	Barton	J26
St. Thomas (Fla.)	D 4	Pfeiffer	J29
Pembroke St.	D 7	Coker■	F 2
Lees-McRae	D11	Belmont Abbey	F 5
Charleston (S.C.)	D18	High Point	F 8
Queens (N.C.) Cl.	J6-8	Barton■	F12
St. Andrews	J12	Longwood	F15
Belmont Abbey■	J15	Pfeiffer■	F19
Coker	J17	St. Andrews■	F26

Colors: Forest Green & White. Nickname: Trojans.
AD: George Whitfield. SID: To be named. II

■ Home games on each schedule.

See pages 405–407 for Division I tournament details

MT. ST. MARY (N.Y.) .... Newburgh, NY 12550
Mike Riger (1ST YR. AS HEAD COACH)

Hartwick Cl. N19-20
John Jay N23
Mt. St. Mary Tr. D4-5
Lehman .... D 7
LeMoyne Tr. D10-11
Molloy■ D13
Oswego St. .... J 8
Stony Brook J11
Lock Haven J13
New Paltz St. Tr. J15-16
CCNY■ J18
Mt. St. Mary Cl. J22-23
Albany (N.Y.)■ J29
Western Conn. St. .... F 1
Utica .... F 5
Manhattanville .... F 7
Old Westbury■ F12
Hunter■ F14
Albany Pharmacy■ F19
Adelphi■ F21

Colors: Royal Blue & Old Gold. Nickname: Knights.
AD: John Wright. SID: Brendan Coyne. III

MT. ST. MARY'S (MD.) ...... Emmitsburg, MD 21727
James Phelan (39 YRS. W-706, L-365)

Mt. St. Mary's Tr. D3-4
Loyola (Md.)■ D11
Bucknell■ D18
Georgia Tech D20
Florida St. D22
West Va. D28
Marist .... J 4
FDU-Teaneck .... J 6
Robert Morris■ .... J 8
St. Francis (Pa.)■ J10
St. Francis (N.Y.) J13
LIU-Brooklyn J15
Wagner■ J18
Monmouth (N.J.)■ J20
Rider■ J22
St. Francis (Pa.) J27
Robert Morris J29
Central Conn. St. .... F 1
LIU-Brooklyn■ .... F 3
St. Francis (N.Y.)■ .... F 5
Wagner F10
Monmouth (N.J.) F12
Rider F19
Marist■ F24
FDU-Teaneck■ F26
Northeast Conf. F28-M6

Colors: Blue & White. Nickname: Mountaineers.
AD: J. Thomas Balistrere. SID: Dave Reeder. I

MT. ST. VINCENT .... Bronx, NY 10471
Chuck Mancuso (12 YRS. W-179, L-118)

Stevens Tech■ N28
Maritime (N.Y.)■ .... D 2
Mt. St. Vincent Tr. D4-5
Bard■ .... D 8
Yeshiva D15
St. Leo D31
Mt. St. Vincent Cl. J7-8
CCNY J11
Maritime (N.Y.) J13
Baruch J15
Albertus Magnus■ J19
Mt. St. Mary Cl. J22-23
Bard J26
Stony Brook J29
Pratt■ .... F 1
New Jersey Tech■ .... F 4
Vassar■ .... F 8
St. Joseph's (N.Y.)■ F10
Stevens Tech F12
Manhattanville F14
Polytechnic (N.Y.)■ F17

Colors: Blue, White & Gold. Nickname: Dolphins.
AD: Chuck Mancuso. SID: Chuck Mancuso. III

MOUNT UNION .... Alliance, OH 44601
Lee Hood (1 YR. W-9, L-16)

Mount Union Cl. N19-20
Thiel N23
Grove City .... D 1
Capital .... D 4
Marietta .... D 8
Hiram■ D11
Heidelberg■ D18
Ogelthorpe Cl. D29-30
Otterbein■ .... J 5
Ohio Northern .... J 8
Baldwin-Wallace J12
John Carroll■ J15
Muskingum J19
Capital■ J22
Marietta■ J26
Hiram J29
John Carroll .... F 2
Heidelberg .... F 5
Otterbein .... F 9
Ohio Northern■ F12
Baldwin-Wallace■ F16
Muskingum■ F19

Colors: Purple & White. Nickname: Purple Raiders.
AD: Larry Kehres. SID: Michael De Matteis. III

MUHLENBERG .... Allentown, PA 18104
Dave Madeira (6 YRS. W-88, L-63)

Muhlenberg Tr. N19-20
Albright N23
Western Md. N30
Frank. & Marsh.■ .... D 4
Washington (Md.)■ .... D 7
Moravian D11
Lehigh D22
King's (Pa.) Cl. D29-30
Wash. & Jeff. Tr. J7-8
Allentown■ J12
Gettysburg■ J15
Haverford J19
Johns Hopkins■ J22
Elizabethtown■ J25
Ursinus J29
Swarthmore■ .... F 2
Washington (Md.) .... F 5
Haverford■ .... F 9
Dickinson F12
Ursinus■ F16
Swarthmore F19

Colors: Cardinal & Gray. Nickname: Mules.
AD: Ralph Kirchenheiter. SID: Gracia Perilli. III

MURRAY ST. .... Murray, KY 42071
Scott Edgar (2 YRS. W-35, L-25)

Arkansas N29
Campbellsville■ .... D 7
Florida Int'l■ D11
St. Louis■ D18
Mississippi■ D22
Pikeville■ D27
Toledo Cl. D29-30
Dayton .... J 2
Morehead St. .... J 8
Eastern Ky. J10
Middle Tenn. St.■ J15
Tennessee Tech■ J17
Memphis St.■ J19
Tenn.-Martin■ J22
Tennessee St.■ J24
Austin Peay J29
Tennessee St. J31
Southeast Mo. St.■ .... F 2
Eastern Ky.■ .... F 5
Morehead St.■ .... F 7
Middle Tenn. St. F12
Tennessee Tech F14
Southeast Mo. St. F19
Austin Peay■ F26
Tenn.-Martin F28
Ohio Valley Conf. M3-5

Colors: Blue & Gold. Nickname: Racers.
AD: Mike Strickland. SID: Tim Tucker. I

MUSKINGUM .... New Concord, OH 43762
Jim Burson (26 YRS. W-391, L-261)

Ohio Wesleyan Tr. N19-20
Otterbein .... D 4
Ohio Northern■ .... D 8
Baldwin-Wallace D11
Capital■ D18
Muskingum Cl. D22-23
Marietta .... J 5
John Carroll■ .... J 8
Hiram■ J12
Heidelberg J15
Mount Union■ J19
Otterbein■ J22
Ohio Northern J26
Capital J29
Baldwin-Wallace■ .... F 2
John Carroll .... F 5
Marietta■ .... F 9
Heidelberg■ F12
Hiram F16
Mount Union F19

Colors: Black & Magenta. Nickname: Fighting Muskies.
AD: Al Christopher. SID: Jacquie Nelson. III

NAVY .... Annapolis, MD 21402
Don DeVoe (20 YRS. W-336, L-247)

Air Force■ N27
St. Bonaventure■ .... D 1
Nebraska Cl. D3-4
Air Force .... D 6
Md.-East. Shore■ D11
Gettysburg■ D22
Florida Int'l D28
Fla. Atlantic D30
William & Mary .... J 3
Army .... J 8
Loyola (Md.) J10
Lehigh■ J12
Colgate■ J15
Brown■ J17
Lafayette J19
Bucknell J22
Holy Cross■ J26
Fordham J29
Army■ .... F 2
Lehigh .... F 5
Colgate .... F 9
Lafayette■ F12
Bucknell■ F16
Holy Cross F19
Fordham■ F26
Patriot Conf. M4-11

Colors: Navy Blue & Gold. Nickname: Midshipmen.
AD: Jack Lengyel. SID: Tom Bates. I

NAZARETH (N.Y.) .... Rochester, NY 14610
Mike Daley (7 YRS. W-109, L-76)

Buffalo St. Cl. N19-20
Rochester■ N23
Nazareth Tr. N27-28
Rochester Cl. D3-4
St. Lawrence .... D 7
Keuka■ D11
Brockport St. .... J 8
Rochester Tr. J12-15
Roberts Wesleyan■ J20
Elmira J26
Merchant Marine J29
Alfred J31
Fredonia St.■ .... F 1
Union (N.Y.) .... F 5
Oswego St.■ .... F 8
Hilbert F12
Rochester Inst. F15
St. John Fisher■ F18
Utica■ F23
Hilbert■ F26

Colors: Purple & Gold. Nickname: Golden Flyers.
AD: Bill Carey. SID: Joe Seil. III

NEBRASKA .... Lincoln, NE 68588
Danny Nee (13 YRS. W-233, L-160)

Texas-San Antonio■ N27
Texas■ N28
Appalachian St. .... D 1
Nebraska Cl. D3-4
Creighton .... D 9
Wichita St.■ D11
Michigan St. D18
Florida A&M■ D20
Northern Iowa■ D31
Iowa St. .... J 3
Southern Utah■ .... J 5
Colorado■ .... J 8
Mo.-Kansas City■ J15
Colorado J19
Missouri■ J24
Oklahoma■ J29
Kansas .... F 6
Kansas St. .... F 9
Iowa St.■ F12
Oklahoma F14
Oklahoma St. F19
Kansas■ F23
Kansas St.■ F26
Oklahoma St.■ .... M 2
Missouri .... M 5
Big Eight Conf. M11-13

Colors: Scarlet & Cream. Nickname: Cornhuskers.
AD: Bill Byrne. SID: Chris Anderson. I

■ Home games on each schedule.

See pages 405–407 for Division I tournament details

NEB. WESLEYAN .... Lincoln, NE 68504
Todd Raridon (4 YRS. W-71, L-35)

Opponent	Date	Opponent	Date
Bethany (Kan.)■	N22	Doane■	J22
Neb. Wesleyan Cl.	N26-27	Midland Lutheran■	J26
Simpson	D 4	Dana	J29
Bellevue	D 7	Concordia (Neb.)	F 2
Central (Iowa)■	D11	N'western (Iowa)■	F 5
Fla. Southern	D27	Peru St.■	F 9
Webber	D30	York (Neb.)	F10
Lynn	J 2	Dordt	F12
Concordia (Neb.)■	J 8	Doane	F15
N'western (Iowa)	J12	Dana■	F17
Hastings■	J15	Midland Lutheran	F19
Bellevue■	J19	Hastings	F26

Colors: Yellow & Brown. Nickname: Plainsmen.
AD: Mary Beth Kennedy. SID: Jim Angele. III

NEB.-KEARNEY .... Kearney, NE 68849
Jerry Hueser (23 YRS. W-458, L-230)

Opponent	Date	Opponent	Date
Nebraska-Omaha	N19	Midland Lutheran■	J15
Bellevue■	N22	Hastings■	J19
Colo. Christian■	N26	Peru St.■	J28
Northern Colo.■	N27	Denver	F 1
Angelo St. Cl.	D3-4	Colo. Christian	F 2
Hastings	D 8	Metropolitan St.■	F 5
Nebraska-Omaha■	D11	Briar Cliff	F 9
North Dak. St.	D17	Chadron St.■	F12
North Dak.	D18	Fort Hays St.■	F14
Mt. Senario■	D30	Chadron St.	F22
Southern Colo.	J 3	Wayne St. (Neb.)	F26
Neb.-Kearney Cl.	J6-8	Wayne St. (Neb.)■	M 2
Fort Hays St.	J10		

Colors: Royal Blue & Light Old Gold. Nickname: Antelopes, Lopers.
AD: Dick Beechner. SID: Brent Robinson. II

NEBRASKA-OMAHA .... Omaha, NE 68182
Bob Hanson (24 YRS. W-378, L-291)

Opponent	Date	Opponent	Date
Neb.-Kearney■	N19	Morningside■	J21
Doane■	N26	South Dak.■	J22
Midland Lutheran■	N27	Mankato St.	J28
Creighton	D 4	St. Cloud St.	J29
Neb.-Kearney	D11	Northern Colo.■	F 5
Grand View■	D17	South Dak. St.	F 8
Peru St.■	D18	North Dak.■	F11
Mt. Senario■	D29	North Dak. St.■	F12
South Dak. St.■	J 2	South Dak.	F18
Augustana (S.D.)■	J 3	Morningside	F19
Northern Colo.	J 8	Augustana (S.D.)	F22
North Dak. St.	J14	St. Cloud St.■	F25
North Dak.	J15	Mankato St.■	F26

Colors: Black & Crimson. Nickname: Mavericks.
AD: Robert Gibson. SID: Gary Anderson. II

NEVADA .... Reno, NV 89557
Pat Foster (13 YRS. W-276, L-122)

Opponent	Date	Opponent	Date
Rice	N28	Nevada-Las Vegas	J20
Baylor■	D 4	New Mexico St.	J22
North Texas	D 9	Utah St.■	J29
Kansas St.	D11	New Mexico St.■	F 3
Fresno St.■	D20	Nevada-Las Vegas■	F 5
Santa Clara■	D22	Cal St. Fullerton	F10
Colorado■	D28	UC Irvine	F12
Cal St. Stanislaus■	D30	UC Santa Barb.■	F17
San Jose St.■	J 3	Long Beach St.■	F19
Pacific (Cal.)■	J 5	Pacific (Cal.)	F24
UC Santa Barb.	J 8	San Jose St.	F26
Long Beach St.	J10	Utah St.	M 5
UC Irvine■	J15	Big West Conf.	M10-13
Cal St. Fullerton■	J17		

Colors: Silver & Blue. Nickname: Wolf Pack.
AD: Chris Ault. SID: Paul Stuart. I

NEVADA-LAS VEGAS .... Las Vegas, NV 89154
Rollie Massimino (22 YRS. W-410 , L-265)

Opponent	Date	Opponent	Date
UCLA	D 4	San Jose St.	J29
Texas A&M	D 8	Utah St.	F 3
Loyola (Cal.)■	D18	Nevada	F 5
Vermont■	D21	Long Beach St.■	F 7
Virginia■	J 3	New Mexico St.	F14
Cal St. Fullerton	J 5	Cal St. Fullerton■	F17
Georgetown	J 8	UC Irvine■	F19
UC Irvine	J11	UC Santa Barb.	F24
New Mexico St.■	J17	Long Beach St.	F26
Nevada■	J20	San Jose St.■	M 3
Utah St.■	J22	Pacific (Cal.)■	M 5
UC Santa Barb.■	J24	Big West Conf.	M10-13
Pacific (Cal.)	J27		

Colors: Scarlet & Gray. Nickname: Runnin' Rebels.
AD: Jim Weaver. SID: Tommy Sheppard. I

NEW ENGLAND COL. .... Henniker, NH 03242
To be named

Opponent	Date	Opponent	Date
Daniel Webster■	N23	Anna Maria	J26
Plymouth St.	N30	Roger Williams■	J29
Colby-Sawyer■	D 2	Gordon	F 1
MIT■	D 4	Eastern Nazarene■	F 3
Johnson St.■	D 7	Curry■	F 5
Rivier	D 9	Wentworth Inst.	F 9
Eastern Nazarene	J15	Roger Williams	F12
Curry	J18	Anna Maria■	F15
Wentworth Inst.■	J20	Gordon■	F17
Salve Regina■	J22	Salve Regina	F19

Colors: Scarlet & Royal Blue. Nickname: Pilgrims.
AD: Mary Ellen Alger. SID: To be named. III

NEW HAMPSHIRE .... Durham, NH 03824
Gib Chapman (1 YR. W-6, L-21)

Opponent	Date	Opponent	Date
Dartmouth■	N27	Northeastern	J27
Providence	D 1	Boston U.■	J29
Yale■	D 8	Harvard■	F 1
Wis.-Milwaukee	D11	Maine	F 5
Brown	D22	Boston U.	F10
Shootout Spokane	D27-28	Northeastern■	F12
Hofstra■	J 5	Vermont	F17
Xavier (Ohio)	J 9	Hartford■	F19
Central Conn. St.	J11	Holy Cross	F22
Delaware■	J14	Drexel	F25
Drexel■	J16	Delaware	F27
Hartford	J20	Maine■	M 2
Vermont■	J22	North Atlantic Conf.	M5-9

Colors: Blue & White. Nickname: Wildcats.
AD: Gib Chapman. SID: Pete Dauphinais. I

NEW HAMP. COL. .... Manchester, NH 03104
Stanley Spirou (8 YRS. W-174, L-72)

Opponent	Date	Opponent	Date
Keene St. Cl.	N19-20	Mass.-Lowell	J26
Assumption■	N23	Sacred Heart■	J29
Bryant	D 2	Franklin Pierce■	F 2
Merrimack■	D 8	New Haven■	F 5
American Int'l■	D11	Bridgeport	F 7
St. Michael's■	D19	Keene St.	F 9
Stonehill	D21	Southern Conn. St.■	F12
New Haven	J 8	Franklin Pierce	F16
St. Anselm	J10	Le Moyne■	F19
Le Moyne	J12	Southern Conn. St.	F21
Bridgeport■	J17	Mass.-Lowell■	F23
Keene St.■	J19	Sacred Heart	F26

Colors: Blue & Gold. Nickname: Penmen.
AD: Joseph Polak. SID: Tom McDermott. II

NEW HAVEN .... West Haven, CT 06516
Stu Grove (18 YRS. W-300, L-198)

Opponent	Date	Opponent	Date
Merrimack Tr.	N20-21	Southern Conn. St.	J26
Quinnipiac	N30	Franklin Pierce	J31
East Stroudsburg Cl.	D3-4	Sacred Heart■	F 2
Springfield■	D 7	New Hamp. Col.	F 5
American Int'l	D 9	Mass.-Lowell■	F 7
St. Michael's Cl.	D29-30	Bridgeport■	F 9
New Hamp. Col.■	J 8	Le Moyne	F12
Keene St.■	J12	Sacred Heart	F16
Mass.-Lowell	J15	Franklin Pierce■	F19
Bridgeport	J19	Southern Conn. St.■	F23
Le Moyne■	J23	Keene St.	F26

Colors: Navy Blue & Gold. Nickname: Chargers.
AD: Deborah Chin. SID: Jack Jones. II

NEW JERSEY TECH .... Newark, NJ 07102
James Catalano (14 YRS. W-286, L-99)

Opponent	Date	Opponent	Date
York (Pa.) Cl.	D4-5	Yeshiva	J25
Stony Brook■	D 8	Hunter■	J29
Merchant Marine	D10	Manhattanville■	F 1
Staten Island	D13	Mt. St. Vincent	F 4
Staten Island■	J 3	Polytechnic (N.Y.)■	F 5
Merchant Marine■	J 5	Yeshiva■	F 8
Wilkes Cl.	J7-8	Stony Brook	F10
York (N.Y.)■	J12	Stevens Tech■	F14
Hunter	J13	Maritime (N.Y.)■	F16
Stevens Tech	J15	Manhattanville	F18
Polytechnic (N.Y.)	J22	Bard■	F19

Colors: Red & White. Nickname: Highlanders.
AD: J. Malcolm Simon. SID: Sal Petruzzi. III

■ Home games on each schedule.

See pages 405–407 for Division I tournament details

NEW MEXICO — Albuquerque, NM 87131
Dave Bliss (18 YRS. W-325, L-218)

Western N. Mex.■	D 1	Colorado St.	J20
New Mexico Lobo Cl.	D3-4	Wyoming	J22
Texas Tech	D 8	UTEP	J29
New Mexico St.■	D11	UTEP■	F 5
Tex.-Pan American■	D18	Wyoming■	F10
New Mexico St.	D20	Colorado St.■	F12
New Mexico Lobo Inv.	D29-30	San Diego St.	F17
Brigham Young■	J 3	Hawaii	F19
Utah■	J 5	Air Force■	F24
Air Force	J 8	Fresno St.■	F26
Fresno St.	J10	Brigham Young	M 3
San Diego St.■	J13	Utah	M 5
Hawaii■	J15	Western Ath. Conf.	M9-12

Colors: Cherry & Silver. Nickname: Lobos.
AD: Rudy Davalos. SID: Greg Remington. I

N.M. HIGHLANDS — Las Vegas, NM 87701
Henry Sanchez (10 YRS. W-128, L-163)

Southern Colo. Cl.	N19-20	Colorado Mines■	J22
Fort Lewis■	N22	Fort Hays St.■	J27
Western N. Mex.	N27	Panhandle St.	J29
New Mexico St.	N29	Chadron St.	F 3
N.M. Highlands Tr.	D3-4	Colorado Mines	F 5
Eastern N. Mex.■	D10	Mesa St.■	F11
Colo. Christian	D11	Western St.■	F12
Fort Lewis	D13	Adams St.■	F15
Eastern N. Mex.	J11	Fort Hays St.	F18
Mesa St.	J14	Panhandle St.■	F24
Western St.	J15	Adams St.	F26
Chadron St.■	J21		

Colors: Purple & White. Nickname: Cowboys.
AD: Robert Evers. SID: Jesse Gallegos. II

NEW MEXICO ST. — Las Cruces, NM 88003
Neil McCarthy (18 YRS. W-370, L-179)

Simon Fraser■	N20	San Jose St.	J27
N.M. Highlands■	N29	Pacific (Cal.)	J29
UTEP■	D 3	Nevada	F 3
UTEP	D 6	Utah St.	F 5
New Mexico	D11	Nevada-Las Vegas■	F14
New Mexico■	D20	UC Irvine■	F17
Southern Utah■	D22	Cal St. Fullerton■	F19
UC Santa Barb.■	J 3	Long Beach St.	F24
Long Beach St.■	J 5	UC Irvine	F26
Cal St. Fullerton	J 8	UC Santa Barb.	F28
East Tenn. St.■	J10	Pacific (Cal.)■	M 3
Nevada-Las Vegas	J17	San Jose St.■	M 5
Utah St.■	J20	Big West Conf.	M10-13
Nevada■	J22		

Colors: Crimson & White. Nickname: Aggies.
AD: Al Gonzales. SID: Steve Shutt. I

NEW ORLEANS — New Orleans, LA 70148
Tim Floyd (7 YRS. W-142, L-73)

Florida A&M■	D 6	South Ala.	J27
Purdue■	D 8	Southwestern La.■	J29
Texas Southern	D11	Ark.-Lit. Rock■	J31
Arizona	D14	Louisiana Tech	F 3
New Orleans Cl.	D20-21	Arkansas St.■	F10
Sugar Bowl Tr.	D27-28	Jacksonville	F14
Lamar■	J 3	Louisiana Tech■	F17
Arkansas St.	J 6	Tex.-Pan American■	F19
Ark.-Lit. Rock	J 8	Southwestern La.	F23
Western Ky.■	J13	Western Ky.	F26
Lamar	J15	South Ala.■	F28
Tex.-Pan American	J17	Sun Belt Conf.	M4-8
Jacksonville■	J22		

Colors: Royal Blue & Silver. Nickname: Privateers.
AD: Ron Maestri. SID: Ed Cassiere. I

NEW PALTZ ST. — New Paltz, NY 12561
Paul Clune (4 YRS. W-40, L-58)

New Paltz St. Cl.	N19-20	Plattsburgh St.	J21
Baruch	N30	Potsdam St.	J22
Plattsburgh St.■	D 3	Cortland St.	J25
Potsdam St.■	D 4	Utica Tech■	J28
Binghamton■	D 7	Oswego St.	J29
Geneseo St.	D10	Oneonta St.	F 1
Brockport St.	D11	Stony Brook	F 9
St. Mary's (Md.)☒	J 6	Fredonia St.■	F11
Newport News App.	J 7	Buffalo St.■	F12
Goucher	J 9	Cortland St.■	F15
New Paltz St. Tr.	J15-16	Binghamton	F19
Oneonta St.■	J18	☒ Upper Marlboro, MD	

Colors: Orange & Blue. Nickname: Hawks.
AD: Margaret Lutze. SID: Fred Francello. III

NEW YORK TECH — Old Westbury, NY 11568
Frank Morris (1 YR. W-8, L-19)

Bloomsburg	N23	Molloy■	J21
Phila. Textile	D 1	St. Rose■	J23
Queens (N.Y.)■	D 4	Adelphi	J26
Mercy■	D 8	Queens (N.Y.)	J29
LIU-C.W. Post	D11	Concordia (N.Y.)	F 2
Bridgeport■	D27	Adelphi■	F 5
Franklin Pierce	D29	Kutztown	F 7
Mass.-Lowell	D30	Molloy	F 9
Dowling■	J 5	LIU-Southampton■	F12
LIU-Southampton	J 8	LIU-C.W. Post■	F16
St. Rose	J10	Pace■	F21
Phila. Textile■	J12	Mercy	F23
Pace	J15	Dowling	F26
Concordia (N.Y.)■	J19		

Colors: Navy Blue & Gold. Nickname: Bears.
AD: Clyde Doughty Jr. SID: To Be Named. II

NEW YORK U. — New York, NY 10012
Joe Nesci (5 YRS. W-83, L-35)

New York U. Tr.	N20-21	Emory	J21
Case Reserve■	N26	Carnegie Mellon	J23
Manhattanville	N29	Rochester■	J30
Johns Hopkins	D 5	Brandeis	F 1
Staten Island■	D 8	Yeshiva	F 2
Rochester	D12	Carnegie Mellon■	F 4
Clark (Mass.)■	J 3	Emory■	F 6
Union (N.Y.) Inv.	J7-8	Brandeis■	F12
Plattsburgh St.■	J10	Chicago	F18
Washington (Mo.)■	J14	Washington (Mo.)	F20
Chicago■	J16	Pratt■	F25
York (N.Y.)	J19		

Colors: Violet & White. Nickname: Violets.
AD: Dan Quilty. SID: Larry Baumann. III

NIAGARA — Niagara University, NY 14109
Jack Armstrong (4 YRS. W-51, L-63)

Valparaiso	D 1	St. Bonaventure■	J22
Canisius College Cl.	D3-4	Loyola (Md.)■	J24
Kent	D 7	St. Peter's	J27
George Mason	D 9	Fairfield	J29
St. Bonaventure	D18	Loyola (Md.)	F 5
St. John's (N.Y.)	D22	Iona■	F10
Boston U.	D28	Fairfield■	F12
Northeastern■	J 6	Canisius	F16
Manhattan■	J 8	Siena■	F19
American	J13	St. Peter's■	F21
Canisius■	J15	Iona	F25
Siena	J17	Manhattan	F27
Buffalo■	J19	Metro Atlantic Conf.	M5-7

Colors: Purple, White & Gold. Nickname: Purple Eagles.
AD: Michael Jankowski. SID: James Mauro. I

NICHOLLS ST. — Thibodaux, LA 70301
Rickey Broussard (3 YRS. W-32, L-50)

LSU-Shreveport■	N27	Texas-San Antonio■	J22
Auburn	N30	Sam Houston St.	J27
Louisiana St.	D 4	Stephen F. Austin	J29
Brigham Young Cl.	D10-11	North Texas	F 3
Southeastern La.	D14	Texas-Arlington	F 5
Bapt. Christian■	D16	Northeast La.■	F10
Louisiana Tech	D30	Northwestern (La.)■	F12
McNeese St.	J 3	Texas-San Antonio	F17
Texas-Arlington■	J 6	Southwest Tex. St.	F19
North Texas■	J 8	Stephen F. Austin■	F24
Northwestern (La.)	J13	Sam Houston St.■	F26
Northeast La.	J15	McNeese St.■	F28
Southwest Tex. St.■	J20	Southland Conf.	M4-6

Colors: Red & Gray. Nickname: Colonels.
AD: Mike Knight. SID: Ron Mears. I

NICHOLS — Dudley, MA 01570
Rich Lengieza (2 YRS. W-19, L-30)

Clark Tr.	N19-20	Roger Williams	J24
Amherst	N23	Rivier	J26
Wentworth Inst.■	D 1	Fitchburg St.	F 3
Anna Maria Inv.	D4-5	Worcester Tech	F 5
Curry■	D 9	Emerson-MCA■	F 8
Framingham St.	J13	Coast Guard■	F10
MIT	J15	Albertus Magnus	F12
Emerson-MCA	J18	Rhode Island Col.■	F17
Worcester St.■	J20	Suffolk	F19
Wheaton (Mass.)■	J22	Western New Eng.■	F22

Colors: Black & Green. Nickname: Bison.
AD: Tom Cafaro. SID: Bob Flannery. III

■ Home games on each schedule.

See pages 405–407 for Division I tournament details

NORFOLK ST. .... Norfolk, VA 23504

Michael Bernard (8 YRS. W-156, L-76)

Opponent	Date	Opponent	Date
Knoxville■	N20	Elizabeth City St.	J22
N.C. Central■	D 1	Bowie St.■	J24
Virginia St.	D 4	Shaw	J26
Augusta■	D11	Virginia St.■	J29
Morehouse	D20	Hampton■	F 1
St. Michael's Cl.	D29-30	Virginia Union■	F 5
Livingstone	J 3	Bowie St.	F 7
Winston-Salem■	J 5	St. Paul's	F 9
Johnson Smith■	J 8	Hampton	F12
St. Paul's■	J15	St. Augustine's■	F16
Fayetteville St.	J17	Elizabeth City St.■	F19
Virginia Union	J20		

Colors: Green & Gold. Nickname: Spartans.
AD: Dick Price. SID: John Holley. II

NORTH ADAMS ST. .... North Adams, MA 01247

Tim Kelly (3 YRS. W-24, L-51)

Opponent	Date	Opponent	Date
Western New Eng.	N23	Worcester St.■	J22
Southern Vt.	N30	Salem St.	J25
Eastern Conn. St.■	D 2	Skidmore	J27
Clark (Mass.)■	D 4	Fitchburg St.■	J29
Castleton St.■	D 7	Westfield St.	F 1
Williams■	D 9	Albany (N.Y.)	F 3
Mass.-Boston	D11	Framingham St.■	F 5
Md.-East. Shore	J 6	Bri'water (Mass.)	F10
Framingham St.	J11	Worcester St.	F12
Keuka■	J15	Salem St.■	F14
Bri'water (Mass.)■	J17	Fitchburg St.	F17
Central Conn. St.	J20	Westfield St.■	F19

Colors: Navy & Gold. Nickname: Mohawks.
AD: Joseph Zavattaro. SID: Tim Kelly. III

NORTH ALA. .... Florence, AL 35631

Gary Elliott (8 YRS. W-122, L-97)

Opponent	Date	Opponent	Date
North Ala. Tr.	N19-20	Athens St.	J24
Tenn. Wesleyan■	N22	Valdosta St.	J29
Bapt. Christian■	N29	Knoxville■	J31
Jacksonville St. Cl.	D3-4	Henderson St.■	F 5
Shorter■	D11	Central Ark.■	F 7
Delta St.	D17	Ala.-Huntsville	F12
Miss. College Inv.	J3-4	Lincoln Memorial	F14
Valdosta St.■	J 8	Delta St.■	F21
West Ga.■	J10	Ala.-Huntsville■	F23
Henderson St.	J15	West Ga.	F26
Central Ark.	J17	Athens St.■	F28
Lincoln Memorial■	J22		

Colors: Purple & Gold. Nickname: Lions.
AD: Bill Jones. SID: Jeff Hodges. II

NORTH CARO. .... Chapel Hill, NC 27514

Dean Smith (32 YRS. W-774, L-223)

Opponent	Date	Opponent	Date
Pre-Season NIT	N17-26	Florida St.	J26
Hawaii■	D 1	Wake Forest■	J30
Charlotte Tr.	D3-4	Duke■	F 3
Colorado St.■	D 9	North Caro. St.	F 5
Ohio St.■	D18	Maryland■	F10
Pittsburgh	D20	Georgia Tech■	F12
Marshall■	J 2	Clemson	F17
North Caro. St.■	J 5	Virginia■	F19
Maryland	J 8	Notre Dame	F23
Georgia Tech	J12	Florida St.■	F26
Clemson■	J15	Wake Forest	M 2
Virginia	J19	Duke	M 5
Louisiana St.☒	J22	Atlantic Coast Conf.	M10-13
Butler■	J24	☒ New Orleans, LA	

Colors: Carolina Blue & White. Nickname: Tar Heels.
AD: John Swofford. SID: Rick Brewer. I

NORTH CARO. A&T .... Greensboro, NC 27411

Jeff Capel (4 YRS. W-63, L-50)

Opponent	Date	Opponent	Date
Georgia Tech	N30	N.C.-Greensboro☒	J26
Fairfield Tr.	D3-4	Florida A&M	J29
N.C.-Charlotte	D 6	Bethune-Cookman	J31
Tennessee St.	D18	Winston-Salem■	F 2
Ohio St.	J 2	Delaware St.	F 5
Howard	J 8	Md.-East. Shore	F 7
Morgan St.	J10	South Caro. St.	F12
Coppin St.■	J13	Howard■	F19
Bethune-Cookman■	J15	Coppin St.	F23
Florida A&M■	J17	Morgan St.■	F28
N.C. Central■	J19	South Caro. St.■	M 5
Delaware St.■	J22	Mid-Eastern Conf.	M9-13
Md.-East. Shore■	J24	☒ Greensboro, NC	

Colors: Blue & Gold. Nickname: Aggies.
AD: Willie J. Burden. SID: Charles Mooney. I

NORTH CARO. ST. .... Raleigh, NC 27695

Les Robinson (19 YRS. W-253, L-280)

Opponent	Date	Opponent	Date
Great Alas. Shootout	N24-27	Clemson	J29
N.C.-Greensboro■	D 2	Wake Forest	F 2
Campbell■	D 4	North Caro.■	F 5
Kansas■	D 8	Tennessee	F 7
N.C.-Asheville■	D11	Virginia■	F 9
Oregon St.	D22	Florida St.	F16
UCLA☒	D28	Duke	F20
Davidson■	J 2	Maryland■	F23
North Caro.	J 5	Georgia Tech	F26
Virginia	J 9	Fla. Atlantic■	F28
Florida St.■	J16	Clemson■	M 2
Duke■	J20	Wake Forest■	M 5
Maryland	J22	Atlantic Coast Conf.	M10-13
Georgia Tech■	J26	☒ Greensboro, NC	

Colors: Red & White. Nickname: Wolfpack.
AD: Todd Turner. SID: Mark Bockelman. I

N.C. CENTRAL .... Durham, NC 27707

Greg Jackson (2 YRS. W-49, L-17)

Opponent	Date	Opponent	Date
N.C. Central Tr.	N26-27	St. Paul's■	J17
Norfolk St.	D 1	North Caro. A&T	J19
St. Augustine's■	D 4	St. Augustine's	J22
Virginia St.■	D 6	Livingstone	J26
Atlantic City Cl.	D16-18	Fayetteville St.	J29
Johnson Smith	J 4	Johnson Smith■	F 3
Hampton■	J 6	Livingstone■	F 5
Fayetteville St.■	J 8	Shaw	F 7
Shaw■	J11	Virginia Union	F10
Bowie St.■	J13	Elizabeth City St.	F12
Winston-Salem	J15	Winston-Salem■	F19

Colors: Maroon & Gray. Nickname: Eagles.
AD: Carey Hughley. SID: J. Michael Wilson. II

N.C. WESLEYAN .... Rocky Mount, NC 27801

Bill Chambers (7 YRS. W-115, L-74)

Opponent	Date	Opponent	Date
Wofford	N20	Methodist	J24
Apprentice	N23	Averett■	J26
Va. Wesleyan Tr.	N27-28	Greensboro■	J29
Chowan■	D 8	Chris. Newport■	F 2
Barton	D11	Shenandoah	F 5
Ogelthorpe Cl.	D29-30	Greensboro	F 9
N.C. Wesleyan Tr.	J7-8	Ferrum	F12
Chris. Newport	J12	Methodist■	F14
Shenandoah■	J15	Averett	F16
Ferrum■	J18	Apprentice■	F19
Chowan	J22		

Colors: Royal Blue & Gold. Nickname: Battling Bishops.
AD: Mike Fox. SID: Patrick Baker. III

N.C.-ASHEVILLE .... Asheville, NC 28804

Randy Wiel (1ST YR. AS HEAD COACH)

Opponent	Date	Opponent	Date
Montreat-Anderson■	N29	Md.-Balt. County	J27
Miami (Fla.)	D 1	Towson St.	J29
Ohio St.	D 4	Radford■	J31
Mars Hill■	D 8	Charleston So.■	F 5
North Caro. St.	D11	Coastal Caro.■	F 7
Erskine■	D18	Liberty	F10
Xavier (Ohio)	D20	Radford	F12
Kansas	J 5	Campbell■	F14
Charleston So.	J 8	N.C.-Greensboro	F17
Coastal Caro.	J10	Winthrop■	F19
Liberty■	J13	Md.-Balt. County■	F24
N.C.-Greensboro■	J15	Towson St.■	F26
Campbell	J17	Big South Conf.	M4-7
Winthrop	J22		

Colors: Royal Blue & White. Nickname: Bulldogs.
AD: Tom Hunnicutt. SID: Mike Gore. I

N.C.-CHARLOTTE .... Charlotte, NC 28223

Jeff Mullins (8 YRS. W-133, L-105)

Opponent	Date	Opponent	Date
East Caro.■	N29	Louisville	F 3
Duquesne■	D 1	Tulane■	F 5
Appalachian St.	D 4	Charleston (S.C.)	F 7
North Caro. A&T■	D 6	Southern Miss.■	F10
Davidson	D11	Va. Commonwealth	F12
Old Dominion■	D20	Davidson■	F15
Santa Clara Cl.	D29-30	Louisville■	F17
Pepperdine	J 4	Geo. Washington	F24
Clemson	J 8	Virginia Tech	F26
South Fla.■	J15	James Madison■	F28
Southern Miss.	J20	Va. Commonwealth■	M 3
Tulane	J22	Virginia Tech■	M 6
South Fla.	J29	Metro Conf.	M11-13

Colors: Green & White. Nickname: 49ers.
AD: Judy W. Rose. SID: Tom Whitestone. I

■ Home games on each schedule.

See pages 405–407 for Division I tournament details

N.C.-GREENSBORO .... Greensboro, NC 27412

Mike Dement (7 YRS. W-84, L-105)

Middle Tenn. St. N27
Austin Peay N29
North Caro. St. .... D 2
Austin Peay■ .... D 6
Virginia Tech .... D 8
William & Mary D21
Citadel D29
Florida St. D30
Radford■ .... J 6
Campbell .... J 8
Coastal Caro. J12
N.C.-Asheville J15
Winthrop■ J17
Md.-Balt. County■ J22
Towson St.■ J24
North Caro. A&T☒ J26
Charleston So.■ J29
Liberty J31
Winthrop .... F 2
Coastal Caro.■ .... F 9
Liberty■ F12
Radford F14
N.C.-Asheville■ F17
Md.-Balt. County F19
Towson St. F21
Campbell■ F24
Charleston So. F26
Big South Conf. M4-7
☒ Greensboro, NC

Colors: Gold, White & Navy. Nickname: Spartans.
AD: Nelson Bobb. SID: Ty Buckner. I

N.C.-WILMINGTON .... Wilmington, NC 28403

Kevin Eastman (6 YRS. W-106, L-65)

Appalachian St.■ N26
Auburn N28
Fla. Int'l Inv. D3-4
N.C.-Wilmington Cl. D17-18
Campbell■ D21
Portland Far West Cl D27-28
Charleston (S.C.) .... J 5
George Mason■ .... J 8
American■ J10
William & Mary J15
Old Dominion J17
James Madison J22
Richmond■ J26
East Caro. J29
Chicago St.■ .... F 2
American .... F 5
George Mason .... F 7
William & Mary■ F12
Old Dominion■ F14
Richmond F19
James Madison■ F23
East Caro.■ F26
Fla. Atlantic■ .... M 1
Colonial Conf. M5-7

Colors: Green, Gold & Navy Blue. Nickname: Seahawks.
AD: Paul A. Miller. SID: Joe Browning. I

NORTH CENTRAL .... Naperville, IL 60566

Bill Warden (12 YRS. W-174, L-142)

North Central Cl. N19-20
Regis (Colo.) .... D 2
Metropolitan St. .... D 4
Colo. Christian .... D 6
Rockford D11
Olivet (Ill.) D14
Ill. Benedictine■ D18
Hope Tr. D28-29
Aurora■ .... J 8
Millikin■ J12
Augustana (Ill.) J15
Ill. Wesleyan■ J18
Carthage■ J22
Elmhurst■ J26
Wheaton (Ill.) J29
North Park■ .... F 1
Millikin .... F 5
Augustana (Ill.)■ .... F 8
Ill. Wesleyan F12
Carthage F16
Elmhurst F19
Wheaton (Ill.)■ F22
North Park F26

Colors: Cardinal & White. Nickname: Cardinals.
AD: Walter Johnson. SID: Mike Koon. III

NORTH DAK. .... Grand Forks, ND 58202

Rich Glas (15 YRS. W-266, L-153)

Northern Ky. Cl. N19-20
Jamestown N30
Southwest St.■ .... D 4
Dakota St.■ D11
Neb.-Kearney■ D18
North Dak. Cl. D29-30
St. Cloud St.■ .... J 2
Mankato St.■ .... J 3
South Dak. St. .... J 7
Augustana (S.D.) .... J 8
Northern Colo.■ J14
Nebraska-Omaha■ J15
St. Cloud St. J18
North Dak. St.■ J22
South Dak. J28
Morningside J29
Augustana (S.D.)■ .... F 4
South Dak. St.■ .... F 5
Nebraska-Omaha F11
Northern Colo. F12
North Dak. St. F19
Mankato St. F22
Morningside■ F25
South Dak.■ F26

Colors: Green & White. Nickname: Sioux.
AD: Terry Wanless. SID: Kathy Howe. II

NORTH DAK. ST. .... Fargo, ND 58105

Tom Billeter (1 YR. W-12, L-17)

Michigan Tech N22
Bemidji St.■ N30
Moorhead St. .... D 7
Southwest St.■ .... D 9
Northeast Mo. St. D11
Teikyo-Westmar■ D15
Neb.-Kearney■ D17
Mt. Senario■ D20
Mankato St.■ .... J 2
St. Cloud St.■ .... J 3
Augustana (S.D.) .... J 7
South Dak. St. .... J 8
Nebraska-Omaha■ J14
Northern Colo.■ J15
Mankato St. J18
North Dak. J22
Morningside J28
South Dak. J29
South Dak. St.■ .... F 4
Augustana (S.D.)■ .... F 5
Northern Colo. F11
Nebraska-Omaha F12
North Dak.■ F19
St. Cloud St. F22
South Dak.■ F25
Morningside■ F26

Colors: Yellow & Green. Nickname: Bison.
AD: Robert Entzion. SID: George Ellis. II

NORTH FLA. .... Jacksonville, FL 32216

Rich Zvosec (4 YRS. W-42, L-68)

North Fla. Cl. N26-27
Embry-Riddle■ .... D 1
Flagler■ .... D 4
Warner Southern■ .... D 7
Western Ky. .... D 8
Webber■ D18
St. Francis (Ill.)■ D28
Milwaukee Engr.■ D30
Graceland (Iowa)■ .... J 2
St. Mary's (Tex.)■ .... J 6
Florida Tech■ J12
St. Leo■ J15
Edward Waters■ J17
Eckerd J19
Barry■ J22
Fla. Southern J26
Tampa J29
Rollins■ .... F 2
St. Leo .... F 5
Eckerd■ .... F 9
Barry F12
Fla. Southern■ F16
Tampa■ F19
Rollins F23
Florida Tech F26

Colors: Navy Blue & Gray. Nickname: Ospreys.
AD: John Ratliff. SID: Bonnie Senappe. II

NORTH TEXAS .... Denton, TX 76203

Tim Jankovich (1ST YR. AS HEAD COACH)

Baylor N27
Colorado N29
Tulsa■ .... D 1
New Mexico Lobo Cl. D3-4
Southern Methodist■ .... D 7
Nevada■ .... D 9
Texas Tech D21
Stephen F. Austin D28
Sam Houston St.■ D30
McNeese St. .... J 6
Nicholls St. .... J 8
Texas-Arlington J15
Northeast La.■ J20
Northwestern (La.)■ J22
Southwest Tex. St. J27
Texas-San Antonio J29
Nicholls St.■ .... F 3
McNeese St.■ .... F 5
Sam Houston St. .... F 7
Texas-Arlington■ F12
Northwestern (La.) F17
Northeast La. F19
Texas-San Antonio■ F24
Southwest Tex. St.■ F26
Stephen F. Austin F28
Southland Conf. M4-6

Colors: Green & White. Nickname: Mean Green Eagles.
AD: To be named. SID: Brian Briscoe. I

NORTHEAST LA. .... Monroe, LA 71209

Mike Vining (12 YRS. W-230, L-126)

Ark.-Monticello■ N29
Montana Cl. D3-4
Wright St. Cl. D17-18
Mississippi St.■ D21
Southern Miss. D23
Southwest Tex. St.■ D28
Texas-San Antonio■ D30
Sam Houston St. .... J 6
Stephen F. Austin .... J 8
McNeese St.■ J13
Nicholls St.■ J15
Southern Miss.■ J17
North Texas J20
Texas-Arlington J22
Northwestern (La.) J29
Stephen F. Austin■ .... F 3
Sam Houston St.■ .... F 5
Texas-San Antonio .... F 7
Nicholls St. F10
McNeese St. F12
Texas-Arlington■ F17
North Texas■ F19
Northwestern (La.)■ F26
Southwest Tex. St. F28
Southland Conf. M4-6

Colors: Maroon & Gold. Nickname: Indians.
AD: Benny Hollis. SID: Bob Anderson. I

NORTHEAST MO. ST. .... Kirksville, MO 63501

Willard Sims (22 YRS. W-274, L-314)

Central (Iowa)■ N20
Florida Tech Cl. N26-27
Quincy .... D 1
Westminster (Mo.)■ .... D 4
North Dak. St.■ D11
Fort Hays St. D18
Mo.-St. Louis■ .... J 5
Emporia St.■ .... J 8
Quincy■ J10
Lincoln (Mo.) J12
Mo. Southern St. J15
Mo. Western St.■ J19
Central Mo. St.■ J22
Southwest Baptist J27
Pittsburg St. J29
Washburn■ .... F 2
Northwest Mo. St. .... F 5
Missouri-Rolla■ .... F 9
Emporia St. F12
Lincoln (Mo.)■ F16
Mo. Southern St.■ F19
Mo. Western St. F23
Central Mo. St. F26

Colors: Purple & White. Nickname: Bulldogs.
AD: Alan Graham. SID: William Cable. II

NORTHEASTERN .... Boston, MA 02115

Karl Fogel (10 YRS. W-159, L-121)

Duke N27
Mass.-Boston■ N30
George Mason■ .... D 4
Central Mich.■ D11
Howard D18
Stetson Cl. D29-30
Siena■ .... J 3
Niagara .... J 6
Canisius .... J 8
Iona J11
Vermont■ J13
Hartford J15
Drexel J21
Delaware J23
New Hampshire■ J27
Maine■ J29
Rhode Island .... F 1
Boston U.■ .... F 5
Maine F10
New Hampshire F12
Delaware■ F18
Drexel■ F20
Vermont F24
Hartford■ F26
Boston U. .... M 1
North Atlantic Conf. M5-9

Colors: Red & Black. Nickname: Huskies.
AD: Barry Gallup. SID: Jack Grinold. I

■ Home games on each schedule.

See pages 405–407 for Division I tournament details

NORTHEASTERN ILL. .... Chicago, IL 60625
Rees Johnson (17 YRS. W-263, L-222)

Opponent	Date	Opponent	Date
Cornell College■	N29	Chicago St.	J13
Oklahoma	D 1	Central Conn. St.	J17
Wis.-Milwaukee	D 4	Buffalo■	J22
Cal St. Sacramento■	D 6	Troy St.	J24
Ill.-Chicago	D 9	Cal St. Northridge■	J29
Eastern Ill.■	D11	Trinity (Ill.)■	F 2
DePaul	D14	Mo.-Kansas City■	F 5
Arizona St.	D18	Clarke■	F 7
Montana	D21	Cal St. Northridge	F10
Jackson St.■	D23	Mo.-Kansas City	F16
Central Mich.	D28	Central Conn. St.■	F19
Minnesota	J 3	Chicago St.■	F24
Wis.-Milwaukee■	J 6	Hofstra■	F28
Grinnell■	J 8	East Coast Conf.	M4-6

Colors: Royal Blue & Gold. Nickname: Golden Eagles.
AD: Vivian Fuller. SID: Mark Johnson. I

NORTHERN ARIZ. .... Flagstaff, AZ 86011
Harold Merritt (6 YRS. W-52, L-110)

Opponent	Date	Opponent	Date
Southwest Tex. St.■	N27	Montana■	J22
Southern Colo.■	N29	Eastern Wash.	J27
Cal St. Sacramento	D 4	Idaho	J29
Southern Utah	D 6	Weber St.	F 4
Wis.-Parkside■	D11	Idaho St.■	F10
UC San Diego■	D18	Boise St.■	F12
Arizona St. Cl.	D28-29	Montana	F17
Cal Poly SLO■	J 3	Montana St.	F19
Cal St. Sacramento■	J 5	Idaho■	F24
Fairfield■	J 7	Eastern Wash.■	F26
Boise St.	J13	Southern Utah■	M 2
Idaho St.	J15	Weber St.■	M 5
Montana St.■	J20	Big Sky Conf.	M10-12

Colors: Blue & Gold. Nickname: Lumberjacks.
AD: Tom Jurich. SID: Chris Burkhalter. I

NORTHERN COLO. .... Greeley, CO 80639
Ken Smith (1 YR. W-12, L-15)

Opponent	Date	Opponent	Date
Colorado-CS■	N23	South Dak.■	J21
Neb.-Kearney	N27	Morningside■	J22
Colo. Christian	N29	St. Cloud St.	J28
Colorado-CS	D 3	Mankato St.	J29
Denver■	D11	Nebraska-Omaha	F 5
Metropolitan St.■	D13	Augustana (S.D.)	F 8
Colo. Christian■	D15	North Dak. St.■	F11
Regis (Colo.)	D29	North Dak.■	F12
Augustana (S.D.)■	J 2	Morningside	F18
South Dak. St.■	J 3	South Dak.	F19
Nebraska-Omaha■	J 8	South Dak. St.	F22
North Dak.	J14	Mankato St.■	F25
North Dak. St.	J15	St. Cloud St.■	F26

Colors: Navy & Gold. Nickname: Bears.
AD: Jim Fallis. SID: Scott Leisinger. II

NORTHERN ILL. .... De Kalb, IL 60115
Brian Hammel (8 YRS. W-117, L-99)

Opponent	Date	Opponent	Date
Aurora■	N27	Youngstown St.	J29
Kent	D 1	Cleveland St.	J31
Akron■	D18	Valparaiso■	F 5
Morehead St.	D21	Eastern Ill.	F 7
Marquette■	D28	Loyola (Ill.)	F10
Chicago St.	D30	Wis.-Green Bay■	F14
Texas A&M■	J 5	Ill.-Chicago	F17
Ill.-Chicago■	J 8	Youngstown St.■	F19
Wis.-Green Bay	J10	Cleveland St.■	F21
Valparaiso	J15	Western Ill.	F24
Eastern Ill.■	J17	Wis.-Milwaukee■	F26
Wis.-Milwaukee	J19	Wright St.	M 1
Wright St.■	J24	Mid-Continent Conf.	M6-8
Western Ill.■	J27		

Colors: Cardinal & Black. Nickname: Huskies.
AD: Gerald O'Dell. SID: Mike Korcek. I

NORTHERN IOWA .... Cedar Falls, IA 50613
Eldon Miller (31 YRS. W-504, L-344)

Opponent	Date	Opponent	Date
Morningside■	N29	Southwest Mo. St.	J24
Iowa St.	D 4	Wichita St.■	J27
Iowa■	D 7	Indiana St.■	J29
Drake■	D12	Southern Ill.	F 3
Illinois St.	D19	Illinois St.■	F 5
LIU-Brooklyn	D21	Bradley■	F 7
Cal St. Fullerton	D28	Drake	F12
Nebraska	D31	Tulsa■	F15
Creighton	J 4	Indiana St.	F19
Tulsa	J 8	Southern Ill.■	F23
St. Bonaventure■	J11	Bradley	F26
Wichita St.	J15	Southwest Mo. St.■	F28
Chicago St.■	J18	Missouri Valley Conf	M5-7
Creighton■	J22		

Colors: Purple & Old Gold. Nickname: Panthers.
AD: Christopher Ritrievi. SID: Nancy Justis. I

NORTHERN KY. .... Highland Heights, KY 41076
Ken Shields (5 YRS. W-62, L-78)

Opponent	Date	Opponent	Date
Northern Ky. Cl.	N19-20	IU/PU-Ft. Wayne	J27
Spalding■	N24	Ashland	J29
Morehead St.	N29	Bellarmine■	F 3
Spalding	D 9	Kentucky St.■	F 5
Ky. Wesleyan■	D20	Oakland City	F 9
Southern Ind.■	D22	Indianapolis■	F12
Gannon Tr.	D29-30	Lewis	F17
Kentucky St.	J 6	St. Joseph's (Ind.)	F19
Bellarmine	J 8	Ashland■	F24
Oakland City■	J12	IU/PU-Ft. Wayne■	F26
Indianapolis	J15	Southern Ind.	M 3
St. Joseph's (Ind.)■	J20	Ky. Wesleyan	M 5
Lewis■	J22		

Colors: Gold, Black & White. Nickname: Norse.
AD: Jane Meier. SID: J.D. Campbell. II

NORTHERN MICH. .... Marquette, MI 49855
Dean Ellis (7 YRS. W-109, L-87)

Opponent	Date	Opponent	Date
Alas. Anchorage	N19	Northwood■	J15
Alas. Anchorage	N20	Wis.-Superior■	J17
Alas. Fairbanks	N22	Oakland	J20
Alas. Fairbanks	N23	Saginaw Valley	J22
Wis.-Stevens Point■	N30	Wayne St. (Mich.)	J27
Wayne St. (Mich.)■	D 2	Hillsdale	J29
Bemidji St.■	D 4	Michigan Tech■	F 5
Minn.-Duluth■	D 6	Ferris St.■	F10
Michigan Tech	D11	Grand Valley St.■	F12
Hillsdale■	D20	Lake Superior St.	F17
Minn.-Duluth	J 2	Northwood	F19
Bemidji St.	J 3	Oakland■	F24
Ferris St.	J 6	Saginaw Valley■	F26
Grand Valley St.	J 8	Mt. Senario■	F28
Lake Superior St.■	J13		

Colors: Old Gold & Olive Green. Nickname: Wildcats.
AD: Rick Comley. SID: Jim Pinar. II

NORTHERN ST. .... Aberdeen, SD 57401
Bob Olson (8 YRS. W-158, L-91)

Opponent	Date	Opponent	Date
Wayne St. (Neb.)	N20	Minn.-Morris	J12
Jamestown	N23	Minn.-Duluth■	J15
Northern St. Tr.	N26-27	Winona St.	J19
Minot St.	D 1	Moorhead St.■	J22
Augustana (S.D.)■	D 4	Valley City St.	J26
South Dak. St.	D 7	Wayne St. (Neb.)■	J29
Dak. Wesleyan	D10	Bemidji St.■	F 2
Huron	D15	Southwest St.	F 5
Jamestown■	D17	Minn.-Morris■	F 9
Mt. Senario■	D18	Minn.-Duluth	F12
Northern St. Inv.	J1-2	Winona St.■	F16
Bemidji St.	J 5	Moorhead St.	F19
Southwest St.■	J 8		

Colors: Maroon & Gold. Nickname: Wolves.
AD: Jim Kretchman. SID: Deb Smith. II

NORTHWEST MO. ST. .... Maryville, MO 64468
Steve Tappmeyer (5 YRS. W-77, L-62)

Opponent	Date	Opponent	Date
Oakland City Inv.	N19-20	Washburn■	J22
Mid-America Naz.■	N23	Mo. Southern St.■	J26
Mankato St. Cl.	N26-27	Emporia St.	J29
SIU-Edwardsville	D 1	Central Mo. St.	F 2
Peru St.■	D 4	Northeast Mo. St.■	F 5
Northwest Mo. St. Cl	D10-11	Lincoln (Mo.)	F 9
Rockhurst■	D18	Missouri-Rolla	F12
Mo. Western St.■	J 5	Pittsburg St.■	F16
Missouri-Rolla■	J 8	Southwest Baptist■	F19
Pittsburg St.	J12	Mo.-St. Louis	F23
Southwest Baptist	J15	Washburn	F26
Mo.-St. Louis■	J19		

Colors: Green & White. Nickname: Bearcats.
AD: Richard Flanagan. SID: Larry Cain. II

NORTHWESTERN .... Evanston, IL 60208
Ricky Byrdsong (5 YRS. W-53, L-87)

Opponent	Date	Opponent	Date
Chicago■	N27	Iowa■	J26
Western Ill.■	N29	Penn St.■	J29
Illinois St.■	D 4	Minnesota	F 5
Loyola (Ill.)	D11	Purdue	F 9
Youngstown St.	D15	Illinois■	F12
Texas A&M	D18	Michigan St.■	F17
Holy Cross■	D20	Wisconsin	F19
Stetson Cl.	D29-30	Indiana■	F24
Purdue■	J 5	Iowa	F26
Minnesota■	J 8	Penn St.	M 2
Illinois	J12	Wisconsin■	M 5
Michigan St.	J15	Ohio St.	M 9
Indiana	J22	Michigan■	M12

Colors: Purple & White. Nickname: Wildcats.
AD: Ken Kraft. SID: Greg Shea. I

■ Home games on each schedule.

See pages 405–407 for Division I tournament details

N'WESTERN (WIS.) .... Watertown, WI 53094

Jerome Kruse (11 YRS. W-92, L-134)

- Beloit■ N20
- Lawrence■ N23
- Ripon■ N29
- Wis. Lutheran D 2
- Edgewood D 4
- Marian (Wis.) D11
- Wis. Lutheran Cl. J7-8
- Concordia (Wis.)■ J12
- Maranatha■ J15
- Milwaukee Engr. J17
- St. Norbert J19
- Cardinal Stritch■ J22
- Lakeland J26
- Wis. Lutheran J29
- Edgewood■ F 2
- Milwaukee Engr.■ F 5
- Marian (Wis.)■ F 9
- Concordia (Wis.) F12
- Carroll (Wis.)■ F14
- Maranatha F17
- Lakeland■ F22
- Cardinal Stritch F24

Colors: Black & Red. Nickname: Trojans.
AD: Jerome Kruse. SID: Tim Dolan. III

NORTHWESTERN (LA.) ...... Natchitoches, LA 71497

Dan Bell (5 YRS. W-57, L-83)

- Ouachita Bapt.■ N26
- Tarleton St.■ D 1
- Arkansas D 4
- Ambassador■ D 6
- Alabama D 9
- Troy St. D11
- Southeastern La.■ D18
- Henderson St.■ D20
- Texas-San Antonio■ D28
- Southwest Tex. St.■ D30
- Stephen F. Austin J 6
- Sam Houston St. J 8
- Nicholls St.■ J13
- McNeese St.■ J15
- Texas-Arlington J20
- North Texas J22
- Northeast La.■ J29
- Sam Houston St.■ F 3
- Stephen F. Austin■ F 5
- Southwest Tex. St. F 7
- McNeese St. F10
- Nicholls St. F12
- North Texas■ F17
- Texas-Arlington■ F19
- Northeast La. F26
- Texas-San Antonio F28
- Southland Conf. M4-6

Colors: Purple, White & Burnt Orange. Nickname: Demons.
AD: Tynes Hildebrand. SID: Doug Ireland. I

NORTHWOOD .... Midland, MI 48640

Dean Lockwood (2 YRS. W-16, L-42)

- Grand Rapids Bapt. N27
- Oakland■ D 2
- Grand Valley St. D 4
- Hillsdale D 9
- Ferris St.■ D11
- Spring Arbor■ D15
- Tri-State■ D18
- Aquinas D21
- Mich.-Dearborn■ J 3
- Saginaw Valley J 6
- Wayne St. (Mich.)■ J 8
- Michigan Tech J13
- Northern Mich. J15
- Lake Superior St. J22
- Concordia (Mich.) J24
- Oakland J27
- Grand Valley St.■ J29
- Hillsdale■ F 3
- Ferris St. F 5
- Alma■ F 7
- Saginaw Valley■ F10
- Wayne St. (Mich.) F12
- Michigan Tech■ F17
- Northern Mich.■ F19
- Siena Heights■ F21
- Lake Superior St.■ F26

Colors: Columbia Blue & White. Nickname: Northmen.
AD: Dave Coffey. SID: Fritz Reznor. II

NOTRE DAME .... Notre Dame, IN 46556

John MacLeod (8 YRS. W-117, L-102)

- Valparaiso■ N28
- Boston College D 2
- San Diego■ D 4
- Indiana D 7
- Southern Cal D11
- Maui Inv. D21-23
- Fordham■ J 2
- Kentucky J 6
- La Salle J 8
- Missouri■ J12
- Duquesne J15
- St. Bonaventure J19
- Manhattan■ J22
- Loyola (Ill.)■ J24
- Duke J26
- Providence■ J29
- Cal St. Northridge■ J31
- UCLA■ F 5
- Georgia☒ F 6
- Butler■ F 8
- Hofstra■ F11
- Marquette F17
- DePaul■ F20
- North Caro.■ F23
- Louisville■ F26
- Loyola (Ill.) M 3
- Dayton■ M 5

☒ Atlanta, GA

Colors: Gold & Blue. Nickname: Fighting Irish.
AD: Richard Rosenthal. SID: John Heisler. I

NOTRE DAME (CAL.) .... Belmont, CA 94002

Pat Fuscaldo (2 YRS. W-16, L-35)

- Bethany (Cal.)■ N23
- St. Mary's (Cal.) N27
- UC Riverside■ D 3
- Cal St. Dom. Hills■ D 4
- Pacific (Cal.) D 7
- Menlo■ D11
- Seattle Pacific■ D18
- Coast Guard■ D21
- Cal St. Los Angeles■ D23
- Christian Heritage D29
- Cal St. San B'dino D30
- Sonoma St.■ J 7
- San Fran. St. J 8
- Cal St. Stanislaus■ J14
- Cal St. Hayward J15
- Cal St. Chico■ J21
- Humboldt St.■ J22
- Menlo J26
- UC Davis J29
- Humboldt St. F 4
- Cal St. Chico F 5
- Cal St. Hayward■ F11
- Cal St. Stanislaus F12
- Sonoma St. F18
- San Fran. St.■ F19
- UC Davis■ F24

Colors: Gold, White & Columbia Blue. Nickname: Argonauts.
AD: Virginia Babel. SID: Virginia Babel. II

OAKLAND .... Rochester, MI 48063

Greg Kampe (9 YRS. W-150, L-103)

- Alma N27
- Lewis■ N29
- Northwood D 2
- Grand Rapids Bapt.■ D 7
- Grand Valley St.■ D 9
- Wayne St. (Mich.) D11
- Toledo D18
- Madonna D20
- Oakland (Mich.) Cl. D29-30
- Saginaw Valley■ J 4
- Lake Superior St. J 8
- Ferris St.■ J13
- Hillsdale J15
- Northern Mich.■ J20
- Michigan Tech■ J22
- Northwood■ J27
- Saginaw Valley J29
- Grand Valley St. F 3
- Wayne St. (Mich.)■ F 5
- Mercyhurst F 7
- Lake Superior St.■ F12
- Ferris St. F17
- Hillsdale■ F19
- Northern Mich. F24
- Michigan Tech F26

Colors: Gold, Black & White. Nickname: Pioneers.
AD: Paul Hartman. SID: Andy Glantzman. II

OAKLAND CITY .... Oakland City, IN 47660

Mike Sandifar (15 YRS. W-242, L-178)

- Oakland City Inv. N19-20
- Hillsdale Free Will N23
- SIU-Edwardsville■ N27
- Bellarmine D 1
- St. Francis (Ill.)■ D 4
- St. Louis Christian■ D 7
- Ohio St.-Newark■ D10
- Ind.-Northwest■ D12
- Ind.-East■ D18
- Ind.-Northwest■ J 8
- Northern Ky. J12
- Purdue-North Cent.■ J15
- Indianapolis J17
- Lane■ J22
- Wis.-Parkside■ J24
- SIU-Edwardsville J29
- Graceland (Ind.)■ F 3
- Jacksonville St. F 6
- Northern Ky.■ F 9
- Lane F12
- Graceland (Ind.) F17
- IU/PU-Indianapolis■ F22
- Sanford Brown■ F26
- Ind.-East■ M 1

Colors: Blue & White. Nickname: Mighty Oaks.
AD: Mike Sandifar. SID: Denise Sandifar. II

OBERLIN .... Oberlin, OH 44074

Gene DeLorenzo (2 YRS. W-15, L-31)

- Colby Tr. N19-20
- Rochester Inv. N27-28
- Denison■ D 1
- Earlham■ D 4
- Allegheny D 8
- Thiel■ D10
- Wash. & Jeff.■ D11
- Kenyon J 3
- Wooster J 5
- Ohio Wesleyan■ J12
- Wittenberg J15
- Case Reserve■ J19
- Earlham J22
- Allegheny■ J26
- Penn St.-Behrend J29
- Bethany (W.Va.)■ J31
- Ohio Wesleyan F 2
- Kenyon■ F 5
- Denison F 9
- Wittenberg■ F12
- Case Reserve F16
- Wooster■ F19

Colors: Crimson & Gold. Nickname: Yeomen.
AD: Jim Foels. SID: Scott Wargo. III

OCCIDENTAL .... Los Angeles, CA 90041

Brian Newhall (5 YRS. W-68, L-58)

- Pacific Christian■ N29
- Cal St. San B'dino D 1
- Westminster Cl. D10-12
- Fontbonne D15
- Occidental Tr. D30-31
- Azusa Pacific Tr. J3-4
- Cal Lutheran J12
- Claremont-M-S■ J15
- Cal Tech■ J19
- La Verne J22
- Pomona-Pitzer J26
- Redlands■ J29
- Whittier■ F 2
- Cal Lutheran■ F 5
- Claremont-M-S F 9
- Cal Tech F12
- La Verne■ F16
- Pomona-Pitzer■ F19
- Redlands F21
- Whittier F24

Colors: Orange & Black. Nickname: Tigers.
AD: Dale Widolff. SID: James Kerman. III

OGLETHORPE .... Atlanta, GA 30319

Jack Berkshire (17 YRS. W-242, L-205)

- Johns Hopkins N19-20
- Emory N27
- Otterbein■ D 1
- Maryville (Tenn.)■ D11
- Davidson D13
- Ogelthorpe Cl. D29-30
- Parks■ J 7
- Emory■ J11
- Fisk J14
- Centre J16
- Rhodes■ J21
- Millsaps■ J23
- Emory■ J26
- Hendrix J28
- Trinity (Tex.) J30
- Sewanee■ F 2
- Fisk■ F 4
- Centre■ F 6
- Hendrix■ F11
- Trinity (Tex.)■ F13
- Rhodes F18
- Millsaps F20
- Sewanee F26

Colors: Black & Gold. Nickname: Stormy Petrels.
AD: Jack Berkshire. SID: Dunn Neugebauer. III

■ Home games on each schedule.

See pages 405–407 for Division I tournament details

OHIO .... Athens, OH 45701

Larry Hunter (17 YRS. W-365, L-127)

Ohio Dominican■	N30	Eastern Mich.■	J26
Nebraska Cl.	D3-4	Toledo	J29
Robert Morris■	D11	Kent■	F 2
Duquesne	D14	Miami (Ohio)	F 5
West Va.	D18	Western Mich.■	F 9
Youngstown St.■	D20	Akron	F12
Wright St.	D22	Central Mich.	F16
Ball St.	J 5	Bowling Green■	F19
Miami (Ohio)■	J 8	Eastern Mich.	F23
Western Mich.	J12	Toledo■	F26
Akron■	J15	Kent	M 2
Central Mich.■	J19	Ball St.■	M 5
Bowling Green	J22	Mid-American Conf.	M8-12

Colors: Kelly Green & White. Nickname: Bobcats.
AD: Harold McElhaney. SID: Glenn Coble. I

OHIO NORTHERN .... Ada, OH 45810

Joe Campoli (1 YR. W-28 , L-2)

Alas. Fairbanks Tr.	N19-20	Marietta	J15
Lake Erie■	N24	Otterbein■	J19
Defiance■	N27	John Carroll	J22
Bluffton	D 1	Muskingum■	J26
Baldwin-Wallace	D 4	Baldwin-Wallace■	J29
Muskingum	D 8	Heidelberg	F 2
John Carroll■	D11	Hiram■	F 5
Hiram	D18	Capital	F 9
Wooster Cl.	D29-30	Mount Union	F12
Heidelberg■	J 5	Otterbein	F16
Mount Union■	J 8	Marietta■	F19
Capital■	J12		

Colors: Orange & Black. Nickname: Polar Bears.
AD: Gale Daugherty. SID: Cort Reynolds. III

OHIO ST. .... Columbus, OH 43210

Randy Ayers (4 YRS. W-85, L-36)

Mo.-St. Louis■	N27	Purdue	J22
Pennsylvania■	N29	Michigan St.■	J26
N.C.-Asheville■	D 4	Indiana	F 2
Marquette	D12	Wisconsin■	F 5
UC Santa Barb.■	D14	Minnesota	F 9
North Caro.	D18	Michigan■	F13
Maui Inv.	D21-23	Illinois	F15
West Va.■	D30	Penn St.	F19
North Caro. A&T■	J 2	Purdue■	F23
Iowa■	J 4	Michigan St.	F26
Wisconsin	J 8	Indiana■	M 6
Michigan	J13	Northwestern■	M 9
Illinois■	J15	Iowa	M12
Penn St.■	J19		

Colors: Scarlet & Gray. Nickname: Buckeyes.
AD: James Jones. SID: Steve Snapp. I

OHIO WESLEYAN .... Delaware, OH 43015

Gene Mehaffey (25 YRS. W-460, L-297)

Ohio Wesleyan Tr.	N20-21	Wooster■	J15
Ohio Dominican■	N24	Earlham■	J19
Capital	N27	Allegheny	J22
Kenyon	D 1	Wittenberg	J26
Allegheny■	D 4	Denison	J29
Wittenberg■	D 8	Oberlin■	F 2
Findlay	D18	Wilmington (Ohio)	F 5
Thomas More■	D30	Kenyon■	F 9
Denison■	J 2	Wooster	F12
Case Reserve	J 5	Earlham	F16
Wilmington (Ohio)■	J 8	Case Reserve■	F19
Oberlin	J12		

Colors: Red & Black. Nickname: Battling Bishops.
AD: Jay Martin. SID: Mark Beckenbach. III

OKLAHOMA .... Norman, OK 73019

Billy Tubbs (19 YRS. W-424, L-189)

Massachusetts■	N28	Nebraska	J29
Northeastern Ill.■	D 1	Southern Methodist■	F 2
Oregon St.	D 4	Missouri■	F 5
Maryland⊠	D 7	Oklahoma St.	F 7
Lamar■	D18	Colorado■	F12
Coppin St.■	D22	Nebraska■	F14
Oklahoma Tr.	D29-30	Kansas St.	F19
Baylor■	J 5	Iowa St.■	F23
Oklahoma St.■	J 8	Missouri	F26
Kansas	J10	Colorado	M 2
Iowa St.	J15	Kansas■	M 6
Va. Commonwealth	J20	Big Eight Conf.	M11-13
Kansas St.■	J26	⊠ Oklahoma City, OK	

Colors: Crimson & Cream. Nickname: Sooners.
AD: Donnie Duncan. SID: Mike Prusinski. I

OKLAHOMA ST. .... Stillwater, OK 74078

Eddie Sutton (23 YRS. W-502, L-189)

Southern Methodist	N27	Kansas	J26
Oral Roberts■	N29	Kansas St.■	F 2
Arizona St.⊠	D 2	Iowa St.■	F 5
Arizona ♦	D 5	Oklahoma■	F 7
Texas Christian■	D 9	Missouri	F12
Louisiana St.@	D11	Kansas■	F16
UC Davis■	D18	Nebraska■	F19
Tulsa	D20	Colorado	F21
Hawaii Rainbow Cl.	D27-30	Iowa St.	F26
Prairie View■	J 4	Nebraska	M 2
Oklahoma	J 8	Colorado■	M 5
West Tex. A&M■	J10	Big Eight Conf.	M11-13
Kansas St.	J15	⊠ Tulsa, OK	
Southwest Mo. St.	J19	♦ Phoenix, AZ	
Missouri■	J22	@ New Orleans, LA	

Colors: Orange & Black. Nickname: Cowboys.
AD: Jim Garner. SID: Steve Buzzard. I

OLD DOMINION .... Norfolk, VA 23529

Oliver Purnell (5 YRS. W-80, L-65)

Richmond	J13	George Mason	J22
South Caro.	N27	American■	J26
Florida A&M■	N29	Va. Commonwealth⊠	J31
U.C.-Santa Barb. Tr.	D2-4	William & Mary■	F 2
Virginia■	D11	James Madison■	F 5
Auburn■	D18	Richmond■	F 9
N.C.-Charlotte	D20	East Caro.	F12
South Fla.	D22	N.C.-Wilmington	F14
Wyoming Cowboy Tr.	D28-29	George Mason■	F19
Howard■	J 5	American	F23
James Madison	J 8	William & Mary	F26
East Caro.■	J15	Colonial Conf.	M5-7
N.C.-Wilmington■	J17	⊠ Hampton, VA	

Colors: Slate Blue & Silver. Nickname: Monarchs.
AD: Jim Jarrett. SID: Carol Hudson. I

OLD WESTBURY .... Long Island, NY 11568

Ron Jackson (2 YRS. W-21, L-26)

John Jay Tr.	N20-21	King's (N.Y.)■	J20
Rutgers-Newark	N29	Mt. St. Mary Cl.	J22-23
Stony Brook	D 1	Centenary (N.J.)■	J26
Hunter	D 3	Baruch	J28
Kean■	D 6	CCNY	F 1
Upsala■	D 8	Albany (N.Y.)	F 5
York (N.Y.)■	D15	John Jay	F 9
Medgar Evers■	D17	Mt. St. Mary (N.Y.)	F12
Bloomsburg Inv.	J7-8	Montclair St.■	F14
Lehman	J13	LIU-Southampton■	F21
Pratt■	J15	Merchant Marine	F23

Colors: Green & White. Nickname: Panthers.
AD: Dora Ierides. SID: Mark Sosna. III

OLIVET .... Olivet, MI 49076

Gary Morrison (26 YRS. W-256, L-335)

Saginaw Valley Tr.	N19-20	Kalamazoo■	J15
Manchester■	N29	Hope■	J19
Aquinas	N30	Calvin	J22
Penn St.-Behrend Tr.	D3-4	Albion■	J26
Goshen	D11	Alma■	F 2
Bluffton■	D15	Adrian■	F 5
Defiance	D18	Kalamazoo	F 9
Albion Tr.	D28-29	Hope	F12
Alma	J 8	Calvin■	F16
Adrian	J12	Albion	F19

Colors: Red & White. Nickname: Comets.
AD: Jackie Shimp. SID: Jerry Rashid. III

ONEONTA ST. .... Oneonta, NY 13820

Jeri Mirabito (2 YRS. W-8, L-41)

Pracitical Bible	N23	Oswego St.■	J28
Potsdam St.■	D 3	Utica Tech	J29
Plattsburgh St.■	D 4	New Paltz St.■	F 1
Cortland St.■	D 7	Dominican (N.Y.)■	F 3
Brockport St.	D10	Hamilton	F 5
Geneseo St.	D11	Albany (N.Y.)■	F 8
Lebanon Valley Tr.	J7-8	Buffalo St.■	F11
Utica	J12	Fredonia St.■	F12
New Paltz St.	J18	Binghamton	F15
Potsdam St.	J21	Cortland St.	F19
Plattsburgh St.	J22	Hartwick	F21
Binghamton■	J25		

Colors: Red & White. Nickname: Red Dragons.
AD: Al Sosa. SID: Barbara Blodgett. III

■ Home games on each schedule.

See pages 405–407 for Division I tournament details

ORAL ROBERTS .... Tulsa, OK 74171

Bill Self (1ST YR. AS HEAD COACH)

Sam Houston St.■	N26
Mississippi Val.■	N27
Oklahoma St.	N29
Middle Tenn. St.	D 1
Tulsa■	D 6
Indiana Cl.	D10-11
Indiana St.■	D18
Marshall■	D20
Texas Christian	J 6
Pepperdine■	J 8
Loyola (Cal.)■	J10
Creighton	J13
Mississippi■	J17
Mississippi Val.	J19
Rice■	J22
Baylor■	J29
Western Ky.	F 1
Southwest Tex. St.	F 3
Texas A&M	F 9
Mo.-Kansas City	F12
Southern Ill.■	F14
Stephen F. Austin	F16
Texas Tech■	F23
Texas Christian■	F26
Texas	F28
Southern Methodist	M 2

Colors: Navy Blue, White & Vegas Gold. Nickname: Golden Eagles.
AD: Bob Brooks. SID: Scott Vallery. I

OREGON .... Eugene, OR 97401

Jerry Green (10 YRS. W-160, L-128)

Humboldt St.■	N26
Pacific (Cal.)■	D 4
Idaho	D12
Santa Clara■	D14
Wis.-Green Bay	D18
Portland Far West Cl	D27-28
St. Mary's (Cal.)	D30
Alas. Fairbanks■	J 3
UCLA	J 6
Southern Cal	J 8
Oregon St.■	J15
Washington St.■	J20
Washington■	J22
Arizona	J27
Arizona St.	J29
Stanford■	F 3
California■	F 5
Oregon St.	F12
Washington	F17
Washington St.	F19
Arizona St.■	F24
Arizona■	F26
California	M 3
Stanford	M 5
Southern Cal■	M10
UCLA■	M12

Colors: Green & Yellow. Nickname: Ducks.
AD: Rich Brooks. SID: Steve Hellyer. I

OREGON ST. .... Corvallis, OR 97331

Jim Anderson (4 YRS. W-64, L-51)

Oklahoma■	D 4
Brigham Young Cl.	D10-11
Bradley■	D16
Fresno St.	D18
North Caro. St.■	D22
Portland Far West Cl	D27-28
Portland■	D31
Southern Cal	J 6
UCLA	J 8
Oregon	J15
Washington■	J20
Washington St.■	J22
Arizona St.	J27
Arizona	J29
California■	F 3
Stanford■	F 5
Oregon■	F12
Washington St.	F17
Washington	F19
Arizona■	F24
Arizona St.■	F26
Stanford	M 3
California	M 5
UCLA■	M10
Southern Cal■	M12

Colors: Orange & Black. Nickname: Beavers.
AD: Dutch Baughman. SID: Hal Cowan. I

OSWEGO ST. .... Oswego, NY 13126

John Meehan (3 YRS. W-8, L-64)

St. Lawrence■	D 1
Mt. St. Mary Tr.	D4-5
Utica Tech■	D 7
Utica	D11
Mt. St. Mary (N.Y.)■	J 8
Hamilton	J11
Cortland St.■	J14
Binghamton	J15
Brockport St.	J18
Fredonia St.■	J21
Buffalo St.■	J22
Geneseo St.	J25
Oneonta St.	J28
New Paltz St.■	J29
Utica■	J31
Utica Tech	F 4
Geneseo St.■	F 5
Nazareth (N.Y.)	F 8
Potsdam St.■	F11
Plattsburgh St.	F12
Brockport St.■	F15
Fredonia St.	F18
Buffalo St.	F19

Colors: Green, Gold & White. Nickname: Great Lakers.
AD: Sandra Moore. SID: Danielle Martin. III

OTTERBEIN .... Westerville, OH 43081

Dick Reynolds (21 YRS. W-381, L-193)

Eckerd	N27
St. Leo	N29
Oglethorpe	D 1
Muskingum■	D 4
Hiram	D 8
Capital	D11
Wittenberg	D14
John Carroll■	D18
Otterbein Cl.	D28-29
Mount Union	J 5
Heidelberg	J 8
Marietta■	J12
Baldwin-Wallace■	J15
Ohio Northern	J19
Muskingum	J22
Hiram■	J26
Heidelberg■	J29
Marietta	F 2
Capital■	F 5
Mount Union■	F 9
John Carroll	F12
Ohio Northern■	F16
Baldwin-Wallace	F19

Colors: Tan & Cardinal. Nickname: Cardinals.
AD: Dick Reynolds. SID: Ed Syguda. III

PACE .... New York, NY 10038

Darrell Halloran (10 YRS. W-162, L-123)

Bridgeport■	N23
Sacred Heart■	N28
Dowling■	D 1
East Stroudsburg Cl.	D3-4
LIU-Southampton■	D11
Mercy	D14
St. Rose	J 5
Concordia (N.Y.)	J 8
LIU-C.W. Post■	J10
Dowling	J12
New York Tech■	J15
Queens (N.Y.)■	J19
Phila. Textile■	J22
LIU-C.W. Post	J24
Molloy	J26
Mercy■	J29
Queens (N.Y.)	F 2
Molloy■	F 5
Phila. Textile	F 9
Concordia (N.Y.)■	F12
LIU-Southampton	F16
Adelphi☒	F19
New York Tech	F21
Adelphi■	F23
St. Rose■	F26

☒ New York, NY

Colors: Blue & Gold. Nickname: Setters.
AD: Christopher Bledsoe. SID: John Balkam. II

PACIFIC (CAL.) .... Stockton, CA 95211

Bob Thomason (8 YRS. W-118, L-104)

San Juan Shootout	N26-28
Cal St. Sacramento■	D 1
Oregon	D 4
Notre Dame (Cal.)■	D 7
Fresno St.■	D11
San Diego	D18
UC Davis■	D21
Washington Tr.	D28-29
Utah St.	J 3
Nevada	J 5
San Jose St.■	J 8
UC Santa Barb.■	J15
Long Beach St.■	J17
UC Irvine	J20
Cal St. Fullerton	J22
Nevada-Las Vegas■	J27
New Mexico St.■	J29
Cal St. Fullerton■	F 3
UC Irvine■	F 5
Long Beach St.	F10
UC Santa Barb.	F12
San Jose St.	F19
Nevada■	F24
Utah St.■	F26
New Mexico St.	M 3
Nevada-Las Vegas	M 5
Big West Conf.	M10-13

Colors: Orange & Black. Nickname: Tigers.
AD: Bob Lee. SID: Kevin Messenger. I

PAINE .... Augusta, GA 30910

Ron Spry (13 YRS. W-285, L-146)

Miles■	N23
Morris Brown■	N30
Tuskegee	D 1
Miles	D11
LeMoyne-Owen	D13
Jacksonville St.	J 3
Alabama A&M■	J 8
Savannah St.	J10
Voorhees■	J13
Jacksonville St.■	J14
Fort Valley St.■	J17
Albany St. (Ga.)■	J19
Morehouse	J22
Morris■	J24
Clark Atlanta	J28
Morris Brown	J29
Albany St. (Ga.)	F 3
Clark Atlanta■	F 6
Tuskegee■	F 7
Savannah St.☒	F12
LeMoyne-Owen■	F14
Fort Valley St.	F15
Alabama A&M	F19
Voorhees	F21
Augusta☒	F25

☒ Augusta, GA

Colors: Purple & White. Nickname: Lions.
AD: Ron Spry. SID: Andre Kent-Bright. II

PARKS .... Cahokia, IL 62206

Doug Rose (1ST YR. AS HEAD COACH)

Lewis	N20
MacMurray	N30
St. Louis Christian	D 2
Southern Cal Col.■	D 4
Lincoln Chrst.■	D 6
Lawrence■	D12
Berry	J 5
Emory	J 6
Oglethorpe	J 7
Westminster (Mo.)	J13
Blackburn■	J15
Lincoln Chrst.	J17
Fontbonne■	J20
Principia■	J22
Concordia (Mo.)	J25
Webster■	J27
MacMurray■	J29
Maryville (Mo.)■	F 3
Westminster (Mo.)■	F 5
Maryville (Mo.)	F 8
Blackburn	F10
Fontbonne	F12
Principia	F17
Webster	F19

Colors: Blue & White. Nickname: Falcons.
AD: Jerry Kurfman. SID: To Be Named. III

PEMBROKE ST. .... Pembroke, NC 28372

John Haskins (1 YR. W-10, L-16)

Gardner-Webb Tr.	N19-20
Queens (N.C.)■	N23
Coker■	D 1
Mount Olive■	D 7
Augusta■	D 9
Fayetteville St.■	D11
Georgia Col.■	J 8
Columbus■	J 9
Francis Marion	J12
S.C.-Spartanburg	J15
Lander	J16
Armstrong St.■	J22
St. Andrews	J24
S.C.-Aiken■	J26
Augusta	J29
Francis Marion■	F 2
S.C.-Aiken	F 5
Barton■	F 7
Georgia Col.	F12
Columbus	F13
Wofford	F16
Armstrong St.	F19
S.C.-Spartanburg■	F26
Lander■	F27

Colors: Black & Gold. Nickname: Braves.
AD: Raymond Pennington. SID: Gary Spitler. II

■ Home games on each schedule.

See pages 405–407 for Division I tournament details

PENNSYLVANIA .... Philadelphia, PA 19104

Fran Dunphy (4 YRS. W-59, L-46)

Southern Cal	N27	Columbia■	F 4
Ohio St.	N29	Cornell■	F 5
FDU-Teaneck	D 4	Brown	F11
St. Joseph's (Pa.)☒	D11	Yale	F12
Haverford■	D18	Dartmouth	F18
Washington Tr.	D28-29	Harvard	F19
Lehigh■	J 3	Yale■	F25
Harvard■	J 7	Brown■	F26
Dartmouth■	J 8	Princeton■	M 2
Temple	J11	Columbia	M 5
Lafayette■	J17	Cornell	M 6
La Salle☒	J25	☒ Philadelphia, PA	
Princeton	J29		

Colors: Red & Blue. Nickname: Quakers.
AD: Paul Rubincam. SID: Brad Hurlbut. I

PENN ST. .... University Park, PA 16802

Bruce Parkhill (16 YRS. W-236, L-219)

Vanderbilt	N26	Purdue■	J27
Vermont■	N29	Northwestern	J29
Duquesne■	D 4	Illinois■	F 2
Akron	D 8	Indiana■	F 5
Columbia■	D11	Wisconsin	F 9
Md.-East. Shore■	D20	Minnesota	F16
Bethune-Cookman■	D22	Ohio St.■	F19
Charleston (S.C.) Cl	D28-29	Iowa■	F23
Wisconsin■	J 6	Purdue	F26
Indiana	J 8	Northwestern■	M 2
Minnesota■	J15	Illinois	M 5
Ohio St.	J19	Michigan	M 9
Iowa	J22	Michigan St.■	M12

Colors: Blue & White. Nickname: Nittany Lions.
AD: Jim Tarman. SID: L. Budd Thalman. I

PENN ST.-BEHREND .... Erie, PA 16563

Joe Shapiro (1ST YR. AS HEAD COACH)

Keuka	N20	Alfred	J18
Allegheny	N23	La Roche	J22
Nazareth Tr.	N27-28	Buffalo St.■	J24
Penn St.-Behrend Tr.	D3-4	Oberlin■	J29
Wash. & Jeff.	D 6	Grove City■	F 2
Fredonia St.■	D10	Bethany (W.Va.)	F 5
Muskingum Cl.	D22-23	Daemen	F 9
Grove City	J 5	Wash. & Jeff.■	F12
Waynesburg■	J 8	Keuka■	F13
Fredonia St.	J12	Hilbert■	F19
Bethany (W.Va.)■	J15	La Roche	F22

Colors: Blue, White & Red. Nickname: Lions.
AD: Herb Lauffer. SID: Paul Benim. III

PEPPERDINE .... Malibu, CA 90263

Tom Asbury (5 YRS. W-106, L-48)

San Fran. St.■	N27	San Francisco	J22
Fresno St.■	D 1	Loyola (Cal.)■	J26
San Diego St.■	D 4	Loyola (Cal.)	J29
Baylor Inv.	D10-11	Portland■	F 4
Cal St. San B'dino■	D14	Gonzaga■	F 5
Geo. Washington	D18	Gonzaga	F10
UC Santa Barb.	D22	Portland	F12
UTEP Cl.	D29-30	San Francisco■	F18
N.C.-Charlotte■	J 4	San Diego■	F19
Oral Roberts	J 8	St. Mary's (Cal.)	F25
Santa Clara■	J14	Santa Clara	F26
St. Mary's (Cal.)■	J15	West Coast Conf.	M5-7
San Diego	J20		

Colors: Blue & Orange. Nickname: Waves.
AD: Wayne Wright. SID: Michael Zapolski. I

PFEIFFER .... Misenheimer, NC 28109

Bob Lutz (7 YRS. W-131, L-75)

Pfeiffer Inv.	N26-27	High Point	J26
West Fla. Tr.	D3-4	Mount Olive■	J29
Catawba	D 8	Coker	J31
Ga. Southwestern■	D11	Belmont Abbey■	F 2
Longwood	D19	Lees-McRae	F 5
Embry Riddle Inv.	D30-31	St. Andrews	F 9
Wheaton (Mass.)■	J 8	High Point■	F12
Clinch Valley■	J12	Barton■	F16
Lees-McRae■	J15	Mount Olive	F19
St. Andrews■	J19	Coker■	F23
Barton	J22	Belmont Abbey	F26

Colors: Black & Gold. Nickname: Falcons.
AD: Bobby Lutz. SID: Julian Domenech. II

PHILA. TEXTILE .... Philadelphia, PA 19144

Herb Magee (26 YRS. W-544, L-205)

Holy Family■	N20	Pace	J22
East Stroudsburg	N29	Adelphi	J24
New York Tech■	D 1	Mercy■	J26
LIU-Southampton	D 4	LIU-Southampton■	J29
La Salle	D 8	LIU-C.W. Post	F 2
Dowling	D11	Mercy	F 5
West Chester	D14	Pace■	F 9
Molloy■	J 5	St. Rose■	F12
St. Rose	J 8	Dowling■	F16
Adelphi■	J10	Queens (N.Y.)■	F19
New York Tech	J12	Eastern (Pa.)	F21
Queens (N.Y.)	J15	Concordia (N.Y.)	F25
LIU-C.W. Post■	J19	Molloy	F26

Colors: Maroon & White. Nickname: Rams.
AD: Tom Shirley. SID: To be named. II

PITTSBURG ST. .... Pittsburg, KS 66762

Dennis Hill (4 YRS. W-56 , L-52)

Mo. Southern St.	N20	Missouri-Rolla■	J19
Cameron	N23	Mo.-St. Louis	J22
Mo. Southern Cl.	N26-27	Mo. Western St.■	J26
William Jewell	N29	Northeast Mo. St.■	J29
Washington St.	D 2	Lincoln (Mo.)	F 2
Seattle Pacific	D 4	Mo. Southern St.■	F 5
Fort Hays St.	D 8	Emporia St.	F 9
Friends	D18	Southwest Baptist■	F12
Central Mo. St.	J 5	Northwest Mo. St.	F16
Southwest Baptist	J 8	Washburn■	F19
Northwest Mo. St.■	J12	Missouri-Rolla	F23
Washburn	J15	Mo.-St. Louis■	F26
Drury	J17		

Colors: Crimson & Gold. Nickname: Gorillas.
AD: Bill Samuels. SID: Shawn Ahearn. II

PITTSBURGH .... Pittsburgh, PA 15213

Paul Evans (20 YRS. W-379, L-194)

Youngstown St.■	N27	Georgetown■	J24
St. Francis (Pa.)■	D 1	Buffalo	J26
Providence■	D 4	Connecticut■	J29
St. John's (N.Y.)	D 7	Miami (Fla.)	F 1
West Va.	D11	Syracuse■	F 5
Duquesne☒	D18	Providence	F 8
North Caro.■	D20	St. John's (N.Y.)■	F12
Robert Morris■	D22	Georgetown	F16
Coppin St.■	D27	Villanova■	F19
Syracuse	J 8	Boston College■	F22
Miami (Fla.)■	J12	Connecticut	F26
Seton Hall■	J15	Seton Hall	M 5
Boston College	J18	Big East Conf.	M10-13
Villanova	J22	☒ Pittsburgh, PA	

Colors: Gold & Blue. Nickname: Panthers.
AD: L. Oval Jaynes. SID: Ron Wahl. I

PITT.-JOHNSTOWN .... Johnstown, PA 15904

Bob Rukavina (4 YRS. W-41, L-64)

Pitt.-Johnstown Tr.	N19-20	Pitt.-Bradford	J24
Davis & Elkins■	N22	Calif. (Pa.)	J26
Fairmont St.	N27	Gannon■	J29
Shippensburg	N29	Wheeling Jesuit	J31
Marshall	N30	West Liberty St.■	F 2
Mansfield■	D 4	Gannon	F 5
Clarion■	D 7	Bloomsburg	F 7
Lynchburg■	J 6	Longwood	F12
Edinboro■	J 8	Slippery Rock	F19
Indiana (Pa.)■	J10	Shippensburg■	F23
Lynchburg	J14	St. Vincent■	F26
Mercyhurst	J19	Mercyhurst■	M 1
Slippery Rock■	J22		

Colors: Gold & Blue. Nickname: Mountain Cats.
AD: Ed Sherlock. SID: To be named. II

PLATTSBURGH ST. .... Plattsburgh, NY 12901

Larry Cowen (6 YRS. W-76, L-75)

Plattsburgh St. Cl.	N19-20	Oneonta St.■	J22
New Paltz St.	D 3	Albany (N.Y.)	J25
Oneonta St.	D 4	Brockport St.■	J28
Potsdam St.	D 7	Geneseo St.■	J29
Cortland St.■	D10	Cortland St.	F 4
Binghamton■	D11	Binghamton	F 5
Stony Brook	J 8	Clarkson	F 8
New York U.	J10	Utica Tech	F11
Buffalo St.	J14	Oswego St.■	F12
Fredonia St.	J15	Potsdam St.■	F15
St. Lawrence■	J18	Castleton St.	F19
New Paltz St.■	J21		

Colors: Cardinal Red & White. Nickname: Cardinals.
AD: Peter Luguri. SID: Brian Micheels. III

■ Home games on each schedule.

See pages 405–407 for Division I tournament details

PLYMOUTH ST. .... Plymouth, NH 03264

Paul Hogan (3 YRS. W-46, L-32)

Plymouth St. Tr.	N19-20	Bates	J20
Johnson St.	N23	Western Conn. St.■	J22
New England Col.■	N30	Castleton St.■	J25
Salem St.■	D 2	Mass.-Dartmouth	J29
Gordon	D 4	Southern Me.	F 1
Rivier	D 7	Bri'water (Mass.)■	F 3
Rhode Island Col.■	D12	Rhode Island Col.	F 5
Roanoke Tr.	J3-4	Mass.-Boston	F 8
Mass.-Dartmouth■	J 8	Eastern Conn. St.■	F12
Southern Me.■	J11	New England■	F16
Eastern Conn. St.	J15	Western Conn. St.	F19
Mass.-Boston■	J18		

Colors: Green & White. Nickname: Panthers.
AD: Steve Bamford. SID: Rick Fabrizio. III

POMONA-PITZER .... Claremont, CA 91711

Charles Katsiaficas (6 YRS. W-81, L-74)

UC San Diego	N19	La Verne■	J19
Concordia-M'head■	N23	Cal Lutheran	J22
Colorado College Tr.	N26-27	Occidental■	J26
San Diego	N29	Claremont-M-S■	J29
Christ-Irvine■	D 2	Redlands	F 2
UC Santa Cruz■	D 4	Cal Tech■	F 5
Southern Cal Col.■	D11	Whittier■	F 9
Chapman	D18	La Verne	F12
Bates■	J 3	Cal Lutheran■	F16
Christ-Irvine	J 4	Occidental	F19
Cal Tech	J12	Claremont-M-S	F21
Whittier	J15	Redlands■	F24

Colors: Blue, Orange & White. Nickname: Sagehens.
AD: Curt Tong. SID: Kirk Reynolds. III

PORTLAND .... Portland, OR 97203

Larry Steele (6 YRS. W-43, L-124)

Great Alas. Shootout	N24-27	St. Mary's (Cal.)	J21
Pac. Lutheran■	N30	Santa Clara	J22
Nebraska Cl.	D3-4	Santa Clara■	J27
Idaho St.■	D 7	St. Mary's (Cal.)■	J29
Eastern Ore.■	D11	Pepperdine	F 4
Weber St.■	D18	Loyola (Cal.)	F 5
Washington■	D21	Loyola (Cal.)■	F10
Portland Far West Cl	D27-28	Pepperdine■	F12
Oregon St.	D31	Gonzaga	F16
Montana	J 3	Gonzaga■	F19
Montana St.	J 5	San Diego	F24
San Francisco■	J13	San Francisco	F26
San Diego■	J15	West Coast Conf.	M5-7

Colors: Purple & White. Nickname: Pilots.
AD: Joe Etzel. SID: Steve Walker. I

POTSDAM ST. .... Potsdam, NY 13676

Bill Mitchell (2 YRS. W-20, L-30)

Potsdam St. Tr.	N19-20	New Paltz St.■	J22
Oneonta St.	D 3	Clarkson	J25
New Paltz St.	D 4	Geneseo St.■	J28
Plattsburgh St.■	D 7	Brockport St.■	J29
Binghamton■	D10	Binghamton	F 4
Cortland St.■	D11	Cortland St.	F 5
Otterbein Cl.	D28-29	St. Lawrence■	F 8
Scranton	J 8	Oswego St.	F11
Fredonia St.	J14	Utica Tech■	F12
Buffalo St.	J15	Plattsburgh St.	F15
Oneonta St.■	J21	Albany (N.Y.)■	F19

Colors: Maroon & Gray. Nickname: Bears.
AD: Jan Reetz. SID: Mark Mende. III

PRAIRIE VIEW .... Prairie View, TX 77445

Elwood Plummer (9 YRS. W-83, L-157)

South Ala.	N27	Southern-B.R.	J22
Jarvis Christian■	N29	Alcorn St.	J24
Baylor	D 1	Huston-Tillotson■	J26
Tulane	D 4	Texas Southern■	J29
Mary Hardin-Baylor■	D 7	Alabama St.■	F 5
Arkansas St. Cl.	D10-11	Jackson St.■	F 7
Wright St. Cl.	D17-18	Mississippi Val.	F12
Akron	D21	Grambling	F14
Oklahoma St.	J 4	Southern-B.R.■	F19
Alabama St.	J 8	Alcorn St.■	F21
Jackson St.	J10	Texas Southern	F26
Mississippi Val.■	J15	Southwestern Conf.	M9-13
Grambling■	J17		

Colors: Purple & Gold. Nickname: Panthers.
AD: Barbara Jacket. SID: Errol Domingue. I

PRESBYTERIAN .... Clinton, SC 29325

Gregg Nibert (4 YRS. W-74, L-47)

Lees-McRae	N22	Carson-Newman■	J22
S.C.-Spartanburg Inv	N26-27	Mars Hill	J26
Newberry	N29	Lenoir-Rhyne	J29
Allen■	D 1	Gardner-Webb■	F 5
Ga. Southern	D 3	Wofford■	F 7
Voorhees■	D 6	Catawba	F 9
Gardner-Webb	D11	Elon	F12
S.C.-Aiken■	D18	Wingate■	F16
Erskine	J 6	Carson-Newman	F19
Wofford	J 8	Newberry■	F21
Catawba■	J12	Mars Hill■	F23
Elon■	J15	Lenoir-Rhyne■	F26
Wingate	J19		

Colors: Garnet & Blue. Nickname: Blue Hose.
AD: Cally Gault. SID: Art Chase. II

PRINCETON .... Princeton, NJ 08544

Pete Carril (27 YRS. W-469, L-248)

La Salle	N27	Cornell■	F 4
Lafayette■	D 1	Columbia■	F 5
Syracuse Carrier Cl.	D3-4	Yale	F11
Rutgers■	D 8	Brown	F12
California Cl.	D10-12	Harvard	F18
Providence	D21	Dartmouth	F19
Indiana Hoosier Cl.	D27-28	Brown■	F25
Dartmouth■	J 7	Yale■	F26
Harvard■	J 8	Pennsylvania	M 2
Frank. & Marsh.■	J24	Columbia	M 4
Pennsylvania■	J29	Cornell	M 7

Colors: Orange & Black. Nickname: Tigers.
AD: Robert Myslik. SID: Mark Panus. I

PRINCIPIA .... Elsah, IL 62028

Bob Beeman (2 YRS. W-13, L-37)

Greenville■	N23	Westminster (Mo.)	J20
Rhodes⊠	N24	Parks	J22
Grinnell■	N27	Fontbonne	J27
Illinois Col.■	N30	Blackburn	J29
Knox■	D 7	Webster	F 3
Wheaton (Ill.)	D 9	MacMurray■	F 5
Harris-Stowe■	J 4	Maryville (Mo.)	F10
Blackburn■	J 6	Westminster (Mo.)■	F12
Webster■	J 8	Parks■	F17
MacMurray	J13	Fontbonne■	F19
Maryville (Mo.)■	J15	⊠ St. Louis, MO	

Colors: Navy Blue & Gold. Nickname: Panthers.
AD: Seth Johnson. SID: Phil Webster. III

PROVIDENCE .... Providence, RI 02918

Rick Barnes (6 YRS. W-108, L-76)

Brown■	N27	Notre Dame	J29
New Hampshire■	D 1	Seton Hall	J31
Pittsburgh	D 4	St. John's (N.Y.)	F 5
Villanova	D 7	Pittsburgh■	F 8
Princeton■	D21	Georgetown■	F12
South Caro.■	D31	Syracuse	F15
Seton Hall■	J 5	Connecticut	F19
Miami (Fla.)■	J 8	St. John's (N.Y.)■	F21
Rhode Island	J11	Miami (Fla.)	F26
Georgetown	J15	Villanova■	M 2
Connecticut■	J19	Boston College■	M 5
Boston College	J22	Big East Conf.	M10-13
Syracuse■	J25		

Colors: Black & White. Nickname: Friars.
AD: John Marinatto. SID: Gregg Burke. I

PURDUE .... West Lafayette, IN 47907

Gene Keady (15 YRS. W-306, L-149)

Great Alas. Shootout	N24-27	Minnesota	J29
Purdue Inv.	D3-4	Michigan■	F 1
New Orleans	D 8	Iowa	F 6
Houston ◆	D10	Northwestern■	F 9
Ga. Southern■	D18	Michigan St.	F12
Tenn.-Chatt.■	D21	Wisconsin■	F16
Weber St.	D30	Indiana	F19
San Francisco⊠	J 2	Ohio St.	F23
Northwestern	J 5	Penn St.■	F26
Seton Hall■	J 9	Minnesota■	M 3
Michigan St.■	J12	Michigan	M 6
Wisconsin	J15	Illinois■	M12
Indiana■	J18	⊠ Daly City, CA	
Ohio St.■	J22	◆ Indianapolis, IN	
Penn St.	J27		

Colors: Old Gold & Black. Nickname: Boilermakers.
AD: Morgan Burke. SID: Mark Adams. I

■ Home games on each schedule.

See pages 405–407 for Division I tournament details

QUEENS (N.Y.) .... Flushing, NY 11367

Norman Roberts (2 YRS. W-14, L-40)

Opponent	Date	Opponent	Date
Bridgeport Cl.	N19-20	Pace	J19
Medgar Evers■	N24	St. Rose■	J22
Kutztown	N29	Concordia (N.Y.)	J24
LIU-C.W. Post■	D 1	New York Tech■	J29
New York Tech	D 4	Pace■	F 2
Molloy	D 8	Dowling	F 5
Adelphi	D11	St. Rose	F 9
Dowling■	D15	Mercy■	F12
LIU-Southampton■	J 5	Adelphi■	F16
Mercy	J 8	Phila. Textile	F19
Concordia (N.Y.)■	J10	Molloy■	F23
LIU-C.W. Post	J12	LIU-Southampton	F26
Phila. Textile■	J15		

Colors: Blue & Silver. Nickname: Knights.
AD: Richard Wettan. SID: Neal Kaufer. II

QUEENS (N.C.) .... Charlotte, NC 28274

Dale Layer (4 YRS. W-65, L-47)

Opponent	Date	Opponent	Date
West Va. Tech■	N20	Elon	J24
Pembroke St.	N23	Newberry■	J29
North Fla. Cl.	N26-27	Wingate■	F 2
Gardner-Webb■	D 1	Longwood	F 5
Belmont Abbey■	D 4	Elon■	F 7
Wingate	D 6	Wofford■	F12
Averett■	D11	Newberry	F16
Winthrop	D15	Erskine	F19
Queens (N.C.) Cl.	J6-8	Longwood■	F23
Belmont Abbey	J10	Wofford	F26
Averett☒	J17	Erskine■	M 2
Johnson Smith	J19	☒ Danville, VA	

Colors: Royal & Light Blue, & White. Nickname: Royals.
AD: Dale Layer. SID: Jeff Aumend. II

QUINCY .... Quincy, IL 62301

Steve Hawkins (2 YRS. W-24, L-31)

Opponent	Date	Opponent	Date
Indianapolis Tr.	N19-20	Southern Ind.	J19
Hannibal-La Grange■	N22	SIU-Edwardsville	J22
Missouri-Rolla	N29	Drury	J29
Northeast Mo. St.■	D 1	Wayne St. (Neb.)	F 2
Mo.-St. Louis	D 4	Wis.-Parkside	F 5
IU/PU-Ft. Wayne■	D11	Mo. Baptist■	F 8
Winona St.■	D18	IU/PU-Indianapolis	F12
St. Francis (Ill.)	D20	Wis.-Parkside■	F14
Franklin Pierce	D30	Ky. Wesleyan■	F16
Assumption	J 6	Rockhurst■	F19
Northeast Mo. St.	J10	Culver-Stockton■	F22
Drury■	J12	SIU-Edwardsville■	F26
IU/PU-Indianapolis■	J15	Wayne St. (Neb.)■	M 5

Colors: Brown, White & Gold. Nickname: Hawks.
AD: Jim Vaumovich. SID: Damiam J. Becker. II

QUINNIPIAC .... Hamden, CT 06518

Bill Mecca (2 YRS. W-23, L-31)

Opponent	Date	Opponent	Date
Sacred Heart■	N23	St. Michael's	J22
Merrimack	N28	St. Anselm	J25
New Haven■	N30	Stonehill■	J27
Bentley■	D 4	Merrimack■	J29
Southern Conn. St.■	D 9	Bentley	F 2
Merrimack	D11	Bryant■	F 5
Bridgeport■	D30	Assumption■	F 9
Mass.-Lowell	J 3	American Int'l	F12
Florida Tech Tr.	J7-8	Springfield	F16
Assumption	J12	St. Michael's■	F19
American Int'l■	J15	St. Anselm■	F22
Bryant	J17	Stonehill	F24
Springfield■	J19		

Colors: Blue & Gold. Nickname: Braves.
AD: Burt Kahn. SID: Bill Chaves. II

RADFORD .... Radford, VA 24142

Ron Bradley (7 YRS. W-131, L-76)

Opponent	Date	Opponent	Date
Cabrini■	N27	Coastal Caro.	J22
Richmond	N29	Charleston So.	J24
Va. Commonwealth	D 1	N.C.-Asheville	J31
Bethany (W.Va.)■	D 4	Towson St.	F 5
George Mason■	D 6	Md.-Balt. County	F 7
Va. Military	D11	Winthrop■	F 9
Western Md.■	D18	N.C.-Asheville■	F12
Louisiana St.	D30	N.C.-Greensboro■	F14
N.C.-Greensboro	J 6	Campbell	F17
Towson St.■	J 8	Coastal Caro.■	F19
Md.-Balt. County■	J10	Charleston So.■	F21
Winthrop	J12	Liberty	F26
Liberty■	J15	Big South Conf.	M4-7
Campbell■	J20		

Colors: Blue, Red, Green & White. Nickname: Highlanders.
AD: Chuck Taylor. SID: Rick Rogers. I

RAMAPO .... Mahwah, NJ 07430

Tom Barrise (1 YR. W-7, L-17)

Opponent	Date	Opponent	Date
Bloomfield■	N20	Rowan	J15
Montclair St.	N23	Kean■	J19
Trenton St.■	N27	Stockton St.■	J22
LIU-C.W. Post	N29	Montclair St.■	J26
Stockton St.	D 1	Trenton St.	J29
Rutgers-Newark	D 4	Wm. Paterson	F 2
Jersey City St.■	D 8	Rutgers-Newark■	F 5
Rutgers-Camden	D11	Jersey City St.	F 9
Western Conn. St. Tr	D29-30	Rutgers-Camden■	F12
Albertus Magnus■	J 5	Kean	F15
Medgar Evers	J10	Rowan■	F19
Wm. Paterson■	J12		

Colors: Red & Gold. Nickname: Roadrunners.
AD: Catherine Collins. SID: Michael Rastelli. III

RANDOLPH-MACON .... Ashland, VA 23005

Hal Nunnally (18 YRS. W-331, L-173)

Opponent	Date	Opponent	Date
Va. Wesleyan Tr.	N27-28	East. Mennonite	J24
Randolph-Macon Tr.	D3-4	Va. Wesleyan■	J26
Roanoke	D12	Guilford■	J28
Bridgewater (Va.)	D15	Emory & Henry	J30
DePauw Inv.	D17-18	East. Mennonite■	F 3
Va. Wesleyan	J 6	Lynchburg	F 5
Lynchburg■	J 8	Bridgewater (Va.)■	F 9
Guilford	J12	Emory & Henry■	F13
Wash. & Lee	J15	Hampden-Sydney■	F16
Hampden-Sydney	J19	Wash. & Lee■	F19
Roanoke■	J22		

Colors: Lemon & Black. Nickname: Yellow Jackets.
AD: Ted Keller. SID: Todd Hilder. III

REDLANDS .... Redlands, CA 92373

Gary Smith (22 YRS. W-297, L-273)

Opponent	Date	Opponent	Date
Trinity (Tex.) Tr.	N19-20	Cal Tech	J22
La Sierra■	N23	La Verne■	J26
Redlands Tr.	D2-4	Occidental	J29
Azusa-Pacific	D 8	Pomona-Pitzer■	F 2
Chapman	D10	Whittier	F 5
UC San Diego	D20	Cal Lutheran	F 9
Chapman■	J 6	Claremont-M-S■	F12
LIFE Bible	J 8	Cal Tech■	F16
Whittier■	J12	La Verne	F19
Cal Lutheran■	J15	Occidental■	F21
Claremont-M-S	J19	Pomona-Pitzer	F24

Colors: Maroon & Gray. Nickname: Bulldogs.
AD: Greg Warzecka. SID: Chuck Sadowski. III

REGIS (COLO.) .... Denver, CO 80221

Lonnie Porter (16 YRS. W-261, L-187)

Opponent	Date	Opponent	Date
Chadron St.■	N20	Southern Colo.■	J13
Jacksonville St.■	N22	Colorado-CS	J15
Colorado Mines■	N30	Fort Lewis■	J20
North Central■	D 2	Metropolitan St.	J27
Texas A&M-Kingsville■	D 6	Colo. Christian■	J29
Lincoln (Mo.)■	D11	Chadron St.	J31
Air Force	D13	Denver■	F 5
Western St.■	D15	Southern Colo.	F10
Elmhurst■	D18	Colorado-CS■	F12
Northern Colo.■	D29	Denver	F15
Stonehill■	D31	Fort Lewis	F18
Valley City St.■	J 3	Metropolitan St.■	F24
Concordia (Wis.)■	J 4	Colo. Christian	F26

Colors: Navy Blue & Gold. Nickname: Rangers.
AD: Tom Dedin. SID: Mike Grose. II

RENSSELAER .... Troy, NY 12181

Mike Griffin (17 YRS. W-185, L-235)

Opponent	Date	Opponent	Date
Union (N.Y.) Tr.	N19-20	Southern Vt.■	F 1
Williams	N30	Hobart	F 4
Skidmore☒	D 4	Rochester Inst.	F 5
LeMoyne Tr.	D10-11	Ithaca	F11
Rochester Inst.■	J 7	Alfred	F12
Hobart■	J 8	Union (N.Y.)■	F15
Hartwick	J13	Clarkson■	F18
Albany (N.Y.)	J18	St. Lawrence■	F19
St. Lawrence	J21	Utica	F21
Clarkson	J22	Hartwick■	F24
Alfred■	J28	☒ Albany, NY	
Ithaca■	J29		

Colors: Cherry & White. Nickname: Engineers.
AD: Bob Ducatte. SID: Kelly Vergin. III

■ Home games on each schedule.

See pages 405–407 for Division I tournament details

RHODE ISLAND .... Kingston, RI 02881

Al Skinner (5 YRS. W-80, L-66)

Brown	D 1	Northeastern■	F 1
Iona	D 8	Temple	F 3
Maine	D11	Wake Forest■	F 5
Kansas City Cl.	D29-30	Rutgers■	F 8
West Va.	J 3	Massachusetts☒	F10
Duquesne	J 5	St. Joseph's (Pa.)	F13
St. Joseph's (Pa.)■	J 8	Hofstra	F17
Providence■	J11	Geo. Washington	F21
Temple■	J15	West Va.■	F24
Duquesne■	J19	St. Bonaventure	F26
Ala.-Birmingham	J22	Geo. Washington■	M 2
Rutgers	J25	Atlantic 10 Conf.	M5-10
Massachusetts	J30	☒ Providence, RI	

Colors: Blue & White. Nickname: Rams.
AD: Ronald Petro. SID: Dawn Wright. I

RHODE ISLAND COL. .... Providence, RI 02908

James Adams (14 YRS. W-173 , L-182)

King's (Pa.) Tr.	N19-20	Bri'water (Mass.)	J22
Colby-Sawyer	N23	Western Conn. St.■	J25
Framingham St.■	N30	Southern Me.	J29
Southern Me.■	D 4	Eastern Conn. St.	F 1
Roger Williams	D 7	Wheaton (Mass.)■	F 3
Salve Regina	D 9	Plymouth St.■	F 5
Plymouth St.	D12	Mass.-Dartmouth	F 8
Eastern Nazarene	J 6	Mass.-Boston■	F12
Eastern Conn. St.■	J11	Western Conn. St.	F15
Mass.-Boston	J15	Nichols	F17
Mass.-Dartmouth■	J18	Stony Brook■	F19
Westfield St.	J20		

Colors: White, Gold & Burgundy. Nickname: Anchormen.
AD: To be named. SID: Edward J. Vaillancourt. III

RHODES .... Memphis, TN 38112

Herb Hilgeman (17 YRS. W-255, L-158)

Rhodes Tr.	N19-20	Centre■	J28
Maryville (Mo.)	N23	Fisk■	J30
Principia☒	N24	Millsaps	F 1
Washington (Mo.)■	N27	Trinity (Tex.)■	F 4
Savannah A&D■	N30	Hendrix■	F 6
Rhodes Cl.	D3-4	Centre	F11
MacMurray■	J 8	Fisk	F13
Trinity (Tex.)	J14	Oglethorpe■	F18
Hendrix	J16	Sewanee■	F20
Oglethorpe	J21	Millsaps■	F25
Sewanee	J23	☒ St. Louis, MO	

Colors: Red, Black & White. Nickname: Lynx.
AD: Mike Clary. SID: Matt Dean. III

RICE .... Houston, TX 77251

Willis Wilson (1 YR. W-18, L-10)

Pre-Season NIT	N17-26	Baylor■	J26
Nevada■	N28	Texas Tech	J29
Sam Houston St.	D 1	Texas	F 1
Virginia	D 4	Houston■	F 5
Colorado St.■	D18	Centenary	F 8
Southern-B.R.■	D20	Southern Methodist	F13
New Mexico Lobo Inv.	D29-30	Texas Christian■	F16
Boise St.■	J 3	Texas A&M	F20
Dayton	J 5	Baylor	F23
Montana■	J 8	Texas Tech■	F26
Southern Methodist■	J11	Texas■	M 2
Texas A&M■	J16	Houston	M 5
Texas Christian	J19	Southwest Conf.	M10-12
Oral Roberts	J22		

Colors: Blue & Gray. Nickname: Owls.
AD: Bobby May. SID: Bill Cousins. I

RICHMOND .... Richmond, VA 23173

Bill Dooley (1ST YR. AS HEAD COACH)

Radford■	N29	George Mason	J19
Va. Military	D 1	East Caro.■	J22
Wake Forest	D 4	N.C.-Wilmington	J26
Va. Commonwealth	D18	James Madison■	J29
San Diego	D21	William & Mary	F 5
California	D23	Army■	F 7
Duquesne■	D30	Old Dominion	F 9
La Salle■	J 3	American■	F12
Delaware	J 5	George Mason■	F16
Siena	J 8	N.C.-Wilmington■	F19
Villanova■	J11	East Caro.	F23
Old Dominion■	J13	James Madison	F26
American	J15	Colonial Conf.	M5-7
William & Mary■	J17		

Colors: Red & Blue. Nickname: Spiders.
AD: Chuck Boone. SID: Phil Stanton. I

RIDER .... Lawrenceville, NJ 08648

Kevin Bannon (11 YRS. W-204, L-106)

Bucknell■	N26	Monmouth (N.J.)■	J18
Maryland	N30	Wagner■	J20
Army■	D 3	Mt. St. Mary's (Md.)	J22
Manhattan	D 6	Robert Morris	J27
Drexel	D 8	St. Francis (Pa.)	J29
Lafayette■	D11	St. Francis (N.Y.)■	F 3
Stetson Cl.	D29-30	LIU-Brooklyn■	F 5
FDU-Teaneck	J 4	Monmouth (N.J.)	F10
Marist	J 6	Wagner	F12
St. Francis (Pa.)■	J 8	Mt. St. Mary's (Md.)■	F19
Robert Morris■	J10	FDU-Teaneck■	F22
LIU-Brooklyn	J13	Marist■	F26
St. Francis (N.Y.)	J15	Northeast Conf.	F28-M6

Colors: Cranberry & White. Nickname: Broncs.
AD: Curtis Blake. SID: Bud Focht. I

RIPON .... Ripon, WI 54971

Bob Gillespie (13 YRS. W-205, L-98)

Ripon Tr.	N19-20	Coe	J23
N'western (Wis.)	N29	Knox■	J29
Lake Forest■	D 4	Illinois Col.■	J30
Barat■	D 8	Lawrence■	F 2
Viterbo	D11	Beloit■	F 5
Bahamas Shootout	J2-9	St. Norbert	F 9
St. Norbert■	J12	Lake Forest	F12
Carroll (Wis.)	J15	Beloit	F16
Ill. Benedictine	J17	Carroll (Wis.)■	F19
Grinnell	J22	Lawrence	F21

Colors: Red. Nickname: Redmen.
AD: Robert Gillespie. SID: Bret Atkins. III

ROANOKE .... Salem, VA 24153

Page Moir (4 YRS. W-63, L-42)

Roanoke Cl.	N20-21	Guilford	J19
Carnegie Mellon Inv.	N26-27	Randolph-Macon	J22
Emory & Henry	D 1	Emory & Henry■	J26
Va. Wesleyan■	D 4	Bridgewater (Va.)■	F 3
Lynchburg■	D 6	Hampden-Sydney	F 5
East. Mennonite■	D 9	Lynchburg	F 7
Randolph-Macon■	D12	East. Mennonite	F 9
Roanoke Tr.	J3-4	Wash. & Lee■	F12
Wash. & Lee	J 8	Guilford■	F16
Bridgewater (Va.)	J13	Hampden-Sydney■	F19
Va. Wesleyan	J15		

Colors: Maroon & Gray. Nickname: Maroons.
AD: Scott Allison. SID: Howard Wimmer. III

ROBERT MORRIS .... Coraopolis, PA 15108

Jarrett Durham (9 YRS. W-134, L-123)

Duquesne	N27	St. Francis (Pa.)	J18
West Va.	D 1	LIU-Brooklyn	J22
Md.-Balt. County	D 4	St. Francis (N.Y.)	J24
American	D 6	Rider■	J27
Ohio	D11	Mt. St. Mary's (Md.)■	J29
Pittsburgh	D22	FDU-Teaneck	F 3
Cincinnati	D29	Marist	F 5
Kentucky	D31	St. Francis (Pa.)■	F12
Wagner■	J 4	St. Francis (N.Y.)■	F17
Monmouth (N.J.)■	J 6	LIU-Brooklyn■	F19
Mt. St. Mary's (Md.)	J 8	Monmouth (N.J.)	F24
Rider	J10	Wagner	F26
Marist■	J13	Northeast Conf.	F28-M6
FDU-Teaneck■	J15		

Colors: Blue & White. Nickname: Colonials.
AD: Bob McBee. SID: Marty Galosi. I

ROCHESTER .... Rochester, NY 14627

Mike Neer (17 YRS. W-266, L-177)

Rochester Tip-Off	N19-20	Chicago■	J23
Nazareth (N.Y.)	N23	Brandeis	J28
Rochester Inv.	N27-28	New York U.	J30
Case Reserve	D 3	Rochester Inst.	F 1
Brandeis■	D 5	Chicago	F 4
Johns Hopkins■	D10	Washington (Mo.)	F 6
New York U.■	D12	Hamilton■	F 9
Carnegie Mellon	J 7	Hobart■	F15
Emory	J 9	Emory■	F18
Rochester Tr.	J12-15	Carnegie Mellon■	F26
Washington (Mo.)■	J21		

Colors: Yellow & Blue. Nickname: Yellowjackets.
AD: Jeff Vennell. SID: Dennis O'Donnell. III

■ Home games on each schedule.

See pages 405–407 for Division I tournament details

ROCHESTER INST. .... Rochester, NY 14623

Bob McVean (15 YRS. W-183, L-186)

Roberts Wesleyan	D 1	St. Lawrence■	J28
Keuka■	D 4	Clarkson■	J29
St. John Fisher■	D 7	Rochester■	F 1
RIT Tr.	D10-11	Hartwick■	F 4
Rensselaer	J 7	Rensselaer■	F 5
Hartwick	J 8	Hobart■	F 8
Rochester Tr.	J12-15	Clarkson	F11
Hobart	J18	St. Lawrence	F12
Ithaca	J21	Nazareth (N.Y.)■	F15
Alfred	J22	Alfred■	F18
Houghton	J25	Ithaca■	F19

Colors: Burnt Umber, Orange & White. Nickname: Tigers.
AD: Lou Spiotti. SID: J. Roger Dykes. III

ROCKFORD .... Rockford, IL 61101

To be named

Wartburg Inv.	N19-20	Trinity (Ill.)■	J15
Eureka	N23	Concordia (Wis.)	J17
Beloit■	N30	Aurora■	J19
Loras■	D 2	Ill. Benedictine■	J22
Manchester	D 4	Concordia (Ill.)	J25
Dubuque■	D 6	Judson	J29
Rosary	D 8	Trinity (Ill.)	F 5
North Central■	D11	Aurora	F 9
Augustana (Ill.)	D18	Ill. Benedictine	F12
Wis.-Oshkosh■	J 7	St. Ambrose■	F14
DePauw	J10	Concordia (Ill.)■	F19
Carroll (Wis.)■	J12	Judson■	F23

Colors: Purple & White. Nickname: Regent Lions.
AD: William Langston. SID: To be named. III

ROGER WILLIAMS .... Bristol, RI 02809

Mike Lunney (1 YR. W-10, L-14)

Coast Guard	N19	New England Col.	J29
Stony Brook Inv.	N20-21	Eastern Nazarene■	F 1
Connecticut Col.■	N30	Gordon	F 3
Rhode Island Col.■	D 7	Salve Regina■	F 5
Rivier■	J11	Suffolk	F 7
Gordon■	J15	Anna Maria	F 9
Salve Regina	J18	New England Col.■	F12
Anna Maria■	J20	Wentworth Inst.■	F15
Curry■	J22	Eastern Nazarene	F17
Nichols■	J24	Curry	F19
Wentworth Inst.	J26		

Colors: Blue & Gold. Nickname: Hawks.
AD: William M. Baird. SID: David Kemmy. III

ROLLINS .... Winter Park, FL 32789

Tom Klusman (13 YRS. W-227, L-134)

Central Fla.	N30	Mississippi	J24
Rollins Inv.	D3-4	Barry	J26
Embry-Riddle■	D 7	Eckerd■	J29
Fla. Southern☒	D18	North Fla.	F 2
Milwaukee Engr.■	D27	Florida Tech	F 5
Denison■	D28	Tampa■	F 9
Hanover■	D29	Fla. Southern	F12
Shippensburg■	J 3	Barry■	F16
Bentley■	J 5	Eckerd	F19
Gardner-Webb■	J 8	North Fla.■	F23
St. Leo	J12	St. Leo■	F26
Florida Tech■	J15	☒ Orlando, FL	
Tampa	J19		

Colors: Royal Blue & Gold. Nickname: Tars.
AD: Phil Roach. SID: Fred Battenfield. II

ROSE-HULMAN .... Terre Haute, IN 47803

Bill Perkins (2 YRS. W-28, L-22)

Ripon Tr.	N19-20	Franklin■	J12
Centre	N22	DePauw	J18
Knox	N28	Anderson	J22
Blackburn	N30	Manchester■	J26
Rose-Hulman Inv.	D3-4	Hanover■	J29
Ill. Wesleyan	D11	Wabash	F 2
Centre■	D13	Franklin	F 9
Earlham	D15	Anderson■	F12
Kalamazoo Tr.	D29-30	DePauw■	F16
Wabash■	J 5	Manchester	F19
Hanover	J 8		

Colors: Old Rose & White. Nickname: Fightin' Engineers.
AD: Scott Duncan. SID: Dale Long. III

ROWAN .... Glassboro, NJ 08028

John Giannini (4 YRS. W-87, L-28)

Eastern (Pa.) Tr.	N19-20	Rutgers-Camden	J19
Jersey City St.	N23	Kean	J22
Montclair St.■	N27	Jersey City St.■	J25
Kean■	N30	Montclair St.	J29
Wm. Paterson	D 3	Trenton St.■	F 1
Stockton St.■	D 7	Wm. Paterson■	F 5
Rutgers-Newark■	D11	Stockton St.	F 9
King's (Pa.) Cl.	D29-30	Rutgers-Newark	F12
N.C. Wesleyan Tr.	J7-8	Rutgers-Camden■	F15
Trenton St.	J12	Ramapo	F19
Ramapo■	J15		

Colors: Brown & Gold. Nickname: Profs.
AD: Joy Reighn. SID: Sheila Stevenson. III

RUST .... Holly Springs, MS 38635

Rodney Stennis (1ST YR. AS HEAD COACH)

Tougaloo■	N22	LeMoyne-Owen	J12
Stillman Tr.	N26-27	Maryville (Tenn.)■	J15
Savannah A&D■	N29	Fisk	J18
Philander Smith	N30	Stillman■	J22
Southern-N.O.	D 3	Tougaloo	J26
Wiley	D 4	Lane	F 1
Philander Smith■	D 7	Stillman	F 4
Wiley■	D11	Knoxville	F11
Christian Bros.	D13	Maryville (Tenn.)	F12
Birm. Southern	D18	LeMoyne-Owen■	F16
Paul Quinn■	J 7	Lane■	F19
Knoxville■	J 8	Savannah A&D	F21

Colors: Blue & White. Nickname: Bearcats.
AD: Ishmell Edwards. SID: Paula Clark. III

RUTGERS .... New Brunswick, NJ 08903

Bob Wenzel (11 YRS. W-172, L-156)

FDU-Teaneck■	D 1	Rhode Island■	J25
Wagner■	D 4	Duquesne■	J29
Princeton	D 8	Temple	F 1
Cincinnati Cl.	D10-11	Duquesne	F 6
James Madison	D22	Rhode Island	F 8
Massachusetts■	J 4	West Va.■	F12
Geo. Washington	J 6	Geo. Washington■	F15
Delaware■	J 8	St. Joseph's (Pa.)■	F19
Drexel■	J11	St. Bonaventure	F21
St. Joseph's (Pa.)	J15	Holy Cross■	F24
Allentown	J17	West Va.	F26
Massachusetts	J20	St. Bonaventure■	M 1
Temple■	J23	Atlantic 10 Conf.	M5-10

Colors: Scarlet. Nickname: Scarlet Knights.
AD: Fred E. Gruninger. SID: Pete Kowalski. I

RUTGERS-CAMDEN .... Camden, NJ 08102

Gregory Ackles (9 YRS. W-72, L-150)

Widener Tr.	N19-20	Rowan■	J19
Trenton St.	N23	Rutgers-Newark	J22
Wm. Paterson■	N27	Trenton St.■	J26
Rutgers-Newark■	D 1	Wm. Paterson	J29
Jersey City St.	D 4	Phila. Pharmacy	J31
Kean	D 8	Stockton St.	F 2
Ramapo■	D11	Jersey City St.■	F 5
Virginia St.■	D30	Kean■	F 9
Lincoln (Pa.)■	J 5	Ramapo	F12
York (N.Y.)■	J 8	Rowan	F15
Stockton St.■	J12	Montclair St.■	F19
Montclair St.	J15		

Colors: Scarlet & Black. Nickname: Pioneers.
AD: Wilbur Wilson. SID: To be named. III

RUTGERS-NEWARK .... Newark, NJ 07102

Jim Hill (3 YRS. W-24, L-48)

Stockton St.■	N23	Rutgers-Camden■	J22
Kean	N27	Stockton St.	J26
Old Westbury■	N29	Kean■	J29
Rutgers-Camden	D 1	Centenary (N.J.)	J31
Ramapo■	D 4	Jersey City St.■	F 2
Wm. Paterson■	D 8	Ramapo	F 5
Rowan	D11	Stevens Tech■	F 7
St. Joseph's (N.Y.)■	D29	Wm. Paterson	F 9
Bloomfield■	J10	Rowan■	F12
Jersey City St.	J12	York (N.Y.)	F14
Trenton St.■	J15	Montclair St.	F16
Montclair St.■	J19	Trenton St.	F19

Colors: Scarlet. Nickname: Raiders.
AD: John K. Adams. SID: Lewis W. Shaine. III

■ Home games on each schedule.

See pages 405–407 for Division I tournament details

SACRED HEART .... Fairfield, CT 06432

Dave Bike (15 YRS. W-296, L-158)

St. Michael's■ ... N21
Quinnipiac ... N23
Pace ... N28
East Stroudsburg Cl. ... D3-4
St. Anselm■ ... D11
Stonehill ... D18
Bentley Tr. ... D28-29
Keene St.■ ... J 8
Assumption■ ... J10
Franklin Pierce■ ... J12
Le Moyne ... J17
Southern Conn. St. ... J19
Mass.-Lowell■ ... J22
Bridgeport■ ... J26
New Hamp. Col. ... J29
New Haven ... F 2
Le Moyne■ ... F 6
Southern Conn. St.■ ... F 9
Mass.-Lowell ... F12
Franklin Pierce ... F14
New Haven■ ... F16
Keene St. ... F21
Bridgeport ... F23
New Hamp. Col.■ ... F26

Colors: Scarlet & White. Nickname: Pioneers.
AD: Don Cook. SID: Don Harrison. II

SAGINAW VALLEY ...... University Center, MI 48710

Robert Pratt (20 YRS. W-327, L-252)

Saginaw Valley Tr. ... N19-20
St. Francis (Ill.) ... N27
Cleveland St. ... D 4
Concordia (Mich.)■ ... D 6
Ferris St. ... D 9
Lake Superior St.■ ... D11
Grand Rapids Bapt.■ ... D16
Washburn Tr. ... D29-30
Oakland ... J 4
Northwood■ ... J 6
Hillsdale■ ... J 8
Wayne St. (Mich.) ... J13
Grand Valley St.■ ... J15
Michigan Tech■ ... J20
Northern Mich.■ ... J22
Oakland■ ... J29
Ferris St.■ ... F 3
Lake Superior St. ... F 5
Northwood ... F10
Hillsdale ... F12
Wayne St. (Mich.)■ ... F17
Grand Valley St. ... F19
Michigan Tech ... F24
Northern Mich. ... F26

Colors: Red, White & Blue. Nickname: Cardinals.
AD: Bob Becker. SID: Tom Waske. II

ST. ANDREWS .... Laurinburg, NC 28352

Ron Lievense (2 YRS. W-24, L-33)

Wingate ... D 1
Methodist Inv. ... D3-4
Warner So. Tr. ... D16-18
Wingate■ ... J 4
Queens (N.C.) Cl. ... J6-8
Mount Olive■ ... J12
High Point■ ... J15
Pfeiffer ... J19
Coker■ ... J22
Pembroke St.■ ... J24
Belmont Abbey ... J26
Lees-McRae■ ... J29
Barton■ ... F 2
High Point ... F 5
Pfeiffer■ ... F 9
Belmont Abbey■ ... F12
Coker ... F16
Lees-McRae ... F19
Barton ... F23
Mount Olive ... F26

Colors: Royal Blue & White. Nickname: Knights.
AD: Lorenzo Canalis. SID: Chad Esposito. II

ST. ANSELM .... Manchester, NH 03102

Keith Dickson (7 YRS. W-123, L-88)

Keene St. Cl. ... N19-20
Bentley ... N28
Southern Conn. St. ... D 2
Bryant■ ... D 4
Mass.-Lowell■ ... D 8
Sacred Heart ... D11
Cal St. Dom. Hills ... D30
Cal St. Los Angeles ... J 3
Assumption ... J 8
New Hamp. Col.■ ... J10
American Int'l■ ... J12
Springfield ... J15
St. Michael's■ ... J19
Stonehill ... J22
Quinnipiac■ ... J25
Merrimack ... J27
Bentley■ ... J29
Bryant ... F 2
Assumption■ ... F 5
American Int'l ... F 9
Springfield■ ... F12
St. Michael's ... F16
Stonehill■ ... F19
Quinnipiac ... F22
Merrimack■ ... F24

Colors: Blue & White. Nickname: Hawks.
AD: Ted Paulauskas. SID: Kristopher Russell. II

ST. AUGUSTINE'S .... Raleigh, NC 27611

Harvey Heartley (22 YRS. W-304, L-282)

Allen■ ... N20
Virginia St. ... N23
Morris■ ... N27
N.C. Central ... D 4
St. Paul's■ ... D 7
Shaw ... D 9
Bowie St.■ ... D11
Livingstone■ ... J 6
Hampton■ ... J 8
Winston-Salem■ ... J11
Johnson Smith■ ... J13
Elizabeth City St.■ ... J18
Fayetteville St.■ ... J20
N.C. Central■ ... J22
Livingstone ... J29
Virginia Union ... F 3
Winston-Salem ... F 7
Johnson Smith ... F 9
Shaw☒ ... F12
Norfolk St. ... F16
Fayetteville St. ... F19
☒ Raleigh, NC

Colors: Blue & White. Nickname: Falcons.
AD: Harvey Heartley. SID: Leon Carrington. II

ST. BONAVENTURE .... St.Bonaventure, NY 14778

Jim Baron (6 YRS. W-84, L-88)

Canisius■ ... N29
Navy ... D 1
Massachusetts■ ... D 4
Seton Hall ... D11
Niagara■ ... D18
New Mexico Lobo Inv. ... D29-30
Geo. Washington■ ... J 3
West Va. ... J 9
Northern Iowa ... J11
Massachusetts ... J15
Notre Dame■ ... J19
Niagara ... J22
Canisius ... J25
West Va.■ ... J29
St. Joseph's (Pa.) ... F 3
Temple ... F 5
St. Joseph's (Pa.)■ ... F10
Duquesne■ ... F12
Temple■ ... F16
Geo. Washington ... F18
Rutgers■ ... F21
Duquesne ... F24
Rhode Island■ ... F26
Rutgers ... M 1
Atlantic 10 Conf. ... M5-10

Colors: Brown & White. Nickname: Bonnies, Indians.
AD: Thomas O'Connor. SID: Jim Engelhardt. I

ST. CLOUD ST. .... St.Cloud, MN 56301

Butch Raymond (23 YRS. W-383, L-256)

Eastern Mont. Inv. ... N26-27
Bemidji St. ... D 2
Mt. Senario■ ... D 6
Moorhead St.■ ... D16
Bemidji St.■ ... D18
Minn.-Duluth ... D21
Carleton■ ... D29
North Dak. ... J 2
North Dak. St. ... J 3
South Dak.■ ... J 7
Morningside■ ... J 8
Mankato St.■ ... J15
North Dak.■ ... J18
South Dak. St. ... J21
Augustana (S.D.) ... J22
Northern Colo.■ ... J28
Nebraska-Omaha■ ... J29
Morningside ... F 4
South Dak. ... F 5
Mankato St. ... F12
Augustana (S.D.)■ ... F18
South Dak. St.■ ... F19
North Dak. St.■ ... F22
Nebraska-Omaha ... F25
Northern Colo. ... F26

Colors: Red & Black. Nickname: Huskies.
AD: Morris Kurtz. SID: Anne Abicht. II

ST. FRANCIS (ILL.) .... Joliet, IL 60435

Pat Sullivan (17 YRS. W-280, L-229)

Hillsdale■ ... N20
Wis.-Parkside ... N23
Saginaw Valley■ ... N27
St. Joseph's (Ind.)■ ... N30
Oakland City ... D 4
Lewis ... D 7
Indianapolis ... D11
Wayne St. (Neb.)■ ... D18
Quincy■ ... D20
North Fla. ... D28
Florida Tech ... D30
Wis.-Parkside■ ... J 4
IU/PU-Indianapolis ... J 6
Olivet (Ill.)■ ... J11
Illinois Tech ... J15
Purdue-Calumet■ ... J19
Trinity Chrst. (Il.) ... J22
St. Xavier■ ... J26
Rosary ... J29
Ind.-South Bend■ ... F 2
Olivet (Ill.) ... F 5
SIU-Edwardsville ... F 9
Purdue-Calumet ... F12
Trinity Chrst. (Il.)■ ... F16
St. Xavier ... F19
Rosary■ ... F23
Ind.-South Bend ... F26

Colors: Brown & Gold. Nickname: Fighting Saints.
AD: Pat Sullivan. SID: Dave Laketa. II

ST. FRANCIS (N.Y.) ..... Brooklyn Heights, NY 11201

Ron Ganulin (4 YRS. W-51, L-55)

Boston U. ... N29
Harvard ... D 4
Delaware St.■ ... D 7
Hartford■ ... D22
Iona College Tr. ... D28-29
LIU-Brooklyn ... J 4
Wagner ... J 8
Monmouth (N.J.) ... J10
Mt. St. Mary's (Md.)■ ... J13
Rider■ ... J15
FDU-Teaneck ... J18
Marist ... J20
St. Francis (Pa.)■ ... J22
Robert Morris■ ... J24
Monmouth (N.J.)■ ... J27
Wagner■ ... J29
Rider ... F 3
Mt. St. Mary's (Md.) ... F 5
Hofstra ... F 8
Marist■ ... F10
FDU-Teaneck■ ... F12
Robert Morris ... F17
St. Francis (Pa.) ... F19
LIU-Brooklyn■ ... F26
Northeast Conf. ... F28-M6

Colors: Red & Blue. Nickname: Terriers.
AD: Tom Thompson. SID: Jim Hoffman. I

ST. FRANCIS (PA.) .... Loretto, PA 15940

Tom McConnell (1 YR. W-9, L-18)

Pittsburgh ... D 1
Fla. Int'l Inv. ... D3-4
Duquesne ... D 8
Marist■ ... D11
Canisius■ ... D19
Akron ... D30
Monmouth (N.J.)■ ... J 4
Wagner■ ... J 6
Rider ... J 8
Mt. St. Mary's (Md.) ... J10
FDU-Teaneck■ ... J13
Robert Morris■ ... J18
St. Francis (N.Y.) ... J22
LIU-Brooklyn ... J24
Mt. St. Mary's (Md.)■ ... J27
Rider■ ... J29
Xavier (Ohio)■ ... J31
Marist ... F 3
FDU-Teaneck ... F 5
Robert Morris ... F12
LIU-Brooklyn■ ... F17
St. Francis (N.Y.)■ ... F19
Bucknell■ ... F21
Wagner ... F24
Monmouth (N.J.) ... F26
Northeast Conf. ... F28-M6

Colors: Red & White. Nickname: Red Flash.
AD: Frank Pergolizzi. SID: Kevin Southard. I

■ Home games on each schedule.

See pages 405–407 for Division I tournament details

ST. JOHN FISHER .... Rochester, NY 14618

Bob Ward (6 YRS. W-102, L-55)

St. John Fisher Tr. N20-21
Houghton■ N23
Clarkson N30
Rochester Cl. D3-4
Rochester Inst. .... D 7
St. John Fisher Inv. J7-8
Rochester Tr. J12-15
Fredonia St.■ J18
Binghamton J22
Roberts Wesleyan J29
Elmira■ .... F 1
Keuka■ .... F 3
Hilbert .... F 5
Brockport St. .... F 8
Geneseo St. F11
Utica■ F12
Allegheny■ F16
Nazareth (N.Y.) F18
Albany (N.Y.) F23
Alfred■ F25

Colors: Cardinal Red & Gold. Nickname: Cardinals.
AD: Bob Ward. SID: Michele Morano. III

ST. JOHN'S (MINN.) .... Collegeville, MN 56321

Jim Smith (29 YRS. W-465, L-311)

Carthage N19
North Park N20
Wis.-La Crosse N27
Augsburg .... D 4
Hamline■ .... D 8
Concordia-M'head D11
Loras D30
St. Mary's (Minn.)■ .... J 5
Carleton■ .... J 8
Macalester J10
St. Thomas (Minn.)■ J12
Gust. Adolphus J15
St. Olaf J17
Bethel (Minn.)■ J19
Augsburg■ J22
Hamline J26
Concordia-M'head■ J29
St. Mary's (Minn.) .... F 2
Carleton .... F 5
Macalester■ .... F 9
St. Thomas (Minn.) F12
Gust. Adolphus■ F14
St. Olaf■ F16
Bethel (Minn.) F19

Colors: Red & White. Nickname: Johnnies.
AD: John Gagliardi. SID: Tom Nelson. III

ST. JOHN'S (N.Y.) .... Jamaica, NY 11439

Brian Mahoney (4 YRS. W-35, L-73)

Pre-Season NIT N17-26
Columbia■ N30
Seton Hall■ .... D 4
Pittsburgh■ .... D 7
St. John's (N.Y.) Tr D11-12
Fordham ♦ D18
Niagara■ D22
ECAC Holiday Tr. D27-29
Villanova■ .... J 8
Georgetown J12
Connecticut■ J15
Syracuse J18
Miami (Fla.) J22
Boston College■ J26
Minnesota■ J30
Villanova .... F 2
Providence■ .... F 5
Miami (Fla.)■ .... F 8
Pittsburgh F12
Seton Hall F14
Georgetown■ F19
Providence F21
Syracuse■ F27
Boston College .... M 1
Connecticut .... M 5
Big East Conf. M10-13
⊠
♦ Uniondale, NY

Colors: Red & White. Nickname: Redmen.
AD: John Kaiser. SID: Frank Racaniello. I

ST. JOSEPH'S (IND.) .... Rensselaer, IN 47978

Bill Bland (1ST YR. AS HEAD COACH)

Grand Valley St. N22
Ind. Wesleyan Tr. N26-27
St. Francis (Ill.) N30
Rosary■ .... D 2
Purdue-Calumet .... D 6
Huntington■ .... D 8
IU/PU-Indianapolis D18
Ashland■ D28
IU/PU-Ft. Wayne■ D30
Marian (Ind.)■ .... J 3
Ky. Wesleyan .... J 6
Southern Ind. .... J 8
Kentucky St.■ J13
Bellarmine■ J15
Northern Ky. J20
Indianapolis J22
Lewis J29
Southern Ind.■ .... F 3
Ky. Wesleyan■ .... F 5
Bellarmine F10
Kentucky St. F12
Indianapolis■ F17
Northern Ky.■ F19
Lewis■ F26
Ashland .... M 3
IU/PU-Ft. Wayne .... M 5

Colors: Cardinal & Purple. Nickname: Pumas.
AD: Keith Freeman. SID: Ron Fredrick. II

ST. JOSEPH'S (ME.) ...... North Windham, ME 04062

Rick Simonds (13 YRS. W-265, L-108)

Gordon■ N23
Me.-Farmington■ N29
Colby-Sawyer■ .... D 4
New England .... D 8
Thomas■ D11
Westbrook■ D13
Merrimack Inv. D28-29
Nat'l Catholic Tr. J5-9
Husson■ J13
Johnson St. J15
Lyndon St. J16
New England■ J20
Me.-Farmington J22
Manhattanville Cl. J29-30
Atlantic Union .... F 3
St. Joseph (Vt.)■ .... F 5
Green Mountain■ .... F 6
Southern Me.⊠ .... F 9
Me.-Presque Isle■ F12
Thomas F14
Husson F16
⊠ Portland, ME

Colors: Royal Blue, Red & White. Nickname: Monks.
AD: Mike McDevitt. SID: Curt Smyth. III

ST. JOSEPH'S (PA.) .... Philadelphia, PA 19131

John Griffin (7 YRS. W-114, L-87)

St. Joseph's(Pa.) Tr N26-27
Arizona .... D 1
Loyola (Md.) .... D 4
Pennsylvania⊠ D11
Drexel■ D20
Duquesne D28
Temple .... J 2
St. Peter's■ .... J 5
Rhode Island .... J 8
La Salle J12
Rutgers■ J15
Geo. Washington■ J19
West Va.■ J22
Temple⊠ J25
Hofstra J27
UC Santa Barb. J31
St. Bonaventure■ .... F 3
Geo. Washington .... F 5
St. Bonaventure F10
Rhode Island■ F13
Massachusetts■ F15
Rutgers F19
Massachusetts F22
Duquesne■ F26
West Va. .... M 2
Atlantic 10 Conf. M5-10
⊠ Philadelphia, PA

Colors: Crimson & Gray. Nickname: Hawks.
AD: Don DiJulia. SID: Ken Krsolovic. I

ST. LAWRENCE .... Canton, NY 13617

Barry Davis (8 YRS. W-45, L-176)

Middlebury N19
Amherst N20
Oswego St. .... D 1
Nazareth (N.Y.)■ .... D 7
Clarkson .... D 9
Ithaca■ J14
Alfred■ J15
Plattsburgh St. J18
Rensselaer■ J21
Hartwick■ J22
Utica■ J26
Rochester Inst. J28
Hobart J29
Le Moyne .... F 2
Alfred .... F 4
Ithaca .... F 5
Potsdam St. .... F 8
Hobart■ F11
Rochester Inst.■ F12
Clarkson■ F15
Hartwick F18
Rensselaer F19
Union (N.Y.)■ F25
Hamilton■ F26

Colors: Scarlet & Brown. Nickname: Saints.
AD: John Clark. SID: Wally Johnson. III

ST. LEO .... St. Leo, FL 33574

Todd Smyly (4 YRS. W-82, L-59)

Webber N22
Francis Marion Tr. N26-27
Otterbein■ N29
Valdosta St. .... D 6
Flagler■ D10
Valdosta St.■ D11
West Fla.■ D18
Mt. St. Vincent■ D31
Queens (N.C.) Cl. J6-8
Rollins■ J12
North Fla. J15
Florida Tech J19
Tampa■ J22
Eckerd J26
Fla. Southern■ J29
Barry .... F 2
North Fla.■ .... F 5
Florida Tech■ .... F 9
Tampa F12
Eckerd■ F16
Fla. Southern F19
Barry■ F23
Rollins F26

Colors: Forest Green & Old Gold. Nickname: Monarchs.
AD: John Schaly. SID: Fran Reidy. II

ST. LOUIS .... St. Louis, MO 63108

Charles Spoonhour (10 YRS. W-209, L-98)

Mercer■ N27
Southern Methodist .... D 1
Cornell■ .... D 4
Creighton .... D 6
Chicago St.■ .... D 8
Augustana (Ill.)■ D15
Murray St. D18
Samford■ D20
Southern Ill.■ D30
Detroit Mercy■ .... J 2
Southwest Mo. St.■ .... J 5
Arizona St.⊠ .... J 8
Memphis St.■ J11
DePaul J15
Marquette J22
Marquette■ J26
Mo.-Kansas City J29
Dayton■ .... F 2
DePaul■ .... F 6
Iowa St.■ .... F 9
Dayton F13
Cincinnati F16
Ala.-Birmingham■ F19
Cincinnati■ F23
Memphis St. F26
Ala.-Birmingham .... M 5
Great Midwest Conf. M10-12
⊠ Tucson, AZ

Colors: Blue & White. Nickname: Billikens.
AD: Deborah Yow. SID: Doug McIlhagga. I

ST. MARY'S (CAL.) .... Moraga, CA 94575

Ernie Kent (2 YRS. W-24, L-33)

Notre Dame (Cal.)■ N27
UC Santa Barb. N30
Sonoma St.■ .... D 4
San Jose St. .... D 7
Cal St. Fullerton■ D10
Villanova D18
UC Irvine■ D21
Oregon■ D30
California .... J 2
Boise St. .... J 8
Cal St. Northridge■ J11
Loyola (Cal.) J14
Pepperdine J15
Cal St. Sacramento■ J18
Portland■ J21
Gonzaga■ J22
Gonzaga J27
Portland J29
San Francisco■ .... F 4
San Diego■ .... F 5
San Diego F10
San Francisco F12
Santa Clara■ F16
Santa Clara F20
Pepperdine■ F25
Loyola (Cal.)■ F26
West Coast Conf. M5-7

Colors: Red & Blue. Nickname: Gaels.
AD: Rick Mazzuto. SID: Steve Janisch. I

■ Home games on each schedule.

See pages 405–407 for Division I tournament details

ST. MARY'S (MD.) .... St. Mary's City, MD 20686

Bob Valvano (10 YRS. W-110, L-160)

New York U. Tr.	N20-21	York (Pa.)	J22
Salisbury St. Cl.	D3-4	Marymount (Va.)■	J26
Wesley	D 7	Gallaudet	J31
Roanoke Tr.	J3-4	Mary Washington■	F 3
New Paltz St.⊠	J 6	Goucher	F 5
Mary Washington■	J 8	Marymount (Va.)	F10
Emerson-MCA	J12	York (Pa.)■	F12
Mary Washington	J13	Western Md.	F15
Goucher■	J15	Gallaudet■	F17
Catholic	J19	Catholic■	F19
Bard■	J21	⊠ Upper Marlboro, MD	

Colors: Navy Blue & Gold. Nickname: Seahawks.
AD: Jay Gardiner. SID: Pam Wojnar. III

ST. MICHAEL'S .... Colchester, VT 05439

Tom Crowley (3 YRS. W-35, L-45)

Sacred Heart	N21	St. Anselm	J19
Middlebury■	N23	Quinnipiac■	J22
Le Moyne■	N27	Merrimack	J25
Vermont	D 2	Bentley	J27
Assumption■	D 4	Bryant■	J29
Mass.-Lowell	D 6	Assumption	F 2
Bentley■	D11	American Int'l■	F 5
New Hamp. Col.	D19	Springfield	F 9
St. Michael's Cl.	D29-30	Stonehill■	F12
Bryant	J 3	St. Anselm■	F16
American Int'l	J 8	Quinnipiac	F19
Springfield■	J12	Merrimack■	F22
Stonehill	J15		

Colors: Purple & Gold. Nickname: Purple Knights.
AD: Edward Markey. SID: Chris Kenny. II

ST. NORBERT .... De Pere, WI 54115

Paul De Noble (4 YRS. W-32, L-56)

Lakeland■	N22	Knox	J22
Lawrence	D 1	Illinois Col.	J23
Beloit■	D 5	Monmouth (Ill.)■	J29
Trinity (Ill.)	D 7	Cornell College■	J30
Carroll (Wis.)■	D11	Lake Forest■	F 2
Edgewood	J 2	Carroll (Wis.)	F 5
Nat'l Catholic Tr.	J5-9	Ripon■	F 9
Ripon	J12	Barat■	F12
Lake Forest	J15	Lawrence■	F15
N'western (Wis.)■	J19	Beloit	F19

Colors: Green & Gold. Nickname: Green Knights.
AD: Larry Van Alstine. SID: Len Wagner. III

ST. OLAF .... Northfield, MN 55057

David Buss (20 YRS. W-368, L-184)

N'western (Minn.)■	N23	Gust. Adolphus	J19
Wis.-Oshkosh Cl.	N26-27	St. Thomas (Minn.)■	J22
Concordia (St. Paul)■	N30	Macalester	J29
St. Thomas (Minn.)	D 4	Carleton■	J31
Macalester■	D11	Bethel (Minn.)	F 2
Carleton	J 3	St. Mary's (Minn.)	F 5
Bethel (Minn.)■	J 5	Concordia-M'head■	F 9
St. Mary's (Minn.)■	J 8	Hamline	F12
Concordia-M'head	J10	Augsburg■	F14
Hamline■	J12	St. John's (Minn.)	F16
Augsburg	J15	Gust. Adolphus■	F19
St. John's (Minn.)■	J17		

Colors: Black & Gold. Nickname: Oles.
AD: Whitey Aus. SID: Nancy Moe. III

ST. PAUL'S .... Lawrenceville, VA 23868

Edward Joyner (1ST YR. AS HEAD COACH)

Benedict	N22	N.C. Central	J17
Johnson Smith	N23	Virginia St.	J22
N.C. Central Tr.	N26-27	Virginia Union	J25
Shaw■	D 1	Elizabeth City St.■	J29
Elizabeth City Inv.	D3-4	Bowie St.■	J31
St. Augustine's	D 7	Elizabeth City St.	F 1
Livingstone■	D12	Hampton■	F 5
Hampton	J 3	Norfolk St.■	F 9
Virginia Union■	J11	Bowie St.	F10
Fayetteville St.	J13	Winston-Salem	F12
Norfolk St.	J15	Virginia St.■	F16

Colors: Black & Orange. Nickname: Tigers.
AD: Harold Williams. SID: Monique A.J. Morgan. II

ST. PETER'S .... Jersey City, NJ 07306

Ted Fiore (7 YRS. W-118, L-86)

Seton Hall	N29	Loyola (Md.)■	J17
Fla. Int'l Inv.	D3-4	Fairfield■	J20
Howard■	D 7	Niagara■	J27
Md.-East. Shore	D 9	Manhattan	J30
George Mason	D11	Loyola (Md.)	F 2
FDU-Teaneck■	D14	Iona■	F 5
American■	D18	Manhattan■	F 8
LIU-Brooklyn■	D23	Siena	F12
Marist Cl.	D29-30	Canisius	F19
St. Joseph's (Pa.)	J 5	Niagara	F21
Fairfield	J10	Siena■	F27
Canisius■	J12	Metro Atlantic Conf.	M5-7
Iona	J15		

Colors: Blue & White. Nickname: Peacocks.
AD: William Stein. SID: Tim Camp. I

ST. ROSE .... Albany, NY 12203

Brian Beaury (7 YRS. W-155 , L-62)

Le Moyne■	N19	LIU-Southampton	J15
Assumption■	N21	Dowling■	J19
Franklin Pierce	N29	Queens (N.Y.)	J22
Mercy■	D 1	New York Tech	J23
Adelphi	D 4	Adelphi■	J29
LIU-C.W. Post■	D 8	Queens (N.Y.)■	F 9
Molloy	D11	Phila. Textile	F12
Bentley■	D18	Molloy■	F16
Pace■	J 5	LIU-Southampton■	F19
Phila. Textile■	J 8	LIU-C.W. Post	F23
New York Tech■	J10	Pace	F26
Mercy	J12		

Colors: Brown, Gold & White. Nickname: Golden Knights.
AD: Catherine Cummings Haker. SID: David Alexander. II

ST. THOMAS (MINN.) .... St.Paul, MN 55105

Steve Fritz (13 YRS. W-212, L-133)

Concordia (St. Paul)	N20	Gust. Adolphus■	J17
Viterbo■	N23	Augsburg	J19
Biola	N27	St. Olaf	J22
UC Riverside	N29	Bethel (Minn.)■	J26
St. Olaf■	D 4	St. Mary's (Minn.)	J29
Bethel (Minn.)	D 8	Hamline	J31
St. Mary's (Minn.)■	D11	Concordia-M'head■	F 2
Hamline■	J 3	Carleton■	F 9
Concordia-M'head	J 5	St. John's (Minn.)■	F12
Carleton	J10	Macalester	F14
St. John's (Minn.)	J12	Gust. Adolphus	F16
Macalester■	J15	Augsburg■	F19

Colors: Purple & Gray. Nickname: Tommies.
AD: Steve Fritz. SID: Greg Capell. III

SALEM ST. .... Salem, MA 01970

Jim Todd (8 YRS. W-141, L-75)

Eastern Conn. Tr.	N19-20	North Adams St.■	J25
UC Irvine	N26	Babson■	J27
Plymouth St.	D 2	Bri'water (Mass.)	J29
Mass.-Boston	D 7	Worcester St.■	F 1
Wheaton (Mass.)■	D 9	Mass.-Dartmouth■	F 3
Colby	D11	Fitchburg St.	F 8
Salem St. Tr.	D29-30	Westfield St.■	F10
Gordon■	J12	Framingham St.	F12
Fitchburg St.■	J15	North Adams St.	F14
Westfield St.	J18	Bri'water (Mass.)■	F17
Tufts■	J20	Worcester St.	F19
Framingham St.■	J22		

Colors: Orange & Brown. Nickname: Vikings.
AD: John Galaris. SID: Thomas Roundy. III

SALEM TEIKYO .... Salem, WV 26426

Michael A. Carey (5 YRS. W-88, L-58)

Fairmont St.■	N29	Wheeling Jesuit	J22
Mercyhurst Cl.	D3-4	West Liberty St.■	J24
Glenville St.■	D 6	Shepherd	J26
Davis & Elkins	D 8	Concord	J29
Mercyhurst■	D14	Alderson-Broaddus■	F 2
Bluefield St. Cl.	D30-31	West Va. Wesleyan■	F 5
Glenville St.	J 5	Fairmont St.	F 9
Bluefield St.■	J 8	West Va. St.	F12
Charleston (W.Va.)	J10	Wheeling Jesuit■	F14
West Va. Wesleyan	J12	West Liberty St.	F16
West Va. Tech■	J15	Shepherd■	F19
West Va. St.■	J19		

Colors: Green & White. Nickname: Tigers.
AD: Michael A. Carey. SID: John Miller. II

■ Home games on each schedule.

See pages 405–407 for Division I tournament details

SALISBURY ST. .... Salisbury, MD 21801

Ward Lambert (23 YRS. W-322, L-284)

Susquehanna Tr.	N19-20
Chris. Newport■	D 1
Salisbury St. Cl.	D3-4
Catholic	D 6
Washington (Md.) Tr.	D10-11
Beaver	J 8
Columbia Union■	J12
Allentown■	J15
Chowan	J17
Va. Wesleyan	J19
Lincoln (Pa.)	J22
Mary Washington	J25
Frostburg St.	J29
Lincoln (Pa.)■	F 5
Wesley	F10
Trenton St.■	F14
Columbia Union	F16
Chowan■	F19
Frostburg St.■	F24

Colors: Maroon & Gold. Nickname: Sea Gulls.
AD: Michael Vienna. SID: Paul Ohanian. III

SALVE REGINA .... Newport, RI 02904

Michael Raffa (14 YRS. W-163, L-184)

Plymouth St. Tr.	N19-20
Mass.-Dartmouth■	N23
Suffolk■	N30
Stony Brook	D 4
Connecticut Col.	D 7
Rhode Island Col.■	D 9
Albertus Magnus■	D12
Worcester Tech■	J11
Anna Maria	J15
Roger Williams■	J18
Gordon	J20
New England Col.	J22
Eastern Nazarene■	J26
Curry■	J29
Wentworth Inst.	F 1
Anna Maria■	F 3
Roger Williams	F 5
Gordon■	F 9
Curry	F12
Eastern Nazarene	F15
Wentworth Inst.■	F17
New England Col.■	F19

Colors: Blue, Green & White. Nickname: Newporters.
AD: Lynn Sheedy. SID: Ed Habershaw. III

SAM HOUSTON ST. .... Huntsville, TX 77341

Jerry Hopkins (10 YRS. W-126, L-152)

Oral Roberts	N26
Rice■	D 1
Colorado Cl.	D3-4
Mary Hardin-Baylor■	D 7
Southwestern La.	D15
Miami (Fla.)	D17
South Fla.	D20
North Texas	D30
Northeast La.■	J 6
Northwestern (La.)■	J 8
Texas-Arlington	J11
Southwest Tex. St.	J14
Texas-San Antonio	J16
Stephen F. Austin■	J22
Nicholls St.■	J27
McNeese St.■	J29
Northwestern (La.)	F 3
Northeast La.	F 5
North Texas■	F 7
Texas-San Antonio■	F10
Southwest Tex. St.■	F12
Stephen F. Austin	F19
McNeese St.	F24
Nicholls St.	F26
Texas-Arlington■	F28
Southland Conf.	M4-6

Colors: Orange & White. Nickname: Bearkats.
AD: Ronnie Choate. SID: Paul Ridings. I

SAMFORD .... Birmingham, AL 35229

John Brady (2 YRS. W-28, L-28)

Berry■	N29
Bapt. Christian■	D 2
Davidson	D 4
Arkansas St. Cl.	D10-11
Winthrop■	D18
St. Louis	D20
Shootout Spokane	D27-28
Charleston (S.C.)	J 3
Central Fla.■	J 6
Stetson■	J 8
Southeastern La.	J13
Centenary	J15
Florida Int'l■	J22
Tex.-Pan American	J24
Mercer■	J27
Georgia St.	J29
Stetson	F 3
Central Fla.	F 5
Centenary■	F10
Southeastern La.■	F12
Florida Int'l	F14
Georgia St.■	F17
Mercer	F24
Charleston (S.C.)■	F28
Trans America Conf.	M3-5

Colors: Red & Blue. Nickname: Bulldogs.
AD: Steve Allgood. SID: Riley Adair. I

SAN DIEGO .... San Diego, CA 92110

Hank Egan (22 YRS. W-285, L-301)

Pomona-Pitzer■	N29
UC Irvine	D 2
Notre Dame	D 4
Cal St. Northridge	D 8
Cal St. Dom. Hills■	D11
Pacific (Cal.)■	D18
Richmond■	D21
Meadowlands Tr.	D29-30
Weber St.	J 3
Drake■	J 7
Gonzaga	J13
Portland	J15
Pepperdine■	J20
Loyola (Cal.)■	J22
San Francisco■	J26
San Francisco	J29
Santa Clara	F 4
St. Mary's (Cal.)	F 5
St. Mary's (Cal.)■	F10
Santa Clara■	F12
Loyola (Cal.)	F18
Pepperdine	F19
Portland■	F24
Gonzaga■	F26
Cal St. Sacramento■	M 1
West Coast Conf.	M5-7

Colors: Columbia Blue, Navy & White. Nickname: Toreros.
AD: Tom Iannacone. SID: Ted Gosen. I

SAN DIEGO ST. .... San Diego, CA 92182

Tony Fuller (1 YR. W-8, L-21)

Westmont■	D 2
Pepperdine	D 4
Southern Cal	D 7
Southern Utah■	D11
Cal St. Northridge	D21
Loyola (Cal.)	D23
Cal Poly Pomona■	D30
Hawaii■	J 3
Colorado St.■	J 8
Wyoming■	J10
New Mexico	J13
UTEP	J15
Brigham Young■	J20
Utah■	J22
Fresno St.	J27
Air Force	J29
Fresno St.■	F 3
Air Force■	F 5
Brigham Young	F10
Utah	F12
New Mexico■	F17
UTEP■	F19
Colorado St.	F24
Wyoming	F26
Cal St. Northridge■	M 3
Hawaii	M 5
Western Ath. Conf.	M9-12

Colors: Scarlet & Black. Nickname: Aztecs.
AD: Fred Miller. SID: John Rosenthal. I

SAN FRANCISCO .... San Francisco, CA 94117

Jim Brovelli (19 YRS. W-261, L-259)

St. Joseph's(Pa.) Tr	N26-27
Cal Poly SLO■	N30
San Francisco Cl.	D3-4
Cal St. Stanislaus■	D 8
Cal St. Sacramento	D11
McNeese St.■	D22
Kentucky	D28
Purdue⊠	J 2
Cal St. Sacramento■	J 8
Portland	J13
Gonzaga	J15
Loyola (Cal.)■	J20
Pepperdine■	J22
San Diego	J26
San Diego■	J29
St. Mary's (Cal.)	F 4
Santa Clara	F 5
Santa Clara■	F10
St. Mary's (Cal.)■	F12
Pepperdine	F18
Loyola (Cal.)	F19
Gonzaga■	F24
Portland■	F26
Marquette	F28
West Coast Conf.	M5-7

⊠ Daly City, CA

Colors: Green & Gold. Nickname: Dons.
AD: Bill Hogan. SID: Peter Simon. I

SAN FRAN. ST. .... San Francisco, CA 94132

Charlie Thomas (6 YRS. W-71, L-96)

Cal St. Bakersfield	N20
Pepperdine	N27
Dominican (Cal.)■	N29
Bethany (Cal.)	N30
Menlo■	D 8
San Jose Christian■	D14
Cal St. San B'dino	D17
Cal Poly Pomona	D18
Azusa Pacific Tr.	J3-4
UC Davis	J 7
Notre Dame (Cal.)■	J 8
Humboldt St.	J14
Cal St. Chico	J15
Cal St. Stanislaus■	J21
Cal St. Hayward	J22
Sonoma St.	J29
Cal St. Hayward■	F 4
Cal St. Stanislaus	F 5
Southern Utah	F 8
Cal St. Chico■	F11
Humboldt St.■	F12
UC Davis■	F18
Notre Dame (Cal.)	F19
Sonoma St.■	F24

Colors: Purple & Gold. Nickname: Gators.
AD: Bill Partlow. SID: Kyle McRae. II

SAN JOSE ST. .... San Jose, CA 95192

Stan Morrison (18 YRS. W-227, L-266)

Stanford Inv.	N26-27
Santa Clara⊠	D 1
Fresno St.	D 4
St. Mary's (Cal.)■	D 7
Loyola (Cal.)■	D11
Minnesota■	D23
Montana St.■	D30
Nevada	J 3
Utah St.	J 5
Pacific (Cal.)	J 8
Long Beach St.■	J15
UC Santa Barb.■	J17
Cal St. Fullerton	J20
UC Irvine	J22
New Mexico St.■	J27
Nevada-Las Vegas■	J29
UC Irvine■	F 3
Cal St. Fullerton■	F 5
UC Santa Barb.	F10
Long Beach St.	F12
Pacific (Cal.)■	F19
Utah St.■	F24
Nevada■	F26
Nevada-Las Vegas	M 3
New Mexico St.	M 5
Big West Conf.	M10-13

⊠ San Jose, CA

Colors: Gold, White & Blue. Nickname: Spartans.
AD: Thomas Brennan. SID: Lawrence Fan. I

SANTA CLARA .... Santa Clara, CA 95053

Dick Davey (1 YR. W-19, L-12)

Pre-Season NIT	N17-26
Cal St. Chico■	N27
San Jose St.⊠	D 1
California	D 4
Stanford■	D11
Oregon	D14
Arizona■	D18
Cal St. Sacramento	D20
Nevada	D22
Santa Clara Cl.	D29-30
Cal St. Hayward■	J 4
Pepperdine	J14
Loyola (Cal.)	J15
Gonzaga■	J21
Portland■	J22
Portland	J27
Gonzaga	J29
San Diego■	F 4
San Francisco■	F 5
San Francisco	F10
San Diego	F12
St. Mary's (Cal.)	F16
St. Mary's (Cal.)■	F20
Loyola (Cal.)■	F25
Pepperdine■	F26
West Coast Conf.	M5-7

⊠ San Jose, CA

Colors: Bronco Red & White. Nickname: Broncos.
AD: Carroll Williams. SID: Jim Young. I

■ Home games on each schedule.

See pages 405–407 for Division I tournament details

SAVANNAH A&D .... Savannah, GA 31402

Wally West (1 YR. W-2, L-23)

Trinity Baptist■	N22
Stillman Tr.	N26-27
Rust	N29
Rhodes	N30
Fisk	D 3
Johnson Bible	D 4
Methodist	D 7
Embry-Riddle	J 1
Methodist■	J 4
Savannah A&D Tr.	J7-8
Warren Wilson	J15
Greensboro	J21
Piedmont Bible	J22
Fisk■	J25
Trinity Baptist	J28
Fla. Bible	J29
Bard Tr.	F5-6
Baruch	F 7
Stillman■	F18
Rust■	F21
La Grange⊠	F25
Warren Wilson■	F26

⊠ Atlanta, GA

Colors: Black, White & Gold. Nickname: Bees.
AD: Karen A. Ryan. SID: To be named. III

SCRANTON .... Scranton, PA 18510

Bob Bessoir (21 YRS. W-430, L-177)

King's (Pa.) Tr.	N19-20
Catholic	N27
Delaware Valley	D 4
Elizabethtown	D 7
Wooster■	D18
Salem St. Tr.	D29-30
Potsdam St.■	J 8
FDU-Madison	J13
Upsala■	J15
Moravian	J17
Lycoming■	J19
King's (Pa.)	J22
Susquehanna■	J24
Drew	J26
Wilkes	J29
FDU-Madison■	F 2
Delaware Valley■	F 5
Lycoming	F 9
Upsala	F12
Wilkes■	F14
Drew■	F16
King's (Pa.)■	F19

Colors: Purple & White. Nickname: Royals.
AD: Gary Wodder. SID: Kenneth Buntz. III

SEATTLE PACIFIC .... Seattle, WA 98119

Ken Bone (4 YRS. W-65, L-48)

Seattle Pacific Cl.	N26-27
Concordia (Ore.)■	N30
Pittsburg St.■	D 4
Cal St. Los Angeles	D13
Cal St. Hayward	D16
Notre Dame (Cal.)	D18
Puget Sound■	D30
Western Wash.■	J 3
Alas. Anchorage■	J 7
Alas. Fairbanks■	J 8
Seattle	J11
Northwest Col.■	J17
Chaminade	J20
Hawaii-Hilo	J21
Eastern Mont.■	J27
Grand Canyon■	J29
Western Wash.	F 1
Alas. Anchorage	F 4
Alas. Fairbanks	F 5
Seattle■	F 8
Central Wash.■	F14
Hawaii-Hilo■	F17
Chaminade■	F21
Eastern Mont.	F24
Grand Canyon	F26

Colors: Maroon & White. Nickname: Falcons.
AD: Keith Phillips. SID: Frank MacDonald. II

SETON HALL .... South Orange, NJ 07079

P.J. Carlesimo (18 YRS. W-274, L-259)

St. Peter's■	N29
St. John's (N.Y.)	D 4
Connecticut■	D 8
St. Bonaventure■	D11
Iona■	D14
Texas A&M■	D22
Meadowlands Tr.	D29-30
Providence	J 5
Purdue	J 9
Boston College■	J12
Pittsburgh	J15
Georgetown■	J17
Syracuse■	J22
Miami (Fla.)	J26
Boston College	J29
Providence■	J31
Georgetown	F 5
Villanova■	F 8
Connecticut	F12
St. John's (N.Y.)■	F14
Miami (Fla.)■	F19
Syracuse	F23
Villanova	F26
Pittsburgh■	M 5
Big East Conf.	M10-13

Colors: Blue & White. Nickname: Pirates.
AD: Larry Keating. SID: John Wooding. I

SEWANEE .... Sewanee, TN 37375

Joe Thoni (1 YR. W-13, L-12)

Free Will Baptist	N23
Davidson	N27
Cumberland (Tenn.)■	D 1
Carnegie Mellon■	D 4
DePauw Inv.	D17-18
Cumberland (Tenn.)	J 8
Loyola (La.)	J11
Centre	J14
Fisk	J16
Emory■	J18
Millsaps■	J21
Rhodes■	J23
Maryville (Tenn.)■	J26
Trinity (Tex.)	J28
Hendrix	J30
Oglethorpe	F 2
Centre■	F 4
Fisk■	F 6
Trinity (Tex.)■	F11
Hendrix■	F13
Millsaps	F18
Rhodes	F20
Emory	F23
Oglethorpe■	F26

Colors: Purple & White. Nickname: Tigers.
AD: Bill Huyck. SID: Joe Thoni. III

SHENANDOAH .... Winchester, VA 22601

Dave Dutton (5 YRS. W-77, L-59)

Frank. & Marsh. Cl.	N19-20
Mary Washington■	D 2
Frostburg St.	D 4
Marymount (Va.)■	D11
Frostburg St.■	D18
Wittenberg Tr.	D29-30
East. Mennonite■	J12
N.C. Wesleyan	J15
Chris. Newport	J16
Greensboro■	J19
Methodist■	J22
Marymount (Va.)	J24
Mary Washington	J27
Ferrum	J29
Averett	J30
Va. Military	F 2
N.C. Wesleyan■	F 5
Chris. Newport■	F 6
Greensboro	F12
Methodist	F13
Ferrum■	F16
Averett■	F19

Colors: Red, White & Blue. Nickname: Hornets.
AD: Dave Dutton. SID: Rob Kulton. III

SHEPHERD .... Shepherdstown, WV 25443

Denny Alexander (12 YRS. W-221, L-130)

Lenoir-Rhyne Tr.	N26-27
Dist. Columbia■	N30
California (Pa.) Inv	D3-4
Wheeling Jesuit	D 6
Indiana (Pa.)■	D11
Indiana (Pa.)	J 3
Charleston (W.Va.)■	J 6
Glenville St.■	J 8
West Va. St.	J10
West Va. Tech	J12
West Va. Wesleyan■	J15
West Liberty St.	J17
Alderson-Broaddus	J19
Fairmont St.■	J22
Davis & Elkins	J24
Salem Teikyo■	J26
Bluefield St.	J29
Wheeling Jesuit■	F 3
Concord■	F 5
West Liberty St.■	F 7
Alderson-Broaddus■	F12
Fairmont St.	F14
Davis & Elkins■	F16
Salem Teikyo	F19

Colors: Blue & Gold. Nickname: Rams.
AD: Monte Cater. SID: Michael L. Straley. II

SHIPPENSBURG .... Shippensburg, PA 17257

Rodger Goodling (23 YRS. W-276, L-316)

Kutztown■	N23
Pitt.-Johnstown■	N29
Bloomsburg■	D 1
Shippensburg Tr.	D3-4
West Chester	D 8
Mansfield■	D11
Fla. Southern	D30
Rollins	J 3
Dickinson Tr.	J7-8
Bloomsburg	J10
Indiana (Pa.)■	J12
Clarion	J15
Calif. (Pa.)	J19
Edinboro■	J22
Lock Haven	J26
Slippery Rock■	J29
Kutztown	J31
Clarion■	F 5
Indiana (Pa.)	F 9
Calif. (Pa.)■	F12
Lock Haven■	F16
Edinboro	F19
Pitt.-Johnstown	F23
Slippery Rock	F26

Colors: Red & Blue. Nickname: Red Raiders.
AD: James Pribula. SID: John R. Alosi. II

SIENA .... Loudonville, NY 12211

Mike Deane (9 YRS. W-165, L-95)

Boise St. Cl.	N26-27
Marist	D 1
Holy Cross■	D 4
Marist■	D 6
Wagner	D 8
Va. Commonwealth■	D11
Hartford	D13
Kent■	D28
Northeastern	J 3
Canisius■	J 5
Richmond■	J 8
Manhattan	J13
Loyola (Md.)	J15
Niagara■	J17
Texas A&M	J22
Fairfield■	J24
Manhattan■	J28
Iona	J31
Fairfield	F 5
Loyola (Md.)■	F 9
St. Peter's■	F12
Iona■	F17
Niagara	F19
Canisius⊠	F21
St. Peter's	F27
Metro Atlantic Conf.	M5-7

⊠ Niagara Falls, NY

Colors: Green & Gold. Nickname: Saints.
AD: John D'Argenio. SID: Christopher Caporale. I

SIMPSON .... Indianola, IA 50125

Bruce Wilson (8 YRS. W-102, L-106)

St. Ambrose	N20
Drake	N27
Midland Lutheran■	N30
Neb. Wesleyan■	D 4
Iowa Wesleyan	D 7
Fla. Southern	J 2
Luther■	J 7
Dubuque■	J 8
Coe	J11
Grand View	J17
Buena Vista	J21
Wartburg	J22
Loras	J28
Central (Iowa)■	J29
William Penn■	F 1
Upper Iowa	F 4
Luther	F 5
Loras■	F11
Central (Iowa)	F12
Buena Vista■	F18
Upper Iowa■	F19
William Penn	F22
Wartburg■	F25
Dubuque	F26

Colors: Red & Gold. Nickname: Storm.
AD: John Sirianni. SID: Jerry Fitzsimmons. III

■ Home games on each schedule.

See pages 405–407 for Division I tournament details

SKIDMORE .... Saratoga, NY 12866
John Quattrocchi (9 YRS. W-100, L-124)

Union (N.Y.) Tr.	N19-20
Hartwick	D 1
Rensselaer☒	D 4
Hobart■	D11
Amherst■	D14
Catholic Tr.	J8-9
Ithaca■	J11
Bowdoin■	J15
Bates■	J16
Norwich■	J20
Manhattanville	J22
North Adams St.■	J27
Wheaton (Mass.)■	J29
Middlebury■	F 2
Vassar	F 5
Union (N.Y.)■	F 8
Utica	F10
Merchant Marine■	F12
Southern Vt.■	F16
Hamilton■	F19
Williams■	F23
Albany (N.Y.)	F26

☒ Albany, NY

Colors: Green, White & Gold. Nickname: Thoroughbreds.
AD: Timothy Brown. SID: Bill Jones. III

SLIPPERY ROCK .... Slippery Rock, PA 16057
Bob Barlett (8 YRS. W-110, L-106)

Hiram■	N27
Mercyhurst	N29
West Va. Wesleyan	D 8
Goucher■	D11
Boise St. Tr.	D29-30
Point Park■	J 4
Florida Tech Tr.	J7-8
Calif. (Pa.)	J12
Lock Haven■	J15
Lake Erie	J17
Indiana (Pa.)■	J19
Pitt.-Johnstown	J22
Clarion■	J26
Shippensburg	J29
Edinboro	F 2
Lock Haven	F 5
Calif. (Pa.)■	F 9
Indiana (Pa.)	F12
Clarion	F16
Pitt.-Johnstown■	F19
Gannon	F21
Edinboro■	F23
Shippensburg■	F26

Colors: Green & White. Nickname: Rockets, The Rock.
AD: Bill Lennox. SID: John Carpenter. II

SONOMA ST. .... Rohnert Park, CA 94928
Dick Walker (16 YRS. W-203, L-250)

Humboldt St. Inv.	N19-20
Dominican (Cal.)■	N23
Azusa-Pacific■	D 3
St. Mary's (Cal.)	D 4
Lewis & Clark■	D 8
Cal Poly Pomona■	D11
UC Riverside	D22
Cal St. Dom. Hills	D23
Cal St. Chico Tr.	D28-30
Notre Dame (Cal.)	J 7
UC Davis■	J 8
Cal St. Chico	J14
Humboldt St.	J15
Cal St. Hayward■	J21
Cal St. Stanislaus	J22
San Fran. St.■	J29
Cal St. Stanislaus■	F 4
Cal St. Hayward	F 5
Humboldt St.■	F11
Cal St. Chico■	F12
Notre Dame (Cal.)■	F18
UC Davis	F19
San Fran. St.	F24

Colors: Columbian Blue, Navy & White. Nickname: Cossacks.
AD: Ralph Barkey. SID: Mitch Cox. II

SOUTH ALA. .... Mobile, AL 36688
Ronnie Arrow (6 YRS. W-100, L-76)

Prairie View■	N27
Ark.-Lit. Rock	D 4
West Va.	D 9
Troy St.■	D14
Western Ky.■	D18
Ala.-Birmingham	D21
Tenn.-Chatt. Tr.	D29-30
Texas A&M■	J 3
Western Ky.	J 6
Southwestern La.■	J 8
Southern Miss.■	J11
Arkansas St.	J15
Lamar■	J17
Jacksonville■	J20
Arkansas St.■	J23
New Orleans■	J27
Louisiana Tech	J29
Lamar	F 3
Tex.-Pan American	F 5
Southwestern La.	F10
Tex.-Pan American■	F17
Louisiana Tech■	F19
Ark.-Lit. Rock■	F21
Jacksonville	F26
New Orleans	F28
Sun Belt Conf.	M4-8

Colors: Red, White, Blue. Nickname: Jaguars.
AD: Joe Gottfried. SID: Fred Huff. I

SOUTH CARO. .... Columbia, SC 29208
Eddie Fogler (7 YRS. W-142, L-80)

Old Dominion■	N27
Charlotte Tr.	D3-4
Ga. Southern■	D 7
Coastal Caro.■	D11
South Caro. St.■	D20
Charleston (S.C.)■	D22
Providence	D31
Alabama■	J 5
Vanderbilt	J 8
Campbell■	J12
Florida■	J15
Tennessee■	J19
Arkansas	J22
Kentucky	J26
Georgia■	J29
Louisiana St.■	F 2
Mississippi	F 5
Clemson	F 9
Vanderbilt■	F12
Auburn	F16
Florida	F19
Mississippi St.■	F23
Tennessee	F26
Georgia	M 2
Kentucky■	M 5
Southeastern Conf.	M10-13

Colors: Garnet & Black. Nickname: Fighting Gamecocks.
AD: Mike McGee. SID: Kerry Tharp. I

SOUTH CARO. ST. .... Orangeburg, SC 29117
Cy Alexander (6 YRS. W-97, L-80)

Bryan■	N27
Charleston (S.C.)	N29
Ball St. Cardinal Cl	D3-4
Duke	D 6
Furman	D 8
Claflin■	D11
Coastal Caro.■	D18
South Caro.	D20
Charleston So.■	J 3
Coppin St.	J 6
Morgan St.	J 8
Howard	J10
Florida A&M■	J15
Bethune-Cookman■	J17
Md.-East. Shore■	J22
Delaware St.■	J24
Bethune-Cookman	J29
Florida A&M	J31
Md.-East. Shore	F 5
Delaware St.	F 7
North Caro. A&T■	F12
Coppin St.■	F17
Howard■	F21
Morgan St.■	F26
North Caro. A&T	M 5
Mid-Eastern Conf.	M9-13

Colors: Garnet & Blue. Nickname: Bulldogs.
AD: James A. Martin. SID: Bill Hamilton. I

S.C.-AIKEN .... Aiken, SC 29801
Larry Epperly (6 YRS. W-87, L-89)

Tenn.-Chatt.	N27
Newberry■	D 1
Erskine	D 4
Savannah St.■	D 7
Wofford■	D16
Presbyterian	D18
S.C.-Spartanburg	J 5
Francis Marion	J10
Lander■	J13
Georgia Col.■	J15
Newberry	J17
Augusta■	J22
Pembroke St.	J26
Armstrong St.	J29
Columbus■	J31
Lander	F 2
Pembroke St.■	F 5
Erskine■	F 9
S.C.-Spartanburg■	F12
Augusta	F14
Georgia Col.	F17
Wofford	F19
Armstrong St.■	F21
Francis Marion■	F23
Columbus	F26

Colors: Cardinal & White. Nickname: Pacers.
AD: Randy Warrick. SID: Terry Garbutt. II

S.C.-SPARTANBURG .... Spartanburg, SC 29303
Jerry Waters (15 YRS. W-308, L-124)

Central Wesleyan■	N20
Kennesaw	N22
S.C.-Spartanburg Inv	N26-27
Lenoir-Rhyne■	D 1
Newberry	D 4
Elon	D 6
S.C.-Aiken■	J 5
Armstrong St.	J 8
Georgia Col.	J13
Pembroke St.■	J15
Central Wesleyan	J17
Francis Marion■	J19
Columbus	J22
Lander	J27
Newberry■	J29
Georgia Col.■	J31
Augusta	F 2
Armstrong St.■	F 5
Lander■	F 9
S.C.-Aiken	F12
Francis Marion	F16
Columbus■	F19
Augusta■	F23
Pembroke St.	F26
Lees-McRae	F28

Colors: Kelly Green, White & Black. Nickname: Rifles.
AD: Sterling Brown. SID: Michael MacEachern. II

SOUTH DAK. .... Vermillion, SD 57069
Dave Boots (11 YRS. W-203, L-105)

Teikyo-Westmar	N20
South Dak. Tech	N26
Black Hills St.	N27
Grand View■	N30
Dakota St.■	D 4
Huron■	D 8
Mt. Marty	D16
Grand Canyon	D27
Morningside	J 2
St. Cloud St.	J 7
Mankato St.	J 8
Augustana (S.D.)■	J14
South Dak. St.■	J15
Northern Colo.	J21
Nebraska-Omaha	J22
North Dak.■	J28
North Dak. St.■	J29
Mankato St.■	F 4
St. Cloud St.■	F 5
South Dak. St.	F11
Augustana (S.D.)	F12
Nebraska-Omaha■	F18
Northern Colo.■	F19
Morningside■	F22
North Dak. St.	F25
North Dak.	F26

Colors: Vermillion & White. Nickname: Coyotes.
AD: Jack Doyle. SID: Kyle Johnson. II

SOUTH DAK. ST. .... Brookings, SD 57007
Brad Soderberg (5 YRS. W-79 , L-45)

Bellevue■	N30
Minn.-Morris■	D 3
Winona St.	D 4
Northern St.■	D 7
Wayne St. (Neb.)	D11
Southwest St.■	D14
Dak. Wesleyan■	D18
Mt. Senario■	D28
Nebraska-Omaha	J 2
Northern Colo.	J 3
North Dak.■	J 7
North Dak. St.■	J 8
Morningside	J14
South Dak.	J15
St. Cloud St.■	J21
Mankato St.■	J22
Augustana (S.D.)■	J29
North Dak. St.	F 4
North Dak.	F 5
Nebraska-Omaha■	F 8
South Dak.■	F11
Morningside■	F12
Mankato St.	F18
St. Cloud St.	F19
Northern Colo.■	F22
Augustana (S.D.)	F26

Colors: Yellow & Blue. Nickname: Jackrabbits.
AD: Fred Oien. SID: Ron Lenz. II

■ Home games on each schedule.

See pages 405–407 for Division I tournament details

SOUTH FLA. .... Tampa, FL 33620

Bobby Paschal (15 YRS. W-240, L-199)

Stetson■	N30	Va. Commonwealth	J22
Fla. Atlantic■	D 3	N.C.-Charlotte■	J29
Florida	D 6	Marquette	J31
Florida St.■	D11	Central Fla.	F 7
N.C.-Wilmington Cl.	D17-18	Louisville■	F10
Sam Houston St.■	D20	Southern Miss.■	F12
Old Dominion■	D22	Stetson☒	F16
Southern Cal■	D28	Virginia Tech■	F19
Ala.-Birmingham	D31	Tulane	F24
Louisville	J 6	Southern Miss.	F26
Tulane■	J 8	Va. Commonwealth■	M 5
Florida☒	J11	Metro Conf.	M11-13
N.C.-Charlotte	J15	☒ Orlando, FL	
Virginia Tech	J20		

Colors: Green & Gold. Nickname: Bulls.
AD: Paul Griffin. SID: John Gerdes. I

SOUTHEAST MO. ST. ..... Cape Girardeau, MO 63701

Ron Shumate (19 YRS. W-402, L-164)

Evansville■	N27	Tennessee St.	J29
Southern Cal Col.■	D 1	Austin Peay	J31
Southeast Mo. St. Cl	D3-4	Murray St.	F 2
Chicago St.■	D 6	Morehead St.■	F 5
Arkansas St. Cl.	D10-11	Eastern Ky.■	F 7
Southern Ill.	D16	Tennessee Tech	F12
Colorado St.	D21	Middle Tenn. St.	F14
Eastern Ky.	J 8	Murray St.■	F19
Morehead St.	J10	Missouri	F23
Tennessee Tech■	J15	Tenn.-Martin	F26
Middle Tenn. St.■	J17	Austin Peay■	F28
Tennessee St.■	J22	Memphis St.	M 2
Tenn.-Martin■	J24	Ohio Valley Conf.	M3-5

Colors: Red & Black. Nickname: Indians.
AD: Richard McDuffie. SID: Ron Hines. I

SOUTHEASTERN LA. .... Hammond, LA 70402

Norm Picou (1 YR. W-12, L-15)

Bapt. Christian■	N30	Central Fla.■	J29
LSU-Shreveport■	D 4	Southern-B.R.■	J31
Mississippi St.	D11	Florida Int'l■	F 3
Nicholls St.■	D14	Tulane	F 7
Northwestern (La.)	D18	Georgia St.	F10
Louisiana St.	D21	Samford	F12
Southern-B.R.	D23	Charleston (S.C.)■	F17
Centenary	J 3	Mercer■	F19
Florida Int'l	J 8	Centenary■	F21
Samford■	J13	Grambling	F23
Georgia St.■	J15	Central Fla.	F26
Mercer	J20	Stetson	F28
Charleston (S.C.)	J22	Trans America Conf.	M3-5
Stetson■	J27		

Colors: Green & Gold. Nickname: Lions.
AD: Tom Douple. SID: Larry Hymel. I

SOUTHERN CAL .... Los Angeles, CA 90089

George Raveling (21 YRS. W-320, L-280)

Pennsylvania■	N27	Arizona■	J22
Loyola (Cal.)■	N30	California	J27
Tenn.-Martin	D 4	Stanford	J29
San Diego St.■	D 7	UCLA	F 3
Notre Dame■	D11	Washington St.■	F10
Cal St. Sacramento■	D18	Washington■	F12
Howard■	D21	Arizona	F17
South Fla.	D28	Arizona St.	F19
Mo.-Kansas City	D31	Stanford■	F24
Oregon St.■	J 6	California■	F26
Oregon■	J 8	UCLA■	M 3
Washington	J13	Oregon	M10
Washington St.	J15	Oregon St.	M12
Arizona St.■	J20		

Colors: Cardinal & Gold. Nickname: Trojans.
AD: Mike Garrett. SID: Tim Tessalone. I

SOUTHERN COLO. .... Pueblo, CO 81001

Joe Folda (9 YRS. W-151, L-109)

Southern Colo. Cl.	N19-20	Colo. Christian	J22
Grand Canyon Inv.	N26-27	Adams St.■	J26
Northern Ariz.	N29	Fort Lewis■	J29
Southern Colo. Tr.	D3-4	Western St.	F 2
Cal St. Bakersfield■	D 9	Colorado-CS	F 5
West Tex. A&M	D18	Regis (Colo.)■	F10
Neb.-Kearney■	J 3	Denver	F12
West Tex. A&M■	J 5	Metropolitan St.	F17
Colorado-CS■	J 8	Colo. Christian■	F19
Regis (Colo.)	J13	Western St.■	F22
Denver■	J15	Fort Lewis	F26
Metropolitan St.■	J20		

Colors: Red & Blue. Nickname: Indians.
AD: Dan DeRose. SID: Todd Kelly. II

SOUTHERN CONN. ST. .... New Haven, CT 06515

Arthur Leary (15 YRS. W-192, L-233)

Springfield	N23	New Haven■	J26
American Int'l	N30	Mass.-Lowell■	J29
St. Anselm■	D 2	Bridgeport	F 2
Bentley	D 7	Franklin Pierce	F 5
Quinnipiac	D 9	Keene St.	F 6
Bryant■	D11	Sacred Heart	F 9
Bahamas Shootout	J2-9	New Hamp. Col.	F12
Franklin Pierce■	J15	Bridgeport■	F16
Mass.-Lowell	J17	New Hamp. Col.■	F21
Sacred Heart■	J19	New Haven	F23
Le Moyne■	J22	Le Moyne	F26
Keene St.■	J23		

Colors: Blue & White. Nickname: Owls.
AD: Raymond DeFrancesco. SID: Richard Leddy. II

SOUTHERN ILL. .... Carbondale, IL 62901

Rich Herrin (8 YRS. W-141, L-107)

Tampa■	N27	Indiana St.	J25
Evansville	D 4	Bradley	J29
Mississippi■	D 8	Creighton■	J31
Austin Peay■	D11	Northern Iowa■	F 3
Southeast Mo. St.■	D16	Southwest Mo. St.	F 5
Wichita St.	D22	Indiana St.■	F 9
St. Louis	D30	Tulsa	F12
Missouri■	J 5	Oral Roberts	F14
Illinois St.■	J 8	Southwest Mo. St.■	F16
Drake	J10	Drake■	F19
Bradley■	J15	Northern Iowa	F23
Creighton	J17	Illinois St.	F27
Tulsa■	J20	Missouri Valley Conf	M5-7
Wichita St.■	J22		

Colors: Maroon & White. Nickname: Salukis.
AD: Jim Hart. SID: Fred Huff. I

SIU-EDWARDSVILLE .... Edwardsville, IL 62026

Jack Margenthaler (16 YRS. W-235, L-214)

Lindenwood■	N20	Drury■	J15
Oakland City	N27	Ky. Wesleyan	J20
Lincoln (Mo.)■	N29	Quincy■	J22
Northwest Mo. St.■	D 1	Oakland City■	J29
Mo. Western Cl.	D3-4	IU/PU-Indianapolis■	F 5
Southwest Baptist■	D 7	St. Francis (Ill.)■	F 9
Ky. Wesleyan■	D11	Eureka■	F12
Mo.-St. Louis■	D18	Southern Ind.	F14
Las Vegas Tr.	D27-28	Wis.-Parkside■	F16
Southern Ind.■	J 4	Drury	F19
IU/PU-Indianapolis	J 8	Quincy	F26
Wis.-Parkside	J12	Bellarmine■	M 2

Colors: Red & White. Nickname: Cougars.
AD: Cindy Jones. SID: Eric Hess. II

SOUTHERN IND. .... Evansville, IN 47712

Bruce Pearl (1 YR. W-22, L-7)

Campbellsville■	D 4	Bellarmine■	J27
Southern Ind. Tr.	D18-19	Kentucky St.■	J29
Northern Ky.	D22	St. Joseph's (Ind.)	F 3
Wis.-Parkside	D28	Lewis	F 5
Indianapolis	D30	IU/PU-Ft. Wayne■	F10
SIU-Edwardsville	J 4	Ashland■	F12
Lewis■	J 6	SIU-Edwardsville■	F14
St. Joseph's (Ind.)■	J 8	Ky. Wesleyan	F19
Ashland	J13	Kentucky St.	F24
IU/PU-Ft. Wayne	J15	Bellarmine	F26
Quincy■	J19	Northern Ky.■	M 3
Ky. Wesleyan■	J22	Indianapolis■	M 5
Wis.-Parkside■	J25		

Colors: Red, White & Blue. Nickname: Screaming Eagles.
AD: Donald Bennett. SID: Ray Simmons. II

SOUTHERN ME. .... Gorham, ME 04038

Al Sokaitis (6 YRS. W-111, L-48)

Southern Maine Tr.	N19-20	Mass.-Dartmouth■	J22
Thomas■	N23	Mass.-Boston■	J25
Bowdoin	N27	Rhode Island Col.■	J29
New England	D 2	Plymouth St.■	F 1
Rhode Island Col.	D 4	Me.-Farmington■	F 3
Colby■	D 8	Eastern Conn. St.	F 5
Eastern Conn. St.■	D11	St. Joseph's (Me.)☒	F 9
Clark (Mass.)	J 8	Western Conn. St.■	F12
Plymouth St.	J11	Mass.-Boston	F15
Western Conn. St.	J15	Mass.-Dartmouth	F19
Wheaton (Mass.)	J17	☒ Portland, ME	
Colby-Sawyer■	J19		

Colors: Crimson, Navy Blue & White. Nickname: Huskies.
AD: Paula Hodgdon. SID: Al Bean. III

■ Home games on each schedule.

See pages 405–407 for Division I tournament details

SOUTHERN METHODIST .... Dallas, TX 75275

John Shumate (8 YRS. W-123, L-110)

Oklahoma St.■	N27	Houston■	J26
St. Louis■	D 1	Texas A&M	J29
Wichita St.■	D 4	Oklahoma	F 2
North Texas	D 7	Baylor■	F 6
Missouri	D11	Texas■	F 9
Arizona St.	D22	Rice■	F13
Kansas City Cl.	D29-30	Texas Tech	F16
Arkansas	J 2	Texas Christian	F19
Kansas	J 8	Houston	F24
Rice	J11	Texas A&M■	F27
Texas	J15	Oral Roberts■	M 2
Texas Tech■	J18	Baylor	M 5
Texas Christian■	J22	Southwest Conf.	M10-12

Colors: Red & Blue. Nickname: Mustangs.
AD: Forrest Gregg. SID: Ed Wisneski. I

SOUTHERN MISS. .... Hattiesburg, MS 39401

M.K. Turk (17 YRS. W-256, L-224)

Kansas St.	N27	Va. Commonwealth	J27
Mississippi St.	D 4	Virginia Tech	J29
Alcorn St.■	D 6	Mississippi Val.■	F 1
Mississippi☒	D18	Virginia Tech■	F 5
Alabama■	D21	N.C.-Charlotte	F10
Northeast La.■	D23	South Fla.	F12
Kansas St.■	D30	Memphis St.■	F16
Tenn.-Chatt.	J 2	Tulane	F19
Southwestern La.■	J 5	Auburn	F22
South Ala.	J11	South Fla.■	F26
Va. Commonwealth■	J15	Louisville■	M 2
Northeast La.	J17	Tulane■	M 5
N.C.-Charlotte■	J20	Metro Conf.	M11-13
Louisville	J22	☒ Biloxi, MS	

Colors: Black & Gold. Nickname: Golden Eagles.
AD: Bill McLellan. SID: M. R. Napier. I

SOUTHERN UTAH .... Cedar City, UT 84720

Bill Evans (2 YRS. W-20, L-15)

Western St.■	N26	Eastern Wash.	J10
Central Wash.■	N29	Idaho St.■	J18
Montana Cl.	D3-4	Troy St.	J22
Northern Ariz.■	D 6	Cal St. Sacramento■	J29
San Diego St.	D11	Butler	F 1
Northwest Nazarene■	D14	Troy St.■	F 5
UTEP	D20	San Fran. St.■	F 8
New Mexico St.	D22	Cal St. Northridge■	F12
Eastern Wash.■	D28	Mo.-Kansas City	F19
Idaho■	D30	Cal St. Northridge	F24
Butler■	J 3	Cal St. Sacramento	F26
Nebraska	J 5	Northern Ariz.	M 2
Montana St.	J 8	Mo.-Kansas City■	M 5

Colors: Scarlet, Royal Blue & White. Nickname: Thunderbirds.
AD: Jack Bishop. SID: Neil Gardner. I

SOUTHERN-B.R. .... Baton Rouge, LA 70813

Ben Jobe (22 YRS. W-422, L-193)

Paul Quinn■	N29	Texas Southern■	J24
Tennessee St.☒	D 4	Alcorn St.	J29
Dillard■	D 6	Southeastern La.	J31
Bapt. Christian■	D18	Mississippi Val.■	F 5
Rice	D20	Grambling■	F 7
Southeastern La.■	D23	Jackson St.	F12
Sugar Bowl Tr.	D27-28	Alabama St.	F14
Middle Tenn. St.■	J 6	Prairie View	F19
Mississippi Val.	J 8	Texas Southern	F21
Grambling	J10	Ala.-Birmingham	F24
Jackson St.■	J15	Alcorn St.■	F26
Alabama St.■	J17	Southwestern Conf.	M9-13
Prairie View■	J22	☒ Cincinnati, OH	

Colors: Blue & Gold. Nickname: Jaguars.
AD: Marino Casem. SID: Rodney Lockett. I

SOUTHWEST BAPTIST .... Bolivar, MO 65613

Jerry Kirksey (10 YRS. W-206, L-82)

East Tex. St.■	N20	Washburn	J19
Central Okla.	N23	Missouri-Rolla■	J22
Missouri Valley■	N27	Northeast Mo. St.■	J27
Mid-America Naz.■	N30	Central Mo. St.	J29
Henderson St.■	D 4	Mo. Western St.■	F 1
SIU-Edwardsville	D 7	Lincoln (Mo.)	F 5
Drury■	D11	Mo. Southern St.■	F 8
Southern Ind. Tr.	D18-19	Pittsburg St.	F12
Emporia St.	J 5	Mo.-St. Louis■	F16
Pittsburg St.■	J 8	Northwest Mo. St.	F19
Mo.-St. Louis	J12	Washburn■	F21
Northwest Mo. St.■	J15	Missouri-Rolla	F26

Colors: Purple & White. Nickname: Bearcats.
AD: John Bryant. SID: Christopher Johnson. II

SOUTHWEST MO. ST. .... Springfield, MO 65804

Mark Bernsen (1 YR. W-20, L-11)

Mo.-Kansas City■	N27	Northern Iowa■	J24
Houston	N30	Creighton	J29
Southwest Mo. St. Cl	D3-4	Indiana St.	F 1
Tulsa	D11	Southern Ill.■	F 5
Wichita St.■	D18	Illinois St.	F 9
Fordham	D21	Wichita St.	F12
Indiana St.■	J 2	Southern Ill.	F16
St. Louis	J 5	Tulsa■	F19
Tennessee St.■	J 8	Bradley■	F21
Illinois St.■	J12	Creighton■	F24
Drake	J15	Drake■	F26
Oklahoma St.■	J19	Northern Iowa	F28
Bradley	J22	Missouri Valley Conf	M5-7

Colors: Maroon & White. Nickname: Bears.
AD: Bill Rowe. SID: Mark Stillwell. I

SOUTHWEST ST. .... Marshall, MN 56258

Anthony Odom (7 YRS. W-88, L-105)

Wis.-River Falls■	N20	Wayne St. (Neb.)	J15
Mayville St.	N23	Minn.-Morris	J19
Briar Cliff■	N26	Minn.-Duluth■	J22
Wis.-Eau Claire■	N27	Mayville St.■	J26
Dakota St.	D 1	Winona St.	J29
North Dak.	D 4	Moorhead St.	F 2
Viterbo	D 7	Northern St.■	F 5
North Dak. St.	D 9	Bemidji St.	F 9
South Dak. St.	D14	Wayne St. (Neb.)■	F12
Briar Cliff	D16	Minn.-Morris■	F16
Moorhead St.■	J 5	Minn.-Duluth	F19
Northern St.	J 8	Mt. Senario	F23
Wis.-Eau Claire	J10	Winona St.■	F26
Bemidji St.■	J12		

Colors: Brown & Gold. Nickname: Golden Mustangs.
AD: Dan Snobl. SID: Bob Otterson. II

SOUTHWEST TEX. ST. .... San Marcos, Tex. 78666

Jim Wooldridge (8 YRS. W-151, L-82)

Northern Ariz.	N27	North Texas■	J27
East Central (Okla.)■	D 2	Texas-Arlington■	J29
Mo.-Kansas City	D 6	Oral Roberts■	F 3
Tarleton St.■	D11	Texas-San Antonio■	F 5
Georgia St.	D15	Northwestern (La.)■	F 7
Hawaii Inv.	D17-18	Stephen F. Austin	F10
Northeast La.	D28	Sam Houston St.	F12
Northwestern (La.)	D30	Mo.-Kansas City■	F14
Missouri Valley■	J 3	McNeese St.■	F17
Texas-San Antonio	J 8	Nicholls St.■	F19
Sam Houston St.■	J14	Texas-Arlington	F24
Stephen F. Austin■	J16	North Texas	F26
Nicholls St.	J20	Northeast La.■	F28
McNeese St.	J22	Southland Conf.	M4-6

Colors: Maroon & Gold. Nickname: Bobcats.
AD: Richard Hannan. SID: Tony Brubaker. I

SOUTHWESTERN LA. .... Lafayette, LA 70506

Marty Fletcher (11 YRS. W-156, L-163)

Tex. Wesleyan■	D 1	Louisiana Tech■	J22
Boise St.■	D 4	Western Ky.	J24
Sam Houston St.■	D15	Arkansas St.■	J27
Baylor	D20	New Orleans	J29
Memphis St.■	D23	Ark.-Lit. Rock■	F 2
Boise St. Tr.	D29-30	Western Ky.■	F 5
Jacksonville	J 3	South Ala.■	F10
Southern Miss.	J 5	Lamar	F12
South Ala.	J 8	Tex.-Pan American	F14
Lamar■	J10	Jacksonville■	F19
Ark.-Lit. Rock	J13	New Orleans■	F23
Tex.-Pan American■	J15	Louisiana Tech	F26
Arkansas St.	J20	Sun Belt Conf.	M4-8

Colors: Vermilion & White. Nickname: Ragin' Cajuns.
AD: Nelson Schexnayder. SID: Dan McDonald. I

SOUTHWESTERN (TEX.) ...... Georgetown, TX 78626

Lloyd Winston (7 YRS. W-100 , L-79)

Millsaps	N20	Austin■	J27
Hardin-Simmons■	N23	Houston Baptist	J29
Claremont Tr.	N26-27	Trinity (Tex.)	F 1
Trinity (Tex.)■	D 1	Dallas■	F 5
Rhodes Cl.	D3-4	Austin	F 7
Colorado College Inv	J2-4	Dallas	F13
Hendrix■	J 7	Mary Hardin-Baylor■	F14
LSU-Shreveport■	J 9	LSU-Shreveport	F18
Hardin-Simmons	J15	LeTourneau	F19
Houston Baptist■	J17	Hendrix	F27
LeTourneau■	J22		

Colors: Black & Yellow. Nickname: Pirates.
AD: Carla Lowry. SID: Lloyd Winston. III

■ Home games on each schedule.

See pages 405–407 for Division I tournament details

SPRINGFIELD .... Springfield, MA 01109

Mike Theulen (3 YRS. W-31, L-49)

Assumption	N19	Bentley■	J25
Southern Conn. St.■	N23	Bryant	J27
Keene St.	D 2	Assumption■	J29
American Int'l■	D 4	American Int'l	F 2
New Haven	D 7	Stonehill	F 5
Franklin Pierce■	D14	Bryant■	F 7
Springfield Cl.	J3-4	St. Michael's■	F 9
Stonehill■	J 8	St. Anselm	F12
St. Michael's	J12	Quinnipiac■	F16
St. Anselm■	J15	Merrimack	F19
Quinnipiac	J19	Bentley	F22
Merrimack■	J22		

Colors: Maroon & White. Nickname: Chiefs.
AD: Edward Bilik. SID: Ken Cerino. II

STANFORD .... Stanford, CA 94305

Mike Montgomery (15 YRS. W-279, L-168)

Stanford Inv.	N26-27	Southern Cal■	J29
UC Riverside■	D 4	Oregon	F 3
Santa Clara	D11	Oregon St.	F 5
McNeese St.■	D20	Arizona■	F10
Virginia■	D22	Arizona St.■	F12
Wisconsin	D27	California	F17
Meadowlands Tr.	D29-30	Southern Cal	F24
Washington■	J 6	UCLA	F26
Washington St.■	J 8	Oregon St.■	M 3
Arizona St.	J13	Oregon■	M 5
Arizona	J15	Washington St.	M10
California■	J20	Washington	M12
UCLA■	J27		

Colors: Cardinal & White. Nickname: Cardinal.
AD: Ted Leland. SID: Bob Vazquez. I

STATEN ISLAND .... Staten Island, NY 10301

Anthony Petosa (4 YRS. W-47, L-58)

Manhattanville	N23	John Jay■	J 8
York (N.Y.)	N29	Merchant Marine	J15
Merchant Marine■	D 1	Hunter■	J18
Stony Brook	D 5	Hamilton Inv.	J22-23
New York U.	D 8	Manhattanville■	J26
FDU-Madison	D11	Medgar Evers	J29
New Jersey Tech■	D13	Hunter	J31
Medgar Evers■	D15	CCNY■	F 7
Staten Island Cl.	D29-30	Lehman	F 9
New Jersey Tech	J 3	Stony Brook■	F12
York (N.Y.)■	J 5	Baruch	F16

Colors: Maroon & Columbia Blue. Nickname: Dolphins.
AD: Joseph Barresi. SID: To be named. III

STEPHEN F. AUSTIN .... Nacogdoches, TX 75962

Ned Fowler (7 YRS. W-108, L-89)

Boise St. Cl.	N26-27	Nicholls St.■	J29
Texas■	D 1	Northeast La.	F 3
Houston■	D 7	Northwestern (La.)	F 5
Baylor Inv.	D10-11	Texas-Arlington■	F 7
Texas-Arlington	D22	Southwest Tex. St.■	F10
North Texas	D28	Texas-San Antonio■	F12
Cameron■	D31	Oral Roberts■	F16
Northwestern (La.)■	J 6	Sam Houston St.■	F19
Northeast La.■	J 8	Nicholls St.	F24
Texas-San Antonio	J14	McNeese St.	F26
Southwest Tex. St.	J16	North Texas■	F28
Sam Houston St.	J22	Southland Conf.	M4-6
McNeese St.■	J27		

Colors: Purple & White. Nickname: Lumberjacks.
AD: Steve McCarty. SID: Gregg Fort. I

STETSON .... DeLand, FL 32720

Dan Hipsher (4 YRS. W-97, L-18)

Jacksonville	N27	Georgia	J31
South Fla.	N30	Samford■	F 3
Florida	D11	Georgia St.■	F 5
Fla. Atlantic■	D13	Fla. Atlantic	F 7
West Fla.■	D18	Florida Int'l■	F10
Stetson Cl.	D29-30	Mercer	F12
Georgia St.	J 6	Charleston (S.C.)	F14
Samford	J 8	South Fla.⊠	F16
Mercer■	J13	Central Fla.	F19
Charleston (S.C.)■	J15	Centenary■	F26
Florida Int'l	J17	Southeastern La.■	F28
Central Fla.■	J22	Trans America Conf.	M3-5
Southeastern La.	J27	⊠ Orlando, FL	
Centenary	J29		

Colors: Green & White. Nickname: Hatters.
AD: Bob Jacoby. SID: Tom McClellan. I

STEVENS TECH .... Hoboken, NJ 07030

Charles Brown (1 YR. W-8, L-17)

Lehman	N23	Centenary (N.J.)■	J22
Mt. St. Vincent	N28	Maritime (N.Y.)■	J25
Maritime (N.Y.)	N30	St. Joseph's-Suffolk	J29
Drew■	D 6	FDU-Madison■	J31
Baruch■	D 9	Polytechnic (N.Y.)	F 3
Yeshiva■	D11	Rutgers-Newark	F 7
Westbrook■	J 7	Bard	F 9
Polytechnic (N.Y.)■	J11	Mt. St. Vincent■	F12
Pratt	J13	New Jersey Tech	F14
New Jersey Tech■	J15	Yeshiva	F16
Vassar	J18	Merchant Marine■	F19
St. Joseph's (N.Y.)■	J20		

Colors: Red & Gray. Nickname: Ducks.
AD: Frank Rotunda. SID: John Lyon. III

STILLMAN .... Tuscaloosa, AL 35403

Larry Robinson (9 YRS. W-112, L-101)

Tougaloo■	N20	West Fla.■	J17
Barber-Scotia■	N22	Rust	J22
Talladega	N24	Lane■	J25
Stillman Tr.	N26-27	West Fla.	J27
Millsaps	D 1	Pensacola Christian	J28
Lane	D 3	Rust■	F 4
Fisk	D 4	Pensacola Christian■	F 5
Millsaps■	D 7	Fisk■	F 8
Mobile	D10	Miles■	F12
Aub.-Montgomery Tr.	D17-18	La Grange■	F16
Savannah A&D Tr.	J7-8	Savannah A&D	F18
La Grange	J15	Barber-Scotia	F21

Colors: Old Gold & Navy Blue. Nickname: Tigers.
AD: Larry Robinson. SID: To be named. III

STOCKTON ST. .... Pomona, NJ 08240

Gerald Matthews (8 YRS. W-161 , L-61)

Allentown■	N20	Ramapo	J22
Rutgers-Newark	N23	Lincoln (Pa.)■	J24
Jersey City St.■	N29	Rutgers-Newark■	J26
Ramapo■	D 1	Jersey City St.	J29
Montclair St.■	D 4	Rutgers-Camden■	F 2
Rowan	D 7	Montclair St.	F 5
Kean■	D11	Rowan■	F 9
St. John Fisher Inv.	J7-8	Kean	F11
Rutgers-Camden	J12	Trenton St.■	F16
Wm. Paterson	J15	Wm. Paterson■	F19
Trenton St.	J19		

Colors: Black & White. Nickname: Ospreys.
AD: Larry James. SID: To be named. III

STONEHILL .... North Easton, MA 02356

Raymond Pepin (9 YRS. W-137, L-118)

Merrimack Tr.	N20-21	St. Anselm■	J22
American Int'l	N28	Assumption■	J25
Merrimack■	D 4	Quinnipiac	J27
Keene St.	D11	American Int'l■	J29
Sacred Heart■	D18	Merrimack	F 2
New Hamp. Col.■	D21	Springfield■	F 5
Colo. Christian	D30	Bentley	F 9
Regis (Colo.)	D31	St. Michael's	F12
Denver	J 3	Bryant■	F16
Springfield	J 8	St. Anselm	F19
Bentley■	J12	Assumption	F22
St. Michael's■	J15	Quinnipiac■	F24
Bryant	J19		

Colors: Purple & White. Nickname: Chieftains.
AD: Ray Pepin. SID: Bob Richards. II

STONY BROOK .... Stony Brook, NY 11794

Bernard Tomlin (4 YRS. W-59, L-50)

Stony Brook Inv.	N20-21	Hunter	J22
Old Westbury■	D 1	York (N.Y.)	J26
Salve Regina■	D 4	Mt. St. Vincent■	J29
Staten Island■	D 5	Manhattanville	F 3
New Jersey Tech	D 8	Hunter■	F 7
Adelphi⊠	D18	New Paltz St.■	F 9
Plattsburgh St.■	J 8	New Jersey Tech■	F10
Carnegie Mellon■	J 9	Staten Island	F12
Mt. St. Mary (N.Y.)■	J11	Merchant Marine	F14
Albany (N.Y.)■	J14	Rhode Island Col.	F19
FDU-Madison	J17	Manhattanville■	F22
Merchant Marine■	J20	⊠ Uniondale, NY	

Colors: Scarlet & Gray. Nickname: Patriots.
AD: Paul Dudzick. SID: Kenneth Alber. III

■ Home games on each schedule.

See pages 405–407 for Division I tournament details

SUFFOLK .... Boston, MA 02114
James Nelson (16 YRS. W-163, L-241)

Opponent	Date	Opponent	Date
Williams Cl.	N19-20	Colby-Sawyer	J22
Bri'water (Mass.)■	N23	Babson	J25
Colby	N27	MIT	J27
Salve Regina	N30	Tufts■	J29
Curry	D 4	Worcester Tech■	F 3
Brandeis■	D 9	Mass.-Boston	F 5
Bates■	D11	Roger Williams■	F 7
Eastern Nazarene	J 8	Clark (Mass.)	F 9
Wentworth Inst.	J13	Mass.-Dartmouth■	F12
Colby-Sawyer■	J15	Wheaton (Mass.)■	F15
New England	J17	Notre Dame (N.H.)■	F17
Fitchburg St.	J20	Nichols■	F19

Colors: Blue & Gold. Nickname: Rams.
AD: James Nelson. SID: Lou Connelly. III

SUSQUEHANNA .... Selinsgrove, PA 17870
Frank Marcinek (4 YRS. W-61, L-43)

Opponent	Date	Opponent	Date
Susquehanna Tr.	N19-20	Scranton	J24
York (Pa.)■	N22	Albright	J26
Elizabethtown	D 2	Elizabethtown■	J29
Rochester Cl.	D3-4	Lycoming	J31
Wilkes■	D 8	Messiah■	F 2
Widener■	D11	Widener	F 5
Messiah	J13	Juniata■	F 9
Lebanon Valley■	J15	Lebanon Valley	F12
King's (Pa.)■	J17	Albright■	F15
Juniata	J19	Moravian	F19
Moravian■	J22		

Colors: Orange & Maroon. Nickname: Crusaders.
AD: Donald Harnum. SID: Mike Ferlazzo. III

SWARTHMORE .... Swarthmore, PA 19081
Lee Wimberly (7 YRS. W-60, L-113)

Opponent	Date	Opponent	Date
Bates☒	N20	Drew	J20
Western Md.■	N23	Frank. & Marsh.	J22
Rochester Inv.	N27-28	Ursinus■	J26
Dickinson■	D 1	Washington (Md.)	J29
Phila. Pharmacy■	D 6	Muhlenberg	F 2
Haverford	D 8	Haverford■	F 5
Union (N.Y.) Inv.	J7-8	Johns Hopkins	F 9
Lafayette	J10	Ursinus	F12
Yale	J11	Washington (Md.)■	F16
Emory■	J15	Muhlenberg■	F19
Gettysburg■	J17	☒ Haverford, PA	

Colors: Garnet, White & Gray. Nickname: Garnet.
AD: Robert William. SID: Rose Smith. III

SYRACUSE .... Syracuse, NY 13244
Jim Boeheim (17 YRS. W-411, L-133)

Opponent	Date	Opponent	Date
Tennessee■	N28	Providence	J25
Cornell■	D 1	Villanova■	J29
Syracuse Carrier Cl.	D3-4	Connecticut■	F 1
Boston College■	D 9	Pittsburgh	F 5
Lafayette■	D13	Georgetown	F 7
Md.-East. Shore■	D18	Kentucky■	F12
Miami (Fla.)■	D22	Providence■	F15
Colgate■	D29	Boston College	F19
Pittsburgh■	J 8	Seton Hall■	F23
Connecticut	J10	St. John's (N.Y.)	F27
Villanova	J15	Miami (Fla.)	M 1
St. John's (N.Y.)■	J18	Georgetown■	M 6
Seton Hall	J22	Big East Conf.	M10-13

Colors: Orange. Nickname: Orangemen.
AD: Jake Crouthamel. SID: Larry Kimball. I

TAMPA .... Tampa, FL 33606
Richard Schmidt (12 YRS. W-260, L-101)

Opponent	Date	Opponent	Date
St. Thomas (Fla.)■	N22	Barry	J15
Central Ark.■	N24	Rollins■	J19
Southern Ill.	N27	St. Leo	J22
Webber■	N30	Florida Tech■	J26
Franklin Pierce■	D 2	North Fla.■	J29
Fla. Memorial■	D 6	Eckerd	F 2
Edward Waters■	D 9	Barry■	F 5
St. Thomas (Fla.)	D11	Rollins	F 9
Talladega■	D18	St. Leo■	F12
Bryant■	D30	Florida Tech	F16
St. Mary's (Tex.)■	J 4	North Fla.	F19
American Int'l■	J 5	Eckerd■	F23
Fla. Southern■	J12	Fla. Southern	F26

Colors: Scarlet, Gold & Black. Nickname: Spartans.
AD: Hindman Wall. SID: Gil Swalls. II

TEMPLE .... Philadelphia, PA 19122
John Chaney (21 YRS. W-478, L-156)

Opponent	Date	Opponent	Date
Kansas	D 1	Rutgers■	F 1
Ala.-Birmingham■	D 4	Rhode Island■	F 3
Villanova☒	D11	St. Bonaventure■	F 5
Cincinnati■	D16	West Va.	F 8
ECAC Holiday Tr.	D27-29	Duquesne■	F10
St. Joseph's (Pa.)■	J 2	Massachusetts	F13
West Va.■	J 6	St. Bonaventure	F16
Geo. Washington■	J 8	Louisville◆	F20
Pennsylvania■	J11	Duquesne	F22
Rhode Island	J15	Massachusetts■	F24
La Salle	J20	Duke	F27
Rutgers	J23	Atlantic 10 Conf.	M5-10
St. Joseph's (Pa.)☒	J25	☒ Philadelphia, PA	
Geo. Washington	J29	◆ Orlando, FL	

Colors: Cherry & White. Nickname: Owls.
AD: To be named. SID: Al Shrier. I

TENNESSEE .... Knoxville, TN 37996
Wade Houston (4 YRS. W-60, L-68)

Opponent	Date	Opponent	Date
Tenn.-Martin■	N26	Vanderbilt	J26
Syracuse	N28	Arkansas■	J29
Memphis St.	D 2	Tennessee Tech■	F 1
Ark.-Lit. Rock■	D 8	Louisiana St.	F 5
Western Caro.■	D17	North Caro. St.■	F 7
Michigan St.■	D21	Georgia	F12
Mercer■	D28	Mississippi■	F16
Virginia Tech	J 2	Alabama	F19
Mississippi St.	J 5	Kentucky■	F23
Florida■	J 8	South Caro.■	F26
Georgia■	J12	Vanderbilt■	M 1
Kentucky	J15	Florida	M 5
South Caro.	J19	Southeastern Conf.	M10-13
Auburn■	J22		

Colors: Orange & White. Nickname: Volunteers.
AD: Doug Dickey. SID: Bud Ford. I

TENNESSEE ST. .... Nashville, TN 37203
Frankie Allen (6 YRS. W-79, L-95)

Opponent	Date	Opponent	Date
Jackson St.	N29	Southeast Mo. St.	J22
Cincinnati	D 1	Murray St.	J24
Wilberforce☒	D 3	Tennessee Tech	J27
Southern-B.R.☒	D 4	Southeast Mo. St.■	J29
Fisk■	D 6	Murray St.■	J31
UCLA	D 8	Tenn.-Martin■	F 2
Hawaii Tip-Off Tr.	D10-11	Middle Tenn. St.■	F 5
North Caro. A&T■	D18	Austin Peay■	F 7
Tulane	D22	Tenn.-Martin	F 9
Florida A&M	D29	Morehead St.	F12
Austin Peay	J 4	Eastern Ky.	F14
Southwest Mo. St.	J 8	Tennessee Tech■	F21
Eastern Ky.■	J13	Alabama	F23
Morehead St.■	J17	Ohio Valley Conf.	M3-5
Middle Tenn. St.	J19	☒ Cincinnati, OH	

Colors: Blue & White. Nickname: Tigers.
AD: William Thomas. SID: Johnny Franks. I

TENNESSEE TECH .... Cookeville, TN 38505
Frank Harrell (7 YRS. W-81, L-119)

Opponent	Date	Opponent	Date
Kentucky	D 1	Tennessee St.■	J27
Bethel (Tenn.)■	D 4	Middle Tenn. St.	J29
Appalachian St.	D 6	Tennessee	F 1
Indiana Cl.	D10-11	Tenn.-Martin	F 7
Maui Inv.	D21-23	Southeast Mo. St.■	F12
Hawaii-Hilo Inv.	D28-30	Murray St.■	F14
Idaho St.■	J 3	Middle Tenn. St.■	F17
Austin Peay■	J 8	Austin Peay	F19
Tenn.-Martin■	J10	Tennessee St.	F21
Southeast Mo. St.	J15	Eastern Ky.■	F26
Murray St.	J17	Morehead St.■	F28
Morehead St.	J22	Ohio Valley Conf.	M3-5
Eastern Ky.	J24		

Colors: Purple & Gold. Nickname: Golden Eagles.
AD: David Larimore. SID: Rob Schabert. I

TENN.-CHATT. .... Chattanooga, TN 37401
Mack McCarthy (8 YRS. W-162, L-81)

Opponent	Date	Opponent	Date
S.C.-Aiken■	N27	Ga. Southern■	J22
Alabama	D 1	Citadel■	J24
Michigan	D 4	East Tenn. St.	J26
Columbus■	D11	Davidson	J29
Purdue	D21	East Tenn. St.■	F 5
Tenn.-Chatt. Tr.	D29-30	Appalachian St.■	F 7
Southern Miss.■	J 2	Va. Military	F12
Furman	J 5	Marshall	F14
Marshall■	J 8	Western Caro.	F19
Va. Military■	J10	Furman■	F23
Davidson■	J13	Citadel	F26
Western Caro.■	J15	Ga. Southern	F28
Appalachian St.	J20	Southern Conf.	M3-6

Colors: Navy Blue & Gold. Nickname: Moccasins.
AD: Ed Farrell. SID: Neil Magnussen. I

■ Home games on each schedule.

See pages 405–407 for Division I tournament details

TENN.-MARTIN .... Martin, TN 38238

Calvin C. Luther (32 YRS. W-443, L-352)

Tennessee N26
Arkansas Col.■ N29
Vanderbilt .... D 1
Southern Cal■ .... D 4
Illinios Cl. D10-11
Georgia St. D13
Middle Tenn. St.■ .... J 3
Ala.-Huntsville .... J 5
Tennessee Tech J10
Morehead St.■ J13
Eastern Ky.■ J15
Alabama J17
Murray St. J22
Southeast Mo. St. J24
Evansville■ J26
Middle Tenn. St. J31
Tennessee St. .... F 2
Austin Peay■ .... F 5
Tennessee Tech■ .... F 7
Tennessee St.■ .... F 9
Austin Peay F16
Morehead St. F19
Eastern Ky. F21
Southeast Mo. St.■ F26
Murray St.■ F28
Evansville .... M 2
Ohio Valley Conf. M3-5

Colors: Orange, White, Royal Blue. Nickname: Pacers.
AD: Don McLeary. SID: Lee Wilmot. I

TEXAS .... Austin, TX 78713

Tom Penders (22 YRS. W-376, L-265)

Louisiana St. N26
Nebraska N28
Stephen F. Austin .... D 1
Florida■ .... D 4
Connecticut D15
Maui Inv. D21-23
Utah■ D29
Illinois .... J 2
Texas-San Antonio .... J 5
Texas A&M J12
Southern Methodist■ J15
Baylor J19
Texas Tech■ J22
Georgia■ J23
Houston J29
Rice■ .... F 1
Texas Christian■ .... F 5
Southern Methodist .... F 9
Texas A&M■ F12
Baylor■ F15
Texas Tech F19
Lamar■ F21
Houston■ F26
Oral Roberts■ F28
Rice .... M 2
Texas Christian .... M 5
Southwest Conf. M10-12

Colors: Burnt Orange & White. Nickname: Longhorns.
AD: Dave Saba. SID: Bill Little. I

TEXAS A&M .... College Station, TX 77843

Tony Barone (8 YRS. W-118, L-121)

Bucknell■ N28
Kansas St. .... D 1
Montana St.■ .... D 6
Nevada-Las Vegas■ .... D 8
Northwestern■ D18
Texas Southern■ D20
Seton Hall D22
Loyola (Cal.) D30
South Ala. .... J 3
Northern Ill. .... J 5
Texas■ J12
Rice J16
Houston J19
Siena■ J22
Texas Christian■ J25
Southern Methodist■ J29
Baylor .... F 2
Texas Tech .... F 5
Oral Roberts■ .... F 9
Texas F12
Houston■ F16
Rice■ F20
Texas Christian F23
Southern Methodist F27
Baylor■ .... M 2
Texas Tech■ .... M 5
Southwest Conf. M10-12

Colors: Maroon & White. Nickname: Aggies.
AD: Wally Groff. SID: Colin Killian. I

TEXAS A&M-KINGSVILLE .... Kingsville, TX 78363

Bill Carter (8 YRS. W-135, L-89)

Tex. Lutheran■ N23
Mankato St. Cl. N26-27
St. Edward's N29
Southern Colo. Tr. D3-4
Regis (Colo.) .... D 6
Texas-San Antonio .... D 9
St. Mary's (Tex.)■ D18
Incarnate Wood Tr. D29-30
Drury Tr. J7-8
Concordia (Tex.) J11
Abilene Christian■ J15
Angelo St.■ J17
East Tex. St. J20
Eastern N. Mex. J22
West Tex. A&M J24
Central Okla.■ J29
Central Okla. .... F 7
Angelo St. F12
Abilene Christian F14
West Tex. A&M■ F19
Eastern N. Mex.■ F21
East Tex. St.■ F24

Colors: Blue & Gold. Nickname: Javelinas.
AD: Ron Harms. SID: Fred Nuesch. II

TEXAS-ARLINGTON .... Arlington, TX 76019

Eddie McCarter (1 YR. W-16, L-12)

Ala.-Birmingham N27
Clemson N29
Southeast Mo. St. Cl D3-4
Abilene Christian■ .... D 7
Angelo St.■ .... D 9
East Tex. St.■ D11
Iowa St. D18
Stephen F. Austin■ D22
Hawaii-Hilo Inv. D28-30
Nicholls St. .... J 6
McNeese St. .... J 8
Sam Houston St.■ J11
North Texas■ J15
Northwestern (La.)■ J20
Northeast La.■ J22
Texas-San Antonio J27
Southwest Tex. St. J29
McNeese St.■ .... F 3
Nicholls St.■ .... F 5
Stephen F. Austin .... F 7
North Texas F12
Northeast La. F17
Northwestern (La.) F19
Southwest Tex. St.■ F24
Texas-San Antonio■ F26
Sam Houston St. F28
Southland Conf. M4-6

Colors: Royal Blue & White. Nickname: Mavericks.
AD: B.J. Skelton. SID: Steve Weller. I

TEXAS CHRISTIAN .... Fort Worth, TX 76129

Moe Iba (16 YRS. W-232, L-224)

Fairfield Tr. D3-4
Middle Tenn. St.■ .... D 7
Oklahoma St. .... D 9
DePaul■ D21
Louisiana Tech■ D23
Indiana Hoosier Cl. D27-28
Louisiana Tech⊠ .... J 3
Oral Roberts■ .... J 6
Virginia Tech■ .... J 9
Houston J12
Baylor■ J15
Rice■ J19
Southern Methodist J22
Texas A&M J25
Texas Tech■ .... F 2
Texas .... F 5
Houston■ .... F 8
Baylor F12
Rice F16
Southern Methodist■ F19
Texas A&M■ F23
Oral Roberts F26
Texas Tech .... M 2
Texas■ .... M 5
Southwest Conf. M10-12
⊠ Shreveport, LA

Colors: Purple & White. Nickname: Horned Frogs.
AD: Frank Windegger. SID: Glen Stone. I

TEX.-PAN AMERICAN .... Edinburg, TX 78539

Mark Adams (10 YRS. W-210, L-99)

Concordia (Tex.)■ .... D 4
St. Edward's■ D11
New Mexico D18
UTEP D22
Texas Southern■ .... J 3
Jacksonville■ .... J 8
Louisiana Tech J13
Southwestern La. J15
New Orleans■ J17
Ark.-Lit. Rock■ J20
Western Ky.■ J22
Samford■ J24
Troy St. J27
Jacksonville J29
Lamar■ J31
Arkansas St. .... F 3
South Ala.■ .... F 5
Ark.-Lit. Rock F10
Louisiana Tech■ F12
Southwestern La.■ F14
South Ala. F17
New Orleans F19
Troy St.■ F21
Arkansas St.■ F23
Lamar F26
Western Ky. .... M 1
Sun Belt Conf. M4-8

Colors: Green & White. Nickname: Broncs.
AD: Gary Gallup. SID: Jim McKone. I

TEXAS-SAN ANTONIO .... San Antonio, TX 78285

Stu Starner (10 YRS. W-167, L-125)

Nebraska N27
Grambling■ .... D 1
Grambling .... D 7
Texas A&M-Kingsville■ .... D 9
Angelo St.■ D11
Memphis St. D20
Northwestern (La.) D28
Northeast La. D30
Texas■ .... J 5
Southwest Tex. St.■ .... J 8
Stephen F. Austin■ J14
Sam Houston St.■ J16
McNeese St. J20
Nicholls St. J22
Texas-Arlington■ J27
North Texas■ J29
Houston■ .... F 2
Southwest Tex. St. .... F 5
Northeast La.■ .... F 7
Sam Houston St. F10
Stephen F. Austin F12
Nicholls St.■ F17
McNeese St.■ F19
North Texas F24
Texas-Arlington F26
Northwestern (La.)■ F28
Southland Conf. M4-6

Colors: Orange, Navy Blue & White. Nickname: Roadrunners.
AD: Bobby Thompson. SID: Rick Nixon. I

TEXAS SOUTHERN .... Houston, TX 77004

Robert Moreland (18 YRS. W-288, L-233)

Tougaloo■ N27
Houston Baptist■ N29
California■ .... D 1
Marquette Tr. D3-4
Paul Quinn■ .... D 8
New Orleans■ D11
Texas A&M D20
Baylor D22
Arkansas D28
Tex.-Pan American .... J 3
Xavier (La.)■ .... J 5
Jackson St. .... J 8
Alabama St. J10
Grambling■ J15
Mississippi Val.■ J17
Alcorn St. J22
Southern-B.R. J24
Prairie View J29
Jackson St.■ .... F 5
Alabama St.■ .... F 7
Grambling F12
Mississippi Val. F14
Alcorn St.■ F19
Southern-B.R.■ F21
Prairie View■ F26
Southwestern Conf. M9-13

Colors: Maroon & Gray. Nickname: Tigers.
AD: To be named. SID: Andre L. Smith. I

TEXAS TECH .... Lubbock, TX 79409

James Dickey (2 YRS. W-33, L-26)

Arkansas St.■ N29
Southwest Mo. St. Cl D3-4
New Mexico■ .... D 8
Wisconsin■ D11
Brigham Young D17
North Texas■ D21
Oklahoma Tr. D29-30
Mo.-Kansas City .... J 8
Baylor J12
Houston■ J15
Southern Methodist J18
Texas J22
Mo.-Kansas City■ J25
Rice■ J29
Texas Christian .... F 2
Texas A&M■ .... F 5
Baylor■ .... F 9
Houston F12
Southern Methodist■ F16
Texas■ F19
Oral Roberts F23
Rice F26
Texas Christian■ .... M 2
Texas A&M .... M 5
Southwest Conf. M10-12

Colors: Scarlet & Black. Nickname: Red Raiders.
AD: Bob Bockrath. SID: Joe Hornaday. I

■ Home games on each schedule.

See pages 405–407 for Division I tournament details

UTEP .... El Paso, TX 79968

Don Haskins (32 YRS. W-627, L-276)

Simon Fraser■	N19	Wyoming	J20
Loyola (La.)■	N27	Colorado St.	J22
New Mexico St.	D 3	New Mexico■	J29
New Mexico St.■	D 6	Western N. Mex.■	F 1
Abilene Christian■	D18	New Mexico	F 5
Southern Utah■	D20	Colorado St.■	F10
Tex.-Pan American■	D22	Wyoming■	F12
UTEP Cl.	D29-30	Hawaii	F17
Utah■	J 3	San Diego St.	F19
Brigham Young■	J 5	Fresno St.■	F24
Fresno St.	J 8	Air Force■	F26
Air Force	J10	Utah	M 3
Hawaii■	J13	Brigham Young	M 5
San Diego St.■	J15	Western Ath. Conf.	M9-12

Colors: Orange, White & Blue. Nickname: Miners.
AD: John Thompson. SID: Eddie Mullens. I

THIEL .... Greenville, PA 16125

Jes Hutson (6 YRS. W-48, L-89)

La Roche■	N20	Grove City	J19
Mount Union■	N23	Wash. & Jeff.■	J21
Hilbert	N30	Bethany (W.Va.)	J26
Hiram	D 1	Hilbert■	J28
Penn St.-Behrend Tr.	D3-4	La Roche	J31
Kenyon■	D 6	Waynesburg■	F 2
Oberlin	D10	Grove City■	F 5
Fredonia St.■	D11	Wash. & Jeff.	F 9
Roberts Wesleyan■	J 6	Bethany (W.Va.)■	F12
Ohio Valley College	J10	Carnegie Mellon	F16
Ohio Valley College■	J13	Waynesburg	F19
Bapt. Bible (Pa.)	J15		

Colors: Navy Blue & Old Gold. Nickname: Tomcats.
AD: John Dickason. SID: Joe Michalski. III

THOMAS MORE .... Crestview Hills, KY 41017

Larry Cox (3 YRS. W-36, L-43)

Northern Ky. Cl.	N19-20	Wilmington (Ohio)■	J19
Earlham■	N23	Bluffton	J22
Hanover	N27	Spalding	J27
Graceland (Ind.)■	N30	St. Francis (Ind.)■	J29
Morehead St.	D 4	Ky. Christian	F 1
Manchester■	D11	Cincinnati Bible	F 3
Adrian	D18	Bluffton■	F 5
Wabash	D20	Wilmington (Ohio)	F 9
Ohio Wesleyan	D30	Defiance	F12
Wittenberg■	J 3	Asbury■	F17
Franklin■	J 8	Anderson	F19
Defiance■	J15		

Colors: Royal Blue & White. Nickname: Rebels.
AD: Vic Clark. SID: Ted Kiep. III

TOLEDO .... Toledo, OH 43606

Larry Gipson (2 YRS. W-19, L-36)

Fairfield■	N27	Western Mich.	J26
Drake	D 4	Ohio■	J29
Colorado St.■	D11	Central Mich.	F 2
Oakland■	D18	Eastern Mich.■	F 5
Alcorn St.■	D20	Akron■	F 9
Cal St. Sacramento	D23	Kent	F12
Toledo Cl.	D29-30	Ball St.■	F16
Bowling Green■	J 5	Miami (Ohio)	F19
Eastern Mich.	J 8	Western Mich.■	F23
Akron	J12	Ohio	F26
Kent■	J15	Central Mich.■	M 2
Ball St.	J19	Bowling Green	M 5
Miami (Ohio)■	J22	Mid-American Conf.	M8-12

Colors: Blue & Gold. Nickname: Rockets.
AD: Allen Bohl. SID: Rod Brandt. I

TOWSON ST. .... Towson, MD 21204

Terry Truax (10 YRS. W-144, L-148)

Pre-Season NIT	N17-26	N.C.-Greensboro	J24
Connecticut⊠	N27	Winthrop■	J27
Loyola (Md.)	D 1	N.C.-Asheville■	J29
Dayton	D 4	Radford■	F 5
Lehigh■	D 7	Liberty■	F 7
Delaware	D11	Coastal Caro.	F12
Coppin St.	D13	Charleston So.	F14
Maryland	D23	Md.-Balt. County	F17
American■	J 4	Campbell■	F19
Radford	J 8	N.C.-Greensboro■	F21
Liberty	J10	Winthrop	F24
Coastal Caro.■	J15	N.C.-Asheville	F26
Charleston So.■	J17	Big South Conf.	M4-7
Md.-Balt. County■	J19	⊠ Hershey, PA	
Campbell	J22		

Colors: Gold, White & Black. Nickname: Tigers.
AD: Bill Hunter. SID: Peter Schlehr. I

TRENTON ST. .... Ewing, NJ 08650

John Castaldo 1ST YR. AS HEAD COACH

Rutgers-Camden■	N23	Stockton St.■	J19
Ramapo	N27	Jersey City St.■	J22
Jersey City St.	D 1	Rutgers-Camden	J26
Kean■	D 4	Ramapo■	J29
Hunter	D 6	Rowan	F 1
Montclair St.	D 8	Kean	F 5
Elizabethtown Cl.	D10-11	Montclair St.■	F 9
Trenton St. Cl.	J7-8	Wm. Paterson■	F12
Wm. Paterson	J10	Salisbury St.	F14
Rowan■	J12	Stockton St.	F16
Rutgers-Newark	J15	Rutgers-Newark■	F19

Colors: Navy Blue & Gold. Nickname: Lions.
AD: Kevin McHugh. SID: Ann Bready. III

TRINITY (CONN.) .... Hartford, CT 06106

Stan Ogrodnik (12 YRS. W-192, L-90)

Coast Guard	N30	Clark (Mass.)■	F 1
Eastern Nazarene	D 9	Bates■	F 4
Middlebury	D11	Bowdoin■	F 5
Merchant Marine	J11	Williams	F 9
Trinity (Conn.) Cl.	J14-15	Manhattanville■	F12
Wesleyan	J18	Amherst	F16
Tufts	J22	Wheaton (Mass.)	F19
Worcester Tech■	J26	Wesleyan■	F22
Connecticut Col.	J29		

Colors: Blue & Gold. Nickname: Bantams.
AD: Rick Hazleton. SID: Kevin F. Kavanagh Jr. III

TRINITY (TEX.) .... San Antonio, TX 78212

Charlie Brock (13 YRS. W-150, L-181)

Trinity (Tex.) Tr.	N19-20	Centre	J23
Dallas	N23	Sewanee■	J28
Colorado College Tr.	N26-27	Oglethorpe■	J30
Southwestern (Tex.)	D 1	Southwestern (Tex.)■	F 1
Austin■	D 4	Rhodes	F 4
Dallas■	D 7	Millsaps	F 6
Loyola (La.)	D18	Sewanee	F11
Austin	J 5	Oglethorpe	F13
Hendrix■	J 9	Fisk■	F18
Rhodes■	J14	Centre■	F20
Millsaps■	J16	Hendrix	F26
Fisk	J21		

Colors: Maroon & White. Nickname: Tigers.
AD: Bob King. SID: James Hill. III

TROY ST. .... Troy, AL 36081

Don Maestri (11 YRS. W-210, L-107)

George Mason	N27	Hofstra	J17
Mississippi St.	N30	Southern Utah■	J22
Southeast Mo. St. Cl	D3-4	Northeastern Ill.■	J24
Mississippi Val.	D 6	Tex.-Pan American■	J27
Auburn	D 9	Buffalo■	J30
Northwestern (La.)■	D11	Alcorn St.■	J31
South Ala.	D14	Alabama St.	F 2
Wright St. Cl.	D17-18	Southern Utah	F 5
New Orleans Cl.	D20-21	Chicago St.■	F12
Mississippi Val.■	J 4	Tex.-Pan American	F21
Alabama St.■	J 6	Alcorn St.	F23
Central Conn. St.	J15	East Coast Conf.	M4-6

Colors: Cardinal, Silver & Black. Nickname: Trojans.
AD: Kenneth Blankenship. SID: Tom Ensey. I

TUFTS .... Medford, MA 02155

Robert Sheldon (5 YRS. W-70, L-52)

Anna Maria■	N23	Wesleyan■	J27
Rochester Inv.	N27-28	Suffolk	J29
Colby	D 3	Babson	F 1
Bowdoin	D 4	Amherst■	F 3
Framingham St.	D 9	MIT	F 8
Clark (Mass.)	D11	Mass.-Boston	F10
Catholic Tr.	J8-9	Williams	F12
Albertus Magnus	J11	Bates■	F16
Middlebury	J15	Middlebury■	F19
Salem St.	J20	Brandeis■	F23
Trinity (Conn.)■	J22	Connecticut Col.■	F26

Colors: Brown & Blue. Nickname: Jumbos.
AD: Rocco Carzo. SID: Paul Sweeney. III

■ Home games on each schedule.

See pages 405–407 for Division I tournament details

TULANE .... New Orleans, LA 70118

Perry Clark (4 YRS. W-63, L-55)

- Centenary■ N27
- Michigan D 2
- Prairie View■ D 4
- Mercer■ D 6
- California Cl. D10-12
- Mississippi St.⊠ D18
- Tennessee St.■ D22
- Lehigh■ D29
- Virginia Tech J 6
- South Fla. J 8
- Va. Commonwealth■ J13
- Cal St. Sacramento■ J15
- Louisville■ J20
- N.C.-Charlotte■ J22
- Fla. Atlantic J27
- Canisius J29
- Virginia Tech■ F 3
- N.C.-Charlotte F 5
- Southeastern La.■ F 7
- Louisville F12
- Ala.-Birmingham■ F16
- Southern Miss.■ F19
- South Fla.■ F24
- Va. Commonwealth F26
- Southern Miss. M 5
- Metro Conf. M11-13
- ⊠ Biloxi, MS

Colors: Olive Green & Sky Blue. Nickname: Green Wave.
AD: Dr. Kevin White. SID: Lenny Vangilder. I

TULSA .... Tulsa, OK 74104

Tubby Smith (2 YRS. W-32, L-27)

- Houston Baptist■ N27
- North Texas D 1
- Oral Roberts D 6
- Southwest Mo. St.■ D11
- Oklahoma St.■ D20
- Arkansas■ D23
- Oklahoma Tr. D29-30
- Va. Commonwealth J 3
- Bradley■ J 6
- Northern Iowa■ J 8
- Drake■ J13
- Creighton J15
- Southern Ill. J20
- Indiana St. J22
- Illinois St.■ J27
- Drake J29
- Bradley F 5
- Illinois St. F 7
- Wichita St.■ F 9
- Southern Ill.■ F12
- Northern Iowa F15
- Southwest Mo. St. F19
- Wichita St. F23
- Creighton■ F26
- Indiana St.■ F28
- Missouri Valley Conf M5-7

Colors: Blue, Red, Gold. Nickname: Golden Hurricane.
AD: Rick Dickson. SID: Don Tomkalski. I

TUSKEGEE .... Tuskegee, AL 36088

Lonnie Williams (3 YRS. W-33, L-49)

- Selma■ N23
- Xavier (La.)■ N29
- Paine■ D 1
- Fort Valley St.■ D 4
- Columbus■ D 6
- Lane■ D 9
- Alabama St. D11
- Albany St. (Ga.)■ J12
- Morehouse J15
- LeMoyne-Owen■ J17
- Clark Atlanta■ J21
- Alabama A&M■ J22
- LeMoyne-Owen J24
- Miles■ J28
- Alabama A&M J29
- Morehouse■ F 1
- Fort Valley St. F 3
- Savannah St. F 5
- Paine F 7
- Alabama St.■ F10
- Morris Brown F14
- Albany St. (Ga.) F16
- Miles F19
- Morris Brown■ F22
- West Ga.■ F24

Colors: Crimson & Gold. Nickname: Golden Tigers.
AD: James Martin. SID: Arnold Houston. II

UCLA .... Los Angeles, CA 90024

Jim Harrick (14 YRS. W-283, L-143)

- Loyola (Cal.)■ N27
- Nevada-Las Vegas■ D 4
- Tennessee St.■ D 8
- Long Beach St.■ D11
- Louisiana St.■ D18
- Houston D20
- North Caro. St.⊠ D28
- Oregon■ J 6
- Oregon St.■ J 8
- Washington St. J13
- Washington J15
- Arizona■ J20
- Arizona St.■ J22
- Stanford J27
- California J30
- Southern Cal■ F 3
- Notre Dame F 5
- Washington■ F10
- Washington St.■ F12
- Arizona St. F17
- Arizona F19
- California■ F24
- Stanford■ F26
- Southern Cal M 3
- Louisville■ M 6
- Oregon St. M10
- Oregon M12
- ⊠ Greensboro, NC

Colors: Navy Blue & Gold. Nickname: Bruins.
AD: Peter Dalis. SID: Marc Dellins. I

UNION (N.Y.) .... Schenectady, NY 12308

Bill Scanlon (20 YRS. W-278, L-214)

- Union (N.Y.) Tr. N19-20
- Vassar■ D 1
- Albany (N.Y.)⊠ D 4
- Wesleyan■ D 8
- Ithaca■ D10
- Williams■ J 4
- Union (N.Y.) Inv. J7-8
- Middlebury J13
- Colby■ J15
- Bowdoin■ J16
- Utica■ J18
- Merchant Marine■ J22
- Hartwick■ J25
- Elmira J29
- Hobart F 1
- Nazareth (N.Y.)■ F 5
- Skidmore F 8
- Hamilton■ F12
- Rensselaer F15
- Williams F19
- Middlebury■ F22
- St. Lawrence F25
- Clarkson F26
- ⊠ Albany, NY

Colors: Garnet. Nickname: Dutchmen.
AD: Dick Sakala. SID: George Cuttita. III

UPPER IOWA .... Fayette, IA 52142

Stu Engen (1 YR. W-11, L-14)

- Iowa Wesleyan■ N23
- Marycrest N27
- Coe■ N30
- N'western (Minn.) D 4
- Pillsbury D 7
- Mt. St. Clare D11
- Clarke D17
- Mt. Mercy■ D18
- Dubuque■ J 7
- Luther■ J 8
- Central (Iowa) J14
- William Penn J15
- Wartburg J21
- Buena Vista■ J22
- N'western (Minn.)■ J29
- Loras F 1
- Simpson■ F 4
- Buena Vista F 5
- Luther F11
- William Penn■ F12
- Central (Iowa)■ F15
- Dubuque F18
- Simpson F19
- Loras■ F25
- Wartburg■ F26

Colors: Blue & White. Nickname: Peacocks.
AD: Mike McCready. SID: Julie Lentz. III

UPSALA .... East Orange, NJ 07019

Hoddy Mahon (7 YRS. W-96, L-81)

- Caldwell N23
- Wilmington (Del.) N30
- King's (Pa.)■ D 2
- Lycoming D 4
- Old Westbury D 8
- Hunter D11
- Montclair St.■ D13
- Jersey City St.■ D15
- Albany (N.Y.)■ J 8
- Drew■ J10
- Scranton J15
- FDU-Madison J19
- Wilkes J22
- Bloomfield J24
- Delaware Valley■ J26
- King's (Pa.) J29
- Drew F 2
- Lycoming■ F 5
- FDU-Madison■ F 9
- Scranton■ F12
- Pratt■ F15
- Delaware Valley F16
- Wilkes■ F19

Colors: Blue & Gray. Nickname: Vikings.
AD: Mike Walsh. SID: Rich Carroll. III

URSINUS .... Collegeville, PA 19426

John Spinella (2 YRS. W-10, L-37)

- Dickinson Cl. N19-20
- Johns Hopkins N23
- Gwynedd Mercy Inv. N26-27
- Phila. Pharmacy N29
- Gettysburg■ D 1
- Frank. & Marsh. J15
- Washington (Md.)■ J18
- Eastern (Pa.) J20
- Dickinson■ J22
- Allentown J24
- Swarthmore J26
- Muhlenberg■ J29
- Western Md. J31
- Haverford F 2
- Wesley■ F 5
- Washington (Md.) F 8
- Alvernia■ F10
- Swarthmore■ F12
- West Chester F14
- Muhlenberg F16
- Haverford■ F19

Colors: Red, Old Gold, Black. Nickname: Bears.
AD: Robert Davidson. SID: Dave Sherman. III

UTAH .... Salt Lake City, UT 84112

Rick Majerus (9 YRS. W-181, L-76)

- Southern Cal Col.■ N27
- UC Irvine■ N30
- Weber St. D 4
- Arizona■ D 9
- Chicago St. D11
- Cardinal Stritch■ D16
- Cal St. Fullerton D18
- Utah St.■ D20
- Texas D29
- UTEP J 3
- New Mexico J 5
- Brigham Young■ J 8
- Air Force■ J13
- Fresno St.■ J15
- Hawaii J20
- San Diego St. J22
- Colorado St.■ J27
- Wyoming■ J29
- Colorado St. F 3
- Wyoming F 5
- Hawaii■ F10
- San Diego St.■ F12
- Fresno St. F17
- Air Force F19
- Brigham Young F26
- UTEP■ M 3
- New Mexico■ M 5
- Western Ath. Conf. M9-12

Colors: Crimson & White. Nickname: Utes.
AD: Chris Hill. SID: Bruce Woodbury. I

UTAH ST. .... Logan, UT 84322

Larry Eustachy (3 YRS. W-61, L-33)

- Colorado St. D 3
- Weber St.■ D 7
- Chadron St.■ D11
- Brigham Young D14
- Lewis & Clark■ D18
- Utah D20
- Wyoming Cowboy Tr. D28-29
- Pacific (Cal.)■ J 3
- San Jose St.■ J 5
- Long Beach St. J 8
- UC Santa Barb. J10
- Cal St. Fullerton■ J15
- UC Irvine■ J17
- New Mexico St. J20
- Nevada-Las Vegas J22
- Nevada J29
- Nevada-Las Vegas■ F 3
- New Mexico St.■ F 5
- UC Irvine F10
- Cal St. Fullerton F12
- Long Beach St.■ F17
- UC Santa Barb.■ F19
- San Jose St. F24
- Pacific (Cal.) F26
- Nevada■ M 5
- Big West Conf. M10-13

Colors: Navy Blue & White. Nickname: Aggies.
AD: Chuck Bell. SID: Craig Hislop. I

■ Home games on each schedule.

See pages 405–407 for Division I tournament details

UTICA .... Utica, NY 13502
Ed Jones (6 YRS. W-84, L-70)

Hamilton Tr.	N20-21	Oswego St.	J31
Clarkson	N23	Hamilton■	F 2
Wilkes■	D 1	Mt. St. Mary (N.Y.)■	F 5
Southern Vt.■	D 3	Hartwick■	F 8
Maritime (N.Y.)■	D 5	Skidmore■	F10
Keuka	D 8	St. John Fisher	F12
Oswego St.■	D11	Ithaca	F15
Oneonta St.■	J12	Keuka■	F19
Union (N.Y.)	J18	Rensselaer■	F21
Elmira	J22	Nazareth (N.Y.)	F23
Pracitical Bible■	J24	Elmira■	F26
St. Lawrence	J26		

Colors: Blue & Orange. Nickname: Pioneers.
AD: James Spartano. SID: Jim Taylor. III

UTICA TECH .... Utica, NY 13502
James Klein (12 YRS. W-140, L-150)

Hamilton Tr.	N20-21	New Paltz St.	J28
Oswego St.	D 7	Oneonta St.■	J29
Buffalo St.■	D11	Oswego St.■	F 4
Warner Southern	J 4	Buffalo St.	F 5
Flagler	J 5	Plattsburgh St.■	F11
Savannah A&D Tr.	J7-8	Potsdam St.	F12
Binghamton■	J14	Geneseo St.■	F15
Cortland St.	J15	Brockport St.	F18
Geneseo St.	J18	Fredonia St.	F19
Brockport St.■	J21	Hamilton■	F23
Fredonia St.■	J22		

Colors: Gold & Brown. Nickname: Wildcats.
AD: Jim Klein. SID: Kevin Grimmer. III

VALDOSTA ST. .... Valdosta, GA 31698
James Dominey (22 YRS. W-348, L-246)

North Fla. Cl.	N26-27	West Ga.	J22
Ala.-Huntsville■	N30	Georgia Col.■	J24
Warner Southern■	D 4	Kennesaw	J26
St. Leo■	D 6	North Ala.■	J29
St. Leo	D11	West Ga.■	J31
Ga. Southern	D14	Mississippi Col.	F 5
Augusta Cl.	D29-30	Livingston	F 7
Kennesaw■	J 5	Lincoln Memorial	F12
North Ala.	J 8	Lincoln Memorial■	F19
Ala.-Huntsville	J10	Georgia Col.	F21
Livingston■	J15	Albany St. (Ga.)	F23
Albany St. (Ga.)■	J17	Mississippi Col.■	F26

Colors: Red & Black. Nickname: Blazers.
AD: Herb Reinhard. SID: Steve Roberts. II

VALPARAISO .... Valparaiso, IN 46383
Homer Drew (17 YRS. W-305, L-225)

Notre Dame	N28	Ill.-Chicago■	J27
Niagara■	D 1	Wis.-Green Bay	J29
Butler■	D 4	Eastern Ill.	J31
Ind.-South Bend■	D 6	Northern Ill.	F 5
Evansville	D11	Wright St.	F 7
Dartmouth■	D18	Wis.-Milwaukee■	F12
Air Force	D30	Western Ill.	F14
Brown■	J 6	Wis.-Green Bay■	F19
Western Ill.■	J10	Eastern Ill.■	F21
Wis.-Milwaukee	J13	Ill.-Chicago	F24
Northern Ill.■	J15	Cleveland St.	F26
Wright St.■	J17	Youngstown St.	F28
Cleveland St.■	J22	Mid-Continent Conf.	M6-8
Youngstown St.■	J24		

Colors: Brown & Gold. Nickname: Crusaders.
AD: William Steinbrecher. SID: Bill Rogers. I

VANDERBILT .... Nashville, TN 37212
Jan van Breda Kolff (2 YRS. W-23, L-29)

Penn St.■	N26	Florida	J29
Tenn.-Martin■	D 1	Arkansas	F 1
Syracuse Carrier Cl.	D3-4	Louisville	F 6
Wake Forest■	D 8	Auburn■	F 9
Georgia Tech⊠	D18	South Caro.	F12
Austin Peay■	D21	Mississippi St.■	F16
Vanderbilt Inv.	D28-29	Kentucky■	F19
Kentucky	J 4	Mississippi	F23
South Caro.■	J 8	Florida■	F26
Alabama	J12	Tennessee	M 1
Louisiana St.■	J15	Georgia■	M 5
Georgia	J19	Southeastern Conf.	M10-13
Tennessee■	J26	⊠ Atlanta, GA	

Colors: Black & Gold. Nickname: Commodores.
AD: Paul Hoolahan. SID: Tony Neely. I

VERMONT .... Burlington, VT 05405
Tom Brennan (12 YRS. W-120, L-204)

Lafayette	N27	New Hampshire	J22
Penn St.	N29	Delaware■	J27
St. Michael's■	D 2	Drexel■	J29
Marist⊠	D 4	American■	F 1
Middlebury■	D 8	Hartford■	F 5
Harvard	D19	Drexel	F11
Nevada-Las Vegas	D21	Delaware	F13
Dartmouth■	D28	New Hampshire■	F17
Yale■	J 2	Maine	F19
Colgate■	J 5	Northeastern■	F24
Dartmouth	J11	Boston U.■	F26
Northeastern	J13	Hartford	M 2
Boston U.	J15	North Atlantic Conf.	M5-9
Maine■	J20	⊠ Albany, NY	

Colors: Green & Gold. Nickname: Catamounts.
AD: Rick Farnham. SID: Dick Whittier. I

VILLANOVA .... Villanova, PA 19085
Steve Lappas (5 YRS. W-64, L-81)

American■	D 1	St. John's (N.Y.)■	F 2
Georgetown	D 4	Boston College■	F 5
Providence■	D 7	Seton Hall	F 8
Temple⊠	D11	Miami (Fla.)	F12
St. Mary's (Cal.)■	D18	Connecticut■	F15
Florida■	D22	Pittsburgh	F19
Arizona St. Cl.	D28-29	Georgetown■	F22
Boston College	J 4	Seton Hall■	F26
St. John's (N.Y.)	J 8	La Salle⊠	F28
Richmond	J11	Providence	M 2
Syracuse■	J15	Miami (Fla.)■	M 5
Pittsburgh■	J22	Big East Conf.	M10-13
Connecticut	J25	⊠ Philadelphia, PA	
Syracuse	J29		

Colors: Blue & White.
Nickname: Wildcats. AD: Gene DeFilippo. SID: James DeLorenzo. I

VIRGINIA .... Charlottesville, VA 22903
Jeff Jones (3 YRS. W-62, L-35)

Connecticut■	N29	Georgia Tech	J23
William & Mary■	D 1	Wake Forest	J26
Rice■	D 4	Maryland■	F 2
Coppin St.■	D 9	Florida St.	F 6
Old Dominion	D11	North Caro. St.	F 9
Stanford	D22	Clemson■	F12
Minnesota■	D28	Duke	F16
Liberty■	D30	North Caro.	F19
Nevada-Las Vegas	J 3	Georgia Tech■	F22
Florida St.■	J 6	Wake Forest■	F26
North Caro. St.■	J 9	Virginia Tech⊠	M 2
Clemson	J12	Maryland	M 5
Duke■	J15	Atlantic Coast Conf.	M10-13
North Caro.■	J19	⊠ Landover, MD	

Colors: Orange & Blue. Nickname: Cavaliers.
AD: Jim Copeland. SID: Rich Murray. I

VA. COMMONWEALTH .... Richmond, VA 23284
Sonny Smith (17 YRS. W-262, L-236)

James Madison■	N27	Southern Miss.■	J27
Radford■	D 1	Louisville■	J29
Liberty	D 3	Old Dominion⊠	J31
Buffalo■	D 7	Evansville	F 2
Siena	D11	Virginia Tech■	F10
Richmond■	D18	N.C.-Charlotte■	F12
George Mason	D22	Virginia Tech	F17
UTEP Cl.	D29-30	Xavier (Ohio)	F23
Tulsa■	J 3	Tulane■	F26
Louisville	J 8	N.C.-Charlotte	M 3
Tulane	J13	South Fla.	M 5
Southern Miss.	J15	Metro Conf.	M11-13
Oklahoma■	J20	⊠ Hampton, VA	
South Fla.■	J22		

Colors: Black & Gold.
Nickname: Rams. AD: Richard Sander. SID: Jim O'Brien. I

VA. MILITARY .... Lexington, VA 24450
Joe Cantafio (7 YRS. W-74, L-124)

Bluefield Col.■	N29	Marshall■	J27
Richmond■	D 1	Appalachian St.	J29
Virginia Tech	D 6	Shenandoah■	F 2
Radford■	D11	East Tenn. St.	F 3
Dayton	D22	Marshall	F 5
Wake Forest	J 5	William & Mary	F 9
Western Caro.	J 8	Tenn.-Chatt.■	F12
Tenn.-Chatt.	J10	Western Caro.■	F14
Appalachian St.■	J12	Ga. Southern■	F19
Citadel	J15	Citadel■	F21
Ga. Southern	J17	Furman■	F26
East Tenn. St.■	J20	Davidson	F28
Davidson■	J22	Southern Conf.	M3-6
Furman	J24		

Colors: Red, White, Yellow. Nickname: Keydets.
AD: Davis Babb. SID: Mike Strickler. I

■ Home games on each schedule.

See pages 405–407 for Division I tournament details

VIRGINIA ST. .... Petersburg, VA 23803
Harold Deane (16 YRS. W-245, L-189)

Fayetteville St.■	N20	Bowie St.	J20
St. Augustine's■	N23	St. Paul's■	J22
Winston-Salem	N26	Dist. Columbia	J26
Johnson Smith	N27	Norfolk St.	J29
Virginia Union	N30	Virginia Union■	F 1
Norfolk St.■	D 4	Elizabeth City St.	F 5
N.C. Central	D 6	Hampton	F 8
Rutgers-Camden	D30	Livingstone	F12
Virginia St. Cl.	J6-8	Bowie St.■	F14
Longwood■	J12	St. Paul's	F16
Elizabeth City St.■	J15	Shaw■	F18
Hampton■	J18		

Colors: Orange & Navy Blue. Nickname: Trojans.
AD: Larry Brooks. SID: Gregory Goings. II

VIRGINIA TECH .... Blacksburg, VA 24061
Bill Foster (26 YRS. W-451, L-283)

West Va.☒	N27	Louisville■	J27
Coastal Caro.■	D 4	Southern Miss.■	J29
Va. Military■	D 6	Tulane	F 3
N.C.-Greensboro■	D 8	Southern Miss.	F 5
Xavier (Ohio)	D18	Va. Commonwealth	F10
East Tenn. St.	D20	Marquette■	F15
Fla. Atlantic	D28	Va. Commonwealth■	F17
Florida Int'l	D30	South Fla.	F19
Tennessee■	J 2	N.C.-Charlotte■	F26
Tulane■	J 6	Virginia ◆	M 2
Texas Christian	J 9	N.C.-Charlotte	M 6
Louisville	J13	Metro Conf.	M11-13
Liberty■	J18	☒ Charleston, WV	
South Fla.■	J20	◆ Landover, MD	
William & Mary	J22		

Colors: Orange & Maroon. Nickname: Hokies, Gobblers.
AD: Dave Braine. SID: Dave Smith. I

VIRGINIA UNION .... Richmond, VA 23220
Dave Robbins (15 YRS. W-371, L-90)

Virginia St.■	N30	Hampton	J22
Va. Union Inv.	D3-4	St. Paul's■	J25
Johnson Smith	D14	Winston-Salem■	J27
Atlantic City Cl.	D17-19	Bowie St.■	J29
Fayetteville St.	J 5	Virginia St.	F 1
Elizabeth City St.■	J 8	St. Augustine's■	F 3
St. Paul's	J11	Norfolk St.	F 5
Hampton■	J15	N.C. Central■	F10
Shaw	J18	Bowie St.	F12
Norfolk St.■	J20	Elizabeth City St.	F16

Colors: Steel & Maroon. Nickname: Panthers.
AD: James Battle. SID: Paul Williams. II

VA. WESLEYAN .... Norfolk, VA 23502
Terry Butterfield (4 YRS. W-57, L-50)

Mary Washington	N20	Salisbury St.■	J19
Chris. Newport■	N23	Lynchburg■	J22
Va. Wesleyan Tr.	N27-28	Bridgewater (Va.)	J24
Roanoke	D 4	Randolph-Macon	J26
East. Mennonite■	D 7	Emory & Henry	J29
Wash. & Lee	J 4	Wash. & Lee■	F 2
Randolph-Macon■	J 6	Guilford	F 5
Guilford■	J 8	Hampden-Sydney■	F 9
Hampden-Sydney	J12	Emory & Henry■	F12
Roanoke■	J15	Bridgewater (Va.)■	F16
East. Mennonite	J17	Lynchburg	F19

Colors: Navy Blue & Silver. Nickname: Blue Marlins.
AD: Donald Forsyth. SID: Tom Palombo. III

WABASH .... Crawfordsville, IN 47933
Mac Petty (20 YRS. W-271, L-219)

Lindenwood	N20	Manchester■	J15
Earlham■	N27	Franklin	J19
Millikin	D 2	Eureka■	J22
Fontbonne	D 4	DePauw■	J26
Wabash Inv.	D10-11	Anderson■	J29
Thomas More■	D20	Rose-Hulman■	F 2
Wabash Tr.	D29-30	Manchester	F 5
Rose-Hulman	J 5	Hanover	F 9
Anderson	J 8	Franklin■	F16
Hanover■	J12	DePauw	F19

Colors: Scarlet & White. Nickname: Little Giants.
AD: Max Servies. SID: Jim Amidon. III

WAGNER .... Staten Island, NY 10301
Tim Capstraw (4 YRS. W-49, L-67)

St. Joseph's(Pa.) Tr	N26-27	Marist■	J22
Manhattan■	D 1	FDU-Teaneck■	J24
Rutgers	D 4	LIU-Brooklyn	J27
Siena■	D 8	St. Francis (N.Y.)	J29
Iona■	D18	Monmouth (N.J.)■	F 5
Miami (Fla.)	D29	Mt. St. Mary's (Md.)■	F10
Robert Morris	J 4	Rider■	F12
St. Francis (Pa.)	J 6	FDU-Teaneck	F16
St. Francis (N.Y.)■	J 8	Marist	F19
LIU-Brooklyn■	J10	St. Francis (Pa.)■	F24
Monmouth (N.J.)	J15	Robert Morris■	F26
Mt. St. Mary's (Md.)	J18	Northeast Conf.	F28-M6
Rider	J20		

Colors: Green & White. Nickname: Seahawks.
AD: Walt Hameline. SID: Scott Morse. I

WAKE FOREST .... Winston-Salem, NC 27109
Dave Odom (7 YRS. W-107, L-90)

Great Alas. Shootout	N24-27	Clemson	J22
Winthrop■	D 1	Virginia■	J26
Richmond■	D 4	North Caro.	J30
Davidson■	D 6	North Caro. St.■	F 2
Vanderbilt	D 8	Rhode Island	F 5
Appalachian St.■	D19	Florida St.■	F10
Marshall■	D22	Duke■	F13
California■	D30	Maryland	F16
Canisius■	J 3	Georgia Tech	F19
Va. Military■	J 5	Clemson■	F22
Florida St.	J 8	Virginia	F26
Duke	J13	North Caro.■	M 2
Maryland■	J15	North Caro. St.	M 5
Georgia Tech■	J19	Atlantic Coast Conf.	M10-13

Colors: Old Gold & Black. Nickname: Demon Deacons.
AD: Ron Wellman. SID: John Justus. I

WARTBURG .... Waverly, IA 50677
Lewis Levick (28 YRS. W-510, L-225)

Wartburg Inv.	N19-20	Buena Vista	J28
Teikyo Westmar Tr.	N26-27	Loras■	J29
Iowa Wesleyan■	N30	Dubuque■	F 1
Dordt■	D 4	Teikyo-Westmar	F 5
N'western (Minn.)	D 7	Central (Iowa)	F11
Marycrest	D11	Luther■	F12
Central (Iowa)■	J 7	William Penn	F18
William Penn■	J 8	Loras	F19
Dubuque	J14	Buena Vista■	F22
Luther	J15	Simpson	F25
Upper Iowa■	J21	Upper Iowa	F26
Simpson■	J22		

Colors: Orange & Black. Nickname: Knights.
AD: Bob Nielson. SID: Duane Schroeder. III

WASHBURN .... Topeka, KS 66621
Bob Chipman (14 YRS. W-331, L-115)

Friends■	N19	Northwest Mo. St.	J22
Hawaii-Hilo Cl.	N26-27	Emporia St.■	J26
Baker■	D 1	Lincoln (Mo.)■	J29
Fort Hays St.■	D 4	Northeast Mo. St.	F 2
Kansas	D 6	Central Mo. St.■	F 5
Mid-America Naz.■	D18	Rockhurst	F 7
Washburn Tr.	D29-30	Mo. Western St.	F 9
Mo. Southern St.	J 5	Mo.-St. Louis	F12
Mo.-St. Louis■	J 8	Missouri-Rolla■	F16
Missouri-Rolla	J12	Pittsburg St.	F19
Pittsburg St.■	J15	Southwest Baptist	F21
Southwest Baptist■	J19	Northwest Mo. St.■	F26

Colors: Yale Blue & White. Nickname: Ichabods.
AD: Rich Johanningmeier. SID: Mary Beth Brutton. II

WASHINGTON .... Seattle, WA 98195
Bob Bender (4 YRS. W-60, L-57)

Montana■	N29	Oregon	J22
Cincinnati	D 3	Washington St.■	J29
Fresno St.	D 7	Arizona St.■	F 3
Idaho■	D18	Arizona■	F 5
Portland	D21	UCLA	F10
Idaho St.	D23	Southern Cal	F12
Washington Tr.	D28-29	Oregon■	F17
Missouri	J 2	Oregon St.■	F19
Stanford	J 6	Washington St.	F26
California	J 8	Arizona	M 3
Southern Cal■	J13	Arizona St.	M 5
UCLA■	J15	California■	M10
Oregon St.	J20	Stanford■	M12

Colors: Purple & Gold. Nickname: Huskies.
AD: Barbara Hedges. SID: Dan Lepse. I

■ Home games on each schedule.

See pages 405–407 for Division I tournament details

WASHINGTON (MD.) .... Chestertown, MD 21620
Tom Finnegan (23 YRS. W-296, L-254)

Opponent	Date	Opponent	Date
Widener Tr.	N19-20	Johns Hopkins■	J20
Frostburg St.■	N23	Gettysburg	J22
Md.-Balt. County	N27	Haverford■	J26
Delaware	N29	Swarthmore■	J29
Western Md.■	D 4	Wesley	F 3
Muhlenberg	D 7	Muhlenberg■	F 5
Washington (Md.) Tr.	D10-11	Ursinus■	F 8
Catholic Tr.	J8-9	Haverford	F12
Gallaudet	J11	Swarthmore	F16
Dickinson	J15	Frank. & Marsh.	F19
Ursinus	J18		

Colors: Maroon & Black. Nickname: Shoremen.
AD: Geoff Miller. SID: Sarah Feyerherm. III

WASHINGTON (MO.) .... St.Louis, MO 63130
Mark Edwards (12 YRS. W-173, L-137)

Opponent	Date	Opponent	Date
Washington (Mo.) Tr.	N19-20	Case Reserve	J23
Millikin☒	N23	Emory■	J28
Rhodes	N27	Carnegie Mellon■	J30
Webster	N30	MacMurray	F 1
Washington (Mo.) Cl.	D3-4	Rochester■	F 6
Maryville (Mo.)■	D11	Mo.-Kansas City	F 9
Chicago	J 4	Carnegie Mellon	F11
Aurora	J 6	Emory	F13
Johns Hopkins■	J 9	Brandeis■	F18
New York U.	J14	New York U.■	F20
Brandeis	J16	Chicago■	F26
Rochester	J21	☒ Centralia, IL	

Colors: Red & Green. Nickname: Bears.
AD: John Schael. SID: Mike Wolf. III

WASHINGTON ST. .... Pullman, WA 99164
Kelvin Sampson (10 YRS. W-156, L-137)

Opponent	Date	Opponent	Date
San Juan Shootout	N26-28	Washington	J29
Pittsburg St.■	D 2	Arizona■	F 3
Alabama☒	D 4	Arizona St.■	F 5
Idaho■	D 7	Southern Cal	F10
Indiana Cl.	D10-11	UCLA	F12
Eastern Mich.■	D19	Oregon St.■	F17
Fresno St. Cl.	D27-28	Oregon■	F19
Alas. Anchorage■	J 3	Washington■	F26
California	J 6	Arizona St.	M 3
Stanford	J 8	Arizona	M 5
UCLA■	J13	Stanford■	M10
Southern Cal■	J15	California■	M12
Oregon	J20	☒ Spokane, WA	
Oregon St.	J22		

Colors: Crimson & Gray. Nickname: Cougars.
AD: Jim Livengood. SID: Donna Murphy. I

WASH. & JEFF. .... Washington, PA 15301
Tom Reiter (1ST YR. AS HEAD COACH)

Opponent	Date	Opponent	Date
Allegheny	N19	Waynesburg■	J19
Carnegie Mellon☒	N20	Thiel	J21
Point Park■	N24	Carnegie Mellon■	J26
St. Vincent■	N29	Grove City	J29
Marietta	D 1	Bethany (W.Va.)■	F 2
La Roche■	D 2	Waynesburg	F 5
Penn St.-Behrend■	D 6	Thiel■	F 9
Oberlin	D11	Penn St.-Behrend	F12
Frostburg St.■	J 5	Grove City■	F16
Wash. & Jeff. Tr.	J7-8	Bethany (W.Va.)	F19
La Roche	J12	☒ Meadville, PA	
Point Park	J17		

Colors: Red & Black. Nickname: Presidents.
AD: John Luckhardt. SID: Susan Isola. III

WASH. & LEE .... Lexington, VA 24450
Verne Canfield (29 YRS. W-441, L-307)

Opponent	Date	Opponent	Date
Johns Hopkins	N19-20	Emory & Henry	J19
Emory	N23	Bridgewater (Va.)■	J21
Bridgewater (Va.)	N27	Catholic■	J23
Hampden-Sydney	D 1	Hampden-Sydney■	J26
Guilford	D 4	Guilford■	J29
Emory & Henry■	D 8	Va. Wesleyan	F 2
Amherst■	J 2	East. Mennonite■	F 5
Va. Wesleyan■	J 4	Lynchburg■	F 9
Roanoke■	J 8	Roanoke	F12
Mary Washington	J10	East. Mennonite	F16
Lynchburg	J12	Randolph-Macon	F19
Randolph-Macon■	J15		

Colors: Royal Blue & White. Nickname: Generals.
AD: Mike Walsh. SID: Brian Logue. III

WAYNE ST. (MICH.) .... Detroit, MI 48202
Ron Hammye (5 YRS. W-76, L-70)

Opponent	Date	Opponent	Date
IU/PU-Ft. Wayne■	N23	Grand Valley St.	J22
Detroit Mercy	N27	Northern Mich.■	J27
Madonna■	N29	Michigan Tech■	J29
Northern Mich.	D 2	Lake Superior St.	F 3
Michigan Tech	D 4	Oakland	F 5
Lake Superior St.■	D 9	Calvin	F 9
Oakland■	D11	Northwood■	F12
Mich.-Dearborn■	J 5	Findlay■	F14
Northwood	J 8	Saginaw Valley	F17
Saginaw Valley■	J13	Ferris St.■	F19
Ferris St.	J15	Hillsdale	F24
Hillsdale■	J20	Grand Valley St.■	F26

Colors: Green & Gold. Nickname: Tartars.
AD: Bob Brennan. SID: Richard Thompson, Jr. II

WAYNE ST. (NEB.) .... Wayne, NE 68787
Mike Brewen (3 YRS. W-25, L-57)

Opponent	Date	Opponent	Date
Northern St.■	N20	Minn.-Morris■	J22
Denver Cl.	N26-27	Briar Cliff	J26
Wis.-Parkside■	D 1	Northern St.	J29
Mankato St.	D 4	Quincy■	F 2
Morningside■	D 8	Bemidji St.	F 5
South Dak. St.■	D11	Winona St.■	F 9
St. Francis (Ill.)	D18	Southwest St.	F12
North Dak. Cl.	D29-30	Briar Cliff■	F16
Bemidji St.■	J 8	Minn.-Morris	F19
Dana■	J10	Neb.-Kearney■	F26
Winona St.	J12	Neb.-Kearney	M 2
Southwest St.■	J15	Quincy	M 5
Moorhead St.	J19		

Colors: Black & Gold. Nickname: Wildcats.
AD: Pete Chapman. SID: Dean Watson. II

WAYNESBURG .... Waynesburg, PA 15370
Rudy Marisa (24 YRS. W-407, L-207)

Opponent	Date	Opponent	Date
Frostburg St. Inv.	N19-20	Grove City■	J26
Valley Forge Chrst.■	D 4	Bethany (W.Va.)■	J29
Lake Erie■	D18	Thiel	F 2
Marietta Tr.	D29-30	Wash. & Jeff.■	F 5
La Roche	J 5	Point Park■	F 7
Penn St.-Behrend	J 8	Frostburg St.■	F 9
Kenyon	J15	Grove City	F12
La Roche■	J17	Bethany (W.Va.)	F16
Wash. & Jeff.	J19	Thiel■	F19
Lake Erie	J22		

Colors: Orange & Black. Nickname: Yellowjackets.
AD: Rudy Marisa. SID: To be named. III

WEBER ST. .... Ogden, UT 84408
Ron Abegglen (7 YRS. W-145, L-66)

Opponent	Date	Opponent	Date
Great Alas. Shootout	N24-27	Montana■	J20
Central Wash.■	D 1	Montana St.■	J22
Utah■	D 4	Idaho	J27
Utah St.	D 7	Eastern Wash.	J29
Baylor Inv.	D10-11	Northern Ariz.■	F 4
Oregon Tech■	D15	Boise St.■	F10
Portland	D18	Idaho St.■	F12
Coast Guard■	D20	Montana St.	F17
Brigham Young	D21	Montana	F19
Purdue■	D30	Eastern Wash.■	F24
San Diego■	J 3	Idaho■	F26
Gonzaga	J 6	Northern Ariz.	M 5
Idaho St.	J13	Big Sky Conf.	M10-12
Boise St.	J15		

Colors: Purple & White. Nickname: Wildcats.
AD: Tom Stewart. SID: Brad Larsen. I

WEBSTER .... Webster Groves, MO 63119
Tom Hart (2 YRS. W-7, L-34)

Opponent	Date	Opponent	Date
Millikin	N20	MacMurray■	J15
Central Meth.■	N23	Fontbonne	J17
Millsaps■	N27	Maryville (Mo.)■	J20
Washington (Mo.)■	N30	Westminster (Mo.)■	J22
DePauw■	D 4	Parks	J27
Harris-Stowe■	D 8	Fontbonne■	J29
Lawrence■	D11	Principia■	F 3
Illinois Col.	D18	Blackburn	F 5
Carroll (Wis.)	J 3	MacMurray	F10
Hanover	J 5	Maryville (Mo.)	F12
Principia	J 8	Westminster (Mo.)	F17
Blackburn■	J13	Parks■	F19

Colors: Gold, Navy Blue & White. Nickname: Gorloks.
AD: Elizabeth Alden. SID: To be named. III

■ Home games on each schedule.

See pages 405–407 for Division I tournament details

WENTWORTH INST. .... Boston, MA 02115

Frank Nestor (12 YRS. W-98, L-184)

St. John Fisher Tr. N20-21
Coast Guard N23
Fitchburg St.■ N29
Nichols .... D 1
Eastern Nazarene .... D 3
Worcester Tech .... D 9
Bri'water (Mass.)■ D11
Suffolk■ J13
Curry■ J15
Eastern Nazarene■ J18
New England Col. J20
Gordon J22
Roger Williams■ J26
Anna Maria J29
Salve Regina■ .... F 1
Curry .... F 3
MIT■ .... F 5
New England Col.■ .... F 9
Anna Maria■ F12
Roger Williams F15
Salve Regina F17
Gordon■ F19

Colors: Black & Gold. Nickname: Leopards.
AD: Lee Conrad. SID: Elaine Johnson. III

WESLEY .... Dover, DE 19901

James Wentworth (8 YRS. W-66, L-117)

Hampden-Sydney Cl. N19-20
Catholic N23
Frostburg St.■ N29
Goucher .... D 2
York (Pa.) Cl. D4-5
St. Mary's (Md.)■ .... D 7
Elizabethtown Cl. D10-11
Western Md. J13
Centenary (N.J.)■ J15
Marymount (Va.) J22
Holy Family J24
Allentown■ J27
Lincoln (Pa.) .... F 1
Washington (Md.)■ .... F 3
Ursinus .... F 5
Salisbury St.■ F10
Chowan■ F12
Frostburg St. F14
Messiah■ F22

Colors: Navy Blue & White. Nickname: Wolverines.
AD: Richard Szlasa. SID: Richard Biscayart. III

WESLEYAN .... Middletown, CT 06457

Herb Kenny (25 YRS. W-290, L-256)

Muhlenberg Tr. N19-20
Middlebury■ N27
Western Conn. St. .... D 2
Worcester Tech .... D 4
Union (N.Y.) .... D 8
Trinity (Conn.) Cl. J14-15
Trinity (Conn.)■ J18
Clark (Mass.) J20
Vassar■ J22
Tufts J27
Williams■ J29
Albertus Magnus .... F 2
Colby■ .... F 4
Bates■ .... F 5
Coast Guard■ .... F 8
Amherst F12
Connecticut Col.■ F15
Western New Eng. F17
Amherst■ F19
Trinity (Conn.) F22
Williams F26

Colors: Red & Black. Nickname: Cardinals.
AD: John Biddiscombe. SID: Brian Katten. III

WEST CHESTER .... West Chester, PA 19380

Dick DeLaney (6 YRS. W-94, L-69)

West Chester Tr. N19-20
Alvernia■ N30
Longwood Tr. D3-4
Eastern (Pa.) .... D 6
Shippensburg■ .... D 8
Holy Names■ D11
Phila. Textile■ D14
Bentley Tr. D28-29
Mercyhurst Tr. J7-8
Kutztown■ J12
Mansfield■ J15
Cheyney J19
Millersville■ J22
Bloomsburg J29
East Stroudsburg■ .... F 2
Mansfield .... F 5
Kutztown .... F 9
Cheyney■ F12
Ursinus■ F14
Millersville F19
East Stroudsburg F23
Bloomsburg■ F26

Colors: Purple & Gold. Nickname: Golden Rams.
AD: William E. Lide. SID: Tom Di Camillo. II

WEST GA. .... Carrollton, GA 30117

Ed Murphy (14 YRS. W-220, L-181)

West Georgia Cl. N19-20
Ga. Southwestern N23
Talladega .... D 4
Ga. Southwestern■ .... D 7
Clayton St.■ D13
Birmingham So. Tr. D30-31
Ala.-Huntsville .... J 8
North Ala. J10
Delta St.■ J15
Livingston■ J17
Wofford J19
Valdosta St.■ J22
Wofford■ J26
Columbus J29
Valdosta St. J31
Lincoln Memorial .... F 5
Talladega■ .... F 7
Columbus■ .... F 9
Delta St. F12
Livingston F14
Ala.-Huntsville■ F19
Lincoln Memorial■ F21
Tuskegee F24
North Ala.■ F26

Colors: Red & Blue. Nickname: Braves.
AD: David Dugan. SID: Ken Skinner. II

WEST LIBERTY ST. .... West Liberty, WV 26074

Dan Petri (1 YR. W-12 , L-15)

Wheeling Jesuit Tr. N26-27
Wheeling Jesuit■ .... D 1
Malone■ .... D 8
Point Park D10
Charleston (W.Va.)■ .... J 8
Glenville St. J10
Concord■ J14
Bluefield St.■ J15
Shepherd■ J17
Fairmont St. J19
Davis & Elkins■ J22
Salem Teikyo J24
Alderson-Broaddus■ J26
West Va. Wesleyan J29
West Va. Tech J31
Pitt.-Johnstown .... F 2
West Va. St.■ .... F 5
Shepherd .... F 7
Wheeling Jesuit .... F 9
Fairmont St.■ F12
Davis & Elkins F14
Salem Teikyo■ F16
Alderson-Broaddus F19

Colors: Gold & Black. Nickname: Hilltoppers.
AD: James Watson. SID: Lynn Ullom. II

WEST TEX. A&M .... Canyon, TX 79016

Rick Cooper (6 YRS. W-152, L-48)

Mary Hardin-Baylor■ N19
Lubbock Chrst. N22
Colorado St. N27
Langston■ D11
Lubbock Chrst.■ D14
Southern Colo.■ D18
Southern Colo. .... J 5
Oklahoma S&A■ .... J 8
Oklahoma St. J10
Tarleton St. J12
Cameron J15
Central Okla. J17
Eastern N. Mex.■ J20
East Tex. St.■ J22
Texas A&M-Kingsville■ J24
Abilene Christian J29
Angelo St. J31
Abilene Christian■ .... F 5
Angelo St.■ .... F 7
Tarleton St.■ F10
Cameron■ F12
Central Okla.■ F14
Texas A&M-Kingsville F19
East Tex. St. F21
Eastern N. Mex. F26

Colors: Maroon & White. Nickname: Buffaloes.
AD: Mike Chandler. SID: To be named. II

WEST VA. .... Morgantown, WV 26507

Gale Catlett (21 YRS. W-429, L-201)

Virginia Tech☒ N27
Robert Morris■ .... D 1
South Ala.■ .... D 9
Pittsburgh■ D11
Ohio■ D18
Mt. St. Mary's (Md.)■ D28
Ohio St. D30
Rhode Island■ .... J 3
Temple .... J 6
St. Bonaventure■ .... J 9
Massachusetts■ J13
Geo. Washington■ J16
Marshall☒ J19
St. Joseph's (Pa.) J22
Duquesne■ J26
St. Bonaventure J29
Geo. Washington .... F 1
Marquette .... F 5
Temple■ .... F 8
Rutgers F12
Fla. Atlantic■ F14
Duquesne F18
Massachusetts F20
Rhode Island F24
Rutgers■ F26
St. Joseph's (Pa.)■ .... M 2
Atlantic 10 Conf. M5-10
☒ Charleston, WV

Colors: Old Gold & Blue. Nickname: Mountaineers.
AD: Ed Pastilong. SID: Shelly Poe. I

WEST VA. ST. .... Institute, WV 25112

Robert Marshall (1 YR. W-5, L-22)

Charleston (W.Va.) N29
Coppin St. .... D 1
West Va. Wesleyan .... D 4
Rio Grande .... D 6
Cheyney .... D 8
Central St. (Ohio)■ D10
Wheeling Jesuit■ .... J 3
Virginia St. Cl. J6-8
Shepherd■ J10
Alderson-Broaddus■ J12
Fairmont St. J15
Salem Teikyo J19
Bluefield St.■ J22
Concord J24
West Va. Tech■ J26
Alderson-Broaddus J29
Glenville St.■ .... F 2
West Liberty St. .... F 5
Davis & Elkins .... F 7
Charleston (W.Va.)■ .... F 9
Salem Teikyo■ F12
Bluefield St. F14
Concord■ F16
West Va. Tech F19

Colors: Old Gold & Black. Nickname: Yellow Jackets.
AD: Gregory K.P. Smith. SID: Steven D. Rader. II

WEST VA. TECH .... Montgomery, WV 25136

Tom Sutherland (12 YRS. W-209, L-155)

Queens (N.C.) N20
David Lipscomb N22
Gannon Cl. N26-27
Concord .... D 1
Mercyhurst Cl. D3-4
Bluefield Col.■ .... D 7
Bluefield St.■ D11
Wheeling Jesuit .... J 8
Davis & Elkins J10
Shepherd■ J12
Salem Teikyo J15
Glenville St.■ J19
Charleston (W.Va.) J22
West Va. Wesleyan■ J24
West Va. St. J26
Fairmont St. J29
West Liberty St.■ J31
Concord■ .... F 2
Alderson-Broaddus■ .... F 5
Bluefield St. .... F 7
Glenville St. F12
Charleston (W.Va.)■ F14
West Va. Wesleyan F16
West Va. St.■ F19

Colors: Royal Blue & Gold. Nickname: Golden Bears.
AD: Terry Rupert. SID: Frank Costa. II

■ Home games on each schedule.

See pages 405–407 for Division I tournament details

WEST VA. WESLEYAN .... Buckhannon, WV 26201

Charles Miller (12 YRS. W-90, L-176)

Clarion Cl.	N26-27	Concord■	J22
Rio Grande	D 1	West Va. Tech	J24
West Va. St.■	D 4	Davis & Elkins■	J26
Fairmont St.	D 6	West Liberty St.■	J29
Slippery Rock■	D 8	Longwood■	J31
Glenville St.	D13	Charleston (W.Va.)	F 2
Alderson-Broaddus	J 8	Salem Teikyo	F 5
Wheeling Jesuit■	J10	Glenville St.■	F 9
Salem Teikyo■	J12	Bluefield St.■	F12
Shepherd	J15	Concord	F14
Fairmont St.■	J17	West Va. Tech■	F16
Bluefield St.	J19	Davis & Elkins	F19

Colors: Orange & Black. Nickname: Bobcats.
AD: George Klebez. SID: Megan Britt. II

WESTERN CARO. .... Cullowhee, NC 28723

Benny Dees (10 YRS. W-171, L-114)

Erskine■	N29	Ga. Southern■	J24
Georgia Tech	D 2	Appalachian St.	J26
Georgia	D 4	Furman■	J29
Coker■	D 6	Davidson■	J31
Tennessee	D17	Appalachian St.■	F 5
Minnesota■	D19	East Tenn. St.■	F 7
Duke	D30	Marshall	F12
East Caro.	J 3	Va. Military	F14
Davidson	J 5	Tenn.-Chatt.■	F19
Va. Military■	J 8	East Tenn. St.	F23
Marshall■	J10	Ga. Southern	F26
Furman	J13	Citadel	F28
Tenn.-Chatt.	J15	Southern Conf.	M3-6
Citadel■	J22		

Colors: Purple & Gold. Nickname: Catamounts.
AD: Larry L. Travis. SID: Steve White. I

WESTERN CONN. ST. .... Danbury, CT 06810

Bob Campbell (9 YRS. W-189, L-54)

Johns Hopkins	N19-20	Eastern Conn. St.■	J18
Westfield St.■	N30	Plymouth St.	J22
Wesleyan■	D 2	Rhode Island Col.	J25
Mass.-Boston	D 4	Albertus Magnus	J27
Manhattanville	D 8	Mass.-Boston■	J29
Mass.-Dartmouth	D11	Mt. St. Mary (N.Y.)■	F 1
Wm. Paterson	D14	Mass.-Dartmouth■	F 5
Western Conn. St. Tr	D29-30	Eastern Conn. St.	F 8
Lehman	J 8	Southern Me.	F12
Clark (Mass.)■	J11	Rhode Island Col.■	F15
Southern Me.■	J15	Plymouth St.■	F19

Colors: Blue & White. Nickname: Colonials.
AD: Ed Farrington. SID: Scott Ames. III

WESTERN ILL. .... Macomb, IL 61455

Jim Kerwin (1 YR. W-7, L-20)

Northwestern	N29	Cleveland St.	J29
Ball St. Cardinal Cl	D3-4	Youngstown St.	J31
Augustana (Ill.)■	D 7	Wright St.	F 5
Dayton	D18	Ill.-Chicago■	F 7
Chicago St.■	D20	Detroit Mercy■	F 9
Iowa St.	J 5	Wis.-Green Bay■	F12
Wis.-Green Bay	J 8	Valparaiso■	F14
Valparaiso	J10	Cleveland St.■	F19
Wright St.■	J15	Youngstown St.■	F21
Ill.-Chicago	J17	Northern Ill.■	F24
Eastern Ill.■	J22	Eastern Ill.	F26
Wis.-Milwaukee■	J24	Wis.-Milwaukee	F28
Northern Ill.	J27	Mid-Continent Conf.	M6-8

Colors: Purple & Gold. Nickname: Leathernecks.
AD: Gil Peterson. SID: Larry Heimburger. I

WESTERN KY. .... Bowling Green, KY 42101

Ralph Willard (3 YRS. W-61, L-31)

Pre-Season NIT	N17-26	Southwestern La.■	J24
North Fla.■	D 8	Lamar■	J29
Ball St.■	D11	Oral Roberts■	F 1
South Ala.	D18	Southwestern La.	F 5
Louisville	D22	Louisiana Tech	F10
Indiana Hoosier Cl.	D27-28	Jacksonville■	F12
Ala.-Birmingham	J 3	Kansas St.■	F15
South Ala.■	J 6	Ark.-Lit. Rock	F17
Arkansas St.■	J 8	Arkansas St.	F19
Ark.-Lit. Rock■	J10	Lamar	F24
New Orleans	J13	New Orleans■	F26
Jacksonville	J15	Tex.-Pan American■	M 1
Louisiana Tech■	J20	Sun Belt Conf.	M4-8
Tex.-Pan American	J22		

Colors: Red & White. Nickname: Hilltoppers.
AD: Jim Richards. SID: Paul Just. I

WESTERN MD. .... Westminster, MD 21157

Nick Zoulias (4 YRS. W-32, L-64)

Frostburg St. Inv.	N19-20	Frank. & Marsh.■	J18
Swarthmore	N23	Haverford■	J22
Muhlenberg■	N30	Johns Hopkins	J26
Washington (Md.)	D 4	Catholic■	J29
Dickinson■	D 7	Ursinus■	J31
Marymount (Va.)	D 9	Gettysburg■	F 2
Gallaudet■	D11	Dickinson	F 5
Radford	D18	Frank. & Marsh.	F 8
Lebanon Valley Tr.	J7-8	Johns Hopkins■	F12
Mary Washington■	J11	St. Mary's (Md.)■	F15
Wesley■	J13	Gettysburg	F19

Colors: Green & Gold. Nickname: Green Terrors.
AD: Richard Carpenter. SID: Scott Deitch. III

WESTERN MICH. .... Kalamazoo, MI 49008

Bob Donewald (15 YRS. W-259, L-183)

Pre-Season NIT	N17-26	Toledo■	J26
Purdue Inv.	D3-4	Kent	J29
Evansville	D 8	Ball St.■	F 2
Ill.-Chicago■	D11	Akron	F 5
Liberty■	D21	Ohio	F 9
Morehead St.■	D27	Central Mich.■	F12
Eastern Ill.	D30	Bowling Green	F16
Chicago St.■	J 2	Eastern Mich.■	F19
Miami (Ohio)	J 5	Toledo	F23
Akron■	J 8	Kent■	F26
Ohio■	J12	Ball St.	M 2
Central Mich.	J15	Miami (Ohio)■	M 5
Bowling Green■	J19	Mid-American Conf.	M8-12
Eastern Mich.	J22		

Colors: Brown & Gold. Nickname: Broncos.
AD: Dan Meinert. SID: John Beatty. I

WESTERN NEW ENG. .... Springfield, MA 01119

Brett Bishop (1ST YR. AS HEAD COACH)

Westfield St.■	N20	Coast Guard■	J27
North Adams St.■	N23	Worcester St.	J29
Gordon	N30	Albertus Magnus■	J31
Fitchburg St.■	D 2	Norwich	F 3
Amherst■	D 7	Coast Guard	F 5
Babson	D10	Connecticut Col.■	F 8
Framingham St.	D13	Babson■	F10
Worcester Tech■	J15	MIT■	F12
MIT	J19	Worcester Tech	F15
Bowdoin	J21	Wesleyan■	F17
Colby	J22	Norwich■	F19
Clark (Mass.)■	J25	Nichols	F22

Colors: Navy Blue & Gold. Nickname: Golden Bears.
AD: Eric Geldart. SID: Gene Gumbs. III

WESTERN ST. .... Gunnison, CO 81230

Jay Helman (4 YRS. W-59, L-56)

Southern Utah	N26	Fort Hays St.	J22
Fort Lewis	N29	Colorado Mines	J27
Southern Colo. Tr.	D3-4	Chadron St.	J29
Regis (Colo.)	D15	Southern Colo.■	F 2
Metro St. Tr.	D17-18	Fort Hays St.■	F 5
Grand Canyon Cl.	D30-31	Adams St.	F11
Eastern N. Mex.■	J 3	N.M. Highlands	F12
Mesa St.■	J 7	Colorado Mines■	F18
Fort Lewis■	J 8	Chadron St.■	F19
Adams St.■	J14	Southern Colo.	F22
N.M. Highlands■	J15	Mesa St.	F26

Colors: Crimson & Slate. Nickname: Mountaineers.
AD: Curtiss Mallory. SID: J.W. Campbell. II

WESTFIELD ST. .... Westfield, MA 01085

Robert Lawless (7 YRS. W-91, L-81)

Western New Eng.	N20	Fitchburg St.	J22
Southern Vt.	N22	Wheaton (Mass.)	J26
Western Conn. St.	N30	Framingham St.	J29
Williams Inv.	D3-4	North Adams St.■	F 1
Mass.-Boston	D 9	Bri'water (Mass.)	F 5
Amherst■	D11	Worcester St.■	F 8
Albertus Magnus	J 8	Salem St.	F10
Bri'water (Mass.)■	J11	Fitchburg St.■	F12
Worcester St.	J15	Framingham St.■	F17
Salem St.■	J18	North Adams St.	F19
Rhode Island Col.■	J20		

Colors: Navy & White. Nickname: Owls.
AD: F. Paul Bogan. SID: Mickey Curtis. III

■ Home games on each schedule.

See pages 405–407 for Division I tournament details

WESTMINSTER (MO.) .... Fulton, MO 65251

Jim McEwen (9 YRS. W-134, L-124)

Rhodes Tr. N19-20
Greenville N29
Northeast Mo. St. .... D 4
Fontbonne .... D 7
Missouri-Rolla .... D 8
Westminster Cl. D10-12
Parks■ J13
Greenville■ J17
Principia■ J20
Webster J22
Blackburn J25
MacMurray■ J27
Maryville (Mo.) J29
Central Bible (Mo.) J31
Blackburn■ .... F 3
Parks .... F 5
Eureka .... F 8
Fontbonne■ F10
Principia F12
Maryville (Mo.)■ F15
Webster■ F17
MacMurray F19

Colors: Blue & White. Nickname: Blue Jays.
AD: Jim McEwen. SID: Bruce Hackmann. III

WHEATON (ILL.) .... Wheaton, IL 60187

Bill Harris (8 YRS. W-150, L-89)

Barat■ N20
Calvin N23
Lake Forest .... D 1
Anderson Tr. D3-4
Hope■ .... D 7
Principia■ .... D 9
Illinois Tech■ D11
Whittier Cl. J7-8
Elmhurst■ J11
Ill. Wesleyan■ J15
North Park J18
Augustana (Ill.) J22
Millikin J26
North Central■ J29
Carthage .... F 1
Elmhurst .... F 4
Ill. Wesleyan .... F 8
Barat F10
North Park■ F12
Augustana (Ill.)■ F15
Millikin■ F19
North Central F22
Carthage■ F26

Colors: Orange & Blue. Nickname: Crusaders.
AD: Tony Ladd. SID: Steve Schwepker. III

WHEATON (MASS.) .... Norton, MA 02766

Roy Dow (4 YRS. W-43, L-60)

Colby Tr. N20-21
Assumption N30
Wheaton (Mass.) Tr. D4-5
Salem St. .... D 9
Framingham St. D11
Ferrum⊠ .... J 5
Pfeiffer .... J 8
Southern Me.■ J17
Eastern Conn. St.■ J20
Nichols J22
Westfield St.■ J26
Skidmore J29
Connecticut Col.■ .... F 1
Rhode Island Col. .... F 3
Brandeis .... F 8
Colby■ F11
Bowdoin■ F12
Suffolk F15
Trinity (Conn.)■ F19
Colby-Sawyer F23
Clark (Mass.)■ F26
⊠ Rocky Mount, VA

Colors: Royal & White. Nickname: Lyons.
AD: Chad Yowell. SID: To be named. III

WHEELING JESUIT .... Wheeling, WV 26003

Jay DeFruscio (6 YRS. W-104, L-75)

West Chester Tr. N19-20
Wheeling Jesuit Tr. N26-27
West Liberty St. .... D 1
Shepherd■ .... D 6
Clarion D11
West Va. St. .... J 3
Ohio Valley College■ .... J 6
West Va. Tech■ .... J 8
West Va. Wesleyan J10
Bluefield St.■ J12
Concord■ J15
Davis & Elkins J19
Salem Teikyo■ J22
Alderson-Broaddus J24
Fairmont St.■ J26
Glenville St. J29
Pitt.-Johnstown■ J31
Shepherd .... F 3
Charleston (W.Va.) .... F 5
West Liberty St.■ .... F 9
Davis & Elkins■ F12
Salem Teikyo F14
Alderson-Broaddus■ F16
Fairmont St. F19

Colors: Crimson & Gold. Nickname: Cardinals.
AD: Jay DeFruscio. SID: Jeff Kepreos. II

WHITTIER .... Whittier, CA 90608

Rock Carter (1ST YR. AS HEAD COACH)

Johns Hopkins Cl. N19-20
Azusa-Pacific■ N23
Pt. Loma Nazarene N30
Chapman .... D 7
La Sierra .... D 9
UC Santa Cruz■ D11
Christ-Irvine■ D20
UC San Diego .... J 4
Whittier Cl. J7-8
Redlands J12
Pomona-Pitzer■ J15
Cal Lutheran J19
Claremont-M-S J22
Cal Tech■ J26
La Verne■ J29
Occidental .... F 2
Redlands■ .... F 5
Pomona-Pitzer .... F 9
Cal Lutheran■ F12
Claremont-M-S■ F16
Cal Tech F19
La Verne F21
Occidental■ F24

Colors: Purple & Gold. Nickname: Poets.
AD: Dave Jacobs. SID: Rock Carter. III

WICHITA ST. .... Wichita, KS 67260

Scott Thompson (6 YRS. W-75, L-96)

Hardin-Simmons■ N27
Southern Methodist .... D 4
Coppin St.■ .... D 6
Nebraska D11
Southwest Mo. St. D18
Southern Ill.■ D22
Wichita St. Tr. D29-30
Mo.-Kansas City .... J 4
Bradley■ .... J 8
Kansas St. J12
Northern Iowa■ J15
Indiana St. J20
Southern Ill. J22
Creighton■ J24
Northern Iowa J27
Illinois St.■ J29
Drake■ .... F 2
Creighton .... F 5
Tulsa .... F 9
Southwest Mo. St.■ F12
Illinois St. F17
Bradley F19
Tulsa■ F23
Indiana St.■ F26
Drake F28
Missouri Valley Conf M5-7

Colors: Yellow & Black. Nickname: Shockers.
AD: Bill Belknap. SID: Scott Schumacher. I

WIDENER .... Chester, PA 19013

C. Alan Rowe (28 YRS. W-465, L-268)

Widener Tr. N19-20
Drexel N27
Albright■ N30
Delaware .... D 8
Susquehanna D11
Staten Island Cl. D29-30
Trenton St. Cl. J7-8
Elizabethtown■ J12
Juniata J15
Lebanon Valley J18
Messiah J22
Moravian■ J26
Albright J29
Elizabethtown .... F 2
Susquehanna■ .... F 5
Lebanon Valley■ .... F 9
Juniata■ F12
Moravian F16
Messiah■ F19

Colors: Widener Blue & Gold. Nickname: Pioneers.
AD: Bruce Bryde. SID: John Douglas. III

WILEY .... Marshall, TX 75670

Mark Cook (4 YRS. W-29, L-68)

La. Christian■ N19
East Tex. Bapt.■ N23
La. Christian N30
Louisiana Tech .... D 1
Rust■ .... D 4
LeTourneau .... D 7
Centenary .... D 9
Rust D11
Jarvis Christian■ J15
Paul Quinn J19
Texas Col. J26
Ambassador■ J27
Philander Smith■ J29
Texas Col.■ .... F 1
Paul Quinn■ .... F 5
Ambassador F10
Ark. Baptist■ F12
Ark. Baptist F14
Philander Smith F15
East Tex. Bapt. F17
Jarvis Christian F19
Southwest Adventist F21

Colors: Purple & White. Nickname: Wildcats.
AD: W.M. Owens. SID: S.A. Anderson. III

WILKES .... Wilkes-Barre, PA 18766

Jerry Rickrode (1 YR. W-16, L-9)

Stony Brook Inv. N20-21
Messiah■ N29
Utica .... D 1
Drew■ .... D 4
Allentown■ .... D 6
Susquehanna .... D 8
Pracitical Bible■ D11
Wilkes Cl. J7-8
Lycoming J12
Delaware Valley J15
King's (Pa.)■ J19
Upsala■ J22
FDU-Madison■ J26
Scranton■ J29
Moravian■ J31
Lycoming■ .... F 2
Drew .... F 5
King's (Pa.) .... F 9
Delaware Valley■ F12
Scranton F14
FDU-Madison F16
Upsala F19

Colors: Navy & Gold. Nickname: Colonels.
AD: Phil Wingert. SID: Tom McGuire. III

WM. PATERSON .... Wayne, NJ 07470

Jerry Dallessio (1 YR. W-11, L-13)

Mount Union Cl. N19-20
Kean■ N23
Rutgers-Camden N27
Montclair St. N30
Rowan■ .... D 3
Rutgers-Newark .... D 8
Western Conn. St.■ D14
Staten Island Cl. D29-30
Bloomfield■ .... J 6
Trenton St.■ J10
Ramapo J12
Stockton St.■ J15
Jersey City St. J19
Montclair St.■ J22
Kean J26
Rutgers-Camden■ J29
Ramapo■ .... F 2
Rowan .... F 5
Rutgers-Newark■ .... F 9
Trenton St. F12
Jersey City St.■ F16
Stockton St. F19

Colors: Orange & Black. Nickname: Pioneers.
AD: Arthur Eason. SID: Joe Martinelli. III

■ Home games on each schedule.

See pages 405–407 for Division I tournament details

WILLIAM PENN .... Oskaloosa, IA 52577

Leon Richardson (28 YRS. W-390, L-298)

Neb. Wesleyan Cl.	N26-27
Mt. Mercy■	D 1
Clarke■	D 3
St. Louis Pharmacy■	D 4
Marycrest	D10
St. Ambrose	D11
Grinnell■	J 5
Buena Vista	J 7
Wartburg	J 8
Loras■	J14
Upper Iowa■	J15
Peru St.	J20
Central (Iowa)■	J28
Luther■	J29
Simpson	F 1
Dubuque	F 4
Loras	F 5
Buena Vista■	F11
Upper Iowa	F12
Wartburg■	F18
Dubuque■	F19
Simpson■	F22
Central (Iowa)	F25
Luther	F26

Colors: Navy Blue & Gold. Nickname: The Statesmen.
AD: Mike Laird. SID: John Eberline. III

WILLIAM & MARY .... Williamsburg, VA 23187

Chuck Swenson (6 YRS. W-58, L-111)

Loyola (Md.)■	N29
Virginia	D 1
Citadel	D 4
N.C.-Greensboro■	D21
Shootout Spokane	D27-28
Navy■	J 3
Holy Cross	J 5
Campbell	J10
James Madison	J12
N.C.-Wilmington■	J15
Richmond	J17
East Caro.■	J19
Virginia Tech■	J22
American	J24
George Mason■	J26
Loyola (Md.)	J30
Old Dominion	F 2
Richmond■	F 5
James Madison■	F 7
Va. Military■	F 9
N.C.-Wilmington	F12
East Caro.	F14
American■	F19
George Mason	F23
Old Dominion■	F26
Colonial Conf.	M5-7

Colors: Green, Gold, Silver. Nickname: Indians Tribe.
AD: John Randolph. SID: Jean Elliott. I

WILLIAMS .... Williamstown, MA 01267

Harry Sheehy (10 YRS. W-162, L-76)

Rensselaer■	N30
Williams Inv.	D3-4
North Adams St.	D 9
Connecticut Col.■	D11
Union (N.Y.)	J 4
Williams Tr.	J7-8
Amherst■	J15
Middlebury■	J18
Bates	J21
Bowdoin	J22
Hamilton■	J25
Wesleyan	J29
Merchant Marine	J31
Amherst	F 5
Trinity (Conn.)■	F 9
Tufts■	F12
Middlebury	F16
Union (N.Y.)■	F19
Skidmore	F23
Wesleyan■	F26

Colors: Purple. Nickname: Ephs.
AD: Robert Peck. SID: Dick Quinn. III

WINGATE .... Wingate, NC 28174

John Thurston (11 YRS. W-127, L-163)

Barry Cl.	N26-27
St. Andrews■	D 1
Shippensburg Tr.	D3-4
Queens (N.C.)■	D 6
Appalachian St.	D11
Lincoln Memorial Cl.	D18-19
St. Andrews	J 4
Elon	J 8
Lenoir-Rhyne■	J12
Carson-Newman	J15
Presbyterian■	J19
Gardner-Webb■	J22
Catawba	J26
Mars Hill	J29
Queens (N.C.)	F 2
Elon■	F 5
Lenoir-Rhyne	F 9
Carson-Newman■	F12
Presbyterian	F16
Gardner-Webb	F19
Catawba■	F23
Mars Hill■	F26

Colors: Navy Blue & Old Gold. Nickname: Bulldogs.
AD: John Thurston. SID: David Sherwood. II

WINONA ST. .... Winona, MN 55987

Les Wothke (17 YRS. W-254, L-217)

North Ala. Tr.	N19-20
Livingston	N22
Wis.-River Falls Cl.	N26-27
St. Mary's (Minn.)	D 1
South Dak. St.■	D 4
Mt. Senario■	D 8
Concordia (St. Paul)■	D14
Quincy	D18
Teikyo Marycrest	D20
Mankato St.	D29
Minn.-Morris	J 5
Minn.-Duluth■	J 8
Wayne St. (Neb.)■	J12
Moorhead St.	J15
Northern St.■	J19
Bemidji St.	J22
Southwest St.■	J29
Minn.-Morris■	F 2
Minn.-Duluth	F 5
Wayne St. (Neb.)	F 9
Moorhead St.■	F12
St. Scholastica■	F14
Northern St.	F16
Bemidji St.■	F19
Southwest St.	F26

Colors: Purple & White. Nickname: Warriors.
AD: Stephen Juaire. SID: Michael R. Herzberg. II

WINTHROP .... Rock Hill, SC 29733

Dan Kenney (8 YRS. W-138, L-94)

Wake Forest	D 1
Central Fla.■	D 4
Tenn. Wesleyan■	D 6
Queens (N.C.)■	D15
Samford	D18
Georgia	D21
Louisiana St.	D28
Connecticut	J 2
Coastal Caro.■	J 8
Charleston So.	J10
Radford■	J12
Campbell■	J15
N.C.-Greensboro	J17
Liberty	J20
N.C.-Asheville■	J22
Towson St.	J27
Md.-Balt. County	J29
N.C.-Greensboro■	F 2
Coastal Caro.	F 5
Charleston So.■	F 7
Radford	F 9
Campbell	F12
Liberty■	F16
N.C.-Asheville	F19
Towson St.■	F24
Md.-Balt. County■	F26
Big South Conf.	M4-7

Colors: Garnet & Gold. Nickname: Eagles.
AD: Steve Vacendak. SID: Jack Frost. I

WISCONSIN .... Madison, WI 53711

Stu Jackson (1 YR. W-14, L-14)

Wis.-Milwaukee■	N27
Loyola (Cal.)	D 4
Wis.-Green Bay■	D 8
Texas Tech	D11
Eastern Mich.■	D13
Mississippi Val.■	D23
Stanford■	D27
Grambling■	D29
Marquette■	J 2
Penn St.	J 6
Ohio St.■	J 8
Minnesota	J12
Purdue■	J15
Michigan St.	J19
Illinois■	J25
Michigan	J29
Michigan St.■	F 2
Ohio St.	F 5
Penn St.■	F 9
Minnesota■	F12
Purdue	F16
Northwestern■	F19
Illinois	F26
Michigan■	M 2
Northwestern	M 5
Iowa■	M 9
Indiana	M12

Colors: Cardinal & White. Nickname: Badgers.
AD: Pat Richter. SID: Steve Malchow. I

WIS.-EAU CLAIRE .... Eau Claire, WI 54702

Ken Anderson (25 YRS. W-597, L-136)

Wis.-Eau Claire Tr.	N19-20
Northland■	N24
Southwest St.	N27
Wis.-Stout	D 4
Wis.-La Crosse■	D10
Wis.-Platteville■	D11
Mt. Senario■	D22
Wis.-Eau Claire Cl.	J2-3
Wis.-Parkside■	J 8
Southwest St.■	J10
Wis.-Superior■	J12
Wis.-River Falls	J15
Wis.-Oshkosh	J21
Wis.-Whitewater	J22
Wis.-Stevens Point■	J26
Wis.-Stout■	F 2
Wis.-Superior	F 5
Wis.-Whitewater■	F 8
Wis.-Stevens Point	F11
Wis.-La Crosse	F12
Wis.-Platteville	F15
Briar Cliff■	F19
Wis.-River Falls■	F23
Wis.-Oshkosh■	F26

Colors: Navy Blue & Old Gold. Nickname: Blugolds.
AD: Mel Lewis. SID: Tim Petermann. III

WIS.-GREEN BAY .... Green Bay, WI 54301

Dick Bennett (17 YRS. W-312, L-173)

Great Alas. Shootout	N24-27
Marquette Tr.	D3-4
Wisconsin	D 8
Bowling Green	D11
Oregon■	D18
Chicago St.■	D27
Wis.-Green Bay Tr.	D30-31
Western Ill.■	J 8
Northern Ill.■	J10
Youngstown St.	J15
Cleveland St.	J17
Wright St.	J22
Eastern Ill.	J24
Wis.-Milwaukee	J26
Valparaiso■	J29
Ill.-Chicago■	J31
Youngstown St.■	F 5
Cleveland St.■	F 7
Western Ill.	F12
Northern Ill.	F14
Valparaiso	F19
Ill.-Chicago	F21
Wis.-Milwaukee■	F24
Wright St.■	F26
Eastern Ill.■	F28
Mid-Continent Conf.	M6-8

Colors: Green, White & Phoenix Red. Nickname: Phoenix.
AD: Dan Spielmann. SID: Terry Powers. I

WIS.-LA CROSSE .... La Crosse, WI 54601

Charlie Gross (4 YRS. W-18, L-77)

Mt. St. Clare	N24
St. John's (Minn.)■	N27
Viterbo⊠	D 1
Wis.-River Falls■	D 4
Loras■	D 7
Wis.-Eau Claire	D10
Wis.-Superior	D11
Wis.-Stout■	D14
Minn.-Morris■	D16
Edgewood	J10
Northland	J12
Wis.-Stevens Point■	J15
Wis.-Whitewater	J18
Marian (Wis.)	J22
Wis.-Oshkosh	J26
Wis.-Platteville■	J29
Wis.-River Falls	F 2
Lakeland	F 7
Wis.-Superior■	F11
Wis.-Eau Claire■	F12
Wis.-Stout	F15
Wis.-Oshkosh■	F18
Wis.-Whitewater■	F19
Wis.-Stevens Point	F23
Wis.-Platteville	F26

⊠ La Crosse, WI

Colors: Maroon & Gray. Nickname: Eagles.
AD: Bridget Belgiovine. SID: Todd Clark. III

■ Home games on each schedule.

See pages 405–407 for Division I tournament details

WIS.-MILWAUKEE .... Milwaukee, WI 53201
Steve Antrim (14 YRS. W-202, L-159)

Opponent	Date	Opponent	Date
Wisconsin	N27	Wis.-Green Bay■	J26
Northeastern Ill.■	D 4	Eastern Ill.	J29
Eastern Mich.■	D 6	Wright St.	F 1
Central Mich.	D 8	Cleveland St.■	F 5
New Hampshire■	D11	Youngstown St.■	F 7
Marquette	D18	Valparaiso	F12
Fairfield	D31	Ill.-Chicago	F14
Northeastern Ill.	J 6	Eastern Ill.■	F19
Ill.-Chicago■	J10	Wright St.■	F21
Valparaiso■	J13	Wis.-Green Bay	F24
Cleveland St.	J15	Northern Ill.	F26
Youngstown St.	J17	Western Ill.■	F28
Northern Ill.■	J19	Chicago St.■	M 2
Western Ill.	J24	Mid-Continent Conf.	M6-8

Colors: Black & Gold. Nickname: Panthers.
AD: Bud Haidet. SID: Paul Helgren. I

WIS.-OSHKOSH .... Oshkosh, WI 54901
Ted Van Dellen (3 YRS. W-41, L-36)

Opponent	Date	Opponent	Date
Marian (Wis.)■	N23	Wis.-Superior■	J22
Wis.-Oshkosh Cl.	N26-27	Wis.-La Crosse■	J26
Wis.-Stevens Point■	D 4	Lakeland	J29
Wis.-River Falls	D10	Wis.-Stevens Point	F 2
Wis.-Stout	D11	Wis.-Whitewater■	F 5
St. Scholastica	D20	Wis.-River Falls■	F11
Edgewood	D30	Wis.-Stout■	F12
North Cent. Bible■	J 3	Wis. Lutheran■	F15
Rockford	J 7	Wis.-La Crosse	F18
Wis.-Whitewater	J12	Wis.-Superior	F19
Wis.-Platteville	J15	Wis.-Platteville■	F23
Wis.-Eau Claire■	J21	Wis.-Eau Claire	F26

Colors: Black, Gold & White. Nickname: Titans.
AD: Allen Ackerman. SID: Kennan Timm. III

WIS.-PARKSIDE .... Kenosha, WI 53141
Marty Gillespie (4 YRS. W-62, L-41)

Opponent	Date	Opponent	Date
St. Francis (Ill.)■	N23	St. Francis (Ill.)	J 4
Wis.-Whitewater■	N27	Wis.-Eau Claire	J 8
Carthage■	N29	SIU-Edwardsville■	J12
Wayne St. (Neb.)	D 1	Ferris St.	J17
Midland Lutheran	D 2	Olivet (Ill.)■	J20
Indianapolis	D 6	Oakland City	J24
IU/PU-Indianapolis	D 7	Southern Ind.	J25
Wis.-Stevens Point■	D 9	IU/PU-Indianapolis■	J29
Northern Ariz.	D11	Quincy■	F 5
Minn.-Duluth	D13	Olivet (Ill.)	F10
Bemidji St.	D14	Quincy	F14
Southern Ind.■	D28	SIU-Edwardsville	F16
Ferris St.■	D30	Bemidji St.■	F21
St. Thomas Aquinas■	J 2	Chicago■	F23

Colors: Green, White & Black. Nickname: Rangers.
AD: Linda Draft. SID: To be named. II

WIS.-PLATTEVILLE .... Platteville, WI 53818
Bo Ryan (9 YRS. W-192, L-63)

Opponent	Date	Opponent	Date
Capital Cl.	N19-20	Wis.-River Falls■	J21
Judson■	N23	Wis.-Stout■	J22
Dubuque Cl.	N26-27	Wis.-La Crosse	J29
Mt. Senario■	N29	Wis.-Whitewater	F 2
Wis.-Whitewater■	D 4	Wis.-Stevens Point■	F 5
Wis.-Superior	D10	Wis.-Eau Claire■	F15
Wis.-Eau Claire	D11	Wis.-River Falls	F18
Teikyo Marycrest Cl.	D29-30	Wis.-Stout	F19
Wis.-Superior■	J 8	Wis.-Oshkosh	F23
Wis.-Stevens Point	J12	Wis.-La Crosse■	F26
Wis.-Oshkosh■	J15		

Colors: Blue & Orange. Nickname: Pioneers.
AD: Daryl Leonard. SID: Becky Bohm. III

WIS.-RIVER FALLS .... River Falls, WI 54022
Rick Bowen (7 YRS. W-93, L-92)

Opponent	Date	Opponent	Date
Southwest St.	N20	N'western (Minn.)■	J25
Wis.-River Falls Cl.	N26-27	Wis.-Superior	J29
Mt. Senario■	D 1	Wis.-La Crosse■	F 2
Wis.-La Crosse	D 4	Wis.-Stout	F 5
Wis.-Oshkosh■	D10	Northland	F 7
Wis.-Whitewater■	D11	Wis.-Oshkosh	F11
St. Scholastica■	D14	Wis.-Whitewater	F12
Edgewood Tr.	J7-8	Wis.-Platteville■	F18
Wis.-Stout■	J12	Wis.-Stevens Point■	F19
Wis.-Eau Claire■	J15	Wis.-Eau Claire	F23
Wis.-Platteville	J21	Wis.-Superior■	F26
Wis.-Stevens Point	J22		

Colors: Red and White. Nickname: Falcons.
AD: Rick Bowen. SID: Jim Thies. III

WIS.-STEVENS POINT ...... Stevens Point, WI 54481
Bob Parker (9 YRS. W-166, L-81)

Opponent	Date	Opponent	Date
Edgewood	N23	Wis.-River Falls■	J22
Wis.-Stevens Pt. Cl.	N26-27	Wis.-Eau Claire	J26
Northern Mich.	N30	Wis.-Whitewater■	J29
Wis.-Oshkosh	D 4	Wis.-Oshkosh■	F 2
Wis.-Parkside	D 9	Wis.-Platteville	F 5
Wis.-Superior	D14	Wis.-Eau Claire■	F11
Bemidji St.■	D20	Wis.-Superior■	F12
Viterbo■	D28	Mt. Senario■	F15
Michigan Tech	J 4	Wis.-Stout	F18
Wis.-Platteville■	J12	Wis.-River Falls	F19
Wis.-La Crosse	J15	Wis.-La Crosse■	F23
Wis.-Stout■	J21	Wis.-Whitewater	F26

Colors: Purple & Gold. Nickname: Pointers.
AD: Frank O'Brien. SID: Terry Owens. III

WIS.-STOUT .... Menomonie, WI 54751
John Muraski (9 YRS. W-110, L-124)

Opponent	Date	Opponent	Date
Bethel (Minn.) Cl.	N19-20	Wis.-Stevens Point	J21
North Cent. Bible■	N23	Wis.-Platteville	J22
St. Scholastica■	N30	Mt. Senario	J28
Wis.-Eau Claire■	D 4	Wis.-Eau Claire	F 2
Wis.-Whitewater■	D10	Wis.-River Falls■	F 5
Wis.-Oshkosh■	D11	Wis.-Whitewater	F11
Wis.-La Crosse	D14	Wis.-Oshkosh	F12
N'western (Minn.)■	D18	Wis.-La Crosse■	F15
Colorado College Inv	J2-4	Wis.-Stevens Point■	F18
Marian (Wis.)	J 8	Wis.-Platteville■	F19
Wis.-River Falls	J12	Wis.-Superior	F23
Wis.-Superior■	J15		

Colors: Royal Blue & White. Nickname: Blue Devils.
AD: Rita Slinden. SID: Glen McMicken. III

WIS.-SUPERIOR .... Superior, WI 54880
Glenn Carlson (6 YRS. W-37, L-116)

Opponent	Date	Opponent	Date
Lakeland■	N10	Wis.-Oshkosh	J22
Cardinal Stritch Tr.	N26-27	Wis.-River Falls■	J29
North Cent. Bible	N30	Minn.-Duluth■	F 1
Minn.-Duluth	D 4	Wis.-Eau Claire■	F 5
Wis.-Platteville■	D10	St. Scholastica■	F 8
Wis.-La Crosse■	D11	Wis.-La Crosse	F11
Wis.-Stevens Point■	D14	Wis.-Stevens Point	F12
Wis.-Platteville	J 8	Wis.-Whitewater■	F18
Wis.-Eau Claire	J12	Wis.-Oshkosh■	F19
Wis.-Stout	J15	Wis.-Stout■	F23
Northern Mich.	J17	Wis.-River Falls	F26
Wis.-Whitewater	J21		

Colors: Orange & Black. Nickname: Yellowjackets.
AD: Steve Becker. SID: John Hack. III

WIS.-WHITEWATER .... Whitewater, WI 53190
Dave Vander Meulen (15 YRS. W-298, L-118)

Opponent	Date	Opponent	Date
St. Ambrose■	N23	Wis.-La Crosse■	J18
Wis.-Parkside	N27	Wis.-Superior■	J21
Carroll (Wis.)■	D 1	Wis.-Eau Claire■	J22
Wis.-Platteville	D 4	Wis.-Stevens Point	J29
Wis.-Stout	D10	Wis.-Platteville■	F 2
Wis.-River Falls	D11	Wis.-Oshkosh	F 5
North Park■	D14	Wis.-Eau Claire	F 8
Viterbo	D21	Wis.-Stout■	F11
Wis.-Whitewater Tr.	D29-30	Wis.-River Falls■	F12
Teikyo Marycrest■	J 5	Wis.-Superior	F18
Wis.-Oshkosh■	J12	Wis.-La Crosse	F19
Mt. Senario	J15	Wis.-Stevens Point■	F26

Colors: Purple & White. Nickname: Warhawks.
AD: Willie Myers. SID: Tom Fick. III

WITTENBERG .... Springfield, OH 45501
Bill L. Brown (6 YRS. W-60, L-99)

Opponent	Date	Opponent	Date
Earlham	D 1	Oberlin■	J15
Wooster■	D 4	Kenyon■	J19
Ohio Wesleyan	D 8	Wooster	J22
Hope Cl.	D10-11	Ohio Wesleyan■	J26
Otterbein■	D14	Case Reserve	J29
Case Reserve■	D16	Defiance■	F 2
Wittenberg Tr.	D29-30	Allegheny	F 5
Thomas More	J 3	Earlham■	F 9
Denison	J 5	Oberlin	F12
Allegheny■	J 8	Kenyon	F16
Wilmington (Ohio)	J12	Denison■	F19

Colors: Red & White. Nickname: Tigers.
AD: Carl Schraibman. SID: Alan Aldinger. III

■ Home games on each schedule.

See pages 405–407 for Division I tournament details

WOFFORD .... Spartanburg, SC 29301

Richard Johnson (8 YRS. W-130, L-89)

N.C. Wesleyan■	N20	Erskine■	J22
Furman	N29	Lenoir-Rhyne	J24
Elon■	N30	West Ga.	J26
East Tenn. St.	D 4	Piedmont■	F 5
S.C.-Aiken	D16	Presbyterian	F 7
Lenoir-Rhyne■	J 3	Newberry■	F10
Presbyterian■	J 8	Queens (N.C.)	F12
Elon	J10	Erskine	F14
Newberry	J12	Pembroke St.■	F16
King (Tenn.)	J15	S.C.-Aiken■	F19
Belmont Abbey	J17	Belmont Abbey■	F21
West Ga.■	J19	Queens (N.C.)■	F26

Colors: Old Gold & Black. Nickname: Terriers.
AD: Danny Morrison. SID: Mark Cohen. II

WOOSTER .... Wooster, OH 44691

Steve Moore (12 YRS. W-212 , L-106)

Wilmington (Ohio)	N20	Allegheny■	J12
Carnegie Mellon Inv.	N26-27	Ohio Wesleyan	J15
Ashland■	D 1	Denison	J19
Wittenberg	D 4	Wittenberg■	J22
Case Reserve■	D 7	Case Reserve	J26
Kenyon	D11	Kenyon■	J29
Scranton	D18	Allegheny	F 2
Allentown	D20	Earlham■	F 5
Wooster Cl.	D29-30	Ohio Wesleyan■	F12
Oberlin■	J 5	Denison■	F16
Earlham	J 8	Oberlin	F19

Colors: Black & Old Gold. Nickname: Fighting Scots.
AD: Bill McHenry. SID: John Finn. III

WORCESTER ST. .... Worcester, MA 01602

Tom Moore (4 YRS. W-58, L-49)

Clark Tr.	N19-20	North Adams St.	J22
Anna Maria■	N29	Bri'water (Mass.)■	J25
St. Thomas Aquin. Tr	D3-4	Western New Eng.■	J29
Eastern Conn. St.	D 7	Salem St.	F 1
Mass.-Dartmouth■	D 9	Fitchburg St.■	F 5
Fitchburg St.	J11	Westfield St.	F 8
Worcester Tech■	J13	Framingham St.■	F10
Westfield St.■	J15	North Adams St.■	F12
Framingham St.	J18	Bri'water (Mass.)	F15
Nichols	J20	Salem St.■	F19

Colors: Royal Blue & Gold. Nickname: Lancers.
AD: Susan Chapman. SID: Bruce Baker. III

WORCESTER TECH .... Worcester, MA 01609

Ken Kaufman (18 YRS. W-222, L-208)

Clark Tr.	N19-20	Clark (Mass.)	J22
MIT	N27	Trinity (Conn.)	J26
Babson■	D 1	Coast Guard■	J29
Wesleyan■	D 4	Norwich■	F 1
Anna Maria■	D 7	Suffolk	F 3
Wentworth Inst.■	D 9	Nichols■	F 5
Norwich	D11	Babson	F12
Salve Regina	J11	Western New Eng.■	F15
Worcester St.	J13	MIT■	F17
Western New Eng.	J15	Coast Guard	F19
Brandeis■	J19	Amherst	F22

Colors: Crimson & Gray. Nickname: Engineers.
AD: Raymond Gilbert. SID: Chris Gonzales. III

WRIGHT ST. .... Dayton, OH 45435

Ralph Underhill (15 YRS. W-317, L-114)

San Juan Shootout	N26-28	Eastern Ill.■	J27
John Carroll■	D 4	Ill.-Chicago	J29
Miami (Ohio)	D 8	Wis.-Milwaukee■	F 1
Dayton	D11	Western Ill.■	F 5
Eastern Ky.	D14	Valparaiso■	F 7
Wright St. Cl.	D17-18	Cleveland St.	F12
Ohio■	D22	Youngstown St.	F14
Cleveland St.■	J 5	Ill.-Chicago■	F19
Dayton■	J 8	Wis.-Milwaukee	F21
Youngstown St.■	J10	Eastern Ill.	F24
Western Ill.	J15	Wis.-Green Bay	F26
Valparaiso	J17	Northern Ill.■	M 1
Wis.-Green Bay■	J22	Mid-Continent Conf.	M6-8
Northern Ill.	J24		

Colors: Green & Gold. Nickname: Raiders.
AD: Mike Cusack. SID: Robert J. Noss. I

WYOMING .... Laramie, WY 82071

Joby Wright (3 YRS. W-61, L-29)

Cincinnati	N29	New Mexico■	J22
Denver■	D 1	Brigham Young	J27
Cal St. Fullerton■	D 4	Utah	J29
Colorado	D 9	Brigham Young■	F 3
Louisville■	D18	Utah■	F 5
Montana St.☒	D21	New Mexico	F10
Houston■	D23	UTEP	F12
Wyoming Cowboy Tr.	D28-29	Colorado St.	F19
Air Force■	J 3	Hawaii■	F24
Fresno St.■	J 5	San Diego St.■	F26
Hawaii	J 8	Air Force	M 3
San Diego St.	J10	Fresno St.	M 5
Colorado St.■	J15	☒ Billings, MT	
UTEP■	J20		

Colors: Brown & Yellow. Nickname: Cowboys.
AD: Paul Roach. SID: Kevin McKinney. I

XAVIER (OHIO) .... Cincinnati, OH 45207

Pete Gillen (8 YRS. W-180, L-67)

Marietta■	N29	Dayton	J24
Duke	D 4	Detroit Mercy■	J26
Hartford■	D 6	Loyola (Ill.)■	J29
Miami (Ohio)	D11	St. Francis (Pa.)	J31
Virginia Tech■	D18	La Salle	F 5
N.C.-Asheville■	D20	Geo. Washington■	F12
Md.-Balt. County	D30	Butler■	F16
East Tenn. St.	J 3	Detroit Mercy	F19
Brown■	J 8	Va. Commonwealth■	F23
New Hampshire■	J 9	Evansville■	F26
Dayton■	J12	Loyola (Ill.)	M 1
Butler	J15	La Salle■	M 3
Cincinnati■	J19	Midwestern Conf.	M6-9
Evansville	J22		

Colors: Blue & White. Nickname: Musketeers.
AD: Jeff Fogelson. SID: Tom Eiser. I

YALE .... New Haven, CT 06520

Dick Kuchen (14 YRS. W-178, L-198)

Colgate■	N27	Cornell	J28
Connecticut	D 1	Columbia	J29
Colorado Cl.	D3-4	Harvard	F 4
New Hampshire	D 8	Dartmouth	F 5
St. John's (N.Y.) Tr	D11-12	Princeton■	F11
Kent■	D30	Pennsylvania■	F12
Vermont	J 2	Columbia■	F18
Lafayette	J 6	Cornell■	F19
Lehigh	J 8	Pennsylvania	F25
Swarthmore■	J11	Princeton	F26
Brown	J15	Dartmouth■	M 4
Brown■	J22	Harvard■	M 5

Colors: Yale Blue & White. Nickname: Elis, Bulldogs.
AD: Harold Woodsum Jr. SID: Steve Conn. I

YESHIVA .... New York, NY 10033

Jonathan Halpert (21 YRS. W-171, L-282)

Molloy Tr.	N26-28	New Jersey Tech■	J25
Bard■	D 2	Purchase St.■	J31
CCNY	D 6	New York U.■	F 2
Maritime (N.Y.)■	D 9	John Jay	F 6
Stevens Tech	D11	New Jersey Tech	F 8
Baruch■	D13	Polytechnic (N.Y.)■	F10
Mt. St. Vincent■	D15	Maritime (N.Y.)	F12
Polytechnic (N.Y.)	D18	St. Joseph's (N.Y.)	F14
St. Joseph's (N.Y.)■	D23	Stevens Tech■	F16

Colors: Blue & White. Nickname: Maccabees.
AD: Stephen Young. SID: Mike Cohen. III

YORK (PA.) .... York, PA 17405

Jeff Gamber (16 YRS. W-201, L-209)

Frank. & Marsh. Cl.	N19-20	Dickinson■	J24
Susquehanna	N22	Gallaudet	J27
Allentown■	D 1	Mary Washington	J29
York (Pa.) Cl.	D4-5	Goucher	J31
Frank. & Marsh.	D 9	Marymount (Va.)	F 3
Catholic■	D11	Gettysburg■	F 5
Dickinson Tr.	J7-8	Gallaudet■	F10
Goucher■	J13	St. Mary's (Md.)	F12
Catholic	J15	Juniata	F15
Marymount (Va.)■	J20	Mary Washington■	F19
St. Mary's (Md.)■	J22		

Colors: Green & White. Nickname: Spartans.
AD: Jeff Gamber. SID: Steve Hevner. III

■ Home games on each schedule.

See pages 405–407 for Division I tournament details

YORK (N.Y.) .... Jamaica, NY 11451

Ronald St. John (5 YRS. W-46, L-78)

Williams Cl.	N19-20	Hunter	J15
Dowling	N23	New York U.■	J19
Staten Island■	N29	CCNY	J21
Hunter■	D 1	Medgar Evers■	J24
York (Pa.) Cl.	D4-5	Stony Brook■	J26
Pratt■	D 8	Lehman■	J28
Old Westbury	D15	Baruch■	F 2
Staten Island	J 5	Medgar Evers	F 4
Rutgers-Camden	J 8	CCNY■	F11
John Jay	J10	Rutgers-Newark■	F14
New Jersey Tech	J12		

Colors: Red & White. Nickname: Cardinals.
AD: Stu Bailin. SID: To be named. III

YOUNGSTOWN ST. .... Youngstown, OH 44555

Dan Peters (7 YRS. W-160, L-53)

Pittsburgh	N27	Northern Ill.■	J29
Akron	D11	Western Ill.■	J31
Northwestern■	D15	Wis.-Green Bay	F 5
Cincinnati	D18	Wis.-Milwaukee	F 7
Ohio	D20	Buffalo	F10
Central Conn. St.■	D29	Eastern Ill.■	F12
Eastern Ill.	J 8	Wright St.■	F14
Wright St.	J10	Northern Ill.	F19
Buffalo■	J12	Western Ill.	F21
Wis.-Green Bay■	J15	Cleveland St.	F24
Wis.-Milwaukee■	J17	Ill.-Chicago■	F26
Ill.-Chicago	J22	Valparaiso■	F28
Valparaiso	J24	Mid-Continent Conf.	M6-8
Cleveland St.■	J27		

Colors: Scarlet and White. Nickname: Penguins.
AD: Joseph Malmisur. SID: Greg Gulas. I

■ Home games on each schedule.

See pages 405–407 for Division I tournament details

1993-94 MEN'S TOURNAMENT ROUNDUP

NATIONAL CHAMPIONSHIPS DATES AND SITES

DIVISION I: First and second rounds, March 17-20—Landover, Maryland; Lexington, Kentucky; Long Island, New York; Ogden, Utah; Oklahoma City, Oklahoma; Sacramento, California; St. Petersburg, Florida; Wichita, Kansas. Regionals, March 24-27—Dallas, Texas; Knoxville, Tennessee; Los Angeles, California; Miami, Florida. Semifinals and final, April 2 and 4—Charlotte, North Carolina.
DIVISION II: First Round, March 9—On-campus sites to be determined. Regionals, March 11-12—On-campus sites to be determined. Quarterfinals, semifinals and final, March 23-26—Springfield, Massachusetts.
DIVISION III: First Round, March 3—On-campus sites to be determined. Second Round, March 5—On-campus sites to be determined. Sectionals, March 11-12—On-campus sites to be determined. Semifinals and final, March 18-19—Buffalo, New York.

DIVISION I CONFERENCE TOURNAMENTS

Dates	Conference	Site of Finals
March 10-13	Atlantic Coast	Charlotte, NC
March 5-10	Atlantic 10	Philadelphia, PA
March 10-13	Big East	New York, NY
March 11-13	Big Eight	Kansas City, MO
March 10-12	Big Sky	Boise, ID
March 4-7	Big South	Charleston, SC
March 10-13	Big West	Las Vegas, NV
March 5-7	Colonial	Richmond, VA
March 4-6	East Coast	Buffalo, NY
March 10-12	Great Midwest	Cincinnati, OH
March 11-13	Metro	Biloxi, MS
March 5-7	Metro Atlantic	Albany, NY
March 6-9	Midwestern	Indianapolis, IN
March 8-12	Mid-American	Columbus, OH
March 6-8	Mid-Continent	Chicago, IL
March 9-13	Mid-Eastern	Baltimore, MD
March 5-7	Missouri Valley	St. Louis, MO
March 5-9	North Atlantic	Campus Sites
February 28-March 6	Northeast	Campus Sites
March 3-5	Ohio Valley	Nashville, TN
March 4-11	Patriot	Annapolis, MD
March 10-13	Southeastern	Memphis, TN
March 3-6	Southern	Asheville, NC
March 4-6	Southland	Highest Seed
March 10-12	Southwest	Dallas, TX
March 9-13	Southwestern	Baton Rouge, LA
March 4-8	Sun Belt	Bowling Green, KY
March 3-5	Trans America	Orlando, FL
March 5-7	West Coast	Santa Clara, CA
March 9-12	Western Athletic	Salt Lake City, UT

(Note: The following conferences do not conduct postseason tournaments: Big Ten, Ivy Group and Pacific-10.)

DIVISION I IN-SEASON TOURNAMENTS

Date	Tournament, Site	Participating Teams
Nov. 17-26	Pre-Season NIT, New York, NY	Alabama St., Butler, California, Cincinnati, Cleveland St., Georgia, Kansas, Massachusetts, Minnesota, North Caro., Rice, St. John's (N.Y.), Santa Clara, Towson St., Western Ky., Western Mich.
Nov. 24-27	Great Alaska Shootout, Anchorage, AK	Alas. Anchorage, Hawaii, North Caro. St., Portland, Purdue, Wake Forest, Weber St., Wis.-Green Bay
Nov. 24-29	San Juan Shootout, San Juan, PR	American (P.R.), Coppin St., East Tenn. St., Marquette, Michigan St., Pacific (Cal.), Washington St., Wright St.
Nov. 26-27	Fry's Inv., Stanford, CA	Gonzaga, Cal St. Northridge, San Jose St., Stanford
Nov. 26-27	Real Dairy Cl., Boise, ID	Boise St., Ill.-Chicago, Siena, Stephen F. Austin
Nov. 26-27	Texaco Hawk Tr., Philadelphia, PA	Delaware St., St. Joseph's (Pa.), San Francisco, Wagner
Dec. 2-4	UC Santa Barbara Tr., Santa Barbara, CA	UC Santa Barb., Hofstra, Monmouth (N.J.), Old Dominion

Date	Tournament, Site	Participating Teams
Dec. 3-4	Ameritas Cl., Lincoln, NE	Navy, Nebraska, Ohio, Portland
Dec. 3-4	Boilermaker Inv., West Lafayette, IN	Indiana St., James Madison, Purdue, Western Mich.
Dec. 3-4	Cardinal Varsity Club Cl., Muncie, IN	Ball St., Maine, South Caro. St., Western Ill.
Dec. 3-4	Carrier Cl., Syracuse, NY	Boston U., Princeton, Syracuse, Vanderbilt
Dec. 3-4	Diet Pepsi Tr. of Champions, Charlotte, NC	Brigham Young, Geo. Washington, North Caro., South Caro.
Dec. 3-4	Lobo Cl., Albuquerque, NM	Centenary, Eastern Wash., New Mexico, North Texas
Dec. 3-4	Mile High Cl., Boulder, CO	Colorado, La Salle, Sam Houston St., Yale
Dec. 3-4	Golden Panther Inv., Miami, FL	Florida Int'l, N.C.-Wilmington, St. Francis (Pa.), St. Peter's
Dec. 3-4	Hawkeye Cl., Iowa City, IA	Houston, Iowa, Lehigh, Long Beach St.
Dec. 3-4	KLYT-Coca-Cola Cl., Missoula, MT	Mo.-Kansas City, Montana, Northeast La., Southern Utah
Dec. 3-4	MetLife Cl., San Francisco, CA	Colgate, Idaho, Miami (Ohio), San Francisco
Dec. 3-4	Mt. St. Mary's Tip-Off Tr., Emmitsburg, MD	Central Conn. St., Columbia, East Caro., Mt. St. Mary's (Md.)
Dec. 3-4	River City Cl., Cape Girardeau, MO	Alabama St., Southeast Mo. St., Texas-Arlington, Troy St.
Dec. 3-4	Pizza Hut Cl., Springfield, MO	Cal St. Northridge, Central Mich., Southwest Mo. St., Texas Tech
Dec. 3-4	First City Bank Cl., Milwaukee, WI	Detroit Mercy, Marquette, Texas Southern, Wis.-Green Bay
Dec. 3-4	Fairfield Tr., Fairfield, CT	Drexel, Fairfield, North Caro. A&T, Texas Christian
Dec. 3-4	Canisius College Tr., Buffalo, NY	Buffalo, Canisius, Gonzaga, Niagara
Dec. 10-11	Cougar Cl., Provo, UT	Brigham Young, Nicholls St., Okla. Baptist, Oregon St.
Dec. 10-11	Dr. Pepper Inv., Waco, TX	Baylor, Pepperdine, Stephen F. Austin, Weber St.
Dec. 10-11	Illini Cl., Champaign, IL	American, Illinois, Morehead St., Tenn.-Martin
Dec. 10-11	Indiana Cl., Bloomington, IN	Indiana, Oral Roberts, Tennessee Tech, Washington St.
Dec. 10-11	Runnin' Joe Cl., Jonesboro, AR	Arkansas St., Prairie View, Samford, Southeast Mo. St.
Dec. 10-11	United Airlines Tip-Off Tr., Honolulu, HI	Ala.-Birmingham, Hawaii, Mo.-Kansas City, Tennessee St.
Dec. 10-11	Delta Airlines Bearcat Cl., Cincinnati, OH	Boise St., Cincinnati, Cleveland St., Rutgers
Dec. 10-11	Red Auerbach Colonial Cl., Washington, DC	Geo. Washington, Howard, Jackson St., LIU-Brooklyn
Dec. 10-12	Otis Spunkmeyer Cl., Berkeley, CA	California, Md.-Balt. County, Princeton, Tulane
Dec. 11-12	Joe Lapchick Memorial Tr., Jamaica, NY	Colgate, Hofstra, St. John's (N.Y.), Yale
Dec. 17-18	Hawaii-Nike Festival, Honolulu, HI	Hawaii, Kansas St., Mercer, Southwest Tex. St.
Dec. 17-18	USAir Cl., Dayton, OH	Northeast La., Prairie View, Troy St., Wright St.
Dec. 17-18	USAir East Coast Cl., Wilmington, NC	Georgia St., Grambling, N.C.-Wilmington, South Fla.
Dec. 20-21	New Orleans Cl., New Orleans, LA	Delaware, Loyola (La.), New Orleans, Troy St.
Dec. 21-23	Maui Inv., Maui, HI	Arizona, Boston College, Chaminade, Kentucky, Notre Dame, Ohio St., Tennessee Tech, Texas
Dec. 27-28	Coors Light Cl., Fresno, CA	Cal St. Northridge, Fresno St., Montana St., Washington St.
Dec. 27-28	Hoosier Cl., Indianapolis, IN	Indiana, Princeton, Texas Christian, Western Ky.
Dec. 27-28	Shootout Spokane, Spokane, WA	Gonzaga, New Hampshire, Samford, William & Mary
Dec. 27-28	Thriftway FarWest Cl., Portland, OR	N.C.-Wilmington, Oregon, Oregon St., Portland
Dec. 27-29	ECAC Holiday Festival Tr., New York City, NY	FDU-Teaneck, Georgia Tech, St. John's (N.Y.), Temple
Dec. 27-30	Kraft Rainbow Cl., Honolulu, HI	Army, UC Santa Barb., Clemson, Evansville, Florida, Hawaii, Louisville, Oklahoma St.
Dec. 28-29	ASU Tribune Cl., Tempe, AZ	Arizona St., Mississippi St., Northern Ariz., Villanova

Date	Tournament, Site	Participating Teams
Dec. 28-29	Cowboy Shootout, Casper, WY	Idaho St., Old Dominion, Utah St., Wyoming
Dec. 28-29	Iona College Tr., New Rochelle, NY	Geo. Mason, Iona, Lafayette, St. Francis (N.Y.)
Dec. 28-29	Jones Intercable Lobo Inv., Albuquerque, NM	Middle Tenn. St., New Mexico, Rice, St. Bonaventure
Dec. 28-29	Lowcountry Cl., Charleston, SC	Alabama, Charleston (S.C.), Delaware St., Penn St.
Dec. 28-29	Music City Inv., Nashville, TN	Bucknell, Harvard, Illinois St., Vanderbilt
Dec. 28-29	USF&G Sugar Bowl Tr., New Orleans, LA	Coastal Caro., Geo. Washington, New Orleans, Southern-B.R.
Dec. 28-29	US West Cellular Air Time Tr., Seattle, WA	Georgia, Pacific (Cal.), Pennsylvania, Washington
Dec. 28-29	Abdow's Hall of Fame Cl., Springfield, MA	Hartford, Hofstra, Maryland, Massachusetts
Dec. 28-30	Big Island Inv., Hilo, HI	Chaminade, Connecticut, Creighton, Hawaii-Hilo, La Salle, Southern Ill., Texas-Arlington, Tennessee Tech
Dec. 28-30	Fiesta Bowl Cl., Tucson, AZ	Arizona, Auburn, Fordham, Michigan
Dec. 29-30	Albertson's Cl., Boise, ID	Alcorn St., Boise St., Slippery Rock, Southwestern La.
Dec. 29-30	All-College Tr., Oklahoma City, OK	Eastern Ky., Oklahoma, Texas Tech, Tulsa
Dec. 29-30	Cable Car Cl., Santa Clara, CA	Butler, Holy Cross, N.C.-Charlotte, Santa Clara
Dec. 29-30	Golden Harvest Cl., Kansas City, MO	East Tenn. St., Kansas, Rhode Island, Southern Methodist
Dec. 29-30	Hatter Cl., DeLand, FL	Northeastern, Northwestern, Rider, Stetson
Dec. 29-30	Medical Value Plan Holiday Cl., Toledo, OH	Columbia, Delaware, Murray St., Toledo
Dec. 29-30	Pepsi-Marist Cl., Poughkeepsie, NY	Buffalo, Drexel, Marist, St. Peter's
Dec. 29-30	Seton Hall/Meadowlands Tr., East Rutherford, NJ	Manhattan, San Diego, Seton Hall, Stanford
Dec. 29-30	Sun Carnival Cl., El Paso, TX	Iowa St., Pepperdine, UTEP, Va. Commonwealth
Dec. 29-30	Wichita St. Tr., Wichita, KS	Arkansas St., Jackson St., Monmouth (N.J.), Wichita St.
Dec. 29-30	Oldsmobile Spartan Cl., East Lansing, MI	Bowling Green, Cornell, Ga. Southern, Michigan St.
Dec. 29-30	Dr. Pepper Cl., Chattanooga, TN	Alabama St., American, South Ala., Tenn.-Chatt.
Dec. 30-31	Great Northern Cl., Green Bay, WI	East Caro., Eastern Mich., Eastern Wash., Wis.-Green Bay

DIVISION I
WOMEN'S RECORDS

Lafayette's Heidi Caruso established records for steals in a season and average steals per game with 168 steals and 6.0 per contest in 1993. Caruso tied the standard for steals in a game with 14 against Kansas State.

DIVISION I WOMEN'S INDIVIDUAL RECORDS

Official NCAA women's basketball records began with the 1981-82 season and are based on information submitted to the NCAA statistics service by institutions participating in the weekly statistics rankings. Official career records include players who played at least three seasons (in a four-season career) or two (in a three-season career) in Division I during the era of official NCAA statistics, which began with the 1981-82 season. Assists were added in 1985-86 and blocked shots and steals were added in 1987-88. Scoring, rebounding, assists, blocked shots and steals are ranked on total number and on per-game average; shooting, on percentage. In statistical rankings, the rounding of percentages and/or averages may indicate ties where none exist. In these cases, the numerical order of the rankings is accurate.

SCORING

Points

Game

60—Cindy Brown, Long Beach St. vs. San Jose St., Feb. 16, 1987 (20 FGs, 20 FTs)

Season

974—Cindy Brown, Long Beach St., 1987 (362 FGs, 250 FTs, 35 games)

Career

3,122—Patricia Hoskins, Mississippi Val., 1985-89 (1,196 FGs, 24 3FGs, 706 FTs, 110 games)

Average Per Game

Season

33.6—Patricia Hoskins, Mississippi Val., 1989 (908 points in 27 games)

Career

28.4—Patricia Hoskins, Mississippi Val., 1985-89 (3,122 in 110)

FIELD GOALS

Field Goals

Game

27—Lorri Bauman, Drake vs. Southwest Mo. St., Jan. 6, 1984 (33 attempts, 82.0%)

Season

392—Barbara Kennedy, Clemson, 1982 (760 attempts, 51.6%)

Career

1,259—Joyce Walker, Louisiana St., 1981-84 (2,238 attempts, 56.8%)

Consecutive Field Goals

Game

17—Dorinda Lindstrom, Santa Clara vs. Fresno St., Nov. 30, 1986

Season

23—Renay Adams, Tennessee Tech (1990-91); Mary Ostrowski, Tennessee (1983-84); Pam Kelly, Louisiana Tech (1981-82)

Field-Goal Attempts

Game

40—Kim Perrot, Southwestern La. vs. Southeastern La., Feb. 5, 1990 (20 made)

Season

863—Lisa McMullen, Alabama St., 1991 (285 made)

Career

2,331—Karen Pelphrey, Marshall, 1983-86 (1,175 made)

Field-Goal Percentage

Game

(Min. 15 made) 100.0%—Kelly Mago, Southwest Mo. St. vs. Bradley, Feb. 18, 1988 (16 of 16)

Season

71.7%—Renay Adams, Tennessee Tech, 1991 (185 of 258)

Career

65.1%—Regina Days, Ga. Southern, 1984-88 (835 of 1,282)

THREE-POINT FIELD GOALS

Three-Point Field Goals

Game

10—By seven players. Most recent: Amy Cherubini, Indiana vs. Ohio St., Feb. 21, 1992

Season

126—Lisa McMullen, Alabama St., 1991 (390 attempts)

Career

317—Karen Middleton, South Caro., 1987-91 (712 attempts)

Three-Point Field Goals Made Per Game

Season

4.5—Lisa McMullen, Alabama St., 1991 (126 in 28 games)

Career

(Min. 150 made) 4.00—Lisa McMullen, Alabama St., 1989-91 (224 in 56 games)

Consecutive Three-Point Field Goals

Game

9—Susan Smith, Eastern Wash. vs. Weber St., Feb. 13, 1988 (made 9 of 10 attempts)

Season

9—Susan Smith, Eastern Wash. vs. Weber St., Feb. 13, 1988 (9 made); Heather Donlon, Fordham vs. Niagara, Feb. 3, 1990 (2 made) and vs. Holy Cross, Feb. 10, 1990 (7 made)

Consecutive Games Making a Three-Point Field Goal

Season
30—Sandy Brown, Middle Tenn. St., 1988

Career
53—Sandy Brown, Middle Tenn. St., 1988-89

Three-Point Field-Goal Attempts

Game
26—Lisa McMullen, Alabama St. vs. Alcorn St., Jan. 14, 1991 (7 made)

Season
390—Lisa McMullen, Alabama St., 1991 (126 made)

Career
813—Kim Kuhn, Niagara, 1989-93 (261 made)

Three-Point Field-Goal Attempts Per Game

Season
13.9—Lisa McMullen, Alabama St., 1991 (390 in 28)

Career
7.86—Brenda Hatchett, Lamar, 1990-92 (440 in 56)

Three-Point Field-Goal Percentage

Game
(Min. 7 made) 100.0%—Kristi Brown, Middle Tenn. St. vs. Tennessee Tech, Feb. 15, 1992 (8 of 8); Angie Evans, William & Mary vs. James Madison, Jan. 16, 1988 (7 of 7)

Season
(Min. 50 made) 57.5%—Heather Donlon, Fordham, 1990 (50 of 87)
(Min. 80 made) 50.0%—Mary Just, Loyola (Ill.), 1988 (87 of 174)

Career
(Min. 150 made) 46.7%—Erin Maher, Harvard, 1989-93 (261 of 559)

FREE THROWS

Free Throws

Game
23—Shaunda Greene, Washington vs. Northern Ill., Nov. 30, 1991 (27 attempts, 85.2%)

Season
275—Lorri Bauman, Drake, 1982 (325 attempts, 84.6%)

Career
907—Lorri Bauman, Drake, 1981-84 (1,090 attempts, 83.2%)

Consecutive Free Throws

Game
18—Chris Starr, Nevada vs. San Diego, Jan. 3, 1984; Holly Jones, Rice vs. UC Santa Barb., Nov. 30, 1985; Beth Shearer, American vs. Lehigh, Dec. 28, 1987; Wendy Scholtens, Vanderbilt vs. Tennessee Tech, Jan. 11, 1989

Season
60—Ginny Doyle, Richmond, 1992

All-Time
66—Ginny Doyle, Richmond, 1991-92

Free-Throw Attempts

Game
31—Renee Daniels, Southeastern La. vs. New Orleans, Jan. 23, 1985 (19 made)

Season
338—Valorie Whiteside, Appalachian St., 1985 (200 made, 59.2%)

Career
1,173—Valorie Whiteside, Appalachian St., 1984-88 (638 made)

Free-Throw Percentage

Game
(Min. 18 made) 100.0%—Chris Starr, Nevada vs. San Diego, Jan. 3, 1984 (18 of 18); Holly Jones, Rice vs. UC Santa Barb., Nov. 30, 1985 (18 of 18); Beth Shearer, American vs. Lehigh, Dec. 28, 1987 (18 of 18); Wendy Scholtens, Vanderbilt vs. Tennessee Tech, Jan. 11, 1989 (18 of 18)

Season
95.0%—Ginny Doyle, Richmond, 1992 (96 of 101)

Career
87.6%—Karen Murray, Washington, 1981-84 (269 of 307)

REBOUNDS

Rebounds

Game
40—Deborah Temple, Delta St. vs. Ala.-Birmingham, Feb. 14, 1983

Season
534—Wanda Ford, Drake, 1985 (30 games, 17.8)

Career
1,887—Wanda Ford, Drake, 1983-86 (117 games, 16.1)

Average Per Game

Season
18.5—Rosina Pearson, Bethune-Cookman, 1985 (480 in 26 games)

Career
16.1—Wanda Ford, Drake, 1983-86 (1,887 in 117)

ASSISTS

Assists

Game
23—Michelle Burden, Kent vs. Ball St., Feb. 6, 1991

Season
355—Suzie McConnell, Penn St., 1987 (30 games, 11.8)

Career
1,307—Suzie McConnell, Penn St., 1984-88 (128 games, 10.2 per game)

Average Per Game

Season
11.8—Suzie McConnell, Penn St., 1987 (355 in 30 games)

Career
10.3—Neacole Hall, Alabama St., 1986-89 (869 in 84 games)

Kent's Michelle Burden set a single-game record for assists with 23 against Ball State in 1991.

BLOCKED SHOTS

Blocked Shots

Game
15—Amy Lundquist, Loyola (Cal.) vs. Western Ill., Dec. 20, 1992

Season
151—Michelle Wilson, Texas Southern, 1989 (27 games, 5.6 per game)

Career
428—Genia Miller, Cal St. Fullerton, 1987-91 (118 games, 3.6 per game)

Average Per Game

Season
5.6—Michelle Wilson, Texas Southern, 1989 (151 in 27 games)

Career
(Min. 250) 3.9—Chris Enger, San Diego, 1989-93 (372 in 96 games)

STEALS

Steals

Game
14—Heidi Caruso, Lafayette vs. Kansas St., Dec. 5, 1992; Natalie White, Florida A&M vs. South Ala., Dec. 13, 1991

Season
168—Heidi Caruso, Lafayette, 1993 (28 games, 6.0 per game)

Career
454—Dawn Staley, Virginia, 1988-92 (131 games, 3.5 per game)

Average Per Game

Season
6.0—Heidi Caruso, Lafayette, 1993 (168 in 28 games)

Career
(Min. 200) 4.9—Neacole Hall, Alabama St., 1987-89 (281 in 57 games)

DIVISION I WOMEN'S TEAM RECORDS

Note: Where records involve both teams, each team must be an NCAA Division I member institution.

SINGLE-GAME SCORING

Most Points
149—Long Beach St. vs. San Jose St. (69), Feb. 16, 1987

Most Points by Losing Team (Including Overtimes)
120—North Caro. St. vs. Virginia (123) (3 ot), Jan. 12, 1991

Most Points by Losing Team (Regulation Time)
114—Georgetown vs. Providence (128), Feb. 4, 1991

Most Points, Both Teams
243—Virginia (123) vs. North Caro. St. (120), Jan. 12, 1991 (3 ot)

Most Points in a Half
80—Long Beach St. (149) vs. San Jose St. (69), Feb. 16, 1987

Fewest Points Allowed
12—North Caro. A&T (85) vs. Bennett, Nov. 21, 1990

Fewest Points Allowed, Two Division I Teams
19—Jackson St. (81) vs. Prairie View, March 3, 1983

Fewest Points, Both Teams
72—Virginia (38) vs. San Diego St. (34), Dec. 29, 1981

Widest Margin of Victory
102—Grambling (139) vs. Jarvis Christian (37), Feb. 12, 1986

Widest Margin, Two Division I Teams
101—Louisiana Tech (126) vs. Tex.-Pan American (25), Feb. 18, 1989

Most Games Scoring 100 Points in Single Season
15—Long Beach St., 1987

SINGLE-GAME FIELD GOALS

Most Field Goals
60—Northwestern (La.) vs. Hawaii Pacific, March 1, 1986 (105 attempts, 57.1%)

Most Field-Goal Attempts
118—N.C.-Wilmington vs. Davidson, Dec. 6, 1983 (59 made)

Highest Field-Goal Percentage
(Min. 18 made) 79.2%—Arkansas St. vs. Memphis St., Jan. 15, 1987 (19 of 24)
(Min. 36 made) 73.7%—Florida Int'l vs. Canisius, Jan. 2, 1992 (42 of 57)

SINGLE-GAME THREE-POINT FIELD GOALS

Most Three-Point Field Goals
16—Harvard vs. Rhode Island, Jan. 12, 1993 (30 attempts); Creighton vs. Oral Roberts, Dec. 6, 1989 (34 attempts)

Most Three-Point Field Goals, Both Teams
22—Southwestern La. (15) vs. South Ala. (7), March 7, 1988; Northwestern (La.) (13) vs. Southwestern La. (9), Jan. 8, 1990

Consecutive Three-Point Field Goals Made Without a Miss
9—Boston College vs. Providence, Jan. 9, 1988; Eastern Wash. vs. Weber St., Feb. 13, 1988; Eastern Ill. vs. Illinois St., March 9, 1988

Most Three-Point Field-Goal Attempts
44—Kent vs. Cleveland St., Nov. 23, 1991 (8 made); Southwestern La. vs. South Ala., March 7, 1988 (15 made)

Most Three-Point Field-Goal Attempts, Both Teams
63—Creighton (34) vs. Oral Roberts (29), Dec. 6, 1989

Highest Three-Point Field-Goal Percentage
(Min. 8 made) 100.0%—Idaho St. vs. Southern Utah, Dec. 4, 1990 (9 of 9)
(Min. 12 made) 81.3%—Creighton vs. Wyoming, Dec. 7, 1992 (13 of 16)

Highest Three-Point Field-Goal Percentage, Both Teams
(Min. 10 made) 76.5%—Eastern Wash. (10 of 12) vs. Weber St. (3 of 5), Feb. 13, 1988 (13 of 17)
(Min. 15 made) 76.2%—Eastern Ky. (9 of 11) vs. Louisville (7 of 10), Dec. 9, 1989 (16 of 21)

SINGLE-GAME FREE THROWS

Most Free Throws (Regulation)
48—East Caro. vs. American, Feb. 15, 1992 (58 attempts, 82.8%)

Most Free Throws (Including Overtimes)
51—Washington vs. Northern Ill., Nov. 30, 1991 (2 ot) (69 attempts, 73.9%)

Most Free Throws, Both Teams
74—Georgetown (39, attempted 49) vs. Providence (35, attempted 50), Feb. 4, 1991

Most Free-Throw Attempts (Regulation)
68—Eastern Ky. vs. Pittsburgh, Dec. 30, 1986 (39 made)

Most Free-Throw Attempts (Including Overtimes)
69—Washington vs. Northern Ill., Nov. 30, 1991 (51 made)

Most Free-Throw Attempts, Both Teams
99—Providence (50, made 35) vs. Georgetown (49, made 39), Feb. 4, 1991

Fewest Free Throws
0—Many teams

Fewest Free-Throw Attempts
0—Many teams

Highest Free-Throw Percentage
(Min. 24 made) 100.0%—Tenn.-Chatt. vs. Ala.-Birmingham, Nov. 24, 1990 (26 of 26); San Diego vs. Nevada, Jan. 25, 1986 (24 of 24)
(Min. 30 made) 97.0%—Wisconsin vs. Michigan, Feb. 8, 1991 (32 of 33)
(Min. 40 made) 86.5%—Providence vs. Pittsburgh, Jan. 9, 1989 (45 of 52)

Highest Free-Throw Percentage, Both Teams
(Min. 30 made) 94.6%—North Caro. St. (19 of 19) vs. Georgia Tech (16 of 18), Jan. 3, 1985 (35 of 37)
(Min. 40 made) 91.5%—Penn St. (20 of 20) vs. Geo. Washington (23 of 27) Feb. 28, 1991 (43 of 47)

SINGLE-GAME REBOUNDS

Most Rebounds
92—Pittsburgh vs. Geo. Washington, Jan. 6, 1982

SINGLE-GAME ASSISTS

Most Assists
43—Nebraska vs. Howard, Dec. 11, 1992; Northwestern (La.) vs. Arkansas Baptist, Jan. 10, 1987

Highest Percentage of Assists to Field Goals Made
(Min. 30) 100.0%—St. Louis vs. Loyola (Ill.), Jan. 6, 1986 (32 assists of 32 field goals by team)

SINGLE-GAME BLOCKED SHOTS

Most Blocked Shots
18—Loyola (Cal.) vs. Western Ill., Dec. 20, 1992; Rutgers vs. Oklahoma St., Dec. 28, 1991; Vanderbilt vs. Tennessee St., Dec. 10, 1991

SINGLE-GAME STEALS

Most Steals
38—Grambling vs. Texas College, Dec. 10, 1987

SINGLE-GAME PERSONAL FOULS

Most Personal Fouls
56—Eastern Mich. vs. Kent, Feb. 26, 1986

SINGLE-GAME OVERTIMES

Most Overtime Periods
4—Drake (112) vs. Northern Iowa (106), Jan. 23, 1993; Texas A&M (101) vs. St. Mary's (Tex.) (95), Dec. 17, 1984; Indiana St. (107) vs. Southwest Mo. St. (101), Jan. 28, 1989; Creighton (117) vs. Loyola (Ill.) (108), Jan. 12, 1986; Columbia-Barnard (114) vs. Pennsylvania (111), March 5, 1988

Most Points in One Overtime Period
22—Maine (86) vs. Stetson (78), Dec. 30, 1989; Oklahoma City (104) vs. New Orleans (91), Feb. 16, 1985; Long Beach St. (91) vs. San Diego St. (73), March 22, 1984

Most Points in One Overtime Period, Both Teams
36—Maine (22) vs. Stetson (14), Dec. 30, 1989

Most Points in Overtime Periods
42—Indiana St. vs. Southwest Mo. St. (4 ot), Jan. 28, 1989

Most Points in Overtime Periods, Both Teams
78—Indiana St. (42) vs. Southwest Mo. St. (36) (4 ot), Jan. 28, 1989

SEASON SCORING

Most Points
3,448—Long Beach St., 1987 (36 games)

Highest Average Per Game
96.7—Providence, 1991 (3,095 in 32)

Highest Average Scoring Margin
33.0—Louisiana Tech, 1982 (87.3 offense, 54.3 defense)

Most Games at Least 100 Points
15—Long Beach St., 1987

Lowest Average Per Game Allowed
51.8—Mo.-Kansas City, 1991 (1,450 in 28)

Most Consecutive Games at Least 100 Points
6—Louisiana Tech, 1982

SEASON FIELD GOALS

Most Field Goals
1,412—Long Beach St., 1987 (2,714 attempted, 52.0%)

Most Field Goals Per Game
39.2—Long Beach St., 1987 (1,412 in 36)

Most Field-Goal Attempts
2,714—Long Beach St., 1987 (1,412 made)

Most Field-Goal Attempts Per Game
79.3—Cheyney, 1984 (2,380 in 30)

Highest Field-Goal Percentage
55.9%—Drake, 1984 (945 of 1,691)

SEASON THREE-POINT FIELD GOALS

Most Three-Point Field Goals
248—Alabama, 1992 (765 attempts, 32.4%)

Most Three-Point Field Goals Per Game
8.3—Alabama, 1992 (248 in 30 games)

Most Three-Point Field-Goal Attempts
765—Alabama, 1992 (248 made)

Most Three-Point Field-Goal Attempts Per Game
25.5—Alabama, 1992 (765 in 30 games)

Highest Three-Point Field-Goal Percentage
(Min. 90 made) 47.1%—Loyola (Ill.), 1988 (96 of 204)
(Min. 120 made) 46.3%—Connecticut, 1989 (137 of 296)

SEASON FREE THROWS

Most Free Throws
815—Western Ky., 1986 (1,108 attempts, 73.6%)

Most Free Throws Per Game
22.6—Western Ky., 1986 (815 in 36)

Most Free-Throw Attempts
1,108—Western Ky., 1986 (815 made)

Most Free-Throw Attempts Per Game
31.1—Morgan St., 1985 (839 in 27)

Highest Free-Throw Percentage
79.8%—La Salle, 1988 (479 of 600)

SEASON REBOUNDS

Most Rebounds
1,997—Texas Southern, 1982 (38 games)

Highest Average Per Game
57.9—Texas Southern, 1984 (1,506 in 26)

Highest Average Rebound Margin
18.3—Louisiana Tech, 1990 (52.9 offense, 34.7 defense)

SEASON ASSISTS

Most Assists
780—Long Beach St., 1986 (34 games)

Highest Average Per Game
24.7—Villanova, 1987 (766 in 31 games)

SEASON BLOCKED SHOTS

Most Blocked Shots
235—Geo. Washington, 1992 (32 games)

Highest Average Per Game
7.7—Northern Ill., 1989 (231 in 30 games)

SEASON STEALS

Most Steals
536—Kent, 1993 (29 games)

Highest Average Per Game
18.5—Kent, 1993 (536 in 29 games)

SEASON PERSONAL FOULS

Most Personal Fouls
942—Loyola (Md.), 1982 (27 games)

Most Personal Fouls Per Game
34.9—Loyola (Md.), 1982 (942 in 27)

Fewest Personal Fouls
261—Boston U., 1987 (27 games)

Fewest Personal Fouls Per Game
9.7—Boston U., 1987 (261 in 27)

SEASON DEFENSE

Lowest Scoring Average Per Game Allowed (Since 1982)
51.8%—Mo.-Kansas City, 1991 (1,450 points in 28 games)

Lowest Field-Goal Percentage Allowed (Since 1982)
31.7%—Montana, 1993 (540 of 1,706)

SEASON OVERTIMES

Most Overtime Games
5—Northwestern (La.), 1990 (won 4, lost 1); Ohio St., 1990 (won 3, lost 2)

Most Consecutive Overtime Games
3—James Madison, 1992 (won 2, lost 1)

GENERAL RECORDS

Most Victories in a Season
35—Texas, 1982; Louisiana Tech, 1982; Tennessee, 1989

Most Consecutive Victories, All-Time
54—Louisiana Tech, from Dec. 1, 1980, through Jan. 27, 1982 (ended Jan. 29, 1982, at Old Dominion, 61-58; last Louisiana Tech defeat before streak came vs. South Caro., 77-69)

Most Consecutive Home-Court Victories
68—Auburn, from Feb. 5, 1986, to Nov. 23, 1991

Most Consecutive Regular-Season Victories (NCAA, NWIT tourneys not included)
52—Vermont (from 1991 to 1993)

Most Defeats in a Season
28—Charleston So., 1991

Most Consecutive Defeats in a Season
28—Charleston So., 1991

Most Consecutive Defeats (All Games)
58—Brooklyn (Feb. 7, 1987 to Feb. 22, 1989)

30-Game Winners
35—Louisiana Tech, 1982
Texas, 1982
Tennessee, 1989
34—Texas, 1986
33—Long Beach St., 1987
32—Texas, 1984, 1988
Western Ky., 1986
Auburn, 1988
Louisiana Tech, 1988
Auburn, 1989
Louisiana Tech, 1989

Louisiana Tech, 1990
Stanford, 1990
31—Louisiana Tech, 1983
Southern Cal, 1983, 1986
Old Dominion, 1985
Auburn, 1987
Texas, 1987
Tennessee, 1988
Virginia, 1991
Texas Tech, 1993
30—Georgia, 1984, 1986
Louisiana Tech, 1984
Texas, 1983
Northeast La., 1985
Rutgers, 1987
Louisiana Tech, 1987
Long Beach St., 1989
Stephen F. Austin, 1989
Tennessee, 1991
Miami (Fla.), 1992
Stanford, 1992
Vanderbilt, 1993

Unbeaten Teams (Since 1982; number of victories in parentheses)
1986 Texas (34)†

† *NCAA champion.*

DIVISION I WOMEN'S ALL-TIME INDIVIDUAL LEADERS

SINGLE-GAME SCORING HIGHS

(Since 1982)

Pts.	Player, Team vs. Opponent	Date
60	Cindy Brown, Long Beach St. vs. San Jose St.	Feb. 16, 1987
58	Lorri Bauman, Drake vs. Southwest Mo. St.	Jan. 6, 1984
58	Kim Perrot, Southwestern La. vs. Southeastern La.	Feb. 5, 1990
55	Patricia Hoskins, Mississippi Val. vs. Southern-B.R.	Feb. 13, 1989
55	Patricia Hoskins, Mississippi Val. vs. Alabama St.	Feb. 25, 1989
54	Wanda Ford, Drake vs. Southwest Mo. St.	Feb. 22, 1986
53	Chris Starr, Nevada vs. Cal St. Sacramento	Feb. 8, 1983
53	Felisha Edwards, Northeast La. vs. Southern Miss.	Mar. 1, 1991
53	Sheryl Swoopes, Texas Tech vs. Texas	Mar. 13, 1993
52	Sheryl Martin, Ga. Southern vs. Stetson	Feb. 18, 1983
52	Deborah Temple, Delta St. vs. Tenn.-Martin	Mar. 4, 1983
52	Lisa Ingram, Northeast La. vs. Louisiana St.	Jan. 18, 1984

SINGLE-GAME FIELD-GOAL PERCENTAGE

(Minimum 13 field goals made)
(Since 1982)

Pct.	Player, Team vs. Opponent (FG-FGA)	Date
100	Kelly Mago, Southwest Mo. St. vs. Bradley (16-16)	Feb. 18, 1988
100	Karen Walker, Cornell vs. Pennsylvania (15-15)	Mar. 3, 1990
100	Emma Jones, Ball St. vs. Indiana St. (14-14)	Dec. 10, 1985
100	Tonya Grant, St. Peter's vs. Loyola (Md.) (14-14)	Feb. 3, 1990
92.9	Kelly Lyons, Old Dominion vs. James Madison (13-14)	Feb. 1, 1989
83.3	Sue Wicks, Rutgers vs. Geo. Washington (20-24)	Dec. 5, 1987
81.8	Lorri Bauman, Drake vs. Southwest Mo. St. (27-33)	Jan. 6, 1984
80.8	Kathy Lightfoot, Colorado St. vs. Southern Colo. (21-26)	Jan. 5, 1982
78.5	Karen Jennings, Nebraska vs. Kansas St. (22-28)	Jan. 21, 1992
78.2	Debbie Beckford, St. John's (N.Y.) vs. Seton Hall (18-23)	Feb. 9, 1983
78.1	Deborah Temple, Delta St. vs. Tenn.-Martin (25-32)	Mar. 4, 1983

SINGLE-GAME THREE-POINT FIELD GOALS MADE

(Since 1988)

3FG	Player, Team vs. Opponent	Date
10	Paige Gulledge, Mississippi Col. vs. Mississippi Val.	Dec. 13, 1988
10	Kathy Halligan, Creighton vs. New Mexico St.	Feb. 10, 1990
10	Sandi Bittler, Princeton vs. Dartmouth	Feb. 23, 1990
10	Kim Kuhn, Niagara vs. Holy Cross	Feb. 24, 1990
10	Brenda Hatchett, Lamar vs. Central Fla.	Feb. 9, 1991
10	Sheila Ethridge, Louisiana Tech vs. Tex.-Pan American	Feb. 23, 1991
10	Amy Cherubini, Indiana vs. Ohio St.	Feb. 21, 1992
9	Fourteen players tied	

SINGLE-GAME REBOUNDING HIGHS

(Since 1982)

Reb.	Player, Team vs. Opponent	Date
40	Deborah Temple, Delta St. vs. Ala.-Birmingham	Feb. 14, 1983
37	Rosina Pearson, Bethune-Cookman vs. Fla. Memorial	Nov. 16, 1984
33	Maureen Formico, Pepperdine vs. Loyola (Cal.)	Feb. 15, 1985
31	Darlene Beale, Howard vs. South Caro. St.	Feb. 23, 1987

Reb.	Player, Team vs. Opponent	Date
30	Cindy Bonaforte, Wagner vs. Queens (N.Y.)	Feb. 15, 1983
30	Wanda Ford, Drake vs. Eastern Ill.	Feb. 16, 1985
29	Joy Kellogg, Oklahoma City vs. Okla. Christian	Nov. 29, 1983
29	Joy Kellogg, Oklahoma City vs. UTEP	Jan. 21, 1984
29	Gail Norris, Alabama St. vs. Texas Southern	Feb. 28, 1992
28	Tracy Claxton, Kansas vs. Pacific Christian	Nov. 21, 1981
28	Carolyn Thompson, Texas Tech vs. Rice	Jan. 29, 1982
28	Kara Audery, Lamar vs. McNeese St.	Feb. 28, 1984
28	Olivia Bradley, West Va. vs. Temple	Jan. 26, 1985
28	Yvette Larkins, Coppin St. vs. Charleston So.	Dec. 9, 1989
28	Tarcha Hollis, Grambling vs. Alcorn St.	Mar. 2, 1991

SINGLE-GAME ASSISTS

(Since 1986)

Ast.	Player, Team vs. Opponent	Date
23	Michelle Burden, Kent vs. Ball St.	Feb. 6, 1991
22	Shawn Monday, Tennessee Tech vs. Morehead St.	Feb. 1, 1988
22	Veronica Pettry, Loyola (Ill.) vs. Detroit Mercy	Mar. 4, 1989
22	Tine Freil, Pacific (Cal.) vs. Wichita St.	Dec. 14, 1990
21	Amy Bauer, Wisconsin vs. Detroit Mercy	Dec. 11, 1988
21	Neacole Hall, Alabama St. vs. Southern-B.R.	Jan. 21, 1989
21	Tine Freil, Pacific (Cal.) vs. Fresno St.	Mar. 8, 1992
20	Anja Bordt, St. Mary's (Cal.) vs. Loyola (Cal.)	Jan. 25, 1991
20	Mimi Harris, La Salle vs. Loyola (Ill.)	Feb. 1, 1992
20	Gaynor O'Donnell, East Caro. vs. N.C.-Asheville	Dec. 13, 1992
20	Ira Fuquay, Alcorn St. vs. Grambling	Feb. 8, 1993

SINGLE-GAME BLOCKED SHOTS

(Since 1988)

Blk.	Player, Team vs. Opponent	Date
15	Amy Lundquist, Loyola (Cal.) vs. Western Ill.	Dec. 20, 1992
13	Stefanie Kasperski, Oregon vs. Western Ky.	Dec. 29, 1987
13	Suzanne Johnson, Monmouth (N.J.) vs. Delaware	Dec. 13, 1990
12	Michelle Wilson, Texas Southern vs. Alcorn St.	Jan. 23, 1988
12	Stefanie Kasperski, Oregon vs. California	Feb. 26, 1988
12	Janetta Johnson, Wisconsin vs. Wis.-Green Bay	Dec. 7, 1988
12	Janetta Johnson, Wisconsin vs. Detroit Mercy	Dec. 11, 1988
12	Janetta Johnson, Wisconsin vs. Indiana	Jan. 6, 1989
12	Ellen Bayer, Texas vs. Texas Tech	Jan. 2, 1990
12	Chris Enger, San Diego vs. Gonzaga	Feb. 3, 1990
12	Simone Srubek, Fresno St. vs. Nevada-Las Vegas	Feb. 24, 1990
12	Denise Hogue, Charleston vs. Georgia St.	Feb. 26, 1992

SINGLE-GAME STEALS

(Since 1988)

Stl.	Player, Team vs. Opponent	Date
14	Natalie White, Florida A&M vs. South Ala.	Dec. 13, 1991
14	Heidi Caruso, Lafayette vs. Kansas St.	Dec. 5, 1992
13	Valorie Whiteside, Appalachian St. vs. Charleston	Jan. 9, 1988
13	Tammy Stover, Wright St. vs. Md.-East. Shore	Jan. 20, 1988
13	Stacy Hunt, Cal St. Fullerton vs. San Jose St.	Feb. 13, 1988
13	Ann Thomas, Tennessee St. vs. Monmouth (N.J.)	Nov. 25, 1989
13	Kim Hill, Northwestern (La.) vs. Northeast La.	Jan. 11, 1992
12	Joy Holmes, Purdue vs. Minnesota	Jan. 13, 1989
12	Diana Vines, DePaul vs. Notre Dame	Jan. 24, 1989
12	Lori Wilson, West Va. vs. Rhode Island	Jan. 22, 1990
12	Tammy Story, Southern Cal vs. California	Feb. 17, 1990
12	Debbie Ponist, Drexel vs. Lafayette	Feb. 21, 1990
12	Michelle Hennessey, Cal St. Fullerton vs. San Jose St.	Jan. 7, 1991
12	Ramona Jones, Lamar vs. Central Fla.	Jan. 14, 1991
12	Shelly Boston, Florida A&M vs. Stetson	Jan. 24, 1991
12	Stacy Coffey, Oklahoma St. vs. Missouri	Feb. 28, 1993

SEASON POINTS

Player, Team	Season	G	FG	3FG	FT	Pts.
Cindy Brown, Long Beach St.	1987	35	362	—	250	974
Genia Miller, Cal St. Fullerton	1991	33	376	0	217	969

Player, Team	Season	G	FG	3FG	FT	Pts.
Sheryl Swoopes, Texas Tech	1993	34	356	32	211	955
Andrea Congreaves, Mercer	1992	28	353	77	142	925
Wanda Ford, Drake	1986	30	390	—	139	919
Barbara Kennedy, Clemson	1982	31	392	—	124	908
Patricia Hoskins, Mississippi Val.	1989	27	345	13	205	908
LaTaunya Pollard, Long Beach St.	1983	31	376	—	155	907
Tina Hutchinson, San Diego St.	1984	30	383	—	132	898
Jan Jensen, Drake	1991	30	358	6	166	888
Deborah Temple, Delta St.	1984	28	373	—	127	873
Dale Hodges, St. Joseph's (Pa.)	1990	31	328	0	199	855
Wendy Scholtens, Vanderbilt	1990	34	309	1	236	855
Anucha Browne, Northwestern	1985	28	341	—	173	855
Lisa Foss, Northern Ill.	1991	35	340	14	159	853
LeChandra LeDay, Grambling	1988	28	334	36	146	850
Clarissa Davis, Texas	1989	32	324	7	188	843
Kim Perrot, Southwestern La.	1990	28	308	95	128	839
Jerilynn Harper, Tennessee Tech	1982	31	343	—	145	831
Pam Hudson, Northwestern (La.)	1990	29	330	1	168	829
Lorri Bauman, Drake	1982	35	273	—	275	821
Sonja Tate, Arkansas St.	1993	33	282	95	161	820
Sandra Hodge, New Orleans	1983	30	331	—	158	820
Lorri Bauman, Drake	1984	29	304	—	211	819
Lisa McMullen, Alabama St.	1991	28	285	126	119	815
Cheryl Miller, Southern Cal	1986	32	308	—	198	814
Deborah Temple, Delta St.	1983	29	311	—	189	811
Karen Jennings, Nebraska	1992	32	337	7	129	810
Tresa Spaulding, Brigham Young	1987	28	347	—	116	810
Patricia Hoskins, Mississippi Val.	1988	29	316	11	167	810
Andrea Congreaves, Mercer	1993	26	302	51	150	805
Cindy Brown, Long Beach St.	1986	33	324	—	157	805
Cheryl Miller, Southern Cal	1985	30	302	—	201	805

SEASON SCORING AVERAGE

Player, Team	Season	G	FG	3FG	FT	Pts.	Avg.
Patricia Hoskins, Mississippi Val.	†1989	27	345	13	205	908	*33.6
Andrea Congreaves, Mercer	†1992	28	353	77	142	925	33.0
Deborah Temple, Delta St.	†1984	28	373	—	127	873	31.2
Andrea Congreaves, Mercer	†1993	26	302	51	150	805	31.0
Wanda Ford, Drake	†1986	30	390	—	139	919	30.6
Anucha Browne, Northwestern	†1985	28	341	—	173	855	30.5
LeChandra LeDay, Grambling	†1988	28	334	36	146	850	30.4
Kim Perrot, Southwestern La.	†1990	28	308	95	128	839	30.0
Tina Hutchinson, San Diego St.	1984	30	383	—	132	898	29.9
Jan Jensen, Drake	†1991	30	358	6	166	888	29.6
Genia Miller, Cal St. Fullerton	1991	33	376	0	217	969	29.4
Barbara Kennedy, Clemson	†1982	31	*392	—	124	908	29.3
LaTaunya Pollard, Long Beach St.	†1983	31	376	—	155	907	29.3
Lisa McMullen, Alabama St.	1991	28	285	126	119	815	29.1
Tresa Spaulding, Brigham Young	†1987	28	347	—	116	810	28.9
Hope Linthicum, Central Conn. St.	1987	23	282	—	101	665	28.9
Pam Hudson, Northwestern (La.)	1990	29	330	1	168	829	28.6
Wanda Hightower, Ala.-Birmingham	1982	24	263	—	158	684	28.5
Lorri Bauman, Drake	1984	29	304	—	211	819	28.2
Sheryl Swoopes, Texas Tech	1993	34	356	32	211	955	28.1
Deborah Temple, Delta St.	1983	29	311	—	189	811	28.0
Dorothy Bowers, Youngstown St.	1988	28	342	0	99	783	28.0
Patricia Hoskins, Mississippi Val.	1988	29	316	11	167	810	27.9
Cindy Brown, Long Beach St.	1987	35	362	—	250	*974	27.8
Linda Grayson, Northwestern (La.)	1988	28	311	0	157	779	27.8

** Record. † National champion.*

SEASON FIELD-GOAL PERCENTAGE

(Based on qualifiers for annual championship)

Player, Team	Season	G	FG	FGA	Pct.
Renay Adams, Tennessee Tech	†1991	30	185	258	*71.7
Regina Days, Ga. Southern	†1986	27	234	332	70.5
Kelly Lyons, Old Dominion	†1990	31	308	444	69.4
Trina Roberts, Ga. Southern	†1982	31	189	277	68.2
Lidiya Varbanova, Boise St.	1991	22	128	188	68.1

Player, Team	Season	G	FG	FGA	Pct.
Lidiya Varbanova, Boise St.	†1993	27	200	294	68.0
Sharon McDowell, N.C.-Wilmington	†1987	28	170	251	67.7
Lidiya Varbanova, Boise St.	†1992	29	228	338	67.5
Mary Raese, Idaho	1986	31	254	380	66.8
Lydia Sawney, Tennessee Tech	†1983	27	167	250	66.8
Michelle Suman, San Diego St.	1992	29	156	234	66.7
Becky Jackson, Auburn	†1984	29	210	317	66.3
Monica Lamb, Houston	†1985	30	228	344	66.3
Becky Jackson, Auburn	1983	30	221	334	66.2
Katrina McClain, Georgia	1986	31	262	396	66.2
Tonya Baucom, Southwest Mo. St.	1992	34	173	263	65.8
Margaret Martinovich, Texas-San Antonio	1985	28	184	280	65.7
Chantelle Dishman, Florida St.	1991	31	191	291	65.6
Realia Davis, Nicholls St.	1985	27	198	303	65.3
Michele Savage, Northwestern	1990	27	178	273	65.2
Deneka Knowles, Southeastern La.	1993	26	133	204	65.2
DeShawne Blocker, East Tenn. St.	1993	25	191	294	65.0
Connie Price, Southern Ill.	1983	27	178	274	65.0
Cinietra Henderson, Texas	1993	30	211	325	64.9
Tresa Spaulding, Brigham Young	1987	28	347	536	64.7
Lisa Dodd, Wake Forest	†1988	31	172	266	64.7

* *Record.* † *National champion.*

SEASON THREE-POINT FIELD GOALS MADE PER GAME

(Based on qualifiers for annual championship)

Player, Team	Season	G	3FG	Avg.
Lisa McMullen, Alabama St.	†1991	28	126	*4.50
Gwen Davis, Bethune-Cookman	†1988	26	111	4.27
Sandi Bittler, Princeton	†1990	22	89	4.05
Kathy Halligan, Creighton	1990	27	102	3.78
Lynda Kukla, Valparaiso	†1992	27	101	3.74
Karen Middleton, South Caro.	1991	31	115	3.71
Marquerite Moran, Hofstra	†1989	29	107	3.69
Suzie Dailer, St. Bonaventure	†1993	27	99	3.67
Brenda Hatchett, Lamar	1991	33	119	3.61
Rhonda McCullough, Southwestern La.	1988	29	102	3.52
Lisa McMullen, Alabama St.	1990	28	98	3.50

* *Record.* † *National champion.*

SEASON THREE-POINT FIELD-GOAL PERCENTAGE

(Based on qualifiers for annual championship)

Player, Team	Season	G	3FG	3FGA	Pct.
Heather Donlon, Fordham	†1990	29	50	87	*57.5
Kathy Halligan, Creighton	†1992	32	72	130	55.4
Erin Maher, Harvard	1990	26	41	78	52.6
Cara Frey, Harvard	†1993	25	50	97	51.5
Alicia Burke, Oklahoma St.	†1989	32	57	111	51.4
Jamie Siess, Oklahoma St.	†1988	28	42	82	51.2
Heather Prather, Middle Tenn. St.	1993	28	46	90	51.1
Krista Treide, Wyoming	†1991	28	57	112	50.9
Joy Galloway, Charleston So.	1989	28	65	128	50.8
Kim Gilchrist, Mississippi	1992	31	53	105	50.5
Diane Starry, Evansville	1991	29	55	109	50.5
Mary Just, Loyola (Ill.)	1988	27	87	174	50.0

* *Record.* † *National champion.*

SEASON FREE-THROW PERCENTAGE

(Based on qualifiers for annual championship)

Player, Team	Season	G	FT	FTA	Pct.
Ginny Doyle, Richmond	†1992	29	96	101	*95.0
Linda Cyborski, Delaware	†1991	29	74	79	93.7
Keely Feeman, Cincinnati	†1986	30	76	82	92.7
Amy Slowikowski, Kent	†1989	27	112	121	92.6
Lea Ann Parsley, Marshall	†1990	28	96	104	92.3
Chris Starr, Nevada	1986	25	119	129	92.2
DeAnn Craft, Central Fla.	†1987	24	94	102	92.2
Tracey Sneed, La Salle	†1988	30	151	165	91.5

Player, Team	Season	G	FT	FTA	Pct.
Jana Crosby, Houston	1990	29	84	92	91.3
Lisa Goodin, Eastern Ky.	†1983	27	147	161	91.3
Lorea Feldman, Michigan	1986	28	72	79	91.1
Kelly Hebler, Eastern Mich.	1990	28	82	90	91.1
Jodi Roberts, Colorado St.	1989	28	112	123	91.1
Jennifer Cole, La Salle	†1993	27	150	165	90.9
Randi Meberg, Yale	1987	26	69	76	90.8
Susan Robinson, Penn St.	1992	31	98	108	90.7
Jody Beerman, Central Mich.	1986	29	133	147	90.5
Linda Page, North Caro. St.	1983	30	113	125	90.4
Lisa Furlin, Indiana	1993	27	75	83	90.4
Jen Nelson, Niagara	1993	27	81	90	90.0
Jenni Kraft, Duke	1989	28	90	100	90.0
Jeanine Radice, Fordham	1989	29	158	176	89.8
Jane Roman, Toledo	1992	32	87	97	89.7
Felisha Edwards, Northeast La.	1989	28	87	97	89.7
Emily McCracken, James Madison	1990	30	78	87	89.7
Julie Howell, Miami (Ohio)	1990	28	78	87	89.7
Jo Ellen Swanson, Ill.-Chicago	1987	27	68	76	89.5
Wendy Scholtens, Vanderbilt	1990	34	236	264	89.4
Kirsten Smith, Arizona	1986	28	100	112	89.3
Beverly Williams, Eastern Ill.	1991	27	108	121	89.3
Anna Pavlikhina, Va. Commonwealth	1992	29	82	92	89.1
Chris Starr, Nevada	1983	26	170	191	89.0
Sarah Behn, Boston College	1991	28	161	181	89.0

* *Record.* † *National champion.*

SEASON REBOUNDS

Player, Team	Season	G	Reb.
Wanda Ford, Drake	1985	30	534
Wanda Ford, Drake	†1986	30	506
Anne Donovan, Old Dominion	1983	35	504
Darlene Jones, Mississippi Val.	1983	31	487
Melanie Simpson, Oklahoma City	1982	37	481
Rosina Pearson, Bethune-Cookman	†1985	26	480
Patricia Hoskins, Mississippi Val.	†1987	28	476
Cheryl Miller, Southern Cal	1985	30	474
Darlene Beale, Howard	1987	29	459
Olivia Bradley, West Va.	1985	30	458
Valerie Still, Kentucky	1982	32	457
Darlene Jones, Mississippi Val.	1982	33	453
Deborah Temple, Delta St.	1983	29	451

† *National champion.*

SEASON REBOUND AVERAGE

Player, Team	Ht.	Season	G	Reb.	Avg.
Rosina Pearson, Bethune-Cookman	6-0	†1985	26	480	18.5
Wanda Ford, Drake	6-0	1985	30	534	17.8
Katie Beck, East Tenn. St.	6-0	†1988	25	441	17.6
Patricia Hoskins, Mississippi Val.	6-3	†1987	28	476	17.0
Wanda Ford, Drake	6-0	†1986	30	506	16.9
Patricia Hoskins, Mississippi Val.	6-3	†1989	27	440	16.3
Joy Kellogg, Oklahoma City	6-1	†1984	23	373	16.2
Deborah Mitchell, Mississippi Col.	6-2	†1983	28	447	16.0
Cheryl Miller, Southern Cal	6-3	1985	30	474	15.8
Darlene Beale, Howard	5-10	1987	29	459	15.8
Darlene Jones, Mississippi Val.	6-1	1983	31	487	15.7
Deborah Temple, Delta St.	5-10	1983	29	451	15.6
Valorie Whiteside, Appalachian St.	5-11	1985	28	435	15.5
Tarcha Hollis, Grambling	6-4	†1991	29	443	15.3
Olivia Bradley, West Va.	6-1	1985	30	458	15.3
Pam Hudson, Northwestern (La.)	5-11	†1990	29	438	15.1
Angela Jenkins, Georgia St.	6-3	1985	26	392	15.1
Darlene Beale, Howard	6-2	1986	28	422	15.1

† *National champion.*

SEASON ASSISTS

Player, Team	Season	G	Ast.
Suzie McConnell, Penn St.	†1987	30	355
Suzie McConnell, Penn St.	†1986	32	338
Tine Freil, Pacific (Cal.)	†1990	29	321
Neacole Hall, Alabama St.	†1989	29	319
Neacole Hall, Alabama St.	†1988	28	318
Faith Mimnaugh, Loyola (Ill.)	†1985	27	316

† *National champion.*

SEASON ASSIST AVERAGE

Player, Team	Season	G	Ast.	Avg.
Suzie McConnell, Penn St.	†1987	30	355	11.8
Faith Mimnaugh, Loyola (Ill.)	†1985	27	316	11.7
Neacole Hall, Alabama St.	†1988	28	318	11.4
Tine Freil, Pacific (Cal.)	†1990	29	321	11.1
Neacole Hall, Alabama St.	†1989	29	319	11.0
Gaynor O'Donnell, East Caro.	†1993	28	300	10.7
Suzie McConnell, Penn St.	†1986	32	338	10.6
Kim Skala, East Tenn. St.	1986	27	285	10.6

† *National champion.*

SEASON BLOCKED SHOTS

Player, Team	Season	G	Blk.
Michelle Wilson, Texas Southern	†1989	27	151
Denise Hogue, Charleston	†1992	28	147
Genia Miller, Cal St. Fullerton	1991	33	146
Simone Srubek, Fresno St.	†1990	31	138
Chris Enger, San Diego	†1993	28	137
Trish Andrew, Michigan	1992	28	136
Heidi Gillingham, Vanderbilt	1992	31	131
Janetta Johnson, Wisconsin	1989	27	130
Simone Srubek, Fresno St.	1989	30	130

† *National champion.*

SEASON BLOCKED-SHOT AVERAGE

Player, Team	Season	G	Blk.	Avg.
Michelle Wilson, Texas Southern	†1989	27	151	5.6
Denise Hogue, Charleston	†1992	28	147	5.3
Suzanne Johnson, Monmouth (N.J.)	†1991	23	117	5.1
Chris Enger, San Diego	†1993	28	137	4.9
Trish Andrew, Michigan	1992	28	136	4.9
Janetta Johnson, Wisconsin	1989	27	130	4.8
Simone Srubek, Fresno St.	†1990	31	138	4.5
Carvie Upshaw, New Orleans	1989	28	125	4.5
Genia Miller, Cal St. Fullerton	1991	33	146	4.4

† *National champion.*

SEASON STEALS

Player, Team	Season	G	Stl.
Heidi Caruso, Lafayette	†1993	28	168
Shelly Boston, Florida A&M	†1990	29	160
Donna McGary, Mississippi Val.	†1989	29	158
Debbie Black, St. Joseph's (Pa.)	1988	32	150
Neacole Hall, Alabama St.	1989	29	148
Heidi Caruso, Lafayette	1992	29	144
Natalie White, Florida A&M	†1992	28	143
Kim Perrot, Southwestern La.	1990	28	143
Shelly Boston, Florida A&M	†1991	28	142

† *National champion.*

SEASON STEAL AVERAGE

Player, Team	Season	G	Stl.	Avg.
Heidi Caruso, Lafayette	†1993	28	168	6.0
Shelly Boston, Florida A&M	†1990	29	160	5.5
Donna McGary, Mississippi Val.	†1989	29	158	5.4
Kim Perrot, Southwestern La.	1990	28	143	5.1
Neacole Hall, Alabama St.	1989	29	148	5.1

Player, Team	Season	G	Stl.	Avg.
Tami Varnado, Alcorn St.	1992	27	136	5.0
Heidi Caruso, Lafayette	1992	29	144	5.0
Liz Holz, Montana St.	1989	26	124	4.8
Neacole Hall, Alabama St.	†1988	28	133	4.8

† *National champion.*

TOP SEASONAL PERFORMANCES BY CLASS

SCORING AVERAGE

Class	Player, Team	Year	G	FG	3FG	FT	Pts.	Avg.
Senior	Patricia Hoskins, Mississippi Val.	1989	27	345	13	205	908	33.6
Junior	Andrea Congreaves, Mercer	1992	28	353	77	142	925	33.0
Sophomore	Deborah Temple, Delta St.	1983	29	311	—	189	811	28.0
Freshman	Tina Hutchinson, San Diego St.	1984	30	383	—	132	898	29.9

FIELD-GOAL PERCENTAGE

Class	Player, Team	Year	G	FG	FGA	Pct.
Senior	Renay Adams, Tennessee Tech	1991	30	185	258	71.7
Junior	Lidiya Varbonova, Boise St.	1993	27	200	294	68.0
Sophomore	Regina Days, Ga. Southern	1986	27	234	332	70.5
Freshman	Michelle Suman, San Diego St.	1992	29	156	234	66.7

THREE-POINT FIELD GOALS MADE

Class	Player, Team	Year	G	3FG	Avg.
Senior	Sandi Bittler, Princeton	1990	22	89	4.05
Junior	Lisa McMullen, Alabama St.	1991	28	126	4.50
Sophomore	Kathy Halligan, Creighton	1990	27	102	3.78
Freshman	Cristi Timmons, South Caro.	1992	28	84	3.00

THREE-POINT FIELD-GOAL PERCENTAGE

Class	Player, Team	Year	G	3FG	3FGA	Pct.
Senior	Kathy Halligan, Creighton	1992	32	72	130	55.4
Junior	Cara Frey, Harvard	1993	25	50	97	51.5
Sophomore	Camille Lowe, Georgia	1991	32	52	107	48.6
Freshman	Heather Donlon, Fordham	1990	29	50	87	57.5

FREE-THROW PERCENTAGE

Class	Player, Team	Year	G	FT	FTA	Pct.
Senior	Ginny Doyle, Richmond	1992	29	96	101	95.0
Junior	Linda Cyborski, Delaware	1991	29	74	79	93.7
Sophomore	Lorea Feldman, Michigan	1986	28	72	79	91.1
Freshman	Lisa Furlin, Indiana	1993	27	75	83	90.4

REBOUND AVERAGE

Class	Player, Team	Year	G	Reb.	Avg.
Senior	Katie Beck, East Tenn. St.	1988	25	441	17.6
Junior	Rosina Pearson, Bethune-Cookman	1985	26	480	18.5
Sophomore	Patricia Hoskins, Mississippi Val.	1987	28	476	17.0
Freshman	Valorie Whiteside, Appalachian St.	1985	28	435	15.5

ASSIST AVERAGE

Class	Player, Team	Year	G	Ast.	Avg.
Senior	Faith Mimnaugh, Loyola (Ill.)	1985	27	316	11.7
Junior	Suzie McConnell, Penn St.	1987	30	355	11.8
Sophomore	Suzie McConnell, Penn St.	1986	32	338	10.6
Freshman	Tine Freil, Pacific (Cal.)	1990	29	321	11.1

BLOCKED-SHOT AVERAGE

Class	Player, Team	Year	G	Blk.	Avg.
Senior	Michelle Wilson, Texas Southern	1989	27	151	5.6
Junior	Denise Hogue, Charleston	1992	28	147	5.3
Sophomore	Stefanie Kasperski, Oregon	1988	28	119	4.3
Freshman	Kathy Gilbert, Columbia-Barnard	1988	25	101	4.0

STEAL AVERAGE

Class	Player, Team	Year	G	Stl.	Avg.
Senior	Kim Perrot, Southwestern La.	1990	28	143	5.1
Junior	Heidi Caruso, Lafayette	1993	28	168	6.0
Sophomore	Shelly Boston, Florida A&M	1990	29	160	5.5
Freshman	Natalie White, Florida A&M	1992	28	143	5.1

[All career leaders include only those players who played at least three seasons (in a four-year career) or two (in a three-season career) in Division I during the era of official NCAA statistics beginning with the 1981-82 season.]

CAREER POINTS

Player, Team	Last Year	G	Pts.
Patricia Hoskins, Mississippi Val.	1989	110	3,122
Lorri Bauman, Drake	1984	120	3,115
Cheryl Miller, Southern Cal	1986	128	3,018
Valorie Whiteside, Appalachian St.	1988	116	2,944
Joyce Walker, Louisiana St.	1984	117	2,906
Sandra Hodge, New Orleans	1984	107	2,860
Andrea Congreaves, Mercer	1993	108	2,796
Karen Pelphrey, Marshall	1986	114	2,746
Cindy Brown, Long Beach St.	1987	128	2,696
Carolyn Thompson, Texas Tech	1984	121	2,655
Sue Wicks, Rutgers	1988	125	2,655
Janet Harris, Georgia	1985	131	2,641
Wanda Ford, Drake	1986	117	2,636
Wendy Scholtens, Vanderbilt	1991	122	2,602
Lisa Ingram, Northeast La.	1986	113	2,601
Deborah Temple, Delta St./Mississippi	1985	118	2,573
Annette Smith, Texas	1986	131	2,535
Tracy Lis, Providence	1992	127	2,534
Cheryl Taylor, Tennessee Tech	1987	120	2,526
Sarah Behn, Boston College	1993	109	2,523
Diana Vines, DePaul	1989	121	2,504
Lisa Foss, Northern Ill.	1991	122	2,500
Judy Mosley, Hawaii	1990	114	2,479
Cherie Nelson, Southern Cal	1989	122	2,474
Bridgette Gordon, Tennessee	1989	137	2,450
Caroline Mast, Ohio	1986	112	2,449
Jeanine Radice, Fordham	1989	111	2,417
Genia Miller, Cal St. Fullerton	1991	118	2,415
Sheila Tighe, Manhattan	1984	113	2,412
Shelly Pennefather, Villanova	1987	117	2,408
Karen Jennings, Nebraska	1993	119	2,405
MaChelle Joseph, Purdue	1992	119	2,405
Rachel Bouchard, Maine	1991	110	2,405
Janice Lawrence, Louisiana Tech	1984	135	2,403
Lorena Legarde, Portland	1985	127	2,393
Regina Kirk, Tenn.-Chatt.	1988	112	2,376
Karen Elsner, Richmond	1985	110	2,367
Cheryl Cook, Cincinnati	1985	114	2,367
Kym Hampton, Arizona St.	1984	120	2,361
Maria Rivera, Miami (Fla.)	1988	112	2,358
Chris Starr, Nevada	1986	101	2,356
Paula McGee, Southern Cal.	1984	127	2,346
Sue Galkantas, Florida St.	1984	120	2,327
Dorothy Bowers, Youngstown St.	1988	108	2,322
Sonja Tate, Arkansas St.	1993	119	2,312
Lorri Johnson, Pittsburgh	1991	113	2,312
Tresa Spaulding, Brigham Young	1987	102	2,309
Linda Page, North Caro. St.	1985	124	2,307
Anucha Browne, Northwestern	1985	110	2,307
Jennifer Bruce, Pittsburgh	1985	112	2,295
Sheila Smith, Murray St.	1989	116	2,287
Adrian Vickers, South Ala.	1990	119	2,285
Lillie Mason, Western Ky.	1986	125	2,262
Mary Currie, Grambling	1987	109	2,256
Alison Lang, Oregon	1984	117	2,254
Susan Robinson, Penn St.	1992	122	2,253
Sherry Levin, Holy Cross	1984	103	2,253
$Shalonda Young, Queens (N.Y.)	1988	103	2,251
LeChandra LeDay, Grambling	1988	111	2,250
Chris Moreland, Duke	1988	111	2,232
Kris Kinney, New Hampshire	1989	108	2,231
Kelly Lyons, Old Dominion	1990	122	2,224
Pam McGee, Southern Cal	1984	127	2,214
Eun Jung Lee, Northeast La.	1986	117	2,208
Katrina McClain, Georgia	1987	125	2,195

Player, Team	Last Year	G	Pts.
Marilyn Stephens, Temple	1984	117	2,194
Penny Toler, San Diego St./Long Beach St.	1989	101	2,193
Vivian Herron, Oral Roberts	1989	109	2,192
Maureen Formico, Pepperdine	1986	112	2,190
Jennifer Gillom, Mississippi	1986	126	2,185
Frances Savage, Miami (Fla.)	1992	94	2,184
Kerry Bascom, Connecticut	1991	120	2,177
Shannon Cate, Montana	1992	116	2,172
Clinette Jordan, Oklahoma St.	1989	119	2,168
Chana Perry, Northeast La./San Diego St.	1989	103	2,163
Kathy Halligan, Creighton	1992	115	2,159
Kim Perrot, Southwestern La.	1990	110	2,157
Liz Coffin, Maine	1988	114	2,153
Katie Beck, East Tenn. St.	1988	105	2,151
Stephanie Howard, Radford	1989	112	2,146
Kim Webb, Middle Tenn. St.	1987	116	2,145
Phylette Blake, Ga. Southern	1989	108	2,140
Andrea Stinson, North Caro. St.	1991	94	2,136
Dawn Staley, Virginia	1992	131	2,135
Maurtice Ivy, Nebraska	1988	111	2,131
Portland McCaskill, Southern Miss.	1985	112	2,130
Joni Davis, Missouri	1985	124	2,126
Jackie Motycka, Bowling Green	1989	117	2,123
Renee Kelly, Missouri	1987	122	2,119
Orphie Moore, South Ala.	1987	117	2,118
Jennifer Walz, Bucknell	1989	111	2,112
Ella Williams, Alcorn St.	1984	109	2,111
Kelly Lane, American/Temple	1990	117	2,104
Carol Owens, Northern Ill	1990	116	2,102
Venus Lacy, Old Dominion/Louisiana Tech	1990	125	2,096
Erma Jones, Bethune-Cookman	1984	87	2,095
Regina Days, Ga. Southern	1988	111	2,091
Val Whiting, Stanford	1993	129	2,077
Dale Hodges, St. Joseph's (Pa.)	1990	94	2,077
Deb Asper, Utah	1984	121	2,074
Bettye Fiscus, Arkansas	1985	112	2,073
Sonya Carter, U.S. Int'l	1989	110	2,071
Becky Jackson, Auburn	1984	116	2,068
Lisa Van Goor, Colorado	1985	115	2,067
Tammy McCarthy, Md.-Balt. County	1987	108	2,063
Antoinette Norris, Stephen F. Austin	1988	120	2,062
Rosemary Kosiorek, West Va.	1992	116	2,061
Heather Burge, Virginia	1993	135	2,058
Tarcha Hollis, Grambling	1991	85	2,058
Gwen Austin, N.C.-Wilmington	1985	109	2,056
Laura Coenen, Minnesota	1985	102	2,044
Regina Street, Memphis St.	1985	121	2,043
Jo Ann Osterkamp, Xavier (Ohio)	1984	111	2,036
Cassandra Pack, Detroit Mercy	1987	106	2,036
Vickie Orr, Auburn	1989	131	2,035
Carol Smith, Alabama	1986	116	2,028
Maggie Stinnett, Baylor	1991	106	2,026
Kahadeejah Herbert, Penn St.	1985	126	2,026
Pam Gradoville, Creighton	1988	110	2,024
Patrinda Toney, Radford	1992	118	2,020
Tonya Grant, St. Peter's	1990	110	2,020
Julie VonDielingen, Butler	1993	112	2,018
Nancy Bernhardt, Villanova	1984	119	2,018
Suzanne Bowen, Colgate	1991	108	2,016
Tammy Tibbles, Gonzaga	1988	111	2,011
Connie Yori, Creighton	1986	99	2,010
Debbie Bolen, Valparaiso	1993	109	2,008
Clarissa Davis, Texas	1989	101	2,008
Jamie Glassford, U.S. Int'l	1984	108	2,007
Pam Leake, North Caro.	1986	124	2,001

$ *Played three seasons in Division I (Division II in 1988).*

CAREER SCORING AVERAGE

(Minimum 75 games played)

Player, Team	Seasons	G	FG	3FG	FT	Pts.	Avg.
Patricia Hoskins, Mississippi Val.	1985-89	110	1,196	24	706	*3,122	*28.4
Sandra Hodge, New Orleans	1981-84	107	1,194	—	472	2,860	26.7
Lorri Bauman, Drake	1981-84	120	1,104	—	*907	3,115	26.0
Andrea Congreaves, Mercer	1989-93	108	1,107	153	429	2,796	25.9
Valorie Whiteside, Appalachian St.	1984-88	116	1,153	0	638	2,944	25.4
Joyce Walker, Louisiana St.	1981-84	117	*1,259	—	388	2,906	24.8
Tarcha Hollis, Grambling	1988-91	85	904	3	247	2,058	24.2
Karen Pelphrey, Marshall	1983-86	114	1,175	—	396	2,746	24.1
Erma Jones, Bethune-Cookman	1982-84	87	961	—	173	2,095	24.1
Cheryl Miller, Southern Cal	1983-86	128	1,159	—	700	3,018	23.6
Chris Starr, Nevada	1983-86	101	881	—	594	2,356	23.3
Frances Savage, Miami (Fla.)	1988-92	94	830	43	481	2,184	23.2
Sarah Behn, Boston College	1989-93	109	867	106	683	2,523	23.1
Lisa Ingram, Northeast La.	1983-86	113	1,093	—	415	2,601	23.0
Andrea Stinson, North Caro. St.	1987-91	94	917	55	247	2,136	22.7
Tresa Spaulding, Brigham Young	1983-87	102	968	—	373	2,309	22.6
Wanda Ford, Drake	1983-86	117	1,132	—	372	2,636	22.5
Dale Hodges, St. Joseph's (Pa.)	1986-90	94	817	0	443	2,077	22.1
Carolyn Thompson, Texas Tech	1981-84	121	1,013	—	629	2,655	21.9
Sherry Levin, Holy Cross	1981-84	103	842	—	569	2,253	21.9
$Shalonda Young, Queens (N.Y.)	1984-88	103	944	9	354	2,251	21.9
Caroline Mast, Ohio	1983-86	112	898	—	653	2,449	21.9
Rachel Bouchard, Maine	1987-91	110	875	0	655	2,405	21.9
Deborah Temple, Delta St./Mississippi	1982-84, 85	118	1,036	—	501	2,573	21.8
Jeanine Radice, Fordham	1985-89	111	929	38	521	2,417	21.8
Judy Mosley, Hawaii	1986-90	114	901	0	677	2,479	21.7
Penny Toler, San Diego St./ Long Beach St.	1984-89	101	933	1	326	2,193	21.7
Karen Elsner, Richmond	1982-85	110	935	—	497	2,367	21.5
Dorothy Bowers, Youngstown St.	1984-88	108	976	0	370	2,322	21.5
Sheila Tighe, Manhattan	1981-84	113	1,000	—	412	2,412	21.3
Wendy Scholtens, Vanderbilt	1987-91	122	959	3	681	2,602	21.3
Sue Wicks, Rutgers	1984-88	125	1,091	0	473	2,655	21.2
Regina Kirk, Tenn.-Chatt.	1984-88	112	964	0	448	2,376	21.2
Angela Moorehead, Tennessee Tech	1987-91	91	781	27	336	1,925	21.2
Anja Bordt, St. Mary's (Cal.)	1988-91	81	503	185	519	1,710	21.1
Cheryl Taylor, Tennessee Tech	1983-87	120	1,025	—	476	2,526	21.1
Cindy Brown, Long Beach St.	1983-87	128	1,048	—	600	2,696	21.1
Maria Rivera, Miami (Fla.)	1984-88	112	892	64	508	2,358	21.1
Chana Perry, Northeast La./ San Diego St.	1984-89	103	847	0	469	2,163	21.0
Anucha Browne, Northwestern	1982-85	110	919	—	469	2,307	21.0
Cheryl Cook, Cincinnati	1982-85	114	962	—	443	2,367	20.8
Mary Currie, Grambling	1983-87	109	851	—	554	2,256	20.7
Diana Vines, DePaul	1985-89	121	960	16	568	2,504	20.7
Kris Kinney, New Hampshire	1985-89	108	929	2	371	2,231	20.7
Jacque Nero, Ala.-Birmingham	1988-92	94	784	2	369	1,939	20.6
Shelly Pennefather, Villanova	1983-87	117	1,073	—	262	2,408	20.6
Jennifer Bruce, Pittsburgh	1982-85	112	896	—	503	2,295	20.5
Lisa Foss, Northern Ill	1987-91	122	1,052	17	379	2,500	20.5
Katie Beck, East Tenn. St.	1984-88	105	897	0	357	2,151	20.5
Genia Miller, Cal St. Fullerton	1987-91	118	914	0	587	2,415	20.5
Lorri Johnson, Pittsburgh	1987-91	113	876	109	451	2,312	20.5
Cherie Nelson, Southern Cal.	1985-89	122	933	0	608	2,474	20.3
LeChandra LeDay, Grambling	1984-88	111	898	60	394	2,250	20.3
Lorena Legarde, Portland	1982-85	127	995	—	578	2,568	20.2
MaChelle Joseph, Purdue	1988-92	119	902	138	463	2,405	20.2
Karen Jennings, Nebraska	1989-93	119	981	17	426	2,405	20.2
Janet Harris, Georgia	1982-85	131	1,127	—	387	2,641	20.2
Vivian Herron, Oral Roberts	1985-89	109	853	1	485	2,192	20.1
Chris Moreland, Duke	1984-88	111	828	0	576	2,232	20.1
Donna Yaffe, Brown	1982-85	89	645	—	489	1,788	20.1
Laura Coenen, Minnesota	1982-85	102	842	—	360	2,044	20.0
Sally Anderson, DePaul	1983-87	86	689	—	342	1,720	20.0
Sue Peters, Massachusetts	1983-87	93	757	—	344	1,858	20.0
Tracy Lis, Providence	1988-92	127	906	182	540	2,534	20.0

$ *Played three seasons in Division I (Division II in 1988).* * *Record.*

CAREER FIELD-GOAL PERCENTAGE

(Minimum 400 field goals made)

Player, Team	Seasons	G	FG	FGA	Pct.
Regina Days, Ga. Southern	1984-88	111	835	1,282	*65.1
Kelly Lyons, Old Dominion	1986-90	122	887	1,373	64.6
Renay Adams, Tennessee Tech	1987-91	120	600	931	64.4
Trina Roberts, Ga. Southern	1981-84	117	695	1,099	63.2
Roschelle Vaughn, Tennessee Tech	1991-93	59	488	780	62.6
Katrina McClain, Georgia	1983-87	125	873	1,407	62.0
Vickie Adkins, Kansas	1983-86	95	696	1,127	61.8
Portia Hill, Stephen F. Austin	1988-90	65	610	990	61.6
Mary Raese, Idaho	1983-86	115	723	1,181	61.2
Sharon McDowell, N.C.-Wilmington	1984-88	96	426	699	60.9
Tresa Spaulding, Brigham Young	1983-87	102	968	1,589	60.9
Delmonica DeHorney, Arkansas	1987-91	115	667	1,096	60.9
Pam Hudson, Northwestern (La.)	1988-90	55	559	919	60.8
Jenny Mitchell, Wake Forest	1987-91	117	763	1,258	60.7
Michele Savage, Northwestern	1988-92	90	653	1,078	60.6
Lorena Legarde, Portland	1982-85	127	995	1,647	60.4
Heidi Bunek, Notre Dame	1985-89	83	509	843	60.4
Chris Starr, Nevada	1983-86	101	881	1,460	60.3
Becky Jackson, Auburn	1981-84	116	864	1,439	60.0
Chantelle Dishman, Florida St.	1989-93	94	483	805	60.0
Tracey Hall, Ohio St.	1984-88	122	807	1,346	60.0
Brenda Souther, Eastern Wash.	1983-87	100	766	1,282	59.8
Realia Davis, Nicholls St.	1983-87	103	724	1,215	59.6
Regina Howard, Rutgers	1983-87	118	736	1,237	59.5
Wanda Guyton, South Fla.	1985-89	97	737	1,240	59.4
Char Warring, Southern Ill.	1981-84	117	602	1,014	59.4
Janice Lawrence, Louisiana Tech	1981-84	135	934	1,577	59.2
Mary K. Nordling, Geo. Washington	1988-92	98	472	797	59.2
Renee Daniels, Southeastern La.	1982-86	107	684	1,156	59.2
Alison Lang, Oregon	1981-84	117	884	1,496	59.1
Sheila Frost, Tennessee	1985-89	138	754	1,276	59.1
Cinietra Henderson, Texas	1989-93	123	779	1,319	59.1
Jean Marie Buckley, Holy Cross	1983-87	94	414	703	58.9
Regina Street, Memphis St.	1982-85	121	831	1,411	58.8
Sandy Botham, Notre Dame	1984-88	114	594	1,010	58.8
Jessie Hicks, Maryland	1989-93	112	649	1,104	58.8
Lisa Ingram, Northeast La.	1983-86	113	1,093	1,861	58.7
Trena Trice, North Caro. St.	1983-87	117	740	1,266	58.5
Nell Knox, Louisville	1989-93	124	803	1,376	58.4
Cindy Brown, Long Beach St.	1983-87	128	1,048	1,798	58.3
Pam McGee, Southern Cal	1981-84	127	935	1,607	58.2

* *Record.*

CAREER THREE-POINT FIELD GOALS MADE

Player, Team	Ht.	Last Year	Yrs.	G	3FG
Karen Middleton, South Caro.	5-10	1991	4	128	317
Kathy Halligan, Creighton	5-10	1992	4	115	309
Julie Jones, Richmond	5-9	1992	4	123	309
Wendy Davis, Connecticut	5-8	1992	4	127	279
Kelly Savage, Toledo	5-9	1990	3	92	273
Lynda Kukla, Valparaiso	5-11	1992	4	114	264
Kim Kuhn, Niagara	5-9	1993	4	109	261
Erin Maher, Harvard	5-8	1993	4	103	261
Rhonda McCullough, McNeese St./Southwestern La.	5-8	1990	3	82	260
Michele Hughes, Portland St.	5-3	1991	4	107	256
Sandi Bittler, Princeton	5-6	1990	3	73	246
Gina Sutko, Ala.-Birmingham	5-9	1991	4	119	245
Heather Donlon, Fordham	5-4	1993	4	116	233
Cynthia Thomson, Liberty	5-7	1993	4	113	227
Lisa McMullen, Alabama St.	5-7	1991	2	56	224
Chris Anderson, Wagner	5-8	1992	4	111	224
Denise Dove, Northern Ill.	5-4	1991	4	121	221
Krista Kirkland, Texas Tech	5-10	1993	4	126	219
Kathy Lizarraga, UC Irvine	5-4	1992	4	95	218

CAREER THREE-POINT FIELD GOALS MADE PER GAME

(Minimum 150 three-point field goals made)

Player, Team	Ht.	Last Year	Yrs.	G	3FG	Avg.
Lisa McMullen, Alabama St.	5-7	1991	2	56	224	4.00
Sandi Bittler, Princeton	5-6	1990	3	73	246	3.37
Brenda Hatchett, Lamar	5-0	1992	2	56	188	3.36
Rhonda McCullough, McNeese St./ Southwestern La.	5-8	1990	3	82	260	3.17
Kelly Savage, Toledo	5-9	1990	3	92	273	2.97
Jana Crosby, Houston	5-6	1990	2	57	161	2.82
Julie Lienert, Santa Clara	5-9	1991	2	57	157	2.75
Kathy Halligan, Creighton	5-10	1992	4	115	309	2.69
Dana Bilyeu, Tennessee Tech	5-7	1993	2	59	155	2.63
Anna Pavlikhina, Va. Commonwealth	6-2	1993	3	76	196	2.58
Erin Maher, Harvard	5-8	1993	4	103	261	2.53
Julie Jones, Richmond	5-9	1992	4	123	309	2.51
Karen Middleton, South Caro.	5-10	1991	4	128	317	2.48
Kim Perrot, Southwestern La.	5-4	1990	3	83	202	2.43
Kim Kuhn, Niagara	5-9	1993	4	109	261	2.39
Michele Hughes, Portland St.	5-3	1991	4	107	256	2.39

CAREER THREE-POINT FIELD-GOAL PERCENTAGE

(Minimum 150 three-point field goals made)

Player, Team	Ht.	Last Year	Yrs.	G	3FG	3FGA	Pct.
Erin Maher, Harvard	5-8	1993	4	103	261	559	46.7
Jana Crosby, Houston	5-6	1990	2	57	161	345	46.7
Heather Donlon, Fordham	5-4	1993	4	116	233	504	46.2
Sandi Bittler, Princeton	5-6	1990	3	73	246	534	46.1
Kathy Halligan, Creighton	5-10	1992	4	115	309	680	45.4
Jennifer Azzi, Stanford	5-9	1990	3	95	191	423	45.2
Angie Snyder, South Fla.	5-6	1992	4	109	159	357	44.5
Karen Middleton, South Caro.	5-10	1991	4	128	317	712	44.5
Wendy Davis, Connecticut	5-8	1992	4	127	279	635	43.9
Julie Jones, Richmond	5-9	1992	4	123	309	712	43.4
Kim Berry, Georgia	5-7	1991	4	113	189	442	42.8
Brenda Hatchett, Lamar	5-0	1992	2	56	188	440	42.7
Krista Kirkland, Texas Tech	5-10	1993	4	126	219	525	42.7
Melanee Ehrhardt, DePaul	5-8	1990	3	94	160	383	41.8
Kim Pehlke, Western Ky.	5-7	1992	4	127	209	502	41.6
Peggy Taylor, Siena	5-10	1992	4	108	205	497	41.2
Rhonda McCullough, McNeese St./ Southwestern La.	5-8	1990	3	82	260	632	41.1
Kris Lamb, Connecticut	5-11	1990	3	83	151	368	41.0
Julie Lienert, Santa Clara	5-9	1991	2	57	157	393	40.0
Kerry Bascom, Connecticut	6-1	1991	4	120	161	404	39.9
Denise Dove, Northern Ill.	5-4	1991	4	121	221	561	39.4
Michele Hughes, Portland St.	5-3	1991	4	107	256	650	39.4
Angie Cox, Eastern Ky.	5-9	1992	4	105	170	435	39.1
Cindy Pruim, Loyola (Ill.)	5-9	1992	4	111	152	389	39.1
Jennifer Shasky, Geo. Washington	5-10	1993	4	117	196	502	39.0
Molly Goodenbour, Stanford	5-6	1993	4	120	178	456	39.0
Anja Bordt, St. Mary's (Cal.)	5-8	1991	3	81	185	475	38.9
Kelly Savage, Toledo	5-9	1990	3	92	273	708	38.6
Anna Pavlikhina, Va. Commonwealth	6-2	1993	3	76	196	509	38.5
Veda McNeal, Mo.-Kansas City	5-6	1993	4	99	174	452	38.5
Angie Dobbs, Navy	5-9	1992	4	100	216	563	38.4
Susan Blakely, Eastern Wash.	5-8	1990	3	82	185	483	38.3

CAREER FREE-THROW PERCENTAGE

(Minimum 250 free throws made)

Player, Team	Seasons	G	FT	FTA	Pct.
Karen Murray, Washington	1981-84	107	269	307	*87.6
Susan Robinson, Penn St.	1988-92	122	487	557	87.4
Lisa Goodin, Eastern Ky.	1981-84	111	526	602	87.4
Jennifer Cole, La Salle	1989-93	116	398	456	87.3
Wendy Scholtens, Vanderbilt	1987-91	122	681	785	86.8
Chris Starr, Nevada	1983-86	101	594	687	86.5

Player, Team	Seasons	G	FT	FTA	Pct.
Linda Page, North Caro. St.	1982-85	124	407	477	85.3
Jeanine Radice, Fordham	1985-89	111	521	612	85.1
Jody Beerman, Central Mich	1983-87	114	491	577	85.1
Angie Snyder, South Fla.	1988-92	109	390	459	85.0
Kelly Hebler, Eastern Mich.	1986-90	106	279	329	84.8
Jodi Roberts, Colorado St.	1985-89	112	351	414	84.8
Sarah Behn, Boston College	1989-93	109	683	808	84.5
Amy Slowikowski, Kent	1986-90	110	327	387	84.5
Sheryl Swoopes, Texas Tech	1991-93	66	346	410	84.4
Tammie Crown, Radford	1989-93	115	279	332	84.0
Anja Bordt, St. Mary's (Cal.)	1988-91	81	519	621	83.6
Julie Howell, Miami (Ohio)	1988-92	111	268	321	83.5
Kathy Schulz, Oklahoma St.	1984-85	57	340	408	83.3
Keely Feeman, Cincinnati	1983-86	116	264	317	83.3
Jane Roman, Toledo	1988-92	94	273	328	83.2
Lorri Bauman, Drake	1981-84	120	907	1,090	83.2
Sally Anderson, DePaul	1983-87	86	342	411	83.2
Cindy Bumgarner, Indiana	1984-88	106	408	491	83.1
Julie Zeilstra, Stanford	1988-91	94	296	358	82.7
Dana Chatman, Louisiana St.	1987-91	120	453	548	82.7
Maggie Timoney, Iona	1985-89	114	518	628	82.5
Kelly Savage, Toledo	1986-90	118	390	474	82.3
Sue Manelski, James Madison	1982-85	105	395	481	82.1
Charity Shira, Southwest Mo. St.	1988-92	117	375	457	82.1
Lisa Foss, Northern Ill.	1987-91	122	379	462	82.0
Randi Meberg, Yale	1985-89	103	250	305	82.0
Debra Taylor, Cleveland St.	1987-91	106	391	477	82.0
Shannon Cate, Montana	1988-92	116	423	517	81.8
Tracy Tripp, Colorado	1985-89	121	262	321	81.6
Sherry Levin, Holy Cross	1981-84	103	569	698	81.5
Karen Lounsbury, Georgia Tech	1988-92	119	320	393	81.4
Debbie Flandermeyer, Harvard	1989-93	103	284	349	81.4
Debbie Hartnett, Seton Hall	1985-89	113	257	316	81.3
Karin Vadelund, Geo. Washington	1986-90	105	328	404	81.2
Tammy Rogers, Oklahoma	1986-90	114	283	349	81.1
Dawn Staley, Virginia	1988-92	131	505	623	81.1
Erin Carson, Colorado	1984-88	112	308	380	81.1
Sandra Hodge, New Orleans	1981-84	107	472	583	81.0
Jackie Motycka, Bowling Green	1985-89	117	431	532	81.0
Lauri Landerholm, Oregon	1983-87	120	379	468	81.0

* *Record.*

CAREER REBOUNDS

Player, Team	Seasons	G	Reb.
Wanda Ford, Drake	1983-86	117	1,887
Patricia Hoskins, Mississippi Val.	1985-89	110	1,662
Cheryl Miller, Southern Cal	1983-86	128	1,534
Cheryl Taylor, Tennessee Tech	1983-87	120	1,532
Marilyn Stephens, Temple	1981-84	117	1,519

CAREER REBOUND AVERAGE

(Minimum 800 rebounds)

Player, Team	Ht.	Seasons	G	Reb.	Avg.
Wanda Ford, Drake	6-0	1983-86	117	1,887	*16.1
Patricia Hoskins, Mississippi Val.	6-3	1985-89	110	1,662	15.1
Tarcha Hollis, Grambling	6-4	1988-91	85	1,185	13.9
Katie Beck, East Tenn. St.	6-0	1984-88	105	1,404	13.4
Marilyn Stephens, Temple	6-2	1981-84	117	1,519	13.0
Cheryl Taylor, Tennessee Tech	6-3	1983-87	120	1,532	12.8
Olivia Bradley, West Va.	6-1	1982-85	117	1,484	12.7
Judy Mosley, Hawaii	6-1	1986-90	114	1,441	12.6
Chana Perry, Northeast La./San Diego St.	6-5	1984-89	103	1,286	12.5
Katrina Fields, Fairfield	6-4	1982-85	99	1,210	12.2
Tracy Claxton, Kansas/Old Dominion	6-1	1982-83, 84-85	118	1,434	12.2
Kristin Wilson, N.C.-Charlotte	6-2	1983-87	107	1,305	12.2
Derunzia Johnson, Northeast La.	6-2	1987-90	83	1,006	12.1
Cheryl Miller, Southern Cal	6-3	1983-86	128	1,534	12.0
Rachel Bouchard, Maine	6-1	1987-91	110	1,309	11.9

Player, Team	Ht.	Seasons	G	Reb.	Avg.
Liz Coffin, Maine	6-1	1984-88	114	1,351	11.9
Gwen Austin, N.C.-Wilmington	6-2	1982-85	109	1,290	11.8
Kym Hampton, Arizona St.	6-2	1981-84	120	1,415	11.8
Valorie Whiteside, Appalachian St.	5-11	1984-88	116	1,369	11.8
Linda Wilson, Monmouth (N.J.)	6-0	1983-87	113	1,336	11.8
Phylette Blake, Ga. Southern	6-0	1985-89	108	1,242	11.5
Christy Greis, Evansville	6-4	1989-93	112	1,286	11.5
Adrian Vickers, South Ala.	6-1	1986-90	119	1,364	11.5
Wanda Pittman, South Caro. St.	6-6	1983-87	107	1,219	11.4

* *Record.*

CAREER ASSISTS

Player, Team	Ht.	Last Year	Yrs.	G	Ast.
Suzie McConnell, Penn St.	5-3	1988	4	128	1,307
Tine Freil, Pacific (Cal.)	5-10	1993	4	111	1,088
Shanya Evans, Providence	5-2	1991	4	121	987
Nancy Kennelly, Northwestern	5-7	1993	4	116	892
Neacole Hall, Alabama St.	5-3	1989	3	84	869
Teresa Weatherspoon, Louisiana Tech	5-8	1988	4	131	858
Stephany Raines, Mercer	5-4	1992	4	109	851
Gaynor O'Donnell, East Caro.	5-6	1993	4	114	833
Shawn Monday, Tennessee Tech	5-6	1990	4	121	823
Camille Ratledge, Florida	5-6	1990	4	111	816
Kim Kawamoto, Army	5-5	1992	4	114	796
Mary Gavin, Notre Dame	5-6	1988	4	112	778
Sonja Henning, Stanford	5-8	1991	4	127	757
Jennifer Azzi, Stanford	5-9	1990	4	122	751
Dawn Staley, Virginia	5-5	1992	4	131	729
Rosemary Kosiorek, West Va.	5-5	1992	4	116	725
Janet Malouf, Rutgers	5-5	1989	4	125	718
Beth Mowins, Lafayette	5-7	1989	4	117	715

CAREER ASSIST AVERAGE

(Minimum 500 assists)

Player, Team	Ht.	Last Year	Yrs.	G	Ast.	Avg.
Neacole Hall, Alabama St.	5-3	1989	3	84	869	10.35
Suzie McConnell, Penn St.	5-3	1988	4	128	1,307	10.21
Tine Freil, Pacific (Cal.)	5-10	1993	4	111	1,088	9.80
Shanya Evans, Providence	5-2	1991	4	121	987	8.16
Anja Bordt, St. Mary's (Cal.)	5-8	1991	3	81	654	8.07
Stephany Raines, Mercer	5-4	1992	4	109	851	7.81
Nancy Kennelly, Northwestern	5-7	1993	4	116	892	7.69
Camille Ratledge, Florida	5-6	1990	4	111	816	7.35
Gaynor O'Donnell, East Caro.	5-6	1993	4	114	833	7.31
Kim Kawamoto, Army	5-5	1992	4	114	796	6.98
Mary Gavin, Notre Dame	5-6	1988	4	112	778	6.95
Shawn Monday, Tennessee Tech	5-6	1990	4	121	823	6.80
Tanya Warren, Creighton	5-5	1988	4	98	650	6.63
Teresa Weatherspoon, Louisiana Tech	5-8	1988	4	131	858	6.55
Veronica Pettry, Loyola (Ill.)	5-5	1990	4	84	539	6.42
Marian Murtaugh, Loyola (Ill.)	5-5	1992	4	103	653	6.34
Rosemary Kosiorek, West Va.	5-5	1992	4	116	725	6.25
Jennifer Azzi, Stanford	5-9	1990	4	122	751	6.16
Beth Mowins, Lafayette	5-7	1989	4	117	715	6.11

CAREER BLOCKED SHOTS

Player, Team	Ht.	Last Year	Yrs.	G	Blk.
Genia Miller, Cal St. Fullerton	6-3	1991	4	118	428
Chris Enger, San Diego	6-4	1993	4	96	372
Trish Andrew, Michigan	6-3	1993	4	113	367
Denise Hogue, Charleston	6-4	1993	4	106	359
Stefanie Kasperski, Oregon	6-7	1990	3	89	322
Kathy Gilbert, Columbia-Barnard	6-3	1991	4	100	305
Melinda Hieber, Southwest Tex. St.	6-3	1992	4	106	304
Pauline Jordan, Nevada-Las Vegas	6-3	1990	3	98	286
Tricia Gibson, Loyola (Cal.)	6-3	1991	4	111	280

Player, Team	Ht.	Last Year	Yrs.	G	Blk.
Suzanne Johnson, Monmouth (N.J.)	6-3	1991	3	73	269
Mary K. Nordling, Geo. Washington	6-4	1992	4	98	264
Darla Simpson, Houston	6-3	1992	4	119	249
Tanya Hansen, Rutgers	6-2	1992	4	116	245
Vanessa Blair, Mt. St. Mary's (Md.)	6-0	1992	4	95	242
Christy Greis, Evansville	6-4	1993	4	112	241
Ann Fitzgerald, Drexel	6-2	1993	4	111	235
Trish Elser, Fairfield	6-3	1992	4	117	231
Rosemary Adams, Portland	6-2	1993	3	77	227
Wendy Scholtens, Vanderbilt	6-4	1991	4	122	217
Val Whiting, Stanford	6-3	1993	4	129	201
Kim Wright, Howard	6-4	1991	4	113	200

CAREER BLOCKED-SHOT AVERAGE

(Minimum 200 blocked shots)

Player, Team	Ht.	Last Year	Yrs.	G	Blk.	Avg.
Chris Enger, San Diego	6-4	1993	4	96	372	3.88
Suzanne Johnson, Monmouth (N.J.)	6-3	1991	3	73	269	3.68
Genia Miller, Cal St. Fullerton	6-3	1991	4	118	428	3.63
Stefanie Kasperski, Oregon	6-7	1990	3	89	322	3.62
Denise Hogue, Charleston	6-4	1993	4	106	359	3.39
Trish Andrew, Michigan	6-3	1993	4	113	367	3.25
Kathy Gilbert, Columbia-Barnard	6-3	1991	4	100	305	3.05
Rosemary Adams, Portland	6-2	1993	3	77	227	2.95
Pauline Jordan, Nevada-Las Vegas	6-3	1990	3	98	286	2.92
Melinda Hieber, Southwest Tex. St.	6-3	1992	4	106	304	2.87
Mary K. Nordling, Geo. Washington	6-4	1992	4	98	264	2.69
Vanessa Blair, Mt. St. Mary's (Md.)	6-0	1992	4	95	242	2.55
Tricia Gibson, Loyola (Cal.)	6-3	1991	4	111	280	2.52
Christy Greis, Evansville	6-4	1993	4	112	241	2.15
Ann Fitzpatrick, Drexel	6-2	1993	4	111	235	2.12
Tanya Hansen, Rutgers	6-2	1992	4	116	245	2.11
Darla Simpson, Houston	6-3	1992	4	119	249	2.09
Trish Elser, Fairfield	6-3	1992	4	117	231	1.97
Wendy Scholtens, Vanderbilt	6-4	1991	4	122	217	1.78
Kim Wright, Howard	6-4	1991	4	113	200	1.77

CAREER STEALS

Player, Team	Ht.	Last Year	Yrs.	G	Stl.
Dawn Staley, Virginia	5-5	1992	4	131	454
Donna McGary, Mississippi Val.	5-7	1991	4	113	425
Shelly Boston, Florida A&M	5-7	1992	4	88	416
Sonja Tate, Arkansas St.	5-6	1993	4	119	402
LaShaina Dickerson, Brooklyn	5-6	1992	4	101	381
Tonya Cardoza, Virginia	5-10	1991	4	121	375
Tami Varnado, Alcorn St.	5-9	1992	4	111	373
Nancy Smith, Tenn.-Chatt.	5-3	1991	4	110	356
Maureen Logan, St. Francis (Pa.)	5-6	1993	4	106	354
Dana Chatman, Louisiana St.	5-5	1991	4	120	346
Kim Perrot, Southwestern La.	5-4	1990	3	83	336
Ramona Jones, Lamar	5-5	1993	4	110	333
Mary Majewsky, Butler	5-5	1993	4	118	332
Missy Kelsen, Vermont	5-6	1992	4	108	328
Tracy Lis, Providence	5-9	1992	4	127	327
Katie Curry, St. Joseph's (Pa.)	5-10	1993	4	117	325
Darcie Vincent, Duquesne	5-7	1992	4	108	323
Tine Freil, Pacific (Cal.)	5-10	1993	4	111	320
Stacie Kane, Niagara	5-6	1992	4	110	316
Debbie Bolen, Valparaiso	5-10	1993	4	109	311
Lorrie Drennen, Buffalo	5-9	1993	4	105	310
Tammy Story, Southern Cal	5-8	1992	4	116	309

CAREER STEAL AVERAGE

(Minimum 200 steals)

Player, Team	Ht.	Last Year	Yrs.	G	Stl.	Avg.
Neacole Hall, Alabama St.	5-3	1989	2	57	281	4.93
Shelly Boston, Florida A&M	5-7	1992	4	88	416	4.73
Kim Perrot, Southwestern La.	5-4	1990	3	83	336	4.05
Kim Hill, Northwestern (La.)	5-7	1993	2	61	238	3.90
LaShaina Dickerson, Brooklyn	5-6	1992	4	101	381	3.77
Donna McGary, Mississippi Val.	5-7	1991	4	113	425	3.76
Lisa McMullen, Alabama St.	5-7	1991	2	56	209	3.73
Tomika Young, Brigham Young	5-10	1993	2	55	205	3.73
Charlene Blake, Northeastern	5-7	1990	3	82	287	3.50
Dawn Staley, Virginia	5-5	1992	4	131	454	3.47
Sonja Tate, Arkansas St.	5-6	1993	4	119	402	3.38
Tami Varnado, Alcorn St.	5-9	1992	4	111	373	3.36
Tammy Williams, DePaul	5-6	1993	2	59	200	3.39
Maureen Logan, St. Francis (Pa.)	5-6	1993	4	106	354	3.34
Shelly Borton, Southwest Tex. St.	5-7	1990	3	80	259	3.24
Nancy Smith, Tenn.-Chatt.	5-3	1991	4	110	356	3.24
Shawn Davis, Sam Houston St.	5-10	1992	3	79	246	3.11
Tonya Cardoza, Virginia	5-10	1991	4	121	375	3.10

CAREER 2,000 POINTS & 1,000 REBOUNDS

Player, Team	Last Year	Pts.	Reb.
Patricia Hoskins, Mississippi Val.	1989	3,122	1,662
Lorri Bauman, Drake	1984	3,115	1,050
Cheryl Miller, Southern Cal	1986	3,019	1,534
Valorie Whiteside, Appalachian St.	1988	2,944	1,369
Andrea Congreaves, Mercer	1993	2,796	1,141
Cindy Brown, Long Beach St.	1987	2,696	1,184
Carolyn Thompson, Texas Tech	1984	2,655	1,247
Sue Wicks, Rutgers	1988	2,655	1,357
Janet Harris, Georgia	1985	2,641	1,398
Wanda Ford, Drake	1986	2,636	1,887
Wendy Scholtens, Vanderbilt	1991	2,602	1,272
Lisa Ingram, Northeast La.	1986	2,601	1,173
Deborah Temple, Delta St./Mississippi	1985	2,573	1,261
Cheryl Taylor, Tennessee Tech	1987	2,526	1,532
Diana Vines, DePaul	1989	2,504	1,269
Judy Mosley, Hawaii	1990	2,479	1,441
Cherie Nelson, Southern Cal	1989	2,474	1,232
Caroline Mast, Ohio	1986	2,449	1,223
Genia Miller, Cal St. Fullerton	1991	2,415	1,162
Shelly Pennefather, Villanova	1987	2,408	1,171
Rachel Bouchard, Maine	1991	2,405	1,309
Karen Jennings, Nebraska	1993	2,405	1,000
Janice Lawrence, Louisiana Tech	1984	2,403	1,097
Lorena Legarde, Portland	1985	2,393	1,393
Regina Kirk, Tenn.-Chatt.	1988	2,376	1,086
Karen Elsner, Richmond	1985	2,367	1,244
Kym Hampton, Arizona St.	1984	2,361	1,415
Paula McGee, Southern Cal	1984	2,346	1,160
Sue Galkantas, Florida St.	1984	2,327	1,006
Dorothy Bowers, Youngstown St.	1988	2,322	1,083
Sonja Tate, Arkansas St.	1993	2,312	1,006
Adrian Vickers, South Ala.	1990	2,285	1,364
Lillie Mason, Western Ky.	1986	2,262	1,006
Alison Lang, Oregon	1984	2,254	1,101
Susan Robinson, Penn St.	1992	2,253	1,070
Chris Moreland, Duke	1988	2,232	1,229
Kelly Lyons, Old Dominion	1990	2,224	1,008
Pam McGee, Southern Cal	1984	2,214	1,255
Katrina McClain, Georgia	1987	2,195	1,193
Marilyn Stephens, Temple	1984	2,194	1,519
Vivian Herron, Oral Roberts	1989	2,192	1,007
Maureen Formico, Pepperdine	1986	2,190	1,188
Clinette Jordan, Oklahoma St.	1989	2,168	1,128
Chana Perry, Northeast La./San Diego St.	1989	2,163	1,286
Liz Coffin, Maine	1988	2,153	1,351

Player, Team	Last Year	Pts.	Reb.
Katie Beck, East Tenn. St.	1988	2,151	1,404
Phylette Blake, Ga. Southern	1989	2,140	1,242
Portland McCaskill, Southern Miss.	1985	2,130	1,064
Renee Kelly, Missouri	1987	2,119	1,098
Orphie Moore, South Ala.	1987	2,118	1,116
Ella Williams, Alcorn St.	1984	2,111	1,102
Carol Owens, Northern Ill.	1990	2,102	1,028
Venus Lacy, Old Dominion/Louisiana Tech	1990	2,096	1,243
Regina Days, Ga. Southern	1988	2,091	1,078
Dale Hodges, St. Joseph's (Pa.)	1990	2,077	1,049
Val Whiting, Stanford	1993	2,077	1,134
Deb Asper, Utah	1984	2,074	1,042
Becky Jackson, Auburn	1984	2,068	1,118
Lisa Van Goor, Colorado	1985	2,067	1,154
Tammy McCarthy, Md.-Balt. County	1987	2,063	1,047
Antoinette Norris, Stephen F. Austin	1988	2,062	1,360
Tarcha Hollis, Grambling	1991	2,058	1,187
Gwen Austin, N.C.-Wilmington	1985	2,056	1,290
Laura Coenen, Minnesota	1985	2,044	1,029
Regina Street, Memphis St.	1985	2,043	1,281
Vickie Orr, Auburn	1989	2,035	1,006
Carol Smith, Alabama	1986	2,028	1,076
Maggie Stinnett, Baylor	1991	2,026	1,011
Kahadeejah Herbert, Penn St.	1985	2,026	1,103

DIVISION I WOMEN'S ANNUAL INDIVIDUAL CHAMPIONS

SCORING AVERAGE

Year	Player, Team	Ht.	Cl.	G	FG	3FG	FT	Pts.	Avg.
1982	Barbara Kennedy, Clemson	6-0	Sr.	31	392	—	124	908	29.3
1983	LaTaunya Pollard, Long Beach St.	5-9	Sr.	31	376	—	155	907	29.3
1984	Deborah Temple, Delta St.	5-10	Jr.	28	373	—	127	873	31.2
1985	Anucha Browne, Northwestern	6-1	Sr.	28	341	—	173	855	30.5
1986	Wanda Ford, Drake	6-0	Sr.	30	390	—	139	919	30.6
1987	Tresa Spaulding, Brigham Young	6-7	Sr.	28	347	—	116	810	28.9
1988	LeChandra LeDay, Grambling	5-6	Sr.	28	334	36	146	850	30.4
1989	Patricia Hoskins, Mississippi Val.	6-3	Sr.	27	345	13	205	908	*33.6
1990	Kim Perrot, Southwestern La.	5-4	Sr.	28	308	95	128	839	30.0
1991	Jan Jensen, Drake	5-10	Sr.	30	358	6	166	888	29.6
1992	Andrea Congreaves, Mercer	6-3	Jr.	28	353	77	142	925	33.0
1993	Andrea Congreaves, Mercer	6-3	Sr.	26	302	51	150	805	31.0

* *Record.*

FIELD-GOAL PERCENTAGE

Year	Player, Team	Cl.	G	FG	FGA	Pct.
1982	Trina Roberts, Ga. Southern	So.	31	189	277	68.2
1983	Lydia Sawney, Tennessee Tech	Sr.	27	167	250	66.8
1984	Becky Jackson, Auburn	Sr.	29	210	317	66.2
1985	Monica Lamb, Houston	So.	30	228	344	66.3
1986	Regina Days, Ga. Southern	So.	27	234	332	70.5
1987	Sharon McDowell, N.C.-Wilmington	Jr.	28	170	251	67.7
1988	Lisa Dodd, Wake Forest	So.	31	172	266	64.7
1989	Sheila Reynolds, Florida Int'l	Jr.	27	214	332	64.5
1990	Kelly Lyons, Old Dominion	Sr.	31	308	444	69.4
1991	Renay Adams, Tennessee Tech	Sr.	30	185	258	*71.7
1992	Lidiya Varbanova, Boise St.	So.	29	228	338	67.5
1993	Lidiya Varbanova, Boise St.	Jr.	27	200	294	68.0

* *Record.*

THREE-POINT FIELD GOALS MADE PER GAME

Year	Player, Team	Cl.	G	3FG	Avg.
1988	Gwen Davis, Bethune-Cookman	Jr.	26	111	4.3
1989	Marguerite Moran, Hofstra	Sr.	29	107	3.7
1990	Sandi Bittler, Princeton	Sr.	22	89	4.0

Year	Player, Team	Cl.	G	3FG	Avg.
1991	Lisa McMullen, Alabama St.	Jr.	28	126	*4.5
1992	Lynda Kukla, Valparaiso	Sr.	27	101	3.7
1993	Suzie Dailer, St. Bonaventure	So.	27	99	3.7

* *Record.*

THREE-POINT FIELD-GOAL PERCENTAGE

Year	Player, Team	Cl.	G	3FG	3FGA	Pct.
1988	Jamie Siess, Oklahoma St.	Sr.	28	42	82	51.2
1989	Alicia Burke, Oklahoma St.	Sr.	32	57	111	51.4
1990	Heather Donlon, Fordham	Fr.	29	50	87	*57.5
1991	Krista Treide, Wyoming	Sr.	28	57	112	50.9
1992	Kathy Halligan, Creighton	Sr.	32	72	130	55.4
1993	Cara Frey, Harvard	Jr.	25	50	97	51.5

* *Record.*

FREE-THROW PERCENTAGE

Year	Player, Team	Cl.	G	FT	FTA	Pct.
1982	Val DePaola, Boston U.	Jr.	27	75	86	87.2
1983	Lisa Goodin, Eastern Ky.	Jr.	27	147	161	91.3
1984	Shelly Brand, Evansville	Jr.	25	92	106	86.8
1985	Linda Page, North Caro. St.	Sr.	30	139	158	88.0
1986	Keely Feeman, Cincinnati	Sr.	30	76	82	92.7
1987	DeAnn Craft, Central Fla.	Sr.	24	94	102	92.2
1988	Tracey Sneed, La Salle	Jr.	30	151	165	91.5
1989	Amy Slowikowski, Kent	Jr.	27	112	121	92.6
1990	Lea Ann Parsley, Marshall	Sr.	28	96	104	92.3
1991	Linda Cyborski, Delaware	Jr.	29	74	79	93.7
1992	Ginny Doyle, Richmond	Sr.	29	96	101	*95.0
1993	Jennifer Cole, La Salle	Sr.	27	150	165	90.9

* *Record.*

REBOUND AVERAGE

Year	Player, Team	Ht.	Cl.	G	Reb.	Avg.
1982	Anne Donovan, Old Dominion	6-8	Jr.	28	412	14.7
1983	Deborah Mitchell, Mississippi Col.	6-2	Jr.	28	447	16.0
1984	Joy Kellogg, Oklahoma City	6-1	Jr.	23	373	16.2
1985	Rosina Pearson, Bethune-Cookman	6-0	Jr.	26	480	*18.5
1986	Wanda Ford, Drake	6-0	Sr.	30	506	16.9
1987	Patricia Hoskins, Mississippi Val.	6-3	So.	28	476	17.0
1988	Katie Beck, East Tenn. St.	6-0	Sr.	25	441	17.6
1989	Patricia Hoskins, Mississippi Val.	6-3	Sr.	27	440	16.3
1990	Pam Hudson, Northwestern (La.)	5-11	Sr.	29	438	15.1
1991	Tarcha Hollis, Grambling	6-4	Sr.	29	443	15.3
1992	Christy Greis, Evansville	6-4	Jr.	28	383	13.7
1993	Ann Barry, Nevada	6-0	Sr.	25	355	14.2

* *Record.*

ASSIST AVERAGE

Year	Player, Team	Cl.	G	Ast.	Avg.
1985	Faith Mimnaugh, Loyola (Ill.)	Sr.	27	316	11.7
1986	Suzie McConnell, Penn St.	So.	32	338	10.6
1987	Suzie McConnell, Penn St.	Jr.	30	355	*11.8
1988	Neacole Hall, Alabama St.	Jr.	28	318	11.4
1989	Neacole Hall, Alabama St.	Sr.	29	319	11.0
1990	Tine Freil, Pacific (Cal.)	Fr.	29	321	11.1
1991	Michelle Burden, Kent	Fr.	29	294	10.1
1992	Mimi Harris, La Salle	Sr.	33	320	9.7
1993	Gaynor O'Donnell, East Caro.	Sr.	28	300	10.7

* *Record.*

BLOCKED-SHOT AVERAGE

Year	Player, Team	Cl.	G	Blk.	Avg.
1988	Stefanie Kasperski, Oregon	So.	28	119	4.3
1989	Michelle Wilson, Texas Southern	Sr.	27	151	*5.6
1990	Simone Srubek, Fresno St.	Sr.	31	138	4.5

Year	Player, Team	Cl.	G	Blk.	Avg.
1991	Suzanne Johnson, Monmouth (N.J.)	Jr.	23	117	5.1
1992	Denise Hogue, Charleston	Jr.	28	147	5.3
1993	Chris Enger, San Diego	Sr.	28	137	4.9

* Record.

STEAL AVERAGE

Year	Player, Team	Cl.	G	Stl.	Avg.
1988	Neacole Hall, Alabama St.	Jr.	28	133	4.8
1989	Donna McGary, Mississippi Val.	So.	29	158	5.4
1990	Shelly Boston, Florida A&M	So.	29	160	5.5
1991	Shelly Boston, Florida A&M	Jr.	28	142	5.1
1992	Natalie White, Florida A&M	Fr.	28	143	5.1
1993	Heidi Caruso, Lafayette	Jr.	28	168	*6.0

* Record.

DIVISION I WOMEN'S ALL-TIME TEAM LEADERS

(Since 1982)

SINGLE-GAME SCORING HIGHS

Pts.	Team vs. Opponent	Date
149	Long Beach St. vs. San Jose St.	Feb. 16, 1987
139	Grambling vs. Jarvis Christian	Feb. 12, 1986
138	N.C.-Wilmington vs. Davidson	Dec. 6, 1983
137	North Caro. St. vs. Western Caro.	Dec. 8, 1990
132	Kent vs. Stetson	Nov. 30, 1990
131	West Va. vs. Indiana (Pa.)	Dec. 7, 1983
130	Loyola (Cal.) vs. Master's	Nov. 23, 1990
129	Purdue vs. Kent	Dec. 8, 1990
128	Providence vs. Georgetown	Feb. 4, 1991
128	Valparaiso vs. Chicago St.	Feb. 3, 1992
127	Southwestern La. vs. Southern-N. O.	Dec. 17, 1983
127	Bowling Green vs. Valparaiso	Jan. 5, 1992
127	North Caro. St. vs. Howard	Jan. 31, 1993

SINGLE-GAME SCORING HIGHS IN A HALF

Pts.	Team vs. Opponent	Date
80	Long Beach St. vs. San Jose St.	Feb. 16, 1987
76	Northern Ill. vs. Valparaiso	Feb. 20, 1990
74	Northwestern (La.) vs. Hawaii Pacific	Mar. 1, 1986
72	Southwestern La. vs. Southern-N. O.	Dec. 7, 1982
71	Kent vs. Stetson	Nov. 30, 1990
70	Georgia Tech vs. Presbyterian	Dec. 2, 1985
68	Cincinnati vs. South Caro.	Feb. 12, 1984
68	Creighton vs. Oral Roberts	Dec. 6, 1989
68	Penn St. vs. Duquesne	Jan. 29, 1990
68	Brigham Young vs. Creighton	Feb. 17, 1990
68	Purdue vs. Kent	Dec. 8, 1990

SINGLE-GAME FIELD-GOAL PERCENTAGE

(Minimum 24 made)

Pct.	Team (FG-FGA) vs. Opponent	Date
73.7	Florida Int'l (42-57) vs. Canisius	Jan. 2, 1992
73.6	Southwest Mo. St. (39-53) vs. Drake	Feb. 16, 1991
71.4	Lamar (35-49) vs. Southern Methodist	Dec. 2, 1989
70.7	Vanderbilt (29-41) vs. Kansas	Nov. 26, 1989
70.2	Fresno St. (33-47) vs. Cal St. Northridge	Nov. 30, 1990
70.2	Southern Ill. (40-57) vs. Western Ill.	Jan. 8, 1990
70.0	Maryland (42-60) vs. Florida St.	Feb. 5, 1992
69.7	Northwestern (46-66) vs. Eastern Ill.	Jan. 4, 1993
69.6	Ga. Southern (39-56) vs. Appalachian St.	Jan. 23, 1993
68.5	San Diego St. (37-54) vs. San Jose St.	Jan. 20, 1990
68.1	Maryland (47-69) vs. Western Mich.	Dec. 2, 1990
68.1	Maryland (32-47) vs. Southwest Mo. St.	Mar. 20, 1993

SINGLE-GAME THREE-POINT FIELD GOALS MADE

(Since 1988)

3FG	Team vs. Opponent	Date
16	Creighton vs. Oral Roberts	Dec. 6, 1989
16	Harvard vs. Rhode Island	Jan. 12, 1993
15	Fresno St. vs. Baylor	Dec. 1, 1989
15	Vanderbilt vs. Oral Roberts	Jan. 14, 1993
14	Creighton vs. Brigham Young	Feb. 1, 1990
14	Evansville vs. St. Louis	Feb. 5, 1990
14	Niagara vs. Loyola (Md.)	Feb. 17, 1991
14	Valparaiso vs. La Salle	Jan. 3, 1992
14	Alabama vs. Mississippi Val.	Jan. 8, 1992
14	Navy vs. Bucknell	Jan. 11, 1992
14	Valparaiso vs. Wright St.	Feb. 27, 1992
14	North Caro. vs. Navy	Dec. 6, 1992
14	Alabama vs. Loyola (Ill.)	Feb. 3, 1993
14	Arkansas St. vs. Southwestern La.	Feb. 13, 1993

SINGLE-GAME FREE-THROW PERCENTAGE

(Minimum 26 made)

Pct.	Team (FT-FTA) vs. Opponent	Date
100	Tenn.-Chatt. (26-26) vs. Ala.-Birmingham	Nov. 24, 1990
97.0	Wisconsin (32-33) vs. Michigan	Feb. 8, 1991
96.8	Northwestern (La.) (30-31) vs. Prairie View	Jan. 28, 1991
96.7	Tennessee St. (29-30) vs. Austin Peay	Feb. 27, 1993
96.6	Niagara (28-29) vs. Princeton	Dec. 4, 1992
95.1	Creighton (39-41) vs. Colorado St.	Feb. 9, 1991
93.9	East Tenn. St. (31-33) vs. Furman	Mar. 9, 1990
93.8	Missouri (30-32) vs. Colorado	Feb. 6, 1991
93.8	Oklahoma St. (30-32) vs. Nebraska	Jan. 8, 1993
93.8	Hawaii (30-32) vs. Southern Methodist	Feb. 27, 1993
93.3	Kansas St. (28-30) vs. Colorado	Jan. 12, 1991

SINGLE-GAME REBOUNDS

Reb.	Team vs. Opponent	Date
92	Pittsburgh vs. Geo. Washington	Jan. 6, 1982
85	Loyola (Cal.) vs. Master's	Nov. 23, 1990
84	Creighton vs. Oral Roberts	Dec. 6, 1989
84	Tennessee St. vs. Knoxville	Jan. 26, 1990
83	Bethune-Cookman vs. Florida Memorial	Dec. 3, 1991
80	South Caro. St. vs. Charleston So.	Dec. 4, 1989
80	St. Francis (N.Y.) vs. LIU-Brooklyn	Feb. 3, 1990
79	Auburn vs. Eastern Ky.	Nov. 25, 1989
79	Texas Southern vs. Texas College	Dec. 10, 1992
78	Tennessee St. vs. East Tenn. St.	Dec. 18, 1989
78	Southern-B. R. vs. Texas College	Dec. 5, 1992
77	Coppin St. vs. Charleston So.	Dec. 9, 1989
77	Georgia Tech vs. Hofstra	Dec. 4, 1992

SINGLE-GAME ASSISTS

Ast.	Team vs. Opponent	Date
43	Northwestern (La.) vs. Arkansas Baptist	Jan. 10, 1987
43	Nebraska vs. Howard	Dec. 11, 1992
40	Tennessee Tech vs. Furman	Dec. 3, 1990
39	DePaul vs. Cleveland St.	Feb. 17, 1992
38	Portland vs. Warner Pacific	Nov. 30, 1990
38	Notre Dame vs. Marquette	Dec. 21, 1990
38	Portland St. vs. Southern Utah	Feb. 8, 1991
37	Marquette vs. Detroit Mercy	Mar. 1, 1990
37	Louisiana Tech vs. Southwestern La.	Mar. 9, 1990
37	Stanford vs. Arkansas	Mar. 24, 1990
37	Arizona St. vs. Marquette	Dec. 5, 1992
37	Vanderbilt vs. Oral Roberts	Jan. 14, 1993

SINGLE-GAME BLOCKED SHOTS

Blk.	Team vs. Opponent	Date
18	Vanderbilt vs. Tennessee St.	Dec. 10, 1991
18	Rutgers vs. Oklahoma St.	Dec. 28, 1991
18	Loyola (Cal.) vs. Western Ill.	Dec. 20, 1992

Blk.	Team vs. Opponent	Date
16	Mt. St. Mary's (Md.) vs. Niagara	Nov. 25, 1989
16	N.C.-Wilmington vs. Coastal Caro.	Jan. 29, 1990
16	Monmouth (N.J.) vs. Delaware	Dec. 13, 1990
15	Monmouth (N.J.) vs. Rider	Nov. 28, 1989
15	San Diego vs. San Diego St.	Dec. 6, 1989
15	Fresno St. vs. Nevada-Las Vegas	Feb. 24, 1990
15	Vanderbilt vs. Middle Tenn. St.	Feb. 6, 1991

SINGLE-GAME STEALS

Stl.	Team vs. Opponent	Date
38	Grambling vs. Texas College	Dec. 10, 1987
37	Stephen F. Austin vs. Tex.-Pan American	Dec. 17, 1990
37	Northern Ill. vs. Wright St.	Feb. 15, 1992
34	Southeastern La. vs. Southern-B.R.	Dec. 17, 1989
34	Florida A&M vs. Stetson	Jan. 24, 1991
34	Delaware St. vs. Lincoln (Pa.)	Jan. 23, 1992
33	Delaware St. vs. Lincoln (Pa.)	Nov. 29, 1989
33	Long Beach St. vs. UC Santa Barb.	Jan. 20, 1990
33	Valparaiso vs. St. Louis	Jan. 3, 1991
33	Southwest Mo. St. vs. Idaho	Dec. 13, 1991
32	Creighton vs. Oral Roberts	Dec. 6, 1989
32	Buffalo vs. Delaware St.	Jan. 25, 1992
32	Southern-B.R. vs. Mississippi	Feb. 10, 1993

SEASON WON-LOST PERCENTAGE

Team	Season	Won	Lost	Pct.
Texas	1986	34	0	1.000
Louisiana Tech	1982	35	1	.972
Louisiana Tech	1990	32	1	.970
Stanford	1990	32	1	.970
Vermont	1992	29	1	.967
Vermont	1993	28	1	.966
Oral Roberts	1983	26	1	.963
Tennessee	1989	35	2	.946
Louisiana Tech	1988	32	2	.941
Auburn	1989	32	2	.941
Virginia	1992	32	2	.941
Louisiana Tech	1983	31	2	.939
Southern Cal	1983	31	2	.939
Auburn	1987	31	2	.939
Texas	1987	31	2	.939
Northeast La.	1985	30	2	.938
Georgia	1986	30	2	.938
Miami (Fla.)	1992	30	2	.938
Iowa	1988	29	2	.935
Penn St.	1991	29	2	.935

SEASON SCORING OFFENSE

Team	Season	G	Pts.	Avg.
Providence	†1991	32	3,095	96.7
Long Beach St.	†1987	36	3,448	95.8
Northern Ill.	†1990	31	2,930	94.5
Kent	1991	29	2,715	93.6
Stanford	1990	33	3,063	92.8
Valparaiso	1991	30	2,743	91.4
Valparaiso	†1993	27	2,467	91.4
North Caro. St.	1991	33	3,001	90.9
Long Beach St.	†1986	34	3,086	90.8
Southern Miss.	†1984	28	2,527	90.3
Brigham Young	†1985	28	2,516	89.9
Texas	1984	35	3,128	89.4
Long Beach St.	†1989	35	3,127	89.3
Penn St.	1985	33	2,946	89.3
Georgia	1986	32	2,855	89.2
Gonzaga	1985	32	2,854	89.2
Missouri	1984	31	2,761	89.1

† *National leader.*

SEASON SCORING DEFENSE

Team	Season	G	Pts.	Avg.
Mo.-Kansas City	†1991	28	1,450	51.8
Cheyney	†1983	30	1,558	51.9
Northeastern	†1985	29	1,519	52.4
Mo.-Kansas City	†1990	28	1,471	52.5
Louisiana Tech	1990	33	1,766	53.5
Army	1991	30	1,606	53.5
Montana	†1982	27	1,444	53.5
Montana	†1988	30	1,610	53.7
Richmond	1990	30	1,610	53.7
Richmond	1988	29	1,558	53.7
Montana	†1986	31	1,667	53.8
Chicago St.	1986	31	1,672	53.9
St. Peter's	1983	28	1,515	54.1
Iowa	†1993	31	1,683	54.3
Louisiana Tech	1982	36	1,955	54.3
Northeastern	1986	29	1,578	54.4
Mo.-Kansas City	†1992	31	1,688	54.5
Auburn	1993	29	1,583	54.6
Montana	†1984	30	1,648	54.9

† *National champion.*

SEASON SCORING MARGIN

Team	Season	Off.	Def.	Margin
Louisiana Tech	†1982	87.3	54.3	33.0
Louisiana Tech	†1990	86.5	53.5	32.9
Long Beach St.	†1987	95.8	64.4	31.4
Auburn	1987	87.1	57.9	29.6
Cheyney	†1983	81.0	51.9	29.0
Penn St.	†1991	87.9	59.7	28.2
Louisiana Tech	†1988	83.6	55.7	27.9
Louisiana Tech	†1989	82.6	55.0	27.6
Texas	†1986	83.9	57.2	26.6
Stanford	1990	92.8	66.2	26.6
Penn St.	†1985	89.3	63.1	26.2
Georgia	1986	89.2	63.2	26.1
Louisiana Tech	†1984	84.8	59.2	25.6
Auburn	1988	84.1	58.6	25.5
Louisiana Tech	1983	81.9	56.7	25.2

† *National champion.*

SEASON FIELD-GOAL PERCENTAGE

Team	Season	FG	FGA	Pct.
Drake	†1984	945	1,691	55.9
Texas	†1986	1,162	2,118	54.9
Georgia	1986	1,193	2,195	54.4
Texas	†1987	1,156	2,142	54.0
Idaho	1986	1,019	1,893	53.8
Idaho	†1985	1,034	1,931	53.5
Maryland	†1989	1,139	2,129	53.5
Texas	1985	1,110	2,082	53.3
Notre Dame	†1988	836	1,572	53.2
Georgia	1985	1,173	2,209	53.1
Ohio St.	1987	960	1,813	53.0

† *National champion.*

SEASON FIELD-GOAL PERCENTAGE DEFENSE

Team	Season	FG	FGA	Pct.
Montana	†1993	540	1,706	31.7
South Caro. St.	†1991	682	2,117	32.2
South Caro. St.	†1986	602	1,822	33.0
South Caro. St.	†1987	681	2,043	33.3
Louisiana Tech	†1990	628	1,883	33.4
South Caro. St.	†1992	669	1,997	33.5
Wagner	1993	566	1,678	33.7
Jackson St.	1992	556	1,652	33.7
Dartmouth	†1988	500	1,480	33.8
Auburn	†1989	722	2,086	34.6

Team	Season	FG	FGA	Pct.
Old Dominion	†1982	648	1,864	34.8
Alcorn St.	1993	632	1,817	34.8
Toledo	1992	708	2,023	35.0
Montana	1988	601	1,712	35.1
Coppin St.	1991	576	1,627	35.4

† *National champion.*

SEASON THREE-POINT FIELD GOALS MADE PER GAME

(Since 1988)

Team	Season	G	3FG	Avg.
Alabama	†1992	30	248	8.3
Creighton	†1990	27	209	7.7
Valparaiso	1992	29	224	7.7
Alabama	†1993	31	237	7.6
Harvard	1993	25	186	7.4
Southwestern La.	1990	28	206	7.4
Evansville	†1991	29	211	7.3
Kent	1991	29	208	7.2
Kent	1993	29	199	6.9
Harvard	1992	26	175	6.7
Niagara	1992	28	187	6.7
Harvard	1991	26	170	6.5
Southwestern La.	†1988	29	188	6.5
Valparaiso	1993	27	175	6.5
New Mexico St.	1992	31	200	6.5

† *National champion.*

SEASON THREE-POINT FIELD-GOAL PERCENTAGE

(Since 1988)

Team	Season	G	3FG	3FGA	Pct.
Fordham	†1990	29	61	129	47.3
Loyola (Ill.)	†1988	27	96	204	47.1
Connecticut	†1989	30	137	296	46.3
Richmond	1989	33	66	144	45.8
Texas Tech	1989	28	75	164	45.7
Princeton	1988	26	81	178	45.5
Creighton	†1992	32	169	374	45.2
Harvard	1990	26	119	265	44.9
Lamar	†1991	33	128	288	44.4
Richmond	1992	29	157	355	44.2
Charleston So.	1988	27	88	199	44.2
Holy Cross	1989	31	102	231	44.2
Stanford	1989	31	135	306	44.1
South Caro.	1990	33	86	195	44.1
New Hampshire	1988	27	67	152	44.1
New Mexico St.	1988	29	63	143	44.1

† *National champion.*

SEASON FREE-THROW PERCENTAGE

Team	Season	FT	FTA	Pct.
La Salle	†1988	479	600	79.8
Richmond	†1992	383	482	79.5
Kentucky	†1984	323	416	78.8
Geo. Washington	1988	443	562	78.8
Drake	1984	443	563	78.7
Indiana St.	†1989	484	618	78.3
Penn St.	†1991	540	692	78.0
Penn St.	1992	515	664	77.6
Northern Ill.	†1990	595	768	77.5
Butler	1991	552	717	77.0
Vanderbilt	1989	541	703	77.0
Miami (Ohio)	1990	297	386	76.9
St. Mary's (Cal.)	1990	465	606	76.7
St. Joseph's (Pa.)	1989	438	571	76.7
Texas-Arlington	1990	476	621	76.7
Penn St.	1990	539	704	76.6
James Madison	†1993	421	550	76.5

Team	Season	FT	FTA	Pct.
Lehigh	1990	475	621	76.5
American	1988	400	523	76.5

† *National champion.*

SEASON REBOUND MARGIN

Team	Season	Off.	Def.	Margin
Louisiana Tech	†1990	52.9	34.7	18.3
Old Dominion	†1983	49.1	31.9	17.3
Bethune-Cookman	†1985	55.3	39.1	16.2
Louisiana Tech	†1989	47.8	31.6	16.2
Louisiana Tech	†1988	48.1	32.5	15.6
Auburn	1988	47.2	31.7	15.5
Louisiana Tech	†1982	46.3	30.8	15.4
Nevada-Las Vegas	1989	47.9	34.0	13.9
Old Dominion	1985	46.4	32.7	13.7
South Caro. St.	†1991	55.1	41.4	13.7
South Caro. St.	†1986	54.1	40.5	13.7
Louisiana Tech	†1987	48.0	34.4	13.6
Howard	1986	47.3	33.8	13.5
Georgia St.	1985	56.1	42.9	13.2
Maine	1987	49.8	36.6	13.2

† *National champion.*

SEASON ASSISTS PER GAME

(Since 1986)

Team	Season	G	Ast.	Avg.
Villanova	†1987	31	766	24.7
Bowling Green	†1992	29	672	23.2
Stanford	†1990	33	758	23.0
Long Beach St.	†1986	34	780	22.9
Marquette	1987	27	613	22.7
Idaho	1986	31	703	22.7
Eastern Wash.	†1991	27	611	22.6
Portland St.	1990	27	602	22.3
Brigham Young	1987	28	609	21.8
Arkansas	1991	32	646	21.7
Bowling Green	†1993	30	646	21.5
Maryland	†1989	32	679	21.2
Georgia	1986	32	678	21.2
Stanford	1989	31	656	21.2

SEASON BLOCKED SHOTS PER GAME

(Since 1988)

Team	Season	G	Blk.	Avg.
Northern Ill.	†1989	30	231	7.7
Geo. Washington	†1992	32	235	7.3
Fresno St.	†1988	28	194	6.9
Nevada-Las Vegas	1989	34	223	6.6
Charleston	1992	28	183	6.5
Nevada-Las Vegas	†1990	311	197	6.4
Fresno St.	1989	30	190	6.3
Montana	1989	31	194	6.3
Rutgers	†1991	30	187	6.2
Columbia-Barnard	1988	26	156	6.0

† *National champion.*

SEASON STEALS PER GAME

(Since 1988)

Team	Season	G	Stl.	Avg.
Kent	†1993	29	536	18.5
Buffalo	†1992	29	490	16.9
Florida A&M	1993	27	453	16.8
Wright St.	†1988	28	450	16.1
Florida A&M	†1989	28	450	16.1
DePaul	1988	31	487	15.7
Dartmouth	†1990	26	398	15.3
DePaul	1989	33	493	14.9

Team	Season	G	Stl.	Avg.
Kent	†1991	29	422	14.6
Dartmouth	1993	26	374	14.4

† National champion.

DIVISION I WOMEN'S ANNUAL TEAM CHAMPIONS

WON-LOST PERCENTAGE

Year	Team	Won	Lost	Pct.
1982	Louisiana Tech	35	1	.972
1983	Oral Roberts	26	1	.963
1984	Texas	32	3	.914
1985	Northeast La.	30	2	.938
1986	Texas	34	0	1.000
1987	Auburn	31	2	.939
	Texas	31	2	.939
1988	Louisiana Tech	32	2	.941
1989	Tennessee	35	2	.946
1990	Louisiana Tech	32	1	.970
	Stanford	32	1	.970
1991	Penn St.	29	2	.935
1992	Vermont	29	1	.967
1993	Vermont	28	1	.966

SCORING OFFENSE

Year	Team	G	(W-L)	Pts.	Avg.
1982	Bradley	27	(19-8)	2,372	87.9
1983	Brigham Young	24	(16-8)	2,123	88.5
1984	Southern Miss.	28	(18-10)	2,527	90.3
1985	Brigham Young	28	(19-9)	2,516	89.9
1986	Long Beach St.	34	(29-5)	3,086	90.8
1987	Long Beach St.	36	(33-3)	3,448	95.8
1988	Tennessee	34	(31-3)	3,021	88.9
1989	Long Beach St.	35	(30-5)	3,127	89.3
1990	Northern Ill.	31	(25-6)	2,930	94.5
1991	Providence	32	(26-6)	3,095	*96.7
1992	Bowling Green	29	(24-5)	2,581	89.0
1993	Valparaiso	27	(15-12)	2,467	91.4

** Record.*

SCORING DEFENSE

Year	Team	G	(W-L)	Pts.	Avg.
1982	Montana	27	(22-5)	1,444	53.5
1983	Cheyney	30	(27-3)	1,558	51.9
1984	Montana	30	(26-4)	1,648	54.9
1985	Northeastern	29	(22-7)	1,519	52.4
1986	Montana	31	(27-4)	1,667	53.8
1987	Louisiana Tech	33	(30-3)	1,822	55.2
1988	Montana	30	(28-2)	1,610	53.7
1989	Louisiana Tech	36	(32-4)	1,980	55.0
1990	Mo.-Kansas City	28	(17-11)	1,471	52.5
1991	Mo.-Kansas City	28	(18-10)	1,450	*51.8
1992	Mo.-Kansas City	31	(24-7)	1,688	54.5
1993	Iowa	31	(27-4)	1,683	54.3

** Record.*

SCORING MARGIN

Year	Team	Off.	Def.	Margin
1982	Louisiana Tech	87.3	54.3	*33.0
1983	Cheyney	81.0	51.9	29.0
1984	Louisiana Tech	84.8	59.2	25.6
1985	Penn St.	89.3	63.1	26.2
1986	Texas	83.9	57.2	26.6
1987	Long Beach St.	95.8	64.4	31.4
1988	Louisiana Tech	83.6	55.7	27.9
1989	Louisiana Tech	82.6	55.0	27.6
1990	Louisiana Tech	86.5	53.5	32.9

Year	Team	Off.	Def.	Margin
1991	Penn St.	87.9	59.7	28.2
1992	Virginia	82.0	59.4	22.6
1993	Texas Tech	86.0	63.0	23.0

* *Record.*

FIELD-GOAL PERCENTAGE

Year	Team	FG	FGA	Pct.
1982	New Orleans	979	1,871	52.3
1983	Maryland	1,049	1,982	52.9
1984	Drake	945	1,691	*55.9
1985	Idaho	1,034	1,931	53.5
1986	Texas	1,162	2,118	54.9
1987	Texas	1,156	2,142	54.0
1988	Notre Dame	836	1,572	53.2
1989	Maryland	1,139	2,129	53.5
1990	Stephen F. Austin	1,070	2,077	51.5
1991	Arkansas	1,061	2,028	52.3
1992	Creighton	974	1,871	52.1
1993	Texas Tech	1,093	2,120	51.6

* *Record.*

FIELD-GOAL PERCENTAGE DEFENSE

Year	Team	FG	FGA	Pct.
1982	Old Dominion	648	1,864	34.8
1983	Cheyney	639	1,792	35.7
1984	Wagner	694	1,865	37.2
1985	South Caro. St.	613	1,674	36.6
1986	South Caro. St.	602	1,822	33.0
1987	South Caro. St.	681	2,043	33.3
1988	Dartmouth	500	1,480	33.8
1989	Auburn	722	2,086	34.6
1990	Louisiana Tech	628	1,883	33.4
1991	South Caro. St.	682	2,117	32.2
1992	South Caro. St.	669	1,997	33.5
1993	Montana	540	1,706	*31.7

**Record.*

THREE-POINT FIELD GOALS MADE PER GAME

Year	Team	G	3FG	Avg.
1988	Southwestern La.	29	188	6.5
1989	Tenn.-Chatt.	31	151	4.9
1990	Creighton	27	209	7.7
1991	Evansville	29	211	7.3
1992	Alabama	30	248	*8.3
1993	Alabama	31	237	7.6

* *Record.*

THREE-POINT FIELD-GOAL PERCENTAGE

Year	Team	G	3FG	3FGA	Pct.
1988	Loyola (Ill.)	27	96	204	47.1
1989	Connecticut	30	137	296	46.3
1990	Fordham	29	61	129	*47.3
1991	Lamar	33	128	288	44.4
1992	Creighton	32	169	374	45.2
1993	Harvard	25	186	430	43.3

* *Record.*

FREE-THROW PERCENTAGE

Year	Team	FT	FTA	Pct.
1982	Illinois	471	630	74.8
1983	Stanford	612	804	76.1
1984	Kentucky	328	416	78.8
1985	Oklahoma St.	487	640	76.1
1986	Central Mich.	546	720	75.8
1987	Colorado	517	682	75.8
1988	La Salle	479	600	*79.8

Year	Team	FT	FTA	Pct.
1989	Indiana St.	484	618	78.3
1990	Northern Ill.	595	768	77.5
1991	Penn St.	540	692	78.0
1992	Richmond	383	482	79.5
1993	James Madison	421	550	76.5

* *Record.*

REBOUND MARGIN

Year	Team	Off.	Def.	Margin
1982	Louisiana Tech	46.3	30.8	15.4
1983	Old Dominion	49.1	31.9	17.3
1984	Old Dominion	44.6	32.5	12.1
1985	Bethune-Cookman	55.3	39.1	16.2
1986	South Caro. St.	54.1	40.5	13.7
1987	Louisiana Tech	48.0	34.4	13.6
1988	Louisiana Tech	48.1	32.5	15.6
1989	Louisiana Tech	47.8	31.6	16.2
1990	Louisiana Tech	52.9	34.7	*18.3
1991	South Caro. St.	55.1	41.4	13.7
1992	Virginia	45.8	32.7	13.1
1993	Virginia	46.6	34.1	12.5

* *Record.*

ASSISTS

Year	Team	G	Ast.	Avg.
1986	Long Beach St.	34	*780	22.9
1987	Villanova	31	766	*24.7
1988	Notre Dame	28	569	20.3
1989	Maryland	32	679	21.2
1990	Stanford	33	758	23.0
1991	Eastern Wash.	27	611	22.6
1992	Bowling Green	29	672	23.2
1993	Bowling Green	30	646	21.5

* *Record.*

BLOCKED SHOTS

Year	Team	G	Blk.	Avg.
1988	Fresno St.	28	194	6.93
1989	Northern Ill.	30	231	*7.70
1990	Nevada-Las Vegas	31	197	6.35
1991	Rutgers	30	187	6.23
1992	Geo. Washington	32	*235	7.34
1993	Alcorn St.	24	129	5.38

* *Record.*

STEALS

Year	Team	G	Stl.	Avg.
1988	Wright St.	28	450	16.1
1989	Florida A&M	28	450	16.1
1990	Dartmouth	26	398	15.3
1991	Kent	29	422	14.6
1992	Buffalo	29	490	16.9
1993	Kent	29	*536	*18.5

* *Record.*

DIVISION I WOMEN'S STATISTICAL TRENDS

Year	Games	FG Made	FG Att.	Pct.	3FG Made	3FG Att.	Pct.	FT Made	FT Att.	Pct.	Pts.
1984	7,395	56.5	128.4	44.0	—	—	—	26.4	40.4	65.3	139.4
1985	7,587	56.3	128.2	43.9	—	—	—	26.1	40.3	64.7	138.6
1986	7,697	56.0	126.6	44.2	—	—	—	26.7	40.6	65.7	138.7
1987	7,914	55.6	126.7	43.9	—	—	—	26.8	40.4	66.3	138.0
1988	7,898	54.4	125.6	43.3	3.0	9.0	33.6	26.3	39.8	66.1	138.0
1989	7,971	53.8	125.2	43.0	3.7	10.9	34.1	27.3	40.6	67.1	138.6

Year	Games	FG Made	FG Att.	Pct.	3FG Made	3FG Att.	Pct.	FT Made	FT Att.	Pct.	Pts.
1990	7,963	53.0	125.1	42.4	4.4	13.2	33.2	27.8	41.5	67.0	138.1
1991	8,058	53.7	127.6	42.1	5.4	16.6	32.6	28.1	41.8	67.2	140.9
1992	8,239	52.4	124.7	42.0	5.9	18.1	32.4	28.6	42.5	67.3	139.1
1993	8,022	51.3	123.6	41.5	6.3	20.0	31.4	27.7	41.7	66.4	136.5

[Note: Averages and percentages are for both teams, per game.]

DIVISION I WOMEN'S ALL-TIME WINNINGEST TEAMS

VICTORIES

No.	School	Yrs.	Won	Lost	Tied	Pct.
1.	Long Beach St.	31	564	171	0	.767
2.	Texas	19	541	108	0	.834
3.	James Madison	71	538	291	5	.648
4.	Louisiana Tech	19	524	108	0	.829
5.	Tennessee Tech	23	519	192	0	.730
6.	Tennessee	19	499	124	0	.801
7.	Stephen F. Austin	21	494	170	0	.744
8.	Ohio St.	28	479	180	0	.727
9.	Old Dominion	24	478	193	0	.712
10.	Kansas St.	25	462	260	0	.640
11.	Southern Ill.	34	455	222	0	.672
12.	Auburn	22	443	158	0	.737
13.	Mississippi	19	438	154	0	.740
14.	Western Ky.	31	434	221	0	.663
15.	Penn St.	29	427	180	0	.703
16.	St. Peter's	26	423	170	0	.713
17.	Maryland	22	409	170	0	.706
18.	North Caro. St.	19	408	153	0	.727
19.	Rutgers	18	406	143	0	.740
20.	Virginia	20	406	162	0	.715
21.	Kansas	25	405	257	0	.612
22.	Nevada-Las Vegas	19	404	135	0	.750
23.	Memphis St.	21	401	264	0	.603
24.	Southwest Tex. St.	27	398	293	0	.576
25.	Dayton	25	393	246	0	.615

PERCENTAGE

(Minimum 300 victories)

No.	School	Yrs.	Won	Lost	Tied	Pct.
1.	Texas	19	541	108	0	.834
2.	Louisiana Tech	19	524	108	0	.829
3.	Tennessee	19	499	124	0	.801
4.	Long Beach St.	31	564	171	0	.767
5.	Mt. St. Mary's (Md.)	19	378	122	0	.756
6.	Nevada-Las Vegas	19	404	135	0	.750
7.	Stephen F. Austin	21	494	170	0	.744
8.	Montana	19	391	136	0	.742
9.	Mississippi	19	438	154	0	.740
10.	Rutgers	18	406	143	0	.740
11.	Auburn	22	443	158	0	.737
12.	Tennessee Tech	23	519	192	0	.730
13.	North Caro. St.	19	408	153	0	.727
14.	Ohio St.	28	479	180	0	.727
15.	Virginia	20	406	162	0	.715
16.	Utah	19	387	155	0	.714
17.	St. Peter's	26	423	170	0	.713
18.	Old Dominion	24	478	193	0	.712
19.	Maryland	22	409	170	0	.706
20.	Washington	19	381	159	0	.706
21.	Penn St.	29	427	180	0	.703
22.	St. Joseph's (Pa.)	20	369	162	0	.695
23.	Southern Cal	17	345	160	0	.683
24.	Southern Ill.	34	455	222	0	.672
25.	Georgia	20	383	188	0	.671

DIVISION I WOMEN'S BASKETBALL ASSOCIATED PRESS NO. 1 VS. NO. 2

(Following is a list of games between the No. 1 and No. 2 ranked teams in women's college basketball. The No. 1 team has won 12 of 23 meetings. These games are reflective of Associated Press polls compiled by Mel Greenberg of the Philadelphia Inquirer based on the votes of women's coaches.)

1979—No. 1 Old Dominion defeated No. 2 Louisiana Tech, 75-65, for the Association of Intercollegiate Athletics for Women (AIAW) championship, at Greensboro, North Carolina.

1980—No. 1 Old Dominion defeated No. 2 Texas, 75-45, at Norfolk, Virginia.

1980—No. 1 Old Dominion defeated No. 2 Tennessee, 68-53, for the AIAW championship, at Mount Pleasant, Michigan.

1981—No. 1 Louisiana Tech defeated No. 2 Old Dominion, 81-47, at Ruston, Louisiana.

1981—No. 1 Louisiana Tech defeated No. 2 Tennessee, 79-59, for the AIAW championship, at Eugene, Oregon.

1981—No. 1 Louisiana Tech defeated No. 2 Old Dominion, 68-51, at New York City.

1982—No. 1 Louisiana Tech defeated No. 2 Cheyney, 76-62, for the first NCAA championship, at Norfolk, Virginia.

1982—No. 1 Southern Cal defeated No. 2 Louisiana Tech, 64-58, at Ruston, Louisiana.

1983—No. 2 Louisiana Tech defeated No. 1 Southern Cal, 58-56, at Los Angeles, California.

1983—No. 2 Southern Cal defeated No. 1 Louisiana Tech, 69-67, for the second NCAA championship, at Norfolk, Virginia.

1984—No. 2 Louisiana Tech defeated No. 1 Southern Cal, 75-66, at Ruston, Louisiana.

1984—No. 2 Louisiana Tech defeated No. 1 Texas, 85-60, in the NCAA Midwest regional, at Ruston, Louisiana.

1985—No. 1 Old Dominion defeated No. 2 Long Beach St., 84-71, at Norfolk, Virginia.

1986—No. 2 Texas defeated No. 1 Tennessee, 88-74, at Miami, Florida.

1987—No. 2 Texas defeated No. 1 Tennessee, 97-78, at Knoxville, Tennessee.

1988—No. 1 Tennessee defeated No. 2 Long Beach St., 88-74, at Knoxville, Tennessee.

1989—No. 2 Tennessee defeated No. 1 Auburn, 66-61, for the Southeastern Conference championship at Albany, Georgia.

1989—No. 1 Tennessee defeated No. 2 Auburn, 76-60, for the eighth NCAA championship, at Tacoma, Washington.

1989—No. 2 Louisiana Tech defeated No. 1 Tennessee, 59-58, at Knoxville, Tennessee.

1992—No. 2 Virginia defeated No. 1 Maryland, 75-74, at College Park, Maryland.

1992—No. 2 Tennessee defeated No. 1 Stanford, 74-73 in overtime, at Honolulu, Hawaii.

1992—No. 1 Tennessee defeated No. 2 Stanford, 84-79, at Knoxville, Tennessee.

1993—No. 2 Tennessee defeated No. 1 Vanderbilt, 73-68, at Nashville, Tennessee.

FINAL NATIONAL POLLS

1977-AP

1. Delta St.
2. Immaculata
3. St. Joseph's (Pa.)
4. Cal St. Fullerton
5. Tennessee
6. Tennessee Tech
7. Wayland Baptist
8. Montclair St.
9. Stephen F. Austin
10. North Caro. St.
11. Louisiana St.
12. Baylor
13. UCLA
14. Old Dominion
15. Southeastern La.
16. Maryland
17. Michigan St.
18. Mississippi Col.
19. Southern Conn. St.
20. Kansas St.

1978-AP

1. Tennessee
2. Wayland Baptist
3. North Caro. St.
4. Montclair St.
5. UCLA
6. Maryland
7. Queens (N.Y.)
8. Valdosta St.
9. Delta St.
10. Louisiana St.
11. St. Joseph's (Pa.)
12. Old Dominion
13. Missouri
14. Stephen F. Austin
15. Texas
16. Ohio St.
17. Penn St.
18. Southern Conn. St.
19. Memphis St.
20. Mississippi

1979-AP

1. Old Dominion
2. Louisiana Tech
3. Tennessee
4. Texas
5. Stephen F. Austin
6. UCLA
7. Rutgers
8. Maryland
9. Cheyney
10. Wayland Baptist
11. North Caro. St.
12. Valdosta St.
13. Penn St.
14. Kansas
15. South Caro.
16. Northwestern
17. Nevada-Las Vegas
18. Long Beach St.
19. Fordham
20. Montclair St.

1980-AP

1. Old Dominion
2. Tennessee
3. Louisiana Tech
4. South Caro.
5. Stephen F. Austin
6. Maryland
7. Texas
8. Rutgers
9. Long Beach St.
10. North Caro. St.
11. Kansas
12. Cheyney
13. Kansas St.
14. Kentucky
15. Northwestern
16. Mercer
17. Oregon
18. Central Mo. St.
19. San Francisco
20. Brigham Young

1981-AP
1. Louisiana Tech
2. Tennessee
3. Old Dominion
4. Southern Cal
5. Cheyney
6. Long Beach St.
7. UCLA
8. Maryland
9. Rutgers
10. Kansas
11. Kentucky
12. Oregon
13. North Caro. St.
14. Stephen F. Austin
15. Illinois St.
16. Texas
17. Jackson St.
18. Minnesota
19. Oregon
20. Clemson

1982-AP
1. Louisiana Tech
2. Cheyney
3. Maryland
4. Tennessee
5. Texas
6. Southern Cal
7. Old Dominion
8. Rutgers
9. Long Beach St.
10. Penn St.
11. Villanova
12. North Caro. St.
13. Kentucky
14. Kansas St.
15. South Caro.
16. Drake
17. Memphis St.
18. Arizona St.
19. Oregon
20. Missouri

1983-AP
1. Southern Cal
2. Louisiana Tech
3. Texas
4. Old Dominion
5. Cheyney
6. Long Beach St.
7. Maryland
8. Penn St.
9. Georgia
10. Tennessee
11. Arizona St.
12. Kentucky
13. Mississippi
14. Auburn
15. Missouri
16. North Caro. St.
17. Kansas St.
18. North Caro.
19. Oregon St.
20. Louisiana St.

1984-AP
1. Texas
2. Louisiana Tech
3. Georgia
4. Old Dominion
5. Southern Cal
6. Long Beach St.
7. Kansas St.
8. Louisiana St.
9. Cheyney
10. Mississippi
11. Missouri
12. Alabama
13. Northeast La.
14. North Caro.
15. Tennessee
16. North Caro. St.
17. Maryland
18. Virginia
19. Ohio St.
20. Tenn.-Chatt.

1985-AP
1. Texas
2. Northeast La.
3. Long Beach St.
4. Louisiana Tech
5. Old Dominion
6. Mississippi
7. Ohio St.
8. Georgia
9. Penn St.
10. Auburn
11. Washington
12. North Caro. St.
13. Tennessee
14. Western Ky.
15. Southern Cal
16. Nevada-Las Vegas
17. St. Joseph's (Pa.)
18. UCLA
19. Texas Tech
20. San Diego St.

1986-AP
1. Texas
2. Georgia
3. Southern Cal
4. Louisiana Tech
5. Western Ky.
6. Virginia
7. Auburn
8. Long Beach St.
9. Louisiana St.
10. Rutgers
11. Mississippi
12. Ohio St.
13. Penn St.
14. Iowa
15. Tennessee
16. North Caro.
17. James Madison
18. Southern Ill.
19. Oklahoma
20. Vanderbilt

1987-AP
1. Texas
2. Auburn
3. Louisiana Tech
4. Long Beach St.
5. Rutgers
6. Georgia
7. Tennessee
8. Mississippi
9. Iowa
10. Ohio St.
11. Virginia
12. James Madison
13. North Caro. St.
14. Louisiana St.
15. Penn St.
16. Southern Ill.
17. Villanova
18. Vanderbilt
19. Southern Cal
20. Washington

1988-AP
1. Tennessee
2. Iowa
3. Auburn
4. Texas
5. Louisiana Tech
6. Ohio St.
7. Long Beach St.
8. Rutgers
9. Maryland
10. Virginia
11. Washington
12. Mississippi
13. Stanford
14. James Madison
15. Southern Cal
16. Montana
17. Georgia
18. New Mexico St.
19. Stephen F. Austin
20. La Salle

1989-AP
1. Tennessee
2. Auburn
3. Louisiana Tech
4. Stanford
5. Maryland
6. Texas
7. Long Beach St.
8. Iowa
9. Colorado
10. Georgia
11. Stephen F. Austin
12. Mississippi
13. North Caro. St.
14. Ohio St.
15. Purdue
16. Nevada-Las Vegas
17. South Caro.
18. La Salle
19. Western Ky.
20. Old Dominion

1990-AP
1. Louisiana Tech
2. Stanford
3. Washington
4. Tennessee
5. Nevada-Las Vegas
6. Stephen F. Austin
7. Georgia
8. Texas
9. Auburn
10. Iowa
11. North Caro. St.
12. Virginia
13. Northwestern
14. Long Beach St.
15. Purdue
16. Hawaii
17. Northern Ill.
18. Providence
19. South Caro.
20. Southern Miss.

1991-AP
1. Penn St.
2. Virginia
3. Georgia
4. Tennessee
5. Purdue
6. Auburn
7. North Caro. St.
8. Louisiana St.
9. Arkansas
10. Western Ky.
11. Stanford
12. Washington
13. Connecticut
14. Stephen F. Austin
15. Providence
16. Texas
17. Nevada-Las Vegas
18. Long Beach St.
19. Mississippi
20. Rutgers

1992-AP
1. Virginia
2. Tennessee
3. Stanford
4. Stephen F. Austin
5. Mississippi
6. Miami (Fla.)
7. Iowa
8. Maryland
9. Penn St.
10. Southwest Mo. St.
11. Purdue
12. Texas Tech
13. Vanderbilt
14. West Va.
15. Western Ky.
16. Geo. Washington
17. Kansas
18. Alabama
19. Texas
20. Clemson
21. Creighton
22. Houston
23. Southern Cal
24. UC Santa Barb.
25. Vermont

1993-AP

(Released before NCAA championship)

1. Vanderbilt
2. Tennessee
3. Ohio St.
4. Iowa
5. Texas Tech
6. Stanford
7. Auburn
8. Penn St.
9. Virginia
10. Colorado
11. Maryland
12. Stephen F. Austin
13. Western Ky.
14. Louisiana Tech
15. Southern Cal
16. Texas
17. North Caro.
18. Vermont
19. Bowling Green
20. Miami (Fla.)
21. Georgia
22. Nebraska
23. Hawaii
24. Kansas
25. Northern Ill.
    Oklahoma St.

1992-93
ASSOCIATED PRESS DIVISION I WOMEN'S BASKETBALL WEEK-BY-WEEK POLLS

	Preseason (11-19)	12-8	12-15	12-22	12-29	1-5	1-12	1-19	1-26	2-2	2-9	2-16	2-23	3-2	3-9	3-16
1.	Stanford	2	2	2	3	4	4	3	5	9	8	10	10	9	8	6
2.	Tennessee	1	1	1	1	2	2	2	2	1	1	1	1	1	2	2
3.	Vanderbilt	3	3	3	2	1	1	1	1	2	2	2	5	3	1	1
4.	Maryland	7	6	6	6	3	3	5	8	7	9	12	12	12	12	11
5.	Western Ky.	4	7	12	13	20	19	17	18	18	18	19	17	16	16	13
6.	Virginia	6	5	5	5	9	8	10	1	1	14	11	11	10	10	9
7.	Iowa	5	4	4	4	5	7	6	3	3	3	3	3	2	4	4
8.	Stephen F. Austin	8	9	7	7	8	11	11	10	10	13	16	13	13	13	12
9.	Southern Cal	16	15	16	14	16	15	14	15	15	16	18	16	15	15	15
10.	Texas	14	12	11	19	17	18	16	13	13	15	13	14	14	14	16
11.	Geo. Washington	17	25	NR	NR	NR	NR	NR	NR	NR	NR	NR	NR	NR	NR	NR
12.	Mississippi	9	18	NR	NR	NR	NR	NR	NR	NR	NR	NR	NR	NR	NR	NR
13.	Southwest Mo. St.	25	NR	NR	NR	NR	NR	NR	NR	NR	NR	NR	NR	NR	NR	NR
14.	Alabama	21	NR	NR	NR	NR	NR	NR	NR	NR	NR	NR	NR	NR	NR	NR
15.	Texas Tech	15	14	14	11	11	14	12	14	14	11	9	9	7	6	5
16.	Kansas	NR	NR	NR	25	NR	NR	NR	NR	NR	NR	NR	NR	NR	NR	24
17.	Purdue	11	8	8	8	10	12	15	20	NR	NR	NR	NR	NR	NR	NR
18.	Georgia	13	20	NR	NR	NR	NR	NR	NR	NR	NR	NR	NR	NR	23	21
19.	Louisiana Tech	10	11	13	16	14	13	13	12	12	10	8	8	11	11	14
20.	Miami (Fla.)	18	16	20	22	NR	NR	NR	NR	NR	NR	NR	NR	NR	24	20
21.	Connecticut	23	23	21	21	21	NR	NR	NR	NR	NR	NR	NR	NR	NR	NR
22.	North Carolina	20	19	17	17	15	21	20	16	16	12	14	18	18	18	17
23.	Penn St.	12	10	9	9	6	5	7	6	4	5	5	6	8	5	8
24.	Auburn	22	17	15	12	12	9	9	9	8	6	6	3	5	7	7
25.	Colorado	19	13	10	10	7	6	4	7	5	4	4	4	6	9	10
NR	DePaul	24	21	19	18	18	16	21	NR	NR	NR	NR	23	24	NR	NR
NR	Nebraska	NR	24	18	15	22	NR	NR	25	22	23	22	21	21	20	22
NR	Tennessee Tech	NR	22	22	NR	NR	NR	NR	NR	NR	NR	NR	NR	NR	NR	NR
NR	Ohio St.	NR	NR	23	20	13	10	8	4	6	7	7	7	4	3	3
NR	North Caro. St.	NR	NR	24	NR	NR	NR	NR	NR	NR	NR	NR	NR	NR	NR	NR
NR	Georgia Tech	NR	NR	25	23	23	23	24	NR	NR	NR	NR	NR	NR	NR	NR
NR	Clemson	NR	NR	NR	24	19	17	18	19	19	21	20	24	NR	NR	NR
NR	California	NR	NR	NR	NR	24	NR	NR	22	23	25	23	NR	NR	NR	NR
NR	Vermont	NR	NR	NR	NR	25	20	19	17	17	17	15	15	17	17	18
NR	San Diego St.	NR	NR	NR	NR	NR	22	NR	NR	NR	NR	NR	NR	NR	NR	NR
NR	Kentucky	NR	NR	NR	NR	NR	24	25	NR	25	NR	NR	NR	NR	NR	NR
NR	Oklahoma St.	NR	NR	NR	NR	NR	25	22	21	21	20	24	22	23	25	25T
NR	Indiana	NR	NR	NR	NR	NR	NR	23	NR	NR	NR	NR	NR	NR	NR	NR
NR	Nevada-Las Vegas	NR	NR	NR	NR	NR	NR	NR	23	20	19	17	19	19	21	NR
NR	Northern Ill.	NR	NR	NR	NR	NR	NR	NR	24	24	22	21	NR	NR	NR	25T
NR	Hawaii	NR	NR	NR	NR	NR	NR	NR	NR	NR	24	24	22	21	NR	NR
NR	Bowling Green	NR	NR	NR	NR	NR	NR	NR	NR	NR	NR	NR	25	22	22	19
NR	Georgetown	NR	NR	NR	NR	NR	NR	NR	NR	NR	NR	NR	NR	25	NR	NR

NR *Not ranked.*

1993-USA Today
(Released after NCAA championship)

1. Texas Tech
2. Ohio St.
3. Iowa
4. Vanderbilt
5. Tennessee
6. Virginia
7. Stanford
8. Louisiana Tech
9. Colorado
10. Auburn
11. Stephen F. Austin
12. Western Ky.
13. Penn St.
14. Southern Cal
15. North Caro.
16. Georgetown
17. Southwest Mo. St.
18. Maryland
19. Texas
20. Miami (Fla.)
21. Georgia
22. Nebraska
23. Vermont
24. Hawaii
25. Alabama

1992-93
USA TODAY DIVISION I WOMEN'S BASKETBALL WEEK-BY-WEEK POLLS

	Preseason	12-8	12-15	12-22	12-29	1-5	1-12	1-19	1-26	2-1	2-9	2-16	2-23	3-2	3-9	3-16	4-5
1.	Stanford	3	2	2	3	4	4	3	4	6T	7	9	9	8	6	5	7
2.	Tennessee	1	1	1	1	2	2	2	2	1	1	1	1	1	2	2	5
3.	Vanderbilt	2	3	3	2	1	1	1	1	2	2	2	4	3	1	1	4
4.	Maryland	7	6	6	6	3	3	5	8	9	10	11	12	12	12	12	18
5.	Western Ky.	6	9	15	16	19	19	16	20	18	19	20	17	17	16	11	12
6.	Iowa	5	4	4	4	5	6	6	3	3	3	3	2	2	4	4	3
7.	Virginia	4	5	5	5	9	8T	10	10	11	14	12	11	10	10	7	6
8.	Stephen F. Austin	11	10	9	8	8	11	11	11	10	12	16	14	13	13	13	11
9.	Texas	16	12	11	19	18	18	17	13	13	16	14	16	16	15	14T	19
10.	Southern Cal	15	15	16	14	16	15	14	15	15	15	18	15	14	14	14T	14
11.	Southwest Mo. St.	23	NR	NR	NR	NR	NR	NR	NR	NR	NR	NR	NR	NR	NR	NR	17
12.	Mississippi	8	20	NR	NR	NR	NR	NR	NR	NR	NR	NR	NR	NR	NR	NR	NR
13.	Purdue	10	7	7	7	10	12	15	21	NR	NR	NR	NR	NR	NR	NR	NR
14.	Texas Tech	14	14	14	12	11	13	12	14	14	13	10	10	9	7	6	1
15.	Georgia	13	21	NR	NR	NR	NR	NR	NR	NR	NR	NR	NR	NR	23	21	21
16.	Geo. Washington	20	NR	NR	NR	NR	NR	NR	NR	NR	NR	NR	NR	NR	NR	NR	NR
16.	Alabama	22	NR	NR	NR	NR	NR	NR	NR	NR	NR	NR	NR	NR	NR	NR	25
18.	Kansas	NR	NR	NR	NR	NR	NR	NR	NR	NR	NR	NR	NR	NR	NR	NR	NR
19.	Penn St.	9	8	8	9	6	5	7	5	4	6	6	6	7	5	9	13
20.	Louisiana Tech	12	11	12	17	15	14	13	12	12	9	8	7	11	11	16	8
20.	Miami (Fla.)	18	19	20	24	NR	NR	NR	NR	NR	NR	NR	NR	NR	24	19	20
22.	Connecticut	NR	25	21	22	21	25T	NR	NR	NR	NR	NR	NR	NR	NR	NR	NR
23.	Auburn	21	16	13	11	12	8T	9	9	6T	5	5	3	4	8	8	10
24.	Colorado	17	13	10	10	7	7	4	7	5	4	4	5	6	9	10	9
25.	Clemson	NR	NR	NR	25	20	17	18	18	19	21	10	24	NR	NR	NR	NR
NR	North Carolina	19	17	17	15	14	21	20	16	16	11	13	18	18	18	18	NR
NR	DePaul	24	18	19	18	17	16	21	24	25	23	NR	23	22	25	25T	NR
NR	Vermont	25	24	22	23	24	20	19	17	17	17	15	13	15	17	17	23
NR	Nebraska	NR	22	18	13	22	NR	NR	NR	22	24	23	22	21	20	22	22
NR	Tennessee Tech	NR	23	24	NR	NR	NR	NR	NR	NR	NR	NR	NR	NR	NR	NR	NR
NR	Ohio St.	NR	NR	23	20	13	10	8	6	6T	8	7	8	5	3	3	2
NR	Georgia Tech	NR	NR	25	21	23	25T	NR	NR	NR	NR	NR	NR	NR	NR	NR	NR
NR	Kentucky	NR	NR	NR	NR	NR	23	23	23	23	NR	NR	NR	NR	NR	NR	NR
NR	San Diego St.	NR	NR	NR	NR	NR	22	NR	NR	NR	NR	NR	NR	NR	NR	NR	NR
NR	Oklahoma St.	NR	NR	NR	NR	NR	24	22	19	20	18	22	21	25	NR	25T	NR
NR	Florida St.	NR	NR	NR	NR	NR	NR	24	NR	NR	NR	NR	NR	NR	NR	NR	NR
NR	Indiana	NR	NR	NR	NR	NR	NR	25	NR	NR	NR	NR	NR	NR	NR	NR	NR
NR	Nevada-Las Vegas	NR	NR	NR	NR	NR	NR	NR	22	21	20	17	19	19	21	24	NR
NR	California	NR	NR	NR	NR	NR	NR	NR	25	24	25	24	NR	NR	NR	NR	NR
NR	Northern Ill.	NR	NR	NR	NR	NR	NR	NR	NR	NR	22	21	NR	NR	NR	NR	NR
NR	Hawaii	NR	NR	NR	NR	NR	NR	NR	NR	NR	NR	NR	20	20	19	23	24
NR	Georgetown	NR	NR	NR	NR	NR	NR	NR	NR	NR	NR	NR	25	24	NR	NR	16
NR	Bowling Green	NR	NR	NR	NR	NR	NR	NR	NR	NR	NR	NR	NR	23	22	20	NR

NR *Not ranked.*

LaTanya Patty finished her career at Delta State with a career field-goal percentage of 63.6. Delta State is the second winning-est team in Division II with 548 vic ories in 26 years of competi

DIVISION II WOMEN'S INDIVIDUAL RECORDS

Official NCAA women's basketball records began with the 1982 season and are based on information submitted to the NCAA statistics service by institutions participating in the weekly statistics rankings. Official career records include players who played at least two seasons in Division II during the era of official NCAA statistics, which began with the 1981-82 season. Three-point field goals were added in 1987-88, assists were added in 1988-89 and blocked shots and steals were added in 1992-93. In statistical rankings, the rounding of percentages and/or averages may indicate ties where none exist. In these cases, the numerical order of the rankings is accurate.

SCORING

Points

Game
67—Jackie Givens, Fort Valley St. vs. Knoxville, Feb. 22, 1991 (25 FGs, 6 3FGs, 11 FTs)

Season
1,075—Jackie Givens, Fort Valley St., 1991 (369 FGs, 120 3FGs, 217 FTs, 28 games)

Career
2,810—Dina Kangas, Minn.-Duluth, 1988-91 (1,170 FGs, 25 3FGs, 445 FTs, 124 games)

Average Per Game

Season
38.4—Jackie Givens, Fort Valley St., 1991 (1,075 in 28)

Career
(Min. 1,300 points) 28.3—Paulette King, Florida Tech, 1992-93 (1,668 in 59)

FIELD GOALS

Field Goals

Game
26—Jackie Givens, Fort Valley St. vs. LeMoyne-Owen, Feb. 2, 1991

Season
389—Dina Kangas, Minn.-Duluth, 1991 (743 attempts)

Career
1,170—Dina Kangas, Minn.-Duluth, 1988-91 (2,207 attempts)

Consecutive Field Goals

Game
17—Maria Teal, Barry vs. Fla. Southern, Feb. 13, 1991

Season
17—Maria Teal, Barry, Feb. 13, 1991; Renee Rice, Armstrong St., Jan. 29-Feb. 1, 1992

Field-Goal Attempts

Game
62—Jackie Givens, Fort Valley St. vs. Knoxville, Feb. 22, 1991 (25 made)

Season
892—Jackie Givens, Fort Valley St., 1991 (369 made)

Career
2,815—Sheila Lindsey, Franklin Pierce, 1985-88 (1,137 made)

Field-Goal Percentage

Game
(Min. 20 made) 90.9%—Renee Rice, Armstrong St. vs. S.C.-Spartanburg, Feb. 1, 1992 (20 of 22)

Season
72.5%—Dalonda Newton, Oakland City, 1991 (198 of 273)

Career
(Min. 400 made) 65.5%—Tracy Payne, St. Joseph's (Ind.), 1986-89 (751 of 1,147)

THREE-POINT FIELD GOALS

Three-Point Field Goals

Game
11—Lisa Blackmon-Phillips, West Ga. vs. Troy St., Feb. 23, 1989 (23 attempts); Christine Keenan, Florida Tech vs. Flagler, Feb. 3, 1992 (16 attempts); Carolyn Brown, St. Augustine's vs. Tampa, Dec. 5, 1992 (17 attempts); Jackie Carter, Virginia St. vs. St. Paul's, Jan. 23, 1993 (18 attempts)

Season
138—Lisa Blackmon-Phillips, West Ga., 1989 (391 attempts)

Career
343—Betsy Bergdoll, Rio Grande/Queens (N.C.), 1989, 91-93 (809 attempts)

Three-Point Field Goals Made Per Game

Season
4.8—Lisa Blackmon-Phillips, West Ga., 1989 (138 in 29)

Career
(Min. 150 made) 4.29—Lisa Blackmon-Phillips, West Ga., 1988-89 (219 in 51)

Consecutive Three-Point Field Goals

Game
9—Diane Dodge, Quinnipiac vs. New Haven, Feb. 6, 1989

Season
11—Shelby Peterson, South Dak., Jan. 8-11, 1992

Consecutive Games Making a Three-Point Field Goal

Season
32—Shannon Coakley, Clarion, from Nov. 16, 1990, to March 16, 1991

Career
51—Amy Coon, Clarion, from Jan. 26, 1991, to Dec. 5, 1992

Three-Point Field-Goal Attempts

Game

26—Lisa Blackmon-Phillips, West Ga. vs. Jacksonville St., Jan. 9, 1989 (9 made)

Season

391—Lisa Blackmon-Phillips, West Ga., 1989 (138 made)

Career

911—Mary Nesbit, Keene St., 1988-91 (340 made)

Three-Point Field-Goal Percentage

Game

(Best perfect game) 100.0%—Denise Nehme, Northern Colo. vs. Mankato St., Jan. 30, 1993 (7 of 7)

Season

(Min. 50 made) 56.3%—Durene Heisler, North Dak., 1990 (63 of 112)

(Min. 75 made) 50.6%—Julie Dabrowski, New Hamp. Col., 1990 (89 of 176)

Career

(Min. 150 made) 46.5%—Greta Fadness, Alas. Anchorage, 1988-91 (164 of 353)

FREE THROWS

Free Throws

Game

21—By six players. Most recent: Jennifer Hillard, Presbyterian vs. Erskine, Dec. 2, 1992 (28 attempts)

Season

266—Lisa Miller, IU/PU-Ft. Wayne, 1992 (336 attempts)

Career

741—Lisa Miller, IU/PU-Ft. Wayne, 1989-92 (922 attempts)

Consecutive Free Throws

Game

21—Candace Fincher, Valdosta St. vs. Livingston, Jan. 25, 1986

Season

37—Bobbi Hardy, Central Okla., Feb. 1-27, 1993

Career

44—Kerri Lang, St. Anselm, Feb. 22-Dec. 2, 1989.

Free-Throw Attempts

Game

28—Amy Crossman, Pace vs. St. Anselm, Nov. 18, 1989 (20 made); Jennifer Hilliard, Presbyterian vs. Erskine, Dec. 2, 1992 (21 made)

Season

336—Lisa Miller, IU/PU-Ft. Wayne, 1992 (266 made)

Career

961—Jennifer DiMaggio, Pace, 1984-88 (557 made)

Free-Throw Percentage

Game

(Best perfect game) 100.0%—Karen Armold, Millersville vs. Phila. Textile, Dec. 11, 1989 (19 of 19)

Season

92.6%—Kelly Jewett, Franklin Pierce, 1992 (112 of 121)

Career

87.6%—Kerri Lang, St. Anselm, 1988-91 (369 of 421)

REBOUNDS

Rebounds

Game

35—Chanel Hamilton, Dist. Columbia vs. New York Tech, Nov. 26, 1982; Kim Ambrose, Shaw vs. St. Augustine's, Jan. 28, 1984

Season

635—Francine Perry, Quinnipiac, 1982 (28 games)

Career

1,626—Francine Perry, Quinnipiac, 1982-85 (103 games)

Average Per Game

Season

22.7—Francine Perry, Quinnipiac, 1982 (635 in 28)

Career

(Min. 900) 18.4—Norma Knight, Norfolk St., 1982-83 (937 in 51)

ASSISTS

Assists

Game

23—Selina Bynum, Albany St. (Ga.) vs. LeMoyne-Owen, Jan. 13, 1993

Season

309—Selina Bynum, Albany St. (Ga.), 1992 (26 games)

Career

927—Selina Bynum, Albany St. (Ga.), 1990-93 (107 games)

Average Per Game

Season

11.9—Selina Bynum, Albany St. (Ga.), 1992 (309 in 26)

Career

(Min. 500) 8.7—Selina Bynum, Albany St. (Ga.), 1990-93 (927 in 107)

BLOCKED SHOTS

Blocked Shots

Game

12—Tonya Roper, Wingate vs. Johnson Smith, Dec. 12, 1992; Sherrie Willis, N.M. Highlands vs. Angelo St., Dec. 12, 1992

Season

142—Rebecca Hanson, Pace, 1993 (30 games)

Average Per Game

Season

4.7—Rebecca Hanson, Pace, 1993 (142 in 30)

STEALS

Steals

Game

13—Debbie Moore, New Haven vs. Quinnipiac, Jan. 18, 1993; Yolanda Gregory, Fla. Atlantic vs. Barry, Feb. 8, 1993; Christine Keenan, Florida Tech vs. Barry, Feb. 13, 1993; Shaun Thomas, Jacksonville St. vs. North Ala., Feb. 15, 1993

Season

156—Christine Keenan, Florida Tech, 1993 (30 games)

Average Per Game

Season

6.1—Valerie Curtis, Dist. Columbia, 1993 (135 in 22)

DIVISION II WOMEN'S TEAM RECORDS

Note: When records involve both teams, each team must be an NCAA Division II member institution.

SINGLE-GAME SCORING

Most Points

148—Clarion vs. Westminster (Pa.) (62), Nov. 20, 1992

Most Points by Losing Team (Including Overtimes)

130—Northern Ky. vs. St. Joseph's (Ind.) (131) (5 ot), Feb. 27, 1988

Most Points by Losing Team (Regulation Time)

106—Lewis vs. St. Joseph's (Ind.) (111), Jan. 13, 1990; Mo.-St. Louis vs. Northeast Mo. St. (109), Jan. 13, 1990

Most Points, Both Teams

261—St. Joseph's (Ind.) (131) vs. Northern Ky. (130) (5 ot), Feb. 27, 1988

Most Points in a Half

78—Norfolk St. (143) vs. Fayetteville St. (43), Nov. 20, 1990; Clarion (148) vs. Westminster (Pa.) (62), Nov. 20, 1992

Fewest Points Allowed

9—Sonoma St. (84) vs. Notre Dame (Cal.), Jan. 14, 1992

Fewest Points, Both Teams

78—Army (53) vs. LIU-Southampton (25), Feb. 1, 1990

Widest Margin of Victory

100—Norfolk St. (143) vs. Fayetteville St. (43), Nov. 20, 1990

SINGLE-GAME FIELD GOALS

Most Field Goals

62—Norfolk St. vs. Fayetteville St., Nov. 20, 1990 (104 attempts)

Most Field-Goal Attempts

134—Lincoln (Mo.) vs. Harris-Stowe, Feb. 12, 1982 (54 made)

Highest Field-Goal Percentage

(Min. 30 made) 77.5%—North Dak. vs. Cal St. Dom. Hills, Nov. 27, 1981 (31 of 40)

Highest Field-Goal Percentage, Half

(Min. 20 made) 84.6%—Northern Ky. vs. Southern Ind., Jan. 7, 1982 (22 of 26); Oakland vs. Lake Superior St., Feb. 10, 1990 (22 of 26)

SINGLE-GAME THREE-POINT FIELD GOALS

Most Three-Point Field Goals

26—Clarion vs. Ashland, Feb. 24, 1992 (52 attempts)

Most Three-Point Field Goals, Both Teams

26—Clarion (26) vs. Ashland (0), Feb. 24, 1992

Consecutive Three-Point Field Goals Made Without a Miss

10—Quinnipiac vs. Bryant, Feb. 4, 1989; Quinnipiac vs. New Haven, Feb. 6, 1989

Most Three-Point Field-Goal Attempts

52—Clarion vs. Ashland, Feb. 24, 1992 (26 made)

Most Three-Point Field-Goal Attempts, Both Teams

65—Clarion (51) vs. West Liberty St. (14), Nov. 22, 1991

Highest Three-Point Field-Goal Percentage

(Best perfect game) 100.0%—Navy vs. Shippensburg, Dec. 6, 1989 (9 of 9)

Highest Three-Point Field-Goal Percentage, Both Teams

(Min. 10 made) 76.5%—New York Tech (9 of 11) vs. Queens (N.Y.) (4 of 6), Dec. 9, 1987 (13 of 17)

SINGLE-GAME FREE THROWS

Most Free Throws

49—Quincy vs. Lincoln (Mo.), Jan. 22, 1990 (64 attempts)

Most Free Throws, Both Teams

67—Valdosta St. (40) vs. Tampa (27), Jan. 11, 1986

Most Free-Throw Attempts

64—Quincy vs. Lincoln (Mo.), Jan. 22, 1990 (49 made); Neb.-Kearney vs. Hastings, Jan. 15, 1991 (40 made)

Most Free-Throw Attempts, Both Teams

94—Mass.-Lowell (52) vs. Bridgeport (42), Jan. 15, 1992

Fewest Free Throws

0—Many teams

Fewest Free-Throw Attempts

0—Many teams

Highest Free-Throw Percentage

(Best perfect game) 100.0%—St. Cloud St. vs. Cal St. Los Angeles, Dec. 17, 1992 (27 of 27)

(Min. 30 made) 96.9%—Central Okla. vs. Eastern N. Mex., Jan. 18, 1992 (31 of 32)

Highest Free-Throw Percentage, Both Teams

(Min. 40 made) 89.4%—St. Cloud St. (27 of 27) vs. Cal St. Los Angeles (15 of 20), Dec. 17, 1992 (42 of 47)

SINGLE-GAME REBOUNDS

Most Rebounds
96—Alabama A&M vs. LeMoyne-Owen, Feb. 26, 1993

Highest Rebound Margin
66—Humboldt St. (77) vs. Dominican (Cal.) (11), Nov. 24, 1990

SINGLE-GAME PERSONAL FOULS

Most Personal Fouls
45—Livingston vs. Ala.-Huntsville, Nov. 27, 1990

Most Personal Fouls, Both Teams
62—St. Anselm (34) vs. Pace (28), Nov. 18, 1989

SINGLE-GAME OVERTIMES

Most Overtime Periods
5—Northern Ky. (130) vs. St. Joseph's (Ind.) (131), Feb. 2, 1988

Most Points in One Overtime Period
21—Central Okla. vs. Texas A&M-Kingsville, Feb. 20, 1989

Most Points in One Overtime Period, Both Teams
36—Catawba (24) vs. Elon (12), Feb. 10, 1993

Most Points in Overtime Periods
36—Angelo St. vs. West Tex. A&M, Jan. 17, 1987

Most Points in Overtime Periods, Both Teams
68—Angelo St. (36) vs. West Tex. A&M (32), Jan. 17, 1987

SEASON SCORING

Most Points
3,357—Hampton, 1988 (34 games)

Highest Average Per Game
98.7—Hampton, 1988 (3,357 in 34)

Highest Average Scoring Margin
36.7—West Tex. A&M, 1991 (86.3 offense, 49.7 defense)

Most Games at Least 100 Points
16—Hampton, 1988

Most Consecutive Games at Least 100 Points
5—Valdosta St., 1987; Hampton, 1988

SEASON FIELD GOALS

Most Field Goals
1,324—Hampton, 1988 (2,887 attempts)

Most Field Goals Per Game
38.9—Hampton, 1988 (1,324 in 34)

Most Field-Goal Attempts
2,887—Hampton, 1988 (1,324 made)

Most Field-Goal Attempts Per Game
84.9—Hampton, 1988 (2,887 in 34)

Highest Field-Goal Percentage
52.4%—West Tex. A&M, 1988 (1,138 of 2,173)

SEASON THREE-POINT FIELD GOALS

Most Three-Point Field Goals
386—Clarion, 1992 (1,068 attempts)

Most Three-Point Field Goals Per Game
13.3—Clarion, 1992 (386 in 29)

Most Three-Point Field-Goal Attempts
1,068—Clarion, 1992 (386 made)

Most Three-Point Field-Goal Attempts Per Game
36.8—Clarion, 1992 (1,068 in 29)

Highest Three-Point Field-Goal Percentage
(Min. 70 made) 54.1%—North Dak., 1990 (73 of 135)
(Min. 100 made) 48.9%—New York Tech, 1988 (111 of 227)

SEASON FREE THROWS

Most Free Throws
666—Jacksonville St., 1991 (935 attempts)

Most Free Throws Per Game
22.2—Jacksonville St., 1991 (666 in 30)

Most Free-Throw Attempts
935—Jacksonville St., 1991 (666 made)

Most Free-Throw Attempts Per Game
31.2—Jacksonville St., 1991 (935 in 30)

Highest Free-Throw Percentage
78.5%—Augustana (S.D.), 1993 (567 of 722)

SEASON REBOUNDS

Most Rebounds
1,875—Quinnipiac, 1982 (28 games)

Highest Average Per Game
67.0—Quinnipiac, 1982 (1,875 in 28)

Highest Average Rebound Margin
29.9—Quinnipiac, 1982 (67.0 offense, 37.1 defense)

SEASON PERSONAL FOULS

Most Personal Fouls
1,040—Mercy, 1988 (26 games)

Most Personal Fouls Per Game
40.0—Mercy, 1988 (1,040 in 26)

Fewest Personal Fouls
213—Sacred Heart, 1987 (26 games)

Fewest Personal Fouls Per Game
8.2—Sacred Heart, 1987 (213 in 26)

SEASON DEFENSE

Lowest Scoring Average Per Game Allowed
44.7—St. John Fisher, 1986 (1,072 in 24)

Lowest Field-Goal Percentage Allowed
32.3%—Albany St. (Ga.), 1991 (581 of 1,797)

GENERAL RECORDS

Most Victories in a Season
34—Fort Hays St., 1991

Most Consecutive Victories
41—New Haven, 1986-88

Most Consecutive Victories, Season
33—West Tex. A&M, 1988; Norfolk St., 1991

Most Consecutive Home-Court Victories
85—West Tex. A&M, from Jan. 9, 1987, to Dec. 6, 1991

Most Consecutive 20-Win Seasons
12—Cal Poly Pomona, 1982-93 (current)

Most Consecutive 30-Win Seasons
5—Bentley, 1989-93 (current)

Most Consecutive Defeats
70—Notre Dame (Cal.), from Dec. 15, 1988, to Feb. 13, 1992

DIVISION II WOMEN'S ALL-TIME INDIVIDUAL LEADERS

SINGLE-GAME SCORING HIGHS

Pts.	Player, Team vs. Opponent	Season
*67	Jackie Givens, Fort Valley St. vs. Knoxville	1991
64	Kim Brewington, Johnson Smith vs. Livingstone	1990
63	Jackie Givens, Fort Valley St. vs. LeMoyne-Owen	1991
58	Carolyn Brown, St. Augustine's vs. Tampa	1993
55	Jackie Givens, Fort Valley St. vs. LeMoyne-Owen	1991
53	Renee Rice, Armstrong St. vs. Brewton-Parker	1992
52	Linda Krawford, Oakland vs. Michigan Tech	1983
52	Carolyn Huntley, Winston-Salem vs. Lenoir-Rhyne	1986
52	Jackie Dolberry, Hampton vs. N.C. Central	1989
52	Jackie Givens, Fort Valley St. vs. Clark Atlanta	1991
52	Gina Flowers, West Ga. vs. Miles	1992
52	Julie Heldt, Northern Mich. vs. Wis.-Parkside	1993
51	Jeannette Yeoman, St. Joseph's (Ind.) vs. Lewis	1990
50	Belinda Hill, Bridgeport vs. Assumption	1987
50	Shannon Williams, Valdosta St. vs. Fla. Southern	1987
50	Jeannette Yeoman, St. Joseph's (Ind.) vs. Northern Ky.	1988
50	Kim Brewington, Johnson Smith vs. Livingstone	1990

* *Record.*

SEASON POINTS

Player, Team	Season	G	FG	3FG	FT	Pts.
Jackie Givens, Fort Valley St.	†1991	28	369	120	217	*1,075
Dina Kangas, Minn.-Duluth	1991	32	*389	9	151	938
Kim Brewington, Johnson Smith	†1990	28	312	62	222	908
Annette Wiles, Fort Hayes St.	1991	36	358	0	164	880
Paulette King, Florida Tech	†1992	29	322	2	209	855
Dina Kangas, Minn.-Duluth	1990	30	338	16	145	837
Paulette King, Florida Tech	1993	30	310	0	193	813
Jeannette Yeoman, St. Joseph's (Ind.)	1990	30	300	45	164	809
Jackie Dolberry, Hampton	1988	34	299	91	114	803
Mary Naughton, Stonehill	†1988	31	291	1	216	799
Beverly Reed, Livingston	1982	36	299	—	197	795
Yvonnie Owens, Clark Atlanta	1985	31	287	—	219	793
Janice Washington, Valdosta St.	1984	33	308	—	155	771
Claudie Schleyer, Abilene Christian	†1986	28	293	—	184	770
Laura Buehning, Cal Poly SLO	1982	33	307	—	143	757
Lisa Miller, IU/PU-Ft. Wayne	1992	29	243	0	*266	752
Amy Wilhelm, Morningside	1986	31	314	—	122	750
Vincene Morris, Phila. Textile	1986	30	290	—	163	743
Stella Cannon, LeMoyne-Owen	1990	25	259	77	147	742
Peggy Taylor, Howard Payne	1983	27	300	—	138	738

† *National champion.* * *Record.*

SEASON SCORING AVERAGE

Player, Team	Season	G	FG	3FG	FT	Pts.	Avg.
Jackie Givens, Fort Valley St.	†1991	28	369	120	217	*1,075	*38.4
Kim Brewington, Johnson Smith	†1990	28	312	62	222	908	32.4
Stacey Cunningham, Shippensburg	†1983	22	266	—	126	658	29.9
Stella Cannon, LeMoyne-Owen	1990	25	259	77	147	742	29.7
Cissy Little, Belmont Abbey	1983	24	318	—	74	710	29.6
Paulette King, Florida Tech	†1992	29	322	2	209	855	29.5
Dina Kangas, Minn.-Duluth	1991	32	*389	9	151	938	29.3
Carmille Barnette, Longwood	1990	21	223	48	102	596	28.4
Rene Jones, St. Paul's	1988	26	266	24	179	735	28.3
Yolanda Griffith, Fla. Atlantic	†1993	22	262	0	97	621	28.2
Dina Kangas, Minn.-Duluth	1990	30	338	16	145	837	27.9
Donna Hammond, UC Riverside	†1982	26	290	—	145	725	27.9
Claudia Schleyer, Abilene Christian	†1986	28	293	—	184	770	27.5
Peggy Taylor, Howard Payne	1983	27	300	—	138	738	27.3
Concetha Smith, Fayetteville St.	1983	23	254	—	118	626	27.2
Paulette King, Florida Tech	1993	30	310	0	193	813	27.1
Jeannette Yeoman, St. Joseph's (Ind.)	1990	30	300	45	164	809	27.0
Shannon Williams, Valdosta St.	†1989	26	251	0	196	698	26.8
Carolyn Brown, St. Augustine's	1993	24	240	90	74	644	26.8
Shelley Altrogge, Eastern Mont.	1990	26	254	0	183	691	26.6

* *Record.* † *National champion.*

SEASON FIELD-GOAL PERCENTAGE

(Based on qualifiers for annual championship)

Player, Team	Season	G	FG	FGA	Pct.
Dalonda Newton, Oakland City	1991	22	198	273	*72.5
Missy Taylor, Oakland City	†1993	29	267	385	69.4
Corinne Vanderwal, Calif. (Pa.)	†1992	26	156	228	68.4
Julie Eymann, Regis (Colo.)	1993	27	186	273	68.1
Darla Leavitt, West Tex. A&M	†1991	27	145	215	67.4
Jackie Andrews, Morris Brown	†1983	22	134	200	67.0
Cynthia Bridges, Fort Valley St.	1993	30	151	226	66.8
Candace Fincher, Valdosta St.	†1986	27	185	277	66.8
Tracy Payne, St. Joseph's (Ind.)	†1989	31	221	333	66.4
Diane Velky, Quinnipiac	†1982	28	146	220	66.4
Tracy Payne, St. Joseph's (Ind.)	†1988	31	242	368	65.8
Julie Coughlin, Minn.-Duluth	1992	30	150	229	65.5
Corinne Vanderwal, Calif. (Pa.)	1993	26	191	293	65.2
Tracy Payne, St. Joseph's (Ind.)	†1987	28	183	282	64.9
LaTanya Patty, Delta St.	1991	30	280	432	64.8
Bridget Lindquist, Augustana (S.D.)	†1990	28	149	230	64.8
Bridget Lindquist, Augustana (S.D.)	1991	29	148	229	64.6
Sharon Lyke, Utica	†1985	26	222	345	64.3
Mabel Sanders, Savannah St.	1992	29	266	414	64.3

* *Record.* † *National champion.*

SEASON THREE-POINT FIELD-GOALS MADE PER GAME

(Based on qualifiers for annual championship)

Player, Team	Season	G	3FG	Avg.
Lisa Blackmon-Phillips, West Ga.	†1989	29	*138	*4.8
Jackie Givens, Fort Valley St.	†1991	28	120	4.3
Jackie Dolberry, Hampton	1989	28	113	4.0
Betsy Bergdoll, Queens (N.C.)	1991	27	104	3.9
Lisa Kurtenback, South Dak. St.	1989	28	107	3.8
Terri Haynes, Mo. Southern St.	1991	27	102	3.8
Carolyn Brown, St. Augustine's	†1993	24	90	3.8
Lisa Blackmon-Phillips, West Ga.	†1988	22	81	3.7
Betsy Bergdoll, Queens (N.C.)	†1992	28	103	3.7
Toni Peterson, LeMoyne-Owen	1991	24	88	3.7
Angie Dobbs, Navy	1991	24	83	3.5
Camelia Bloodsaw, Alabama A&M	1992	30	102	3.4
Carolyn Brown, St. Augustine's	1992	23	78	3.4
Mary Nesbit, Keene St.	1988	29	98	3.4
Dionka Davis, Fort Valley St.	1993	30	101	3.4

Player, Team	Season	G	3FG	Avg.
Betsy Bergdoll, Queens (N.C.)	1993	26	87	3.3
Shannon Coakley, Clarion	1991	32	107	3.3
Shelby Petersen, South Dak.	1992	27	89	3.3
Lara Thornton, Calif. (Pa.)	1993	26	85	3.3
Tori Lindbeck, Tampa	1993	26	85	3.3
Michelle Butler, Livingston	†1990	27	88	3.3
Armeda Flores, Adams St.	1993	27	88	3.3

† *National champion.* * *Record.*

SEASON THREE-POINT FIELD-GOAL PERCENTAGE

(Based on qualifiers for annual championship)

Player, Team	Season	G	3FG	3FGA	Pct.
Durene Heisler, North Dak.	†1990	31	63	112	*56.3
Jeannette Yeoman, St. Joseph's (Ind.)	1990	30	45	81	55.6
Trish Van Diggelen, Missouri-Rolla	†1989	25	43	81	53.1
Monica Steinhoff, Mo.-St. Louis	1989	27	60	117	51.3
Kelly Tomlin, Livingston	†1993	26	56	110	50.9
Jackie Farnan, New York Tech	†1988	26	58	114	50.9
Julie Dabrowski, New Hamp. Col.	1990	30	89	176	50.6
Kim Francis, Southwest Baptist	1993	27	45	89	50.6
Darlene Hildebrand, Phila. Textile	†1992	32	48	95	50.5
Greta Fadness, Alas. Anchorage	†1991	25	63	127	49.6
Margaret Thomas, Paine	1988	30	75	152	49.3
Patty Costa, Bridgeport	1989	30	61	124	49.2
Darlene Hildebrand, Phila. Textile	1993	29	73	149	49.0
Tara Jackson, Elizabeth City St.	1990	22	40	82	48.8
Carol Kloecker, Gannon	1989	27	64	132	48.5
Donna Wheeler, Southern Conn. St.	1988	25	66	138	47.8
Sandy Vincent, Bellarmine	1993	28	43	90	47.8
Marilyn Chung, New York Tech	1988	26	42	89	47.2
Greta Fadness, Alas. Anchorage	1990	27	49	104	47.1

† *National champion.* * *Record.*

SEASON FREE-THROW PERCENTAGE

(Based on qualifiers for annual championship)

Player, Team	Season	G	FT	FTA	Pct.
Kelly Jewett, Franklin Pierce	†1992	31	112	121	*92.6
Teena Merrell, IU/PU Ft. Wayne	†1987	26	69	76	90.8
Sarah Howard, St. Cloud St.	†1988	28	111	123	90.2
Kerri Lang, St. Anselm	†1991	31	92	102	90.2
Kelly Legler, Southern Ore.	†1982	21	53	59	89.8
Denise Nehme, Northern Colo.	†1990	28	88	98	89.8
Darlene Hildebrand, Phila. Textile	1992	32	119	133	89.5
Kaye Klotzer, Mo.-St. Louis	1987	28	92	103	89.3
Mary Fisher, Michigan Tech	1987	27	92	103	89.3
Margie Speaks, Ky. Wesleyan	†1984	23	58	65	89.2
Lisa McGhee, West Ga.	†1985	26	81	91	89.0
Dixie Horn, SIU-Edwardsville	†1989	27	89	100	89.0
Jennifer Demby, Mass.-Lowell	1988	26	72	81	88.9
Debbie Leffler, Wright St.	1984	26	71	80	88.8
Karmen MacLean, Angelo St.	1992	22	63	71	88.7
Kim Martin, Central Okla.	1992	28	70	79	88.6
Stefanie Quayle, Emporia St.	1991	24	61	69	88.4
Kerri Lang, St. Anselm	1990	29	144	163	88.3
Renae Aschoff, Portland St.	†1993	29	75	85	88.2
Michele Coyle, Mercy	1992	27	82	93	88.2

* *Record.* † *National champion.*

SEASON REBOUNDS

Player, Team	Season	G	Reb.
Francine Perry, Quinnipiac	†1982	28	*635
Toni Goodman, Hampton	1982	33	507
Yvonnie Owens, Clark Atlanta	†1985	31	502
Francine Perry, Quinnipiac	1985	32	481
Tracy Linton, Jacksonville St.	1993	29	480

Player, Team	Season	G	Reb.
Norma Knight, Norfolk St.	1983	26	472
Norma Knight, Norfolk St.	1982	25	465
Von Fulmore, N.C. Central	†1986	26	464
Rachel Rosario, UC Riverside	1993	28	456
Kim Zornow, Pace	1989	30	438
Darlene Chaney, Hampton	1985	34	436
Tammy Walker-Strode, Edinboro	1992	30	436
Vanessa White, Tuskegee	†1993	25	433
Francine Perry, Quinnipiac	1984	31	430
Joy Jeter, New Haven	1989	32	429
Sue Salg, LIU-C.W. Post	1982	32	428
Mabel Sanders, Savannah St.	†1992	29	426
Kimberly Oates, Fort Valley St.	†1989	28	424
Sylvia Walker, Virginia Union	1986	27	423
Antoinette Goode, Cal St. Hayward	1987	28	418

*† National champion. * Record.*

SEASON REBOUND AVERAGE

Player, Team	Season	G	Reb.	Avg.
Francine Perry, Quinnipiac	†1982	28	*635	*22.7
Chanel Hamilton, Dist. Columbia	†1983	19	399	21.0
Norma Knight, Norfolk St.	1982	25	465	18.6
Norma Knight, Norfolk St.	1983	26	472	18.2
Von Fulmore, N.C. Central	†1986	26	464	17.8
Vanessa White, Tuskegee	†1993	25	433	17.3
Kim Ambrose, Shaw	†1984	23	383	16.7
Tracy Linton, Jacksonville St.	1993	29	480	16.6
Rachel Rosario, UC Riverside	1993	28	456	16.3
Tracy Fidler, Keene St.	1983	22	357	16.2
Yvonnie Owens, Clark Atlanta	†1985	31	502	16.2
Yolanda Griffith, Fla. Atlantic	1993	22	352	16.0
Sylvia Walker, Virginia Union	1986	27	423	15.7
Jean Millen, Bloomsburg	1984	25	390	15.6
Lorain Truesdale, Lander	1993	26	404	15.5
Toni Goodman, Hampton	1982	33	507	15.4
Kay Goodwin, Texas A&M-Kingsville	1982	27	413	15.3
Lynnetta Dority, Morris Brown	1986	24	365	15.2
Kimberly Oates, Fort Valley St.	†1989	28	424	15.1

** Record. † National champion.*

SEASON ASSISTS

Player, Team	Season	G	Ast.
Selina Bynum, Albany St. (Ga.)	†1992	26	*309
Lisa Rice, Norfolk St.	1993	31	305
Angela Hewlett, Portland St.	1992	34	296
Denise Holm, Minn.-Duluth	†1989	32	291
Jennifer Radosevic, St. Joseph's (Ind.)	†1990	30	281
Selina Bynum, Albany St. (Ga.)	†1993	26	280
Katrina Lofton, Barry	1991	30	279
Paula Kline, St. Joseph's (Ind.)	1992	31	278
Selina Bynum, Albany St. (Ga.)	†1991	26	274
Monica Odoy, Bentley	1991	35	262
Nikki Leibold, Northern Mich.	1992	30	248
Eileen Prendergast, Bentley	1992	32	245
Nikki Leibold, Northern Mich.	1993	28	243
Mindy Young, Pitt.-Johnstown	1991	29	242
Missy Wolfe, Bentley	1989	34	240
Lori Richelderfer, Calif. (Pa.)	1993	26	239
Jeannette Yeoman, St. Joseph's (Ind.)	1989	31	238
Andrea Martre, Edinboro	1990	30	238
Lisa Rice, Norfolk St.	1992	32	237
Jody Hill, Pace	1993	31	236

*† National champion. * Record.*

SEASON ASSIST AVERAGE

Player, Team	Season	G	Ast.	Avg.
Selina Bynum, Albany St. (Ga.)	†1992	26	*309	*11.9
Selina Bynum, Albany St. (Ga.)	†1993	26	280	10.8
Selina Bynum, Albany St. (Ga.)	†1991	26	274	10.5
Lisa Rice, Norfolk St.	1993	31	305	9.8
Jennifer Radosevic, St. Joseph's (Ind.)	†1990	30	281	9.4
Katrina Lofton, Barry	1991	30	279	9.3
Lori Richelderfer, Calif. (Pa.)	1993	26	239	9.2
Tammy Wood, Calif. (Pa.)	1992	24	220	9.2
Denise Holm, Minn.-Duluth	†1989	32	291	9.1
Paula Kline, St. Joseph's (Ind.)	1992	31	278	9.0
Angela Hewlett, Portland St.	1992	34	296	8.7
Nikki Leibold, Northern Mich.	1993	28	243	8.7
Shaunda Hill, Alabama A&M	1989	27	233	8.6
Tara Reardon, Queens (N.Y.)	1989	26	221	8.5
Tara Reardon, Queens (N.Y.)	1993	20	169	8.5
Tara Reardon, Queens (N.Y.)	1990	27	226	8.4
Pat Neder, Winona St.	1990	25	209	8.4
Mindy Young, Pitt.-Johnstown	1991	29	242	8.3
Nikki Leibold, Northern Mich.	1992	30	248	8.3
Elnita Curtis, Bowie St.	1990	22	180	8.2

† *National champion.* * *Record.*

SEASON BLOCKED SHOTS

Player, Team	Season	G	Blk.
Rebecca Hanson, Pace	†1993	30	*142
Tonya Roper, Wingate	1993	31	140
Missy Taylor, Oakland City	1993	29	127
Sherry Willis, N.M. Highlands	1993	29	122
Bobbi Jo Austin, LIU-C. W. Post	1993	27	97
Andrea Sunday, St. Anselm	1993	29	97
Jeanette Polk, Augusta	1993	28	90
Jen Andersson, Florida Tech	1993	30	76
Terri Ayers, Edinboro	1993	30	76
Jenn Hamilton, Quinnipiac	1993	27	76
Holly Roberts, Metropolitan St.	1993	27	76
Karin Kane, Adelphi	1993	27	73
Vicki Carlisle, Franklin Pierce	1993	30	70
Yolanda Griffith, Fla. Atlantic	1993	22	69
Darlene Orlando-Ciarcia, Mass.-Lowell	1993	30	67

† *National champion.* * *Record.*

SEASON BLOCKED-SHOT AVERAGE

Player, Team	Season	G	Blk.	Avg.
Rebecca Hanson, Pace	†1993	30	*142	*4.7
Tonya Roper, Wingate	1993	31	140	4.5
Missy Taylor, Oakland City	1993	29	127	4.4
Sherry Willis, N.M. Highlands	1993	29	122	4.2
Bobbi Jo Austin, LIU-C. W. Post	1993	27	97	3.6
Andrea Sunday, St. Anselm	1993	29	97	3.3
Jeanette Polk, Augusta	1993	28	90	3.2
Yolanda Griffith, Fla. Atlantic	1993	22	69	3.1
Holly Roberts, Metropolitan St.	1993	27	76	2.8
Jenn Hamilton, Quinnipiac	1993	27	76	2.8
Karin Kane, Adelphi	1993	27	73	2.7
Terri Ayers, Edinboro	1993	30	76	2.5
Jen Andersson, Florida Tech	1993	30	76	2.5
Vicki Carlisle, Franklin Pierce	1993	30	70	2.3
Jennifer Sullivan, Northern Colo.	1993	27	63	2.3

† *National champion.* * *Record.*

SEASON STEALS

Player, Team	Season	G	Stl.
Christine Keenan, Florida Tech	1993	30	*156
Patrena Wilson, Limestone	1993	29	155
Carolyn Brown, St. Augustine's	1993	24	145
Dionka Davis, Fort Valley St.	1993	30	138

Player, Team	Season	G	Stl.
Tammy Greene, Phila. Textile	1993	29	138
Debbie Moore, New Haven	1993	27	138
Valerie Curtis, Dist. Columbia	†1993	22	135
Jody Buck, North Dak. St.	1993	32	131
Shaun Thomas, Jacksonville St.	1993	29	129
Necole Watts, Pfeiffer	1993	25	123
Ebonie Simmons, American Int'l	1993	28	119
Queenie Edwards, Quinnipiac	1993	27	118
DeShonna Anderson, Norlfolk St.	1993	32	116
Yolanda Gregory, Fla. Atlantic	1993	25	113
Jennine Tanks, Norfolk St.	1993	30	113

† *National champion.* * *Record.*

SEASON STEAL AVERAGE

Player, Team	Season	G	Stl.	Avg.
Valerie Curtis, Dist. Columbia	†1993	22	135	*6.1
Carolyn Brown, St. Augustine's	1993	24	145	6.0
Patrena Wilson, Limestone	1993	29	155	5.3
Christine Keenan, Florida Tech	1993	30	*156	5.2
Tara Reardon, Queens (N.Y.)	1993	20	103	5.2
Debbie Moore, New Haven	1993	27	138	5.1
Yolanda Griffith, Fla. Atlantic	1993	22	109	5.0
Necole Watts, Pfeiffer	1993	25	123	4.9
Tammy Greene, Phila. Textile	1993	29	138	4.8
Dionka Davis, Fort Valley St.	1993	30	138	4.6
Yolanda Gregory, Fla. Atlantic	1993	25	113	4.5
Shaun Thomas, Jacksonville St.	1993	29	129	4.4
Queenie Edwards, Quinnipiac	1993	27	118	4.4
Selina Bynum, Albany St. (Ga.)	1993	26	112	4.3
Ebonie Simmons, American Int'l	1993	28	119	4.3

† *National champion.* * *Record.*

CAREER POINTS

Player, Team	Seasons	Pts.
Dina Kangas, Minn.-Duluth	1988-91	*2,810
Claudia Schleyer, Abilene Christian	1983-86	2,770
Shannon Williams, Valdosta St.	1987-90	2,636
Brenda Shaffer-Dahl, Washburn	1987-90	2,613
Sheila Lindsey, Franklin Pierce	1985-88	2,564
Annette Wiles, Fort Hays St.	1988-91	2,407
Lisa Miller, IU/PU-Ft. Wayne	1989-92	2,358
Amy Wilhelm, Morningside	1984-87	2,332
Joy Jeter, New Haven	1986-89	2,299
Jeannette Yeoman, St. Joseph's (Ind.)	1987-90	2,280
Jackie Givens, Fort Valley St.	1988-91	2,277
Niki Bracken, Cal Poly Pomona	1987-90	2,246
Kammy Brown, Virginia St.	1987-90	2,242
Robin Graul, Alas. Anchorage	1986-89	2,237
Linda Schnitzler, Wayne St. (Neb.)	1986-89	2,224
Lynette Richardson, Florida Int'l	1983-86	2,187
Vincene Morris, Phila. Textile	1983-86	2,180
Theresa Lorenzi, Bloomsburg	1986-89	2,173
Velisa Levett, West Ga.	1988-91	2,172
Sandy Skaisgir, Hillsdale	1987-90	2,160
Tina Martin, Lock Haven	1983-86	2,157
Mary Naughton, Stonehill	1986-89	2,144
Barbara Green, Pembroke St.	1982-85	2,133
Malissa Stephenson, Dist. Columbia	1986-89	2,131
Dana Bright, Jacksonville St.	1988-91	2,128

* *Record.*

CAREER SCORING AVERAGE

(Minimum 1,300 points)

Player, Team	Seasons	G	FG	3FG	FT	Pts.	Avg.
Paulette King, Florida Tech	1992-93	59	632	2	402	1,668	*28.3
Shannon Williams, Valdosta St.	1987-90	105	1,003	0	630	2,636	25.1
Shelley Altrogge, Eastern Mont.	1989-91	56	536	0	310	1,382	24.7
Claudia Schleyer, Abilene Christian	1983-86	114	1,074	—	622	2,770	24.3
Stacey Cunningham, Shippensburg	1981-84	89	816	—	425	2,057	23.1

Player, Team	Seasons	G	FG	3FG	FT	Pts.	Avg.
Dina Kangas, Minn.-Duluth	1988-91	124	*1,170	25	445	*2,810	22.7
Malissa Stephenson, Dist. Columbia	1986-89	97	807	1	516	2,131	22.0
Theresa Lorenzi, Bloomsburg	1986-89	100	975	0	223	2,173	21.7
Jackie Givens, Fort Valley St.	1988-91	107	832	245	368	2,277	21.3
Lisa Miller, IU/PU-Ft. Wayne	1989-92	111	808	1	*741	2,358	21.2
Sheila Lindsey, Franklin Pierce	1985-88	121	1,137	—	290	2,564	21.2
Kim Brewington, Johnson Smith	1987-90	82	625	139	335	1,724	21.0
Tina Martin, Lock Haven	1983-86	103	918	—	321	2,157	20.9
Lynette Richardson, Florida Int'l	1983-86	105	893	—	401	2,187	20.8
Brenda Shaffer-Dahl, Washburn	1987-90	126	1,061	110	381	2,613	20.7
Velisa Levett, West Ga.	1988-91	105	848	5	471	2,172	20.7
Amy Wilhelm, Morningside	1984-87	114	988	—	356	2,332	20.5
Annette Wiles, Fort Hays St.	1988-91	118	993	0	421	2,407	20.4
Kammy Brown, Virginia St.	1987-90	110	887	56	412	2,242	20.4
Sandy Skaisgir, Hillsdale	1987-90	107	827	2	504	2,160	20.2
Robin Graul, Alas. Anchorage	1986-89	111	819	1	598	2,237	20.2
Tisha England, S.C.-Aiken	1989-92	104	747	74	516	2,084	20.0
Keenan Menefee, Winston-Salem	1983-86	86	733	—	247	1,713	19.9
Vincene Morris, Phila. Textile	1983-86	110	876	—	428	2,180	19.8
Cathy Cox, Alas. Fairbanks	1987-90	106	719	45	592	2,075	19.6

* *Record.*

CAREER FIELD-GOAL PERCENTAGE

(Minimum 400 field goals made)

Player, Team	Seasons	G	FG	FGA	Pct.
Tracy Payne, St. Joseph's (Ind.)	1986-89	118	751	1,147	*65.5
Candace Fincher, Valdosta St.	1984-87	111	594	931	63.8
LaTanya Patty, Delta St.	1990-93	123	866	1,361	63.6
Shelly Trego, Shippensburg	1989-92	102	401	654	61.3
Mabel Sanders, Savannah St.	1989-92	106	817	1,343	60.8
Sharonda O'Bannon, Bellarmine	1989-92	77	466	772	60.4
Janice Washington, Valdosta St.	1981-84	112	689	1,144	60.2
Bridget Lindquist, Augustana (S.D.)	1988-91	107	427	709	60.2
Karyn Marshall, Bryant	1983-86	111	824	1,379	59.8
Pat Colon, Southeast Mo. St.	1984-87	117	875	1,462	59.8
Tammy Wilson, Central Mo. St.	1986-89	122	835	1,408	59.3
Dani Fronabarger, Pittsburg St.	1990-93	111	575	977	58.9
Colleen Chaske, North Dak.	1987-89	55	402	688	58.4
Annette Wiles, Fort Hays St.	1988-91	118	993	1,700	58.4
Donna Burks, Dayton	1981-84	107	769	1,329	57.9
Connie James, Navy	1987-90	101	698	1,207	57.8
Debbie Delie, Oakland	1987-90	113	818	1,415	57.8
Velisa Levett, West Ga.	1988-91	105	848	1,476	57.5
Tammy Walker-Strode, Edinboro	1991-92	57	521	909	57.3
Karen Sayers, Pitt.-Johnstown	1984-87	109	539	942	57.2
Crystal Hardy, Delta St.	1987-90	130	675	1,182	57.1
Jennifer Johnson, South Dak. St.	1982-85	103	688	1,209	56.9
Laura Regal, Niagara	1983-86	103	662	1,171	56.5
Staci Stevens, UC Davis	1985-88	84	595	1,054	56.5
Peggy McCoy, Texas Woman's	1988-91	102	715	1,268	56.4

* *Record.*

CAREER THREE-POINT FIELD GOALS MADE

Player, Team	Seasons	G	3FG
Betsy Bergdoll, Rio Grande/Queens (N.C.)	1989, 91-93	108	*343
Mary Nesbit, Keene St.	1988-91	118	340
Kelli Ritzer, Minn.-Duluth	1988-91	128	325
Nancy Somers, Ozarks (Mo.)/Mo. Southern St.	1990-91, 92-93	120	288
#Shannon Coakley, Clarion	1991-93	89	257
#Amy Coon, Clarion	1991-93	91	255
Monica Steinhoff, Mo.-St. Louis	1989-92	108	247
Jackie Givens, Fort Valley St.	1988-91	107	245
Tricia Lukawski, Chadron St.	1990-93	100	238
Julie Krauth, Augustana (S.D.)	1990-93	100	230
Shaunda Hill, Alabama A&M	1989-91	108	227
Christine Keenan, Florida Tech	1989-90, 92-93	106	223
Lisa Blackmon-Phillips, West Ga.	1988-89	51	219
$Angie Dobbs, Navy	1989-92	100	219
Trish Van Diggelen, Missouri-Rolla	1989-92	108	219

Player, Team	Seasons	G	3FG
Teresa Ramos, Eastern N. Mex.	1989-92	107	218
Melissa Hammond, West Liberty St.	1990-93	105	216
Kellie Wyatt, Clark Atlanta	1989-92	99	210
Jackie Dolberry, Hampton	1988-89	62	204

*# Active player. * Record. $ Played three seasons in Division II (Division I in 1992).*

CAREER THREE-POINT FIELD GOALS MADE PER GAME

(Minimum 150 three-point field goals made)

Player, Team	Seasons	G	3FG	Avg.
Lisa Blackmon-Phillips, West Ga.	1988-89	51	219	*4.29
Terri Haynes, Mo. Southern St.	1990-91	54	180	3.33
Jackie Dolberry, Hampton	1988-89	62	204	3.29
Betsy Bergdoll, Rio Grande/Queens (N.C.)	1989, 91-93	108	*343	3.18
Lisa Kurtenbach, South Dak. St.	1988-89	58	179	3.09
Michelle Butler, Livingston	1989-90	54	157	2.91
Mary Nesbit, Keene St.	1988-91	118	340	2.88
Bell Powell, Fort Valley St.	1990-91	57	153	2.68
Kelli Ritzer, Minn.-Duluth	1988-91	128	325	2.54
Val Sewald, Regis (Colo.)	1988-90	79	191	2.42
Nancy Somers, Ozarks (Mo.)/Mo. Southern St.	1990-91, 92-93	120	288	2.40
Tricia Lukawski, Chadron St.	1990-93	100	238	2.38
Julie Krauth, Augustana (S.D.)	1990-93	100	230	2.30
Jackie Givens, Fort Valley St.	1988-91	107	245	2.29
Monica Steinhoff, Mo.-St. Louis	1989-92	108	247	2.29

** Record.*

CAREER THREE-POINT FIELD-GOAL PERCENTAGE

(Minimum 150 three-point field goals made)

Player, Team	Seasons	G	3FG	3FGA	Pct.
Greta Fadness, Alas. Anchorage	1988-91	105	164	353	*46.5
Trish Van Diggelen, Missouri-Rolla	1989-92	108	219	499	43.9
$Angie Dobbs, Navy	1989-92	100	219	502	43.6
Tricia Floyd, Nebraska-Omaha	1989-92	108	155	357	43.4
Betsy Bergdoll, Rio Grande/Queens (N.C.)	1989, 91-93	108	*343	809	42.4
Terri Haynes, Mo. Southern St.	1990-91	54	180	427	42.2
Julie Dale, Southern Conn. St.	1988-90	81	150	356	42.1
Lisa Kurtenbach, South Dak. St.	1988-89	58	179	427	41.9
Teena Merrell, IU/PU-Ft. Wayne	1988-90	80	151	363	41.6
Nancy Somers, Ozarks (Mo.)/Mo. Southern St.	1990-91, 92-93	120	288	706	40.8
Anita Vigil, Abilene Christian	1988-92	105	175	435	40.2

** Record. $ Played three seasons in Division II (Division I in 1992).*

CAREER FREE-THROW PERCENTAGE

(Minimum 250 free throws made)

Player, Team	Seasons	G	FT	FTA	Pct.
Kerri Lang, St. Anselm	1988-91	116	369	421	*87.6
Anita Cooper, Hampton	1983-86	118	271	313	86.6
Sarah Howard, St. Cloud St.	1985-88	113	382	447	85.5
Mary Fisher, Michigan Tech	1984-87	95	250	293	85.3
Amy Kessler, Pitt.-Johnstown	1989-92	111	291	344	84.6
Bridgett Moore, Valdosta St.	1984-87	113	264	316	83.5
Paulette King, Florida Tech	1992-93	59	402	482	83.4
Amy Wilhelm, Morningside	1984-87	114	356	427	83.4
Julie Eisenschenk, St. Cloud St.	1986-89	109	277	333	83.2
Melissa Jones, Bridgeport/Sacred Heart	1990-92, 93	105	387	466	83.0
Sherry Vallejos, Southern Colo.	1989-92	94	454	547	83.0
Petrece Faulkner, Fort Hays St.	1990-93	122	295	360	81.9
Pat Smykowski, North Dak. St.	1986-89	124	348	426	81.7
Robin Graul, Alas. Anchorage	1986-89	111	598	736	81.3
Dani Fronabarger, Pittsburg St.	1990-93	111	537	661	81.2
Anita Vigil, Abilene Christian	1988-92	106	355	439	80.9
Brenda Shaffer-Dahl, Washburn	1987-90	126	381	472	80.7
Julie Dabrowski, New Hamp. Col.	1987-90	111	360	446	80.7
Jill Halapin, Pitt.-Johnstown	1985-88	111	290	360	80.6
Deonna Moore, Abilene Christian	1983-86	112	268	333	80.5

Player, Team	Seasons	G	FT	FTA	Pct.
Lisa Miller, IU/PU-Ft. Wayne	1989-92	111	*741	922	80.4
Diane Hoch, Mo. Southern St.	1989-92	94	298	371	80.3
Peggy Taylor, Howard Payne	1981-84	56	280	349	80.2
Cathy Fox, Tampa	1984-87	101	349	436	80.0
Corinne Deters, Regis (Colo.)	1990-93	111	379	474	80.0

* *Record.*

CAREER REBOUNDS

Player, Team	Seasons	G	Reb.
Francine Perry, Quinnipiac	1982-85	103	1,626
Stacey Gillespie, Mercy	1983-86	117	1,617
Tracy Linton, Jacksonville St.	1990-93	116	1,530
Joy Jeter, New Haven	1986-89	122	1,486
Kimberly Oates, Fort Valley St.	1986-89	110	1,448
Kay Goodwin, Texas A&M-Kingsville	1981-84	108	1,441
Mabel Sanders, Savannah St.	1989-92	106	1,405
Shelia Lindsey, Franklin Pierce	1985-88	121	1,404

* *Record.*

CAREER REBOUND AVERAGE

(Minimum 900 rebounds)

Player, Team	Seasons	G	Reb.	Avg.
Norma Knight, Norfolk St.	1982-83	51	937	*18.4
Francine Perry, Quinnipiac	1982-85	103	*1,626	15.8
Stacey Gillespie, Mercy	1983-86	117	1,617	13.8
Kim Ambrose, Shaw	1982-85	89	1,191	13.4
Kay Goodwin, Texas A&M-Kingsville	1981-84	108	1,441	13.3
Mabel Sanders, Savannah St.	1989-92	106	1,405	13.3
Tracy Linton, Jacksonville St.	1990-93	116	1,530	13.2
Kimberly Oates, Fort Valley St.	1986-89	110	1,448	13.2
Deb Schneider, Mansfield	1983-86	99	1,207	12.2
Joy Jeter, New Haven	1986-89	122	1,486	12.2
Vincene Morris, Phila. Textile	1983-86	110	1,335	12.1
Shelia Seward, Fayetteville St.	1987-90	100	1,211	12.1
Mary Kay Lynch, Gannon	1982-85	99	1,194	12.1

* *Record.*

CAREER ASSISTS

Player, Team	Seasons	G	Ast.
Selina Bynum, Albany St. (Ga.)	1990-93	107	*927
Missy Wolfe, Bentley	1989-92	115	709
Jennifer Radosevic, St. Joseph's (Ind.)	1989-91	88	692
Tammy Wood, Calif. (Pa.)	1989-92	105	656
Jennifer Edgar, Troy St.	1990-93	107	644
Paula Kline, St. Joseph's (Ind.)	1989-92	117	629
Tara Reardon, Queens (N.Y.)	1989-90, 93	73	617
Josephine Longoria, West Tex. A&M	1989-92	122	606
Paula Light, Millersville	1990-93	98	597
#Jody Hill, Pace	1991-93	93	586
Mindy Young, Pitt.-Johnstown	1989-92	111	577
Kathy Warner, Rollins	1989-91	116	576
Roseann Rutledge, Saginaw Valley	1990-93	107	570
Jody Buck, North Dak. St.	1990-93	128	560
Jan Bolton, Seattle Pacific	1989-92	107	552
Diana Odoardi, New Hamp. Col.	1990-93	117	546
Nadine Schmidt, North Dak. St.	1990-93	126	546
#Lisa Rice, Norfolk St.	1992-93	63	542
Shorlone Crockam, Delta St.	1990-93	127	541
Sherry Mitchell, Southeast Mo. St.	1989-91	94	530
Holly Sallden, South Dak. St.	1990-93	111	521
#Shani Baraka, Johnson Smith	1991-93	86	519
Candee Zepka, Florida Tech	1990-93	113	511
Toni Wimer, Gannon	1990-93	100	509
Jodi Pipes, South Dak.	1989-92	112	507

 # Active player. * *Record.*

CAREER ASSIST AVERAGE

(Minimum 500 assists)

Player, Team	Seasons	G	Ast.	Avg.
Selina Bynum, Albany St. (Ga.)	1990-93	107	*927	*8.7
Tara Reardon, Queens (N.Y.)	1989-90, 93	73	617	8.5
Jennifer Radosevic, St. Joseph's (Ind.)	1989-91	88	692	7.9
Tammy Wood, Calif. (Pa.)	1989-92	105	656	6.2
Lisa Houska, Mo.-St. Louis	1989-91	81	502	6.2
Missy Wolfe, Bentley	1989-92	115	709	6.2
Paula Light, Millersville	1990-93	98	597	6.1
Jennifer Edgar, Troy St.	1990-93	107	644	6.0
Becky Pigga, Bloomsburg	1989-91	87	503	5.8
Sherry Mitchell, Southeast Mo. St.	1989-91	94	530	5.6
Paula Kline, St. Joseph's (Ind.)	1989-92	117	629	5.4
Roseann Rutledge, Saginaw Valley	1990-93	107	570	5.3
Mindy Young, Pitt.-Johnstown	1989-92	111	577	5.2
Jan Bolton, Seattle Pacific	1989-92	107	552	5.2
Toni Wimer, Gannon	1990-93	100	509	5.1
Josephine Longoria, West Tex. A&M	1989-92	122	606	5.0
Kathy Warner, Rollins	1989-92	116	576	5.0

* *Record.*

DIVISION II WOMEN'S ANNUAL INDIVIDUAL CHAMPIONS

SCORING AVERAGE

Year	Player, Team	G	FG	3FG	FT	Pts.	Avg.
1982	Donna Hammond, UC Riverside	26	290	—	145	725	27.9
1983	Stacey Cunningham, Shippensburg	22	266	—	126	658	29.9
1984	Claudia Schleyer, Abilene Christian	26	250	—	153	653	25.1
1985	Yvonnie Owens, Clark Atlanta	31	287	—	219	793	25.6
1986	Claudia Schleyer, Abilene Christian	28	293	—	184	770	27.5
1987	Theresa Lorenzi, Bloomsburg	25	282	—	84	648	25.9
1988	Mary Naughton, Stonehill	31	291	1	216	799	25.8
1989	Shannon Williams, Valdosta St.	26	251	0	196	698	26.8
1990	Kim Brewington, Johnson Smith	28	312	62	222	908	32.4
1991	Jackie Givens, Fort Valley St.	28	369	120	217	*1,075	*38.4
1992	Paulette King, Florida Tech	29	322	2	209	855	29.5
1993	Yolanda Griffith, Fla. Atlantic	22	262	0	97	621	28.2

* *Record.*

FIELD-GOAL PERCENTAGE

Year	Player, Team	G	FG	FGA	Pct.
1982	Diane Velky, Quinnipiac	28	146	220	66.4
1983	Jackie Andrews, Morris Brown	22	134	200	67.0
1984	Janice Washington, Valdosta St.	33	308	489	63.0
1985	Sharon Lyke, Utica	26	222	345	64.3
1986	Candace Fincher, Valdosta St.	27	185	277	66.8
1987	Tracy Payne, St. Joseph's (Ind.)	28	183	282	64.9
1988	Tracy Payne, St. Joseph's (Ind.)	31	242	368	65.8
1989	Tracy Payne, St. Joseph's (Ind.)	31	221	333	66.4
1990	Bridget Lindquist, Augustana (S.D.)	28	149	230	64.8
1991	Darla Leavitt, West Tex. A&M	27	145	215	67.4
1992	Corinne Vanderwal, Calif. (Pa.)	26	156	228	68.4
1993	Missy Taylor, Oakland City	29	267	385	69.4

THREE-POINT FIELD GOALS MADE PER GAME

Year	Player, Team	G	3FG	Avg.
1988	Lisa Blackmon-Phillips, West Ga.	22	81	3.7
1989	Lisa Blackmon-Phillips, West Ga.	29	*138	*4.8
1990	Michelle Butler, Livingston	27	88	3.3
1991	Jackie Givens, Fort Valley St.	28	120	4.3
1992	Betsy Bergdoll, Queens (N.C.)	28	103	3.7
1993	Carolyn Brown, St. Augustine's	24	90	3.8

* *Record.*

THREE-POINT FIELD-GOAL PERCENTAGE

Year	Player, Team	G	3FG	3FGA	Pct.
1988	Jackie Farnan, New York Tech	26	58	114	50.9
1989	Tricia Van Diggelen, Missouri-Rolla	25	43	81	53.1
1990	Durene Heisler, North Dak.	31	63	112	*56.3
1991	Greta Fadness, Alas. Anchorage	25	63	127	49.6
1992	Darlene Hildebrand, Phila. Textile	32	48	95	50.5
1993	Kelly Tomlin, Livingston	26	56	110	50.9

* *Record.*

FREE-THROW PERCENTAGE

Year	Player, Team	G	FT	FTA	Pct.
1982	Kelly Legler, Southern Ore.	21	53	59	89.8
1983	Cindy Pavell, New Haven	27	76	87	87.4
1984	Margie Speaks, Ky. Wesleyan	23	58	65	89.2
1985	Lisa McGee, West Ga.	26	81	91	89.0
1986	Kim Scamman, Northwest Mo. St.	27	96	109	88.1
1987	Teena Merrell, IU/PU-Ft. Wayne	26	69	76	90.8
1988	Sarah Howard, St. Cloud St.	28	111	123	90.2
1989	Dixie Horn, SIU-Edwardsville	27	89	100	89.0
1990	Denise Nehme, Northern Colo.	28	88	98	89.8
1991	Kerri Lang, St. Anselm	31	92	102	90.2
1992	Kelly Jewett, Franklin Pierce	31	112	121	*92.6
1993	Renae Aschoff, Portland St.	29	75	85	88.2

* *Record.*

REBOUND AVERAGE

Year	Player, Team	G	Reb.	Avg.
1982	Francine Perry, Quinnipiac	28	*635	*22.7
1983	Chanel Hamilton, Dist. Columbia	19	399	21.0
1984	Kim Ambrose, Shaw	23	383	16.7
1985	Yvonnie Owens, Clark Atlanta	31	502	16.2
1986	Von Fulmore, N.C. Central	26	464	17.8
1987	Jackie Anderson, Livingstone	22	331	15.0
1988	Jackie Anderson, Livingstone	23	325	14.1
1989	Kimberly Oates, Fort Valley St.	28	424	15.1
1990	Stephanie Palmer, Norfolk St.	25	370	14.8
1991	Mabel Sanders, Savannah St.	28	407	14.5
1992	Mabel Sanders, Savannah St.	29	426	14.7
1993	Vanessa White, Tuskegee	25	433	17.3

* *Record.*

ASSIST AVERAGE

Year	Player, Team	G	Ast.	Avg.
1989	Denise Holm, Minn.-Duluth	32	291	9.1
1990	Jennifer Radosevic, St. Joseph's (Ind.)	30	281	9.4
1991	Selina Bynum, Albany St. (Ga.)	26	274	10.5
1992	Selina Bynum, Albany St. (Ga.)	26	*309	*11.9
1993	Selina Bynum, Albany St. (Ga.)	26	280	10.8

* *Record.*

BLOCKED-SHOT AVERAGE

Year	Player, Team	G	Blk.	Avg.
1993	Rebecca Hanson, Pace	30	142	4.7

STEAL AVERAGE

Year	Player, Team	G	Stl.	Avg.
1993	Valerie Curtis, Dist. Columbia	22	135	6.1

DIVISION II WOMEN'S ANNUAL TEAM CHAMPIONS

WON-LOST PERCENTAGE

Year	Team	Won	Lost	Pct.
1982	Springfield	23	3	.885
1983	Virginia Union	27	2	.931
1984	Saginaw Valley	30	1	.968
1985	Saginaw Valley	32	1	.970
1986	Florida Int'l	26	2	.929
1987	Albany St. (Ga.)	28	1	.966
1988	Hampton	33	1	*.971
	West Tex. A&M	33	1	*.971
1989	Bloomsburg	28	2	.933
1990	Delta St.	32	1	.970
1991	Fort Hays St.	*34	2	.944
1992	Bentley	31	2	.939
1993	Washburn	31	1	.969

* *Record.*

SCORING OFFENSE

Year	Team	G	(W-L)	Pts.	Avg.
1982	Charleston (W.Va.)	34	(27-7)	2,767	81.4
1983	Valdosta St.	31	(27-4)	2,610	84.2
1984	Dayton	31	(27-4)	2,597	83.8
1985	Hampton	34	(30-4)	3,021	88.9
1986	Delta St.	31	(28-3)	2,765	89.2
1987	Morningside	30	(20-10)	2,626	87.5
1988	Hampton	34	(33-1)	*3,357	*98.7
1989	St. Augustine's	27	(18-9)	2,297	85.1
1990	St. Joseph's (Ind.)	30	(28-2)	2,745	91.5
1991	Jacksonville St.	30	(26-4)	2,780	92.7
1992	Clarion	29	(25-4)	2,730	94.1
1993	Augustana (S.D.)	29	(24-5)	2,612	90.1

* *Record.*

SCORING DEFENSE

Year	Team	G	(W-L)	Pts.	Avg.
1982	St. John Fisher	24	(20-4)	1,262	52.6
1983	IU/PU-Ft. Wayne	21	(17-4)	1,135	54.0
1984	Saginaw Valley	31	(30-1)	1,720	55.5
1985	Chapman	29	(25-4)	1,496	51.6
1986	St. John Fisher	24	(21-3)	1,072	*44.7
1987	Fla. Atlantic	26	(21-5)	1,226	47.2
1988	West Tex. A&M	34	(33-1)	1,818	53.5
1989	UC Davis	26	(20-6)	1,399	53.8
1990	Army	29	(19-10)	1,431	49.3
1991	West Tex. A&M	32	(30-2)	1,589	49.7
1992	Oakland City	25	(17-8)	1,337	53.5
1993	Minn.-Duluth	30	(22-8)	1,701	56.7

* *Record.*

SCORING MARGIN

Year	Team	Off.	Def.	Margin
1982	Pitt.-Johnstown	76.7	56.0	20.7
1983	Florida Int'l	83.6	60.2	23.4
1984	Saginaw Valley	83.6	55.5	28.1
1985	Saginaw Valley	83.4	56.2	27.3
1986	Florida Int'l	80.8	53.5	27.3
1987	Delta St.	83.0	58.5	24.5
1988	Hampton	*98.7	65.1	33.6
1989	Central Mo. St.	81.1	59.9	21.2
1990	Delta St.	85.6	59.6	26.0
1991	West Tex. A&M	86.3	49.7	*36.7
1992	Norfolk St.	90.3	66.2	24.1
1993	North Dak. St.	89.3	58.5	30.8

* *Record.*

FIELD-GOAL PERCENTAGE

Year	Team	FG	FGA	Pct.
1982	Cal Poly Pomona	1,194	2,382	50.1
1983	Cal Poly Pomona	1,088	2,100	51.8
1984	Pembroke St.	981	1,925	51.0
1985	Mercer	1,129	2,305	49.0
1986	Valdosta St.	853	1,659	51.4
1987	Delta St.	1,068	2,072	51.5
1988	West Tex. A&M	1,138	2,173	*52.4
1989	St. Joseph's (Ind.)	1,030	2,022	50.9
1990	St. Joseph's (Ind.)	1,058	2,052	51.6
1991	West Tex. A&M	1,095	2,148	51.0
1992	Portland St.	1,119	2,224	50.3
1993	Oakland City	929	1,806	51.4

* *Record.*

FIELD-GOAL PERCENTAGE DEFENSE

Year	Team	FG	FGA	Pct.
1982	St. John Fisher	516	1,526	33.8
1983	Dist. Columbia	575	1,708	33.7
1984	Virginia Union	593	1,683	35.2
1985	New Haven	668	2,004	33.3
1986	Concordia (N.Y.)	470	1,313	35.8
1987	Virginia St.	669	1,858	36.0
1988	Fort Valley St.	621	1,773	35.0
1989	Calif. (Pa.)	675	1,878	35.9
1990	Virginia St.	674	1,977	34.1
1991	Albany St. (Ga.)	581	1,797	*32.3
1992	Oakland City	515	1,555	33.1
1993	Pace	659	1,962	33.6

* *Record.*

THREE-POINT FIELD GOALS MADE PER GAME

Year	Team	G	3FG	Avg.
1988	Keene St.	29	239	8.2
1989	Keene St.	31	204	6.6
1990	Fort Valley St.	29	184	6.3
1991	Clarion	32	317	9.9
1992	Clarion	29	*386	*13.3
1993	Clarion	30	337	11.2

* *Record.*

THREE-POINT FIELD-GOAL PERCENTAGE

Year	Team	G	3FG	3FGA	Pct.
1988	New York Tech	26	111	227	¢48.9
1989	Augustana (S.D.)	28	72	156	46.2
1990	North Dak.	31	73	135	*54.1
1991	Alas. Anchorage	28	83	197	42.1
1992	Indianapolis	28	77	182	42.3
1993	Phila. Textile	29	114	266	42.9

* *Record.* ¢ *Record for minimum 100 made.*

FREE-THROW PERCENTAGE

Year	Team	FT	FTA	Pct.
1982	Cal Poly Pomona	451	580	77.8
1983	Minn.-Duluth	441	601	73.4
1984	Ky. Wesleyan	378	498	75.9
1985	Niagara	323	432	74.8
1986	New Hamp. Col.	466	611	76.3
1987	IU/PU-Ft. Wayne	396	525	75.4
1988	Mo.-St. Louis	361	483	74.7
1989	IU/PU-Ft. Wayne	463	605	76.5
1990	Lake Superior St.	448	598	74.9
1991	Augustana (S.D.)	418	557	75.0
1992	Pitt.-Johnstown	491	633	77.6
1993	Augustana (S.D.)	567	722	*78.5

* *Record.*

REBOUND MARGIN

Year	Team	Off.	Def.	Margin
1982	Quinnipiac	*67.0	37.1	*29.9
1983	Norfolk St.	62.9	46.1	16.8
1984	Quinnipiac	51.5	41.0	10.5
1985	Alabama A&M	65.6	48.6	17.0
1986	Alabama A&M	62.0	45.6	16.4
1987	Alabama A&M	57.0	39.3	17.7
1988	Pace	51.9	36.0	15.9
1989	Fort Valley St.	54.6	41.7	12.9
1990	Elizabeth City St.	58.5	40.6	17.9
1991	Fla. Atlantic	51.9	38.3	13.7
1992	West Ga.	46.2	31.4	14.8
1993	Oakland City	49.8	33.0	16.8

* *Record.*

DIVISION II WOMEN'S ALL-TIME WINNINGEST TEAMS

Includes records as a senior college only; minimum 10 seasons of competition. Postseason games are included.

PERCENTAGE

Team	Yrs.	Won	Lost	Pct.
Pitt.-Johnstown	18	404	70	.852
Cal Poly Pomona	19	498	113	.815
Bentley	19	414	107	.795
Delta St.	26	548	141	*.794
West Tex. A&M	13	300	83	.783
Central Mo. St.	23	478	150	.761
Saginaw Valley	18	421	135	.757
Stonehill	21	406	142	.741
Carson-Newman	15	348	122	.740
Francis Marion	20	441	164	.729
Norfolk St.	19	374	140	.728
Lincoln Memorial	18	365	152	.706
Northern Ky.	19	382	163	.701
Oakland	19	344	161	.681
Bellarmine	22	364	173	.678
Pace	15	292	143	.671
Air Force	17	287	144	.666
St. Anselm	17	273	139	.663
Northwest Mo. St.	22	374	198	.654
Phila. Textile	19	289	153	.654
Pembroke St.	19	320	170	.653
Valdosta St.	19	346	185	.652
Fla. Southern	16	252	136	.649
North Dak. St.	27	407	224	.645
Bloomsburg	23	276	158	.636

* *Includes three ties.*

VICTORIES

Team	Yrs.	Wins
East Stroudsburg	67	555
Delta St.	26	548
Cal Poly Pomona	19	498
Central Mo. St.	23	478
Francis Marion	20	441
Saginaw Valley	18	421
Bentley	19	414
North Dak. St.	27	407
Southern Conn. St.	31	407
Stonehill	21	406
Pitt.-Johnstown	18	404
West Ga.	33	385
Northern Ky.	19	382
Norfolk St.	19	374
Northwest Mo. St.	22	374
Grand Valley St.	24	365
Lincoln Memorial	18	365
Bellarmine	22	364
Fort Hays St.	24	363
Abilene Christian	22	362
Mankato St.	26	354
Millersville	48	349
Carson-Newman	15	348
Valdosta St.	19	346
Washburn	24	345

DIVISION III
WOMEN'S RECORDS

St. Benedict's Tina Kampa (41) set a record for season field-goal percentage. Kampa shot 68.4 percent in 1992-93 and led the Blazers to a 28-2 record.

DIVISION III WOMEN'S INDIVIDUAL RECORDS

Official NCAA women's basketball records began with the 1982 season and are based on information submitted to the NCAA statistics service by institutions participating in the weekly statistics rankings. Official career records include players who played at least two seasons in Division III during the era of official NCAA statistics, which began with the 1981-82 season. Three-point field goals were added in 1987-88, assists were added in 1988-89 and blocked shots and steals were added in 1992-93. In statistical rankings, the rounding of percentages and/or averages may indicate ties where none exist. In these cases, the numerical order of the rankings is accurate.

SCORING

Points

Game
61—Ann Gilbert, Oberlin vs. Allegheny, Feb. 6, 1991 (28 FGs, 2 3FGs, 3FTs)

Season
891—Jeannie Demers, Buena Vista, 1987 (385 FGs, 121 FTs, 26 games)

Career
3,171—Jeannie Demers, Buena Vista, 1984-87 (1,386 FGs, 399 FTs, 105 games)

Average Per Game

Season
34.3—Jeannie Demers, Buena Vista, 1987 (891 in 26)

Career
(Min. 1,200 points) 30.2—Jeannie Demers, Buena Vista, 1984-87 (3,171 in 105)

Consecutive Games Scoring in Double Figures

Career
113—Laurie Trow, St. Thomas (Minn.), from Nov. 17, 1989, to March 5, 1993

FIELD GOALS

Field Goals

Game
28—Ann Gilbert, Oberlin vs. Allegheny, Feb. 6, 1991 (55 attempts)

Season
385—Jeannie Demers, Buena Vista, 1987 (816 attempts)

Career
1,386—Jeannie Demers, Buena Vista, 1984-87 (2,838 attempts)

Consecutive Field Goals

Game
13—Susan Brogna, Regis (Mass.) vs. Colby-Sawyer, Jan. 28, 1988; Anne Krumrine, Frank. & Marsh. vs. Gettysburg, Jan. 17, 1989; Mary Lou Kimball, St. Joseph's (Me.) vs. St. Joseph's (Vt.), Feb. 17, 1989

Season
16—Mary Lou Kimball, St. Joseph's (Me.), Feb. 15-17, 1989

Field-Goal Attempts

Game
55—Ann Gilbert, Oberlin vs. Allegheny, Feb. 6, 1991 (28 made)

Season
816—Jeannie Demers, Buena Vista, 1987 (385 made)

Career
2,838—Jeannie Demers, Buena Vista, 1984-87 (1,386 made)

Field-Goal Percentage

Game
(Min. 20 made) 81.3%—Terry Cole, Rutgers-Camden vs. Ramapo, Feb. 26, 1983 (26 of 32)

Season
68.4%—Tina Kampa, St. Benedict, 1993 (158 of 231)

Career
(Min. 400 made) 63.4%—Linda Rose, Nichols, 1989-91, (629 of 992)

THREE-POINT FIELD GOALS

Three-Point Field Goals

Game
15—Michelle Jones, Wm. Paterson vs. Jersey City St., Jan. 9, 1991 (33 attempts)

Season
100—Brenda Straight, Neb. Wesleyan, 1991 (247 attempts)

Career
286—Michelle Jones, Wm. Paterson, 1988-91 (685 attempts)

Three-Point Field Goals Made Per Game

Season
3.9—Kate Peterson, Wis.-Stevens Point, 1991 (77 in 20)

Career
(Min. 125 made) 3.65—Vicki Fuess, Utica Tech, 1992-93 (179 in 49)

Consecutive Three-Point Field Goals

Game
9—Stacie Robey, Wis.-River Falls vs. Wis.-La Crosse, Feb. 18, 1989

Season
13—Jane Ruliffson, Macalester, from Dec. 31, 1990, to Jan. 2, 1991

Consecutive Games Making a Three-Point Goal

Season
22—Brenda Straight, Neb. Wesleyan, from Nov. 17, 1990, to Feb. 9, 1991

Career
29—Brenda Straight, Neb. Wesleyan, from Jan. 31, 1990, to Feb. 9, 1991

Three-Point Field-Goal Attempts

Game
33—Michelle Jones, Wm. Paterson vs. Jersey

City St., Jan. 9, 1991 (15 made)
Season
257—Vicki Fuess, Utica Tech, 1993 (95 made)
Career
748—Jill Brower, William Smith, 1990-93 (251 made)

Three-Point Field-Goal Percentage

Game
(Best perfect game) 100.0%—Melissa Young, Gust. Adolphus vs. Macalester, Jan. 25, 1992 (8 of 8)
Season
(Min. 50 made) 60.0%—Ellen Thompson, Rhodes, 1989 (54 of 90)
(Min. 75 made) 43.4%—Michelle Jones, Wm. Paterson, 1990 (75 of 173)
Career
(Min. 125 made) 49.0%—Ellen Thompson, Rhodes, 1989-92 (204 of 416)

FREE THROWS

Free Throws

Game
23—Mary Engel, New England Col. vs. Rivier, Feb. 19, 1986 (27 attempts); Eileen Spear, Mt. St. Vincent vs. Dowling, Dec. 15, 1987 (27 attempts)
Season
238—Simone Edwards, FDU-Madison, 1991 (315 attempts)
Career
789—Simone Edwards, FDU-Madison, 1990-93 (1,078 attempts)

Consecutive Free Throws

Game
20—Sharon Rines, St. Joseph's (Me.) vs. Emmanuel, Jan. 26, 1993
Season
61—Valerie Kepner, Baldwin-Wallace, from Nov. 18, 1988, to Feb. 18, 1989
Career
69—Valerie Kepner, Lake Erie/Baldwin-Wallace, from Feb. 15, 1987, to Feb. 18, 1989

Free-Throw Attempts

Game
27—Mary Engel, New England Col. vs. Rivier, Feb. 19, 1986 (23 made); Eileen Spear, Mt. St. Vincent vs. Dowling, Dec. 15, 1987 (23 made); Mary Ellen Kennedy, Curry vs. Mass.-Boston, Feb. 10, 1992 (16 made); Molly Lackman, Immaculata vs. Ursinus, Feb. 11, 1993 (19 made)
Season
315—Simone Edwards, FDU-Madison, 1991 (238 made)
Career
1,078—Simone Edwards, FDU-Madison, 1990-93 (789 made)

Free-Throw Percentage

Game
(Best perfect game) 100.0%—Annette Hoffman, Juniata vs. Waynesburg, Jan. 25, 1993 (19 of 19)
Season
95.5%—Valerie Kepner, Baldwin-Wallace, 1989 (63 of 66)
Career
(Min. 250 made) 83.0%—Tammy Anair, Southern Me., 1984-87 (279 of 336)

REBOUNDS

Rebounds

Game
35—Terry Cole, Rutgers-Camden vs. Rowan, Jan. 13, 1983; Malane Perry, Fitchburg St. vs. Worcester St., Feb. 8, 1992
Season
579—Carla Gadsden, Jersey City St., 1982 (27 games)
Career
1,452—Tina Shaw, Bishop, 1981-84 (88 games)

Average Per Game

Season
22.0—Terry Lockwood, St. Elizabeth, 1989 (461 in 21)
Career
(Min. 1,000) 18.4—Terry Lockwood, St. Elizabeth, 1986-89 (1,343 in 73)

ASSISTS

Assists

Game
21—Tricia Andres, Mills vs. Dominican (Cal.), Nov. 21, 1991
Season
303—Tonja Sanders, Rust, 1990 (26 games)
Career
729—Karen Barefoot, Chris. Newport, 1991-93 (83 games)

Average Per Game

Season
11.7—Tonja Sanders, Rust, 1990 (303 in 26)
Career
(Min. 450) 9.8—Tonja Sanders, Rust, 1989-92 (669 in 68)

BLOCKED SHOTS

Blocked Shots

Game
12—Liza Janssen, Wellesley vs. Worcester St., Nov. 24, 1992; Liza Janssen, Wellesley vs. Wesleyan (Conn.), Dec. 10, 1992
Season
145—Liza Janssen, Wellesley, 1993 (27 games)

Average Per Game

Season
5.4—Liza Janssen, Wellesley, 1993 (145 in 27)

STEALS

Steals

Game
14—Angel Esposito, Elms vs. Regis (Mass.), Dec. 5, 1992

Season
149—Alicia LaValley, Plattsburgh St., 1993 (24 games)

Average Per Game

Season
6.2—Alicia LaValley, Plattsburgh St., 1993 (149 in 24)

DIVISION III WOMEN'S TEAM RECORDS

Note: Where records include both teams, each team must be an NCAA Division III member institution.

SINGLE-GAME SCORING

Most Points
140—Plymouth St. vs. Hawthorne (41), Feb. 14, 1983; Bishop vs. Concordia (Tex.) (75), Feb. 21, 1986

Most Points by Losing Team
107—Albany (N.Y.) vs. New York U. (114) (2 ot), Feb. 2, 1988; Carthage vs. North Central (113) (2 ot), Feb. 25, 1992

Most Points, Both Teams
221—New York U. (114) vs. Albany (N.Y.) (107) (2 ot), Feb. 2, 1988

Most Points in a Half
71—Chris. Newport (120) vs. Averett (23), Jan. 19, 1991

Fewest Points Allowed
10—LeMoyne-Owen (44) vs. Philander Smith, Dec. 6, 1985; Middlebury (102) vs. Trinity (Vt.), Nov. 30, 1988; Hunter (79) vs. John Jay, Jan. 23, 1991

Fewest Points Allowed in a Half
0—New York U. (73) vs. CCNY (18), Dec. 13, 1991 (New York U. outscored CCNY 40-0 in second half)

Fewest Points, Both Teams
48—Beloit (28) vs. Cornell College (20), Jan. 19, 1985

Widest Margin of Victory
114—Kean (134) vs. Rutgers-Newark (20), Nov. 30, 1983

SINGLE-GAME FIELD GOALS

Most Field Goals
65—Plymouth St. vs. Hawthorne, Feb. 14, 1983 (100 attempts)

Most Field-Goal Attempts
125—Colby-Sawyer vs. Hawthorne, Nov. 19, 1983 (55 made)

Highest Field-Goal Percentage
77.4%—Millsaps vs. Judson, Feb. 11, 1986 (41 of 53)

Highest Field-Goal Percentage, Half
(Min. 20 made) 80.0%—St. John Fisher vs. Buffalo St., Jan. 11, 1988 (20 of 25); Cal St. Stanislaus vs. Bethel (Minn.), Dec. 2, 1988 (24 of 30)

SINGLE-GAME THREE-POINT FIELD GOALS

Most Three-Point Field Goals
15—Wm. Paterson vs. Jersey City St., Jan. 9, 1991 (33 attempts)

Most Three-Point Field Goals, Both Teams
18—Rockford (10) vs. Aurora (8), Feb. 8, 1992; Calvin (12) vs. Olivet (6), Jan. 20, 1993

Consecutive Three-Point Field Goals Made
10—Cal St. Stanislaus vs. Point Loma, Dec. 10, 1988

Most Three-Point Field-Goal Attempts
47—Neb. Wesleyan vs. Concordia (Neb.), Feb. 19, 1991 (12 made)

Most Three-Point Field-Goal Attempts, Both Teams
47—Neb. Wesleyan (47) vs. Concordia (Neb.), Feb. 19, 1991*

Highest Three-Point Field-Goal Percentage
(Best perfect game) 100.0%—Utica Tech vs. Skidmore, Feb. 5, 1992 (8 of 8)

Highest Three-Point Field-Goal Percentage, Both Teams
(Min. 10 made) 82.4%—Pine Manor (14 of 17) vs. Framingham St. (0 of 0), Feb. 6, 1988 (14 of 17)

** Note: Concordia (Neb.), a non-NCAA member institution, attempted eight three-point field goals that are not credited as part of the NCAA Division III record for both teams.*

SINGLE-GAME FREE THROWS

Most Free Throws
46—Elizabethtown vs. Moravian, Jan. 14, 1993 (51 attempts)

Most Free Throws, Both Teams
64—Elizabethtown (46) vs. Moravian (18), Jan. 14, 1993

Most Free-Throw Attempts
63—Hartwick vs. Alfred, Jan. 30, 1993 (43 made)

Most Free-Throw Attempts, Both Teams
84—Delaware Valley (51) vs. Lycoming (33), Feb. 9, 1991

Highest Free-Throw Percentage
(Min. 30 made) 96.9%—St. Mary's (Ind.) vs. Denver, Dec. 19, 1989 (31 of 32); Juniata vs. Waynesburg, Jan. 25, 1993 (31 of 32)

Highest Free-Throw Percentage, Both Teams
(Min. 40 made) 93.5%—Juniata (31 of 32) vs.

Waynesburg (12 of 14), Jan. 25, 1993 (43 of 46)
(Min. 60 made) 86.5%—Elizabethtown (46 of 51) vs. Moravian (18 of 23), Jan. 14, 1993 (64 of 74)

SINGLE-GAME REBOUNDS

Most Rebounds
96—Grove City vs. Villa Maria, Feb. 20, 1984; Lehman vs. St. Joseph's (N.Y.), Jan. 9, 1985

Highest Rebound Margin
52—Hunter (68) vs. York (Pa.) (16), Dec. 5, 1990

SINGLE-GAME PERSONAL FOULS

Most Personal Fouls
51—Knoxville vs. Fisk, Jan. 23, 1985

Most Personal Fouls, Both Teams
64—Westfield St. vs. Bri'water (Mass.), Feb. 8, 1992

SINGLE-GAME OVERTIMES

Most Overtime Periods
3—Ohio Northern vs. Marietta, Jan. 12, 1991; Berea vs. Albion, Dec. 5, 1992; Delaware Valley vs. FDU-Madison, Jan. 30, 1993

Most Points in One Overtime Period
21—Utica Tech vs. Brockport St., Feb. 19, 1993

Most Points in One Overtime Period, Both Teams
35—Anna Maria (18) vs. Regis (Mass.) (17), Jan. 24, 1991; Millikin (18) vs. Ill. Wesleyan (17), Feb. 19, 1991

Most Points in Overtime Periods
28—Marietta vs. Ohio Northern, Jan. 12, 1991 (3 ot)

Most Points in Overtime Periods, Both Teams
53—Marietta (28) vs. Ohio Northern (25), Jan. 12, 1991 (3 ot)

SEASON SCORING

Most Points
3,023—North Central, 1982 (38 games)

Highest Average Per Game
96.6—Bishop, 1985 (2,995 in 31)

Highest Average Scoring Margin
34.2—St. John Fisher, 1988 (80.3 offense, 46.1 defense)

Most Games at Least 100 Points
10—St. Joseph's (Me.), 1990

Most Consecutive Games at Least 100 Points
5—Marymount (Va.), Feb. 17-March 6, 1993

SEASON FIELD GOALS

Most Field Goals
1,287—Bishop, 1986 (2,900 attempts)

Most Field-Goal Attempts
2,900—Bishop, 1986 (1,287 made)

Highest Field-Goal Percentage
54.6%—Wilkes, 1984 (730 of 1,338)

SEASON THREE-POINT FIELD GOALS

Most Three-Point Field Goals
202—Neb. Wesleyan, 1991 (588 attempts)

Most Three-Point Field Goals Per Game
7.8—Neb. Wesleyan, 1991 (202 in 26)

Most Three-Point Field-Goal Attempts
588—Neb. Wesleyan, 1991 (202 made)

Most Three-Point Field-Goal Attempts Per Game
22.6—Neb. Wesleyan, 1991 (588 in 26)

Highest Three-Point Field-Goal Percentage
(Min. 50 made) 60.4%—Rhodes, 1989 (55 of 91)
(Min. 100 made) 45.9%—Cal St. Stanislaus, 1989 (111 of 242)

SEASON FREE THROWS

Most Free Throws
631—Moravian, 1992 (861 attempts)

Most Free-Throw Attempts
861—Moravian, 1992 (631 made)

Highest Free-Throw Percentage
78.3%—St. John Fisher, 1990 (483 of 617)

SEASON REBOUNDS

Most Rebounds
1,776—Bishop, 1986 (31 games)

Highest Average Per Game
60.2—Mills, 1992 (1,203 in 20)

Highest Average Rebound Margin
30.4—Norwich, 1984 (57.2 offense, 26.7 defense)

SEASON PERSONAL FOULS

Most Personal Fouls
710—Bishop, 1984 (28 games)

Fewest Personal Fouls
100—Webster, 1987 (6 games)

SEASON DEFENSE

Lowest Scoring Average Per Game Allowed
32.6—Mt. St. Mary (N.Y.), 1990 (620 in 19)

Lowest Field-Goal Percentage Allowed
28.5%—Mills, 1992 (367 of 1,288)

GENERAL RECORDS

Most Victories in a Season
31—Scranton, 1985; Scranton, 1987; St. John Fisher, 1988; St. John Fisher, 1990; Moravian, 1992

Most Consecutive Victories
40—St. Thomas (Minn.), from Jan. 30, 1991, to March 7, 1992

Most Consecutive Victories in a Season
31—St. John Fisher, from Nov. 20, 1987, to March 18, 1988

Most Consecutive Home-Court Victories
88—Rust, from Jan. 23, 1982, to Nov. 20, 1989

Most Consecutive 20-Win Seasons
12—Southern Me., 1982-93 (current)*

*Note: Also had 20 wins in 1981, one year before official NCAA women's basketball records began.

DIVISION III WOMEN'S ALL-TIME INDIVIDUAL LEADERS

SINGLE-GAME SCORING HIGHS

Pts.	Player, Team vs. Opponent	Season
61	Ann Gilbert, Oberlin vs. Allegheny	1991
55	Michelle Jones, Wm. Paterson vs. Jersey City St.	1991
53	Terry Cole, Rutgers-Camden vs. Ramapo	1983
51	Ann Gilbert, Oberlin vs. Case Reserve	1990
51	Ann Gilbert, Oberlin vs. Allegheny	1990
50	Laura Johnson, Shenandoah vs. Delaware Valley	1984
50	Valerie Brown, Stockton St. vs. Rutgers-Camden	1985
50	Crystal Coleman, Bishop vs. Texas College	1986
50	Crystal Coleman, Bishop vs. Concordia (Minn.)	1986
50	Jill Weisner, Principia vs. Blackburn	1989
50	Kristi Hardy, Me.-Farmington vs. Southeastern Fla.	1990
50	Missy Sharer, Grinnell vs. Cornell College	1991
50	Sylvia Newman, Meredith vs. Bennett	1991
49	Tammy Steele, Rowan vs. Rutgers-Newark	1984
49	Annette Hoffman, Juniata vs. Elizabethtown	1993

SEASON POINTS

Player, Team	Season	G	FG	3FG	FT	Pts.
Jeannie Demers, Buena Vista	†1987	26	*385	—	121	*891
Jeannie Demers, Buena Vista	†1985	28	375	—	108	858
Missy Sharer, Grinnell	†1991	24	272	33	217	794
Jody Lavin, Rochester	1982	31	323	—	133	779
Ann Gilbert, Oberlin	†1990	25	319	7	133	778
Jeannie Demers, Buena Vista	†1986	25	324	—	129	777
Jody Imbrie, Grove City	†1983	27	285	—	200	770
Susan Heidt, St. John Fisher	1990	33	269	0	228	766
Susan Heidt, St. John Fisher	1989	30	270	0	213	753
Ann Gilbert, Oberlin	1991	24	309	17	114	749
Crystal Coleman, Bishop	1986	29	319	—	104	742
Bonnie Hansen, North Central	1983	32	329	—	74	732
Karla Robinson, Rutgers-Camden	1992	29	285	6	136	712
Terri Schumacher, Wis.-Oshkosh	1985	26	330	—	50	710
Amy Simpson, Va. Wesleyan	1986	29	260	—	182	702
Laurie Trow, St. Thomas (Minn.)	1991	31	276	4	143	699
Fredia Gibbs, Cabrini	1986	24	286	—	121	693
Merry Beth Ryan, Kean	1988	29	277	56	79	689
Michelle Jones, Wm. Paterson	1991	228	216	83	174	689
Merry Beth Ryan, Kean	1989	28	277	58	75	687

* *Record.* † *National champion.*

SEASON SCORING AVERAGE

Player, Team	Season	G	FG	3FG	FT	Pts.	Avg.
Jeannie Demers, Buena Vista	†1987	26	*385	—	121	*891	*34.3
Catie Cleary, Pine Manor	†1988	20	228	43	175	674	33.7
Missy Sharer, Grinnell	†1991	24	272	33	217	794	33.1
Ann Gilbert, Oberlin	1991	24	309	17	114	749	31.2
Ann Gilbert, Oberlin	†1990	25	319	7	133	778	31.1
Jeannie Demers, Buena Vista	†1986	25	324	—	129	777	31.1
Sladja Kovijanic, Middlebury	†1993	21	235	80	98	648	30.9
Jeannie Demers, Buena Vista	†1985	28	375	—	108	858	30.6
Missy Hensley, East. Mennonite	†1992	23	251	0	183	685	29.8
Annette Hoffman, Juniata	1993	22	197	21	228	643	29.2

Player, Team	Season	G	FG	3FG	FT	Pts.	Avg.
Christel Brown, Upper Iowa	1986	20	214	—	151	579	29.0
Fredia Gibbs, Cabrini	1986	24	286	—	121	693	28.9
Jody Imbrie, Grove City	†1983	27	285	—	200	770	28.5
Sylvia Newman, Meredith	1992	21	220	0	158	598	28.5
Melissa Hensley, East. Mennonite	1991	23	235	0	184	654	28.4
Tricia Kosenina, Thiel	1992	24	222	50	173	667	27.8
Terri Schumacher, Wis.-Oshkosh	1985	26	330	—	50	710	27.3
Tricia Rasmussen, St. Mary's (Minn.)	1993	24	270	2	103	645	26.9
Lisa Halloran, Framingham St.	†1989	25	235	59	141	670	26.8
Hilary Williams, Baruch	1990	25	280	0	108	668	26.7
Laura Johnson, Shenandoah	†1984	16	176	—	75	427	26.7

* *Record.* † *National champion.*

SEASON FIELD-GOAL PERCENTAGE

(Based on qualifiers for annual championship)

Player, Team	Season	G	FG	FGA	Pct.
Tina Kampa, St. Benedict	†1993	30	158	231	*68.4
Laurie Trow, St. Thomas (Minn.)	†1992	28	276	411	67.2
Lanett Stephen, Franklin	1993	25	147	222	66.2
Laurie Trow, St. Thomas (Minn.)	1993	26	271	413	65.6
Sabrina Moody, Va. Wesleyan	†1984	29	163	249	65.5
Arlene Eagan, Buffalo St.	†1990	28	223	344	64.8
Linda Mason, Rust	†1987	28	244	377	64.7
Doris Nicholson, Jersey City St.	†1989	27	205	317	64.7
Linda Rose, Nichols	1990	25	197	305	64.6
Deanna Kyle, Wilkes	1984	22	195	304	64.1
Sherry Patterson, Wm. Paterson	1987	25	234	365	64.1
Linda Rose, Nichols	†1991	24	225	351	64.1
Lesa Dennis, Emmanuel	†1988	21	191	298	64.1
Melissa Hayes, Rhodes	1984	22	201	315	63.8
Laurie Trow, St. Thomas (Minn.)	1991	31	276	433	63.7
Karen Porath, Ohio Wesleyan	1992	25	137	215	63.7
Linda Mason, Rust	1988	24	188	296	63.5
Doris Nicholson, Jersey City St.	1988	22	173	273	63.4
Chris Holec, N.C.-Greensboro	1988	32	163	259	62.9
Louise MacDonald, St. John Fisher	1988	32	225	358	62.8
Mary Schultz, St. Mary's (Minn.)	†1985	26	221	352	62.8

* *Record.* † *National champion.*

SEASON THREE-POINT FIELD GOALS MADE PER GAME

(Based on qualifiers for annual championship)

Player, Team	Season	G	3FG	Avg.
Kate Peterson, Wis.-Stevens Point	†1991	20	77	*3.9
Brenda Straight, Neb. Wesleyan	1991	26	*100	3.8
Sladja Kovijanic, Middlebury	†1993	21	80	3.8
Vicki Fuess, Utica Tech	1993	25	95	3.8
MaryKate Fannon, Cabrini	†1992	25	93	3.7
Shannon Stobel, N.C. Wesleyan	†1989	24	87	3.6
MaryKate Fannon, Cabrini	1993	26	92	3.5
Vicki Fuess, Utica Tech	1992	24	84	3.5
Heather Toma, Maryville (Mo.)	1989	26	86	3.3
Martha Sainz, Va. Wesleyan	1992	28	92	3.3
Kristin Nielsen, Thomas	†1990	25	82	3.3
Sona Bedenian, Aurora	1992	23	73	3.2
Dana Painter, Shenandoah	1991	20	63	3.2
Julie Radke, St. Mary's (Ind.)	1990	18	55	3.1
Sue Bavineau, Pine Manor	1989	24	73	3.0
Martha Sainz, Va. Wesleyan	1993	26	79	3.0
Michelle Jones, Wm. Paterson	1991	28	83	3.0
Kim Prewitt, Thomas More	1993	26	77	3.0
Debbi Pearson, Notre Dame (Md.)	1993	23	67	2.9
Sladja Kovijanic, Middlebury	1992	22	64	2.9
Mandy Jackson, Emory	1992	26	75	2.9

* *Record.* † *National champion.*

SEASON THREE-POINT FIELD-GOAL PERCENTAGE

(Based on qualifiers for annual championship)

Player, Team	Season	G	3FG	3FGA	Pct.
Ellen Thompson, Rhodes	†1989	23	54	90	*60.0
Missie Burns, Berea	†1993	20	56	99	56.6
Tracy Ragatz, UC San Diego	†1988	25	48	86	55.8
Honey Brown, Maryville (Tenn.)	1993	26	40	73	54.8
Lori Towle, Bowdoin	†1992	17	31	58	53.4
Catie Cleary, Pine Manor	1988	20	43	81	53.1
Ellen Thompson, Rhodes	†1991	24	50	95	52.6
Missy Sharer, Grinnell	†1990	23	42	80	52.5
Dawn Hill, Ohio Northern	1990	23	38	74	51.4
Ellen Thompson, Rhodes	1990	26	54	106	50.9
Jane Ruliffson, Macalester	1991	26	59	116	50.9
Kristen Crawley, St. Mary's (Ind.)	1993	21	40	80	50.0
Jody Normandin, Worcester Tech	1988	25	64	129	49.6
Sladja Kovijanic, Middlebury	1990	20	37	75	49.3
Paula Fritz, Messiah	1988	23	57	116	49.1
JoEllen Dickert, Carthage	1991	26	54	110	49.1
Kris Jacobsen, Wis.-Platteville	1989	30	58	120	48.3
Dee Ann Mell, Muskingum	1988	28	43	90	47.8
Kathy Roberts, Wartburg	1993	28	43	90	47.8

* *Record.* † *National champion.*

SEASON FREE-THROW PERCENTAGE

(Based on qualifiers for annual championship)

Player, Team	Season	G	FT	FTA	Pct.
Valerie Kepner, Baldwin-Wallace	†1989	25	63	66	*95.5
Stacy Schmidt, Beloit	†1992	22	57	62	91.9
Kim Bartman, Calvin	1992	21	80	88	90.9
Anne Bennett, Lake Forest	†1991	22	55	61	90.2
Joann D'Alessandro, Rhode Island Col.	†1985	26	78	87	89.7
Jill Kathmann, William Smith	†1993	25	66	74	89.2
Shannon Collins, Centre	1989	31	177	200	88.5
Jill Morrison, Lake Forest	†1990	24	86	98	87.8
Katie Anderson, Luther	1993	20	57	65	87.7
Lissa Nienhuis, Hope	1990	26	85	97	87.6
Jill Morrison, Lake Forest	1989	22	95	109	87.2
Jen Gray, Elms	1990	22	61	70	87.1
Deana Moren, East. Mennonite	†1984	23	60	69	87.0
Sandy Eilertson, Wis.-Superior	1984	23	73	84	86.9
Mary Kay Babcock, Elmira	†1982	19	53	61	86.9
Angie Miller, Wilkes	1989	23	66	76	86.8
Jenny Taylor, Whittier	1989	25	72	83	86.7
Jillayn Quaschnick, Concordia-M'head	1989	27	103	119	86.6
Cindy Vigurs, Hartwick	†1986	22	57	66	86.4
Ellen Martinovic, Wis.-Whitewater	†1988	22	57	66	86.4

* *Record.* † *National champion.*

SEASON REBOUNDS

Player, Team	Season	G	Reb.
Carla Gadsden, Jersey City St.	†1982	27	*579
Sandra Ivory, Rust	1984	31	493
Stacy Carr, Va. Wesleyan	†1990	27	489
Dawn Webb, Salisbury St.	1989	27	480
Wanda Davis, New York U.	†1986	28	474
Carolyn Savio, Montclair St.	1990	29	473
Tina Shaw, Bishop	†1984	28	470
Brenda Sanders, North Central	1982	38	462
Terry Lockwood, St. Elizabeth	†1989	21	461
Cindy Lonneman, Minn.-Morris	1983	35	457
Stacy Carr, Va. Wesleyan	1989	29	448
Carolyn Savio, Montclair St.	1989	29	448
Malane Perry, Fitchburg St.	†1992	25	443
Tina Griffiths, Norwich	1992	26	423
Melanie Alston, Bishop	†1987	25	418

Player, Team	Season	G	Reb.
Ruth Bonner, Mary Washington	1985	27	411
Liza Janssen, Wellesley	1993	27	407
Margie O'Brien, Clark (Mass.)	1983	29	406
Hilary Williams, Baruch	1990	25	405
Lillian Goree, Susquehanna	1982	25	402
Caroline Leary, Middlebury	†1991	20	402

** Record. † National champion.*

SEASON REBOUND AVERAGE

Player, Team	Season	G	Reb.	Avg.
Terry Lockwood, St. Elizabeth	†1989	21	461	*22.0
Carla Gadsen, Jersey City St.	†1982	27	*579	21.4
Caroline Leary, Middlebury	†1991	20	402	20.1
Stacy Carr, Va. Wesleyan	†1990	27	489	18.1
Dawn Webb, Salisbury St.	1989	27	480	17.8
Malane Perry, Fitchburg St.	†1992	25	443	17.7
Tina Shaw, Bishop	1982	18	308	17.1
Wanda Davis, New York U.	†1986	28	474	16.9
Regina Reed, Incarnate Word	1983	23	389	16.9
Tina Shaw, Bishop	†1984	28	470	16.8
Molly Lackman, Immaculata	1991	23	384	16.7
Jennifer Allen, Mass.-Boston	†1983	18	300	16.7
Melanie Alston, Bishop	†1987	25	418	16.7
Giovanni Licorish, Baruch	†1993	19	317	16.7
Dion McMillian, New Jersey Tech	1987	19	316	16.6
Tina Griffiths, Norwich	1991	24	397	16.5
Colleen Lemanski, Fredonia St.	1989	23	379	16.5
Susan Burns, Skidmore	1990	24	395	16.5
Carol Johnson, Illinois Col.	1984	21	345	16.4
Carla Cannon, Wesley	1991	24	394	16.4
Wendy Merk, Connecticut Col.	†1988	20	327	16.4

** Record. † National champion.*

SEASON ASSISTS

Player, Team	Season	G	Ast.
Tonja Sanders, Rust	†1990	26	*303
Eleanor Wykpisz, Kean	1989	29	283
Kristie Delbrugge, Frostburg St.	†1989	25	273
Karen Barefoot, Chris. Newport	†1991	27	265
Karen Barefoot, Chris. Newport	†1993	28	236
Allison Gagnon, Southern Me.	1991	30	232
Karen Barefoot, Chris. Newport	†1992	28	228
Allison Gagnon, Southern Me.	1993	29	221
Kate Titus, Muskingum	1991	32	217
Beth Bacon, Clarkson	1989	33	216
Jody Krueger, Wis.-Eau Claire	1992	28	215
Tonja Sanders, Rust	1989	21	211
Marlo Foley, Binghamton	1993	27	211
Kristi Schultz, Concordia-M'head	1991	29	210
Tammie McDowell, Salem St.	1991	29	210
Cathy Clark, Marietta	1990	27	209
Allison Gagnon, Southern Me.	1992	30	207
Laura Beeman, Cal St. San B'dino	1990	28	203
Tammie McDowell, Salem St.	1990	28	202
Meredith Grenier, Marymount (Va.)	1991	28	190
Kristi Schultz, Concordia-M'head	1993	27	190

** Record. † National champion.*

SEASON ASSIST AVERAGE

Player, Team	Season	G	Ast.	Avg.
Tonja Sanders, Rust	†1990	26	*303	*11.7
Kristie Delbrugge, Frostburg St.	†1989	25	273	10.9
Tonja Sanders, Rust	1989	21	211	10.0
Karen Barefoot, Chris. Newport	†1991	27	265	9.8
Eleanor Wykpisz, Kean	1989	29	283	9.8

Player, Team	Season	G	Ast.	Avg.
Karen Barefoot, Chris. Newport	†1993	28	236	8.4
Karen Barefoot, Chris. Newport	†1992	28	228	8.1
Marlo Foley, Binghamton	1993	27	211	7.8
Cathy Clark, Marietta	1990	27	209	7.7
Allison Gagnon, Southern Me.	1991	30	232	7.7
Lynn Elliott, Connecticut Col.	1989	22	170	7.7
Jody Krueger, Wis.-Eau Claire	1992	28	215	7.7
Allison Gagnon, Southern Me.	1993	29	221	7.6
Kim Wood, Lycoming	1989	23	175	7.6
Kileen Kertesz, Marietta	1991	25	189	7.6
Cathy Hayes, Bowdoin	1989	24	181	7.5
Lynn Elliott, Connecticut Col.	1990	23	173	7.5
Barb Milligan, Cabrini	1991	23	172	7.5
Missy Daniels, Thomas	1990	25	186	7.4
Carol Hile, Berea	1989	23	171	7.4
Tonja Sanders, Rust	1992	21	155	7.4

** Record. † National champion.*

SEASON BLOCKED SHOTS

Player, Team	Season	G	Blk.
Liza Janssen, Wellesley	†1993	27	*145
Janet Kasinger, Ill. Benedictine	1993	22	113
Kim Stumpf, Whittier	1993	24	110
Tamiko Martin, Ferrum	1993	25	97
Kim McCabe, Wentworth Inst.	1993	22	90
Wendy Gibbs, La Verne	1993	24	76
Jen Tregoning, St. Mary's (Md.)	1993	20	74
Sheila Retcher, Defiance	1993	24	71
Keisha Brown, John Jay	1993	23	70
Liliana Alvarez, New Jersey Tech	1993	21	66
Heather Dawkins, Wash. & Jeff.	1993	21	65
Megan Wilrett, Elmhurst	1993	24	64
Emma Bascom, Drew	1993	21	63
Sylvia Newman, Meredith	1993	20	61
Tracy Wilson, Central (Iowa)	1993	29	61

** Record. † National champion.*

SEASON BLOCKED-SHOT AVERAGE

Player, Team	Season	G	Blk.	Avg.
Liza Janssen, Wellesley	†1993	27	*145	*5.4
Janet Kasinger, Ill. Benedictine	1993	22	113	5.1
Kim Stumpf, Whittier	1993	24	110	4.6
Kim McCabe, Wentworth Inst.	1993	22	90	4.1
Tamiko Martin, Ferrum	1993	25	97	3.9
Jen Tregoning, St. Mary's (Md.)	1993	20	74	3.7
Wendy Gibbs, La Verne	1993	24	76	3.2
Liliana Alvarez, New Jersey Tech	1993	21	66	3.1
Heather Dawkins, Wash. & Jeff.	1993	21	65	3.1
Sylvia Newman, Meredith	1993	20	61	3.0
Keisha Brown, John Jay	1993	23	70	3.0
Emma Bascom, Drew	1993	21	63	3.0
Sheila Retcher, Defiance	1993	24	71	3.0
Megan Wilrett, Elmhurst	1993	24	64	2.7
Julie Snyder, St. Mary's (Ind.)	1993	20	52	2.6

** Record. † National champion.*

SEASON STEALS

Player, Team	Season	G	Stl.
Alicia LaValley, Plattsburgh St.	†1993	24	*149
Rose Addison, York (N.Y.)	1993	23	137
Julie Rando, Regis (Mass.)	1993	25	132
Angel Esposito, Elms	1993	23	129
Karen Barefoot, Chris. Newport	1993	28	128
Nicole Albert, Cal Lutheran	1993	25	124
Lisa Villata, Montclair St.	1993	25	123
Annelise Houston, New England Col.	1993	25	112
Melissa Bryce, Plymouth St.	1993	25	108
Amy Endler, Moravian	1993	29	107

ayer, Team	Season	G	Stl.
issy Kowolenko, Eastern Conn. St.	1993	27	107
egina Austin, Buffalo St.	1993	27	106
sa Trujillo, Norwich	1993	28	106
sa Matukaitis, Eastern Conn. St.	1993	25	103
enie Amoss, Goucher	1993	25	102

Record. † *National champion.*

SEASON STEAL AVERAGE

layer, Team	Season	G	Stl.	Avg.
licia LaValley, Plattsburgh St.	†1993	24	*149	*6.2
ose Addison, York (N.Y.)	1993	23	137	6.0
ngel Esposito, Elms	1993	23	129	5.6
ulie Rando, Regis (Mass.)	1993	25	132	5.3
indy Leeds, St. Mary's (Md.)	1993	20	100	5.0
icole Albert, Cal Lutheran	1993	25	124	5.0
isa Villata, Montclair St.	1993	25	123	4.9
aren Barefoot, Chris. Newport	1993	28	128	4.6
nnelise Houston, New England Col.	1993	25	112	4.5
atricia Frost, Upsala	1993	20	88	4.4
mily Edson, Rhodes	1993	22	96	4.4
elissa Bryce, Plymouth St.	1993	25	108	4.3
racy Salciccia, Mt. St. Vincent	1993	23	97	4.2
etty Perez, Gallaudet	1993	24	100	4.2
eisha Brown, John Jay	1993	23	95	4.1

Record. † *National champion.*

CAREER POINTS

Player, Team	Seasons	Pts.
Jeannie Demers, Buena Vista	1984-87	*3,171
Laurie Trow, St. Thomas (Minn.)	1990-93	2,607
Julie Curtis, Whittier	1984-87	2,433
Maureen Burchill, Southern Me.	1982-85	2,357
Kim Wallner, North Central	1981-84	2,324
Cathy Clark, Marietta	1987-90	2,311
Annette Hoffman, Juniata	1990-93	2,269
Sandy Buddelmeyer, Capital	1990-93	2,248
Renie Amoss, Goucher	1990-93	2,220
Simone Edwards, FDU-Madison	1990-93	2,205
Lynn Butler, Allentown	1984-87	2,193
Michele White, Stony Brook	1984-87	2,183
Missy Hensley, East. Mennonite	1989-92	2,163
Kathy Roberts, Wartburg	1990-93	2,144
Becky Inman, William Penn	1984-87	2,139
Jessica Beachy, Concordia-M'head	1985-88	2,101
Lois Salto, New Rochelle	1981-84	2,087
Tricia Kosenina, Thiel	1990-93	2,086
Eva Pittman, St. Andrews	1981-84	2,079
Lisa Halloran, Framingham St.	1986-89	2,077
Deb Yeasted, Susquehanna	1982-85	2,075
Suzanne Coyne, Wilmington (Ohio)	1989-92	2,065
Lisa Ekmekjian, Upsala	1981-84	2,061
Michelle Jones, Wm. Paterson	1988-91	2,048
Amy Vanden Langenberg, Carroll (Wis.)	1983-86	2,040

* *Record.*

CAREER SCORING AVERAGE

(Minimum 1,200 points)

Player, Team	Seasons	G	FG	3FG	FT	Pts.	Avg.
Jeannie Demers, Buena Vista	1984-87	105	*1,386	—	399	*3,171	*30.2
Missy Sharer, Grinnell	1990-91	47	436	75	318	1,265	26.9
Terri Schumacher, Wis.-Oshkosh	1984-85	47	551	—	107	1,209	25.7
Sladja Kovijanic, Middlebury	1990-93	65	591	185	235	1,602	24.6
Renie Amoss, Goucher	1990-93	91	860	115	385	2,220	24.4
Julie Curtis, Whittier	1984-87	100	988	—	457	2,433	24.3
Annette Hoffman, Juniata	1990-93	94	744	58	723	2,269	24.1
Leslie Rushton, Drew	1981-84	83	778	—	442	1,998	24.1
Sylvia Newman, Meredith	1990-93	79	679	0	490	1,848	23.4
Laurie Trow, St. Thomas (Minn.)	1990-93	113	1,022	4	559	2,607	23.1

Player, Team	Seasons	G	FG	3FG	FT	Pts.	A
Gretchen Gates, Chicago	1983-86	84	847	—	230	1,924	2
Simone Edwards, FDU-Madison	1990-93	97	687	42	*789	2,205	2
Laura Johnson, Shenandoah	1982-85	75	720	—	264	1,704	2
Eva Pittman, St. Andrew's	1981-84	92	885	—	309	2,079	2
Missy Hensley, East. Mennonite	1989-92	96	796	4	567	2,163	22
Tricia Kosenina, Thiel	1990-93	93	709	150	518	2,086	22
April Owen, Staten Island	1991-93	55	526	5	149	1,206	21
Cathy Clark, Marietta	1987-90	106	939	51	382	2,311	21
Lisa Ekmekjian, Upsala	1981-84	95	820	—	421	2,061	21
Suzanne Coyne, Wilmington (Ohio)	1989-92	98	945	0	175	2,065	21
Laura VanSickle, Grinnell	1987-90	86	751	0	308	1,810	21
Tina Shaw, Bishop	1981-84	88	832	—	183	1,847	21
Jill Morrison, Lake Forest	1988-91	90	774	8	329	1,885	20
Terry Lockwood, St. Elizabeth	1986-89	73	624	0	274	1,522	20
Pauline Therriault, Thomas	1986-89	89	845	1	159	1,850	20

* *Record.*

CAREER FIELD-GOAL PERCENTAGE

(Minimum 400 field goals made)

Player, Team	Seasons	G	FG	FGA	Pc
Linda Rose, Nichols	1989-91	74	629	992	*63
Laurie Trow, St. Thomas (Minn.)	1990-93	113	1,022	1,615	63.
Linda Mason, Rust	1985-88	86	580	920	63.
Sabrina Moody, Va. Wesleyan	1982-85	97	581	971	59.
Sherry Patterson, Wm. Paterson	1984-87	90	620	1,038	59.
Sylvia Newman, Meredith	1990-93	79	679	1,142	59.
Mary Schultz, St. Mary's (Minn.)	1983-86	96	812	1,384	58.
Audrey Seymour, Adrian	1990-93	101	566	969	58.
Sandy Buddelmeyer, Capital	1990-93	116	859	1,495	57.
Carri Metzler, St. Norbert	1988-91	92	687	1,196	57.
Pat Garcia, Whittier	1981-84	71	469	821	57.
Jodene Heldt, Wis.-River Falls	1989-90, 92	74	525	922	56.
Elise Cromack, Mount Holyoke	1983-87	89	475	835	56.
Dawn Hevel, Illinois Col.	1989-92	86	444	781	56.
Anne Krumrine, Frank. & Marsh.	1987-90	105	779	1,378	56.5
Kaye Cross, Colby	1981-84	84	572	1,012	56.5
Michelle Thykeson, Concordia-M'head	1988-91	116	697	1,239	56.3
Vickie Meiners, Illinois Col.	1990-93	93	686	1,221	56.2
Mickey Jurewicz, St. Benedict	1988-91	106	574	1,026	55.9
Sue Eilerman, Blackburn	1984-87	101	491	878	55.9
Gretchen Gates, Chicago	1983-86	84	847	1,519	55.8
Karen Porath, Ohio Wesleyan	1990-93	104	441	799	55.2
Arlene Eagan, Buffalo St.	1988-91	109	706	1,284	55.0
Susan Heidt, St. John Fisher	1987-90	127	723	1,317	54.9
Julie Curtis, Whittier	1984-87	100	988	1,809	54.6
Kathy Beck, Moravian	1989-92	109	774	1,418	54.6

* *Record.*

CAREER THREE-POINT FIELD GOALS MADE

Player, Team	Seasons	G	3FG
Michelle Jones, Wm. Paterson	1988-91	107	*286
Martha Sainz, Va. Wesleyan	1990-93	108	258
Jill Brower, William Smith	1990-93	103	251
Heather Toma, Maryville (Mo.)	1988-91	89	231
Sue Bavineau, Pine Manor	1988-91	93	224
Shannon Stobel, N.C. Wesleyan	1988-90	73	207
Sona Bedenian, Aurora	1990-93	92	205
Paula Fritz, Messiah	1988-91	94	204
Ellen Thompson, Rhodes	1989-92	99	204
MaryKate Fannon, Cabrini	1990-93	81	198
Sladja Kovijanic, Middlebury	1990-93	65	185
Michelle Snow, Muskingum	1989-92	103	182
Vicki Fuess, Utica Tech	1992-93	49	179
Julie Sheldon, Hamilton	1990-93	99	176
Richelle Reilly, Albion	1989-92	90	175
Beth Shapiro, New York U.	1990-93	99	175

* *Record.*

CAREER THREE-POINT FIELD GOALS MADE PER GAME

(Minimum 125 three-point field goals made)

Player, Team	Seasons	G	3FG	Avg.
Vicki Fuess, Utica Tech	1992-93	49	179	*3.65
Sladja Kovijanic, Middlebury	1990-93	65	185	2.85
Shannon Stobel, N.C. Wesleyan	1988-90	73	207	2.84
Michelle Jones, Wm. Paterson	1988-91	107	*286	2.67
Heather Toma, Maryville (Mo.)	1988-91	89	231	2.60
MaryKate Fannon, Cabrini	1990-93	81	198	2.44
Jill Brower, William Smith	1990-93	103	251	2.44
Sue Bavineau, Pine Manor	1988-91	93	224	2.41
Martha Sainz, Va. Wesleyan	1990-93	108	258	2.39
Sona Bedenian, Aurora	1990-93	92	205	2.23
Barb Milligan, Cabrini	1989-91	61	134	2.20
Paula Fritz, Messiah	1988-91	94	204	2.17
Shannon Dwyer, Nazareth (N.Y.)	1988-90	80	167	2.09
Ellen Thompson, Rhodes	1989-92	99	204	2.06
Stacie Robey, Wis.-River Falls	1988-89, 91	81	165	2.04

* *Record.*

CAREER THREE-POINT FIELD-GOAL PERCENTAGE

(Minimum 125 three-point field goals made)

Player, Team	Seasons	G	3FG	3FGA	Pct.
Ellen Thompson, Rhodes	1989-92	99	204	416	*49.0
JoEllen Dickert, Carthage	1989-92	102	139	300	46.3
Sladja Kovijanic, Middlebury	1990-93	65	185	413	44.8
Jody Normandin, Worcester Tech	1988-90	79	147	349	42.1
Michelle Jones, Wm. Paterson	1988-91	107	*286	685	41.8
Shannon Dwyer, Nazareth (N.Y.)	1988-90	80	167	401	41.6
Paula Fritz, Messiah	1988-91	94	204	494	41.3
Barb Milligan, Cabrini	1989-91	61	134	328	40.9
Kate Peterson, Wis.-Stevens Point	1988-91	90	169	422	40.0

* *Record.*

CAREER FREE-THROW PERCENTAGE

(Minimum 250 free throws made)

Player, Team	Seasons	G	FT	FTA	Pct.
Tammy Anair, Southern Me.	1984-87	113	279	336	*83.0
Missy Sharer, Grinnell	1990-91	47	318	383	83.0
Carla Weaver, DePauw	1989-92	100	277	334	82.9
Annette Hoffman, Juniata	1990-93	94	723	883	81.9
Cathy Clark, Marietta	1987-90	106	382	468	81.6
Jill Morrison, Lake Forest	1988-91	90	329	406	81.0
Susan Heidt, St. John Fisher	1987-90	127	573	708	80.9
Linda Atiyeh, Moravian	1985-88	99	278	345	80.6
Jane Ruliffson, Macalester	1989-92	101	380	474	80.2
Penny Wehrs, Dubuque	1985-88	101	450	563	79.9
Susan Yates, Centre	1987-90	114	353	442	79.9
Christy Evans, Wooster	1989-92	105	287	360	79.7
Valery Broadwater, Frostburg St.	1983-86	98	305	384	79.4
Jillayn Quaschnick, Concordia-M'head	1986-89	112	255	321	79.4
Michelle Jones, Wm. Paterson	1988-91	108	466	587	79.4
Jessica Beachy, Concordia-M'head	1985-88	118	369	465	79.4
Charlotte Smith, Capital	1988-91	88	295	373	79.1
Pam Conk, Randolph-Macon	1989-92	95	452	572	79.0
Sally Gangell, Hartwick	1981-84	96	259	328	79.0
Malane Perry, Fitchburg St.	1992-93	48	392	498	78.7
Tricia Kosenina, Thiel	1990-93	93	518	659	78.6
Shannon Dwyer, Nazareth (N.Y.)	1987-90	83	292	372	78.5
Juliana Klocek, John Carroll	1989-92	103	318	407	78.1
Ann Osborne, Ohio Wesleyan	1985-88	97	427	549	77.8
A. J. DeRoo, Connecticut Col.	1988-91	87	280	360	77.8

* *Record.*

CAREER REBOUNDS

Player, Team	Seasons	G	Reb.
Tina Shaw, Bishop	1981-84	88	*1,452
Arlene Eagan, Buffalo St.	1988-91	109	1,419
Sandy Buddelmeyer, Capital	1990-93	116	1,365
Caroline Leary, Middlebury	1989-92	81	1,364
Ruth Bonner, Mary Washington	1982-85	100	1,362
Terry Lockwood, St. Elizabeth	1986-89	73	1,343
Sherry Patterson, Wm. Paterson	1984-87	90	1,289
Dawn Webb, Salisbury St.	1986-89	101	1,254
Lorretta Thomas, Ramapo	1983-86	96	1,244
Kristan Radak, Rochester	1982-85	109	1,229
Rebecca Hooker, Colby-Sawyer	1981-84	91	1,222
Eileen Fenton, Mass.-Boston	1988-91	98	1,220
Jill Myers, Ohio Wesleyan	1985-88	101	1,217
Laurie Trow, St. Thomas (Minn.)	1990-93	113	1,204

* *Record.*

CAREER REBOUND AVERAGE

(Minimum 1,000 rebounds)

Player, Team	Seasons	G	Reb.	Avg.
Terry Lockwood, St. Elizabeth	1986-89	73	1,343	*18.4
Caroline Leary, Middlebury	1989-92	81	1,364	16.8
Tina Shaw, Bishop	1981-84	88	*1,452	16.5
Sherry Patterson, Wm. Paterson	1984-87	90	1,289	14.3
Leslie Rushton, Drew	1981-84	83	1,165	14.0
Ruth Bonner, Mary Washington	1982-85	100	1,362	13.6
Rebecca Hooker, Colby-Sawyer	1981-84	91	1,222	13.4
Kelly White, Norwich	1983-86	77	1,027	13.3
Arlene Eagan, Buffalo St.	1988-91	109	1,419	13.0
Lorretta Thomas, Ramapo	1983-86	96	1,244	13.0
Carolyn Cochrane, Grove City	1986-89	86	1,110	12.9
Linda Mason, Rust	1985-88	86	1,103	12.8
Gretchen Gates, Chicago	1983-86	84	1,056	12.6
Eileen Fenton, Mass.-Boston	1988-91	98	1,220	12.4
Dawn Webb, Salisbury St.	1986-89	101	1,254	12.4
Carolyn Savio, Montclair St.	1987-90	90	1,088	12.1
Jill Myers, Ohio Wesleyan	1985-88	101	1,217	12.0
Sally Gangell, Hartwick	1981-84	96	1,145	11.9
Pauline Therriault, Thomas	1986-89	89	1,058	11.9
Karen Kinsella, Elmhurst	1983-86	94	1,112	11.8
Linda DeRyke, Oswego St.	1983-86	95	1,123	11.8
Sandy Buddelmeyer, Capital	1990-93	116	1,365	11.8
Leslie Hathaway, Stony Brook	1986-89	96	1,098	11.4
Carrie Kaczmarski, New York U.	1990-93	94	1,075	11.4
Courtney Wildung, Hamline	1990-93	103	1,176	11.4
Melanie Thistle, Regis (Mass.)	1988-91	91	1,036	11.4

* *Record.*

CAREER ASSISTS

Player, Team	Seasons	G	Ast.
#Karen Barefoot, Chris. Newport	1991-93	83	*729
Allison Gagnon, Southern Me.	1990-93	115	673
Tonja Sanders, Rust	1989-92	68	669
Kristi Schultz, Concordia-M'head	1990-93	104	650
Sheri McCarthy, St. Joseph's (Me.)	1990-93	117	603
Regina Austin, Buffalo St.	1990-93	108	585
Wendy Rogers, Bri'water (Mass.)/Eastern Conn. St.	1988, 90-92	108	566
Dana Patete, Juniata	1989-92	85	560
Tammie McDowell, Salem St.	1989-91	85	554
Karen Walker, Beloit	1990-93	90	532
Christy Evans, Wooster	1989-92	105	529
Lynn Elliott, Connecticut Col.	1989-91	68	497
Kileen Kertesz, Marietta	1989-92	103	497
Cathy Hayes, Bowdoin	1989-92	82	481
Jill Thomas, Carthage	1990-93	103	479

Player, Team	Seasons	G	Ast.
Jodi Condron, Adrian	1989-91	74	477
Sherri Ervin, Fredonia St.	1989-90, 92	73	471
Juli Maki, Wis.-Stout	1990-93	107	469
Kate Titus, Muskingum	1989-91	85	460
Stacy Scudder, Heidelberg	1990-93	113	458
Gina Pizzimento, Clark (Mass.)	1989-92	111	450
Amy Russell, Wheaton (Ill.)	1990-93	103	450

*# Active player. * Record.*

CAREER ASSIST AVERAGE

(Minimum 450 assists)

Player, Team	Seasons	G	Ast.	Avg.
Tonja Sanders, Rust	1989-92	68	669	*9.8
Lynn Elliott, Connecticut Col.	1989-91	68	497	7.3
Dana Patete, Juniata	1989-92	85	560	6.6
Tammie McDowell, Salem St.	1989-91	85	554	6.5
Sherri Ervin, Fredonia St.	1989-90, 92	73	471	6.5
Jodi Condron, Adrian	1989-91	74	477	6.4
Kristi Schultz, Concordia-M'head	1990-93	104	650	6.3
Karen Walker, Beloit	1990-93	90	532	5.9
Cathy Hayes, Bowdoin	1989-92	82	481	5.9
Allison Gagnon, Southern Me.	1990-93	115	673	5.9
Regina Austin, Buffalo St.	1990-93	108	585	5.4
Kate Titus, Muskingum	1989-91	85	460	5.4
Wendy Rogers, Bri'water (Mass.)/Eastern Conn. St.	1988, 90-92	108	566	5.2
Sheri McCarthy, St. Joseph's (Me.)	1990-93	117	603	5.2
Christy Evans, Wooster	1989-92	105	529	5.0
Kileen Kertesz, Marietta	1989-92	103	497	4.8

** Record.*

DIVISION III WOMEN'S ANNUAL INDIVIDUAL CHAMPIONS

SCORING AVERAGE

Year	Player, Team	G	FG	3FG	FT	Pts.	Avg.
1982	Mary Beth Bowler, King's (Pa.)	25	246	—	150	642	25.7
1983	Jody Imbrie, Grove City	27	285	—	200	770	28.5
1984	Laura Johnson, Shenandoah	16	176	—	75	427	26.7
1985	Jeannie Demers, Buena Vista	28	375	—	108	858	30.6
1986	Jeannie Demers, Buena Vista	25	324	—	129	777	31.1
1987	Jeannie Demers, Buena Vista	26	*385	—	121	*891	*34.3
1988	Catie Cleary, Pine Manor	20	228	43	175	674	33.7
1989	Lisa Halloran, Framingham St.	25	235	59	141	670	26.8
1990	Ann Gilbert, Oberlin	25	319	7	133	778	31.1
1991	Missy Sharer, Grinnell	24	272	33	217	794	33.1
1992	Missy Hensley, East Mennonite	23	251	0	183	685	29.8
1993	Sladja Kovijanic, Middlebury	21	235	80	98	648	30.9

** Record.*

FIELD-GOAL PERCENTAGE

Year	Player, Team	G	FG	FGA	Pct.
1982	Terese Kwiatkowski, Worcester Tech	23	225	365	61.6
1983	Debbie Litten, Bridgewater (Va.)	26	193	320	60.3
1984	Sabrina Moody, Va. Wesleyan	29	163	249	65.5
1985	Mary Schultz, St. Mary's (Minn.)	26	221	352	62.8
1986	Queen Dickerson, Millikin	23	123	197	62.4
1987	Linda Mason, Rust	28	244	377	64.7
1988	Lesa Dennis, Emmanuel	21	191	298	64.1
1989	Doris Nicholson, Jersey City St.	27	205	317	64.7
1990	Arlene Eagan, Buffalo St.	28	223	344	64.8
1991	Linda Rose, Nichols	24	255	351	64.1
1992	Laurie Trow, St. Thomas (Minn.)	28	276	411	67.2
1993	Tina Kampa, St. Benedict	30	158	231	*68.4

** Record.*

THREE-POINT FIELD GOALS MADE PER GAME

Year	Player, Team	G	3FG	Avg.
1988	Debbie Gertsch, Redlands	22	60	2.7
1989	Shannon Stobel, N.C. Wesleyan	24	87	3.6
1990	Kristin Nielsen, Thomas	25	82	3.3
1991	Kate Peterson, Wis.-Stevens Point	20	77	*3.9
1992	MaryKate Fannon, Cabrini	25	93	3.7
1993	Sladja Kovijanic, Middlebury	21	80	3.8

* *Record.*

THREE-POINT FIELD-GOAL PERCENTAGE

Year	Player, Team	G	3FG	3FGA	Pct.
1988	Tracy Ragatz, UC San Diego	25	48	86	55.8
1989	Ellen Thompson, Rhodes	23	54	90	*60.0
1990	Missy Sharer, Grinnell	23	42	80	52.5
1991	Ellen Thompson, Rhodes	24	50	95	52.6
1992	Lori Towle, Bowdoin	17	31	58	53.4
1993	Missie Burns, Berea	20	56	99	56.6

* *Record.*

FREE-THROW PERCENTAGE

Year	Player, Team	G	FT	FTA	Pct.
1982	Mary Kay Babcock, Elmira	19	53	61	86.9
1983	Tammy Metcalf, St. Olaf	21	53	62	85.5
1984	Deana Moren, East. Mennonite	23	60	69	87.0
1985	Joann D'Alessandro, Rhode Island Col.	26	78	87	89.7
1986	Cindy Vigurs, Hartwick	22	57	66	86.4
1987	Katie Lokits, Berea	23	87	101	86.1
1988	Ellen Martinkovic, Wis.-Whitewater	22	57	66	86.4
1989	Valerie Kepner, Baldwin-Wallace	25	63	66	*95.5
1990	Jill Morrison, Lake Forest	24	86	98	87.8
1991	Anne Bennett, Lake Forest	22	55	61	90.2
1992	Stacy Schmidt, Beloit	22	57	62	91.9
1993	Jill Kathmann, William Smith	25	66	74	89.2

* *Record.*

REBOUND AVERAGE

Year	Player, Team	G	Reb.	Avg.
1982	Carla Gadsden, Jersey City St.	27	*579	21.4
1983	Jennifer Allen, Mass.-Boston	18	300	16.7
1984	Tina Shaw, Bishop	28	470	16.8
1985	Carla Williams, Bishop	20	312	15.6
1986	Wanda Davis, New York U.	28	474	16.9
1987	Melanie Alston, Bishop	25	418	16.7
1988	Wendy Merk, Connecticut Col.	20	327	16.4
1989	Terry Lockwood, St. Elizabeth	21	461	*22.0
1990	Stacy Carr, Va. Wesleyan	27	489	18.1
1991	Caroline Leary, Middlebury	20	402	20.1
1992	Malane Perry, Fitchburg St.	25	443	17.7
1993	Giovanni Licorish, Baruch	19	317	16.7

* *Record.*

ASSIST AVERAGE

Year	Player, Team	G	Ast.	Avg.
1989	Kristie Delbrugge, Frostburg St.	25	273	10.9
1990	Tonja Sanders, Rust	26	*303	*11.7
1991	Karen Barefoot, Chris. Newport	27	265	9.8
1992	Karen Barefoot, Chris. Newport	28	228	8.1
1993	Karen Barefoot, Chris. Newport	28	236	8.4

* *Record.*

BLOCKED-SHOT AVERAGE

Year	Player, Team	G	Blk.	Avg.
1993	Liza Janssen, Wellesley	27	*145	*5.4

STEAL AVERAGE

Year	Player, Team	G	Stl.	Avg.
1993	Alicia LaValley, Plattsburgh St.	24	*149	*6.2

DIVISION III WOMEN'S ANNUAL TEAM CHAMPIONS

WON-LOST PERCENTAGE

Year	Team	Won	Lost	Pct.
1982	Elizabethtown	26	1	.963
1983	Pitt.-Johnstown	24	2	.923
	Susquehanna	24	2	.923
1984	Elizabethtown	29	2	.935
1985	Scranton	*31	1	*.969
1986	Salem St.	29	1	.967
1987	Scranton	*31	2	.939
1988	St. John Fisher	*31	1	*.969
1989	Clark (Mass.)	28	1	.966
1990	St. John Fisher	*31	2	.939
1991	St. Thomas (Minn.)	29	2	.935
1992	St. Thomas (Minn.)	27	1	.964
1993	Geneseo St.	27	1	.964

* *Record.*

SCORING OFFENSE

Year	Team	Games	(W-L)	Pts.	Avg.
1982	King's (Pa.)	25	(17-8)	1,989	79.6
1983	Bishop	25	(18-7)	2,038	81.5
1984	Millikin	25	(19-6)	2,153	86.1
1985	Pitt.-Johnstown	29	(26-3)	2,370	81.7
1986	Bishop	31	(28-3)	2,995	*96.6
1987	Bishop	25	(20-5)	2,210	88.4
1988	Concordia-M'head	31	(29-2)	2,737	88.3
1989	Bridgewater (Va.)	28	(19-9)	2,386	85.2
1990	St. Joseph's (Me.)	30	(25-5)	2,677	89.2
1991	Neb. Wesleyan	26	(15-11)	2,300	88.5
1992	Moravian	33	(31-2)	2,871	87.0
1993	Marymount (Va.)	28	(23-5)	2,588	92.4

* *Record.*

SCORING DEFENSE

Year	Team	Games	(W-L)	Pts.	Avg.
1982	CCNY	27	(19-8)	1,241	46.0
1983	Cornell College	21	(14-7)	1,024	48.8
1984	Pine Manor	24	(20-4)	1,170	48.8
1985	Pomona-Pitzer	29	(27-2)	1,440	49.7
1986	Centre	21	(17-4)	1,052	50.1
1987	St. John Fisher	31	(28-3)	1,367	44.1
1988	St. John Fisher	32	(31-1)	1,475	46.1
1989	Bryn Mawr	18	(11-7)	847	47.1
1990	Montclair St.	29	(23-6)	1,320	45.5
1991	Albertus Magnus	20	(10-10)	922	46.1
1992	Wittenberg	28	(21-7)	1,367	48.8
1993	York (N.Y.)	25	(15-10)	1,200	48.0

SCORING MARGIN

Year	Team	Off.	Def.	Margin
1982	Elizabethtown	74.3	49.9	24.4
1983	Susquehanna	73.8	51.8	22.0
1984	Allegheny	79.3	52.7	26.6
1985	CCNY	75.1	50.3	24.9
1986	Allegheny	82.9	52.2	30.7
1987	St. John Fisher	74.1	44.1	30.0
1988	St. John Fisher	80.3	46.1	*34.2
1989	Concordia-M'head	84.5	59.7	24.9
1990	St. John Fisher	77.3	51.8	25.5
1991	Roanoke	79.2	51.1	28.1
1992	Moravian	87.0	60.1	26.9
1993	Geneseo St.	82.8	53.8	29.1

* *Record.*

FIELD-GOAL PERCENTAGE

Year	Team	FG	FGA	Pct
1982	Worcester Tech	658	1,321	49.
1983	Central (Iowa)	751	1,528	49.
1984	Wilkes	730	1,338	*54
1985	Millikin	890	1,814	49
1986	Whittier	816	1,533	53.
1987	Rust	1,008	1,911	52.
1988	Concordia-M'head	1,122	2,097	53.
1989	Concordia-M'head	942	1,818	51.
1990	St. John Fisher	1,029	2,049	50.
1991	Illinois Col.	786	1,559	50.
1992	St. Thomas (Minn.)	864	1,754	49.
1993	Meredith	635	1,244	51.

* *Record.*

FIELD-GOAL PERCENTAGE DEFENSE

Year	Team	FG	FGA	Pct
1982	Elizabethtown	540	1,725	31.
1983	Bridgewater (Va.)	559	1,663	33.
1984	Oneonta St.	503	1,525	33.
1985	Colby-Sawyer	518	1,650	31.
1986	St. Norbert	466	1,511	30.
1987	Bryn Mawr	327	981	33.
1988	Emmanuel	423	1,368	30.
1989	Bryn Mawr	340	1,011	33.6
1990	Rhodes	552	1,760	31.4
1991	Albertus Magnus	386	1,324	29.2
1992	Mills	367	1,288	*28.5
1993	Wellesley	551	1,744	31.6

* *Record.*

THREE-POINT FIELD GOALS MADE PER GAME

Year	Team	Games	3FG	Avg.
1988	Ferrum	26	111	4.3
1989	Marywood	27	131	4.9
1990	Neb. Wesleyan	24	122	5.1
1991	Neb. Wesleyan	26	*202	*7.8
1992	Catholic	23	149	6.5
1993	Calvin	26	162	6.2

* *Record.*

THREE-POINT FIELD-GOAL PERCENTAGE

Year	Team	Games	3FG	3FGA	Pct.
1988	UC San Diego	25	51	94	54.3
1989	Rhodes	23	55	91	*60.4
1990	Rhodes	26	60	123	48.8
1991	Rhodes	24	64	128	50.0
1992	Vassar	24	63	141	44.7
1993	Southern Me.	29	82	194	42.3

* *Record.*

FREE-THROW PERCENTAGE

Year	Team	FT	FTA	Pct.
1982	King's (Pa.)	379	539	70.3
1983	Rutgers-Camden	322	431	74.7
1984	Whittier	319	429	74.4
1985	Connecticut Col.	308	430	71.6
1986	William Penn	487	669	72.8
1987	Susquehanna	242	330	73.3
1988	Centre	493	640	77.0
1989	Centre	524	680	77.1
1990	St. John Fisher	483	617	*78.3
1991	Allentown	395	515	76.7
1992	Juniata	472	627	75.3
1993	Juniata	430	567	75.8

* *Record.*

REBOUND MARGIN

Year	Team	Off.	Def.	Margin
1982	Lane	58.7	39.3	19.4
1983	Grove City	57.8	38.2	19.6
1984	Norwich	57.2	26.7	*30.4
1985	Bri'water (Mass.)	45.3	28.8	16.6
1986	Spring Garden	40.5	19.8	20.7
1987	Bishop	58.4	34.6	23.8
1988	Rust	53.1	34.7	18.4
1989	Middlebury	49.7	33.8	16.0
1990	Frostburg St.	56.1	41.7	14.4
1991	UC San Diego	49.3	32.1	17.2
1992	Mills	*60.2	43.8	16.3
1993	Immaculata	52.9	36.4	16.5

* *Record.*

DIVISION III WOMEN'S ALL-TIME WINNINGEST TEAMS

Includes records as a senior college only; minimum 10 seasons of competition. Postseason games are included.

PERCENTAGE

Team	Yrs.	Won	Lost	Pct.
St. John Fisher	19	460	86	.842
Salem St.	12	274	67	.804
Scranton	18	408	108	.791
Concordia-M'head	19	404	125	.764
Moravian	14	278	96	.743
Buffalo St.	12	227	79	.742
Kean	20	360	127	.739
St. Thomas (Minn.)	16	315	114	.734
Southern Me.	31	452	166	.731
Marymount (Va.)	10	209	80	.723
St. Norbert	16	271	105	.721
William Penn	61	477	187	.718
Wis.-Oshkosh	22	360	153	.702
Capital	19	307	131	.701
Augustana (Ill.)	18	309	137	.693
Muskingum	19	305	136	.692
Montclair St.	24	392	175	.691
Elizabethtown	65	675	308	.687
Washington (Mo.)	14	210	98	.682
St. Joseph's (Me.)	16	283	133	.680
Pomona-Pitzer	24	357	169	.679
Eastern Conn. St.	22	349	166	.678
Bridgewater (Va.)	45	530	261	.670
Connecticut Col.	15	208	103	.669
St. Benedict	12	199	102	.661

VICTORIES

Team	Yrs.	Wins
Elizabethtown	65	675
Bridgewater (Va.)	45	530
Ursinus	76	501
William Penn	61	477
St. John Fisher	19	460
Southern Me.	31	452
Scranton	18	408
Concordia-M'head	19	404
New York U.	70	399
Montclair St.	24	392
Frostburg St.	29	370
Wheaton (Ill.)	33	364
Wheaton (Mass.)	33	361
Kean	20	360
Wis.-Oshkosh	22	360
Pomona-Pitzer	24	357
Wis.-Whitewater	27	350
Eastern Conn. St.	22	349
Worcester St.	26	339
St. Thomas (Minn.)	16	315
Augustana (Ill.)	18	309
Capital	19	307
Carthage	35	306
Muskingum	19	305
Hartwick	26	294

AWARD WINNERS

Natalie Williams of UCLA was named to the U.S. Basketball Writers Association's 1993 all-America team. The 6-1 junior was 12th in the nation in Division I scoring with 21.2 points per game. Williams is a two-sport standout for the Bruins; she is a member of UCLA's national championship volleyball team in addition to

WOMEN'S ALL-AMERICAN SELECTIONS

KODAK

1975

Carolyn Bush, Wayland Baptist; Marianne Crawford, Immaculata; Nancy Dunkle, Cal St. Fullerton; Lusia Harris, Delta St.; Jan Irby, William Penn; Ann Meyers, UCLA; Brenda Moeller, Wayland Baptist; Debbie Oing, Indiana; Sue Rojcewicz, Southern Conn. St.; Susan Yow, Elon.

1976

Carol Blazejowski, Montclair St.; Cindy Brogdon, Mercer; Nancy Dunkle, Cal St. Fullerton; Doris Felderhoff, Stephen F. Austin; Lusia Harris, Delta St.; Ann Meyers, UCLA; Marianne Crawford Stanley, Immaculata; Pearl Worrell, Wayland Baptist; Susan Yow, North Caro. St.; Susie Kudrna, William Penn.

1977

Carol Blazejowski, Montclair St.; Nancy Dunkle, Cal St. Fullerton; Rita Easterling, Mississippi Col.; Susie Snider Eppers, Baylor; Doris Felderhoff, Stephen F. Austin; Lusia Harris, Delta St.; Charlotte Lewis, Illinois St.; Ann Meyers, UCLA; Patricia Roberts, Tennessee; Mary Scharff, Immaculata.

1978

Genia Beasley, North Caro. St.; Carol Blazejowski, Montclair St.; Debbie Brock, Delta St.; Cindy Brogdon, Tennessee; Julie Gross, Louisiana St.; Althea Gwyn, Queens (N.Y.); Kathy Harston, Wayland Baptist; Nancy Lieberman, Old Dominion; Ann Meyers, UCLA; Lynette Woodard, Kansas.

1979

Cindy Brogdon, Tennessee; Carol Chason, Valdosta St.; Pat Colasardo, Montclair St.; Denise Curry, UCLA; Nancy Lieberman, Old Dominion; Jill Rankin, Wayland Baptist; Susan Taylor, Valdosta St.; Rosie Walker, Stephen F. Austin; Franci Washington, Ohio St.; Lynette Woodard, Kansas.

1980

Denise Curry, UCLA; Tina Gunn, Brigham Young; Pam Kelly, Louisiana Tech; Nancy Lieberman, Old Dominion; Inge Nissen, Old Dominion; Jill Rankin, Tennessee; Susan Taylor, Valdosta St.; Rosie Walker, Stephen F. Austin; Holly Warlick, Tennessee; Lynette Woodard, Kansas.

1981

Denise Curry, UCLA; Anne Donovan, Old Dominion; Pam Kelly, Louisiana Tech; Kris Kirchner, Rutgers; Carol Menken, Oregon St.; Cindy Noble, Tennessee; LaTaunya Pollard, Long Beach St.; Bev Smith, Oregon; Valerie Walker, Cheyney; Lynette Woodard, Kansas.

1982

Pam Kelly, Louisiana Tech; Angela Turner, Louisiana Tech; Valerie Walker, Cheyney; Bev Smith, Oregon; Jerilynn Harper, Tennessee Tech; Janet Harris, Georgia; Barbara Kennedy, Clemson; June Olkowski, Rutgers; Mary Ostrowski, Tennessee; Valerie Still, Kentucky.

1983

University Division: Anne Donovan, Old Dominion; Valerie Still, Kentucky; LaTaunya Pollard, Long Beach St.; Paula McGee, Southern Cal; Cheryl Miller, Southern Cal; Janice Lawrence, Louisiana Tech; Tanya Haave, Tennessee; Joyce Walker, Louisiana St.; Jasmina Perazic, Maryland; Priscilla Gary, Kansas St.
College Division: Carol Welch, Cal Poly Pomona; Jackie White, Cal Poly Pomona; Mary Beasley, Berry; Regina Brown, Charleston; Daphne Donnelly, Francis Marion; Carla Eades, Central Mo. St.; Alison Fay, Bentley; Linda Krawford, Oakland; Kelli Litsch, Southwestern Okla.; Robin Mortensen, St. John Fisher.

1984

Division I: Pam McGee, Southern Cal; Cheryl Miller, Southern Cal; Janice Lawrence, Louisiana Tech; Yolanda Laney, Cheyney; Tresa Brown, North Caro.; Janet Harris, Georgia; Becky Jackson, Auburn; Annette Smith, Texas; Marilyn Stephens, Temple; Joyce Walker, Louisiana St.
Division II: Carla Eades, Central Mo. St.; Francine Perry, Quinnipiac; Stacey Cunningham, Shippensburg; Claudia Schleyer, Abilene Christian; Lorena Legarde, Portland; Janice Washington, Valdosta St.; Donna Burks, Dayton; Beth Couture, Erskine; Candy Crosby, Northeast Ill.; Kelli Litsch, Southwestern Okla.
Division III: Evelyn Oquendo, Salem St.; Kaye Cross, Colby; Sallie Maxwell, Kean; Page Lutz, Elizabethtown; Deanna Kyle, Wilkes; Laurie Sankey, Simpson; Eva Marie Pittman, St. Andrews; Lois Salto, New Rochelle; Sally Gangell, Hartwick.

1985

Division I: Anucha Browne, Northwestern; Sheila Collins, Tennessee; Kirsten Cummings, Long Beach St.; Medina Dixon, Old Dominion; Teresa Edwards, Georgia; Kamie Ethridge, Texas; Pam Gant, Louisiana Tech; Janet Harris, Georgia; Eun Jung Lee, Northeast La.; Cheryl Miller, Southern Cal.
Division II: Darlene Chaney, Hampton; Anita Cooper, Hampton; Julie Fruendt, Lewis; Rosie Jones, Central Mo. St.; Rachel Jackson, St. Anselm; Sharon Lyke, Utica; Vincene Morris, Phila. Textile; Francine Perry, Quinnipiac; Lynette Richardson, Florida Int'l; Claudia Schleyer, Abilene Christian.
Division III: Deanna Kyle, Scranton; Ann Fitzpatrick, New Rochelle; Terri Schumacher, Wis.-Oshkosh; Tracy Weaver, Muskingum; Jeannie Demers, Buena Vista; Shontel Sherwood, Pomona-Pitzer; Evelyn Oquendo, Salem St.; Maureen Burchill, Southern Me.; Wendy Engelmann, N.C.-Greensboro; Dawn Cillo, New Rochelle.

1986

Division I: Cheryl Miller, Southern Cal; Kamie Ethridge, Texas; Lillie Mason, Western Ky.; Teresa Edwards, Georgia; Cindy Brown, Long Beach St.; Wanda Ford, Drake; Jennifer Gillom, Mississippi; Pam Leake, North Caro.; Katrina McClain, Georgia; Sue Wicks, Rutgers.
Division II: Von Fulmore, N.C. Central; Jackie Harris, Central Mo. St.; Hope Linthicum, Central Conn. St.; Vickie Mitchell, Cal Poly Pomona; Vincene Morris, Phila. Textile; Leone Patterson, Chapman; Delinda Samuel, Delta St.; Claudia Schleyer, Abilene Christian; Diane Walker, Slippery Rock; Lisa Walters, Mankato St.
Division III: Jane Meyer, Elizabethtown; Jeannie Demers, Buena Vista; Cathy Lanni, Rhode Island

Col.; Rinny Lesane, Albany (N.Y.); Una Espenkotter, Scranton; Evelyn Oquendo, Salem St.; Amy Proctor, St. Norbert; Connie Sanford, Heidelberg; Mary Schultz, St. Mary's (Minn.); Pam Stewart, Chris. Newport.

1987

Division I: Cindy Brown, Long Beach St.; Clarissa Davis, Texas; Tracey Hall, Ohio St.; Donna Holt, Virginia; Andrea Lloyd, Texas; Katrina McClain, Georgia; Vickie Orr, Auburn; Shelly Pennefather, Villanova; Teresa Weatherspoon, Louisiana Tech; Sue Wicks, Rutgers.
Division II: Candace Fincher, Valdosta St.; Kim Disbro, Fla. Southern; Jennifer DiMaggio, Pace; Vanessa Wells, West Tex. A&M; Joy Jeter, New Haven; Jackie Dolberry, Hampton; Lisa Walters, Mankato St.; Laura Anderson, Nebraska-Omaha; Debra Larsen, Cal Poly Pomona; Michelle McCoy, Cal Poly Pomona.
Division III: Shelley Parks, Scranton; Torrie Rumph, Kean; Sonja Sorenson, Wis.-Stevens Point; Jessica Beachy, Concordia-M'head; Jeannie Demers, Buena Vista; Michele White, Stony Brook; Trish Neary, Western Conn. St.; Robin Brooks, N.C. Wesleyan; Becky Inman, William Penn; Alfredia Gibbs, Cabrini.

1988

Division I: Michelle Edwards, Iowa; Bridgette Gordon, Tennessee; Tracey Hall, Ohio St.; Donna Holt, Virginia; Suzie McConnell, Penn St.; Vickie Orr, Auburn; Penny Toler, Long Beach St.; Teresa Weatherspoon, Louisiana Tech; Beverly Williams, Texas; Sue Wicks, Rutgers.
Division II: Jennifer DiMaggio, Pace; Jackie Dolberry, Hampton; Cathy Gooden, Cal Poly Pomona; Jill Halapin, Pitt.-Johnstown; Joy Jeter, New Haven; Mary Naughton, Stonehill; Julie Wells, Northern Ky.; Vanessa Wells, West Tex. A&M; Shannon Williams, Valdosta St.; Tammy Wilson, Central Mo. St.
Division III: Jessica Beachy, Concordia-M'head; Catie Cleary, Pine Manor; Lesa Dennis, Emmanuel; Kimm Lacken, Trenton St.; Louise MacDonald, St. John Fisher; Linda Mason, Rust; Patti McCrudden, New York U.; Angie Polk, N.C.-Greensboro; Sonja Sorenson, Wis.-Stevens Point; Michelle Swantner, Elizabethtown.

1989

Division I: Jennifer Azzi, Stanford; Vicky Bullett, Maryland; Clarissa Davis, Texas; Bridgette Gordon, Tennessee; Nora Lewis, Louisiana Tech; Nikita Lowry, Ohio St.; Vickie Orr, Auburn; Chana Perry, San Diego St.; Deanna Tate, Maryland; Penny Toler, Long Beach St.
Division II: Cathy Gooden, Cal Poly Pomona; Jackie Dolberry, Hampton; Joy Jeter, New Haven; Shannon Williams, Valdosta St.; Tammy Wilson, Central Mo. St.; Pat Smykowski, North Dak. St.; Niki Bracken, Cal Poly Pomona; Charlene Taylor, New Haven; Velisa Levett, West Ga.; Teresa Tinner, West Tex. A&M
Division III: Shannon Collins, Centre; Diana Duff, Southern Me.; Kirsten Dumford, Cal St. Stanislaus; Susan Heidt, St. John Fisher; Mona Henriksen, Luther; Nancy Keene, Elizabethtown; Patti McCrudden, New York U.; Tara McGuire, Clark (Mass.); Jillayn Quaschnick, Concordia-M'head; Joan Watzka, St. Norbert.

1990

Division I: Venus Lacy, Louisiana Tech; Jennifer Azzi, Stanford; Dawn Staley, Virginia; Carolyn Jones, Auburn; Andrea Stinson, North Caro. St.; Franthea Price, Iowa; Daedra Charles, Tennessee; Dale Hodges, St. Joseph's (Pa.); Portia Hill, Stephen F. Austin; Wendy Scholtens, Vanderbilt.
Division II: Crystal Hardy, Delta St.; Carmille Barnette, Longwood; Niki Bracken, Cal Poly Pomona; Kammy Brown, Virginia St.; Julie Dabrowski, New Hamp. Col.; Debbie Delie, Oakland; Durene Heisler, North Dak.; Bridget Hale, Pitt.-Johnstown; Shannon Williams, Valdosta St.; Jeannette Yeoman, St. Joseph's (Ind.).
Division III: Kim Beckman, Buena Vista; Cathy Clark, Marietta; Arlene Eagan, Buffalo St.; Robin Gaby, Eastern Conn. St.; Ann Gilbert, Oberlin; Anestine Hector, Clark (Mass.); Susan Heidt, St. John Fisher; Anne Krumrine, Frank. & Marsh.; Michelle Thykeson, Concordia-M'head; Susan Yates, Centre.

1991

Division I: Daedra Charles, Tennessee; Sonja Henning, Stanford; Kerry Bascom, Connecticut; Joy Holmes, Purdue; Andrea Stinson, North Caro. St.; Dawn Staley, Virginia; Genia Miller, Cal St. Fullerton; Delmonica DeHorney, Arkansas; Carolyn Jones, Auburn; Dana Chatman, Louisiana St.
Division II: Joy Barry, Assumption; Dana Bright, Jacksonville St.; Stephanie Coons, Cal Poly Pomona; Jackie Givens, Fort Valley St.; Pat McDonald, West Tex. A&M; Whitney Meier, North Dak.; Sharonda O'Bannon, Bellarmine; Kim Penwell, Bentley; Tracy Saunders, Norfolk St.; Jerri Wiley, Southeast Mo. St.
Division III: Laura Pate, Southern Me.; Arlene Eagan, Buffalo St.; Ann Gilbert, Oberlin; Kathy Beck, Moravian; Karen Jenkins, Roanoke; Lisa Kirchenwitz, Wis.-Oshkosh; Karen Hermann, Washington (Mo.); Missy Sharer, Grinnell; Joyce Spanier, St. Benedict; Laurie Trow, St. Thomas (Minn.).

1992

Division I: Shannon Cate, Montana; Dena Head, Tennessee; MaChelle Joseph, Purdue; Rosemary Kosiorek, West Va.; Tammi Reiss, Virginia; Susan Robinson, Penn St.; Frances Savage, Miami (Fla.); Dawn Staley, Virginia; Sheryl Swoopes, Texas Tech; Val Whiting, Stanford.
Division II: Pat McDonald, West Text. A&M; Lisa Miller, IU/PU-Ft. Wayne; Dana Neilsen, Augustana (S. D.); Laurie Northrop, Portland St.; LaTanya Patty, Delta St.; Kim Penwell, Bentley; Tracie Seymour, Bentley; Nadine Schmidt, North Dak. St.; Tammy Walker-Strode, Edinboro; Mindy Young, Pitt.-Johnstown.
Division III: Kathy Beck, Moravian; Laurie Trow, St. Thomas (Minn.); Sandy Buddelmeyer, Capital; Kathy Roberts, Wartburg; Caryn Cranston, Pomona-Pitzer; Kristen Curtis, Western Conn. St.; Diane Ring, Wis.-Eau Claire; Donna Cogar, Roanoke; Stephanie Sullivan, Wis.-Platteville; Trish Harvey, Luther.

1993

Division I: Andrea Congreaves, Mercer; Toni Foster, Iowa; Lauretta Freeman, Auburn; Heidi Gillingham, Vanderbilt; Lisa Harrison, Tennessee; Katie Smith, Ohio St.; Karen Jennings, Nebraska; Sheryl Swoopes, Texas Tech; Milica Vukadinovic, California; Val Whiting, Stanford.
Division II: Carolyn Brown, St. Augustine's; Jody Buck, North Dak. St.; Shelley Foster, Washburn; Yolanda Griffith, Fla. Atlantic; Jeannine Jean-Pierre, Edinboro; Amy Molina, St. Michael's;

Dana Nielsen, Augustana (S. D.); LaTanya Patty, Delta St.; Rachel Rosario, UC Riverside; Courtney Sands, Indianapolis.

Division III: Laurie Trow, St. Thomas (Minn.); Sandy Buddelmeyer, Capital; Julie Maki, Wis.-Stout; Lynne Kempski, Scranton; Kelly Mahlum, St. Benedict; Tracy Wilson, Central (Iowa); Leah Onks, Maryville (Tenn.); Sladja Kovijanic, Middlebury; Kathy Roberts, Wartburg; Donna Layne, New York U.

WBCA

1982

University Division: Pam Kelly, Louisiana Tech; Angela Turner, Louisiana Tech; Barbara Kennedy, Clemson; Valerie Walker, Cheyney; June Olkowski, Rutgers; Cathy Boswell, Illinois St.; Anne Donovan, Old Dominion; Sheila Foster, South Caro.; Paula McGee, Southern Cal; LaTaunya Pollard, Long Beach St.

College Division: Pam Brisby, Mo. Southern St.; Sherry Raney-Lovaas, Arkansas Tech; Laura Buehning, Cal Poly SLO; Holly Stilley, Charleston; Donna Hammond, UC Riverside; Robin Mortensen, St. John Fisher; Carol Welch, Cal Poly Pomona; Jackie White, Cal Poly Pomona; Alison Fay, Bentley; Kelli Litsch, Southwestern Okla.

U. S. BASKETBALL WRITERS ASSOCIATION

1988

Suzie McConnell, Penn St.; Michelle Edwards, Iowa; Vickie Orr, Auburn; Sue Wicks, Rutgers; Bridgette Gordon, Tennessee.

1989

Clarissa Davis, Texas; Chana Perry, San Diego St.; Bridgette Gordon, Tennessee; Vickie Orr, Auburn; Vicky Bullett, Maryland.

1990

Jennifer Azzi, Stanford; Dale Hodges, St. Joseph's (Pa.); Venus Lacy, Louisiana Tech; Andrea Stinson, North Caro. St.; Portia Hill, Stephen F. Austin.

1991

Dawn Staley, Virginia; Dana Chatman, Louisiana St.; Genia Miller, Cal St. Fullerton; Delmonica DeHorney, Arkansas; Andrea Stinson, North Caro. St.

1992

Dawn Staley, Virginia; Sheryl Swoopes, Texas Tech; Val Whiting, Stanford; Dena Head, Tennessee; Susan Robinson, Penn St.; MaChelle Joseph, Purdue.

1993

Sheryl Swoopes, Texas Tech; Heidi Gillingham, Vanderbilt; Val Whiting, Stanford; Natalie Williams, UCLA; Lisa Leslie, Southern Cal.

NAISMITH TROPHY FINALISTS

These teams represent the five finalists for the Naismith Trophy presented by the Atlanta Tip-Off Club.

1983

Anne Donovan, Old Dominion; Valerie Still, Kentucky; Cheryl Miller, Southern Cal; LaTaunya Pollard, Long Beach St.; Janice Lawrence, Louisiana Tech.

1984

Cheryl Miller, Southern Cal; Janet Harris, Georgia; Janice Lawrence, Louisiana Tech; Kim Mulkey, Louisiana Tech; Medina Dixon, Old Dominion.

1985

Cheryl Miller, Southern Cal; Janet Harris, Georgia; Medina Dixon, Old Dominion; Andrea Lloyd, Texas; Pam Gant, Louisiana Tech.

1986

Cheryl Miller, Southern Cal; Cindy Brown, Long Beach St.; Teresa Edwards, Georgia; Kamie Ethridge, Texas; Andrea Lloyd, Texas.

1987

Clarissa Davis, Texas; Cindy Brown, Long Beach St.; Katrina McClain, Georgia; Andrea Lloyd, Texas; Clemette Haskins, Western Ky.

1988

Michelle Edwards, Iowa; Bridgette Gordon, Tennessee; Vickie Orr, Auburn; Teresa Weatherspoon, Louisiana Tech; Sue Wicks, Rutgers.

1989

Vickie Orr, Auburn; Vicky Bullett, Maryland; Bridgette Gordon, Tennessee; Clarissa Davis, Texas; Penny Toler, Long Beach St.

1990

Jennifer Azzi, Stanford; Venus Lacy, Louisiana Tech; Dale Hodges, St. Joseph's (Pa.); Paulette Jordan, Nevada-Las Vegas; Andrea Stinson, North Caro. St.

1992

Susan Robinson, Penn St.; MaChelle Joseph, Purdue; Val Whiting, Stanford; Dena Head, Tennessee; Dawn Staley, Virginia.

NAISMITH TROPHY

First presented in 1983 by the Atlanta Tip-Off Club and voted on by a panel of media and coaches. Named after Dr. James Naismith, inventor of basketball.

Year	Player, Team
1983	Anne Donovan, Old Dominion
1984	Cheryl Miller, Southern Cal
1985	Cheryl Miller, Southern Cal
1986	Cheryl Miller, Southern Cal
1987	Clarissa Davis, Texas
1988	Sue Wicks, Rutgers
1989	Clarissa Davis, Texas
1990	Jennifer Azzi, Stanford
1991	Dawn Staley, Virginia
1992	Dawn Staley, Virginia
1993	Sheryl Swoopes, Texas Tech

NAISMITH LIFETIME ACHIEVEMENT AWARD

Presented by the Atlanta Tip-Off Club.

Year	Recipient
1992	Margaret Wade

WADE TROPHY

First presented in 1978 by the National Association for Girls and Women in Sport (NAGWS). Named after former Delta State head coach Margaret Wade.

Year	Player, Team
1978	Carol Blazejowski, Montclair St.
1979	Nancy Lieberman, Old Dominion

1980 Nancy Lieberman, Old Dominion
1981 Lynette Woodard, Kansas
1982 Pam Kelly, Louisiana Tech
1983 LaTaunya Pollard, Long Beach St.
1984 Janice Lawrence, Louisiana Tech
1985 Cheryl Miller, Southern Cal
1986 Kamie Ethridge, Texas
1987 Shelly Pennefather, Villanova
1988 Teresa Weatherspoon, Louisiana Tech
1989 Clarissa Davis, Texas
1990 Jennifer Azzi, Stanford
1991 Daedra Charles, Tennessee
1992 Susan Robinson, Penn St.
1993 To be announced November 1993

FRANCES POMEROY NAISMITH AWARD

First presented in 1984 to the outstanding female senior collegian under 5-6 in height.

Year	Player, Team
1984	Kim Mulkey, Louisiana Tech
1985	Maria Stack, Georgia
1986	Kamie Ethridge, Texas
1987	Rhonda Windham, Southern Cal
1988	Suzie McConnell, Penn St.
1989	Paulette Backstrom, Bowling Green
1990	Julie Dabrowski, New Hampshire
1991	Shanya Evans, Providence
1992	Rosemary Kosiorek, West Va.
1993	Dena Evans, Virginia

BRODERICK AWARD

First presented in 1977 by the late Thomas Broderick. Honda has presented the award since 1987. The winner of the award is nominated for the Honda Award, which recognizes the collegiate woman athlete of the year.

Year	Player, Team
1977	Lusia Harris, Delta St.
1978	Ann Meyers, UCLA
1979	Nancy Lieberman, Old Dominion
1980	Nancy Lieberman, Old Dominion
1981	Lynette Woodard, Kansas
1982	Pam Kelly, Louisiana Tech
1983	Anne Donovan, Old Dominion
1984	Cheryl Miller, Southern Cal
1985	Cheryl Miller, Southern Cal
1986	Cheryl Miller, Southern Cal
1987	Kamie Ethridge, Texas
1988	Katrina McClain, Georgia
1989	Teresa Weatherspoon, Louisiana Tech
1990	Bridgette Gordon, Tennessee
1991	Dawn Staley, Virginia

WBCA PLAYER OF THE YEAR

First presented in 1983 by Champion athletics manufacturer. Voted on by Women's Basketball Coaches Association membership.

Year	Player, Team
1983	Div. I: Anne Donovan, Old Dominion Div. II: Jackie White, Cal Poly Pomona Div. III: Margie O'Brien, Clark (Mass.)
1984	Div. I: Janice Lawrence, Louisiana Tech Div. II: Carla Eades, Central Mo. St. Div. III: Page Lutz, Elizabethtown
1985	Div. I: Cheryl Miller, Southern Cal Div. II: Rosie Jones, Central Mo. St. Div. III: Deanna Kyle, Scranton
1986	Div. I: Cheryl Miller, Southern Cal Div. II: Vickie Mitchell, Cal Poly Pomona Div. III: Jane Meyer, Elizabethtown
1987	Div. I: Katrina McClain, Georgia Div. II: Debra Larsen, Cal Poly Pomona Div. III: Shelley Parks, Scranton
1988	Div. I: Michelle Edwards, Iowa Div. II: Vanessa Wells, West Tex. A&M Div. III: Jessica Beachy, Concordia-M'head
1989	Div. I: Clarissa Davis, Texas Div. II: Cathy Gooden, Cal Poly Pomona Div. III: Kirsten Dumford, Cal St. Stanislaus
1990	Div. I: Venus Lacy, Louisiana Tech Div. II: Crystal Hardy, Delta St. Div. III: Susan Heidt, St. John Fisher
1991	Div. I: Dawn Staley, Virginia Div. II: Tracy Saunders, Norfolk St. Div. III: Ann Gilbert, Oberlin
1992	Div. I: Dawn Staley, Virginia Div. II: Mindy Young, Pitt.-Johnstown Div. III: Kathy Beck, Moravian
1993	Div. I: Sheryl Swoopes, Texas Tech Div. II: Yolanda Griffith, Fla. Atlantic Div. III: Laurie Trow, St. Thomas (Minn.)

NCAA TEAM OF THE DECADE—1980s

Selected in 1991 by a panel of media and former and current members of the NCAA Division I Women's Basketball Committee. Players must have played in a Women's Final Four.

Cheryl Miller, Southern Cal, captain; Janice Lawrence, Louisiana Tech; Teresa Weatherspoon, Louisiana Tech; Clarissa Davis, Texas; Bridgette Gordon, Tennessee.

NAISMITH COACH OF THE YEAR

Year	Coach, Team
1987	Pat Summitt, Tennessee
1988	Leon Barmore, Louisiana Tech
1989	Pat Summitt, Tennessee
1990	Tara VanDerveer, Stanford
1991	Debbie Ryan, Virginia
1992	Chris Weller, Maryland
1993	Vivian Stringer, Iowa

WBCA COACH OF THE YEAR

First presented in 1983 by Converse athletics manufacturer. Voted on by Women's Basketball Coaches Association membership.

Year		Coach, Team
1983	Div. I:	Pat Summitt, Tennessee
	Div. II:	Jorja Hoehn, Central Mo. St.
	Div. III:	Wayne Morgan, North Central
1984	Div. I:	Jody Conradt, Texas
	Div. II:	Linda Makowski, Dayton
	Div. III:	A. J. Stovall, Rust
1985	Div. I:	Jim Foster, St. Joseph's (Pa.)
	Div. II:	Jorja Hoehn, Central Mo. St.
	Div. III:	Mike Strong, Scranton
1986	Div. I:	Jody Conradt, Texas
	Div. II:	Brenda Reilly, Central Conn. St.
	Div. III:	Tim Shea, Salem St.
1987	Div. I:	Theresa Grentz, Rutgers
	Div. II:	Nancy Winstel, Northern Ky.
	Div. III:	Linda Wunder, Wis.-Stevens Point

1988 Div. I: Vivian Stringer, Iowa
Div. II: Darlene May, Cal Poly Pomona
Div. III: Duane Siverson, Concordia-M'head

1989 Div. I: Tara VanDerveer, Stanford
Div. II: Jane Williamson, West Ga.
Div. III: LeAnn Heinrich, Cal St. Stanislaus

1990 Div. I: Kay Yow, North Caro. St.
Div. II: Darlene May, Cal Poly Pomona
Div. III: Sue Wise, Hope

1991 Div. I: Rene Portland, Penn St.
Div. II: James Sweat, Norfolk St.
Div. III: Donna Newberry, Muskingum

1992 Div. I: Ferne Labati, Miami (Fla.)
Div. II: Barbara Stevens, Bentley
Div. III: Mary Beth Spirk, Moravian

1993 Div. I: Vivian Stringer, Iowa
Div. II: Amy Ruley, North Dak. St.
Div. III: Mike Durbin, St. Benedict

CAROL ECKMAN AWARD

First presented in 1983 to the coach that shows spirit, integrity and courage in coaching women's basketball. The award is named in honor of the late Carol Eckman, former West Chester coach, who died in 1985.

Year	Coach, Team
1986	Laura Mapp, Bridgewater (Va.)
1987	Jody Conradt, Texas
1988	Kay Yow, North Caro. St.
1989	Linda Hill-MacDonald, Minnesota
1990	Maryalyce Jeremiah, Cal St. Fullerton
1991	Marian Washington, Kansas
1992	Jill Hutchison, Illinois St.
1993	Vivian Stringer, Iowa

UNITED STATES OLYMPIC TEAMS

1976 in Montreal, Canada (Silver Medal)
Cindy Brogdon, Mercer
Nancy Dunkle, Cal St. Fullerton
Lusia Harris, Delta St.
Pat Head, Tennessee
Charlotte Lewis, Illinois St.
Nancy Lieberman, Far Rockaway, Queens, N. Y.
Gail Marquis, Queens (N.Y.)
Ann Meyers, UCLA
Mary Anne O'Connor, Southern Conn. St.
Patricia Roberts, Emporia St.
Sue Rojcewicz, Southern Conn. St.
Juliene Simpson, John F. Kennedy
Coach: Billie Moore, Cal St. Fullerton
Assistant: Sue Gunter, Stephen F. Austin

1980 in Moscow, Russia (boycotted Moscow Games)
Carol Blazejowski, Montclair St.
Denise Curry, UCLA
Anne Donovan, Old Dominion
Tara Heiss, Maryland
Kris Kirchner, Maryland
Debra Miller, Boston U.
Cindy Noble, Tennessee
LaTaunya Pollard, Long Beach St.
Jill Rankin, Tennessee
Rosie Walker, Stephen F. Austin
Holly Warlick, Tennessee
Lynette Woodard, Kansas
Coach: Sue Gunter, Stephen F. Austin
Assistant; Pat Head, Tennessee

1984 in Los Angeles, California (Gold Medal)
Cathy Boswell, Illinois St.
Denise Curry, UCLA
Anne Donovan, Old Dominion
Teresa Edwards, Georgia
Lea Henry, Tennessee
Janice Lawrence, Louisiana Tech
Pam McGee, Southern Cal
Cheryl Miller, Southern Cal
Kim Mulkey, Louisiana Tech
Cindy Noble, Tennessee
Carol Menken Schaudt, Oregon St.
Lynette Woodard, Kansas
Coach: Pat Head Summitt, Tennessee
Assistants: Kay Yow, North Caro. St.; Nancy Darsch, Tennessee

1988 in Seoul, South Korea (Gold Medal)
Cindy Brown, Long Beach St.
Vicky Bullett, Maryland
Cynthia Cooper, Southern Cal
Anne Donovan, Old Dominion
Teresa Edwards, Georgia
Kamie Ethridge, Texas
Jennifer Gillom, Mississippi
Bridgette Gordon, Tennessee
Andrea Lloyd, Texas
Katrina McClain, Georgia
Suzie McConnell, Penn St.
Teresa Weatherspoon, Louisiana Tech
Coach: Kay Yow, North Caro. St.
Assistants; Susan Yow, Drake; Sylvia Hatchell, North Caro.

1992 in Barcelona, Spain (Bronze Medal)
Vicky Bullett, Maryland
Deadra Charles, Tennessee
Cynthia Cooper, Southern Cal
Clarissa Davis, Texas
Medina Dixon, Old Dominion
Teresa Edwards, Georgia
Tammy Jackson, Florida
Carolyn Jones, Auburn
Katrina McClain, Georgia
Suzie McConnell, Penn St.
Vickie Orr, Auburn
Teresa Weatherspoon, Louisiana Tech
Coach: Theresa Grentz, Rutgers
Assistants: Lin Dunn, Purdue; Jim Foster, Vanderbilt; Linda Hargrove, Wichita St.

DIVISION I WOMEN'S FIRST-TEAM ALL-AMERICANS BY COLLEGE

ARKANSAS
91—Delmonica DeHorney

AUBURN
84—Becky Jackson
87—Vickie Orr
88—Vickie Orr
89—Vickie Orr
90—Carolyn Jones
91—Carolyn Jones
93—Lauretta Freeman

BAYLOR
77—Susie Snider Eppers

BRIGHAM YOUNG
80—Tina Gunn

CALIFORNIA
93—Milica Vukadinovic

CAL ST. FULLERTON
75—Nancy Dunkle
76—Nancy Dunkle
77—Nancy Dunkle
91—Genia Miller

CHEYNEY
81—Valerie Walker
82—Valerie Walker
84—Yolanda Laney

CLEMSON
82—Barbara Kennedy

CONNECTICUT
91—Kerry Bascom

DELTA ST.
75—Lusia Harris
76—Lusia Harris
77—Lusia Harris
78—Debbie Brock

DRAKE
86—Wanda Ford

ELON
75—Susan Yow

GEORGIA
82—Janet Harris
84—Janet Harris
85—Janet Harris
Teresa Edwards
86—Teresa Edwards
Katrina McClain
87—Katrina McClain

ILLINOIS ST.
77—Charlotte Lewis
82—Cathy Boswell

IMMACULATA
75—Marianne Crawford
76—Marianne
Crawford Stanley
77—Mary Scharff

INDIANA
75—Debbie Oing

IOWA
88—Michelle Edwards
90—Franthea Price
93—Toni Foster

KANSAS
78—Lynette Woodard
79—Lynette Woodard
80—Lynette Woodard
81—Lynette Woodard

KANSAS ST.
83—Priscilla Gary

KENTUCKY
82—Valerie Still
83—Valerie Still

LONG BEACH ST.
81—LaTaunya Pollard
82—LaTaunya Pollard
83—LaTaunya Pollard
85—Kirsten Cummings
86—Cindy Brown
87—Cindy Brown
88—Penny Toler
89—Penny Toler

LOUISIANA ST.
78—Julie Gross
83—Joyce Walker
84—Joyce Walker
91—Dana Chatman

LOUISIANA TECH
80—Pam Kelly
81—Pam Kelly
82—Pam Kelly
Angela Turner
83—Janice Lawrence
84—Janice Lawrence
Kim Mulkey
85—Pam Gant
87—Teresa Weatherspoon
88—Teresa Weatherspoon
89—Nora Lewis
90—Venus Lacy

MARYLAND
83—Jasmina Perazic
89—Deanna Tate
Vicky Bullet

MERCER
76—Cindy Brogdon
93—Andrea Congreaves

MIAMI (FLA.)
92—Frances Savage

MISSISSIPPI
86—Jennifer Gillom

MISSISSIPPI COL.
77—Rita Easterling

MONTANA
92—Shannon Cate

MONTCLAIR ST.
76—Carol Blazejowski
77—Carol Blazejowski
78—Carol Blazejowski
79—Pat Colasardo

NEBRASKA
93—Karen Jennings

NORTH CARO.
84—Tresa Brown
86—Pam Leake

NORTH CARO. ST.
76—Susan Yow
78—Genia Beasley
90—Andrea Stinson
91—Andrea Stinson

NORTHEAST LA.
85—Eun Jung Lee

NORTHWESTERN
85—Anucha Browne

OHIO ST.
79—Franci Washington
87—Tracey Hall
88—Tracey Hall
89—Nikita Lowry
93—Katie Smith

OLD DOMINION
78—Nancy Lieberman
79—Nancy Lieberman
80—Nancy Lieberman
Inge Nissen
81—Anne Donovan
82—Anne Donovan
83—Anne Donovan
84—Medina Dixon
85—Medina Dixon

OREGON
81—Bev Smith
82—Bev Smith

OREGON ST.
81—Carol Menken

PENN ST.
88—Suzie McConnell
92—Susan Robinson

PURDUE
91—Joy Holmes
92—MaChelle Joseph

QUEENS (N.Y.)
78—Althea Gwyn

RUTGERS
81—Kris Kirchner
82—June Olkowski
86—Sue Wicks
87—Sue Wicks
88—Sue Wicks

ST. JOSEPH'S (PA.)
90—Dale Hodges

SAN DIEGO ST.
89—Chana Perry

SOUTH CARO.
82—Sheila Foster

SOUTHERN CAL
82—Paula McGee
83—Paula McGee
Cheryl Miller
84—Cheryl Miller
Pam McGee
85—Cheryl Miller
86—Cheryl Miller

SOUTHERN CONN. ST.
75—Sue Rojcewicz

STANFORD
89—Jennifer Azzi
90—Jennifer Azzi
91—Sonja Henning
92—Val Whiting
93—Val Whiting

STEPHEN F. AUSTIN
76—Doris Felderhoff
77—Doris Felderhoff
79—Rosie Walker
80—Rosie Walker
90—Portia Hill

TEMPLE
84—Marilyn Stephens

TENNESSEE
77—Patricia Roberts
78—Cindy Brogdon
79—Cindy Brogdon
80—Jill Rankin
Holly Warlick
81—Cindy Noble
82—Mary Ostrowski
83—Tanya Haave
85—Sheila Collins
88—Bridgette Gordon
89—Bridgette Gordon
90—Daedra Charles
91—Daedra Charles
92—Dena Head
93—Lisa Harrison

TENNESSEE TECH
82—Jerilynn Harper

TEXAS
84—Annette Smith
85—Kamie Ethridge
86—Kamie Ethridge
87—Andrea Lloyd
Clarissa Davis
88—Beverly Williams
89—Clarissa Davis

TEXAS TECH
92—Sheryl Swoopes
93—Sheryl Swoopes

UCLA
75—Ann Meyers
76—Ann Meyers
77—Ann Meyers
78—Ann Meyers
79—Denise Curry

80—Denise Curry
81—Denise Curry

VALDOSTA ST.
79—Carol Chason
Susan Taylor
80—Susan Taylor

VANDERBILT
90—Wendy Scholtens
93—Heidi Gillingham

VILLANOVA
87—Shelly Pennefather

VIRGINIA
87—Donna Holt
88—Donna Holt
90—Dawn Staley
91—Dawn Staley
92—Tammi Reiss
Dawn Staley

WAYLAND BAPTIST
75—Carolyn Bush
Brenda Moeller
76—Pearl Worrell
78—Kathy Harston
79—Jill Rankin

WEST VA.
92—Rosemary Kosiorek

WESTERN KY.
86—Lillie Mason
87—Clemette Haskins

WILLIAM PENN
75—Jan Irby
76—Susie Kudrna

Teams Used for Selections:
Women's Basketball Coaches Assn. (KODAK)—1975-93
Naismith—1982-90, 92-93
U. S. Basketball Writers—1988-93

DIVISIONS II AND III WOMEN'S FIRST-TEAM ALL-AMERICANS BY COLLEGE

ABILENE CHRISTIAN
84—Claudia Schleyer
85—Claudia Schleyer
86—Claudia Schleyer

ALBANY (N.Y.)
86—Rinny Lesane

ARKANSAS TECH
82—Sherry Raney Lovaas

ASSUMPTION
91—Joy Barry

AUGUSTANA (S. D.)
92—Dana Nielsen
93—Dana Nielsen

BELLARMINE
91—Sharonda O'Bannon

BENTLEY
82—Alison Fay
83—Alison Fay
91—Kim Penwell
92—Kim Penwell
Tracie Seymour

BERRY
83—Mary Beasley

BUENA VISTA
85—Jeannie Demers
86—Jeannie Demers
87—Jeannie Demers
90—Kim Beckman

BUFFALO ST.
90—Arlene Eagan
91—Arlene Eagan

CABRINI
87—Alfredia Gibbs

CAL POLY POMONA
82—Carol Welch
Jackie White
83—Carol Welch
Jackie White
86—Vickie Mitchell
87—Debra Larsen
Michelle McCoy
88—Cathy Gooden
89—Cathy Gooden
Niki Bracken
90—Niki Bracken
91—Stephanie Coons

CAL POLY SLO
82—Laura Buehning

CAL ST. STANISLAUS
89—Kirsten Dumford

UC RIVERSIDE
82—Donna Hammond
93—Rachel Rosario

CAPITAL
92—Sandy Buddelmeyer
93—Sandy Buddelmeyer

CENTRAL CONN. ST.
86—Hope Linthicum

CENTRAL (IOWA)
93—Tracy Wilson

CENTRAL MO. ST.
83—Carla Eades
84—Carla Eades
85—Rosie Jones
86—Jackie Harris
88—Tammy Wilson
89—Tammy Wilson

CENTRE
89—Shannon Collins
90—Susan Yates

CHAPMAN
86—Leone Patterson

CHARLESTON
82—Holly Stilley
83—Regina Brown

CHRIS. NEWPORT
86—Pam Stewart

CLARK (MASS.)
83—Margie O'Brien
89—Tara McGuire
90—Anestine Hector

COLBY
84—Kaye Cross

CONCORDIA-M'HEAD
87—Jessica Beachy
88—Jessica Beachy
89—Jillayn Quaschnick
90—Michelle Thykeson

DAYTON
84—Donna Burks

DELTA ST.
86—Delinda Samuel
90—Crystal Hardy
92—LaTanya Patty
93—LaTanya Patty

EASTERN CONN. ST.
90—Robin Gaby

EDINBORO
92—Tammy Walker-Strode
93—Jeannine Jean-Pierre

ELIZABETHTOWN
84—Page Lutz
Sherri Kinsey
86—Jane Meyer
88—Michelle Swantner
89—Nancy Keene

EMMANUEL
88—Lesa Dennis

ERSKINE
84—Beth Couture

FLA. ATLANTIC
93—Yolanda Griffith

FLORIDA INT'L
85—Lynette Richardson

FLA. SOUTHERN
87—Kim Disbro

FORT VALLEY ST.
91—Jackie Givens

FRANCIS MARION
83—Daphne Donnelly

FRANK. & MARSH.
90—Anne Krumrine

GRINNELL
91—Missy Sharer

GROVE CITY
83—Jody Imbrie

HAMPTON
85—Darlene Chaney
Anita Cooper
87—Jackie Dolberry
88—Jackie Dolberry
89—Jackie Dolberry

HARTWICK
84—Sandy Gangell

HEIDELBERG
86—Connie Sanford

INDIANAPOLIS
93—Courtney Sands

IU/PU-FT. WAYNE
92—Lisa Miller

JACKSONVILLE ST.
91—Dana Bright

KEAN
84—Sallie Maxwell
87—Torrie Rumph

LEWIS
85—Julie Fruendt

LONGWOOD
90—Carmille Barnette

LUTHER
89—Mona Henriksen
92—Trish Harvey

LYNCHBURG
83—Betty Jackson

MANKATO ST.
86—Lisa Walters
87—Lisa Walters

MARIETTA
90—Cathy Clark

MARYVILLE (TENN.)
93—Leah Onks

MIDDLEBURY
93—Sladja Kovijanic

MO. SOUTHERN ST.
82—Pam Brisby

MORAVIAN
91—Kathy Beck
92—Kathy Beck

MUSKINGUM
85—Tracy Weaver

NEBRASKA-OMAHA
87—Laura Anderson

NEW HAMP. COL.
90—Julie Dabrowski

NEW HAVEN
87—Joy Jeter
88—Joy Jeter
89—Joy Jeter
Charlene Taylor

NEW ROCHELLE
84—Lois Salto
85—Dawn Cillo
Ann Fitzpatrick

NEW YORK U.
88—Patti McCrudden
89—Patti McCrudden
93—Donna Layne

NORFOLK ST.
91—Tracy Saunders

N.C. CENTRAL
86—Von Fulmore

N.C.-GREENSBORO
83—Michele Blazevich
85—Wendy Engelmann
88—Angie Polk

N.C. WESLEYAN
87—Robin Brooks

NORTH CENTRAL
83—Bonnie Jansen

NORTH DAK.
90—Durene Heisler
91—Whitney Meier

NORTH DAK. ST.
89—Pat Smykowski
92—Nadine Schmidt
93—Jody Buck

NORTHERN ILL.
84—Candy Crosby

NORTHERN KY.
88—Julie Wells

OAKLAND
83—Linda Krawford
90—Debbie Delie

OBERLIN
90—Ann Gilbert
91—Ann Gilbert

PACE
87—Jennifer DiMaggio
88—Jennifer DiMaggio

PHILA. TEXTILE
85—Vincene Morris
86—Vincene Morris

PINE MANOR
88—Catie Cleary

PITT.-JOHNSTOWN
88—Jill Halapin
90—Bridget Hale
92—Mindy Young

POMONA-PITZER
83—Carol Ferren
85—Shontel Sherwood
92—Caryn Cranston

PORTLAND
84—Lorena Legarde

PORTLAND ST.
92—Laurie Northrop

QUINNIPIAC
84—Francine Perry
85—Francine Perry

RHODE ISLAND COL.
86—Cathy Lanni

ROANOKE
91—Karen Jenkins
92—Donna Cogar

RUST
88—Linda Mason

ST. ANDREWS
84—Eva Marie Pittman

ST. ANSELM
85—Rachel Jackson

ST. AUGUSTINE'S
93—Carolyn Brown

ST. BENEDICT
91—Joyce Spanier
93—Kelly Mahlum

ST. JOHN FISHER
82—Robin Mortensen
83—Robin Mortensen
88—Louise MacDonald
89—Susan Heidt
90—Susan Heidt

ST. JOSEPH'S (IND.)
90—Jeannette Yeoman

ST. MARY'S (MINN.)
86—Mary Schultz

ST. MICHAEL'S
93—Amy Molina

ST. NORBERT
86—Amy Proctor
89—Joan Watzka

ST. THOMAS (MINN.)
91—Laurie Trow
92—Laurie Trow
93—Laurie Trow

SALEM ST.
84—Evelyn Oquendo
85—Evelyn Oquendo
86—Evelyn Oquendo

SCRANTON
83—Fran Harkins
85—Deanna Kyle
86—Una Espenkotter
87—Shelley Parks
93—Lynne Kempski

SHIPPENSBURG
84—Stacey Cunningham

SIMPSON
83—Laurie Sankey
84—Laurie Sankey

SLIPPERY ROCK
86—Diane Walker

SOUTHEAST MO. ST.
91—Jerri Wiley

SOUTHERN ME.
83—Maureen Burchill
85—Maureen Burchill
89—Diana Duff
91—Laura Pate

STONEHILL
88—Mary Naughton

STONY BROOK
87—Michele White

SOUTHWESTERN OKLA.
83—Kelli Litsch
84—Kelli Litsch

TRENTON ST.
88—Kimm Lacken

UTICA
85—Sharon Lyke

VALDOSTA ST.
84—Janice Washington
87—Candace Fincher
88—Shannon Williams
89—Shannon Williams
90—Shannon Williams

VIRGINIA ST.
90—Kammy Brown

WARTBURG
92—Kathy Roberts
93—Kathy Roberts

WASHBURN
93—Shelley Foster

WASHINGTON (MO.)
91—Karen Hermann

WEST GA.
89—Velisa Levett

WEST TEX. A&M
87—Vanessa Wells
88—Vanessa Wells
89—Teresa Tinner
91—Pat McDonald
92—Pat McDonald

WESTERN CONN. ST.
87—Trish Neary
92—Kristen Curtis

WILKES
84—Deanna Kyle

WILLIAM PENN
83—Leslie Spencer
87—Becky Inman

WIS.-EAU CLAIRE
92—Diane Ring

WIS.-OSHKOSH
85—Terri Schumacher
91—Lisa Kirchenwitz

WIS.-PLATTEVILLE
92—Stephanie Sullivan

WIS.-STEVENS POINT
87—Sonja Sorenson
88—Sonja Sorenson

WIS.-STOUT
93—Julie Maki

NCAA POSTGRADUATE SCHOLARSHIP WINNERS BY COLLEGE

Following are women basketball players who are NCAA Postgraduate Scholarship winners, whether or not they were able to accept the grant, plus all alternates indicated by (*) who accepted grants. The program began with the 1982 season. To qualify, student-athletes must maintain a 3.000 grade-point average (on a 4.000 scale) during their collegiate careers and perform with distinction in varsity basketball.

ABILENE CHRISTIAN
86—Claudia Schleyer
90—Sheryl Johnson
92—Terry Crow

AIR FORCE
85—Mary Manning
87—Amy Hartfield

ALBION
93—Jennifer Kennedy

ALMA
90—Kelly Spalding

APPALACHIAN ST.
88—Jane Dalton

ASHLAND
91—Jodi Ireland

AUGUSTANA (S. D.)
91—Bridget Lindquist

BENTLEY
93—Kimberly Penwell

BETHANY (W. VA.)
91—Denise Doster

BOWLING GREEN
90—Angelene Bonner

BROWN
86—Christa Champion

BUFFALO
85—Michelle Stiles

UC DAVIS
83—Carol Rische

CAL POLY POMONA
83—Carol Welch

CAL POLY SLO
82—Laura Buehning
90—*Jody Hasselfield

CAL ST. SACRAMENTO
86—Heidi Carroll

CAPITAL
93—Sandy Buddelmeyer

CENTRAL MICH.
86—*Betsy Yonkman
87—Jody Beerman
91—Sue Nissen

CENTRAL MO. ST.
84—Carla Eades

CHEYNEY
84—Yolanda Laney

CHICAGO
91—Kristin Maschka

COLORADO COL.
84—Deborah Nalty

CONCORDIA-M'HEAD
88—Jessica Beachy

CONNECTICUT
85—Leigh Curl
92—Wendy Davis

CREIGHTON
88—Pamela Gradoville
92—Kathy Halligan

DARTMOUTH
82—Gail Koziara
90—*Sophia Neely

DELTA ST.
90—Crystal Hardy

DRAKE
82—Connie Newlin
91—Jan Jensen

EAST CARO.
83—Mary Denkler

EAST TENN. ST.
83—Marsha Cowart
91—Nicole Hopson

ELIZABETHTOWN
86—Jane Meyer

EVANSVILLE
85—Michelle Adlard

FDU-MADISON
89—Daria Klachko

FORDHAM
92—Nicole Williams

FRESNO ST.
87—Wendy Martell

GEORGE MASON
92—Deborah Taneyhill

GEORGIA ST.
88—Tracy Cheek

GEO. WASHINGTON
85—Kathleen Marshall
93—Jennifer Shasky

GORDON
93—Carrie Dahl

GRINNELL
90—Laura Van Sickle

HAMILTON
88—Dawn Roselli

HARTWICK
84—Sally Gangell

HARVARD
93—Erin Maher

IU/PU-FT. WAYNE
92—Lisa Miller

IOWA
88—Jolynn Schneider

JACKSON ST.
84—Vanetta Robinson

KANSAS
92—Geri Hart

LA SALLE
93—Jennifer Cole

LOUISIANA ST.
85—*Madeline Doucet

LOUISIANA TECH
82—Angela Turner
83—Jennifer White
84—Kim Mulkey
86—Kay Konerza

LUTHER
83—Desiree Kempcke
87—Anne Smith
92—Trish Harvey

MAINE
91—Rachel Bouchard

MANHATTAN
87—Stacia Jack

MANHATTANVILLE
82—Theresa Carey

MARSHALL
93—Tracy Krueger

MIAMI (FLA.)
90—*Elaine Harlow

MICHIGAN ST.
86—*Kelly Belanger

MISSOURI
85—Joni Davis

MIT
90—Maureen Fahey
93—Portia Lewis

MUHLENBERG
82—Rebecca Zuurbier

MURRAY ST.
90—*Melissa Huffman

NAVY
87—*Shelly Laurilla

NEBRASKA
93—Karen Jennings

NEB. WESLEYAN
86—*Kimberly Hissong

NEW MEXICO ST.
83—Tana Fallon

NORTH CARO. ST.
84—*Claudia Kreicker

NORTH DAK.
92—Jennifer Walter

NORTHWEST MO. ST.
84—*Diane Kloewer

OAKLAND
90—Debbie Delie

OHIO
86—Caroline Mast

OHIO ST.
84—*Kelly Robinson

OHIO WESLEYAN
88—Ann Osborne

OLD DOMINION
83—Anne Donovan

OREGON
90—Stefanie Kasperski

OREGON ST.
93—Margo Evashevski

PACE
88—Amy Acker

PENN ST.
92—Susan Robinson

POMONA-PITZER
83—Carol Ferren

PORTLAND ST.
92—Martha Shelton

PRINCETON
90—Sandi Bittler

PURDUE
82—Susan Bartz

REGIS (COLO.)
85—Waverly Dodrill

ROCHESTER
82—Josephine Lavin

ROLLINS
85—Mary McDaniel

RUTGERS
87—Kristen Foley

ST. FRANCIS (PA.)
82—Colleen Curley

ST. MARY'S (CAL.)
91—Anja Bordt

SCRANTON
87—Una Espenkotter

SKIDMORE
93—Deirdre Passarello

SOUTH DAK.
87—Jean Misterek

SOUTH DAK. ST.
88—Tara Tessier
91—Laurie Kruse

SPRINGFIELD
82—Anita Thomas

TAMPA
87—Catherine Fox

TENNESSEE
83—Ludi Henry
84—Tanya Haave

TEXAS-SAN ANTONIO
85—Margaret Martinovich

TEXAS TECH
92—Jennifer Buck

TOLEDO
84—Mitzi Hallinan

UPSALA
84—Elizabeth Ekmekjian

VIRGINIA
85—Cathy Grimes

WAKE FOREST
87—Amy Privette

WASHBURN
93—Jannica Beam

WELLESLEY
86—Elizabeth Murphy
88—Catherine Christensen
89—Louise McCleary

WEST LIBERTY ST.
93—Melissa Hammond

WILMINGTON (OHIO)
92—Suzanne Coyne

WINGATE
92—Elizabeth Hancock

YALE
86—Susan Johnson
90—Tonya Lawrence

FIRST-TEAM ACADEMIC ALL-AMERICANS BY COLLEGE

Since 1952, academic all-American teams have been selected by the College Sports Information Directors of America. To be eligible, student-athletes must be regular performers and have at least a 3.200 grade-point average (on a 4.000 scale) during their collegiate careers. The women's basketball players have been selected since 1980. Here are the CoSIDA/GTE first-team selections:

ABILENE CHRISTIAN
86—Claudia Schleyer

ADAMS ST.
82—Pamela Bond

AIR FORCE
80—Michelle Johnson
81—Michelle Johnson
83—Mary Manning

ALAS. FAIRBANKS
89—Jennifer S. Lin

ALMA
90—Kelly Spalding

ANGELO ST.
90—Lisa Klein

ASHLAND
83—Cindy Dorsey

AUGUSTANA (ILL.)
93—Andrea Magyar

BALL ST.
82—Karen Bauer
83—Karen Bauer
Donna Lamping
84—Donna Lamping
85—Donna Lamping

BELLARMINE
89—Stephanie Ann Tracy

BENTLEY
92—Kim Penwell

BETHANY (W. VA.)
91—Denise Doster

BOISE ST.
80—Ruth Fugleberg

BOWLING GREEN
87—Stephnie Coe

BRADLEY
83—Judy Burns

BRIDGEWATER (VA.)
91—Melody Derrow

BROWN
84—Christa Champion
Donna Yaffe
85—Christa Champion
86—Christa Champion

BUCKNELL
81—Jill Henry
86—Ann Kirwin
87—Jennifer Walz
88—Jennifer Walz
89—Jennifer Walz

BUENA VISTA
85—Jeannie Demers
86—Jeannie Demers
91—Dana Janning

BUTLER
93—Julie VonDielingen

CAL POLY SLO
82—Laura Buehning

CAL ST. SACRAMENTO
86—Heidi Carroll

CAPITAL
82—Shelley Blackburn
83—Shelley Blackburn

CARTHAGE
80—Sandy Burkhardt

CATAWBA
93—Angela Harbour

CENTRAL (IOWA)
83—Denise Boll
84—Denise Boll
85—Sue Poppens

CENTRAL MICH.
87—Jody Beerman

CENTRAL MO. ST.
84—Carla Eades

CHICAGO
86—Gretchen Gates

COLORADO COL.
84—Debbie Nalty

CONNECTICUT
84—Leigh Curl
85—Leigh Curl

DARTMOUTH
81—Gail Koziara
82—Gail Koziara
90—Sophia Neely

DAYTON
81—Carol Lammers

DIST. COLUMBIA
81—Alice Butler

DRAKE
82—Connie Newlin
90—Jan Jensen
91—Jan Jensen

ELIZABETHTOWN
84—Sherri Kinsey
Page Lutz
86—Jane Meyer

EVANSVILLE
90—Amy Humphries
91—Amy Humphries

FORDHAM
80—Anne Gregory

FORT HAYS ST.
85—Stacey Wells

GANNON
81—Rona Nesbit

GEORGIA ST.
88—Traci Lynne Cheek

GOUCHER
93—Corene Amoss

GREENVILLE
80—Carolyn Parker

GRINNELL
82—Paula Moon
90—Laura Van Sickle
91—Melissa Sharer

GROVE CITY
83—Jody Imbrie

HAMLINE
86—Pat Summers

HOFSTRA
86—Hilarie Cranmer

HOLY CROSS
82—Sherry Levin
83—Sherry Levin

HOPE
93—Jamie Crooks

ILLINOIS
80—Liz Brauer
82—Lisa Robinson

ILL. WESLEYAN
82—Terri Friedman

INDIANA ST.
89—Amy Vanderkolk

JAMESTOWN
80—Kathi Fischer
81—Kathi Fischer

KANSAS
80—Lynette Woodard
81—Lynette Woodard
84—Angie Snider

LA SALLE
92—Jennifer Cole

LAWRENCE
83—Carol Arnosti
84—Carol Arnosti

LOUISIANA TECH
83—Kim Mulkey
Jennifer White
84—Kim Mulkey

LUTHER
83—Desiree Kempcke

MAINE
91—Rachel Bouchard

MANKATO ST.
82—Lori Klammer
88—Lisa Walters

MICHIGAN
81—Diane Dietz
82—Diane Dietz

MICHIGAN ST.
82—Deb Traxinger
85—Kelly Belanger
86—Julie Polakowski

MIDDLE TENN. ST.
88—Lianne Beck

MILLIKIN
92—Barb Blume-Love

MISSISSIPPI COL.
90—Katrina Bibb

MISSOURI
84—Joni Davis

MIT
84—Louise Jandura
87—Martha Beverage
90—Maureen Fahey

MT. ST. JOSEPH
80—Julie Biermann

MURPHY
82—Patience Vanderbush

NEBRASKA
88—Stephanie Bolli
91—Karen Jennings
92—Karen Jennings
93—Karen Jennings

NEVADA
86—Chris Starr

NEVADA-LAS VEGAS
84—Misty Thomas
85—Misty Thomas
86—Misty Thomas

NIAGARA
80—Joan Thornton
81—Nancy Egerton

NORTH DAK.
85—Lori Carriere
92—Jennifer Walter

NORTHERN ARIZ.
87—Tracey Barnes

NORTHWOOD
92—Jennifer Wood-Hetherington

NOTRE DAME
83—Mary Beth Schueth

OAKLAND
80—Helen Shereda

OHIO
85—Caroline Mast
86—Caroline Mast

OKLAHOMA CHRISTIAN
91—Kim Golden

OLD DOMINION
82—Anne Donovan
83—Anne Donovan

OREGON
89—Stefanie Kasperski
90—Stefanie Kasperski

OREGON ST.
84—Juli Coleman
85—Juli Coleman
88—Michelle Flamoe
89—Michelle Flamoe

PACE
87—Amy Acker
88—Amy Acker

PENN ST.
92—Susan Robinson

PENNSYLVANIA
80—Carol Kuna

PERU ST.
89—Connie Viner

PITTSBURG ST.
93—Dani Fronabarger

POINT PARK
86—Darlene Brusco

PORTLAND
92—Martha Shelton

PROVIDENCE
83—Kathy Finn
90—Dottie Van Gheem

PURDUE
82—Carol Emanuel
Sue Bartz
83—Carol Emanuel

REGIS (COLO.)
85—Waverly Dodrill

RIO GRANDE COLLEGE
83—Robin Hagen

ROCHESTER
80—Jody Lavin

ROCKFORD
84—Tina Palmieri

ROLLINS
89—Kirsten Dellinger

ST. BONAVENTURE
93—Jodi Urich

ST. CLOUD ST.
88—Sarah Howard

ST. JOHN FISHER
83—Robin Mortensen

ST. JOSEPH'S (IND.)
81—Jennifer Voreis

ST. JOSEPH'S (PA.)
89—Kim Foley

ST. LOUIS
86—Arlene Lampe

ST. MARY'S (CAL.)
91—Anja Bordt

ST. MARY OF THE PLAINS
80—Diane Mannebach

ST. NORBERT
85—Amy Spielbauer

SAGINAW VALLEY
81—Diane Dockus

SAN DIEGO ST.
80—Susan Shue

SAN FRANCISCO
80—Mary Hile
81—Mary Hile

SCRANTON
86—Shelly Ritz

SEATTLE
85—Kelly Brewe

SIENA
80—Victoria Aromando
85—Ann Marie Graney

SIMPSON
92—Michelle Mackie

SOUTH DAK.
81—Deb Petersen
84—Karrie Wallen
87—Jean Misterek

SOUTH DAK. ST.
88—Tara Tessier

SPRINGFIELD
82—Anita Thomas

SYRACUSE
93—Erin Kenneally

TAMPA
85—Penny Dickos
86—Penny Dickos
Catherine Fox
87—Catherine Fox
Penny Dickos

TARLETON ST.
84—Patti Phillips

TENNESSEE
80—Jill Rankin
84—Tanya Haave

TENN.-MARTIN
88—Mary Kate Long

89—Mary Kate Long

TEX.-PAN AMERICAN
85—Becky Dube

TEXAS-SAN ANTONIO
84—Margaret Martinovich

TUFTS
85—Kathy Amoroso

UCLA
81—Denise Curry
86—Anne Dean

VIRGINIA
81—Val Ackerman
93—Dena Evans

WAGNER
81—Mary Gormley

WAKE FOREST
86—Amy Privette
87—Amy Privette

WARTBURG
80—Jill Crouse

WEST VA.
92—Rosemary Kosiorek

WESTERN KY.
81—Alicia Polson

WESTERN NEW ENG.
82—Roma St. George

WILLIAM & MARY
80—Lynn Norenberg
81—Lynn Norenberg

WILMINGTON (OHIO)
92—Suzanne Coyne

WIS.-MILWAUKEE
83—Jaci Clark

WITTENBERG
82—Melinda Wigton
Pamela Evans

WORCESTER ST.
81—Jacqueline Shakar

WOMEN'S COACHES' RECORDS

North Dakota State coach Amy Ruley is ninth on the list of winningest active Division II coaches. In 14 seasons, Ruley has compiled a record of 321-103. Her .757 winning percentage is 13th among her Division II peers. Her North Dakota State squads have won two NCAA championships.

WINNINGEST ACTIVE 1993-94 DIVISION I WOMEN'S COACHES

BY PERCENTAGE

(Minimum five years as major-college head coach; includes record at four-year colleges only.)

	Name, Institution	Yrs.	Won	Lost	Pct.
1.	#Leon Barmore, Louisiana Tech	11	307	52	.885
2.	Gary Blair, Arkansas	8	210	43	.830
3.	Bill Sheahan, Mt. St. Mary's (Md.)	12	272	60	.819
4.	Vivian Stringer, Iowa	21	488	111	.814
5.	Robin Selvig, Montana	15	357	88	.802
6.	Jody Conradt, Texas	24	620	153	.802
7.	Pat Summitt, Tennessee	19	499	124	.801
8.	Joe Ciampi, Auburn	16	389	101	.794
9.	*Jim Bolla, Nevada-Las Vegas	11	262	77	.773
10.	Tara VanDerveer, Stanford	15	348	104	.770
11.	Andy Landers, Georgia	14	344	103	.770
12.	Joan Bonvicini, Arizona	14	347	104	.769
13.	Paul Sanderford, Western Ky.	11	272	84	.764
14.	Theresa Grentz, Rutgers	19	422	134	.759
15.	Van Chancellor, Mississippi	15	360	115	.758
16.	Bill Fennelly, Toledo	5	118	38	.756
17.	Rene Portland, Penn St.	17	384	132	.744
18.	Bill Worrell, Tennessee Tech	7	156	54	.743
19.	Debbie Ryan, Virginia	16	359	130	.734
20.	Kay Yow, North Caro. St.	22	454	168	.730
21.	Mike Granelli, St. Peter's	21	389	147	.726
22.	Joe McKeown, Geo. Washington	7	150	59	.718
23.	Sue Gunter, Louisiana St.	23	483	193	.715
24.	Marsha Sharp, Texas Tech	11	241	97	.713
25.	Nancy Darsch, Ohio St.	8	170	69	.711
26.	Chris Weller, Maryland	18	375	153	.710
27.	John Miller, La Salle	7	146	60	.709
28.	Jean Burr, Brown	5	92	38	.708
29.	Lewis Bivens, Middle Tenn. St.	15	324	135	.706
30.	Linda Sharp, Southwest Tex. St.	16	337	143	.702
31.	Nancy Wilson, South Caro.	17	370	158	.701
32.	Bill Gibbons, Holy Cross	8	165	71	.699
33.	Vince Goo, Hawaii	6	125	54	.698
34.	Shelia Moorman, James Madison	11	224	97	.698
35.	Cindy Russo, Florida Int'l	16	315	140	.692
36.	Bob Foley, Providence	8	171	76	.692
37.	Sylvia Hatchell, North Caro.	18	381	174	.686
38.	Jim Foster, Vanderbilt	15	300	138	.685
39.	Elaine Elliott, Utah	10	200	92	.685
40.	Kay James, Southern Miss.	21	381	178	.682
41.	Jim Izard, Indiana	12	239	114	.677
42.	Geno Auriemma, Connecticut	8	162	78	.675
43.	Marynell Meadors, Florida St.	23	473	228	.675
44.	Jim Davis, Clemson	7	144	70	.673
45.	Cindy Scott, Southern Ill.	16	312	152	.672
46.	Carol Hammerle, Wis.-Green Bay	20	360	177	.670
47.	Linda Wunder, Fresno St.	8	146	73	.667
48.	Marsha Reall, Ohio	11	216	109	.665
49.	Don Perrelli, Northwestern	17	333	169	.663
50.	Doug Bruno, DePaul	7	132	67	.663
51.	James Smith, Northwestern (La.)	6	116	59	.663
52.	Joann Rutherford, Missouri	18	359	183	.662
53.	Muffet McGraw, Notre Dame	11	204	104	.662
54.	!Scott Harrelson, West Va.	5	98	50	.662
55.	Wanda Watkins, Campbell	12	214	111	.658
56.	Joey Favaloro, New Orleans	13	250	130	.658
57.	Drema Greer, Ga. Southern	8	156	82	.655
58.	Ed Baldwin, N.C.-Charlotte	5	95	50	.655
59.	Linda Robinson, Appalachian St.	14	258	138	.652
60.	Stephanie Gaitley, St. Joseph's (Pa.)	8	154	83	.650
61.	Cheryl Burnett, Southwest Mo. St.	6	115	62	.650
62.	Harry Perretta, Villanova	15	280	153	.647
63.	Chris Gobrecht, Washington	14	265	151	.637

	Name, Institution	Yrs.	Won	Lost	Pct.
64.	Ceal Barry, Colorado	14	266	155	.632
65.	%Jill Hutchison, Illinois St.	22	385	229	.627
66.	Larry Inman, Eastern Ky.	13	231	138	.626
67.	Ferne Labati, Miami (Fla.)	14	256	154	.624
68.	Kathy Sanborn, New Hampshire	12	195	118	.623
69.	Gooch Foster, California	20	338	205	.622
70.	Marian Washington, Kansas	20	368	225	.621
71.	Terri Rubenstein, St. Mary's (Cal.)	10	175	107	.621
72.	Patricia Bibbs, Grambling	9	155	96	.618
73.	Lynn Hickey, Texas A&M	14	256	159	.617
74.	Lin Dunn, Purdue	22	374	233	.616
75.	Craig Parrott, Tenn.-Chatt.	6	107	67	.615
76.	Jane Albright-Dieterle, Northern Ill.	9	164	104	.612
77.	Pat Fisher, Lafayette	13	217	139	.610
78.	Dick Halterman, Oklahoma St.	10	182	118	.607
79.	Chad Lavin, Wyoming	11	191	124	.606
80.	Wendy Larry, Old Dominion	9	157	102	.606
81.	Christina Wielgus, Fordham	10	144	94	.605
82.	Jerry Winters, Arkansas St.	9	154	101	.604
83.	Joyce Perry, Delaware	20	286	188	.603
84.	Alvin Wyatt, Bethune-Cookman	15	222	147	.602

*# Cohead coach with Sonja Hogg for 1983-85. * Cohead coach with Sheila Strike for 1982-88. ! Cohead coach with Kittie Blakemore for 1989-92. % Cohead coach with Melinda Fischer for 1980-85.*

(Coaches with less than five years as a Division I head coach; includes record at four-year colleges only.)

	Name, Institution	Yrs.	Won	Lost	Pct.
1.	Ed Arnzen, Southeast Mo. St.	10	225	72	.758
2.	Lynne Agee, N. C.-Greensboro	15	306	101	.752
3.	Lisa Bluder, Drake	9	208	81	.720
4.	Wayne Allen, Fla. Atlantic	6	114	55	.675
5.	Scooter Barnette, Charleston	9	170	90	.654
6.	Brian Agler, Kansas St.	5	87	51	.630
7.	Mary Ann Kelling, Wis.-Milwaukee	17	289	177	.620

BY VICTORIES

(Minimum five years as major-college head coach; includes record at four-year colleges only.)

	Name, Institution (Pct.)	Years	Wins
1.	Jody Conradt, Texas (.802)	24	620
2.	Pat Summitt, Tennessee (.801)	19	499
3.	Vivian Stringer, Iowa (.815)	21	488
4.	Sue Gunter, Louisiana St. (.715)	23	483
5.	Marynell Meadors, Florida St. (.675)	23	473
6.	Kay Yow, North Caro. St. (.730)	22	454
7.	Theresa Grentz, Rutgers (.759)	19	422
8.	Joe Ciampi, Auburn (.794)	16	389
9.	Mike Granelli, St. Peter's (.726)	21	389
10.	&Jill Hutchison, Illinois St. (.627)	22	385
11.	Rene Portland, Penn St. (.744)	17	384
12.	Sylvia Hatchell, North Caro. (.686)	18	381
13.	Kay James, Southern Miss. (.682)	21	381
14.	Chris Weller, Maryland (.710)	18	375
15.	Lin Dunn, Purdue (.616)	22	374
16.	Nancy Wilson, South Caro. (.701)	17	370
17.	Marian Washington, Kansas (.621)	20	368
18.	Van Chancellor, Mississippi (.758)	15	360
19.	Carol Hammerle, Wis.-Green Bay (.670)	20	360
20.	Debbie Ryan, Virginia (.734)	16	359
21.	Joann Rutherford, Missouri (.662)	18	359
22.	Robin Selvig, Montana (.802)	15	357
23.	Tara VanDerveer, Stanford (.770)	15	348
24.	Joan Bonvicini, Arizona (.769)	14	347
25.	Andy Landers, Georgia (.770)	14	344
26.	Gooch Foster, California (.622)	20	338
27.	Linda Sharp, Southwest Tex. St. (.702)	16	337

	Name, Institution (Pct.)	Years	Wins
28.	Don Perrelli, Northwestern (.663)	17	333
29.	Lewis Bivens, Middle Tenn. St. (.706)	15	324
30.	Cindy Russo, Florida Int'l (.692)	16	315
31.	Cindy Scott, Southern Ill. (.672)	16	312
32.	#Leon Barmore, Louisiana Tech (.855)	11	307
33.	Jim Foster, Vanderbilt (.685)	15	300
34.	Brenda Reilly, Central Conn. St. (.518)	22	299
35.	Dianne Nolan, Fairfield (.570)	19	297
36.	Sharon Fanning, Kentucky (.592)	17	292
37.	Joyce Perry, Delaware (.603)	20	286
38.	Barbara Jacobs, Syracuse (.550)	22	285
39.	Bill Smithpeters, Eastern Wash. (.573)	17	282
40.	Harry Perretta, Villanova (.647)	15	280
41.	Bill Sheahan, Mt. St. Mary's (Md.) (.819)	12	272
42.	Paul Sanderford, Western Ky. (.764)	11	272
43.	Jessie Harris, Mississippi Val. (.556)	17	271
44.	Ceal Barry, Colorado (.632)	14	266
45.	Chris Gobrecht, Washington (.637)	14	265
46.	*Jim Bolla, Nevada-Las Vegas (.773)	11	262
47.	Karen Langeland, Michigan St. (.564)	17	261
48.	Brenda Paul, Georgia St. (.586)	15	260
49.	Jeannie Milling, Ala.-Birmingham (.579)	16	260
50.	Linda Robinson, Appalachian St. (.652)	14	258
51.	Ferne Labati, Miami (Fla.) (.624)	14	256
52.	Lynn Hickey, Texas A&M (.617)	14	256
53.	Terry Hall, Wright St. (.573)	16	252
54.	Joey Favaloro, New Orleans (.658)	13	250
55.	Marsha Sharp, Texas Tech (.713)	11	241
56.	Jim Izard, Indiana (.677)	12	239
57.	Kathy Marpe, San Diego (.478)	19	238
58.	Aki Hill, Oregon St. (.558)	15	236
59.	Paulette Stein, Butler (.581)	15	233
60.	Joy Malchodi, Northeastern (.495)	17	233
61.	Larry Inman, Eastern Ky. (.626)	13	231
62.	Shirley Walker, Alcorn St. (.569)	15	231
63.	Shelia Moorman, James Madison (.698)	11	224
64.	Alvin Wyatt, Bethune-Cookman (.602)	15	222
65.	Pat Fisher, Lafayette (.610)	13	217
66.	Marsha Reall, Ohio (.665)	11	216
67.	Angela Beck, Nebraska (.573)	13	215
68.	Wanda Watkins, Campbell (.658)	12	214
69.	Carol Alfano, Virginia Tech (.502)	15	211
70.	Gary Blair, Arkansas (.830)	8	210
71.	Frank Schneider, Southeast La. (.522)	14	210
72.	Juliene Simpson, Bucknell (.532)	14	207
73.	Joe Mullaney Jr., St. John's (N.Y.) (.582)	12	205
74.	Muffet McGraw, Notre Dame (.662)	11	204
75.	Elaine Elliott, Utah (.685)	10	200
76.	Susan Yow, N.C.-Wilmington (.488)	15	200

*# Cohead coach with Sonja Hogg for 1983-85. & Cohead coach with Melinda Fischer for 1980-85. * Cohead coach with Sheila Strike for 1982-88.*

(Coaches with less than five years as major-college head coach; includes record at four-year colleges only.)

	Name, Institution (Pct.)	Years	Wins
1.	Lynne Agee, N. C.-Greensboro (.752)	15	306
2.	Mary Ann Kelling, Wis.-Milwaukee (.620)	17	289
3.	Joyce Sorrell, Troy St. (.508)	18	252
4.	Andrew Pennington, Jackson St. (.599)	14	240
5.	Ed Arnzen, Southeast Mo. St. (.758)	10	225
6.	Lisa Bluder, Drake (.720)	9	208

WINNINGEST ACTIVE 1993-94 DIVISION II WOMEN'S COACHES

BY PERCENTAGE

(Minimum five years as a head coach; includes record at four-year colleges only.)

	Name, Institution	Yrs.	Won	Lost	Pct.
1.	Lloyd Clark, Delta St.	10	267	45	.856

	Name, Institution	Yrs.	Won	Lost	Pct.
2.	Jodi Gault, Pitt.-Johnstown	11	265	45	.855
3.	Curt Fredrickson, Northern St.	14	339	74	.821
4.	Darlene May, Cal Poly Pomona	19	498	113	.815
5.	Gene Roebuck, North Dak.	6	143	33	.813
6.	Joe Bressi, Bloomsburg	7	158	37	.810
7.	James Sweat, Norfolk St.	12	311	74	.808
8.	Jon Pye, Central Mo. St.	8	193	49	.798
9.	Mike Geary, Northern Mich.	7	155	45	.775
10.	Bob Schneider, West Tex. A&M	15	344	109	.759
11.	Barbara Stevens, Bentley	16	365	116	.759
12.	Keith Freeman, St. Joseph's (Ind.)	5	113	36	.758
13.	Amy Ruley, North Dak. St.	14	321	103	.757
14.	Johnny Jacumin, Wingate	13	297	99	.750
15.	Eddie Carter, Carson-Newman	6	132	47	.737
16.	Paula Sullivan, Stonehill	22	390	139	.737
17.	Charlie Just, Bellarmine	9	190	70	.731
18.	David Smith, Shippensburg	11	210	81	.722
19.	Bob Taylor, Oakland	10	203	79	.720
20.	Jorja Hoehn, UC Davis	13	265	107	.712
21.	Roger Vannoy, Lincoln Memorial	11	23	94	.712
22.	Claudette Charney, Saginaw Valley	9	185	75	.712
23.	Ron Marvel, Central Ark.	13	269	110	.710
24.	Glenn Wilkes, Rollins	7	141	58	.709
25.	Bertha Cummings, Virginia St.	5	96	40	.706
26.	Thomas Jessee, Bluefield St.	5	102	43	.703
27.	Norm Benn, Fla. Southern	8	156	69	.693
28.	Nancy Winstel, Northern Ky.	13	248	111	.691
29.	Karen Stromme, Minn.-Duluth	9	184	84	.687
30.	Kevin Borseth, Michigan Tech	6	118	55	.682
31.	Tom Shirley, Phila. Textile	12	230	109	.678
32.	Denise Sandifar, Oakland City	5	88	42	.677
33.	Press Parham, Alabama A&M	11	207	99	.676
34.	Pat Dick, Washburn	16	308	148	.675
35.	Elaine Kebbe, Belmont Abbey	10	194	94	.674
36.	John Reynolds, Florida Tech	6	112	55	.671
37.	Donna Guimont, St. Anselm	17	273	139	.663
38.	LeAnn Millar, Cal St. Stanislaus	12	221	113	.662
39.	Gordy Presnell, Seattle Pacific	6	113	60	.653
40.	Tiny Laster, Hampton	21	391	209	.652
41.	Stan Swank, Edinboro	6	110	59	.651
42.	Steve Kirkham, Mesa St.	5	92	51	.643
43.	John Klein, Fort Hays St.	11	205	114	.643
44.	Mary Fleig, Millersville	10	165	92	.642
45.	Joe Sanchez, Neb.-Kearney	15	288	165	.636
46.	Don Hustead, Wheeling Jesuit	5	92	53	.634
47.	Lonnie Bartley, Fort Valley St.	9	154	89	.634
48.	Margaret Parsons, Clarion	12	188	109	.633
49.	Cindy Tudehope, Morningside	9	150	87	.633
50.	Nancy Neiber, South Dak. St.	9	158	92	.632
51.	Charles Cooper, Valdosta St.	12	204	123	.624
52.	Todd Cotton, Adams St.	9	167	101	.623
53.	Gregory Bruce, Portland St.	7	122	75	.619
54.	Lisa Hicks, Indianapolis	5	82	52	.612
55.	Hythia Evans-Liebert, Johnson Smith	6	103	66	.609
56.	Jane Williamson, West Ga.	6	111	52	.609
57.	Wayne Winstead, Northwest Mo. St.	14	240	156	.606
58.	Frank Scarfo, Lock Haven	7	123	80	.606
59.	Russ Shepherd, Glenville St.	5	86	56	.606
60.	Marti Gasser, Air Force	14	238	155	.606
61.	Bev Downing, St. Augustine's	11	181	118	.605
62.	Jim Brinkman, Fairmont St.	11	203	135	.601
63.	Gary Schwartz, Northern Colo.	11	180	120	.600
64.	Bob Nichols, Eckerd	26	350	245	.588
65.	Paul Flores, Calif. (Pa.)	10	156	111	.584
66.	Wayne Moore, Eastern N. Mex.	13	195	142	.579
67.	Robert Skinner, Albany (Ga.)	13	197	144	.578
68.	John Carrick, Georgia Col.	10	163	120	.576
69.	Gail Johnson, S.C.-Aiken	7	115	85	.575
70.	Jan Kiger, Indiana (Pa.)	7	106	79	.573
71.	Cherri Mankenberg, Nebraska-Omaha	17	279	209	.572

	Name, Institution	Yrs.	Won	Lost	Pct.
72.	Teri Sheridan, Winona St.	5	74	57	.565
73.	Bobby Sanders, Shaw	6	87	68	.561
74.	Val Schierling, Emporia St.	12	193	151	.561
75.	Sue Duprat, St. Michael's	17	231	181	.561
76.	Lowell Barnhart, Augusta	7	107	84	.560
77.	Sue Lauder, Assumption	13	181	143	.559
78.	Pat Baker-Grzyb, Grand Valley St.	14	211	168	.557
79.	Kelly Kruger, Southwest St.	8	121	97	.555
80.	Wayne Byrd, North Ala.	11	165	134	.552
81.	Linda Roberts, Missouri-Rolla	14	186	152	.550
82.	Susan Zachensky-Walthall, Sonoma St.	14	197	161	.550
83.	Nancy Dreffs, New Hamp. Col.	11	167	137	.549
84.	Steve Hancock, Franklin Pierce	5	79	65	.549
85.	Kathy O'Neil, Mass.-Lowell	8	123	105	.539
86.	Anthony Barone, Southern Conn. St.	14	207	182	.532
87.	Ed Nixon, Mississippi Col.	23	345	305	.531
88.	Wendy Hedberg, SIU-Edwardsville	14	202	182	.526
89.	Tom York, Kutztown	6	85	77	.525
90.	Joe Ellenburg, High Point	5	74	68	.521
91.	Beth Palmer, East Tex. St.	7	104	97	.517
92.	Deirdre Kane, West Chester	9	127	119	.516
93.	Cheryl Kennedy, Slippery Rock	8	109	103	.514
94.	Crystal Sharpe, Wofford	9	117	112	.511
95.	Mary Ortelee, North Fla.	8	105	102	.507
96.	Ed Fincham, Shepherd	11	145	141	.507
97.	John Keely, Central Okla.	15	220	217	.503
98.	Patrick Houlihan, Molloy	7	98	98	.500

BY VICTORIES

(Includes record at four-year colleges only.)

	Name, Institution (Pct.)	Years	Wins
1.	Darlene May, Cal Poly Pomona (.815)	19	498
2.	Tiny Laster, Hampton (.652)	21	391
3.	Paula Sullivan, Stonehill (.737)	22	390
4.	Barbara Stevens, Bentley (.759)	16	365
5.	Bob Nichols, Eckerd (.588)	26	350
6.	Ed Nixon, Mississippi Col. (.531)	23	345
7.	Bob Schneider, West Tex. A&M (.759)	15	344
8.	Curt Fredrickson, Northern St. (.821)	14	339
9.	Amy Ruley, North Dak. St. (.757)	14	321
10.	James Sweat, Norfolk St. (.808)	12	311
11.	Pat Dick, Washburn (.675)	16	308
12.	Johnny Jacumin, Wingate (.750)	13	297
13.	Joe Sanchez, Neb.-Kearney (.636)	15	288
14.	Cherri Mankenberg, Nebraska-Omaha (.572)	17	279
15.	Donna Guimont, St. Anselm (.663)	17	273
16.	Ron Marvel, Central Ark. (.710)	13	269
17.	Lloyd Clark, Delta St. (.856)	10	267
18.	Jodi Gault, Pitt.-Johnstown (.855)	11	265
19.	Jorja Hoehn, UC Davis (.712)	13	265
20.	Nancy Winstel, Northern Ky. (.691)	13	248
21.	Wayne Winstead, Northwest Mo. St. (.606)	14	240
22.	Marti Gasser, Air Force (.606)	14	238
23.	Roger Vannoy, Lincoln Memorial (.712)	11	232
24.	Sue Duprat, St. Michael's (.561)	17	231
25.	Moses Golatt, Virginia Union (.422)	21	231
26.	Tom Shirley, Phila. Textile (.678)	12	230
27.	LeAnn Millar, Cal St. Stanislaus (.662)	12	221
28.	John Keely, Central Okla. (.503)	15	220
29.	Pat Baker-Grzyb, Grand Valley St. (.557)	14	211
30.	David Smith, Shippensburg (.722)	11	210
31.	Press Parham, Alabama A&M (.676)	11	207
31.	Anthony Barone, Southern Conn. St. (.532)	14	207
33.	John Klein, Fort Hays St. (.643)	11	205
34.	Charles Cooper, Valdosta St. (.624)	12	204
35.	Bob Taylor, Oakland (.720)	10	203
35.	Jim Brinkman, Fairmont St. (.601)	11	203
37.	Wendy Hedberg, SIU-Edwardsville (.526)	14	202

WINNINGEST ACTIVE 1993-94 DIVISION III WOMEN'S COACHES

BY PERCENTAGE

(Minimum five years as a head coach; includes record at four-year colleges only.)

	Name, Institution	Yrs.	Won	Lost	Pct.
1.	Gary Fifield, Southern Me.	6	151	26	.853
2.	Phillip Kahler, St. John Fisher	19	462	86	.843
3.	Mary Beth Spirk, Moravian	6	149	29	.837
4.	Nancy Fahey, Washington (Mo.)	7	149	35	.810
5.	Tim Shea, Salem St.	12	276	66	.807
6.	Monica Severson, Wartburg	5	109	27	.801
7.	Mike Strong, Scranton	14	328	82	.800
8.	Wes Moore, Maryville (Tenn.)	6	131	36	.784
9.	Robert Guy, Geneseo St.	9	181	51	.780
10.	Michael McDevitt, St. Joseph's (Me.)	6	137	40	.774
11.	Dixie Jeffers, Capital	10	206	63	.766
12.	Ted Riverso, St. Thomas (Minn.)	9	188	58	.764
13.	Glenn Begley, William Smith	5	97	31	.758
14.	Yvonne Kauffman, Elizabethtown	23	402	129	.757
15.	Rich Wilson, Kean	7	145	48	.751
16.	Susan Dunagan, Roanoke	12	238	79	.751
17.	Patricia Glispin, Clark (Mass.)	9	180	60	.750
18.	Andy Yosinoff, Emmanuel	16	266	95	.737
19.	Jody Rajcula, Western Conn. St.	12	219	82	.728
20.	Connie Tilley, St. Norbert	16	271	105	.721
21.	Gail Maloney, Buffalo St.	14	246	98	.715
22.	Kathi Bennett, Wis.-Oshkosh	5	90	36	.714
23.	Mike Durbin, St. Benedict	8	155	63	.711
24.	Mari Warner, Albany (N.Y.)	10	177	72	.711
25.	Donald Crist, Hamilton	8	134	55	.709
26.	Bill Finney, Marymount (Va.)	10	185	76	.709
27.	Lisa Stone, Wis.-Eau Claire	8	139	61	.695
28.	Jim Crawley, Frostburg St.	15	273	120	.695
29.	Donna Newberry, Muskingum	19	305	136	.692
30.	Jacqueline Slaats, Lake Forest	7	109	49	.690
31.	Karen McConnell, Heidelberg	5	97	44	.688
32.	Charles Goffnett, Alma	6	98	45	.685
33.	Sharon Dawley, Tufts	9	137	63	.685
34.	Janice Quinn, New York U.	6	110	52	.679
35.	Carl Hatchell, Meredith	5	76	36	.679
36.	Cindy Elliott, Defiance	6	102	49	.675
37.	Ronda Seagraves, Southwestern (Tex.)	7	123	60	.672
38.	Cathy Parson, Chris. Newport	5	90	44	.672
39.	Nan Carney-DeBord, Ohio Wesleyan	8	136	68	.667
40.	Mike Decillis, Nazareth (N.Y.)	9	154	78	.664
41.	Judy Blinstrub, Babson	9	152	79	.658
42.	Diane Schumacher, Augustana (Ill.)	12	202	105	.658
43.	Mark Hribar, Susquehanna	6	99	52	.656
44.	Jim Stukel, Wis.-Superior	8	138	73	.654
45.	Amy Proctor, Lawrence	5	78	42	.650
46.	Laura Mapp, Bridgewater (Va.)	32	447	244	.647
47.	Bonnie Foley, Cortland St.	12	197	108	.646
48.	Declan McMullen, Stony Brook	11	185	104	.640
49.	Mika Ryan, Trenton St.	9	147	83	.639
50.	Garey Smith, William Penn	11	187	107	.636
51.	Beth Baker, Wheaton (Ill.)	7	113	65	.635
52.	Pam Evans, Wittenberg	7	119	69	.633
53.	Brenna Kelly, Illinois Col.	6	87	51	.630
54.	Lori Kerans, Millikin	7	111	66	.627
55.	Dick Kelly, Curry	10	153	92	.624
56.	Nancy Binion, Rust	5	73	44	.624
57.	Jane Hildebrand, Luther	9	146	89	.621
58.	Amy Backus, Middlebury	12	173	110	.611
59.	Gene White, Franklin	7	90	58	.608
60.	Brian Niemuth, Simpson	5	76	49	.608
61.	Maureen Pine, Trinity (Conn.)	6	80	53	.602
62.	Carol Simon, Brandeis	6	98	65	.601
63.	Deb Hunter, Bethel (Minn.)	7	104	70	.598

	Name, Institution	Yrs.	Won	Lost	Pct.
64.	Dave Swanson, Ill. Benedictine	13	181	123	.595
65.	Dan Welde, Cabrini	6	91	62	.595
66.	Jodie Burton, Claremont-M-S	14	204	140	.593
67.	Joy Scruggs, Emory & Henry	12	168	117	.589
68.	Christine Hart, Wooster	7	104	73	.588
69.	Mark Thomas, Wis.-Stout	6	90	66	.577
70.	Susan Zawacki, Chicago	15	195	144	.575
71.	Harvey Shapiro, Bowdoin	14	173	130	.571
72.	Gary Boeyink, Central (Iowa)	20	274	207	.570
73.	Del Malloy, Wheaton (Mass.)	9	126	96	.568
74.	Robert Meomartino, Anna Maria	12	148	118	.556
75.	Nancy Clelan-Blank, Johns Hopkins	21	240	197	.549
76.	Rob Phillips, Waynesburg	5	67	55	.549
77.	Gerri Seidl, Carnegie Mellon	9	115	95	.548
78.	Joyce Wong, Rochester	18	248	205	.547
79.	Christine Pritchard, Ithaca	12	155	129	.546
80.	Judith Sullivan, Mass.-Dartmouth	16	200	167	.545
81.	Ray Tharan, Bryn Mawr	5	49	41	.544
82.	Donna Tanner, Regis (Mass.)	6	77	65	.542
83.	Lisa Cornish, Ursinus	7	93	80	.538
84.	Kevin Grimmer, Utica Tech	5	65	58	.528
85.	Mary Ellen Alger, New England Col.	5	68	62	.523
86.	Kitty Baldridge, Gallaudet	17	205	187	.523
87.	Ted Furman, Beaver	9	106	97	.522
88.	Sarah Hatgas, Rhodes	16	174	161	.519
89.	Gary Pento, Delaware Valley	9	116	108	.518
89.	Marvin Wood, St. Mary's (Ind.)	8	87	81	.518
91.	Vicki Staton, Wash. & Jeff.	18	180	169	.516
92.	Connie Gallahan, Mary Washington	16	192	187	.507
93.	Ken Hopkins, Rhode Island Col.	8	104	102	.505
94.	Bill Craig, Nichols	8	99	98	.503

BY VICTORIES

(Includes record at four-year colleges only.)

	Name, Institution (Pct.)	Years	Wins
1.	Phillip Kahler, St. John Fisher (.843)	19	462
2.	Laura Mapp, Bridgewater (Va.) (.647)	32	447
3.	Yvonne Kauffman, Elizabethtown (.757)	23	402
4.	Mike Strong, Scranton (.800)	14	328
5.	Donna Newberry, Muskingum (.692)	19	305
6.	Tim Shea, Salem St. (.807)	12	276
7.	Gary Boeyink, Central (Iowa) (.570)	20	274
8.	Jim Crawley, Frostburg St. (.695)	15	273
9.	Connie Tilley, St. Norbert (.721)	16	271
10.	Andy Yosinoff, Emmanuel (.737)	16	266
11.	Joyce Wong, Rochester (.547)	18	248
12.	Gail Maloney, Buffalo St. (.715)	14	246
13.	Nancy Clelan-Blank, Johns Hopkins (.549)	21	240
14.	Susan Dunagan, Roanoke (.751)	12	238
15.	Jody Rajcula, Western Conn. St. (.728)	12	219
16.	Judy Malone, UC San Diego (.494)	17	209
17.	Dixie Jeffers, Capital (.766)	10	206
18.	Kitty Baldridge, Gallaudet (.523)	17	205
19.	Jodie Burton, Claremont-M-S (.593)	14	204
20.	Diane Schumacher, Augustana (Ill.) (.658)	12	202
21.	Judith Sullivan, Mass.-Dartmouth (.545)	16	200

CHAMPIONSHIPS

Bentley's Kim Penwell helped her team advance to the semifinals of the 1993 Division II Women's Basketball Championship. Penwell had 12 points in a 79-57 loss to North Dakota State. She tallied 12 points and nine rebounds in a consolation-game loss to Michigan Tech. North Dakota State won the title with a 95-63 vic

1993 DIVISION I WOMEN'S CHAMPIONSHIP RESULTS

FIRST ROUND
Rutgers 80, Vermont 74
Miami (Fla.) 61, St. Peter's 44
Georgetown 76, Northern Ill. 74
Florida 69, Bowling Green 67
Northwestern 90, Georgia Tech 62
Alabama 102, Ga. Southern 70
Louisville 74, Connecticut 71
Old Dominion 77, Tennessee Tech 60
California 62, Kansas 47
Clemson 70, Xavier (Ohio) 64
Louisiana Tech 70, DePaul 59
Southwest Mo. St. 86, Oklahoma St. 71
Georgia 85, San Diego St. 68
UC Santa Barb. 88, Brigham Young 79
Nebraska 81, San Diego 58
Washington 80, Montana St. 51

SECOND ROUND
Ohio St. 91, Rutgers 60
Western Ky. 78, Miami (Fla.) 63
Georgetown 68, Penn St. 67
Virginia 69, Florida 55
Tennessee 89, Northwestern 66
North Caro. 74, Alabama 73 (ot)
Auburn 66, Louisville 61
Iowa 82, Old Dominion 56
Vanderbilt 82, California 63
Stephen F. Austin 89, Clemson 78
Louisiana Tech 82, Texas 78
Southwest Mo. St. 86, Maryland 82
Stanford 93, Georgia 60
Colorado 81, UC Santa Barb. 54
Southern Cal 78, Nebraska 60
Texas Tech 70, Washington 64

REGIONAL SEMIFINALS
Ohio St. 86, Western Ky. 73
Virginia 77, Georgetown 57
Tennessee 74, North Caro. 54
Iowa 63, Auburn 50
Vanderbilt 59, Stephen F. Austin 56
Louisiana Tech 59, Southwest Mo. St. 43
Colorado 80, Stanford 67
Texas Tech 87, Southern Cal 67

REGIONAL CHAMPIONSHIPS
Ohio St. 75, Virginia 73
Iowa 72, Tennessee 56
Vanderbilt 58, Louisiana Tech 53
Texas Tech 79, Colorado 54

SEMIFINALS
Ohio St. 73, Iowa 72 (ot)
Texas Tech 60, Vanderbilt 46

CHAMPIONSHIP
Texas Tech 84, Ohio St. 82

WOMEN'S FINAL FOUR BOX SCORES

SEMIFINALS

Ohio St. 73, Iowa 72 (ot)

Iowa	FG-FGA	FT-FTA	RB	PF	TP
Necole Tunsil	4- 9	2- 2	6	4	10
Toni Foster	5-15	0- 0	10	3	10
Andrea Harmon	2- 2	3- 3	6	3	7
Laurie Aaron	6-16	8-10	5	3	21
Tia Jackson	10-17	2- 2	10	2	22
Cathy Marx	1- 2	0- 2	1	3	2
Molly Tideback	0- 1	0- 0	1	1	0
Virgie Dillingham	0- 1	0- 0	3	0	0
Arneda Yarbrough	0- 0	0- 1	0	1	0
Karen Clayton	0- 0	0- 0	0	0	0
Team			3		
TOTALS	28-63	15-20	45	20	72

Ohio St.	FG-FGA	FT-FTA	RB	PF	TP
Katie Smith	4-11	3- 5	5	3	11
Nikki Keyton	4-11	5- 9	13	4	14
Stacie Howard	2- 6	2- 3	1	1	6
Audrey Burcy	5-12	0- 2	9	3	13
Averrill Roberts	7-15	1- 2	2	4	16
Adrienne Johnson	2- 4	0- 0	1	0	4
Lisa Negri	3- 3	2- 2	2	3	9
Erin Ingwersen	0- 1	0- 0	1	1	0
Kelly Fergus	0- 0	0- 0	0	0	0
Lisa Sebastian	0- 0	0- 0	0	1	0
Team			0		
TOTALS	27-63	13-23	34	20	73

Half time: Ohio St. 33, Iowa 29. End of regulation: Tied at 61. Three-point field goals: Iowa 1-2 (Aaron 1-2); Ohio St. 6-15 (Smith 0-1, Ketyon 1-1, Burcy 3-5, Roberts 1-6, Negri 1-1, Ingwersen 0-1). Officials: Bob Gallagher, Carla Fugimoto. Attendance: 16,141.

Texas Tech 60, Vanderbilt 46

Texas Tech	FG-FGA	FT-FTA	RB	PF	TP
Krista Kirkland	5- 9	2- 3	7	1	14
Sheryl Swoopes	11-24	8- 9	11	0	31
Cynthia Clinger	2- 6	0- 0	7	1	4
Noel Johnson	1- 2	4- 4	6	2	6
Stephanie Scott	1- 7	1- 2	5	2	3
Michi Atkins	1- 2	0- 0	1	2	2
Team			5		
TOTALS	21-50	15-18	42	8	60

Vanderbilt	FG-FGA	FT-FTA	RB	PF	TP
Misty Lamb	2- 3	0- 0	2	0	4
Shelley Jarrard	1-11	0- 3	6	3	3
Heidi Gillingham	12-18	0- 0	12	4	24
Rhonda Blades	2- 8	0- 0	3	4	5
Julie Powell	1- 9	0- 0	1	3	3
Mara Cunningham	0- 1	0- 0	0	0	0
Ginger Jared	0- 3	0- 0	0	0	0
Renee Allen	0- 0	0- 0	0	1	0
Lisa King	3- 6	1- 2	1	1	7
Team			2		
TOTALS	21-59	1- 5	27	16	46

Half time: Texas Tech 28, Vanderbilt 26. Three-point field goals: Texas Tech 3-11 (Kirkland 2-5, Swoopes 1-3, Scott 0-3); Vanderbilt 3-26 (Jarrard 1-8, Blades 1-7, Powell 1-7, Jared 0-3, King 0-1). Officials: June Courteau, Larry Sheppard. Attendance: 16,141.

CHAMPIONSHIP

Texas Tech 84, Ohio St. 82

Texas Tech	FG-FGA	FT-FTA	RB	PF	TP
Krista Kirkland	5-10	1- 5	3	2	14
Sheryl Swoopes	16-24	11-11	5	4	47
Cynthia Clinger	3- 5	1- 1	5	5	7

Player	FG-FGA	FT-FTA	RB	PF	TP
Noel Johnson	2- 7	4- 4	0	1	8
Stephanie Scott	2- 3	0- 0	3	3	4
Michi Atkins	1- 3	2- 2	6	2	4
Janice Farris	0- 1	0- 0	0	2	0
Team			2		
TOTALS	29-53	19-23	24	19	84

Ohio St.	**FG-FGA**	**FT-FTA**	**RB**	**PF**	**TP**
Katie Smith	11-20	5- 7	11	3	28
Nikki Keyton	6-12	7- 7	8	4	19
Stacie Howard	0- 0	2- 2	1	1	2
Audrey Burcy	3-15	3- 4	5	4	12
Averrill Roberts	5-11	1- 1	3	4	13
Lisa Negri	2- 2	1- 1	5	3	5
Erin Ingwersen	0- 0	0- 0	0	0	0
Adrienne Johnson	0- 0	0- 0	0	0	0
Lisa Sebastian	0- 1	0- 0	0	2	0
Alysiah Bond	1- 3	0- 0	2	4	3
Team			6		
TOTALS	28-64	19-22	41	25	82

Half time: Texas Tech 40, Ohio St. 31. Three-point field goals: Texas Tech 7-17 (Kirkland 3-6, Swoopes 4-6, Johnson 0-4, Scott 0-1); Ohio St. 7-22 (Smith 1-2, Keyton 0-2, Burcy 3-11, Roberts 2-5, Bond 1-2). Officials: Sally Bell, Dee Kantner. Attendance: 16,141.

DIVISION I WOMEN'S CHAMPIONSHIP RECORDS

ALL-TIME RESULTS

Year	Champion	Coach	Score	Runner-Up	Site
1982	Louisiana Tech	Sonja Hogg	76-62	Cheyney	Norfolk, Va.
1983	Southern Cal	Linda Sharp	69-67	Louisiana Tech	Norfolk, Va.
1984	Southern Cal	Linda Sharp	72-61	Tennessee	Los Angeles, Calif.
1985	Old Dominion	Marianne Stanley	70-65	Georgia	Austin, Tex.
1986	Texas	Jody Conradt	97-81	Southern Cal	Lexington, Ky.
1987	Tennessee	Pat Summitt	67-44	Louisiana Tech	Austin, Tex.
1988	Louisiana Tech	Leon Barmore	56-54	Auburn	Tacoma, Wash.
1989	Tennessee	Pat Summitt	76-60	Auburn	Tacoma, Wash.
1990	Stanford	Tara VanDerveer	88-81	Auburn	Knoxville, Tenn.
1991	Tennessee	Pat Summitt	70-67*	Virginia	New Orleans, La.
1992	Stanford	Tara VanDerveer	78-62	Western Ky.	Los Angeles, Calif.
1993	Texas Tech	Marsha Sharp	84-82	Ohio St.	Atlanta, Ga.

* *Overtime.*

OUTSTANDING PLAYER AWARDS

1982—Janice Lawrence, Louisiana Tech; 1983—Cheryl Miller, Southern Cal; 1984—Cheryl Miller, Southern Cal; 1985—Tracy Claxton, Old Dominion; 1986—Clarissa Davis, Texas; 1987—Tonya Edwards, Tennessee; 1988—Erica Westbrooks, Louisiana Tech; 1989—Bridgette Gordon, Tennessee; 1990—Jennifer Azzi, Stanford; 1991—Dawn Staley, Virginia; 1992—Molly Goodenbour, Stanford; 1993—Sheryl Swoopes, Texas Tech.

LEADING SCORER

Year	Player, School	G	FG	3FG	FT	Pts.	Avg.
1982	Lorri Bauman, Drake	3	36	—	38	110	36.7
1983	Janice Lawrence, Louisiana Tech	5	41	—	32	114	22.8
1984	Mary Ostrowski, Tennessee	5	43	—	27	113	22.6
1985	Lillie Mason, Western Ky.	4	34	—	25	93	23.3
1986	Clarissa Davis, Texas	5	43	—	17	103	20.6
1987	Bridgette Gordon, Tennessee	5	41	—	29	111	22.2
1988	Penny Toler, Long Beach St.	4	41	0	17	99	24.8
1989	Bridgette Gordon, Tennessee	5	53	0	28	134	26.8
1990	Trisha Stevens, Stanford	5	46	0	18	110	22.0
	Delmonica DeHorney, Arkansas	4	42	0	26	110	27.5
1991	Kerry Bascom, Connecticut	4	35	8	20	98	19.6
1992	Kim Pehlke, Western Ky.	5	40	15	19	114	22.8
1993	Sheryl Swoopes, Texas Tech	5	56	8	57	177	35.4

CAREER SCORING

Player, School (Years Competed)	G	FG	3FG	FT	Pts.	Avg.
Bridgette Gordon, Tennessee (1986-87-88-89)	18	155	0	78	388	21.6
Cheryl Miller, Southern Cal (1983-84-85-86)	16	121	—	91	333	20.8
Janice Lawrence, Louisiana Tech (1982-83-84)	14	118	—	76	312	22.3
Penny Toler, Long Beach St. (1985-87-88-89)*	13	128	0	35	291	22.4
Dawn Staley, Virginia (1989-90-91-92)	15	102	11	59	274	18.3
Cindy Brown, Long Beach St. (1984-85-86-87)	12	98	—	67	263	21.9
Venus Lacy, Louisiana Tech (1988-89-90)	14	102	1	58	263	18.8
Clarissa Davis, Texas (1986-87-89)	12	108	2	43	261	21.8
Janet Harris, Georgia (1982-83-84-85)	13	108	—	38	254	19.5
Val Whiting, Stanford (1990-91-92-93)	16	99	1	50	249	15.6

Player, School (Years Competed)	G	FG	3FG	FT	Pts.	Avg.
Teresa Edwards, Georgia (1983-84-85-86)	14	100	—	49	249	17.8
Heather Burge, Virginia (1990-91-92-93)	16	103	0	41	247	15.4
Paula McGee, Southern Cal (1982-83-84)	13	102	—	33	237	18.2
Tori Harrison, Louisiana Tech (1984-85-86-87)	15	103	—	27	233	15.5
Nora Lewis, Louisiana Tech (1987-88-89)	14	88	0	56	232	16.6
Pam McGee, Southern Cal (1982-83-84)	13	98	—	35	231	17.8
Medina Dixon, Old Dominion (1983-84-85)	12	101	—	23	225	18.8
Sheryl Swoopes, Texas Tech (1992-93)	7	74	11	63	222	31.7

* *Played for San Diego St. in 1985 tournament.*

BEST SINGLE-GAME SCORING PERFORMANCES

Player, School vs. Opponent, Year	Round	FG	3FG	FT	Pts.
Lorri Bauman, Drake vs. Maryland, 1982	RC	21	—	8	50
Sheryl Swoopes, Texas Tech vs. Ohio St., 1993	F	16	4	11	47
Barbara Kennedy, Clemson vs. Penn St., 1982	1st	20	—	3	43
LaTaunya Pollard, Long Beach St. vs. Howard, 1982	1st	13	—	14	40
Cindy Brown, Long Beach St. vs. Ohio St., 1987	RF	15	—	10	40
Kerry Bascom, Connecticut vs. Toledo, 1991	2nd	13	5	8	39
Portia Hill, Stephen F. Austin vs. Arkansas, 1990	RS	17	0	5	39
Delmonica DeHorney, Arkansas vs. Stanford, 1990	RC	15	0	9	39
LaTaunya Pollard, Long Beach St. vs. Southern Cal, 1983	RC	14	—	9	37
Teresa Edwards, Georgia vs. Tennessee, 1986	RS	14	—	9	37
Sheryl Swoopes, Texas Tech vs. Colorado, 1993	RC	10	1	15	36
Shannon Cate, Montana vs. Iowa, 1991	1st	16	2	2	36
Lisa Ingram, Northeast La. vs. Texas, 1984	RS	17	—	2	36
Eileen Shea, Michigan St. vs. Oklahoma St., 1991	2nd	12	3	8	35
Mary Ostrowski, Tennessee vs. Cheyney, 1984	SF	13	—	9	35
Wanda Ford, Drake vs. Kentucky, 1986	1st	15	—	5	35
Vicki Link, Penn St. vs. Mississippi, 1987	2nd	15	—	5	35
Dale Hodges, St. Joseph's (Pa.) vs. Long Beach St., 1989	2nd	13	0	9	35
Kim Foley, St. Joseph's (Pa.) vs. Vanderbilt, 1989	1st	13	2	7	35
Trisha Stevens, Stanford vs. Hawaii, 1990	2nd	13	0	9	35
Shannon Cate, Montana vs. Wisconsin, 1992	1st	15	0	4	34
Trise Jackson, Long Beach St. vs. Creighton, 1992	1st	14	5	1	34
Tanya Hansen, Rutgers vs. Tennessee, 1992	1st	14	0	6	34
Beth Hasenmiller, DePaul vs. Oklahoma St., 1991	1st	16	0	2	34
Lorri Bauman, Drake vs. Ohio St., 1982	1st	9	—	16	34
Lisa Ingram, Northeast La. vs. Montana, 1983	1st	15	—	4	34
Cheryl Taylor, Tennessee Tech vs. Tennessee, 1987	1st	14	—	6	34
Clinette Jordan, Oklahoma St. vs. Miami (Fla.), 1989	1st	16	0	2	34
Sheryl Swoopes, Texas Tech vs. Southern Cal, 1993	RS	11	2	9	33
Tracy Lis, Providence vs. Fairfield, 1991	1st	10	1	12	33
Delmonica DeHorney, Arkansas vs. Lamar, 1991	RS	14	0	5	33
LaTaunya Pollard, Long Beach St. vs. Drake, 1982	RC	15	—	3	33
LaTaunya Pollard, Long Beach St. vs. Oregon St., 1983	1st	14	—	5	33
Tina Hutchinson, San Diego St. vs. Oregon, 1984	1st	15	—	3	33
Kim Webb, Middle Tenn. St. vs. Western Ky., 1985	1st	13	—	7	33
Sue Wicks, Rutgers vs. North Caro. St., 1987	RS	11	—	11	33
Vicky Bullett, Maryland vs. Ohio St., 1988	RS	14	0	5	33
Nikita Lowry, Ohio St. vs. Long Beach St., 1989	RS	11	2	9	33
Bridgette Gordon, Tennessee vs. Long Beach St., 1989	RC	8	0	17	33

[Key: 1st—first round; 2nd—second round; RS—regional semifinal; RC—regional championship; SF—national semifinal; F—national championship.]

LEADING REBOUNDER

Year	Player, School	G	Reb.	Avg.
1982	Debra Walker, Cheyney	5	44	8.8
1983	Cheryl Miller, Southern Cal	5	59	11.8
1984	Mary Ostrowski, Tennessee	5	59	11.8
1985	Tracy Claxton, Old Dominion	5	72	14.4
1986	Clarissa Davis, Texas	5	56	11.2
1987	Sheila Frost, Tennessee	5	45	9.0
1988	Nora Lewis, Louisiana Tech	5	52	10.4
1989	Venus Lacy, Louisiana Tech	4	54	13.5
1990	Venus Lacy, Louisiana Tech	4	48	12.0
1991	Daedra Charles, Tennessee	5	67	13.4
1992	Val Whiting, Stanford	5	58	11.6
1993	Sheryl Swoopes, Texas Tech	5	48	9.6

CAREER REBOUNDING

Player, School (Years Competed)	G	Reb.	Avg.
Cheryl Miller, Southern Cal (1983-84-85-86)	16	170	10.6
Sheila Frost, Tennessee (1986-87-88-89)	18	162	9.0
Val Whiting, Stanford (1990-91-92-93)	16	161	10.1
Venus Lacy, Louisiana Tech (1988-89-90)	14	148	10.6
Bridgette Gordon, Tennessee (1986-87-88-89)	18	142	7.9
Kirsten Cummings, Long Beach St. (1982-83-84-85)	13	136	10.5
Nora Lewis, Louisiana Tech (1987-88-89)	14	130	9.3
Pam McGee, Southern Cal (1982-83-84)	13	127	9.8
Daedra Charles, Tennessee (1989-90-91)	13	125	9.6
Paula McGee, Southern Cal (1982-83-84)	13	125	9.6
Heather Burge, Virginia (1990-91-92-93)	16	119	7.4
Tracy Claxton, Old Dominion (1984-85)	8	117	14.6
Cindy Brown, Long Beach St. (1984-85-86-87)	12	116	9.7
Clarissa Davis, Texas (1986-87-89)	12	116	9.7
Janice Lawrence, Louisiana Tech (1982-83-84-85)	14	112	8.0
Paula Towns, Tennessee (1982-83-84)	12	112	9.3
Medina Dixon, Old Dominion (1983-84-85)	12	111	9.3

BEST SINGLE-GAME REBOUNDING PERFORMANCES

Player, School vs. Opponent, Year	Round	Reb.
Cheryl Taylor, Tennessee Tech vs. Georgia, 1985	1st	23
Daedra Charles, Tennessee vs. Southwest Mo. St., 1991	2nd	22
Cherie Nelson, Southern Cal vs. Western Ky., 1987	2nd	21
Alison Lang, Oregon vs. Missouri, 1982	1st	20
Shelda Arceneaux, San Diego St. vs. Long Beach St., 1984	RS	20
Tracy Claxton, Old Dominion vs. Georgia, 1985	F	20
Brigette Combs, Western Ky. vs. West Va., 1989	1st	20
Tandreia Green, Western Ky. vs. West Va., 1989	1st	20
Jackie Farmer, Clemson vs. Providence, 1991	2nd	19
Anne Donovan, Old Dominion vs. St. Peter's, 1982	1st	19
Sheila Foster, South Caro. vs. Kentucky, 1982	RC	19
Sheila Foster, South Caro. vs. East Caro., 1982	1st	19
Brantley Southers, South Caro. vs. East Caro., 1982	1st	19
Debra Walker, Cheyney vs. Monmouth (N.J.), 1982	1st	19
Kirsten Cummings, Long Beach St. vs. Oregon St., 1983	1st	18
Pearl Wells, South Caro. St. vs. La Salle, 1983	OR	18
Clarissa Davis, Texas vs. Western Ky., 1986	SF	18
Cindy Brown, Long Beach St. vs. Tennessee, 1987	SF	18
Sharon Stewart, Auburn vs. Penn St., 1988	1st	18
Vicky Bullett, Maryland vs. Bowling Green, 1989	RS	18

[Key: OR—opening round; 1st—first round; 2nd—second round; RS—regional semifinal; RC—regional championship; SF—national semifinal; F—national championship.]

INDIVIDUAL RECORDS

Most Points, One Game
50—Lorri Bauman, Drake (78) vs. Maryland (89), 1982

Most Points, Series
177—Sheryl Swoopes, Texas Tech, 1993 (30 vs. Washington, 33 vs. Southern Cal, 36 vs. Colorado, 31 vs. Vanderbilt, 47 vs. Ohio St.)

Most Points, Career
388—Bridgette Gordon, Tennessee (1986-87-88-89)

Most Field Goals, One Game
21—Lorri Bauman, Drake (78) vs. Maryland (89), 1982

Most Field Goals, Series
56—Sheryl Swoopes, Texas Tech, 1993 (8 vs. Washington, 11 vs. Southern Cal, 10 vs. Colorado, 11 vs. Vanderbilt, 16 vs. Ohio St.)

Most Field Goals, Career
155—Bridgette Gordon, Tennessee (1986-87-88-89)

Most Field Goals Attempted, One Game
35—Lorri Bauman, Drake (78) vs. Maryland (89), 1982

Most Field Goals Attempted, Series
110—Sheryl Swoopes, Texas Tech, 1993 (19 vs. Washington, 22 vs. Southern Cal, 21 vs. Colorado, 24 vs. Vanderbilt, 24 vs. Ohio St.)

Highest Field-Goal Percentage, One Game (minimum 10 made)
100.0%—Terry Carmichael, St. Joseph's (Pa.) (63) vs. North Caro. St. (67), 1985 (11-11); Genia Miller, Cal St. Fullerton (84) vs. Louisiana Tech (80), 1991 (10-10)

Highest Field-Goal Percentage, Series
(Minimum 40 made) 71.2%—Pam McGee, Southern Cal, 1983 (42-59)

Most Three-Point Field Goals, One Game
6—Mozell Brooks, Stephen F. Austin (84) vs. Louisiana St. (62), 1988; Katy Steding, Stanford (88) vs. Auburn (81), 1990; Brenda Hatchett, Lamar (91) vs. Arkansas (75), 1991; Molly Goodenbour, Stanford (82) vs. Southern Cal (62), 1992; Tara Saunooke, Clemson (70) vs. Xavier (Ohio) (64), 1993.

Most Three-Point Field Goals, Series
18—Molly Goodenbour, Stanford, 1992 (2 vs.

UC Santa Barb., 5 vs. Texas Tech, 6 vs. Southern Cal, 4 vs. Virginia, 1 vs. Western Ky.)

Most Three-Point Field Goals Attempted, One Game
15—Katy Steding, Stanford (88) vs. Auburn (81), 1990

Most Three-Point Field Goals Attempted, Series
39—Molly Goodenbour, Stanford, 1992 (5 vs. UC Santa Barb., 11 vs. Texas Tech, 9 vs. Southern Cal, 7 vs. Virginia, 7 vs. Western Ky.)

Highest Three-Point Field-Goal Percentage, One Game (minimum 5 made)
100.0%—Donna Holt, Virginia (85) vs. St. John's (N.Y.) (64), 1988 (5-5); Karen Middleton, South Caro. (76) vs. Northwestern (67), 1990 (5-5)

Highest Three-Point Field-Goal Percentage, Series (minimum 10 made)
73.3%—Amber Nicholas, Arkansas, 1990 (11-15)

Most Free Throws, One Game
17—Bridgette Gordon, Tennessee (94) vs. Long Beach St. (80), 1989

Most Free Throws, Series
57—Sheryl Swoopes, Texas Tech, 1993 (14 vs. Washington, 9 vs. Southern Cal, 15 vs. Colorado, 8 vs. Vanderbilt, 11 vs. Ohio St.)

Most Free Throws, Career
91—Cheryl Miller, Southern Cal (1983-84-85-86)

Most Free Throws Attempted, One Game
20—Bridgette Gordon, Tennessee (94) vs. Long Beach St. (80), 1989

Most Free Throws Attempted, Series
61—Sheryl Swoopes, Texas Tech, 1993 (15 vs. Washington, 10 vs. Southern Cal, 16 vs. Colorado, 9 vs. Vanderbilt, 11 vs. Ohio St.)

Highest Free-Throw Percentage, One Game (minimum 16 made)
100.0%—Lorri Bauman, Drake (90) vs. Ohio St. (79), 1982 (16-16)

Highest Free-Throw Percentage, Series (minimum 20 made)
93.4%—Sheryl Swoopes, Texas Tech, 1993 (57-61)

Most Rebounds, One Game
23—Cheryl Taylor, Tennessee Tech (74) vs. Georgia (91), 1985

Most Rebounds, Series
72—Tracy Claxton, Old Dominion, 1985 (13 vs. Syracuse, 11 vs. North Caro. St., 11 vs. Ohio St., 17 vs. Northeast La., 20 vs. Georgia)

Most Rebounds, Career
170—Cheryl Miller, Southern Cal (1983-84-85-86)

Most Assists, One Game (since 1985)
17—Suzie McConnell, Penn St. (98) vs. North Caro. (79), 1985; McConnell, Penn St. (72) vs. Rutgers (85), 1986

Most Assists, Series (since 1985)
42—Teresa Weatherspoon, Louisiana Tech, 1987 (11 vs. Northwestern, 11 vs. Southern Ill., 6 vs. Iowa, 11 vs. Texas, 3 vs. Tennessee)

Most Steals, One Game (since 1988)
10—Ruthie Bolton, Auburn (68) vs. Long Beach St. (55), 1988

Most Blocked Shots, One Game (since 1988)
11—Pauline Jordan, Nevada-Las Vegas (84) vs. Colorado (74), 1989

TEAM RECORDS

Most Points, One Game
116—Ohio St. vs. Syracuse (75), 1988

Most Points, Series
461—Stanford, 1990 (106 vs. Hawaii, 78 vs. Mississippi, 114 vs. Arkansas, 75 vs. Virginia, 88 vs. Auburn)

Most Field Goals, One Game
50—Georgia (112) vs. Louisville (69), 1984

Most Field Goals, Series
181—Southern Cal, 1983 (43 vs. Northeast La., 40 vs. Arizona St., 33 vs. Long Beach St., 37 vs. Georgia, 28 vs. Louisiana Tech)

Most Field Goals Attempted, One Game
89—San Diego St. (73) vs. Long Beach St. (91) (ot), 1984

Highest Field-Goal Percentage, One Game
75.0%—Texas (108) vs. Missouri (67), 1986 (42-56)

Most Three-Point Field Goals, One Game
12—Stanford (82) vs. Southern Cal (62), 1992

Most Three-Point Field Goals, Series
31—Stanford, 1992 (6 vs. UC Santa Barb., 6 vs. Texas Tech, 12 vs. Southern Cal, 4 vs. Virginia, 3 vs. Western Ky.)

Most Three-Point Field Goals Attempted, One Game
34—Alabama (68) vs. Western Ky. (98), 1992

Highest Three-Point Field-Goal Percentage, One Game (minimum 5 made)
100.0%—South Caro. (76) vs. Northwestern (67), 1990 (5-5)

Highest Three-Point Field-Goal Percentage, Series (minimum 15 made)
66.7%—Stanford, 1989 (22-33)

Most Free Throws, One Game
38—Tennessee (94) vs. Long Beach St. (80), 1989

Most Free Throws, Series
108—Texas Tech, 1993 (23 vs. Washington, 30 vs. Southern Cal, 21 vs. Colorado, 15 vs. Vanderbilt, 19 vs. Ohio St.)

Most Free Throws Attempted, One Game
48—Tennessee (94) vs. Long Beach St. (80), 1989

Highest Free-Throw Percentage, One Game (minimum 14 made)
100.0%—Virginia (76) vs. Memphis St. (75), 1987 (14-14)

Highest Free-Throw Percentage, Series (minimum 75 made)
81.2%—Texas Tech, 1993 (108-133)

Most Rebounds, One Game
66—Clemson (103) vs. Providence (91), 1991

Most Rebounds, Series
242—Old Dominion, 1985 (43 vs. Syracuse, 49 vs. North Caro. St., 36 vs. Ohio St., 57 vs. Northeast La., 57 vs. Georgia)

Most Assists, One Game (since 1985)
37—Stanford (114) vs. Arkansas (87), 1990

Most Steals, One Game (since 1988)
25—Maryland (89) vs. Stephen F. Austin (54), 1989

Most Blocked Shots, One Game (since 1988)
15—Nevada-Las Vegas (84) vs. Colorado (74), 1989

NCAA DIVISION I WOMEN'S TOURNAMENT

ALL-TIME RECORD OF EACH COLLEGE COACH-BY-COACH, 1982-1993

(126 COLLEGES)

	Yrs.	Won	Lost	Pct.	Final Four CH	2nd	3rd
ALABAMA							
Ken Weeks (Mississippi St. '67) 84	1	1	1	.500	0	0	0
Lois Myers (Ga. Southern '75) 88	1	0	1	.000	0	0	0
Rick Moody (Troy St. '76) 93	2	2	2	.500	0	0	0
TOTAL	4	3	4	.429	0	0	0
APPALACHIAN ST.							
Linda Robinson (Mars Hill '78) 90, 91	2	0	2	.000	0	0	0
TOTAL	2	0	2	.000	0	0	0
ARIZONA ST.							
Juliene Simpson (John Kennedy '74) 82, 83	2	2	2	.500	0	0	0
Maura McHugh (Old Dominion '75) 92	1	0	1	.000	0	0	0
TOTAL	3	2	3	.400	0	0	0
ARKANSAS							
John Sutherland (Kent '81) 86, 89, 90, 91	4	4	4	.500	0	0	0
TOTAL	4	4	4	.500	0	0	0
AUBURN							
Joe Ciampi (Mansfield St. '68) 82, 83, 85, 86, 87, 88, 89, 90, 91, 93	10	20	10	.667	0	3	0
TOTAL	10	20	10	.667	0	3	0
BOWLING GREEN							
Fran Voll (Bowling Green '68) 87, 88, 89, 90	4	1	4	.200	0	0	0
Jaci Clark (Wis.-Milwaukee '84) 93	1	0	1	.000	0	0	0
TOTAL	5	1	5	.167	0	0	0
BRIGHAM YOUNG							
Courtney Leishman (Utah St. '76) 84, 85	2	0	2	.000	0	0	0
Jeanie Wilson (Brigham Young '74) 93	1	0	1	.000	0	0	0
TOTAL	3	0	3	.000	0	0	0
CALIFORNIA							
Gooch Foster (Geo. Peabody '63) 90, 92, 93	3	1	3	.250	0	0	0
TOTAL	3	1	3	.250	0	0	0
UC SANTA BARB.							
Mark French (UC Santa Barb. '73) 92, 93	2	2	2	.500	0	0	0
TOTAL	2	2	2	.500	0	0	0
CAL ST. FULLERTON							
Maryalyce Jeremiah (Cedarville '65) 89, 91	2	1	2	.333	0	0	0
TOTAL	2	1	2	.333	0	0	0
CENTRAL MICH.							
Laura Golden (Florida St. '64) 83, 84	2	0	2	.000	0	0	0
TOTAL	2	0	2	.000	0	0	0
CHEYNEY							
Vivian Stringer (Slippery Rock '70) 82, 83	2	5	2	.714	0	1	0
Winthrop McGriff (Wisconsin '62) 84	1	3	1	.750	0	0	1
TOTAL	3	8	3	.727	0	1	1
CINCINNATI							
Laurie Pirtle (Ohio St. '80) 89	1	0	1	.000	0	0	0
TOTAL	1	0	1	.000	0	0	0
CLEMSON							
Annie Tribble (Clemson '66) 82	1	0	1	.000	0	0	0
Jim Davis (Tenn. Wesleyan '70) 88, 89, 90, 91, 92, 93	6	7	6	.538	0	0	0
TOTAL	7	7	7	.500	0	0	0
COLORADO							
Ceal Barry (Kentucky '77) 88, 89, 92, 93	4	3	4	.429	0	0	0
TOTAL	4	3	4	.429	0	0	0

	Yrs.	Won	Lost	Pct.	Final Four CH	2nd	3rd
CONNECTICUT							
Geno Auriemma (West Chester '81) 89, 90, 91, 92, 93	5	4	5	.444	0	0	1
TOTAL	5	4	5	.444	0	0	1
CREIGHTON							
Bruce Rasmussen (Northern Iowa '71) 92	1	1	1	.500	0	0	0
TOTAL	1	1	1	.500	0	0	0
DARTMOUTH							
Chris Wielgus (Springfield '74) 83	1	0	1	.000	0	0	0
TOTAL	1	0	1	.000	0	0	0
DEPAUL							
Doug Bruno (DePaul '73) 90, 91, 92, 93	4	2	4	.333	0	0	0
TOTAL	4	2	4	.333	0	0	0
DRAKE							
Carole Baumgarten (Northern Iowa '70) 82, 84, 86	3	3	3	.500	0	0	0
TOTAL	3	3	3	.500	0	0	0
DUKE							
Debbie Leonard (High Point '74) 87	1	1	1	.500	0	0	0
TOTAL	1	1	1	.500	0	0	0
EAST CARO.							
Cathy Andruzzi (Queens '68) 82	1	0	1	.000	0	0	0
TOTAL	1	0	1	.000	0	0	0
EASTERN ILL.							
Barbara Hilke (Western Ore. '74) 88	1	0	1	.000	0	0	0
TOTAL	1	0	1	.000	0	0	0
EASTERN WASH.							
Bill Smithpeters (Otterbein '57) 87	1	0	1	.000	0	0	0
TOTAL	1	0	1	.000	0	0	0
FAIRFIELD							
Dianne Nolan (Rowan '73) 88, 91	2	0	2	.000	0	0	0
TOTAL	2	0	2	.000	0	0	0
FLORIDA							
Carol Ross (Mississippi '82) 93	1	1	1	.500	0	0	0
TOTAL	1	1	1	.500	0	0	0
FLORIDA ST.							
Janice Dykehouse-Allen (Grand Valley St. '76) 83	1	0	1	.000	0	0	0
Marynell Meadors (Middle Tenn. St. '65) 90, 91	2	1	2	.333	0	0	0
TOTAL	3	1	3	.250	0	0	0
GEO. WASHINGTON							
Joe McKeown (Kent '78) 91, 92	2	2	2	.500	0	0	0
TOTAL	2	2	2	.500	0	0	0
GEORGETOWN							
Patrick Knapp (Widener '75) 93	1	2	1	.667	0	0	0
TOTAL	1	2	1	.667	0	0	0
GEORGIA							
Andy Landers (Tennessee Tech '74) 82, 83, 84, 85, 86, 87, 88, 89, 90, 91, 93	11	16	11	.593	0	1	1
TOTAL	11	16	11	.593	0	1	1
GA. SOUTHERN							
Drema Greer (Clemson '79) 93	1	0	1	.000	0	0	0
TOTAL	1	0	1	.000	0	0	0
GEORGIA TECH							
Agnus Berenato [Mt. St. Mary's (Md.) '80] 93	1	0	1	.000	0	0	0
TOTAL	1	0	1	.000	0	0	0
HAWAII							
Vince Goo (Southern Ore. '69) 89, 90	2	1	2	.333	0	0	0
TOTAL	2	1	2	.333	0	0	0
HOLY CROSS							
Togo Palazzi (Holy Cross '54) 85	1	0	1	.000	0	0	0
Bill Gibbons Jr. [Clark (Mass.) '81] 89, 91	2	1	2	.333	0	0	0
TOTAL	3	1	3	.250	0	0	0
HOUSTON							
Greg Williams (Rice '70) 88	1	0	1	.000	0	0	0
Jessie Kenlaw (Savannah St. '75) 92	1	0	1	.000	0	0	0
TOTAL	1	0	1	.000	0	0	0

	Yrs.	Won	Lost	Pct.	Final Four CH	2nd	3rd
HOWARD							
Sanya Tyler (Howard '79) 82	1	0	1	.000	0	0	0
TOTAL	1	0	1	.000	0	0	0
IDAHO							
Pat Dobratz (South Dak. St. '73) 85	1	0	1	.000	0	0	0
TOTAL	1	0	1	.000	0	0	0
ILLINOIS							
Jane Schroeder (Kansas St. '71) 82	1	0	1	.000	0	0	0
Laura Golden (Florida St. '64) 86, 87	2	2	2	.500	0	0	0
TOTAL	3	2	3	.400	0	0	0
ILLINOIS ST.							
Melinda Fischer (Illinois St. '72) 83, 85	2	0	2	.000	0	0	0
Jill Hutchison (New Mexico '68) 83, 85, 89	3	1	3	.250	0	0	0
TOTAL	5	1	5	.167	0	0	0
INDIANA							
Maryalyce Jeremiah (Cedarville '65) 83	1	1	1	.500	0	0	0
TOTAL	1	1	1	.500	0	0	0
IOWA							
Vivian Stringer (Slippery Rock '70) 86, 87, 88, 89, 90, 91, 92, 93	8	9	8	.529	0	0	1
TOTAL	8	9	8	.529	0	0	1
JACKSON ST.							
Sadie Magee (Alcorn St. '52) 82, 83	2	0	2	.000	0	0	0
TOTAL	2	0	2	.000	0	0	0
JAMES MADISON							
Shelia Moorman (Brigham Young '68) 86, 87, 88, 89, 91	5	7	5	.583	0	0	0
TOTAL	5	7	5	.583	0	0	0
KANSAS							
Marian Washington (West Chester '70) 87, 88, 92, 93	4	2	4	.333	0	0	0
TOTAL	4	2	4	.333	0	0	0
KANSAS ST.							
Lynn Hickey (Ouachita Baptist '73) 82, 83, 84	3	3	3	.500	0	0	0
Matilda Mossman (Western Ky. '79) 87	1	0	1	.000	0	0	0
TOTAL	4	3	4	.429	0	0	0
KENT							
Laurel Wartluft (John Kennedy '75) 82	1	0	1	.000	0	0	0
TOTAL	1	0	1	.000	0	0	0
KENTUCKY							
Terry Hall (Indiana St. '66) 82, 83, 86	3	2	3	.400	0	0	0
Sharon Fanning (Tenn.-Chatt. '75) 91	1	0	1	.000	0	0	0
TOTAL	4	2	4	.333	0	0	0
LAMAR							
Al Barbre (Stephen F. Austin '69) 91	1	3	1	.750	0	0	0
TOTAL	1	3	1	.750	0	0	0
LA SALLE							
Kevin Gallagher (Rider '72) 83	1	0	1	.000	0	0	0
Bill "Speedy" Morris [St. Joseph's (Pa.) '73] 86	1	0	1	.000	0	0	0
John Miller (St. Charles Seminary '69) 88, 89	2	1	2	.333	0	0	0
TOTAL	4	1	4	.200	0	0	0
LONG BEACH ST.							
Joan Bonvicini (Southern Conn. St. '75) 82, 83, 84, 85, 86, 87, 88, 89, 90, 91	10	18	10	.643	0	0	2
Glenn McDonald (Long Beach St. '84) 92	1	0	1	.000	0	0	0
TOTAL	11	18	11	.621	0	0	2
LOUISIANA ST.							
Sue Gunter (Peabody '62) 84, 86, 87, 88, 89, 90, 91	7	4	7	.364	0	0	0
TOTAL	7	4	7	.364	0	0	0
LOUISIANA TECH							
Sonja Hogg* (Louisiana Tech '68) 82, 83, 84, 85	4	14	3	.824	1	1	1
Leon Barmore* (Louisiana Tech '67) 83, 84, 85, 86, 87, 88, 89, 90, 91, 92, 93	11	29	10	.744	1	2	3
TOTAL	15	43	13	.768	2	3	4
LOUISVILLE							
Peggy Fiehrer (Spalding '72) 83, 84	2	0	2	.000	0	0	0
Bud Childers (Charleston So. '79) 93	1	1	1	.500	0	0	0
Total	3	1	3	.250	0	0	0

	Yrs.	Won	Lost	Pct.	Final Four CH	2nd	3rd
MANHATTAN							
Kathy Solano (Cortland St. '78) 87, 90	2	0	2	.000	0	0	0
TOTAL	2	0	2	.000	0	0	0
MARYLAND							
Chris Weller (Maryland '66) 82, 83, 84, 86, 88, 89, 90, 91 92, 93	10	12	10	.545	0	0	2
TOTAL	10	12	10	.545	0	0	2
MEMPHIS ST.							
Mary Lou Johns (Memphis St. '64) 82, 85, 87	3	1	3	.250	0	0	0
TOTAL	3	1	3	.250	0	0	0
MIAMI (FLA.)							
Ferne Labati (East Stroudsburg '66) 89, 92, 93	3	2	3	.400	0	0	0
TOTAL	3	2	3	.400	0	0	0
MICHIGAN							
Bud Van De Wege (Michigan '80) 90	1	1	1	.500	0	0	0
TOTAL	1	1	1	.500	0	0	0
MICHIGAN ST.							
Karen Langeland (Calvin '70) 91	1	0	1	.000	0	0	0
TOTAL	1	0	1	.000	0	0	0
MIDDLE TENN. ST.							
Larry Inman (Austin Peay '70) 83, 84, 85, 86	4	2	4	.333	0	0	0
Lewis Bivens (Tenn. Wesleyan '74) 88	1	0	1	.000	0	0	0
TOTAL	5	2	5	.286	0	0	0
MISSISSIPPI							
Van Chancellor (Mississippi St. '66) 82, 83, 84, 85, 86, 87, 88, 89, 90, 91, 92	11	14	11	.560	0	0	0
TOTAL	11	14	11	.560	0	0	0
MISSOURI							
Joann Rutherford (Pittsburg St. '71) 82, 83, 84, 85, 86	5	2	5	.286	0	0	0
TOTAL	5	2	5	.286	0	0	0
MONMOUTH (N.J.)							
Milton Parker (N.C. Central '65) 83	1	1	1	.500	0	0	0
TOTAL	1	1	1	.500	0	0	0
MONTANA							
Robin Selvig (Montana '74) 83, 84, 86, 88, 89, 90, 91, 92	8	4	8	.333	0	0	0
TOTAL	8	4	8	.333	0	0	0
MONTANA ST.							
Judy Spoelstra (Oregon St. '83) 93	1	0	1	.000	0	0	0
TOTAL	1	0	1	.000	0	0	0
NEBRASKA							
Angela Beck (Millikin '79) 88, 93	2	1	2	.333	0	0	0
TOTAL	2	1	2	.333	0	0	0
NEVADA-LAS VEGAS							
Jim Bolla** (Pittsburgh '75) 84, 85, 86, 89, 90, 91	6	3	6	.333	0	0	0
Sheila Strike Bolla** (Laurentian '75) 84, 85, 86	3	0	3	.000	0	0	0
TOTAL	9	3	9	.250	0	0	0
NEW MEXICO ST.							
Joe McKeown (Kent '78) 87, 88	2	0	2	.000	0	0	0
TOTAL	2	0	2	.000	0	0	0
NEW ORLEANS							
Joey Favaloro (Tulane '73) 87	1	0	1	.000	0	0	0
TOTAL	1	0	1	.000	0	0	0
NORTH CARO.							
Jennifer Alley (Appalachian St. '59) 83, 84, 85, 86	4	2	4	.333	0	0	0
Sylvia Hatchell (Carson-Newman '74) 87, 92, 93	3	2	3	.400	0	0	0
TOTAL	7	4	7	.364	0	0	0
NORTH CARO. ST.							
Kay Yow (East Caro. '64) 82, 83, 84, 85, 86, 87, 89, 90, 91	9	7	9	.438	0	0	0
TOTAL	9	7	9	.438	0	0	0
NORTH TEXAS							
Judy Nelson (Oklahoma '72) 86	1	0	1	.000	0	0	0
TOTAL	1	0	1	.000	0	0	0
NORTHEAST LA.							
Linda Harper [Northwestern (La.) '65] 83, 84, 85, 87	4	5	4	.556	0	0	1
TOTAL	4	5	4	.556	0	0	1

	Yrs.	Won	Lost	Pct.	Final Four CH	2nd	3rd
NORTHERN ILL.							
Jane Albright-Dieterle (Appalachian St. '77) 90, 92, 93	3	2	3	.400	0	0	0
TOTAL	3	2	3	.400	0	0	0
NORTHWESTERN							
Annette Lynch (Illinois St. '68) 82	1	0	1	.000	0	0	0
Don Perrelli (Southen Conn. St. '61) 87, 90, 91, 93	4	3	4	.429	0	0	0
TOTAL	5	3	5	.375	0	0	0
NORTHWESTERN (LA.)							
James Smith (Northeast La. '75) 89	1	0	1	.000	0	0	0
TOTAL	1	0	1	.000	0	0	0
NOTRE DAME							
Muffet McGraw [St. Joseph's, (Pa.) '77] 92	1	0	1	.000	0	0	0
TOTAL	1	0	1	.000		0	0
OHIO							
Amy Pritchard (Northwestern '83) 86	1	0	1	.000	0	0	0
TOTAL	1	0	1	.000	0	0	0
OHIO ST.							
Tara VanDerveer (Indiana '75) 82, 84, 85	3	2	3	.400	0	0	0
Nancy Darsch (Springfield '73) 86, 87, 88, 89, 90, 93	6	10	6	.625	0	1	0
TOTAL	9	12	9	.571	0	1	0
OKLAHOMA							
Maura McHugh (Old Dominion '75) 86	1	1	1	.500	0	0	0
TOTAL	1	1	1	.500	0	0	0
OKLAHOMA ST.							
Dick Halterman (Northeast Mo. St. '74) 89, 90, 91, 93	4	3	4	.429	0	0	0
TOTAL	4	3	4	.429	0	0	0
OLD DOMINION							
Marianne Stanley (Immaculata '76) 82, 83, 84, 85, 87	5	12	4	.750	1	0	1
Wendy Larry (Old Dominion '77) 88, 89, 90, 92, 93	5	3	5	.375	0	0	0
TOTAL	10	15	9	.625	1	0	1
OREGON							
Elwin Heiny (German Sports U. '69) 82, 84, 87	3	1	3	.250	0	0	0
TOTAL	3	1	3	.250	0	0	0
OREGON ST.							
Aki Hill (Japan AAU, John Wooden Program '72) 83, 84	2	1	2	.333	0	0	0
TOTAL	2	1	2	.333	0	0	0
PENN ST.							
Rene Portland (Immaculata '75) 82, 83, 84, 85, 86, 87, 88, 90, 91, 92, 93	11	8	11	.421	0	0	0
TOTAL	11	8	11	.421	0	0	0
PROVIDENCE							
Bob Foley (Villanova '74) 86, 89, 90, 91, 92	5	2	5	.286	0	0	0
TOTAL	5	2	5	.286	0	0	0
PURDUE							
Lin Dunn (Tenn.-Martin '69) 89, 90, 91, 92	4	3	4	.429	0	0	0
TOTAL	4	3	4	.429	0	0	0
RICHMOND							
Stephanie Gaitley (Villanova '82) 90, 91	2	0	2	.000	0	0	0
TOTAL	2	0	2	.000	0	0	0
RUTGERS							
Theresa Grentz (Immaculata '74) 86, 87, 88, 89, 90, 91, 92, 93	8	8	8	.500	0	0	0
TOTAL	8	8	8	.500	0	0	0
ST. JOHN'S (N.Y.)							
Don Perrelli (Southern Conn. St. '61) 83, 84	2	0	2	.000	0	0	0
Joe Mullaney Jr. (Providence '78) 88	1	1	1	.500	0	0	0
TOTAL	3	1	3	.250	0	0	0
ST. JOSEPH'S (PA.)							
Jim Foster (Temple '80) 85, 86, 87, 88, 89, 90	6	3	6	.333	0	0	0
TOTAL	6	3	6	.333	0	0	0
ST. PETER'S							
Mike Granelli [Mt. St. Mary's (Md.) '61] 82, 92, 93	3	0	3	.000	0	0	0
TOTAL	3	0	3	.000	0	0	0
SAN DIEGO							
Kathy Marpe (Minnesota '71) 93	1	0	1	.000	0	0	0
TOTAL	1	0	1	.000	0	0	0

	Yrs.	Won	Lost	Pct.	Final Four CH	2nd	3rd
SAN DIEGO ST.							
Earnest Riggins (Mississippi Val. '58) 84, 85	2	2	2	.500	0	0	0
Beth Burns (Ohio Wesleyan '79) 93	1	0	1	.000	0	0	0
TOTAL	3	2	3	.400	0	0	0
SANTA CLARA							
Caren Horstmeyer (Santa Clara '84) 92	1	1	1	.500	0	0	0
TOTAL	1	1	1	.500	0	0	0
SOUTH ALA.							
Charles Branum (Livingston '64) 87	1	0	1	.000	0	0	0
TOTAL	1	0	1	.000	0	0	0
SOUTH CARO.							
Terry Kelly (Covenant '76) 82	1	1	1	.500	0	0	0
Nancy Wilson (Coker '73) 86, 88, 89, 90, 91	5	3	5	.375	0	0	0
TOTAL	6	4	6	.400	0	0	0
SOUTH CARO. ST.							
Willie Simon (Allen '58) 83	1	1	1	.500	0	0	0
TOTAL	1	1	1	.500	0	0	0
SOUTHERN CAL							
Linda Sharp (Cal St. Fullerton '73) 82, 83, 84, 85, 86, 87, 88	7	19	5	.792	2	1	0
Marianne Stanley (Immaculata '76) 91, 92, 93	3	4	3	.571	0	0	0
TOTAL	10	23	8	.742	2	1	0
SOUTHERN ILL.							
Cindy Scott (Memphis St. '75) 86, 87, 90, 92	4	2	4	.333	0	0	0
TOTAL	4	2	4	.333	0	0	0
SOUTHERN MISS.							
Kay James (Mississippi Women's '69) 85, 87, 89, 90, 92	5	1	5	.167	0	0	0
TOTAL	5	1	5	.167	0	0	0
SOUTHWEST MO. ST.							
Cheryl Burnett (Kansas '81) 91, 92, 93	3	7	3	.700	0	0	1
TOTAL	3	7	3	.700	0	0	1
STANFORD							
Dotty McCrea [Monmouth (N.J.) '73]	1	0	1	.000	0	0	0
Tara VanDerveer (Indiana '75) 88, 89, 90, 91, 92, 93	6	17	4	.810	2	0	1
TOTAL	7	17	5	.773	2	0	1
STEPHEN F. AUSTIN							
Mary Ann Otwell (Ouachita Baptist '64) 82, 83	2	0	2	.000	0	0	0
Gary Blair (Texas Tech '72) 88, 89, 90, 91, 92, 93	6	6	6	.500	0	0	0
TOTAL	8	6	8	.429	0	0	0
SYRACUSE							
Barbara Jacobs (Wis.-La Crosse '71) 85, 88	2	0	2	.000	0	0	0
TOTAL	2	0	2	.000	0	0	0
TEMPLE							
Linda Hill-MacDonald (West Chester '70) 89	1	1	1	.500	0	0	0
TOTAL	1	1	1	.500	0	0	0
TENNESSEE							
Pat Summitt (Tenn.-Martin '74) 82, 83, 84, 85, 86, 87, 88, 89, 90, 91, 92, 93	12	36	9	.800	3	1	3
TOTAL	12	36	9	.800	3	1	3
TENN.-CHATT.							
Craig Parrott (Southern Miss. '79) 89, 92	2	0	2	.000	0	0	0
TOTAL	2	0	2	.000	0	0	0
TENNESSEE TECH							
Marynell Meadors (Middle Tenn. St. '65) 82, 85	2	0	2	.000	0	0	0
Bill Worrell (Tennessee Tech '68) 87, 89, 90, 91, 92, 93	6	3	6	.333	0	0	0
TOTAL	8	3	8	.273	0	0	0
TEXAS							
Jody Conradt (Baylor '63) 83, 84, 85, 86, 87, 88, 89, 90, 91, 92, 93	11	19	10	.655	1	0	1
TOTAL	11	19	10	.655	1	0	1
TEXAS TECH							
Marsha Sharp (Wayland Baptist '74) 84, 86, 90, 91, 92, 93	6	6	5	.545	1	0	0
TOTAL	6	6	4	.545	1	0	0
TOLEDO							
Bill Fennelly (William Penn '79) 91, 92	2	2	2	.500	0	0	0
TOTAL	2	2	2	.500	0	0	0

	Yrs.	Won	Lost	Pct.	Final Four		
					CH	2nd	3rd
UCLA							
Billie Moore (Washburn '66) 83, 85, 90, 92	4	3	4	.429	0	0	0
TOTAL	4	3	4	.429	0	0	0
UTAH							
Fern Gardner (Utah St. '61) 83	1	0	1	.000	0	0	0
Elaine Elliott (Boise St. '77) 86, 89, 90, 91	4	0	4	.000	0	0	0
TOTAL	5	0	5	.000	0	0	0
VANDERBILT							
Phil Lee (Campbell '70) 86, 87, 89, 90, 91	5	4	5	.444	0	0	0
Jim Foster (Temple '80) 92, 93	2	5	2	.714	0	0	1
TOTAL	7	9	7	.563	0	0	1
VERMONT							
Cathy Inglese (Southern Conn. St. '80) 92, 93	2	0	2	.000	0	0	0
TOTAL	2	0	2	.000	0	0	0
VILLANOVA							
Harry Perretta (Lycoming '78) 86, 87, 88, 89	4	1	4	.200	0	0	0
TOTAL	4	1	4	.200	0	0	0
VIRGINIA							
Debbie Ryan (Ursinus '75) 84, 85, 86, 87, 88, 89, 90, 91, 92, 93	10	16	10	.615	0	1	2
TOTAL	10	16	10	.615	0	1	2
WAKE FOREST							
Joe Sanchez (Corpus Christi '70) 88	1	1	1	.500	0	0	0
TOTAL	1	1	1	.500	0	0	0
WASHINGTON							
Joyce Sake (San Diego St. '85) 85	1	0	1	.000	0	0	0
Chris Gobrecht (Southern Cal '77) 86, 87, 88, 89, 90, 91, 93	7	8	7	.533	0	0	0
TOTAL	8	8	8	.500	0	0	0
WASHINGTON ST.							
Harold Rhodes (Washington St. '77) 91	1	0	1	.000	0	0	0
TOTAL	1	0	1	.000	0	0	0
WEST VA.							
Kittie Blakemore% (James Madison '50) 89, 92	2	2	2	.500	0	0	0
Scott Harrelson% (Southwest Tex. St. '79) 89, 92	2	2	2	.500	0	0	0
TOTAL	4	4	4	.000	0	0	0
WESTERN KY.							
Paul Sanderford (Methodist '72) 85, 86, 87, 88, 89, 90, 91, 92, 93	9	12	9	.571	0	1	2
TOTAL	9	12	9	.571	0	1	2
WESTERN MICH.							
Jim Hess (Eastern Mich. '85) 85	1	0	1	.000	0	0	0
TOTAL	1	0	1	.000	0	0	0
WISCONSIN							
Mary Murphy (Northwestern '80) 92	1	0	1	.000	0	0	0
TOTAL	1	0	1	.000	0	0	0
XAVIER (OHIO)							
Mark Ehlen (Ohio St. '75) 93	1	0	1	.000	0	0	0
TOTAL	1	0	1	.000	0	0	0

** Hogg and Barmore were co-head coaches from 1983-85. ** Bolla and Strike-Bolla were co-head coaches from 1982-88. % Blakemore and Harrelson were co-head coaches from 1989-92.*

WOMEN'S FINAL FOUR ALL-TOURNAMENT TEAMS

(First player listed on each team was the outstanding player of the championship)

1982—Janice Lawrence, Louisiana Tech
Pam Kelly, Louisiana Tech
Valerie Walker, Cheyney
Kim Mulkey, Louisiana Tech
Yolanda Laney, Cheyney

1983—Cheryl Miller, Southern Cal
Paula McGee, Southern Cal
Janice Lawrence, Louisiana Tech
Jennifer White, Louisiana Tech
Anne Donovan, Old Dominion

1984—Cheryl Miller, Southern Cal
Pam McGee, Southern Cal
Paula McGee, Southern Cal
Janice Lawrence, Louisiana Tech
Mary Ostrowski, Tennessee

1985—Tracy Claxton, Old Dominion
Medina Dixon, Old Dominion
Teresa Edwards, Georgia
Katrina McClain, Georgia
Lillie Mason, Western Ky.

1986—Clarissa Davis, Texas
Cheryl Miller, Southern Cal
Cynthia Cooper, Southern Cal
Fran Harris, Texas
Clemette Haskins, Western Ky.

1987—Tonya Edwards, Tennessee
Bridgette Gordon, Tennessee
Teresa Weatherspoon, Louisiana Tech
Clarissa Davis, Texas
Cindy Brown, Long Beach St.

1988—Erica Westbrooks, Louisiana Tech
Teresa Weatherspoon, Louisiana Tech
Diann McNeil, Auburn
Ruthie Bolton, Auburn
Penny Toler, Long Beach St.

1989—Bridgette Gordon, Tennessee
Sheila Frost, Tennessee
Vickie Orr, Auburn
Deanna Tate, Maryland
Venus Lacy, Louisiana Tech

1990—Jennifer Azzi, Stanford
Katy Steding, Stanford
Chantel Tremitiere, Auburn
Carolyn Jones, Auburn
Venus Lacy, Louisiana Tech

1991—Dawn Staley, Virginia
Tonya Cardoza, Virginia
Daedra Charles, Tennessee
Dena Head, Tennessee
Sonja Henning, Stanford

1992—Molly Goodenbour, Stanford
Rachel Hemmer, Stanford
Val Whiting, Stanford
Kim Pehlke, Western Ky.
Dawn Staley, Virginia

1993—Sheryl Swoopes, Texas Tech
Krista Kirkland, Texas Tech
Nikki Keyton, Ohio St.
Katie Smith, Ohio St.
Heidi Gillingham, Vanderbilt

AIAW CHAMPIONSHIP FINALS RESULTS

For historical purposes, the results of the Association of Intercollegiate Athletics for Women (AIAW) championships are listed below. The AIAW championships served as the national women's large-college playoff for the 10 years preceding the NCAA championship in 1982.

Year	Finals Teams	Championship Game Score	Site of Championship
1972	Immaculata West Chester Cal St. Fullerton Mississippi-Women	Immaculata 52, West Chester 48	Normal, Ill.
1973	Immaculata Queens (N.Y.) Southern Conn. St. Indiana	Immaculata 59, Queens (N.Y.) 52	Flushing, N.Y.
1974	Immaculata Mississippi Col. Southern Conn. St. William Penn	Immaculata 68, Mississippi Col. 53	Manhattan, Kan.
1975	Delta St. Immaculata Cal St. Fullerton Southern Conn. St.	Delta St. 90, Immaculata 81	Harrisonburg, Va.
1976	Delta St. Immaculata Wayland Baptist William Penn	Delta St. 69, Immaculata 64	University Park, Pa.
1977	Delta St. Louisiana St. Tennessee Immaculata	Delta St. 68, Louisiana St. 55	Minneapolis, Minn.
1978	UCLA Maryland Montclair St. Wayland Baptist	UCLA 90, Maryland 74	Los Angeles, Calif.
1979	Old Dominion Louisiana Tech Tennessee UCLA	Old Dominion 75, Louisiana Tech 65	Greensboro, N.C.
1980	Old Dominion Tennessee South Caro. Louisiana Tech	Old Dominion 68, Tennessee 53	Mt. Pleasant, Mich.
1981	Louisiana Tech Tennessee Old Dominion Southern Cal	Louisiana Tech 79, Tennessee 59	Eugene, Ore.
1982	Rutgers Texas Villanova Wayland Baptist	Rutgers 83, Texas 77	Philadelphia, Pa.

1993 DIVISION II WOMEN'S CHAMPIONSHIP RESULTS

FIRST ROUND
Bentley 71, Franklin Pierce 46
Mass.-Lowell 84, Stonehill 78
Norfolk St. 90, Fort Valley St. 76
S.C.-Spartanburg 71, St. Augustine's 69
North Dak. St. 92, Denver 77
Augustana (S.D.) 79, North Dak. 67
Cal Poly Pomona 62, UC Riverside 49
Portland St. 64, UC Davis 61
Clarion 67, Phila. Textile 64
Pitt.-Johnstown 88, Edinboro 76 (ot)
Florida Tech 86, Fla. Atlantic 74
Delta St. 90, Jacksonville 61
Mo. Southern St. 82, Pittsburg St. 67
Washburn 77, Central Mo. St. 67
Saginaw Valley 81, Indianapolis 76
Michigan Tech 92, Bellarmine 73

REGIONAL CHAMPIONSHIPS
Bentley 68, Mass.-Lowell 60
Norfolk St. 75, S.C.-Spartanburg 68
North Dak. St. 91, Augustana (S.D.) 82
Cal Poly Pomona 59, Portland St. 51
Pitt.-Johnstown 70, Clarion 64
Delta St. 75, Florida Tech 51
Washburn 75, Mo. Southern St. 62
Michigan Tech 77, Saginaw Valley 58

QUARTERFINALS
Bentley 84, Norfolk St. 66
North Dak. St. 91, Cal Poly Pomona 55
Delta St. 96, Pitt.-Johnstown 63
Michigan Tech 78, Washburn 77 (ot)

SEMIFINALS
Delta St. 71, Michigan Tech 67
North Dak. St. 79, Bentley 57

THIRD PLACE
Michigan Tech 74, Bentley 60

CHAMPIONSHIP
North Dak. St. 95, Delta St. 63

DIVISION II WOMEN'S CHAMPIONSHIP BOX SCORES

SEMIFINALS

Delta St. 71, Michigan Tech 67

Michigan Tech	FG-FGA	FT-FTA	RB	PF	TP
Connie Pleshe	2-10	0- 0	0	2	6
Terri Sorenson	3- 5	0- 0	8	2	6
Darla Innes	3- 6	0- 0	3	4	6
Leigh Murphy	0- 0	0- 0	0	0	0
Dawn Zarling	7-12	5- 9	8	3	19
Traci Vinopal	5-11	4- 4	5	2	15
Jenny Postlewaite	6-22	2- 2	7	5	15
Team			4		
TOTALS	26-66	11-15	35	18	67

Delta St.	FG-FGA	FT-FTA	RB	PF	TP
Theresa Perry	6-13	2- 2	6	1	17
Dawn Chism	1- 5	2- 2	1	2	5
LaTanya Patty	5-10	3- 4	13	0	13
Marieia Wright	1- 4	3- 4	3	4	6
Shorlone Crockam	6-17	3- 5	7	4	16
Leslie McKiernon	4- 8	0- 1	10	0	8
Shelley Murrell	2- 3	0- 0	2	2	4
Sonya Marshall	1- 2	0- 0	0	0	2
Mary Margaret Vandevender	0- 0	0- 0	3	2	0
Team			3		
TOTALS	26-62	13-18	48	15	71

Half time: Delta St. 37, Michigan Tech 34. Three-point field goals: Michigan Tech 4-17 (Pleshe 2-8, Postlewaite 1-4, Vinopal 1-5); Delta St. 6-19 (Perry 3-7, Chism 1-2, Wright 1-2, Crockam 1-8). Officials: Joanne Aldrich, Curt Seter. Attendance: 4,000.

North Dak. St. 79, Bentley 57

North Dak. St.	FG-FGA	FT-FTA	RB	PF	TP
Nadine Schmidt	5-13	0- 0	5	2	10
Jody Buck	5- 6	2- 2	5	1	12
Jenni Rademacher	3- 8	1- 2	5	1	7
Lori Roufs	2- 3	0- 0	3	2	4
Darci Steere	4- 7	1- 5	11	2	9
Jackie Parsley	9-21	1- 2	6	1	19
Linda Davis	0- 1	0- 0	0	2	0
Lynette Mund	2-12	7- 9	4	3	12
Dawn Mattern	0- 1	0- 0	1	2	0
Slone Benson	2- 4	0- 0	5	2	4
Jessica DeRemer	1- 1	0- 0	0	0	2
Team			3		
TOTALS	33-77	12-20	48	18	79

Bentley	FG-FGA	FT-FTA	RB	PF	TP
Tracy Pomerenke	2- 6	0- 0	1	1	5
Sharon Conway	1- 4	0- 2	3	3	3
Kim Cummings	3- 8	6- 6	6	1	12
Kim Penwell	3- 6	6- 6	7	3	12
Karen Mishelof	2- 3	0- 1	2	1	4
Patrice Misiano	5- 9	2- 2	7	4	12
Beth Biasotti	1- 5	0- 0	2	1	3
Janet Kerrigan	1- 4	4- 8	9	3	6
Carlini Guest	0- 3	0- 0	3	3	0
Team			0		
TOTALS	18-48	18-25	40	20	57

Half time: Bentley 36, North Dak. St. 34. Three-point field goals: North Dak. St. 1-7 (Mund 1-5, Schmidt 0-1, Mattern 0-1); Bentley 3-8 (Conway 1-2, Pomerenke 1-3, Biasotti 1-3). Officials: Ed Miller, Ron Dressander. Attendance: 4,000.

THIRD PLACE

Michigan Tech 74, Bentley 60

Michigan Tech	FG-FGA	FT-FTA	RB	PF	TP
Kristin Hager	0- 3	2- 2	2	0	2
Connie Pleshe	2-10	1- 2	3	3	7
Chaunda Shaw	0- 1	0- 0	0	0	0
Terri Sorenson	7-10	7- 9	5	3	22
Darla Innes	4- 8	0- 0	6	3	8
Leigh Murphy	0- 1	0- 0	2	1	0
Dawn Zarling	2- 6	0- 0	3	5	4
Traci Vinopal	4-11	2- 3	8	3	10
Jenny Postlewaite	6-12	9- 9	5	3	21
Team			2		
TOTALS	25-62	21-25	36	21	74

Bentley	FG-FGA	FT-FTA	RB	PF	TP
Tracy Pomerenke	0- 5	0- 0	3	1	0
Sharon Conway	1- 4	1- 2	0	1	3
Kim Cummings	2- 7	2- 3	2	3	6
Kim Penwell	1- 7	10-13	9	2	12
Marcy Spahr	0- 1	0- 0	0	0	0

Karen Mishelof...	3- 6	4- 4	3	2	10
Patrice Misiano ..	6-11	0- 0	5	5	12
Beth Biasotti	1- 8	0- 0	2	5	3
Janet Kerrigan ...	3- 3	4- 4	10	1	10
Beth Pilgrim	0- 0	0- 0	2	1	0
Carlini Guest	2- 2	0- 1	3	0	4
Team			4		
TOTALS	19-54	21-27	43	21	60

Half time: Michigan Tech 35, Bentley 31. Three-point field goals: Michigan Tech 3-14 (Pleshe 2-6, Sorenson 1-1, Postlewaite 0-1, Shaw 0-1, Hager 0-2, Vinopal 0-3); Bentley 1-11 (Biasotti 1-4, Spahr 0-1, Conway 0-2, Pomerenke 0-4). Officials: Ed Miller, Ron Dressander. Attendance: 4,000.

CHAMPIONSHIP

North Dak. St. 95, Delta St. 63

North Dak. St.	**FG-FGA**	**FT-FTA**	**RB**	**PF**	**TP**
Patty Jo VandenBurg	0- 1	2- 2	0	0	2
Theresa Berger ..	1- 1	0- 0	0	0	2
Nadine Schmidt ..	10-16	3- 4	6	0	24
Jody Buck	3- 6	1- 2	4	0	7
Jenni Rademacher ...	6-10	2- 2	2	1	14
Lori Roufs	2- 2	0- 0	2	1	4
Darci Steere	5-13	0- 0	7	1	10
Jackie Parsley	7-15	3- 4	6	3	17
Linda Davis	3- 3	0- 0	1	0	6
Lynette Mund	2-12	3- 4	5	2	7
Dawn Mattern	0- 1	0- 0	1	1	0
Slone Benson	1- 2	0- 0	5	1	2
Jessica DeRemer	0- 1	0- 0	3	1	0
Team			7		
TOTALS	40-83	14-18	49	11	95

Delta St.	**FG-FGA**	**FT-FTA**	**RB**	**PF**	**TP**
Theresa Perry	2- 8	0- 0	4	1	5
Dawn Chism	3- 5	1- 1	4	2	8
Charisse Stratton	0- 1	0- 0	0	0	0
LaTanya Patty	6-10	2- 2	6	3	14
Marieia Wright ...	2- 8	2- 3	5	3	6
Shorlone Crockam	4-16	0- 0	6	2	8
Mechelli Lollar ...	0- 0	0- 0	0	0	0
Leslie McKeirnon	4-16	3- 6	12	0	11
Shelley Murrell ...	3- 3	0- 0	1	0	6
Sonya Marshall ..	1- 2	0- 0	0	2	2
Mary Margaret Vandevender ...	1- 2	1- 2	1	1	3
Team			7		
TOTALS	26-71	9-14	46	14	63

Half time: North Dak. St. 40, Delta St. 26. Three-point field goals: North Dak. St. 1-3 (Schmidt 1-1, Buck 0-1, Mund 0-1); Delta St. 2-12 (Perry 1-2, Chism 1-3, Stratton 0-1, Wright 0-2, Crockam 0-4). Officials: Joanne Aldrich, Curt Seter. Attendance: 4,000.

DIVISION II WOMEN'S CHAMPIONSHIP RECORDS

ALL-TIME RESULTS

Year	Champion	Coach	Score	Runner-Up	Site
1982	Cal Poly Pomona	Darlene May	93-74	Tuskegee	Springfield, Mass.
1983	Virginia Union	Louis Hearn	73-60	Cal Poly Pomona	Springfield, Mass.
1984	Central Mo. St.	Jorja Hoehn	80-73	Virginia Union	Springfield, Mass.
1985	Cal Poly Pomona	Darlene May	80-69	Central Mo. St.	Springfield, Mass.
1986	Cal Poly Pomona	Darlene May	70-63	North Dak. St.	Springfield, Mass.
1987	New Haven	Jan Rossman	77-75	Cal Poly Pomona	Springfield, Mass.
1988	Hampton	James Sweat	65-48	West Tex. A&M	Fargo, N.D.
1989	Delta St.	Lloyd Clark	88-58	Cal Poly Pomona	Cleveland, Miss.
1990	Delta St.	Lloyd Clark	77-43	Bentley	Pomona, Calif.
1991	North Dak. St.	Amy Ruley	81-74	Southeast Mo. St.	Cape Girardeau, Mo.
1992	Delta St.	Lloyd Clark	65-63	North Dak. St.	Fargo, N.D.
1993	North Dak. St.	Amy Ruley	95-63	Delta St.	Waltham, Mass.

OUTSTANDING PLAYER AWARDS

1982—Jackie White, Cal Poly Pomona; 1983—Paris McWhirter, Virginia Union; 1984—Carla Eades, Central Mo. St.; 1985—Vickie Mitchell, Cal Poly Pomona; 1986—Debra Larsen, Cal Poly Pomona; 1987—Joy Jeter, New Haven; 1988—Jackie Dolberry, Hampton; 1989—Pam Lockett, Delta St; 1990—Crystal Hardy, Delta St; 1991—Nadine Schmidt, North Dak. St.; 1992—Leslie McKiernon, Delta St.; 1993—Nadine Schmidt, North Dak. St.

INDIVIDUAL RECORDS

Most Points, One Game
44—Niki Bracken, Cal Poly Pomona (103) vs. Alas. Anchorage (77), 1988

Most Points, Series
132—Debbie Delie, Oakland, 1990 [33 vs. IU/PU-Ft. Wayne, 33 vs. St. Joseph's (Ind.), 28 vs. Central Mo. St., 27 vs. Bentley, 11 vs. Cal Poly Pomona]

Most Field Goals, One Game
18—Niki Bracken, Cal Poly Pomona (103) vs. Alas. Anchorage (77), 1988

Most Field Goals, Series
54—Niki Bracken, Cal Poly Pomona, 1989 [15 vs. Cal St. Hayward, 12 vs. Cal St. Northridge, 8 vs. St. Joseph's (Ind.), 8 vs. Bentley, 11 vs. Delta St.]

Highest Field-Goal Percentage, One Game (minimum 11 made)
100.0%—Cathy Gooden, Cal Poly Pomona (88) vs. UC Davis (52), 1988 (11-11)

Most Three-Point Field Goals, One Game
7—Durene Heisler, North Dak. (93) vs. Augustana (S.D.) (78), 1990; Serenda Valdez, Cal Poly Pomona (67) vs. North Dak. (64), 1990; Amy Coon, Clarion (80) vs. Bloomsburg (76), 1991

Most Three-Point Field Goals, Series
21—Lori Bender, Bentley, 1989 (2 vs. Bridgeport, 5 vs. New Haven, 5 vs. Bloomsburg, 4 vs. Cal Poly Pomona, 5 vs. Central Mo. St.)

Highest Three-Point Field-Goal Percentage, One Game (minimum 5 made)
85.7%—Missy Wolfe, Bentley (97) vs. Jacksonville St. (92), 1991 (6-7)

Highest Three-Point Field-Goal Percentage, Series (minimum 10 made)
59.1%—Tracie Seymour, Bentley, 1992 (13-22)

Most Free Throws, One Game
16—Whitney Meier, North Dak. (94) vs. Fla. Atlantic (78), 1991

Most Free Throws, Series
41—Kim Penwell, Bentley, 1992 (4 vs. Franklin Pierce, 7 vs. Stonehill, 15 vs. Pitt.-Johnstown, 6 vs. Delta St., 9 vs. Portland St.)

Highest Free-Throw Percentage, One Game (minimum 14 made)
100.0%—Pat Smykowski, North Dak. (77) vs. Central Mo. St. (60), 1986 (14-14)

Most Rebounds, One Game
23—Michelle Weakley, Bellarmine (67) vs. Wright St. (80), 1987; Yolanda Griffith, Fla. Atlantic (74) vs. Florida Tech (86), 1993

Most Rebounds, Series
57—Venice Frazer, Hampton, 1988 (10 vs. Dist. Columbia, 12 vs. Virginia St., 13 vs. Pitt.-Johnstown, 10 vs. North Dak. St., 12 vs. West Tex. A&M); Jerri Wiley, Southeast Mo. St., 1991 (14 vs. Central Mo. St., 13 vs. West Tex. A&M, 11 vs. Cal Poly Pomona, 11 vs. Norfolk St., 8 vs. North Dak. St.)

TEAM RECORDS

Most Points, One Game
108—Pitt.-Johnstown vs. Indiana (Pa.) (55), 1988; Norfolk St. vs. Johnson Smith (71), 1992

Most Points, Series
448—North Dak. St., 1993 [92 vs. Denver, 91 vs. Augustana (S.D.), 91 vs. Cal Poly Pomona, 79 vs. Bentley, 95 vs. Delta St.]

Most Field Goals, One Game
47—Delta St. (100) vs. Clark Atlanta (54), 1986

Most Field Goals, Series
172—North Dak. St., 1991 [36 vs. Augustana (S.D.), 31 vs. North Dak., 38 vs. Bellarmine, 33 vs. Bentley, 34 vs. Southeast Mo. St.]; North Dak. St., 1992 [40 vs. South Dak. St., 39 vs. Augustana (S.D.), 30 vs. Washburn, 34 vs. Portland St., 29 vs. Delta St.]

Most Three-Point Field Goals, One Game
13—Clarion (73) vs. Pitt.-Johnstown (75), 1992

Most Three-Point Field Goals, Series
26—Bentley, 1991 (2 vs. Stonehill, 9 vs. St. Anselm, 8 vs. Jacksonville St, 5 vs. North Dak. St., 2 vs. Norfolk St.); Clarion, 1991 (11 vs. Bloomsburg, 6 vs. Lock Haven, 9 vs. Norfolk St.)

Highest Three-Point Field-Goal Percentage, One Game (minimum 5 made)
77.8%—St. Anselm (82) vs. Mass.-Lowell (65), 1991 (7-9)

Highest Three-Point Field-Goal Percentage, Series (minimum 10 made)
58.3%—Bentley, 1992 (14-24)

Most Free Throws, One Game
34—Augustana (S.D.) (79) vs. North Dak. (67), 1993

Most Free Throws, Series
104—Bentley, 1992 (18 vs. Franklin Pierce, 15 vs. Stonehill, 32 vs. Pitt.-Johnstown, 14 vs. Delta St., 25 vs. Portland St.)

Most Rebounds, One Game
68—North Dak. St. (104) vs. Augustana (S.D.) (69), 1992

Most Rebounds, Series
281—North Dak. St., 1992 [52 vs. South Dak St., 68 vs. Augustana (S.D.), 60 vs. Washburn, 55 vs. Portland St., 46 vs. Delta St.]

Most Personal Fouls, One Game
36—Tuskegee (83) vs. Central Fla. (68), 1983

DIVISION II WOMEN'S ALL-TOURNAMENT TEAMS

(First player listed on each team was the outstanding player of the championship)

1982—Jackie White, Cal Poly Pomona
Annette Chester, Tuskegee
Carol Welch, Cal Poly Pomona
Brenda McLean, Oakland
Becky Lovett, Mt. St. Mary's (Md.)

1983—Paris McWhirter, Virginia Union
Barvenia Wooten, Virginia Union
Jackie White, Cal Poly Pomona
Lisa Ulmer, Cal Poly Pomona
Carla Eades, Central Mo. St.

1984—Carla Eades, Central Mo. St.
Veta Williams, Virginia Union
Janice Washington, Valdosta St.
Rosie Jones, Central Mo. St.
Donna Burks, Dayton

1985—Vickie Mitchell, Cal Poly Pomona
Kelley Fraser, Cal Poly Pomona
Sheri Jennum, Cal Poly Pomona
Rosie Jones, Central Mo. St.
Anita Meadows, Mercer

1986—Debra Larsen, Cal Poly Pomona
Michelle McCoy, Cal Poly Pomona
Vickie Mitchell, Cal Poly Pomona
Janice Woods, North Dak. St.
Pat Smykowski, North Dak. St.
Vincene Morris, Phila. Textile

1987—Joy Jeter, New Haven
Niki Bracken, Cal Poly Pomona
Michelle McCoy, Cal Poly Pomona
Charlene Taylor, New Haven
Jill Halapin, Pitt.-Johnstown

1988—Jackie Dolberry, Hampton
Venice Frazer, Hampton
Karen Drewry, Hampton
Teresa Tinner, West Tex. A&M
Kristi Kremer, North Dak. St.

1989—Pam Lockett, Delta St.
Jo Lynn Davis, Delta St.
Niki Bracken, Cal Poly Pomona
Lori Bender, Bentley
Tammy Wilson, Central Mo. St.

1990—Crystal Hardy, Delta St.
Pam Lockett, Delta St.
Tracie Seymour, Bentley
Niki Bracken, Cal Poly Pomona
Debbie Delie, Oakland

1991—Nadine Schmidt, North Dak. St.
Jill DeVries, North Dak. St.
Jerri Wiley, Southeast Mo. St.
Sarita Wesley, Southeast Mo. St.
Kim Penwell, Bentley

1992—Leslie McKiernon, Delta St.
LaTanya Patty, Delta St.
Nadine Schmidt, North Dak. St.
Sherri Stemple, Portland St.
Jody Buck, North Dak. St.
Tracie Seymour, Bentley

1993—Nadine Schmidt, North Dak. St.
Jody Buck, North Dak. St.
Jackie Parsley, North Dak. St.
LaTanya Patty, Delta St.
Jenny Postlewaite, Michigan Tech

DIVISION III WOMEN'S CHAMPIONSHIP

1993 DIVISION III WOMEN'S CHAMPIONSHIP RESULTS

REGIONALS
Southern Me. 67, Salem St. 63
Rowan 65, Wm. Paterson 55
Babson 86, Western Conn. St. 68
Capital 93, Wittenberg 50
Geneseo St. 84, Buffalo St. 69
Moravian 56, Susquehanna 55
New York U. 64, St. John Fisher 57 (ot)
Scranton 103, Waynesburg 76
Maryville (Tenn.) 85, Roanoke 67
Concordia-M'head 78, Muskingum 64
Marymount (Va.) 115, Chris. Newport 96
St. Benedict 78, St. Thomas (Minn.) 65
Wis.-Eau Claire 95, Wis.-Stout 89
Central (Iowa) 81, Augustana (Ill.) 68
Wis.-Whitewater 76, Calvin 68
Wartburg 75, Washington (Mo.) 60

SECTIONAL SEMIFINALS
Southern Me. 75, Rowan 48
Capital 68, Babson 56
Geneseo St. 80, Moravian 57
Scranton 82, New York U. 54
Concordia-M'head 87, Maryville (Tenn.) 69
St. Benedict 108, Marymount (Va.) 75
Central (Iowa) 70, Wis.-Eau Claire 63
Wartburg 83, Wis.-Whitewater 77

SECTIONAL CHAMPIONSHIPS
Capital 66, Southern Me. 56
Scranton 79, Geneseo St. 70
St. Benedict 84, Concordia-M'head 57
Central (Iowa) 62, Wartburg 60

SEMIFINALS
Capital 65, Scranton 61
Central (Iowa) 60, St. Benedict 59

THIRD PLACE
Scranton 89, St. Benedict 69

CHAMPIONSHIP
Central (Iowa) 71, Capital 63

DIVISION III WOMEN'S CHAMPIONSHIP BOX SCORES

SEMIFINALS

Capital 65, Scranton 61

Capital	FG-FGA	FT-FTA	RB	PF	TP
Lora Vandenbark	3- 3	6- 6	2	1	12
Teresa Kelly	1- 1	1- 1	1	0	3
Carmen Ellis	4- 9	0- 0	2	4	8
Jacque Mattox	2- 4	0- 0	1	0	5
Robyne Fogle	3- 7	0- 0	1	4	8
Laura Schmelzer	3- 5	0- 0	0	5	6
Sandy Buddelmeyer	7-15	3- 4	15	3	17
Katie Mang	0- 2	4- 4	1	0	4
Darcy Lyons	0- 0	0- 0	1	0	0
Jane Rausch	1- 1	0- 1	1	0	2
Team			2		
TOTALS	24-47	14-16	27	17	65

Scranton	FG-FGA	FT-FTA	RB	PF	TP
Sue Sitnik	0- 0	0- 0	1	0	0
Kenella Lester	0- 1	0- 0	0	0	0
Anne Gooley	6-10	0- 0	2	3	15
Katie Geiger	6- 9	0- 1	7	5	14
Jackie Dougherty	3- 9	1- 2	7	4	7
Lynne Kempski	4- 8	3- 5	2	3	12
Regan McGorry	2- 7	1- 2	3	2	5
Ann Turlip	2- 5	4- 4	3	3	8
Team			1		
TOTALS	23-49	9-14	26	20	61

Half time: Scranton 32, Capital 28. Three-point field goals: Capital 3-7 (Fogle 2-3, Mattox 1-2, Mang 0-2); Scranton 6-9 (Gooley 3-5, Geiger 2-3, Kempski 1-1). Officials: Donna Wegner, Dan Fitzgerald. Attendance: 2,200.

Central (Iowa) 60, St. Benedict 59

St. Benedict	FG-FGA	FT-FTA	RB	PF	TP
Melissa Harren	0- 0	0- 0	1	0	0
Kelly Mahlum	5-15	0- 0	8	1	13
Janine Mettling	5- 9	4- 4	5	0	14
Colleen Casey	1- 5	0- 0	2	4	2
Lynn Nielsen	4- 5	1- 2	6	1	9
Danielle Guse	0- 6	2- 2	3	0	2
Amy Hergott	2- 5	0- 0	4	2	4
Tina Kampa	7-11	1- 2	7	3	15
Team			4		
TOTALS	24-56	8-10	40	11	59

Central (Iowa)	FG-FGA	FT-FTA	RB	PF	TP
Jayna Blom	1- 5	0- 0	2	2	2
Emilie Hanson	5-14	0- 0	1	0	10
Tiffanie Corey	4- 9	1- 4	5	1	10
Teresa McGovern	2- 4	0- 0	5	0	4
Tracy Wilson	9-21	0- 0	10	3	18
Brenda Rempe	0- 0	0- 0	1	0	0
Wendy Rinehart	0- 0	0- 0	0	1	0
Chris Rogers	7-11	2- 4	7	3	16
Team			2		
TOTALS	28-64	3- 8	33	10	60

Half time: St. Benedict 29, Central (Iowa) 27. Three-point field goals: St. Benedict 3-10 (Mahlum 3-5, Mettling 0-1, Guse 0-1, Casey 0-3); Central

(Iowa) 1-5 (Corey 1-4, McGovern 0-1). Officials: Kathy Lynch, Angela Sanseviro. Attendance: 2,200.

THIRD PLACE

Scranton 89, St. Benedict 69

Scranton	FG-FGA	FT-FTA	RB	PF	TP
Sue Sitnik	0- 2	0- 0	1	0	0
Kenella Lester	0- 1	0- 0	3	2	0
Anne Gooley	8-13	0- 0	2	1	19
Katie Geiger	8-14	2- 2	6	3	20
Jackie Dougherty	7-13	2- 4	7	4	16
Lynne Kempski	4- 7	0- 2	3	2	11
Regan McGorry	2- 4	5- 8	4	1	9
Ann Turlip	5-10	4- 4	5	4	14
Joelle Hudak	0- 1	0- 0	0	0	0
Team			1		
TOTALS	34-65	13-20	32	17	89

St. Benedict	FG-FGA	FT-FTA	RB	PF	TP
Kelly Mahlum	6-20	0- 0	6	3	12
Janine Mettling	2- 4	0- 0	6	4	6
Colleen Casey	1- 3	0- 0	4	3	2
Lynn Nielsen	9-14	4- 4	5	2	22
Danielle Guse	2- 5	2- 2	2	2	6
Amy Hergott	0- 3	2- 2	2	0	2
Tina Kampa	7-12	0- 1	8	4	14
Glennis Werner	2- 2	1- 2	4	0	5
Team			1		
TOTALS	29-63	9-11	38	18	69

Half time: Scranton 34, St. Benedict 27. Three-point field goals: Scranton 8-12 (Kempski 3-3, Gooley 3-4, Geiger 2-5); St. Benedict 2-7 (Mettling 2-3, Casey 0-1, Mahlum 0-3). Officials: Dan Fitzgerald, Donna Wegner. Attendance: 2,200.

CHAMPIONSHIP

Central (Iowa) 71, Capital 63

Capital	FG-FGA	FT-FTA	RB	PF	TP
Lora Vandenbark	1- 3	0- 0	2	5	2
Teresa Kelly	0- 0	0- 0	0	0	0
Carmen Ellis	2- 7	1- 2	6	4	5
Jacque Mattox	5- 7	1- 2	3	1	13
Betty Cameron	0- 0	0- 0	1	0	0
Robyne Fogle	1- 4	0- 0	0	3	2
Laura Schmelzer	4-13	1- 2	4	2	9
Sandy Buddelmeyer	9-14	7- 8	12	4	25
Katie Mang	1- 2	4- 5	1	1	7
Kelly Kerscher	0- 0	0- 0	0	0	0
Jane Rausch	0- 0	0- 0	0	0	0
Team			0		
TOTALS	23-50	14-19	29	20	63

Central (Iowa)	FG-FGA	FT-FTA	RB	PF	TP
Jayna Blom	0- 5	0- 0	2	2	0
Emilie Hanson	7-13	12-14	2	2	26
Tiffanie Corey	3- 7	3- 3	1	1	10
Teresa McGovern	1- 2	0- 0	2	1	2
Tracy Wilson	4- 9	9- 9	7	4	17
Brenda Rempe	0- 0	0- 0	2	1	0
Chris Rogers	8-14	0- 0	10	3	16
Team			2		
TOTALS	23-50	24-26	28	14	71

Half time: Central (Iowa) 37, Capital 33. Three-point field goals: Capital 3-6 (Mattox 2-3, Mang 1-2, Fogle 0-1); Central (Iowa) 1-3 (Corey 1-3). Officials: Angela Sanseviro, Kathy Lynch. Attendance: 2,200.

DIVISION III WOMEN'S CHAMPIONSHIP RECORDS

ALL-TIME RESULTS

Year	Champion	Coach	Score	Runner-Up	Site
1982	Elizabethtown	Yvonne Kauffman	67-66†	N.C.-Greensboro	Elizabethtown, Pa.
1983	North Central	Wayne Morgan	83-71	Elizabethtown	Worcester, Mass.
1984	Rust	A. J. Stovall	51-49	Elizabethtown	Scranton, Pa.
1985	Scranton	Mike Strong	68-59	New Rochelle	DePere, Wis.
1986	Salem St.	Tim Shea	89-85	Bishop	Salem, Mass.
1987	Wis.-Stevens Point	Linda Wunder	81-74	Concordia-M'head	Scranton, Pa.
1988	Concordia-M'head	Duane Siverson	65-57	St. John Fisher	Moorhead, Minn.
1989	Elizabethtown	Yvonne Kauffman	66-65	Cal St. Stanislaus	Danville, Ky.
1990	Hope	Sue Wise	65-63	St. John Fisher	Holland, Mich.
1991	St. Thomas (Minn.)	Ted Riverso	73-55	Muskingum	St. Paul, Minn.
1992	Alma	Charlie Goffnet	79-75	Moravian	Bethlehem, Pa.
1993	Central (Iowa)	Gary Boeyink	71-63	Capital	Pella, Iowa

† *Overtime.*

OUTSTANDING PLAYER AWARD

(Discontinued after 1984 championship)

1982—Bev Hall, Elizabethtown; 1983—Page Lutz, Elizabethtown; 1984—Page Lutz, Elizabethtown.

INDIVIDUAL RECORDS

Most Points, One Game
50—Crystal Coleman, Bishop (90) vs. Concordia-M'head (86), 1986

Most Points, Series
162—Crystal Coleman, Bishop, 1986 (26 vs. Pomona-Pitzer, 50 vs. Concordia-M'head, 28 vs. William Penn, 39 vs. Capital, 19 vs. Salem St.)

Most Field Goals, One Game
20—Crystal Coleman, Bishop (90) vs. Concordia-M'head (86), 1986

Most Field Goals, Series
68—Crystal Coleman, Bishop, 1986 (12 vs. Pomona-Pitzer, 20 vs. Concordia-M'head, 10 vs. William Penn, 18 vs. Capital, 8 vs. Salem St.)

Highest Field-Goal Percentage, One Game (minimum 10 made)
93.3%—Cynthia Allen, Chris Newport (96) vs. Marymount (Va.) (115), 1993 (14-15)

Most Three-Point Field Goals, One Game
8—Susan Swanson, North Park (60) vs. William Penn (87), 1988

Most Three-Point Field Goals, Series
18—Nancy Keene, Elizabethtown, 1989 (3 vs. Carnegie Mellon, 4 vs. Allentown, 4 vs. Muskingum, 2 vs. Centre, 5 vs. Cal St. Stanislaus)

Highest Three-Point Field-Goal Percentage, One Game (minimum 5 made)
75.0%—Michelle Snow, Muskingum (85) vs. Washington (Mo.) (60), 1991 (6-8)

Highest Three-Point Field-Goal Percentage, Series (minimum 10 made)
56.5%—Anne Gooley, Scranton, 1993 (13-23)

Most Free Throws, One Game
16—Karin Povish, Allentown (74) vs. Frank. & Marsh. (58), 1989

Most Free Throws, Series
59—Susan Heidt, St. John Fisher, 1990 (11 vs. Buffalo St., 13 vs. Hartwick, 11 vs. Scranton, 15 vs. Heidelberg, 9 vs. Hope)

Most Rebounds, One Game
23—Amy Spielbauer, St. Norbert (78) vs. Simpson (81), 1983; Shelley Parks, Scranton (85) vs. Salem St. (59), 1985

Most Rebounds, Series
76—Kirsten Dumford, Cal St. Stanislaus, 1989 [10 vs. St. Thomas (Minn.), 17 vs. Concordia-M'head, 11 vs. Luther, 20 vs. Clarkson, 18 vs. Elizabethtown]

TEAM RECORDS

Most Points, One Game
115—Marymount (Va.) vs. Chris. Newport (96), 1993

Most Points, Series
422—Moravian, 1992 (84 vs. Western Conn. St., 104 vs. Muskingum, 85 vs. Capital, 74 vs. Eastern Conn. St., 75 vs. Alma)

Most Field Goals, One Game
44—Pitt.-Johnstown (101) vs. North Central (105), 1984

Most Field Goals, Series
173—Bishop, 1986 (36 vs. Pomona-Pitzer, 37 vs. Concordia-M'head, 31 vs. William Penn, 35 vs. Capital, 34 vs. Salem St.)

Most Three-Point Field Goals, One Game
11—Alma (81) vs. Luther (80), 1992

Most Three-Point Field Goals, Series
33—Moravian, 1992 (5 vs. Western Conn. St., 7 vs. Muskingum, 7 vs. Capital, 7 vs. Eastern Conn. St., 7 vs. Alma)

Highest Three-Point Field-Goal Percentage, One Game (minimum 5 made)
77.8%—Moravian (85) vs. Capital (76), 1992 (7-9)

Highest Three-Point Field-Goal Percentage, Series (minimum 15 made)
58.5%—Scranton, 1993 (24-41)

Most Free Throws, One Game
36—Centre (73) vs. Maryville (Tenn.) (63), 1990

Most Free Throws, Series
117—Salem St., 1986 [18 vs. Bri'water (Mass.), 21 vs. Emmanuel, 34 vs. Albany (N.Y.), 17 vs. Rust, 27 vs. Bishop]

Most Rebounds, One Game
69—North Central (85) vs. Gettysburg (74), 1984

Most Rebounds, Series
241—Cal St. Stanislaus, 1989 [39 vs. St. Thomas (Minn.), 54 vs. Concordia-M'head, 51 vs. Luther, 51 vs. Clarkson, 46 vs. Elizabethtown]

Most Personal Fouls, One Game
35—Rowan (51) vs. Capital (106), 1992

DIVISION III WOMEN'S ALL-TOURNAMENT TEAMS

(First player listed on the 1982, 1983 and 1984 teams was the outstanding player of the championship. The award was discontinued after the 1984 championship.)

1982—Bev Hall, Elizabethtown
Page Lutz, Elizabethtown
Carol Peschel, N.C.-Greensboro
Carol Ferrin, Pomona-Pitzer
Sherry Sydney, N.C.-Greensboro

1983—Page Lutz, Elizabethtown
Kim Wallner, North Central
Brenda Sanders, North Central
Judy Hodge, Clark (Mass.)
Jackie Moore, Knoxville

1984—Page Lutz, Elizabethtown
Shelley Parks, Elizabethtown
Brenda Christian, Rust
Evelyn Oquendo, Salem St.
Cheryl Juris, North Central

1985—Dawn Cillo, New Rochelle
Lori Kerans, Millikin
Deanna Kyle, Scranton
Shelley Parks, Scranton
Amy Proctor, St. Norbert

1986—Evelyn Oquendo, Salem St.
Beth Kapnis, Salem St.
Crystal Coleman, Bishop
Batavia Evans, Bishop
Mary Fuhr, Capital

1987—Jessica Beachy, Concordia-M'head
Una Espenkotter, Scranton
Wendy Norris, Kean
Donna Pivonka, Wis.-Stevens Point
Karla Miller, Wis.-Stevens Point

1988—Jessica Beachy, Concordia-M'head
Jillayn Quaschnick, Concordia-M'head
Michelle Thykeson, Concordia-M'head
Diana Duff, Southern Me.
Shelly Bayhurst, St. John Fisher

1989—Nancy Keene, Elizabethtown
Kirsten Dumford, Cal St. Stanislaus
Lisa Minturn, Cal St. Stanislaus
Amy Huestis, Clarkson
Susan Yates, Centre

1990—Dina Disney, Hope
Holly VandenBerg, Hope
Susan Heidt, St. John Fisher
Michelle Skovrinski, St. John Fisher
Dortha Ford, Heidelberg

1991—Tonja Englund, St. Thomas (Minn.)
Laurie Trow, St. Thomas (Minn.)
Michelle Snow, Muskingum
Kate Titus, Muskingum
Bernice Laferriere, Eastern Conn. St.

1992—Lauri LaBeau, Alma
Kathy Beck, Moravian
Pam Porter, Moravian
Trish Harvey, Luther
Wendy Rogers, Eastern Conn. St.

1993—Sandy Buddelmeyer, Capital
Katie Geiger, Scranton
Emilie Hanson, Central (Iowa)
Tina Kampa, St. Benedict
Chris Rogers, Central (Iowa)

STATISTICAL LEADERS

Vanderbilt center Heidi Gillingham was 11th in the nation in Division I with 3.2 blocked shots per game. The 6-10 junior recorded 105 blocks in 33 games and also shot 62.5 percent from the field.

1993 DIVISION I WOMEN'S INDIVIDUAL LEADERS

SCORING

	CL	HT	G	TFG	FGA	PCT.	3FG	FGA	PCT.	FT	FTA	PCT.	REB	AVG.	PTS.	AVG.
1. Andrea Congreaves, Mercer	Sr	6-3	26	302	550	54.9	51	158	32.3	150	180	83.3	266	10.2	805	31.0
2. Sheryl Swoopes, Texas Tech	Sr	6-0	34	356	652	54.6	32	78	41.0	211	243	86.8	312	9.2	955	28.1
3. Sarah Behn, Boston College	Sr	5-10	27	227	473	48.0	27	68	39.7	203	244	83.2	142	5.3	684	25.3
4. Sonja Tate, Arkansas St.	Sr	5-6	33	282	670	42.1	95	263	36.1	161	257	62.6	327	9.9	820	24.8
5. Albena Branzova, Florida Int'l	So	6-4	31	308	501	61.5	23	58	39.7	109	139	78.4	344	11.1	748	24.1
6. T. Jackson, Nevada-Las Vegas	Sr	5-11	31	278	539	51.6	6	23	26.1	156	195	80.0	237	7.6	718	23.2
7. Roschelle Vaughn, Tenn.Tech	Sr	5-9	29	272	421	64.6	1	4	25.0	118	165	71.5	291	10.0	663	22.9
8. Carol Ann Shudlick, Minnesota	Jr	6-0	26	253	470	53.8	0	2	0.0	81	104	77.9	215	8.3	587	22.6
9. Travesa Gant, Lamar	Jr	6-1	26	239	449	53.2	11	43	25.6	93	134	69.4	348	13.4	582	22.4
10. Samantha David, Niagara	Sr	5-11	27	240	452	53.1	0	0	0.0	104	136	76.5	260	9.6	584	21.6
11. Angie Crosby, Appalachian St.	Jr	6-1	27	221	347	63.7	0	0	0.0	138	198	69.7	225	8.3	580	21.5
12. Natalie Williams, UCLA	Jr	6-1	23	201	425	47.3	0	0	0.0	86	115	74.8	310	13.5	488	21.2
13. Angela Gilbert, Ill.-Chicago	Sr	6-0	28	231	427	54.1	0	0	0.0	128	175	73.1	286	10.2	590	21.1
13. Latoja Harris, Toledo	Jr	6-0	28	221	347	63.7	0	0	0.0	148	199	74.4	279	10.0	590	21.1
15. Tonya Sampson, North Caro.	Jr	5-9	30	217	468	46.4	60	174	34.5	137	186	73.7	245	8.2	631	21.0
16. Karen Jennings, Nebraska	Sr	6-2	31	251	456	55.0	10	32	31.3	135	167	80.8	249	8.0	647	20.9
17. Caryn Brune, Illinois St.	Sr	6-4	27	227	446	50.9	1	3	33.3	107	144	74.3	243	9.0	562	20.8
18. Tracy Connor, Wake Forest	Fr	6-2	28	223	413	54.0	0	0	0.0	130	197	66.0	316	11.3	576	20.6
19. Cornelia Gayden, Louisiana St.	Jr	5-9	27	179	475	37.7	74	240	30.8	120	146	82.2	232	8.6	552	20.4
20. Debbie Bolen, Valparaiso	Sr	5-10	27	208	439	47.4	17	62	27.4	117	172	68.0	168	6.2	550	20.4
21. Nell Knox, Louisville	Sr	6-0	31	261	420	62.1	0	0	0.0	108	151	71.5	222	7.2	630	20.3
22. Janice Felder, Southern Miss.	Jr	6-1	28	221	413	53.5	0	0	0.0	127	166	76.5	287	10.3	569	20.3
23. Jennifer Parker, Murray St.	Jr	5-6	25	183	369	49.6	26	86	30.2	116	137	84.7	107	4.3	508	20.3
24. Tammy Gibson, North Caro. St.	Jr	5-8	27	194	441	44.0	86	207	41.5	73	103	70.9	115	4.3	547	20.3
25. Mikki Kane-Barton, Utah	Sr	6-0	29	224	461	48.6	10	24	41.7	129	166	77.7	255	8.8	587	20.2
26. Melissa King, Santa Clara	Sr	5-7	28	209	410	51.0	31	71	43.7	115	151	76.2	180	6.4	564	20.1
27. Julie VonDielingen, Butler	Sr	6-0	31	233	550	42.4	7	16	43.8	149	185	80.5	267	8.6	622	20.1
28. Sheri Turnbull, Vermont	Jr	5-11	29	231	427	54.1	1	1	100.0	117	153	76.5	277	9.6	580	20.0
29. Jennifer Cole, La Salle	Sr	5-8	27	172	439	39.2	42	141	29.8	150	165	90.9	156	5.8	536	19.9
30. Carol Madsen, Xavier (Ohio)	Jr	6-0	30	227	484	46.9	65	161	40.4	76	91	83.5	174	5.8	595	19.8
31. Angela Hill, North Caro. A&T	Jr	5-10	28	189	392	48.2	13	34	38.2	164	223	73.5	230	8.2	555	19.8
32. Patty Stoffey, Loyola (Md.)	So	5-10	29	227	447	50.8	0	1	0.0	116	163	71.2	242	8.3	570	19.7
33. Connie Swift, Tennessee St.	Fr	5-9	27	190	306	62.1	0	2	0.0	147	201	73.1	201	7.4	527	19.5
33. Tangela McAlister, McNeese St.	Sr	5-10	27	195	467	41.8	16	57	28.1	121	169	71.6	162	6.0	527	19.5
35. Kris Witfill, Georgetown	Sr	5-7	30	224	437	51.3	13	44	29.5	124	156	79.5	151	5.0	585	19.5
36. Tia Paschal, Florida St.	Sr	6-1	27	219	418	52.4	3	9	33.3	83	116	71.6	200	7.4	524	19.4
36. Suzie Dailer, St. Bonaventure	So	5-6	27	163	460	35.4	99	285	34.7	99	117	84.6	154	5.7	524	19.4
38. Tracey Lynn, Kent	Jr	6-0	28	167	343	48.7	20	67	29.9	187	242	77.3	203	7.3	541	19.3
39. Beverly Smith, Morehead St.	Sr	6-1	26	189	327	57.8	0	0	0.0	123	181	68.0	256	9.8	501	19.3
40. Anita Maxwell, New Mexico St.	Fr	5-11	28	236	422	55.9	0	0	0.0	66	101	65.3	287	10.3	538	19.2
40. Kate Abromovitch, Fairfield	Sr	5-10	28	170	444	38.3	62	177	35.0	136	170	80.0	166	5.9	538	19.2
42. Allison Jackson, Cal St. Fullerton	Sr	5-5	27	164	468	35.0	23	88	26.1	167	206	81.1	107	4.0	518	19.2
42. Thelma Wilhite, Southern-B.R.	Sr	5-10	27	206	480	42.9	10	35	28.6	96	156	61.5	233	8.6	518	19.2
44. Heather Burge, Virginia	Sr	6-5	32	258	414	62.3	0	0	0.0	96	192	50.0	245	7.7	612	19.1
44. Joyce Pierce, Georgia Tech	Sr	6-0	24	159	321	49.5	3	14	21.4	138	164	84.1	219	9.1	459	19.1
44. Cassandra Anderson, Alcorn St.	Sr	5-6	24	187	407	45.9	10	40	25.0	75	105	71.4	130	5.4	459	19.1
47. Tonya McJimson, Texas Southern	Sr	5-9	27	184	402	45.8	3	12	25.0	144	214	67.3	276	10.2	515	19.1
48. Trish Andrew, Michigan	Sr	6-3	27	198	480	41.3	7	24	29.2	111	138	80.4	311	11.5	514	19.0
49. Robin Threatt, Wisconsin	Sr	5-7	27	209	444	47.1	40	114	35.1	51	72	70.8	138	5.1	509	18.9
50. Rushia Brown, Furman	Jr	6-3	28	231	384	60.2	0	3	0.0	65	119	54.6	269	9.6	527	18.8
51. Lisa Leslie, Southern Cal	Jr	6-5	29	211	378	55.8	2	8	25.0	119	162	73.5	285	9.8	543	18.7
51. Lauretta Freeman, Auburn	Sr	6-1	29	237	466	50.9	0	3	0.0	69	92	75.0	401	13.8	543	18.7
53. Shandy Bryan, Clemson	Sr	6-2	30	224	411	54.5	0	0	0.0	113	152	74.3	258	8.6	561	18.7
54. Clara Jackson, Mississippi	Jr	5-10	29	229	417	54.9	8	20	40.0	76	121	62.8	237	8.2	542	18.7
55. Val Whiting, Stanford	Sr	6-3	32	239	466	51.3	5	13	38.5	114	162	70.4	286	8.9	597	18.7
56. P. Robinson, Middle Tenn. St.	Jr	5-10	26	177	329	53.8	8	19	42.1	123	155	79.4	199	7.7	485	18.7
57. Monique Collier, Delaware St.	So	5-9	27	198	419	47.3	13	50	26.0	94	145	64.8	187	6.9	503	18.6
58. Kristy Ryan, Cal St. Sacramento	Jr	6-0	27	171	426	40.1	3	19	15.8	157	205	76.6	208	7.7	502	18.6
59. Amy Claboe, Portland	So	6-2	22	153	349	43.8	1	13	7.7	102	140	72.9	133	6.0	409	18.6
60. Jodi Urich, St. Bonaventure	Sr	5-10	27	176	362	48.6	1	12	8.3	146	177	82.5	149	5.5	499	18.5
61. San Kegler, Georgia St.	Sr	6-2	28	212	419	50.6	5	12	41.7	86	117	73.5	254	9.1	515	18.4
62. Melody Howard, S'west Mo. St.	Jr	5-9	32	209	451	46.3	67	159	42.1	102	125	81.6	110	3.4	587	18.3
63. Lori Lyons, Western Caro.	Sr	5-10	27	176	347	50.7	12	30	40.0	130	166	78.3	176	6.5	494	18.3
64. Lisa Russell, Army	So	5-9	27	191	378	50.5	1	1	100.0	109	149	73.2	192	7.1	492	18.2
65. Cass Bauer, Montana St.	Jr	6-3	29	172	338	50.9	1	2	50.0	181	215	84.2	249	8.6	526	18.1
65. Kim Wood, Wis.-Green Bay	Jr	6-3	29	198	348	56.9	0	0	0.0	130	163	79.8	334	11.5	526	18.1
67. Lisa McGill, Oklahoma St.	Sr	6-0	32	226	437	51.7	0	2	0.0	128	208	61.5	272	8.5	580	18.1
68. Katie Smith, Ohio St.	Fr	5-11	32	189	375	50.4	36	80	45.0	164	203	80.8	186	5.8	578	18.1
69. Val Agee, Hawaii	Sr	5-11	32	216	496	43.5	21	63	33.3	123	188	65.4	156	4.9	576	18.0
69. DeShawne Blocker, East Tenn. St.	So	6-0	25	191	294	65.0	0	0	0.0	68	138	49.3	326	13.0	450	18.0

FIELD-GOAL PERCENTAGE

(Min. 5 FG Made Per Game)	CL	HT	G	FG	FGA	PCT.
1. Lidiya Varbanova, Boise St.	Jr	6-4	27	200	294	68.0
2. Deneka Knowles, Southeastern La	Fr	6-0	26	133	204	65.2
3. DeShawne Blocker, East Tenn. St	So	6-0	25	191	294	65.0
4. Cinietra Henderson, Texas	Sr	6-4	30	211	325	64.9
5. Roschelle Vaughn, Tennessee Tech	Sr	5-9	29	272	421	64.6

(Min. 5 FG Made Per Game)	CL	HT	G	FG	FGA	PCT.
6. Crystal Steward, Northeast La.	Jr	6-2	28	171	266	64.3
7. Latoja Harris, Toledo	Jr	6-0	28	221	347	63.7
7. Angie Crosby, Appalachian St.	Jr	6-1	27	221	347	63.7
9. Keisha Johnson, Tulane	Jr	5-11	27	178	280	63.6
10. Talita Scott, Bowling Green	Jr	5-10	30	197	311	63.3
11. Jessie Hicks, Maryland	Sr	6-4	30	205	324	63.3
12. Tonya Baucom, Southwest Mo. St.	Sr	6-0	25	147	234	62.8
13. Heidi Gillingham, Vanderbilt	Jr	6-10	33	212	339	62.5
14. Heather Burge, Virginia	Sr	6-5	32	258	414	62.3
15. Nell Knox, Louisville	Sr	6-0	31	261	420	62.1
16. Connie Swift, Tennessee St.	Fr	5-9	27	190	306	62.1
17. Monique McClelland, Ga. Southern	Jr	5-11	30	160	258	62.0
18. Albena Branzova, Florida Int'l	So	6-4	31	308	501	61.5
19. Wendy Palmer, Virginia	Fr	6-2	31	156	254	61.4
20. Debbie Sporcich, Oregon	Jr	6-4	21	124	206	60.2
21. Rushia Brown, Furman	Jr	6-3	28	231	384	60.2
22. Kesha Martin, California	Sr	6-2	29	187	311	60.1
23. Donna Groh, Northwestern	Sr	6-1	29	153	258	59.3
24. Patricia Babcock, Northwestern	Jr	6-2	29	160	271	59.0
25. Nickie Hilton, George Mason	Jr	6-2	27	142	241	58.9
26. Monique Ambers, Arizona St.	Sr	6-6	27	143	243	58.8
27. Vickie Henson, N.C.-Greensboro	Jr	6-2	29	199	339	58.7
28. Tammie Crown, Radford	Sr	6-1	28	148	253	58.5
29. Jenny Root, Virginia Tech	So	6-3	28	163	281	58.0
30. Beverly Smith, Morehead St.	Sr	6-1	26	189	327	57.8

THREE-POINT FIELD GOALS MADE PER GAME

	CL	HT	G	NO.	AVG.
1. Suzie Dailer, St. Bonaventure	So	5-6	27	99	3.7
2. Veda McNeal, Mo.-Kansas City	Sr	5-6	27	87	3.2
3. Heather Donlon, Fordham	Sr	5-4	29	93	3.2
4. Tammy Gibson, North Caro. St.	Jr	5-8	27	86	3.2
5. Erin Maher, Harvard	Sr	5-8	25	78	3.1
6. Kristen Follis, Stetson	Jr	5-5	25	77	3.1
7. Anna Pavlikhina, Va. Commonwealth	Sr	6-2	27	79	2.9
8. Sonja Tate, Arkansas St.	Sr	5-6	33	95	2.9
9. Betsy Harris, Alabama	Jr	5-10	31	89	2.9
10. Tiffany Adams, Youngstown St.	Sr	5-6	27	77	2.9
11. Katie Curry, St. Joseph's (Pa.)	Sr	5-10	29	82	2.8
12. Cornelia Gayden, Louisiana St.	Jr	5-9	27	74	2.7
13. Kelli Dufficy, Nevada	So	5-9	20	53	2.7
14. Alisha Cole, New Mexico St.	Sr	5-5	28	73	2.6
15. Latricia McDole, Alabama St.	Jr	5-9	27	69	2.6
15. Carolyn Aldridge, Tennessee St.	So	5-8	27	69	2.6
17. Dana Bilyeu, Tennessee Tech	Sr	5-7	29	74	2.6
18. Marilyn Robinson, Grambling	Sr	5-8	25	63	2.5
19. Shelly Hurst, Northeastern Ill.	Jr	5-5	28	69	2.5
20. Zelda Bowman, Texas Southern	Sr	5-6	27	66	2.4
21. Alyson Habetz, Southwestern La.	Jr	5-5	26	63	2.4
22. Kim Kuhn, Niagara	Sr	5-9	27	64	2.4
23. Sonya Wilson, South Caro. St.	Jr	5-7	29	68	2.3
24. Julie Rittgers, Drake	So	5-8	28	65	2.3
24. Stacey Reed, Kentucky	So	5-7	28	65	2.3
26. Molly Goodenbour, Stanford	Sr	5-6	32	74	2.3
27. Neisha Williams, Long Beach St.	Jr	5-7	26	60	2.3
28. Shelley Jarrard, Vanderbilt	Sr	6-1	33	76	2.3
29. Julie Jenson, Mo.-Kansas City	Sr	5-7	27	62	2.3
30. Shelley Sheetz, Colorado	So	5-6	31	71	2.3
30. Gwynn Hobbs, Nevada-Las Vegas	So	5-6	31	71	2.3

THREE-POINT FIELD-GOAL PERCENTAGE

(Min. 1.5 3FG Made Per Game)	CL	HT	G	FG	FGA	PCT.
1. Cara Frey, Harvard	Jr	5-8	25	50	97	51.5
2. Heather Prater, Middle Tenn. St.	Fr	5-8	28	46	90	51.1
3. Heather Donlon, Fordham	Sr	5-4	29	93	198	47.0
4. Julie Meier, Southeast Mo. St.	So	5-10	26	52	114	45.6
5. Tara Saunooke, Clemson	So	5-6	29	59	130	45.4
6. Krista Kirkland, Texas Tech	Sr	5-10	34	71	159	44.7
6. Shelley Sheetz, Colorado	So	5-6	31	71	159	44.7
8. Latricia McDole, Alabama St.	Jr	5-9	27	69	155	44.5
9. Missy Miller, Creighton	Fr	6-1	28	51	115	44.3
10. Kristin Mattox, Louisville	Fr	6-1	31	61	139	43.9
11. Erin Maher, Harvard	Sr	5-8	25	78	178	43.8
12. Gail Wilkins, American	Fr	5-8	28	54	125	43.2
13. Shannon Kite, Kansas	Sr	5-9	30	62	144	43.1
14. Betsy Harris, Alabama	Jr	5-10	31	89	208	42.8
15. Kelli Dufficy, Nevada	So	5-9	20	53	124	42.7

(Min. 1.5 3FG Made Per Game)	CL	HT	G	FG	FGA	PCT.
16. Julie Powell, Vanderbilt	Jr	5-11	32	49	115	42.6
17. Jennifer Lipinski, Delaware	Sr	5-6	28	43	101	42.6
17. Robin Verschneider, Yale	Jr	5-11	26	43	101	42.6
19. Tara Tansil, Tenn.-Martin	So	5-6	25	56	132	42.4
20. Melody Howard, Southwest Mo. St.	Jr	5-9	32	67	159	42.1
21. Tammy Gibson, North Caro. St.	Jr	5-8	27	86	207	41.5
22. Jen Nelson, Niagara	So	5-0	27	54	131	41.2
23. Tammy Gilliam, N.C.-Charlotte	Sr	5-9	27	49	120	40.8
24. Renee Westmoreland, Western Ky.	Sr	5-10	29	46	113	40.7
25. Patrice Martin, Detroit Mercy	Sr	5-9	27	48	118	40.7
26. Gwynn Hobbs, Nevada-Las Vegas	So	5-6	31	71	175	40.6
27. Carol Madsen, Xavier (Ohio)	Jr	6-0	30	65	161	40.4
28. Jen Niebling, Vermont	Sr	5-6	29	44	109	40.4
29. Julie Jenson, Mo.-Kansas City	Sr	5-7	27	62	154	40.3
30. Laura Moore, Washington	Sr	5-9	29	64	159	40.3

FREE-THROW PERCENTAGE

(Min. 2.5 FT Made Per Game)	CL	HT	G	FT	FTA	PCT.
1. Jennifer Cole, La Salle	Sr	5-8	27	150	165	90.9
2. Lisa Furlin, Indiana	Fr	5-10	27	75	83	90.4
3. Jen Nelson, Niagara	So	5-0	27	81	90	90.0
4. Shelley Sheetz, Colorado	So	5-6	31	123	139	88.5
5. Jennifer Clary, Idaho	So	5-8	27	76	86	88.4
6. Sheryl Swoopes, Texas Tech	Sr	6-0	34	211	243	86.8
7. Julie Powell, Vanderbilt	Jr	5-11	32	85	98	86.7
8. Tammie Crown, Radford	Sr	6-1	28	121	140	86.4
9. Helen Holloway, Penn St.	Jr	6-0	28	70	81	86.4
10. Erin Kenneally, Syracuse	Sr	5-9	27	104	121	86.0
11. Holly Rilinger, Miami (Fla.)	Fr	5-4	28	90	105	85.7
12. Kris Sebastian, Duquesne	Jr	5-7	26	65	76	85.5
13. Beth Mollerup, Va. Commonwealth	Sr	5-11	27	86	101	85.1
14. Debbie Teske, Northern Ill.	Sr	5-10	30	84	99	84.8
15. Patti Winterfeldt, Wagner	Jr	5-9	27	72	85	84.7
16. Jennifer Parker, Murray St.	Jr	5-6	25	116	137	84.7
17. Suzie Dailer, St. Bonaventure	So	5-6	27	99	117	84.6
18. Moira Kennelly, Northwestern	Jr	5-7	29	104	123	84.6
19. Kim Kristofik, Massachusetts	Sr	6-0	26	71	84	84.5
20. Carla Beattie, Montana	So	5-7	28	76	90	84.4
21. Pam Davis, McNeese St.	Sr	5-8	27	81	96	84.4
22. Cass Bauer, Montana St.	Jr	6-3	29	181	215	84.2
23. Amy Burnett, Wyoming	So	5-11	27	133	158	84.2
24. Joyce Pierce, Georgia Tech	Sr	6-0	24	138	164	84.1
25. Kim Brungardt, Southern Methodist	Fr	6-2	30	99	118	83.9
26. Deborah Reese, Georgia	Jr	5-10	31	93	111	83.8
27. Kim Roberts, Eastern Ky.	Jr	5-7	27	77	92	83.7
28. Carol Madsen, Xavier (Ohio)	Jr	6-0	30	76	91	83.5
29. Peggy Yingling, Wright St.	Sr	6-3	27	81	97	83.5
30. Christine Silvernail, Santa Clara	Jr	6-1	28	136	163	83.4

REBOUNDING

	CL	HT	G	NO.	AVG.
1. Ann Barry, Nevada	Sr	6-0	25	355	14.2
2. Lauretta Freeman, Auburn	Sr	6-1	29	401	13.8
3. Natalie Williams, UCLA	Jr	6-1	23	310	13.5
4. Travesa Gant, Lamar	Jr	6-1	26	348	13.4
5. DeShawne Blocker, East Tenn. St.	So	6-0	25	326	13.0
6. Cammie Williams, LIU-Brooklyn	Sr	5-8	26	334	12.8
7. Christy Greis, Evansville	Sr	6-4	28	359	12.8
8. Deneka Knowles, Southeastern La.	Fr	6-0	26	332	12.8
9. Erin Butcher, Davidson	Fr	6-0	20	246	12.3
10. Natasha Rezek, Pennsylvania	So	6-1	25	293	11.7
11. Trish Andrew, Michigan	Sr	6-3	27	311	11.5
12. Kim Wood, Wis.-Green Bay	Jr	6-3	29	334	11.5
13. Paulina Blunt, New Mexico St.	Jr	6-1	27	310	11.5
14. Tammy Butler, Harvard	So	6-1	25	285	11.4
15. Tracy Connor, Wake Forest	Fr	6-2	28	316	11.3
16. Rebecca Lobo, Connecticut	So	6-4	29	326	11.2
17. Darlene Saar, Geo. Washington	So	6-0	31	346	11.2
18. Robin Massari, Fairfield	Jr	5-10	28	312	11.1
19. Albena Branzova, Florida Int'l	So	6-4	31	344	11.1
20. Jessica Davis, Southern-B.R.	Jr	5-10	27	298	11.0
21. Tonya Scott, Ala.-Birmingham	Jr	5-11	27	294	10.9
22. Marsha Williams, South Caro.	Sr	6-4	24	256	10.7
23. Wendy Talbot, Weber St.	Jr	6-2	20	210	10.5
24. Amy Mallon, St. Joseph's (Pa.)	Sr	5-10	29	304	10.5
25. Tabitha Barber, South Caro. St.	Sr	6-0	28	293	10.5
26. Leni Wilson, Georgetown	Sr	5-10	30	313	10.4
27. Kim Bradley, Toledo	Sr	5-11	28	289	10.3
28. Sheri Brown, Loyola (Cal.)	Jr	6-1	26	268	10.3
29. Tera Sheriff, Jackson St.	So	6-1	23	237	10.3
30. Nickie Hilton, George Mason	Jr	6-2	27	278	10.3

	CL	HT	G	NO.	AVG.
31. Janice Felder, Southern Miss.	Jr	6-1	28	287	10.3
31. Anita Maxwell, New Mexico St.	Fr	5-11	28	287	10.3

ASSISTS

	CL	HT	G	NO.	AVG.
1. Gaynor O'Donnell, East Caro.	Sr	5-6	28	300	10.7
2. Tine Freil, Pacific (Cal.)	Sr	5-10	26	272	10.5
3. Ira Fuquay, Alcorn St.	So	5-5	24	223	9.3
4. Andrea Nagy, Florida Int'l	So	5-7	31	270	8.7
5. Nancy Kennelly, Northwestern	Sr	5-7	29	252	8.7
6. Cori Close, UC Santa Barb.	Sr	5-6	31	257	8.3
7. Lori Pasceri, Canisius	Sr	5-6	26	214	8.2
8. Michelle Bouldin, Duquesne	So	5-4	27	201	7.4
9. Niesa Johnson, Alabama	So	5-9	31	226	7.3
10. Ramona Jones, Lamar	Sr	5-5	26	189	7.3
11. LaShawn Scott, Coppin St.	Sr	5-5	29	210	7.2
12. Ryneldi Becenti, Arizona St.	Sr	5-7	27	195	7.2
13. Andrea Higgins, Boston U.	Sr	5-6	27	191	7.1
14. Kathy Adelman, Portland	Sr	5-9	29	202	7.0
15. Debbie Bolen, Valparaiso	Sr	5-10	27	187	6.9
16. Maureen Logan, St. Francis (Pa.)	Sr	5-6	26	177	6.8
17. Shonta Tabourn, Campbell	Sr	5-4	26	176	6.8
18. Dena Evans, Virginia	Sr	5-5	31	209	6.7
19. Mindy Hendrickson, Creighton	Sr	5-4	28	188	6.7
20. Amy Fordham, Missouri	Jr	5-9	27	177	6.6
21. Carrie LaPine, Vermont	So	5-6	29	188	6.5
22. Sherri Harris, Alabama St.	Jr	5-0	24	155	6.5
23. Tomika Young, Brigham Young	Sr	5-10	29	183	6.3
24. Susie Cassell, Bowling Green	Jr	5-4	30	185	6.2
25. Kristen Von Netzer, North Texas	Sr	5-10	26	159	6.1
26. Alisha Cole, New Mexico St.	Sr	5-5	28	171	6.1
27. Milica Vukadinovic, California	Sr	6-1	29	177	6.1
28. Sheila Jackson, Tennessee St.	Sr	5-10	26	158	6.1
29. Dana Bilyeu, Tennessee Tech	Sr	5-7	29	176	6.1
30. Suzie Dailer, St. Bonaventure	So	5-6	27	163	6.0
30. Diane Hobin, Hofstra	So	5-5	27	163	6.0

BLOCKED SHOTS

	CL	HT	G	NO.	AVG.
1. Chris Enger, San Diego	Sr	6-4	28	137	4.9
2. Kim Wood, Wis.-Green Bay	Jr	6-3	29	113	3.9
3. Denise Hogue, Charleston	Sr	6-4	27	101	3.7
4. Deb Flandermeyer, Harvard	Sr	6-3	25	85	3.4
5. Amy Lundquist, Loyola (Cal.)	Fr	6-5	26	88	3.4
6. Rebecca Lobo, Connecticut	So	6-4	29	97	3.3
6. Rosemary Adams, Portland	Sr	6-2	29	97	3.3
8. Tammi Barksdale, Alcorn St.	Sr	6-1	24	79	3.3
9. Kelly Roche, Fordham	Sr	6-5	29	95	3.3
9. Lisa Leslie, Southern Cal	Jr	6-5	29	95	3.3
11. Heidi Gillingham, Vanderbilt	Jr	6-10	33	105	3.2
12. Cassandra Barker, Northeast La.	Sr	6-1	25	79	3.2
13. Holly Oslander, Syracuse	Sr	6-5	27	84	3.1
14. Jill Frohlich, Montana	Jr	6-3	28	85	3.0
15. Donna Djorovic, Youngstown St.	Sr	6-2	27	81	3.0
16. Lisa Tate, Kansas	Jr	6-3	30	88	2.9
17. Trish Andrew, Michigan	Sr	6-3	27	79	2.9
18. Debbie Dimond, Brigham Young	So	6-3	29	84	2.9
19. Nichelle Hardy, Prairie View	So	5-7	27	74	2.7
20. Martha Williams, Geo. Washington	So	6-5	30	80	2.7
21. Lori Toomey, Manhattan	Jr	6-4	27	68	2.5
22. Katasha Artis, Northeastern	So	6-0	28	70	2.5
23. Albena Branzova, Florida Int'l	So	6-4	31	77	2.5
24. Dawn Johnson, Seton Hall	So	6-3	27	65	2.4
25. LaNae Jones, Oklahoma	Fr	6-5	27	64	2.4
26. Mechelle Shelton, Murray St.	Sr	6-4	25	58	2.3
27. Christy Greis, Evansville	Sr	6-4	28	64	2.3
28. Tammie Crown, Radford	Sr	6-1	28	63	2.3
29. Katarina Poulsen, Pennsylvania	Jr	6-3	22	49	2.2
30. Pam Clemente, Iona	Sr	6-1	23	49	2.1

STEALS

	CL	HT	G	NO.	AVG.
1. Heidi Caruso, Lafayette	Jr	5-5	28	168	6.0
2. Toina Coley, East Caro.	Sr	5-6	26	123	4.7
3. Natalie White, Florida A&M	So	5-5	27	118	4.4
4. Tracy Krueger, Marshall	Sr	5-9	28	122	4.4
5. Stacy Coffey, Oklahoma St.	Fr	5-10	32	135	4.2

	CL	HT	G	NO.	AVG.
6. Yolunda Oatis, Southwest Tex. St.	Sr	5-5	27	111	4.1
7. Thelma Wilhite, Southern-B.R.	Sr	5-10	27	109	4.0
8. Shonta Tabourn, Campbell	Sr	5-4	26	103	4.0
9. Laurie Aaron, Iowa	Sr	5-6	31	122	3.9
10. Lori Pasceri, Canisius	Sr	5-6	26	99	3.8
11. Sonja Tate, Arkansas St.	Sr	5-6	33	125	3.8
12. Valerie Vincent, Western Ill.	So	5-6	24	90	3.8
13. Nadira Ricks, Georgetown	Jr	5-7	30	112	3.7
14. Nicole Anderson, UCLA	Sr	5-5	27	100	3.7
15. Tonya Sampson, North Caro.	Jr	5-9	30	111	3.7
16. Tia Paschal, Florida St.	Sr	6-1	27	96	3.6
17. Tomika Young, Brigham Young	Sr	5-10	29	103	3.6
18. Rachel Hesse, Texas Christian	Sr	5-7	27	95	3.5
19. Kimberly Hill, Northwestern (La.)	Sr	5-7	32	112	3.5
20. Sheryl Swoopes, Texas Tech	Sr	6-0	34	116	3.4
21. Maureen Logan, St. Francis (Pa.)	Sr	5-6	26	88	3.4
22. Tammy Williams, DePaul	Sr	5-6	29	98	3.4
23. Rushia Brown, Furman	Jr	6-3	28	94	3.4
24. E. C. Hill, Northern Ill.	Jr	5-7	30	100	3.3
24. Jennifer McGowan, La Salle	Sr	5-7	27	90	3.3
26. Suzanne Spencer, Cincinnati	Sr	5-8	28	93	3.3
26. Becky Flynn, Creighton	Fr	5-11	28	93	3.3
28. Katie Curry, St. Joseph's (Pa.)	Sr	5-10	29	96	3.3
29. Pam Bartnik, Wis.-Milwaukee	Jr	5-9	26	86	3.3
29. Ramona Jones, Lamar	Sr	5-5	26	86	3.3

1993 DIVISION I WOMEN'S BASKETBALL GAME HIGHS

INDIVIDUAL HIGHS

SCORING

Pts.	Player, Team vs. Opponent	Date
53	Sheryl Swoopes, Texas Tech vs. Texas	March 13
50	Sonja Tate, Arkansas St. vs. Southwestern La.	Feb. 13
48	Sheryl Swoopes, Texas Tech vs. Washington	Jan. 2
48	Lori Lyons, Western Caro. vs. East Tenn. St.	Jan. 30
47	Andrea Congreaves, Mercer vs. Boston U.	Dec. 4
47	Sheryl Swoopes, Texas Tech vs. Ohio St.	April 4
44	Sonja Tate, Arkansas St. vs. Tex.-Pan American	Jan. 18
43	Caryn Brune, Illinois St. vs. Marquette	Dec. 11
43	Tomika Secrest, Austin Peay vs. Bethel (Tenn.)	Dec. 12
43	Sheryl Swoopes, Texas Tech vs. Southern Methodist	Feb. 13
43	Andrea Congreaves, Mercer vs. South Fla.	Feb. 13

THREE-POINT FIELD GOALS

3FG	Player, Team vs. Opponent	Date
9	Stacy Carver, Minnesota vs. Boise St.	Dec. 20
9	Molly Goodenbour, Stanford vs. Tennessee	Dec. 21
9	Carol Madsen, Xavier (Ohio) vs. Indiana St.	Dec. 28
9	Marilyn Robinson, Grambling vs. Murray St.	Jan. 2
9	Dana Bilyeu, Tennessee Tech vs. Tenn.-Martin	Jan. 16
9	Danielle Featherston, Arkansas St. vs. Ala.-Birmingham	Feb. 9
8	Nine tied	

FREE THROWS

FT	Player, Team vs. Opponent	Date
17	Tina Geis, Portland vs. Western Oregon St.	Dec. 1
17	Sarah Behn, Boston College vs. Georgetown	Jan. 14
17	Revonda Whitley, Winthrop vs. Towson St.	Jan. 30
17	Sonja Tate, Arkansas St. vs. Southwestern La.	Feb. 13
16	10 tied	

REBOUNDS

Reb.	Player, Team vs. Opponent	Date
25	DeShawne Blocker, East Tenn. St. vs. Marshall	Feb. 13
25	Ann Barry, Nevada vs. San Jose St.	March 4
25	Travesa Gant, Lamar vs. Oral Roberts	March 8
24	Travesa Gant, Lamar vs. Cleveland St.	Dec. 5
24	Michelle Diener, Wagner vs. Monmouth (N.J.)	Jan. 16
24	Natasha Rezek, Pennsylvania vs. American	March 2
24	Rebecca Lobo, Connecticut vs. Seton Hall	March 6
23	Theresa Bream, Liberty vs. St. Peter's	Dec. 4
23	Jennette Reed, Marshall vs. Campbell	Dec. 28
23	Deneka Knowles, Southeastern La. vs. Grambling	Jan. 6
23	Erin Butcher, Davidson vs. Lynchburg	Jan. 30

ASSISTS

Ast.	Player, Team vs. Opponent	Date
20	Gaynor O'Donnell, East Caro. vs. N.C.-Asheville	Dec. 13
20	Ira Fuquay, Alcorn St. vs. Grambling	Feb. 8
19	Andrea Nagy, Florida Int'l vs. Southeastern La.	Jan. 21
19	Lisa Branch, Texas A&M vs. Texas Christian	Jan. 23
17	Ryneldi Becenti, Arizona St. vs. Marquette	Dec. 5
17	Andrea Nagy, Florida Int'l vs. Mercer	Jan. 28
17	Tine Freil, Pacific (Cal.) vs. UC Santa Barb	Feb. 13
17	Tine Freil, Pacific (Cal.) vs. Nevada	March 6
16	Nancy Kennelly, Northwestern vs. Eastern Ill.	Jan. 4
16	Kay Tucker, Purdue vs. Illinois	Jan. 31
15	Nine tied	

BLOCKED SHOTS

Blk.	Player, Team vs. Opponent	Date
*15	Amy Lundquist, Loyola (Cal.) vs. Western Ill.	Dec. 20
11	Tammi Barksdale, Alcorn St. vs. Mississippi Val.	Jan. 9
10	Rosemary Adams, Portland vs. Weber St.	Dec. 11
10	Teresa James, Colorado St. vs. Baylor	Dec. 12
10	Holly Oslander, Syracuse vs Marquette	Dec. 28
10	Trish Andrew, Michigan vs. Old Dominion	Dec. 30
10	Chris Enger, San Diego vs. St. Mary's (Cal.)	Jan. 14
9	Kelly Roche, Fordham vs. Fairfield	Jan. 5
9	Lisa Tate, Kansas vs. Iowa St.	Jan. 17
9	Rosemary Adams, Portland vs. San Franciso	Feb. 13

* NCAA record.

STEALS

St.	Player, Team vs. Opponent	Date
#14	Heidi Caruso, Lafayette vs. Kansas St.	Dec. 5
12	Stacy Coffey, Oklahoma St. vs. Missouri	Feb. 28
11	Katie Curry, St. Joseph's (Pa.) vs. Wagner	Dec. 12
11	Jessica Davis, Southern-B.R. vs. Bethune-Cookman	Jan. 4
11	Moira Kennelly, Northwestern vs. Wis.-Milwaukee	Jan. 12
11	Stacy Coffey, Oklahoma St. vs. Kansas	Jan. 24
11	Sherrall Bass, Florida A&M vs. Spelman	Feb. 18
11	Heidi Caruso, Lafayette vs. Lehigh	Feb. 24
10	10 tied	

Ties NCAA record.

TEAM HIGHS

SCORING

Pts.	Team vs. Opponent	Date
127	North Caro. St. vs. Howard	Jan. 31
125	Valparaiso vs. Wright St.	Feb. 9
124	Vanderbilt vs. Oral Roberts	Jan. 14
123	Nebraska vs. Howard	Dec. 11
122	Alabama vs. Oral Roberts	Feb. 25
121	Maryland vs. Drexel	Dec. 1
119	Arizona St. vs. Marquette	Dec. 5
119	Northwestern (La.) vs. Prairie View	Dec. 8
117	Alabama vs. Grambling	Dec. 18
116	Georgia vs. Oral Roberts	Jan. 25

FIELD-GOAL PERCENTAGE

Pct.		Team vs. Opponent	Date
70.2%	(33-47)	Pacific (Cal.) vs. UC Irvine	Feb. 27
69.7%	(46-66)	Northwestern vs. Eastern Ill.	Jan. 4
69.6%	(39-56)	Ga. Southern vs. Appalachian St.	Jan. 23
68.1%	(32-47)	Maryland vs. Southwest Mo. St.	March 20
67.9%	(55-81)	North Caro. St. vs. Howard	Jan. 31
66.7%	(32-48)	Maryland vs. Florida St.	Jan. 23
66.1%	(39-59)	Va. Commonwealth vs. Kent	Dec. 31
65.5%	(36-55)	Southwest Mo. St. vs. Illinois St.	Feb. 11
65.2%	(45-69)	Virginia vs. Morgan St.	Dec. 10
64.9%	(37-57)	St. Mary's (Cal.) vs. Pepperdine	Jan. 29

THREE-POINT FIELD GOALS

3FG	Team vs. Opponent	Date
#16	Harvard vs. Rhode Island	Jan. 12
15	Vanderbilt vs. Oral Roberts	Jan. 14
14	Alabama vs. Loyola (Ill.)	Feb. 3
14	Arkansas St. vs. Southwestern La.	Feb. 13
13	Creighton vs. Wyoming	Dec. 7
13	Grambling vs. Tenn.-Chatt.	Jan. 1
13	Grambling vs. Murray St.	Jan. 2
13	Bradley vs. Indiana St.	Feb. 21
13	Kent vs. Akron	Feb. 24
12	12 tied	

Ties NCAA record.

1993 DIVISION I WOMEN'S TEAM LEADERS

SCORING OFFENSE

	G	W-L	PTS.	AVG.
1. Valparaiso	27	15-12	2,467	91.4
2. Alabama	31	22-9	2,688	86.7
3. Texas Tech	34	31-3	2,923	86.0
4. Kent	29	20-9	2,476	85.4
5. Northern Ill.	30	24-6	2,541	84.7
6. Ohio St.	32	28-4	2,662	83.2
7. Northwestern (La.)	32	24-8	2,659	83.1
8. Bowling Green	30	25-5	2,481	82.7
9. Penn St.	28	22-6	2,313	82.6
10. Virginia	32	26-6	2,595	81.1
11. Marquette	31	22-9	2,503	80.7
12. Nevada-Las Vegas	31	24-7	2,499	80.6
13. Tennessee	32	29-3	2,570	80.3
14. Boise St.	27	19-8	2,161	80.0
15. Hawaii	32	28-4	2,548	79.6
16. Middle Tenn. St.	28	21-7	2,229	79.6
17. Tennessee Tech	29	22-7	2,303	79.4
18. Texas	30	22-8	2,377	79.2
19. Florida Int'l	31	26-5	2,450	79.0
20. Stanford	32	26-6	2,527	79.0
21. Georgia Tech	27	16-11	2,125	78.7
22. Maryland	30	22-8	2,359	78.6
23. Western Ky.	31	24-7	2,435	78.5
24. Butler	31	23-8	2,434	78.5
25. Northwestern	29	20-9	2,271	78.3
26. Southern-B.R.	27	20-7	2,113	78.3
27. Arizona St.	27	17-10	2,106	78.0
28. Harvard	25	16-9	1,948	77.9
29. Tennessee St.	27	18-9	2,101	77.8
30. Xavier (Ohio)	30	21-9	2,333	77.8

SCORING DEFENSE

	G	W-L	PTS.	AVG.
1. Iowa	31	27-4	1,683	54.3
2. Auburn	29	25-4	1,583	54.6
3. Mo.-Kansas City	27	17-10	1,488	55.1
4. Montana	28	23-5	1,556	55.6
5. Missouri	27	19-8	1,535	56.9
6. Lafayette	28	19-9	1,601	57.2
6. UTEP	28	18-10	1,601	57.2
8. Colorado	31	27-4	1,775	57.3
9. Utah	29	19-10	1,674	57.7
10. Army	27	12-15	1,560	57.8
11. Louisiana Tech	32	26-6	1,863	58.2
12. St. Joseph's (Pa.)	29	21-8	1,698	58.6
13. San Diego St.	28	19-9	1,647	58.8
14. Miami (Fla.)	31	24-7	1,827	58.9
15. Old Dominion	30	22-8	1,771	59.0
16. Coppin St.	29	20-9	1,712	59.0
17. Northeastern	28	14-14	1,655	59.1
18. N.C.-Charlotte	28	16-12	1,656	59.1
19. Oklahoma St.	32	23-9	1,896	59.3
20. Vanderbilt	33	30-3	1,961	59.4
21. Arkansas St.	33	25-8	1,964	59.5
22. Connecticut	29	18-11	1,728	59.6
23. DePaul	29	20-9	1,729	59.6
24. Montana St.	29	22-7	1,730	59.7
25. New Orleans	28	18-10	1,672	59.7
26. Southern Cal	29	22-7	1,733	59.8
27. Kentucky	28	18-10	1,675	59.8
28. Wagner	27	11-16	1,620	60.0
29. Yale	26	15-11	1,564	60.2
30. Florida Int'l	31	26-5	1,867	60.2

SCORING MARGIN

	OFF.	DEF.	MAR.
1. Texas Tech	86.0	63.0	23.0
2. Louisiana Tech	77.3	58.2	19.1
3. Florida Int'l	79.0	60.2	18.8
4. Iowa	72.8	54.3	18.5
5. Tennessee	80.3	62.1	18.2
6. Bowling Green	82.7	65.5	17.2
7. Vermont	77.7	60.6	17.2
8. Colorado	74.3	57.3	17.0
9. Western Ky.	78.5	61.8	16.7
10. Montana	72.0	55.6	16.4
11. Virginia	81.1	65.0	16.1
12. Stanford	79.0	63.3	15.6
13. Nevada-Las Vegas	80.6	65.5	15.1
14. Ohio St.	83.2	68.1	15.1
15. Vanderbilt	74.5	59.4	15.1
16. Penn St.	82.6	68.0	14.6
17. Northwestern (La.)	83.1	69.0	14.1
18. Northern Ill.	84.7	70.7	14.0
19. Maryland	78.6	64.7	13.9
20. Alabama	86.7	73.1	13.6
21. Miami (Fla.)	71.7	58.9	12.8
22. Stephen F. Austin	77.1	64.4	12.8
23. Arizona St.	78.0	65.4	12.6
24. North Caro.	74.1	61.6	12.5
25. Southern-B.R.	78.3	65.7	12.5
26. Hawaii	79.6	67.4	12.3
27. Texas	79.2	67.0	12.2
28. Auburn	66.7	54.6	12.1
29. Kansas	72.8	60.7	12.1
30. Nebraska	77.6	65.6	12.0

WON-LOST PERCENTAGE

	W-L	PCT.
1. Vermont	28-1	.966
2. Texas Tech	31-3	.912
3. Vanderbilt	30-3	.909
4. Tennessee	29-3	.906
5. Hawaii	28-4	.875
5. Ohio St.	28-4	.875
7. Colorado	27-4	.871
7. Iowa	27-4	.871

	W-L	PCT.
9. Auburn	25-4	.862
10. Stephen F. Austin	28-5	.848
11. Florida Int'l	26-5	.839
12. Bowling Green	25-5	.833
13. Brigham Young	24-5	.828
14. Montana	23-5	.821
15. Louisiana Tech	26-6	.813
15. Stanford	26-6	.813
15. Virginia	26-6	.813
18. Northern Ill.	24-6	.600
19. Penn St.	22-6	.786
20. Mt. St. Mary's (Md.)	21-6	.778
21. Miami (Fla.)	24-7	.774
21. Nevada-Las Vegas	24-7	.774
21. Western Ky.	24-7	.774
24. Georgetown	23-7	.767
24. North Caro.	23-7	.767
26. Holy Cross	22-7	.759
26. Montana St.	22-7	.759
26. Southern Cal	22-7	.759
26. Tennessee Tech	22-7	.759
30. Arkansas St.	25-8	.758

FIELD-GOAL PERCENTAGE

	FG	FGA	PCT.
1. Texas Tech	1,093	2,120	51.6
2. Bowling Green	995	1,943	51.2
3. Northwestern	848	1,678	50.5
4. Vanderbilt	916	1,851	49.5
5. Southwest Mo. St.	848	1,715	49.4
6. Tennessee Tech	856	1,741	49.2
7. Virginia	1,020	2,077	49.1
8. Maryland	926	1,886	49.1
9. Florida Int'l	948	1,938	48.9
10. Nevada-Las Vegas	962	2,012	47.8
11. Harvard	742	1,554	47.7
12. Virginia Tech	792	1,662	47.7
13. Western Ky.	895	1,885	47.5
14. N.C.-Greensboro	804	1,698	47.3
15. Appalachian St.	791	1,671	47.3
16. Ga. Southern	928	1,971	47.1
17. Texas	915	1,951	46.9
18. East Tenn. St.	704	1,502	46.9
19. Ohio St.	957	2,043	46.8
20. Louisville	873	1,874	46.6
21. Florida St.	722	1,551	46.6
22. Pacific (Cal.)	746	1,605	46.5
23. Penn St.	874	1,892	46.2
24. Hawaii	932	2,018	46.2
25. California	837	1,815	46.1
26. Xavier (Ohio)	900	1,959	45.9
27. Iowa	890	1,943	45.8
28. Colorado	847	1,851	45.8
29. Pepperdine	818	1,788	45.7
30. Oregon	646	1,414	45.7

FIELD-GOAL PERCENTAGE DEFENSE

	FG	FGA	PCT.
1. Montana	540	1,706	31.7
2. Wagner	566	1,678	33.7
3. Alcorn St.	632	1,817	34.8
4. Louisiana Tech	644	1,796	35.9
5. Northeast La.	652	1,811	36.0
6. Fordham	682	1,873	36.4
7. Texas Southern	730	2,000	36.5
8. Coppin St.	622	1,700	36.6
9. Alabama St.	618	1,685	36.7
10. Connecticut	658	1,793	36.7
11. Auburn	583	1,586	36.8
12. Geo. Washington	706	1,915	36.9
13. Mo.-Kansas City	529	1,433	36.9
14. Florida Int'l	718	1,941	37.0
15. Loyola (Cal.)	585	1,577	37.1
16. Mt. St. Mary's (Md.)	647	1,741	37.2
17. Delaware	703	1,889	37.2
18. Kansas	654	1,755	37.3
19. Jackson St.	639	1,709	37.4
20. Utah	592	1,580	37.5
21. Vanderbilt	760	2,027	37.5
22. Southern Cal	636	1,696	37.5
23. Rider	630	1,679	37.5
24. FDU-Teaneck	655	1,743	37.6
25. Nevada-Las Vegas	737	1,960	37.6
26. Massachusetts	574	1,526	37.6
27. Bethune-Cookman	667	1,772	37.6
28. Charleston	677	1,797	37.7
29. Texas Tech	819	2,167	37.8
30. UTEP	560	1,477	37.9

THREE-POINT FIELD GOALS MADE PER GAME

	G	NO.	AVG.
1. Alabama	31	237	7.6
2. Harvard	25	186	7.4
3. Kent	29	199	6.9
4. Valparaiso	27	175	6.5
5. Niagara	27	170	6.3
6. Arkansas St.	33	203	6.2
7. Tenn.-Martin	25	148	5.9
8. Mo.-Kansas City	27	156	5.8
9. Bradley	27	155	5.7
9. Oregon	27	155	5.7
11. Vanderbilt	33	187	5.7
12. Evansville	28	157	5.6
13. Toledo	28	156	5.6
14. Fordham	29	160	5.5
15. Kentucky	28	154	5.5
16. Baylor	28	152	5.4
17. Austin Peay	26	141	5.4
18. Youngstown St.	27	146	5.4
19. North Caro.	30	161	5.4
20. Marquette	31	166	5.4
21. Creighton	28	149	5.3
22. Clemson	30	159	5.3
23. Middle Tenn. St.	28	147	5.3
24. Connecticut	29	151	5.2
25. Grambling	26	133	5.1
26. Texas Tech	34	173	5.1
27. Western Ky.	31	156	5.0
28. Liberty	28	140	5.0
29. Boise St.	27	132	4.9
30. Brigham Young	29	139	4.8

THREE-POINT FIELD-GOAL PERCENTAGE

(Min. 3.0 3FG Made Per Game)	G	FG	FGA	PCT.
1. Harvard	25	186	430	43.3
2. Texas Tech	34	173	404	42.8
3. Vermont	29	108	258	41.9
4. Creighton	28	149	359	41.5
5. Southwest Mo. St.	32	109	264	41.3
6. Fordham	29	160	391	40.9
7. Western Ky.	31	156	388	40.2
8. Colorado	31	85	214	39.7
9. Bowling Green	30	65	168	38.7
10. Southeast Mo. St.	26	68	177	38.4
11. Xavier (Ohio)	30	136	355	38.3
12. Virginia Tech	28	93	243	38.3
13. Akron	26	120	315	38.1
14. Northwestern	29	122	322	37.9
15. American	28	81	216	37.5
16. Duke	27	58	155	37.4
17. San Francisco	26	111	298	37.2
18. Mo.-Kansas City	27	156	420	37.1
19. Kansas	30	131	354	37.0
20. Drake	28	90	244	36.9
21. Fresno St.	27	75	204	36.8
22. Nevada-Las Vegas	31	117	320	36.6
23. Evansville	28	157	430	36.5
24. Wyoming	27	77	211	36.5
25. Miami (Fla.)	31	99	272	36.4
26. Southern Methodist	30	131	360	36.4
27. Hawaii	32	68	187	36.4
27. Appalachian St.	27	116	319	36.4
29. Vanderbilt	33	187	516	36.2
30. Oregon	27	155	429	36.1

FREE-THROW PERCENTAGE

	FT	FTA	PCT.
1. James Madison	421	550	76.5
2. Drake	445	583	76.3

	FT	FTA	PCT.
3. St. Bonaventure	476	627	75.9
4. La Salle	404	533	75.8
5. St. Mary's (Cal.)	396	524	75.6
6. Siena	395	524	75.4
7. Va. Commonwealth	409	544	75.2
8. Miami (Ohio)	403	537	75.0
9. Northeastern Ill.	275	372	73.9
10. Bowling Green	426	577	73.8
11. Marquette	513	696	73.7
12. Penn St.	470	638	73.7
13. Radford	518	704	73.6
14. Niagara	412	560	73.6
15. Harvard	278	379	73.4
16. Duquesne	288	393	73.3
17. Wyoming	360	492	73.2
18. Notre Dame	330	452	73.0
19. Mercer	346	475	72.8
20. Boston College	410	563	72.8
21. New Hampshire	426	585	72.8
22. Hartford	299	411	72.7
23. Pepperdine	525	722	72.7
24. Butler	559	769	72.7
25. Ohio St.	608	838	72.6
26. Montana St.	463	641	72.2
27. Santa Clara	439	609	72.1
28. Southwest Mo. St.	495	688	71.9
29. Middle Tenn. St.	464	645	71.9
30. Wis.-Milwaukee	430	598	71.9

REBOUND MARGIN

	OFF.	DEF.	MAR.
1. Virginia	46.6	34.1	12.5
2. Tennessee	47.0	35.3	11.8
3. Western Ky.	43.4	32.6	10.8
4. Louisiana Tech	46.7	37.0	9.8
5. Auburn	43.2	33.8	9.3
6. St. Peter's	44.8	35.7	9.1
7. Florida Int'l	44.2	35.2	9.0
8. Wagner	48.1	39.1	9.0
9. Cal St. Sacramento	47.9	39.6	8.3
10. Iowa	41.8	33.7	8.1
11. Southern Ill.	40.5	32.7	7.8
12. Loyola (Cal.)	43.5	35.8	7.7
13. Connecticut	42.9	35.6	7.3
14. St. Joseph's (Pa.)	40.7	33.5	7.2
15. Brown	46.0	38.9	7.1
16. Penn St.	43.1	36.5	6.6
17. UTEP	43.0	36.5	6.5
18. Coppin St.	45.4	39.0	6.4
19. Southern-B.R.	48.3	42.0	6.4
20. Northwestern (La.)	49.3	43.1	6.2
21. Montana	48.9	42.9	6.1
22. Robert Morris	45.8	39.8	6.0
23. Bowling Green	40.6	34.6	6.0
24. Illinois	44.5	38.5	6.0
25. New Orleans	42.4	36.6	5.8
26. Missouri	40.0	34.4	5.6
27. Maryland	40.2	34.9	5.3
28. Northern Ill.	49.0	43.8	5.3
29. George Mason	41.1	35.8	5.3
30. St. John's (N.Y.)	48.1	42.8	5.3

1993 DIVISION II WOMEN'S INDIVIDUAL LEADERS

SCORING

	CL	G	TFG	3FG	FT	PTS.	AVG.
1. Yolanda Griffith, Fla. Atlantic	Jr	22	262	0	97	621	28.2
2. Paulette King, Florida Tech	Sr	30	310	0	193	813	27.1
3. Carolyn Brown, St. Augustine's	Jr	24	240	90	74	644	26.8
4. Julie Heldt, Northern Mich.	Sr	28	263	0	189	715	25.5
5. Kathy Comeaux, Henderson	So	24	242	0	106	590	24.6
6. Veronica Freeman, Paine	Jr	27	251	0	134	636	23.6
7. Carmelia Bloodsaw, Alabama A&M	Jr	26	207	72	118	604	23.2
8. Lorain Truesdale, Lander	Sr	26	227	34	108	596	22.9
9. Kristy O'Hara, Shippensburg	Sr	26	221	35	118	595	22.9
10. Rachel Rosario, UC Riverside	Sr	28	250	0	134	634	22.6
11. Vanessa White, Tuskegee	So	25	226	1	113	566	22.6
12. Marie Thomas, Grand Valley St.	Jr	26	209	24	136	578	22.2
13. Jeanette Polk, Augusta	Jr	28	285	0	51	621	22.2
14. Ana Litton, Longwood	Jr	27	242	46	65	595	22.0
15. Tia Glass, St. Joseph's (Ind.)	Sr	27	227	0	135	589	21.8
16. Aimee Conner, UC Davis	Sr	26	238	4	81	561	21.6
17. Teresa Szumigala, Mercyhurst	So	25	194	14	137	539	21.6
18. Jeannine Jean-Pierre, Edinboro	Sr	29	257	9	99	622	21.4
19. Sandy Skradski, Nebraska-Omaha	Sr	26	217	1	115	550	21.2
20. Missy Taylor, Oakland City	Fr	29	267	0	60	594	20.5
21. Tonya Stites, Mesa St.	Jr	28	208	0	156	572	20.4
22. Cathy Torchia, Indiana (Pa.)	Sr	23	185	10	79	459	20.0
23. Diahann Tabor, Bridgeport	Sr	21	162	0	95	419	20.0
24. Stacey Ungashick, Fla. Southern	Sr	28	227	33	69	556	19.9
25. Debbie Moore, New Haven	Sr	27	204	15	110	533	19.7
26. Amy Molina, St. Michael's	Sr	27	194	10	134	532	19.7
26. Tricia Lukawski, Chadron St.	Sr	27	191	78	72	532	19.7
28. Holly Kozlowski, Lock Haven	Jr	26	183	14	132	512	19.7
29. Sheri Stemple, Portland St.	Sr	29	209	0	153	571	19.7
30. Angela Harbour, Catawba	Sr	33	221	72	134	648	19.6
31. Joddie Vossler, Cal St. Chico	Sr	26	206	3	94	509	19.6
32. Kim Young, Cal St. San B'dino	Jr	28	240	25	43	548	19.6
33. Clare McInerney, Merrimack	Sr	26	161	2	183	507	19.5
33. Tammi Julch, Texas Woman's	Jr	24	153	9	153	468	19.5
35. Darlene Ciarcia, Mass.-Lowell	Jr	30	240	0	101	581	19.4
36. Shawna Paskert, Morningside	Sr	27	213	0	96	522	19.3
37. Shannon Smart, Western St.	Sr	24	167	1	126	461	19.2
38. Shelly Leonard, Queens (N.C.)	Sr	26	171	64	93	499	19.2
39. HiCynthia Spells, Norfolk St.	Jr	27	194	5	123	516	19.1
40. Tracy Bruno, Saginaw Valley	Jr	29	216	0	121	553	19.1

SCORING

	CL	G	TFG	3FG	FT	PTS.	AVG.
41. Robin Minehart, West Chester	Sr	25	184	13	95	476	19.0
42. Tammy Greene, Phila. Textile	Jr	29	201	25	121	548	18.9
43. Anita Foskuhl, Regis (Colo.)	Sr	27	191	42	85	509	18.9
44. Shelby Petersen, South Dak. St.	Jr	27	162	71	113	508	18.8
45. Sherry McQuinn, Eastern Mont.	Sr	27	192	0	121	505	18.7
46. Dawn Miner, Humboldt St.	Sr	26	167	0	152	486	18.7
46. Lisa Chamberlin, Wayne St. (Neb.)	Jr	26	186	24	90	486	18.7
46. Nicole Covi, Dowling	Jr	26	167	1	151	486	18.7
49. Lori McClellan, Northern Ky.	Sr	27	180	47	97	504	18.7
50. Rolanda Gladen, Mo. Southern St.	Sr	31	221	7	128	577	18.6
51. Kory Fielitz, Slippery Rock	Jr	25	181	0	100	462	18.5
52. Debbie Ray, Fort Valley St.	Sr	30	251	0	51	553	18.4
53. Joee Kvetensky, Missouri-Rolla	Jr	27	179	8	130	496	18.4
54. Mildred Conston, Cal Poly Pomona	Jr	30	227	1	96	551	18.4
55. Deedra Howard, S.C.-Spartanburg	Sr	31	260	19	30	569	18.4
56. Corinne Vanderwal, Calif. (Pa.)	Sr	26	191	0	94	476	18.3
57. Tareon Kelsey, West Ga.	Sr	27	198	0	98	494	18.3
58. Marnie Wiegman, St. Leo	Sr	24	166	16	90	438	18.3
59. Deeadra Brown, Cameron	Sr	25	196	0	62	454	18.2
60. Rose Rutledge, Saginaw Valley	Sr	29	201	21	103	526	18.1
61. Renae Aschoff, Portland St.	Sr	29	224	2	75	525	18.1
62. Courtney Sands, Indianapolis	Sr	28	179	1	146	505	18.0
63. LeAnn Bryan, SIU-Edwardsville	So	27	206	0	74	486	18.0
64. Petrece Faulkner, Fort Hays St.	Sr	29	183	62	91	519	17.9
65. Melanie Johnson, Presbyterian	So	26	190	0	83	463	17.8
66. Christine Keenan, Florida Tech	Sr	30	192	76	74	534	17.8
67. Jessica Morris, Oakland City	Sr	29	208	1	98	515	17.8
68. LaTanya Patty, Delta St.	Sr	33	240	0	106	586	17.8
69. Dionka Davis, Ft. Valley St.	Sr	30	182	101	65	530	17.7
70. Melissa Hammond, West Liberty St.	Sr	29	182	64	83	511	17.6

FIELD-GOAL PERCENTAGE

(Min. 5 FG Made Per Game)	CL	G	FG	FGA	PCT.
1. Missy Taylor, Oakland City	Fr	29	267	385	69.4
2. Julie Eymann, Regis (Colo.)	Sr	27	186	273	68.1
3. Cynthia Bridges, Fort Valley St.	So	30	151	226	66.8
4. Corinne Vanderwal, Calif. (Pa.)	Sr	26	191	293	65.2
5. LaTanya Patty, Delta St.	Sr	33	240	375	64.0
6. Kathy Comeaux, Henderson St.	So	24	242	381	63.5
7. Yolanda Griffith, Fla. Atlantic	Jr	22	262	415	63.1
8. Jeanette Polk, Augusta	Jr	28	285	453	62.9
9. Tia Glass, St. Joseph's (Ind.)	Sr	27	227	365	62.2
10. Stephanie Anderson, Northern Colo.	Sr	27	150	243	61.7
11. Renata Kuchowicz, Bellarmine	Sr	28	176	288	61.1
12. Jen Cazeault, Stonehill	Sr	30	171	280	61.1
13. Shelly Havard, Northern Mich.	So	28	141	231	61.0
14. Traci Cox, Calif. (Pa.)	Jr	26	181	302	59.9
15. Carrie Schmidt, Cal Poly SLO	Sr	23	163	277	58.8
16. Stacy Mathes, Missouri-Rolla	Sr	27	180	306	58.8
17. Makesha Sampson, Troy St.	Jr	26	168	287	58.5
18. Julie Coughlin, Minn.-Duluth	Jr	30	155	265	58.5
19. Rachel Rosario, UC Riverside	Sr	28	250	433	57.7
20. Shelley Foster, Washburn	So	32	214	371	57.7
21. Dani Fronabarger, Pittsburg St.	Sr	28	144	250	57.6
22. Deeadra Brown, Cameron	Sr	25	196	341	57.5
23. Valerie Scott, S.C.-Spartanburg	Jr	31	232	407	57.0
24. Julie Schlimm, Pitt.-Johnstown	Sr	29	197	347	56.8
25. Jodi Bergemann, South Dak. St.	Jr	27	135	238	56.7
26. Yvonne Boeckmann, SIU-Edwardsville	Sr	25	168	298	56.4
27. Jackie Parsley, North Dak. St.	Sr	32	187	333	56.2
28. Laura Case, Elon	Sr	24	151	269	56.1
29. Susie Hopson, Mars Hill	Fr	22	156	278	56.1
30. Angela Faulk, Hampton	Jr	29	184	328	56.1
31. Tonya Stites, Mesa St.	Jr	28	208	371	56.1
32. Shawna Paskert, Morningside	Sr	27	213	380	56.1
33. Darlene Ciarcia, Mass.-Lowell	Jr	30	240	431	55.7
34. Diahann Tabor, Bridgeport	Sr	21	162	294	55.1
35. Tracy Linton, Jacksonville St.	Sr	29	193	351	55.0

THREE-POINT FIELD GOALS MADE PER GAME

	CL	G	NO.	AVG.
1. Carolyn Brown, St. Augustine's	Sr	24	90	3.8
2. Dionka Davis, Fort Valley St.	Sr	30	101	3.4
3. Betsy Bergdoll, Queens (N.C.)	Sr	26	87	3.3
4. Lara Thornton, Calif. (Pa.)	Jr	26	85	3.3
4. Tori Lindbeck, Tampa	So	26	85	3.3
6. Armeda Flores, Adams St.	Jr	27	88	3.3
7. Keisha Bostic, Albany St. (Ga.)	So	27	87	3.2
8. April Haskins, Columbus	Fr	27	80	3.0
9. Tricia Lukawski, Chadron St.	Sr	27	78	2.9
10. Christina Ortega, Mo Southern St.	Sr	30	85	2.8

	CL	G	NO.	AVG.
11. Tami Matheny, Lenoir-Rhyne	Sr	24	67	2.8
12. Carmelia Bloodsaw, Alabama A&M	Jr	26	72	2.8
12. Odessa Wallace, Troy St.	Sr	26	72	2.8
14. Cindy Dalton, Metropolitan St.	Sr	27	74	2.7
14. Kristi Coffee, West Ga.	So	27	74	2.7
16. Roslyn Stevenson, St. Paul's	So	23	63	2.7
17. Julie Krauth, Augustana (S.D.)	Sr	29	79	2.7
18. Kristin Hillery, Air Force	Sr	27	73	2.7
19. Amy Coon, Clarion	Jr	30	81	2.7
20. Jackie Carter, Virginia St.	Jr	22	59	2.7
21. Sue Williams, Mercy	Jr	27	72	2.7
22. Karee Bonde, Cal St. Dom. Hills	Jr	26	69	2.7
23. Shelby Petersen, South Dak.	Jr	27	71	2.6
24. Christine Keenan, Florida Tech	Sr	30	76	2.5
25. Darlene Hildebrand, Phila. Textile	So	29	73	2.5
25. Kristin Sullivan, St. Anselm	Jr	29	73	2.5
27. Beth Thiebaut, Southern Colo.	Jr	27	67	2.5
28. Javorah Dallas, West Ga.	Jr	21	52	2.5
29. Rhnea Ellenburg, North Ala.	Sr	26	64	2.5
29. Shelly Leonard, Queens (N.C.)	Sr	26	64	2.5
31. Jennifer Teeple, Armstrong St.	Fr	24	59	2.5
32. Stacie Cook, Mansfield	Fr	24	58	2.4
33. Amy Boynton, Northern Mich.	Jr	28	67	2.4
33. Doreen Belkowski, Oakland	Jr	28	67	2.4
35. Brandi Bosley, Texas Woman's	Fr	19	45	2.4

THREE-POINT FIELD-GOAL PERCENTAGE

(Min. 1.5 3FG Made Per Game)	CL	G	FG	FGA	PCT.
1. Kelly Tomlin, Livingston	Fr	26	56	110	50.9
2. Kim Francis, Southwest Baptist	So	27	45	89	50.6
3. Darlene Hildebrand, Phila. Textile	So	29	73	149	49.0
4. Sandy Vincent, Bellarmine	Sr	28	43	90	47.8
5. Julie Filpus, Wayne St. (Mich.)	Jr	26	57	123	46.3
6. Karee Bonde, Cal St. Dom. Hills	Jr	26	69	151	45.7
7. Melissa Graham, Indianapolis	So	28	60	136	44.1
8. Tricia Lukawski, Chadron St.	Sr	27	78	179	43.6
9. Kristin Sullivan, St. Anselm	Jr	29	73	169	43.2
10. Treena Royston, Eastern N. Mex.	So	28	49	114	43.0
11. Connie Pleshe, Michigan Tech	Sr	33	75	176	42.6
12. Rosalyn Phillips, Livingston	Jr	26	61	144	42.4
13. Cindy Phillips, N.M. Highlands	Sr	28	50	119	42.0
14. Patty Skelton, Keene St.	Fr	25	54	129	41.9
15. Tori Lindbeck, Tampa	So	26	85	206	41.3
16. Anita Foskuhl, Regis (Colo.)	Sr	27	42	102	41.2
17. Tracey Pudenz, North Dak.	Jr	23	44	107	41.1
18. Kim Black, Le Moyne	Sr	27	62	152	40.8
19. Paula Blackwell, S.C.-Spartanburg	Jr	27	63	155	40.6
20. Brandi Bosley, Texas Woman's	Fr	19	45	111	40.5
21. Bonnie Richrath, Lewis	Jr	27	57	141	40.4
22. Odessa Wallace, Troy St.	Sr	26	72	179	40.2
23. Paige Hargrove, Bloomsburg	Fr	26	44	110	40.0
24. Jana Flanagan, Central Okla.	Sr	28	45	113	39.8
25. Shorlone Crockam, Delta St.	Sr	33	70	176	39.8
26. Kathleen Murphy, Molloy	Sr	27	61	154	39.6
27. Cindy Dalton, Metropolitan St.	Sr	27	74	190	38.9
28. Pam Mountsier, Clarion	Jr	30	62	161	38.5
29. Carmelia Bloodsaw, Alabama A&M	Jr	26	72	187	38.5
30. Debra Wells, Livingston	Sr	26	43	112	38.4
31. Julie Krauth, Augustana (S.D.)	Sr	29	79	206	38.3
32. Cathy Brawner, Bellarmine	So	28	61	160	38.1
33. Amy Boynton, Northern Mich.	Jr	28	67	176	38.1
34. Jennifer Teeple, Armstrong St.	Fr	24	59	155	38.1
35. Brenda Ryan, Bloomsburg	Jr	26	39	103	37.9
35. Christine Rodness, Cal Poly SLO	So	23	39	103	37.9

FREE-THROW PERCENTAGE

(Min. 2.5 FT Made Per Game)	CL	G	FT	FTA	PCT.
1. Renae Aschoff, Portland St.	Sr	29	75	85	88.2
2. Julie Filpus, Wayne St. (Mich.)	Jr	26	71	82	86.6
3. Joyce Dimond, Phila. Textile	Sr	25	96	111	86.5
4. Dawn Murphy, Hillsdale	Jr	26	116	135	85.9
5. Darlene Hildebrand, Phila. Textile	So	29	109	127	85.8
6. Paulette King, Florida Tech	Sr	30	193	226	85.4
7. Jamie Long, Northwest Mo. St.	Sr	27	102	120	85.0
8. Sara Belanger, Minn.-Duluth	Fr	30	83	98	84.7
9. Julie Krauth, Augustana (S.D.)	Sr	29	74	88	84.1
10. Keisha Bostic, Albany St. (Ga.)	So	27	68	81	84.0

(Min. 2.5 FT Made Per Game)	CL	G	FT	FTA	PCT.
11. Corinne Deters, Regis (Colo.)	Sr	27	88	105	83.8
12. Shelby Petersen, South Dak.	Jr	27	113	135	83.7
13. Jill Frederick, Northwood	So	25	77	92	83.7
14. Dani Fronabarger, Pittsburg St.	Sr	28	162	194	83.5
15. Robin Minehart, West Chester	Sr	25	95	114	83.3
16. Tina Bisegger, West Chester	Sr	24	69	83	83.1
17. Chrissy Elliott, Lenoir-Rhyne	Fr	24	93	113	82.3
18. Petrece Faulkner, Fort Hays St.	Sr	29	91	111	82.0
19. Shelley Foster, Washburn	So	32	99	121	81.8
19. Dana Nielson, Augustana (S.D.)	Sr	28	81	99	81.8
21. Missy Grimes, Ashland	Jr	20	58	71	81.7
22. Bobbi Hardy, Central Okla.	Sr	28	92	113	81.4
23. Kristi Brown, Northeast Mo. St.	Fr	21	69	85	81.2
24. Kelly O'Brien, Cal St. San B'dino	Sr	25	64	79	81.0
25. Ruby Fullard, Newberry	So	24	63	78	80.8
26. Katie Laidley, Shepherd	Jr	26	78	97	80.4
27. Anita Foskuhl, Regis (Colo.)	Sr	27	85	106	80.2
28. Rhonda Matzke, Washburn	Jr	32	105	131	80.2
28. Laura Case, Elon	Sr	24	105	131	80.2
30. Missy Swanson, St. Cloud St.	Jr	26	72	90	80.0
30. Sandy Zupetz, St. Rose	Jr	26	120	150	80.0
30. Heidi Alderman, Alas. Anchorage	Fr	25	84	105	80.0
33. Terri Ingalls, Wis.-Parkside	Sr	27	71	89	79.8
34. Heidi Morlock, Augustana (S.D.)	Jr	29	125	157	79.6
35. Stephanie Anderson, Northern Colo.	Sr	27	78	98	79.6

REBOUNDING

	CL	G	NO.	AVG.
1. Vanessa White, Tuskegee	So	25	433	17.3
2. Tracy Linton, Jacksonville St.	Sr	29	480	16.6
3. Rachel Rosario, UC Riverside	Sr	28	456	16.3
4. Yolanda Griffith, Fla. Atlantic	Jr	22	352	16.0
5. Lorain Truesdale, Lander	Sr	26	404	15.5
6. Holly Roberts, Metropolitan St.	Sr	27	349	12.9
7. Rebecca Hanson, Pace	Jr	30	380	12.7
8. Erica Taylor, Virginia St.	So	26	327	12.6
9. Lorraine Morrissey, Dowling	So	22	269	12.2
10. Carrolyn Burke, Queens (N.Y.)	Fr	25	296	11.8
11. Vicki Carlisle, Franklin Pierce	Sr	30	355	11.8
12. TaReon Kelsey, West Ga.	Sr	27	319	11.8
13. Allison Heisler, Eckerd	So	25	294	11.8
14. Jeannine Jean-Pierre, Edinboro	Sr	29	339	11.7
15. Tonya Roper, Wingate	Jr	31	362	11.7
16. Sylvia Howard, St. Paul's	Sr	23	268	11.7
17. Regina Darden, Pembroke St.	So	27	308	11.4
18. Jen Harrington, Assumption	Jr	21	238	11.3
19. Amy Washington, Virginia Union	Jr	28	314	11.2
20. Sharon Manning, N.C. Central	Jr	24	269	11.2
21. Kay Sanders, Augusta	Sr	29	325	11.2
22. Arlevia Samuel, New Haven	So	26	287	11.0
23. Courtney Sands, Indianapolis	Sr	28	309	11.0
24. Brenda Jackson, Wofford	Jr	27	297	11.0
24. Breda Flynn, Concordia (N.Y.)	Fr	23	253	11.0
26. Sandy Skradski, Nebraska-Omaha	Sr	26	285	11.0
27. Missy Taylor, Oakland City	Fr	29	317	10.9
28. Ton'Nea Williams, Central Okla.	Sr	26	283	10.9
29. Kathleen Davis, Virginia St.	So	28	304	10.9
30. Shawna Paskert, Morningside	Sr	27	289	10.7
31. Carlita Jones, Clarion	So	30	320	10.7
32. Bobbi Jo Austin, LIU-C. W. Post	Sr	27	287	10.6
33. Schwanda Walker, West Ga.	Jr	26	273	10.5
34. Lanita Turner, Lincoln (Mo.)	Sr	26	272	10.5
35. Kathy Comeaux, Henderson St.	So	24	251	10.5

ASSISTS

	CL	G	NO.	AVG.
1. Selina Bynum, Albany St. (Ga.)	Sr	26	280	10.8
2. Lisa Rice, Norfolk St.	So	31	305	9.8
3. Lori Richelderfer, Calif. (Pa.)	Jr	26	239	9.2
4. Nikki Leibold, Northern Mich.	Sr	28	243	8.7
5. Tara Reardon, Queens (N.Y.)	Sr	20	169	8.4
6. Beth Browning, Tampa	Sr	25	202	8.1
7. Paula Light, Millersville	Sr	25	201	8.0
8. Jody Hill, Pace	Jr	31	236	7.6
9. Roseann Rutledge, Saginaw Valley	Sr	29	214	7.4
10. Amy McMullen, Seattle Pacific	Sr	26	184	7.1
11. Jennifer Edgar, Troy St.	Sr	26	182	7.0
11. Melissa Church, Emporia St.	So	26	182	7.0
13. Camille Iverson, Cal St. Stanislaus	Sr	27	186	6.9
14. Juanita Gordon, Hampton	So	29	197	6.8
15. Shani Baraka, Johnson Smith	Jr	28	186	6.6

	CL	G	NO.	AVG.
16. Candee Zepka, Florida Tech	Sr	30	197	6.6
17. Kathleen Shippee, St. Anselm	So	29	190	6.6
18. Margaret Farley, Florida Tech	Sr	30	196	6.5
19. Melissa Graham, Indianapolis	So	28	178	6.4
20. Kim Ross, Bryant	Sr	27	167	6.2
21. Darcy Deutsch, North Dak.	Sr	28	171	6.1
22. Shunda Barkley, West Ga.	Jr	27	163	6.0
23. Dottie Hibbs, West Liberty St.	Sr	29	175	6.0
24. Angela Harbour, Catawba	Sr	33	195	5.9
25. Kristen Morast, Stonehill	Jr	25	147	5.9
26. Susan Worman, SIU-Edwardsville	So	27	157	5.8
27. Toni Wimer, Gannon	Sr	25	145	5.8
28. Stephanie Brockman, Eastern N. Mex.	Sr	28	162	5.8
29. Queenie Edwards, Quinnipiac	So	27	156	5.8
30. Julie Giles, Lewis	Jr	27	155	5.7
31. Krissy Wegman, Rollins	Jr	27	154	5.7
32. Lynne Liebhauser, St. Michael's	Jr	27	153	5.7
33. Diana Odoardi, New Hamp. Col.	Sr	26	146	5.6
34. Mickie Drum, Gardner-Webb	Jr	25	139	5.6
35. Kathleen Shriver, Columbus	Jr	27	150	5.6
35. Trisa Fisher, Southwest Baptist	Jr	27	150	5.6

BLOCKED SHOTS

	CL	HT	G	NO.
1. Rebecca Hanson, Pace	Jr	30	142	4.7
2. Tonya Roper, Wingate	Jr	31	140	4.5
3. Missy Taylor, Oakland City	Fr	29	127	4.4
4. Sherry Willis, N.M. Highlands	Jr	29	122	4.2
5. Bobbi Jo Austin, LIU-C. W. Post	Sr	27	97	3.6
6. Andrea Sunday, St. Anselm	So	29	97	3.3
7. Jeanette Polk, Augusta	Jr	28	90	3.2
8. Yolanda Griffith, Fla. Atlantic	Jr	22	69	3.1
9. Holly Roberts, Metropolitan St.	Sr	27	76	2.8
9. Jenn Hamilton, Quinnipiac	Sr	27	76	2.8
11. Karin Kane, Adelphi	Sr	27	73	2.7
12. Terri Ayers, Edinboro	Jr	30	76	2.5
12. Jen Andersson, Florida Tech	Sr	30	76	2.5
14. Vicki Carlisle, Franklin Pierce	Sr	30	70	2.3
14. Jennifer Sullivan, Northern Colo.	Jr	27	63	2.3
16. Erica Taylor, Virginia St.	So	26	59	2.3
16. Hallie Byfield, Adams St.	Jr	26	59	2.3
16. Tes Spahr, Chadron St.	So	26	59	2.3
19. Darlene Ciarcia, Mass.-Lowell	Jr	30	67	2.2
20. Christy Wessell, Slippery Rock	Jr	25	55	2.2
20. Stephanie Childers, Fort Lewis	Sr	25	55	2.2
22. Courtney Sands, Indianapolis	Sr	28	61	2.2
23. Kamala Sherman, Central Mo. St.	Sr	29	62	2.1
24. Brandai Prince, Angelo St.	Jr	22	47	2.1
25. Cindy Capesius, Quincy	So	27	57	2.1
26. Candi Black, Augusta	Jr	23	48	2.1
27. Crystal Ashley, Tampa	So	26	54	2.1
28. Jen Cazeault, Stonehill	Sr	30	60	2.0
29. Amy Washington, Virginia Union	Jr	28	55	2.0
30. Kim Brigham, Mass.-Lowell	Sr	27	53	2.0
31. Darcee Nienkamp, Neb.-Kearney	Sr	26	50	1.9
32. Jen Harrington, Assumption	Jr	21	40	1.9
33. Renae Aschoff, Portland St.	Sr	29	54	1.9
34. Emily Anspach, Le Moyne	Fr	27	50	1.9
34. Ellen O'Day, Rollins	Sr	27	50	1.9

STEALS

	CL	HT	G	NO.
1. Valerie Curtis, Dist. Columbia	Jr	22	135	6.1
2. Carolyn Brown, St. Augustine's	Jr	24	145	6.0
3. Patrena Wilson, Limestone	Sr	29	155	5.3
4. Christine Keenan, Florida Tech	Sr	30	156	5.2
5. Tara Reardon, Queens (N.Y.)	Sr	20	103	5.2
6. Debbie Moore, New Haven	Sr	27	138	5.1
7. Yolanda Griffith, Fla. Atlantic	Jr	22	109	5.0
8. Necole Watts, Pfeiffer	Sr	25	123	4.9
9. Tammy Greene, Phila. Textile	Jr	29	138	4.8
10. Dionka Davis, Fort Valley St.	Sr	30	138	4.6
11. Yolanda Gregory, Fla. Atlantic	Sr	25	113	4.5
12. Shaun Thomas, Jacksonville St.	Jr	29	129	4.4
13. Queenie Edwards, Quinnipiac	So	27	118	4.4
14. Selina Bynum, Albany St. (Ga.)	Sr	26	112	4.3
15. Ebonie Simmons, American Int'l	So	28	119	4.3

	CL	HT	G	NO.
16. Jody Buck, North Dak. St.	Sr	32	131	4.1
17. Cheryl Bogues, N.C. Central	Sr	24	97	4.0
18. Kay Sanders, Augusta	Sr	29	110	3.8
18. Natoshia Williams, Fort Valley St	Fr	29	110	3.8
18. Kim Manifesto, Portland St.	Fr	29	110	3.8
21. Marnie Wiegman, St. Leo	Sr	24	91	3.8
21. Alanda Danner, Lenoir-Rhyne	Fr	24	91	3.8
23. Jennine Tanks, Norfolk St.	Sr	30	113	3.8
24. Shaunte' Matthews, Bowie St.	Jr	24	90	3.8
25. Marva Lindsay, Armstrong St.	Jr	26	97	3.7
25. Karen Donahue, Assumption	Jr	26	97	3.7
27. Jeannine Jean-Pierre, Edinboro	Sr	29	108	3.7
28. Denise Broun, Mercy	Jr	27	100	3.7
29. Katie Laidley, Shepherd	Jr	26	96	3.7
30. DeShonna Anderson, Norfolk St.	Sr	32	116	3.6
31. Lisa Rice, Norfolk St.	So	31	111	3.6
32. Lisa Jones, Georgia Col.	Sr	27	96	3.6
33. Kelly Charron, Fla. Southern	So	28	98	3.5
33. Melissa Graham, Indianapolis	So	28	98	3.5
35. Stacey Ungashick, Fla. Southern	Sr	28	97	3.5

1993 DIVISION II WOMEN'S BASKETBALL GAME HIGHS

INDIVIDUAL HIGHS

SCORING

Pts.	Player, Team vs. Opponent	Date
58	Carolyn Brown, St. Augustine's vs. Tampa	Dec. 5
52	Julie Heldt, Northern Mich. vs. Wis.-Parkside	Feb. 27
46	Petrece Faulkner, Fort Hays St. vs. Adams St.	Feb. 6
46	Jodi Raab, Ferris St. vs. Wayne St. (Mich.)	Feb. 6
46	Yolanda Griffith, Fla. Atlantic vs. West Ga.	Jan. 22
46	Carmelia Bloodsaw, Alabama A&M vs. LeMoyne-Owen	Dec. 7
45	Kristy O'Hara, Shippensburg vs. Cheyney	Feb. 11
44	Marie Thomas, Grand Valley St. vs. Lewis	Dec. 22
43	Ana Litton, Longwood vs. Converse	Jan. 14
43	Carlita Jones, Clarion vs. Mercyhurst	Dec. 8

THREE-POINT FIELD GOALS

3FG	Player, Team vs. Opponent	Date
#11	Jackie Carter, Virginia St. vs. St. Paul's	Jan. 23
#11	Carolyn Brown, St. Augustine's vs. Tampa	Dec. 5
9	Amy Boynton, Northern Mich. vs. Michigan Tech	Feb. 8
9	Sharon Harris, Morris Brown vs. Alabama A&M	Jan. 27
9	Annette Bergman, Slippery Rock vs. Oakland	Dec. 21
9	Dionka Davis, Fort Valley St. vs. Ga. Southwestern	Nov. 20

Ties Division II record.

FREE THROWS

FT	Player, Team vs. Opponent	Date
#21	Jennifer Hilliard, Presbyterian vs. Erskine	Dec. 2
19	Natoshia Williams, Fort Valley St. vs. LeMoyne-Owen	Feb. 8
18	Julie Heldt, Northern Mich. vs. Wis.-Parkside	Feb. 27
18	Michelle Doonan, Stonehill vs. St. Michael's	Jan. 19
16	Amy Molina, St. Michael's vs. American Int'l	Feb. 25
16	Clare McInerney, Merricmack vs. Quinnipiac	Feb. 13
16	Clare McInerney, Merrimack vs. Assumption	Jan. 9
16	Dani Fronabarger, Pittsburg St. vs. Okla. Christian	Nov. 21

Ties Division II record.

REBOUNDS

Reb.	Player, Team vs. Opponent	Date
33	Yolanda Griffith, Fla. Atlantic vs. Florida Int'l	Feb. 27
28	Vanessa White, Tuskegee vs. Paine	Feb. 8
27	Tracy Linton, Jacksonville St. vs. Mississippi-Women	Jan. 28
27	Dione Stephens, Miles vs. LeMoyne-Owen	Jan. 26
26	Vicki Carlisle, Franklin Pierce vs. Keene St.	March 5
26	Lorraine Morrissey, Dowling vs. Adelphi	Feb. 11
26	Erica Taylor, Virginia St. vs. Longwood	Feb. 11

ASSISTS

Ast.	Player, Team vs. Opponent	Date
*23	Selina Bynum, Albany St. (Ga.) vs. LeMoyne-Owen	Jan. 13
19	Lisa Rice, Norfolk St. vs. Virginia Union	Feb. 26
16	Jennifer Goble, Eastern N. Mex. vs. Texas Woman's	Feb. 28
16	Lori Richelderfer, Calif. (Pa.) vs. Clarion	Jan. 20
16	Tara Reardon, Queens (N.Y.) vs. Concordia (N.Y.)	Jan. 11
16	Selina Bynum, Albany St. (Ga.) vs. Morris Brown	Jan. 9
16	Lisa Rice, Norfolk St. vs. N.C. Central	Dec. 2

* Division II record.

BLOCKED SHOTS

Blk.	Player, Team vs. Opponent	Date
12	Tonya Roper, Wingate vs. Johnson Smith	Dec. 12
12	Sherrie Willis, N.M. Highlands vs. Angelo St.	Dec. 12
10	Andrea Sunday, St. Anselm vs. Assumption	Feb. 20
10	Yolanda Griffith, Fla. Atlantic vs. West Ga.	Jan. 22
10	Tonya Roper, Wingate vs. Catawba	Jan. 20
10	Bobbi Jo Austin, LIU-C. W. Post vs. Mercy	Dec. 15
10	Joy Barry, Assumption vs. Sacred Heart	Nov. 24

STEALS

St.	Player, Team vs. Opponent	Date
13	Shaun Thomas, Jacksonville St. vs. North Ala.	Feb. 15
13	Christine Keenan, Florida Tech vs. Barry	Feb. 13
13	Yolanda Gregory, Fla. Atlantic vs. Barry	Feb. 8
13	Debbie Moore, New Haven vs. Quinnipiac	Jan. 18
12	Linda Schabloske, Nebraska-Omaha vs. St. Cloud St.	Feb. 26
12	Lisa Rice, Norfolk St. vs. Dist. Columbia	Feb. 18
12	Shaun Thomas, Jacksonville St. vs. Delta St.	Feb. 13
12	Marnie Wiegman, St. Leo vs. Southeastern Bible	Feb. 1
12	Necole Watts, Pfeiffer vs. Coker	Jan. 13
12	Yolanda Gregory, Fla. Atlantic vs. Johnson Smith	Dec. 18
12	Carolyn Brown, St. Augustine's vs. St. Paul's	Dec. 10
12	Shaun Thomas, Jacksonville St. vs. Piedmont	Dec. 3

TEAM HIGHS

SCORING

Pts.	Team vs. Opponent	Date
*148	Clarion vs. Westminster (Pa.)	Nov. 20
138	Clarion vs. Bethany (W. Va.)	Nov. 21
133	Alabama A&M vs. LeMoyne-Owen	Dec. 7
129	Augustana (S.D.) vs. St. Cloud St.	Feb. 19
127	Augustana (S.D.) vs. Sioux Falls	Nov. 24
124	Central Ark. vs. Ark. Baptist	Dec. 5
121	Savannah St. vs. LeMoyne-Owen	Jan. 2
121	Henderson St. vs. Ark. Baptist	Dec. 3
121	Catawba vs. Mount Olive	Nov. 21
119	Grand Canyon vs. Fort Lewis	Jan. 1

* Division II record.

FIELD-GOAL PERCENTAGE

Pct.	Team vs. Opponent	Date
72.1%	(31-43) Pittsburg St. vs. Southwest Baptist	Feb. 3
70.7%	(41-58) Oakland City vs. Ind.-South Bend	Jan. 16
70.0%	(28-40) Elizabeth City St. vs. Winston-Salem	Jan. 18
67.4%	(29-43) Mississippi Col. vs. Livingston	Feb. 1
67.3%	(35-52) Clarion vs. Bethany (W. Va.)	Nov. 21
67.2%	(43-64) Denver vs. St. Cloud St.	Dec. 5
66.7%	(28-42) Northern Colo. vs. Mankato St.	Jan. 30

THREE-POINT FIELD GOALS

3FG	Team vs. Opponent	Date
18	Clarion vs. Bethany (W. Va.)	Nov. 21
17	Clarion vs. Gannon	Feb. 12
17	Oakland vs. Northern Mich.	Feb. 11
17	Clarion vs. Calif. (Pa.)	Feb. 10
17	Oakland vs. Aquinas	Nov. 22
16	Clarion vs. Indiana (Pa.)	Feb. 6
15	Northern Mich. vs. Oakland	Jan. 7

1993 DIVISION II WOMEN'S TEAM LEADERS

SCORING OFFENSE

	G	W-L	PTS.	AVG.
1. Augustana (S.D.)	29	24-5	2,612	90.1
2. Northern Mich.	28	22-6	2,512	89.7
3. North Dak. St.	32	30-2	2,858	89.3
4. Norfolk St.	32	29-3	2,777	86.8
5. St. Augustine's	29	23-6	2,508	86.5
6. Clarion	30	24-6	2,591	86.4
7. Florida Tech	30	26-4	2,577	85.9
7. Fort Valley St.	30	27-3	2,577	85.9
9. Alabama A&M	26	17-9	2,190	84.2
10. Chadron St.	27	18-9	2,241	83.0
10. Troy St.	26	19-7	2,158	83.0
12. Eastern N. Mex.	28	23-5	2,312	82.6
13. Delta St.	33	27-6	2,710	82.1
14. Indianapolis	28	24-4	2,295	82.0
15. Fla. Atlantic	28	20-8	2,275	81.3
16. Catawba	33	24-9	2,681	81.2
17. Southern Ind.	30	15-15	2,428	80.9
18. Denver	28	24-4	2,266	80.9
19. Henderson St.	24	12-12	1,932	80.5
20. Fla. Southern	28	25-3	2,252	80.4
21. Bellarmine	28	18-10	2,228	79.6
22. Saginaw Valley	29	20-9	2,305	79.5
23. Morningside	27	18-9	2,140	79.3
24. Livingston	26	17-9	2,053	79.0
25. Oakland	28	19-9	2,209	78.9
26. Edinboro	30	18-12	2,350	78.3
27. Oakland City	29	20-9	2,261	78.0
28. Shippensburg	26	14-12	2,026	77.9
29. Lincoln Memorial	27	18-9	2,103	77.9
30. Jacksonville St.	29	18-11	2,257	77.8
31. North Ala.	26	14-12	2,021	77.7
32. Calif. (Pa.)	26	18-8	2,019	77.7
33. Central Okla.	28	18-10	2,172	77.6
34. Mo. Southern St.	31	27-4	2,403	77.5
35. Wofford	27	23-4	2,088	77.3

SCORING DEFENSE

	G	W-L	PTS.	AVG.
1. Minn.-Duluth	30	22-8	1,701	56.7
2. Phila. Textile	29	27-2	1,646	56.8
3. Pace	31	24-7	1,760	56.8
4. Cal Poly Pomona	30	27-3	1,725	57.5
5. Washburn	32	31-1	1,846	57.7
6. UC Davis	26	19-7	1,501	57.7
7. Pitt.-Johnstown	30	25-5	1,745	58.2
8. Metropolitan St.	27	21-6	1,572	58.2
9. Bentley	34	30-4	1,987	58.4
10. Fla. Southern	28	25-3	1,637	58.5
11. North Dak. St.	32	30-2	1,871	58.5
12. Colorado-CS	27	18-9	1,581	58.6
13. Armstrong St.	26	16-10	1,535	59.0
14. Bloomsburg	26	20-6	1,536	59.1
15. Savannah St.	29	24-5	1,730	59.7
16. Cal St. Dom. Hills	26	15-11	1,559	60.0
17. North Dak.	28	23-5	1,694	60.5
18. Pittsburg St.	28	21-7	1,696	60.6
19. Franklin Pierce	30	21-9	1,823	60.8
20. Cal St. San B'dino	28	17-11	1,702	60.8
21. Augusta	29	24-5	1,768	61.0
22. Denver	28	24-4	1,721	61.5
23. Fort Hays St.	29	18-11	1,787	61.6
24. St. Rose	26	14-12	1,605	61.7
25. Le Moyne	27	16-11	1,671	61.9
25. Paine	27	12-15	1,671	61.9
27. Central Mo. St.	29	19-10	1,797	62.0
27. Oakland City	29	20-9	1,797	62.0
29. S.C.-Spartanburg	31	28-3	1,924	62.1
30. Albany St. (Ga.)	27	17-10	1,678	62.1
31. Eastern Mont.	27	18-9	1,682	62.3
32. San Fran. St.	25	8-17	1,560	62.4
33. South Dak. St.	27	17-10	1,687	62.5
34. Carson-Newman	30	22-8	1,875	62.5
35. Michigan Tech	33	30-3	2,064	62.5

SCORING MARGIN

	OFF.	DEF.	MAR.
1. North Dak. St.	89.3	58.5	30.8
2. Fort Valley St.	85.9	62.8	23.1
3. Fla. Southern	80.4	58.5	22.0
4. Florida Tech	85.9	64.7	21.2
5. Augustana (S.D.)	90.1	68.9	21.1
6. Norfolk St.	86.8	66.0	20.8
7. Denver	80.9	61.5	19.5
8. Washburn	76.5	57.7	18.8
9. Pitt.-Johnstown	76.9	58.2	18.7
10. Delta St.	82.1	63.6	18.5
11. Phila. Textile	73.8	56.8	17.0
12. Oakland City	78.0	62.0	16.0
13. Metropolitan St.	74.0	58.2	15.8
14. Alabama A&M	84.2	68.6	15.6
15. UC Davis	73.2	57.7	15.5
16. Savannah St.	75.1	59.7	15.5
17. St. Augustine's	86.5	71.1	15.3
18. Northern Mich.	89.7	74.5	15.2
19. S.C.-Spartanburg	77.2	62.1	15.1
20. Clarion	86.4	71.6	14.8
21. Mo. Southern St.	77.5	63.1	14.5
22. Michigan Tech	76.8	62.5	14.3
23. Eastern N. Mex.	82.6	68.8	13.8
24. Cal Poly Pomona	70.6	57.5	13.1
25. Indianapolis	82.0	69.0	13.0
26. Troy St.	83.0	70.0	13.0
27. Wofford	77.3	64.4	12.9
28. Pace	69.6	56.8	12.8
29. Fla. Atlantic	81.3	68.6	12.6
30. Chadron St.	83.0	70.6	12.4

	OFF.	DEF.	MAR.
31. North Dak.	72.4	60.5	11.9
32. Bentley	70.3	58.4	11.8
33. Carson-Newman	74.3	62.5	11.8
34. Pittsburg St.	72.2	60.6	11.6
35. Colorado-CS	69.7	58.6	11.1

WON-LOST PERCENTAGE

	W-L	PCT.
1. Washburn	31-1	.969
2. North Dak. St.	30-2	.938
3. Phila. Textile	27-2	.931
4. Michigan Tech	30-3	.909
5. Norfolk St.	29-3	.906
6. S.C.-Spartanburg	28-3	.903
7. Cal Poly Pomona	27-3	.900
7. Fort Valley St.	27-3	.900
9. Fla. Southern	25-3	.893
10. Bentley	30-4	.882
11. Mo. Southern St.	27-4	.871
12. Florida Tech	26-4	.867
13. Denver	24-4	.857
13. Indianapolis	24-4	.857
15. Wofford	23-4	.852
16. Pitt.-Johnstown	25-5	.833
17. Augusta	24-5	.828
17. Augustana (S.D.)	24-5	.828
17. Savannah St.	24-5	.828
20. Eastern N. Mex.	23-5	.821
20. North Dak.	23-5	.821
22. Delta St.	27-6	.818
23. Clarion	24-6	.800
23. Mass.-Lowell	24-6	.800
25. St. Augustine's	23-6	.793
26. Northern Mich.	22-6	.786
27. Metropolitan St.	21-6	.778
28. Pace	24-7	.774
29. Bloomsburg	20-6	.769
30. Pittsburg St.	21-7	.750
31. St. Joseph's (Ind.)	20-7	.741
31. SIU-Edwardsville	20-7	.741
33. Minn.-Duluth	22-8	.733
33. Stonehill	22-8	.733
33. Carson-Newman	22-8	.733

FIELD-GOAL PERCENTAGE

	FG	FGA	PCT.
1. Oakland City	929	1,806	51.4
2. Washburn	930	1,859	50.0
3. Pittsburg St.	747	1,500	49.8
4. St. Joseph's (Ind.)	784	1,606	48.8
5. Denver	908	1,885	48.2
6. Henderson St.	740	1,549	47.8
7. Lincoln Memorial	839	1,763	47.6
8. Tampa	723	1,534	47.1
9. Indianapolis	856	1,818	47.1
10. SIU-Edwardsville	766	1,627	47.1
11. Delta St.	1,057	2,246	47.1
12. Northern Ky.	788	1,675	47.0
13. S.C.-Spartanburg	936	1,996	46.9
14. Pace	877	1,874	46.8
15. Calif. (Pa.)	766	1,641	46.7
16. North Dak. St.	1,125	2,412	46.6
17. Pitt.-Johnstown	943	2,022	46.6
18. Northern Mich.	921	1,984	46.4
19. Eastern N. Mex.	831	1,793	46.3
20. Hampton	838	1,812	46.2
21. Norfolk St.	1,089	2,357	46.2
22. Regis (Colo.)	739	1,609	45.9
23. Augustana (S.D.)	959	2,091	45.9
24. Chadron St.	834	1,822	45.8
25. West Tex. St.	734	1,606	45.7
26. Bellarmine	802	1,772	45.3
27. Stonehill	804	1,779	45.2
28. Florida Tech	977	2,162	45.2
29. Fla. Southern	889	1,969	45.1
30. Millersville	803	1,783	45.0
31. Colorado-CS	709	1,575	45.0
32. UC Davis	757	1,689	44.8
33. Minn.-Duluth	782	1,745	44.8
34. Augusta	798	1,783	44.8
35. Indiana (Pa.)	655	1,464	44.7

FIELD-GOAL PERCENTAGE DEFENSE

	FG	FGA	PCT.
1. Pace	659	1,962	33.6
2. Oakland City	660	1,934	34.1
3. Wingate	685	1,964	34.9
4. Hampton	647	1,847	35.0
5. Alabama A&M	637	1,811	35.2
6. Bentley	739	2,099	35.2
7. Virginia Union	653	1,844	35.4
8. Adelphi	613	1,730	35.4
9. Wofford	624	1,761	35.4
10. North Dak. St.	700	1,972	35.5
11. Augustana (S.D.)	696	1,959	35.5
12. St. Rose	579	1,624	35.7
13. Savannah St.	595	1,655	36.0
14. Carson-Newman	684	1,897	36.1
15. Virginia St.	667	1,841	36.2
16. LIU-C. W. Post	633	1,734	36.5
17. Delta St.	787	2,152	36.6
18. Lander	663	1,812	36.6
19. Johnson Smith	754	2,045	36.9
20. Metropolitan St.	567	1,534	37.0
21. Le Moyne	606	1,638	37.0
22. Mississippi Col.	632	1,705	37.1
23. Augusta	695	1,868	37.2
24. Phila. Textile	619	1,663	37.2
25. Washburn	718	1,928	37.2
26. Seattle Pacific	637	1,709	37.3
27. Paine	672	1,791	37.5
28. Cal St. San B'dino	600	1,598	37.5
29. Chadron St.	660	1,756	37.6
30. Mass.-Lowell	734	1,950	37.6
31. Minn.-Duluth	577	1,527	37.8
32. Norfolk St.	812	2,141	37.9
33. Ashland	619	1,626	38.1
34. N.C. Central	710	1,864	38.1
35. Central Mo. St.	664	1,742	38.1

THREE-POINT FIELD GOALS MADE PER GAME

	G	NO.	AVG.
1. Clarion	30	337	11.2
2. Oakland	28	282	10.1
3. Southern Ind.	30	217	7.2
4. Livingston	26	168	6.5
4. Troy St.	26	168	6.5
6. Queens (N.C.)	26	165	6.3
7. Bellarmine	28	174	6.2
8. Metropolitan St.	27	164	6.1
9. Adams St.	27	163	6.0
10. Northern Mich.	28	166	5.9
11. Central Okla.	28	160	5.7
12. Keene St.	29	158	5.4
13. West Ga.	27	146	5.4
14. North Dak.	28	148	5.3
15. Catawba	33	174	5.3
16. Mo. Southern St.	31	163	5.3
17. Bloomsburg	26	128	4.9
17. Calif. (Pa.)	26	128	4.9
19. Grand Valley St.	26	125	4.8
20. Michigan Tech	33	158	4.8
21. St. Anselm	29	135	4.7
22. Wayne St. (Neb.)	26	118	4.5
23. Saginaw Valley	29	131	4.5
24. Fort Valley St.	30	134	4.5
25. Angelo St.	27	120	4.4
26. Shippensburg	26	114	4.4
27. Augustana (S.D.)	29	127	4.4
27. Jacksonville St.	29	127	4.4
29. Chapman	25	109	4.4
30. Texas Woman's	24	104	4.3
31. Florida Tech	30	128	4.3
32. St. Michael's	27	115	4.3
33. Albany St. (Ga.)	27	114	4.2
34. St. Augustine's	29	122	4.2
35. Southwest Baptist	27	112	4.1

THREE-POINT FIELD-GOAL PERCENTAGE

(Min. 2.0 3FG Made Per Game)	G	FG	FGA	PCT.
1. Phila. Textile	29	114	266	42.9
2. Cal St. Dom. Hills	26	102	250	40.8
3. Livingston	26	168	413	40.7
4. Chadron St.	27	88	221	39.8
5. Le Moyne	27	101	255	39.6
6. Bloomsburg	26	128	331	38.7
7. Wayne St. (Mich.)	26	91	237	38.4
8. Colorado-CS	27	68	178	38.2
9. Eastern N. Mex.	28	109	286	38.1
10. Indianapolis	28	87	229	38.0
11. Delta St.	33	134	357	37.5
12. Bellarmine	28	174	464	37.5
13. Southwest Baptist	27	112	299	37.5
14. Mo. Southern St.	31	163	436	37.4
15. St. Anselm	29	135	363	37.2
16. Tampa	26	92	248	37.1
17. Texas Woman's	24	104	285	36.5
18. Regis (Colo.)	27	54	148	36.5
19. Lewis	27	103	283	36.4
20. Alabama A&M	26	72	198	36.4
21. St. Augustine's	29	122	336	36.3
22. Cal St. Stanislaus	28	62	172	36.0
23. Central Ark.	28	98	273	35.9
24. Oakland	28	282	788	35.8
25. S.C.-Spartanburg	31	128	358	35.8
26. North Dak.	28	148	414	35.7
27. Millersville	26	95	266	35.7
28. Saginaw Valley	29	131	367	35.7
29. Michigan Tech	33	158	443	35.7
30. Northern Mich.	28	166	466	35.6
31. Keene St.	29	158	445	35.5
32. Norfolk St.	32	91	257	35.4
33. Morningside	27	70	199	35.2
34. Southern Ind.	30	217	623	34.8
35. Augustana (S.D.)	29	127	366	34.7

FREE-THROW PERCENTAGE

	FT	FTA	PCT.
1. Augustana (S.D.)	567	722	78.5*
2. Phila. Textile	500	647	77.3
3. Pittsburg St.	486	643	75.6
4. Central Okla.	544	722	75.3
5. Portland St.	482	647	74.5
6. West Chester	430	585	73.5
7. Central Ark.	518	707	73.3
8. Washburn	526	718	73.3
9. Florida Tech	495	684	72.4
10. Stonehill	480	666	72.1
11. Mo. Southern St.	514	715	71.9
12. Eastern N. Mex.	541	753	71.8
13. Minn.-Duluth	406	567	71.6
14. Assumption	335	468	71.6
15. Queens (N.C.)	375	524	71.6
16. Abilene Christian	483	677	71.3
17. Gannon	291	408	71.3
18. Oakland	379	532	71.2
19. St. Rose	433	608	71.2
20. Alas. Anchorage	417	586	71.2
21. Henderson St.	366	517	70.8
22. Regis (Colo.)	379	536	70.7
23. East Tex. St.	531	755	70.3
24. Southwest Baptist	391	556	70.3
25. Bellarmine	450	640	70.3
26. Franklin Pierce	432	615	70.2
27. Central Mo. St.	348	497	70.0
28. St. Cloud St.	380	543	70.0
29. Hillsdale	428	612	69.9
30. North Dak.	416	597	69.7
31. South Dak.	432	621	69.6
32. Mo. Western St.	365	526	69.4
33. Denver	409	591	69.2
34. Michigan Tech	483	698	69.2
35. Shepherd	384	555	69.2

* NCAA Divison II record.

REBOUND MARGIN

	OFF.	DEF.	MAR.
1. Oakland City	49.8	33.0	16.8
2. North Dak. St.	54.4	37.7	16.7
3. Alabama A&M	57.3	43.8	13.4
4. West Ga.	48.1	35.2	12.9
5. Northern Ky.	45.1	33.5	11.6
6. Savannah St.	51.2	40.5	10.8
7. Washburn	41.9	32.0	9.9
8. Carson-Newman	47.5	38.1	9.4
9. Hampton	49.3	40.2	9.1
10. Neb.-Kearney	48.8	39.8	9.0
10. UC Davis	44.2	35.2	9.0
12. Mesa St.	45.5	37.4	8.1
13. Ferris St.	46.4	38.5	8.0
14. Calif. (Pa.)	45.7	37.8	7.8
15. Pace	44.5	36.7	7.8
16. Wofford	50.3	42.6	7.7
17. St. Joseph's (Ind.)	42.2	34.9	7.3
18. Fla. Atlantic	48.7	41.4	7.3
19. Johnson Smith	56.9	49.8	7.1
20. Henderson St.	43.2	36.1	7.1
21. Florida Tech	47.0	40.2	6.8
22. Angelo St.	46.3	39.6	6.7
23. Pitt.-Johnstown	42.4	35.7	6.6
24. Delta St.	46.6	40.0	6.6
25. Columbus	53.1	46.6	6.6
26. Virginia Union	53.3	46.8	6.5
27. Minn.-Duluth	39.6	33.3	6.3
28. Bentley	45.9	39.7	6.2
29. Central Ark.	41.1	34.9	6.2
30. Abilene Christian	45.3	39.3	6.1
31. Troy St.	48.5	42.5	5.9
32. Jacksonville St.	51.8	45.9	5.9
33. St. Michael's	45.9	40.0	5.9
34. Valdosta St.	49.2	43.4	5.8
35. Indiana (Pa.)	43.9	38.4	5.5

1993 DIVISION III WOMEN'S INDIVIDUAL LEADERS

SCORING

	CL	G	TFG	3FG	FT	PTS.	AVG.
1. Sladja Kovijanic, Middlebury	Sr	21	235	80	98	648	30.9
2. Annette Hoffman, Juniata	Sr	22	197	21	228	643	29.2
3. Tricia Rasmussen, St. Mary's (Minn.)	Sr	24	270	2	103	645	26.9
4. Laurie Trow, St. Thomas (Minn.)	Sr	26	271	0	137	679	26.1
5. Tricia Kosenina, Thiel	Sr	24	214	42	152	622	25.9
6. Renie Amoss, Goucher	Sr	25	244	39	85	612	24.5
7. Patricia Frost, Upsala	So	20	200	32	47	479	24.0
8. Simone Edwards, FDU-Madison	Sr	25	183	20	206	592	23.7
9. Brenda Davis, Guilford	Jr	25	238	0	108	584	23.4
10. Kim Coia, Western New Eng.	So	21	184	44	76	488	23.2
11. Julie Maki, Wis.-Stout	Sr	25	224	33	94	575	23.0
12. Vangela Crowe, Rutgers-Newark	Jr	26	223	0	151	597	23.0
13. Leah Onks, Maryville (Tenn.)	Jr	26	218	39	120	595	22.9
14. Erin Adamson, Bryn Mawr	Jr	17	139	1	109	388	22.8
15. Jerilynn Johnson, Rhode Island Col.	Sr	23	189	0	144	522	22.7

	CL	G	TFG	3FG	FT	PTS.	AVG.
16. Molly Lackman, Immaculata	Jr	25	187	0	192	566	22.6
17. Shannon Ferguson, Earlham	Jr	23	173	14	151	511	22.2
18. Jill Coleman, Wesley	Sr	25	227	4	89	547	21.9
19. Debbie Filipek, Rowan	Jr	23	192	0	118	502	21.8
20. Laura Williams, Principia	Jr	21	152	15	136	455	21.7
21. Anessa Lourensz, Utica Tech	Jr	25	187	16	148	538	21.5
22. Tracie Rieder, Marywood	Sr	23	219	0	56	494	21.5
23. Missie Burns, Berea	Jr	20	159	56	52	426	21.3
24. Wendy Gibbs, La Verne	Sr	24	204	1	100	509	21.2
25. Kim Prewitt, Thomas More	Fr	26	166	77	130	539	20.7
26. Lisa Grudzinski, Wis.-Stevens Point	Jr	24	195	0	105	495	20.6
27. Chris Pagano, Middlebury	Jr	21	167	20	79	433	20.6
28. Robin Gobeille, Rhode Island Col.	Sr	23	157	39	117	470	20.4
29. Vickie Meiners, Illinois Col	Sr	24	192	1	105	490	20.4
30. Michelle Frisby, Rust	Sr	24	212	0	62	486	20.3
31. Julie Rando, Regis (Mass.)	Jr	25	184	11	127	506	20.2
32. Katina Johnson, Ramapo	Jr	27	227	0	90	544	20.1
33. Liza Janssen, Wellesley	Jr	27	214	0	115	543	20.1
34. Sylvia Newman, Meredith	Sr	20	149	0	104	402	20.1
35. Carrie Bowen, Frank.& Marsh	Sr	24	207	7	61	482	20.1
36. Kathy Roberts, Wartburg	Sr	28	177	43	164	561	20.0
37. Heather Dawkins, Wash. & Jeff.	Jr	21	172	0	75	419	20.0
38. Laura Schultz, Bowdoin	Fr	20	175	3	46	399	20.0
39. Peggy Hoops, Defiance	Sr	25	202	0	93	497	19.9
40. Peggie Sweeney, Pine Manor	Fr	27	182	0	172	536	19.9
41. Kiki Seago, Cortland St.	Sr	25	182	3	129	496	19.8
42. Erica Scholl, UC San Diego	Sr	25	214	0	65	493	19.7
43. Theresa Berg, Grove City	Sr	22	170	21	71	432	19.6
44. Kim McCabe, Wentworth Inst.	So	22	168	25	70	431	19.6
45. Traci Butler, Ill. Wesleyan	Fr	25	193	42	59	487	19.5
46. Tamara Carey, Rutgers-Camden	So	23	174	20	79	447	19.4
47. Missy Kowolenko, Eastern Conn. St.	Sr	27	191	13	126	521	19.3
48. Vicki Fuess, Utica Tech	Sr	25	149	95	87	480	19.2
49. Tracy Salciccia, Mt. St. Vincent	Sr	23	151	34	105	441	19.2
50. April Owen, Staten Island	Sr	18	148	1	46	343	19.1
51. Julie Diehl, Hamilton	Sr	26	200	0	94	494	19.0
52. Keesha Brooks, Augustana (Ill.)	Sr	26	204	0	84	492	18.9
53. Sylke Knuppel, Johns Hopkins	Sr	22	145	23	102	415	18.9
54. Evelyn Albert, Cal Lutheran	Sr	25	182	0	106	470	18.8
55. Sarah Hackl, St. Norbert	So	21	162	0	70	394	18.8
56. Emily Grana, Maryville (Mo.)	Fr	27	203	0	100	506	18.7
57. Christi Clay, Denison	Jr	25	187	26	67	467	18.7
58. Sharon Rines, St. Joseph's (Me.)	Jr	29	179	0	182	540	18.6
59. Sandy Buddelmeyer, Capital	Sr	32	225	0	145	595	18.6
60. Jenn. Hadfield, Trinity (Conn.)	Jr	23	153	0	121	427	18.6
61. Violaine Romans, Marymont (Va.)	Jr	28	212	3	90	517	18.5
62. Donna Layne, New York U.	Jr	24	178	0	87	443	18.5
63. Jackie Oliver, Rutgers-Newark	Jr	25	173	33	80	459	18.4
64. Regina Washington, Berea	Sr	20	147	0	71	365	18.3
65. Jen Taubenheim, St. Mary's (Ind.)	Fr	21	166	0	51	383	18.2
66. Tracy Wilson, Central (Ill.)	Sr	29	204	0	118	526	18.1
67. Martha Cleary, Catholic	So	25	161	45	86	453	18.1
68. Holly Larkin, Hendrix	Jr	23	144	0	128	416	18.1
69. Courtney Wildung, Hamline	Sr	25	199	0	54	452	18.1
70. Malane Perry, Fitchburg	Sr	23	114	0	186	414	18.0

FIELD-GOAL PERCENTAGE

(Min. 5 FG Made Per Game)	CL	G	FG	FGA	PCT.
1. Tina Kampa, St. Benedict	So	30	158	231	68.4*
2. Lanett Stephan, Franklin	Fr	25	147	222	66.2
3. Laurie Trow, St. Thomas (Minn.)	Sr	26	271	413	65.6
4. Sylvia Newman, Meredith	Sr	20	149	238	62.6
5. Arlene Meinholz, Wis.-Eau Claire	So	26	192	313	61.3
6. Jerilynn Johnson, Rhode Island Col.	Sr	23	189	314	60.2
7. Liza Janssen, Wellesley	Jr	27	214	357	59.9
8. Audrey Seymour, Adrian	Sr	26	163	274	59.5
9. Jamie Parrott, Maryville (Tenn.)	Fr	26	145	245	59.2
10. Jill Coleman, Wesley	Sr	25	227	384	59.1
11. Jennifer Norris, Meredith	Sr	20	138	235	58.7
12. Sarah Hackl, St. Norbert	So	21	162	276	58.7
13. Heather Dawkins, Wash. & Jeff.	Jr	21	172	294	58.5
14. Dawn Krupp, Wis.-Whitewater	Sr	25	128	220	58.2
15. Missie Burns, Berea	Jr	20	159	274	58.0
16. Erica Hanson; Concordia-M'head	Jr	27	201	348	57.8
17. Angie Horner, Hiram	Jr	25	154	268	57.5
18. Sue Grack, St. Olaf	Sr	23	143	249	57.4
19. Sandy Buddelmeyer, Capital	Sr	32	225	392	57.4
20. Lisa Grudzinski, Wis.-Stevens Point	Jr	24	195	340	57.4

(Min. 5 FG Made Per Game)	CL	G	FG	FGA	PCT.
21. Katina Johnson, Ramapo	Jr	27	227	401	56.6
22. Chris Neibert, Trenton St.	Sr	24	150	266	56.4
23. Dawn Rattray, Wis.-Eau Claire	Sr	26	174	309	56.3
24. Keesha Brooks, Augustana (Ill.)	Sr	26	204	364	56.0
25. Vickie Meiners, Illinois Col.	Sr	24	192	346	55.5
26. Brenda Davis, Guilford	Jr	25	238	429	55.5
27. Chris Gleisner, Mary Washington	Jr	26	171	309	55.3
28. Katie Mans, Alma	Jr	25	141	255	55.3
29. Meridith McKnight, Carnegie Mellon	So	25	136	246	55.3
29. Tina Breithaupt, Frank. & Marsh.	Jr	24	136	246	55.3
31. Angie Haas, Elizabethtown	Fr	25	162	294	55.1
32. Tricia Rasmussen, St. Mary's (Minn.)	Sr	24	270	492	54.9
33. Emily Grana, Maryville (Mo.)	Fr	27	203	370	54.9
34. Katie Smith, Geneseo St.	So	27	198	361	54.8
35. Julie Westcott, Centre	Jr	25	137	250	54.8

* Division III record.

THREE-POINT FIELD GOALS MADE PER GAME

	CL	G	NO.	AVG.
1. Sladja Kovijanic, Middlebury	Sr	21	80	3.8
2. Vicki Fuess, Utica Tech	Sr	25	95	3.8
3. MaryKate Fannon, Cabrini	Sr	26	92	3.5
4. Martha Sainz, Va. Wesleyan	Sr	26	79	3.0
5. Kim Prewitt, Thomas More	Fr	26	77	3.0
6. Debbi Pearson, Notre Dame (Md.)	Jr	23	67	2.9
7. Missie Burns, Berea	Jr	20	56	2.8
8. Molly Geisen, Olivet	Jr	22	60	2.7
9. Michelle Stuart, Rhodes	Fr	22	58	2.6
10. Tina Forth, Monmouth (Ill.)	So	26	66	2.5
11. Leanne Bajema, Calvin	Sr	26	66	2.5
12. Sona Bedenian, Aurora	Sr	25	62	2.5
13. Sherry Bradley, Gallaudet	So	24	59	2.5
14. Beth Shapiro, New York U.	Sr	26	63	2.4
15. Jill Irland, Alfred	So	25	59	2.4
16. Jill Brower, William Smith	Sr	26	61	2.3
17. Angie Dale, Millikin	Sr	24	56	2.3
18. Katie Kowalczyk, Hope	Sr	22	50	2.3
19. Tami Bobst, Upper Iowa	Jr	22	48	2.2
20. Mandy Jackson, Emory	So	24	52	2.2
20. Amy Jo Leonard, Potsdam St.	Jr	24	52	2.2
22. Brenda Robertson, Brockport St.	So	25	54	2.2
22. Kerry Driver, Worcester St.	Sr	25	54	2.2
24. Tara O'Riordan, Mass.-Boston	Fr	23	49	2.1
25. Katrina Roggenbaum, Binghamton	Jr	25	53	2.1
25. Annelise Houston, New Eng. Col.	Sr	25	53	2.1
25. Cindy Hovet, Wis.-Stout	Jr	25	53	2.1
28. Michele Maxwell, Clark (Mass.)	Sr	26	55	2.1
29. Jennie Kirk, Berea	Fr	20	42	2.1
30. Kim Coia, Western New Eng.	So.	21	44	2.1
31. Sandi Hedden, Oswego St.	Jr	23	48	2.1
32. Karlyn Dalsing, Loras	Sr	24	50	2.1
33. Lori Towle, Southern Me.	So	29	60	2.1
34. Julie Ludden, Bates	Sr	22	45	2.0
35. Cathy Silva, Wheaton (Mass.)	Jr	26	52	2.0
35. Barbara Toolan, Trinity (Conn.)	So	23	46	2.0

THREE-POINT FIELD-GOAL PERCENTAGE

(Min. 1.5 3FG Made Per Game)	CL	G	FG	FGA	PCT.
1. Missie Burns, Berea	Jr	20	56	99	56.6
2. Honey Brown, Maryville (Tenn.)	Jr	26	40	73	54.8
3. Kristen Crawly, St. Mary's (Ind.)	Sr	21	40	80	50.0
4. Kathy Roberts, Wartburg	Sr	28	43	90	47.8
5. Anne Gooley, Scranton	Jr	32	53	113	46.9
6. Lori Towle, Southern Me.	So	29	60	129	46.5
7. Kelly Mahlum, St. Benedict	Sr	30	52	112	46.4
8. Cindi Neanen, Wilmington (Ohio)	Fr	24	42	94	44.7
9. Joslin Stanton, Jersey City St.	Sr	24	47	107	43.9
10. Leanne Bajema, Calvin	Sr	26	66	151	43.7
11. Kim Bartman, Calvin	Sr	26	48	110	43.6
12. Vicki Wittman, Chicago	So	25	47	108	43.5
13. Michelle Stuart, Rhodes	Fr	22	58	134	43.3
14. Katie Mang, Capital	So	32	48	113	42.5
15. Angie Dale, Millikin	Sr	24	56	135	41.5
16. Neile Joler, St. Joseph's (Me.)	So	29	45	109	41.3
17. Sladja Kovijanic, Middlebury	Sr	21	80	195	41.0
18. Traci Butler, Ill. Wesleyan	Fr	25	42	103	40.8
19. Heidi Metzger, Elizabethtown	So	24	41	101	40.6
20. Mandy Jackson, Emory	So	24	52	130	40.0

(Min. 1.5 3FG Made Per Game)	CL	G	FG	FGA	PCT.
21. Janice Kemp, Fontbonne	Sr	25	49	126	38.9
22. Tina Forth, Monmouth (Ill.)	So	22	56	146	38.4
23. Michele Maxwell, Clark (Mass.)	Sr	26	55	14	38.2
24. Debbi Pearson, Notre Dame (Md.)	Jr	23	67	176	38.1
25. Kerry Driver, Worcester St.	Sr	25	54	143	37.8
26. Jill Thomas, Carthage	Sr	25	49	131	37.4
27. Andrea Bertini, Westfield St.	Fr	26	43	115	37.4
28. Terri Tubbs, Southwestern (Tex.)	Sr	24	38	102	37.3
29. Cissi White, Hanover	So	19	35	94	37.2
30. Linda Carlson, Wheaton (Ill.)	Sr	25	46	124	37.1
31. Vicki Fuess, Utica Tech	Sr	25	95	257	37.0
32. Barbara Toolan, Trinity (Conn.)	So	23	46	125	36.8
33. Naomi Jordan, New York U.	Jr	24	36	98	36.7
34. Sona Bedenian, Aurora	Sr	25	62	169	36.7
35. MaryKate Fannon, Cabrini	Sr	26	92	252	36.5

FREE-THROW PERCENTAGE

(Min. 2.5 FT Made Per Game)	CL	G	FT	FTA	PCT.
1. Jill Kathmann, William Smith	Fr	25	66	74	89.2
2. Katie Anderson, Luther	Sr	20	57	65	87.7
3. Jen Olsen, Wellesley	Sr	27	70	82	85.4
4. Annette Hoffman, Juniata	Sr	22	228	268	85.1
5. Chris Pagano, Middlebury	Jr	21	79	93	84.9
6. Tricia Kosenina, Thiel	Sr	24	152	179	84.9
7. Eileen Horaitis, Lake Forest	So	22	61	73	83.6
8. Heidi Metzger, Elizabethtown	So	24	91	109	83.5
9. Colleen Tribby, Claremont-M-S	Fr	25	94	113	83.2
9. Pam Porter, Moravian	Jr	24	94	113	83.2
11. Cindi Neanen, Wilmington (Ohio)	Fr	24	113	136	83.1
12. Christa Goetz, Carthage	So	25	98	118	83.1
13. Kim Bartman, Calvin	Sr	26	71	86	82.6
14. Michelle Harkness, Muskingum	Sr	26	93	113	82.3
15. Karen Trojanowski, Allentown	Jr	26	102	124	82.3
16. Ana Cayro, Loras	Sr	24	80	98	81.6
17. Malane Perry, Fitchburg St.	Sr	23	186	228	81.6
18. Michelle Kulbitsky, King's (Pa.)	Fr	22	65	80	81.3
19. Laurie Trow, St. Thomas (Minn.)	Sr	26	137	169	81.1
20. Joan Gandolf, Stony Brook	Jr	25	106	131	80.9
21. Pamela Dumond, William Smith	Fr	26	80	99	80.8
22. Jill Bachonski, Wm. Paterson	Sr	26	117	145	80.7
23. Tricia Rasmussen, St. Mary's (Minn.)	Sr	24	103	128	80.5
24. Melissa Hay, Trenton St.	So	24	70	87	80.5
25. Julie Schindler, Wis.-Stevens Point	Jr	24	102	127	80.3
26. Stephanie Sealer, Clarkson	So	24	76	95	80.0
26. Kim Coia, Western New Eng.	So	21	76	95	80.0
28. Roe Falcone, Dickinson	So	26	111	139	79.9
29. Sharon Rines, St. Joseph's (Me.)	Jr	29	182	228	79.8
30. Tiffany Lockett, Baldwin-Wallace	Sr	25	93	117	79.5
31. Standish Stewart, Case Reserve	Fr	25	81	102	79.4
32. Angie Horner, Hiram	Jr	25	104	131	79.4
33. Kerry Delk, Wis.-La Crosse	Jr	25	88	111	79.3
34. Corinne May, Mary Washington	So	26	76	96	79.2
35. Krista Hershner, Penn St.-Behrend	Jr	25	87	110	79.1

REBOUNDING

	CL	G	NO.	AVG.
1. Giovanni Licorish, Baruch	Fr	19	317	16.7
2. Shannon Shaffer, Montclair St.	Sr	25	382	15.3
3. Liza Janssen, Wellesley	Jr	27	407	15.1
4. Kim Roth, Salisbury St.	So	23	340	14.8
5. Erica Scholl, UC San Diego	Sr	25	368	14.7
6. Molly Lackman, Immaculata	Jr	25	359	14.4
7. Wendy Gruenewald, New Jersey Tech	Fr	22	314	14.3
8. Erin Adamson, Bryn Mawr	Jr	17	242	14.2
9. Wendy Howard, Utica Tech	Jr	25	354	14.2
10. Brenda Davis, Guilford	Jr	25	341	13.6
11. Marianne Kelm, Concordia (Ill.)	Sr	22	300	13.6
12. Heather Dawkins, Wash. & Jeff.	Jr	21	281	13.4
13. Kristin Kahle, Pine Manor	Jr	26	344	13.2
14. Nancy Rosenbaum, Swarthmore	Fr	22	291	13.2
15. Wendy Gibbs, La Verne	Sr	24	316	13.2
16. Tamara Carey, Rutgers-Camden	So	23	301	13.1
17. Jill Coleman, Wesley	Sr	25	322	12.9
18. Allison Palmer, Wesleyan	So	23	295	12.8
19. Esty Wood, Connecticut Col.	Sr	24	306	12.8
20. Melissa Small, Old Westbury	Jr	15	191	12.7
21. Johanna McGourty, Suffolk	Sr	22	280	12.7
22. Courtney Wildung, Hamline	Sr	25	316	12.6
23. Pam Dabbs, Averett	Fr	24	299	12.5
24. Kimbra Braithwaite, Oswego St.	Sr	20	248	12.4
25. Becky Rodriguez, Trinity (Tex.)	Fr	20	246	12.3

	CL	G	NO.	AVG.
26. Michelle Milot, Skidmore	Jr	25	305	12.2
27. Jerilynn Johnson, Rhode Island Col.	Sr	23	280	12.2
28. Kelly James, Hartwick	Sr	24	291	12.1
29. Ayanna Parker, CCNY	Fr	25	303	12.1
30. Dana Maul, New Paltz St.	So	26	315	12.1
31. Tracie Rieder, Marywood	Sr	23	278	12.1
32. Katina Johnson, Ramapo	Jr	27	322	11.9
33. Julie Harvilchuck, King's (Pa.)	Jr	25	298	11.9
34. Karen Scibetta, Grove City	Sr	22	262	11.9
35. Tracy Wilson, Central (Iowa)	Sr	29	345	11.9

ASSISTS

	CL	G	NO.	AVG.
1. Karen Barefoot, Chris. Newport	Jr	28	236	8.4
2. Marlo Foley, Binghamton	Sr	27	211	7.8
3. Allison Gagnon, Southern Me.	Sr	29	221	7.6
4. Renie Amoss, Goucher	Sr	25	182	7.3
5. Kristi Schultz, Concordia-M'head	Sr	27	190	7.0
6. Regina Austin, Buffalo St.	Sr	27	188	7.0
7. Chris Lavery, Immaculata	Jr	23	157	6.8
8. Leslie Cox, Meredith	So	20	136	6.8
9. Maureen Andrews, Gettysburg	So	24	162	6.8
10. Mary Keegan, Loras	So	24	159	6.6
11. Lynne Unice, Wash. & Jeff.	Jr	22	144	6.5
12. Lisa Pliskin, Blackburn	Jr	28	180	6.4
13. Julie Schindler, Wis.-Stevens Point	Jr	24	153	6.4
14. Robyn Wainwright, Westfield St.	Jr	29	178	6.1
15. Stacy Willard, Ill. Wesleyan	Sr	25	153	6.1
16. Danielle Moorehead, Brockport St.	Jr	25	144	5.8
17. Stacy Scudder, Heidelberg	Sr	27	155	5.7
18. Jen Kelley, Grinnell	Sr	23	131	5.7
19. Amy Russell, Wheaton (Ill.)	Sr	25	142	5.7
20. Dana Mills, Cabrini	Fr	24	133	5.5
21. Carey Janis, Geneseo St.	So	28	155	5.5
22. Amy Wilson, Illinois Col.	Sr	24	132	5.5
23. Amy Heit, Maryville (Mo.)	So	27	148	5.5
24. Karen Walker, Beloit	Sr	24	129	5.4
25. Gen Washington, Juniata	Fr	22	118	5.4
26. Lisa Matukaitis, Eastern Conn. St	Sr	25	133	5.3
27. Libbie Tobin, Rochester	Jr	25	132	5.3
28. Emily Edson, Rhodes	So	22	116	5.3
29. Michelle Harkness, Muskingum	Sr	26	136	5.2
29. Jody Krueger, Wis.-Eau Claire	Sr	26	136	5.2
31. Danielle Spanski, Baldwin-Wallace	So	25	130	5.2
32. Amy Jo Leonard, Potsdam St.	Jr	24	124	5.2
33. Jill Thomas, Carthage	Sr	25	129	5.2
34. Sara Purdom, Hendrix	So	23	117	5.1
35. Amy Sullivan, Brandeis	Sr	25	126	5.0
35. Jill Anderson, St. Olaf	Jr	25	126	5.0

BLOCKED SHOTS

	CL	G	NO.	AVG.
1. Liza Janssen, Wellesley	Jr	27	145	5.4
2. Janet Kasinger, Ill. Benedictine	Jr	22	113	5.1
3. Kim Stumpf, Whittier	Jr	24	110	4.6
4. Kim McCabe, Wentworth Inst.	So	22	90	4.1
5. Tamiko Martin, Ferrum	So	25	97	3.9
6. Jen Tregoning, St. Mary's (Md.)	Jr	20	74	3.7
7. Wendy Gibbs, La Verne	Sr	24	76	3.2
8. Liliana Alvarez, New Jersey Tech	Jr	21	66	3.1
9. Heather Dawkins, Wash. & Jeff.	Jr	21	65	3.1
10. Sylvia Newman, Meredith	Sr	20	61	3.0
11. Keisha Brown, John Jay	Jr	23	70	3.0
12. Emma Bascom, Drew	Fr	21	63	3.0
13. Sheila Retcher, Defiance	Jr	24	71	3.0
14. Megan Wilrett, Elmhurst	So	24	64	2.7
15. Julie Snyder, St. Mary's (Ind.)	Sr	20	52	2.6
16. Marianne Kelm, Concordia (Ill.)	Sr	22	56	2.5
17. Marlene Neal, Upsala	Fr	23	55	2.4
18. Tracie Rieder, Marywood	Sr	23	52	2.3
18. Laura Lavery, Wesleyan	Sr	23	52	2.3
20. Caroline Duffy, Immaculata	Sr	25	55	2.2
20. Monica Mills, Westminster (Mo.)	Sr	20	44	2.2
22. Laurie Trow, St. Thomas (Minn.)	Sr	26	57	2.2
23. Jennifer Mantione, FDU-Madison	Jr	25	54	2.2
23. Lanett Stephan, Franklin	Fr	25	54	2.2
25. Annie Guzek, Dickinson	Fr	26	55	2.1

	CL	G	NO.	AVG.
26. Paula Keith, St. John Fisher	Sr	28	59	2.1
27. Tracy Wilson, Central (Iowa)	Sr	29	61	2.1
28. Tracey Buettgens, Rochester	Jr	22	46	2.1
29. Tina Breithaupt, Frank. & Marsh.	Jr	24	50	2.1
30. Carla Cannon, Wesley	Jr	25	51	2.0
31. Michelle Milot, Skidmore	Jr	25	50	2.0
31. Lynn Haden, Averett	Jr	23	46	2.0
31. Kathleen Abbott, Chicago	So	22	44	2.0
34. Tia Johnson, Chris. Newport	Sr	28	55	2.0
35. Emily Grana, Maryville (Mo.)	Fr	27	53	2.0

STEALS

	CL	G	NO.	AVG.
1. Alicia LaValley, Plattsburgh St.	Sr	24	149	6.2
2. Rose Addison, York (N.Y.)	So	23	137	6.0
3. Angel Esposito, Elms	So	23	129	5.6
4. Julie Rando, Regis (Mass.)	Jr	25	132	5.3
5. Cindy Leeds, St. Mary's (Md.)	So	20	100	5.0
6. Nicole Albert, Cal Lutheran	Fr	25	124	5.0
7. Lisa Villalta, Montclair St.	Fr	25	123	4.9
8. Karen Barefoot, Chris. Newport	Jr	28	128	4.6
9. Annelise Houston, New Eng. Col.	Sr	25	112	4.5
10. Patricia Frost, Upsala	So	20	88	4.4
11. Emily Edson, Rhodes	So	22	96	4.4
12. Melissa Bryce, Plymouth St.	Sr	25	108	4.3
13. Tracy Salciccia, Mt. St. Vincent	Sr	23	97	4.2
14. Letty Perez, Gallaudet	Fr	24	100	4.2
15. Keisha Brown, John Jay	Jr	23	95	4.1
16. Lisa Matukaitis, Eastern Conn. St.	Sr	25	103	4.1
17. Renie Amoss, Goucher	Sr	25	102	4.1
18. Jen Erickson, Regis (Mass.)	So	25	100	4.0
19. Missy Kowolenko, Eastern Conn. St.	Sr	27	107	4.0
20. Karen Walker, Beloit	Sr	24	95	4.0
21. Natasha Upson, Delaware Valley	So	22	87	4.0
22. Regina Austin, Buffalo St.	Sr	27	106	3.9
23. Sakari Morrison, Pomona-Pitzer	Fr	25	97	3.9
24. Erika Enomoto, Whittier	Fr	24	93	3.9
25. Shannon Martin, St. Mary's (Minn.)	Sr	24	92	3.8
26. Pam Barton, North Adams St.	Jr	21	80	3.8
27. Shannon Shaffer, Montclair St.	Sr	25	95	3.8
27. Roxanne Chiang, Baruch	Jr	20	76	3.8
29. Lisa Trujillo, Norwich	Jr	28	106	3.8
30. Hillary Davis, Jersey City St.	Fr	24	90	3.8
30. Sylvia Newman, Meredith	Sr	20	75	3.8
32. Jen Esposito, Albright	Sr	23	85	3.7
33. Amy Endler, Moravian	Sr	29	107	3.7
34. Shannon Osborne, Pomona-Pitzer	So	24	87	3.6
35. Shannon English, Elmhurst	Jr	20	72	3.6

1993 DIVISION III WOMEN'S BASKETBALL GAME HIGHS

INDIVIDUAL HIGHS

SCORING

Pts.	Player, Team vs. Opponent	Date
49	Annette Hoffman, Juniata vs. Elizabethtown	Nov. 30
47	Sladja Kovijanic, Middlebury vs. Tufts	Feb. 20
47	Annette Hoffman, Juniata vs. Wash. & Jeff.	Nov. 24
46	Sladja Kovijanic, Middlebury vs. Thomas	Feb. 12
44	Sladja Kovijanic, Middlebury vs. Hamilton	Jan. 16
43	Peggie Sweeney, Pine Manor vs. Regis (Mass.)	March 3
43	Sladja Kovijanic, Middlebury vs. Bates	Feb. 13
43	Melanie Payne, Medgar Evers vs. Staten Island	Nov. 28
42	Laurie Trow, St. Thomas (Minn.) vs. St. Olaf	Jan. 23
42	Simone Edwards, FDU-Madison vs. Drew	Jan. 9
42	Tricia Rasmussen, St. Mary's (Minn.) vs. Wis.-Oshkosh	Jan. 3
42	Terri Hogg, Otterbein vs. Ohio Dominican	Dec. 30
42	Kelly Lewis, Albion vs. Berea	Dec. 5
42	Sladja Kovijanic, Middlebury vs. Norwich	Dec. 3

THREE-POINT FIELD GOALS

3FG	Player, Team vs. Opponent	Date
9	Tricia Stilwell, UC San Diego vs. Cal Baptist	Feb. 5
8	Missie Burns, Berea vs. Wilmington (Ohio)	Feb. 6
8	Jennie Kirk, Berea vs. Midway	Feb. 3
8	Sherry Bradley, Gallaudet vs. Goucher	Jan. 30
8	MaryKate Fannon, Cabrini vs. Eastern (Pa.)	Jan. 23
8	Angie Dale, Millikin vs. Ind.-South Bend	Dec. 5

FREE THROWS

FT	Player, Team vs. Opponent	Date
22	Sharon Rines, St. Joseph's (Me.) vs. Emmauel	Jan. 26
19	Molly Lackman, Immaculata vs. Ursinus	Feb. 11
19	Annette Hoffman, Juniata vs. Waynesburg	Jan. 25
19	Cindi Neanen, Wilmington (Ohio) vs. Thomas More	Jan. 13
18	Heidi Metzger, Elizabethtown vs. Moravian	Jan. 14
17	Simone Edwards, FDU-Madison vs. Ramapo	March 5
17	Malane Perry, Fitchburg St. vs. Worcester St.	Jan. 12
17	Shannon Ferguson, Earlham vs. DePauw	Nov. 23

REBOUNDS

Reb.	Player, Team vs. Opponent	Date
30	Erica Scholl, UC San Diego vs. Southern Cal Col.	Dec. 5
29	Marianne Kelm, Concordia (Ill.) vs. Aurora	Feb. 20
28	Allison Palmer, Wesleyan vs. Bates	Feb. 5
28	Liza Janssen, Wellesley vs. Williams	Jan. 23

Reb.	Player, Team vs. Opponent	Date
27	Giovanni Licorish, Baruch vs. CCNY	Jan. 27
27	Chris Boos, Wis.-Eau Claire vs. Wis.-Stout	Dec. 5

ASSISTS

Ast.	Player, Team vs. Opponent	Date
18	Laureen Barnett, York (N.Y.) vs. Mt. St. Vincent	Dec. 12
16	Karyn Murphy, Notre Dame (Md.) vs. Mary Baldwin	Feb. 26
16	Karen Barefoot, Chris. Newport vs. Averett	Feb. 23
16	Danielle Moorehead, Brockport St. vs. Hilbert	Dec. 1
15	Karen Barefoot, Chris. Newport vs. N.C. Wesleyan	Feb. 20
15	Denise Ortiz, New Paltz St. vs. CCNY	Feb. 6

BLOCKED SHOTS

Blk.	Player, Team vs. Opponent	Date
12	Liza Jannsen, Wellesley vs. Wesleyan	Dec. 10
12	Liza Janssen, Wellesley vs. Worcester St.	Nov. 24
11	Caroline Duffy, Immaculata vs. Misericordia	Jan. 23
10	Mary Burch Harmon, Notre Dame (Md.) vs. Mary Baldwin	Jan. 16
9	Janet Kasinger, Ill. Benedictine vs. Concordia (Ill.)	Feb. 4
9	Janet Kasinger, Ill. Benedictine vs. Aurora	Jan. 23
9	Janet Kasinger, Ill. Benedictine vs. Judson	Jan. 16

STEALS

St.	Player, Team vs. Opponent	Date
14	Angel Esposito, Elms vs. Regis (Mass.)	Dec. 5
13	Nicole Albert, Cal Lutheran vs. Whittier	Feb. 23
13	Sonya Jones, Goucher vs. Lancaster Bible	Nov. 23
12	Alicia LaValley, Plattsburgh St. vs. Oswego St.	Feb. 14
12	Angela Thomas, Aurora vs. North Central	Dec. 4

TEAM HIGHS

SCORING

Pts.	Team vs. Opponent	Date
124	Millikin vs. Ind.-South Bend	Dec. 5
124	Emory vs. Wesleyan (Ga.)	Nov. 20
122	Rust vs. Stillman	Feb. 1
115	Marymount (Va.) vs. Chris. Newport	March 6
114	Wilmington (Ohio) vs. Asbury	Feb. 11
114	York (Pa.) vs. St. Mary's (Md.)	Jan. 23
113	Marymount (Va.) vs. Gallaudet	Feb. 2
113	Adrian vs. Taylor	Dec. 19
112	Scranton vs. Upsala	Feb. 6
112	Elizabethtown vs. Albright	Jan. 18
112	St. Mary's (Ind.) vs. Ind.-South Bend	Dec. 4
112	Staten Island vs. New Rochelle	Nov. 20

FIELD-GOAL PERCENTAGE

Pct.		Team vs. Opponent	Date
70.6%	(36-51)	Meredith vs. Guilford	Feb. 10
69.8%	(37-53)	Wis.-Eau Claire vs. Wis.-Platteville	Feb. 12
69.4%	(25-36)	Washington (Mo.) vs. Johns Hopkins	Jan. 17
67.4%	(29-43)	Simpson vs. Wartburg	Feb. 26
65.8%	(25-38)	Wilkes vs. Penn St.-Behrend	Jan. 10
65.4%	(34-52)	Luther vs. Loras	Feb. 19

THREE-POINT FIELD GOALS

3FG	Team vs. Opponent	Date
14	Berea vs. Maryville (Tenn.)	Feb. 12
12	Calvin vs. Kalamazoo	Feb. 20
12	Wis.-Stout vs. Wis.-La Crosse	Feb. 6
12	Calvin vs. Olivet	Jan. 20
11	Rowan vs. Rutgers-Newark	Feb. 15
11	Utica Tech vs. New Paltz St.	Jan. 29
11	DePauw vs. Fontbonne	Jan. 23
11	Calvin vs. Kalamazoo	Jan. 9

1993 DIVISION III WOMEN'S TEAM LEADERS

SCORING OFFENSE

	G	W-L	PTS.	AVG.
1. Marymount (Va.)	28	23-5	2,588	92.4
2. Wis.-Stout	25	21-4	2,163	86.5
3. Scranton	32	30-2	2,747	85.8
4. Maryville (Tenn.)	26	23-3	2,199	84.6
5. Elizabethtown	25	16-9	2,113	84.5
6. Moravian	29	24-5	2,414	83.2
7. Geneseo St.	28	27-1	2,319	82.8
8. Meredith	20	19-1	1,623	81.2
9. Chris. Newport	28	19-9	2,262	80.8
10. Emmanuel	25	18-7	2,012	80.5
11. Adrian	26	19-7	2,080	80.0
12. Berea	20	9-11	1,595	79.8
13. St. Benedict	30	28-2	2,387	79.6
14. Eureka	26	19-7	2,067	79.5
15. St. Joseph's (Me.)	29	24-5	2,282	78.7
16. Wis.-Eau Claire	26	22-4	2,045	78.7
17. Concordia-M'head	27	20-7	2,113	78.3
18. Middlebury	22	19-3	1,721	78.2
18. Wash. & Jeff.	22	17-5	1,721	78.2
20. Southern Me.	29	25-4	2,266	78.1
21. Rhode Island Col.	23	16-7	1,766	76.8
22. Waynesburg	25	19-6	1,913	76.5
23. Wilmington (Ohio)	24	16-8	1,836	76.5
24. Buffalo St.	27	19-8	2,063	76.4
25. Muskingum	27	24-3	2,061	76.3
26. Rowan	28	23-5	2,132	76.1
27. Illinois Col.	24	20-4	1,827	76.1
28. Juniata	22	15-7	1,673	76.0
29. Wheaton (Mass.)	26	18-8	1,977	76.0
30. Babson	28	23-5	2,124	75.9
31. Salisbury St.	23	10-13	1,740	75.7
32. Thomas More	26	12-14	1,962	75.5
33. Wartburg	28	23-5	2,111	75.4
34. Rust	24	10-14	1,778	74.1
35. William Smith	26	20-6	1,915	73.7

SCORING DEFENSE

	G	W-L	PTS.	AVG.
1. York (N.Y.)	25	15-10	1,200	48.0
2. Western New Eng.	21	20-1	1,029	49.0
3. Curry	25	15-10	1,253	50.1
4. Wesley	25	22-3	1,255	50.2
5. Cabrini	26	21-5	1,316	50.6
6. Wellesley	27	24-3	1,370	50.7
7. Anna Maria	26	18-8	1,342	51.6
8. Albertus Magnus	23	16-7	1,194	51.9
9. Montclair St.	25	16-9	1,302	52.1
10. New Jersey Tech	22	8-14	1,148	52.2
11. Skidmore	25	15-10	1,306	52.2
12. Westfield St.	29	23-6	1,520	52.4
13. Wis.-Oshkosh	24	16-8	1,269	52.9
14. Wittenberg	27	23-4	1,428	52.9
15. Connecticut Col.	24	22-2	1,272	53.0
16. Old Westbury	20	9-11	1,064	53.2
17. Jersey City St.	24	12-12	1,279	53.3
18. St. John Fisher	28	22-6	1,499	53.5
19. Geneseo St.	28	27-1	1,505	53.8
20. Meredith	20	19-1	1,076	53.8
21. Ohio Wesleyan	27	21-6	1,454	53.9
22. Baruch	20	8-12	1,089	54.5
23. Hunter	26	15-11	1,422	54.7
24. Stony Brook	25	16-9	1,369	54.8

	G	W-L	PTS.	AVG.
25. Regis (Mass.)	25	16-9	1,370	54.8
26. Mt. St. Vincent	23	9-14	1,261	54.8
27. New York U.	26	20-6	1,426	54.8
28. New England Col.	26	20-6	1,433	55.1
29. Williams	21	10-11	1,159	55.2
30. Rhodes	22	9-13	1,216	55.3
31. Heidelberg	27	19-8	1,493	55.3
32. Binghamton	28	22-6	1,549	55.3
33. Millsaps	25	19-6	1,386	55.4
34. Hamilton	26	21-5	1,442	55.5
35. Blackburn	30	23-7	1,665	55.5

SCORING MARGIN

	OFF.	DEF.	MAR.
1. Geneseo St.	82.8	53.8	29.1
2. Meredith	81.2	53.8	27.4
3. Scranton	85.8	60.5	25.3
4. Maryville (Tenn.)	84.6	62.3	22.3
5. Southern Me.	78.1	57.1	21.0
6. Moravian	83.2	62.3	20.9
7. St. Benedict	79.6	58.7	20.9
8. Marymount (Va.)	92.4	72.6	19.9
9. Wittenberg	72.6	52.9	19.7
10. Wellesley	68.9	50.7	18.1
11. Western New Eng.	67.0	49.0	18.0
12. Wis.-Stout	86.5	68.6	17.9
13. Wartburg	75.4	57.8	17.6
14. Rowan	76.1	58.9	17.2
15. Ohio Wesleyan	70.9	53.9	17.0
16. Connecticut Col.	69.9	53.0	16.9
17. Wis.-Eau Claire	78.7	62.3	16.4
18. St. Thomas (Minn.)	72.0	55.8	16.2
19. Wesley	65.8	50.2	15.6
20. Illinois Col.	76.1	61.1	15.0
21. William Smith	73.7	58.7	14.9
22. St. John Fisher	68.4	53.5	14.9
23. Muskingum	76.3	61.7	14.7
24. Middlebury	78.2	63.6	14.6
25. Penn St.-Behrend	71.0	56.8	14.2
26. Capital	70.5	56.3	14.2
27. Millsaps	69.4	55.4	14.0
28. Lake Forest	73.5	59.5	14.0
29. Babson	75.9	61.9	13.9
30. Eureka	79.5	65.7	13.8
31. Cabrini	64.0	50.6	13.4
32. Millikin	72.5	59.1	13.4
33. Wheaton (Mass.)	76.0	62.7	13.3
34. Roanoke	71.3	58.1	13.2
35. Westfield St.	65.5	52.4	13.1

WON-LOST PERCENTAGE

	W-L	PCT.
1. Geneseo St.	27-1	.964
2. Western New Eng.	20-1	.952
3. Meredith	19-1	.950
4. Scranton	30-2	.938
5. St. Benedict	28-2	.933
6. Connecticut Col.	22-2	.917
7. Muskingum	24-3	.889
7. Wellesley	24-3	.889
9. Maryville (Tenn.)	23-3	.885
10. Wesley	22-3	.880
11. Capital	28-4	.875
12. Middlebury	19-3	.864
13. Southern Me.	25-4	.862
14. Wittenberg	23-4	.852
15. Washington (Mo.)	22-4	.846
15. Wis.-Eau Claire	22-4	.846
17. Wis.-Stout	21-4	.840
18. Illinois Col.	20-4	.833
19. Central (Iowa)	24-5	.828
19. Moravian	24-5	.828
19. St. Joseph's (Me.)	24-5	.828
22. Lawrence	19-4	.826
23. Babson	23-5	.821
23. Rowan	23-5	.821
23. Marymount (Va.)	23-5	.821
23. Wartburg	23-5	.821
27. Lake Forest	18-4	.818
28. Cabrini	21-5	.808
28. Hamilton	21-5	.808
30. Western Conn. St.	20-5	.800
31. Westfield St.	23-6	.793
32. Frank. & Marsh.	19-5	.792
33. Binghamton	22-6	.786
34. Manchester	18-5	.783
35. Ohio Wesleyan	21-6	.778
35. Roanoke	21-6	.778

FIELD-GOAL PERCENTAGE

	FG	FGA	PCT.
1. Meredith	635	1,244	51.0
2. Maryville (Tenn.)	849	1,721	49.3
3. St. Benedict	937	1,919	48.8
4. Illinois Col.	706	1,457	48.5
5. Concordia-M'head	882	1,830	48.2
6. Luther	690	1,454	47.5
7. Millsaps	687	1,458	47.1
8. Wis.-Eau Claire	824	1,749	47.1
9. Scranton	1,067	2,292	46.6
10. St. Thomas (Minn.)	759	1,633	46.5
11. Central (Iowa)	814	1,755	46.4
12. Southern Me.	866	1,875	46.2
13. Geneseo St.	914	1,984	46.1
14. Calvin	716	1,561	45.9
15. Simpson	642	1,406	45.7
16. Gust. Adolphus	659	1,449	45.5
17. Tufts	695	1,532	45.4
18. Elizabethtown	816	1,805	45.2
19. Capital	834	1,847	45.2
20. Babson	839	1,870	44.9
21. Wellesley	734	1,636	44.9
22. St. Mary's (Ind.)	621	1,388	44.7
23. St. Norbert	561	1,256	44.7
24. Lake Forest	631	1,416	44.6
25. Centre	723	1,634	44.2
26. Manchester	667	1,513	44.1
27. Ohio Wesleyan	795	1,807	44.0
28. St. Joseph's (Me.)	854	1,942	44.0
29. Adrian	776	1,765	44.0
30. Bethel (Minn.)	626	1,425	43.9
31. Muskingum	795	1,813	43.8
32. Trenton St.	590	1,348	43.8
33. Marymount (Va.)	1,030	2,366	43.5
34. Beloit	642	1,475	43.5
35. Berea	615	1,414	43.5

FIELD-GOAL PERCENTAGE DEFENSE

	FG	FGA	PCT.
1. Wellesley	551	1,744	31.6
2. Geneseo St.	560	1,753	31.9
3. Connecticut Col.	493	1,535	32.1
4. Meredith	404	1,256	32.2
5. Curry	465	1,442	32.2
6. New Jersey Tech	462	1,431	32.3
7. Mary Washington	615	1,866	33.0
8. Westfield St.	575	1,742	33.0
9. Immaculata	533	1,608	33.1
10. Frostburg St.	568	1,708	33.3
11. Hunter	558	1,674	33.3
12. Albertus Magnus	441	1,320	33.4
13. Baruch	435	1,302	33.4
14. Salem St.	537	1,601	33.5
15. Stony Brook	516	1,535	33.6
16. Ithaca	593	1,758	33.7
17. Hamilton	531	1,567	33.9
18. Frank. & Marsh.	501	1,476	33.9
19. Wesley	485	1,425	34.0
20. Southern Me.	609	1,788	34.1
21. Colby-Sawyer	503	1,475	34.1
22. Rensselaer	491	1,438	34.1
23. Utica Tech	643	1,868	34.4
24. Ill. Benedictine	485	1,398	34.7
25. Notre Dame (Md.)	517	1,490	34.7
26. Wis.-Eau Claire	581	1,673	34.7
27. Anna Maria	521	1,490	35.0
28. Bri'water (Mass.)	601	1,708	35.2
29. Wittenberg	538	1,526	35.3
30. Washington (Mo.)	542	1,527	35.5

	FG	FGA	PCT.
31. Staten Island	594	1,670	35.6
32. Binghamton	595	1,672	35.6
33. Skidmore	517	1,451	35.6
34. Millsaps	546	1,529	35.7
35. Williams	445	1,245	35.7

THREE-POINT FIELD GOALS MADE PER GAME

	G	NO.	AVG.
1. Calvin	26	162	6.2
2. Berea	20	121	6.1
3. Utica Tech	25	143	5.7
4. Middlebury	22	123	5.6
5. Cabrini	26	144	5.5
6. Alma	25	128	5.1
6. Wis.-Stout	25	128	5.1
8. Maryville (Tenn.)	26	132	5.1
9. William Smith	26	130	5.0
10. Va. Wesleyan	25	121	4.8
11. Rowan	28	133	4.8
12. New England Col.	26	122	4.7
13. Moravian	29	130	4.5
14. Oswego St.	24	104	4.3
15. Thomas More	26	112	4.3
16. Aurora	25	106	4.2
16. Worcester St.	25	106	4.2
18. Monmouth (Ill.)	22	93	4.2
19. Wilmington (Ohio)	24	101	4.2
20. New York U.	26	108	4.2
21. Western New Eng.	21	85	4.0
22. DePauw	24	96	4.0
22. Wheaton (Mass.)	26	104	4.0
24. Mass.-Boston	25	98	3.9
25. Western Conn. St.	25	97	3.9
26. Olivet	23	87	3.8
27. Shenandoah	24	90	3.8
28. St. Benedict	30	112	3.7
29. St. Joseph's (Me.)	29	108	3.7
30. Neb. Wesleyan	25	93	3.7
31. Catholic	25	91	3.6
32. Alfred	25	90	3.6
32. Ferrum	25	90	3.6
34. Wis.-Whitewater	26	93	3.6
35. Gettysburg	24	85	3.5

THREE-POINT FIELD-GOAL PERCENTAGE

(Min. 2.0 3FG Made Per Game)	G	FG	FGA	PCT.
1. Southern Me.	29	82	194	42.3
2. Calvin	26	162	386	42.0
3. Scranton	32	96	233	41.2
4. Millikin	25	79	200	39.5
5. Maryville (Tenn.)	26	132	335	39.4
6. Middlebury	22	123	313	39.3
7. Berea	20	121	319	37.9
8. St. Benedict	30	112	296	37.8
9. Wheaton (Ill.)	25	72	191	37.7
10. St. Mary's (Ind.)	21	70	186	37.6
11. Wittenberg	27	60	162	37.0
12. Wis.-Whitewater	26	93	252	36.9
13. Hanover	20	67	182	36.8
14. St. Joseph's (Me.)	29	108	295	36.6
15. Elizabethtown	25	65	182	35.7
16. Wilmington (Ohio)	24	101	283	35.7
17. Southwestern (Tex.)	24	51	143	35.7
18. Kean	24	53	149	35.6
19. Capital	32	81	228	35.5
20. Cabrini	26	144	407	35.4
21. Carthage	25	66	188	35.1
22. Utica Tech	25	143	408	35.0
23. Muskingum	27	83	238	34.9
24. Wheaton (Mass.)	26	104	300	34.7
25. Notre Dame (Md.)	23	81	236	34.3
26. DePauw	24	96	280	34.3
27. Rhodes	22	73	213	34.3
28. Clark (Mass.)	26	86	251	34.3
29. Mass.-Boston	25	98	287	34.1
30. Simpson	24	66	194	34.0
31. Luther	25	51	151	33.8
32. Chicago	25	74	220	33.6
33. New England Col.	26	122	363	33.6
34. Coe	22	69	206	33.5
35. Ill. Wesleyan	25	61	183	33.3
35. Elmira	20	59	177	33.3

FREE-THROW PERCENTAGE

	FT	FTA	PCT.
1. Juniata	430	567	75.8
2. St. Benedict	401	534	75.1
3. Elizabethtown	416	557	74.7
4. Moravian	532	715	74.4
5. Penn St.-Behrend	405	555	73.0
6. Baldwin-Wallace	338	470	71.9
7. William Smith	387	539	71.8
8. Carthage	334	468	71.4
9. Lake Forest	319	447	71.4
10. Kalamazoo	316	443	71.3
11. Calvin	312	438	71.2
12. Middlebury	314	441	71.2
13. Otterbein	353	497	71.0
14. Eureka	407	575	70.8
15. Trinity (Conn.)	367	519	70.7
16. Bethel (Minn.)	318	450	70.7
17. Wartburg	501	710	70.6
18. St. Joseph's (Me.)	466	662	70.4
19. Adrian	443	630	70.3
20. Macalester	266	379	70.2
21. Luther	327	466	70.2
22. Wellesley	352	502	70.1
23. Dickinson	368	525	70.1
24. Loras	300	429	69.9
25. Meredith	333	477	69.8
26. Scranton	517	743	69.6
27. Maryville (Tenn.)	369	531	69.5
28. Stony Brook	344	496	69.4
29. Fitchburg St.	491	709	69.3
30. Heidelberg	412	596	69.1
31. Wm. Paterson	433	627	69.1
32. St. Thomas (Minn.)	281	407	69.0
33. North Park	370	536	69.0
34. Thiel	302	438	68.9
35. Gordon	242	353	68.6

REBOUND MARGIN

	OFF	DEF	MAR
1. Immaculata	52.9	36.4	16.5
2. Wellesley	50.2	34.0	16.1
3. UC San Diego	55.7	39.9	15.8
4. Wittenberg	47.9	34.5	13.4
5. Wesley	47.5	34.5	13.0
6. Susquehanna	51.2	38.3	12.9
7. Geneseo St.	51.8	39.9	11.9
8. Frostburg St.	51.7	41.0	10.7
9. Marymount (Va.)	53.9	43.3	10.7
10. Wilmington (Ohio)	48.5	38.4	10.2
11. Hunter	52.0	42.7	9.3
12. Augustana (Ill.)	47.8	38.5	9.2
13. St. Benedict	42.7	33.8	8.8
14. Averett	52.8	44.0	8.8
15. Connecticut Col.	48.8	40.1	8.7
16. Colby-Sawyer	49.6	41.1	8.5
17. Ithaca	50.3	41.8	8.5
18. Bryn Mawr	49.4	41.1	8.4
19. Grinnell	44.4	36.0	8.4
20. Redlands	47.8	39.4	8.4
21. Utica Tech	56.1	47.8	8.3
22. Ohio Wesleyan	43.2	35.0	8.2
23. Emory	45.6	37.5	8.2
24. Buffalo St.	53.2	45.1	8.1
25. Southern Me.	47.0	38.9	8.0
26. St. John Fisher	43.7	35.7	8.0
27. Pine Manor	52.4	44.5	7.9
28. Cabrini	43.7	35.9	7.8
29. Stony Brook	49.9	42.1	7.8
30. Trenton St.	42.0	34.3	7.7
31. Lake Forest	43.6	36.0	7.6
32. Scranton	47.6	40.2	7.4
33. Tufts	44.3	37.1	7.2
34. Wooster	47.0	39.8	7.2
35. New Jersey Tech	52.2	45.1	7.1

Ohio State guard Katie Smith paced the Buckeyes to a 16-2 record in the Big Ten Conference and a 28-4 record overall. The Buckeyes lost to Texas Tech in the championship game of the Women's Final Four. Smith led Ohio State in scoring with 28 points versus the Red Raiders.

1993 WOMEN'S CONFERENCE STANDINGS

DIVISION I

ATLANTIC COAST CONFERENCE

	CONFERENCE			FULL SEASON		
	W	L	Pct.	W	L	Pct.
Virginia #	13	3	.813	26	6	.813
Maryland	11	5	.688	22	8	.733
North Caro.	11	5	.688	23	7	.767
Clemson	8	8	.500	19	11	.633
Georgia Tech	8	8	.500	16	11	.593
North Caro. St.	8	8	.500	14	13	.519
Florida St.	6	10	.375	13	14	.481
Wake Forest	4	12	.250	14	14	.500
Duke	3	13	.188	12	15	.444

ATLANTIC 10 CONFERENCE

	CONFERENCE			FULL SEASON		
	W	L	Pct.	W	L	Pct.
Rutgers #	12	2	.857	22	9	.710
Geo. Washington	11	3	.786	20	11	.645
St. Joseph's (Pa.)	10	4	.714	21	8	.724
West Va.	7	7	.500	12	16	.429
Massachusetts	6	8	.429	11	15	.423
Rhode Island	5	9	.357	11	16	.407
Temple	3	11	.214	8	19	.296
St. Bonaventure	2	12	.143	13	14	.481

BIG EAST CONFERENCE

	CONFERENCE			FULL SEASON		
	W	L	Pct.	W	L	Pct.
Miami (Fla.) #	15	3	.833	24	7	.774
Georgetown	15	3	.833	23	7	.767
Connecticut	12	6	.667	18	11	.621
Villanova	10	8	.556	15	13	.536
Pittsburgh	9	9	.500	15	12	.556
Seton Hall	8	10	.444	14	13	.519
Providence	7	11	.389	15	15	.500
St. John's (N.Y.)	5	13	.278	12	16	.429
Boston College	4	14	.222	10	17	.370
Syracuse	4	14	.222	6	21	.222

BIG EIGHT CONFERENCE

	CONFERENCE			FULL SEASON		
	W	L	Pct.	W	L	Pct.
Colorado	12	2	.857	27	4	.871
Nebraska	10	4	.714	23	8	.742
Oklahoma St.	9	5	.643	23	9	.719
Kansas #	9	5	.643	21	9	.700
Missouri	8	6	.571	19	8	.704
Oklahoma	6	8	.429	12	15	.444
Kansas St.	1	13	.071	10	17	.370
Iowa St.	1	13	.071	2	25	.074

BIG SKY CONFERENCE

	CONFERENCE			FULL SEASON		
	W	L	Pct.	W	L	Pct.
Montana St. #	13	1	.929	22	7	.759
Montana	13	1	.929	23	5	.821
Boise St.	9	5	.643	19	8	.704
Idaho	7	7	.500	12	15	.444
Idaho St.	6	8	.429	10	16	.385
Eastern Wash.	5	9	.357	9	16	.360
Weber St.	3	11	.214	4	22	.154
Northern Ariz.	0	14	.000	2	24	.077

BIG SOUTH CONFERENCE

	CONFERENCE			FULL SEASON		
	W	L	Pct.	W	L	Pct.
N.C.-Greensboro	14	2	.875	19	10	.655
Radford	12	4	.750	17	11	.607
Campbell	11	5	.688	16	10	.615
Liberty	10	6	.625	16	12	.571
Towson St.	10	6	.625	12	16	.429
Md.-Balt. County	10	6	.625	11	16	.407
Coastal Caro.	8	8	.500	11	17	.393
Charleston So.	6	10	.353	10	18	.357
Winthrop	5	11	.313	6	21	.222
N. C.-Asheville	0	16	.000	0	27	.000

Won conference tournament.

BIG TEN CONFERENCE

(No postseason tournament)

	CONFERENCE			FULL SEASON		
	W	L	Pct.	W	L	Pct.
Ohio St.	16	2	.889	28	4	.875
Iowa	16	2	.889	27	4	.871
Penn St.	14	4	.778	22	6	.786
Northwestern	13	5	.722	20	9	.690
Minnesota	9	9	.500	14	12	.538
Purdue	8	10	.444	16	11	.593
Illinois	7	11	.389	12	15	.444
Michigan St.	6	12	.333	10	17	.370
Indiana	5	13	.278	14	13	.519
Wisconsin	4	14	.222	7	20	.259
Michigan	1	17	.056	2	25	.074

BIG WEST CONFERENCE

	CONFERENCE			FULL SEASON		
	W	L	Pct.	W	L	Pct.
Hawaii	17	1	.944	28	4	.875
Nevada-Las Vegas	15	3	.833	24	7	.774
UC Santa Barb. #	13	5	.722	19	12	.613
Pacific (Cal.)	12	6	.667	19	8	.704
New Mexico St.	11	7	.611	17	11	.607
Long Beach St.	8	10	.444	9	17	.346
Cal St. Fullerton	5	13	.278	8	19	.296
San Jose St.	4	14	.222	5	21	.192
Nevada	4	14	.222	4	22	.154
UC Irvine	1	17	.056	2	24	.077

COLONIAL ATHLETIC ASSOCIATION

	CONFERENCE			FULL SEASON		
	W	L	Pct.	W	L	Pct.
Old Dominion #	14	0	1.000	22	8	.733
James Madison	9	5	.643	16	11	.593
Richmond	8	6	.571	11	15	.423
George Mason	8	6	.571	17	10	.630
East Caro.	7	7	.500	16	12	.571
American	7	7	.500	15	13	.536
William & Mary	3	11	.214	11	17	.393
N. C.-Wilmington	0	14	.000	4	23	.148

GREAT MIDWEST CONFERENCE

	CONFERENCE			FULL SEASON		
	W	L	Pct.	W	L	Pct.
Marquette	10	0	1.000	22	9	.710
DePaul	8	2	.800	20	9	.690
Cincinnati	4	6	.400	13	15	.464
Ala.-Birmingham	4	6	.400	9	18	.333
Memphis St.	3	7	.300	12	16	.429
St. Louis	1	9	.100	5	21	.192

IVY GROUP

	CONFERENCE			FULL SEASON		
	W	L	Pct.	W	L	Pct.
Brown	13	1	.929	19	7	.731
Harvard	11	3	.786	16	9	.640
Yale	8	6	.571	15	11	.577
Princeton	7	7	.500	13	13	.500
Dartmouth	6	8	.429	8	18	.308
Pennsylvania	6	8	.429	8	18	.308
Cornell	4	10	.286	10	16	.385
Columbia	1	13	.071	7	19	.269

METRO ATLANTIC ATHLETIC CONFERENCE

	CONFERENCE			FULL SEASON		
	W	L	Pct.	W	L	Pct.
St. Peter's #	9	5	.643	18	11	.621
Niagara	9	5	.643	17	10	.630
Fairfield	8	6	.571	14	14	.500
Loyola (Md.)	8	6	.571	14	15	.483
Manhattan	6	8	.429	12	15	.444
Canisius	6	8	.429	9	18	.333
Iona	5	9	.357	12	15	.444
Siena	5	9	.357	11	16	.407

METROPOLITAN COLLEGIATE ATHLETIC CONFERENCE

	CONFERENCE W	L	Pct.	FULL SEASON W	L	Pct.
Southern Miss.	10	2	.833	20	8	.714
Virginia Tech	8	4	.667	20	8	.714
Louisville #	7	5	.583	19	12	.613
N. C.-Charlotte	6	6	.500	16	12	.571
Tulane	6	6	.500	14	13	.519
Va. Commonwealth	5	7	.417	15	12	.556
South Fla.	0	12	.000	10	17	.370

MID-AMERICAN ATHLETIC CONFERENCE

	CONFERENCE W	L	Pct.	FULL SEASON W	L	Pct.
Bowling Green #	17	1	.944	25	5	.833
Miami (Ohio)	13	5	.722	19	9	.679
Kent	12	6	.667	20	9	.690
Toledo	12	6	.667	18	10	.643
Central Mich.	10	8	.556	15	12	.556
Western Mich.	10	8	.556	14	13	.519
Ohio	10	8	.556	13	14	.481
Ball St.	3	15	.167	3	23	.115
Eastern Mich.	2	16	.111	3	22	.120
Akron	1	17	.056	4	22	.154

MID-CONTINENT CONFERENCE

	CONFERENCE W	L	Pct.	FULL SEASON W	L	Pct.
Northern Ill. #	15	1	.938	24	6	.800
Wis.-Green Bay	14	2	.875	19	10	.655
Youngstown St.	11	5	.688	17	11	.607
Valparaiso	10	6	.625	15	12	.556
Ill.-Chicago	8	8	.500	15	13	.536
Cleveland St.	6	10	.375	7	20	.259
Wright St.	5	11	.313	9	18	.333
Eastern Ill.	2	14	.125	3	24	.111
Western Ill.	1	15	.063	3	21	.125

MID-EASTERN ATHLETIC CONFERENCE

	CONFERENCE W	L	Pct.	FULL SEASON W	L	Pct.
South Caro. St.	12	4	.750	18	11	.621
Coppin St.	12	4	.750	20	9	.690
Florida A&M	12	4	.750	17	10	.630
Morgan St.	11	5	.688	16	12	.571
Delaware St.	6	10	.375	10	17	.370
North Caro. A&T	5	11	.313	9	19	.321
Howard	5	11	.313	5	22	.185
Bethune-Cookman	4	12	.250	9	19	.321
Md.-East. Shore	4	12	.250	7	19	.269

MIDWESTERN COLLEGIATE CONFERENCE

	CONFERENCE W	L	Pct.	FULL SEASON W	L	Pct.
Butler	14	2	.875	23	8	.742
Xavier (Ohio) #	11	5	.688	21	9	.700
Notre Dame	11	5	.688	15	12	.556
La Salle	10	6	.625	16	11	.593
Evansville	9	7	.563	18	10	.643
Dayton	7	9	.438	15	13	.536
Detroit Mercy	5	11	.313	11	16	.407
Loyola (Ill.)	3	13	.188	6	21	.222
Duquesne	2	14	.125	7	20	.259

MISSOURI VALLEY CONFERENCE

	CONFERENCE W	L	Pct.	FULL SEASON W	L	Pct.
Southwest Mo. St. #	14	2	.875	23	9	.719
Southern Ill.	12	4	.750	19	10	.655
Creighton	12	4	.750	20	8	.714
Wichita St.	8	8	.500	15	12	.556
Drake	8	8	.500	15	13	.536
Illinois St.	6	10	.375	11	16	.407
Northern Iowa	4	12	.250	10	17	.370
Indiana St.	4	12	.250	8	18	.308
Bradley	4	12	.250	7	20	.259

Won conference tournament.

NORTH ATLANTIC CONFERENCE

	CONFERENCE W	L	Pct.	FULL SEASON W	L	Pct.
Vermont	14	0	1.000	28	1	.966
New Hampshire	10	4	.714	18	8	.692
Northeastern	9	5	.643	14	14	.500
Delaware	8	6	.571	17	11	.607
Hartford	6	8	.429	11	16	.407
Boston U.	4	10	.286	10	17	.370
Maine	4	10	.286	9	20	.310
Drexel	1	13	.071	5	22	.185

NORTHEAST CONFERENCE

	CONFERENCE W	L	Pct.	FULL SEASON W	L	Pct.
Mt. St. Mary's (Md.)	14	4	.778	21	6	.778
FDU-Teaneck	14	4	.778	15	12	.556
Rider	13	5	.722	17	10	.630
Marist	12	6	.667	19	10	.655
Wagner	9	9	.500	11	16	.407
Monmouth (N. J.)	8	10	.444	11	17	.393
Robert Morris	7	11	.389	8	18	.308
St. Francis (Pa.)	7	11	.389	8	18	.308
LIU-Brooklyn	6	12	.333	9	17	.346
St. Francis (N.Y.)	0	18	.000	3	23	.115

OHIO VALLEY CONFERENCE

	CONFERENCE W	L	Pct.	FULL SEASON W	L	Pct.
Tennessee Tech #	14	2	.875	22	7	.759
Middle Tenn. St.	13	3	.813	21	7	.750
Eastern Ky.	10	6	.625	12	15	.444
Tennessee St.	10	6	.625	18	9	.667
Southeast Mo. St.	8	8	.500	13	13	.500
Morehead St.	8	8	.500	10	16	.385
Murray St.	4	12	.250	6	19	.240
Austin Peay	4	12	.250	5	21	.192
Tenn.-Martin	1	15	.063	2	23	.080

PACIFIC-10 CONFERENCE

(No postseason tournament)

	CONFERENCE W	L	Pct.	FULL SEASON W	L	Pct.
Stanford	15	3	.833	26	6	.813
Southern Cal	14	4	.778	22	7	.758
Washington	11	7	.611	17	12	.586
California	10	8	.556	19	10	.655
Arizona St.	10	8	.556	17	10	.630
Oregon St.	9	9	.500	15	12	.556
UCLA	8	10	.444	13	14	.481
Arizona	7	11	.389	13	14	.481
Oregon	3	15	.167	9	18	.333
Washington St.	3	15	.167	7	20	.259

PATRIOT LEAGUE

	CONFERENCE W	L	Pct.	FULL SEASON W	L	Pct.
Holy Cross	12	2	.857	22	7	.759
Lafayette	10	4	.714	19	9	.679
Fordham	9	5	.643	16	13	.552
Army	8	6	.571	12	15	.444
Bucknell	8	6	.571	11	17	.393
Navy	5	9	.357	11	15	.423
Colgate	3	11	.214	4	23	.148
Lehigh	1	13	.071	1	26	.037

SOUTHEASTERN CONFERENCE

	CONFERENCE W	L	Pct.	FULL SEASON W	L	Pct.
Tennessee	11	0	1.000	29	3	.906
Vanderbilt #	9	2	.818	30	3	.909
Auburn	9	2	.818	25	4	.862
Alabama	8	6	.571	22	9	.710
Florida	6	5	.545	19	10	.655
Kentucky	5	6	.455	18	10	.643
South Caro.	5	6	.455	17	10	.630
Mississippi	4	7	.364	19	10	.655
Georgia	4	7	.364	21	13	.618
Arkansas	4	7	.364	13	14	.481
Mississippi St.	3	8	.273	14	13	.519
Louisiana St.	0	11	.000	9	18	.333

SOUTHERN CONFERENCE

	CONFERENCE			FULL SEASON		
	W	L	Pct.	W	L	Pct.
Furman	10	2	.833	17	11	.607
Ga. Southern #	9	3	.750	21	9	.700
Tenn.-Chatt.	9	3	.750	15	13	.536
Marshall	5	7	.417	15	13	.536
Appalachian St.	4	8	.333	10	17	.370
East Tenn. St.	4	8	.333	7	18	.280
Western Caro.	1	11	.083	7	20	.259

SOUTHLAND CONFERENCE

	CONFERENCE			FULL SEASON		
	W	L	Pct.	W	L	Pct.
Stephen F. Austin #	17	1	.944	28	5	.848
Southwest Tex. St.	15	3	.833	19	8	.704
Northwestern (La.)	14	4	.778	24	8	.750
Northeast La.	13	5	.722	19	9	.679
McNeese St.	8	10	.444	14	13	.519
Texas-Arlington	7	11	.389	11	16	.407
Texas-San Antonio	6	12	.333	11	15	.423
North Texas	6	12	.333	9	17	.346
Sam Houston St.	3	15	.167	6	20	.231
Nicholls St.	1	17	.056	2	24	.077

SOUTHWEST CONFERENCE

	CONFERENCE			FULL SEASON		
	W	L	Pct.	W	L	Pct.
Texas Tech #	13	1	.929	31	3	.912
Texas	13	1	.929	22	8	.733
Southern Methodist	8	6	.571	20	10	.667
Texas A&M	7	7	.500	15	12	.556
Baylor	6	8	.429	12	16	.429
Houston	5	9	.357	11	16	.407
Rice	3	11	.214	13	14	.481
Texas Christian	1	13	.071	10	17	.370

SOUTHWESTERN ATHLETIC CONFERENCE

	CONFERENCE			FULL SEASON		
	W	L	Pct.	W	L	Pct.
Southern-B.R.	12	2	.857	20	7	.741
Alcorn St.	12	2	.857	16	8	.667
Grambling	8	6	.571	12	14	.462
Jackson St.	7	7	.500	10	18	.357
Mississippi Val.	6	8	.429	11	17	.393
Alabama St.	6	8	.429	8	19	.296
Texas Southern	5	9	.357	11	16	.407
Prairie View	0	14	.000	2	25	.074

SUN BELT CONFERENCE

	CONFERENCE			FULL SEASON		
	W	L	Pct.	W	L	Pct.
Western Ky. #	13	1	.929	24	7	.774
Louisiana Tech	13	1	.929	26	6	.813
Arkansas St.	10	4	.714	25	8	.758
New Orleans	7	7	.500	18	10	.643
Lamar	4	10	.286	10	16	.385
South Ala.	4	10	.286	9	18	.333
Tex.-Pan American	3	11	.214	6	21	.222
Southwestern La.	2	12	.143	4	22	.154

Won conference tournament.

TRANS AMERICA ATHLETIC CONFERENCE

	CONFERENCE			FULL SEASON		
	W	L	Pct.	W	L	Pct.
Florida Int'l	12	0	1.000	25	6	.806
Georgia St.	7	5	.583	12	16	.429
Southeastern La.	6	6	.500	9	18	.333
Charleston	5	7	.417	12	15	.444
Stetson	5	7	.417	8	19	.296
Mercer	4	8	.333	11	18	.379
Central Fla.	3	9	.250	4	24	.143

WEST COAST CONFERENCE

	CONFERENCE			FULL SEASON		
	W	L	Pct.	W	L	Pct.
Santa Clara	12	2	.857	19	9	.679
San Diego #	8	6	.571	16	12	.571
Pepperdine	7	7	.500	15	15	.500
San Francisco	6	8	.429	14	12	.538
St. Mary's (Cal.)	6	8	.429	12	14	.462
Gonzaga	6	8	.429	11	15	.423
Portland	6	8	.429	12	17	.414
Loyola (Cal.)	5	9	.357	14	12	.538

WESTERN ATHLETIC CONFERENCE

	CONFERENCE			FULL SEASON		
	W	L	Pct.	W	L	Pct.
Brigham Young #	13	1	.929	24	5	.828
Utah	9	5	.643	19	10	.655
San Diego St.	9	5	.643	19	9	.679
UTEP	8	6	.571	18	10	.643
Wyoming	6	8	.429	14	13	.519
Colorado St.	4	10	.286	13	14	.481
Fresno St.	4	10	.286	10	17	.370
New Mexico	3	11	.214	5	22	.185

DIVISION I INDEPENDENTS

	FULL SEASON		
	W	L	Pct.
Cal St. Sacramento	17	10	.630
Mo.-Kansas City	17	10	.630
Wis.-Milwaukee	15	12	.556
Buffalo	13	13	.500
Southern Utah	12	15	.444
Davidson	9	13	.409
Chicago St.	9	18	.333
Hofstra	8	19	.296
Central Conn. St.	6	20	.231
Cal St. Northridge	6	21	.222
Northeastern Ill.	5	23	.179

DIVISION II

ARKANSAS INTERCOLLEGIATE CONFERENCE

	CONFERENCE			FULL SEASON		
	W	L	Pct.	W	L	Pct.
Ark.-Monticello	13	3	.813	23	11	.676
Arkansas Tech	12	4	.750	31	5	.861
Central Ark.	11	5	.688	16	12	.571
Ozarks (Ark.)	10	6	.625	22	9	.710
Harding	6	10	.375	18	12	.600
Henderson St.	6	10	.375	12	12	.500
Ouachita Baptist	6	10	.375	13	13	.500
Arkansas Col.	5	11	.313	11	15	.423
Southern Ark.	3	13	.188	8	15	.348
*John Brown	—	—	—	10	19	.345

* Not eligible for conference title.

Won conference tournament.

CALIFORNIA COLLEGIATE ATHLETIC ASSOCIATION

	CONFERENCE			FULL SEASON		
	W	L	Pct.	W	L	Pct.
Cal Poly Pomona #	11	1	.917	27	3	.900
UC Riverside	9	3	.750	17	11	.607
Cal St. San B'dino	7	5	.583	18	10	.643
Cal St. Dom. Hills	7	5	.583	15	11	.577
Cal Poly SLO	6	6	.500	10	13	.435
Cal St. Los Angeles	2	10	.167	5	21	.192
Chapman	0	12	.000	2	23	.080

CAROLINAS INTERCOLLEGIATE ATHLETIC CONFERENCE

	CONFERENCE			FULL SEASON		
	W	L	Pct.	W	L	Pct.
Belmont Abbey #	11	1	.917	23	5	.821

	CONFERENCE			FULL SEASON		
	W	L	Pct.	W	L	Pct.
Mount Olive	8	4	.667	19	11	.633
High Point	8	4	.667	16	13	.552
Barton	6	6	.500	11	14	.440
St. Andrews	5	7	.417	9	14	.391
Pfeiffer	4	8	.333	8	17	.320
Coker	0	12	.000	2	25	.074
*Lees-McRae	—	—	—	26	5	.838

* Not eligible for conference title.

CENTRAL INTERCOLLEGIATE ATHLETIC ASSOCIATION

	CONFERENCE			FULL SEASON		
Northern Division	W	L	Pct.	W	L	Pct.
Norfolk St. #	11	1	.917	29	3	.906
Hampton	10	2	.833	20	9	.690
Virginia Union	8	4	.667	19	9	.679
Virginia St.	5	7	.417	17	11	.607
Bowie St.	4	8	.333	6	18	.250
Elizabeth City St.	3	9	.250	8	15	.348
St. Paul's	1	11	.083	4	19	.174
Southern Division						
St. Augustine's	11	1	.917	23	6	.793
Johnson Smith	10	2	.833	16	12	.571
Shaw	8	4	.667	16	10	.615
Fayetteville St.	7	5	.583	13	10	.565
N.C. Central	3	9	.250	5	19	.208
Winston-Salem	2	10	.167	3	20	.130
Livingstone	1	11	.083	3	23	.115

COLORADO ATHLETIC CONFERENCE

	CONFERENCE			FULL SEASON		
	W	L	Pct.	W	L	Pct.
Denver	14	0	1.000	24	4	.857
Colorado-CS	11	3	.786	18	9	.667
Metropolitan St.	10	4	.714	21	6	.778
Regis (Colo.)	7	7	.500	16	11	.593
Air Force	7	7	.500	14	13	.519
Southern Colo.	4	10	.286	7	20	.259
Colo. Christian	3	11	.214	7	19	.269
Fort Lewis	0	14	.000	4	22	.154

GREAT LAKES INTERCOLLEGIATE ATHLETIC CONFERENCE

	CONFERENCE			FULL SEASON		
	W	L	Pct.	W	L	Pct.
Michigan Tech #	15	1	.938	30	3	.909
Northern Mich.	12	4	.750	22	6	.786
Saginaw Valley	11	5	.688	20	9	.690
Oakland	10	6	.625	19	9	.679
Ferris St.	7	9	.438	14	12	.538
Wayne St. (Mich.)	6	10	.375	13	13	.500
Lake Superior St.	6	10	.375	10	15	.400
Grand Valley St.	4	12	.250	8	18	.308
Hillsdale	1	15	.063	7	19	.269

GREAT LAKES VALLEY CONFERENCE

	CONFERENCE			FULL SEASON		
	W	L	Pct.	W	L	Pct.
Indianapolis	16	2	.889	24	4	.857
Bellarmine	15	3	.833	18	10	.643
St. Joseph's (Ind.)	13	5	.722	20	7	.741
Northern Ky.	12	6	.667	19	8	.704
Southern Ind.	9	9	.500	15	15	.500
Ashland	7	11	.389	13	13	.500
Lewis	7	11	.389	12	15	.444
IU/PU-Ft. Wayne	7	11	.389	10	17	.370
Ky. Wesleyan	4	14	.222	9	18	.333
Kentucky St.	0	18	.000	2	25	.074

GULF SOUTH CONFERENCE

	CONFERENCE			FULL SEASON		
	W	L	Pct.	W	L	Pct.
Delta St.	12	0	1.000	27	6	.818
Jacksonville St.	8	4	.667	18	11	.621
Livingston	7	5	.593	17	9	.654
West Ga.	5	7	.417	13	14	.481
Mississippi Col.	5	7	.417	11	15	.423

\# Won conference tournament.

	CONFERENCE			FULL SEASON		
	W	L	Pct.	W	L	Pct.
North Ala.	4	8	.333	14	12	.538
Valdosta St.	1	11	.083	9	17	346
*Lincoln Memorial	—	—	—	18	9	.667

* Not eligible for conference title.

LONE STAR CONFERENCE

	CONFERENCE			FULL SEASON		
	W	L	Pct.	W	L	Pct.
Eastern N. Mex.	12	2	.857	23	5	.821
Abilene Christian #	9	5	.643	18	9	.667
Central Okla.	9	5	.643	18	10	.643
East Tex. St.	9	5	.643	13	15	.464
Cameron	7	7	.500	8	17	.320
Angelo St.	6	8	.429	11	16	.407
Texas A&M-Kingsville	3	11	.214	6	20	.231
Texas Woman's	1	13	.071	5	19	.208

MID-AMERICA INTERCOLLEGIATE ATHLETICS ASSOCIATION

	CONFERENCE			FULL SEASON		
	W	L	Pct.	W	L	Pct.
Washburn #	16	0	1.000	31	1	.969
Mo. Southern St.	14	2	.875	27	4	.871
Pittsburg St.	12	4	.750	21	7	.750
Central Mo. St.	10	6	.625	19	10	.655
Mo. Western St.	10	6	.625	16	11	.593
Missouri-Rolla	8	8	.500	14	13	.519
Northwest Mo. St.	7	9	.438	13	14	.481
Southwest Baptist	7	9	.438	13	14	.481
Emporia St.	6	10	.375	10	16	.385
Mo.-St. Louis	4	12	.250	9	17	.346
Lincoln (Mo.)	1	15	.063	4	22	.154
Northeast Mo. St.	1	15	.063	2	24	.077

NEW ENGLAND COLLEGIATE CONFERENCE

	CONFERENCE			FULL SEASON		
	W	L	Pct.	W	L	Pct.
Mass.-Lowell #	13	1	.929	24	6	.800
Keene St.	11	3	.786	19	10	.655
Franklin Pierce	10	4	.714	21	9	.700
Sacred Heart	7	7	.500	16	13	.552
Le Moyne	6	8	.429	16	11	.593
New Hamp. Col.	5	9	.357	8	18	.308
New Haven	4	10	.286	10	17	.370
Southern Conn. St.	0	14	.000	4	23	.148
*Bridgeport	—	—	—	4	20	.167

* Not eligible for conference title.

NEW YORK COLLEGIATE ATHLETIC CONFERENCE

	CONFERENCE			FULL SEASON		
	W	L	Pct.	W	L	Pct.
Phila. Textile #	17	1	.944	27	2	.931
Pace	15	3	.833	24	7	.774
Adelphi	13	5	.722	17	10	.630
St. Rose	12	6	.667	14	12	.538
Molloy	10	8	.556	14	13	.519
Mercy	7	11	.389	12	15	.444
LIU-C. W. Post	7	11	.389	11	16	.407
Queens (N.Y.)	5	13	278	7	18	.280
Dowling	3	15	.167	5	21	.192
LIU-Southampton	1	17	.056	3	21	.125
*Concordia (N.Y.)	—	—	—	5	21	.192

* Not eligible for conference title.

NORTH CENTRAL INTERCOLLEGIATE ATHLETIC CONFERENCE

	CONFERENCE			FULL SEASON		
	W	L	Pct.	W	L	Pct.
North Dak. St.	16	2	.889	30	2	.938
North Dak.	16	2	.889	23	5	.821
Augustana (S.D.)	14	4	.778	24	5	.828
Morningside	10	8	.556	18	9	.667
South Dak. St.	10	8	.556	17	10	.630
South Dak.	9	9	.500	16	11	.593
Northern Colo.	6	12	.333	9	18	.333

	CONFERENCE W	L	Pct.	FULL SEASON W	L	Pct.
Mankato St.	5	13	.278	12	15	.444
Nebraska-Omaha	4	14	.222	7	19	.269
St. Cloud St.	0	18	.000	3	23	.115

NORTHEAST-10 CONFERENCE

	CONFERENCE W	L	Pct.	FULL SEASON W	L	Pct.
Bentley #	16	2	.889	30	4	.882
Stonehill	16	2	.889	22	8	.733
American Int'l	11	7	.611	18	11	.621
St. Anselm	11	7	.611	17	12	.586
St. Michael's	9	9	.500	16	11	.593
Quinnipiac	8	10	.444	10	17	.370
Bryant	7	11	.389	12	15	.444
Merrimack	6	12	.333	9	17	.346
Assumption	5	13	.278	10	16	.385
Springfield	1	17	.056	3	22	.120

NORTHERN CALIFORNIA ATHLETIC CONFERENCE

	CONFERENCE W	L	Pct.	FULL SEASON W	L	Pct.
UC Davis #	9	3	.750	19	7	.731
Cal St. Chico	9	3	.750	16	10	.615
Cal St. Stanislaus	8	4	.667	19	9	.679
Humboldt St.	8	4	.667	12	14	.462
Sonoma St.	5	7	.417	11	14	.440
Cal St. Hayward	3	9	.250	6	20	.231
San Fran. St.	0	12	.000	8	17	.346

NORTHERN SUN INTERCOLLEGIATE CONFERENCE

	CONFERENCE W	L	Pct.	FULL SEASON W	L	Pct.
Minn.-Duluth	11	1	.917	22	8	.733
Moorhead St.	9	3	.750	20	9	.690
Northern St.	8	4	.667	28	7	.800
Southwest St.	5	7	.417	16	12	.571
Bemidji St.	4	8	.333	10	17	.370
Winona St.	3	9	.250	11	16	.407
Minn.-Morris	2	10	.167	13	14	481

PACIFIC WEST CONFERENCE

	CONFERENCE W	L	Pct.	FULL SEASON W	L	Pct.
Portland St.	9	1	.900	21	8	.724
Seattle Pacific	7	3	.700	17	10	.630
Eastern Mont.	6	4	.600	18	9	.667
Alas. Anchorage	4	6	.400	11	15	.423
Grand Canyon	3	7	.300	7	20	.259
Alas. Fairbanks	1	9	.100	9	17	.346

PEACH BELT ATHLETIC CONFERENCE

	CONFERENCE W	L	Pct.	FULL SEASON W	L	Pct.
S.C.-Spartanburg	16	0	1.000	28	3	.903
Augusta #	14	2	.875	24	5	828
Armstrong St.	10	6	.625	16	10	.615
Georgia Col.	8	8	.500	17	11	.607
Lander	7	9	.438	11	16	.407
Columbus	6	10	.375	12	15	.444
Pembroke St.	5	11	.313	10	17	.370
Francis Marion	3	13	.188	11	17	.393
S.C.-Aiken	3	13	.188	8	18	.308
*Kennesaw St.	—	—	—	19	11	.633

* Did not compete for conference title.

PENNSYLVANIA STATE ATHLETIC CONFERENCE

Eastern Division	CONFERENCE W	L	Pct.	FULL SEASON W	L	Pct.
Bloomsburg	10	2	.833	20	6	.769
Millersville	10	2	.833	17	9	.654
East Stroudsburg	9	3	.750	16	9	.640
West Chester	7	5	.583	14	11	.560
Kutztown	3	9	.250	11	15	.423
Mansfield	3	9	.250	6	18	.250

Won conference tournament.

	CONFERENCE W	L	Pct.	FULL SEASON W	L	Pct.
Cheyney	0	12	.000	2	21	.087
Western Division						
Clarion #	11	1	.917	24	6	.800
Edinboro	9	3	.750	18	12	.600
Calif. (Pa.)	7	5	.583	18	8	.692
Indiana (Pa.)	5	7	.417	13	10	.565
Slippery Rock	4	8	.333	10	15	.400
Shippensburg	3	9	.250	14	12	.538
Lock Haven	3	9	.250	13	13	.500

ROCKY MOUNTAIN ATHLETIC CONFERENCE

	CONFERENCE W	L	Pct.	FULL SEASON W	L	Pct.
Chadron St.	10	2	.833	18	9	.667
Mesa St.	10	2	.833	17	11	.607
N.M. Highlands	8	4	.667	19	10	.655
Fort Hays St. #	8	4	.667	18	11	.621
Adams St.	3	9	.250	9	18	.333
Western St.	2	10	.167	4	20	.167
Colorado Mines	1	11	.083	1	22	.043

SOUTH ATLANTIC CONFERENCE

	CONFERENCE W	L	Pct.	FULL SEASON W	L	Pct.
Wingate	12	2	.857	23	8	.742
Carson-Newman	12	2	.857	22	8	.733
Catawba #	10	4	.714	24	9	.727
Presbyterian	7	7	.500	16	10	.615
Mars Hill	6	8	.429	11	15	.423
Elon	5	9	.357	11	13	.458
Gardner-Webb	4	10	.286	10	17	.370
Lenoir-Rhyne	0	14	.000	6	18	.250

SOUTHERN INTERCOLLEGIATE ATHLETIC CONFERENCE

Eastern Region	CONFERENCE W	L	Pct.	FULL SEASON W	L	Pct.
Fort Valley St. #	12	1	.923	27	3	.900
Savannah St.	10	3	.769	24	5	.828
Albany St. (Ga.)	8	5	.615	17	10	.630
Paine	5	8	.385	12	15	.444
Clark Atlanta	2	11	.154	7	16	.304
Western Region						
Tuskegee	11	2	.846	17	8	.680
Alabama A&M	10	3	.769	17	9	.654
Miles	4	9	.308	7	19	.269
Morris Brown	3	10	.231	6	21	.222
LeMoyne-Owen	0	13	.000	1	25	.038

SUNSHINE STATE CONFERENCE

	CONFERENCE W	L	Pct.	FULL SEASON W	L	Pct.
Florida Tech #	12	0	1.000	26	4	.867
Fla. Southern	10	2	.833	25	3	.893
Tampa	6	6	.500	14	12	.538
Rollins	5	7	.417	14	13	.519
Barry	4	8	.333	7	18	.280
Eckerd	4	8	.333	7	19	.269
St. Leo	1	11	.083	3	21	.125
*North Fla.	—	—	—	10	17	.370

* Not eligible for conference title.

WEST VIRGINIA INTERCOLLEGIATE ATHLETIC CONFERENCE

	CONFERENCE W	L	Pct.	FULL SEASON W	L	Pct.
Bluefield St. #	19	0	1.000	26	3	.897
Wheeling Jesuit	16	3	.842	24	5	.828
Salem-Teikyo	16	3	.842	22	7	.759
Glenville St.	14	7	.667	20	9	.690
Charleston (W.Va.)	11	7	.611	13	14	.481
Fairmont St.	11	8	.579	12	15	.444
Shepherd	8	10	.444	12	14	.462
Concord	8	11	.421	12	14	.462
West Liberty St.	6	12	.333	10	19	.345
West Va. Wesleyan	6	12	.333	6	18	.250
West Va. St.	5	14	.263	6	20	.231
Alderson-Broaddus	5	15	.250	8	18	.308

	CONFERENCE W	L	Pct.	FULL SEASON W	L	Pct.
West Va. Tech	4	14	.222	8	18	.308
Davis & Elkins	3	16	.158	4	22	.154

DIVISION II INDEPENDENTS

	FULL SEASON W	L	Pct.
Wofford	23	4	.852
Pitt.-Johnstown	25	5	.833
SIU-Edwardsville	20	7	.741
Troy St.	19	7	.731
Fla. Atlantic	20	8	.714
West Tex. A&M	18	8	.692
Oakland City	20	9	.690
Mercyhurst	15	10	.600
Neb.-Kearney	15	12	.556
Wayne St. (Neb.)	14	12	.538
Queens (N.C.)	13	13	.500
Limestone	14	15	.483
Quincy	12	15	.444
Wis.-Parkside	12	15	.444
Gannon	10	15	.400
Longwood	8	19	.296
Mississippi-Women	8	19	.296
Ala.-Huntsville	6	18	.250
Erskine	6	20	.231
Notre Dame (Cal.)	5	18	.217
Newberry	5	19	.208
Northwood	5	22	.185
Dist. Columbia	4	18	.182

DIVISION III

ASSOCIATION OF MIDEAST COLLEGES

	CONFERENCE W	L	Pct.	FULL SEASON W	L	Pct.
Defiance #	6	0	1.000	17	8	.680
Wilmington (Ohio)	3	3	.500	16	8	.667
Bluffton	2	4	.333	8	17	.320
Thomas More	1	5	.167	12	14	.462

CAPITAL ATHLETIC CONFERENCE

	CONFERENCE W	L	Pct.	FULL SEASON W	L	Pct.
Marymount (Va.) #	11	1	.917	23	5	.821
Mary Washington	10	2	.833	19	7	.731
York (Pa.)	7	5	.583	13	12	.520
Catholic	6	6	.500	9	16	.360
Goucher	5	7	.417	12	13	.480
Gallaudet	3	9	.250	9	15	.375
St. Mary's (Md.)	0	12	.000	1	21	.045

CITY UNIVERSITY OF NEW YORK ATHLETIC CONFERENCE

	CONFERENCE W	L	Pct.	FULL SEASON W	L	Pct.
Hunter #	5	1	.833	15	11	.577
Staten Island	5	1	.833	9	15	.375
CCNY	4	2	.667	12	14	.462
York (N.Y.)	3	3	.500	15	10	.600
John Jay	3	3	.500	6	17	.261
Baruch	1	5	.167	8	12	.400
Medgar Evers	0	6	.000	2	22	.083

COLLEGE CONFERENCE OF ILLINOIS AND WISCONSIN

	CONFERENCE W	L	Pct.	FULL SEASON W	L	Pct.
Augustana (Ill.)	12	2	.857	19	7	.760
Millikin	11	3	.786	19	6	.760
North Park	9	5	.643	15	10	.600
Wheaton (Ill.)	8	6	.571	16	9	.640
Ill. Wesleyan	6	8	.429	14	11	.560
Carthage	6	8	.429	9	16	.360
Elmhurst	2	12	.143	6	18	.250
North Central	2	12	.143	4	20	.167

COMMONWEALTH COAST CONFERENCE

	CONFERENCE W	L	Pct.	FULL SEASON W	L	Pct.
Regis (Mass.)	12	2	.857	16	9	.640
New England Col. #	11	3	.786	20	6	.769
Curry	10	4	.714	15	10	.600
Anna Maria	9	5	.643	18	8	.692
Salve Regina	7	7	.500	8	15	.348
Eastern Nazarene	4	10	.286	6	19	.240
Roger Williams	2	12	.143	2	21	.087
Wentworth Inst.	1	13	.071	1	21	.045

Won conference tournament.

DIXIE INTERCOLLEGIATE ATHLETIC CONFERENCE

	CONFERENCE W	L	Pct.	FULL SEASON W	L	Pct.
Methodist	8	2	.800	15	11	.577
Chris. Newport #	7	3	.700	19	9	.679
Greensboro	7	3	.700	11	14	.440
N.C. Wesleyan	5	5	.500	11	15	.423
Ferrum	3	7	.300	9	16	.360
Averett	0	10	.000	6	18	.250

EASTERN STATES ATHLETIC CONFERENCE

	CONFERENCE W	L	Pct.	FULL SEASON W	L	Pct.
Frostburg St. #	7	1	.875	18	8	.692
Allentown	6	2	.750	14	12	.538
Shenandoah	4	4	.500	10	14	.417
Salisbury St.	3	5	.375	10	13	.435
Lincoln (Pa.)	0	8	.000	1	23	.042

EMPIRE ATHLETIC ASSOCIATION

	CONFERENCE W	L	Pct.	FULL SEASON W	L	Pct.
William Smith	13	1	.929	20	6	.769
Ithaca	10	4	.714	20	8	.714
Hartwick	9	5	.643	15	9	.625
Clarkson	8	6	.571	11	13	.458
Rensselaer	6	8	.429	12	11	.522
Rochester Inst.	5	9	.357	6	16	.273
St. Lawrence	3	11	.214	5	17	.227
Alfred	2	12	.143	4	21	.160

HUDSON VALLEY WOMEN'S ATHLETIC CONFERENCE

	CONFERENCE W	L	Pct.	FULL SEASON W	L	Pct.
Mt. St. Mary (N.Y.) #	8	0	1.000	19	7	.731
Vassar	6	1	.857	12	10	.545
York (N.Y.)	5	3	.625	15	10	.600
Old Westbury	5	3	.625	9	11	.450
Mt. St. Vincent	5	3	.625	9	14	.391
John Jay	3	5	.375	6	17	.261
New Rochelle	2	6	.250	2	17	.105
Baruch	1	6	.143	8	12	.400
Medgar Evers	0	8	.000	2	22	.083

INDIANA COLLEGIATE ATHLETIC CONFERENCE

	CONFERENCE W	L	Pct.	FULL SEASON W	L	Pct.
Franklin	8	0	1.000	14	11	.560
Manchester	6	2	.750	18	5	.783
Hanover	3	5	.375	6	14	.300
Anderson	2	6	.250	4	17	.191
DePauw	1	7	.125	7	17	.292

IOWA INTERCOLLEGIATE ATHLETIC CONFERENCE

	CONFERENCE			FULL SEASON		
	W	L	Pct.	W	L	Pct.
Central (Iowa)	14	2	.875	24	5	.828
Wartburg	13	3	.813	23	5	.821
Luther	13	3	.813	16	9	.640
Loras	8	8	.500	12	12	.500
William Penn	7	9	.438	14	11	.560
Simpson	7	9	.438	11	13	.458
Buena Vista	7	9	.438	8	17	.320
Upper Iowa	2	14	.125	4	19	.174
Dubuque	1	15	.063	4	21	.160

LITTLE EAST CONFERENCE

	CONFERENCE			FULL SEASON		
	W	L	Pct.	W	L	Pct.
Southern Me. #	10	0	1.000	25	4	.862
Rhode Island Col.	6	4	.600	16	7	.696
Eastern Conn. St.	6	4	.600	15	12	.556
Mass.-Dartmouth	4	6	.400	13	12	.520
Plymouth St.	4	6	.400	11	14	.440
Mass.-Boston	0	10	.000	8	17	.320

MASSACHUSETTS STATE COLLEGE ATHLETIC CONFERENCE

	CONFERENCE			FULL SEASON		
	W	L	Pct.	W	L	Pct.
Westfield St.	11	1	.917	23	6	.793
Salem St. #	9	3	.750	18	8	.692
Fitchburg St.	9	3	.750	17	10	.630
Worcester St.	7	5	.583	11	14	.440
Bri'water (Mass.)	4	8	.333	10	16	.385
Framingham St.	1	11	.083	3	22	.120
North Adams St.	1	11	.083	3	22	.120

MICHIGAN INTERCOLLEGIATE ATHLETIC ASSOCIATION

	CONFERENCE			FULL SEASON		
	W	L	Pct.	W	L	Pct.
Calvin #	11	1	.917	18	8	.692
Adrian	10	2	.833	19	7	.731
Alma	9	3	.750	16	9	.640
Albion	6	6	.500	12	13	.480
Hope	3	9	.250	8	15	.348
Kalamazoo	3	9	.250	6	18	.250
Olivet	0	12	.000	0	23	.000

MIDDLE ATLANTIC STATES COLLEGIATE ATHLETIC CONFERENCE

	CONFERENCE			FULL SEASON		
NORTHERN DIVISION	W	L	Pct.	W	L	Pct.
Northeast Section						
Scranton #	10	0	1.000	30	2	.938
King's (Pa.)	6	4	.600	14	11	.560
Delaware Valley	6	4	.600	13	11	.542
Upsala	4	6	.400	14	9	.609
FDU-Madison	4	6	.400	13	12	.520
Drew	0	10	.000	4	18	.182
Northwest Section						
Susquehanna	9	1	.900	19	7	.731
Elizabethtown	7	3	.700	16	9	.640
Juniata	6	4	.600	15	7	.682
Wilkes	4	6	.400	18	8	.692
Messiah	3	7	.300	9	15	.375
Lycoming	1	9	.100	5	19	.208
SOUTHERN DIVISION						
Southeast Section						
Moravian	12	0	1.000	24	5	.828
Muhlenberg	9	3	.750	15	10	.600
Ursinus	9	3	.750	11	13	.458
Albright	6	6	.500	10	13	.435
Widener	4	8	.333	5	19	.208
Swarthmore	1	11	.083	4	18	.182
Haverford	1	11	.083	2	22	.083
Southwest Section						
Frank. & Marsh.	10	0	1.000	19	5	.792
Dickinson	8	2	.800	18	8	.692
Johns Hopkins	5	5	.500	11	11	.500
Western Md.	4	6	.400	9	15	.375
Gettysburg	3	7	.300	10	14	417
Lebanon Valley	0	10	.000	2	22	.083

Won conference tournament.

MIDWEST ATHLETIC CONFERENCE FOR WOMEN

	CONFERENCE			FULL SEASON		
North Division	W	L	Pct.	W	L	Pct.
Lawrence	11	3	.786	19	4	.826
Beloit	10	4	.714	16	8	.667
Lake Forest	10	4	.714	18	4	.818
St. Norbert	9	5	.643	11	10	.524
Carroll (Wis.)	7	7	.500	12	10	.545
Ripon	3	11	.214	7	15	.318
South Division						
Illinois Col. #	12	2	.857	20	4	.833
Grinnell	10	4	.714	13	11	.542
Coe	6	8	.429	9	13	.409
Knox	4	10	.286	6	15	.286
Monmouth (Ill.)	2	12	.143	5	17	.227
Cornell College	0	14	.000	0	22	.000

MINNESOTA INTERCOLLEGIATE ATHLETIC CONFERENCE

	CONFERENCE			FULL SEASON		
	W	L	Pct.	W	L	Pct.
St. Benedict	20	0	1.000	28	2	.933
Concordia-M'head	17	3	.850	20	7	.741
St. Thomas (Minn.)	15	5	.750	19	7	.731
Bethel (Minn.)	13	7	.650	15	9	.625
Gust. Adolphus	12	8	.600	14	11	.560
St. Olaf	11	9	.550	14	11	.560
Macalester	6	14	.300	10	15	.400
Hamline	6	14	.300	9	16	.360
Carleton	5	15	.250	8	17	.320
St. Mary's (Minn.)	4	16	.200	5	19	.208
Augsburg	1	19	.050	2	23	.080

NEBRASKA-IOWA ATHLETIC CONFERENCE

	CONFERENCE			FULL SEASON		
	W	L	Pct.	W	L	Pct.
Hastings	12	0	1.000	28	1	.966
Doane	9	3	.750	22	9	.710
Concordia (Neb.)	6	6	.500	26	11	.703
Dana	5	7	.417	13	12	.520
Midland Lutheran	5	7	.417	9	17	.346
Neb. Wesleyan	3	9	.250	13	12	.520
N'western (Iowa)	2	10	.167	9	17	.346

NEW ENGLAND SMALL COLLEGE ATHLETIC CONFERENCE

(Did not compete for a regular-season conference title.)

	FULL SEASON		
	W	L	Pct.
Connecticut Col.	22	2	.917
Middlebury	19	3	.864
Hamilton	21	5	.808
Trinity (Conn.)	14	9	.609
Colby	13	9	.591
Tufts	14	11	.560
Williams	10	11	.476
Wesleyan (Conn.)	10	13	.435
Bates	9	13	.409
Bowdoin	6	14	.300
Amherst	6	17	.261

NEW ENGLAND WOMEN'S EIGHT CONFERENCE

	CONFERENCE			FULL SEASON		
	W	L	Pct.	W	L	Pct.
Wellesley	6	1	.857	24	3	.889
Babson #	6	1	.857	23	5	.821
Wheaton (Mass.)	5	2	.714	18	8	.692

	CONFERENCE			FULL SEASON		
	W	L	Pct.	W	L	Pct.
Brandeis	4	3	.571	11	14	.440
Smith	3	4	.429	8	15	.348
Worcester Tech	2	5	.286	9	14	.391
Mount Holyoke	1	6	.143	3	20	.130
MIT	1	6	.143	8	15	.348

NEW JERSEY ATHLETIC CONFERENCE

	CONFERENCE			FULL SEASON		
	W	L	Pct.	W	L	Pct.
Rowan	17	1	.944	23	5	.821
Wm. Paterson #	13	5	.722	18	9	.667
Ramapo	13	5	.722	19	8	.704
Montclair St.	13	5	.722	16	9	.640
Trenton St.	9	9	.500	13	11	.542
Kean	9	9	.500	11	13	.458
Rutgers-Newark	8	10	.444	14	12	.538
Jersey City St.	6	12	.333	12	12	.500
Rutgers-Camden	2	16	.111	4	20	.167
Stockton St.	0	18	.000	2	22	.083

NORTH COAST ATHLETIC CONFERENCE

	CONFERENCE			FULL SEASON		
	W	L	Pct.	W	L	Pct.
Ohio Wesleyan	15	1	.938	21	6	.778
Wittenberg #	14	2	.875	23	4	.852
Wooster	10	6	.625	13	11	.542
Denison	9	7	.563	13	12	.520
Case Reserve	9	7	.563	12	13	.480
Allegheny	7	9	.438	11	15	.423
Earlham	6	10	.375	11	12	.478
Kenyon	2	14	.125	2	20	.091
Oberlin	0	16	.000	0	21	.000

NORTHERN ILLINOIS INTERCOLLEGIATE CONFERENCE

	CONFERENCE			FULL SEASON		
	W	L	Pct.	W	L	Pct.
Aurora	9	1	.900	16	9	.640
Ill. Benedictine	9	1	.900	13	9	.591
Trinity (Ill.)	6	4	.600	20	7	.741
Concordia (Ill.)	4	6	.400	7	18	.280
Judson	2	8	.200	7	20	.259
Rockford	0	10	.000	0	25	.000

OHIO ATHLETIC CONFERENCE

	CONFERENCE			FULL SEASON		
	W	L	Pct.	W	L	Pct.
Muskingum	17	1	.944	24	3	.889
Capital #	16	2	.889	28	4	.875
John Carroll	14	4	.778	19	6	.768
Heidelberg	11	7	.611	19	8	.704
Baldwin-Wallace	9	9	.500	15	10	.600
Mount Union	8	10	.444	13	12	.520
Marietta	6	12	.333	11	15	.423
Ohio Northern	4	14	.222	8	18	.308
Otterbein	3	15	.167	5	20	.200
Hiram	2	16	.111	5	20	.200

OLD DOMINION ATHLETIC CONFERENCE

	CONFERENCE			FULL SEASON		
	W	L	Pct.	W	L	Pct.
Roanoke #	15	3	.833	21	6	.778
Va. Wesleyan	13	5	.722	16	10	.615
Bridgewater (Va.)	13	5	.722	15	12	.556
Emory & Henry	12	6	.667	14	12	.538
Randolph-Macon	12	6	.667	14	11	.560
Guilford	9	9	.500	12	13	.480
Hollins	8	10	.444	12	13	.480
East. Mennonite	4	14	.222	8	17	.320
Lynchburg	3	15	.167	4	18	.182
R.-Macon Woman's	1	17	.056	4	20	.167

PENNSYLVANIA ATHLETIC CONFERENCE

	CONFERENCE			FULL SEASON		
Northern Division	W	L	Pct.	W	L	Pct.
Marywood	7	1	.875	9	14	.391
Alvernia	6	2	.750	15	10	.600
Misericordia	4	4	.500	11	11	.500
Beaver	2	6	.250	8	10	.444
*Cedar Crest	0	8	.000	2	4	.333
Southern Division						
Cabrini #	8	0	1.000	21	5	.808
Immaculata	6	2	.750	17	8	.680
Gwynedd Mercy	4	4	.500	10	9	.526
Eastern	3	5	.375	5	18	.217
Rosemont	0	8	.000	0	18	.000

Won conference tournament.

* Forfeited six conference games (does not affect full-season record).

PRESIDENTS' ATHLETIC CONFERENCE

	CONFERENCE			FULL SEASON		
	W	L	Pct.	W	L	Pct.
Waynesburg	7	1	.875	19	6	.760
Wash. & Jeff.	6	2	.750	17	5	.773
Grove City	4	4	.500	10	12	.455
Bethany (W. Va.)	3	5	.375	12	12	.500
Thiel	0	8	.000	7	17	.292

ST. LOUIS INTERCOLLEGIATE ATHLETIC CONFERENCE

	CONFERENCE			FULL SEASON		
	W	L	Pct.	W	L	Pct.
Blackburn #	12	0	1.000	23	7	.767
Maryville (Mo.)	7	5	.583	10	17	.370
Webster	6	6	.500	13	9	.591
Fontbonne	6	6	.500	10	15	.400
Principia	5	7	.417	9	13	.409
MacMurray	4	8	.333	8	17	.320
Westminster (Mo.)	2	10	.167	3	17	.150

SOUTHERN CALIFORNIA INTERCOLLEGIATE ATHLETIC CONFERENCE

	CONFERENCE			FULL SEASON		
	W	L	Pct.	W	L	Pct.
Redlands	10	2	.833	13	12	.520
Claremont-M-S	8	4	.667	17	8	.680
La Verne	7	5	.583	13	12	.520
Occidental	7	5	.583	13	12	.520
Pomona-Pitzer	6	6	.500	13	12	.520
Cal Lutheran	3	9	.250	8	17	.320
Whittier	1	11	.083	5	19	.208

SOUTHERN COLLEGIATE ATHLETIC CONFERENCE

	CONFERENCE			FULL SEASON		
	W	L	Pct.	W	L	Pct.
Centre	14	0	1.000	19	6	.760
Millsaps	12	2	.857	19	6	.760
Trinity (Tex.)	8	6	.571	10	11	.476
Rhodes	7	7	.500	9	13	.409
Hendrix	7	7	.500	7	16	.304
Oglethorpe	4	10	.286	9	15	.375
Sewanee	4	10	.286	8	17	.320
Fisk	0	14	.000	0	24	.000

STATE UNIVERSITY OF NEW YORK ATHLETIC CONFERENCE

	CONFERENCE			FULL SEASON		
East Division	W	L	Pct.	W	L	Pct.
Binghamton	12	4	.750	22	6	.786
Potsdam St.	11	5	.688	16	8	.667
Cortland St.	8	8	.500	12	13	.480
New Paltz St.	6	10	.375	13	13	.500
Plattsburgh St.	3	13	.188	6	18	.250
Oneonta St.	2	14	.125	4	20	.167
West Division						
Geneseo St. #	16	0	1.000	27	1	.964
Buffalo St.	13	3	.813	19	8	.704
Utica Tech	9	7	.563	15	10	.600

	CONFERENCE			FULL SEASON		
	W	L	Pct.	W	L	Pct.
Brockport St.	9	7	.563	14	11	.560
Oswego St.	4	12	.250	6	18	.250
Fredonia St.	3	13	.188	5	19	.208

UNIVERSITY ATHLETIC ASSOCIATION

	CONFERENCE			FULL SEASON		
	W	L	Pct.	W	L	Pct.
Washington (Mo.)	12	2	.857	22	4	.846
New York U.	10	4	.714	20	6	.769
Carnegie Mellon	8	6	.571	13	12	.520
Chicago	7	7	.500	14	11	.560
Emory	5	9	.357	14	10	.583
Brandeis	5	9	.357	11	14	.440
Rochester	4	10	.286	11	15	.423
*Johns Hopkins	3	5	.375	11	11	.500
*Case Reserve	3	5	.375	12	13	.480

* Not eligible for conference title.

WESTERN MAINE ATHLETIC CONFERENCE

	CONFERENCE			FULL SEASON		
	W	L	Pct.	W	L	Pct.
Husson	7	1	.875	28	3	.903
St. Joseph's (Me.)	7	1	.875	24	5	.828
New England	4	4	.500	20	7	.741
Me.-Farmington	2	6	.250	14	8	.636
Thomas	0	8	.000	9	15	.375

WISCONSIN WOMEN'S INTERCOLLEGIATE ATHLETIC CONFERENCE

	CONFERENCE			FULL SEASON		
	W	L	Pct.	W	L	Pct.
Wis.-Eau Claire	14	2	.875	22	4	.846
Wis.-Stout	13	3	.813	21	4	.840
Wis.-Whitewater	12	4	.750	19	7	.731
Wis.-Oshkosh	12	4	.750	16	8	.667
Wis.-Stevens Point	9	7	.563	16	8	.667
Wis.-Superior	5	11	.313	9	15	.375
Wis.-La Crosse	4	12	.250	9	16	.360
Wis.-Platteville	2	14	.125	5	20	.200
Wis.-River Falls	1	15	.063	5	20	.200

WOMEN'S INTERCOLLEGIATE ATHLETIC CONFERENCE

	CONFERENCE			FULL SEASON		
	W	L	Pct.	W	L	Pct.
FDU-Madison	9	1	.900	13	12	.520
Upsala	8	2	.800	14	9	.609
Mt. St. Mary (N.Y.)	6	4	.600	19	7	.731
Centenary (N.J.)	4	6	.400	13	12	.520
St. Elizabeth	3	7	.300	8	15	.348
New Jersey Tech	0	10	.000	8	14	.364

DIVISION III INDEPENDENTS

	FULL SEASON		
	W	L	Pct.
Western New Eng.	20	1	.952
Meredith	19	1	.950
Maryville (Tenn.)	23	3	.885
Wesley	22	3	.880
Western Conn. St.	20	5	.800
St. John Fisher	22	6	.786
Eureka	19	7	.731
Emmanuel	18	7	.720
Albertus Magnus	16	7	.696
Penn St.-Behrend	18	8	.692
St. Mary's (Ind.)	14	7	.667
Clark (Mass.)	17	9	.654
Stony Brook	16	9	.640
Bryn Mawr	11	7	.611
Albany (N.Y.)	14	9	.609
Skidmore	15	10	.600
Nazareth (N.Y.)	13	10	.565
Southwestern (Tex.)	13	11	.542
Elms	12	11	.522
UC San Diego	13	12	.520
Norwich	14	13	.519
Notre Dame (Md.)	11	12	.478
Berea	9	11	.450
Rust	10	14	.417
Elmira	8	12	.400
Keuka	9	14	.391
Suffolk	9	14	.391
Colby-Sawyer	9	15	.375
Gordon	9	15	.375
Pine Manor	10	17	.370
Union (N.Y.)	6	17	.261
Coast Guard	5	18	.217
Nichols	4	20	.167
Hilbert	3	20	.130
Utica	3	20	.130
Asbury	3	21	.125
Castleton St.	2	21	.087
Colorado Col.	2	23	.080
Mary Baldwin	1	17	.056
Manhattanville	1	21	.048

ATTENDANCE RECORDS

Southwest Missouri State led the nation in attendance in 1993 for Division I. The Bears averaged 7,421 fans per home game. Ohio State and Tennessee were second and third with 6,146 and 6,002 fans per game, respectively. North Dakota State led Division II.

1993 WOMEN'S COLLEGE BASKETBALL ATTENDANCE

(Home attendance does not include double-headers with men)

	Total Teams	G/S	$1993 Net Attendance	Av. PG Or Sess.	Change @ In Avg.		Change @ In Total	
Home Attendance, NCAA Division I	*294	2,627	*2,831,319	*1,078	Up	207	Up	278,910
NCAA Championship Tournament	—	42	*231,367	*5,509	Up	708	Up	29,707
Other Division I Neutral-Site Attendance	—	103	110,345	1,071	Down	27	Down	22,522
NCAA DIVISION I TOTALS	*294	2,772	*3,173,031	*1,145	Up	212	Up	286,095
Home Attendance, NCAA Division II	*289	*1,655	478,035	289	Down	3	Up	89,532
Home Attendance, NCAA Division III	*311	2,420	443,307	*183	Up	6	Down	12,869
Home Attendance, All Nonmembers #	329	2,277	438,282	192	Up	2	Down	94,808
NCAA Division II Tournament	—	22	36,397	1,654	Down	328	Down	7,210
NCAA Division III Tournament	—	26	28,080	1,080	Up	272	Up	7,080
NAIA Dist. Tournaments, Divisions I & II	—	163	35,956	221	Down	44	Down	7,019
NAIA Nat'l Tournaments, Divisions I & II	—	11	46,339	4,212	Up	1,080	Up	8,755
NCCAA, NSCAA, NBCAA Tournaments, Other Neutral-Site Games for All 929 Teams Below NCAA Division I	—	155	58,766	379	Down	21	Down	8,019
NATIONAL FIGURES FOR 1993	*1,223	9,501	*4,738,193	*499	Up	60	Up	261,537

* Record high. $ Women's net attendance excludes double-headers with men. @ The 1992 figures used for comparison reflect 1993 changes in association and divisional lineups to provide parallel comparisons (i.e., 1993 lineups vs. same teams in 1992, whether members or not). # Nonmembers include all NAIA (National Association of Intercollegiate Athletics) teams that are not also in the NCAA, plus teams in the NCCAA (National Christian College Athletic Association), NSCAA (National Small College Athletic Association) and NBCAA (National Bible College Athletic Association).

1993 NCAA DIVISION I WOMEN'S CONFERENCE ATTENDANCE

	Total Teams	Games Or Sessions	1993 Attendance	Av. PG Or Sess.	Change @ In Avg.		Change @ In Total	
Big Ten #	11	146	n379,418	n2,599	Up	555	Up	66,734
Southeastern	12	136	*284,246	*2,090	Up	312	Up	35,270
Southwest	8	98	*190,043	1,939	Up	239	Up	18,331
Pacific-10	10	133	*225,351	*1,694	Up	246	Up	29,886
Atlantic Coast	9	117	197,893	1,691	Down	330	Down	38,533
Missouri Valley**	9	103	164,447	1,597	Up	417	Up	28,791
Big Sky#	8	90	*142,288	*1,581	Up	277	Up	24,549
Southland	10	57	*86,614	*1,520	Up	119	Up	10,958
Big Eight	8	104	*148,884	*1,432	Up	472	Up	51,889
Sun Belt#	8	77	100,834	*1,310	Up	204	Down	931
Mid-American#	10	36	*30,568	*849	Up	281	Up	2,166
Big East	10	140	117,447	838	Down	63	Down	6,015
Western Athletic#	8	81	*65,083	*803	Up	212	Up	7,751
Ohio Valley	8	34	26,829	789	Up	104	Down	1,950
North Atlantic	8	90	*70,235	*780	Up	231	Up	18,645
Mid-Eastern Athletic#	9	60	*43,521	725	Up	323	Up	27,457
Mid-Continent**	9	90	61,436	683	Up	86	Up	5,303
Atlantic 10#	8	91	61,187	672	Down	116	Down	26,285
Metropolitan Collegiate	7	80	46,918	*586	Up	222	Up	15,980
Great Midwest	6	80	46,690	584	Down	107	Down	3,091
Colonial Athletic	8	94	50,012	532	Down	10	Down	399
Midwestern Collegiate#	9	94	*47,317	503	Down	12	Down	3,138
Big West	10	109	53,728	493	Down	8	Up	2,649
Southern#	7	60	22,675	*378	Up	4	Down	5,720
West Coast	8	45	14,154	315	Down	42	Down	1,908
Patriot	8	32	8,983	281	Up	69	Up	504
Northeast#	10	71	*19,072	*269	Up	11	Up	1,248
Ivy Group	8	86	22,855	*266	Up	40	Up	2,735
Southwestern Athletic	8	20	5,308	265	Down	145	Down	6,987
Big South#	10	109	*27,664	254	Up	6	Up	169
Metro Atlantic#	8	81	19,140	236	Up	15	Up	1,702
Trans America#	7	69	14,041	203	Up	9	Down	119
Division I Independents#	11	116	23,646	204	Up	27	Up	4,673

* Record high for that conference. n Indicates national record. @ All figures used in this report reflect 1993 changes in conference lineups, to provide valid comparisons (i.e., the 1993 lineup vs. same teams in 1992, whether or not members in 1992 or whether or not conference existed in 1992); conferences marked (#) had different lineups in 1992. ** New conference.

LEADING 1993 NCAA DIVISION II WOMEN'S CONFERENCE ATTENDANCE

	Total Teams	Games Or Sessions	1993 Attendance	Av. PG Or Sess.	Change @ In Avg.		Change @ In Total	
North Central Intercollegiate	10	66	65,179	988	Down	291	Down	69
Southern Intercollegiate	10	26	13,786	530	Up	214	Up	6,836
Mid-America	12	43	20,760	483	Up	131	Up	5,611
Northeast-10	10	44	20,105	457	Up	115	Up	8,486
Central Intercollegiate	14	29	12,902	445	Down	116	Down	3,379
Gulf South	7	36	15,983	444	Down	39	Up	517
South Atlantic	8	38	15,822	416	Down	29	Down	1,527
Northern California	7	46	18,326	398	Up	91	Up	7,277
Rocky Mountain	7	32	12,481	390	Up	84	Up	3,009
Great Lakes Intercollegiate	9	30	9,830	328	Up	35	Down	4,810
Pacific West	6	59	18,692	317	Up	24	Down	938
Great Lakes Valley	10	28	8,377	299	Down	81	Down	6,046
Lone Star	8	37	10,528	285	Down	51	Down	3,245
Pennsylvania State	14	62	15,949	257	Down	23	Down	9,559
Peach Belt	9	52	11,802	227	Up	24	Down	2,188

	Total Teams	Games Or Sessions	1993 Attendance	Av. PG Or Sess.	Change @ In Avg.		Change @ In Total	
California Collegiate	7	71	14,943	210	Up	72	Up	4,866
Colorado Athletic	8	70	13,393	191	Down	18	Down	1,204
Sunshine State	8	61	9,824	161	Up	19	Down	3
New England Collegiate	7	20	3,034	152	Up	28	Down	449
New York Collegiate	10	103	12,960	126	Up	15	Up	1,461

@ All 1992 figures used in this compilation reflect 1993 changes in conference lineups, to provide parallel comparisons (i.e., the 1993 lineup vs. same teams in 1992, whether or not members in 1992).

LEADING 1993 NCAA DIVISION III WOMEN'S CONFERENCE ATTENDANCE

	Total Teams	Games Or Sessions	1993 Attendance	Av. PG Or Sess.	Change @ In Avg.		Change @ In Total	
Little East	6	36	11,736	326	Down	58	Up	228
Ohio Athletic	10	124	35,302	285	Down	37	Down	3,978
Southern California	7	83	22,402	270	Up	111	Up	10,782
Michigan	7	74	17,557	237	Down	2	Up	814
Minnesota	11	118	27,603	234	Up	62	Up	7,263
Wisconsin Women's	9	90	20,530	228	Up	11	Up	104
Midwest	12	112	23,445	209	Down	2	Down	1,270
Middle Atlantic	25	234	47,127	201	Down	2	Down	2,119
University Athletic	9	52	10,260	197	Up	28	Down	700
Massachusetts	7	28	5,450	195	Down	13	Down	2,235
SUNY	12	40	7,693	192	Up	82	Up	2,106
NESCAC	11	70	13,388	191	Up	1	Down	3,860
Eastern States	5	33	5,490	166	Down	15	Down	1,405
Illinois & Wisconsin	8	89	14,515	163	Up	12	Up	155
North Coast	9	84	13,537	161	Up	7	Up	576
Association of Mid-East	4	37	5,821	157	Down	71	Down	1,007
St. Louis Intercollegiate	7	48	7,020	146	Up	52	Up	3,183
Southern Collegiate	8	33	4,773	145	Down	99	Down	7,203
Old Dominion Athletic	10	108	15,525	144	Up	2	Up	379
Hoosier	5	49	6,985	143	Up	3	Down	415
New Jersey	10	43	6,074	141	Down	24	Down	1,850
New England	8	81	11,142	138	Down	15	Down	2,508
Capital	7	52	7,121	137	Down	16	Down	47
Dixie	6	48	6,376	133	Down	43	Down	840
Empire	8	41	5,108	125	Up	22	Up	1,283

@ All 1992 figures used in this compilation reflect 1993 changes in conference lineups, to provide parallel comparisons (i.e., the 1993 lineup vs. same teams in 1992, whether or not members in 1992).

1993 NCAA DIVISION I WOMEN'S BASKETBALL ATTENDANCE LEADERS

(Min. 4 home games)	G/S	Attend.	Avg.	Change in Avg.	
1. Southwest Mo. St.	15	111,318	7,421	Up	2,522
2. Ohio St.	16	98,328	6,146	Up	3,351
3. Tennessee	13	78,025	6,002	Down	677
4. Texas	15	86,493	5,766	Up	26
5. Iowa	15	76,092	5,073	Up	644
6. Stanford	15	74,118	4,941	Up	1,176
7. Virginia	15	69,134	4,609	Down	1,683
8. Vanderbilt	16	73,115	4,570	Up	2,152
9. Texas Tech	14	61,871	4,419	Up	218
10. Connecticut	14	54,652	3,904	Up	656
11. Stephen F. Austin	18	68,640	3,813	Up	191
12. Washington	14	49,719	3,551	Down	97
13. Montana	14	49,593	3,542	Down	258
14. Colorado	14	48,620	3,473	Up	1,999
15. Penn St.	15	51,241	3,416	Up	628
16. Purdue	14	45,067	3,219	Down	385
17. Louisiana Tech	13	40,414	3,109	Up	1,159
18. Boise St.	11	33,108	3,010	Down	32
19. Vermont	14	40,459	2,890	Up	1,186
20. Western Ky.	13	34,570	2,659	Up	408
21. Auburn	12	31,692	2,641	Up	1,308
22. Arkansas	14	35,106	2,508	Down	389
23. Tennessee Tech	6	14,596	2,433	Up	143
24. Montana St.	15	34,183	2,279	Up	700
25. Nebraska	13	29,295	2,253	Up	308
26. Maryland	15	32,709	2,181	Down	362
27. UTEP	9	17,610	1,957	Up	1,554
28. Minnesota	13	24,745	1,903	Up	940
29. Utah	9	17,059	1,895	Up	581
30. Georgia Tech	13	24,103	1,854	Up	381
31. Rutgers	14	25,709	1,836	Up	127
32. Northern Ill.	13	23,856	1,835	Up	104
33. Arizona	16	27,363	1,710	Up	346
34. Wisconsin	11	18,310	1,665	Down	1,094
35. Bethune-Cookman	7	11,621	1,660	Up	1,310
36. New Mexico St.	10	16,529	1,653	Up	930
37. DePaul	14	22,916	1,637	Down	197
38. Clemson	10	16,196	1,620	Up	830
39. Oklahoma	10	16,174	1,617	Up	400
40. Northeast La.	4	6,260	1,565	Up	1
41. Michigan St.	11	16,922	1,538	Down	342
42. Kentucky	13	19,511	1,501	Up	187
43. Oklahoma St.	13	19,104	1,470	Up	760
44. North Caro. St.	12	17,594	1,466	Down	536
45. Bowling Green	5	7,091	1,418	Up	805
46. Louisville	14	18,827	1,345	Up	719
47. Southeast Mo. St.	4	5,070	1,268	Up	200
48. Old Dominion	16	19,991	1,249	Up	227
49. Northwestern	14	17,249	1,232	Up	494
50. Drake	13	15,537	1,195	Up	525
51. California	13	15,528	1,194	Up	404
52. Arkansas St.	9	10,734	1,193	Up	162
53. Wake Forest	11	12,954	1,178	Up	127
54. Texas A&M	10	10,979	1,098	Up	479
55. St. Joseph's (Pa.)	10	10,373	1,037	Up	271
56. Kansas	16	16,425	1,027	Up	192
57. Maine	10	10,107	1,011	Up	67
58. Florida A&M	11	10,901	991	Up	465
59. Arizona St.	13	12,812	986	Up	204
60. Notre Dame	13	12,581	968	Down	808
61. Michigan	12	11,238	937	Up	42
62. Ohio	8	7,437	930	Up	684
63. Youngstown St.	9	8,352	928	Up	256
64. James Madison	13	11,970	921	Down	333
65. Southern Methodist	12	10,865	905	Up	69
66. Xavier (Ohio)	13	11,726	902	Up	421
67. Georgia	13	11,589	891	Down	471
68. Illinois	13	10,813	832	Up	84
69. South Caro.	9	7,422	825	Down	8
70. Washington St.	13	10,618	817	Up	167
71. South Caro. St.	11	8,976	816	Up	59
72. Eastern Wash.	11	8,834	803	Up	130
73. Alabama	12	9,622	802	Down	275
74. Illinois St.	12	9,557	796	Down	116
75. Southern Cal	14	11,126	795	Up	47
76. Indiana	12	9,413	784	Up	78
77. San Diego St.	9	6,894	766	Up	54
78. Brigham Young	7	5,276	754	Up	346
79. Providence	18	13,164	731	Down	249
80. Florida	11	7,937	722	Up	55
81. Idaho St.	13	9,320	717	Up	358
82. North Caro.	15	10,621	708	Down	434
83. Geo. Washington	10	6,999	700	Up	38
84. Oregon St.	10	6,981	698	Up	203
84. UCLA	12	8,371	698	Down	28

1993 NCAA DIVISION II WOMEN'S BASKETBALL ATTENDANCE LEADERS

(Min. 4 home games)	G/S	Attend.	Avg.	Change in Avg.	
1. North Dak. St.	11	31,363	2,851	Down	447
2. North Dak.	7	12,480	1,783	Up	1,163
3. Mesa St.	4	7,000	1,750	Up	1,250
4. LeMoyne-Owen	4	5,826	1,457	Up	1,457
5. Washburn	6	8,558	1,426	Up	721
6. Delta St.	7	9,252	1,322	Down	86
7. Bentley	11	13,350	1,214	Up	371
8. Michigan Tech	5	4,904	981	Up	274
9. Nebraska-Omaha	7	5,650	807	Up	323
10. Georgia Col.	4	3,200	800	Up	420
10. Northern St.	5	4,000	800	Down	367
12. Elizabeth City St.	7	5,156	737	Up	158
13. Catawba	7	5,000	714	Up	614
14. Cal St. Chico	13	9,273	713	Up	355
15. West Tex. A&M	9	6,197	689	Down	170
15. South Dak. St.	4	2,754	689	Down	1,371

1993 NCAA DIVISION III WOMEN'S BASKETBALL ATTENDANCE LEADERS

(Min. 4 home games)	G/S	Attend.	Avg.	Change in Avg.	
1. Moravian	12	8,790	733	No change	
2. Wis.-Eau Claire	11	7,600	*691	Up	287
3. Claremont-M-S	13	8,450	650	Up	333
4. Scranton	10	5,550	555	Up	226
5. Mass.-Dartmouth	6	3,199	533	Up	8
6. Illinois Col.	10	5,200	520	Up	290
7. Capital	15	7,773	518	Down	320
8. Southern Me.	10	5,099	510	Down	49
9. Alma	11	5,600	509	Up	165
10. Central (Iowa)	9	4,200	467	Up	367
11. Williams	8	3,520	440	Up	21
12. St. Benedict	*14	6,099	436	Up	252
13. Muskingum	14	5,540	396	Up	9
14. Fontbonne	10	3,900	390	Up	290
15. Geneseo St.	7	2,725	389	Up	226

ANNUAL TEAM HOME ATTENDANCE CHAMPIONS

Year	Division I Champion	#Net Avg.	Division II Champion	#Net Avg.	Division III Champion	#Net Avg.
1983	Louisiana Tech	4,241	Slippery Rock	1,563	Susquehanna	638
1984	Louisiana Tech	5,285	Savannah St.	1,750	Bishop	971
1985	Iowa	4,363	Shaw	1,725	Rust	1,154
1986	Texas	5,289	Augustana (S.D.)	1,964	Bishop	*1,190
1987	Texas	6,639	Missouri-Rolla	774	Rust	984
1988	Texas	7,663	North Dak. St.	2,177	Concordia-M'head	1,124
1989	Texas	*8,481	Jacksonville St.	1,742	Centre	669
1990	Texas	7,525	Lincoln Memorial	1,817	Hope	879
1991	Texas	6,161	Southeast Mo. St.	2,225	Muskingum	779
1992	Tennessee	6,679	North Dak. St.	*3,298	Capital	838
1993	Southwest Mo. St.	7,421	North Dak. St.	2,851	Moravian	733

* Record. # Excluding double-headers with men.

ALL-TIME NCAA WOMEN'S BASKETBALL ATTENDANCE+

Year	Division I Teams	Division I Attendance	Per Game Average	Change In Avg.		All Divisions Teams	All Divisions Attendance	Per Game Average	Change In Avg.	
1982	272	1,923,792	624	—		764	2,675,193	375	—	
1983	274	2,112,075	675	Up	51	764	3,017,377	407	Up	32
1984	267	1,233,403	520	Down	155	749	2,047,550	336	Down	71
1985	276	1,327,056	510	Down	10	746	2,071,531	330	Down	6
1986	275	1,333,578	498	Down	12	760	2,092,296	323	Down	7
1987	283	1,464,678	530	Up	32	756	2,156,405	337	Up	14
1988	280	1,623,806	576	Up	46	754	2,324,613	363	Up	26
1989	281	1,812,802	632	Up	56	765	2,502,114	388	Up	25
1990	279	2,003,915	705	Up	73	782	2,776,695	422	Up	34
1991	284	2,118,402	729	Up	24	806	3,012,723	435	Up	13
1992	288	2,552,409	871	Up	142	815	3,397,088	496	Up	61
1993	294	2,831,319	1,078	Up	207	894	4,094,373	598	Up	102

+ Does not include double-headers with men.

Division I Conference Leader by Per-Game Average

Year	Conference	Teams	Attendance	P/G Avg.
1982	Southeastern	10	154,176	1,186
1983	Southeastern	10	182,250	1,494
1984	Southeastern	10	128,170	1,176
1985	Sun Belt	7	92,416	1,141
1986	Southwest	9	105,806	1,275
1987	Southwest	9	131,364	1,752
1988	Southwest	9	165,418	1,838
1989	Southwest	9	179,223	2,037
1990	Southwest	9	179,092	2,012
1991	Southwest	9	172,438	1,938
1992	Atlantic Coast	9	236,426	2,021
1993	Big Ten	11	379,418	2,599

Division II Conference Leader by Per-Game Average

(From 1984)

Year	Conference	Teams	Attendance	P/G Avg.
1984	Central Intercollegiate	14	48,995	557
1985	Central Intercollegiate	14	44,212	582
1986	North Central	8	31,771	836
1987	Central States	8	27,889	664
1988	North Central	8	21,975	733
1989	Lone Star	8	28,311	577
1990	Central Intercollegiate	14	48,022	1,044
1991	North Central	10	47,690	954
1992	North Central	10	65,248	1,279
1993	North Central	10	65,179	988

Division III Conference Leader by Per-Game Average

(From 1984)

Year	Conference	Teams	Attendance	P/G Avg.
1984	Upstate New York	8	18,168	249
1985	Iowa Intercollegiate	8	8,346	278
1986	Massachusetts	7	14,515	382
1987	Massachusetts	7	5,050	281
1988	Iowa Intercollegiate	9	14,536	291
1989	Ohio Athletic	9	29,808	264
1990	Ohio Athletic	11	35,423	253
1991	Ohio Athletic	10	42,160	335
1992	Little East	6	11,508	384
1993	Little East	6	11,736	326

NCAA Division I Championship Tournament

Year	Teams	G/S	%Attendance	P/G Avg.
1982	32	26	66,924	2,574
1983	36	30	73,687	2,456
1984	32	25	85,158	3,406
1985	32	26	98,804	3,800
1986	40	34	96,822	2,848
1987	40	34	121,912	3,586
1988	40	34	133,742	3,934
1989	48	42	167,585	3,990
1990	48	42	191,519	4,560
1991	48	42	153,939	3,665
1992	48	42	197,664	4,706
1993	48	42	231,367	5,509
TOTALS		419	1,619,123	3,864

% Figures taken from official box scores.

NCAA Division II Championship Tournament

Year	Teams	G/S	%Attendance	P/G Avg.
1982	16	16	12,614	788
1983	23	22	19,174	872
1984	24	+20	15,869	793
1985	24	+21	13,737	654
1986	24	+21	32,976	1,570
1987	24	22	26,536	1,206
1988	32	22	30,079	1,367
1989	32	22	20,731	942
1990	32	22	20,904	950
1991	32	22	47,066	2,139
1992	32	22	43,607	1,982
1993	32	22	36,397	1,654
TOTALS		254	319,690	1,259

% Figures taken from official box scores. + Division II tournament double-header with men not included.

NCAA Division III Championship Tournament

Year	Teams	G/S	%Attendance	P/G Avg.
1982	16	16	7,908	494
1983	32	22	15,704	714
1984	32	22	12,900	586
1985	32	22	20,966	953
1986	32	22	21,038	956
1987	32	22	18,231	829
1988	32	22	25,375	1,153
1989	32	22	17,625	801
1990	32	22	25,040	1,138
1991	32	26	23,834	917
1992	32	26	21,000	808
1993	32	26	28,080	1,080
TOTALS		270	237,701	880

% Figures taken from official box scores.

ALL-TIME WOMEN'S DIVISION I CONFERENCE BASKETBALL ATTENDANCE

(#Net Home Attendance Excludes Double-headers With Men)

ATLANTIC COAST CONFERENCE

Year	All Home Teams	G/S	Attendance	#Net Home G/S	Attendance	Per Game		Change Net Total
1984	8	101	69,254	79	48,643	616	Up	12,387
1985	8	100	63,570	84	42,328	504	Down	6,315
1986	8	112	92,139	88	63,441	721	Up	21,113
1987	8	111	126,657	85	66,439	782	Up	2,998
1988	8	108	78,411	100	71,068	711	Up	4,629
1989	8	109	102,414	96	91,586	954	Up	20,518
1990	8	109	113,079	98	99,656	1,017	Up	8,070
1991	8	110	164,411	102	156,324	1,533	Up	56,668
1992	9	124	249,518	117	236,426	2,021	Up	73,988
1993	9	121	202,204	117	197,893	1,691	Down	38,533

ATLANTIC 10 CONFERENCE

Year	All Home Teams	G/S	Attendance	#Net Home G/S	Attendance	Per Game		Change Net Total
1984	9	101	98,219	67	44,496	664	Up	1,417
1985	9	104	184,883	70	49,745	711	Up	5,249
1986	9	111	103,082	87	59,176	680	Up	9,431
1987	10	134	129,053	99	85,907	868	Up	25,231
1988	10	139	171,070	104	82,657	794	Down	3,250
1989	10	137	131,366	118	99,938	847	Up	17,281
1990	10	128	123,500	110	93,169	847	Down	6,769
1991	10	134	125,708	112	106,881	954	Up	13,712
1992	9	121	112,938	111	87,472	788	Up	11,124
1993	8	95	78,189	91	61,187	672	Down	26,285

BIG EAST CONFERENCE

Year	All Home Teams	G/S	Attendance	#Net Home G/S	Attendance	Per Game		Change Net Total
1984	9	112	38,670	91	28,379	312	Down	1,729
1985	9	123	82,498	116	34,093	294	Up	5,714
1986	9	118	123,920	100	31,212	312	Down	2,881
1987	9	122	61,493	115	40,829	355	Up	9,617
1988	9	117	55,650	116	37,397	322	Down	3,432
1989	9	120	52,019	112	34,742	310	Down	2,655
1990	9	117	79,742	108	56,932	527	Up	22,190
1991	9	117	87,389	114	68,208	598	Up	11,276
1992	10	138	153,890	137	123,462	901	Up	49,614
1993	10	140	117,447	140	117,447	838	Down	6,015

BIG EIGHT CONFERENCE

Year	All Home Teams	G/S	Attendance	#Net Home G/S	Attendance	Per Game		Change Net Total
1984	8	104	110,712	46	41,781	908	Up	6,637
1985	8	105	106,292	52	40,778	784	Down	1,003
1986	8	110	92,161	64	39,093	611	Down	1,685
1987	8	106	100,465	70	54,789	783	Up	15,696
1988	8	99	103,417	76	59,437	782	Up	4,648
1989	8	102	100,662	88	78,728	895	Up	19,291
1990	8	107	83,498	97	77,586	800	Down	1,142
1991	8	95	84,912	89	79,527	894	Up	1,941
1992	8	105	102,937	101	96,995	960	Up	17,468
1993	8	108	152,871	104	148,884	1,432	Up	51,889

BIG SKY CONFERENCE

(Members before 1989 were in Mountain West Athletic Conference)

Year	All Home Teams	G/S	Attendance	#Net Home G/S	Attendance	Per Game		Change Net Total
1989	9	120	97,194	94	78,949	840	Up	9,173
1990	9	108	111,449	89	93,826	1,054	Up	14,877
1991	9	113	108,032	96	94,515	985	Up	689
1992	9	110	129,475	104	121,009	1,164	Up	26,487
1993	8	110	149,121	101	145,558	1,441	Up	24,549

BIG SOUTH CONFERENCE

Year	All Home Teams	G/S	Attendance	#Net Home G/S	Attendance	Per Game		Change Net Total
1987	7	92	21,270	52	13,020	250	Down	3,835
1988	7	97	23,132	79	18,545	235	Up	5,525
1989	7	100	26,142	84	21,380	255	Up	2,835
1990	7	89	18,219	72	10,567	147	Down	10,813
1991	7	92	21,423	85	16,983	200	Up	6,416
1992	7	89	21,616	81	19,473	240	Down	2,040
1993	10	120	33,723	109	27,664	254	Up	8,191

BIG TEN CONFERENCE

Year	All Home Teams	G/S	Attendance	#Net Home G/S	Attendance	Per Game		Change Net Total
1984	10	134	118,446	127	110,125	867	Up	36,136
1985	10	133	139,169	132	138,469	1,049	Up	28,344
1986	10	146	146,848	144	145,845	1,013	Up	7,376
1987	10	138	164,533	137	162,363	1,185	Up	16,518
1988	10	136	225,342	136	225,342n	1,657	Up	62,979
1989	10	138	228,193	136	219,393	1,613	Down	5,949
1990	10	144	260,339	143	256,864n	1,796	Up	37,471
1991	10	140	238,212	140	238,212	1,702	Down	18,652
1992	10	143	285,959	142	282,015n	1,986	Up	43,803
1993	11	152	384,962	146	379,418n	2,599n	Up	97,403

n—*National record.*

BIG WEST CONFERENCE

(Before 1988, members were in Pacific Coast Athletic Conference)

Year	All Home Teams	G/S	Attendance	#Net Home G/S	Attendance	Per Game		Change Net Total
1988	10	139	209,147	115	77,522	674	Up	30,821
1989	10	146	96,112	122	57,253	469	Up	534
1990	10	136	77,963	125	58,613	469	Up	1,360
1991	10	142	97,372	123	59,268	482	Up	655
1992	10	135	63,248	102	51,079	501	Down	8,189
1993	10	137	86,140	109	53,728	493	Up	2,649

COLONIAL ATHLETIC ASSOCIATION

(Before 1986, members were in ECAC South Conference)

Year	All Home Teams	G/S	Attendance	#Net Home G/S	Attendance	Per Game		Change Net Total
1986	7	92	28,775	84	20,849	248	Up	4,606
1987	7	92	31,718	88	30,367	345	Up	9,518
1988	7	91	36,237	85	30,101	354	Down	266
1989	7	89	32,324	75	28,036	374	Down	2,065
1990	7	89	30,995	74	26,922	364	Down	1,114
1991	7	92	40,616	82	33,610	410	Up	6,688
1992	8	100	53,212	93	50,411	542	Up	6,612
1993	8	100	62,320	94	50,012	532	Down	399

GREAT MIDWEST CONFERENCE

Year	All Home Teams	G/S	Attendance	#Net Home G/S	Attendance	Per Game		Change Net Total
1992	6	75	51,257	72	49,781	691	Up	2,102
1993	6	81	47,733	80	46,690	584	Down	3,091

IVY GROUP

Year	All Home Teams	G/S	Attendance	#Net Home G/S	Attendance	Per Game		Change Net Total
1984	8	89	25,961	85	16,374	193	Up	1,779
1985	7	87	26,927	81	15,694	194	Up	520
1986	7	88	20,223	84	14,547	173	Down	1,147
1987	8	93	17,325	88	15,995	182	Up	1,448
1988	8	97	26,194	89	21,206	236	Up	5,211
1989	8	93	22,392	86	20,462	238	Down	744
1990	8	102	26,129	95	23,432	247	Up	2,970
1991	8	93	25,275	83	18,811	227	Down	4,621
1992	8	96	25,074	89	20,120	226	Up	1,309
1993	8	92	34,063	86	22,855	266	Up	2,735

METRO ATLANTIC CONFERENCE

Year	All Home Teams	G/S	Attendance	#Net Home G/S	Attendance	Per Game		Change Net Total
1984	8	106	32,325	79	23,152	293	Up	6,912
1985	7	86	35,095	75	25,130	335	Up	6,188
1986	7	93	37,151	76	21,872	288	Down	3,258
1987	7	92	28,450	82	20,901	255	Down	971
1988	7	88	48,837	72	23,216	322	Up	2,315
1989	7	88	43,874	70	21,012	300	Down	2,204
1990	11	138	51,840	108	30,040	278	Up	3,798
1991	9	117	30,333	112	24,092	215	Down	5,948
1992	9	107	32,949	92	21,590	235	Down	1,502
1993	8	78	29,490	81	19,140	236	Down	2,450

METROPOLITAN COLLEGIATE ATHELTIC CONFERENCE

Year	All Home Teams	G/S	Attendance	#Net Home G/S	Attendance	Per Game		Change Net Total
1984	8	106	47,453	76	31,053	409	Up	1,776
1985	8	106	62,181	92	51,060	555	Up	20,007
1986	7	93	46,750	76	37,461	493	Down	12,212
1987	7	95	58,422	79	40,853	517	Up	3,392
1988	7	86	106,129	71	27,951	394	Down	12,902
1989	7	97	54,749	92	48,132	523	Up	20,181

Year	All Home Teams	G/S	Attendance	#Net Home G/S	Attendance	Per Game		Change Net Total
1990	8	107	57,733	89	41,929	471	Down	6,203
1991	8	112	55,427	97	43,903	453	Up	1,974
1992	7	99	73,152	85	30,938	364	Up	904
1993	7	90	57,056	80	46,918	586	Up	15,910

MID-AMERICAN ATHLETIC CONFERENCE

Year	All Home Teams	G/S	Attendance	#Net Home G/S	Attendance	Per Game		Change Net Total
1984	10	123	57,773	28	16,083	574	Down	812
1985	10	121	125,336	28	10,400	371	Down	5,683
1986	10	124	136,031	27	11,703	433	Up	1,303
1987	9	102	80,163	28	15,292	546	Up	4,815
1988	9	110	128,521	43	19,644	456	Up	4,352
1989	9	111	61,469	37	19,955	539	Up	311
1990	9	108	150,483	39	20,237	519	Up	282
1991	9	110	137,556	43	21,395	498	Up	1,158
1992	9	103	91,508	37	25,382	686	Up	3,987
1993	10	122	96,732	50	28,402	568	Up	3,020

MID-CONTINENT CONFERENCE

(Before 1993, six members were in North Star Conference)

Year	All Home Teams	G/S	Attendance	#Net Home G/S	Attendance	Per Game		Change Net Total
1984	6	75	27,994	57	18,694	328	Up	1,329
1985	8	107	46,537	89	23,198	261	Down	2,767
1986	8	104	32,940	95	21,662	228	Down	1,536
1987	4	56	16,603	50	14,678	294	Up	1,224
1988	6	74	28,213	64	23,870	373	Up	9,192
1989	8	102	55,019	94	41,514	442	Up	17,644
1990	7	90	61,163	85	53,752	632	Up	16,336
1991	8	98	62,251	88	53,675	610	Down	77
1992	7	93	57,843	76	48,155	634	Up	18,195
1993	9	108	69,378	90	61,436	683	Up	13,281

MID-EASTERN ATHLETIC CONFERENCE

Year	All Home Teams	G/S	Attendance	#Net Home G/S	Attendance	Per Game		Change Net Total
1984	7	79	69,988	44	31,500	716	Up	9,691
1985	7	76	54,314	35	26,200	749	Down	5,300
1986	8	100	101,722	38	13,790	363	Down	12,410
1987	8	96	82,865	40	16,785	420	Up	2,995
1988	8	93	63,663	42	26,666	635	Up	9,881
1989	8	95	100,658	36	17,785	494	Down	8,881
1990	8	93	71,482	43	22,078	513	Up	4,293
1991	8	87	85,128	40	18,316	458	Down	3,762
1992	8	86	63,720	26	8,699	335	Down	9,617
1993	9	102	88,852	60	43,521	725	Up	34,822

MIDWESTERN COLLEGIATE CONFERENCE

Year	All Home Teams	G/S	Attendance	#Net Home G/S	Attendance	Per Game		Change Net Total
1987	7	94	18,401	72	11,408	158	Down	397
1988	6	76	74,867	62	8,737	141	Down	2,135
1989	8	105	23,248	78	17,833	229	Up	9,096
1990	9	108	32,705	78	22,627	290	Up	696
1991	9	120	45,479	85	33,749	397	Up	11,122
1992	7	88	48,872	74	44,038	595	Up	15,037
1993	9	110	52,399	94	47,317	503	Up	3,279

MISSOURI VALLEY CONFERENCE

(Before 1993, teams were members of Gateway Collegiate Conference.)

Year	All Home Teams	G/S	Attendance	#Net Home G/S	Attendance	Per Game		Change Net Total
1984	10	124	48,599	107	37,231	348	Down	5,820
1985	10	138	51,886	119	42,869	360	Up	5,638
1986	10	134	58,407	116	52,565	453	Up	9,696
1987	10	130	59,101	117	55,156	471	Up	2,591
1988	10	131	63,217	120	58,356	486	Up	3,200
1989	10	126	67,145	116	59,189	510	Up	833
1990	10	121	72,310	111	62,995	568	Up	3,806
1991	10	130	92,375	119	88,818	746	Up	25,823
1992	10	134	135,263	125	131,048	1,048	Up	42,230
1993	9	114	169,062	103	164,447	1,597	Up	33,399

NORTH ATLANTIC CONFERENCE

(Before 1990, members were in Seaboard Conference)

Year	All Home Teams	G/S	Attendance	#Net Home G/S	Attendance	Per Game		Change Net Total
1990	7	88	30,409	82	27,060	330	Down	551
1991	6	72	30,195	70	26,764	382	Down	296
1992	8	99	60,830	94	51,590	549	Up	22,118
1993	8	98	82,039	90	70,235	780	Up	18,645

NORTHEAST CONFERENCE

(Before 1989, members were in ECAC Metro Conference)

Year	All Home Teams	G/S	Attendance	#Net Home G/S	Attendance	Per Game		Change Net Total
1989	9	114	28,734	84	14,064	167	Down	566
1990	9	114	29,382	60	9,925	165	Down	6,174
1991	9	113	21,004	62	11,561	186	Up	1,636
1992	9	115	26,475	63	15,763	250	Up	4,202
1993	10	125	49,437	71	19,072	269	Up	3,309

OHIO VALLEY CONFERENCE

Year	All Home Teams	G/S	Attendance	#Net Home G/S	Attendance	Per Game		Change Net Total
1984	8	102	41,405	44	16,841	383	Down	1,124
1985	8	100	59,154	31	16,995	548	Up	154
1986	8	97	62,998	29	15,480	534	Down	1,515
1987	8	108	77,990	41	29,896	729	Up	14,416
1988	8	99	90,196	37	13,047	353	Down	16,849
1989	7	77	74,970	34	22,425	660	Up	9,378
1990	7	89	101,786	45	39,454	877	Up	17,029
1991	7	82	81,166	37	31,261	845	Down	8,193
1992	8	101	98,087	42	28,779	685	Down	35,779
1993	8	99	89,831	34	26,829	789	Down	1,950

PACIFIC-10 CONFERENCE

(Members before 1987 were in Northern Pacific & Pacific West Conferences)

Year	All Home Teams	G/S	Attendance	#Net Home G/S	Attendance	Per Game		Change Net Total
1987	10	145	112,626	132	92,078	698	Up	20,278
1988	10	135	125,206	126	108,645	862	Up	16,567
1989	10	137	116,596	129	109,604	850	Up	959
1990	10	142	197,372	139	189,720	515	Up	80,116
1991	10	141	179,384	141	177,425	1,276	Down	12,295
1992	10	140	201,302	135	195,465	1,448	Up	18,040
1993	10	137	228,776	133	225,351	1,694	Up	29,886

PATRIOT LEAGUE

Year	All Home Teams	G/S	Attendance	#Net Home G/S	Attendance	Per Game		Change Net Total
1991	7	80	59,568	44	16,358	372	Up	1,344
1992	8	95	62,349	40	8,479	212	Down	10,444
1993	8	94	34,076	32	8,983	281	Up	504

SOUTHEASTERN CONFERENCE

Year	All Home Teams	G/S	Attendance	#Net Home G/S	Attendance	Per Game		Change Net Total
1984	10	134	152,074	109	128,170	1,176	Down	28,740
1985	10	130	154,652	111	126,577	1,140	Down	1,593
1986	10	133	141,141	104	119,718	1,151	Down	6,859
1987	10	136	205,583	120	178,761	1,490	Up	59,043
1988	10	134	191,810	113	142,802	1,264	Down	35,959
1989	10	134	212,266	111	174,649	1,573	Up	31,847
1990	10	131	235,611	106	194,571	1,836	Up	19,922
1991	10	131	214,846	111	179,931	1,621	Down	14,640
1992	12	160	287,797	140	248,976	1,778	Up	21,579
1993	12	160	320,433	136	284,246	2,090	Up	35,270

SOUTHERN CONFERENCE

Year	All Home Teams	G/S	Attendance	#Net Home G/S	Attendance	Per Game		Change Net Total
1985	6	77	28,460	57	21,305	374	Down	10,682
1986	7	88	44,606	62	22,588	364	Up	283
1987	7	74	36,547	59	26,327	446	Up	3,739
1988	6	79	33,912	61	26,972	442	Up	645
1989	6	76	37,511	67	20,775	310	Down	6,197
1990	6	76	25,631	67	19,545	292	Down	1,230
1991	6	75	31,188	67	23,595	352	Up	4,050
1992	6	69	25,620	63	22,488	357	Down	1,107
1993	7	77	38,733	60	22,675	378	Down	187

SOUTHLAND CONFERENCE

(Most teams came from Gulf Star in 1987)

Year	All Home Teams	G/S	Attendance	#Net Home G/S	Attendance	Per Game		Change Net Total
1984	7	88	43,724	65	31,164	479	Up	4,097
1985	7	84	67,059	70	60,108	859	Up	28,944
1986	7	87	51,941	68	38,841	589	Down	21,267
1987	7	86	37,892	63	23,678	376	Down	15,163
1988	8	108	69,814	89	53,141	597	Up	29,463
1989	8	103	129,371	40	33,582	858	Down	19,694
1990	8	97	83,427	45	40,268	895	Up	6,686
1991	8	97	91,490	38	43,837	1,154	Up	3,569
1992	10	129	127,194	54	75,656	1,401	Up	25,396
1993	10	130	125,090	57	86,614	1,520	Up	10,958

SOUTHWEST CONFERENCE

Year	All Home Teams	G/S	Attendance	#Net Home G/S	Attendance	Per Game		Change Net Total
1984	9	112	82,564	76	63,543	836	Up	28,243
1985	9	111	81,075	83	70,186	846	Up	6,643
1986	9	118	127,431	83	105,806	1,275	Up	35,620
1987	9	118	151,846	75	131,364	1,752	Up	25,558
1988	9	119	170,448	90	165,418	1,838	Up	29,094
1989	9	112	187,189	88	179,223	2,037n	Up	13,805
1990	9	118	187,551	89	179,092	2,012	Down	131
1991	9	117	181,165	89	172,438	1,938	Down	6,654
1992	8	103	172,301	101	171,712	1,700	Up	40,771
1993	8	101	199,524	98	190,043	1,939	Up	18,331

n—*National record.*

SOUTHWESTERN ATHLETIC CONFERENCE

Year	All Home Teams	G/S	Attendance	#Net Home G/S	Attendance	Per Game		Change Net Total
1984	8	103	158,317	47	36,472	776	Up	14,455
1985	8	89	138,464	31	31,656	1,021	Down	4,816
1986	8	107	122,918	35	32,418	926	Up	762
1987	8	90	126,390	30	17,334	578	Down	15,084
1988	8	85	116,822	32	26,004	813	Up	8,670
1989	8	93	109,147	40	20,347	509	Down	5,657
1990	8	87	74,745	26	5,003	192	Down	15,344
1991	8	87	96,171	43	29,472	685	Up	24,469
1992	8	87	87,638	30	12,295	410	Down	17,177
1993	8	81	95,017	20	5,308	265	Down	6,987

SUN BELT CONFERENCE

(Combined with American South in 1992)

Year	All Home Teams	G/S	Attendance	#Net Home G/S	Attendance	Per Game		Change Net Total
1984	7	96	149,382	71	72,345	1,019	Up	18,774
1985	7	95	131,056	81	92,416	1,141	Up	20,071
1986	7	92	105,102	77	69,469	902	Down	22,947
1987	7	99	98,120	89	72,663	816	Up	3,194
1988	7	86	84,785	82	60,982	744	Down	11,681
1989	7	95	88,314	90	65,774	731	Up	4,792
1990	7	89	73,412	85	58,880	693	Down	6,894
1991	7	85	66,253	81	58,853	727	Down	27
1992	9	120	149,303	106	103,090	973	Up	19,652
1993	8	98	147,762	77	100,834	1,310	Down	2,256

TRANS AMERICA CONFERENCE

(New in 1992, formerly New South Women's Athletic Conference)

Year	All Home Teams	G/S	Attendance	#Net Home G/S	Attendance	Per Game		Change Net Total
1992	7	97	35,213	82	23,982	292	Up	3,963
1993	7	97	23,951	69	14,041	203	Down	9,941

WEST COAST ATHLETIC CONFERENCE

Year	All Home Teams	G/S	Attendance	#Net Home G/S	Attendance	Per Game		Change Net Total
1986	7	102	15,739	92	13,479	147	Down	704
1987	7	95	10,013	89	9,240	43	Down	4,189
1988	8	113	22,033	108	16,943	157	Up	892
1989	8	112	27,159	109	16,824	154	Down	119
1990	8	120	35,595	111	23,457	211	Up	6,633
1991	8	116	32,718	57	12,987	228	Down	10,470
1992	8	107	34,463	45	16,062	357	Up	3,075
1993	8	107	37,938	45	14,154	315	Down	1,908

WESTERN ATHLETIC CONFERENCE

(Before 1991, members were in High Country Athletic Conference)

Year	All Home Teams	G/S	Attendance	#Net Home G/S	Attendance	Per Game		Change Net Total
1991	7	90	40,480	82	33,029	403	Up	898
1992	8	109	66,174	97	60,116	620	Up	27,087
1993	8	98	75,905	81	65,083	803	Up	4,967

WOMEN'S ALL-TIME CONFERENCE BASKETBALL ATTENDANCE

(Conferences that either discontinued or changed names)

AMERICAN SOUTH CONFERENCE

(Combined with Sun Belt Conference after 1991 season)

Year	All Home Teams	G/S	Attendance	#Net Home G/S	Attendance	Per Game		Change Net Total
1988	6	72	51,509	53	37,890	715	Down	17,800
1989	6	81	123,875	58	62,824	1,083	Up	24,934
1990	6	73	90,596	57	43,340	760	Down	19,484
1991	7	91	116,922	61	52,204	856	Up	8,864

COSMOPOLITAN CONFERENCE

Year	All Home Teams	G/S	Attendance	#Net Home G/S	Attendance	Per Game		Change Net Total
1984	8	104	24,369	90	21,059	234	Up	4,216
1985	8	111	28,408	89	21,757	244	Up	698
1986	9	110	19,069	93	12,872	138	Down	9,939

EAST COAST CONFERENCE

(Some teams joined Northeast Conference in 1993)

Year	All Home Teams	G/S	Attendance	#Net Home G/S	Attendance	Per Game		Change Net Total
1984	9	102	20,045	75	12,525	167	Up	602
1985	8	107	31,748	71	14,764	208	Up	4,238
1986	8	104	33,403	63	10,496	167	Down	4,268
1987	8	102	40,295	60	12,203	203	Up	1,707
1988	8	93	33,508	51	7,669	150	Down	4,309
1989	8	98	34,509	51	9,918	194	Up	2,249
1990	8	102	33,935	54	9,199	170	Down	719
1991	7	80	22,555	49	9,886	202	Up	687
1992	7	89	20,114	63	13,953	221	Up	2,457

ECAC METRO CONFERENCE

(Before 1987, most members were in Cosmopolitan Conference)

Year	All Home Teams	G/S	Attendance	#Net Home G/S	Attendance	Per Game		Change Net Total
1987	9	118	27,838	87	17,302	199	Up	4,521
1988	9	120	41,126	82	14,630	178	Down	2,672

ECAC SOUTH CONFERENCE

(Became Colonial Athletic Association in 1986)

Year	All Home Teams	G/S	Attendance	#Net Home G/S	Attendance	Per Game		Change Net Total
1984	4	52	9,988	45	9,018	200	Down	4,524
1985	7	88	20,042	82	16,243	198	Up	3,522

GATEWAY COLLEGIATE CONFERENCE

(Teams became members of Missouri Valley Conference in 1993)

Year	All Home Teams	G/S	Attendance	#Net Home G/S	Attendance	Per Game		Change Net Total
1984	10	124	48,599	107	37,231	348	Down	5,820
1985	10	138	51,886	119	42,869	360	Up	5,638
1986	10	134	58,407	116	52,565	453	Up	9,696
1987	10	130	59,101	117	55,156	471	Up	2,591
1988	10	131	63,217	120	58,356	486	Up	3,200
1989	10	126	67,145	116	59,189	510	Up	833
1990	10	121	72,310	111	62,995	568	Up	3,806
1991	10	130	92,375	119	88,818	746	Up	25,823
1992	10	134	135,263	125	131,048	1,048	Up	42,230

GULF STAR CONFERENCE

(After 1987, most members were in Southland Conference)

Year	All Home Teams	G/S	Attendance	#Net Home G/S	Attendance	Per Game		Change Net Total
1985	6	75	26,128	63	17,833	283	Down	926
1986	6	76	38,633	69	28,187	409	Up	10,354
1987	6	77	69,112	36	24,725	687	Down	3,462

HIGH COUNTRY ATHLETIC CONFERENCE

(In 1991, became the Western Athletic Conference)

Year	All Home Teams	G/S	Attendance	#Net Home G/S	Attendance	Per Game		Change Net Total
1984	7	85	33,317	70	24,640	352	Up	7,955
1985	7	83	36,093	60	17,841	297	Down	5,002
1986	7	85	29,414	70	23,178	331	Up	5,337
1987	7	90	47,513	76	26,914	354	Up	3,736
1988	6	84	51,048	68	37,951	558	Up	11,037
1989	6	86	38,664	71	26,694	376	Down	11,257
1990	6	87	43,667	71	32,131	453	Up	5,437

MIDDLE EASTERN COLLEGE CONFERENCE

Year	All Home Teams	G/S	Attendance	#Net Home G/S	Attendance	Per Game		Change Net Total
1987	6	84	19,796	64	8,758	137	Up	191

MOUNTAIN WEST CONFERENCE

Year	All Home Teams	G/S	Attendance	#Net Home G/S	Attendance	Per Game		Change Net Total
1984	9	107	49,865	90	39,615	440	Up	5,272
1985	8	91	55,117	55	28,338	515	Down	6,277
1986	8	102	57,353	96	48,627	507	Up	20,289
1987	7	82	56,082	75	41,209	549	Down	5,628
1988	9	124	105,752	106	69,776	658	Up	28,657

NEW SOUTH WOMEN'S ATHLETIC CONFERENCE

(Started as New South Conference in 1986, became Trans America in 1992)

Year	All Home Teams	G/S	Attendance	#Net Home G/S	Attendance	Per Game		Change Net Total
1986	6	82	40,940	62	28,484	459	Down	74
1987	6	84	29,854	66	19,792	300	Down	8,692
1988	7	98	43,785	73	29,499	404	Up	9,707
1989	7	97	37,648	73	27,711	380	Down	1,788
1990	7	97	40,191	72	27,680	384	Down	31
1991	7	93	39,603	77	23,834	310	Down	3,846

NORTH STAR CONFERENCE

(Six teams formed Mid-Continent Conference in 1993)

Year	All Home Teams	G/S	Attendance	#Net Home G/S	Attendance	Per Game		Change Net Total
1984	6	75	27,994	57	18,694	328	Up	1,329
1985	8	107	46,537	89	23,198	261	Down	2,767
1986	8	104	32,940	95	21,662	228	Down	1,536
1987	4	56	16,603	50	14,678	294	Up	1,224
1988	6	74	28,213	64	23,870	373	Up	9,192
1989	8	102	55,019	94	41,514	442	Up	17,644
1990	7	90	61,163	85	53,752	632	Up	16,336
1991	8	98	62,251	88	53,675	610	Down	77
1992	7	93	57,843	76	48,155	634	Up	18,195

NORTHERN PACIFIC CONFERENCE

(Some members joined Pacific-10 Conference in 1987)

Year	All Home Teams	G/S	Attendance	#Net Home G/S	Attendance	Per Game		Change Net Total
1984	10	118	44,985	94	37,420	398	Down	4,365
1985	9	111	66,444	104	45,433	437	Up	9,438
1986	7	84	49,079	76	46,249	609	Up	7,396

OIL COUNTRY CONFERENCE

Year	All Home Teams	G/S	Attendance	#Net Home G/S	Attendance	Per Game		Change Net Total
1984	6	74	38,978	55	16,252	295	Up	5,675
1985	6	72	61,161	55	16,050	292	Down	202

PACIFIC COAST ATHLETIC CONFERENCE

Year	All Home Teams	G/S	Attendance	#Net Home G/S	Attendance	Per Game		Change Net Total
1985	5	77	31,447	65	19,888	306	Up	5,012
1986	8	104	40,598	92	31,520	343	Down	18,583
1987	10	146	58,907	118	46,701	396	Up	15,181

PACIFIC WEST CONFERENCE

(After 1986, members were in Pacific-10 Conference)

Year	All Home Teams	G/S	Attendance	#Net Home G/S	Attendance	Per Game		Change Net Total
1986	5	61	50,767	47	33,957	722	Down	1,130

SEABOARD CONFERENCE
(Started in 1985 as ECAC Seaboard)

Year	All Home Teams	G/S	Attendance	#Net Home G/S	Attendance	Per Game		Change Net Total
1985	7	67	12,814	64	11,750	184	Down	828
1986	8	97	20,134	86	15,291	178	Up	2,508
1987	8	95	23,614	91	21,404	235	Up	6,113
1988	8	104	38,817	99	35,837	362	Up	14,433
1989	8	94	33,096	90	29,776	331	Down	7,801

WESTERN COLLEGIATE CONFERENCE

Year	All Home Teams	G/S	Attendance	#Net Home G/S	Attendance	Per Game		Change Net Total
1984	8	113	113,436	85	72,403	852	Down	722
1985	8	106	103,919	90	65,302	726	Down	7,101

ALL-TIME TOP WOMEN'S DIVISION I ATTENDANCE GAMES
(Excluding double-headers with men/includes NCAA tournament games)
(Paid Attendance)

23,912—Texas (97) vs. Tennessee (78), December 9, 1987, at Thompson-Boling Arena, Knoxville, Tennessee. Total attendance was 24,563.

20,023—Stanford (88) vs. Auburn (81), April 1, 1990, at Thompson-Boling Arena, Knoxville, Tennessee (NCAA final).

19,467—Auburn (81) vs. Louisiana Tech (69) and Stanford (75) vs. Virginia (66), March 30, 1990, at Thompson-Boling Arena, Knoxville, Tennessee, (NCAA semifinals).

16,141—Ohio St. (73) vs. Iowa (72) (ot) and Texas Tech (60) vs. Vanderbilt (46), April 3, 1993, at The Omni, Atlanta, Georgia (NCAA semifinals) and Texas Tech (84) vs. Ohio St. (82), April 4, 1993, at The Omni, Atlanta, Georgia (NCAA final).

15,615—Louisiana Tech (79) vs. Texas (75) and Tennessee (74) vs. Long Beach St. (64), March 27, 1987, at Erwin Special Events Center, Austin, Texas (NCAA semifinals) and Tennessee (67) vs. Louisiana Tech (44), March 29, 1987, at Erwin Special Events Center, Austin, Texas (NCAA final). The turnstile count was 15,303 March 27 and 9,823 March 29.

15,500—Iowa (75) vs. Ohio St. (64), January 31, 1988, at Carver-Hawkeye Arena, Iowa City, Iowa.

15,317—Tennessee (73) vs. Vanderbilt (68), January 30, 1993, at Memorial Gymnasium, Nashville, Tennessee.

14,821—Ohio St. (56) vs. Iowa (47), February 3, 1985, at Carver-Hawkeye Arena, Iowa City, Iowa. Total attendance was 22,157 (which included 7,876 free admissions).

14,500—Virginia (75) vs. Maryland (74), February 12, 1992, at Cole Field House, College Park, Maryland.

13,498—Iowa (70) vs. Purdue (67), February 11, 1990, at Mackey Arena, West Lafayette, Indiana.

13,276—Ohio St. (72) vs. Iowa (60), March 7, 1993, at St. John Arena, Columbus, Ohio.

12,951—Western Ky. (74) vs. Old Dominion (64), February 12, 1986, at Diddle Arena, Bowling Green, Kentucky.

12,874—Maryland (79) vs. Texas (71), March 25, 1989, at Erwin Special Events Center, Austin, Texas (NCAA West regional).

12,531—Arkansas (73) vs. Texas (68), February 9, 1991, at Erwin Special Events Center, Austin, Texas.

12,421—Stanford (66) vs. Virginia (65) and Western Ky. (84) vs. Southwest Mo. St. (72), April 4, 1992, at Los Angeles Sports Arena, Los Angeles, California (NCAA semifinals)

12,390—Louisiana Tech (71) vs. Texas (57), March 24, 1990, at Erwin Special Events Center, Austin, Texas (NCAA Midwest regional).

12,343—Iowa (72) vs. Tennessee (56), March 27, 1993, at Carver-Hawkeye Arena, Iowa City, Iowa (NCAA Mideast regional).

12,336—Montclair St. (102) vs. Queen's (N. Y.) (91) and Delta St. (76) vs. Immaculata ((62), March 6, 1977, at Madison Square Garden, New York, New York.

12,288—Louisiana Tech (83) vs. Texas (80), March 26, 1988, at Erwin Special Events Center, Austin, Texas (NCAA Midwest regional).

12,187—Brigham Young (75) vs. Utah (66), February 26, 1993, at Huntsman Center, Salt Lake City, Utah.

12,131—Vanderbilt (70) vs. Ohio St. (67), January 8, 1993, at Memorial Gymnasium, Nashville, Tennessee.

12,072—Stanford (78) vs. Western Ky. (62), April 5, 1992, at Los Angeles Sports Arena, Los Angeles, California (NCAA final).

12,000—Ohio St. (91) vs. Rutgers (60), March 21, 1993, at St. John Arena, Columbus, Ohio (NCAA second round).

1992 SEASON ATTENDANCE HIGHS
Single-Game Highs
(Excludes double-headers with men/includes NCAA tournament games)

Attendance	Teams (Site)	Date
16,141	Texas Tech vs. Ohio St. (Atlanta, Ga.)*	April 4, 1993
16,141	Iowa vs. Ohio St. and Vanderbilt vs. Texas Tech (Atlanta, Ga.)#	April 3, 1993
15,317	Tennessee at Vanderbilt (Nashville, Tenn.)	January 30, 1993
13,276	Iowa at Ohio St. (Columbus, Ohio)	March 7, 1993
12,343	Tennessee at Iowa (Iowa City, Iowa)%	March 27, 1993

Attendance	Teams (Site)	Date
12,187	Brigham Young at Utah (Salt Lake City, Utah)	February 26, 1993
12,131	Ohio St. at Vanderbilt (Nashville, Tenn.)	January 8, 1993
12,000	Rutgers at Ohio St. (Columbus, Ohio)†	March 21, 1993
11,858	Stanford at Tennessee (Knoxville, Tenn.)	December 21, 1992
10,358	Tennessee at Texas (Austin, Texas)	February 2, 1993

** NCAA final. # NCAA semifinals. % NCAA Mideast regional final. † NCAA East second round.*

PLAYING-RULES HISTORY

Boise State center Lidiya Varbanova blocks an opponent's shot. After two major research studies, women's basketball rules makers legislated a slightly smaller and lighter ball. Since the 1984-85 season, women have played with the smaller ball (28½ to 29 inches in circumference; 18 to 20 ounces in weight).

IMPORTANT COLLEGE RULES CHANGES FOR WOMEN'S BASKETBALL

1891-92 - Basketball is invented by Dr. James Naismith, instructor at YMCA Training School in Springfield, Massachusetts, in December 1891. His 13 original rules and description of the game are published in January 1892 and read by Senda Berenson, physical education instructor at nearby Smith College. She immediately creates new rules for women to discourage roughness and introduces basketball to Smith women. Peach baskets and the soccer ball are used, but she divides the court into three equal sections and requires players to stay in their section. Stealing the ball is prohibited, players may not hold the ball more than three seconds and there is a three-bounce limit on dribbles. Berenson's rules, often modified somewhat, spread rapidly across the country via YMCAs and colleges, but many women also used men's rules.

1894-95 - Berenson's article describing her game and its benefits in general terms is published in the September 1894 issue of the magazine, Physical Education. Clara Gregory Baer, physical culture instructor at Sophie Newcomb College in New Orleans, publishes the first women's basketball rules book, calling her game "Basquette" (this name is dropped in her first revision in 1908, called Newcomb College Basketball Rules). Her women stage a demonstration game March 13, 1895, before an all-female audience of 560 at the Southern Athletic Club (the first publicly played basketball game in the South by men or women). Baer's rules, much different than Berenson's, divide the court according to number of players on a side—11 sections if 11 players, seven sections if seven on a side, etc. No dribbling or guarding is allowed. A player is given six seconds to aim and shoot the ball (later four). No backboards are allowed. Players may run only when the ball is in the air, and then only a few steps within their area. Goals are changed after each score so that offensive and defensive roles are reversed. Uniquely, the one-handed push shot is required (more than 40 years before the one-handed shot becomes popular in the men's game). A two-handed shot (and a two-handed pass) is a foul in Baer's game. Baer's rules are used widely across the South and in widely scattered places elsewhere until 1922, when Newcomb adopts "official" rules.

1901-02 - Noting the different sets of rules, Luther Gulick and other leaders at an 1899 physical training meeting in Springfield appoint four women at the meeting to form a Women's Basketball Committee to incorporate all modifications into one set of rules, with the health of the players the most important factor. Berenson heads the committee. It decides on Berenson's original three-court rules (in which only certain players play offense), plus five to 10 players on a side. These rules, edited by Berenson, are published in 1901 by Spalding Athletic Library. However, Baer's rules and men's rules also are used.

1903-04 - Halves are shortened to 15 minutes (from 20) in the first revised rules by the committee. To avoid the rush to retrieve the ball out of bounds, which had been allowed, the ball is awarded to an opponent of the player who caused it to go out. Six to nine players are on a side, 11 officials.

1905-06 - The National Women's Basketball Committee becomes part of the American Physical Education Association, known today as American Alliance for Health, Physical Education, Recreation and Dance (AAHPERD).

1906-07 - Five to nine players are on a side. Description of backboard follows design of present backboards.

1908-09 - Boxing up (two opponents guarding a player in the act of shooting) is a foul. Placing one hand on a ball already held by an opponent is a foul. Player is warned after third foul, sent to bench after fourth. Committee notes that some are using open-bottom baskets, and notes that officials must make certain the ball has passed through the basket.

1910-11 - Dribbling is eliminated.

1913-14 - Single dribble returns, retaining requirement that ball must bounce knee-high. If the court is small, the court can be divided in half and the center on five-player team (center had special markings) could play entire court but not shoot for a basket.

1916-17 - No coaching from sidelines during game—only at half time (a hardship since there still were no timeouts and no substitutions).

1917-18 - Player is warned after four fouls, disqualified after five. Center in small two-court game can shoot if she plays full court. Shooting foul now yields two free throws.

1918-19 - Substitutes can be used, but they may not re-enter the game. Bounce pass now legal. Throw-in from out of bounds awarded opponent for a violation (instead of free throw). Freedom to shoot reversed for roving center in small two-court game. Basket with open bottom now required (instead of closed basket with pull chain). Three timeouts of five minutes each are available. Rules are rewritten to conform with wording and sequence of men's rules "without in any way altering the spirit of the women's rules."

1921-22 - Two-handed overhead field goal now is worth one point (instead of two, because only vertical guarding is allowed and this shot has been perfected).

1922-23 - Must be at least six players on a side; maximum of nine remains. Tie games are allowed to stand, "to minimize the emphasis on winning."

1924-25 - Eight-minute quarters with two minutes between quarters and a 10-minute half time, no coaching is allowed in the two minutes between quarters.

1925-26 - Goals scored by one-hand overhand throw, two-hand underhand throw, the shot-put throw and the throw with back to the basket also count as one point. Timeouts also used for injuries.

1926-27 - Timeouts reduced to two minutes (still five minutes for an injury).

1927-28 - Timeouts reduced from three to two per game.

1932-33 - Guarding on any plane is made legal (making the game much more exciting and skillful). All field goals now count two points. Two options to start the game—a center throw-in or a jump-up.

1933-34 - Must be two complete passes after a center throw-in (to prevent quick move on the basket).

1935-36 - Timeouts one minute each (still two per game).

1936-37 - Center throw-in mandatory (no jump-up to start game).

1938-39 - Two-court game with six players on a side is made mandatory (used experimentally for the two previous seasons by selected teams and proved highly popular). A team is three guards and three forwards; only forwards can score but all players are part of action.

1939-40 - Timeouts increased to three per game (number increased afterward until by mid-1970s five per game and one for each overtime, reflecting coach's greater importance).

1942-43 - Team scored against, either by field goal or free throw, gets ball at center court (previously, possession alternated after each goal, also at center court).

1945-46 - Team has choice of taking free throw, or getting ball out of bounds at free-throw line.

1947-48 - Players must wear numbers both front and back (since 1927, only on back).

1949-50 - Three rules that had been experimental for one season become mandatory. They are a limited two-bounce dribble with no height definition, a timeout for all fouls and free throws, and guarding is redefined—one or both arms, legs or body in any plane now permitted. (The continuous dribble also had been allowed the experimental season, but respondents to a questionnaire prefer the limited dribble.)

1951-52 - Players can receive coaching during all timeouts and intermissions.

1953-54 - Tie game is permitted to continue for one or more extra periods with "sudden death" (scoring a total of two points) after the first extra period.

1955-56 - Three seconds in the lane is a violation.

1956-57 - Ball can be tied up with "both hands held firmly around the ball held by an opponent."

1959-60 - Mandatory (after two seasons as an experiment) that missed free throw continues in play (bringing back the art of rebounding).

1960-61 - Tie ball permitted by either one or two hands held firmly on ball (making it possible to block a shot and encouraging faster passing and shooting).

1961-62 - After successful field goal or free throw, other team gets ball at the end line. Three-bounce dribble allowed.

1962-63 - After one experimental season, each team is permitted two players to rove the entire court and "snatching" the ball once again is permitted. Committee explains the former "provides more opportunity for team play and encourages all players to develop skills of shooting and both defensive and offensive tactics."

1964-65 - Player can hold ball indefinitely if not closely guarded; five seconds if closely guarded (instead of three seconds). Part of old vertical guarding rule returns as "holding both arms extended horizontally" is prohibited. Two free throws awarded last two minutes of each half "to make it unprofitable to deliberately foul." Officials now can remove a coach from the playing area for unsportsmanlike conduct. All these changes are made by a joint committee of the Division of Girls' and Women's Sports [now the National Association for Girls and Women in Sport (NAGWS)] and the Amateur Athletic Union (AAU). Its charge was to select the best from each group of rules to arrive at one set.

1966-67 - Continuous, unlimited dribble, used experimentally previous two seasons, becomes the official rule, making game much faster. Another two-season experiment, the 30-second clock, is made optional.

1968-69 - Coaching from the sidelines is no longer a foul.

1969-70 - Experimental use of five player, full-court game, in combination with 30-second clock, is permitted for the first time, continues for a second season, and is highly popular.

1971-72 - Five player, full-court game and 30-second clock is made official, with little fanfare. Thus the women's game comes almost (but not quite) full circle back to the game designed by Dr. Naismith.

1975-76 - After one experimental season, 20-minute halves and the bonus free throw rule both become official. The latter awards no free throws on the first six common fouls of each half, then a free throw is awarded plus a bonus if it is made. Free throws never are taken for offensive fouls and always taken if against a player in the act of shooting—or in case of a flagrant foul. Half time is increased to 15 minutes.

1977-78 - Coach may call timeout—only on dead ball.

1978-79 - Injured player must be replaced, otherwise team must take timeout.

1979-80 - Mandatory that shot clocks be visible by 1980-81 season. Three free throws are awarded for intentional or flagrant foul on player in act of shooting, if attempt is missed.

1982-83 - It is a violation if the ball goes over the backboard from out of bounds.

1983-84 - Held ball becomes violation, not jump ball. Warning for first slap on hand of inbounder, then technical foul. Coach may call timeout after made field goal until opponent is positioned out of bounds. Bench selection is by home team, not coin toss. Women's Basketball Coaches Association has membership on U. S. Girls' and Women's Basketball Rules Committee, which had been formed in 1979.

1984-85 - After two major research studies, committee legislates a smaller ball, about one inch less in circumference (becoming 28½ to 29 inches) and two ounces lighter (18 to 20 ounces) than the previous ball. (This is the same weight recommended by the original women's committee in 1899.) Also, slapping ball in hand of inbounder is technical foul—no warning. Technical foul on bench also charged to head coach. All three and four free-throw awards are deleted.

1985-86 - Formation of the NCAA Women's Basketball Rules Committee is approved at the 1985 NCAA Convention. The first changes determined by this group include: Offensive fouls only are on the player with ball—not the entire team. Fumble, dribble, fumble is allowed. Bottom lane space on free throw must be filled—no longer optional.

1986-87 - Coaches must stay in the coaching box and may not leave without the chance of a technical foul. Alternating possession arrow is introduced—jump ball to start game and overtimes. Only head coach may stand during live ball.

1987-88 - Three-point field goal is introduced and set at 19 feet, 9 inches from center of basket (after a year of experimentation). No goal is allowed when personal foul is committed by airborne shooter. Interrupted dribble is legal. Only the four marked lane spaces on the free-throw lane may be occupied. Men's and women's rules are in one rule book for first time.

1988-89 - Intentional foul is two shots plus possession. Any squad member who participates in a fight will be ejected from the game and will be placed on probation. If that player participates in a second fight during the season, she will be suspended for one game. A third fight involving the same person results in suspension for the rest of the season including championship competition.

1989-90 - Closely-guarded distance while holding the ball is six feet, not three. Timeouts 75 seconds, not 60. Technical fouls of any kind are two shots.

1990-91 - Three free throws for foul in act of shooting three-pointer if shot is missed. All alternating possessions inbound at closest spot. Goaltending a free throw is a technical foul.

1991-92 - Contact technical fouls count toward a player's five fouls for disqualification and toward the bonus. The shot clock will be reset when the ball hits the rim instead of when the ball leaves the shooter's hand. The fighting rule is amended. The first time any squad member or bench personnel participates in a fight she will be suspended for the team's next game. If that same person participates in a second fight, she will be suspended for the rest of the season including championship competition.

1992-93 - Unsporting technical fouls, in addition to contact technical fouls, count toward the five fouls for player disqualification and toward the team fouls in reaching bonus free-throw situations.

1993-94 - A foul shall be ruled intentional if, while playing the ball, a player causes excessive contact (hard foul) with an opponent.

- The game clock will be stopped after successful field goals in the last minute of the game and the last minute of any overtime period with no substitution allowed.
- The rule concerning the use of profanity is expanded to include abusive and obscene language in an effort to curtail verbal misconduct by players and coaches.

RESULTS/SCHEDULES

Loyola Marymount's Amy Lundquist led the Lions to a 14-12 record in 1992-93. Lundquist set a Division I record for blocked shots in a game when she rejected 15 shots against Western Illinios. The Lions had 18 blocks in that game, tying the Division I

1993 Women's Basketball Scores

Following is an alphabetical listing of the 1992-93 season's game-by-game scores for the women's teams of the member colleges and universities of the National Collegiate Athletic Association whose records were available at press time.

Squares (■) indicate home games, daggers (†) indicate neutral-site games and section symbols (§) forfeits. Games played and subsequently forfeited do not alter records.

All records are restricted to games between four-year college institutions.

ABILENE CHRISTIAN 18-9
71 † Southwest Baptist .. 69
49 † Arkansas Tech 86
73 ■ Adams St. 68
69 ■ Mississippi Col. 60
56 Wayland Bapt. 83
48 † Pittsburg St. 53
67 Southwest Baptist .. 62
90 ■ Northeast Mo. St. .. 47
60 Fort Lewis 64
80 Adams St. 76
87 Southern Colo. 69
80 ■ Texas A&I 62
84 ■ East Tex. St. 79
81 Cameron 63
91 Central Okla. 98
66 Angelo St. 71
72 Texas Woman's 70
68 Eastern N. Mex. 70
64 ■ Eastern N. Mex. 88
92 ■ Texas Woman's 75
84 East Tex. St. 74
74 Texas A&I 85
102 ■ Central Okla. 93
82 ■ Cameron 77
75 ■ Angelo St. 59
85 ■ Central Okla. 80
90 ■ Eastern N. Mex. 79

ADAMS ST. 9-18
70 Western N. Mex. ... 90
83 Fort Lewis 77
68 Abilene Christian ... 73
76 † Texas A&I 94
56 Wyoming 74
78 Air Force 63
57 Colo. Christian 68
94 ■ Fort Lewis 64
105 ■ Colorado Col. 51
78 ■ Western N. Mex. .. 111
76 ■ Abilene Christian ... 80
80 ■ Colo. Christian 67
65 Mesa St. 81
79 Western St. 85
67 ■ N.M. Highlands 77
87 ■ Colorado Mines 56
74 ■ Chadron St. 85
70 ■ Fort Hays St. 80
62 ■ Tarleton St. 64
74 Colorado Col. 71
78 Colorado Mines 68
79 N.M. Highlands 86
56 Chadron St. 84
62 Fort Hays St. 76
83 ■ Western St. 73
73 ■ Mesa St. 78
51 † Fort Hays St. 58

ADELPHI 17-10
60 West Chester 76
63 Bloomsburg 87
69 ■ Southern Conn. St. . 47
68 St. Rose 58
47 Stonehill 82
62 † Franklin Pierce 88
55 ■ Queens (N.Y.) 49
59 Phila. Textile 73
74 Mercy 58
43 Pace 66
61 ■ LIU-C.W. Post 58
68 Concordia (N.Y.) ... 53
72 ■ Dowling 41
80 LIU-Southampton .. 65
81 ■ Molloy 56
61 ■ Phila. Textile 71
79 ■ St. Rose 76
80 ■ LIU-Southampton .. 50
72 Queens (N.Y.) 67
55 Dowling 65
45 ■ Pace 67
57 LIU-C.W. Post 48
75 ■ Concordia (N.Y.) ... 57
61 Molloy 58
73 ■ Mercy 58
77 ■ LIU-C.W. Post 64
56 † Pace 84

ADRIAN 19-7
102 ■ Bethel (Ind.) 55
94 ■ Spring Arbor 84
97 ■ Concordia (Mich.) .. 77
67 Ohio Northern 73
81 ■ Siena Heights 60
56 † Defiance 59
76 † Bethany (W.Va.) 53
81 † Indiana Tech 83
113 † Taylor 60
79 Saginaw Valley 97
66 ■ Northwood 51
82 ■ Alma 71
71 ■ Calvin 82
76 Albion 66
74 ■ Hope 60
104 ■ Olivet 52
79 Bluffton 54
76 Kalamazoo 60
71 ■ Kalamazoo 64
86 Olivet 47
76 Hope 66
81 Calvin 88
75 ■ Albion 74
76 Alma 74
86 ■ Olivet 55
55 ■ Alma 80

AIR FORCE 14-13
64 Northern Colo. 56
87 ■ Colorado Mines 42
68 † Cal St. Stanislaus .. 72
52 Cal St. Hayward 36
63 ■ Adams St. 78
61 New Mexico 76
72 ■ Eastern N. Mex. 77
81 Rollins 69
60 Florida Tech 102
64 † Bryant 74
89 ■ Western St. 47
60 ■ Denver 72
50 ■ Metropolitan St. 58
69 Colo. Christian 56
58 ■ Colorado-CS 66
47 Regis (Colo.) 64
81 Southern Colo. 65
79 ■ Fort Lewis 66
80 ■ Colorado Col. 37
69 Denver 75
43 Metropolitan St. 71
59 ■ Colo. Christian 51
64 Colorado-CS 90
63 ■ Regis (Colo.) 60
71 ■ Southern Colo. 61
63 Fort Lewis 58
73 ■ West Tex. St. 50

AKRON 4-22
78 Niagara 97
45 American 54
70 ■ Buffalo 60
50 † N.C.-Greensboro ... 68
62 † Western Caro. 66
65 ■ Austin Peay 63
64 Youngstown St. 71
48 ■ Bowling Green 84
38 ■ Miami (Ohio) 70
65 Eastern Mich. 54
61 ■ Western Mich. 63
50 Toledo 64
52 ■ Ohio 77
55 Kent 83
50 ■ Central Mich. 80
47 Ball St. 66
58 Miami (Ohio) 77
60 ■ Eastern Mich. 67
67 Western Mich. 78
69 ■ Toledo 84
61 Ohio 70
64 ■ Kent 109
64 Central Mich. 78
87 ■ Cincinnati 85
47 ■ Ball St. 50
57 Bowling Green 102

ALABAMA 22-9
91 † Delta St. 71
72 Louisiana Tech 93
70 ■ Vanderbilt 87
111 ■ Austin Peay 79
117 ■ Grambling 51
68 ■ Clemson 79
103 † Georgia Tech 101
71 St. Joseph's (Pa.) .. 64
75 Florida 81
95 ■ Xavier (Ohio) 76
82 ■ South Caro. 67
74 Louisiana St. 69
94 South Ala. 65
91 Mercer 69
74 ■ Tennessee 86
90 ■ Tulane 74
73 Kentucky 77
107 ■ Loyola (Ill.) 64
102 Mississippi St. 89
94 ■ Appalachian St. 64
93 ■ Mississippi 74
67 Auburn 93
66 ■ Arkansas 56
122 ■ Oral Roberts 52
67 Georgia 50
80 Alabama St. 57
106 † Louisiana St. 86
88 † Florida 73
72 † Georgia 76
102 ■ Ga. Southern 70
73 North Caro. 74

ALABAMA A&M 17-9
77 Miles 45
64 Livingston 79
77 ■ Albany St. (Ga.) 65
133 LeMoyne-Owen 55
73 Mississippi Col. 89
80 Paine 65
63 Albany St. (Ga.) 64
74 Jacksonville St. ... 112
66 ■ Savannah St. 69
74 ■ Fort Valley St. 85
94 ■ Tuskegee 89
95 Clark Atlanta 49
90 ■ Morris Brown 70
83 Tuskegee 84
93 ■ Miles 65
85 ■ Jacksonville St. 70
90 ■ Mississippi-Women 53
92 Morris Brown 71
101 ■ Ala.-Huntsville 87
80 ■ Talladega 60
92 ■ Knoxville 48
80 ■ Paine 55
100 ■ Lane 67
73 Mississippi-Women 75
97 ■ LeMoyne-Owen 44
64 † Albany St. (Ga.) 69

ALABAMA ST. 8-19
68 Florida A&M 74
59 † Toledo 68
52 † Tennessee St. 71
32 Florida 95
68 Ala.-Birmingham ... 86
60 † Mercer 77
68 Texas Southern 47
74 Prairie View 47
68 Troy St. 73
55 ■ Southern-B.R. 68
57 ■ Alcorn St. 66
35 Clemson 92
67 Mississippi Val. 50
68 ■ Grambling 69
80 ■ Jackson St. 61
58 Aub.-Montgomery .. 83
59 ■ Southeastern La. 53
58 ■ Texas Southern 61
70 ■ Prairie View 34
69 Southern-B.R. 62
57 Alcorn St. 73
62 ■ Troy St. 44
57 ■ Mississippi Val. 58
77 Grambling 87
50 Jackson St. 51
57 ■ Alabama 80
63 † Jackson St. 64

ALA.-BIRMINGHAM 9-18
71 † San Diego 68
65 Nevada-Las Vegas . 80
48 Southern Miss. 72
46 Auburn 65
77 South Ala. 74

83 ■ Mississippi Val. 65
63 ■ Wake Forest 72
52 Arkansas St. 80
86 ■ Alabama St. 68
63 ■ N.C.-Charlotte 72
60 ■ Southern Miss. 61
49 ■ Mississippi 66
65 Memphis St. 67
53 ■ Auburn 63
71 St. Louis 46
72 ■ Marquette 86
61 ■ DePaul 77
75 Cincinnati 76
70 Marquette 81
72 ■ Arkansas St. 74
91 ■ Memphis St. 72
78 Mississippi St. 81
47 DePaul 74
68 ■ St. Louis 46
91 Cincinnati 62
67 ■ South Ala. 61
69 Memphis St. 79

ALA.-HUNTSVILLE 6-18

71 Bryan 61
44 Mobile 75
57 Spring Hill 70
72 ■ Livingston 88
70 ■ Troy St. 99
62 Belmont 84
65 Ga. Southwestern 75
49 † Valdosta St. 71
61 Jacksonville St. 87
64 West Fla. 66
64 ■ Shorter 63
65 North Ala. 92
58 ■ Aub.-Montgomery 85
60 Lincoln Memorial 79
66 Talladega 58
59 Shorter 78
70 ■ Mississippi-Women 73
77 ■ Talladega 59
87 Alabama A&M 101
50 ■ Lincoln Memorial 73
72 ■ North Ala. 87
67 Troy St. 94
100 Stillman 44
72 Mississippi-Women 70

ALAS. ANCHORAGE 11-15

77 ■ Edinboro 76
64 ■ Edinboro 73
82 ■ Eastern N. Mex. 93
59 ■ Eastern N. Mex. 83
67 † St. Martin's 74
58 Pac. Lutheran 62
85 ■ Southern Ind. 93
102 ■ Southern Ind. 84
97 Cal St. Hayward 62
56 † Washburn 67
81 † Cal Poly SLO 65
98 ■ Norwich 51
95 ■ Norwich 49
74 ■ Alas. Fairbanks 57
76 Portland St. 92
54 Seattle Pacific 80
64 Alas. Fairbanks 59
90 ■ Grand Canyon 77
65 ■ Eastern Mont. 67
69 Eastern Mont. 53
47 Grand Canyon 75
51 ■ Portland St. 65
64 ■ Seattle Pacific 77
65 ■ Hawaii 80
73 ■ Northeastern Ill. 69
60 ■ Southern Methodist 68

ALAS. FAIRBANKS 9-17

73 ■ Sheldon Jackson 52
89 ■ Edinboro 66
85 ■ Edinboro 78
61 ■ Eastern N. Mex. 80
75 ■ Eastern N. Mex. 74
52 Northern Ky. 91
44 † North Dak. 76
81 ■ Southern Ind. 59
74 ■ Southern Ind. 66
59 Cal Poly Pomona 74
65 UC Riverside 76
59 Christ-Irvine 76
58 Cal St. Los Angeles 68
59 Seattle Pacific 92
75 ■ Norwich 66
93 ■ Norwich 59
57 Alas. Anchorage 74
58 Seattle Pacific 63
35 Portland St. 86
59 ■ Alas. Anchorage 64
72 ■ Grand Canyon 54
59 ■ Eastern Mont. 66
74 Grand Canyon 77
54 Eastern Mont. 78
62 ■ Seattle Pacific 64
67 ■ Portland St. 82

ALBANY (N.Y.) 14-9

72 † Rensselaer 56
55 Skidmore 67
61 Binghamton 69
97 ■ William Smith 91
56 ■ New York U. 64
66 Ithaca 63
63 Plattsburgh St. 67
73 Buffalo St. 66
60 New York U. 76
66 ■ Hunter 41
56 Rensselaer 70
74 ■ Staten Island 38
66 ■ Norwich 64
80 ■ Union (N.Y.) 50
77 ■ Cortland St. 48
70 Stony Brook 63
85 ■ Utica 38
53 ■ Western Conn. St. 60
103 Keuka 85
51 Hamilton 65
76 ■ Nazareth (N.Y.) 69
53 ■ Skidmore 43
51 † Rochester 61

ALBANY ST. (GA.) 17-10

62 † Talladega 49
87 † Knoxville 59
77 Hampton 72
49 † Fort Valley St. 76
68 Augusta 65
104 LeMoyne-Owen 45
65 Alabama A&M 77
86 Clark Atlanta 40
76 Morris Brown 58
64 ■ Alabama A&M 63
91 ■ LeMoyne-Owen 37
75 Fort Valley St. 66
64 ■ Fla. Atlantic 74
69 Paine 54
92 ■ Morris Brown 46
71 Troy St. 89
45 ■ Clark Atlanta 35
55 ■ Paine 46
71 ■ Fort Valley St. 76
75 Miles 50
63 Savannah St. 66
65 Tuskegee 69
50 ■ Savannah St. 63
59 Fla. Atlantic 84
70 ■ Troy St. 69
69 † Alabama A&M 64
75 † Fort Valley St. 86

ALBERTUS MAGNUS 16-7

84 ■ Salve Regina 42
51 ■ Trinity (Conn.) 68
59 John Jay 30
54 Norwich 67
73 † Old Westbury 49
76 Teiko Post 60
84 ■ Johnson & Wales 43
73 ■ Notre Dame (N.H.) 32
40 ■ Ramapo 83
40 ■ Southern Conn. St. 57
39 Westfield St. 53
61 Teiko Post 54
57 Connecticut Col. 59
58 Rivier 47
68 ■ Bridgeport 53
58 ■ Mt. St. Vincent 45
58 ■ Colby-Sawyer 31
71 ■ Wesleyan 67
60 Bridgeport 48
63 ■ Coast Guard 51
64 ■ Rivier 43
54 ■ Elms 48
50 Western New Eng. 66

ALBION 12-13

49 † Mount Union 51
47 † Brockport St. 58
65 Spring Arbor 85
48 † Manchester 51
102 † Berea 104
68 ■ Manchester 62
55 † St. John Fisher 59
62 † Bluffton 54
70 ■ Madonna 62
67 ■ Calvin 74
76 ■ Olivet 61
71 Hope 69
66 ■ Adrian 76
76 Kalamazoo 71
45 Alma 58
64 St. Mary's (Ind.) 62
70 Calvin 77
78 ■ Siena Heights 56
68 ■ Alma 71
75 ■ Kalamazoo 62
79 ■ Hope 67
74 Adrian 75
66 Olivet 57
72 ■ Hope 62
70 Calvin 86

ALBRIGHT 10-13

57 † Juniata 91
62 † York (Pa.) 55
75 ■ Dickinson 79
59 ■ Ursinus 83
55 Muhlenberg 73
77 ■ Widener 45
71 ■ Western Md. 60
50 Moravian 67
60 Swarthmore 38
66 ■ Delaware Valley 52
57 ■ Haverford 35
60 ■ Elizabethtown 112
64 Wilkes 70
46 Ursinus 66
75 ■ Swarthmore 40
65 Messiah 55
75 ■ Susquehanna 87
62 Widener 47
81 Lebanon Valley 87
59 ■ Moravian 91
57 ■ Muhlenberg 64
54 Haverford 42
65 Gettysburg 74

ALCORN ST. 16-8

70 Louisiana Tech 110
70 † Delta St. 69
93 ■ Texas Col. 51
50 Mississippi 54
54 † McNeese St. 78
79 South Ala. 90
74 † Howard 54
73 ■ Mississippi Val. 57
72 ■ Grambling 68
75 Jackson St. 67
66 Alabama St. 57
89 Prairie View 66
61 Texas Southern 58
76 Southern-B.R. 75
97 Mississippi Val. 90
86 Grambling 82
89 ■ Jackson St. 76
73 ■ Alabama St. 57
104 Texas Col. 64
82 ■ Prairie View 39
73 ■ Texas Southern 76
64 ■ Arkansas St. 65
69 ■ Southern-B.R. 70
88 † Texas Southern 90

ALFRED 4-21

46 ■ Binghamton 61
61 ■ Nazareth (N.Y.) 79
42 † Colby 60
51 Nichols 54
33 ■ Houghton 75
34 ■ Clarkson 53
63 ■ St. Lawrence 49
50 ■ Buffalo St. 77
52 Nazareth (N.Y.) 67
67 Ithaca 63
66 ■ Russell Sage 59
43 Penn St.-Behrend 74
54 William Smith 78
40 Rochester Inst. 61
65 ■ Keuka 73
45 ■ Rensselaer 57
91 ■ Hartwick 99
60 St. Lawrence 65
44 Clarkson 52
44 ■ Ithaca 60
47 Hartwick 87
43 Rensselaer 64
54 ■ Elmira 51
52 ■ Rochester Inst. 65
44 ■ William Smith 60

ALLEGHENY 11-15

70 † King's (Pa.) 72
71 † Phila. Pharmacy 45
60 ■ Penn St.-Behrend 76
76 † Dickinson 71
54 Marietta 78
75 Case Reserve 64
59 ■ Ohio Wesleyan 71
57 Thiel 60
90 ■ Oberlin 49
87 Wash. & Jeff. 98
82 Earlham 80
71 Kenyon 46
60 ■ Wittenberg 79
62 Wooster 85
75 ■ Denison 60
44 Ohio Wesleyan 72
88 Oberlin 28
76 ■ Earlham 77
56 ■ Wooster 64
51 Wittenberg 64
52 ■ Case Reserve 67
56 Denison 70
59 Carnegie Mellon 56
76 ■ Kenyon 35
69 Wooster 50
51 † Wittenberg 70

ALLENTOWN 14-12

74 † Potsdam St. 70
67 Muhlenberg 66
54 Kutztown 70
98 ■ Widener 41
56 † Scranton 77
50 Ithaca 67
96 ■ Lycoming 82
60 Delaware Valley 81
74 ■ Hunter 52
73 Muhlenberg 85
63 Wilkes 74
97 ■ Haverford 37
73 ■ Salisbury St. 75
78 ■ Lincoln (Pa.) 43
51 Frostburg St. 59
67 Shenandoah 39
69 ■ King's (Pa.) 73
61 ■ Moravian 68
86 ■ Elizabethtown 95

79 Salisbury St. 74
97 Lincoln (Pa.) 54
88 ■ Ursinus 71
72 ■ Frostburg St. 62
75 ■ Shenandoah 57
81 † Shenandoah 50
64 Frostburg St. 72

ALMA 16-9
63 ■ Capital 66
78 Northern Mich. 81
80 ■ Concordia (Mich.) 66
56 † Indiana Tech 70
61 Oakland 101
59 ■ Madonna 49
75 ■ Spring Arbor 63
69 † Northwood 47
45 † Ferris St. 57
91 Olivet 52
72 Hope 56
58 ■ Albion 45
59 ■ Hope 50
97 ■ Olivet 47
71 Adrian 82
66 Kalamazoo 42
85 ■ Calvin 70
62 Aquinas 47
71 Albion 68
75 ■ Kalamazoo 46
61 Calvin 62
74 ■ Adrian 76
61 ■ Kalamazoo 39
80 Adrian 55
64 Calvin 72

AMERICAN 15-13
78 ■ Md.-East. Shore 56
54 Maryland 93
54 ■ Akron 45
74 Md.-Balt. County 71
74 ■ Rider 67
66 Georgetown 69
47 † Towson St. 48
58 St. Francis (Pa.) 69
67 ■ Charleston 38
52 Geo. Washington 75
76 William & Mary 70
56 ■ Old Dominion 66
62 East Caro. 70
79 N.C.-Wilmington 76
68 George Mason 57
75 ■ James Madison 69
70 Richmond 52
73 ■ Drexel 53
78 ■ William & Mary 68
49 Old Dominion 75
61 ■ East Caro. 71
76 ■ N.C.-Wilmington 56
42 ■ George Mason 57
53 James Madison 60
84 ■ Pennsylvania 80
62 ■ Richmond 68
59 † Richmond 57
60 † William & Mary 83

AMERICAN INT'L 18-11
79 Southern Conn. St. 62
62 Franklin Pierce 63
63 Stonehill 60
68 ■ Quinnipiac 58
70 New Haven 49
58 ■ New Hamp. Col. 53
68 † Sacred Heart 61
84 † East Stroudsburg 55
71 Mass.-Lowell 91
58 St. Michael's 74
88 ■ Merrimack 81
68 ■ Springfield 42
76 St. Anselm 71
64 Assumption 63
90 ■ Bryant 71
51 Quinnipiac 70
62 ■ Bentley 76
57 ■ Stonehill 60
88 Merrimack 68
68 Springfield 60
98 ■ St. Anselm 77
70 ■ Keene St. 84
71 ■ Assumption 51
78 Bryant 82
52 Bentley 56
69 ■ St. Michael's 72
83 ■ Quinnipiac 65
71 † Stonehill 86
86 † St. Anselm 73

AMHERST 6-17
51 ■ Westfield St. 59
57 North Adams St. 56
54 ■ Williams 58
56 Western New Eng. 62
50 † Western Conn. St. 55
56 UC San Diego 82
54 † Stony Brook 76
63 ■ Wheaton (Mass.) 86
57 ■ Mount Holyoke 40
52 ■ Babson 65
47 Gordon 42
50 Williams 65
53 Connecticut Col. 55
50 Worcester Tech 54
45 ■ Clark (Mass.) 64
62 Rensselaer 60
68 ■ Wellesley 79
53 ■ Coast Guard 40
64 Smith 55
47 Wesleyan 82
50 ■ Wesleyan 67
52 Trinity (Conn.) 67
53 Tufts 69

ANDERSON 4-17
48 Marian (Ind.) 65
100 Cedarville 71
64 Olivet (Ill.) 74
65 Purdue-Calumet 72
64 ■ Huntington 103
70 Earlham 71
72 ■ Taylor 77
54 ■ Franklin 74
72 Manchester 90
65 Hanover 92
71 ■ Goshen 59
64 DePauw 73
59 ■ Ind. Wesleyan 72
60 Taylor 76
49 ■ Manchester 72
44 Franklin 74
63 ■ Defiance 94
49 ■ Hanover 48
39 Goshen 58
53 ■ DePauw 38
72 ■ Thomas More 80

ANGELO ST. 11-16
59 Lubbock Chrst. 80
65 ■ St. Mary's (Tex.) 68
75 Lubbock Chrst. 59
64 † Portland St. 66
76 † Cal Poly SLO 69
55 † Cal St. Chico 43
57 Southern Colo. 66
60 † N.M. Highlands 74
98 ■ Northeast Mo. St. 77
78 Mary Hardin-Baylor 85
63 ■ Tex. Lutheran 56
84 St. Mary's (Tex.) 88
72 ■ East Tex. St. 76
74 ■ Texas A&I 56
72 Central Okla. 79
70 Cameron 79
71 ■ Abilene Christian 66
69 Eastern N. Mex. 87
59 Texas Woman's 52
77 ■ Texas Woman's 61
73 ■ Eastern N. Mex. 76
65 Texas A&I 46
75 East Tex. St. 91
71 ■ Cameron 77
76 ■ Central Okla. 61
59 Abilene Christian 75
69 † Central Okla. 72

ANNA MARIA 18-8
69 Nichols 50
54 Suffolk 50
56 ■ Worcester St. 45
52 Simmons 36
76 ■ Emerson-MCA 35
78 ■ Green Mountain 54
58 ■ Coast Guard 46
49 Fitchburg St. 95
55 Roger Williams 42
75 Wentworth Inst. 46
47 ■ Regis (Mass.) 49
59 ■ Salve Regina 50
62 ■ MIT 50
75 ■ Eastern Nazarene 57
51 New England Col. 66
47 ■ Curry 46
61 ■ Wentworth Inst. 40
79 ■ New England Col. 69
65 Rivier 63
40 Regis (Mass.) 58
51 Salve Regina 59
39 Curry 41
50 Eastern Nazarene 36
79 ■ Roger Williams 45
46 ■ Salve Regina 60
39 Elms 54

APPALACHIAN ST. 10-17
100 ■ N.C.-Asheville 49
70 † Evansville 79
74 † St. Peter's 64
90 ■ Campbell 84
72 Georgia Tech 110
76 Duke 79
79 † Michigan 71
63 Miami (Fla.) 80
64 † Florida Int'l 93
94 ■ Tenn.-Martin 67
65 Wake Forest 78
77 East Tenn. St. 75
61 Marshall 71
91 ■ N.C.-Greensboro 61
77 Ga. Southern 96
77 Tenn.-Chatt. 84
81 ■ Furman 85
88 ■ Western Caro. 80
64 Alabama 94
91 ■ East Tenn. St. 94
80 ■ Marshall 47
64 ■ Ga. Southern 72
67 ■ Tenn.-Chatt. 68
73 Furman 92
108 Western Caro. 74
87 ■ East Caro. 89
56 † Ga. Southern 66

ARIZONA 13-14
63 ■ Vanderbilt 73
57 Texas 81
77 Southwest Tex. St. 83
84 ■ UC Irvine 64
80 ■ Northern Ill. 75
76 ■ Western Mich. 48
70 ■ Providence 68
89 ■ Michigan St. 46
54 ■ Southern Cal 68
77 ■ UCLA 91
75 ■ San Diego St. 58
68 Washington 82
64 Washington St. 55
72 ■ Arizona St. 73
79 ■ Oregon 70
69 ■ Oregon St. 62
52 Stanford 69
73 California 72
72 ■ Washington St. 64
69 ■ Washington 72
58 Arizona St. 75
63 Oregon St. 49
63 Oregon 77
74 ■ California 81
60 ■ Stanford 79
91 UCLA 83
62 Southern Cal 78

ARIZONA ST. 17-10
79 Nebraska 86
83 ■ Grand Canyon 30
119 ■ Marquette 72
91 New Mexico 36
72 ■ Southern Ill. 43
71 † Mississippi 72
97 † Northeastern 54
79 ■ Western Mich. 69
81 ■ Montana St. 42
63 ■ UCLA 81
72 ■ Southern Cal 86
70 Washington St. 59
82 Washington 77
73 Arizona 72
79 ■ Oregon St. 66
79 ■ Oregon 42
66 California 70
80 Stanford 85
74 ■ Washington 61
88 ■ Washington St. 68
75 ■ Arizona 58
77 Oregon 63
71 Oregon St. 81
76 ■ Stanford 86
74 ■ California 79
64 Southern Cal 55
71 UCLA 72

ARKANSAS 13-14
55 Southwest Mo. St. 64
102 ■ North Texas 58
80 ■ Butler 66
67 Colorado 94
47 DePaul 71
75 Loyola (Ill.) 70
70 ■ Texas-Arlington 43
84 ■ Washington St. 62
73 ■ Mississippi 72
47 Oklahoma St. 62
49 Auburn 68
71 Georgia 91
60 ■ Florida 68
63 ■ Oklahoma 70
45 ■ Kentucky 43
73 South Caro. St. 59
51 South Caro. 76
82 ■ Memphis St. 60
59 ■ Vanderbilt 80
69 Louisiana St. 66
80 ■ Mississippi St. 51
62 Northwestern (La.) 77
56 Alabama 66
82 ■ Jackson St. 39
55 ■ Tennessee 72
96 ■ Oral Roberts 60
73 † Georgia 84

ARKANSAS ST. 25-8
58 † Stephen F. Austin 78
60 † Oklahoma St. 61
82 † Portland 56
62 ■ Mississippi 61
82 Northeast La. 79
80 ■ Mississippi Val. 62
85 ■ Southern-B.R. 59
76 ■ Oklahoma 63
80 ■ Ala.-Birmingham 52
63 South Ala. 42
68 ■ Southwestern La. 51
74 ■ Tex.-Pan American 44
66 ■ New Orleans 54
57 Lamar 49
93 Tex.-Pan American 43
86 Mississippi Val. 59
53 ■ Louisiana Tech 54
58 New Orleans 55
57 ■ Lamar 40
74 Ala.-Birmingham 72
77 Mississippi St. 72

102	Southwestern La.	63
66	Louisiana Tech	72
83	■ South Ala.	34
67	Western Ky.	77
65	Alcorn St.	64
63	Oklahoma St.	71
53	■ Western Ky.	63
70	† Tex.-Pan American	53
70	† Western Ky.	73
68	† Geo. Washington	60
80	† Marquette	65
67	† Southern Methodist	54

ARMSTRONG ST. 16-10

68	North Ga.	53
67	† Cumberland (Ky.)	68
62	■ Brewton Parker	55
70	■ Presbyterian	74
58	Brewton Parker	80
75	■ St. Leo	53
69	■ North Ga.	65
58	Voorhees	33
67	St. Leo	49
68	■ Georgia Col.	51
57	S.C.-Spartanburg	83
63	Lander	53
62	Columbus	69
49	■ Augusta	62
73	■ Pembroke St.	61
56	Francis Marion	39
65	S.C.-Aiken	57
57	Augusta	69
68	■ S.C.-Spartanburg	79
82	■ Columbus	56
52	■ Francis Marion	42
75	■ Lander	44
74	Pembroke St.	42
71	■ S.C.-Aiken	59
63	Georgia Col.	69
60	† Columbus	70

ARMY 12-15

46	Hartford	73
58	Duquesne	62
69	Robert Morris	64
43	■ Marist	51
57	Princeton	61
67	† Tex.-Pan American	57
48	Rice	55
63	■ Columbia-Barnard	56
60	Navy	50
54	■ Holy Cross	52
49	Fordham	59
37	Bucknell	51
72	■ Lehigh	60
42	Yale	52
68	Colgate	54
50	■ Lafayette	51
67	■ Navy	62
44	Holy Cross	57
54	■ Fordham	68
63	■ Hofstra	48
59	■ Bucknell	50
37	Rutgers	63
63	Lehigh	59
76	■ Colgate	62
69	Harvard	78
54	Lafayette	55
46	■ Bucknell	50

ASBURY 2-21

45	Thomas More	89
40	Heidelberg	91
39	† Waynesburg	98
60	■ Transylvania	97
79	■ Wilmington (Ohio)	84
60	■ Alice Lloyd	69
73	■ Malone	86
59	Berea	81
84	■ Lake Erie	69
91	■ Thomas More	99
55	Midway	73
72	Hanover	81
43	Transylvania	100
63	St. Catherine	81
42	Franklin	93
79	Ky. Christian	82
51	Capital	91
80	■ Ky. Christian	65
57	Wilmington (Ohio)	114
70	■ Berea	107
84	■ Midway	97
69	Brescia	89
71	■ St. Catherine	77

ASHLAND 13-13

62	Wayne St. (Mich.)	60
61	Findlay	79
65	Mercyhurst	59
62	■ Gannon	56
62	Pitt.-Johnstown	53
79	■ Clarion	88
54	■ Northern Ky.	63
60	■ Indianapolis	78
62	Southern Ind.	79
71	Ky. Wesleyan	60
66	■ Edinboro	61
69	■ IU/PU-Ft. Wayne	64
83	■ Kentucky St.	55
57	■ Bellarmine	73
62	St. Joseph's (Ind.)	78
67	Lewis	73
58	■ Ky. Wesleyan	64
72	■ Southern Ind.	70
68	Hillsdale	58
51	IU/PU-Ft. Wayne	67
63	Bellarmine	76
101	Kentucky St.	51
66	■ Lewis	50
84	■ St. Joseph's (Ind.)	74
56	Indianapolis	68
49	Northern Ky.	74

ASSUMPTION 10-16

82	■ New Haven	90
82	■ Sacred Heart	61
55	Quinnipiac	56
83	■ Springfield	59
73	Mass.-Lowell	66
61	■ Franklin Pierce	68
46	Fla. Atlantic	100
62	Barry	54
76	■ New Hamp. Col.	75
68	Merrimack	80
89	■ Bridgeport	74
66	St. Michael's	82
55	■ Bentley	76
67	Bryant	70
63	■ American Int'l	64
68	■ St. Anselm	84
84	Springfield	67
75	Stonehill	77
68	■ Quinnipiac	61
62	■ St. Michael's	73
50	Bentley	62
75	■ Bryant	69
51	American Int'l	71
76	St. Anselm	77
46	■ Stonehill	82
71	■ Merrimack	60

AUBURN 25-4

78	■ Aub.-Montgomery	58
59	Richmond	56
54	Va. Commonwealth	53
65	■ Ala.-Birmingham	46
57	Mississippi	47
68	Northeastern Ill.	42
56	DePaul	52
74	■ Furman	61
68	■ Wis.-Milwaukee	41
81	■ Houston	51
68	■ Arkansas	49
59	■ Tennessee	70
52	Kentucky	49
63	Ala.-Birmingham	53
83	Louisiana St.	59
54	■ New Orleans	50
72	■ Mississippi St.	64
62	■ Florida Int'l	50
84	■ South Ala.	41
82	Georgia	56
71	■ Southern Miss.	57
79	Florida	64
93	■ Alabama	67
55	■ Vanderbilt	53
78	■ Oral Roberts	42
47	South Caro.	59
55	† Mississippi	69
66	■ Louisville	61
50	Iowa	63

AUGSBURG 2-23

63	Wis.-Superior	94
56	St. Scholastica	70
59	■ St. Benedict	93
43	■ St. Mary's (Minn.)	70
59	Macalester	76
65	Hamline	83
51	■ Neb. Wesleyan	79
65	St. Mary's (Minn.)	60
88	■ N'western (Minn.)	75
48	Concordia-M'head	79
40	Gust. Adolphus	62
27	■ Bethel (Minn.)	60
47	■ St. Olaf	77
56	Carleton	58
30	■ St. Thomas (Minn.)	77
53	St. Benedict	91
44	■ Macalester	60
62	■ Hamline	73
52	■ Concordia-M'head	108
65	■ Gust. Adolphus	79
59	Bethel (Minn.)	73
58	■ Carleton	64
48	St. Thomas (Minn.)	87
65	St. Olaf	94
64	■ Concordia (St. Paul)	66

AUGUSTA 24-5

71	† Valdosta St.	62
63	Fort Valley St.	69
74	■ Gardner-Webb	70
80	■ Erskine	40
65	■ Albany St. (Ga.)	68
76	■ Jacksonville St.	73
64	Pembroke St.	52
97	■ Troy St.	63
64	Troy St.	80
94	■ Fort Valley St.	79
74	Lander	48
59	Georgia Col.	54
68	Francis Marion	55
62	Armstrong St.	49
67	■ S.C.-Aiken	58
73	■ Pembroke St.	54
69	■ Armstrong St.	57
56	S.C.-Spartanburg	80
76	Columbus	69
59	■ Georgia Col.	58
64	■ Lander	54
65	S.C.-Aiken	49
70	■ Francis Marion	51
70	† Paine	66
70	■ S.C.-Spartanburg	80
73	■ Columbus	52
66	■ Pembroke St.	60
73	■ Columbus	60
69	■ S.C.-Spartanburg	60

AUGUSTANA (ILL.) 19-7

54	Northeast Mo. St.	58
56	■ Illinois Col.	67
71	■ Teiko-Marycrest	61
77	North Central	62
70	■ Wis.-Whitewater	61
61	† St. Benedict	68
73	† Stony Brook	58
58	UC San Diego	46
68	■ Wheaton (Ill.)	53
60	North Park	71
64	Carthage	44
71	■ Millikin	59
68	Elmhurst	56
72	■ North Park	59
57	■ Ill. Benedictine	39
69	■ Ill. Wesleyan	40
71	■ Carthage	52
67	■ St. Ambrose	83
81	■ Rockford	28
67	■ North Central	56
63	Ill. Wesleyan	67
76	Millikin	63
79	Aurora	70
64	Wheaton (Ill.)	56
55	■ Elmhurst	40
68	Central (Iowa)	81

AUGUSTANA (S.D.) 24-5

95	Neb.-Kearney	78
127	■ Sioux Falls	69
107	■ Briar Cliff	46
94	Moorhead St.	79
78	Wayne St. (Neb.)	55
67	Cal St. San B'dino	62
106	UC Riverside	61
96	■ Bemidji St.	60
99	■ Nebraska-Omaha	72
92	■ Northern Colo.	54
68	North Dak. St.	95
59	North Dak.	68
94	■ South Dak.	73
96	■ Morningside	73
75	Mankato St.	66
115	St. Cloud St.	52
73	South Dak. St.	76
82	Northwest Mo. St.	70
90	■ North Dak.	67
92	■ North Dak. St.	83
101	Morningside	67
84	South Dak.	88
129	■ St. Cloud St.	62
79	■ Mankato St.	69
84	■ South Dak. St.	62
80	Nebraska-Omaha	60
89	Northern Colo.	74
79	† North Dak.	67
82	North Dak. St.	91

AURORA 16-9

57	Washington (Mo.)	70
81	■ Fontbonne	55
80	■ Ill. Wesleyan	60
57	North Central	55
68	† Carroll (Wis.)	77
58	■ Wheaton (Ill.)	62
76	Beloit	71
54	Carroll (Wis.)	75
81	■ Knox	59
73	■ Elmhurst	63
77	Rockford	40
78	■ Trinity (Ill.)	65
66	Ill. Benedictine	75
83	Concordia (Ill.)	75
90	■ Eureka	74
87	■ Judson	48
62	Millikin	84
57	Carthage	74
80	■ Rockford	29
78	Trinity (Ill.)	63
81	■ Ill. Benedictine	61
70	■ Augustana (Ill.)	79
74	St. Mary's (Ind.)	81
81	■ Concordia (Ill.)	71
69	Judson	57

AUSTIN PEAY 5-21

76	■ Louisville	83
61	Indiana	77
70	† Colorado St.	77
108	■ Bethel (Tenn.)	84
79	Alabama	111
65	Wright St.	70
63	Akron	65
76	Cleveland St.	89
71	■ Tenn.-Chatt.	98
87	■ Murray St.	75

63 ■ Southeast Mo. St. 70
70 ■ Tennessee Tech 109
75 Eastern Ky. 100
76 Morehead St. 64
90 ■ Tenn.-Martin 95
70 Middle Tenn. St. 91
68 Tennessee St. 85
57 Chicago St. 61
67 ■ Eastern Ky. 59
63 ■ Morehead St. 87
62 Tennessee Tech 91
65 Tenn.-Martin 55
76 Murray St. 94
45 Southeast Mo. St. 77
71 ■ Middle Tenn. St. 100
74 ■ Tennessee St. 91

AVERETT 6-18
89 St. Mary's (Md.) 76
50 † Hollins 60
68 Meredith 87
50 St. Andrews 63
45 Pfeiffer 76
63 ■ Bennett 51
58 East. Mennonite 66
55 Hollins 50
52 ■ Meredith 84
69 ■ Pfeiffer 83
50 Ferrum 74
44 ■ N.C. Wesleyan 54
87 ■ Mary Baldwin 53
57 Chris. Newport 85
74 ■ Greensboro 87
61 Methodist 75
77 ■ Ferrum 78
53 ■ Hollins 48
52 N.C. Wesleyan 78
55 ■ Chris. Newport 84
83 Mary Baldwin 53
50 Greensboro 61
63 ■ Methodist 73
51 Chris. Newport 92

BABSON 23-5
78 ■ Framingham St. 31
90 ■ Salve Regina 58
57 ■ Tufts 60
85 ■ Union (N.Y.) 57
84 ■ Clark (Mass.) 77
71 Curry 43
71 ■ Coast Guard 52
85 Pine Manor 74
65 Amherst 52
69 Brandeis 70
74 ■ Bowdoin 40
74 ■ St. Joseph's (Me.) 75
96 Emmanuel 80
60 ■ Wellesley 51
66 Salem St. 78
74 ■ Bates 63
83 ■ Smith 63
83 ■ Wheaton (Mass.) 73
88 ■ Regis (Mass.) 57
71 Mount Holyoke 60
72 MIT 52
96 Trinity (Conn.) 84
61 ■ Worcester Tech 60
85 ■ MIT 63
81 † Brandeis 69
63 † Wellesley 56
86 Western Conn. St. 68
56 ■ Capital 68

BALDWIN-WALLACE 15-10
80 ■ Grove City 69
62 † Alvernia 59
43 St. John Fisher 42
59 John Carroll 75
73 ■ Muskingum 78
49 Ohio Northern 62
66 ■ Marietta 49
58 ■ Defiance 50
79 ■ Bluffton 62
65 ■ Hiram 34
40 Capital 67
63 ■ Mount Union 56
76 Otterbein 62
64 ■ Heidelberg 67
85 Wilberforce 48
64 Hiram 50
68 ■ John Carroll 70
76 ■ Ohio Northern 65
68 Muskingum 71
92 Marietta 81
63 Heidelberg 59
50 ■ Capital 67
58 Mount Union 76
82 ■ Otterbein 50
61 Heidelberg 78

BALL ST. 3-23
52 Eastern Ky. 72
41 St. Louis 52
47 ■ Indiana 74
51 ■ Purdue 70
53 Stetson 73
54 South Fla. 70
54 Miami (Ohio) 68
62 ■ Western Mich. 64
31 Ohio 42
48 ■ Central Mich. 51
51 Marquette 75
58 Bowling Green 87
41 ■ Eastern Mich. 56
38 Toledo 53
81 ■ Kent 92
66 ■ Akron 47
49 Western Mich. 68
42 ■ Ohio 68
59 Central Mich. 66
52 ■ Bowling Green 62
57 Eastern Mich. 45
46 ■ Toledo 75
40 Kent 89
50 Akron 47
56 ■ Miami (Ohio) 75
39 Bowling Green 75

BARRY 7-18
61 Fla. Memorial 78
46 Rollins 73
71 † Tampa 76
57 ■ Fla. Atlantic 89
65 ■ Fla. Memorial 53
63 ■ Northern Mich. 104
65 ■ Stonehill 85
54 ■ Assumption 62
52 ■ Molloy 58
44 ■ Transylvania 56
45 Fla. Southern 85
79 North Fla. 71
49 ■ Rollins 66
44 Florida Tech 107
78 ■ St. Leo 66
76 Eckerd 79
64 ■ Tampa 63
73 ■ North Fla. 65
40 Fla. Atlantic 103
68 Rollins 85
55 ■ Florida Tech 88
68 St. Leo 82
65 ■ Eckerd 47
63 Tampa 48
52 ■ Fla. Southern 90

BATES 9-13
43 † Wilkes 67
62 † Russell Sage 44
72 Bowdoin 51
83 ■ MIT 66
65 New England 76
80 ■ New England Col. 67
58 ■ Gordon 56
60 Southern Me. 93
77 Colby-Sawyer 37
61 Smith 49
45 † Western New Eng. 63
58 ■ Colby 68
63 Babson 74
61 ■ Me.-Farmington 66
76 ■ Wesleyan 80
79 ■ Trinity (Conn.) 78
80 ■ Bowdoin 64
75 ■ Norwich 88
70 ■ Middlebury 100
64 ■ Tufts 84
65 Connecticut Col. 77
63 Colby 70

BAYLOR 12-16
70 New Mexico St. 83
55 UTEP 71
68 † Wichita St. 70
88 † Eastern Ill. 37
76 Wyoming 67
79 Colorado St. 81
58 ■ Colorado 84
84 † Va. Commonwealth 91
110 Central Fla. 67
71 † Navy 81
81 ■ Idaho 76
83 Texas Christian 74
66 Texas 82
78 ■ Houston 54
72 Rice 71
115 ■ Prairie View 45
73 ■ Texas A&M 89
89 Southern Methodist 91
76 ■ Texas Tech 96
103 ■ Texas Christian 78
75 ■ Texas 89
73 Houston 72
77 ■ Rice 75
70 Texas A&M 92
84 ■ Southern Methodist 88
72 Texas Tech 104
63 † Texas A&M 61
67 † Texas Tech 91

BELLARMINE 18-10
53 ■ Lincoln Memorial 56
98 ■ Florida Tech 90
67 Georgetown (Ky.) 76
86 † Cal Poly SLO 68
74 † Portland St. 77
74 † Saginaw Valley 76
75 ■ Tiffin 64
71 ■ St. Joseph's (Ind.) 59
89 ■ Lewis 71
74 Indianapolis 67
80 Northern Ky. 82
90 ■ Ky. Wesleyan 61
95 ■ Southern Ind. 87
64 IU/PU-Ft. Wayne 61
73 Ashland 57
89 Campbellsville 93
90 Kentucky St. 58
75 ■ Northern Ky. 72
84 ■ Indianapolis 96
70 Southern Ind. 71
86 Ky. Wesleyan 76
76 ■ Ashland 63
86 ■ IU/PU-Ft. Wayne 68
56 Quincy 69
111 ■ Kentucky St. 47
82 St. Joseph's (Ind.) 79
87 Lewis 59
73 † Michigan Tech 92

BELOIT 16-8
46 Wis.-Whitewater 59
53 ■ Wheaton (Ill.) 55
61 ■ Ripon 40
68 ■ Carroll (Wis.) 64
71 ■ Aurora 76
73 Carthage 64
75 † Bethel (Ind.) 52
78 † Warner Southern 64
83 † Rhode Island Col. 62
86 Carroll (Wis.) 69
60 St. Norbert 68
61 Illinois Col. 63
76 Knox 62
63 Ripon 59
58 ■ Monmouth (Ill.) 50
96 ■ Cornell College 34
75 ■ Lake Forest 65
69 ■ Lawrence 60
73 ■ St. Norbert 55
64 ■ St. Mary's (Ind.) 48
67 Lake Forest 72
57 Lawrence 61
51 Illinois Col. 77
74 † Grinnell 67

BEMIDJI ST. 10-17
74 Northern Mich. 89
73 Wis.-Parkside 81
69 Lewis 71
56 Michigan Tech 77
79 ■ St. Scholastica 60
71 ■ St. Cloud St. 66
66 ■ South Dak. St. 68
71 ■ Southern Colo. 64
51 North Dak. St. 99
60 Augustana (S.D.) 96
45 South Dak. St. 73
74 ■ Wis.-Parkside 71
38 ■ Northern St. 77
65 ■ Southwest St. 67
62 ■ Minn.-Duluth 63
87 Winona St. 91
63 Northern St. 98
67 Southwest St. 56
84 ■ Moorhead St. 88
85 ■ Minn.-Morris 77
43 Minn.-Duluth 71
87 ■ Winona St. 72
92 ■ Wayne St. (Neb.) 91
87 Minn.-Morris 68
60 Moorhead St. 77
70 † Neb.-Kearney 82
75 Wayne St. (Neb.) 71

BENTLEY 30-4
69 Merrimack 53
91 ■ Bryant 43
62 Mass.-Lowell 57
75 † Lock Haven 50
60 West Chester 50
64 ■ New Haven 57
81 Keene St. 56
75 ■ Clarion 70
67 ■ Pace 57
63 New Hamp. Col. 58
84 ■ Quinnipiac 56
73 St. Anselm 72
76 Assumption 55
69 Springfield 45
70 ■ Stonehill 51
83 ■ St. Michael's 79
74 ■ Merrimack 56
76 American Int'l 62
78 Bryant 57
59 ■ St. Anselm 66
62 ■ Assumption 50
70 ■ Springfield 41
59 Stonehill 71
74 St. Michael's 66
56 ■ American Int'l 52
60 Quinnipiac 57
72 ■ Merrimack 62
72 ■ St. Anselm 49
75 ■ Stonehill 64
71 ■ Franklin Pierce 46
68 ■ Mass.-Lowell 60
84 ■ Norfolk St. 66
57 ■ North Dak. St. 79
60 ■ Michigan Tech 74

BEREA 9-11
44 Bluffton 53
104 † Albion 102
84 ■ Ind.-Southeast 88
82 ■ Centre 75
79 ■ Thomas More 84
82 Thomas More 110
64 Fisk 19

94 Ky. Christian 77
81 ■ Asbury 59
73 ■ Wilmington (Ohio) 75
79 Centre 76
48 Alice Lloyd 77
66 ■ Alice Lloyd 70
81 ■ Maryville (Tenn.) 87
81 ■ Midway 67
77 Wilmington (Ohio) 88
89 Maryville (Tenn.) 99
79 ■ Fisk 37
107 Asbury 70
81 Hanover 88

BETHANY (W.VA.) 12-12
72 Alderson-Broaddus 69
56 Clarion 138
98 Oberlin 54
67 ■ Davis & Elkins 55
83 ■ Westminster (Pa.) 56
58 ■ Point Park 55
53 Wittenberg 84
53 † Adrian 76
50 Wheeling Jesuit 92
73 Point Park 68
64 Point Park 78
76 ■ Ohio Belmont 62
79 Carlow 73
52 Penn St.-Behrend 63
49 ■ Grove City 63
81 ■ Thiel 58
57 Waynesburg 67
78 ■ Oberlin 34
70 Wash. & Jeff. 95
58 ■ Penn St.-Behrend 72
72 Grove City 76
82 Thiel 72
70 ■ Waynesburg 56
75 ■ Wash. & Jeff. 78

BETHEL (MINN.) 15-9
57 ■ Wis.-River Falls 62
75 ■ Wis.-La Crosse 53
61 ■ Minn.-Morris 69
62 Macalester 70
59 ■ St. Thomas (Minn.) 79
84 ■ Neb. Wesleyan 75
56 Concordia-M'head 88
66 St. Olaf 70
68 ■ Gust. Adolphus 53
67 St. Mary's (Minn.) 63
60 Augsburg 27
72 ■ Carleton 51
81 ■ Hamline 63
64 St. Benedict 83
62 ■ Macalester 60
62 St. Thomas (Minn.) 45
85 ■ St. Olaf 82
45 Gust. Adolphus 53
73 ■ St. Mary's (Minn.) 49
73 ■ Augsburg 59
71 Hamline 58
45 ■ St. Benedict 76
69 ■ Concordia-M'head 65
75 Carleton 55

BETHUNE-COOKMAN 9-19
72 ■ Stetson 67
65 Edward Waters 30
56 ■ Florida 64
71 Fla. Memorial 60
41 Florida Int'l 86
54 ■ Southern-B.R. 69
46 ■ George Mason 77
53 † George Mason 62
71 ■ Delaware St. 37
51 ■ Md.-East. Shore 53
72 ■ Fla. Atlantic 77
41 ■ South Caro. St. 72
72 ■ North Caro. A&T 73
76 Howard 78
44 Morgan St. 62
43 Coppin St. 56
62 South Caro. St. 73
58 North Caro. A&T 60
61 Florida A&M 74
67 ■ Howard 61
51 ■ Morgan St. 63
71 ■ Coppin St. 63
56 Delaware St. 64
49 Md.-East. Shore 51
75 ■ Fla. Memorial 68
54 ■ Florida A&M 51
62 † Md.-East. Shore 61
50 † South Caro. St. 81

BINGHAMTON 22-6
61 Alfred 46
69 ■ Albany (N.Y.) 61
66 Brockport St. 52
56 Fredonia St. 63
75 ■ New Paltz St. 61
74 ■ Plattsburgh St. 48
66 † Concordia (Mich.) 63
73 † Marian (Wis.) 68
73 Elmira 59
69 ■ Utica Tech 60
72 Oswego St. 62
71 Cortland St. 40
76 ■ Union (N.Y.) 38
58 ■ Stony Brook 61
70 ■ Oneonta St. 36
55 ■ Buffalo St. 56
72 ■ Utica 31
74 Potsdam St. 64
64 Plattsburgh St. 43
78 ■ Cortland St. 62
66 ■ Marywood 49
50 ■ Geneseo St. 65
75 Oneonta St. 48
66 ■ Hamilton 46
74 New Paltz St. 66
69 ■ Potsdam St. 72
81 ■ William Smith 77
51 ■ Ithaca 52

BLACKBURN 23-7
50 † Loras 81
64 † Graceland (Iowa) 68
75 Ill. Wesleyan 70
62 Illinois Col. 78
66 † Webster 54
65 DePauw 57
66 McKendree 69
61 ■ Eureka 65
63 ■ Maryville (Mo.) 54
84 ■ Rockford 39
59 Washington (Mo.) 70
57 Westminster 43
72 ■ Webster 58
80 ■ Principia 47
57 MacMurray 42
63 Fontbonne 45
57 Maryville (Mo.) 34
67 ■ Greenville 45
73 Principia 43
59 ■ Westminster 44
60 Webster 55
46 SIU-Edwardsville 68
65 ■ Graceland (Ind.) 56
70 ■ MacMurray 48
52 ■ Fontbonne 47
61 ■ Midway 45
84 † Webster 60
58 † Maryville (Mo.) 55
69 † Trinity (Ill.) 53
81 † Wilmington (Del.) 72

BLOOMSBURG 20-6
97 † LIU-Southampton 43
64 Kutztown 49
68 Lock Haven 62
73 ■ Phila. Textile 76
75 ■ Mercyhurst 74
87 ■ Adelphi 63
88 ■ Alvernia 48
62 Slippery Rock 67
67 Shippensburg 63
65 ■ Clarion 56
54 ■ Millersville 47
55 West Chester 63
73 Cheyney 39
75 ■ Kutztown 52
60 Susquehanna 54
64 ■ Indiana (Pa.) 47
61 Mansfield 50
74 ■ East Stroudsburg 59
73 Millersville 83
85 ■ West Chester 74
78 ■ Cheyney 48
64 Kutztown 47
59 Pitt.-Johnstown 80
72 ■ Mansfield 58
68 East Stroudsburg 58
62 ■ Edinboro 76

BLUFFTON 8-17
34 Hiram 35
53 ■ St. Francis (Ind.) 52
53 ■ Berea 44
50 ■ Manchester 49
41 Ohio Northern 52
57 Cedarville 72
43 Defiance 55
54 † Albion 62
47 ■ Heidelberg 64
62 Baldwin-Wallace 79
68 ■ Thomas More 71
50 ■ Defiance 69
40 Huntington 80
41 ■ Findlay 67
54 Wilmington (Ohio) 76
54 ■ Adrian 79
75 Thomas More 64
59 Defiance 68
66 ■ Ohio Wesleyan 54
78 ■ Grace 69
81 ■ Olivet 61
65 Denison 70
71 ■ Wilmington (Ohio) 62
74 † Wilmington (Ohio) 76
63 † Thomas More 67

BOISE ST. 19-8
82 ■ Washington 78
82 † La Salle 65
76 † Tulane 79
78 ■ California 76
87 St. Mary's (Cal.) 76
96 † UC Santa Barb. 75
91 † Minnesota 95
80 Cal St. Sacramento 69
91 ■ Oregon 78
72 Washington St. 69
75 ■ Gonzaga 69
85 ■ Northern Ariz. 48
90 ■ Weber St. 67
85 ■ Idaho St. 61
63 Montana 75
78 Montana St. 87
82 ■ Eastern Wash. 55
83 ■ Idaho 60
94 Weber St. 72
78 Northern Ariz. 70
101 Southern Utah 89
80 Idaho St. 68
70 ■ Montana 81
66 ■ Montana St. 69
64 Idaho 66
72 Eastern Wash. 59
68 † Montana 70

BOSTON COLLEGE 10-17
80 ■ Maine 65
54 † Oregon St. 89
73 † Iowa St. 45
82 Boston U. 81
65 ■ Ohio St. 104
75 Holy Cross 74
64 ■ Northeastern 59
81 ■ Iona 63
63 ■ St. John's (N.Y.) 52
51 ■ Villanova 63
69 Connecticut 81
92 Georgetown 101
72 ■ Seton Hall 64
64 Pittsburgh 69
79 Providence 103
59 ■ Syracuse 67
67 ■ Miami (Fla.) 80
58 Seton Hall 65
58 Villanova 70
52 ■ Connecticut 79
82 ■ Georgetown 95
55 Miami (Fla.) 84
59 ■ Pittsburgh 57
77 ■ Providence 70
77 St. John's (N.Y.) 79
60 Syracuse 73
71 Providence 81

BOSTON U. 10-17
75 Providence 87
53 † Mercer 71
85 † Hofstra 48
81 ■ Boston College 82
72 Harvard 81
59 Western Ky. 70
80 ■ Lafayette 58
71 ■ Brown 67
68 ■ Hartford 69
62 ■ Vermont 84
70 Dartmouth 56
59 Delaware 60
86 Drexel 66
61 ■ Maine 52
55 New Hampshire 66
76 ■ Central Conn. St. 53
48 Northeastern 52
83 Colgate 63
59 ■ New Hampshire 62
64 Maine 57
66 ■ Drexel 76
70 ■ Delaware 76
55 Hartford 67
70 Vermont 80
56 Massachusetts 63
71 ■ Northeastern 53
52 Northeastern 65

BOWDOIN 6-14
73 † Mass.-Boston 42
53 † MIT 52
51 ■ Bates 72
39 Tufts 83
65 Westbrook 56
56 ■ Me.-Presque Isle 66
64 Salem St. 87
45 † Simpson 86
40 Babson 74
60 Colby 78
61 ■ Colby-Sawyer 47
71 ■ Middlebury 75
74 ■ Thomas 79
63 ■ New England 61
62 Southern Me. 92
46 Me.-Farmington 82
64 Bates 80
65 ■ Wheaton (Mass.) 75
57 ■ Connecticut Col. 75
60 ■ Colby 52

BOWIE ST. 6-18
51 Gannon 81
51 † Saginaw Valley 83
44 Winston-Salem 38
46 Shaw 59
66 Livingstone 57
62 Md.-East. Shore 79
44 ■ Hampton 66
55 ■ St. Augustine's 72
58 ■ Fayetteville St. 75
44 Kutztown 65
48 ■ N.C. Central 63
65 ■ Johnson Smith 73
58 ■ St. Paul's 64
58 Virginia St. 73
44 ■ Norfolk St. 86

58	■ Elizabeth City St.	57
45	■ Virginia Union	58
60	Elizabeth City St.	50
69	St. Paul's	57
49	Norfolk St.	97
53	Virginia Union	79
64	■ Virginia St.	58
37	Hampton	75
60	† Fayetteville St.	61

BOWLING GREEN 25-5

65	Ohio St.	76
88	■ Wis.-Milwaukee	69
66	Vanderbilt	69
94	Dayton	68
105	† Marquette	103
78	Purdue	81
84	■ Illinois St.	70
105	■ Cincinnati	78
84	Akron	48
81	Eastern Mich.	42
88	■ Toledo	77
94	Kent	99
87	■ Ball St.	58
77	Miami (Ohio)	75
84	■ Western Mich.	59
68	Ohio	58
81	■ Central Mich.	62
93	■ Eastern Mich.	54
70	Toledo	46
81	■ Kent	78
62	Ball St.	52
77	■ Miami (Ohio)	74
91	Western Mich.	64
82	■ Ohio	55
73	Central Mich.	62
102	■ Akron	57
75	■ Ball St.	39
83	† Toledo	55
96	† Kent	68
67	■ Florida	69

BRADLEY 7-20

56	Dayton	75
47	† Central Mich.	53
75	† Texas Southern	38
58	Purdue	84
81	† Furman	87
68	† Dartmouth	59
49	■ Kentucky	78
44	■ Wake Forest	56
49	Loyola (Ill.)	54
53	■ Creighton	75
67	■ Drake	68
79	■ Northern Iowa	73
43	Southern Ill.	73
81	Indiana St.	84
94	■ Chicago St.	55
68	■ Illinois St.	83
53	Southwest Mo. St.	76
44	Wichita St.	76
77	Illinois St.	66
57	■ Wichita St.	72
53	■ Southwest Mo. St.	95
54	■ Southern Ill.	77
98	■ Indiana St.	79
83	Drake	75
75	Northern Iowa	87
59	Creighton	74
55	Southwest Mo. St.	80

BRANDEIS 11-14

73	■ Case Reserve	72
51	■ Nichols	38
56	Johns Hopkins	63
67	Rochester	55
50	Tufts	71
48	Chicago	60
50	Washington (Mo.)	71
80	■ MIT	53
70	■ Babson	69
52	■ Rochester	57
55	Smith	57
59	■ New York U.	60

63	■ Emory	69
82	■ Mount Holyoke	34
68	■ Carnegie Mellon	38
76	■ Worcester Tech	43
55	Emory	49
41	New York U.	62
56	Wheaton (Mass.)	77
51	Carnegie Mellon	59
54	■ Wellesley	61
43	■ Washington (Mo.)	58
54	■ Chicago	46
70	■ Smith	66
69	† Babson	81

BRIDGEPORT 4-20

43	St. Michael's	77
39	LIU-Southampton	70
78	Molloy	76
33	■ Pitt.-Johnstown	73
70	Teiko Post	66
38	† Rollins	76
52	† New Haven	64
62	■ Mercy	74
48	Montclair St.	56
56	■ Dominican (N.Y.)	39
43	■ Franklin Pierce	69
74	Assumption	89
66	■ Teiko Post	34
63	Lock Haven	89
39	Susquehanna	74
55	New Haven	74
29	Franklin Pierce	74
53	Albertus Magnus	68
57	LIU-C.W. Post	64
47	■ Southern Conn. St.	71
82	■ St. Thomas Aquinas	85
48	■ Albertus Magnus	60
51	Keene St.	83
43	Northeastern	77

BRIDGEWATER (VA.) 15-12

44	Marymount (Va.)	93
47	† Roanoke	60
45	† Va. Wesleyan	59
71	■ R.-M. Woman's	36
53	Hollins	45
64	Lynchburg	77
50	■ Marymount (Va.)	90
55	Guilford	49
54	■ Randolph-Macon	62
43	■ Roanoke	66
58	■ East. Mennonite	48
49	Emory & Henry	39
60	■ Frostburg St.	71
55	■ Emory & Henry	51
52	■ Guilford	47
52	Roanoke	66
68	R.-M. Woman's	35
59	■ Lynchburg	50
61	■ Va. Wesleyan	58
63	East. Mennonite	51
54	Mary Washington	64
78	■ Hollins	67
54	Randolph-Macon	74
56	Va. Wesleyan	53
73	■ Hollins	54
57	† Va. Wesleyan	47
65	† Roanoke	75

BRI'WATER (MASS.) 10-16

51	Plymouth St.	76
57	† Mount Holyoke	39
63	■ Emmanuel	99
64	■ Worcester Tech	59
56	■ Wheaton (Mass.)	75
72	Rhode Island Col.	77
52	Mass.-Dartmouth	79
61	■ Westfield St.	64
77	■ Roger Williams	33
69	Framingham St.	46
72	■ North Adams St.	60
85	■ Pine Manor	65
71	Mass.-Boston	62
62	■ Worcester St.	70

33	Salem St.	50
44	■ Fitchburg St.	61
34	■ Clark (Mass.)	86
44	Westfield St.	70
76	■ Framingham St.	27
83	North Adams St.	66
45	■ Western Conn. St.	78
64	Worcester St.	67
58	■ Salem St.	62
59	Fitchburg St.	73
77	Worcester St.	56
45	† Westfield St.	70

BRIGHAM YOUNG 24-5

89	■ Southern Utah	74
56	Montana	61
60	Montana St.	48
63	Oregon	77
74	Oregon St.	60
76	Portland	69
79	Weber St.	70
62	■ Pacific (Cal.)	65
79	■ Weber St.	42
77	■ Iowa St.	54
79	Idaho St.	70
60	■ New Mexico	48
80	■ UTEP	55
74	Colorado St.	61
78	Wyoming	75
65	■ Utah	49
72	■ Fresno St.	61
82	■ San Diego St.	73
61	UTEP	57
70	New Mexico	64
83	■ Wyoming	67
84	■ Colorado St.	71
75	Utah	66
57	San Diego St.	73
81	Fresno St.	68
82	† New Mexico	61
63	† UTEP	48
53	Utah	50
79	UC Santa Barb.	88

BROCKPORT ST. 14-11

65	Penn St.-Behrend	73
58	† Albion	47
83	■ Hilbert	53
52	■ Binghamton	66
52	Geneseo St.	77
58	■ Buffalo St.	82
55	Oneonta St.	52
71	New Paltz St.	57
60	Nazareth (N.Y.)	79
72	■ Utica	36
66	Oswego St.	52
89	■ Utica Tech	81
47	Fredonia St.	45
71	■ Plattsburgh St.	42
58	■ Potsdam St.	67
58	Buffalo St.	78
59	■ Fredonia St.	49
69	St. John Fisher	83
54	■ Roberts Wesleyan	48
61	Cortland St.	55
63	■ Oswego St.	49
74	Utica Tech	89
51	■ Geneseo St.	90
76	■ Elmira	49
68	† Cortland St.	70

BROWN 19-7

61	Rhode Island	77
60	■ Villanova	59
69	■ Vermont	81
82	Providence	65
59	† Eastern Ky.	75
80	† Lehigh	55
61	† Temple	55
67	Boston U.	71
59	New Hampshire	67
64	■ Central Conn. St.	54
69	Yale	65
52	Northeastern	61

71	■ Yale	65
77	■ Hartford	71
82	■ Cornell	63
68	■ Columbia-Barnard	46
69	Pennsylvania	40
68	Princeton	63
76	■ Dartmouth	57
77	■ Harvard	64
79	Columbia-Barnard	66
70	Cornell	66
87	Harvard	81
62	Dartmouth	57
57	■ Princeton	56
68	■ Pennsylvania	78

BRYANT 12-15

74	■ Rhode Island Col.	64
43	Bentley	91
69	New Hamp. Col.	74
75	Sacred Heart	90
80	■ Keene St.	78
55	■ Stonehill	64
102	■ Southern Conn. St.	56
57	† Michigan Tech	79
74	† Air Force	64
66	■ Mass.-Lowell	64
64	Springfield	75
84	■ Quinnipiac	50
80	■ St. Michael's	73
70	■ Assumption	67
80	St. Anselm	95
71	American Int'l	90
52	Stonehill	76
68	■ Merrimack	64
57	■ Bentley	78
69	Quinnipiac	71
77	St. Michael's	84
69	Assumption	75
78	■ St. Anselm	66
82	■ American Int'l	78
67	Merrimack	71
82	■ Springfield	53
63	Stonehill	68

BRYN MAWR 11-7

65	Goucher	82
77	Neumann	60
65	■ Beaver	46
68	† Simmons	35
64	† Smith	66
59	Mount Holyoke	53
68	■ Ursinus	71
75	Immaculata	85
54	■ St. Elizabeth	45
53	Widener	62
64	Haverford	46
72	■ Gwynedd Mercy	47
73	Phila. Pharmacy	77
52	Swarthmore	50
77	Rosemont	23
92	■ Chestnut Hill	52
58	Wesley	68
88	† Mary Baldwin	48

BUCKNELL 11-17

82	St. Bonaventure	84
48	Iona	56
75	† Marist	80
70	■ Cornell	58
48	■ Hofstra	51
54	Miami (Fla.)	74
77	† Michigan	83
60	† Oklahoma	84
39	† Iowa	97
53	† Temple	67
89	† Lehigh	75
87	■ Colgate	66
69	Fordham	85
54	■ Lafayette	62
69	■ Buffalo	84
51	■ Army	37
55	Navy	47
90	■ Lehigh	56
50	Holy Cross	80

69 Colgate 52
64 ■ Fordham 58
68 Lafayette 84
50 Army 59
90 ■ Navy 63
73 Lehigh 60
65 ■ Holy Cross 77
50 Army 46
63 Holy Cross 75

BUFFALO 13-13
50 ■ Cornell 47
55 ■ Cincinnati 73
54 Cornell 70
60 Akron 70
85 Niagara 87
55 † Princeton 78
68 Navy 74
63 ■ Morgan St. 55
53 ■ Loyola (Cal.) 60
65 ■ Marquette 100
76 Colgate 74
68 Marist 78
65 ■ Canisius 51
67 Delaware St. 55
84 Bucknell 69
62 St. Francis (N.Y.) 64
79 Fairfield 96
74 Stetson 71
87 ■ Hofstra 56
80 ■ Central Conn. St. 62
77 ■ Colgate 50
88 ■ Md.-East. Shore 50
60 Robert Morris 47
62 Central Conn. St. 63
75 Hofstra 57
49 Canisius 75

BUFFALO ST. 19-8
97 ■ East. Mennonite 56
73 ■ St. Norbert 71
67 ■ Fredonia St. 65
73 ■ Cortland St. 62
82 Brockport St. 58
74 ■ Utica Tech 60
66 ■ Albany (N.Y.) 73
88 ■ Keuka 68
77 Alfred 50
76 Plattsburgh St. 52
105 Potsdam St. 109
55 Nazareth (N.Y.) 67
64 Geneseo St. 69
87 ■ Oswego St. 68
79 ■ Penn St.-Behrend 67
76 St. John Fisher 82
56 Binghamton 55
78 ■ Brockport St. 58
88 Utica Tech 58
76 ■ Oneonta St. 53
106 ■ New Paltz St. 84
79 Fredonia St. 60
68 ■ Geneseo St. 76
68 Oswego St. 47
73 † Potsdam St. 60
78 Geneseo St. 95
69 Geneseo St. 84

BUTLER 23-8
80 ■ Cincinnati 66
75 † West Va. 59
66 Arkansas 80
91 ■ Indiana St. 68
89 Eastern Mich. 72
81 Michigan 50
76 Loyola (Ill.) 68
80 † Houston 72
64 Louisville 84
90 ■ La Salle 64
87 ■ Duquesne 67
64 Evansville 62
91 Xavier (Ohio) 87
72 Dayton 65
76 ■ Kentucky 83
82 ■ Notre Dame 70

82 ■ Detroit Mercy 65
78 ■ Loyola (Ill.) 59
79 Duquesne 66
68 La Salle 84
73 Detroit Mercy 74
70 ■ Evansville 57
82 ■ Dayton 71
89 ■ Xavier (Ohio) 80
80 Notre Dame 69
84 † Duquesne 74
79 † Evansville 51
72 † Xavier (Ohio) 82
75 † Florida Int'l 79
74 † Nevada-Las Vegas 71
85 † Northwestern (La.) 89

CABRINI 21-5
37 † Mansfield 57
57 † Delaware Valley 56
60 ■ Marywood 56
64 Notre Dame (Md.) 62
89 Rosemont 13
87 ■ Gwynedd Mercy 29
50 ■ Delaware Valley 59
64 Immaculata 57
44 † Holy Family 40
65 † Phila. Pharmacy 58
71 Beaver 55
36 Alvernia 84
82 ■ Eastern (Pa.) 42
68 Gwynedd Mercy 38
69 ■ Immaculata 64
59 Wilmington (Del.) 62
80 ■ Rosemont 11
79 Eastern (Pa.) 58
62 ■ Swarthmore 43
69 ■ Beaver 47
71 Neumann 50
65 ■ Hunter 48
50 ■ Bloomfield 59
54 ■ Alvernia 44
62 ■ Immaculata 56
71 Salisbury St. 68

CAL LUTHERAN 8-17
39 Fresno Pacific 104
46 † Cal Baptist 73
105 ■ Mt. St. Mary (N.Y.) 48
47 San Fran. St. 70
66 Mills 63
69 ■ Pac. Christian 37
63 Christ-Irvine 86
55 ■ Azusa-Pacific 56
69 ■ Pt. Loma Nazarene 88
61 ■ Mills 51
68 ■ Southern Cal Col. 78
73 ■ La Verne 74
47 ■ Redlands 54
69 ■ Pomona-Pitzer 70
69 Claremont-M-S 81
69 ■ Whittier 65
59 ■ Occidental 54
68 La Verne 67
95 ■ La Sierra 31
47 Redlands 72
62 UC San Diego 94
59 Pomona-Pitzer 87
66 ■ Claremont-M-S 91
72 Whittier 84
50 Occidental 61

CAL POLY POMONA 27-3
81 ■ Southern Colo. 71
71 ■ Biola 61
72 † Central Mo. St. 63
80 Grand Canyon 76
79 † San Fran. St. 71
63 Cal St. Stanislaus 73
68 ■ Cal St. Chico 62
69 ■ Denver 65
55 ■ St. Ambrose 44
68 ■ UC Davis 51
74 ■ Alas. Fairbanks 59
63 ■ Sonoma St. 51
99 Cal Baptist 50

86 Cal St. Los Angeles 47
86 ■ Cal St. San B'dino 55
53 UC Riverside 60
67 Cal Poly SLO 61
84 Chapman 54
74 ■ Cal St. Dom. Hills 47
84 ■ Cal St. Los Angeles 49
45 Cal St. San B'dino 42
70 ■ UC Riverside 65
77 ■ Cal Poly SLO 60
77 ■ Chapman 31
55 Cal St. Dom. Hills 48
62 ■ Cal St. Dom. Hills 46
80 † Cal St. San B'dino 72
62 ■ UC Riverside 49
59 ■ Portland St. 51
55 North Dak. St. 91

CAL POLY SLO 10-13
68 † Bellarmine 86
69 † Angelo St. 76
72 † Fort Lewis 58
71 Fresno Pacific 66
68 San Fran. St. 63
66 Cal St. Stanislaus 69
65 † Alas. Anchorage 81
52 ■ UC Davis 84
78 ■ Fresno St. 81
70 ■ Cal St. Stanislaus 90
86 Cal St. San B'dino 75
84 ■ UC Riverside 77
88 ■ Chapman 49
61 ■ Cal Poly Pomona 67
54 Cal St. Dom. Hills 61
85 ■ Cal St. Los Angeles 68
61 ■ West Tex. St. 56
55 ■ Cal St. San B'dino 81
72 UC Riverside 81
96 Chapman 53
60 Cal Poly Pomona 77
52 ■ Cal St. Dom. Hills 61
82 Cal St. Los Angeles 60

CAL ST. CHICO 16-10
69 ■ Whitworth (Wash.) 62
68 ■ Metropolitan St. 78
70 ■ Humboldt St. 59
75 Southern Ore. St. 69
67 Southern Ore. St. 68
73 † Saginaw Valley 80
83 † Fort Lewis 56
43 † Angelo St. 55
62 Cal Poly Pomona 68
85 UC Riverside 78
99 ■ Portland St. 88
74 ■ Southern Ore. St. 64
63 ■ Washburn 76
63 UC Davis 72
75 Sonoma St. 52
86 ■ San Fran. St. 52
69 Cal St. Stanislaus 58
68 Cal St. Hayward 71
72 Humboldt St. 73
97 ■ Cal St. Hayward 63
72 ■ Cal St. Stanislaus 58
64 San Fran. St. 51
88 ■ Sonoma St. 70
102 ■ UC Davis 78
83 ■ Humboldt St. 66
78 ■ Cal St. Stanislaus 81

CAL ST. DOM. HILLS 15-11
64 Biola 72
79 † Western N. Mex. 82
78 † Cal Baptist 42
75 ■ Southern Cal Col. 46
53 Pt. Loma Nazarene 58
78 ■ Christ-Irvine 48
69 ■ Biola 59
59 † Sonoma St. 65
72 Humboldt St. 71
60 Cal St. Hayward 34
37 UC Davis 65
61 ■ San Fran. St. 57

75 Chapman 34
61 ■ Cal St. Los Angeles 60
64 Cal St. San B'dino 70
57 Cal St. Northridge 50
67 ■ UC Riverside 77
61 ■ Cal Poly SLO 54
47 Cal Poly Pomona 74
76 ■ Chapman 58
65 Cal St. Los Angeles 63
80 ■ Cal St. San B'dino 77
63 UC Riverside 74
61 Cal Poly SLO 52
48 ■ Cal Poly Pomona 55
46 Cal Poly Pomona 62

CAL ST. FULLERTON 8-19
66 UCLA 99
64 ■ San Diego 87
79 ■ Fresno St. 76
46 Southern Cal 85
46 † San Francisco 69
76 San Jose St. 75
64 UC Santa Barb. 87
78 Long Beach St. 80
63 ■ Nevada-Las Vegas 82
58 ■ New Mexico St. 66
65 Hawaii 87
68 Hawaii 85
82 Nevada 67
88 ■ San Jose St. 66
44 ■ Pacific (Cal.) 70
62 New Mexico St. 65
48 Nevada-Las Vegas 84
55 ■ UC Irvine 72
74 ■ Cal St. Northridge 63
85 ■ Nevada 65
68 Pepperdine 100
57 Pacific (Cal.) 73
68 San Jose St. 85
96 UC Irvine 91
73 ■ Long Beach St. 99
68 ■ UC Santa Barb. 64
68 † Nevada-Las Vegas 98

CAL ST. HAYWARD 6-20
48 † Biola 57
61 † Southern Colo. 73
52 ■ Cal St. Los Angeles 62
36 ■ Air Force 52
50 UC Davis 94
65 † UC Santa Cruz 42
46 Eastern Mont. 62
48 Eastern Mont. 73
62 ■ Alas. Anchorage 97
64 ■ Fresno Pacific 65
47 Cal St. San B'dino 67
60 UC Riverside 56
34 ■ Cal St. Dom. Hills 60
39 ■ Texas Woman's 37
49 ■ San Fran. St. 47
39 ■ UC Davis 77
44 Sonoma St. 63
43 ■ Humboldt St. 52
71 ■ Cal St. Chico 68
62 Cal St. Stanislaus 80
63 Cal St. Chico 97
46 Humboldt St. 52
40 ■ Sonoma St. 54
46 UC Davis 76
74 San Fran. St. 73
57 ■ Cal St. Stanislaus 81

CAL ST. NORTHRIDGE 6-21
36 Loyola (Cal.) 67
39 ■ Pacific (Cal.) 69
76 Grand Canyon 50
59 Northern Ariz. 53
59 ■ Pepperdine 66
63 ■ Rice 72
74 ■ Northern Ariz. 52
58 UC Irvine 57
52 ■ Colorado St. 67
61 Loyola (Ill.) 66
51 Northeastern Ill. 55
54 Chicago St. 60

61	Santa Clara	96
59	Fresno St.	79
48	■ Cal St. Sacramento	86
60	■ UC Santa Barb.	71
50	■ Cal St. Dom. Hills	57
46	Cal St. Sacramento	68
69	Southern Utah	87
72	Pepperdine	80
63	Cal St. Fullerton	74
62	■ Cal St. Los Angeles	53
36	■ Southern Cal	78
51	■ Southern Utah	59
63	† Chicago St.	69
76	† Northeastern Ill.	55
46	Mo.-Kansas City	71

CAL ST. SACRAMENTO		**17-10**
74	San Jose St.	56
58	Houston	65
67	† Jackson St.	52
77	■ San Francisco	75
54	Pacific (Cal.)	67
83	Nevada	65
82	† Fresno St.	63
69	■ Boise St.	80
75	■ Biola	43
59	■ Idaho	64
52	San Diego	66
63	■ Northern Ariz.	55
80	Southern Utah	70
86	Cal St. Northridge	48
66	UC Irvine	62
76	Idaho	81
64	Eastern Wash.	67
90	■ Santa Clara	71
68	■ Cal St. Northridge	46
74	Northern Ariz.	80
103	Fresno St.	105
70	■ Mo.-Kansas City	62
82	■ Nevada	67
82	■ Southern Utah	62
93	† Northeastern Ill.	67
85	† Wis.-Milwaukee	72
67	Mo.-Kansas City	70

CAL ST. SAN B'DINO		**18-10**
103	■ UC Santa Cruz	31
58	■ Cal St. Stanislaus	72
78	■ East Tex. St.	69
78	■ Cal Baptist	54
72	Pepperdine	90
67	■ Whittier	31
65	Metropolitan St.	76
82	Regis (Colo.)	78
69	■ UC Davis	61
62	■ Augustana (S.D.)	67
67	■ Cal St. Hayward	47
69	Southern Cal Col.	50
70	■ Occidental	55
75	■ UC Riverside	53
75	■ Cal Poly SLO	86
55	Cal Poly Pomona	86
70	■ Cal St. Dom. Hills	64
78	Cal St. Los Angeles	60
72	■ Azusa-Pacific	61
69	■ Chapman	44
73	UC Riverside	76
81	Cal Poly SLO	55
42	■ Cal Poly Pomona	45
77	Cal St. Dom. Hills	80
81	■ Cal St. Los Angeles	71
71	Chapman	59
74	† UC Riverside	72
72	† Cal Poly Pomona	80

CAL ST. STANISLAUS		**19-9**
68	† Pembroke St.	55
72	Cal St. San B'dino	58
72	† Air Force	68
81	† Cal St. Los Angeles	56
63	■ UC Riverside	79
84	■ Chapman	67
73	■ Cal Poly Pomona	63
57	■ Fresno Pacific	67
60	UC Santa Cruz	39
60	■ Pt. Loma Nazarene	67
69	■ Cal Poly SLO	66
58	■ Washburn	82
82	■ Texas Woman's	65
68	San Fran. St.	51
90	Cal Poly SLO	70
66	■ Sonoma St.	50
53	UC Davis	70
58	■ Cal St. Chico	69
72	■ Humboldt St.	75
80	■ Cal St. Hayward	62
82	Humboldt St.	76
58	Cal St. Chico	72
61	■ UC Davis	59
62	Sonoma St.	45
75	■ San Fran. St.	47
81	Cal St. Hayward	57
81	Cal St. Chico	78
68	UC Davis	77

CALIFORNIA		**19-10**
70	San Francisco	64
80	■ Santa Clara	67
78	■ UC Santa Barb.	63
76	Boise St.	78
74	Utah	59
81	■ Northwestern	78
69	■ Florida St.	50
83	■ Seton Hall	67
69	Pepperdine	65
75	Oregon	63
73	Oregon St.	75
63	Stanford	89
68	■ Southern Cal	55
78	■ UCLA	70
61	Washington	62
75	Washington St.	65
70	■ Arizona St.	66
72	■ Arizona	73
64	■ Stanford	59
71	Southern Cal	76
68	UCLA	85
79	■ Washington St.	65
66	■ Washington	73
81	Arizona	74
79	Arizona St.	74
61	■ Oregon St.	73
90	■ Oregon	74
62	Kansas	47
63	Vanderbilt	82

CALIF. (PA.)		**18-8**
81	■ West Liberty St.	60
63	■ Mercyhurst	73
75	■ Fairmont St.	53
79	■ Millersville	68
77	■ Seton Hill	64
95	† Holy Family	63
65	Mansfield	54
62	West Va. Wesleyan	48
88	■ East Stroudsburg	78
83	Salem-Teikyo	69
88	Davis & Elkins	56
74	Gannon	86
84	Columbia Union	78
81	■ Clarion	91
73	■ Indiana (Pa.)	63
76	Slippery Rock	60
79	Shippensburg	69
75	Edinboro	77
77	St. Vincent	96
72	■ Lock Haven	66
80	Clarion	87
80	Indiana (Pa.)	61
83	■ Slippery Rock	70
90	■ Shippensburg	73
76	■ Edinboro	78
63	Lock Haven	67

UC DAVIS		**19-7**
76	† Puget Sound	65
73	† Pacific (Ore.)	58
89	■ UC Riverside	76
67	■ Humboldt St.	42
94	■ Cal St. Hayward	50
96	■ UC Santa Cruz	22
46	■ Portland St.	60
61	Cal St. San B'dino	69
51	Cal Poly Pomona	68
65	■ Cal St. Dom. Hills	37
84	Cal Poly SLO	52
72	■ Cal St. Chico	63
70	■ Humboldt St.	78
77	Cal St. Hayward	39
70	■ Cal St. Stanislaus	53
79	■ San Fran. St.	39
77	■ Sonoma St.	52
74	San Fran. St.	59
59	Cal St. Stanislaus	61
76	■ Cal St. Hayward	46
90	Humboldt St.	76
78	Cal St. Chico	102
72	Sonoma St.	50
70	■ Humboldt St.	52
77	■ Cal St. Stanislaus	68
61	† Portland St.	64

UC IRVINE		**2-24**
60	■ Pepperdine	82
48	■ Tulane	64
66	■ La Salle	68
64	Arizona	84
50	■ Texas A&M	75
83	■ Western Ill.	76
57	■ Cal St. Northridge	58
74	Long Beach St.	82
51	UC Santa Barb.	76
61	■ New Mexico St.	80
44	■ Nevada-Las Vegas	86
75	■ San Jose St.	85
62	■ Cal St. Sacramento	66
45	Hawaii	78
71	Hawaii	79
58	■ Pacific (Cal.)	74
71	Nevada-Las Vegas	100
68	New Mexico St.	79
72	Cal St. Fullerton	55
74	Nevada	81
73	■ Nevada	82
81	■ Long Beach St.	90
62	San Jose St.	80
73	Pacific (Cal.)	90
91	■ Cal St. Fullerton	96
61	■ UC Santa Barb.	66

UC RIVERSIDE		**17-11**
70	† Eastern Mont.	69
74	† Mesa St.	81
67	■ Southern Colo.	61
76	UC Davis	89
96	† UC Santa Cruz	39
79	Cal St. Stanislaus	63
78	■ Cal St. Chico	85
82	■ Denver	78
80	Grand Canyon	63
61	† N.M. Highlands	62
61	■ Augustana (S.D.)	106
56	■ Cal St. Hayward	60
76	■ Alas. Fairbanks	65
79	■ San Fran. St.	62
53	Cal St. San B'dino	75
78	■ Chapman	62
77	Cal Poly SLO	84
60	■ Cal Poly Pomona	53
77	Cal St. Dom. Hills	67
69	Cal St. Los Angeles	67
76	■ Cal St. San B'dino	73
84	Chapman	64
81	■ Cal Poly SLO	72
65	Cal Poly Pomona	70
74	■ Cal St. Dom. Hills	63
84	■ Cal St. Los Angeles	66
72	† Cal St. San B'dino	74
49	Cal Poly Pomona	62

UC SAN DIEGO		**13-12**
85	† Colorado Col.	60
67	† Neb. Wesleyan	79
75	■ Pt. Loma Nazarene	76
50	■ St. Martin's	100
77	■ Claremont-M-S	61
75	Azusa-Pacific	84
66	■ Southern Cal Col.	61
78	Whittier	51
72	■ North Park	85
82	■ Amherst	56
46	■ Augustana (Ill.)	58
55	■ Whitman	78
60	■ Master's	49
87	Pac. Christian	34
79	UC Santa Cruz	39
77	Mills	67
63	Sonoma St.	87
48	■ Christ-Irvine	74
55	Pomona-Pitzer	50
61	■ La Verne	70
67	■ Cal Baptist	76
59	Redlands	54
94	■ Cal Lutheran	62
76	■ Occidental	56
72	La Verne	80

UC SANTA BARB.		**19-12**
63	California	78
78	■ Pepperdine	84
52	Stanford	85
63	Fresno St.	70
75	† Boise St.	96
51	Santa Clara	82
74	■ Colorado St.	66
87	■ Cal St. Fullerton	64
76	■ UC Irvine	51
64	■ Hawaii	60
66	■ Hawaii	75
76	■ Pacific (Cal.)	75
77	■ San Jose St.	49
71	Cal St. Northridge	60
72	■ Long Beach St.	67
70	New Mexico St.	68
51	Nevada-Las Vegas	89
76	■ Nevada	49
88	San Jose St.	60
79	Pacific (Cal.)	88
67	Nevada	61
88	Long Beach St.	72
66	■ New Mexico St.	61
79	■ Nevada-Las Vegas	86
66	UC Irvine	61
64	Cal St. Fullerton	68
74	Long Beach St.	46
62	† Nevada-Las Vegas	58
80	† Hawaii	77
88	■ Brigham Young	79
54	Colorado	81

CAMERON		**8-17**
71	West Tex. St.	83
82	† Chapman	69
64	Southwestern Okla.	86
70	† Texas Woman's	71
62	† Mo. Southern St.	89
38	Midwestern St.	97
49	West Tex. St.	92
71	■ Oklahoma City	74
67	■ West Tex. St.	89
71	■ Central Okla.	58
60	Texas Woman's	64
58	Eastern N. Mex.	101
63	■ Abilene Christian	81
79	■ Angelo St.	70
71	■ East Tex. St.	78
83	■ Texas A&I	67
90	Texas A&I	88
56	East Tex. St.	78
62	■ Eastern N. Mex.	60
61	■ Texas Woman's	55
63	■ Midwestern St.	70
77	Angelo St.	71
77	Abilene Christian	82
63	Central Okla.	74
78	† East Tex. St.	80

CAMPBELL		16-10
58	North Caro. A&T	52
88	■ Mt. Olive	61
84	Appalachian St.	90
58	† Marshall	68
71	† Drexel	52
78	■ North Caro. A&T	70
84	N.C.-Wilmington	72
95	■ N.C.-Asheville	67
52	Radford	63
52	Liberty	73
60	East Caro.	75
57	■ Towson St.	37
52	■ Md.-Balt. County	42
55	Md.-Balt. County	70
65	Towson St.	49
78	■ Liberty	81
60	■ Radford	73
54	■ Charleston So.	45
74	■ N.C.-Greensboro	87
58	Winthrop	46
81	■ Coastal Caro.	79
74	Charleston So.	58
75	■ Winthrop	43
63	Coastal Caro.	60
55	N.C.-Asheville	52
57	† Liberty	66

CANISIUS		9-18
72	Wichita St.	76
71	■ Colgate	54
62	Temple	84
86	Duquesne	92
55	■ Loyola (Cal.)	64
68	■ Marquette	90
76	■ St. Bonaventure	88
55	Detroit Mercy	77
51	Buffalo	65
82	Drake	75
71	■ Manhattan	61
58	Siena	63
76	Fairfield	69
49	St. Peter's	64
67	■ Niagara	69
63	■ Siena	58
72	■ Iona	70
70	■ St. Peter's	77
67	Loyola (Md.)	79
51	North Caro.	80
63	■ Loyola (Md.)	55
63	■ Fairfield	81
68	Niagara	72
59	Iona	67
81	Manhattan	64
75	■ Buffalo	49
65	† Loyola (Md.)	74

CAPITAL		28-4
71	Calvin	59
66	Alma	63
79	■ Tiffin	65
67	Mount Union	59
86	■ Heidelberg	57
81	■ Otterbein	44
63	Muskingum	82
51	Wittenberg	56
73	■ Ohio Wesleyan	48
83	John Carroll	84
67	■ Baldwin-Wallace	40
72	Ohio Northern	42
78	Hiram	46
61	■ Marietta	44
71	■ Mount Union	49
61	Heidelberg	60
81	■ Muskingum	74
76	■ Hiram	51
91	■ Asbury	51
76	Otterbein	56
70	■ Ohio Northern	56
67	Baldwin-Wallace	50
43	Marietta	42
69	■ John Carroll	68
63	■ Marietta	46
63	■ John Carroll	58
73	† Heidelberg	59
93	■ Wittenberg	50
68	Babson	56
66	† Southern Me.	56
65	† Scranton	61
63	Central (Iowa)	71

CARLETON		8-17
53	■ South Dak. Tech	73
57	Grinnell	65
69	† Phila. Pharmacy	51
67	Gallaudet	57
61	■ Gust. Adolphus	67
69	St. Mary's (Minn.)	86
51	Concordia-M'head	80
57	St. Olaf	90
32	Macalester	65
34	St. Benedict	70
36	■ St. Thomas (Minn.)	80
75	■ Dr. Martin Luther	43
51	Bethel (Minn.)	72
58	■ Augsburg	56
59	Hamline	75
56	■ Concordia-M'head	83
68	■ St. Mary's (Minn.)	56
68	Gust. Adolphus	69
62	■ Macalester	57
62	■ St. Benedict	89
46	St. Thomas (Minn.)	72
64	Augsburg	58
62	■ Hamline	61
47	■ St. Olaf	60
55	■ Bethel (Minn.)	75

CARNEGIE MELLON		13-12
70	† Lebanon Valley	52
67	Susquehanna	64
55	Case Reserve	66
60	■ Waynesburg	71
48	■ Frostburg St.	52
61	Wash. & Jeff.	72
60	■ Chicago	56
68	■ Johns Hopkins	61
65	Haverford	44
73	† Davidson	59
73	■ New York U.	59
52	■ Emory	86
44	Grove City	56
75	Washington (Mo.)	81
72	Chicago	68
52	Rochester	54
38	Brandeis	68
59	■ Washington (Mo.)	53
64	Juniata	82
55	■ Rochester	46
59	■ Brandeis	51
56	■ Allegheny	59
55	New York U.	60
83	Thiel	65
81	Emory	62

CARROLL (WIS.)		12-10
59	Lawrence	52
58	■ Lake Forest	76
73	† Luther	59
77	† Aurora	68
64	Beloit	68
75	■ Aurora	54
48	Ohio Northern	57
65	† DePauw	39
65	Wis.-La Crosse	69
59	St. Norbert	57
69	■ Beloit	86
64	Lake Forest	75
55	Grinnell	65
70	Coe	61
80	■ Knox	52
82	■ Illinois Col.	72
59	Ripon	56
72	■ St. Norbert	76
61	Wis.-Whitewater	69
81	■ St. Mary's (Ind.)	56
72	■ Lawrence	73
67	■ Ripon	57

CARSON-NEWMAN		22-8
88	† Francis Marion	62
63	† Virginia Union	56
71	■ Cumberland (Ky.)	62
68	† Union (Tenn.)	66
58	† Lambuth	74
64	Catawba	72
79	■ Lincoln Memorial	74
83	Lees-McRae	88
74	■ Gardner-Webb	52
49	■ Wingate	52
80	■ Elon	62
77	Mars Hill	45
70	■ Presbyterian	58
66	Lincoln Memorial	68
94	■ Lenoir-Rhyne	70
75	Elon	73
87	■ Lees-McRae	61
79	■ Catawba	67
85	Gardner-Webb	47
67	Wingate	60
86	Cumberland (Ky.)	67
73	■ Mars Hill	43
77	Presbyterian	52
80	Lenoir-Rhyne	46
88	† Gardner-Webb	61
84	† Catawba	88
94	Belmont Abbey	66
50	Wingate	46
70	Catawba	75
49	† Minn.-Duluth	62

CARTHAGE		9-16
74	Rockford	35
83	■ Trinity Chrst. (Il.)	86
79	† Madonna	95
77	† Trinity Chrst. (Il.)	84
64	■ Beloit	73
50	National Louis	66
79	■ Olivet (Ill.)	82
69	Ill. Wesleyan	66
59	Lake Forest	78
56	■ Millikin	58
44	■ Augustana (Ill.)	64
54	Marian (Wis.)	73
71	■ Ill. Wesleyan	58
70	North Park	71
52	Augustana (Ill.)	71
47	Wheaton (Ill.)	68
74	■ Aurora	57
63	Millikin	95
68	■ North Park	69
69	■ Elmhurst	62
55	■ North Central	50
73	■ Wheaton (Ill.)	79
88	Edgewood	72
75	North Central	62
91	Elmhurst	53

CASE RESERVE		12-13
66	■ Carnegie Mellon	55
72	Brandeis	73
64	■ Allegheny	75
59	Rochester	66
72	■ Emory	53
47	Wooster	60
43	Wittenberg	72
80	■ Johns Hopkins	60
56	■ Ohio Wesleyan	75
58	Denison	71
52	■ New York U.	73
73	■ Kenyon	38
96	■ Earlham	78
64	Oberlin	36
51	Chicago	58
40	Washington (Mo.)	57
61	■ Wooster	58
48	■ Wittenberg	82
69	Kenyon	28
63	■ Denison	49
67	Allegheny	52
65	Earlham	61
84	■ Oberlin	35
65	Ohio Wesleyan	87
63	Denison	78

CASTLETON ST.		2-21
56	† Endicott	68
42	Pine Manor	81
57	Russell Sage	74
35	† Worcester Tech	63
73	† Roger Williams	26
56	■ North Adams St.	69
29	† Lyndon St.	66
29	■ Plymouth St.	89
41	Westbrook	81
52	■ Westbrook	64
51	Lyndon St.	81
38	Johnson St.	58
63	■ Notre Dame (N.H.)	34
44	■ Green Mountain	55
53	■ St. Joseph (Vt.)	55
50	■ Lyndon St.	59
37	Colby-Sawyer	56
41	St. Joseph (Vt.)	67
41	Green Mountain	71
32	■ Johnson St.	48
32	■ Skidmore	88
44	Norwich	80
41	■ Plattsburgh St.	75

CATAWBA		24-9
121	■ Mt. Olive	65
72	■ Lees-McRae	86
103	■ Pfeiffer	60
62	Limestone	59
74	† Pikeville	58
75	Lees-McRae	95
72	■ Carson-Newman	64
74	High Point	73
99	Queens (N.C.)	89
68	† Berry	80
106	† Gardner-Webb	86
58	■ Presbyterian	59
70	Pfeiffer	44
96	Lenoir-Rhyne	78
87	■ Elon	66
107	Mars Hill	73
77	Wingate	84
81	■ Gardner-Webb	71
72	■ Queens (N.C.)	74
67	Carson-Newman	79
81	Presbyterian	83
93	■ Lenoir-Rhyne	83
64	■ Wingate	61
107	Elon	95
79	■ Mars Hill	68
78	Gardner-Webb	55
83	† Elon	62
88	† Carson-Newman	84
60	† Wingate	57
87	■ High Point	75
88	Lees-McRae	80
75	■ Carson-Newman	70
57	† Wayland Bapt.	74

CATHOLIC		9-16
48	Johns Hopkins	67
58	† Ursinus	57
52	Randolph-Macon	70
40	■ St. Thomas (Minn.)	76
62	■ Dist. Columbia	70
71	Gettysburg	86
84	■ Immaculata	69
84	■ Marymount (Va.)	103
50	■ Washington (Mo.)	69
75	York (Pa.)	106
65	Western Md.	69
79	St. Mary's (Md.)	43
79	Gallaudet	61
73	Goucher	62
51	■ Notre Dame (Md.)	53
53	■ Mary Washington	72
60	■ Goucher	65
65	■ York (Pa.)	50
67	Marymount (Va.)	94
60	Salisbury St.	82
64	■ Gallaudet	54

57 Mary Washington 78
68 ■ St. Mary's (Md.) 41
82 ■ Goucher 76
61 Marymount (Va.) 106

CENTRAL (IOWA) 24-5
65 ■ Washington (Mo.) 57
73 ■ Graceland (Iowa) 58
55 Grand View 65
70 ■ Mt. Mercy 66
52 Midland Lutheran 62
81 † Kan. Newman 77
52 Central Mo. St. 89
83 ■ Wartburg 64
89 ■ Buena Vista 61
81 Upper Iowa 61
65 Loras 67
92 Dubuque 40
71 Luther 60
80 ■ William Penn 48
61 ■ Simpson 51
67 Buena Vista 53
70 ■ Luther 60
83 ■ Dubuque 46
58 Wartburg 64
82 Simpson 68
99 ■ Upper Iowa 38
80 Dordt 56
79 William Penn 52
79 ■ Loras 56
81 ■ Augustana (Ill.) 68
70 ■ Wis.-Eau Claire 63
62 ■ Wartburg 60
60 ■ St. Benedict 59
71 ■ Capital 63

CENTRAL ARK. 16-12
78 ■ Northeastern Okla. 62
74 ■ Southern Nazarene 90
82 ■ Ozarks (Mo.) 63
90 Williams Bapt. 74
63 Mo. Southern St. 78
68 † Pittsburg St. 76
71 Ozarks (Ark.) 75
90 ■ Southern St. 74
124 ■ Ark. Baptist 44
82 Northeastern Okla. 69
74 Southern Nazarene 91
91 Northwestern (La.) 111
66 Louisiana Col. 67
60 Arkansas Tech 59
81 ■ Ouachita Bapt. 71
79 ■ Arkansas Col. 57
65 Ark.-Monticello 75
70 ■ Harding 50
88 Henderson St. 97
46 ■ Ozarks (Ark.) 44
83 Southern St. 65
70 ■ Arkansas Tech 82
66 Ouachita Bapt. 62
70 Arkansas Col. 57
66 ■ Ark.-Monticello 68
78 Harding 74
92 ■ Henderson St. 75
65 ■ Henderson St. 70

CENTRAL CONN. ST. 6-20
62 ■ Yale 69
68 ■ Fairfield 67
73 Harvard 93
73 Md.-East. Shore 91
87 ■ Md.-East. Shore 61
59 ■ Wagner 52
63 La Salle 96
61 † James Madison 92
45 ■ Massachusetts 59
95 St. Francis (N.Y.) 76
63 ■ Northeastern 72
54 Brown 64
62 ■ Temple 64
68 ■ Holy Cross 85
50 Hofstra 68
55 ■ Vermont 76
41 Dartmouth 61

53 Boston U. 76
52 ■ Maine 79
63 Hartford 65
50 Rhode Island 74
62 Buffalo 80
67 ■ Hofstra 57
70 ■ Colgate 71
63 ■ Buffalo 62
60 ■ New Hampshire 76

CENTRAL FLA. 4-24
55 South Fla. 110
83 ■ Nicholls St. 76
41 ■ Memphis St. 79
47 Ga. Southern 101
46 New Orleans 85
39 Louisiana Tech 90
67 ■ Louisiana St. 77
66 ■ Kent 112
67 ■ Baylor 110
73 ■ Monmouth (N.J.) 81
78 ■ South Fla. 81
61 ■ Southeastern La. 60
45 Florida 96
60 ■ Mercer 61
69 Stetson 79
59 Florida Int'l 88
64 ■ Charleston 57
60 ■ Georgia St. 68
71 ■ Fla. Atlantic 100
42 Southeastern La. 69
37 ■ Louisiana Tech 93
49 ■ New Orleans 69
66 Mercer 68
66 ■ Stetson 75
62 ■ Florida Int'l 81
54 Charleston 52
47 Georgia St. 80
61 † Georgia St. 81

CENTRAL MICH. 15-12
59 Michigan St. 66
53 † Bradley 47
47 Washington St. 58
69 ■ Detroit Mercy 67
65 Ohio St. 97
68 † Mo.-Kansas City 56
81 ■ Maine 56
91 ■ Siena 65
66 ■ Eastern Mich. 55
69 Toledo 81
97 ■ Kent 72
51 Ball St. 48
59 ■ Miami (Ohio) 63
56 Western Mich. 61
59 ■ Ohio 61
80 Akron 50
62 Bowling Green 81
60 ■ Toledo 54
64 Kent 81
66 ■ Ball St. 59
69 Miami (Ohio) 70
62 ■ Western Mich. 50
55 Ohio 45
78 ■ Akron 64
62 ■ Bowling Green 73
53 Eastern Mich. 51
57 Kent 71

CENTRAL MO. ST. 19-10
63 † Cal Poly Pomona 72
85 † Western St. 73
66 ■ Avila 44
68 ■ Lindenwood 52
64 † Moorhead St. 74
77 † Cal St. Los Angeles 42
78 ■ Quincy 67
89 ■ Central (Iowa) 52
86 ■ SIU-Edwardsville 68
70 Emporia St. 84
73 Lincoln (Mo.) 43
60 ■ Washburn 74
66 ■ Missouri-Rolla 73
83 ■ Northeast Mo. St. 58
53 Northwest Mo. St. 60

65 SIU-Edwardsville 61
65 ■ Emporia St. 50
58 ■ Mo. Western St. 43
60 Washburn 76
69 Mo.-St. Louis 57
74 Northeast Mo. St. 48
73 ■ Northwest Mo. St. 62
62 Mo. Western St. 56
64 ■ Pittsburg St. 63
66 Mo. Southern St. 73
74 ■ Southwest Baptist 62
67 ■ Mo. Western St. 49
71 Washburn 84
67 Washburn 77

CENTRAL OKLA. 18-10
83 † Tex. Wesleyan 62
91 † Concordia (Tex.) 81
68 † Pittsburg St. 80
76 Mo. Southern St. 82
67 ■ Mo. Southern St. 89
79 ■ Texas Woman's 66
82 Southwest Baptist 79
61 † IU/PU-Ft. Wayne 58
53 SIU-Edwardsville 65
78 ■ Emporia St. 75
81 † West Tex. St. 64
64 † Oklahoma City 62
58 Cameron 71
77 Eastern N. Mex. 89
85 Texas Woman's 66
79 ■ Angelo St. 72
98 ■ Abilene Christian 91
67 ■ Texas A&I 64
88 ■ East Tex. St. 85
95 East Tex. St. 91
94 Texas A&I 64
80 ■ Texas Woman's 67
88 ■ Eastern N. Mex. 94
93 Abilene Christian 102
61 Angelo St. 76
74 ■ Cameron 63
72 † Angelo St. 69
80 Abilene Christian 85

CENTRE 19-6
57 ■ Georgetown (Ky.) 77
82 ■ Midway 63
97 ■ Fisk 29
64 ■ Transylvania 65
75 Berea 82
83 † DePauw 54
65 Ohio Northern 62
56 ■ Maryville (Tenn.) 73
64 † Hanover 63
75 Maryville (Tenn.) 85
70 Trinity (Tex.) 66
70 Hendrix 56
76 ■ Berea 79
71 Oglethorpe 62
71 Sewanee 51
68 ■ Millsaps 52
72 ■ Rhodes 54
82 ■ Oglethorpe 48
73 ■ Sewanee 56
76 Thomas More 63
81 Fisk 19
72 Millsaps 59
66 Rhodes 48
71 ■ Trinity (Tex.) 64
73 ■ Hendrix 65

CHADRON ST. 18-9
72 ■ Minot St. 59
78 South Dak. Tech 88
81 † Jamestown 88
101 † Teiko Post 56
84 ■ South Dak. Tech 70
86 ■ Black Hills St. 62
84 Wayne St. (Neb.) 92
64 ■ Wayne St. (Neb.) 67
85 Dickinson St. 93
95 † Dana 75
72 ■ Doane 67
66 Fort Hays St. 69

99 Colorado Mines 67
92 ■ Neb.-Kearney 69
84 ■ Mesa St. 71
88 ■ Western St. 51
82 Black Hills St. 57
85 Adams St. 74
78 N.M. Highlands 63
65 Mesa St. 77
93 Western St. 79
74 Neb.-Kearney 82
84 ■ Adams St. 56
93 ■ N.M. Highlands 74
72 ■ Fort Hays St. 64
108 ■ Colorado Mines 58
76 † Fort Hays St. 78

CHAPMAN 2-23
64 † Texas A&I 89
69 † Cameron 82
55 West Tex. St. 90
63 ■ Southwest Baptist 99
65 ■ East Tex. St. 97
43 Fresno Pacific 71
67 Cal St. Stanislaus 84
64 † San Fran. St. 69
62 Pt. Loma Nazarene 84
69 Cal Baptist 65
60 ■ St. Ambrose 91
45 ■ Occidental 44
34 ■ Cal St. Dom. Hills 75
62 UC Riverside 78
64 ■ Cal St. Los Angeles 75
49 Cal Poly SLO 88
54 ■ Cal Poly Pomona 84
44 Cal St. San B'dino 69
58 Cal St. Dom. Hills 76
44 ■ West Tex. St. 91
64 ■ UC Riverside 84
54 Cal St. Los Angeles 75
53 ■ Cal Poly SLO 96
31 Cal Poly Pomona 77
59 ■ Cal St. San B'dino 71

CHARLESTON 12-15
52 South Caro. 54
69 Charleston So. 49
91 ■ Coastal Caro. 73
76 ■ South Caro. St. 63
59 ■ Wake Forest 82
60 ■ N.C.-Wilmington 61
56 North Caro. 99
38 American 67
65 Mercer 67
91 ■ Coker 50
87 ■ Stetson 85
48 ■ Florida Int'l 80
89 Coastal Caro. 74
56 ■ Georgia St. 51
57 Central Fla. 64
52 Southeastern La. 62
61 South Caro. St. 73
69 ■ Mercer 51
58 Stetson 47
56 Florida Int'l 78
46 ■ Ga. Southern 61
63 ■ Charleston So. 58
64 Georgia St. 51
52 ■ Central Fla. 54
52 ■ Southeastern La. 53
76 † Stetson 56
60 Florida Int'l 84

CHARLESTON SO. 10-18
41 North Caro. 80
49 ■ Charleston 69
49 Ga. Southern 77
43 South Caro. 75
84 ■ N.C.-Wilmington 70
63 ■ Webber 45
76 ■ Radford 69
50 ■ Liberty 57
89 Md.-Balt. County 91
42 Towson St. 68
58 ■ Winthrop 50

56 ■ Md.-Balt. County 65
54 ■ Towson St. 48
52 Liberty 77
57 Radford 67
63 ■ Coastal Caro. 76
64 ■ N.C.-Asheville 61
45 Campbell 54
44 Davidson 57
49 N.C.-Asheville 45
70 ■ Coker 56
58 Charleston 63
58 ■ Campbell 74
59 N.C.-Greensboro 83
67 Winthrop 87
84 Coastal Caro. 82
61 † Winthrop 57
55 † N.C.-Greensboro 58

CHEYNEY 2-21
62 † Dist. Columbia 81
71 Columbia Union 85
74 † Lincoln (Pa.) 34
96 Medgar Evers 21
43 Morgan St. 74
46 Md.-East. Shore 65
52 Phila. Pharmacy 58
46 Clark Atlanta 65
52 Spelman 61
27 Kutztown 65
39 ■ Bloomsburg 73
46 ■ West Chester 78
43 East Stroudsburg 58
26 Pitt.-Johnstown 87
54 ■ Millersville 74
41 Mansfield 68
66 ■ Shippensburg 101
41 ■ Kutztown 75
48 Bloomsburg 78
41 West Chester 79
47 ■ East Stroudsburg 67
28 Millersville 94
58 ■ Mansfield 72

CHICAGO 14-11
65 † Trinity (Ill.) 85
74 † St. Mary's (Ind.) 73
53 Wis.-Whitewater 74
98 ■ Fontbonne 59
77 ■ North Central 59
56 Carnegie Mellon 60
74 Concordia (Ill.) 73
101 ■ Rockford 28
60 ■ Brandeis 48
66 ■ Rochester 47
55 Rosary 78
54 Johns Hopkins 60
62 ■ St. Mary's (Ind.) 63
58 ■ Case Reserve 51
68 ■ Carnegie Mellon 72
68 ■ Wheaton (Ill.) 40
46 New York U. 58
64 Emory 60
46 ■ Washington (Mo.) 52
69 ■ Emory 66
70 ■ New York U. 66
77 Wis. Lutheran 74
56 Rochester 53
46 Brandeis 54
53 Washington (Mo.) 74

CHICAGO ST. 9-18
44 Creighton 65
58 ■ Southeast Mo. St. 69
66 Wisconsin 82
63 ■ Evansville 81
59 ■ Ill.-Chicago 74
65 Wichita St. 75
33 † Kentucky 95
58 ■ Utah 72
60 ■ Cal St. Northridge 54
70 ■ St. Louis 68
91 ■ Silver Lake 50
96 Judson 53
69 ■ Northeastern Ill. 76
55 Bradley 94

60 Central St. (Ohio) 77
53 Wis.-Milwaukee 65
61 ■ Austin Peay 57
58 ■ La Salle 76
69 Northeastern Ill. 82
66 St. Francis (Ill.) 58
58 St. Louis 66
58 ■ Wis.-Milwaukee 76
61 Northern Iowa 95
70 ■ Eastern Ill. 66
69 † Cal St. Northridge 63
77 † Northeastern Ill. 65
48 Mo.-Kansas City 80

CHRIS. NEWPORT 19-9
99 † Va. Wesleyan 59
75 † Maryville (Tenn.) 81
76 † Elizabethtown 83
74 ■ Salisbury St. 81
50 ■ St. Thomas (Minn.) 81
79 ■ Va. Wesleyan 51
76 † Wilmington (Del.) 89
111 † St. Mary's (Md.) 45
87 Marymount (Va.) 74
72 ■ Hampton 68
94 † Marymount (Va.) 73
80 Frostburg St. 71
104 Shenandoah 56
70 ■ Mary Washington 61
67 Greensboro 69
72 Methodist 79
81 ■ Ferrum 79
85 ■ Averett 57
69 N.C. Wesleyan 55
78 ■ Methodist 75
52 ■ Greensboro 62
84 Averett 55
81 Ferrum 72
81 ■ N.C. Wesleyan 60
92 ■ Averett 51
92 ■ Greensboro 74
85 ■ Methodist 83
96 Marymount (Va.) 115

CINCINNATI 13-15
66 Butler 80
67 † Delaware St. 48
73 Buffalo 55
66 ■ Wright St. 51
72 ■ Ohio 59
78 ■ Cleveland St. 55
69 Illinois 82
43 Miami (Ohio) 58
78 Bowling Green 105
66 ■ Dayton 68
82 ■ Eastern Ky. 80
87 ■ St. Louis 62
71 Tennessee Tech 93
83 Marquette 109
59 ■ DePaul 62
75 Memphis St. 72
76 ■ Ala.-Birmingham 75
60 St. Louis 71
72 ■ Kentucky 69
55 DePaul 79
65 ■ Morehead St. 60
76 ■ Marquette 85
48 ■ Xavier (Ohio) 81
66 ■ Memphis St. 65
85 Akron 87
62 ■ Ala.-Birmingham 91
79 † St. Louis 39
57 † DePaul 73

CCNY 12-14
47 ■ Mt. St. Vincent 46
46 ■ Dominican (N.Y.) 60
33 Kean 80
54 † Otterbein 84
57 ■ York (N.Y.) 68
46 John Jay 51
44 Caldwell 69
41 Bloomfield 75
42 New Jersey Tech 62
58 ■ Baruch 55

72 Maritime (N.Y.) 20
71 ■ Medgar Evers 50
28 Stony Brook 84
51 York (N.Y.) 46
44 Hunter 62
68 Baruch 56
54 ■ John Jay 39
51 Old Westbury 76
66 ■ Maritime (N.Y.) 13
51 Manhattanville 49
64 New Paltz St. 92
66 ■ Staten Island 44
40 ■ Hunter 67
68 Medgar Evers 35
67 ■ Baruch 64
50 Hunter 57

CLAREMONT-M-S 17-8
47 ■ UC Santa Cruz 30
57 ■ Neb. Wesleyan 82
61 UC San Diego 77
46 Southern Cal Col. 64
66 ■ Master's 60
70 Pac. Christian 24
77 ■ Azusa-Pacific 56
51 ■ Millikin 64
75 ■ Willamette 70
59 ■ Colorado Col. 51
59 UC Santa Cruz 39
54 Notre Dame (Cal.) 30
73 Mills 33
62 Whittier 60
49 Occidental 64
46 La Verne 62
81 ■ Cal Lutheran 69
60 ■ Redlands 57
79 Pomona-Pitzer 63
66 ■ Whittier 50
67 ■ Occidental 64
62 ■ La Verne 65
91 Cal Lutheran 66
60 Redlands 72
79 ■ Pomona-Pitzer 69

CLARION 24-6
148 ■ Westminster (Pa.) 62
138 ■ Bethany (W.Va.) 56
58 Pitt.-Johnstown 69
93 Gannon 78
112 ■ Mercyhurst 85
88 Ashland 79
70 Bentley 75
89 † Pace 73
61 Mass.-Lowell 78
86 Mercyhurst 78
56 Bloomsburg 65
74 Kutztown 60
91 Calif. (Pa.) 81
105 ■ Edinboro 84
77 Lock Haven 64
95 Shippensburg 85
75 ■ Slippery Rock 73
93 ■ Indiana (Pa.) 82
77 St. Vincent 60
87 ■ Calif. (Pa.) 80
91 ■ Gannon 53
64 Edinboro 76
107 ■ Lock Haven 67
78 ■ Shippensburg 68
74 Slippery Rock 63
75 Indiana (Pa.) 73
94 † Millersville 65
104 † Edinboro 81
67 † Phila. Textile 64
64 Pitt.-Johnstown 70

CLARK (MASS.) 17-9
75 Worcester St. 60
78 † Worcester Tech 55
77 Babson 84
67 † St. Joseph's (Me.) 82
81 † Lincoln (Pa.) 38
69 ■ Eastern Conn. St. 65
61 ■ Williams 60

51 Southern Me. 65
55 ■ Springfield 62
65 ■ Rochester 56
80 Colby 61
68 Wheaton (Mass.) 83
79 ■ Worcester St. 61
65 ■ Connecticut Col. 70
68 Wesleyan 66
64 Amherst 45
61 ■ Trinity (Conn.) 48
86 Bri'water (Mass.) 34
72 ■ Middlebury 57
64 ■ Tufts 62
71 Worcester Tech 58
66 ■ Mass.-Dartmouth 51
60 Stony Brook 74
65 Gordon 54
65 ■ Western Conn. St. 71
68 Westfield St. 70

CLARKSON 11-13
46 Cortland St. 53
52 † Wm. Paterson 67
64 ■ Keuka 67
73 ■ Utica 41
50 † Wheaton (Mass.) 64
60 Nazareth (N.Y.) 48
69 St. Lawrence 54
53 Alfred 34
58 Ithaca 79
68 ■ Hamilton 69
58 Skidmore 70
54 Hartwick 64
58 Rensselaer 59
72 Potsdam St. 76
68 ■ William Smith 78
67 ■ Rochester Inst. 49
49 ■ Ithaca 54
52 ■ Alfred 44
69 Plattsburgh St. 56
64 Rochester Inst. 61
46 William Smith 79
76 ■ St. Lawrence 57
72 ■ Rensselaer 60
56 ■ Hartwick 48

CLEMSON 19-11
72 Furman 58
87 ■ South Caro. St. 60
68 Georgia Tech 86
94 † Eastern Ill. 58
79 Alabama 68
78 † Texas 75
68 Rutgers 67
89 ■ North Caro. St. 66
60 ■ Maryland 64
61 ■ Virginia 60
56 ■ North Caro. 59
71 Wake Forest 51
92 ■ Alabama St. 35
71 North Caro. St. 79
85 ■ Georgia Tech 80
74 ■ Tenn.-Chatt. 60
88 ■ Duke 63
54 South Caro. 55
83 Florida St. 69
68 ■ Wake Forest 58
65 Duke 67
73 Maryland 81
70 Virginia 87
70 ■ Florida St. 63
63 North Caro. 70
75 ■ N.C.-Greensboro 66
87 † Georgia Tech 66
71 † Virginia 79
70 ■ Xavier (Ohio) 64
78 Stephen F. Austin 89

CLEVELAND ST. 7-20
97 Kent 108
55 DePaul 94
79 † Lamar 100
72 Ohio 81
55 Cincinnati 78

69	Pittsburgh	83
52	† FDU-Teaneck	72
89	■ Austin Peay	76
71	■ Robert Morris	75
64	Toledo	86
81	Eastern Ill.	61
95	Western Ill.	75
65	■ Youngstown St.	83
66	■ Wright St.	69
54	■ Northern Ill.	85
53	■ Wis.-Green Bay	87
66	Ill.-Chicago	86
84	Valparaiso	108
53	Youngstown St.	66
89	■ Eastern Ill.	59
78	■ Western Ill.	69
93	Wright St.	83
77	Northern Ill.	88
55	Wis.-Green Bay	65
87	■ Ill.-Chicago	66
81	■ Valparaiso	88
74	† Youngstown St.	89

COAST GUARD 5-18

53	Stony Brook	72
70	† Drew	62
73	■ Roger Williams	18
52	Babson	71
46	Anna Maria	58
71	■ Pine Manor	69
52	■ Rutgers-Newark	65
46	Worcester Tech	47
66	Norwich	70
55	Norwich	65
46	■ Wheaton (Mass.)	75
64	■ Trinity (Conn.)	69
47	Connecticut Col.	81
49	■ MIT	71
49	■ Western New Eng.	69
40	Amherst	53
51	Albertus Magnus	63
35	Wesleyan	76
51	■ Pine Manor	59
34	■ Connecticut Col.	86
67	■ Suffolk	40
59	Emmanuel	67
40	■ Nichols	39

COASTAL CARO. 11-17

73	Charleston	91
69	Georgia St.	92
46	Mercer	68
88	■ Webber	55
53	N.C.-Wilmington	83
68	■ North Caro. A&T	61
35	■ North Caro.	83
45	Furman	86
75	■ Liberty	71
66	■ Radford	59
66	Towson St.	85
61	Md.-Balt. County	62
74	■ Charleston	89
45	Liberty	60
79	■ N.C.-Asheville	56
56	Radford	83
52	■ N.C.-Greensboro	87
76	Charleston So.	63
52	■ Towson St.	67
70	■ Md.-Balt. County	68
82	■ Winthrop	62
80	N.C.-Asheville	61
79	Campbell	81
83	Winthrop	72
60	■ Campbell	63
82	■ Charleston So.	84
72	† N.C.-Asheville	49
62	Radford	81

COE 9-13

74	Webster	45
73	Fontbonne	66
48	Wartburg	79
57	■ Loras	73
46	■ Mt. Mercy	88
50	Grinnell	74
55	■ Teiko-Marycrest	70
77	■ Iowa Wesleyan	47
68	■ Illinois Col.	77
73	Monmouth (Ill.)	54
66	Knox	62
41	■ Grinnell	55
62	■ Ripon	67
61	■ Carroll (Wis.)	70
53	Upper Iowa	55
50	Lawrence	66
73	St. Norbert	80
98	■ Cornell College	45
70	Illinois Col.	85
83	■ Monmouth (Ill.)	60
82	■ Knox	57
76	Cornell College	52

COLBY 13-9

58	Tufts	88
60	Plymouth St.	54
73	■ Husson	87
60	† Alfred	42
56	† Colby-Sawyer	49
55	■ Southern Me.	81
65	Thomas	53
61	■ Clark (Mass.)	80
78	■ Bowdoin	60
53	Middlebury	65
66	■ Colby-Sawyer	44
68	Bates	58
75	Me.-Farmington	56
69	Emmanuel	81
57	St. Joseph's (Me.)	67
70	■ Trinity (Conn.)	62
59	■ Wesleyan	51
62	■ Wheaton (Mass.)	67
52	Bowdoin	60
55	■ Gordon	45
81	■ Mass.-Boston	74
70	■ Bates	63

COLBY-SAWYER 9-15

32	† Mt. St. Mary (N.Y.)	61
57	† Rivier	45
44	Rivier	42
52	■ New England Col.	58
36	Nichols	31
49	† Colby	56
42	Green Mountain	71
59	Thomas	75
47	Russell Sage	63
74	■ MIT	79
37	■ Bates	77
47	Bowdoin	61
44	Colby	66
35	Middlebury	80
54	Johnson St.	46
31	Albertus Magnus	58
56	■ Castleton St.	37
48	■ St. Joseph (Vt.)	43
82	■ Endicott	27
38	■ Southern Me.	88
51	Simmons	50
67	■ Notre Dame (N.H.)	53
52	■ Norwich	67
52	■ Gordon	58

COLGATE 4-23

43	Cornell	55
54	Canisius	71
48	Dartmouth	81
36	† William & Mary	73
56	Hofstra	69
74	■ Buffalo	76
65	■ Niagara	77
66	Bucknell	87
46	Lafayette	70
50	■ Navy	64
53	■ Columbia-Barnard	64
57	Holy Cross	79
53	Fordham	64
54	■ Army	68
71	■ St. Bonaventure	90
65	Lehigh	74
52	■ Bucknell	69
51	■ Lafayette	50
63	■ Boston U.	83
52	Navy	61
53	■ Holy Cross	71
50	Buffalo	77
50	■ Fordham	48
62	Army	76
71	Central Conn. St.	70
84	■ Lehigh	64
60	Lafayette	79

COLORADO 27-4

86	New Mexico	37
95	■ Mississippi St.	59
64	■ Southern Ill.	52
94	■ Arkansas	67
90	Colorado St.	69
78	■ Southwest Tex. St.	51
84	Baylor	58
72	■ Wyoming	56
92	■ Texas A&M	61
64	† Temple	35
72	† Iowa	70
74	Florida Int'l	71
61	■ Kansas St.	33
80	■ Kansas	71
67	Missouri	53
50	Nebraska	62
92	Iowa St.	52
80	■ Oklahoma	49
78	■ Oklahoma St.	76
77	Kansas	60
61	Kansas St.	51
75	■ Missouri	52
79	■ Iowa St.	29
71	■ Nebraska	63
49	Oklahoma St.	48
69	Oklahoma	74
63	† Kansas St.	56
78	† Kansas	81
81	■ UC Santa Barb.	54
80	† Stanford	67
54	† Texas Tech	79

COLO. CHRISTIAN 7-19

60	N.M. Highlands	76
77	■ Doane	88
77	■ Colorado Col.	51
66	■ South Dak. Tech	74
68	■ Adams St.	57
46	■ Fort Hays St.	67
56	■ N.M. Highlands	81
38	Doane	79
67	Adams St.	80
53	■ Denver	101
56	■ Air Force	69
89	■ Colorado Mines	66
70	Southern Colo.	79
54	Regis (Colo.)	75
63	■ Colorado-CS	78
56	■ Neb.-Kearney	89
38	■ Metropolitan St.	69
65	† Fort Lewis	62
38	Denver	71
51	Air Force	59
55	Colorado Mines	47
75	■ Fort Lewis	67
60	■ Southern Colo.	58
55	■ Regis (Colo.)	70
53	Colorado-CS	81
46	Metropolitan St.	83

COLORADO COL. 2-23

60	† UC San Diego	85
50	Redlands	48
48	Regis (Colo.)	75
53	■ La Verne	54
44	■ William Penn	63
51	Colo. Christian	77
54	† Dana	71
35	Colorado-CS	86
67	Western St.	94
51	Adams St.	105
64	■ Judson	79
54	■ Gordon	70
50	La Verne	84
57	Pomona-Pitzer	76
51	Claremont-M-S	59
77	Colorado Mines	73
47	Sterling	81
67	■ Panhandle St.	72
56	Neb. Wesleyan	87
59	Hastings	104
37	Air Force	80
48	■ Western St.	68
53	■ Colorado-CS	82
71	■ Adams St.	74
48	■ N.M. Highlands	75

COLORADO MINES 1-22

43	Bethany (Kan.)	72
32	Colorado-CS	79
42	Air Force	87
47	Regis (Colo.)	78
52	■ Denver	93
55	■ St. Cloud St.	72
75	■ Wayne St. (Neb.)	104
73	■ Colorado Col.	77
66	Colo. Christian	89
67	■ Chadron St.	99
55	Fort Hays St.	91
56	Adams St.	87
59	N.M. Highlands	77
95	Western St.	98
64	Mesa St.	98
68	■ Adams St.	78
63	■ N.M. Highlands	87
47	■ Colo. Christian	55
67	■ Western St.	65
59	■ Mesa St.	66
49	■ Fort Hays St.	92
58	Chadron St.	108
52	† Mesa St.	83

COLORADO ST. 13-14

91	■ Northern Colo.	62
53	† Ohio	58
77	† Austin Peay	70
69	■ Colorado	90
81	■ Baylor	79
82	■ Loyola (Cal.)	70
85	■ Toledo	80
66	UC Santa Barb.	74
67	Cal St. Northridge	52
106	■ Southern Colo.	42
66	Idaho St.	52
78	Weber St.	73
69	Wyoming	83
61	■ Brigham Young	74
54	■ Utah	81
59	San Diego St.	82
71	Fresno St.	65
73	■ New Mexico	48
41	■ UTEP	54
70	■ Wyoming	58
55	Utah	71
71	Brigham Young	84
76	■ Fresno St.	60
60	■ San Diego St.	64
48	UTEP	72
73	New Mexico	74
48	Utah	62

COLORADO-CS 18-9

79	■ Colorado Mines	32
45	† Northwest Mo. St.	55
44	Washburn	80
63	Neb.-Kearney	70
75	† Hastings	99
59	† Wayne St. (Neb.)	67
86	■ Colorado Col.	35
55	Fla. Southern	64
72	† Quinnipiac	53
87	■ McKendree	44
71	■ Regis (Colo.)	62
74	Western St.	50

74 Southern Colo. 54
78 ■ Fort Lewis 46
66 Air Force 58
43 ■ Denver 64
68 ■ Metropolitan St. 65
78 Colo. Christian 63
76 ■ N.M. Highlands 63
74 Regis (Colo.) 58
82 Colorado Col. 53
78 ■ Southern Colo. 49
64 Fort Lewis 46
90 ■ Air Force 64
54 Denver 66
65 Metropolitan St. 68
81 ■ Colo. Christian 53

COLUMBIA-BARNARD 7-19
65 ■ Manhattan 56
45 Wagner 77
75 FDU-Teaneck 65
38 ■ Fordham 69
57 † Hartford 66
61 † Coppin St. 58
61 Rice 71
63 † Tex.-Pan American 60
56 Army 63
66 ■ Hofstra 61
51 Cornell 64
64 Colgate 53
46 ■ Cornell 60
60 Marist 77
65 Yale 78
46 Brown 68
36 Dartmouth 72
53 Harvard 85
70 ■ Pennsylvania 69
44 ■ Princeton 58
66 ■ Brown 79
46 ■ Yale 70
55 Princeton 73
57 Pennsylvania 64
69 ■ Harvard 85
58 ■ Dartmouth 69

COLUMBUS 12-15
80 ■ Morris Brown 65
70 Tuskegee 74
71 ■ Shorter 65
71 ■ Ga. Southwestern 80
90 Flagler 52
89 North Fla. 100
107 ■ LeMoyne-Owen 57
73 ■ Tuskegee 76
68 ■ S.C.-Aiken 70
74 ■ Francis Marion 62
75 ■ Pembroke St. 52
69 ■ Armstrong St. 62
69 Georgia Col. 66
69 S.C.-Spartanburg 81
61 Lander 51
79 Ga. Southwestern 58
68 ■ Georgia Col. 76
69 ■ Augusta 76
56 Armstrong St. 82
76 Francis Marion 77
69 Pembroke St. 77
44 ■ S.C.-Spartanburg 77
65 ■ Lander 67
62 S.C.-Aiken 59
52 Augusta 73
70 † Armstrong St. 60
60 Augusta 73

CONCORDIA (ILL.) 7-18
47 Millikin 79
73 Moody Bible 42
73 ■ Chicago 74
55 Spring Arbor 94
73 Concordia (Mich.) 74
57 † North Park 85
67 † Iowa Wesleyan 64
53 Elmhurst 73
81 ■ North Park 80
67 ■ St. Mary's (Ind.) 82

59 Olivet (Ill.) 78
58 ■ Trinity (Ill.) 60
71 Judson 51
57 ■ Rockford 37
75 ■ Aurora 83
50 ■ Concordia (Wis.) 60
71 ■ Concordia (St. Paul) 82
60 Ill. Benedictine 75
47 Trinity (Ill.) 80
71 ■ Judson 66
43 ■ Lake Forest 76
73 Rockford 58
63 ■ Ill. Benedictine 70
55 Eureka 88
71 Aurora 81

CONCORDIA-M'HEAD 20-7
77 Minn.-Morris 78
69 ■ Moorhead St. 75
83 Valley City St. 74
77 ■ Gust. Adolphus 51
56 St. Benedict 79
37 North Dak. St. 102
80 ■ Carleton 51
88 ■ Bethel (Minn.) 56
47 St. Thomas (Minn.) 46
79 ■ Augsburg 48
79 ■ St. Olaf 70
84 ■ Macalester 64
97 ■ Hamline 59
95 ■ St. Mary's (Minn.) 59
83 Carleton 56
82 Gust. Adolphus 71
69 ■ St. Benedict 71
70 ■ St. Thomas (Minn.) 57
108 Augsburg 52
91 St. Olaf 68
87 Macalester 60
95 St. Mary's (Minn.) 61
65 Bethel (Minn.) 69
93 Hamline 83
78 ■ Muskingum 64
87 † Maryville (Tenn.) 69
57 St. Benedict 84

CONNECTICUT 18-11
95 ■ Fairfield 58
58 † Geo. Washington 56
54 Kentucky 75
53 ■ Lafayette 36
53 ■ St. Joseph's (Pa.) 51
70 Seton Hall 64
37 † Vanderbilt 57
54 † N.C.-Charlotte 44
78 Syracuse 50
51 St. John's (N.Y.) 54
81 ■ Boston College 69
66 ■ Miami (Fla.) 69
74 Providence 58
72 ■ Seton Hall 53
73 ■ Pittsburgh 52
44 ■ Villanova 50
81 Georgetown 78
71 ■ St. John's (N.Y.) 59
85 ■ Syracuse 54
79 Boston College 52
51 Miami (Fla.) 69
76 ■ Providence 47
54 ■ Stanford 68
74 Pittsburgh 76
62 ■ Georgetown 64
60 Villanova 50
56 † Seton Hall 54
73 Providence 87
71 ■ Louisville 74

CONNECTICUT COL. 22-2
53 ■ Tufts 50
63 Wesleyan 61
71 † Salve Regina 40
84 ■ Westfield St. 85
60 ■ Wellesley 39
80 Mount Holyoke 42
55 ■ Amherst 53
59 ■ Albertus Magnus 57

70 Clark (Mass.) 65
75 ■ Mass.-Dartmouth 60
81 ■ Coast Guard 47
62 Trinity (Conn.) 59
63 ■ Eastern Conn. St. 52
80 Elms 46
68 ■ Skidmore 53
67 ■ Wesleyan 58
75 Bowdoin 57
86 Coast Guard 34
77 ■ Bates 65
80 ■ Pine Manor 47
69 Nichols 52
74 Manhattanville 29
70 ■ Wheaton (Mass.) 64
55 † Westfield St. 57

COPPIN ST. 20-9
56 † Towson St. 45
75 † Md.-Balt. County 55
76 ■ St. Francis (N.Y.) 59
68 Fairfield 70
58 † Columbia-Barnard 61
75 Hofstra 57
56 LIU-Brooklyn 47
59 Louisville 98
47 † Houston 70
55 South Caro. St. 58
74 East Caro. 60
51 ■ North Caro. A&T 42
70 Md.-East. Shore 56
61 ■ Florida A&M 58
56 ■ Bethune-Cookman 43
56 ■ Morgan St. 71
76 Howard 47
67 Delaware St. 59
58 ■ Howard 50
82 Morgan St. 73
77 ■ Delaware St. 63
68 Florida A&M 77
63 Bethune-Cookman 71
67 ■ South Caro. St. 64
58 North Caro. A&T 49
64 ■ Md.-East. Shore 42
70 † Howard 53
51 † North Caro. A&T 49
54 † South Caro. St. 65

CORNELL 10-16
55 ■ Colgate 43
47 Buffalo 50
64 † Delaware St. 58
58 Bucknell 70
70 ■ Buffalo 54
62 ■ Niagara 77
61 N.C.-Greensboro 70
76 † East Tenn. St. 65
45 Lafayette 54
79 ■ St. Bonaventure 87
64 ■ Columbia-Barnard 51
70 ■ Delaware St. 56
60 Columbia-Barnard 46
64 ■ Hofstra 58
63 Brown 82
62 Yale 72
71 Harvard 84
50 Dartmouth 64
68 ■ Princeton 67
65 ■ Pennsylvania 69
63 ■ Yale 74
66 ■ Brown 70
63 Pennsylvania 75
63 Princeton 84
66 ■ Dartmouth 60
75 ■ Harvard 97

CORNELL COLLEGE 0-22
54 † Clarke 76
48 ■ William Penn 67
53 Grinnell 79
71 Mt. St. Clare 90
38 ■ Wartburg 93
57 ■ Upper Iowa 66
53 ■ Illinois Col. 83
33 Grand View 108

49 Knox 80
51 Monmouth (Ill.) 76
49 ■ St. Norbert 99
40 ■ Lawrence 76
46 ■ Grinnell 81
55 Lake Forest 97
34 Beloit 96
45 Coe 98
40 ■ Monmouth (Ill.) 77
39 ■ Teiko-Marycrest 89
59 ■ Knox 74
52 ■ Coe 76
54 Illinois Col. 91
52 Iowa Wesleyan 53

CORTLAND ST. 12-13
53 ■ Clarkson 46
61 ■ Le Moyne 69
38 Geneseo St. 66
62 Buffalo St. 73
62 ■ Oneonta St. 41
57 ■ Plattsburgh St. 49
57 ■ Potsdam St. 61
52 ■ Ithaca 46
57 ■ Oswego St. 56
62 Utica Tech 73
40 ■ Binghamton 71
57 Scranton 103
55 ■ Stony Brook 53
66 New Paltz St. 60
69 ■ Fredonia St. 67
48 Albany (N.Y.) 77
65 Plattsburgh St. 52
73 Potsdam St. 56
62 Binghamton 78
55 ■ Brockport St. 61
93 ■ New Paltz St. 64
56 Oneonta St. 59
58 St. John Fisher 77
70 † Brockport St. 68
53 Geneseo St. 77

CREIGHTON 20-8
71 Iowa St. 55
65 ■ Chicago St. 44
98 ■ Wyoming 61
70 Missouri 65
69 Texas 86
58 ■ Nebraska 79
64 † Mo.-Kansas City 51
54 Oklahoma St. 64
75 Kansas 60
85 ■ Western Ill. 52
75 Bradley 53
68 Illinois St. 69
58 ■ Southwest Mo. St. 55
76 ■ Wichita St. 45
83 ■ Drake 72
90 Northern Iowa 66
82 ■ Southern Ill. 76
83 ■ Indiana St. 51
76 ■ Northern Iowa 41
71 Drake 60
80 Indiana St. 65
73 Southern Ill. 76
74 Wichita St. 82
59 Southwest Mo. St. 73
80 ■ Illinois St. 57
74 ■ Bradley 59
86 ■ Northern Iowa 73
69 ■ Southern Ill. 71

CURRY 15-10
50 Gordon 57
66 Simmons 30
43 ■ Babson 71
46 ■ Fitchburg St. 62
59 ■ Suffolk 26
51 Framingham St. 48
42 Nichols 39
46 ■ Regis (Mass.) 50
65 Roger Williams 51
55 Salve Regina 44
72 ■ Wentworth Inst. 60

30 Elms 51
53 ■ New England Col. 49
68 ■ Eastern Nazarene 48
46 Anna Maria 47
65 ■ Roger Williams 26
68 Eastern Nazarene 51
52 Mass.-Boston 58
63 ■ Salve Regina 46
55 Wentworth Inst. 33
41 ■ Anna Maria 39
47 New England Col. 57
53 Regis (Mass.) 58
64 ■ Eastern Nazarene 49
39 † New England Col. 53

DARTMOUTH 8-18

58 ■ Vermont 76
47 New Hampshire 67
52 Vanderbilt 90
83 Stetson 86
59 † Bradley 68
81 ■ Colgate 48
57 ■ Manhattan 58
49 ■ Hartford 57
66 ■ Pennsylvania 76
68 ■ Princeton 59
57 Siena 63
66 Harvard 99
56 ■ Boston U. 70
59 Maine 60
61 ■ Central Conn. St. 41
72 ■ Columbia-Barnard 36
64 ■ Cornell 50
57 Brown 76
49 Yale 67
49 Princeton 67
63 Pennsylvania 57
78 ■ Yale 51
57 ■ Brown 62
60 Cornell 66
69 Columbia-Barnard 58
77 ■ Harvard 88

DAVIDSON 9-13

64 ■ Ferrum 40
62 N.C.-Asheville 48
40 Liberty 74
71 ■ Lenoir-Rhyne 84
70 N.C.-Wilmington 78
53 † New Hampshire 91
51 Frank. & Marsh. 56
84 † Phila. Pharmacy 60
59 † Carnegie Mellon 73
52 ■ Western Caro. 76
63 Wofford 73
62 ■ Pfeiffer 49
64 ■ Winthrop 62
65 ■ Barton 58
56 ■ Gardner-Webb 81
67 Lynchburg 49
54 ■ Liberty 71
61 ■ Wofford 70
57 Western Caro. 71
57 ■ Charleston So. 44
58 Francis Marion 85
59 ■ N.C.-Asheville 49

DAVIS & ELKINS 4-22

55 Alderson-Broaddus 67
55 Bethany (W.Va.) 67
57 † Ohio Belmont 51
70 ■ Glenville St. 85
66 West Va. Wesleyan 49
56 ■ Shepherd 61
52 Salem-Teikyo 67
70 ■ Alderson-Broaddus 68
56 ■ Calif. (Pa.) 88
65 West Va. Tech 82
65 Fairmont St. 79
75 West Va. St. 77
45 Shippensburg 74
38 Pitt.-Johnstown 90
50 Wheeling Jesuit 62
48 ■ Elon 65
68 ■ West Va. Wesleyan 65
59 ■ Concord 68
57 ■ Wheeling Jesuit 64
62 Bluefield St. 80
57 Glenville St. 98
54 ■ Charleston (W.Va.) 65
58 Shepherd 68
55 West Liberty St. 74
54 ■ Salem-Teikyo 73
52 † Wheeling Jesuit 69

DAYTON 15-13

75 ■ Bradley 56
92 † Radford 90
86 † Manhattan 70
68 ■ Bowling Green 94
58 Wright St. 54
66 ■ St. Francis (Pa.) 50
50 Miami (Ohio) 83
57 ■ Missouri 68
61 ■ Xavier (Ohio) 76
61 ■ Ohio 45
60 ■ Notre Dame 72
68 Cincinnati 66
71 Duquesne 67
67 La Salle 100
65 ■ Evansville 67
65 ■ Butler 72
84 Loyola (Ill.) 80
57 Detroit Mercy 43
65 Xavier (Ohio) 78
80 Notre Dame 92
81 ■ La Salle 65
69 ■ Duquesne 45
71 Butler 82
55 Evansville 59
67 ■ Detroit Mercy 64
70 ■ Loyola (Ill.) 63
78 Notre Dame 74
57 † Xavier (Ohio) 67

DEPAUL 20-9

94 ■ Cleveland St. 55
62 ■ Southern Cal 54
65 Oregon 62
87 Northeastern Ill. 49
71 ■ Arkansas 47
52 ■ Auburn 56
78 ■ Penn St. 85
65 Wis.-Green Bay 54
82 ■ Memphis St. 73
76 ■ Marquette 82
69 Northern Ill. 73
48 Tennessee 60
71 ■ Notre Dame 55
62 Cincinnati 59
77 Ala.-Birmingham 61
87 ■ St. Louis 57
62 Memphis St. 52
61 Vanderbilt 71
73 ■ Loyola (Ill.) 60
79 ■ Cincinnati 55
84 ■ Northern Ill. 68
74 ■ Ala.-Birmingham 47
62 Georgia 74
82 ■ Ill.-Chicago 43
65 Marquette 67
76 St. Louis 40
73 † Cincinnati 57
70 † Marquette 53
59 Louisiana Tech 70

DEPAUW 7-17

55 † Ill. Wesleyan 74
38 † Washington (Mo.) 79
57 Earlham 64
66 ■ Hanover 67
57 ■ Blackburn 65
67 ■ Webster 72
54 † Centre 83
39 † Carroll (Wis.) 65
61 ■ Thomas More 55
58 ■ Oakland City 55
72 † Lynchburg 36
55 † Whittier 48
36 ■ Franklin 51
73 ■ Anderson 64
79 ■ Fontbonne 74
69 Maryville (Mo.) 68
46 Manchester 79
71 ■ Taylor 76
46 Hanover 64
43 Franklin 63
59 Oakland City 81
60 ■ Manchester 62
38 Anderson 53
60 Thomas More 71

DEFIANCE 17-8

56 Hillsdale 67
81 ■ Earlham 62
70 † Waynesburg 53
58 Heidelberg 60
59 † Adrian 56
42 Wittenberg 87
55 ■ Bluffton 43
51 ■ St. John Fisher 37
50 Baldwin-Wallace 58
67 ■ Wilmington (Ohio) 61
69 Bluffton 50
70 Findlay 81
66 ■ St. Francis (Ind.) 70
82 ■ Thomas More 70
71 Manchester 72
66 ■ Hiram 35
69 Wilmington (Ohio) 67
68 ■ Bluffton 59
94 Anderson 63
68 ■ Wooster 53
78 Thomas More 69
57 ■ Kalamazoo 41
53 Franklin 68
74 ■ Thomas More 64
74 ■ Wilmington (Ohio) 61

DELAWARE 17-11

78 Lehigh 55
74 ■ Temple 53
51 ■ Lafayette 42
81 Delaware St. 56
59 ■ Towson St. 49
45 George Mason 80
72 † FDU-Teaneck 68
51 Pittsburgh 68
38 St. Joseph's (Pa.) 57
68 Princeton 63
59 ■ Pennsylvania 70
63 New Hampshire 89
56 Maine 53
81 ■ Md.-Balt. County 63
60 ■ Boston U. 59
60 ■ Northeastern 52
60 Vermont 83
59 Hartford 75
68 Drexel 62
70 ■ Hartford 57
55 ■ Vermont 77
57 Northeastern 72
76 Boston U. 70
53 ■ Maine 58
73 ■ New Hampshire 67
68 ■ Drexel 67
73 ■ Hartford 64
62 Vermont 75

DELAWARE ST. 10-17

59 ■ Va. Commonwealth 81
48 † Cincinnati 67
58 † Cornell 64
71 ■ FDU-Teaneck 69
56 ■ Delaware 81
70 Dist. Columbia 55
60 ■ Md.-East. Shore 51
37 Bethune-Cookman 71
70 Florida A&M 85
55 ■ Buffalo 67
77 Howard 70
53 Morgan St. 80
56 Cornell 70
54 ■ North Caro. A&T 56
75 ■ South Caro. St. 87
75 ■ Dist. Columbia 46
59 ■ Coppin St. 67
84 North Caro. A&T 71
61 South Caro. St. 80
63 Coppin St. 77
64 † Md.-East. Shore 58
58 ■ Morgan St. 62
77 ■ Howard 56
64 ■ Bethune-Cookman 56
51 ■ Florida A&M 70
77 Hofstra 74
70 † Morgan St. 83

DELAWARE VALLEY 13-11

39 Phila. Textile 66
56 † Cabrini 57
91 Upsala 75
95 Drew 55
59 Ursinus 48
59 Cabrini 50
81 ■ Allentown 60
91 ■ Hilbert 58
66 ■ New Paltz St. 69
86 Widener 41
52 Albright 66
73 ■ King's (Pa.) 67
81 ■ Drew 43
62 ■ Lebanon Valley 58
61 ■ Holy Family 63
45 ■ Scranton 71
74 FDU-Madison 70
61 ■ Lycoming 74
69 King's (Pa.) 81
52 ■ FDU-Madison 59
64 Scranton 84
89 ■ Upsala 72
63 ■ King's (Pa.) 59
58 Susquehanna 80

DELTA ST. 27-6

95 † Florida Tech 61
87 † Lincoln Memorial 70
100 Montevallo 98
95 ■ Ark.-Monticello 84
71 † Alabama 91
69 † Alcorn St. 70
100 ■ North Ala. 50
61 Arkansas Tech 70
82 Valdosta St. 61
86 West Ga. 62
103 Mississippi Val. 72
62 ■ Arkansas Tech 65
73 ■ Jacksonville St. 66
86 Ark.-Pine Bluff 45
88 ■ Mississippi Col. 60
92 ■ Livingston 67
91 ■ Ark.-Pine Bluff 64
73 North Ala. 41
95 ■ Mississippi-Women 43
79 Livingston 56
63 Mississippi Col. 61
92 ■ Mississippi Val. 68
91 Jacksonville St. 78
84 ■ Valdosta St. 48
82 ■ West Ga. 56
75 Mississippi-Women 43
75 ■ West Ga. 46
65 ■ Jacksonville St. 67
90 ■ Jacksonville St. 61
75 ■ Florida Tech 51
96 ■ Pitt.-Johnstown 63
71 † Michigan Tech 67
63 † North Dak. St. 95

DENISON 13-12

54 † Rosary 89
74 † Taylor 85
72 ■ Malone 75
94 Oberlin 56
71 ■ Kenyon 27
57 ■ Wash. & Jeff. 79

65 Wooster 64
81 ■ Thomas More 71
36 Ohio Wesleyan 62
61 ■ Wittenberg 56
71 ■ Case Reserve 58
70 ■ Earlham 53
60 Allegheny 75
48 ■ Wooster 56
65 Kenyon 32
84 Wilberforce 52
59 ■ Ohio Wesleyan 64
55 Earlham 60
49 Case Reserve 63
77 ■ Oberlin 34
70 ■ Allegheny 56
70 ■ Bluffton 65
74 Wittenberg 82
78 ■ Case Reserve 63
55 Ohio Wesleyan 56

DENVER 24-4
77 ■ Northern Colo. 52
81 Mesa St. 87
93 Colorado Mines 52
92 ■ Mesa St. 57
102 ■ St. Cloud St. 70
79 ■ Emporia St. 42
65 Cal Poly Pomona 69
78 UC Riverside 82
71 Nebraska-Omaha 64
89 ■ Midland Lutheran 56
77 ■ Wayne St. (Neb.) 64
72 Air Force 60
101 Colo. Christian 53
68 Metropolitan St. 59
79 ■ Regis (Colo.) 44
64 Colorado-CS 43
95 ■ Fort Lewis 51
81 Southern Colo. 78
75 Northern Colo. 68
75 ■ Air Force 69
71 ■ Colo. Christian 38
68 ■ Metropolitan St. 66
92 Regis (Colo.) 73
66 ■ Colorado-CS 54
99 Fort Lewis 66
87 ■ Southern Colo. 50
94 ■ West Tex. St. 62
77 North Dak. St. 92

DETROIT MERCY 11-16
70 ■ Wis.-Milwaukee 45
71 Western Mich. 73
67 Central Mich. 69
70 Toledo 78
63 ■ Syracuse 45
77 Temple 64
76 † Illinois 85
76 † Florida A&M 68
77 Michigan 73
77 ■ Canisius 55
63 Loyola (Ill.) 60
55 Notre Dame 80
69 ■ Evansville 79
64 Duquesne 80
76 La Salle 77
75 ■ Xavier (Ohio) 70
43 ■ Dayton 57
65 Butler 82
42 Evansville 62
75 ■ Loyola (Ill.) 52
74 ■ Butler 73
55 ■ Notre Dame 68
69 ■ La Salle 88
82 ■ Duquesne 79
64 Dayton 67
75 Xavier (Ohio) 83
72 † Xavier (Ohio) 74

DICKINSON 18-8
69 † Houghton 83
94 † Widener 44
71 † Allegheny 76
60 † Point Park 58
79 Albright 75
70 Lycoming 45
64 ■ Frank. & Marsh. 73
76 ■ York (Pa.) 66
67 Western Md. 56
71 Lebanon Valley 42
79 Gettysburg 75
64 ■ Wash. & Jeff. 73
71 ■ Wilkes 69
72 ■ Western Md. 47
66 Widener 36
71 ■ Johns Hopkins 67
78 Moravian 87
69 ■ Gettysburg 55
52 Frank. & Marsh. 59
65 ■ Lebanon Valley 49
63 Johns Hopkins 62
70 ■ Juniata 53
62 Messiah 58
58 Moravian 67
63 † Penn St.-Behrend 61
43 † Wilkes 44

DIST. COLUMBIA 4-18
61 Columbia Union 74
81 † Cheyney 62
75 ■ Virginia Union 61
53 ■ Pembroke St. 68
59 ■ Longwood 64
70 Catholic 62
55 Morgan St. 69
70 ■ Columbia Union 61
55 ■ Delaware St. 70
46 Elizabeth City St. 62
55 Kutztown 66
64 Columbia Union 68
59 Virginia St. 63
46 Delaware St. 75
53 Hampton 78
55 ■ Elizabeth City St. 74
53 ■ Morgan St. 56
59 Pembroke St. 78
56 ■ Hampton 82
53 ■ Norfolk St. 73
55 Virginia Union 64
46 Longwood 55

DOWLING 5-21
36 Mercyhurst 86
72 † West Liberty St. 73
37 Phila. Textile 75
50 Tampa 71
64 † St. Augustine's 82
53 Molloy 62
50 Pace 70
68 ■ Southern Conn. St. 60
65 Mercy 66
63 ■ LIU-C.W. Post 73
64 Concordia (N.Y.) 53
41 Adelphi 72
45 LIU-C.W. Post 71
55 ■ St. Rose 63
55 ■ Phila. Textile 73
59 ■ Queens (N.Y.) 57
50 ■ Pace 71
71 ■ Mercy 81
75 LIU-Southampton 58
76 ■ Molloy 93
65 ■ Adelphi 55
63 ■ Concordia (N.Y.) 67
57 ■ LIU-Southampton 65
68 St. Rose 71
63 Southern Conn. St. 65
57 Queens (N.Y.) 60

DRAKE 15-13
59 ■ Montana St. 54
68 Northeastern Ill. 67
57 Iowa St. 43
44 Iowa 90
73 ■ Loyola (Ill.) 65
58 † Duke 71
74 † Princeton 63
61 Portland 77
90 ■ Montana 83
71 Illinois St. 62
68 Bradley 67
75 ■ Canisius 82
53 ■ Southwest Mo. St. 69
81 ■ Wichita St. 60
72 Creighton 83
112 ■ Northern Iowa 106
83 ■ Indiana St. 74
61 ■ Southern Ill. 56
78 Northern Iowa 71
60 ■ Creighton 71
57 Southern Ill. 82
76 Indiana St. 78
79 Wichita St. 92
64 Southwest Mo. St. 95
75 ■ Bradley 83
69 ■ Illinois St. 65
77 ■ Wichita St. 68
53 Southwest Mo. St. 83

DREW 4-18
62 † Coast Guard 70
67 Stony Brook 97
55 ■ Delaware Valley 95
67 New Jersey Tech 59
60 ■ Caldwell 63
56 Muhlenberg 97
30 ■ FDU-Madison 85
54 ■ King's (Pa.) 78
45 ■ Wheaton (Mass.) 81
55 Scranton 99
43 Delaware Valley 81
63 Upsala 83
50 ■ Rutgers-Newark 69
57 Haverford 55
59 Dominican (N.Y.) 74
69 ■ Upsala 71
48 FDU-Madison 68
39 ■ Scranton 91
64 ■ Widener 49
42 King's (Pa.) 78
76 ■ St. Elizabeth 69
51 Centenary (N.J.) 59

DREXEL 5-22
52 ■ Maryland 121
82 Pennsylvania 67
75 Princeton 79
60 Towson St. 55
86 ■ FDU-Teaneck 71
63 Georgetown 92
41 Virginia Tech 92
52 † Campbell 71
61 La Salle 77
64 ■ Lafayette 67
70 ■ Hofstra 53
50 Maine 56
54 New Hampshire 64
59 ■ Northeastern 72
66 ■ Boston U. 86
49 Hartford 65
56 Vermont 96
62 ■ Delaware 68
53 American 73
58 ■ Vermont 80
72 ■ Hartford 76
76 Boston U. 66
52 Northeastern 70
59 ■ New Hampshire 73
53 ■ Maine 66
67 Delaware 68
56 Vermont 75

DUKE 12-15
88 N.C.-Wilmington 52
64 ■ Northeastern 53
85 ■ Virginia Tech 63
114 ■ East Tenn. St. 74
80 N.C.-Greensboro 76
79 ■ Appalachian St. 76
71 † Drake 58
48 Washington 72
72 ■ Florida St. 84
61 ■ Loyola (Md.) 52
57 Virginia 76
60 North Caro. St. 77
51 ■ Maryland 82
54 North Caro. 66
59 Radford 58
60 ■ Wake Forest 64
80 ■ Georgia Tech 86
63 Clemson 88
71 Maryland 90
82 ■ North Caro. St. 65
61 ■ Virginia 97
67 ■ Clemson 65
71 Wake Forest 59
63 ■ North Caro. 84
67 Georgia Tech 72
67 Florida St. 74
69 † Wake Forest 70

DUQUESNE 7-20
67 ■ Pittsburgh 80
62 ■ Army 58
65 ■ North Caro. 81
73 Niagara 78
86 † Loyola (Md.) 76
43 Geo. Washington 55
92 ■ Canisius 86
86 St. Francis (Pa.) 76
71 † Towson St. 37
59 Evansville 74
67 Butler 87
67 ■ Dayton 71
65 ■ Xavier (Ohio) 80
80 ■ Detroit Mercy 64
63 ■ Loyola (Ill.) 66
71 ■ La Salle 81
80 West Va. 90
67 Notre Dame 95
66 ■ Butler 79
66 ■ Evansville 65
69 Xavier (Ohio) 102
45 Dayton 69
63 Loyola (Ill.) 77
79 Detroit Mercy 82
63 ■ Notre Dame 91
60 La Salle 96
74 † Butler 84

EARLHAM 11-12
83 Miami (Middletown) 61
62 Defiance 81
64 ■ DePauw 57
61 ■ Wittenberg 99
86 Oberlin 51
82 Thomas More 80
76 ■ Kenyon 42
71 ■ Anderson 70
84 ■ Graceland (Ind.) 77
80 ■ Allegheny 82
54 ■ Wooster 73
53 Denison 70
78 Case Reserve 96
63 Ohio Wesleyan 86
78 ■ Oberlin 33
58 Kenyon 40
77 Allegheny 76
60 ■ Denison 55
50 Wooster 83
63 Wittenberg 74
61 ■ Case Reserve 65
60 ■ Ohio Wesleyan 89
58 Wittenberg 83

EAST CARO. 16-12
72 † Virginia Tech 86
71 † Northeastern 61
92 ■ N.C.-Asheville 58
79 North Caro. St. 94
86 Winthrop 59
91 † East Tenn. St. 83
76 N.C.-Greensboro 59
60 ■ Coppin St. 74
53 James Madison 60
73 Richmond 76
75 ■ Campbell 60
70 ■ American 62
61 ■ George Mason 73

39	Old Dominion	75
62	William & Mary	60
45	N.C.-Charlotte	78
87	N.C.-Wilmington	67
69	■ James Madison	67
60	■ Richmond	61
71	■ North Caro. A&T	56
71	American	61
57	George Mason	77
59	■ Old Dominion	71
81	■ William & Mary	73
89	Appalachian St.	87
82	■ N.C.-Wilmington	56
72	† George Mason	50
67	Old Dominion	85

EAST STROUDSBURG		16-9
60	† Northern Ky.	68
88	† Fairmont St.	59
60	■ New Haven	57
68	■ Rollins	60
78	■ LIU-Southampton	44
78	Calif. (Pa.)	88
60	St. Rose	55
55	† American Int'l	84
57	■ Mercyhurst	82
84	Edinboro	87
63	Le Moyne	67
86	■ Centenary (N.J.)	45
86	West Chester	81
75	■ Mansfield	62
59	Millersville	86
58	■ Cheyney	43
77	■ LIU-C.W. Post	41
80	■ Kutztown	66
59	Bloomsburg	74
61	■ West Chester	59
67	Mansfield	49
74	■ Millersville	59
67	Cheyney	47
84	Kutztown	69
58	■ Bloomsburg	68

EAST TENN. ST.		7-18
51	■ Wake Forest	76
94	† N.C.-Asheville	73
66	† Winthrop	61
74	Duke	114
62	Liberty	73
59	Virginia Tech	91
102	■ Tenn.-Martin	94
83	† East Caro.	91
65	† Cornell	76
58	Wake Forest	71
75	■ Appalachian St.	77
72	Marshall	78
79	Tenn.-Chatt.	66
83	Ga. Southern	82
53	South Caro.	86
91	■ Western Caro.	83
72	■ Furman	88
55	Georgia Tech	88
94	Appalachian St.	91
81	■ Marshall	86
72	■ Tenn.-Chatt.	85
72	■ Ga. Southern	73
67	Western Caro.	104
80	Furman	96
55	■ Marshall	74

EAST TEX. ST.		13-15
69	■ Arkansas Tech	91
54	■ Southwest Baptist	62
69	Cal St. San B'dino	78
97	Chapman	65
68	Midwestern St.	82
82	Tarleton St.	72
67	Southwest Baptist	79
58	† Pittsburg St.	71
64	† West Tex. St.	88
70	■ Wayland Bapt.	104
84	■ Midwestern St.	107
76	Angelo St.	72
79	Abilene Christian	84

76	Texas A&I	66
81	■ Texas Woman's	63
72	■ Eastern N. Mex.	85
78	Cameron	71
85	Central Okla.	88
91	■ Central Okla.	95
78	■ Cameron	56
74	■ Abilene Christian	84
91	■ Angelo St.	75
78	Eastern N. Mex.	73
71	Texas Woman's	59
78	■ Tarleton St.	74
76	■ Texas A&I	69
80	† Cameron	78
84	† Eastern N. Mex.	98

EASTERN CONN. ST.		15-12
74	■ Teiko Post	55
55	■ Montclair St.	53
59	■ Emmanuel	71
90	† Concordia (N.Y.)	52
48	Western Conn. St.	70
65	Clark (Mass.)	69
74	■ Norwich	50
58	■ Trinity (Conn.)	67
74	■ Wesleyan	66
57	Worcester St.	67
74	■ Mass.-Dartmouth	54
52	■ Southern Me.	53
76	■ Wheaton (Mass.)	71
79	■ Rhode Island Col.	84
66	Plymouth St.	58
52	Connecticut Col.	63
64	Mass.-Dartmouth	66
77	Mass.-Boston	51
68	■ Western New Eng.	56
99	Rhode Island Col.	81
67	■ Plymouth St.	60
73	■ Mass.-Boston	57
44	Southern Me.	78
83	■ Mass.-Boston	61
63	† Rhode Island Col.	56
55	Southern Me.	77
63	Middlebury	76

EASTERN ILL.		3-24
45	Missouri	68
49	Texas-Arlington	64
37	† Baylor	88
57	■ Evansville	67
58	† Clemson	94
75	† Grambling	68
44	■ Indiana St.	61
57	Northwestern	104
61	■ Cleveland St.	81
50	■ Youngstown St.	66
54	Wright St.	65
58	■ Northern Ill.	85
65	Valparaiso	112
68	■ Ill.-Chicago	61
74	Murray St.	91
54	Wis.-Green Bay	68
72	Western Ill.	80
58	■ Wright St.	75
59	Cleveland St.	89
56	Youngstown St.	71
57	Northern Ill.	103
77	■ Western Ill.	71
78	■ Valparaiso	89
57	Ill.-Chicago	82
66	Chicago St.	70
41	■ Wis.-Green Bay	71
51	† Northern Ill.	102

EASTERN KY.		12-15
72	■ Ball St.	52
66	Louisville	74
77	Indiana St.	80
75	† Brown	59
68	Florida Int'l	82
63	† Iowa	67
59	Tennessee Tech	68
62	Middle Tenn. St.	76
80	Cincinnati	82

100	■ Austin Peay	75
90	■ Tennessee St.	85
79	Murray St.	66
66	Southeast Mo. St.	60
72	Morehead St.	60
92	■ Tenn.-Martin	61
80	■ Marshall	84
59	Austin Peay	67
84	Tennessee St.	65
106	■ Morehead St.	110
108	■ Murray St.	102
85	■ Southeast Mo. St.	58
56	Kentucky	74
75	■ Tennessee Tech	84
66	■ Middle Tenn. St.	80
58	■ Tennessee	95
95	Tenn.-Martin	76
74	† Middle Tenn. St.	87

EAST. MENNONITE		8-17
56	Buffalo St.	97
58	† Salem St.	70
65	■ Lynchburg	67
59	■ Va. Wesleyan	70
81	R.-M. Woman's	48
44	Roanoke	74
66	■ Averett	58
78	■ Shenandoah	64
84	Hollins	76
48	Bridgewater (Va.)	58
53	■ Randolph-Macon	55
56	■ Guilford	78
56	■ Emory & Henry	70
62	■ Roanoke	77
58	Emory & Henry	63
97	■ Mary Baldwin	37
68	Lynchburg	58
50	Guilford	58
51	■ Bridgewater (Va.)	63
84	Mary Baldwin	53
55	■ Hollins	63
79	■ R.-M. Woman's	57
57	Va. Wesleyan	87
56	Randolph-Macon	72
55	Roanoke	66

EASTERN MICH.		3-22
78	■ Wis.-Milwaukee	76
51	Illinois	80
78	† Texas A&M	80
72	■ Butler	89
68	■ Ill.-Chicago	74
68	Valparaiso	106
63	† Vermont	82
55	Central Mich.	66
42	■ Bowling Green	81
54	■ Akron	65
58	Toledo	75
67	■ Kent	79
56	Ball St.	41
56	■ Miami (Ohio)	78
53	Western Mich.	76
56	■ Ohio	58
54	Bowling Green	93
67	Akron	60
52	■ Toledo	62
71	Kent	101
45	■ Ball St.	57
61	Miami (Ohio)	76
63	■ Western Mich.	67
53	Ohio	65
51	■ Central Mich.	53

EASTERN MONT.		18-9
69	† UC Riverside	70
83	Cal St. Los Angeles	60
78	Rocky Mountain	62
51	† North Dak. St.	82
68	† Sonoma St.	48
64	■ Western Mont.	57
62	■ Cal St. Hayward	46
73	■ Cal St. Hayward	48
62	Montana St.	77
60	■ Northern Mont.	59
67	Montana Tech	56

61	Carroll (Mont.)	55
49	Northern Mont.	65
63	Grand Canyon	71
76	Grand Canyon	79
72	■ Portland St.	58
68	■ Seattle Pacific	58
71	■ Seattle Pacific	61
67	■ Rocky Mountain	57
67	Alas. Anchorage	65
66	Alas. Fairbanks	59
53	■ Alas. Anchorage	69
78	■ Alas. Fairbanks	54
78	■ Montana Tech	63
63	■ Grand Canyon	48
64	Portland St.	83
56	Seattle Pacific	72

EASTERN NAZARENE		6-19
41	King's (N.Y.)	64
55	Nyack	64
34	■ Regis (Mass.)	70
45	■ Mass.-Dartmouth	72
61	■ Suffolk	48
46	■ Nichols	50
52	† Emerson-MCA	45
39	Simmons	51
38	Wellesley	80
69	■ Mass.-Boston	79
68	Wentworth Inst.	59
43	New England Col.	72
60	■ Roger Williams	46
45	Regis (Mass.)	75
63	■ Wentworth Inst.	65
57	Anna Maria	75
48	Curry	68
68	■ Salve Regina	69
50	■ New England Col.	72
51	■ Curry	68
47	■ Gordon	56
47	Roger Williams	38
68	Salve Regina	62
36	■ Anna Maria	50
49	Curry	64

EASTERN N. MEX.		23-5
80	Alas. Fairbanks	61
74	Alas. Fairbanks	75
93	Alas. Anchorage	82
83	Alas. Anchorage	59
77	Air Force	72
76	■ Grand Canyon	65
93	Cal St. Los Angeles	56
70	Grand Canyon	60
86	■ Lubbock Chrst.	47
71	West Tex. St.	80
86	N.M. Highlands	75
76	■ Texas Woman's	54
89	■ Central Okla.	77
101	■ Cameron	58
94	Texas A&I	51
85	East Tex. St.	72
87	■ Angelo St.	69
70	■ Abilene Christian	68
88	Abilene Christian	64
76	Angelo St.	73
60	Cameron	62
94	Central Okla.	88
73	■ East Tex. St.	78
78	■ Texas A&I	65
80	■ Neb.-Kearney	74
95	Texas Woman's	66
98	† East Tex. St.	84
79	Abilene Christian	90

EASTERN WASH.		9-16
77	■ Seattle Pacific	72
55	■ Wis.-Green Bay	67
79	† St. Mary's (Cal.)	64
50	Nebraska	94
54	Gonzaga	69
61	Xavier (Ohio)	69
55	Purdue	68
58	† Marquette	64
66	Portland	67
70	■ Gonzaga	69

59 Montana St. 76
50 Montana 81
66 Idaho 59
67 ■ Cal St. Sacramento 64
79 ■ Northern Ariz. 65
65 ■ Weber St. 56
55 Boise St. 82
66 Idaho St. 73
35 ■ Montana 61
65 ■ Montana St. 77
81 ■ Idaho 82
65 Northern Ariz. 52
70 Weber St. 82
76 ■ Idaho St. 73
59 ■ Boise St. 72

ECKERD 7-19
69 Warner Southern 44
66 ■ Lindsey Wilson 77
62 ■ Florida A&M 79
43 ■ Morningside 98
51 ■ Seattle Pacific 78
65 ■ Southern Me. 73
63 ■ Shippensburg 81
67 ■ Lee 78
90 ■ Holy Family 79
60 ■ Millersville 75
59 ■ North Fla. 66
38 ■ Florida Tech 90
71 ■ Webber 54
83 ■ St. Leo 56
77 Rollins 87
52 ■ Tampa 81
79 ■ Barry 76
54 Webber 69
59 Fla. Southern 93
44 Florida Tech 98
69 St. Leo 68
56 ■ Rollins 48
48 Tampa 75
47 Barry 65
64 ■ Fla. Southern 94
61 North Fla. 69

EDINBORO 18-12
76 Alas. Anchorage 77
73 Alas. Anchorage 64
66 Alas. Fairbanks 89
78 Alas. Fairbanks 85
104 ■ Mich.-Dearborn 76
61 ■ Central St. (Ohio) 67
80 ■ Gannon 64
79 ■ Mercyhurst 54
113 Ohio Dominican 72
70 IU/PU-Ft. Wayne 68
77 Indiana Tech 81
61 Mercyhurst 85
87 ■ East Stroudsburg 84
61 Ashland 66
78 Gannon 71
81 ■ Slippery Rock 66
86 ■ Lock Haven 69
84 Clarion 105
77 ■ Calif. (Pa.) 75
73 Indiana (Pa.) 68
99 ■ Shippensburg 87
74 Slippery Rock 64
95 Lock Haven 56
76 ■ Clarion 64
78 Calif. (Pa.) 76
72 ■ Indiana (Pa.) 86
58 Shippensburg 77
76 Bloomsburg 62
81 † Clarion 104
76 Pitt.-Johnstown 88

ELIZABETH CITY ST. 8-15
57 Fayetteville St. 72
47 ■ Livingstone 48
47 † St. Paul's 61
52 ■ Shaw 67
79 Johnson Smith 63
97 ■ Virginia Union 94
62 ■ Dist. Columbia 46
63 ■ Hampton 77
62 ■ Virginia St. 65
84 ■ St. Augustine's 91
66 Norfolk St. 77
57 Bowie St. 58
43 Hampton 64
68 ■ St. Paul's 62
74 Dist. Columbia 55
67 ■ St. Paul's 56
72 ■ Winston-Salem 45
50 ■ Bowie St. 60
53 Virginia St. 66
77 N.C. Central 56
63 Virginia Union 68
60 ■ Norfolk St. 91
67 † Shaw 80

ELIZABETHTOWN 16-9
79 † Roanoke 68
82 Marymount (Va.) 88
83 † Chris. Newport 76
73 Juniata 84
86 Messiah 54
62 Scranton 77
106 ■ St. Mary's (Md.) 48
68 Ursinus 72
81 Johns Hopkins 90
93 ■ Moravian 83
54 Frank. & Marsh. 61
112 Albright 60
93 ■ Lycoming 61
96 ■ Kean 56
86 Wilkes 70
69 Susquehanna 73
107 ■ Juniata 104
75 ■ Messiah 62
79 Lycoming 66
95 Allentown 86
82 Gettysburg 61
85 ■ Susquehanna 86
97 ■ Wilkes 65
97 ■ Western Md. 51
73 Scranton 102

ELMHURST 6-18
55 † William Penn 49
64 † Mt. St. Clare 55
40 Wheaton (Ill.) 66
39 Ill. Benedictine 68
79 ■ Ill. Wesleyan 72
69 ■ Iowa Wesleyan 49
57 ■ North Park 73
73 ■ Concordia (Ill.) 53
55 Southern Cal Col. 58
60 Occidental 82
63 Aurora 73
81 ■ Millikin 75
69 Ill. Wesleyan 77
56 ■ Augustana (Ill.) 68
55 ■ North Central 56
44 Millikin 63
55 North Park 69
59 North Central 63
62 Carthage 69
63 ■ North Park 66
40 Augustana (Ill.) 55
50 Wis.-Oshkosh 85
52 ■ Wheaton (Ill.) 75
53 ■ Carthage 91

ELMIRA 8-12
44 † Upsala 59
66 † Haverford 45
97 ■ Oneonta St. 55
51 Houghton 81
81 ■ Oswego St. 63
65 ■ Daemen 61
59 ■ Binghamton 73
78 ■ Russell Sage 66
66 Hartwick 75
67 ■ Utica 55
74 Ithaca 82
54 Nazareth (N.Y.) 61
36 † Hamilton 57
67 † Nichols 51
61 ■ St. John Fisher 76
66 Roberts Wesleyan 80
56 ■ Geneseo St. 86
51 Alfred 54
69 Keuka 55
49 Brockport St. 76

ELON 11-13
79 ■ Longwood 55
83 ■ Lees-McRae 97
58 Wingate 68
75 Slippery Rock 86
72 † Tri-State 54
63 S.C.-Spartanburg 79
79 Pfeiffer 60
89 High Point 68
76 ■ Mars Hill 66
62 ■ Presbyterian 61
62 Carson-Newman 80
66 Catawba 87
80 Lenoir-Rhyne 73
81 ■ Gardner-Webb 68
73 ■ Carson-Newman 75
65 Davis & Elkins 48
57 Longwood 48
61 ■ Wingate 77
84 Mars Hill 90
75 Presbyterian 85
67 Gardner-Webb 70
95 ■ Catawba 107
88 ■ Lenoir-Rhyne 69
62 † Catawba 83

EMORY 14-10
124 ■ Wesleyan (Ga.) 27
54 ■ Tenn. Temple 65
79 † Principia 42
71 Rhodes 58
70 New York U. 69
53 Case Reserve 72
81 ■ Millsaps 70
95 ■ Johns Hopkins 73
85 Barton 39
86 Carnegie Mellon 52
58 ■ Sewanee 48
75 Rochester 90
69 Brandeis 63
85 ■ Oglethorpe 51
70 ■ Washington (Mo.) 77
60 ■ Chicago 64
49 ■ Brandeis 55
70 ■ Rochester 47
73 Sewanee 51
66 Chicago 69
64 Washington (Mo.) 85
87 Agnes Scott 25
64 ■ New York U. 74
62 ■ Carnegie Mellon 81

EMORY & HENRY 14-12
65 Ferrum 74
62 † Methodist 71
58 ■ Maryville (Tenn.) 75
69 ■ Ky. Christian 61
56 ■ Hollins 59
58 Va. Wesleyan 66
68 Randolph-Macon 52
55 Guilford 52
49 ■ R.-M. Woman's 31
39 ■ Bridgewater (Va.) 49
57 Lynchburg 54
51 Bridgewater (Va.) 55
70 East. Mennonite 56
65 Roanoke 60
63 ■ East. Mennonite 58
52 ■ Guilford 36
47 Maryville (Tenn.) 95
57 R.-M. Woman's 42
55 ■ Randolph-Macon 54
48 Hollins 54
56 ■ Ferrum 65
62 ■ Va. Wesleyan 47
48 ■ Roanoke 60
62 ■ Lynchburg 39
63 ■ Randolph-Macon 57
67 † Roanoke 78

EMPORIA ST. 10-16
64 Fort Hays St. 74
91 † Regis (Colo.) 87
80 ■ Northeastern Okla. 76
92 ■ Kan. Wesleyan 60
42 Denver 79
74 Neb.-Kearney 80
66 ■ Fort Hays St. 79
79 ■ Friends 65
75 Central Okla. 78
84 ■ Central Mo. St. 70
68 ■ Mo. Southern St. 79
62 Mo. Western St. 70
87 ■ Mo.-St. Louis 66
62 Washburn 75
68 Northeast Mo. St. 54
50 Central Mo. St. 65
66 Northwest Mo. St. 72
34 Mo.-Kansas City 70
69 ■ Mo. Western St. 74
68 Southwest Baptist 63
64 ■ Washburn 74
87 ■ Northeast Mo. St. 53
74 ■ Northwest Mo. St. 82
71 ■ Lincoln (Mo.) 63
53 Missouri-Rolla 75
75 Pittsburg St. 86

ERSKINE 6-20
54 ■ Lander 42
40 Augusta 80
55 ■ S.C.-Aiken 63
69 Presbyterian 86
63 † Newberry 65
65 ■ Limestone 58
44 ■ Wingate 75
55 Presbyterian 81
45 ■ Wofford 75
71 ■ Queens (N.C.) 83
64 Wingate 76
30 Lander 59
72 ■ Francis Marion 74
57 S.C.-Aiken 64
56 Converse 36
51 Limestone 79
71 ■ Newberry 51
77 ■ Central Wesleyan 69
57 Queens (N.C.) 67
71 ■ Clayton St. 78
59 ■ Piedmont 79
66 Wofford 99
67 Central Wesleyan 78
82 ■ Converse 55
66 Piedmont 81
56 Newberry 61

EUREKA 19-7
71 † Wis.-Stout 93
97 Grace 88
69 ■ Trinity Chrst. (Il.) 67
75 ■ Principia 55
102 ■ MacMurray 61
62 Ind. Wesleyan 58
67 Mt. Vernon Naz. 92
85 ■ Olivet (Ill.) 66
65 Blackburn 61
90 Purdue-Calumet 86
78 ■ Knox 54
77 Judson 61
90 ■ Monmouth (Ill.) 54
88 ■ Rockford 45
91 Greenville 36
70 ■ Mo. Baptist 78
74 Aurora 90
83 Moody Bible 38
58 Trinity (Ill.) 80
67 Maryville (Mo.) 48
68 ■ McKendree 71
76 ■ Iowa Wesleyan 62
88 ■ Ill. Wesleyan 77

88 ■ Concordia (Ill.) 55
103 ■ Greenville 58
58 Trinity (Ill.) 72

EVANSVILLE 18-10
63 ■ Indiana St. 62
79 † Appalachian St. 70
74 Liberty 66
67 Eastern Ill. 57
63 Loyola (Ill.) 74
62 ■ St. Louis 42
76 ■ Northeastern Ill. 59
54 Indiana 70
81 Chicago St. 63
55 Murray St. 57
74 ■ Duquesne 59
70 ■ La Salle 53
62 ■ Butler 64
79 Detroit Mercy 69
67 Dayton 65
76 Xavier (Ohio) 71
73 ■ Notre Dame 69
81 ■ Louisville 71
54 ■ Loyola (Ill.) 36
62 ■ Detroit Mercy 42
54 La Salle 70
65 Duquesne 66
57 Butler 70
59 ■ Dayton 55
69 ■ Xavier (Ohio) 79
62 Notre Dame 74
71 † La Salle 68
51 † Butler 79

FAIRFIELD 14-14
58 Connecticut 95
55 St. John's (N.Y.) 69
67 Central Conn. St. 68
50 ■ Seton Hall 61
70 ■ Coppin St. 68
69 ■ Hartford 61
79 † Providence 82
69 † Western Mich. 77
66 Fordham 60
49 ■ Richmond 54
69 ■ Niagara 64
56 Loyola (Md.) 74
73 ■ Yale 66
58 ■ St. Peter's 52
69 ■ Canisius 76
58 Iona 66
96 ■ Buffalo 79
68 Siena 79
57 St. Peter's 58
91 Manhattan 77
71 ■ Siena 70
69 ■ Iona 54
76 ■ Manhattan 75
74 Niagara 83
81 Canisius 63
72 ■ Loyola (Md.) 69
93 † Manhattan 84
75 † St. Peter's 77

FDU-MADISON 13-12
53 † Bloomfield 65
47 Scranton 100
59 ■ Wilkes 62
58 King's (Pa.) 74
71 New Jersey Tech 46
45 Mt. St. Mary (N.Y.) 36
85 Drew 30
51 ■ Bloomfield 54
31 ■ Trenton St. 59
56 Caldwell 62
55 ■ Mt. St. Mary (N.Y.) 49
62 ■ King's (Pa.) 78
52 Upsala 72
70 ■ Delaware Valley 74
77 ■ New Jersey Tech 45
69 ■ St. Elizabeth 47
62 Centenary (N.J.) 52
68 ■ Drew 48
59 Delaware Valley 52
70 ■ Upsala 67
65 ■ Centenary (N.J.) 40
58 ■ Scranton 81
66 ■ Manhattanville 22
75 St. Elizabeth 44
61 Ramapo 73

FDU-TEANECK 15-12
57 Seton Hall 65
65 ■ Columbia-Barnard 75
69 Delaware St. 71
65 Manhattan 67
57 Princeton 83
71 Drexel 86
68 † Delaware 72
72 † Cleveland St. 52
78 Mt. St. Mary's (Md.) 71
66 ■ Rider 59
70 ■ St. Francis (N.Y.) 53
65 ■ LIU-Brooklyn 56
58 ■ Wagner 56
76 Monmouth (N.J.) 49
74 ■ Robert Morris 54
68 ■ St. Francis (Pa.) 57
60 ■ Marist 62
72 Rider 79
82 ■ Mt. St. Mary's (Md.) 67
74 LIU-Brooklyn 63
91 St. Francis (N.Y.) 62
77 ■ Monmouth (N.J.) 53
61 Wagner 58
81 St. Francis (Pa.) 57
54 Robert Morris 70
71 Marist 72
67 ■ Marist 81

FAYETTEVILLE ST. 13-10
57 ■ Virginia St. 70
96 ■ Hampton 102
70 St. Augustine's 90
72 ■ Elizabeth City St. 57
75 Pembroke St. 73
75 Bowie St. 58
61 Norfolk St. 76
81 Virginia Union 97
87 ■ N.C. Central 69
87 St. Paul's 83
85 Livingstone 77
82 ■ St. Augustine's 96
67 ■ Shaw 81
83 Winston-Salem 58
67 Johnson Smith 78
86 N.C. Central 82
88 ■ Livingstone 66
66 Shaw 84
76 Methodist 68
79 ■ Johnson Smith 77
83 ■ Winston-Salem 63
61 † Bowie St. 60
73 † Norfolk St. 93

FERRIS ST. 14-12
66 Aquinas 78
75 † Lake Superior St. 52
74 † Oakland 77
72 ■ Quincy 61
52 ■ Indiana (Pa.) 79
69 Northern Mich. 92
67 Michigan Tech 89
51 Wayne St. (Mich.) 64
88 Mich.-Dearborn 44
72 Calvin 62
57 † Alma 45
76 ■ Hillsdale 60
79 Grand Valley St. 72
85 ■ Lake Superior St. 83
67 Saginaw Valley 76
80 ■ Northwood 46
73 ■ Northern Mich. 91
57 ■ Michigan Tech 68
69 Oakland 78
91 ■ Wayne St. (Mich.) 79
70 Northwood 51
68 Hillsdale 57
57 ■ Oakland 70
79 ■ Grand Valley St. 59
65 Lake Superior St. 59
68 ■ Saginaw Valley 74

FERRUM 9-16
74 ■ Emory & Henry 65
57 ■ Mary Washington 71
74 Guilford 78
40 Davidson 64
64 ■ Roanoke 79
70 ■ Marymount (Va.) 74
60 ■ Rowan 80
61 Lynchburg 44
67 † New Paltz St. 82
87 † Hilbert 61
74 ■ Averett 50
52 Mary Washington 49
49 N.C. Wesleyan 57
79 Chris. Newport 81
62 Shenandoah 61
60 Methodist 76
76 ■ Greensboro 91
78 Averett 77
59 ■ N.C. Wesleyan 56
52 Maryville (Tenn.) 97
65 Emory & Henry 56
72 ■ Chris. Newport 81
41 Greensboro 70
60 ■ Methodist 83
56 N.C. Wesleyan 79

FISK 0-24
38 ■ Bristol 42
38 ■ Spelman 51
30 ■ Maryville (Tenn.) 79
29 Centre 97
38 Spelman 68
34 Bristol 64
19 ■ Berea 64
13 Lane 88
31 Hendrix 81
35 Trinity (Tex.) 82
30 Sewanee 87
34 Oglethorpe 59
21 ■ Rhodes 74
17 ■ Millsaps 73
31 ■ Stillman 53
19 Sewanee 61
32 ■ Oglethorpe 56
19 ■ Centre 81
37 Berea 79
27 Rhodes 86
18 Millsaps 96
31 Stillman 58
16 Maryville (Tenn.) 95
37 ■ Hendrix 82

FITCHBURG ST. 17-10
58 † Scranton 89
92 † Nazareth (N.Y.) 82
72 ■ Western New Eng. 78
58 Worcester Tech 67
67 ■ Rhode Island Col. 82
62 Curry 46
56 † Pac. Lutheran 80
58 † Concordia (Mich.) 70
81 Worcester St. 64
95 ■ Anna Maria 49
75 ■ Salem St. 60
69 ■ Mass.-Dartmouth 50
77 Elms 62
57 Westfield St. 68
71 ■ Framingham St. 41
85 ■ Suffolk 50
74 ■ North Adams St. 59
61 Bri'water (Mass.) 44
62 Nichols 36
74 ■ Worcester St. 67
59 Salem St. 74
57 ■ Westfield St. 61
73 Framingham St. 41
73 North Adams St. 54
73 ■ Bri'water (Mass.) 59
62 ■ North Adams St. 41
50 † Salem St. 63

FLORIDA 19-10
58 Mississippi St. 74
61 Tennessee Tech 81
101 ■ Furman 56
95 ■ Alabama St. 32
64 Bethune-Cookman 56
57 † Utah 51
66 Stanford 76
92 ■ Florida A&M 66
72 ■ Illinois 57
81 ■ Alabama 75
66 West Va. 59
69 Mississippi 65
96 ■ Central Fla. 45
68 Arkansas 60
64 Georgia 70
63 ■ Vanderbilt 69
92 Ga. Southern 78
89 ■ Louisiana St. 65
81 ■ Florida St. 78
74 South Caro. 53
80 ■ South Fla. 66
64 ■ Auburn 79
63 Fla. Atlantic 84
75 ■ Tennessee 88
87 Stetson 55
72 Kentucky 69
73 † Alabama 88
69 Bowling Green 67
55 Virginia 69

FLORIDA A&M 17-10
74 ■ Alabama St. 68
79 Eckerd 62
73 Fla. Memorial 64
53 † Western Ky. 76
67 † Ga. Southern 82
71 Tennessee St. 88
66 Florida 92
68 † Detroit Mercy 76
73 ■ Tennessee St. 65
98 ■ Stetson 66
84 ■ Md.-East. Shore 45
85 ■ Delaware St. 70
95 ■ North Caro. A&T 91
59 ■ South Caro. St. 79
80 Morgan St. 79
58 Coppin St. 61
58 Florida St. 79
83 North Caro. A&T 60
85 South Caro. St. 70
74 ■ Bethune-Cookman 61
80 ■ Morgan St. 64
77 ■ Coppin St. 68
95 Spelman 35
67 Md.-East. Shore 59
70 Delaware St. 51
51 Bethune-Cookman 54
68 † North Caro. A&T 75

FLA. ATLANTIC 20-8
67 Florida St. 97
37 Miami (Fla.) 94
89 Barry 57
50 † Mo.-Kansas City 62
53 Kansas 99
78 ■ Seattle Pacific 62
98 ■ Johnson Smith 59
76 ■ Florida Tech 63
100 ■ Assumption 46
80 North Caro. St. 106
85 ■ Stonehill 60
92 ■ Transylvania 57
77 Bethune-Cookman 72
103 ■ St. Thomas Aquinas 70
74 Albany St. (Ga.) 64
82 Georgia St. 60
94 West Ga. 88
56 Mercer 73
111 Fla. Memorial 68
100 Central Fla. 71

104 Stetson 70
83 ■ Southwestern La. 45
103 ■ Barry 40
84 ■ Florida 63
86 ■ Fla. Memorial 52
84 ■ Albany St. (Ga.) 59
55 Florida Int'l 78
74 † Florida Tech 86

FLORIDA TECH 26-4
61 † Delta St. 95
90 Bellarmine 98
93 Edward Waters 74
80 ■ Fla. Memorial 54
102 ■ St. Augustine's 82
89 ■ Seattle Pacific 61
84 † Virginia St. 68
63 Fla. Atlantic 76
102 ■ Air Force 60
68 ■ Michigan Tech 66
105 ■ Slippery Rock 68
88 Fla. Memorial 59
82 North Fla. 66
106 ■ St. Leo 50
90 Eckerd 38
77 Tampa 63
107 ■ Barry 44
74 Fla. Southern 68
80 ■ North Fla. 50
83 Rollins 69
98 ■ Eckerd 44
102 ■ Tampa 68
88 Barry 55
64 ■ Fla. Southern 56
85 ■ Rollins 69
105 St. Leo 52
87 ■ Rollins 63
87 † Fla. Southern 75
86 † Fla. Atlantic 74
51 Delta St. 75

FLORIDA INT'L 25-6
68 † Mississippi 78
75 Maine 61
58 ■ Miami (Fla.) 80
77 ■ Louisiana St. 64
78 ■ Texas Southern 64
86 ■ Bethune-Cookman 41
71 † Old Dominion 67
66 † Texas Tech 70
93 † Appalachian St. 64
101 ■ Lehigh 42
82 ■ Eastern Ky. 68
71 ■ Colorado 74
97 Stetson 50
66 Georgia St. 40
80 Charleston 48
88 ■ Southeastern La. 40
88 ■ Central Fla. 59
86 Mercer 64
50 Auburn 62
102 ■ Stetson 55
88 ■ Georgia St. 51
78 ■ Charleston 56
77 Southeastern La. 61
81 Central Fla. 62
73 ■ Mercer 53
78 ■ Fla. Atlantic 55
84 ■ Charleston 60
77 ■ Mercer 52
79 † Butler 75
59 † Southern Methodist 60
93 † Marquette 87

FLA. SOUTHERN 25-3
73 † Tampa 51
69 Rollins 56
79 ■ Morningside 68
61 ■ West Ga. 57
92 ■ Queens (N.C.) 73
108 ■ Fontbonne 44
64 ■ Colorado-CS 55
63 ■ Missouri-Rolla 52
81 ■ Merrimack 59

86 ■ Culver-Stockton 50
88 ■ Lee 55
73 ■ Millersville 57
85 ■ Barry 45
71 Rollins 49
98 ■ North Fla. 66
93 St. Leo 52
68 ■ Florida Tech 74
106 Tampa 60
93 ■ Eckerd 59
77 ■ Rollins 63
78 North Fla. 68
93 ■ St. Leo 46
56 Florida Tech 64
80 ■ Tampa 57
94 Eckerd 64
90 Barry 52
58 † Tampa 54
75 † Florida Tech 87

FLORIDA ST. 13-14
97 ■ Fla. Atlantic 67
87 ■ South Fla. 68
79 ■ Louisiana St. 59
67 North Caro. St. 75
64 Miami (Fla.) 61
88 † Tennessee Tech 72
50 California 69
84 Duke 72
66 ■ Virginia 78
85 North Caro. 66
68 ■ Maryland 61
53 Wake Forest 57
79 Georgia Tech 71
66 ■ North Caro. 73
61 Maryland 74
79 ■ Florida A&M 58
68 Virginia 76
78 Florida 81
69 ■ Clemson 83
80 Northern Ill. 86
46 ■ Georgia Tech 61
77 ■ Wake Forest 73
74 ■ Oral Roberts 53
47 ■ North Caro. St. 57
63 Clemson 70
74 ■ Duke 67
68 † Maryland 91

FONTBONNE 10-15
66 ■ Coe 73
55 Aurora 81
59 Chicago 98
49 † Millsaps 62
65 Rhodes 57
39 ■ Washington (Mo.) 83
77 ■ Dubuque 69
44 Fla. Southern 108
75 Principia 46
75 Webster 44
63 ■ Ripon 67
54 ■ Maryville (Mo.) 55
77 ■ MacMurray 62
70 Westminster 53
74 DePauw 79
45 ■ Blackburn 63
60 ■ Principia 65
62 ■ Webster 69
68 MacMurray 61
62 ■ Westminster 58
71 Monmouth (Ill.) 69
82 Maryville (Mo.) 84
47 Blackburn 52
66 † MacMurray 63
55 † Maryville (Mo.) 62

FORDHAM 16-13
75 Monmouth (N.J.) 70
100 ■ St. Francis (N.Y.) 45
69 Columbia-Barnard 38
77 Seton Hall 88
68 St. Peter's 81
51 St. Joseph's (Pa.) 96
68 † Georgia Tech 69

58 ■ Iona 72
60 ■ Fairfield 66
75 Holy Cross 80
85 ■ Bucknell 69
59 ■ Army 49
76 ■ Hofstra 58
86 Lehigh 65
64 ■ Colgate 53
71 ■ Manhattan 54
54 ■ Lafayette 38
64 Navy 56
73 ■ Holy Cross 69
58 Bucknell 64
68 Army 54
64 ■ Lehigh 57
48 Colgate 50
63 Lafayette 65
67 Marist 77
61 ■ Navy 63
55 ■ Navy 41
61 Lafayette 49
63 Holy Cross 82

FORT HAYS ST. 18-11
74 ■ Emporia St. 64
61 ■ Washburn 65
34 Washburn 71
80 † Northwest Mo. St. 69
74 ■ Tabor 60
77 ■ Friends 55
67 Colo. Christian 46
68 Regis (Colo.) 74
79 Emporia St. 66
58 ■ Bethany (Kan.) 30
59 Wayne St. (Neb.) 76
67 ■ Wayne St. (Neb.) 72
66 Neb.-Kearney 81
69 ■ Chadron St. 66
91 ■ Colorado Mines 55
89 ■ Western St. 39
59 ■ Mesa St. 69
55 N.M. Highlands 61
80 Adams St. 70
62 ■ Neb.-Kearney 63
88 Western St. 51
53 Mesa St. 58
63 ■ N.M. Highlands 54
76 ■ Adams St. 62
92 Colorado Mines 49
64 Chadron St. 72
58 † Adams St. 51
78 † Chadron St. 76
68 † N.M. Highlands 62

FORT LEWIS 4-22
68 ■ Western St. 64
77 ■ Adams St. 83
63 West Tex. St. 80
56 † Cal St. Chico 83
58 † Cal Poly SLO 72
64 Adams St. 94
83 Western St. 74
66 Grand Canyon 119
86 † Cal St. Los Angeles 77
64 ■ Abilene Christian 60
52 Mesa St. 70
44 Regis (Colo.) 88
46 Colorado-CS 78
71 ■ Mesa St. 79
50 ■ Metropolitan St. 101
51 Denver 95
66 Air Force 79
85 Southern Colo. 89
62 † Colo. Christian 65
52 ■ Regis (Colo.) 72
46 ■ Colorado-CS 64
67 Colo. Christian 75
45 Metropolitan St. 91
66 ■ Denver 99
58 ■ Air Force 63
68 ■ Southern Colo. 91

FORT VALLEY ST. 27-3
102 ■ Ga. Southwestern 77

69 ■ Augusta 63
86 † Virginia Union 62
76 † Albany St. (Ga.) 49
99 ■ Tuskegee 60
89 Valdosta St. 71
96 ■ LeMoyne-Owen 56
79 Augusta 94
84 ■ Miles 58
90 Savannah St. 75
66 ■ Albany St. (Ga.) 75
87 Morris Brown 55
85 Alabama A&M 74
97 Miles 60
95 Spelman 41
86 ■ Savannah St. 75
70 Paine 65
76 Albany St. (Ga.) 71
118 LeMoyne-Owen 54
79 Tuskegee 63
91 ■ Clark Atlanta 50
83 ■ Paine 73
102 ■ Morris Brown 32
74 Clark Atlanta 62
97 ■ Spelman 33
67 West Ga. 59
97 † Morris Brown 44
86 † Albany St. (Ga.) 75
75 † Savannah St. 67
76 † Norfolk St. 90

FRAMINGHAM ST. 3-22
31 Babson 78
28 Mass.-Dartmouth 79
51 ■ Worcester Tech 66
30 ■ Western New Eng. 46
33 Nichols 60
59 Mass.-Boston 67
37 Rhode Island Col. 82
48 ■ Curry 51
45 North Adams St. 58
54 Pine Manor 73
46 ■ Bri'water (Mass.) 69
54 Worcester St. 76
47 Plymouth St. 79
42 ■ Salem St. 61
41 Fitchburg St. 71
41 Westfield St. 68
33 ■ Emmanuel 73
64 Suffolk 61
56 ■ North Adams St. 41
27 Bri'water (Mass.) 76
66 ■ Worcester St. 68
30 Salem St. 84
41 ■ Fitchburg St. 73
25 ■ Westfield St. 64
56 ■ Endicott 36

FRANCIS MARION 11-17
62 † Carson-Newman 88
67 Longwood 73
83 ■ Newberry 62
85 ■ Converse 56
66 ■ Wofford 88
92 ■ Coker 66
55 Pembroke St. 65
62 Columbus 74
55 ■ Augusta 68
50 ■ Lander 70
86 Coker 78
51 ■ S.C.-Spartanburg 82
74 Erskine 72
39 ■ Armstrong St. 56
91 Newberry 52
68 ■ Georgia Col. 67
62 S.C.-Aiken 69
66 ■ Pembroke St. 71
63 Georgia Col. 82
42 Armstrong St. 52
77 ■ Columbus 76
42 S.C.-Spartanburg 68
51 Augusta 70
85 ■ Davidson 58
60 ■ S.C.-Aiken 52

57 Lander 62
93 † S.C.-Aiken 89
60 † S.C.-Spartanburg .. 73

FRANKLIN 14-11
74 ■ Huntington 78
62 ■ Mo.-St. Louis 68
60 Marian (Ind.) 68
57 Kalamazoo 49
60 St. Francis (Ind.) ... 65
52 Tri-State 54
58 ■ Indianapolis 70
70 ■ Rosary 68
48 ■ Huntington 60
74 Anderson 54
83 Hanover 53
71 ■ Ind.-Southeast 78
51 DePauw 36
78 ■ Manchester 58
73 ■ Taylor 65
65 ■ Hanover 53
93 ■ Asbury 42
74 ■ Anderson 44
63 ■ DePauw 43
76 IU/PU-Indianapolis . 82
84 Taylor 81
64 Indiana Tech 80
81 Manchester 55
68 ■ Defiance 53
71 Thomas More 74

FRANKLIN PIERCE 21-9
54 ■ New Hamp. Col. ... 49
72 ■ Keene St. 58
63 ■ American Int'l 62
87 St. Joseph's (Me.) .. 76
68 Assumption 61
67 ■ Springfield 66
75 † St. Anselm 85
88 † Adelphi 62
72 St. Michael's 77
79 ■ Le Moyne 58
69 Bridgeport 43
64 Merrimack 66
75 Sacred Heart 64
77 Southern Conn. St. . 38
73 ■ Mass.-Lowell 75
74 ■ Bridgeport 29
66 Keene St. 61
74 Le Moyne 53
83 ■ New Haven 69
56 New Hamp. Col. ... 47
91 ■ Southern Conn. St. . 42
68 Mass.-Lowell 80
66 ■ New Hamp. Col. ... 53
76 ■ Sacred Heart 53
67 New Haven 85
60 ■ Keene St. 74
66 ■ New Hamp. Col. ... 53
60 † Keene St. 57
55 Mass.-Lowell 56
46 Bentley 71

FRANK. & MARSH. 19-5
84 ■ York (Pa.) 61
66 ■ Juniata 68
51 ■ Johns Hopkins 44
62 Lebanon Valley 51
73 Dickinson 64
56 ■ Davidson 51
69 Widener 49
69 Moravian 76
68 ■ Western Md. 53
61 ■ Elizabethtown 54
85 ■ Gettysburg 64
71 Johns Hopkins 55
77 ■ Muhlenberg 58
72 ■ Lebanon Valley 44
64 Messiah 48
73 Ursinus 56
67 Western Md. 51
59 ■ Dickinson 52
81 ■ Lycoming 49
77 Gettysburg 70

60 Susquehanna 61
86 ■ Muhlenberg 36
60 Moravian 67
56 ■ Wilkes 59

FREDONIA ST. 5-19
67 † Concordia (N.Y.) ... 41
48 St. John Fisher 67
57 Rochester Inst. 41
65 Buffalo St. 67
63 ■ Binghamton 56
45 Geneseo St. 72
31 ■ Penn St.-Behrend .. 69
43 Penn St.-Behrend .. 63
70 Potsdam St. 80
64 Plattsburgh St. 54
53 ■ St. John Fisher 69
66 ■ Oswego St. 49
57 ■ Utica Tech 70
45 ■ Brockport St. 47
39 Roberts Wesleyan .. 59
67 Cortland St. 69
38 ■ Geneseo St. 93
49 Brockport St. 59
47 Nazareth (N.Y.) 85
53 ■ New Paltz St. 54
40 ■ Oneonta St. 56
60 ■ Buffalo St. 79
41 Oswego St. 56
59 Utica Tech 88

FRESNO ST. 10-17
74 Northern Ill. 93
58 Ill.-Chicago 59
73 Northeastern Ill. 68
76 Cal St. Fullerton 79
70 ■ UC Santa Barb. 63
80 † McNeese St. 65
63 † Cal St. Sacramento . 82
57 Pacific (Cal.) 72
81 Cal Poly SLO 78
55 Pepperdine 86
79 ■ Cal St. Northridge .. 59
40 San Diego St. 63
58 New Mexico 71
48 UTEP 65
99 ■ Wyoming 70
65 ■ Colorado St. 71
61 Brigham Young 72
61 Utah 94
105 ■ Cal St. Sac. 103
53 ■ San Diego St. 58
64 ■ UTEP 51
64 ■ New Mexico 60
60 Colorado St. 76
73 Wyoming 89
77 ■ Utah 74
68 ■ Brigham Young 81
38 † San Diego St. 62

FROSTBURG ST. 18-8
72 ■ Lycoming 37
56 ■ Gettysburg 63
50 Marietta 63
45 † Penn St.-Behrend .. 66
52 Carnegie Mellon ... 48
82 Goucher 36
62 Columbia Union 80
64 ■ N.C. Wesleyan 58
71 ■ Chris. Newport 80
54 ■ Waynesburg 76
74 Shenandoah 53
63 Salisbury St. 49
81 Lincoln (Pa.) 40
71 Bridgewater (Va.) .. 60
59 Caldwell 53
85 ■ Notre Dame (Md.) .. 55
60 Mary Washington .. 50
59 ■ Allentown 51
61 ■ Shenandoah 50
93 ■ Salisbury St. 65
73 ■ Lincoln (Pa.) 36
80 † Emmanuel 69
67 Marymount (Va.) ... 97

62 Allentown 72
89 ■ Salisbury St. 64
72 ■ Allentown 64

FURMAN 17-11
58 ■ Clemson 72
56 Florida 101
76 North Caro. 94
87 † Bradley 81
105 Stetson 86
61 Auburn 74
82 † Jackson St. 69
69 ■ Md.-Balt. County ... 50
34 ■ Indiana 39
86 ■ Coastal Caro. 45
93 Marshall 70
89 ■ Ga. Southern 84
76 ■ Tenn.-Chatt. 80
49 ■ South Caro. 56
68 ■ Marshall 65
85 Appalachian St. 81
88 East Tenn. St. 72
86 ■ Western Caro. 59
101 Western Caro. 84
74 Winthrop 58
84 Ga. Southern 90
72 Georgia Tech 86
66 Georgia 90
92 ■ Appalachian St. 73
96 ■ East Tenn. St. 80
90 Tenn.-Chatt. 75
74 † Marshall 58
73 † Ga. Southern 76

GALLAUDET 9-15
84 Randolph-Macon ... 78
67 † Shenandoah 71
66 ■ Shenandoah 58
72 ■ Lebanon Valley 62
57 ■ Carleton 67
88 ■ Washington Bible .. 29
52 Messiah 70
74 St. Mary's (Md.) 66
75 ■ Marymount (Va.) .. 102
81 Notre Dame (Md.) .. 76
69 Mary Washington .. 71
77 ■ Wesley 79
61 ■ Catholic 79
64 York (Pa.) 75
84 Goucher 87
76 Marymount (Va.) .. 113
60 Western Md. 67
90 ■ St. Mary's (Md.) 65
52 ■ Mary Washington .. 73
74 ■ York (Pa.) 66
90 ■ Mary Baldwin 60
54 Catholic 64
59 ■ Goucher 76
72 York (Pa.) 97

GANNON 10-15
81 ■ Bowie St. 51
69 ■ Findlay 77
66 ■ Lock Haven 84
62 Indiana (Pa.) 73
56 Ashland 62
78 ■ Clarion 93
64 Edinboro 80
77 ■ Point Park 36
70 ■ Wayne St. (Mich.) .. 75
86 ■ Calif. (Pa.) 74
47 Slippery Rock 69
71 ■ Edinboro 78
67 ■ Mercyhurst 60
62 Malone 53
62 Pitt.-Johnstown 75
88 ■ West Liberty St. 57
78 ■ Houghton 67
71 Point Park 49
72 Hilbert 35
58 Mercyhurst 81
53 Clarion 91
53 Notre Dame (Ohio) . 61
72 ■ Wis.-Parkside 82

64 ■ Madonna 63
37 ■ Pitt.-Johnstown 46

GARDNER-WEBB 10-17
85 ■ Central Wesleyan .. 55
70 Augusta 74
53 ■ Lander 52
76 ■ Lincoln Memorial .. 74
72 Presbyterian 69
52 ■ Clayton St. 53
62 Lincoln Memorial .. 79
86 † Catawba 106
59 Virginia Tech 89
89 North Ga. 87
52 Carson-Newman ... 74
80 ■ Mars Hill 82
67 Queens (N.C.) 97
72 ■ Lenoir-Rhyne 59
54 ■ Wingate 58
68 Elon 81
71 Catawba 81
81 Davidson 56
61 ■ Presbyterian 79
63 ■ North Ga. 55
47 ■ Carson-Newman ... 85
69 Mars Hill 76
70 ■ Elon 67
90 Lenoir-Rhyne 77
54 Wingate 71
55 ■ Catawba 78
61 † Carson-Newman ... 88

GENESEO ST. 27-1
105 ■ D'youville 30
66 ■ Cortland St. 38
77 ■ Brockport St. 52
72 ■ Fredonia St. 45
90 New Paltz St. 45
80 Oneonta St. 48
105 ■ Utica 32
105 ■ Hilbert 43
90 † Utica Tech 63
69 ■ Buffalo St. 64
76 ■ Roberts Wesleyan .. 62
79 Oswego St. 65
76 ■ Potsdam St. 53
107 ■ Plattsburgh St. 60
68 Rochester Inst. 25
93 Fredonia St. 38
76 ■ Oswego St. 52
71 Rochester 63
86 Elmira 56
65 Binghamton 50
91 ■ Utica Tech 66
76 Buffalo St. 68
90 Brockport St. 51
77 ■ Cortland St. 53
95 ■ Buffalo St. 78
84 ■ Buffalo St. 69
80 ■ Moravian 57
70 ■ Scranton 79

GEORGE MASON 17-10
73 ■ Georgetown 70
63 † Montana 78
83 † Siena 72
74 ■ Towson St. 58
68 ■ Morgan St. 36
80 ■ Delaware 45
76 ■ Howard 56
74 Md.-Balt. County ... 72
77 Bethune-Cookman . 46
62 † Bethune-Cookman . 53
64 South Fla. 66
48 ■ Old Dominion 81
56 William & Mary 53
78 N.C.-Wilmington ... 61
73 East Caro. 61
50 ■ Va. Commonwealth 69
57 ■ American 68
60 ■ Richmond 66
53 James Madison 56
57 Old Dominion 64
72 ■ William & Mary 67

81 ■ N.C.-Wilmington ... 62
77 ■ East Caro. ... 57
57 American ... 42
57 Richmond ... 61
52 ■ James Madison ... 49
50 † East Caro. ... 72

GEO. WASHINGTON 20-11
56 † Connecticut ... 58
87 † Murray St. ... 56
50 ■ Georgetown ... 51
55 ■ Duquesne ... 43
74 ■ Loyola (Md.) ... 53
85 ■ North Caro. St. ... 79
53 † Tennessee ... 73
91 † Howard ... 32
65 St. Peter's ... 63
75 ■ American ... 52
72 ■ Towson St. ... 51
80 St. Joseph's (Pa.) ... 77
71 West Va. ... 82
65 ■ Massachusetts ... 51
78 ■ Temple ... 39
72 North Caro. St. ... 90
68 ■ Rhode Island ... 62
63 ■ Rutgers ... 76
71 St. Bonaventure ... 67
87 ■ West Va. ... 61
57 Massachusetts ... 59
82 Rhode Island ... 72
83 Temple ... 64
72 ■ St. Joseph's (Pa.) ... 52
83 ■ St. Bonaventure ... 66
85 Rutgers ... 62
73 ■ Temple ... 55
67 ■ St. Joseph's (Pa.) ... 74
60 † Arkansas St. ... 68
77 † Northwestern (La.) ... 93
70 † Nevada-Las Vegas ... 71

GEORGETOWN 23-7
70 George Mason ... 73
100 ■ Navy ... 74
87 ■ Mt. St. Mary's (Md.) ... 81
51 Geo. Washington ... 50
81 St. Francis (Pa.) ... 61
69 ■ American ... 66
92 ■ Drexel ... 63
72 Notre Dame ... 78
88 ■ Villanova ... 81
63 Syracuse ... 49
55 Miami (Fla.) ... 62
101 ■ Boston College ... 92
70 Pittsburgh ... 74
105 ■ Providence ... 76
66 Seton Hall ... 62
74 St. John's (N.Y.) ... 72
78 ■ Connecticut ... 81
69 Villanova ... 68
84 ■ Pittsburgh ... 74
90 ■ Miami (Fla.) ... 88
95 Boston College ... 82
75 ■ Syracuse ... 64
96 Providence ... 86
68 ■ Seton Hall ... 65
64 Connecticut ... 62
80 ■ St. John's (N.Y.) ... 69
81 Providence ... 82
76 ■ Northern Ill. ... 74
68 Penn St. ... 67
57 † Virginia ... 77

GEORGIA 21-13
80 ■ Middle Tenn. St. ... 65
62 † Santa Clara ... 64
79 † Oregon St. ... 81
72 † Mo.-Kansas City ... 63
72 Ohio St. ... 89
81 Notre Dame ... 75
63 † San Diego St. ... 70
97 † Rider ... 57
66 ■ Vanderbilt ... 90
78 ■ Georgia St. ... 63
108 ■ Winthrop ... 58
60 Kentucky ... 69
91 ■ Arkansas ... 71
57 South Caro. ... 77
70 ■ Florida ... 64
65 Mississippi St. ... 76
116 ■ Oral Roberts ... 49
75 ■ Mississippi ... 60
65 Mercer ... 57
78 Ga. Southern ... 64
56 ■ Auburn ... 82
72 ■ South Caro. St. ... 61
68 Tennessee ... 71
82 ■ Wis.-Green Bay ... 60
88 Louisiana St. ... 53
74 ■ DePaul ... 62
90 ■ Furman ... 66
50 ■ Alabama ... 67
84 † Arkansas ... 73
73 † Tennessee ... 72
76 † Alabama ... 72
64 † Vanderbilt ... 78
85 ■ San Diego St. ... 68
60 Stanford ... 93

GEORGIA COL. 17-11
83 ■ Clark Atlanta ... 37
71 Kennesaw ... 68
70 Valdosta St. ... 57
75 ■ Paine ... 68
61 ■ Kennesaw ... 77
85 Midway ... 40
76 Lee ... 72
88 Ga. Southwestern ... 77
51 Armstrong St. ... 68
86 ■ Pembroke St. ... 52
54 ■ Augusta ... 59
67 S.C.-Spartanburg ... 81
80 S.C.-Aiken ... 53
66 ■ Columbus ... 69
73 Lander ... 68
67 ■ Valdosta St. ... 71
67 Francis Marion ... 68
59 ■ S.C.-Spartanburg ... 62
76 Columbus ... 68
82 ■ Francis Marion ... 63
58 Augusta ... 59
64 Pembroke St. ... 62
63 ■ S.C.-Aiken ... 48
68 ■ Lander ... 72
69 ■ Armstrong St. ... 63
82 North Fla. ... 69
64 † Lander ... 54
63 † S.C.-Spartanburg ... 80

GA. SOUTHERN 21-9
77 ■ Charleston So. ... 49
101 ■ Central Fla. ... 47
63 Tennessee Tech ... 71
82 † Florida A&M ... 67
63 † New Orleans ... 75
67 Georgia St. ... 63
79 ■ Morehead St. ... 53
80 ■ South Ala. ... 70
97 ■ Stetson ... 43
63 South Fla. ... 72
56 ■ Tenn.-Chatt. ... 65
84 Furman ... 89
65 Western Caro. ... 49
93 ■ Mercer ... 51
96 ■ Appalachian St. ... 77
82 ■ East Tenn. St. ... 83
78 ■ Florida ... 92
86 Marshall ... 65
64 ■ Georgia ... 78
66 Tenn.-Chatt. ... 61
90 ■ Furman ... 84
76 ■ Western Caro. ... 72
61 Charleston ... 46
72 Appalachian St. ... 64
73 East Tenn. St. ... 72
74 ■ Marshall ... 61
66 † Appalachian St. ... 56
83 † Tenn.-Chatt. ... 73
76 † Furman ... 73
70 Alabama ... 102

GEORGIA ST. 12-16
82 ■ Tenn.-Martin ... 63
74 ■ Tennessee St. ... 79
92 ■ Coastal Caro. ... 69
70 ■ Mississippi St. ... 91
63 ■ Ga. Southern ... 67
77 Tennessee St. ... 83
63 Tenn.-Chatt. ... 81
60 Nevada-Las Vegas ... 78
53 † Lamar ... 56
63 Georgia ... 78
56 Mercer ... 53
78 Tenn.-Martin ... 76
40 ■ Florida Int'l ... 66
65 ■ Stetson ... 59
60 ■ Fla. Atlantic ... 82
51 Charleston ... 56
59 Southeastern La. ... 58
68 Central Fla. ... 60
78 ■ Mercer ... 52
51 Florida Int'l ... 88
47 Stetson ... 58
56 ■ Tenn.-Chatt. ... 61
51 ■ Charleston ... 64
70 ■ Southeastern La. ... 60
80 ■ Central Fla. ... 47
102 ■ Morris Brown ... 42
81 † Central Fla. ... 61
60 † Mercer ... 64

GEORGIA TECH 16-11
111 ■ Hofstra ... 62
82 ■ Mercer ... 59
82 Minnesota ... 62
86 ■ Clemson ... 68
110 ■ Appalachian St. ... 72
101 † Alabama ... 103
69 † Fordham ... 68
73 ■ North Caro. ... 63
86 North Caro. St. ... 79
70 Wake Forest ... 85
66 ■ Maryland ... 77
71 ■ Florida St. ... 79
81 ■ Virginia ... 107
80 Clemson ... 85
86 Duke ... 80
68 North Caro. ... 72
88 ■ East Tenn. St. ... 55
53 Virginia ... 88
70 Maryland ... 75
61 Florida St. ... 46
86 ■ Furman ... 72
92 ■ North Caro. St. ... 89
85 ■ Wake Forest ... 72
68 Tenn.-Chatt. ... 67
72 ■ Duke ... 67
66 † Clemson ... 87
62 Northwestern ... 90

GETTYSBURG 10-14
79 Glenville St. ... 76
63 Frostburg St. ... 56
71 ■ Susquehanna ... 65
90 ■ Moravian ... 105
86 ■ Catholic ... 71
69 York (Pa.) ... 63
77 ■ Juniata ... 82
72 ■ Messiah ... 77
75 ■ Dickinson ... 79
69 Juniata ... 81
64 Frank. & Marsh. ... 85
77 ■ Lebanon Valley ... 70
82 Lycoming ... 77
71 Muhlenberg ... 87
73 ■ Western Md. ... 79
66 ■ Johns Hopkins ... 59
69 Messiah ... 78
83 Lebanon Valley ... 63
55 Dickinson ... 69
64 Johns Hopkins ... 80
61 ■ Elizabethtown ... 82
59 Western Md. ... 63
70 ■ Frank. & Marsh. ... 77
74 ■ Albright ... 65

GONZAGA 11-15
67 ■ Central Wash. ... 43
53 † Mo.-Kansas City ... 67
66 † Nevada ... 63
95 ■ Whitworth (Wash.) ... 66
71 ■ Washington St. ... 69
72 ■ Idaho ... 76
69 ■ Eastern Wash. ... 54
71 Montana St. ... 80
52 Montana ... 68
64 Washington ... 94
69 Boise St. ... 75
69 Eastern Wash. ... 70
72 Pepperdine ... 93
56 Loyola (Cal.) ... 71
71 ■ Santa Clara ... 68
55 ■ San Diego ... 53
88 ■ Portland ... 77
70 Portland ... 72
61 St. Mary's (Cal.) ... 76
58 San Francisco ... 80
88 ■ San Francisco ... 69
87 ■ St. Mary's (Cal.) ... 71
62 San Diego ... 87
59 Santa Clara ... 72
65 ■ Loyola (Cal.) ... 59
67 ■ Pepperdine ... 70

GORDON 9-15
57 ■ Curry ... 50
66 MIT ... 54
65 ■ Roger Williams ... 26
60 ■ Worcester Tech ... 58
47 Elms ... 59
54 ■ Western New Eng. ... 70
39 † Wis.-Eau Claire ... 103
70 Colorado Col. ... 54
56 Bates ... 58
42 ■ Salem St. ... 69
66 ■ Suffolk ... 45
42 ■ Amherst ... 47
66 ■ Nichols ... 44
67 Pine Manor ... 72
45 ■ Tufts ... 79
45 Norwich ... 66
57 ■ Rhode Island Col. ... 63
47 New England Col. ... 63
56 Eastern Nazarene ... 47
55 Emmanuel ... 75
45 Colby ... 55
45 Me.-Farmington ... 64
54 ■ Clark (Mass.) ... 65
58 Colby-Sawyer ... 52

GOUCHER 12-13
82 ■ Bryn Mawr ... 65
86 Lancaster Bible ... 13
40 ■ Wesley ... 57
36 ■ Frostburg St. ... 82
58 Manhattanville ... 31
69 † Emmanuel ... 71
75 Neumann ... 54
42 ■ Notre Dame (Md.) ... 58
35 † Ohio Wesleyan ... 75
77 † Hunter ... 60
67 ■ York (Pa.) ... 77
70 ■ St. Mary's (Md.) ... 40
87 Salisbury St. ... 77
36 Mary Washington ... 70
58 Marymount (Va.) ... 96
62 ■ Catholic ... 73
87 ■ Gallaudet ... 84
62 York (Pa.) ... 67
65 Catholic ... 60
83 St. Mary's (Md.) ... 73
77 ■ Western Md. ... 70
63 ■ Mary Washington ... 67
73 ■ Marymount (Va.) ... 110
76 Gallaudet ... 59
76 Catholic ... 82

GRAMBLING 12-14

106	■ Texas Col.	48
90	† Tougaloo	50
90	† Paul Quinn	73
52	† Southwestern La.	55
86	† Southern-B.R.	95
51	Alabama	117
68	† Eastern Ill.	75
83	† Tenn.-Chatt.	91
89	† Murray St.	80
62	Southeastern La.	68
55	Southern-B.R.	68
68	Alcorn St.	72
89	■ Prairie View	61
79	■ Texas Southern	63
69	Jackson St.	67
69	Alabama St.	68
83	■ Mississippi Val.	84
61	■ Southern-B.R.	82
82	■ Alcorn St.	86
80	■ Lamar	85
82	Prairie View	60
85	Texas Southern	90
77	■ Jackson St.	58
87	■ Alabama St.	77
81	Mississippi Val.	80
56	† Mississippi Val.	64

GRAND CANYON 7-20

74	† Cal Baptist	65
48	Fresno Pacific	74
104	■ Western St.	65
76	■ Cal Poly Pomona	80
66	Northern Ariz.	78
30	Arizona St.	83
56	† James Madison	83
50	■ Cal St. Northridge	76
65	Eastern N. Mex.	76
63	■ UC Riverside	80
73	■ N.M. Highlands	76
66	■ Panhandle St.	71
119	■ Fort Lewis	66
60	■ Eastern N. Mex.	70
68	Southern Utah	84
71	■ Eastern Mont.	63
79	■ Eastern Mont.	76
69	■ Seattle Pacific	70
64	■ Portland St.	74
77	Alas. Anchorage	90
54	Alas. Fairbanks	72
77	■ Alas. Fairbanks	74
75	■ Alas. Anchorage	47
48	Eastern Mont.	63
56	Seattle Pacific	75
53	Portland St.	105
56	■ Southern Utah	67

GRAND VALLEY ST. 8-18

55	■ Wis.-Parkside	77
63	† Calvin	75
62	Aquinas	69
71	■ Calvin	70
69	■ Madonna	71
69	■ St. Joseph's (Ind.)	62
67	Michigan Tech	81
77	Northern Mich.	96
77	■ Saginaw Valley	86
72	Lewis	76
62	Aquinas	72
74	Wayne St. (Mich.)	97
78	■ Lake Superior St.	67
72	■ Ferris St.	79
66	Northwood	62
69	■ Oakland	84
68	Hillsdale	52
64	■ Michigan Tech	71
71	■ Northern Mich.	89
84	■ Northwood	68
62	Saginaw Valley	82
82	Lake Superior St.	73
76	■ Wayne St. (Mich.)	89
59	Ferris St.	79
64	Oakland	82
69	■ Hillsdale	53

GREENSBORO 11-14

44	† Maryville (Tenn.)	81
85	† Va. Wesleyan	71
58	† Roanoke	92
61	High Point	70
82	■ Mt. Olive	97
68	Guilford	74
66	Bennett	68
92	■ Pfeiffer	71
66	N.C. Wesleyan	61
69	■ Chris. Newport	67
79	Maryville (Tenn.)	76
73	Mt. Olive	84
50	Meredith	71
64	■ Methodist	79
49	■ High Point	67
87	Averett	74
91	Ferrum	76
71	■ Guilford	64
62	Chris. Newport	52
57	■ Meredith	67
71	Methodist	93
59	■ N.C. Wesleyan	72
70	■ Ferrum	41
61	■ Averett	50
74	Chris. Newport	92

GRINNELL 13-11

62	■ Graceland (Iowa)	58
60	■ Loras	49
65	William Penn	73
61	Hamline	70
49	Macalester	73
65	■ Carleton	57
79	■ Cornell College	53
74	■ Coe	50
67	Clarke	80
57	Teiko-Marycrest	81
63	Illinois Col.	73
55	Coe	41
65	■ Carroll (Wis.)	55
66	■ Ripon	55
81	Cornell College	46
51	St. Norbert	70
73	Lawrence	74
76	■ Knox	59
69	■ Monmouth (Ill.)	59
63	■ Illinois Col.	78
81	Monmouth (Ill.)	78
57	Knox	45
48	† Lawrence	61
67	† Beloit	74

GROVE CITY 10-12

56	Ohio Wesleyan	64
69	Baldwin-Wallace	80
58	John Carroll	101
72	■ Geneva	53
76	■ Westminster (Pa.)	54
58	Carlow	61
51	Geneva	53
70	Pitt-Bradford	57
56	■ Carnegie Mellon	44
75	Thiel	50
63	Bethany (W.Va.)	49
78	Westminster (Pa.)	56
65	Waynesburg	89
78	Wash. & Jeff.	83
65	■ Penn St.-Behrend	81
63	■ Thiel	53
97	■ Pitt-Bradford	69
76	■ Bethany (W.Va.)	72
66	■ Waynesburg	80
71	St. Vincent	80
85	■ Wash. & Jeff.	94
75	Penn St.-Behrend	82

GUILFORD 12-13

46	■ N.C. Wesleyan	52
78	■ Ferrum	74
71	Methodist	70
48	Roanoke	63
74	■ Greensboro	68
49	■ Bridgewater (Va.)	55
67	Randolph-Macon	72
71	Va. Wesleyan	76
52	■ Emory & Henry	55
68	■ Lynchburg	40
62	R.-M. Woman's	35
78	East. Mennonite	56
47	Bridgewater (Va.)	52
49	■ Va. Wesleyan	53
66	Hollins	56
36	Emory & Henry	52
64	Greensboro	71
80	■ Roanoke	68
58	■ East. Mennonite	50
71	■ R.-M. Woman's	48
65	Meredith	85
54	■ Randolph-Macon	68
74	Lynchburg	47
50	■ Hollins	45
64	† Va. Wesleyan	65

GUST. ADOLPHUS 14-11

44	■ Wartburg	59
51	Mankato St.	65
73	Wis.-River Falls	62
67	Carleton	61
51	Concordia-M'head	77
44	† Arkansas Tech	77
82	† Southwestern (Tex.)	51
76	Hamline	53
53	Bethel (Minn.)	68
62	■ Augsburg	40
72	St. Mary's (Minn.)	63
49	■ St. Benedict	73
59	St. Thomas (Minn.)	73
54	■ St. Olaf	60
71	■ Concordia-M'head	82
69	■ Carleton	68
64	■ Macalester	59
87	■ Hamline	61
53	■ Bethel (Minn.)	45
79	Augsburg	65
73	■ St. Mary's (Minn.)	57
55	■ St. Thomas (Minn.)	65
69	St. Olaf	62
69	Macalester	57
52	St. Benedict	86

HAMILTON 21-5

58	† Heidelberg	78
62	† Skidmore	53
60	Oswego St.	54
79	■ St. Lawrence	58
66	■ Utica	46
64	Rochester Inst.	47
87	■ Skidmore	64
74	Rensselaer	62
69	Clarkson	68
79	■ Middlebury	83
60	■ Utica	41
70	■ Union (N.Y.)	60
64	■ Nazareth (N.Y.)	53
55	William Smith	60
57	† Elmira	36
44	Skidmore	36
66	Hartwick	58
80	Oneonta St.	62
64	■ Williams	53
57	■ Utica Tech	55
61	Le Moyne	60
65	■ Albany (N.Y.)	51
46	Binghamton	66
78	Russell Sage	46
54	† Skidmore	41
45	† St. John Fisher	51

HAMLINE 9-16

73	Trinity (Tex.)	69
74	† Pomona-Pitzer	62
52	■ St. Scholastica	74
70	■ Grinnell	61
65	St. Mary's (Minn.)	87
48	■ Wittenberg	77
51	St. Benedict	90
83	■ Augsburg	65
49	St. Thomas (Minn.)	96
53	■ Gust. Adolphus	76
62	■ Macalester	43
62	St. Olaf	71
59	Concordia-M'head	97
63	Bethel (Minn.)	81
75	■ Carleton	59
79	■ St. Mary's (Minn.)	66
62	■ St. Benedict	82
73	Augsburg	62
61	Gust. Adolphus	87
63	Macalester	62
61	■ St. Olaf	68
58	■ Bethel (Minn.)	71
61	Carleton	62
69	■ St. Thomas (Minn.)	71
83	■ Concordia-M'head	93

HAMPTON 20-9

102	Fayetteville St.	96
72	■ Albany St. (Ga.)	77
70	■ Virginia Union	91
85	Johnson Smith	82
95	St. Augustine's	94
61	■ Shaw	71
66	Bowie St.	44
68	Chris. Newport	72
77	St. Paul's	52
60	† Claflin	70
45	† Spelman	46
77	Elizabeth City St.	63
88	■ Winston-Salem	52
61	Virginia Union	59
71	■ Virginia St.	60
57	■ Virginia Union	62
80	■ Livingstone	42
64	■ Elizabeth City St.	43
78	■ Dist. Columbia	53
61	■ Norfolk St.	85
76	■ St. Paul's	66
57	Virginia St.	55
65	Norfolk St.	58
82	Dist. Columbia	56
74	■ N.C. Central	60
75	■ Bowie St.	37
75	† Livingstone	62
69	† Shaw	43
63	† St. Augustine's	79

HANOVER 6-14

92	† Wilberforce	56
68	Cedarville	56
79	■ Ind.-Southeast	81
67	DePauw	66
65	■ Marian (Ind.)	70
65	■ Brescia	77
54	Mt. St. Joseph's	77
53	■ Franklin	83
63	† Centre	64
92	■ Anderson	65
62	Manchester	83
65	Taylor	79
81	■ Asbury	72
53	Franklin	65
79	Ind. Wesleyan	89
64	■ DePauw	46
56	■ Manchester	83
48	Anderson	49
81	■ Taylor	90
88	■ Berea	81

HARTFORD 11-16

73	■ Army	46
57	† Louisiana St.	59
59	† South Fla.	63
66	† Columbia-Barnard	57
61	Fairfield	69
64	■ Morgan St.	60
59	■ Yale	66
57	Dartmouth	49
60	■ St. Peter's	68
54	■ Holy Cross	55
69	Boston U.	68
42	■ Northeastern	53
79	New Hampshire	82
50	Maine	51

71 Brown 77
65 ■ Drexel 49
75 ■ Delaware 59
63 Vermont 83
65 ■ Central Conn. St. 63
57 Delaware 70
76 Drexel 72
66 ■ Maine 63
63 New Hampshire 81
67 ■ Boston U. 55
53 Northeastern 70
61 ■ Vermont 75
64 Delaware 73

HARTWICK 15-9
87 ■ Russell Sage 49
47 ■ Wilkes 62
71 Utica 61
51 St. John Fisher 73
68 ■ Nazareth (N.Y.) 73
71 William Smith 82
70 Rochester Inst. 50
65 ■ Rensselaer 60
50 ■ Skidmore 47
75 ■ Elmira 66
64 ■ Clarkson 54
71 ■ St. Lawrence 61
68 ■ Union (N.Y.) 43
56 Ithaca 79
99 Alfred 91
58 ■ Hamilton 66
67 ■ Rochester Inst. 33
51 ■ William Smith 59
70 Oneonta St. 47
87 ■ Alfred 47
57 ■ Ithaca 48
71 St. Lawrence 59
48 Clarkson 56
54 Rensselaer 57

HARVARD 16-9
81 ■ Lehigh 58
72 ■ Texas Christian 80
93 ■ Central Conn. St. 73
81 ■ Boston U. 72
63 Stanford 85
49 † Utah 60
64 Vermont 77
70 Northeastern 60
68 ■ Princeton 59
92 ■ Pennsylvania 69
82 Rhode Island 83
99 ■ Dartmouth 66
84 New Hampshire 87
84 ■ Cornell 71
85 ■ Columbia-Barnard 53
75 Yale 69
64 Brown 77
77 Pennsylvania 80
72 Princeton 58
78 ■ Army 69
81 ■ Brown 87
69 ■ Yale 61
85 Columbia-Barnard 69
97 Cornell 75
88 Dartmouth 77

HAVERFORD 2-22
47 Hunter 49
45 † Elmira 66
40 ■ Moravian 103
38 † Smith 69
62 † Simmons 39
48 † Vassar 57
44 ■ Carnegie Mellon 65
44 ■ Phila. Pharmacy 59
47 ■ Widener 49
35 Albright 57
55 ■ Ursinus 74
37 Allentown 97
38 ■ Swarthmore 35
46 ■ Bryn Mawr 64
55 ■ Drew 57
38 Moravian 105

50 Ursinus 89
47 ■ Muhlenberg 81
41 Widener 51
34 Immaculata 62
53 Muhlenberg 68
46 Eastern (Pa.) 49
42 ■ Albright 54
32 Swarthmore 48

HAWAII 28-4
80 ■ Portland 54
56 ■ Stanford 85
63 ■ Stephen F. Austin 67
72 ■ Oregon St. 71
80 ■ Santa Clara 78
80 ■ Southwest Mo. St. 74
80 ■ Pepperdine 66
80 ■ Washington 67
87 New Mexico St. 79
62 New Mexico St. 57
69 Long Beach St. 67
60 UC Santa Barb. 64
75 UC Santa Barb. 66
91 Long Beach St. 90
87 ■ Cal St. Fullerton 65
85 ■ Cal St. Fullerton 68
78 ■ UC Irvine 45
79 ■ UC Irvine 71
85 ■ Nevada 52
85 ■ Nevada 63
64 Pacific (Cal.) 61
79 San Jose St. 66
91 San Jose St. 54
72 Pacific (Cal.) 59
80 Alas. Anchorage 65
90 † Southern Methodist 68
98 † Northeastern Ill. 59
100 ■ Nevada-Las Vegas 85
82 ■ Nevada-Las Vegas 69
88 † Nevada 71
93 † New Mexico St. 70
77 † UC Santa Barb. 80

HEIDELBERG 19-8
78 † Hamilton 58
56 Rochester 52
67 Hiram 41
91 ■ Asbury 40
60 ■ Defiance 58
57 Capital 86
77 Kenyon 30
53 ■ Marietta 51
61 ■ Mount Union 55
64 Bluffton 47
62 Ohio Northern 40
65 ■ Otterbein 49
51 John Carroll 70
58 ■ Muskingum 61
67 Baldwin-Wallace 64
51 Marietta 41
60 ■ Capital 61
58 Otterbein 44
71 ■ Ohio Northern 51
62 Mount Union 67
59 ■ Baldwin-Wallace 63
65 Muskingum 72
59 ■ John Carroll 51
72 ■ Hiram 50
78 ■ Baldwin-Wallace 61
75 Muskingum 57
59 † Capital 73

HENDERSON ST. 12-12
121 ■ Ark. Baptist 51
75 ■ Harding 81
67 Arkansas Col. 69
96 Ark. Baptist 34
89 † West Fla. 72
92 † St. Mary's (Tex.) 62
86 † Dillard 74
73 ■ Ozarks (Ark.) 77
89 Southern St. 68
70 ■ Arkansas Tech 90
67 Ouachita Bapt. 69
97 ■ Central Ark. 88

72 Ark.-Monticello 91
80 Harding 63
93 ■ Arkansas Col. 67
61 West Tex. St. 86
64 Ozarks (Ark.) 76
90 ■ Southern St. 67
64 Arkansas Tech 70
90 ■ Ouachita Bapt. 76
75 Central Ark. 92
83 Ark.-Monticello 101
70 Central Ark. 65
68 Arkansas Tech 78

HILBERT 3-20
48 Utica Tech 79
89 Medgar Evers 30
53 Thiel 91
53 Brockport St. 83
64 ■ Thiel 77
53 Daemen 80
50 St. John Fisher 88
43 ■ Sewanee 57
58 Delaware Valley 91
61 † Ferrum 87
43 Geneseo St. 105
60 † Western New Eng. 81
47 Smith 60
38 Houghton 80
63 D'youville 42
35 ■ Gannon 72
63 ■ Daemen 65
48 Houghton 92
39 ■ Pitt.-Johnstown 84
40 Roberts Wesleyan 69
24 Keuka 84
54 D'youville 47
43 † Nazareth (N.Y.) 79

HILLSDALE 7-19
79 Spring Arbor 55
67 ■ Defiance 56
76 IU/PU-Ft. Wayne 98
60 ■ Aquinas 39
63 Urbana 50
56 ■ Lake Superior St. 73
70 ■ Saginaw Valley 94
78 Oakland 94
64 ■ Wayne St. (Mich.) 62
60 Ferris St. 76
79 Siena Heights 67
72 ■ Michigan Tech 83
80 ■ Northern Mich. 99
69 Northwood 78
52 ■ Grand Valley St. 68
48 Lake Superior St. 59
65 Saginaw Valley 88
59 ■ Oakland 78
58 ■ Ashland 68
79 Wayne St. (Mich.) 91
57 ■ Ferris St. 68
77 ■ Northwood 79
60 Michigan Tech 75
86 Northern Mich. 102
62 ■ Tri-State 57
53 Grand Valley St. 69

HIRAM 5-20
35 ■ Bluffton 34
41 ■ Heidelberg 67
63 Penn St.-Behrend 72
71 ■ Otterbein 62
44 Mount Union 62
60 ■ Mt. Vernon Naz. 54
59 ■ Ohio Northern 45
58 ■ Walsh 60
34 Baldwin-Wallace 65
76 Thiel 54
48 ■ Marietta 61
50 Muskingum 98
46 ■ Capital 78
55 John Carroll 76
50 ■ Baldwin-Wallace 64
59 Otterbein 75
35 Defiance 66
57 ■ Mount Union 63

51 Capital 76
57 Ohio Northern 69
62 ■ John Carroll 66
47 Marietta 70
61 ■ Muskingum 78
50 Heidelberg 72
65 Marietta 67

HOFSTRA 8-19
77 Lehigh 65
62 Georgia Tech 111
48 † Boston U. 85
51 Bucknell 48
78 ■ St. Francis (N.Y.) 55
57 ■ Coppin St. 75
47 ■ Lafayette 62
69 ■ Colgate 56
47 ■ Monmouth (N.J.) 60
97 Wagner 95
61 Columbia-Barnard 66
53 ■ Massachusetts 88
53 Drexel 70
58 Fordham 76
68 ■ Central Conn. St. 50
58 Cornell 64
76 Siena 90
70 ■ Md.-East. Shore 53
56 Buffalo 87
69 St. Bonaventure 92
48 Army 63
77 Monmouth (N.J.) 67
57 Central Conn. St. 67
50 ■ Iona 79
74 ■ Delaware St. 77
57 ■ Buffalo 75
59 ■ Loyola (Md.) 73

HOLLINS 12-13
60 † Stockton St. 46
60 † Averett 50
64 ■ Mary Baldwin 27
45 ■ Bridgewater (Va.) 53
34 ■ Roanoke 52
59 Emory & Henry 56
52 ■ R.-M. Woman's 32
50 ■ Averett 55
76 ■ East. Mennonite 84
80 Mary Baldwin 40
55 Roanoke 82
42 Randolph-Macon 51
65 Va. Wesleyan 71
91 ■ Lynchburg 74
56 ■ Guilford 66
58 R.–M. Woman's 45
75 Lynchburg 49
62 ■ Randolph-Macon 53
48 Averett 53
54 ■ Emory & Henry 48
66 ■ Va. Wesleyan 75
63 East. Mennonite 55
67 Bridgewater (Va.) 78
45 Guilford 50
54 Bridgewater (Va.) 73

HOLY CROSS 22-7
73 ■ New Hampshire 71
53 ■ St. John's (N.Y.) 55
61 Rhode Island 60
74 ■ Boston College 75
74 † South Caro. 66
60 St. Peter's 68
54 † Indiana 79
75 † Md.-Balt. County 50
63 ■ Vermont 65
80 ■ Fordham 75
55 Hartford 54
52 Army 54
80 ■ Lehigh 42
85 Central Conn. St. 68
79 ■ Colgate 57
67 Lafayette 61
76 ■ Navy 46
80 ■ Bucknell 50

69	Fordham	73
57	■ Army	44
65	Lehigh	55
71	Colgate	53
74	■ Lafayette	66
76	Navy	61
75	Siena	61
77	Bucknell	65
84	■ Lehigh	58
75	■ Bucknell	63
82	■ Fordham	63

HOPE		8-15
87	■ Concordia (Mich.)	77
49	† Olivet (Ill.)	55
70	† Bethel (Ind.)	51
72	■ St. Mary's (Ind.)	77
64	■ Trinity Chrst. (Il.)	57
74	■ Madonna	64
59	Madonna	75
96	Taylor	88
49	Valdosta St.	77
47	Clayton St.	52
50	Alma	59
69	■ Albion	71
91	Olivet	47
60	Adrian	74
65	■ Kalamazoo	60
66	■ Calvin	69
56	■ Alma	72
58	Calvin	73
51	Kalamazoo	54
66	■ Adrian	76
67	Albion	79
83	■ Olivet	42
62	Albion	72

HOUSTON		11-16
70	■ Stephen F. Austin	81
58	■ Southern Miss.	61
65	■ Cal St. Sacramento	58
64	Sam Houston St.	71
76	■ Southern-B.R.	62
68	■ Southwestern La.	48
60	Lamar	59
57	Southwestern La.	44
71	■ Oklahoma St.	74
70	† Coppin St.	47
72	† Butler	80
51	Auburn	81
41	Texas Tech	93
60	■ Texas A&M	58
54	Baylor	78
76	Southern Methodist	68
66	■ Texas	70
63	Rice	56
86	■ Texas Christian	73
70	■ Texas Tech	88
61	Texas A&M	66
72	■ Baylor	73
63	■ Southern Methodist	73
68	Texas	97
74	■ Rice	70
60	Texas Christian	76
80	Southern Methodist	96

HOWARD		5-22
50	† Massachusetts	70
75	† Rider	76
56	Richmond	87
62	Nebraska	123
61	† St. Mary's (Cal.)	67
65	† Northeast La.	86
54	† Alcorn St.	74
56	George Mason	76
46	Maryland	101
32	† Geo. Washington	91
58	■ Navy	71
54	† North Caro. A&T	53
50	South Caro. St.	54
64	Md.-East. Shore	44
70	■ Delaware St.	77
78	■ Bethune-Cookman	76
57	■ Md.-East. Shore	59
47	■ Coppin St.	76
50	■ North Caro. St.	127
62	■ Morgan St.	59
50	Coppin St.	58
61	Bethune-Cookman	67
56	Delaware St.	77
62	■ North Caro. A&T	61
56	■ South Caro. St.	82
63	Morgan St.	76
53	† Coppin St.	70

HUMBOLDT ST.		12-14
76	† Seattle	57
49	† Western Wash.	68
59	Cal St. Chico	70
72	† UC Santa Cruz	38
42	UC Davis	67
86	■ Notre Dame (Cal.)	18
88	■ Southern Ore. St.	92
64	■ Portland St.	74
60	■ Western Ore.	72
71	■ Cal St. Dom. Hills	72
64	George Fox	60
75	Puget Sound	82
69	Seattle Pacific	89
75	Sonoma St.	53
78	UC Davis	70
79	■ San Fran. St.	68
52	Cal St. Hayward	43
75	Cal St. Stanislaus	72
73	■ Cal St. Chico	72
76	■ Cal St. Stanislaus	82
52	■ Cal St. Hayward	46
62	San Fran. St.	47
76	■ UC Davis	90
72	■ Sonoma St.	73
66	Cal St. Chico	83
52	UC Davis	70

HUNTER		15-11
49	■ Haverford	47
66	■ Upsala	75
63	St. Elizabeth	68
58	■ Concordia (N.Y.)	56
53	John Jay	27
72	■ Mt. St. Vincent	37
52	Allentown	74
45	Staten Island	49
58	† Rutgers-Newark	69
93	Medgar Evers	30
76	■ Russell Sage	59
64	St. John Fisher	85
60	† Goucher	77
41	Albany (N.Y.)	66
54	Manhattanville	32
69	■ John Jay	42
62	■ CCNY	44
53	York (N.Y.)	49
72	■ Baruch	54
41	■ Stony Brook	70
44	New York U.	74
67	CCNY	40
48	Cabrini	65
73	■ Medgar Evers	32
57	■ CCNY	50
84	■ Staten Island	51

IDAHO		12-15
79	■ Nevada	64
55	■ Mo.-Kansas City	56
76	Gonzaga	72
59	Portland	72
65	Portland St.	87
74	San Jose St.	58
49	† San Francisco	51
64	Cal St. Sacramento	59
57	Pacific (Cal.)	68
54	Texas Christian	72
76	Baylor	81
58	Montana	77
45	Montana St.	74
59	■ Eastern Wash.	66
81	■ Cal St. Sacramento	76
65	■ Weber St.	62
78	■ Northern Ariz.	44
64	Idaho St.	76
60	Boise St.	83
56	■ Montana St.	67
50	■ Montana	67
82	Eastern Wash.	81
59	Northern Ariz.	44
61	Weber St.	60
66	■ Boise St.	64
57	■ Idaho St.	52
43	Montana St.	57

IDAHO ST.		10-16
55	† Southern Ill.	70
63	† Mississippi St.	72
49	Utah	55
71	■ Seattle Pacific	67
61	† Marist	60
49	San Francisco	78
53	Southern Utah	50
61	■ Oregon	83
70	■ Brigham Young	79
52	■ Colorado St.	66
59	■ Wyoming	61
74	■ Weber St.	56
76	■ Northern Ariz.	64
71	■ Southern Utah	58
61	Boise St.	85
52	Montana St.	74
54	Montana	74
76	■ Idaho	64
73	■ Eastern Wash.	66
77	Northern Ariz.	57
78	Weber St.	57
68	■ Boise St.	80
46	■ Montana St.	59
45	■ Montana	70
73	Eastern Wash.	76
52	Idaho	57

ILLINOIS		12-15
73	Illinois St.	49
80	■ Eastern Mich.	51
65	■ Louisville	51
67	Nebraska	84
70	■ Southern Ill.	74
82	■ Cincinnati	69
85	† Detroit Mercy	76
57	Florida	72
54	■ Missouri	80
71	Penn St.	101
57	Ohio St.	87
57	■ Iowa	65
56	Minnesota	66
76	■ Northwestern	85
81	■ Wisconsin	74
53	Indiana	72
84	■ Purdue	78
82	■ Michigan	62
78	■ Michigan St.	65
58	Iowa	77
76	Northwestern	80
84	Wisconsin	74
63	■ Indiana	55
92	Michigan	70
69	Michigan St.	85
62	■ Penn St.	78
78	■ Ohio St.	94

ILL. BENEDICTINE		13-9
51	■ Wheaton (Ill.)	52
57	■ MacMurray	34
67	North Central	58
68	■ Elmhurst	39
42	Lake Forest	74
41	Millikin	68
53	■ North Park	60
51	† Rosary	94
57	† St. Joseph's (Me.)	87
57	† Avila	48
57	■ Judson	38
56	Rockford	40
75	■ Aurora	66
39	Augustana (Ill.)	57
61	Trinity (Ill.)	56
75	■ Concordia (Ill.)	60
68	Judson	54
58	■ Ill. Wesleyan	69
61	■ Rockford	43
61	Aurora	81
70	Concordia (Ill.)	63
67	■ Trinity (Ill.)	52

ILLINOIS COL.		20-4
93	MacMurray	35
72	† Wis.-Platteville	82
84	† Millsaps	66
78	■ Blackburn	62
82	Monmouth (Ill.)	45
79	■ Knox	44
67	Augustana (Ill.)	56
83	Cornell College	53
77	Coe	68
76	■ Maryville (Mo.)	53
73	■ Grinnell	63
63	■ Beloit	61
77	■ Lake Forest	65
90	■ Principia	54
51	Ripon	81
72	Carroll (Wis.)	82
66	Knox	61
85	■ Coe	70
71	Millikin	76
78	Grinnell	63
72	■ Monmouth (Ill.)	57
91	■ Cornell College	54
77	■ Beloit	51
70	■ Lawrence	64

ILLINOIS ST.		11-16
49	■ Illinois	73
50	† Stanford	72
81	† Portland	68
76	† Oklahoma St.	68
94	■ Marquette	68
76	■ Northwestern	68
43	Michigan St.	63
56	Missouri	66
70	Bowling Green	84
69	■ Iowa St.	53
62	■ Drake	71
72	■ Northern Iowa	67
69	■ Creighton	68
64	Southern Ill.	73
72	Indiana St.	73
83	Bradley	68
53	Wichita St.	64
47	Southwest Mo. St.	83
66	■ Bradley	77
46	■ Southwest Mo. St.	91
71	■ Wichita St.	53
71	■ Indiana St.	50
65	■ Southern Ill.	77
57	Creighton	80
65	Drake	69
67	Northern Iowa	66
57	Southern Ill.	68

ILL. WESLEYAN		14-11
74	† DePauw	55
75	Maryville (Mo.)	60
70	■ Blackburn	75
60	Aurora	80
108	■ Rockford	35
93	■ MacMurray	82
72	Elmhurst	79
83	■ Monmouth (Ill.)	67
74	■ Principia	47
66	■ Carthage	69
66	■ North Central	58
77	■ Elmhurst	69
74	Knox	66
58	Carthage	71
49	■ Millikin	72
40	Augustana (Ill.)	69
60	North Park	71
38	Wheaton (Ill.)	70
69	Ill. Benedictine	58
67	■ Augustana (Ill.)	63
70	■ Wheaton (Ill.)	68

77 Eureka 88
69 ■ North Park 66
85 Millikin 92
79 North Central 72

ILL.-CHICAGO 15-13
72 ■ Northeastern Ill. 59
59 ■ Fresno St. 58
71 ■ Notre Dame 76
62 Toledo 72
74 Eastern Mich. 68
63 Kansas 94
61 Kansas St. 60
74 Chicago St. 59
62 ■ Wis.-Green Bay 71
64 ■ Wright St. 45
65 ■ Loyola (Ill.) 57
76 ■ Western Ill. 61
84 Valparaiso 111
61 Eastern Ill. 68
86 ■ Cleveland St. 66
59 ■ Youngstown St. 68
53 Northern Ill. 79
89 Western Ill. 58
59 Wis.-Green Bay 76
75 Wright St. 60
91 ■ Valparaiso 81
81 ■ Northern Ill. 76
43 DePaul 82
82 ■ Eastern Ill. 57
66 Cleveland St. 87
62 Youngstown St. 74
101 † Valparaiso 100
47 † Northern Ill. 81

IMMACULATA 17-8
48 † Salisbury St. 83
53 † Western Md. 67
72 ■ Widener 60
60 ■ Eastern (Pa.) 48
78 ■ Neumann 63
70 ■ Gwynedd Mercy 43
95 Rosemont 39
57 ■ Cabrini 64
69 Catholic 84
66 Notre Dame (Md.) 62
73 Eastern (Pa.) 45
85 ■ Bryn Mawr 75
64 Gwynedd Mercy 46
62 ■ Misericordia 53
63 ■ Alvernia 66
64 Cabrini 69
63 Marywood 57
75 ■ Rosemont 37
49 Wesley 71
62 ■ Haverford 34
69 ■ Ursinus 66
65 Shenandoah 50
77 Beaver 36
58 † Marywood 55
56 Cabrini 62

INDIANA 14-13
88 Wright St. 44
77 ■ Austin Peay 61
70 ■ Ohio 54
74 Ball St. 47
87 † Indiana St. 70
59 ■ Miami (Ohio) 48
70 ■ Evansville 54
79 † Holy Cross 54
39 Furman 34
65 Michigan 61
71 ■ Penn St. 65
67 ■ Ohio St. 81
50 Iowa 79
70 Minnesota 80
72 ■ Illinois 53
58 ■ Northwestern 77
56 Purdue 57
58 Ohio St. 99
69 Penn St. 94
59 ■ Minnesota 60
46 ■ Iowa 68
65 Northwestern 77
55 Illinois 63
60 ■ Purdue 65
79 Wisconsin 72
54 ■ Michigan 67
74 ■ Michigan St. 54

INDIANA (PA.) 13-10
93 ■ Fairmont St. 54
63 ■ Northern Ky. 71
73 ■ Gannon 62
72 Salem-Teikyo 65
96 † Indianapolis 83
79 Ferris St. 52
57 ■ St. Vincent 53
78 Wayne St. (Mich.) 77
63 ■ Pitt.-Johnstown 66
63 ■ Mercyhurst 60
78 Lock Haven 63
63 Calif. (Pa.) 73
70 ■ Shippensburg 74
87 ■ Slippery Rock 65
47 Bloomsburg 64
68 ■ Edinboro 73
82 Clarion 93
71 ■ Lock Haven 65
61 ■ Calif. (Pa.) 80
98 Shippensburg 95
61 Slippery Rock 71
86 Edinboro 72
73 ■ Clarion 75

INDIANA ST. 8-18
62 Evansville 63
79 ■ Michigan 68
68 Butler 91
70 † Indiana 87
45 Missouri 63
70 Xavier (Ohio) 82
80 ■ Eastern Ky. 77
61 Eastern Ill. 44
60 Wichita St. 70
49 Southwest Mo. St. 77
84 ■ Bradley 81
73 ■ Illinois St. 72
59 ■ Wis.-Milwaukee 56
46 ■ Southern Ill. 70
74 Drake 83
69 Northern Iowa 74
51 Creighton 83
59 ■ Wright St. 70
69 Southern Ill. 83
59 ■ Northern Iowa 78
65 ■ Creighton 80
78 ■ Drake 76
50 Illinois St. 71
79 Bradley 98
59 ■ Wichita St. 66
63 ■ Southwest Mo. St. 58

IU/PU-FT. WAYNE 10-17
86 Taylor 73
98 ■ Hillsdale 76
59 ■ Wayne St. (Mich.) 63
56 ■ Mo.-St. Louis 60
46 Tri-State 59
58 † Central Okla. 61
61 † Lincoln (Mo.) 58
68 ■ Edinboro 70
64 ■ Indianapolis 76
60 ■ Northern Ky. 56
61 Ky. Wesleyan 57
72 Southern Ind. 78
61 ■ St. Francis (Ind.) 63
64 Ashland 69
61 ■ Bellarmine 64
99 ■ Kentucky St. 58
55 Lewis 65
72 St. Joseph's (Ind.) 81
63 ■ Southern Ind. 65
58 ■ Ky. Wesleyan 54
67 ■ Ashland 51
107 Kentucky St. 41
68 Bellarmine 86
61 ■ St. Joseph's (Ind.) 69
73 ■ Lewis 59
60 Northern Ky. 70
62 Indianapolis 84

INDIANAPOLIS 24-4
83 † Indiana (Pa.) 96
79 † Quincy 59
99 IU/PU-Indianapolis 71
81 Oakland City 67
70 Franklin 58
76 IU/PU-Ft. Wayne 64
78 Ashland 60
67 ■ Bellarmine 74
92 ■ Kentucky St. 65
83 Lewis 71
70 St. Joseph's (Ind.) 54
86 ■ IU/PU-Indianapolis 65
89 ■ Quincy 81
72 Northern Ky. 69
88 ■ Oakland City 71
79 ■ Ky. Wesleyan 63
81 ■ Southern Ind. 60
98 Kentucky St. 60
96 Bellarmine 84
67 ■ St. Joseph's (Ind.) 65
96 ■ Lewis 77
78 ■ Northern Ky. 81
82 Ky. Wesleyan 67
97 Southern Ind. 82
80 ■ SIU-Edwardsville 69
68 ■ Ashland 56
84 ■ IU/PU-Ft. Wayne 62
76 ■ Saginaw Valley 81

IONA 12-15
50 ■ St. John's (N.Y.) 63
56 ■ Bucknell 48
83 ■ New Hampshire 62
65 St. Bonaventure 75
70 ■ Northeastern 54
70 ■ St. Francis (N.Y.) 59
63 Boston College 81
72 Fordham 58
49 Tulane 86
68 Nicholls St. 59
48 ■ St. Joseph's (Pa.) 68
55 St. Peter's 68
52 ■ Niagara 65
66 ■ Fairfield 58
47 ■ Loyola (Md.) 56
73 Manhattan 77
70 Canisius 72
69 Niagara 75
61 ■ Manhattan 45
54 Fairfield 69
59 Loyola (Md.) 67
67 Siena 57
52 ■ St. Peter's 62
79 Hofstra 50
67 ■ Canisius 59
67 ■ Siena 57
53 † St. Peter's 67

IOWA 27-4
70 Pittsburgh 59
53 Maryland 50
74 ■ West Va. 44
60 ■ N.C.-Charlotte 38
90 ■ Drake 44
97 † Bucknell 39
70 † Colorado 72
67 † Eastern Ky. 63
65 ■ Wisconsin 39
75 Minnesota 47
65 Illinois 57
60 Northwestern 55
79 ■ Indiana 50
92 ■ Northern Ill. 59
84 Michigan 54
75 Michigan St. 55
79 ■ Ohio St. 62
84 ■ Penn St. 59
68 ■ Northwestern 62
77 ■ Illinois 58
63 Purdue 55
68 Indiana 46
76 ■ Michigan St. 46
71 ■ Michigan 34
64 Penn St. 70
54 Ohio St. 58
83 ■ Minnesota 59
82 Old Dominion 56
63 ■ Auburn 50
72 ■ Tennessee 56
72 † Ohio St. 73

IOWA ST. 2-25
55 ■ Creighton 71
62 ■ Montana St. 61
53 Michigan St. 76
45 † Boston College 73
56 Wichita St. 68
43 ■ Drake 57
51 Wis.-Milwaukee 76
50 Northern Iowa 68
54 Brigham Young 77
51 † St. Mary's (Cal.) 72
53 Illinois St. 69
36 ■ Montana 65
55 ■ Oklahoma 66
56 ■ Oklahoma St. 67
67 Kansas St. 61
33 Kansas 92
52 ■ Missouri 83
52 ■ Colorado 92
52 ■ Nebraska 82
38 Oklahoma St. 75
57 Oklahoma 79
45 ■ Kansas 77
43 ■ Kansas St. 67
29 Colorado 79
41 Missouri 64
40 Nebraska 89
39 † Nebraska 87

ITHACA 20-8
78 † Oneonta St. 47
86 Rochester 67
88 Keuka 60
60 ■ Stony Brook 61
67 ■ Allentown 50
63 ■ Albany (N.Y.) 66
64 ■ St. Lawrence 30
79 ■ Clarkson 58
46 Cortland St. 52
73 St. John Fisher 76
63 ■ Alfred 67
72 Rochester Inst. 40
70 William Smith 68
82 ■ Elmira 74
79 ■ Hartwick 56
68 ■ Rensselaer 37
54 Clarkson 49
83 St. Lawrence 59
60 Alfred 44
65 Rensselaer 52
48 Hartwick 57
68 ■ William Smith 69
51 ■ Rochester Inst. 55
59 ■ William Smith 54
75 ■ Rochester 68
59 ■ St. John Fisher 49
71 † Potsdam St. 68
52 Binghamton 51

JACKSON ST. 10-18
46 ■ Belhaven 47
42 † Southern Miss. 79
52 † Cal St. Sacramento 67
66 ■ Ark. Baptist 33
72 ■ Texas Col. 36
51 Memphis St. 85
52 † Wis.-Milwaukee 79
69 † Furman 82
45 † Okla. Baptist 60
45 Mo.-Kansas City 65
40 St. Louis 58
54 Prairie View 43
55 Texas Southern 51

67 ■ Alcorn St. 75
66 ■ Southern-B.R. 82
67 ■ Grambling 69
75 Mississippi Val. 61
61 Alabama St. 80
73 ■ Prairie View 47
65 ■ Texas Southern 63
76 Alcorn St. 89
63 Southern-B.R. 75
58 Grambling 77
63 ■ Mississippi Val. 47
39 Arkansas 82
51 ■ Alabama St. 50
64 † Alabama St. 63
56 Southern-B.R. 59

JACKSONVILLE ST. 18-11
98 ■ Piedmont 92
73 Augusta 76
74 S.C.-Aiken 59
87 ■ Ala.-Huntsville 61
81 ■ Kennesaw 63
88 † Ark.-Monticello 102
78 ■ Montevallo 89
86 ■ Livingston 85
78 ■ Mississippi Col. 62
112 ■ Alabama A&M 74
62 North Ala. 64
66 Delta St. 73
68 Montevallo 72
89 ■ Valdosta St. 76
81 ■ West Ga. 61
81 Mississippi-Women 59
68 Troy St. 81
70 Alabama A&M 85
72 Valdosta St. 65
66 West Ga. 58
78 ■ Delta St. 91
95 ■ North Ala. 82
78 ■ Mississippi-Women 48
55 Mississippi Col. 54
70 Livingston 91
83 ■ Troy St. 74
79 † Livingston 74
67 Delta St. 65
61 Delta St. 90

JAMES MADISON 16-11
80 ■ Morgan St. 47
79 † Marquette 92
83 † Grand Canyon 56
80 Radford 84
88 ■ Md.-Balt. County 58
62 ■ Vermont 84
63 † Nebraska 87
92 † Central Conn. St. 61
84 ■ St. Peter's 61
65 ■ Va. Commonwealth 62
63 ■ N.C.-Greensboro 45
60 ■ East Caro. 53
66 ■ N.C.-Wilmington 55
55 William & Mary 49
42 ■ Old Dominion 71
76 ■ Richmond 59
69 American 75
56 ■ George Mason 53
60 Virginia Tech 81
67 East Caro. 69
78 N.C.-Wilmington 63
66 ■ William & Mary 64
44 Old Dominion 67
60 ■ American 53
52 Richmond 47
49 George Mason 52
58 † William & Mary 60

JERSEY CITY ST. 12-12
60 John Jay 31
53 † Dominican (N.Y.) 46
28 Rowan 61
62 ■ Stockton St. 55
36 Trenton St. 54
71 Rutgers-Camden 51
49 ■ Ramapo 50
91 ■ Medgar Evers 11

43 Montclair St. 59
43 Staten Island 42
72 ■ York (N.Y.) 34
56 Rutgers-Newark 62
59 ■ Kean 82
51 Wm. Paterson 68
44 ■ Trenton St. 64
44 ■ Rowan 84
53 Stockton St. 32
70 ■ Rutgers-Newark 61
62 ■ Rutgers-Camden 52
45 Ramapo 69
49 ■ Montclair St. 42
78 ■ St. Elizabeth 50
52 ■ Wm. Paterson 56
60 Kean 63

JOHN CARROLL 19-6
79 † Ursinus 61
81 Johns Hopkins 50
72 Otterbein 50
101 ■ Grove City 58
75 ■ Marietta 43
75 ■ Baldwin-Wallace 59
75 Ohio Northern 55
81 † North Central 55
58 † Doane 86
84 ■ Capital 83
73 Muskingum 91
70 ■ Heidelberg 51
52 Mount Union 51
76 ■ Hiram 55
71 ■ Ohio Northern 64
70 Baldwin-Wallace 68
75 Marietta 51
64 ■ Mount Union 63
68 ■ Muskingum 74
66 Hiram 62
82 ■ Otterbein 61
51 Heidelberg 59
68 Capital 69
69 ■ Mount Union 59
58 Capital 63

JOHN JAY 6-17
31 ■ Jersey City St. 60
35 ■ Old Westbury 60
30 ■ Mt. St. Mary (N.Y.) 56
30 ■ Albertus Magnus 59
51 ■ Baruch 31
33 ■ York (N.Y.) 47
27 ■ Hunter 53
26 New York U. 91
51 ■ CCNY 46
63 Medgar Evers 52
53 ■ Mt. St. Vincent 45
59 ■ Medgar Evers 31
25 Stony Brook 68
43 Staten Island 45
42 Hunter 69
36 Vassar 75
39 CCNY 54
46 Old Westbury 62
31 ■ Manhattanville 34
48 Baruch 61
70 New Rochelle 27
42 York (N.Y.) 56
43 † York (N.Y.) 59

JOHNS HOPKINS 11-11
67 ■ Catholic 48
50 ■ John Carroll 81
44 Frank. & Marsh. 51
66 ■ Western Md. 38
63 ■ Brandeis 56
61 Carnegie Mellon 68
60 ■ Rochester 47
60 Case Reserve 80
52 New York U. 58
73 Emory 95
90 ■ Elizabethtown 81
60 ■ Chicago 54
56 ■ Washington (Mo.) 71
64 ■ Lebanon Valley 41
55 ■ Frank. & Marsh. 71

73 Widener 38
75 Lebanon Valley 55
59 Gettysburg 66
67 Dickinson 71
64 Western Md. 46
80 ■ Gettysburg 64
62 ■ Dickinson 63

JOHNSON SMITH 16-12
51 Virginia St. 62
81 ■ Norfolk St. 95
82 ■ Hampton 85
62 Virginia Union 72
69 Wingate 81
63 ■ Elizabeth City St. 79
59 Fla. Atlantic 98
67 † Virginia St. 60
79 N.C. Central 59
85 St. Augustine's 80
76 ■ Barber-Scotia 62
79 ■ Livingstone 51
73 Bowie St. 65
73 ■ Queens (N.C.) 91
93 Winston-Salem 49
84 ■ Shaw 75
75 Barber-Scotia 65
78 ■ Fayetteville St. 67
100 St. Paul's 75
71 ■ N.C. Central 65
78 ■ Winston-Salem 62
66 ■ St. Augustine's 69
77 Fayetteville St. 79
68 Shaw 60
75 Livingstone 70
70 Queens (N.C.) 89
67 † St. Paul's 50
72 † Virginia Union 80

JUNIATA 15-7
91 † Albright 57
68 Frank. & Marsh. 66
77 Wash. & Jeff. 85
84 ■ Elizabethtown 73
75 Susquehanna 72
68 Lebanon Valley 49
71 ■ Messiah 60
82 Gettysburg 77
72 † York (Pa.) 73
64 Lycoming 66
85 ■ Wash. & Jeff. 61
81 ■ Gettysburg 69
74 ■ Wilkes 64
80 ■ Waynesburg 75
89 Messiah 69
104 Elizabethtown 107
98 ■ Lycoming 72
58 ■ Susquehanna 72
82 ■ Carnegie Mellon 64
48 Wilkes 80
69 Western Md. 55
53 Dickinson 70

KALAMAZOO 6-18
73 ■ Taylor 66
55 ■ Rosary 80
62 ■ Grand Rapids Bapt. 63
50 Bethel (Ind.) 51
49 ■ Franklin 57
60 St. Mary's (Ind.) 72
72 Madonna 55
77 Ind.-South Bend 54
43 Aquinas 61
47 Spring Arbor 85
77 Olivet 39
62 Calvin 80
42 ■ Alma 66
71 ■ Albion 76
60 Hope 65
60 ■ Adrian 76
68 ■ Olivet 42
64 Adrian 71
54 ■ Hope 51
62 Albion 75
46 Alma 75

41 Defiance 57
46 ■ Calvin 66
39 Alma 61

KANSAS 21-9
76 Minnesota 82
65 ■ Southwest Mo. St. 51
86 ■ Mo.-Kansas City 52
99 ■ Fla. Atlantic 53
94 ■ Ill.-Chicago 63
106 ■ West Va. 64
60 Southwest Mo. St. 54
61 Kentucky 71
60 ■ Creighton 75
62 Missouri 64
71 Colorado 80
109 ■ Oral Roberts 53
69 ■ Nebraska 62
92 ■ Iowa St. 33
70 Oklahoma 64
54 Oklahoma St. 56
58 Kansas St. 51
60 ■ Colorado 77
62 ■ Missouri 52
75 Northern Iowa 73
77 Iowa St. 45
52 Nebraska 66
84 ■ Lamar 56
73 ■ Oklahoma St. 69
76 ■ Oklahoma 54
77 ■ Kansas St. 45
63 † Missouri 56
81 † Colorado 78
64 † Nebraska 60
47 ■ California 62

KANSAS ST. 10-17
70 ■ Missouri-Rolla 59
61 ■ Northern Iowa 55
48 ■ Lafayette 41
77 ■ Oral Roberts 44
75 ■ Mo. Western St. 55
60 ■ Ill.-Chicago 61
44 ■ Minnesota 58
69 † New Hampshire 60
69 N.C.-Wilmington 51
33 Colorado 61
49 Missouri 62
61 ■ Iowa St. 67
57 ■ Nebraska 74
54 Oklahoma St. 72
60 Oklahoma 68
54 ■ Wichita St. 66
62 ■ Quincy 44
51 ■ Kansas 58
51 ■ Missouri 67
51 ■ Colorado 61
50 Nebraska 69
67 Iowa St. 43
65 ■ Oklahoma 87
53 ■ Oklahoma St. 63
63 Loyola (Ill.) 52
45 Kansas 77
56 † Colorado 63

KEAN 11-13
80 ■ Wm. Paterson 57
47 Rutgers-Newark 71
66 ■ Rowan 81
80 ■ CCNY 33
58 ■ Susquehanna 71
68 Rutgers-Camden 56
63 Stockton St. 48
57 ■ Trenton St. 62
57 Rowan 86
68 ■ Stockton St. 51
59 Montclair St. 67
82 Jersey City St. 59
92 ■ Ramapo 94
56 Elizabethtown 96
62 Wm. Paterson 65
87 ■ Rutgers-Newark 54
47 ■ Montclair St. 59
86 Trenton St. 70
88 ■ Rutgers-Camden 75

81	Marymount (Va.)	90
78	† Emmanuel	89
69	Ramapo	77
63	■ Jersey City St.	60
71	■ Western Conn. St.	69

KEENE ST.		19-10
88	† St. Anselm	69
58	Franklin Pierce	72
59	† Pace	63
73	† Mansfield	57
89	■ Merrimack	76
85	Springfield	75
78	Bryant	80
57	Quinnipiac	67
56	■ Bentley	81
71	■ Le Moyne	61
55	Sacred Heart	61
81	Southern Conn. St.	43
66	New Haven	48
76	Le Moyne	61
76	New Hamp. Col.	60
61	■ Franklin Pierce	66
59	Mass.-Lowell	81
62	■ Southern Conn. St.	50
56	■ New Hamp. Col.	50
83	■ Bridgeport	51
84	American Int'l	70
85	■ Mass.-Lowell	76
76	■ Sacred Heart	53
74	Franklin Pierce	60
86	■ New Haven	69
75	■ New Haven	64
57	† Franklin Pierce	60
70	† St. Michael's	67
64	Pace	74

KENT		20-9
108	■ Cleveland St.	97
75	† Vermont	107
87	† Villanova	68
82	■ Youngstown St.	69
77	■ Pittsburgh	61
112	Central Fla.	66
91	† Va. Common.	101
106	† Texas Christian	90
74	Western Mich.	88
93	■ Ohio	61
72	Central Mich.	97
99	■ Bowling Green	94
79	Eastern Mich.	67
79	■ Toledo	58
83	■ Akron	55
92	Ball St.	81
63	■ Miami (Ohio)	65
65	Ohio	75
81	■ Central Mich.	64
78	Bowling Green	81
101	■ Eastern Mich.	71
79	Toledo	68
109	Akron	64
89	■ Ball St.	40
87	Miami (Ohio)	92
97	■ Western Mich.	79
71	■ Central Mich.	57
79	† Miami (Ohio)	69
68	† Bowling Green	96

KENTUCKY		18-10
79	■ Marshall	44
89	■ Murray St.	55
75	■ Connecticut	54
76	■ South Caro.	55
54	† N.C.-Charlotte	57
73	† West Va.	63
57	† Oklahoma St.	61
95	† Chicago St.	33
78	Bradley	49
71	■ Kansas	61
73	Mississippi St.	53
58	Louisville	53
69	■ Georgia	60
66	■ Morehead St.	38
49	■ Auburn	52
62	■ Western Ky.	60
43	Arkansas	45
83	Butler	76
77	■ Alabama	73
61	Tennessee	85
69	Cincinnati	72
72	Louisiana St.	65
74	■ Eastern Ky.	56
65	Mississippi	77
52	■ Vanderbilt	65
69	■ Florida	72
84	† Mississippi St.	73
61	† Vanderbilt	68

KENTUCKY ST.		2-25
77	■ Ind.-Southeast	73
61	Transylvania	85
73	■ Central St. (Ohio)	83
65	Lindsey Wilson	102
74	■ Lewis	76
58	■ St. Joseph's (Ind.)	73
44	Northern Ky.	74
65	Indianapolis	92
76	■ Transylvania	72
59	■ Southern Ind.	87
57	■ Ky. Wesleyan	82
55	Ashland	83
58	IU/PU-Ft. Wayne	99
60	Ind.-Southeast	86
51	Central St. (Ohio)	122
58	■ Bellarmine	90
36	■ Lindsey Wilson	88
60	■ Indianapolis	98
46	■ Northern Ky.	117
60	Ky. Wesleyan	93
74	Southern Ind.	116
41	■ IU/PU-Ft. Wayne	107
51	■ Ashland	101
64	Lincoln Memorial	102
47	Bellarmine	111
47	Lewis	99
57	St. Joseph's (Ind.)	111

KY. WESLEYAN		9-18
80	Midway	79
77	■ Oakland City	74
77	Brescia	75
88	■ Midway	50
69	■ Campbellsville	72
52	SIU-Edwardsville	64
75	Southern Ind.	89
57	■ IU/PU-Ft. Wayne	61
60	■ Ashland	71
64	Oakland City	77
61	Bellarmine	90
82	Kentucky St.	57
58	■ Lewis	73
62	■ St. Joseph's (Ind.)	64
63	Indianapolis	79
48	Northern Ky.	62
64	Ashland	58
54	IU/PU-Ft. Wayne	58
93	■ Kentucky St.	60
76	■ Bellarmine	86
44	St. Joseph's (Ind.)	66
66	Lewis	80
72	■ Quincy	56
77	■ Northern Ky.	87
67	■ Indianapolis	82
66	■ SIU-Edwardsville	83
107	■ Southern Ind.	94

KENYON		2-20
20	Waynesburg	87
28	■ Mt. Vernon Naz.	64
42	■ Ohio Wesleyan	87
27	Denison	71
30	■ Heidelberg	77
42	Earlham	76
38	■ Wooster	74
46	■ Allegheny	71
57	Oberlin	42
38	Case Reserve	73
44	■ Notre Dame (Ohio)	64
35	Wittenberg	68
32	■ Denison	65
40	■ Earlham	58
31	Wooster	75
28	■ Case Reserve	69
57	■ Oberlin	43
51	■ Lake Erie	68
41	Ohio Wesleyan	72
26	■ Wittenberg	99
35	Allegheny	76
26	Ohio Wesleyan	85

KEUKA		9-14
64	Emmanuel	75
62	† Moravian	86
67	Clarkson	64
60	■ Ithaca	88
58	■ Rochester Inst.	55
58	■ Roberts Wesleyan	53
58	D'youville	44
50	■ Sewanee	49
58	■ William Smith	84
68	Buffalo St.	88
65	Nazareth (N.Y.)	80
45	Roberts Wesleyan	78
66	■ Houghton	85
73	Alfred	65
54	† St. John Fisher	72
74	Manhattanville	43
68	Houghton	90
65	■ St. John Fisher	83
78	Utica	67
64	■ Nazareth (N.Y.)	69
85	■ Albany (N.Y.)	103
84	■ Hilbert	24
55	■ Elmira	69

KING'S (PA.)		14-11
72	† Allegheny	70
72	† Muskingum	83
66	■ Muhlenberg	57
56	Scranton	96
74	■ FDU-Madison	58
70	■ William Smith	69
54	Lebanon Valley	40
58	■ Wilkes	70
69	■ Lycoming	57
78	Drew	54
79	■ Scranton	91
85	Upsala	64
67	Delaware Valley	73
81	■ Misericordia	67
78	FDU-Madison	62
62	■ Lycoming	63
56	Wilkes	57
77	■ Upsala	79
71	■ Moravian	84
73	Allentown	69
64	■ Marywood	55
81	■ Delaware Valley	69
78	■ Drew	42
48	Susquehanna	84
59	Delaware Valley	63

KNOX		6-15
81	■ Maryville (Mo.)	77
82	■ Iowa Wesleyan	61
42	■ Washington (Mo.)	80
44	Illinois Col.	79
60	Webster	64
59	Aurora	81
54	Eureka	78
80	■ Cornell College	49
62	■ Coe	66
66	■ Ill. Wesleyan	74
43	■ Lake Forest	79
62	■ Beloit	76
70	■ Monmouth (Ill.)	68
52	Carroll (Wis.)	80
45	Ripon	79
61	■ Illinois Col.	66
59	Grinnell	76
73	Monmouth (Ill.)	71
74	Cornell College	59
57	Coe	82
45	■ Grinnell	57

KUTZTOWN		11-15
81	■ Mercy	59
49	■ Bloomsburg	64
66	■ Shippensburg	92
71	■ St. Rose	66
70	■ Allentown	54
53	Le Moyne	69
58	† Queens (N.Y.)	44
61	■ Phila. Textile	74
62	Alvernia	57
79	Holy Family	54
65	■ Bowie St.	44
52	Rowan	70
66	■ Dist. Columbia	55
60	■ Clarion	74
70	Mansfield	46
65	■ Cheyney	27
57	■ West Chester	67
52	Bloomsburg	75
53	Millersville	70
66	East Stroudsburg	80
62	■ Mansfield	69
75	Cheyney	41
58	West Chester	77
47	■ Bloomsburg	64
62	■ Millersville	73
69	■ East Stroudsburg	84

LA SALLE		16-11
83	Pennsylvania	77
65	† Boise St.	82
68	UC Irvine	66
79	† Temple	88
56	St. Joseph's (Pa.)	67
60	Villanova	62
96	■ Central Conn. St.	63
92	■ Nebraska	88
69	■ Notre Dame	63
77	■ Drexel	61
64	Butler	90
53	Evansville	70
75	■ Xavier (Ohio)	86
100	■ Dayton	67
79	■ Loyola (Ill.)	49
77	■ Detroit Mercy	76
81	Duquesne	71
58	Notre Dame	61
76	Chicago St.	58
70	■ Evansville	54
84	■ Butler	68
65	Dayton	81
54	Xavier (Ohio)	79
88	Detroit Mercy	69
70	Loyola (Ill.)	54
96	■ Duquesne	60
68	† Evansville	71

LA VERNE		13-12
50	■ Southern Cal Col.	78
55	■ Neb. Wesleyan	69
54	Colorado Col.	53
68	Hastings	115
72	■ La Sierra	19
61	Pt. Loma Nazarene	66
80	La Sierra	25
60	■ Azusa-Pacific	61
61	■ Manchester	74
48	■ Whitman	66
84	■ Colorado Col.	50
74	Cal Lutheran	73
54	Redlands	58
73	■ Pomona-Pitzer	45
62	■ Claremont-M-S	46
68	Whittier	58
54	Occidental	61
70	UC San Diego	61
67	■ Cal Lutheran	68
63	■ Redlands	71
64	Pomona-Pitzer	76
65	Claremont-M-S	62
66	■ Whittier	58

60 ■ Occidental 55
80 ■ UC San Diego 72

LAFAYETTE 19-9
79 ■ Princeton 72
66 ■ Towson St. 57
41 Kansas St. 48
42 Delaware 51
36 Connecticut 53
65 † Wagner 64
62 Hofstra 47
58 Boston U. 80
67 Drexel 64
54 ■ Cornell 45
57 Yale 42
70 ■ Colgate 46
62 Bucknell 54
58 Navy 47
61 ■ Holy Cross 67
38 Fordham 54
51 Army 50
75 ■ Pennsylvania 62
69 ■ Lehigh 42
50 Colgate 51
84 ■ Bucknell 68
72 ■ Navy 67
66 Holy Cross 74
65 ■ Fordham 63
87 Lehigh 64
55 ■ Army 54
79 ■ Colgate 60
49 ■ Fordham 61

LAKE FOREST 18-4
74 ■ St. Mary's (Ind.) 64
89 ■ Trinity (Ill.) 58
73 † Teiko-Marycrest 59
90 † Clarke 59
76 Carroll (Wis.) 58
74 ■ Ill. Benedictine 42
78 ■ Carthage 59
41 Lawrence 56
75 ■ Carroll (Wis.) 64
79 Knox 43
65 Illinois Col. 77
75 North Central 67
97 ■ Cornell College 55
66 ■ Monmouth (Ill.) 47
65 Beloit 75
74 ■ Ripon 62
69 St. Norbert 73
76 Concordia (Ill.) 43
81 ■ Lawrence 67
70 Ripon 62
72 ■ Beloit 67
59 ■ St. Norbert 53

LAMAR 10-16
84 Oral Roberts 75
43 † Southern Cal 78
100 † Cleveland St. 79
80 † Sam Houston St. 62
58 Stephen F. Austin 84
59 ■ Houston 60
62 † Youngstown St. 72
56 † Georgia St. 53
54 ■ Western Ky. 83
47 Louisiana Tech 71
81 ■ Southwestern La. 41
49 ■ Arkansas St. 57
47 ■ Louisiana Tech 85
77 ■ South Ala. 66
65 New Orleans 52
40 Arkansas St. 57
66 Mississippi 75
85 Grambling 80
54 ■ Tex.-Pan American 58
56 Kansas 84
43 Western Ky. 92
75 Tex.-Pan American 62
64 Southwestern La. 71
70 South Ala. 73
47 ■ New Orleans 65
85 ■ Oral Roberts 52

LANDER 11-16
80 Newberry 48
42 Erskine 54
79 Converse 72
52 Gardner-Webb 53
61 † North Ga. 76
48 ■ Presbyterian 57
48 ■ Augusta 74
53 ■ Armstrong St. 63
60 ■ S.C.-Aiken 59
70 Francis Marion 50
63 Pembroke St. 69
59 ■ Erskine 30
68 ■ Georgia Col. 73
51 ■ Columbus 61
42 S.C.-Spartanburg 86
65 Presbyterian 80
61 ■ Converse 68
58 S.C.-Aiken 51
55 ■ S.C.-Spartanburg 72
54 Augusta 64
44 Armstrong St. 75
67 ■ Newberry 57
72 Georgia Col. 68
67 Columbus 65
62 ■ Francis Marion 57
57 ■ Pembroke St. 52
54 † Georgia Col. 64

LAWRENCE 19-4
58 Marian (Wis.) 51
52 ■ Carroll (Wis.) 59
67 ■ Wis.-Whitewater 61
49 Occidental 47
60 Pomona-Pitzer 52
58 ■ Lakeland 55
68 ■ Silver Lake 51
56 ■ Lake Forest 41
70 Monmouth (Ill.) 55
76 Cornell College 40
79 St. Norbert 64
66 ■ Coe 50
74 ■ Grinnell 73
83 ■ Wis. Lutheran 69
60 Beloit 69
75 ■ Ripon 66
67 Lake Forest 81
68 ■ St. Norbert 61
73 Carroll (Wis.) 72
61 ■ Beloit 57
56 Ripon 45
61 † Grinnell 48
64 Illinois Col. 70

LE MOYNE 16-11
54 † Wm. Paterson 53
69 Cortland St. 61
64 Queens (N.Y.) 46
74 St. Rose 53
69 ■ Kutztown 53
62 ■ Mercy 53
61 Keene St. 71
58 Franklin Pierce 79
66 ■ Mass.-Lowell 81
66 ■ St. Lawrence 29
67 ■ East Stroudsburg 63
61 ■ Keene St. 76
77 ■ Sacred Heart 76
75 New Haven 74
77 Southern Conn. St. 45
53 ■ Franklin Pierce 74
65 ■ New Hamp. Col. 59
65 Sacred Heart 68
60 ■ Hamilton 61
70 ■ New Haven 69
72 Lock Haven 86
74 Utica 33
50 New Hamp. Col. 79
57 † Mass.-Lowell 77
71 ■ Oswego St. 45
68 ■ Southern Conn. St. 39
59 Sacred Heart 68

LEMOYNE-OWEN 1-25
72 Mississippi-Women 79
66 Lane 78
55 ■ Miles 73
45 ■ Albany St. (Ga.) 104
55 ■ Alabama A&M 133
57 Columbus 107
77 ■ Morris Brown 79
55 Savannah St. 121
56 Fort Valley St. 96
37 ■ Mississippi-Women 73
61 Clark Atlanta 63
37 Albany St. (Ga.) 91
54 ■ Tuskegee 79
52 Rust 85
47 Tuskegee 84
51 Miles 90
45 Paine 87
47 ■ Lane 53
22 Mississippi Col. 90
52 Ark.-Pine Bluff 70
54 ■ Fort Valley St. 118
53 ■ Rust 82
61 ■ Ark.-Pine Bluff 54
76 Morris Brown 91
62 ■ Clark Atlanta 74
44 Alabama A&M 97

LEBANON VALLEY 2-22
52 † Carnegie Mellon 70
58 † Wash. & Jeff. 93
55 Alvernia 81
51 ■ Frank. & Marsh. 62
62 Gallaudet 72
49 Phila. Pharmacy 63
49 ■ Juniata 68
40 ■ King's (Pa.) 54
55 Notre Dame (Md.) 56
42 ■ Dickinson 71
47 Swarthmore 60
57 ■ Western Md. 79
41 Johns Hopkins 64
70 Gettysburg 77
58 Delaware Valley 62
55 ■ Johns Hopkins 75
44 Frank. & Marsh. 72
63 ■ Gettysburg 83
87 ■ Albright 81
46 Susquehanna 70
72 Moravian 101
49 Dickinson 65
68 ■ Messiah 67
63 Western Md. 65

LEHIGH 1-26
65 ■ Hofstra 77
55 ■ Delaware 78
58 Harvard 81
64 † LIU-Brooklyn 69
56 Rider 70
34 Princeton 74
42 Florida Int'l 101
55 † Brown 80
75 † Bucknell 89
55 Yale 68
70 Navy 77
42 Holy Cross 80
65 ■ Pennsylvania 73
65 ■ Fordham 86
60 Army 72
56 ■ Mt. St. Mary's (Md.) 78
56 Bucknell 90
74 ■ Colgate 65
42 Lafayette 69
68 ■ Navy 80
55 ■ Holy Cross 65
57 Fordham 64
59 ■ Army 63
60 ■ Bucknell 73
64 ■ Lafayette 87
64 Colgate 84
58 Holy Cross 84

LENOIR-RHYNE 6-18
94 † Barton 88
79 † Lees-McRae 86
67 † Mt. Olive 64
67 ■ High Point 88
60 Belmont Abbey 70
58 Mars Hill 86
84 Davidson 71
65 High Point 57
61 ■ Queens (N.C.) 47
66 ■ Presbyterian 84
73 ■ Wingate 78
78 ■ Catawba 96
59 Gardner-Webb 72
73 ■ Elon 80
70 Carson-Newman 94
63 Presbyterian 80
77 ■ Mars Hill 83
60 Wingate 102
83 Catawba 93
94 ■ Pfeiffer 66
77 ■ Gardner-Webb 90
69 Elon 88
46 ■ Carson-Newman 80
58 † Wingate 79

LEWIS 12-15
48 ■ SIU-Edwardsville 83
71 ■ Bemidji St. 69
69 St. Francis (Ill.) 54
64 Rosary 76
76 ■ Grand Valley St. 72
76 Kentucky St. 74
71 Bellarmine 89
60 St. Joseph's (Ind.) 84
71 ■ Indianapolis 83
66 ■ Northern Ky. 80
45 Quincy 58
73 Ky. Wesleyan 58
71 Southern Ind. 89
79 Wis.-Parkside 68
65 ■ IU/PU-Ft. Wayne 55
73 ■ Ashland 67
58 SIU-Edwardsville 74
62 ■ St. Joseph's (Ind.) 74
78 Northern Ky. 86
77 Indianapolis 96
76 ■ Wis.-Parkside 59
76 ■ Southern Ind. 73
80 ■ Ky. Wesleyan 66
50 Ashland 66
59 IU/PU-Ft. Wayne 73
99 ■ Kentucky St. 47
59 ■ Bellarmine 87

LIBERTY 16-12
48 ■ N.C.-Greensboro 50
69 ■ St. Peter's 66
66 ■ Evansville 74
45 ■ Navy 54
73 ■ East Tenn. St. 62
74 ■ Davidson 40
84 ■ Columbia Union 56
71 Coastal Caro. 75
57 Charleston So. 50
82 ■ Winthrop 51
59 Va. Commonwealth 78
73 ■ Campbell 52
60 ■ Coastal Caro. 45
65 ■ Radford 74
77 ■ Charleston So. 52
68 ■ N.C.-Asheville 50
71 Davidson 54
81 Campbell 78
62 Winthrop 59
77 ■ Towson St. 72
56 ■ Md.-Balt. County 64
57 Towson St. 69
53 Md.-Balt. County 65
52 N.C.-Greensboro 77
66 Radford 77
49 N.C.-Asheville 48
66 † Campbell 57
62 Radford 70

LIMESTONE 14-15
84 ■ Voorhees 69

61 Pfeiffer 58
76 ■ Barber-Scotia 53
66 S.C.-Spartanburg 78
76 † Converse 64
59 ■ Catawba 62
58 Erskine 65
83 Barber-Scotia 76
63 ■ Benedict 67
64 Voorhees 51
77 Converse 62
78 Central Wesleyan 81
65 ■ Claflin 76
90 ■ Warren Wilson 30
48 Wofford 69
83 Newberry 50
82 ■ Converse 59
68 Benedict 78
79 ■ Erskine 51
55 Morris 56
55 ■ Central Wesleyan 58
65 ■ Morris 76
76 ■ Wofford 84
78 ■ Newberry 60
61 Lees-McRae 99
71 Claflin 77
90 Warren Wilson 26
52 Benedict 42
71 Claflin 82

LINCOLN (MO.) 4-22
53 Quincy 72
58 † Oklahoma City 75
45 ■ Bethany (Kan.) 64
69 William Woods 60
47 Rockhurst 70
46 SIU-Edwardsville 70
58 † IU/PU-Ft. Wayne 61
48 Mo.-St. Louis 73
43 ■ Central Mo. St. 73
66 Mo. Southern St. 82
56 ■ Mo. Western St. 86
84 Harris-Stowe 59
49 Pittsburg St. 91
65 Southwest Baptist 77
55 Peru St. 70
70 ■ Mo.-St. Louis 77
58 Missouri-Rolla 73
47 ■ Mo. Southern St. 70
86 ■ Northeast Mo. St. 63
53 ■ Pittsburg St. 75
66 ■ Southwest Baptist 73
79 ■ William Woods 49
44 ■ Missouri-Rolla 69
63 Emporia St. 71
53 Washburn 79
66 Northwest Mo. St. 72

LINCOLN MEMORIAL 18-9
56 Bellarmine 53
70 † Delta St. 87
73 Bluefield St. 77
77 † North Ga. 69
74 Gardner-Webb 76
74 Carson-Newman 79
93 Kennesaw 79
79 ■ Gardner-Webb 62
67 ■ Berry 61
79 Longwood 60
82 ■ Bluefield St. 41
77 ■ North Ga. 63
68 ■ Carson-Newman 66
98 ■ Lees-McRae 73
79 ■ Ala.-Huntsville 60
77 ■ S.C.-Spartanburg 82
77 Wofford 83
94 ■ Newberry 62
99 Newberry 52
78 ■ Union (Ky.) 65
73 Lees-McRae 98
73 Ala.-Huntsville 50
57 Berry 79
66 ■ Wofford 59
102 ■ Kentucky St. 64
99 ■ Longwood 67

73 S.C.-Spartanburg 83

LIVINGSTON 17-9
75 William Carey 91
77 Miles 49
88 Ala.-Huntsville 72
79 ■ Alabama A&M 64
88 Southern-N.O. 53
78 ■ William Carey 81
77 ■ Mississippi-Women 62
64 Mississippi Col. 65
85 Jacksonville St. 86
77 ■ Miles 42
80 ■ Valdosta St. 63
71 ■ West Ga. 62
92 ■ West Fla. 79
90 ■ Judson 51
76 North Ala. 74
67 Delta St. 92
77 ■ Mississippi Col. 72
83 Mississippi St. 106
56 ■ Delta St. 79
97 ■ North Ala. 87
69 West Ga. 81
94 Valdosta St. 70
86 ■ Southern-N.O. 54
62 Mississippi-Women 57
91 ■ Jacksonville St. 70
74 † Jacksonville St. 79

LIVINGSTONE 3-23
39 Norfolk St. 113
57 ■ Bowie St. 66
52 † Edward Waters 61
48 † Voorhees 67
48 Elizabeth City St. 47
44 † Savannah St. 57
39 ■ Virginia Union 96
57 St. Augustine's 83
39 Shaw 53
51 Johnson Smith 79
77 ■ Fayetteville St. 85
62 Morris 74
42 Barber-Scotia 59
58 ■ Shaw 68
42 Hampton 80
71 ■ N.C. Central 72
59 Winston-Salem 68
66 Fayetteville St. 88
90 N.C. Central 98
65 ■ St. Paul's 86
82 ■ Morris 48
45 Virginia St. 77
70 ■ Johnson Smith 75
83 ■ Winston-Salem 77
79 ■ St. Augustine's 95
62 † Hampton 75

LOCK HAVEN 13-13
99 ■ Concordia (N.Y.) 40
84 ■ St. Vincent 75
84 Gannon 66
62 ■ Bloomsburg 68
72 Millersville 91
50 † Bentley 75
66 † Longwood 56
68 Mercyhurst 53
75 ■ Georgian Court 37
66 ■ Montclair St. 51
71 ■ Mansfield 43
89 ■ Bridgeport 63
63 ■ Indiana (Pa.) 78
69 Edinboro 86
64 ■ Clarion 77
79 ■ Slippery Rock 72
87 Shippensburg 76
66 Calif. (Pa.) 72
74 ■ Mercyhurst 79
65 Indiana (Pa.) 71
56 ■ Edinboro 95
86 ■ Le Moyne 72
67 Clarion 107
79 Slippery Rock 83
59 ■ Shippensburg 68

67 ■ Calif. (Pa.) 63

LONG BEACH ST. 9-17
57 North Caro. St. 75
82 † South Ala. 66
50 Southwest Tex. St. 69
48 Southern Cal 101
76 ■ St. John's (N.Y.) 82
78 ■ Oregon St. 92
61 ■ Stanford 98
82 ■ UC Irvine 74
80 ■ Cal St. Fullerton 78
67 ■ Hawaii 69
72 Nevada 80
90 ■ Hawaii 91
69 ■ Pacific (Cal.) 64
67 UC Santa Barb. 72
67 Nevada-Las Vegas 94
64 New Mexico St. 73
63 ■ Nevada 61
55 Pacific (Cal.) 75
59 San Jose St. 58
90 UC Irvine 81
72 ■ UC Santa Barb. 88
62 ■ New Mexico St. 64
55 ■ Nevada-Las Vegas 68
99 Cal St. Fullerton 73
87 ■ San Jose St. 73
46 ■ UC Santa Barb. 74

LIU-BROOKLYN 9-17
67 † Texas Christian 80
69 † Lehigh 64
62 ■ Georgian Court 58
47 ■ Coppin St. 56
45 † Yale 78
60 † Morgan St. 75
67 ■ St. Bonaventure 77
50 Wagner 73
63 ■ Monmouth (N.J.) 65
53 Marist 51
56 FDU-Teaneck 65
48 ■ Robert Morris 68
62 St. Francis (N.Y.) 59
59 ■ St. Francis (Pa.) 56
83 Georgian Court 68
45 Rider 76
60 Mt. St. Mary's (Md.) 84
53 Monmouth (N.J.) 67
57 ■ Wagner 56
63 ■ FDU-Teaneck 74
61 ■ Marist 56
66 St. Francis (Pa.) 81
54 Robert Morris 58
77 ■ St. Francis (N.Y.) 66
50 ■ Mt. St. Mary's (Md.) 76
57 ■ Rider 75

LIU-C.W. POST 11-16
71 Concordia (N.Y.) 60
62 St. Francis (N.Y.) 73
56 ■ Southern Conn. St. 53
61 Queens (N.Y.) 76
51 ■ Mercy 52
48 ■ New Haven 51
40 West Chester 87
73 Dowling 63
60 Mercy 56
58 Adelphi 61
48 ■ St. Rose 58
71 ■ Dowling 45
58 Phila. Textile 79
73 ■ Concordia (N.Y.) 57
58 ■ LIU-Southampton 49
64 ■ Bridgeport 57
41 East Stroudsburg 77
67 Molloy 71
60 ■ Queens (N.Y.) 48
38 ■ Pace 72
58 St. Rose 76
48 ■ Adelphi 57
66 ■ Molloy 73
62 ■ Phila. Textile 52
46 Pace 75

74 LIU-Southampton 65
64 Adelphi 77

LIU-SOUTHAMPTON 3-21
43 † Bloomsburg 97
65 † Mercy 66
70 ■ Bridgeport 39
40 ■ Pace 74
44 East Stroudsburg 78
49 Queens (N.Y.) 75
51 ■ Molloy 67
51 ■ Phila. Textile 82
66 ■ St. Rose 70
68 Concordia (N.Y.) 75
61 ■ Mercy 74
65 ■ Adelphi 80
55 Pace 95
49 LIU-C.W. Post 58
56 Molloy 63
50 Adelphi 80
58 ■ Dowling 75
64 ■ Queens (N.Y.) 70
65 Dowling 57
45 Mercy 63
49 St. Rose 86
89 ■ Concordia (N.Y.) 63
65 ■ LIU-C.W. Post 74
57 Phila. Textile 89

LONGWOOD 8-19
77 ■ Virginia Union 78
73 ■ Francis Marion 67
55 Elon 79
65 ■ Pembroke St. 57
64 Dist. Columbia 59
65 West Chester 101
56 † Lock Haven 66
51 ■ High Point 70
60 ■ Lincoln Memorial 79
64 ■ West Chester 62
99 ■ Converse 77
66 ■ Millersville 99
52 Barton 82
59 ■ Wofford 70
80 Pfeiffer 100
48 ■ Elon 57
56 Queens (N.C.) 79
79 ■ Mt. Olive 85
79 Columbia Union 74
61 ■ Pitt.-Johnstown 97
67 Virginia St. 80
51 ■ Queens (N.C.) 62
74 Mt. Olive 88
82 Converse 66
76 Wofford 91
55 ■ Dist. Columbia 46
67 Lincoln Memorial 99

LORAS 12-12
81 † Blackburn 50
49 Grinnell 60
67 Wis.-Platteville 71
73 Coe 57
71 ■ Teiko-Westmar 54
64 † Carroll (Mont.) 67
41 † Xavier (La.) 85
82 † St. Scholastica 73
69 ■ William Penn 68
67 ■ Central (Iowa) 65
66 ■ Luther 89
90 Dubuque 39
62 Simpson 74
64 ■ Wartburg 95
65 Upper Iowa 58
67 ■ Buena Vista 53
68 William Penn 73
65 ■ Simpson 60
69 Buena Vista 77
67 Luther 78
47 Wartburg 84
101 ■ Dubuque 64
81 ■ Upper Iowa 59
56 Central (Iowa) 79

LOUISIANA ST. 9-18

100	■	Southeastern La.	55
59	†	Hartford	57
59		Florida St.	79
49	■	Nevada-Las Vegas	71
64		Florida Int'l	77
77		Central Fla.	67
76	■	Southwest Tex. St.	63
56		South Caro.	66
68	■	Southwestern La.	41
61	■	Tennessee	95
61		Vanderbilt	87
69	■	Alabama	74
57		Texas A&M	58
59	■	Auburn	83
89		Southern Miss.	82
65		Florida	89
92	■	Southern-B.R.	71
86	■	Tulane	74
62		Mississippi	95
66	■	Arkansas	69
65	■	Kentucky	72
68		Stephen F. Austin	81
72	■	Nicholls St.	42
53	■	Georgia	88
71		Mississippi St.	76
61		New Orleans	77
86	†	Alabama	106

LOUISIANA TECH 26-6

110	■	Alcorn St.	70
93	■	Alabama	72
51		Northeast La.	62
88	†	McNeese St.	52
68		Mississippi	64
90	■	Central Fla.	39
76	■	Tennessee	83
71		Texas Tech	74
96	■	Louisiana Col.	61
71		New Orleans	62
71	■	Lamar	47
76	■	Northeast La.	49
102	■	South Ala.	55
85		Lamar	47
83		Tex.-Pan American	43
94	■	Southwestern La.	50
54		Arkansas St.	53
78		Stephen F. Austin	63
82	■	Tex.-Pan American	42
93		Central Fla.	37
86	■	Western Ky.	77
72	■	Arkansas St.	66
74		South Ala.	53
54	■	New Orleans	47
62		Western Ky.	63
89		Southwestern La.	53
67	■	New Orleans	60
73	■	Western Ky.	81
70	■	DePaul	59
82		Texas	78
59	†	Southwest Mo. St.	43
53	†	Vanderbilt	58

LOUISVILLE 19-12

83		Austin Peay	76
63	†	Texas A&M	59
51		Illinois	65
74	■	Eastern Ky.	66
79	†	North Texas	53
71		Middle Tenn. St.	70
70		Oregon	81
62	■	Purdue	65
98	■	Coppin St.	59
84	■	Butler	64
53	■	Kentucky	58
79		Tulane	85
72		Southern Miss.	77
94	■	South Fla.	46
100		Va. Commonwealth	63
75	■	Virginia Tech	79
71	■	N.C.-Charlotte	55
71		Evansville	81
69		South Fla.	44
87	■	Tulane	74
59	■	Va. Commonwealth	54
69		Western Ky.	76
86		N.C.-Charlotte	82
61		Virginia Tech	82
65	■	Southern Miss.	71
93		Northeastern Ill.	61
70	■	Va. Commonwealth	62
92	■	Virginia Tech	73
84	■	Southern Miss.	73
74		Connecticut	71
61		Auburn	66

LOYOLA (ILL.) 6-21

60	■	Northwestern	82
74	■	Evansville	63
70	■	Arkansas	75
65		Drake	73
68	■	Butler	76
66	■	Cal St. Northridge	61
54	■	Bradley	49
72	■	Manhattan	56
60	■	Detroit Mercy	63
57		Ill.-Chicago	65
50		Notre Dame	76
49		La Salle	79
66		Duquesne	63
80	■	Dayton	84
52	■	Xavier (Ohio)	73
64		Alabama	107
36		Evansville	54
59		Butler	78
60		DePaul	73
52		Detroit Mercy	75
60	■	Notre Dame	74
77		Wis.-Milwaukee	88
52	■	Kansas St.	63
77	■	Duquesne	63
54	■	La Salle	70
57		Xavier (Ohio)	96
63		Dayton	70

LOYOLA (MD.) 14-15

49		Rutgers	66
66	†	Towson St.	51
72	†	Md.-Balt. County	66
63	■	Mt. St. Mary's (Md.)	45
76	†	Duquesne	86
53		Geo. Washington	74
48	■	Notre Dame	55
44	■	Maryland	75
51		North Caro.	87
45	■	William & Mary	50
52		Duke	61
58	■	Niagara	52
78	■	Siena	59
74	■	Fairfield	56
60	■	Manhattan	63
56		Iona	47
50		St. Peter's	67
48		Manhattan	60
69		Siena	55
79	■	Canisius	67
67	■	Iona	59
55		Canisius	63
93		Niagara	97
64	■	St. Peter's	59
69		Fairfield	72
73		Hofstra	59
74	†	Canisius	65
68	†	Siena	66
64	†	St. Peter's	72

LOYOLA (CAL.) 14-12

67	■	Cal St. Northridge	36
45		San Diego St.	59
53		Wyoming	51
70		Colorado St.	82
66	■	Rice	55
71	■	Western Ill.	52
50	■	Utah	48
64		Canisius	55
60		Buffalo	53
47		UCLA	81
60	■	New Mexico	53
68	■	Southern Utah	60
74	■	Portland	61
71	■	Gonzaga	56
52		St. Mary's (Cal.)	54
51		San Francisco	66
54	■	San Francisco	51
72	■	St. Mary's (Cal.)	61
49		San Diego	63
47		Santa Clara	67
63	■	Santa Clara	83
45	■	San Diego	40
70	■	Pepperdine	82
59		Gonzaga	65
62		Portland	78
56		Pepperdine	85

LUTHER 16-9

62	■	Wis.-Stevens Point	64
62		St. Olaf	63
68		Wis.-La Crosse	71
59	†	Carroll (Wis.)	73
59		North Central	55
68	■	Winona St.	76
75		Wis.-Platteville	72
80	■	Southwestern (Tex.)	55
57	■	Arkansas Tech	76
73	■	Simpson	50
72	■	Upper Iowa	29
94		Buena Vista	54
72		Wartburg	76
89		Loras	66
60	■	Central (Iowa)	71
77	■	Dubuque	36
77	■	William Penn	56
60		Central (Iowa)	70
67		Simpson	66
61		Upper Iowa	58
72	■	Wartburg	58
78	■	Loras	67
75	■	Buena Vista	42
80		Dubuque	59
60		William Penn	54

LYCOMING 5-19

37		Frostburg St.	72
59	†	Glenville St.	90
50		Wilkes	72
49	■	Susquehanna	59
45	■	Dickinson	70
53	■	Messiah	63
82		Allentown	96
48	†	Penn St.-Behrend	60
57		King's (Pa.)	69
66	■	Juniata	64
41	■	Marywood	39
63		Susquehanna	72
57		Scranton	78
61		Elizabethtown	93
77	■	Gettysburg	82
63		King's (Pa.)	62
52		Mansfield	57
66	■	Wilkes	75
74		Delaware Valley	61
72		Juniata	98
66	■	Elizabethtown	79
78		Messiah	79
49		Frank. & Marsh.	81
60	■	Misericordia	59

LYNCHBURG 4-18

67		East. Mennonite	65
77	■	Bridgewater (Va.)	64
44	■	Ferrum	61
36	†	DePauw	72
50		Rhodes	36
60		Va. Wesleyan	77
53	■	Randolph-Macon	72
40		Guilford	68
54	■	Emory & Henry	57
52	■	R.-M. Woman's	53
51	■	Roanoke	77
74		Hollins	91
66	■	Va. Wesleyan	83
49	■	Davidson	67
49	■	Hollins	75
50		Bridgewater (Va.)	59
58	■	East. Mennonite	68
58		R.-M. Woman's	50
59		Randolph-Macon	72
54		Roanoke	70
47	■	Guilford	74
39		Emory & Henry	62

MACMURRAY 8-17

35	■	Illinois Col.	93
50	■	Sewanee	76
34		Ill. Benedictine	57
61		Eureka	102
36		Judson	66
64	†	Moody Bible	56
82		Ill. Wesleyan	93
55	■	Westminster	50
59	■	Mo. Baptist	81
66	■	Rockford	46
67		Iowa Wesleyan	73
59		Principia	60
62		Fontbonne	77
61	■	Webster	54
42	■	Blackburn	57
57	■	Greenville	55
53		Maryville (Mo.)	71
53		Westminster	46
60	■	Lincoln Chrst.	37
61	■	Fontbonne	68
61	■	Principia	74
61		Webster	59
48		Blackburn	70
59	■	Maryville (Mo.)	64
63	†	Fontbonne	66

MACALESTER 10-15

78	■	Dr. Martin Luther	34
73	■	Grinnell	49
83		Concordia (St. Paul)	67
70	■	Bethel (Minn.)	62
76	■	Augsburg	59
92		St. Olaf	86
65	■	Carleton	32
43		Hamline	62
61	■	St. Benedict	74
64		Concordia-M'head	84
59	■	St. Thomas (Minn.)	75
85		St. Mary's (Minn.)	65
57		N'western (Minn.)	72
60		Bethel (Minn.)	62
83		Wis.-River Falls	70
60		Augsburg	44
66	■	St. Olaf	71
59		Gust. Adolphus	64
57		Carleton	62
62	■	Hamline	63
50		St. Benedict	82
60	■	Concordia-M'head	87
59	■	St. Mary's (Minn.)	67
57	■	Gust. Adolphus	69
40		St. Thomas (Minn.)	70

MAINE 9-20

65		Boston College	80
61	■	Florida Int'l	75
50	■	Mississippi	64
55		St. Peter's	65
51	†	Rhode Island	62
43		Rutgers	71
34	†	Texas	72
56		Central Mich.	81
72	†	Valparaiso	73
56	■	Drexel	50
53	■	Delaware	56
63		Vermont	94
51	■	Hartford	50
60	■	Dartmouth	59
52		Boston U.	61
43		Northeastern	45
79		Central Conn. St.	52
63	■	New Hampshire	68
51	■	Northeastern	57
57	■	Boston U.	64
63		Hartford	66

67 ■ Vermont 68
79 ■ Md.-East. Shore 44
58 Delaware 53
66 Drexel 53
38 New Hampshire 58
59 New Hampshire 55
44 † Northeastern 43
45 Vermont 62

MANCHESTER 18-5
66 ■ Ohio Northern 49
81 ■ Grace 48
51 † Albion 48
49 Bluffton 50
62 Albion 68
97 ■ Purdue-Calumet 72
68 ■ Marian (Ind.) 63
73 † Rio Grande 88
61 Redlands 58
74 La Verne 61
86 ■ Goshen 52
90 ■ Anderson 72
85 Taylor 46
83 ■ Hanover 62
58 Franklin 78
67 St. Mary's (Ind.) 63
72 ■ Defiance 71
79 ■ DePauw 46
72 Anderson 49
83 Hanover 56
84 ■ Taylor 79
62 DePauw 60
55 ■ Franklin 81

MANHATTAN 12-15
56 Columbia-Barnard 65
73 Syracuse 58
70 † Dayton 86
80 ■ Monmouth (N.J.) 63
67 ■ FDU-Teaneck 65
63 † William & Mary 57
58 Dartmouth 57
62 ■ Rhode Island 61
56 Northern Ill. 109
56 Loyola (Ill.) 72
64 ■ St. Joseph's (Pa.) 86
53 St. Peter's 77
61 Canisius 71
69 Niagara 78
82 ■ Siena 76
63 Loyola (Md.) 60
54 Fordham 71
77 ■ Iona 73
60 ■ Loyola (Md.) 48
77 ■ Fairfield 91
45 Iona 61
75 ■ St. Peter's 68
75 Fairfield 76
54 Siena 81
68 ■ Niagara 57
64 ■ Canisius 81
84 † Fairfield 93

MANHATTANVILLE 1-21
23 St. John Fisher 91
27 † Concordia (Mich.) 58
33 ■ New Paltz St. 80
23 New York U. 73
53 ■ Vassar 56
31 ■ Goucher 58
42 ■ Russell Sage 57
35 ■ Dominican (N.Y.) 36
32 ■ Hunter 54
26 Skidmore 60
60 ■ Staten Island 62
36 ■ St. Elizabeth 51
43 ■ Keuka 74
49 ■ CCNY 51
34 John Jay 31
38 ■ Ramapo 71
21 ■ Trinity (Conn.) 73
28 Union (N.Y.) 65
46 Utica 58
51 Mt. St. Vincent 55

22 FDU-Madison 66
29 ■ Connecticut Col. 74

MANKATO ST. 12-15
77 ■ St. Scholastica 48
65 ■ Gust. Adolphus 51
60 Minn.-Duluth 68
77 ■ Viterbo 53
58 Hastings 75
74 Neb.-Kearney 62
76 ■ Cal St. Los Angeles 41
59 ■ Moorhead St. 57
81 ■ Mt. Senario 38
60 ■ North Dak. 72
50 ■ North Dak. St. 92
59 Morningside 78
73 South Dak. 83
81 ■ St. Cloud St. 38
66 ■ Augustana (S.D.) 75
73 ■ South Dak. St. 61
63 Nebraska-Omaha 68
74 Northern Colo. 81
81 ■ South Dak. 67
65 ■ Morningside 84
80 St. Cloud St. 57
67 South Dak. St. 80
69 Augustana (S.D.) 79
63 ■ Northern Colo. 47
65 ■ Nebraska-Omaha 73
78 North Dak. St. 95
50 North Dak. 71

MANSFIELD 6-18
57 † Cabrini 37
54 Phila. Textile 75
43 St. Michael's 90
57 † Keene St. 73
65 Pitt-Bradford 67
70 ■ Seton Hill 69
54 ■ Calif. (Pa.) 65
60 Mercyhurst 81
51 ■ Pitt.-Johnstown 67
48 Shippensburg 63
43 Lock Haven 71
46 ■ Kutztown 70
62 ■ Millersville 68
62 East Stroudsburg 75
57 ■ Lycoming 52
38 West Chester 57
50 ■ Bloomsburg 61
68 ■ Cheyney 41
69 Kutztown 62
58 Millersville 82
49 ■ East Stroudsburg 67
67 ■ West Chester 70
58 Bloomsburg 72
72 Cheyney 58

MARIETTA 11-15
63 ■ Frostburg St. 50
60 ■ Point Park 52
78 ■ Allegheny 54
70 Greenville 83
66 ■ Mount Union 56
43 John Carroll 75
51 Heidelberg 53
49 Baldwin-Wallace 66
73 ■ Walsh 42
49 ■ Muskingum 56
40 Mt. St. Joseph's 82
61 Hiram 48
66 Otterbein 45
55 ■ Ohio Northern 45
44 Capital 61
41 ■ Heidelberg 51
46 Mount Union 58
51 ■ John Carroll 75
64 ■ Otterbein 50
81 ■ Baldwin-Wallace 92
57 Muskingum 67
70 ■ Hiram 47
42 ■ Capital 43
58 Ohio Northern 68

67 ■ Hiram 65
46 Capital 63

MARIST 19-10
40 † New Hampshire 76
80 † Bucknell 75
51 Army 43
60 † Idaho St. 61
59 † Southern Utah 79
78 ■ Buffalo 68
58 Rider 69
69 Mt. St. Mary's (Md.) 76
51 ■ LIU-Brooklyn 53
87 ■ St. Francis (N.Y.) 67
72 Monmouth (N.J.) 66
71 ■ Robert Morris 68
77 ■ Columbia-Barnard 60
70 ■ St. Francis (Pa.) 79
60 ■ Wagner 61
62 FDU-Teaneck 60
76 ■ Mt. St. Mary's (Md.) 73
78 ■ Rider 75
79 St. Francis (N.Y.) 62
56 LIU-Brooklyn 61
62 Wagner 59
63 ■ Monmouth (N.J.) 51
77 ■ Fordham 67
72 Robert Morris 69
82 St. Francis (Pa.) 73
72 ■ FDU-Teaneck 71
61 ■ Wagner 57
81 FDU-Teaneck 67
61 † Mt. St. Mary's (Md.) 82

MARQUETTE 22-9
66 ■ Notre Dame 62
92 † James Madison 79
72 Arizona St. 119
68 Illinois St. 94
103 † Bowling Green 105
64 † Eastern Wash. 58
74 Syracuse 86
90 Canisius 68
100 Buffalo 65
89 Minnesota 87
97 ■ Memphis St. 84
73 ■ Wis.-Milwaukee 60
82 DePaul 76
75 ■ Ball St. 51
109 ■ Cincinnati 83
69 ■ Wis.-Green Bay 72
86 Ala.-Birmingham 72
79 ■ St. Louis 51
64 Missouri 77
81 ■ Ala.-Birmingham 70
100 Memphis St. 76
77 St. Louis 58
93 ■ Northeastern Ill. 73
85 Cincinnati 76
76 Wis.-Milwaukee 70
67 ■ DePaul 65
90 Memphis St. 78
53 † DePaul 70
77 † Northwestern (La.) 74
65 † Arkansas St. 80
87 † Florida Int'l 93

MARS HILL 11-15
80 † Claflin 99
58 † Charleston (W.Va.) 56
64 Lees-McRae 86
55 Kennesaw 65
80 Piedmont 89
96 Milligan 65
56 ■ Wingate 60
86 ■ Lenoir-Rhyne 58
66 Elon 76
82 Gardner-Webb 80
69 ■ Wofford 59
45 ■ Carson-Newman 77
73 ■ Catawba 107
56 Presbyterian 72
61 Wingate 82
87 ■ Queens (N.C.) 80

83 Lenoir-Rhyne 77
80 ■ Lees-McRae 92
90 ■ Elon 84
76 ■ Gardner-Webb 69
73 ■ Presbyterian 69
43 Carson-Newman 73
68 Catawba 79
74 ■ S.C.-Spartanburg 80
70 † Presbyterian 68
60 † Wingate 69

MARSHALL 15-13
44 Kentucky 79
76 ■ Winthrop 60
92 ■ N.C.-Asheville 37
57 Wright St. 71
65 ■ Youngstown St. 62
75 ■ Ohio 55
60 ■ St. Francis (Pa.) 42
68 † Campbell 58
78 Virginia Tech 84
42 † North Caro. 67
71 † North Caro. A&T 59
65 Furman 68
70 ■ Furman 93
78 ■ East Tenn. St. 72
71 ■ Appalachian St. 61
79 Western Caro. 63
65 ■ Ga. Southern 86
64 ■ Tenn.-Chatt. 71
84 Eastern Ky. 80
47 Appalachian St. 80
86 East Tenn. St. 81
92 † West Va. 81
84 ■ Western Caro. 65
61 Ga. Southern 74
60 Tenn.-Chatt. 77
63 ■ Morehead St. 65
74 East Tenn. St. 55
58 † Furman 74

MARY BALDWIN 1-17
27 Hollins 64
40 ■ Hollins 80
28 ■ Meredith 103
41 ■ Notre Dame (Md.) 73
53 Averett 87
43 Wash. & Lee 77
42 ■ Bennett 72
52 Sweet Briar 67
49 ■ R.-M. Woman's 82
37 East. Mennonite 97
53 ■ Wash. & Lee 70
53 ■ East. Mennonite 84
60 Gallaudet 90
53 ■ Averett 83
45 ■ R.-M. Woman's 76
64 ■ Sweet Briar 53
35 Notre Dame (Md.) 79
48 † Bryn Mawr 88

MARY WASHINGTON 19-7
76 † Methodist 70
71 Ferrum 57
62 Western Md. 66
97 ■ Notre Dame (Md.) 55
81 Salisbury St. 78
60 St. Mary's (Md.) 36
61 Chris. Newport 70
49 ■ Ferrum 52
72 ■ Marymount (Va.) 86
71 ■ Gallaudet 69
70 ■ Goucher 36
63 ■ N.C. Wesleyan 53
50 ■ Frostburg St. 60
66 York (Pa.) 84
72 Catholic 53
78 ■ St. Mary's (Md.) 42
88 Marymount (Va.) 85
73 Gallaudet 52
64 ■ Bridgewater (Va.) 54
67 Goucher 63
71 ■ Shenandoah 49
78 ■ Catholic 57

83	■ York (Pa.)	68
77	■ St. Mary's (Md.)	32
93	■ York (Pa.)	70
79	Marymount (Va.)	103

	MARYLAND	**22-8**
121	Drexel	52
93	■ American	54
50	■ Iowa	53
59	Rutgers	52
83	■ Old Dominion	54
75	Loyola (Md.)	44
101	■ Howard	46
77	■ Tennessee	72
73	† Purdue	69
64	Clemson	60
61	Florida St.	68
77	Georgia Tech	66
82	Duke	51
70	■ Virginia	66
80	North Caro.	85
74	■ Florida St.	61
92	■ North Caro. St.	52
65	Wake Forest	67
90	■ Duke	71
75	■ Georgia Tech	70
67	■ Miami (Fla.)	57
72	North Caro. St.	74
81	■ Clemson	73
73	■ North Caro.	52
73	Virginia	87
80	■ Wake Forest	65
91	† Florida St.	68
75	† North Caro.	61
103	† Virginia	106
82	■ Southwest Mo. St.	86

	MD.-BALT. COUNTY	**11-16**
78	■ Richmond	73
66	† Loyola (Md.)	72
55	† Coppin St.	75
71	■ American	74
58	James Madison	88
72	■ George Mason	74
50	Furman	69
50	† Holy Cross	75
80	N.C.-Asheville	57
57	Winthrop	62
91	■ Charleston So.	89
62	■ Coastal Caro.	61
63	Delaware	81
65	Charleston So.	56
42	Campbell	52
70	■ Campbell	55
78	■ Winthrop	46
60	Towson St.	70
68	Coastal Caro.	70
57	■ Radford	61
64	Liberty	56
58	■ Mt. St. Mary's (Md.)	82
65	■ Liberty	53
70	■ N.C.-Asheville	55
78	Radford	71
58	■ Towson St.	59
55	† Towson St.	70

	MD.-EAST. SHORE	**7-19**
56	American	78
79	■ Bowie St.	62
65	■ Cheyney	46
91	■ Central Conn. St.	73
61	Central Conn. St.	87
51	Delaware St.	60
45	Florida A&M	84
53	Bethune-Cookman	51
44	■ Howard	64
50	Morgan St.	60
56	■ Coppin St.	70
57	William & Mary	78
61	■ South Caro. St.	63
57	■ North Caro. A&T	50
59	Howard	57
63	■ Morgan St.	66
53	Hofstra	70
43	South Caro. St.	70
45	North Caro. A&T	63
58	† Delaware St.	64
50	Buffalo	88
59	■ Florida A&M	67
51	■ Bethune-Cookman	49
44	Maine	79
42	Coppin St.	64
61	† Bethune-Cookman	62

	MARYMOUNT (VA.)	**23-5**
93	■ Bridgewater (Va.)	44
88	■ Elizabethtown	82
85	■ Maryville (Tenn.)	74
74	Ferrum	70
70	† Maryville (Tenn.)	83
90	Bridgewater (Va.)	50
77	N.C. Wesleyan	64
74	■ Chris. Newport	87
73	† Chris. Newport	94
99	† N.C. Wesleyan	75
103	Catholic	84
102	Gallaudet	75
86	Mary Washington	72
91	■ York (Pa.)	60
96	■ Goucher	58
113	■ Gallaudet	76
99	York (Pa.)	87
85	■ Mary Washington	88
94	■ Catholic	67
95	St. Mary's (Md.)	40
90	■ Kean	81
97	■ Frostburg St.	67
110	Goucher	73
105	■ St. Mary's (Md.)	36
106	■ Catholic	61
103	■ Mary Washington	79
115	■ Chris. Newport	96
75	St. Benedict	108

	MARYVILLE (MO.)	**10-17**
56	■ Washington (Mo.)	94
60	■ Ill. Wesleyan	75
77	Knox	81
57	Monmouth (Ill.)	64
55	Rhodes	67
50	† Millsaps	90
64	■ Dubuque	77
55	Rockford	54
54	Blackburn	63
53	Illinois Col.	76
46	■ Ripon	73
55	Fontbonne	54
60	■ Principia	46
55	■ Webster	69
68	■ DePauw	69
71	■ MacMurray	53
34	■ Blackburn	57
62	Westminster	48
48	■ Eureka	67
68	Principia	73
63	■ Westminster	49
64	Webster	73
64	MacMurray	59
84	■ Fontbonne	82
58	† Westminster	56
62	† Fontbonne	55
55	† Blackburn	58

	MARYVILLE (TENN.)	**23-3**
81	† Greensboro	44
81	† Chris. Newport	75
74	Marymount (Va.)	85
79	Fisk	30
75	Emory & Henry	58
94	† Rowan	90
83	† Marymount (Va.)	70
78	■ Tusculum	63
68	Spelman	63
73	Centre	56
85	■ Centre	75
104	Milligan	65
76	■ Greensboro	79
94	Knoxville	72
90	■ Sewanee	35
87	Berea	81
95	■ Emory & Henry	47
80	Bennett	34
79	Roanoke	69
97	■ Ferrum	52
99	■ Berea	89
89	Sewanee	55
89	■ Knoxville	65
95	■ Fisk	16
85	■ Roanoke	67
69	† Concordia-M'head	87

	MARYWOOD	**9-14**
91	Gwynedd Mercy	52
56	Cabrini	60
59	Neumann	52
50	Alvernia	77
46	■ Wilkes	71
59	■ William Smith	69
51	Scranton	84
39	Lycoming	41
77	■ St. Elizabeth	47
60	■ Wesley	62
61	■ Misericordia	58
48	■ Moravian	77
63	■ Alvernia	52
68	Bapt. Bible (Pa.)	72
55	■ Phila. Pharmacy	66
57	■ Immaculata	63
73	Beaver	58
69	Misericordia	65
55	King's (Pa.)	64
63	■ Beaver	57
49	Binghamton	66
73	■ Eastern (Pa.)	68
55	† Immaculata	58

	MASS.-LOWELL	**24-6**
79	■ Stonehill	61
79	■ Merrimack	67
79	Mercy	46
57	■ Bentley	62
66	■ Assumption	73
69	St. Michael's	76
84	■ St. Anselm	69
91	■ American Int'l	71
78	■ Clarion	61
64	Bryant	66
81	Le Moyne	66
78	Quinnipiac	76
84	■ New Haven	54
78	■ Southern Conn. St.	54
75	Franklin Pierce	73
70	Sacred Heart	65
77	■ New Hamp. Col.	73
82	Southern Conn. St.	61
81	■ Keene St.	59
66	New Haven	65
80	■ Franklin Pierce	68
77	† Sacred Heart	75
76	Keene St.	85
77	† Le Moyne	57
85	New Hamp. Col.	64
88	■ Southern Conn. St.	62
72	■ Sacred Heart	62
56	■ Franklin Pierce	55
84	† Stonehill	78
60	Bentley	68

	MASSACHUSETTS	**11-15**
63	Northeastern	64
70	† Howard	50
60	Seton Hall	66
49	New Hampshire	71
48	■ Ohio St.	81
52	Wagner	58
54	† Yale	56
59	Central Conn. St.	45
60	■ Siena	43
66	Temple	63
88	Hofstra	53
40	■ Temple	46
74	■ St. Bonaventure	54
51	Geo. Washington	65
65	■ St. Joseph's (Pa.)	56
76	■ West Va.	68
63	St. Bonaventure	90
51	West Va.	67
47	■ Rutgers	65
60	■ Rhode Island	76
59	■ Geo. Washington	57
57	St. Joseph's (Pa.)	68
63	Rutgers	71
63	■ Boston U.	56
70	Rhode Island	69
56	† West Va.	68

	MIT	**8-15**
52	† Bowdoin	53
51	Regis (Mass.)	71
54	■ Gordon	66
61	Elms	81
66	Bates	83
73	■ Simmons	45
82	■ Wentworth Inst.	51
53	Brandeis	80
79	Colby-Sawyer	74
63	Mount Holyoke	67
62	■ Nichols	57
50	Anna Maria	62
53	Wellesley	83
71	Coast Guard	49
57	■ Rivier	76
56	■ Wheaton (Mass.)	82
58	■ Western New Eng.	76
52	Worcester Tech	81
76	Suffolk	60
52	■ Babson	72
53	Pine Manor	51
54	■ Smith	48
63	Babson	85

	MASS.-BOSTON	**8-17**
64	Regis (Mass.)	62
42	† Bowdoin	73
67	■ Framingham St.	59
62	Salem St.	66
49	Westfield St.	85
66	North Adams St.	64
69	Suffolk	66
79	Eastern Nazarene	69
71	■ Pine Manor	67
54	Emmanuel	93
50	■ Southern Me.	100
62	■ Bri'water (Mass.)	71
58	Rhode Island Col.	81
52	Mass.-Dartmouth	67
47	Southern Me.	77
65	■ Simmons	41
52	■ Plymouth St.	64
51	■ Eastern Conn. St.	77
58	■ Curry	52
50	■ Mass.-Dartmouth	73
75	■ Rhode Island Col.	84
57	Eastern Conn. St.	73
74	Colby	81
75	Plymouth St.	86
61	Eastern Conn. St.	83

	MCNEESE ST.	**14-13**
79	Louisiana Col.	59
52	† Louisiana Tech	88
78	† Alcorn St.	54
75	Southeastern La.	44
65	† Fresno St.	80
90	Nevada	80
72	■ Texas-San Antonio	61
55	■ Southwest Tex. St.	81
58	Northeast La.	74
54	Northwestern (La.)	76
59	■ Texas-Arlington	51
84	■ North Texas	81
65	Nicholls St.	57
77	Sam Houston St.	58
60	Stephen F. Austin	86
60	■ Northwestern (La.)	73
59	Texas-San Antonio	63
80	North Texas	89

69 Texas-Arlington 80
80 ■ Southwestern La. .. 56
84 ■ Nicholls St. 77
75 ■ Northeast La. 70
68 ■ Stephen F. Austin .. 81
70 ■ Sam Houston St. ... 50
82 ■ Tulane 80
72 Southwest Tex. St. . 91
72 Northeast La. 84

MEMPHIS ST. 12-16
70 ■ Middle Tenn. St. ... 83
92 † Stetson 63
79 Central Fla. 41
95 ■ Tenn.-Martin 69
64 ■ Oklahoma St. 75
85 ■ Jackson St. 51
106 Murray St. 70
59 ■ Tulane 60
57 Vanderbilt 91
84 Marquette 97
73 DePaul 82
67 ■ Ala.-Birmingham ... 65
67 ■ Mississippi 69
86 ■ Oral Roberts 55
68 ■ South Caro. 73
82 St. Louis 47
72 ■ Cincinnati 75
60 Arkansas 82
52 ■ DePaul 62
76 ■ Marquette 100
72 Ala.-Birmingham ... 91
46 Tennessee 90
101 Tenn.-Martin 89
85 ■ St. Louis 55
65 Cincinnati 66
62 ■ Southeastern La. ... 51
79 ■ Ala.-Birmingham ... 69
78 ■ Marquette 90

MERCER 11-18
71 † Boston U. 53
59 Georgia Tech 82
68 ■ Coastal Caro. 46
60 † Oklahoma 69
64 † Southern-B.R. 72
73 ■ Tennessee St. 84
57 † N.C.-Charlotte 75
77 † Alabama St. 60
53 ■ Georgia St. 56
67 ■ Charleston 65
61 Southeastern La. ... 69
61 Central Fla. 60
51 Ga. Southern 93
69 ■ Alabama 91
73 ■ Fla. Atlantic 56
64 ■ Florida Int'l 86
75 ■ Stetson 68
57 ■ Georgia 65
52 Georgia St. 78
51 Charleston 69
41 ■ Southeastern La. ... 59
68 ■ Central Fla. 66
73 ■ South Fla. 72
66 Tennessee St. 70
53 Florida Int'l 73
80 Stetson 85
67 † Southeastern La. ... 65
64 † Georgia St. 60
52 Florida Int'l 77

MERCY 12-15
59 Kutztown 81
66 † LIU-Southampton .. 65
46 ■ Mass.-Lowell 79
71 † Queens (N.Y.) 66
53 Le Moyne 62
74 Bridgeport 62
76 Concordia (N.Y.) ... 67
52 LIU-C.W. Post 51
66 ■ Dowling 65
58 ■ Adelphi 74
56 ■ LIU-C.W. Post 60
58 ■ Phila. Textile 90
63 ■ Queens (N.Y.) 56

74 LIU-Southampton .. 61
59 ■ St. Rose 61
60 Pace 75
81 Dowling 71
56 Molloy 73
57 ■ Concordia (N.Y.) ... 43
47 Queens (N.Y.) 63
67 ■ Molloy 62
47 Phila. Textile 75
63 ■ LIU-Southampton .. 45
56 St. Rose 63
58 Adelphi 73
62 ■ Pace 82
54 Pace 82

MERCYHURST 15-10
86 ■ Dowling 36
73 Calif. (Pa.) 63
59 ■ Ashland 65
74 Slippery Rock 86
74 Bloomsburg 75
85 Clarion 112
54 Edinboro 79
81 ■ Mansfield 60
77 ■ West Va. Wesleyan . 46
88 ■ Norfolk St. 60
85 ■ Edinboro 61
53 ■ Lock Haven 68
82 East Stroudsburg .. 57
78 ■ Clarion 86
60 Indiana (Pa.) 63
60 Gannon 67
81 ■ Seton Hill 66
64 Oakland 62
59 Pitt-Bradford 50
79 Lock Haven 74
81 ■ Gannon 58
66 Pitt.-Johnstown 70
70 Westminster (Pa.) .. 45
87 ■ Wis.-Parkside 85
71 ■ Pitt.-Johnstown 67

MEREDITH 19-1
77 † Shenandoah 39
90 Randolph-Macon ... 71
88 ■ R.-M. Woman's 28
94 ■ Mt. Olive 92
87 ■ Averett 68
72 ■ N.C. Wesleyan 53
84 Averett 52
85 ■ Methodist 60
103 Mary Baldwin 28
71 St. Andrews 41
71 ■ Greensboro 50
83 Mt. Olive 59
79 ■ St. Andrews 48
61 Methodist 64
73 N.C. Wesleyan 63
82 ■ Bennett 35
67 Greensboro 57
85 ■ Guilford 65
68 Bennett 32
108 † R.-M. Woman's 53

MERRIMACK 9-17
78 † Sacred Heart 88
67 Mass.-Lowell 79
53 ■ Bentley 69
67 St. Anselm 82
76 Keene St. 89
55 ■ New Hamp. Col. ... 41
59 Fla. Southern 81
88 Rollins 82
80 ■ Assumption 68
66 ■ Franklin Pierce 64
81 American Int'l 88
57 Stonehill 59
60 ■ Quinnipiac 63
67 ■ St. Michael's 69
79 ■ Springfield 48
56 Bentley 74
64 Bryant 68
78 ■ St. Anselm 101
68 ■ American Int'l 88
56 ■ Stonehill 79

71 Quinnipiac 62
78 St. Michael's 77
79 Springfield 67
71 ■ Bryant 67
60 Assumption 71
62 Bentley 72

MESA ST. 17-11
79 Cal St. Los Angeles 60
81 † UC Riverside 74
62 ■ Metropolitan St. 78
87 ■ Denver 81
50 † South Dak. St. 73
63 † Northern Colo. 83
57 Denver 92
42 Metropolitan St. 76
70 ■ Fort Lewis 52
58 ■ Western N. Mex. ... 53
54 ■ Neb.-Kearney 84
67 † Western N. Mex. ... 87
71 † Wayland Bapt. 95
79 Fort Lewis 71
81 ■ Adams St. 65
74 ■ N.M. Highlands 69
71 Chadron St. 84
69 Fort Hays St. 59
74 Western St. 62
98 ■ Colorado Mines 64
77 ■ Chadron St. 65
58 ■ Fort Hays St. 53
92 ■ Western St. 78
66 Colorado Mines 59
44 N.M. Highlands 59
78 Adams St. 73
83 † Colorado Mines 52
55 † N.M. Highlands 77

MESSIAH 9-15
80 ■ Widener 49
65 ■ Houghton 73
67 ■ Notre Dame (Md.) .. 53
54 York (Pa.) 56
54 ■ Elizabethtown 86
63 Lycoming 53
70 ■ Gallaudet 52
63 † North Central 76
60 Juniata 71
57 † York (Pa.) 64
77 Gettysburg 72
56 Wilkes 65
60 ■ Susquehanna 66
63 ■ Western Md. 50
69 ■ Juniata 89
55 ■ Albright 65
62 Elizabethtown 75
78 ■ Gettysburg 69
48 ■ Frank. & Marsh. ... 64
57 Susquehanna 73
79 ■ Lycoming 78
67 Lebanon Valley 68
72 ■ Wilkes 69
58 ■ Dickinson 62

METHODIST 15-11
70 † Mary Washington .. 76
71 † Emory & Henry 62
81 ■ St. Andrews 73
88 Mt. Olive 97
70 ■ Guilford 71
80 ■ Randolph-Macon ... 63
60 St. Andrews 61
71 Bennett 57
75 ■ Mt. Olive 88
60 Meredith 85
79 ■ Chris. Newport 72
81 ■ Va. Wesleyan 87
60 ■ N.C. Wesleyan 57
79 Greensboro 64
76 ■ Ferrum 60
75 ■ Averett 61
64 ■ Meredith 61
75 Chris. Newport 78
68 ■ Fayetteville St. 76
93 ■ Greensboro 71
79 ■ Bennett 33

73 N.C. Wesleyan 77
83 Ferrum 60
73 Averett 63
70 † N.C. Wesleyan 64
83 Chris. Newport 85

METROPOLITAN ST. 21-6
78 † Lewis-Clark St. 70
78 Cal St. Chico 68
59 † Western Wash. 42
78 Mesa St. 62
89 † Hastings 83
66 † Wayne St. (Neb.) ... 70
71 Neb.-Kearney 69
74 ■ Northern Colo. 65
76 ■ Cal St. San B'dino .. 65
88 ■ Christ-Irvine 52
76 ■ Mesa St. 42
52 Utah 56
58 Air Force 50
59 ■ Denver 68
101 Fort Lewis 50
83 ■ Southern Colo. 37
65 Colorado-CS 68
67 ■ Regis (Colo.) 55
98 ■ Neb.-Kearney 68
69 Colo. Christian 38
71 ■ Air Force 43
66 Denver 68
72 Southern Colo. 54
91 ■ Fort Lewis 45
68 ■ Colorado-CS 65
63 Regis (Colo.) 73
83 ■ Colo. Christian 46

MIAMI (FLA.) 24-7
94 ■ Fla. Atlantic 37
80 Florida Int'l 58
98 ■ Texas Southern 41
61 ■ Florida St. 64
74 ■ Bucknell 54
80 ■ Appalachian St. 63
74 ■ Texas Tech 75
59 Seton Hall 73
64 Providence 52
62 ■ Georgetown 55
69 Connecticut 66
65 Syracuse 53
64 ■ Villanova 53
59 ■ St. John's (N.Y.) 65
55 Pittsburgh 50
80 Boston College 67
60 ■ Syracuse 40
85 ■ Providence 65
88 Georgetown 90
57 Maryland 67
69 ■ Connecticut 51
84 ■ Boston College 55
57 Villanova 52
84 St. John's (N.Y.) 68
72 ■ Seton Hall 60
77 ■ Pittsburgh 65
84 † St. John's (N.Y.) 61
67 † Villanova 49
77 Providence 56
61 ■ St. Peter's 44
63 Western Ky. 78

MIAMI (OHIO) 19-9
81 † Valparaiso 57
56 St. Bonaventure 63
65 Wright St. 53
71 Xavier (Ohio) 60
48 Indiana 59
83 ■ Dayton 50
58 ■ Cincinnati 43
56 Wis.-Milwaukee ... 66
68 ■ Ball St. 54
70 Akron 38
58 Western Mich. 61
60 ■ Ohio 53
63 Central Mich. 59
75 ■ Bowling Green 77
78 Eastern Mich. 56
66 ■ Toledo 46

65 Kent 63
77 ■ Akron 58
67 ■ Western Mich. 72
76 Ohio 66
70 ■ Central Mich. 69
74 Bowling Green 77
76 ■ Eastern Mich. 61
65 Toledo 84
92 ■ Kent 87
75 Ball St. 56
67 ■ Western Mich. 61
69 † Kent 79

MICHIGAN 2-25

67 ■ Toledo 90
68 Indiana St. 79
54 Notre Dame 62
62 Pittsburgh 64
50 ■ Butler 81
71 † Appalachian St. 79
83 † Bucknell 77
63 † Old Dominion 71
73 ■ Detroit Mercy 77
61 ■ Indiana 65
64 ■ Purdue 99
62 ■ Michigan St. 65
67 Wisconsin 73
73 Ohio St. 90
61 Penn St. 81
54 ■ Iowa 84
62 ■ Minnesota 71
62 Illinois 82
63 Michigan St. 67
75 ■ Wisconsin 79
59 ■ Ohio St. 79
69 Minnesota 85
34 Iowa 71
70 ■ Illinois 92
58 ■ Northwestern 98
67 Indiana 54
56 Purdue 59

MICHIGAN ST. 10-17

66 ■ Central Mich. 59
76 ■ Iowa St. 53
65 ■ Oregon St. 86
64 † Montana St. 76
61 † Wis.-Milwaukee 48
63 ■ Illinois St. 43
57 † UCLA 82
50 Southern Cal 66
46 Arizona 89
60 ■ Purdue 56
65 Michigan 62
67 Wisconsin 75
57 Ohio St. 78
61 ■ Minnesota 70
55 ■ Iowa 75
58 Northwestern 78
65 Illinois 78
67 ■ Michigan 63
81 ■ Wisconsin 67
51 ■ Ohio St. 88
54 ■ Penn St. 87
46 Iowa 76
71 Minnesota 54
103 ■ Northwestern 109
85 ■ Illinois 69
45 Purdue 60
54 Indiana 74

MICHIGAN TECH 30-3

76 Minn.-Duluth 60
86 ■ North Dak. 71
77 ■ Bemidji St. 56
85 ■ Minn.-Duluth 58
72 ■ Wis.-Parkside 70
81 ■ Grand Valley St. 67
89 ■ Ferris St. 67
81 Northwood 35
77 Lake Superior St. 65
79 † Bryant 57
66 Florida Tech 68
73 ■ Saginaw Valley 70
90 ■ Oakland 66

83 Hillsdale 72
75 Wayne St. (Mich.) 40
71 Northern Mich. 70
71 Grand Valley St. 64
68 Ferris St. 57
81 ■ Northwood 52
64 ■ Lake Superior St. 56
73 ■ Northern Mich. 80
86 Saginaw Valley 70
68 Oakland 62
75 ■ Hillsdale 60
79 ■ Wayne St. (Mich.) 50
71 Wis.-Parkside 48
80 ■ Oakland 71
70 ■ Saginaw Valley 63
92 † Bellarmine 73
77 † Saginaw Valley 58
78 Washburn 77
67 † Delta St. 71
74 Bentley 60

MIDDLE TENN. ST. 21-7

83 Memphis St. 70
65 Georgia 80
79 Tenn.-Chatt. 73
88 ■ Troy St. 65
70 ■ Louisville 71
84 ■ Tenn.-Chatt. 72
66 † Yale 50
73 Wagner 53
79 ■ Morehead St. 49
76 ■ Eastern Ky. 62
72 ■ Tennessee St. 78
77 ■ Western Ky. 97
76 Tenn.-Martin 54
72 Tennessee Tech 91
91 ■ Austin Peay 70
65 Southeast Mo. St. 58
96 Murray St. 63
81 ■ Tenn.-Martin 73
105 Tennessee St. 103
77 ■ Tennessee Tech 71
73 Morehead St. 85
80 Eastern Ky. 66
100 Austin Peay 71
75 ■ Southeast Mo. St. 65
79 ■ Murray St. 56
89 ■ Southern Ind. 77
87 † Eastern Ky. 74
73 Tennessee Tech 80

MIDDLEBURY 19-3

62 ■ Williams 48
65 St. Michael's 86
92 ■ Wesleyan 60
92 ■ Norwich 65
81 North Adams St. 51
79 ■ Nazareth (N.Y.) 59
67 Williams 57
83 Hamilton 79
65 ■ Colby 53
75 Bowdoin 71
80 ■ Colby-Sawyer 35
79 ■ Western Conn. St. 75
75 ■ Union (N.Y.) 31
57 Clark (Mass.) 72
89 Norwich 76
92 Thomas 79
100 Bates 70
72 ■ Skidmore 49
89 ■ Tufts 74
80 ■ Emmanuel 67
76 ■ Eastern Conn. St. 63
71 ■ Wellesley 80

MILLERSVILLE 17-9

73 ■ Holy Family 61
79 ■ St. Augustine's 92
68 Calif. (Pa.) 79
91 ■ Lock Haven 72
77 Shippensburg 68
82 ■ Houghton 55
72 Rollins 74
57 Fla. Southern 73
75 Eckerd 60

99 Longwood 66
47 Bloomsburg 54
68 Mansfield 62
86 ■ East Stroudsburg 59
70 ■ Kutztown 53
102 ■ Holy Family 60
74 Cheyney 54
65 ■ West Chester 63
71 Phila. Textile 79
83 ■ Bloomsburg 73
82 ■ Mansfield 58
76 Wilmington (Del.) 94
59 East Stroudsburg 74
73 Kutztown 62
94 ■ Cheyney 28
77 West Chester 65
65 † Clarion 94

MILLIKIN 19-6

79 ■ Concordia (Ill.) 47
124 † Ind.-South Bend 71
54 St. Mary's (Ind.) 69
68 ■ Ill. Benedictine 41
59 Wheaton (Ill.) 52
59 North Central 46
64 Claremont-M-S 51
59 Occidental 68
52 Redlands 59
75 Elmhurst 81
58 Carthage 56
68 North Park 58
59 Augustana (Ill.) 71
88 ■ McKendree 64
77 ■ North Central 55
72 Ill. Wesleyan 49
63 ■ Elmhurst 44
84 ■ Aurora 62
95 ■ Carthage 63
76 ■ Illinois Col. 71
64 ■ Wheaton (Ill.) 52
63 ■ Augustana (Ill.) 76
82 ■ Rockford 38
78 ■ North Park 48
92 ■ Ill. Wesleyan 85

MILLSAPS 19-6

77 ■ Southwestern (Tex.) 59
65 ■ Judson 61
56 Washington (Mo.) 70
66 † Illinois Col. 84
94 ■ La. St.-Shreveport 77
62 † Fontbonne 49
90 † Maryville (Mo.) 50
65 Judson 58
44 ■ Spring Hill 58
70 Emory 81
67 ■ Mississippi-Women 54
86 ■ Oglethorpe 50
66 ■ Sewanee 45
69 ■ Trinity (Tex.) 58
71 ■ Hendrix 44
52 Centre 68
73 Fisk 17
61 Trinity (Tex.) 53
74 Hendrix 62
55 Rhodes 46
65 ■ Rhodes 48
59 ■ Centre 72
96 ■ Fisk 18
83 Oglethorpe 51
68 Sewanee 53

MINNESOTA 14-12

82 ■ Kansas 76
64 ■ Western Ky. 92
62 ■ Georgia Tech 82
82 Santa Clara 80
95 † Boise St. 91
79 Wis.-Green Bay 66
58 Kansas St. 44
87 ■ Marquette 89
47 ■ Iowa 75
72 Wisconsin 75
66 ■ Illinois 56

67 ■ Purdue 51
80 ■ Indiana 70
70 Michigan St. 61
71 Michigan 62
62 ■ Penn St. 77
68 Northwestern 76
72 ■ Northwestern 70
60 Indiana 59
64 Purdue 72
85 ■ Michigan 69
54 ■ Michigan St. 71
76 Ohio St. 95
78 Penn St. 99
91 ■ Wisconsin 56
59 Iowa 83

MINN.-DULUTH 22-8

60 ■ Michigan Tech 76
93 ■ St. Scholastica 43
56 ■ North Dak. St. 72
58 Michigan Tech 85
86 Wis.-Superior 51
68 ■ Mankato St. 60
77 ■ Northern Mich. 94
71 St. Cloud St. 39
73 ■ South Dak. St. 56
50 North Dak. St. 76
44 North Dak. 55
65 † St. Joseph's (Ind.) 53
62 Wis.-Parkside 58
79 ■ Southwest St. 41
67 ■ Northern St. 46
63 Bemidji St. 62
74 Winona St. 46
60 Southwest St. 41
60 Northern St. 67
69 ■ Minn.-Morris 50
68 ■ Moorhead St. 56
71 ■ Bemidji St. 43
82 ■ Winona St. 43
57 Moorhead St. 56
65 Minn.-Morris 61
69 St. Scholastica 42
71 ■ Winona St. 42
70 ■ Moorhead St. 66
62 † Carson-Newman 49
61 † Southern Nazarene 72

MISERICORDIA 11-11

70 † Utica 71
67 † Lincoln (Pa.) 46
65 ■ Scranton 107
52 Wilkes 75
49 York (Pa.) 73
68 † Western Md. 57
87 Cedar Crest 51
63 ■ Bapt. Bible (Pa.) 59
76 Upsala 77
63 St. Elizabeth 51
60 ■ Neumann 54
74 ■ Caldwell 73
74 ■ Alvernia 71
58 Marywood 61
67 King's (Pa.) 81
53 Immaculata 62
80 ■ Centenary (N.J.) 77
63 Beaver 49
65 ■ Marywood 69
55 Alvernia 91
67 ■ Widener 51
59 Lycoming 60

MISSISSIPPI 19-10

78 † Florida Int'l 68
64 Maine 50
61 Arkansas St. 62
54 ■ Alcorn St. 50
64 ■ Louisiana Tech 68
47 ■ Auburn 57
72 † Arizona St. 71
62 St. John's (N.Y.) 56
72 Arkansas 73
70 ■ Tennessee Tech 68
65 ■ Florida 69
66 Ala.-Birmingham 49

53 Tennessee 64
69 Memphis St. 67
81 ■ South Caro. 57
69 ■ Northeast La. 44
60 Georgia 75
87 ■ Oral Roberts 53
95 ■ Louisiana St. 62
75 ■ Lamar 66
73 Southern-B.R. 63
74 Alabama 93
81 Southeastern La. 55
77 ■ Kentucky 65
83 ■ Mississippi St. 77
62 Vanderbilt 77
59 † South Caro. 57
69 † Auburn 55
54 † Vanderbilt 79

MISSISSIPPI COL. 11-15
63 Belhaven 68
64 Mississippi-Women 42
75 † Texas A&I 63
60 Abilene Christian 69
56 ■ Paul Quinn 64
42 ■ Belhaven 52
75 Louisiana Col. 79
71 Blue Mountain 64
89 ■ Alabama A&M 73
65 ■ Livingston 64
62 Jacksonville St. 78
60 ■ Mississippi-Women 52
59 ■ West Ga. 51
75 ■ Valdosta St. 72
59 Paul Quinn 67
60 Delta St. 88
47 North Ala. 55
72 Livingston 77
90 ■ LeMoyne-Owen 22
81 ■ North Ala. 73
61 ■ Delta St. 63
71 Valdosta St. 58
62 West Ga. 67
54 ■ Jacksonville St. 55
49 Montevallo 82
51 Mississippi St. 86

MISSISSIPPI ST. 14-13
74 ■ Florida 58
59 Colorado 95
72 † Idaho St. 63
69 ■ Belhaven 56
85 ■ Christian Bros. 54
91 Georgia St. 70
63 † New Orleans 76
72 † Wake Forest 79
106 † Mississippi Val. 69
97 † Monmouth (N.J.) 62
108 † Texas Christian 85
89 † Va. Commonwealth 74
53 ■ Kentucky 73
61 South Caro. 72
62 Tennessee 109
44 Vanderbilt 108
76 ■ Georgia 65
64 Auburn 72
106 ■ Livingston 83
89 ■ Alabama 102
72 ■ Arkansas St. 77
51 Arkansas 80
81 ■ Ala.-Birmingham 78
77 Mississippi 83
76 ■ Louisiana St. 71
86 ■ Mississippi Col. 51
73 † Kentucky 84

MISSISSIPPI-WOMEN 8-19
79 ■ LeMoyne-Owen 72
72 Christian Bros. 81
42 ■ Mississippi Col. 64
90 ■ Blue Mountain 72
85 ■ Christian Bros. 67
55 † Arkansas Tech 104
73 Belhaven 72
62 Livingston 77
73 LeMoyne-Owen 37
54 Millsaps 67
52 Mississippi Col. 60
75 ■ Troy St. 87
70 Blue Mountain 63
65 ■ North Ala. 85
58 Aub.-Montgomery 80
59 ■ Jacksonville St. 81
73 Ala.-Huntsville 70
43 Delta St. 95
70 North Ala. 76
53 Alabama A&M 90
53 Troy St. 112
60 ■ Aub.-Montgomery 89
48 Jacksonville St. 78
57 ■ Livingston 62
75 ■ Alabama A&M 73
43 ■ Delta St. 75
70 ■ Ala.-Huntsville 72

MISSISSIPPI VAL. 11-17
64 South Ala. 82
35 Southern Miss. 95
62 Arkansas St. 80
65 Ala.-Birmingham 83
69 † Mississippi St. 106
95 ■ Tougaloo 42
57 Alcorn St. 73
78 Southern-B.R. 97
72 ■ Delta St. 103
90 ■ Texas Southern 77
74 ■ Prairie View 52
50 ■ Alabama St. 67
61 ■ Jackson St. 75
59 ■ Arkansas St. 86
84 Grambling 83
64 ■ South Ala. 84
90 ■ Alcorn St. 97
77 ■ Southern-B.R. 84
68 Delta St. 92
87 Texas Southern 77
72 Prairie View 56
85 Tougaloo 46
58 Alabama St. 57
47 Jackson St. 63
80 ■ Grambling 81
64 † Grambling 56
74 † Texas Southern 63
72 Southern-B.R. 68

MISSOURI 19-8
68 ■ Eastern Ill. 45
67 ■ Tennessee St. 60
68 ■ Toledo 38
65 ■ Creighton 70
63 ■ Indiana St. 45
66 ■ Illinois St. 56
77 Wright St. 38
68 Dayton 57
80 Illinois 54
64 ■ Kansas 62
62 ■ Kansas St. 49
62 Mo.-Kansas City 49
53 ■ Colorado 67
75 ■ Oral Roberts 53
83 Iowa St. 52
66 Nebraska 86
49 ■ Oklahoma St. 58
69 ■ Oklahoma 63
77 ■ Marquette 64
67 Kansas St. 51
52 Kansas 62
52 Colorado 75
64 ■ Iowa St. 41
64 ■ Nebraska 65
68 Oklahoma 49
64 Oklahoma St. 63
56 † Kansas 63

MO. SOUTHERN ST. 27-4
91 † Okla. Christian 89
81 † John Brown 34
90 Evangel 51
78 ■ Central Ark. 63
82 ■ Central Okla. 76
89 Central Okla. 67
89 † Cameron 62
92 ■ Ozarks (Mo.) 55
66 Avila 56
106 ■ Oral Roberts 64
58 ■ Pittsburg St. 52
79 Emporia St. 68
82 ■ Lincoln (Mo.) 66
90 Northeast Mo. St. 60
66 ■ Missouri-Rolla 63
82 Mo.-St. Louis 56
65 Pittsburg St. 81
78 ■ Southwest Baptist 56
70 Lincoln (Mo.) 47
79 ■ Northwest Mo. St. 55
71 Missouri-Rolla 52
76 ■ Mo.-St. Louis 65
59 Southwest Baptist 57
82 Mo. Western St. 70
73 ■ Central Mo. St. 66
82 ■ Washburn 83
67 ■ Northwest Mo. St. 64
71 ■ Pittsburg St. 57
65 Washburn 78
82 † Pittsburg St. 67
62 Washburn 75

MO. WESTERN ST. 16-11
71 † Morningside 76
68 † Peru St. 49
70 † Missouri-Rolla 71
66 Nebraska-Omaha 64
62 ■ Midland Lutheran 51
61 ■ Nebraska-Omaha 63
76 Park 54
78 ■ Doane 67
55 Kansas St. 75
66 ■ Okla. Baptist 58
85 ■ Northeast Mo. St. 48
57 Missouri-Rolla 55
70 ■ Emporia St. 62
86 Lincoln (Mo.) 56
78 ■ Northwest Mo. St. 67
60 ■ Washburn 65
67 Northeast Mo. St. 46
43 Central Mo. St. 58
74 Emporia St. 69
63 ■ Pittsburg St. 78
74 Northwest Mo. St. 71
54 Washburn 71
56 ■ Central Mo. St. 62
70 ■ Mo. Southern St. 82
65 Southwest Baptist 60
69 ■ Mo.-St. Louis 61
49 Central Mo. St. 67

MO.-KANSAS CITY 17-10
57 ■ Northern Iowa 41
67 † Gonzaga 53
56 Idaho 55
52 Kansas 86
62 † Fla. Atlantic 50
63 † Georgia 72
56 † Central Mich. 68
63 ■ Oklahoma St. 66
51 † Creighton 64
64 † Oral Roberts 35
92 ■ Western Ill. 58
65 ■ Jackson St. 45
66 ■ Texas-Arlington 46
49 ■ Missouri 62
45 Texas 72
78 ■ Northeastern Ill. 44
70 ■ Emporia St. 34
75 Southeast Mo. St. 50
62 Cal St. Sacramento 70
60 ■ Texas A&M 61
45 Wis.-Milwaukee 57
68 Northeastern Ill. 65
64 St. Louis 31
80 ■ Chicago St. 48
63 ■ Wis.-Milwaukee 42
70 ■ Cal St. Sacramento 67
71 ■ Cal St. Northridge 46

MISSOURI-ROLLA 14-13
59 † Oklahoma City 67
60 Quincy 56
71 † Mo. Western St. 70
65 † SIU-Edwardsville 75
59 Kansas St. 70
75 ■ William Jewell 69
68 ■ Mo. Baptist 50
53 ■ Lindenwood 51
68 † Quinnipiac 56
52 Fla. Southern 63
77 ■ Southwest Baptist 60
55 ■ Mo. Western St. 57
83 ■ Mo.-St. Louis 72
73 Central Mo. St. 66
63 Mo. Southern St. 66
68 ■ Pittsburg St. 77
69 Southwest Baptist 75
73 ■ Lincoln (Mo.) 58
54 Mo.-St. Louis 56
53 ■ Washburn 68
52 ■ Mo. Southern St. 71
53 Pittsburg St. 75
69 Lincoln (Mo.) 44
72 Northwest Mo. St. 63
75 ■ Emporia St. 53
75 Northeast Mo. St. 59
53 Pittsburg St. 70

MO.-ST. LOUIS 9-17
73 ■ Mo. Baptist 53
76 ■ SIU-Edwardsville 75
68 Franklin 62
73 ■ Harris-Stowe 42
63 † Lake Superior St. 85
60 IU/PU-Ft. Wayne 56
58 Southeast Mo. St. 81
68 ■ Washington (Mo.) 70
73 ■ Lincoln (Mo.) 48
67 Northeast Mo. St. 49
72 Missouri-Rolla 83
66 Emporia St. 87
63 ■ Southwest Baptist 78
56 ■ Mo. Southern St. 82
75 Quincy 94
77 Lincoln (Mo.) 70
54 ■ Pittsburg St. 65
56 ■ Missouri-Rolla 54
57 ■ Central Mo. St. 69
55 Southwest Baptist 57
65 Mo. Southern St. 76
50 Pittsburg St. 91
54 ■ Washburn 81
60 SIU-Edwardsville 77
84 ■ Northwest Mo. St. 85
61 Mo. Western St. 69

MOLLOY 14-13
76 ■ Bridgeport 78
70 ■ St. Rose 71
49 Pace 70
62 ■ Dowling 53
46 St. Francis (N.Y.) 65
54 Fla. Memorial 69
58 Barry 52
67 LIU-Southampton 51
53 St. Rose 52
65 ■ Queens (N.Y.) 54
57 ■ Phila. Textile 72
69 ■ Southern Conn. St. 46
77 ■ Concordia (N.Y.) 51
56 Adelphi 81
75 ■ Sacred Heart 76
63 ■ LIU-Southampton 56
63 Concordia (N.Y.) 49
71 ■ LIU-C.W. Post 67
73 ■ Mercy 56
93 Dowling 76
66 Phila. Textile 74
62 Mercy 67
60 ■ Pace 77
73 LIU-C.W. Post 66

62 Queens (N.Y.) 52
58 ■ Adelphi 61
65 St. Rose 73

MONMOUTH (ILL.) 5-17
38 Teiko-Marycrest 84
72 ■ Iowa Wesleyan 63
64 ■ Maryville (Mo.) 57
67 ■ Dubuque 43
45 ■ Illinois Col. 82
67 Ill. Wesleyan 83
54 Eureka 90
54 ■ Coe 73
76 ■ Cornell College 51
55 ■ Lawrence 70
57 ■ St. Norbert 70
68 Knox 70
50 Beloit 58
47 Lake Forest 66
59 Iowa Wesleyan 60
59 Grinnell 69
77 Cornell College 40
71 ■ Knox 73
60 Coe 83
69 ■ Fontbonne 71
57 Illinois Col. 72
78 ■ Grinnell 81

MONMOUTH (N.J.) 11-17
70 ■ Fordham 75
63 Manhattan 80
66 ■ Seton Hall 69
62 † Mississippi St. 97
72 † Navy 78
81 Central Fla. 73
60 Hofstra 47
56 St. Francis (N.Y.) 54
65 LIU-Brooklyn 63
73 ■ Wagner 71
66 ■ Marist 72
49 ■ FDU-Teaneck 76
58 Rider 73
68 ■ Mt. St. Mary's (Md.) 90
61 Robert Morris 54
77 St. Francis (Pa.) 63
67 ■ LIU-Brooklyn 53
73 ■ St. Francis (N.Y.) 64
51 Wagner 76
67 ■ Hofstra 77
53 FDU-Teaneck 77
51 Marist 63
52 Mt. St. Mary's (Md.) 69
94 ■ Rider 67
64 ■ St. Francis (Pa.) 82
45 ■ Robert Morris 66
67 Rider 64
63 † Mt. St. Mary's (Md.) 74

MONTANA 23-5
61 ■ Brigham Young 56
78 † George Mason 63
63 Providence 74
46 Southwest Mo. St. 49
68 ■ Gonzaga 52
68 ■ Washington St. 63
89 ■ Western Caro. 41
81 ■ Rhode Island 54
83 Drake 90
65 Iowa St. 36
70 ■ Portland 67
77 ■ Idaho 58
81 ■ Eastern Wash. 50
98 Weber St. 76
80 Northern Ariz. 31
75 ■ Boise St. 63
74 ■ Idaho St. 54
88 ■ Southern Utah 69
65 ■ Montana St. 49
61 Eastern Wash. 35
67 Idaho 50
71 ■ Northern Ariz. 29
81 ■ Weber St. 47
81 Boise St. 70
70 Idaho St. 45
48 Montana St. 53
70 † Boise St. 68
57 Montana St. 64

MONTANA ST. 22-7
54 Drake 59
61 Iowa St. 62
48 ■ Brigham Young 60
76 † Michigan St. 64
65 Wis.-Green Bay 51
80 ■ Gonzaga 71
77 ■ Eastern Mont. 62
91 ■ St. Mary's (Cal.) 57
42 Arizona St. 81
49 Utah 68
86 ■ Portland 67
76 ■ Eastern Wash. 59
74 ■ Idaho 45
60 Northern Ariz. 53
69 Weber St. 59
74 ■ Idaho St. 52
87 ■ Boise St. 78
71 ■ Southern Utah 57
49 Montana 65
67 Idaho 56
77 Eastern Wash. 65
65 ■ Weber St. 47
72 ■ Northern Ariz. 52
59 Idaho St. 46
69 Boise St. 66
53 ■ Montana 48
57 ■ Idaho 43
64 ■ Montana 57
51 Washington 80

MONTCLAIR ST. 16-9
58 † Caldwell 47
53 Eastern Conn. St. 55
37 Ramapo 44
56 ■ Rowan 59
49 Wm. Paterson 61
92 ■ Lincoln (Pa.) 29
66 ■ St. Joseph's (Me.) 75
64 Trenton St. 53
56 ■ Bridgeport 48
59 ■ Jersey City St. 43
76 ■ Stockton St. 28
51 Lock Haven 66
67 ■ Kean 59
76 Rutgers-Camden 43
67 Rutgers-Newark 61
61 ■ Wm. Paterson 54
71 ■ Ramapo 55
52 Rowan 70
59 Kean 47
66 ■ Trenton St. 50
42 Jersey City St. 49
63 Stockton St. 26
71 ■ Rutgers-Newark 70
86 ■ Rutgers-Camden 44
54 Rowan 66

MORAVIAN 24-5
74 † Trenton St. 77
86 † Keuka 62
103 Haverford 40
105 Gettysburg 90
86 ■ Muhlenberg 66
94 Widener 48
71 Scranton 65
84 Wilkes 87
67 ■ Albright 50
76 ■ Frank. & Marsh. 69
83 Elizabethtown 93
83 ■ Ursinus 57
77 Marywood 48
107 ■ Widener 50
84 Swarthmore 26
105 ■ Haverford 38
84 King's (Pa.) 71
87 ■ Dickinson 78
68 Allentown 61
91 Albright 59
101 ■ Lebanon Valley 72
83 Ursinus 74
95 ■ Swarthmore 27
91 Muhlenberg 57
67 ■ Dickinson 58
67 ■ Frank. & Marsh. 60
82 Scranton 89
56 ■ Susquehanna 55
57 Geneseo St. 80

MOREHEAD ST. 10-16
54 ■ Xavier (Ohio) 103
63 Wright St. 70
63 ■ Northern Ky. 75
72 ■ Radford 77
53 Ga. Southern 79
72 † N.C.-Greensboro 61
49 Middle Tenn. St. 79
49 Tennessee Tech 82
38 Kentucky 66
76 ■ Tennessee St. 69
64 ■ Austin Peay 76
75 Southeast Mo. St. 80
79 Murray St. 71
60 ■ Eastern Ky. 72
84 ■ Tenn.-Martin 76
67 Tennessee St. 76
87 Austin Peay 63
110 Eastern Ky. 106
62 ■ Southeast Mo. St. 74
101 ■ Murray St. 86
60 Cincinnati 65
85 ■ Middle Tenn. St. 73
73 ■ Tennessee Tech 89
88 ■ Virginia Tech 94
77 Tenn.-Martin 69
65 Marshall 63

MORGAN ST. 16-12
47 James Madison 80
69 ■ Dist. Columbia 55
74 ■ Cheyney 43
49 Virginia 110
36 George Mason 68
55 Buffalo 63
60 Hartford 64
75 † LIU-Brooklyn 60
60 South Caro. St. 70
61 † North Caro. A&T 57
60 ■ Md.-East. Shore 50
80 ■ Delaware St. 53
79 ■ Florida A&M 80
62 ■ Bethune-Cookman 44
71 Coppin St. 56
66 Md.-East. Shore 63
59 Howard 62
69 ■ Richmond 73
56 Dist. Columbia 53
73 ■ Coppin St. 82
64 Florida A&M 80
63 Bethune-Cookman 51
62 Delaware St. 58
60 ■ South Caro. St. 55
59 ■ North Caro. A&T 55
76 ■ Howard 63
83 † Delaware St. 70
60 † South Caro. St. 81

MORNINGSIDE 18-9
76 † Mo. Western St. 71
70 Northwest Mo. St. 63
82 ■ Wayne St. (Neb.) 68
101 Briar Cliff 36
68 Fla. Southern 79
98 Eckerd 43
74 ■ Northwest Mo. St. 58
86 South Dak. 70
78 ■ Mankato St. 59
96 ■ St. Cloud St. 41
92 ■ Briar Cliff 74
68 South Dak. St. 64
73 Augustana (S.D.) 96
88 ■ Nebraska-Omaha 41
98 ■ Northern Colo. 65
70 North Dak. St. 111
69 North Dak. 100
72 St. Cloud St. 61
84 Mankato St. 65
86 Wayne St. (Neb.) 66
67 ■ Augustana (S.D.) 101
67 ■ South Dak. St. 84
95 Northern Colo. 79
81 Nebraska-Omaha 57
65 ■ North Dak. 68
59 ■ North Dak. St. 88
77 ■ South Dak. 78

MORRIS BROWN 6-21
65 Columbus 80
49 ■ Valdosta St. 93
68 Spelman 54
69 ■ Miles 59
46 ■ Paine 60
79 LeMoyne-Owen 77
58 ■ Albany St. (Ga.) 76
64 ■ S.C.-Aiken 66
71 ■ Tuskegee 97
54 ■ Clark Atlanta 74
55 ■ Fort Valley St. 87
54 ■ Clayton St. 51
46 Albany St. (Ga.) 92
26 Valdosta St. 94
70 Alabama A&M 90
61 Clark Atlanta 64
61 Miles 65
71 ■ Alabama A&M 92
77 S.C.-Aiken 76
62 Savannah St. 70
54 Paine 61
32 Fort Valley St. 102
91 ■ LeMoyne-Owen 76
61 Tuskegee 75
77 ■ Savannah St. 78
42 Georgia St. 102
44 † Fort Valley St. 97

MOUNT HOLYOKE 3-20
25 † St. Joseph's (Me.) 69
39 † Bri'water (Mass.) 57
39 ■ Trinity (Conn.) 68
48 ■ Vassar 46
28 ■ Wellesley 69
53 ■ Bryn Mawr 59
66 Suffolk 50
40 Amherst 57
52 ■ Wesleyan 68
56 ■ North Adams St. 75
42 ■ Connecticut Col. 80
67 ■ MIT 63
41 Western New Eng. 72
34 Brandeis 82
55 ■ Worcester Tech 56
64 ■ Elms 83
46 Smith 59
33 Wellesley 71
28 Tufts 61
60 ■ Babson 71
64 Wheaton (Mass.) 101
46 ■ Williams 76
37 Wellesley 78

MT. ST. MARY'S (MD.) 21-6
73 ■ Towson St. 51
81 Georgetown 87
45 Loyola (Md.) 63
71 Radford 59
66 ■ William & Mary 50
71 ■ FDU-Teaneck 78
76 ■ Marist 69
65 St. Francis (Pa.) 58
71 Robert Morris 61
93 ■ Rider 79
78 Lehigh 56
63 Wagner 62
90 Monmouth (N.J.) 68
104 ■ St. Francis (N.Y.) 60
84 ■ LIU-Brooklyn 60
73 Marist 76
67 FDU-Teaneck 82
62 ■ Robert Morris 46
87 ■ St. Francis (Pa.) 67

82 Md.-Balt. County 58
57 Rider 69
69 ■ Monmouth (N.J.) 52
64 ■ Wagner 48
76 LIU-Brooklyn 50
89 St. Francis (N.Y.) 59
74 † Monmouth (N.J.) 63
82 † Marist 61

MT. ST. VINCENT 9-14

46 CCNY 47
39 ■ New York U. 68
42 ■ Mt. St. Mary (N.Y.) 55
40 ■ Stony Brook 82
37 Hunter 72
73 ■ New Rochelle 31
47 ■ York (N.Y.) 50
45 John Jay 53
47 ■ York (N.Y.) 41
56 Staten Island 46
45 New Jersey Tech 71
56 ■ Baruch 51
41 Vassar 62
72 Marymount (N.Y.) 41
45 Albertus Magnus 58
65 ■ Medgar Evers 56
65 New Rochelle 44
52 Old Westbury 68
39 ■ New Jersey Tech 37
51 Centenary (N.J.) 59
38 Nyack 50
55 ■ Manhattanville 51
32 Mt. St. Mary (N.Y.) 68

MOUNT UNION 13-12

51 † Albion 49
50 Penn St.-Behrend 49
77 Oberlin 23
69 Notre Dame (Ohio) 45
59 ■ Capital 67
56 Marietta 66
62 ■ Hiram 44
55 Heidelberg 61
69 ■ Wooster 60
52 Waynesburg 64
74 ■ Otterbein 56
63 ■ Ohio Northern 44
56 Baldwin-Wallace 63
51 ■ John Carroll 52
44 Muskingum 56
49 Capital 71
58 ■ Marietta 46
63 Hiram 57
63 John Carroll 64
67 ■ Heidelberg 62
67 Otterbein 70
63 Ohio Northern 59
76 ■ Baldwin-Wallace 58
63 ■ Muskingum 84
59 John Carroll 69

MUHLENBERG 15-10

71 ■ Oswego St. 60
66 ■ Allentown 67
57 King's (Pa.) 66
64 ■ Ursinus 54
66 Moravian 86
73 ■ Albright 55
68 Trenton St. 62
97 ■ Drew 56
59 Occidental 60
63 Pomona-Pitzer 71
79 Redlands 81
85 ■ Allentown 73
90 Swarthmore 28
87 Widener 68
67 Ursinus 73
87 ■ Gettysburg 71
58 Frank. & Marsh. 77
60 ■ Widener 55
81 Haverford 47
68 ■ Swarthmore 32
68 ■ Haverford 53
64 Albright 57
57 ■ Moravian 91
81 ■ Ursinus 74
36 Frank. & Marsh. 86

MURRAY ST. 6-19

55 Kentucky 89
56 † Geo. Washington 87
75 ■ Southern Ill. 94
70 ■ Memphis St. 106
59 Southern Miss. 91
80 † Grambling 89
57 ■ Evansville 55
75 Austin Peay 87
74 Tennessee St. 80
88 ■ Tenn.-Martin 85
67 Southeast Mo. St. 70
66 ■ Eastern Ky. 79
71 ■ Morehead St. 79
91 ■ Eastern Ill. 74
71 ■ Tennessee Tech 93
63 ■ Middle Tenn. St. 96
62 Southern Ill. 77
72 ■ Southeast Mo. St. 86
80 Tenn.-Martin 68
102 Eastern Ky. 10
86 Morehead St. 101
94 ■ Austin Peay 76
72 ■ Tennessee St. 83
85 Tennessee Tech 76
56 Middle Tenn. St. 79

MUSKINGUM 24-3

86 † Phila. Pharmacy 49
83 † King's (Pa.) 72
104 ■ Olivet 38
76 ■ Ohio Wesleyan 71
87 Otterbein 49
75 ■ Ohio Northern 53
82 Walsh 73
78 Baldwin-Wallace 73
82 ■ Capital 63
89 ■ Waynesburg 80
56 Marietta 49
91 ■ John Carroll 73
98 ■ Hiram 50
61 Heidelberg 58
56 ■ Mount Union 44
80 ■ Otterbein 63
75 Ohio Northern 45
74 Capital 81
71 ■ Baldwin-Wallace 68
74 John Carroll 68
67 ■ Marietta 57
72 ■ Heidelberg 65
78 Hiram 61
84 Mount Union 63
61 ■ Ohio Northern 46
57 ■ Heidelberg 75
64 Concordia-M'head 78

NAVY 11-15

82 St. Francis (Pa.) 69
74 Georgetown 100
60 Western Caro. 63
54 Liberty 45
40 ■ William & Mary 55
74 ■ Buffalo 68
60 † Texas Christian 91
78 † Monmouth (N.J.) 72
81 † Baylor 71
71 Howard 58
77 ■ St. Bonaventure 84
50 ■ Army 60
77 ■ Lehigh 70
64 Colgate 50
47 ■ Lafayette 58
47 ■ Bucknell 55
46 Holy Cross 76
56 ■ Fordham 64
62 Army 67
80 Lehigh 68
61 ■ Colgate 52
67 Lafayette 72
63 Bucknell 90
61 ■ Holy Cross 76
63 Fordham 61
41 Fordham 55

NAZARETH (N.Y.) 13-10

65 Wheaton (Mass.) 90
82 † Fitchburg St. 92
64 Rochester 70
79 Alfred 61
58 ■ Wooster 65
48 ■ Clarkson 60
59 Middlebury 79
73 Hartwick 68
79 ■ Brockport St. 60
80 ■ Keuka 65
67 ■ Alfred 52
90 ■ Rochester Inst. 43
67 ■ Buffalo St. 55
64 Roberts Wesleyan 78
53 Hamilton 64
61 ■ Elmira 54
74 ■ Roberts Wesleyan 72
72 ■ Utica 40
85 ■ Fredonia St. 47
69 Keuka 64
55 ■ St. John Fisher 76
69 Albany (N.Y.) 76
79 † Hilbert 43

NEB.-KEARNEY 15-12

75 ■ Northeast Mo. St. 63
78 ■ Augustana (S.D.) 95
70 ■ Colorado-CS 63
67 ■ South Dak. 70
69 ■ Metropolitan St. 71
81 ■ Nebraska-Omaha 80
80 ■ Emporia St. 74
62 ■ Mankato St. 74
75 Doane 76
62 Hastings 70
78 † Western N. Mex. 70
84 Mesa St. 54
88 ■ Wayne St. (Neb.) 58
81 ■ Fort Hays St. 66
83 ■ Doane 80
69 Chadron St. 92
77 Wayne St. (Neb.) 82
91 ■ Hastings 96
68 Metropolitan St. 98
89 Colo. Christian 56
63 Fort Hays St. 62
63 ■ Quincy 57
82 ■ Chadron St. 74
82 † Bemidji St. 70
88 † Briar Cliff 42
74 Eastern N. Mex. 80
72 West Tex. St. 74

NEBRASKA 23-8

86 ■ Arizona St. 79
63 † South Caro. 51
83 Northwestern 71
84 ■ Illinois 67
123 ■ Howard 62
94 ■ Eastern Wash. 50
79 Creighton 58
87 † James Madison 63
88 La Salle 92
66 Penn St. 102
81 Wis.-Green Bay 78
69 ■ Oklahoma St. 77
87 ■ Oklahoma 78
62 Kansas 69
74 Kansas St. 57
62 ■ Colorado 50
86 ■ Missouri 66
82 Iowa St. 52
88 ■ Southwest Mo. St. 84
97 Oklahoma 83
58 Oklahoma St. 64
69 ■ Kansas St. 50
66 ■ Kansas 52
63 Colorado 71
65 Missouri 64
89 ■ Iowa St. 40
87 † Iowa St. 39
66 † Oklahoma St. 64
60 † Kansas 64
81 ■ San Diego 58
60 Southern Cal 78

NEB. WESLEYAN 13-12

66 Redlands 63
79 † UC San Diego 67
69 La Verne 55
82 Claremont-M-S 57
75 Buena Vista 65
52 ■ Peru St. 78
77 Graceland (Iowa) 64
52 ■ Simpson 69
79 Augsburg 51
75 Bethel (Minn.) 84
77 ■ Buena Vista 53
73 ■ Dana 77
65 ■ Doane 93
64 ■ Concordia (Neb.) 66
65 N'western (Iowa) 63
74 Hastings 91
57 ■ Midland Lutheran 64
87 ■ Colorado Col. 56
71 Dana 75
57 Doane 97
68 ■ N'western (Iowa) 65
62 Midland Lutheran 76
43 ■ Hastings 64
66 Concordia (Neb.) 64
87 ■ Graceland (Iowa) 53

NEBRASKA-OMAHA 7-19

66 ■ SIU-Edwardsville 69
64 ■ Mo. Western St. 66
63 Mo. Western St. 61
57 Northwest Mo. St. 75
80 Neb.-Kearney 81
79 ■ Midland Lutheran 43
64 ■ Denver 71
61 ■ Peru St. 47
72 Augustana (S.D.) 99
51 South Dak. St. 60
54 ■ Northern Colo. 56
56 ■ North Dak. St. 88
57 ■ North Dak. 64
41 Morningside 88
70 South Dak. 79
68 ■ Mankato St. 63
95 ■ St. Cloud St. 51
68 Northern Colo. 69
50 North Dak. 82
52 North Dak. St. 88
64 ■ South Dak. 66
57 ■ Morningside 81
104 St. Cloud St. 61
73 Mankato St. 65
60 ■ Augustana (S.D.) 80
59 ■ South Dak. St. 75

NEVADA 4-22

64 Idaho 79
63 † Gonzaga 66
65 ■ Cal St. Sacramento 83
80 ■ McNeese St. 90
51 Pacific (Cal.) 79
49 San Jose St. 55
80 ■ Long Beach St. 72
46 New Mexico St. 83
66 Nevada-Las Vegas 99
44 Southern Utah 61
67 ■ Cal St. Fullerton 82
72 ■ New Mexico St. 85
52 Hawaii 85
63 Hawaii 85
49 UC Santa Barb. 76
61 Long Beach St. 63
81 ■ Nevada-Las Vegas 88
81 ■ UC Irvine 74
61 ■ UC Santa Barb. 67
65 Cal St. Fullerton 85
82 UC Irvine 73
67 Cal St. Sacramento 82

73 ■ Southern Utah 78
76 ■ San Jose St. 63
69 ■ Pacific (Cal.) 73
71 † Hawaii 88

NEVADA-LAS VEGAS 24-7
83 ■ Tenn.-Chatt. 69
80 ■ Ala.-Birmingham 65
59 Tulane 65
71 Louisiana St. 49
78 ■ Georgia St. 60
84 ■ Youngstown St. 64
99 ■ Valparaiso 67
68 New Mexico St. 51
82 Cal St. Fullerton 63
86 UC Irvine 44
99 ■ Nevada 66
67 Pacific (Cal.) 54
84 San Jose St. 69
94 ■ Long Beach St. 67
89 ■ UC Santa Barb. 51
100 ■ UC Irvine 71
84 ■ Cal St. Fullerton 48
88 Nevada 81
67 ■ New Mexico St. 63
84 ■ Southern Utah 62
95 ■ San Jose St. 52
78 ■ Pacific (Cal.) 83
68 Long Beach St. 55
86 UC Santa Barb. 79
85 Hawaii 100
69 Hawaii 82
98 † Cal St. Fullerton 68
58 † UC Santa Barb. 62
74 † Southern Methodist 76
71 † Butler 74
71 † Geo. Washington 70

NEW ENGLAND COL. 20-6
61 Pine Manor 60
63 Endicott 51
58 Colby-Sawyer 52
80 ■ Notre Dame (N.H.) 31
67 Bates 80
75 ■ Rivier 68
48 ■ Lyndon St. 57
69 Salve Regina 73
72 ■ Eastern Nazarene 43
72 Wentworth Inst. 55
89 ■ Roger Williams 40
73 ■ Plymouth St. 90
49 Curry 53
66 ■ Anna Maria 51
74 Regis (Mass.) 67
72 Eastern Nazarene 50
69 Anna Maria 79
63 ■ Gordon 47
75 ■ Wentworth Inst. 58
66 Roger Williams 44
57 ■ Curry 47
80 ■ Salve Regina 57
54 ■ Regis (Mass.) 41
68 ■ Roger Williams 40
53 † Curry 39
70 † Regis (Mass.) 60

NEW HAMPSHIRE 18-8
71 Holy Cross 73
76 † Marist 40
62 Iona 83
71 ■ Massachusetts 49
67 ■ Dartmouth 47
60 † Kansas St. 69
91 † Davidson 53
88 ■ Rhode Island 69
67 ■ Brown 59
89 ■ Delaware 63
64 ■ Drexel 54
82 ■ Hartford 79
70 ■ Vermont 75
64 Northeastern 62
66 ■ Boston U. 55
87 ■ Harvard 84
68 Maine 63
62 Boston U. 59
58 ■ Northeastern 67
55 Vermont 70
81 ■ Hartford 63
73 Drexel 59
67 Delaware 73
76 Central Conn. St. 60
58 ■ Maine 38
55 ■ Maine 59

NEW HAMP. COL. 8-18
49 Franklin Pierce 54
65 † St. Anselm 54
74 ■ Bryant 69
77 Springfield 62
55 ■ Stonehill 73
41 Merrimack 55
53 American Int'l 58
62 ■ St. Michael's 81
58 ■ Bentley 63
75 Assumption 76
58 New Haven 76
70 ■ St. Anselm 81
85 ■ Southern Conn. St. 45
60 ■ Keene St. 76
73 Mass.-Lowell 77
72 ■ Sacred Heart 69
59 Le Moyne 65
47 ■ Franklin Pierce 56
74 ■ New Haven 56
50 Keene St. 56
74 Southern Conn. St. 61
53 Franklin Pierce 66
79 ■ Le Moyne 50
64 ■ Mass.-Lowell 85
69 Sacred Heart 71
53 Franklin Pierce 66

NEW HAVEN 10-17
90 Assumption 82
58 St. Anselm 90
63 Pace 66
57 East Stroudsburg 60
64 † Bridgeport 52
49 ■ American Int'l 70
57 Bentley 64
51 LIU-C.W. Post 48
76 ■ New Hamp. Col. 58
65 ■ Stonehill 70
48 ■ Keene St. 66
54 Mass.-Lowell 84
70 ■ Quinnipiac 63
74 ■ Bridgeport 55
74 ■ Le Moyne 75
66 Southern Conn. St. 65
69 Franklin Pierce 83
56 ■ Sacred Heart 66
56 New Hamp. Col. 74
65 ■ Mass.-Lowell 66
69 Le Moyne 70
78 Springfield 67
66 Sacred Heart 88
85 ■ Franklin Pierce 67
98 ■ Southern Conn. St. 62
69 Keene St. 86
64 Keene St. 75

NEW JERSEY TECH 8-14
52 ■ York (N.Y.) 50
49 Upsala 81
56 ■ Old Westbury 65
43 ■ St. Elizabeth 53
59 ■ Drew 67
46 ■ FDU-Madison 71
79 New Rochelle 37
62 ■ CCNY 42
37 York (N.Y.) 39
71 ■ Mt. St. Vincent 45
52 Centenary (N.J.) 74
57 St. Elizabeth 64
41 Mt. St. Mary (N.Y.) 67
57 Stevens Tech 28
64 Maritime (N.Y.) 16
57 ■ Upsala 62
45 FDU-Madison 77
71 ■ Stevens Tech 25
37 Mt. St. Vincent 39
62 Yeshiva 17
38 ■ Centenary (N.J.) 65
47 ■ Mt. St. Mary (N.Y.) 63

NEW MEXICO 5-22
37 ■ Colorado 86
56 New Mexico St. 77
76 ■ Air Force 61
36 ■ Arizona St. 91
47 Texas-Arlington 64
38 Texas Tech 96
43 ■ San Diego 64
49 ■ New Mexico St. 63
86 ■ Northern Ariz. 66
53 Southern Utah 64
53 Loyola (Cal.) 60
48 Brigham Young 60
41 Utah 68
71 ■ Fresno St. 58
44 ■ San Diego St. 55
45 UTEP 60
48 Colorado St. 73
57 Wyoming 69
48 ■ Utah 68
64 ■ Brigham Young 70
51 San Diego St. 78
60 Fresno St. 64
55 N.M. Highlands 68
73 ■ UTEP 70
52 ■ Wyoming 75
74 ■ Colorado St. 73
61 † Brigham Young 82

N.M. HIGHLANDS 19-10
76 ■ Colo. Christian 60
74 ■ Lubbock Chrst. 57
62 † Okla. Baptist 77
64 Southern Nazarene 88
73 † West Tex. St. 76
74 † Angelo St. 60
81 Colo. Christian 56
62 † UC Riverside 61
76 Grand Canyon 73
85 ■ Southern Colo. 63
75 ■ Eastern N. Mex. 86
89 Western St. 73
69 Mesa St. 74
77 Adams St. 67
77 ■ Colorado Mines 59
63 Colorado-CS 76
61 ■ Fort Hays St. 55
63 ■ Chadron St. 78
75 Colorado Col. 48
87 Colorado Mines 63
86 ■ Adams St. 79
54 Fort Hays St. 63
74 Chadron St. 93
68 ■ New Mexico 55
59 ■ Mesa St. 44
92 ■ Western St. 70
83 † Western St. 61
77 † Mesa St. 55
62 † Fort Hays St. 68

NEW MEXICO ST. 17-11
83 ■ Baylor 70
77 ■ New Mexico 56
58 ■ UTEP 51
70 Stephen F. Austin 84
45 † Sam Houston St. 55
47 UTEP 69
63 New Mexico 49
51 ■ Nevada-Las Vegas 68
79 ■ Hawaii 87
57 ■ Hawaii 62
80 UC Irvine 61
66 Cal St. Fullerton 58
83 ■ Nevada 46
71 San Jose St. 56
73 Pacific (Cal.) 83
85 Nevada 72
68 ■ UC Santa Barb. 70
73 ■ Long Beach St. 64
65 ■ Cal St. Fullerton 62
79 ■ UC Irvine 68
63 Nevada-Las Vegas 67
68 ■ Pacific (Cal.) 66
80 ■ San Jose St. 72
64 Long Beach St. 62
61 UC Santa Barb. 66
77 ■ Oral Roberts 54
73 † Pacific (Cal.) 72
70 † Hawaii 93

NEW ORLEANS 18-10
85 ■ Central Fla. 46
93 Southeastern La. 55
75 † Ga. Southern 63
76 † Mississippi St. 63
75 Southern Miss. 62
98 ■ Tex.-Pan American 55
69 ■ Pennsylvania 49
62 ■ Louisiana Tech 71
67 ■ South Ala. 54
54 Arkansas St. 66
79 ■ Tulane 61
67 South Ala. 55
85 ■ Southern Miss. 64
50 Auburn 54
70 ■ Western Ky. 94
52 ■ Lamar 65
55 ■ Arkansas St. 58
50 Western Ky. 71
69 Central Fla. 49
78 ■ Southwestern La. 56
64 Tulane 75
47 Louisiana Tech 54
76 Southwestern La. 47
77 ■ Louisiana St. 61
66 Tex.-Pan American 52
65 Lamar 47
66 † South Ala. 58
60 Louisiana Tech 67

NEW PALTZ ST. 13-13
36 Southern Me. 87
70 † Norwich 78
80 Manhattanville 33
68 Plattsburgh St. 42
52 Potsdam St. 69
61 Binghamton 75
45 ■ Geneseo St. 90
57 ■ Brockport St. 71
82 † Ferrum 67
69 Delaware Valley 66
70 ■ St. Joseph (Vt.) 58
63 Vassar 52
76 Oneonta St. 67
68 ■ Plattsburgh St. 54
74 ■ Potsdam St. 66
60 ■ Cortland St. 66
69 Utica Tech 97
58 ■ Oswego St. 66
77 ■ Oneonta St. 60
79 ■ Russell Sage 62
92 ■ CCNY 64
54 Fredonia St. 53
84 Buffalo St. 106
64 Cortland St. 93
66 ■ Binghamton 74
78 † Rutgers-Newark 79

NEW YORK U. 20-6
74 Staten Island 48
68 Mt. St. Vincent 39
73 ■ Manhattanville 23
69 ■ Emory 70
64 Albany (N.Y.) 56
91 ■ John Jay 26
58 ■ Johns Hopkins 52
76 ■ Albany (N.Y.) 60
73 Case Reserve 52
59 Carnegie Mellon 73
64 ■ Wheaton (Mass.) 54
60 Brandeis 59

66 Rochester 59
69 ■ Stony Brook 39
58 ■ Chicago 46
73 ■ Washington (Mo.) 65
64 ■ Rochester 56
62 ■ Brandeis 41
74 ■ Hunter 44
52 Washington (Mo.) 58
66 Chicago 70
61 ■ Western Conn. St. 73
60 ■ Carnegie Mellon 55
74 Emory 64
64 ■ St. John Fisher 57
54 † Scranton 82

NEWBERRY 5-19
48 ■ Lander 80
62 Francis Marion 83
62 † Wofford 98
65 † Erskine 63
69 ■ Presbyterian 67
59 Voorhees 55
52 ■ Voorhees 73
73 Pfeiffer 86
72 ■ Converse 64
50 ■ Limestone 83
57 Belmont Abbey 75
52 ■ Francis Marion 91
62 Lincoln Memorial 94
51 Erskine 71
72 Wofford 73
52 ■ Lincoln Memorial 99
81 Lees-McRae 101
60 Limestone 78
68 Converse 75
59 ■ Belmont Abbey 87
57 Lander 67
74 S.C.-Aiken 88
61 ■ Erskine 56
70 ■ S.C.-Aiken 81

NIAGARA 17-10
97 ■ Akron 78
84 † Princeton 91
86 † Pennsylvania 78
78 ■ Duquesne 73
87 ■ Buffalo 85
77 Cornell 62
83 St. Bonaventure 91
63 † Rhode Island 79
78 † Western Caro. 70
91 Robert Morris 78
77 Colgate 65
52 Loyola (Md.) 58
64 Fairfield 69
83 ■ Rutgers 85
78 ■ Manhattan 69
65 Iona 52
66 Siena 83
69 Canisius 67
68 ■ St. Peter's 66
75 ■ Iona 69
84 ■ Siena 64
83 ■ Fairfield 74
97 ■ Loyola (Md.) 93
72 ■ Canisius 68
57 Manhattan 68
76 St. Peter's 98
73 † Siena 77

NICHOLLS ST. 2-24
76 ■ Xavier (La.) 91
76 Central Fla. 83
60 † Stetson 84
65 Xavier (La.) 74
66 Southwestern La. 73
58 ■ Southwest Tex. St. 80
78 ■ Texas-San Antonio 60
59 ■ Iona 68
79 Northwestern (La.) 105
60 Northeast La. 95
61 ■ Southeastern La. 57
69 ■ North Texas 72
44 ■ Texas-Arlington 59
57 ■ McNeese St. 65

48 Stephen F. Austin 89
43 Sam Houston St. 84
63 ■ Northeast La. 77
66 ■ Northwestern (La.) 98
49 Texas-Arlington 72
56 North Texas 85
42 Louisiana St. 72
77 McNeese St. 84
59 ■ Sam Houston St. 64
53 ■ Stephen F. Austin 93
42 Texas-San Antonio 58
59 Southwest Tex. St. 68

NICHOLS 4-20
52 † Worcester Tech 73
54 Worcester St. 72
50 ■ Anna Maria 69
38 Brandeis 51
60 ■ Framingham St. 33
31 ■ Colby-Sawyer 36
54 ■ Alfred 51
50 Eastern Nazarene 46
39 ■ Curry 42
39 ■ Trinity (Conn.) 59
57 MIT 62
44 Gordon 66
51 † Elmira 67
27 Skidmore 28
45 Elms 54
36 ■ Fitchburg St. 62
48 Pine Manor 54
52 Suffolk 54
45 ■ Western New Eng. 55
51 ■ Worcester Tech 50
27 Wellesley 58
32 ■ Wesleyan 82
52 ■ Connecticut Col. 69
39 Coast Guard 40

NORFOLK ST. 29-3
90 † Queens (N.C.) 67
102 † Concord 62
113 ■ Livingstone 39
95 Johnson Smith 81
74 ■ St. Thomas (Minn.) 71
106 N.C. Central 43
87 Virginia St. 68
111 † St. Vincent 81
60 Mercyhurst 88
76 ■ Fayetteville St. 61
104 Winston-Salem 60
70 ■ West Chester 65
84 St. Paul's 55
83 ■ Virginia Union 45
77 ■ Elizabeth City St. 66
86 Bowie St. 44
105 ■ Shaw 86
91 ■ Virginia St. 76
85 Hampton 61
70 Virginia Union 65
97 ■ Bowie St. 49
86 ■ St. Paul's 60
58 ■ Hampton 65
104 St. Augustine's 71
73 Dist. Columbia 53
91 Elizabeth City St. 60
93 † Fayetteville St. 73
97 † Virginia Union 91
78 † St. Augustine's 77
90 † Fort Valley St. 76
75 S.C.-Spartanburg 68
66 Bentley 84

NORTH ADAMS ST. 3-22
45 Smith 50
56 ■ Amherst 57
61 Russell Sage 72
51 ■ Middlebury 81
69 Castleton St. 56
64 ■ Mass.-Boston 66
58 ■ Framingham St. 45
75 Mount Holyoke 56
55 Union (N.Y.) 75
60 Bri'water (Mass.) 72
69 Green Mountain 72

54 Worcester St. 68
51 ■ Salem St. 84
46 ■ Western New Eng. 59
59 Fitchburg St. 74
41 ■ Westfield St. 62
40 Williams 72
41 Framingham St. 56
39 Skidmore 65
66 ■ Bri'water (Mass.) 83
52 ■ Worcester St. 84
47 Salem St. 65
54 ■ Fitchburg St. 73
33 Westfield St. 77
41 Fitchburg St. 62

NORTH ALA. 14-12
94 Bethel (Tenn.) 89
87 ■ Freed-Hardeman 52
69 ■ David Lipscomb 83
79 ■ Troy St. 76
68 Freed-Hardeman 66
84 ■ Bethel (Tenn.) 70
87 ■ Belmont 79
50 Delta St. 100
64 David Lipscomb 85
60 Belmont 71
91 West Ga. 97
91 Valdosta St. 99
92 ■ Ala.-Huntsville 65
64 ■ Jacksonville St. 62
85 Mississippi-Women 65
74 ■ Livingston 76
55 ■ Mississippi Col. 47
41 ■ Delta St. 73
76 ■ Mississippi-Women 70
73 Mississippi Col. 81
87 Livingston 97
80 Troy St. 82
82 Jacksonville St. 95
87 Ala.-Huntsville 72
70 ■ West Ga. 69
91 ■ Valdosta St. 74

NORTH CARO. 23-7
80 ■ Charleston So. 41
54 Robert Morris 39
81 Duquesne 65
94 ■ Furman 76
97 ■ Stetson 42
99 ■ Charleston 56
87 ■ Loyola (Md.) 51
67 † Marshall 42
83 Coastal Caro. 35
63 Georgia Tech 73
66 ■ Florida St. 85
92 ■ Wake Forest 68
59 Clemson 56
66 ■ Duke 54
73 Florida St. 66
85 ■ Maryland 80
71 ■ North Caro. St. 47
72 ■ Georgia Tech 68
72 ■ Virginia 65
77 Wake Forest 69
67 Virginia 73
80 ■ Canisius 51
55 North Caro. St. 60
52 Maryland 73
84 Duke 63
70 ■ Clemson 63
89 † North Caro. St. 71
61 † Maryland 75
74 ■ Alabama 73
54 † Tennessee 74

NORTH CARO. A&T 9-19
52 ■ N.C.-Charlotte 80
89 ■ Winston-Salem 49
52 ■ Campbell 58
61 Coastal Caro. 68
59 † Marshall 71
70 Campbell 78
53 † Howard 54
57 † Morgan St. 61
42 Coppin St. 51

91 Florida A&M 95
73 Bethune-Cookman 72
55 † N.C. Central 49
56 Delaware St. 54
50 Md.-East. Shore 57
48 N.C.-Greensboro 64
60 ■ Florida A&M 83
60 ■ Bethune-Cookman 58
61 Winston-Salem 51
71 ■ Delaware St. 84
63 ■ Md.-East. Shore 45
56 ■ South Caro. St. 51
56 East Caro. 71
61 Howard 62
55 Morgan St. 59
49 ■ Coppin St. 58
53 South Caro. St. 80
75 † Florida A&M 68
49 † Coppin St. 51

N.C. CENTRAL 5-19
80 † Mt. Olive 92
81 † Barton 85
43 St. Augustine's 101
43 ■ Norfolk St. 106
48 Virginia St. 90
59 ■ Johnson Smith 79
69 Fayetteville St. 87
61 Shaw 67
63 Bowie St. 48
67 ■ Winston-Salem 54
69 St. Paul's 53
49 † North Caro. A&T 55
42 ■ St. Augustine's 74
72 Livingstone 71
82 ■ Fayetteville St. 86
65 Johnson Smith 71
98 ■ Livingstone 90
59 ■ Shaw 74
47 ■ Virginia Union 62
56 ■ Elizabeth City St. 77
42 Clark Atlanta 47
60 Hampton 74
59 Winston-Salem 67
52 † Virginia St. 75

NORTH CARO. ST. 14-13
75 ■ Long Beach St. 57
80 Washington 83
75 ■ Florida St. 67
94 ■ East Caro. 79
82 ■ Western Ky. 75
79 Geo. Washington 85
77 Va. Commonwealth 79
106 ■ Fla. Atlantic 80
66 Clemson 89
79 ■ Georgia Tech 86
77 ■ Duke 60
73 Virginia 79
75 ■ Wake Forest 72
79 ■ Clemson 71
47 North Caro. 71
52 Maryland 92
127 Howard 50
90 ■ Geo. Washington 72
67 Old Dominion 81
65 Duke 82
74 ■ Maryland 72
60 ■ North Caro. 55
89 Georgia Tech 92
57 Florida St. 47
84 Wake Forest 80
75 ■ Virginia 76
71 † North Caro. 89

N.C.-ASHEVILLE 0-27
49 Appalachian St. 100
73 † East Tenn. St. 94
37 Marshall 92
63 ■ Western Caro. 68
48 ■ Davidson 62
58 East Caro. 92
57 ■ Md.-Balt. County 80
49 Towson St. 81
67 Campbell 95

64 Winthrop 72
57 Radford 79
67 N.C.-Greensboro 81
56 Coastal Caro. 79
64 Western Caro. 90
50 Liberty 68
51 ■ Winthrop 67
61 Charleston So. 64
41 ■ N.C.-Greensboro 80
45 ■ Charleston So. 49
61 ■ Coastal Caro. 80
46 ■ Radford 82
53 ■ Towson St. 83
55 Md.-Balt. County 70
49 Davidson 59
48 ■ Liberty 49
52 ■ Campbell 55
49 † Coastal Caro. 72

N.C.-CHARLOTTE 16-12

80 North Caro. A&T 52
64 Wake Forest 62
45 Tennessee 89
57 † Kentucky 54
38 Iowa 60
78 ■ South Caro. St. 41
74 † Virginia 77
44 † Connecticut 54
75 † Mercer 57
72 Ala.-Birmingham 63
76 South Fla. 56
69 ■ Va. Commonwealth 60
59 ■ Southern Miss. 63
77 ■ Tulane 48
69 ■ Western Caro. 48
90 Winthrop 43
55 Louisville 71
81 ■ Virginia Tech 44
78 ■ East Caro. 45
52 ■ South Caro. 62
58 Tulane 62
45 Southern Miss. 62
82 ■ Louisville 86
72 ■ South Fla. 48
92 Va. Commonwealth 61
70 Virginia Tech 76
69 † Tulane 44
64 † Southern Miss. 68

N.C.-GREENSBORO 19-10

56 Southwest Tex. St. 80
70 † South Ala. 73
76 ■ Duke 80
69 ■ Stetson 62
68 † Akron 50
74 South Fla. 67
62 † South Ala. 66
61 † Morehead St. 72
50 Liberty 48
70 ■ Cornell 61
59 ■ East Caro. 76
63 ■ Virginia Tech 54
72 ■ N.C.-Wilmington 54
45 James Madison 63
61 Appalachian St. 91
81 ■ N.C.-Asheville 67
64 ■ North Caro. A&T 48
87 Coastal Caro. 52
70 N.C.-Wilmington 56
80 N.C.-Asheville 41
87 Campbell 74
88 ■ Winthrop 48
77 ■ Liberty 52
83 ■ Charleston So. 59
66 Clemson 75
74 ■ Radford 57
58 † Charleston So. 55
81 † Towson St. 69
57 Radford 62

N.C.-WILMINGTON 4-23

52 ■ Duke 88
66 Rice 81
61 † Sam Houston St. 87
70 Charleston So. 84

61 Charleston 60
83 ■ Coastal Caro. 53
78 ■ Davidson 70
51 ■ Kansas St. 69
75 Western Caro. 66
54 N.C.-Greensboro 72
72 ■ Campbell 84
58 Richmond 63
55 James Madison 66
61 ■ George Mason 78
76 ■ American 79
61 William & Mary 79
54 Old Dominion 71
56 ■ N.C.-Greensboro 70
67 ■ East Caro. 87
61 ■ Richmond 66
63 ■ James Madison 78
62 George Mason 81
56 American 76
65 ■ William & Mary 85
59 ■ Old Dominion 83
56 East Caro. 82
42 Old Dominion 75

NORTH CENTRAL 4-20

58 ■ Ill. Benedictine 67
59 Chicago 77
55 ■ Aurora 57
55 ■ Luther 59
46 ■ Millikin 59
62 ■ Augustana (Ill.) 77
55 † John Carroll 81
49 † Huron 70
76 † Messiah 63
84 Rockford 24
58 Ill. Wesleyan 66
34 Wheaton (Ill.) 61
42 ■ Wheaton (Ill.) 56
45 ■ North Park 60
55 Millikin 77
67 ■ Lake Forest 75
56 Elmhurst 55
56 ■ St. Mary's (Ind.) 63
56 Augustana (Ill.) 67
63 ■ Elmhurst 59
58 North Park 60
50 Carthage 55
62 ■ Carthage 75
72 ■ Ill. Wesleyan 79

NORTH DAK. 23-5

71 Michigan Tech 86
63 † Pittsburg St. 79
76 † Alas. Fairbanks 44
71 Moorhead St. 68
79 ■ Mayville St. 46
91 ■ Southern Colo. 58
55 ■ Minn.-Duluth 44
73 ■ Valley City St. 55
78 ■ Portland St. 46
72 Mankato St. 60
72 St. Cloud St. 50
67 ■ South Dak. St. 58
68 ■ Augustana (S.D.) 59
61 Northern Colo. 46
64 Nebraska-Omaha 57
55 North Dak. St. 78
85 ■ South Dak. 66
100 ■ Morningside 69
67 Augustana (S.D.) 90
79 South Dak. St. 78
82 ■ Nebraska-Omaha 50
69 ■ Northern Colo. 57
62 ■ North Dak. St. 56
68 Morningside 65
72 South Dak. 56
88 ■ St. Cloud St. 44
71 ■ Mankato St. 50
67 † Augustana (S.D.) 79

NORTH DAK. ST. 30-2

95 ■ Wayne St. (Neb.) 55
97 ■ Moorhead St. 64
72 Minn.-Duluth 56
82 † Eastern Mont. 51

86 Regis (Colo.) 67
101 ■ Minn.-Morris 55
102 ■ Concordia-M'head 37
76 ■ Minn.-Duluth 50
99 ■ Bemidji St. 51
100 St. Cloud St. 35
92 Mankato St. 50
95 ■ Augustana (S.D.) 68
77 ■ South Dak. St. 59
88 Nebraska-Omaha 56
81 Northern Colo. 57
78 ■ North Dak. 55
111 ■ Morningside 70
87 ■ South Dak. 45
88 South Dak. St. 71
83 Augustana (S.D.) 92
91 ■ Northern Colo. 51
88 ■ Nebraska-Omaha 52
56 North Dak. 62
85 South Dak. 50
88 Morningside 59
95 ■ Mankato St. 78
117 ■ St. Cloud St. 41
92 ■ Denver 77
91 ■ Augustana (S.D.) 82
91 ■ Cal Poly Pomona 55
79 Bentley 57
95 † Delta St. 63

NORTH FLA. 10-17

70 ■ Edward Waters 57
77 Webber 54
75 ■ Valdosta St. 70
59 Flagler 71
82 ■ Warner Southern 72
100 ■ Columbus 89
46 ■ Mt. Mercy 75
47 Valdosta St. 84
66 ■ Southern Me. 70
67 ■ High Point 78
66 ■ Florida Tech 82
66 Eckerd 59
71 ■ Barry 79
66 Fla. Southern 98
70 ■ Tampa 77
68 ■ Rollins 73
50 Florida Tech 80
68 ■ Flagler 60
69 ■ St. Leo 56
65 Barry 73
56 ■ Savannah St. 69
68 ■ Fla. Southern 78
64 Tampa 79
53 Rollins 83
80 St. Leo 64
69 ■ Eckerd 61
69 ■ Georgia Col. 82

NORTH TEXAS 9-17

68 Texas Christian 86
58 Arkansas 102
80 † West Va. 86
57 Southern Methodist 96
53 † Louisville 79
107 † Troy St. 77
69 ■ Northern Ariz. 48
66 ■ Texas Christian 61
87 ■ Northwestern (La.) 94
67 ■ Northeast La. 69
59 Texas-Arlington 62
72 Nicholls St. 69
81 McNeese St. 84
59 ■ Stephen F. Austin 83
52 ■ Sam Houston St. 54
60 Southwest Tex. St. 77
64 Texas-San Antonio 65
59 ■ Texas-Arlington 46
89 ■ McNeese St. 80
85 ■ Nicholls St. 56
74 Sam Houston St. 53
64 Stephen F. Austin 82
66 ■ Texas-San Antonio 63
54 ■ Southwest Tex. St. 75

79 Northeast La. 81
60 Northwestern (La.) 102

NORTHEAST LA. 19-9

85 ■ Louisiana Col. 60
62 ■ Louisiana Tech 51
79 ■ Arkansas St. 82
76 Southwestern La. 53
86 † Howard 65
74 South Ala. 61
69 North Texas 67
74 Texas-Arlington 53
74 ■ McNeese St. 58
95 ■ Nicholls St. 60
49 Louisiana Tech 76
59 Stephen F. Austin 70
60 Sam Houston St. 51
67 ■ Southwest Tex. St. 61
65 ■ Texas-San Antonio 58
44 Mississippi 69
64 Northwestern (La.) 67
77 Nicholls St. 63
76 ■ Sam Houston St. 60
77 ■ Stephen F. Austin 73
74 Texas-San Antonio 50
66 Southwest Tex. St. 81
70 McNeese St. 75
82 ■ Northwestern (La.) 84
81 ■ North Texas 79
56 ■ Texas-Arlington 46
84 ■ McNeese St. 72
53 Stephen F. Austin 72

NORTHEAST MO. ST. 2-24

63 Neb.-Kearney 75
64 Culver-Stockton 84
61 ■ St. Cloud St. 79
55 SIU-Edwardsville 64
65 ■ Mt. Mercy 79
58 ■ Augustana (Ill.) 54
55 ■ Quincy 65
42 ■ St. Ambrose 84
47 Abilene Christian 90
77 Angelo St. 98
48 Mo. Western St. 85
49 ■ Mo.-St. Louis 67
59 Northwest Mo. St. 64
60 ■ Mo. Southern St. 90
58 Central Mo. St. 83
54 ■ Emporia St. 68
46 ■ Mo. Western St. 67
44 Washburn 81
65 ■ Northwest Mo. St. 62
63 Lincoln (Mo.) 86
48 ■ Central Mo. St. 74
53 Emporia St. 87
44 ■ Washburn 71
57 Southwest Baptist 85
35 Pittsburg St. 97
59 ■ Missouri-Rolla 75

NORTHEASTERN 14-14

64 ■ Massachusetts 63
53 Duke 64
61 † East Caro. 71
53 Rhode Island 56
54 Iona 70
59 Boston College 64
48 St. John's (N.Y.) 65
54 † Arizona St. 97
60 ■ Harvard 70
72 Central Conn. St. 63
50 ■ Vermont 73
53 Hartford 42
61 ■ Brown 52
72 Drexel 59
52 Delaware 60
62 ■ New Hampshire 64
45 ■ Maine 43
52 ■ Boston U. 48
57 Maine 51
67 New Hampshire 58
77 ■ Bridgeport 43
72 ■ Delaware 57
70 ■ Drexel 52

40 Vermont 50
70 ■ Hartford 53
53 Boston U. 71
65 ■ Boston U. 52
43 † Maine 44

NORTHEASTERN ILL. 5-23
59 Ill.-Chicago 72
67 ■ Drake 68
68 ■ Fresno St. 73
58 ■ Northern Iowa 66
72 Western Mich. 85
49 ■ DePaul 87
42 ■ Auburn 68
59 Evansville 76
86 Western Ill. 90
55 ■ Cal St. Northridge 51
53 St. Louis 72
64 Southeast Mo. St. 75
76 Chicago St. 69
69 Wis.-Milwaukee 79
44 Mo.-Kansas City 78
71 National Louis 60
82 ■ Chicago St. 69
68 ■ St. Louis 49
38 ■ Wis.-Milwaukee 61
73 Marquette 93
65 ■ Mo.-Kansas City 68
73 † Southern Meth. 106
69 Alas. Anchorage 73
59 † Hawaii 98
61 ■ Louisville 93
67 † Cal St. Sacramento 93
65 † Chicago St. 77
55 † Cal St. Northridge 76

NORTHERN ARIZ. 2-24
78 ■ Grand Canyon 66
61 St. Mary's (Cal.) 73
50 † San Jose St. 62
53 ■ Cal St. Northridge 59
48 North Texas 69
52 Cal St. Northridge 74
79 ■ Valparaiso 101
66 New Mexico 86
55 Cal St. Sacramento 63
48 Boise St. 85
64 Idaho St. 76
53 ■ Montana St. 60
31 ■ Montana 80
65 Eastern Wash. 79
44 Idaho 78
80 ■ Cal St. Sacramento 74
68 ■ Weber St. 70
63 Southern Utah 80
57 ■ Idaho St. 77
70 ■ Boise St. 78
29 Montana 71
52 Montana St. 72
44 ■ Idaho 59
52 ■ Eastern Wash. 65
60 ■ Southern Utah 76
70 Weber St. 81

NORTHERN COLO. 9-18
56 ■ Air Force 64
52 Denver 77
66 ■ Regis (Colo.) 70
62 Colorado St. 91
77 Southern Colo. 53
83 † Mesa St. 63
65 Metropolitan St. 74
48 South Dak. St. 65
54 Augustana (S.D.) 92
77 ■ Southern Colo. 48
56 Nebraska-Omaha 54
46 ■ North Dak. 61
57 ■ North Dak. St. 81
61 South Dak. 63
65 Morningside 98
96 ■ St. Cloud St. 46
81 ■ Mankato St. 74
68 ■ Denver 75
69 ■ Nebraska-Omaha 68
51 North Dak. St. 91
57 North Dak. 69
79 ■ Morningside 95
59 ■ South Dak. 60
47 Mankato St. 63
82 St. Cloud St. 58
75 ■ South Dak. St. 67
74 ■ Augustana (S.D.) 89

NORTHERN ILL. 24-6
84 Southern Ill. 80
93 ■ Fresno St. 74
64 Southern Cal 91
75 Arizona 80
85 ■ Utah 69
109 ■ Manhattan 56
102 ■ Valparaiso 85
85 ■ Wis.-Green Bay 76
85 Eastern Ill. 58
73 ■ DePaul 69
85 Cleveland St. 54
91 Youngstown St. 75
59 Iowa 92
95 ■ Western Ill. 75
78 ■ Wright St. 61
79 ■ Ill.-Chicago 53
71 Wis.-Green Bay 68
86 ■ Florida St. 80
91 Valparaiso 80
68 DePaul 84
103 ■ Eastern Ill. 57
76 Ill.-Chicago 81
88 ■ Cleveland St. 77
105 ■ Youngstown St. 92
102 Western Ill. 70
77 Wright St. 51
102 † Eastern Ill. 51
81 † Ill.-Chicago 47
75 Wis.-Green Bay 58
74 Georgetown 76

NORTHERN IOWA 10-17
41 Mo.-Kansas City 57
55 Kansas St. 61
52 ■ Wyoming 62
65 Western Ill. 62
66 Northeastern Ill. 58
82 Valparaiso 72
68 ■ Iowa St. 50
67 Illinois St. 72
73 Bradley 79
75 ■ Wichita St. 69
63 ■ Southwest Mo. St. 84
78 St. Louis 59
106 Drake 112
66 ■ Creighton 90
62 ■ Southern Ill. 86
74 ■ Indiana St. 69
41 Creighton 76
71 ■ Drake 78
73 ■ Kansas 75
78 Indiana St. 59
68 Southern Ill. 92
54 Southwest Mo. St. 84
52 Wichita St. 87
95 ■ Chicago St. 61
87 ■ Bradley 75
66 ■ Illinois St. 67
73 Creighton 86

NORTHERN KY. 19-8
68 † East Stroudsburg 60
71 Indiana (Pa.) 63
94 ■ IU/PU-Indianapolis 61
91 ■ Alas. Fairbanks 52
64 ■ Pittsburg St. 62
75 Morehead St. 63
63 Ashland 54
56 IU/PU-Ft. Wayne 60
74 ■ Kentucky St. 44
82 ■ Bellarmine 80
51 St. Joseph's (Ind.) 53
80 Lewis 66
60 ■ SIU-Edwardsville 67
69 ■ Indianapolis 72
87 IU/PU-Indianapolis 67
71 ■ Southern Ind. 73
62 ■ Ky. Wesleyan 48
72 Bellarmine 75
117 Kentucky St. 46
86 ■ Lewis 78
65 ■ St. Joseph's (Ind.) 67
68 SIU-Edwardsville 77
81 Indianapolis 78
87 Ky. Wesleyan 77
91 Southern Ind. 79
70 ■ IU/PU-Ft. Wayne 60
74 ■ Ashland 49

NORTHERN MICH. 22-6
89 ■ Bemidji St. 74
93 ■ Mich.-Dearborn 63
81 ■ Alma 78
79 ■ Wis.-Parkside 63
94 Minn.-Duluth 77
92 ■ Ferris St. 69
96 ■ Grand Valley St. 77
83 Northwood 60
99 Rollins 64
104 Barry 63
106 ■ Oakland 73
111 ■ Saginaw Valley 96
84 Wayne St. (Mich.) 66
99 Hillsdale 80
70 ■ Michigan Tech 71
91 Ferris St. 73
89 Grand Valley St. 71
86 ■ Lake Superior St. 71
101 ■ Northwood 54
80 Michigan Tech 73
99 Oakland 105
69 Saginaw Valley 72
79 Lake Superior St. 88
90 ■ Wayne St. (Mich.) 77
102 ■ Hillsdale 86
96 Wis.-Parkside 87
69 † Saginaw Valley 72
81 † Oakland 83

NORTHWEST MO. ST. 13-14
59 ■ Peru St. 44
63 ■ Morningside 70
81 Quincy 69
55 † Colorado-CS 45
69 † Fort Hays St. 80
75 ■ Nebraska-Omaha 57
87 ■ William Jewell 59
58 Morningside 74
53 ■ Washburn 70
51 Pittsburg St. 71
64 ■ Northeast Mo. St. 59
81 ■ Southwest Baptist 79
70 ■ Rockhurst 63
67 Mo. Western St. 78
60 ■ Central Mo. St. 53
47 Washburn 72
72 ■ Emporia St. 66
70 ■ Augustana (S.D.) 82
62 Northeast Mo. St. 65
55 Mo. Southern St. 79
71 ■ Mo. Western St. 74
62 Central Mo. St. 73
82 Emporia St. 74
63 ■ Missouri-Rolla 72
85 Mo.-St. Louis 84
72 ■ Lincoln (Mo.) 66
64 Mo. Southern St. 67

NORTHWESTERN 20-9
82 Loyola (Ill.) 60
73 ■ Yale 56
71 ■ Nebraska 83
68 Illinois St. 76
63 St. Mary's (Cal.) 49
78 California 81
72 † Tennessee Tech 58
104 ■ Eastern Ill. 57
63 Penn St. 75
89 ■ Wis.-Milwaukee 46
55 ■ Iowa 60
85 Illinois 76
82 ■ Wisconsin 65
73 Purdue 62
77 Indiana 58
78 ■ Michigan St. 58
76 ■ Minnesota 68
62 Iowa 68
70 Minnesota 72
80 ■ Illinois 76
103 Wisconsin 90
77 ■ Indiana 65
70 ■ Purdue 62
109 Michigan St. 103
98 Michigan 58
66 ■ Ohio St. 76
99 ■ Penn St. 84
90 ■ Georgia Tech 62
66 Tennessee 89

NORTHWESTERN (LA.) 24-8
94 † Oral Roberts 61
67 Texas Tech 91
119 ■ Prairie View 42
76 San Francisco 80
84 San Jose St. 62
94 North Texas 87
71 Texas-Arlington 58
111 ■ Central Ark. 91
105 ■ Nicholls St. 79
76 ■ McNeese St. 54
74 Stephen F. Austin 77
80 ■ Texas-San Antonio 52
77 ■ Southwest Tex. St. 84
72 Southeastern La. 62
67 ■ Northeast La. 64
73 McNeese St. 60
98 Nicholls St. 66
75 ■ Stephen F. Austin 80
101 ■ Sam Houston St. 51
77 ■ Arkansas 62
71 Southwest Tex. St. 88
93 Texas-San Antonio 65
74 Sam Houston St. 64
84 Northeast La. 82
76 ■ Texas-Arlington 66
102 ■ North Texas 60
65 ■ Texas-Arlington 47
78 † Southwest Tex. St. 58
75 Stephen F. Austin 77
74 † Marquette 77
93 † Geo. Washington 77
89 † Butler 85

NORTHWOOD 5-22
78 ■ Grand Rapids Bapt. 67
52 Aquinas 50
53 † Calvin 73
53 ■ Aquinas 75
64 Saginaw Valley 82
49 Wayne St. (Mich.) 69
35 ■ Michigan Tech 81
60 ■ Northern Mich. 83
47 † Alma 69
56 Calvin 77
51 Adrian 66
57 ■ Lake Superior St. 69
57 Oakland 69
62 ■ Grand Valley St. 66
70 Mich.-Dearborn 77
78 ■ Hillsdale 69
46 Ferris St. 80
56 ■ Saginaw Valley 91
74 ■ Wayne St. (Mich.) 73
68 Grand Valley St. 84
52 Michigan Tech 81
54 Northern Mich. 101
51 ■ Ferris St. 70
42 Lake Superior St. 84
79 Hillsdale 77
43 ■ Oakland 79
63 Shawnee St. 85

NORWICH 14-13
46 † Western Conn. St. 98

78 † New Paltz St. 70
53 ■ Smith 39
65 Middlebury 92
67 ■ Albertus Magnus ... 54
70 ■ Westfield St. 81
70 Lyndon St. 63
50 Eastern Conn. St. .. 74
51 Alas. Anchorage ... 98
49 Alas. Anchorage ... 95
66 Alas. Fairbanks 75
59 Alas. Fairbanks 93
70 ■ Coast Guard 66
65 ■ Coast Guard 55
81 ■ Plymouth St. 66
64 Albany (N.Y.) 66
66 ■ Western Conn. St. .. 75
98 ■ Emmanuel 81
66 ■ Gordon 45
66 ■ St. Joseph's (Me.) .. 85
76 ■ Middlebury 89
88 Bates 75
93 Thomas 76
80 ■ Castleton St. 44
69 ■ St. Joseph (Vt.) 55
45 Williams 55
67 Colby-Sawyer 52

NOTRE DAME 15-12
62 Marquette 66
41 ■ Purdue 74
76 Ill.-Chicago 71
62 ■ Michigan 54
75 ■ Georgia 81
55 Loyola (Md.) 48
78 ■ Georgetown 72
63 La Salle 69
48 Tennessee 79
72 Dayton 60
64 Xavier (Ohio) 56
80 ■ Detroit Mercy 55
76 ■ Loyola (Ill.) 50
66 Penn St. 87
55 DePaul 71
69 Evansville 73
70 Butler 82
61 ■ La Salle 58
95 ■ Duquesne 67
68 ■ Xavier (Ohio) 70
92 ■ Dayton 80
74 Loyola (Ill.) 60
68 Detroit Mercy 55
91 Duquesne 63
69 ■ Butler 80
74 ■ Evansville 62
74 ■ Dayton 78

NOTRE DAME (CAL.) 5-18
37 Dominican (Cal.) ... 72
34 Holy Names 33
18 Humboldt St. 86
24 † Lewis & Clark 89
43 ■ Simpson (Cal.) 32
23 ■ Southern Ore. St. .. 84
42 ■ Mills 39
47 ■ Dominican (Cal.) ... 49
35 UC Santa Cruz 44
35 ■ Sheldon Jackson ... 75
30 ■ Claremont-M-S 54
36 Simpson (Cal.) 23
20 Master's 77
41 La Sierra 47
40 ■ Pac. Christian 41
42 San Fran. St. 102
38 ■ UC Santa Cruz 41
64 ■ Holy Names 21
44 Mills 48
35 † Pac. Christian 50
51 † Holy Names 52
44 ■ Master's 80
24 ■ San Fran. St. 69

NOTRE DAME (MD.) 11-12
59 ■ Western Md. 51
53 ■ Salisbury St. 73

53 Messiah 67
62 ■ Cabrini 64
55 Mary Washington .. 97
69 Shenandoah 72
67 † Christendom 78
58 Goucher 42
56 ■ Lebanon Valley 55
62 ■ Immaculata 66
73 Mary Baldwin 41
76 ■ Gallaudet 81
86 ■ Rosemont 34
55 Frostburg St. 85
77 Salisbury St. 93
53 Catholic 51
94 ■ Washington (Md.) .. 20
76 ■ Shenandoah 53
52 Swarthmore 33
63 St. Mary's (Md.) 46
44 ■ Wesley 47
79 ■ Mary Baldwin 35
46 ■ Wesley 73

OAKLAND 19-9
86 ■ Central St. (Ohio) ... 64
86 ■ Aquinas 73
82 † Madonna 59
77 † Ferris St. 74
63 ■ Calvin 73
101 ■ Alma 61
79 ■ Lake Superior St. .. 76
94 ■ Hillsdale 78
86 ■ Slippery Rock 79
73 Northern Mich. ... 106
66 Michigan Tech 90
69 ■ Northwood 57
71 Saginaw Valley 83
84 Grand Valley St. 69
95 ■ Wayne St. (Mich.) .. 85
62 ■ Mercyhurst 64
66 Lake Superior St. .. 75
78 ■ Ferris St. 69
78 Hillsdale 59
105 ■ Northern Mich. 99
62 ■ Michigan Tech 68
70 Ferris St. 57
79 Northwood 43
77 ■ Saginaw Valley 85
82 ■ Grand Valley St. 64
84 Wayne St. (Mich.) .. 82
71 Michigan Tech 80
83 † Northern Mich. 81

OAKLAND CITY 20-9
63 ■ Ind. Wesleyan 69
106 St. Mary-Woods ... 10
74 Ky. Wesleyan 77
74 Greenville 43
67 ■ Indianapolis 81
83 ■ Spalding 51
61 Ind.-Southeast 60
55 DePauw 58
72 ■ Missouri Valley 66
69 ■ Clinch Valley 57
77 ■ Ky. Wesleyan 64
98 Ind.-South Bend ... 60
74 Midway 58
101 ■ Greenville 47
92 Wilberforce 57
71 Indianapolis 88
70 Spalding 58
78 Brescia 85
79 ■ Ind.-Southeast 75
81 ■ DePauw 59
78 ■ SIU-Edwardsville ... 91
91 ■ Ind.-South Bend ... 35
77 ■ Concordia (Mich.) ... 48
77 Cedarville 63
63 Huntington 73
86 ■ Wilberforce 28
75 † Covenant 64
97 † Lee 91
69 † Williams Bapt. 81

OBERLIN 0-21
23 ■ Mount Union 77
54 ■ Bethany (W.Va.) 98
56 ■ Denison 94
51 ■ Earlham 86
49 Allegheny 90
41 Thiel 92
46 Wooster 92
42 ■ Kenyon 57
37 ■ Ohio Wesleyan 94
15 Wittenberg 84
36 ■ Case Reserve 64
33 Earlham 78
28 ■ Allegheny 88
36 ■ Penn St.-Behrend . 101
34 Bethany (W.Va.) 78
29 Ohio Wesleyan 90
43 Kenyon 57
34 Denison 77
21 ■ Wittenberg 65
35 Case Reserve 84
54 ■ Wooster 74

OCCIDENTAL 13-12
68 ■ Pt. Loma Nazarene . 66
75 Pac. Christian 28
33 Christ-Irvine 65
47 ■ Lawrence 49
71 ■ Master's 61
60 ■ Muhlenberg 59
82 ■ Elmhurst 60
44 Chapman 45
68 ■ Millikin 59
55 Cal St. San B'dino .. 70
60 ■ Willamette 74
48 ■ Redlands 55
67 Pomona-Pitzer 72
64 ■ Claremont-M-S 49
68 ■ Whittier 47
57 ■ Southern Cal Col. .. 75
61 ■ La Verne 54
54 Cal Lutheran 59
59 Redlands 49
69 ■ Pomona-Pitzer 66
64 Claremont-M-S 67
66 Whittier 57
56 UC San Diego 76
55 La Verne 60
61 ■ Cal Lutheran 50

OGLETHORPE 9-15
57 ■ Spelman 65
73 Tenn. Temple 88
85 ■ Agnes Scott 17
72 Wesleyan (Ga.) 44
50 Sewanee 54
59 † Southwestern (Tex.) 74
82 ■ Tenn. Temple 65
50 Millsaps 86
56 Rhodes 63
59 Agnes Scott 24
62 ■ Centre 71
59 ■ Fisk 34
51 Emory 85
55 ■ Trinity (Tex.) 59
72 ■ Hendrix 70
48 Centre 82
56 Fisk 32
74 ■ Wesleyan (Ga.) 33
51 ■ Sewanee 49
62 ■ Judson 65
53 Trinity (Tex.) 67
54 Hendrix 73
51 ■ Millsaps 83
40 ■ Rhodes 56

OHIO 13-14
58 † Colorado St. 53
54 Indiana 70
81 ■ Cleveland St. 72
59 Cincinnati 72
55 Marshall 75
52 ■ Xavier (Ohio) 51
64 ■ Youngstown St. 83
45 Dayton 61
58 ■ Toledo 64
61 Kent 93
42 ■ Ball St. 31
53 Miami (Ohio) 60
62 ■ Western Mich. 53
77 Akron 52
61 Central Mich. 59
58 ■ Bowling Green 68
58 Eastern Mich. 56
75 ■ Kent 65
68 Ball St. 42
66 ■ Miami (Ohio) 76
59 Western Mich. 53
70 ■ Akron 61
45 ■ Central Mich. 55
55 Bowling Green 82
65 ■ Eastern Mich. 53
57 Toledo 72
65 Toledo 77

OHIO NORTHERN 8-18
49 Manchester 66
47 Mt. St. Joseph's ... 88
73 ■ Adrian 67
53 Muskingum 75
52 ■ Bluffton 41
55 ■ John Carroll 75
62 ■ Baldwin-Wallace ... 49
45 Hiram 59
57 ■ Carroll (Wis.) 48
62 ■ Centre 65
40 ■ Heidelberg 62
44 Mount Union 63
42 ■ Capital 72
45 Marietta 55
54 ■ Otterbein 55
64 John Carroll 71
45 ■ Muskingum 75
65 Baldwin-Wallace ... 76
51 Heidelberg 71
69 ■ Hiram 57
56 Capital 70
59 ■ Mount Union 63
66 Otterbein 63
68 ■ Marietta 58
75 ■ Otterbein 71
46 Muskingum 61

OHIO ST. 28-4
76 ■ Bowling Green 65
104 Boston College 65
81 Massachusetts 48
97 ■ Central Mich. 65
89 ■ Georgia 72
91 ■ UCLA 80
84 ■ Syracuse 55
91 ■ Virginia 84
67 Vanderbilt 70
87 ■ Illinois 57
84 Purdue 78
81 Indiana 67
90 ■ Michigan 73
78 ■ Michigan St. 57
80 Penn St. 97
70 Wisconsin 66
62 Iowa 79
99 ■ Indiana 58
72 ■ Purdue 61
88 Michigan St. 51
79 Michigan 59
73 ■ Penn St. 71
95 ■ Wisconsin 50
95 ■ Minnesota 76
58 ■ Iowa 54
76 Northwestern 66
94 Illinois 78
91 ■ Rutgers 60
86 † Western Ky. 73
75 † Virginia 73
73 † Iowa 72
82 † Texas Tech 84

OHIO WESLEYAN 21-6
64 ■ Grove City 56
74 † Wilmington (Ohio) 56
71 Muskingum 76
87 Kenyon 42
71 Allegheny 59
54 ■ Wittenberg 64
73 ■ Thomas More 63
48 Capital 73
62 ■ Denison 36
75 Case Reserve 56
75 † Goucher 35
57 St. John Fisher 59
94 Oberlin 37
66 ■ Wooster 58
86 ■ Earlham 63
72 ■ Allegheny 44
60 Wittenberg 57
64 Denison 59
90 ■ Oberlin 29
54 Bluffton 66
72 ■ Kenyon 41
68 Wooster 52
89 Earlham 60
87 ■ Case Reserve 65
85 ■ Kenyon 26
56 ■ Denison 55
60 ■ Wittenberg 67

OKLAHOMA 12-15
66 ■ Southern Methodist 72
101 ■ Prairie View 41
69 † Mercer 60
63 Arkansas St. 76
56 † Texas Tech 93
54 † Old Dominion 60
84 † Bucknell 60
84 ■ Oral Roberts 62
66 Iowa St. 55
78 Nebraska 87
92 Prairie View 56
44 Oklahoma St. 65
70 Arkansas 63
64 ■ Kansas 70
68 ■ Kansas St. 60
49 Colorado 80
63 Missouri 69
59 Texas-Arlington 80
83 ■ Nebraska 97
79 ■ Iowa St. 57
64 ■ Oklahoma St. 55
87 Kansas St. 65
54 Kansas 76
76 Texas Christian 79
49 ■ Missouri 68
74 ■ Colorado 69
70 † Oklahoma St. 85

OKLAHOMA ST. 23-9
69 ■ Texas A&M 55
60 † Tennessee 69
61 † Arkansas St. 60
68 † Illinois St. 76
65 † Wisconsin 59
75 Memphis St. 64
61 † Kentucky 57
70 Wichita St. 53
66 Mo.-Kansas City 63
105 ■ Oral Roberts 31
64 ■ Creighton 54
74 Houston 71
74 ■ Phillips (Okla.) 49
62 ■ Arkansas 47
77 Nebraska 69
67 Iowa St. 56
65 ■ Oklahoma 44
72 ■ Kansas St. 54
56 ■ Kansas 54
58 Missouri 49
76 Colorado 78
75 ■ Iowa St. 38
64 ■ Nebraska 58
55 Oklahoma 64
69 Kansas 73
63 Kansas St. 53
48 ■ Colorado 49
63 ■ Missouri 64
71 ■ Arkansas St. 63
85 † Oklahoma 70
64 † Nebraska 66
71 Southwest Mo. St. 86

OLD DOMINION 22-8
67 Va. Commonwealth 72
54 Maryland 83
63 ■ Virginia Tech 76
67 † Florida Int'l 71
60 † Oklahoma 54
71 † Michigan 63
60 ■ Tennessee 68
66 ■ Rutgers 58
65 ■ South Caro. 67
81 George Mason 48
66 American 56
75 ■ Richmond 51
71 James Madison 42
75 ■ East Caro. 39
71 ■ N.C.-Wilmington 54
64 William & Mary 48
81 ■ North Caro. St. 67
60 St. Peter's 66
64 ■ George Mason 57
75 ■ American 49
91 Richmond 66
67 ■ James Madison 44
71 East Caro. 59
83 N.C.-Wilmington 59
79 ■ William & Mary 52
75 ■ N.C.-Wilmington 42
85 ■ East Caro. 67
65 ■ William & Mary 51
77 ■ Tennessee Tech 60
56 ■ Iowa 82

OLD WESTBURY 9-11
49 † Dominican (N.Y.) 74
60 John Jay 35
65 New Jersey Tech 56
37 ■ Stony Brook 67
28 † Westfield St. 74
49 † Albertus Magnus 73
62 ■ Staten Island 70
59 Medgar Evers 22
44 ■ Dominican (N.Y.) 74
53 Mt. St. Mary (N.Y.) 76
55 ■ Vassar 65
61 ■ Baruch 35
83 ■ New Rochelle 27
80 Marymount (N.Y.) 33
52 ■ York (N.Y.) 54
76 ■ CCNY 51
62 ■ John Jay 46
54 Centenary (N.J.) 68
68 ■ Mt. St. Vincent 52
58 † Vassar 65

OLIVET 0-23
53 Madonna 100
38 Muskingum 104
45 † Wilmington (Ohio) 69
46 ■ Grand Rapids Bapt. 71
60 † Grace 76
55 Siena Heights 72
44 ■ St. Mary's (Ind.) 68
56 ■ Madonna 80
47 ■ Spring Arbor 111
39 ■ Kalamazoo 77
61 Albion 76
47 ■ Hope 91
55 Calvin 102
52 Adrian 104
52 ■ Alma 91
42 Kalamazoo 68
47 Alma 97
47 ■ Adrian 86
62 ■ Calvin 99
61 Bluffton 81
42 Hope 83
57 ■ Albion 66
55 Adrian 86

ONEONTA ST. 4-20
50 Rochester 75
47 † Ithaca 78
55 Elmira 97
56 Potsdam St. 65
50 Plattsburgh St. 63
41 Cortland St. 62
52 ■ Brockport St. 55
48 ■ Geneseo St. 80
67 ■ New Paltz St. 76
60 ■ Potsdam St. 72
64 ■ Plattsburgh St. 66
36 Binghamton 70
43 Oswego St. 60
53 ■ Utica Tech 75
60 New Paltz St. 77
62 ■ Hamilton 80
53 † Russell Sage 52
43 Union (N.Y.) 53
47 ■ Hartwick 70
53 Buffalo St. 76
56 Fredonia St. 40
48 ■ Binghamton 75
47 ■ Union (N.Y.) 43
59 ■ Cortland St. 56

OREGON 9-18
58 † Southwest Mo. St. 56
68 Vanderbilt 72
77 ■ Brigham Young 63
62 ■ DePaul 65
84 ■ Weber St. 45
81 ■ Louisville 70
85 Portland 77
83 Idaho St. 61
78 Boise St. 91
63 ■ California 75
72 ■ Stanford 91
75 UCLA 79
69 Southern Cal 78
54 ■ Washington St. 66
74 ■ Washington 87
70 Arizona 79
42 Arizona St. 79
63 ■ Oregon St. 67
61 ■ Southern Cal 80
89 ■ UCLA 78
51 Washington 59
88 Washington St. 75
63 ■ Arizona St. 77
77 ■ Arizona 63
56 Oregon St. 66
52 Stanford 86
74 California 90

OREGON ST. 15-12
62 Portland 59
89 † Boston College 54
86 Michigan St. 65
60 ■ Brigham Young 74
71 Hawaii 72
81 † Georgia 79
77 Pepperdine 60
50 San Diego St. 61
92 Long Beach St. 78
60 ■ Stanford 70
75 ■ California 73
57 Southern Cal 82
71 UCLA 67
57 ■ Washington 71
75 ■ Washington St. 55
66 Arizona St. 79
62 Arizona 69
67 Oregon 63
71 ■ UCLA 68
64 ■ Southern Cal 59
67 Washington St. 68
71 Washington 81
49 ■ Arizona 63
81 ■ Arizona St. 71
66 ■ Oregon 56
73 California 61
69 Stanford 84

OSWEGO ST. 6-18
60 Muhlenberg 71
65 † Potsdam St. 71
54 ■ Hamilton 60
63 Elmira 81
68 Utica Tech 85
66 ■ William Smith 92
56 Cortland St. 57
62 ■ Binghamton 72
52 ■ Brockport St. 66
49 Fredonia St. 66
68 Buffalo St. 87
65 ■ Geneseo St. 79
60 ■ Oneonta St. 43
66 New Paltz St. 58
78 ■ St. Lawrence 55
74 ■ Utica Tech 59
52 Geneseo St. 76
55 ■ Roberts Wesleyan 52
64 Potsdam St. 68
50 ■ Plattsburgh St. 54
49 Brockport St. 63
56 ■ Fredonia St. 41
47 ■ Buffalo St. 68
45 Le Moyne 71

OTTERBEIN 5-20
50 ■ John Carroll 72
49 ■ Muskingum 87
68 † Susquehanna 74
84 † CCNY 54
62 Hiram 71
44 Capital 81
80 Thomas More 84
61 ■ Wittenberg 72
99 Ohio Dominican 85
56 Mount Union 74
49 Heidelberg 65
45 ■ Marietta 66
62 ■ Baldwin-Wallace 76
55 Ohio Northern 54
66 ■ Mt. St. Joseph's 71
63 Muskingum 80
75 ■ Hiram 59
44 ■ Heidelberg 58
50 Marietta 64
56 ■ Capital 76
70 ■ Mount Union 67
61 John Carroll 82
63 ■ Ohio Northern 66
50 Baldwin-Wallace 82
71 Ohio Northern 75

ELMS 12-11
56 ■ Rivier 35
64 ■ Mt. St. Mary (N.Y.) 59
81 ■ MIT 61
67 ■ Regis (Mass.) 54
59 ■ Gordon 47
53 † Rutgers-Newark 70
73 † Pine Manor 47
51 Wesleyan 77
62 ■ Fitchburg St. 77
51 ■ Curry 30
42 ■ Westfield St. 77
83 Mount Holyoke 64
54 ■ Nichols 45
46 ■ Connecticut Col. 80
47 Russell Sage 61
51 Western New Eng. 67
79 Simmons 53
62 Pine Manor 68
64 Suffolk 65
48 Albertus Magnus 54
63 ■ Emmanuel 73
54 ■ Anna Maria 39
62 ■ Pine Manor 48

PACE 24-7
63 † Keene St. 59
61 St. Michael's 72
66 ■ New Haven 63

74 LIU-Southampton 40
70 ■ Molloy 49
78 ■ Sacred Heart 62
97 ■ Concordia (N.Y.) 48
70 ■ Dowling 50
73 † Clarion 89
57 Bentley 67
66 ■ St. Rose 56
46 Queens (N.Y.) 45
66 ■ Adelphi 43
59 Phila. Textile 61
62 ■ Pitt.-Johnstown 59
95 ■ LIU-Southampton 55
75 ■ Mercy 60
56 ■ Queens (N.Y.) 48
71 Dowling 50
58 St. Rose 61
72 LIU-C.W. Post 38
67 Adelphi 45
77 Molloy 60
55 ■ Phila. Textile 70
75 ■ LIU-C.W. Post 46
82 Mercy 62
82 ■ Mercy 54
84 † Adelphi 56
54 Phila. Textile 62
73 ■ Sacred Heart 66
74 ■ Keene St. 64

PACIFIC (CAL.) 19-8
86 ■ Santa Clara 90
69 Cal St. Northridge 39
67 ■ Cal St. Sacramento 54
65 Brigham Young 62
68 Weber St. 49
72 ■ Fresno St. 57
79 ■ Nevada 51
68 ■ Idaho 57
71 ■ St. Mary's (Cal.) 66
57 ■ San Jose St. 45
75 UC Santa Barb. 76
64 Long Beach St. 69
54 ■ Nevada-Las Vegas 67
83 ■ New Mexico St. 73
74 UC Irvine 58
70 Cal St. Fullerton 44
61 ■ Hawaii 64
59 ■ Hawaii 72
75 ■ Long Beach St. 55
88 ■ UC Santa Barb. 79
66 New Mexico St. 68
83 Nevada-Las Vegas 78
73 ■ Cal St. Fullerton 57
90 ■ UC Irvine 73
69 San Jose St. 51
73 Nevada 69
72 † New Mexico St. 73

PAINE 12-15
92 ■ Knoxville 52
60 ■ Talladega 62
66 ■ Morris 53
68 Georgia Col. 75
42 † West Ga. 59
104 Morris 63
60 Morris Brown 46
75 Talladega 60
66 Troy St. 97
65 ■ Alabama A&M 80
61 ■ Savannah St. 68
77 Spelman 51
54 ■ Albany St. (Ga.) 69
48 Savannah St. 74
60 ■ Clark Atlanta 48
87 ■ LeMoyne-Owen 45
65 ■ Fort Valley St. 70
46 Albany St. (Ga.) 55
71 Clark Atlanta 39
57 Tuskegee 61
61 ■ Morris Brown 54
73 Fort Valley St. 83
100 Miles 54
55 Alabama A&M 80
66 † Augusta 70
68 † Tuskegee 48
43 † Savannah St. 55

PEMBROKE ST. 10-17
55 † Cal St. Stanislaus 68
64 UC Santa Cruz 38
68 Dist. Columbia 53
57 Longwood 65
73 Coker 69
52 ■ Augusta 64
73 ■ Fayetteville St. 75
65 ■ Francis Marion 55
52 Georgia Col. 86
52 Columbus 75
71 ■ S.C.-Spartanburg 78
69 ■ Lander 63
61 Armstrong St. 73
59 ■ Wingate 79
72 S.C.-Aiken 74
54 Augusta 73
71 Francis Marion 66
67 ■ S.C.-Aiken 54
77 ■ Coker 56
78 ■ Dist. Columbia 59
62 ■ Georgia Col. 64
77 ■ Columbus 69
68 ■ St. Andrews 71
42 ■ Armstrong St. 74
51 S.C.-Spartanburg 77
52 Lander 57
60 Augusta 66

PENN ST. 22-6
85 ■ Texas 76
79 ■ Rutgers 66
82 Pittsburgh 69
67 Syracuse 43
108 Temple 48
85 DePaul 78
102 ■ Nebraska 66
101 ■ Illinois 71
75 ■ Northwestern 63
65 Indiana 71
73 Purdue 59
87 ■ Notre Dame 66
81 ■ Michigan 61
97 ■ Ohio St. 80
90 Wisconsin 73
77 Minnesota 62
59 Iowa 84
96 ■ Purdue 69
94 ■ Indiana 69
57 ■ Vanderbilt 66
87 Michigan St. 54
71 Ohio St. 73
95 ■ Wisconsin 66
70 ■ Iowa 64
99 ■ Minnesota 78
78 Illinois 62
84 Northwestern 99
67 ■ Georgetown 68

PENN ST.-BEHREND 18-8
73 ■ Brockport St. 65
49 ■ Mount Union 50
76 Allegheny 60
66 † Frostburg St. 45
63 ■ Waynesburg 68
99 ■ D'youville 31
72 ■ Hiram 63
69 Fredonia St. 31
70 Westminster (Pa.) 50
60 † Lycoming 48
62 † Wilkes 69
63 ■ Fredonia St. 43
63 ■ Bethany (W.Va.) 52
74 ■ Alfred 43
60 Waynesburg 67
67 Buffalo St. 79
63 ■ Wash. & Jeff. 67
101 Oberlin 36
71 ■ Thiel 50
81 Grove City 65
72 Bethany (W.Va.) 58
80 ■ Waynesburg 66
72 Wash. & Jeff. 83
78 Thiel 51
82 ■ Grove City 75
61 † Dickinson 63

PENNSYLVANIA 8-18
77 ■ La Salle 83
67 ■ Drexel 82
78 † Niagara 86
52 Temple 91
68 Tulane 72
49 New Orleans 69
76 Dartmouth 66
69 Harvard 92
70 Delaware 59
73 Lehigh 65
52 ■ St. Joseph's (Pa.) 78
49 ■ Villanova 59
57 ■ Princeton 74
62 Lafayette 75
40 ■ Brown 69
44 ■ Yale 71
69 Columbia-Barnard 70
69 Cornell 65
80 ■ Harvard 77
57 ■ Dartmouth 63
67 Princeton 74
75 ■ Cornell 63
64 ■ Columbia-Barnard 57
80 American 84
44 Yale 55
78 Brown 68

PEPPERDINE 15-15
82 UC Irvine 60
90 ■ Cal St. San B'dino 72
84 UC Santa Barb. 78
66 Cal St. Northridge 59
60 ■ Oregon St. 77
64 † Washington 84
76 † Southwest Mo. St. 80
66 Hawaii 80
61 Southern Cal 76
52 † UCLA 100
65 ■ California 69
86 ■ Fresno St. 55
112 ■ Cal Baptist 44
93 ■ Gonzaga 72
91 ■ Portland 66
77 San Francisco 69
79 St. Mary's (Cal.) 90
79 ■ St. Mary's (Cal.) 92
80 ■ San Francisco 87
60 Santa Clara 64
63 San Diego 54
80 ■ Cal St. Northridge 72
63 ■ San Diego 68
61 ■ Santa Clara 75
82 Loyola (Cal.) 70
100 ■ Cal St. Fullerton 68
64 Portland 69
70 Gonzaga 67
85 ■ Loyola (Cal.) 56
67 † San Diego 83

PFEIFFER 8-17
60 Catawba 103
58 ■ Limestone 61
93 Barton 79
73 ■ Mt. Olive 84
76 ■ Averett 45
60 ■ Elon 79
53 ■ Wofford 74
71 Greensboro 92
44 ■ Catawba 70
57 ■ Belmont Abbey 78
83 Averett 69
72 Coker 64
86 ■ Newberry 73
49 Davidson 62
74 St. Andrews 76
80 ■ Barton 87
100 ■ Longwood 80
60 ■ High Point 69
81 Mt. Olive 93
80 ■ Coker 65
68 Belmont Abbey 80
66 Lenoir-Rhyne 94
64 ■ St. Andrews 48
53 High Point 65
70 Mt. Olive 71

PHILA. TEXTILE 27-2
66 ■ Delaware Valley 39
75 ■ Mansfield 54
75 ■ Dowling 37
76 Bloomsburg 73
74 Kutztown 61
92 ■ West Chester 70
80 ■ Concordia (N.Y.) 43
66 ■ St. Rose 49
73 ■ Adelphi 59
82 LIU-Southampton 51
90 Mercy 58
61 ■ Pace 59
72 Molloy 57
79 ■ LIU-C.W. Post 58
71 Adelphi 61
73 Dowling 55
83 ■ Queens (N.Y.) 51
73 St. Rose 64
79 ■ Millersville 71
74 ■ Molloy 66
75 ■ Mercy 47
70 Pace 55
52 LIU-C.W. Post 62
68 Queens (N.Y.) 48
89 ■ LIU-Southampton 57
83 ■ Queens (N.Y.) 51
65 ■ St. Rose 62
62 ■ Pace 54
64 † Clarion 67

PINE MANOR 10-17
60 ■ New England Col. 61
81 ■ Castleton St. 42
69 ■ Rhode Island Col. 76
85 Salve Regina 83
52 Western New Eng. 99
75 ■ Roger Williams 44
74 ■ Babson 85
69 Coast Guard 71
47 † Elms 73
69 ■ Plymouth St. 76
73 ■ Framingham St. 54
67 Mass.-Boston 71
65 Trinity (Conn.) 85
65 Bri'water (Mass.) 85
46 ■ Worcester Tech 56
77 ■ Emerson-MCA 33
72 ■ Gordon 67
54 ■ Nichols 48
79 ■ Emmanuel 96
59 Coast Guard 51
51 ■ MIT 53
68 ■ Elms 62
47 Connecticut Col. 80
56 ■ Suffolk 59
54 Tufts 100
97 ■ Regis (Mass.) 79
48 Elms 62

PITTSBURG ST. 21-7
46 ■ John Brown 45
86 ■ Okla. Christian 82
80 † Central Okla. 68
76 † Central Ark. 68
79 † North Dak. 63
62 Northern Ky. 64
53 † Abilene Christian 48
71 † East Tex. St. 58
59 Northeastern Okla. 53
52 Mo. Southern St. 58
71 ■ Northwest Mo. St. 51
59 Southwest Baptist 61
77 Washburn 81
91 ■ Lincoln (Mo.) 49
77 Missouri-Rolla 68
81 ■ Mo. Southern St. 65

65	Mo.-St. Louis	54
77	■ Southwest Baptist	61
78	Mo. Western St.	63
75	Lincoln (Mo.)	53
75	■ Missouri-Rolla	53
91	■ Mo.-St. Louis	50
63	Central Mo. St.	64
97	■ Northeast Mo. St.	35
86	■ Emporia St.	75
70	■ Missouri-Rolla	53
57	Mo. Southern St.	71
67	† Mo. Southern St.	82

PITTSBURGH 15-12

80	Duquesne	67
59	■ Iowa	70
69	■ Penn St.	82
70	Robert Morris	50
64	■ Michigan	62
61	Kent	77
83	■ Cleveland St.	69
68	■ Delaware	51
81	■ Providence	67
64	■ Seton Hall	60
61	Villanova	56
59	Syracuse	61
74	■ Georgetown	70
69	■ Boston College	64
52	Connecticut	73
50	■ Miami (Fla.)	55
64	St. John's (N.Y.)	77
85	Providence	84
74	Georgetown	84
53	■ Villanova	70
60	■ St. John's (N.Y.)	54
59	Seton Hall	47
57	Boston College	59
76	■ Connecticut	74
57	■ Syracuse	48
65	Miami (Fla.)	77
59	† Villanova	74

PITT.-JOHNSTOWN 25-5

84	† St. Augustine's	96
107	† Holy Family	43
79	St. Thomas Aquinas	65
73	Bridgeport	33
69	■ Clarion	58
53	■ Ashland	62
89	■ Slippery Rock	50
67	Mansfield	51
65	■ Charleston (W.Va.)	63
66	Indiana (Pa.)	63
87	■ West Chester	52
87	St. Vincent	70
90	■ Davis & Elkins	38
59	Pace	62
85	Queens (N.Y.)	45
75	■ Gannon	62
65	Central St. (Ohio)	64
87	■ Cheyney	26
97	Longwood	61
82	■ West Va. Wesleyan	51
91	Notre Dame (Ohio)	60
70	■ Mercyhurst	66
84	Hilbert	39
82	West Liberty St.	62
80	■ Bloomsburg	59
46	Gannon	37
67	Mercyhurst	71
88	■ Edinboro	76
70	■ Clarion	64
63	Delta St.	96

PLATTSBURGH ST. 6-18

41	Johnson St.	54
45	■ Lyndon St.	55
42	■ New Paltz St.	68
63	■ Oneonta St.	50
57	■ Potsdam St.	85
49	Cortland St.	57
48	Binghamton	74
67	■ Albany (N.Y.)	63
61	Union (N.Y.)	58
56	Skidmore	63
52	■ Buffalo St.	76
54	■ Fredonia St.	64
56	St. Lawrence	60
54	New Paltz St.	68
66	Oneonta St.	64
42	Brockport St.	71
60	Geneseo St.	107
52	■ Cortland St.	65
43	■ Binghamton	64
56	■ Clarkson	69
60	■ Utica Tech	78
54	Oswego St.	50
62	Potsdam St.	63
75	Castleton St.	41

PLYMOUTH ST. 11-14

76	■ Bri'water (Mass.)	51
65	■ St. Joseph's (Me.)	92
54	■ Colby	60
66	■ Johnson St.	54
65	Salem St.	66
74	Emmanuel	90
84	■ Thomas	78
89	Castleton St.	29
76	Pine Manor	69
64	Southern Me.	86
74	Rhode Island Col.	82
66	Norwich	81
79	■ Framingham St.	47
75	■ Rhode Island Col.	77
90	New England Col.	73
62	■ Southern Me.	96
58	■ Eastern Conn. St.	66
64	Mass.-Boston	52
64	Mass.-Dartmouth	56
70	New England	76
60	Eastern Conn. St.	67
56	Husson	81
75	■ Mass.-Dartmouth	56
86	■ Mass.-Boston	75
45	■ Mass.-Dartmouth	52

POMONA-PITZER 13-12

88	† Dallas	68
62	† Hamline	74
47	Christ-Irvine	74
58	■ Azusa-Pacific	77
60	■ Master's	50
82	■ Pac. Christian	31
67	Pt. Loma Nazarene	87
52	■ Lawrence	60
71	■ Muhlenberg	63
76	■ Colorado Col.	57
88	UC Santa Cruz	53
62	Mills	45
72	■ Whittier	54
72	■ Occidental	67
45	La Verne	73
70	Cal Lutheran	69
64	■ Redlands	73
50	■ UC San Diego	55
63	■ Claremont-M-S	79
76	Whittier	59
66	Occidental	69
76	■ La Verne	64
87	■ Cal Lutheran	59
52	Redlands	68
69	Claremont-M-S	79

PORTLAND 12-17

97	■ Western Ore.	89
59	■ Oregon St.	62
54	Hawaii	80
68	† Illinois St.	81
56	† Arkansas St.	82
56	■ Weber St.	45
69	■ Brigham Young	76
72	■ Idaho	59
77	■ Oregon	85
77	■ Drake	61
67	■ Eastern Wash.	66
83	Portland St.	77
67	Montana St.	86
67	Montana	70
61	Loyola (Cal.)	74
66	Pepperdine	91
63	■ San Diego	65
55	■ Santa Clara	74
77	Gonzaga	88
72	■ Gonzaga	70
75	San Francisco	77
75	St. Mary's (Cal.)	58
60	■ St. Mary's (Cal.)	54
73	■ San Francisco	62
53	Santa Clara	59
52	San Diego	71
69	■ Pepperdine	64
78	■ Loyola (Cal.)	62
65	Santa Clara	87

PORTLAND ST. 21-8

99	■ St. Martin's	71
74	■ Simon Fraser	72
79	■ Pacific (Ore.)	53
72	† Northern Mont.	80
100	† Concordia (Ore.)	55
66	† Angelo St.	64
77	† Bellarmine	74
83	West Tex. St.	92
74	Humboldt St.	64
60	UC Davis	46
88	Cal St. Chico	99
87	■ Idaho	65
71	South Dak.	87
46	North Dak.	78
77	■ Portland	83
76	St. Martin's	63
78	Seattle Pacific	57
92	■ Alas. Anchorage	76
86	■ Alas. Fairbanks	35
58	Eastern Mont.	72
74	Grand Canyon	64
80	■ Western Ore.	60
82	■ Seattle Pacific	71
65	Alas. Anchorage	51
82	Alas. Fairbanks	67
83	■ Eastern Mont.	64
105	■ Grand Canyon	53
64	† UC Davis	61
51	Cal Poly Pomona	59

POTSDAM ST. 16-8

70	† Allentown	74
71	† Oswego St.	65
81	■ St. Lawrence	56
65	■ Oneonta St.	56
69	■ New Paltz St.	52
85	Plattsburgh St.	57
61	Cortland St.	57
80	■ Fredonia St.	70
109	■ Buffalo St.	105
72	Oneonta St.	60
66	New Paltz St.	74
76	■ Clarkson	72
53	Geneseo St.	76
67	Brockport St.	58
64	■ Binghamton	74
56	■ Cortland St.	73
77	St. Lawrence	57
68	■ Oswego St.	64
77	Utica Tech	78
63	■ Plattsburgh St.	62
72	Binghamton	69
72	† Utica Tech	69
60	† Buffalo St.	73
68	† Ithaca	71

PRAIRIE VIEW 2-25

28	Rice	96
42	Paul Quinn	82
65	† Tougaloo	52
42	Northwestern (La.)	119
41	Oklahoma	101
36	■ Southeastern La.	82
43	■ Jackson St.	54
47	■ Alabama St.	74
56	■ Oklahoma	92
61	Grambling	89
52	Mississippi Val.	74
98	■ Wiley	51
66	■ Alcorn St.	89
55	■ Southern-B.R.	100
45	Baylor	115
54	■ Texas Southern	71
47	Jackson St.	73
34	Alabama St.	70
69	Wiley	91
60	■ Grambling	82
56	■ Mississippi Val.	72
57	■ Rice	83
39	Alcorn St.	82
54	Southern-B.R.	81
53	■ Tex.-Pan American	57
63	Texas Southern	83
42	Southern-B.R.	84

PRESBYTERIAN 16-10

92	Converse	56
100	Flagler	47
74	Armstrong St.	70
86	■ Erskine	69
74	■ Wofford	66
67	Newberry	69
69	■ Gardner-Webb	72
57	Lander	48
84	Lenoir-Rhyne	66
59	Catawba	58
61	Elon	62
81	■ Erskine	55
72	■ Wingate	76
58	Carson-Newman	70
72	■ Mars Hill	56
80	■ Lenoir-Rhyne	63
67	Wofford	72
79	Gardner-Webb	61
80	■ Lander	65
83	■ Catawba	81
85	■ Elon	75
69	Mars Hill	73
61	Wingate	73
52	■ Carson-Newman	77
79	■ Converse	65
68	† Mars Hill	70

PRINCETON 13-13

72	Lafayette	79
91	† Niagara	84
79	■ Drexel	75
61	■ Army	57
74	■ Lehigh	34
83	■ FDU-Teaneck	57
78	† Buffalo	55
55	† William & Mary	57
43	Washington	79
63	† Drake	74
63	■ Delaware	68
59	Harvard	68
59	Dartmouth	68
63	Rider	74
74	Pennsylvania	57
68	■ Yale	62
63	■ Brown	68
67	Cornell	68
58	Columbia-Barnard	44
67	■ Dartmouth	49
58	■ Harvard	72
74	■ Pennsylvania	67
73	■ Columbia-Barnard	55
84	■ Cornell	63
56	Brown	57
60	Yale	67

PRINCIPIA 9-13

63	■ Lincoln Chrst.	56
48	Rhodes	67
42	† Emory	79
55	Eureka	75
48	■ Iowa Wesleyan	45
47	Ill. Wesleyan	74
46	■ Fontbonne	75
62	Webster	63
60	■ MacMurray	59
47	Blackburn	80

46		Maryville (Mo.)	60
60	■	Westminster	64
54		Illinois Col.	90
74	■	Greenville	45
65		Fontbonne	60
43	■	Blackburn	73
52	■	Webster	59
75		Greenville	73
74		MacMurray	61
73	■	Maryville (Mo.)	68
64		Westminster	48
61	†	Webster	81

PROVIDENCE			**15-15**
87	■	Boston U.	75
85	■	Siena	67
74	■	Montana	63
65	■	Brown	82
85	■	Rhode Island	84
82	†	Fairfield	79
68		Arizona	70
67		Pittsburgh	81
52	■	Miami (Fla.)	64
70		St. John's (N.Y.)	58
71		Villanova	69
58	■	Connecticut	74
76		Georgetown	105
103	■	Boston College	79
50		Tennessee	93
80	■	Seton Hall	77
68		Syracuse	56
84	■	Pittsburgh	85
65		Miami (Fla.)	85
88	■	St. John's (N.Y.)	82
74	■	Syracuse	65
47		Connecticut	76
86	■	Georgetown	96
70		Boston College	77
80	■	Villanova	84
68		Seton Hall	80
81	■	Boston College	71
82	■	Georgetown	81
87	■	Connecticut	73
56	■	Miami (Fla.)	77

PURDUE			**16-11**
74		Notre Dame	41
92	■	Western Mich.	64
84	■	Bradley	58
83	■	Wichita St.	75
70		Ball St.	51
68	■	Eastern Wash.	55
81	■	Bowling Green	78
65		Louisville	62
69	†	Maryland	73
56		Michigan St.	60
99		Michigan	64
78	■	Ohio St.	84
59	■	Penn St.	73
51		Minnesota	67
62	■	Northwestern	73
78		Illinois	84
57	■	Indiana	56
72	■	Wisconsin	49
69		Penn St.	96
61		Ohio St.	72
55	■	Iowa	63
72	■	Minnesota	64
62		Northwestern	70
65		Indiana	60
77		Wisconsin	57
60	■	Michigan St.	45
59	■	Michigan	56

QUEENS (N.Y.)			**7-18**
46	■	Le Moyne	64
44	†	Kutztown	58
66	†	Mercy	71
76	■	LIU-C.W. Post	61
49		Adelphi	55
75	■	LIU-Southampton	49
45	■	Pace	46
74		Concordia (N.Y.)	56
49		St. Rose	63
52		Molloy	65
56		Mercy	63
45	■	Pitt.-Johnstown	85
57		Dowling	59
48		Pace	56
58		Houghton	83
48		LIU-C.W. Post	60
67	■	Adelphi	72
63	■	Mercy	47
70		LIU-Southampton	64
64	■	Concordia (N.Y.)	48
52	■	Molloy	62
60	■	Dowling	57
48	■	Phila. Textile	68
45	■	St. Rose	46
51		Phila. Textile	83

QUEENS (N.C.)			**13-13**
67	†	Norfolk St.	90
93		Shippensburg	96
64		Belmont Abbey	79
59	■	S.C.-Spartanburg	82
60		West Va. Tech	81
86		Concord	64
73	■	Wingate	64
89	■	Catawba	99
73		Fla. Southern	92
75		Rollins	80
47		Lenoir-Rhyne	61
74	■	Winthrop	64
100	■	St. Leo	62
57		Wofford	71
97	■	Gardner-Webb	67
83		Erskine	71
66	■	Belmont Abbey	81
91		Johnson Smith	73
74		Catawba	72
80		Mars Hill	87
79	■	Longwood	56
76		Wingate	73
67	■	Erskine	57
81		S.C.-Spartanburg	83
62		Longwood	51
89	■	Johnson Smith	70

QUINCY			**12-15**
72	■	Lincoln (Mo.)	53
56	■	Missouri-Rolla	60
69	■	Northwest Mo. St.	81
79	■	St. Cloud St.	60
56		Culver-Stockton	68
61		Ferris St.	72
59	†	Indianapolis	79
65		Northeast Mo. St.	55
67		Central Mo. St.	78
73		Winona St.	76
50		Southwest Baptist	68
83		Lindenwood	68
77		Missouri Valley	64
82	■	McKendree	53
45		SIU-Edwardsville	67
58	■	Lewis	45
81		Indianapolis	89
94	■	Mo.-St. Louis	75
44		Kansas St.	62
87	■	IU/PU-Indianapolis	64
86	■	Winona St.	62
63		Wayne St. (Neb.)	74
57		Neb.-Kearney	63
64	■	SIU-Edwardsville	69
56		Ky. Wesleyan	72
69	■	Bellarmine	56
62	■	Wayne St. (Neb.)	57

QUINNIPIAC			**10-17**
56	■	Assumption	55
56		Sacred Heart	57
58		American Int'l	68
67	■	Keene St.	57
56	†	Missouri-Rolla	68
53	†	Colorado-CS	72
82	†	Mt. Mercy	101
70	■	St. Michael's	72
56		Bentley	84
76	■	Mass.-Lowell	78
50		Bryant	84
64	■	St. Anselm	60
63		New Haven	70
63		Merrimack	60
57		Springfield	52
58	■	Stonehill	70
70	■	American Int'l	51
66		St. Michael's	52
61		Assumption	68
71	■	Bryant	69
47		St. Anselm	72
62	■	Merrimack	71
64	■	Springfield	45
73		Stonehill	77
67		Southern Conn. St.	53
57	■	Bentley	60
65		American Int'l	83

RADFORD			**17-11**
90	†	Dayton	92
55		Syracuse	59
84	■	James Madison	80
59	■	Mt. St. Mary's (Md.)	71
73	■	Va. Commonwealth	86
77		Morehead St.	72
69		Charleston So.	76
59		Coastal Caro.	66
63	■	Campbell	52
79	■	N.C.-Asheville	57
68		Virginia Tech	81
58	■	Duke	59
84	■	Winthrop	63
74		Liberty	65
83	■	Coastal Caro.	56
67	■	Charleston So.	57
73		Campbell	60
61		Md.-Balt. County	57
68	■	Towson St.	60
82		N.C.-Asheville	46
81		Winthrop	74
55		Towson St.	71
71	■	Md.-Balt. County	78
77	■	Liberty	66
57		N.C.-Greensboro	74
81	■	Coastal Caro.	62
70	■	Liberty	62
62	■	N.C.-Greensboro	57

RAMAPO			**19-8**
94	■	Lincoln (Pa.)	42
71	■	Utica	48
44	■	Montclair St.	37
75	■	Stockton St.	45
54	■	Rutgers-Newark	51
50		Jersey City St.	49
79	■	Rutgers-Camden	54
83		Albertus Magnus	40
55		Trenton St.	66
68		Wm. Paterson	60
59	■	Rowan	82
94		Kean	92
65		Stockton St.	52
55		Montclair St.	71
64	■	Trenton St.	60
62		Bloomfield	64
59	■	Wm. Paterson	72
71		Manhattanville	38
69	■	Jersey City St.	45
76		Rutgers-Camden	60
49	■	Western Conn. St.	64
77	■	Kean	69
57		Rowan	78
73		Rutgers-Newark	64
58		Wm. Paterson	62
73	■	FDU-Madison	61
79	■	Rutgers-Newark	78

RANDOLPH-MACON			**14-11**
78	■	Gallaudet	84
71	■	Meredith	90
70	■	Catholic	52
91	■	St. Mary's (Md.)	59
63		Methodist	80
51		N.C. Wesleyan	59
62		Bridgewater (Va.)	54
72	■	Guilford	67
52	■	Emory & Henry	68
67	■	Roanoke	66
72		Lynchburg	53
76	■	R.-M. Woman's	34
55		East. Mennonite	53
62	■	Va. Wesleyan	65
51	■	Hollins	42
68		R.-M. Woman's	51
61		Va. Wesleyan	66
53		Hollins	62
54		Emory & Henry	55
72	■	Lynchburg	59
68		Guilford	54
69		Roanoke	74
74	■	Bridgewater (Va.)	54
72	■	East. Mennonite	56
57		Emory & Henry	63

R.-M. WOMAN'S			**4-20**
49	■	Bennett	53
28		Meredith	88
36		Bridgewater (Va.)	71
27	■	Roanoke	84
31	■	Va. Wesleyan	61
48	■	East. Mennonite	81
32		Hollins	52
31		Emory & Henry	49
27		Va. Wesleyan	81
34		Randolph-Macon	76
35	■	Guilford	62
40		Roanoke	83
53		Lynchburg	52
51	■	Randolph-Macon	68
82		Mary Baldwin	49
45	■	Hollins	58
35	■	Bridgewater (Va.)	68
42	■	Emory & Henry	57
50	■	Lynchburg	58
48		Guilford	71
57		East. Mennonite	79
76		Mary Baldwin	45
53	†	Meredith	108
57	†	Bennett	54

REDLANDS			**13-12**
63	■	Neb. Wesleyan	66
48	■	Colorado Col.	50
64	■	Biola	71
57		San Fran. St.	63
55		Sonoma St.	67
56		Azusa-Pacific	87
61	■	Cal Baptist	40
58	■	Manchester	61
81	■	Muhlenberg	79
56	■	Whitman	74
59	■	Millikin	52
55		Occidental	48
58	■	La Verne	54
54		Cal Lutheran	47
64	■	Southern Cal Col.	67
73		Pomona-Pitzer	64
57		Claremont-M-S	60
47	■	Whittier	33
49	■	Occidental	59
54	■	UC San Diego	59
71		La Verne	63
72	■	Cal Lutheran	47
68	■	Pomona-Pitzer	52
72	■	Claremont-M-S	60
62		Whittier	48

REGIS (COLO.)			**16-11**
49	†	Washburn	80
87	†	Emporia St.	91
75	■	Colorado Col.	48
70		Northern Colo.	66
78	■	Colorado Mines	47
56	■	Sonoma St.	50
67	■	North Dak. St.	86
74	■	Fort Hays St.	68
78	■	Cal St. San B'dino	82
71		Western St.	58

70 ■ Midland Lutheran 59
83 ■ Christ-Irvine 76
100 ■ McKendree 45
62 Colorado-CS 71
88 ■ Fort Lewis 44
99 ■ Southern Colo. 56
44 Denver 79
64 ■ Air Force 47
75 ■ Colo. Christian 54
55 Metropolitan St. 67
58 ■ Colorado-CS 74
72 Fort Lewis 52
60 Southern Colo. 67
73 ■ Denver 92
60 Air Force 63
70 Colo. Christian 55
73 ■ Metropolitan St. 63

REGIS (MASS.) 16-9
62 ■ Mass.-Boston 64
71 ■ MIT 51
55 Suffolk 58
70 Eastern Nazarene 34
54 Elms 67
39 Wellesley 66
55 ■ Simmons 49
50 Curry 46
65 ■ Salve Regina 56
49 Anna Maria 47
75 ■ Eastern Nazarene 45
80 ■ Roger Williams 35
81 ■ Wentworth Inst. 51
67 ■ New England Col. 74
61 Salve Regina 47
72 Wentworth Inst. 42
57 Babson 88
58 ■ Anna Maria 40
69 Roger Williams 34
58 ■ Curry 53
41 New England Col. 54
70 ■ Wentworth Inst. 47
66 † Salve Regina 55
60 † New England Col. 70
79 Pine Manor 97

RENSSELAER 12-11
56 † Albany (N.Y.) 72
63 † Union (N.Y.) 54
67 Russell Sage 61
74 St. Joseph (Vt.) 40
68 ■ Union (N.Y.) 59
73 Utica 47
55 Rochester Inst. 48
54 William Smith 71
62 ■ Hamilton 74
60 Hartwick 65
70 ■ Albany (N.Y.) 56
63 ■ St. Lawrence 41
59 ■ Clarkson 58
57 Alfred 45
37 Ithaca 68
60 ■ Amherst 62
46 ■ William Smith 66
60 ■ Rochester Inst. 61
52 ■ Ithaca 65
64 ■ Alfred 43
60 Clarkson 72
60 St. Lawrence 68
57 ■ Hartwick 54

RHODE ISLAND 11-16
77 ■ Brown 61
60 ■ Holy Cross 61
56 ■ Northeastern 53
62 † Maine 51
84 Providence 85
79 † Niagara 63
54 Montana 81
61 Manhattan 62
71 ■ Rutgers 75
69 New Hampshire 88
61 Vermont 75
83 ■ Harvard 82
54 ■ Temple 50
78 ■ St. Bonaventure 71
58 Rutgers 73
74 ■ West Va. 78
48 ■ St. Joseph's (Pa.) 67
62 Geo. Washington 68
76 Temple 62
74 ■ Central Conn. St. 50
76 Massachusetts 60
61 St. Joseph's (Pa.) 62
72 ■ Geo. Washington 82
90 St. Bonaventure 74
80 West Va. 87
69 ■ Massachusetts 70
57 † St. Joseph's (Pa.) 72

RHODE ISLAND COL. 16-7
64 Bryant 74
76 Pine Manor 69
99 Roger Williams 46
82 Fitchburg St. 67
77 ■ Bri'water (Mass.) 72
82 ■ Framingham St. 37
104 ■ Salve Regina 69
82 † Centenary (N.J.) 60
76 † Webber 71
62 † Beloit 83
64 Mass.-Dartmouth 66
82 ■ Plymouth St. 74
87 ■ Southern Me. 95
65 ■ Westfield St. 62
77 Plymouth St. 75
81 ■ Mass.-Boston 58
84 Eastern Conn. St. 79
77 ■ Mass.-Dartmouth 55
63 Gordon 57
60 Southern Me. 74
81 ■ Eastern Conn. St. 99
84 Mass.-Boston 75
56 † Eastern Conn. St. 63

RHODES 9-13
59 † Judson (Ala.) 84
59 † Southwestern (Tex.) 70
67 ■ Principia 48
58 ■ Emory 71
67 ■ Maryville (Mo.) 55
57 ■ Fontbonne 65
45 ■ Whittier 58
36 ■ Lynchburg 50
49 ■ Sewanee 42
63 ■ Oglethorpe 56
57 ■ Hendrix 60
62 ■ Trinity (Tex.) 50
74 Fisk 21
54 Centre 72
47 Hendrix 56
45 Trinity (Tex.) 59
46 ■ Millsaps 55
48 Millsaps 65
86 ■ Fisk 27
48 ■ Centre 66
70 Sewanee 46
56 Oglethorpe 40

RICE 13-14
96 ■ Prairie View 28
81 ■ N.C.-Wilmington 66
69 ■ UTEP 64
55 Loyola (Cal.) 66
72 Cal St. Northridge 63
79 St. Mary's (Cal.) 85
71 ■ Columbia-Barnard 61
55 ■ Army 48
77 ■ Texas Southern 53
73 ■ Texas A&M 83
65 Texas Christian 59
61 Tulane 59
71 ■ Baylor 72
48 Texas Tech 101
61 Texas 74
56 ■ Houston 63
60 ■ Southern Methodist 68
61 Texas A&M 73
69 ■ Texas Christian 66
68 ■ Sam Houston St. 56
83 Prairie View 57
75 Baylor 77
53 ■ Texas Tech 89
53 ■ Texas 76
70 Houston 74
65 Southern Methodist 64
61 † Texas 87

RICHMOND 11-15
73 Md.-Balt. County 78
56 ■ Auburn 59
41 ■ Wake Forest 89
87 ■ Howard 56
66 Virginia 93
60 West Va. 73
55 ■ Vermont 66
54 Fairfield 49
55 Siena 70
57 ■ William & Mary 54
63 ■ N.C.-Wilmington 58
76 ■ East Caro. 73
51 Old Dominion 75
59 James Madison 76
66 George Mason 60
73 Morgan St. 69
52 ■ American 70
49 Va. Commonwealth 73
66 N.C.-Wilmington 61
61 East Caro. 60
66 ■ Old Dominion 91
62 William & Mary 74
61 ■ George Mason 57
47 ■ James Madison 52
68 American 62
57 † American 59

RIDER 17-10
66 St. Peter's 65
56 Seton Hall 95
76 † Howard 75
70 ■ Lehigh 56
67 American 74
55 Villanova 70
57 † Georgia 97
69 ■ Marist 58
59 FDU-Teaneck 66
60 Robert Morris 48
75 St. Francis (Pa.) 60
79 Mt. St. Mary's (Md.) 93
74 ■ Princeton 63
73 ■ Monmouth (N.J.) 58
58 Wagner 50
76 ■ LIU-Brooklyn 45
92 St. Francis (N.Y.) 69
79 ■ FDU-Teaneck 72
75 Marist 78
80 ■ St. Francis (Pa.) 61
58 ■ Robert Morris 49
69 ■ Mt. St. Mary's (Md.) 57
58 ■ Wagner 61
67 Monmouth (N.J.) 94
74 ■ St. Francis (N.Y.) 62
75 LIU-Brooklyn 57
64 ■ Monmouth (N.J.) 67

RIPON 7-15
54 Edgewood 60
49 ■ Wis.-Oshkosh 66
69 North Park 59
40 Beloit 61
51 ■ St. Norbert 63
61 ■ Marian (Wis.) 46
67 Fontbonne 63
73 Maryville (Mo.) 46
66 Silver Lake 74
67 Coe 62
55 Grinnell 66
59 ■ Beloit 63
81 ■ Illinois Col. 51
79 ■ Knox 45
62 Lake Forest 74
56 ■ Carroll (Wis.) 59
66 Lawrence 75
48 St. Norbert 64
62 ■ Lake Forest 70
79 Rosary 97
57 Carroll (Wis.) 67
45 ■ Lawrence 56

ROANOKE 21-6
68 † Elizabethtown 79
60 † Bridgewater (Va.) 47
92 † Greensboro 58
79 Ferrum 64
84 R.-M. Woman's 27
52 Hollins 34
63 ■ Guilford 48
74 ■ East. Mennonite 44
66 Bridgewater (Va.) 43
66 Randolph-Macon 67
74 Va. Wesleyan 65
82 ■ Hollins 55
83 ■ R.-M. Woman's 40
77 Lynchburg 51
60 ■ Emory & Henry 65
77 East. Mennonite 62
66 ■ Bridgewater (Va.) 52
68 Guilford 80
69 ■ Maryville (Tenn.) 79
74 ■ Va. Wesleyan 61
70 ■ Lynchburg 54
74 ■ Randolph-Macon 69
60 Emory & Henry 48
66 ■ East. Mennonite 55
78 † Emory & Henry 67
75 † Bridgewater (Va.) 65
67 Maryville (Tenn.) 85

ROBERT MORRIS 8-18
64 ■ Army 69
39 ■ North Caro. 54
50 ■ Pittsburgh 70
66 Youngstown St. 74
75 Cleveland St. 71
78 ■ Niagara 91
79 ■ St. Francis (Pa.) 62
72 ■ West Va. 99
48 ■ Rider 60
61 ■ Mt. St. Mary's (Md.) 71
68 LIU-Brooklyn 48
68 Marist 71
54 FDU-Teaneck 74
64 St. Francis (N.Y.) 50
54 ■ Monmouth (N.J.) 61
50 ■ Wagner 51
68 St. Francis (Pa.) 82
46 Mt. St. Mary's (Md.) 62
49 Rider 58
60 ■ St. Francis (N.Y.) 57
58 ■ LIU-Brooklyn 54
47 ■ Buffalo 60
69 ■ Marist 72
70 ■ FDU-Teaneck 54
53 Wagner 68
66 Monmouth (N.J.) 45

ROCHESTER 11-15
75 ■ Oneonta St. 50
67 ■ Ithaca 86
70 ■ Nazareth (N.Y.) 64
64 ■ Skidmore 42
52 ■ Heidelberg 56
66 ■ Case Reserve 59
55 ■ Brandeis 67
82 ■ Roberts Wesleyan 75
47 Johns Hopkins 60
37 Washington (Mo.) 44
47 Chicago 66
56 Clark (Mass.) 65
57 Brandeis 52
53 St. John Fisher 44
90 ■ Emory 75
59 ■ New York U. 66
54 ■ Carnegie Mellon 52
56 New York U. 64
47 Emory 70
63 ■ Geneseo St. 71
46 Carnegie Mellon 55
53 ■ Chicago 56
66 ■ Washington (Mo.) 70

70 ■ William Smith 67
61 † Albany (N.Y.) 51
68 Ithaca 75

ROCHESTER INST. 6-16
41 ■ Fredonia St. 57
55 Keuka 58
58 ■ Union (N.Y.) 37
47 ■ Hamilton 64
48 ■ Rensselaer 55
50 ■ Hartwick 70
45 Roberts Wesleyan 88
43 Nazareth (N.Y.) 90
49 ■ William Smith 79
40 ■ Ithaca 72
61 ■ Alfred 40
56 St. Lawrence 67
49 Clarkson 67
25 ■ Geneseo St. 68
33 Hartwick 67
61 Rensselaer 60
42 William Smith 68
61 ■ Clarkson 64
61 ■ St. Lawrence 57
66 ■ Roberts Wesleyan 72
65 Alfred 52
55 Ithaca 51

ROCKFORD 0-25
40 ■ Mt. St. Clare 71
35 ■ William Penn 82
35 ■ Carthage 74
18 Wis.-Whitewater 100
35 Ill. Wesleyan 108
45 ■ North Park 92
38 Dubuque 85
28 Chicago 101
54 ■ Maryville (Mo.) 55
24 ■ North Central 84
46 MacMurray 66
39 Blackburn 84
35 ■ Judson 79
45 Eureka 88
40 ■ Aurora 77
40 ■ Ill. Benedictine 56
37 Concordia (Ill.) 57
47 Judson 64
33 ■ Trinity (Ill.) 85
28 Augustana (Ill.) 81
29 Aurora 80
43 Ill. Benedictine 61
58 ■ Concordia (Ill.) 73
38 Millikin 82
31 Trinity (Ill.) 74

ROGER WILLIAMS 2-21
36 ■ Suffolk 52
18 Coast Guard 73
46 ■ Rhode Island Col. 99
26 Gordon 65
26 † Castleton St. 73
44 Pine Manor 75
33 Bri'water (Mass.) 77
42 ■ Anna Maria 55
27 Rivier 61
51 ■ Curry 65
46 Eastern Nazarene 60
40 New England Col. 89
35 Regis (Mass.) 80
23 Salve Regina 68
49 ■ Wentworth Inst. 48
26 Curry 65
37 ■ Salve Regina 77
38 ■ Eastern Nazarene 47
44 ■ New England Col. 66
48 Wentworth Inst. 44
34 ■ Regis (Mass.) 69
45 Anna Maria 79
40 New England Col. 68

ROLLINS 14-13
73 ■ Barry 46
56 ■ Fla. Southern 69
76 † Bridgeport 38
60 East Stroudsburg 68
80 ■ Queens (N.C.) 75
64 ■ Northern Mich. 99
69 ■ Air Force 81
68 ■ Slippery Rock 63
82 ■ Merrimack 88
84 ■ Lee 68
74 ■ Millersville 72
56 Tampa 63
49 ■ Fla. Southern 71
66 Barry 49
87 ■ Eckerd 77
73 North Fla. 68
61 ■ St. Leo 37
69 ■ Florida Tech 83
63 Fla. Southern 77
85 ■ Barry 68
48 Eckerd 56
83 ■ North Fla. 53
79 St. Leo 41
96 ■ Converse 51
69 Florida Tech 85
68 ■ Tampa 82
63 Florida Tech 87

ROWAN 23-5
61 ■ Jersey City St. 28
59 Montclair St. 56
81 Kean 66
90 † Maryville (Tenn.) 94
80 Ferrum 60
95 Stockton St. 29
77 Rutgers-Newark 59
80 † Simpson 69
87 Salem St. 64
86 ■ Kean 57
77 ■ Wm. Paterson 74
70 ■ Kutztown 52
76 ■ Trenton St. 45
82 Ramapo 59
81 ■ Rutgers-Camden 43
84 Jersey City St. 44
70 ■ Montclair St. 52
78 Trenton St. 67
73 Wm. Paterson 87
72 ■ Stockton St. 46
86 ■ Rutgers-Newark 63
96 Rutgers-Camden 53
78 ■ Ramapo 57
64 ■ West Chester 69
66 ■ Montclair St. 54
70 ■ Wm. Paterson 73
65 ■ Wm. Paterson 55
48 † Southern Me. 75

RUST 10-14
49 ■ Lambuth 61
79 ■ Philander Smith 87
54 Ark. Baptist 70
60 Wiley 57
81 ■ Southern-N.O. 30
84 ■ Blue Mountain 66
99 ■ Wiley 62
72 ■ Xavier (La.) 90
72 Lambuth 88
71 ■ Paul Quinn 75
107 ■ Knoxville 55
53 Lane 68
69 Williams Bapt. 82
43 Arkansas Tech 98
63 Xavier (La.) 84
85 ■ LeMoyne-Owen 52
70 ■ Williams Bapt. 81
73 Philander Smith 86
67 Paul Quinn 79
122 ■ Stillman 50
82 LeMoyne-Owen 53
61 ■ Lane 65
81 Knoxville 59
84 Stillman 65

RUTGERS 22-9
66 ■ Loyola (Md.) 49
66 Penn St. 79
52 ■ Maryland 59
61 Syracuse 59
71 ■ UCLA 56
71 ■ Maine 43
67 ■ Clemson 68
80 ■ West Va. 68
75 Rhode Island 71
58 Old Dominion 66
84 St. Bonaventure 82
85 Niagara 83
74 Tennessee 93
73 ■ Rhode Island 58
60 ■ St. John's (N.Y.) 73
76 Temple 56
60 ■ St. Joseph's (Pa.) 59
76 Geo. Washington 63
65 Massachusetts 47
79 ■ Temple 42
63 ■ Army 37
94 ■ St. Bonaventure 82
76 West Va. 75
58 St. Joseph's (Pa.) 60
71 ■ Massachusetts 63
62 ■ Geo. Washington 85
88 † St. Bonaventure 72
71 † West Va. 66
59 † St. Joseph's (Pa.) 51
80 Vermont 74
60 Ohio St. 91

RUTGERS-CAMDEN 4-20
54 ■ Trenton St. 74
56 Wm. Paterson 81
51 Rutgers-Newark 65
51 ■ Jersey City St. 71
47 ■ Georgian Court 78
56 ■ Kean 68
54 Ramapo 79
60 Wilmington (Del.) 92
70 ■ Upsala 65
91 Lincoln (Pa.) 63
62 Stockton St. 55
50 Virginia St. 86
43 ■ Montclair St. 76
43 Rowan 81
67 Phila. Pharmacy 72
74 ■ Rutgers-Newark 77
52 Trenton St. 77
49 ■ Wm. Paterson 68
57 ■ Stockton St. 50
52 Jersey City St. 62
75 Kean 88
60 ■ Ramapo 76
53 ■ Rowan 96
44 Montclair St. 86

RUTGERS-NEWARK 14-12
84 ■ St. Elizabeth 59
70 Stockton St. 60
71 ■ Kean 47
65 ■ Rutgers-Camden 51
51 Ramapo 54
51 Wm. Paterson 60
59 ■ Rowan 77
62 † Wilmington (Del.) 71
69 † Hunter 58
70 † Elms 53
65 Coast Guard 52
62 ■ Jersey City St. 56
57 Trenton St. 68
61 ■ Montclair St. 67
77 Rutgers-Camden 74
69 Drew 50
74 ■ Stockton St. 55
54 Kean 87
61 Jersey City St. 70
80 ■ Wm. Paterson 73
63 Rowan 86
70 Montclair St. 71
81 ■ Trenton St. 68
64 ■ Ramapo 73
79 † New Paltz St. 78
78 Ramapo 79

SACRED HEART 16-13
88 † Merrimack 78
75 † Stonehill 68
61 Assumption 82
81 ■ St. Rose 66
57 ■ Quinnipiac 56
90 ■ Bryant 75
62 Pace 78
65 St. Anselm 86
61 † American Int'l 68
65 St. Rose 54
81 ■ Springfield 45
61 ■ Keene St. 55
64 ■ Franklin Pierce 75
76 Le Moyne 77
74 Southern Conn. St. 56
65 ■ Mass.-Lowell 70
76 Molloy 75
69 New Hamp. Col. 72
66 New Haven 56
68 ■ Le Moyne 65
80 ■ Southern Conn. St. 62
75 † Mass.-Lowell 77
53 Franklin Pierce 76
88 ■ New Haven 66
53 Keene St. 76
71 ■ New Hamp. Col. 69
68 ■ Le Moyne 59
62 Mass.-Lowell 72
66 Pace 73

SAGINAW VALLEY 20-9
62 † Findlay 74
83 † Bowie St. 51
85 Siena Heights 62
80 † Cal St. Chico 73
69 West Tex. St. 73
76 † Bellarmine 74
72 ■ Wayne St. (Mich.) 91
82 ■ Northwood 64
94 Hillsdale 70
86 Grand Valley St. 77
97 ■ Adrian 79
70 Michigan Tech 73
96 Northern Mich. 111
83 ■ Oakland 71
76 ■ Ferris St. 67
98 Lake Superior St. 96
91 Northwood 56
88 ■ Hillsdale 65
69 Wayne St. (Mich.) 87
82 ■ Grand Valley St. 62
70 ■ Michigan Tech 86
72 ■ Northern Mich. 69
85 Oakland 77
74 Ferris St. 68
91 ■ Lake Superior St. 75
72 † Northern Mich. 69
63 Michigan Tech 70
81 Indianapolis 76
58 † Michigan Tech 77

SALEM ST. 18-8
72 † St. Norbert 84
70 † East. Mennonite 58
77 ■ Southern Me. 74
66 ■ Plymouth St. 65
66 ■ Mass.-Boston 62
87 ■ Bowdoin 64
64 ■ Rowan 87
67 Mass.-Dartmouth 70
69 Gordon 42
60 Fitchburg St. 75
50 ■ Westfield St. 48
61 Framingham St. 42
84 North Adams St. 51
78 ■ Babson 66
50 ■ Bri'water (Mass.) 33
61 Worcester St. 65
63 Emmanuel 89
74 ■ Fitchburg St. 59
53 Westfield St. 56
84 ■ Framingham St. 30
65 ■ North Adams St. 47

62 Bri'water (Mass.) ... 58
72 ■ Worcester St. ... 50
63 † Fitchburg St. ... 50
57 † Westfield St. ... 47
63 Southern Me. ... 67

SALISBURY ST. 10-13
83 † Immaculata ... 48
73 Notre Dame (Md.) ... 53
81 Chris. Newport ... 74
95 ■ St. Mary's (Md.) ... 61
94 ■ Wilmington (Del.) ... 103
76 ■ Widener ... 40
78 ■ Mary Washington ... 81
62 Stockton St. ... 71
49 ■ Frostburg St. ... 63
65 ■ Shenandoah ... 66
77 ■ Goucher ... 87
75 Allentown ... 73
63 Wilmington (Del.) ... 105
93 ■ Notre Dame (Md.) ... 77
95 ■ Lincoln (Pa.) ... 39
65 Frostburg St. ... 93
63 Shenandoah ... 64
82 ■ Catholic ... 60
74 ■ Allentown ... 79
76 ■ Wesley ... 80
87 Lincoln (Pa.) ... 59
68 ■ Cabrini ... 71
64 Frostburg St. ... 89

SALVE REGINA 8-15
42 Albertus Magnus ... 84
58 Babson ... 90
83 ■ Pine Manor ... 85
40 † Connecticut Col. ... 71
36 Mass.-Dartmouth ... 71
69 Rhode Island Col. ... 104
73 ■ New England Col. ... 69
56 Regis (Mass.) ... 65
44 ■ Curry ... 55
50 Anna Maria ... 59
60 Wentworth Inst. ... 41
68 ■ Roger Williams ... 23
69 Eastern Nazarene ... 68
47 ■ Regis (Mass.) ... 61
77 Roger Williams ... 37
40 ■ Skidmore ... 56
46 Curry ... 63
59 ■ Anna Maria ... 51
62 ■ Eastern Nazarene ... 68
66 ■ Wentworth Inst. ... 59
57 New England Col. ... 80
60 Anna Maria ... 46
55 † Regis (Mass.) ... 66

SAM HOUSTON ST. 6-20
51 † UTEP ... 64
87 † N.C.-Wilmington ... 61
71 ■ Houston ... 64
62 † Lamar ... 80
55 † New Mexico St. ... 45
41 Stephen F. Austin ... 88
52 Southwest Tex. St. ... 56
64 Texas-San Antonio ... 66
51 ■ Northeast La. ... 60
49 ■ Texas A&M ... 63
51 Texas-Arlington ... 69
54 North Texas ... 52
58 ■ McNeese St. ... 77
84 ■ Nicholls St. ... 43
58 ■ Southern Methodist 79
54 ■ Texas-San Antonio ... 70
59 ■ Southwest Tex. St. ... 75
60 Northeast La. ... 76
51 Northwestern (La.) 101
56 Rice ... 68
53 ■ North Texas ... 74
55 ■ Texas-Arlington ... 59
64 ■ Northwestern (La.) ... 74
64 Nicholls St. ... 59
50 McNeese St. ... 70
53 ■ Stephen F. Austin ... 68

SAN DIEGO 16-12
66 San Diego St. ... 72
68 † Ala.-Birmingham ... 71
61 † Tenn.-Chatt. ... 75
87 Cal St. Fullerton ... 64
56 Texas Tech ... 99
64 New Mexico ... 43
90 ■ Fresno Pacific ... 61
49 ■ Stanford ... 71
56 ■ Southern Nazarene ... 55
66 ■ Cal St. Sacramento ... 52
83 ■ Cal St. Los Angeles 48
70 ■ St. Mary's (Cal.) ... 57
66 ■ San Francisco ... 49
65 Portland ... 63
53 Gonzaga ... 55
57 ■ Santa Clara ... 63
63 ■ Loyola (Cal.) ... 49
54 ■ Pepperdine ... 63
68 Pepperdine ... 63
40 Loyola (Cal.) ... 45
87 ■ Gonzaga ... 62
71 ■ Portland ... 52
63 San Francisco ... 61
54 St. Mary's (Cal.) ... 76
45 Santa Clara ... 67
83 † Pepperdine ... 67
64 Santa Clara ... 57
58 Nebraska ... 81

SAN DIEGO ST. 19-9
72 ■ San Diego ... 66
59 ■ Loyola (Cal.) ... 45
77 UCLA ... 52
51 ■ St. John's (N.Y.) ... 42
61 ■ Oregon St. ... 50
62 ■ Texas A&M ... 63
70 † Georgia ... 63
56 Villanova ... 54
63 ■ Southern Cal ... 61
78 San Francisco ... 56
58 Arizona ... 75
63 ■ Fresno St. ... 40
59 UTEP ... 70
55 New Mexico ... 44
82 ■ Colorado St. ... 59
53 ■ Wyoming ... 48
42 Utah ... 68
73 Brigham Young ... 82
58 Fresno St. ... 53
78 ■ New Mexico ... 51
53 ■ UTEP ... 54
72 Wyoming ... 78
64 Colorado St. ... 60
73 ■ Brigham Young ... 57
63 ■ Utah ... 57
62 † Fresno St. ... 38
56 Utah ... 74
68 Georgia ... 85

SAN FRANCISCO 14-12
64 ■ California ... 70
66 † St. Joseph's (Pa.) ... 80
78 † William & Mary ... 62
75 Cal St. Sacramento ... 77
57 ■ San Jose St. ... 41
80 ■ Northwestern (La.) ... 76
70 ■ Southern Utah ... 60
78 ■ Idaho St. ... 49
69 † Cal St. Fullerton ... 46
51 † Idaho ... 49
71 ■ Wisconsin ... 69
56 ■ San Diego St. ... 78
71 Santa Clara ... 69
49 San Diego ... 66
69 ■ Pepperdine ... 77
66 ■ Loyola (Cal.) ... 51
51 Loyola (Cal.) ... 54
87 Pepperdine ... 80
77 ■ Portland ... 75
80 ■ Gonzaga ... 58
69 Gonzaga ... 88
62 Portland ... 73
60 St. Mary's (Cal.) ... 78

61 ■ San Diego ... 63
61 ■ Santa Clara ... 77
72 ■ St. Mary's (Cal.) ... 68

SAN FRAN. ST. 8-17
57 ■ Cal St. Los Angeles 68
63 ■ Redlands ... 57
70 ■ Cal Lutheran ... 47
71 † Cal Poly Pomona ... 79
69 † Chapman ... 64
73 ■ UC Santa Cruz ... 38
63 ■ Cal Poly SLO ... 68
64 ■ Pt. Loma Nazarene ... 53
57 Cal St. Dom. Hills ... 61
62 UC Riverside ... 79
51 ■ Cal St. Stanislaus ... 68
47 Cal St. Hayward ... 49
68 Humboldt St. ... 79
52 Cal St. Chico ... 86
63 ■ Sonoma St. ... 66
39 UC Davis ... 79
75 ■ Mills ... 28
102 ■ Notre Dame (Cal.) ... 42
68 Sonoma St. ... 76
59 ■ UC Davis ... 74
51 ■ Cal St. Chico ... 64
47 ■ Humboldt St. ... 62
47 Cal St. Stanislaus ... 75
73 ■ Cal St. Hayward ... 74
69 Notre Dame (Cal.) ... 24

SAN JOSE ST. 5-21
56 ■ Cal St. Sacramento ... 74
63 † Southern Utah ... 64
62 † Northern Ariz. ... 50
41 San Francisco ... 57
62 ■ Northwestern (La.) ... 84
58 ■ Idaho ... 74
75 ■ Cal St. Fullerton ... 76
55 ■ Nevada ... 49
55 ■ St. Mary's (Cal.) ... 60
45 Pacific (Cal.) ... 57
85 UC Irvine ... 75
49 UC Santa Barb. ... 77
56 ■ New Mexico St. ... 71
69 ■ Nevada-Las Vegas ... 84
66 Cal St. Fullerton ... 88
66 ■ Hawaii ... 79
54 ■ Hawaii ... 91
60 ■ UC Santa Barb. ... 88
58 ■ Long Beach St. ... 59
52 Nevada-Las Vegas ... 95
72 New Mexico St. ... 80
80 ■ UC Irvine ... 62
85 ■ Cal St. Fullerton ... 68
51 ■ Pacific (Cal.) ... 69
63 Nevada ... 76
73 Long Beach St. ... 87

SANTA CLARA 19-9
90 Pacific (Cal.) ... 86
67 California ... 80
64 † Georgia ... 62
78 Hawaii ... 80
80 ■ Minnesota ... 82
82 ■ UC Santa Barb. ... 51
77 ■ Seton Hall ... 68
81 ■ Wisconsin ... 71
54 UCLA ... 63
66 ■ Texas ... 69
96 ■ Cal St. Northridge ... 61
69 ■ San Francisco ... 71
67 ■ St. Mary's (Cal.) ... 54
68 Gonzaga ... 71
74 Portland ... 55
71 Cal St. Sacramento ... 90
63 San Diego ... 57
64 ■ Pepperdine ... 60
67 ■ Loyola (Cal.) ... 47
83 Loyola (Cal.) ... 63
75 Pepperdine ... 61
59 ■ Portland ... 53
72 ■ Gonzaga ... 59
70 St. Mary's (Cal.) ... 67

77 San Francisco ... 61
67 ■ San Diego ... 45
87 ■ Portland ... 65
57 ■ San Diego ... 64

SAVANNAH ST. 24-5
66 ■ Fla. Memorial ... 48
103 ■ Voorhees ... 53
82 † Voorhees ... 59
90 † Edward Waters ... 44
93 † St. Paul's ... 55
57 † Livingstone ... 44
63 Fla. Memorial ... 36
80 ■ Edward Waters ... 47
121 ■ LeMoyne-Owen ... 55
87 ■ Wofford ... 78
68 Paine ... 61
75 ■ Fort Valley St. ... 90
69 Alabama A&M ... 66
67 Voorhees ... 56
72 ■ Clark Atlanta ... 42
74 ■ Paine ... 48
75 Fort Valley St. ... 86
72 Tuskegee ... 84
62 Clark Atlanta ... 58
69 North Fla. ... 56
70 ■ Morris Brown ... 62
66 ■ Albany St. (Ga.) ... 63
97 ■ Miles ... 65
63 Albany St. (Ga.) ... 50
60 Wofford ... 68
78 Morris Brown ... 77
78 † Miles ... 63
55 † Paine ... 43
67 † Fort Valley St. ... 75

SCRANTON 30-2
89 † Fitchburg St. ... 58
79 Wheaton (Mass.) ... 59
107 Misericordia ... 65
100 ■ FDU-Madison ... 47
96 ■ King's (Pa.) ... 56
77 † Allentown ... 56
65 † Stony Brook ... 46
77 ■ Elizabethtown ... 62
65 ■ Moravian ... 71
73 Holy Family ... 62
84 ■ Marywood ... 51
89 Upsala ... 52
91 King's (Pa.) ... 79
99 ■ Drew ... 55
78 ■ Lycoming ... 57
103 ■ Cortland St. ... 57
74 Susquehanna ... 68
71 Delaware Valley ... 45
79 Stony Brook ... 65
112 ■ Upsala ... 46
93 ■ Wilkes ... 74
91 Drew ... 39
84 ■ Delaware Valley ... 64
81 FDU-Madison ... 58
102 ■ Elizabethtown ... 73
86 ■ Susquehanna ... 55
89 ■ Moravian ... 82
103 ■ Waynesburg ... 76
82 † New York U. ... 54
79 Geneseo St. ... 70
61 † Capital ... 65
89 † St. Benedict ... 69

SEATTLE PACIFIC 17-10
88 Northwest (Wash.) ... 49
89 ■ Columbia Chrst. ... 41
95 ■ West Fla. ... 71
72 Eastern Wash. ... 77
74 ■ Western Wash. ... 63
78 Eckerd ... 51
61 Florida Tech ... 89
62 Fla. Atlantic ... 78
67 Idaho St. ... 71
89 ■ Humboldt St. ... 69
92 ■ Alas. Fairbanks ... 59
71 ■ Northwest (Wash.) ... 47
63 Puget Sound ... 55

57	■	Portland St.	78
63	■	Alas. Fairbanks	58
80	■	Alas. Anchorage	54
70		Grand Canyon	69
58		Eastern Mont.	68
61		Eastern Mont.	71
67	■	Puget Sound	77
66		Western Wash.	65
71		Portland St.	82
74	■	Seattle	82
64		Alas. Fairbanks	62
77		Alas. Anchorage	64
75	■	Grand Canyon	56
72	■	Eastern Mont.	56

SETON HALL			**14-13**
65	■	FDU-Teaneck	57
95	■	Rider	56
66	■	Massachusetts	60
61		Fairfield	50
88	■	Fordham	77
69		Monmouth (N.J.)	66
64	■	Connecticut	70
68		Santa Clara	77
67		California	83
73	■	Miami (Fla.)	59
60		Pittsburgh	64
69	■	Syracuse	41
78	■	St. John's (N.Y.)	40
64		Boston College	72
53		Connecticut	72
62	■	Georgetown	66
77		Providence	80
63		Villanova	67
65	■	Boston College	58
72		St. John's (N.Y.)	58
62		Syracuse	59
70	■	Villanova	69
47	■	Pittsburgh	59
65		Georgetown	68
60		Miami (Fla.)	72
80	■	Providence	68
54	†	Connecticut	56

SEWANEE			**8-17**
76		MacMurray	50
55		Webster	59
85		Agnes Scott	29
54	■	Oglethorpe	50
34	■	Southwestern (Tex.)	66
49		Keuka	50
57		Hilbert	43
75	■	Wesleyan (Ga.)	26
42		Rhodes	49
45		Millsaps	66
48		Emory	58
87	■	Fisk	30
51	■	Centre	71
35		Maryville (Tenn.)	90
61	■	Hendrix	52
43	■	Trinity (Tex.)	56
61	■	Fisk	19
56		Centre	73
51	■	Emory	73
49		Oglethorpe	51
55	■	Maryville (Tenn.)	89
45		Hendrix	60
55		Trinity (Tex.)	68
46	■	Rhodes	70
53	■	Millsaps	68

SHAW			**16-10**
81	■	Morris	60
46		Barber-Scotia	59
59	■	Bowie St.	46
80		Morris	63
71		Hampton	61
67		Elizabeth City St.	52
60	■	Winston-Salem	49
50	■	St. Paul's	45
53	■	Livingstone	39
67	■	N.C. Central	61
67		Voorhees	69
72	■	St. Augustine's	76
51		Virginia Union	64
68		Livingstone	58
81		Fayetteville St.	67
75		Johnson Smith	84
86		Norfolk St.	105
59	■	Voorhees	50
69		Winston-Salem	63
84	■	Fayetteville St.	66
74		N.C. Central	59
55		St. Augustine's	82
60	■	Johnson Smith	68
57	■	Virginia St.	84
80	†	Elizabeth City St.	67
43	†	Hampton	69

SHENANDOAH			**10-14**
39	†	Meredith	77
71	†	Gallaudet	67
58		Gallaudet	66
86		Washington Bible	36
41	■	Wesley	85
72	■	Notre Dame (Md.)	69
64		East. Mennonite	78
56	■	Chris. Newport	104
53	■	Frostburg St.	74
62		Lincoln (Pa.)	56
66		Salisbury St.	65
86	■	Washington (Md.)	29
61	■	Ferrum	62
82		St. Mary's (Md.)	71
66	■	Va. Intermont	62
39	■	Allentown	67
50		Frostburg St.	61
61	■	Lincoln (Pa.)	49
64	■	Salisbury St.	63
53		Notre Dame (Md.)	76
50	■	Immaculata	65
49		Mary Washington	71
57		Allentown	75
50	†	Allentown	81

SHEPHERD			**12-14**
81	■	West Va. St.	53
88	■	St. Thomas Aquinas	77
74	■	West Va. Tech	70
61	■	Wesley	69
60		Georgian Court	66
92		Caldwell	79
73	■	West Liberty St.	66
61		Davis & Elkins	56
55	■	Bluefield St.	85
61		West Va. Wesleyan	77
73		Charleston (W.Va.)	84
61		West Va. St.	62
72	■	Columbia Union	60
74		Fairmont St.	84
56	■	Wheeling Jesuit	55
75	■	Glenville St.	71
74	■	Concord	77
60		Columbia Union	67
64		West Liberty St.	66
50		Wheeling Jesuit	63
64	■	Salem-Teikyo	70
58		Alderson-Broaddus	75
68	■	Davis & Elkins	58
84	■	Fairmont St.	72
61		Concord	53
58	†	West Va. Wesleyan	71

SHIPPENSBURG			**14-12**
89	■	Concord	91
96	■	Queens (N.C.)	93
92		Kutztown	66
61		Georgian Court	50
76		Holy Family	61
68	■	Millersville	77
78	■	West Chester	67
90		Tampa	70
79		St. Leo	54
81		Eckerd	63
63	■	Mansfield	48
63	■	Bloomsburg	67
74	■	Davis & Elkins	45
58		Slippery Rock	71
74		Indiana (Pa.)	70
69	■	Calif. (Pa.)	79
85	■	Clarion	95
76	■	Lock Haven	87
87		Edinboro	99
101		Cheyney	66
85	■	Slippery Rock	89
95	■	Indiana (Pa.)	98
73		Calif. (Pa.)	90
68		Clarion	78
68		Lock Haven	59
77	■	Edinboro	58

SIENA			**11-16**
64	■	Syracuse	52
67		Providence	85
72	†	George Mason	83
58		Vermont	91
105	†	Valparaiso	97
65		Central Mich.	91
43		Massachusetts	60
70	■	Richmond	55
63	■	Dartmouth	57
59		Loyola (Md.)	78
72		St. Peter's	66
63	■	Canisius	58
76		Manhattan	82
83	■	Niagara	66
69	■	St. Peter's	72
79	■	Fairfield	68
90	■	Hofstra	76
58		Canisius	63
55	■	Loyola (Md.)	69
70		Fairfield	71
64		Niagara	84
57	■	Iona	67
81	■	Manhattan	54
61	■	Holy Cross	75
57		Iona	67
77	†	Niagara	73
66	†	Loyola (Md.)	68

SIMPSON			**11-13**
92	■	Mt. St. Clare	49
77		Grand View	97
70	■	Iowa Wesleyan	38
70		Midland Lutheran	72
69		Neb. Wesleyan	52
69	†	Rowan	80
86	†	Bowdoin	45
50		Luther	73
95		Dubuque	40
45		Rockhurst	75
76	■	Buena Vista	62
60	■	Wartburg	71
74	■	Loras	62
51		Central (Iowa)	61
70		William Penn	56
74	■	Upper Iowa	51
66	■	Luther	67
60		Loras	65
68	■	Central (Iowa)	82
60		Buena Vista	62
50		Upper Iowa	53
61	■	William Penn	71
75		Wartburg	69
83	■	Dubuque	58

SKIDMORE			**15-10**
74	■	Union (N.Y.)	52
67	■	Albany (N.Y.)	55
55		Williams	61
42		Rochester	64
53	†	Hamilton	62
61		Green Mountain	58
64		Hamilton	87
61	■	Smith	60
63	■	Plattsburgh St.	56
60		Union (N.Y.)	54
47		Hartwick	50
70	■	Clarkson	58
60	■	Manhattanville	26
49		Utica	40
28	■	Nichols	27
36	■	Hamilton	44
55		Vassar	48
53		Connecticut Col.	68
56		Salve Regina	40
65	■	North Adams St.	39
88		Castleton St.	32
68		Russell Sage	46
49		Middlebury	72
43		Albany (N.Y.)	53
41	†	Hamilton	54

SLIPPERY ROCK			**10-15**
84		Seton Hill	70
60	†	Wis.-Parkside	64
83	†	Spring Arbor	74
86	■	Mercyhurst	74
86	■	Elon	75
66	■	St. Vincent	69
61		Findlay	77
79		Oakland	86
50		Pitt.-Johnstown	89
63		Rollins	68
68		Florida Tech	105
67	■	Bloomsburg	62
69	■	Gannon	47
66		Edinboro	81
71	■	Shippensburg	58
60	■	Calif. (Pa.)	76
65		Indiana (Pa.)	87
72		Lock Haven	79
73		Clarion	75
64	■	Edinboro	74
89		Shippensburg	85
70		Calif. (Pa.)	83
71	■	Indiana (Pa.)	61
83	■	Lock Haven	79
63	■	Clarion	74

SMITH			**8-15**
50	■	North Adams St.	45
39		Norwich	53
69	†	Haverford	38
66	†	Bryn Mawr	64
57	†	Wellesley	66
70	■	Trinity (Conn.)	73
60		Skidmore	61
51		Union (N.Y.)	67
78	■	Wesleyan	75
45		Western New Eng.	47
57	■	Brandeis	55
49	■	Bates	61
60	■	Hilbert	47
43	■	Williams	60
50		Worcester Tech	47
59	■	Mount Holyoke	46
63		Babson	83
32		Tufts	75
55	■	Amherst	64
38		Wellesley	68
56	■	Wheaton (Mass.)	80
48		MIT	54
66		Brandeis	70

SONOMA ST.			**11-14**
60	†	Seattle	93
39	†	Western Wash.	62
55	†	Whitworth (Wash.)	72
67	■	Redlands	55
105		Dominican (Cal.)	42
50		Regis (Colo.)	56
48	†	Eastern Mont.	68
72	■	UC Santa Cruz	49
65	†	Cal St. Dom. Hills	59
48	†	Western Ore.	74
63		Cal St. Los Angeles	57
51		Cal Poly Pomona	63
53	■	Humboldt St.	75
52	■	Cal St. Chico	75
50		Cal St. Stanislaus	66
63	■	Cal St. Hayward	44
66		San Fran. St.	63
87	■	UC San Diego	63
52		UC Davis	77
76	■	San Fran. St.	68
54		Cal St. Hayward	40
45	■	Cal St. Stanislaus	62
70		Cal St. Chico	88

73 Humboldt St. 72
50 ■ UC Davis 72

SOUTH ALA. 9-18
82 ■ Mississippi Val. 64
66 † Long Beach St. 82
73 † N.C.-Greensboro 70
74 ■ Ala.-Birmingham 77
90 ■ Alcorn St. 79
61 ■ Northeast La. 74
66 † N.C.-Greensboro 62
70 Ga. Southern 80
79 Southwestern La. 67
42 ■ Arkansas St. 63
54 New Orleans 67
65 ■ Western Ky. 82
55 Louisiana Tech 102
55 ■ New Orleans 67
65 ■ Alabama 94
72 ■ Southwestern La. 62
66 Lamar 77
71 Tex.-Pan American 68
84 Mississippi Val. 64
41 Auburn 84
34 Arkansas St. 83
53 ■ Louisiana Tech 74
61 Western Ky. 92
58 ■ Tex.-Pan American 59
73 ■ Lamar 70
61 Ala.-Birmingham 67
58 † New Orleans 66

SOUTH CARO. 17-10
54 ■ Charleston 52
51 † Nebraska 63
64 † Yale 57
75 ■ Charleston So. 43
55 Kentucky 76
66 † Holy Cross 74
55 St. Peter's 67
66 ■ Louisiana St. 56
81 ■ South Caro. St. 63
72 ■ Mississippi St. 61
67 Alabama 82
67 Old Dominion 65
77 ■ Georgia 57
56 Furman 49
57 Mississippi 81
73 Memphis St. 68
86 ■ East Tenn. St. 53
76 ■ Arkansas 51
55 ■ Clemson 54
53 ■ Florida 74
62 N.C.-Charlotte 52
48 Vanderbilt 58
69 ■ Western Caro. 54
57 Tennessee 100
58 South Caro. St. 55
59 ■ Auburn 47
57 † Mississippi 59

SOUTH CARO. ST. 18-11
87 ■ Benedict 60
60 Clemson 87
76 Claflin 73
63 Charleston 76
41 N.C.-Charlotte 78
63 South Caro. 81
58 ■ Coppin St. 55
70 ■ Morgan St. 60
54 ■ Howard 50
72 Bethune-Cookman 41
79 Florida A&M 59
63 Md.-East. Shore 61
87 Delaware St. 75
59 ■ Arkansas 73
73 ■ Bethune-Cookman 62
70 ■ Florida A&M 85
73 ■ Charleston 61
70 ■ Md.-East. Shore 43
80 ■ Delaware St. 61
61 Georgia 72
51 North Caro. A&T 56
64 Coppin St. 67
55 Morgan St. 60
82 Howard 56
55 ■ South Caro. 58
80 ■ North Caro. A&T 53
81 † Bethune-Cookman 50
81 † Morgan St. 60
65 † Coppin St. 54

S.C.-AIKEN 8-18
63 Erskine 55
62 ■ Claflin 69
44 ■ S.C.-Spartanburg 67
59 ■ Jacksonville St. 74
70 Columbus 68
66 Morris Brown 64
59 Lander 60
53 ■ Georgia Col. 80
66 Claflin 83
58 Augusta 67
64 ■ Erskine 57
74 ■ Pembroke St. 72
57 ■ Armstrong St. 65
69 ■ Francis Marion 62
54 Pembroke St. 67
51 ■ Lander 58
76 ■ Morris Brown 77
60 S.C.-Spartanburg 95
49 ■ Augusta 65
48 Georgia Col. 63
88 ■ Newberry 74
59 Armstrong St. 71
52 Francis Marion 60
59 ■ Columbus 62
81 Newberry 70
89 † Francis Marion 93

S.C.-SPARTANBURG 28-3
78 ■ Limestone 66
82 ■ Wofford 84
82 Queens (N.C.) 59
67 S.C.-Aiken 44
79 ■ Elon 63
83 ■ Armstrong St. 57
70 ■ Kennesaw 57
81 ■ Georgia Col. 67
78 Pembroke St. 71
82 Francis Marion 51
81 ■ Columbus 69
82 Lincoln Memorial 77
86 ■ Lander 42
74 Converse 48
62 Georgia Col. 59
80 ■ Augusta 56
79 Armstrong St. 68
83 ■ Queens (N.C.) 81
72 Lander 55
95 ■ S.C.-Aiken 60
80 Mars Hill 74
68 ■ Francis Marion 42
77 Columbus 44
80 Augusta 70
77 ■ Pembroke St. 51
83 ■ Lincoln Memorial 73
73 † Francis Marion 60
80 † Georgia Col. 63
60 Augusta 69
71 ■ St. Augustine's 69
68 ■ Norfolk St. 75

SOUTH DAK. 16-11
94 ■ Mt. Marty 61
87 † Huron 56
68 Southwest St. 75
74 † Wayne St. (Neb.) 68
70 Neb.-Kearney 67
69 † Hastings 91
85 Wayne St. (Neb.) 68
90 ■ Peru St. 38
87 ■ Portland St. 71
70 ■ Morningside 86
75 ■ St. Cloud St. 44
83 ■ Mankato St. 73
73 Augustana (S.D.) 94
60 South Dak. St. 75
63 ■ Northern Colo. 61
79 ■ Nebraska-Omaha 70
66 North Dak. 85
45 North Dak. St. 87
67 Mankato St. 81
75 St. Cloud St. 55
61 ■ South Dak. St. 79
88 ■ Augustana (S.D.) 84
66 Nebraska-Omaha 64
60 Northern Colo. 59
50 ■ North Dak. St. 85
56 ■ North Dak. 72
78 Morningside 77

SOUTH DAK. ST. 17-10
72 ■ Moorhead St. 74
90 ■ Briar Cliff 43
92 ■ Dakota St. 26
73 † Mesa St. 50
75 Southern Colo. 55
56 Minn.-Duluth 73
68 Bemidji St. 66
84 Sioux Falls 59
73 ■ Bemidji St. 45
65 ■ Northern Colo. 48
60 ■ Nebraska-Omaha 51
58 North Dak. 67
59 North Dak. St. 77
64 ■ Morningside 68
75 ■ South Dak. 60
88 St. Cloud St. 55
61 Mankato St. 73
76 ■ Augustana (S.D.) 73
71 ■ North Dak. St. 88
78 ■ North Dak. 79
79 South Dak. 61
84 Morningside 67
80 ■ Mankato St. 67
90 ■ St. Cloud St. 44
62 Augustana (S.D.) 84
67 Northern Colo. 75
75 Nebraska-Omaha 59

SOUTH FLA. 10-17
110 ■ Central Fla. 55
68 Florida St. 87
63 † Hartford 59
72 ■ Western Caro. 58
67 ■ N.C.-Greensboro 74
69 ■ Texas-Arlington 62
70 ■ Ball St. 54
81 Central Fla. 78
72 ■ Ga. Southern 63
56 ■ N.C.-Charlotte 76
66 ■ George Mason 64
46 Louisville 94
76 Stetson 68
72 Tulane 89
63 Southern Miss. 91
83 ■ Virginia Tech 85
70 Va. Commonwealth 84
91 ■ Southwestern La. 58
44 ■ Louisville 69
66 Florida 80
72 Mercer 73
62 Virginia Tech 82
48 N.C.-Charlotte 72
69 ■ Tulane 89
66 ■ Southern Miss. 81
49 ■ Va. Commonwealth 87
50 † Virginia Tech 74

SOUTHEAST MO. ST. 13-13
86 ■ Southern Ind. 94
69 Chicago St. 58
60 Wis.-Milwaukee 73
81 ■ Mo.-St. Louis 58
63 Tex.-Pan American 64
64 St. Louis 51
54 ■ Wis.-Milwaukee 56
59 Tennessee St. 68
70 Austin Peay 63
75 ■ Northeastern Ill. 64
70 ■ Murray St. 67
58 ■ St. Louis 52
80 ■ Morehead St. 75
60 ■ Eastern Ky. 66
69 Tenn.-Martin 50
58 ■ Middle Tenn. St. 65
67 ■ Tennessee Tech 79
50 ■ Mo.-Kansas City 75
86 Murray St. 72
74 Morehead St. 62
58 Eastern Ky. 85
67 ■ Tennessee St. 71
77 ■ Austin Peay 45
80 ■ Tenn.-Martin 56
65 Middle Tenn. St. 75
53 Tennessee Tech 73

SOUTHEASTERN LA. 9-18
55 Louisiana St. 100
55 ■ New Orleans 93
44 ■ McNeese St. 75
55 ■ Southern Miss. 75
60 ■ Southern Methodist 71
82 Prairie View 36
68 ■ Grambling 62
60 Central Fla. 61
57 Nicholls St. 61
69 ■ Mercer 61
59 William Carey 70
40 Florida Int'l 88
62 Stetson 86
62 ■ Northwestern (La.) 72
58 ■ Georgia St. 59
62 ■ Charleston 52
53 Alabama St. 59
69 ■ Central Fla. 42
65 ■ Southwestern La. 54
59 Mercer 41
55 ■ Mississippi 81
61 ■ Florida Int'l 77
58 ■ Stetson 55
60 Georgia St. 70
53 Charleston 52
51 Memphis St. 62
65 † Mercer 67

SOUTHERN CAL 22-7
78 † Lamar 43
54 DePaul 62
101 ■ Long Beach St. 48
91 ■ Northern Ill. 64
85 ■ Cal St. Fullerton 46
76 ■ Pepperdine 61
66 ■ Michigan St. 50
61 San Diego St. 63
68 Arizona 54
86 Arizona St. 72
82 ■ Oregon St. 57
78 ■ Oregon 69
67 ■ Stanford 55
55 California 68
67 Stanford 76
73 UCLA 60
69 ■ Washington St. 63
74 ■ Washington 61
80 Oregon 61
59 Oregon St. 64
76 ■ California 71
78 Cal St. Northridge 36
66 ■ UCLA 57
46 Washington 45
55 Washington St. 52
55 ■ Arizona St. 64
78 ■ Arizona 62
78 ■ Nebraska 60
67 † Texas Tech 87

SOUTHERN COLO. 7-20
71 Cal Poly Pomona 81
73 † Cal St. Hayward 61
61 UC Riverside 67
53 ■ Northern Colo. 77
55 ■ South Dak. St. 75
66 ■ Angelo St. 57
66 ■ West Tex. St. 62
58 North Dak. 91
64 Bemidji St. 71
42 Colorado St. 106

48 Northern Colo. 77
69 ■ Abilene Christian 87
63 N.M. Highlands 85
54 ■ Colorado-CS 74
56 Regis (Colo.) 99
37 Metropolitan St. 83
79 ■ Colo. Christian 70
65 ■ Air Force 81
78 ■ Denver 81
89 ■ Fort Lewis 85
49 Colorado-CS 78
67 ■ Regis (Colo.) 60
54 ■ Metropolitan St. 72
58 Colo. Christian 60
61 Air Force 71
50 Denver 87
91 Fort Lewis 68

SOUTHERN CONN. ST. 4-23

62 ■ American Int'l 79
72 ■ Springfield 80
53 LIU-C.W. Post 56
76 ■ Concordia (N.Y.) 42
47 Adelphi 69
56 Bryant 102
60 Dowling 68
57 Albertus Magnus 40
43 ■ Keene St. 81
45 New Hamp. Col. 85
38 ■ Franklin Pierce 77
54 Mass.-Lowell 78
56 ■ Sacred Heart 74
46 Molloy 69
45 ■ Le Moyne 77
65 ■ New Haven 66
61 ■ Mass.-Lowell 82
71 Bridgeport 47
42 Franklin Pierce 91
50 Keene St. 62
62 Sacred Heart 80
61 ■ New Hamp. Col. 74
65 ■ Dowling 63
53 ■ Quinnipiac 67
62 New Haven 98
39 Le Moyne 68
62 Mass.-Lowell 88

SOUTHERN ILL. 19-10

80 ■ Northern Ill. 84
70 † Idaho St. 55
52 Colorado 64
65 ■ Tennessee Tech 66
94 Murray St. 75
74 Illinois 70
43 Arizona St. 72
81 ■ Wisconsin 79
58 Southwest Mo. St. 65
74 Wichita St. 61
73 ■ Bradley 43
73 ■ Illinois St. 64
55 Vanderbilt 85
70 Indiana St. 46
86 Northern Iowa 62
76 Creighton 82
56 Drake 61
77 ■ Murray St. 62
83 ■ Indiana St. 69
82 ■ Drake 57
92 ■ Northern Iowa 68
76 ■ Creighton 73
77 Bradley 54
77 Illinois St. 65
57 ■ Southwest Mo. St. 68
68 ■ Wichita St. 56
68 ■ Illinois St. 57
71 Creighton 69
53 Southwest Mo. St. 54

SIU-EDWARDSVILLE 20-7

83 Lewis 48
63 ■ Southern Ind. 62
75 Mo.-St. Louis 76
69 Nebraska-Omaha 66
75 † Missouri-Rolla 65
64 ■ Northeast Mo. St. 55
59 † Southwest Baptist 56
71 † Southern Ind. 75
70 ■ Lincoln (Mo.) 46
65 ■ Central Okla. 53
64 ■ Ky. Wesleyan 52
68 Central Mo. St. 86
93 Southern Ind. 102
67 ■ Quincy 45
67 Northern Ky. 60
61 ■ Central Mo. St. 65
62 ■ Wis.-Parkside 70
74 ■ Lewis 58
91 Oakland City 78
68 ■ Blackburn 46
77 ■ Northern Ky. 68
94 McKendree 69
69 Quincy 64
77 ■ Mo.-St. Louis 60
81 ■ Wayne St. (Neb.) 79
69 Indianapolis 80
83 Ky. Wesleyan 66

SOUTHERN IND. 15-15

62 SIU-Edwardsville 63
74 ■ David Lipscomb 93
94 Southeast Mo. St. 86
98 IU/PU-Indianapolis 89
75 † SIU-Edwardsville 71
93 Alas. Anchorage 85
84 Alas. Anchorage 102
59 Alas. Fairbanks 81
66 Alas. Fairbanks 74
107 ■ IU/PU-Indianapolis 85
89 ■ Ky. Wesleyan 75
79 ■ Ashland 62
78 ■ IU/PU-Ft. Wayne 72
102 ■ SIU-Edwardsville 93
87 Kentucky St. 59
87 Bellarmine 95
69 ■ St. Joseph's (Ind.) 92
89 ■ Lewis 71
73 Northern Ky. 71
60 Indianapolis 81
65 IU/PU-Ft. Wayne 63
70 Ashland 72
71 ■ Bellarmine 70
116 ■ Kentucky St. 74
73 Lewis 76
76 St. Joseph's (Ind.) 79
79 ■ Northern Ky. 91
82 ■ Indianapolis 97
77 Middle Tenn. St. 89
94 Ky. Wesleyan 107

SOUTHERN ME. 25-4

87 ■ New Paltz St. 36
71 ■ Western Conn. St. 40
86 Thomas 40
74 Salem St. 77
88 ■ New England 60
75 Husson 82
81 Colby 55
73 Eckerd 65
70 North Fla. 66
65 ■ Clark (Mass.) 51
93 ■ Bates 60
86 ■ Plymouth St. 64
72 Mass.-Dartmouth 53
95 Rhode Island Col. 87
100 Mass.-Boston 50
53 Eastern Conn. St. 52
96 Plymouth St. 62
77 ■ Mass.-Boston 47
92 ■ Bowdoin 62
74 ■ Rhode Island Col. 60
64 ■ St. Joseph's (Me.) 66
78 ■ Mass.-Dartmouth 58
88 Colby-Sawyer 38
78 ■ Eastern Conn. St. 44
73 ■ Mass.-Dartmouth 50
77 ■ Eastern Conn. St. 55
67 ■ Salem St. 63
75 † Rowan 48
56 † Capital 66

SOUTHERN METH. 20-10

70 ■ Texas-Arlington 66
72 Oklahoma 66
96 ■ North Texas 57
107 ■ Oral Roberts 72
58 Tulane 82
71 Southeastern La. 60
78 ■ Stephen F. Austin 69
69 ■ Texas 93
64 ■ Texas Tech 100
86 ■ Texas Christian 82
68 ■ Houston 76
77 Texas A&M 74
79 Sam Houston St. 58
91 ■ Baylor 89
68 Rice 60
77 Texas 99
78 Texas Tech 83
89 Texas Christian 69
73 Houston 63
90 ■ Texas A&M 77
106 † Northeastern Ill. 73
68 † Hawaii 90
68 Alas. Anchorage 60
88 Baylor 84
64 ■ Rice 65
96 ■ Houston 80
76 ■ Texas 95
76 † Nevada-Las Vegas 74
60 † Florida Int'l 59
54 † Arkansas St. 67

SOUTHERN MISS. 20-8

79 † Jackson St. 42
61 Houston 58
72 ■ Ala.-Birmingham 48
95 ■ Mississippi Val. 35
75 Southeastern La. 55
62 ■ New Orleans 75
91 ■ Murray St. 59
75 ■ Tenn.-Chatt. 70
61 Ala.-Birmingham 60
77 ■ Louisville 72
77 ■ Southwestern La. 60
63 N.C.-Charlotte 59
70 Virginia Tech 85
64 New Orleans 85
91 ■ South Fla. 63
82 ■ Louisiana St. 89
69 Tulane 71
68 Va. Commonwealth 49
57 Auburn 71
89 ■ Virginia Tech 80
62 ■ N.C.-Charlotte 45
67 ■ Va. Commonwealth 57
71 ■ Stephen F. Austin 72
71 Louisville 65
81 South Fla. 66
78 ■ Tulane 61
68 † N.C.-Charlotte 64
73 Louisville 84

SOUTHERN UTAH 12-15

74 Brigham Young 89
64 † San Jose St. 63
57 St. Mary's (Cal.) 69
63 UTEP 67
60 San Francisco 70
79 † Marist 59
78 ■ Weber St. 63
50 ■ Idaho St. 53
57 ■ Wyoming 63
64 ■ New Mexico 53
60 Loyola (Cal.) 68
70 ■ Cal St. Sacramento 80
84 ■ Grand Canyon 68
61 ■ Nevada 44
58 Idaho St. 71
65 ■ UTEP 77
69 Montana 88
57 Montana St. 71
87 ■ Cal St. Northridge 69
80 ■ Northern Ariz. 63
62 Nevada-Las Vegas 84
89 ■ Boise St. 101
59 Cal St. Northridge 51
62 Cal St. Sacramento 82
78 Nevada 73
76 Northern Ariz. 60
67 Grand Canyon 56

SOUTHERN-B.R. 20-7

99 ■ Tougaloo 59
105 Texas Col. 98
62 Houston 76
95 † Grambling 86
59 Arkansas St. 85
72 † Mercer 64
69 Bethune-Cookman 54
68 ■ Grambling 55
97 ■ Mississippi Val. 78
68 Alabama St. 55
82 Jackson St. 66
85 Texas Southern 67
100 Prairie View 55
75 ■ Alcorn St. 76
71 Louisiana St. 92
82 Grambling 61
84 Mississippi Val. 77
63 ■ Mississippi 73
62 ■ Alabama St. 69
75 ■ Jackson St. 63
111 ■ Texas Col. 50
68 ■ Texas Southern 62
81 ■ Prairie View 54
70 Alcorn St. 69
84 ■ Prairie View 42
59 ■ Jackson St. 56
68 ■ Mississippi Val. 72

SOUTHWEST BAPTIST 13-14

69 † Abilene Christian 71
62 East Tex. St. 54
108 Cal Baptist 59
99 Chapman 63
56 † SIU-Edwardsville 59
90 IU/PU-Indianapolis 78
79 ■ Central Okla. 82
79 ■ East Tex. St. 67
62 ■ Abilene Christian 67
68 ■ Quincy 50
60 Missouri-Rolla 77
58 Washburn 76
61 ■ Pittsburg St. 59
79 Northwest Mo. St. 81
78 Mo.-St. Louis 63
77 ■ Lincoln (Mo.) 65
75 ■ Missouri-Rolla 69
56 Mo. Southern St. 78
61 Pittsburg St. 77
63 ■ Emporia St. 68
57 ■ Mo.-St. Louis 55
73 Lincoln (Mo.) 66
57 ■ Mo. Southern St. 59
85 ■ Northeast Mo. St. 57
60 ■ Mo. Western St. 65
62 Central Mo. St. 74
47 Washburn 66

SOUTHWEST MO. ST. 23-9

64 ■ Arkansas 55
56 † Oregon 58
59 Vanderbilt 72
51 Kansas 65
49 ■ Montana 46
74 Hawaii 80
80 † Pepperdine 76
54 ■ Kansas 60
60 Western Ky. 59
65 ■ Southern Ill. 58
77 ■ Indiana St. 49
55 Creighton 58
69 Drake 53
84 Northern Iowa 63
94 ■ Wichita St. 64

76 ■ Bradley 53
83 ■ Illinois St. 47
84 Nebraska 88
70 Wichita St. 60
91 Illinois St. 46
95 Bradley 53
84 ■ Northern Iowa 54
73 ■ Creighton 59
95 ■ Drake 64
68 Southern Ill. 57
58 Indiana St. 63
80 ■ Bradley 55
83 ■ Drake 53
54 ■ Southern Ill. 53
86 ■ Oklahoma St. 71
86 Maryland 82
43 † Louisiana Tech 59

SOUTHWEST TEX. ST. 19-8

72 ■ Wayland Bapt. 58
80 ■ N.C.-Greensboro 56
69 ■ Long Beach St. 50
83 ■ Arizona 77
51 Colorado 78
66 Wyoming 71
63 Louisiana St. 76
80 Nicholls St. 58
81 McNeese St. 55
56 ■ Sam Houston St. 52
62 ■ Stephen F. Austin 71
47 Texas Tech 78
78 Texas-San Antonio 48
61 Northeast La. 67
84 Northwestern (La.) 77
77 ■ North Texas 60
73 ■ Texas-Arlington 57
67 Stephen F. Austin 74
75 Sam Houston St. 59
96 ■ Texas-San Antonio 43
88 ■ Northwestern (La.) 71
81 ■ Northeast La. 66
59 Texas-Arlington 51
75 North Texas 54
68 ■ Nicholls St. 59
91 ■ McNeese St. 72
58 † Northwestern (La.) 78

SOUTHWESTERN (TEX.) 13-11

59 Millsaps 77
70 † Rhodes 59
70 ■ Austin 45
57 ■ McMurry 68
74 † Oglethorpe 59
66 Sewanee 34
55 Luther 80
51 † Gust. Adolphus 82
56 ■ Hardin-Simmons 77
79 Hendrix 61
65 ■ Howard Payne 52
67 Austin 60
70 Trinity (Tex.) 69
65 ■ Huston-Tillotson 72
75 Ambassador 57
69 ■ Concordia (Tex.) 84
83 ■ Ambassador 44
72 ■ Trinity (Tex.) 56
60 ■ Hendrix 45
57 Howard Payne 81
68 McMurry 73
76 Dallas 65
46 Hardin-Simmons 78
76 Huston-Tillotson 78

SOUTHWESTERN LA. 4-22

55 † Grambling 52
48 Houston 68
53 ■ Northeast La. 76
73 ■ Nicholls St. 66
44 ■ Houston 57
67 ■ South Ala. 79
41 Louisiana St. 68
51 Arkansas St. 68
41 Lamar 81
60 Southern Miss. 77

45 Western Ky. 83
68 ■ Tex.-Pan American 55
62 South Ala. 72
50 Louisiana Tech 94
65 ■ Western Ky. 92
58 South Fla. 91
45 Fla. Atlantic 83
54 Southeastern La. 65
63 ■ Arkansas St. 102
56 New Orleans 78
56 McNeese St. 80
71 ■ Lamar 64
47 ■ New Orleans 76
53 ■ Louisiana Tech 89
61 Tex.-Pan Am. 108
37 † Western Ky. 96

SPRINGFIELD 3-22

80 Southern Conn. St. 72
59 Assumption 83
75 ■ Keene St. 85
62 ■ New Hamp. Col. 77
67 ■ New Haven 78
56 ■ St. Michael's 77
66 Franklin Pierce 67
45 Sacred Heart 81
75 ■ Bryant 64
62 Clark (Mass.) 55
41 Stonehill 66
42 American Int'l 68
45 ■ Bentley 69
52 ■ Quinnipiac 57
48 Merrimack 79
67 ■ Assumption 84
61 St. Anselm 86
64 St. Michael's 69
54 ■ Stonehill 77
60 ■ American Int'l 68
41 Bentley 70
45 Quinnipiac 64
67 ■ Merrimack 79
79 ■ St. Anselm 81
53 Bryant 82

ST. ANSELM 17-12

69 † Keene St. 88
54 † New Hamp. Col. 65
90 ■ New Haven 58
82 ■ Merrimack 67
92 St. Michael's 80
69 Mass.-Lowell 84
86 ■ Sacred Heart 65
85 † Franklin Pierce 75
77 Stonehill 70
68 ■ Stonehill 78
81 New Hamp. Col. 70
72 ■ Bentley 73
60 Quinnipiac 64
71 ■ American Int'l 76
95 ■ Bryant 80
84 Assumption 68
70 ■ St. Michael's 60
86 ■ Springfield 61
101 Merrimack 78
66 Bentley 59
72 ■ Quinnipiac 47
77 American Int'l 98
66 Bryant 78
77 ■ Assumption 76
81 Springfield 79
51 Stonehill 75
74 ■ St. Michael's 71
49 Bentley 72
73 † American Int'l 86

ST. AUGUSTINE'S 23-6

96 † Pitt.-Johnstown 84
92 Millersville 79
101 ■ N.C. Central 43
87 ■ Virginia St. 68
90 ■ Fayetteville St. 70
94 ■ Hampton 95
82 † Dowling 64
111 Tampa 95
82 Florida Tech 102

105 St. Paul's 71
72 Bowie St. 55
83 ■ Livingstone 57
80 ■ Johnson Smith 85
86 ■ Winston-Salem 47
76 Shaw 72
91 Elizabeth City St. 84
96 Fayetteville St. 82
74 N.C. Central 42
88 Voorhees 57
82 ■ Virginia Union 61
118 Winston-Salem 69
69 Johnson Smith 66
82 ■ Shaw 55
71 ■ Norfolk St. 104
95 Livingstone 79
80 † Virginia St. 65
79 † Hampton 63
77 † Norfolk St. 78
69 S.C.-Spartanburg 71

ST. BENEDICT 28-2

92 ■ Wis.-River Falls 62
88 ■ Wittenberg 70
93 Augsburg 59
90 ■ Hamline 51
79 ■ Concordia-M'head 56
68 † Augustana (Ill.) 61
74 † Wartburg 55
80 † Western Conn. St. 50
91 ■ St. Mary's (Minn.) 58
70 ■ Carleton 34
74 Macalester 61
83 ■ St. Thomas (Minn.) 66
73 Gust. Adolphus 49
66 St. Olaf 62
83 ■ Bethel (Minn.) 64
91 ■ Augsburg 53
82 Hamline 62
71 Concordia-M'head 69
74 St. Mary's (Minn.) 43
89 Carleton 62
82 ■ Macalester 50
66 St. Thomas (Minn.) 60
66 ■ St. Olaf 60
76 Bethel (Minn.) 45
86 ■ Gust. Adolphus 52
78 ■ St. Thomas (Minn.) 65
108 ■ Marymount (Va.) 75
84 ■ Concordia-M'head 57
59 Central (Iowa) 60
69 † Scranton 89

ST. BONAVENTURE 13-14

84 ■ Bucknell 82
80 ■ St. Francis (Pa.) 72
63 ■ Miami (Ohio) 56
75 ■ Iona 65
68 West Va. 75
91 ■ Niagara 83
88 Canisius 76
77 LIU-Brooklyn 67
84 Navy 77
65 William & Mary 68
87 Cornell 79
82 ■ Rutgers 84
95 ■ West Va. 77
71 Rhode Island 78
54 Massachusetts 74
90 Colgate 71
90 ■ Massachusetts 63
92 ■ Hofstra 69
67 ■ Geo. Washington 71
56 ■ St. Joseph's (Pa.) 91
82 Rutgers 94
70 Temple 80
74 ■ Rhode Island 90
76 ■ Temple 78
66 Geo. Washington 83
59 St. Joseph's (Pa.) 88
72 † Rutgers 88

ST. CLOUD ST. 3-23

60 Quincy 79
79 Northeast Mo. St. 61

72 Colorado Mines 55
70 Denver 102
39 ■ Minn.-Duluth 71
66 Bemidji St. 71
46 ■ Moorhead St. 78
76 ■ Cal St. Los Angeles 69
35 ■ North Dak. St. 100
50 ■ North Dak. 72
44 South Dak. 75
41 Morningside 96
38 Mankato St. 81
55 ■ South Dak. St. 88
52 ■ Augustana (S.D.) 115
46 Northern Colo. 96
51 Nebraska-Omaha 95
61 ■ Morningside 72
55 ■ South Dak. 75
57 ■ Mankato St. 80
62 Augustana (S.D.) 129
44 South Dak. St. 90
61 ■ Nebraska-Omaha 104
58 ■ Northern Colo. 82
44 North Dak. 88
41 North Dak. St. 117

ST. ELIZABETH 8-15

59 Rutgers-Newark 84
68 ■ Hunter 63
56 ■ Trenton St. 72
53 New Jersey Tech 43
59 ■ Cedar Crest 54
77 ■ Centenary (N.J.) 71
51 ■ Misericordia 63
45 Upsala 87
47 Marywood 77
45 Bryn Mawr 54
47 Centenary (N.J.) 73
64 ■ New Jersey Tech 57
39 Mt. St. Mary (N.Y.) 67
51 Manhattanville 36
55 † St. John Fisher 87
53 ■ Mt. St. Mary (N.Y.) 71
47 FDU-Madison 69
61 ■ Upsala 83
73 ■ Staten Island 68
50 Jersey City St. 78
69 Drew 76
71 ■ Dominican (N.Y.) 63
44 ■ FDU-Madison 75

ST. FRANCIS (N.Y.) 3-23

73 ■ LIU-C.W. Post 62
45 Fordham 100
59 Coppin St. 76
65 ■ Molloy 46
55 Hofstra 78
59 Iona 70
76 ■ Central Conn. St. 95
54 ■ Monmouth (N.J.) 56
49 ■ Wagner 67
59 ■ LIU-Brooklyn 62
53 FDU-Teaneck 70
67 Marist 87
52 ■ St. Francis (Pa.) 76
64 ■ Buffalo 62
50 ■ Robert Morris 64
60 Mt. St. Mary's 104
69 ■ Rider 92
57 Wagner 66
64 Monmouth (N.J.) 73
62 ■ Marist 79
62 ■ FDU-Teaneck 91
57 Robert Morris 60
52 St. Francis (Pa.) 81
66 LIU-Brooklyn 77
62 Rider 74
59 ■ Mt. St. Mary's (Md.) 89

ST. FRANCIS (PA.) 8-18

69 ■ Navy 82
72 St. Bonaventure 80
89 † Valparaiso 99
61 ■ Georgetown 81
50 Dayton 66

42 Marshall 60
76 ■ Duquesne 86
69 ■ American 58
62 Robert Morris 79
58 ■ Mt. St. Mary's (Md.) 65
60 ■ Rider 75
76 St. Francis (N.Y.) 52
56 LIU-Brooklyn 59
79 Marist 70
57 FDU-Teaneck 68
59 ■ Wagner 54
63 ■ Monmouth (N.J.) 77
82 ■ Robert Morris 68
61 Rider 80
67 Mt. St. Mary's (Md.) 87
81 ■ LIU-Brooklyn 66
81 ■ St. Francis (N.Y.) 52
57 ■ FDU-Teaneck 81
73 ■ Marist 82
82 Monmouth (N.J.) 64
57 Wagner 69

ST. JOHN FISHER 22-6
91 ■ Manhattanville 23
67 ■ Fredonia St. 48
68 ■ Roberts Wesleyan 37
86 ■ Dominican (N.Y.) 48
42 ■ Baldwin-Wallace 43
73 ■ Hartwick 51
88 ■ Hilbert 50
59 † Albion 55
37 Defiance 51
85 ■ Hunter 64
59 ■ Ohio Wesleyan 57
76 ■ Ithaca 73
44 ■ Rochester 53
69 Fredonia St. 53
82 ■ Buffalo St. 76
72 † Keuka 54
87 † St. Elizabeth 55
76 Elmira 61
83 Keuka 65
83 ■ Brockport St. 69
76 Nazareth (N.Y.) 55
56 Houghton 58
65 ■ Utica 21
77 ■ Cortland St. 58
57 † Stony Brook 54
51 † Hamilton 45
49 Ithaca 59
57 New York U. 64

ST. JOHN'S (N.Y.) 12-16
63 Iona 50
69 ■ Fairfield 55
55 Holy Cross 53
42 San Diego St. 51
82 Long Beach St. 76
65 ■ Northeastern 48
56 ■ Mississippi 62
52 Boston College 63
54 ■ Connecticut 51
58 ■ Providence 70
40 Seton Hall 78
47 Villanova 65
69 ■ Syracuse 54
65 Miami (Fla.) 59
72 ■ Georgetown 74
73 Rutgers 60
77 ■ Pittsburgh 64
59 Connecticut 71
58 ■ Seton Hall 72
82 Providence 88
54 Pittsburgh 60
46 ■ Villanova 56
56 Syracuse 74
68 ■ Miami (Fla.) 84
79 ■ Boston College 77
69 Georgetown 80
67 † Syracuse 50
61 † Miami (Fla.) 84

ST. JOSEPH'S (IND.) 20-7
79 ■ IU/PU-Indianapolis 65
62 Grand Valley St. 69
69 ■ Huntington 63
87 Indiana Tech 79
88 Tenn.-Martin 70
92 Wis.-Parkside 75
53 † Minn.-Duluth 65
59 Bellarmine 71
73 Kentucky St. 58
84 ■ Lewis 60
53 ■ Northern Ky. 51
54 ■ Indianapolis 70
92 Southern Ind. 69
64 Ky. Wesleyan 62
78 ■ Ashland 62
81 ■ IU/PU-Ft. Wayne 72
79 IU/PU-Indianapolis 62
71 ■ Wis.-Parkside 54
74 Lewis 62
65 Indianapolis 67
67 Northern Ky. 65
66 ■ Ky. Wesleyan 44
79 ■ Southern Ind. 76
69 IU/PU-Ft. Wayne 61
74 Ashland 84
79 ■ Bellarmine 82
111 ■ Kentucky St. 57

ST. JOSEPH'S (ME.) 24-5
69 † Mount Holyoke 25
92 Plymouth St. 65
96 ■ Me.-Farmington 75
76 ■ Franklin Pierce 87
82 † Clark (Mass.) 67
75 Montclair St. 66
94 New England 86
89 ■ Thomas 63
62 † Viterbo 64
87 † Ill. Benedictine 57
72 † St. Ambrose 68
67 ■ Husson 70
71 Johnson St. 44
68 Lyndon St. 57
75 Babson 74
96 ■ New England 80
76 Me.-Farmington 62
98 ■ Emmanuel 84
78 ■ St. Thomas Aquinas 66
67 ■ Colby 57
85 Norwich 66
66 Southern Me. 64
96 ■ Me.-Presque Isle 71
85 Thomas 74
76 Husson 66
90 ■ Lyndon St. 56
72 † Me.-Farmington 58
58 † Husson 64
64 † Peru St. 81

ST. JOSEPH'S (PA.) 21-8
83 ■ Villanova 57
80 † San Francisco 66
53 Virginia 64
68 † Wagner 50
51 Connecticut 53
67 ■ La Salle 56
96 ■ Fordham 51
64 ■ Alabama 71
57 ■ Delaware 38
68 Iona 48
86 Manhattan 64
77 ■ Geo. Washington 80
78 Pennsylvania 52
83 West Va. 67
56 Massachusetts 65
67 Rhode Island 48
59 Rutgers 60
69 ■ Temple 47
91 St. Bonaventure 56
62 ■ Rhode Island 61
61 Temple 54
68 ■ Massachusetts 57
60 ■ Rutgers 58
52 Geo. Washington 72
77 ■ West Va. 61
88 ■ St. Bonaventure 59
72 † Rhode Island 57
74 Geo. Washington 67
51 † Rutgers 59

ST. LAWRENCE 5-17
56 Potsdam St. 81
58 Hamilton 79
43 † Utica Tech 78
54 ■ Clarkson 69
30 Ithaca 64
49 Alfred 63
29 Le Moyne 66
60 ■ Plattsburgh St. 56
41 Rensselaer 63
61 Hartwick 71
60 Utica 58
67 ■ Rochester Inst. 56
44 ■ William Smith 86
55 Oswego St. 78
65 ■ Alfred 60
59 ■ Ithaca 83
57 ■ Potsdam St. 77
57 Rochester Inst. 61
55 William Smith 81
57 Clarkson 76
59 ■ Hartwick 71
68 ■ Rensselaer 60

ST. LEO 3-21
66 ■ Lindsey Wilson 85
61 Flagler 71
53 Armstrong St. 75
77 Webber 71
49 ■ Armstrong St. 67
54 ■ Shippensburg 79
62 Queens (N.C.) 100
74 Belmont Abbey 97
50 Florida Tech 106
57 ■ Tampa 82
56 Eckerd 83
52 ■ Fla. Southern 93
66 Barry 78
37 Rollins 61
81 ■ Southeastern Bible 46
56 North Fla. 69
63 Tampa 83
70 ■ Webber 74
68 ■ Eckerd 69
46 Fla. Southern 93
82 ■ Barry 68
41 ■ Rollins 79
64 ■ North Fla. 80
52 ■ Florida Tech 105

ST. LOUIS 5-21
57 ■ Western Ill. 61
52 ■ Ball St. 41
42 Evansville 62
51 ■ Southeast Mo. St. 64
63 ■ Wis.-Milwaukee 76
58 ■ Jackson St. 40
72 ■ Northeastern Ill. 53
68 Chicago St. 70
62 Cincinnati 87
52 Southeast Mo. St. 58
59 ■ Northern Iowa 78
46 ■ Ala.-Birmingham 71
61 ■ Valparaiso 90
47 ■ Memphis St. 82
51 Marquette 79
61 Wis.-Milwaukee 72
57 DePaul 87
71 ■ Cincinnati 60
49 Northeastern Ill. 68
58 ■ Marquette 77
66 ■ Chicago St. 58
55 Memphis St. 85
46 Ala.-Birmingham 68
31 ■ Mo.-Kansas City 64
40 ■ DePaul 76
39 † Cincinnati 79

ST. MARY'S (CAL.) 12-14
73 ■ Northern Ariz. 61
69 ■ Southern Utah 57
64 † Eastern Wash. 79
67 † Howard 61
76 ■ Boise St. 87
49 ■ Northwestern 63
85 ■ Rice 79
57 Montana St. 91
67 † Weber St. 69
72 † Iowa St. 51
66 Pacific (Cal.) 71
60 San Jose St. 55
57 San Diego 70
54 Santa Clara 67
54 ■ Loyola (Cal.) 52
90 ■ Pepperdine 79
92 Pepperdine 79
61 Loyola (Cal.) 72
76 ■ Gonzaga 61
58 ■ Portland 75
54 Portland 60
71 Gonzaga 87
78 ■ San Francisco 60
67 ■ Santa Clara 70
76 ■ San Diego 54
68 San Francisco 72

ST. MARY'S (IND.) 14-7
64 Lake Forest 74
73 † Chicago 74
103 Ind.-South Bend 63
77 Hope 72
112 ■ Ind.-South Bend 56
69 ■ Millikin 54
68 Olivet 44
72 ■ Kalamazoo 60
82 Concordia (Ill.) 67
77 ■ St. Francis (Ind.) 61
63 Chicago 62
63 ■ Manchester 67
62 ■ Albion 64
63 North Central 56
89 Bethel (Ind.) 85
82 ■ Grace 74
85 ■ Goshen 52
48 Beloit 64
56 Carroll (Wis.) 81
81 ■ Aurora 74
53 ■ Wheaton (Ill.) 67

ST. MARY'S (MD.) 1-21
76 ■ Averett 89
94 ■ Stockton St. 82
59 Randolph-Macon 91
61 Salisbury St. 95
45 † Chris. Newport 111
48 Elizabethtown 106
36 ■ Mary Washington 60
66 ■ Gallaudet 74
25 Wesley 74
40 Goucher 70
43 ■ Catholic 79
52 ■ York (Pa.) 114
71 ■ Shenandoah 82
42 Mary Washington 78
65 Gallaudet 90
73 ■ Goucher 83
40 ■ Marymount (Va.) 95
48 York (Pa.) 77
46 ■ Notre Dame (Md.) 63
41 Catholic 68
36 Marymount (Va.) 105
32 Mary Washington 77

ST. MICHAEL'S 16-11
77 ■ Bridgeport 43
86 ■ Middlebury 65
90 ■ Mansfield 43
72 ■ Pace 61
80 ■ St. Anselm 92
76 ■ Mass.-Lowell 69
77 Springfield 56
81 New Hamp. Col. 62
77 ■ Franklin Pierce 72

72 Quinnipiac 70
74 ■ American Int'l 58
82 ■ Assumption 66
73 Bryant 80
75 ■ Stonehill 88
69 Merrimack 67
79 Bentley 83
60 St. Anselm 70
52 ■ Quinnipiac 66
69 ■ Springfield 64
73 Assumption 62
84 ■ Bryant 77
59 Stonehill 79
77 ■ Merrimack 78
66 ■ Bentley 74
72 American Int'l 69
71 St. Anselm 74
67 † Keene St. 70

ST. NORBERT 11-10

84 † Salem St. 72
71 Buffalo St. 73
61 ■ Wis.-Eau Claire 79
39 Wis.-Oshkosh 71
63 Ripon 51
62 ■ Wis.-Whitewater 63
57 ■ Carroll (Wis.) 59
66 ■ Wis.-La Crosse 60
68 ■ Beloit 60
99 Cornell College 49
70 Monmouth (Ill.) 57
64 ■ Lawrence 79
70 ■ Grinnell 51
80 ■ Coe 73
76 Carroll (Wis.) 72
73 ■ Lake Forest 69
55 Beloit 73
64 ■ Ripon 48
61 Lawrence 68
53 Lake Forest 59
74 Wis.-Stevens Point 79

ST. OLAF 14-11

82 ■ Dr. Martin Luther 36
63 ■ Luther 62
73 ■ South Dak. Tech 76
59 ■ N'western (Minn.) 54
55 St. Thomas (Minn.) 80
72 ■ Wis.-Stout 82
86 ■ Macalester 92
90 ■ Carleton 57
70 ■ Bethel (Minn.) 66
80 ■ St. Mary's (Minn.) 56
70 Concordia-M'head 79
71 ■ Hamline 62
77 Augsburg 47
62 ■ St. Benedict 66
60 Gust. Adolphus 54
70 ■ St. Thomas (Minn.) 74
71 Macalester 66
82 Bethel (Minn.) 85
77 St. Mary's (Minn.) 55
68 ■ Concordia-M'head 91
68 Hamline 61
60 St. Benedict 66
62 ■ Gust. Adolphus 69
60 Carleton 47
94 ■ Augsburg 65

ST. PAUL'S 4-19

50 ■ Benedict 76
55 † Savannah St. 93
61 † Elizabeth City St. 47
67 ■ Winston-Salem 50
71 ■ St. Augustine's 105
52 ■ Hampton 77
45 Shaw 50
51 Virginia Union 78
83 ■ Fayetteville St. 87
55 ■ Norfolk St. 84
53 ■ N.C. Central 69
64 Bowie St. 58
48 ■ Virginia St. 95
72 ■ Virginia Union 79

62 Elizabeth City St. 68
75 ■ Johnson Smith 100
56 Elizabeth City St. 67
57 ■ Bowie St. 69
66 Hampton 76
86 Livingstone 65
60 Norfolk St. 86
42 Virginia St. 74
50 † Johnson Smith 67

ST. PETER'S 18-11

65 ■ Rider 66
66 Liberty 69
64 † Appalachian St. 74
65 ■ Maine 55
81 ■ Fordham 68
67 ■ South Caro. 55
68 ■ Holy Cross 60
61 James Madison 84
63 ■ Geo. Washington 65
68 Hartford 60
77 ■ Manhattan 53
66 ■ Siena 72
68 ■ Iona 55
52 Fairfield 58
64 ■ Canisius 49
72 Siena 69
67 ■ Loyola (Md.) 50
58 ■ Fairfield 57
66 Niagara 68
77 Canisius 70
66 ■ Old Dominion 60
68 Manhattan 75
62 Iona 52
59 Loyola (Md.) 64
98 ■ Niagara 76
67 † Iona 53
77 † Fairfield 75
72 † Loyola (Md.) 64
44 Miami (Fla.) 61

ST. ROSE 14-12

66 Kutztown 71
66 Sacred Heart 81
53 ■ Le Moyne 74
71 Molloy 70
58 ■ Adelphi 68
55 ■ East Stroudsburg 60
54 ■ Sacred Heart 65
49 Phila. Textile 66
56 Pace 66
52 ■ Molloy 53
63 ■ Queens (N.Y.) 49
70 LIU-Southampton 66
58 LIU-C.W. Post 48
63 Dowling 55
61 Mercy 59
76 Adelphi 79
61 ■ Pace 58
64 ■ Phila. Textile 73
66 ■ Concordia (N.Y.) 38
76 ■ LIU-C.W. Post 58
71 ■ Dowling 68
86 ■ LIU-Southampton 49
63 ■ Mercy 56
46 Queens (N.Y.) 45
73 ■ Molloy 65
62 Phila. Textile 65

ST. THOMAS (MINN.) 19-7

82 ■ Wis.-Stevens Point 51
81 Chris. Newport 50
71 Norfolk St. 74
76 Catholic 40
80 ■ St. Olaf 55
79 Bethel (Minn.) 59
81 ■ St. Mary's (Minn.) 54
76 ■ Wis.-River Falls 53
96 ■ Hamline 49
46 ■ Concordia-M'head 47
80 Carleton 36
66 St. Benedict 83
75 Macalester 59
73 ■ Gust. Adolphus 59
77 Augsburg 30

74 St. Olaf 70
45 ■ Bethel (Minn.) 62
68 St. Mary's (Minn.) 49
57 Concordia-M'head 70
72 ■ Carleton 46
60 ■ St. Benedict 66
65 Gust. Adolphus 55
87 ■ Augsburg 48
71 Hamline 69
70 ■ Macalester 40
65 St. Benedict 78

STANFORD 26-6

75 ■ Texas Tech 67
72 † Illinois St. 50
85 Hawaii 56
73 † Tennessee 74
85 ■ UC Santa Barb. 52
85 ■ Harvard 63
76 ■ Florida 66
79 Tennessee 84
98 Long Beach St. 61
71 San Diego 49
87 ■ Texas 64
70 Oregon St. 60
91 Oregon 72
89 ■ California 63
55 Southern Cal 67
79 ■ UCLA 70
76 ■ Southern Cal 67
78 Washington St. 44
70 Washington 73
69 ■ Arizona 52
85 ■ Arizona St. 80
59 California 64
71 UCLA 54
68 Connecticut 54
86 ■ Washington 62
100 ■ Washington St. 56
86 Arizona St. 76
79 Arizona 60
86 ■ Oregon 52
84 ■ Oregon St. 69
93 ■ Georgia 60
67 † Colorado 80

STATEN ISLAND 9-15

112 ■ New Rochelle 22
48 ■ New York U. 74
98 Medgar Evers 57
43 Stony Brook 79
52 Worcester St. 67
55 † Mass.-Dartmouth 67
70 Old Westbury 62
65 Baruch 54
49 ■ Hunter 45
54 ■ Wilmington (Del.) 96
42 ■ Jersey City St. 43
46 ■ Mt. St. Vincent 56
45 ■ John Jay 43
39 ■ Concordia (N.Y.) 69
38 Albany (N.Y.) 74
57 † Emmanuel 87
62 Manhattanville 60
60 ■ King's (N.Y.) 87
46 Georgian Court 79
55 ■ York (N.Y.) 48
44 CCNY 66
68 St. Elizabeth 73
73 ■ York (N.Y.) 54
51 Hunter 84

STEPHEN F. AUSTIN 28-5

81 Houston 70
78 † Arkansas St. 58
71 † Tennessee 94
67 Hawaii 63
84 ■ New Mexico St. 70
84 ■ Lamar 58
70 ■ Tennessee Tech 56
88 ■ Sam Houston St. 41
69 Southern Methodist 78
96 Texas-San Antonio 63
71 Southwest Tex. St. 62

70 ■ Northeast La. 59
77 ■ Northwestern (La.) 74
83 North Texas 59
70 Texas-Arlington 52
89 ■ Nicholls St. 48
86 ■ McNeese St. 60
63 ■ Louisiana Tech 78
74 ■ Southwest Tex. St. 67
76 ■ Texas-San Antonio 60
80 Northwestern (La.) 75
73 Northeast La. 77
81 ■ Louisiana St. 68
74 ■ Texas-Arlington 60
82 ■ North Texas 64
72 Southern Miss. 71
81 McNeese St. 68
93 Nicholls St. 53
68 Sam Houston St. 53
72 ■ Northeast La. 53
77 ■ Northwestern (La.) 75
89 ■ Clemson 78
56 ■ Vanderbilt 59

STETSON 8-19

67 Bethune-Cookman 72
63 † Memphis St. 92
84 † Nicholls St. 60
42 North Caro. 97
62 N.C.-Greensboro 69
86 ■ Dartmouth 83
86 ■ Furman 105
73 ■ Ball St. 53
43 Ga. Southern 97
66 Florida A&M 98
50 ■ Florida Int'l 97
85 Charleston 87
59 Georgia St. 65
68 ■ South Fla. 76
79 ■ Central Fla. 69
86 ■ Southeastern La. 62
68 Mercer 75
71 ■ Buffalo 74
70 ■ Fla. Atlantic 104
55 Florida Int'l 102
47 ■ Charleston 58
58 ■ Georgia St. 47
75 Central Fla. 66
55 Southeastern La. 58
55 ■ Florida 87
85 ■ Mercer 80
56 † Charleston 76

STOCKTON ST. 2-22

82 St. Mary's (Md.) 94
46 † Hollins 60
60 ■ Rutgers-Newark 70
55 Jersey City St. 62
45 Ramapo 75
29 ■ Rowan 95
48 ■ Kean 63
66 ■ Georgian Court 76
28 Montclair St. 76
55 ■ Rutgers-Camden 62
71 ■ Salisbury St. 62
51 Kean 68
48 ■ Wm. Paterson 67
40 ■ Trenton St. 76
52 ■ Ramapo 65
42 ■ Wesley 56
55 Rutgers-Newark 74
32 ■ Jersey City St. 53
87 Lincoln (Pa.) 46
50 Rutgers-Camden 57
46 Rowan 72
26 ■ Montclair St. 63
40 Trenton St. 76
49 Wm. Paterson 65

STONEHILL 22-8

61 Mass.-Lowell 79
68 † Sacred Heart 75
60 ■ American Int'l 63
73 New Hamp. Col. 55
64 Bryant 55

82	■ Adelphi	47
70	■ St. Anselm	77
85	Barry	65
60	Fla. Atlantic	85
78	St. Anselm	68
70	New Haven	65
66	■ Springfield	41
59	■ Merrimack	57
88	St. Michael's	75
51	Bentley	70
70	Quinnipiac	58
76	■ Bryant	52
77	■ Assumption	75
60	American Int'l	57
77	Springfield	54
79	Merrimack	56
79	■ St. Michael's	59
71	■ Bentley	59
77	■ Quinnipiac	73
82	Assumption	46
75	■ St. Anselm	51
68	■ Bryant	63
86	† American Int'l	71
64	Bentley	75
78	† Mass.-Lowell	84

STONY BROOK		**16-9**
72	■ Coast Guard	53
97	■ Drew	67
79	■ Staten Island	43
67	Old Westbury	37
61	Ithaca	60
46	† Scranton	65
82	Mt. St. Vincent	40
59	† Wartburg	76
58	† Augustana (Ill.)	73
76	† Amherst	54
68	■ John Jay	25
40	Western Conn. St.	70
58	■ Mt. St. Mary (N.Y.)	47
84	■ CCNY	28
53	Cortland St.	55
61	Binghamton	58
39	New York U.	69
65	■ Scranton	79
70	Hunter	41
63	■ Albany (N.Y.)	70
67	■ Vassar	37
84	■ York (N.Y.)	42
67	Wm. Paterson	63
74	■ Clark (Mass.)	60
54	† St. John Fisher	57

SUSQUEHANNA		**19-7**
67	■ Wash. & Jeff.	58
64	■ Carnegie Mellon	67
65	Gettysburg	71
59	Lycoming	49
72	■ Juniata	75
74	† Otterbein	68
71	Kean	58
65	■ Wilkes	47
72	■ Lycoming	63
74	■ Bridgeport	39
66	Messiah	60
68	■ Scranton	74
81	■ York (Pa.)	50
73	■ Elizabethtown	69
54	■ Bloomsburg	60
87	Albright	75
72	Wilkes	56
73	■ Messiah	57
72	Juniata	58
70	■ Lebanon Valley	46
86	Elizabethtown	85
84	■ King's (Pa.)	48
61	■ Frank. & Marsh.	60
80	■ Delaware Valley	58
55	Scranton	86
55	Moravian	56

SWARTHMORE		**4-18**
56	■ Chestnut Hill	28
50	■ Ursinus	80
51	Widener	53
35	† Wellesley	62
34	† Vassar	51
32	† Simmons	41
38	■ Albright	60
60	■ Lebanon Valley	47
28	■ Muhlenberg	90
35	Haverford	38
26	■ Moravian	84
40	Albright	75
53	■ Eastern (Pa.)	43
50	■ Bryn Mawr	52
34	Ursinus	83
32	Muhlenberg	68
43	Cabrini	62
33	■ Notre Dame (Md.)	52
27	Moravian	95
45	■ Widener	67
48	■ Haverford	32
35	Neumann	49

SYRACUSE		**6-21**
52	Siena	64
58	■ Manhattan	73
59	■ Radford	55
43	■ Penn St.	67
59	■ Rutgers	61
45	Detroit Mercy	63
86	■ Marquette	74
55	Ohio St.	84
50	■ Connecticut	78
49	■ Georgetown	63
41	Seton Hall	69
61	■ Pittsburgh	59
53	■ Miami (Fla.)	65
54	St. John's (N.Y.)	69
50	Villanova	60
67	Boston College	59
56	■ Providence	68
40	Miami (Fla.)	60
54	Connecticut	85
59	■ Seton Hall	62
65	Providence	74
64	Georgetown	75
74	■ St. John's (N.Y.)	56
37	■ Villanova	64
48	Pittsburgh	57
73	■ Boston College	60
50	† St. John's (N.Y.)	67

TAMPA		**14-12**
74	Flagler	56
51	† Fla. Southern	73
76	† Barry	71
82	■ Webber	70
71	■ Dowling	50
95	■ St. Augustine's	111
55	■ West Ga.	65
84	■ Mich.-Dearborn	53
70	■ Shippensburg	90
106	■ Flagler	43
68	■ Husson	74
63	■ Rollins	56
82	St. Leo	57
63	■ Florida Tech	77
77	North Fla.	70
81	Eckerd	52
60	■ Fla. Southern	106
63	Barry	64
83	■ St. Leo	63
68	Florida Tech	102
79	■ North Fla.	64
75	■ Eckerd	48
57	Fla. Southern	80
48	■ Barry	63
82	Rollins	68
54	† Fla. Southern	58

TEMPLE		**8-19**
30	Virginia	74
53	Delaware	74
88	† La Salle	79
91	■ Pennsylvania	52
84	■ Canisius	62
64	■ Detroit Mercy	77
48	■ Penn St.	108
35	† Colorado	64
67	† Bucknell	53
55	† Brown	61
63	■ Massachusetts	66
49	■ Villanova	54
50	Rhode Island	54
64	Central Conn. St.	62
46	Massachusetts	40
55	West Va.	72
39	Geo. Washington	78
56	■ Rutgers	76
47	St. Joseph's (Pa.)	69
62	■ Rhode Island	76
42	Rutgers	79
54	■ St. Joseph's (Pa.)	61
80	■ St. Bonaventure	70
64	■ Geo. Washington	83
78	St. Bonaventure	76
71	■ West Va.	78
55	Geo. Washington	73

TENNESSEE		**29-3**
69	† Oklahoma St.	60
94	† Stephen F. Austin	71
74	† Stanford	73
89	■ N.C.-Charlotte	45
83	Louisiana Tech	76
84	■ Stanford	79
73	† Geo. Washington	53
72	Maryland	77
68	Old Dominion	60
79	■ Notre Dame	48
95	Louisiana St.	61
109	■ Mississippi St.	62
70	Auburn	59
64	■ Mississippi	53
93	■ Rutgers	74
60	■ DePaul	48
86	Alabama	74
93	■ Providence	50
73	Vanderbilt	68
72	Texas	58
85	■ Kentucky	61
78	Youngstown St.	54
71	■ Georgia	68
90	■ Memphis St.	46
100	■ South Caro.	57
88	Florida	75
95	Eastern Ky.	58
72	Arkansas	55
72	† Georgia	73
89	■ Northwestern	66
74	† North Caro.	54
56	Iowa	72

TENNESSEE ST.		**18-9**
60	Missouri	67
71	† Alabama St.	52
79	Georgia St.	74
88	■ Florida A&M	71
83	■ Georgia St.	77
82	Tenn.-Chatt.	77
84	Mercer	73
65	Florida A&M	73
68	■ Southeast Mo. St.	59
80	■ Murray St.	74
78	Middle Tenn. St.	72
69	Morehead St.	76
85	Eastern Ky.	90
80	■ Tenn.-Chatt.	66
84	■ Tenn.-Martin	66
64	Tennessee Tech	82
85	■ Austin Peay	68
76	■ Morehead St.	67
65	■ Eastern Ky.	84
103	■ Middle Tenn. St.	105
85	Tenn.-Martin	62
70	■ Mercer	66
71	Southeast Mo. St.	67
83	Murray St.	72
70	■ Tennessee Tech	83
91	Austin Peay	74
80	Tennessee Tech	85

TENNESSEE TECH		**22-7**
82	■ Tenn.-Chatt.	72
81	■ Florida	61
66	Southern Ill.	65
71	■ Ga. Southern	63
65	■ Western Ky.	49
56	Stephen F. Austin	70
72	† Florida St.	88
58	† Northwestern	72
68	Mississippi	70
68	■ Eastern Ky.	59
82	■ Morehead St.	49
109	Austin Peay	70
101	Tenn.-Martin	59
93	■ Cincinnati	71
91	■ Middle Tenn. St.	72
82	■ Tennessee St.	64
93	Murray St.	71
79	Southeast Mo. St.	67
94	■ Tenn.-Martin	62
91	■ Austin Peay	62
71	Middle Tenn. St.	77
84	Eastern Ky.	75
89	Morehead St.	73
83	Tennessee St.	70
76	■ Murray St.	85
73	■ Southeast Mo. St.	53
85	■ Tennessee St.	80
80	■ Middle Tenn. St.	73
60	Old Dominion	77

TENN.-CHATT.		**15-13**
72	Tennessee Tech	82
69	Nevada-Las Vegas	83
75	† San Diego	61
73	■ Middle Tenn. St.	79
72	Middle Tenn. St.	84
81	■ Georgia St.	63
77	■ Tennessee St.	82
91	† Grambling	83
70	Southern Miss.	75
98	Austin Peay	71
65	Ga. Southern	56
82	Western Caro.	56
80	Furman	76
66	Tennessee St.	80
66	■ East Tenn. St.	79
84	■ Appalachian St.	77
60	Clemson	74
71	Marshall	64
61	■ Ga. Southern	66
69	■ Western Caro.	65
61	Georgia St.	56
85	East Tenn. St.	72
68	Appalachian St.	67
67	■ Georgia Tech	68
77	■ Marshall	60
75	■ Furman	90
91	† Western Caro.	66
73	† Ga. Southern	83

TENN.-MARTIN		**2-23**
103	■ Bethel (Tenn.)	88
63	Georgia St.	82
69	Memphis St.	95
63	† Wisconsin	83
70	■ St. Joseph's (Ind.)	88
94	East Tenn. St.	102
67	Appalachian St.	94
76	■ Georgia St.	78
85	Murray St.	88
59	■ Tennessee Tech	101
54	■ Middle Tenn. St.	76
95	Austin Peay	90
66	Tennessee St.	84
50	■ Southeast Mo. St.	69
61	Eastern Ky.	92
76	Morehead St.	84
62	Tennessee Tech	94
73	Middle Tenn. St.	81
68	■ Murray St.	80

55 ■ Austin Peay 65
62 ■ Tennessee St. 85
89 ■ Memphis St. 101
56 Southeast Mo. St. .. 80
76 ■ Eastern Ky. 95
69 ■ Morehead St. 77

TEXAS 22-8
76 Penn St. 85
81 ■ Arizona 57
86 ■ Creighton 69
109 ■ Oral Roberts 68
73 ■ Vanderbilt 78
75 † Clemson 78
72 † Maine 34
76 ■ Washington St. 51
64 Stanford 87
69 Santa Clara 66
82 ■ Texas Christian 59
93 Southern Methodist 69
82 ■ Baylor 66
76 Texas Tech 75
72 ■ Mo.-Kansas City ... 45
70 Houston 66
74 ■ Rice 61
58 ■ Tennessee 72
79 Texas A&M 63
99 ■ Southern Methodist 77
89 Baylor 75
67 ■ Texas Tech 77
97 ■ Houston 68
76 Rice 53
75 Texas Christian 50
76 ■ Texas A&M 64
87 † Rice 61
95 Southern Methodist 76
71 † Texas Tech 78
78 ■ Louisiana Tech 82

TEXAS A&M 15-12
55 Oklahoma St. 69
59 † Louisville 63
80 † Eastern Mich. 78
84 ■ Tulane 67
75 UC Irvine 50
63 San Diego St. 62
61 Colorado 92
66 Wyoming 75
96 ■ Oral Roberts 49
83 Rice 73
58 Houston 60
63 Sam Houston St. ... 49
58 ■ Louisiana St. 57
79 ■ Texas Christian 74
74 ■ Southern Methodist 77
89 Baylor 73
68 Texas Tech 91
63 ■ Texas 79
73 ■ Rice 61
66 ■ Houston 61
61 Mo.-Kansas City ... 60
70 Texas Christian 60
77 Southern Methodist 90
92 ■ Baylor 70
59 ■ Texas Tech 89
64 Texas 76
61 † Baylor 63

TEXAS A&I 6-20
89 † Chapman 64
55 West Tex. St. 62
53 Wayland Bapt. 97
63 † Mississippi Col. 75
94 † Adams St. 76
77 Texas Southern 86
46 Texas-San Antonio . 73
48 St. Edward's 78
71 Incarnate Word 57
62 ■ Texas Southern 72
68 Tex.-Pan American . 76
68 ■ St. Edward's 73
62 Abilene Christian ... 80
56 Angelo St. 74
66 ■ East Tex. St. 76

51 ■ Eastern N. Mex. 94
69 ■ Texas Woman's 62
64 Central Okla. 67
67 Cameron 83
88 ■ Cameron 90
64 ■ Central Okla. 94
46 ■ Angelo St. 65
85 ■ Abilene Christian ... 74
76 Texas Woman's 58
65 Eastern N. Mex. 78
69 East Tex. St. 76

TEXAS CHRISTIAN 10-17
86 ■ North Texas 68
80 † LIU-Brooklyn 67
80 Harvard 72
85 ■ Tex.-Pan American . 52
69 ■ UTEP 61
61 North Texas 66
91 † Navy 60
85 † Mississippi St. 108
90 † Kent 106
72 ■ Idaho 54
59 Texas 82
74 ■ Baylor 83
59 ■ Rice 65
82 Southern Methodist 86
74 Texas A&M 79
76 ■ Oral Roberts 62
65 ■ Texas Tech 111
73 Houston 86
78 Baylor 103
66 Rice 69
69 ■ Southern Methodist 89
60 ■ Texas A&M 70
79 ■ Oklahoma 76
74 Texas Tech 103
50 ■ Texas 75
76 ■ Houston 60
50 † Texas Tech 107

TEXAS SOUTHERN 11-16
86 ■ Texas A&I 77
64 Washington St. 84
38 † Bradley 75
90 ■ Texas Col. 61
78 ■ Texas-San Antonio . 62
63 Texas-San Antonio . 76
41 Miami (Fla.) 98
64 Florida Int'l 78
72 Texas A&I 62
53 Rice 77
47 ■ Alabama St. 68
51 ■ Jackson St. 55
77 Mississippi Val. 90
63 Grambling 79
67 ■ Southern-B.R. 85
58 ■ Alcorn St. 61
85 Texas Col. 45
71 Prairie View 54
61 Alabama St. 58
63 Jackson St. 65
77 ■ Mississippi Val. 87
90 ■ Grambling 85
62 Southern-B.R. 68
76 Alcorn St. 73
83 ■ Prairie View 63
90 † Alcorn St. 88
63 † Mississippi Val. 74

TEXAS TECH 31-3
67 Stanford 75
79 ■ Tex.-Pan American . 36
91 ■ Northwestern (La.) . 67
96 ■ New Mexico 38
99 ■ San Diego 56
74 ■ Louisiana Tech 71
93 † Oklahoma 56
70 † Florida Int'l 66
75 Miami (Fla.) 74
90 † Washington 74
55 Utah 72
78 ■ Southwest Tex. St. . 47
93 ■ Houston 41

100 Southern Methodist 64
75 ■ Texas 76
101 ■ Rice 48
111 Texas Christian 65
91 ■ Texas A&M 68
96 Baylor 76
88 Houston 70
83 ■ Southern Methodist 78
77 Texas 67
89 Rice 53
103 ■ Texas Christian 74
89 Texas A&M 59
104 ■ Baylor 72
107 † Texas Christian 50
91 † Baylor 67
78 † Texas 71
70 ■ Washington 64
87 † Southern Cal 67
79 † Colorado 54
60 † Vanderbilt 46
84 † Ohio St. 82

TEXAS WOMAN'S 5-19
81 ■ Concordia (Tex.) ... 71
69 ■ Tex. Wesleyan 71
66 Tex. Wesleyan 69
65 ■ St. Mary's (Tex.) ... 64
71 † Cameron 70
66 Central Okla. 79
43 ■ West Tex. St. 72
37 Cal St. Hayward 39
65 Cal St. Stanislaus .. 82
76 ■ Mary Hardin-Baylor 70
54 Eastern N. Mex. 76
64 ■ Cameron 60
66 ■ Central Okla. 85
63 East Tex. St. 81
62 Texas A&I 69
70 ■ Abilene Christian ... 72
52 ■ Angelo St. 59
61 Angelo St. 77
75 Abilene Christian ... 92
67 Central Okla. 80
55 Cameron 61
58 ■ Texas A&I 76
59 ■ East Tex. St. 71
66 ■ Eastern N. Mex. 95

TEXAS-ARLINGTON 11-16
66 Southern Methodist 70
64 ■ Eastern Ill. 49
68 ■ Wichita St. 61
64 ■ New Mexico 47
43 Arkansas 70
62 South Fla. 69
58 ■ Northwestern (La.) . 71
53 ■ Northeast La. 74
46 Mo.-Kansas City ... 66
62 ■ North Texas 59
51 McNeese St. 59
59 Nicholls St. 44
69 ■ Sam Houston St. ... 51
52 ■ Stephen F. Austin .. 70
63 Texas-San Antonio . 70
57 Southwest Tex. St. . 73
80 ■ Oklahoma 59
46 North Texas 59
72 ■ Nicholls St. 49
80 ■ McNeese St. 69
60 Stephen F. Austin .. 74
59 Sam Houston St. ... 55
51 ■ Southwest Tex. St. . 59
53 ■ Texas-San Antonio . 44
66 Northwestern (La.) . 76
46 Northeast La. 56
47 Northwestern (La.) . 65

UTEP 18-10
71 ■ Baylor 55
64 † Sam Houston St. ... 51
64 Rice 69
51 New Mexico St. 58
61 Texas Christian 69
75 ■ Texas-San Antonio . 47

67 ■ Southern Utah 63
69 ■ New Mexico St. 47
70 Western Mich. 44
60 ■ Oral Roberts 50
54 Texas-San Antonio . 32
75 Utah 71
55 Brigham Young 80
70 ■ San Diego St. 59
65 ■ Fresno St. 48
77 Southern Utah 65
60 ■ New Mexico 45
73 Wyoming 69
54 Colorado St. 41
57 ■ Brigham Young 61
51 ■ Utah 55
51 Fresno St. 64
54 San Diego St. 53
70 New Mexico 73
72 ■ Colorado St. 48
64 ■ Wyoming 66
68 † Wyoming 55
48 † Brigham Young 63

TEX.-PAN AMERICAN 6-21
51 ■ Texas-San Antonio . 54
36 Texas Tech 79
59 † Oral Roberts 85
52 Texas Christian 85
47 Texas-San Antonio . 50
64 ■ Southeast Mo. St. .. 63
59 ■ St. Mary's (Tex.) ... 60
55 New Orleans 98
52 ■ Wichita St. 72
57 † Army 67
60 † Columbia-Barnard . 63
76 ■ Texas A&I 68
44 Arkansas St. 74
43 ■ Arkansas St. 93
55 Southwestern La. .. 68
43 ■ Louisiana Tech 83
33 Western Ky. 87
68 ■ South Ala. 71
42 Louisiana Tech 82
60 ■ Western Ky. 90
58 Lamar 54
62 ■ Lamar 75
57 Prairie View 53
59 South Ala. 58
52 ■ New Orleans 66
108 ■ Southwestern La. .. 61
53 † Arkansas St. 70

TEXAS-SAN ANTONIO 11-15
54 Tex.-Pan American . 51
73 ■ Texas A&I 46
50 ■ Tex.-Pan American . 47
62 Texas Southern 78
76 ■ Texas Southern 63
47 UTEP 75
61 McNeese St. 72
60 Nicholls St. 78
63 ■ Stephen F. Austin .. 96
66 ■ Sam Houston St. ... 64
32 ■ UTEP 54
48 ■ Southwest Tex. St. . 78
52 Northwestern (La.) . 80
58 Northeast La. 65
70 ■ Texas-Arlington 63
65 ■ North Texas 64
60 ■ Schreiner 49
70 Sam Houston St. ... 54
60 Stephen F. Austin .. 76
63 ■ McNeese St. 59
43 Southwest Tex. St. . 96
50 ■ Northeast La. 74
65 ■ Northwestern (La.) . 93
63 North Texas 66
44 Texas-Arlington 53
58 ■ Nicholls St. 42

THIEL 7-17
67 Lake Erie 78
91 ■ Hilbert 53
72 ■ Carlow 67
64 Westminster (Pa.) .. 65

77 Hilbert 64
60 ■ Allegheny 57
92 ■ Oberlin 41
54 ■ Hiram 76
55 Geneva 78
65 ■ Lake Erie 57
77 ■ Malone 87
50 ■ Grove City 75
65 Wash. & Jeff. 81
58 Bethany (W.Va.) 81
59 ■ Geneva 66
50 Penn St.-Behrend 71
49 Waynesburg 93
53 Grove City 63
64 Carlow 53
56 ■ Wash. & Jeff. 79
72 ■ Bethany (W.Va.) 82
51 ■ Penn St.-Behrend 78
55 ■ Waynesburg 76
65 ■ Carnegie Mellon 83

THOMAS MORE 12-14
89 ■ Asbury 45
47 † Findlay 90
93 † Va. Intermont 65
80 ■ Earlham 82
84 Berea 79
84 ■ Otterbein 80
63 Ohio Wesleyan 73
78 Ohio Dominican 89
71 Denison 81
55 DePauw 61
110 ■ Berea 82
71 Bluffton 68
87 ■ Wilmington (Ohio) 94
77 ■ Brescia 82
99 Asbury 91
70 Defiance 82
64 ■ Bluffton 75
71 Wilmington (Ohio) 84
63 ■ Centre 76
69 ■ Defiance 78
83 ■ Ky. Christian 50
71 ■ DePauw 60
80 Anderson 72
74 ■ Franklin 71
64 Defiance 74
67 † Bluffton 63

TOLEDO 18-10
90 Michigan 67
68 † Alabama St. 59
38 Missouri 68
78 ■ Detroit Mercy 70
72 ■ Ill.-Chicago 62
63 Wyoming 64
80 Colorado St. 85
86 ■ Cleveland St. 64
64 Ohio 58
81 ■ Central Mich. 69
77 Bowling Green 88
75 ■ Eastern Mich. 58
64 ■ Akron 50
58 Kent 79
53 ■ Ball St. 38
46 Miami (Ohio) 66
59 ■ Western Mich. 49
54 Central Mich. 60
46 ■ Bowling Green 70
62 Eastern Mich. 52
84 Akron 69
68 ■ Kent 79
75 Ball St. 46
84 ■ Miami (Ohio) 65
70 Western Mich. 51
72 ■ Ohio 57
77 ■ Ohio 65
55 † Bowling Green 83

TOWSON ST. 12-16
51 Mt. St. Mary's (Md.) 73
57 Lafayette 66
45 † Coppin St. 56
51 † Loyola (Md.) 66
58 George Mason 74
49 Delaware 59
55 ■ Drexel 60
48 † American 47
37 † Duquesne 71
67 Winthrop 50
81 ■ N.C.-Asheville 49
51 Geo. Washington 72
85 ■ Coastal Caro. 66
68 ■ Charleston So. 42
37 Campbell 57
48 Charleston So. 54
68 ■ Winthrop 87
49 ■ Campbell 65
70 ■ Md.-Balt. County 60
67 Coastal Caro. 52
72 Liberty 77
60 Radford 68
69 ■ Liberty 57
83 N.C.-Asheville 53
71 ■ Radford 55
59 Md.-Balt. County 58
70 † Md.-Balt. County 55
69 † N.C.-Greensboro 81

TRENTON ST. 13-11
77 † Moravian 74
59 Emmanuel 80
74 Rutgers-Camden 54
72 St. Elizabeth 56
54 ■ Jersey City St. 36
62 ■ Muhlenberg 68
53 ■ Montclair St. 64
53 ■ Wm. Paterson 57
62 Kean 57
66 ■ Ramapo 55
45 Rowan 76
59 FDU-Madison 31
68 ■ Rutgers-Newark 57
76 Stockton St. 40
64 Jersey City St. 44
67 ■ Ursinus 50
77 ■ Rutgers-Camden 52
60 Ramapo 64
67 ■ Rowan 78
70 ■ Kean 86
50 Montclair St. 66
56 Wm. Paterson 61
76 ■ Stockton St. 40
68 Rutgers-Newark 81

TRINITY (CONN.) 14-9
68 Albertus Magnus 51
68 Mount Holyoke 39
85 ■ Wesleyan 53
73 Smith 70
67 Eastern Conn. St. 58
65 Western Conn. St. 79
65 ■ Worcester Tech 55
64 ■ Wellesley 73
85 ■ Pine Manor 65
59 Nichols 39
69 Coast Guard 64
69 ■ Western Conn. St. 74
72 Wesleyan 70
59 ■ Connecticut Col. 62
48 Clark (Mass.) 61
62 Colby 70
78 Bates 79
68 ■ Williams 64
73 Manhattanville 21
54 Tufts 89
84 ■ Babson 96
67 ■ Amherst 52
65 ■ Vassar 61

TRINITY (TEX.) 10-11
69 ■ Hamline 73
81 ■ Dallas 72
58 ■ Dallas 66
55 Austin 52
64 Hendrix 80
63 Dallas 79
66 ■ Centre 70
82 ■ Fisk 35
69 ■ Southwestern (Tex.) 70
58 Millsaps 69
50 Rhodes 62
59 Oglethorpe 55
56 Sewanee 43
53 ■ Millsaps 61
59 ■ Rhodes 45
56 Southwestern (Tex.) 72
62 ■ Hendrix 52
63 ■ Austin 49
67 ■ Oglethorpe 53
68 ■ Sewanee 55
64 Centre 71

TROY ST. 19-7
76 North Ala. 79
99 Ala.-Huntsville 70
98 Miles 64
65 Middle Tenn. St. 88
77 † North Texas 107
63 Augusta 97
80 ■ Augusta 64
97 ■ Paine 66
98 ■ Tuskegee 60
73 ■ Alabama St. 68
87 Mississippi-Women 75
103 Ga. Southwestern 80
98 ■ Talladega 52
89 ■ Albany St. (Ga.) 71
70 ■ West Ga. 59
81 ■ Jacksonville St. 68
80 Talladega 45
112 ■ Mississippi-Women 53
78 West Ga. 76
82 ■ North Ala. 80
88 Tuskegee 70
44 Alabama St. 62
94 ■ Ala.-Huntsville 67
74 Jacksonville St. 83
83 ■ Miles 48
69 Albany St. (Ga.) 70

TUFTS 14-11
88 ■ Colby 58
60 Babson 57
54 † Western Conn. St. 75
50 Connecticut Col. 53
83 ■ Bowdoin 39
71 ■ Brandeis 50
38 Sheldon Jackson 55
58 Sheldon Jackson 57
33 St. Martin's 79
76 Seattle 93
72 Seattle 92
67 Wesleyan 76
39 Wellesley 43
90 ■ Mass.-Dartmouth 54
60 ■ Williams 58
64 Wheaton (Mass.) 76
79 Gordon 45
75 ■ Smith 32
61 ■ Mount Holyoke 28
62 Clark (Mass.) 64
89 ■ Trinity (Conn.) 54
84 Bates 64
74 Middlebury 89
69 ■ Amherst 53
100 ■ Pine Manor 54

TULANE 14-13
64 UC Irvine 48
79 † Boise St. 76
67 Texas A&M 84
65 ■ Nevada-Las Vegas 59
82 ■ Southern Methodist 58
72 ■ Pennsylvania 68
60 Memphis St. 59
86 ■ Iona 49
85 ■ Louisville 79
61 New Orleans 79
57 Virginia Tech 80
48 N.C.-Charlotte 77
59 ■ Rice 61
89 ■ South Fla. 72
74 Alabama 90
60 Va. Commonwealth 75
71 ■ Southern Miss. 69
74 Louisiana St. 86
74 Louisville 87
62 ■ N.C.-Charlotte 58
79 ■ Virginia Tech 65
75 ■ New Orleans 64
71 ■ Va. Commonwealth 77
89 South Fla. 69
80 McNeese St. 82
61 Southern Miss. 78
44 † N.C.-Charlotte 69

TUSKEGEE 17-8
54 ■ West Ga. 67
84 † Talladega 78
74 ■ Columbus 70
60 Fort Valley St. 99
39 West Ga. 58
76 Columbus 73
60 Troy St. 98
97 Morris Brown 71
70 ■ Spelman 54
79 LeMoyne-Owen 54
66 ■ Clark Atlanta 58
89 Alabama A&M 94
84 ■ LeMoyne-Owen 47
78 Miles 75
84 ■ Alabama A&M 83
74 ■ Talladega 40
81 Spelman 55
84 ■ Savannah St. 72
61 ■ Paine 57
63 ■ Fort Valley St. 79
70 ■ Troy St. 88
69 ■ Albany St. (Ga.) 65
80 ■ Miles 55
75 ■ Morris Brown 61
48 † Paine 68

UCLA 13-14
99 ■ Cal St. Fullerton 66
52 ■ San Diego St. 77
55 Western Ky. 73
56 Rutgers 71
80 Ohio St. 91
82 † Michigan St. 57
100 † Pepperdine 52
81 ■ Loyola (Cal.) 47
63 ■ Santa Clara 54
81 Arizona St. 63
91 Arizona 77
79 ■ Oregon 75
67 ■ Oregon St. 71
70 Stanford 79
70 California 78
60 ■ Southern Cal 73
68 ■ Washington 59
82 ■ Washington St. 75
68 Oregon St. 71
78 Oregon 89
54 ■ Stanford 71
85 ■ California 68
57 Southern Cal 66
77 Washington St. 74
72 Washington 80
83 ■ Arizona 91
72 ■ Arizona St. 71

UNION (N.Y.) 6-17
52 Skidmore 74
54 † Rensselaer 63
44 † Western Conn. St. 78
57 Babson 85
52 ■ William Smith 87
59 Rensselaer 68
37 Rochester Inst. 58
58 ■ Plattsburgh St. 61
67 ■ Smith 51
54 ■ Skidmore 60
75 ■ North Adams St. 55
79 ■ Russell Sage 65
60 Hamilton 70
38 Binghamton 76
43 Hartwick 68

50 Albany (N.Y.) 80
31 Middlebury 75
71 ■ Mt. St. Mary (N.Y.) . 65
53 ■ Oneonta St. 43
60 ■ Vassar 72
65 ■ Manhattanville 28
43 Oneonta St. 47
57 ■ Williams 63

UPPER IOWA 4-19
51 Culver-Stockton ... 90
35 † Teikyo-Westmar ... 43
53 Viterbo 66
66 ■ Clarke 77
55 Iowa Wesleyan 57
66 Cornell College 57
62 Dubuque 53
29 Luther 72
61 ■ Central (Iowa) 81
56 ■ William Penn 78
46 ■ Wartburg 75
56 Buena Vista 67
55 ■ Coe 53
58 ■ Loras 65
51 Simpson 74
60 ■ Buena Vista 73
58 ■ Luther 61
48 William Penn 55
38 Central (Iowa) 99
59 ■ Dubuque 61
53 ■ Simpson 50
59 Loras 81
63 Wartburg 99

UPSALA 14-9
59 † Elmira 44
75 Hunter 66
81 ■ New Jersey Tech .. 49
75 ■ Delaware Valley 91
50 Mt. St. Mary (N.Y.) . 46
65 Rutgers-Camden ... 70
77 ■ Misericordia 76
87 ■ St. Elizabeth 45
52 ■ Scranton 89
64 ■ King's (Pa.) 85
56 ■ Bloomfield 68
83 ■ Drew 63
70 ■ Centenary (N.J.) ... 55
72 ■ FDU-Madison 52
79 King's (Pa.) 77
62 New Jersey Tech .. 57
71 Drew 69
46 Scranton 112
83 St. Elizabeth 61
74 Mt. St. Mary (N.Y.) . 70
67 FDU-Madison 70
72 Delaware Valley 89
57 Centenary (N.J.) ... 70

URSINUS 11-13
61 † John Carroll 79
57 † Catholic 58
80 Swarthmore 50
54 Muhlenberg 64
83 Albright 59
48 ■ Delaware Valley 59
71 Bryn Mawr 68
72 ■ Elizabethtown 68
66 Western Md. 75
57 Moravian 83
74 Haverford 55
73 ■ Muhlenberg 67
66 ■ Albright 46
50 Trenton St. 67
49 Wesley 70
86 ■ Widener 71
89 ■ Haverford 50
83 ■ Swarthmore 34
56 ■ Frank. & Marsh. ... 73
66 Immaculata 69
74 ■ Moravian 83
73 Widener 58
71 Allentown 88
74 Muhlenberg 81

UTAH 19-10
78 Weber St. 67
54 ■ Weber St. 52
55 ■ Idaho St. 49
59 ■ California 74
51 † Florida 57
60 † Harvard 49
48 Loyola (Cal.) 50
72 Chicago St. 58
69 Northern Ill. 85
68 ■ Montana St. 49
56 ■ Metropolitan St. 52
72 ■ Texas Tech 55
71 ■ UTEP 75
68 ■ New Mexico 41
75 Wyoming 55
81 Colorado St. 54
49 Brigham Young 65
68 ■ San Diego St. 42
94 ■ Fresno St. 61
68 New Mexico 48
55 UTEP 51
71 ■ Colorado St. 55
62 ■ Wyoming 58
66 ■ Brigham Young 75
74 Fresno St. 77
57 San Diego St. 63
62 ■ Colorado St. 48
74 ■ San Diego St. 56
50 ■ Brigham Young 53

UTICA 3-20
71 † Misericordia 70
48 Ramapo 71
61 ■ Hartwick 71
41 Clarkson 73
56 † Utica Tech 55
46 Hamilton 66
47 ■ Rensselaer 73
56 ■ Utica Tech 62
36 Brockport St. 72
32 Geneseo St. 105
41 Hamilton 60
55 Elmira 67
40 ■ Skidmore 49
58 ■ St. Lawrence 60
51 ■ Russell Sage 56
31 Binghamton 72
40 Nazareth (N.Y.) 72
67 ■ Keuka 78
38 Albany (N.Y.) 85
37 Roberts Wesleyan .. 66
58 ■ Manhattanville 46
33 ■ Le Moyne 74
21 St. John Fisher 65

UTICA TECH 15-10
79 ■ Hilbert 48
71 ■ Vassar 59
55 † Utica 56
78 † St. Lawrence 43
85 ■ Oswego St. 68
62 Utica 56
60 Buffalo St. 74
70 Russell Sage 60
60 Binghamton 69
73 ■ Cortland St. 62
63 † Geneseo St. 90
81 Brockport St. 89
70 Fredonia St. 57
91 ■ Russell Sage 58
97 ■ New Paltz St. 69
75 Oneonta St. 53
59 Oswego St. 74
58 ■ Buffalo St. 88
55 Hamilton 57
78 Plattsburgh St. 60
78 ■ Potsdam St. 77
66 Geneseo St. 91
89 ■ Brockport St. 74
88 ■ Fredonia St. 59
69 † Potsdam St. 72

VALDOSTA ST. 9-17
62 † Augusta 71
94 † Ga. Southwestern .. 73
93 Morris Brown 49
57 ■ Georgia Col. 70
70 North Fla. 75
71 ■ Fort Valley St. 89
72 † Piedmont 74
71 † Ala.-Huntsville 49
70 Kennesaw 80
77 ■ Hope 49
84 ■ North Fla. 47
66 West Ga. 68
61 ■ Delta St. 82
99 ■ North Ala. 91
63 Livingston 80
72 Mississippi Col. 75
76 Jacksonville St. 89
94 ■ Morris Brown 26
71 Georgia Col. 67
69 ■ West Ga. 74
65 ■ Jacksonville St. 72
103 ■ Ga. Southwestern .. 80
58 ■ Mississippi Col. 71
70 ■ Livingston 94
48 Delta St. 84
74 North Ala. 91

VALPARAISO 15-12
91 ■ Western Mich. 104
57 † Miami (Ohio) 81
99 † St. Francis (Pa.) 89
72 ■ Northern Iowa 82
106 ■ Eastern Mich. 68
67 Nevada-Las Vegas . 99
101 Northern Ariz. 79
97 † Siena 105
73 † Maine 72
70 Wright St. 68
85 Northern Ill. 102
111 ■ Ill.-Chicago 84
112 ■ Eastern Ill. 65
112 Western Ill. 85
90 St. Louis 61
107 ■ Youngstown St. 99
108 ■ Cleveland St. 84
69 Wis.-Green Bay 87
125 ■ Wright St. 87
80 ■ Northern Ill. 91
81 Ill.-Chicago 91
77 ■ Wis.-Green Bay 86
89 Eastern Ill. 78
94 ■ Western Ill. 73
106 Youngstown St. 117
88 Cleveland St. 81
100 † Ill.-Chicago 101

VANDERBILT 30-3
73 Arizona 63
72 ■ Southwest Mo. St. . 59
72 ■ Oregon 68
69 ■ Bowling Green 66
87 Alabama 70
90 ■ Dartmouth 52
78 Texas 73
57 † Connecticut 37
66 † Virginia 62
90 Georgia 66
91 ■ Memphis St. 57
70 ■ Ohio St. 67
87 ■ Louisiana St. 61
124 ■ Oral Roberts 58
108 ■ Mississippi St. 44
85 ■ Southern Ill. 55
69 Florida 63
68 ■ Tennessee 73
62 ■ Western Ky. 59
80 Arkansas 59
71 ■ DePaul 61
58 ■ South Caro. 48
66 Penn St. 57
53 Auburn 55
65 Kentucky 52
77 ■ Mississippi 62

68 † Kentucky 61
79 † Mississippi 54
78 † Georgia 64
82 ■ California 63
59 Stephen F. Austin .. 56
58 † Louisiana Tech 53
46 † Texas Tech 60

VASSAR 12-10
90 † Medgar Evers 26
59 Utica Tech 71
80 ■ New Rochelle 26
56 Manhattanville 53
46 Mount Holyoke 48
51 † Swarthmore 34
57 † Haverford 48
52 ■ New Paltz St. 63
55 York (N.Y.) 43
65 Old Westbury 55
41 Williams 63
62 ■ Mt. St. Vincent 41
75 ■ John Jay 36
49 Mt. St. Mary (N.Y.) . 62
58 ■ Russell Sage 69
48 ■ Skidmore 55
37 Stony Brook 67
72 Union (N.Y.) 60
65 † Old Westbury 58
40 Mt. St. Mary (N.Y.) . 53
61 Trinity (Conn.) 65
83 ■ Medgar Evers 26

VERMONT 28-1
76 Dartmouth 58
107 † Kent 75
81 Brown 69
91 ■ Siena 58
84 James Madison 62
77 ■ Harvard 64
82 † Eastern Mich. 63
66 Richmond 55
65 Holy Cross 63
75 ■ Rhode Island 61
73 Northeastern 50
84 Boston U. 62
94 ■ Maine 63
75 New Hampshire 70
76 Central Conn. St. ... 55
83 ■ Delaware 60
96 ■ Drexel 56
83 ■ Hartford 63
80 Drexel 58
77 Delaware 55
70 ■ New Hampshire 55
68 Maine 67
50 ■ Northeastern 40
80 ■ Boston U. 70
75 Hartford 61
75 ■ Drexel 56
75 ■ Delaware 62
62 ■ Maine 45
74 ■ Rutgers 80

VILLANOVA 15-13
57 St. Joseph's (Pa.) .. 83
59 Brown 60
68 † Kent 87
62 ■ La Salle 60
70 ■ Rider 55
54 ■ San Diego St. 56
81 Georgetown 88
63 Boston College 51
56 ■ Pittsburgh 61
54 Temple 49
69 ■ Providence 71
65 ■ St. John's (N.Y.) 47
53 Miami (Fla.) 64
60 ■ Syracuse 50
59 Pennsylvania 49
50 Connecticut 44
67 ■ Seton Hall 63
68 ■ Georgetown 69
70 ■ Boston College 58
70 Pittsburgh 53
69 Seton Hall 70

56	St. John's (N.Y.)	46
52	■ Miami (Fla.)	57
64	Syracuse	37
84	Providence	80
50	■ Connecticut	60
74	† Pittsburgh	59
49	† Miami (Fla.)	67

VIRGINIA 26-6

74	■ Temple	30
82	■ William & Mary	40
64	■ St. Joseph's (Pa.)	53
93	Virginia Tech	59
110	■ Morgan St.	49
94	■ Va. Commonwealth	53
93	■ Richmond	66
77	† N.C.-Charlotte	74
62	† Vanderbilt	66
84	Ohio St.	91
78	Florida St.	66
76	■ Duke	57
60	Clemson	61
79	■ North Caro. St.	73
66	Maryland	70
107	Georgia Tech	81
82	Wake Forest	78
76	■ Florida St.	68
65	North Caro.	72
88	■ Georgia Tech	53
73	■ North Caro.	67
97	Duke	61
87	■ Wake Forest	67
87	■ Clemson	70
87	■ Maryland	73
76	North Caro. St.	75
74	† Wake Forest	46
79	† Clemson	71
106	† Maryland	103
69	■ Florida	55
77	† Georgetown	57
73	† Ohio St.	75

VA. COMMONWEALTH 15-12

81	Delaware St.	59
53	■ Auburn	54
72	■ Old Dominion	67
53	Virginia	94
86	Radford	73
64	■ William & Mary	61
79	■ North Caro. St.	77
91	† Baylor	84
101	† Kent	91
74	† Mississippi St.	89
62	James Madison	65
67	Virginia Tech	70
60	N.C.-Charlotte	69
78	■ Liberty	59
63	■ Louisville	100
69	George Mason	50
75	■ Tulane	60
84	■ South Fla.	70
49	■ Southern Miss.	68
73	■ Richmond	49
54	Louisville	59
57	Southern Miss.	67
77	Tulane	71
61	■ N.C.-Charlotte	92
71	■ Virginia Tech	69
87	South Fla.	49
62	Louisville	70

VIRGINIA ST. 17-11

70	Fayetteville St.	57
62	■ Johnson Smith	51
68	St. Augustine's	87
75	■ Virginia Union	78
68	■ Norfolk St.	87
90	■ N.C. Central	48
68	Winston-Salem	60
68	† Florida Tech	84
60	† Johnson Smith	67
75	■ Spelman	49
59	■ Claflin	57
86	■ Rutgers-Camden	50
65	Elizabeth City St.	62
60	Hampton	71
73	■ Bowie St.	58
95	St. Paul's	48
63	■ Dist. Columbia	59
76	Norfolk St.	91
80	Virginia Union	92
66	■ Elizabeth City St.	53
55	■ Hampton	57
80	■ Longwood	67
77	■ Livingstone	45
58	Bowie St.	64
74	■ St. Paul's	42
84	Shaw	57
75	† N.C. Central	52
65	† St. Augustine's	80

VIRGINIA TECH 20-8

58	■ Wingate	43
86	† East Caro.	72
63	Duke	85
59	■ Virginia	93
76	Old Dominion	63
91	■ East Tenn. St.	59
92	■ Drexel	41
84	■ Marshall	78
89	■ Gardner-Webb	59
54	N.C.-Greensboro	63
70	■ Va. Commonwealth	67
74	Western Caro.	48
80	■ Tulane	57
85	■ Southern Miss.	70
81	■ Radford	68
79	Louisville	75
85	South Fla.	83
44	N.C.-Charlotte	81
81	■ James Madison	60
80	Southern Miss.	89
65	Tulane	79
82	■ South Fla.	62
82	■ Louisville	61
94	Morehead St.	88
69	Va. Commonwealth	71
76	■ N.C.-Charlotte	70
74	† South Fla.	50
73	Louisville	92

VIRGINIA UNION 19-9

56	† Carson-Newman	63
78	Longwood	77
61	Dist. Columbia	75
62	† Fort Valley St.	86
91	Hampton	70
78	Virginia St.	75
72	■ Johnson Smith	62
96	Livingstone	39
97	■ Fayetteville St.	81
94	Elizabeth City St.	97
78	■ St. Paul's	51
59	■ Hampton	61
64	■ Shaw	51
45	Norfolk St.	83
62	Hampton	57
79	St. Paul's	72
67	Winston-Salem	58
58	Bowie St.	45
92	■ Virginia St.	80
61	St. Augustine's	82
65	■ Norfolk St.	70
62	N.C. Central	47
79	■ Bowie St.	53
68	■ Elizabeth City St.	63
64	■ Dist. Columbia	55
80	† Johnson Smith	72
64	† Winston-Salem	57
91	† Norfolk St.	97

VA. WESLEYAN 16-10

59	† Chris. Newport	99
71	† Greensboro	85
59	† Bridgewater (Va.)	45
51	Chris. Newport	79
61	R.-M. Woman's	31
70	East. Mennonite	59
66	■ Emory & Henry	58
76	■ Guilford	71
77	■ Lynchburg	60
65	■ Roanoke	74
81	■ R.-M. Woman's	27
87	Methodist	81
65	Randolph-Macon	62
71	■ Hollins	65
53	Guilford	49
55	■ N.C. Wesleyan	57
83	Lynchburg	66
66	■ Randolph-Macon	61
58	Bridgewater (Va.)	61
61	Roanoke	74
75	Hollins	66
47	Emory & Henry	62
87	■ East. Mennonite	57
53	■ Bridgewater (Va.)	56
65	† Guilford	64
47	† Bridgewater (Va.)	57

WAGNER 11-16

77	■ Columbia-Barnard	45
51	Yale	60
50	† St. Joseph's (Pa.)	68
64	† Lafayette	65
52	Central Conn. St.	59
58	■ Massachusetts	52
53	■ Middle Tenn. St.	73
95	■ Hofstra	97
73	■ LIU-Brooklyn	50
67	St. Francis (N.Y.)	49
71	Monmouth (N.J.)	73
56	FDU-Teaneck	58
62	■ Mt. St. Mary's (Md.)	63
50	■ Rider	58
61	Marist	60
54	St. Francis (Pa.)	59
51	Robert Morris	50
66	■ St. Francis (N.Y.)	57
56	LIU-Brooklyn	57
76	■ Monmouth (N.J.)	51
59	■ Marist	62
58	■ FDU-Teaneck	61
61	Rider	58
48	Mt. St. Mary's (Md.)	64
68	■ Robert Morris	53
69	■ St. Francis (Pa.)	57
57	Marist	61

WAKE FOREST 14-14

76	East Tenn. St.	51
62	■ N.C.-Charlotte	64
89	Richmond	41
82	Charleston	59
79	† Mississippi St.	72
72	Ala.-Birmingham	63
93	Wisconsin	67
56	Bradley	44
78	■ Appalachian St.	65
71	■ East Tenn. St.	58
85	■ Georgia Tech	70
68	North Caro.	92
57	■ Florida St.	53
51	■ Clemson	71
72	North Caro. St.	75
64	Duke	60
78	■ Virginia	82
67	■ Maryland	65
69	■ North Caro.	77
58	Clemson	68
73	Florida St.	77
67	Virginia	87
59	■ Duke	71
72	Georgia Tech	85
80	■ North Caro. St.	84
65	Maryland	80
70	† Duke	69
46	† Virginia	74

WARTBURG 23-5

57	■ Wis.-Platteville	42
59	Gust. Adolphus	44
79	■ Coe	48
77	Dordt	53
93	Cornell College	38
69	Iowa Wesleyan	24
76	† Stony Brook	59
55	† St. Benedict	74
94	North Park	56
64	Central (Iowa)	83
73	William Penn	64
82	■ Dubuque	59
76	■ Luther	72
75	Upper Iowa	46
71	Simpson	60
88	■ Buena Vista	58
95	Loras	64
85	Dubuque	38
64	■ Central (Iowa)	58
58	Luther	72
73	■ William Penn	62
84	■ Loras	47
78	Buena Vista	59
69	■ Simpson	75
99	■ Upper Iowa	63
75	Washington (Mo.)	60
83	† Wis.-Whitewater	77
60	Central (Iowa)	62

WASHBURN 31-1

80	† Regis (Colo.)	49
65	Fort Hays St.	61
71	■ Fort Hays St.	34
80	■ Colorado-CS	44
91	William Jewell	51
94	■ Doane	71
89	■ Baker	44
67	† Alas. Anchorage	56
82	Cal St. Stanislaus	58
76	Cal St. Chico	63
70	Northwest Mo. St.	53
76	■ Southwest Baptist	58
74	Central Mo. St.	60
81	■ Pittsburg St.	77
75	■ Emporia St.	62
65	Mo. Western St.	60
72	■ Northwest Mo. St.	47
81	■ Northeast Mo. St.	44
76	■ Central Mo. St.	60
68	Missouri-Rolla	53
74	Emporia St.	64
71	■ Mo. Western St.	54
71	Northeast Mo. St.	44
81	Mo.-St. Louis	54
79	■ Lincoln (Mo.)	53
83	Mo. Southern St.	82
66	■ Southwest Baptist	47
84	■ Central Mo. St.	71
78	■ Mo. Southern St.	65
77	■ Central Mo. St.	67
75	■ Mo. Southern St.	62
77	■ Michigan Tech	78

WASHINGTON 17-12

78	Boise St.	82
83	■ North Caro. St.	80
55	Western Ky.	93
84	† Pepperdine	64
67	Hawaii	80
79	■ Princeton	43
72	■ Duke	48
74	† Texas Tech	90
94	■ Gonzaga	64
72	■ Washington St.	75
82	■ Arizona	68
77	■ Arizona St.	82
71	Oregon St.	57
87	Oregon	74
62	■ California	61
73	■ Stanford	70
59	UCLA	68
61	Southern Cal	74
61	Arizona St.	74
72	Arizona	69
59	■ Oregon	51
81	■ Oregon St.	71
62	Stanford	86
73	California	66
45	■ Southern Cal	46
80	■ UCLA	72

77 Washington St. 62
80 ■ Montana St. 51
64 Texas Tech 70

WASHINGTON (MO.) 22-4
94 Maryville (Mo.) 56
79 † DePauw 38
70 ■ Aurora 57
70 ■ Millsaps 56
65 ■ Wis.-Platteville 56
57 Central (Iowa) 65
80 Knox 42
83 Fontbonne 39
70 Mo.-St. Louis 68
44 ■ Rochester 37
71 ■ Brandeis 50
70 ■ Blackburn 59
69 Catholic 50
71 Johns Hopkins 56
81 ■ Carnegie Mellon 75
57 ■ Case Reserve 40
77 Emory 70
65 New York U. 73
53 Carnegie Mellon 59
52 Chicago 46
58 ■ New York U. 52
85 ■ Emory 64
58 Brandeis 43
70 Rochester 66
74 ■ Chicago 53
60 ■ Wartburg 75

WASHINGTON ST. 7-20
84 ■ Texas Southern 64
58 ■ Central Mich. 47
59 ■ Wis.-Green Bay 52
69 Gonzaga 71
66 Weber St. 50
63 Montana 68
62 Arkansas 84
51 Texas 76
69 ■ Boise St. 72
75 Washington 72
59 ■ Arizona St. 70
55 ■ Arizona 64
66 Oregon 54
55 Oregon St. 75
44 ■ Stanford 78
65 ■ California 75
63 Southern Cal 69
75 UCLA 82
64 Arizona 72
68 Arizona St. 88
68 ■ Oregon St. 67
75 ■ Oregon 88
65 California 79
56 Stanford 100
74 ■ UCLA 77
52 ■ Southern Cal 55
62 ■ Washington 77

WASH. & JEFF. 17-5
58 Susquehanna 67
93 † Lebanon Valley 58
85 ■ Juniata 77
72 ■ Carnegie Mellon 61
64 Carlow 36
79 Denison 57
98 ■ Allegheny 87
84 ■ Point Park 72
69 ■ Carlow 67
61 Juniata 85
73 Dickinson 64
79 Waynesburg 82
81 ■ Thiel 65
67 Penn St.-Behrend 63
83 ■ Grove City 78
95 ■ Bethany (W.Va.) 70
72 ■ Waynesburg 84
79 Thiel 56
83 ■ Penn St.-Behrend 72
74 Alderson-Broaddus 78
94 Grove City 85
78 Bethany (W.Va.) 75

WAYNE ST. (MICH.) 13-13
60 ■ Ashland 62
79 ■ Spring Arbor 61
91 ■ Wis.-Parkside 83
63 IU/PU-Ft. Wayne 59
57 † Lake Superior St. 44
91 Saginaw Valley 72
77 ■ Siena Heights 59
69 ■ Northwood 49
64 ■ Ferris St. 51
77 ■ Indiana (Pa.) 78
75 Gannon 70
62 Hillsdale 64
97 ■ Grand Valley St. 74
66 ■ Northern Mich. 84
40 ■ Michigan Tech 75
67 Lake Superior St. 75
85 Oakland 95
73 Northwood 74
87 ■ Saginaw Valley 69
79 Ferris St. 91
91 ■ Hillsdale 79
89 Grand Valley St. 76
77 Northern Mich. 90
50 Michigan Tech 79
52 ■ Lake Superior St. 69
82 ■ Oakland 84

WAYNE ST. (NEB.) 14-12
55 North Dak. St. 95
68 Morningside 82
68 † South Dak. 74
70 † Metropolitan St. 66
67 † Colorado-CS 59
87 ■ Concordia (Neb.) 53
68 ■ South Dak. 85
55 ■ Augustana (S.D.) 78
84 ■ Southwest St. 64
92 ■ Chadron St. 84
64 Denver 77
104 Colorado Mines 75
67 Chadron St. 64
76 ■ Fort Hays St. 59
58 Neb.-Kearney 88
72 Fort Hays St. 67
78 Mt. Marty 71
82 ■ Neb.-Kearney 77
95 Dakota St. 71
91 Bemidji St. 92
66 ■ Morningside 86
74 ■ Quincy 63
105 ■ Briar Cliff 73
71 ■ Bemidji St. 75
57 Quincy 62
79 SIU-Edwardsville 81

WAYNESBURG 19-6
87 ■ Kenyon 20
71 Carnegie Mellon 60
68 Penn St.-Behrend 63
82 ■ Wheeling Jesuit 78
53 † Defiance 70
98 † Asbury 39
96 ■ Ohio Dominican 56
80 Muskingum 89
64 ■ Mount Union 52
76 Frostburg St. 54
90 Notre Dame (Ohio) 63
61 ■ Fairmont St. 49
76 ■ Point Park 62
82 ■ Wash. & Jeff. 79
67 ■ Penn St.-Behrend 60
75 Juniata 80
89 ■ Grove City 65
67 ■ Bethany (W.Va.) 57
93 ■ Thiel 49
84 Wash. & Jeff. 72
66 Penn St.-Behrend 80
80 Grove City 66
56 Bethany (W.Va.) 70
76 Thiel 55
76 Scranton 103

WEBER ST. 4-22
67 ■ Utah 78
52 Utah 54
45 Portland 56
45 Oregon 84
70 ■ Brigham Young 79
50 ■ Washington St. 66
49 ■ Pacific (Cal.) 68
63 Southern Utah 78
69 † St. Mary's (Cal.) 67
42 Brigham Young 79
61 ■ Wyoming 72
73 ■ Colorado St. 78
56 Idaho St. 74
67 Boise St. 90
76 ■ Montana 98
59 ■ Montana St. 69
62 Idaho 65
56 Eastern Wash. 65
70 Northern Ariz. 68
72 ■ Boise St. 94
57 ■ Idaho St. 78
47 Montana St. 65
47 Montana 81
60 ■ Idaho 61
82 ■ Eastern Wash. 70
81 ■ Northern Ariz. 70

WEBSTER 13-9
45 ■ Coe 74
59 ■ Sewanee 55
54 † Blackburn 66
72 DePauw 67
64 Lincoln Chrst. 56
64 ■ Knox 60
44 ■ Fontbonne 75
63 ■ Principia 62
58 Blackburn 72
54 MacMurray 61
69 Maryville (Mo.) 55
64 ■ Lincoln Chrst. 45
64 Westminster 63
56 ■ Moody Bible 46
69 Fontbonne 62
59 Principia 52
55 ■ Blackburn 60
59 ■ MacMurray 61
73 ■ Maryville (Mo.) 64
63 ■ Westminster 66
81 † Principia 61
60 † Blackburn 84

WELLESLEY 24-3
80 ■ Worcester St. 59
62 † Swarthmore 35
69 Mount Holyoke 28
66 † Smith 57
66 ■ Regis (Mass.) 39
76 ■ Wesleyan 61
80 ■ Eastern Nazarene 38
39 Connecticut Col. 60
73 Trinity (Conn.) 64
43 ■ Tufts 39
66 Williams 47
51 Babson 60
83 ■ MIT 53
71 ■ Simmons 27
62 Wheaton (Mass.) 59
79 Amherst 68
71 ■ Mount Holyoke 33
80 Worcester Tech 48
68 ■ Smith 38
61 Brandeis 54
58 ■ Nichols 27
78 ■ Mount Holyoke 37
75 † Wheaton (Mass.) 69
56 † Babson 63
86 ■ Emmanuel 75
80 Middlebury 71
81 † Westfield St. 61

WENTWORTH INST. 1-21
38 † Suffolk 49
52 Rivier 73
38 † Emerson-MCA 39
61 ■ Suffolk 63
65 Eastern Nazarene 63
51 MIT 82
51 Suffolk 53
51 Simmons 52
59 ■ Eastern Nazarene 68
46 ■ Anna Maria 75
55 ■ New England Col. 72
60 Curry 72
41 ■ Salve Regina 60
51 Regis (Mass.) 81
48 Roger Williams 49
40 Anna Maria 61
42 ■ Regis (Mass.) 72
58 New England Col. 75
33 ■ Curry 55
44 ■ Roger Williams 48
59 Salve Regina 66
47 Regis (Mass.) 70

WESLEY 22-3
85 ■ Washington (Md.) 32
57 Goucher 40
69 Shepherd 61
85 Shenandoah 41
57 Christendom 39
65 ■ Wilmington (Del.) 79
80 Washington (Md.) 17
66 ■ Lincoln (Pa.) 28
74 ■ St. Mary's (Md.) 25
62 Marywood 60
73 Wilmington (Del.) 67
56 Columbia Union 67
79 Gallaudet 77
56 Stockton St. 42
70 ■ Ursinus 49
55 Neumann 46
71 ■ Immaculata 49
53 Lincoln (Pa.) 42
70 ■ Alvernia 68
71 ■ Holy Family 60
80 Salisbury St. 76
46 ■ Phila. Pharmacy 47
47 Notre Dame (Md.) 44
68 ■ Bryn Mawr 58
73 Notre Dame (Md.) 46

WESLEYAN 10-13
60 Middlebury 92
61 ■ Connecticut Col. 63
53 Trinity (Conn.) 85
61 Wellesley 76
48 † Western Conn. St. 62
66 Eastern Conn. St. 74
68 Mount Holyoke 52
75 Smith 78
77 ■ Elms 51
76 ■ Tufts 67
65 Wheaton (Mass.) 80
66 ■ Clark (Mass.) 68
70 ■ Trinity (Conn.) 72
55 Williams 48
67 Albertus Magnus 71
80 Bates 76
51 Colby 59
58 Connecticut Col. 67
76 ■ Coast Guard 35
82 ■ Amherst 47
67 Amherst 50
82 Nichols 32
67 ■ Williams 63

WEST CHESTER 14-11
76 ■ Adelphi 60
101 ■ Longwood 65
50 ■ Bentley 60
67 Shippensburg 78
70 Phila. Textile 92
87 ■ LIU-C.W. Post 40
80 Columbia Union 75
65 Norfolk St. 70
62 Longwood 64
75 Holy Family 63
52 Pitt.-Johnstown 87
81 ■ East Stroudsburg 86
63 ■ Bloomsburg 55
67 Kutztown 57

78	Cheyney	46
57	■ Mansfield	38
60	Alvernia	45
63	Millersville	65
59	East Stroudsburg	61
74	Bloomsburg	85
77	■ Kutztown	58
79	■ Cheyney	41
70	Mansfield	67
69	Rowan	64
65	■ Millersville	77
99	■ North Ala.	91
63	Livingston	80
72	Mississippi Col.	75
76	Jacksonville St.	89
94	■ Morris Brown	26
71	Georgia Col.	67
69	■ West Ga.	74
65	■ Jacksonville St.	72
103	■ Ga. Southwestern	80
58	■ Mississippi Col.	71
70	■ Livingston	94
48	Delta St.	84
74	North Ala.	91

WEST GA.		**13-14**
67	Tuskegee	54
65	Miles	43
89	■ Clark Atlanta	50
62	† Kennesaw	78
59	† Paine	42
57	Fla. Southern	61
65	Tampa	55
58	■ Tuskegee	39
68	■ Valdosta St.	66
97	■ North Ala.	91
62	■ Delta St.	86
51	Mississippi Col.	59
62	Livingston	71
88	■ Fla. Atlantic	94
61	Jacksonville St.	81
59	Troy St.	70
79	Clark Atlanta	42
74	Valdosta St.	69
86	■ Miles	42
58	■ Jacksonville St.	66
76	■ Troy St.	78
81	■ Livingston	69
67	■ Mississippi Col.	62
69	North Ala.	70
56	Delta St.	82
59	■ Fort Valley St.	67
46	Delta St.	75

WEST LIBERTY ST.		**10-19**
60	Calif. (Pa.)	81
73	† Dowling	72
58	■ Tiffin	87
68	Ohio Valley	70
60	Charleston (W.Va.)	80
66	Shepherd	73
60	Wheeling Jesuit	73
71	■ Point Park	66
54	Wheeling Jesuit	85
64	■ West Va. St.	48
65	West Va. Tech	55
81	Concord	82
65	Bluefield St.	86
79	■ Fairmont St.	69
72	Salem-Teikyo	78
65	■ Ohio Valley	55
84	■ West Va. Wesleyan	88
76	■ Alderson-Broaddus	73
57	Glenville St.	83
58	Fairmont St.	72
66	■ Shepherd	64
57	Gannon	88
68	West Va. St.	72
60	■ Wheeling Jesuit	63
65	Alderson-Broaddus	72
74	■ Davis & Elkins	55
62	■ Pitt.-Johnstown	82
64	† Concord	62
60	† Bluefield St.	82

WEST TEX. A&M		**18-8**
83	■ Cameron	71
62	■ Texas A&I	55
90	■ Chapman	55
78	■ Langston	47
49	■ Oklahoma City	63
80	■ Fort Lewis	63
73	■ Saginaw Valley	69
92	■ Portland St.	83
76	† N.M. Highlands	73
62	Southern Colo.	66
72	Texas Woman's	43
88	† East Tex. St.	64
92	■ Cameron	49
64	† Central Okla.	81
89	Cameron	67
80	■ Eastern N. Mex.	71
65	■ Midwestern St.	72
74	Western N. Mex.	83
86	■ Henderson St.	61
56	Cal Poly SLO	61
91	Chapman	44
59	■ Western N. Mex.	56
92	■ Panhandle St.	73
74	■ Neb.-Kearney	72
62	Denver	94
50	Air Force	73

WEST VA.		**12-16**
72	■ Youngstown St.	92
59	† Butler	75
86	† North Texas	80
68	Xavier (Ohio)	99
44	Iowa	74
63	† Kentucky	73
75	■ St. Bonaventure	68
64	Kansas	106
73	■ Richmond	60
68	Rutgers	80
59	■ Florida	66
99	Robert Morris	72
77	St. Bonaventure	95
82	■ Geo. Washington	71
67	■ St. Joseph's (Pa.)	83
72	■ Temple	55
78	Rhode Island	74
68	Massachusetts	76
90	■ Duquesne	80
67	■ Massachusetts	51
61	Geo. Washington	87
81	† Marshall	92
75	■ Rutgers	76
87	■ Rhode Island	80
61	St. Joseph's (Pa.)	77
78	Temple	71
68	† Massachusetts	56
66	† Rutgers	71

WESTERN CARO.		**7-20**
65	Winthrop	71
63	■ Navy	60
68	N.C.-Asheville	63
58	South Fla.	72
66	† Akron	62
41	Montana	89
70	† Niagara	78
66	■ N.C.-Wilmington	75
48	■ Virginia Tech	74
76	Davidson	52
56	■ Tenn.-Chatt.	82
49	■ Ga. Southern	65
48	N.C.-Charlotte	69
63	■ Marshall	79
90	■ N.C.-Asheville	64
83	East Tenn. St.	91
80	Appalachian St.	88
59	Furman	86
84	■ Furman	101
71	■ Davidson	57
65	Tenn.-Chatt.	69
72	Ga. Southern	76
54	South Caro.	69
65	Marshall	84
104	■ East Tenn. St.	67
74	■ Appalachian St.	108
66	† Tenn.-Chatt.	91

WESTERN CONN. ST.		**20-5**
98	† Norwich	46
40	Southern Me.	71
78	† Union (N.Y.)	44
75	† Tufts	54
68	Westfield St.	56
62	■ Williams	50
70	■ Eastern Conn. St.	48
84	■ Worcester St.	41
55	† Amherst	50
75	† North Park	70
50	† St. Benedict	80
55	Wm. Paterson	51
62	† Wesleyan	48
79	■ Trinity (Conn.)	65
70	■ Stony Brook	40
74	Trinity (Conn.)	69
75	Norwich	66
75	Middlebury	79
60	Albany (N.Y.)	53
78	Bri'water (Mass.)	45
64	Ramapo	49
73	New York U.	61
69	Kean	71
71	Clark (Mass.)	65
68	■ Babson	86

WESTERN ILL.		**3-21**
61	St. Louis	57
62	■ Northern Iowa	65
69	■ Wichita St.	83
52	Loyola (Cal.)	71
76	UC Irvine	83
90	■ Northeastern Ill.	86
58	Mo.-Kansas City	92
52	Creighton	85
75	■ Youngstown St.	95
75	■ Cleveland St.	95
61	Ill.-Chicago	76
52	Wis.-Green Bay	92
72	Wright St.	95
85	■ Valparaiso	112
75	Northern Ill.	95
80	■ Eastern Ill.	72
58	■ Ill.-Chicago	89
64	Youngstown St.	80
69	Cleveland St.	78
60	■ Wis.-Green Bay	81
71	Eastern Ill.	77
57	■ Wright St.	79
73	Valparaiso	94
70	■ Northern Ill.	102

WESTERN KY.		**24-7**
92	Minnesota	64
93	■ Washington	55
76	† Florida A&M	53
49	Tennessee Tech	65
73	■ UCLA	55
75	North Caro. St.	82
70	■ Boston U.	59
59	■ Southwest Mo. St.	60
83	Lamar	54
82	South Ala.	65
97	Middle Tenn. St.	77
83	■ Southwestern La.	45
60	Kentucky	62
87	■ Tex.-Pan American	33
94	New Orleans	70
92	Southwestern La.	65
59	Vanderbilt	62
71	■ New Orleans	50
90	Tex.-Pan American	60
77	Louisiana Tech	86
76	■ Louisville	69
92	■ Lamar	43
77	■ Arkansas St.	67
92	■ South Ala.	61
63	■ Louisiana Tech	62
63	Arkansas St.	53
96	† Southwestern La.	37
73	† Arkansas St.	70
81	Louisiana Tech	73
78	■ Miami (Fla.)	63
73	† Ohio St.	86

WESTERN MD.		**9-15**
51	Notre Dame (Md.)	59
67	† Immaculata	53
51	York (Pa.)	62
66	■ Mary Washington	62
38	Johns Hopkins	66
42	† William Smith	71
57	† Misericordia	68
60	Albright	71
56	■ Dickinson	67
75	■ Ursinus	66
53	Frank. & Marsh.	68
79	Lebanon Valley	57
69	■ Catholic	65
50	Messiah	63
47	Dickinson	72
79	Gettysburg	73
67	■ Gallaudet	60
46	■ Johns Hopkins	64
51	■ Frank. & Marsh.	67
70	Goucher	77
63	■ Gettysburg	59
55	■ Juniata	69
65	■ Lebanon Valley	63
51	Elizabethtown	97

WESTERN MICH.		**14-13**
104	Valparaiso	91
73	■ Detroit Mercy	71
64	Purdue	92
85	■ Northeastern Ill.	72
48	Arizona	76
69	Arizona St.	79
44	■ UTEP	70
77	† Fairfield	69
88	■ Kent	74
64	Ball St.	62
61	■ Miami (Ohio)	58
63	Akron	61
53	Ohio	62
61	■ Central Mich.	56
59	Bowling Green	84
76	■ Eastern Mich.	53
49	Toledo	59
68	■ Ball St.	49
72	Miami (Ohio)	67
78	■ Akron	67
53	■ Ohio	59
50	Central Mich.	62
64	■ Bowling Green	91
67	Eastern Mich.	63
51	■ Toledo	70
79	Kent	97
61	Miami (Ohio)	67

WESTERN NEW ENG.		**20-1**
58	■ Westfield St.	52
78	Fitchburg St.	72
46	Framingham St.	30
99	■ Pine Manor	52
62	■ Amherst	56
70	Gordon	54
79	■ Rivier	29
47	■ Smith	45
60	Worcester Tech	46
72	■ Mount Holyoke	41
81	† Hilbert	60
63	† Bates	45
59	North Adams St.	46
66	■ Worcester St.	54
69	Coast Guard	49
77	■ Simmons	26
76	MIT	58
56	Eastern Conn. St.	68
67	■ Elms	51
55	Nichols	45
66	■ Albertus Magnus	50

WESTERN ST.		**4-20**
64	Fort Lewis	68

65		Grand Canyon	104
73	†	Central Mo. St.	85
94	■	Colorado Col.	67
74	■	Fort Lewis	83
58	■	Regis (Colo.)	71
62	■	Wis.-Eau Claire	94
47		Air Force	89
50	■	Colorado-CS	74
73	■	N.M. Highlands	89
85	■	Adams St.	79
39		Fort Hays St.	89
51		Chadron St.	88
62	■	Mesa St.	74
98	■	Colorado Mines	95
68		Colorado Col.	48
57	■	Tarleton St.	74
51	■	Fort Hays St.	88
79	■	Chadron St.	93
78		Mesa St.	92
65		Colorado Mines	67
73		Adams St.	83
70		N.M. Highlands	92
61	†	N.M. Highlands	83

WESTFIELD ST.			23-6
52		Western New Eng.	58
59		Amherst	51
56	■	Western Conn. St.	68
74	†	Old Westbury	28
81		Norwich	70
85		Connecticut Col.	84
85	■	Mass.-Boston	49
53		Williams	47
64		Bri'water (Mass.)	61
53	■	Albertus Magnus	39
72	■	Worcester St.	29
48		Salem St.	50
62		Rhode Island Col.	65
68	■	Fitchburg St.	57
77		Elms	42
68	■	Framingham St.	41
62		North Adams St.	41
81	■	Emmanuel	70
70	■	Bri'water (Mass.)	44
67		Worcester St.	52
56	■	Salem St.	53
61		Fitchburg St.	57
64		Framingham St.	25
77	■	North Adams St.	33
70	†	Bri'water (Mass.)	45
47	†	Salem St.	57
70	■	Clark (Mass.)	68
57	†	Connecticut Col.	55
61	†	Wellesley	81

WESTMINSTER			3-17
52	■	Greenville	37
41		Central Meth.	92
31	■	Mo. Baptist	67
50		MacMurray	55
45	■	Central Meth.	99
43	■	Blackburn	57
47		Avila	78
64		Principia	60
53	■	Fontbonne	70
63	■	Webster	64
46	■	MacMurray	53
48	■	Maryville (Mo.)	62
44		Blackburn	59
51		Mo. Baptist	83
58		Fontbonne	62
62		Greenville	65
49		Maryville (Mo.)	63
48	■	Principia	64
66		Webster	63
56	†	Maryville (Mo.)	58

WHEATON (ILL.)			16-9
52		Ill. Benedictine	51
49	■	Rosary	81
55		Beloit	53
66	■	Elmhurst	40
69		Rosary	78
65	†	St. Francis (Ind.)	57
62		Aurora	58
52	■	Millikin	59
66	■	Olivet (Ill.)	59
53		Augustana (Ill.)	68
60		North Park	65
61	■	North Central	34
56		North Central	42
60	■	Calvin	56
40		Chicago	68
71	■	North Park	62
68	■	Carthage	47
70	■	Ill. Wesleyan	38
52		Millikin	64
68		Ill. Wesleyan	70
56	■	Augustana (Ill.)	64
79		Carthage	73
70	■	Trinity Chrst. (Il.)	58
75		Elmhurst	52
67		St. Mary's (Ind.)	53

WHEATON (MASS.)			18-8
90	■	Nazareth (N.Y.)	65
59	■	Scranton	79
67	■	Mass.-Dartmouth	71
75		Bri'water (Mass.)	56
64	†	Clarkson	50
74	†	Wooster	60
86		Amherst	63
81		Drew	45
54		New York U.	64
83	■	Clark (Mass.)	68
75		Coast Guard	46
80	■	Wesleyan	65
71		Eastern Conn. St.	76
76	■	Tufts	64
59	■	Wellesley	62
82		MIT	56
73		Babson	83
77	■	Brandeis	56
67		Colby	62
75		Bowdoin	65
78	■	Worcester Tech	60
80		Smith	56
101	■	Mount Holyoke	64
97	■	Worcester Tech	59
69	†	Wellesley	75
64		Connecticut Col.	70

WHEELING JESUIT			24-5
85	■	West Va. Tech	59
78		Waynesburg	82
94		Ohio Valley	40
76	■	Fairmont St.	58
73	■	West Liberty St.	60
92	■	Bethany (W.Va.)	50
85	■	West Liberty St.	54
85	■	West Va. St.	56
102		Glenville St.	99
82	■	Alderson-Broaddus	60
58		Bluefield St.	90
76		Concord	69
57	■	West Va. Wesleyan	46
74	■	Charleston (W.Va.)	69
62	■	Davis & Elkins	50
55		Shepherd	56
65		Fairmont St.	59
61	■	Salem-Teikyo	60
90	■	Ohio Valley	48
64		Davis & Elkins	57
63	■	Shepherd	50
75	■	Seton Hill	64
63		West Liberty St.	60
52		Salem-Teikyo	66
69		Alderson-Broaddus	59
69	†	Davis & Elkins	52
72	†	Fairmont St.	62
61	†	Salem-Teikyo	60
48	†	Bluefield St.	66

WHITTIER			5-19
69	■	Mills	48
52		Southern Cal Col.	58
78	■	Pac. Christian	24
97	■	Mt. St. Mary (N.Y.)	43
54	■	Master's	74
31		Cal St. San B'dino	67
63	■	Panhandle St.	66
58		Rhodes	45
48	†	DePauw	55
54		Pomona-Pitzer	72
50		Claremont-M-S	66
64	■	Southern Cal Col.	76
57	■	Occidental	66
58		La Verne	66
84	■	Cal Lutheran	72
48	■	Redlands	62
51	■	UC San Diego	78

WICHITA ST.			15-12
76	■	Canisius	72
70	†	Baylor	68
61		Texas-Arlington	68
68	■	Iowa St.	56
75		Purdue	83
83		Western Ill.	69
75	■	Chicago St.	65
53	■	Oklahoma St.	70
72		Tex.-Pan American	52
70	■	Indiana St.	60
61	■	Southern Ill.	74
69		Northern Iowa	75
45		Creighton	76
60		Drake	81
64		Southwest Mo. St.	94
66		Kansas St.	54
64	■	Illinois St.	53
76	■	Bradley	44
60	■	Southwest Mo. St.	70
72		Bradley	57
53		Illinois St.	71
82	■	Creighton	74
92	■	Drake	79
87	■	Northern Iowa	52
66		Indiana St.	59
56		Southern Ill.	68
68		Drake	77

WIDENER			5-19
49		Messiah	80
44	†	Dickinson	94
60		Immaculata	72
53	■	Swarthmore	51
41		Allentown	98
48	■	Moravian	94
45		Albright	77
40		Salisbury St.	76
49	■	Frank. & Marsh.	69
41	■	Delaware Valley	86
49		Haverford	47
68	■	Muhlenberg	87
62	■	Bryn Mawr	53
50		Moravian	107
38	■	Johns Hopkins	73
36	■	Dickinson	66
71		Ursinus	86
55		Muhlenberg	60
47	■	Albright	62
51	■	Haverford	41
51		Misericordia	67
49		Drew	64
58	■	Ursinus	73
67		Swarthmore	45

WILKES			18-8
67	†	Bates	43
62		Hartwick	47
72	■	Lycoming	50
75	■	Misericordia	52
62		FDU-Madison	59
71		Marywood	46
90		Bapt. Bible (Pa.)	49
47		Susquehanna	65
87	■	Moravian	84
70		King's (Pa.)	58
69	†	Penn St.-Behrend	62
65	■	Messiah	56
74	■	Allentown	63
69		Dickinson	71
70	■	Albright	64
64		Juniata	74
70	■	Elizabethtown	86
57	■	King's (Pa.)	56
75		Lycoming	66
56	■	Susquehanna	72
74		Scranton	93
80	■	Juniata	48
65		Elizabethtown	97
69		Messiah	72
59		Frank. & Marsh.	56
44	†	Dickinson	43

WM. PATERSON			18-9
53	†	Le Moyne	54
67	†	Clarkson	52
57		Kean	80
81	■	Rutgers-Camden	56
61	■	Montclair St.	49
68	†	Mass.-Dartmouth	53
73		Worcester St.	66
60	■	Rutgers-Newark	51
57		Trenton St.	53
51	■	Western Conn. St.	55
74		Rowan	77
60	■	Ramapo	68
67		Stockton St.	48
68	■	Jersey City St.	51
54		Montclair St.	61
65	■	Kean	62
68		Rutgers-Camden	49
72		Ramapo	59
87	■	Rowan	73
73		Rutgers-Newark	80
61	■	Trenton St.	56
63	■	Stony Brook	67
56		Jersey City St.	52
65	■	Stockton St.	49
62	■	Ramapo	58
73		Rowan	70
55		Rowan	65

WILLIAM PENN			14-11
49	†	Elmhurst	55
82		Rockford	35
73	■	Grinnell	65
58	†	Hastings	88
63		Colorado Col.	44
67		Cornell College	48
80		Grand View	64
71	■	Teiko-Marycrest	66
60	■	Graceland (Iowa)	49
70	■	Buena Vista	47
64	■	Wartburg	73
68		Loras	69
78		Upper Iowa	56
48		Central (Iowa)	80
56		Luther	77
56	■	Simpson	70
71	■	Dubuque	59
73	■	Loras	68
66		Buena Vista	73
55	■	Upper Iowa	48
62		Wartburg	73
66		Dubuque	57
71		Simpson	61
52	■	Central (Iowa)	79
54	■	Luther	60

WILLIAM SMITH			20-6
87		Union (N.Y.)	52
91		Albany (N.Y.)	97
71	†	Western Md.	42
70		York (Pa.)	56
69		King's (Pa.)	70
69		Marywood	59
84		Keuka	58
82	■	Hartwick	71
71	■	Rensselaer	54
92		Oswego St.	66
79		Rochester Inst.	49
78	■	Alfred	54
68	■	Ithaca	70
60	■	Hamilton	55
78		Clarkson	68
86		St. Lawrence	44

66 Rensselaer 46
59 Hartwick 51
68 ■ Rochester Inst. 42
79 ■ Clarkson 46
81 ■ St. Lawrence 55
69 Ithaca 68
60 Alfred 44
67 Rochester 70
54 Ithaca 59
77 Binghamton 81

WILLIAM & MARY 11-17
40 Virginia 82
62 † San Francisco 78
55 Navy 40
57 † Princeton 55
61 Va. Commonwealth 64
57 † Manhattan 63
73 † Colgate 36
50 Loyola (Md.) 45
50 Mt. St. Mary's (Md.) 66
68 ■ St. Bonaventure 65
54 Richmond 57
70 ■ American 76
53 ■ George Mason 56
78 ■ Md.-East. Shore 57
49 ■ James Madison 55
79 ■ N.C.-Wilmington 61
60 ■ East Caro. 62
48 ■ Old Dominion 64
68 American 78
67 George Mason 72
64 James Madison 66
74 ■ Richmond 62
85 N.C.-Wilmington 65
73 East Caro. 81
52 Old Dominion 79
60 † James Madison 58
83 † American 60
51 Old Dominion 65

WILLIAMS 10-11
48 Middlebury 62
61 ■ Skidmore 55
58 Amherst 54
50 Western Conn. St. 62
53 † Concordia (N.Y.) 43
60 Clark (Mass.) 61
47 ■ Westfield St. 53
57 ■ Middlebury 67
65 ■ Amherst 50
63 ■ Vassar 41
47 ■ Wellesley 66
58 Tufts 60
60 Smith 43
48 ■ Wesleyan 55
72 ■ North Adams St. 40
53 Hamilton 64
64 Trinity (Conn.) 68
76 Mount Holyoke 46
63 Union (N.Y.) 57
55 ■ Norwich 45
63 Wesleyan 67

WILMINGTON (OHIO) 16-8
83 ■ Wilberforce 51
61 ■ Cedarville 88
64 Rio Grande 100
56 † Ohio Wesleyan 74
69 † Olivet 45
78 ■ Walsh 59
96 ■ Ohio Dominican 76
84 Asbury 79
67 Urbana 61
81 ■ Urbana 76
61 Defiance 67
94 Thomas More 87
75 Berea 73
73 Mt. St. Joseph's 81
76 ■ Bluffton 54
67 ■ Defiance 69
84 ■ Thomas More 71
88 ■ Berea 77
114 ■ Asbury 57

77 Malone 67
89 ■ Wooster 87
62 Bluffton 71
76 † Bluffton 74
61 Defiance 74

WINONA ST. 11-16
80 ■ Concordia (St. Paul) 62
70 ■ Wis.-La Crosse 61
57 † Wis.-Stevens Point 60
84 † Concordia (St. Paul) 68
70 ■ Mt. Senario 56
76 Luther 68
59 St. Ambrose 76
63 St. Scholastica 70
76 ■ Quincy 73
61 Wis.-Parkside 83
83 ■ Minn.-Morris 54
68 ■ Moorhead St. 88
91 ■ Bemidji St. 87
46 ■ Minn.-Duluth 74
49 Minn.-Morris 68
52 Moorhead St. 89
77 ■ St. Scholastica 53
57 ■ Southwest St. 49
55 ■ Northern St. 83
61 ■ Viterbo 57
72 Bemidji St. 87
43 Minn.-Duluth 82
62 Quincy 86
69 Northern St. 101
59 Southwest St. 60
62 ■ Wis.-Stout 90
42 Minn.-Duluth 71

WINSTON-SALEM 3-20
38 ■ Bowie St. 44
49 North Caro. A&T 89
50 St. Paul's 67
60 ■ Virginia St. 68
49 Shaw 60
60 ■ Norfolk St. 104
47 St. Augustine's 86
52 Hampton 88
54 N.C. Central 67
45 Elizabeth City St. 72
49 ■ Johnson Smith 93
58 ■ Fayetteville St. 83
58 ■ Virginia Union 67
68 ■ Livingstone 59
63 ■ Shaw 69
51 ■ North Caro. A&T 61
62 Johnson Smith 78
72 ■ Bennett 36
69 ■ St. Augustine's 118
77 Livingstone 83
63 Fayetteville St. 83
67 ■ N.C. Central 59
57 † Virginia Union 64

WINTHROP 6-21
62 Davidson 64
71 ■ Western Caro. 65
60 Marshall 76
61 † East Tenn. St. 66
59 ■ East Caro. 86
64 Queens (N.C.) 74
58 Georgia 108
50 ■ Towson St. 67
62 ■ Md.-Balt. County 57
51 Liberty 82
72 ■ N.C.-Asheville 64
50 Charleston So. 58
63 Radford 84
43 ■ N.C.-Charlotte 90
87 Towson St. 68
46 Md.-Balt. County 78
67 N.C.-Asheville 51
59 ■ Liberty 62
58 ■ Furman 74
62 Coastal Caro. 82
46 ■ Campbell 58
48 N.C.-Greensboro 88
74 ■ Radford 81

43 Campbell 75
72 ■ Coastal Caro. 83
87 ■ Charleston So. 67
57 † Charleston So. 61

WISCONSIN 7-20
63 ■ Wis.-Green Bay 62
82 ■ Chicago St. 66
59 † Oklahoma St. 65
83 † Tenn.-Martin 63
77 ■ Wis.-Milwaukee 78
67 ■ Wake Forest 93
79 Southern Ill. 81
71 Santa Clara 81
69 San Francisco 71
39 Iowa 65
75 ■ Minnesota 72
75 ■ Michigan St. 67
73 ■ Michigan 67
74 Illinois 81
65 Northwestern 82
66 ■ Ohio St. 70
73 ■ Penn St. 90
49 Purdue 72
79 Michigan 75
67 Michigan St. 81
90 ■ Northwestern 103
74 ■ Illinois 84
50 Ohio St. 95
66 Penn St. 95
72 ■ Indiana 79
57 ■ Purdue 77
56 Minnesota 91

WIS.-EAU CLAIRE 22-4
80 ■ Mt. Senario 40
79 St. Norbert 61
83 Viterbo 69
75 ■ Northland 30
74 Wis.-Stout 77
69 Wis.-Oshkosh 52
66 Wis.-Whitewater 64
66 ■ Wis.-La Crosse 48
103 † Gordon 39
84 † Judson 45
94 Western St. 62
72 ■ Wis.-Superior 62
82 Wis.-River Falls 66
86 ■ Wis.-Platteville 59
77 ■ Wis.-Stevens Point 61
70 Wis.-Parkside 73
81 ■ Wis.-Stout 103
68 Wis.-Superior 59
47 ■ Wis.-Oshkosh 42
76 ■ Wis.-Whitewater 75
85 Wis.-La Crosse 73
93 Wis.-Platteville 67
85 Wis.-Stevens Point 63
96 ■ Wis.-River Falls 67
95 ■ Wis.-Stout 89
63 Central (Iowa) 70

WIS.-GREEN BAY 19-10
62 Wisconsin 63
67 Eastern Wash. 55
52 Washington St. 59
71 ■ Wis.-Milwaukee 70
51 ■ Montana St. 65
66 ■ Minnesota 79
78 ■ Nebraska 81
71 Ill.-Chicago 62
54 ■ DePaul 65
76 Northern Ill. 85
92 ■ Western Ill. 52
67 Youngstown St. 54
87 Cleveland St. 53
72 Marquette 69
70 ■ Wright St. 65
68 ■ Eastern Ill. 54
87 ■ Valparaiso 69
68 ■ Northern Ill. 71
76 ■ Ill.-Chicago 59
60 Georgia 82
81 Western Ill. 60

86 Valparaiso 77
73 ■ Youngstown St. 58
65 ■ Cleveland St. 55
53 Wright St. 49
71 Eastern Ill. 41
76 ■ Wright St. 60
73 ■ Youngstown St. 63
58 ■ Northern Ill. 75

WIS.-LA CROSSE 9-16
80 † Viterbo 57
61 Winona St. 70
53 Bethel (Minn.) 75
71 ■ Luther 68
65 Wis.-Superior 69
71 ■ Wis.-Stout 93
63 ■ Wis.-River Falls 56
48 Wis.-Eau Claire 66
69 ■ Carroll (Wis.) 65
67 Wis.-Platteville 71
47 ■ Wis.-Oshkosh 67
60 St. Norbert 66
64 ■ Wis.-Parkside 65
65 Wis.-Stevens Point 76
67 ■ Wis.-Superior 65
73 ■ Cardinal Stritch 68
68 ■ Viterbo 61
65 ■ Wis.-Whitewater 73
85 Wis.-River Falls 77
87 Wis.-Stout 109
73 ■ Wis.-Eau Claire 85
52 Wis.-Whitewater 75
37 Wis.-Oshkosh 73
74 ■ Wis.-Platteville 64
68 ■ Wis.-Stevens Point 81

WIS.-MILWAUKEE 15-12
76 Eastern Mich. 78
45 Detroit Mercy 70
73 ■ Southeast Mo. St. 60
69 Bowling Green 88
48 † Michigan St. 61
78 Wisconsin 77
76 ■ Iowa St. 51
79 † Jackson St. 52
41 Auburn 68
66 ■ Miami (Ohio) 56
76 St. Louis 63
56 Southeast Mo. St. 54
70 Wis.-Green Bay 71
46 Northwestern 89
60 Marquette 73
79 ■ Northeastern Ill. 69
56 Indiana St. 59
65 ■ Chicago St. 53
72 ■ St. Louis 61
78 ■ Wis.-Parkside 67
61 Northeastern Ill. 38
57 ■ Mo.-Kansas City 45
88 ■ Loyola (Ill.) 77
70 ■ Marquette 76
76 Chicago St. 58
42 Mo.-Kansas City 63
72 † Cal St. Sacramento 85

WIS.-OSHKOSH 16-8
66 Ripon 49
57 St. Francis (Ill.) 71
71 ■ St. Norbert 39
57 ■ Wis.-Stevens Point 66
52 ■ Wis.-Eau Claire 69
63 ■ Wis.-Superior 55
55 ■ Marian (Wis.) 56
46 † Cardinal Stritch 48
83 † St. Mary's (Minn.) 55
71 ■ Wis.-Whitewater 49
67 Wis.-La Crosse 47
67 Wis.-River Falls 45
68 Wis.-Stout 67
51 Concordia (Wis.) 54
80 ■ Wis.-Platteville 42
69 Wis.-Stevens Point 56
53 Wis.-Whitewater 59
82 ■ Wis.-Stout 67
42 Wis.-Eau Claire 47

66 Wis.-Superior 45
70 ■ Wis.-River Falls 43
73 ■ Wis.-La Crosse 37
74 Wis.-Platteville 53
85 ■ Elmhurst 50

WIS.-PARKSIDE 12-15
77 Grand Valley St. 55
81 ■ Bemidji St. 73
64 † Slippery Rock 60
83 Wayne St. (Mich.) 91
63 Northern Mich. 79
70 Michigan Tech 72
55 Wis.-Stevens Point 67
85 ■ St. Francis (Ill.) 57
72 National Louis 60
75 ■ St. Joseph's (Ind.) 92
58 ■ Minn.-Duluth 62
83 ■ Winona St. 61
71 Bemidji St. 74
81 Wis.-Platteville 57
65 Wis.-La Crosse 64
73 ■ Wis.-Eau Claire 70
68 ■ Lewis 79
70 SIU-Edwardsville 62
65 McKendree 66
54 St. Joseph's (Ind.) 71
67 Wis.-Milwaukee 78
90 Purdue-Calumet 47
59 Lewis 76
85 Mercyhurst 87
82 Gannon 72
87 ■ Northern Mich. 96
48 ■ Michigan Tech 71

WIS.-PLATTEVILLE 5-20
42 Wartburg 57
56 St. Ambrose 101
82 † Illinois Col. 72
56 Washington (Mo.) 65
71 ■ Loras 67
47 Wis.-Whitewater 67
81 Viterbo 86
72 ■ Luther 75
69 Wis.-Stevens Point 75
71 ■ Wis.-La Crosse 67
57 ■ Wis.-Parkside 81
59 Wis.-Eau Claire 86
66 Wis.-Superior 79
54 ■ Wis.-Stout 80
42 Wis.-Oshkosh 80
47 ■ Wis.-Whitewater 82
65 ■ Wis.-Stevens Point 74
74 Wis.-Stout 102
68 Wis.-River Falls 75
73 ■ Clarke 66
67 ■ Wis.-Eau Claire 93
70 ■ Wis.-Superior 82
64 Wis.-La Crosse 74
53 ■ Wis.-Oshkosh 74
74 ■ Wis.-River Falls 66

WIS.-RIVER FALLS 5-20
62 Bethel (Minn.) 57
50 Southwest St. 70
54 † Huron 40
62 St. Benedict 92
62 ■ Gust. Adolphus 73
59 Wis.-Stevens Point 67
56 Wis.-La Crosse 63
80 ■ N'western (Minn.) 50
53 St. Thomas (Minn.) 76
74 ■ Wis.-Stout 88
66 ■ Wis.-Eau Claire 82
45 ■ Wis.-Oshkosh 67
64 ■ Wis.-Whitewater 84
83 Wis.-Superior 86
70 ■ Macalester 83
73 St. Scholastica 70
67 Wis.-Stout 92
49 ■ Wis.-Stevens Point 61
77 ■ Wis.-La Crosse 85
75 ■ Wis.-Platteville 68
43 Wis.-Oshkosh 70
63 Wis.-Whitewater 85
67 Wis.-Eau Claire 96
70 ■ Wis.-Superior 74
66 Wis.-Platteville 74

WIS.-STEVENS POINT 16-8
64 Luther 62
51 St. Thomas (Minn.) 82
72 ■ Marian (Wis.) 60
60 † Winona St. 57
72 St. Mary's (Minn.) 59
79 Viterbo 71
66 Wis.-Oshkosh 57
67 ■ Wis.-Parkside 55
67 ■ Wis.-River Falls 59
47 ■ Wis.-Stout 69
75 ■ Wis.-Platteville 69
52 Wis.-Whitewater 78
84 Wis.-Superior 66
61 Wis.-Eau Claire 77
76 ■ Wis.-La Crosse 65
56 ■ Wis.-Oshkosh 69
74 Wis.-Platteville 65
61 Wis.-River Falls 49
40 Wis.-Stout 88
74 ■ Wis.-Superior 52
63 ■ Wis.-Eau Claire 85
61 ■ Wis.-Whitewater 67
81 Wis.-La Crosse 68
79 ■ St. Norbert 74

WIS.-STOUT 21-4
93 † Eureka 71
83 St. Francis (Ill.) 61
83 Northland 44
92 ■ Mt. Senario 73
77 ■ Wis.-Eau Claire 74
82 St. Olaf 72
93 Wis.-La Crosse 71
69 Wis.-Stevens Point 47
87 Minn.-Morris 83
88 Wis.-River Falls 74
103 ■ Concordia (St. Paul) 63
85 ■ Wis.-Superior 59
81 ■ Wis.-Whitewater 54
67 ■ Wis.-Oshkosh 68
80 Wis.-Platteville 54
103 Wis.-Eau Claire 81
92 ■ Wis.-River Falls 67
67 Wis.-Oshkosh 82
102 ■ Wis.-Platteville 74
109 ■ Wis.-La Crosse 87
88 ■ Wis.-Stevens Point 40
90 Winona St. 62
84 Wis.-Superior 62
76 Wis.-Whitewater 97
89 Wis.-Eau Claire 95

WIS.-SUPERIOR 9-15
94 ■ Augsburg 63
64 ■ Mt. Senario 61
51 ■ Minn.-Duluth 86
69 ■ Wis.-La Crosse 65
64 ■ Northland 48
61 Wis.-Whitewater 66
55 Wis.-Oshkosh 63
70 Mt. Senario 88
62 Wis.-Eau Claire 72
59 Wis.-Stout 85
73 St. Scholastica 76
66 ■ Wis.-Stevens Point 84
79 ■ Wis.-Platteville 66
70 ■ St. Scholastica 59
86 ■ Wis.-River Falls 83
65 Wis.-La Crosse 67
59 ■ Wis.-Eau Claire 68
64 Northland 66
77 ■ Wis.-Whitewater 87
45 ■ Wis.-Oshkosh 66
52 Wis.-Stevens Point 74
82 Wis.-Platteville 70
62 ■ Wis.-Stout 84
74 Wis.-River Falls 70

WIS.-WHITEWATER 19-7
59 ■ Beloit 46
74 ■ Chicago 53
100 ■ Rockford 18
61 Lawrence 67
67 ■ Wis.-Platteville 47
63 St. Norbert 62
66 ■ Wis.-Superior 61
64 ■ Wis.-Eau Claire 66
61 Augustana (Ill.) 70
49 Wis.-Oshkosh 71
78 ■ Wis.-Stevens Point 52
72 ■ Edgewood 50
54 Wis.-Stout 81
84 Wis.-River Falls 64
82 Wis.-Platteville 47
59 ■ Wis.-Oshkosh 53
73 Wis.-La Crosse 65
87 Wis.-Superior 77
75 Wis.-Eau Claire 76
69 ■ Carroll (Wis.) 61
75 ■ Wis.-La Crosse 52
85 ■ Wis.-River Falls 63
67 Wis.-Stevens Point 61
97 ■ Wis.-Stout 76
76 Calvin 68
77 † Wartburg 83

WITTENBERG 23-4
76 ■ Wooster 41
99 Earlham 61
70 St. Benedict 88
77 Hamline 48
64 Ohio Wesleyan 54
84 ■ Bethany (W.Va.) 53
87 ■ Defiance 42
56 ■ Capital 51
72 Otterbein 61
72 ■ Case Reserve 43
56 Denison 61
79 Allegheny 60
84 ■ Oberlin 15
68 ■ Kenyon 35
52 Wooster 41
57 ■ Ohio Wesleyan 60
82 Case Reserve 48
72 ■ Mt. St. Joseph's 69
64 ■ Allegheny 51
74 ■ Earlham 63
65 Oberlin 21
99 Kenyon 26
82 ■ Denison 74
83 ■ Earlham 58
70 † Allegheny 51
67 Ohio Wesleyan 60
50 Capital 93

WOFFORD 23-4
100 ■ Coker 61
80 ■ Belmont Abbey 71
85 † Converse 61
84 S.C.-Spartanburg 82
98 † Newberry 62
66 Presbyterian 74
88 Francis Marion 66
74 Pfeiffer 53
78 Converse 43
78 Savannah St. 87
71 ■ Queens (N.C.) 57
59 Mars Hill 69
75 Erskine 45
73 ■ Davidson 63
69 ■ Limestone 48
70 Longwood 59
72 ■ Presbyterian 67
83 ■ Lincoln Memorial 77
71 ■ Converse 52
73 ■ Newberry 72
70 Davidson 61
84 Limestone 76
99 ■ Erskine 66
70 Coker 65
59 Lincoln Memorial 66
91 ■ Longwood 76
68 ■ Savannah St. 60

WOOSTER 13-11
82 ■ Urbana 77
41 Wittenberg 76
65 Nazareth (N.Y.) 58
60 † Wheaton (Mass.) 74
60 ■ Case Reserve 47
64 ■ Denison 65
76 ■ Notre Dame (Ohio) 51
60 Mount Union 69
74 Kenyon 38
92 ■ Oberlin 46
73 Earlham 54
85 ■ Allegheny 62
58 Ohio Wesleyan 66
56 Denison 48
41 ■ Wittenberg 52
58 Case Reserve 61
75 ■ Kenyon 31
64 Allegheny 56
83 ■ Earlham 50
53 Defiance 68
52 ■ Ohio Wesleyan 68
87 Wilmington (Ohio) 89
74 Oberlin 54
50 ■ Allegheny 69

WORCESTER TECH 9-14
73 † Nichols 52
55 † Clark (Mass.) 78
67 ■ Fitchburg St. 58
66 Framingham St. 51
59 Bri'water (Mass.) 64
63 † Castleton St. 35
58 Gordon 60
47 ■ Mass.-Dartmouth 66
47 ■ Coast Guard 46
55 Trinity (Conn.) 65
46 ■ Western New Eng. 60
56 Pine Manor 46
54 ■ Amherst 50
56 Mount Holyoke 55
47 ■ Smith 50
43 Brandeis 76
48 ■ Wellesley 80
81 ■ MIT 52
58 ■ Clark (Mass.) 71
60 Wheaton (Mass.) 78
50 Nichols 51
60 Babson 61
59 Wheaton (Mass.) 97

WORCESTER ST. 11-14
60 ■ Clark (Mass.) 75
72 ■ Nichols 54
59 Wellesley 80
45 Anna Maria 56
84 ■ Suffolk 60
67 ■ Staten Island 52
66 ■ Wm. Paterson 73
41 Western Conn. St. 84
64 ■ Fitchburg St. 81
67 ■ Eastern Conn. St. 57
29 Westfield St. 72
76 ■ Framingham St. 54
61 Clark (Mass.) 79
68 ■ North Adams St. 54
70 Bri'water (Mass.) 62
83 ■ Emmanuel 92
54 Western New Eng. 66
65 ■ Salem St. 61
67 Fitchburg St. 74
52 ■ Westfield St. 67
68 Framingham St. 66
84 North Adams St. 52
67 ■ Bri'water (Mass.) 64
50 Salem St. 72
56 ■ Bri'water (Mass.) 77

WRIGHT ST. 9-18
44 ■ Indiana 88
70 ■ Morehead St. 63
71 ■ Marshall 57
53 ■ Miami (Ohio) 65
51 Cincinnati 66

54 ■ Dayton 58
70 ■ Austin Peay 65
38 ■ Missouri 77
54 Xavier (Ohio) 77
68 ■ Valparaiso 70
45 Ill.-Chicago 64
65 ■ Eastern Ill. 54
59 Youngstown St. 66
69 Cleveland St. 66
95 ■ Western Ill. 72
65 Wis.-Green Bay 70
61 Northern Ill. 78
70 Indiana St. 59
75 Eastern Ill. 58
87 Valparaiso 125
60 ■ Ill.-Chicago 75
83 ■ Cleveland St. 93
62 ■ Youngstown St. 66
79 Western Ill. 57
49 ■ Wis.-Green Bay 53
51 ■ Northern Ill. 77
60 Wis.-Green Bay 76

WYOMING 14-13
74 ■ Adams St. 56
62 Northern Iowa 52
61 Creighton 98
67 ■ Baylor 76
51 ■ Loyola (Cal.) 53
64 ■ Toledo 63
71 ■ Southwest Tex. St. . 66
56 Colorado 72
75 ■ Texas A&M 66
63 Southern Utah 57
72 Weber St. 61
61 Idaho St. 59
83 ■ Colorado St. 69
55 ■ Utah 75
75 ■ Brigham Young 78
70 Fresno St. 99
48 San Diego St. 53
69 ■ UTEP 73
69 ■ New Mexico 57
58 Colorado St. 70
67 Brigham Young 83
58 Utah 62
78 ■ San Diego St. 72
89 ■ Fresno St. 73
75 New Mexico 52
66 UTEP 64
55 † UTEP 68

XAVIER (OHIO) 21-9
103 Morehead St. 54
99 ■ West Va. 68
60 ■ Miami (Ohio) 71
69 ■ Eastern Wash. 61
51 Ohio 52
82 ■ Indiana St. 70
77 ■ Wright St. 54
76 Dayton 61
76 Alabama 95
56 ■ Notre Dame 64
86 La Salle 75
80 Duquesne 65
87 ■ Butler 91
71 ■ Evansville 76
70 Detroit Mercy 75
73 Loyola (Ill.) 52
82 Youngstown St. 79
78 ■ Dayton 65
70 Notre Dame 68
102 ■ Duquesne 69
79 ■ La Salle 54
81 Cincinnati 48
80 Butler 89
79 Evansville 69
96 ■ Loyola (Ill.) 57
83 ■ Detroit Mercy 75
74 † Detroit Mercy 72
67 † Dayton 57
82 † Butler 72
64 Clemson 70

YALE 15-11
69 Central Conn. St. ... 62
56 Northwestern 73
57 † South Caro. 64
60 ■ Wagner 51
50 † Middle Tenn. St. ... 66
56 † Massachusetts 54
78 † LIU-Brooklyn 45
66 Hartford 59
68 ■ Lehigh 55
42 ■ Lafayette 57
65 ■ Brown 69
66 Fairfield 73
65 Brown 71
52 ■ Army 42
78 ■ Columbia-Barnard . 65
72 ■ Cornell 62
62 Princeton 68
71 Pennsylvania 44
69 ■ Harvard 75
67 ■ Dartmouth 49
74 Cornell 63
70 Columbia-Barnard . 46
51 Dartmouth 78
61 Harvard 69
55 ■ Pennsylvania 44
67 ■ Princeton 60

YORK (N.Y.) 15-10
50 New Jersey Tech .. 52
82 Medgar Evers 19
47 John Jay 33
68 CCNY 57
71 † Medgar Evers 17
50 Mt. St. Vincent 47
69 Baruch 63
34 Jersey City St. 72
41 Mt. St. Vincent 47
39 ■ New Jersey Tech .. 37
43 ■ Vassar 55
78 ■ Marymount (N.Y.) .. 41
46 ■ CCNY 51
70 ■ Medgar Evers 40
49 ■ Hunter 53
68 New Rochelle 32
54 Old Westbury 52
51 ■ Baruch 42
48 Staten Island 55
60 ■ Yeshiva 16
42 Stony Brook 84
44 Mt. St. Mary (N.Y.) . 76
56 ■ John Jay 42
59 † John Jay 43
54 Staten Island 73

YORK (PA.) 13-12
61 Frank. & Marsh. ... 84
55 † Albright 62
62 ■ Western Md. 51
56 ■ Messiah 54
73 ■ Misericordia 49
56 ■ William Smith 70
63 ■ Gettysburg 69
66 Dickinson 76
64 † Messiah 57
73 † Juniata 72
77 Goucher 67
106 ■ Catholic 75
60 Marymount (Va.) ... 91
114 St. Mary's (Md.) 52
50 Susquehanna 81
75 ■ Gallaudet 64
84 ■ Mary Washington .. 66
67 ■ Goucher 62
87 ■ Marymount (Va.) ... 99
50 Catholic 65
77 ■ St. Mary's (Md.) 48
66 Gallaudet 74
68 Mary Washington .. 83
97 ■ Gallaudet 72
70 Mary Washington .. 93

YOUNGSTOWN ST. 17-11
92 West Va. 72
69 Kent 82
62 Marshall 65
74 ■ Robert Morris 66
72 † Lamar 62
64 Nevada-Las Vegas . 84
83 Ohio 64
71 ■ Akron 64
95 Western Ill. 75
66 Eastern Ill. 50
83 Cleveland St. 65
66 ■ Wright St. 59
54 ■ Wis.-Green Bay 67
75 ■ Northern Ill. 91
99 Valparaiso 107
68 Ill.-Chicago 59
79 ■ Xavier (Ohio) 82
66 ■ Cleveland St. 53
54 ■ Tennessee 78
80 ■ Western Ill. 64
71 ■ Eastern Ill. 56
66 Wright St. 62
58 Wis.-Green Bay 73
92 Northern Ill. 105
117 ■ Valparaiso 106
74 ■ Ill.-Chicago 62
89 † Cleveland St. 74
63 Wis.-Green Bay 73

1993-94 WOMEN'S SCHEDULES

Listed alphabetically in this section are the 1993-94 schedules for women's teams that were available from NCAA member institutions at press time.

Below each institution's name and location appear the name of its head coach and his or her complete won-lost record as a college head coach.

Divisional designation for each institution is indicated in the lower right-hand corner of each schedule.

Schedules are subject to change.

ABILENE CHRISTIAN .... Abilene, TX 79699

Suzanne Fox (1 YR. W-18, L-9)

East Tex. St. Tr. N19-20
Abilene Chrst. Cl. N26-27
UTEP .... D 4
Schreiner■ .... D 6
Incarnate Word■ D18
New Mexico St. Cl. D21-22
North Fla. .... J 3
St. Leo .... J 4
Fla. Southern .... J 6
Angelo St.■ J11
Texas A&I J15
East Tex. St. J17
Texas Woman's■ J22
Central Okla.■ J24
West Tex. St.■ J29
Eastern N. Mex.■ J31
West Tex. St. .... F 5
Eastern N. Mex. .... F 7
East Tex. St.■ F12
Texas A&I■ F14
Central Okla. F19
Texas Woman's F21
Angelo St. F26

Colors: Purple & White. Nickname: Wildcats.
AD: Cecil Eager. SID: Garner Roberts.

II

ADAMS ST. .... Alamosa, CO 81102

Todd Cotton (9 YRS. W-167, L-101)

Air Force■ N20
Colo. Christian N23
Southern Colo. Tr. D3-4
Fort Lewis .... D 7
Colorado Col. D10
Colorado-CS D11
Pt. Loma Nazarene .... J 6
La Verne .... J 7
Western St. J14
Mesa St. J15
Chadron St.■ J20
Colorado Mines■ J21
Colorado Col.■ J28
Fort Hays St.■ J29
Colo. Christian■ .... F 2
Colorado Mines .... F 3
Chadron St. .... F 5
Southern Colo.■ .... F 8
Western St.■ F11
Mesa St.■ F12
N.M. Highlands F15
Fort Hays St. F19
Fort Lewis■ F22
N.M. Highlands■ F26

Colors: Green & Gold. Nickname: Lady Indians.
AD: Vivian Frausto. SID: Lloyd Engen.

II

ADELPHI .... Garden City, NY 11530

Bill Zatulskis (3 YRS. W-42, L-42)

St. Michael's N29
St. Rose■ .... D 4
Molloy■ .... D 6
Pace .... D 8
Queens (N.Y.) D11
Southern Conn. St. D13
Phila. Textile D19
St. Michael's■ D30
Sacred Heart■ .... J 3
Concordia (N.Y.)■ .... J 5
LIU-Southampton■ .... J 8
Molloy J12
LIU-C.W. Post J15
Mercy J19
Albany (N.Y.) Tr. J21-22
Phila. Textile■ J24
St. Rose J29
Mercy■ .... F 2
LIU-Southampton .... F 9
Dowling F12
LIU-C.W. Post■ F14
Queens (N.Y.)■ F16
Dowling■ F21
Pace■ F23
Concordia (N.Y.) F26

Colors: Brown & Gold. Nickname: Panthers.
AD: Bob Hartwell. SID: S. Andrew Baumbach.

II

ADRIAN .... Adrian, MI 49221

Kathy Lee (1 YR. W-19, L-7)

Capital■ N20
Spring Arbor N23
Wis.-Oshkosh Cl. N26-27
Ohio Northern■ N30
St. Mary's (In.) Cl. D3-4
Northwood .... D 7
Concordia (Mich.) D18
Madonna■ D30
Calvin■ .... J 5
Albion .... J 8
Olivet J12
Alma■ J15
Bluffton■ J19
Kalamazoo J22
Hope■ J26
Calvin J29
Albion■ .... F 2
Olivet■ .... F 5
Alma .... F 9
Siena Heights F12
Kalamazoo■ F16
Hope F19

Colors: Gold & Black. Nickname: Bulldogs.
AD: C. Henry Mensing. SID: Darcy Gifford.

III

AGNES SCOTT .... Decatur, GA 30030

Nancy Rast (1 YR. W-1, L-18)

Emory Tr. N19-20
Tenn. Temple■ .... D 2
Oglethorpe .... D 4
Sewanee .... D 6
Spelman .... D 9
Toccoa Falls Inst.■ J15
Oglethorpe■ J19
Savannah A&D J22
Savannah A&D■ J29
Wesleyan (Ga.) .... F 1
Spelman■ .... F 3
Tenn. Temple F11
Wesleyan (Ga.)■ F21
Wesleyan (Ga.) Tr. F26-27

Colors: Purple & White.
AD: To be named. SID: Nancy Rast.

III

AIR FORCE .... USAF Academy, CO 80840

Marti Gasser (14 YRS. W-238, L-155)

Adams St. N20
Colorado Mines N23
Texas Woman's Tr. N26-27
Northern Colo.■ .... D 1
UC Davis Inv. D3-4
Western St.■ D11
Florida Tech Tr. J2-3
Fort Lewis .... J 8
Metropolitan St.■ J12
Colo. Christian■ J15
Denver J19
Regis (Colo.) J22
Southern Colo. J26
Colorado-CS J29
Colorado Col. .... F 2
Fort Lewis■ .... F 5
Metropolitan St. .... F 9
Colo. Christian F12
Denver■ F16
Regis (Colo.)■ F19
Southern Colo.■ F23
Colorado-CS■ F28

Colors: Blue & Silver. Nickname: Falcons.
AD: Col. Ken Schweitzer. SID: Dave Kellogg.

II

AKRON .... Akron, OH 44325

To be named

Cincinnati N26
Niagara■ N29
Buffalo Tr. D3-4
Valparaiso .... D 8
Austin Peay D11
Youngstown St.■ D18
American■ D30
Eastern Mich. .... J 5
Western Mich. .... J 8
Toledo■ J12
Ohio J15
Kent■ J19
Central Mich. J22
Ball St.■ J26
Bowling Green J29
Miami (Ohio)■ .... F 2
Western Mich.■ .... F 5
Toledo .... F 9
Ohio■ F12
Kent F16
Central Mich.■ F19
Ball St. F23
Bowling Green■ F26
Miami (Ohio) .... M 2
Eastern Mich.■ .... M 5
Mid-American Tr. M11-12

Colors: Blue & Gold. Nickname: Lady Zips.
AD: Dick Aynes (Interim). SID: Joey Arrietta.

I

ALABAMA .... University, AL 35486

Rick Moody (4 YRS. W-78, L-40)

Iowa St. Cl. N26-27
Alabama Cl. D3-4
East Tenn. St.■ .... D 8
Louisiana Tech■ D11
Central Fla. Cl. D29-31
Georgia■ .... J 5
Illinois .... J 7
Vanderbilt .... J 9
Troy St. J12
Florida■ J16
Mercer■ J18
South Caro. J22
South Ala.■ J26
Louisiana St.■ J29
Arkansas .... F 1
Tennessee .... F 5
Kentucky■ F13
Auburn■ F16
Mississippi St.■ F19
Alabama St.■ F23
Mississippi F26
Troy St.■ F28
Southeastern Tr. M4-7

Colors: Crimson & White. Nickname: Crimson Tide.
AD: Cecil Ingram. SID: Larry White.

I

■ Home games on each schedule.

See pages 735-738 for Division I tournament details

ALA.-BIRMINGHAM .... Birmingham, AL 35294
Jeannie Milling (16 YRS. W-200, L-189)

Mississippi St. Tr. D3-4
Southern Miss. .... D 7
Ala.-Birmingham Tr. D10-11
South Ala. D15
Ala.-Birmingham Cl. D20-21
South Ala.■ D30
Florida Int'l Tr. J2-4
St. Louis .... J 8
Auburn■ J12
Memphis St.■ J15
Mississippi St.■ J19
St. Louis■ J22
Marquette J29
Cincinnati■ .... F 3
Marquette■ .... F 5
Memphis St. F12
Dayton F15
DePaul■ F19
Dayton■ F21
DePaul F26
Cincinnati .... M 5
Great Midwest Tr. M9-12

Colors: Green, Gold & White. Nickname: Lady Blazers.
AD: Gene Bartow. SID: Chris Pika. I

ALA.-HUNTSVILLE .... Huntsville, AL 35899
Tia Sossamon (1ST YR. AS HEAD COACH)

Valdosta St. N30
West Fla.■ .... D 4
Ga. Southwestern■ .... D 8
Aub.-Montgomery D13
Belhaven D17
Mississippi Col. D18
Livingston .... J 3
Mississippi-Women■ .... J 5
West Ga.■ .... J 8
Valdosta St.■ J10
Central Ark. J15
Henderson St. J17
Livingston■ J20
Mississippi-Women J22
Lincoln Memorial■ J24
Mississippi Col.■ J27
Montevallo J29
Aub.-Montgomery■ J31
Central Ark.■ .... F 5
Henderson St.■ .... F 7
North Ala.■ F12
Alabama A&M F16
West Ga. F19
Montevallo■ F21
North Ala. F23
Lincoln Memorial F26

Colors: Royal Blue & White. Nickname: Chargers.
AD: Paul Brand. SID: Julie Woltjen. II

ALABAMA A&M .... Normal, AL 35762
Press Parham (11 YRS. W-207, L-99)

Jacksonville St. N22
Miles N28
Livingston■ N30
Lane■ .... D 2
Albany St. (Ga.)■ .... D 4
LeMoyne-Owen .... D 6
Morris Brown D11
Savannah St. .... J 7
Paine .... J 8
Albany St. (Ga.) J10
Savannah St.■ J14
LeMoyne-Owen■ J19
Tuskegee J22
Clark Atlanta J24
Tuskegee■ J29
Fort Valley St. J31
Miles■ .... F 2
Fort Valley St.■ .... F 7
Clark Atlanta■ .... F 9
Morris Brown■ F11
Ala.-Huntsville■ F16
Paine■ F19
Knoxville■ F21
Talladega■ F23
Jacksonville St.■ F26

Colors: Maroon & White. Nickname: Lady Bulldogs.
AD: Gene Bright. SID: Antoine Bell. II

ALABAMA ST. .... Montgomery, AL 36101
Ron Mitchell (8 YRS. W-87, L-122)

Georgia St. N26
Florida A&M■ .... D 1
Georgia St.■ .... D 8
Tennessee Tech Cl. D11-12
Tuskegee■ .... J 6
Prairie View■ .... J 8
Texas Southern■ J10
Alcorn St. J15
Southern-B.R. J17
Troy St.■ J19
Grambling J22
Mississippi Val.■ J24
Florida A&M J26
Jackson St. J29
Prairie View .... F 5
Texas Southern .... F 7
Troy St. F10
Alcorn St.■ F12
Southern-B.R.■ F14
Aub.-Montgomery■ F16
Grambling■ F19
Mississippi Val. F21
Alabama F23
Jackson St.■ F26
Southeastern La. .... M 1
SWAC Tr. M10-13

Colors: Black & Gold. Nickname: Hornets.
AD: Arthur Barnett. SID: Peter Forest. I

ALAS. ANCHORAGE .... Anchorage, AK 99508
Milt Raugust (3 YRS. W-51, L-31)

Morningside■ N19
Morningside■ N19
Colorado-CS■ N22
Colorado-CS■ N23
Mo.-St. Louis■ N29
Mo.-St. Louis■ N30
Hawaii Tr. D3-5
Slippery Rock■ D10
Slippery Rock■ D11
Cal St. Chico D17
Fresno Pacific D18
UC San Diego Inv. D28-30
Alas. Anchorage Inv. J6-8
Seattle Pacific■ J20
Portland St.■ J22
Alas. Fairbanks J29
Grand Canyon .... F 3
Eastern Mont. .... F 5
Seattle Pacific F10
Portland St. F12
Alas. Fairbanks■ F19
Grand Canyon■ F24
Eastern Mont.■ F26

Colors: Green & Gold. Nickname: Seawolves.
AD: Timothy Dillon. SID: Dave Mateer. II

ALAS. FAIRBANKS .... Fairbanks, AK 99775
Joe Tremarello (3 YRS. W-34, L-44)

Colorado-CS■ N19
Colorado-CS■ N20
Morningside■ N22
Morningside■ N23
Mo.-St. Louis■ N26
Mo.-St. Louis■ N27
Regis (Colo.) Cl. D3-4
Slippery Rock■ .... D 7
Slippery Rock■ .... D 8
St. Martin's D20
Seattle D22
Seattle D23
UC Davis .... J 4
Portland St.■ J20
Seattle Pacific■ J22
Seattle Pacific■ J23
Alas. Anchorage■ J29
Eastern Mont. .... F 3
Grand Canyon .... F 5
Portland St. F10
Seattle Pacific F12
Alas. Anchorage F19
Eastern Mont.■ F24
Grand Canyon■ F26

Colors: Blue & Gold. Nickname: Nanooks.
AD: Tom Wells. SID: Jodi Hoatson. II

ALBANY (N.Y.) .... Albany, NY 12222
Mari Warner (10 YRS. W-177, L-72)

Albany (N.Y.) Tr. N20-21
Binghamton■ N23
William Smith .... D 1
Worcester St. Tr. D4-5
Buffalo St.■ D12
New York U. .... J 3
Skidmore .... J 6
Wilkes J10
Hunter J15
Ithaca■ J18
Albany (N.Y.) Tr. J21-22
Plattsburgh St.■ J25
Union (N.Y.) J27
Stony Brook■ J29
Cortland St. .... F 2
Old Westbury■ .... F 5
Utica .... F 7
Elmira■ F12
Hamilton■ F15
Nazareth (N.Y.) F19
Rensselaer■ F22

Colors: Purple & Gold. Nickname: Great Danes.
AD: Milt Richards. SID: Kyle Serba. III

ALBERTUS MAGNUS .... New Haven, CT 06511
Jim Ferraro (3 YRS. W-40, L-28)

Eastern Conn. Tr. N19
Trinity (Conn.) N23
John Jay■ N29
Eastern Conn. St.■ .... D 1
Norwich■ .... D 4
Elms■ .... D 9
Salve Regina D12
Westfield St.■ .... J 8
Simmons■ J15
Ramapo J17
Mt. St. Vincent J19
Suffolk J29
Wesleyan .... F 1
Colby-Sawyer .... F 5
Coast Guard .... F 7
Endicott F12
Western New Eng.■ F15
Teiko Post■ F17

Colors: Royal Blue & White. Nickname: Falcons.
AD: Thomas Blake. SID: Joseph Tonelli. III

ALBION .... Albion, MI 49224
Sally Konkle (3 YRS. W-34, L-38)

John Carroll Tr. N19-20
Manchester N23
Bluffton Tr. D3-4
Concordia (Mich.) .... D 7
Spring Arbor■ .... D 9
Defiance Cl. D17-18
Northwood■ D29
Alma .... J 5
Adrian■ .... J 8
Kalamazoo J12
Hope J15
Calvin■ J19
Olivet■ J26
Alma■ J29
Adrian .... F 2
Kalamazoo■ .... F 5
Hope■ .... F 9
Calvin F12
Hillsdale■ F17
Olivet F19

Colors: Purple & Gold. Nickname: Britons.
AD: Sally Konkle. SID: Robin Hartman. III

ALBRIGHT .... Reading, PA 19604
Sally Miller (15 YRS. W-136, L-173)

Frank. & Marsh. Tr. N20-21
Widener N30
Ursinus .... D 2
Lebanon Valley■ .... D 4
Drew■ .... D 7
Delaware Valley .... D 9
Tampa Tr. J7-8
Moravian■ J13
Elizabethtown J15
Messiah J18
Wilkes■ J20
Juniata■ J22
Susquehanna■ J27
Widener■ J29
Allentown .... F 1
Moravian .... F 3
Lebanon Valley .... F 5
Messiah■ .... F 9
Elizabethtown■ F12
Susquehanna F15
Juniata F19
Gettysburg■ F22

Colors: Cardinal & White. Nickname: Lady Lions.
AD: William Helm Jr. SID: Elliot Tannenbaum. III

■ Home games on each schedule.

See pages 735-738 for Division I tournament details

ALCORN ST. .... Lorman, MS 39096

Shirley Walker (14 YRS. W-215, L-167)

Houston Cl. N26-27
Tennessee St.■ N29
Texas Tech Cl. D4-5
Tennessee St. D18
Grambling .... J 8
Mississippi Val. J10
Alabama St.■ J15
Jackson St.■ J17
Texas Southern■ J22
Prairie View■ J24
Southern-B.R. J29
Grambling■ .... F 5
Mississippi Val.■ .... F 7
Alabama St. F12
Jackson St. F14
Texas Southern F19
Prairie View F21
Southern-B.R. F26
South Ala.■ F28

Colors: Purple & Gold. Nickname: Lady Braves.
AD: Cardell Jones. SID: Gus Howard. I

ALDERSON-BROADDUS .... Phillippi, WV 26146

Carolyn Mair (2 YRS. W-19, L-34)

Ohio Valley N22
Davis & Elkins N29
Fairmont St. .... D 4
West Va. Wesleyan .... D 6
Wash. & Jeff. .... D 9
Mercyhurst Tr. D17-18
Bluefield St. .... J 5
Concord .... J 6
West Va. Wesleyan■ .... J 8
Wheeling Jesuit J10
West Liberty St.■ J12
Charleston (W.Va.)■ J15
Salem-Teikyo■ J17
Glenville St. J22
West Liberty St. J26
West Va. St.■ J29
Fairmont St.■ J31
Salem-Teikyo .... F 2
West Va. Tech■ .... F 5
Shepherd .... F 7
Davis & Elkins■ .... F 9
Ohio Valley■ F10
Glenville St.■ F14
Wheeling Jesuit■ F16

Colors: Royal Blue, Gold & Gray. Nickname: Battlers.
AD: Allen Cassell. SID: Dave Stingo. II

ALFRED .... Alfred, NY 14802

Sarah Burdsall (3 YRS. W-11 , L-62)

Binghamton N30
Nazareth (N.Y.) .... D 1
Houghton .... D 8
Russell Sage D10
Skidmore D11
Nazareth (N.Y.)■ .... J 8
Buffalo St. J11
Clarkson J14
St. Lawrence J15
Penn St.-Behrend■ J18
William Smith■ J21
Rochester Inst.■ J22
Ithaca■ J25
Rensselaer J28
Hartwick J29
St. Lawrence■ .... F 4
Clarkson■ .... F 5
Ithaca .... F 8
Hartwick■ F11
Rensselaer■ F12
Elmira F15
Rochester Inst. F18
William Smith F19
Keuka F22

Colors: Purple & Gold. Nickname: Saxons.
AD: Hank Ford. SID: Paul Vecchio. III

ALLEGHENY .... Meadville, PA 16335

Laurel Heilman (1 YR. W-11, L-15)

Frostburg St. Inv. N19-20
Wash. & Jeff.■ N23
Carnegie Mellon Inv. N27-28
Case Reserve■ .... D 1
Ohio Wesleyan .... D 4
Thiel■ .... D 6
Oberlin .... D 8
Earlham■ D11
Kenyon■ .... J 5
Wittenberg .... J 8
Wooster■ J12
Denison J15
Ohio Wesleyan■ J22
Oberlin■ J26
Earlham J29
Wooster .... F 2
Wittenberg■ .... F 5
Grove City .... F 7
Case Reserve .... F 9
Denison■ F12
Penn St.-Behrend F14
Kenyon F19

Colors: Blue & Gold. Nickname: Gators.
AD: Rick Creehan. SID: To be named. III

ALLENTOWN .... Center Valley, PA 18034

Fred Richter (3 YRS. W-42, L-36)

Muhlenberg Tr. N20-21
Moravian N23
Kutztown■ N30
Widener .... D 2
Cabrini .... D 7
Scranton Cl. D10-11
Messiah■ .... J 5
King's (Pa.) Tr. J7-8
Alvernia J10
Muhlenberg■ J12
Salisbury St. J15
Frank. & Marsh.■ J20
Montclair St.■ J24
Marywood J27
Albright■ .... F 1
Caldwell■ .... F 5
Misericordia .... F 7
Catholic■ F10
Delaware Valley■ F14
Ursinus F17
Rowan■ F19

Colors: Red & Blue. Nickname: Centaurs.
AD: Joy Richman. SID: John Gump. III

ALMA .... Alma, MI 48801

Charles Goffnett (6 YRS. W-98 , L-45)

Northwood■ N20
Muskingum Tr. N27-28
Spring Arbor■ .... D 1
Aquinas■ .... D 4
Concordia (Mich.) .... D 9
Mich.-Dearborn■ D11
Capital D30
John Carroll D31
Albion■ .... J 5
Olivet .... J 8
Grand Rapids Bapt.■ J11
Adrian J15
Kalamazoo■ J19
Hope■ J22
Calvin J26
Albion J29
Olivet■ .... F 2
Adrian■ .... F 9
Kalamazoo F12
Hope F16
Calvin■ F19

Colors: Maroon & Cream. Nickname: Scots.
AD: Debra Mapes. SID: Greg Baadte/Skip Traynor. III

AMERICAN .... Washington, DC 20016

Jeff Thatcher (4 YRS. W-49, L-63)

Maryland N27
Fordham■ .... D 1
Duke Tr. D4-5
Liberty■ .... D 8
St. Francis (Pa.)■ D11
Winthrop■ D20
Akron D30
Bucknell .... J 2
La Salle .... J 4
Duquesne■ J10
N.C.-Wilmington J14
East Caro. J16
Richmond■ J20
James Madison■ J23
William & Mary■ J27
Old Dominion J30
George Mason .... F 3
Geo. Washington■ .... F 8
East Caro.■ F11
N.C.-Wilmington■ F13
Richmond F16
James Madison F20
William & Mary F24
Old Dominion■ F27
George Mason■ .... M 3
CAA Tr. M10-12

Colors: Red, White & Blue. Nickname: Eagles.
AD: Joseph F. O'Donnell. SID: Joan von Thron. I

AMERICAN INT'L .... Springfield, MA 01109

Peter Cinella (1ST YR. AS HEAD COACH)

Franklin Pierce■ N23
Stonehill■ N28
Southern Conn. St.■ N30
Hunter .... D 1
Springfield .... D 4
New Haven■ .... D 9
New Hamp. Col. D11
Barry D28
Lynn D29
West Chester■ .... J 6
St. Michael's■ .... J 8
St. Anselm J12
Quinnipiac J15
Merrimack■ J19
Bentley J22
Bryant■ J25
Assumption J27
Stonehill J29
Springfield■ .... F 2
St. Michael's .... F 5
Assumption■ .... F 7
St. Anselm■ .... F 9
Quinnipiac■ F12
Merrimack F16
Bentley■ F19
Bryant F22

Colors: Gold & White. Nickname: Yellow Jackets.
AD: Bob Burke. SID: Frank Polera. II

AMHERST .... Amherst, MA 01002

Billy McBride (1ST YR. AS HEAD COACH)

Tufts Tr. N20-21
Westfield St. N23
North Adams St.■ N30
Middlebury■ .... D 4
Western New Eng.■ .... D 7
Wheaton (Mass.) D11
Mount Holyoke .... J 8
Babson J11
Elms■ J13
Williams■ J15
Connecticut Col.■ J18
Gordon■ J22
Worcester Tech■ J25
Clark (Mass.) J29
Wellesley .... F 3
Coast Guard .... F 5
Smith■ .... F 8
Wesleyan■ F12
Trinity (Conn.)■ F15
Wesleyan F19
Tufts■ F23
Williams F26

Colors: Purple & White. Nickname: Lord Jeffs.
AD: Peter Gooding. SID: Kirstin Thorne. III

ANDERSON .... Anderson, IN 46012

Marcie Taylor (3 YRS. W-18, L-50)

Goshen■ N20
Hanover■ N30
Ind.-South Bend .... D 7
Purdue-Calumet■ D11
Earlham■ .... J 5
Asbury .... J 8
DePauw■ J11
Manchester J15
Defiance J19
St. Mary's (Ind.)■ J22
Kenyon J24
Taylor■ J27
Franklin■ J29
DePauw .... F 1
Hanover .... F 5
Cincinnati Bible■ .... F 8
Manchester■ F12
Franklin F19

Colors: Orange & Black. Nickname: Lady Ravens.
AD: A. Barrett Bates. SID: Marcie Taylor. II

■ Home games on each schedule.

See pages 735-738 for Division I tournament details

ANGELO ST. .... San Angelo, TX 76901
Peggy Davis (5 YRS. W-62, L-74)

Fort Hays St. Cl. N19-20
Southern Colo.■ N23
St. Mary's (Tex.) N30
Wayland Bapt.■ .... D 2
St. Mary's (Tex.)■ .... D 7
Cameron D10
Texas-San Antonio D27
Fort Hays St.■ .... J 7
Tex. Lutheran .... J 8
Abilene Christian J11
East Tex. St. J15
Texas A&I J17
Central Okla.■ J22
Texas Woman's■ J24
Eastern N. Mex.■ J29
West Tex. St.■ J31
Eastern N. Mex. .... F 5
West Tex. St. .... F 7
Texas A&I■ F12
East Tex. St.■ F14
Cameron■ F17
Texas Woman's F19
Central Okla. F21
Abilene Christian■ F26

Colors: Blue & Gold. Nickname: Rambelles.
AD: Kathleen Brasfield. SID: Sean Johnson. II

ANNA MARIA .... Paxton, MA 01512
Robert Meomartino (12 YRS. W-148, L-118)

Nichols■ N23
Suffolk■ N27
Worcester St. N29
Simmons■ .... D 1
Anna Maria Inv. D3-4
Worcester Tech .... D 7
Fitchburg St.■ J13
Salve Regina■ J15
Regis (Mass.) J18
Roger Williams J20
Eastern Nazarene J22
MIT■ J24
New England Col.■ J26
Wentworth Inst.■ J29
Curry .... F 1
Salve Regina .... F 3
Regis (Mass.)■ .... F 5
Roger Williams■ .... F 9
Wentworth Inst. F12
New England Col. F15
Curry■ F17
Eastern Nazarene■ F19

Colors: Royal Blue & White. Nickname: Amcats.
AD: Stephen C. Washkevich. SID: To be named. III

APPALACHIAN ST. .... Boone, NC 28608
Linda Robinson (14 YRS. W-258, L-138)

Radford N27
Wake Forest■ .... D 1
Arizona St. Cl. D3-4
Duke■ .... D 8
Virginia Tech Cl. D29-30
N.C.-Charlotte■ .... J 4
N.C.-Wilmington Tr. J7-8
Furman J13
Western Caro.■ J19
Marshall J22
East Tenn. St. J24
Ga. Southern■ J29
Tenn.-Chatt.■ J31
Western Caro. .... F 5
Furman■ .... F 9
Davidson■ F14
Marshall■ F19
East Tenn. St.■ F21
Davidson F23
Ga. Southern F26
Tenn.-Chatt. F28
N.C.-Wilmington .... M 4
East Caro. .... M 6
Southern Tr. M10-12

Colors: Black & Gold. Nickname: Lady Mountaineers.
AD: Roachel Laney. SID: Rick Covington. I

ARIZONA .... Tucson, AZ 85721
Joan Bonvicini (14 YRS. W-347, L-104)

Cal St. Fullerton N26
UC Irvine N28
Arizona Cl. D3-5
Tennessee■ .... D 7
San Diego St. D11
Texas■ D21
Weber St. D28
Arizona St. .... J 8
California J13
Stanford J15
Southern Cal■ J20
UCLA■ J22
Oregon J27
Oregon St. J29
Washington St.■ .... F 3
Washington■ .... F 5
Stanford■ F10
California■ F12
Cal St. Northridge■ F16
UCLA F18
Southern Cal F20
Oregon St.■ F24
Oregon■ F26
Washington .... M 3
Washington St. .... M 5
Arizona St.■ M12

Colors: Cardinal & Navy. Nickname: Wildcats.
AD: Cedric Dempsey. SID: Butch Henry. I

ARIZONA ST. .... Tempe, AZ 85287
Jacqueline Hullah (9 YRS. W-138, L-95)

Texas A&M■ N27
Arizona St. Cl. D3-4
San Diego St. .... D 7
Northern Iowa■ D18
Southern Ill. D20
Montana St. Tr. D31-J1
Nebraska■ .... J 4
Arizona■ .... J 8
Stanford J13
California J15
UCLA■ J20
Southern Cal■ J22
Oregon St. J27
Oregon J29
Washington■ .... F 3
Washington St.■ .... F 5
California■ F10
Stanford■ F12
Southern Cal F18
UCLA F20
Oregon■ F24
Oregon St.■ F26
Washington St. .... M 3
Washington .... M 5
Arizona M12

Colors: Maroon & Gold. Nickname: Sun Devils.
AD: Charles S. Harris. SID: Heather Loll. I

ARKANSAS .... Fayetteville, AR 72701
Gary Blair (8 YRS. W-210, L-43)

Kent N30
Hawaii Tr. D3-6
DePaul■ .... D 8
Arkansas Cl. D17-18
Southern Methodist D21
Texas-Arlington D22
Southwest Mo. St.■ D29
Tennessee .... J 2
Georgia■ .... J 8
Butler J10
Dayton J12
Mississippi J15
Tulane■ J19
Auburn■ J22
Oklahoma J26
Florida J30
Alabama■ .... F 1
Kentucky .... F 5
Louisiana St.■ .... F 8
South Caro.■ F12
Tex.-Pan American■ F15
Vanderbilt F20
Oral Roberts■ F23
Mississippi St. F26
Oklahoma St.■ .... M 1
Southeastern Tr. M4-7

Colors: Cardinal & White. Nickname: Lady Razorbacks.
AD: Bev Lewis. SID: Bill Smith. I

ARKANSAS ST. .... State University, AR 72467
Jerry Ann Winters (9 YRS. W-154 , L-101)

Nebraska■ N30
Mississippi .... D 1
Arkansas St. Cl. D3-4
Nebraska D12
Northeast La.■ D15
Washington Cl. D20-21
Florida Int'l Tr. J2-4
Lamar J13
South Ala.■ J15
Louisiana Tech J20
Lamar■ J22
Southwestern La. J27
New Orleans J29
Louisiana Tech■ .... F 5
South Ala. .... F 7
New Orleans■ .... F 9
Tex.-Pan American■ F13
Southwestern La.■ F17
Western Ky. F20
Tex.-Pan American F26
Grambling■ .... M 3
Western Ky.■ .... M 5
Sun Belt Tr. M10-12

Colors: Scarlet & Black. Nickname: Lady Indians.
AD: Brad Hovious. SID: Sunnie Ewing. I

ARMSTRONG ST. .... Savannah, GA 31419
Lenny Passink (4 YRS. W-55, L-46)

North Ga. Cl. N19-20
Savannah St. N23
Brewton Parker■ .... D 2
Brewton Parker .... D 6
Coker .... D 8
Florida Tech■ D11
Georgia Col. .... J 6
S.C.-Spartanburg■ .... J 8
Lander■ J10
Columbus■ J15
Augusta J17
Pembroke St. J22
Francis Marion J24
Savannah St.■ J26
S.C.-Aiken■ J29
Augusta■ J31
S.C.-Spartanburg .... F 5
Columbus .... F 7
Francis Marion■ F10
Lander F14
Pembroke St.■ F19
S.C.-Aiken F21
Georgia Col.■ F26

Colors: Maroon & Gold. Nickname: Lady Pirates.
AD: Roger Counsil. SID: Darrell Stephens. II

ARMY .... West Point, NY 10996
Lynn Chiavaro (6 YRS. W-98, L-75)

DePaul Inv. N26-27
Harvard■ .... D 1
Maine Cl. D3-4
Marist .... D 8
Dartmouth Inv. D29-30
Hartford■ .... J 5
Navy■ .... J 8
Holy Cross J12
Fordham■ J15
Columbia-Barnard J17
Bucknell■ J19
Lehigh J22
Colgate■ J26
Lafayette J29
Duquesne■ J31
Navy .... F 3
Holy Cross■ .... F 5
Fordham .... F 9
Bucknell F12
Lehigh■ F16
Colgate F19
Hofstra F22
Lafayette■ F26
Patriot Tr. M3-12

Colors: Black, Gold, Gray. Nickname: Lady Knights.
AD: Al Vanderbush. SID: Mady Salvani. I

ASBURY .... Lexington, KY 40390
Donna Murphy (2 YRS. W-5, L-33)

Franklin Inv. D3-4
Spalding .... D 7
Sue Bennett■ .... D 9
Transylvania D11
St. Catherine■ .... J 6
Anderson■ .... J 8
Thomas More■ J11
Kenyon J15
Ky. Christian J18
Transylvania■ J20
Georgetown (Ky.) J22
Berea J25
Sue Bennett J27
Midway■ J29
Kenyon■ J31
Thomas More .... F 3
Ky. Christian■ .... F 8
Franklin■ F10
Hanover■ F12
Midway F17
Berea■ F19
Graceland (Ind.)■ F22
Spalding■ F26

Colors: Purple & White. Nickname: Eagles.
AD: Rita Pritchett. SID: Ken Pickerill. III

■ Home games on each schedule.

See pages 735-738 for Division I tournament details

ASHLAND .... Ashland, OH 44805

Melanie Balcomb (1ST YR. AS HEAD COACH)

Wayne St. (Mich.)■	N20	Indianapolis■	J27
Tampa	N24	Northern Ky.■	J29
Eckerd	N28	Gannon	F 1
Hillsdale Cl.	D3-4	IU/PU-Ft. Wayne	F 5
Tiffin	D 7	Ky. Wesleyan	F10
St. Joseph's (Ind.)	D28	Southern Ind.	F12
Lewis	D30	Mercyhurst■	F15
Pitt.-Johnstown■	J 5	Kentucky St.■	F17
IU/PU-Ft. Wayne■	J 8	Bellarmine■	F19
Southern Ind.■	J13	Northern Ky.	F24
Ky. Wesleyan■	J15	Indianapolis	F26
Bellarmine	J20	St. Joseph's (Ind.)■	M 3
Kentucky St.	J22	Lewis■	M 5

Colors: Purple & Gold. Nickname: Lady Eagles.
AD: Alan Platt. SID: Al King. II

ASSUMPTION .... Worcester, MA 01615

Sue Lauder (13 YRS. W-181, L-143)

Springfield■	N19	Bryant■	J22
Sacred Heart	N21	Stonehill	J25
New Hamp. Col.	N30	American Int'l■	J27
Mass.-Lowell■	D 4	Springfield	J29
Franklin Pierce■	D 7	St. Michael's■	F 2
St. Michael's	D18	St. Anselm	F 5
Stonehill Cl.	D27-28	American Int'l	F 7
Bridgeport	J 3	Quinnipiac	F 9
St. Anselm■	J 8	Merrimack■	F12
New Haven	J10	Bentley■	F16
Quinnipiac■	J12	Bryant	F19
Merrimack	J15	Stonehill■	F22
Bentley	J19		

Colors: Royal Blue & White. Nickname: Lady Hounds.
AD: Rita Castagna. SID: Steve Morris. II

AUBURN .... Auburn, AL 36830

Joe Ciampi (16 YRS. W-389 , L-101)

Houston Cl.	N26-27	Arkansas	J22
Jackson St.■	D 1	New Orleans	J25
Southwest Tex. Cl.	D3-4	Kentucky■	J29
Connecticut■	D 8	Aub.-Montgomery■	F 2
Vanderbilt	D17	Louisiana St.■	F 5
Florida Int'l	D19	Southern Miss.	F 7
Auburn Cl.	D29-30	Mississippi St.	F12
South Caro.■	J 5	Alabama	F16
Mississippi■	J 8	Georgia■	F20
Ala.-Birmingham	J12	South Ala.	F23
Tennessee	J15	Florida■	F26
DePaul■	J19	Southeastern Tr.	M4-7

Colors: Orange & Blue. Nickname: Lady Tigers.
AD: Mike Lude. SID: Scott Stricklin. I

AUGSBURG .... Minneapolis, MN 55454

To be named

Northland■	N19	St. Benedict■	J22
Wis.-Superior■	N23	Macalester	J26
St. Scholastica■	D 1	Hamline	J29
St. Benedict	D 4	Concordia-M'head	F 5
Macalester■	D 8	Gust. Adolphus	F 9
Hamline■	D11	Bethel (Minn.)■	F12
St. Mary's (Minn.)■	J 3	N'western (Minn.)	F14
Concordia-M'head■	J 8	Carleton	F16
Gust. Adolphus■	J10	St. Thomas (Minn.)■	F19
Bethel (Minn.)	J12	Concordia (St. Paul)	F22
St. Olaf	J15	St. Mary's (Minn.)	F23
Carleton■	J17	St. Olaf■	F26
St. Thomas (Minn.)	J19		

Colors: Maroon & Gray. Nickname: Auggies.
AD: Marilyn Florian. SID: Gene McGivern. III

AUGUSTANA (ILL.) .... Rock Island, IL 61201

Diane Schumacher (12 YRS. W-202, L-105)

Trinity (Tex.) Inv.	N20-21	North Park	J19
Southwestern (Tex.)	N23	Elmhurst■	J22
Illinois Col.	N27	William Penn■	J24
Blackburn■	D 4	Millikin	J29
Ill. Wesleyan■	D 7	Wheaton (Ill.)■	F 3
Carthage■	D11	North Park■	F 5
North Central■	D15	St. Ambrose	F 7
Wis.-Whitewater	D18	Elmhurst	F 9
Teiko-Marycrest■	J 5	Carthage	F12
Ill. Wesleyan	J 8	Millikin■	F15
Aurora■	J13	Wheaton (Ill.)	F19
North Central	J15	Ill. Benedictine	F26

Colors: Gold & Blue. Nickname: Vikings.
AD: Diane Schumacher. SID: Dave Wrath. III

AUGUSTANA (S.D.) .... Sioux Falls, SD 57197

Dave Krauth (4 YRS. W-92, L-25)

Sioux Falls■	N23	Mankato St.■	J21
Wayne St. (Neb.)■	D 2	St. Cloud St.■	J22
Moorhead St.■	D 4	Neb.-Kearney■	J26
Dak. Wesleyan	D 9	South Dak. St.	J29
Northwest Mo. St.■	D11	North Dak.	F 4
Bemidji St.	D19	North Dak. St.	F 5
Southwest St.■	D29	Morningside■	F11
Winona St.■	D30	South Dak.■	F12
Northern Colo.	J 2	St. Cloud St.	F18
Nebraska-Omaha	J 3	Mankato St.	F19
North Dak. St.■	J 7	South Dak. St.■	F26
North Dak.■	J 8	Nebraska-Omaha■	M 4
South Dak.	J14	Northern Colo.■	M 5
Morningside	J15		

Colors: Blue & Yellow. Nickname: Vikings.
AD: Bill Gross. SID: Andy Ludwig. II

AURORA .... Aurora, IL 60506

James Lancaster (3 YRS. W-36, L-37)

Carroll (Wis.)■	N23	Rockford■	J18
Beloit■	N30	Trinity (Ill.)	J22
Ill. Wesleyan	D 3	Ill. Benedictine■	J25
Millikin■	D 7	Carthage■	J27
Fontbonne	D10	Knox	F 1
Blackburn	D11	Concordia (Ill.)	F 3
Elmhurst Tr.	D17-18	Judson■	F 5
Washington (Mo.)■	J 6	Rockford	F 8
North Central■	J 8	Trinity (Ill.)■	F12
St. Mary's (Ind.)■	J11	Concordia (Ill.)■	F15
Augustana (Ill.)	J13	Ill. Benedictine	F19
Judson	J15	Wheaton (Ill.)	F25

Colors: Royal & White. Nickname: Spartans.
AD: Sam Bedrosian. SID: Dave Beyer. III

AUSTIN PEAY .... Clarksville, TN 37044

LaDonna Wilson (3 YRS. W-14, L-65)

Valparaiso■	N27	Murray St.■	J29
Cleveland St.■	D 1	Southeast Mo. St.■	J31
Wright St.■	D 6	Tenn.-Martin	F 5
Akron■	D11	Tennessee St.	F 7
Southern Miss. Cl.	D20-21	Eastern Ky.	F12
Coastal Caro. Cl.	D29-30	Morehead St.	F14
Tennessee St.■	J 3	Tenn.-Martin■	F16
Tennessee Tech	J 8	Tennessee Tech■	F19
Middle Tenn. St.	J12	Middle Tenn. St.■	F22
Morehead St.■	J15	Murray St.	F26
Eastern Ky.■	J17	Southeast Mo. St.	F28
Tenn.-Chatt.	J20	Ohio Valley Tr.	M3-5
Troy St.■	J23		

Colors: Red & White. Nickname: Lady Govs.
AD: Tim Weiser. SID: Brad Kirtley. I

AVERETT .... Danville, VA 24541

Kathy Babcock (1 YR. W-6, L-18)

Goucher Tr.	N19-20	Maryville (Tenn.)■	J23
St. Andrews■	D 2	N.C. Wesleyan	J26
Meredith■	D 6	Meredith	J28
Pfeiffer■	D 8	Shenandoah■	J30
Maryville (Tenn.)	D11	Ferrum■	F 1
St. Mary's (Md.)■	J 9	East. Mennonite■	F 2
Ferrum	J11	Greensboro	F 5
Wesley■	J14	Methodist■	F 8
Greensboro■	J16	Chris. Newport	F12
Hollins■	J17	N.C. Wesleyan■	F16
Methodist	J20	Shenandoah	F19
Chris. Newport■	J22		

Colors: Navy & Gold. Nickname: Cougars.
AD: Vesa Hiltunen. SID: Steve Ballard. III

BABSON .... Babson Park, MA 02157

Judy Blinstrub (9 YRS. W-152, L-79)

Bryant	N21	Wellesley	J25
Salve Regina	N23	Bowdoin	J28
Curry■	D 1	Bates	J29
Nazareth (N.Y.) Inv.	D4-5	Smith	F 3
Bri'water (Mass.)	D 7	Wheaton (Mass.)	F 5
Pine Manor■	D 9	Brandeis■	F10
Amherst■	J11	Mount Holyoke■	F12
Coast Guard	J18	MIT■	F15
Emmanuel■	J20	Clark (Mass.)	F17
Connecticut Col.	J22	Worcester Tech	F19

Colors: Green & White. Nickname: Beavers.
AD: Steve Stirling. SID: Christine Merlo. III

■ Home games on each schedule.

See pages 735-738 for Division I tournament details

BALDWIN-WALLACE .... Berea, OH 44017
Cheri Harrer (3 YRS. W-34, L-44)

Penn St.-Behrend■	N30	Otterbein■	J15
Ohio Northern	D 4	Heidelberg	J18
John Carroll■	D 7	Hiram■	J22
Muskingum	D11	John Carroll	J25
Grove City	D14	Ohio Northern■	J29
Marietta■	D18	Muskingum■	F 1
Defiance	D21	Marietta	F 5
Ohio Wesleyan■	D29	Heidelberg■	F 8
Bluffton	D31	Capital	F12
Hiram	J 4	Mount Union■	F15
Capital■	J 8	Otterbein	F19
Mount Union	J11		

Colors: Brown & Gold. Nickname: Yellow Jackets.
AD: Marcia French. SID: Kevin Ruple. III

BALL ST. .... Muncie, IN 47306
Robyn Markey (4 YRS. W-28, L-73)

Eastern Ky.■	N27	Miami (Ohio)■	J29
Chicago St.	D 4	Western Mich.	F 2
Butler■	D 8	Central Mich.■	F 5
Purdue Cl.	D11	Bowling Green	F 9
Marquette■	D21	Eastern Mich.■	F12
Pittsburgh Inv.	D29-30	Toledo	F16
Ohio■	J 5	Kent■	F19
Central Mich.	J 8	Akron■	F23
Bowling Green■	J12	Miami (Ohio)	F26
Eastern Mich.	J15	Western Mich.■	M 2
Toledo■	J19	Ohio	M 5
Kent	J22	Mid-American Tr.	M11-12
Akron	J26		

Colors: Cardinal & White. Nickname: Cardinals.
AD: Andrea Seger. SID: Joe Hernandez. I

BARRY .... Miami Shores, FL 33161
Patricia Ficenec (2 YRS. W-10, L-42)

Pembroke St.■	N28	North Fla.	J22
Fla. Atlantic	D 1	Rollins■	J26
Lynn■	D 8	Florida Tech■	J29
St. Ambrose■	D16	St. Leo■	F 2
Bethune-Cookman■	D18	Tampa	F 5
North Park■	D21	Fla. Southern■	F 9
American Int'l■	D28	North Fla.■	F12
Barry Cl.	J2-3	Lynn	F14
Mass.-Dartmouth■	J 6	Rollins	F16
Eckerd■	J12	Florida Tech	F19
Tampa■	J15	St. Leo	F23
Fla. Southern	J19	Eckerd	F26

Colors: Black, Red & Grey. Nickname: Lady Buccaneers.
AD: G. Jean Cerra. SID: Robert McKinney. II

BATES .... Lewiston, ME 04240
Marti Kingsley (1 YR. W-9, L-13)

Williams Tr.	N19-20	Babson■	J29
Bowdoin■	N30	Me.-Farmington	F 1
New England■	D 6	Trinity (Conn.)	F 4
New England Col.	D11	Wesleyan	F 5
Gordon	J 6	Bowdoin	F 8
Southern Me.■	J13	Norwich	F11
Hamilton	J15	Middlebury	F12
Skidmore	J16	Tufts	F16
Colby	J25	Connecticut Col.■	F19
Colby-Sawyer■	J28	Colby■	F23

Colors: Garnet. Nickname: Bobcats.
AD: Suzanne Coffey. SID: Anne Whittemore. III

BAYLOR .... Waco, TX 76711
Pam Bowers (14 YRS. W-155, L-243)

Prairie View■	D 1	Oral Roberts	J29
Southwest/Ivy Chall.	D3-4	Texas A&M	F 2
New Mexico	D 9	Southern Methodist■	F 5
Northern Ariz.	D11	Texas Tech■	F 9
Louisiana Tech☒	D20	Texas Christian	F12
Baylor Cl.	D29-30	Texas■	F16
Rice Cl.	J3-4	Houston■	F19
Iona■	J 6	Rice	F23
Texas Tech	J12	Texas A&M■	M 2
Texas Christian■	J15	Southern Methodist	M 5
Texas	J19	Southwest Tr.	M9-12
Houston	J22	☒ Shreveport, LA	
Rice■	J26		

Colors: Green & Gold. Nickname: Bears.
AD: To be named. SID: Julie Bennett. I

BELLARMINE .... Louisville, KY 40205
Charlie Just (9 YRS. W-190, L-70)

IU/PU-Indianapolis■	N23	Ky. Wesleyan	J29
Kentucky St.■	D11	Northern Ky.	F 3
Portland St. Cl.	D16-18	Indianapolis	F 5
Bellarmine Cl.	D29-30	St. Joseph's (Ind.)■	F10
Indianapolis■	J 6	Lewis■	F12
Northern Ky.■	J 8	IU/PU-Ft. Wayne	F17
Lewis	J13	Ashland	F19
St. Joseph's (Ind.)	J15	Ky. Wesleyan■	F24
Georgetown (Ky.)■	J18	Southern Ind.■	F26
Ashland■	J20	SIU-Edwardsville	M 2
IU/PU-Ft. Wayne■	J22	Kentucky St.	M 5
Southern Ind.	J27		

Colors: Scarlet & Silver. Nickname: Lady Knights.
AD: James Spalding. SID: Mark Mulloy. II

BELMONT ABBEY .... Belmont, NC 28012
Eliane Kebbe (10 YRS. W-194, L-94)

Limestone	N23	High Point	J22
Queens (N.C.)■	N27	Converse	J24
Lenoir-Rhyne	N29	St. Andrews■	J26
Converse■	D 1	Barton	J29
Lees-McRae Tr.	D3-4	Lees-McRae	J31
Newberry■	D 8	Pfeiffer	F 2
St. Leo■	J 6	Mt. Olive■	F 5
Pfeiffer■	J 8	Coker■	F 9
Barber-Scotia	J10	St. Andrews	F12
Lees-McRae■	J12	High Point■	F16
Mt. Olive	J15	Barton■	F19
Limestone■	J17	Queens (N.C.)	F21
Coker	J19		

Colors: Red & White. Nickname: Lady Crusaders.
AD: Michael Reidy. SID: Frank Mercogliano. II

BELOIT .... Beloit, WI 53511
Mimi Walters (3 YRS. W-43, L-25)

Wis.-Stevens Point	N20	Grinnell■	J22
Carthage■	N23	Lake Forest	J25
Aurora	N30	Cornell College	J28
Lawrence	D 4	Monmouth (Ill.)	J29
Carroll (Wis.)■	D 8	Ripon■	F 5
Wis.-Whitewater■	D14	Carroll (Wis.)	F 8
Maryville (Tn.) Tr.	J8-9	Lawrence■	F12
St. Norbert■	J12	Lake Forest■	F15
St. Mary's (Ind.)	J15	Rockford■	F17
Ripon	J17	St. Norbert	F19
Coe■	J21		

Colors: Gold & Navy Blue. Nickname: Buccaneers.
AD: Ed DeGeorge. SID: Paul Erickson. III

BEMIDJI ST. .... Bemidji, MN 56601
Doreen Zierer (3 YRS. W-42, L-41)

South Dak. St.	N19	Southwest St.	J12
South Dak.	N20	Minn.-Morris■	J15
Michigan Tech■	N26	Minn.-Duluth	J19
Northern Mich.■	N27	Winona St.■	J22
Nebraska-Omaha Tr.	D3-4	Moorhead St.	J29
North Dak. St.■	D10	Northern St.	F 2
St. Scholastica	D16	Wayne St. (Neb.)■	F 5
Neb.-Kearney■	D17	Southwest St.■	F 9
Augustana (S.D.)■	D19	Minn.-Morris	F12
St. Cloud St.	D21	Minn.-Duluth■	F16
Wis.-Parkside■	J 3	Winona St.	F19
Northern St.■	J 5	Wis.-Parkside	F21
Wayne St. (Neb.)	J 8	Moorhead St.■	F26

Colors: Green & White. Nickname: Beavers.
AD: Marion Christianson. SID: Jeff Swanson. II

BENTLEY .... Waltham, MA 02154
Barbara Stevens (16 YRS. W-365, L-116)

New Hamp. Col.■	N23	American Int'l■	J22
St. Anselm■	N28	Springfield	J25
Mass.-Lowell■	D 1	St. Michael's■	J27
Clarion Cl.	D3-4	St. Anselm	J29
Quinnipiac	D 7	Quinnipiac■	F 2
New Haven	D11	Merrimack	F 5
Keene St.■	D18	Stonehill■	F 9
Fla. Southern	J 3	Bryant■	F12
Tampa	J 5	Assumption	F16
Merrimack■	J 8	American Int'l	F19
Stonehill	J12	Springfield■	F22
Bryant	J15	St. Michael's	F25
Assumption■	J19		

Colors: Royal Blue & Gold. Nickname: Falcons.
AD: Bob DeFelice. SID: Dick Lipe. II

■ Home games on each schedule.

See pages 735-738 for Division I tournament details

BEREA .... Berea, KY 40404

Martha Beagle (9 YRS. W-81, L-101)

Sewanee Inv.	N19-20
Hanover■	D 7
Alice Lloyd■	D 9
Lawrence■	D11
Earlham Inv.	D17-18
Georgetown (Ky.)■	J 8
Transylvania	J11
Thomas More■	J13
Midway	J20
Asbury■	J25
Alice Lloyd	F 3
Maryville (Tenn.)■	F 5
Ky. Christian	F17
Asbury	F19
Midway■	F22
Maryville (Tenn.)	F26

Colors: Royal Blue & White. Nickname: Lady Mountainers.
AD: Joy Hager. SID: Ann Ford. III

BETHANY (W.VA.) .... Bethany, WV 26032

Lisa Campanell-Komara (8 YRS. W-55, L-131)

Wilming. (Ohio) Tr.	N19-20
LaRoche	N30
Bethany (W.Va.) Tr.	D3-4
Ohio Dominican■	D 8
Ohio Belmont■	D11
Point Park	D30
Wheeling Jesuit Tr.	J2-3
Frostburg St. Cl.	J7-8
Penn St.-Behrend	J15
Point Park■	J19
Grove City	J22
Thiel	J26
Waynesburg■	J29
Wash. & Jeff.■	F 2
Penn St.-Behrend■	F 5
Grove City■	F 9
Thiel■	F12
Waynesburg	F16
Wash. & Jeff.	F19
Carlow■	F23

Colors: Kelly Green & White. Nickname: Bison.
AD: Wally Neel. SID: Cole Vulgamore. III

BETHEL (MINN.) .... St. Paul, MN 55112

Deb Hunter (7 YRS. W-104, L-70)

Wis.-Eau Claire Tr.	N26-27
Macalester	D 4
St. Thomas (Minn.)	D 8
Concordia-M'head	J 3
St. Olaf■	J 5
Gust. Adolphus	J 8
St. Mary's (Minn.)■	J10
Augsburg■	J12
Carleton	J15
Hamline	J17
St. Benedict■	J19
Macalester■	J22
St. Thomas (Minn.)■	J26
St. Olaf	F 2
Gust. Adolphus■	F 5
St. Mary's (Minn.)	F 9
Augsburg	F12
Hamline■	F16
St. Benedict	F19
Concordia-M'head■	F21
Carleton■	F26

Colors: Royal Blue & Gold. Nickname: Royals.
AD: Dave Klostriech. SID: Leland Christanson. III

BETHUNE-COOKMAN ...... Daytona Beach, FL 32015

Alvin Wyatt (15 YRS. W-222, L-147)

Florida A&M	N26
Fla. Atlantic■	D 4
Florida Int'l■	D11
Fla. Memorial	D17
Barry	D18
Stetson	J 4
Delaware St.	J 8
Md.-East. Shore	J10
North Caro. A&T	J15
South Caro. St.	J17
Howard■	J20
Morgan St.■	J22
Coppin St.■	J24
South Caro. St.■	J29
North Caro. A&T■	J31
Florida	F 2
Florida A&M■	F 4
Howard	F10
Morgan St.	F12
Coppin St.	F14
Edward Waters■	F17
Delaware St.■	F19
Md.-East. Shore■	F21
Florida A&M	M 5
MEAC Tr.	M9-13

Colors: Maroon & Gold. Nickname: Wildcats.
AD: Lynn Thompson. SID: W. Earl Kitchings. I

BINGHAMTON .... Binghamton, NY 13902

David Wilson (3 YRS. W-49, L-29)

Albany (N.Y.)	N23
Alfred■	N30
Brockport St.■	D 3
Fredonia St.■	D 4
New Paltz St.	D 7
Potsdam St.	D10
Plattsburgh St.	D11
Elmira	J11
Utica Tech	J14
Oswego St.■	J15
Cortland St.■	J18
Stony Brook	J21
Union (N.Y.)	J22
Oneonta St.	J25
Buffalo St.	J29
William Smith■	F 1
Potsdam St.■	F 4
Plattsburgh St.■	F 5
Cortland St.	F 8
Geneseo St.	F12
Utica	F14
Oneonta St.■	F15
New Paltz St.■	F19

Colors: Green & White. Nickname: Colonials.
AD: Joel Thirer. SID: John Hartrick. III

BLACKBURN .... Carlinville, IL 62626

James Sexton (12 YRS. W-124, L-175)

Rockford Tr.	N19-20
Washington (Mo.)■	N23
McKendree■	N30
Eureka	D 3
Augustana (Ill.)	D 4
Aurora■	D11
Illinois Col.■	D14
Principia	J 6
Grinnell■	J11
Webster	J13
Quincy	J15
MacMurray■	J20
Fontbonne■	J22
Westminster■	J25
Maryville (Mo.)	J27
Principia■	J29
Greenville	F 1
Westminster	F 3
Webster■	F 5
Millikin■	F 8
MacMurray	F12
Fontbonne	F17
Maryville (Mo.)■	F19

Colors: Scarlet & Black. Nickname: Beavers.
AD: Fra Zeff. SID: Tom Emery. III

BLOOMSBURG .... Bloomsburg, PA 17815

Joe Bressi (7 YRS. W-158, L-37)

Bloomfield	N21
Mercyhurst	N23
Phila. Textile	N29
Alvernia■	D 1
Rowan■	D 5
Lock Haven■	D 7
Bloomsburg Inv.	D10-11
Clarion	J 5
Slippery Rock■	J 8
Shippensburg■	J10
Cheyney■	J12
Pitt.-Johnstown■	J15
Kutztown	J19
East Stroudsburg	J22
Mansfield■	J26
West Chester■	J29
Millersville	F 2
Indiana (Pa.)	F 5
Susquehanna■	F 7
Cheyney	F 9
Kutztown■	F12
Mansfield	F16
East Stroudsburg■	F19
Millersville■	F23
West Chester	F26

Colors: Maroon & Gold. Nickname: Huskies.
AD: Mary Gardner. SID: Jim Hollister. II

BLUEFIELD ST. .... Bluefield, WV 24701

Thomas Jessee (5 YRS. W-102, L-43)

Wingate Tr.	N19-21
Bluefield St. Tr.	N26-27
Lincoln Memorial■	N30
West Va. Tech	D 4
Charleston (W.Va.)■	D10
Alderson-Broaddus■	J 5
West Va. St.	J 7
Lincoln Memorial	J11
Wheeling Jesuit	J14
West Liberty St.	J15
Concord■	J17
West Va. Wesleyan■	J19
Fairmont St.	J21
Salem-Teikyo	J22
Glenville St.■	J24
Davis & Elkins	J29
Shepherd■	J31
West Va. Wesleyan	F 4
West Va. Tech■	F 7
Concord	F 9
Charleston (W.Va.)	F11
West Va. St.■	F14
Glenville St.	F16

Colors: Blue & Gold. Nickname: Blues.
AD: Terry Brown. SID: Terry Brown. II

BLUFFTON .... Bluffton, OH 45817

Michele Durand (3 YRS. W-34, L-41)

Olivet	N23
Hiram■	N27
Bluffton Tr.	D3-4
Cedarville■	D 7
Wittenberg Cl.	D10-11
Huntington■	D17
Heidelberg	D20
Baldwin-Wallace■	D31
Manchester	J 4
St. Francis (Ind.)	J 8
Defiance■	J11
Adrian	J19
Wilmington (Ohio)	J22
Urbana■	J27
Thomas More	J29
Findlay	F 1
Ohio Wesleyan	F 5
Otterbein■	F10
Wilmington (Ohio)■	F12
Defiance	F16
Thomas More■	F19

Colors: Purple & White. Nickname: Beavers.
AD: Carlin Carpenter. SID: Ron Geiser. III

BOISE ST. .... Boise, ID 83725

June Daugherty (3 YRS. W-52, L-35)

Southern Utah■	N29
Hawaii Tr.	D3-6
Minnesota Cl.	D11-12
Oregon St.■	D16
UCLA	D19
Brigham Young	J 6
St. Mary's (Cal.)■	J 9
Northern Ariz.	J13
Weber St.	J15
Eastern Wash.■	J19
Idaho St.	J22
Montana■	J29
Eastern Wash.	F 4
Idaho	F 5
Weber St.■	F10
Northern Ariz.■	F12
Idaho St.■	F19
Montana	F25
Idaho■	M 6
Big Sky Tr.	M11-12

Colors: Orange & Blue. Nickname: Broncos.
AD: Carol Ladwig. SID: Lori Orr Hays. I

■ Home games on each schedule.

See pages 735-738 for Division I tournament details

BOSTON COLLEGE .... Chestnut Hill, MA 02167

Margo Plotzke (12 YRS. W-167, L-161)

Maine	N28	Seton Hall	J19
Holy Cross■	D 1	Syracuse■	J22
St. Peter's■	D 8	Miami (Fla.)■	J25
Connecticut■	D13	Pittsburgh	J29
Northeastern	D19	Villanova	F 1
Northwestern■	D21	Georgetown■	F 5
Iona	D30	Syracuse	F 9
Pittsburgh■	J 3	Providence	F13
Georgetown	J 5	Connecticut	F16
Providence■	J 8	Seton Hall■	F19
St. John's (N.Y.)	J12	St. John's (N.Y.)■	F23
Villanova■	J16	Miami (Fla.)	F26

Colors: Maroon & Gold. Nickname: Eagles.
AD: Chet Gladchuk. SID: Reid Oslin. I

BOSTON U. .... Boston, MA 02215

Chris Basile (10 YRS. W-147, L-131)

Providence■	N30	New Hampshire■	J29
Seton Hall Cl.	D4-5	Central Conn. St.	F 1
Brown	D 8	Northeastern■	F 5
Harvard■	D14	New Hampshire	F10
Wagner Tr.	D28-29	Maine■	F12
Lafayette	J 6	Holy Cross	F14
Dartmouth■	J10	Drexel	F18
Hartford	J13	Delaware	F20
Vermont	J15	Hartford■	F24
Delaware■	J21	Vermont■	F26
Drexel■	J23	Northeastern	M 2
Maine	J27	North Atlantic Tr.	M6-12

Colors: Scarlet & White. Nickname: Terriers.
AD: Gary Strickler. SID: Ed Carpenter. I

BOWDOIN .... Brunswick, ME 04011

Harvey Shapiro (14 YRS. W-173, L-130)

Tufts Tr.	N20-21	New England	J31
Bates	N30	Clark (Mass.)	F 4
Tufts■	D 4	Trinity (Conn.)	F 5
Westbrook■	D 8	Bates■	F 8
Me.-Machias■	D11	Connecticut Col.	F11
Skidmore	J15	Wheaton (Mass.)	F12
Union (N.Y.)	J16	Me.-Farmington■	F15
Colby-Sawyer	J21	Colby■	F16
Middlebury	J22	Me.-Presque Isle■	F19
Thomas	J25	New England■	F21
Babson■	J28	Colby	F26

Colors: White. Nickname: Polar Bears.
AD: Sidney Watson. SID: Craig Cheslog. III

BOWIE ST. .... Bowie, MD 20715

Edward Davis (1 YR. W-6, L-18)

West Tex. A&M Inv.	N19-20	Virginia St.■	J20
Winston-Salem■	N27	Norfolk St.	J24
Shaw■	N29	Elizabeth City St.	J25
West Chester■	N30	Virginia Union	J29
Md.-East. Shore■	D 2	St. Paul's	J31
Livingstone■	D 4	Elizabeth City St.■	F 3
Hampton	D 7	Norfolk St.■	F 7
St. Augustine's	D11	St. Paul's■	F10
Fayetteville St.	D13	Virginia Union■	F12
N.C. Central	J13	Virginia St.	F14
Johnson Smith	J15	Dist. Columbia■	F16
Cheyney	J17	Hampton■	F18

Colors: Black & Gold. Nickname: Bulldogs.
AD: Charles Guilford. SID: Troy Macon. II

BOWLING GREEN .... Bowling Green, OH 43403

Jaci Clark (2 YRS. W-49, L-10)

Xavier (Ohio)■	N30	Central Mich.	J26
Louisiana Tech Cl.	D3-4	Akron■	J29
Michigan St.■	D 8	Eastern Mich.■	F 2
Vanderbilt	D11	Kent	F 5
Wis.-Green Bay	D22	Ball St.■	F 9
Wis.-Milwaukee	D23	Miami (Ohio)	F12
Youngstown St.	J 3	Western Mich.■	F16
Toledo	J 5	Ohio	F19
Kent■	J 8	Central Mich.■	F23
Ball St.	J12	Akron	F26
Miami (Ohio)■	J15	Eastern Mich.	M 2
Western Mich.	J19	Toledo■	M 5
Ohio■	J22	Mid-American Tr.	M11-12

Colors: Orange & Brown. Nickname: Falcons.
AD: Jack Gregory. SID: Steve Barr. I

BRADLEY .... Peoria, IL 61625

Lisa Boyer (7 YRS. W-89, L-103)

Loyola (Ill.)■	N26	Illinois St.	J22
Missouri■	N28	Drake■	J27
Northwestern Inv.	D3-4	Creighton■	J29
St. Louis	D 8	Wichita St.	F 4
Stetson Cl.	D17-18	Southwest Mo. St.	F 6
Purdue■	D30	Northern Iowa	F12
Southern Ill.	J 4	Illinois St.■	F17
Southwest Mo. St.■	J 6	Drake	F24
Wichita St.■	J 9	Creighton	F26
Virginia Tech	J12	Southern Ill.■	M 3
Northern Iowa■	J15	Indiana St.■	M 5
Chicago St.	J18	Missouri Valley Tr.	M8-12
Indiana St.	J20		

Colors: Red & White. Nickname: Lady Braves.
AD: Ron Ferguson. SID: Bo Ryan. I

BRANDEIS .... Waltham, MA 02254

Carol Simon (6 YRS. W-98, L-65)

Case Reserve	N28	Emory	J23
Johns Hopkins■	D 3	Mount Holyoke	J25
Rochester	D 5	Rochester■	J28
Tufts■	D 8	Worcester Tech	F 2
Nichols	D11	Emory■	F 4
New York U.■	J 8	Carnegie Mellon■	F 6
MIT	J11	Wheaton (Mass.)■	F 8
Chicago■	J14	Babson	F10
Washington (Mo.)■	J16	New York U.	F12
Smith■	J18	Wellesley	F15
Carnegie Mellon	J21	Chicago	F20

Colors: Blue & White. Nickname: Judges.
AD: Jeff Cohen. SID: Jack Molloy. III

BRIDGEPORT .... Bridgeport, CT 06602

Harvey Herer (1 YR. W-4, L-20)

Bridgeport Inv.	N20-21	Sacred Heart	J26
Molloy■	N29	Keene St.	J29
Quinnipiac	D 2	Southern Conn. St.■	F 2
Husson Cl.	D4-5	Le Moyne■	F 5
Clarion Cl.	D10-11	New Hamp. Col.■	F 7
Montclair St.■	D13	New Haven	F 9
Assumption■	J 3	Franklin Pierce■	F12
Le Moyne	J10	Mass.-Lowell	F14
Mass.-Lowell■	J12	Southern Conn. St.	F16
New Hamp. Col.	J17	Keene St.■	F19
New Haven■	J19	Sacred Heart■	F23
Franklin Pierce	J22		

Colors: Purple & White. Nickname: Purple Knights.
AD: Ann Fariss. SID: Bob Baird. II

BRIDGEWATER (VA.) .... Bridgewater, VA 22812

Laura Mapp (32 YRS. W-447, L-244)

Bri'water (Va.) Inv.	N19-20	East. Mennonite	J18
Ferrum	N22	Emory & Henry	J22
Rand.-Macon Woman's	N30	Roanoke	J29
Hollins■	D 2	Rand.-Macon Woman's■	F 1
Lynchburg■	D 4	Lynchburg	F 3
Marymount (Va.)	D 7	Va. Wesleyan	F 5
Guilford	D11	East. Mennonite■	F 8
Randolph-Macon■	D14	Randolph-Macon	F10
Roanoke■	J 8	Guilford■	F12
Mary Washington■	J11	Hollins	F15
Frostburg St.	J13	Va. Wesleyan■	F19
Emory & Henry■	J15		

Colors: Crimson & Gold. Nickname: Eagles.
AD: Tom Kinder. SID: Rob Marchiony. III

BRI'WATER (MASS.) .... Bridgewater, MA 02324

Paul Bonitto (1ST YR. AS HEAD COACH)

Wheaton (Mass.) Tr.	N19-20	Worcester St.	J25
Emmanuel	N23	Clark (Mass.)	J27
Worcester Tech	N30	Salem St.■	J29
Pine Manor	D 2	Fitchburg St.■	F 1
Babson■	D 7	Plymouth St.	F 3
Mass.-Dartmouth■	D 9	Westfield St.■	F 5
Westfield St.	J11	Framingham St.	F 8
Framingham St.■	J15	North Adams St.■	F10
North Adams St.	J17	Worcester St.■	F15
Mass.-Boston■	J20	Salem St.	F17
Rhode Island Col.■	J22	Fitchburg St.	F19

Colors: Crimson & White. Nickname: Bears.
AD: John C. Harper. SID: Mike Storey. III

■ Home games on each schedule.

See pages 735-738 for Division I tournament details

BRIGHAM YOUNG .... Provo, UT 84602

Jeanie Wilson (4 YRS. W-63, L-51)

St. Mary's Cl.	N26-27	Wyoming■	J22
Idaho Cl.	D3-4	New Mexico	J27
Montana St.■	D10	UTEP	J29
Montana■	D11	UTEP■	F 3
Southwest Tex. St.	D17	New Mexico■	F 5
Texas	D18	Wyoming	F11
Brigham Young Cl.	D29-30	Colorado St.	F12
Weber St.■	J 4	Utah	F18
Boise St.■	J 6	San Diego St.■	F24
Fresno St.	J13	Fresno St.■	F26
San Diego St.	J15	Utah■	M 4
Colorado St.■	J20	Western Athletic Tr.	M9-12

Colors: Royal Blue & White. Nickname: Cougars.
AD: Lu Wallace. SID: Ellen A. Larsen. I

BROCKPORT ST. .... Brockport, NY 14420

Michele Carron (1 YR. W-14, L-11)

Hilbert	N30	Plattsburgh St.	J28
Binghamton	D 3	Potsdam St.	J29
Geneseo St.■	D 4	Roberts Wesleyan	F 1
Buffalo St.	D 7	Buffalo St.■	F 4
Oneonta St.■	D10	Fredonia St.	F 5
New Paltz St.■	D11	St. John Fisher■	F 8
St. John Fisher Inv.	J8-9	Cortland St.■	F12
Nazareth (N.Y.)■	J13	Oswego St.	F15
Utica	J15	Utica Tech■	F18
Oswego St.■	J18	Geneseo St.	F19
Utica Tech	J21	Elmira	F22
Fredonia St.■	J25		

Colors: Green & Gold. Nickname: Golden Eagles.
AD: Edward Matejkovic. SID: Mike Andriatch. III

BROWN .... Providence, RI 02912

Jean Marie Burr (5 YRS. W-92, L-38)

Fairfield	N27	Cornell■	J29
Northeastern■	N28	Dartmouth■	F 4
Rhode Island■	D 1	Harvard■	F 5
Brown Cl.	D4-5	Pennsylvania	F11
Boston U.■	D 8	Princeton	F12
Rice Cl.	J3-4	Cornell	F18
Hartford	J 8	Columbia-Barnard	F19
New Hampshire■	J11	Princeton■	F25
Central Conn. St.	J13	Pennsylvania■	F26
Massachusetts	J19	Harvard	M 4
Yale	J22	Dartmouth	M 5
Columbia-Barnard■	J28	Yale■	M 8

Colors: Brown, Cardinal & White. Nickname: Bears.
AD: Dave Roach. SID: Chris Humm. I

BRYANT .... Smithfield, RI 02917

Mary Burke (2 YRS. W-23, L-32)

Babson■	N21	Assumption	J22
Teiko Post■	N23	American Int'l	J25
Mass.-Lowell	N27	Springfield■	J27
St. Anselm	D 4	St. Michael's	J29
Keene St.	D 6	St. Anselm■	F 2
Sacred Heart	D 8	Quinnipiac	F 5
St. Rose Cl.	D28-29	Springfield	F 7
St. Michael's■	J 3	Merrimack■	F 9
Rhode Island Col.	J 5	Bentley	F12
Merrimack	J12	Stonehill	F16
Bentley■	J15	Assumption■	F19
Quinnipiac■	J17	American Int'l■	F22
Stonehill■	J19		

Colors: Black & Gold. Nickname: Indians.
AD: Linda Hackett. SID: None. II

BUCKNELL .... Lewisburg, PA 17837

Juliene Simpson (14 YRS. W-207, L-182)

Monmouth (N.J.)	D 1	Lehigh	J26
Hartford Cl.	D4-5	Holy Cross■	J29
Rider	D 7	Colgate■	F 2
Mt. St. Mary's (Md.)■	D21	Fordham	F 5
St. Francis Cl.	D30-31	Hofstra	F 6
American■	J 2	Lafayette■	F 9
Drexel	J 6	Army■	F12
Colgate	J 8	Navy	F16
Yale■	J 9	Lehigh■	F19
Fordham■	J12	Towson St.■	F21
Lafayette	J15	Holy Cross	F26
Army	J19	Patriot Tr.	M3-12
Navy■	J22		

Colors: Orange & Blue. Nickname: Bison.
AD: Rick Hartzell. SID: Bo Smolka. I

BUENA VISTA .... Storm Lake, IA 50588

Janet Allgood (1 YR. W-8, L-17)

Winona St. Inv.	N19-20	Upper Iowa	J22
Coe	D 3	Wartburg■	J28
Clarke	D 4	Dubuque■	J29
N'western (Iowa)■	D 7	Central (Iowa)	F 1
Briar Cliff	D13	Loras■	F 4
Buena Vista Tr.	D29-30	Upper Iowa■	F 5
William Penn■	J 7	William Penn	F11
Central (Iowa)■	J 8	Loras	F12
Neb. Wesleyan	J11	Simpson	F18
Luther	J14	Luther■	F19
Dubuque	J15	Wartburg	F22
Simpson■	J21		

Colors: Navy Blue & Gold. Nickname: Beavers.
AD: Jim Hershberger. SID: Jay Miller. III

BUFFALO .... Buffalo, NY 14260

Sal Buscaglia (3 YRS. W-52, L-30)

Drexel■	N30	Hofstra	J21
Buffalo Tr.	D3-4	Niagara	J26
Cornell	D 8	Troy St.	J30
Colgate■	D10	Chicago St.■	F 3
Md.-East. Shore■	D13	Colgate	F 7
Niagara■	D18	Cleveland St.■	F10
Maine■	D28	Central Conn. St.■	F13
St. Francis Cl.	D30-31	Canisius■	F15
Coppin St.■	J 3	Chicago St.	F17
Fairfield■	J 9	Northeastern Ill.	F19
Marist■	J17	Marquette	F21
Md.-East. Shore	J19	Duquesne■	F28

Colors: Royal Blue, White & Red. Nickname: Royals.
AD: Nelson E. Townsend. SID: Mike Rowland. I

BUFFALO ST. .... Buffalo, NY 14222

Gail F. Maloney (14 YRS. W-246, L-98)

Buffalo St. Inv.	N20-21	Penn St.-Behrend	J24
Fredonia St.	D 3	St. John Fisher■	J26
Cortland St.	D 4	Binghamton■	J29
Brockport St.■	D 7	Keuka	F 1
Utica Tech	D11	Brockport St.	F 4
Albany (N.Y.)	D12	Utica Tech■	F 5
Alfred■	J11	Oneonta St.	F11
Plattsburgh St.■	J14	New Paltz St.	F12
Potsdam St.■	J15	Fredonia St.■	F15
Nazareth (N.Y.)■	J18	Geneseo St.	F18
Geneseo St.■	J21	Oswego St.■	F19
Oswego St.	J22		

Colors: Orange & Black. Nickname: Lady Bengals.
AD: Fred Hartrick. SID: Keith Bullion. III

BUTLER .... Indianapolis, IN 46208

June Olkowski (4 YRS. W-34, L-82)

Iowa Cl.	N27-28	Dayton■	J17
Louisville■	N30	Loyola (Ill.)	J20
Northwestern Inv.	D3-4	Notre Dame	J22
Ball St.	D 8	La Salle	J29
Michigan■	D11	Evansville■	F 5
Ala.-Birmingham Cl.	D20-21	Notre Dame■	F10
Purdue	D28	Loyola (Ill.)■	F12
Miami (Ohio)■	D30	Xavier (Ohio)	F17
Indiana St.	J 2	Detroit Mercy	F19
Arkansas■	J10	La Salle■	F24
Detroit Mercy■	J13	Evansville	M 2
Xavier (Ohio)■	J15	MCC Tr.	M5-8

Colors: Blue & White. Nickname: Bulldogs.
AD: John Parry. SID: Gina Grueneberg. I

CALIFORNIA .... Berkeley, CA 94720

Gooch Foster (20 YRS. W-338, L-205)

Cal St. Sacramento■	N27	UCLA	J29
St. Mary's (Cal.)■	D 1	Oregon St.■	F 3
Hawaii Tr.	D3-6	Oregon■	F 5
San Francisco■	D18	Arizona St.	F10
California Cl.	D20-21	Arizona	F12
Southern Methodist	D28	Stanford	F18
Texas	D30	UCLA■	F24
Washington St.	J 6	Southern Cal■	F26
Washington	J 8	Oregon	M 3
Arizona■	J13	Oregon St.	M 5
Arizona St.■	J15	Washington■	M10
Stanford■	J21	Washington St.■	M12
Southern Cal	J27		

Colors: Blue & Gold. Nickname: Golden Bears.
AD: To be named. SID: Beth Breyer. I

■ Home games on each schedule.

See pages 735-738 for Division I tournament details

CALIF. (PA.) .... California, PA 15419
Paul Flores (11 YRS. W-156, L-111)

Calif. (Pa.) Tr.	N19-20
Point Park■	N24
Northern Ky.■	N28
St. Vincent■	D 1
Seton Hill	D 3
Gannon■	D 7
Millersville	D10
East Stroudsburg	D12
Salem-Teikyo■	D15
Georgetown (Ky.)■	D18
Fairmont St.	J 7
Slippery Rock■	J12
Edinboro	J15
Shippensburg■	J19
Lock Haven	J22
Davis & Elkins■	J25
Indiana (Pa.)■	J29
Clarion	F 2
Edinboro■	F 5
Slippery Rock	F 9
Shippensburg	F12
Columbia Union■	F14
Lock Haven■	F19
Clarion■	F23
Indiana (Pa.)	F26

Colors: Red & Black. Nickname: Vulcans.
AD: Tom Pucci. SID: Bruce Wald. II

CAL LUTHERAN .... Thousand Oaks, CA 91360
Tim La Kose (1ST YR. AS HEAD COACH)

Biola	N23
Concordia-M'head■	N26
Pac. Christian■	N30
Mills	D 3
San Fran. St.	D 4
Azusa-Pacific■	D 7
Pt. Loma Nazarene	D10
Chapman■	J 7
Mills■	J 9
Pomona-Pitzer■	J11
Redlands	J14
Occidental■	J21
Claremont-M-S	J25
La Verne■	J28
Whittier■	F 1
Pomona-Pitzer	F 4
Redlands■	F 8
Southern Cal Col.	F11
UC San Diego■	F12
Occidental	F15
Claremont-M-S■	F18
La Verne	F22
Whittier	F25

Colors: Purple & Gold. Nickname: Regals.
AD: Bob Doering. SID: John Czimbal. III

CAL POLY POMONA .... Pomona, CA 91768
Darlene May (19 YRS. W-498, L-113)

Cal Poly Pomona Cl.	N19-20
San Diego■	N26
St. Cloud St.■	N27
CCAA/NCAC Challenge	D3-4
Cal Baptist■	D11
Northern Colo.	D15
Denver	D17
Regis (Colo.)	D18
Loyola (Cal.)■	D21
Wayne St. (Neb.)■	D31
Wayland Bapt.■	J 3
Western N. Mex.■	J 5
Azusa-Pacific■	J 8
Cal St. Los Angeles■	J13
Cal St. Dom. Hills	J15
Cal St. San B'dino■	J20
Cal Poly SLO	J22
UC Riverside■	J29
Cal St. Los Angeles	F 5
Cal St. Dom. Hills■	F10
Cal St. San B'dino	F12
Cal Poly SLO■	F18
UC Riverside	F24

Colors: Green & Gold. Nickname: Broncos.
AD: Karen Miller. SID: Ron Fremont. II

CAL POLY SLO .... San Luis Obispo, CA 93407
Jill Orrock (7 YRS. W-87, L-97)

Cal Poly SLO Tr.	N26-27
Southern Colo. Tr.	D3-4
Cal St. Sacramento	D11
UC Davis■	D15
Fresno St.	D17
Cal St. Stanislaus	D18
Cal Poly SLO Cl.	D29-30
Sonoma St.	J 7
UC Davis	J 8
Cal St. Stanislaus■	J12
Chapman	J15
Cal St. Dom. Hills■	J20
Cal Poly Pomona■	J22
UC Riverside■	J27
Cal St. Los Angeles	J29
Cal St. San B'dino■	F 3
Cal St. Northridge	F 5
Cal St. Dom. Hills	F12
Cal Poly Pomona	F18
UC Riverside	F19
Cal St. Los Angeles■	F24
Cal St. San B'dino	F26

Colors: Green & Gold. Nickname: Mustangs.
AD: John McCutcheon. SID: Eric McDowell. II

CAL ST. DOM. HILLS .... Carson, CA 90747
Van Girard (5 YRS. W-65, L-67)

Cal St. Chico Tr.	N19-20
Pt. Loma Nazarene■	N23
UC Davis■	N26
Biola■	N30
Cal Baptist Tr.	D3-4
Christ-Irvine	D11
Azusa-Pacific■	D17
San Fran. St.	D20
Cal St. Stanislaus	D21
Sonoma St.	D22
McKendree■	J 8
Cal St. Northridge	J10
Cal Poly Pomona■	J15
Cal Poly SLO	J20
UC Riverside■	J22
Cal St. Los Angeles	J27
Cal St. San B'dino	J29
Chapman■	F 5
Cal Poly Pomona	F10
Cal Poly SLO■	F12
UC Riverside	F18
Cal St. Los Angeles■	F19
Cal St. San B'dino■	F21

Colors: Cardinal & Gold. Nickname: Toros.
AD: Kay Don. SID: Kevin Gilmore. II

CAL ST. FULLERTON .... Fullerton, CA 92634
Deborah Ayres (1 YR. W-8, L-19)

Arizona■	N26
Cal St. Northridge	D 1
Fresno St.	D 3
Stephen F. Austin■	D18
California Cl.	D20-21
UC Santa Barb.	J 3
Long Beach St.■	J 6
Nevada-Las Vegas	J 8
New Mexico St.	J10
UC Irvine■	J15
San Diego St.	J18
Long Beach St.	J20
New Mexico St.■	J27
Nevada-Las Vegas■	J29
San Jose St.	F 3
Pacific (Cal.)	F 5
Hawaii■	F11
Hawaii■	F12
Nevada	F17
UC Santa Barb.■	F19
San Jose St.■	F24
Nevada■	F26
UC Irvine	F28
Pacific (Cal.)■	M 5
Big West Tr.	M9-12

Colors: Blue, Orange & White. Nickname: Titans.
AD: Bill Shumard. SID: Mel Franks. I

CAL ST. HAYWARD .... Hayward, CA 94542
Dennis Frese (5 YRS. W-54, L-80)

Cal St. LA Tr.	N19-20
Notre Dame (Cal.)■	N26
CCAA/NCAC Challenge	D3-4
Fresno Pacific	D10
Cal St. San B'dino■	D11
Portland St. Cl.	D16-18
Seattle■	D20
Cal St. Stanis. Tr.	D29-30
Lake Superior St.■	J 2
Cal St. Chico■	J 7
Humboldt St.■	J 8
San Fran. St.■	J14
Sonoma St.	J21
UC Davis■	J22
UC Davis	F 4
Sonoma St.■	F 5
San Fran. St.	F12
Humboldt St.	F18
Cal St. Chico	F19
Cal St. Stanislaus■	F24

Colors: Red & White. Nickname: Pioneers.
AD: Doug Weiss. SID: Marty Valdez. II

CAL ST. LOS ANGELES .... Los Angeles, CA 90032
Marcia Murota (2 YRS. W-14, L-39)

Cal St. LA Tr.	N19-20
Cal Poly SLO Tr.	N26-27
West Tex. A&M Tr.	D2-4
Pepperdine	D11
Grand Canyon■	D15
UC Davis■	D18
Cal St. Stanis. Tr.	D29-30
Wayne St. (Neb.)■	J 5
Cal Poly Pomona	J13
Cal St. San B'dino■	J15
Cal St. Dom. Hills■	J27
Cal Poly SLO■	J29
UC Riverside	F 3
Cal Poly Pomona■	F 5
Cal St. Northridge	F 8
Cal St. San B'dino	F10
Cal St. Dom. Hills	F19
Cal Poly SLO	F24
UC Riverside■	F26

Colors: Black & Gold. Nickname: Golden Eagles.
AD: Carol M. Dunn. SID: John Czimbal. II

CAL ST. NORTHRIDGE .... Northridge, CA 91330
Kim Chandler (2 YRS. W-8, L-36)

St. Mary's Cl.	N26-27
Cal St. Fullerton■	D 1
Nevada■	D 4
Southern Cal	D 7
Fresno St.■	D10
San Diego	D18
Pepperdine■	D21
UC Santa Barb.	D28
San Jose St.■	D30
Northern Ariz.■	J 2
Loyola (Cal.)	J 6
Cal St. Dom. Hills■	J10
Nevada	J13
Cal St. Sacramento	J15
Southern Utah■	J18
Pacific (Cal.)	J25
San Francisco	J26
Northern Ariz.	F 2
Cal Poly SLO■	F 5
Cal St. Los Angeles■	F 8
Southern Utah	F12
Arizona	F16
Cal St. Sacramento■	F19
Mo.-Kansas City	F26

Colors: Red, White & Black. Nickname: Matadors.
AD: Judith M. Brame. SID: Barry Smith. I

CAL ST. SACRAMENTO .... Sacramento, CA 95819
Sue Huffman (7 YRS. W-107, L-81)

California	N27
Pacific (Cal.)■	N30
UC Irvine Cl.	D3-4
San Jose St.■	D10
Cal Poly SLO■	D11
Stanford Cl.	D17-18
San Francisco	D20
Nevada	D29
Santa Clara	J 2
St. Mary's (Cal.)	J 4
San Diego■	J 7
Cal St. Northridge■	J15
Southern Utah■	J20
Texas A&M	J23
Sam Houston St.	J25
Northeastern Ill.	F 5
Chicago St.	F 7
Nevada■	F14
Cal St. Northridge	F19
Southern Utah	F21
UC Davis■	F25
Kansas St.	M 2

Colors: Green & Gold. Nickname: Hornets.
AD: Lee McElroy. SID: Jeff Minahan. I

■ Home games on each schedule.

See pages 735-738 for Division I tournament details

CAL ST. SAN B'DINO ..... San Bernardino, CA 92407

Luvina Beckley (2 YRS. W-21, L-18)

San Fran. St.■	N22	UC Riverside■	J13
Cal Baptist	N23	Cal St. Los Angeles	J15
Grand Canyon Inv.	N26-27	Cal Poly Pomona	J20
Pt. Loma Nazarene■	N30	Cal St. Dom. Hills■	J29
Pomona-Pitzer■	D 4	Wayne St. (Neb.)■	J31
Cal St. Hayward	D11	Cal Poly SLO	F 3
UC Davis	D13	UC Riverside	F 5
Cal St. Stanislaus	D14	Cal St. Los Angeles■	F10
Chapman■	D20	Cal Poly Pomona■	F12
Occidental	D22	Azusa-Pacific	F19
Pepperdine	D30	Cal St. Dom. Hills	F21
Harding■	J 6	Cal Poly SLO■	F26

Colors: Light Blue & Brown. Nickname: Coyotes.
AD: David Suenram. SID: Dave Beyer. II

CAL ST. STANISLAUS .... Turlock, CA 95380

Leann Millar (12 YRS. W-221, L-113)

Southern Ore. Tr.	N19-20	Cal Poly SLO	J12
Cal St. Stanis. Inv.	N26-27	UC Davis	J15
CCAA/NCAC Challenge	D3-4	San Fran. St.	J21
Fresno Pacific	D 8	Sonoma St.■	J22
Cal St. San B'dino■	D14	Sonoma St.	F 4
Southern Ore. St.■	D16	San Fran. St.■	F 5
Cal Poly SLO■	D18	UC Davis■	F11
Cal St. Dom. Hills■	D21	Cal St. Chico	F18
Cal St. Stanis. Tr.	D29-30	Humboldt St.	F19
Humboldt St.■	J 7	Cal St. Hayward	F24
Cal St. Chico■	J 8		

Colors: Red & Gold. Nickname: Warriors.
AD: Joe Donahue. SID: Will Keener. II

UC DAVIS .... Davis, CA 95616

Jorja Hoehn (13 YRS. W-265, L-107)

Cal St. Dom. Hills	N26	Humboldt St.	J14
UC Riverside	N27	Cal St. Stanislaus■	J15
UC Davis Inv.	D3-4	Cal St. Chico	J21
Cal St. San B'dino■	D13	Cal St. Hayward	J22
Cal Poly SLO	D15	Cal St. Hayward■	F 4
Cal St. Los Angeles	D18	Cal St. Chico■	F 5
Portland St. Tr.	D29-30	Cal St. Stanislaus	F11
Alas. Fairbanks■	J 4	Humboldt St.■	F12
San Fran. St.■	J 7	San Fran. St.	F18
Cal Poly SLO■	J 8	Sonoma St.■	F19
Sonoma St.	J 9	Cal St. Sacramento	F25

Colors: Blue & Gold. Nickname: Aggies.
AD: Keith Williams. SID: Doug Dull. II

UC IRVINE .... Irvine, CA 92717

Colleen Matsuhara (5 YRS. W-53, L-90)

Arizona■	N28	Nevada-Las Vegas■	J27
UC Irvine Cl.	D3-4	New Mexico St.■	J29
Pepperdine	D14	Pacific (Cal.)	F 3
Rice	D19	San Jose St.	F 5
Texas A&M	D21	Hawaii■	F 8
Drake■	D28	Hawaii■	F 9
Colorado■	D30	UC Santa Barb.	F17
Long Beach St.	J 4	Nevada	F19
UC Santa Barb.■	J 6	San Jose St.■	F26
New Mexico St.	J 8	Cal St. Fullerton■	F28
Nevada-Las Vegas	J10	Pacific (Cal.)■	M 3
Cal St. Fullerton	J15	Long Beach St.■	M 5
Nevada■	J22	Big West Tr.	M9-12

Colors: Blue & Gold. Nickname: Anteaters.
AD: Dan Guerrero. SID: Bob Olson. I

UC SAN DIEGO .... La Jolla, CA 92093

Judy Malone (17 YRS. W-209, L-214)

Claremont-M-S	N23	Southern Cal Col.	J18
Rochester Inv.	N27-28	Chapman	J21
La Verne■	D 3	Whittier■	J22
Redlands■	D 4	Pomona-Pitzer■	J29
Pt. Loma Nazarene	D11	Redlands	F 4
Christ-Irvine	D14	UC Santa Cruz■	F 5
UC San Diego Inv.	D28-30	Chapman■	F11
Azusa-Pacific■	J 4	Cal Lutheran	F12
McKendree■	J 6	Occidental	F18
Harding■	J 8	Pt. Loma Nazarene■	F19
La Verne	J14		

Colors: Blue & Gold. Nickname: Tritons.
AD: Judith Sweet. SID: Bill Gannon. III

UC SANTA BARB. .... Santa Barbara, CA 93106

Mark French (14 YRS. W-194, L-195)

UCLA	N27	Long Beach St.■	J22
San Francisco	N30	Hawaii	J28
Pepperdine	D 4	Hawaii	J30
Fresno St.■	D12	New Mexico St.■	F 3
Oregon St.	D18	Nevada-Las Vegas■	F 5
Washington Cl.	D20-21	San Jose St.■	F10
Cal St. Northridge■	D28	Pacific (Cal.)■	F13
Cal St. Fullerton■	J 3	UC Irvine■	F17
UC Irvine	J 6	Cal St. Fullerton	F19
Long Beach St.	J 9	New Mexico St.■	F24
Pacific (Cal.)	J13	Nevada-Las Vegas	F26
San Jose St.	J15	Nevada	M 5
Nevada■	J20	Big West Tr.	M9-12

Colors: Blue & Gold. Nickname: Gauchos.
AD: Alice Henry. SID: Bill Mahoney. I

UC SANTA CRUZ .... Santa Cruz, CA 95064

Diane Morgenstern (1ST YR. AS HEAD COACH)

Cal St. Stanis. Inv.	N26-27	Humboldt St.■	J22
Mills	N30	Dominican (Cal.)	J23
San Fran. St.■	D11	Dominican (Cal.)■	J28
Notre Dame (Cal.)	D18	Mills■	F 4
Whittier■	J 5	UC San Diego	F 5
Notre Dame (Cal.)■	J 8	Mills Tr.	F17-19

Colors: Blue & Gold. Nickname: Banana Slugs.
AD: Dan Wood. SID: Cori Houston. III

CALVIN .... Grand Rapids, MI 49546

Gregg Afman (1ST YR. AS HEAD COACH)

Oakland Tr.	N19-20	Albion	J19
Wheaton (Ill.)■	N23	Olivet	J22
Grand Rapids Tr.	N26-27	Alma■	J26
Grand Valley St.■	N30	Adrian■	J29
Aquinas■	D 2	Kalamazoo	F 2
North Central■	D 8	Hope	F 4
Ohio Northern Inv.	D29-30	St. Mary's (Ind.)	F 9
Adrian	J 5	Albion■	F12
Kalamazoo■	J 8	Olivet■	F16
Hope■	J11	Alma	F19

Colors: Maroon & Gold. Nickname: Lady Knights.
AD: Doris Zuidema. SID: Phil de Haan. III

CAMERON .... Lawton, OK 73505

Laina McDonald (4 YRS. W-28, L-78)

West Tex. A&M Inv.	N19-20	Eastern N. Mex.	J20
Texas Woman's Tr.	N26-27	Oklahoma S&A	J24
Southwestern Okla.■	N30	Texas A&I	J27
Central Okla. Cl.	D3-4	Tarleton St.	J29
Midwestern St.	D 8	Western N. Mex.■	F 3
Angelo St.■	D10	Tarleton St.■	F 8
Lubbock Chrst.■	D11	Midwestern St.■	F 9
Texas Woman's■	D18	Angelo St.	F17
Southwest Baptist	J 3	Oklahoma S&A■	F19
East Tex. St.■	J 8	Western N. Mex.	F21
Lubbock Chrst.	J10	Central Okla.■	F26
Central Okla.	J12		

Colors: Gold & Black. Nickname: Lady Aggies.
AD: Jerry Hrnciar. SID: David Siegel. II

CAMPBELL .... Buies Creek, NC 27506

Wanda Watkins (12 YRS. W-214, L-111)

East Caro.■	N30	Coastal Caro.	J29
Barton■	D 7	N.C.-Greensboro	F 5
N.C.-Greensboro■	D18	North Caro. A&T	F 9
Ga. Southern Inv.	D29-30	Winthrop■	F11
North Caro. A&T■	J 4	N.C.-Asheville■	F12
Winthrop	J 7	Radford	F18
N.C.-Asheville	J 8	Liberty	F19
Radford■	J14	Towson St.	F25
Liberty■	J15	Md.-Balt. County	F27
Davidson	J19	Charleston So.■	M 4
Towson St.■	J21	Coastal Caro.■	M 5
Md.-Balt. County■	J22	Big South Tr.	M9-12
Charleston So.	J28		

Colors: Orange & Black. Nickname: Lady Camels.
AD: Tom Collins. SID: Stan Cole. I

■ Home games on each schedule.

See pages 735-738 for Division I tournament details

CANISIUS .... Buffalo, NY 14208

Kara Rehbaum (1ST YR. AS HEAD COACH)

Detroit Mercy■	D 4	Colgate	J30
Eastern Mich.■	D 6	Siena	F 2
Navy Cl.	D18-19	St. Peter's	F 5
Pittsburgh Inv.	D29-30	Iona	F 7
New Hampshire	J 6	Siena■	F11
Fairfield■	J 8	Manhattan■	F13
Marquette	J11	Buffalo	F15
Iona■	J13	Loyola (Md.)■	F19
St. Peter's■	J15	Niagara	F21
St. Bonaventure	J18	Loyola (Md.)	F25
Fairfield	J22	Manhattan	F27
Temple■	J24	Metro Atlantic Tr.	M4-6
Niagara■	J28		

Colors: Blue & Gold. Nickname: Golden Griffins.
AD: Daniel P. Starr. SID: John Maddock. I

CAPITAL .... Columbus, OH 43209

Dixie Jeffers (10 YRS. W-206, L-63)

Adrian	N20	Hiram■	J15
Ohio Wesleyan	N22	Marietta	J18
Mount Union■	D 4	Mount Union	J22
Heidelberg	D 7	Heidelberg■	J25
Wittenberg Cl.	D10-11	Muskingum	J29
Otterbein	D15	Hiram	F 1
Muskingum■	D20	Otterbein■	F 5
Alma■	D30	Ohio Northern	F 8
John Carroll■	J 4	Baldwin-Wallace■	F12
Baldwin-Wallace	J 8	Marietta■	F15
Ohio Northern■	J11	John Carroll	F19

Colors: Purple & White. Nickname: Crusaders.
AD: Roger Welsh. SID: Dave Graham. III

CARLETON .... Northfield, MN 55057

Eileen Reading (8 YRS. W-60, L-135)

Dr. Martin Luther	D 2	Hamline■	J19
St. Scholastica	D 4	Concordia-M'head	J22
Concordia-M'head■	D 6	St. Mary's (Minn.)	J26
St. Mary's (Minn.)■	D 8	Gust. Adolphus■	J29
Gust. Adolphus	D10	Macalester	F 2
St. Olaf■	J 3	St. Benedict	F 5
Macalester■	J 5	St. Thomas (Minn.)■	F 9
St. Benedict■	J 8	Augsburg■	F16
St. Thomas (Minn.)	J10	Hamline	F19
N'western (Minn.)■	J13	St. Olaf	F23
Bethel (Minn.)■	J15	Bethel (Minn.)	F26
Augsburg	J17		

Colors: Maize & Blue. Nickname: Carls.
AD: Leon Lunder. SID: Joe Hargis. III

CARNEGIE MELLON .... Pittsburgh, PA 15213

Gerri Seidl (9 YRS. W-115 , L-95)

Muskingum	N20	Johns Hopkins	J16
Case Reserve■	N23	Brandeis■	J21
Carnegie Mellon Inv.	N27-28	New York U.■	J23
Wash. & Jeff.■	N30	Chicago	J28
Emory	D 3	Washington (Mo.)	J30
Sewanee	D 4	New York U.	F 4
LaRoche	D 6	Brandeis	F 6
Waynesburg	J 4	Washington (Mo.)■	F11
Rochester■	J 7	Chicago■	F13
Grove City■	J10	Frostburg St.■	F15
Thiel■	J12	Emory■	F20
Catholic	J14	Rochester	F26

Colors: Cardinal, White & Gray. Nickname: Lady Tartans.
AD: John Harvey. SID: Bruce Gerson. III

CARROLL (WIS.) .... Waukesha, WI 53186

Sue Hansen (4 YRS. W-55, L-41)

Aurora	N23	Cornell College■	J22
Carthage■	N30	Knox	J28
Lake Forest	D 4	Illinois Col.	J29
Beloit	D 8	Lake Forest■	F 2
St. Norbert■	D11	St. Mary's (Ind.)	F 5
Colorado Col. Tr.	D29-31	Beloit■	F 8
Lawrence	J 5	Wis. Lutheran	F10
Ripon■	J15	Ripon	F12
Wis.-Platteville	J18	St. Norbert	F16
Monmouth (Ill.)■	J21	Lawrence■	F21

Colors: Orange & White. Nickname: Pioneers.
AD: Merle Masonholder. SID: Shawn Ama. III

CARSON-NEWMAN .... Jefferson City, TN 37760

Eddie Carter (6 YRS. W-132, L-47)

Longwood Inv.	N19-20	Elon■	J29
Francis Marion	N30	Lincoln Memorial■	F 2
Lincoln Memorial	D 7	Catawba	F 5
Carson-Newman Cl.	J5-6	Gardner-Webb■	F 9
Catawba■	J 8	Wingate	F12
Gardner-Webb	J12	Cumberland (Ky.)	F14
Wingate■	J15	Mars Hill	F16
Erskine	J17	Presbyterian■	F19
Mars Hill■	J19	Lenoir-Rhyne■	F23
Presbyterian	J22	Elon	F26
Lenoir-Rhyne	J26		

Colors: Orange & Blue. Nickname: Lady Eagles.
AD: David Barger. SID: Eric Trainer. II

CARTHAGE .... Kenosha, WI 53140

Rich Fanning (1 YR. W-9, L-16)

Marian (Wis.)■	N20	North Park■	J25
Beloit	N23	Aurora	J27
Carroll (Wis.)	N30	Wheaton (Ill.)■	J29
St. Mary's (In.) Cl.	D3-4	Wheaton (Ill.)	F 1
Wis. Lutheran	D 7	Elmhurst■	F 5
Augustana (Ill.)	D11	North Park	F10
North Central■	D18	Augustana (Ill.)■	F12
Olivet (Ill.)	J 6	Lawrence	F17
North Central	J11	Ill. Wesleyan	F19
Millikin■	J15	Edgewood■	F21
Lakeland■	J18	Elmhurst	F24
Ill. Wesleyan■	J21	Millikin	F26

Colors: Red & White. Nickname: Lady Reds.
AD: Bob Bonn. SID: Greg Sorenson. III

CASE RESERVE .... Cleveland, OH 44106

To be named

Carnegie Mellon	N23	Earlham■	J15
New York U.	N26	Oberlin■	J19
Brandeis■	N28	Chicago■	J21
Allegheny	D 1	Washington (Mo.)■	J23
Rochester■	D 3	Wooster	J26
Emory	D 5	Wittenberg■	J29
Wooster■	D 7	Kenyon■	F 2
Wittenberg	D16	Denison	F 5
Johns Hopkins	J 3	Allegheny■	F 9
Ohio Wesleyan	J 5	Earlham	F12
Denison■	J 8	Oberlin	F16
Kenyon	J12	Ohio Wesleyan■	F19

Colors: Blue, Gray & White. Nickname: Lady Spartans.
AD: Dave Hutter. SID: Sue Penicka. III

CASTLETON ST. .... Castleton, VT 05735

Patrick Whalen (2 YRS. W-6, L-43)

Buffalo St. Inv.	N20-21	Notre Dame (N.H.)	J22
Russell Sage■	N30	Plymouth St.	J25
Southern Vt.	D 2	Green Mountain■	J27
North Adams St.	D 7	St. Joseph (Vt.)	J29
Trinity (Vt.)■	D 9	Albany Pharmacy■	F 1
Westbrook■	D11	Notre Dame (N.H.)■	F 5
Lyndon St.■	D14	Green Mountain	F 8
Me.-Presque Isle■	J10	Johnson St.	F10
Utica■	J12	Skidmore■	F12
Lyndon St.	J15	Norwich■	F15
Westbrook	J16	St. Joseph (Vt.)■	F17
Johnson St.■	J20	Plattsburgh St.■	F19

Colors: Green & White. Nickname: Spartans.
AD: To be named. SID: Carrie Zahm. III

CATHOLIC .... Washington, DC 20064

Jack Sullivan (4 YRS. W-33, L-65)

Johns Hopkins Cl.	N20-21	Gallaudet■	J25
Scranton■	N27	Goucher	J27
Randolph-Macon■	D 4	Notre Dame (Md.)	J29
Salisbury St.■	D 6	Mary Washington■	F 1
Catholic Tr.	J8-9	Goucher■	F 3
Marymount (Va.)	J12	York (Pa.)	F 5
Washington (Md.)■	J13	Marymount (Va.)■	F 7
Carnegie Mellon■	J14	Allentown	F10
York (Pa.)■	J15	Gallaudet	F15
St. Mary's (Md.)■	J19	Mary Washington	F17
Western Md.■	J20	St. Mary's (Md.)	F19

Colors: Cardinal, Red & Black. Nickname: Cardinals.
AD: Bob Talbot. SID: Gabe Romano. III

■ Home games on each schedule.

See pages 735-738 for Division I tournament details

CATAWBA .... Salisbury, NC 28144

Cindy Connelly (5 YRS. W-65, L-68)

Catawba Cl.	N19-20	Wingate■	J26
S.C.-Spart. Inv.	N26-27	Gardner-Webb	J29
High Point■	N30	Livingstone■	J31
Johnson Smith Inv.	D3-4	Carson-Newman■	F 5
Longwood	D 7	Presbyterian■	F 9
Queens (N.C.)	D14	Longwood■	F10
Carson-Newman	J 8	Lenoir-Rhyne	F12
Presbyterian	J12	Elon■	F16
Lenoir-Rhyne■	J15	Mars Hill	F19
Elon	J19	Wingate	F23
Mars Hill■	J22	Gardner-Webb■	F26

Colors: Blue & White. Nickname: Lady Indians.
AD: Tom Childress (Interim). SID: Dennis Davidson. II

CENTRAL (IOWA) .... Pella, IA 50219

Gary Boeyink (20 YRS. W-274, L-207)

Monmouth (Ill.)	N27	Simpson	J29
Knox	N28	Buena Vista■	F 1
St. Ambrose■	D 1	Luther	F 4
Midland Lutheran Tr.	D17-18	Dubuque	F 5
Wartburg	J 7	Wartburg■	F11
Buena Vista	J 8	Simpson■	F12
Upper Iowa■	J14	Upper Iowa	F15
Loras■	J15	Dordt■	F19
Dubuque■	J21	William Penn■	F25
Luther■	J22	Loras	F26
William Penn	J28		

Colors: Red & White. Nickname: Flying Dutchmen.
AD: Ron Schipper. SID: Larry Happel. III

CENTRAL ARK. .... Conway, AR 72032

Ron Marvel (13 YRS. W-269, L-110)

Livingston Cl.	N19-20	Mississippi-Women	J24
Ozarks (Mo.)■	D 2	Henderson St.	J27
Northeastern Okla.■	D 3	Livingston■	J29
Ouachita Bapt.■	D 4	Delta St.■	J31
Northeast Okla. Cl.	D10-11	Ala.-Huntsville	F 5
Harding	D17	North Ala.	F 7
Olivet (Ill.)☒	D30	Mississippi-Women■	F12
Arkansas Tech	J 4	Mississippi Col.■	F14
Mississippi Col.	J 8	Henderson St.■	F19
Livingston	J10	Tex.-Pan American	F22
Ala.-Huntsville■	J15	Delta St.	F26
North Ala.■	J17	☒ Pensacola, FL	

Colors: Purple & Gray. Nickname: Sugar Bears.
AD: Bill Stephens. SID: Darrell Walsh. II

CENTRAL CONN. ST. .... New Britain, CT 06050

Brenda Reilly (22 YRS. W-299, L-278)

Siena■	N27	Temple	J18
Yale	N30	Dartmouth■	J23
Liberty Cl.	D3-4	Harvard■	J29
Fairfield■	D 7	Boston U.■	F 1
Wagner	D11	Hofstra	F 4
Delaware St.■	D12	Vermont	F 8
Drexel■	D21	Buffalo	F13
Hartford■	D29	Chicago St.	F21
Florida Int'l Tr.	J2-4	Northeastern Ill.■	F25
Northeastern	J 8	Holy Cross	F28
Maine	J11	East Coast Tr.	M3-6
Brown■	J13		

Colors: Blue & White. Nickname: Blue Devils.
AD: Judith Davidson. SID: Kathleen Pulek. I

CENTRAL FLA. .... Orlando, FL 32816

Jerry Richardson (1 YR. W-4, L-24)

Memphis St. Cl.	D10-11	Florida Int'l■	J29
South Fla.■	D20	South Fla.	F 2
Central Fla. Cl.	D29-31	Stetson■	F 5
Northwestern (La.)	J 3	Mercer	F10
Grambling	J 5	Charleston	F12
Florida■	J11	Southeastern La.■	F17
Charleston■	J13	Georgia St.■	F19
Mercer■	J15	Fla. Atlantic	F22
Georgia St.	J20	Florida Int'l	F24
Southeastern La.	J22	Stetson	M 5
Louisiana St.	J24	Trans America Tr.	M10-12
Fla. Atlantic■	J27		

Colors: Black & Gold. Nickname: Lady Knights.
AD: Steve Sloan. SID: Bob Cefalo. I

CENTRAL MICH. .... Mt. Pleasant, MI 48858

Donita Davenport (9 YRS. W-147, L-109)

Michigan St.■	N29	Eastern Mich.	J29
Kansas Cl.	D3-4	Toledo■	F 2
Wis.-Green Bay Cl.	D10-11	Ball St.	F 5
Detroit Mercy	D17	Miami (Ohio)■	F 9
Central Mich. Cl.	D29-30	Western Mich.	F12
Kent	J 5	Ohio■	F16
Ball St.■	J 8	Akron	F19
Miami (Ohio)	J12	Bowling Green	F23
Western Mich.■	J15	Eastern Mich.■	F26
Ohio	J19	Toledo	M 2
Akron■	J22	Kent■	M 5
Bowling Green■	J26	Mid-American Tr.	M11-12

Colors: Maroon & Gold. Nickname: Chippewas.
AD: Marcy Weston. SID: Fred Stabley Jr. I

CENTRAL MO. ST. .... Warrensburg, MO 64093

Jon Pye (8 YRS. W-193, L-49)

SIU-Edwardsville■	N23	Northeast Mo. St.	J22
Washburn Cl.	N26-27	Missouri-Rolla	J26
SIU-Edwardsville Tr.	D3-4	Southwest Baptist■	J29
Avila■	D18	Northwest Mo. St.■	F 2
Quincy	D21	Washburn	F 5
High Desert Cl.	D27-28	Mo.-St. Louis	F 9
Pittsburg St.■	J 5	Mo. Western St.	F12
Mo. Western St.■	J 8	Emporia St.■	F16
Emporia St.	J12	Lincoln (Mo.)	F19
Lincoln (Mo.)■	J15	Mo. Southern St.	F23
Mo. Southern St.■	J19	Northeast Mo. St.■	F26

Colors: Cardinal & Black. Nickname: Jennies.
AD: Jerry Hughes. SID: Bill Turnage. II

CENTRAL OKLA. .... Edmond, OK 73034

John Keely (15 YRS. W-220, L-217)

Texas Woman's Inv.	N19-20	Abilene Christian	J24
Southwest Baptist■	N23	Texas A&I	J29
Pittsburg St. Cl.	N26-27	East Tex. St.	J31
Central Okla. Cl.	D3-4	East Tex. St.■	F 5
Emporia St.	D 7	Texas A&I■	F 7
Southwest Bapt. Cl.	D10-11	Eastern N. Mex.	F12
Texas Woman's	J 6	West Tex. St.	F14
Cameron■	J12	Abilene Christian■	F19
Eastern N. Mex.■	J15	Angelo St.■	F21
West Tex. St.■	J17	Texas Woman's■	F24
Angelo St.	J22	Cameron	F26

Colors: Bronze & Blue. Nickname: Lady Bronchos.
AD: Skip Wagnon. SID: Mike Kirk. II

CENTRE .... Danville, KY 40422

Cindy Noble-Hauserman (4 YRS. W-75, L-30)

Marymount (Va.) Tr.	N19-21	Rhodes	J28
Maryville (Tenn.)■	N28	Millsaps	J30
Hanover	D11	Midway	F 2
Thomas More■	D13	Sewanee	F 4
Lawrence■	D15	Oglethorpe	F 6
Franklin■	J 4	Rhodes■	F11
Fisk	J 9	Millsaps■	F13
Maryville (Tenn.)	J12	Hendrix	F18
Sewanee■	J14	Trinity (Tex.)	F20
Oglethorpe■	J16	Transylvania	F23
Hendrix■	J21	Fisk■	F26
Trinity (Tex.)■	J23		

Colors: Gold & White. Nickname: Colonels.
AD: Ray Hammond. SID: Cheryl Hart. III

CHADRON ST. .... Chadron, NE 69337

Bunny Rider (2 YRS. W-25, L-31)

South Dak. Tech■	N19	Adams St.	J20
Colo. Christian■	N20	N.M. Highlands	J21
Minot St.	N26-27	Mesa St.■	J27
Northern Colo.	N30	Western St.■	J29
Regis (Colo.) Cl.	D3-4	N.M. Highlands■	F 3
South Dak. Tech	D 7	Adams St.■	F 5
Dickinson St.■	D10	Fort Hays St.	F11
Denver	J 4	Neb.-Kearney	F12
Colorado Mines	J 5	Black Hills St.■	F15
Black Hills St.	J11	Mesa St.	F18
Fort Hays St.■	J13	Western St.	F19
Neb.-Kearney■	J14	Colorado Mines■	F26

Colors: Cardinal & White. Nickname: Lady Eagles.
AD: Brad Smith. SID: Con Marshall. II

■ Home games on each schedule.

See pages 735-738 for Division I tournament details

CHAPMAN .... **Orange, CA 92666**

Mary Hegarty (1ST YR. AS HEAD COACH)

Cal St. Stanis. Inv. N26-27
Cal Baptist■ N30
Cal Baptist Tr. D3-4
La Verne D 7
Redlands■ D10
Pomona-Pitzer■ D18
Cal St. San B'dino D20
Phillips (Okla.)■ J 4
Occidental J 5
Cal Lutheran J 7
Fresno Pacific■ J 8
Redlands J11
Cal Poly SLO■ J15
UC San Diego■ J21
Christ-Irvine J27
Claremont-M-S F 1
Pac. Christian■ F 4
Cal St. Dom. Hills F 5
UC San Diego F11
Southern Cal Col. F15
Biola F18

Colors: Cardinal & Gray. Nickname: Panthers.
AD: Dave Currey. SID: Derek Anderson. II

CHARLESTON .... **Charleston, SC 29424**

Scooter Barnette (9 YRS. W-170, L-90)

Charleston So.■ N27
Coastal Caro.■ D 1
N.C.-Wilmington■ D 3
Wake Forest D16
North Caro. D18
South Caro. J 3
Coker■ J 8
Central Fla. J13
Stetson J15
Charleston So. J17
Fla. Atlantic■ J20
Mercer■ J22
Coastal Caro. J24
Georgia St.■ J27
Southeastern La.■ J29
Florida Int'l F 3
Fla. Atlantic F 5
Stetson■ F10
Central Fla.■ F12
Furman■ F16
Mercer F19
Southeastern La. F24
Georgia St. F26
Florida Int'l■ M 5
Trans America Tr. M10-12

Colors: Maroon & White. Nickname: Lady Cougars.
AD: Jerry Baker. SID: Tony Ciuffo. I

CHARLESTON SO. .... **Charleston, SC 29411**

Jack Jordan (2 YRS. W-12, L-44)

Charleston N27
Coker■ D 1
Navy■ D 3
Webber■ D 4
Radford D 9
Liberty D10
Towson St.■ J 7
Md.-Balt. County■ J 8
Coastal Caro.■ J11
Winthrop J14
N.C.-Asheville J15
Charleston■ J17
Davidson■ J22
Campbell■ J28
N.C.-Greensboro■ J29
Radford■ F 4
Liberty■ F 5
Towson St. F11
Md.-Balt. County F12
Winthrop■ F18
N.C.-Asheville■ F19
N.C.-Wilmington■ F23
Coastal Caro. F26
Campbell M 4
N.C.-Greensboro M 5
Big South Tr. M9-12

Colors: Blue & Gold. Nickname: Lady Bucs.
AD: Howard Bagwell. SID: Michael Meyer. I

CHEYNEY .... **Cheyney, PA 19319**

Fred Dukes (1 YR. W-2, L-21)

Calif. (Pa.) Tr. N19-20
Clarion■ N22
Lincoln (Pa.)■ N27
Medgar Evers■ D 3
CCNY■ D 4
Virginia St. Cl. J7-8
Bloomsburg J12
East Stroudsburg■ J15
Bowie St.■ J17
West Chester■ J19
Mansfield■ J22
Dist. Columbia■ J24
Millersville J26
Kutztown■ J29
Columbia Union■ J31
Pitt.-Johnstown■ F 3
East Stroudsburg F 5
Bloomsburg■ F 9
West Chester F12
Dist. Columbia F14
Millersville■ F16
Mansfield F19
Shippensburg F23
Kutztown F26

Colors: Blue & White. Nickname: Lady Wolves.
AD: Andrew Hinson. SID: To be named. II

CHICAGO .... **Chicago, IL 60637**

Susan Zawacki (15 YRS. W-195, L-144)

Lake Forest Tr. N19-20
Wis.-Whitewater■ N23
North Central N30
Wheaton (Ill.) D 2
North Park■ D 4
Concordia (Ill.)■ D 7
Judson■ D 9
Washington (Mo.)■ J 4
Johns Hopkins■ J 7
Rockford J11
Brandeis J14
New York U. J16
St. Mary's (Ind.)■ J18
Case Reserve J21
Rochester J23
Carnegie Mellon■ J28
Emory■ J30
Rochester■ F 4
Emory F11
Carnegie Mellon F13
New York U.■ F18
Brandeis■ F20
Wis. Lutheran■ F22
Washington (Mo.) F26

Colors: White & Maroon. Nickname: Maroons.
AD: Tom Weingartner. SID: Dave Hilbert. III

CHICAGO ST. .... **Chicago, IL 60628**

Mike Clark (3 YRS. W-20, L-63)

Ill.-Chicago N29
St. Louis D 2
Ball St.■ D 4
Creighton■ D 6
Eastern Mich. D 8
Minnesota Cl. D11-12
National Louis■ D14
Stetson■ D30
St. Louis■ J 2
Northeastern Ill. J 5
Silver Lake■ J 7
Northeastern Ill.■ J12
Central St. (Ohio)■ J15
Bradley■ J18
Wright St. J20
Northern Iowa■ J22
Mo.-Kansas City J29
Buffalo F 3
Cal St. Sacramento■ F 7
Troy St. F12
Buffalo■ F17
Silver Lake F19
Central Conn. St.■ F21
Mo.-Kansas City■ F24
Hofstra■ F26
East Coast Tr. M3-6

Colors: Green & White. Nickname: Cougars.
AD: Al Avant. SID: Lisette Allison-Moore. I

CHRIS. NEWPORT .... **Newport News, VA 23606**

Cathy Parson (5 YRS. W-90, L-44)

Marymount (Va.) Tr. N19-21
Salisbury St. N23
Hampton Tr. N26-27
Salisbury St. Cl. D3-4
Frank. & Marsh.■ J10
N.C. Wesleyan■ J12
Va. Wesleyan J15
Shenandoah■ J16
Ferrum J21
Averett J22
Mary Washington J27
Methodist■ J29
Greensboro■ J30
N.C. Wesleyan F 2
Shenandoah F 6
Ferrum■ F 9
Averett■ F12
Greensboro F18
Methodist F19

Colors: Blue & Silver. Nickname: Lady Captains.
AD: C.J. Woollum. SID: Wayne Block. III

CINCINNATI .... **Cincinnati, OH 45221**

Laurie Pirtle (11 YRS. W-163, L-134)

Akron■ N26
Texas A&M Inv. D4-5
Wright St. D11
Ohio D14
Washington Cl. D20-21
Miami (Ohio)■ D28
Yale■ D30
Louisville Cl. J2-3
Dayton■ J 7
St. Louis J15
Xavier (Ohio) J18
Marquette■ J21
DePaul J27
Memphis St.■ J29
Ala.-Birmingham F 3
St. Louis■ F 5
Kentucky F 8
DePaul■ F11
Marquette F19
Memphis St. F26
Dayton M 1
Ala.-Birmingham■ M 5
Great Midwest Tr. M9-12

Colors: Red & Black. Nickname: Bearcats.
AD: Rick Taylor. SID: Tom Hathaway. I

CCNY .... **New York, NY 10031**

Stephanie English (2 YRS. W-15, L-33)

Bridgeport Inv. N20-21
Mt. St. Vincent N30
Lincoln (Pa.) D 3
Cheyney D 4
York (N.Y.) D10
Dowling J 3
Caldwell■ J 5
New Jersey Tech■ J10
Baruch■ J13
Lehman■ J15
Rutgers-Newark J17
Dominican (N.Y.)■ J19
York (N.Y.)■ J21
Hunter■ J24
Baruch J27
John Jay■ J29
Old Westbury■ F 1
Manhattanville■ F 3
Medgar Evers F 5
Staten Island F 7
Hunter F10
John Jay F12
Maritime (N.Y.) F14

Colors: Lavender & Black. Nickname: Beavers.
AD: Paul Bobb. SID: Carlos Alejandro. III

CLARION .... **Clarion, PA 16214**

Margaret Parsons (12 YRS. W-188, L-109)

Millersville Cl. N19-20
Cheyney N22
Mansfield Tr. N26-27
Point Park■ D 1
Clarion Cl. D3-4
Gannon D10
Mercyhurst D11
Bloomsburg■ J 5
Mercyhurst■ J 8
Edinboro J12
Shippensburg■ J15
Lock Haven■ J19
Indiana (Pa.) J22
Slippery Rock J26
Pace J29
Calif. (Pa.)■ F 2
Shippensburg F 5
Edinboro■ F 9
Lock Haven F12
Slippery Rock■ F16
Indiana (Pa.)■ F19
Calif. (Pa.) F23
Gannon■ F26

Colors: Blue & Gold. Nickname: Golden Eagles.
AD: Bob Carlson. SID: Rich Herman. II

■ Home games on each schedule.

See pages 735-738 for Division I tournament details

CLARK (MASS.) .... Worcester, MA 01610

Patricia Glispin (9 YRS. W-180, L-60)

Worcester City Tr. N20-21
Rochester Inv. N27-28
Springfield N30
Eastern Conn. St. D 8
Middlebury J 4
Southern Me.■ J 8
Western Conn. St.■ J11
Williams J13
Mass.-Dartmouth J15
Wheaton (Mass.)■ J18
Worcester St. J20
Western New Eng. J24
Bri'water (Mass.)■ J27
Amherst■ J29
Trinity (Conn.) F 1
Bowdoin■ F 4
Colby■ F 5
Tufts F10
Worcester Tech■ F12
Babson■ F17
Stony Brook■ F19
Gordon■ F22
Wesleyan■ F26

Colors: Scarlet & White. Nickname: Cougars.
AD: Linda Moulton. SID: Kathryn Smith. III

CLARKSON .... Potsdam, NY 13676

Jeanne Johnston (3 YRS. W-44, L-32)

Elmira N19
Utica N20
Keuka N23
Union (N.Y.)■ D 3
Skidmore■ D 4
St. Lawrence■ D 9
Potsdam St. Inv. J7-8
Alfred■ J14
Ithaca■ J15
Hamilton J18
Hartwick■ J21
Rensselaer■ J22
Potsdam St.■ J25
William Smith J28
Rochester Inst. J29
Ithaca F 4
Alfred F 5
Plattsburgh St.■ F 8
Rochester Inst.■ F11
William Smith■ F12
St. Lawrence F15
Rensselaer F18
Hartwick F19

Colors: Green & Gold. Nickname: Golden Knights.
AD: Bill O'Flaherty. SID: Gary Mikel. III

CLEMSON .... Clemson, SC 29631

Jim Davis (7 YRS. W-144, L-70)

Furman■ D 1
Western Caro.■ D 4
Coppin St.■ D11
South Caro. St. D15
Hilton Head Shootout D29-30
Virginia J 3
North Caro. St. J 5
Maryland■ J 8
Wake Forest■ J13
Winthrop■ J18
Duke■ J22
Georgia Tech■ J26
Duke J28
North Caro. J30
North Caro. St.■ F 3
Florida St.■ F 7
Wake Forest F 9
Maryland F11
South Caro.■ F16
Virginia■ F19
Florida St. F23
Georgia Tech F25
North Caro.■ F27
ACC Tr. M4-7

Colors: Purple & Orange. Nickname: Tigers.
AD: Bobby Robinson. SID: Sam Blackman. I

CLEVELAND ST. .... Cleveland, OH 44115

Loretta Hummeldorf (2 YRS. W-15, L-41)

Robert Morris N26
Southeast Mo. St. N29
Austin Peay D 1
Toledo■ D15
Xavier (Ohio) D18
Evansville■ D21
Kent■ D23
Wis.-Green Bay D30
Wis.-Milwaukee J 2
Youngstown St. J 8
Wright St.■ J13
Eastern Ill.■ J15
Valparaiso J21
Ill.-Chicago J23
Western Ill.■ J27
Northern Ill.■ J29
Wis.-Milwaukee■ F 3
Wis.-Green Bay■ F 5
Buffalo F10
Youngstown St.■ F12
Wright St. F17
Eastern Ill. F19
Valparaiso■ F24
Ill.-Chicago■ F26
Western Ill. M 3
Northern Ill. M 5
Mid-Continent Tr. M10-12

Colors: Green & White. Nickname: Vikings.
AD: John Konstantinos. SID: Paulette Welch. I

COAST GUARD .... New London, CT 06320

Alex Simonka (1ST YR. AS HEAD COACH)

Smith D 1
Anna Maria Inv. D3-4
Wheaton (Mass.) D 7
Coast Guard Cl. J8-9
Worcester Tech■ J11
Norwich■ J14
Norwich■ J15
Babson■ J18
Trinity (Conn.) J22
Connecticut Col.■ J25
Nichols J27
MIT J29
Western New Eng. F 1
Amherst■ F 5
Albertus Magnus■ F 7
Wesleyan■ F10
Pine Manor F12
Connecticut Col. F15
Emmanuel■ F17
Suffolk F19

Colors: Blue, Orange & White. Nickname: Cadets, Bears.
AD: Chuck Mills. SID: Shaun May. III

COASTAL CARO. .... Conway, SC 29526

Regina Markland (7 YRS. W-52, L-137)

Charleston D 1
Webber■ D 3
North Caro. D 8
Davidson D11
Liberty D18
Radford D20
Coastal Caro. Cl. D29-30
Md.-Balt. County■ J 7
Towson St.■ J 8
Charleston So. J11
N.C.-Asheville J14
Winthrop J15
N.C.-Wilmington■ J19
Charleston■ J24
N.C.-Greensboro■ J28
Campbell■ J29
Liberty■ F 4
Radford■ F 5
Md.-Balt. County F11
Towson St. F12
N.C.-Asheville■ F18
Winthrop■ F19
Charleston So.■ F26
N.C.-Greensboro M 4
Campbell M 5
Big South Tr. M9-12

Colors: Scarlet & Black. Nickname: Lady Chants.
AD: Andy Hendrick. SID: Davis Fisher. I

COE .... Cedar Rapids, IA 52402

John Klein (2 YRS. W-16, L-26)

Coe Cl. N20-21
Dubuque Tr. N26-27
Iowa Wesleyan N30
Buena Vista■ D 3
Grinnell■ D 7
Wartburg■ D10
Knox■ J 7
Illinois Col.■ J 8
Cornell College J11
Monmouth (Ill.)■ J15
Beloit J21
Lake Forest J22
Upper Iowa■ J26
Lawrence■ J28
St. Norbert■ J29
Grinnell F 8
Illinois Col. F12
Cornell College■ F15
Monmouth (Ill.) F18
Knox F19

Colors: Crimson & Gold. Nickname: Kohawks.
AD: Barron Bremner. SID: Alice Davidson. III

COKER .... Hartsville, SC 29550

Suzanne McBride (2 YRS. W-7, L-43)

Converse N19
Newberry■ N20
Erskine N29
Charleston So. D 1
Armstrong St.■ D 8
Berry D10
Mt. Olive■ J 5
Charleston J 8
Erskine■ J10
Pfeiffer J12
Barton■ J15
Francis Marion J17
Belmont Abbey■ J19
St. Andrews J22
Newberry J24
Lees-McRae■ J26
High Point■ J29
Pfeiffer■ J31
Mt. Olive F 2
Barton F 5
Converse■ F 7
Belmont Abbey F 9
Lees-McRae F12
St. Andrews■ F16
High Point F19
Francis Marion■ F21

Colors: Navy Blue & Gold. Nickname: Lady Cobras.
AD: Ed Clark. SID: Greg Grissom. II

COLBY-SAWYER .... New London, NH 03257

Bill Warnken (2 YRS. W-18, L-31)

Rivier■ N23
Green Mountain■ N30
New England Col. D 2
Western Conn. Cl. D4-5
Regis (Mass.)■ D10
Coast Guard Cl. J8-9
Russell Sage■ J12
MIT J15
Suffolk J17
Southern Me. J19
Bowdoin■ J21
Colby■ J22
Middlebury■ J25
Bates J28
Thomas■ J30
Simmons■ F 1
Norwich F 3
Albertus Magnus■ F 5
Endicott F 8
Elmira■ F11
Notre Dame (N.H.) F13
Connecticut Col.■ F18

Colors: Blue & White. Nickname: Chargers.
AD: Deborah Field McGrath. SID: Bill Warnken. III

COLGATE .... Hamilton, NY 13346

Liz Feeley (1 YR. W-4, L-23)

Connecticut N27
Cornell■ N29
Harvard Inv. D4-5
Buffalo D10
Niagara D12
Virginia Tech Cl. D29-30
Bucknell■ J 8
Hofstra■ J10
Lafayette■ J12
Navy J15
Holy Cross■ J19
Fordham■ J22
Army J26
Lehigh■ J29
Canisius■ J30
Bucknell F 2
Lafayette F 5
Buffalo■ F 7
Navy■ F 9
Holy Cross F12
Fordham F16
Army■ F19
St. Bonaventure F22
Lehigh F26
Patriot Tr. M3-12

Colors: Maroon, Gray & White. Nickname: Red Raiders.
AD: Mark Murphy. SID: Bob Cornell. I

■ Home games on each schedule.

See pages 735-738 for Division I tournament details

COLORADO .... Boulder, CO 80309

Ceal Barry (14 YRS. W-266, L-155)

Colorado Cl.	N26-27	Nebraska■	J21
Colorado St.■	D 1	Iowa St.■	J23
S.F. Austin Cl.	D3-4	Oklahoma	J28
Texas Christian	D 7	Oklahoma St.	J30
Northern Ariz.■	D18	Kansas■	F 4
Tennessee	D20	Kansas St.■	F 6
Rutgers Tr.	D28-29	Missouri	F12
UC Irvine	D30	Iowa St.	F18
Long Beach St.	J 2	Nebraska	F20
Kansas St.	J 7	Oklahoma St.■	F25
Kansas	J 9	Oklahoma■	F27
Missouri■	J16	Big Eight Tr.	M5-7

Colors: Silver, Gold & Black. Nickname: Buffs.
AD: Bill Marolt. SID: Colleen Reilly. I

COLO. CHRISTIAN .... Lakewood, CO 80226

Judy Vaughn (7 YRS. W-85, L-87)

Chadron St.	N20	Southern Colo.■	J22
Adams St.■	N23	Denver■	J26
Grand Canyon Inv.	N26-27	Regis (Colo.)	J29
Colorado Mines■	N30	Colorado Mines	J31
Colo. Christian Tr.	D3-4	Adams St.	F 2
Fort Hays St.	D11	Metropolitan St.■	F 5
UC Riverside■	D13	Fort Lewis■	F11
N.M. Highlands	J 6	Air Force■	F12
Metropolitan St.	J 8	Southern Colo.	F19
Fort Lewis	J13	Denver	F23
Air Force	J15	Regis (Colo.)■	F26
Colorado-CS	J19		

Colors: Blue & White. Nickname: Cougars.
AD: Frank Evans. SID: Judy Vaughn. II

COLORADO COL. .... Colorado Springs, CO 80903

Roxanne Dale (13 YRS. W-102, L-177)

Grinnell Tr.	N19-20	Bethany (Kan.)	J17
Sterling■	N23	Kan. Wesleyan	J18
Western St.	D 3	Colorado-CS■	J24
Colorado-CS	D 7	Adams St.	J28
Adams St.■	D10	Air Force■	F 2
Colorado Mines■	D11	Neb. Wesleyan■	F 5
Colorado Col. Tr.	D29-31	Kan. Wesleyan■	F12
La Verne	J 3	Panhandle St.	F18
Pomona-Pitzer	J 5	Bethany (Kan.)■	F21
Claremont-M-S	J 6	Colorado Mines	F24
Panhandle St.■	J13		

Colors: Black & Gold. Nickname: Tigers.
AD: Max Taylor. SID: Dave Moross. III

COLORADO MINES .... Golden, CO 80401

Gail Klock (18 YRS. W-97, L-287)

Sterling■	N22	N.M. Highlands	J22
Air Force■	N23	Western St.■	J27
Colo. Christian	N30	Mesa St.■	J29
Neb.-Kearney Cl.	D2-4	Colo. Christian■	J31
Regis (Colo.)■	D 7	Adams St.■	F 3
Colorado Col.	D11	N.M. Highlands■	F 5
Chadron St.■	J 5	Colorado-CS	F 8
Bethany (Kan.)■	J 8	Fort Hays St.	F12
Northern Colo.	J11	Western St.	F18
Fort Hays St.■	J15	Mesa St.	F19
Colorado-CS■	J17	Colorado Col.■	F24
Adams St.	J21	Chadron St.	F26

Colors: Silver & Blue. Nickname: Orediggers.
AD: R. Bruce Allison. SID: Steve Smith. II

COLORADO ST. .... Fort Collins, CO 80523

Greg Williams (8 YRS. W-125, L-100)

Southern Utah■	N26	Utah	J22
Colorado	D 1	San Diego St.■	J27
UNLV Cl.	D3-4	Fresno St.■	J29
Colorado-CS■	D 9	Fresno St.	F 4
Texas Christian■	D11	San Diego St.	F 6
Pepperdine Tr.	D18-19	Utah■	F11
Northern Ariz.	D28	Brigham Young■	F12
Southern Utah	D30	Wyoming	F19
Weber St.■	J 7	New Mexico	F25
Idaho St.■	J 8	UTEP	F27
New Mexico■	J13	Wyoming■	M 5
UTEP■	J15	Western Athletic Tr.	M9-12
Brigham Young	J20		

Colors: Green & Gold. Nickname: Rams.
AD: Corey Johnson. SID: Gary Ozzello. I

COLORADO-CS .... Colorado Springs, CO 80933

Celia Slater (4 YRS. W-41, L-64)

Alas. Fairbanks	N19	Colo. Christian■	J19
Alas. Fairbanks	N20	Metropolitan St.	J22
Alas. Anchorage	N22	Colorado Col.	J24
Alas. Anchorage	N23	Fort Lewis■	J28
West Tex. A&M Tr.	D2-4	Air Force■	J29
Colorado Col.■	D 7	Western St.■	F 1
Colorado St.	D 9	Southern Colo.■	F 5
Adams St.■	D11	Colorado Mines■	F 8
Grand Canyon Cl.	D30-31	Denver■	F10
Neb.-Kearney■	J 5	Regis (Colo.)	F12
Southern Colo.	J 8	Metropolitan St.■	F19
Denver	J12	Fort Lewis	F24
Regis (Colo.)■	J15	Air Force	F28
Colorado Mines	J17		

Colors: Gold & Blue. Nickname: Gold.
AD: Theophilus Gregory. SID: Nanette Anderson. II

COLUMBIA-BARNARD .... New York, NY 10027

Kerry Phayre (2 YRS. W-11, L-41)

Wagner■	D 1	Yale	J29
Seton Hall Cl.	D4-5	Pennsylvania■	F 4
Iona■	D 8	Princeton■	F 5
FDU-Teaneck■	D11	Dartmouth	F11
Fordham	D14	Harvard	F12
Florida Int'l Tr.	J2-4	Yale■	F18
Maine■	J 7	Brown■	F19
Hofstra	J12	Harvard■	F25
Cornell■	J15	Dartmouth■	F26
Army■	J17	Princeton	M 4
Cornell	J22	Pennsylvania	M 5
Brown	J28		

Colors: Columbia Blue & White. Nickname: Lions.
AD: Dr. John Reeves. SID: Bill Steinman. I

CONCORD .... Athens, WV 24712

Will Johnson (1ST YR. AS HEAD COACH)

Shepherd Tr.	N19-20	Fairmont St.	J22
West Va. Tech■	D 1	Clinch Valley■	J24
Glenville St.	D 4	Charleston (W.Va.)	J26
West Va. St.	D 6	Clinch Valley	J29
Shepherd	D11	West Va. St.■	J31
Alderson-Broaddus■	J 6	West Va. Tech	F 2
Ohio Valley■	J 8	Davis & Elkins■	F 5
West Liberty St.	J14	Charleston (W.Va.)■	F 7
Wheeling Jesuit	J15	Bluefield St.■	F 9
Bluefield St.	J17	West Va. Wesleyan■	F14
Salem-Teikyo	J21	Shepherd■	F17

Colors: Maroon & Gray. Nickname: Mountain Lions.
AD: Don Christie. SID: Tom Bone. II

CONCORDIA (ILL.) .... River Forest, IL 60305

Jan Fisher (2 YRS. W-12, L-38)

Wheaton (Ill.)	N30	Trinity (Ill.)■	J18
Lake Forest	D 2	Moody Bible■	J20
Chicago	D 7	Judson■	J22
Concordia (Mich.)■	D11	Conc. (St.Paul) Inv.	J28-29
Rockford	D14	Aurora■	F 3
Elmhurst Tr.	D17-18	Ill. Benedictine	F 5
Webber Tr.	D29-30	Trinity (Ill.)	F 8
Eureka■	J 8	Judson	F12
Ill. Wesleyan■	J11	Aurora	F15
Olivet (Ill.)■	J13	St. Mary's (Ind.)	F17
Ill. Benedictine■	J15	Rockford■	F19

Colors: Maroon & Gold. Nickname: Cougars.
AD: Thomas Faszholz. SID: Jim Egan. III

CONCORDIA-M'HEAD .... Moorhead, MN 56560

Robert Kohler (3 YRS. W-56, L-24)

Pomona-Pitzer	N23	St. Mary's (Minn.)	J19
Cal Lutheran	N26	Carleton■	J22
Moorhead St.	D 1	Gust. Adolphus■	J26
Gust. Adolphus	D 4	St. Benedict	J29
Carleton	D 6	St. Thomas (Minn.)	F 2
St. Benedict■	D11	Augsburg■	F 5
Valley City St.■	D13	St. Olaf■	F 9
Bethel (Minn.)■	J 3	Macalester	F12
St. Thomas (Minn.)■	J 5	Moorhead St.■	F15
Augsburg	J 8	St. Mary's (Minn.)■	F19
St. Olaf	J10	Bethel (Minn.)	F21
Macalester■	J12	Hamline	F26
Hamline■	J15		

Colors: Maroon & Gold. Nickname: Cobbers.
AD: Armin Pipho. SID: Jerry Pyle. III

■ Home games on each schedule.

See pages 735-738 for Division I tournament details

CONNECTICUT .... Storrs, CT 06269

Geno Auriemma (8 YRS. W-162, L-78)

Colgate■	N27	Pittsburgh	J19
Vermont■	D 1	Miami (Fla.)■	J23
Connecticut Cl.	D4-5	St. John's (N.Y.)■	J26
Auburn	D 8	Providence	J29
Virginia■	D11	Georgetown	F 2
Boston College	D13	Seton Hall■	F 6
Stanford	D28	Villanova■	F 9
San Francisco	D30	Miami (Fla.)	F13
Syracuse■	J 3	Boston College■	F16
Seton Hall	J 5	Pittsburgh■	F20
Georgetown■	J 9	Syracuse	F23
Villanova	J12	St. John's (N.Y.)	F27
Providence■	J16	Big East Tr.	M4-7

Colors: Blue & White. Nickname: Huskies.
AD: Lew Perkins. SID: Barbara Kowal. I

COPPIN ST. .... Baltimore, MD 21216

Tori Harrison (1 YR. W-20, L-9)

Geo. Washington	N27	Morgan St.	J27
James Madison	N29	Howard■	J29
Alabama Cl.	D3-4	Delaware St.■	F 2
Clemson	D11	Howard	F 5
George Mason■	D18	Morgan St.■	F 7
Columbia Union■	D21	Florida A&M■	F12
St. John's Inv.	D29-30	Bethune-Cookman■	F14
Buffalo	J 3	South Caro. St.	F17
South Caro. St.■	J 6	North Caro. A&T■	F23
North Caro. A&T	J13	Md.-East. Shore	F26
Md.-East. Shore■	J17	Delaware St.	M 5
Florida A&M	J22	MEAC Tr.	M9-13
Bethune-Cookman	J24		

Colors: Royal Blue & Gold. Nickname: Eagles.
AD: Clayton McNeill (interim). SID: Jesse Batten. I

CORNELL .... Ithaca, NY 14853

Kim Jordan (11 YRS. W-85, L-167)

Colgate	N29	Yale	J28
St. Bonaventure	D 1	Brown	J29
Cornell Cl.	D3-4	Princeton■	F 4
Buffalo■	D 8	Pennsylvania■	F 5
Lafayette■	D11	Harvard	F11
Georgetown	D20	Dartmouth	F12
San Jose St.	J 5	Brown■	F18
Santa Clara	J 6	Yale■	F19
San Francisco	J 8	Dartmouth■	F25
Niagara	J12	Harvard■	F26
Columbia-Barnard	J15	Pennsylvania	M 4
Hofstra	J17	Princeton	M 5
Columbia-Barnard■	J22		

Colors: Carnelian & White. Nickname: Big Red.
AD: Laing Kennedy. SID: Dave Wohlhueter. I

CORNELL COLLEGE .... Mt. Vernon, IA 52314

Wanda Schwartz (2 YRS. W-6, L-38)

Teiko-Marycrest	N23	Carroll (Wis.)	J22
Monmouth (Ill.)■	D 2	Beloit■	J28
William Penn	D 4	Lake Forest■	J29
Upper Iowa	D 7	Grinnell	F 2
New Rochelle	D 9	Wartburg	F 5
Cornell College Inv.	D10-11	Eureka■	F 9
Illinois Col.■	J 7	Monmouth (Ill.)	F11
Knox■	J 8	Knox	F12
Coe■	J11	Coe	F15
Iowa Wesleyan■	J15	Illinois Col.	F18
New Rochelle■	J20	Grinnell■	F21
Ripon	J21		

Colors: Purple & White. Nickname: Rams.
AD: Ellen Whale. SID: Mick Kulikowski. III

CORTLAND ST. .... Cortland, NY 13045

Bonnie Foley (12 YRS. W-197, L-108)

Southern Me. Cl.	N20-21	Stony Brook	J22
Geneseo St.■	D 3	New Paltz St.■	J25
Buffalo St.■	D 4	Fredonia St.	J29
Oneonta St.	D 7	Albany (N.Y.)■	F 2
Plattsburgh St.	D10	Plattsburgh St.■	F 4
Potsdam St.	D11	Potsdam St.■	F 5
Kean Tr.	J7-8	Binghamton■	F 8
Ithaca■	J11	Brockport St.	F12
Oswego St.	J14	New Paltz St.	F15
Utica Tech■	J15	St. John Fisher■	F17
Binghamton	J18	Oneonta St.■	F19

Colors: Red & White. Nickname: Red Dragons.
AD: Lee Roberts. SID: Fran Elia. III

CREIGHTON .... Omaha, NE 68178

Connie Yori (3 YRS. W-45, L-33)

Kansas■	N26	Southwest Mo. St.■	J22
Iowa St.■	N30	Northern Iowa	J27
Chicago St.	D 6	Bradley	J29
Western Ill.	D 7	Oklahoma St.■	F 2
Nebraska	D10	Drake	F 5
Mo.-Kansas City	D20	Southern Ill.■	F11
St. Joseph's Cl.	D29-30	Indiana St.■	F13
Illinois St.■	J 2	Southwest Mo. St.	F17
Drake■	J 6	Wichita St.	F19
Missouri■	J11	Northern Iowa■	F24
Indiana St.	J13	Bradley■	F26
Southern Ill.	J15	Illinois St.	F28
Wichita St.■	J20	Missouri Valley Tr.	M8-12

Colors: Blue & White. Nickname: Lady Jays.
AD: Thomas Moore. SID: Vince Lodl. I

CURRY .... Milton, MA 02186

Richard Kelly (10 YRS. W-153, L-92)

Gordon■	N20	Regis (Mass.)	J26
Babson	D 1	Salve Regina	J29
Fitchburg St.	D 4	Anna Maria■	F 1
Suffolk	D 6	Wentworth Inst.■	F 3
Framingham St.■	D 9	New England Col.	F 5
Nichols■	D13	Mass.-Boston■	F 7
Wentworth Inst.	J15	Eastern Nazarene■	F 9
New England Col.■	J18	Salve Regina■	F12
Eastern Nazarene	J20	Regis (Mass.)■	F15
Roger Williams	J22	Anna Maria	F17
Elms■	J24	Roger Williams■	F19

Colors: Purple & White. Nickname: Colonels.
AD: Tom Stephens. SID: Joe Hunter. III

DARTMOUTH .... Hanover, NH 03755

Christina Wielgus (10 YRS. W-144, L-94)

Vermont	N27	Maine■	J31
Siena■	D11	Brown	F 4
Hartford	D13	Yale	F 5
Stanford Cl.	D17-18	Columbia-Barnard■	F11
Dartmouth Inv.	D29-30	Cornell■	F12
Princeton■	J 7	Pennsylvania	F18
Pennsylvania■	J 8	Princeton	F19
Boston U.	J10	Cornell	F25
Harvard■	J15	Columbia-Barnard	F26
Rhode Island■	J18	Yale■	M 4
Hofstra	J22	Brown■	M 5
Central Conn. St.	J23	Harvard	M 8

Colors: Green & White. Nickname: Big Green.
AD: Dick Jaeger. SID: Kathy Slattery. I

DAVIDSON .... Davidson, NC 28036

John Filar (1 YR. W-9, L-13)

Mars Hill■	N27	Wash. & Lee■	J29
Winthrop	D 1	Gardner-Webb■	F 2
Cornell Cl.	D3-4	Furman■	F 5
N.C.-Asheville	D 8	Radford	F 8
Coastal Caro.■	D11	Western Caro.	F12
N.C.-Wilmington■	J 3	Appalachian St.	F14
Navy	J 6	Ga. Southern■	F17
Loyola (Md.)	J 8	Tenn.-Chatt.■	F19
William & Mary■	J11	Appalachian St.■	F23
Campbell■	J19	East Tenn. St.	F26
Charleston So.	J22	Marshall	F28
Ga. Southern	J24	Southern Tr.	M10-12
Western Caro.■	J26		

Colors: Red & Black. Nickname: Wildcats.
AD: Terry Holland. SID: Kristie Cowan. I

DAYTON .... Dayton, OH 45469

Sue Ramsey (7 YRS. W-87, L-109)

St. Francis (Pa.)	N28	Memphis St.■	J27
Florida St. Cl.	D3-4	Xavier (Ohio)	F 2
Miami (Ohio)■	D11	Louisville■	F 5
Michigan St.	D18	St. Louis■	F 7
Wright St.■	D20	Detroit Mercy	F10
Ohio	D22	DePaul■	F13
N.C.-Greensboro■	D30	Ala.-Birmingham■	F15
Notre Dame■	J 4	Ala.-Birmingham	F21
Cincinnati	J 7	Memphis St.	F24
DePaul	J 9	St. Louis	F26
Arkansas■	J12	Cincinnati■	M 1
Butler	J17	Marquette	M 5
Marquette■	J23	Great Midwest Tr.	M9-12

Colors: Red & Blue. Nickname: Lady Flyers.
AD: Ted Kissell. SID: Doug Hauschild. I

■ Home games on each schedule.

See pages 735-738 for Division I tournament details

DEPAUL .... Chicago, IL 60614
Doug Bruno (7 YRS. W-132, L-67)

DePaul Inv.	N26-27	St. Louis	F 3
Georgia■	D 5	Memphis St.■	F 5
Arkansas	D 8	Western Ky.■	F 8
Loyola (Ill.)	D11	Cincinnati	F11
San Juan Shootout	D20-22	Dayton	F13
Tennessee■	J 5	Northern Ill.	F15
Dayton■	J 9	Ala.-Birmingham	F19
Notre Dame	J11	Northeastern Ill.■	F21
Marquette	J15	Vanderbilt■	F23
Auburn	J19	Ala.-Birmingham■	F26
Memphis St.	J22	Marquette■	M 3
Wis.-Green Bay■	J25	St. Louis■	M 5
Cincinnati■	J27	Great Midwest Tr.	M9-12
Ill.-Chicago	F 1		

Colors: Scarlet & Royal Blue. Nickname: Blue Demons.
AD: Bill Bradshaw. SID: John Lanctot. I

DEPAUW .... Greencastle, IN 46135
Kris Huffman (1ST YR. AS HEAD COACH)

DePauw Tr.	N19-20	Hanover	J22
Earlham■	N27	Millikin	J25
St. Mary's (In.) Cl.	D3-4	St. Mary's (Ind.)■	J29
Marian (Ind.)■	D 7	Anderson■	F 1
Defiance Cl.	D17-18	Manchester	F 5
Thomas More	D30	Franklin	F12
IU/PU-Indianapolis	J 6	Hanover■	F15
Manchester■	J 8	Webster	F19
Anderson	J11	Fontbonne	F20
Franklin■	J15	Thomas More■	F23
Taylor	J18		

Colors: Old Gold & Black. Nickname: Tigers.
AD: Ted Katula. SID: Bill Wagner. III

DEFIANCE .... Defiance, OH 43512
Cindy Elliott (6 YRS. W-102, L-49)

Earlham	N20	Anderson■	J19
Hillsdale■	N23	Thomas More■	J22
Wooster	N30	Kalamazoo	J26
Heidelberg Tr.	D3-4	Wilmington (Ohio)	J29
Taylor■	D 8	Siena Heights■	F 1
Defiance Cl.	D17-18	St. Francis (Ind.)■	F 5
Baldwin-Wallace■	D21	Manchester■	F 8
Findlay■	J 8	Thomas More	F12
Bluffton	J11	Bluffton■	F16
Franklin■	J13	Wilmington (Ohio)■	F19
St. Francis (Ind.)	J15		

Colors: Purple & Gold. Nickname: Lady Jackets.
AD: Marvin Hohenberger. SID: Cindy Elliott. III

DELAWARE .... Newark, DE 19716
Joyce Perry (20 YRS. W-286, L-188)

Temple	D 1	Vermont■	J28
Delaware St.■	D 4	Hartford■	J30
Lafayette	D 7	La Salle■	F 3
Towson St.	D 9	Drexel■	F 5
Pennsylvania	D11	George Mason■	F 8
Princeton■	D15	Hartford	F11
St. Joseph's Cl.	D29-30	Vermont	F13
Lehigh■	J 5	Northeastern■	F18
Siena■	J12	Boston U.■	F20
New Hampshire■	J14	Maine	F25
Maine■	J16	New Hampshire	F27
Boston U.	J21	Drexel	M 2
Northeastern	J23	North Atlantic Tr.	M6-12

Colors: Blue & Gold. Nickname: Fightin' Blue Hens.
AD: Edgar N. Johnson. SID: Scott Selheimer. I

DELAWARE ST. .... Dover, DE 19901
Mary Lamb-Bowman (11 YRS. W-155, L-154)

Elizabeth City St.■	D 1	South Caro. St.	J24
Delaware	D 4	Dist. Columbia■	J29
FDU-Teaneck	D 7	Coppin St.	F 2
Hartford	D11	North Caro. A&T■	F 5
Central Conn. St.	D12	South Caro. St.■	F 7
Atlantic City Cl.	D18-19	Md.-East. Shore■	F12
Drexel	J 4	Morgan St.	F17
William & Mary	J 6	Bethune-Cookman	F19
Bethune-Cookman■	J 8	Florida A&M	F21
Florida A&M■	J10	Howard	F24
Howard■	J15	Md.-East. Shore	M 3
Morgan St.■	J17	Coppin St.■	M 5
North Caro. A&T	J22	MEAC Tr.	M9-13

Colors: Red & Blue. Nickname: Hornets.
AD: John Martin. SID: Craig Cotton. I

DELAWARE VALLEY .... Doylestown, PA 18901
Gary Pento (9 YRS. W-116, L-108)

Alvernia	N29	Lycoming	J22
FDU-Madison	D 1	Holy Family	J24
Scranton■	D 4	Upsala	J26
Widener■	D 7	FDU-Madison■	J29
Albright■	D 9	King's (Pa.)■	F 2
Caldwell	D11	Scranton	F 5
Delaware Valley Cl.	J7-8	Drew	F 9
King's (Pa.)	J12	Wilkes	F12
Wilkes■	J15	Allentown	F14
Drew■	J18	Upsala■	F16
Lebanon Valley	J20	Lycoming■	F19

Colors: Green & Gold. Nickname: Aggies.
AD: Frank Wolfgang. SID: Matthew Levy. III

DELTA ST. .... Cleveland, MS 38733
Lloyd Clark (10 YRS. W-267, L-45)

East Tex. St. Tr.	N19-20	Mississippi-Women■	J27
Ark.-Monticello	N23	Henderson St.	J29
Lane■	D 1	Central Ark.	J31
Lincoln Memorial	D 4	Ark.-Pine Bluff	F 2
East Tex. St.■	D11	Livingston■	F 5
North Ala.■	D17	Mississippi Col.	F 7
Ark.-Pine Bluff■	J 6	Mississippi Val.	F 9
Lincoln Memorial■	J 8	West Ga.■	F12
Mississippi-Women	J10	Livingston	F19
Mississippi Val.■	J12	North Ala.	F21
West Ga.	J15	Lane	F23
Mississippi Col.■	J19	Central Ark.■	F26
Henderson St.■	J22		

Colors: Green & White. Nickname: Lady Statesmen.
AD: Jim Jordan. SID: Jody Correro. II

DENISON .... Granville, OH 43023
Sara Lee (5 YRS. W-41, L-79)

Kalamazoo Tr.	N19-20	Allegheny■	J15
Malone	N23	Wooster	J19
Oberlin■	D 1	Kenyon■	J22
Kenyon	D 4	Wilberforce■	J26
Wash. & Jeff.	D 7	Ohio Wesleyan	J29
Thomas More	D11	Earlham■	F 2
Mt. Vernon Naz.	D30	Case Reserve■	F 5
Ohio Wesleyan■	J 2	Oberlin	F 9
Wittenberg	J 5	Allegheny	F12
Case Reserve	J 8	Wooster■	F16
Earlham	J12	Wittenberg■	F19

Colors: Red & White. Nickname: Big Red.
AD: Larry Scheiderer. SID: Jack Hire. III

DENVER .... Denver, CO 80208
Tracey Sheehan (4 YRS. W-78, L-36)

Mesa St.■	N19	Air Force■	J19
Lincoln (Mo.)☒	N26	Fort Lewis■	J22
Concordia (St. Paul)☒	N27	Colo. Christian	J26
Nebraska-Omaha Tr.	D3-4	Metropolitan St.■	J29
Wayne St. (Neb.)	D 6	Regis (Colo.)	F 5
Northern Colo.	D11	Colorado-CS	F10
UC Riverside■	D14	Southern Colo.■	F12
Cal Poly Pomona■	D17	Air Force	F16
Puget Sound■	D30	Fort Lewis	F19
Eastern Mont.■	J 2	Colo. Christian■	F23
Chadron St.■	J 4	N.M. Highlands■	F24
Regis (Colo.)■	J 8	Metropolitan St.	F26
Colorado-CS■	J12	☒ Denver, CO	
Southern Colo.	J15		

Colors: Crimson & Gold. Nickname: Pioneers.
AD: Jack McDonald. SID: Amy Turner. II

DETROIT MERCY .... Detroit, MI 48221
Fred Procter (5 YRS. W-69, L-69)

Kansas St.	N27	Notre Dame	J29
Toledo■	D 1	Kentucky■	F 2
Canisius	D 4	Xavier (Ohio)	F 5
Western Mich.■	D11	Dayton■	F10
Central Mich.■	D17	La Salle	F12
California Cl.	D20-21	Evansville■	F17
Syracuse	D30	Butler■	F19
Michigan St.	J 2	Kansas St.■	F22
Michigan■	J 5	Notre Dame■	F24
Butler	J13	Loyola (Ill.)	F26
Evansville	J15	Wis.-Milwaukee	F28
La Salle■	J20	Xavier (Ohio)■	M 3
Loyola (Ill.)■	J26	MCC Tr.	M5-8

Colors: Red, White & Blue. Nickname: Lady Titans.
AD: Brad Kinsman. SID: Mark Engel. I

■ Home games on each schedule.

See pages 735-738 for Division I tournament details

DICKINSON .... Carlisle, PA 17013

Anne Haynam (3 YRS. W-27, L-48)

Susquehanna Tr. N20-21
Muhlenberg N23
Swarthmore■ N30
Wash. & Jeff. .... D 4
Western Md.■ .... D 7
Moravian■ .... D 9
Lycoming■ D11
King's (Pa.) Tr. J7-8
Messiah■ J11
Washington (Md.) J15
Gettysburg J18
Bryn Mawr J20
Ursinus■ J22
Haverford■ J24
Frank. & Marsh. J29
Johns Hopkins■ .... F 2
Western Md. .... F 5
Gettysburg■ .... F 8
Frostburg St.■ F10
Wesley F12
Frank. & Marsh.■ F15
Johns Hopkins F19

Colors: Red & White. Nickname: Red Devils.
AD: Les J. Poolman. SID: Matt Howell. III

DIST. COLUMBIA .... Washington, DC 20008

Britt King (1 YR. W-4, L-18)

Dist. Columbia Tr. N26-27
Elizabeth City St. N29
Shippensburg Tr. D3-4
Johnson Smith D16
Norfolk St.■ D21
Cal Poly SLO Cl. D29-30
Virginia St. J12
Virginia Union J13
Longwood J15
Norfolk St. J17
Elizabeth City St.■ J20
Cheyney J24
Virginia St.■ J26
Delaware St. J29
Md.-East. Shore■ J31
Columbia Union■ .... F 2
Morgan St.■ .... F 5
Longwood■ .... F 7
Millersville■ .... F 9
Cheyney■ F14
Bowie St. F16
Virginia Union■ F18
Md.-East. Shore F24

Colors: Red & Gold. Nickname: Lady Firebirds.
AD: Dwight Datcher. SID: Donald Huff. II

DRAKE .... Des Moines, IA 50311

Lisa Bluder (9 YRS. W-208, L-81)

Northeastern Ill.■ N28
Iowa■ .... D 1
Montana St. .... D 3
Montana .... D 5
Iowa St.■ .... D 9
Mo.-Kansas City D14
UC Irvine D28
San Diego D30
Loyola (Ill.) .... J 2
Illinois St.■ .... J 4
Creighton .... J 6
Mo.-Kansas City■ .... J 9
Southern Ill. J13
Indiana St. J15
Southwest Mo. St.■ J20
Wichita St.■ J22
Bradley J27
Northern Iowa J29
Creighton■ .... F 5
Indiana St.■ F11
Southern Ill.■ F13
Wichita St. F17
Southwest Mo. St. F19
Bradley■ F24
Northern Iowa■ F26
Illinois St. .... M 2
Missouri Valley Tr. M8-12

Colors: Blue & White. Nickname: Bulldogs.
AD: Lynn King. SID: Jean Berger. I

DREW .... Madison, NJ 07940

Terry Murphy (1 YR. W-4, L-18)

Wheaton (Mass.) Tr. N19-20
Lycoming■ .... D 1
Wilkes .... D 4
Albright .... D 7
Caldwell .... D 9
Bloomfield⊠ .... J 8
Upsala■ J11
Haverford J13
King's (Pa.)■ J15
Delaware Valley J18
FDU-Madison J22
Rutgers-Newark J24
Scranton■ J26
Lycoming J29
Upsala .... F 2
Wilkes■ .... F 5
Delaware Valley■ .... F 9
King's (Pa.) F12
Cedar Crest■ F14
Scranton F16
FDU-Madison■ F19
Centenary (N.J.)■ F23
St. Elizabeth F25
⊠ Caldwell, NJ

Colors: Lincoln Green & Oxford Blue. Nickname: Rangers.
AD: Vernon Mummert. SID: Ernie Larossa. III

DREXEL .... Philadelphia, PA 19104

Kristen Foley (1 YR. W-5, L-22)

Buffalo N30
Manhattan Cl. D4-5
La Salle■ D11
FDU-Teaneck D19
Central Conn. St. D21
Rutgers Tr. D28-29
Delaware St.■ .... J 4
Bucknell■ .... J 6
Lafayette J10
Maine■ J14
New Hampshire■ J16
Northeastern J21
Boston U. J23
Hartford■ J28
Vermont■ J30
Iona■ .... F 2
Delaware .... F 5
Hofstra .... F 8
Vermont F11
Hartford F13
Boston U.■ F18
Northeastern■ F20
New Hampshire F25
Maine F27
Delaware■ .... M 2
North Atlantic Tr. M6-12

Colors: Navy Blue & Gold. Nickname: Lady Dragons.
AD: Barbara Kilgour. SID: Jan Giel. I

DUBUQUE .... Dubuque, IA 52001

Jay Schiesl (2 YRS. W-7, L-44)

Coe Cl. N20-21
Rockford N23
Dubuque Tr. N26-27
Grand View .... D 4
Clarke■ .... D 7
Peru St.■ D18
Teiko-Marycrest D20
Upper Iowa .... J 7
Simpson .... J 8
Wartburg■ J14
Buena Vista■ J15
Central (Iowa) J21
Loras J22
Luther■ J28
Buena Vista J29
Wartburg .... F 1
William Penn■ .... F 4
Central (Iowa)■ .... F 5
Upper Iowa■ F18
William Penn F19
Loras■ F22
Luther F25
Simpson■ F26

Colors: Blue and White. Nickname: Lady Spartans.
AD: Jon Davison. SID: Rick Hecker. III

DUKE .... Durham, NC 27706

Gail Goestenkors (1ST YR. AS HEAD COACH)

Morgan St.■ N26
Loyola (Md.) N29
Duke Tr. D4-5
Appalachian St. .... D 8
McNeese St.■ D11
California Cl. D20-21
North Caro. St.■ D31
Wake Forest .... J 2
East Caro. .... J 5
North Caro. St. J12
Georgia Tech■ J14
Florida St.■ J16
North Caro.■ J19
Clemson J22
Virginia■ J25
Clemson■ J28
Wake Forest■ .... F 1
Maryland .... F 5
Western Caro.■ .... F 9
Virginia F12
Maryland■ F18
North Caro. F22
Florida St. F25
Georgia Tech F27
ACC Tr. M4-7

Colors: Royal Blue & White. Nickname: Blue Devils.
AD: Tom Butters. SID: Mike Cragg. I

DUQUESNE .... Pittsburgh, PA 15282

Dan Durkin (1ST YR. AS HEAD COACH)

Pittsburgh N27
Ohio■ .... D 2
Howard■ D11
Marshall■ D22
Central Mich. Cl. D29-30
Geo. Washington■ .... J 8
American J10
Temple J15
St. Joseph's (Pa.) J17
Rutgers■ J20
Rhode Island J22
Massachusetts J24
Army J31
Geo. Washington .... F 5
West Va.■ .... F 7
Temple■ F10
St. Joseph's (Pa.)■ F12
St. Bonaventure F14
Massachusetts■ F19
Rutgers F22
Rhode Island■ F24
St. Bonaventure■ F26
Buffalo F28
West Va. .... M 5

Colors: Red & Blue. Nickname: Lady Dukes.
AD: Brian Colleary. SID: Sue Ryan. I

EARLHAM .... Richmond, IN 47374

Jill Butcher (2 YRS. W-15, L-32)

Defiance■ N20
DePauw N27
Wittenberg .... D 1
Oberlin .... D 4
Cincinnati Bible■ .... D 6
Kenyon .... D 8
Allegheny D11
Earlham Inv. D17-18
Anderson .... J 5
Wooster■ .... J 8
Denison■ J12
Case Reserve J15
Ohio Wesleyan■ J19
Oberlin■ J22
Kenyon■ J26
Allegheny■ J29
Denison .... F 2
Wooster .... F 5
Wittenberg■ .... F 9
Case Reserve■ F12
Ohio Wesleyan F16

Colors: Maroon & White. Nickname: Hustlin' Quakers.
AD: Porter Miller. SID: Pat Thomas. III

EAST CARO. .... Greenville, NC 27834

Rosie Thompson (1 YR. W-16, L-12)

Campbell N30
North Caro. A&T .... D 6
Furman D17
Central Fla. Cl. D29-31
Duke■ .... J 5
Western Caro. .... J 8
George Mason■ J14
American■ J16
William & Mary J20
N.C.-Charlotte■ J22
Old Dominion J24
Richmond J27
James Madison■ J30
N.C.-Wilmington■ .... F 3
North Caro. St.■ .... F 9
American F11
George Mason F13
William & Mary■ F18
Old Dominion■ F20
Richmond■ F24
James Madison F27
N.C.-Wilmington .... M 2
Appalachian St.■ .... M 6
CAA Tr. M10-12

Colors: Purple & Gold. Nickname: Lady Pirates.
AD: Dave Hart Jr. SID: Carolyn Hinson. I

■ Home games on each schedule.

See pages 735-738 for Division I tournament details

EAST STROUDSBURG ..... E. Stroudsburg, PA 18301
Rose Haller (2 YRS. W-29, L-23)

Pace N23
Pitt.-Johnstown Tr. N27-28
Shippensburg■ .... D 1
East Stroudsburg Cl. D3-4
LIU-C.W. Post D10
Calif. (Pa.)■ D12
LIU-Southampton D14
Gannon D30
Rollins .... J 6
Fla. Southern .... J 8
Mansfield J12
Cheyney J15
Millersville■ J19
Bloomsburg■ J22
Kutztown J26
Lock Haven■ J31
West Chester .... F 2
Cheyney■ .... F 5
Mansfield■ .... F 9
Millersville F12
Phila. Textile■ F14
Kutztown■ F16
Bloomsburg F19
West Chester■ F23

Colors: Red & Black. Nickname: Warriors.
AD: Earl Edwards. SID: Peter Nevins. II

EAST TENN. ST. .... Johnson City, TN 37614
Debbie Richardson (7 YRS. W-66, L-117)

Mars Hill■ N30
North Caro. Inv. D3-4
Alabama .... D 8
N.C.-Asheville■ D11
Tenn.-Martin D30
Marshall .... J 8
Tenn.-Chatt. J15
Ga. Southern J17
Western Caro.■ J22
Appalachian St.■ J24
South Caro.■ J26
Furman J30
Marshall■ .... F 6
Georgia Tech■ .... F 9
Tenn.-Chatt.■ F12
Ga. Southern■ F14
Western Caro. F19
Appalachian St. F21
Davidson■ F26
Furman■ .... M 1
Southern Tr. M10-12

Colors: Old Gold & Navy. Nickname: Buccaneers.
AD: Janice Shelton. SID: John Cathey. I

EAST TEX. ST. .... Commerce, TX 75429
Beth Palmer (7 YRS. W-104, L-97)

East Tex. St. Tr. N19-20
Texas Woman's Tr. N26-27
Pittsburg St. N29
Mo. Southern St. N30
Tarleton St.■ .... D 4
Rocky Mountain■ .... D 7
Delta St. D11
Eastern Mont.■ 20
Regis (Colo.)☒ .... J 1
Ouachita Bapt. .... J 3
Henderson St. .... J 4
Cameron .... J 8
Montana Tech■ J10
Rocky Mountain J12
Angelo St.■ J15
Abilene Christian■ J17
Northern Mont.■ J18
West Tex. St. J22
Eastern N. Mex. J24
Texas Woman's■ J29
Central Okla.■ J31
Central Okla. .... F 5
Texas Woman's .... F 7
Abilene Christian F12
Angelo St. F14
Eastern N. Mex.■ F19
West Tex. St.■ F21
☒ Denton, TX

Colors: Blue & Gold. Nickname: Lady Lions.
AD: Margo Harbison. SID: Bill Powers. II

EASTERN CONN. ST. .... Willimantic, CT 06226
Steve Siegrist (1ST YR. AS HEAD COACH)

Eastern Conn. Tr. N19-20
Albertus Magnus .... D 1
Montclair St. Cl. D3-4
Clark (Mass.)■ .... D 8
Southern Me. D11
Wm. Paterson D29
Rhode Island Col. J11
Worcester St.■ J13
Plymouth St.■ J15
Western Conn. St. J18
Wheaton (Mass.) J20
Mass.-Boston■ J22
Mass.-Dartmouth J25
Connecticut Col.■ J27
Rhode Island Col.■ .... F 1
Southern Me.■ .... F 5
Western Conn. St.■ .... F 8
Plymouth St. F12
Mass.-Dartmouth■ F15
Western New Eng. F17
Mass.-Boston F19

Colors: Blue & White. Nickname: Warriors.
AD: Sharlene Peter. SID: Bob Molta. III

EASTERN ILL. .... Charleston, IL 61920
John Klein (1ST YR. AS HEAD COACH)

Rice Cl. D3-4
Murray St.■ .... D 6
Indiana St. .... D 9
Evansville D17
Missouri■ D19
Indiana D22
Northern Ill. D30
Western Ill. .... J 2
Wis.-Green Bay■ .... J 6
Wis.-Milwaukee■ .... J 8
Youngstown St. J13
Cleveland St. J15
Wright St. J22
Ill.-Chicago■ J27
Valparaiso■ J29
Northern Ill.■ .... F 3
Western Ill.■ .... F 5
Wis.-Green Bay F10
Wis.-Milwaukee F12
Youngstown St.■ F17
Cleveland St.■ F19
St. Louis■ F23
Wright St.■ F26
Ill.-Chicago .... M 3
Valparaiso .... M 5
Mid-Continent Tr. M10-12

Colors: Blue & Gray. Nickname: Lady Panthers.
AD: Mike Ryan. SID: Darin Bryan. I

EASTERN KY. .... Richmond, KY 40475
Larry Inman (13 YRS. W-231, L-138)

Ball St. N27
Thomas More■ N30
Marshall .... D 7
Stetson Cl. D17-18
Indiana St.■ D30
Indiana Cl. J2-3
Southeast Mo. St.■ .... J 8
Murray St.■ .... J 9
Tennessee St. J13
Tenn.-Martin J15
Austin Peay J17
Middle Tenn. St.■ J22
Tennessee Tech■ J24
Morehead St.■ J29
Kentucky .... F 1
Murray St. .... F 5
Southeast Mo. St. .... F 7
Austin Peay■ F12
Tennessee St.■ F14
Tenn.-Martin■ F21
Morehead St. F24
Tennessee Tech F26
Middle Tenn. St. F28
Ohio Valley Tr. M3-5

Colors: Maroon & White. Nickname: Colonels.
AD: Roy Kidd. SID: Karl Park. I

EAST. MENNONITE .... Harrisonburg, VA 22801
Ted Kinder (2 YRS. W-11, L-37)

Wash. & Lee■ N19
Shenandoah N23
Lynchburg .... D 1
Hollins■ .... D 4
Roanoke■ .... D 7
Rand.-Macon Woman's .... D 9
Emory & Henry D11
Frostburg St. Cl. J7-8
Randolph-Macon■ J11
Ferrum■ J13
Emory & Henry■ J14
Bridgewater (Va.)■ J18
Lynchburg■ J20
Guilford J22
Roanoke J26
Hollins J28
Averett .... F 2
Rand.-Macon Woman's■ .... F 3
Bridgewater (Va.) .... F 8
Guilford■ F11
Randolph-Macon F15
Va. Wesleyan■ F18

Colors: Royal Blue & White. Nickname: Royals.
AD: Roger Mast/Ted Kinder. SID: Larry Guengerich. III

EASTERN MICH. .... Ypsilanti, MI 48197
To be named

Michigan N30
Buffalo Tr. D3-4
Canisius .... D 6
Chicago St.■ .... D 8
Ala.-Birmingham Tr. D10-11
Akron■ .... J 5
Toledo■ .... J 8
Kent J12
Ball St.■ J15
Miami (Ohio) J19
Western Mich.■ J22
Ohio J26
Central Mich.■ J29
Bowling Green .... F 2
Toledo .... F 5
Kent■ .... F 9
Ball St. F12
Miami (Ohio)■ F16
Western Mich. F19
Ohio■ F23
Central Mich. F26
Bowling Green■ .... M 2
Akron .... M 5
Mid-American Tr. M11-12

Colors: Green & White. Nickname: Eagles.
AD: To be named. SID: Jim Streeter. I

EASTERN NAZARENE .... Quincy, MA 02170
Tom Dagley (6 YRS. W-43, L-91)

Mass.-Dartmouth .... D 2
Suffolk .... D 4
Nichols .... D 7
Emerson-MCA■ .... D 9
Simmons .... J 8
Wellesley J11
Mass.-Boston■ J13
New England Col.■ J15
Wentworth Inst.■ J18
Curry■ J20
Anna Maria■ J22
Salve Regina J26
Regis (Mass.) J29
Roger Williams .... F 1
New England Col. .... F 3
Wentworth Inst.■ .... F 5
Gordon .... F 8
Curry .... F 9
Regis (Mass.)■ F12
Salve Regina■ F15
Roger Williams■ F17
Anna Maria F19

Colors: Red & White. Nickname: Crusaders.
AD: Carroll Bradley. SID: Carroll Bradley. III

EASTERN N. MEX. .... Portales, NM 88130
Wayne Moore (13 YRS. W-195, L-142)

Eastern N. Mex. Cl. N25-26
Neb.-Kearney Cl. D2-4
Southern Colo. Inv. D10-11
West Tex. St. .... J 8
Central Okla. J15
Texas Woman's J17
Cameron■ J20
Texas A&I■ J22
East Tex. St.■ J24
Angelo St. J29
Abilene Christian J31
Angelo St.■ .... F 5
Abilene Christian■ .... F 7
Central Okla.■ F12
Texas Woman's■ F14
East Tex. St. F19
Texas A&I F21
Lubbock Chrst. F24
West Tex. St.■ F26

Colors: Green & Silver. Nickname: Zias.
AD: Chris Gage. SID: Wendel Sloan. II

■ Home games on each schedule.

See pages 735-738 for Division I tournament details

EASTERN WASH. .... Cheney, WA 99004

Bill Smithpeters (17 YRS. W-282, L-210)

Simon Fraser■ ... N21
Iowa St. Cl. ... N26-27
Arizona Cl. ... D3-5
Utah■ ... D18
Portland■ ... D19
Washington ... D31
Oregon St. ... J 2
Lewis-Clark St.■ ... J 6
Gonzaga■ ... J 8
Montana St.■ ... J14
Montana■ ... J15
Boise St. ... J19
Idaho■ ... J22
Northern Ariz. ... J27
Weber St. ... J29
Boise St.■ ... F 4
Idaho St.■ ... F 5
Montana ... F11
Montana St. ... F12
Idaho ... F17
Southern Utah■ ... F19
Weber St.■ ... F24
Northern Ariz.■ ... F26
Idaho St. ... M 5
Big Sky Tr. ... M11-12

Colors: Red & White. Nickname: Eagles.
AD: John Johnson. SID: Dave Cook. I

ECKERD .... St. Petersburg, FL 33733

Bob Nichols (26 YRS. W-350, L-245)

Wingate Tr. ... N19-21
Ashland■ ... N28
Northwest Mo. St.■ ... N29
Warner Southern ... D 1
Flagler ... D 7
Savannah A&D■ ... D18
St. Francis (Ill.)■ ... J 4
Wheaton (Mass.)■ ... J 6
Barry ... J12
Fla. Southern ... J15
Warner Southern■ ... J17
North Fla.■ ... J19
Florida Tech ... J22
St. Leo■ ... J26
Rollins ... J29
Tampa■ ... F 2
Fla. Southern■ ... F 5
North Fla. ... F 9
Florida Tech■ ... F12
St. Leo ... F16
Webber■ ... F17
Rollins■ ... F19
Tampa ... F23
Barry■ ... F26

Colors: Red, White & Black. Nickname: Tritons.
AD: James R. Harley. SID: Bill Thornton. II

EDINBORO .... Edinboro, PA 16444

Stan Swank (6 YRS. W-110, L-59)

Ohio Dominican■ ... N20
Seton Hill■ ... N21
Mansfield Tr. ... N26-27
Lake Erie■ ... N29
Edinboro Inv. ... D3-4
Mercyhurst■ ... D 8
Gannon■ ... D18
Mercyhurst ... J 5
Pitt.-Johnstown ... J 8
Clarion■ ... J12
Calif. (Pa.)■ ... J15
Gannon ... J19
Shippensburg ... J22
Indiana (Pa.) ... J26
Lock Haven ... J29
Slippery Rock■ ... F 2
Calif. (Pa.) ... F 5
Clarion ... F 9
Pitt.-Johnstown■ ... F11
Indiana (Pa.)■ ... F16
Shippensburg■ ... F19
Slippery Rock ... F23
Lock Haven■ ... F26

Colors: Red & White. Nickname: Fighting Scots.
AD: Jim McDonald. SID: Todd Jay. II

ELIZABETH CITY ST. .... Elizabeth City, NC 27909

Wanda Crump (1 YR. W-8, L-15)

Calif. (Pa.) Tr. ... N19-20
Hampton Tr. ... N26-27
Dist. Columbia■ ... N29
Delaware St. ... D 1
Eliz. City St. Inv. ... D3-4
Virginia Union ... J 8
Hampton ... J12
Virginia St. ... J15
Livingstone ... J17
St. Augustine's ... J18
Dist. Columbia ... J20
Norfolk St.■ ... J22
Bowie St.■ ... J25
Hampton■ ... J27
St. Paul's ... J29
St. Paul's■ ... F 1
Bowie St. ... F 3
Virginia St.■ ... F 5
Johnson Smith■ ... F 7
Shaw ... F 9
N.C. Central■ ... F12
Fayetteville St.■ ... F14
Virginia Union■ ... F16
Norfolk St. ... F19

Colors: Royal Blue & White. Nickname: Vikings.
AD: Willie Shaw. SID: Glen Mason. II

ELIZABETHTOWN .... Elizabethtown, PA 17022

Yvonne Kauffman (23 YRS. W-402, L-129)

Marymount (Va.) Tr. ... N19-20
Susquehanna■ ... D 2
Messiah ... D 4
Scranton■ ... D 7
Lycoming ... D 9
King's (Pa.) ... D11
Widener ... J12
Albright■ ... J15
Moravian ... J19
Lebanon Valley ... J22
Frank. & Marsh.■ ... J24
Juniata■ ... J27
Susquehanna ... J29
Widener■ ... F 2
Messiah■ ... F 5
Moravian■ ... F 8
Gettysburg■ ... F10
Albright ... F12
Western Md. ... F15
Juniata ... F17
Lebanon Valley■ ... F19

Colors: Blue & Grey. Nickname: Lady Jays.
AD: D. Kenneth Ober. SID: Matt Mackowski. III

ELMHURST .... Elmhurst, IL 60126

Jeri Findlay (1 YR. W-6, L-18)

Lake Forest Tr. ... N19-20
Ill. Benedictine■ ... D 7
Wis.-Stevens Pt. Tr. ... D10-11
Elmhurst Tr. ... D17-18
National Louis ... D21
Hope ... D29
Kalamazoo ... D30
Ill. Wesleyan ... J 5
North Park■ ... J 8
Millikin■ ... J11
Wheaton (Ill.)■ ... J18
Augustana (Ill.) ... J22
Ill. Wesleyan■ ... J26
Wis.-Oshkosh■ ... J29
North Central ... F 2
Carthage ... F 5
Augustana (Ill.)■ ... F 9
Millikin ... F12
North Park ... F15
North Central■ ... F18
Wheaton (Ill.) ... F22
Carthage■ ... F24

Colors: Navy & White. Nickname: Bluejays.
AD: Christopher Ragsdale. SID: John Quigley. III

ELMIRA .... Elmira, NY 14901

Jim Scheible (2 YRS. W-30, L-16)

Clarkson■ ... N19
St. Lawrence■ ... N20
Oneonta St. ... N23
Hamilton■ ... D 2
Williams Inv. ... D4-5
Ithaca■ ... D 7
Oswego St. ... D11
Binghamton■ ... J11
Rochester Inst.■ ... J13
Russell Sage ... J15
Hartwick■ ... J17
Utica ... J19
Houghton■ ... J22
Nazareth (N.Y.)■ ... J26
Skidmore Inv. ... J28-29
St. John Fisher ... F 1
Stony Brook ... F 5
Geneseo St. ... F 9
Colby-Sawyer ... F11
Albany (N.Y.) ... F12
Alfred■ ... F15
Brockport St.■ ... F22

Colors: Purple & Gold. Nickname: Soaring Eagles.
AD: Patricia Thompson. SID: Jim Scheible. III

ELON .... Elon College, NC 27244

Jackie Myers (11 YRS. W-103, L-146)

High Point Cl. ... N19-20
Longwood ... N23
N.C.-Asheville ... N29
Shippensburg Tr. ... D3-4
Mt. Olive■ ... D 7
High Point■ ... D11
Barton■ ... D15
Davis & Elkins■ ... J 6
Wingate■ ... J 8
Mars Hill ... J12
Presbyterian ... J15
Catawba■ ... J19
Lenoir-Rhyne■ ... J22
Gardner-Webb ... J26
Carson-Newman ... J29
Longwood■ ... F 2
Wingate ... F 5
Mars Hill■ ... F 9
Presbyterian■ ... F12
Catawba ... F16
Lenoir-Rhyne ... F19
Gardner-Webb■ ... F23
Carson-Newman■ ... F26

Colors: Maroon & Gold. Nickname: Fightin' Christians.
AD: Alan White. SID: David Hibbard. II

EMERSON-MCA .... Boston, MA 02116

To be named

Westbrook■ ... N14
Lasell ... N17
Rivier ... N20
Endicott ... N23
Regis (Mass.)■ ... D 2
Wentworth Inst. ... D 7
Eastern Nazarene ... D 9
Southern Vt. ... D11
Mass. Pharmacy■ ... D15
Pine Manor■ ... J25
Suffolk■ ... J31
Lasell■ ... F 4
Mass. Pharmacy ... F10
Rivier ... F12
Newberry ... F14
Westbrook ... F20

Colors: Purple & Gold. Nickname: Lady Lions.
AD: James C. Peckham. SID: None. III

EMMANUEL .... Boston, MA 02115

Andy Yosinoff (16 YRS. W-266, L-95)

Emmanuel Tr. ... N20-21
Bri'water (Mass.)■ ... N23
Westfield St.■ ... D 2
Manhattanville Tr. ... D4-5
Plymouth St. ... D 8
Nat'l Catholic Tr. ... J5-9
Babson ... J20
Western New Eng.■ ... J22
St. Joseph's (Me.)■ ... J25
Worcester St.■ ... J27
Norwich■ ... J29
Middlebury■ ... J30
Nichols■ ... F 3
Salem St. ... F 5
Pine Manor■ ... F 8
Husson■ ... F12
Gordon ... F15
Coast Guard ... F17
Wellesley ... F19

Colors: Royal & Gold. Nickname: Saints.
AD: Andy Yosinoff. SID: To be named. III

■ Home games on each schedule.

See pages 735-738 for Division I tournament details

EMORY .... Atlanta, GA 30322

Myra Sims (5 YRS. W-54, L-69)

Emory Tr.	N19-20	New York U.■	J21
Wash. & Lee■	N23	Brandeis■	J23
Millsaps	N27	Barton■	J25
Sewanee■	D 1	Washington (Mo.)	J28
Carnegie Mellon■	D 3	Chicago	J30
Case Reserve■	D 5	Brandeis	F 4
Ferrum■	J 6	New York U.	F 6
Rochester■	J 9	Chicago■	F11
Oglethorpe	J11	Washington (Mo.)■	F13
Johns Hopkins	J14	Rochester	F18
Swarthmore	J15	Carnegie Mellon	F20
Sewanee	J18	Millsaps■	F23

Colors: Blue & Gold. Nickname: Eagles.
AD: Chuck Gordon. SID: John Arenberg. III

EMORY & HENRY .... Emory, VA 24327

Joy Scruggs (12 YRS. W-168, L-117)

Ferrum Tr.	N19-20	Lynchburg■	J25
Hollins■	D 7	Guilford■	J28
Ferrum■	D 9	Va. Wesleyan■	J29
East. Mennonite■	D11	Maryville (Tenn.)	F 3
Va. Wesleyan	J 7	Randolph-Macon■	F 5
Randolph-Macon	J 8	Liberty	F 8
Rand.-Macon Woman's■	J12	Rand.-Macon Woman's	F11
East. Mennonite	J14	Lynchburg	F12
Bridgewater (Va.)	J15	Roanoke■	F15
Maryville (Tenn.)■	J18	Guilford	F17
Roanoke	J20	Hollins■	F19
Bridgewater (Va.)■	J22		

Colors: Blue & Gold. Nickname: Wasps.
AD: Joy Scruggs. SID: Nathan Graybeal. III

EMPORIA ST. .... Emporia, KS 66801

Val Schierling (12 YRS. W-193, L-151)

Fort Hays St. Cl.	N19-20	Mo. Southern St.	J22
Ottawa■	N22	Washburn	J26
Baker■	N27	Northwest Mo. St.■	J29
Southern Colo. Tr.	D3-4	Missouri-Rolla	F 3
Central Okla.■	D 7	Mo.-St. Louis	F 5
Fort Hays St.■	D18	Pittsburg St.■	F 9
Grand Canyon Cl.	D30-31	Northeast Mo. St.■	F12
Southwest Baptist■	J 5	Central Mo. St.	F16
Northeast Mo. St.	J 8	Mo. Western St.	F19
Central Mo. St.■	J12	Lincoln (Mo.)■	F23
Mo. Western St.■	J15	Mo. Southern St.■	F26
Lincoln (Mo.)	J19		

Colors: Black & Gold. Nickname: Lady Hornets.
AD: William Quayle. SID: Brian Pracht. II

ENDICOTT .... Beverly, MA 01915

Lorinda Visnick (1 YR. W-4, L-12)

Pine Manor Tr.	N19-20	Trinity (Vt.)■	F 2
Emerson-MCA■	N23	Colby-Sawyer■	F 8
Westbrook■	N30	Rivier	F10
Utica Tech Cl.	D4-5	Albertus Magnus■	F12
Rivier■	D 7	Westbrook	F13
Notre Dame (N.H.)■	D 8	Simmons	F16
Suffolk■	D11	Framingham St.■	F19

Colors: Royal & Kelly. Nickname: Powergulls.
AD: Stephen Woodcock. SID: Nancy Bias. III

ERSKINE .... Due West, SC 29639

Rosalind Jennings (2 YRS. W-12, L-37)

Piedmont■	N22	Queens (N.C.)	J22
Francis Marion	N27	Central Wesleyan	J24
Coker■	N29	Wofford	J26
Newberry Tr.	D1-2	Converse	J29
Georgia Col.■	D 4	Newberry	F 3
Linc. Memorial Cl.	D10-11	Wofford■	F 5
S.C.-Aiken	D15	S.C.-Aiken■	F 9
Presbyterian■	J 6	Queens (N.C.)■	F12
Lander	J 8	Georgia Col.	F14
Coker	J10	Central Wesleyan■	F16
Clayton St.	J15	Piedmont	F21
Carson-Newman■	J17	Newberry■	F23
Lander■	J19	Converse■	F26

Colors: Maroon & Gold. Nickname: Lady Fleet.
AD: Bill Lesesne. SID: Dick Haldeman. II

EUREKA .... Eureka, IL 61530

Sandy Schuster (2 YRS. W-38, L-14)

Mt. St. Clare	N19	McKendree	J15
Clarke	N20	Moody Bible■	J18
Illinois Tech■	N22	National Louis■	J20
Trinity Chrst. (Il.)■	N30	Greenville	J25
Blackburn■	D 3	St. Francis (Ind.)	J29
Olivet (Ill.)	D 7	Trinity (Ill.)■	F 1
Trinity (Ill.) Tr.	D10-11	Rockford	F 3
Purdue-Calumet■	D14	Monmouth (Ill.)	F 7
Judson■	J 7	Cornell College	F 9
Concordia (Ill.)	J 8	Ill. Wesleyan	F15
MacMurray	J11	Principia	F17
Mo. Baptist■	J13	Greenville■	F19

Colors: Maroon & Gold. Nickname: Red Devils.
AD: Warner McCullom. SID: Becky Duffield. III

EVANSVILLE .... Evansville, IN 47722

Faith Mimnaugh (1ST YR. AS HEAD COACH)

Nebraska Cl.	N26-27	Detroit Mercy■	J15
Murray St.■	N29	Notre Dame	J20
Wis.-Milwaukee	D 4	Loyola (Ill.)	J22
Wright St.■	D 8	La Salle	J27
St. Louis	D11	Butler	F 5
Eastern Ill.■	D17	Loyola (Ill.)■	F10
Cleveland St.	D21	Notre Dame■	F12
Indiana St.	D28	Detroit Mercy	F17
Southern Ill.■	D30	Xavier (Ohio)	F19
Southeast Mo. St.	J 3	La Salle■	F26
Mo.-Kansas City	J 5	Butler■	M 2
Vanderbilt	J 7	MCC Tr.	M5-8
Xavier (Ohio)■	J13		

Colors: Purple & White. Nickname: Lady Aces.
AD: Jim Byers. SID: Bob Boxell. I

FAIRFIELD .... Fairfield, CT 06430

Dianne Nolan (19 YRS. W-297, L-224)

Brown■	N27	Canisius■	J22
Seton Hall■	D 1	St. Peter's	J26
Central Conn. St.	D 7	Loyola (Md.)■	J29
Fairfield Cl.	D10-11	Manhattan■	F 4
St. John's (N.Y.)■	D13	Niagara■	F 6
St. Francis (N.Y.)■	D22	Iona■	F10
Tulane	D28	Loyola (Md.)	F12
New Orleans	D30	Manhattan	F16
Fordham■	J 6	Siena■	F19
Canisius	J 8	St. Peter's■	F21
Buffalo	J 9	Iona	F26
Niagara	J10	Metro Atlantic Tr.	M4-6
Siena	J18		

Colors: Scarlet Red. Nickname: Lady Stags.
AD: Harold Menninger. SID: Christopher Tetro. I

FDU-MADISON .... Madison, NJ 07940

Denise Fiore (8 YRS. W-98, L-113)

Delaware Valley■	D 1	New Jersey Tech	J27
King's (Pa.)■	D 4	Delaware Valley	J29
New Jersey Tech■	D 6	St. Elizabeth	J31
Mt. St. Mary (N.Y.)■	D 8	Scranton	F 2
St. Elizabeth■	D10	King's (Pa.)	F 5
New York U.	J11	Upsala	F 8
Scranton■	J13	Centenary (N.J.)■	F10
Lycoming	J15	Lycoming■	F12
Upsala■	J18	Centenary (N.J.)	F14
Mt. St. Mary (N.Y.)	J20	Wilkes■	F17
Drew■	J22	Drew	F19
Wilkes	J25		

Colors: Navy, Columbia Blue & White. Nickname: Jersey Devils.
AD: William Klika. SID: Tom Bonerbo. III

FDU-TEANECK .... Teaneck, NJ 07666

Sharon Beverly (15 YRS. W-187, L-219)

Manhattan■	D 1	Monmouth (N.J.)	J22
Geo. Washington Cl.	D3-4	Wagner	J24
Delaware St.■	D 7	Marist	J29
Columbia-Barnard	D11	Robert Morris■	F 3
Princeton■	D14	St. Francis (Pa.)■	F 5
Drexel■	D19	LIU-Brooklyn	F10
Seton Hall■	D22	St. Francis (N.Y.)	F12
Mt. St. Mary's (Md.)■	J 3	Wagner■	F16
Rider■	J 6	Monmouth (N.J.)■	F18
Marist■	J 8	Rider	F24
St. Francis (Pa.)	J13	Mt. St. Mary's (Md.)	F26
Robert Morris	J15	St. Francis (N.Y.)■	M 2
LIU-Brooklyn■	J20	Northeast Tr.	M5-12

Colors: Maroon, White, Blue. Nickname: Lady Knights.
AD: Roy Danforth. SID: Carmine Faccenda. I

■ Home games on each schedule.

See pages 735-738 for Division I tournament details

FAIRMONT ST. .... Fairmont, WV 26554

Jim Brinkman (11 YRS. W-203, L-135)

- Rio Grande■ N23
- Bluefield St. Tr. N26-27
- St. Vincent N29
- Gannon■ D 1
- Alderson-Broaddus■ D 4
- Davis & Elkins D 7
- Waynesburg■ D11
- Shepherd D20
- West Va. Wesleyan J 5
- Calif. (Pa.)■ J 7
- Salem-Teikyo J 8
- Glenville St.■ J12
- West Va. St. J15
- West Liberty St.■ J19
- Bluefield St.■ J21
- Concord■ J22
- Wheeling Jesuit J26
- West Va. Tech■ J29
- Alderson-Broaddus J31
- Wheeling Jesuit■ F 2
- Glenville St. F 5
- Salem-Teikyo■ F 9
- West Liberty St. F12
- Shepherd■ F14
- Charleston (W.Va.) F16

Colors: Maroon & White. Nickname: Falcons.
AD: Colin Cameron. SID: Jim Brinkman. II

FAYETTEVILLE ST. .... Fayetteville, NC 28301

Eric Tucker (1 YR. W-13, L-10)

- Virginia St. N20
- Hampton N23
- Claflin N29
- Johnson Smith Inv. D3-4
- Pembroke St. D11
- Bowie St.■ D13
- Virginia Union■ J 5
- N.C. Central J 8
- Methodist■ J10
- St. Paul's■ J13
- Livingstone J15
- Norfolk St.■ J16
- St. Augustine's J20
- Shaw■ J22
- Winston-Salem J24
- Johnson Smith■ J27
- N.C. Central■ J29
- Livingstone■ F 2
- Shaw F 5
- Claflin■ F 7
- Johnson Smith F12
- Elizabeth City St. F14
- Winston-Salem■ F17
- St. Augustine's■ F19

Colors: White & Blue. Nickname: Broncos.
AD: Ralph Burns. SID: John Hinton. II

FERRIS ST. .... Big Rapids, MI 49307

Lori Hyman (9 YRS. W-112, L-118)

- Hope■ N20
- Aquinas■ N23
- Grand Rapids Tr. N26-27
- Ferris St. Cl. D3-4
- Saginaw Valley■ D 9
- Northwood D11
- Lake Superior St. D18
- Fla. Southern Cl. D30-31
- Northern Mich.■ J 6
- Michigan Tech■ J 8
- Oakland J13
- Wayne St. (Mich.)■ J15
- Hillsdale J22
- Grand Valley St. J27
- Lake Superior St.■ J29
- Saginaw Valley F 3
- Northwood■ F 5
- Northern Mich. F10
- Michigan Tech F12
- Oakland■ F17
- Wayne St. (Mich.) F19
- Grand Valley St.■ F21
- Hillsdale■ F26

Colors: Crimson & Gold. Nickname: Bulldogs.
AD: Tom Kirinovic (Interim). SID: Becky Olsen. II

FERRUM .... Ferrum, VA 24088

Donna Doonan (17 YRS. W-185, L-187)

- Ferrum Tr. N19-20
- Bridgewater (Va.)■ N22
- Ferrum Inv. D4-5
- Emory & Henry D 9
- Roanoke D11
- Emory J 6
- Maryville (Tn.) Tr. J8-9
- Averett■ J11
- East. Mennonite J13
- Methodist■ J15
- N.C. Wesleyan J19
- Chris. Newport■ J21
- Greensboro J25
- Shenandoah■ J29
- Averett F 1
- Hollins■ F 3
- Methodist F 5
- Chris. Newport F 9
- N.C. Wesleyan■ F12
- Greensboro■ F14
- Shenandoah F16

Colors: Black & Gold. Nickname: Panthers.
AD: Hank Norton. SID: Gary Holden. III

FITCHBURG ST. .... Fitchburg, MA 01420

To be named

- Worcester Tech■ N23
- Western New Eng. D 2
- Curry■ D 4
- Worcester St.■ J11
- Anna Maria J13
- Salem St. J15
- Nichols■ J18
- Elms■ J20
- Westfield St.■ J22
- Framingham St. J25
- Suffolk J27
- North Adams St. J29
- Bri'water (Mass.) F 1
- Worcester St. F 5
- Salem St.■ F 8
- Mass.-Dartmouth F10
- Westfield St. F12
- Framingham St.■ F15
- North Adams St.■ F17
- Bri'water (Mass.)■ F19

Colors: Green, Gold & White. Nickname: Falcons.
AD: Elizabeth Kruczek. SID: David Marsh. III

FLORIDA .... Gainesville, FL 32604

Carol Ross (2 YRS. W-32, L-24)

- Miami (Fla.)■ N26
- Southern Miss. N29
- S.F. Austin Cl. D3-4
- Furman D 8
- South Ala.■ D12
- Tennessee D18
- Tennessee Tech■ D20
- Florida Tr. D28-29
- Kentucky■ J 2
- Fla. Atlantic■ J 5
- Mississippi St.■ J 8
- Central Fla. J11
- Alabama J16
- Stetson■ J17
- Mississippi■ J22
- Miami (Fla.)■ J27
- Arkansas■ J30
- Bethune-Cookman■ F 2
- Vanderbilt F 6
- Georgia■ F 9
- Louisiana St. F12
- Florida St. F15
- South Caro.■ F19
- South Fla. F23
- Auburn F26
- Southeastern Tr. M4-7

Colors: Orange & Blue. Nickname: Lady Gators.
AD: Jeremy Foley. SID: Debbi Edwards. I

FLORIDA A&M .... Tallahassee, FL 32307

Claudette Farmer (3 YRS. W-44, L-41)

- Bethune-Cookman■ N26
- Troy St. N29
- Alabama St. D 1
- Florida St.■ D10
- Keene St.■ J 1
- Mercer■ J 5
- Md.-East. Shore J 8
- Delaware St. J10
- Tuskegee■ J13
- South Caro. St. J15
- North Caro. A&T J17
- Morgan St.■ J20
- Coppin St.■ J22
- Alabama St.■ J26
- North Caro. A&T■ J29
- South Caro. St.■ J31
- Bethune-Cookman F 4
- Troy St.■ F 8
- Morgan St. F10
- Coppin St. F12
- Md.-East. Shore■ F19
- Delaware St.■ F21
- Stetson F24
- Bethune-Cookman■ M 5

Colors: Orange & Green. Nickname: Rattlerettes.
AD: Walter Reed. SID: Michelle Jinks. I

FLA. ATLANTIC .... Boca Raton, FL 33431

Wayne Allen (6 YRS. W-114, L-55)

- Florida Tech■ N27
- Barry■ D 1
- Bethune-Cookman D 4
- South Fla. D12
- Florida St. D14
- South Ala. Cl. D17-18
- Miami (Fla.) Tr. D28-30
- North Caro. St.■ J 2
- Florida J 5
- Georgia J12
- Georgia St.■ J15
- Charleston J20
- Florida Int'l J22
- Central Fla. J27
- Stetson J29
- Mercer■ F 3
- Charleston■ F 5
- New Orleans F12
- Southwestern La. F14
- Florida Int'l■ F19
- Central Fla.■ F22
- Stetson■ F28
- Georgia St. M 3
- Mercer M 5

Colors: Blue & Gray. Nickname: Owls.
AD: Tom Scott. SID: Katrina McCormick. I

FLORIDA TECH .... Melbourne, FL 32901

John Reynolds Jr. (6 YRS. W-112, L-55)

- Fla. Memorial■ N23
- Fla. Atlantic N27
- Southern Ind.■ N29
- Fla. Memorial D 1
- Lynn■ D 4
- Edward Waters■ D 8
- Armstrong St. D11
- Keene St.■ D29
- Merrimack■ D30
- Florida Tech Tr. J2-3
- Gardner-Webb■ J 6
- North Fla. J12
- Rollins J15
- St. Leo■ J19
- Eckerd■ J22
- Tampa J26
- Barry J29
- Fla. Southern F 2
- Rollins■ F 5
- St. Leo F 9
- Eckerd F12
- Tampa■ F16
- Barry■ F19
- Fla. Southern■ F23
- North Fla.■ F26

Colors: Crimson & Gray. Nickname: Panthers.
AD: William Jurgens. SID: Mike Stern. II

FLORIDA INT'L .... Miami, FL 33199

Cindy Russo (16 YRS. W-315, L-140)

- Texas Tech Cl. D4-5
- Bethune-Cookman D11
- Auburn■ D19
- Valparaiso■ D20
- Miami (Fla.) Tr. D28-30
- Florida Int'l Tr. J2-4
- Georgia St.■ J13
- Southeastern La.■ J15
- Fla. Atlantic■ J22
- Stetson J27
- Central Fla. J29
- Charleston■ F 3
- Mercer■ F 5
- Southeastern La. F10
- Georgia St. F12
- Georgia F14
- Fla. Atlantic F19
- Central Fla.■ F24
- Stetson■ F26
- Mercer M 3
- Charleston M 5
- Trans America Tr. M10-12

Colors: Blue & Yellow. Nickname: Golden Panthers.
AD: Ted Aceto. SID: Eddie Mills. I

■ Home games on each schedule.

See pages 735-738 for Division I tournament details

FLA. SOUTHERN .... Lakeland, FL 33801
Norm Benn (8 YRS. W-156, L-69)

Nassau Cl. N26-27
Augusta D 4
Kennesaw St.■ D 7
Webber■ D 9
Warner Southern■ D17
Fla. Southern Cl. D30-31
Bentley■ J 3
Gardner-Webb■ J 5
Abilene Christian■ J 6
East Stroudsburg■ J 8
Tampa J12
Eckerd■ J15
Barry■ J19
Rollins J22
North Fla.■ J26
St. Leo J29
Florida Tech■ F 2
Eckerd F 5
Barry F 9
Rollins■ F12
North Fla. F16
St. Leo■ F19
Florida Tech F23
Tampa■ F26

Colors: Scarlet & White. Nickname: Moccasins.
AD: Hal Smeltzly. SID: Wayne Koehler. II

FORT LEWIS .... Durango, CO 81301
Cathy Simbeck (8 YRS. W-85, L-127)

Western St. N19
West Tex. A&M Tr. D2-4
Adams St.■ D 7
Western St.■ D10
Mesa St.■ D11
Southern Ore. St. D30
Cal St. Chico D31
Neb.-Kearney■ J 2
Mesa St. J 5
Air Force■ J 8
Colo. Christian■ J13
Metropolitan St.■ J15
Regis (Colo.) J21
Denver J22
Colorado-CS J28
Southern Colo. J29
Air Force F 5
Colo. Christian F11
Metropolitan St. F12
Regis (Colo.)■ F17
Denver■ F19
Adams St. F22
Colorado-CS■ F24
Southern Colo.■ F26

Colors: Blue & Gold. Nickname: Raiders.
AD: Bruce Grimes. SID: Chris Aaland. II

FLORIDA ST. .... Tallahassee, FL 32306
Marynell Meadors (23 YRS. W-473, L-228)

Middle Tenn. St. N18
Tenn.-Chatt. N26
Florida St. Cl. D3-4
Florida A&M D10
North Caro. D12
Fla. Atlantic■ D14
Georgia Tech■ D18
Virginia D21
Central Fla. Cl. D29-31
Maryland■ J 5
North Caro.■ J14
Duke J16
Wake Forest■ J22
North Caro. St.■ J24
Maryland J28
Georgia Tech F 1
Virginia■ F 4
Clemson F 7
Florida■ F15
Wake Forest F18
North Caro. St. F20
Clemson■ F23
Duke■ F25
ACC Tr. M4-7

Colors: Garnet & Gold. Nickname: Lady Seminoles.
AD: Bob Goin. SID: Kim McWilliams. I

FORT VALLEY ST. .... Ft. Valley, GA 31030
Lonnie Bartley (9 YRS. W-154, L-89)

Fla. Memorial■ N20
LeMoyne-Owen N27
Tuskegee N29
Fort Valley St. Inv. D3-4
Fla. Memorial D11
Valdosta St. D13
Savannah St.■ J 8
Morris Brown J12
Albany St. (Ga.)■ J15
Paine J17
Miles J19
Savannah St. J22
Morris Brown■ J26
LeMoyne-Owen■ J29
Alabama A&M■ J31
Tuskegee■ F 3
Albany St. (Ga.) F 4
Alabama A&M F 7
Clark Atlanta F12
Paine■ F15
Valdosta St.■ F17
Clark Atlanta■ F19
Jacksonville St. F21
West Ga.■ F23
Miles■ F26

Colors: Old Gold & Blue. Nickname: Lady Wildcats.
AD: Douglas Porter. SID: Russell Boone. II

FONTBONNE .... St. Louis, MO 63105
Linda Haley (1ST YR. AS HEAD COACH)

Sewanee Inv. N20-21
McKendree N23
Brescia■ N27
Rhodes Tr. D4-5
Washington (Mo.) D 7
Aurora■ D10
Oakland City■ D15
Maryville (Mo.) J11
MacMurray J15
Webster■ J17
Blackburn J22
Principia■ J27
Webster J29
MacMurray■ F 3
Maryville (Mo.)■ F 5
Greenville■ F 8
Westminster F10
Westminster■ F15
Blackburn■ F17
Principia F19
DePauw■ F20

Colors: Purple & Gold. Nickname: Griffins.
AD: Lee McKinney. SID: None. III

FRAMINGHAM ST. .... Framingham, MA 01701
Ellen Thompson (2 YRS. W-3, L-47)

Worcester Tech N27
Western New Eng. N30
Nichols■ D 2
Mass.-Boston■ D 4
Rhode Island Col.■ D 7
Curry D 9
North Adams St.■ J11
Pine Manor■ J13
Bri'water (Mass.) J15
Worcester St.■ J18
Salem St. J22
Fitchburg St.■ J25
Westfield St.■ J29
Suffolk■ F 3
North Adams St. F 5
Bri'water (Mass.)■ F 8
Worcester St. F10
Salem St.■ F12
Fitchburg St. F15
Westfield St. F17
Endicott F19

Colors: Black & Gold. Nickname: Rams.
AD: Lawrence Boyd. SID: Scott Kavanagh. III

FORDHAM .... New York, NY 10458
To be named

Iona N27
American D 1
Providence■ D 3
Manhattan D 8
Marist■ D11
Columbia-Barnard■ D14
St. Peter's■ D18
Villanova Tr. D28-29
Southern Methodist D31
Fairfield J 6
Holy Cross■ J 8
Bucknell J12
Army J15
Lehigh■ J19
Colgate J22
Lafayette J26
Navy■ J29
Holy Cross F 2
Bucknell■ F 5
Army■ F 9
Lehigh F12
Hofstra F14
Colgate■ F16
Lafayette■ F19
Navy F26
Patriot Tr. M3-12

Colors: Maroon & White. Nickname: Lady Rams.
AD: Frank McLaughlin. SID: Joe Favorito. I

FRANCIS MARION .... Florence, SC 29501
Steven Garber (3 YRS. W-46, L-41)

Lincoln Memorial N20
Gardner-Webb N21
Lees-McRae■ N23
Erskine■ N27
Carson-Newman■ N30
Wofford D 4
Augusta■ D 7
Columbus■ J 8
S.C.-Aiken■ J10
Pembroke St.■ J12
Lander J15
Coker■ J17
S.C.-Spartanburg J19
Newberry■ J22
Armstrong St.■ J24
Georgia Col.■ J29
Pembroke St. F 2
Georgia Col. F 5
Newberry F 7
Armstrong St. F10
Columbus F12
S.C.-Spartanburg■ F16
Augusta F19
Coker F21
S.C.-Aiken F23
Lander■ F26

Colors: Red, White & Blue. Nickname: Lady Patriots.
AD: Gerald Griffin. SID: Michael Hawkins. II

FORT HAYS ST. .... Hays, KS 67601
John Klein (11 YRS. W-205, L-114)

Fort Hays St. Cl. N19-20
Washburn Cl. N26-27
Neb.-Kearney Cl. D2-4
Washburn■ D 8
Colo. Christian■ D11
Emporia St. D18
Bethel (Kan.)■ J 5
Angelo St. J 7
Chadron St. J13
Colorado Mines J15
Mesa St.■ J21
Western St.■ J22
N.M. Highlands J27
Adams St. J29
Mesa St. F 4
Western St. F 5
Neb.-Kearney■ F 8
Chadron St.■ F11
Colorado Mines■ F12
N.M. Highlands■ F18
Adams St.■ F19
Neb.-Kearney F23

Colors: Black & Gold. Nickname: Lady Tigers.
AD: Tom Spicer. SID: Jack Kuestermeyer. II

FRANKLIN .... Franklin, IN 46131
Gene White (7 YRS. W-90, L-58)

Rollins N22
Lambuth☒ N24
Franklin Inv. D3-4
Ind.-Southeast D 7
Ind. Wesleyan■ D 9
Kalamazoo■ D11
Indianapolis D18
Wilmington (Ohio) D20
Huntington J 1
Centre J 4
Millikin J 8
Hanover■ J11
Defiance J13
DePauw J15
Mt. St. Joseph's J20
Manchester■ J22
IU/PU-Indianapolis■ J25
Anderson J29
Hanover F 1
Taylor■ F 5
Asbury F10
DePauw■ F12
Manchester F15
Anderson■ F19
St. Mary's (Ind.) F26
☒ Babson Park, FL

Colors: Blue & Gold. Nickname: Grizzlies.
AD: Jenny Johnson-Kappes. SID: Kevin Elixman. III

■ Home games on each schedule.

See pages 735-738 for Division I tournament details

FRANKLIN PIERCE .... Rindge, NH 03461

Steve Hancock (5 YRS. W-79, L-65)

New Hamp. Col. Cl.	N20-21	Bridgeport■	J22
American Int'l	N23	Keene St.	J26
St. Michael's■	D 1	Le Moyne	J29
Assumption	D 7	New Haven■	J31
Quinnipiac■	D11	New Hamp. Col.	F 2
Springfield	D14	Southern Conn. St.■	F 5
St. Rose Cl.	D28-29	Mass.-Lowell	F 9
Le Moyne■	J 5	Bridgeport	F12
Merrimack■	J10	Sacred Heart■	F14
Sacred Heart	J12	New Hamp. Col.■	F16
Southern Conn. St.	J15	New Haven	F19
Mass.-Lowell■	J19	Keene St.■	F23

Colors: Crimson & Gray. Nickname: Lady Ravens.
AD: Bruce Kirsh. SID: Jon Tirone. II

FRANK. & MARSH. .... Lancaster, PA 17604

Noreen Pecsok (1 YR. W-19, L-5)

Frank. & Marsh. Tr.	N20-21	Swarthmore	J22
Haverford■	N23	Elizabethtown	J24
Washington (Md.)	N30	Gettysburg■	J26
Muhlenberg■	D 4	Dickinson■	J29
Johns Hopkins	D 7	Moravian■	F 1
Messiah■	D 9	Johns Hopkins■	F 5
Bryn Mawr■	D11	Western Md.	F 8
Shenandoah	J 8	Lebanon Valley■	F10
Chris. Newport	J10	Gettysburg	F12
Ursinus	J15	Dickinson	F15
Western Md.■	J18	Susquehanna■	F17
Allentown	J20		

Colors: Blue & White. Nickname: Diplomats.
AD: William A. Marshall. SID: Tom Byrnes. III

FREDONIA ST. .... Fredonia, NY 14063

Cathy Flanders (6 YRS. W-58 , L-87)

St. John Fisher Tr.	N19-20	Roberts Wesleyan■	J27
Buffalo St.■	D 3	Cortland St.■	J29
Binghamton	D 4	Geneseo St.	F 4
Geneseo St.■	D 7	Brockport St.■	F 5
Penn St.-Behrend	D10	Nazareth (N.Y.)■	F 8
Potsdam St.■	J14	New Paltz St.	F11
Plattsburgh St.■	J15	Oneonta St.	F12
St. John Fisher	J18	Buffalo St.	F15
Oswego St.	J21	Oswego St.■	F18
Utica Tech	J22	Utica Tech■	F19
Brockport St.	J25		

Colors: Blue & White. Nickname: Blue Devils.
AD: Thomas Prevet. SID: Donna Hart. III

FRESNO ST. .... Fresno, CA 93740

Linda Wunder (8 YRS. W-146, L-73)

San Jose St.	N30	Wyoming	J27
Cal St. Fullerton■	D 3	Colorado St.	J29
Pacific (Cal.)■	D 8	Colorado St.■	F 4
Cal St. Northridge	D10	Wyoming■	F 6
UC Santa Barb.	D12	UTEP	F11
Santa Clara■	D15	New Mexico	F13
Cal Poly SLO■	D17	New Mexico■	F18
Oklahoma St. Tr.	D31-J1	UTEP■	F20
San Diego■	J 5	Utah	F24
Pepperdine■	J 8	Brigham Young	F26
Brigham Young■	J13	San Diego St.	M 5
Utah■	J15	Western Athletic Tr.	M9-12
San Diego St.■	J22		

Colors: Cardinal & Blue. Nickname: Bulldogs.
AD: Gary Cunningham. SID: Scott Johnson. I

FROSTBURG ST. .... Frostburg, MD 21532

Jim Crawley (15 YRS. W-273, L-120)

Frostburg St. Inv.	N19-20	Columbia Union■	J18
Waynesburg	N23	Salisbury St.	J21
Wesley■	N30	Gallaudet	J22
Mary Washington■	D 2	Notre Dame (Md.)	J25
York (Pa.) Tr.	D3-4	Salisbury St.■	J29
Frostburg St. Cl.	J7-8	Shenandoah■	F 2
Shenandoah	J11	Waynesburg■	F 7
Bridgewater (Va.)■	J13	Dickinson	F10
Lincoln (Pa.)	J15	Carnegie Mellon	F15
Wesley	J16	Lincoln (Pa.)■	F19

Colors: Red, White & Black. Nickname: Bobcats.
AD: Loyal Park. SID: Jeff Krone. III

FURMAN .... Greenville, SC 29613

Sherry Carter (11 YRS. W-153, L-143)

Georgia■	N28	Marshall■	J29
Clemson	D 1	East Tenn. St.■	J30
Southwest Tex. Cl.	D3-4	South Caro.	F 2
Florida■	D 8	Davidson	F 5
East Caro.■	D17	Tenn.-Chatt.■	F 7
New Orleans	D28	Appalachian St.	F 9
Southeastern La.	D30	Western Caro.■	F14
Winthrop■	J11	Charleston	F16
Appalachian St.■	J13	Ga. Southern	F22
Western Caro.	J16	Marshall	F26
Georgia Tech■	J19	East Tenn. St.	M 1
Ga. Southern■	J22	Southern Tr.	M10-12
Tenn.-Chatt.	J26		

Colors: Purple & White. Nickname: Lady Paladins.
AD: Ray Parlier. SID: Teri Brinkman. I

GANNON .... Erie, PA 16541

Doug Zimmerman (3 YRS. W-35, L-42)

Gannon Tr.	N19-20	Davis & Elkins■	J15
Lock Haven	N23	Edinboro■	J19
Indiana (Pa.)■	N27	Slippery Rock■	J22
Fairmont St.	D 1	Pitt.-Johnstown■	J29
Le Moyne Tr.	D4-5	Ashland■	F 1
Calif. (Pa.)	D 7	Mercyhurst	F 5
Clarion■	D10	Hilbert■	F 8
Edinboro	D18	Mercyhurst■	F12
East Stroudsburg■	D30	Notre Dame (Ohio)■	F16
Oakland	J 4	Point Park■	F21
Wayne St. (Mich.)	J 5	Pitt.-Johnstown	F23
Columbia Union■	J 9	Clarion	F26

Colors: Maroon & Gold. Nickname: Lady Knights.
AD: Howard Elwell. SID: Bob Shreve. II

GARDNER-WEBB .... Boiling Springs, NC 28017

Brenda Halford (3 YRS. W-42, L-41)

Clayton St.	N20	Lenoir-Rhyne	J19
Francis Marion■	N21	Wingate	J22
Wofford	N23	Elon■	J26
Queens (N.C.)	N29	Catawba■	J29
Gardner-Webb Tr.	D3-4	Davidson	F 2
Presbyterian■	D 8	Presbyterian	F 5
Linc. Memorial Cl.	D10-11	Carson-Newman	F 9
Fla. Southern	J 5	Mars Hill■	F12
Florida Tech	J 6	Lenoir-Rhyne■	F16
Queens (N.C.)■	J10	Wingate■	F19
Carson-Newman■	J12	Elon	F23
Mars Hill	J15	Catawba	F26

Colors: Scarlet & Red. Nickname: Bulldogs.
AD: Ozzie McFarland. SID: Mark Wilson. II

GENESEO ST. .... Geneseo, NY 14454

Robert Guy (9 YRS. W-181, L-51)

Ithaca■	D 1	Oswego St.■	J25
Cortland St.	D 3	Potsdam St.	J28
Brockport St.	D 4	Plattsburgh St.	J29
Fredonia St.	D 7	Rochester Inst.■	F 1
New Paltz St.■	D10	Fredonia St.■	F 4
Oneonta St.■	D11	Oswego St.	F 5
UC San Diego Inv.	D28-30	Elmira■	F 9
Hilbert	J14	Binghamton■	F12
Rochester■	J16	Utica Tech	F15
Utica Tech■	J18	Buffalo St.■	F18
Buffalo St.	J21	Brockport St.■	F19

Colors: Blue & White. Nickname: Lady Knights.
AD: John Spring. SID: Fred Bright. III

GEORGE MASON .... Fairfax, VA 22030

Jim Lewis (9 YRS. W-134, L-121)

Winthrop■	N27	Richmond■	J23
Georgetown	N30	Old Dominion■	J27
Hawaii Tr.	D3-5	William & Mary	J30
Loyola (Md.)■	D 9	American■	F 3
Md.-Balt. County■	D11	La Salle	F 5
Coppin St.	D18	Delaware	F 8
Howard	D22	N.C.-Wilmington■	F11
Princeton■	D29	East Caro.■	F13
Monmouth (N.J.)■	D31	James Madison	F17
Va. Commonwealth	J 5	Richmond	F20
Siena■	J 9	Old Dominion	F24
East Caro.	J14	William & Mary■	F27
N.C.-Wilmington	J16	American	M 3
James Madison■	J20	CAA Tr.	M10-12

Colors: Green & Gold. Nickname: Patriots.
AD: Jack Kvancz. SID: Carl Sell. I

■ Home games on each schedule.

See pages 735-738 for Division I tournament details

GEO. WASHINGTON .... Washington, DC 20052

Joe McKeown (7 YRS. W-150, L-59)

Coppin St.■ N27
Geo. Washington Cl. D3-4
Georgetown .... D 8
Vanderbilt■ D21
Florida Int'l Tr. J2-4
Duquesne .... J 8
Maryland■ J12
West Va. J15
Rhode Island■ J20
St. Joseph's (Pa.)■ J22
Massachusetts J26
Rutgers J29
Temple■ .... F 2
Duquesne■ .... F 5
American .... F 8
Rhode Island F12
Rutgers■ F15
St. Bonaventure■ F17
St. Joseph's (Pa.) F19
Temple F23
Massachusetts■ F26
St. Bonaventure F28
West Va.■ .... M 3

Colors: Buff & Blue. Nickname: Colonial Women.
AD: Steve Bilsky. SID: Brad Bower. I

GEORGETOWN .... Washington, DC 20057

Patrick Knapp (10 YRS. W-140, L-141)

Kentucky Inv. N26-27
George Mason■ N30
Mt. St. Mary's (Md.) .... D 4
Geo. Washington■ .... D 8
Miami (Fla.) D11
Cornell■ D20
Notre Dame■ D30
Princeton■ D31
Villanova .... J 3
Boston College■ .... J 5
Connecticut .... J 9
Pittsburgh■ J12
Syracuse J15
St. John's (N.Y.)■ J20
Providence■ J22
Seton Hall J26
Villanova■ J29
Connecticut■ .... F 2
Boston College .... F 5
Providence .... F 9
Syracuse■ F12
Miami (Fla.)■ F17
St. John's (N.Y.) F19
Pittsburgh F23
Seton Hall■ F26
Big East Tr. M4-7

Colors: Blue & Gray. Nickname: Hoyas.
AD: Francis X. Rienzo. SID: Bill Hurd. I

GEORGIA .... Athens, GA 30613

Andy Landers (14 YRS. W-344, L-103)

Furman N28
DePaul .... D 5
Loyola (Ill.) .... D 7
Marquette .... D 8
Stephen F. Austin■ D11
Georgia St. Inv. D14-15
Southern-B.R.■ D18
St. John's Inv. D29-30
Alabama .... J 5
Arkansas .... J 8
Mercer■ J10
Fla. Atlantic■ J12
Vanderbilt J16
Louisiana St.■ J18
Kentucky■ J23
South Caro.■ J29
Tennessee Tech■ .... F 2
Mississippi St.⊠ .... F 6
Florida .... F 9
Mississippi F12
Florida Int'l■ F14
Auburn F20
South Caro. St. F23
Tennessee■ F27
Southeastern Tr. M4-7
⊠ Atlanta, GA

Colors: Red & Black. Nickname: Lady Bulldogs.
AD: Vince Dooley. SID: Claude Felton. I

GEORGIA COL. .... Milledgeville, GA 31061

John Carrick (10 YRS. W-163, L-120)

Kennesaw St. N24
Clark Atlanta■ .... D 1
Erskine .... D 4
Georgia Col. Cl. D10-11
Kennesaw St.■ D15
Clayton St.■ .... J 3
Armstrong St.■ .... J 6
Pembroke St. .... J 8
S.C.-Spartanburg■ J13
S.C.-Aiken J15
Columbus J19
Lander■ J22
Valdosta St. J24
Augusta J26
Francis Marion J29
S.C.-Spartanburg J31
Columbus■ .... F 3
Francis Marion■ .... F 5
Augusta■ .... F 7
Pembroke St.■ F12
Erskine■ F14
S.C.-Aiken■ F17
Lander F19
Valdosta St.■ F21
Armstrong St. F26

Colors: Brown & Gold. Nickname: Lady Colonials.
AD: Stan Aldridge. SID: Don Carswell. II

GA. SOUTHERN .... Statesboro, GA 30460

Drema Greer (8 YRS. W-156, L-82)

South Caro. .... D 6
Ala.-Birmingham Tr. D10-11
Georgia St. Inv. D14-15
Ga. Southern Inv. D29-30
Tenn.-Chatt.■ .... J 3
N.C.-Wilmington Tr. J7-8
N.C.-Charlotte■ J11
Marshall■ J15
East Tenn. St.■ J17
Furman J22
Davidson■ J24
South Fla.■ J26
Appalachian St. J29
Western Caro. J31
Tenn.-Chatt. .... F 5
Marshall F12
East Tenn. St. F14
Davidson F17
Furman■ F22
Appalachian St.■ F26
Western Caro.■ F28
Mercer .... M 7
Southern Tr. M10-12

Colors: Blue & White. Nickname: Lady Eagles.
AD: David Wagner. SID: To be named. I

GEORGIA ST. .... Atlanta, GA 30303

Brenda Paul (15 YRS. W-260, L-184)

Alabama St.■ N26
Georgia St. Cl. N27
Alabama St. .... D 8
Troy St. D11
Georgia St. Inv. D14-15
Coastal Caro. Cl. D29-30
Maine Shootout J2-3
Troy St.■ .... J 6
Florida Int'l J13
Fla. Atlantic J15
Central Fla.■ J20
Stetson■ J22
Charleston J27
Mercer J29
Western Caro.■ .... F 2
Southeastern La.■ .... F 5
Florida Int'l■ F12
Stetson F17
Central Fla. F19
Mercer■ F24
Charleston■ F26
Fla. Atlantic■ .... M 3
Southeastern La. .... M 5

Colors: Royal & Crimson. Nickname: Lady Panther.
AD: Orby Moss. SID: Martin Harmon. I

GEORGIA TECH .... Atlanta, GA 30332

Agnus Berenato (9 YRS. W-138, L-123)

Minnesota■ .... D 1
Georgia Tech Cl. D3-4
Georgia St. Inv. D14-15
Florida St. D18
Rider D29
Maryland .... J 2
Tenn.-Chatt.■ .... J 5
North Caro. St.■ .... J 8
Wake Forest■ J10
Duke J14
North Caro. J16
Furman J19
Virginia J22
Clemson J26
Maryland■ J30
Florida St.■ .... F 1
Virginia■ .... F 6
East Tenn. St. .... F 9
North Caro.■ F12
Mercer F14
North Caro. St. F18
Wake Forest F20
Clemson■ F25
Duke■ F27
ACC Tr. M4-7

Colors: Old Gold & White. Nickname: Lady Jackets.
AD: Homer Rice. SID: Mike Finn. I

GETTYSBURG .... Gettysburg, PA 17325

Michael Kirkpatrick (4 YRS. W-40, L-52)

Frostburg St. Inv. N19-20
Bryn Mawr N23
Ursinus■ N30
York (Pa.)■ .... D 7
Messiah■ D11
Gettysburg Tr. J7-8
Swarthmore■ J13
Muhlenberg■ J15
Dickinson■ J18
Washington (Md.) J22
Frank. & Marsh. J26
Johns Hopkins J29
Western Md.■ .... F 1
Lebanon Valley .... F 3
Dickinson .... F 8
Elizabethtown F10
Frank. & Marsh.■ F12
Johns Hopkins■ F15
Haverford F17
Western Md. F19
Albright F22

Colors: Orange & Blue. Nickname: Lady Bullets.
AD: Charles Winters. SID: Robert Kenworthy. III

GLENVILLE ST. .... Glenville, WV 26351

Russ Shepherd (5 YRS. W-86, L-56)

Shepherd Tr. N19-20
Marietta Tr. N27
Charleston (W.Va.)■ .... D 1
Concord■ .... D 4
Salem-Teikyo .... D 6
West Va. Wesleyan■ .... D 8
Davis & Elkins D11
Fairmont St. J12
Ohio Valley■ J13
Charleston (W.Va.) J17
West Va. Tech J19
Alderson-Broaddus■ J22
Bluefield St. J24
Ohio Valley J27
Davis & Elkins■ J31
West Va. St. .... F 2
Fairmont St.■ .... F 5
West Liberty St. .... F 7
West Va. Wesleyan .... F 9
West Va. Tech■ F12
Alderson-Broaddus F14
Bluefield St.■ F16

Colors: Blue & White. Nickname: Lady Pioneers.
AD: Russ Shepherd. SID: Mark Loudin. II

GONZAGA .... Spokane, WA 99202

Julie Holt (11 YRS. W-115, L-184)

Idaho N26
Whitworth (Wash.)■ .... D 1
Lewis-Clark St.■ .... D 7
Washington St. D11
Washington■ D18
Brigham Young Cl. D29-30
Montana St.■ .... J 4
Montana■ .... J 6
Eastern Wash. .... J 8
San Diego St. J11
San Diego J13
San Francisco J15
Santa Clara■ J20
St. Mary's (Cal.)■ J22
St. Mary's (Cal.) J28
Santa Clara J29
Loyola (Cal.)■ .... F 3
Pepperdine■ .... F 5
Pepperdine F11
Loyola (Cal.) F12
Portland■ F16
Portland F19
San Francisco■ F24
San Diego■ F26
West Coast Tr. M11-12

Colors: Blue, White & Red. Nickname: Bulldogs.
AD: Dan Fitzgerald. SID: Oliver Pierce. I

■ Home games on each schedule.

See pages 735-738 for Division I tournament details

GORDON .... Wenham, MA 01984

Amy Reiter (2 YRS. W-23, L-29)

Curry	N20
MIT■	N23
Tufts	D 1
Worcester Tech	D 4
New England Col.■	D 7
Western New Eng.	D 9
Southern Me.	D14
Western Conn. Tr.	D28-29
St. Joseph's (Me.)	J 4
Bates■	J 6
Salem St.	J12
Suffolk	J14
Elms■	J18
Amherst	J22
Pine Manor■	J27
Nichols	J29
Norwich■	F 1
Rhode Island Col.	F 3
Eastern Nazarene■	F 8
New England	F10
Emmanuel■	F15
Colby■	F18
Me.-Farmington■	F19
Clark (Mass.)	F22

Colors: Blue, Gold & White. Nickname: The Fighting Scots.
AD: Walter Bowman. SID: None. III

GOUCHER .... Towson, MD 21204

Noelle Navarro (3 YRS. W-28, L-41)

Goucher Tr.	N19-20
Immaculata	N22
Columbia Union■	N30
Montclair St. Cl.	D3-4
Shepherd■	D 6
Holy Family	D10
St. John Fisher Inv.	J8-9
York (Pa.)	J13
St. Mary's (Md.)	J15
Gallaudet	J18
Mary Washington■	J22
Salisbury St.■	J24
Catholic■	J27
Marymount (Va.)	J29
York (Pa.)■	F 1
Catholic	F 3
St. Mary's (Md.)■	F 5
Wesley	F 9
Gallaudet■	F12
Mary Washington	F15
Marymount (Va.)■	F17

Colors: Royal Blue & Gold. Nickname: Gophers.
AD: William J. Kaiser. SID: Kevin Fillman. III

GRAMBLING .... Grambling, LA 71245

Pat Bibbs (9 YRS. W-155, L-96)

Southern-N.O.	N26
Ark.-Pine Bluff■	N29
Alabama Cl.	D3-4
Texas Col.■	D11
Mississippi	D13
McNeese St.■	D16
Morgan St.■	D18
Central Fla.■	J 5
Alcorn St.■	J 8
Southern-B.R.■	J10
Texas Southern	J15
Prairie View	J17
Southern-N.O.■	J19
Alabama St.■	J22
Jackson St.■	J24
Mississippi Val.	J29
Southeastern La.■	F 1
Alcorn St.	F 5
Southern-B.R.	F 7
Texas Southern■	F12
Prairie View■	F14
Mississippi■	F16
Alabama St.	F19
Jackson St.	F21
Mississippi Val.■	F26
Arkansas St.	M 3
SWAC Tr.	M10-13

Colors: Black & Gold. Nickname: Tigers.
AD: Fred Hobdy. SID: Stanley Lewis. I

GRAND CANYON .... Phoenix, AZ 85017

Julie Hanks (1ST YR. AS HEAD COACH)

Cal Poly Pomona Cl.	N19-20
Grand Canyon Inv.	N26-27
Northern Ariz.	D 3
Southern Utah■	D 6
Humboldt St.■	D 9
Western N. Mex.■	D11
Cal St. Los Angeles	D15
Cal Baptist	D16
UC Riverside	D17
Grand Canyon Cl.	D30-31
Southern Utah	J 5
Western N. Mex.	J15
Eastern Mont.	J21
Eastern Mont.	J22
Portland St.	J27
Seattle Pacific	J29
Alas. Anchorage■	F 3
Alas. Fairbanks■	F 5
Eastern Mont.■	F10
Portland St.■	F17
Seattle Pacific■	F19
Alas. Anchorage	F24
Alas. Fairbanks	F26

Colors: Purple & White. Nickname: Antelopes.
AD: Gil Stafford. SID: Elizabeth Warner. II

GRAND VALLEY ST. .... Allendale, MI 49401

Pat Baker-Grzyb (14 YRS. W-211, L-168)

Grand Rapids Bapt.■	N20
Grand Rapids Tr.	N26-27
Calvin	N30
Northwood■	D 4
Aquinas	D 7
Oakland	D 9
Hillsdale	D11
St. Francis (Ill.)	D20
Wis.-Parkside	D30
Michigan Tech■	J 6
Northern Mich.■	J 8
Saginaw Valley	J15
Lake Superior St.	J20
Wayne St. (Mich.)■	J22
Ferris St.■	J27
Northwood	J29
Oakland■	F 3
Hillsdale■	F 5
Michigan Tech	F10
Northern Mich.	F12
Saginaw Valley■	F19
Ferris St.	F21
Lake Superior St.■	F24
Wayne St. (Mich.)	F26

Colors: Blue, Black & White. Nickname: Lakers.
AD: Michael Kovalchik. SID: Don Thomas. II

GREENSBORO .... Greensboro, NC 27420

Steve Johnson (1 YR. W-11, L-14)

Marymount (Va.) Tr.	N19-21
Guilford	N23
Roanoke	N30
Greensboro Tr.	D3-4
Lynchburg■	D 7
Hollins	J 8
Methodist■	J12
Averett	J16
Shenandoah	J19
Maryville (Tenn.)■	J22
Ferrum■	J25
N.C. Wesleyan	J29
Chris. Newport	J30
Methodist	F 3
Averett■	F 5
Meredith	F 7
N.C. Wesleyan■	F 9
Shenandoah■	F12
Ferrum	F14
Chris. Newport■	F18

Colors: Green & White. Nickname: Pride.
AD: Kim Strable. SID: Samuel Hanger. III

GRINNELL .... Grinnell, IA 50112

Marti Kingsley (1ST YR. AS HEAD COACH)

Grinnell Tr.	N19-20
William Penn■	N23
Maryville (Mo.)	N28
Teiko-Marycrest■	N30
Loras	D 4
Coe	D 7
North Park	J 7
Blackburn	J11
Illinois Col.■	J15
Knox	J18
Lake Forest	J21
Beloit	J22
Monmouth (Ill.)■	J25
St. Norbert■	J28
Lawrence■	J29
Cornell College■	F 2
Knox■	F 5
Coe■	F 8
Monmouth (Ill.)	F12
Illinois Col.	F19
Cornell College	F21

Colors: Scarlet & Black. Nickname: Pioneers.
AD: Dee Fairchild. SID: Andy Hamilton. III

GROVE CITY .... Grove City, PA 16127

Melissa VanHeukelem (1ST YR. AS HEAD COACH)

John Carroll■	D 2
Carlow■	D 4
Geneva■	D 8
Westminster (Pa.)	D11
Baldwin-Wallace■	D14
Geneva	J 8
Carnegie Mellon	J10
Hiram	J13
Pitt-Bradford■	J17
Thiel■	J19
Bethany (W.Va.)■	J22
Westminster (Pa.)■	J24
Waynesburg■	J26
Wash. & Jeff.■	J29
St. Vincent■	J31
Penn St.-Behrend	F 2
Thiel	F 5
Allegheny■	F 7
Bethany (W.Va.)	F 9
Waynesburg	F12
Wash. & Jeff.	F16
Penn St.-Behrend■	F19

Colors: Crimson & White. Nickname: Lady Wolverines.
AD: R. Jack Behringer. SID: Joe Klimchak. III

GUILFORD .... Greensboro, NC 27410

To be named

N.C. Wesleyan	N20
Greensboro■	N23
Methodist■	N30
Greensboro Tr.	D3-4
Rand.-Macon Woman's	D 7
Hollins■	D 9
Bridgewater (Va.)■	D11
Randolph-Macon	J 7
Va. Wesleyan	J 8
Roanoke■	J11
Rand.-Macon Woman's■	J14
Lynchburg■	J15
Hollins	J18
East. Mennonite■	J22
Meredith■	J26
Emory & Henry	J28
Roanoke	F 2
Lynchburg	F 5
Va. Wesleyan■	F 8
East. Mennonite	F11
Bridgewater (Va.)	F12
Emory & Henry■	F17
Randolph-Macon■	F19

Colors: Crimson & Gray. Nickname: Quakers.
AD: Gayle Currie. SID: Brett Ayers. III

GUST. ADOLPHUS .... St. Peter, MN 56082

Peg Moline (1 YR. W-14, L-11)

Mankato St.■	N23
Concordia-M'head■	D 4
Wartburg	D 7
Carleton■	D10
Colorado Col. Tr.	D29-31
Hamline■	J 5
Bethel (Minn.)■	J 8
Augsburg	J10
St. Mary's (Minn.)■	J12
St. Benedict	J15
St. Thomas (Minn.)■	J17
St. Olaf	J19
Concordia-M'head	J26
Carleton	J29
Macalester	J31
Hamline	F 2
Bethel (Minn.)	F 5
Augsburg■	F 9
St. Mary's (Minn.)	F12
St. Thomas (Minn.)	F16
St. Olaf■	F19
Macalester■	F23
St. Benedict■	F26

Colors: Black & Gold. Nickname: Golden Gusties.
AD: James Malmquist. SID: Tim Kennedy. III

■ Home games on each schedule.

See pages 735-738 for Division I tournament details

HAMILTON .... Clinton, NY 13323

Donald Crist (8 YRS. W-134, L-55)

Trinity (Conn.) Tr.	N20-21	St. Lawrence	J25
Oswego St.■	N30	Le Moyne■	J27
Elmira	D 2	Hartwick■	F 1
Utica Tech Cl.	D4-5	Oneonta St.■	F 3
Skidmore	D 9	Williams	F 5
Rensselaer■	J11	Utica Tech	F 8
William Smith■	J13	Utica	F10
Bates■	J15	Union (N.Y.)	F12
Colby■	J16	Albany (N.Y.)	F15
Clarkson■	J18	Russell Sage■	F19
Nazareth (N.Y.)	J22		

Colors: Buff & Blue. Nickname: Continentals.
AD: Thomas Murphy. SID: Russell Christ. III

HAMPTON .... Hampton, VA 23668

Tiny Laster (21 YRS. W-391, L-209)

Columbia Union■	N20	Virginia Union■	J15
Fayetteville St.■	N23	Virginia St.	J18
Hampton Tr.	N26-27	Columbia Union	J20
Johnson Smith■	N29	Virginia Union	J22
Fort Valley St. Inv.	D3-4	Livingstone	J24
Bowie St.■	D 7	Elizabeth City St.	J27
Winston-Salem	D 9	Norfolk St.	F 1
Shaw	D11	St. Paul's	F 5
St. Paul's■	J 3	Virginia St.■	F 8
N.C. Central	J 6	Norfolk St.■	F12
St. Augustine's■	J 8	Bowie St.	F18
Elizabeth City St.■	J12		

Colors: Royal Blue & White. Nickname: Lady Pirates.
AD: Dennis Thomas. SID: LeCounte Conaway. II

HARTFORD .... West Hartford, CT 06117

Allison Jones (4 YRS. W-85, L-33)

Holy Cross	N28	Maine	J22
Siena	D 1	Lehigh	J24
Hartford Cl.	D4-5	Drexel	J28
Yale	D 8	Delaware	J30
Delaware St.■	D11	Vermont■	F 5
Dartmouth■	D13	Delaware■	F11
St. Peter's	D15	Drexel■	F13
Central Conn. St.	D29	Maine■	F17
Army	J 5	New Hampshire■	F19
Brown■	J 8	Boston U.	F24
Boston U.■	J13	Northeastern■	F26
Northeastern	J15	Vermont	M 2
New Hampshire	J20	North Atlantic Tr.	M6-12

Colors: Scarlet & White. Nickname: Lady Hawks.
AD: Pat Meiser-McKnett. SID: Andy Bean. I

HARTWICK .... Oneonta, NY 13820

Daphne Joy (1 YR. W-15, L-9)

Hartwick Inv.	N20-21	Alfred■	J29
Utica■	D 1	Hamilton	F 1
Nazareth (N.Y.)	D 8	Rochester Inst.	F 4
William Smith■	J 7	William Smith	F 5
Rochester Inst.■	J 8	Oneonta St.■	F 8
St. John Fisher■	J11	Alfred	F11
Rensselaer■	J13	Ithaca	F12
Elmira	J17	Rensselaer	F15
Clarkson	J21	St. Lawrence■	F18
St. Lawrence	J22	Clarkson■	F19
Union (N.Y.)	J25	Skidmore	F21
Ithaca■	J28		

Colors: Royal Blue & White. Nickname: Warriors.
AD: Ken Kutler. SID: Tim Markey. III

HARVARD .... Cambridge, MA 02138

Kathleen Delaney Smith (11 YRS. W-150, L-136)

William & Mary	N27	New Hampshire■	F 1
Army	D 1	Yale	F 4
Harvard Inv.	D4-5	Brown	F 5
Rhode Island■	D11	Cornell■	F11
Boston U.	D14	Columbia-Barnard■	F12
Vermont Tr.	D21-22	Princeton	F18
Vanderbilt■	D30	Pennsylvania	F19
Northeastern	J 3	Columbia-Barnard	F25
Pennsylvania■	J 7	Cornell	F26
Princeton■	J 8	Brown■	M 4
Dartmouth	J15	Yale■	M 5
Central Conn. St.	J29	Dartmouth■	M 8

Colors: Crimson, Black & White. Nickname: Crimson.
AD: William Cleary. SID: John Veneziano. I

HAWAII .... Honolulu, HI 96822

Vince Goo (6 YRS. W-125, L-54)

Hawaii Cl.	N26-27	UC Santa Barb.■	J30
Hawaii Tr.	D3-6	UC Irvine	F 8
Southern Utah■	D17	UC Irvine	F 9
Southern Utah■	D18	Cal St. Fullerton	F11
Oregon St.	D20	Cal St. Fullerton	F12
Oregon	D22	Long Beach St.■	F18
Nevada-Las Vegas	J 3	Long Beach St.■	F20
Nevada-Las Vegas	J 5	Pacific (Cal.)■	F25
Nevada	J 7	Pacific (Cal.)■	F26
Nevada	J 8	San Jose St.■	M 4
New Mexico St.■	J13	San Jose St.■	M 6
New Mexico St.■	J15	Big West Tr.	M9-12
UC Santa Barb.■	J28		

Colors: Green & White. Nickname: Rainbow Wahine.
AD: Marilyn Kahoohanohano. SID: Lois Manin. I

HEIDELBERG .... Tiffin, OH 44883

Karen McConnell (5 YRS. W-97, L-44)

Frostburg St. Inv.	N19-20	Muskingum	J15
Hiram■	N30	Baldwin-Wallace■	J18
Heidelberg Tr.	D3-4	Marietta■	J22
Capital■	D 7	Capital	J25
Marietta	D11	Otterbein■	J29
Mount Union	D18	Ohio Northern	F 1
Bluffton■	D20	Mount Union■	F 5
Thomas More	D22	Baldwin-Wallace	F 8
Ohio Northern■	J 4	Muskingum■	F12
Otterbein	J 8	John Carroll	F15
John Carroll■	J11	Hiram	F17

Colors: Red, Orange, Black. Nickname: Student Princes.
AD: John Hill. SID: Dick Edmond. III

HENDERSON ST. .... Arkadelphia, AR 71923

David Thigpen (4 YRS. W-46, L-63)

Arkansas Tech	N19	Ala.-Huntsville■	J17
Arkansas Col.■	N22	Delta St.	J22
Ark.-Monticello	N27	Central Ark.■	J27
Southern St.	N29	Delta St.■	J29
West Tex. A&M Tr.	D2-4	Livingston■	J31
Southwest Bapt. Cl.	D10-11	North Ala.	F 5
East Tex. St.■	J 4	Ala.-Huntsville	F 7
Arkansas Tech■	J 6	Mississippi Col.■	F12
Livingston	J 8	Mississippi-Women■	F14
Mississippi Col.	J11	Central Ark.	F19
North Ala.■	J15	Mississippi-Women	F24

Colors: Red & Gray. Nickname: Lady Reddies.
AD: Ken Turner. SID: Steve Eddington. II

HENDRIX .... Conway, AR 72032

Mike Ritchie (1 YR. W-7, L-16)

Westminst. (Mo.) Cl.	N19-20	Fisk	J23
La. St.-Shreveport■	N22	Oglethorpe■	J28
John Brown	N29	Sewanee■	J30
Maryville (Mo.)	D 3	Millsaps	F 4
Webster	D 4	Rhodes	F 6
Philander Smith■	D11	Oglethorpe	F11
La. St.-Shreveport	J 5	Sewanee	F13
Southwestern (Tex.)	J 8	Centre■	F18
Trinity (Tex.)	J 9	Fisk■	F20
Millsaps■	J14	Philander Smith	F22
Rhodes■	J16	Trinity (Tex.)■	F26
Centre	J21	Southwestern (Tex.)■	F27

Colors: Black & Orange. Nickname: Warriors.
AD: Cliff Garrison. SID: Ann Turney. III

HIGH POINT .... High Point, NC 27262

Joe Ellenburg (5 YRS. W-74, L-68)

High Point Cl.	N19-20	Belmont Abbey■	J22
Lenoir-Rhyne■	N23	Pfeiffer■	J26
Catawba	N30	Coker	J29
Pembroke St.	D 2	Lees-McRae■	F 2
Lenoir-Rhyne	D 4	Wingate	F 3
Lees-McRae	D 7	St. Andrews■	F 5
Elon	D11	Mt. Olive■	F 8
Davis & Elkins■	J 8	Pfeiffer	F12
Barton	J12	Belmont Abbey	F16
St. Andrews	J15	Coker■	F19
Longwood■	J17	Barton■	F21
Mt. Olive	J19		

Colors: Purple & White. Nickname: Panthers.
AD: Jerry Steele. SID: Woody Gibson. II

■ Home games on each schedule.

See pages 735-738 for Division I tournament details

HILLSDALE .... Hillsdale, MI 49242

Rose Antrim (1 YR. W-7, L-19)

Spring Arbor■	N20	Wayne St. (Mich.)	J20
Defiance	N23	Ferris St.■	J22
Aquinas	N30	Michigan Tech■	J27
Hillsdale Cl.	D3-4	Northern Mich.■	J29
Northwood■	D 9	Northwood	F 3
Grand Valley St.■	D11	Grand Valley St.	F 5
Michigan Tech	D18	Lake Superior St.■	F10
Northern Mich.	D20	Saginaw Valley■	F12
IU/PU-Indianapolis	D30	Albion	F17
Lake Superior St.	J 6	Oakland	F19
Saginaw Valley	J 8	Wayne St. (Mich.)■	F24
Findlay■	J10	Ferris St.	F26
Oakland■	J15		

Colors: Royal Blue & White. Nickname: Chargers.
AD: Jack McAvoy. SID: Brian Boyse. II

HIRAM .... Hiram, OH 44234

Cindy McKnight (6 YRS. W-67, L-87)

Bluffton	N27	Capital	J15
Heidelberg	N30	John Carroll■	J18
Penn St.-Behrend■	D 2	Baldwin-Wallace	J22
Otterbein	D 7	Otterbein■	J25
Mount Union■	D11	Mount Union	J29
Ohio Northern	D14	Capital■	F 1
Defiance Cl.	D17-18	Ohio Northern■	F 5
Baldwin-Wallace■	J 4	John Carroll	F 8
Thiel■	J 6	Marietta■	F12
Marietta	J 8	Muskingum	F15
Muskingum■	J11	Heidelberg■	F17
Grove City■	J13		

Colors: Red & Blue. Nickname: Terriers.
AD: Cindy McKinight. SID: Renee Arnold. III

HOFSTRA .... Hempstead, NY 11550

Margaret McKeon (1ST YR. AS HEAD COACH)

Lafayette	N27	Yale■	J19
LIU-Brooklyn	D 1	Buffalo■	J21
Harvard Inv.	D4-5	Dartmouth■	J22
Lehigh■	D 8	Md.-East. Shore	J27
Monmouth (N.J.)	D11	Loyola (Md.)	F 2
Wagner■	D20	Central Conn. St.■	F 4
St. Francis (N.Y.)	D30	Bucknell■	F 6
Siena■	J 3	Drexel■	F 8
Northeastern	J 5	Fordham■	F14
Colgate	J10	Army■	F22
Columbia-Barnard■	J12	Chicago St.	F26
Troy St.■	J14	Northeastern Ill.	F28
Cornell■	J17	East Coast Tr.	M3-6

Colors: Blue, White & Gold. Nickname: Flying Dutchwomen.
AD: Jim Garvey. SID: Jim Sheehan. I

HOLLINS .... Hollins, VA 24019

Laura Williges (2 YRS. W-22, L-25)

Bridgewater (Va.)	D 2	Roanoke■	J24
East. Mennonite	D 4	Rand.-Macon Woman's	J27
Emory & Henry	D 7	East. Mennonite■	J28
Guilford	D 9	Lynchburg■	F 1
Rand.-Macon Woman's■	D10	Ferrum	F 3
Greensboro■	J 8	Randolph-Macon■	F 4
Lynchburg	J10	Roanoke	F 6
Va. Wesleyan	J14	Wash. & Lee■	F 9
Randolph-Macon	J15	Va. Wesleyan■	F11
Averett	J17	Bridgewater (Va.)■	F15
Guilford■	J18	Wash. & Lee	F16
Bennett■	J20	Emory & Henry	F19

Colors: Green & Gold.
AD: Lynda J. Calkins. SID: None. III

HOLY CROSS .... Worcester, MA 01610

Bill Gibbons Jr. (8 YRS. W-165, L-71)

Hartford■	N28	Navy	J26
Boston College	D 1	Bucknell	J29
Connecticut Cl.	D4-5	Fordham■	F 2
Siena■	D 9	Army	F 5
Northwestern■	D19	Lehigh	F 9
Iowa St.	D30	Colgate■	F12
Nebraska	J 2	Boston U.■	F14
Vermont	J 6	Lafayette	F16
Fordham	J 8	Navy■	F19
Army■	J12	New Hampshire	F22
Lehigh■	J15	Bucknell■	F26
Colgate	J19	Central Conn. St.■	F28
Lafayette■	J22	Patriot Tr.	M3-12

Colors: Royal Purple & White. Nickname: Crusaders.
AD: Ron Perry. SID: Rose Shea. I

HOPE .... Holland, MI 49423

Tod Gugino (1ST YR. AS HEAD COACH)

Ferris St.	N20	Calvin	J11
Concordia (Mich.)	N23	Albion■	J15
Grand Rapids Tr.	N26-27	Olivet■	J19
St. Mary's (Ind.)	N30	Alma	J22
Hope Cl.	D3-4	Adrian	J26
North Central■	D 9	Kalamazoo	J29
Taylor■	D11	Calvin■	F 4
Saginaw Valley	D18	Albion	F 9
Elmhurst■	D29	Olivet	F12
Northwood	D31	Alma■	F16
Kalamazoo■	J 5	Adrian■	F19

Colors: Blue & Orange. Nickname: Flying Dutch.
AD: Anne Irwin. SID: Tom Renner. III

HOUSTON .... Houston, TX 77204

Jessie Kenlaw (3 YRS. W-53, L-36)

Houston Cl.	N26-27	Southern Methodist■	J26
Texas Southern	D 1	Texas	J29
Manhattan Cl.	D4-5	Rice■	F 5
Stephen F. Austin	D 8	Texas Christian	F 9
Lamar■	D12	Texas Tech	F12
Oklahoma St.	D19	Texas A&M■	F16
Southern Cal Cl.	D29-30	Baylor	F19
Texas Christian	J12	Southern Methodist	F23
Texas Tech■	J15	Texas■	F26
Texas A&M	J19	Rice	M 5
Baylor■	J22	Southwest Tr.	M9-12

Colors: Scarlet & White. Nickname: Lady Cougars.
AD: Bill Carr. SID: John Sullivan. I

HOWARD .... Washington, DC 20059

Sanya Tyler (12 YRS. W-160, L-174)

Richmond■	N26	Delaware St.	J15
Maryland	N29	Bethune-Cookman	J20
North Caro. St.	D 1	Coppin St.	J29
Navy	D 7	Va. Commonwealth■	F 2
Mt. St. Mary's (Md.)	D 9	Coppin St.■	F 5
Duquesne	D11	Bethune-Cookman■	F10
George Mason■	D22	North Caro. A&T	F19
Wagner Tr.	D28-29	South Caro. St.	F21
North Caro. A&T■	J 8	Delaware St.■	F24
South Caro. St.■	J10	MEAC Tr.	M9-13
Md.-East. Shore■	J13		

Colors: Blue & White. Nickname: Bisonettes.
AD: David Simmons. SID: Edward Hill, Jr. I

HUNTER .... New York, NY 10021

Jackee Meadow (1ST YR. AS HEAD COACH)

Hunter Tr.	N19-20	Concordia (N.Y.)	J18
St. Elizabeth■	N23	Manhattanville■	J20
Dominican (N.Y.)■	N29	John Jay■	J22
American Int'l■	D 1	CCNY	J24
Old Westbury■	D 3	York (N.Y.)■	J26
John Jay	D 6	Baruch	J28
Staten Island Tr.	D29-30	Stony Brook	F 1
Medgar Evers■	J 4	Mt. St. Vincent	F 4
Russell Sage	J 8	New York U.■	F 8
New Paltz St.	J13	CCNY■	F10
Albany (N.Y.)■	J15	Staten Island■	F16

Colors: Purple, White & Gold. Nickname: Hawks.
AD: Terry Ann Wansart. SID: Ron Ratner. III

IDAHO .... Moscow, ID 83843

Laurie Turner (11 YRS. W-171 , L-135)

Gonzaga■	N26	Weber St.	J27
Simon Fraser■	N29	Northern Ariz.	J29
Idaho Cl.	D3-4	Idaho St.■	F 4
Washington St.■	D17	Boise St.■	F 5
Portland■	D18	Montana St.	F11
Santa Clara■	D28	Montana	F12
Lewis-Clark St.■	D30	Eastern Wash.■	F17
Southern Utah	J 3	Southern Utah■	F18
Utah	J 4	Northern Ariz.■	F24
St. Mary's (Cal.)■	J 7	Weber St.■	F26
Montana■	J14	Idaho St.	M 4
Montana St.■	J15	Boise St.	M 6
Eastern Wash.	J22	Big Sky Tr.	M11-12

Colors: Silver & Gold. Nickname: Vandals.
AD: Pete Liske. SID: Rance Pugmire. I

■ Home games on each schedule.

See pages 735-738 for Division I tournament details

IDAHO ST. — Pocatello, ID 83209

Ted Anderson (12 YRS. W-168, L-152)

- Kentucky Inv. N26-27
- Southern Utah D 1
- Utah■ D 4
- Portland D 9
- Oregon D11
- New Mexico St. Cl. D21-22
- Western Mont.■ D30
- Wyoming J 7
- Colorado St. J 8
- Weber St. J13
- Northern Ariz. J15
- Boise St.■ J22
- Montana■ J28
- Montana St.■ J29
- Idaho F 4
- Eastern Wash. F 5
- Northern Ariz.■ F10
- Weber St.■ F12
- Southern Utah■ F16
- Boise St. F19
- Montana St. F25
- Montana F26
- Idaho■ M 4
- Eastern Wash.■ M 5
- Big Sky Tr. M11-12

Colors: Orange & Black. Nickname: Bengals.
AD: Randy Hoffman. SID: Dave Geringer. I

ILLINOIS — Champaign, IL 61820

Kathy Lindsey (3 YRS. W-30, L-53)

- Illinois St.■ D 1
- Loyola (Ill.)■ D 4
- Ill.-Chicago D 7
- Southern Ill. D11
- Miami (Ohio)■ D19
- Missouri D21
- Maine Shootout J2-3
- Ohio St.■ J 5
- Alabama■ J 7
- Penn St.■ J 9
- Iowa J14
- Minnesota■ J16
- Northwestern J19
- Wisconsin J21
- Indiana■ J28
- Purdue J30
- Michigan F 4
- Michigan St. F 6
- Iowa■ F13
- Northwestern■ F16
- Wisconsin■ F20
- Indiana F27
- Michigan■ M 4
- Michigan St.■ M 6
- Penn St. M10
- Ohio St. M12

Colors: Orange & Blue. Nickname: Fighting Illini.
AD: Ron Guenther. SID: Mike Pearson. I

ILL. BENEDICTINE — Lisle, IL 60532

Dave Swanson (13 YRS. W-181, L-123)

- Ill. Wesleyan N23
- North Park N27
- Lake Forest■ N30
- Wheaton (Ill.) D 4
- Elmhurst D 7
- MacMurray D11
- Loras■ D21
- Nat'l Catholic Tr. J5-9
- Concordia (Ill.) J15
- Judson J18
- North Central■ J20
- Rockford■ J22
- Aurora J25
- Trinity (Ill.)■ J29
- Millikin■ F 1
- Concordia (Ill.)■ F 5
- Judson■ F 8
- Rockford F12
- Aurora■ F19
- Trinity (Ill.) F22
- Augustana (Ill.)■ F26

Colors: Cardinal & White. Nickname: Eagles.
AD: Tony Lascala. SID: Keith Bernkenberg. III

ILLINOIS COL. — Jacksonville, IL 62650

Brenna Kelly (6 YRS. W-87, L-51)

- SIU-Edwardsville■ N19
- Augustana (Ill.)■ N27
- Washington (Mo.)■ N30
- Monmouth (Ill.) D 7
- Knox■ D11
- Blackburn D14
- Cornell College J 7
- Coe J 8
- Grinnell J15
- Lawrence J21
- St. Norbert J22
- Principia J25
- Ripon■ J28
- Carroll (Wis.)■ J29
- Monmouth (Ill.)■ F 1
- Millikin■ F 3
- MacMurray■ F 6
- Knox F 9
- Coe■ F12
- Cornell College■ F18
- Grinnell■ F19

Colors: Blue & White. Nickname: Lady Blues.
AD: William Anderson. SID: James T. Murphy. III

ILLINOIS ST. — Normal, IL 61761

Jill Hutchison (22 YRS. W-385, L-229)

- Michigan St.■ N26
- Northwestern N28
- Illinois D 1
- Geo. Washington Cl. D3-4
- Missouri■ D 8
- Iowa St. D18
- Old Dominion■ D20
- Marquette D29
- South Fla.■ D31
- Creighton J 2
- Drake J 4
- Indiana St.■ J 7
- Southern Ill.■ J 9
- Wichita St. J13
- Southwest Mo. St. J15
- Northern Iowa■ J20
- Bradley■ J22
- Indiana St. F 4
- Southern Ill. F 7
- Wichita St.■ F10
- Southwest Mo. St.■ F12
- Bradley F17
- Northern Iowa F19
- Creighton■ F28
- Drake■ M 2
- Missouri Valley Tr. M8-12

Colors: Red & White. Nickname: Redbirds.
AD: Rick Greenspan. SID: Tom Lamonica. I

ILL. WESLEYAN — Bloomington, IL 61702

Mandy Neal (5 YRS. W-51, L-77)

- DePauw Tr. N19-20
- Ill. Benedictine■ N23
- Knox■ D 1
- Aurora■ D 3
- Augustana (Ill.) D 7
- MacMurray D10
- Elmhurst■ J 5
- Augustana (Ill.)■ J 8
- Concordia (Ill.) J11
- Wheaton (Ill.) J14
- North Park J15
- Millikin■ J19
- Carthage J21
- Elmhurst J26
- Judson (Ala.) J28
- Southern-N.O. F 1
- Principia F 7
- North Central F 9
- Wheaton (Ill.)■ F12
- Eureka■ F15
- North Park■ F18
- Carthage■ F19
- Millikin F23
- North Central■ F26

Colors: Green & White. Nickname: Lady Titans.
AD: Dennis Bridges. SID: Stew Salowitz. III

ILL.-CHICAGO — Chicago, IL 60680

Eileen McMahon (3 YRS. W-30, L-54)

- Notre Dame N27
- Chicago St.■ N29
- Illinois■ D 7
- Wisconsin■ D13
- Loyola (Ill.) D18
- Michigan D20
- South Fla.■ D29
- Valparaiso■ J 2
- Northern Ill.■ J 6
- Western Ill.■ J 8
- Wis.-Green Bay J13
- Wis.-Milwaukee J15
- Youngstown St.■ J21
- Cleveland St.■ J23
- Eastern Ill. J27
- Wright St. J29
- DePaul■ F 1
- Valparaiso F 5
- Northern Ill. F10
- Western Ill. F12
- Wis.-Green Bay■ F17
- Wis.-Milwaukee■ F19
- Youngstown St. F24
- Cleveland St. F26
- Eastern Ill.■ M 3
- Wright St.■ M 5
- Mid-Continent Tr. M10-12

Colors: Indigo & Flame. Nickname: Flames.
AD: Tom Russo. SID: Anne Schoenherr. I

IMMACULATA — Immaculata, PA 19345

Mary Scharff (7 YRS. W-54, L-120)

- Phila. Pharmacy■ N20
- Goucher■ N22
- Eastern (Pa.)■ D 1
- Gwynedd Mercy D 7
- Rosemont■ D 9
- Neumann■ D11
- Catholic Tr. J8-9
- Eastern (Pa.) J11
- Notre Dame (Md.)■ J15
- Gwynedd Mercy■ J18
- Beaver■ J20
- Misericordia J22
- Neumann J24
- Cabrini J27
- Marywood■ J29
- Rosemont F 3
- Cabrini■ F 5
- Widener F10
- Alvernia■ F12
- Notre Dame (Md) Inv. F18-19
- Ursinus F22

Colors: Blue & White. Nickname: Mighty Macs.
AD: Lynn Reichert. SID: None. III

INDIANA — Bloomington, IN 47405

Jim Izard (12 YRS. W-239, L-114)

- Wright St. D 1
- Indiana Cl. D3-4
- Kentucky D 7
- Purdue Cl. D11
- Tenn.-Martin D20
- Eastern Ill.■ D22
- Indiana Cl. J2-3
- Michigan■ J 7
- Penn St. J14
- Ohio St. J16
- Iowa■ J21
- Minnesota■ J23
- Illinois J28
- Northwestern J30
- Purdue■ F 4
- Ohio St.■ F11
- Penn St.■ F13
- Minnesota F18
- Iowa F20
- Northwestern■ F25
- Illinois■ F27
- Purdue M 2
- Wisconsin■ M 4
- Michigan M10
- Michigan St.■ M12

Colors: Cream & Crimson. Nickname: Hoosiers.
AD: Clarence Doninger. SID: Shelli Stewart. I

INDIANA (PA.) — Indiana, PA 15705

Jan Kiger (7 YRS. W-106, L-79)

- Indiana (Pa.) Inv. N20-21
- St. Vincent N23
- Gannon N27
- Northern Ky. Cl. D3-4
- Pitt.-Johnstown D 7
- Clarion Cl. D10-11
- Central St. (Ohio)■ D16
- Columbia Union■ J 5
- Central St. (Ohio) J 8
- Shippensburg J12
- Mercyhurst J15
- Slippery Rock J19
- Clarion■ J22
- Edinboro■ J26
- Calif. (Pa.) J29
- Lock Haven■ F 2
- Bloomsburg■ F 5
- Shippensburg■ F 9
- Slippery Rock■ F12
- Edinboro F16
- Clarion F19
- Lock Haven F23
- Calif. (Pa.)■ F26

Colors: Crimson & Gray. Nickname: Indians.
AD: Frank Cignetti. SID: Larry Judge. II

■ Home games on each schedule.

See pages 735-738 for Division I tournament details

INDIANA ST. .... Terre Haute, IN 47809

Kay Riek (4 YRS. W-39, L-68)

Wis.-Milwaukee	N27	Southern Ill.■	J22
Xavier (Ohio)■	D 4	Wichita St.	J27
Eastern Ill.■	D 9	Southwest Mo. St.	J29
Purdue Cl.	D11	Northeastern Ill.	F 2
South Ala. Cl.	D17-18	Illinois St.■	F 4
Evansville■	D28	Drake	F11
Eastern Ky.	D30	Creighton	F13
Butler■	J 2	Southern Ill.	F19
Northern Iowa■	J 4	Southwest Mo. St.■	F24
Illinois St.	J 7	Wichita St.■	F26
Creighton■	J13	Northern Iowa	M 3
Drake■	J15	Bradley	M 5
Bradley■	J20	Missouri Valley Tr.	M8-12

Colors: Royal Blue & White. Nickname: Sycamores.
AD: Brian Faison. SID: Jackie Fischer. I

IU/PU-FT. WAYNE .... Ft. Wayne, IN 46805

Eileen Kleinfelter (2 YRS. W-32, L-24)

Taylor■	N23	Bellarmine	J22
West Tex. A&M Tr.	D2-4	Northern Ky.■	J27
IU/PU-Ft. Wayne Tr.	D10-11	Indianapolis■	J29
Voorhees■	D18	Ashland■	F 5
St. Francis (Ind.)	D20	Southern Ind.	F10
St. Joseph's (Ind.)	D30	Ky. Wesleyan	F12
Lewis	J 2	Bellarmine■	F17
SIU-Edwardsville■	J 6	Kentucky St.■	F19
Ashland	J 8	Indianapolis	F24
Ky. Wesleyan■	J13	Northern Ky.	F26
Southern Ind.■	J15	Lewis■	M 3
Kentucky St.	J20	St. Joseph's (Ind.)■	M 5

Colors: Blue & White. Nickname: Mastodons.
AD: Arnie Ball. SID: Matt Delong. II

INDIANAPOLIS .... Indianapolis, IN 46227

Lisa Hicks (5 YRS. W-82, L-52)

Northeast Mo. Tr.	N26-27	Ashland	J27
IU/PU-Ind. Cl.	D3-4	IU/PU-Ft. Wayne	J29
Oakland City■	D11	Kentucky St.■	F 3
Franklin■	D18	Bellarmine■	F 5
Quincy	D20	SIU-Edwardsville	F 7
Southern Ind.■	D30	Northern Ky.	F12
Ky. Wesleyan■	J 1	St. Joseph's (Ind.)	F17
Bellarmine	J 6	Lewis	F19
Kentucky St.	J 8	IU/PU-Ft. Wayne■	F24
IU/PU-Indianapolis■	J13	Ashland■	F26
Northern Ky.■	J15	Ky. Wesleyan	M 3
Lewis■	J20	Southern Ind.	M 5
St. Joseph's (Ind.)■	J22		

Colors: Crimson & Grey. Nickname: Lady Greyhounds.
AD: Bill Bright. SID: Joe Gentry. II

IONA .... New Rochelle, NY 10801

Harry Hart (1ST YR. AS HEAD COACH)

Fordham■	N27	St. Peter's■	J22
St. Francis (N.Y.)	D 1	Loyola (Md.)■	J26
Iona Tr.	D4-5	Drexel	F 2
Columbia-Barnard	D 8	Niagara■	F 4
Northeastern	D11	Canisius■	F 7
Boston College■	D30	Fairfield	F10
Texas Christian	J 5	St. Peter's	F12
Baylor	J 6	Manhattan■	F19
St. Bonaventure■	J 8	Loyola (Md.)	F21
Canisius	J13	Siena	F24
Niagara	J15	Fairfield■	F26
Manhattan	J18	Metro Atlantic Tr.	M4-6
Siena■	J20		

Colors: Maroon & Gold. Nickname: Gaels.
AD: Rich Petriccione. SID: David Torromeo. I

IOWA .... Iowa City, IA 52242

Vivian Stringer (20 YRS. W-461, L-107)

Iowa Cl.	N27-28	Indiana	J21
Drake	D 1	Michigan■	J28
Indiana Cl.	D3-4	Michigan St.	J30
Southwest Mo. St.■	D 5	Ohio St.	F 4
James Madison	D19	Northwestern	F11
West Va.	D21	Illinois	F13
Southern Cal Cl.	D29-30	Indiana■	F20
Minnesota■	J 5	Michigan St.■	F25
Wisconsin	J 7	Michigan	F27
Illinois■	J14	Ohio St.■	M 6
Northwestern■	J15	Minnesota	M11
Northern Ill.	J16		

Colors: Gold & Black. Nickname: Hawkeyes.
AD: Christine Grant. SID: Beth Weber. I

IOWA ST. .... Ames, IA 50011

Theresa Becker (1 YR. W-2, L-25)

Iowa St. Cl.	N26-27	Kansas■	J16
Creighton	N30	Missouri	J21
Montana	D 4	Colorado	J23
Montana St.	D 5	Nebraska	J30
Drake	D 9	Oklahoma St.■	F 4
Wis.-Milwaukee■	D11	Oklahoma■	F 6
Illinois St.■	D18	Kansas	F11
Wichita St.■	D28	Kansas St.	F13
Holy Cross■	D30	Colorado■	F18
N.C.-Greensboro Cl.	J2-3	Missouri■	F20
Oklahoma	J 7	Nebraska■	F27
Oklahoma St.	J 9	Big Eight Tr.	M5-7
Kansas St.■	J14		

Colors: Cardinal & Gold. Nickname: Cyclones.
AD: Gene Smith. SID: Beth Haag. I

ITHACA .... Ithaca, NY 14850

Christine Pritchard (8 YRS. W-155, L-129)

Stony Brook Tr.	N19-20	Alfred	J25
Keuka■	N29	Hartwick	J28
Geneseo St.	D 1	Rensselaer	J29
Elmira	D 7	Clarkson■	F 4
Scranton Cl.	D10-11	St. Lawrence■	F 5
Cortland St.	J11	Alfred■	F 8
St. Lawrence	J14	Rensselaer■	F11
Clarkson	J15	Hartwick■	F12
Albany (N.Y.)	J18	Nazareth (N.Y.)	F15
Rochester Inst.■	J21	William Smith	F18
William Smith■	J22	Rochester Inst.	F19

Colors: Blue & Gold. Nickname: Bombers.
AD: Robert Deming. SID: Pete Moore. III

JACKSON ST. .... Jackson, MS 39217

Andrew Pennington (14 YRS. W-240, L-161)

Ark. Baptist■	N27	Mississippi Val.■	J22
Auburn	D 1	Grambling	J24
Kansas Cl.	D3-4	Alabama St.■	J29
Tougaloo■	D 6	Texas Southern	F 5
Tulane Cl.	D10-11	Prairie View	F 7
Belhaven■	D18	Southern-B.R.■	F12
Louisiana St.	D21	Alcorn St.■	F14
Missouri■	D31	Louisiana St.■	F16
Southeastern La.	J 2	Mississippi Val.	F19
Texas Southern■	J 8	Grambling■	F21
Prairie View■	J10	Alabama St.	F26
Southern-B.R.	J15	SWAC Tr.	M10-13
Alcorn St.	J17		

Colors: Blue & White. Nickname: Tigers.
AD: W.C. Gorden. SID: Sam Jefferson. I

JACKSONVILLE ST. .... Jacksonville, AL 36265

Tony Mabrey (3 YRS. W-62, L-24)

Alabama A&M■	N22	Aub.-Montgomery■	J22
S.C.-Aiken■	N29	West Ga.	J24
North Fla. Tr.	D3-4	Montevallo■	J27
Converse■	D 6	Shorter■	J29
North Ala.■	D11	Converse	J31
Talladega■	D13	Kennesaw St.	F 5
Paine■	J 3	Montevallo	F12
Carson-Newman Cl.	J5-6	Freed-Hardeman■	F14
Augusta■	J 8	North Ala.	F19
Kennesaw St.■	J10	Fort Valley St.■	F21
Paine	J14	Alabama A&M	F26
Augusta	J15	West Ga.■	F28
Valdosta St.	J17		

Colors: Red & White. Nickname: Gamecocks.
AD: Jerry Cole. SID: Mike Galloway. II

JAMES MADISON .... Harrisonburg, VA 22807

Shelia Moorman (11 YRS. W-224, L-97)

Va. Commonwealth	N26	Virginia Tech■	J25
Coppin St.■	N29	N.C.-Wilmington	J28
Syracuse Cl.	D4-5	East Caro.	J30
Ohio St.■	D11	Richmond■	F 3
Iowa■	D19	William & Mary	F11
St. Peter's	D22	Old Dominion	F13
Robert Morris■	D30	George Mason■	F17
Florida Int'l Tr.	J2-4	American■	F20
William & Mary■	J14	N.C.-Wilmington■	F25
Old Dominion■	J16	East Caro.■	F27
George Mason	J20	Richmond	M 3
American	J23	CAA Tr.	M10-12

Colors: Purple & Gold. Nickname: Dukes.
AD: Dean Ehlers. SID: Milla Sue Wisecarver. I

■ Home games on each schedule.

See pages 735-738 for Division I tournament details

JERSEY CITY ST. .... Jersey City, NJ 07305

Cathy Decker (2 YRS. W-15, L-34)

Hunter Tr.	N19-20	Wm. Paterson■	J19
Rowan■	N23	Trenton St.	J22
Stockton St.	N29	Rowan	J25
Trenton St.■	D 1	Stockton St.■	J29
Rutgers-Camden■	D 4	Rutgers-Newark	F 2
Ramapo	D 8	Rutgers-Camden	F 5
Montclair St.■	D11	Ramapo■	F 9
Staten Island	D17	Montclair St.	F12
Webber Cl.	J6-8	Wm. Paterson	F16
Rutgers-Newark■	J12	Kean■	F19
Kean	J14		

Colors: Green & Gold. Nickname: Lady Gothics.
AD: Larry Schiner. SID: John Stallings. III

JOHN CARROLL .... Cleveland, OH 44118

Roxanne Allen (4 YRS. W-58, L-44)

John Carroll Tr.	N19-20	Mount Union■	J15
Carnegie Mellon Inv.	N27-28	Hiram	J18
Grove City	D 2	Ohio Northern	J22
Marietta	D 4	Baldwin-Wallace■	J25
Baldwin-Wallace	D 7	Marietta■	J29
Ohio Northern■	D11	Mount Union	F 1
Otterbein■	D29	Muskingum	F 5
Alma■	D31	Hiram■	F 8
Capital	J 4	Otterbein	F12
Muskingum■	J 8	Heidelberg■	F15
Heidelberg	J11	Capital■	F19

Colors: Blue & Gold. Nickname: Blue Streaks.
AD: Tony DeCarlo. SID: Chris Wenzler. III

JOHN JAY .... New York, NY 10019

Ulana Lysniak (2 YRS. W-24, L-23)

John Jay Tr.	N20-21	Manhattanville	J24
Mt. St. Mary (N.Y.)	N23	Lehman	J26
Molloy Tr.	N26-27	CCNY	J29
Albertus Magnus	N29	Baruch	J31
York (N.Y.)■	D 2	Stony Brook	F 3
Hunter■	D 6	Medgar Evers	F 7
New York U.■	D 8	Old Westbury■	F 9
Staten Island	J 7	CCNY■	F12
Baruch■	J10	York (N.Y.)	F14
Mt. St. Vincent	J17	Vassar■	F16
Hunter	J22		

Colors: Blue & Gold. Nickname: Bloodhounds.
AD: Susan Larkin. SID: Jeff Risener. III

JOHNS HOPKINS .... Baltimore, MD 21218

Nancy Clelan-Blank (21 YRS. W-240, L-197)

Johns Hopkins Cl.	N20-21	Carnegie Mellon■	J16
Ursinus	N23	Washington (Md.)	J20
Bryn Mawr■	N30	Muhlenberg	J22
Brandeis	D 3	Western Md.	J25
New York U.■	D 5	Gettysburg■	J29
Frank. & Marsh.■	D 7	Dickinson	F 2
Rochester	D10	Frank. & Marsh.	F 5
Case Reserve■	J 3	Swarthmore	F10
Chicago	J 7	Western Md.■	F12
Washington (Mo.)	J 9	Gettysburg	F15
Haverford■	J11	Dickinson■	F19
Emory■	J14		

Colors: Blue & Black. Nickname: Blue Jays.
AD: Robert Scott. SID: Andy Bilello. III

JOHNSON SMITH .... Charlotte, NC 28208

Hythia Evans-Liebert (6 YRS. W-103, L-66)

St. Paul's■	N23	Winston-Salem■	J22
Barber-Scotia	N24	St. Augustine's	J24
Virginia St.■	N27	Fayetteville St.	J27
Hampton	N29	Shaw	J29
Johnson Smith Inv.	D3-4	N.C. Central	F 2
Wingate■	D11	Winston-Salem	F 5
Virginia Union■	D14	Elizabeth City St.	F 7
Dist. Columbia■	D16	St. Augustine's■	F 9
N.C. Central■	J 4	Fayetteville St.■	F12
Norfolk St.	J 8	Shaw■	F15
Livingstone■	J11	Livingstone	F17
Bowie St.■	J15	Queens (N.C.)■	F19
Queens (N.C.)	J20		

Colors: Blue & Gold. Nickname: Lady Golden Bulls.
AD: Horace Small. SID: James Cuthbertson. II

JOHNSON ST. .... Johnson, VT 05656

Barbara Lougec (3 YRS. W-25, L-44)

Teiko Post■	N19	Trinity (Vt.)■	J22
Plattsburgh St.	N20	Bishop■	J24
Plymouth St.■	N23	Lyndon St.■	J26
St. Joseph (Vt.)	N29	Green Mountain■	J29
Bishop	D 4	St. Joseph (Vt.)■	F 2
Me.-Machias■	D12	Lyndon St.	F 5
Westbrook	J12	Me.-Farmington	F 7
Notre Dame (N.H.)	J13	Castleton St.■	F10
St. Joseph's (Me.)■	J15	Green Mountain	F12
Trinity (Vt.)	J16	Notre Dame (N.H.)■	F15
Norwich	J18	Westbrook■	F19
Castleton St.	J20		

Colors: Green & White. Nickname: Badgers.
AD: Peter Albright. SID: To be named. III

JUNIATA .... Huntingdon, PA 16652

Stan Risser (2 YRS. W-29, L-12)

Frank. & Marsh. Tr.	N20-21	Albright	J22
Waynesburg	N27	Elizabethtown	J27
Misericordia■	N29	Messiah	J29
Messiah■	D 1	Lebanon Valley■	F 1
Moravian	D 4	Moravian■	F 5
Lycoming■	D 7	Susquehanna	F 9
Wash. & Jeff.	J 8	Widener	F12
Lebanon Valley	J11	York (Pa.)■	F15
Widener■	J15	Elizabethtown■	F17
Susquehanna■	J19	Albright■	F19

Colors: Yale Blue & Old Gold. Nickname: Indians.
AD: William F. Berrier. SID: Joseph Scialabba. III

KALAMAZOO .... Kalamazoo, MI 49006

Jim Hess (10 YRS. W-115, L-149)

Kalamazoo Tr.	N19-20	Olivet■	J15
Grand Rapids Bapt.	N23	Alma	J19
Concordia (Mich.)■	N27	Adrian■	J22
Bethel (Ind.)■	D 1	Defiance■	J26
Franklin	D11	Hope■	J29
Spring Arbor■	D18	Calvin■	F 2
Madonna■	D20	Albion	F 5
Aquinas■	D28	Olivet	F 9
Elmhurst■	D30	Alma■	F12
Hope	J 5	Adrian	F16
Calvin	J 8	St. Mary's (Ind.)■	F19
Albion■	J12		

Colors: Orange & Black. Nickname: Hornets.
AD: Lyn Maurer. SID: John Greenhoe. III

KANSAS .... Lawrence, KS 66045

Marian Washington (20 YRS. W-368, L-225)

Creighton	N26	Oklahoma■	J21
Wichita St.	D 1	Oklahoma St.■	J23
Kansas Cl.	D3-4	Kansas St.■	J30
Morgan St.■	D 8	Colorado	F 4
Lamar	D19	Missouri	F 6
Mo.-Kansas City	D22	Iowa St.■	F11
St. John's Inv.	D29-30	Nebraska■	F13
West Va.	J 2	Oklahoma St.	F18
Missouri■	J 7	Oklahoma	F20
Colorado■	J 9	Kansas St.	F27
Nebraska	J14	Big Eight Tr.	M5-7
Iowa St.	J16		

Colors: Crimson & Blue. Nickname: Jayhawks.
AD: Bob Frederick. SID: Ginger Miller. I

KANSAS ST. .... Manhattan, KS 66506

Brian Agler (5 YRS. W-87, L-51)

Detroit Mercy■	N27	Oklahoma■	J23
Missouri-Rolla■	N29	Northeastern Ill.■	J27
Wichita St.	D 7	Kansas	J30
Fairfield Cl.	D10-11	Missouri	F 2
Ohio St.	D19	Colorado	F 6
Minnesota	D21	Nebraska■	F11
Mo.-St. Louis■	D30	Iowa St.■	F13
Utah■	J 1	Oklahoma	F18
Colorado■	J 7	Oklahoma St.	F20
Missouri■	J 9	Detroit Mercy	F22
Iowa St.	J14	Kansas■	F27
Nebraska	J16	Cal St. Sacramento■	M 2
Oklahoma St.■	J21	Big Eight Tr.	M5-7

Colors: Purple & White. Nickname: Wildcats.
AD: Max Urick. SID: Jenifer Scheibler. I

■ Home games on each schedule.

See pages 735-738 for Division I tournament details

KEENE ST. .... Keene, NH 03431
Keith Boucher (4 YRS. W-67, L-47)

New Hamp. Col. Cl. N20-21
Merrimack N30
Springfield■ .... D 2
Bryant■ .... D 6
Stonehill■ D11
Bentley D18
Florida Tech D29
Florida A&M .... J 1
Le Moyne■ .... J 4
Sacred Heart .... J 8
New Haven J12
Le Moyne J15
New Hamp. Col. J19
Southern Conn. St. J23
Franklin Pierce■ J26
Bridgeport■ J29
Mass.-Lowell .... F 2
Southern Conn. St.■ .... F 6
New Hamp. Col.■ .... F 9
Mass.-Lowell■ F16
Bridgeport F19
Sacred Heart■ F21
Franklin Pierce F23
New Haven■ F26

Colors: Red & White. Nickname: Owls.
AD: Joanne Fortunato. SID: Stuart Kaufman. II

KENNESAW ST. .... Marietta, GA 30061
Susan Montgomery (1 YR. W-19, L-11)

Lander N20
Valdosta St. N22
Georgia Col.■ N24
Georgia St. Cl. N27
Lander■ .... D 4
Tampa .... D 6
Fla. Southern .... D 7
Georgia Col. D15
Kennesaw St. Tr. D17-18
Albany St. (Ga.)■ .... J 3
Ga. Southwestern .... J 6
Portland St.■ .... J 8
Jacksonville St. J10
Brewton Parker■ J17
North Ga.■ J19
Montevallo J22
Clayton St. J24
Shorter J26
Berry J31
Jacksonville St.■ .... F 5
Clayton St.■ .... F 9
Shorter■ F12
North Ga. F16
Ga. Southwestern■ F19
Brewton Parker F22
Berry■ F26

Colors: Black & Gold. Nickname: Lady Owls.
AD: Dave Waples. SID: Scott Whitlock. II

KENT .... Kent, OH 44242
Bob Lindsay (4 YRS. W-60, L-55)

Arkansas■ N30
Rice Cl. D3-4
N.C.-Greensboro■ .... D 9
Youngstown St. D11
Cleveland St. D23
Maine Shootout J2-3
Central Mich.■ .... J 5
Bowling Green .... J 8
Eastern Mich.■ J12
Toledo J15
Akron J19
Ball St.■ J22
Miami (Ohio) J26
Western Mich.■ J29
Ohio .... F 2
Bowling Green■ .... F 5
Eastern Mich. .... F 9
Toledo■ F12
Akron■ F16
Ball St. F19
Miami (Ohio)■ F23
Western Mich. F26
Ohio■ .... M 2
Central Mich. .... M 5
Mid-American Tr. M8-12

Colors: Blue & Gold. Nickname: Lady Flashes.
AD: Paul Amodio. SID: Dale Gallagher. I

KENTUCKY .... Lexington, KY 40506
Sharon Fanning (17 YRS. W-292, L-201)

Kentucky Inv. N26-27
Memphis St.■ .... D 4
Indiana■ .... D 7
Western Ky. D10
Mississippi■ D18
Ohio St.■ D21
Central Fla. Cl. D29-31
Florida .... J 2
South Caro. .... J 8
Vanderbilt J12
Mississippi St.■ J16
Louisville■ J19
Georgia J23
Auburn J29
Eastern Ky.■ .... F 1
Detroit Mercy .... F 2
Arkansas■ .... F 5
Cincinnati■ .... F 8
Alabama F13
Marshall F16
Tennessee■ F20
Murray St. F23
Louisiana St.■ F27
Southeastern Tr. M4-7

Colors: Blue & White. Nickname: Lady Kats.
AD: C.M. Newton. SID: Gail Dent. I

KENTUCKY ST. .... Frankfort, KY 40601
To be named

Lindsey Wilson■ N23
Cumberland (Ky.) Tr. N26-27
Oakland City .... D 1
Bellarmine D11
Northern Ky.■ .... J 6
Indianapolis■ .... J 8
Central St. (Ohio)■ J11
St. Joseph's (Ind.) J13
Lewis J15
Lincoln Memorial■ J18
IU/PU-Ft. Wayne■ J20
Ashland■ J22
Ky. Wesleyan J27
Southern Ind. J29
Oakland City■ .... F 1
Indianapolis .... F 3
Northern Ky. .... F 5
Lewis■ F10
St. Joseph's (Ind.)■ F12
Ashland F17
IU/PU-Ft. Wayne F19
Central St. (Ohio) F22
Southern Ind.■ F24
Ky. Wesleyan■ F26
Lincoln Memorial F28
Bellarmine■ .... M 5

Colors: Green & Gold. Nickname: Thorobrettes.
AD: Don Lyons. SID: Ron Braden. II

KY. WESLEYAN .... Owensboro, KY 42301
Ty Stauffer (1 YR. W-9, L-18)

Southeast Mo. St. .... D 1
Oakland City■ .... D 4
SIU-Edwardsville D11
Oakland City D18
Northern Ky. D20
Spalding D28
Indianapolis .... J 1
St. Joseph's (Ind.)■ .... J 6
Lewis■ .... J 8
IU/PU-Ft. Wayne J13
Ashland J15
Spalding■ J17
SIU-Edwardsville■ J20
Southern Ind. J22
Brescia■ J25
Kentucky St.■ J27
Bellarmine■ J29
Lewis .... F 3
St. Joseph's (Ind.) .... F 5
Ashland■ F10
IU/PU-Ft. Wayne■ F12
Quincy F16
Southern Ind.■ F19
Bellarmine F24
Kentucky St. F26
Indianapolis■ .... M 3
Northern Ky.■ .... M 5

Colors: Purple & White. Nickname: Lady Panthers.
AD: Wayne Boultinghouse. SID: Roy Pickerill. II

KEUKA .... Keuka Park, NY 14478
Sherri Nowatzki (1 YR. W-10, L-14)

Emmanuel Tr. N20-21
Clarkson■ N23
Ithaca N29
Rochester Inst. .... D 4
D'youville .... D 9
Misericordia D11
Sewanee■ .... J 4
Nazareth (N.Y.) J11
William Smith J15
Houghton■ J21
Buffalo St.■ .... F 1
Houghton .... F 2
St. John Fisher .... F 3
Utica■ .... F 5
Albany St. (Ga.)■ F13
Nazareth (N.Y.)■ F17
Hilbert■ F20
Alfred■ F22

Colors: Green & Gold. Nickname: Warriors.
AD: David Sweet. SID: Alan Loucks. III

KNOX .... Galesburg, IL 61401
Jane Marie Stangl (3 YRS. W-29, L-34)

Webster■ N27
Central (Iowa)■ N28
Ill. Wesleyan .... D 1
Rhodes Tr. D4-5
Maryville (Mo.) D10
Illinois Col. D11
Coe .... J 7
Cornell College .... J 8
Monmouth (Ill.) J12
Grinnell■ J18
St. Norbert J21
Lawrence J22
Carroll (Wis.)■ J28
Ripon■ J29
Aurora■ .... F 1
Grinnell .... F 5
Illinois Col.■ .... F 9
Cornell College■ F12
Monmouth (Ill.)■ F15
Coe■ F19
Teiko-Marycrest■ F22

Colors: Purple & Gold. Nickname: Prairie Fire.
AD: Harlan Knosher. SID: Jay Redfern. III

KUTZTOWN .... Kutztown, PA 19530
Tom York (6 YRS. W-85, L-77)

Kutztown Cl. N19-20
Shippensburg N23
Pitt.-Johnstown Tr. N27-28
Allentown N30
Phila. Textile .... D 2
Holy Family■ .... D 8
Alvernia■ D11
Lock Haven .... J 5
Longwood■ .... J 8
West Chester J12
Millersville J15
Bloomsburg■ J19
Pitt.-Johnstown■ J22
East Stroudsburg■ J26
Cheyney J29
Shippensburg■ J31
Mansfield .... F 2
Millersville■ .... F 5
West Chester■ .... F 9
Bloomsburg F12
East Stroudsburg F16
Rowan■ F21
Mansfield■ F23
Cheyney■ F26

Colors: Maroon & Gold. Nickname: Golden Bears.
AD: Clark Yeager. SID: Matt Santos. II

LA SALLE .... Philadelphia, PA 19141
John Miller (7 YRS. W-146, L-60)

Pennsylvania■ N30
Seton Hall Cl. D4-5
Temple .... D 8
Drexel D11
St. Joseph's (Pa.)■ D14
Villanova■ D23
La Salle Inv. D28-29
American■ .... J 4
N.C.-Wilmington Tr. J7-8
Loyola (Ill.)■ J13
Notre Dame■ J15
Detroit Mercy J20
Xavier (Ohio) J22
Evansville■ J27
Butler■ J29
Delaware .... F 3
George Mason■ .... F 5
Xavier (Ohio)■ F10
Detroit Mercy■ F12
Notre Dame F17
Loyola (Ill.) F19
Butler F24
Evansville F26
MCC Tr. M5-8

Colors: Blue & Gold. Nickname: Explorers.
AD: Bob Mullen. SID: Colleen Corace. I

■ Home games on each schedule.

See pages 735-738 for Division I tournament details

LA VERNE .... La Verne, CA 91750

Julie Curtis (1 YR. W-13, L-12)

- Trinity (Tex.) Inv. N20-21
- Southern Cal Col. N30
- UC San Diego .... D 3
- Chapman■ .... D 7
- Azusa-Pacific D18
- Colorado Col.■ .... J 3
- Adams St.■ .... J 7
- Wheaton (Ill.)■ .... J 8
- Claremont-M-S■ J11
- UC San Diego■ J14
- Whittier J18
- Pomona-Pitzer■ J21
- Redlands J25
- Cal Lutheran J28
- Occidental■ .... F 1
- Claremont-M-S .... F 4
- Whittier■ F11
- Pomona-Pitzer F15
- Redlands■ F18
- Cal Lutheran■ F22
- Occidental F25

Colors: Dark Green & Orange. Nickname: Leopards.
AD: Jim Paschal. SID: Pam Maunakea.

III

LAFAYETTE .... Easton, PA 18042

Pat Fisher (13 YRS. W-217, L-139)

- Hofstra■ N27
- Princeton .... D 1
- Syracuse Cl. D4-5
- Delaware■ .... D 7
- Cornell D11
- Seton Hall D13
- Miami (Fla.) Tr. D28-30
- Boston U.■ .... J 6
- Drexel■ J10
- Colgate J12
- Bucknell■ J15
- Pennsylvania J17
- Navy■ J19
- Holy Cross J22
- Fordham■ J26
- Army■ J29
- Lehigh .... F 2
- Colgate■ .... F 5
- Bucknell .... F 9
- Navy F12
- Holy Cross■ F16
- Fordham F19
- Lehigh■ F23
- Army F26
- Patriot Tr. M3-12

Colors: Maroon & White. Nickname: Leopards.
AD: Eve Atkinson. SID: Steve Pulver.

I

LAKE FOREST .... Lake Forest, IL 60045

Jackie Slaats (7 YRS. W-109, L-49)

- Lake Forest Tr. N19-20
- Ill. Benedictine N30
- Concordia (Ill.)■ .... D 2
- Carroll (Wis.)■ .... D 4
- UC San Diego Inv. D28-30
- Ripon J12
- St. Norbert■ J15
- Lawrence J18
- Grinnell■ J21
- Coe■ J22
- Beloit■ J25
- Monmouth (Ill.) J28
- Cornell College J29
- Carroll (Wis.) .... F 2
- Lawrence■ .... F 5
- North Central■ .... F 7
- St. Norbert F12
- Beloit F15
- Ripon■ F19

Colors: Red & Black. Nickname: Foresters.
AD: Jackie Slaats. SID: To be named.

III

LAKE SUPERIOR ST. ...... Sault Ste. Marie, MI 49783

Erica Ledy (3 YRS. W-42, L-38)

- Grand Rapids Tr. N26-27
- Ferris St. Cl. D3-4
- Wayne St. (Mich.) .... D 9
- Saginaw Valley D11
- Ferris St.■ D18
- Sonoma St. D29
- Sonoma St. D30
- Cal St. Hayward .... J 2
- Hillsdale■ .... J 6
- Oakland■ .... J 8
- Northern Mich. J13
- Michigan Tech J18
- Grand Valley St.■ J20
- Northwood■ J22
- Ferris St. J29
- Wayne St. (Mich.)■ .... F 3
- Saginaw Valley■ .... F 5
- Hillsdale F10
- Oakland F12
- Northern Mich.■ F17
- Michigan Tech■ F19
- Grand Valley St. F24
- Northwood F26

Colors: Royal Blue & Gold. Nickname: Lakers.
AD: Jeff Jackson. SID: Scott Monaghan.

II

LAMAR .... Beaumont, TX 77710

Liz McQuitter (4 YRS. W-51, L-45)

- Stephen F. Austin■ N30
- Southwest Tex. Cl. D3-4
- Texas A&M .... D 7
- Houston D12
- Kansas■ D19
- Baylor Cl. D29-30
- Texas Tech .... J 2
- South Ala. .... J 6
- New Orleans■ .... J 8
- Arkansas St.■ J13
- Louisiana Tech J15
- Tex.-Pan American J17
- Western Ky.■ J20
- Arkansas St. J22
- Southwestern La.■ J29
- Mississippi■ .... F 2
- Tex.-Pan American■ .... F 5
- Western Ky. F13
- South Ala.■ F17
- Southwestern La. F19
- Louisiana St.■ F24
- New Orleans F26
- Louisiana Tech■ .... M 5
- Sun Belt Tr. M10-12

Colors: Red & White. Nickname: Lady Cardinals.
AD: To be named. SID: Tim McMurray.

I

LANDER .... Greenwood, SC 29649

Anne Williamson (5 YRS. W-62, L-69)

- Kennesaw St.■ N20
- Central Wesleyan■ N22
- Newberry■ N24
- Converse■ N29
- Kennesaw St. .... D 4
- Pfeiffer■ D11
- Augusta■ .... J 4
- Erskine■ .... J 8
- Armstrong St. J10
- S.C.-Aiken J13
- Francis Marion■ J15
- Pembroke St.■ J16
- Erskine J19
- Georgia Col. J22
- Columbus J23
- S.C.-Spartanburg■ J27
- S.C.-Aiken■ .... F 2
- Newberry .... F 5
- S.C.-Spartanburg .... F 9
- Augusta F12
- Armstrong St.■ F14
- Georgia Col.■ F19
- Columbus■ F20
- Francis Marion F26
- Pembroke St. F27

Colors: Royal Blue & Gold. Nickname: Senators.
AD: Finis Horne. SID: Bob Stoner.

II

LANE .... Jackson, TN 38301

James Shaw (2 YRS. W-27, L-23)

- LeMoyne-Owen N18
- Fisk N20
- Bethel (Tenn.) N22
- Union (Tenn.)■ N29
- Delta St. .... D 1
- Alabama A&M .... D 2
- Stillman■ .... D 3
- Lambuth■ .... J 6
- Virginia St. Cl. J7-8
- Union (Tenn.) J10
- Lambuth J17
- Oakland City J21
- Oakland City J22
- Stillman J25
- Morris Brown J28
- Rust■ .... F 1
- Morris Brown■ .... F 4
- LeMoyne-Owen■ .... F 8
- Oakland City■ F11
- Oakland City■ F12
- Rust F19
- Delta St.■ F23

Colors: Blue & Red. Nickname: Dragons.
AD: J.L. Perry. SID: Sherrill Scott.

II

LAWRENCE .... Appleton, WI 54911

Amy Proctor (6 YRS. W-78, L-42)

- Wis.-Platteville■ N20
- Marian (Wis.)■ N23
- Ripon .... D 1
- Beloit■ .... D 4
- Berea D11
- Centre D15
- Carroll (Wis.)■ .... J 5
- Wis.-Whitewater .... J 8
- Wis. Lutheran J13
- Lake Forest■ J18
- Illinois Col.■ J21
- Knox■ J22
- St. Norbert J25
- Coe J28
- Grinnell J29
- Ripon■ .... F 2
- Lake Forest .... F 5
- Silver Lake F10
- Beloit F12
- St. Norbert■ F14
- Carthage■ F17
- Carroll (Wis.) F21

Colors: Navy & White. Nickname: Vikings.
AD: Amy Proctor. SID: Jeff School.

III

LE MOYNE .... Syracuse, NY 13214

Tom Cooney (16 YRS. W-198, L-199)

- Kutztown Cl. N19-20
- Mansfield N23
- St. Rose■ N29
- Le Moyne Tr. D4-5
- Oswego St. .... D 9
- Keene St. .... J 4
- Franklin Pierce .... J 5
- Mass.-Lowell■ .... J 8
- Bridgeport■ J10
- St. Lawrence■ J11
- New Hamp. Col.■ J12
- Keene St.■ J15
- Sacred Heart■ J17
- Southern Conn. St. J22
- New Haven J23
- Hamilton J27
- Franklin Pierce■ J29
- Bridgeport .... F 5
- Sacred Heart .... F 6
- New Haven■ F12
- Utica■ F16
- New Hamp. Col. F19
- Mass.-Lowell F20
- Southern Conn. St.■ F26

Colors: Green & Gold. Nickname: Dolphins.
AD: Richard Rockwell. SID: Kim McAuliff.

II

LEMOYNE-OWEN .... Memphis, TN 38126

Eddie Cook (1 YR. W-11, L-37)

- Lane■ N18
- Miles■ N20
- Stillman N22
- Fort Valley St.■ N27
- Savannah St. N30
- Alabama A&M■ .... D 6
- Albany St. (Ga.)■ D11
- Paine■ D13
- Mississippi-Women .... J 7
- Rust■ J12
- Savannah St.■ J15
- Tuskegee J17
- Alabama A&M J19
- Morris Brown J21
- Tuskegee■ J24
- Miles J27
- Fort Valley St. J29
- Morris Brown■ .... F 5
- Lane .... F 8
- Clark Atlanta F11
- Albany St. (Ga.) F12
- Paine F14
- Rust F16
- Mississippi-Women■ F21
- Clark Atlanta■ F23
- Stillman■ F26

Colors: Purple & Old Gold. Nickname: Lady Magicians.
AD: E.D. Wilkens. SID: Eddie Cook.

II

■ Home games on each schedule.

See pages 735-738 for Division I tournament details

LEBANON VALLEY .... Annville, PA 17003

Peg Kauffman (1ST YR. AS HEAD COACH)

Notre Dame (Md.) Tr. N19-20
Moravian■ .... D 2
Albright .... D 4
King's (Pa.) .... J 4
Juniata■ J11
Western Md. J13
Susquehanna J15
Widener■ J18
Delaware Valley■ J20
Elizabethtown■ J22
Messiah J25
Notre Dame (Md.)■ J27
Moravian J29
Juniata .... F 1
Gettysburg■ .... F 3
Albright■ .... F 5
Widener .... F 8
Frank. & Marsh. F10
Susquehanna■ F12
Messiah■ F15
Muhlenberg F17
Elizabethtown F19

Colors: Royal Blue & White. Nickname: Flying Dutchmen.
AD: Louis Sorrentino. SID: John Deamer. III

LEHIGH .... Bethlehem, PA 18015

Jocelyn Beck (11 YRS. W-107, L-174)

Towson St. N27
LIU-Brooklyn N29
Rider■ .... D 1
Iona Tr. D4-5
Hofstra .... D 8
Princeton■ D11
Pittsburgh Inv. D29-30
Delaware .... J 5
Yale■ .... J 8
Navy J12
Holy Cross J15
Fordham J19
Army■ J22
Hartford■ J24
Bucknell■ J26
Colgate J29
Pennsylvania J31
Lafayette■ .... F 2
Navy■ .... F 5
Holy Cross■ .... F 9
Fordham■ F12
Army F16
Bucknell F19
Lafayette F23
Colgate■ F26
Patriot Tr. M3-12

Colors: Brown & White. Nickname: Engineers.
AD: Joe Sterrett. SID: Glenn Hofmann. I

LENOIR-RHYNE .... Hickory, NC 28603

Janet Greene (13 YRS. W-126, L-163)

Catawba Cl. N19-20
High Point N23
Belmont Abbey■ N29
High Point■ .... D 4
Pfeiffer .... D 6
Queens (N.C.) .... J 5
Mars Hill■ .... J 8
Wingate J12
Catawba J15
Pfeiffer■ J17
Gardner-Webb■ J19
Elon J22
Carson-Newman■ J26
Presbyterian■ J29
Mars Hill .... F 5
Wingate■ .... F 9
Catawba■ F12
Queens (N.C.)■ F14
Gardner-Webb F16
Elon■ F19
Carson-Newman F23
Presbyterian F26

Colors: Red & Black. Nickname: Lady Bears.
AD: Keith Ochs. SID: Thomas Neff. II

LEWIS .... Romeoville, IL 60441

To be named

Olivet (Ill.)■ N30
Ferris St. Cl. D3-4
St. Francis (Ill.)■ .... D 8
National Louis■ D10
Winona St.■ D14
Rosary■ D18
Ashland■ D30
IU/PU-Ft. Wayne■ .... J 2
Southern Ind. .... J 6
Ky. Wesleyan .... J 8
Bellarmine■ J13
Kentucky St.■ J15
Indianapolis J20
Northern Ky. J22
Wis.-Parkside J27
St. Joseph's (Ind.)■ J29
Ky. Wesleyan■ .... F 3
Southern Ind.■ .... F 5
Kentucky St. F10
Bellarmine F12
Northern Ky.■ F17
Indianapolis■ F19
Wis.-Parkside■ F24
St. Joseph's (Ind.) F26
IU/PU-Ft. Wayne .... M 3
Ashland .... M 5

Colors: Red & White. Nickname: Lady Flyers.
AD: Paul Ruddy. SID: Mark Buerger. II

LIBERTY .... Lynchburg, VA 24506

Rick Reeves (7 YRS. W-103, L-87)

Liberty Cl. D3-4
American .... D 8
Charleston So.■ D10
Coastal Caro.■ D18
St. Peter's Tr. D29-30
Cedarville .... J 6
Radford .... J 8
N.C.-Greensboro J14
Campbell J15
Va. Commonwealth■ J18
Winthrop■ J21
N.C.-Asheville■ J22
Towson St. J28
Md.-Balt. County J29
Coastal Caro. .... F 4
Charleston So. .... F 5
Emory & Henry■ .... F 8
Radford■ F12
N.C.-Greensboro■ F18
Campbell■ F19
Winthrop F25
N.C.-Asheville F26
Towson St.■ .... M 4
Md.-Balt. County■ .... M 5
Big South Tr. M9-12

Colors: Red, White & Blue. Nickname: Lady Flames.
AD: Chuck Burch. SID: Mitch Goodman. I

LINCOLN MEMORIAL .... Harrogate, TN 37752

Roger Vannoy (11 YRS. W-232, L-94)

Francis Marion■ N20
Queens (N.C.) N23
Bluefield St. N30
Delta St.■ .... D 4
Carson-Newman■ .... D 7
Linc. Memorial Cl. D10-11
North Ga.■ .... J 3
Mississippi Col. .... J 6
Delta St. .... J 8
Bluefield St.■ J11
Mississippi Col.■ J15
Kentucky St. J18
Union (Ky.) J20
North Ala. J22
Ala.-Huntsville J24
Mississippi-Women■ J30
Carson-Newman .... F 2
West Ga.■ .... F 5
Mississippi-Women .... F 7
Valdosta St.■ F12
North Ala.■ F14
Valdosta St. F19
West Ga. F21
Ala.-Huntsville■ F26
Kentucky St.■ F28

Colors: Blue & Gray. Nickname: Lady Railsplitters.
AD: Dave Hyatt. SID: Tom Amis. II

LIVINGSTON .... Livingston, AL 35470

Tom Jernigan (1 YR. W-17, L-9)

Livingston Cl. N19-20
Mississippi St. N26
Alabama A&M N30
Ouachita Bapt.⊠ .... D 3
Northeastern Okla.⊠ .... D 4
Southern-N.O. .... D 6
Ala.-Huntsville■ .... J 3
William Carey■ .... J 4
Henderson St.■ .... J 8
Central Ark.■ J10
Mississippi-Women■ J12
Valdosta St. J15
West Ga. J17
Ala.-Huntsville J20
Mississippi Col.■ J24
Central Ark. J29
Henderson St. J31
Delta St. .... F 5
Valdosta St.■ .... F 7
West Fla. F12
West Ga.■ F14
Mississippi-Women F17
Delta St.■ F19
Mississippi Col. F22
West Fla.■ F25
⊠ Conway, AR

Colors: Red & White. Nickname: Lady Tigers.
AD: Billy Slay. SID: Dee Outlaw. II

LOCK HAVEN .... Lock Haven, PA 17745

Frank Scarfo (7 YRS. W-123, L-80)

Lock Haven Cl. N19-20
Gannon■ N23
Mansfield N29
Millersville■ .... D 1
West Chester Cl. D3-4
Bloomsburg .... D 7
Kutztown■ .... J 5
Montclair St. .... J 8
Mercyhurst■ J12
Slippery Rock J15
Clarion J19
Calif. (Pa.)■ J22
Shippensburg■ J26
Edinboro■ J29
East Stroudsburg J31
Indiana (Pa.) .... F 2
Slippery Rock■ .... F 5
Mercyhurst .... F 8
Clarion■ F12
Shippensburg F16
Calif. (Pa.) F19
Indiana (Pa.)■ F23
Edinboro F26

Colors: Crimson & White. Nickname: Lady Eagles.
AD: Sharon E. Taylor. SID: Pat Donghia. II

LONG BEACH ST. .... Long Beach, CA 90840

Glenn McDonald (2 YRS. W-30, L-27)

Loyola (Cal.) .... D 4
Stanford .... D 8
Oregon St. Cl. D10-11
Rice■ D21
Western Mich.■ D27
Colorado■ .... J 2
UC Irvine■ .... J 4
Cal St. Fullerton .... J 6
UC Santa Barb.■ .... J 9
San Jose St. J13
Pacific (Cal.) J15
Cal St. Fullerton■ J20
UC Santa Barb. J22
Louisiana Tech J26
Nevada J29
Nevada-Las Vegas■ .... F 3
New Mexico St.■ .... F 5
Pacific (Cal.)■ F11
San Jose St.■ F13
Hawaii F18
Hawaii F20
Nevada■ F24
New Mexico St.■ F26
Nevada-Las Vegas F28
UC Irvine .... M 5
Big West Tr. M9-12

Colors: Black & Gold. Nickname: Forty Niners.
AD: Dave O'Brien. SID: Tony Gervase. I

LIU-BROOKLYN .... Brooklyn, NY 11201

Marguerite Moran (4 YRS. W-34, L-64)

Lehigh■ N29
Hofstra■ .... D 1
Maine Cl. D3-4
Princeton .... D 8
Md.-East. Shore■ D11
San Juan Shootout D20-22
Dartmouth Inv. D29-30
St. Francis (N.Y.)■ .... J 4
Monmouth (N.J.) .... J 8
Wagner J10
Rider■ J13
Mt. St. Mary's (Md.)■ J15
FDU-Teaneck J20
Robert Morris■ J22
St. Francis (Pa.)■ J24
Wagner■ J27
Monmouth (N.J.)■ J29
Mt. St. Mary's (Md.) .... F 3
Rider .... F 5
FDU-Teaneck■ F10
Marist■ F12
St. Francis (Pa.) F17
Robert Morris F19
St. Francis (N.Y.) F26
Marist .... M 2
Northeast Tr. M6-12

Colors: Blue & White. Nickname: Lady Blackbirds.
AD: Paul Lizzo. SID: Bob Gesslein. I

■ Home games on each schedule.

See pages 735-738 for Division I tournament details

LIU-C.W. POST .... Greenvale, NY 11548

Patrice Walker (3 YRS. W-42, L-44)

Dist. Columbia Tr.	N26-27
Concordia (N.Y.)■	N29
Queens (N.Y.)	D 1
New Haven	D 3
St. Rose	D 8
East Stroudsburg■	D10
Mercy	J 5
West Chester■	J 8
Queens (N.Y.)■	J12
Adelphi■	J15
Molloy	J17
Phila. Textile	J19
St. Rose■	J22
Pace■	J24
LIU-Southampton■	J26
Dowling	J29
Southern Conn. St.	J31
Phila. Textile■	F 2
LIU-Southampton	F 5
Dowling■	F 7
Concordia (N.Y.)	F 9
Molloy■	F12
Adelphi	F14
Pace	F18
Mercy■	F26

Colors: Green & Gold. Nickname: Lady Pioneers.
AD: Vin Salamone. SID: To be named. II

LIU-SOUTHAMPTON .... Southampton, NY 11968

Anthony Bozzella (1 YR. W-3, L-21)

Kutztown Cl.	N19-20
Concordia (N.Y.)	D 1
Phila. Textile■	D 4
Dowling	D 7
Pace	D11
East Stroudsburg■	D14
Queens (N.Y.)	J 5
Adelphi	J 8
Mercy	J10
Concordia (N.Y.)■	J12
St. Rose■	J15
Molloy	J19
Mercy■	J24
LIU-C.W. Post	J26
Phila. Textile	J29
Molloy■	F 1
LIU-C.W. Post■	F 5
Adelphi■	F 9
Bloomfield	F12
Georgian Court	F13
Pace■	F16
St. Rose	F19
Dowling■	F23
Queens (N.Y.)■	F26

Colors: Blue & Gold. Nickname: Colonials.
AD: Mary Topping. SID: Cindy Corwith. II

LONGWOOD .... Farmville, VA 23909

Shirley Duncan (14 YRS. W-158, L-204)

Longwood Inv.	N19-20
Elon■	N23
Pfeiffer■	N29
West Chester Cl.	D3-4
Catawba■	D 7
Queens (N.C.)	D16
Kutztown	J 8
Millersville	J 9
Dist. Columbia■	J15
High Point	J17
Converse	J21
Wofford	J22
Columbia Union	J29
Elon	F 2
Queens (N.C.)■	F 5
Dist. Columbia	F 7
Catawba	F10
Wofford■	F12
Barton	F14
Columbia Union■	F16
Pitt.-Johnstown	F20
Wofford Tr.	F25-26
Converse■	F28

Colors: Blue & White. Nickname: Lancers.
AD: Emily Harsh. SID: Greg Prouty. II

LORAS .... Dubuque, IA 52003

Lyn Baber (2 YRS. W-15, L-32)

Lake Forest Tr.	N19-20
Grinnell■	D 4
Wis.-Platteville■	D 7
Ill. Benedictine	D21
Nat'l Catholic Tr.	J5-9
William Penn	J14
Central (Iowa)	J15
Luther	J21
Dubuque■	J22
Simpson■	J28
Wartburg	J29
Upper Iowa■	F 1
Buena Vista	F 4
William Penn■	F 5
Simpson	F11
Buena Vista■	F12
Luther■	F18
Wartburg■	F19
Dubuque	F22
Upper Iowa	F25
Central (Iowa)■	F26

Colors: Purple & Gold. Nickname: Duhawks.
AD: Bob Bierie. SID: Howard Thomas. III

LOUISIANA ST. .... Baton Rouge, LA 70893

Sue Gunter (23 YRS. W-483, L-193)

Southeastern La.	N30
Southwest Tex. St.	D15
Nicholls St.■	D17
Notre Dame	D19
Jackson St.■	D21
Texas A&M■	D29
Louisville Cl.	J2-3
Mississippi St.■	J 5
Tennessee	J 9
Southern-B.R.	J12
South Caro.■	J15
Georgia	J18
Vanderbilt■	J22
Central Fla.■	J24
Southern Miss.■	J26
Alabama	J29
Southwestern La.■	F 2
Auburn	F 5
Arkansas	F 8
Florida■	F12
Jackson St.	F16
Mississippi■	F19
Tulane	F21
Lamar	F24
Kentucky	F27
Southeastern Tr.	M4-7

Colors: Purple & Gold. Nickname: Fighting Tigers.
AD: Joe Dean. SID: Michael Bonnette. I

LOUISIANA TECH .... Ruston, LA 71272

Leon Barmore (11 YRS. W-307, L-52)

Iowa Cl.	N27-28
Louisiana Tech Cl.	D3-4
Northeast La.■	D 7
Alabama	D11
Baylor⊠	D20
Tennessee	D22
Texas-Arlington■	J 4
Southwestern La.	J 6
Tex.-Pan American■	J 8
New Orleans	J13
Lamar■	J15
Arkansas St.■	J20
Western Ky.	J23
Long Beach St.■	J26
South Ala.■	J29
South Ala.	F 3
Arkansas St.	F 5
Northeast La.	F 8
Southwestern La.■	F12
New Orleans■	F19
Western Ky.■	F24
Tex.-Pan American	M 3
Lamar	M 5
Sun Belt Tr.	M10-12

⊠ Shreveport, LA

Colors: Red & Blue. Nickname: Lady Techsters.
AD: Jerry Stovall. SID: Hank Largin. I

LOUISVILLE .... Louisville, KY 40292

Bud Childers (10 YRS. W-177 , L-120)

Butler	N30
Texas Tech Cl.	D4-5
Purdue	D10
Louisville Cl.	J2-3
Western Caro.■	J 5
Tulane■	J 8
Southern Miss.■	J10
South Fla.	J15
Kentucky	J19
Va. Commonwealth■	J23
Virginia Tech	J28
N.C.-Charlotte	J30
Dayton	F 5
Virginia Tech■	F 7
Southern Miss.	F11
Tulane	F13
N.C.-Charlotte■	F19
Notre Dame■	F21
Va. Commonwealth	F25
South Fla.■	M 3
Metro Tr.	M8-11

Colors: Red, Black, White. Nickname: Cardinals.
AD: William Olsen. SID: Andy Dumstorf. I

LOYOLA (CAL.) .... Los Angeles, CA 90045

Todd Corman (8 YRS. W-85, L-138)

Hawaii Cl.	N26-27
San Diego St.■	D 1
Long Beach St.■	D 4
Nevada-Las Vegas■	D11
Texas	D14
Weber St.	D16
Cal Poly Pomona	D21
New Mexico■	D22
San Jose St.■	D29
Wayland Bapt.■	D31
Cal St. Northridge■	J 6
Southern Utah	J 8
St. Mary's (Cal.)	J14
Santa Clara	J15
San Francisco■	J21
San Diego■	J22
Pepperdine	J28
Gonzaga	F 3
Portland	F 5
Portland■	F11
Gonzaga■	F12
San Diego	F17
San Francisco	F19
Santa Clara■	F25
St. Mary's (Cal.)■	F26
Pepperdine■	M 2
West Coast Tr.	M11-12

Colors: Crimson & Blue. Nickname: Lions.
AD: Brian Quinn. SID: Bruce Meyers. I

LOYOLA (ILL.) .... Chicago, IL 60626

Tracy Manuel (1 YR. W-12, L-15)

Bradley	N26
Toledo■	N28
Northwestern	N30
Illinois	D 4
Georgia■	D 7
DePaul■	D11
Ill.-Chicago■	D18
Toledo	D21
Stetson■	D28
Drake■	J 2
Xavier (Ohio)	J 8
La Salle	J13
St. Joseph's (Pa.)	J15
Butler■	J20
Evansville■	J22
Detroit Mercy	J26
Xavier (Ohio)■	J29
Northern Ill.■	J31
Notre Dame■	F 5
Evansville	F10
Butler	F12
La Salle■	F19
Valparaiso	F22
Detroit Mercy■	F26
Notre Dame	M 3
MCC Tr.	M5-8

Colors: Maroon & Gold. Nickname: Lady Ramblers.
AD: Chuck Schwarz. SID: Ian Solomon. I

LOYOLA (MD.) .... Baltimore, MD 21210

Pat Coyle (1 YR. W-14, L-15)

Duke■	N29
Towson St.■	D 1
Vanderbilt Cl.	D4-5
George Mason	D 9
Maryland Cl.	D28-29
St. Peter's■	J 6
Davidson■	J 8
Rutgers■	J11
Siena■	J15
Mt. St. Mary's (Md.)	J17
St. Peter's	J20
Manhattan■	J22
Iona	J26
Fairfield	J29
Manhattan	J31
Hofstra■	F 2
Siena	F 5
William & Mary	F 7
Fairfield■	F12
Niagara	F17
Canisius	F19
Iona■	F21
Canisius■	F25
Niagara■	F27
Metro Atlantic Tr.	M4-6

Colors: Green & Grey. Nickname: Lady Greyhounds.
AD: Joe Boylan. SID: Steve Jones. I

■ Home games on each schedule.

See pages 735-738 for Division I tournament details

LUTHER .... Decorah, IA 52101

Jane Hildebrand (9 YRS. W-146, L-89)

St. Olaf■	N20	Central (Iowa)	J22
Viterbo■	N21	Dubuque	J28
Wis.-Stevens Point	N27	William Penn	J29
Montclair St. Cl.	D3-4	Central (Iowa)■	F 4
Mt. Mercy	D 8	Simpson■	F 5
Luther Inv.	D30-31	Upper Iowa■	F11
Wis.-La Crosse■	J 3	Wartburg	F12
Simpson	J 7	Loras	F18
Upper Iowa	J 8	Buena Vista	F19
Buena Vista■	J14	Dubuque■	F25
Wartburg■	J15	William Penn■	F26
Loras■	J21		

Colors: Blue & White. Nickname: Norse.
AD: Andrea Wickerham. SID: Dave Blanchard. III

LYCOMING .... Williamsport, PA 17701

Christen Ditzler (1ST YR. AS HEAD COACH)

Emmanuel Tr.	N20-21	King's (Pa.)	J26
Marywood	N29	Drew■	J29
Drew	D 1	Susquehanna■	J31
Upsala■	D 4	Wilkes	F 2
Juniata	D 7	Upsala	F 5
Elizabethtown■	D 9	Scranton■	F 9
Dickinson	D11	FDU-Madison	F12
Wilkes■	J12	Misericordia	F15
FDU-Madison■	J15	King's (Pa.)■	F17
Scranton	J19	Delaware Valley	F19
Delaware Valley■	J22		

Colors: Blue & Gold. Nickname: Warriors.
AD: Frank Girardi. SID: Ken Weingartner. III

LYNCHBURG .... Lynchburg, VA 24501

Charles Stevens (1 YR. W-4, L-18)

Ferrum Tr.	N19-20	Va. Wesleyan■	J22
Roanoke	N23	Emory & Henry	J25
Shenandoah■	N30	Rand.-Macon Woman's	J28
East. Mennonite■	D 1	Hollins	F 1
Bridgewater (Va.)	D 4	Bridgewater (Va.)■	F 3
Greensboro	D 7	Guilford■	F 5
Gallaudet	D15	Rand.-Macon Woman's■	F 8
Salisbury St.	D16	Emory & Henry■	F12
Hollins■	J10	Va. Wesleyan	F15
Randolph-Macon	J13	Randolph-Macon■	F17
Guilford	J15	Roanoke■	F19
East. Mennonite	J20		

Colors: Grey & Crimson. Nickname: Hornets.
AD: Jack Toms. SID: Lee Ashby. III

MACALESTER .... St. Paul, MN 55105

John Hershey (7 YRS. W-77, L-98)

N'western (Minn.)■	N30	Bethel (Minn.)	J22
Bethel (Minn.)■	D 4	Augsburg■	J26
Concordia (St. Paul)■	D 6	St. Olaf	J29
Augsburg	D 8	Gust. Adolphus■	J31
St. Olaf■	D11	Carleton■	F 2
UC San Diego Inv.	D28-30	Hamline	F 5
Carleton	J 5	St. Benedict■	F 9
Hamline■	J 8	Concordia-M'head■	F12
St. Benedict	J10	St. Mary's (Minn.)	F16
Concordia-M'head	J12	Gust. Adolphus	F23
St. Thomas (Minn.)■	J15	St. Thomas (Minn.)	F26
St. Mary's (Minn.)■	J17		

Colors: Orange & Blue. Nickname: Scots.
AD: Ken Andrews. SID: Andy Johnson. III

MAINE .... Orono, ME 04469

Joanne Palombo (1 YR. W-9, L-20)

Boston College■	N28	Boston U.■	J27
Maine Cl.	D3-4	Northeastern■	J29
Minnesota Cl.	D11-12	Dartmouth	J31
Buffalo	D28	New Hampshire	F 5
St. Bonaventure	D29	Northeastern	F10
Maine Shootout	J2-3	Boston U.	F12
Columbia-Barnard	J 7	Hartford	F17
Manhattan	J 9	Vermont	F19
Central Conn. St.■	J11	Delaware■	F25
Drexel	J14	Drexel■	F27
Delaware	J16	New Hampshire■	M 2
Vermont■	J20	North Atlantic Tr.	M6-12
Hartford■	J22		

Colors: Blue & White. Nickname: Black Bears.
AD: Michael Ploszek. SID: Matt Bourque. I

MANHATTAN .... Riverdale, NY 10471

Michele Sharp (1 YR. W-12, L-15)

FDU-Teaneck	D 1	Loyola (Md.)■	J31
Manhattan Cl.	D4-5	Fairfield	F 4
Fordham■	D 8	St. Peter's■	F 9
Rhode Island	D14	Niagara	F11
St. John's (N.Y.)☒	D18	Canisius	F13
Villanova Tr.	D28-29	Fairfield■	F16
South Fla.	J 3	Iona	F19
Stetson	J 5	Siena■	F21
Maine■	J 9	St. Peter's	F23
St. Joseph's (Pa.)	J12	Niagara■	F25
Iona■	J18	Canisius■	F27
Loyola (Md.)	J22	Metro Atlantic Tr.	M4-6
Siena	J28	☒ Uniondale, NY	

Colors: Kelly Green & White. Nickname: Lady Jaspers.
AD: Robert J. Byrnes. SID: Jeff Bernstein. I

MANHATTANVILLE .... Purchase, NY 10577

Lisa Graf (2 YRS. W-10, L-33)

Rochester Tr.	N19-20	Staten Island	J26
New Paltz St.	N23	Manhattanville Inv.	J29-30
New York U.■	N29	King's (N.Y.)■	F 1
Vassar	D 1	CCNY	F 3
Manhattanville Tr.	D4-5	Connecticut Col.	F 5
Medgar Evers	D 9	Mt. St. Mary (N.Y.)■	F 7
Dominican (N.Y.)■	D11	Trinity (Conn.)	F10
New Rochelle	J18	Old Westbury	F12
Hunter	J20	Mt. St. Vincent■	F14
Skidmore■	J22	Baruch	F17
John Jay■	J24	New Jersey Tech■	F22

Colors: Red & White. Nickname: Valiants.
AD: Ted Kolva. SID: Susan Eichner. III

MANKATO ST. .... Mankato, MN 56001

Joan Anderson (9 YRS. W-137, L-140)

Wis.-Parkside■	N20	Augustana (S.D.)	J21
Gust. Adolphus	N23	South Dak. St.	J22
St. Scholastica	N27	Nebraska-Omaha■	J28
Minn.-Duluth■	D 4	Northern Colo.■	J29
Winona St.■	D 7	South Dak.	F 4
IU/PU-Ft. Wayne Tr.	D10-11	Morningside	F 5
Mankato St. Cl.	D17-18	South Dak. St.■	F18
North Dak. St.	J 2	Augustana (S.D.)■	F19
North Dak.	J 3	Northern Colo.	F25
Morningside■	J 7	Nebraska-Omaha	F26
South Dak.■	J 8	North Dak.■	M 4
St. Cloud St.■	J12	North Dak. St.■	M 5
St. Cloud St.	J15		

Colors: Purple & Gold. Nickname: Mavericks.
AD: Georgene Brock. SID: Paul Allan. II

MANSFIELD .... Mansfield, PA 16933

Karen Bogues (2 YRS. W-12, L-37)

Gannon Tr.	N19-20	Cheyney	J22
Le Moyne■	N23	Bloomsburg	J26
Mansfield Tr.	N26-27	Millersville	J29
Lock Haven■	N29	Kutztown■	F 2
Northern Ky. Cl.	D3-4	West Chester■	F 5
Pitt-Bradford■	D 8	East Stroudsburg	F 9
Slippery Rock■	J 6	Bloomsburg■	F16
Shippensburg■	J 8	Cheyney■	F19
East Stroudsburg■	J12	Kutztown	F23
West Chester	J15	Millersville■	F26
Mercyhurst■	J18		

Colors: Red, Black & White. Nickname: Mountaineers.
AD: Roger Maisner. SID: Steve McCloskey. II

MARIETTA .... Marietta, OH 45750

Suzanne Helfant (1 YR. W-11, L-15)

Penn St.-Behrend	N23	Ohio Northern	J15
Marietta Tr.	N27-28	Capital■	J18
Waynesburg	D 1	Heidelberg	J22
John Carroll■	D 4	Mount Union■	J25
Mount Union	D 7	John Carroll	J29
Heidelberg■	D11	Otterbein	F 1
Baldwin-Wallace	D18	Baldwin-Wallace■	F 5
Wittenberg■	D28	Muskingum■	F 8
Muskingum	J 4	Hiram	F12
Wash. & Jeff.■	J 6	Capital	F15
Hiram■	J 8	Ohio Northern■	F19
Otterbein■	J11		

Colors: Navy Blue & White. Nickname: Pioneers.
AD: Debora Lazorik. SID: Mike McNamara. III

■ Home games on each schedule.

See pages 735-738 for Division I tournament details

MARIST .... Poughkeepsie, NY 12601
Ken Babineau (7 YRS. W-91, L-105)

Opponent	Date	Opponent	Date
Kentucky Inv.	N26-27	FDU-Teaneck■	J29
Connecticut Cl.	D4-5	St. Francis (Pa.)■	F 3
Army■	D 8	Robert Morris■	F 5
Fordham	D11	Siena■	F 7
Mt. St. Mary's (Md.)■	J 4	St. Francis (N.Y.)	F10
Rider■	J 5	LIU-Brooklyn	F12
FDU-Teaneck	J 8	Monmouth (N.J.)■	F16
Robert Morris	J13	Wagner■	F19
St. Francis (Pa.)	J15	Mt. St. Mary's (Md.)	F24
Buffalo	J17	Rider	F26
St. Francis (N.Y.)■	J20	LIU-Brooklyn■	M 2
Wagner	J22	Northeast Tr.	M5-12
Monmouth (N.J.)	J24		

Colors: Red & White. Nickname: Red Foxes.
AD: Gene Doris. SID: Dan Sullivan. I

MARQUETTE .... Milwaukee, WI 53233
Jim Jabir (6 YRS. W-87, L-73)

Opponent	Date	Opponent	Date
Minnesota■	N27	Cincinnati	J21
Notre Dame	D 1	Dayton	J23
Wis.-Green Bay	D 4	Wis.-Milwaukee	J25
Georgia■	D 8	St. Louis	J27
Southwest Mo. St.	D11	Ala.-Birmingham■	J29
Michigan	D18	Memphis St.■	F 3
Ball St.	D21	Ala.-Birmingham	F 5
Syracuse■	D27	St. Louis■	F12
Illinois St.■	D29	Northeastern Ill.	F14
Texas	J 5	Cincinnati■	F19
Memphis St.	J 8	Buffalo■	F21
Canisius■	J11	DePaul	M 3
DePaul■	J15	Dayton■	M 5

Colors: Royal Blue & Gold. Nickname: Warriors.
AD: Bill Cords. SID: Kathleen Hohl. I

MARS HILL .... Mars Hill, NC 28754
Sylvia White (1 YR. W-11, L-15)

Opponent	Date	Opponent	Date
Davidson	N27	Lees-McRae	J24
East Tenn. St.	N30	Presbyterian■	J26
Tusculum■	D 2	Wingate■	J29
Mt. Olive■	D 9	Limestone■	J31
Queens (N.C.)	D11	Limestone	F 2
Kennesaw St. Tr.	D17-18	Lenoir-Rhyne■	F 5
Carson-Newman Cl.	J5-6	Elon	F 9
Lenoir-Rhyne	J 8	Gardner-Webb	F12
Wofford	J10	Carson-Newman■	F16
Elon■	J12	Catawba■	F19
Gardner-Webb■	J15	Presbyterian	F23
Carson-Newman	J19	Wingate	F26
Catawba	J22		

Colors: Royal Blue & Gold. Nickname: Lady Lions.
AD: Ed Hoffmeyer. SID: To be named. II

MARSHALL .... Huntington, WV 25701
Sarah Evans (1 YR. W-14, L-10)

Opponent	Date	Opponent	Date
Youngstown St.	N27	Western Caro.■	J24
Virginia Cl.	D3-4	Furman	J29
Eastern Ky.■	D 7	Morehead St.	F 2
Ohio	D 9	East Tenn. St.	F 6
Radford■	D11	Ga. Southern■	F12
Robert Morris	D18	Tenn.-Chatt.■	F14
St. Francis (Pa.)	D20	Kentucky■	F16
Duquesne	D22	Appalachian St.	F19
St. Peter's	J 3	Western Caro.	F21
East Tenn. St.■	J 8	Furman■	F26
Ga. Southern	J15	Davidson■	F28
Tenn.-Chatt.	J17	Southern Tr.	M10-12
West Va.☒	J19	☒ Charleston, WV	
Appalachian St.■	J22		

Colors: Green & White. Nickname: Lady Herd.
AD: Lee Moon. SID: Clark Haptonstall. I

MARY WASHINGTON ..... Fredericksburg, VA 22401
Connie Gallahan (16 YRS. W-192, L-187)

Opponent	Date	Opponent	Date
Ferrum Tr.	N19-20	Chris. Newport■	J27
Notre Dame (Md.)	N23	York (Pa.)■	J29
Randolph-Macon	N30	Catholic	F 1
Frostburg St.	D 2	St. Mary's (Md.)	F 3
N.C. Wesleyan	J 8	Marymount (Va.)	F 5
Bridgewater (Va.)	J11	Gallaudet■	F 8
St. Mary's (Md.)■	J13	Salisbury St.■	F10
Marymount (Va.)■	J18	Goucher■	F15
Gallaudet	J20	Catholic■	F17
Goucher	J22	York (Pa.)	F19
Shenandoah	J25		

Colors: Navy, Gray & White. Nickname: Eagles.
AD: Ed Hegmann. SID: Vince Benigni. III

MARYLAND .... College Park, MD 20740
Chris Weller (18 YRS. W-375, L-153)

Opponent	Date	Opponent	Date
American■	N27	North Caro.■	J24
Howard■	N29	Florida St.■	J28
Richmond Inv.	D3-4	Georgia Tech	J30
Old Dominion	D 8	Duke■	F 5
Tennessee	D12	Rutgers■	F 8
Maryland Cl.	D28-29	Clemson■	F11
Georgia Tech■	J 2	North Caro. St.■	F13
Florida St.	J 5	Wake Forest■	F16
Clemson	J 8	Duke	F18
Geo. Washington	J12	North Caro.	F20
Wake Forest	J15	Virginia■	F23
Virginia	J18	ACC Tr.	M4-7
North Caro. St.	J22		

Colors: Red & White, Black & Gold. Nickname: Terps.
AD: Andy Geiger. SID: Chuck Walsh. I

MD.-BALT. COUNTY .... Baltimore, MD 21228
Kathy Solano (11 YRS. W-179, L-143)

Opponent	Date	Opponent	Date
North Caro. Inv.	D3-4	Towson St.■	F 1
George Mason	D11	N.C.-Asheville	F 4
N.C.-Asheville■	D17	Winthrop	F 5
Winthrop■	D18	Coastal Caro.■	F11
Florida Int'l Tr.	J2-4	Charleston So.■	F12
Coastal Caro.	J 7	Navy■	F22
Charleston So.	J 8	N.C.-Greensboro■	F25
Richmond	J12	Campbell■	F27
N.C.-Greensboro	J21	Towson St.	M 1
Campbell	J22	Radford	M 4
Radford■	J28	Liberty	M 5
Liberty■	J29	Big South Tr.	M9-12

Colors: Black, Gold & Red. Nickname: Retrievers.
AD: Charles Brown. SID: Jerry Milani. I

MD.-EAST. SHORE .... Princess Anne, MD 21853
Lisa Jones (1ST YR. AS HEAD COACH)

Opponent	Date	Opponent	Date
St. Peter's	N27	Hofstra■	J27
Bowie St.	D 2	Morgan St.	J29
Va. Commonwealth	D 8	Dist. Columbia	J31
LIU-Brooklyn	D11	South Caro. St.■	F 5
Buffalo	D13	North Caro. A&T■	F 7
Florida A&M■	J 8	Delaware St.	F12
Bethune-Cookman■	J10	Florida A&M	F19
Howard	J13	Bethune-Cookman	F21
Morgan St.■	J15	Dist. Columbia■	F24
Coppin St.	J17	Coppin St.■	F26
Buffalo■	J19	Delaware St.■	M 3
South Caro. St.	J22	MEAC Tr.	M9-13
North Caro. A&T	J24		

Colors: Maroon & Gray. Nickname: Hawks.
AD: Hallie Gregory. SID: Shelia Benton. I

MARYMOUNT (VA.) .... Arlington, VA 22207
Bill Finney (10 YRS. W-185, L-76)

Opponent	Date	Opponent	Date
Marymount (Va.) Tr.	N19-21	St. Mary's (Md.)	J26
Ferrum Inv.	D4-5	Goucher■	J29
Bridgewater (Va.)■	D 7	York (Pa.)■	F 3
Notre Dame (Md.)	D11	Mary Washington■	F 5
Maryville (Tn.) Tr.	J8-9	Catholic	F 7
Catholic■	J12	St. Mary's (Md.)■	F10
Gallaudet■	J15	Marymount (Va.) Inv.	F12-13
Mary Washington	J18	Goucher	F17
York (Pa.)	J20	Gallaudet	F19

Colors: Blue, White & Green. Nickname: Saints.
AD: Bill Finney. SID: Webb Hatch. III

MARYVILLE (MO.) .... Creve Coeur, MO 63141
Lonnie Folks (6 YRS. W-54 , L-93)

Opponent	Date	Opponent	Date
Westminst. (Mo.) Cl.	N19-20	Webster	J20
Rhodes■	N27	MacMurray	J22
Grinnell■	N28	Blackburn■	J27
Greenville■	N30	Westminster■	J29
Hendrix■	D 3	Washington (Mo.)■	F 3
Westminster	D 6	Fontbonne	F 5
Knox■	D10	Webster■	F12
Monmouth (Ill.)■	D11	Principia■	F14
Rockford■	J 8	MacMurray■	F17
Fontbonne■	J11	Blackburn	F19
Principia	J15		

Colors: Red & White. Nickname: Saints.
AD: Dave Pierce. SID: Lonnie Folks. III

■ Home games on each schedule.

See pages 735-738 for Division I tournament details

MARYVILLE (TENN.) — Maryville, TN 37801
Wes Moore (6 YRS. W-131, L-36)

Marymount (Va.) Tr. N19-21
Centre N28
Ferrum Inv. D4-5
Tusculum D 9
Averett■ D11
Thomas More■ J 5
Maryville (Tn.) Tr. J8-9
Centre■ J12
Roanoke■ J15
Emory & Henry J18
Greensboro J22
Averett J23
Bennett■ J28
Emory & Henry■ F 3
Berea F 5
Thomas More F 6
Sewanee■ F 9
Knoxville F12
Milligan■ F14
Sewanee F23
Berea■ F26

Colors: Orange & Garnet. Nickname: Scots.
AD: Randy Lambert. SID: Wes Moore. III

MARYWOOD — Scranton, PA 18509
John Seitzinger (1ST YR. AS HEAD COACH)

Marywood Tr. N19-20
Scranton■ N23
Lycoming■ N29
Bapt. Bible (Pa.) D 2
Alvernia■ D 4
Cedar Crest D 9
Wesley D11
Phila. Pharmacy J13
St. Elizabeth J15
Misericordia J18
King's (Pa.)■ J20
Alvernia J22
Bapt. Bible (Pa.)■ J25
Allentown■ J27
Immaculata J29
Beaver■ J31
Misericordia■ F 2
Neumann■ F 5
Wilkes F10
Cedar Crest■ F12
Eastern (Pa.) F15
Beaver F17
Gwynedd Mercy■ F19

Colors: Green & White. Nickname: Pacers.
AD: Mary Jo Gunning. SID: John Seitzinger. III

MASSACHUSETTS — Amherst, MA 01003
Joanie O'Brien (2 YRS. W-15, L-39)

Ohio St. N28
Northeastern■ D 1
New Hampshire■ D 8
Providence D11
St. Peter's Tr. D29-30
Vanderbilt■ J 2
St. Bonaventure J 4
Siena J 6
Vermont■ J 9
Rhode Island J11
St. Bonaventure■ J15
Brown■ J19
West Va.■ J22
Duquesne■ J24
Geo. Washington■ J26
Temple J29
St. Joseph's (Pa.) J31
Rhode Island■ F 5
Rutgers■ F12
West Va. F17
Duquesne F19
Geo. Washington F26
Rutgers F28
St. Joseph's (Pa.)■ M 3
Temple■ M 5

Colors: Maroon & White. Nickname: Minutewomen.
AD: Bob Marcum. SID: Lamar Chance. I

MASS.-BOSTON — Boston, MA 02125
Dana Brown (3 YRS. W-18, L-54)

Regis (Mass.) Tr. N20-21
Framingham St. D 4
Western Conn. St.■ D 7
Westfield St.■ D 9
North Adams St.■ D11
Redlands J 5
Whittier J 8
Mass.-Dartmouth■ J11
Eastern Nazarene J13
Pine Manor■ J15
Plymouth St. J18
Bri'water (Mass.) J20
Eastern Conn. St. J22
Southern Me. J25
Western Conn. St. J29
Mass.-Dartmouth F 1
Suffolk■ F 5
Curry F 7
Plymouth St.■ F 8
Rhode Island Col. F12
Southern Me.■ F15
Eastern Conn. St.■ F19

Colors: Blue & White. Nickname: Beacons.
AD: Charlie Titus. SID: Kevin Dolan. III

MASS.-LOWELL — Lowell, MA 01854
Kathy O'Neil (8 YRS. W-123, L-105)

Mass.-Lowell Tr. N20-21
Bryant■ N27
Bentley D 1
Assumption D 4
St. Michael's■ D 6
St. Anselm D 8
Le Moyne J 8
Quinnipiac■ J10
Bridgeport J12
New Haven■ J15
Southern Conn. St.■ J17
Franklin Pierce J19
Sacred Heart J22
New Hamp. Col.■ J26
Southern Conn. St. J29
Keene St.■ F 2
New Haven F 7
Franklin Pierce■ F 9
Sacred Heart■ F12
Bridgeport■ F14
Keene St. F16
Le Moyne■ F20
New Hamp. Col. F23

Colors: Red, White & Blue. Nickname: Chiefs.
AD: Wayne Edwards. SID: B.L. Elfring. II

MIT — Cambridge, MA 02139
Suzan Rowe (6 YRS. W-60, L-85)

MIT Tr. N20-21
Gordon N23
Elms■ D 1
Wentworth Inst. D 4
Simmons D 8
Catholic Tr. J8-9
Brandeis■ J11
Colby-Sawyer■ J15
Mount Holyoke■ J18
Anna Maria J24
Wellesley■ J27
Coast Guard■ J29
Rivier■ F 1
Wheaton (Mass.) F 3
Western New Eng. F 5
Nichols F 8
Worcester Tech■ F10
Suffolk■ F12
Babson F15
Pine Manor■ F17
Smith F19

Colors: Cardinal & Gray. Nickname: Engineers.
AD: Richard Hill. SID: Roger Crosley. III

MCNEESE ST. — Lake Charles, LA 70601
B.Martin & S. Watkins (3 YRS. W-32, L-50)

Louisiana Col.■ N27
Southeastern La.■ D 7
Duke D11
Va. Commonwealth D13
Grambling D16
Southern Miss. Cl. D20-21
Nicholls St.■ J 3
North Texas■ J 6
Texas-Arlington■ J 8
Northeast La. J13
Northwestern (La.) J15
Texas-San Antonio■ J20
Southwest Tex. St.■ J22
Stephen F. Austin J27
Sam Houston St. J29
Texas-Arlington F 3
North Texas F 5
Southwestern La. F 7
Northwestern (La.)■ F10
Northeast La.■ F12
Southwest Tex. St. F17
Texas-San Antonio F19
Sam Houston St.■ F24
Stephen F. Austin■ F26
Nicholls St. F28
Southland Tr. M8-12

Colors: Blue & Gold. Nickname: Cowgirls.
AD: Robert Hayes. SID: Louis Bonnette. I

MEMPHIS ST. — Memphis, TN 38152
Joye Lee-McNelis (2 YRS. W-24, L-33)

Tenn.-Martin■ D 1
Kentucky D 4
Mississippi D 7
Memphis St. Cl. D10-11
Santa Clara Shootout D18-19
Tennessee■ D30
Missouri■ J 2
Middle Tenn. St. J 5
Marquette■ J 8
Oral Roberts■ J11
Ala.-Birmingham J15
DePaul■ J22
Dayton J27
Cincinnati J29
St. Louis■ J31
Marquette F 3
DePaul F 5
Mississippi St.■ F 9
Ala.-Birmingham■ F12
Tenn.-Martin F14
St. Louis F19
Dayton■ F24
Cincinnati■ F26
Mississippi St. M 1
Great Midwest Tr. M9-12

Colors: Blue & Gray. Nickname: Lady Tigers.
AD: Charles Cavagnaro. SID: Sherilyn Fiveash. I

MERCER — Macon, GA 31207
Lea Henry (3 YRS. W-49, L-35)

New Orleans■ D 2
Tennessee Tech Cl. D11-12
South Fla. D15
Columbus■ J 3
Florida A&M J 5
Troy St.■ J 8
Georgia J10
Stetson J13
Central Fla. J15
Alabama J18
Charleston J22
Southeastern La.■ J27
Georgia St.■ J29
Fla. Atlantic F 3
Florida Int'l F 5
Central Fla.■ F10
Stetson■ F12
Georgia Tech■ F14
Charleston■ F19
Troy St. F21
Georgia St. F24
Southeastern La. F26
Florida Int'l■ M 3
Fla. Atlantic■ M 5
Ga. Southern■ M 7
Trans America Tr. M10-12

Colors: Orange & Black. Nickname: Lady Bears.
AD: Bobby Pope. SID: Bobby Pope. I

MERCYHURST — Erie, PA 16546
Paul Demyanovich (3 YRS. W-42, L-35)

Indiana (Pa.) Inv. N20-21
Bloomsburg■ N23
Houghton■ D 1
Le Moyne Tr. D4-5
Edinboro D 8
Clarion■ D11
Mercyhurst Tr. D17-18
Edinboro■ J 5
Clarion J 8
Lock Haven J12
Indiana (Pa.)■ J15
Mansfield J18
Columbia Union■ J22
Pitt.-Johnstown■ J26
Pitt.-Bradford■ J30
Houghton F 2
Gannon■ F 5
Lock Haven■ F 8
Westminster (Pa.)■ F10
Gannon F12
Ashland F15
Notre Dame (Ohio) F19
Central St. (Ohio) F26
Pitt.-Johnstown M 3

Colors: Blue & Green. Nickname: Lakers.
AD: Pete Russo. SID: Joe Jordano. II

■ Home games on each schedule.

See pages 735-738 for Division I tournament details

MEREDITH .... Raleigh, NC 27611

Carl Hatchell (5 YRS. W-76, L-36)

Opponent	Date	Opponent	Date
Ursinus	N20	Mary Baldwin	J22
Rand.-Macon Woman's	N22	St. Andrews■	J24
Methodist	D 1	Guilford	J26
Greensboro Tr.	D3-4	Averett■	J28
Averett	D 6	Methodist■	F 1
N.C. Wesleyan■	D 8	Bennett	F 2
Bennett■	J14	Mary Baldwin■	F 4
N.C. Wesleyan	J17	Greensboro■	F 7
Wash. & Lee	J21	Marymount (Va.) Inv.	F12-13

Colors: Maroon, White & Grey. Nickname: Angels.
AD: Jay Massey. SID: None. III

MERRIMACK .... N. Andover, MA 01845

Debbie Cogan (7 YRS. W-59, L-126)

Opponent	Date	Opponent	Date
Mass.-Lowell Tr.	N20-21	Springfield	J22
Quinnipiac■	N28	St. Michael's■	J25
Keene St.■	N30	St. Anselm■	J27
Stonehill	D 4	Quinnipiac	J29
New Hamp. Col.	D 8	Stonehill■	F 2
Florida Tech	D30	Bentley■	F 5
Tampa	D31	Bryant	F 9
Bentley	J 8	Assumption	F12
Franklin Pierce	J10	American Int'l■	F16
Bryant■	J12	Springfield■	F19
Assumption■	J15	St. Michael's	F22
American Int'l	J19	St. Anselm	F24

Colors: Navy Blue & Gold. Nickname: Warriors.
AD: Robert DeGregorio. SID: Jim Seavey. II

MESA ST. .... Grand Junction, CO 81501

Steve Kirkham (5 YRS. W-92, L-51)

Opponent	Date	Opponent	Date
Denver	N19	N.M. Highlands■	J14
Metropolitan St.	N20	Adams St.■	J15
Cal Poly SLO Tr.	N26-27	Fort Hays St.	J21
Neb.-Kearney Cl.	D2-4	Chadron St.	J27
Southern Colo.■	D 7	Colorado Mines	J29
Fort Lewis	D11	Fort Hays St.■	F 4
Northern Colo.■	D30	N.M. Highlands	F11
Metropolitan St.■	J 2	Adams St.	F12
Fort Lewis■	J 5	Chadron St.■	F18
Western St.	J 7	Colorado Mines■	F19
Southern Colo.	J11	Western St.■	F26

Colors: Maroon, Gold & White. Nickname: Mavericks.
AD: Jay Jefferson. SID: To be named. II

MESSIAH .... Grantham, PA 17027

Michael Miller (7 YRS. W-81, L-82)

Opponent	Date	Opponent	Date
Messiah Tr.	N19-20	Albright■	J18
York (Pa.)■	N23	Widener■	J22
Juniata	D 1	Lebanon Valley■	J25
Elizabethtown■	D 4	Juniata■	J29
Frank. & Marsh.	D 9	Susquehanna	F 3
Gettysburg	D11	Elizabethtown	F 5
Allentown	J 5	Albright	F 9
Gettysburg Tr.	J7-8	Moravian■	F12
Dickinson	J11	Lebanon Valley	F15
Susquehanna■	J13	Western Md.	F17
Moravian	J15	Widener	F19

Colors: Royal Blue & White. Nickname: Falcons.
AD: Layton Shoemaker. SID: Mike D'Virgilio. III

METHODIST .... Fayetteville, NC 28301

Rita Sue Wiggs (7 YRS. W-81, L-94)

Opponent	Date	Opponent	Date
Randolph-Macon Tr.	N20-21	N.C. Wesleyan■	J24
Guilford	N30	Bennett■	J26
Meredith■	D 1	Chris. Newport	J29
Ferrum Inv.	D4-5	Meredith	F 1
Savannah A&D■	D 7	Greensboro■	F 3
Wis.-Oshkosh■	J 7	Ferrum■	F 5
Fayetteville St.	J10	Averett	F 8
Greensboro	J12	Shenandoah■	F13
Ferrum	J15	N.C. Wesleyan	F14
Averett■	J20	Bennett	F16
Shenandoah	J22	Chris. Newport■	F19

Colors: Green & Gold. Nickname: Monarchs.
AD: Rita Wiggs. SID: Michael Hogan. III

METROPOLITAN ST. .... Denver, CO 80204

Darryl Smith (3 YRS. W-60, L-22)

Opponent	Date	Opponent	Date
Mesa St.■	N20	Southern Colo.	J20
Wyoming	N26	Colorado-CS■	J22
West Tex. A&M Tr.	D2-4	Regis (Colo.)■	J27
Northern Colo.	D13	Denver	J29
Portland St. Cl.	D16-17	Colo. Christian	F 5
Puget Sound■	D28	Air Force■	F 9
Mesa St.	J 2	Fort Lewis■	F12
Eastern Mont.■	J 4	Southern Colo.■	F17
Colo. Christian■	J 8	Colorado-CS	F19
Air Force	J12	Regis (Colo.)	F23
Fort Lewis	J15	Denver■	F26

Colors: Navy Blue & Columbia Blue. Nickname: Roadrunners.
AD: William Helman. SID: Gregory Smith. II

MIAMI (FLA.) .... Coral Gables, FL 33124

Ferne Labati (14 YRS. W-256, L-154)

Opponent	Date	Opponent	Date
Florida	N26	Boston College	J25
Old Dominion Cl.	N27-28	Florida	J27
Florida St. Cl.	D3-4	St. John's (N.Y.)■	J30
Georgetown■	D11	Pittsburgh■	F 2
Valparaiso■	D18	Villanova	F 6
Miami (Fla.) Tr.	D28-29	Seton Hall■	F 9
Providence	J 3	Connecticut■	F13
Villanova■	J 6	Georgetown	F17
Pittsburgh	J 9	Syracuse	F20
Seton Hall	J13	Providence■	F23
St. John's (N.Y.)	J15	Boston College■	F26
Syracuse■	J19	Big East Tr.	M4-7
Connecticut	J23		

Colors: Orange, Green & White. Nickname: Hurricanes.
AD: Paul Dee. SID: David Tratner. I

MIAMI (OHIO) .... Oxford, OH 45056

To be named

Opponent	Date	Opponent	Date
Wis.-Milwaukee■	N30	Kent■	J26
Duke Tr.	D4-5	Ball St.	J29
Xavier (Ohio)■	D 9	Akron	F 2
Dayton	D11	Ohio■	F 5
Illinois	D19	Central Mich.	F 9
Cincinnati	D28	Bowling Green■	F12
Butler	D30	Eastern Mich.	F16
Western Mich.■	J 5	Toledo■	F19
Ohio	J 8	Kent	F23
Central Mich.■	J12	Ball St.■	F26
Bowling Green	J15	Akron■	M 2
Eastern Mich.■	J19	Western Mich.	M 5
Toledo	J22	Mid-American Tr.	M8-12

Colors: Red & White. Nickname: Redskins.
AD: R.C. Johnson. SID: Brian Teter. I

MICHIGAN .... Ann Arbor, MI 48109

Trish Roberts (5 YRS. W-84, L-57)

Opponent	Date	Opponent	Date
Eastern Mich.■	N30	Iowa	J28
UC Irvine Cl.	D3-4	Minnesota	J30
Butler	D11	Illinois■	F 4
Marquette■	D18	Michigan St.■	F 9
Ill.-Chicago■	D20	Wisconsin	F11
Oklahoma Cl.	D28-29	Ohio St.	F20
Detroit Mercy	J 5	Minnesota■	F25
Indiana	J 7	Iowa■	F27
Purdue	J 9	Illinois	M 4
Michigan St.	J12	Northwestern	M 6
Wisconsin■	J16	Indiana■	M10
Ohio St.■	J21	Purdue■	M12
Penn St.■	J23		

Colors: Maize & Blue. Nickname: Wolverines.
AD: Jack Weidenbach. SID: Bruce Madej. I

MICHIGAN ST. .... East Lansing, MI 48824

Karen Langeland (17 YRS. W-261 , L-202)

Opponent	Date	Opponent	Date
Illinois St.	N26	Northwestern■	F 4
Central Mich.	N29	Illinois■	F 6
Michigan St. Cl.	D3-4	Michigan	F 9
Bowling Green	D 8	Wisconsin	F13
Dayton■	D18	Ohio St.	F18
Central Mich. Cl.	D29-30	Penn St.■	F20
Detroit Mercy■	J 2	Iowa	F25
Purdue■	J 7	Minnesota■	F27
Michigan■	J12	Northwestern	M 4
Wisconsin■	J14	Illinois	M 6
Ohio St.■	J23	Purdue	M10
Minnesota	J28	Indiana	M12
Iowa■	J30		

Colors: Green & White. Nickname: Spartans.
AD: Merrily Dean Baker. SID: Lori Schulze. I

■ Home games on each schedule.

See pages 735-738 for Division I tournament details

MICHIGAN TECH .... Houghton, MI 49931
Kevin Borseth (6 YRS. W-118, L-55)

Minn.-Duluth N23
Bemidji St. N26
North Dak. N27
Wayne St. (Mich.)■ .... D 4
Northern Mich.■ D11
Wis.-Parkside D16
Hillsdale■ D18
St. Ambrose■ D30
Minn.-Duluth■ .... J 2
Grand Valley St. .... J 6
Ferris St. .... J 8
Northwood■ J13
Lake Superior St.■ J18
Saginaw Valley J20
Oakland J22
Hillsdale J27
Wayne St. (Mich.) J29
Northern Mich. .... F 5
Grand Valley St.■ F10
Ferris St.■ F12
Northwood F17
Lake Superior St. F19
Saginaw Valley■ F24
Oakland■ F26
Wis.-Parkside■ F28

Colors: Silver & Gold. Nickname: Huskies.
AD: Rick Yeo. SID: Dave Fischer. II

MIDDLE TENN. ST. .... Murfreesboro, TN 37132
Lewis Bivens (15 YRS. W-324, L-135)

Florida St.■ N18
Tenn.-Chatt.■ .... D 1
Texas-Arlington Cl. D3-4
Middle Tenn. St. Cl. D10-11
Tenn.-Chatt. D21
Mo.-Kansas City D30
Tenn.-Martin .... J 3
Memphis St.■ .... J 5
Austin Peay■ J12
Murray St. J15
Southeast Mo. St. J17
Tennessee St.■ J19
Eastern Ky. J22
Morehead St. J24
Tennessee Tech■ J29
Tenn.-Martin■ J31
Tennessee St. .... F 5
Murray St.■ F12
Southeast Mo. St.■ F14
Tennessee Tech F17
Troy St. F19
Austin Peay F22
Morehead St.■ F26
Eastern Ky.■ F28
Ohio Valley Tr. M3-5

Colors: Blue & White. Nickname: Blue Raiders.
AD: John Stanford. SID: Ed Given. I

MIDDLEBURY .... Middlebury, VT 05753
Amy Backus (12 YRS. W-173, L-110)

Trinity (Conn.) Tr. N20-21
St. Michael's■ N23
Wesleyan N27
Norwich .... D 1
Amherst .... D 4
Trinity (Vt.)■ D11
Western Conn. Tr. D28-29
Clark (Mass.)■ .... J 4
Williams■ .... J 8
New England■ .... J 9
Wheaton (Mass.)■ J14
North Adams St.■ J15
Colby■ J21
Bowdoin■ J22
Colby-Sawyer J25
Emmanuel J30
Union (N.Y.) .... F 2
Norwich■ .... F 8
Bates■ F12
Skidmore F16
Tufts F19

Colors: Blue & White. Nickname: Panthers.
AD: G. Thomas Lawson. SID: Peter Lardner. III

MILLERSVILLE .... Millersville, PA 17551
Mary Fleig (10 YRS. W-165, L-92)

Millersville Cl. N19-20
Wilmington (Del.)■ N23
Phila. Textile■ N27
Lock Haven .... D 1
Le Moyne Tr. D4-5
Calif. (Pa.)■ D10
Longwood■ .... J 9
Pitt.-Johnstown J13
Kutztown■ J15
Shippensburg■ J17
East Stroudsburg J19
West Chester J22
Cheyney■ J26
Mansfield■ J29
Bloomsburg■ .... F 2
Kutztown .... F 5
Dist. Columbia .... F 9
East Stroudsburg■ F12
Cheyney F16
West Chester■ F19
Bloomsburg F23
Mansfield F26

Colors: Black & Gold. Nickname: Marauders.
AD: Marjorie A. Trout. SID: Greg Wright. II

MILLIKIN .... Decatur, IL 62522
Lori Kerans (7 YRS. W-111, L-66)

Washington (Mo.)■ .... D 4
Aurora .... D 7
McKendree D11
Luther Inv. D30-31
Culver-Stockton■ .... J 6
Franklin■ .... J 8
Elmhurst J11
North Park J14
Carthage J15
Ill. Wesleyan J19
Wheaton (Ill.) J21
North Central J22
DePauw■ J25
Augustana (Ill.)■ J29
Ill. Benedictine .... F 1
Illinois Col. .... F 3
North Central■ .... F 5
Blackburn .... F 8
Wheaton (Ill.)■ F11
Elmhurst■ F12
Augustana (Ill.) F15
North Park■ F19
Ill. Wesleyan■ F23
Carthage■ F26

Colors: Royal & White. Nickname: Big Blue.
AD: Merle Chapman. SID: Mickey Smith. III

MILLS .... Oakland, CA 94613
Cheryl Campbell (1ST YR. AS HEAD COACH)

Claremont-M-S N19
Holy Names N23
UC Santa Cruz■ N30
Cal Lutheran■ .... D 3
Simpson (Cal.)■ .... D 7
Notre Dame (Cal.) .... J 5
Whittier■ .... J 6
Master's .... J 7
Cal Lutheran .... J 9
La Sierra J11
Whittier J12
Dominican (Cal.) J19
Simpson (Cal.) J21
San Fran. St.■ J25
Dominican (Cal.)■ .... F 1
UC Santa Cruz .... F 4
Notre Dame (Cal.)■ .... F 8
Holy Names■ F15
Mills Tr. F17-19

Colors: Gold, Navy Blue & White. Nickname: Cyclones.
AD: Helen Carroll. SID: Karen Smyte. III

MILLSAPS .... Jackson, MS 39210
Cindy Hannon (3 YRS. W-54, L-15)

Millsaps Tr. N20-21
Emory■ N27
Judson (Ala.)■ N29
Rhodes Tr. D4-5
Mississippi-Women .... D 7
Blue Mountain■ .... J 4
Southwestern (Tex.) .... J 7
La. St.-Shreveport .... J 9
Hendrix J14
Trinity (Tex.) J16
Sewanee J21
Oglethorpe J23
Fisk■ J28
Centre■ J30
Rhodes■ .... F 1
Hendrix■ .... F 4
Trinity (Tex.)■ .... F 6
Fisk F11
Centre F13
Sewanee■ F18
Oglethorpe■ F20
Emory F23
Rhodes F25

Colors: Purple & White. Nickname: Lady Majors.
AD: Ron Jurney. SID: Trey Porter. III

MINNESOTA .... Minneapolis, MN 55455
Linda Hill-MacDonald (13 YRS. W-194, L-183)

Marquette N27
Georgia Tech .... D 1
Minnesota Cl. D11-12
Wis.-Green Bay■ D14
Wichita St. Shootout D18-19
Kansas St.■ D21
Northern Iowa D30
Iowa .... J 5
Wisconsin■ .... J 9
Illinois J16
Purdue J21
Indiana J23
Michigan St.■ J28
Michigan■ J30
Penn St. .... F 4
Northwestern■ .... F 6
Northwestern F13
Indiana■ F18
Purdue■ F20
Michigan F25
Michigan St. F27
Ohio St.■ .... M 4
Penn St.■ .... M 6
Wisconsin .... M 8
Iowa■ M11

Colors: Maroon & Gold. Nickname: Gophers.
AD: Chris Voelz. SID: Dianne Boyer. I

MINN.-MORRIS .... Morris, MN 56267
Michelle Woodard (2 YRS. W-28, L-27)

Minn.-Morris Tr. N19-20
South Dak. Tech Inv. N26-27
Concordia (St. Paul) N30
Jamestown .... D 2
Valley City St.■ .... D 3
South Dak. D10
Sioux Falls D11
South Dak. St. D30
Wis.-River Falls .... J 2
Winona St.■ .... J 5
Moorhead St. .... J 8
Wis.-Stout J10
Northern St.■ J12
Bemidji St. J15
Southwest St.■ J19
Wayne St. (Mich.) J22
Minn.-Duluth■ J29
Winona St. .... F 2
Moorhead St.■ .... F 5
Northern St. .... F 9
St. Scholastica■ F11
Bemidji St.■ F12
Southwest St. F16
Wayne St. (Neb.)■ F19
Minn.-Duluth F26

Colors: Maroon & Gold. Nickname: Cougars.
AD: Mark Fohl. SID: Judy Riley. II

MISERICORDIA .... Dallas, PA 18612
Julie Oja (1 YR. W-11, L-11)

Centenary (N.J.) N23
Juniata N29
Oneonta St.■ .... D 1
York (Pa.) Tr. D3-4
Bapt. Bible (Pa.) .... D 7
King's (Pa.)■ .... D 9
Keuka■ D11
Neumann J11
St. Elizabeth■ J12
Alvernia■ J15
Marywood■ J18
Cedar Crest■ J20
Immaculata■ J22
Wilkes■ J27
Beaver J29
Marywood .... F 2
Alvernia .... F 5
Allentown■ .... F 7
Cedar Crest .... F 9
Beaver■ F12
Lycoming■ F15
Holy Family F17

Colors: Royal Blue & Gold. Nickname: Lady Cougars.
AD: Michael Mould. SID: Scott Crispell. III

■ Home games on each schedule.

See pages 735-738 for Division I tournament details

MISSISSIPPI .... University, MS 38677

Van Chancellor (15 YRS. W-360, L-115)

Texas Christian N26
Texas-Arlington N28
Arkansas St.■ .... D 1
Washington .... D 4
Memphis St.■ .... D 7
Mississippi Cl. D10-11
Grambling■ D13
Kentucky D18
San Juan Shootout D20-22
Brigham Young Cl. D29-30
Tennessee Tech .... J 2
Auburn .... J 8
South Caro. J11
Arkansas■ J15
Vanderbilt■ J19
Florida J22
Northeast La. J25
Tennessee■ J29
Lamar .... F 2
Southern-B.R.■ .... F 9
Georgia■ F12
Grambling F16
Louisiana St. F19
Mississippi St. F23
Alabama■ F26
Southeastern Tr. M4-7

Colors: Red & Blue. Nickname: Lady Rebels.
AD: Warner Alford. SID: Bonnie Bishop. I

MISSISSIPPI COL. .... Clinton, MS 39058

Ed Nixon (23 YRS. W-345, L-305)

Tuskegee■ N27
Louisiana Col.■ .... D 2
Mississippi-Women .... D 4
Blue Mountain■ .... D 7
Selma■ D16
Ala.-Huntsville■ D18
Tougaloo■ .... J 3
Lincoln Memorial■ .... J 6
Central Ark.■ .... J 8
Henderson St.■ J11
Lincoln Memorial J15
Delta St. J19
Belhaven■ J22
Livingston J24
Ala.-Huntsville J27
Xavier (La.)■ J29
Valdosta St.■ .... F 5
Delta St.■ .... F 7
Henderson St. F12
Central Ark. F14
Mississippi-Women■ F19
Livingston■ F22
Miles■ F24
Valdosta St. F26

Colors: Blue & Gold. Nickname: Lady Chocs.
AD: Terry McMillan. SID: Norman Gough. II

MISSISSIPPI ST. .... Mississippi State, MS 39762

Jerry Henderson (4 YRS. W-45, L-65)

Livingston■ N26
Belhaven■ N30
Mississippi St. Tr. D3-4
South Caro.■ .... D 8
Nicholls St.■ D11
Pepperdine Tr. D18-19
Southern-B.R. .... J 3
Louisiana St. .... J 5
Florida .... J 8
William Carey■ J11
Kentucky J16
Ala.-Birmingham J19
Tennessee■ J22
Tulane■ J25
Vanderbilt■ J29
Southern-B.R.■ .... F 1
Georgia☒ .... F 6
Memphis St. .... F 9
Auburn■ F12
Northeast La. F15
Alabama F19
Mississippi■ F23
Arkansas■ F26
Memphis St.■ .... M 1
Southeastern Tr. M4-7
☒ Atlanta, GA

Colors: Maroon & White. Nickname: Lady Bulldogs.
AD: Larry Templeton. SID: Johnita Johnston. I

MISSISSIPPI-WOMEN .... Columbus, MS 39701

Glenn Schmidt (1 YR. W-8, L-19)

Christian Bros.■ N23
Ga. Southwestern N29
Blue Mountain .... D 2
Mississippi Col.■ .... D 4
Millsaps■ .... D 7
Ala.-Huntsville .... J 5
LeMoyne-Owen■ .... J 7
Christian Bros. .... J 8
Delta St.■ J10
Livingston J12
Rust J14
North Ala. J20
Ala.-Huntsville■ J22
Central Ark.■ J24
Delta St. J27
Lincoln Memorial J30
Queens (N.C.) J31
Rust■ .... F 3
Lincoln Memorial■ .... F 7
North Ala.■ F10
Central Ark. F12
Henderson St. F14
Livingston■ F17
Mississippi Col. F19
LeMoyne-Owen F21
Henderson St.■ F24
Blue Mountain■ F26

Colors: Columbia Blue & Navy Blue. Nickname: Blues.
AD: Dorothy Burdeshaw. SID: Keith Gaskin. II

MISSISSIPPI VAL. .... Itta Bena, MS 38941

Jessie Harris (17 YRS. W-271, L-216)

Oral Roberts N27
Southern Miss.■ .... D 1
Arkansas St. Cl. D3-4
Mississippi Cl. D10-11
Arkansas Cl. D17-18
Southern-B.R.■ .... J 8
Alcorn St.■ J10
Delta St. J12
Prairie View J15
Texas Southern J17
Oral Roberts■ J19
Jackson St. J22
Alabama St. J24
Troy St. J25
Grambling■ J29
Troy St.■ .... F 2
Southern-B.R. .... F 5
Alcorn St. .... F 7
Delta St.■ .... F 9
Prairie View■ F12
Texas Southern■ F14
Jackson St.■ F19
Alabama St.■ F21
Grambling F26
SWAC Tr. M10-13

Colors: Green & White. Nickname: Delta Devils.
AD: Charles Prophet. SID: Charles Prophet. I

MISSOURI .... Columbia, MO 65205

Joann Rutherford (18 YRS. W-359, L-183)

Northeastern Ill. N26
Bradley N28
Missouri Cl. D3-4
Illinois St. .... D 8
Southeast Mo. St.■ D11
Eastern Ill. D19
Illinois■ D21
Jackson St. D31
Memphis St. .... J 2
Kansas .... J 7
Kansas St. .... J 9
Creighton J11
Mo.-Kansas City■ J13
Colorado J16
Iowa St.■ J21
Nebraska■ J23
Oklahoma St. J28
Oklahoma J30
Kansas St.■ .... F 2
Kansas■ .... F 6
Colorado■ F12
Nebraska F16
Iowa St. F20
Oklahoma■ F25
Oklahoma St.■ F27
Big Eight Tr. M5-7

Colors: Old Gold & Black. Nickname: Tigers.
AD: Dan Devine. SID: Bob Brendel. I

MO.-KANSAS CITY .... Kansas City, MO 64110

David Glass (1ST YR. AS HEAD COACH)

Okla. Baptist■ N26
Northern Iowa N28
Peru St.■ .... D 2
Texas A&M Inv. D4-5
Middle Tenn. St. Cl. D10-11
Drake■ D14
Creighton■ D20
Kansas■ D22
Middle Tenn. St.■ D30
Louisville Cl. J2-3
Evansville■ .... J 5
Drake .... J 9
Missouri J13
Western Ky. J16
Oral Roberts J22
Texas-Arlington J24
Chicago St.■ J29
Oral Roberts■ .... F 5
Southwest Mo. St. .... F 9
Western Ill. F15
Southeast Mo. St.■ F21
Chicago St. F24
Cal St. Northridge■ F26

Colors: Blue & Gold. Nickname: Kangaroos.
AD: Lee Hunt. SID: Jeff Rogers. I

MISSOURI-ROLLA .... Rolla, MO 65401

Linda Roberts (14 YRS. W-186, L-152)

East Tex. St. Tr. N19-20
Texas Woman's Tr. N26-27
Kansas St. N29
SIU-Edwardsville Tr. D3-4
Quincy■ .... D 7
Ozarks (Mo.)■ D10
Harding■ D11
Lincoln (Mo.)■ .... J 5
Northwest Mo. St. .... J 8
Washburn■ J12
Mo.-St. Louis■ J15
Pittsburg St. J19
Southwest Baptist J22
Central Mo. St.■ J26
Mo. Southern St. J29
Emporia St.■ .... F 3
Mo. Western St. .... F 5
Northeast Mo. St. .... F 9
Northwest Mo. St.■ F12
Washburn F16
Mo.-St. Louis F19
Pittsburg St.■ F23
Southwest Baptist■ F26

Colors: Silver & Gold. Nickname: Miners.
AD: Mark Mullin. SID: John Kean. II

MO. SOUTHERN ST. .... Joplin, MO 64801

Scott Ballard (3 YRS. W-57, L-29)

Pittsburg St.■ N23
Pittsburg St. Cl. N26-27
East Tex. St.■ N30
Central Okla. Cl. D3-4
Oral Roberts .... D 6
Lincoln (Mo.)■ .... D 8
Washburn■ D11
Bahamas Tr. J3-8
Mo. Western St. J12
Northeast Mo. St.■ J15
Central Mo. St. J19
Emporia St.■ J22
Northwest Mo. St. J26
Missouri-Rolla■ J29
Mo.-St. Louis■ .... F 2
Pittsburg St. .... F 5
Southwest Baptist .... F 8
Lincoln (Mo.) F12
Mo. Western St.■ F16
Northeast Mo. St. F19
Central Mo. St.■ F23
Emporia St. F26

Colors: Green & Gold. Nickname: Lady Lions.
AD: Sallie Beard. SID: Dennis Slusher. II

MO. WESTERN ST. .... St. Joseph, MO 64507

Jeff Mittie (1 YR. W-16, L-11)

Hastings Tr. N20-21
Neb.-Kearney Cl. D2-4
Ozarks (Ark.)■ .... D 9
Doane D11
Quincy■ D18
High Desert Cl. D27-28
Northwest Mo. St. .... J 5
Central Mo. St. .... J 8
Mo. Southern St.■ J12
Emporia St. J15
Northeast Mo. St. J19
Lincoln (Mo.)■ J22
Pittsburg St. J26
Mo.-St. Louis■ J29
Southwest Baptist .... F 1
Missouri-Rolla■ .... F 5
Washburn■ .... F 9
Central Mo. St.■ F12
Mo. Southern St. F16
Emporia St.■ F19
Northeast Mo. St.■ F23
Lincoln (Mo.) F26

Colors: Black & Gold. Nickname: Lady Griffons.
AD: Ed Harris. SID: Paul Sweetgall. II

■ Home games on each schedule.

See pages 735-738 for Division I tournament details

MOLLOY .... Rockville Center, NY 11570
Bob Houlihan (7 YRS. W-98, L-98)

West Chester	N23	LIU-C.W. Post■	J17
Molloy Tr.	N26-27	LIU-Southampton■	J19
Bridgeport	N29	Dowling	J24
Sacred Heart	D 1	Pace■	J26
Southern Conn. St.	D 2	Concordia (N.Y.)■	J29
Concordia (N.Y.)	D 4	LIU-Southampton	F 1
Adelphi	D 6	Pace	F 9
Queens (N.Y.)■	D 8	LIU-C.W. Post	F12
St. Rose■	D11	St. Rose	F16
Dowling■	D29	Mercy■	F19
Phila. Textile	J 5	Queens (N.Y.)	F23
Adelphi■	J12	Phila. Textile■	F26
Mercy	J15		

Colors: Maroon & White. Nickname: Lions.
AD: Robert Houlihan. SID: To be named. II

MONMOUTH (ILL.) .... Monmouth, IL 61462
Dennis Mann (1 YR. W-5, L-17)

Central (Iowa)■	N27	Ripon	J22
Webster■	N28	Grinnell	J25
Cornell College	D 2	Lake Forest■	J28
Illinois Col.■	D 7	Beloit■	J29
Webster	D10	Illinois Col.	F 1
Maryville (Mo.)	D11	Eureka■	F 7
Rollins	D27	Cornell College■	F11
Knox■	J12	Grinnell■	F12
Iowa Wesleyan■	J14	Knox	F15
Coe	J15	Coe■	F18
Carroll (Wis.)	J21		

Colors: Crimson & White. Nickname: Fighting Scots.
AD: Terry Glasgow. SID: Chris Pio. III

MONMOUTH (N.J.) .... W. Long Branch, NJ 07764
Susan Dekalb (7 YRS. W-71, L-114)

Seton Hall	N27	Marist■	J24
Bucknell■	D 1	St. Francis (N.Y.)	J27
Iona Tr.	D4-5	LIU-Brooklyn	J29
Hofstra■	D11	Wagner	F 5
Villanova Tr.	D28-29	Rider■	F10
George Mason	D31	Mt. St. Mary's (Md.)■	F12
St. Francis (Pa.)	J 4	Marist	F16
Robert Morris	J 6	FDU-Teaneck	F18
LIU-Brooklyn■	J 8	Robert Morris■	F24
St. Francis (N.Y.)■	J10	St. Francis (Pa.)■	F26
Wagner■	J15	Mt. St. Mary's (Md.)	M 2
Rider	J20	Northeast Tr.	M5-12
FDU-Teaneck■	J22		

Colors: Royal Blue & White. Nickname: Hawks.
AD: Wayne Szoke. SID: Bernie Greenberg. I

MONTANA .... Missoula, MT 59812
Robin Selvig (15 YRS. W-357, L-88)

Tennessee	N28	Weber St.■	J20
Eastern Mont.■	D 2	Northern Ariz.■	J22
Iowa St.■	D 4	Idaho St.	J28
Drake■	D 5	Boise St.	J29
Southern Utah	D10	Montana St.■	F 4
Brigham Young	D11	Eastern Wash.■	F11
Utah■	D20	Idaho■	F12
Southwest Mo. St.■	D21	Northern Ariz.	F17
Montana Tr.	D29	Weber St.	F19
Gonzaga	J 6	Boise St.■	F25
Portland	J 8	Idaho St.■	F26
Idaho	J14	Montana St.	M 4
Eastern Wash.	J15	Big Sky Tr.	M11-12

Colors: Copper, Silver, Gold. Nickname: Lady Griz.
AD: Kathy Noble. SID: Linda McCarthy. I

MONTANA ST. .... Bozeman, MT 59717
Judy Spoelstra (4 YRS. W-67, L-45)

Drake■	D 3	Weber St.■	J22
Iowa St.■	D 5	Idaho St.	J29
Brigham Young	D10	Montana	F 4
Southern Utah	D11	Idaho■	F11
Montana St. Tr.	D31-J1	Eastern Wash.■	F12
Gonzaga	J 4	Weber St.	F17
Alas. Anchorage Inv.	J6-8	Northern Ariz.	F19
Eastern Wash.	J14	Idaho St.■	F25
Idaho	J15	Montana■	M 4
Northern Ariz.■	J20	Big Sky Tr.	M11-12

Colors: Blue & Gold. Nickname: Bobcats.
AD: Doug Fullerton. SID: Tom Schulz. I

MONTCLAIR ST. .... Upper Montclair, NJ 07043
To be named

Scranton	N19	Rutgers-Camden■	J15
Ramapo■	N23	Rutgers-Newark	J19
Rowan	N27	Wm. Paterson	J22
Wm. Paterson■	N30	Allentown	J24
Montclair St. Cl.	D3-4	Ramapo	J26
Trenton St.■	D 8	Rowan■	J29
Jersey City St.	D11	Kean■	F 2
Bridgeport	D13	Stockton St.■	F 5
Husson■	D28	Trenton St.	F 9
Lock Haven■	J 8	Jersey City St.■	F12
Stockton St.	J10	Rutgers-Newark■	F16
Kean	J12	Rutgers-Camden	F19

Colors: Scarlet & White. Nickname: Red Hawks.
AD: Gregory L. Lockard. SID: Al Langer. III

MOORHEAD ST. .... Moorhead, MN 56560
Lori Ulferts (4 YRS. W-64, L-51)

North Dak. St.■	N19	Southwest St.	J 5
Valley City St.■	N20	Minn.-Morris■	J 8
Southwest St. Cl.	N26-27	Minn.-Duluth	J12
Concordia-M'head■	D 1	Winona St.■	J15
Dakota St.	D 3	Northern St.	J22
Augustana (S.D.)	D 4	Bemidji St.■	J29
Jamestown■	D 8	Southwest St.■	F 2
North Dak.■	D10	Minn.-Morris	F 5
St. Cloud St.■	D11	Minn.-Duluth■	F 9
Minot St.	D13	Winona St.	F12
South Dak. St.■	D16	Concordia-M'head	F15
St. Cloud St.	D18	Northern St.■	F19
North Dak.	D20	Bemidji St.	F26

Colors: Scarlet & White. Nickname: Dragons.
AD: Katy Wilson. SID: Larry Scott. II

MORAVIAN .... Bethlehem, PA 18018
Mary Beth Spirk (6 YRS. W-149, L-29)

Allentown■	N23	Elizabethtown■	J19
Lebanon Valley	D 2	Susquehanna	J22
Juniata■	D 4	Widener	J26
King's (Pa.)■	D 7	Lebanon Valley■	J29
Dickinson	D 9	Frank. & Marsh.	F 1
Muhlenberg■	D11	Albright■	F 3
UC San Diego Inv.	D28-30	Juniata	F 5
Wilkes■	J 8	Elizabethtown	F 8
Albright	J13	Messiah	F12
Messiah■	J15	Widener■	F15
Scranton■	J17	Susquehanna■	F19

Colors: Blue & Grey. Nickname: Greyhounds.
AD: John Makuvek. SID: Mike Warwick. III

MOREHEAD ST. .... Morehead, KY 40351
Janet Gabriel (5 YRS. W-58, L-80)

Indiana Cl.	D3-4	Middle Tenn. St.■	J24
Northern Ky.	D 8	Eastern Ky.	J29
Xavier (Ohio)	D11	Marshall■	F 2
Wright St.■	D22	Southeast Mo. St.	F 5
La Salle Inv.	D28-29	Murray St.	F 7
Western Caro.■	J 3	Tennessee St.■	F12
Virginia Tech	J 5	Austin Peay■	F14
Murray St.■	J 8	Tenn.-Martin■	F19
Southeast Mo. St.■	J10	Eastern Ky.■	F24
Tenn.-Martin	J13	Middle Tenn. St.	F26
Austin Peay	J15	Tennessee Tech	F28
Tennessee St.	J17	Ohio Valley Tr.	M3-5
Tennessee Tech■	J22		

Colors: Blue & Gold. Nickname: Lady Eagles.
AD: Steve Hamilton. SID: Randy Stacy. I

MORGAN ST. .... Baltimore, MD 21239
Anderson Powell (8 YRS. W-76, L-139)

Duke	N26	Coppin St.■	J27
Mt. Olive	N28	Md.-East. Shore■	J29
Va. Commonwealth	D 1	Dist. Columbia	F 5
Temple■	D 4	Coppin St.	F 7
Kansas	D 8	Florida A&M■	F10
Grambling	D18	Bethune-Cookman■	F12
Hilton Head Shootout	D29-30	Point Park■	F14
South Caro. St.■	J 8	Delaware St.■	F17
North Caro. A&T■	J10	South Caro. St.	F26
Md.-East. Shore	J15	North Caro. A&T	F28
Delaware St.	J17	Point Park	M 5
Florida A&M	J20	MEAC Tr.	M9-13
Bethune-Cookman	J22		

Colors: Blue & Orange. Nickname: Lady Bears.
AD: Kenneth McBryde. SID: Joseph McIver. I

■ Home games on each schedule.

See pages 735-738 for Division I tournament details

MORRIS BROWN .... Atlanta, GA 30314

Steve Daniels (1ST YR. AS HEAD COACH)

Morris Brown Tr.	N19-20	Lane■	J28
Ga. Southwestern■	N23	Paine■	J29
Paine	N30	Clark Atlanta	F 2
Miles■	D 6	Lane	F 4
Albany St. (Ga.)	D 8	LeMoyne-Owen	F 5
Alabama A&M■	D11	Ga. Southwestern	F 9
Fort Valley St.■	J12	Alabama A&M	F11
Clark Atlanta■	J15	Tuskegee■	F14
Miles	J17	Savannah St.■	F18
LeMoyne-Owen■	J21	Clayton St.■	F19
Albany St. (Ga.)■	J22	Spelman	F21
Savannah St.	J24	Tuskegee	F22
Fort Valley St.	J26		

Colors: Purple & Black. Nickname: Lady Wolverettes.
AD: Greg Thompson. SID: Cecil McKay. II

MOUNT HOLYOKE .... South Hadley, MA 01075

Janice Savitz (12 YRS. W-113, L-151)

Trinity (Conn.)	N30	Brandeis■	J25
Bryn Mawr Tr.	D3-5	Worcester Tech	J27
Gallaudet Tr.	D10-12	Smith■	F 1
Suffolk■	J 6	Wellesley■	F 5
Amherst■	J 8	Tufts■	F 8
Wesleyan■	J11	Williams	F10
North Adams St.	J13	Babson	F12
Connecticut Col.	J15	Elms	F15
MIT	J18	Wheaton (Mass.)■	F19
Western New Eng.■	J20		

Colors: Columbia Blue & White. Nickname: Lyons.
AD: Laurie Priest. SID: Janice Savitz. III

MT. ST. MARY'S (MD.) ...... Emmitsburg, MD 21727

Bill Sheahan (12 YRS. W-272, L-60)

Georgetown■	D 4	Rider■	J22
Towson St.	D 6	St. Francis (Pa.)	J27
Howard■	D 9	Robert Morris	J29
Bucknell	D21	LIU-Brooklyn■	F 3
La Salle Inv.	D28-29	St. Francis (N.Y.)■	F 5
FDU-Teaneck	J 3	Wagner	F10
Marist	J 4	Monmouth (N.J.)	F12
Robert Morris■	J 8	William & Mary	F15
St. Francis (Pa.)■	J10	Rider	F19
St. Francis (N.Y.)	J13	Marist■	F24
LIU-Brooklyn	J15	FDU-Teaneck■	F26
Loyola (Md.)■	J17	Monmouth (N.J.)■	M 2
Wagner■	J20	Northeast Tr.	M5-12

Colors: Blue & White. Nickname: Lady Mountaineers.
AD: J. Thomas Balistrere. SID: Dave Reeder. I

MT. ST. MARY (N.Y.) .... Newburgh, NY 12550

J. Randall Ognibene (14 YRS. W-278, L-114)

Elms Tr.	N20-21	FDU-Madison■	J20
John Jay■	N23	St. Elizabeth	J24
Upsala	N30	Vassar	J27
New York U.■	D 3	Centenary (N.J.)■	J29
New Jersey Tech■	D 4	Staten Island■	F 5
FDU-Madison	D 8	Manhattanville	F 7
Centenary (N.J.)	D10	New Jersey Tech	F 9
Mt. St. Vincent■	J10	Stony Brook	F12
Baruch■	J12	New Rochelle	F14
Old Westbury	J13	St. Elizabeth■	F16
York (N.Y.)■	J17	Vassar T..	F18-19
Medgar Evers	J18	Upsala■	F23

Colors: Royal Blue & Gold. Nickname: Lady Knights.
AD: John Wright. SID: Brendan Coyne. III

MOUNT UNION .... Alliance, OH 44601

Deanne Knoblauch (6 YRS. W-66, L-85)

Penn St.-Behrend Tr.	N19-20	John Carroll	J15
Oberlin■	N23	Muskingum■	J18
Notre Dame (Ohio)■	D 1	Capital■	J22
Capital	D 4	Marietta	J25
Marietta■	D 7	Hiram■	J29
Hiram	D11	John Carroll■	F 1
Heidelberg■	D18	Heidelberg	F 5
Wooster	D30	Otterbein■	F 8
Otterbein	J 4	Ohio Northern■	F12
Waynesburg■	J 6	Baldwin-Wallace	F15
Ohio Northern	J 8	Muskingum	F19
Baldwin-Wallace■	J11		

Colors: Purple & White. Nickname: Purple Raiders.
AD: Larry Kehres. SID: Michael De Matteis. III

MUHLENBERG .... Allentown, PA 18104

Karl Foerster (11 YRS. W-126, L-130)

Muhlenberg Tr.	N20-21	Bryn Mawr	J25
Dickinson■	N23	Ursinus■	J29
Western Md.■	N30	Swarthmore	F 1
Frank. & Marsh.	D 4	Centenary (N.J.)■	F 3
Washington (Md.)■	D 7	Washington (Md.)	F 5
Moravian	D11	Haverford	F 8
Frostburg St. Cl.	J7-8	King's (Pa.)■	F10
Allentown	J12	Bryn Mawr■	F12
Gettysburg	J15	Ursinus	F15
Haverford■	J18	Lebanon Valley■	F17
Johns Hopkins■	J22	Swarthmore■	F19

Colors: Cardinal & Gray. Nickname: Mules.
AD: Ralph Kirchenheiter. SID: Gracia Perilli. III

MURRAY ST. .... Murray, KY 42071

Eddie Fields (1ST YR. AS HEAD COACH)

Evansville	N29	Austin Peay	J29
Arkansas St. Cl.	D3-4	Tennessee St.	J31
Eastern Ill.	D 6	Southeast Mo. St.■	F 2
Southern Ill.	D 8	Eastern Ky.■	F 5
Memphis St. Cl.	D10-11	Morehead St.■	F 7
Campbellsville■	D18	Middle Tenn. St.	F12
Morehead St.	J 8	Tennessee Tech	F14
Eastern Ky.	J 9	Southeast Mo. St.	F19
Middle Tenn. St.■	J15	Kentucky■	F23
Tennessee Tech■	J17	Austin Peay■	F26
Southern Ill.■	J19	Tenn.-Martin	F28
Tenn.-Martin■	J22	Ohio Valley Tr.	M3-5
Tennessee St.■	J24		

Colors: Blue & Gold. Nickname: Lady Racers.
AD: Michael D. Strickland. SID: Tim Tucker. I

MUSKINGUM .... New Concord, OH 43762

Donna Newberry (19 YRS. W-305, L-136)

Carnegie Mellon■	N20	Heidelberg■	J15
Muskingum Tr.	N27-28	Mount Union	J18
Otterbein■	D 1	Otterbein	J22
Nazareth (N.Y.) Inv.	D4-5	Ohio Northern■	J25
Ohio Northern	D 8	Capital■	J29
Baldwin-Wallace■	D11	Baldwin-Wallace	F 1
Capital	D20	John Carroll■	F 5
Waynesburg	D30	Marietta	F 8
Marietta■	J 4	Heidelberg	F12
John Carroll	J 8	Hiram■	F15
Hiram	J11	Mount Union■	F19

Colors: Black & Magenta. Nickname: Fighting Muskies.
AD: Al Christopher. SID: Jacquie Nelson. III

NAVY .... Annapolis, MD 21402

Debra Schlegel (12 YRS. W-177, L-127)

William & Mary	N30	Lafayette	J19
Charleston So.	D 3	Bucknell	J22
N.C.-Wilmington	D 5	Holy Cross■	J26
Howard■	D 7	Fordham	J29
St. Francis (Pa.)■	D 9	Army■	F 3
Navy Cl.	D18-19	Lehigh	F 5
Southeastern La.	D28	Colgate	F 9
Nicholls St.	D30	Lafayette■	F12
Towson St.	J 4	Bucknell■	F16
Davidson■	J 6	Holy Cross	F19
Army	J 8	Md.-Balt. County	F22
Lehigh■	J12	Fordham■	F26
Colgate■	J15	Patriot Tr.	M3-12

Colors: Navy Blue & Gold. Nickname: Midshipmen.
AD: Jack Lengyel. SID: Susan Fumagalli. I

NAZARETH (N.Y.) .... Rochester, NY 14610

Mike Decillis (9 YRS. W-154, L-78)

Rochester Tr.	N19-20	Hamilton■	J22
Alfred■	D 1	Elmira	J26
Nazareth (N.Y.) Inv.	D4-5	Hilbert■	J29
Hartwick■	D 8	Utica	F 3
St. John Fisher	D11	Fredonia St.	F 8
Alfred	J 8	Nazareth (N.Y.) Tr.	F11-12
Keuka■	J11	Ithaca■	F15
Brockport St.	J13	Keuka	F17
Rochester Inst.	J15	Albany (N.Y.)■	F19
Buffalo St.	J18	Hilbert	F22
Roberts Wesleyan■	J20		

Colors: Purple & Gold. Nickname: Golden Flyers.
AD: Bill Carey. SID: Joe Seil. III

■ Home games on each schedule.

See pages 735-738 for Division I tournament details

NEB.-KEARNEY .... Kearney, NE 68849
Joe Sanchez (15 YRS. W-288, L-165)

Fort Hays St. Cl. N19-20
Western St.■ N22
Abilene Chrst. Cl. N26-27
Hastings N29
Neb.-Kearney Cl. D2-4
Northwest Mo. St.■ .... D 7
Nebraska-Omaha .... D 8
South Dak. St.■ D12
Bemidji St. D17
North Dak. D18
Pittsburg St. D31
Fort Lewis .... J 2
Western St. .... J 4
Colorado-CS .... J 5
Chadron St. J14
Hastings■ J19
Peru St. J21
Augustana (S.D.) J26
Fort Hays St. .... F 8
Chadron St.■ F12
Peru St.■ F15
Fort Hays St.■ F23
Wayne St. (Neb.) F26
Wayne St. (Neb.)■ .... M 2

Colors: Royal Blue & Old Gold. Nickname: Lady Lopers.
AD: Dick Beechner. SID: Brent Robinson. II

NEBRASKA .... Lincoln, NE 68588
Angela Beck (13 YRS. W-215, L-160)

Nebraska Cl. N26-27
Arkansas St. N30
Idaho Cl. D3-4
Southwest Mo. St. .... D 8
Creighton■ D10
Arkansas St.■ D12
San Juan Shootout D20-22
Northern Iowa D28
Holy Cross■ .... J 2
Arizona St. .... J 4
Oklahoma St. .... J 7
Oklahoma .... J 9
Kansas■ J14
Kansas St.■ J16
Colorado J21
Missouri J23
Southern Utah■ J28
Iowa St.■ J30
Oklahoma■ .... F 4
Oklahoma St.■ .... F 6
Kansas St. F11
Kansas F13
Missouri■ F16
Colorado■ F20
Iowa St. F27
Big Eight Tr. M5-7

Colors: Scarlet & Cream. Nickname: Cornhuskers.
AD: Bill Byrne. SID: Terry Beek. I

NEB. WESLEYAN .... Lincoln, NE 68504
Mary Beth Kennedy (8 YRS. W-86, L-109)

Graceland (Iowa) N20
Peru St. .... D 4
Graceland (Iowa)■ .... D 7
William Penn Cl. D10-11
UC San Diego Inv. D28-30
Dana■ .... J 4
N'western (Iowa)■ .... J 7
Buena Vista■ J11
Concordia (Neb.) J14
Hastings■ J18
Doane J21
Midland Lutheran J26
Dana J28
N'western (Iowa) .... F 1
Colorado Col. .... F 5
Concordia (Neb.)■ .... F 8
Hastings F11
Doane■ F15
Midland Lutheran■ F19

Colors: Yellow & Brown. Nickname: Plainswomen.
AD: Mary Beth Kennedy. SID: Jim Angele. III

NEBRASKA-OMAHA .... Omaha, NE 68182
Cherri Mankenberg (17 YRS. W-279, L-209)

Avila■ N19
St. Leo N26
Rollins N27
Nebraska-Omaha Tr. D3-4
Neb.-Kearney■ .... D 8
Midland Lutheran D11
Hastings■ D17
South Dak. St.■ .... J 2
Augustana (S.D.)■ .... J 3
Northern Colo. .... J 8
North Dak. St. J14
North Dak. J15
Morningside■ J21
South Dak.■ J22
Mankato St. J28
St. Cloud St. J29
Northern Colo.■ .... F 5
North Dak.■ F11
North Dak. St.■ F12
South Dak. F18
Morningside F19
St. Cloud St.■ F25
Mankato St.■ F26
Augustana (S.D.) .... M 4
South Dak. St. .... M 5

Colors: Black & Red. Nickname: Lady Mavericks.
AD: Connie Claussen. SID: Gary Anderson. II

NEVADA .... Reno, NV 89557
Ada Gee (1 YR. W-2, L-1)

Fresno Pacific■ .... D 1
Cal St. Northridge .... D 4
Oregon St. Cl. D10-11
Cal St. Sacramento■ D29
Northern Ariz.■ D30
Pacific (Cal.)■ .... J 3
Hawaii■ .... J 7
Hawaii■ .... J 8
Cal St. Northridge■ J13
Nevada-Las Vegas■ J15
San Jose St. J17
UC Santa Barb. J20
UC Irvine J22
San Jose St.■ J27
Long Beach St.■ J29
Pacific (Cal.) J31
Nevada-Las Vegas F10
New Mexico St. F12
Cal St. Sacramento F14
Cal St. Fullerton■ F17
UC Irvine■ F19
Long Beach St. F24
Cal St. Fullerton F26
New Mexico St.■ .... M 3
UC Santa Barb.■ .... M 5
Big West Tr. M9-12

Colors: Blue & Silver. Nickname: Wolf Pack.
AD: Angie Taylor. SID: Michael Connors. I

NEVADA-LAS VEGAS .... Las Vegas, NV 89154
Jim Bolla (11 YRS. W-262, L-77)

UNLV Cl. D3-4
Loyola (Cal.) D11
Pepperdine D12
Stanford D30
Hawaii■ .... J 3
Hawaii■ .... J 5
Cal St. Fullerton■ .... J 8
UC Irvine■ J10
Nevada J15
Pacific (Cal.)■ J20
San Jose St.■ J22
UC Irvine J27
Cal St. Fullerton J29
Long Beach St. .... F 3
UC Santa Barb. .... F 5
Nevada■ F10
New Mexico St. F14
San Jose St. F17
Pacific (Cal.) F19
Southern Utah F22
UC Santa Barb.■ F26
Long Beach St.■ F28
New Mexico St.■ .... M 5
Big West Tr. M9-12

Colors: Scarlet & Gray. Nickname: Rebels.
AD: Jim Weaver. SID: Jim Gemma. I

NEW ENGLAND COL. .... Henniker, NH 03242
Mary Ellen Alger (5 YRS. W-69 , L-62)

Elms Tr. N20-21
Plymouth St. N30
Colby-Sawyer■ .... D 2
Worcester St. Tr. D4-5
Gordon .... D 7
Rivier .... D 9
Bates■ D11
Eastern Nazarene J15
Curry J18
Wentworth Inst.■ J20
Salve Regina■ J22
Anna Maria J26
Roger Williams■ J29
Regis (Mass.)■ .... F 1
Eastern Nazarene■ .... F 3
Curry■ .... F 5
Wentworth Inst. .... F 9
Roger Williams F12
Anna Maria■ F15
Regis (Mass.) F17
Salve Regina F19

Colors: Scarlet, White & Royal Blue. Nickname: Pilgrims.
AD: Mary Ellen Alger. SID: None. III

NEW HAMPSHIRE .... Durham, NH 03824
Kathleen Sanborn (12 YRS. W-195, L-118)

Rhode Island N28
Cornell Cl. D3-4
Massachusetts .... D 8
Dartmouth Inv. D29-30
N.C.-Greensboro Cl. J2-3
Canisius■ .... J 6
Brown J11
Delaware J14
Drexel J16
Hartford■ J20
Vermont J22
Northeastern■ J27
Boston U. J29
Harvard .... F 1
Maine■ .... F 5
Boston U.■ F10
Northeastern F12
Vermont■ F17
Hartford F19
Holy Cross■ F22
Drexel■ F25
Delaware■ F27
Maine .... M 2
North Atlantic Tr. M6-12

Colors: Blue & White. Nickname: Wildcats.
AD: Judith Ray. SID: Lisa Markley. I

NEW HAMP. COL. .... Manchester, NH 03104
Nancy Dreffs (11 YRS. W-167, L-137)

New Hamp. Col. Cl. N20-21
Bentley N23
Assumption■ N30
West Chester Cl. D3-4
Stonehill .... D 6
Merrimack■ .... D 8
American Int'l■ D11
New Haven .... J 8
St. Anselm J10
Le Moyne J12
Bridgeport■ J17
Keene St.■ J19
Mass.-Lowell J26
Sacred Heart■ J29
Franklin Pierce■ .... F 2
New Haven■ .... F 5
Bridgeport .... F 7
Keene St. .... F 9
Southern Conn. St.■ F12
Franklin Pierce F16
Le Moyne■ F19
Southern Conn. St. F21
Mass.-Lowell■ F23
Sacred Heart F26

Colors: Blue & Gold. Nickname: Penmen.
AD: Joseph Polak. SID: Tom McDermott. II

NEW HAVEN .... West Haven, CT 06516
Mary Ann Palazzi (1ST YR. AS HEAD COACH)

Mass.-Lowell Tr. N20-21
St. Anselm■ N23
Quinnipiac N30
LIU-C.W. Post■ .... D 3
Springfield■ .... D 7
American Int'l .... D 9
Bentley■ D11
Pace■ D13
New Hamp. Col.■ .... J 8
Assumption■ J10
Keene St.■ J12
Mass.-Lowell J15
Bridgeport J19
Le Moyne■ J23
Southern Conn. St. J26
Franklin Pierce J31
Sacred Heart■ .... F 2
New Hamp. Col. .... F 5
Mass.-Lowell■ .... F 7
Bridgeport■ .... F 9
Le Moyne F12
Sacred Heart F16
Franklin Pierce■ F19
Southern Conn. St.■ F23
Keene St. F26

Colors: Blue & Gold. Nickname: Chargers.
AD: William Leete. SID: Jack Jones. II

■ Home games on each schedule.

See pages 735-738 for Division I tournament details

NEW JERSEY TECH .... Newark, NJ 07102

Brenda Zabriskie (3 YRS. W-19, L-47)

Upsala■	N23	St. Elizabeth■	J19
St. Elizabeth	D 1	Staten Island	J24
Mt. St. Mary (N.Y.)	D 4	FDU-Madison■	J27
FDU-Madison	D 6	Lehman	F 2
Mt. St. Vincent Tr.	D10-11	Mt. St. Mary (N.Y.)■	F 9
CCNY	J10	York (N.Y.)■	F11
Baruch■	J14	Upsala	F14
Mt. St. Vincent■	J15	Centenary (N.J.)	F16
Centenary (N.J.)■	J17	Manhattanville	F22

Colors: Red & White. Nickname: Highlanders.
AD: J. Malcolm Simon. SID: Sal Petruzzi. III

NEW MEXICO .... Albuquerque, NM 87131

Maureen Eckroth (2 YRS. W-7, L-48)

New Mexico St.■	N27	UTEP■	J22
Northern Ariz.	N29	Brigham Young■	J27
New Mexico St.	D 4	Utah■	J29
Texas-Arlington■	D 7	Utah	F 3
Baylor■	D 9	Brigham Young	F 5
North Texas■	D18	San Diego St.■	F11
Pacific (Cal.)	D20	Fresno St.■	F13
Loyola (Cal.)	D22	Fresno St.	F18
Montana St. Tr.	D31-J1	San Diego St.	F20
Portland	J 4	Colorado St.■	F25
N.M. Highlands■	J 8	Wyoming■	F27
Colorado St.	J13	UTEP	M 5
Wyoming	J15	Western Athletic Tr.	M9-12

Colors: Cherry & Silver. Nickname: Lobos.
AD: Rudy Davalos. SID: Steve Carr. I

N.M. HIGHLANDS .... Las Vegas, NM 87701

Cindy Roybal (8 YRS. W-102, L-113)

West Tex. A&M Inv.	N19-20	Lubbock Chrst.■	J25
Eastern N. Mex. Cl.	N25-26	Fort Hays St.■	J27
Regis (Colo.) Cl.	D3-4	Chadron St.	F 3
Southern Colo. Inv.	D10-11	Colorado Mines	F 5
Colo. Christian■	J 6	Mesa St.■	F11
New Mexico	J 8	Western St.■	F12
Mesa St.	J14	Adams St.■	F15
Western St.	J15	Fort Hays St.	F18
Southern Colo.■	J18	Denver	F24
Chadron St.■	J21	Adams St.	F26
Colorado Mines■	J22		

Colors: Purple & White. Nickname: Cowgirls.
AD: Robert Evers. SID: Jesse Gallegos. II

NEW MEXICO ST. .... Las Cruces, NM 88003

Mike Petersen (5 YRS. W-82, L-59)

New Mexico	N27	Cal St. Fullerton	J27
UTEP■	D 1	UC Irvine	J29
New Mexico■	D 4	UC Santa Barb.	F 3
Western N. Mex.■	D 8	Long Beach St.	F 5
UTEP	D17	Nevada■	F12
New Mexico St. Cl.	D21-22	Nevada-Las Vegas■	F14
Baylor Cl.	D29-30	Pacific (Cal.)	F17
Texas	J 2	San Jose St.	F19
UC Irvine■	J 8	UC Santa Barb.	F24
Cal St. Fullerton■	J10	Long Beach St.	F26
Hawaii	J13	Nevada	M 3
Hawaii	J15	Nevada-Las Vegas	M 5
San Jose St.■	J20	Big West Tr.	M9-12
Pacific (Cal.)■	J22		

Colors: Crimson & White. Nickname: Roadrunners.
AD: Al Gonzales. SID: Brian McCann. I

NEW ORLEANS .... New Orleans, LA 70148

Joey Favaloro (13 YRS. W-250, L-130)

Mercer	D 2	Tulane■	J31
Washington St. Cl.	D3-4	Western Ky.■	F 3
Arkansas Cl.	D17-18	South Ala.■	F 5
Furman■	D28	Arkansas St.	F 9
Fairfield■	D30	Fla. Atlantic■	F12
Rice Cl.	J3-4	Tulane	F16
Tex.-Pan American	J 6	Louisiana Tech	F19
Lamar	J 8	Southwestern La.	F24
Louisiana Tech■	J13	Lamar■	F26
Tex.-Pan American■	J20	Western Ky.	M 2
South Ala.	J22	Southwestern La.■	M 5
Auburn■	J25	Sun Belt Tr.	M10-12
Arkansas St.■	J29		

Colors: Royal Blue & Silver. Nickname: Buc-kettes.
AD: Ron Maestri. SID: Ed Cassiere. I

NEW PALTZ ST. .... New Paltz, NY 12561

Fred Francello (4 YRS. W-41, L-59)

Regis (Mass.) Tr.	N20-21	Potsdam St.	J22
Manhattanville■	N23	Cortland St.	J25
Plattsburgh St.■	D 3	Utica Tech■	J28
Potsdam St.■	D 4	Oswego St.	J29
Binghamton■	D 7	Oneonta St.	F 1
Geneseo St.	D10	Vassar■	F 4
Brockport St.	D11	Fredonia St.■	F11
Bahamas Tr.	J3-8	Buffalo St.■	F12
Hunter■	J13	Cortland St.■	F15
Oneonta St.■	J18	Binghamton	F19
Plattsburgh St.	J21		

Colors: Orange & Blue. Nickname: Lady Hawks.
AD: Jim Zalacca. SID: Joe Donovan. III

NEW ROCHELLE .... New Rochelle, NY 10805

Brian Flynn (1 YR. W-2, L-17)

John Jay Tr.	N20-21	Old Westbury■	J26
Vassar■	N23	York (N.Y.)	J31
King's (N.Y.)	N29	Yeshiva	F 2
Marymount (N.Y.)■	D 2	Baruch	F 4
Medgar Evers	D 7	Maritime (N.Y.)	F 5
Cornell College■	D 9	Marymount (N.Y.)	F 9
Manhattanville■	J18	Mt. St. Vincent	F11
Cornell College	J20	Mt. St. Mary (N.Y.)■	F14
Maritime (N.Y.)■	J24	Yeshiva■	F16

Colors: Blue & White. Nickname: Blue Angels.
AD: Kathleen Levache. SID: Kathleen LeVache. III

NEW YORK U. .... New York, NY 10012

Janice Quinn (6 YRS. W-110, L-52)

Staten Island■	N23	Emory	J21
Case Reserve■	N26	Carnegie Mellon	J23
Manhattanville	N29	Stony Brook	J26
Mt. St. Mary (N.Y.)	D 3	Rochester■	J30
Johns Hopkins	D 5	Carnegie Mellon■	F 4
John Jay	D 8	Emory■	F 6
Rochester	D12	Hunter	F 8
Albany (N.Y.)■	J 3	Brandeis■	F12
Brandeis	J 8	Old Westbury■	F15
FDU-Madison■	J11	Chicago	F18
Washington (Mo.)■	J14	Washington (Mo.)	F20
Chicago■	J16	Mt. Marty■	F23

Colors: Violet & White. Nickname: Violets.
AD: Dan Quilty. SID: Larry Baumann. III

NIAGARA .... Niagara University, NY 14109

Bill Agronin (1 YR. W-17, L-10)

Akron	N29	St. Peter's■	J17
North Caro. Inv.	D3-4	Siena	J22
Pittsburgh■	D 8	Buffalo■	J26
Colgate■	D12	Canisius	J28
St. Bonaventure■	D14	Iona	F 4
Buffalo	D18	Fairfield	F 6
Penn St.■	D21	Manhattan■	F11
Toledo	J 2	Siena■	F13
Rutgers	J 6	Loyola (Md.)■	F17
St. Peter's	J 8	Canisius■	F21
Fairfield■	J10	Manhattan	F25
Cornell■	J12	Loyola (Md.)	F27
Iona■	J15	Metro Atlantic Tr.	M4-6

Colors: Purple, White & Gold. Nickname: Lady Eagles.
AD: Michael Jankowski. SID: James Mauro. I

NICHOLLS ST. .... Thibodaux, LA 70301

Ben Abadie (9 YRS. W-87, L-148)

Mississippi St.	D11	Stephen F. Austin	J29
Louisiana St.	D17	North Texas	F 3
Navy■	D30	Texas-Arlington	F 5
McNeese St.	J 3	Southeastern La.■	F 7
Texas-Arlington■	J 6	Northeast La.■	F10
North Texas■	J 8	Northwestern (La.)■	F12
Northwestern (La.)	J13	Texas-San Antonio	F17
Northeast La.	J15	Southwest Tex. St.	F19
Southwest Tex. St.■	J20	Stephen F. Austin■	F24
Texas-San Antonio■	J22	Sam Houston St.■	F26
Southeastern La.	J24	McNeese St.■	F28
Sam Houston St.	J27		

Colors: Red & Gray. Nickname: Lady Colonels.
AD: Phil Greco. SID: Jim Silverberg. I

■ Home games on each schedule.

See pages 735-738 for Division I tournament details

NICHOLS .... Dudley, MA 01570

Bill Craig (8 YRS. W-99, L-98)

Worcester City Tr. N20-21
Anna Maria N23
Framingham St. D 2
Nichols Tr. D4-5
Eastern Nazarene■ D 7
Brandeis■ D11
Curry D13
Fitchburg St. J18
Trinity (Conn.) J20
Norwich J22
Coast Guard■ J27
Gordon■ J29
Elms■ F 1
Emmanuel F 3
Pine Manor■ F 5
MIT■ F 8
Rhode Island Col.■ F10
Western New Eng.■ F12
Worcester Tech F17
Wesleyan F21

Colors: Black & Green. Nickname: Lady Bison.
AD: Tom Cafaro. SID: Bob Flannery. III

NORFOLK ST. .... Norfolk, VA 23504

James Sweat (12 YRS. W-311, L-74)

N.C. Central■ D 1
Norfolk St. Inv. D3-4
Clarion Cl. D10-11
Atlantic City Cl. D18-19
Dist. Columbia D21
Livingstone J 3
Johnson Smith■ J 8
St. Paul's■ J15
Fayetteville St. J16
Dist. Columbia■ J17
Virginia Union J20
Elizabeth City St. J22
Bowie St.■ J24
Shaw J26
Virginia St.■ J29
Hampton■ F 1
Virginia St. F 3
Virginia Union■ F 5
Bowie St. F 7
St. Paul's F 9
Hampton F12
St. Augustine's■ F17
Elizabeth City St.■ F19

Colors: Green & Gold. Nickname: Spartanettes.
AD: Dick Price. SID: John Holley. II

NORTH ADAMS ST. .... North Adams, MA 01247

Dorothy Houston (4 YRS. W-16, L-81)

Regis (Mass.) Tr. N20-21
Amherst N30
Russell Sage■ D 2
Castleton St.■ D 7
Williams■ D 9
Mass.-Boston D11
Smith■ J 6
Framingham St. J11
Mount Holyoke■ J13
Middlebury J15
Bri'water (Mass.)■ J17
Green Mountain J20
Worcester St.■ J22
Salem St. J25
Western New Eng. J27
Fitchburg St.■ J29
Westfield St. F 1
Framingham St.■ F 5
Bri'water (Mass.) F10
Worcester St. F12
Salem St.■ F14
Fitchburg St. F17
Westfield St.■ F19

Colors: Navy & Gold. Nickname: Mohawks.
AD: Joseph Zavattaro. SID: Tim Kelly. III

NORTH ALA. .... Florence, AL 35630

Wayne Byrd (11 YRS. W-165, L-134)

Freed-Hardeman N20
David Lipscomb■ N23
Bethel (Tenn.) N24
Freed-Hardeman■ N29
Belmont■ N30
Jacksonville St. D11
Delta St. D17
David Lipscomb J 3
Belmont J 4
Valdosta St.■ J 8
West Ga.■ J10
Henderson St. J15
Central Ark. J17
Mississippi-Women■ J20
Lincoln Memorial■ J22
Valdosta St. J29
Bethel (Tenn.)■ J31
Henderson St.■ F 5
Central Ark.■ F 7
Mississippi-Women F10
Ala.-Huntsville F12
Lincoln Memorial F14
Jacksonville St.■ F19
Delta St.■ F21
Ala.-Huntsville■ F23
West Ga. F26

Colors: Purple & Gold. Nickname: Lady Lions.
AD: Bill Jones. SID: Jeff Hodges. II

NORTH CARO. .... Chapel Hill, NC 27514

Sylvia Rhyne Hatchell (18 YRS. W-381, L-174)

N.C.-Asheville■ D 1
North Caro. Inv. D3-4
Coastal Caro.■ D 8
Florida St.■ D12
Charleston■ D18
Central Fla. Cl. D29-31
Wake Forest■ J 5
Northwestern☒ J 8
Virginia■ J12
Florida St. J14
Georgia Tech■ J16
Duke J19
Maryland J24
North Caro. St. J27
Clemson■ J30
Winthrop■ F 1
Wake Forest F 3
Virginia F 9
Georgia Tech F12
North Caro. St.■ F16
Maryland■ F20
Duke■ F22
Clemson F27
ACC Tr. M4-7
☒ Charlottesville, VA

Colors: Carolina Blue & White. Nickname: Tar Heels.
AD: John Swofford. SID: Rick Brewer. I

NORTH CARO. A&T .... Greensboro, NC 27411

Tim Abney (7 YRS. W-109, L-86)

Liberty Cl. D3-4
East Caro.■ D 6
North Caro. St.■ D 8
Campbell J 4
Howard J 8
Morgan St. J10
Coppin St.■ J13
Bethune-Cookman■ J15
Florida A&M■ J17
N.C. Central■ J19
Delaware St.■ J22
Md.-East. Shore■ J24
N.C.-Greensboro■ J26
Florida A&M J29
Bethune-Cookman J31
Winston-Salem■ F 2
Delaware St. F 5
Md.-East. Shore F 7
Campbell■ F 9
South Caro. St. F12
N.C.-Charlotte F16
Howard■ F19
Coppin St. F23
Morgan St.■ F28
South Caro. St.■ M 5
MEAC Tr. M9-13

Colors: Blue & Gold. Nickname: Aggies.
AD: Willie Burden. SID: Charles Mooney. I

NORTH CARO. ST. .... Raleigh, NC 27650

Kay Yow (22 YRS. W-454, L-168)

Howard■ D 1
Arizona St. Cl. D3-4
North Caro. A&T D 8
Va. Commonwealth■ D11
Southwest Tex. St.■ D21
UCLA☒ D28
Duke D31
Fla. Atlantic J 2
Clemson■ J 5
Georgia Tech J 8
Duke■ J12
Virginia■ J15
Wake Forest J18
Maryland■ J22
Florida St. J24
North Caro.■ J27
Clemson F 3
Old Dominion■ F 5
East Caro. F 9
Maryland F13
North Caro. F16
Georgia Tech■ F18
Florida St.■ F20
Wake Forest■ F24
Virginia F26
ACC Tr. M4-7
☒ Greensboro, NC

Colors: Red & White. Nickname: Wolfpack.
AD: Todd Turner. SID: Ann Wheelwright. I

N.C.-ASHEVILLE .... Asheville, NC 28804

Ray Ingram (1ST YR. AS HEAD COACH)

Elon■ N29
North Caro. D 1
Limestone■ D 4
Western Caro. D 6
Davidson■ D 8
East Tenn. St. D11
Md.-Balt. County D17
Towson St. D18
N.C.-Greensboro■ J 7
Campbell■ J 8
Coastal Caro.■ J14
Charleston So.■ J15
Wofford■ J18
Radford J21
Liberty J22
Winthrop J29
Md.-Balt. County■ F 4
Towson St.■ F 5
N.C.-Greensboro F11
Campbell F12
Coastal Caro. F18
Charleston So. F19
Radford■ F25
Liberty■ F26
Winthrop■ M 2
Big South Tr. M9-12

Colors: Royal Blue & White. Nickname: Bulldogs.
AD: Tom Hunnicutt. SID: Mike Gore. I

N.C.-CHARLOTTE .... Charlotte, NC 28223

Ed Baldwin (5 YRS. W-95, L-50)

N.C.-Greensboro■ D 1
Michigan St. Cl. D3-4
Western Caro. D11
Wake Forest■ D19
UCLA■ D30
Winthrop■ J 2
Appalachian St. J 4
South Fla.■ J 8
Ga. Southern J11
Southern Miss. J15
Tulane J17
East Caro. J22
Va. Commonwealth J28
Louisville■ J30
Virginia Tech F 3
South Fla. F 7
South Caro. St. F10
Va. Commonwealth■ F14
North Caro. A&T■ F16
Louisville F19
South Caro. F23
Southern Miss.■ F26
Tulane■ F28
Virginia Tech■ M 3
Metro Tr. M8-11

Colors: Green & White. Nickname: 49ers.
AD: Judy Rose. SID: Thomas Whitestone. I

N.C.-GREENSBORO .... Greensboro, NC 27412

Lynne Agee (15 YRS. W-306, L-101)

N.C.-Wilmington■ N28
N.C.-Charlotte D 1
Kent D 9
Campbell D18
Southwest Tex. St.■ D20
Dayton D30
N.C.-Greensboro Cl. J2-3
N.C.-Asheville J 7
Winthrop J 8
Liberty■ J14
Radford■ J15
Md.-Balt. County■ J21
Towson St.■ J22
North Caro. A&T J26
Coastal Caro. J28
Charleston So. J29
Campbell■ F 5
N.C.-Asheville■ F11
Winthrop■ F12
Liberty F18
Radford F19
Md.-Balt. County F25
Towson St. F26
Coastal Caro.■ M 4
Charleston So.■ M 5
Big South Tr. M9-12

Colors: Gold, White & Navy. Nickname: Spartans.
AD: Nelson Bobb. SID: Ty Buckner. I

■ Home games on each schedule.

See pages 735-738 for Division I tournament details

N.C.-WILMINGTON .... Wilmington, NC 28403
Susan Yow (15 YRS. W-200, L-210)

- N.C.-Greensboro N28
- Charleston D 3
- Navy■ D 5
- South Fla. Tr. D17-18
- Davidson J 3
- N.C.-Wilmington Tr. J7-8
- American■ J14
- George Mason■ J16
- Coastal Caro. J19
- Old Dominion J21
- William & Mary J23
- James Madison■ J28
- Richmond■ J30
- East Caro. F 3
- George Mason F11
- American F13
- Old Dominion■ F18
- William & Mary■ F20
- Charleston So. F23
- James Madison F25
- Richmond F27
- East Caro.■ M 2
- Appalachian St.■ M 4
- CAA Tr. M10-12

Colors: Green & Gold. Nickname: Seahawks.
AD: Paul A. Miller. SID: Joe Browning. I

NORTH CENTRAL .... Naperville, IL 60566
Kim Hansen (5 YRS. W-47, L-78)

- Chicago■ N30
- North Central Tr. D3-4
- Calvin D 8
- Hope D 9
- Augustana (Ill.) D15
- Carthage D18
- Colorado Col. Tr. D29-31
- Aurora J 8
- Carthage■ J11
- Augustana (Ill.)■ J15
- Ill. Benedictine J20
- Millikin■ J22
- Wheaton (Ill.)■ J25
- North Park J29
- Elmhurst■ F 2
- Millikin F 5
- Lake Forest F 7
- Ill. Wesleyan■ F 9
- Wheaton (Ill.) F16
- Elmhurst F18
- North Park■ F23
- Ill. Wesleyan F26

Colors: Cardinal & White. Nickname: Cardinals.
AD: Walter Johnson. SID: Mike Koon. III

NORTH DAK. .... Grand Forks, ND 58201
Gene Roebuck (6 YRS. W-143, L-33)

- Dickinson St. N20
- Michigan Tech■ N27
- Portland St. D 2
- Seattle Pacific D 4
- Moorhead St. D10
- Mayville St.■ D15
- Neb.-Kearney■ D18
- Moorhead St.■ D20
- Minn.-Duluth D29
- St. Cloud St.■ J 2
- Mankato St.■ J 3
- South Dak. St. J 7
- Augustana (S.D.) J 8
- Northern Colo.■ J14
- Nebraska-Omaha■ J15
- North Dak. St.■ J21
- South Dak. J28
- Morningside J29
- Augustana (S.D.)■ F 4
- South Dak. St.■ F 5
- Nebraska-Omaha F11
- Northern Colo. F12
- North Dak. St. F18
- Morningside■ F25
- South Dak.■ F26
- Mankato St. M 4
- St. Cloud St. M 5

Colors: Green & White. Nickname: Sioux.
AD: Terry Wanless. SID: Kathy Howe. II

NORTH DAK. ST. .... Fargo, ND 58105
Amy Ruley (14 YRS. W-321, L-103)

- Moorhead St. N19
- Northeast Mo. Tr. N26-27
- Clarion Cl. D3-4
- Bemidji St. D10
- Minn.-Duluth D11
- Minn.-Duluth■ D18
- Valley City St.■ D19
- Mankato St.■ J 2
- St. Cloud St.■ J 3
- Augustana (S.D.) J 7
- South Dak. St. J 8
- Nebraska-Omaha■ J14
- Northern Colo.■ J15
- North Dak. J21
- Morningside J28
- South Dak. J29
- South Dak. St.■ F 4
- Augustana (S.D.)■ F 5
- Northern Colo. F11
- Nebraska-Omaha F12
- North Dak.■ F18
- South Dak.■ F25
- Morningside■ F26
- St. Cloud St. M 4
- Mankato St. M 5

Colors: Yellow & Green. Nickname: Bison.
AD: Lynn Dorn. SID: Jeff Schwartz. II

NORTH FLA. .... Jacksonville, FL 32216
Mary Ortelee (8 YRS. W-105, L-102)

- Nassau Cl. N26-27
- North Fla. Tr. D3-4
- Warner Southern D 7
- Savannah St. D10
- Kennesaw St. Tr. D17-18
- Walsh■ D30
- Abilene Christian■ J 3
- Florida Tech■ J12
- St. Leo■ J15
- Eckerd J19
- Barry■ J22
- Fla. Southern J26
- Tampa J29
- Rollins■ F 2
- St. Leo F 5
- Eckerd■ F 9
- Barry F12
- Valdosta St. F14
- Fla. Southern■ F16
- Tampa■ F19
- Rollins F23
- Florida Tech F26

Colors: Navy Blue & Gray. Nickname: Lady Ospreys.
AD: John Ratliff. SID: Bonnie Senappe. II

NORTH TEXAS .... Denton, TX 76203
Tina Slinker (4 YRS. W-39, L-66)

- Southern Methodist■ N27
- Oklahoma St. D 1
- UC Irvine Cl. D3-4
- Oklahoma D 8
- UTEP D11
- New Mexico D18
- Texas Christian■ D21
- Stephen F. Austin■ J 3
- McNeese St. J 6
- Nicholls St. J 8
- Texas-Arlington J15
- Northeast La.■ J20
- Northwestern (La.)■ J22
- Southwest Tex. St. J27
- Texas-San Antonio J29
- Nicholls St.■ F 3
- McNeese St.■ F 5
- Sam Houston St. F 7
- Texas-Arlington■ F12
- Northwestern (La.) F17
- Northeast La. F19
- Texas-San Antonio■ F24
- Southwest Tex. St.■ F26
- Stephen F. Austin F28
- Sam Houston St.■ M 2
- Southland Tr. M8-12

Colors: Green & White. Nickname: Lady Eagles.
AD: Steve Sloan. SID: Brian Hollen. I

NORTHEAST LA. .... Monroe, LA 71209
Roger Stockton (3 YRS. W-49, L-36)

- Ark.-Monticello■ N29
- Mississippi St. Tr. D3-4
- Louisiana Tech D 7
- Arkansas St. D15
- Southwest Tex. St.■ D28
- Texas-San Antonio■ D30
- Alas. Anchorage Inv. J6-8
- McNeese St.■ J13
- Nicholls St.■ J15
- Stephen F. Austin J18
- North Texas J20
- Texas-Arlington J22
- Mississippi■ J25
- Northwestern (La.) J29
- Stephen F. Austin■ F 3
- Sam Houston St.■ F 5
- Louisiana Tech■ F 8
- Nicholls St. F10
- McNeese St. F12
- Mississippi St.■ F15
- Texas-Arlington■ F17
- North Texas■ F19
- Sam Houston St. F22
- Northwestern (La.)■ F26
- Southwest Tex. St. F28
- Texas-San Antonio M 2
- Southland Tr. M8-12

Colors: Maroon & Gold. Nickname: Indians.
AD: Benny Hollis. SID: Robby Edwards. I

NORTHEAST MO. ST. .... Kirksville, MO 63501
Jan Conner (1 YR. W-2, L-24)

- Northeast Mo. Tr. N26-27
- IU/PU-Ind. Cl. D3-4
- SIU-Edwardsville■ D 8
- Mankato St. Cl. D17-18
- UC San Diego Inv. D28-30
- Mo.-St. Louis■ J 5
- Emporia St.■ J 8
- Lincoln (Mo.) J12
- Mo. Southern St. J15
- Mo. Western St.■ J19
- Central Mo. St.■ J22
- Southwest Baptist J27
- Pittsburg St. J29
- Washburn■ F 2
- Northwest Mo. St. F 5
- Missouri-Rolla■ F 9
- Emporia St. F12
- Lincoln (Mo.)■ F16
- Mo. Southern St.■ F19
- Mo. Western St. F23
- Central Mo. St. F26

Colors: Purple & White. Nickname: Bulldogs.
AD: Alan Graham. SID: William Cable. II

NORTHEASTERN .... Boston, MA 02115
Joy Malchodi (17 YRS. W-233, L-238)

- Brown N28
- Massachusetts D 1
- Rhode Island■ D 8
- Iona■ D11
- Boston College■ D19
- Northwestern■ D22
- Auburn Cl. D29-30
- Harvard■ J 3
- Hofstra■ J 5
- Central Conn. St.■ J 8
- Vermont J13
- Hartford■ J15
- Drexel■ J21
- Delaware■ J23
- New Hampshire J27
- Maine J29
- St. Peter's F 2
- Boston U. F 5
- Maine■ F10
- New Hampshire■ F12
- Delaware F18
- Drexel F20
- Vermont■ F24
- Hartford F26
- Boston U.■ M 2
- North Atlantic Tr. M6-12

Colors: Red & Black. Nickname: Huskies.
AD: Irwin Cohen. SID: Jack Grinold. I

NORTHEASTERN ILL. .... Chicago, IL 60625
Denise Taylor (2 YRS. W-32, L-23)

- Missouri■ N26
- Drake N28
- Western Mich.■ D 1
- Buffalo Tr. D3-4
- National Louis D 6
- Wisconsin D11
- Wis.-Milwaukee D14
- Auburn Cl. D29-30
- St. Louis■ J 3
- Chicago St.■ J 5
- Trinity (Ill.)■ J11
- Chicago St. J12
- Troy St.■ J22
- Kansas St. J27
- Indiana St.■ F 2
- Cal St. Sacramento■ F 5
- St. Louis F 9
- Marquette■ F14
- Buffalo■ F19
- DePaul F21
- Central Conn. St. F25
- Hofstra■ F28
- East Coast Tr. M3-6

Colors: Royal Blue & Gold. Nickname: Golden Eagles.
AD: Vivian Fuller. SID: Mark Johnson. I

■ Home games on each schedule.

See pages 735-738 for Division I tournament details

NORTHERN ARIZ. .... Flagstaff, AZ 86011
Charli Turner (1ST YR. AS HEAD COACH)

- New Mexico■ N29
- Grand Canyon■ D 3
- Southern Utah■ D 4
- Baylor■ D11
- Colorado D18
- Northern Iowa■ D20
- Colorado St.■ D28
- Nevada D30
- Cal St. Northridge J 2
- Texas-San Antonio■ J 5
- Boise St.■ J13
- Idaho St.■ J15
- Montana St. J20
- Montana J22
- Eastern Wash.■ J27
- Idaho■ J29
- Cal St. Northridge■ F 2
- Weber St.■ F 5
- Idaho St. F10
- Boise St. F12
- Montana■ F17
- Montana St.■ F19
- Idaho F24
- Eastern Wash. F26
- Southern Utah M 3
- Weber St. M 5
- Big Sky Tr. M11-12

Colors: Blue & Gold. Nickname: Lady Jacks.
AD: Kelly Patton-Woodard. SID: Kim Tompkins. I

NORTHERN COLO. .... Greeley, CO 80639
Gary Schwartz (11 YRS. W-180, L-120)

- Regis (Colo.) N23
- Chadron St.■ N30
- Air Force D 1
- Denver■ D11
- Metropolitan St.■ D13
- Cal Poly Pomona■ D15
- Wyoming D18
- Mesa St. D30
- Augustana (S.D.)■ J 2
- South Dak. St.■ J 3
- Nebraska-Omaha■ J 8
- Colorado Mines■ J11
- North Dak. J14
- North Dak. St. J15
- South Dak.■ J21
- Morningside■ J22
- St. Cloud St. J28
- Mankato St. J29
- Nebraska-Omaha F 5
- North Dak. St.■ F11
- North Dak.■ F12
- Morningside F18
- South Dak. F19
- Mankato St.■ F25
- St. Cloud St.■ F26
- South Dak. St. M 4
- Augustana (S.D.) M 5

Colors: Navy & Gold. Nickname: Bears.
AD: Jim Fallis. SID: Scott Leisinger. II

NORTHERN ILL. .... De Kalb, IL 60115
Jane Albright-Dieterle (9 YRS. W-164, L-104)

- Hawaii Cl. N26-27
- Southern Cal■ D 1
- Southern Ill.■ D17
- Eastern Ill.■ D30
- Wright St.■ J 3
- Ill.-Chicago J 6
- Valparaiso J 9
- Western Ill.■ J13
- Iowa■ J16
- Wis.-Green Bay■ J20
- Wis.-Milwaukee■ J22
- Youngstown St. J27
- Cleveland St. J29
- Loyola (Ill.) J31
- Eastern Ill. F 3
- Wright St. F 5
- Northwestern F 8
- Ill.-Chicago■ F10
- Valparaiso■ F12
- DePaul■ F15
- Western Ill. F19
- Wis.-Green Bay F23
- Wis.-Milwaukee F26
- Youngstown St.■ M 3
- Cleveland St.■ M 5
- Mid-Continent Tr. M10-12

Colors: Cardinal & Black. Nickname: Huskies.
AD: Gerald K. O'Dell. SID: Kari Brackett. I

NORTHERN IOWA .... Cedar Falls, IA 50613
Terri Lasswell (4 YRS. W-25, L-83)

- Mo.-Kansas City■ N28
- Indiana Cl. D3-4
- Arizona St. D18
- Northern Ariz. D20
- Nebraska■ D28
- Minnesota■ D30
- Southern Ill. J 2
- Indiana St. J 4
- Wichita St.■ J 7
- Southwest Mo. St.■ J 9
- Bradley J15
- St. Louis■ J17
- Illinois St. J20
- Chicago St. J22
- Creighton■ J27
- Drake■ J29
- Southwest Mo. St. F 4
- Wichita St. F 6
- Bradley■ F12
- Illinois St.■ F19
- Creighton F24
- Drake F26
- Indiana St.■ M 3
- Southern Ill.■ M 5
- Missouri Valley Tr. M8-12

Colors: Purple & Old Gold. Nickname: Panthers.
AD: Christopher Ritrievi. SID: Nancy Justis. I

NORTHERN KY. .... Highland Heights, KY 41076
Nancy Winstel (13 YRS. W-248, L-111)

- Salem-Teikyo N27
- Calif. (Pa.) N28
- Northern Ky. Cl. D3-4
- Morehead St.■ D 8
- Ky. Wesleyan■ D20
- Southern Ind.■ D22
- IU/PU-Indianapolis■ J 4
- Kentucky St. J 6
- Bellarmine J 8
- Oakland City■ J12
- Indianapolis J15
- St. Joseph's (Ind.)■ J20
- Lewis■ J22
- IU/PU-Ft. Wayne J27
- Ashland J29
- Bellarmine■ F 3
- Kentucky St.■ F 5
- Oakland City F 9
- Indianapolis■ F12
- Lewis F17
- St. Joseph's (Ind.) F19
- IU/PU-Indianapolis F22
- Ashland■ F24
- IU/PU-Ft. Wayne■ F26
- Southern Ind. M 3
- Ky. Wesleyan M 5

Colors: Gold, Black & White. Nickname: The Lady Norse.
AD: Jane Meier. SID: J.D. Campbell. II

NORTHERN MICH. .... Marquette, MI 49855
Mike Geary (7 YRS. W-155 , L-45)

- Siena Heights■ N20
- Bemidji St. N27
- Wayne St. (Mich.)■ D 2
- Wis.-Superior■ D 4
- Wis.-Parkside D 7
- Michigan Tech D11
- Hillsdale■ D20
- Minn.-Duluth■ J 3
- Ferris St. J 6
- Grand Valley St. J 8
- Lake Superior St.■ J13
- Northwood■ J15
- Oakland J20
- Saginaw Valley J22
- Wayne St. (Mich.) J27
- Hillsdale J29
- Michigan Tech■ F 5
- Ferris St.■ F10
- Grand Valley St.■ F12
- Lake Superior St. F17
- Northwood F19
- Winona St.■ F21
- Oakland■ F24
- Saginaw Valley■ F26
- Wis.-Parkside■ M 1

Colors: Old Gold & Olive Green. Nickname: Wildcats.
AD: Rick Comley. SID: Jim Pinar. II

NORTHERN ST. .... Aberdeen, SD 57401
Curt Fredrickson (14 YRS. W-339 , L-74)

- Wayne St. (Neb.) N20
- Minot St. N23
- Mary N24
- Mayville St. N30
- Jamestown■ D 2
- Valley City St. D 7
- Dakota St. D11
- Mt. Marty D14
- Huron D15
- Sioux Falls■ D18
- Bemidji St. J 5
- Southwest St.■ J 8
- Minn.-Morris J12
- Minn.-Duluth■ J15
- Dak. Wesleyan J17
- Winona St. J19
- Moorhead St.■ J22
- Huron■ J26
- Valley City St.■ J28
- Wayne St. (Neb.)■ J29
- Minot St.■ J31
- Bemidji St.■ F 2
- Southwest St. F 5
- Minn.-Morris■ F 9
- Minn.-Duluth F12
- Winona St.■ F16
- Moorhead St. F19

Colors: Maroon & Gold. Nickname: Wolves.
AD: Jim Kretchman. SID: Deb Smith. II

NORTHWEST MO. ST. .... Maryville, MO 64468
Wayne Winstead (14 YRS. W-240, L-156)

- Northwest Mo. Cl. N19-20
- Lynn N28
- Eckerd N29
- Nebraska-Omaha Tr. D3-4
- Neb.-Kearney D 7
- Augustana (S.D.) D11
- Mo. Western St.■ J 5
- Missouri-Rolla■ J 8
- William Jewell J10
- Pittsburg St. J12
- Southwest Baptist J15
- Rockhurst J17
- Mo.-St. Louis■ J19
- Washburn■ J22
- Mo. Southern St.■ J26
- Emporia St. J29
- Central Mo. St. F 2
- Northeast Mo. St.■ F 5
- Lincoln (Mo.) F 9
- Missouri-Rolla F12
- Pittsburg St.■ F16
- Southwest Baptist■ F19
- Mo.-St. Louis F23
- Washburn F26

Colors: Green & White. Nickname: Bearkittens.
AD: Sherri Reeves. SID: Larry Cain. II

NORTHWESTERN .... Evanston, IL 60208
Don Perrelli (17 YRS. W-333, L-169)

- Illinois St.■ N28
- Loyola (Ill.)■ N30
- Northwestern Inv. D3-4
- Holy Cross D19
- Boston College D21
- Northeastern D22
- Penn St.■ J 6
- North Caro.☒ J 8
- Iowa J15
- Illinois■ J19
- Wisconsin J23
- Purdue■ J28
- Indiana■ J30
- Michigan St. F 4
- Minnesota F 6
- Northern Ill.■ F 8
- Iowa■ F11
- Minnesota■ F13
- Illinois F16
- Wisconsin■ F18
- Indiana F25
- Purdue F27
- Michigan St.■ M 4
- Michigan■ M 6
- Ohio St. M10
- Penn St. M12

☒ Charlottesville, VA

Colors: Purple & White. Nickname: Wildcats.
AD: Bill Foster (interim). SID: Greg Shea. I

NORTHWESTERN (LA.) ...... Natchitoches, LA 71457
James Smith (6 YRS. W-116, L-59)

- East Texas Bapt.■ N26
- Maine Cl. D3-4
- Arkansas Cl. D17-18
- Texas-San Antonio■ D28
- Southwest Tex. St.■ D30
- Central Fla.■ J 3
- Stephen F. Austin J 6
- Sam Houston St. J 8
- Nicholls St.■ J13
- McNeese St.■ J15
- Texas-Arlington J20
- North Texas J22
- Northeast La.■ J29
- Sam Houston St.■ F 3
- Stephen F. Austin■ F 5
- McNeese St. F10
- Nicholls St. F12
- North Texas■ F17
- Texas-Arlington■ F19
- Northeast La. F26
- Texas-San Antonio F28
- Southwest Tex. St. M 2
- Southern Miss.■ M 5
- Southland Tr. M8-12

Colors: Purple, White & Orange. Nickname: Lady Demons.
AD: James Smith. SID: Doug Ireland. I

■ Home games on each schedule.

See pages 735-738 for Division I tournament details

NORTHWOOD .... Midland, MI 48640

Debbie Norman (1 YR. W-5, L-22)

Alma	N20	Concordia (Mich.)■	J18
Grand Rapids Tr.	N26-27	Lake Superior St.	J22
Oakland■	D 2	Spring Arbor■	J25
Grand Valley St.	D 4	Oakland	J27
Adrian■	D 7	Grand Valley St.■	J29
Hillsdale	D 9	Hillsdale■	F 3
Ferris St.■	D11	Ferris St.	F 5
Albion	D29	Saginaw Valley■	F10
Hope■	D31	Wayne St. (Mich.)	F12
Saginaw Valley	J 6	Michigan Tech■	F17
Wayne St. (Mich.)■	J 8	Northern Mich.■	F19
Michigan Tech	J13	Lake Superior St.■	F26
Northern Mich.	J15		

Colors: Columbia Blue & White. Nickname: Northwomen.
AD: Dave Coffey. SID: Fritz Reznor. II

NOTRE DAME .... Notre Dame, IN 46556

Muffet McGraw (10 YRS. W-204, L-104)

Ill.-Chicago■	N27	Evansville■	J20
Marquette■	D 1	Butler■	J22
Brown Cl.	D4-5	Xavier (Ohio)■	J27
Purdue	D 8	Detroit Mercy■	J29
Seton Hall■	D11	Loyola (Ill.)	F 5
Louisiana St.■	D19	Butler	F10
Temple■	D21	Evansville	F12
Georgetown	D30	La Salle■	F17
Old Dominion	J 2	Louisville	F21
Dayton	J 4	Detroit Mercy	F24
Tennessee■	J 7	Xavier (Ohio)	F26
DePaul■	J11	Loyola (Ill.)■	M 3
La Salle	J15		

Colors: Gold & Blue. Nickname: Fighting Irish.
AD: Richard Rosenthal. SID: John Heisler. I

NOTRE DAME (CAL.) .... Belmont, CA 94002

Steve Picchi (2 YRS. W-8, L-39)

Holy Names	N17	San Fran. St.	J11
Bethany (Cal.)■	N23	Simpson (Cal.)■	J15
Cal St. Hayward	N26	Dominican (Cal.)	J22
Claremont-M-S	D 2	Pac. Christian■	J27
Pac. Christian	D 3	Holy Names■	F 2
La Sierra	D 4	Dominican (Cal.)■	F 4
Simpson (Cal.)	D11	Mills	F 8
UC Santa Cruz■	D18	La Sierra■	F12
Mills■	J 5	Mills Tr.	F17-19
UC Santa Cruz	J 8		

Colors: Yellow & White. Nickname: Argonauts.
AD: Virginia Babel. SID: Virginia Babel. II

NOTRE DAME (MD.) .... Baltimore, MD 21210

Tim Engle (4 YRS. W-34, L-56)

Notre Dame (Md.) Tr.	N19-20	Frostburg St.■	J25
Mary Washington■	N23	Lebanon Valley	J27
Western Md.	D 1	Catholic■	J29
Nichols Tr.	D4-5	Washington (Md.)	F 3
Marymount (Va.)■	D11	Wesley	F 5
Bahamas Tr.	J3-8	Shenandoah	F 9
Gallaudet	J12	Randolph-Macon	F12
Mary Baldwin■	J14	St. Mary's (Md.)■	F15
Immaculata	J15	Notre Dame (Md) Inv.	F18-19
Salisbury St.■	J19	Eastern (Pa.)	F23
Rosemont	J22	Lincoln (Pa.)■	F25

Colors: Royal Blue & White. Nickname: Gators.
AD: Donna Ledwin. SID: Donna Ledwin. III

OAKLAND .... Rochester, MI 48063

Bob Taylor (10 YRS. W-203, L-79)

Oakland Tr.	N19-20	Northern Mich.■	J20
Grand Rapids Tr.	N26-27	Michigan Tech■	J22
Northwood	D 2	Northwood■	J27
Saginaw Valley■	D 4	Saginaw Valley	J29
Grand Valley St.■	D 9	Grand Valley St.	F 3
Wayne St. (Mich.)	D11	Wayne St. (Mich.)■	F 5
Madonna■	D18	Lake Superior St.■	F12
Bellarmine Cl.	D29-30	Ferris St.	F17
Gannon■	J 4	Hillsdale■	F19
Lake Superior St.	J 8	Northern Mich.	F24
Ferris St.■	J13	Michigan Tech	F26
Hillsdale	J15		

Colors: Gold, White & Black. Nickname: Pioneers.
AD: Paul Hartman. SID: Andy Glantzman. II

OAKLAND CITY .... Oakland City, IN 47660

Denise Sandifar (5 YRS. W-88, L-42)

Hillsdale Free Will	N22	Lane■	J21
Hillsdale Free Will	N23	Lane■	J22
Kentucky St.■	D 1	Manchester■	J27
Ky. Wesleyan	D 4	SIU-Edwardsville	J29
Ind. Wesleyan	D 7	Kentucky St.	F 1
Indianapolis	D11	Graceland (Ind.)	F 5
Fontbonne	D15	Northern Ky.■	F 9
Ky. Wesleyan■	D18	Lane	F11
Oakland City Cl.	J7-8	Lane	F12
Northern Ky.	J12	SIU-Edwardsville■	F24
Westminster■	J15	Graceland (Ind.)■	F26

Colors: Blue & White. Nickname: Lady Oaks.
AD: Mike Sandifar. SID: Denise Sandifar. II

OCCIDENTAL .... Los Angeles, CA 90041

Kathleen Connell (1 YR. W-13, L-12)

St. Thomas (Minn.)■	N28	Cal Lutheran	J21
Pac. Christian■	N29	Southern Cal Col.■	J25
Christ-Irvine■	D 2	Claremont-M-S■	J28
Cal Baptist■	D 6	La Verne	F 1
Biola	D18	Whittier■	F 4
Southern Cal Col.	D20	Pomona-Pitzer■	F 8
Cal St. San B'dino■	D22	Redlands	F11
UC San Diego Inv.	D28-30	Cal Lutheran■	F15
Chapman■	J 5	UC San Diego■	F18
Whittier	J11	Claremont-M-S	F22
Pomona-Pitzer	J14	La Verne■	F25
Redlands■	J18		

Colors: Orange & Black. Nickname: Tigers.
AD: Dale Widolff. SID: James Kerman. III

OHIO .... Athens, OH 45701

Marsha Reall (11 YRS. W-216, L-109)

Duquesne	D 2	Eastern Mich.■	J26
Virginia Tech	D 4	Toledo	J29
Western Ky.■	D 6	Kent■	F 2
Marshall■	D 9	Miami (Ohio)	F 5
Cincinnati■	D14	Western Mich.■	F 9
Dayton■	D22	Akron	F12
Hilton Head Shootout	D29-30	Central Mich.	F16
Ball St.	J 5	Bowling Green■	F19
Miami (Ohio)■	J 8	Eastern Mich.	F23
Western Mich.	J12	Toledo■	F26
Akron■	J15	Kent	M 2
Central Mich.■	J19	Ball St.■	M 5
Bowling Green	J22		

Colors: Kelly Green & White. Nickname: Bobcats.
AD: Harold McElhaney. SID: Glenn Coble. I

OHIO NORTHERN .... Ada, OH 45810

Theresa Conroy (2 YRS. W-16, L-37)

Buffalo St. Inv.	N20-21	Marietta■	J15
Adrian	N30	Otterbein	J18
Baldwin-Wallace■	D 4	John Carroll■	J22
Muskingum■	D 8	Muskingum	J25
John Carroll	D11	Baldwin-Wallace	J29
Hiram■	D14	Heidelberg■	F 1
Manchester■	D18	Hiram	F 5
Ohio Northern Inv.	D29-30	Capital■	F 8
Heidelberg	J 4	Mount Union	F12
Mount Union■	J 8	Otterbein■	F15
Capital	J11	Marietta	F19

Colors: Orange & Black. Nickname: Polar Bears.
AD: Gale Daugherty. SID: Cort Reynolds. III

OHIO ST. .... Columbus, OH 43210

Nancy Darsch (8 YRS. W-170, L-69)

Tennessee☒	N21	Penn St.■	J25
Massachusetts■	N28	Wisconsin■	J28
Vanderbilt■	D 1	Iowa■	F 4
James Madison	D11	Indiana	F11
Syracuse	D14	Purdue	F13
Kansas St.■	D19	Michigan St.■	F18
Kentucky	D21	Michigan■	F20
Florida Tr.	D28-29	Penn St.	F25
Illinois	J 5	Wisconsin	F27
Virginia	J 8	Minnesota	M 4
Purdue■	J14	Iowa	M 6
Indiana■	J16	Northwestern■	M10
Michigan	J21	Illinois■	M12
Michigan St.	J23	☒ Jackson, TN	

Colors: Scarlet & Gray. Nickname: Buckeyes.
AD: James L. Jones. SID: Liz Cook. I

■ Home games on each schedule.

See pages 735-738 for Division I tournament details

OHIO WESLEYAN .... Delaware, OH 43015

Nan Carney-DeBord (8 YRS. W-136, L-68)

Urbana■ N20
Capital■ N22
Kenyon■ .... D 1
Allegheny■ .... D 4
Wittenberg .... D 8
Baldwin-Wallace D29
Denison .... J 2
Case Reserve■ .... J 5
Thomas More .... J 8
Oberlin■ J12
Wooster J15
Earlham J19
Allegheny J22
Wittenberg■ J26
Denison■ J29
Lake Erie■ J31
Oberlin .... F 2
Bluffton■ .... F 5
Kenyon .... F 9
Wooster■ F12
Earlham■ F16
Case Reserve F19

Colors: Red & Black. Nickname: Battling Bishops.
AD: Jay Martin. SID: Mark Beckenbach. III

OKLAHOMA .... Norman, OK 73019

Burl Plunkett (1ST YR. AS HEAD COACH)

Tex.-Pan American■ N27
Texas N30
Geo. Washington Cl. D3-4
North Texas■ .... D 8
Texas A&M■ D18
Oklahoma Cl. D28-29
Southern Methodist .... J 2
Iowa St.■ .... J 7
Nebraska■ .... J 9
Oklahoma St.■ J16
Kansas J21
Kansas St. J23
Arkansas■ J26
Colorado■ J28
Missouri■ J30
Nebraska .... F 4
Iowa St. .... F 6
Oral Roberts■ F10
Oklahoma St. F13
Kansas St.■ F18
Kansas■ F20
Missouri F25
Colorado F27
Big Eight Tr. M5-7

Colors: Crimson & Cream. Nickname: Sooners.
AD: Don Jimerson. SID: Mike Prusinski. I

OKLAHOMA ST. .... Stillwater, OK 74074

Dick Halterman (10 YRS. W-182, L-118)

North Texas■ .... D 1
Louisiana Tech Cl. D3-4
Houston■ D19
Oklahoma St. Tr. D31-J1
Texas A&M .... J 3
Nebraska■ .... J 7
Iowa St.■ .... J 9
Oral Roberts■ J14
Oklahoma J16
Kansas St. J21
Kansas J23
Missouri■ J28
Colorado■ J30
Creighton .... F 2
Iowa St. .... F 4
Nebraska .... F 6
Oklahoma■ F13
Kansas■ F18
Kansas St.■ F20
Colorado F25
Missouri F27
Arkansas .... M 1
Big Eight Tr. M5-7

Colors: Orange & Black. Nickname: Cowgirls.
AD: Dave Martin (Interim). SID: Steve Buzzard. I

OLD DOMINION .... Norfolk, VA 23529

Wendy Larry (9 YRS. W-157, L-102)

Old Dominion Cl. N27-28
Rutgers .... D 2
Radford■ .... D 4
Maryland■ .... D 8
Va. Commonwealth■ D18
Illinois St. D20
Montana Tr. D29-30
Notre Dame■ .... J 2
Richmond .... J 8
Tennessee J13
James Madison J16
N.C.-Wilmington■ J21
East Caro.■ J24
George Mason J27
American■ J30
William & Mary■ .... F 3
North Caro. St. .... F 5
Richmond■ F10
James Madison■ F13
N.C.-Wilmington F18
East Caro. F20
George Mason■ F24
American F27
William & Mary .... M 3
CAA Tr. M10-12

Colors: Slate Blue & Silver. Nickname: Lady Monarchs.
AD: James Jarrett. SID: Linda Turner. I

OLD WESTBURY .... Old Westbury, NY 11568

To be named

John Jay Tr. N20-21
Stony Brook N23
Dowling N29
Centenary (N.J.)■ .... D 1
Hunter .... D 3
York (N.Y.) .... D 8
Medgar Evers■ D17
Staten Island Tr. D29-30
Dominican (N.Y.)■ J11
Mt. St. Mary (N.Y.)■ J13
Vassar J17
Baruch J20
Wesley■ J22
New Rochelle J26
Marymount (N.Y.)■ J28
CCNY .... F 1
Albany (N.Y.) .... F 5
Mt. St. Vincent .... F 7
John Jay .... F 9
Manhattanville■ F12
New York U. F15

Colors: Green & White. Nickname: Panthers.
AD: Dora Icrides. SID: Mark Sosna. III

OLIVET .... Olivet, MI 49076

Nancy Van Hoozier (1 YR. W-0, L-23)

Wilming. (Ohio) Tr. N19-20
Bluffton■ N23
Heidelberg Tr. D3-4
Manchester Tr. D10-11
Madonna D14
Walsh Tr. D17-18
Grand Rapids Bapt. .... J 4
Alma■ .... J 8
Adrian■ J12
Kalamazoo J15
Hope J19
Calvin■ J22
St. Mary's (Ind.)■ J24
Albion J26
Alma .... F 2
Adrian .... F 5
Kalamazoo■ .... F 9
Hope■ F12
Calvin F16
Albion■ F19

Colors: Red & White. Nickname: Comets.
AD: Jackie Shimp. SID: Jerry Rashid. III

ONEONTA ST. .... Oneonta, NY 13820

Steven Garner (1ST YR. AS HEAD COACH)

Stony Brook Tr. N19-20
Elmira■ N23
Misericordia .... D 1
Potsdam St.■ .... D 3
Plattsburgh St.■ .... D 4
Cortland St.■ .... D 7
Brockport St. D10
Geneseo St. D11
New Paltz St. J18
Potsdam St. J21
Plattsburgh St. J22
Binghamton■ J25
Oswego St.■ J28
Utica Tech J29
New Paltz St.■ .... F 1
Hamilton .... F 3
Russell Sage■ .... F 5
Hartwick .... F 8
Buffalo St.■ F11
Fredonia St.■ F12
Binghamton F15
Union (N.Y.) F17
Cortland St. F19

Colors: Red & White. Nickname: Red Dragons.
AD: Al Sosa. SID: Barbara Blodgett. III

ORAL ROBERTS .... Tulsa, OK 74171

Cletus Green (1ST YR. AS HEAD COACH)

Tex.-Pan American■ N26
Mississippi Val.■ N27
Kansas Cl. D3-4
Mo. Southern St.■ .... D 6
Southeast Mo. St. .... D 9
Middle Tenn. St. Cl. D10-11
Tenn.-Martin■ D18
Oklahoma Cl. D28-29
Southeast Mo. St.■ .... J 5
Texas Christian■ .... J 8
Memphis St. J11
Oklahoma St. J14
Wichita St.■ J17
Mississippi Val. J19
Mo.-Kansas City■ J22
Tenn.-Martin J27
Baylor■ J29
Tex.-Pan American .... F 1
Mo.-Kansas City .... F 5
East Texas Bapt.■ .... F 7
Oklahoma F10
Texas A&M■ F18
Arkansas F23
Okla. Baptist■ F26

Colors: Navy Blue, White & Vegas Gold. Nickname: Golden Eagles.
AD: Bob Brooks. SID: Scott Valley. I

OREGON .... Eugene, OR 97401

Jody Runge (1ST YR. AS HEAD COACH)

Hawaii Cl. N26-27
Texas-Arlington Cl. D3-4
Idaho St.■ D11
Weber St. D13
Hawaii■ D22
San Diego D28
San Diego St. D30
UTEP■ .... J 3
UCLA■ .... J 6
Southern Cal■ .... J 8
Oregon St. J13
Washington St. J20
Washington J22
Arizona■ J27
Arizona St.■ J29
Stanford .... F 3
California .... F 5
Oregon St.■ F11
Washington■ F17
Washington St.■ F19
Arizona St. F24
Arizona F26
California■ .... M 3
Stanford■ .... M 5
Southern Cal M11
UCLA M12

Colors: Green & Yellow. Nickname: Ducks.
AD: Rich Brooks. SID: David Williford. I

OREGON ST. .... Corvallis, OR 97331

Aki Hill (15 YRS. W-236, L-187)

St. Mary's Cl. N26-27
Oregon St. Cl. D10-11
Utah D14
Boise St. D16
UC Santa Barb.■ D18
Hawaii■ D20
Eastern Wash.■ .... J 2
Southern Cal■ .... J 6
UCLA■ .... J 8
Oregon■ J13
Washington J20
Washington St. J22
Arizona St.■ J27
Arizona■ J29
California .... F 3
Stanford .... F 5
Oregon F11
Washington St.■ F17
Washington■ F19
Arizona F24
Arizona St. F26
Stanford■ .... M 3
California■ .... M 5
UCLA M10
Southern Cal M13

Colors: Orange & Black. Nickname: Beavers.
AD: Dutch Baughman. SID: Hal Cowan. I

■ Home games on each schedule.

See pages 735-738 for Division I tournament details

OSWEGO ST. .... Oswego, NY 13126
To be named

Hamilton N30
St. John Fisher Cl. D3-4
Utica Tech■ .... D 7
Le Moyne■ .... D 9
Elmira■ D11
William Smith J11
Cortland St.■ J14
Binghamton J15
Brockport St. J18
Fredonia St.■ J21
Buffalo St.■ J22
Geneseo St. J25
Oneonta St. J28
New Paltz St.■ J29
St. Lawrence .... F 2
Utica Tech .... F 4
Geneseo St.■ .... F 5
Roberts Wesleyan .... F 9
Potsdam St.■ F11
Plattsburgh St. F12
Brockport St.■ F15
Fredonia St. F18
Buffalo St. F19

Colors: Green, Gold & White. Nickname: Great Lakers.
AD: Sandra Moore. SID: Danielle Martin. III

OTTERBEIN .... Westerville, OH 43081
Connie Richardson (2 YRS. W-12, L-37)

Muskingum .... D 1
Ohio Dominican Tr. D3-4
Hiram■ .... D 7
Manchester Tr. D10-11
Capital■ D15
Mt. St. Joseph's D20
John Carroll D29
Mount Union■ .... J 4
Heidelberg■ .... J 8
Marietta J11
Baldwin-Wallace J15
Ohio Northern■ J18
Muskingum■ J22
Hiram J25
Heidelberg J29
Marietta■ .... F 1
Capital .... F 5
Mount Union .... F 8
Bluffton F10
John Carroll■ F12
Ohio Northern F15
Baldwin-Wallace■ F19

Colors: Tan & Cardinal. Nickname: Cardinals.
AD: Marilyn Day. SID: Ed Syguda. III

PACE .... Pleasantville, NY 10570
Carrie Seymour (1 YR. W-24, L-7)

East Stroudsburg■ N23
Concordia (N.Y.) N27
Dowling■ .... D 1
Mercy■ .... D 4
Adelphi■ .... D 8
LIU-Southampton■ D11
New Haven D13
Stonehill Cl. D27-28
St. Rose .... J 5
West Chester■ .... J 9
Dowling J12
Mercy J17
Queens (N.Y.)■ J19
Phila. Textile J22
LIU-C.W. Post J24
Molloy J26
Clarion■ J29
Queens (N.Y.) .... F 2
Phila. Textile■ .... F 4
Molloy■ .... F 9
Pitt.-Johnstown F13
LIU-Southampton F16
LIU-C.W. Post■ F18
Adelphi F23
St. Rose■ F26

Colors: Blue & Gold. Nickname: Setters.
AD: Christopher Bledsoe. SID: John Balkam. II

PACIFIC (CAL.) .... Stockton, CA 95211
Melissa DeMarchi (5 YRS. W-68, L-73)

Cal St. Sacramento N30
Idaho Cl. D3-4
Fresno St. .... D 8
Santa Clara■ D11
New Mexico■ D20
St. Mary's (Cal.) D29
Nevada .... J 3
San Jose St.■ .... J 8
UC Santa Barb.■ J13
Long Beach St.■ J15
Nevada-Las Vegas J20
New Mexico St. J22
Cal St. Northridge■ J25
San Jose St. J29
Nevada■ J31
UC Irvine■ .... F 3
Cal St. Fullerton■ .... F 5
Long Beach St. F11
UC Santa Barb. F13
New Mexico St.■ F17
Nevada-Las Vegas■ F19
Hawaii F25
Hawaii F26
UC Irvine .... M 3
Cal St. Fullerton .... M 5
Big West Tr. M9-12

Colors: Orange & Black. Nickname: Tigers.
AD: Bob Lee. SID: Mike Millerick. I

PAINE .... Augusta, GA 30901
Rodney Minggia (2 YRS. W-19, L-35)

Miles■ N23
Morris Brown■ N30
Tuskegee .... D 2
Spelman■ .... D 4
Miles D11
LeMoyne-Owen D13
Tampa D17
Rollins D18
Jacksonville St. .... J 3
Alabama A&M■ .... J 8
Savannah St. J10
Jacksonville St.■ J14
Fort Valley St.■ J17
Albany St. (Ga.)■ J19
Morris■ J24
Clark Atlanta J28
Morris Brown J29
Albany St. (Ga.) .... F 3
Clark Atlanta■ .... F 6
Tuskegee■ .... F 7
Savannah St.☒ F12
LeMoyne-Owen■ F14
Fort Valley St. F15
Alabama A&M F19
Voorhees F21
Augusta☒ F25
☒ Augusta, GA

Colors: Purple & White. Nickname: Lady Lions.
AD: Ronnie Spry. SID: To be named. II

PEMBROKE ST. .... Pembroke, NC 28372
Linda Pitts (6 YRS. W-73, L-89)

Lynn N26
Barry N28
High Point■ .... D 2
St. Andrews .... D 4
Augusta■ .... D 9
Fayetteville St.■ D11
Georgia Col.■ .... J 8
Columbus■ .... J 9
Francis Marion J12
S.C.-Spartanburg J15
Lander J16
N.C. Central J20
Armstrong St.■ J22
Wingate J24
S.C.-Aiken■ J26
Augusta J29
Francis Marion■ .... F 2
S.C.-Aiken .... F 5
Connecticut Col. .... F 9
Georgia Col. F12
Columbus F13
N.C. Central■ F16
Armstrong St. F19
S.C.-Spartanburg■ F26
Lander■ F27

Colors: Black & Gold. Nickname: Lady Braves.
AD: Raymond Pennington. SID: Gary Spitler. II

PENNSYLVANIA .... Philadelphia, PA 19104
Julie Soriero (12 YRS. W-169, L-152)

Virginia N27
La Salle N30
Southwest/Ivy Chall. D3-4
St. Joseph's (Pa.) ♦ .... D 8
Delaware■ D11
Florida Tr. D28-29
Harvard .... J 7
Dartmouth .... J 8
Temple J11
Lafayette■ J17
Villanova J24
Princeton J29
Lehigh■ J31
Columbia-Barnard .... F 4
Cornell .... F 5
Brown■ F11
Yale■ F12
Princeton■ F15
Dartmouth■ F18
Harvard■ F19
Yale F25
Brown F26
Cornell■ .... M 4
Columbia-Barnard■ .... M 5
♦ Philadelphia, PA

Colors: Red & Blue. Nickname: Quakers.
AD: Paul Rubincam. SID: To be named. I

PENN ST. .... University Park, PA 16802
Rene Portland (17 YRS. W-384, L-132)

Providence■ .... D 5
Rutgers D11
Pittsburgh■ D19
Niagara D21
Hilton Head Shootout D29-30
St. Joseph's (Pa.) .... J 2
Northwestern .... J 6
Illinois .... J 9
Indiana■ J14
Michigan J23
Ohio St. J25
Vanderbilt J25
Wisconsin■ J30
Minnesota■ .... F 4
Indiana F13
Michigan St. F20
Wisconsin F23
Ohio St.■ F25
Minnesota .... M 6
Illinois■ M10
Northwestern■ M12

Colors: Blue & White. Nickname: Lady Lions.
AD: Jim Tarman. SID: Mary Jo Haverbeck. I

PENN ST.-BEHREND .... Erie, PA 16563
To be named

Penn St.-Behrend Tr. N19-20
Marietta■ N23
Muskingum Tr. N27-28
Baldwin-Wallace N30
Hiram .... D 2
Westminster (Pa.)■ .... D 7
Fredonia St.■ D10
Bethany (W.Va.)■ J15
Alfred J18
Hilbert■ J20
Buffalo St.■ J24
Wash. & Jeff. J26
Thiel J31
Grove City■ .... F 2
Bethany (W.Va.) .... F 5
Wash. & Jeff.■ F12
Allegheny■ F14
Thiel■ F16
Grove City F19

Colors: White, Blue & Red. Nickname: Lions.
AD: Herb Lauffer. SID: Paul Benim. III

PEPPERDINE .... Malibu, CA 90263
Mark Trakh (1ST YR. AS HEAD COACH)

Nebraska Cl. N26-27
UC Santa Barb.■ .... D 4
Cal St. Los Angeles■ D11
Nevada-Las Vegas■ D12
UC Irvine■ D14
Pepperdine Tr. D18-19
Cal St. Northridge D21
Cal St. San B'dino■ D30
Fresno St. .... J 8
Santa Clara J14
St. Mary's (Cal.) J15
San Diego■ J21
San Francisco■ J22
Loyola (Cal.)■ J28
Portland .... F 3
Gonzaga .... F 5
Gonzaga■ F11
Portland■ F12
San Francisco F17
San Diego F19
St. Mary's (Cal.)■ F25
Santa Clara■ F26
Loyola (Cal.) .... M 2
West Coast Tr. M11-12

Colors: Blue & Orange. Nickname: Waves.
AD: Wayne Wright. SID: Michael Zapolski. I

■ Home games on each schedule.

See pages 735-738 for Division I tournament details

PFEIFFER .... Misenheimer, NC 28109
Edie Sayewich (3 YRS. W-34, L-46)

Barber-Scotia■ N27
Longwood N29
Limestone D 1
Clinch Valley■ D 4
Lenoir-Rhyne■ D 6
Averett D 8
Lander D11
Belmont Abbey J 8
Coker■ J12
Lees-McRae■ J15
Lenoir-Rhyne J17
St. Andrews■ J19
Barton J22
High Point J26
Mt. Olive■ J29
Coker J31
Belmont Abbey■ F 2
Lees-McRae F 5
St. Andrews F 9
High Point■ F12
Newberry F14
Barton■ F16
Mt. Olive F19
Barber-Scotia F21

Colors: Black & Gold. Nickname: Falcons.
AD: Bobby Lutz. SID: Julian Domenech. II

PHILA. TEXTILE .... Philadelphia, PA 19144
Tom Shirley (12 YRS. W-230, L-109)

St. Michael's■ N20
Millersville N27
Bloomsburg■ N29
Kutztown■ D 2
LIU-Southampton D 4
Dowling D11
West Chester D14
Adelphi■ D19
Rollins D29
Molloy■ J 5
St. Rose J 8
Queens (N.Y.) J15
LIU-C.W. Post■ J19
Pace■ J22
Adelphi J24
Mercy■ J26
LIU-Southampton■ J29
LIU-C.W. Post F 2
Pace F 4
Mercy F 5
St. Rose■ F12
East Stroudsburg F14
Dowling■ F16
Queens (N.Y.)■ F19
Concordia (N.Y.) F25
Molloy F26

Colors: Maroon & White. Nickname: Lady Rams.
AD: Tom Shirley. SID: To be named. II

PINE MANOR .... Chestnut Hill MA 02167
Kathy Stockman (3 YRS. W-33, L-43)

Pine Manor Tr. N19-20
Rhode Island Col. N23
Connecticut Col.■ N30
Bri'water (Mass.)■ D 2
Western New Eng.■ D 4
Roger Williams D 7
Babson D 9
Rivier D11
Framingham St. J13
Mass.-Boston J15
Trinity (Conn.)■ J18
Worcester Tech J22
Emerson-MCA J25
Gordon J27
Norwich■ J30
Tufts■ F 3
Nichols F 5
Emmanuel F 8
Plymouth St. F10
Coast Guard■ F12
Suffolk F14
MIT F17
Elms F19

Colors: Dartmouth Green & White. Nickname: Gators.
AD: Colleen Queally. SID: Kathy Stockman. III

PITTSBURG ST. .... Pittsburg, KS 66762
Steve High (4 YRS. W-67, L-44)

Mo. Southern St. N23
Pittsburg St. Cl. N26-27
East Tex. St.■ N29
John Brown D 7
Southwest Bapt. Cl. D10-11
Northeastern Okla.■ D18
Neb.-Kearney■ D31
Central Mo. St. J 5
Southwest Baptist J 8
Northwest Mo. St.■ J12
Washburn J15
Missouri-Rolla■ J19
Mo.-St. Louis J22
Mo. Western St.■ J26
Northeast Mo. St.■ J29
Lincoln (Mo.) F 2
Mo. Southern St.■ F 5
Emporia St. F 9
Southwest Baptist■ F12
Northwest Mo. St. F16
Washburn■ F19
Missouri-Rolla F23
Mo.-St. Louis■ F26

Colors: Crimson & Gold. Nickname: Gorillas.
AD: Bill Samuels. SID: Shawn Ahearn. II

PITTSBURGH .... Pittsburgh, PA 15213
Kirk Bruce (8 YRS. W-100, L-130)

Duquesne■ N27
Robert Morris■ N30
Vanderbilt Cl. D4-5
Niagara D 8
Villanova D11
Penn St. D19
Pittsburgh Inv. D29-30
Boston College J 3
Syracuse J 5
Miami (Fla.)■ J 9
Georgetown J12
Seton Hall■ J16
Connecticut■ J19
St. John's (N.Y.) J23
Providence■ J26
Boston College■ J29
Miami (Fla.) F 2
Syracuse■ F 5
St. John's (N.Y.)■ F 9
Seton Hall F12
Villanova■ F16
Connecticut F20
Georgetown■ F23
Providence F26
Big East Tr. M4-7

Colors: Gold & Blue. Nickname: Lady Panthers.
AD: L. Oval Jaynes. SID: Sam Sciullo. I

PITT.-JOHNSTOWN .... Johnstown, PA 15904
Jodi Gault (11 YRS. W-265, L-45)

Slippery Rock N23
Pitt.-Johnstown Tr. N27-28
Clarion Cl. D3-4
Indiana (Pa.)■ D 7
Columbia Union■ D 9
Ashland J 5
Edinboro■ J 8
Millersville■ J13
Bloomsburg J15
Queens (N.Y.)■ J17
St. Vincent■ J20
Kutztown J22
Virginia Union J24
Mercyhurst J26
Gannon J29
Cheyney F 3
Hilbert■ F 5
Virginia Union■ F 7
Edinboro F11
Pace■ F13
West Chester F15
Longwood■ F20
Gannon■ F23
Charleston (W.Va.) F25
Mercyhurst■ M 3

Colors: Gold & Blue. Nickname: Lady Mountain Cats.
AD: Ed Sherlock. SID: To be named. II

PLATTSBURGH ST. .... Plattsburgh, NY 12901
Phoebe Sturm (19 YRS. W-146, L-229)

Johnson St.■ N20
Lyndon St. N30
New Paltz St. D 3
Oneonta St. D 4
Potsdam St. D 7
Cortland St.■ D10
Binghamton■ D11
Union (N.Y.)■ J 8
Skidmore■ J11
Buffalo St. J14
Fredonia St. J15
St. Lawrence■ J18
New Paltz St.■ J21
Oneonta St.■ J22
Albany (N.Y.) J25
Brockport St.■ J28
Geneseo St.■ J29
Cortland St. F 4
Binghamton F 5
Clarkson F 8
Utica Tech F11
Oswego St.■ F12
Potsdam St.■ F15
Castleton St. F19

Colors: Cardinal Red & White. Nickname: Cardinals.
AD: Peter Luguri. SID: Brian Micheels. III

PLYMOUTH ST. .... Plymouth, NH 03264
Nancy Feldman (3 YRS. W-44, L-33)

Hartwick Inv. N20-21
Johnson St. N23
New England Col.■ N30
Salem St.■ D 2
Mass.-Dartmouth■ D 5
Emmanuel■ D 8
Rhode Island Col.■ D11
Colby J 8
Southern Me.■ J11
Eastern Conn. St. J15
Mass.-Boston■ J18
Norwich■ J20
Western Conn. St.■ J22
Castleton St.■ J25
Mass.-Dartmouth J29
Southern Me. F 1
Bri'water (Mass.)■ F 3
Rhode Island Col. F 5
Mass.-Boston F 8
Pine Manor■ F10
Eastern Conn. St.■ F12
New England■ F16
Western Conn. St. F19

Colors: Green & White. Nickname: Panthers.
AD: Steve Bamford. SID: Mike Moffett. III

POMONA-PITZER .... Claremont, CA 91711
Barbara Krieger (1ST YR. AS HEAD COACH)

San Fran. St.■ N20
Concordia-M'head■ N23
Master's N27
Christ-Irvine■ N30
Cal St. San B'dino D 4
Southern Cal Col.■ D 7
Azusa-Pacific D10
Chapman D18
Colorado Col.■ J 5
Rhodes■ J 7
Cal Lutheran J11
Occidental■ J14
Claremont-M-S■ J18
La Verne J21
Whittier■ J25
UC San Diego J29
Redlands F 1
Cal Lutheran■ F 4
Occidental F 8
Claremont-M-S F11
La Verne■ F15
Whittier F18
Redlands■ F25

Colors: Blue, White & Orange. Nickname: Sagehens.
AD: Curtis Tong. SID: Kirk Reynolds. III

PORTLAND .... Portland, OR 97203
Jim Sollars (10 YRS. W-100, L-176)

Portland St.■ N27
Texas A&M Inv. D4-5
Idaho St.■ D 9
Western Ore.■ D11
Idaho D18
Eastern Wash. D19
St. Francis Cl. D30-31
New Mexico■ J 4
UTEP■ J 6
Montana■ J 8
San Francisco J13
San Diego J15
St. Mary's (Cal.)■ J20
Santa Clara■ J22
Santa Clara J28
St. Mary's (Cal.) J29
Pepperdine■ F 3
Loyola (Cal.)■ F 5
Loyola (Cal.) F11
Pepperdine F12
Gonzaga F16
Gonzaga■ F19
San Diego■ F24
San Francisco■ F26
West Coast Tr. M11-12

Colors: Purple & White. Nickname: Pilots.
AD: Joe Etzel. SID: Loren Wohlgemuth. I

■ Home games on each schedule.

See pages 735-738 for Division I tournament details

PORTLAND ST. .... Portland, OR 97207

Greg Bruce (7 YRS. W-122, L-75)

Cal St. Chico Tr.	N19-21	Alas. Anchorage	J22
Portland	N27	Grand Canyon■	J27
Pacific (Ore.)■	N30	Eastern Mont.■	J29
North Dak.■	D 2	Northwest Nazarene■	F 5
Cal St. Chico■	D11	Western Ore.■	F 7
Portland St. Cl.	D16-18	Alas. Fairbanks■	F10
Portland St. Tr.	D29-30	Alas. Anchorage■	F12
West Ga.	J 6	Grand Canyon	F17
Kennesaw St.	J 8	Eastern Mont.	F19
Seattle Pacific■	J15	Seattle Pacific	F26
Alas. Fairbanks	J20		

Colors: Green & White. Nickname: Vikings.
AD: Randy Nordlof. SID: Mike Lund. II

POTSDAM ST. .... Potsdam, NY 13676

Joseph Vaadi (1 YR. W-16, L-8)

Muhlenberg Tr.	N20-21	New Paltz St.■	J22
St. Lawrence	N30	Clarkson	J25
Oneonta St.	D 3	Geneseo St.■	J28
New Paltz St.	D 4	Brockport St.■	J29
Plattsburgh St.■	D 7	Binghamton	F 4
Binghamton■	D10	Cortland St.	F 5
Cortland St.■	D11	St. Lawrence■	F 8
Potsdam St. Inv.	J7-8	Oswego St.	F11
Fredonia St.	J14	Utica Tech■	F12
Buffalo St.	J15	Plattsburgh St.	F15
Oneonta St.■	J21	Houghton	F19

Colors: Maroon, Gray & White. Nickname: Bears.
AD: Jan Reetz. SID: Mark Mende. III

PRAIRIE VIEW .... Prairie View, TX 77445

Bob Atkins (9 YRS. W-64, L-176)

Sam Houston St.	N28	Southern-B.R.	J22
Baylor	D 1	Alcorn St.	J24
Paul Quinn Tr.	D3-4	Huston-Tillotson■	J26
Texas-San Antonio	D 7	Texas Southern■	J29
Tulane Cl.	D10-11	Alabama St.■	F 5
South Ala. Cl.	D17-18	Jackson St.■	F 7
Rice	J 6	Mississippi Val.	F12
Alabama St.	J 8	Grambling	F14
Jackson St.	J10	Southern-B.R.■	F19
Mississippi Val.■	J15	Alcorn St.■	F21
Grambling■	J17	Texas Southern	F26
Sam Houston St.■	J19	SWAC Tr.	M10-13

Colors: Purple & Gold. Nickname: Panthers.
AD: George Stafford. SID: Rickey Walker. I

PRESBYTERIAN .... Clinton, SC 29325

Beth Couture (4 YRS. W-66, L-44)

Converse■	N23	Carson-Newman■	J22
Newberry Tr.	D1-2	Wofford■	J24
S.C.-Spartanburg■	D 5	Mars Hill	J26
Gardner-Webb	D 8	Lenoir-Rhyne	J29
Newberry■	D11	Gardner-Webb■	F 5
UC San Diego Inv.	D28-30	Catawba	F 9
Erskine	J 6	Elon	F12
Converse	J 8	Wingate■	F16
Catawba■	J12	Carson-Newman	F19
Elon■	J15	Mars Hill■	F23
Wingate	J19	Lenoir-Rhyne■	F26

Colors: Garnet & Blue. Nickname: Lady Blue Hose.
AD: Cally Gault. SID: Art Chase. II

PRINCETON .... Princeton, NJ 08544

Joan Kowalik (9 YRS. W-185, L-130)

Nebraska Cl.	N26-27	Pennsylvania■	J29
Lafayette■	D 1	Cornell	F 4
Southwest/Ivy Chall.	D3-4	Columbia-Barnard	F 5
LIU-Brooklyn■	D 8	Yale■	F11
Lehigh	D11	Brown■	F12
FDU-Teaneck	D14	Pennsylvania	F15
Delaware	D15	Harvard■	F18
Santa Clara Shootout	D18-19	Dartmouth■	F19
George Mason	D29	Brown	F25
Georgetown	D31	Yale	F26
Dartmouth	J 7	Columbia-Barnard■	M 4
Harvard	J 8	Cornell■	M 5
Rider■	J24		

Colors: Orange & Black. Nickname: Tigers.
AD: Bob Myslik. SID: Mark Panus. I

PROVIDENCE .... Providence, RI 02918

Bob Foley (8 YRS. W-171, L-76)

Boston U.	N30	Pittsburgh	J26
Fordham	D 3	Connecticut■	J29
Penn St.	D 5	Syracuse	F 2
Seton Hall■	D 9	St. John's (N.Y.)	F 6
Massachusetts■	D11	Georgetown■	F 9
Montana Tr.	D29-30	Tennessee■	F11
Miami (Fla.)■	J 3	Boston College■	F13
St. John's (N.Y.)■	J 6	Seton Hall	F16
Boston College	J 8	Villanova	F20
Syracuse■	J12	Miami (Fla.)	F23
Connecticut	J16	Pittsburgh■	F26
Villanova■	J18	Big East Tr.	M4-7
Georgetown	J22		

Colors: Black & White. Nickname: Lady Friars.
AD: John Marinatto. SID: Bernadette Cafarelli. I

PURDUE .... West Lafayette, IN 47907

Lin Dunn (22 YRS. W-374, L-233)

DePaul Inv.	N26-27	Northwestern	J28
Notre Dame■	D 8	Illinois■	J30
Louisville■	D10	Indiana	F 4
Vanderbilt Cl.	D11	Wisconsin	F 6
Purdue Cl.	D20-22	Ohio St.■	F13
Butler■	D28	Minnesota	F20
Bradley	D30	Northwestern■	F27
Michigan St.	J 7	Indiana■	M 2
Michigan■	J 9	Wisconsin■	M 6
Ohio St.	J14	Michigan St.■	M10
Minnesota■	J21	Michigan	M12

Colors: Old Gold & Black. Nickname: Boilermakers.
AD: Morgan Burke. SID: Tom Schott. I

QUEENS (N.Y.) .... Flushing, NY 11367

Robert Graf (5 YRS. W-53, L-78)

Bridgeport Inv.	N20-21	Pace	J19
LIU-C.W. Post■	D 1	St. Rose■	J23
Molloy	D 8	Concordia (N.Y.)	J24
Adelphi■	D11	Dowling■	J26
Mankato St. Cl.	D17-18	Pace■	F 2
St. Rose Cl.	D28-29	Dowling	F 4
LIU-Southampton■	J 5	Mercy	F12
Mercy■	J 8	Adelphi	F16
Concordia (N.Y.)■	J10	Phila. Textile	F19
LIU-C.W. Post	J12	Molloy■	F23
Phila. Textile■	J15	LIU-Southampton	F26
Pitt.-Johnstown	J17		

Colors: Blue & Silver. Nickname: Knights.
AD: Richard Wettan. SID: Neal Kaufer. II

QUEENS (N.C.) .... Charlotte, NC 28274

Jeannie King (3 YRS. W-40, L-36)

Lincoln Memorial■	N23	Erskine■	J22
Belmont Abbey	N27	S.C.-Spartanburg	J24
Gardner-Webb■	N29	Limestone■	J29
Johnson Smith Inv.	D3-4	Mississippi-Women■	J31
Wingate	D 6	Wingate■	F 2
Mars Hill■	D11	Longwood	F 5
Catawba■	D14	Erskine	F12
Longwood■	D16	Lenoir-Rhyne	F14
Lenoir-Rhyne■	J 5	Limestone	F17
St. Leo■	J 8	Johnson Smith	F19
Gardner-Webb	J10	Belmont Abbey■	F21
Wofford■	J13	Wofford Tr.	F25-26
Johnson Smith■	J20		

Colors: Royal Blue, Light Blue & Whte. Nickname: Royals.
AD: Dale Layer. SID: Jeff Aumend. II

QUINCY .... Quincy, IL 62301

Penny Lewis (1ST YR. AS HEAD COACH)

Cal St. LA Tr.	N19-20	St. Francis (Ill.)	J13
St. Francis (Ill.)■	N23	Blackburn■	J15
Southwest Baptist■	N30	SIU-Edwardsville	J22
Northern Ky. Cl.	D3-4	Mo.-St. Louis	J24
Missouri-Rolla	D 7	Teiko-Marycrest■	J29
Mt. Mercy■	D10	IU/PU-Indianapolis	F 5
Lindenwood■	D11	Culver-Stockton■	F 7
Mo. Western St.	D18	Lincoln (Mo.)	F14
Indianapolis■	D20	Ky. Wesleyan■	F16
Central Mo. St.■	D21	Wis.-Parkside	F18
Bellarmine Cl.	D29-30	SIU-Edwardsville■	F26
Missouri Valley■	J11	Wis.-Parkside■	M 5

Colors: Brown & White. Nickname: Lady Hawks.
AD: Jim Naumovich. SID: Damian Becker. II

■ Home games on each schedule.

See pages 735-738 for Division I tournament details

QUINNIPIAC .... Hamden, CT 06518

Bill Dixon (7 YRS. W-69, L-122)

Sacred Heart■	N23	St. Michael's	J22
Merrimack	N28	St. Anselm	J25
New Haven■	N30	Stonehill■	J27
Bridgeport■	D 2	Merrimack■	J29
Bentley■	D 7	Bentley	F 2
Southern Conn. St.■	D 9	Bryant■	F 5
Franklin Pierce	D11	Assumption■	F 9
Tampa Tr.	J7-8	American Int'l	F12
Mass.-Lowell	J10	Springfield	F16
Assumption	J12	St. Michael's■	F20
American Int'l■	J15	St. Anselm■	F22
Bryant	J17	Stonehill	F24
Springfield■	J19		

Colors: Blue & Gold. Nickname: Lady Braves.
AD: Burt Kahn. SID: Bill Chaves. II

RADFORD .... Radford, VA 24142

Lubomyr Lichonczak (3 YRS. W-50, L-37)

Appalachian St.■	N27	Virginia Tech■	F 1
Old Dominion	D 4	Charleston So.	F 4
Charleston So.■	D 9	Coastal Caro.	F 5
Marshall	D11	Davidson■	F 8
Coastal Caro.■	D20	Liberty	F12
Central Fla. Cl.	D29-31	Campbell■	F18
Liberty■	J 8	N.C.-Greensboro■	F19
Campbell	J14	Winthrop	F22
N.C.-Greensboro	J15	N.C.-Asheville	F25
N.C.-Asheville■	J21	Md.-Balt. County■	M 4
Winthrop■	J22	Towson St.■	M 5
Md.-Balt. County	J28	Big South Tr.	M9-12
Towson St.	J29		

Colors: Blue, Red, Green & White. Nickname: Highlanders.
AD: Chuck Taylor. SID: Rick Rogers. I

RAMAPO .... Mahwah, NJ 07430

Ben Allen (5 YRS. W-36, L-89)

Bloomfield■	N20	Albertus Magnus■	J17
Montclair St.	N23	Kean■	J19
Trenton St.■	N27	Smith Inv.	J22-23
Stockton St.	D 1	Montclair St.■	J26
Worcester St. Tr.	D4-5	Trenton St.	J29
Jersey City St.■	D 8	Wm. Paterson	F 2
Rutgers-Camden	D11	Rutgers-Newark■	F 5
Rutgers-Newark	J 4	Jersey City St.	F 9
Stockton St.	J 5	Rutgers-Camden■	F12
Wm. Paterson■	J12	Kean	F15
Rowan	J15	Rowan■	F17

Colors: Red & Gold. Nickname: Roadrunners.
AD: Catherine Collins. SID: Michael Rastelli. III

RANDOLPH-MACON .... Ashland, VA 23005

Carroll LaHaye (11 YRS. W-120, L-155)

Randolph-Macon Tr.	N20-21	Roanoke	J22
Mary Washington■	N30	Rand.-Macon Woman's■	J25
Wesley	D 3	Va. Wesleyan	F 1
Catholic	D 4	Hollins	F 4
Bridgewater (Va.)	D14	Emory & Henry	F 5
Guilford■	J 7	Roanoke■	F 8
Emory & Henry■	J 8	Bridgewater (Va.)■	F10
East. Mennonite	J11	Notre Dame (Md.)■	F12
Lynchburg■	J13	East. Mennonite■	F15
Hollins■	J15	Lynchburg	F17
Va. Wesleyan■	J18	Guilford	F19
Rand.-Macon Woman's	J20		

Colors: Lemon & Black. Nickname: Yellow Jackets.
AD: Ted Keller. SID: Todd Hilder. III

REDLANDS .... Redlands, CA 92373

D. Mickey McAulay (4 YRS. W-50, L-51)

Pac. Christian■	N20	Claremont-M-S■	J21
Washing. (Mo.) Inv.	N25-27	La Verne■	J25
St. Thomas (Minn.)■	N30	Whittier	J28
UC San Diego	D 4	Pomona-Pitzer■	F 1
Cal Baptist	D 7	UC San Diego■	F 4
Chapman	D10	Cal Lutheran	F 8
Mass.-Boston■	J 5	Occidental■	F11
Pac. Christian	J 7	Claremont-M-S	F15
Chapman■	J11	La Verne	F18
Cal Lutheran■	J14	Whittier■	F22
Occidental	J18	Pomona-Pitzer	F25

Colors: Maroon & Gray. Nickname: Bulldogs.
AD: Greg Warzecka. SID: Chuck Sadowski. III

REGIS (COLO.) .... Denver, CO 80221

Linda Raunig (3 YRS. W-41, L-41)

Western St.■	N20	Colorado-CS	J15
Northern Colo.■	N23	Fort Lewis■	J21
Concordia (St. Paul)■	N26	Air Force■	J22
Lincoln (Mo.)■	N27	Metropolitan St.	J27
Regis (Colo.) Cl.	D3-4	Colo. Christian■	J29
Colorado Mines	D 7	Denver■	F 5
UC Riverside■	D11	Southern Colo.	F10
Cal Poly Pomona■	D18	Colorado-CS■	F12
Puget Sound■	D29	Fort Lewis	F17
East Tex. St.☒	J 1	Air Force	F19
Texas Woman's	J 3	Metropolitan St.■	F23
Denver	J 8	Colo. Christian	F26
Southern Colo.■	J13	☒ Denton, TX	

Colors: Navy Blue & Gold. Nickname: Rangers.
AD: Tom Dedin. SID: Mike Grose. II

REGIS (MASS.) .... Weston, MA 02193

Donna Tanner (6 YRS. W-77, L-65)

Regis (Mass.) Tr.	N20-21	Curry■	J26
Suffolk■	N23	Eastern Nazarene■	J29
Emerson-MCA	D 2	New England Col.	F 1
Elms■	D 4	Roger Williams	F 3
Wellesley■	D 8	Anna Maria	F 5
Colby-Sawyer	D10	Salve Regina■	F 9
Simmons	J12	Eastern Nazarene	F12
Roger Williams■	J15	Curry	F15
Anna Maria■	J18	New England Col.■	F17
Salve Regina	J20	Wentworth Inst.■	F19
Wentworth Inst.	J22		

Colors: Crimson & Gold. Nickname: Beacons.
AD: Judy Burling. SID: To be named. III

RENSSELAER .... Troy, NY 12180

Kathleen Ryan (4 YRS. W-51, L-44)

Albany (N.Y.) Tr.	N20-21	Clarkson	J22
Russell Sage■	N23	Alfred■	J28
St. Joseph (Vt.)■	D 2	Ithaca■	J29
Utica■	D 7	William Smith	F 4
Union (N.Y.)	D 9	Rochester Inst.	F 5
St. Leo	D31	Ithaca	F11
Barry Cl.	J2-3	Alfred	F12
Rochester Inst.■	J 7	Hartwick■	F15
William Smith■	J 8	Clarkson■	F18
Hamilton	J11	St. Lawrence■	F19
Hartwick	J13	Albany (N.Y.)	F22
St. Lawrence	J21		

Colors: Cherry & White. Nickname: Engineers.
AD: Bob Ducatte. SID: Kelly Vergin. III

RHODE ISLAND .... Kingston, RI 02881

Linda Ziemke (14 YRS. W-156, L-200)

New Hampshire■	N28	Geo. Washington	J20
Brown	D 1	Duquesne■	J22
Florida St. Cl.	D3-4	West Va.■	J24
Northeastern	D 8	St. Joseph's (Pa.)	J29
Harvard	D11	Temple	J31
Manhattan■	D14	Massachusetts	F 5
Rutgers Tr.	D28-29	St. Bonaventure	F 8
Vermont■	J 3	Geo. Washington■	F12
Alas. Anchorage Inv.	J6-8	Temple■	F17
Massachusetts■	J11	Duquesne	F24
St. Bonaventure■	J13	West Va.	F26
Rutgers■	J15	St. Joseph's (Pa.)■	M 5
Dartmouth	J18	Atlantic-10 Tr.	M9-10

Colors: Blue & White. Nickname: Rams.
AD: Ronald Petro. SID: Dawn Wright. I

RHODES .... Memphis, TN 38112

Sarah Risser-Hatgas (16 YRS. W-174 , L-161)

Millsaps Tr.	N20-21	Centre■	J28
Maryville (Mo.)	N27	Fisk■	J30
Principia	N29	Millsaps	F 1
Savannah A&D■	N30	Trinity (Tex.)■	F 4
Rhodes Tr.	D4-5	Hendrix■	F 6
Pomona-Pitzer	J 7	Centre	F11
Claremont-M-S	J 9	Fisk	F13
Trinity (Tex.)	J14	Oglethorpe■	F18
Hendrix	J16	Sewanee■	F20
Oglethorpe	J21	Millsaps■	F25
Sewanee	J23	Southwestern (Tex.)■	F26

Colors: Red & Black. Nickname: Lady Lynx.
AD: Mike Clary. SID: Matt Dean. III

■ Home games on each schedule.

See pages 735-738 for Division I tournament details

RICE .... Houston, TX 77001

Cristy McKinney (2 YRS. W-27, L-28)

Texas Southern	N27	Baylor	J26
Rice Cl.	D3-4	Texas Tech■	J29
Sam Houston St.	D17	Texas■	F 2
UC Irvine■	D19	Houston	F 5
Long Beach St.	D21	Southern Methodist	F 8
San Diego	D22	Texas A&M■	F12
Ga. Southern Inv.	D29-30	Texas Christian	F16
Rice Cl.	J3-4	Baylor■	F23
Prairie View■	J 6	Texas Tech	F26
Southern Methodist■	J12	Texas	M 2
Texas A&M	J15	Houston■	M 5
Texas Christian■	J19	Southwest Tr.	M9-12

Colors: Blue & Gray. Nickname: Owls.
AD: Bobby May. SID: Mark Sanders. I

RICHMOND .... Richmond, VA 23173

Tammy Holder (5 YRS. W-80, L-57)

Howard	N26	East Caro.■	J27
Richmond Inv.	D3-4	N.C.-Wilmington	J30
Va. Commonwealth	D21	James Madison	F 3
Central Fla. Cl.	D29-31	Old Dominion	F10
West Va.■	J 4	William & Mary	F13
Old Dominion■	J 8	American■	F16
Md.-Balt. County■	J12	Va. Commonwealth■	F18
William & Mary■	J16	George Mason■	F20
Towson St.	J18	East Caro.	F24
American	J20	N.C.-Wilmington■	F27
George Mason	J23	James Madison■	M 3
Wake Forest	J25	CAA Tr.	M10-12

Colors: Red & Blue. Nickname: Spiders.
AD: Chuck Boone. SID: Phil Stanton. I

RIDER .... Lawrenceville, NJ 08648

Eldon Price (4 YRS. W-49, L-63)

Lehigh	D 1	Mt. St. Mary's (Md.)	J22
Cornell Cl.	D3-4	Princeton	J24
Bucknell■	D 7	Robert Morris	J27
St. Peter's■	D10	St. Francis (Pa.)	J29
Syracuse	D18	St. Francis (N.Y.)■	F 3
Georgia Tech■	D29	LIU-Brooklyn■	F 5
Marist	J 5	Monmouth (N.J.)	F10
FDU-Teaneck	J 6	Wagner	F12
St. Francis (Pa.)■	J 8	Mt. St. Mary's (Md.)■	F19
Robert Morris■	J10	FDU-Teaneck■	F24
LIU-Brooklyn	J13	Marist■	F26
St. Francis (N.Y.)	J15	Wagner■	M 2
Monmouth (N.J.)■	J20	Northeast Tr.	M5-12

Colors: Cranberry & White. Nickname: Broncs.
AD: Curtis Blake. SID: Bud Focht. I

RIPON .... Ripon, WI 54971

Julie Heinz (3 YRS. W-27, L-36)

Ripon Inv.	N20-21	Monmouth (Ill.)■	J22
Wis.-Oshkosh Cl.	N26-27	Illinois Col.	J28
Lawrence■	D 1	Knox	J29
Lakeland■	D 4	Lawrence	F 2
Marian (Wis.)	D 8	Beloit	F 5
Bahamas Tr.	J3-8	St. Norbert	F 9
Lake Forest■	J12	Carroll (Wis.)■	F12
Carroll (Wis.)	J15	Lake Forest	F19
Beloit■	J17	St. Norbert■	F21
Cornell College■	J21		

Colors: Red. Nickname: Redmen.
AD: Robert Gillespie. SID: Bret Atkins. III

ROANOKE .... Salem, VA 24153

Susan Dunagan (12 YRS. W-238, L-79)

Marymount (Va.) Tr.	N19-21	Randolph-Macon■	J22
Lynchburg■	N23	Hollins	J24
Greensboro■	N30	East. Mennonite■	J26
Va. Wesleyan	D 4	Bridgewater (Va.)■	J29
East. Mennonite	D 7	Guilford■	F 2
Ferrum■	D11	Rand.-Macon Woman's	F 5
Bridgewater (Va.)	J 8	Hollins■	F 6
Guilford	J11	Randolph-Macon	F 8
Maryville (Tenn.)	J15	Va. Wesleyan■	F12
Rand.-Macon Woman's■	J18	Emory & Henry	F15
Emory & Henry■	J20	Lynchburg	F19

Colors: Maroon & Gray. Nickname: Maroons.
AD: Scott Allison. SID: Howard Wimmer. III

ROBERT MORRIS .... Coraopolis, PA 15108

Renate' Costner (2 YRS. W-18, L-35)

Cleveland St.■	N26	LIU-Brooklyn	J22
Virginia	N28	St. Francis (N.Y.)	J24
Pittsburgh	N30	Rider■	J27
St. Bonaventure	D 7	Mt. St. Mary's (Md.)■	J29
West Va.	D 9	FDU-Teaneck	F 3
Marshall■	D18	Marist	F 5
Youngstown St.■	D21	St. Francis (Pa.)■	F12
James Madison	D30	St. Francis (N.Y.)■	F17
Wagner■	J 4	LIU-Brooklyn■	F19
Monmouth (N.J.)■	J 6	Monmouth (N.J.)	F24
Mt. St. Mary's (Md.)	J 8	Wagner	F26
Rider	J10	St. Francis (Pa.)	M 4
Marist■	J13	Northeast Tr.	M5-12
FDU-Teaneck■	J15		

Colors: Blue & White. Nickname: Colonials.
AD: Bob McBee. SID: Marty Galosi. I

ROCHESTER .... Rochester, NY 14627

Joyce Wong (17 YRS. W-248, L-205)

Penn St.-Behrend Tr.	N19-20	Geneseo St.	J16
Rochester Inv.	N27-28	Washington (Mo.)■	J21
Case Reserve	D 3	Chicago■	J23
Brandeis■	D 5	Brandeis	J28
Rochester Inst.	D 8	New York U.	J30
Johns Hopkins■	D10	Chicago	F 4
New York U.■	D12	Washington (Mo.)	F 6
Carnegie Mellon	J 7	Nazareth (N.Y.) Tr.	F11-12
Emory	J 9	Emory■	F18
Trinity (Tex.)	J12	William Smith	F23
Southwestern (Tex.)	J14	Carnegie Mellon■	F26

Colors: Yellow & Blue. Nickname: Yellowjackets.
AD: Jeff Vennell. SID: Dennis O'Donnell. III

ROCHESTER INST. .... Rochester, NY 14623

Nelson Miles (4 YRS. W-12, L-82)

Keuka■	D 4	St. Lawrence■	J28
Rochester■	D 8	Clarkson■	J29
Union (N.Y.)	D11	Geneseo St.	F 1
Rensselaer	J 7	Hartwick■	F 4
Hartwick	J 8	Rensselaer■	F 5
Roberts Wesleyan	J11	William Smith■	F 8
Elmira	J13	Clarkson	F11
Nazareth (N.Y.)■	J15	St. Lawrence	F12
William Smith	J18	Roberts Wesleyan■	F15
Ithaca	J21	Alfred■	F18
Alfred	J22	Ithaca■	F19

Colors: Burnt Umber,Orange & White. Nickname: Tigers.
AD: Lou Spiotti. SID: J. Roger Dykes. III

ROCKFORD .... Rockford, IL 61101

Kristyn King (1 YR. W-0, L-25)

Rockford Tr.	N19-20	Aurora	J18
Dubuque■	N23	Ill. Benedictine	J22
Clarke	N30	Edgewood	J24
MacMurray■	D 4	Judson■	J29
North Park	D 7	Eureka■	F 3
Cornell College Inv.	D10-11	Trinity (Ill.)■	F 5
Concordia (Ill.)■	D14	Aurora■	F 8
Greenville	J 6	Ill. Benedictine■	F12
Maryville (Mo.)	J 8	Beloit	F17
Chicago■	J11	Concordia (Ill.)	F19
Trinity (Ill.)	J15	Judson	F22

Colors: Purple & White. Nickname: Regents.
AD: William Langston. SID: To be named. III

ROGER WILLIAMS .... Bristol, RI 02809

Patricia Bedard (2 YRS. W-7, L-37)

Johns Hopkins Cl.	N20-21	New England Col.	J29
Rhode Island Col.	N30	Eastern Nazarene■	F 1
Pine Manor■	D 7	Regis (Mass.)■	F 3
Simmons■	D11	Salve Regina■	F 5
Rivier■	J11	Anna Maria	F 9
Regis (Mass.)	J15	New England Col.■	F12
Salve Regina	J18	Wentworth Inst.■	F15
Anna Maria■	J20	Eastern Nazarene	F17
Curry■	J22	Curry	F19
Wentworth Inst.	J26		

Colors: Blue & Gold. Nickname: Hawks.
AD: Dwight Datcher. SID: David Kemmy. III

■ Home games on each schedule.

See pages 735-738 for Division I tournament details

ROLLINS .... Winter Park, FL 32789
Glenn Wilkes Jr. (7 YRS. W-141, L-58)

Franklin■	N22
Barton■	N24
Nebraska-Omaha■	N27
Brewton Parker■	D11
Paine■	D18
Monmouth (Ill.)■	D27
Phila. Textile■	D29
Clinch Valley■	J 3
East Stroudsburg■	J 6
St. Francis (Ill.)■	J 8
St. Leo	J12
Florida Tech■	J15
Tampa	J19
Fla. Southern■	J22
Flagler	J24
Barry	J26
Eckerd■	J29
North Fla.	F 2
Florida Tech	F 5
Tampa■	F 9
Fla. Southern	F12
Lynn■	F14
Barry■	F16
Eckerd	F19
North Fla.■	F23
St. Leo■	F26

Colors: Royal Blue & Gold. Nickname: Lady Tars.
AD: Phil Roach. SID: Fred Battenfield. II

ROWAN .... Glassboro, NJ 08028
Candace Crabtree (1ST YR. AS HEAD COACH)

Jersey City St.	N23
Montclair St.■	N27
Kean■	N30
Wm. Paterson	D 3
Bloomsburg	D 5
Stockton St.■	D 7
Rutgers-Newark■	D11
Trenton St.	J12
Ramapo■	J15
Rutgers-Camden	J19
Kean	J22
Jersey City St.■	J25
West Chester	J26
Montclair St.	J29
Trenton St.■	F 1
Salisbury St.	F 3
Wm. Paterson■	F 5
Stockton St.	F 9
Rutgers-Newark	F12
Rutgers-Camden■	F15
Ramapo	F17
Allentown	F19
Kutztown	F21

Colors: Brown & Gold. Nickname: Profs.
AD: Joy Reighn. SID: Sheila Stevenson. III

RUSSELL SAGE .... Troy, NY 12180
Julie Goodenough (2 YRS. W-18, L-31)

Rensselaer	N23
Castleton St.	N30
North Adams St.	D 2
Manhattanville Tr.	D4-5
Alfred■	D10
Hunter■	J 8
Colby-Sawyer	J12
Elmira■	J15
Union (N.Y.)■	J18
Albany Pharmacy	J20
Southern Vt.■	J22
Utica Tech■	J25
Stony Brook■	J28
Utica■	J29
Vassar■	J31
Skidmore■	F 2
Oneonta St.	F 5
Western New Eng.	F 8
Green Mountain	F13
Elms	F17
Hamilton	F19

Colors: Green & White. Nickname: Lady Gators.
AD: Beth Matfield. SID: To be named. III

RUST .... Holly Springs, MS 38635
Nancy Binion (5 YRS. W-73, L-44)

Philander Smith■	N20
Tougaloo■	N22
Savannah A&D■	N29
Philander Smith	N30
Southern-N.O.	D 3
Wiley	D 4
Blue Mountain	D 9
Wiley■	D11
Paul Quinn■	J 7
Knoxville■	J 8
Arkansas Tech■	J10
LeMoyne-Owen	J12
Mississippi-Women■	J14
Williams Bapt.■	J18
Stillman■	J22
Williams Bapt.	J25
Tougaloo	J26
Paul Quinn	J29
Lane	F 1
Mississippi-Women	F 3
Stillman	F 4
Knoxville	F11
LeMoyne-Owen■	F16
Lane■	F19
Savannah A&D	F21

Colors: Blue & White. Nickname: Lady Bearcats.
AD: Ishmell Edward. SID: Paula Clark. III

RUTGERS .... Piscataway, NJ 08855
Theresa Grentz (19 YRS. W-422, L-134)

Old Dominion■	D 2
St. John's (N.Y.)	D 8
Penn St.■	D11
Rutgers Tr.	D28-29
UCLA	J 3
Niagara■	J 6
West Va.	J 8
Loyola (Md.)	J11
Rhode Island	J15
Tennessee■	J17
Duquesne	J20
Temple■	J27
Geo. Washington■	J29
West Va.■	F 2
St. Joseph's (Pa.)■	F 5
Maryland	F 8
Massachusetts	F12
Geo. Washington	F15
St. Bonaventure	F19
Duquesne■	F22
St. Joseph's (Pa.)	F26
Massachusetts■	F28
Temple	M 3
St. Bonaventure■	M 5

Colors: Scarlet. Nickname: Lady Knights.
AD: Frederick E. Gruninger. SID: Maureen Coyle. I

RUTGERS-CAMDEN .... Camden, NJ 08102
Merry Carole Ellerbe (4 YRS. W-44, L-59)

Trenton St.	N23
Wm. Paterson■	N27
Rutgers-Newark■	D 1
Jersey City St.	D 4
Georgian Court■	D 6
Kean	D 8
Ramapo■	D11
Lincoln (Pa.)■	J 5
York (N.Y.)■	J 8
Stockton St.■	J12
Montclair St.	J15
Rowan■	J19
Rutgers-Newark	J22
Trenton St.■	J26
Wm. Paterson	J29
Stockton St.	F 2
Jersey City St.■	F 5
Kean■	F 9
Ramapo	F12
Rowan	F15
Montclair St.■	F19

Colors: Scarlet & Black. Nickname: Lady Pioneers.
AD: Wilbur Wilson. SID: To be named. III

RUTGERS-NEWARK .... Newark, NJ 07102
To be named

Stockton St.■	N23
Kean	N27
Rutgers-Camden	D 1
Wm. Paterson■	D 8
Rowan	D11
Ramapo■	J 4
Coast Guard Cl.	J8-9
Jersey City St.	J12
Trenton St.■	J15
CCNY■	J17
Montclair St.■	J19
Rutgers-Camden■	J22
Drew■	J24
Stockton St.	J26
Kean■	J29
Jersey City St.■	F 2
Ramapo	F 5
St. Elizabeth	F 7
Wm. Paterson	F 9
Rowan■	F12
Montclair St.	F16
Trenton St.	F19

Colors: Scarlet. Nickname: Raiders.
AD: John Adams. SID: Lewis Shaine. III

SACRED HEART .... Fairfield, CT 06432
Ed Swanson (3 YRS. W-35, L-48)

Assumption■	N21
Quinnipiac	N23
Molloy■	D 1
East Stroudsburg Cl.	D3-4
Bryant■	D 8
St. Anselm■	D11
Stonehill	D18
St. Rose	D21
Adelphi	J 3
Keene St.■	J 8
Franklin Pierce■	J12
Le Moyne	J17
Southern Conn. St.	J19
Mass.-Lowell■	J22
Bridgeport■	J26
New Hamp. Col.	J29
New Haven	F 2
Le Moyne■	F 6
Southern Conn. St.■	F 9
Mass.-Lowell	F12
Franklin Pierce	F14
New Haven■	F16
Keene St.	F21
Bridgeport	F23
New Hamp. Col.■	F26

Colors: Scarlet & White. Nickname: Pioneers.
AD: Don Cook. SID: Don Harrison. II

SAGINAW VALLEY ...... University Center, MI 48710
Claudette Charney (9 YRS. W-185, L-75)

Indiana (Pa.) Inv.	N20-21
Washburn	N24
Pitt.-Johnstown Tr.	N27-28
Oakland	D 4
Ferris St.	D 9
Lake Superior St.■	D11
Hope■	D18
Cal St. Stanis. Tr.	D29-30
Northwood■	J 6
Hillsdale■	J 8
Wayne St. (Mich.)	J13
Grand Valley St.■	J15
Michigan Tech■	J20
Northern Mich.■	J22
Oakland■	J29
Ferris St.■	F 3
Lake Superior St.	F 5
Northwood	F10
Hillsdale	F12
Wayne St. (Mich.)■	F17
Grand Valley St.	F19
Michigan Tech	F24
Northern Mich.	F26

Colors: Red, White & Blue. Nickname: Lady Cardinals.
AD: Bob Becker. SID: Tom Waske. II

SALEM ST. .... Salem, MA 01970
Tim Shea (12 YRS. W-276, L-66)

Emmanuel Tr.	N20-21
Southern Me.	N30
Plymouth St.	D 2
Colby	D11
Gordon■	J12
Fitchburg St.■	J15
Westfield St.	J18
Framingham St.■	J22
North Adams St.■	J25
Bri'water (Mass.)	J29
Worcester St.■	F 1
Mass.-Dartmouth■	F 3
Emmanuel■	F 5
Fitchburg St.	F 8
Westfield St.■	F10
Framingham St.	F12
North Adams St.	F14
Bri'water (Mass.)■	F17
Worcester St.	F19

Colors: Orange & Brown. Nickname: Lady Vikings.
AD: John Galaris. SID: Thomas Roundy. III

■ Home games on each schedule.

See pages 735-738 for Division I tournament details

SALEM-TEIKYO .... Salem, WV 26426

Tammy Biesenthal (1ST YR. AS HEAD COACH)

Northern Ky.■	N27
Edinboro Inv.	D3-4
Glenville St.■	D 6
Davis & Elkins	D 9
Calif. (Pa.)	D15
Fairmont St.■	J 8
Charleston (W.Va.)	J10
West Va. Wesleyan	J12
West Va. Tech■	J15
Alderson-Broaddus	J17
West Va. St.■	J19
Concord■	J21
Bluefield St.■	J22
Shepherd■	J24
Davis & Elkins■	J26
Wheeling Jesuit	J31
Alderson-Broaddus■	F 2
West Va. Wesleyan■	F 5
Fairmont St.	F 9
West Va. St.	F12
Wheeling Jesuit■	F14
West Liberty St.	F16

Colors: Green & White. Nickname: Tigers.
AD: Michael Carey. SID: John Miller. II

SALISBURY ST. .... Salisbury, MD 21801

Bridget Benshetler (3 YRS. W-31, L-42)

Bri'water (Va.) Inv.	N19-20
Chris. Newport■	N23
Salisbury St. Cl.	D3-4
Catholic	D 6
Wilmington (Del.)	D 8
Lynchburg■	D16
Wm. Paterson	J 5
Kean Tr.	J7-8
Allentown■	J15
Notre Dame (Md.)	J19
Frostburg St.■	J21
Stockton St.■	J22
Goucher	J24
Va. Wesleyan■	J26
Frostburg St.	J29
Wesley■	F 1
Rowan■	F 3
Trenton St.	F 7
Mary Washington	F10
Marymount (Va.) Inv.	F12-13
Wesley	F16
Cabrini	F21

Colors: Maroon & Gold. Nickname: Sea Gulls.
AD: Michael Vienna. SID: Paul Ohanian. III

SALVE REGINA .... Newport, RI 02840

John Klitzner (1 YR. W-8, L-15)

MIT Tr.	N20-21
Babson■	N23
Rhode Island Col.■	D 2
Simmons	D 4
Connecticut Col.	D 7
Worcester Tech■	D 9
Albertus Magnus■	D12
Anna Maria	J15
Roger Williams■	J18
Regis (Mass.)■	J20
New England Col.	J22
Eastern Nazarene■	J26
Curry■	J29
Wentworth Inst.	F 1
Anna Maria■	F 3
Roger Williams	F 5
Regis (Mass.)	F 9
Curry	F12
Eastern Nazarene	F15
Wentworth Inst.■	F17
New England Col.■	F19

Colors: Blue, White & Green. Nickname: The Newporters.
AD: Lynn Sheedy. SID: Ed Habershaw. III

SAM HOUSTON ST. .... Huntsville, TX 77341

Vic Schaefer (3 YRS. W-26, L-54)

Prairie View■	N28
Missouri Cl.	D3-4
Texas Southern■	D 9
Rice■	D17
Texas Southern	J 6
Northwestern (La.)■	J 8
Texas-Arlington	J11
Southwest Tex. St.	J14
Texas-San Antonio	J16
Prairie View	J19
Stephen F. Austin■	J22
Cal St. Sacramento■	J25
Nicholls St.■	J27
McNeese St.■	J29
Northwestern (La.)	F 3
Northeast La.	F 5
North Texas■	F 7
Texas-San Antonio■	F10
Southwest Tex. St.■	F12
Stephen F. Austin	F19
Northeast La.■	F22
McNeese St.	F24
Nicholls St.	F26
Texas-Arlington■	F28
North Texas	M 2
Southland Tr.	M8-12

Colors: Orange & White. Nickname: Ladykats.
AD: Ronnie Choate. SID: Paul Ridings Jr. I

SAN DIEGO .... San Diego, CA 92110

Kathleen Marpe (19 YRS. W-238, L-260)

Cal Poly Pomona	N26
UCLA	D 1
San Diego St.■	D 4
Oregon St. Cl.	D10-11
Cal St. Northridge■	D18
Rice■	D22
Oregon■	D28
Drake■	D30
Fresno Pacific	J 4
Fresno St.	J 5
Cal St. Sacramento	J 7
Gonzaga■	J13
Portland■	J15
Pepperdine	J21
Loyola (Cal.)	J22
San Francisco■	J29
Santa Clara■	F 3
St. Mary's (Cal.)■	F 5
St. Mary's (Cal.)	F11
Santa Clara	F12
Loyola (Cal.)■	F17
Pepperdine■	F19
Portland	F24
Gonzaga	F26
San Francisco	M 2
West Coast Tr.	M11-12

Colors: Columbia Blue, Navy & White. Nickname: Toreros.
AD: Tom Iannacone. SID: Ted Gosen. I

SAN DIEGO ST. .... San Diego, CA 92182

Beth Burns (4 YRS. W-58, L-57)

DePaul Inv.	N26-27
Loyola (Cal.)	D 1
San Diego	D 4
Arizona St.■	D 7
Arizona■	D11
Santa Clara Shootout	D18-19
Oregon■	D30
Southern Cal	J 2
Gonzaga■	J11
Utah■	J13
Brigham Young■	J15
Cal St. Fullerton■	J18
Fresno St.	J22
Colorado St.	J27
Wyoming	J29
Wyoming■	F 4
Colorado St.■	F 6
New Mexico	F11
UTEP	F13
UTEP■	F18
New Mexico■	F20
Brigham Young	F24
Utah	F26
Fresno St.■	M 5
Western Athletic Tr.	M9-12

Colors: Scarlet & Black. Nickname: Aztecs.
AD: Fred Miller. SID: Lisa Vad. I

SAN FRANCISCO .... San Francisco, CA 94117

Mary Hile-& Bill Nepfel (15 YRS. W-217, L-197)

UC Santa Barb.■	N30
Hawaii Tr.	D3-5
San Jose St.	D 8
UCLA■	D10
San Fran. St.■	D12
California	D18
Cal St. Sacramento■	D20
Connecticut■	D30
Cornell■	J 8
Portland■	J13
Gonzaga■	J15
Loyola (Cal.)	J21
Pepperdine	J22
Cal St. Northridge■	J26
San Diego	J29
St. Mary's (Cal.)■	F 3
Santa Clara■	F 5
Santa Clara	F11
St. Mary's (Cal.)	F12
Pepperdine■	F17
Loyola (Cal.)■	F19
Gonzaga	F24
Portland	F26
San Diego■	M 2
West Coast Tr.	M11-12

Colors: Green & Gold. Nickname: Lady Dons.
AD: Bill Hogan. SID: Pete LaFleur. I

SAN FRAN. ST. .... San Francisco, CA 94132

Arden Kragalott (9 YRS. W-109, L-117)

Pomona-Pitzer	N20
Cal St. San B'dino	N22
Cal St. Stanis. Inv.	N26-27
Cal Lutheran■	D 4
UC Santa Cruz	D11
San Francisco	D12
Southern Ore. St.■	D17
Seattle Pacific■	D18
Cal St. Dom. Hills■	D20
Whitman■	J 3
UC Davis	J 7
Notre Dame (Cal.)■	J11
Humboldt St.	J13
Cal St. Hayward	J14
Cal St. Chico	J15
Cal St. Stanislaus■	J21
Mills	J25
Sonoma St.	J29
Humboldt St.■	F 4
Cal St. Stanislaus	F 5
Cal St. Chico■	F11
Cal St. Hayward■	F12
UC Davis■	F18
Sonoma St.■	F24

Colors: Purple & Gold. Nickname: Gators.
AD: Bill Partlow. SID: Kyle McRae. II

SAN JOSE ST. .... San Jose, CA 95192

Karen Smith (1 YR. W-5, L-21)

Fresno St.■	N30
Santa Clara■	D 1
San Francisco■	D 8
Cal St. Sacramento	D10
St. Mary's (Cal.)	D20
Loyola (Cal.)	D29
Cal St. Northridge	D30
Cornell■	J 5
Pacific (Cal.)	J 8
Long Beach St.■	J13
UC Santa Barb.■	J15
Nevada■	J17
New Mexico St.	J20
Nevada-Las Vegas	J22
Nevada	J27
Pacific (Cal.)■	J29
Cal St. Fullerton■	F 3
UC Irvine■	F 5
UC Santa Barb.	F10
Long Beach St.	F13
Nevada-Las Vegas■	F17
New Mexico St.■	F19
Cal St. Fullerton	F24
UC Irvine	F26
Hawaii	M 4
Hawaii	M 6
Big West Tr.	M9-12

Colors: Gold, White & Blue. Nickname: Spartans.
AD: Thomas Brennan. SID: Lawrence Fan. I

SANTA CLARA .... Santa Clara, CA 95053

Caren Horstmeyer (5 YRS. W-84, L-60)

San Jose St.	D 1
Pacific (Cal.)	D11
UCLA■	D12
Fresno St.	D15
Santa Clara Shootout	D18-19
Idaho	D28
Washington St.	D30
Cal St. Sacramento■	J 2
Stanford■	J 3
Cornell■	J 6
Texas	J 8
Pepperdine■	J14
Loyola (Cal.)■	J15
Gonzaga	J20
Portland	J22
Portland■	J28
Gonzaga■	J29
San Diego	F 3
San Francisco	F 5
San Francisco■	F11
San Diego■	F12
St. Mary's (Cal.)■	F18
Loyola (Cal.)	F25
Pepperdine	F26
St. Mary's (Cal.)	M 2
West Coast Tr.	M11-12

Colors: Bronco Red & White. Nickname: Broncos.
AD: Carroll Williams. SID: Lee Klusky. I

■ Home games on each schedule.

See pages 735-738 for Division I tournament details

SCRANTON .... Scranton, PA 18510

Michael Strong (14 YRS. W-328, L-82)

Montclair St.■ N19
Marywood N23
Catholic N27
Wilkes■ .... D 1
Delaware Valley .... D 4
Elizabethtown .... D 7
Scranton Cl. D10-11
Tampa Tr. J7-8
FDU-Madison J13
Upsala■ J15
Moravian J17
Lycoming■ J19
King's (Pa.) J22
Susquehanna■ J24
Drew J26
Wilkes J29
FDU-Madison■ .... F 2
Delaware Valley■ .... F 5
Lycoming .... F 9
Upsala F12
Drew■ F16
King's (Pa.)■ F19

Colors: Purple & White. Nickname: Lady Royals.
AD: Gary Wodder. SID: Kenneth Buntz. III

SEATTLE PACIFIC .... Seattle, WA 98119

Gordy Presnell (6 YRS. W-113, L-60)

Pac. Lutheran■ N23
Humboldt St. Cl. N26-27
Northwest (Wash.)■ N30
Seattle■ .... D 1
North Dak.■ .... D 4
Puget Sound■ D11
San Fran. St. D18
Portland St. Tr. D29-30
Seattle .... J 4
St. Martin's■ .... J 5
Portland St. J15
Alas. Anchorage J20
Alas. Fairbanks J22
Alas. Fairbanks J23
Eastern Mont.■ J27
Grand Canyon■ J29
Western Wash.■ .... F 4
Puget Sound .... F 7
Alas. Anchorage■ F10
Alas. Fairbanks■ F12
Eastern Mont. F17
Grand Canyon F19
St. Martin's F22
Portland St.■ F26

Colors: Maroon & White. Nickname: Falcons.
AD: Keith Phillips. SID: Frank MacDonald. II

SETON HALL .... South Orange, NJ 07079

Phyllis Mangina (8 YRS. W-112 , L-115)

Monmouth (N.J.)■ N27
Fairfield .... D 1
Seton Hall Cl. D4-5
Providence .... D 9
Notre Dame D11
Lafayette■ D13
FDU-Teaneck D22
Texas Tech■ D28
St. John's (N.Y.) .... J 3
Connecticut■ .... J 5
Syracuse .... J 8
Miami (Fla.)■ J13
Pittsburgh J16
Boston College■ J19
Villanova J22
Georgetown■ J26
Syracuse■ J29
St. John's (N.Y.)■ .... F 2
Connecticut .... F 6
Miami (Fla.) .... F 9
Pittsburgh■ F12
Providence■ F16
Boston College F19
Villanova■ F23
Georgetown F26
Big East Tr. M4-7

Colors: Blue & White. Nickname: Pirates.
AD: Larry Keating. SID: Marie Wozinak. I

SHENANDOAH .... Winchester, VA 22601

Kathy Orsini (2 YRS. W-24, L-23)

Bri'water (Va.) Inv. N19-20
East. Mennonite■ N23
Lynchburg N30
Heidelberg Tr. D3-4
St. Mary's (Md.)■ .... D 9
Frank. & Marsh.■ .... J 8
Frostburg St.■ J11
N.C. Wesleyan J15
Chris. Newport J16
Greensboro■ J19
Methodist■ J22
Mary Washington■ J25
Ferrum J29
Averett J30
Frostburg St. .... F 2
N.C. Wesleyan■ .... F 5
Chris. Newport■ .... F 6
Notre Dame (Md.)■ .... F 9
Greensboro F12
Methodist F13
Ferrum■ F16
Averett■ F19

Colors: Red, White & Blue. Nickname: Hornets.
AD: Dave Dutton. SID: Rob Kulton. III

SHEPHERD .... Shepherdstown, WV 25443

Ed Fincham (11 YRS. W-145, L-141)

Shepherd Tr. N19-20
West Va. Tech N23
Davis & Elkins .... D 1
St. Thomas Aq. Tr. D3-4
Goucher .... D 6
West Liberty St.■ .... D 8
Concord■ D11
Fairmont St.■ D20
Gettysburg Tr. J7-8
West Va. St.■ J10
West Va. Wesleyan■ J15
Salem-Teikyo J24
Ohio Valley J25
Charleston (W.Va.)■ J29
Bluefield St. J31
West Liberty St. .... F 4
Wheeling Jesuit .... F 5
Alderson-Broaddus■ .... F 7
Wheeling Jesuit■ F11
Davis & Elkins■ F12
Fairmont St. F14
Concord F17

Colors: Blue & Gold. Nickname: Lady Rams.
AD: Monte Cater. SID: Michael Straley. II

SHIPPENSBURG .... Shippensburg, PA 17257

David Smith (11 YRS. W-210, L-81)

Longwood Inv. N19-20
Kutztown■ N23
East Stroudsburg .... D 1
Shippensburg Tr. D3-4
Phila. Pharmacy■ .... D 6
West Chester .... D 8
Georgian Court■ D11
Mansfield .... J 8
Bloomsburg J10
Indiana (Pa.)■ J12
Clarion J15
Millersville J17
Calif. (Pa.) J19
Edinboro■ J22
Lock Haven J26
Slippery Rock■ J29
Kutztown J31
Clarion■ .... F 5
Indiana (Pa.) .... F 9
Calif. (Pa.)■ F12
Lock Haven■ F16
Edinboro F19
Cheyney■ F23
Slippery Rock F26

Colors: Red & Blue. Nickname: Lady Raiders.
AD: Jane Goss. SID: John R. Alosi. II

SIENA .... Loudonville, NY 12211

Gina Castelli (3 YRS. W-43, L-40)

Central Conn. St. N27
Hartford■ .... D 1
Vermont■ .... D 4
Holy Cross .... D 9
Dartmouth D11
Brigham Young Cl. D29-30
Hofstra .... J 3
Massachusetts■ .... J 6
George Mason .... J 9
Delaware J12
Loyola (Md.) J15
Fairfield■ J18
Iona J20
Niagara■ J22
Manhattan■ J28
Canisius■ .... F 2
Loyola (Md.)■ .... F 5
Marist .... F 7
Canisius F11
Niagara F13
St. Peter's■ F16
Fairfield F19
Manhattan F21
Iona■ F24
St. Peter's F26
Metro Atlantic Tr. M4-6

Colors: Green & Gold. Nickname: Saints.
AD: John D'Argenio. SID: Meg Culhane. I

SIMMONS .... Boston, MA 02115

Petra Farias (1ST YR. AS HEAD COACH)

MIT Tr. N20-21
Wentworth Inst.■ N23
Anna Maria .... D 1
Salve Regina■ .... D 4
MIT■ .... D 8
Roger Williams D11
New England■ .... J 5
Eastern Nazarene■ .... J 8
Regis (Mass.)■ J12
Albertus Magnus J15
Suffolk J19
Rivier J26
Colby-Sawyer .... F 1
Elms■ F12
Endicott■ F16
Western New Eng. F19

Colors: Blue & Gold. Nickname: Thunderbolts.
AD: Sheila Brown. SID: None. III

SIMPSON .... Indianola, IA 50125

Brian Niemuth (5 YRS. W-76, L-49)

Culver-Stockton Tr. N19-20
Midland Lutheran■ .... D 4
Mt. St. Clare .... D 7
Park■ D11
Teiko-Marycrest D18
St. Benedict Cl. D29-30
Luther■ .... J 7
Dubuque■ .... J 8
Rockhurst■ J15
Buena Vista J21
Wartburg J22
Loras J28
Central (Iowa)■ J29
William Penn■ .... F 1
Upper Iowa .... F 4
Luther .... F 5
Loras■ F11
Central (Iowa) F12
Buena Vista■ F18
Upper Iowa■ F19
William Penn F22
Wartburg■ F25
Dubuque F26

Colors: Red & Gold. Nickname: Storm.
AD: John Sirianni. SID: Jerry Fitzsimmons. III

SKIDMORE .... Saratoga Springs, NY 12866

Jamie Bautochka (1ST YR. AS HEAD COACH)

Albany (N.Y.) Tr. N20-21
Williams■ N30
St. Lawrence .... D 3
Clarkson .... D 4
Hamilton■ .... D 9
Alfred■ D11
Albany (N.Y.)■ .... J 6
Smith .... J 8
Plattsburgh St. J11
Union (N.Y.)■ J13
Bowdoin■ J15
Bates■ J16
Manhattanville J22
Utica■ J24
Skidmore Inv. J28-29
Russell Sage .... F 2
Castleton St. F12
Vassar■ F14
Middlebury■ F16
Green Mountain F19
Hartwick■ F21

Colors: Green, White & Gold. Nickname: Thoroughbreds.
AD: Tim Brown. SID: Bill Jones. III

■ Home games on each schedule.

See pages 735-738 for Division I tournament details

SLIPPERY ROCK .... Slippery Rock, PA 16057

Cheryl Kennedy (8 YRS. W-109, L-103)

Wayne St. (Mich.)■	N19	Lock Haven■	J15
Pitt.-Johnstown■	N23	Indiana (Pa.)■	J19
Seton Hill■	N30	Gannon	J22
Alas. Fairbanks	D 7	Clarion■	J26
Alas. Fairbanks	D 8	Shippensburg	J29
Alas. Anchorage	D10	Edinboro	F 2
Alas. Anchorage	D11	Lock Haven	F 5
Mercyhurst Tr.	D17-18	Calif. (Pa.)■	F 9
Lynn	D31	Indiana (Pa.)	F12
Florida Tech Tr.	J2-3	Clarion	F16
Mansfield	J 6	Edinboro■	F23
Bloomsburg	J 8	Shippensburg■	F26
Calif. (Pa.)	J12		

Colors: Green & White. Nickname: Rockets, The Rock.
AD: Bill Lennox. SID: John Carpenter. II

SMITH .... Northampton, MA 01063

James Babyak (12 YRS. W-137, L-159)

Coast Guard■	D 1	Williams	J27
Bryn Mawr Tr.	D3-5	Worcester Tech■	J29
Trinity (Conn.)	D 9	Mount Holyoke	F 1
North Adams St.	J 6	Babson■	F 3
Skidmore■	J 8	Tufts■	F 5
Union (N.Y.)■	J10	Amherst	F 8
Wesleyan	J13	Wellesley■	F12
Western New Eng.■	J16	Wheaton (Mass.)	F17
Brandeis	J18	MIT■	F19
Smith Inv.	J22-23		

Colors: Yellow,White & Blue. Nickname: Pioneers.
AD: Lynn Oberbillig. SID: Carole A. Grills. III

SONOMA ST. .... Rohnert Park, CA 94928

Susan Zachensky-Walthall (14 YRS. W-197, L-161)

Dominican (Cal.)■	N20	Humboldt St.	J15
Eastern Mont.■	N23	Cal St. Hayward■	J21
Humboldt St. Cl.	N26-27	Cal St. Stanislaus	J22
UC Davis Inv.	D3-4	San Fran. St.■	J29
Cal St. Dom. Hills■	D22	Cal St. Stanislaus■	F 4
Lake Superior St.■	D29	Cal St. Hayward	F 5
Lake Superior St.■	D30	Humboldt St.■	F11
Whitman■	J 4	Cal St. Chico■	F12
Cal Poly SLO■	J 7	UC Davis	F19
UC Davis■	J 9	San Fran. St.	F24
Cal St. Chico	J14		

Colors: Blue & White. Nickname: Cossacks.
AD: Ralph Barkey. SID: Mitch Cox. II

SOUTH ALA. .... Mobile, AL 36688

Butch Stockton (2 YRS. W-17, L-38)

Michigan St. Cl.	D3-4	Louisiana Tech■	F 3
Troy St.■	D 8	New Orleans	F 5
Florida	D12	Arkansas St.■	F 7
Ala.-Birmingham■	D15	Southwestern La.	F10
South Ala. Cl.	D17-18	Lamar	F17
Ala.-Birmingham	D30	Tex.-Pan American	F19
Lamar■	J 6	Auburn■	F23
Troy St.	J10	Western Ky.■	F26
Western Ky.	J13	Alcorn St.	F28
Arkansas St.	J15	Southwestern La.■	M 3
New Orleans■	J22	Tex.-Pan American■	M 5
Alabama	J26	Sun Belt Tr.	M10-12
Louisiana Tech	J29		

Colors: Red, White, Blue. Nickname: Lady Jaguars.
AD: Joe Gottfried. SID: Fred Huff. I

SOUTH CARO. .... Columbia, SC 29208

Nancy Wilson (17 YRS. W-370, L-158)

Old Dominion Cl.	N27-28	South Caro. St.	J20
South Caro. St.■	N30	Alabama■	J22
Arizona St. Cl.	D3-4	East Tenn. St.	J26
Ga. Southern■	D 6	Georgia	J29
Mississippi St.	D 8	Furman■	F 2
Coastal Caro. Cl.	D29-30	Tennessee■	F 8
Charleston■	J 3	Arkansas	F12
Auburn	J 5	Clemson	F16
Kentucky■	J 8	Florida	F19
Mississippi■	J11	N.C.-Charlotte■	F23
Western Caro.	J13	Vanderbilt■	F26
Louisiana St.	J15	Southeastern Tr.	M4-7

Colors: Garnet & Black. Nickname: Lady Gamecocks.
AD: Mike McGee. SID: Erika Austin. I

SOUTH CARO. ST. .... Orangeburg, SC 29117

Lyman Foster (5 YRS. W-79, L-68)

South Caro.	N30	Florida A&M	J31
Liberty Cl.	D3-4	Md.-East. Shore	F 5
Claflin■	D11	Delaware St.	F 7
Clemson■	D15	N.C.-Charlotte■	F10
Coppin St.	J 6	North Caro. A&T■	F12
Morgan St.	J 8	Benedict	F14
Howard	J10	Coppin St.■	F17
Florida A&M■	J15	Howard■	F21
Bethune-Cookman■	J17	Georgia■	F23
South Caro.■	J20	Morgan St.■	F26
Md.-East. Shore■	J22	North Caro. A&T	M 5
Delaware St.■	J24	MEAC Tr.	M9-13
Bethune-Cookman	J29		

Colors: Garnet & Blue. Nickname: Lady Bulldogs.
AD: James Martin. SID: Bill Hamilton. I

S.C.-AIKEN .... Aiken, SC 29801

Gail Johnson (7 YRS. W-115, L-85)

Catawba Cl.	N19-20	Armstrong St.	J29
Newberry	N22	Columbus	J31
Jacksonville St.	N29	Lander	F 2
Voorhees■	D 7	Pembroke St.■	F 5
Erskine■	D15	Savannah St.■	F 7
S.C.-Spartanburg	J 5	Erskine	F 9
Voorhees	J 8	S.C.-Spartanburg■	F12
Francis Marion	J10	Augusta	F14
Lander■	J13	Georgia Col.	F17
Georgia Col.■	J15	Armstrong St.■	F21
Newberry■	J17	Francis Marion■	F23
Augusta■	J22	Columbus	F26
Pembroke St.	J26		

Colors: Cardinal & White. Nickname: Lady Pacers.
AD: Randy Warrick. SID: Terry Garbutt. II

S.C.-SPARTANBURG .... Spartanburg, SC 29303

Peggy Sells (1 YR. W-28, L-3)

Central Wesleyan■	N20	Queens (N.C.)■	J24
S.C.-Spart. Inv.	N26-27	Lander	J27
Presbyterian	D 5	Georgia Col.■	J31
Kennesaw St. Tr.	D17-18	Augusta	F 2
S.C.-Aiken■	J 5	Armstrong St.■	F 5
Armstrong St.	J 8	Lander■	F 9
Converse■	J10	S.C.-Aiken	F12
Georgia Col.	J13	Francis Marion	F16
Pembroke St.■	J15	Columbus■	F19
Central Wesleyan	J17	Lees-McRae■	F21
Francis Marion■	J19	Augusta■	F23
Columbus	J22	Pembroke St.	F26

Colors: Kelly Green, White & Black. Nickname: Lady Rifles.
AD: Jerry Waters. SID: Michael MacEachern. II

SOUTH DAK. .... Vermillion, SD 57069

Gary Larson (4 YRS. W-66, L-41)

Bemidji St.■	N20	Northern Colo.	J21
Wayne St. (Neb.)■	N23	Nebraska-Omaha	J22
Wis.-Parkside	D 2	North Dak.■	J28
Wis.-Oshkosh	D 3	North Dak. St.■	J29
Doane■	D 7	Mankato St.■	F 4
Minn.-Morris■	D10	St. Cloud St.■	F 5
Southwest St.■	D11	South Dak. St.	F11
Mt. Marty	D18	Augustana (S.D.)	F12
Winona St.■	D29	Nebraska-Omaha■	F18
Morningside	J 2	Northern Colo.■	F19
St. Cloud St.	J 7	North Dak. St.	F25
Mankato St.	J 8	North Dak.	F26
Augustana (S.D.)■	J14	Morningside■	M 5
South Dak. St.■	J15		

Colors: Red & White. Nickname: Coyotes.
AD: Jack Doyle. SID: Kyle Johnson. II

SOUTH DAK. ST. .... Brookings, SD 57007

Nancy Neiber (9 YRS. W-158, L-92)

Bemidji St.■	N19	South Dak.	J15
Dak. Wesleyan■	N23	St. Cloud St.■	J21
Grand Canyon Inv.	N26-27	Mankato St.■	J22
Minn.-Duluth■	D 3	Augustana (S.D.)■	J29
Southwest St.	D 7	North Dak. St.	F 4
Neb.-Kearney	D12	North Dak.	F 5
Moorhead St.	D16	South Dak.■	F11
Minn.-Morris■	D30	Morningside■	F12
Nebraska-Omaha	J 2	Mankato St.	F18
Northern Colo.	J 3	St. Cloud St.	F19
North Dak.■	J 7	Augustana (S.D.)	F26
North Dak. St.■	J 8	Northern Colo.■	M 4
Morningside	J14	Nebraska-Omaha■	M 5

Colors: Yellow & Blue. Nickname: Jackrabbits.
AD: Fred Oien. SID: Ron Lenz. II

■ Home games on each schedule.

See pages 735-738 for Division I tournament details

SOUTH FLA. .... Tampa, FL 33620

Trudi Lacey (7 YRS. W-112 , L-90)

Stetson■	D 1	Va. Commonwealth■	J21
Texas-Arlington Cl.	D3-4	Ga. Southern	J26
Southwest Tex. St.	D 6	Southern Miss.■	J31
Fla. Atlantic■	D12	Central Fla.■	F 2
Mercer■	D15	Tulane■	F 5
South Fla. Tr.	D17-18	N.C.-Charlotte■	F 7
Central Fla.	D20	Tulane	F11
Ill.-Chicago	D29	Southern Miss.	F13
Illinois St.	D31	Virginia Tech■	F20
Manhattan■	J 3	Florida■	F23
N.C.-Charlotte	J 8	Va. Commonwealth	F27
Virginia Tech	J10	Louisville	M 3
Louisville■	J15	Metro Tr.	M8-11

Colors: Green & Gold. Nickname: Bulls.
AD: Paul Griffin. SID: Tracy Judd. I

SOUTHEAST MO. ST. ..... Cape Girardeau, MO 63701

Ed Arnzen (10 YRS. W-225, L-72)

Cleveland St.■	N29	Tenn.-Martin■	J24
Ky. Wesleyan■	D 1	Tennessee St.	J29
Oral Roberts■	D 9	Austin Peay	J31
Missouri	D11	Murray St.	F 2
Western Ill.	D28	Morehead St.■	F 5
St. Louis	D30	Eastern Ky.■	F 7
Evansville■	J 3	Tennessee Tech	F12
Oral Roberts	J 5	Middle Tenn. St.	F14
Eastern Ky.	J 8	Murray St.■	F19
Morehead St.	J10	Mo.-Kansas City	F21
St. Louis■	J13	Tenn.-Martin	F26
Tennessee Tech■	J15	Austin Peay■	F28
Middle Tenn. St.■	J17	Ohio Valley Tr.	M3-5
Tennessee St.■	J22		

Colors: Red & Black. Nickname: Otahkians.
AD: Richard McDuffie. SID: Ron Hines. I

SOUTHEASTERN LA. .... Hammond, LA 70402

Frank Schneider (14 YRS. W-210, L-192)

Louisiana St.■	N30	Charleston	J29
Troy St.■	D 4	Grambling	F 1
McNeese St.	D 7	Georgia St.	F 5
Mississippi Cl.	D10-11	Nicholls St.	F 7
Southwestern La.	D18	Florida Int'l■	F10
Navy■	D28	Troy St.	F16
Furman■	D30	Central Fla.	F17
Jackson St.■	J 2	Stetson	F19
Florida Int'l	J15	Charleston■	F24
Stetson■	J20	Mercer■	F26
Central Fla.■	J22	Alabama St.■	M 1
Nicholls St.■	J24	Georgia St.■	M 5
Mercer	J27	Trans America Tr.	M10-12

Colors: Green & Gold. Nickname: Lady Lions.
AD: Tom Douple. SID: Larry Hymel. I

SOUTHERN CAL .... Los Angeles, CA 90089

Cheryl Miller (1ST YR. AS HEAD COACH)

Northern Ill.	D 1	California■	J27
Richmond Inv.	D3-4	Stanford■	J29
Cal St. Northridge■	D 7	UCLA■	F 5
Stephen F. Austin■	D20	Washington St.	F10
Southern Cal Cl.	D29-30	Washington	F12
San Diego St.■	J 2	Arizona St.■	F18
Oregon St.	J 6	Arizona■	F20
Oregon	J 8	Stanford	F24
Washington■	J14	California	F26
Washington St.■	J16	UCLA	M 3
Arizona	J20	Oregon■	M11
Arizona St.	J22	Oregon St.■	M13

Colors: Cardinal & Gold. Nickname: Trojans.
AD: Mike Garrett. SID: Linda Dodge. I

SOUTHERN COLO. .... Pueblo, CO 81001

Sue Richardson (1ST YR. AS HEAD COACH)

Angelo St.	N23	Colo. Christian	J22
Abilene Chrst. Cl.	N26-27	Air Force■	J26
Southern Colo. Tr.	D3-4	Fort Lewis■	J29
Mesa St.	D 7	Colorado-CS	F 5
Southern Colo. Inv.	D10-11	Adams St.	F 8
Western St.■	D13	Regis (Colo.)■	F10
Colorado-CS■	J 8	Denver	F12
Mesa St.■	J11	Metropolitan St.	F17
Regis (Colo.)	J13	Colo. Christian■	F19
Denver■	J15	Air Force	F23
N.M. Highlands	J18	Fort Lewis	F26
Metropolitan St.■	J20		

Colors: Red & Blue. Nickname: Indians.
AD: Dan DeRose. SID: Todd Kelly. II

SOUTHERN CONN. ST. .... New Haven, CT 06515

Anthony Barone (14 YRS. W-207, L-182)

Millersville Cl.	N19-20	New Haven■	J26
Springfield	N23	Mass.-Lowell■	J29
American Int'l	N30	LIU-C.W. Post■	J31
Molloy■	D 2	Bridgeport	F 2
Concordia (N.Y.)	D 6	Franklin Pierce	F 5
Quinnipiac	D 9	Keene St.	F 6
Adelphi■	D13	Sacred Heart	F 9
Dowling■	J 8	New Hamp. Col.	F12
Franklin Pierce■	J15	Bridgeport■	F16
Mass.-Lowell	J17	New Hamp. Col.■	F21
Sacred Heart■	J19	New Haven	F23
Le Moyne■	J22	Le Moyne	F26
Keene St.■	J23		

Colors: Blue & White. Nickname: Owls.
AD: To be named. SID: Richard Leddy. II

SOUTHERN ILL. .... Carbondale, IL 62901

Cindy Scott (16 YRS. W-312, L-152)

Tennessee Tech	N28	Indiana St.	J22
Virginia Cl.	D3-4	Southwest Mo. St.	J27
Murray St.■	D 8	Wichita St.	J29
Illinois■	D11	Vanderbilt■	F 2
Northern Ill.	D17	Illinois St.■	F 7
Arizona St.■	D20	Creighton	F11
Evansville	D30	Drake	F13
Northern Iowa■	J 2	Indiana St.■	F19
Bradley■	J 4	Wichita St.■	F24
Illinois St.	J 9	Southwest Mo. St.■	F26
Drake■	J13	Bradley	M 3
Creighton■	J15	Northern Iowa	M 5
Murray St.	J19	Missouri Valley Tr.	M8-12

Colors: Maroon & White. Nickname: Salukis.
AD: Jim Hart. SID: Mitch Parkinson. I

SIU-EDWARDSVILLE .... Edwardsville, IL 62026

Wendy Hedberg (14 YRS. W-202, L-182)

Illinois Col.	N19	Ky. Wesleyan	J20
Harris-Stowe	N20	Quincy■	J22
Central Mo. St.	N23	Oakland City■	J29
Southwest Baptist	N27	Indianapolis■	F 7
SIU-Edwardsville Tr.	D3-4	St. Francis (Ill.)■	F 9
Northeast Mo. St.	D 8	Wis.-Parkside■	F13
Ky. Wesleyan■	D11	Southern Ind.	F14
Mo.-St. Louis■	D18	McKendree■	F22
High Desert Cl.	D27-28	Oakland City	F24
IU/PU-Ft. Wayne	J 6	Quincy	F26
Wis.-Parkside	J12	Bellarmine■	M 2
St. Ambrose	J17		

Colors: Red & White. Nickname: Cougars.
AD: Cindy Jones. SID: Eric Hess. II

SOUTHERN IND. .... Evansville, IN 47712

Chancellor Dugan (2 YRS. W-22, L-36)

Lynn	N27	Bellarmine■	J27
Florida Tech	N29	Kentucky St.■	J29
SIU-Edwardsville Tr.	D3-4	St. Joseph's (Ind.)	F 3
Mo.-St. Louis	D 7	Lewis	F 5
Middle Tenn. St. Cl.	D10	IU/PU-Ft. Wayne■	F10
Northern Ky.	D22	Ashland■	F12
IU/PU-Indianapolis■	D28	SIU-Edwardsville■	F14
Indianapolis	D30	Ky. Wesleyan	F19
Lewis■	J 6	Kentucky St.	F24
St. Joseph's (Ind.)■	J 8	Bellarmine	F26
Ashland	J13	Northern Ky.■	M 3
IU/PU-Ft. Wayne	J15	Indianapolis■	M 5
Ky. Wesleyan■	J22		

Colors: Red, White & Blue. Nickname: Screaming Eagles.
AD: Donald Bennett. SID: Ray Simmons. II

SOUTHERN ME. .... Gorham, ME 04038

Gary Fifield (6 YRS. W-151, L-26)

Southern Me. Cl.	N20-21	Western Conn. St.	J15
Thomas■	N23	Colby-Sawyer■	J19
Salem St.■	N30	Mass.-Dartmouth■	J22
New England	D 2	Mass.-Boston■	J25
Rhode Island Col.	D 4	Rhode Island Col.■	J29
Colby■	D 8	Plymouth St.■	F 1
Eastern Conn. St.■	D11	Eastern Conn. St.	F 5
Gordon■	D14	St. Joseph's (Me.)☒	F 9
Husson■	J 3	Western Conn. St.■	F12
Clark (Mass.)	J 8	Mass.-Boston	F15
Plymouth St.	J11	Mass.-Dartmouth	F19
Bates	J13	☒ Portland, ME	

Colors: Navy, Crimson & White. Nickname: Huskies.
AD: Paula Hogdon. SID: Al Bean. III

■ Home games on each schedule.

See pages 735-738 for Division I tournament details

SOUTHERN METHODIST .... Dallas, TX 75275

Rhonda Rompola (2 YRS. W-37, L-22)

North Texas	N27	Houston	J26
Southwest/Ivy Chall.	D3-4	Texas A&M■	J29
Wis.-Green Bay Cl.	D10-11	Southwest Tex. St.■	F 1
Arkansas■	D21	Baylor	F 5
California■	D28	Rice■	F 8
Fordham■	D31	Texas	F12
Oklahoma■	J 2	Texas Tech■	F16
Tulane■	J 5	Texas Christian■	F19
Rice	J12	Houston■	F23
Texas■	J15	Texas A&M	F26
Texas Tech	J19	Baylor■	M 5
Texas Christian	J22	Southwest Tr.	M9-12

Colors: Red & Blue. Nickname: Mustangs.
AD: Forrest Gregg. SID: Charley Green. I

SOUTHERN MISS. .... Hattiesburg, MS 39401

Kay James (21 YRS. W-381, L-178)

Florida■	N29	Tulane	J29
Mississippi Val.	D 1	South Fla.	J31
Ala.-Birmingham■	D 7	Auburn■	F 7
Ala.-Birmingham Tr.	D10-11	Louisville■	F11
Southern Miss. Cl.	D20-21	South Fla.■	F13
Florida Tr.	D28-29	Tulane■	F19
Va. Commonwealth	J 8	N.C.-Charlotte	F26
Louisville	J10	Virginia Tech	F28
N.C.-Charlotte■	J15	Va. Commonwealth■	M 3
Virginia Tech■	J17	Northwestern (La.)	M 5
Southwestern La.	J20	Metro Tr.	M8-11
Louisiana St.	J26		

Colors: Black & Gold. Nickname: Lady Golden Eagles.
AD: Bill McLellan. SID: M.R. Napier. I

SOUTHERN UTAH .... Cedar City, UT 84720

Larry Shurtliff (2 YRS. W-18, L-36)

Colorado St.	N26	Loyola (Cal.)■	J 8
Wyoming	N27	UC Riverside	J15
Boise St.	N29	Cal St. Northridge	J18
Idaho St.■	D 1	Cal St. Sacramento	J20
Northern Ariz.	D 4	Nebraska	J28
Grand Canyon	D 6	Weber St.	F 3
Montana■	D10	Cal St. Northridge■	F12
Montana St.■	D11	Idaho St.	F16
Hawaii	D17	Idaho	F18
Hawaii	D18	Eastern Wash.	F19
Colorado St.■	D30	Cal St. Sacramento■	F21
Weber St.■	D31	Nevada-Las Vegas■	F22
Idaho■	J 3	Northern Ariz.■	M 3
Grand Canyon■	J 5		

Colors: Scarlett, Royal Blue & White. Nickname: Thunderbirds.
AD: Jack Bishop. SID: Jim Robinson. I

SOUTHERN-B.R. .... Baton Rouge, LA 70813

Herman Hartman (1 YR. W-20, L-7)

Paul Quinn■	N27	Texas Southern■	J24
Tougaloo	D 1	Alcorn St.■	J29
Arkansas St. Cl.	D3-4	Mississippi St.	F 1
Xavier (La.)■	D 9	Mississippi Val.■	F 5
Georgia	D18	Grambling■	F 7
Oklahoma Cl.	D28-29	Mississippi	F 9
Mississippi St.■	J 3	Jackson St.	F12
Mississippi Val.	J 8	Alabama St.	F14
Grambling	J10	Prairie View	F19
Louisiana St.■	J12	Texas Southern	F21
Jackson St.■	J15	Alcorn St.■	F26
Alabama St.■	J17	SWAC Tr.	M10-13
Prairie View■	J22		

Colors: Blue & Gold. Nickname: Jaguars.
AD: Marino Casem. SID: Rodney Lockett. I

SOUTHWEST BAPTIST .... Bolivar, MO 65613

Kip Drown (5 YRS. W-61, L-76)

Northwest Mo. Cl.	N19-20	Washburn	J19
Central Okla.	N23	Missouri-Rolla■	J22
SIU-Edwardsville■	N27	Northeast Mo. St.■	J27
Quincy	N30	Central Mo. St.	J29
Belmont	D 4	Mo. Western St.■	F 1
Evangel■	D 7	Lincoln (Mo.)	F 5
Southwest Bapt. Cl.	D10-11	Mo. Southern St.■	F 8
Cameron■	J 3	Pittsburg St.	F12
Emporia St.	J 5	Mo.-St. Louis■	F16
Pittsburg St.■	J 8	Northwest Mo. St.	F19
Mo.-St. Louis	J12	Washburn■	F23
Northwest Mo. St.■	J15	Missouri-Rolla	F26

Colors: Purple & White. Nickname: Bearcats.
AD: John Bryant. SID: Christopher Johnson. II

SOUTHWEST MO. ST. .... Springfield, MO 65804

Cheryl Burnett (6 YRS. W-115, L-62)

Western Ky.■	N30	Southern Ill.■	J27
Iowa	D 5	Indiana St.■	J29
Nebraska■	D 8	Northern Iowa■	F 4
Marquette■	D11	Bradley■	F 6
Stanford Cl.	D17-18	Mo.-Kansas City■	F 9
Montana	D21	Illinois St.	F12
Arkansas	D29	Creighton■	F17
Wichita St.	J 4	Drake■	F19
Bradley	J 6	Indiana St.	F24
Northern Iowa	J 9	Southern Ill.	F26
Illinois St.■	J15	Wichita St.■	M 5
Drake	J20	Missouri Valley Tr.	M8-12
Creighton	J22		

Colors: Maroon & White. Nickname: Bears.
AD: Mary Jo Wynn. SID: Jon Ripperger. I

SOUTHWEST ST. .... Marshall, MN 56258

Kelly Kruger (8 YRS. W-121, L-97)

Huron■	N20	Bemidji St.■	J12
Jamestown■	N23	Wayne St. (Neb.)	J15
Southwest St. Cl.	N26-27	Minn.-Morris	J19
Sioux Falls	N30	Minn.-Duluth■	J22
Valley City St.■	D 4	Winona St.	J29
South Dak. St.■	D 7	Moorhead St.	F 2
Morningside	D10	Northern St.■	F 5
South Dak.	D11	Bemidji St.	F 9
Dakota St.■	D14	Wayne St. (Neb.)■	F12
Mankato St. Cl.	D17-18	Minn.-Morris■	F16
Augustana (S.D.)	D29	Minn.-Duluth	F19
Moorhead St.■	J 5	Winona St.■	F26
Northern St.	J 8		

Colors: Brown & Gold. Nickname: Mustangs.
AD: Dan Snobl (Interim). SID: Bob Otterson. II

SOUTHWEST TEX. ST. .... San Marcos, TX 78666

Linda Sharp (16 YRS. W-337, L-143)

Southwest Tex. Cl.	D3-4	North Texas■	J27
South Fla.■	D 6	Texas-Arlington■	J29
Louisiana St.■	D15	Southern Methodist	F 1
Brigham Young■	D17	Texas-San Antonio■	F 5
N.C.-Greensboro	D20	Stephen F. Austin	F10
North Caro. St.	D21	Sam Houston St.	F12
Northeast La.	D28	McNeese St.■	F17
Northwestern (La.)	D30	Nicholls St.■	F19
Texas-San Antonio	J 8	Texas-Arlington	F24
Sam Houston St.■	J14	North Texas	F26
Stephen F. Austin■	J16	Northeast La.■	F28
Nicholls St.	J20	Northwestern (La.)■	M 2
McNeese St.	J22	Southland Tr.	M8-12

Colors: Maroon & Gold. Nickname: Bobcats.
AD: Richard Hannan. SID: Tony Brubaker. I

SOUTHWESTERN (TEX.) ...... Georgetown, TX 78626

Ronda Seagraves (7 YRS. W-123, L-60)

Millsaps Tr.	N20-21	Hardin-Simmons	J22
Augustana (Ill.)■	N23	Trinity (Tex.)	J25
Trinity (Tex.)■	N30	Austin■	J27
Hardin-Simmons■	D 6	Concordia (Tex.)	F 1
Colorado Col. Tr.	D29-31	Dallas■	F 5
Millsaps■	J 7	Austin	F 7
Hendrix■	J 8	Marymount (Va.) Inv.	F12-13
Rochester■	J14	McMurry■	F16
Howard Payne	J17	Rhodes	F26
McMurry	J21	Hendrix	F27

Colors: Black & Yellow. Nickname: Pirates.
AD: Carla Lowry. SID: Lloyd Winston. III

SOUTHWESTERN LA. .... Lafayette, LA 70506

Dwayne Searle (3 YRS. W-7, L-73)

Texas Christian	D 1	Louisiana St.	F 2
S.F. Austin Cl.	D3-4	Western Ky.■	F 5
Southeastern La.■	D18	McNeese St.■	F 7
Ala.-Birmingham Cl.	D20-21	South Ala.■	F10
Louisiana Tech■	J 6	Louisiana Tech	F12
Western Ky.	J 9	Fla. Atlantic■	F14
Tulane■	J12	Arkansas St.	F17
Tex.-Pan American■	J15	Lamar■	F19
Southern Miss.■	J20	New Orleans■	F24
Tex.-Pan American	J22	South Ala.	M 3
Arkansas St.■	J27	New Orleans	M 5
Lamar	J29	Sun Belt Tr.	M10-12

Colors: Vermilion & White. Nickname: Ragin' Cajuns.
AD: Nelson Schexnayder. SID: None. I

■ Home games on each schedule.

See pages 735-738 for Division I tournament details

SPRINGFIELD .... **Springfield, MA 01109**
Naomi Graves (8 YRS. W-73, L-128)

Assumption	N19	Bentley■	J25
Southern Conn. St.■	N23	Bryant	J27
Clark (Mass.)■	N30	Assumption■	J29
Keene St.	D 2	American Int'l	F 2
American Int'l■	D 4	Stonehill	F 5
New Haven	D 7	Bryant■	F 7
Franklin Pierce■	D14	St. Michael's■	F 9
Stonehill■	J 8	St. Anselm	F12
St. Michael's	J12	Quinnipiac■	F16
St. Anselm■	J15	Merrimack	F19
Quinnipiac	J19	Bentley	F22
Merrimack■	J22		

Colors: Maroon & White. Nickname: Maroons.
AD: Edward Bilik. SID: Ken Cerino. II

ST. ANDREWS .... **Laurinburg, NC 28352**
Nancy Swain (5 YRS. W-23, L-76)

N.C. Wesleyan■	N29	Barber-Scotia■	J27
Averett	D 2	Lees-McRae■	J29
Pembroke St.■	D 4	Mt. Olive	J31
Barton	J 8	Barton■	F 2
Mt. Olive■	J12	High Point	F 5
High Point■	J15	Lees-McRae	F 7
Converse■	J17	Pfeiffer■	F 9
Pfeiffer	J19	Belmont Abbey■	F12
Coker■	J22	Coker	F16
Meredith	J24	Barber-Scotia	F17
Belmont Abbey	J26		

Colors: Royal Blue & White. Nickname: Knights.
AD: Lorenzo Canalis. SID: Chad Esposito. II

ST. ANSELM .... **Manchester, NH 03102**
Donna Guimont (17 YRS. W-273, L-139)

New Hamp. Col. Cl.	N20-21	Stonehill	J22
New Haven	N23	Quinnipiac■	J25
Bentley	N28	Merrimack	J27
Bryant■	D 4	Bentley■	J29
Mass.-Lowell■	D 8	Bryant	F 2
Sacred Heart	D11	Assumption■	F 5
Barry Cl.	J2-3	American Int'l	F 9
Assumption	J 8	Springfield■	F12
New Hamp. Col.■	J10	St. Michael's	F16
American Int'l■	J12	Stonehill■	F19
Springfield	J15	Quinnipiac	F22
St. Michael's■	J19	Merrimack■	F24

Colors: Blue & White. Nickname: Hawks.
AD: Ted Paulauskas. SID: Kristopher Russell. II

ST. AUGUSTINE'S .... **Raleigh, NC 27611**
Bev Downing (11 YRS. W-181, L-118)

Calif. (Pa.) Tr.	N19-20	Fayetteville St.■	J20
Virginia St.	N23	N.C. Central■	J22
Dist. Columbia Tr.	N26-27	Johnson Smith■	J24
St. Paul's■	D 7	Livingstone	J29
Shaw	D 9	N.C. Central	J31
Bowie St.■	D11	Virginia Union	F 3
Atlantic City Cl.	D18-19	Winston-Salem■	F 7
Livingstone■	J 6	Johnson Smith	F 9
Hampton	J 8	Shaw⊠	F12
Winston-Salem■	J11	Norfolk St.	F17
Elizabeth City St.■	J18	Fayetteville St.	F19

Colors: Blue & White. Nickname: Falcons.
AD: Harvey Heartley. SID: Leon Carrington. II

ST. BENEDICT .... **St. Joseph, MN 56374**
Michael Durbin (8 YRS. W-155, L-63)

Wis.-River Falls	N30	St. Olaf■	J17
Wis.-Stout■	D 2	Bethel (Minn.)	J19
Augsburg■	D 4	Augsburg	J22
St. Scholastica■	D 6	Hamline■	J26
Hamline	D 8	Concordia-M'head■	J29
Concordia-M'head	D11	St. Mary's (Minn.)■	F 2
St. Benedict Cl.	D29-30	Carleton■	F 5
St. Mary's (Minn.)	J 5	Macalester	F 9
Carleton	J 8	St. Thomas (Minn.)■	F12
Macalester■	J10	St. Olaf	F16
St. Thomas (Minn.)	J12	Bethel (Minn.)■	F19
Gust. Adolphus■	J15	Gust. Adolphus	F26

Colors: Red & White. Nickname: Blazers.
AD: Carol Howe-Veenstra. SID: Mike Durbin. III

ST. BONAVENTURE .... **St.Bonaventure, NY 14778**
Mark Whitmore (1ST YR. AS HEAD COACH)

Cornell■	D 1	Temple■	J22
St. Francis (Pa.)	D 4	West Va.	J29
Robert Morris■	D 7	St. Joseph's (Pa.)	F 3
Fairfield Cl.	D10-11	Temple	F 5
Niagara	D14	Rhode Island■	F 8
Maine■	D29	Duquesne■	F14
Massachusetts■	J 4	Geo. Washington	F17
St. Joseph's (Pa.)■	J 6	Rutgers■	F19
Iona	J 8	Colgate■	F22
West Va.■	J11	Duquesne	F26
Rhode Island	J13	Geo. Washington■	F28
Massachusetts	J15	Rutgers	M 5
Canisius■	J18		

Colors: Brown & White. Nickname: Bonnies.
AD: Thomas O'Connor. SID: Jim Engelhardt. I

ST. CLOUD ST. .... **St.Cloud, MN 56301**
To be named

UC Riverside	N26	Mankato St.■	J15
Cal Poly Pomona	N27	South Dak. St.	J21
Mt. Senario■	D 2	Augustana (S.D.)	J22
Wis.-Parkside	D 5	Northern Colo.■	J28
Moorhead St.	D11	Nebraska-Omaha■	J29
Minn.-Duluth	D15	Morningside	F 4
Moorhead St.■	D18	South Dak.	F 5
Bemidji St.■	D21	Augustana (S.D.)■	F18
North Dak.	J 2	South Dak. St.■	F19
North Dak. St.	J 3	Nebraska-Omaha	F25
South Dak.■	J 7	Northern Colo.	F26
Morningside■	J 8	North Dak. St.■	M 4
Mankato St.	J12	North Dak.■	M 5

Colors: Red & Black. Nickname: Huskies.
AD: Gladys Ziemer. SID: Anne Abicht. II

ST. ELIZABETH .... **Convent Station, NJ 07961**
Frank Sturm (4 YRS. W-25, L-64)

St. John Fisher Tr.	N19-20	Dominican (N.Y.)⊠	J17
Hunter	N23	New Jersey Tech	J19
Trenton St.	N29	Centenary (N.J.)■	J21
New Jersey Tech■	D 1	Mt. St. Mary (N.Y.)■	J24
Cedar Crest■	D 4	FDU-Madison■	J31
Centenary (N.J.)	D 8	Bryn Mawr■	F 3
FDU-Madison	D10	Rutgers-Newark■	F 7
Catholic Tr.	J8-9	Upsala■	F10
Misericordia	J12	Staten Island	F12
Upsala	J13	Mt. St. Mary (N.Y.)	F16
Marywood■	J15	Drew■	F25

Colors: Blue & Gold. Nickname: Eagles.
AD: Patricia Singiser. SID: None. III

ST. FRANCIS (ILL.) .... **Joliet, IL 60435**
John Barkoski (2 YRS. W-29, L-28)

Quincy	N23	National Louis	J22
IU/PU-Ind. Cl.	D3-4	Ind.-South Bend■	J25
Lewis	D 8	Illinois Tech	J29
IU/PU-Ft. Wayne Tr.	D10-11	Rosary■	F 1
Grand Valley St.■	D20	Wis.-Parkside■	F 3
Florida Tech Tr.	J2-3	Purdue-Calumet■	F 5
Eckerd	J 4	Trinity Chrst. (Il.)	F 8
Rollins	J 8	SIU-Edwardsville	F 9
Purdue-Calumet	J11	Olivet (Ill.)■	F12
Quincy■	J13	Ind.-South Bend	F19
Trinity Chrst. (Il.)■	J15	Illinois Tech■	F22
Olivet (Ill.)	J18	Rosary	F26

Colors: Brown & Gold. Nickname: Lady Saints.
AD: Pat Sullivan. SID: Dave Laketa. II

ST. FRANCIS (N.Y.) .... **Brooklyn, NY 11201**
Irma Garcia (5 YRS. W-18, L-115)

Iona■	D 1	Robert Morris■	J24
Hartford Cl.	D4-5	Monmouth (N.J.)■	J27
Navy Cl.	D18-19	Wagner■	J29
Fairfield	D22	Rider	F 3
Hofstra■	D30	Mt. St. Mary's (Md.)	F 5
LIU-Brooklyn	J 4	Marist■	F10
Wagner	J 8	FDU-Teaneck■	F12
Monmouth (N.J.)	J10	Robert Morris	F17
Mt. St. Mary's (Md.)■	J13	St. Francis (Pa.)	F19
Rider■	J15	LIU-Brooklyn■	F26
Marist	J20	FDU-Teaneck	M 2
St. Francis (Pa.)■	J22		

Colors: Red & Blue. Nickname: Lady Terriers.
AD: To be named. SID: Patrick Horne. I

■ Home games on each schedule.

See pages 735-738 for Division I tournament details

ST. FRANCIS (PA.) .... Loretto, PA 15940
Jenny Przekwas (2 YRS. W-19, L-35)

Dayton■ N28
St. Bonaventure■ .... D 4
Navy .... D 9
American D11
Marshall■ D20
St. Francis Cl. D30-31
Monmouth (N.J.)■ .... J 4
Wagner■ .... J 6
Rider .... J 8
Mt. St. Mary's (Md.) J10
FDU-Teaneck■ J13
Marist■ J15
St. Francis (N.Y.) J22
LIU-Brooklyn J24
Mt. St. Mary's (Md.)■ J27
Rider■ J29
Marist .... F 3
FDU-Teaneck .... F 5
Robert Morris F12
LIU-Brooklyn■ F17
St. Francis (N.Y.)■ F19
Wagner F24
Monmouth (N.J.) F26
Robert Morris■ .... M 4
Northeast Tr. M5-12

Colors: Red & White. Nickname: Red Flash.
AD: Frank Pergolizzi. SID: Kevin Southard. I

ST. JOHN FISHER .... Rochester, NY 14618
Phillip I. Kahler (19 YRS. W-462, L-86)

St. John Fisher Tr. N19-20
Houghton■ N23
St. John Fisher Cl. D3-4
Hilbert .... D 8
Nazareth (N.Y.)■ D11
St. John Fisher Inv. J8-9
Hartwick J11
Fredonia St.■ J18
Albany (N.Y.) Tr. J21-22
Buffalo St. J26
Skidmore Inv. J28-29
Elmira■ .... F 1
Keuka■ .... F 3
Brockport St. .... F 8
Nazareth (N.Y.) Tr. F11-12
Cortland St. F17
Utica F19
Roberts Wesleyan F22

Colors: Cardinal Red & Gold. Nickname: Cardinals.
AD: Phil Kahler. SID: Michele Morano. III

ST. JOHN'S (N.Y.) .... Jamaica, NY 11439
Joe Mullaney, Jr. (12 YRS. W-205, L-147)

St. Peter's■ .... D 1
Washington St. Cl. D3-4
Rutgers■ .... D 8
Syracuse D11
Fairfield D13
Manhattan☒ D18
St. John's Inv. D29-30
Seton Hall■ .... J 3
Providence .... J 6
Villanova■ .... J 9
Boston College■ J12
Miami (Fla.)■ J15
Georgetown J20
Pittsburgh■ J23
Connecticut J26
Miami (Fla.) J30
Seton Hall .... F 2
Providence■ .... F 6
Pittsburgh .... F 9
Villanova F13
Syracuse■ F16
Georgetown■ F19
Boston College F23
Connecticut■ F27
Big East Tr. M4-7
☒ Uniondale, NY

Colors: Red & White. Nickname: The Express.
AD: John Kaiser. SID: Mary Donovan. I

ST. JOSEPH'S (IND.) .... Rensselaer, IN 47978
Keith Freeman (5 YRS. W-113, L-36)

Wis.-Parkside N23
IU/PU-Indianapolis N30
Ferris St. Cl. D3-4
Grace■ .... D 7
Indiana Tech■ D10
St. Francis (Ind.)■ D17
Ashland■ D28
IU/PU-Ft. Wayne■ D30
Ky. Wesleyan .... J 6
Southern Ind. .... J 8
Kentucky St.■ J13
Bellarmine■ J15
Northern Ky. J20
Indianapolis J22
Wis.-Parkside■ J25
IU/PU-Indianapolis■ J27
Lewis J29
Southern Ind.■ .... F 3
Ky. Wesleyan■ .... F 5
Bellarmine F10
Kentucky St. F12
Indianapolis■ F17
Northern Ky.■ F19
Lewis■ F26
Ashland .... M 3
IU/PU-Ft. Wayne .... M 5

Colors: Cardinal & Purple. Nickname: Pumas.
AD: Keith Freeman. SID: Ron Fredrick. II

ST. JOSEPH'S (ME.) ...... North Windham, ME 04062
Michael McDevitt (6 YRS. W-137, L-40)

Wheaton (Mass.) Tr. N19-20
Me.-Farmington■ N29
Western Conn. Cl. D4-5
New England .... D 8
Thomas■ D11
Westbrook■ D13
Gordon■ .... J 4
Husson■ J13
Johnson St. J15
Lyndon St. J16
New England■ J20
Me.-Farmington J22
Emmanuel J25
Manhattanville Inv. J29-30
Norwich■ .... F 5
Southern Me.☒ .... F 9
Me.-Presque Isle■ F12
Thomas F14
Husson F16
☒ Portland, ME

Colors: Royal Bl., Red & White. Nickname: Monks.
AD: Rick Simonds. SID: Curt Smyth. III

ST. JOSEPH'S (PA.) .... Philadelphia, PA 19131
Stephanie Gaitley (8 YRS. W-154 , L-83)

Villanova N30
Georgia Tech Cl. D3-4
Pennsylvania☒ .... D 8
La Salle D14
St. Joseph's Cl. D29-30
Penn St.■ .... J 2
St. Bonaventure .... J 6
Temple■ .... J 8
Manhattan■ J12
Loyola (Ill.)■ J15
Duquesne■ J17
Geo. Washington J22
Rhode Island■ J29
Massachusetts■ J31
St. Bonaventure■ .... F 3
Rutgers .... F 5
West Va. F10
Duquesne F12
Geo. Washington■ F19
West Va.■ F21
Rutgers■ F26
Temple F28
Massachusetts .... M 3
Rhode Island .... M 5
☒ Philadelphia, PA

Colors: Crimson & Gray. Nickname: Hawks.
AD: Don DiJulia. SID: Larry Dougherty. I

ST. LAWRENCE .... Canton, NY 13617
Fran Grembowicz (2 YRS. W-9, L-38)

Utica N19
Elmira N20
Potsdam St.■ N30
Skidmore■ .... D 3
Union (N.Y.)■ .... D 4
Clarkson .... D 9
Le Moyne J11
Ithaca■ J14
Alfred■ J15
Plattsburgh St. J18
Rensselaer■ J21
Hartwick■ J22
Hamilton■ J25
Rochester Inst. J28
William Smith J29
Oswego St.■ .... F 2
Alfred .... F 4
Ithaca .... F 5
Potsdam St. .... F 8
William Smith■ F11
Rochester Inst.■ F12
Clarkson■ F15
Hartwick F18
Rensselaer F19

Colors: Scarlet & Brown. Nickname: Saints.
AD: John Clark. SID: Wally Johnson. III

ST. LEO .... St.Leo, FL 33574
Rob Oppedisano (1 YR. W-3, L-21)

Nebraska-Omaha■ N26
Lynn .... D 1
Warner Southern■ .... D 4
Georgia Col. Cl. D10-11
Savannah A&D■ D14
Rensselaer■ D31
Southeastern Bapt. ....
Abilene Christian■ .... J 4
Belmont Abbey .... J 6
Queens (N.C.) .... J 8
Rollins■ J12
North Fla. J15
Florida Tech J19
Tampa J22
Eckerd J26
Fla. Southern■ J29
Barry .... F 2
North Fla.■ .... F 5
Florida Tech■ .... F 9
Tampa■ F12
Webber F14
Eckerd■ F16
Fla. Southern F19
Barry■ F23
Rollins F26

Colors: Forest Green & Old Gold. Nickname: Monarchs.
AD: John Schaly. SID: Fran Reidy. II

ST. LOUIS .... St.Louis, MO 63108
Sharon Allen (2 YRS. W-7, L-46)

Chicago St.■ .... D 2
Tenn.-Martin .... D 4
Bradley■ .... D 8
Evansville■ D11
Stetson Cl. D17-18
Southeast Mo. St.■ D30
Chicago St. .... J 2
Northeastern Ill. .... J 3
Tenn.-Martin■ .... J 6
Ala.-Birmingham■ .... J 8
Southeast Mo. St. J13
Cincinnati■ J15
Northern Iowa J17
Ala.-Birmingham J22
Marquette■ J27
Memphis St. J31
DePaul■ .... F 3
Cincinnati .... F 5
Dayton .... F 7
Northeastern Ill.■ .... F 9
Marquette F12
Memphis St.■ F19
Eastern Ill. F23
Dayton■ F26
DePaul .... M 5
Great Midwest Tr. M9-12

Colors: Blue & White. Nickname: Billikens.
AD: Debbie Yow. SID: Russell Brightman. I

ST. MARY'S (CAL.) .... Moraga, CA 94575
Terri Rubenstein (10 YRS. W-175, L-107)

St. Mary's Cl. N26-27
California .... D 1
Arizona Cl. D3-5
Fairfield Cl. D10-11
San Jose St.■ D20
Pacific (Cal.)■ D29
Cal St. Sacramento■ .... J 4
Idaho .... J 7
Boise St. .... J 9
Loyola (Cal.)■ J14
Pepperdine■ J15
Portland J20
Gonzaga J22
Gonzaga■ J28
Portland■ J29
San Francisco .... F 3
San Diego .... F 5
San Diego■ F11
San Francisco■ F12
Santa Clara F18
Pepperdine F25
Loyola (Cal.) F26
Santa Clara■ .... M 2
West Coast Tr. M11-12

Colors: Blue, White & Red. Nickname: Gaels.
AD: Rick Mazzuto. SID: Steve Janisch. I

■ Home games on each schedule.

See pages 735-738 for Division I tournament details

ST. MARY'S (IND.) .... Notre Dame, IN 46556

Marvin Wood (8 YRS. W-87, L-81)

Kalamazoo Tr.	N19-20	Bethel (Ind.)■	J27
Ind.-South Bend■	N23	DePauw	J29
Hope■	N30	Carroll (Wis.)■	F 5
St. Mary's (In.) Cl.	D3-4	Calvin■	F 9
Wheaton (Ill.)	D 8	St. Francis (Ind.)	F11
Aurora	J11	Goshen	F15
Beloit■	J15	Concordia (Ill.)■	F17
Chicago	J18	Kalamazoo	F19
Anderson	J22	Manchester	F22
Olivet	J24	Franklin■	F26

Colors: Columbia Blue & White. Nickname: The Belles.
AD: Jo-Ann Nester. SID: To be named. III

ST. MICHAEL'S .... Colchester, VT 05439

Sue Duprat (17 YRS. W-231, L-181)

Phila. Textile	N20	Quinnipiac■	J22
Middlebury	N23	Merrimack	J25
Adelphi■	N29	Bentley	J27
Franklin Pierce	D 1	Bryant■	J29
East Stroudsburg Cl.	D3-4	Assumption	F 2
Mass.-Lowell	D 6	American Int'l■	F 5
Assumption■	D18	Springfield	F 9
Adelphi	D30	Stonehill■	F12
Bryant	J 3	St. Anselm■	F16
American Int'l	J 8	Quinnipiac	F20
Springfield■	J12	Merrimack■	F22
Stonehill	J15	Bentley■	F25
St. Anselm	J19		

Colors: Purple & Gold. Nickname: Purple Knights.
AD: Edward Markey. SID: Chris Kenny. II

ST. NORBERT .... De Pere, WI 54115

Connie L. Tilley (16 YRS. W-271, L-105)

Wis.-Oshkosh■	N20	Illinois Col.■	J22
Wis.-Stevens Point■	N23	Lawrence■	J25
Wis.-Whitewater	N30	Grinnell	J28
Wis.-La Crosse	D 8	Coe	J29
Carroll (Wis.)	D11	Ripon■	F 9
Nat'l Catholic Tr.	J5-9	Lake Forest■	F12
Beloit	J12	Lawrence	F14
Lake Forest	J15	Carroll (Wis.)■	F16
Wis.-Eau Claire	J18	Beloit■	F19
Knox■	J21	Ripon	F21

Colors: Green & Gold. Nickname: Green Knights.
AD: Larry Van Alstine. SID: Len Wagner. III

ST. OLAF .... Northfield, MN 55057

Pat Buresh (9 YRS. W-103, L-140)

Dr. Martin Luther■	N19	St. Benedict	J17
Luther	N20	Gust. Adolphus■	J19
N'western (Minn.)	N23	St. Thomas (Minn.)■	J22
Viterbo■	N27	Macalester■	J29
St. Thomas (Minn.)	D 4	Bethel (Minn.)■	F 2
Wis.-Stout	D 7	St. Mary's (Minn.)■	F 5
Macalester	D11	Concordia-M'head	F 9
Carleton	J 3	Hamline■	F12
Bethel (Minn.)	J 5	St. Benedict■	F16
St. Mary's (Minn.)	J 8	Gust. Adolphus	F19
Concordia-M'head■	J10	Carleton■	F23
Hamline	J12	Augsburg	F26
Augsburg■	J15		

Colors: Black & Gold. Nickname: Oles.
AD: Whitey Aus. SID: Nancy Moe. III

ST. PAUL'S .... Lawrenceville, VA 23868

Juliana Freeman (2 YRS. W-10, L-37)

Benedict	N22	N.C. Central	J17
Johnson Smith	N23	Virginia St.	J22
Shaw■	D 1	Virginia Union	J25
Norfolk St. Inv.	D3-4	Elizabeth City St.■	J29
St. Augustine's	D 7	Bowie St.■	J31
Livingstone■	D12	Elizabeth City St.	F 1
St. Rose■	D30	Hampton■	F 5
Hampton	J 3	Norfolk St.■	F 9
Virginia Union■	J11	Bowie St.	F10
Fayetteville St.	J13	Winston-Salem	F12
Norfolk St.	J15	Virginia St.■	F16

Colors: Black & Orange. Nickname: Tigers.
AD: Harold Williams. SID: Monique Morgan. II

ST. PETER'S .... Jersey City, NJ 07306

Mike Granelli (21 YRS. W-389, L-147)

Md.-East. Shore■	N27	Niagara	J17
St. John's (N.Y.)	D 1	Loyola (Md.)■	J20
Boston College	D 8	Iona	J22
Rider	D10	Fairfield■	J26
Hartford■	D15	Northeastern■	F 2
Fordham	D18	Canisius■	F 5
James Madison■	D22	Manhattan	F 9
St. Peter's Tr.	D29-30	Iona■	F12
Marshall■	J 3	Siena	F16
Loyola (Md.)	J 6	Fairfield	F21
Niagara■	J 8	Manhattan■	F23
Canisius	J15	Siena■	F26

Colors: Blue & White. Nickname: Peahens.
AD: William Stein. SID: Tim Camp. I

ST. ROSE .... Albany, NY 12203

Curt Bailey (4 YRS. W-57, L-48)

Le Moyne	N29	Mercy	J12
Mercy■	D 1	LIU-Southampton	J15
Adelphi	D 4	Dowling■	J19
LIU-C.W. Post■	D 8	LIU-C.W. Post	J22
Molloy	D11	Queens (N.Y.)	J23
Sacred Heart■	D21	Adelphi■	J29
St. Rose Cl.	D28-29	Concordia (N.Y.)	F 5
St. Paul's	D30	Dowling	F 6
Virginia Union	J 1	Phila. Textile	F12
Virginia St.	J 2	Molloy■	F16
Pace■	J 5	LIU-Southampton■	F19
Phila. Textile■	J 8	Pace	F26

Colors: Brown, Gold & White. Nickname: Golden Knights.
AD: Cathy Cummings-Haker. SID: David Alexander. II

ST. THOMAS (MINN.) .... St.Paul, MN 55105

Ted Riverso (9 YRS. W-188, L-58)

Wis.-Stevens Point	N19	Gust. Adolphus	J17
Wis.-Eau Claire■	N22	Augsburg■	J19
Occidental	N28	St. Olaf	J22
Redlands	N30	Bethel (Minn.)	J26
St. Olaf■	D 4	St. Mary's (Minn.)	J29
Bethel (Minn.)■	D 8	Concordia-M'head■	F 2
St. Mary's (Minn.)■	D11	Carleton	F 9
Hamline	J 3	St. Benedict	F12
Concordia-M'head	J 5	Gust. Adolphus■	F16
Carleton■	J10	Augsburg	F19
St. Benedict■	J12	Hamline■	F23
Macalester	J15	Macalester■	F26

Colors: Purple & Gray. Nickname: Tommies.
AD: Steve Fritz. SID: Greg Capell. III

STANFORD .... Stanford, CA 94305

Tara VanDerveer (15 YRS. W-348, L-104)

Texas Tech	N27	UCLA	J27
Utah	N29	Southern Cal	J29
Tennessee■	D 3	Oregon■	F 3
Long Beach St.■	D 8	Oregon St.■	F 5
Stanford Cl.	D17-18	Arizona	F10
Connecticut■	D28	Arizona St.	F12
Nevada-Las Vegas■	D30	California■	F18
Santa Clara	J 3	Southern Cal■	F24
Washington	J 6	UCLA■	F26
Washington St.	J 8	Oregon St.	M 3
Arizona St.■	J13	Oregon	M 5
Arizona■	J15	Washington St.■	M10
California	J21	Washington■	M12

Colors: Cardinal & White. Nickname: Cardinal.
AD: Ted Leland. SID: Steve Raczynski. I

STATEN ISLAND .... Staten Island, NY 10301

Gerry Mosley (4 YRS. W-54, L-41)

New York U.	N23	Medgar Evers■	J14
Stony Brook■	D 1	Concordia (N.Y.)	J20
Nazareth (N.Y.) Inv.	D4-5	New Jersey Tech■	J24
Baruch■	D 8	Manhattanville■	J26
York (N.Y.)	D13	King's (N.Y.)	J28
Jersey City St.■	D17	Lehman■	J31
Staten Island Tr.	D29-30	Mt. St. Mary (N.Y.)	F 5
Kean■	J 5	CCNY■	F 7
John Jay■	J 7	St. Elizabeth■	F12
Mt. St. Vincent	J12	Hunter	F16

Colors: Maroon & Columbia Blue. Nickname: Dolphins.
AD: Joseph Barresi. SID: Jim Hoffman. III

■ Home games on each schedule.

See pages 735-738 for Division I tournament details

STEPHEN F. AUSTIN .... Nacogdoches, TX 75962

Joe Curl (1ST YR. AS HEAD COACH)

Lamar	N30
S.F. Austin Cl.	D3-4
Houston■	D 8
Georgia	D11
Cal St. Fullerton	D18
Southern Cal	D20
North Texas	J 3
Northwestern (La.)■	J 6
Texas Tech■	J 9
Texas-San Antonio	J14
Southwest Tex. St.	J16
Northeast La.■	J18
Sam Houston St.	J22
McNeese St.■	J27
Nicholls St.■	J29
Northeast La.	F 3
Northwestern (La.)	F 5
Southwest Tex. St.■	F10
Texas-San Antonio■	F12
Texas-Arlington	F14
Sam Houston St.■	F19
Nicholls St.	F24
McNeese St.	F26
North Texas■	F28
Texas-Arlington■	M 3
Southland Tr.	M8-12

Colors: Purple & White. Nickname: Ladyjacks.
AD: Steve McCarty. SID: Joni James. I

STETSON .... Deland, FL 32720

Dee Romine (9 YRS. W-122, L-104)

South Fla.	D 1
Georgia Tech Cl.	D3-4
Tenn.-Martin■	D14
Stetson Cl.	D17-18
Loyola (Ill.)	D28
Chicago St.	D30
Bethune-Cookman■	J 4
Manhattan■	J 5
Mercer■	J13
Charleston■	J15
Florida	J17
Southeastern La.	J20
Georgia St.	J22
Florida Int'l■	J27
Fla. Atlantic■	J29
Central Fla.	F 5
Charleston	F10
Mercer	F12
Georgia St.■	F17
Southeastern La.■	F19
Florida A&M■	F24
Florida Int'l	F26
Fla. Atlantic	F28
Central Fla.■	M 5
Trans America Tr.	M10-12

Colors: Green & White. Nickname: Hatters.
AD: Robert Jacoby. SID: Tom McClellan. I

STOCKTON ST. .... Pomona, NJ 08240

Jill Bush (1ST YR. AS HEAD COACH)

Messiah Tr.	N19-20
Rutgers-Newark	N23
Jersey City St.■	N29
Ramapo■	D 1
Rowan	D 7
Kean■	D11
Ramapo■	J 5
Bloomfield■	J 6
Lincoln (Pa.)■	J 8
Montclair St.■	J10
Rutgers-Camden	J12
Wm. Paterson	J15
Trenton St.	J19
Salisbury St.	J22
Rutgers-Newark■	J26
Jersey City St.	J29
Georgian Court	J31
Rutgers-Camden■	F 2
Montclair St.	F 5
Rowan■	F 9
Kean	F11
Trenton St.■	F16
Wm. Paterson■	F19

Colors: Black & White. Nickname: Ospreys.
AD: Larry James. SID: None. III

STONEHILL .... North Easton, MA 02356

Paula J. Sullivan (22 YRS. W-390, L-139)

Mass.-Lowell Tr.	N20-21
American Int'l	N28
Merrimack■	D 4
New Hamp. Col.■	D 6
Keene St.	D11
Sacred Heart■	D18
Stonehill Cl.	D27-28
Barry Cl.	J2-3
Springfield	J 8
Bentley■	J12
St. Michael's■	J15
Bryant	J19
St. Anselm■	J22
Assumption■	J25
Quinnipiac	J27
American Int'l■	J29
Merrimack	F 2
Springfield■	F 5
Bentley	F 9
St. Michael's	F12
Bryant■	F16
St. Anselm	F19
Assumption	F22
Quinnipiac■	F24

Colors: Purple & White. Nickname: Chieftains.
AD: Raymond P. Pepin. SID: Bob Richards. II

STONY BROOK .... Stony Brook, NY 11790

Declan McMullen (11 YRS. W-185, L-104)

Stony Brook Tr.	N19-20
Old Westbury■	N23
Staten Island	D 1
Western Conn. Cl.	D4-5
Mt. St. Vincent■	D 7
Scranton Cl.	D10-11
Wesley■	J19
Binghamton■	J21
Cortland St.■	J22
New York U.■	J26
Russell Sage	J28
Albany (N.Y.)	J29
Hunter■	F 1
John Jay■	F 3
Elmira■	F 5
Vassar	F 6
York (N.Y.)	F 9
Mt. St. Mary (N.Y.)■	F12
Wm. Paterson■	F14
Kean■	F17
Clark (Mass.)	F19

Colors: Scarlet & Gray. Nickname: Lady Patriots.
AD: Sandra Weeden. SID: Kenneth Alber. III

SUSQUEHANNA .... Selinsgrove, PA 17870

Mark Hribar (6 YRS. W-99, L-52)

Susquehanna Tr.	N20-21
Elizabethtown	D 2
Widener■	D 4
Wilkes■	D 9
York (Pa.)	D11
Messiah	J13
Lebanon Valley■	J15
Juniata	J19
Moravian■	J22
Scranton	J24
Albright	J27
Elizabethtown■	J29
Lycoming	J31
Messiah■	F 3
Widener	F 5
Bloomsburg	F 7
Juniata■	F 9
Lebanon Valley	F12
Albright■	F15
Frank. & Marsh.	F17
Moravian	F19

Colors: Orange & Maroon. Nickname: Crusaders.
AD: Donald Harnum. SID: Mike Ferlazzo. III

SYRACUSE .... Syracuse, NY 13244

Marianna Freeman (2 YRS. W-21, L-27)

Syracuse Cl.	D4-5
St. John's (N.Y.)■	D11
Ohio St.■	D14
Rider■	D18
Marquette	D27
Detroit Mercy■	D30
Connecticut	J 3
Pittsburgh■	J 5
Seton Hall■	J 8
Providence	J12
Georgetown■	J15
Miami (Fla.)	J19
Boston College	J22
Villanova■	J26
Seton Hall	J29
Providence■	F 2
Pittsburgh	F 5
Boston College■	F 9
Georgetown	F12
St. John's (N.Y.)	F16
Miami (Fla.)■	F20
Connecticut■	F23
Villanova	F27
Big East Tr.	M4-7

Colors: Orange. Nickname: Orangewomen.
AD: Jake Crouthamel. SID: Sue Cornelius. I

TAMPA .... Tampa, FL 33606

Tom Mosca (4 YRS. W-57, L-52)

Lynn■	N16
Webber	N20
Ashland■	N24
Wingate■	N26
Troy St.	D 1
Kennesaw St.■	D 6
Paine■	D17
Walsh■	D28
Merrimack■	D31
Bentley■	J 5
Tampa Tr.	J7-8
Fla. Southern■	J12
Barry	J15
Rollins■	J19
St. Leo■	J22
Florida Tech■	J26
North Fla.■	J29
Eckerd	F 2
Barry■	F 5
Rollins	F 9
St. Leo	F12
Florida Tech	F16
North Fla.	F19
Eckerd■	F23
Fla. Southern	F26

Colors: Scarlett, Black & Gold. Nickname: Spartans.
AD: Hindman Wall. SID: Gil Swalls. II

TEMPLE .... Philadelphia, PA 19122

Charlene Curtis (9 YRS. W-152, L-104)

Delaware■	D 1
Morgan St.	D 4
La Salle■	D 8
Villanova	D19
Notre Dame	D21
N.C.-Greensboro Cl.	J2-3
St. Joseph's (Pa.)	J 8
Pennsylvania■	J11
Duquesne■	J15
Central Conn. St.■	J18
St. Bonaventure	J22
Canisius	J24
Rutgers	J27
Massachusetts■	J29
Rhode Island■	J31
Geo. Washington	F 2
St. Bonaventure■	F 5
Duquesne	F10
West Va.	F12
Rhode Island	F17
West Va.■	F19
Geo. Washington■	F23
St. Joseph's (Pa.)■	F28
Rutgers■	M 3
Massachusetts	M 5

Colors: Cherry & White. Nickname: Owls.
AD: Jim Brown. SID: Marla Rodriguez. I

TENNESSEE .... Knoxville, TN 37916

Pat Summitt (19 YRS. W-499, L-124)

Ohio St.☒	N21
Montana■	N28
Stanford	D 3
Arizona	D 7
Maryland■	D12
Florida■	D18
Colorado■	D20
Louisiana Tech■	D22
Memphis St.	D30
Arkansas■	J 2
DePaul	J 5
Notre Dame	J 7
Louisiana St.■	J 9
Old Dominion■	J13
Auburn■	J15
Rutgers	J17
Virginia Tech■	J20
Mississippi St.	J22
Texas■	J25
Mississippi	J29
Vanderbilt	J31
Alabama■	F 5
South Caro.	F 8
Providence	F11
Vanderbilt■	F13
Kentucky	F20
Georgia	F27
Southeastern Tr.	M4-7

☒ Jackson, TN

Colors: Orange & White. Nickname: Lady Volunteers.
AD: Joan Cronan. SID: Debby Jennings. I

■ Home games on each schedule.

See pages 735-738 for Division I tournament details

TENNESSEE ST. .... Nashville, TN 37203

Teresa Lawrence-Phillips (8 YRS. W-118, L-91)

Alcorn St.	N29	Murray St.	J24
Alabama Cl.	D3-4	Tennessee Tech	J27
Tenn.-Chatt.	D 8	Southeast Mo. St.■	J29
Memphis St. Cl.	D10-11	Murray St.■	J31
Alcorn St.■	D18	Middle Tenn. St.■	F 5
Ga. Southern Inv.	D29-30	Austin Peay■	F 7
Austin Peay	J 3	Tenn.-Martin	F 9
Tenn.-Martin■	J 8	Morehead St.	F12
Eastern Ky.■	J13	Eastern Ky.	F14
Morehead St.■	J17	Tennessee Tech■	F21
Middle Tenn. St.	J19	Tenn.-Chatt.■	F23
Southeast Mo. St.	J22	Ohio Valley Tr.	M3-5

Colors: Blue & White. Nickname: Lady Tigers.
AD: William Thomas. SID: Johnny Franks. I

TENNESSEE TECH .... Cookeville, TN 38505

Bill Worrell (7 YRS. W-156, L-54)

Southern Ill.■	N28	Tennessee St.■	J27
UNLV Cl.	D3-4	Middle Tenn. St.	J29
Tennessee Tech Cl.	D11-12	Georgia	F 2
Florida	D20	Tenn.-Martin	F 7
Mississippi■	J 2	Southeast Mo. St.■	F12
Western Ky.■	J 6	Murray St.■	F14
Austin Peay■	J 8	Middle Tenn. St.■	F17
Tenn.-Martin■	J10	Austin Peay	F19
Tenn.-Chatt.	J12	Tennessee St.	F21
Southeast Mo. St.	J15	Eastern Ky.■	F26
Murray St.	J17	Morehead St.■	F28
Morehead St.	J22	Ohio Valley Tr.	M3-5
Eastern Ky.	J24		

Colors: Purple & Gold. Nickname: Golden Eaglettes.
AD: David Larimore. SID: Jeff Patton. I

TENN.-CHATT. .... Chattanooga, TN 37401

Craig Parrott (6 YRS. W-107, L-67)

Florida St.■	N26	Furman■	J26
Middle Tenn. St.	D 1	Western Caro.	J29
Mississippi St. Tr.	D3-4	Appalachian St.	J31
Tennessee St.■	D 8	Ga. Southern■	F 5
South Fla. Tr.	D17-18	Furman	F 7
Middle Tenn. St.■	D21	East Tenn. St.	F12
Ga. Southern	J 3	Marshall	F14
Georgia Tech	J 5	Davidson	F19
Virginia Tech	J 8	Tennessee St.	F23
Tennessee Tech■	J12	Western Caro.■	F26
East Tenn. St.■	J15	Appalachian St.■	F28
Marshall■	J17	Southern Tr.	M10-12
Austin Peay■	J20		

Colors: Navy Blue & Gold. Nickname: Moccasins.
AD: Ed Farrell. SID: Neil Magnussen. I

TENN.-MARTIN .... Martin, TN 38238

Sharman Coley (4 YRS. W-38, L-67)

Bethel (Tenn.)■	N29	Southeast Mo. St.	J24
Memphis St.	D 1	Oral Roberts■	J27
St. Louis■	D 4	Middle Tenn. St.	J31
Stetson	D14	Austin Peay■	F 5
Oral Roberts	D18	Tennessee Tech■	F 7
Indiana■	D20	Tennessee St.■	F 9
East Tenn. St.■	D30	Memphis St.■	F14
Middle Tenn. St.■	J 3	Austin Peay	F16
St. Louis	J 6	Morehead St.	F19
Tennessee St.	J 8	Eastern Ky.	F21
Tennessee Tech	J10	Southeast Mo. St.■	F26
Morehead St.■	J13	Murray St.■	F28
Eastern Ky.■	J15	Ohio Valley Tr.	M3-5
Murray St.	J22		

Colors: Orange, White, Royal Blue. Nickname: Lady Pacers.
AD: Bettye Giles. SID: Lee Wilmot. I

TEXAS .... Austin, TX 78712

Jody Conradt (24 YRS. W-620, L-153)

Vanderbilt	N26	Texas Tech■	J22
Oklahoma■	N30	Tennessee	J25
Richmond Inv.	D3-4	Houston■	J29
Loyola (Cal.)■	D14	Rice	F 2
Brigham Young■	D18	Texas Christian	F 6
Arizona	D21	Texas A&M■	F 9
California■	D30	Southern Methodist■	F12
New Mexico St.■	J 2	Baylor	F16
Marquette■	J 5	Texas Tech	F19
Santa Clara■	J 8	Houston	F26
Texas A&M	J12	Rice■	M 2
Southern Methodist	J15	Texas Christian■	M 6
Baylor■	J19	Southwest Tr.	M9-12

Colors: Orange & White. Nickname: Longhorns.
AD: Jody Conradt. SID: Kim Stone. I

TEXAS A&M .... College Station, TX 77843

Lynn Hickey (14 YRS. W-256, L-159)

Arizona St.	N27	Texas Christian	J26
Texas Southern■	N30	Southern Methodist	J29
Texas A&M Inv.	D4-5	Baylor■	F 2
Lamar■	D 7	Texas Tech■	F 5
Oklahoma	D18	Texas	F 9
UC Irvine■	D21	Rice	F12
Louisiana St.	D29	Houston	F16
Tulane	D31	Oral Roberts	F18
Oklahoma St.■	J 3	Texas Christian■	F23
Texas■	J12	Southern Methodist■	F26
Rice■	J15	Baylor	M 2
Houston■	J19	Texas Tech	M 5
Cal St. Sacramento■	J23	Southwest Tr.	M9-12

Colors: Maroon & White. Nickname: Lady Aggies.
AD: Wally Groff (Interim). SID: Debbie Darrah. I

TEXAS A&M - KINGSVILLE ...... Kingsville, TX 78363

Jill Willson (1 YR. W-6, L-20)

Tarleton St.	N22	West Tex. St.	J24
Abilene Chrst. Cl.	N26-27	Cameron■	J27
Incarnate Word■	N29	Central Okla.■	J29
West Tex. A&M Tr.	D2-4	Texas Woman's■	J31
Concordia (Tex.)■	D 9	Texas Woman's	F 5
Texas-San Antonio	D11	Central Okla.	F 7
Tex.-Pan American	D31	Angelo St.	F12
Incarnate Word	J11	Abilene Christian	F14
Abilene Christian■	J15	West Tex. St.■	F19
Angelo St.■	J17	Eastern N. Mex.■	F21
Eastern N. Mex.	J22		

Colors: Blue & Gold. Nickname: Javelinas.
AD: Ron Harms. SID: Fred Nuesch. II

TEXAS CHRISTIAN .... Fort Worth, TX 76129

Shell Robinson (1ST YR. AS HEAD COACH)

Mississippi■	N26	Southern Methodist■	J22
Southwestern La.■	D 1	Texas A&M■	J26
Colorado■	D 7	Texas Tech	F 2
Wyoming	D 9	Texas■	F 6
Colorado St.	D11	Houston■	F 9
UTEP	D13	Baylor■	F12
North Texas	D21	Rice■	F16
Oklahoma St. Tr.	D30-J1	Southern Methodist	F19
Iona■	J 5	Texas A&M	F23
Oral Roberts	J 8	Texas Tech■	M 2
Houston■	J12	Texas	M 6
Baylor	J15	Southwest Tr.	M9-12
Rice	J19		

Colors: Purple & White. Nickname: Lady Frogs.
AD: Frank Windegger. SID: Glen Stone. I

TEXAS SOUTHERN .... Houston, TX 77004

Robert Gatlin (7 YRS. W-82, L-109)

Rice■	N27	UTEP	J19
Texas A&M	N30	Alcorn St.	J22
Houston■	D 1	Southern-B.R.	J24
Louisiana Tech Cl.	D3-4	Prairie View	J29
Vanderbilt	D 7	Jackson St.■	F 5
Sam Houston St.	D 9	Alabama St.■	F 7
Baylor Cl.	D29-30	Grambling	F12
Tex.-Pan American■	J 3	Mississippi Val.	F14
Sam Houston St.■	J 6	Alcorn St.■	F19
Jackson St.	J 8	Southern-B.R.■	F21
Alabama St.	J10	Prairie View■	F26
Grambling■	J15	SWAC Tr.	M10-13
Mississippi Val.■	J17		

Colors: Maroon & Gray. Nickname: Lady Tigers.
AD: To be named. SID: Andre Smith. I

TEXAS TECH .... Lubbock, TX 79409

Marsha Sharp (11 YRS. W-241, L-97)

Vanderbilt☒	N21	Rice	J29
Stanford■	N27	Texas Christian■	F 2
Texas Tech Cl.	D4-5	Texas A&M	F 5
UTEP■	D 7	Baylor	F 9
Wichita St. Shootout	D18-19	Houston■	F12
Seton Hall	D28	Southern Methodist	F16
St. Peter's Tr.	D29-30	Texas■	F19
Lamar■	J 2	Rice■	F26
Stephen F. Austin	J 9	Texas Christian	M 2
Baylor■	J12	Texas A&M■	M 5
Houston	J15	Southwest Tr.	M9-12
Southern Methodist■	J19	☒ Jackson, TN	
Texas	J22		

Colors: Scarlet & Black. Nickname: Lady Raiders.
AD: To be named. SID: Walt McAlexander. I

■ Home games on each schedule.

See pages 735-738 for Division I tournament details

TEXAS-ARLINGTON .... Arlington, TX 76019

Mike Dean (1 YR. W-11, L-16)

Mississippi■	N28	Texas-San Antonio	J27
Texas-Arlington Cl.	D3-4	Southwest Tex. St.	J29
New Mexico	D 7	McNeese St.■	F 3
Wichita St.	D11	Nicholls St.■	F 5
Arkansas■	D22	North Texas	F12
Louisiana Tech	J 4	Stephen F. Austin■	F14
Nicholls St.	J 6	Northeast La.	F17
McNeese St.	J 8	Northwestern (La.)	F19
Sam Houston St.■	J11	Southwest Tex. St.■	F24
North Texas■	J15	Texas-San Antonio■	F26
Northwestern (La.)■	J20	Sam Houston St.	F28
Northeast La.■	J22	Stephen F. Austin	M 3
Mo.-Kansas City■	J24	Southland Tr.	M8-12

Colors: Royal Blue & White. Nickname: Mavericks.
AD: B.J. Skelton. SID: Steve Weller. I

UTEP .... El Paso, TX 79968

Sandra Rushing (4 YRS. W-47, L-57)

New Mexico St.	D 1	Utah■	J27
Abilene Christian■	D 4	Brigham Young■	J29
Texas Tech	D 7	Brigham Young	F 3
North Texas■	D11	Utah	F 5
Texas Christian■	D13	Fresno St.■	F11
New Mexico St.■	D17	San Diego St.■	F13
Southern Miss. Cl.	D20-21	San Diego St.	F18
Oregon	J 3	Fresno St.	F20
Portland	J 6	Wyoming■	F25
Wyoming	J13	Colorado St.■	F27
Colorado St.	J15	New Mexico■	M 5
Texas Southern■	J19	Western Athletic Tr.	M9-12
New Mexico	J22		

Colors: Orange, White & Blue. Nickname: Lady Miners.
AD: John Thompson. SID: Frank de Santos. I

TEX.-PAN AMERICAN .... Edinburg, TX 78539

Tracie Garner (1 YR. W-4, L-10)

Oral Roberts	N26	Western Ky.■	J27
Oklahoma	N27	Oral Roberts■	F 1
Missouri Cl.	D3-4	Lamar	F 5
South Fla. Tr.	D17-18	Western Ky.	F11
Texas A&I■	D31	Arkansas St.	F13
Texas Southern	J 3	Arkansas	F15
New Orleans■	J 6	South Ala.■	F19
Louisiana Tech	J 8	Central Ark.■	F22
Southwestern La.	J15	Arkansas St.■	F26
Lamar■	J17	Louisiana Tech■	M 3
New Orleans	J20	South Ala.	M 5
Southwestern La.■	J22	Sun Belt Tr.	M10-12

Colors: Green & White. Nickname: Lady Broncs.
AD: Gary Gallup. SID: Jim McKone. I

TEXAS-SAN ANTONIO .... San Antonio, TX 78285

Mary Ann McLaughlin (4 YRS. W-45, L-66)

Rice Cl.	D3-4	North Texas■	J29
Prairie View■	D 7	Schreiner■	F 3
Texas A&I■	D11	Southwest Tex. St.	F 5
Angelo St.■	D27	Sam Houston St.	F10
Northwestern (La.)	D28	Stephen F. Austin	F12
Northeast La.	D30	Nicholls St.■	F17
Northern Ariz.	J 5	McNeese St.■	F19
Southwest Tex. St.■	J 8	North Texas	F24
Stephen F. Austin■	J14	Texas-Arlington	F26
Sam Houston St.■	J16	Northwestern (La.)■	F28
McNeese St.	J20	Northeast La.■	M 2
Nicholls St.	J22	Southland Tr.	M8-12
Texas-Arlington■	J27		

Colors: Orange, White & Navy Blue. Nickname: Lady Roadrunners.
AD: Bobby Thompson. SID: Rick Nixon. I

THIEL .... Greenville, PA 16125

Gloria Pacsi (4 YRS. W-29, L-66)

Geneva■	N20	Grove City	J19
Hilbert	N23	Wash. & Jeff.■	J21
Carlow	N29	LaRoche	J24
Westminster (Pa.)■	D 1	Bethany (W.Va.)■	J26
Hilbert■	D 3	Lake Erie	J29
Allegheny	D 6	Penn St.-Behrend■	J31
Oberlin	D10	Waynesburg■	F 2
Hiram	J 6	Grove City■	F 5
Lake Erie■	J 8	Wash. & Jeff.	F 9
Carnegie Mellon	J12	Bethany (W.Va.)	F12
LaRoche■	J13	Penn St.-Behrend	F16
Malone	J15	Waynesburg	F19

Colors: Navy Blue & Old Gold. Nickname: Lady Cats.
AD: Dale Liston. SID: William Ross. III

THOMAS MORE .... Crestview Hills, KY 41017

Sharri Brumfield (6 YRS. W-55, L-98)

Eastern Ky.	N30	Hanover■	J19
St. John Fisher Cl.	D3-4	Defiance	J22
Denison■	D11	Wilmington (Ohio)■	J26
Centre	D13	Bluffton■	J29
Ohio Dominican■	D16	Ky. Christian	F 1
Brescia	D18	Asbury■	F 3
Heidelberg■	D22	Maryville (Tenn.)■	F 6
DePauw■	D30	Hanover	F 9
Maryville (Tenn.)	J 5	Defiance■	F12
Ohio Wesleyan■	J 8	Wilmington (Ohio)	F16
Asbury	J11	Bluffton	F19
Berea	J13	DePauw	F23

Colors: Royal Blue & White. Nickname: Blue Rebels.
AD: Vic Clark. SID: Ted Kiep. III

TOLEDO .... Toledo, OH 43606

Bill Fennelly (5 YRS. W-118, L-38)

Wisconsin	N26	Western Mich.	J26
Loyola (Ill.)	N28	Ohio■	J29
Detroit Mercy	D 1	Central Mich.	F 2
Virginia Cl.	D3-4	Eastern Mich.■	F 5
Cleveland St.	D15	Akron■	F 9
Loyola (Ill.)■	D21	Kent	F12
Niagara■	J 2	Ball St.■	F16
Bowling Green■	J 5	Miami (Ohio)	F19
Eastern Mich.	J 8	Western Mich.■	F23
Akron	J12	Ohio	F26
Kent■	J15	Central Mich.■	M 2
Ball St.	J19	Bowling Green	M 5
Miami (Ohio)■	J22	Mid-American Tr.	M8-12

Colors: Blue & Gold. Nickname: Rockets.
AD: Allen Bohl. SID: John McNamara. I

TOWSON ST. .... Towson, MD 21204

Ellen Fitzkee (5 YRS. W-55, L-81)

Lehigh■	N27	Radford■	J29
Loyola (Md.)	D 1	Md.-Balt. County	F 1
Mt. St. Mary's (Md.)■	D 6	Winthrop	F 4
Delaware■	D 9	N.C.-Asheville	F 5
Winthrop■	D17	Charleston So.■	F11
N.C.-Asheville■	D18	Coastal Caro.■	F12
La Salle Inv.	D28-29	Bucknell	F21
Navy■	J 4	Campbell■	F25
Charleston So.	J 7	N.C.-Greensboro■	F26
Coastal Caro.	J 8	Md.-Balt. County■	M 1
Richmond■	J18	Liberty	M 4
Campbell	J21	Radford	M 5
N.C.-Greensboro	J22	Big South Tr.	M9-12
Liberty■	J28		

Colors: Gold, White & Black. Nickname: Tigers.
AD: Bill Hunter. SID: Peter Schlehr. I

TRENTON ST. .... Ewing, NJ 08650

Mika Ryan (9 YRS. W-147, L-83)

Muhlenberg Tr.	N20-21	Stockton St.■	J19
Rutgers-Camden■	N23	Jersey City St.■	J22
Ramapo	N27	Rutgers-Camden	J26
St. Elizabeth■	N29	Ramapo■	J29
Jersey City St.	D 1	Rowan	F 1
Kean■	D 4	Kean	F 5
Montclair St.	D 8	Salisbury St.■	F 7
Wm. Paterson	D11	Montclair St.■	F 9
Western Conn. Tr.	D28-29	Wm. Paterson■	F12
Rowan■	J12	Stockton St.	F16
Rutgers-Newark	J15	Rutgers-Newark■	F19

Colors: Navy Blue & Gold. Nickname: Lions.
AD: Kevin McHugh. SID: Ann Bready. III

TRINITY (TEX.) .... San Antonio, TX 78212

Becky Geyer (1 YR. W-10, L-11)

Trinity (Tex.) Inv.	N20-21	Southwestern (Tex.)■	J25
Austin	N23	Sewanee■	J28
Southwestern (Tex.)	N30	Oglethorpe■	J30
Schreiner■	D 4	Schreiner	F 1
St. Benedict Cl.	D29-30	Rhodes	F 4
Hendrix■	J 9	Millsaps	F 6
Rochester■	J12	Sewanee	F11
Rhodes■	J14	Oglethorpe	F13
Millsaps■	J16	Fisk■	F18
Fisk	J21	Centre■	F20
Centre	J23	Hendrix	F26

Colors: Maroon & White. Nickname: Tigers.
AD: Bob King. SID: James Hill. III

■ Home games on each schedule.

See pages 735-738 for Division I tournament details

TROY ST. .... Troy, AL 36082

Joyce Sorrell (18 YRS. W-252, L-244)

Florida A&M■	N29	Austin Peay	J23
Tampa■	D 1	Mississippi Val.■	J25
Southeastern La.	D 4	Buffalo■	J30
Tulane	D 7	Mississippi Val.	F 2
South Ala.	D 8	Florida A&M	F 8
Georgia St.■	D11	Alabama St.■	F10
Georgia St.	J 6	Chicago St.■	F12
Mercer	J 8	Southeastern La.■	F16
South Ala.■	J10	Middle Tenn. St.■	F19
Alabama■	J12	Mercer■	F21
Hofstra	J14	Alabama	F28
Alabama St.	J19	East Coast Tr.	M3-6
Northeastern Ill.	J22		

Colors: Cardinal, Gray & Black. Nickname: Lady Trojans.
AD: Kennith Blakenship. SID: Tom Ensey. I

TUFTS .... Medford, MA 02155

Sharon Dawley (9 YRS. W-137, L-63)

Tufts Tr.	N20-21	Williams	F 1
Western New Eng.■	N23	Pine Manor	F 3
Rochester Inv.	N27-28	Smith	F 5
Gordon■	D 1	Mount Holyoke	F 8
Colby	D 3	Clark (Mass.)■	F10
Bowdoin	D 4	Trinity (Conn.)	F12
Brandeis	D 8	Bates■	F16
Wesleyan■	J18	Middlebury■	F19
Wellesley■	J20	Amherst	F23
Mass.-Dartmouth	J27	Connecticut Col.■	F26
Wheaton (Mass.)■	J29		

Colors: Blue & Brown. Nickname: Jumbos.
AD: Rocco Carzo. SID: Paul Sweeney. III

TULANE .... New Orleans, LA 70118

Candi Harvey (3 YRS. W-29, L-54)

Harvard Inv.	D3-4	New Orleans	J31
Troy St.■	D 7	South Fla.	F 5
Tulane Cl.	D10-11	Va. Commonwealth	F 7
Fairfield■	D28	South Fla.■	F11
Texas A&M■	D31	Louisville■	F13
Southern Methodist	J 5	New Orleans■	F16
Louisville	J 8	Southern Miss.	F19
Southwestern La.	J12	Louisiana St.■	F21
Virginia Tech■	J15	Virginia Tech	F26
N.C.-Charlotte■	J17	N.C.-Charlotte	F28
Arkansas	J19	Va. Commonwealth■	M 5
Mississippi St.	J25	Metro Tr.	M8-11
Southern Miss.■	J29		

Colors: Olive Green & Sky Blue. Nickname: Green Wave.
AD: Kevin White. SID: Wendi McLendon. I

TUSKEGEE .... Tuskegee, AL 36088

Angelia Nelson (1 YR. W-17, L-8)

Selma■	N23	LeMoyne-Owen	J24
Mississippi Col.	N27	Miles■	J28
Fort Valley St.■	N29	Alabama A&M	J29
Paine■	D 2	Spelman■	F 1
Talladega	D 7	Fort Valley St.	F 3
Atlantic City Cl.	D18-19	Savannah St.	F 5
Alabama St.	J 6	Paine	F 7
Talladega■	J10	Spelman	F 9
Albany St. (Ga.)■	J12	Morris Brown	F14
Florida A&M	J13	Albany St. (Ga.)	F16
LeMoyne-Owen■	J17	Miles	F19
Clark Atlanta■	J21	Morris Brown■	F22
Alabama A&M■	J22	Clark Atlanta	F25

Colors: Crimson & Gold. Nickname: Tigerettes.
AD: James Martin Sr. SID: Arnold Houston. II

UCLA .... Los Angeles, CA 90024

Kathy Olivier (1ST YR. AS HEAD COACH)

UC Santa Barb.■	N27	Arizona	J22
San Diego■	D 1	Stanford■	J27
Western Ky.■	D 4	California■	J29
San Francisco	D10	Southern Cal	F 5
Santa Clara	D12	Washington	F10
Boise St.■	D19	Washington St.	F12
North Caro. St.☒	D28	Arizona■	F18
N.C.-Charlotte	D30	Arizona St.■	F20
Rutgers■	J 3	California	F24
Oregon	J 6	Stanford	F26
Oregon St.	J 8	Southern Cal■	M 3
Washington St.■	J13	Oregon St.■	M10
Washington■	J16	Oregon■	M12
Arizona St.	J20	☒ Greensboro, NC	

Colors: Navy Blue & Gold. Nickname: Bruins.
AD: Judith Holland. SID: Marc Dellins. I

UNION (N.Y.) .... Schenectady, NY 12308

Joanne Little (4 YRS. W-37, L-57)

Albany (N.Y.) Tr.	N20-21	Russell Sage	J18
William Smith	N30	Binghamton■	J22
Clarkson	D 3	Hartwick■	J25
St. Lawrence	D 4	Albany (N.Y.)■	J27
Rensselaer■	D 9	Middlebury■	F 2
Rochester Inst.■	D11	Vassar	F 9
Plattsburgh St.	J 8	Hamilton■	F12
Smith	J10	Oneonta St.■	F17
Skidmore	J13	Williams	F19
Colby■	J15	Utica■	F22
Bowdoin■	J16		

Colors: Garnet. Nickname: Dutchwomen.
AD: Dick Sakala. SID: George Cuttita. III

UPPER IOWA .... Fayette, IA 52142

Linda Olson (1 YR. W-4, L-19)

Teiko-Marycrest■	N19	Buena Vista■	J22
Clarke	N22	Coe	J26
Winona St.	N30	Loras	F 1
Viterbo■	D 3	Simpson■	F 4
Cornell College■	D 7	Buena Vista	F 5
Wis.-Stevens Pt. Tr.	D10-11	Luther	F11
St. Mary's (Minn.)	D15	William Penn■	F12
Dubuque■	J 7	Central (Iowa)■	F15
Luther■	J 8	Dubuque	F18
Central (Iowa)	J14	Simpson	F19
William Penn	J15	Loras■	F25
Wartburg	J21	Wartburg■	F26

Colors: Blue & White. Nickname: Lady Peacocks.
AD: Mike McCready. SID: Julie Lentz. III

UPSALA .... East Orange, NJ 07019

William McGrady (2 YRS. W-25, L-22)

New Jersey Tech	N23	King's (Pa.)	J29
Mt. St. Mary (N.Y.)■	N30	Drew■	F 2
King's (Pa.)■	D 1	Lycoming■	F 5
Lycoming	D 4	FDU-Madison■	F 8
Drew	J11	St. Elizabeth	F10
St. Elizabeth■	J13	Scranton■	F12
Scranton	J15	New Jersey Tech■	F14
FDU-Madison	J18	Delaware Valley	F16
Bloomfield	J20	Wilkes■	F19
Wilkes	J22	Centenary (N.J.)■	F21
Centenary (N.J.)	J24	Mt. St. Mary (N.Y.)	F23
Delaware Valley■	J26		

Colors: Blue & Gray. Nickname: Lady Vikings.
AD: Mike Walsh. SID: Rich Carroll. III

URSINUS .... Collegeville, PA 19426

Lisa Ortlip-Cornish (7 YRS. W-93, L-80)

Meredith■	N20	Swarthmore	J25
Rand.-Macon Woman's	N21	Western Md.■	J27
Johns Hopkins■	N23	Muhlenberg	J29
Gettysburg	N30	Haverford■	F 2
Albright■	D 2	Bryn Mawr	F 5
Holy Family■	D 4	Washington (Md.)■	F 8
Bryn Mawr■	D 7	Swarthmore■	F12
Widener	D 9	Muhlenberg■	F15
King's (Pa.) Tr.	J7-8	Allentown■	F17
Frank. & Marsh.■	J15	Haverford	F19
Washington (Md.)	J18	Immaculata■	F22
Dickinson	J22		

Colors: Red, Old Gold, Black. Nickname: Bears.
AD: Robert Davidson. SID: Dave Sherman. III

UTAH .... Salt Lake City, UT 84112

Elaine Elliott (10 YRS. W-200, L-92)

Western Ky.	N26	Colorado St.■	J22
Stanford■	N29	UTEP	J27
Idaho St.	D 4	New Mexico	J29
Weber St.	D10	New Mexico■	F 3
Oregon St.■	D14	UTEP■	F 5
Eastern Wash.	D18	Colorado St.	F11
Montana	D20	Wyoming	F12
Wisconsin	D30	Brigham Young■	F18
Kansas St.	J 1	Fresno St.■	F24
Idaho■	J 4	San Diego St.■	F26
San Diego St.	J13	Brigham Young	M 4
Fresno St.	J15	Western Athletic Tr.	M9-12
Wyoming■	J20		

Colors: Crimson & White. Nickname: Lady Utes.
AD: Fern Gardner. SID: Liz Abel. I

■ Home games on each schedule.

See pages 735-738 for Division I tournament details

UTICA .... Utica, NY 13502

To be named

St. Lawrence■ N19
Clarkson■ N20
Hartwick D 1
Utica Tech Cl. D4-5
Rensselaer D 7
Utica Tech D 9
Castleton St. J12
St. Joseph (Vt.) J13
Brockport St.■ J15
Elmira■ J19
Roberts Wesleyan■ J22
Skidmore J24
Russell Sage J29
Nazareth (N.Y.)■ F 3
Keuka F 5
Albany (N.Y.)■ F 7
Hamilton■ F10
Binghamton■ F14
Le Moyne F16
St. John Fisher■ F19
Union (N.Y.) F22

Colors: Blue & Orange. Nickname: Pioneers.
AD: James Spartano. SID: Jim Taylor. III

UTICA TECH .... Utica, NY 13504

Kevin Grimmer (5 YRS. W-65, L-58)

Utica Tech Cl. D4-5
Oswego St. D 7
Utica■ D 9
Buffalo St.■ D11
Webber Cl. J6-8
Binghamton■ J14
Cortland St. J15
Geneseo St. J18
Brockport St.■ J21
Fredonia St.■ J22
Russell Sage J25
New Paltz St. J28
Oneonta St.■ J29
Oswego St.■ F 4
Buffalo St. F 5
Hamilton■ F 8
Plattsburgh St.■ F11
Potsdam St. F12
Geneseo St.■ F15
Brockport St. F18
Fredonia St. F19

Colors: Gold & Brown. Nickname: Lady Wildcats.
AD: Jim Klein. SID: Kevin Grimmer. III

VALDOSTA ST. .... Valdosta, GA 31698

Charles Cooper (12 YRS. W-204, L-123)

Kennesaw St.■ N22
Ga. Southwestern■ N27
Ala.-Huntsville■ N30
North Fla. Tr. D3-4
Fort Valley St.■ D13
Trinity (Ill.)■ J 6
North Ala. J 8
Ala.-Huntsville J10
Ga. Southwestern J13
Livingston■ J15
Jacksonville St.■ J17
West Ga. J22
Georgia Col.■ J24
North Ala.■ J29
West Ga.■ J31
Mississippi Col. F 5
Livingston F 7
Lincoln Memorial F12
North Fla.■ F14
Fort Valley St. F17
Lincoln Memorial■ F19
Georgia Col. F21
Mississippi Col.■ F26

Colors: Red & Black. Nickname: Lady Blazers.
AD: Herb Reinhard. SID: Steve Roberts. II

VALPARAISO .... Valparaiso, IN 46383

Dave Wolter (6 YRS. W-76, L-94)

Austin Peay N27
Michigan St. Cl. D3-4
Akron■ D 8
Miami (Fla.) D18
Florida Int'l D20
Ill.-Chicago J 2
Western Ill.■ J 6
Northern Ill.■ J 9
Wis.-Milwaukee J13
Wis.-Green Bay J15
Cleveland St.■ J21
Youngstown St.■ J23
Wright St. J27
Eastern Ill. J29
Ill.-Chicago■ F 5
Western Ill. F10
Northern Ill. F12
Wis.-Milwaukee■ F17
Wis.-Green Bay■ F19
Loyola (Ill.)■ F22
Cleveland St. F24
Youngstown St. F26
Wright St.■ M 3
Eastern Ill.■ M 5
Mid-Continent Tr. M10-12

Colors: Brown & Gold. Nickname: Crusaders.
AD: William Steinbrecher. SID: Bill Rogers. I

VANDERBILT .... Nashville, TN 37212

Jim Foster (15 YRS. W-300, L-138)

Texas Tech☒ N21
Texas■ N26
Ohio St. D 1
Vanderbilt Cl. D4-5
Texas Southern■ D 7
Bowling Green■ D11
Auburn■ D17
Geo. Washington D21
Harvard D30
Massachusetts J 2
Evansville■ J 7
Alabama■ J 9
Kentucky■ J12
Georgia■ J16
Mississippi J19
Louisiana St. J22
Penn St.■ J25
Mississippi St. J29
Tennessee■ J31
Southern Ill. F 2
Florida■ F 6
Tennessee F13
Western Ky. F17
Arkansas■ F20
DePaul F23
South Caro. F26
Southeastern Tr. M4-7
☒ Jackson, TN

Colors: Black & Gold. Nickname: Commodores.
AD: Paul Hoolahan. SID: Rod Williamson. I

VERMONT .... Burlington, VT 05401

Pam Borton (1ST YR. AS HEAD COACH)

Dartmouth■ N27
Connecticut D 1
Siena D 4
Vermont Tr. D21-22
Central Mich. Cl. D29-30
Rhode Island J 3
Holy Cross■ J 6
Massachusetts J 9
Northeastern■ J13
Boston U.■ J15
Maine J20
New Hampshire■ J22
Delaware J28
Drexel J30
Hartford F 5
Central Conn. St.■ F 8
Drexel■ F11
Delaware■ F13
New Hampshire F17
Maine■ F19
Northeastern F24
Boston U. F26
Hartford■ M 2
North Atlantic Tr. M6-12

Colors: Green & Gold. Nickname: Catamounts.
AD: Rick Farnham. SID: Dick Whittier. I

VILLANOVA .... Villanova, PA 19085

Harry Perretta (15 YRS. W-280, L-153)

St. Joseph's (Pa.)■ N30
UNLV Cl. D3-4
Pittsburgh■ D11
Temple■ D19
La Salle D23
Villanova Tr. D28-29
Georgetown■ J 3
Miami (Fla.) J 6
St. John's (N.Y.) J 9
Connecticut■ J12
Boston College J16
Providence J18
Seton Hall■ J22
Pennsylvania■ J24
Syracuse J26
Georgetown J29
Boston College■ F 1
Miami (Fla.)■ F 6
Connecticut F 9
St. John's (N.Y.)■ F13
Pittsburgh F16
Providence■ F20
Seton Hall F23
Syracuse■ F27
Big East Tr. M4-7

Colors: Blue & White. Nickname: Wildcats.
AD: Gene DeFilippo. SID: Jim DeLorenzo. I

VIRGINIA .... Charlottesville, VA 22903

Debbie Ryan (16 YRS. W-359, L-130)

Pennsylvania■ N27
Robert Morris■ N28
Virginia Cl. D3-4
Virginia Tech■ D 8
Connecticut D11
Florida St.■ D21
St. Joseph's Cl. D29-30
Clemson■ J 3
Ohio St.■ J 8
North Caro. J12
North Caro. St. J15
Maryland■ J18
Georgia Tech■ J22
Duke J25
Wake Forest■ J29
Va. Commonwealth J31
Florida St. F 4
Georgia Tech F 6
North Caro.■ F 9
Duke■ F12
Wake Forest F15
Clemson F19
Maryland F23
North Caro. St.■ F26
ACC Tr. M4-7

Colors: Orange & Blue. Nickname: Cavaliers.
AD: Jim Copeland. SID: Rich Murray. I

VA. COMMONWEALTH .... Richmond, VA 23284

Susan Walvius (3 YRS. W-44, L-40)

James Madison■ N26
Morgan St.■ D 1
Syracuse Cl. D4-5
Md.-East. Shore■ D 8
North Caro. St. D11
McNeese St.■ D13
Old Dominion D18
Richmond■ D21
George Mason■ J 5
Southern Miss.■ J 8
Liberty J18
South Fla. J21
Louisville J23
N.C.-Charlotte■ J28
Virginia■ J31
Howard F 2
William & Mary F 5
Tulane■ F 7
Virginia Tech F12
N.C.-Charlotte F14
Richmond F18
Virginia Tech■ F22
Louisville■ F25
South Fla.■ F27
Southern Miss. M 3
Tulane M 5
Metro Tr. M8-11

Colors: Black & Gold. Nickname: Lady Rams.
AD: Richard Sander. SID: Joe Onderko. I

VIRGINIA ST. .... Petersburg, VA 23803

Bertha Cummings (5 YRS. W-96, L-40)

Fayetteville St.■ N20
St. Augustine's■ N23
Winston-Salem N26
Johnson Smith N27
Virginia Union N30
East Stroudsburg Cl. D3-4
N.C. Central D 6
St. Rose■ J 2
Virginia St. Cl. J7-8
Dist. Columbia■ J12
Elizabeth City St.■ J15
Hampton■ J18
Bowie St. J20
St. Paul's■ J22
Dist. Columbia J26
Norfolk St. J29
Virginia Union■ F 1
Norfolk St.■ F 3
Elizabeth City St. F 5
Hampton F 8
Livingstone F12
Bowie St.■ F14
St. Paul's F16
Shaw■ F18

Colors: Orange & Navy Blue. Nickname: Trojanettes.
AD: Larry Brooks. SID: Gregory Goings. II

■ Home games on each schedule.

See pages 735-738 for Division I tournament details

VIRGINIA TECH .... Blacksburg, VA 24061
Carol Alfano (15 YRS. W-211, L-209)

Western Caro.■	D 1	James Madison	J25
Ohio■	D 4	Louisville■	J28
Virginia	D 8	Radford	F 1
Pepperdine Tr.	D18-19	N.C.-Charlotte■	F 3
Buffalo Tr.	D29-30	Louisville	F 7
Morehead St.■	J 5	Va. Commonwealth■	F12
Tenn.-Chatt.■	J 8	South Fla.	F20
South Fla.■	J10	Va. Commonwealth	F22
Bradley■	J12	Tulane■	F26
Tulane	J15	Southern Miss.■	F28
Southern Miss.	J17	N.C.-Charlotte	M 3
Tennessee	J20	Metro Tr.	M8-11

Colors: Orange & Maroon. Nickname: Lady Hokies.
AD: Dave Braine. SID: Ed Moore. I

VIRGINIA UNION .... Richmond, VA 23220
Moses Golatt (21 YRS. W-231, L-316)

Virginia St.■	N30	Pitt.-Johnstown■	J24
Livingstone■	D11	St. Paul's■	J25
Johnson Smith	D14	Winston-Salem■	J27
Mercyhurst Tr.	D17-18	Bowie St.■	J29
St. Rose■	J 1	Virginia St.	F 1
Fayetteville St.	J 5	St. Augustine's■	F 3
Elizabeth City St.■	J 8	Norfolk St.	F 5
St. Paul's	J11	Pitt.-Johnstown	F 7
Dist. Columbia■	J13	N.C. Central■	F10
Hampton	J15	Bowie St.	F12
Shaw	J18	Elizabeth City St.	F16
Norfolk St.■	J20	Dist. Columbia	F18
Hampton■	J22		

Colors: Steel & Maroon. Nickname: Panthers.
AD: James Battle. SID: Paul Williams. II

VA. WESLEYAN .... Norfolk, VA 23502
Tom Palombo (3 YRS. W-43, L-34)

Marymount (Va.) Tr.	N19-21	Salisbury St.	J26
Rand.-Macon Woman's■	D 3	Emory & Henry	J29
Roanoke■	D 4	Randolph-Macon■	F 1
Emory & Henry■	J 7	Bridgewater (Va.)■	F 5
Guilford■	J 8	Guilford	F 8
Wash. & Lee■	J 9	Hollins	F11
Hollins■	J14	Roanoke	F12
Chris. Newport■	J15	Lynchburg■	F15
Randolph-Macon	J18	East. Mennonite	F18
Rand.-Macon Woman's	J21	Bridgewater (Va.)	F19
Lynchburg	J22		

Colors: Navy Blue & Silver. Nickname: Blue Marlins.
AD: Donald Forsyth. SID: Tom Palombo. III

WAGNER .... Staten Island, NY 10301
Pam Roecker (3 YRS. W-41, L-45)

Yale■	N27	FDU-Teaneck■	J24
Columbia-Barnard	D 1	LIU-Brooklyn	J27
Brown Cl.	D4-5	St. Francis (N.Y.)	J29
Central Conn. St.■	D11	Monmouth (N.J.)■	F 5
Hofstra	D20	Mt. St. Mary's (Md.)■	F10
Wagner Tr.	D28-29	Rider■	F12
Robert Morris	J 4	FDU-Teaneck	F16
St. Francis (Pa.)	J 6	Marist	F19
St. Francis (N.Y.)■	J 8	St. Francis (Pa.)■	F24
LIU-Brooklyn■	J10	Robert Morris■	F26
Monmouth (N.J.)	J15	Rider	M 2
Mt. St. Mary's (Md.)	J20	Northeast Tr.	M5-12
Marist■	J22		

Colors: Green & White. Nickname: Seahawks.
AD: Walt Hameline. SID: Scott Morse. I

WAKE FOREST .... Winston-Salem, NC 27109
Karen Freeman (1 YR. W-14, L-14)

Old Dominion Cl.	N27-28	Florida St.	J22
Appalachian St.	D 1	Richmond■	J25
Northwestern Inv.	D3-4	Virginia	J29
Charleston■	D16	Duke	F 1
N.C.-Charlotte	D19	North Caro.■	F 3
Vermont Tr.	D21-22	Clemson■	F 9
Duke■	J 2	Virginia■	F15
North Caro.	J 5	Maryland	F16
Georgia Tech	J10	Florida St.■	F18
Clemson	J13	Georgia Tech■	F20
Maryland■	J15	North Caro. St.	F24
North Caro. St.■	J18	ACC Tr.	M4-7

Colors: Old Gold & Black. Nickname: Demon Deacons.
AD: Ron Wellman. SID: John Justus. I

WARTBURG .... Waverly, IA 50677
Monica Severson (5 YRS. W-109, L-27)

Ripon Inv.	N20-21	Buena Vista	J28
Dordt■	N27	Loras■	J29
Wis.-Platteville	N30	Dubuque■	F 1
North Central Tr.	D3-4	Cornell College■	F 5
Gust. Adolphus■	D 7	Central (Iowa)	F11
Coe	D10	Luther■	F12
Central (Iowa)■	J 7	William Penn	F18
William Penn■	J 8	Loras	F19
Dubuque	J14	Buena Vista■	F22
Luther	J15	Simpson	F25
Upper Iowa■	J21	Upper Iowa	F26
Simpson■	J22		

Colors: Orange & Black. Nickname: Lady Knights.
AD: Bob Nielson. SID: Duane Schroeder. III

WASHBURN .... Topeka, KS 66621
Pat Dick (16 YRS. W-308, L-148)

Baker■	N20	Southwest Baptist■	J19
Saginaw Valley■	N24	Northwest Mo. St.	J22
Washburn Cl.	N26-27	Emporia St.■	J26
Texas Woman's	N30	Lincoln (Mo.)■	J29
Tabor■	D 4	Northeast Mo. St.	F 2
Fort Hays St.	D 8	Central Mo. St.■	F 5
Mo. Southern St.	D11	Mo. Western St.	F 9
Bellarmine Cl.	D29-30	Mo.-St. Louis	F12
Doane	J 4	Missouri-Rolla■	F16
Mo.-St. Louis■	J 8	Pittsburg St.	F19
Missouri-Rolla	J12	Southwest Baptist	F23
Pittsburg St.■	J15	Northwest Mo. St.■	F26

Colors: Yale Blue & White. Nickname: Lady Blues.
AD: Rich Johanningmeier. SID: Mary Beth Brutton. II

WASHINGTON .... Seattle, WA 98195
Chris Gobrecht (14 YRS. W-265, L-151)

Colorado Cl.	N26-27	Washington St.	J29
Mississippi■	D 4	Arizona St.	F 3
Gonzaga	D18	Arizona	F 5
Washington Cl.	D20-21	UCLA■	F10
Maryland Cl.	D28-29	Southern Cal■	F12
Eastern Wash.■	D31	Oregon	F17
Stanford■	J 6	Oregon St.	F19
California■	J 8	Washington St.■	F26
Southern Cal	J14	Arizona■	M 3
UCLA	J16	Arizona St.■	M 5
Oregon St.■	J20	California	M10
Oregon■	J22	Stanford	M12

Colors: Purple & Gold. Nickname: Huskies.
AD: Barbara Hedges. SID: Jim Daves. I

WASH. & LEE .... Lexington, VA 24450
Terri Dadio (1ST YR. AS HEAD COACH)

East. Mennonite	N19	Meredith■	J21
Emory	N23	Bennett	J22
Wesley■	D 6	Davidson	J29
Wesley	D 8	Mary Baldwin	F 2
Va. Wesleyan	J 9	Midway■	F 5
Sewanee■	J11	Hollins	F 9
Sweet Briar	J13	Hollins■	F16
Mary Baldwin■	J19		

Colors: Royal Blue & White. Nickname: Generals.
AD: Michael Walsh. SID: Brian Logue. III

WASHINGTON (MO.) .... St.Louis, MO 63130
Nancy Fahey (7 YRS. W-149, L-35)

DePauw Tr.	N19-20	Brandeis	J16
Blackburn	N23	Rochester	J21
Washing. (Mo.) Inv.	N26-27	Case Reserve	J23
Illinois Col.	N30	Emory■	J28
Millikin	D 4	Carnegie Mellon■	J30
Fontbonne■	D 7	Maryville (Mo.)	F 3
Mo.-St. Louis■	D11	Rochester■	F 6
Chicago	J 4	Carnegie Mellon	F11
Aurora	J 6	Emory	F13
Johns Hopkins■	J 9	New York U.■	F20
New York U.	J14	Chicago■	F26

Colors: Red & Green. Nickname: Bears.
AD: John Schael. SID: Dave Moessner. III

■ Home games on each schedule.

See pages 735-738 for Division I tournament details

WASHINGTON ST. .... Pullman, WA 99164
Harold Rhodes (10 YRS. W-113, L-161)

- Washington St. Cl. ... D3-4
- Gonzaga■ ... D11
- Idaho ... D17
- Ala.-Birmingham Cl. ... D20-21
- Santa Clara■ ... D30
- California■ ... J 6
- Stanford■ ... J 8
- UCLA ... J13
- Southern Cal ... J16
- Oregon■ ... J20
- Oregon St.■ ... J22
- Washington■ ... J29
- Arizona ... F 3
- Arizona St. ... F 5
- Southern Cal■ ... F10
- UCLA■ ... F12
- Oregon St. ... F17
- Oregon ... F19
- Washington ... F26
- Arizona St.■ ... M 3
- Arizona■ ... M 5
- Stanford ... M10
- California ... M12

Colors: Crimson & Gray. Nickname: Cougars.
AD: Jim Livengood. SID: Rod Commons. I

WASH. & JEFF. .... Washington, PA 15301
Vicki L. Staton (20 YRS. W-180, L-169)

- Malone Tr. ... N19-20
- Allegheny ... N23
- Carnegie Mellon ... N30
- Dickinson■ ... D 4
- Denison■ ... D 7
- Alderson-Broaddus■ ... D 9
- Marietta ... J 6
- Juniata■ ... J 8
- Point Park ... J10
- Carlow ... J12
- Ohio Eastern■ ... J15
- Waynesburg■ ... J19
- Thiel ... J21
- Penn St.-Behrend■ ... J26
- Grove City ... J29
- Bethany (W.Va.) ... F 2
- Waynesburg ... F 5
- Thiel■ ... F 9
- Penn St.-Behrend ... F12
- Grove City■ ... F16
- Bethany (W.Va.)■ ... F19

Colors: Red & Black. Nickname: Presidents.
AD: John Luckhardt. SID: Susan Isola. III

WAYNE ST. (NEB.) .... Wayne, NE 68787
Mike Barry (4 YRS. W-46, L-60)

- Northern St.■ ... N20
- South Dak. ... N23
- Northeast Mo. Tr. ... N26-27
- Augustana (S.D.) ... D 2
- Morningside■ ... D 4
- Denver■ ... D 6
- Dakota St.■ ... D10
- Concordia (Neb.)■ ... D11
- Morningside ... D18
- Cal Poly Pomona ... D31
- Cal St. Los Angeles ... J 5
- Bemidji St.■ ... J 8
- Winona St. ... J12
- Southwest St.■ ... J15
- Mt. Marty■ ... J17
- Briar Cliff ... J22
- Northern St. ... J29
- Cal St. San B'dino ... J31
- Bemidji St. ... F 5
- Winona St.■ ... F 9
- Southwest St. ... F12
- Briar Cliff■ ... F16
- Minn.-Morris ... F19
- Neb.-Kearney■ ... F26
- Neb.-Kearney ... M 2

Colors: Black & Gold. Nickname: Wildcats.
AD: Pete Chapman. SID: Dean Watson. II

WAYNESBURG .... Waynesburg, PA 15370
Rob Phillips (5 YRS. W-67, L-55)

- John Carroll Tr. ... N19-20
- Frostburg St.■ ... N23
- Juniata■ ... N27
- Marietta■ ... D 1
- Wheeling Jesuit ... D 4
- LaRoche■ ... D10
- Fairmont St. ... D11
- Muskingum■ ... D30
- Carnegie Mellon■ ... J 4
- Mount Union ... J 6
- West Va. Wesleyan■ ... J10
- Kenyon ... J15
- Wash. & Jeff. ... J19
- LaRoche ... J21
- Grove City ... J26
- Bethany (W.Va.) ... J29
- Thiel ... F 2
- Wash. & Jeff.■ ... F 5
- Frostburg St. ... F 7
- Grove City■ ... F12
- Bethany (W.Va.)■ ... F16
- Thiel■ ... F19
- Point Park■ ... F23

Colors: Orange & Black. Nickname: Yellow Jackets.
AD: Rudy Marisa. SID: None. III

WEBER ST. .... Ogden, UT 84408
Carla Taylor (5 YRS. W-57, L-78)

- Colorado Cl. ... N26-27
- Utah■ ... D10
- Oregon■ ... D13
- Loyola (Cal.)■ ... D16
- Eastern Mont.■ ... D18
- Arizona■ ... D28
- Southern Utah ... D31
- Brigham Young ... J 4
- Colorado St. ... J 7
- Wyoming ... J 8
- Idaho St.■ ... J13
- Boise St.■ ... J15
- Montana ... J20
- Montana St. ... J22
- Idaho■ ... J27
- Eastern Wash.■ ... J29
- Southern Utah■ ... F 3
- Northern Ariz. ... F 5
- Boise St. ... F10
- Idaho St. ... F12
- Montana St.■ ... F17
- Montana■ ... F19
- Eastern Wash. ... F24
- Idaho ... F26
- Northern Ariz.■ ... M 5
- Big Sky Tr. ... M11-12

Colors: Purple & White. Nickname: Wildcats.
AD: Tom Stewart. SID: Nan Holyoak. I

WEBSTER .... Webster Groves, MO 63119
Randy Kriewall (4 YRS. W-21, L-57)

- Knox ... N27
- Monmouth (Ill.) ... N28
- Greenville■ ... D 3
- Hendrix■ ... D 4
- Harris-Stowe■ ... D 7
- Monmouth (Ill.)■ ... D10
- Principia ... J 8
- Blackburn■ ... J13
- MacMurray■ ... J15
- Fontbonne ... J17
- Maryville (Mo.)■ ... J20
- Westminster■ ... J22
- Lincoln Chrst.■ ... J25
- Fontbonne■ ... J29
- Principia■ ... F 3
- Blackburn ... F 5
- MacMurray ... F10
- Maryville (Mo.) ... F12
- Greenville ... F15
- Westminster ... F17
- DePauw■ ... F19

Colors: Gold, White & Navy Blue. Nickname: Gorloks.
AD: Elizabeth Alden. SID: Bob Delaney. III

WENTWORTH INST. .... Boston, MA 02115
Melissa Hodgdon (1 YR. W-2, L-20)

- MIT Tr. ... N20-21
- Simmons ... N23
- Rivier■ ... D 1
- MIT■ ... D 4
- Emerson-MCA■ ... D 7
- Suffolk■ ... J12
- Curry■ ... J15
- Eastern Nazarene ... J18
- New England Col. ... J20
- Regis (Mass.)■ ... J22
- Roger Williams■ ... J26
- Anna Maria ... J29
- Salve Regina■ ... F 1
- Curry ... F 3
- Eastern Nazarene ... F 5
- New England Col.■ ... F 9
- Anna Maria■ ... F12
- Roger Williams ... F15
- Salve Regina ... F17
- Regis (Mass.) ... F19

Colors: Black & Gold. Nickname: Leopards.
AD: Lee Conrad. SID: Elaine Johnson. III

WESLEY .... Dover, DE 19901
Jim Howard (2 YRS. W-35 , L-17)

- Penn St.-Behrend Tr. ... N19-20
- Frostburg St. ... N30
- Randolph-Macon■ ... D 3
- Wash. & Lee ... D 6
- Wash. & Lee■ ... D 8
- Marywood■ ... D11
- Washington (Md.)■ ... J 8
- Averett ... J14
- Frostburg St.■ ... J16
- Stony Brook ... J19
- Old Westbury ... J22
- Lincoln (Pa.) ... J25
- Manhattanville Inv. ... J29-30
- Salisbury St. ... F 1
- Notre Dame (Md.)■ ... F 5
- Lincoln (Pa.)■ ... F 7
- Goucher■ ... F 9
- Dickinson■ ... F12
- Salisbury St.■ ... F16
- Phila. Pharmacy ... F19

Colors: Navy, Blue & White. Nickname: Wolverines.
AD: Richard Szlasa. SID: Richard Biscayart. III

WESLEYAN .... Middletown, CT 06457
Kate Mullen (12 YRS. W-123, L-144)

- Williams Tr. ... N19-20
- Middlebury■ ... N27
- Connecticut Col. ... D 2
- Trinity (Conn.)■ ... D 4
- Wellesley■ ... D11
- Elms ... J 8
- Mount Holyoke ... J11
- Smith■ ... J13
- Tufts ... J18
- Wheaton (Mass.)■ ... J22
- Trinity (Conn.) ... J27
- Williams ... J29
- Albertus Magnus■ ... F 1
- Colby■ ... F 4
- Bates■ ... F 5
- Coast Guard ... F10
- Amherst ... F12
- Williams■ ... F16
- Amherst■ ... F19
- Nichols■ ... F21
- Clark (Mass.) ... F26

Colors: Red & Black. Nickname: Cardinals.
AD: John Biddiscombe. SID: Brian Katten. III

WEST CHESTER .... West Chester, PA 19380
Deirdre Kane (9 YRS. W-127, L-119)

- Millersville Cl. ... N19-20
- Molloy■ ... N23
- Bowie St. ... N30
- West Chester Cl. ... D3-4
- Shippensburg■ ... D 8
- Lewis & Clark■ ... D11
- Phila. Textile■ ... D14
- American Int'l ... J 6
- LIU-C.W. Post ... J 8
- Pace ... J 9
- Kutztown■ ... J12
- Mansfield■ ... J15
- Cheyney ... J19
- Millersville■ ... J22
- Rowan■ ... J26
- Bloomsburg ... J29
- East Stroudsburg■ ... F 2
- Mansfield ... F 5
- Kutztown ... F 9
- Cheyney■ ... F12
- Pitt.-Johnstown■ ... F15
- Millersville ... F19
- East Stroudsburg ... F23
- Bloomsburg■ ... F26

Colors: Purple & Gold. Nickname: Golden Rams.
AD: William Lide. SID: Tom Di Camillo. II

■ Home games on each schedule.

See pages 735-738 for Division I tournament details

WEST GA. .... Carrollton, GA 30118

Jane Williamson (6 YRS. W-111, L-52)

Columbus■	N27	Valdosta St.■	J22
Miles■	N30	Jacksonville St.■	J24
Clark Atlanta■	D 3	West Fla.■	J29
Georgia Col. Cl.	D10-11	Valdosta St.	J31
West Fla.	D14	Lincoln Memorial	F 5
Barry Cl.	J2-3	Delta St.	F12
Portland St.■	J 6	Livingston	F14
Ala.-Huntsville	J 8	Ala.-Huntsville■	F19
North Ala.	J10	Lincoln Memorial■	F21
Delta St.■	J15	Fort Valley St.	F23
Livingston■	J17	North Ala.■	F26
Clark Atlanta	J20	Jacksonville St.	F28

Colors: Red & Blue. Nickname: Lady Braves.
AD: David Dugan. SID: Ken Skinner. II

WEST LIBERTY ST. .... West Liberty, WV 26074

Lynn Ullom (2 YRS. W-22, L-35)

Tiffin Cl.	N20-21	Ohio Valley	J17
Rio Grande■	N27	Fairmont St.	J19
Wheeling Jesuit■	N29	Alderson-Broaddus■	J26
Walsh	D 1	West Va. Wesleyan	J29
Charleston (W.Va.)■	D 3	Carlow	F 1
Shepherd	D 8	Shepherd■	F 4
West Va. Tech■	D11	West Va. St.■	F 5
Ohio Valley■	J 5	Glenville St.■	F 7
West Va. St.	J 8	Wheeling Jesuit	F 9
Alderson-Broaddus	J12	Fairmont St.■	F12
Concord■	J14	Davis & Elkins	F14
Bluefield St.■	J15	Salem-Teikyo■	F16

Colors: Gold & Black. Nickname: Hilltoppers.
AD: James Watson. SID: Lynn Ullom. II

WEST TEX. A&M .... Canyon, TX 79016

Bob Schneider (15 YRS. W-344, L-109)

West Tex. A&M Inv.	N19-20	Texas A&I■	J24
Cal Poly SLO Tr.	N26-27	Abilene Christian	J29
West Tex. A&M Tr.	D2-4	Angelo St.	J31
Western N. Mex.■	D18	Abilene Christian■	F 5
Grand Canyon Cl.	D30-31	Angelo St.■	F 7
Eastern N. Mex.■	J 8	Texas Woman's■	F12
Western N. Mex.	J10	Central Okla.■	F14
Texas Woman's	J15	Texas A&I	F19
Central Okla.	J17	East Tex. St.	F21
East Tex. St.■	J22	Eastern N. Mex.	F26

Colors: Maroon & White. Nickname: Lady Buffs.
AD: Mike Chandler. SID: Rick Thompson. II

WEST VA. .... Morgantown, WV 26505

Scott Harrelson (5 YRS. W-98, L-50)

Colorado Cl.	N26-27	St. Bonaventure■	J29
Youngstown St.	N30	Rutgers	F 2
Robert Morris■	D 9	Duquesne	F 7
Iowa■	D21	St. Joseph's (Pa.)■	F10
Auburn Cl.	D29-30	Temple■	F12
Kansas■	J 2	Massachusetts■	F17
Richmond	J 4	Temple	F19
Rutgers■	J 8	St. Joseph's (Pa.)	F21
St. Bonaventure	J11	Rhode Island■	F26
Geo. Washington■	J15	Geo. Washington	M 3
Marshall☒	J19	Duquesne■	M 5
Massachusetts	J22	☒ Charleston, WV	
Rhode Island	J24		

Colors: Old Gold & Blue. Nickname: Mountaineers.
AD: Ed Pastilong. SID: John Antonik. I

WEST VA. ST. .... Institute, WV 25112

Barbara Burke (8 YRS. W-72, L-91)

West Va. St. Inv.	N19-20	West Va. Wesleyan■	J17
Davis & Elkins■	N23	Salem-Teikyo	J19
Ohio Valley■	N27	Charleston (W.Va.)■	J22
Wheeling Jesuit■	D 1	West Va. Tech■	J26
West Va. Wesleyan	D 4	Alderson-Broaddus	J29
Concord■	D 6	Concord	J31
Charleston (W.Va.)	D 8	Glenville St.■	F 2
Ohio Valley	D16	West Liberty St.	F 5
Bluefield St.■	J 7	Davis & Elkins	F 7
West Liberty St.■	J 8	Salem-Teikyo■	F12
Shepherd	J10	Bluefield St.	F14
Fairmont St.■	J15	West Va. Tech	F16

Colors: Old Gold & Black. Nickname: Lady Jackets.
AD: Gregory Smith. SID: Steven Rader. II

WEST VA. TECH .... Montgomery, WV 25136

Tom Watkins (9 YRS. W-115, L-124)

Rio Grande Tr.	N19-20	Glenville St.■	J19
Shepherd■	N23	Davis & Elkins	J22
Bluefield St. Tr.	N26-27	Charleston (W.Va.)	J24
Ohio Valley	N29	West Va. St.	J26
Concord	D 1	Fairmont St.	J29
Bluefield St.■	D 4	Concord■	F 2
Ohio Valley■	D 9	Alderson-Broaddus	F 5
West Liberty St.	D11	Bluefield St.	F 7
West Va. Wesleyan■	D13	Glenville St.	F12
Shawnee St. Tr.	D17-18	Charleston (W.Va.)■	F14
Salem-Teikyo	J15	West Va. St.■	F16
Wheeling Jesuit■	J17		

Colors: Royal Blue & Gold. Nickname: Lady Bears.
AD: Terry Rupert. SID: Frank Costa. II

WEST VA. WESLEYAN .... Buckhannon, WV 26201

Lori Flaherty (1ST YR. AS HEAD COACH)

Rio Grande Tr.	N19-20	Bluefield St.	J19
West Va. St.■	D 4	Wheeling Jesuit■	J22
Alderson-Broaddus■	D 6	Davis & Elkins■	J24
Glenville St.	D 8	West Liberty St.■	J29
West Va. Tech	D13	Ohio Valley■	J31
Fairmont St.■	J 5	Charleston (W.Va.)■	F 2
Alderson-Broaddus	J 8	Bluefield St.■	F 4
Waynesburg	J10	Salem-Teikyo	F 5
Salem-Teikyo■	J12	Glenville St.■	F 9
Shepherd	J15	Concord	F14
West Va. St.	J17	Davis & Elkins	F16

Colors: Orange & Black. Nickname: Bobcats.
AD: George Klebez. SID: Megan Britt. II

WESTERN CARO. .... Cullowhee, NC 28723

Gary Peters (6 YRS. W-86, L-74)

Virginia Tech	D 1	Davidson	J26
Clemson	D 4	Tenn.-Chatt.■	J29
N.C.-Asheville■	D 6	Ga. Southern■	J31
N.C.-Charlotte■	D11	Georgia St.	F 2
Navy Cl.	D18-19	Appalachian St.■	F 5
Morehead St.	J 3	Duke	F 9
Louisville	J 5	Davidson■	F12
East Caro.■	J 8	Furman	F14
South Caro.■	J13	East Tenn. St.■	F19
Furman■	J16	Marshall■	F21
Appalachian St.	J19	Tenn.-Chatt.	F26
East Tenn. St.	J22	Ga. Southern	F28
Marshall	J24	Southern Tr.	M10-12

Colors: Purple & Gold. Nickname: Lady Catamounts.
AD: Larry Travis. SID: Craig Wells. I

WESTERN CONN. ST. .... Danbury, CT 06810

Jody Rajcula (12 YRS. W-219, L-82)

Rochester Tr.	N19-20	Eastern Conn. St.■	J18
Westfield St.■	N30	Plymouth St.	J22
Western Conn. Cl.	D4-5	Rhode Island Col.	J25
Mass.-Boston	D 7	Mass.-Boston■	J29
Mass.-Dartmouth	D11	Mass.-Dartmouth■	F 5
Wm. Paterson■	D14	Eastern Conn. St.	F 8
Western Conn. Tr.	D28-29	Southern Me.	F12
Kean Tr.	J7-8	Rhode Island Col.■	F15
Clark (Mass.)	J11	Trinity (Conn.)	F17
Southern Me.■	J15	Plymouth St.■	F19

Colors: Blue & White. Nickname: Colonials.
AD: Ed Farrington. SID: Scott Ames. III

WESTERN ILL. .... Macomb, IL 61455

Regina Miller (1 YR. W-3, L-21)

Wisconsin	N28	Youngstown St.	J29
Arizona Cl.	D3-5	Wright St.	F 3
Creighton■	D 7	Eastern Ill.	F 5
Wichita St. Shootout	D18-19	Valparaiso■	F10
Southeast Mo. St.■	D28	Ill.-Chicago■	F12
Wright St.■	D30	Mo.-Kansas City■	F15
Eastern Ill.■	J 2	Northern Ill.■	F19
Valparaiso	J 6	Wis.-Milwaukee	F24
Ill.-Chicago	J 8	Wis.-Green Bay	F26
Northern Ill.	J13	Cleveland St.■	M 3
Wis.-Milwaukee■	J20	Youngstown St.■	M 5
Wis.-Green Bay■	J22	Mid-Continent Tr.	M10-12
Cleveland St.	J27		

Colors: Purple & Gold. Nickname: Westerwinds.
AD: Helen Smiley. SID: Mike McFarland. I

■ Home games on each schedule.

See pages 735-738 for Division I tournament details

WESTERN KY. .... Bowling Green, KY 42101

Paul Sanderford (11 YRS. W-272, L-84)

Utah■	N26	Tex.-Pan American	J27
Southwest Mo. St.	N30	New Orleans	F 3
UCLA	D 4	Southwestern La.	F 5
Ohio	D 6	DePaul	F 8
Kentucky■	D10	Tex.-Pan American■	F11
Wright St.■	D17	Lamar■	F13
San Juan Shootout	D20-22	Vanderbilt■	F17
Tennessee Tech	J 6	Arkansas St.■	F20
Southwestern La.■	J 9	Louisiana Tech	F24
South Ala.■	J13	South Ala.	F26
Mo.-Kansas City■	J16	New Orleans■	M 2
Lamar	J20	Arkansas St.	M 5
Louisiana Tech■	J23	Sun Belt Tr.	M10-12

Colors: Red & White. Nickname: Lady Toppers.
AD: Jim Richards. SID: Dan Wallenburg. I

WESTERN MD. .... Westminster, MD 21157

Becky Martin (12 YRS. W-134, L-135)

Swarthmore■	N23	Johns Hopkins■	J25
Muhlenberg	N30	Ursinus	J27
Notre Dame (Md.)■	D 1	Gettysburg	F 1
York (Pa.) Tr.	D3-4	Gallaudet	F 3
Dickinson	D 7	Dickinson■	F 5
York (Pa.)■	D 9	Frank. & Marsh.■	F 8
Lebanon Valley■	J13	Washington (Md.)■	F10
Bryn Mawr■	J15	Johns Hopkins	F12
Frank. & Marsh.	J18	Elizabethtown■	F15
Catholic	J20	Messiah■	F17
Haverford	J22	Gettysburg■	F19

Colors: Green & Gold. Nickname: Green Terrors.
AD: Richard Carpenter. SID: Scott E. Deitch. III

WESTERN MICH. .... Kalamazoo, MI 49008

Pat Charity (3 YRS. W-25, L-56)

Northeastern Ill.	D 1	Kent	J29
Indiana Cl.	D3-4	Ball St.■	F 2
Detroit Mercy	D11	Akron	F 5
Long Beach St.	D27	Ohio	F 9
Southern Cal Cl.	D29-30	Central Mich.■	F12
Miami (Ohio)	J 5	Bowling Green	F16
Akron■	J 8	Eastern Mich.■	F19
Ohio■	J12	Toledo	F23
Central Mich.	J15	Kent■	F26
Bowling Green■	J19	Ball St.	M 2
Eastern Mich.	J22	Miami (Ohio)■	M 5
Toledo■	J26	Mid-American Tr.	M8-12

Colors: Brown & Gold. Nickname: Broncos.
AD: Dan Meinert. SID: John Beatty. I

WESTERN NEW ENG. .... Springfield, MA 01119

Michael Thompson (4 YRS. W-52, L-33)

Tufts	N23	Emmanuel	J22
Framingham St.■	N30	Clark (Mass.)■	J24
Fitchburg St.■	D 2	North Adams St.■	J27
Pine Manor	D 4	Worcester St.	J29
Amherst	D 7	Coast Guard■	F 1
Gordon■	D 9	MIT■	F 5
Norwich	D11	Russell Sage■	F 8
Westfield St.	D13	Elms	F10
Rivier	J14	Nichols	F12
Smith	J16	Albertus Magnus	F15
Worcester Tech■	J18	Eastern Conn. St.■	F17
Mount Holyoke	J20	Simmons■	F19

Colors: Navy Blue & Gold. Nickname: Golden Bears.
AD: Eric Geldart. SID: Gene Gumbs. III

WESTERN ST. .... Gunnison, CO 81230

Mary Schrad (4 YRS. W-56, L-55)

Fort Lewis■	N19	N.M. Highlands■	J15
Regis (Colo.)	N20	Panhandle St.■	J18
Neb.-Kearney	N22	Fort Hays St.	J22
Eastern N. Mex. Cl.	N25-26	Colorado Mines	J27
Colorado Col.■	D 3	Chadron St.	J29
Fort Lewis	D10	Colorado-CS	F 1
Air Force	D11	Fort Hays St.■	F 5
Southern Colo.	D13	Adams St.	F11
Colorado Col. Tr.	D29-31	N.M. Highlands	F12
Neb.-Kearney■	J 4	Colorado Mines■	F18
Mesa St.■	J 7	Chadron St.■	F19
Adams St.■	J14	Mesa St.	F26

Colors: Crimson & Slate. Nickname: Mountaineers.
AD: Curtiss Mallory. SID: J.W. Campbell. II

WESTFIELD ST. .... Westfield, MA 01085

Rick Berger (3 YRS. W-60, L-24)

Southern Me. Cl.	N20-21	Rhode Island Col.■	J20
Amherst■	N23	Fitchburg St.	J22
Western Conn. St.	N30	Elms■	J26
Emmanuel	D 2	Framingham St.	J29
Connecticut Col.■	D 4	North Adams St.■	F 1
Mass.-Boston	D 9	Bri'water (Mass.)	F 5
Western New Eng.■	D13	Worcester St.■	F 8
Williams■	J 6	Salem St.	F10
Albertus Magnus	J 8	Fitchburg St.■	F12
Bri'water (Mass.)■	J11	Framingham St.■	F17
Worcester St.	J15	North Adams St.	F19
Salem St.■	J18		

Colors: Navy & White. Nickname: Owls.
AD: F. Paul Bogan. SID: Mickey Curtis. III

WESTMINSTER .... Fulton, MO 65251

Judy Tegtmeyer (1 YR. W-3, L-17)

Westminst. (Mo.) Cl.	N19-20	MacMurray■	J27
Evangel■	N23	Maryville (Mo.)	J29
Greenville	D 4	Blackburn■	F 3
Maryville (Mo.)■	D 6	Greenville■	F 5
Avila■	D 8	Fontbonne■	F10
Oakland City	J15	Principia	F12
Principia■	J20	Fontbonne	F15
Webster	J22	Webster■	F17
Blackburn	J25	MacMurray	F19

Colors: Blue & White. Nickname: Blue Jays.
AD: Jim McEwen. SID: Bruce Hackman. III

WHEATON (ILL.) .... Wheaton, IL 60187

Beth Baker (8 YRS. W-113, L-65)

Calvin	N23	North Central	J25
Washing. (Mo.) Inv.	N26-27	Carthage	J29
Concordia (Ill.)■	N30	Carthage■	F 1
Chicago■	D 2	Augustana (Ill.)	F 3
Ill. Benedictine■	D 4	North Park■	F 8
St. Mary's (Ind.)■	D 8	Millikin	F11
Claremont-M-S	J 7	Ill. Wesleyan	F12
La Verne	J 8	North Central■	F16
North Park	J11	Augustana (Ill.)■	F19
Ill. Wesleyan■	J14	Elmhurst■	F22
Elmhurst	J18	Aurora■	F25
Millikin■	J21		

Colors: Orange & Blue. Nickname: Crusaders.
AD: Tony Ladd. SID: Steve Schwepker. III

WHEATON (MASS.) .... Norton, MA 02766

Del Malloy (9 YRS. W-126, L-96)

Wheaton (Mass.) Tr.	N19-20	Tufts	J29
Williams Inv.	D4-5	Wellesley	F 1
Coast Guard■	D 7	MIT■	F 3
Amherst■	D11	Babson■	F 5
Eckerd	J 6	Brandeis	F 8
Lynn	J 9	Colby■	F11
Middlebury	J14	Bowdoin■	F12
Clark (Mass.)	J18	Worcester Tech	F15
Eastern Conn. St.■	J20	Smith■	F17
Wesleyan	J22	Mount Holyoke	F19

Colors: Blue & White. Nickname: Lyons.
AD: Chad Yowell. SID: Lynn Miller. III

WHEELING JESUIT .... Wheeling, WV 26003

Don Hustead (5 YRS. W-92, L-53)

West Liberty St.	N29	West Va. Tech	J17
West Va. St.	D 1	Davis & Elkins	J19
Waynesburg■	D 4	West Va. Wesleyan	J22
Charleston (W.Va.)	D 6	Fairmont St.■	J26
Malone■	D 9	Salem-Teikyo■	J31
Notre Dame (Ohio)	D10	Fairmont St.	F 2
Wheeling Jesuit Tr.	J2-3	Shepherd■	F 5
Alderson-Broaddus■	J10	West Liberty St.■	F 9
Davis & Elkins■	J12	Shepherd	F11
Bluefield St.■	J14	Salem-Teikyo	F14
Concord■	J15	Alderson-Broaddus	F16

Colors: Crimson & Gold. Nickname: Cardinals.
AD: Jay DeFruscio. SID: Jeff Kepreos. II

■ Home games on each schedule.

See pages 735-738 for Division I tournament details

WHITTIER .... Whittier, CA 90608

Trish Van Oosbree (1ST YR. AS HEAD COACH)

Master's■ .... D 3
Pac. Christian■ .... D 6
Biola .... D 8
Southern Cal Col. D18
Phillips (Okla.)■ .... J 3
UC Santa Cruz .... J 5
Mills .... J 6
Mass.-Boston■ .... J 8
Occidental■ J11
Mills■ J12
Claremont-M-S J14
La Verne■ J18
UC San Diego J22
Pomona-Pitzer J25
Redlands■ J28
Cal Lutheran .... F 1
Occidental .... F 4
Pac. Christian .... F 7
Claremont-M-S■ .... F 8
La Verne F11
Master's F15
Pomona-Pitzer■ F18
Redlands F22
Cal Lutheran■ F25

Colors: Purple & Gold. Nickname: Poets.
AD: Dave Jacobs. SID: Rock Carter. III

WICHITA ST. .... Wichita, KS 67208

Linda Hargrove (4 YRS. W-41, L-69)

Kansas■ .... D 1
Washington St. Cl. D3-4
Kansas St.■ .... D 7
Texas-Arlington■ D11
Wichita St. Shootout D18-19
Iowa St. D28
Wyoming■ .... J 2
Southwest Mo. St.■ .... J 4
Northern Iowa .... J 7
Bradley .... J 9
Illinois St.■ J13
Oral Roberts J17
Creighton J20
Drake J22
Indiana St.■ J27
Southern Ill.■ J29
Bradley■ .... F 4
Northern Iowa■ .... F 6
Illinois St. F10
Drake■ F17
Creighton■ F19
Southern Ill. F24
Indiana St. F26
Southwest Mo. St. .... M 5
Missouri Valley Tr. M8-12

Colors: Black & Yellow. Nickname: Shockers.
AD: Darlene Bailey (Interim). SID: Scott Schumacher. I

WIDENER .... Chester, PA 19013

Maureen Susko (8 YRS. W-66, L-124)

Johns Hopkins Cl. N20-21
Albright■ N30
Allentown■ .... D 2
Susquehanna .... D 4
Delaware Valley .... D 7
Ursinus■ .... D 9
Elizabethtown■ J12
Juniata J15
Lebanon Valley J18
Swarthmore■ J20
Messiah J22
Haverford J24
Moravian■ J26
Albright J29
Elizabethtown .... F 2
Susquehanna■ .... F 5
Lebanon Valley■ .... F 8
Immaculata■ F10
Juniata■ F12
Moravian F15
Messiah■ F19

Colors: Widener Blue & Gold. Nickname: Pioneers.
AD: Bruce Bryde. SID: John Douglas. III

WILEY .... Marshall, TX 75601

W.M. Owens

La. Christian■ N19
Bapt. Christian N23
La. Christian N30
Austin■ .... D 1
Rust■ .... D 4
Huston-Tillotson■ .... D 6
Rust D11
Bapt. Christian■ D17
Jarvis Christian■ J15
Austin J17
Paul Quinn J19
Ambassador J22
Texas Col. J25
Philander Smith■ J29
Texas Col.■ .... F 1
Huston-Tillotson .... F 3
Paul Quinn■ .... F 5
Ark.-Pine Bluff .... F 7
Panhandle St.■ F10
Ark. Baptist■ F12
Ark. Baptist F14
Philander Smith F15
Jarvis Christian F19
Ambassador■ F21

Colors: Purple & White. Nickname: Wildcats.
AD: W.M. Owens. SID: S.A. Anderson. III

WILKES .... Wilkes-Barre, PA 18766

Karen Haag (2 YRS. W-26, L-22)

Hartwick Inv. N20-21
Scranton .... D 1
Drew■ .... D 4
Bapt. Bible (Pa.)■ .... D 7
Susquehanna .... D 9
Moravian .... J 8
Albany (N.Y.)■ J10
Lycoming J12
Delaware Valley J15
King's (Pa.)■ J18
Albright J20
Upsala■ J22
FDU-Madison■ J25
Misericordia J27
Scranton■ J29
Lycoming■ .... F 2
Drew .... F 5
King's (Pa.) .... F 8
Marywood■ F10
Delaware Valley■ F12
FDU-Madison F17
Upsala F19

Colors: Navy & Gold. Nickname: Lady Colonels.
AD: Phil Wingert. SID: Tom McGuire. III

WM. PATERSON .... Wayne, NJ 07470

Erin Shaughnessy (1 YR. W-18, L-9)

Susquehanna Tr. N20-21
Kean■ N23
Rutgers-Camden N27
Montclair St. N30
Rowan■ .... D 3
Rutgers-Newark .... D 8
Trenton St.■ D11
Western Conn. St. D14
Eastern Conn. St.■ D29
Salisbury St.■ .... J 5
Ramapo J12
Stockton St.■ J15
Jersey City St. J19
Montclair St.■ J22
Kean J26
Rutgers-Camden■ J29
Ramapo■ .... F 2
Rowan .... F 5
Rutgers-Newark■ .... F 9
Trenton St. F12
Stony Brook F14
Jersey City St.■ F16
Stockton St. F19

Colors: Orange & Black. Nickname: Pioneers.
AD: Arthur Eason. SID: Joe Martinelli. III

WILLIAM PENN .... Oskaloosa, IA 52577

Garey Smith (11 YRS. W-187, L-107)

Culver-Stockton Tr. N19-20
Grinnell N23
Washing. (Mo.) Inv. N26-27
Cornell College■ .... D 4
William Penn Cl. D10-11
Buena Vista .... J 7
Wartburg .... J 8
Loras■ J14
Upper Iowa■ J15
Augustana (Ill.) J24
Central (Iowa)■ J28
Luther■ J29
Simpson .... F 1
Dubuque .... F 4
Loras .... F 5
Buena Vista■ F11
Upper Iowa F12
Wartburg■ F18
Dubuque■ F19
Simpson■ F22
Central (Iowa) F25
Luther F26

Colors: Navy Blue & Gold. Nickname: Lady Statesmen.
AD: Mike Laird. SID: John Eberline. III

WILLIAM SMITH .... Geneva, NY 14456

Glenn C. Begley (5 YRS. W-97, L-31)

Union (N.Y.)■ N30
Albany (N.Y.)■ .... D 1
Nichols Tr. D4-5
Elms .... D 7
Hartwick .... J 7
Rensselaer .... J 8
Oswego St.■ J11
Hamilton J13
Keuka■ J15
Rochester Inst.■ J18
Alfred J21
Ithaca J22
Clarkson■ J28
St. Lawrence■ J29
Binghamton .... F 1
Rensselaer■ .... F 4
Hartwick■ .... F 5
Rochester Inst. .... F 8
St. Lawrence F11
Clarkson F12
Ithaca■ F18
Alfred■ F19
Rochester■ F23

Colors: Forest Green & White. Nickname: Herons.
AD: Connee Zotos. SID: Eric Reuscher. III

WILLIAM & MARY .... Williamsburg, VA 23187

Trina Thomas (2 YRS. W-18, L-37)

Harvard■ N27
Navy■ N30
Manhattan Cl. D4-5
Virginia Tech Cl. D29-30
Delaware St.■ .... J 6
Davidson J11
James Madison J14
Richmond J16
East Caro.■ J20
N.C.-Wilmington■ J23
American J27
George Mason■ J30
Old Dominion .... F 3
Va. Commonwealth■ .... F 5
Loyola (Md.)■ .... F 7
James Madison■ F11
Richmond■ F13
Mt. St. Mary's (Md.)■ F15
East Caro. F18
N.C.-Wilmington F20
American■ F24
George Mason F27
Old Dominion■ .... M 3
CAA Tr. M10-12

Colors: Green, Gold, Silver. Nickname: Tribe.
AD: John Randolph. SID: Jean Elliott. I

WINGATE .... Wingate, NC 28174

Johnny Jacumin (13 YRS. W-297, L-99)

Wingate Tr. N19-21
Tampa N26
Shippensburg Tr. D3-4
Queens (N.C.)■ .... D 6
Johnson Smith D11
Elon .... J 8
Lenoir-Rhyne■ J12
Carson-Newman J15
Presbyterian■ J19
Gardner-Webb■ J22
Pembroke St.■ J24
Catawba J26
Mars Hill J29
Queens (N.C.) .... F 2
High Point■ .... F 3
Elon■ .... F 5
Lenoir-Rhyne .... F 9
Carson-Newman■ F12
Presbyterian F16
Gardner-Webb F19
Catawba■ F23
Mars Hill■ F26

Colors: Navy & Old Gold. Nickname: Lady Bulldogs.
AD: John Thurston. SID: David Sherwood. II

■ Home games on each schedule.

See pages 735-738 for Division I tournament details

WINONA ST. .... Winona, MN 55987

Teri Sheridan (5 YRS. W-74, L-57)

Winona St. Inv.	N19-20	Viterbo	J17
Upper Iowa■	N30	Northern St.■	J19
Concordia (St. Paul)	D 3	Bemidji St.	J22
Mankato St.	D 7	Southwest St.■	J29
Wis.-Parkside■	D11	Minn.-Morris■	F 2
Lewis	D14	Minn.-Duluth	F 5
Mt. Senario■	D16	Wayne St. (Neb.)	F 9
South Dak.	D29	Moorhead St.■	F12
Augustana (S.D.)	D30	Northern St.	F16
Minn.-Morris	J 5	Bemidji St.■	F19
Minn.-Duluth■	J 8	Northern Mich.	F21
Wayne St. (Neb.)■	J12	Southwest St.	F26
Moorhead St.	J15		

Colors: Purple & White. Nickname: Warriors.
AD: Stephen Juaire. SID: Michael Herzberg. II

WINTHROP .... Rock Hill. SC 29733

Robin Muller (1ST YR. AS HEAD COACH)

George Mason	N27	Newberry■	J26
Davidson■	D 1	N.C.-Asheville■	J29
Towson St.	D17	North Caro.	F 1
Md.-Balt. County	D18	Towson St.■	F 4
American	D20	Md.-Balt. County■	F 5
N.C.-Charlotte	J 2	Campbell	F11
Campbell■	J 7	N.C.-Greensboro	F12
N.C.-Greensboro■	J 8	Charleston So.	F18
Furman	J11	Coastal Caro.	F19
Charleston So.■	J14	Radford■	F22
Coastal Caro.■	J15	Liberty■	F25
Clemson	J18	N.C.-Asheville	M 2
Liberty	J21	Big South Tr.	M9-12
Radford	J22		

Colors: Garnet & Gold. Nickname: Eagles.
AD: Steve Vacendak. SID: Jack Frost. I

WISCONSIN .... Madison, WI 53711

Mary Murphy (7 YRS. W-75, L-121)

Toledo■	N26	Northwestern■	J23
Western Ill.■	N28	Ohio St.	J28
Brown Cl.	D4-5	Penn St.	J30
Wis.-Milwaukee■	D 8	Purdue■	F 6
Northeastern Ill.■	D11	Michigan■	F11
Ill.-Chicago	D13	Michigan St.■	F13
Utah■	D30	Northwestern	F18
Wis.-Green Bay■	J 3	Illinois	F20
Iowa■	J 7	Penn St.■	F23
Minnesota	J 9	Ohio St.■	F27
Michigan St.	J14	Indiana	M 4
Michigan	J16	Purdue	M 6
Illinois■	J21	Minnesota■	M 8

Colors: Cardinal & White. Nickname: Badgers.
AD: Pat Richter. SID: Tamara Flarup. I

WIS.-EAU CLAIRE .... Eau Claire, WI 54702

Lisa Stone (8 YRS. W-139, L-61)

St. Thomas (Minn.)	N22	Wis.-Whitewater■	J22
Wis.-Eau Claire Tr.	N26-27	Wis.-Stevens Point	J26
Wis.-Stout■	D 4	Northland■	J29
Wis.-La Crosse	D10	Wis.-Stout	F 2
Wis.-Platteville	D11	Wis.-Superior■	F 5
St. Benedict Cl.	D29-30	Wis.-Whitewater	F 8
Wis.-Superior	J12	Wis.-Stevens Point■	F11
Wis.-Parkside■	J14	Wis.-La Crosse■	F12
Wis.-River Falls■	J15	Wis.-Platteville■	F15
St. Norbert■	J18	Wis.-River Falls	F23
Wis.-Oshkosh■	J21	Wis.-Oshkosh	F26

Colors: Navy Blue & Old Gold. Nickname: Blugolds.
AD: Marilyn Skrivseth. SID: Tim Petermann. III

WIS.-GREEN BAY .... Green Bay, WI 54302

Carol Hammerle (20 YRS. W-360, L-177)

Xavier (Ohio)	N27	Western Ill.	J22
Marquette■	D 4	DePaul	J25
Wis.-Green Bay Cl.	D10-11	Wis.-Milwaukee■	J29
Minnesota	D14	Youngstown St.	F 3
Bowling Green■	D22	Cleveland St.	F 5
Youngstown St.■	D28	Eastern Ill.■	F10
Cleveland St.■	D30	Wright St.■	F12
Wisconsin	J 3	Ill.-Chicago	F17
Eastern Ill.	J 6	Valparaiso	F19
Wright St.	J 8	Northern Ill.■	F23
Ill.-Chicago■	J13	Western Ill.■	F26
Valparaiso■	J15	Wis.-Milwaukee	M 5
Northern Ill.	J20	Mid-Continent Tr.	M10-12

Colors: Cardinal, White & Green. Nickname: Phoenix.
AD: Dan Spielmann. SID: Sue Bodilly. I

WIS.-LA CROSSE .... LaCrosse, WI 54601

Alice Simpson (7 YRS. W-56, L-118)

St. Mary's (Minn.)■	N23	Wis.-Parkside	J22
Cardinal Stritch	N27	Wis.-Oshkosh■	J26
Viterbo■	D 1	Wis.-Platteville	J29
Wis.-River Falls	D 4	Wis.-River Falls■	F 2
St. Norbert■	D 8	St. Ambrose■	F 4
Wis.-Eau Claire■	D10	Wis.-Superior	F11
Wis.-Superior■	D11	Wis.-Eau Claire	F12
Wis.-Stout	D14	Wis.-Stout■	F15
Luther	J 3	Wis.-Oshkosh	F18
Concordia (St. Paul)	J 8	Wis.-Whitewater	F19
Northland	J12	Wis.-Stevens Point■	F23
Wis.-Stevens Point	J15	Wis.-Platteville■	F26
Wis.-Whitewater■	J18		

Colors: Maroon & Gray. Nickname: Eagles.
AD: Bridget Belgiovine. SID: Todd Clark. III

WIS.-MILWAUKEE .... Milwaukee, WI 53201

Mary Ann Kelling (17 YRS. W-289, L-177)

Indiana St.■	N27	Northern Ill.	J22
Miami (Ohio)	N30	Marquette■	J25
Evansville■	D 4	Wis.-Green Bay	J29
Wisconsin	D 8	Cleveland St.	F 3
Iowa St.	D11	Youngstown St.	F 5
Northeastern Ill.■	D14	Wright St.■	F10
Bowling Green■	D23	Eastern Ill.■	F12
Youngstown St.■	D30	Valparaiso	F17
Cleveland St.■	J 2	Ill.-Chicago	F19
Wright St.	J 6	Western Ill.■	F24
Eastern Ill.	J 8	Northern Ill.■	F26
Valparaiso■	J13	Detroit Mercy■	F28
Ill.-Chicago■	J15	Wis.-Green Bay■	M 5
Western Ill.	J20	Mid-Continent Tr.	M10-12

Colors: Black & Gold. Nickname: Panthers.
AD: Bud K. Haidet. SID: Paul Helgren. I

WIS.-OSHKOSH .... Oshkosh, WI 54901

Kathi Bennett (5 YRS. W-90, L-36)

St. Norbert	N20	Wis.-Superior	J22
Wis.-Oshkosh Cl.	N26-27	Wis.-La Crosse	J26
South Dak.■	D 3	Elmhurst	J29
Wis.-Stevens Point	D 7	Wis.-Stevens Point■	F 2
Wis.-River Falls■	D10	Wis.-Whitewater	F 5
Wis.-Stout■	D11	Wis.-River Falls	F11
Marian (Wis.)	D30	Wis.-Stout	F12
N.C. Wesleyan	J 6	Wis.-La Crosse■	F18
Methodist	J 7	Wis.-Superior■	F19
Wis.-Whitewater■	J12	Wis.-Platteville	F23
Wis.-Platteville■	J15	Wis.-Eau Claire■	F26
Concordia (Wis.)☒	J18	☒ Oshkosh, WI	
Wis.-Eau Claire	J21		

Colors: Gold, Black & White. Nickname: Titans.
AD: Al Ackerman. SID: Kennan Timm. III

WIS.-PARKSIDE .... Kenosha, WI 53141

Wendy Miller (14 YRS. W-138, L-199)

Mankato St.	N20	Wis.-La Crosse■	J22
St. Joseph's (Ind.)■	N23	St. Joseph's (Ind.)	J25
Wayne St. Tr.	N26-27	Lewis■	J27
Wis.-Stevens Point■	N30	St. Francis (Ill.)	F 3
South Dak.■	D 2	Wis.-Platteville■	F10
St. Cloud St.■	D 5	SIU-Edwardsville	F13
Northern Mich.■	D 7	Quincy■	F18
Winona St.	D11	Bemidji St.■	F21
Michigan Tech■	D16	Lewis	F24
Grand Valley St.■	D30	Michigan Tech	F28
Bemidji St.	J 3	Northern Mich.	M 1
SIU-Edwardsville■	J12	Quincy	M 5
Wis.-Eau Claire	J14		

Colors: Green, White & Black. Nickname: Rangers.
AD: Linda Draft. SID: None. II

WIS.-PLATTEVILLE .... Platteville, WI 53818

Mary Otten (2 YRS. W-18, L-32)

Lawrence	N20	Wis.-River Falls	J21
Wis.-Platteville Tr.	N26-27	Wis.-Stout	J22
Wartburg■	N30	Wis.-La Crosse■	J29
Wis.-Whitewater	D 4	Wis.-Whitewater■	F 2
Loras	D 7	Wis.-Stevens Point	F 5
Wis.-Superior■	D10	Clarke	F 8
Wis.-Eau Claire■	D11	Wis.-Parkside	F10
Teiko-Marycrest	D14	Wis.-Eau Claire	F15
Wis.-Superior	J 7	Wis.-River Falls■	F18
Wis.-Stevens Point■	J12	Wis.-Stout■	F19
Wis.-Oshkosh	J15	Wis.-Oshkosh■	F23
Carroll (Wis.)■	J18	Wis.-La Crosse	F26

Colors: Blue & Orange. Nickname: Pioneers.
AD: Daryl Leonard. SID: Becky Bohm. III

■ Home games on each schedule.

See pages 735-738 for Division I tournament details

WIS.-RIVER FALLS .... River Falls, WI 54022
Carol Thelen (2 YRS. W-9, L-41)

Northland■	N20	Wis.-Stevens Point■	J22
Mt. Senario	N24	St. Scholastica■	J26
St. Benedict■	N30	Wis.-Superior■	J29
Wis.-La Crosse■	D 4	Wis.-La Crosse	F 2
Wis.-Oshkosh	D10	Wis.-Stout■	F 5
Wis.-Whitewater	D11	St. Scholastica	F 8
Mt. Senario■	D18	Wis.-Oshkosh■	F11
Minn.-Morris■	J 2	Wis.-Whitewater■	F12
N'western (Minn.)	J 7	Wis.-Platteville	F18
Wis.-Stout	J12	Wis.-Stevens Point	F19
Wis.-Eau Claire	J15	Wis.-Eau Claire■	F23
Wis.-Platteville■	J21	Wis.-Superior	F26

Colors: Red and White. Nickname: Falcons.
AD: Connie Foster. SID: Jim Thies. III

WIS.-STEVENS POINT ...... Stevens Point, WI 54481
Shirley Egner (4 YRS. W-60, L-35)

St. Thomas (Minn.)■	N19	Wis.-River Falls	J22
Beloit■	N20	Wis.-Eau Claire■	J26
St. Norbert	N23	Wis.-Whitewater	J29
Luther■	N27	Wis.-Oshkosh	F 2
Wis.-Parkside	N30	Wis.-Platteville■	F 5
Wis.-Oshkosh■	D 7	Wis.-Eau Claire	F11
Wis.-Stevens Pt. Tr.	D10-11	Wis.-Superior	F12
Wis.-Superior■	D14	Wis.-Stout■	F18
UC San Diego Inv.	D28-30	Wis.-River Falls■	F19
Wis.-Platteville	J12	Wis.-La Crosse	F23
Wis.-La Crosse■	J15	Wis.-Whitewater■	F26
Wis.-Stout	J21		

Colors: Purple & Gold. Nickname: Pointers.
AD: Frank O'Brien. SID: Terry Owens. III

WIS.-STOUT .... Menomonie, WI 54751
Mark Thomas (6 YRS. W-90, L-66)

Minn.-Morris Tr.	N19-20	Wis.-Stevens Point■	J21
Northland■	N23	Wis.-Platteville■	J22
St. Benedict	D 2	Mt. Senario■	J26
Wis.-Eau Claire	D 4	Wis.-Eau Claire■	F 2
St. Olaf■	D 7	Wis.-River Falls	F 5
Wis.-Whitewater	D10	Wis.-Whitewater■	F11
Wis.-Oshkosh	D11	Wis.-Oshkosh■	F12
Wis.-La Crosse■	D14	Wis.-La Crosse	F15
Luther Inv.	D30-31	Wis.-Stevens Point	F18
Minn.-Morris■	J10	Wis.-Platteville	F19
Wis.-River Falls■	J12	Wis.-Superior■	F23
Wis.-Superior	J15		

Colors: Navy Blue & White. Nickname: Blue Devils.
AD: Rita Slinden. SID: Glen McMicken. III

WIS.-WHITEWATER .... Whitewater, WI 53190
Julia Yeater (9 YRS. W-118, L-127)

Ripon Inv.	N20-21	Wis.-Superior	J21
Chicago	N23	Wis.-Eau Claire	J22
St. Norbert■	N30	Wis.-Stevens Point■	J29
Wis.-Platteville■	D 4	Wis.-Platteville	F 2
Wis.-Stout■	D10	Wis.-Oshkosh■	F 5
Wis.-River Falls■	D11	Wis.-Eau Claire■	F 8
Beloit	D14	Wis.-Stout	F11
Augustana (Ill.)■	D18	Wis.-River Falls	F12
Lawrence■	J 8	Edgewood	F15
Wis.-Oshkosh	J12	Wis.-Superior■	F18
Wis. Lutheran■	J15	Wis.-La Crosse■	F19
Wis.-La Crosse	J18	Wis.-Stevens Point	F26

Colors: Purple & White. Nickname: Warhawks.
AD: Dianne Jones. SID: Tom Fick. III

WITTENBERG .... Springfield, OH 45501
Pam Evans (7 YRS. W-119, L-69)

Muskingum Tr.	N27-28	Kenyon	J19
Earlham■	D 1	Wooster■	J22
North Central Tr.	D3-4	Ohio Wesleyan	J26
Ohio Wesleyan■	D 8	Case Reserve	J29
Wittenberg Cl.	D10-11	Mt. St. Joseph's	F 2
Case Reserve■	D16	Allegheny	F 5
Wooster	D18	Earlham	F 9
Marietta	D28	Oberlin■	F12
Denison■	J 5	Kenyon■	F16
Allegheny■	J 8	Denison	F19
Oberlin	J15		

Colors: Red & White. Nickname: Tigers.
AD: Carl Schraibman. SID: Alan Aldinger. III

WOFFORD .... Spartanburg, SC 29303
Crystal Sharpe (9 YRS. W-117, L-112)

Wingate Tr.	N19-21	N.C.-Asheville	J18
Gardner-Webb■	N23	Longwood■	J22
S.C.-Spart. Inv.	N26-27	Presbyterian	J24
Newberry Tr.	D1-2	Erskine■	J26
Francis Marion■	D 4	Converse	F 3
Fla. Southern Cl.	D30-31	Erskine	F 5
Converse■	J 6	Limestone■	F 8
Mars Hill■	J10	Longwood	F12
Queens (N.C.)	J13	Limestone	F15
Newberry	J15	Wofford Tr.	F25-26

Colors: Old Gold & Black. Nickname: Lady Terriers.
AD: Daniel Morrison. SID: Mark Cohen. II

WOOSTER .... Wooster, OH 44691
Christine Hart (7 YRS. W-104, L-73)

Trinity (Tex.) Inv.	N20-21	Denison■	J19
Defiance■	N30	Wittenberg	J22
Bluffton Tr.	D3-4	Case Reserve■	J26
Case Reserve	D 7	Kenyon	J29
Kenyon■	D11	Allegheny■	F 2
Wittenberg■	D18	Earlham■	F 5
Mount Union■	D30	Wilmington (Ohio)■	F 9
Oberlin	J 5	Ohio Wesleyan	F12
Earlham	J 8	Denison	F16
Allegheny	J12	Oberlin■	F19
Ohio Wesleyan■	J15		

Colors: Black & Old Gold. Nickname: Lady Scots.
AD: Nan Nichols. SID: John Finn. III

WORCESTER ST. .... Worcester, MA 01602
Sandra Gentile (3 YRS. W-40, L-39)

Worcester City Tr.	N20-21	Bri'water (Mass.)■	J25
Wellesley	N23	Emmanuel	J27
Anna Maria■	N29	Western New Eng.■	J29
Suffolk	D 1	Salem St.	F 1
Worcester St. Tr.	D4-5	Fitchburg St.■	F 5
Fitchburg St.	J11	Westfield St.	F 8
Eastern Conn. St.	J13	Framingham St.■	F10
Westfield St.■	J15	North Adams St.■	F12
Framingham St.	J18	Bri'water (Mass.)	F15
Clark (Mass.)■	J20	Salem St.■	F19
North Adams St.	J22		

Colors: Royal Blue & Gold. Nickname: Lancers.
AD: Susan E. Chapman. SID: Bruce Baker. III

WORCESTER TECH .... Worcester, MA 01609
Megan Henry (2 YRS. W-17, L-29)

Worcester City Tr.	N20-21	Pine Manor■	J22
Fitchburg St.	N23	Amherst	J25
Framingham St.■	N27	Mount Holyoke■	J27
Bri'water (Mass.)■	N30	Smith	J29
Gordon■	D 4	Brandeis■	F 2
Anna Maria■	D 7	Wellesley	F 8
Salve Regina	D 9	MIT	F10
Mass.-Dartmouth	J 9	Clark (Mass.)	F12
Coast Guard	J11	Wheaton (Mass.)■	F15
Trinity (Conn.)■	J13	Nichols■	F17
Western New Eng.	J18	Babson■	F19

Colors: Maroon & Grey. Nickname: Engineers.
AD: Raymond R. Gilbert. SID: Chris Gonzales. III

WRIGHT ST. .... Dayton, OH 45435
Terry Hall (16 YRS. W-252, L-188)

Indiana■	D 1	Eastern Ill.■	J22
Austin Peay	D 6	Valparaiso■	J27
Evansville	D 8	Ill.-Chicago■	J29
Cincinnati■	D11	Western Ill.■	F 3
Western Ky.	D17	Northern Ill.■	F 5
Dayton	D20	Wis.-Milwaukee	F10
Morehead St.	D22	Wis.-Green Bay	F12
Western Ill.	D30	Cleveland St.■	F17
Northern Ill.	J 3	Youngstown St.■	F19
Wis.-Milwaukee■	J 6	Eastern Ill.	F26
Wis.-Green Bay■	J 8	Valparaiso	M 3
Cleveland St.	J13	Ill.-Chicago	M 5
Youngstown St.	J15	Mid-Continent Tr.	M10-12
Chicago St.■	J20		

Colors: Green & Gold. Nickname: Raiders.
AD: Mike Cusack. SID: Robert Noss. I

■ Home games on each schedule.

See pages 735-738 for Division I tournament details

WYOMING .... Laramie, WY 82071

Chad Lavin (11 YRS. W-191, L-124)

Idaho St.■	J 7	Brigham Young	J22
Metropolitan St.■	N26	Fresno St.■	J27
Southern Utah■	N27	San Diego St.■	J29
Hawaii Tr.	D3-5	San Diego St.	F 4
Texas Christian■	D 9	Fresno St.	F 6
Northern Colo.■	D18	Brigham Young■	F11
Oklahoma St. Tr.	D31-J1	Utah■	F12
Wichita St.	J 2	Colorado St.■	F19
Weber St.■	J 8	UTEP	F25
UTEP■	J13	New Mexico	F27
New Mexico■	J15	Colorado St.	M 5
Utah	J20	Western Athletic Tr.	M9-12

Colors: Brown & Yellow. Nickname: Cowgirls.
AD: Paul Roach. SID: Kevin McKinney. I

XAVIER (OHIO) .... Cincinnati, OH 45207

Mark Ehlen (7 YRS. W-88, L-107)

Wis.-Green Bay■	N27	Cincinnati■	J18
Bowling Green	N30	La Salle■	J22
Indiana St.	D 4	Notre Dame	J27
Miami (Ohio)	D 9	Loyola (Ill.)	J29
Morehead St.■	D11	Dayton■	F 2
Cleveland St.■	D18	Detroit Mercy■	F 5
Vermont Tr.	D21-22	La Salle	F10
Wagner Tr.	D28-29	Butler■	F17
Indiana Cl.	J2-3	Evansville■	F19
Loyola (Ill.)■	J 8	Notre Dame■	F26
Evansville	J13	Detroit Mercy	M 3
Butler	J15	MCC Tr.	M5-8

Colors: Blue & White. Nickname: Lady Musketeers.
AD: Jeff Fogelson. SID: Tom Eiser. I

YALE .... New Haven, CT 06520

Cecelia DeMarco (12 YRS. W-169, L-131)

Wagner	N27	Harvard■	F 4
Central Conn. St.■	N30	Dartmouth■	F 5
Connecticut Cl.	D4-5	Princeton	F11
Hartford■	D 8	Pennsylvania	F12
Cincinnati	D30	Columbia-Barnard	F18
Indiana Cl.	J2-3	Cornell	F19
Lehigh	J 8	Pennsylvania■	F25
Bucknell	J 9	Princeton■	F26
Hofstra	J19	Dartmouth	M 4
Brown■	J22	Harvard	M 5
Cornell■	J28	Brown	M 8
Columbia-Barnard■	J29		

Colors: Yale Blue & White. Nickname: Elis, Bulldogs.
AD: Harold E. Woodsum Jr. SID: Steve Conn. I

YORK (N.Y.) .... Jamaica, NY 11432

Rick McPhun (2 YRS. W-20, L-27)

Marywood Tr.	N19-20	Nyack■	J19
Vassar	N29	CCNY	J21
John Jay	D 2	Medgar Evers■	J24
Manhattanville Tr.	D4-5	Hunter	J26
Old Westbury■	D 8	New Rochelle■	J31
CCNY■	D10	Baruch	F 2
Staten Island■	D13	Medgar Evers	F 4
Baruch■	J 5	Stony Brook■	F 9
Rutgers-Camden	J 8	New Jersey Tech	F11
Lehman■	J10	John Jay■	F14
Mt. St. Mary (N.Y.)	J17	Mt. St. Vincent■	F16

Colors: Red & White. Nickname: Lady Cardinals.
AD: Stu Bailin. SID: To be named. III

YORK (PA.) .... York, PA 17405

Donna Wise (6 YRS. W-65, L-75)

Frank. & Marsh. Tr.	N20-21	Alvernia■	J24
Messiah	N23	Gallaudet	J27
York (Pa.) Tr.	D3-4	Mary Washington	J29
Gettysburg	D 7	Goucher	F 1
Western Md.	D 9	Marymount (Va.)	F 3
Susquehanna■	D11	Catholic■	F 5
Gettysburg Tr.	J7-8	Gallaudet■	F10
Goucher■	J13	St. Mary's (Md.)	F12
Catholic	J15	Juniata	F15
Marymount (Va.)■	J20	Mary Washington■	F19
St. Mary's (Md.)■	J22		

Colors: Green & White. Nickname: Spartans.
AD: Jeff Gamber. SID: Steve Hevner. III

YOUNGSTOWN ST. .... Youngstown, OH 44555

Ed DiGregorio (10 YRS. W-155 , L-118)

Marshall■	N27	Valparaiso	J23
West Va.■	N30	Northern Ill.■	J27
Missouri Cl.	D3-4	Western Ill.■	J29
Kent■	D11	Wis.-Green Bay■	F 3
Akron	D18	Wis.-Milwaukee■	F 5
Robert Morris	D21	Cleveland St.	F12
Wis.-Green Bay	D28	Eastern Ill.	F17
Wis.-Milwaukee	D30	Wright St.	F19
Bowling Green■	J 3	Ill.-Chicago■	F24
Cleveland St.■	J 8	Valparaiso■	F26
Eastern Ill.■	J13	Northern Ill.	M 3
Wright St.■	J15	Western Ill.	M 5
Ill.-Chicago	J21	Mid-Continent Tr.	M10-12

Colors: Scarlet and White. Nickname: Penguins.
AD: Joseph Malmisur. SID: Greg Gulas. I

■ Home games on each schedule.

See pages 735-738 for Division I tournament details

1993-94 WOMEN'S TOURNAMENT ROUNDUP

NATIONAL CHAMPIONSHIPS DATES AND SITES

DIVISION I: First round, March 16—On-campus site to be determined. Second round, March 19 or 20—On-campus sites to be determined. Regionals, March 24 and 26—East, New Brunswick, New Jersey; Mideast, Fayetteville, Arkansas; Midwest, Austin, Texas; West, Palo Alto, California. Semifinals and final, April 2 & 3—Richmond, Virginia.
DIVISION II: First rounds, March 9—On-campus sites to be determined. Regionals, March 11-12—On-campus sites to be determined. Finals, March 23-26—On-campus site to be determined.
DIVISION III: First rounds, March 2—On-campus sites to be determined. Regionals, March 5—On-campus sites to be determined. Sectionals, March 11-12—On-campus sites to be determined. Semifinals and final March 18-19—On-campus site to be determined.

DIVISION I CONFERENCE TOURNAMENTS

Dates	Conference	Site of Finals
March 4-7	Atlantic Coast	Rock Hill, SC
March 9-10	Atlantic 10	Philadelphia, PA
March 4-7	Big East	Storrs, CT
March 5-7	Big Eight	Salina, KS
March 11-12	Big Sky	To Be Determined
March 9-12	Big South	Harrisonburg, VA
March 9-10, 12	Big West	Las Vegas, NV
March 10-12	Colonial	Norfolk, VA
March 3, 5-6	East Coast	Buffalo, NY
March 9-12	Great Midwest	Cincinnati, OH
March 8-9, 11	Metropolitan	Biloxi, MS
March 4-6	Metro Atlantic	Albany, NY
March 8, 11-12	Mid-American	Columbus, OH
March 10-12	Mid-Continent	DeKalb, IL
March 9-13	Mid-Eastern	Baltimore, MD
March 5-6, 8	Midwestern	Indianapolis, IN
March 8-9, 12	Missouri Valley	To Be Determined
March 5, 7, 10, 12	Northeast	To Be Determined
March 3-5	Ohio Valley	Nashville, TN
March 6, 10, 12	North Atlantic	To Be Determined
March 3, 5, 12	Patriot	Annapolis, MD
March 4-7	Southeastern	Chattanooga,TN
March 10-12	Southern	Greenville, SC
March 8, 11-12	Southland	To Be Determined
March 9-10, 12	Southwest	Dallas, TX
March 10-13	Southwestern	Baton Rouge, LA
March 10-12	Sun Belt	Bowling Green, KY
March 10-12	Trans America	Hammond, LA
March 11-12	West Coast	To Be Determined
March 9-12	Western Athletic	Salt Lake City, UT

[Note: The following do not conduct postseason tournaments: Big Ten, Ivy Group, Pacific-10.]

DIVISION I IN-SEASON TOURNAMENTS

Date	Tournament, Site	Participating Teams
Nov. 26-27	Cablevision Classic, Lincoln, NE	Nebraska, Evansville, Pepperdine, Princeton
Nov. 26-27	Coopers and Lybrand Invitational, Chicago, IL	DePaul, Army, Purdue, San Diego St.
Nov. 26-27	Coors Classic, Boulder, CO	Colorado, Washington, Weber St., West Va.
Nov. 26-27	Cyclone Classic, Ames, IA	Iowa St., Alabama, Eastern Wash.
Nov. 26-27	Lady Kats Invitational, Lexington, KY	Kentucky, Georgetown, Idaho St., Marist
Nov. 26-27	Paradise Classic, Honolulu, HI	Hawaii, Loyola (Cal.), Northern Ill., Oregon
Nov. 26-27	St. Mary's (Cal.) Tip Off Classic, Moraga, CA	St. Mary's (Cal.), Brigham Young, Cal St. Northridge, Oregon St.
Nov. 27	Metro Atlantic Classic, Atlanta, GA	Georgia St., Clayton St., Kennesaw St., Spelman
Nov. 27-28	Iowa Hawkeye Classic, Iowa City, IA	Iowa, Butler, Louisiana Tech
Nov. 27-28	Old Dominion Dial Classic, Norfolk, VA	Old Dominion, Miami (Fla.), South Caro., Wake Forest
Dec. 3-4	Alabama Shoney's Classic, Tuscaloosa, AL	Alabama, Coppin St., Grambling, Tennessee St.
Dec. 3-5	Arizona Classic, Tucson, AZ	Arizona, Eastern Wash., St. Mary's (Cal.), Western Ill.

Date	Tournament, Site	Participating Teams
Dec. 3-4	Arizona St. Dial Classic, Tempe, AZ	Arizona St., Appalachian St., North Caro. St., South Caro.
Dec. 3-4	Arkansas St. Pizza Inn Classic, Jonesboro, AR	Arkansas St., Mississippi Val., Murray St., Southern-B.R.
Dec. 3-4	Buffalo Tournament Buffalo, NY	Buffalo, Akron, Eastern Mich., Northeastern Ill.
Dec. 3-4	Capital Classic, Washington, DC	Geo. Washington, FDU-Teaneck, Illinois St., Oklahoma
Dec. 3-4	Carolina Invitational, Chapel Hill, NC	North Caro., East Tenn. St., Md.-Balt. County, Niagara
Dec. 3-4	Central Fidelity Women's Invitational, Richmond, VA	Richmond, Maryland, Southern Cal, Texas
Dec. 3-4	Coca Cola/Holiday Inn Classic, Charlottesville, VA	Virginia, Marshall, Southern Ill., Toledo
Dec. 3-4	Comfort Inn Downtown Classic, Atlanta, GA	Georgia Tech, St. Joseph's (Pa.), Stetson
Dec. 3-4	Cornell Sheraton Classic, Ithaca, NY	Cornell, Davidson, New Hampshire, Rider
Dec. 3-4	Felpausch/Michigan St. Holiday Classic, East Lansing, MI	Michigan St., N.C.-Charlotte, South Ala., Valparaiso
Dec. 3-4	Florida St. Dial Classic, Tallahassee, FL	Florida St., Dayton, Miami (Fla.), Rhode Island
Dec. 3-6	Hawaii/Rainbow Wahine Tournament, Honolulu, HI	Hawaii, Alas. Anchorage, Arkansas, Boise St., California, George Mason, San Francisco, Wyoming
Dec. 3-4	Idaho Classic, Moscow, ID	Idaho, Brigham Young, Nebraska, Pacific (Cal.)
Dec. 3-4	Indiana Full-O-Pep Classic, Bloomington, IN	Indiana, Morehead St., Northern Iowa, Western Mich.
Dec. 3-4	Kansas Dial Classic, Lawrence, KS	Kansas, Central Mich., Jackson St., Oral Roberts
Dec. 3-4	Lady Flames Classic, Lynchburg, VA	Liberty, Central Conn. St., North Caro. A&T, South Caro. St.
Dec. 3-4	Lady Techsters Dial Classic, Ruston, LA	Louisiana Tech, Bowling Green, Oklahoma St., Texas Southern
Dec. 3-4	Ladyjack Dial Classic, Nacogdoches, TX	Stephen F. Austin, Colorado, Florida, Southwestern La.
Dec. 3-4	Maine Tip Off Classic, Orono, ME	Maine, Army, LIU-Brooklyn, Northwestern (La.)
Dec. 3-4	Marriott/Freedom Bowl Classic, Irvine, CA	UC Irvine, Cal St. Sacramento, Michigan, North Texas
Dec. 3-4	Mid-America Classic, Columbia, MO	Missouri, Sam Houston St., Tex.-Pan American, Youngstown St.
Dec. 3-4	Mississippi St. Tournament, Starkville, MS	Mississippi St., Ala.-Birmingham, Northeast La., Tenn.-Chatt.
Dec. 3-4	Rice Classic, Houston, TX	Rice, Eastern Ill., Kent, Tex.-San Antonio
Dec. 3-4	Roger White Invitational, Evanston, IL	Northwestern, Bradley, Butler, Wake Forest
Dec. 3-4	Southwest Conference/Ivy League Challenge, Philadelphia, PA	Princeton, Baylor, Pennsylvania, Southern Methodist
Dec. 3-4	Southwest Texas Classic, San Marcos, TX	Southwest Tex. St., Auburn, Furman, Lamar
Dec. 3-4	Texas-Arlington/Marriott Classic, Arlington, TX	Texas-Arlington, Middle Tenn. St., Oregon, South Fla.
Dec. 3-4	UNLV/7-UP Desert Classic, Las Vegas, NV	Nevada-Las Vegas, Colorado St., Tennessee Tech, Villanova
Dec. 3-4	Washington St. Dial Classic, Pullman, WA	Washington St., New Orleans, St. John's (N.Y.), Wichita St.
Dec. 4-5	Brown Classic, Providence, RI	Brown, Notre Dame, Wagner, Wisconsin
Dec. 4-5	Carrier Classic, Syracuse, NY	Syracuse, James Madison, Lafayette, Va. Commonwealth
Dec. 4-5	Duke Tournament, Durham, NC	Duke, American, Miami (Ohio)
Dec. 4-5	Fila Big Apple Classic, Riverdale, NY	Manhattan, Drexel, Houston, William & Mary
Dec. 4-5	Hartford Courant Classic, Storrs, CT	Connecticut, Holy Cross, Marist, Yale
Dec. 4-5	Harvard Invitational, Boston, MA	Harvard, Colgate, Hofstra, Tulane
Dec. 4-5	Iona Tournament, New Rochelle, NY	Iona, Lehigh, Monmouth (N.J.), Nicholls St.
Dec. 4-5	Lady Raider Classic, Lubbock, TX	Texas Tech, Alcorn St., Florida Int'l., Louisville
Dec. 4-5	MCI/First American Classic, Nashville, TN	Vanderbilt, Loyola (Md.), Pittsburgh, Purdue

Date	Tournament, Site	Participating Teams
Dec. 4-5	Pal's/Mayfair Farms Classic, South Orange, NJ	Seton Hall, Boston U., Columbia, La Salle
Dec. 4-5	Target Lady Aggie Invitational, College Station, TX	Texas A&M, Cincinnati, Mo.-Kansas City, Portland
Dec. 4-5	Wellesley Inn Classic, West Hartford, CT	Hartford, Bucknell, St. Francis (N.Y.)
Dec. 10-11	Alabama-Birmingham Tournament, Birmingham, AL	Ala.-Birmingham, Eastern Mich., Ga. Southern, Southern Miss.
Dec. 10-11	Days Inn Phoenix Classic, Green Bay, WI	Wis.-Green Bay, Central Mich., Southern Methodist, Winnepeg
Dec. 10-11	Domino's Lady Rebel Classic, Oxford, MS	Mississippi, Mississippi Val., Southeastern La.
Dec. 10-11	Fairfield Warner's Classic, Fairfield, CT	Fairfield, Kansas St., St. Bonaventure, St. Mary's (Cal.)
Dec. 10-11	Fisher Implement Classic, Corvalis, OR	Oregon St., Long Beach St., Nevada, San Diego
Dec. 10-11	Green Wave Classic, New Orleans, LA	Tulane, Jackson St., Nicholls St., Prairie View
Dec. 10-11	Lady Raider/Garden Plaza Classic, Murfreesboro, TN	Middle Tenn. St., Mo.-Kansas City, Oral Roberts, Southern Ind.
Dec. 10-11	Memphis St. Classic, Memphis, TN	Memphis St., Central Fla., Murray St., Tennessee St.
Dec. 10-11	Tennessee Tech/Krystal Holiday Classic, Cookeville, TN	Tennessee Tech, Alabama St., Mercer
Dec. 11	Big Four Classic, West Lafayette, IN	Purdue, Ball St., Indiana, Indiana St.
Dec. 11-12	Minnesota Dial Classic, Minneapolis, MN	Minnesota, Boise St., Chicago St., Maine
Dec. 14-15	ISES Southern Invitational, Atlanta, GA	Georgia St., Georgia, Ga. Southern, Georgia Tech
Dec. 17-18	Arkansas Dial Classic, Fayetteville, AR	Arkansas, Mississippi Val., New Orleans, Northwestern (La.)
Dec. 17-18	Fry's/Cardinal Classic, Stanford, CA	Stanford, Cal St. Sacramento, Dartmouth, Southwest Mo. St.
Dec. 17-18	Hatter Classic, DeLand, FL	Stetson, Bradley, Eastern Ky., St. Louis
Dec. 17-18	Lady Jaguar Classic, Mobile, AL	South Ala., Fla. Atlantic, Indiana St., Prairie View
Dec. 17-18	South Florida Tournament, Tampa, FL	South Fla., N.C.-Wilmington, Tenn.-Chatt., Tex.-Pan American
Dec. 18-19	Navy Classic, Annapolis, MD	Navy, Canisius, St. Francis (N.Y.), Western Caro.
Dec. 18-19	Pepperdine Tournament, Malibu, CA	Pepperdine, Colorado St., Mississippi St., Virginia Tech
Dec. 18-19	Pizza Hut Shocker Shootout, Wichita, KS	Wichita St., Minnesota, Texas Tech, Western Ill.
Dec. 18-19	Santa Clara Diet Pepsi Shootout, Santa Clara, CA	Santa Clara, Memphis St., Princeton, San Diego St.
Dec. 20-21	California Tribune Classic, Berkeley, CA	California, Cal St. Fullerton, Detroit Mercy, Duke
Dec. 20-21	Lady Blazer Classic, Birmingham, AL	Ala.-Birmingham, Butler, Southwestern La., Washington St.
Dec. 20-21	Lady Eagle Classic, Hattiesburg, MS	Southern Miss., Austin Peay, McNeese St., UTEP
Dec. 20-22	San Juan Shootout, San Juan, PR	American (P.R.), DePaul, LIU-Brooklyn, Mississippi, Nebraska, Purdue, Western Ky.
Dec. 20-21	Seattle Times Husky Classic, Seattle, WA	Washington, Arkansas St., UC Santa Barb., Cincinnati
Dec. 21-22	L'eggs Classic, Las Cruces, NM	New Mexico St., Abilene Christian, Idaho St.
Dec. 21-22	Showboat Shootout, Las Vegas, NV	Nevada-Las Vegas, Clemson, Louisville, Oklahoma St.
Dec. 21-22	Vermont Holiday Tournament, Burlington, VT	Vermont, Harvard, Wake Forest, Xavier (Ohio)
Dec. 28-29	Florida Tournament, Gainesville, FL	Florida, Ohio St., Pennsylvania, Southern Miss.
Dec. 28-29	La Salle Invitational, Philadelphia, PA	La Salle, Morehead St., Mt. St. Mary's (Md.), Towson St.
Dec. 28-29	Maryland Dial Classic, College Park, MD	Maryland, Loyola (Md.), Washington
Dec. 28-30	Miami (Fla.) Christmas Tournament, Miami, FL	Miami (Fla.), Fla. Atlantic, Florida Int'l., Lafayette
Dec. 28-29	Oklahoma Holiday Classic, Norman, OK	Oklahoma, Michigan, Oral Roberts, Southern-B.R.
Dec. 28-29	Rutgers Tournament, New Brunswick, NJ	Rutgers, Colorado, Drexel

Date	Tournament, Site	Participating Teams
Dec. 28-29	Villanova Tournament, Villanova, PA	Villanova, Fordham, Manhattan, Monmouth (N.J.)
Dec. 28-29	Wagner Christmas Tournament, Staten Island, NY	Wagner, Boston U., Howard, Xavier (Ohio)
Dec. 29-30	Auburn Dial Classic, Auburn, AL	Auburn, Northeastern Ill., West Va.
Dec. 29-30	Baylor Lady Bear Classic, Waco, TX	Baylor, Lamar, New Mexico St., Texas Southern
Dec. 29-30	Brigham Young Holiday Classic, Provo, UT	Brigham Young, Gonzaga, Mississippi, Siena
Dec. 29-31	Central Florida Holiday Classic, Orlando, FL	Central Fla., Alabama, East Caro., Florida St., Kentucky, North Caro., Radford, Richmond
Dec. 29-30	Chippewa Classic, Mt. Pleasant, MI	Central Mich., Duquesne, Michigan St., Vermont
Dec. 29-30	Coastal Carolina Classic, Conway, SC	Coastal Caro., Austin Peay, Georgia St., South Caro.
Dec. 29-30	Dartmouth Invitational, Hanover, NH	Dartmouth, Army, LIU-Brooklyn, New Hampshire
Dec. 29-30	Ga. Southern/Days Inn Invitational, Statesboro, GA	Ga. Southern, Campbell, Rice, Tennessee St.
Dec. 29-30	Hilton Head Super Shootout, Hilton Head, SC	Clemson, Morgan St., Ohio, Penn St.
Dec. 29-30	Pitt Invitational, Pittsburgh, PA	Pittsburgh, Ball St., Canisius, Lehigh
Dec. 29-30	Rev. Joseph Cahill Invitational, Jamaica, NY	St. John's (N.Y.), Coppin St., Georgia, Kansas
Dec. 29-30	St. Peter's Tournament, Jersey City, NJ	St. Peter's, Liberty, Massachusetts, Texas Tech
Dec. 29-30	Southern Cal Christmas Classic, Los Angeles, CA	Southern Cal, Houston, Iowa, Western Mich.
Dec. 29-30	Texaco Hawk Classic, Philadelphia, PA	St. Joseph's (Pa.), Creighton, Delaware, Virginia
Dec. 29-30	Virginia Tech/Diamond Club Classic, Blacksburg, VA	Virginia Tech, Alabama St., Colgate, William & Mary
Dec. 29-30	Western States Showdown, Missoula, MT	Montana, Old Dominion, Providence
Dec. 30-31	Hoss's/Red Flash Classic, Loretto, PA	St. Francis (Pa.), Bucknell, Buffalo, Portland
Dec. 31-Jan. 1	Bertha Teague Tournament, Stillwater, OK	Oklahoma St., Fresno St., Texas Christian, Wyoming
Dec. 31-Jan. 1	Montana St. Tournament, Boseman, MT	Montana St., Arizona St., New Mexico
Jan. 2-3	Marriott Hoosier Classic, Bloomington, IN	Indiana, Eastern Ky., Xavier (Ohio), Yale
Jan. 2-3	N.C.-Greensboro Marriott Classic, Greensboro, NC	N.C.-Greensboro, Iowa St., New Hampshire, Temple
Jan. 2-3	Portland Shootout, Portland, ME	Maine, Georgia St., Illinois, Kent
Jan. 2-4	Sun and Fun Tournament, Miami, FL	Florida Int'l, Ala.-Birmingham, Arkansas St., Central Conn. St., Columbia, Geo. Washington, James Madison, Md.-Balt. County
Jan. 2-3	US Air/Seelbach Cardinal Classic, Louisville, KY	Louisville, Cincinnati, Louisiana St., Mo.-Kansas City
Jan. 3-4	Rice Holiday Classic, Houston, TX	Rice, Baylor, Brown, New Orleans
Jan. 6-8	Northern Lights Invitational, Anchorage, AK	Alas. Anchorage, Montana St., Northeast La., Rhode Island
Jan. 7-8	N.C.-Wilmington/Holiday Inn Beach Blast, Wilmington, NC	N.C.-Wilmington, Appalachian St., Ga. Southern, La Salle